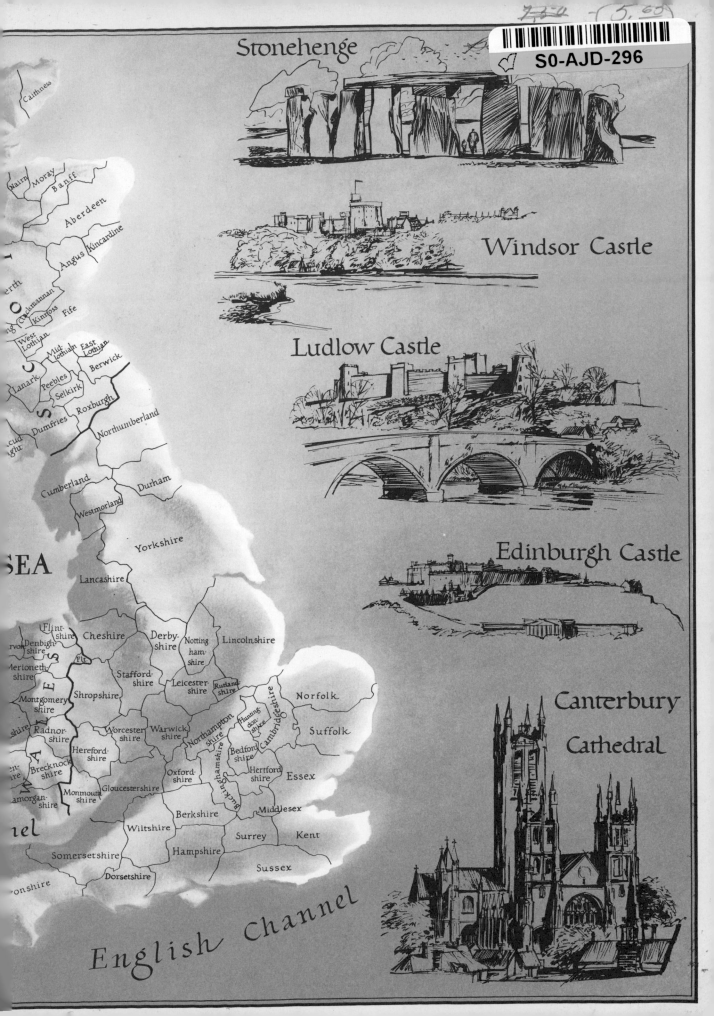

Stonehenge

Windsor Castle

Ludlow Castle

Edinburgh Castle

Canterbury Cathedral

English Channel

SEA

BRITISH LITERATURE

from Blake *to the* Present Day

BRITISH LITERATURE

I. *From* Beowulf *to Sheridan*

EDITED BY *Hazelton Spencer*

II. *From* Blake *to the Present Day*

EDITED BY *Hazelton Spencer*

Walter E. Houghton

Herbert Barrows

British Literature

from
BLAKE
to the
PRESENT DAY

Edited by
HAZELTON SPENCER
WALTER E. HOUGHTON
HERBERT BARROWS

D. C. Heath and Company BOSTON

PUBLISHERS' PREFACE

THE EDITORS of this book have been mindful that literature has always been addressed to what is today called the "general reader" and his enjoyment. The student's intelligent enjoyment of the literature of the British people has been their first concern, both in selecting the texts and in providing explanatory comment. The introductions and notes are designed to supply the information which will most readily remove the barriers of space and time and allow the reader to confront without obstacle the permanence of the literature's thought and art. The explanatory material constitutes a large body of scholarship, historical and critical; no pain has been spared to make this a work of sound and accurate learning. But the scholarship has constantly been directed to the primary end of making the literature speak for itself.

The first volume, BRITISH LITERATURE FROM BEOWULF TO SHERIDAN, is entirely the work of Hazelton Spencer, late of The Johns Hopkins University. The second volume, BRITISH LITERATURE FROM BLAKE TO THE PRESENT DAY, is the work of Mr. Spencer, Walter E. Houghton of Wellesley College, and Herbert Barrows of the University of Michigan. Mr. Spencer edited and annotated the texts which appear in "The Romantic Period" and wrote the biographical introductions in that section. (For slight changes in this material and for the General Introduction the publishers' editors assume responsibility.) Mr. Houghton, with the valuable aid of his wife, Esther Rhoads Houghton, contributed "The Victorian Period"; Mr. Barrows, "The Modern Period." Mr. Karl Shapiro wrote the essay on prosody which stands at the end of each volume.

In the whole course of his work on the book, Mr. Spencer asked, and received generously, the opinions and advice of his colleagues at The Johns Hopkins University: Messrs. Don C. Allen, Charles R. Anderson, Raymond D. Havens, Kemp Malone, and Edward T. Norris. Mr. Spencer's appreciation and gratitude for their help, so frequently and heartily expressed to his publishers, he would wish to be recorded in the warmest terms. For their continued interest and helpfulness after his death, the publishers here record their own gratitude.

CONTENTS

THE ROMANTIC PERIOD

A GROUP OF LESSER ROMANTICS

ILLUSTRATIONS AND MAPS

The end papers and the map following page 416 have been designed and drawn especially for this book by Mr. Aldren A. Watson.

The Romantic Period

THE ROMANTIC PERIOD

J. H. RANDALL, in his valuable book *The Making of the Modern Mind*, quotes a statement by Goethe that makes a useful starting point for our consideration of Romanticism. Goethe has been describing the unfavorable reaction of his circle in 1770 to Holbach's *System of Nature*, a book typifying the methods and results of eighteenth-century rationalism. He concludes:

... We took a hearty dislike to all philosophy, and especially metaphysics, and remained in that dislike; while, on the other hand, we threw ourselves into living knowledge, experience, action, and poetizing, with all the more liveliness and passion.

If we take "philosophy" here to mean the rational ordering of experience into a coherent and systematic whole, we have in this statement the essence of the difference between the eighteenth century and the period that followed it. The men of the earlier age had wanted primarily to draw rational conclusions about life, to discern behind the welter of experience the general principles that would enable them to control it. Encouraged by the results of applying reason to the fields of mathematics and physics, they had come to trust reason as an instrument which could perceive all necessary truth and had striven to extend its sway over the whole of life. The Romantics, in reaction, wanted to turn from abstract speculation to immediate experience. As Randall goes on to say, Romanticism was fundamentally

an emphasis on the less rational side of human nature, on everything that differentiates man from the coldly calculating thinking machine; and correspondingly a revolt against viewing the world as nothing but a vast mechanical order. It was the voicing of the conviction that life is broader than intelligence, and that the world is more than what physics can find in it. It was the appeal from science alone to the whole breadth and expanse of man's experience; its creed, if so formless a persuasion can be said to have a creed, has been admirably summed up by him who is perhaps the foremost living romanticist, Bergson: "We cannot sacrifice experience to the requirements of any system." Experience, in its infinite richness and color and warmth and complexity, is something greater than any intelligible formulation of it; it is primary, and all science, all art, all religion, is but a selection from a whole that must inevitably slip through whatever human net is set to catch it.

It follows that Romantic literature will center on the individual and his personal experience, in contrast to the eighteenth-century focus on Man and his general or typical character. The *Tatler* and the *Spectator*, for example, assume the existence of a "reasonable" code of manners, morals, and taste, and crusade seriously or humorously against such deviations as those of duelists and Mohocks, coquettes and coffee-house politicians. Lamb, on the other hand, exploits his personal and peculiar preferences or aversions with regard to old china, roast pig, or classical music. At the beginning of his essay "Imperfect Sympathies" he quotes a passage from Sir Thomas Browne's *Religio Medici:* "I am of a constitution so general, that it consorts and sympathiseth with all things; I have no antipathy, or rather idiosyncrasy in anything"—but quotes it only to reject it. "For myself," he confesses, " . . . I do feel the differences of mankind, national or individual"; and he gladly admits that he himself is a very special person with a full supply of "sympathies, apathies, antipathies." The result is that where the essays of Addison and Steele are social and didactic, Lamb's are almost entirely autobiographical. Again, the Romantic taste for individuality leads to admiration for the *great* man as well as for the eccentric man. The Byronic hero, for example, is as different from the typical or ordinary person as Lamb himself, but in this case because his knowledge and courage, his joys and miseries, and his dynamic energy lift him above the common herd:

> This man
> Is of no common order, as his port
> And presence here denote; his sufferings
> Have been of an immortal nature . . . ;
> . . . his knowledge, and his powers and will,
> As far as is compatible with clay,
> Which clogs the ethereal essence, have been such
> As clay hath seldom borne; his aspirations
> Have been beyond the dwellers of the earth.
> *(Manfred, II, iv, 51–59)*

In contrast to the eighteenth-century ideal of conformity, the Romantic period places a new emphasis on individualism.

Such individualism in the realm of personality was of course not new. It was, in fact, almost the dominant trait of the Renaissance; and it has often been pointed out that Romanticism was not essentially a new creation in the nineteenth century but a reassertion of the value of certain elements of human experience that had been subordinated during the Age of Reason. But in the Romantic recurrence of individualism there was something unknown before. It now included more than individuality; it also meant the value of every individual as such. Renaissance individualism, in literature and in life, had been for the few; the lower classes did not count. Shakespeare's common people are almost always "clowns"; Wordsworth finds particular virtues in "rustic and humble life." Spenser's solution of the "Irish problem" was simply the liquidation of the populace; Shelley's crusade on behalf of the oppressed Irish was the first of many concrete, if often highly impractical, efforts to improve the lot of the lowly. Manfred, and Byron's other heroes, may appear to constitute an exception. But though Byron might sometimes behave in private life as a snob and in literature as a self-isolated cynic, his maiden speech in the House of Lords was an eloquent defense of some poor workmen sentenced to death for rioting against the introduction of machinery that seemed to them to mean starvation; and he died as a result of his dogged determination to bring the Greek people freedom (little, perhaps, as many of them and their leaders seemed to deserve it) from the alien rule of the Turks. Despite the air of misanthropy that his personal troubles sometimes made him affect, he exemplified in much of his life the creed that Wordsworth exemplified in literature: that of the worth of *every* human being, however mean his social status.

THE FRENCH REVOLUTION

THIS kind of individualism is inevitably associated with the "Liberty, Equality, Fraternity" that became the watchwords of the great social upheaval called the French Revolution—an upheaval that is often regarded as the political counterpart of Romanticism in literature. So profound was its effect upon England that some account of it must be given here.

The extravagance and incompetence of the Bourbon kings (whose power was absolute) and of their favorites, together with the strain of two world wars, had left the French government bankrupt; and in desperation the dull-witted though well-meaning Louis XVI sanctioned in 1789 the calling together of the Estates General for the first time in nearly two hundred years. This medieval institution, made up of the nobility, the clergy, and the Third Estate (which was supposed to represent all the rest of the population), could hardly be expected to solve the problems of a society in which most of the intelligence, energy, and economic initiative belonged to a newly

risen middle class, and in which the lower classes, long ruthlessly exploited by a parasitic nobility, were at last developing a determination to have their grievances righted. It was therefore probably inevitable that the Third Estate, supported by a small minority of public-spirited nobility and by many of the lower clergy among the representatives of the Church, should presently take control, and so make possible some of the reforms that were so desperately needed and intensely desired. Serfdom was abolished, the special privileges of the nobility and clergy were sharply limited, and civil liberties were guaranteed by a Declaration of the Rights of Man similar to the Bill of Rights embodied at almost the same time in the first ten amendments to the Constitution of the United States.

These reforms were moderate enough. Revolutions, however, generate or let loose unforeseen and uncontrollable forces. The fierce resentment of the nobility, the arrogance of Marie Antoinette, the stubborn stupidity of Louis, the threats and intrigues of uniformly hostile neighboring monarchies, made the halfway measures of the moderate party (the Girondists) seem inadequate; and presently the extreme radicals (the Jacobins) began to gain the whip hand. During this period the spirit of the Revolution underwent a basic change. The sporadic and spontaneous outbursts of violence, like the storming of the notorious prison for political offenders known as the Bastille, on July 14, 1789, and the forcible removal of the King from Versailles by the Paris mob toward the end of the same year, were succeeded by the horrible "September Massacres" of imprisoned nobility in 1792, by the execution of the royal family in 1793 (an act as shocking to all Europe as had been the execution of Charles I by the followers of Cromwell), and by the calculated slaughters of the Reign of Terror under Robespierre, which have been made familiar by Carlyle's *The French Revolution* and Dickens's *A Tale of Two Cities*. But the Reign of Terror also had results unforeseen by those who instituted and directed it; they themselves were swept to destruction, leaving a vacuum into which Napoleon stepped in 1795.

THE ENGLISH REACTION

THE effect of these events upon England cannot be overstated. At the beginning the Revolution was widely welcomed by liberal thinkers as a long-overdue correction of flagrant political abuses. Blake and Burns were ardent partisans. Wordsworth and Coleridge were both fired with passionate enthusiasm. Coleridge, still a schoolboy at Christ's Hospital in

1789, wrote an "Ode on the Destruction of the Bastile" which hailed the event as a symbol of man rebelling against entrenched tyranny and recovering his original freedom. Wordsworth was in France during most of 1792, was actively associated with the Girondists, and on his return to England, when the Reign of Terror was already under way, wrote (although he did not publish) a long *Letter to the Bishop of Llandaff* upbraiding the latter for his abandonment of the Revolutionary cause and urging eloquently and in detail an extreme republican form of government for England. Looking back a decade later, he described the hopes of men like himself in the outcome of the Revolution:

> I . . . believed
> That a benignant spirit was abroad
> Which might not be withstood, that poverty
> Abject . . . would in a little time
> Be found no more, that we should see the earth
> Unthwarted in her wish to recompense
> The meek, the lowly, patient child of toil,
> All institutes for ever blotted out
> That legalised exclusion, empty pomp
> Abolished, sensual state and cruel power,
> Whether by edict of the one or few;
> And finally, as sum and crown of all,
> Should see the people having a strong hand
> In framing their own laws; whence better days
> To all mankind.

But even at the beginning many of the older generation of Englishmen looked askance at what was happening across the Channel. Most influential among them was Edmund Burke, who, in his *Reflections on the Revolution in France* (1790), accurately predicted the violence which was to ensue and warned England against following the course of France (see above, I, 911–17). As the progress of the Revolution made it increasingly clear that one form of tyranny was being replaced by another, disaffection toward the French cause grew among English liberals. Moreover, the Revolution soon ceased to be merely a domestic issue and became an active threat to other countries. The revolutionary "people's army" in France, formed to repel the attempts of neighboring monarchs to restore by force the old regime, became imbued with the desire to spread the benefits of the new order throughout Europe, and invited the masses in other countries to rebel against their rulers. By 1793 England was at war with France.

The Tory government, under the leadership of the able but inflexible William Pitt the younger, was convinced that it had to combat not only the growing military power of France but the danger of revolt at home. Fearful lest the scenes of violence in France might be re-enacted in England if the discontent of the lower classes were fed by revolutionary agitators, it took strongly repressive measures. Any expression of liberal sympathy was liable to interpretation as treason. Spies were set to watch men regarded as dangerous, and various liberals were brought to trial. Public meetings were strictly regulated; freedom of speech was muzzled; freedom of the press was curtailed. No proposal for internal reform by parliamentary action, however urgently needed, was listened to. Everywhere in England reaction reigned.

This reaction continued throughout the twenty years of turmoil which Europe suffered as a result of Napoleon's grandiose dream of empire. The Corsican was not a monster of the Hitler type; in his early years, at least, he could with some justice claim to be the heir of the Revolution, the bringer of liberty and justice to peoples still oppressed by feudal institutions. He was also able to appeal to the spirit of nationalism which the Revolution kindled—a spirit which, outside of Britain, had scarcely been known in Europe before the latter part of the eighteenth century. The political power that a progressively greater part of the population was now beginning to demand had to be exercised within definite limits set by geography, language, economic interest, and other ties; and the masses of people began to identify themselves with the state, as only their rulers had done before. This new spirit of patriotism Napoleon cultivated in France and elsewhere as an instrument in the destruction of the old monarchies.

What he did not see, because of his growing megalomania, was that nationalism was a two-edged sword: that men in whose minds personal liberty and national sovereignty had become closely linked would have as little liking for his dictatorship as for that of their former rulers. As France had been made a nation, in the modern sense, by the attacks of her neighbors in the early years of the Revolution, so now French aggression against Prussia, Russia, and Spain provoked a similar response. Britain, too, despite the cross currents of internal politics, was unified in a fight for life. And Napoleon was finally destroyed by the power that at first he had exploited so successfully. Defeated at Waterloo (1815), he was exiled to Saint Helena, and the Congress of Vienna re-established the heirs of "legitimate" rulers on all the thrones of Europe.

THE INDUSTRIAL REVOLUTION

IN ENGLAND, where the Tories remained in power and continued their resistance to change, change was long overdue. Even before the war the beginnings of the Industrial Revolution had created serious economic and social problems. During the war the government had refused to give them enlightened consideration, and at the war's end they were aggravated by the usual aftermath of war—unemployment resulting from the collapse of war industry and from the return of many soldiers to civilian life, heavy taxation to meet war debts, soaring prices, and the like.

The impact of the Industrial Revolution—a revolution less sudden and spectacular than the political explosion in France, but even more heavily laden with significance for the future—is considered in detail in the introduction to the Victorian period, since it is in that period rather than in the Romantic period that its effects make themselves most conspicuously felt in literature; but something needs to be said of it here. The event that undoubtedly provided the greatest impetus in this revolution was James Watt's invention, about 1765, following the discovery of how to make use of coal, of a really practical steam engine. Thus was opened up what is still, despite the development of hydroelectric power and of the petroleum industry, by far the greatest source of the world's industrial power. The most spectacular use of this new resource began about 1785 in the textile industry, in which the eighteenth century had seen a rapid succession of mechanical improvements in spinning and weaving alternately, each technological triumph in one branch of the industry demanding a corresponding improvement in the other. The invention of the cotton gin by the American Eli Whitney in 1782, making possible the rapid separation of fiber from seed, was the last important link in a chain of inventions which brought about the expansion of the industry at a speed hitherto unimagined.

Perhaps never in human history, however, have technological advantages of such immense ultimate benefit to man been accompanied by such terrible evils. The insatiable demand for cotton gave a new and malignant vitality to what had been the dying system of Negro slavery in America—just at the time when the long-sustained efforts of a little band of unselfish men under the leadership of William Wilberforce (1759–1833), struggling against the inertia of the many and the greed of the few, had at last (1807) succeeded in outlawing the monstrous anachronism of slave-trading by English merchants. And it brought to a vast number of the English people themselves a slavery nearly as abominable.

The need for hands to tend the new machines drew laborers from the rural districts (where the enclosure movement was still going on) to huge new "mill towns" like Manchester, which emerged like sores upon the face of England, where human life spawned, festered, and was destroyed. For it was not only, or mainly, the hands of *men* that were wanted; hands of women and children would do as well, and could be bought more cheaply. Their spirit could also be more easily broken; and if the flesh of ten-year-old tots became weak toward the end of a sixteen-hour working day, there were chains to hold them at their machines, and whips in the hands of overseers to keep them awake.

One might suppose that the fathers would have objected; but the family had to eat—or, all too often, the father had to be able to buy the alcohol that would enable him to forget his humiliating helplessness to support his family. Some millowners, also, depended for labor on orphan or pauper children, whom they bought in London or elsewhere of officials who were commendably concerned to save money for the taxpayers, while at the same time lining their own pockets. Where the children went or what happened to them, it was to nobody's interest to inquire. It was not even to the millowners' interest to keep them in decent health. It was cheaper to work them to death and buy more.

These evils were not universal, but they afflicted a vast number of "freeborn Englishmen." They existed in other industries, such as coal mining, and are documented in grisly detail by report after report of Royal Commissions, from the pages of which emerges an appalling picture of ill-paid drudgery, slum housing, malnutrition, disease, and a high death rate which is all the uglier by contrast with the luxury and extravagance of aristocratic Regency life. As Shelley in *A Defence of Poetry* (1821) was among the first to point out, "all inventions for abridging and combining labour" had led only "to the exasperation of the inequality of mankind"; "the discoveries which should have lightened, have added a weight to the curse imposed on Adam," and "man, having enslaved the elements, remains himself a slave." His words anticipate the grave fears of many in the age of atomic power that man's scientific achievements have outstripped his moral capacity to control them.

Still, twentieth-century Americans may ask with sincere astonishment and horror why such injustices were tolerated in a supposedly Christian country. Answers are not difficult to find—aside from the normal capacity of human beings to bear with fortitude the misfortunes of their fellows. The Anglican Church, supported largely by the upper classes and their dependents, strongly favored the status quo. Methodism, influential among the laboring classes, turned their thoughts to compensation in a future life. The great Protestant middle class in England in the nineteenth century inherited the Puritan belief that God helps those who help themselves, and that people are poor only because they are lazy and improvident, and therefore neither deserving nor capable of being helped.

Possibly the most potent obstacle to reform, however, was a philosophical one—the application to economic problems of the concept of natural universal law that had dominated eighteenth-century thought: the notion of a clockwork universe created and set in motion by a divine Watchmaker, whose work it was not only futile but wrong to try to alter. "Thou shalt not tamper with the law of supply and demand" was a sort of Eleventh Commandment, resting on the authority of England's first great economist, Adam Smith, who had published *The Wealth of Nations* in 1776. By no means all the captains of industry conformed to the Marxian stereotype that later developed; many sincerely deplored the sufferings of the workers in their factories. But most of them believed with equal sincerity that nothing could be done to mitigate the evil.

The workers themselves were helpless. Unions were outlawed in 1800 and did not become legal until 1825. The ballot box was a weapon far beyond their reach—not until toward the end of the nineteenth century were ordinary laborers allowed to vote. Moreover, the great new industrial cities like Manchester were entirely unrepresented in Parliament. No reapportionment of the seats in the House of Commons had been made for generations. Areas once thinly populated might now be metropolises; localities once populous enough to deserve a representative might now be almost uninhabited (the notorious "rotten boroughs") and the seat be openly for sale by the wealthy nobleman (as a rule) who owned the land, part of the price, of course, being the member's willingness to vote as he was told.

The only resort, therefore, seemed to be mass protest, peaceful or violent as circumstances might dictate. But of such meetings the government naturally took a dim view. Violence drew harsh reprisals from the authorities—for example, the death penalty for smashing machines. Even a peaceful gathering might be treated as if it were an insurrection—as when a cavalry charge on a perfectly orderly mass meeting in St. Peter's Field, near Manchester, in 1819, resulted in the death of nine of the crowd and injuries to hundreds (the "Peterloo Massacre," which inspired the burning eloquence of Shelley's "The Masque of Anarchy"). A vicious circle was constantly in motion —the callousness of the authorities led to demonstrations of popular discontent, and such demonstrations convinced the authorities that repressive measures must be strengthened in the interests of public safety.

But underneath the iron lid of reaction the pressure of a general desire for change was steadily rising. Even during the most critical periods of the war there had been outspoken critics of the government's policy, who could not be silenced by prosecutions, fines, and imprisonment. After the war the protests became louder, and more widespread. Gradually the extremity of the sufferings of the lower classes stimulated the growth of a social conscience in the middle and upper classes, of the humanitarian principles that had brought about the abolition of the slave trade and were working (though the great leader in the work, John Howard, had died in 1790) for the reform of a penal code and of a prison system unsurpassed in senseless barbarity by anything in English history. In the late 1820's the tide began to turn. The Great Reform Bill of 1832, forced through Parliament under threat of a popular revolution, corrected the most glaring inequalities in parliamentary representation and thus laid the groundwork for subsequent reforms. It did little to alleviate directly the sufferings of the populace; even yet the vote was given only to owners of a substantial amount of property. Its greatest significance lay in its acceptance of the principle of change. No longer was it to be assumed that the established way of life, the established political, social, and economic system, accorded with changeless laws which man was not to try to tamper with but only to obey. The world was not static but dynamic, not a mechanism but an evolving organism, the future of which was not yet determined, and in the shaping of which men themselves might play a part.

THE NATURE OF ROMANTIC LITERATURE

How was the literature of the time related to these political and social conditions? None of the Romantic writers was indifferent to them. The reader has only to turn to the selections below to note the many points at which they touch, with awareness and sympathy, on contemporary problems. Yet it will also be obvious that the achievement by which the Romantic writers rank high in literature is in areas quite separate from direct social criticism and protest. The reforms, when they came, were brought about by nonliterary men.

By some this fact is regarded as a reproach, as a ground for indicting Romantic literature for triviality and escapism. Such an attitude stems largely from the conception of the function of literature that grew up in the next age. When we come to study the Victorian period we shall see the influence of a widespread conviction that prose literature should center upon contemporary problems and offer answers for them, and that poetry should be the vehicle of moral guidance or inspiration—a belief that literature which does not justify its existence by serving such useful ends is sheer escapism, or a luxury that has no rightful place in the serious business of life. We shall see how severely some of the Victorian writers, trapped between the popular demand for didacticism and their own leanings toward a purer or broader aestheticism, suffered from the conflict of divided aims. Such a conflict the Romantic writers, by and large, escaped. But not by turning their backs upon reality. They were keenly alive to the suffering in the world. Keats, speaking of "sharpening one's vision into the heart and nature of Man," equated the process with "convincing one's nerves that the world is full of Misery and Heartbreak, Pain, Sickness and oppression." Shelley, sharing the same vision, was more fully aware of the political blundering and the economic injustices that produced much of the suffering, and at times he attacked them directly. But the supposition that poetry should combat the evil in the world by trying to reform such external wrongs, he said in *A Defence of Poetry,* "rests upon a misconception of the manner in which poetry acts to produce the moral improvement of man." It is not "for want of admirable doctrines that men hate, and despise, and censure, and deceive, and subjugate one another," and a didactic poetry that simply multiplies such doctrines is therefore useless. What we lack is the imaginative awareness that will stimulate us to put our knowledge into action, and it is this that poetry must create. "A man, to be greatly good, must imagine intensely and comprehensively; he must put himself in the place of another and of many others; the pains and pleasures of his species must become his own. The great instrument of moral good is the imagination; and poetry administers to the effect by acting upon the cause. . . . Poetry strengthens the faculty which is the organ of the moral nature of man, in the same manner as exercise strengthens a limb." So far as literature serves a moral purpose, then, it should quicken the sentiments which are the springs of moral action, rather than teach explicit moral lessons. More broadly, its purpose is to make available to a reader a broader and richer range of experience than he could otherwise have access to, and hence heighten and intensify his awareness of life—his awareness both of his own nature and of his relation to what lies outside himself. A literature which achieves this end needs no other justification, and is far more valuable than any specific social "reform."

Such a literature the Romantic writers produced. Their broad aim was to open men's eyes to new vistas of experience, by exploring and recording life in all its fullness and diversity, especially (as has already been made clear) in areas which the preceding age had neglected as possessing slight value or none at all. Their works took two main directions. On the one hand, they sought to give an accurate picture of the everyday life that men lead in the world. On the other hand, they sought to broaden the range of experience to its utmost limits by looking beyond everyday life to less familiar regions—to the strange, the remote, the mysterious. These two manifestations lie side by side in the first great landmark of Romantic literature, *Lyrical Ballads,* in which, as Coleridge tells us (see p. 118, below), Wordsworth's "subjects were to be chosen from ordinary life; the characters and incidents were to be such, as will be found in every village and its vicinity, where there is a meditative and feeling mind to seek after them, or to notice them, when they present themselves"; while Coleridge was to concern himself with "persons and characters supernatural, or at least romantic."

These two provinces of Romantic literature we may consider in turn.

1. The first often receives less attention in discussions of Romanticism than its prominence in the literature warrants. We are familiar with the use of the word "romantic" as an antonym for "realistic"— as Coleridge employs it, in the passage just quoted, when he speaks of "characters supernatural, or at least romantic," that is, of a type not ordinarily encountered—and therefore we think of Coleridge's proposed contribution to *Lyrical Ballads* as closer to the spirit of Romanticism than Wordsworth's. Or we call eighteenth-century literature realistic because it centers on the contemporary scene, and assume too hastily that the literature which broke with it and established a new tradition must be most typical when it deals with the far away and long ago. The fact is that one whole side of Romantic literature is concerned with everyday life, but the resulting picture differs from that of the eighteenth-century writers in two main points: (a) in its close and accurate observation of the particular details of actual nature, both the outer world of physical nature and

the inner world of consciousness; and (b) in its reliance on "natural" or spontaneous feelings as the guide to what is valuable in experience.

(a) Romantic literature is a literature of direct, immediate experience. Because one cannot experience an abstraction or a generalization, such a literature must center on the concrete and the particular. This was directly contrary to neoclassical practice. "The business of a poet," Dr. Johnson had said in *Rasselas* (see I, 865, above), "is to examine not the individual but the species; to remark general properties and large appearances. He does not number the streaks of the tulip, or describe the different shades in the verdure of the forest. He is to exhibit in his portraits of nature such prominent and striking features as recall the original to every mind; and must neglect the minuter discriminations, which one may have remarked and another have neglected, for those characteristics which are alike obvious to vigilance and carelessness." To which Hazlitt energetically replies (see p. 165, below): "I hate people who have no notion of anything but generalities, and forms, and creeds, and naked propositions, even worse than I dislike those who cannot for the soul of them arrive at the comprehension of an abstract idea. There are those (even among philosophers) who, deeming that all truth is contained within certain outlines and common topics, if you proceed to add colour or relief from individuality, protest against the use of rhetoric as an illogical thing. . . ." For the mere map of life which contented such people, Hazlitt and the other Romantics wanted to substitute a detailed picture. Fidelity to the precise quality of the individual experience was a primary article in their literary creed.

Hence the sharp accuracy of the sense imagery with which Romantic poetry abounds. Wordsworth, explicitly rejecting the blurring effects of the conventional epithet and the generalized personification which had been popular with his predecessors, "at all times endeavoured to look steadily at my subject"; and the concrete realism of countless scenes, characters, and incidents in his poems amply confirms the success of his endeavor. Not that Wordsworth's aim is pictorial accuracy for its own sake. He paints a scene or a character because his own reaction to it later proved to be unexpectedly meaningful, and it is this meaning that he wants to communicate to the reader. But he begins a poem as he began the experience behind it—with the sense impression. Coleridge pays tribute to Wordsworth in chapter 22 of *Biographia Literaria* for "the perfect truth of nature in his images and descriptions as taken immediately from

nature, and proving a long and genial intimacy with the very spirit which gives the physiognomic expression to all the works of nature. . . . Genius . . . brings out many a vein and many a tint, which escape the eye of common observation, thus raising to the rank of gems what had been often kicked away by the hurrying foot of the traveller on the dusty high road of custom." The statement, it will be observed, implicitly rejects the assumption on which Dr. Johnson's dictum is based.

Each poet responds to external impressions according to his own sensibility. Very different from the plain and simple images of much of Wordsworth's poetry is the rich and luxuriant imagery of Keats. His was an organism almost painfully susceptible to the inrush of sense impressions, yet exquisitely accurate in recording their precise quality. Some of his early poems seem choked with images; in his later work they are no less opulent, only better integrated in the unity of the individual poem. One of his maxims for poetry was that "its touches of Beauty should never be half way," and he advised Shelley to "load every rift of your subject with ore." It is important to understand that such a practice does not spring from a mere love of decoration for its own sake, but reflects an insight into the nature of reality that was shared by many Romantic writers. It is true to the Romantic conviction of the plenitude of experience—the sense that the world is filled to overflowing with possibilities for experience, and the corollary that the rewarding existence is one packed with as many different kinds of experience as possible. We see the same belief reflected in Hazlitt's "gusto" for the color and flavor of life as he encountered it everywhere—in a book or on a solitary walk or at a prize fight—and especially in Lamb's enchantment with the varied joys of existence:

Sun, and sky, and breeze, and solitary walks, and summer holidays, and the greenness of fields, and the delicious juices of meats and fishes, and society, and the cheerful glass, and candle-light, and fire-side conversations, and innocent vanities, and jests, and *irony itself*—do these things go out with life?

The men of the eighteenth century, too, had had their doctrine of plenitude—the doctrine, rationally arrived at, that God's perfection makes it impossible for him to deny existence to any conceivable form. But, as we have seen in Pope's *An Essay on Man,* they imposed a schematic arrangement upon this plenitude by constructing a Chain of Being, a hierarchy of creatures in which each had its appointed station between two others, from which it was distinguished by infinitesimal differences that rendered it superior to one neighbor, inferior to another. Thus they avoided disquieting possibilities of confusion and conflict, and placed emphasis where they liked it to be—on order and harmony. The Romantics, instead, reveled in their sense of the variety and complexity of existence, and strove to do justice to it in their writing.

Reality includes, of course, what takes place within the consciousness as well as what lies outside. That subjective experience will naturally be an important part of the subject matter of Romantic poetry is implied in Wordsworth's description of a poet as "a man pleased with his own passions and volitions, and who rejoices more than other men in the spirit of life that is in him." Romantic literature abounds in mental and spiritual autobiography, both verse and prose, ranging from Wordsworth's full-length study of the "growth of a poet's mind" in *The Prelude* to such brief records of transitory moods as Shelley's "Stanzas Written in Dejection, near Naples." Nor do the writers look only into their own minds; beside the literature of introspection stands the literature, equally rich, of imaginative penetration into other minds, the product of what Keats called the "chameleon poet," who immerses himself in the personality of others and loses his own identity in theirs. These two strands of psychological exploration comprise one of the most permanently valuable parts of Romantic literature.

In their wide range the Romantics enter into areas which the eighteenth century would have ignored as too trivial for serious treatment or deplored as morbid deviations from a rational norm of behavior. Freakish quirks of personality; "unedifying" feelings of inexplicable melancholy, delight in indolence, wounded pride, discontent with the limitations of existence, longing for death; irrational prejudices and paradoxical feelings; the vagaries of reverie; the psychology of dreams and nightmares; abnormal and neurotic states of mind; glimmerings of what a later age was to call the subconscious—all these find a place in the Romantic record of human consciousness because they all find a place in that consciousness itself. At times the Romantic writers seem to be striving to record feelings and impressions so vague and elusive that they defy complete articulation. Coleridge speaks in *Biographia Literaria* of readers who "had been accustomed to watch the flux and reflux of their inmost nature, to venture at times into the twilight realms of consciousness, and to feel a deep interest in modes of inmost being." The writers of the eighteenth century had not envisaged such

readers, nor did they invite their readers to embark on voyages of such profound inner discovery. Their successors wanted to develop in every reader the potential capacity for such self-contemplation and self-understanding. At times, no doubt, one or another was motivated by a desire to startle or a need to gratify his ego by parading his own personality. But at best their study of the "modes of inmost being" is serious and profound.

(b) If primary emphasis is laid upon immediate experience, all of the faculties are involved together: feeling, imagination, memory, and reason. The insights or ideas about life which take their rise from such fullness of response are therefore never the products of purely logical thought. They spring from what is variously called "instinct," imagination, the "feelings of the heart"—in short, from intuition. This is the guide to truth and conduct, not rational analysis and formal logic. In a letter of Jane Carlyle's we hear the Romantic protest against eighteenth-century rationalism:

A woman is constantly getting warned against following "the impulses of her heart"! Why, I never could imagine: for all the grand blunders I am conscious of having committed in life have resulted from neglecting or gainsaying the impulses of my heart, to follow the insights of my understanding, or, still worse, of other understandings. And so . . . I have flung my understanding to the dogs; and think, do, say, and feel just exactly as nature prompts me.

It must be recognized that this is no plea to follow one's passions; and only the extremists among the Romantics advocated an anti-intellectual life of sheer emotion. "The impulses of the heart" plainly means that "sixth sense" or intuitive insight which women in particular are supposed to possess, but which, in fact, everyone relies on, and must rely on, for all human judgments and decisions. In view of our present-day life in a world where science and the logical methods of science are so constantly stressed and so often assumed to be the one and only source of truth, the Romantic insistence on the limitations of reason, in the area of human values, and on the central importance of intuition is of the greatest relevance. So too is the underlying requirement of patient and sensitive observation. Only by lying open to life with what Wordsworth called "wise passiveness" and Keats "diligent indolence" can one store up the experience and create the state of mind which are the prerequisites for valid and effective intuition. Wordsworth's "Expostulation and Reply" and "The Tables Turned" (p. 47, below) are a lasting protest against a too exclusive emphasis on strenuous action and

intellectual analysis. In much the same vein Keats wrote to his friend Reynolds: "Let us not . . . go hurrying about and collecting honey, bee-like buzzing here and there impatiently from a knowledge of what is to be aimed at; but let us open our leaves like a flower and be passive and receptive . . . —sap will be given us for meat and dew for drink."

We are not to be troubled if our intuitive glimpses of truth are fragmentary and incoherent; their full implications and their relations to other fragments may eventually emerge, but we must in any case avoid a premature forcing of them into a scheme that will satisfy the requirements of reason. Keats praises Negative Capability—"when a man is capable of being in uncertainties, mysteries, doubts, without any irritable reaching after fact and reason," when he is capable "of remaining content with half-knowledge." In Lamb's essay on "Imperfect Sympathies," this Romantic character is placed in significant contrast to that of a rationalistic philosopher, here identified with a typical Scotsman:

I have been trying all my life to like Scotchmen, and am obliged to desist from the experiment in despair. . . . There is an order of imperfect intellects (under which mine must be content to rank) which in its constitution is essentially anti-Caledonian. The owners of the sort of faculties I allude to, have minds rather suggestive than comprehensive. They have no pretences to much clearness or precision in their ideas, or in their manner of expressing them. Their intellectual wardrobe (to confess fairly) has few whole pieces in it. They are content with fragments and scattered pieces of Truth. She presents no full front to them—a feature or side-face at the most. Hints and glimpses, germs and crude essays at a system, is the utmost they pretend to. They beat up a little game peradventure—and leave it to knottier heads, more robust constitutions, to run it down. The light that lights them is not steady and polar, but mutable and shifting; waxing, and again waning. . . . They seldom wait to mature a proposition, but e'en bring it to market in the green ear. They delight to impart their defective discoveries as they arise, without waiting for their full development. They are no systematisers, and would but err more by attempting it. Their minds, as I said before, are suggestive merely.

The brain of a true Caledonian (if I am not mistaken) is constituted upon quite a different plan. His Minerva is born in panoply. You are never admitted to see his ideas in their growth—if, indeed, they do grow, and are not rather put together upon principles of clockwork. You never catch his mind in an undress. He never hints or suggests any thing, but unlades his stock of ideas in perfect order and completeness. . . . You never witness his first apprehension of a thing. His understanding is always at its meridian—you never see the first dawn, the early streaks.—He has no falterings of self-suspicion. Surmises, guesses, misgivings, half-intuitions, semi-consciousnesses, partial illuminations, dim instincts, embryo conceptions, have no place in his brain, or vocabulary. The twilight of dubiety never falls upon him. Is he orthodox—he has no doubts. Is he an infidel—he has none either. Between the affirmative and the negative there is no border-land with him. You cannot hover with him upon the confines of truth, or wander in the maze of a probable argument. . . . He cannot compromise, or understand middle actions. There can be but a right and a wrong. . . .

By virtue of their reliance on natural feelings, the Romantics regarded as particularly admirable certain types of personality. Primitive peoples and peasants who have always lived close to nature are unaffected by the artificialities of rational systems. The vision of children is similarly unclouded, and we are therefore wise to learn from children, or to turn back to learn from the memories of our own childhood. The man who understands with his heart rather than with his head is found in many guises. He is the peddler who wanders through life learning from all he sees; the "idler" who has not laid waste his powers in striving for what the world calls success; the individualist who scorns convention; the critic whose first principle is to start with what he himself unaffectedly sees in literature or art; the humanitarian whose ethic is based on his spontaneous indignation at the sight of cruelty and his instinctive sympathy with suffering.

2. If one side of Romantic literature fastens attention on the immediate world of external and internal experience, another side—the one we are accustomed to think of as "Romantic"—answers the deep desire, long frustrated by eighteenth-century common sense, for "other worlds and other seas." Here again we may distinguish two main characteristics: (a) a taste for whatever is rare and remote, strange, fantastic, thereby transcending the humdrum, half-alive, monotonous character of daily life; and (b) a longing for whatever suggests the Ideal and the Infinite in contrast to the imperfections and finite limitations of ordinary life or painful reality.

(a) In large part the Romantic love for the extraordinary, which at first glance seems opposed to Romantic naturalism, is on the contrary rooted directly in it. The psychological penetration which reveals the novelty in oneself ("I am not made like any one else I have ever known," said Rousseau; "and, if I am not better, at least I am different") leads easily to an interest in what is novel to the point of being singular, eccentric, bizarre. The acceptance of whatever actually *occurs* in experience, whether rational explanation can account for it or not, leads to serious scrutiny of the mysterious. The belief that earlier ages and remoter scenes may yield a picture of men less corrupted by the false systematizations of reason leads to an interest in the exotic and the long ago. This whole side of the work of the Romantic writers is a further assertion of their refusal to accept any limitation upon experience, their conviction that we can be bound by no preconceived ideas as to the places and times where we may find truth.

To be sure, the motive behind such interests may be mere escapism. On one level the period carried on the tradition of Gothic romance, with its sensational and supernatural trappings intended merely to excite pleasurable suspense and surprise. Byron's Eastern tales are of scarcely greater value. But the Romantic literature of strangeness and remoteness has far more serious manifestations than these. A medieval setting may provide a more favorable frame for exhibiting "the essential passions of the heart" than a contemporary one could afford. An exotic setting may permit new scope for imaginative probing into the way in which man reacts to his situation. A supernatural setting may provide a writer with the only satisfactory symbolic language he can devise to render concrete his deepest and most elusive insights into the depths of the human spirit. "The Ancient Mariner" and "Christabel" contain much to remind us that Coleridge conceived it to be his task not merely to present "persons and characters supernatural, or at least romantic," but to transfer to them "from our inward nature a human interest and a semblance of truth." At its best the Romantic literature of the strange is no less richly suggestive of real truths of human nature than is the Romantic literature of the familiar.

(b) Using the term in a broad sense, the Romantics were idealists. "In different ways," says C. M. Bowra, "each of them believed in an order of things which is not that which we can see and know, and this was the goal of their passionate search." In part this preoccupation was a natural extension of their rejection of any sort of closed system—their desire to push always farther into experience and their refusal to set any limits to its potential range. At one end of the scale the pursuit of the ideal may manifest itself in their writing merely as a longing for greater happiness than the everyday world affords. At the other end there is Blake's direct mystical access to the sphere of the eternal and the absolute ("I have conversed with the spiritual Sun," he could say; "I saw him on Primrose Hill").

Shelley's apprehension of the ideal was scarcely less tangible, at its moments of greatest intensity, than Blake's. He *felt* with almost a physical awareness the presence of a Spirit of Beauty, which appears and disappears in life at identifiable times and in identifiable places to inform material things with transitory beauty. The Spirits of Love and Reason were similarly real to him; he believed that they could and must become the saviors of mankind. Such spirits he addressed directly in his poetry, as in his "Hymn to Intellectual Beauty"; or he gave them forms like those of the gods of Greek myth, as in *Prometheus Unbound*; or, again, he expressed his perception of their nature through the symbolic use of some natural object, as in "To a Skylark." It is natural that Shelley, like others of the Romantics, should have found Plato's philosophy congenial; but it is important to remember that his idealism was rooted first of all not in abstract speculation but in direct experience.

An important, if difficult, passage in one of Keats's letters (see p. 336, below) describes the Romantic imagination as an idealizing faculty:

I am certain of nothing but the holiness of the Heart's affections and the truth of Imagination—What the imagination seizes as Beauty must be truth—whether it existed before or not—for I have the same Idea of all our Passions as of Love: they are all, in their sublime, creative of essential Beauty.

As the capital B of "Beauty" suggests, Keats did not mean "sensuous beauty" in the concrete, but, as he elsewhere says, "the principle of Beauty in all things." This is close to Shelley's "Intellectual Beauty," but there is an important distinction to notice. Where Shelley actually felt or apprehended a *Spirit* of Beauty in the universe, Keats, who never had such mystical experiences, speaks only of a *Principle* of Beauty. This Principle is simply the Ideal of anything which he, like all of us, could imagine from what he had seen or known. All our passions "in their sublime"—that is, at their highest and fullest—are creative of, suggestive of, their ultimate perfection, their ideal form, their essential Beauty. Not by themselves, but in conjunction with the idealizing Imagination: for example, from love at its best we can imagine Ideal Love. Thus, when Keats says that what the imagination seizes as Beauty must be truth, he means that the imaginative Vision of the Ideal is not an illusion, not a fancy daydream, but the ultimate truth. It *must* be, though we cannot prove that it is by actual experience in this life. "The Imagination," he continues, "may be compared to Adam's dream [of Eve]—he awoke and found it truth." So we too will some day awake in a Platonic heaven and find true the ideal Beauties that we imagined:

Have you never by being Surprised with an old Melody—in a delicious place—by a delicious voice, felt over again your very Speculations and Surmises at the time it first operated on your Soul—do you not remember forming to yourself the Singer's face more beautiful than it was possible and yet with the elevation of the Moment you did not think so? Even then you were mounted on the Wings of Imagination so high—that the Prototype must be hereafter—that delicious face you will see.

This does not mean that Keats's poetry, or Romantic poetry in general under this motivation, presents merely "beautiful idealisms." Sometimes, to be sure, it does; the poet seems unable to face the ugliness of the world, and he makes a futile attempt to escape from it by devising pretty pictures of a world that would suit him better. But primarily the Ideal is presented in significant contrast to the Real, either in melancholy contrast (as seen in Keats and Shelley) or in ironic contrast (as in Byron).

The natural form which this often takes is a contrast between the Present and the Past or the Future. If the Romantic love of the past had one source, as we have seen, in the belief that earlier ages were less affected by erroneous systems of thought, it had another in the quest for an ideal image to place against the far-from-ideal realities of the present. The opening paragraph of Lamb's essay on "Blakesmoor in H——shire" is a fine revelation of the Romantic imagination in the very act of idealizing the past.

I do not know a pleasure more affecting than to range at will over the deserted apartments of some fine old family mansion. The traces of extinct grandeur admit of a better passion than envy: and contemplations on the great and good, whom we fancy in succession to have been its inhabitants, weave for us illusions, incompatible with the bustle of modern occupancy, and vanities of foolish present aristocracy. The same difference of feeling, I think, attends us between entering an empty and a crowded church. In the latter it is chance but some present human frailty—an act of inattention on the part of some of the auditory—or a trait of affectation, or worse, vainglory, on that of the preacher—puts us by our best thoughts, disharmonising the place and the occasion. But wouldst thou know the beauty of holiness?—go alone on some week-day, borrowing the keys of good Master Sexton, traverse the cool aisles of some country church: think of the piety that has kneeled there—the congregations, old and young, that have found consolation there—the meek pastor—the docile parishioner. With no disturbing emotions, no cross conflicting comparisons, drink in the tranquillity of the place, till thou thyself become as fixed and motionless as the marble effigies that kneel and weep around thee.

In similar fashion it was possible to view the future as a complementary point of ideal fulfillment, both for the individual and for society, so that Romantic literature is full of glowing visions of personal happiness to come, or Utopian visions (in Shelley especially) of the perfectibility of man.

But the Ideal was not always thought of as beyond the present limits of human experience. It often meant what was rare but possible, what man can see or can be when the potentialities of life are realized at their finest: the beauty of nature and of love (in Keats's ode "To Autumn" and "The Eve of St. Agnes," for example), and the grandeur of nature and of the human spirit (in a poem like Wordsworth's "Michael").

Nature, it will be noticed, is looked at in both ways, but especially in its grandeur. Though gardens and streams and the spring countryside are treated by the Romantic poets with a fineness of perception that was new in English poetry, their taste turned more toward the sublime, to whatever by its vast size, height, and potential or actual power suggested the Infinite: mountains, the ocean, thunderstorms, the expanse of the night sky. This taste had both an aesthetic and a religious basis. In the presence of sublimity, one can feel an excited release from the limitations and anxieties of finite, daily life. But that experience readily passed, for the Romantics, into a mystical sense of an Infinite and Sublime Spirit. The development from the first to the second is clearly revealed in a passage from Carlyle's *Sartor Resartus:*

A hundred and a hundred savage peaks, in the last light of Day; all glowing, of gold and amethyst, like giant spirits of the wilderness; there in their silence, in their solitude, even as on the night when Noah's Deluge first dried! Beautiful, nay solemn, was the sudden aspect to our Wanderer. He gazed over those stupendous masses with wonder, almost with longing desire; never till this hour had he known Nature, that she was One, that she was his Mother and divine. And as the ruddy glow was fading into clearness in the sky, and the Sun had now departed, a murmur of Eternity and Immensity, of Death and Life, stole through his soul; and he felt as if Death and Life were one, as if the Earth were not dead, as if the Spirit of the Earth had its throne in that splendour, and his own spirit were therewith holding communion.

This is Romantic Pantheism. When the tradition of orthodox Christianity began to lose its hold on the eighteenth-century intellectuals, they found a substitute in natural theology, with its conception of nature as the work of God, revealing the Divine Hand in its ordered beauty. One looked at nature, so to speak, and *reasoned* back to a Creator and Architect. When the Romantics turned to nature, they too had the same religious motive, but true to their principles, they relied on immediate experience and intuitive perception: they *felt* the presence of God *in* nature, above all in its grandest forms, where his sublime power was most fully suggested:

> And I have felt
> A presence that disturbs me with the joy
> Of elevated thoughts; a sense sublime
> Of something far more deeply interfused,
> Whose dwelling is the light of setting suns,
> And the round ocean and the living air,
> And the blue sky, and in the mind of man:
> A motion and a spirit, that impels
> All thinking things, all objects of all thought,
> And rolls through all things.

GENERAL REFERENCES

The political and social background is well treated in G. M. Trevelyan's *British History in the Nineteenth Century* (2d ed., 1938) and *English Social History* (1942). The intellectual background is discussed in D. C. Somervell's *English Thought in the Nineteenth Century* (1929); more specifically focused on our period is H. N. Brailsford's *Shelley, Godwin, and Their Circle* (1913), which, however, overemphasizes the influence of Godwin. The concept of Romanticism is well analyzed in A. O. Lovejoy's *Romanticism and the History of Ideas* (1948); J. H. Randall, Jr., gives a briefer account in *The Making of the Modern Mind* (1926), chap. 16. Despite the vast number of books on English Romantic literature (the most important are listed in the extensive bibliographies in Ernest Bernbaum's *Guide through the Romantic Movement* [2d ed., 1949]), there is no thoroughly satisfactory general study. Perhaps the best critical account, making its approach largely through individual authors, is Oliver Elton's *A Survey of English Literature, 1780–1880* (4 vols., 1920), vols. I and II. Much helpful material is included in H. N. Fairchild's *The Romantic Quest* (1939). Douglas Bush's *Mythology and the Romantic Tradition in English Poetry* (1937) contains excellent criticism, of wider range than the title may suggest. Two stimulating recent studies are C. M. Bowra's *The Romantic Imagination* (1949) and Basil Willey's *Nineteenth Century Studies: Coleridge to Matthew Arnold* (1949). The most important books relating to single writers are mentioned in the separate introductions below.

William Blake

1757–1827

BLAKE was one of those rare men whose inner strength is so rugged and so spiritual that they are able, not only to catch sight of an ideal, but to keep it steadily before their eyes and to pursue it unswervingly, without being diverted so much as a hair's breadth by current conventions or by any misunderstanding of their own purposes. The whole of his mature life was devoted to an attempt, through his writing and his engraving and painting, to rouse men to cast off the shackles of conventional beliefs and institutions and to realize their spiritual potentialities. The unorthodoxy of his ideas frequently caused his aims and motives to be misunderstood. He was often saddened, sometimes infuriated, by the blindness of his contemporaries to his message, but he was sustained throughout his long life by his certainty of its truth.

He had, to be sure, special reason for his certainty. Blake was a mystic, a visionary in the literal sense. From his childhood he saw visions—angels, the prophet Ezekiel, the apostles, Christ himself. The spiritual world was more real to him than the sensations produced by the physical objects about him. While ordinary men argue about the psychology of the mystical experience, the mystic himself can rest secure in his conviction that he has been vouchsafed a direct revelation of the truth. Blake had the strongest possible personal grounds for his faith that the essential reality is spiritual and that the avenue to eternal truth is "imagination heightened to vision." This faith is the key to Blake's most strikingly romantic trait—his abhorrence of the rationalistic philosophy of his own age and his lifelong attempt to free the human spirit from the evils that it had created.

Blake exhorted the young artists of his time, painters and sculptors as well as writers, to abandon the worship of the classical models and trust their own intuition and imagination. But his conviction that men and women need and thrive on liberty was by no means confined to his creed as an artist; it went far beyond the limits of artistic theory into the fields of social and political reform. He was a hot sympathizer with the French Revolution, in which he optimistically saw freedom beginning its struggle to cast off enslaving and deadening custom. Though a deeply religious man, he was outspokenly impatient with the restraints and the formalism of organized, codified religion and ethics. In every area of life he believed profoundly in unshackling the human spirit for free expression and development.

Blake was a shopkeeper's son, born in London in 1757. His father soon perceived that his second son was meant for art, not trade, and sent him at the age of ten to drawing school. At fourteen, there being no money for staking him to the study of painting, he was apprenticed to an engraver. In due time Blake became an engraver himself; it was principally by commissions for book illustrations and engravings of pictures that he was to earn his meager living. After his apprenticeship he briefly attended the art school of the Royal Academy. He made friends with several well-known artists; but his own productions went without any wide recognition, even after he became, as we now think, one of the greatest artists England has had. He did find one loyal patron in Thomas Butts, who engaged Blake at £26 a year as drawing master to his son and bought paintings and drawings so regularly that his house was crammed with them. Otherwise Blake's painting encountered general neglect.

Meanwhile the artist was educating himself by reading many of the standard books, always with independent judgment. He was twenty-four when he married an illiterate girl of twenty who proved an ideal helpmeet. Though childless, they had a long and happy life together; poverty was no barrier to their happiness. Blake taught her to read and write; she grew intellectually, worked with him, understood him, and sustained him with her belief in his visions. By a small circle of friends his genius was, if not understood, at least recognized; but his occasional exhibition of a drawing at the Academy attracted little attention. His sole determined bid for public notice, a one-man show at his brother's shop and dwelling in 1809, was reviewed in the *Examiner* as the work of a lunatic; and Robert Southey, who thought well of both the painting and the poetry, nevertheless considered him "evidently insane." Blake set forth his theories of art in the *Descriptive Catalogue* of this exhibition, his most important prose work. Of the numerous illustrations in which his genius found scope, the most famous are those for the Book of Job; they are now ranked among the most remarkable things in British art, "the quintessence of mystical, unreal beauty." They were executed toward the end of his life.

In his own books Blake habitually combined his two mediums. Only the first, *Poetical Sketches,* was printed from type. Of the others he personally manufactured every copy by a laborious process of his own invention, engraving text and illustrations, printing from the engraved plates, and then illuminating the pages in water colors. Needless to say, only a few copies were ever made; they now command fabulous prices. As an artist, Blake was ahead of his time; after his death in 1827 his work was ignored till the Pre-Raphaelites, in their rebellion against traditionalism, took him up about the middle of the nineteenth century. He had less in common with the Romantic school of his own day than with the postrealist and neo-Romantic of recent decades, who scorns the *appearance* of things and conceives the artist's aim as something higher than either realism for its own sake or a use of natural objects merely as a means of inspiration. He sought in both his mediums to get through to the spiritual reality of which the outward form is merely a sign, and this quest for the essence beyond literal expression links him to some extent with the expressionists of our own century.

Except in some of his earliest verse, in the *Poetical Sketches* (1783), written with the Elizabethan and Caroline lyrics as models, Blake is trying in all his best poetry for that essential reality. His reputation as a poet today rests mainly on *Songs of Innocence* (1789) and *Songs of Experience* (1794), which contain some of the greatest lyrics in our language. In the long series of "Prophetic Books" which followed them, he endeavored with small success to make a communicable pattern of his ideas by means of an elaborate system of symbols drawn from his own visions and from his reading in Neoplatonic, cabalistic, alchemical, and other out-of-the-way books. Almost all of Blake's poetry is more or less symbolic. If much of his later work is obscure, it is because he abandoned the conventional symbols for others that seemed to him more adequate to communicate his message. Modern scholars have devoted much time and ingenuity to unraveling the "Prophetic Books," and some claim to find Blake's greatest work in them. Perhaps most critics regard them on the whole as artistic failures. In any event, they are not mediocre; even at their murkiest they reveal the daring and grandeur of Blake's imagination.

The standard edition is *The Writings of William Blake,* edited by G. Keynes (3 vols., 1925). Of the one-volume editions, *Poetry and Prose of William Blake* (1927), by the same editor, is complete; but a new reader is likely to find J. Sampson's edition of *The Poetical Works* (1913) more satisfactory. Mona Wilson has written a good Life (1927; incomplete but revised ed., 1932). Blake's ideas are discussed in S. F. Damon's *William Blake: His Philosophy and Symbols* (1924), D. Saurat's *Blake and Modern Thought* (1929), M. O. Percival's *William Blake's Circle of Destiny* (1938), and M. Schorer's *William Blake: The Politics of Vision* (1946).

William Blake

from POETICAL SKETCHES

This volume, which appeared in 1783, was privately printed at the expense of friends. The first of the following selections is said to have been written before Blake was fourteen.

SONG

How sweet I roam'd from field to field,
    And tasted all the summer's pride,
Till I the prince of love beheld,
    Who in the sunny beams did glide!

He shew'd me lilies for my hair,   5
    And blushing roses for my brow;
He led me through his gardens fair,
    Where all his golden pleasures grow.

With sweet May dews my wings were wet,
    And Phoebus fir'd my vocal rage;[1]   10

He caught me in his silken net,
    And shut me in his golden cage.

He loves to sit and hear me sing,
    Then, laughing, sports and plays with me;
Then stretches out my golden wing,   15
    And mocks my loss of liberty.

SONG

My silks and fine array,
    My smiles and languish'd air,
By love are driv'n away;
    And mournful lean Despair
Brings me yew to deck my grave: 5
Such end true lovers have.

His face is fair as heav'n,
    When springing buds unfold;

---

[1] Fervor.

O why to him was't giv'n
  Whose heart is wintry cold?   10
His breast is love's all worship'd tomb,
Where all love's pilgrims come.

Bring me an ax and spade,
  Bring me a winding sheet;
When I my grave have made,   15
  Let winds and tempests beat:
Then down I'll lie as cold as clay.
True love doth pass away!

MAD SONG

The wild winds weep,
  And the night is a-cold;
Come hither, Sleep,
  And my griefs unfold:
But lo! the morning peeps   5
Over the eastern steeps,
And the rustling beds of dawn
The earth do scorn.

Lo! to the vault
  Of pavèd heaven,   10
With sorrow fraught
  My notes are driven:
They strike the ear of night,
Make weep the eyes of day;
They make mad the roaring winds,   15
And with tempests play.

Like a fiend in a cloud,
  With howling woe
After night I do croud,[2]
  And with night will go;   20
I turn my back to the east,
From whence comforts have increas'd;
For light doth seize my brain
With frantic pain.

TO THE MUSES

Whether on Ida's[3] shady brow,
  Or in the chambers of the East,
The chambers of the sun, that now
  From antient melody have ceas'd;

---

[2] Crowd, press on.
[3] The gods of classical mythology visited Mt. Ida, near Troy;
Blake is unwarranted, however, in making it a haunt of the
Muses.—The complaint of the final stanza is against the neoclassical poetry of the century.

Whether in Heav'n ye wander fair,   5
  Or the green corners of the earth,
Or the blue regions of the air
  Where the melodious winds have birth;

Whether on chrystal rocks ye rove,
  Beneath the bosom of the sea   10
Wand'ring in many a coral grove,
  Fair Nine, forsaking Poetry!

How have you left the antient love
  That bards of old enjoy'd in you!
The languid strings do scarcely move!   15
  The sound is forc'd, the notes are few!

from SONGS OF INNOCENCE

This was the first important example of Blake's "illuminated printing," as he termed his method. He etched the
text and the surrounding designs on thirty-one copper
plates, printed from these in monochrome, and then illuminated the pages in water color. *Songs of Innocence* was
offered for sale in 1789; *Songs of Experience,* produced in
the same way, was ready in 1794. Blake soon added a
general title page and issued the two sets together as *Songs
of Innocence and Experience: Shewing the Two Contrary
States of the Human Soul.*

INTRODUCTION

Piping down the valleys wild,
  Piping songs of pleasant glee,
On a cloud I saw a child,
  And he laughing said to me:

"Pipe a song about a Lamb!"   5
  So I piped with merry chear.
"Piper, pipe that song again";
  So I piped: he wept to hear.

"Drop thy pipe, thy happy pipe;
  Sing thy songs of happy chear!"   10
So I sang the same again,
  While he wept with joy to hear.

"Piper, sit thee down and write
  In a book, that all may read."
So he vanish'd from my sight,   15
  And I pluck'd a hollow reed,

And I made a rural pen,
  And I stain'd the water clear,
And I wrote my happy songs
  Every child may joy to hear.   20

THE LAMB

Little Lamb, who made thee?
  Dost thou know who made thee?
Gave thee life, and bid thee feed,
By the stream and o'er the mead;
Gave thee clothing of delight,   5
Softest clothing, wooly, bright;
Gave thee such a tender voice,
Making all the vales rejoice?
  Little Lamb, who made thee?
  Dost thou know who made thee?   10

  Little Lamb, I'll tell thee,
  Little Lamb, I'll tell thee:
He is callèd by thy name,
For he calls himself a Lamb,
He is meek, and he is mild;   15
He became a little child.
I a child, and thou a lamb,
We are callèd by his name.
  Little Lamb, God bless thee!
  Little Lamb, God bless thee!   20

INFANT JOY

"I have no name:
I am but two days old."
  What shall I call thee?
"I happy am,
Joy is my name."   5
  Sweet joy befall thee!

Pretty joy!
Sweet joy, but two days old.
  Sweet joy I call thee:
Thou dost smile,   10
I sing the while,
  Sweet joy befall thee!

THE LITTLE BLACK BOY

My mother bore me in the southern wild,
And I am black, but O my soul is white;
White as an angel is the English child,
But I am black, as if bereav'd of light.

My mother taught me underneath a tree,   5
And sitting down before the heat of day,
She took me on her lap and kissèd me,
And, pointing to the east, began to say:

"Look on the rising sun—there God does live,
And gives his light, and gives his heat away;   10
And flowers and trees and beasts and men receive
Comfort in morning, joy in the noonday.

"And we are put on earth a little space,
That we may learn to bear the beams of love;
And these black bodies and this sunburnt face   15
Is but a cloud, and like a shady grove.

"For when our souls have learn'd the heat to bear,
The cloud will vanish; we shall hear his voice,
Saying: 'Come out from the grove, my love and care,
And round my golden tent like lambs rejoice.'"   20

Thus did my mother say, and kissèd me;
And thus I say to little English boy.
When I from black and he from white cloud free,
And round the tent of God like lambs we joy,

I'll shade him from the heat, till he can bear   25
To lean in joy upon our father's knee;
And then I'll stand and stroke his silver hair,
And be like him, and he will then love me.

A CRADLE SONG

Sweet dreams, form a shade
O'er my lovely infant's head;
Sweet dreams of pleasant streams
By happy, silent, moony beams.

Sweet sleep, with soft down   5
Weave thy brows an infant crown.
Sweet sleep, Angel mild,
Hover o'er my happy child.

Sweet smiles, in the night
Hover over my delight;   10
Sweet smiles, Mother's smiles,
All the livelong night beguiles.

Sweet moans, dovelike sighs,
Chase not slumber from thy eyes.
Sweet moans, sweeter smiles,   15
All the dovelike moans beguiles.

Sleep, sleep, happy child,
All creation slept and smil'd;
Sleep, sleep, happy sleep,
While o'er thee thy mother weep.   20

Sweet babe, in thy face
Holy image I can trace.
Sweet babe, once like thee,
Thy maker lay and wept for me,

Wept for me, for thee, for all,   25
When he was an infant small.
Thou his image ever see,
Heavenly face that smiles on thee,

Smiles on thee, on me, on all;
Who became an infant small.   30
Infant smiles are his own smiles;
Heaven and earth to peace beguiles.

THE CHIMNEY SWEEPER

When my mother died I was very young,
And my father sold me while yet my tongue
Could scarcely cry "'weep! 'weep! 'weep! 'weep!"
So your chimneys I sweep, and in soot I sleep.

There's little Tom Dacre, who cried when his head,   5
That curl'd like a lamb's back, was shav'd: so I said
"Hush, Tom! never mind it, for when your head's bare
You know that the soot cannot spoil your white hair."

And so he was quiet, and that very night,
As Tom was a-sleeping, he had such a sight!   10
That thousands of sweepers, Dick, Joe, Ned, and Jack,
Were all of them lock'd up in coffins of black.

And by came an Angel who had a bright key,
And he open'd the coffins and set them all free;
Then down a green plain leaping, laughing, they run,   15
And wash in a river, and shine in the Sun.

Then naked and white, all their bags left behind,
They rise upon clouds and sport in the wind;
And the Angel told Tom, if he'd be a good boy,
He'd have God for his father, and never want joy.   20

And so Tom awoke; and we rose in the dark,
And got with our bags and our brushes to work.
Tho' the morning was cold, Tom was happy and warm:
So if all do their duty they need not fear harm.

from SONGS OF EXPERIENCE

THE TYGER

Tyger! Tyger! burning bright
In the forests of the night,

What immortal hand or eye
Could frame thy fearful symmetry?

In what distant deeps or skies   5
Burnt the fire of thine eyes?
On what wings dare he aspire?
What the hand dare seize the fire?

And what shoulder, and what art,
Could twist the sinews of thy heart?   10
And when thy heart began to beat,
What dread hand? and what dread feet?[4]

What the hammer? what the chain?
In what furnace was thy brain?
What the anvil? what dread grasp   15
Dare its deadly terrors clasp?

When the stars threw down their spears,
And water'd heaven with their tears,
Did he smile his work to see?
Did he who made the Lamb make thee?   20

Tyger! Tyger! burning bright
In the forests of the night,
What immortal hand or eye
Dare frame thy fearful symmetry?

THE CLOD AND THE PEBBLE

"Love seeketh not Itself to please,
    Nor for itself hath any care,
But for another gives its ease,
    And builds a Heaven in Hell's despair."

So sung a little Clod of Clay,   5
    Trodden with the cattle's feet,
But a Pebble of the brook
    Warbled out these metres meet:

"Love seeketh only Self to please,
    To bind another to Its delight,   10
Joys in another's loss of ease,
    And builds a Hell in Heaven's despite."

[4] Blake's manuscript shows that he originally intended the sentence beginning in lines 11 and 12 to run on into another stanza, opening "Could fetch it from the furnace deep?" Although he decided to cancel that stanza, he was unwilling to discard the powerful but now incomplete line 12, the punctuation of which he therefore altered to two question marks.

A POISON TREE

I was angry with my friend:
I told my wrath, my wrath did end.
I was angry with my foe:
I told it not, my wrath did grow.

And I water'd it in fears,   5
Night and morning with my tears;
And I sunnèd it with smiles,
And with soft deceitful wiles.

And it grew both day and night,
Till it bore an apple bright;   10
And my foe beheld it shine,
And he knew that it was mine,

And into my garden stole
When the night had veil'd the pole:
In the morning glad I see   15
My foe outstretch'd beneath the tree.

AH, SUN-FLOWER

Ah, Sun-flower! weary of time,
   Who countest the steps of the Sun,
Seeking after that sweet golden clime
   Where the traveller's journey is done:

Where the Youth pined away with desire,   5
   And the pale Virgin shrouded in snow,
Arise from their graves, and aspire
   Where my Sun-flower wishes to go.

THE GARDEN OF LOVE

I went to the Garden of Love,
   And saw what I never had seen:
A Chapel was built in the midst,
   Where I used to play on the green.

And the gates of this Chapel were shut,   5
   And "Thou shalt not" writ over the door;
So I turn'd to the Garden of Love
   That so many sweet flowers bore;

And I saw it was fillèd with graves,
   And tomb-stones where flowers should be;   10
And Priests in black gowns were walking their
      rounds,
And binding with briars my joys and desires.

A LITTLE BOY LOST

"Nought loves another as itself,
   Nor venerates another so,
Nor is it possible to Thought
   A greater than itself to know:

"And Father, how can I love you   5
   Or any of my brothers more?
I love you like the little bird
   That picks up crumbs around the door."

The Priest sat by and heard the child,
   In trembling zeal he seiz'd his hair: 10
He led him by his little coat,
   And all admir'd the priestly care.

And standing on the altar high,
   "Lo! what a fiend is here," said he,
"One who sets reason up for judge   15
   Of our most holy Mystery."

The weeping child could not be heard,
   The weeping parents wept in vain;
They strip'd him to his little shirt,
   And bound him in an iron chain;   20

And burn'd him in a holy place,
   Where many had been burn'd before:
The weeping parents wept in vain.
   Are such things done on Albion's[5] shore?

INFANT SORROW

My mother groan'd! my father wept.
Into the dangerous world I leapt:
Helpless, naked, piping loud:
Like a fiend hid in a cloud.

Struggling in my father's hands,   5
Striving against my swadling bands,
Bound and weary I thought best
To sulk upon my mother's breast.

LONDON

I wander thro' each charter'd street,
   Near where the charter'd Thames does flow,
And mark in every face I meet
   Marks of weakness, marks of woe.

---

[5] England's.

In every cry of every Man,   5
    In every Infant's cry of fear,
In every voice, in every ban,
    The mind-forg'd manacles I hear.

How the Chimney sweeper's cry
    Every black'ning Church appalls;   10
And the hapless Soldier's sigh
    Runs in blood down Palace walls.

But most thro' midnight streets I hear
    How the youthful Harlot's curse
Blasts the new-born Infant's tear,   15
    And blights with plagues the Marriage hearse.

THE CHIMNEY SWEEPER

A little black thing among the snow,
    Crying "'weep! 'weep!" in notes of woe!
"Where are thy father and mother? say?"
    "They are both gone up to the church to pray.

"Because I was happy upon the heath,   5
    And smil'd among the winter's snow,
They clothèd me in the clothes of death,
    And taught me to sing the notes of woe.

"And because I am happy and dance and sing,
    They think they have done me no injury,   10
And are gone to praise God and his Priest and King,
    Who make up a heaven of our misery."

POEMS FROM MANUSCRIPTS

The Rossetti Manuscript (so called because it belonged for
a time to the Victorian poet Dante Gabriel Rossetti) is the
commonplace-book in which Blake composed many of
his poems (cf. note 4). Some he never printed, among
them the first three of the following. Although an editor
should normally accept his author's final wording,
"Never seek to tell thy love" is given as it stood before
Blake's alterations. The earlier version is far better, and
we have no reason to suppose that Blake's revision was
final. "A Cradle Song" was evidently intended for *Songs
of Experience,* as a contrast to the poem with the same
title in *Songs of Innocence;* but for some reason the poet did
not use it.

NEVER SEEK TO TELL THY LOVE

Never seek to tell thy love,
    Love that never told can be;
For the gentle wind doth move
    Silently, invisibly.

I told my love, I told my love,   5
    I told her all my heart,
Trembling, cold, in ghastly fears,
    Ah! she doth depart.

Soon as she was gone from me,
    A traveller came by,   10
Silently, invisibly:
    He took her with a sigh.

A CRADLE SONG

Sleep! sleep! beauty bright,
Dreaming o'er the joys of night;
Sleep! sleep! in thy sleep
Little sorrows sit and weep.

Sweet Babe, in thy face   5
Soft desires I can trace,
Secret joys and secret smiles,
Little pretty infant wiles.

As thy softest limbs I feel,
Smiles as of the morning steal   10
O'er thy cheek, and o'er thy breast
Where thy little heart does rest.

O! the cunning wiles that creep
In thy little heart asleep.
When thy little heart does wake   15
Then the dreadful lightnings break,

From thy cheek and from thy eye,
O'er the youthful harvests nigh.
Infant wiles and infant smiles
Heaven and Earth of peace beguiles.   20

ETERNITY

He who bends to himself a Joy
Does the wingèd life destroy;
But he who kisses the Joy as it flies
Lives in Eternity's sunrise.

AUGURIES OF INNOCENCE

This disjointed but powerful poem was left unfinished and unpublished by Blake. The Pickering Manuscript, in which it appears, gets its name from an owner. These couplets were probably written about 1803. They may have been intended simply as jottings from which several poems might later be drawn.

To see a World in a Grain of Sand
And a Heaven in a Wild Flower,
Hold Infinity in the palm of your hand
And Eternity in an hour.

A Robin Redbreast in a Cage   5
Puts all Heaven in a Rage.
A dove-house fill'd with Doves and Pigeons
Shudders Hell thro' all its regions.
A dog starv'd at his Master's Gate
Predicts the ruin of the State.   10
A Horse misus'd upon the Road
Calls to Heaven for Human blood.
Each outcry of the hunted Hare
A fibre from the Brain does tear.
A Skylark wounded in the wing,   15
A Cherubim does cease to sing;
The Game Cock clip'd and arm'd for fight
Does the Rising Sun affright.
Every Wolf's and Lion's howl
Raises from Hell a Human Soul.   20
The wild Deer, wand'ring here and there,
Keeps the Human Soul from Care.
The Lamb misus'd breeds Public Strife
And yet forgives the Butcher's Knife.
The Bat that flits at close of Eve   25
Has left the Brain that won't Believe.
The Owl that calls upon the Night
Speaks the Unbeliever's fright.
He who shall hurt the little Wren
Shall never be belov'd by Men.   30
He who the Ox[6] to wrath has mov'd
Shall never be by Woman lov'd.
The wanton Boy that kills the Fly
Shall feel the Spider's enmity.
He who torments the Chafer's Sprite[7]   35
Weaves a Bower in endless Night.
The Caterpillar on the Leaf
Repeats to thee thy Mother's grief.

[6] A London custom, which persisted as late as the second quarter of the nineteenth century, was to turn an ox loose in the street, torment it into a frenzy, and finally hunt it down and kill it.
[7] Beetle's spirit.

Kill not the Moth nor Butterfly,
For the Last Judgment draweth nigh.   40
He who shall train the Horse to War
Shall never pass the Polar Bar.
The Beggar's Dog and Widow's Cat,
Feed them and thou wilt grow fat.
The Gnat that sings his Summer's Song   45
Poison gets from Slander's tongue.
The poison of the Snake and Newt
Is the sweat of Envy's Foot.
The poison of the Honey Bee
Is the Artist's Jealousy.   50
The Prince's Robes and Beggar's Rags
Are Toadstools on the Miser's Bags.
A Truth that's told with bad intent
Beats all the Lies you can invent.
It is right it should be so;   55
Man was made for Joy and Woe;
And when this we rightly know,
Thro' the World we safely go.
Joy and Woe are woven fine,
A Clothing for the Soul divine.   60
Under every grief and pine
Runs a joy with silken twine.
The Babe is more than Swadling Bands;
Throughout all these Human Lands
Tools were made, and Born were hands,   65
Every Farmer Understands.
Every Tear from Every Eye
Becomes a Babe in Eternity;
This is caught by Females bright,
And return'd to its own delight.   70
The Bleat, the Bark, Bellow, and Roar
Are Waves that beat on Heaven's Shore.
The Babe that weeps the Rod beneath
Writes Revenge in realms of Death.
The Beggar's Rags, fluttering in Air,   75
Does to Rags the Heavens tear.
The Soldier, arm'd with Sword and Gun,
Palsied strikes the Summer's Sun.
The poor Man's Farthing is worth more
Than all the Gold on Afric's Shore.   80
One Mite wrung from the Lab'rer's hands
Shall buy and sell the Miser's Lands;
Or, if protected from on high,
Does that whole Nation sell and buy.
He who mocks the Infant's Faith   85
Shall be mock'd in Age and Death.
He who shall teach the Child to Doubt
The rotting Grave shall ne'er get out.
He who respects the Infant's faith
Triumphs over Hell and Death.   90

The Child's Toys and the Old Man's Reasons
Are the Fruits of the Two Seasons.
The Questioner, who sits so sly,
Shall never know how to Reply.
He who replies to words of Doubt   95
Doth put the Light of Knowledge out.
The Strongest Poison ever known
Came from Caesar's Laurel Crown.
Nought can Deform the Human Race
Like to the Armour's iron brace.   100
When Gold and Gems adorn the Plow
To peaceful Arts shall Envy bow.
A Riddle or the Cricket's Cry
Is to Doubt a fit Reply.
The Emmet's[8] Inch and Eagle's Mile   105
Make Lame Philosophy to smile.
He who Doubts from what he sees
Will ne'er Believe, do what you Please.
If the Sun and Moon should Doubt,
They'd immediately Go Out.   110
To be in a Passion you Good may do,
But no Good if a Passion is in you.
The Whore and Gambler, by the State
Licens'd, build that Nation's Fate.
The Harlot's cry from Street to Street   115
Shall weave Old England's winding Sheet.
The Winner's shout, the Loser's Curse,
Dance before dead England's Hearse.
Every Night and every Morn
Some to Misery are Born.   120
Every Morn and every Night
Some are Born to Sweet Delight.
Some are Born to Sweet Delight,
Some are Born to Endless Night.
We are led to Believe a Lie   125
When we see not Thro' the Eye,
Which was Born in a Night to perish in a Night,
When the Soul Slept in Beams of Light.

God appears and God is light
To those poor Souls who dwell in Night,   130
But does a Human Form Display
To those who Dwell in Realms of Day.

from MILTON

*Milton: A Poem in 2 Books: To Justify the Ways of God to
Men* was "written and etched, 1804–1808." It is one of
Blake's "Prophetic Books," which are frankly didactic as
well as obscurely symbolical. The Preface denounces the
literature of pagan antiquity: "Rouze up, O Young Men
of the New Age! . . . We do not want either Greek or
Roman Models if we are but just and true to our own
Imaginations, those Worlds of Eternity in which we shall
live for ever in JESUS OUR LORD." The flaming stanzas
which follow, also from the Preface, have been set to
music and are often sung at public meetings of liberals in
England.

And did those feet in ancient time
    Walk upon England's mountains green?
And was the holy Lamb of God
    On England's pleasant pastures seen?

And did the Countenance Divine   5
    Shine forth upon our clouded hills?
And was Jerusalem builded here
    Among these dark Satanic mills?

Bring me my Bow of burning gold!
    Bring me my Arrows of desire!   10
Bring me my Spear! O clouds, unfold!
    Bring me my Chariot of fire!

I will not cease from Mental Fight,
    Nor shall my Sword sleep in my hand,
Till we have built Jerusalem   15
    In England's green and pleasant Land.

Robert Burns

1759–1796

BURNS lived only thirty-seven years, but long enough to
become indisputably Scotland's foremost poet. His life
falls entirely within the latter half of the eighteenth century. Yet, despite occasional conformity to neoclassical
literary patterns, he usually rejected them; and in his
passion for freedom, his respect for the common man, his
knowledge of nature and love of natural beauty, his

interest in local traditions and folklore, and, above all, his
faith in emotion and instinct as higher guides than reason,
he is thoroughly Romantic. Though he was familiar with
many of the earlier English writers, especially those of his
own century, his art was derived less from them than
from Scottish poets whose names are now almost or quite
forgotten. Sometimes an old song would strike his fancy,

---

[8] Ant's.

and he would make it his own through rewriting it with the indescribable touch by which genius turns mediocre things into perfection. The traditional airs of his country deeply moved him; some of his finest lyrics were inspired by them. Aside from the songs, his best verse sprang as directly as any art can from the soil, straight out of the life he knew in his native Ayrshire.

That Burns is greatly loved wherever English is read or sung is the more remarkable because his poems are full of words strange to most readers. The braid (broad) Scots is not a separate language, but a Scottish form of English; it has nothing to do with Gaelic, a Celtic tongue spoken in the Highlands. Burns's idiom is simply that dialect of English commonly used in southern Scotland. A special effort is required to get behind the linguistic veil. First, you are advised to go slowly through a poem, looking when necessary at the glosses in the footnotes. Then, with the meaning of the Scottish words well in mind, read it again rapidly, for its swing and savor, its humor or beauty. If you adopt this simple method, the dialect will soon cease to hamper enjoyment and may even become an additional source of pleasure.

Along with many Scottish liberals, Burns hated the iron hand of Calvinism, or at any rate of the state church that John Knox had established. It was, subject to the Parliament in far-off Westminster, the dominant force in Scotland. Over the private lives of his parishioners the local minister, appointed for life, exercised a tyrannical power. Offenders against the prevailing concepts of morality and orthodoxy were tried by a church court called the Session, consisting of the minister and two of his assistants, the Elders. Delegates from the churches of a district formed the Presbytery, which could excommunicate. Over a group of Presbyteries was the Synod, and over the Synods the annual General Assembly at Edinburgh. This system was able to put tremendous pressure on an individual; but already a relatively liberal group, the New Lichts, was opposing the rigid conservatism of the Auld Lichts. With some of the New Licht ministers Burns was on excellent terms. A good deal of his verse will be better understood if viewed in relation to this ecclesiastical background. However he rebelled against it, Burns was in part a product of Presbyterianism; his father was a religious man and brought his children up in it. For all his satirical freedom with the clergy, the poet was a believer to the extent of being a Deist. His shafts were aimed at hypocrisy, not religion.

As for his political views, he was obliged for his children's sake to keep quiet in public when, toward the close of his life, an expression of sympathy with France might have cost any government employee his job and even his liberty. But his approval of the French Revolution, and consequently his desire for reform at home, appear in a private letter as late as 1794. "What is there,"

he wrote of the execution of Louis and his queen, "in delivering over a perjured blockhead and an unprincipled prostitute to the hands of the hangman, that it should arrest . . . attention?" He was stirred to a nobler expression of his revolutionary sentiments in "Scots, wha hae"; and Liberty, Equality, and Fraternity, as well as the reading of Tom Paine, lurk behind "For A' That." As a romantic Scot, Burns sometimes indulged a sentimental and highly inconsistent Jacobitism. Yet he professed loyalty to the principles of 1688, and in an endorsement of our own Revolution predicted that July 4 would be a sacred date to American posterity.

The oldest of seven children, he was born in 1759 in southwestern Scotland at Alloway, two miles south of Ayr, in a two-room cottage still standing. His father, a gardener on a near-by estate, had built it of clay and thatch with his own hands. The cow shed and stable were under the same roof as the dwelling. Mrs. Burns was illiterate, but her head was well stocked with the old songs and ballads. Her husband was a man of character, who took the lead in finding a youth to keep school in the neighborhood, and later, when no schooling was procurable, did his best to teach his children himself. Robert was seven at the time of the first of several removals, never far from Ayr, to places where his father tried to find subsistence as a tenant farmer. From time to time, when their services could be spared, Robert and the next son, Gilbert, got a few weeks at school somewhere. Of more importance were their father's talk and their reading under his guidance. By the time he was fourteen Robert was doing, to the permanent injury of his health, a man's work on the farm. Land rents were inflated. The whole family labored; but faithful toil and acceptance of grinding poverty were not enough to avert bankruptcy and a forced sale of their goods shortly before the poet's father died in 1784. That event left Robert head of the family; and he and Gilbert decided to move again, to make a fresh start at a farm called Mossgiel in the parish of Mauchline, ten miles northeast of Ayr.

Meanwhile, though he had known cruel hardship, and never received much formal instruction, Burns had not been growing up a mere clodhopper. All his life he read widely and intelligently. Wherever he went, the brilliance of his conversation fascinated everyone. In Tarbolton, a village near the farm where he lived in his early twenties, he helped organize a convivial and debating society known as the Bachelors' Club. Later he joined the Masons. His instincts were warmly social; he liked people, and they liked him. His friends, even before the publication of his first book, included men of professional standing as well as reputable businessmen in and near Ayr.

Many of Burns's best poems were written at Mossgiel. In the town of Mauchline his amorous propensities soon brought him a notoriety less pleasing than the local fame achieved by the circulation of his manuscripts. Sensitive, responsive, and passionate, he was always entangled with one or more women. His youthful attitude, though graced by his talent for verse, was essentially the simple, earthy realism of the peasant, with all the peasant's ignorance that love is not a simple thing. Burns was twenty-six when the first of his illegitimate children was born; the mother was a servant in his own household. Even before the birth of this child, Burns had begun another and much more serious affair with Jean Armour, the daughter of a Mauchline contractor. Under Scottish law a promise, even without witnesses, could constitute a legal marriage. Burns seems to have given Jean some sort of written acknowledgment; but to his chagrin her father thought that wedlock with him was likely to prove more calamitous than the prospect of a child born out of wedlock. Armour induced a lawyer to mutilate the document; Robert and Jean underwent public penance at the Mauchline church; and Daddy Auld, the minister, formally pronounced Burns a bachelor.

Meanwhile the poet had decided to emigrate to Jamaica. He wished to leave a name behind him in Scotland; and in 1786 at the Ayrshire town of Kilmarnock he published by subscription the 612 copies of *Poems, Chiefly in the Scottish Dialect*. It attracted more attention than he expected. He dropped the idea of leaving Scotland, and decided to seek a wider audience in the capital. At Edinburgh that winter he scored a personal success. He was received in the best society, was made much of in academic circles, found influential friends, and in 1787 brought out another subscription edition of his poems with some new ones added. This book was also published in London; its popularity throughout Great Britain was immediate, and within two years pirated editions appeared in Ireland and the United States. Burns spent a good deal of the following summer touring the Border country and the Highlands, and then returned to Edinburgh for a second winter. During his brief career there he became acquainted with James Johnson, an engraver who was an enthusiast for Scottish folksong. Johnson was publishing the first of six volumes entitled *The Scots Musical Museum*. Of this work Burns became, purely as a labor of love and patriotism, practically the editor; and for tunes unfurnished with suitable words he composed, or adapted from old songs, a number of lyrics, including some of his best. He also contributed (among other pieces "Scots, wha hae") to another enterprise, *A Select Collection of Scottish Airs*. The adulation he received in Edinburgh did not spoil him. He estimated its worth shrewdly, well aware that with a few exceptions his flatterers were principally interested in the novelty of a plowman poet, and that their interest would soon languish.

Meanwhile the liaison with Jean had continued; now that Burns was famous, the Armours wanted him to marry her. She had already borne him two sets of twins, of whom only one child had survived. Jean was in no respect the poet's equal, nor had she any comprehension of his genius. But in his fashion he loved her, and in 1788 he decided to set matters right by marrying her. Although she could not share his inner life, she made him a faithful wife. Friends got him a post in the Excise as a gauger; he was what we would call an internal revenue agent. He took Jean to the farm of Ellisland, six miles outside the shire town of Dumfries, hoping to make a livelihood by combining his duties as Exciseman with farming, and yet retain enough leisure to go on with his poetry. Unfortunately, economic conditions were then extremely unfavorable to the tenant farmer; Ellisland's 170 acres drained Burns of his little capital. (He had managed to keep for his own use only a small amount of the proceeds from his books, and on bad advice had sold the copyright for all future printings at the absurd figure of a hundred guineas.) He was a skillful and intelligent agriculturalist, and he worked hard; but by 1791 he knew he was beaten, and moved into Dumfries. He now had three surviving sons by Jean; later on there were a daughter and another son, and two of Burns's illegitimate children were also reared in the household. Burns was promoted to a better place in the Excise and his salary was increased, but it was still small, and it was all he had during the five years that remained to him. Though his duties were also increased, he went on writing poetry to the end. A two-volume edition came out in 1793; among the new poems, for which he received nothing from the publisher, was the immortal "Tam o' Shanter."

Early biographers spread the legend that Burns was brought to his early grave by drink. His faults certainly included some fondness for the bottle, then a universal failing, but Burns was not a drunkard. His high reputation for efficiency and reliability is on record in the Excise Office. During the final years in Dumfries he was honored by official and semiofficial acts of recognition; he was esteemed as a distinguished citizen, and for a time was Senior Warden of the Masonic lodge. He was a hard-working man, devoted to his children, and in money matters both generous and responsible. His death in 1796 was from heart disease, probably caused by the hardships of his youth, and certainly not alleviated by the financial worries that constantly pressed upon him. He had his first attack at Mossgiel when he was twenty-five.

The poems are available in many reprints, some of which incorporate liberties taken with the text by early editors. The standard edition is by W. E. Henley and T. F. Henderson (4 vols., 1896–97). The best Life is by F. B. Snyder (1932). De L. Ferguson's *Pride and Passion* (1939) is an important biographical study. See also D. Daiches, *Robert Burns* (1951). Professor Ferguson has edited the letters (2 vols., 1931).

Robert Burns

MARY MORISON

The following selections appear in the order of their composition, as far as that is known. This poem was written when Burns was about twenty-one.

O Mary, at thy window be!
  It is the wish'd, the trysted hour.
Those smiles and glances let me see,
  That make the miser's treasure poor.
How blythely wad I bide the stoure,[1]   5
A weary slave frae[2] sun to sun,
  Could I the rich reward secure—
  The lovely Mary Morison!

Yestreen, when to the trembling string
  The dance gaed[3] thro' the lighted ha',[4]   10
To thee my fancy took its wing,
  I sat, but neither heard or saw:
Tho' this was fair, and that was braw,[5]
  And yon the toast of a'[6] the town,
I sigh'd and said amang them a':—   15
  "Ye are na Mary Morison!"

O Mary, canst thou wreck his peace
  Wha[7] for thy sake wad gladly die?[8]
Or canst thou break that heart of his
  Whase only faut[9] is loving thee?   20
If love for love thou wilt na gie,[10]
  At least be pity to me shown:
A thought ungentle canna be
  The thought o' Mary Morison.

GREEN GROW THE RASHES, O

Among the inspirations of this gay lyric, composed when Burns was about twenty-five, was an old song describing how "green grow the rashes, O" and how superior they are to feather beds.

CHORUS

Green grow the rashes,[1] O;
  Green grow the rashes, O;
The sweetest hours that e'er I spend,
  Are spent among the lasses, O.

There's nought but care on ev'ry han',   5
  In every hour that passes, O:
What signifies the life o' man,
  An' 'twere na for the lasses, O.

The war'ly race[2] may riches chase,
  An' riches still may fly them, O;   10
An' tho' at last they catch them fast,
  Their hearts can ne'er enjoy them, O.

But gie me a cannie[3] hour at e'en,
  My arms about my dearie, O,
An' war'ly cares an' war'ly men   15
  May a' gae tapsalteerie,[4] O!

For you sae douce,[5] ye sneer at this;
  Ye're nought but senseless asses, O;
The wisest man the warl' e'er saw,[6]
  He dearly lov'd the lasses, O.   20

Auld[7] Nature swears, the lovely dears
  Her noblest work she classes, O:
Her prentice han' she try'd on man,
  An' then she made the lasses, O.

HOLY WILLIE'S PRAYER

The subject of this brilliant satire (unpublished till after Burns's death) is William Fisher (1737–1809), an elder and a meddling member of the Session of the church at Mauchline. Burns explains in a note that in 1785 Gavin Hamilton, whom Fisher and the minister had accused of "habitual neglect of church ordinances," appealed to the Presbytery of Ayr, which proceeded to acquit him. Fisher having lost his case, "the Muse overheard him at his devotions." It was from Hamilton, a friend, that Burns subleased the farm of Mossgiel.

O Thou, that in the Heavens does dwell,
  Wha, as it pleases best Thysel',
Sends ane[1] to Heaven and ten to Hell,
    A' for Thy glory,
And no for ony guid[2] or ill   5
    They've done before Thee!

I bless and praise Thy matchless might,
  When thousands Thou hast left in night,

---

[1] Would I abide the dust, i.e., endure the struggle.   [2] From.
[3] Went.   [4] Hall.
[5] Fine, handsome (in person or dress).   [6] All.   [7] Who.
[8] Pronounce *dee*.   [9] Fault.   [10] Give.
[1] Rushes.

[2] Worldly folk.   [3] Quiet.   [4] Go topsy-turvy.
[5] As for you, so serious.   [6] I.e., Solomon.   [7] Old.
[1] One.   [2] Any good.

That I am here before Thy sight,
      For gifts an' grace   10
A burning an' a shining light,
      To a' this place.

What was I, or my generation,
That I should get sic[3] exaltation?
I, wha deserv'd most just damnation   15
      For broken laws
Sax thousand years ere my creation,
      Thro' Adam's cause!

When frae my mither's womb I fell,
Thou might hae plung'd me deep in hell,   20
To gnash my gooms, and weep, and wail
      In burning lakes,
Where damnèd devils roar and yell,
      Chain'd to their stakes.

Yet I am here a chosen sample,
To show Thy grace is great and ample: 25
I'm here a pillar o' Thy temple,
      Strong as a rock,
A guide, a buckler, and example
      To a' Thy flock!   30

O Lord, Thou kens[4] what zeal I bear
When drinkers drink, an' swearers swear,
An' singin' here and dancin' there
      Wi' great an' sma';
For I am keepit by Thy fear[5]   35
      Free frae them a'.

But yet, O Lord! confess I must:
At times I'm fash'd[6] wi' fleshy lust;
An' sometimes, too, in warldly trust,
      Vile self gets in;   40
But Thou remembers we are dust,
      Defiled wi' sin.

O Lord! yestreen, Thou kens, wi' Meg—
Thy pardon I sincerely beg—
O, may 't ne'er be a living plague   45
      To my dishonor!
An' I'll ne'er lift a lawless leg
      Again upon her.

Besides, I farther maun[7] avow—
Wi' Leezzie's lass, three times, I trow—   50

But, Lord, that Friday I was fou,[8]
      When I cam near her,
Or else, Thou kens, Thy servant true
      Wad[9] never steer[10] her.

May be Thou lets this fleshly thorn   55
Buffet Thy servant e'en and morn,
Lest he owre[11] proud and high should turn
      That he's sae gifted:
If sae, Thy han' maun e'en be borne
      Until Thou lift it.   60

Lord, bless Thy chosen in this place,
For here Thou has a chosen race!
But God confound their stubborn face
      An' blast their name,
Wha bring Thy elders to disgrace,   65
      An' open shame!

Lord, mind Gau'n Hamilton's deserts:
He drinks, an' swears, an' plays at cartes,
Yet has sae monie takin[12] arts
      Wi' great and sma',   70
Frae God's ain Priest[13] the people's hearts
      He steals awa'.

And when we chasten'd him therefore,
Thou kens how he bred sic a splore,[14]
And set the warld[15] in a roar   75
      O' laughin at us:
Curse Thou his basket and his store,
      Kail[16] an' potatoes!

Lord, hear my earnest cry and pray'r
Against that Presbyt'ry o' Ayr!   80
Thy strong right hand, Lord, make it bare
      Upo' their heads!
Lord, visit them, an' dinna[17] spare,
      For their misdeeds!

O Lord, my God! that glib-tongu'd Aiken,[18]   85
My vera heart and flesh are quakin,
To think how we stood sweatin, shakin,
      An' pish'd[19] wi' dread,
While he, wi' hingin[20] lip an' snakin,[21]
      Held up his head.   90

---

[8] Full, drunk.   [9] Would.   [10] Touch.
[11] Over, too.   [12] So many taking.
[13] William Auld, the minister at Mauchline.   [14] Row.
[15] Pronounce as a dissyllable by trilling the r.
[16] Cabbage.—One of the charges against Hamilton was that he had ordered his servants to dig potatoes on a Sunday.
[17] Do not.   [18] Robert Aiken, of Ayr, Hamilton's counsel.
[19] Subjected to contempt.   [20] Hanging.   [21] Sneering.

---

[3] Such.   [4] Knowest.   [5] Kept by fear of Thee.
[6] Troubled.   [7] Must.

Lord, in Thy day o' vengeance try him!
Lord, visit him wha did employ him!
And pass not in Thy mercy by them,
      Nor hear their pray'r,
But for Thy people's sake destroy them,   95
      An' dinna spare!

But, Lord, remember me and mine
Wi' mercies temporal and divine,
That I for grace an' gear[22] may shine
      Excell'd by nane;   100
And a' the glory shall be Thine—
      Amen, Amen!

EPISTLE TO J. LAPRAIK

AN OLD SCOTTISH BARD, APRIL 1, 1785

This is the first of three poetic epistles to John Lapraik
(1727–1807), a poet who owned an estate in Ayrshire.

While briers an' woodbines budding green,
And paitricks scraichin[1] loud at e'en,
An' morning poussie[2] whiddin[3] seen,
      Inspire my Muse,
This freedom, in an unknown frien'   5
      I pray excuse.

On Fasten-e'en[4] we had a rockin,[5]
To ca' the crack[6] and weave our stockin;
And there was muckle[7] fun and jokin,
      Ye need na doubt;   10
At length we had a hearty yokin,[8]
      At "sang[9] about."

There was ae[10] sang, among the rest,
Aboon[11] them a' it pleas'd me best,
That some kind husband had addrest   15
      To some sweet wife:
It thirled[12] the heart-strings thro' the breast,
      A' to the life.

I've scarce heard ought describ'd sae weel,[13]
What gen'rous, manly bosoms feel;   20
Thought I, "Can this be Pope or Steele,
      Or Beattie's wark?"[14]

They tald me 'twas an odd kind chiel[15]
      About[16] Muirkirk.

It pat me fidgin-fain[17] to hear 't,   25
An' sae about him there I spier't;[18]
Then a' that kent[19] him round declar'd
      He had ingíne;[20]
That nane excell'd it, few cam near 't,
      It was sae fine: 30

That, set him to a pint of ale,
An' either douce or merry tale,
Or rhymes an' sangs he'd made himsel,
      Or witty catches,
'Tween Inverness an' Teviotdale,   35
      He had few matches.

Then up I gat, an' swoor an aith,[21]
Tho' I should pawn my pleugh an' graith,[22]
Or die a cadger pownie's[23] death,
      At some dyke-back,[24]   40
A pint an' gill I'd gie them baith,[25]
      To hear your crack.

But, first an' foremost, I should tell,
Amaist[26] as soon as I could spell,
I to the crambo-jingle[27] fell;   45
      Tho' rude an' rough—
Yet crooning to a body's sel,[28]
      Does weel eneugh.[29]

I am nae poet, in a sense;
But just a rhymer like by chance,   50
An' hae[30] to learning nae pretence;
      Yet, what the matter?
Whene'er my Muse does on me glance,
      I jingle at her.

Your critic-folk may cock their nose,   55
And say, "How can you e'er propose,
You wha ken hardly verse frae prose,
      To mak a sang?"
But, by your leaves, my learned foes,
      Ye're maybe wrang.   60

---

[22] Wealth.

[1] Partridges screeching.   [2] Pussy, hare.   [3] Scudding.
[4] The eve of Ash Wednesday, the first day of Lent.
[5] Social gathering. The women spin on the rock or distaff.
[6] Have ("call") a chat.   [7] Much.
[8] "Yoking," spell, bout.   [9] Song.   [10] One.
[11] Above.   [12] Thrilled.   [13] Which described so well.
[14] Work.—James Beattie (1735–1803), a Scottish poet and philosopher.

[15] Kind of fellow ("child").   [16] Near.
[17] It put me fidgeting with eagerness.   [18] Asked.
[19] Knew.   [20] Genius.   [21] Oath.
[22] Plow and implements.   [23] Hawker's pony's.
[24] Behind some fence.   [25] Both.   [26] Almost.
[27] Riming. *Crambo* is a riming game.   [28] One's self.
[29] Well enough.   [30] Have.

What's a' your jargon o' your Schools,
Your Latin names for horns an' stools?
If honest Nature made you fools,
      What sairs[31] your grammers?
Ye'd better taen[32] up spades and shools,[33]   65
      Or knappin-hammers.[34]

A set o' dull, conceited hashes[35]
Confuse their brains in college-classes,
They gang in stirks,[36] and come out asses,
      Plain truth to speak;   70
An' syne[37] they think to climb Parnassus[38]
      By dint o' Greek!

Gie me ae spark o' Nature's fire,
That's a' the learning I desire;
Then, tho' I drudge thro' dub[39] an' mire   75
      At pleugh or cart,
My Muse, tho' hamely[40] in attire,
      May touch the heart.

O for a spunk[41] o' Allan's[42] glee,[43]
Or Fergusson's,[44] the bauld an' slee,   80
Or bright Lapraik's, my friend to be,
      If I can hit it!
That would be lear[45] eneugh for me,
      If I could get it.

Now, sir, if ye hae friends enow,   85
Tho' real friends, I b'lieve, are few,
Yet, if your catalogue be fou,
      I'se no[46] insist:
But gif[47] ye want ae friend that's true
      I'm on your list.   90

I winna blaw[48] about mysel,
As ill I like my fauts to tell;
But friends, an' folks that wish me well,
      They sometimes roose[49] me;
Tho', I maun own, as mony still   95
      As far abuse me.

There's ae wee faut they whyles[50] lay to me,
I like the lasses—Gude[51] forgie me!
For mony a plack[52] they wheedle frae me,
      At dance or fair;   100
Maybe some ither thing they gie me,
      They weel can spare.

But Mauchline Race, or Mauchline Fair,
I should be proud to meet you there;
We'se gie ae night's discharge to care,   105
      If we forgather,
An' hae a swap o' rhymin'-ware
      Wi' ane anither.

The four-gill chap,[53] we'se gar[54] him clatter,
An' kirsen[55] him wi' reekin[56] water;   110
Syne we'll sit down an' tak our whitter,[57]
      To cheer our heart;
An' faith, we'se be acquainted better   *realistic*
      Before we part.

Awa, ye selfish war'ly race,   115
Wha think that havins,[58] sense, an' grace,
E'en love an' friendship, should give place
      To catch-the-plack![59]
I dinna like to see your face,
      Nor hear your crack.   120

But ye whom social pleasure charms,
Whose hearts the tide of kindness warms,
Who hold your being on the terms
      "Each aid the others,"
Come to my bowl, come to my arms,   125
      My friends, my brothers!

But to conclude my lang epistle,
As my auld pen's worn to the gristle;
Twa lines frae you wad gar me fissle,[60]
      Who am, most fervent,   130
While I can either sing or whistle,
      Your friend and servant.

---

[31] Serves, avails.   [32] Have taken.   [33] Shovels.
[34] Hammers for stone breaking.   [35] Oafs.
[36] Yearling cattle.   [37] Then.   [38] I.e., become poets.
[39] Puddle.   [40] Homely.   [41] Spark.
[42] Allan Ramsay. See under "Lesser Augustans," I, 824, above.
[43] Song.
[44] Robert Fergusson (1750–74), a Scottish poet who wrote some
  humorous verse; hence "bold and sly."   [45] Lore, learning.
[46] I'll not.   [47] If.   [48] I will not brag ("blow").
[49] Praise.

[50] Sometimes.   [51] God.
[52] An old Scottish coin, worth one-sixth of a cent.
[53] Fellow; i.e., the pint cup.   [54] We'll make.
[55] Christen.
[56] Smoking. Burns suggests a steaming hot toddy.
[57] Draught.   [58] Manners.   [59] I.e., dollar chasing.
[60] Make me fizz, effervesce, be exhilarated.

TO A MOUSE

ON TURNING HER UP IN HER NEST
WITH THE PLOUGH, NOVEMBER, 1785

Wee, sleekit,[1] cow'rin', tim'rous beastie,
O, what a panic's in thy breastie!
Thou need na start awa sae hasty,
    Wi' bickering brattle![2]
I wad be laith to rin[3] an' chase thee,   5
    Wi' murdering pattle![4]

I'm truly sorry man's dominion
Has broken Nature's social union,
An' justifies that ill opinion
    Which makes thee startle   10
At me, thy poor earth-born companion,
    An' fellow-mortal!

I doubt na, whyles,[5] but thou may thieve;
What then? poor beastie, thou maun live!
A daimen icker[6] in a thrave[7]   15
    'S a sma' request;
I'll get a blessin wi' the lave,[8]
    And never miss 't!

Thy wee-bit housie, too, in ruin!
Its silly wa's the win's are strewin'!   20
An' naething, now, to big[9] a new ane,
    O' foggage[10] green!
An' bleak December's win's ensuin',
    Baith snell[11] an' keen!

Thou saw the fields laid bare an' waste,   25
An' weary winter comin' fast,
An' cozie here, beneath the blast,
    Thou thought to dwell,
Till crash! the cruel coulter past
    Out thro' thy cell.   30

That wee bit heap o' leaves an' stibble[12]
Has cost thee monie a weary nibble!
Now thou's turned out, for a' thy trouble,
    But[13] house or hald,[14]
To thole[15] the winter's sleety dribble,   35
    An' cranreuch[16] cauld!

But, Mousie, thou art no thy lane,[17]
In proving foresight may be vain:
The best-laid schemes o' mice an' men
    Gang aft agley,[18]   40
An' lea'e us nought but grief an' pain,
    For promis'd joy!

Still thou art blest, compared wi' me!
The present only toucheth thee:
But och! I backward cast my e'e,   45
    On prospects drear!
An' forward, tho' I canna see,
    I guess an' fear!

THE COTTER'S SATURDAY NIGHT

Cotters or cottagers were small tenant-farmers. Composed in 1785, this homely glimpse of peasant life is one of Burns's best-loved poems. It is not, however, one of his masterpieces, being far from characteristic of his genius and among the most imitative of his writings. It is more English and less Scottish than his best things, with its reminiscences of Goldsmith, Thomson, Pope, Milton, and Gray. From the famous *Elegy* he prefixed, as a motto for his own poem, the stanza ending "The short and simple annals of the poor." Burns adopted an unfamiliar form, the Spenserian stanza; he had not yet read Spenser, but knew his Scottish imitators. The poem is dedicated to Robert Aiken, the "writer," i.e., lawyer, whose defense of Hamilton had frustrated the designs of Holy Willie.

My lov'd, my honor'd, much respected friend!
    No mercenary bard his homage pays;
With honest pride, I scorn each selfish end,
    My dearest meed, a friend's esteem and praise:
    To you I sing, in simple Scottish lays,   5
The lowly train in life's sequester'd scene;
    The native feelings strong, the guileless ways;
What Aiken in a cottage would have been;
Ah! tho' his worth unknown, far happier there I ween!

November chill blaws loud wi' angry sugh;[1]   10
    The short'ning winter-day is near a close;
The miry beasts retreating frae the pleugh;
    The black'ning trains o' craws to their repose:
    The toil-worn Cotter frae his labor goes—
This night his weekly moil is at an end,   15
    Collects his spades, his mattocks, and his hoes,
Hoping the morn in ease and rest to spend,
And weary, o'er the moor, his course does hameward
    bend.

---

[1] Sleek.   [2] Hasty scamper.   [3] Loath to run.
[4] Paddle, a kind of narrow spade for digging weeds, cleaning the plowshare, etc.   [5] At times.   [6] Occasional ear of grain.
[7] Twenty-four sheaves.   [8] Remnant.   [9] Build.
[10] Moss.   [11] Both harsh.   [12] Stubble.   [13] Without.
[14] Holding, possession.   [15] Endure.   [16] Hoarfrost.

[17] Not alone.   [18] Go often askew.

[1] Sough, moan.

At length his lonely cot appears in view,
    Beneath the shelter of an agèd tree;   20
Th' expectant wee-things, toddlin, stacher[2] through
    To meet their dad, wi' flichterin[3] noise and glee.
His wee bit ingle,[4] blinkin bonilie,
His clean hearth-stane, his thrifty wifie's smile,
    The lisping infant, prattling on his knee,   25
Does a' his weary kiaugh[5] and care beguile,
And makes him quite forget his labor and his toil.

Belyve,[6] the elder bairns[7] come drapping in,
    At service out, amang the farmers roun';
Some ca'[8] the pleugh, some herd, some tentie rin[9]   30
    A cannie[10] errand to a neebor[11] town:
Their eldest hope, their Jenny, woman grown,
    In youthfu' bloom, love sparkling in her e'e,
    Comes hame: perhaps, to shew a braw new gown,
Or déposite her sair-won penny-fee,[12]   35
To help her parents dear, if they in hardship be.

With joy unfeign'd, brothers and sisters meet,
    And each for other's weelfare kindly spiers:
The social hours, swift-wing'd, unnotic'd fleet;
    Each tells the uncos[13] that he sees or hears.   40
The parents partial eye their hopeful years;
Anticipation forward points the view;
    The mother, wi' her needle and her sheers,
Gars auld claes[14] look amaist as weel's the new;
The father mixes a'[15] wi' admonition due.   45

Their master's and their mistress's command
    The younkers a' are warnèd to obey;
And mind their labors wi' an eydent[16] hand,
    And ne'er, tho' out o' sight, to jauk[17] or play:
"And O! be sure to fear the Lord alway,   50
And mind your duty, duly, morn and night;
    Lest in temptation's path ye gang astray,
Implore His counsel and assisting might:
They never sought in vain that sought the Lord aright."

But hark! a rap comes gently to the door;   55
    Jenny, wha kens the meaning o' the same,
Tells how a neebor lad came o'er the moor,
    To do some errands, and convoy her hame.
The wily mother sees the conscious flame
Sparkle in Jenny's e'e, and flush her cheek;   60

With heart-struck anxious care, enquires his name,
While Jenny hafflins[18] is afraid to speak;
Weel-pleas'd the mother hears, it's nae wild, worthless
    rake.

With kindly welcome, Jenny brings him ben;[19]
    A strappin' youth, he takes the mother's eye;   65
Blythe Jenny sees the visit's no ill taen;
    The father cracks of horses, pleughs, and kye.[20]
    The youngster's artless heart o'erflows wi' joy,
But blate and laithfu',[21] scarce can weel behave;
    The mother, wi' a woman's wiles, can spy   70
What makes the youth sae bashfu' and sae grave;
Weel-pleas'd to think her bairn's respected like the
    lave.[22]

O happy love! where love like this is found:
    O heart-felt raptures! bliss beyond compare!
I've pacèd much this weary, mortal round,   75
    And sage experience bids me this declare:—
    "If Heaven a draught of heavenly pleasure spare,
One cordial in this melancholy vale,
    'Tis when a youthful, loving, modest pair,
In other's arms, breathe out the tender tale   80
Beneath the milk-white thorn that scents the ev'ning
    gale."

Is there, in human form, that bears a heart,
    A wretch! a villain! lost to love and truth!
That can, with studied, sly, ensnaring art,
    Betray sweet Jenny's unsuspecting youth?   85
Curse on his perjur'd arts! dissembling, smooth!
Are honor, virtue, conscience, all exil'd?
    Is there no pity, no relenting ruth,
Points to the parents fondling o'er their child?
Then paints the ruin'd maid, and their distraction
    wild?   90

But now the supper crowns their simple board,
    The healsome parritch,[23] chief o' Scotia's food;
The soupe[24] their only hawkie[25] does afford,
    That 'yont the hallan[26] snugly chows her cood;
    The dame brings forth, in complimental mood,   95
To grace the lad, her weel-hained kebbuck,[27] fell;[28]
    And aft he's prest, and aft he ca's it guid;

---

[18] Half.
[19] Inside; i.e., all the way in through the but (the kitchen end of the cottage) into the ben (the inner apartment).
[20] Cattle.
[21] Bashful and sheepish ("loathful").
[22] The rest; i.e., other girls.
[23] Wholesome porridge—oatmeal, of course.   [24] Sup, drink.
[25] Cow (especially a white-faced one).   [26] Beyond the wall.
[27] Well-saved cheese.   [28] Pungent.

[2] Stagger, toddle.   [3] Fluttering.   [4] Fire.
[5] Worry.   [6] By and by.   [7] Children.   [8] Drive.
[9] Heedful run.   [10] Careful.   [11] Neighboring.
[12] Hard-won wages.   [13] Uncouth (= unknown) things; news.
[14] Clothes.   [15] All, everything.   [16] Diligent.
[17] Dally.

The frugal wifie, garrulous, will tell,
How 'twas a towmond[29] auld, sin' lint was i' the bell.[30]

The chearfu' supper done, wi' serious face,   100
  They, round the ingle, form a circle wide;
The sire turns o'er, wi' patriarchal grace,
  The big ha'-Bible,[31] ance[32] his father's pride.
His bonnet rev'rently is laid aside,
His lyart haffets[33] wearing thin and bare;   105
  Those strains that once did sweet in Zion glide,
He wales[34] a portion with judicious care,
And "Let us worship God!" he says, with solemn air.

They chant their artless notes in simple guise,
  They tune their hearts, by far the noblest aim;   110
Perhaps *Dundee's* wild-warbling measures rise,
  Or plaintive *Martyrs,* worthy of the name;
Or noble *Elgin*[35] beets[36] the heaven-ward flame,
  The sweetest far of Scotia's holy lays:
Compar'd with these, Italian trills are tame;   115
The tickl'd ears no heart-felt raptures raise;
Nae unison hae they, with our Creator's praise.

The priest-like father reads the sacred page,
  How Abram was the friend of God on high;[37]
Or, Moses bade eternal warfare wage   120
  With Amalek's ungracious progeny;[38]
Or how the royal bard[39] did groaning lie
Beneath the stroke of Heaven's avenging ire;
  Or Job's pathetic plaint, and wailing cry;
Or rapt Isaiah's wild, seraphic fire;   125
Or other holy Seers that tune the sacred lyre.

Perhaps the Christian volume is the theme:
  How guiltless blood for guilty man was shed;
How He, who bore in Heaven the second name,
  Had not on earth whereon to lay His head;   130
  How His first followers and servants sped;[40]
The precepts sage they wrote to many a land:
  How he, who lone in Patmos[41] banishèd,
Saw in the sun a mighty angel stand,
And heard great Bab'lon's doom pronounc'd
  by Heaven's command.[42]   135

Then kneeling down to Heaven's Eternal King,
  The saint, the father, and the husband prays:
Hope "springs exulting on triumphant wing"[43]
  That thus they all shall meet in future days,
  There ever bask in uncreated rays,   140
No more to sigh, or shed the bitter tear,
  Together hymning their Creator's praise,
In such society, yet still more dear;
While circling Time moves round in an eternal sphere.

Compar'd with this, how poor Religion's pride,   145
  In all the pomp of method, and of art;
When men display to congregations wide
  Devotion's ev'ry grace, except the heart,
  The Power, incens'd, the pageant will desert,
The pompous strain, the sacerdotal stole:[44]   150
  But haply, in some cottage far apart,
May hear, well-pleas'd, the language of the soul,
And in His Book of Life the inmates poor enroll.

Then homeward all take off their sev'ral way;
  The youngling cottagers retire to rest: 155
The parent-pair their secret homage pay,
  And proffer up to Heaven the warm request,
  That He who stills the raven's clam'rous nest,
And decks the lily fair in flow'ry pride,
  Would, in the way His wisdom sees the best,   160
For them and for their little ones provide;
But, chiefly, in their hearts with Grace Divine preside.

From scenes like these, old Scotia's grandeur springs,
  That makes her lov'd at home, rever'd abroad:
Princes and lords are but the breath of kings,   165
  "An honest man's the noblest work of God";[45]
  And certes, in fair Virtue's heavenly road,
The cottage leaves the palace far behind;
  What is a lordling's pomp? a cumbrous load,
Disguising oft the wretch of human kind,   170
Studied in arts of Hell, in wickedness refin'd!

O Scotia! my dear, my native soil!
  For whom my warmest wish to Heaven is sent!
Long may thy hardy sons of rustic toil
  Be blest with health, and peace, and sweet
    content!   175
  And O! may Heaven their simple lives prevent
From Luxury's contagion, weak and vile!

---

[29] Twelvemonth.   [30] Since the flax was in bloom.
[31] Hall Bible; thus called because in great houses family worship
  was held in the central hall.   [32] Once.   [33] Gray temples.
[34] Chooses.   [35] Psalm tunes.   [36] Kindles.
[37] Genesis 12 ff.   [38] Exodus 17:8 ff.
[39] King David. See 2 Samuel 12:15 ff.   [40] Fared.
[41] The island in the Dodecanese where St. John was exiled.
[42] Revelation 18.

[43] Slightly misquoted from Pope's "Windsor Forest," lines 111 f.
[44] The priestly band (worn around the neck and falling from the
  shoulders).   [45] Pope, *Essay on Man,* IV, 248.

Then, howe'er crowns and coronets be rent,
A virtuous populace may rise the while,
And stand a wall of fire around their much-lov'd
    Isle.   180

O Thou! who pour'd the patriotic tide
  That stream'd thro' Wallace's[46] undaunted heart,
Who dar'd to, nobly, stem tyrannic pride,
  Or nobly die, the second glorious part.
  (The patriot's God, peculiarly thou art,   185
His friend, inspirer, guardian, and reward!)
    O never, never, Scotia's realm desert;
But still the patriot, and the patriot-bard,
In bright succession raise, her ornament and guard!

ADDRESS TO THE DEIL

The humor of the familiar tone Burns takes with his
decidedly un-Miltonic Satan is heightened by his prefixing to this poem, which he wrote about the same time as
"The Cotter's Saturday Night," two lines from *Paradise
Lost* (I, 128-9):

    O prince, O chief of many thronèd powers,
    That led the embattled seraphim to war.

O Thou! whatever title suit thee—
Auld Hornie, Satan, Nick, or Clootie[1]—
Wha in yon cavern grim an' sootie,
    Clos'd under hatches,
Spairges[2] about the brunstane cootie,[3]   5
    To scaud[4] poor wretches!

Hear me, auld Hangie,[5] for a wee,[6]
An' let poor damnèd bodies be;
I'm sure sma' pleasure it can gie,
    Ev'n to a deil,   10
To skelp[7] an' scaud poor dogs like me
    An' hear us squeel!

Great is thy pow'r, an' great thy fame;
Far kend an' noted is thy name;
An' tho' yon lowin heugh's[8] thy hame,   15
    Thou travels far;
An' faith! thou's neither lag,[9] nor lame,
    Nor blate, nor scaur.[10]

Whyles, ranging like a roarin lion,
For prey, a' holes an' corners trying;   20
Whyles, on the strong-wing'd tempest flyin',
    Tirlin the kirks;[11]
Whyles, in the human bosom pryin,
    Unseen thou lurks.

I've heard my rev'rend graunie say,   25
In lanely glens ye like to stray;
Or, where auld ruin'd castles grey
    Nod to the moon,
Ye fright the nightly wand'rer's way,
    Wi' eldritch[12] croon.   30

When twilight did my graunie summon,
To say her pray'rs, douce,[13] honest woman!
Aft yont the dyke she's heard you bummin,[14]
    Wi' eerie drone;
Or, rustlin, through the boortrees[15] comin,   35
    Wi' heavy groan.

Ae dreary, windy, winter night,
The stars shot down wi' sklentin[16] light,
Wi' you mysel, I gat a fright;
    Ayont the lough,[17]   40
Ye, like a rash-buss,[18] stood in sight,
    Wi' waving sugh.[19]

The cudgel in my nieve[20] did shake,
Each bristl'd hair stood like a stake;
When, wi' an eldritch, stoor[21] "quaick, quaick,"   45
    Amang the springs,
Awa ye squatter'd like a drake,
    On whistling wings.

Let warlocks[22] grim, an' wither'd hags,
Tell how wi' you, on ragweed nags,
They skim the muirs[23] an' dizzy crags,   50
    Wi' wicked speed;
And in kirk-yards renew their leagues,
    Owre howkit[24] dead.

Thence countra wives, wi' toil an' pain,   55
May plunge an' plunge the kirn[25] in vain;
For O! the yellow treasure's taen
    By witching skill;

---

[46] William Wallace, national hero of Scotland. Having fought for her independence, he was executed by Edward I in 1305.

[1] Hoofie.   [2] Splashes.   [3] Brimstone bowl.
[4] Scald.   [5] Hangman, executioner.   [6] Bit, jiffy.
[7] Spank.   [8] Flaming pit is.   [9] Backward.
[10] Bashful nor timid ("scared").

[11] Stripping (i.e., unroofing) the churches.   [12] Unearthly.
[13] Grave.   [14] Humming.   [15] Elderbushes.
[16] Slanting.   [17] Beyond the lake or pond ("loch").
[18] Clump of rushes.   [19] Moan.   [20] Fist.   [21] Harsh.
[22] Sorcerers.   [23] Moors, wastelands.   [24] Over dug-up.
[25] Churn.

An' dawtit, twal-pint hawkie's gane
    As yell 's the bill.[26]   60

Thence mystic knots mak great abuse
On young guidmen,[27] fond, keen, an' croose;[28]
When the best wark-lume[29] i' the house,
    By cantraip[30] wit,
Is instant made no worth a louse,   65
    Just at the bit.[31]

When thowes[32] dissolve the snawy hoord,[33]
An' float the jinglin icy boord,[34]
Then water-kelpies[35] haunt the foord,
    By your direction,   70
An' nighted trav'llers are allur'd
    To their destruction.

An' aft your moss-traversing spunkies[36]
Decoy the wight that late an' drunk is:
The bleezin, curst, mischievous monkies   75
    Delude his eyes,
Till in some miry slough he sunk is,
    Ne'er mair to rise.

When masons'[37] mystic word an' grip
In storms an' tempests raise you up,   80
Some cock or cat your rage maun stop,[38]
    Or, strange to tell!
The youngest brother ye wad whip
    Aff straught[39] to hell.

Lang syne in Eden's bonie yard,[40]   85
When youthfu' lovers first were pair'd,
An' all the soul of love they shar'd,
    The raptur'd hour,
Sweet on the fragrant flow'ry swaird,
    In shady bow'r;   90

Then you, ye auld, snick-drawing[41] dog!
Ye cam to Paradise incog,
An' play'd on man a cursèd brogue,[42]
    (Black be your fa'!)[43]

An' gied[44] the infant warld a shog,[45]   95
    'Maist ruin'd a'.

D'ye mind[46] that day, when in a bizz,[47]
Wi' reekit duds, an' reestit gizz,[48]
Ye did present your smoutie phiz[49]
    'Mang better folk,   100
An' sklented on the man of Uzz[50]
    Your spitefu' joke?

An' how ye gat him i' your thrall,
An' brak him out o' house an' hal',
While scabs an' blotches did him gall,   105
    Wi' bitter claw;
An' lowsed[51] his ill-tongued, wicked scawl[52]—
    Was warst ava?[53]

But a' your doings to rehearse,
Your wily snares an' fechtin[54] fierce,   110
Sin' that day Michael did you pierce,[55]
    Down to this time,
Wad ding a Lallan tongue, or Erse,[56]
    In prose or rhyme.

An' now, auld Cloots, I ken ye're thinkin,   115
A certain Bardie's[57] rantin,[58] drinkin,
Some luckless hour will send him linkin,[59]
    To your black Pit;
But faith! he'll turn a corner jinkin',[60]
    An' cheat you yet.   120

But fare-you-weel, auld Nickie-Ben!
O, wad ye tak a thought an' men'![61]
Ye aiblins[62] might—I dinna ken—
    Still hae a stake:[63]
I'm wae[64] to think upo' yon den,   125
    Ev'n for your sake!

---

26 And the petted, twelve-pint cow has gone as dry as the bull. (A Scots pint equaled two English quarts.)
27 Goodmen, husbands.   28 Cocksure.
29 Tool ("work loom").   30 Magic.
31 Crucial moment (of love-making).   32 Thaws.
33 Hoard.   34 Board, i.e., surface ice.   35 Water demons.
36 Bog-crossing will-o'-the-wisps.
37 Burns was a Freemason, but his reference here is jocose.
38 Must stop (by being sacrificed to you.)   39 Off straight.
40 Long since in Eden's pretty garden.
41 I.e., burglarizing. *Snick* = latch.   42 Trick.
43 What falls to you, your lot.

44 Gave.   45 Jog, shake.
46 Remember.   47 Bustle, hurry.
48 With smoky clothes and scorched wig.   49 Smutty face.
50 Job.   51 Loosed.   52 Scold.   53 Worst of all.
54 Fighting.
55 Described by Milton in *Paradise Lost*, VI, 321 ff.
56 Would be too much for a Lowland tongue, or a Gaelic one.
57 Bardlet, little poet.   58 Indulgence in high jinks.
59 Skipping.   60 Dodging.   61 Mend (your ways).
62 Perhaps.   63 Gambler's chance.   64 Woeful.

ADDRESS TO THE UNCO GUID,[1]
OR THE RIGIDLY RIGHTEOUS

My Son, these maxims make a rule,
An' lump them ay thegither:
The Rigid Righteous is a fool,
The Rigid Wise anither:
The cleanest corn that e'er was dight,[2]
May hae some pyles o' caff[3] in;
So ne'er a fellow-creature slight
For random fits o' daffin.[4]
　　　　　—SOLOMON (Ecclesiastes 7:16).

O ye, wha are sae guid yoursel,
　　Sae pious and sae holy,
Ye've nought to do but mark and tell
　　Your neebour's fauts and folly;
Whase life is like a weel-gaun[5] mill,　　　5
　　Supplied wi' store o' water;
The heapet happer's[6] ebbing still,
　　An' still the clap[7] plays clatter!

Hear me, ye venerable core,[8]
　　As counsel for poor mortals　　　10
That frequent pass douce Wisdom's door
　　For glaikit[9] Folly's portals:
I for their thoughtless, careless sakes,
　　Would here propone[10] defences,—
Their donsie[11] tricks, their black mistakes,　15
　　Their failings and mischances.

Ye see your state wi' theirs compared,
　　And shudder at the niffer;[12]
But cast a moment's fair regard,
　　What makes the mighty differ?[13]　　　20
Discount what scant occasion gave;
　　That purity ye pride in;
And (what's aft mair than a' the lave)
　　Your better art o' hidin'.

Think, when your castigated[14] pulse　　　25
　　Gies[15] now and then a wallop,
What ragings must his veins convulse,
　　That still eternal gallop!

Wi' wind and tide fair i' your tail,
　　Right on ye scud your sea-way;　　　30
But in the teeth o' baith to sail,
　　It makes an unco lee-way.

See Social-life and Glee sit down
　　All joyous and unthinking,
Till, quite transmugrify'd,[16] they're grown　35
　　Debauchery and Drinking:
O, would they stay to calculate
　　Th' eternal consequences,
Or—your more dreaded hell to state—
　　Damnation of expenses!　　　40

Ye high, exalted, virtuous dames,
　　Tied up in godly laces,
Before ye gie poor Frailty names,
　　Suppose a change o' cases:
A dear-lov'd lad, convenience snug,　　　45
　　A treach'rous inclination—
But, let me whisper i' your lug,[17]
　　Ye're aiblins[18] nae temptation.

Then gently scan your brother man,
　　Still gentler sister woman;　　　50
Tho' they may gang a kennin[19] wrang,
　　To step aside is human:
One point must still be greatly dark,
　　The moving *why* they do it;
And just as lamely can ye mark　　　55
　　How far perhaps they rue it.

Who made the heart, 'tis He alone
　　Decidedly can try us:
He knows each chord, its various tone,
　　Each spring, its various bias:　　　60
Then at the balance let's be mute,
　　We never can adjust it;
What's done we partly may compute,
　　But know not what's resisted.

---

[1] Extraordinarily good.　　[2] Grain that was ever winnowed.
[3] Bits of chaff.　　[4] Larking.　　[5] Well-going.
[6] Heaped-up hopper.
[7] Clapper; the device which, by shaking the hopper, keeps the grain moving down to the grinding stones.　　[8] Corps.
[9] Giddy.　　[10] Propound.　　[11] Perverse.
[12] Exchange.　　[13] Big difference.　　[14] I.e., disciplined.
[15] Gives.

[16] Transmogrified, transformed.　　[17] Ear.　　[18] Perhaps.
[19] A tiny bit, the least perceptible bit.

TO A LOUSE

ON SEEING ONE ON A LADY'S BONNET AT CHURCH

Ha! whare ye gaun, ye crowlin' ferlie?[1]
Your impudence protects you sairly:[2]
I canna say but ye strunt rarely,[3]
    Owre gauze and lace;
Tho' faith! I fear ye dine but sparely   5
    On sic a place.

Ye ugly, creepin, blastit wonner,[4]
Detested, shunn'd by saunt an' sinner,
How daur ye set your fit[5] upon her,
    Sae fine a lady?   10
Gae somewhere else, and seek your dinner
    On some poor body.

Swith![6] in some beggar's hauffet squattle;[7]
There ye may creep, and sprawl, and sprattle,[8]
Wi' ither kindred, jumping cattle,
    In shoals and nations;   15
Where horn nor bane[9] ne'er daur unsettle
    Your thick plantations.

Now haud[10] ye there! ye're out o' sight
Below the fatt'rils,[11] snug an' tight;   20
Na, faith ye yet! ye'll no be right,
    Till ye've got on it—
The vera tapmost tow'ring height
    O' Miss's bonnet.

My sooth![12] right bauld[13] ye set your nose out,   25
As plump an' grey as onie grozet:[14]
O for some rank, mercurial rozet,[15]
    Or fell, red smeddum![16]
I'd gie ye sic a hearty dose o't,
    Wad dress your droddum![17]   30

I wad na been surpris'd to spy
You on an auld wife's flainen toy;[18]
Or aiblins some bit duddie[19] boy,
    On's wyliecoat;[20]
But Miss's fine Lunardi![21] fye,   35
    How daur ye do't?

O Jenny, dinna toss your head,
An' set your beauties a' abroad![22]
Ye little ken what cursèd speed
    The blastie's makin![23]   40
Thae[24] winks and finger-ends, I dread,
    Are notice takin!

O wad some Power the giftie[25] gie us
To see oursels as ithers see us!
It wad frae monie a blunder free us,   45
    An' foolish notion:
What airs in dress an' gait wad lea'e us,
    An' ev'n devotion!

TO A MOUNTAIN DAISY

ON TURNING ONE DOWN WITH THE PLOUGH IN APRIL, 1786

This is merely an imitation, sentimental though not without charm, of the much finer "To a Mouse."

Wee, modest, crimson-tippèd[1] flow'r,
Thou's met me in an evil hour;
For I maun crush amang the stoure[2]
    Thy slender stem:
To spare thee now is past my pow'r,   5
    Thou bonie gem.

Alas! it's no thy neebor sweet,
The bonie lark, companion meet,
Bending thee 'mang the dewy weet,[3]
    Wi' spreckled breast!   10
When upward-springing, blythe, to greet
    The purpling east.

Cauld blew the bitter-biting north
Upon thy early, humble birth;
Yet cheerfully thou glinted forth   15
    Amid the storm,
Scarce rear'd above the parent-earth
    Thy tender form.

The flaunting flow'rs our gardens yield,
High shelt'ring woods and wa's maun[4] shield: 20
But thou, beneath the random bield[5]
    O' clod or stane,[6]
Adorns the histie[7] stibble-field,
    Unseen, alane.

---

[1] Where are you going, you crawling marvel?   [2] Grievously.
[3] Strut in fine style.   [4] Blasted wonder.   [5] Foot.
[6] Instantly; i.e., be off!   [7] Temple settle.   [8] Scramble.
[9] Bone; i.e., no comb, of horn or bone.   [10] Hold.
[11] Ribbon ends.   [12] Faith.   [13] Bold.
[14] Gooseberry.   [15] Rosin.   [16] Deadly red powder.
[17] Beat your buttocks.   [18] Flannel trifle, i.e., headdress.
[19] Little ragged.   [20] Undershirt.
[21] "Balloon" bonnet; from the name of a well-known aeronaut.

[22] Abroad.   [23] The blasted thing is making.   [24] Those.
[25] Small gift.

[1] Burns's flower is the European variety, with short, tight petals; we call it the *English* daisy. Another name for it in Scotland is the gowan.   [2] Dust.   [3] Wet, moisture.
[4] Walls must.   [5] Shelter.   [6] Stone.   [7] Bare.

There, in thy scanty mantle clad,   25
Thy snawie bosom sun-ward spread,
Thou lifts thy unassuming head
    In humble guise;
But now the share uptears thy bed,
    And low thou lies!   30

Such is the fate of artless maid,
Sweet flow'ret of the rural shade!
By love's simplicity betray'd,
    And guileless trust;
Till she, like thee, all soil'd, is laid   35
    Low i' the dust.

Such is the fate of simple Bard,
On Life's rough ocean luckless starr'd!
Unskilful he to note the card[8]
    Of prudent lore,   40
Till billows rage, and gales blow hard,
    And whelm him o'er!

Such fate to suffering Worth is giv'n,
Who long with wants and woes has striv'n,
By human pride or cunning driv'n   45
    To mis'ry's brink;
Till, wrench'd of ev'ry stay but Heav'n,
    He, ruin'd, sink!

Ev'n thou who mourn'st the Daisy's fate,
That fate is thine no distant date;   50
Stern Ruin's plough-share drives elate,
    Full on thy bloom,
Till crush'd beneath the furrow's weight
    Shall be thy doom!

O, MY LUVE IS LIKE A RED, RED ROSE

We come now to examples of Burns's greatness as a writer of songs. That the first adapts most of its lines from earlier poets is of interest but scarcely of importance, for the result is one of the most exquisite lyrics in existence.

O, my luve is like a red, red rose,
    That's newly sprung in June.
O, my luve is like the melodie,
    That's sweetly play'd in tune.

As fair art thou, my bonie lass,   5
    So deep in luve am I;
And I will luve thee still, my dear,
    Till a' the seas gang dry.

[8] Chart.

Till a' the seas gang dry, my dear,
    And the rocks melt wi' the sun!   10
And I will luve thee still, my dear,
    While the sands o' life shall run.

And fare thee weel, my only luve,
    And fare thee weel a while!
And I will come again, my luve,   15
    Tho' it were ten thousand mile!

OF A' THE AIRTS

"This song I composed out of compliment to Mrs. Burns . . . during the honeymoon.—R.B."

Of a' the airts[9] the wind can blaw,
    I dearly like the west,
For there the bonie lassie lives,
    The lassie I lo'e best.
There wild woods grow, and rivers row,[10]   5
    And monie a hill between,
But day and night my fancy's flight
    Is ever wi' my Jean.

I see her in the dewy flowers—
    I see her sweet and fair.   10
I hear her in the tunefu' birds—
    I hear her charm the air:
There's not a bonie flower that springs
    By fountain, shaw,[11] or green,
There's not a bonie bird that sings,   15
    But minds me o' my Jean.

AULD LANG SYNE

The three words chiefly responsible for the popularity of this song were already associated in Scottish balladry. Burns produced his lyric, in 1788, for an older tune than the one to which it is now sung. He never claimed authorship of this poem, but repeatedly stated that he wrote it down after hearing an old man sing it. Nevertheless no earlier trace of it has ever been discovered.

Should auld acquaintance be forgot,
    And never brought to mind?
Should auld acquaintance be forgot,
    And auld lang syne![1]

Chorus. For auld lang syne, my dear,   5
    For auld lang syne,
We'll tak a cup o' kindness yet
    For auld lang syne!

[9] Directions.   [10] Roll.   [11] Wood.
[1] Old long ago, old times.

And surely ye'll be your pint-stowp,[2]
  And surely I'll be mine,   10
And we'll tak a cup o' kindness yet
  For auld lang syne!

We twa hae run about the braes,[3]
  And pou'd[4] the gowans[5] fine,
But we've wander'd monie a weary fit[6]   15
  Sin' auld lang syne.

We twa hae paidl'd in the burn[7]
  From morning sun till dine;[8]
But seas between us braid[9] hae roar'd
  Sin' auld lang syne.   20

And there's a hand, my trusty fiere,[10]
  And gie's a hand o' thine!
And we'll tak a right guid-willie waught,[11]
  For auld lang syne!

SWEET AFTON

The heroine of this lovely song, written in 1789, is not
the unknown Mary but an Ayrshire stream, identified by
Burns as "the small river Afton that flows into [the]
Nith, near New Cumnock, which has some charming
wild romantic scenery on its banks," that is, its braes or
hillsides.

Flow gently, sweet Afton, among thy green braes!
Flow gently, I'll sing thee a song in thy praise!
My Mary's asleep by thy murmuring stream—
Flow gently, sweet Afton, disturb not her dream!

Thou stock dove whose echo resounds thro' the glen, 5
Ye wild whistling blackbirds in yon thorny den,
Thou green-crested lapwing, thy screaming forbear—
I charge you, disturb not my slumbering fair!

How lofty, sweet Afton, thy neighbouring hills,
Far mark'd with the courses of clear, winding rills! 10
There daily I wander, as noon rises high,
My flocks and my Mary's sweet cot in my eye.

How pleasant thy banks and green vallies below,
Where wild in the woodlands the primroses blow!
There oft, as mild Ev'ning weeps over the lea,   15
The sweet-scented birk shades my Mary and me.

Thy crystal stream, Afton, how lovely it glides,
And winds by the cot where my Mary resides!
How wanton thy waters her snowy feet lave,
As, gathering sweet flowerets, she stems thy clear
      wave!   20

Flow gently, sweet Afton, among thy green braes!
Flow gently, sweet river, the theme of my lays!
My Mary's asleep by thy murmuring stream—
Flow gently, sweet Afton, disturb not her dream!

WILLIE BREWED A PECK O' MAUT

The trio mentioned in this drinking song were, besides
Burns, William Nicol and Allan Masterton, respectively
classics and writing teachers at the Edinburgh High
School. The occasion was during the fall vacation of 1789.

O, Willie brewed a peck o' maut,[1]
  And Rob an' Allan cam to see.
Three blyther hearts that lee-lang[2] night
  Ye wad na found in Christendie.

Chorus. We are na fou,[3] we're nae that fou,   5
  But just a drappie in our e'e![4]
The cock may craw, the day may daw,
  And ay we'll taste the barley-bree![5]

Here are we met three merry boys,
  Three merry boys, I trow, are we;   10
And monie a night we've merry been,
  And monie mae[6] we hope to be!

It is the moon, I ken her horn,
  That's blinkin in the lift sae hie:[7]
She shines sae bright to wyle us hame,[8]   15
  But, by my sooth, she'll wait a wee!

Wha first shall rise to gang awa,
  A cuckold, coward loun[9] is he!
Wha first beside his chair shall fa',
  He is the King amang us three!   20

TAM O' SHANTER

A TALE

Burns considered this his most finished poem, and such
was also the opinion of Sir Walter Scott. It was written
at Ellisland in 1790 for a volume on Scottish antiquities

---

2 I.e., pay for your drink.
3 Hillsides.   4 Pulled.   5 Daisies.   6 Foot.
7 Waded ("paddled") in the brook.   8 Dinner time, noon.
9 Broad.   10 Comrade.
11 Good-will drink. Cf. "cup o' kindness," line 7.

1 Malt.   2 Livelong.   3 Full, drunk.
4 Little drop in our eye.   5 Brew.   6 More.
7 Sky so high.   8 Entice us home.   9 Loon, lout.

by Francis Grose (1731–91),[1] to whom Burns had suggested the inclusion of a drawing of the old ruined church near his birthplace at Alloway, a few miles south of Ayr. Grose agreed, on condition that Burns provide a witch story to accompany the engraving. Already roofless before Burns was born, the haunted kirk is only a couple of hundred yards from the bank of the little river Doon and the "Auld Brig," then the only way of getting over. Fortunately for Tam, no witch could cross running water.

Of Brownyis and of Bogillis full is this Buke.
GAWIN DOUGLAS[2]

When chapman billies[3] leave the street,
And drouthy[4] neebors neebors meet;
As market-days are wearing late,
An' folk begin to tak the gate;[5]
While we sit bousing at the nappy,[6]   5
An' gettin fou and unco happy,
We think na on the lang Scots miles,[7]
The mosses,[8] waters, slaps, and styles,[9]
That lie between us and our hame,
Whare sits our sulky, sullen dame,   10
Gathering her brows like gathering storm,
Nursing her wrath to keep it warm.

This truth fand[10] honest Tam o' Shanter,[11]
As he frae Ayr ae[12] night did canter:
(Auld Ayr, wham ne'er a town surpasses,   15
For honest men and bonie lasses).

O Tam, had'st thou but been sae wise,
As taen thy ain wife Kate's advice!
She tauld thee weel thou was a skellum,[13]
A blethering,[14] blustering, drunken blellum;[15]   20
That frae November till October,
Ae market-day thou was nae sober;
That ilka melder[16] wi' the miller,
Thou sat as lang as thou had siller;[17]
That ev'ry naig was ca'd a shoe on,[18]   25

The smith and thee gat roaring fou on;
That at the Lord's house, even on Sunday,
Thou drank wi' Kirkton Jean[19] till Monday.
She prophesied, that, late or soon,
Thou would be found deep drown'd in Doon,   30
Or catch'd wi' warlocks in the mirk[20]
By Alloway's auld, haunted kirk.

Ah! gentle dames, it gars me greet,[21]
To think how monie counsels sweet,
How monie lengthen'd, sage advices   35
The husband frae the wife despises!

But to our tale:—Ae market-night,
Tam had got planted unco right,
Fast by an ingle, bleezing[22] finely,
Wi' reaming swats,[23] that drank divinely;   40
And at his elbow, Souter[24] Johnie,
His ancient, trusty, drouthy cronie:
Tam lo'ed him like a very brither;
They had been fou for weeks thegither.
The night drave on wi' sangs and clatter;   45
And ay the ale was growing better:
The landlady and Tam grew gracious
Wi' secret favors, sweet and precious:
The Souter tauld his queerest stories;
The landlord's laugh was ready chorus: 50
The storm without might rair[25] and rustle,
Tam did na mind the storm a whistle.

Care, mad to see a man sae happy,
E'en drown'd himsel amang the nappy.
As bees flee hame wi' lades o' treasure,   55
The minutes wing'd their way wi' pleasure:
Kings may be blest but Tam was glorious,
O'er a' the ills o' life victorious!

But pleasures are like poppies spread:
You seize the flow'r, its bloom is shed;   60
Or like the snow falls[26] in the river,
A moment white—then melts for ever;
Or like the borealis race,[27]
That flit ere you can point their place;
Or like the rainbow's lovely form   65
Evanishing amid the storm.
Nae man can tether time or tide;
The hour approaches Tam maun ride:

1 Now best known for *A Classical Dictionary of the Vulgar Tongue* (1785). He drew his own illustrations for his antiquarian works.
2 The Scottish poet Gavin Douglas (d. 1522); the line, meaning "Of brownies and bogies full is this book," is from the prologue to his translation of Vergil's *Aeneid*.
3 Peddler fellows.   4 Thirsty.   5 Road.
6 Boozing at the ale.
7 The Scotch mile was longer than the English, sometimes by 216 yards.   8 Bogs.
9 Openings in fences, and stiles.   10 Found.
11 The name of a farm in southern Ayrshire.—The cap called tam-o'-shanter gets its name from the poem.   12 One.
13 A good-for-nothing.   14 Foolish-talking.   15 Babbler.
16 Grinding; i.e., every time you took a quantity of grain to be ground.   17 Silver, money.
18 Every nag that was knocked a shoe on; i.e., every time you took a horse to be shod.

19 At Jean's tavern near the church.
20 By sorcerers in the dark.   21 Makes me weep.
22 A fireplace, blazing.   23 Foaming new ale.
24 Cobbler.   25 Roar.   26 That falls.
27 Species, kind (of phenomena).

That hour, o' night's black arch the key-stane,
That dreary hour Tam mounts his beast in;   70
And sic a night he taks the road in,
As ne'er poor sinner was abroad in.

The wind blew as 't wad[28] blawn its last;
The rattling showers rose on the blast;
The speedy gleams the darkness swallow'd;   75
Loud, deep, and lang the thunder bellow'd;
That night, a child might understand,
The Deil had business on his hand.

Weel mounted on his gray mare Meg,
A better never lifted leg,   80
Tam skelpit[29] on thro' dub[30] and mire,
Despising wind, and rain, and fire;
Whiles[31] holding fast his guid blue bonnet,
Whiles crooning o'er some auld Scots sonnet,[32]
Whiles glow'ring round wi' prudent cares,   85
Lest bogles[33] catch him unawares:
Kirk-Alloway was drawing nigh,
Whare ghaists and houlets[34] nightly cry.

By this time he was cross the ford,
Whare in the snaw the chapman smoor'd;[35]   90
And past the birks and meikle stane,[36]
Whare drunken Charlie brak's neck-bane;
And thro' the whins,[37] and by the cairn,[38]
Whare hunters fand the murder'd bairn;
And near the thorn, aboon[39] the well,   95
Whare Mungo's mither hang'd hersel.
Before him Doon pours all his floods;
The doubling storm roars thro' the woods;
The lightnings flash from pole to pole;
Near and more near the thunders roll: 100
When, glimmering thro' the groaning trees,
Kirk-Alloway seem'd in a bleeze;
Thro' ilka bore[40] the beams were glancing,
And loud resounded mirth and dancing.

Inspiring bold John Barleycorn!   105
What dangers thou canst make us scorn!
Wi' tippenny,[41] we fear nae evil;
Wi' usquebae,[42] we'll face the Devil!
The swats sae ream'd in Tammie's noddle,

Fair play, he car'd na deils a boddle.[43]   110
But Maggie stood right sair astonish'd,
Till, by the heel and hand admonish'd,
She ventur'd forward on the light;
And, wow! Tam saw an unco[44] sight!

Warlocks and witches in a dance: 115
Nae cótillion brent-new frae[45] France,
But hornpipes, jigs, strathspeys,[46] and reels,
Put life and mettle in their heels.
A winnock-bunker[47] in the east,
There sat Auld Nick, in shape o' beast;   120
A tousie tyke,[48] black, grim, and large,
To gie them music was his charge;
He screw'd the pipes and gart them skirl,[49]
Till roof and rafters a' did dirl.[50]
Coffins stood round like open presses,[51]   125
That shaw'd[52] the dead in their last dresses;
And by some devilish cantraip sleight,[53]
Each in its cauld hand held a light:
By which heroic Tam was able
To note upon the haly[54] table   130
A murderer's banes in gibbet-airns;[55]
Twa span-lang, wee, unchristen'd bairns;
A thief, new-cutted frae a rape[56]—
Wi' his last gasp his gab[57] did gape;
Five tomahawks wi' bluid red-rusted;   135
Five scymitars wi' murder crusted;
A garter which a babe had strangled;
A knife a father's throat had mangled—
Whom his ain son o' life bereft—
The grey-hairs yet stack to the heft;[58]   140
Wi' mair o' horrible and awefu',
Which even to name wad be unlawfu':
Three Lawyers' tongues, turned inside out,
Wi' lies seamed like a beggar's clout;[59]
Three Priests'[60] hearts, rotten black as muck, 145
Lay stinking, vile, in every neuk.[61]

As Tammie glower'd,[62] amaz'd, and curious,
The mirth and fun grew fast and furious:

[43] Given fair play, he cared not for devils so much as twopence (that is, a Scotch coin worth one-third of an English penny).
[44] Uncommon, wondrous.   [45] Brand-new from.
[46] A relatively slow kind of reel.   [47] Window seat.
[48] Shaggy dog.   [49] Made them squeal.   [50] Ring.
[51] Cupboards.   [52] Showed.   [53] Magic trick.
[54] Holy.
[55] Gallows-irons. The bodies of malefactors were sometimes hung up in chains till only the bones remained.
[56] Newly cut down from a rope.   [57] Mouth.
[58] Stuck to the handle.
[59] Patch.—Burns yielded to the advice of friends and omitted from his books lines 143–6, though they had appeared in Grose's volume and in periodicals.   [60] Ministers'.   [61] Nook.
[62] Stared.

---

[28] As if it would have.   [29] Went along at a spanking pace.
[30] Puddle.   [31] Sometimes.   [32] Song.
[33] Bogies, goblins.   [34] Ghosts and owls.   [35] Smothered.
[36] Birches and big stone.   [37] Furze, gorse.
[38] Pile of stones.   [39] Above.   [40] Every chink.
[41] Twopenny ale.   [42] Whisky.

The piper loud and louder blew,
The dancers quick and quicker flew;
They reel'd, they set,[63] they cross'd,[64] they cleekit,[65]   150
Till ilka carlin swat and reekit,[66]
And coost her duddies to the wark[67]
And linket[68] at it in her sark![69]

Now Tam, O Tam! had thae been queans,[70]   155
A' plump and strapping in their teens!
Their sarks, instead o' creeshie flannen,[71]
Been snaw-white seventeen hunder[72] linen!—
Thir breeks[73] o' mine, my only pair,
That ance were plush, o' guid blue hair,   160
I wad hae gi'en them off my hurdies,[74]
For ae blink o'[75] the bonie burdies![76]

But wither'd beldams, auld and droll,
Rigwoodie[77] hags wad spean[78] a foal,
Louping and flinging on a crummock,[79]   165
I wonder didna turn thy stomach!

But Tam kend what was what fu' brawlie;[80]
There was ae winsome wench and wawlie,[81]
That night enlisted in the core[82]
Lang after kend on Carrick[83] shore   170
(For monie a beast to dead she shot,
An' perish'd monie a bonie boat,
And shook baith meikle corn and bear,[84]
And kept the country-side in fear).
Her cutty[85] sark, o' Paisley harn,[86]   175
That while a lassie she had worn,
In longitude tho' sorely scanty,
It was her best, and she was vauntie.—[87]
Ah! little kend thy reverend grannie,
That sark she coft[88] for her wee Nannie,   180
Wi' twa pund Scots[89] ('twas a' her riches),
Wad ever grac'd a dance of witches!

But here my Muse her wing maun cour;[90]
Sic flights are far beyond her power:
To sing how Nannie lap and flang,[91]   185
(A souple jad[92] she was and strang),
And how Tam stood like ane bewitch'd,
And thought his very een enrich'd;
Even Satan glower'd, and fidged fu' fain,[93]
And hotched[94] and blew wi' might and main;   190
Till first ae caper, syne[95] anither,
Tam tint[96] his reason a' thegither,[97]
And roars out; "Weel done, Cutty-sark!"
And in an instant all was dark;
And scarcely had he Maggie rallied,   195
When out the hellish legion sallied.

As bees bizz out wi' angry fyke,[98]
When plundering herds[99] assail their byke;[1]
As open[2] pussie's[3] mortal foes,
When, pop! she starts before their nose;   200
As eager runs the market-crowd,
When "Catch the thief!" resounds aloud:
So Maggie runs, the witches follow,
Wi' monie an eldritch skriech and hollo.

Ah, Tam! Ah, Tam! thou'll get thy fairin![4]   205
In hell they'll roast thee like a herrin!
In vain thy Kate awaits thy comin!
Kate soon will be a woefu' woman!
Now, do thy speedy utmost, Meg,
And win the key-stane of the brig;   210
There, at them thou thy tail may toss,
A running stream they dare na cross!
But ere the key-stane she could make,
The fient[5] a tail she had to shake;
For Nannie, far before the rest,   215
Hard upon noble Maggie prest,
And flew at Tam wi' furious ettle;[6]
But little wist[7] she Maggie's mettle!
Ae spring brought off her master hale,[8]
But left behind her ain grey tail: 220
The carlin claught[9] her by the rump,
And left poor Maggie scarce a stump.

Now, wha this tale o' truth shall read,
Ilk man, and mother's son, take heed:

---

63 Executed a balancing step facing their partners.
64 Crossed over to exchange places with their partners.
65 Seized; i.e., linked arms.   66 Each hag sweat and steamed.
67 Cast her duds (threw off her clothes) for the work.
68 Skipped.   69 Shirt, shift, chemise.
70 These been lasses.   71 Greasy flannels.
72 I.e., finely woven (a 1700-thread) fabric.   73 These breeches.
74 Buttocks.   75 Glance at.   76 Maidens.
77 Ropelike, scrawny.
78 Wean; i.e., a hungry foal would turn away from them in disgust.
79 Leaping and kicking on a stick.   80 Full finely, very well.
81 Choice.   82 Corps; i.e., she had just become a witch.
83 The southern district of Ayrshire.
84 Both much wheat and barley.   85 Short.
86 A coarse linen woven in the famous shawl-town of Paisley, near
   Glasgow.   87 Proud.   88 Bought.
89 A pound Scots equaled 20 pence, an English pound 20 shillings.

90 Must cower, i.e., lower.   91 Leaped and kicked.
92 Supple jade.   93 Fidgeted full fondly.
94 Jerked (his arm, in playing the bagpipes).   95 Then.
96 Lost.   97 Altogether.   98 Fuss.
99 Herdsmen (or boys).

1 Hive.   2 Begin (barking).   3 The hare's.
4 Present at a fair, i.e., reward.   5 Devil ("fiend").
6 Aim.   7 Knew.   8 Whole.   9 Clutched.

Whene'er to drink you are inclin'd,   225
Or cutty sarks run in your mind,
Think! ye may buy the joys o'er dear:
Remember Tam o' Shanter's mare.

YE FLOWERY BANKS

This is the second version of a lyric that Burns wrote
while living in Dumfries "to sing to a Strathspey reel of
which I am very fond." Often reprinted is a third and
inferior version beginning "Ye banks and braes o' bonny
Doon."

Ye flowery banks o' bonie Doon,
    How can ye blume sae fair?
How can ye chant, ye little birds,
    And I sae fu' o' care?

Thou'll break my heart, thou bonie bird,   5
    That sings upon the bough:
Thou minds me o' the happy days
    When my fause Luve was true!

Thou'll break my heart, thou bonie bird,
    That sings beside thy mate: 10
For sae I sat, and sae I sang,
    And wist na o' my fate!

Aft hae I roved by bonie Doon
    To see the woodbine twine,
And ilka[1] bird sang o' its luve,   15
    And sae did I o' mine.

Wi' lightsome heart I pu'd a rose
    Frae aff its thorny tree,
And my fause luver staw[2] my rose,
    But left the thorn wi' me.   20

AE FOND KISS

This poem came out of a love affair with the beautiful
Mrs. M'Lehose during Burns's second winter in Edinburgh. She was separated but not divorced from her husband, and though she returned Burns's love, prudence
and piety forbade her yielding. He sent the poem to her
at the end of 1791.

Ae fond kiss, and then we sever!
Ae farewell, and then for ever!
Deep in heart-wrung tears I'll pledge thee,
Warring sighs and groans I'll wage[3] thee.

Who shall say that Fortune grieves him,   5
While the star of hope she leaves him?
Me, nae cheerfu' twinkle lights me,
Dark despair around benights me.

I'll ne'er blame my partial fancy:
Naething could resist my Nancy!   10
But to see her was to love her,
Love but her, and love for ever.
Had we never lov'd sae kindly,
Had we never lov'd sae blindly,
Never met—or never parted—   15
We had ne'er been broken-hearted.

Fare-thee-weel, thou first and fairest!
Fare-thee-weel, thou best and dearest!
Thine be ilka joy and treasure,
Peace, Enjoyment, Love and Pleasure!   20
Ae fond kiss, and then we sever!
Ae farewell, alas, for ever!
Deep in heart-wrung tears I'll pledge thee,
Warring signs and groans I'll wage thee.

SCOTS, WHA HAE

At the battle of Bannockburn in 1314 King Robert Bruce,
fighting for Scottish independence, cut to pieces an English army under Edward II. This unhistorical but stirring
address of the hero to his troops was inspired in 1793 by
Burns's liking for a tune which, according to tradition,
played the Scots into the battle. In a letter Burns discloses
that he was moved "by the glowing ideas of some other
struggles of the same nature *not quite so ancient*," that is,
by the French Revolution.

Scots, wha hae wi' Wallace bled,
Scots, wham Bruce has aften led,
Welcome to your gory bed
        Or to victorie!

Now's the day, and now's the hour: 5
See the front o' battle lour,
See approach proud Edward's power—
        Chains and slaverie!

Wha will be a traitor knave?
Wha can fill a coward's grave?   10
Wha sae base as be a slave?—
        Let him turn, and flee!

Wha for Scotland's King and Law
Freedom's sword will strongly draw,
Freeman stand or freeman fa',   15
        Let him follow me!

---

[1] Each.   [2] Stole.   [3] Pledge.

By Oppression's woes and pains,
By your sons in servile chains,
We will drain our dearest veins,
    But they shall be free!   20

Lay the proud usurpers low!
Tyrants fall in every foe!
Liberty's in every blow!
    Let us do, or die!

FOR A' THAT

These verses of 1795 mark the rising tide of democracy, the same tide which had swept away the Bourbon monarchy in France, and was soon to carry Jefferson into the White House. Burns told a friend, "The piece is not really poetry." This statement was probably meant ironically; if not, he was quite wrong.

Is there for[1] honest poverty
    That hings his head, an' a' that?
That coward slave, we pass him by—
    We dare be poor for a' that!
      For a' that, an' a' that,   5
      Our toils obscure, an' a' that,
    The rank is but the guinea's stamp;
    The man's the gowd[2] for a' that.

What tho' on hamely fare we dine,
    Wear hoddin grey,[3] an' a' that?   10
Gie fools their silks, and knaves their wine—
    A man's a man for a' that.
      For a' that, an' a' that,
      Their tinsel show, an' a' that,
    The honest man, tho' e'er sae poor,   15
    Is king o' men for a' that.

Ye see yon birkie,[4] ca'd[5] "a lord,"
    Wha struts, an' stares, an' a' that?
Tho' hundreds worship at his word,
    He's but a cuif[6] for a' that.   20
      For a' that, an' a' that,
      His ribband, star, an' a' that,
    The man o' independent mind,
    He looks and laughs at a' that.

A prince can mak a belted knight,   25
    A marquis, duke, an' a' that!
But an honest man's aboon his might[7]—
    Guid faith, he mauna fa'[8] that!
      For a' that, an' a' that,
      Their dignities, an' a' that,   30
    The pith o' sense an' pride o' worth
    Are higher rank than a' that.

Then let us pray that come it may,
    (As come it will for a' that)
That Sense and Worth o'er a' the earth   35
    May bear the gree[9] an' a' that!
      For a' that, an' a' that,
      It's comin yet for a' that,
    That man to man, the world o'er,
    Shall brithers be for a' that.   40

O, WERT THOU IN THE CAULD BLAST

This song was written a few weeks before Burns died, in honor of Jessy Lewars (d. 1855). She was the young sister of a friend, one of the Excise officers, and had been a great help in the household during the poet's illness. One day he asked her to play him her favorite tune, and immediately composed these words to it. Thus music, always for Burns a primary source of inspiration, stood by him to the end.

O, wert thou in the cauld blast
    On yonder lea, on yonder lea,
My plaidie[1] to the angry airt,[2]
    I'd shelter thee, I'd shelter thee.
Or did Misfortune's bitter storms   5
    Around thee blaw, around thee blaw,
Thy bield[3] should be my bosom,
    To share it a', to share it a'.

Or were I in the wildest waste,
    Sae black and bare, sae black and bare,   10
The desert were a Paradise,
    If thou wert there, if thou wert there.
Or were I monarch o' the globe,
    Wi' thee to reign, wi' thee to reign,
The brightest jewel in my crown   15
    Wad be my queen, wad be my queen.

---

[1] Is there anyone on account of.   [2] Gold.
[3] I.e., coarse gray cloth.   [4] Forward chap.   [5] Called.
[6] Ninny.

[7] Beyond ("above") his power.
[8] Must not claim.   [9] Have first place.

[1] Plaid; the Scot's substitute for a cloak or overcoat.
[2] Quarter, direction of the wind.   [3] Shelter.

William Wordsworth

1770–1850

Parts of three northwestern English counties constitute the Lake District: Cumberland, Westmorland, and Lancashire. In the most northerly of them, at Cockermouth on the Derwent River, Wordsworth was born in 1770. He tells us in *The Prelude* how, normal boy that he seemed in family relations, school life, and sports (he was always one of the best skaters of the region), the beauty and majesty of nature gave him, from early childhood, raptures that are not to be had by everyone or for the mere asking. How much his poetic development owed to the accident of his birth in Cumberland and his boyhood among lakes and mountains, how much to the ferment of ideas and aspirations which precipitated the French Revolution and the Romantic Movement, cannot be known. It is evident in *The Prelude* that he believed he owed a great deal. Earlier poets, his reading in general, the discipline of love, the daily round of experience and observation—no doubt all these helped to form a poet. But above all, behind all, was the mystery of genius, that rare, inexplicable capacity to receive life intensely and, having exerted upon it certain mental and spiritual processes which remain inscrutable, to transmute its impermanent and puzzling phenomena into the permanence and significance of art.

A lawyer's son, Wordsworth was the second of five children, all boys except one sister nearly two years younger than he. Dorothy Wordsworth (1771–1855) was to be his spiritual companion, and to some extent his instructor in his responsiveness to nature. To many hers seems a tragic story, though she did not regard it as a tragedy. That her mind gave way twenty years before her death is not the chief reason for calling it that. Dorothy was one of countless gifted women who have deliberately chosen to work for the success of those they love instead of for triumphs of their own, and have found their happiness there. To his great profit, William absorbed her life. It may have been an injustice; but we cannot regret it, seeing how great was his need of her and also what he gave the world. Her genius, except in molding him, remained latent; her life, unexpressed. She never married. Her *Journals,* as well as her brother's poetic tributes, show something of her quality. His was, if not the finer spirit, the more powerful mind. It was masculine, and unconsciously somewhat ruthless, as artists' minds often are.

When William was eight, his mother died; when he was thirteen, his father died. Uncles assumed guardianship of the children. Money was not lacking, and in 1787 the poet entered St. John's College, Cambridge. He was already a poet; the earliest of his surviving verses had been composed two years before, when he was fifteen. Not, however, till he was in his late twenties did he begin writing great poetry. He took his B.A. in 1791. He had spent the previous summer in France and Switzerland on a walking tour. The end of 1791 found him again in France, where he stayed a little over a year, at Paris, Orleans, and Blois. First Nature, in Cumberland; then Books, at Cambridge; then revolutionary France, Man, and the Rights of Man. And Woman. For besides forming a close friendship with the soldier-patriot Michel Beaupuy, he fell in love with a girl four years older than himself, Marie Anne Vallon, daughter of a French surgeon at Blois. In that dawn of a new, free world, as Wordsworth supposed it was to be, established institutions were collapsing under the revolutionists' assault. The lovers did not marry; but late in 1792, when Wordsworth was back in Paris thinking of joining the Girondin or moderate wing of the Revolutionists, and just before lack of funds compelled his return to England, Annette bore a daughter. Though he did not shirk his financial obligations, this affair, as a love affair, soon became a closed chapter in Wordsworth's life, so much so that public knowledge of it is of recent date. For one thing, England declared war on France early in 1793, and for several years that barred a reunion with Annette. Presumably their feelings changed during the enforced separation.

Nor was it many years before Wordsworth's ardor as a radical abated. Like most men, he moved politically from left to right as he grew older. He was, however, still hopeful of the Revolution when in 1794 Robespierre fell and the Reign of Terror ended; and throughout the period of his best literary work he continued on the radical side. In London, not long after his return from France, he came for a time under the influence of William Godwin (1756–1836), the leading English exponent of philosophical radicalism and atheism, though Godwin's ideas made no permanent appeal to him. Meanwhile he had been subject to the common worry of young poets about finding his place in the world. With Dorothy he went to live on his small capital, a legacy from a friend, in a house on the coast of Dorsetshire. A meeting with Coleridge proved a turning point, for talk with that extraordinary man spurred Wordsworth further on into poetry. Soon they were planning a joint volume of poetry; and in the summer of 1797 William and Dorothy moved to Alfoxden in Somersetshire to be near Coleridge, who was three miles away at Nether Stowey.

Lyrical Ballads came out in the fall of 1798. It was the trumpet call which summoned English literature back from a century and a half of neoclassicism to its normal, romantic attitude toward life and toward art. Wordsworth had already published two longish poems but nothing comparable to the contents of this volume. Not that it swept everything before it. Eighteenth-century standards did not topple like the walls of Jericho at one poetic blast. There were savage reviews, and such ridicule as we shall soon be sampling in Byron's derisive allusions. Wordsworth's genius was understood in this country long before Britain accepted him; though he had ardent admirers there, general recognition was delayed till he was nearly fifty. But whether or not the garrison knew it in 1798, the blast had been blown and the bastions had begun to vibrate.

The volume was jointly conceived; yet, even though it included "The Ancient Mariner," it is Wordsworth's book. In these and their subsequent poems the partners' romanticism usually took different turnings. Coleridge was more attracted by the marvelous and the melodramatically supernatural. Wordsworth's stimulus was just the opposite. For him the common and familiar strikes deep—not dreams of stately pleasure domes built near sacred rivers with exotic names, but this lake or that valley known to him since boyhood, the peasant in his field, the shepherd on his hills. Coleridge *begins* with wonders and, in his best poems, draws them close to us so artfully that he produces in us a "willing suspension of disbelief." Wordsworth leads us gently from the plain forms and facts of Nature, and of Man her child, into the eternal mystery of which to the eye of inspiration they are the symbols. In Coleridge's masterpiece, a voyage of marvels arrives at a homely, touching injunction to kindness. In Wordsworth's "Michael" a simple story of a boy's leaving home takes us into the secret places of the human heart; and "Tintern Abbey" lifts us from the physical beauty of the Wye Valley, perceptible by every tourist, to

> a sense sublime
> Of something far more deeply interfused,
> Whose dwelling is the light of setting suns,
> And the round ocean and the living air,
> And the blue sky, and in the mind of man.

In short, Coleridge would, as Vachel Lindsay enjoins, "bring the wonders down"; Wordsworth shows us that they are already present.

In that fall of 1798 the two Wordsworths went to Germany, where the Romantic cause had already triumphed. There they stayed nine months; and there William wrote some of his best poems. He now resolved to devote all his energies to poetry. Not for the reading public, but as a kind of stocktaking and accounting with himself, he decided to launch out on a long poem which should review those of his experiences which had contributed to equipping his mind for a poetic career. Such was the genesis of *The Prelude*. To secure freedom for the writing of it and to guard that state of tranquillity in which, according to his theory of composition, the mind can best recollect and artistically record emotions previously felt too intensely for immediate poetic use, he settled with Dorothy in 1799 at Dove Cottage in Grasmere, a Westmorland village of the Lake District; and there he went on writing great poetry. It was in 1802 that he began composing the sonnets which were ultimately to reveal him as the greatest sonneteer since Shakespeare and Milton.

In the summer of that year, accompanied by Dorothy, he went over to Calais and spent a month near Annette and their daughter Caroline in order to make certain arrangements before his marriage that autumn to Mary Hutchinson, his first love, whom he had known since childhood. Marriage was now feasible because the Wordsworths had at last received payment of a large debt owed by the owner of an estate their father had managed. Why William and Annette had decided against marriage is uncertain. Her family and perhaps she herself may have thought union with an Englishman, a Protestant, and a radical an unpromising outlook. Correspondence between the families continued without rancor. The affair was known to Wordsworth's wife; she and Dorothy appear to have regarded Annette as a sister. Wordsworth acknowledged his paternity of Caroline, visited her whenever he was in Paris, and stood godfather to her first child. Of his own marriage three sons and two daughters were born. The family, which included Dorothy, lived at Dove Cottage till 1808. From 1813 till the end of his long life Wordsworth lived at Rydal Mount, a large house a few miles away from Dove Cottage. With his wife and sister he often traveled, in the British Isles and on the Continent.

In the second edition (1801) of *Lyrical Ballads* first appeared Wordsworth's famous Preface, the principal Romantic manifesto. A large part of it is reprinted below. While it is explicit in declaring against "poetic diction" and in favor of a return to "the real language of men," Wordsworth's successful poems fall stylistically into two classes. It is true that the language of some of his greatest passages is utterly simple, but in others he writes in an elevated strain, much loftier than the level of common speech. Moreover, his attempts at simplicity sometimes produce what is merely prosaic, sometimes even ludicrous.

One may wish that the saving grace of humor had been Wordsworth's; it would have kept him from numerous falls into bathos. Yet it must be remembered that the great things in art are usually produced by boldness, not caution. If Wordsworth's failures are more depressing than a minor poet's steady maintenance of a respectable standard, his successes have won him a lofty place among English poets.

By the close of the year 1807 most of his best work was finished. He continued writing, and a fraction of what he wrote is of great value; but he seldom equaled his earlier work. Nor are the external events of his later years comparable in interest to those of his youth or of much significance for his poetry. In 1812 the death of two of his children brought suffering. Need of money took him in 1813 to London in search of employment by the government; he was appointed revenue-stamp distributor for Westmorland. He resigned this office in favor of one of his sons in 1842, when in recognition of his attainment in literature he was awarded an annual pension of £300. In the following year he succeeded Southey as poet laureate. As is usually the case, the office proved no stimulus to the production of poetry. Wordsworth was now a thoroughgoing conservative; and some of the younger poets, mindful of what he had stood for in the past, thought he had sold out to the enemies of freedom. The charge was unjust; his Toryism was rooted in conviction, not self-interest. But his mind had hardened;[1] he was now a confirmed opponent of change, hostile to the Reform Bill and to Catholic Emancipation: his view of the national indispensability of the Church of England was as rockribbed as his political opinions. Three years before his death he suffered the deepest sorrow of his life in the loss of his daughter Dora, in her forty-third year. He died in 1850 and was buried, not in Westminster Abbey, but far more appropriately in the churchyard at Grasmere.

Excepting *The Prelude,* Wordsworth's greatness lies in his shorter poems. In successive collected editions he grouped his works according to a scheme he considered "corresponding with the course of human life." This unhappy arrangement has been followed by most editors, but not here. Since Wordsworth's personal experience will be of more interest to a reader already acquainted with some of his greatest poems and with the aims set forth in the Preface to *Lyrical Ballads,* our selections from *The Prelude* come last, though it was a fairly early poem. The sonnets have been placed together, preceded by a number of the other short poems, which are given in order of composition.

The standard edition is *The Poetical Works,* by E. de Selincourt and Helen Darbishire (5 vols., 1940–50). Of the one-volume editions, *The Poetical Works,* edited by T. Hutchinson (1904, later revised by E. de Selincourt), preserves Wordsworth's own grouping. Hutchinson's text has also been reprinted in this country with an introduction by G. M. Harper (1933). One of the best of the chronologically arranged editions is by A. J. George (1904). All these one-volume editions contain the Preface to *Lyrical Ballads.* De Selincourt brought out the letters of William and Dorothy (6 vols., 1935–39); he also wrote a Life of Dorothy (1933) and edited her *Journals* (2 vols., 1941). The standard biography of the poet is by G. M. Harper (2 vols., 1916). A good short Life is C. H. Herford's (1930). Valuable general studies are H. W. Garrod's *Wordsworth* (1923) and Part I of R. D. Havens's *The Mind of a Poet* (1941).

William Wordsworth

LINES WRITTEN IN EARLY SPRING

The first four of the following poems were composed in 1798 and published in *Lyrical Ballads.*

    I heard a thousand blended notes,
    While in a grove I sate reclined,
    In that sweet mood when pleasant thoughts
    Bring sad thoughts to the mind.

    To her fair works did Nature link   5
    The human soul that through me ran;
    And much it grieved my heart to think
    What man has made of man.

    Through primrose tufts, in that green bower,
    The periwinkle trailed its wreaths;   10
    And 'tis my faith that every flower
    Enjoys the air it breathes.

    The birds around me hopped and played,
    Their thoughts I cannot measure:—

---

[1] For an argument to the contrary, see Edith J. Batho, *The Later Wordsworth* (1933).

But the least motion which they made,   15
It seemed a thrill of pleasure.

The budding twigs spread out their fan,
To catch the breezy air;
And I must think, do all I can,
That there was pleasure there.   20

If this belief from heaven be sent,
If such be Nature's holy plan,
Have I not reason to lament
What man has made of man?

EXPOSTULATION AND REPLY

"Why, William, on that old grey stone,
Thus for the length of half a day,
Why, William, sit you thus alone,
And dream your time away?

"Where are your books?—that light bequeathed 5
To Beings else forlorn and blind!
Up! up! and drink the spirit breathed
From dead men to their kind.

"You look round on your Mother Earth,
As if she for no purpose bore you;   10
As if you were her first-born birth,
And none had lived before you!"

One morning thus, by Esthwaite lake,[1]
When life was sweet, I knew not why,
To me my good friend Matthew[2] spake,   15
And thus I made reply:

"The eye—it cannot choose but see;
We cannot bid the ear be still;
Our bodies feel, where'er they be,
Against or with our will.   20

"Nor less I deem that there are Powers
Which of themselves our minds impress;
That we can feed this mind of ours
In a wise passiveness.

"Think you, 'mid all this mighty sum   25
Of things for ever speaking,

---

[1] Esthwaite Water is a lake near Hawkshead, where Wordsworth went to school.
[2] Wordsworth explains that this poem and the next resulted from conversation with "a friend who was somewhat unreasonably attached to modern books of moral philosophy."

That nothing of itself will come,
But we must still be seeking?

"—Then ask not wherefore, here, alone,
Conversing as I may,   30
I sit upon this old grey stone,
And dream my time away."

THE TABLES TURNED

AN EVENING SCENE ON THE SAME SUBJECT

Up! up! my Friend, and quit your books;
Or surely you'll grow double:
Up! up! my Friend, and clear your looks;
Why all this toil and trouble?

The sun, above the mountain's head,   5
A freshening lustre mellow
Through all the long green fields has spread,
His first sweet evening yellow.

Books! 'tis a dull and endless strife:
Come, hear the woodland linnet,   10
How sweet his music! on my life,
There's more of wisdom in it.

And hark! how blithe the throstle sings!
He, too, is no mean preacher:
Come forth into the light of things,   15
Let Nature be your Teacher.

She has a world of ready wealth,
Our minds and hearts to bless—
Spontaneous wisdom breathed by health,
Truth breathed by cheerfulness.   20

One impulse from a vernal wood
May teach you more of man,
Of moral evil and of good,
Than all the sages can.

Sweet is the lore which Nature brings;   25
Our meddling intellect
Mis-shapes the beauteous forms of things:—
We murder to dissect.

Enough of Science and of Art;
Close up those barren leaves;   30
Come forth, and bring with you a heart
That watches and receives.

LINES

COMPOSED A FEW MILES ABOVE TINTERN ABBEY,
ON REVISITING THE BANKS OF THE WYE
DURING A TOUR. JULY 13, 1798

In this great poem Wordsworth elaborates the attitude
toward nature which is suggested in the first three of our
selections. The noble ruins of Tintern Abbey stand in a
lovely valley in Monmouthshire.

Five years have past; five summers, with the length
Of five long winters! and again I hear
These waters, rolling from their mountain-springs
With a soft inland murmur.—Once again
Do I behold these steep and lofty cliffs, 5
That on a wild secluded scene impress
Thoughts of more deep seclusion; and connect
The landscape with the quiet of the sky.
The day is come when I again repose
Here, under this dark sycamore, and view 10
These plots of cottage-ground, these orchard-tufts,
Which at this season, with their unripe fruits,
Are clad in one green hue, and lose themselves
'Mid groves and copses. Once again I see
These hedge-rows, hardly hedge-rows, little lines 15
Of sportive wood run wild: these pastoral farms,
Green to the very door; and wreaths of smoke
Sent up, in silence, from among the trees!
With some uncertain notice, as might seem
Of vagrant dwellers in the houseless woods, 20
Or of some Hermit's cave, where by his fire
The Hermit sits alone.
                    These beauteous forms,
Through a long absence, have not been to me
As is a landscape to a blind man's eye:
But oft, in lonely rooms, and 'mid the din 25
Of towns and cities, I have owed to them,
In hours of weariness, sensations sweet,
Felt in the blood, and felt along the heart;
And passing even into my purer mind,
With tranquil restoration:—feelings too 30
Of unremembered pleasure: such, perhaps,
As have no slight or trivial influence
On that best portion of a good man's life,
His little, nameless, unremembered, acts
Of kindness and of love. Nor less, I trust, 35
To them I may have owed another gift,
Of aspect more sublime; that blessèd mood,
In which the burthen of the mystery,
In which the heavy and the weary weight
Of all this unintelligible world, 40
Is lightened:—that serene and blessèd mood,
In which the affections gently lead us on,—

Until, the breath of this corporeal frame
And even the motion of our human blood
Almost suspended, we are laid asleep 45
In body, and become a living soul:
While with an eye made quiet by the power
Of harmony, and the deep power of joy,
We see into the life of things.
                        If this
Be but a vain belief, yet, oh! how oft— 50
In darkness and amid the many shapes
Of joyless daylight; when the fretful stir
Unprofitable, and the fever of the world,
Have hung upon the beatings of my heart—
How oft, in spirit, have I turned to thee, 55
O sylvan Wye! thou wanderer thro' the woods,
How often has my spirit turned to thee!

     And now, with gleams of half-extinguished thought,
With many recognitions dim and faint,
And somewhat of a sad perplexity, 60
The picture of the mind revives again:
While here I stand, not only with the sense
Of present pleasure, but with pleasing thoughts
That in this moment there is life and food
For future years. And so I dare to hope, 65
Though changed, no doubt, from what I was when first
I came among these hills; when like a roe
I bounded o'er the mountains, by the sides
Of the deep rivers, and the lonely streams,
Wherever nature led: more like a man 70
Flying from something that he dreads than one
Who sought the thing he loved. For nature then
(The coarser pleasures of my boyish days,
And their glad animal movements all gone by)
To me was all in all.—I cannot paint 75
What then I was. The sounding cataract
Haunted me like a passion: the tall rock,
The mountain, and the deep and gloomy wood,
Their colours and their forms, were then to me
An appetite; a feeling and a love, 80
That had no need of a remoter charm,
By thought supplied, nor any interest
Unborrowed from the eye.—That time is past,
And all its aching joys are now no more,
And all its dizzy raptures. Not for this 85
Faint I, nor mourn nor murmur; other gifts
Have followed; for such loss, I would believe,
Abundant recompense. For I have learned
To look on nature, not as in the hour
Of thoughtless youth; but hearing oftentimes 90
The still, sad music of humanity,
Nor harsh nor grating, though of ample power
To chasten and subdue. And I have felt

48 THE ROMANTIC PERIOD

A presence that disturbs me with the joy
Of elevated thoughts; a sense sublime   95
Of something far more deeply interfused,
Whose dwelling is the light of setting suns,
And the round ocean and the living air,
And the blue sky, and in the mind of man:
A motion and a spirit, that impels   100
All thinking things, all objects of all thought,
And rolls through all things. Therefore am I still
A lover of the meadows and the woods,
And mountains; and of all that we behold
From this green earth; of all the mighty world   105
Of eye, and ear,—both what they half create,
And what perceive; well pleased to recognise
In nature and the language of the sense
The anchor of my purest thoughts, the nurse,
The guide, the guardian of my heart, and soul   110
Of all my moral being.
                                    Nor perchance,
If I were not thus taught, should I the more
Suffer my genial spirits to decay:
For thou[1] art with me here upon the banks
Of this fair river; thou my dearest Friend,   115
My dear, dear Friend; and in thy voice I catch
The language of my former heart, and read
My former pleasures in the shooting lights
Of thy wild eyes. Oh! yet a little while
May I behold in thee what I was once,   120
My dear, dear Sister! and this prayer I make,
Knowing that Nature never did betray
The heart that loved her; 'tis her privilege,
Through all the years of this our life, to lead
From joy to joy: for she can so inform[2]   125
The mind that is within us, so impress
With quietness and beauty, and so feed
With lofty thoughts, that neither evil tongues,
Rash judgments, nor the sneers of selfish men,
Nor greetings where no kindness is, nor all   130
The dreary intercourse of daily life,
Shall e'er prevail against us, or disturb
Our cheerful faith, that all which we behold
Is full of blessings. Therefore let the moon
Shine on thee in thy solitary walk;   135
And let the misty mountain-winds be free
To blow against thee: and, in after years,
When these wild ecstasies shall be matured
Into a sober pleasure; when thy mind
Shall be a mansion for all lovely forms,   140
Thy memory be as a dwelling-place
For all sweet sounds and harmonies; oh! then,
If solitude, or fear, or pain, or grief,

_____
[1] His sister Dorothy.   [2] Animate, inspire.

Should be thy portion, with what healing thoughts
Of tender joy wilt thou remember me,   145
And these my exhortations! Nor, perchance—
If I should be where I no more can hear
Thy voice, nor catch from thy wild eyes these gleams
Of past existence[3]—wilt thou then forget
That on the banks of this delightful stream   150
We stood together; and that I, so long
A worshipper of Nature, hither came
Unwearied in that service: rather say
With warmer love—oh! with far deeper zeal
Of holier love. Nor wilt thou then forget   155
That after many wanderings, many years
Of absence, these steep woods and lofty cliffs,
And this green pastoral landscape, were to me
More dear, both for themselves and for thy sake!

STRANGE FITS OF PASSION
HAVE I KNOWN

This poem and the four that follow it constitute the
"Lucy poems," written in 1799, while Wordsworth was
in Germany. He never explained them, and no one knows
whether this little cycle elegizes someone the poet actually
knew or, as seems more likely, is wholly imaginative.

Strange fits of passion have I known:
And I will dare to tell,
But in the Lover's ear alone,
What once to me befell.

When she I loved looked every day   5
Fresh as a rose in June,
I to her cottage bent my way,
Beneath an evening-moon.

Upon the moon I fixed my eye,
All over the wide lea;[1]   10
With quickening pace my horse drew nigh
Those paths so dear to me.

And now we reached the orchard-plot;
And, as we climbed the hill,
The sinking moon to Lucy's cot   15
Came near, and nearer still.

In one of those sweet dreams I slept,
Kind Nature's gentlest boon!
And all the while my eyes I kept
On the descending moon.   20

_____
[3] The poet's own past.
[1] Meadow or pastureland.

My horse moved on; hoof after hoof
He raised, and never stopped:
When down behind the cottage roof,
At once, the bright moon dropped.

What fond and wayward thoughts will slide   25
Into a Lover's head!
"O mercy!" to myself I cried,
"If Lucy should be dead!"[2]

SHE DWELT AMONG THE
UNTRODDEN WAYS

She dwelt among the untrodden ways
    Beside the springs of Dove,[3]
A Maid whom there were none to praise
    And very few to love:

A violet by a mossy stone   5
    Half hidden from the eye!
—Fair as a star, when only one
    Is shining in the sky.

She lived unknown, and few could know
    When Lucy ceased to be;   10
But she is in her grave, and, oh,
    The difference to me!

I TRAVELLED
AMONG UNKNOWN MEN

I travelled among unknown men,
    In lands beyond the sea;
Nor, England! did I know till then
    What love I bore to thee.

'Tis past, that melancholy dream!   5
    Nor will I quit thy shore
A second time; for still I seem
    To love thee more and more.

Among thy mountains did I feel
    The joy of my desire;   10
And she I cherished turned her wheel
    Beside an English fire.

Thy mornings showed, thy nights concealed,
    The bowers where Lucy played;
And thine too is the last green field   15
    That Lucy's eyes surveyed.

THREE YEARS SHE GREW IN
SUN AND SHOWER

Three years she grew in sun and shower,
Then Nature said, "A lovelier flower
On earth was never sown;
This Child I to myself will take;
She shall be mine, and I will make   5
A Lady of my own.

"Myself will to my darling be
Both law and impulse: and with me
The Girl, in rock and plain,
In earth and heaven, in glade and bower,   10
Shall feel an overseeing power
To kindle or restrain.

"She shall be sportive as the fawn
That wild with glee across the lawn
Or up the mountain springs;   15
And hers shall be the breathing balm,
And hers the silence and the calm
Of mute insensate things.

"The floating clouds their state shall lend
To her; for her the willow bend;   20
Nor shall she fail to see
Even in the motions of the Storm
Grace that shall mould the Maiden's form
By silent sympathy.

"The stars of midnight shall be dear   25
To her; and she shall lean her ear
In many a secret place
Where rivulets dance their wayward round,
And beauty born of murmuring sound
Shall pass into her face.   30

"And vital feelings of delight
Shall rear her form to stately height,
Her virgin bosom swell;
Such thoughts to Lucy I will give
While she and I together live   35
Here in this happy dell."

Thus Nature spake—The work was done—
How soon my Lucy's race was run!

---

[2] The poem originally ended with a stanza that Wordsworth later
canceled (see *The Early Letters*, ed. E. de Selincourt, pp. 205–6):
        "I told her this; her laughter light
        Is ringing in my ears;
        And when I think upon that night
        My eyes are dim with tears."
[3] A river between Derbyshire and Staffordshire.

She died, and left to me
This heath, this calm, and quiet scene;   40
The memory of what has been,
And never more will be.

A SLUMBER DID MY SPIRIT SEAL

A slumber did my spirit seal;
    I had no human fears:
She seemed a thing that could not feel
    The touch of earthly years.

No motion has she now, no force;   5
    She neither hears nor sees;
Rolled round in earth's diurnal course,
    With rocks, and stones, and trees.

LUCY GRAY
OR SOLITUDE

This poem was also written in 1799, in Germany. Dorothy
had told her brother about a little Yorkshire girl drowned
in the lock of a canal during a snowstorm. Wordsworth's
aim was to tell this story with the simplicity of the old
ballads, and yet (as he says in a note) to treat "common
life" imaginatively.

Oft I had heard of Lucy Gray:
And, when I crossed the wild,
I chanced to see at break of day
The solitary child.

No mate, no comrade Lucy knew;   5
She dwelt on a wide moor,
—The sweetest thing that ever grew
Beside a human door!

You yet may spy the fawn at play,
The hare upon the green;   10
But the sweet face of Lucy Gray
Will never more be seen.

"To-night will be a stormy night—
You to the town must go;
And take a lantern, Child, to light   15
Your mother through the snow."

"That, Father! will I gladly do:
'Tis scarcely afternoon—
The minster-clock has just struck two,
And yonder is the moon!"   20

At this the Father raised his hook,
And snapped a faggot-band;
He plied his work;—and Lucy took
The lantern in her hand.

Not blither is the mountain roe: 25
With many a wanton stroke
Her feet disperse the powdery snow,
That rises up like smoke.

The storm came on before its time:
She wandered up and down;   30
And many a hill did Lucy climb:
But never reached the town.

The wretched parents all that night
Went shouting far and wide;
But there was neither sound nor sight   35
To serve them for a guide.

At day-break on a hill they stood
That overlooked the moor;
And thence they saw the bridge of wood,
A furlong from their door.   40

They wept—and, turning homeward, cried,
"In heaven we all shall meet";
—When in the snow the mother spied
The print of Lucy's feet.

Then downwards from the steep hill's edge   45
They tracked the footmarks small;
And through the broken hawthorn hedge,
And by the long stone-wall;

And then an open field they crossed:
The marks were still the same;   50
They tracked them on, nor ever lost;
And to the bridge they came.

They followed from the snowy bank
Those footmarks, one by one,
Into the middle of the plank;   55
And further there were none!

—Yet some maintain that to this day
She is a living child;
That you may see sweet Lucy Gray
Upon the lonesome wild.   60

O'er rough and smooth she trips along,
And never looks behind;
And sings a solitary song
That whistles in the wind.

THE FOUNTAIN

A CONVERSATION

The character of Matthew (who appears also in two other poems, "Matthew" and "The Two April Mornings") is copied at least in part from that of a master in the Hawkshead grammar school, to which Wordsworth was sent at the age of eight. All three poems were composed in 1799 and published in the second edition of *Lyrical Ballads*.

We talked with open heart, and tongue
Affectionate and true,
A pair of friends, though I was young,
And Matthew seventy-two.

We lay beneath a spreading oak,   5
Beside a mossy seat;
And from the turf a fountain[1] broke,
And gurgled at our feet.

"Now Matthew!" said I, "let us match
This water's pleasant tune   10
With some old border-song, or catch
That suits a summer's noon;

"Or of the church-clock and the chimes
Sing here beneath the shade,
That half-mad thing of witty rhymes   15
Which you last April made!"

In silence Matthew lay, and eyed
The spring beneath the tree;
And thus the dear old Man replied,
The grey-haired man of glee: 20

"No check, no stay, this Streamlet fears;
How merrily it goes!
'T will murmur on a thousand years,
And flow as now it flows.

"And here, on this delightful day,   25
I cannot choose but think
How oft, a vigorous man, I lay
Beside this fountain's brink.

"My eyes are dim with childish tears,
My heart is idly stirred,   30
For the same sound is in my ears
Which in those days I heard.

"Thus fares it still in our decay:
And yet the wiser mind
Mourns less for what age takes away   35
Than what it leaves behind.

"The blackbird amid leafy trees,
The lark above the hill,
Let loose their carols when they please,
Are quiet when they will.   40

"With Nature never do *they* wage
A foolish strife; they see
A happy youth, and their old age
Is beautiful and free:

"But we are pressed by heavy laws;   45
And often, glad no more,
We wear a face of joy, because
We have been glad of yore.

"If there be one who need bemoan
His kindred laid in earth,   50
The household hearts that were his own,
It is the man of mirth.

"My days, my Friend, are almost gone,
My life has been approved,
And many love me; but by none   55
Am I enough beloved."

"Now both himself and me he wrongs,
The man who thus complains!
I live and sing my idle songs
Upon these happy plains;   60

"And, Matthew, for thy children dead
I'll be a son to thee!"
At this he grasped my hand, and said,
"Alas! that cannot be."

We rose up from the fountain-side,   65
And down the smooth descent
Of the green sheep-track did we glide;
And through the wood we went;

And, ere we came to Leonard's rock,
He sang those witty rhymes   70
About the crazy old church-clock,
And the bewildered chimes.

---

[1] Spring.

MICHAEL

A PASTORAL POEM

In "Michael" Wordsworth tells a story of humble folk,
and tells it with a masterly simplicity. He has attempted,
he says in a letter, "to give a picture of a man, of strong
mind and lively sensibility, agitated by two of the most
powerful affections of the human heart: the parental
affection and the love of property (*landed* property), including the feelings of inheritance, home, and personal
and family independence." His success may be judged
by the intensity of tragic pathos reached in the quiet line
(466), "And never lifted up a single stone." "Michael"
was composed in 1800; Wordsworth was living at
Grasmere, in the northern lake country.

If from the public way you turn your steps
Up the tumultuous brook of Greenhead Ghyll,[1]
You will suppose that with an upright path
Your feet must struggle; in such bold ascent
The pastoral mountains front you, face to face.
But, courage! for around that boisterous brook
The mountains have all opened out themselves,
And made a hidden valley of their own.
No habitation can be seen; but they
Who journey thither find themselves alone
With a few sheep, with rocks and stones, and kites[2]
That overhead are sailing in the sky.
It is in truth an utter solitude;
Nor should I have made mention of this Dell
But for one object which you might pass by,   15
Might see and notice not. Beside the brook
Appears a straggling heap of unhewn stones!
And to that simple object appertains
A story—unenriched with strange events,
Yet not unfit, I deem, for the fireside,   20
Or for the summer shade. It was the first
Of those domestic tales that spake to me
Of Shepherds, dwellers in the valleys, men
Whom I already loved;—not verily
For their own sakes, but for the fields and hills   25
Where was their occupation and abode.
And hence this Tale, while I was yet a Boy
Careless of books, yet having felt the power
Of Nature, by the gentle agency
Of natural objects, led me on to feel   30
For passions that were not my own, and think
(At random and imperfectly indeed)
On man, the heart of man, and human life.
Therefore, although it be a history
Homely and rude, I will relate the same   35

_____

[1] Gully.   [2] A kind of hawk.

For the delight of a few natural hearts;
And, with yet fonder feeling, for the sake
Of youthful Poets, who among these hills
Will be my second self when I am gone.

Upon the forest-side in Grasmere Vale   40
There dwelt a Shepherd, Michael was his name;
An old man, stout of heart, and strong of limb.
His bodily frame had been from youth to age
Of an unusual strength: his mind was keen,
Intense, and frugal, apt for all affairs,   45
And in his shepherd's calling he was prompt
And watchful more than ordinary men.
Hence had he learned the meaning of all winds,
Of blasts of every tone; and oftentimes,
When others heeded not, he heard the South   50
Make subterraneous music, like the noise
Of bagpipers on distant Highland hills.
The Shepherd, at such warning, of his flock
Bethought him, and he to himself would say,
"The winds are now devising work for me!"   55
And, truly, at all times, the storm, that drives
The traveller to a shelter, summoned him
Up to the mountains: he had been alone
Amid the heart of many thousand mists,
That came to him, and left him, on the heights.   60
So lived he till his eightieth year was past.
And grossly that man errs who should suppose
That the green valleys, and the streams and rocks,
Were things indifferent to the Shepherd's thoughts.
Fields, where with cheerful spirits he had breathed 65
The common air; hills, which with vigorous step
He had so often climbed; which had impressed
So many incidents upon his mind
Of hardship, skill or courage, joy or fear;
Which, like a book, preserved the memory   70
Of the dumb animals, whom he had saved,
Had fed or sheltered, linking to such acts
The certainty of honourable gain;
Those fields, those hills—what could they less? had laid
Strong hold on his affections, were to him   75
A pleasurable feeling of blind love,
The pleasure which there is in life itself.

His days had not been passed in singleness.
His Helpmate was a comely matron, old—
Though younger than himself full twenty years.   80
She was a woman of a stirring life,
Whose heart was in her house: two wheels she had
Of antique form; this large, for spinning wool;
That small, for flax; and, if one wheel had rest,
It was because the other was at work.   85
The Pair had but one inmate in their house,

An only Child, who had been born to them
When Michael, telling o'er[3] his years, began
To deem that he was old,—in shepherd's phrase,
With one foot in the grave. This only Son, 90
With two brave sheep-dogs tried in many a storm,
The one of an inestimable worth,
Made all their household. I may truly say,
That they were as a proverb in the vale
For endless industry. When day was gone, 95
And from their occupations out of doors
The Son and Father were come home, even then,
Their labour did not cease; unless when all
Turned to the cleanly supper-board, and there,
Each with a mess of pottage and skimmed milk, 100
Sat round the basket piled with oaten cakes,
And their plain home-made cheese. Yet when the meal
Was ended, Luke (for so the Son was named)
And his old Father both betook themselves
To such convenient work as might employ 105
Their hands by the fire-side; perhaps to card
Wool for the Housewife's spindle, or repair
Some injury done to sickle, flail, or scythe,
Or other implement of house or field.

Down from the ceiling, by the chimney's edge, 110
That in our ancient uncouth country style
With huge and black projection overbrowed
Large space beneath, as duly as the light
Of day grew dim the Housewife hung a lamp;
An aged utensil, which had performed 115
Service beyond all others of its kind.
Early at evening did it burn—and late,
Surviving comrade of uncounted hours,
Which, going by from year to year, had found,
And left, the couple neither gay perhaps 120
Nor cheerful, yet with objects and with hopes,
Living a life of eager industry.
And now, when Luke had reached his eighteenth year,
There by the light of this old lamp they sate,
Father and Son, while far into the night 125
The Housewife plied her own peculiar[4] work,
Making the cottage through the silent hours
Murmur as with the sound of summer flies.
This light was famous in its neighbourhood,
And was a public symbol of the life 130
That thrifty Pair had lived. For, as it chanced,
Their cottage on a plot of rising ground
Stood single, with large prospect, north and south,
High into Easedale, up to Dunmail-Raise,[5]

And westward to the village near the lake; 135
And from this constant light, so regular,
And so far seen, the House itself, by all
Who dwelt within the limits of the vale,
Both old and young, was named THE EVENING STAR.

Thus living on through such a length of years, 140
The Shepherd, if he loved himself, must needs
Have loved his Helpmate; but to Michael's heart
This son of his old age was yet more dear—
Less from instinctive tenderness, the same
Fond spirit that blindly works in the blood of all— 145
Than that a child, more than all other gifts
That earth can offer to declining man,
Brings hope with it, and forward-looking thoughts,
And stirrings of inquietude, when they
By tendency of nature needs must fail. 150
Exceeding was the love he bare to him,
His heart and his heart's joy! For oftentimes
Old Michael, while he was a babe in arms,
Had done him female service, not alone
For pastime and delight, as is the use 155
Of fathers, but with patient mind enforced
To acts of tenderness; and he had rocked
His cradle, as with a woman's gentle hand.

And in a later time, ere yet the Boy
Had put on boy's attire, did Michael love, 160
Albeit of a stern unbending mind,
To have the Young-one in his sight, when he
Wrought in the field, or on his shepherd's stool
Sate with a fettered sheep before him stretched
Under the large old oak, that near his door 165
Stood single, and, from matchless depth of shade,
Chosen for the Shearer's covert from the sun,
Thence in our rustic dialect was called
The CLIPPING TREE, a name which yet it bears.
There, while they two were sitting in the shade, 170
With others round them, earnest all and blithe,
Would Michael exercise his heart with looks
Of fond correction and reproof bestowed
Upon the Child, if he disturbed the sheep
By catching at their legs, or with his shouts 175
Scared them, while they lay still beneath the shears.

And when by Heaven's good grace the boy grew up
A healthy Lad, and carried in his cheek
Two steady roses that were five years old;
Then Michael from a winter coppice cut 180
With his own hand a sapling, which he hooped
With iron, making it throughout in all
Due requisites a perfect shepherd's staff,
And gave it to the Boy; wherewith equipt

---

[3] Counting.   [4] Special.
[5] A hill south of Thirlmere, on the road between Keswick and
    Grasmere. Easedale Tarn (pond) lies among the hills southwest
    of it.

He as a watchman oftentimes was placed   185
At gate or gap, to stem or turn the flock;
And, to his office prematurely called,
There stood the urchin, as you will divine,
Something between a hindrance and a help;
And for this cause not always, I believe,   190
Receiving from his Father hire of praise;
Though nought was left undone which staff, or voice,
Or looks, or threatening gestures, could perform.

But soon as Luke, full ten years old, could stand
Against the mountain blasts; and to the heights,   195
Not fearing toil, nor length of weary ways,
He and his Father daily went, and they
Were as companions, why should I relate
That objects which the Shepherd loved before
Were dearer now? that from the Boy there came   200
Feelings and emanations—things which were
Light to the sun and music to the wind;
And that the old Man's heart seemed born again?

Thus in his Father's sight the Boy grew up:
And now, when he had reached his eighteenth year, 205
He was his comfort and his daily hope.

While in this sort the simple household lived
From day to day, to Michael's ear there came
Distressful tidings. Long before the time
Of which I speak, the Shepherd had been bound   210
In surety for his brother's son, a man
Of an industrious life, and ample means;
But unforeseen misfortunes suddenly
Had prest upon him; and old Michael now
Was summoned to discharge the forfeiture,   215
A grievous penalty, but little less
Than half his substance. This unlooked-for claim,
At the first hearing, for a moment took
More hope out of his life than he supposed
That any old man ever could have lost.   220
As soon as he had armed himself with strength
To look his trouble in the face, it seemed
The Shepherd's sole resource to sell at once
A portion of his patrimonial fields.
Such was his first resolve; he thought again,   225
And his heart failed him. "Isabel," said he,
Two evenings after he had heard the news,
"I have been toiling more than seventy years,
And in the open sunshine of God's love
Have we all lived; yet, if these fields of ours   230
Should pass into a stranger's hand, I think
That I could not lie quiet in my grave.
Our lot is a hard lot; the sun himself
Has scarcely been more diligent than I;

And I have lived to be a fool at last   235
To my own family. An evil man
That was, and made an evil choice, if he
Were false to us; and, if he were not false,
There are ten thousand to whom loss like this
Had been no sorrow. I forgive him;—but   240
'Twere better to be dumb than to talk thus.

"When I began, my purpose was to speak
Of remedies and of a cheerful hope.
Our Luke shall leave us, Isabel; the land
Shall not go from us, and it shall be free;   245
He shall possess it, free as is the wind
That passes over it. We have, thou know'st,
Another kinsman—he will be our friend
In this distress. He is a prosperous man,
Thriving in trade—and Luke to him shall go,   250
And with his kinsman's help and his own thrift
He quickly will repair this loss, and then
He may return to us. If here he stay,
What can be done? Where every one is poor,
What can be gained?"
                    At this the old Man paused,   255
And Isabel sat silent, for her mind
Was busy, looking back into past times.
There's Richard Bateman, thought she to herself,
He was a parish-boy—at the church-door
They made a gathering for him, shillings, pence,   260
And halfpennies, wherewith the neighbours bought
A basket, which they filled with pedlar's wares;
And, with this basket on his arm, the lad
Went up to London, found a master there,
Who, out of many, chose the trusty boy   265
To go and overlook his merchandise
Beyond the seas; where he grew wondrous rich,
And left estates and monies to the poor,
And, at his birth-place, built a chapel floored
With marble, which he sent from foreign lands.   270
These thoughts, and many others of like sort,
Passed quickly through the mind of Isabel,
And her face brightened. The old Man was glad,
And thus resumed:—"Well, Isabel! this scheme
These two days has been meat and drink to me.   275
Far more than we have lost is left us yet.
—We have enough—I wish indeed that I
Were younger;—but this hope is a good hope.
Make ready Luke's best garments, of the best
Buy for him more, and let us send him forth   280
To-morrow, or the next day, or to-night:
—If he could go, the Boy should go to-night."

Here Michael ceased, and to the fields went forth
With a light heart. The Housewife for five days

Was restless morn and night, and all day long   285
Wrought on with her best fingers to prepare
Things needful for the journey of her son.
But Isabel was glad when Sunday came
To stop her in her work: for, when she lay
By Michael's side, she through the last two nights   290
Heard him, how he was troubled in his sleep:
And when they rose at morning she could see
That all his hopes were gone. That day at noon
She said to Luke, while they two by themselves
Were sitting at the door, "Thou must not go: 295
We have no other Child but thee to lose,
None to remember—do not go away,
For if thou leave thy Father he will die."
The Youth made answer with a jocund voice;
And Isabel, when she had told her fears,   300
Recovered heart. That evening her best fare
Did she bring forth, and all together sat
Like happy people round a Christmas fire.

With daylight Isabel resumed her work;
And all the ensuing week the house appeared   305
As cheerful as a grove in Spring: at length
The expected letter from their Kinsman came,
With kind assurances that he would do
His utmost for the welfare of the Boy;
To which, requests were added, that forthwith   310
He might be sent to him. Ten times or more
The letter was read over; Isabel
Went forth to show it to the neighbours round;
Nor was there at that time on English land
A prouder heart than Luke's. When Isabel   315
Had to her house returned, the old Man said,
"He shall depart to-morrow." To this word
The Housewife answered, talking much of things
Which, if at such short notice he should go,
Would surely be forgotten. But at length   320
She gave consent, and Michael was at ease.

Near the tumultuous brook of Greenhead Ghyll,
In that deep valley, Michael had designed
To build a Sheep-fold; and, before he heard
The tidings of his melancholy loss,   325
For this same purpose he had gathered up
A heap of stones, which by the streamlet's edge
Lay thrown together, ready for the work.
With Luke that evening thitherward he walked:
And soon as they had reached the place he stopped,   330
And thus the old Man spake to him:—"My Son,
To-morrow thou wilt leave me: with full heart
I look upon thee, for thou art the same
That wert a promise to me ere thy birth,
And all thy life hast been my daily joy.   335

I will relate to thee some little part
Of our two histories; 'twill do thee good
When thou art from me, even if I should touch
On things thou canst not know of.—After thou
First cam'st into the world—as oft befalls   340
To new-born infants—thou didst sleep away
Two days, and blessings from thy Father's tongue
Then fell upon thee. Day by day passed on,
And still I loved thee with increasing love.
Never to living ear came sweeter sounds   345
Than when I heard thee by our own fire-side
First uttering, without words, a natural tune;
While thou, a feeding babe, didst in thy joy
Sing at thy Mother's breast. Month followed month,
And in the open fields my life was passed   350
And on the mountains; else I think that thou
Hadst been brought up upon thy Father's knees.
But we were playmates, Luke: among these hills,
As well thou knowest, in us the old and young
Have played together, nor with me didst thou   355
Lack any pleasure which a boy can know."
Luke had a manly heart; but at these words
He sobbed aloud. The old Man grasped his hand,
And said, "Nay, do not take it so—I see
That these are things of which I need not speak.   360
—Even to the utmost I have been to thee
A kind and a good Father: and herein
I but repay a gift which I myself
Received at others' hands; for, though now old
Beyond the common life of man, I still   365
Remember them who loved me in my youth.
Both of them sleep together: here they lived,
As all their Forefathers had done; and, when
At length their time was come, they were not loth
To give their bodies to the family mould.   370
I wished that thou shouldst live the life they lived,
But 'tis a long time to look back, my Son,
And see so little gain from threescore years.
These fields were burthened when they came to me;
Till I was forty years of age, not more   375
Than half of my inheritance was mine.
I toiled and toiled; God blessed me in my work,
And till these three weeks past the land was free.
—It looks as if it never could endure
Another Master. Heaven forgive me, Luke,   380
If I judge ill for thee, but it seems good
That thou shouldst go."
                    At this the old Man paused;
Then, pointing to the stones near which they stood,
Thus, after a short silence, he resumed:
"This was a work for us; and now, my Son,   385
It is a work for me. But, lay one stone—
Here, lay it for me, Luke, with thine own hands.

Nay, Boy, be of good hope;—we both may live
To see a better day. At eighty-four
I still am strong and hale;—do thou thy part;   390
I will do mine.—I will begin again
With many tasks that were resigned to thee:
Up to the heights, and in among the storms,
Will I without thee go again, and do
All works which I was wont to do alone,   395
Before I knew thy face.—Heaven bless thee, Boy!
Thy heart these two weeks has been beating fast
With many hopes; it should be so—yes—yes—
I knew that thou couldst never have a wish
To leave me, Luke: thou hast been bound to me   400
Only by links of love: when thou art gone,
What will be left to us!—But I forget
My purposes. Lay now the corner-stone,
As I requested; and hereafter, Luke,
When thou art gone away, should evil men   405
Be thy companions, think of me, my Son,
And of this moment; hither turn thy thoughts,
And God will strengthen thee: amid all fear
And all temptation, Luke, I pray that thou
May'st bear in mind the life thy Fathers lived,   410
Who, being innocent, did for that cause
Bestir them in good deeds. Now, fare thee well—
When thou return'st, thou in this place wilt see
A work which is not here: a covenant
'Twill be between us; but, whatever fate   415
Befall thee, I shall love thee to the last,
And bear thy memory with me to the grave."

The Shepherd ended here; and Luke stooped down,
And, as his Father had requested, laid
The first stone of the Sheep-fold. At the sight   420
The old Man's grief broke from him; to his heart
He pressed his Son, he kissèd him and wept;
And to the house together they returned.
—Hushed was that House in peace, or seeming peace,
Ere the night fell:—with morrow's dawn the Boy   425
Began his journey, and, when he had reached
The public way, he put on a bold face;
And all the neighbours, as he passed their doors,
Came forth with wishes and with farewell prayers,
That followed him till he was out of sight.   430

A good report did from their Kinsman come,
Of Luke and his well-doing: and the Boy
Wrote loving letters, full of wondrous news,
Which, as the Housewife phrased it, were throughout
"The prettiest letters that were ever seen."   435

Both parents read them with rejoicing hearts.
So, many months passed on: and once again
The Shepherd went about his daily work
With confident and cheerful thoughts; and now
Sometimes when he could find a leisure hour   440
He to that valley took his way, and there
Wrought at the Sheep-fold. Meantime Luke began
To slacken in his duty; and, at length,
He in the dissolute city gave himself
To evil courses: ignominy and shame   445
Fell on him, so that he was driven at last
To seek a hiding-place beyond the seas.

There is a comfort in the strength of love;
'Twill make a thing endurable, which else
Would overset the brain, or break the heart: 450
I have conversed with more than one who well
Remember the old Man, and what he was
Years after he had heard this heavy news.
His bodily frame had been from youth to age
Of an unusual strength. Among the rocks   455
He went, and still looked up to sun and cloud,
And listened to the wind; and, as before,
Performed all kinds of labour for his sheep,
And for the land, his small inheritance.
And to that hollow dell from time to time   460
Did he repair, to build the Fold of which
His flock had need. 'Tis not forgotten yet
The pity which was then in every heart
For the old Man—and 'tis believed by all
That many and many a day he thither went,   465
And never lifted up a single stone.

There, by the Sheep-fold, sometimes was he seen
Sitting alone, or with his faithful Dog,
Then old, beside him, lying at his feet.
The length of full seven years, from time to time,   470
He at the building of this Sheep-fold wrought,
And left the work unfinished when he died.
Three years, or little more, did Isabel
Survive her Husband: at her death the estate
Was sold, and went into a stranger's hand.   475
The cottage which was named the EVENING STAR
Is gone—the ploughshare has been through the
    ground
On which it stood; great changes have been wrought
In all the neighbourhood:—yet the oak is left
That grew beside their door; and the remains   480
Of the unfinished Sheep-fold may be seen
Beside the boisterous brook of Greenhead Ghyll.

MY HEART LEAPS UP

My heart leaps up when I behold
  A rainbow in the sky:
So was it when my life began;
So is it now I am a man;
So be it when I shall grow old,   5
  Or let me die!
The Child is father of the Man;
And I could wish my days to be
Bound each to each by natural piety.[1]

RESOLUTION AND INDEPENDENCE

Wordsworth wrote this poem and the preceding one at
Grasmere in 1802. "This old Man I met a few hundred
yards from my cottage; and the account of him is taken
from his own mouth. I was in the state of feeling described in the beginning of the poem." At first in high
spirits, the poet has become depressed as he thinks of how
precarious human happiness is, especially the happiness
of poets. Then he meets the leech gatherer. "I cannot," he
wrote in a letter, "conceive a figure more impressive than
that of an old man like this . . . travelling alone . . . carrying with him his own fortitude, and the necessities which
an unjust state of society has laid upon him."

There was a roaring in the wind all night;
The rain came heavily and fell in floods;
But now the sun is rising calm and bright;
The birds are singing in the distant woods;
Over his own sweet voice the Stock-dove broods;   5
The Jay makes answer as the Magpie chatters;
And all the air is filled with pleasant noise of waters.

All things that love the sun are out of doors;
The sky rejoices in the morning's birth;
The grass is bright with rain-drops;—on the moors   10
The hare is running races in her mirth;
And with her feet she from the plashy earth
Raises a mist; that, glittering in the sun,
Runs with her all the way, wherever she doth run.

I was a Traveller then upon the moor;   15
I saw the hare that raced about with joy;
I heard the woods and distant waters roar;
Or heard them not, as happy as a boy:
The pleasant season did my heart employ:
My old remembrances went from me wholly;   20
And all the ways of men, so vain and melancholy.

---

[1] Reverence for nature.

But, as it sometimes chanceth, from the might
Of joy in minds that can no further go,
As high as we have mounted in delight
In our dejection do we sink as low;   25
To me that morning did it happen so;
And fears and fancies thick upon me came;
Dim sadness—and blind thoughts, I knew not, nor could
    name.

I heard the sky-lark warbling in the sky;
And I bethought me of the playful hare: 30
Even such a happy Child of earth am I;
Even as these blissful creatures do I fare;
Far from the world I walk, and from all care;
But there may come another day to me—
Solitude, pain of heart, distress, and poverty.   35

My whole life I have lived in pleasant thought,
As if life's business were a summer mood;
As if all needful things would come unsought
To genial faith, still rich in genial good;
But how can He expect that others should   40
Build for him, sow for him, and at his call
Love him, who for himself will take no heed at all?

I thought of Chatterton,[1] the marvellous Boy,
The sleepless Soul that perished in his pride;
Of Him who walked in glory and in joy   45
Following his plough, along the mountain-side:[2]
By our own spirits are we deified:
We Poets in our youth begin in gladness;
But thereof come in the end despondency and madness.

Now, whether it were by peculiar grace,   50
A leading from above, a something given,
Yet it befell that, in this lonely place,
When I with these untoward[3] thoughts had striven,
Beside a pool bare to the eye of heaven
I saw a Man before me unawares: 55
The oldest man he seemed that ever wore grey hairs.

As a huge stone is sometimes seen to lie
Couched on the bald top of an eminence;
Wonder to all who do the same espy,
By what means it could thither come, and whence;   60
So that it seems a thing endued with sense:

---

[1] Thomas Chatterton (1752–70) was fascinated by medieval
poetry. He died at eighteen, having won fame with his imitations of it; for a time he succeeded in tricking readers into
accepting them as genuine relics of former times. Their merit is
slight, but remarkable for his years.   [2] Robert Burns.
[3] Perverse, wrong.

Like a sea-beast crawled forth, that on a shelf
Of rock or sand reposeth, there to sun itself;

Such seemed this Man, not all alive nor dead,
Nor all asleep—in his extreme old age: 65
His body was bent double, feet and head
Coming together in life's pilgrimage;
As if some dire constraint of pain, or rage
Of sickness felt by him in times long past,
A more than human weight upon his frame had cast.   70

Himself he propped, limbs, body, and pale face,
Upon a long grey staff of shaven wood:
And, still as I drew near with gentle pace,
Upon the margin of that moorish flood[4]
Motionless as a cloud the old Man stood,   75
That heareth not the loud winds when they call;
And moveth all together, if it move at all.

At length, himself unsettling, he the pond
Stirred with his staff, and fixedly did look
Upon the muddy water, which he conned,   80
As if he had been reading in a book:
And now a stranger's privilege I took;
And, drawing to his side, to him did say,
"This morning gives us promise of a glorious day."

A gentle answer did the old Man make,   85
In courteous speech which forth he slowly drew:
And him with further words I thus bespake,
"What occupation do you there pursue?
This is a lonesome place for one like you."
Ere he replied, a flash of mild surprise   90
Broke from the sable orbs of his yet-vivid eyes.

His words came feebly, from a feeble chest,
But each in solemn order followed each,
With something of a lofty utterance drest—
Choice word and measured phrase, above the reach   95
Of ordinary men; a stately speech;
Such as grave Livers do in Scotland use,
Religious men, who give to God and man their dues.

He told, that to these waters he had come
To gather leeches,[5] being old and poor: 100
Employment hazardous and wearisome!
And he had many hardships to endure:
From pond to pond he roamed, from moor to moor;
Housing, with God's good help, by choice or chance;
And in this way he gained an honest maintenance.   105

The old Man still stood talking by my side;
But now his voice to me was like a stream
Scarce heard; nor word from word could I divide;
And the whole body of the Man did seem
Like one whom I had met with in a dream;   110
Or like a man from some far region sent,
To give me human strength, by apt admonishment.

My former thoughts returned: the fear that kills;
And hope that is unwilling to be fed;
Cold, pain, and labour, and all fleshly ills;   115
And mighty Poets in their misery dead.
—Perplexed, and longing to be comforted,
My question eagerly did I renew,
"How is it that you live, and what is it you do?"

He with a smile did then his words repeat;   120
And said that, gathering leeches, far and wide
He travelled; stirring thus about his feet
The waters of the pools where they abide.
"Once I could meet with them on every side;
But they have dwindled long by slow decay;   125
Yet still I persevere, and find them where I may."

While he was talking thus, the lonely place,
The old Man's shape, and speech—all troubled me:
In my mind's eye I seemed to see him pace
About the weary moors continually,   130
Wandering about alone and silently.
While I these thoughts within myself pursued,
He, having made a pause, the same discourse renewed.

And soon with this he other matter blended,
Cheerfully uttered, with demeanour kind,   135
But stately in the main; and, when he ended,
I could have laughed myself to scorn to find
In that decrepit Man so firm a mind.
"God," said I, "be my help and stay secure;
I'll think of the Leech-gatherer on the lonely moor!"   140

TO THE CUCKOO

O blithe New-comer! I have heard,
I hear thee and rejoice.
O Cuckoo! shall I call thee Bird,
Or but a wandering Voice?

While I am lying on the grass
Thy twofold shout I hear;
From hill to hill it seems to pass
At once far off, and near.

---

[4] Stream on the moor.
[5] Physicians used them for bleeding patients.

Though babbling only to the Vale,
Of sunshine and of flowers,   10
Thou bringest unto me a tale
Of visionary hours.

Thrice welcome, darling of the Spring!
Even yet thou art to me
No bird, but an invisible thing,   15
A voice, a mystery;

The same whom in my schoolboy days
I listened to; that Cry
Which made me look a thousand ways
In bush, and tree, and sky.   20

To seek thee did I often rove
Through woods and on the green;
And thou wert still a hope, a love;
Still longed for, never seen.

And I can listen to thee yet;   25
Can lie upon the plain
And listen, till I do beget
That golden time again.

O blessèd Bird! the earth we pace
Again appears to be   30
An unsubstantial, faery place,
That is fit home for Thee!

SHE WAS A PHANTOM OF DELIGHT

A tribute to the poet's wife, and through her to noble
womanhood. Like the foregoing poem and the next, this
was written in 1804.

She was a Phantom of delight
When first she gleamed upon my sight;
A lovely Apparition, sent
To be a moment's ornament;
Her eyes as stars of Twilight fair;   5
Like Twilight's, too, her dusky hair;
But all things else about her drawn
From May-time and the cheerful Dawn;
A dancing Shape, an Image gay,
To haunt, to startle, and way-lay.   10

I saw her upon nearer view,
A Spirit, yet a Woman too!
Her household motions light and free,
And steps of virgin-liberty;
A countenance in which did meet   15
Sweet records, promises as sweet;

A Creature not too bright or good
For human nature's daily food;
For transient sorrows, simple wiles,
Praise, blame, love, kisses, tears, and smiles.   20

And now I see with eye serene
The very pulse of the machine;[1]
A Being breathing thoughtful breath,
A Traveller between life and death;
The reason firm, the temperate will,   25
Endurance, foresight, strength, and skill;
A perfect Woman, nobly planned,
To warn, to comfort, and command;
And yet a Spirit still, and bright
With something of angelic light.   30

I WANDERED LONELY AS A CLOUD

"The Daffodils grew and still grow on the margin of
Ullswater, and probably may be seen to this day as beautiful in the month of March, nodding their golden heads
beside the dancing and foaming waves" (Wordsworth's
note). Ullswater, the second largest of the lakes, lies
between Cumberland and Westmorland.

I wandered lonely as a cloud
That floats on high o'er vales and hills,
When all at once I saw a crowd,
A host, of golden daffodils;
Beside the lake, beneath the trees,   5
Fluttering and dancing in the breeze.

Continuous as the stars that shine
And twinkle on the milky way,
They stretched in never-ending line
Along the margin of a bay: 10
Ten thousand saw I at a glance,
Tossing their heads in sprightly dance.

The waves beside them danced; but they
Out-did the sparkling waves in glee:
A poet could not but be gay,   15
In such a jocund company:
I gazed—and gazed—but little thought
What wealth the show to me had brought:

For oft, when on my couch I lie
In vacant or in pensive mood,   20
They flash upon that inward eye
Which is the bliss of solitude;
And then my heart with pleasure fills,
And dances with the daffodils.

------

[1] I.e., the whole intricate organism.

ODE

INTIMATIONS OF IMMORTALITY FROM
RECOLLECTIONS OF EARLY CHILDHOOD

This poem was begun at Grasmere in 1802. "Two years at least," Wordsworth tells us, "passed between the writing of the four first stanzas and the remaining part." As a child, he explains, he was imbued with "a sense of the indomitableness of the Spirit within me. . . . I was often unable to think of external things as having external existence, and I communed with all that I saw as something not apart from, but inherent in, my own immaterial nature. Many times while going to school have I grasped at a wall or tree to recall myself from this abyss of idealism to the reality." That as they grow older the tendency of most men is to reverse their ideas and to become subjugated by material things, Wordsworth goes on to deplore. He does not, however, wish us to take literally his suggestion that the child's consciousness of the ideal may be evidence for a previous state of existence; it is, he says, "far too shadowy a notion to be recommended to faith, as more than an element in our instincts of immortality." But since the idea of pre-existence "has entered into the popular creeds of many nations," he feels authorized "to make for my purpose the best use of it I could as a poet." This is a poet's way of emphasizing the importance of spiritual considerations.

> The Child is father of the Man;
> And I could wish my days to be
> Bound each to each by natural piety.[1]

I

There was a time when meadow, grove, and stream,
The earth, and every common sight,
  To me did seem
  Apparelled in celestial light,
The glory and the freshness of a dream. 5
It is not now as it hath been of yore;—
  Turn wheresoe'er I may,
   By night or day,
The things which I have seen I now can see no more.

II

  The Rainbow comes and goes, 10
  And lovely is the Rose,
  The Moon doth with delight
Look round her when the heavens are bare,
  Waters on a starry night
  Are beautiful and fair; 15
  The sunshine is a glorious birth;
  But yet I know, where'er I go,
That there hath past away a glory from the earth.

---

[1] The conclusion of "My heart leaps up" (see p. 58, above).

III

Now, while the birds thus sing a joyous song,
  And while the young lambs bound 20
   As to the tabor's[2] sound,
To me alone there came a thought of grief:
A timely utterance gave that thought relief,
  And I again am strong:
The cataracts blow their trumpets[3] from the steep; 25
No more shall grief of mine the season wrong;
I hear the Echoes through the mountains throng,
The Winds come to me from the fields of sleep,
  And all the earth is gay;
   Land and sea 30
  Give themselves up to jollity,
   And with the heart of May
  Doth every Beast keep holiday;—
   Thou Child of Joy,
Shout round me, let me hear thy shouts, thou happy
  Shepherd-boy! 35

IV

Ye blessèd Creatures, I have heard the call
  Ye to each other make; I see
The heavens laugh with you in your jubilee;
  My heart is at your festival,
  My head hath its coronal, 40
The fulness of your bliss, I feel—I feel it all.
  Oh evil day! if I were sullen
  While Earth herself is adorning,
   This sweet May morning,
  And the Children are culling 45
   On every side,
  In a thousand valleys far and wide,
  Fresh flowers; while the sun shines warm,
And the Babe leaps up on his Mother's arm:—
  I hear, I hear, with joy I hear! 50
  —But there's a Tree, of many, one,
A single Field which I have looked upon,
Both of them speak of something that is gone:
  The Pansy at my feet
  Doth the same tale repeat: 55
Whither is fled the visionary gleam?
Where is it now, the glory and the dream?

V

Our birth is but a sleep and a forgetting:
The Soul that rises with us, our life's Star,
  Hath had elsewhere its setting, 60
  And cometh from afar:

---

[2] Little drum's.
[3] I.e., are sounding. On the hillsides of the Lake District beautiful little streams dash down, often precipitously.

Not in entire forgetfulness,
And not in utter nakedness,
But trailing clouds of glory do we come
    From God, who is our home:
Heaven lies about us in our infancy!
Shades of the prison-house begin to close
    Upon the growing Boy,
But He beholds the light, and whence it flows,
    He sees it in his joy;   70
The Youth, who daily farther from the east
    Must travel, still is Nature's Priest,
    And by the vision splendid
    Is on his way attended;
At length the Man perceives it die away,   75
And fade into the light of common day.

VI

Earth fills her lap with pleasures of her own;
Yearnings she hath in her own natural kind,
And, even with something of a Mother's mind,
    And no unworthy aim,   80
    The homely Nurse doth all she can
To make her Foster-child, her Inmate Man,
    Forget the glories he hath known,
And that imperial palace whence he came.

VII

Behold the Child among his new-born blisses,   85
A six years' Darling of a pigmy size!
See, where 'mid work of his own hand he lies,
Fretted by sallies of his mother's kisses,
With light upon him from his father's eyes!
See, at his feet, some little plan or chart,   90
Some fragment from his dream of human life,
Shaped by himself with newly-learnèd art;
    A wedding or a festival,
    A mourning or a funeral;
        And this hath now his heart,   95
    And unto this he frames his song:
        Then will he fit his tongue
To dialogues of business, love, or strife;
    But it will not be long
    Ere this be thrown aside,   100
    And with new joy and pride
The little Actor cons another part;
Filling from time to time his "humorous stage"[4]
With all the Persons, down to palsied Age,
That Life brings with her in her equipage;   105
    As if his whole vocation
    Were endless imitation.

---

[4] I.e., all the world's a stage, filled with "persons" or characters
of various "humors" or types.

VIII

Thou, whose exterior semblance doth belie
    Thy Soul's immensity;
Thou best Philosopher, who yet dost keep   110
Thy heritage, thou Eye among the blind,
That, deaf and silent, read'st the eternal deep,
Haunted for ever by the eternal mind,—
    Mighty Prophet! Seer blest!
    On whom those truths do rest,   115
Which we are toiling all our lives to find,
In darkness lost, the darkness of the grave;
Thou, over whom thy Immortality
Broods like the Day, a Master o'er a Slave,
A Presence which is not to be put by;   120
    To whom the grave
Is but a lonely bed without the sense or sight
    Of day or the warm light,
A place of thought where we in waiting lie;
Thou little Child, yet glorious in the might   125
Of heaven-born freedom on thy being's height,
Why with such earnest pains dost thou provoke
The years to bring the inevitable yoke,
Thus blindly with thy blessedness at strife?
Full soon thy Soul shall have her earthly freight,   130
And custom lie upon thee with a weight,
Heavy as frost, and deep almost as life!

IX

    O joy! that in our embers
    Is something that doth live,
    That nature yet remembers   135
    What was so fugitive!
The thought of our past years in me doth breed
Perpetual benediction: not indeed
For that which is most worthy to be blest;
Delight and liberty, the simple creed   140
Of Childhood, whether busy or at rest,
With new-fledged hope still fluttering in his breast:—
    Not for these I raise
    The song of thanks and praise;
    But for those obstinate questionings   145
    Of sense and outward things,
    Fallings from us, vanishings;
    Blank misgivings of a Creature
Moving about in worlds not realised,
High instincts before which our mortal Nature   150
Did tremble like a guilty Thing surprised:
    But for those first affections,
    Those shadowy recollections,
    Which, be they what they may,
Are yet the fountain-light of all our day,   155
Are yet a master-light of all our seeing;

Uphold us, cherish, and have power to make
Our noisy years seem moments in the being
Of the eternal Silence: truths that wake,
        To perish never: 160
Which neither listlessness, nor mad endeavour,
        Nor Man nor Boy,
Nor all that is at enmity with joy,
Can utterly abolish or destroy!
  Hence in a season of calm weather   165
    Though inland far we be,
Our Souls have sight of that immortal sea
    Which brought us hither,
    Can in a moment travel thither,
And see the Children sport upon the shore,   170
And hear the mighty waters rolling evermore.

                    X

Then sing, ye Birds, sing, sing a joyous song!
    And let the young Lambs bound
    As to the tabor's sound!
We in thought will join your throng,   175
    Ye that pipe and ye that play,
    Ye that through your hearts to-day
    Feel the gladness of the May!
What though the radiance which was once so bright
Be now for ever taken from my sight,   180
  Though nothing can bring back the hour
Of splendour in the grass, of glory in the flower;
    We will grieve not, rather find
    Strength in what remains behind;
    In the primal sympathy   185
    Which having been must ever be;
    In the soothing thoughts that spring
    Out of human suffering;
    In the faith that looks through death,
In years that bring the philosophic mind.   190

                    XI

And O, ye Fountains, Meadows, Hills, and Groves,
Forebode not any severing of our loves!
Yet in my heart of hearts I feel your might;
I only have relinquished one delight
To live beneath your more habitual sway.   195
I love the Brooks which down their channels fret,
Even more than when I tripped lightly as they;
The innocent brightness of a new-born Day
        Is lovely yet;
The Clouds that gather round the setting sun   200
Do take a sober colouring from an eye
That hath kept watch o'er man's mortality;
Another race hath been, and other palms are won.
Thanks to the human heart by which we live,
Thanks to its tenderness, its joys, and fears,   205
To me the meanest flower that blows can give
Thoughts that do often lie too deep for tears.

ODE TO DUTY[1]

Stern Daughter of the Voice of God!
O Duty! if that name thou love
Who art a light to guide, a rod
To check the erring, and reprove;
Thou, who art victory and law   5
When empty terrors overawe;
From vain temptations dost set free;
And calm'st the weary strife of frail humanity!

There are who ask not if thine eye
Be on them; who, in love and truth,   10
Where no misgiving is, rely
Upon the genial sense of youth:
Glad Hearts! without reproach or blot;
Who do thy work, and know it not:
Oh! if through confidence misplaced   15
They fail, thy saving arms, dread Power! around them
    cast.

Serene will be our days and bright,
And happy will our nature be,
When love is an unerring light,
And joy its own security.   20
And they a blissful course may hold
Even now, who, not unwisely bold,
Live in the spirit of this creed;
Yet seek thy firm support, according to their need.

I, loving freedom, and untried;   25
No sport of every random gust,
Yet being to myself a guide,
Too blindly have reposed my trust:
And oft, when in my heart was heard
Thy timely mandate, I deferred   30
The task, in smoother walks to stray;
But thee I now would serve more strictly, if I may.

Through no disturbance of my soul,
Or strong compunction in me wrought,
I supplicate for thy control;   35
But in the quietness of thought:
Me this unchartered freedom tires;
I feel the weight of chance-desires:

---

[1] Written in 1804.

My hopes no more must change their name,
I long for a repose that ever is the same.   40

Stern Lawgiver! yet thou dost wear
The Godhead's most benignant grace;
Nor know we anything so fair
As is the smile upon thy face:
Flowers laugh before thee on their beds   45
And fragrance in thy footing treads;
Thou dost preserve the stars from wrong;
And the most ancient heavens, through Thee, are fresh
    and strong.

To humbler functions, awful Power!
I call thee: I myself commend   50
Unto thy guidance from this hour;
Oh, let my weakness have an end!
Give unto me, made lowly wise,
The spirit of self-sacrifice;
The confidence of reason give;   55
And in the light of truth thy Bondman let me live!

THE SOLITARY REAPER

Wordsworth traveled in Scotland in 1803; but this poem,
composed in 1805, "was suggested by a beautiful sentence
in a MS *Tour in Scotland* written by a friend," Thomas
Wilkinson: "Passed a female who was reaping alone; she
sung in Erse as she bended over her sickle; the sweetest
human voice I ever heard: her strains were tenderly
melancholy, and felt delicious long after they were heard
no more."

Behold her, single in the field,
Yon solitary Highland Lass!
Reaping and singing by herself;
Stop here, or gently pass!
Alone she cuts and binds the grain,   5
And sings a melancholy strain;
O listen! for the Vale profound
Is overflowing with the sound.

No Nightingale did ever chaunt
More welcome notes to weary bands   10
Of travellers in some shady haunt,
Among Arabian sands:
A voice so thrilling ne'er was heard
In spring-time from the Cuckoo-bird,
Breaking the silence of the seas   15
Among the farthest Hebrides.

Will no one tell me what she sings?—[1]
Perhaps the plaintive numbers flow
For old, unhappy, far-off things,
And battles long ago: 20
Or is it some more humble lay,
Familiar matter of to-day?
Some natural sorrow, loss, or pain,
That has been, and may be again?

Whate'er the theme, the Maiden sang   25
As if her song could have no ending;
I saw her singing at her work,
And o'er the sickle bending;—
I listened, motionless and still;
And, as I mounted up the hill,   30
The music in my heart I bore,
Long after it was heard no more.

STEPPING WESTWARD

This poem, inspired by an incident during Wordsworth's
visit to Scotland in 1803, was composed in 1805. Wordsworth in a note describes how he and Dorothy, "walking
by the side of Loch Ketterine, one fine evening after sunset, . . . met, in one of the loneliest parts of that solitary
region, two well-dressed Women, one of whom said to
us, by way of greeting, 'What, you are stepping westward?' "

"What, you are stepping westward?"—"*Yea.*"
—'T would be a *wildish* destiny,
If we, who thus together roam
In a strange Land, and far from home,
Were in this place the guests of Chance: 5
Yet who would stop, or fear to advance,
Though home or shelter he had none,
With such a sky to lead him on?

The dewy ground was dark and cold;
Behind, all gloomy to behold;   10
And stepping westward seemed to be
A kind of *heavenly* destiny:
I liked the greeting; 't was a sound
Of something without place or bound;
And seemed to give me spiritual right   15
To travel through that region bright.

The voice was soft, and she who spake
Was walking by her native lake:
The salutation had to me
The very sound of courtesy: 20

---

[1] Her song is in Erse, i.e., Gaelic.

Its power was felt; and while my eye
Was fixed upon the glowing Sky,
The echo of the voice enwrought
A human sweetness with the thought
Of travelling through the world that lay   25
Before me in my endless way.

ELEGIAC STANZAS

SUGGESTED BY A PICTURE OF PEELE CASTLE, IN A
STORM, PAINTED BY SIR GEORGE BEAUMONT

Beaumont (1753–1827), a landscape painter and art collector, was a friend of Wordsworth and of other poets.
The castle is on Piel Island near Walney Island, off the
coast of northern Lancashire, where Wordsworth seems
to have spent part of a college vacation. This poem was
written in 1805.

I was thy neighbour once, thou rugged Pile!
Four summer weeks I dwelt in sight of thee:
I saw thee every day; and all the while
Thy Form was sleeping on a glassy sea.

So pure the sky, so quiet was the air!   5
So like, so very like, was day to day!
Whene'er I looked, thy Image still was there;
It trembled, but it never passed away.

How perfect was the calm! it seemed no sleep;
No mood, which season takes away, or brings: 10
I could have fancied that the mighty Deep
Was even the gentlest of all gentle Things.

Ah! THEN, if mine had been the Painter's hand,
To express what then I saw; and add the gleam,
The light that never was, on sea or land,   15
The consecration, and the Poet's dream;

I would have planted thee, thou hoary Pile,
Amid a world how different from this!
Beside a sea that could not cease to smile;
On tranquil land, beneath a sky of bliss.   20

Thou shouldst have seemed a treasure-house divine
Of peaceful years; a chronicle of heaven;—
Of all the sunbeams that did ever shine
The very sweetest had to thee been given.

A Picture had it been of lasting ease,   25
Elysian[1] quiet, without toil or strife;

No motion but the moving tide, a breeze,
Or merely silent Nature's breathing life.

Such, in the fond illusion of my heart,
Such Picture would I at that time have made: 30
And seen the soul of truth in every part,
A steadfast peace that might not be betrayed.

So once it would have been,—'tis so no more;
I have submitted to a new control:
A power is gone, which nothing can restore;   35
A deep distress[2] hath humanised my Soul.

Not for a moment could I now behold
A smiling sea, and be what I have been:
The feeling of my loss will ne'er be old;
This, which I know, I speak with mind serene.   40

Then, Beaumont, Friend! who would have been the
     Friend,
If he had lived, of Him whom I deplore,
This work of thine I blame not, but commend;
This sea in anger, and that dismal shore.

O 'tis a passionate Work!—yet wise and well,   45
Well chosen is the spirit that is here;
That Hulk which labours in the deadly swell,
This rueful sky, this pageantry of fear!

And this huge Castle, standing here sublime,
I love to see the look with which it braves,   50
Cased in the unfeeling armour of old time,
The lightning, the fierce wind, and trampling waves.

Farewell, farewell the heart that lives alone,
Housed in a dream, at distance from the Kind!
Such happiness, wherever it be known,   55
Is to be pitied; for 'tis surely blind.

But welcome fortitude, and patient cheer,
And frequent sights of what is to be borne!
Such sights, or worse, as are before me here.—
Not without hope we suffer and we mourn.   60

---

[1] Like Elysium, in classical mythology the abode of the happy
dead.

[2] Wordsworth's brother John had been lost at sea early in the
year in which this poem was composed (1805); see the headnote to "Character of a Happy Warrior" on the next page.

CHARACTER OF A HAPPY WARRIOR

In composing this poem Wordsworth had in mind the
qualities of two seamen; both died in 1805, the year before he wrote it. On February 6 his brother John was
lost in the wreck of the East Indiaman he commanded.
The other was Lord Nelson, England's greatest admiral,
who fell on October 21 in the battle off Cape Trafalgar,
at the moment of victory over the combined French and
Spanish fleets. The poet is also thinking, however, of the
way we all have to face up to life's difficulties; the
"happy warrior" of the title may be any man who does
his duty.

Who is the happy Warrior? Who is he
That every man in arms should wish to be?
—It is the generous Spirit, who, when brought
Among the tasks of real life, hath wrought
Upon the plan that pleased his boyish thought: 5
Whose high endeavours are an inward light
That makes the path before him always bright:
Who, with a natural instinct to discern
What knowledge can perform, is diligent to learn;
Abides by this resolve, and stops not there,   10
But makes his moral being his prime care;
Who, doomed to go in company with Pain,
And Fear, and Bloodshed, miserable train!
Turns his necessity to glorious gain;
In face of these doth exercise a power   15
Which is our human nature's highest dower;
Controls them and subdues, transmutes, bereaves
Of their bad influence, and their good receives:
By objects, which might force the soul to abate
Her feeling, rendered more compassionate;   20
Is placable—because occasions rise
So often that demand such sacrifice;
More skilful in self-knowledge, even more pure,
As tempted more; more able to endure,
As more exposed to suffering and distress;   25
Thence, also, more alive to tenderness.
—'Tis he whose law is reason; who depends
Upon that law as on the best of friends;
Whence, in a state where men are tempted still
To evil for a guard against worse ill,   30
And what in quality or act is best
Doth seldom on a right foundation rest,
He labours good on good to fix, and owes
To virtue every triumph that he knows:
—Who, if he rise to station of command,   35
Rises by open means; and there will stand

On honourable terms, or else retire,
And in himself possess his own desire;
Who comprehends his trust, and to the same
Keeps faithful with a singleness of aim;   40
And therefore does not stoop, nor lie in wait
For wealth, or honours, or for worldly state;
Whom they must follow; on whose head must fall,
Like showers of manna, if they come at all:
Whose powers shed round him in the common strife, 45
Or mild concerns of ordinary life,
A constant influence, a peculiar grace;
But who, if he be called upon to face
Some awful moment to which Heaven has joined
Great issues, good or bad for human kind,   50
Is happy as a Lover; and attired
With sudden brightness, like a Man inspired;
And, through the heat of conflict, keeps the law
In calmness made, and sees what he foresaw;
Or if an unexpected call succeed,   55
Come when it will, is equal to the need:
—He who, though thus endued as with a sense
And faculty for storm and turbulence,
Is yet a Soul whose master-bias leans
To homefelt pleasures and to gentle scenes;   60
Sweet images! which, wheresoe'er he be,
Are at his heart; and such fidelity
It is his darling passion to approve;
More brave for this, that he hath much to love:—
'Tis, finally, the Man, who, lifted high,   65
Conspicuous object in a Nation's eye,
Or left unthought-of in obscurity,—
Who, with a toward or untoward lot,
Prosperous or adverse, to his wish or not—
Plays, in the many games of life, that one   70
Where what he most doth value must be won:
Whom neither shape of danger can dismay,
Nor thought of tender happiness betray;
Who, not content that former worth stand fast,
Looks forward, persevering to the last,   75
From well to better, daily self-surpast:
Who, whether praise of him must walk the earth
For ever, and to noble deeds give birth,
Or he must fall, to sleep without his fame,
And leave a dead unprofitable name—   80
Finds comfort in himself and in his cause;
And, while the mortal mist is gathering, draws
His breath in confidence of Heaven's applause:
This is the happy Warrior; this is He
That every Man in arms should wish to be.   85

UPON WESTMINSTER BRIDGE

This sonnet and the next eight are connected with
Wordsworth's trip to France in August, 1802. Accompanied by his sister Dorothy, he spent four weeks at Calais
in order to see Annette Vallon and Caroline, now nine
years old. This beautiful poem was written on the roof
of the coach by which, over Westminster Bridge, he left
London in the early morning of July 31.

Earth has not anything to show more fair:
Dull would he be of soul who could pass by
A sight so touching in its majesty:
This City now doth, like a garment, wear
The beauty of the morning; silent, bare,   5
Ships, towers, domes, theatres, and temples lie
Open unto the fields, and to the sky;
All bright and glittering in the smokeless air.
Never did sun more beautifully steep
In his first splendour, valley, rock, or hill;   10
Ne'er saw I, never felt, a calm so deep!
The river glideth at his own sweet will:
Dear God! the very houses seem asleep;
And all that mighty heart is lying still!

BY THE SEA-SIDE, NEAR CALAIS

In Wordsworth's own arrangement of his collected verse,
this sonnet stands first in the section entitled "Poems
Dedicated to National Independence and Liberty." In the
month when it was written (August, 1802) Napoleon
was made consul for life, and it became clearer than ever
that the French Revolution was to end in a dictatorship.

Fair Star of evening, Splendour of the west,
Star of my Country!—on the horizon's brink
Thou hangest, stooping, as might seem, to sink
On England's bosom; yet well pleased to rest,
Meanwhile, and be to her a glorious crest   5
Conspicuous to the Nations. Thou, I think,
Shouldst be my Country's emblem; and shouldst
     wink,
Bright Star! with laughter on her banners, drest
In thy fresh beauty. There! that dusky spot
Beneath thee, that is England; there she lies.   10
Blessings be on you both! one hope, one lot,
One life, one glory!—I, with many a fear
For my dear Country, many heartfelt sighs,
Among men who do not love her, linger here.

IT IS A BEAUTEOUS EVENING

This sonnet was also written at Calais in August, 1802.
The child is Wordsworth's French daughter, Caroline.

It is a beauteous evening, calm and free,
The holy time is quiet as a Nun
Breathless with adoration; the broad sun
Is sinking down in its tranquillity;
The gentleness of heaven broods o'er the Sea: 5
Listen! the mighty Being is awake,
And doth with his eternal motion make
A sound like thunder—everlastingly.
Dear Child! dear Girl! that walkest with me here,
If thou appear untouched by solemn thought,   10
Thy nature is not therefore less divine:
Thou liest in Abraham's bosom[1] all the year;
And worshipp'st at the Temple's inner shrine,
God being with thee when we know it not.

ON THE EXTINCTION OF THE
VENETIAN REPUBLIC

The colonial empire of Venice once extended along a
chain of islands all the way to Crete and Cyprus. These
outposts and her naval power were a main bulwark of
Christendom against Turkish expansion. Though her decline had begun in the sixteenth century, Venice maintained her independence in Italy till 1797, when Napoleon
seized her and then ceded her to Austria in return for
territorial concessions elsewhere.

Once did She hold the gorgeous east in fee;
And was the safeguard of the west: the worth
Of Venice did not fall below her birth,
Venice, the eldest Child of Liberty.
She was a maiden City, bright and free;   5
No guile seduced, no force could violate;
And, when she took unto herself a Mate,
She must espouse the everlasting Sea.[2]
And what if she had seen those glories fade,
Those titles vanish, and that strength decay;   10
Yet shall some tribute of regret be paid
When her long life hath reached its final day:
Men are we, and must grieve when even the Shade
Of that which once was great is passed away.

---

[1] I.e., in God's presence. See Luke 16:22.
[2] In an annual ceremony dating from the twelfth century, the
doge or chief magistrate renewed the city's wedding to the
Adriatic by throwing a ring into that sea.

TO TOUSSAINT L'OUVERTURE

Like the preceding poem, this great sonnet, with its closing lines of reassurance to all who fight to make a better world, protests against French imperialism and tyranny. Toussaint L'Ouverture (1743–1803—his real name was Pierre Dominique) was the heroic Negro general who liberated the oppressed people of Haiti. He resisted Napoleon's attempt to re-establish slavery there but was finally defeated and, shortly before this poem was written, arrived as a prisoner in France, where he died less than a year later.

Toussaint, the most unhappy man of men!
Whether the whistling Rustic tend his plough
Within thy hearing, or thy head be now
Pillowed in some deep dungeon's earless den;—
O miserable Chieftain! where and when   5
Wilt thou find patience! Yet die not; do thou
Wear rather in thy bonds a cheerful brow:
Though fallen thyself, never to rise again,
Live, and take comfort. Thou hast left behind
Powers that will work for thee; air, earth, and skies;   10
There's not a breathing of the common wind
That will forget thee; thou hast great allies;
Thy friends are exultations, agonies,
And love, and man's unconquerable mind.

NEAR DOVER

This sonnet and the next three were composed soon after Wordsworth returned to England in the autumn of 1802. All were inspired by his realization that France was again a menace to Europe and by his hope that England would guard her heritage of freedom.

Inland, within a hollow vale, I stood;
And saw, while sea was calm and air was clear,
The coast of France—the coast of France how near!
Drawn almost into frightful neighbourhood.
I shrunk; for verily the barrier flood   5
Was like a lake, or river bright and fair,
A span of waters; yet what power is there!
What mightiness for evil and for good!
Even so doth God protect us if we be
Virtuous and wise. Winds blow, and waters roll,   10
Strength to the brave, and Power, and Deity;
Yet in themselves are nothing! One decree
Spake laws to *them,* and said that by the soul
Only, the Nations shall be great and free.

LONDON, SEPTEMBER 1802

O Friend![3] I know not which way I must look
For comfort, being, as I am, opprest,
To think that now our life is only drest
For show; mean handy-work of craftsman, cook,
Or groom!—We must run glittering like a brook   5
In the open sunshine, or we are unblest:
The wealthiest man among us is the best:
No grandeur now in nature or in book
Delights us. Rapine, avarice, expense,
This is idolatry; and these we adore: 10
Plain living and high thinking are no more:
The homely beauty of the good old cause[4]
Is gone; our peace, our fearful innocence,
And pure religion breathing household laws.

LONDON, 1802

Milton! thou shouldst be living at this hour:
England hath need of thee: she is a fen
Of stagnant waters: altar, sword, and pen,
Fireside, the heroic wealth of hall and bower,
Have forfeited their ancient English dower   5
Of inward happiness. We are selfish men;
Oh! raise us up, return to us again;
And give us manners, virtue, freedom, power.
Thy soul was like a Star, and dwelt apart;
Thou hadst a voice whose sound was like the sea: 10
Pure as the naked heavens, majestic, free,
So didst thou travel on life's common way,
In cheerful godliness; and yet thy heart
The lowliest duties on herself did lay.

IT IS NOT TO BE THOUGHT OF

It is not to be thought of that the Flood
Of British freedom, which, to the open sea
Of the world's praise, from dark antiquity
Hath flowed, "with pomp of waters, unwithstood."[5]
Roused though it be full often to a mood   5
Which spurns the check of salutary bands,[6]
That this most famous Stream in bogs and sands
Should perish; and to evil and to good
Be lost for ever. In our halls is hung
Armoury of the invincible Knights of old: 10

---

[3] Coleridge.
[4] The cause of English liberty in the seventeenth-century rebellions against the Stuart monarchy.
[5] From Samuel Daniel's *The Civil Wars,* Book II, stanza 7.
[6] Bonds, restraints.

We must be free or die, who speak the tongue
That Shakespeare spake; the faith and morals hold
Which Milton held.—In every thing we are sprung
Of Earth's first blood, have titles manifold.

THE WORLD IS TOO MUCH WITH US

This sonnet dates from 1806.

The world is too much with us; late and soon,
Getting and spending, we lay waste our powers:
Little we see in Nature that is ours;
We have given our hearts away, a sordid boon!
This Sea that bares her bosom to the moon;   5
The winds that will be howling at all hours,
And are up-gathered now like sleeping flowers;
For this, for everything, we are out of tune;
It moves us not.—Great God! I'd rather be
A Pagan suckled in a creed outworn;   10
So might I, standing on this pleasant lea,
Have glimpses that would make me less forlorn;
Have sight of Proteus rising from the sea;
Or hear old Triton[7] blow his wreathèd horn.

This sonnet stands last in a series of forty-eight poems
"composed or suggested" during a tour, chiefly of Scotland, in the summer of 1833.

Most sweet it is with unuplifted eyes
To pace the ground, if path be there or none,
While a fair region round the traveller lies
Which he forbears again to look upon;
Pleased rather with some soft ideal scene,   5
The work of Fancy, or some happy tone
Of meditation, slipping in between
The beauty coming and the beauty gone.
If Thought and Love desert us, from that day
Let us break off all commerce with the Muse: 10
With Thought and Love companions of our way,
Whate'er the senses take or may refuse,
The Mind's internal heaven shall shed her dews
Of inspiration on the humblest lay.

PREFACE TO THE SECOND EDITION OF *LYRICAL BALLADS*

As long as tastes and judgments differ, men and women
of taste and judgment will debate the nature, aims, and
methods of art. Wordsworth's manifesto is one of the
few that have actually had a share in making an epoch.
As the considered view of a great poet at the moment   5
when he was engaged in demolishing the literary standards of the day, it is bound to interest everyone who cares
about any sort of artistic expression in any era, past or
present. For revolutions in art never stay won. The new
man rebels against current practice; as Emerson says, he   10
adorns nature with a new thing; and then, after he is
dead and gone, his imitators run the new thing into the
ground—till it in turn takes root as a convention, flourishes, withers, and at last is and ought to be attacked by
the next rebellious generation.

The second edition of *Lyrical Ballads* came out in 1801   15
(misdated 1800) in the first of two volumes, the second
of which added new poems by Wordsworth. The essay
was altered and expanded in subsequent editions of his
poems; eventually it was printed as an appendix. The
present text incorporates changes but not all the added   20
material.

THE first Volume of these Poems has already been
submitted to general perusal. It was published, as an
experiment, which, I hoped, might be of some use to
ascertain, how far, by fitting to metrical arrangement
a selection of the real language of men in a state of
vivid sensation, that sort of pleasure and that quantity
of pleasure may be imparted, which a Poet may
rationally endeavour to impart.

I had formed no very inaccurate estimate of the
probable effect of those Poems: I flattered myself that   10
they who should be pleased with them would read
them with more than common pleasure: and, on the
other hand, I was well aware, that by those who
should dislike them, they would be read with more
than common dislike. The result has differed from   15
my expectation in this only, that a greater number
have been pleased than I ventured to hope I should
please. . . .[1]

The principal object, then, proposed in these Poems
was to choose incidents and situations from common   20

---

[7] Sea gods of classical mythology. Proteus had the faculty of assuming any shape. Triton, son of Neptune, raised and calmed
the waves by blasts on his conch-shell trumpet. *Wreathed*=spiral.

[1] At this point Wordsworth mentions Coleridge's contribution
of "The Ancient Mariner" and three other poems, and goes on
to declare his own unwillingness to engage in an elaborate defense of the new poetic theory.

life, and to relate or describe them, throughout, as far as was possible in a selection of language really used by men, and, at the same time, to throw over them a certain colouring of imagination, whereby ordinary things should be presented to the mind in an unusual aspect; and, further, and above all, to make these incidents and situations interesting by tracing in them, truly though not ostentatiously, the primary laws of our nature: chiefly, as far as regards the manner in which we associate ideas in a state of excitement. Humble and rustic life was generally chosen, because, in that condition, the essential passions of the heart find a better soil in which they can attain their maturity, are less under restraint, and speak a plainer and more emphatic language; because in that condition of life our elementary feelings coexist in a state of greater simplicity, and, consequently, may be more accurately contemplated, and more forcibly communicated; because the manners of rural life germinate from those elementary feelings, and, from the necessary character of rural occupations, are more easily comprehended, and are more durable; and, lastly, because in that condition the passions of men are incorporated with the beautiful and permanent forms of nature. The language, too, of these men has been adopted (purified indeed from what appear to be its real defects, from all lasting and rational causes of dislike or disgust) because such men hourly communicate with the best objects from which the best part of language is originally derived; and because, from their rank in society and the sameness and narrow circle of their intercourse, being less under the influence of social vanity, they convey their feelings and notions in simple and unelaborated expressions. Accordingly, such a language, arising out of repeated experience and regular feelings, is a more permanent, and a far more philosophical language, than that which is frequently substituted for it by Poets, who think that they are conferring honour upon themselves and their art, in proportion as they separate themselves from the sympathies of men, and indulge in arbitrary and capricious habits of expression, in order to furnish food for fickle tastes, and fickle appetites, of their own creation.[2]

I cannot, however, be insensible to the present outcry against the triviality and meanness, both of thought and language, which some of my contemporaries have occasionally introduced into their metrical compositions; and I acknowledge that this defect, where it exists, is more dishonourable to the Writer's own character than false refinement or arbitrary innovation, though I should contend at the same time, that it is far less pernicious in the sum of its consequences. From such verses the Poems in these volumes will be found distinguished at least by one mark of difference, that each of them has a worthy *purpose*. Not that I always began to write with a distinct purpose formally conceived; but habits of meditation have, I trust, so prompted and regulated my feelings, that my descriptions of such objects as strongly excite those feelings, will be found to carry along with them a *purpose*. If this opinion be erroneous, I can have little right to the name of a Poet. For all good poetry is the spontaneous overflow of powerful feelings: and though this be true, Poems to which any value can be attached were never produced on any variety of subjects but by a man who, being possessed of more than usual organic sensibility, had also thought long and deeply. For our continued influxes of feeling are modified and directed by our thoughts, which are indeed the representatives of all our past feelings; and, as by contemplating the relation of these general representatives to each other, we discover what is really important to men, so, by the repetition and continuance of this act, our feelings will be connected with important subjects, till at length, if we be originally possessed of much sensibility, such habits of mind will be produced, that, by obeying blindly and mechanically the impulses of those habits, we shall describe objects, and utter sentiments, of such a nature, and in such connection with each other, that the understanding of the Reader must necessarily be in some degree enlightened, and his affections strengthened and purified.

It has been said that each of these Poems has a purpose. Another circumstance must be mentioned which distinguishes these Poems from the popular Poetry of the day; it is this, that the feeling therein developed gives importance to the action and situation, and not the action and situation to the feeling.

A sense of false modesty shall not prevent me from asserting, that the Reader's attention is pointed to this mark of distinction, far less for the sake of these particular Poems than from the general importance of the subject. The subject is indeed important! For the human mind is capable of being excited without the application of gross and violent stimulants; and he must have a very faint perception of its beauty and dignity who does not know this, and who does not further know, that one being is elevated above

2 Wordsworth's note: "It is worth while here to observe, that the affecting parts of Chaucer are almost always expressed in language pure and universally intelligible even to this day."

another, in proportion as he possesses this capability. It has therefore appeared to me, that to endeavour to produce or enlarge this capability is one of the best services in which, at any period, a Writer can be engaged; but this service, excellent at all times, is especially so at the present day. For a multitude of causes, unknown to former times, are now acting with a combined force to blunt the discriminating powers of the mind, and, unfitting it for all voluntary exertion, to reduce it to a state of almost savage torpor. The most effective of these causes are the great national events which are daily taking place,[3] and the increasing accumulation of men in cities, where the uniformity of their occupations produces a craving for extraordinary incident, which the rapid communication of intelligence[4] hourly gratifies. To this tendency of life and manners the literature and theatrical exhibitions of the country have conformed themselves. The invaluable works of our elder writers, I had almost said the works of Shakspeare and Milton, are driven into neglect by frantic novels,[5] sickly and stupid German Tragedies,[6] and deluges of idle and extravagant stories in verse.[7]— When I think upon this degrading thirst after outrageous stimulation, I am almost ashamed to have spoken of the feeble endeavour made in these volumes to counteract it; and, reflecting upon the magnitude of the general evil, I should be oppressed with no dishonourable melancholy, had I not a deep impression of certain inherent and indestructible qualities of the human mind, and likewise of certain powers in the great and permanent objects that act upon it, which are equally inherent and indestructible; and were there not added to this impression a belief, that the time is approaching when the evil will be systematically opposed, by men of greater powers, and with far more distinguished success.

Having dwelt thus long on the subjects and aim of these Poems, I shall request the Reader's permission to apprise him of a few circumstances relating to their *style,* in order, among other reasons, that he may not censure me for not having performed what I never attempted. The Reader will find that personifications of abstract ideas rarely occur in these volumes; and are utterly rejected, as an ordinary device to elevate the style, and raise it above prose. My purpose was to imitate, and, as far as possible, to adopt the very language of men; and assuredly such personifications do not make any natural or regular part of that language. They are, indeed, a figure of speech occasionally prompted by passion, and I have made use of them as such; but have endeavoured utterly to reject them as a mechanical device of style, or as a family language which Writers in metre seem to lay claim to by prescription. I have wished to keep the Reader in the company of flesh and blood, persuaded that by so doing I shall interest him. Others who pursue a different track will interest him likewise; I do not interfere with their claim, but wish to prefer[8] a claim of my own. There will also be found in these volumes little of what is usually called poetic diction; as much pains has been taken to avoid it as is ordinarily taken to produce it; this has been done for the reason already alleged, to bring my language near to the language of men; and further, because the pleasure which I have proposed to myself to impart, is of a kind very different from that which is supposed by many persons to be the proper object of poetry. Without being culpably particular, I do not know how to give my Reader a more exact notion of the style in which it was my wish and intention to write, than by informing him that I have at all times endeavoured to look steadily at my subject; consequently, there is I hope in these Poems little falsehood of description, and my ideas are expressed in language fitted to their respective importance. Something must have been gained by this practice, as it is friendly to one property of all good poetry, namely, good sense: but it has necessarily cut me off from a large portion of phrases and figures of speech which from father to son have long been regarded as the common inheritance of Poets. I have also thought it expedient to restrict myself still further, having abstained from the use of many expressions, in themselves proper and beautiful, but which have been foolishly repeated by bad Poets, till such feelings of disgust are connected with them as it is scarcely possible by any art of association to overpower.

If in a poem there should be found a series of lines, or even a single line, in which the language, though naturally arranged, and according to the strict laws of metre, does not differ from that of prose, there is a numerous class of critics, who, when they stumble upon these prosaisms, as they call them, imagine that they have made a notable discovery, and exult over

---

[3] The war with France, for example. [4] News.

[5] I.e., the Gothic novels or romances, such as Ann Radcliffe's *The Mysteries of Udolpho* (1794).

[6] Such as the sentimental plays of August von Kotzebue (1761–1819), which were extremely popular in England.

[7] Perhaps an allusion to the earliest work of Scott, written under the influence of German romanticism, as well as the work of some of his predecessors.

[8] Set forth.

the Poet as over a man ignorant of his own profession. Now these men would establish a canon of criticism which the Reader will conclude he must utterly reject, if he wishes to be pleased with these volumes. And it would be a most easy task to prove to him, that not only the language of a large portion of every good poem, even of the most elevated character, must necessarily, except with reference to the metre, in no respect differ from that of good prose, but likewise that some of the most interesting parts of the best poems will be found to be strictly the language of prose when prose is well written. The truth of this assertion might be demonstrated by innumerable passages from almost all the poetical writings, even of Milton himself. To illustrate the subject in a general manner, I will here adduce a short composition[9] of Gray, who was at the head of those who, by their reasonings, have attempted to widen the space of separation betwixt Prose and Metrical composition, and was more than any other man curiously elaborate in the structure of his own poetic diction.

> In vain to me the smiling mornings shine,
> And reddening Phoebus lifts his golden fire:
> The birds in vain their amorous descant join,
> Or cheerful fields resume their green attire.
> These ears, alas! for other notes repine;
> *A different object do these eyes require;*
> *My lonely anguish melts no heart but mine;*
> *And in my breast the imperfect joys expire;*
> Yet morning smiles the busy race to cheer,
> And new-born pleasure brings to happier men;
> The fields to all their wonted tribute bear;
> To warm their little loves the birds complain.
> *I fruitless mourn to him that cannot hear,*
> *And weep the more because I weep in vain.*

It will easily be perceived, that the only part of this Sonnet which is of any value is the lines printed in Italics; it is equally obvious, that, except in the rhyme, and in the use of the single word "fruitless" for fruitlessly, which is so far a defect, the language of these lines does in no respect differ from that of prose.

By the foregoing quotation it has been shown that the language of Prose may yet be well adapted to Poetry; and it was previously asserted, that a large portion of the language of every good poem can in no respect differ from that of good Prose. We will go further. It may be safely affirmed, that there neither is, nor can be, any *essential* difference between the language of prose and metrical composition. We are fond of tracing the resemblance between Poetry and Painting, and, accordingly, we call them Sisters: but where shall we find bonds of connection sufficiently strict to typify the affinity betwixt metrical and prose composition? They both speak by and to the same organs; the bodies in which both of them are clothed may be said to be of the same substance, their affections are kindred, and almost identical, not necessarily differing even in degree; Poetry[10] sheds no tears "such as Angels weep," but natural and human tears; she can boast of no celestial ichor[11] that distinguishes her vital juices from those of prose; the same human blood circulates through the veins of them both.

If it be affirmed that rhyme and metrical arrangement of themselves constitute a distinction which overturns what has just been said on the strict affinity of metrical language with that of prose, and paves the way for other artificial distinctions which the mind voluntarily admits, I answer that the language of such Poetry as is here recommended is, as far as is possible, a selection of the language really spoken by men; that this selection, wherever it is made with true taste and feeling, will of itself form a distinction far greater than would at first be imagined, and will entirely separate the composition from the vulgarity and meanness of ordinary life; and, if metre be superadded thereto, I believe that a dissimilitude will be produced altogether sufficient for the gratification of a rational mind. What other distinction would we have? Whence is it to come? And where is it to exist? Not, surely, where the Poet speaks through the mouths of his characters: it cannot be necessary here, either for elevation of style, or any of its supposed ornaments: for, if the Poet's subject be judiciously chosen, it will naturally, and upon fit occasion, lead him to passions the language of which, if selected truly and judiciously, must necessarily be dignified and variegated, and alive with metaphors and figures. I forbear to speak of an incongruity

---

9 Sonnet "On the Death of Richard West." West, who was Gray's best friend at Eton, died young in 1742.

10 Wordsworth's note: "I here use the word 'Poetry' (though against my own judgment) as opposed to the word Prose, and synonymous with metrical composition. But much confusion has been introduced into criticism by this contradistinction of Poetry and Prose, instead of the more philosophical one of Poetry and Matter of Fact, or Science. The only strict antithesis to Prose is Metre; nor is this, in truth, a *strict* antithesis, because lines and passages of metre so naturally occur in writing prose, that it would be scarcely possible to avoid them, even were it desirable."

11 In classical mythology, the fluid which flowed instead of blood in the veins of the gods.

which would shock the intelligent Reader, should the Poet interweave any foreign splendour of his own with that which the passion naturally suggests: it is sufficient to say that such addition is unnecessary. And, surely, it is more probable that those passages, which with propriety abound with metaphors and figures, will have their due effect, if, upon other occasions where the passions are of a milder character, the style also be subdued and temperate.

But, as the pleasure which I hope to give by the Poems now presented to the Reader must depend entirely on just notions upon this subject, and, as it is in itself of high importance to our taste and moral feelings, I cannot content myself with these detached remarks. And if, in what I am about to say, it shall appear to some that my labour is unnecessary, and that I am like a man fighting a battle without enemies, such persons may be reminded, that, whatever be the language outwardly holden by men, a practical faith in the opinions which I am wishing to establish is almost unknown. If my conclusions are admitted, and carried as far as they must be carried if admitted at all, our judgments concerning the works of the greatest Poets both ancient and modern will be far different from what they are at present, both when we praise, and when we censure: and our moral feelings influencing and influenced by these judgments will, I believe, be corrected and purified.

Taking up the subject, then, upon general grounds, let me ask, what is meant by the word Poet? What is a Poet? To whom does he address himself? And what language is to be expected from him?—He is a man speaking to men: a man, it is true, endowed with more lively sensibility, more enthusiasm and tenderness, who has a greater knowledge of human nature, and a more comprehensive soul, than are supposed to be common among mankind; a man pleased with his own passions and volitions, and who rejoices more than other men in the spirit of life that is in him; delighting to contemplate similar volitions and passions as manifested in the goings-on of the Universe, and habitually impelled to create them where he does not find them. To these qualities he has added a disposition to be affected more than other men by absent things as if they were present; an ability of conjuring up in himself passions, which are indeed far from being the same as those produced by real events, yet (especially in those parts of the general sympathy which are pleasing and delightful) do more nearly resemble the passions produced by real events, than anything which, from the motions of their own minds merely, other men are accustomed to feel in themselves:—whence, and from

practice, he has acquired a greater readiness and power in expressing what he thinks and feels, and especially those thoughts and feelings which, by his own choice, or from the structure of his own mind, arise in him without immediate external excitement.

But whatever portion of this faculty we may suppose even the greatest Poet to possess, there cannot be a doubt that the language which it will suggest to him, must often, in liveliness and truth, fall short of that which is uttered by men in real life, under the actual pressure of those passions, certain shadows of which the Poet thus produces, or feels to be produced, in himself.

However exalted a notion we would wish to cherish of the character of a Poet, it is obvious, that while he describes and imitates passions, his employment is in some degree mechanical, compared with the freedom and power of real and substantial action and suffering. So that it will be the wish of the Poet to bring his feelings near to those of the persons whose feelings he describes, nay, for short spaces of time, perhaps, to let himself slip into an entire delusion, and even confound and identify his own feelings with theirs; modifying only the language which is thus suggested to him by a consideration that he describes for a particular purpose, that of giving pleasure. Here, then, he will apply the principle of selection which has been already insisted upon. He will depend upon this for removing what would otherwise be painful or disgusting in the passion; he will feel that there is no necessity to trick out or to elevate nature: and, the more industriously he applies this principle, the deeper will be his faith that no words, which *his* fancy or imagination can suggest, will be to be compared with those which are the emanations of reality and truth.

But it may be said by those who do not object to the general spirit of these remarks, that, as it is impossible for the Poet to produce upon all occasions language as exquisitely fitted for the passion as that which the real passion itself suggests, it is proper that he should consider himself as in the situation of a translator, who does not scruple to substitute excellencies of another kind for those which are unattainable by him; and endeavours occasionally to surpass his original, in order to make some amends for the general inferiority to which he feels that he must submit. But this would be to encourage idleness and unmanly despair. Further, it is the language of men who speak of what they do not understand; who talk of Poetry as of a matter of amusement and idle pleasure; who will converse with us as gravely about a *taste* for Poetry, as they express it, as if it were a thing as indifferent as a taste for rope-dancing, or Frontiniac[12] or Sherry. Aristotle, I have been told, has said, that Poetry is the most philosophic of all writing:[13] it is so: its object is truth, not individual and local, but general, and operative; not standing upon external testimony, but carried alive into the heart by passion; truth which is its own testimony, which gives competence and confidence to the tribunal to which it appeals, and receives them from the same tribunal. Poetry is the image of man and nature. The obstacles which stand in the way of the fidelity of the Biographer and Historian, and of their consequent utility, are incalculably greater than those which are to be encountered by the Poet who comprehends the dignity of his art. The Poet writes under one restriction only, namely, the necessity of giving immediate pleasure to a human Being possessed of that information which may be expected from him, not as a lawyer, a physician, a mariner, an astronomer, or a natural philosopher,[14] but as a Man. Except this one restriction, there is no object standing between the Poet and the image of things; between this, and the Biographer and Historian, there are a thousand.

Nor let this necessity of producing immediate pleasure be considered as a degradation of the Poet's art. It is far otherwise. It is an acknowledgment of the beauty of the Universe, an acknowledgment the more sincere, because not formal, but indirect; it is a task light and easy to him who looks at the world in the spirit of love: further, it is a homage paid to the native and naked dignity of man, to the grand elementary principle of pleasure, by which he knows, and feels, and lives, and moves. We have no sympathy but what is propagated by pleasure: I would not be misunderstood; but wherever we sympathise with pain, it will be found that the sympathy is produced and carried on by subtle combinations with pleasure. We have no knowledge, that is, no general principles drawn from the contemplation of particular facts, but what has been built up by pleasure, and exists in us by pleasure alone. The Man of science, the Chemist and Mathematician, whatever difficulties and disgusts they may have had to struggle with, know and feel this. However painful may be the objects with which the Anatomist's knowledge is connected, he feels that his knowledge is pleasure;

and where he has no pleasure he has no knowledge. What then does the Poet? He considers man and the objects that surround him as acting and re-acting upon each other, so as to produce an infinite complexity of pain and pleasure; he considers man in his own nature and in his ordinary life as contemplating this with a certain quantity of immediate knowledge, with certain convictions, intuitions, and deductions, which from habit acquire the quality of intuitions; he considers him as looking upon this complex scene of ideas and sensations, and finding everywhere objects that immediately excite in him sympathies which, from the necessities of his nature, are accompanied by an overbalance of enjoyment.

To this knowledge which all men carry about with them, and to these sympathies in which, without any other discipline than that of our daily life, we are fitted to take delight, the Poet principally directs his attention. He considers man and nature as essentially adapted to each other, and the mind of man as naturally the mirror of the fairest and most interesting properties of nature. And thus the Poet, prompted by this feeling of pleasure, which accompanies him through the whole course of his studies, converses with general nature, with affections akin to those, which, through labour and length of time, the Man of science has raised up in himself, by conversing with those particular parts of nature which are the objects of his studies. The knowledge both of the Poet and the Man of science is pleasure; but the knowledge of the one cleaves to us as a necessary part of our existence, our natural and unalienable inheritance; the other is a personal and individual acquisition, slow to come to us, and by no habitual and direct sympathy connecting us with our fellow-beings. The Man of science seeks truth as a remote and unknown benefactor; he cherishes and loves it in his solitude: the Poet, singing a song in which all human beings join with him, rejoices in the presence of truth as our visible friend and hourly companion. Poetry is the breath and finer spirit of all knowledge; it is the impassioned expression which is in the countenance of all Science. Emphatically may it be said of the Poet, as Shakspeare hath said of man, "that he looks before and after."[15] He is the rock of defence for human nature; an upholder and preserver, carrying everywhere with him relationship and love. In spite of difference of soil and climate, of language and manners, of laws and customs: in spite of things silently gone out of mind, and things

---

12 Frontignac, a sweet wine of southern France.
13 Aristotle (*Poetics*, IX) says that the truth of poetry is more serious and philosophical than that of history, since the latter deals with the particular and the former with the universal.
14 Student of the natural sciences.

15 Cf. *Hamlet*, IV, iv, 37.

violently destroyed; the Poet binds together by passion and knowledge the vast empire of human society, as it is spread over the whole earth, and over all time. The objects of the Poet's thoughts are everywhere; though the eyes and senses of man are, it is true, his favourite guides, yet he will follow wheresoever he can find an atmosphere of sensation in which to move his wings. Poetry is the first and last of all knowledge—it is as immortal as the heart of man. If the labours of Men of science should ever create any material revolution, direct or indirect, in our condition, and in the impressions which we habitually receive, the Poet will sleep then no more than at present; he will be ready to follow the steps of the Man of science, not only in those general indirect effects, but he will be at his side, carrying sensation into the midst of the objects of the science itself. The remotest discoveries of the Chemist, the Botanist, or Mineralogist, will be as proper objects of the Poet's art as any upon which it can be employed, if the time should ever come when these things shall be familiar to us, and the relations under which they are contemplated by the followers of these respective sciences shall be manifestly and palpably material to us as enjoying and suffering beings. If the time should ever come when what is now called science, thus familiarised to men, shall be ready to put on, as it were, a form of flesh and blood, the Poet will lend his divine spirit to aid the transfiguration, and will welcome the Being thus produced, as a dear and genuine inmate of the household of man.—It is not, then, to be supposed that any one, who holds that sublime notion of Poetry which I have attempted to convey, will break in upon the sanctity and truth of his pictures by transitory and accidental ornaments, and endeavour to excite admiration of himself by arts, the necessity of which must manifestly depend upon the assumed meanness of his subject.

What has been thus far said applies to Poetry in general; but especially to those parts of composition where the Poet speaks through the mouths of his characters; and upon this point it appears to authorise the conclusion that there are few persons of good sense, who would not allow that the dramatic parts of composition are defective, in proportion as they deviate from the real language of nature, and are coloured by a diction of the Poet's own, either peculiar to him as an individual Poet or belonging simply to Poets in general; to a body of men who, from the circumstance of their compositions being in metre, it is expected will employ a particular language.

It is not, then, in the dramatic parts of composition that we look for this distinction of language; but still it may be proper and necessary where the Poet speaks to us in his own person and character. To this I answer by referring the Reader to the description before given of a Poet. Among the qualities there enumerated as principally conducing to form a Poet, is implied nothing differing in kind from other men, but only in degree. The sum of what was said is, that the Poet is chiefly distinguished from other men by a greater promptness to think and feel without immediate external excitement, and a greater power in expressing such thoughts and feelings as are produced in him in that manner. But these passions and thoughts and feelings are the general passions and thoughts and feelings of men. And with what are they connected? Undoubtedly with our moral sentiments and animal sensations, and with the causes which excite these; with the operations of the elements, and the appearances of the visible universe; with storm and sunshine, with the revolutions of the seasons, with cold and heat, with loss of friends and kindred, with injuries and resentments, gratitude and hope, with fear and sorrow. These, and the like, are the sensations and objects which the Poet describes, as they are the sensations of other men, and the objects which interest them. The Poet thinks and feels in the spirit of human passions. How, then, can his language differ in any material degree from that of all other men who feel vividly and see clearly? It might be *proved* that it is impossible. But supposing that this were not the case, the Poet might then be allowed to use a peculiar language when expressing his feelings for his own gratification, or that of men like himself. But Poets do not write for Poets alone, but for men. Unless therefore we are advocates for that admiration which subsists upon ignorance, and that pleasure which arises from hearing what we do not understand, the Poet must descend from this supposed height; and, in order to excite rational sympathy, he must express himself as other men express themselves. To this it may be added, that while he is only selecting from the real language of men, or, which amounts to the same thing, composing accurately in the spirit of such selection, he is treading upon safe ground, and we know what we are to expect from him. Our feelings are the same with respect to metre; for, as it may be proper to remind the Reader, the distinction of metre is regular and uniform, and not, like that which is produced by what is usually called POETIC DICTION, arbitrary, and subject to infinite caprices upon which no calculation whatever can be made. In the one case, the Reader is utterly at the mercy of the Poet, respecting what imagery or diction he may choose to connect with the passion; whereas, in the other, the metre obeys certain laws, to which the Poet and Reader both willingly submit because they are certain, and because no interference is made by them with the passion, but such as the concurring testimony of ages has shown to heighten and improve the pleasure which co-exists with it.

It will now be proper to answer an obvious question, namely, Why, professing these opinions, have I written in verse? To this, in addition to such answer as is included in what has been already said, I reply, in the first place, Because, however I may have restricted myself, there is still left open to me what confessedly constitutes the most valuable object of all writing, whether in prose or verse; the great and universal passions of men, the most general and interesting of their occupations, and the entire world of nature before me—to supply endless combinations of forms and imagery. Now, supposing for a moment that whatever is interesting in these objects may be as vividly described in prose, why should I be condemned for attempting to superadd to such description the charm which, by the consent of all nations, is acknowledged to exist in metrical language? To this, by such as are yet unconvinced, it may be answered that a very small part of the pleasure given by Poetry depends upon the metre, and that it is injudicious to write in metre, unless it be accompanied with the other artificial distinctions of style with which metre is usually accompanied, and that, by such deviation, more will be lost from the shock which will thereby be given to the Reader's associations than will be counterbalanced by any pleasure which he can derive from the general power of numbers.[16] In answer to those who still contend for the necessity of accompanying metre with certain appropriate colours of style in order to the accomplishment of its appropriate end, and who also, in my opinion, greatly underrate the power of metre in itself, it might, perhaps, as far as relates to these Volumes, have been almost sufficient to observe, that poems are extant, written upon more humble subjects, and in a still more naked and simple style, which have continued to give pleasure from generation to generation. Now, if nakedness and simplicity be a defect, the fact here mentioned affords a strong presumption that poems somewhat less naked and simple are capable of affording pleasure at the present day; and, what I wished *chiefly* to attempt, at

present, was to justify myself for having written under the impression of this belief. . . .[17]

I have said that poetry is the spontaneous overflow of powerful feelings: it takes its origin from emotion recollected in tranquillity: the emotion is contemplated till, by a species of reaction, the tranquillity gradually disappears, and an emotion, kindred to that which was before the subject of contemplation, is gradually produced, and does itself actually exist in the mind. In this mood successful composition generally begins, and in a mood similar to this it is carried on; but the emotion, of whatever kind, and in whatever degree, from various causes, is qualified by various pleasures, so that in describing any passions whatsoever, which are voluntarily described, the mind will, upon the whole, be in a state of enjoyment. If Nature be thus cautious to preserve in a state of enjoyment a being so employed, the Poet ought to profit by the lesson held forth to him, and ought especially to take care, that, whatever passions he communicates to his Reader, those passions, if his Reader's mind be sound and vigorous, should always be accompanied with an overbalance of pleasure. Now the music of harmonious metrical language, the sense of difficulty overcome, and the blind association of pleasure which has been previously received from works of rhyme or metre of the same or similar construction, an indistinct perception perpetually renewed of language closely resembling that of real life, and yet, in the circumstance of metre, differing from it so widely—all these imperceptibly make up a complex feeling of delight, which is of the most important use in tempering the painful feeling always found intermingled with powerful descriptions of the deeper passions. This effect is always produced in pathetic and impassioned poetry; while, in lighter compositions, the ease and gracefulness with which the Poet manages his numbers are themselves confessedly a principal source of the gratification of the Reader. All that it is *necessary* to say, however, upon this subject, may be effected by affirming, what few persons will deny, that, of two descriptions, either of passions, manners, or characters, each of them equally well executed, the one in prose and the other in verse, the verse will be read a hundred times where the prose is read once.

Having thus explained a few of my reasons for writing in verse, and why I have chosen subjects from common life, and endeavoured to bring my language near to the real language of men, if I have been too minute in pleading my own cause, I have

---

[16] Meter, versification.

[17] A passage on the importance of meter is here omitted.

at the same time been treating a subject of general interest; and for this reason a few words shall be added with reference solely to these particular poems, and to some defects which will probably be found in them. I am sensible that my associations must have sometimes been particular instead of general, and that, consequently, giving to things a false importance, I may have sometimes written upon unworthy subjects; but I am less apprehensive on this account, than that my language may frequently have suffered from those arbitrary connections of feelings and ideas with particular words and phrases, from which no man can altogether protect himself. Hence I have no doubt, that, in some instances, feelings, even of the ludicrous, may be given to my Readers by expressions which appeared to me tender and pathetic. Such faulty expressions, were I convinced they were faulty at present, and that they must necessarily continue to be so, I would willingly take all reasonable pains to correct. But it is dangerous to make these alterations on the simple authority of a few individuals, or even of certain classes of men; for where the understanding of an Author is not convinced, or his feelings altered, this cannot be done without great injury to himself: for his own feelings are his stay and support; and, if he set them aside in one instance, he may be induced to repeat this act till his mind shall lose all confidence in itself, and become utterly debilitated. To this it may be added, that the critic ought never to forget that he is himself exposed to the same errors as the Poet, and, perhaps, in a much greater degree: for there can be no presumption in saying of most readers, that it is not probable they will be so well acquainted with the various stages of meaning through which words have passed, or with the fickleness or stability of the relations of particular ideas to each other; and, above all, since they are so much less interested in the subject, they may decide lightly and carelessly.

Long as the Reader has been detained, I hope he will permit me to caution him against a mode of false criticism which has been applied to Poetry, in which the language closely resembles that of life and nature. Such verses have been triumphed over in parodies, of which Dr. Johnson's stanza is a fair specimen:—

> I put my hat upon my head
> And walked into the Strand,[18]
> And there I met another man
> Whose hat was in his hand.

Immediately under these lines let us place one of the most justly-admired stanzas of the "Babes in the Wood."[19]

> These pretty Babes with hand in hand
> Went wandering up and down;
> But never more they saw the Man
> Approaching from the Town.

In both these stanzas the words, and the order of the words, in no respect differ from the most unimpassioned conversation. There are words in both, for example, "the Strand," and "the Town," connected with none but the most familiar ideas; yet the one stanza we admit as admirable, and the other as a fair example of the superlatively contemptible. Whence arises this difference? Not from the metre, not from the language, not from the order of the words; but the *matter* expressed in Dr. Johnson's stanza is contemptible. The proper method of treating trivial and simple verses, to which Dr. Johnson's stanza would be a fair parallelism, is not to say, this is a bad kind of poetry, or, this is not poetry; but, this wants sense; it is neither interesting in itself, nor can *lead* to anything interesting; the images neither originate in that sane state of feeling which arises out of thought, nor can excite thought or feeling in the Reader. This is the only sensible manner of dealing with such verses. Why trouble yourself about the species till you have previously decided upon the genus? Why take pains to prove that an ape is not a Newton, when it is self-evident that he is not a man? One request I must make of my Reader, which is, that in judging these Poems he would decide by his own feelings genuinely, and not by reflection upon what will probably be the judgment of others. How common is it to hear a person say, I myself do not object to this style of composition, or this or that expression, but, to such and such classes of people it will appear mean or ludicrous! This mode of criticism, so destructive of all sound unadulterated judgment, is almost universal: let the Reader then abide, independently, by his own feelings, and, if he finds himself affected, let him not suffer such conjectures to interfere with his pleasure.

If an Author, by any single composition, has impressed us with respect for his talents, it is useful to consider this as affording a presumption, that on other occasions where we have been displeased, he, nevertheless, may not have written ill or absurdly; and further, to give him so much credit for this one composition as may induce us to review what has displeased us, with more care than we should other-

---

18 One of London's most famous streets.

19 Reprinted in *The Oxford Book of Ballads,* pp. 854–9.

wise have bestowed upon it. This is not only an act of justice, but, in our decisions upon poetry especially, may conduce, in a high degree, to the improvement of our own taste; for an *accurate* taste in poetry, and in all the other arts, as Sir Joshua Reynolds has observed,[20] is an *acquired* talent, which can only be produced by thought and a long-continued intercourse with the best models of composition. This is mentioned, not with so ridiculous a purpose as to prevent the most inexperienced Reader from judging for himself, (I have already said that I wish him to judge for himself;) but merely to temper the rashness of decision, and to suggest, that, if Poetry be a subject on which much time has not been bestowed, the judgment may be erroneous; and that, in many cases, it necessarily will be so.

Nothing would, I know, have so effectually contributed to further the end which I have in view, as to have shown of what kind the pleasure is, and how that pleasure is produced, which is confessedly produced by metrical composition essentially different from that which I have here endeavoured to recommend: for the Reader will say that he has been pleased by such composition; and what more can be done for him? The power of any art is limited; and he will suspect, that, if it be proposed to furnish him with new friends, that can be only upon condition of his abandoning his old friends. Besides, as I have said, the Reader is himself conscious of the pleasure which he has received from such composition, composition to which he has peculiarly attached the endearing name of Poetry; and all men feel an habitual gratitude, and something of an honourable bigotry, for

the objects which have long continued to please them: we not only wish to be pleased, but to be pleased in that particular way in which we have been accustomed to be pleased. There is in these feelings enough to resist a host of arguments; and I should be the less able to combat them successfully, as I am willing to allow, that, in order entirely to enjoy the Poetry which I am recommending, it would be necessary to give up much of what is ordinarily enjoyed. But, would my limits have permitted me to point out how this pleasure is produced, many obstacles might have been removed, and the Reader assisted in perceiving that the powers of language are not so limited as he may suppose; and that it is possible for poetry to give other enjoyments, of a purer, more lasting, and more exquisite nature. This part of the subject has not been altogether neglected, but it has not been so much my present aim to prove, that the interest excited by some other kinds of poetry is less vivid, and less worthy of the nobler powers of the mind, as to offer reasons for presuming, that if my purpose were fulfilled, a species of poetry would be produced, which is genuine poetry; in its nature well adapted to interest mankind permanently, and likewise important in the multiplicity and quality of its moral relations.

From what has been said, and from a perusal of the Poems, the Reader will be able clearly to perceive the object which I had in view: he will determine how far it has been attained; and, what is a much more important question, whether it be worth attaining: and upon the decision of these two questions will rest my claim to the approbation of the Public.

---

20 In the seventh of the *Discourses* of this eminent eighteenth-century painter.

---

from THE PRELUDE
OR GROWTH OF A POET'S MIND

AN AUTOBIOGRAPHICAL POEM

WORDSWORTH'S preface to *The Excursion* (1814) states: "Several years ago, when the Author retired to his native mountains, with the hope of being able to construct a literary Work that might live, it was a reasonable thing that he should take a review of his own mind, and examine how far Nature and Education had qualified him for such employment. As subsidiary to this preparation, he undertook to record, in verse, the origin and progress of his own powers, as far as he was acquainted with them. . . . The result . . . was a determination to compose

a philosophical poem, containing views of Man, Nature, and Society; and to be entitled 'The Recluse'; as having for its principal subject the sensations and opinions of a poet living in retirement. The preparatory poem [*The Prelude*] is biographical, and conducts the history of the Author's mind to the point when he was emboldened to hope that his faculties were sufficiently matured for entering upon the arduous labour which he had proposed to himself. . . ." *The Recluse* was never completed; *The Excursion,* a long and unsuccessful poem in nine books, was intended as the second part of it.

As he states in a letter to a friend, Wordsworth's motive in writing about himself a poem of such length

as *The Prelude* was "not self-conceit . . . but real humility;
I began the work because I was unprepared to treat any
more arduous subject, and diffident of my own powers.
Here, at least, I hoped that . . . I should be sure of succeeding, as I had nothing to do but describe what I had
felt and thought; therefore could not easily be bewildered." Begun in 1798, *The Prelude* was all written
by 1805 but not published till 1850, after Wordsworth's
death. Meanwhile, it had undergone many revisions. The
text of the following extracts is from the final version.
The most useful edition is by E. de Selincourt (1926).
The most thorough and illuminating treatise is R. D.
Havens's *The Mind of a Poet: A Study of Wordsworth's
Thought with Particular Reference to "The Prelude"* (1941).

from BOOK FIRST

INTRODUCTION—CHILDHOOD AND SCHOOL-TIME

. . . Sometimes it suits me better to invent
A tale from my own heart, more near akin
To my own passions and habitual thoughts;[1]
Some variegated story, in the main
Lofty, but the unsubstantial structure melts   225
Before the very sun that brightens it,
Mist into air dissolving! Then a wish,
My last and favourite aspiration, mounts
With yearning toward some philosophic song
Of Truth that cherishes our daily life;   230
With meditations passionate from deep
Recesses in man's heart, immortal verse
Thoughtfully fitted to the Orphean[2] lyre;
But from this awful burthen I full soon
Take refuge and beguile myself with trust   235
That mellower years will bring a riper mind
And clearer insight. Thus my days are past
In contradiction; with no skill to part
Vague longing, haply[3] bred by want of power,
From paramount impulse not to be withstood,   240
A timorous capacity from prudence,
From circumspection, infinite delay.
Humility and modest awe themselves
Betray me, serving often for a cloak
To a more subtle selfishness; that now   245
Locks every function up in blank reserve,
Now dupes me, trusting to an anxious eye
That with intrusive restlessness beats off

Simplicity and self-presented truth.
Ah! better far than this, to stray about   250
Voluptuously through fields and rural walks,
And ask no record of the hours, resigned
To vacant musing, unreproved neglect
Of all things, and deliberate holiday.
Far better never to have heard the name   255
Of zeal and just ambition, than to live
Baffled and plagued by a mind that every hour
Turns recreant to her task; takes heart again,
Then feels immediately some hollow[4] thought
Hang like an interdict upon her hopes.   260
This is my lot; for either still I find
Some imperfection in the chosen theme,
Or see of absolute accomplishment
Much wanting, so much wanting, in myself,
That I recoil and droop, and seek repose   265
In listlessness from vain perplexity,
Unprofitably travelling toward the grave,
Like a false steward[5] who hath much received
And renders nothing back.
                              Was it for this
That one, the fairest of all rivers, loved   270
To blend his murmurs with my nurse's song,
And, from his alder shades and rocky falls,
And from his fords and shallows, sent a voice
That flowed along my dreams? For this, didst thou,
O Derwent! winding among grassy holms[6]   275
Where I was looking on, a babe in arms,
Make ceaseless music that composed my thoughts
To more than infant softness, giving me
Amid the fretful dwellings of mankind
A foretaste, a dim earnest, of the calm   280
That Nature breathes among the hills and groves.
    When he had left the mountains and received
On his smooth breast the shadow of those towers[7]
That yet survive, a shattered monument
Of feudal sway, the bright blue river passed   285
Along the margin of our terrace walk;
A tempting playmate whom we dearly loved.
Oh, many a time have I, a five years' child,
In a small mill-race severed from his stream,
Made one long bathing of a summer's day;   290
Basked in the sun, and plunged and basked again
Alternate, all a summer's day, or scoured
The sandy fields, leaping through flowery groves
Of yellow ragwort; or when rock and hill,

---

[1] Wordsworth has been reviewing the various subjects he had
thought of writing about.
[2] Exalted. The phrase is from Milton, *Paradise Lost,* III, 17. In
Greek mythology the musician Orpheus, son of Apollo, had
extraordinary powers.   [3] Perhaps.

[4] Unsound.
[5] See the parable of the talents, Matthew 25:14–30.
[6] Bottoms, low flatlands.—Wordsworth was born at Cockermouth, Cumberland, where the Cocker flows into the Derwent.
[7] Of Cockermouth Castle.

The woods, and distant Skiddaw's lofty height,[8]   295
Were bronzed with deepest radiance, stood alone
Beneath the sky, as if I had been born
On Indian plains, and from my mother's hut
Had run abroad in wantonness, to sport,
A naked savage, in the thunder shower.   300

    Fair seed-time had my soul, and I grew up
Fostered alike by beauty and by fear:
Much favoured in my birthplace, and no less
In that belovèd Vale[9] to which erelong
We were transplanted—there were we let loose   305
For sports of wider range. Ere I had told
Ten birth-days, when among the mountain-slopes
Frost, and the breath of frosty wind, had snapped
The last autumnal crocus, 'twas my joy
With store of springes[10] o'er my shoulder hung   310
To range the open heights where woodcocks run
Among the smooth green turf. Through half the night,
Scudding away from snare to snare, I plied
That anxious visitation;—moon and stars
Were shining o'er my head. I was alone,   315
And seemed to be a trouble to the peace
That dwelt among them. Sometimes it befell
In these night wanderings, that a strong desire
O'erpowered my better reason, and the bird
Which was the captive of another's toil   320
Became my prey; and when the deed was done
I heard among the solitary hills
Low breathings coming after me, and sounds
Of undistinguishable motion, steps
Almost as silent as the turf they trod.   325

    Nor less when spring had warmed the cultured[11] Vale
Moved we as plunderers where the mother-bird
Had in high places built her lodge; though mean
Our object and inglorious, yet the end
Was not ignoble.[12] Oh! when I have hung   330
Above the raven's nest, by knots of grass
And half-inch fissures in the slippery rock
But ill sustained, and almost (so it seemed)
Suspended by the blast that blew amain,
Shouldering the naked crag, oh, at that time   335
While on the perilous ridge I hung alone,
With what strange utterance did the loud dry wind
Blow through my ear! the sky seemed not a sky
Of earth—and with what motion moved the clouds!

---

[8] The fourth highest (3054 feet) of the peaks in the Lake District.
[9] In northern Lancashire, near Lake Windermere; after his mother's death Wordsworth was sent to school at the village of Hawkshead in Esthwaite Vale.
[10] Snares, traps.
[11] Cultivated, farmed. Probably the valley of Yewdale, near Hawkshead.
[12] Because these expeditions were adventurous and brought him close to nature.

Dust as we are, the immortal spirit grows   340
Like harmony in music; there is a dark
Inscrutable workmanship that reconciles
Discordant elements, makes them cling together
In one society. How strange that all
The terrors, pains, and early miseries,   345
Regrets, vexations, lassitudes interfused
Within my mind, should e'er have borne a part,
And that a needful part, in making up
The calm existence that is mine when I
Am worthy of myself! Praise to the end!   350
Thanks to the means which Nature deigned to employ;
Whether her fearless visitings, or those
That came with soft alarm, like hurtless light
Opening the peaceful clouds; or she may use
Severer interventions, ministry   355
More palpable, as best might suit her aim.

    One summer evening (led by her) I found
A little boat tied to a willow tree
Within a rocky cave, its usual home.
Straight I unloosed her chain, and stepping in   360
Pushed from the shore. It was an act of stealth
And troubled pleasure, nor without the voice
Of mountain-echoes did my boat move on;
Leaving behind her still, on either side,
Small circles glittering idly in the moon,   365
Until they melted all into one track
Of sparkling light. But now, like one who rows,
Proud of his skill, to reach a chosen point
With an unswerving line, I fixed my view
Upon the summit of a craggy ridge,   370
The horizon's utmost boundary; for above
Was nothing but the stars and the grey sky.
She was an elfin pinnace; lustily
I dipped my oars into the silent lake,
And, as I rose upon the stroke, my boat   375
Went heaving through the water like a swan;
When, from behind that craggy steep till then
The horizon's bound, a huge peak, black and huge,
As if with voluntary power instinct
Upreared its head. I struck and struck again,   380
And growing still in stature the grim shape
Towered up between me and the stars, and still,
For so it seemed, with purpose of its own
And measured motion like a living thing,
Strode after me. With trembling oars I turned,   385
And through the silent water stole my way
Back to the covert of the willow tree;
There in her mooring-place I left my bark,—
And through the meadows homeward went, in grave
And serious mood; but after I had seen   390
That spectacle, for many days, my brain

I want! I want!

BLAKE'S *THE GATES OF PARADISE*, 1793

This small book (reproductions are actual size) consists chiefly of pictures, simple in conception but strongly symbolic of elemental emotions. (Harvard College Library)

Death's Door

WILLIAM BLAKE

A life mask made in 1809, when Blake was 51 or 52 years old, by the phrenologist J. S. Deville. A life mask is made from a mold obtained by spreading plaster over the subject's face. (National Portrait Gallery, London)

SONGS OF EXPERIENCE, 1794

This page shows Blake's practice of engraving words and illustrations in a single design. (Pierpont Morgan Library)

VISION OF THE BOOK OF JOB, 1825

Blake's illustrations for the Book of Job, engraved by him toward the end of his life, show the full capacity of his imagination in handling ideas of power and grandeur. (Boston Public Library)

THE ENGLISH LAKE DISTRICT

Above is Lake Windermere, the largest lake in England, on the boundary between Westmorland and Lancashire. (British Travel and Holidays Association; photograph by J. Allan Cash) At near-by Hawkshead Wordsworth went to school; shown at the left is the house where he lodged. (G. P. Abraham, Ltd., Keswick) Below, Langdale Pikes at Dungeon Ghyll, a Westmorland scene to which Coleridge refers in *Christabel*, lines 350 f. (British Travel and Holidays Association)

Worked with a dim and undetermined sense
Of unknown modes of being; o'er my thoughts
There hung a darkness, call it solitude
Or blank desertion. No familiar shapes   395
Remained, no pleasant images of trees,
Of sea or sky, no colours of green fields;
But huge and mighty forms, that do not live
Like living men, moved slowly through the mind
By day, and were a trouble to my dreams.   400
    Wisdom and Spirit of the universe![13]
Thou Soul that art the eternity of thought,
That givest to forms and images a breath
And everlasting motion, not in vain
By day or star-light thus from my first dawn   405
Of childhood didst thou intertwine for me
The passions that build up our human soul;
Not with the mean and vulgar works of man,
But with high objects, with enduring things—
With life and nature—purifying thus   410
The elements of feeling and of thought,
And sanctifying, by such discipline,
Both pain and fear, until we recognise
A grandeur in the beatings of the heart.[14]
Nor was this fellowship vouchsafed to me   415
With stinted kindness. In November days,
When vapours rolling down the valley made
A lonely scene more lonesome, among woods
At noon, and 'mid the calm of summer nights,
When, by the margin of the trembling lake,   420
Beneath the gloomy hills homeward I went
In solitude, such intercourse was mine;
Mine was it in the fields both day and night,
And by the waters, all the summer long.
    And in the frosty season, when the sun   425
Was set, and visible for many a mile
The cottage windows blazed through twilight gloom,
I heeded not their summons: happy time
It was indeed for all of us—for me
It was a time of rapture! Clear and loud   430
The village clock tolled six,—I wheeled about,
Proud and exulting like an untired horse
That cares not for his home. All shod with steel,
We hissed along the polished ice in games
Confederate, imitative of the chase   435
And woodland pleasures,—the resounding horn,
The pack loud chiming, and the hunted hare.
So through the darkness and the cold we flew,
And not a voice was idle; with the din
Smitten, the precipices rang aloud;   440
The leafless trees and every icy crag

Tinkled like iron; while far distant hills
Into the tumult sent an alien sound
Of melancholy not unnoticed, while the stars
Eastward were sparkling clear, and in the west   445
The orange sky of evening died away.
Not seldom from the uproar I retired
Into a silent bay, or sportively
Glanced sideway, leaving the tumultuous throng,
To cut across the reflex of a star   450
That fled, and, flying still before me, gleamed
Upon the glassy plain; and oftentimes,
When we had given our bodies to the wind,
And all the shadowy banks on either side
Came sweeping through the darkness, spinning still 455
The rapid line of motion, then at once
Have I, reclining back upon my heels,
Stopped short; yet still the solitary cliffs
Wheeled by me—even as if the earth had rolled
With visible motion her diurnal round!   460
Behind me did they stretch in solemn train,
Feebler and feebler, and I stood and watched
Till all was tranquil as a dreamless sleep.
    Ye Presences of Nature in the sky
And on the earth! Ye Visions of the hills!   465
And Souls of lonely places! can I think
A vulgar hope was yours when ye employed
Such ministry, when ye through many a year
Haunting me thus among my boyish sports,
On caves and trees, upon the woods and hills,   470
Impressed upon all forms the characters
Of danger or desire; and thus did make
The surface of the universal earth
With triumph and delight, with hope and fear,
Work like a sea?
                Not uselessly employed,   475
Might I pursue this theme through every change
Of exercise and play, to which the year
Did summon us in his delightful round.
    We were a noisy crew; the sun in heaven
Beheld not vales more beautiful than ours;   480
Nor saw a band in happiness and joy
Richer, or worthier of the ground they trod.
I could record with no reluctant voice
The woods of autumn, and their hazel bowers
With milk-white clusters hung; the rod and line,   485
True symbol of hope's foolishness, whose strong
And unreproved enchantment led us on
By rocks and pools shut out from every star,
All the green summer, to forlorn cascades
Among the windings hid of mountain brooks.   490
—Unfading recollections! at this hour
The heart is almost mine with which I felt,

---

[13] I.e., God, the Eternal Spirit.
[14] I.e., our simple emotions.

From some hill-top on sunny afternoons,
The paper kite high among fleecy clouds
Pull at her rein like an impetuous courser;   495
Or, from the meadows sent on gusty days,
Beheld her breast the wind, then suddenly
Dashed headlong, and rejected by the storm.

    Ye lowly cottages wherein we dwelt,
A ministration of your own was yours;   500
Can I forget you, being as you were
So beautiful among the pleasant fields
In which ye stood? or can I here forget
The plain and seemly countenance with which
Ye dealt out your plain comforts? Yet had ye   505
Delights and exultations of your own.
Eager and never weary we pursued
Our home-amusements by the warm peat-fire
At evening, when with pencil, and smooth slate
In square divisions parcelled out and all   510
With crosses and with cyphers scribbled o'er,
We schemed and puzzled, head opposed to head
In strife[15] too humble to be named in verse:
Or round the naked table, snow-white deal,[16]
Cherry or maple, sate in close array,   515
And to the combat, Loo[17] or Whist, led on
A thick-ribbed army; not, as in the world,
Neglected and ungratefully thrown by
Even for the very service they had wrought,
But husbanded through many a long campaign.   520
Uncouth assemblage was it, where no few
Had changed their functions; some, plebeian cards
Which Fate, beyond the promise of their birth,
Had dignified, and called to represent
The persons of departed potentates.[18]   525
Oh, with what echoes[19] on the board they fell!
Ironic diamonds,—clubs, hearts, diamonds, spades,
A congregation piteously akin!
Cheap matter offered they to boyish wit,
Those sooty knaves, precipitated down   530
With scoffs and taunts, like Vulcan out of heaven:
The paramount ace, a moon in her eclipse,
Queens gleaming through their splendour's last decay,
And monarchs surly at the wrongs sustained
By royal visages. Meanwhile abroad   535
Incessant rain was falling, or the frost
Raged bitterly, with keen and silent tooth;
And, interrupting oft that eager game,

From under Esthwaite's[20] splitting fields of ice
The pent-up air, struggling to free itself,   540
Gave out to meadow-grounds and hills a loud
Protracted yelling, like the noise of wolves
Howling in troops along the Bothnic Main.[21]

    Nor, sedulous as I have been to trace
How Nature by extrinsic passion first   545
Peopled the mind with forms sublime or fair,
And made me love them, may I here omit
How other pleasures have been mine, and joys
Of subtler origin; how I have felt,
Not seldom even in that tempestuous time,   550
Those hallowed and pure motions of the sense
Which seem, in their simplicity, to own
An intellectual charm; that calm delight
Which, if I err not, surely must belong
To those first-born affinities that fit   555
Our new existence to existing things,
And, in our dawn of being, constitute
The bond of union between life and joy.

    Yes, I remember when the changeful earth,
And twice five summers on my mind had stamped   560
The faces of the moving year, even then
I held unconscious intercourse with beauty
Old as creation, drinking in a pure
Organic pleasure from the silver wreaths
Of curling mist, or from the level plain   565
Of waters coloured by impending clouds.
    The sands of Westmoreland, the creeks and bays
Of Cumbria's[22] rocky limits, they can tell
How, when the Sea threw off his evening shade
And to the shepherd's hut on distant hills   570
Sent welcome notice of the rising moon,
How I have stood, to fancies such as these
A stranger, linking with the spectacle
No conscious memory of a kindred sight,
And bringing with me no peculiar sense   575
Of quietness or peace; yet have I stood,
Even while mine eye hath moved o'er many a league
Of shining water, gathering as it seemed,
Through every hair-breadth in that field of light,
New pleasure like a bee among the flowers.   580
    Thus oft amid those fits of vulgar joy
Which, through all seasons, on a child's pursuits
Are prompt attendants, 'mid that giddy bliss
Which, like a tempest, works along the blood
And is forgotten; even then I felt   585
Gleams like the flashing of a shield;—the earth
And common face of Nature spake to me

---

[15] The game of ticktacktoe.
[16] I.e., of plain, unvarnished boards.   [17] A card game.
[18] The pack was not a dainty one ("thick-ribbed," line 517). Some
    face cards had been lost, and some low cards (supplied from
    another deck) had been marked as replacements.
[19] I.e., the sounds of the cards slapped down on the table.

[20] Esthwaite Water is a lake near Hawkshead.
[21] Sea. I.e., the Gulf of Bothnia, between Sweden and Finland.
[22] Cumberland's.

Rem, Rememberable things; sometimes, 'tis true,
By chance collisions and quaint accidents
(Like those ill-sorted unions, work supposed   590
Of evil-minded fairies), yet not vain
Nor profitless, if haply they impressed
Collateral objects and appearances,
Albeit lifeless then, and doomed to sleep
Until maturer seasons called them forth   595
To impregnate and to elevate the mind.
—And if the vulgar joy by its own weight
Wearied itself out of the memory,
The scenes which were a witness of that joy
Remained in their substantial lineaments   600
Depicted on the brain, and to the eye
Were visible, a daily sight; and thus
By the impressive discipline of fear,
By pleasure and repeated happiness,
So frequently repeated, and by force   605
Of obscure feelings representative
Of things forgotten, these same scenes so bright,
So beautiful, so majestic in themselves,
Though yet the day was distant, did become
Habitually dear, and all their forms   610
And changeful colours by invisible links
Were fastened to the affections.

               I began
My story early—not misled, I trust,
By an infirmity of love for days
Disowned by memory—ere the birth of spring   615
Planting my snowdrops[23] among winter snows;[24]
Nor will it seem to thee, O Friend![25] so prompt
In sympathy, that I have lengthened out
With fond[26] and feeble tongue a tedious tale.
Meanwhile, my hope has been, that I might fetch   620
Invigorating thoughts from former years;
Might fix the wavering balance of my mind,
And haply meet reproaches too, whose power
May spur me on, in manhood now mature,
To honourable toil. Yet should these hopes   625
Prove vain, and thus should neither I be taught
To understand myself, nor thou to know
With better knowledge how the heart was framed
Of him thou lovest; need I dread from thee
Harsh judgments, if the song be loth to quit   630
Those recollected hours that have the charm
Of visionary things, those lovely forms
And sweet sensations that throw back our life,

And almost make remotest infancy
A visible scene, on which the sun is shining?   635
One end at least hath been attained; my mind
Hath been revived, and if this genial mood
Desert me not, forthwith shall be brought down
Through later years the story of my life.
The road lies plain before me;—'tis a theme   640
Single and of determined bounds; and hence
I choose it rather at this time, than work
Of ampler or more varied argument,
Where I might be discomfited and lost.
And certain hopes are with me, that to thee   645
This labour will be welcome, honoured Friend!

from BOOK THIRD

RESIDENCE AT CAMBRIDGE[27]

... I was the Dreamer, they the Dream; I roamed   30
Delighted through the motley spectacle;
Gowns grave, or gaudy, doctors, students, streets,
Courts, cloisters, flocks of churches, gateways, towers:
Migration strange for a stripling of the hills,
A northern villager.

            As if the change   35
Had waited on some Fairy's wand, at once
Behold me rich in monies, and attired
In splendid garb, with hose of silk, and hair
Powdered like rimy trees, when frost is keen.
My lordly dressing gown, I pass it by,   40
With other signs of manhood that supplied
The lack of beard.—The weeks went roundly on,
With invitations, suppers, wine and fruit,
Smooth housekeeping within, and all without
Liberal, and suiting gentleman's array.   45
  The Evangelist St. John my patron was:
Three Gothic courts are his, and in the first
Was my abiding-place, a nook obscure;
Right underneath, the College kitchens made
A humming sound, less tuneable than bees,   50
But hardly less industrious; with shrill notes
Of sharp command and scolding intermixed.
Near me hung Trinity's loquacious clock,
Who never let the quarters, night or day,
Slip by him unproclaimed, and told the hours   55
Twice over with a male and female voice.
Her pealing organ was my neighbour too;
And from my pillow, looking forth by light

---

23 This European flower often blossoms while snow is still on the
   ground.
24 I.e., I began this account of my life with my childhood.
25 Coleridge.   26 Foolish.

27 Book II continues the subject "School-time." Book III opens
   with the morning of Wordsworth's arrival at the university and
   his feelings of being grown up and independent; the change
   was so sudden that it seemed like a dream. He was seventeen
   when he entered St. John's College.

Of moon or favouring stars, I could behold
The antechapel where the statue stood   60
Of Newton with his prism and silent face,
The marble index of a mind for ever
Voyaging through strange seas of Thought, alone. . . .

from BOOK FOURTH

SUMMER VACATION[28]

. . . Among the favourites whom it pleased me well
To see again, was one by ancient right
Our inmate, a rough terrier of the hills;   95
By birth and call of nature pre-ordained
To hunt the badger and unearth the fox
Among the impervious crags, but having been
From youth our own adopted, he had passed
Into a gentler service. And when first   100
The boyish spirit flagged, and day by day
Along my veins I kindled with the stir,
The fermentation, and the vernal heat
Of poesy, affecting private shades
Like a sick Lover, then this dog was used[29]   105
To watch me, an attendant and a friend,
Obsequious to my steps early and late,
Though often of such dilatory walk
Tired, and uneasy at the halts I made.
A hundred times when, roving high and low,   110
I have been harassed with the toil of verse,
Much pains and little progress, and at once
Some lovely Image in the song rose up
Full-formed, like Venus rising from the sea;
Then have I darted forwards to let loose   115
My hand upon his back with stormy joy,
Caressing him again and yet again.
And when at evening on the public way
I sauntered, like a river murmuring
And talking to itself when all things else   120
Are still, the creature trotted on before;
Such was his custom; but whene'er he met
A passenger approaching, he would turn
To give me timely notice, and straightway,
Grateful for that admonishment, I hushed   125
My voice, composed my gait, and, with the air
And mien of one whose thoughts are free, advanced
To give and take a greeting that might save
My name from piteous rumours, such as wait
On men suspected to be crazed in brain.   130

Those walks well worthy to be prized and loved—
Regretted!—that word, too, was on my tongue,
But they were richly laden with all good,
And cannot be remembered but with thanks
And gratitude, and perfect joy of heart—   135
Those walks in all their freshness now came back
Like a returning Spring. When first I made
Once more the circuit of our little lake,
If ever happiness hath lodged with man,
That day consummate happiness was mine,   140
Wide-spreading, steady, calm, contemplative.
The sun was set, or setting, when I left
Our cottage door, and evening soon brought on
A sober hour, not winning or serene,
For cold and raw the air was, and untuned;[30]   145
But as a face we love is sweetest then
When sorrow damps it, or, whatever look
It chance to wear, is sweetest if the heart
Have fulness in herself; even so with me
It fared that evening. Gently did my soul   150
Put off her veil, and, self-transmuted, stood
Naked, as in the presence of her God.
While on I walked, a comfort seemed to touch
A heart that had not been disconsolate:
Strength came where weakness was not known to be,
At least not felt; and restoration came   156
Like an intruder knocking at the door
Of unacknowledged weariness. I took
The balance, and with firm hand weighed myself.
—Of that external scene which round me lay,   160
Little, in this abstraction, did I see;
Remembered less; but I had inward hopes
And swellings of the spirit, was rapt and soothed,
Conversed with promises, had glimmering views
How life pervades the undecaying mind;   165
How the immortal soul with God-like power
Informs,[31] creates, and thaws the deepest sleep
That time can lay upon her;[32] how on earth
Man, if he do but live within the light
Of high endeavours, daily spreads abroad   170
His being armed with strength that cannot fail.
Nor was there want of milder thoughts, of love,
Of innocence, and holiday repose;
And more than pastoral quiet, 'mid the stir
Of boldest projects, and a peaceful end   175
At last, or glorious, by endurance won.
Thus musing, in a wood I sate me down
Alone, continuing there to muse: the slopes

---

[28] Book IV, dealing with the poet's first "long vacation," from July to October, 1788, opens with his joy in being at home again. The walks with the dog, described in the following lines, came earlier, during adolescence.   [29] Accustomed.

[30] I.e., not in tune with the poet's happiness.
[31] Forms inwardly. This verb and also *creates* are intransitive; *sleep* is the object only of *thaws*.
[32] I.e., the creative power of the human spirit ("soul," line 166) overcomes the deadening effect of life's routine.

And heights meanwhile were slowly overspread
With darkness, and before a rippling breeze   180
The long lake lengthened out its hoary line,
And in the sheltered coppice where I sate,
Around me from among the hazel leaves,
Now here, now there, moved by the straggling wind,
Came ever and anon a breath-like sound,   185
Quick as the pantings of the faithful dog,
The off and on companion of my walk;
And such, at times, believing them to be,
I turned my head to look if he were there;
Then into solemn thought I passed once more. . . .   190

               Yes, that heartless chase
Of trivial pleasures[33] was a poor exchange
For books and nature at that early age.
'Tis true, some casual knowledge might be gained   300
Of character or life; but at that time,
Of manners put to school I took small note,
And all my deeper passions lay elsewhere.
Far better had it been to exalt the mind
By solitary study, to uphold   305
Intense desire through meditative peace;
And yet for chastisement of these regrets,
The memory of one particular hour
Doth here rise up against me. 'Mid a throng
Of maids and youths, old men, and matrons staid,   310
A medley of all tempers, I had passed
The night in dancing, gaiety, and mirth,
With din of instruments and shuffling feet,
And glancing forms, and tapers glittering,
And unaimed prattle flying up and down;   315
Spirits upon the stretch, and here and there
Slight shocks of young love-liking interspersed,
Whose transient pleasure mounted to the head,
And tingled through the veins. Ere we retired,
The cock had crowed, and now the eastern sky   320
Was kindling, not unseen, from humble copse
And open field, through which the pathway wound,
And homeward led my steps. Magnificent
The morning rose, in memorable pomp,
Glorious as e'er I had beheld—in front,   325
The sea lay laughing at a distance; near,
The solid mountains shone, bright as the clouds,
Grain-tinctured,[34] drenched in empyrean light;
And in the meadows and the lower grounds
Was all the sweetness of a common dawn—   330
Dews, vapours, and the melody of birds,
And labourers going forth to till the fields.

Ah! need I say, dear Friend! that to the brim
My heart was full; I made no vows, but vows
Were then made for me; bond unknown to me   335
Was given, that I should be, else sinning greatly,
A dedicated Spirit. On I walked
In thankful blessedness, which yet survives. . . .

from BOOK FIFTH

BOOKS

               . . . Yet is it just
That here, in memory of all books which lay
Their sure foundations in the heart of man,
Whether by native prose, or numerous verse,   200
That in the name of all inspirèd souls—
From Homer the great Thunderer, from the voice
That roars along the bed of Jewish song,
And that more varied and elaborate,
Those trumpet-tones of harmony that shake   205
Our shores in England,—from those loftiest notes
Down to the low and wren-like warblings, made
For cottages and spinners at the wheel,
And sun-burnt travellers resting their tired limbs
Stretched under wayside hedge-rows, ballad tunes,   210
Food for the hungry ears of little ones,
And of old men who have survived their joys—
'Tis just that in behalf of these,[35] the works,
And of the men that framed them, whether known,
Or sleeping nameless in their scattered graves,   215
That I should here assert their rights, attest
Their honours, and should, once for all, pronounce
Their benediction; speak of them as Powers
For ever to be hallowed; only less,
For what we are and what we may become,   220
Than Nature's self, which is the breath of God,
Or His pure Word[36] by miracle revealed. . . .

               Twice five years
Or less I might have seen, when first my mind
With conscious pleasure opened to the charm
Of words in tuneful order, found them sweet   555
For their own *sakes,* a passion, and a power;
And phrases pleased me chosen for delight,
For pomp, or love. Oft, in the public roads
Yet unfrequented, while the morning light
Was yellowing the hill tops, I went abroad   560
With a dear friend,[37] and for the better part
Of two delightful hours we strolled along
By the still borders of the misty lake,

---

[33] The poet has just mentioned the distractions which at this time
    often occasioned "an inner falling off" from his true nature and
    purposes.   [34] Crimson.

[35] The "all books" of line 198.   [36] Or only less than the Bible.
[37] His name was John Fleming; he became a clergyman.

Repeating favourite verses with one voice,
Or conning more, as happy as the birds   565
That round us chaunted. Well might we be glad,
Lifted above the ground by airy fancies,
More bright than madness or the dreams of wine;
And, though full oft the objects of our love
Were false, and in their splendour over-wrought,   570
Yet was there surely then no vulgar power
Working within us,—nothing less, in truth,
Than that most noble attribute of man,
Though yet untutored and inordinate,
That wish for something loftier, more adorned,   575
Than is the common aspect, daily garb,
Of human life. What wonder, then, if sounds
Of exultation echoed through the groves!
For, images, and sentiments, and words,
And everything encountered or pursued   580
In that delicious world of poesy,
Kept holiday, a never-ending show,
With music, incense, festival, and flowers!

   Here must we pause: this only let me add,
From heart-experience, and in humblest sense   585
Of modesty, that he, who in his youth
A daily wanderer among woods and fields
With living Nature hath been intimate,
Not only in that raw unpractised time
Is stirred to ecstasy, as others are,   590
By glittering verse; but further, doth receive,
In measure only dealt out to himself,
Knowledge and increase of enduring joy
From the great Nature that exists in works
Of mighty Poets. Visionary power   595
Attends the motions of the viewless winds,
Embodied in the mystery of words:
There, darkness[38] makes abode, and all the host
Of shadowy things work endless changes,—there,
As in a mansion like their proper home,   600
Even forms and substances are circumfused
By that transparent veil with light divine,
And, through the turnings intricate of verse,
Present themselves as objects recognised,
In flashes, and with glory not their own.   605

---

[38] What Wordsworth elsewhere (XII, 279) calls "the hiding-places
of man's power."

from BOOK NINTH

RESIDENCE IN FRANCE[39]

                          . . . And when we chanced
One day to meet a hunger-bitten girl,   510
Who crept along fitting her languid gait
Unto a heifer's motion, by a cord
Tied to her arm, and picking thus from the lane
Its sustenance, while the girl with pallid hands
Was busy knitting in a heartless[40] mood   515
Of solitude, and at the sight my friend
In agitation said, " 'Tis against that
That we are fighting," I with him believed
That a benignant spirit was abroad
Which might not be withstood, that poverty   520
Abject as this would in a little time
Be found no more, that we should see the earth
Unthwarted in her wish to recompense
The meek, the lowly, patient child of toil,
All institutes for ever blotted out   525
That legalised exclusion, empty pomp
Abolished, sensual state and cruel power,
Whether by edict of the one or few;
And finally, as sum and crown of all,
Should see the people having a strong hand   530
In framing their own laws; whence better days
To all mankind. . . .

from BOOK ELEVENTH

FRANCE.—(CONCLUDED)

. . . O pleasant exercise of hope and joy![41]   105
For mighty were the auxiliars which then stood
Upon our side, us who were strong in love!
Bliss was it in that dawn to be alive,
But to be young was very Heaven! O times,
In which the meagre, stale, forbidding ways   110

---

[39] The titles of the intervening books are: VI, "Cambridge and
the Alps"; VII, "Residence in London"; and VIII, "Retrospect.
—Love of Nature Leading to Love of Man." In the preceding
lines of Book IX Wordsworth tells how "France lured me
forth," how as he watched the progress of the Revolution he
"became a patriot," how his heart "was all given to the people"
even though his associates were army officers who with but one
exception held royalist opinions, and how he used to talk
politics with that friend. This was Michel Beaupuy, afterwards
a general; he was killed in action.   [40] Disheartened.
[41] Book X continues "Residence in France" and ends with the
death of Robespierre.—This line refers to the enthusiasm with
which Wordsworth, now that the Terror was over and the
Revolution seemed purified, devoted himself to the study of
political theory.

Of custom, law, and statute took at once
The attraction of a country in romance!
When Reason seemed the most to assert her rights,
When most intent on making of herself
A prime enchantress—to assist the work,   115
Which then was going forward in her name!
Not favoured spots alone, but the whole Earth,
The beauty wore of promise—that which sets
(As at some moments might not be unfelt
Among the bowers of Paradise itself)   120
The budding rose above the rose full blown.
What temper at the prospect did not wake
To happiness unthought of? The inert
Were roused, and lively natures rapt away!
They who had fed their childhood upon dreams,   125
The play-fellows of fancy, who had made
All powers of swiftness, subtilty, and strength

Their ministers, who in lordly wise had stirred
Among the grandest objects of the sense,
And dealt with whatsoever they found there   130
As if they had within some lurking right
To wield it;—they, too, who of gentle mood
Had watched all gentle motions, and to these
Had fitted their own thoughts, schemers more mild,
And in the region of their peaceful selves;—[42]   135
Now was it that *both* found, the meek and lofty
Did both find, helpers to their heart's desire,
And stuff at hand, plastic as they could wish,—
Were called upon to exercise their skill,
Not in Utopia,—subterranean fields,—   140
Or some secreted island, Heaven knows where![43]
But in the very world, which is the world
Of all of us,—the place where, in the end,
We find our happiness, or not at all! . . . [44]

Samuel Taylor Coleridge
1772–1834

IT HAS been said that Coleridge's major work was Wordsworth, but that statement comes closer to being the truth
about Coleridge than it does to accounting for the greater
poet. Wordsworth began writing great poems after
stimulating talks with Coleridge concerning the nature
of poetry; but Coleridge or no Coleridge, he would
eventually have found himself. Coleridge, on the other
hand, never quite found himself or, as we say, got organized. His mind was capable of short flights of astounding
elevation in poetry and of momentary flashes of illumination in criticism; what it lacked was stability and the
power of steady application. For all that, he is one of the
most fascinating of writers. In the art of living he failed,
and most of his works come far short of his intentions;
but he interests his readers, as he interested his hearers,
because his potentialities seem boundless. We are always
expecting some apparition of wonder in the next stanza,
some penetrating observation on the next page.

His life was a tragedy, in which pain made its entrance
early. His father was vicar of Ottery St. Mary on the
Devon coast; there in 1772 the poet was born, the last of
fourteen children, only four of whom reached maturity.
The Reverend Mr. Coleridge was also master of the local
grammar school and eked out his income by boarding
some of the pupils. He died when his youngest son was
nine. One of his former students secured the child's admission to a famous London school. Its headmaster, the
Reverend James Boyer, was as noted for the soundness of

his instruction as for the whimsicality of his floggings;
but Christ's Hospital was a dismal change from beautiful
Devonshire. The food was bad, discipline was cruel and
unintelligent, and for Coleridge there were few of those
delightful vacations which can make absence from family
life bearable to a sensitive little boy. As a rule he spent
his holidays at the school, for want of money to travel
home. Charles Lamb was a fellow pupil and became a
fast friend, but their intimacy does not seem to have begun
during their schooldays. No wonder that a youngster who
cared nothing for games plunged into books far beyond
his years, and found a better world in them. It was the
world of philosophy, of abstract speculation instead of the
facts of life and history. More especially, it was the world
of idealistic philosophy. Coleridge read Plato and even
the Neoplatonic philosophers, and he developed a way of
speaking about the superiority of their world to the world
of physical phenomena which enabled him to hold at
least a number of his fellow students spellbound. The fact
is, Coleridge became too accomplished a talker for his
own good. Brilliant talkers are rare; and sensible boys,
as well as men, are ready to listen when one turns up. In

---

42 I.e., men whose speculations were limited to their inner selves.
43 Utopias or ideal commonwealths were usually located by their
   inventors somewhere under the earth or on some unknown
   island.
44 Books XII and XIII are entitled "Imagination and Taste, How
   Impaired and Restored"; Book XIV is "Conclusion."

conversational monologues, which some compared to Niagara, Coleridge continued throughout his life to expend creative powers that might better have gone to the shaping of tangible, permanent works.

He entered Cambridge on a scholarship in 1791. He was a diligent student, for a while, and won a medal with a Greek poem on the slave trade. Political philosophy, naturally enough in those years of revolution, was soon one of the subjects uppermost in his mind and talk. No less naturally, he was a radical; while still in school he had written an ode on the fall of the Bastille. He praised the French, called for English reform, and detested the prime minister, Pitt. All this was proper for a young poet in the early 1790's; but Coleridge's next enthusiasms do not suggest that he owned any knack for leavening his idealism with a pinch of common sense. Depressed over some debts, Coleridge withdrew from the university and, although he disliked military affairs, enlisted in the army under an assumed name. More than that, he chose the cavalry, in spite of a particular aversion to horses. As one of His Majesty's 15th Light Dragoons, Private Silas Tomkyn Comberbacke was not a success; but he was soon rescued by his brothers, who got him out of the army and arranged for the payment of his debts. Back to the university he meekly went, only to leave it again in 1794, without a degree.

This time the attraction was a vague program for living on a high intellectual plane in a proposed colony of choice spirits who would "combine the innocence of the patriarchal age with the knowledge and genuine refinements of European culture." "Pantisocracy" was the pretentious name chosen for this fantastic project—the term was compounded of three Greek roots, and signified an all-equal rule. Coleridge went in for Pantisocracy under the influence of Robert Southey, at whose poetry we shall glance below. Coleridge had met him during a visit to Oxford. The Pantisocratic planners talked of setting up a little utopia in the United States, on the banks of the Susquehanna. Economic security was to be obtained through a few hours' daily labor by everyone, leaving plenty of time for the pursuit of culture. There were to be twelve male Pantisocrats, and each must have a wife. Accordingly, certainly not as the result of any grand passion, but partly on the rebound from an unhappy boyish love affair, Coleridge found himself in 1795 married to Sara Fricker, one of the four sisters-in-law of Southey. Funds for going on with the Pantisocratic scheme were not forthcoming; and Southey, to the great indignation of Coleridge, soon withdrew from it. The project collapsed, and several years went by before the brothers-in-law were reconciled. Though it was eventually clear that his wife was unsuited for marriage with a

genius, and that Coleridge was unsuited for marriage with anyone, he had a long and happy honeymoon, his first taste of home life since he was a child of nine. The Pantisocratic solution to what he called the bread-and-cheese problem having evaporated, he bestirred himself to find ways and means; but he never managed to take adequate care of his wife and the four children born to them. Friends and relatives saw to it that his gifted sons, Hartley and Derwent, were educated; a daughter also grew up and made a satisfactory marriage.

At first Coleridge tried lecturing on political questions, preaching for a Unitarian congregation at Bath, and publishing a magazine, the *Watchman,* most of which he wrote himself—its scope embraced news, politics, and poetry. Friends rallied round, Coleridge took a long swing through the Midlands to drum up subscriptions, and the first number came out in 1796 with over a thousand subscribers on the list. With the appearance of the second, half the subscribers sent in cancellations; the tenth number was the last. Coleridge was left with a wife and baby son, debts, and no prospects. His mental distress can be imagined; he began taking opium to relieve it. At this juncture, Thomas Poole, a well-to-do tanner, who despite Coleridge's failure to talk him into Pantisocracy recognized his genius, arranged with a group of admirers to stake him to about $200 a year for seven years. Coleridge was full of plans and projects; but in the upshot he went to live near Poole at Nether Stowey in Somersetshire, with the resolution of making a livelihood by raising vegetables.

Then came the decisive meeting with the Wordsworths, and their removal to Alfoxden (see pp. 44 f.). To the destruction of ways and means but to the lasting benefit of the world, there was more talk of poetry than of vegetables. Soon the two geniuses were planning *Lyrical Ballads.* Bread and cheese remained a problem. Off to Drury Lane went a tragedy in verse, but Coleridge was offended when Sheridan suggested the need of revision. Wordsworth knew the Wedgwoods and had introduced Coleridge. Just as the latter was about to accept a Unitarian pulpit at Shrewsbury, a letter came from Josiah Wedgwood, head of the great pottery firm, offering on behalf of himself and his brother Thomas £150 a year for life. It was accepted, and Coleridge withdrew his candidacy at Shrewsbury, where he had made a strong impression with his first trial sermon. This discourse was the occasion of his original acquaintance with young William Hazlitt, destined to be a leader among the Romantic critics. Most of Hazlitt's essay describing their meeting is reprinted later on in this section.

It was now midwinter of 1797–98. Wordsworth was launched on his great creative decade. For Coleridge their association was even more vital, since to those two years at Nether Stowey belong his two best poems, "Kubla Khan" and "The Ancient Mariner." There is nothing comparable to them in either of the little volumes (1796, 1797) in which some of his poems had already appeared. By the end of 1798 nearly all the poetry on which his reputation is based had been composed. The aims of the two poets in *Lyrical Ballads* (1798) have already been compared (p. 45). Only four of Coleridge's poems were in that volume, and the Preface to the second edition (1801) was Wordsworth's. Coleridge presents his own views in Chapter XIV of his *Biographia Literaria* (1817), reprinted below.

He went to Germany with the Wordsworths in the fall of 1798 but did not continue in their company. Their purposes were different: William and Dorothy went as tourists, Coleridge to perfect himself in the language, which he had already studied. With German literature and the idealism of the new German philosophy he was entranced, and he became the principal pipeline through which the influence of German Romanticism flowed to England. He entered the University of Göttingen, made numerous friends, and did not get home till the summer of 1799. Next came walking trips, with Southey in Devonshire, with William and Dorothy in the Lake District, and then three months as editorial writer in London on the *Morning Post*. The owner offered to make him a shareholder if he would stay; but with the explanation that he could not "give up the country and the lazy reading of old folios," Coleridge threw up this job early in 1800 and settled with his family in a house called Greta Hall at Keswick in the Lake District, thirteen miles from the Wordsworths' cottage at Grasmere. He saw much of them, and also of Sara, sister of the future Mrs. Wordsworth.

Coleridge's marriage was extremely unhappy; a hopeless incompatibility of temperaments was obvious even before he fell in love with Sara Hutchinson. She inspired a number of his poems, admired his genius, and pitied him; but she was evidently too aware of his weaknesses to think seriously of uniting her life with his. For that matter, he had himself strong views on the indissolubility of marriage. His love for Sara Hutchinson was none the less the central emotion of the next ten years. By the end of 1800 his health had broken down; the trouble was mainly rheumatic and extremely painful; he was driven to taking opium in ever larger doses. Southey and his family now came to share Greta Hall; it proved to be their permanent home. In 1804, convinced that his recovery required a sojourn in a milder climate, Coleridge raised enough money through gifts and loans from relatives and friends to go to Malta—alone. There, with excursions to Sicily and Italy, he remained two years. For a few months he was acting secretary to the government of the island. This interlude marks the beginning of his actual separation from his wife. He returned to England in 1806 completely the opium addict, though brandy was also a devastating weakness. From time to time he roused himself, with the Wordsworths' help, and Sara's, sufficiently to work. In 1809-10 he got out a new magazine, the *Friend,* and then he dropped it.

It must now be evident that Coleridge's life after the two great years at Nether Stowey was an anticlimax. Like Wordsworth he had changed his mind about the French Revolution (see, below, "France: an Ode") and gone over to the conservatives. In 1810 he became estranged from Wordsworth. Coleridge had left the Lakes, and the remainder of his life was passed chiefly in or near London. A friend who had taken him in was foolish enough to tell him that Wordsworth disapproved of the arrangement and had warned that Coleridge was in a hopeless state, was a drunkard, and had made himself a nuisance to the Wordsworths, with whom he had been living. Naturally, he was deeply hurt. In 1812 Wordsworth went up to London to seek an explanation of his silence, and a reconciliation. Wordsworth denied the imputed phraseology. Eventually the trouble was patched up by the intervention of friends, but never again were the two poets on quite the old terms.

The problem of subsistence remained acute, especially after Josiah Wedgwood's share of the annuity was regretfully withdrawn in 1812. It had been offered conditionally on the continued prosperity of the business, and the Napoleonic wars had brought grave losses. In an effort to capitalize on his genius for talk, Coleridge gave several courses of more or less extemporaneous lectures. The most remarkable was a series of seventeen in 1811-12 on Shakespeare and Milton, in which brilliantly acute observations stand side by side with impressionistic criticism that has no firm basis in the text. In 1812 he made a tidy sum with his old tragedy, now called *Remorse,* which he had previously objected to revising; in its new form it had a substantial run of twenty nights. But Coleridge's will power showed progressive deterioration. Sometimes an audience would assemble for a lecture, and he would not appear. In desperation he finally put himself in the hands of a physician, Dr. James Gillman, who lived in Highgate, a northern suburb of London. To his house Coleridge went in 1816, with the intention of remaining for a month; it became his home for the remainder of his life. Dr. and Mrs. Gillman were devoted to him; and though he never completely freed himself from opium, the habit was brought under medical control. This partial victory soon bore fruit in the most important of Coleridge's prose writings, *Biographia Literaria* (1817), a chaotic but often stimulating blend of literary criticism and philosophy. Generous excerpts from it have been reprinted below.

The latter years were relatively peaceful. In 1824 Coleridge was elected in the Royal Society of Literature to an honorary rank which carried an annual stipend of £100. His last writings were chiefly philosophical and theological. He had long since abandoned Unitarianism, and his pen was much employed in the defense of Trinitarian orthodoxy. Old friends were faithful, especially the Lambs. In 1828 came a trip to Belgium, the Rhineland, and Holland with Wordsworth and his daughter Dora. The Gillmans' house in Highgate became a literary center, for the poet-philosopher was much visited. Emerson and Cooper were among the American pilgrims. Coleridge died in 1834, after a brief illness.

The standard edition of the poems is by E. H. Coleridge (2 vols., 1912); this gives the plays as well. Good one-volume editions of the poems alone are by J. D. Campbell (1893) and E. H. Coleridge (Oxford Standard Authors). Cheap reprints are numerous, e.g., in Everyman's Library and The World's Classics. Editions of *Biographia Literaria* are mentioned in the headnote to our selections from it. The *Shakespearean Criticism* (2 vols., 1930) and *Miscellaneous Criticism* (1936) have been ably edited by T. M. Raysor. Three complementary collections of Coleridge's letters have been published, edited by E. H. Coleridge (2 vols., 1895), A. Turnbull (2 vols., 1911), and E. L. Griggs (2 vols., 1932). Good volumes of selections are S. Potter's *Coleridge: Select Poetry and Prose* (1933) and E. L. Griggs's *The Best of Coleridge* (1934). As for books about Coleridge and his work, they are many; some are listed in the following headnotes. The most authoritative compilation of the biographical facts is by E. K. Chambers (1938); a more readable Life is H. I'A. Fausset's (1926). The first volume of L. Hanson's projected biography, *The Early Years* (1939), is on a broader scale than either. A good book on Coleridge's ideas is J. H. Muirhead's *Coleridge as Philosopher* (1930).

Samuel Taylor Coleridge

KUBLA KHAN

THIS amazing poem came into being by no ordinary method of composition. Coleridge dreamed it during a sleep induced by opium, subconsciously fusing a number of details from various books (see J. L. Lowes, *The Road to Xanadu*). A prefatory note by Coleridge explains that "in consequence of a slight indisposition, an anodyne had been prescribed, from the effects of which he fell asleep in his chair" while reading Samuel Purchas (d. 1626), the compiler of travel books. In the *Purchas his Pilgrimage* of that devoted follower of Hakluyt (see I, 281, above) occurs this sentence about the enlightened conqueror Kublai Khan (1216-94), founder of the Mongol dynasty in China; Coleridge's eye was on it when he dozed off: "In Xamdu did Cublai Can build a stately Palace, encompassing sixteene miles of plaine ground with a wall, wherein are fertile Meddowes, pleasant springs, delightful Streames, and all sorts of beasts of chase and game, and in the middest thereof a sumptuous house of pleasure, which may be removed from place to place."

"The Author," proceeds Coleridge, "continued for about three hours in a profound sleep, at least of the external senses, during which time he has the most vivid confidence, that he could not have composed less than from two to three hundred lines; if that indeed can be called composition in which all the images rose up before him as *things,* with a parallel production of the correspondent expressions, without any sensation or conscious-ness of effort. On awaking he appeared to himself to have a distinct recollection of the whole, and taking his pen, ink, and paper, instantly and eagerly wrote down the lines that are here preserved. At this moment he was unfortunately called out by a person on business from Porlock,[1] and detained by him above an hour, and on his return to his room, found, to his no small surprise and mortification, that though he still retained some vague and dim recollection of the general purport of the vision, yet, with the exception of some eight or ten scattered lines and images, all the rest had passed away like the images on the surface of a stream into which a stone has been cast, but, alas! without the after restoration of the latter!"

This extraordinary but not unique experience took place probably in the summer of 1797. The poem was published with *Christabel* and another in 1816; the original title was "Kubla Khan: Or, A Vision in a Dream. A Fragment."

In Xanadu did Kubla Khan
A stately pleasure-dome decree:
Where Alph, the sacred river, ran
Through caverns measureless to man
　　Down to a sunless sea.　　　　　　　　　5
So twice five miles of fertile ground

---

[1] A near-by village.

With walls and towers were girdled round:
And there were gardens bright with sinuous rills,
Where blossomed many an incense-bearing tree;
And here were forests ancient as the hills,   10
Enfolding sunny spots of greenery.

But oh! that deep romantic chasm which slanted
Down the green hill athwart a cedarn cover!
A savage place! as holy and enchanted
As e'er beneath a waning moon was haunted   15
By woman wailing for her demon-lover!
And from this chasm, with ceaseless turmoil seething,
As if this earth in fast thick pants were breathing,
A mighty fountain momently was forced:
Amid whose swift half-intermitted burst   20
Huge fragments vaulted like rebounding hail,
Or chaffy grain beneath the thresher's flail:
And 'mid these dancing rocks at once and ever
It flung up momently the sacred river.
Five miles meandering with a mazy motion   25
Through wood and dale the sacred river ran,
Then reached the caverns measureless to man,
And sank in tumult to a lifeless ocean:
And 'mid this tumult Kubla heard from far
Ancestral voices prophesying war!   30

The shadow of the dome of pleasure
Floated midway on the waves;
Where was heard the mingled measure
From the fountain and the caves.
It was a miracle of rare device,   35
A sunny pleasure-dome with caves of ice!

A damsel with a dulcimer
In a vision once I saw:
It was an Abyssinian maid,
And on her dulcimer she played,   40
Singing of Mount Abora.[2]
Could I revive within me
Her symphony and song,
To such a deep delight 'twould win me,
That with music loud and long,   45
I would build that dome in air,
That sunny dome! those caves of ice!
And all who heard should see them there,
And all should cry, Beware! Beware!
His flashing eyes, his floating hair!   50
Weave a circle round him thrice,[3]
And close your eyes with holy dread,
For he on honey-dew hath fed,
And drunk the milk of Paradise.

THE RIME OF THE ANCIENT MARINER

IN SEVEN PARTS

This poem, composed in 1797-8, was Coleridge's only important contribution to the *Lyrical Ballads* of 1798. Intended as a ballad and to some extent inspired by the specimens in Percy's *Reliques of Ancient English Poetry*, it is closer to that genre than any of the poems from Wordsworth's pen. The marginal gloss was not printed till 1817. In *The Road to Xanadu* (1927) J. L. Lowes has shown how bits of Coleridge's reading coalesced in his subconscious to produce some of the most striking details of the poem. Our text incorporates the poet's revisions.

ARGUMENT

How a Ship, having first sailed to the Equator, was driven by Storms to the cold Country towards the South Pole; how the Ancient Mariner cruelly and in contempt of the laws of hospitality killed a Seabird and how he was followed by many and strange Judgements: and in what manner he came back to his own Country.

PART I

It is an ancient Mariner,
And he stoppeth one of three.
'By thy long grey beard and glittering eye,
Now wherefore stopp'st thou me?

An ancient Mariner meeteth three Gallants bidden to a wedding-feast, and detaineth one.

The Bridegroom's doors are opened wide,   5
And I am next of kin;
The guests are met, the feast is set:
May'st hear the merry din.'

He holds him with his skinny hand,
'There was a ship,' quoth he.   10
'Hold off! unhand me, grey-beard loon!'
Eftsoons[1] his hand dropt he.

[2] Probably derived from the name of a tributary of the Nile, the river Abola, which Coleridge had met in his reading.

[3] As a magic protection against his influence.

[1] Soon after. This and other archaisms are intended to suggest the style of the medieval ballads.—Wordsworth tells us that he contributed the next stanza.

He holds him with his glittering eye—
The Wedding-Guest stood still,
And listens like a three years' child:
The Mariner hath his will.   15

The Wedding-Guest is spellbound by the eye of the old sea-faring man, and constrained to hear his tale.

The Wedding-Guest sat on a stone:
He cannot choose but hear;
And thus spake on that ancient man,
The bright-eyed Mariner.   20

'The ship was cheered, the harbour cleared,
Merrily did we drop
Below the kirk,[2] below the hill,
Below the lighthouse top.

The Mariner tells how the ship sailed southward with a good wind and fair weather, till it reached the Line.[3]

The Sun came up upon the left,
Out of the sea came he!   25
And he shone bright, and on the right
Went down into the sea.

Higher and higher every day,
Till over the mast at noon—'
The Wedding-Guest here beat his breast,   30
For he heard the loud bassoon.

The bride hath paced into the hall,
Red as a rose is she;
Nodding their heads before her goes
The merry minstrelsy.   35

The Wedding-Guest heareth the bridal music; but the Mariner continueth his tale.

The Wedding-Guest he beat his breast,
Yet he cannot choose but hear;
And thus spake on that ancient man,
The bright-eyed Mariner.   40

'And now the STORM-BLAST came, and he
Was tyrannous and strong:
He struck with his o'ertaking wings,
And chased us south along.

The ship driven by a storm toward the south pole.

With sloping masts and dipping prow,   45
As who pursued with yell and blow
Still treads the shadow of his foe,
And forward bends his head,
The ship drove fast, loud roared the blast,
And southward aye we fled.   50

And now there came both mist and snow,
And it grew wondrous cold:
And ice, mast-high, came floating by,
As green as emerald.

[2] Church.   [3] Equator.

And through the drifts the snowy clifts[4]   55
Did send a dismal sheen:
Nor shapes of men nor beasts we ken—
The ice was all between.

The land of ice, and of fearful sounds where no living thing was to be seen.

The ice was here, the ice was there,
The ice was all around: 60
It cracked and growled, and roared and howled,
Like noises in a swound![5]

At length did cross an Albatross,
Thorough[6] the fog it came;
As if it had been a Christian soul,
We hailed it in God's name.   65

Till a great sea-bird, called the Albatross, came through the snow-fog, and was received with great joy and hospitality.

It ate the food it ne'er had eat,[7]
And round and round it flew.
The ice did split with a thunder-fit;
The helmsman steered us through!   70

And a good south wind sprung up
behind;
The Albatross did follow,
And every day, for food or play,
Came to the mariners' hollo!

And lo! the Albatross proveth a bird of good omen, and followeth the ship as it returned northward through fog and floating ice.

In mist or cloud, on mast or shroud,[8]   75
It perched for vespers nine;
Whiles all the night, through fog-smoke white,
Glimmered the white Moon-shine.'

'God save thee, ancient Mariner!
From the fiends, that plague thee thus!—
Why look'st thou so?'—With my cross-
bow
I shot the ALBATROSS.[9]

The ancient Mariner inhospitably killeth the pious bird of good omen.   80

PART II

The Sun now rose upon the right:
Out of the sea came he,
Still hid in mist, and on the left   85
Went down into the sea.

And the good south wind still blew behind,
But no sweet bird did follow,
Nor any day for food or play
Came to the mariners' hollo!   90

[4] Cliffs.   [5] Swoon.
[6] Through.   [7] Eaten; pronounced ĕt.
[8] One of the ropes running from the ship's side up to the mast, to secure it laterally.
[9] From this point the text we follow omits quotation marks for the Mariner's story.

And I had done a hellish thing,
And it would work 'em woe:
For all averred, I had killed the bird
That made the breeze to blow.
Ah wretch! said they, the bird to slay,   95
That made the breeze to blow!

His shipmates cry out against the ancient Mariner, for killing the bird of good luck.

Nor dim nor red, like God's own head,
The glorious Sun uprist:[10]
Then all averred, I had killed the bird
That brought the fog and mist.   100
'Twas right, said they, such birds to slay,
That bring the fog and mist.

But when the fog cleared off, they justify the same, and thus make themselves accomplices in the crime.

The fair breeze blew, the white foam flew,
The furrow followed free;
We were the first[11] that ever burst   105
Into that silent sea.

The fair breeze continues; the ship enters the Pacific Ocean, and sails northward, even till it reaches the Line.

Down dropt the breeze, the sails dropt down,
'Twas sad as sad could be;
And we did speak only to break
The silence of the sea!   110

The ship hath been suddenly becalmed.

good weather *killing ship*

All in a hot and copper sky,
The bloody Sun, at noon,
Right up above the mast did stand,
No bigger than the Moon.

Day after day, day after day,   115
We stuck, nor breath nor motion;
As idle as a painted ship
Upon a painted ocean.

Water, water, every where,
And all the boards did shrink;   120
Water, water, every where,
Nor any drop to drink.

And the Albatross begins to be avenged.

The very deep did rot: O Christ!
That ever this should be!
Yea, slimy things did crawl with legs   125
Upon the slimy sea.

About, about, in reel and rout
The death-fires[12] danced at night;
The water, like a witch's oils,
Burnt green and blue and white.   130

And some in dreams assurèd were
Of the Spirit that plagued us so;
Nine fathom deep he had followed us
From the land of mist and snow.

A Spirit had followed them; one of the invisible inhabitants of this planet, neither departed souls nor angels; concerning whom the learned Jew, Josephus, and the Platonic Constantinopolitan, Michael Psellus,[13] may be consulted. They are very numerous, and there is no climate or element without one or more.

And every tongue, through utter drought,
Was withered at the root;   135
We could not speak, no more than if
We had been choked with soot.

Ah! well a-day! what evil looks
Had I from old and young!
Instead of the cross, the Albatross   140
About my neck was hung.

guilt recognized

punishment... *possible* *SALVATION*

The shipmates, in their sore distress, would fain throw the whole guilt on the ancient Mariner: in sign whereof they hang the dead sea-bird round his neck.

PART III

There passed a weary time. Each throat
Was parched, and glazed each eye.
A weary time! a weary time!   145
How glazed each weary eye,
When looking westward, I beheld
A something in the sky.

The ancient Mariner beholdeth a sign in the element[14] afar off.

At first it seemed a little speck,
And then it seemed a mist;   150
It moved and moved, and took at last
A certain shape, I wist.[15]

A speck, a mist, a shape, I wist!
And still it neared and neared:
As if it dodged a water-sprite,   155
It plunged and tacked and veered.

With throats unslaked, with black lips baked,
We could nor laugh nor wail;
Through utter drought all dumb we stood!
I bit my arm, I sucked the blood,   160
And cried, A sail, a sail!

At its nearer approach, it seemeth him to be a ship; and at a dear ransom he freeth his speech from the bonds of thirst.

Realism

With throats unslaked, with black lips baked,
Agape they heard me call:
Gramercy![16] they for joy did grin,
And all at once their breath drew in,   165
As[17] they were drinking all.

A flash of joy;

---

10 I.e., rose. Actually this word is an old form of the present tense.
11 Another medieval hint; Magellan did not enter the Pacific till 1520.   12 I.e., phosphorescent lights.

13 Josephus was a famous first-century historian, Psellus a well-known eleventh-century Byzantine philosopher and politician.
14 Sky.   15 Knew.
16 An exclamation of surprise or thanks.   17 As if.

→ denial of world's larger meaning

See! see! (I cried) she tacks no more!
Hither to work us weal;
Without a breeze, without a tide,
She steadies with upright keel!   170

And horror follows. For can it be a ship that comes onward without wind or tide?

The western wave was all a-flame.
The day was well nigh done!
Almost upon the western wave
Rested the broad bright Sun;
When that strange shape drove suddenly   175
Betwixt us and the Sun.

And straight the Sun was flecked with bars,
(Heaven's Mother send us grace!)
As if through a dungeon-grate he peered
With broad and burning face.   180

It seemeth him but the skeleton of a ship.

Alas! (thought I, and my heart beat loud)
How fast she nears and nears!
Are those *her* sails that glance in the Sun,
Like restless gossameres?[18]

Are those *her* ribs through which the Sun   185
Did peer, as through a grate?
And is that Woman all her crew?
Is that a DEATH?[19] and are there two?
Is DEATH that woman's mate?

And its ribs are seen as bars on the face of the setting Sun.

The Spectre-Woman and her Death-mate, and no other on board the skeleton ship.

Her lips were red, *her* looks were free,   190
Her locks were yellow as gold:
Her skin was as white as leprosy,
The Night-mare LIFE-IN-DEATH was she,
Who thicks man's blood with cold.

Like vessel, like crew!

The naked hulk alongside came,
And the twain were casting dice;   195
'The game is done! I've won!
    I've won!'
Quoth she, and whistles thrice.

Death and Life-in-Death have diced for the ship's crew, and she (the latter) winneth the ancient Mariner.

The Sun's rim dips; the stars rush out:
At one stride comes the dark;   200
With far-heard whisper, o'er the sea,
Off shot the spectre-bark.

No twilight within the courts of the Sun.

We listened and looked sideways up!
Fear at my heart, as at a cup,
My life-blood seemed to sip!   205
The stars were dim, and thick the night,
The steersman's face by his lamp gleamed white;
From the sails the dew did drip—

At the rising of the Moon,

---

[18] Filmy cobwebs which float in calm air.   [19] Skeleton.

Till clomb above the eastern bar
The hornèd Moon, with one bright star   210
Within the nether tip.[20]

One after one, by the star-dogged Moon,
Too quick for groan or sigh,
Each turned his face with a ghastly pang,
And cursed me with his eye.   215

One after another,

Four times fifty living men,
(And I heard nor sigh nor groan)
With heavy thump, a lifeless lump,
They dropped down one by one.

His shipmates drop down dead.

The souls did from their bodies fly,—
They fled to bliss or woe!   220
And every soul, it passed me by,
Like the whizz of my cross-bow!

But Life-in-Death begins her work on the ancient Mariner.

PART IV

'I fear thee, ancient Mariner!
I fear thy skinny hand!
And thou art long, and lank, and brown,
As is the ribbed sea-sand.[21]

The Wedding-Guest feareth that a Spirit is talking to him;   225

I fear thee and thy glittering eye,
And thy skinny hand, so brown.'—
Fear not, fear not, thou Wedding-Guest!   230
This body dropt not down.

But the ancient Mariner assureth him of his bodily life, and proceedeth to relate his horrible penance.

Alone, alone, all, all alone,
Alone on a wide wide sea!
And never a saint took pity on
My soul in agony.   235

The many men, so beautiful!
And they all dead did lie:
And a thousand thousand slimy things
Lived on; and so did I.

He despiseth the creatures of the calm,

I looked upon the rotting sea,
And drew my eyes away;   240
I looked upon the rotting deck,
And there the dead men lay.

And envieth that they should live, and so many lie dead.

---

[20] In a manuscript note Coleridge refers to a sailors' superstition that it is an omen of evil when a star "dogs the moon."

[21] Note by Coleridge: "For the last two lines of this stanza, I am indebted to Mr. Wordsworth. It was on a delightful walk from Nether Stowey to Dulverton, with him and his sister, in the Autumn of 1797, that this Poem was planned, and in part composed."

I looked to heaven, and tried to pray;
But or ever a prayer had gusht,   245
A wicked whisper came, and made
My heart as dry as dust.

I closed my lids, and kept them close,
And the balls like pulses beat;
For the sky and the sea, and the sea and the sky   250
Lay like a load on my weary eye,
And the dead were at my feet.

The cold sweat melted from their limbs,   *But the curse liveth*
Nor rot nor reek did they: *for him in the eye*
The look with which they looked on me   255 *of the dead men.*
Had never passed away.

An orphan's curse would drag to hell
A spirit from on high;
But oh! more horrible than that
Is the curse in a dead man's eye!   260
Seven days, seven nights, I saw that   *In his loneliness and*
    curse,   *fixedness he yearneth*
And yet I could not die.   *towards the journey-*
                                               ing Moon, and the
                                               stars that still so-
The moving Moon went up the sky,   *journ, yet still move*
And no where did abide: *onward; and every*
Softly she was going up,   *HOPE*   *where the blue sky*
And a star or two beside—   *belongs to them, and*
                                               is their appointed
                                               rest, and their native
                                               country and their
                                               own natural
                                               homes, which 265
                                               they enter unan-
                                               nounced, as lords that
                                               are certainly expected
                                               and yet there is a
                                               silent joy at their
                                               arrival.

Her beams bemocked the sultry main,
Like April hoar-frost spread;
But where the ship's huge shadow lay,
The charmèd water burnt alway   270
A still and awful red.

Beyond the shadow of the ship,   *By the light of the*
I watched the water-snakes: *Moon he beholdeth*
They moved in tracks of shining white, *God's creatures of*
And when they reared, the elfish light 275 *the great calm.*
Fell off in hoary flakes.

Within the shadow of the ship
I watched their rich attire:
Blue, glossy green, and velvet black,
They coiled and swam; and every track   280
Was a flash of golden fire.

O happy living things! no tongue   *Their beauty and*
Their beauty might declare: *their happiness.*
A spring of love gushed from my heart,
And I blessed them unaware: *He blesseth*
Sure my kind saint took pity on me,   *them in his* 285
And I blessed them unaware.   *heart.*

The self-same moment I could pray;   *The spell begins*
And from my neck so free   *to break.*
The Albatross fell off, and sank   290
Like lead into the sea.

PART V

Oh sleep! it is a gentle thing,
Beloved from pole to pole!
To Mary Queen the praise be given!
She sent the gentle sleep from Heaven,   295
That slid into my soul.

The silly[22] buckets on the deck,   *By grace of the*
That had so long remained,   *holy Mother, the*
I dreamt that they were filled with dew; *ancient Mariner is*
And when I awoke, it rained.   300 *refreshed with rain.*

My lips were wet, my throat was cold,
My garments all were dank;
Sure I had drunken in my dreams,
And still my body drank.

I moved, and could not feel my limbs: 305
I was so light—almost
I thought that I had died in sleep,
And was a blessèd ghost.

And soon I heard a roaring wind;   *He heareth sounds*
It did not come anear;   *and seeth strange*
But with its sound it shook the sails, 310 *sights and*
That were so thin and sere.   *commotions*
                                        in the sky
                                        and the element.

The upper air burst into life!
And a hundred fire-flags sheen,[23]
To and fro they were hurried about!   315
And to and fro, and in and out,
The wan stars danced between.

And the coming wind did roar more loud,
And the sails did sigh like sedge;
And the rain poured down from one black cloud;   320
The Moon was at its edge.

The thick black cloud was cleft, and still
The Moon was at its side:
Like waters shot from some high crag,
The lightning fell with never a jag,   325
A river steep and wide.

---

22 Useless, because empty.   23 Bright.

The loud wind never reached the ship,
Yet now the ship moved on!
Beneath the lightning and the Moon
The dead men gave a groan.   330

The bodies of the ship's crew are inspired, and the ship moves on;

They groaned, they stirred, they all uprose,
Nor spake, nor moved their eyes;
It had been strange, even in a dream,
To have seen those dead men rise.

The helmsman steered, the ship moved on;   335
Yet never a breeze up-blew;
The mariners all 'gan work the ropes,
Where they were wont to do;
They raised their limbs like lifeless tools—
We were a ghastly crew.   340

The body of my brother's son
Stood by me, knee to knee:
The body and I pulled at one rope,
But he said nought to me.

'I fear thee, ancient Mariner!'
Be calm, thou Wedding-Guest!   345
'Twas not those souls that fled in pain,
Which to their corses[25] came again,
But a troop of spirits blest:

But not by the souls of the men, nor by daemons[24] of the earth or middle air, but by a blessed troop of angelic spirits, sent down by the invocation of the guardian saint.

For when it dawned—they dropped their arms,   350
And clustered round the mast;
Sweet sounds rose slowly through their mouths,
And from their bodies passed.

Around, around, flew each sweet sound,
Then darted to the Sun;   355
Slowly the sounds came back again,
Now mixed, now one by one.

Sometimes a-dropping from the sky
I heard the sky-lark sing;
Sometimes all little birds that are,   360
How they seemed to fill the sea and air
With their sweet jargoning!

And now 'twas like all instruments,
Now like a lonely flute;
And now it is an angel's song,   365
That makes the heavens be mute.

It ceased; yet still the sails made on
A pleasant noise till noon,

A noise like of a hidden brook
In the leafy month of June,
That to the sleeping woods all night   370
Singeth a quiet tune.

Till noon we quietly sailed on,
Yet never a breeze did breathe:
Slowly and smoothly went the ship,   375
Moved onward from beneath.

Under the keel nine fathom deep,
From the land of mist and snow,
The spirit slid: and it was he
That made the ship to go.
The sails at noon left off their tune,   380
And the ship stood still also.

The lonesome Spirit from the south-pole carries on the ship as far as the Line, in obedience to the angelic troop, but still requireth vengeance.

The Sun, right up above the mast,
Had fixed her to the ocean:
But in a minute she 'gan stir,   385
With a short uneasy motion—
Backwards and forwards half her length
With a short uneasy motion.

Then like a pawing horse let go,
She made a sudden bound: 390
It flung the blood into my head,
And I fell down in a swound.

How long in that same fit I lay,
I have not[26] to declare;
But ere my living life returned,   395
I heard and in my soul discerned
Two voices in the air.

The Polar Spirit's fellow-daemons, the invisible inhabitants of the element, take part in his wrong; and two of them relate, one to the other, that penance long and heavy for the ancient Mariner hath been accorded to the Polar Spirit, who returneth southward.

'Is it he?' quoth one, 'Is this the man?
By him who died on cross,
With his cruel bow he laid full low
The harmless Albatross.   400

The spirit who bideth by himself
In the land of mist and snow,
He loved the bird that loved the man
Who shot him with his bow.'   405

The other was a softer voice,
As soft as honey-dew:
Quoth he, 'The man hath penance done,
And penance more will do.'

---

[24] Not demons, but spirits.   [25] Corpses.   [26] I.e., no power.

PART VI

FIRST VOICE

'But tell me, tell me! speak again,   410
Thy soft response renewing—
What makes that ship drive on so fast?
What is the ocean doing?'

SECOND VOICE

'Still as a slave before his lord,
The ocean hath no blast;   415
His great bright eye most silently
Up to the Moon is cast—

If he may know which way to go;
For she guides him smooth or grim.
See, brother, see! how graciously   420
She looketh down on him.'

FIRST VOICE

'But why drives on that ship so fast,
Without or wave or wind?'

The Mariner hath been cast into a trance; for the angelic power causeth the vessel to drive northward faster than human life could endure.

SECOND VOICE

'The air is cut away before,
And closes from behind.   425

Fly, brother, fly! more high, more high!
Or we shall be belated:
For slow and slow that ship will go,
When the Mariner's trance is abated.'

I woke, and we were sailing on   430
As in a gentle weather:
'Twas night, calm night, the moon
        was high;
The dead men stood together.

The supernatural motion is retarded; the Mariner awakes, and his penance begins anew.

All stood together on the deck,
For a charnel-dungeon[27] fitter: 435
All fixed on me their stony eyes,
That in the Moon did glitter.

The pang, the curse, with which they died,
Had never passed away:
I could not draw my eyes from theirs,   440
Nor turn them up to pray.

------

[27] When the digging of a new grave in the churchyard necessitated removal of old bones, they were deposited in the charnel house, or vault. Bodies were sometimes temporarily laid there when the ground was too deeply frozen for digging.

And now this spell was snapt: once more
I viewed the ocean green,
And looked far forth, yet little saw
Of what had else been seen—   445

The curse is finally expiated.

Like one, that on a lonesome road
Doth walk in fear and dread,
And having once turned round walks on,
And turns no more his head;
Because he knows, a frightful fiend   450
Doth close behind him tread.

But soon there breathed a wind on me,
Nor sound nor motion made:
Its path was not upon the sea,
In ripple or in shade.   455

It raised my hair, it fanned my cheek
Like a meadow-gale of spring—
It mingled strangely with my fears,
Yet it felt like a welcoming.

Swiftly, swiftly flew the ship,   460
Yet she sailed softly too:
Sweetly, sweetly blew the breeze—
On me alone it blew.

Oh! dream of joy! is this indeed
The light-house top I see?   465
Is this the hill? is this the kirk?
Is this mine own countree?

And the ancient Mariner beholdeth his native country.

We drifted o'er the harbour-bar,
And I with sobs did pray—
O let me be awake, my God!   470
Or let me sleep alway.

The harbour-bay was clear as glass,
So smoothly it was strewn!
And on the bay the moonlight lay,
And the shadow of the Moon.   475

The rock shone bright, the kirk no less,
That stands above the rock:
The moonlight steeped in silentness
The steady weathercock.

And the bay was white with silent light.   480
Till rising from the same,
Full many shapes, that shadows were,
In crimson colours came.

The angelic spirits leave the dead bodies,

A little distance from the prow   *And appear in their*
Those crimson shadows were: *own forms of light.* 485
I turned my eyes upon the deck—
Oh, Christ! what saw I there!

Each corse lay flat, lifeless and flat,
And, by the holy rood![28]
A man all light, a seraph-man,   490
On every corse there stood.

This seraph-band, each waved his hand:
It was a heavenly sight!
They stood as signals to the land,
Each one a lovely light;   495

This seraph-band, each waved his hand,
No voice did they impart—
No voice; but oh! the silence sank
Like music on my heart.

But soon I heard the dash of oars,   500
I heard the Pilot's cheer;
My head was turned perforce away,
And I saw a boat appear.

The Pilot and the Pilot's boy,
I heard them coming fast: 505
Dear Lord in Heaven! it was a joy
The dead men could not blast.

I saw a third—I heard his voice:
It is the Hermit good!
He singeth loud his godly hymns   510
That he makes in the wood.
He'll shrieve[29] my soul, he'll wash away
The Albatross's blood.

PART VII

This Hermit good lives in that wood   *The Hermit of the*
Which slopes down to the sea.   *Wood,* 515
How loudly his sweet voice he rears!
He loves to talk with marineres
That come from a far countree.

He kneels at morn, and noon, and eve—
He hath a cushion plump: 520
It is the moss that wholly hides
The rotted old oak-stump.

The skiff-boat neared: I heard them talk,
'Why, this is strange, I trow!
Where are those lights so many and fair,   525
That signal made but now?'

'Strange, by my faith!' the Hermit said— *Approacheth the ship*
'And they answered not our cheer!   *with wonder.*
The planks look warped! and see those sails,
How thin they are and sere!   530
I never saw aught like to them,
Unless perchance it were

Brown skeletons of leaves that lag
My forest-brook along;
When the ivy-tod[30] is heavy with snow,   535
And the owlet whoops to the wolf below,
That eats the she-wolf's young.'

'Dear Lord! it hath a fiendish look—
(The Pilot made reply)
I am a-feared'—'Push on, push on!'   540
Said the Hermit cheerily.

The boat came closer to the ship,
But I nor spake nor stirred;
The boat came close beneath the ship,
And straight a sound was heard.   545

Under the water it rumbled on,   *The ship suddenly*
Still louder and more dread: *sinketh.*
It reached the ship, it split the bay;
The ship went down like lead.

Stunned by that loud and dreadful   *The ancient*
    sound,   *Mariner is*
                             saved in the
Which sky and ocean smote,   *Pilot's boat.* 550
Like one that hath been seven days drowned
My body lay afloat;
But swift as dreams, myself I found
Within the Pilot's boat.   555

Upon the whirl, where sank the ship,
The boat spun round and round;
And all was still, save that the hill
Was telling of the sound.

I moved my lips—the Pilot shrieked   560
And fell down in a fit;
The holy Hermit raised his eyes,
And prayed where he did sit.

---

[28] Cross.   [29] Hear confession and give absolution to.   [30] Bush, clump.

I took the oars: the Pilot's boy,
Who now doth crazy go,   565
Laughed loud and long, and all the while
His eyes went to and fro.
'Ha! ha!' quoth he, 'full plain I see,
The Devil knows how to row.'

And now, all in my own countree,   570
I stood on the firm land!
The Hermit stepped forth from the boat,
And scarcely he could stand.

'O shrieve me, shrieve me, holy man!'   *The ancient Mariner*
The Hermit crossed[31] his brow.   *earnestly entreateth*
                                          the Hermit
'Say quick,' quoth he, 'I bid thee say—   *to shrieve* 575
What manner of man art thou?'   *him; and the*
                                          penance of life falls
                                          on him.

Forthwith this frame of mine was wrenched
With a woful agony,
Which forced me to begin my tale;   580
And then it left me free.

Since then, at an uncertain hour,   *And ever and anon*
That agony returns: *throughout his future*
                                          life an agony con-
And till my ghastly tale is told,   *straineth him to*
                                          travel from land to
This heart within me burns.   585 *land;*

I pass, like night, from land to land;
I have strange power of speech;
That moment that his face I see,
I know the man that must hear me:
To him my tale I teach.   590

What loud uproar bursts from that door!
The wedding-guests are there:
But in the garden-bower the bride
And bride-maids singing are:

And hark the little vesper bell,   595
Which biddeth me to prayer!

O Wedding-Guest! this soul hath been
Alone on a wide wide sea:
So lonely 'twas, that God himself
Scarce seemèd there to be.   600

O sweeter than the marriage-feast,
'Tis sweeter far to me,
To walk together to the kirk
With a goodly company!—

To walk together to the kirk,   605
And all together pray,
While each to his great Father bends,
Old men, and babes, and loving friends
And youths and maidens gay!

Farewell, farewell! but this I tell   *And to teach,* 610
                                          by his own
To thee, thou Wedding-Guest!   *example, love*
He prayeth well, who loveth well   *and reverence to all*
                                          things that God
Both man and bird and beast.   *made and loveth.*

He prayeth best, who loveth best
All things both great and small;   615
For the dear God who loveth us,
He made and loveth all.—

The Mariner, whose eye is bright,
Whose beard with age is hoar,
Is gone: and now the Wedding-Guest   620
Turned from the bridegroom's door.

He went like one that hath been stunned,
And is of sense forlorn:[32]
A sadder and a wiser man,
He rose the morrow morn.   625

CHRISTABEL

THIS strange fragment is one of the numerous projects Coleridge failed to complete. Part I was written at Nether Stowey in 1797–98, Part II at Keswick in 1800; the poet appears to have planned three more. In atmosphere and atmosphere alone lies the merit of these lines, for the story remains obscure and the characters are not very convincing. For imitating that once popular genre of story-telling, the metrical romance, Coleridge had poetry enough but not the power to sustain a long narrative.

Coleridge was unable to get *Christabel* ready in time for the second edition of *Lyrical Ballads;* it remained in manuscript till 1816, when Byron persuaded his own publisher to bring it out. A preface mentions the date of composition; for, now that Scott and Byron were in full blast, Coleridge was afraid he might be accused of following their lead. He also explains that the meter is less irregular than it looks, "being founded on a new principle, namely, that of counting in each line the accents, not the syllables. Though the latter may vary from seven to twelve, yet in each line the accents will be found to be only four." The principle was, of course, not new at all; it had been used, as we have seen, by medieval writers of

---

[31] Made the sign of the cross on.

[32] Bereft of his senses.

alliterative verse. Nor does Coleridge stick consistently to it.

The key to understanding the poem is the unpleasant but delicately handled fact that "Geraldine" is at least in part a vampire, that is, a demon which sucks its victims' blood while they sleep. An account Coleridge was subsequently alleged to have given of his intentions may or may not be accurate; Wordsworth doubted whether a settled plan had ever been framed. It seems probable, however, that the vampire is not the actual Geraldine, daughter of Lord Roland de Vaux, but has taken her form. Christabel is good and entirely innocent; her helplessness arises from the spell cast upon her powers of utterance (lines 267 ff., 473 f., 619 f.). Coleridge may have intended to rescue his heroine through the return of her absent fiancé. An interesting "study of the history, background, and purposes" of the poem is A. H. Nethercot's *The Road to Tryermaine* (1939).

PART I

'Tis the middle of night by the castle clock,
And the owls have awakened the crowing cock,
Tu—whit!——Tu—whoo!
And hark, again! the crowing cock,
How drowsily it crew.   5

Sir Leoline, the Baron rich,
Hath a toothless mastiff bitch.
From her kennel beneath the rock
She maketh answer to the clock,
Four for the quarters, and twelve for the hour;   10
Ever and aye, by shine and shower,
Sixteen short howls, not over loud;
Some say, she sees my lady's shroud.

Is the night chilly and dark?
The night is chilly, but not dark.   15
The thin grey cloud is spread on high,
It covers but not hides the sky.
The moon is behind, and at the full;
And yet she looks both small and dull.
The night is chill, the cloud is grey: 20
'Tis a month before the month of May,
And the Spring comes slowly up this way.

The lovely lady, Christabel,
Whom her father loves so well,
What makes her in the wood so late,   25
A furlong from the castle gate?
She had dreams all yesternight
Of her own betrothèd knight;
And she in the midnight wood will pray
For the weal of her lover that's far away.   30

She stole along, she nothing spoke,
The sighs she heaved were soft and low,
And naught was green upon the oak
But moss and rarest mistletoe:
She kneels beneath the huge oak tree,   35
And in silence prayeth she.

The lady sprang up suddenly,
The lovely lady, Christabel!
It moaned as near, as near can be,
But what it is she cannot tell.—   40
On the other side it seems to be,
Of the huge, broad-breasted, old oak tree.

The night is chill; the forest bare;
Is it the wind that moaneth bleak?
There is not wind enough in the air   45
To move away the ringlet curl
From the lovely lady's cheek—
There is not wind enough to twirl
The one red leaf, the last of its clan,
That dances as often as dance it can,   50
Hanging so light, and hanging so high,
On the topmost twig that looks up at the sky.

Hush, beating heart of Christabel!
Jesu, Maria, shield her well!
She folded her arms beneath her cloak,   55
And stole to the other side of the oak.
        What sees she there?

There she sees a damsel bright,
Drest in a silken robe of white,
That shadowy in the moonlight shone: 60
The neck that made that white robe wan,
Her stately neck, and arms were bare;
Her blue-veined feet unsandal'd were,
And wildly glittered here and there
The gems entangled in her hair.   65
I guess, 'twas frightful there to see
A lady so richly clad as she—
Beautiful exceedingly!

Mary mother, save me now!
(Said Christabel,) And who art thou?   70

The lady strange made answer meet,
And her voice was faint and sweet:—
Have pity on my sore distress,
I scarce can speak for weariness:
Stretch forth thy hand, and have no fear!   75
Said Christabel, How camest thou here?

And the lady, whose voice was faint and sweet,
Did thus pursue her answer meet:—

My sire is of a noble line,
And my name is Geraldine: 80
Five warriors seized me yestermorn,
Me, even me, a maid forlorn:
They choked my cries with force and fright,
And tied me on a palfrey white.
The palfrey was as fleet as wind,   85
And they rode furiously behind.
They spurred amain, their steeds were white:
And once we crossed the shade of night.
As sure as Heaven shall rescue me,
I have no thought what men they be;   90
Nor do I know how long it is
(For I have lain entranced I wis[1])
Since one, the tallest of the five,
Took me from the palfrey's back,
A weary woman, scarce alive.   95
Some muttered words his comrades spoke:
He placed me underneath this oak;
He swore they would return with haste;
Whither they went I cannot tell—
I thought I heard, some minutes past,   100
Sounds as of a castle bell.
Stretch forth thy hand (thus ended she),
And help a wretched maid to flee.

Then Christabel stretched forth her hand,
And comforted fair Geraldine: 105
O well, bright dame! may you command
The service of Sir Leoline;
And gladly our stout chivalry[2]
Will he send forth and friends withal[3]
To guide and guard you safe and free   110
Home to your noble father's hall.

She rose: and forth with steps they passed
That strove to be, and were not, fast.
Her gracious stars the lady blest,
And thus spake on sweet Christabel: 115
All our household are at rest,
The hall as silent as the cell;
Sir Leoline is weak in health,
And may not well awakened be,
But we will move as if in stealth,   120
And I beseech your courtesy,
This night, to share your couch with me.

They crossed the moat, and Christabel
Took the key that fitted well;

A little door she opened straight,   125
All in the middle of the gate;
The gate that was ironed within and without,
Where an army in battle array had marched out.
The lady sank, belike through pain,
And Christabel with might and main   130
Lifted her up, a weary weight,
Over the threshold of the gate: *evil spirit*
Then the lady rose again,
And moved, as she were not in pain.[4]

So free from danger, free from fear,   135
They crossed the court: right glad they were.
And Christabel devoutly cried
To the lady by her side,
Praise we the Virgin all divine
Who hath rescued thee from thy distress!   140
Alas, alas! said Geraldine,
I cannot speak for weariness.
So free from danger, free from fear,
They crossed the court: right glad they were.

Outside her kennel, the mastiff old   145
Lay fast asleep, in moonshine cold.
The mastiff old did not awake,
Yet she an angry moan did make!
And what can ail the mastiff bitch?
Never till now she uttered yell   *auib*   150
Beneath the eye of Christabel.
Perhaps it is the owlet's scritch:
For what can ail the mastiff bitch?

They passed the hall, that echoes still,
Pass as lightly as you will!   155
The brands were flat, the brands were dying,
Amid their own white ashes lying;
But when the lady passed, there came   *evil*
A tongue of light, a fit of flame;
And Christabel saw the lady's eye,   160
And nothing else saw she thereby,
Save the boss of the shield of Sir Leoline tall,
Which hung in a murky old niche in the wall.
O softly tread, said Christabel,
My father seldom sleepeth well.   165

Sweet Christabel her feet doth bare,
And jealous of the listening air
They steal their way from stair to stair,
Now in glimmer, and now in gloom,
And now they pass the Baron's room,   170

[4] The point being that she could not of herself cross a threshold
which had been blessed to keep out evil spirits. Other hints that
"Geraldine" is an evil being come in lines 139–42, 148, and 156–9.

[1] Know.   [2] Men-at-arms.   [3] With them.

As still as death, with stifled breath!
And now have reached her chamber door;
And now doth Geraldine press down
The rushes of the chamber floor.

The moon shines dim in the open air,   175
And not a moonbeam enters here.
But they without its light can see
The chamber carved so curiously,[5]
Carved with figures strange and sweet,
All made out of the carver's brain,   180
For a lady's chamber meet:
The lamp with twofold silver chain
Is fastened to an angel's feet.

The silver lamp burns dead and dim;
But Christabel the lamp will trim.   185
She trimmed the lamp, and made it bright,
And left it swinging to and fro,
While Geraldine, in wretched plight,
Sank down upon the floor below.

O weary lady, Geraldine,   190
I pray you, drink this cordial wine!
It is a wine of virtuous[6] powers;
My mother made it of wild flowers.

And will your mother pity me,
Who am a maiden most forlorn?   195
Christabel answered—Woe is me!
She died the hour that I was born.
I have heard the grey-haired friar tell
How on her death-bed she did say,
That she should hear the castle-bell   200
Strike twelve upon my wedding-day.
O mother dear! that thou wert here!
I would, said Geraldine, she were!

But soon with altered voice, said she—
'Off, wandering mother! Peak and pine![7]   205
I have power to bid thee flee.'
Alas! what ails poor Geraldine?
Why stares she with unsettled eye?
Can she the bodiless dead espy?
And why with hollow voice cries she,   210
'Off, woman, off! this hour is mine—
Though thou her guardian spirit be,
Off, woman, off! 'tis given to me.'

Then Christabel knelt by the lady's side,
And raised to heaven her eyes so blue—   215
Alas! said she, this ghastly ride—
Dear lady! it hath wildered you!
The lady wiped her moist cold brow,
And faintly said, ''Tis over now!'

Again the wild-flower wine she drank: 220
Her fair large eyes 'gan glitter bright,
And from the floor whereon she sank,
The lofty lady stood upright:
She was most beautiful to see,
Like a lady of a far countree.   225

And thus the lofty lady spake—
'All they who live in the upper sky,
Do love you, holy Christabel!
And you love them, and for their sake
And for the good which me befel,   230
Even I in my degree will try,
Fair maiden, to requite you well.
But now unrobe yourself; for I
Must pray, ere yet in bed I lie.'

Quoth Christabel, So let it be!   235
And as the lady bade, did she.
Her gentle limbs did she undress,
And lay down in her loveliness.

But through her brain of weal and woe
So many thoughts moved to and fro,   240
That vain it were her lids to close;
So half-way from the bed she rose,
And on her elbow did recline
To look at the lady Geraldine.

Beneath the lamp the lady bowed,   245
And slowly rolled her eyes around;
Then drawing in her breath aloud,
Like one that shuddered, she unbound
The cincture[8] from beneath her breast:
Her silken robe, and inner vest,   250
Dropt to her feet, and full in view,
Behold! her bosom and half her side——
A sight to dream of, not to tell![9]
O shield her! shield sweet Christabel!

Yet Geraldine nor speaks nor stirs;   255
Ah! what a stricken look was hers!

---

[5] Exquisitely.   [6] Potent.

[7] Dwindle away. "Geraldine" is driving off the spirit of Christabel's mother, which desires to aid her daughter.—Note that the text we follow is inconsistent in its use of quotation marks.

[8] Belt.

[9] Failure to specify is more effective than the specific detail in an earlier version of this line: "Are lean and old and foul of hue," i.e., because it is time for her to renew her vitality by sucking blood.

Deep from within she seems half-way
To lift some weight with sick assay,[10]
And eyes the maid and seeks delay;
Then suddenly, as one defied,   260
Collects herself in scorn and pride,
And lay down by the Maiden's side!—
And in her arms the maid she took,
  Ah wel-a-day!
And with low voice and doleful look   265
These words did say:
'In the touch of this bosom there worketh a spell,
Which is lord of thy utterance, Christabel!
Thou knowest to-night, and wilt know to-morrow,
This mark of my shame, this seal of my sorrow; 270
  But vainly thou warrest,
   For this is alone in
   Thy power to declare,
   That in the dim forest
  Thou heard'st a low moaning,   275
And found'st a bright lady, surpassingly fair;
And didst bring her home with thee in love and in charity,
To shield her and shelter her from the damp air.'

The Conclusion to Part I

It was a lovely sight to see
The lady Christabel, when she   280
Was praying at the old oak tree.
  Amid the jaggèd shadows
  Of mossy leafless boughs,
  Kneeling in the moonlight,
  To make her gentle vows;   285
Her slender palms together prest,
Heaving sometimes on her breast;
Her face resigned to bliss or bale—
Her face, oh call it fair not pale,
And both blue eyes more bright than clear,   290
Each about to have a tear.

With open eyes (ah woe is me!)
Asleep, and dreaming fearfully,
Fearfully dreaming, yet, I wis,
Dreaming that alone, which is—   295
O sorrow and shame! Can this be she,
The lady, who knelt at the old oak tree?
And lo! the worker of these harms,
That holds the maiden in her arms,
Seems to slumber still and mild,   300
As a mother with her child.

A star hath set, a star hath risen,
O Geraldine! since arms of thine

Have been the lovely lady's prison.
O Geraldine! one hour was thine—   305
Thou'st had thy will![11] By tairn[12] and rill,
The night-birds all that hour were still.
But now they are jubilant anew,
From cliff and tower, tu—whoo! tu—whoo!
Tu—whoo! tu—whoo! from wood and fell![13]   310

And see! the lady Christabel
Gathers herself from out her trance;
Her limbs relax, her countenance
Grows sad and soft; the smooth thin lids
Close o'er her eyes; and tears she sheds—   315
Large tears that leave the lashes bright!
And oft the while she seems to smile
As infants at a sudden light!

Yea, she doth smile, and she doth weep,
Like a youthful hermitess,   320
Beauteous in a wilderness,
Who, praying always, prays in sleep.
And, if she move unquietly,
Perchance, 'tis but the blood so free
Comes back and tingles in her feet.   325
No doubt, she hath a vision sweet.
What if her guardian spirit 'twere,
What if she knew her mother near?
But this she knows, in joys and woes,
That saints will aid if men will call: 330
For the blue sky bends over all!

PART II

Each matin bell, the Baron saith,
Knells us back to a world of death.
These words Sir Leoline first said,
When he rose and found his lady dead: 335
These words Sir Leoline will say
Many a morn to his dying day!

And hence the custom and law began
That still at dawn the sacristan,
Who duly pulls the heavy bell,   340
Five and forty beads must tell
Between each stroke—a warning knell,
Which not a soul can choose but hear
From Bratha Head[14] to Wyndermere.

---

10 Essay, attempt.

11 As a vampire, "Geraldine" has been sucking Christabel's blood.
Cf. lines 374-80 and 453.   12 Tarn, pool.   13 Hill.
14 Source. Coleridge was living in the Lake District when he composed Part II. The Brathay River flows into the northern end of
Lake Windermere. The other place-names are from the same
region.

Saith Bracy the bard, So let it knell!   345
And let the drowsy sacristan
Still count as slowly as he can!
There is no lack of such, I ween,
As well fill up the space between.
In Langdale Pike[15] and Witch's Lair,   350
And Dungeon-ghyll[16] so foully rent,
With ropes of rock and bells of air
Three sinful sextons' ghosts are pent,
Who all give back, one after t'other,
The death-note to their living brother;   355
And oft too, by the knell offended,
Just as their one! two! three! is ended,
The devil mocks the doleful tale
With a merry peal from Borodale.[17]

The air is still! through mist and cloud   360
That merry peal comes ringing loud;
And Geraldine shakes off her dread,
And rises lightly from the bed;
Puts on her silken vestments white,
And tricks her hair in lovely plight,[18]   365
And nothing doubting of her spell
Awakens the lady Christabel.
'Sleep you, sweet lady Christabel?
I trust that you have rested well.'

And Christabel awoke and spied   370
The same who lay down by her side—
O rather say, the same whom she
Raised up beneath the old oak tree!
Nay, fairer yet! and yet more fair!
For she belike hath drunken deep   375
Of all the blessedness of sleep!
And while she spake, her looks, her air
Such gentle thankfulness declare,
That (so it seemed) her girded vests
Grew tight beneath her heaving breasts.   380
'Sure I have sinn'd!' said Christabel,
'Now heaven be praised if all be well!'
And in low faltering tones, yet sweet,
Did she the lofty lady greet
With such perplexity of mind   385
As dreams too lively leave behind.

So quickly she rose, and quickly arrayed
Her maiden limbs, and having prayed
That He, who on the cross did groan,
Might wash away her sins unknown,   390
She forthwith led fair Geraldine
To meet her sire, Sir Leoline.

The lovely maid and the lady tall
Are pacing both into the hall,
And pacing on through page and groom,   395
Enter the Baron's presence-room.

The Baron rose, and while he prest
His gentle daughter to his breast,
With cheerful wonder in his eyes
The lady Geraldine espies,   400
And gave such welcome to the same,
As might beseem so bright a dame!

But when he heard the lady's tale,
And when she told her father's name,
Why waxed Sir Leoline so pale,   405
Murmuring o'er the name again,
Lord Roland de Vaux of Tryermaine?

Alas! they had been friends in youth;
But whispering tongues can poison truth;
And constancy lives in realms above;   410
And life is thorny; and youth is vain;
And to be wroth with one we love
Doth work like madness in the brain.
And thus it chanced, as I divine,
With Roland and Sir Leoline.   415
Each spake words of high disdain
And insult to his heart's best brother:
They parted—ne'er to meet again!
But never either found another
To free the hollow heart from paining—   420
They stood aloof, the scars remaining,
Like cliffs which had been rent asunder;
A dreary sea now flows between;—
But neither heat, nor frost, nor thunder,
Shall wholly do away, I ween,   425
The marks of that which once hath been.

Sir Leoline, a moment's space,
Stood gazing on the damsel's face:
And the youthful Lord of Tryermaine
Came back upon his heart again.   430

O then the Baron forgot his age,
His noble heart swelled high with rage;
He swore by the wounds in Jesu's side
He would proclaim it far and wide,
With trump and solemn heraldry,   435
That they, who thus had wronged the dame,
Were base as spotted infamy!
'And if they dare deny the same,
My herald shall appoint a week,
And let the recreant traitors seek   440
My tourney court—that there and then

---

[15] Peak.   [16] Gorge.
[17] Borrowdale, perhaps the most beautiful valley of the District.
[18] Plait.

I may dislodge their reptile souls
From the bodies and forms of men!'
He spake: his eye in lightning rolls!
For the lady was ruthlessly seized; and he kenned   445
In the beautiful lady the child of his friend!

And now the tears were on his face,
And fondly in his arms he took
Fair Geraldine, who met the embrace,
Prolonging it with joyous look.   450
Which when she viewed, a vision fell
Upon the soul of Christabel,
The vision of fear, the touch and pain!
She shrunk and shuddered, and saw again—
(Ah, woe is me! Was it for thee,   455
Thou gentle maid! such sights to see?)

Again she saw that bosom old,
Again she felt that bosom cold,
And drew in her breath with a hissing sound:[19]
Whereat the Knight turned wildly round,   460
And nothing saw, but his own sweet maid
With eyes upraised, as one that prayed.

The touch, the sight, had passed away,
And in its stead that vision blest,
Which comforted her after-rest   465
While in the lady's arms she lay,
Had put a rapture in her breast,
And on her lips and o'er her eyes
Spread smiles like light!
                             With new surprise,
'What ails then my belovèd child?'   470
The Baron said—His daughter mild
Made answer, 'All will yet be well!'
I ween, she had no power to tell
Aught else: so mighty was the spell.

Yet he, who saw this Geraldine,   475
Had deemed her sure a thing divine:
Such sorrow with such grace she blended,
As if she feared she had offended
Sweet Christabel, that gentle maid!
And with such lowly tones she prayed   480
She might be sent without delay
Home to her father's mansion.
                             'Nay!
Nay, by my soul!' said Leoline.
'Ho! Bracy the bard, the charge be thine!
Go thou, with music sweet and loud,   485
And take two steeds with trappings proud,
And take the youth whom thou lov'st best

To bear thy harp, and learn thy song,
And clothe you both in solemn vest,
And over the mountains haste along,   490
Lest wandering folk, that are abroad,
Detain you on the valley road.

'And when he has crossed the Irthing flood,
My merry bard! he hastes, he hastes
Up Knorren Moor, through Halegarth Wood,   495
And reaches soon that castle good
Which stands and threatens Scotland's wastes.

'Bard Bracy! bard Bracy! your horses are fleet,
Ye must ride up the hall, your music so sweet,
More loud than your horses' echoing feet!   500
And loud and loud to Lord Roland call,
Thy daughter is safe in Langdale hall!
Thy beautiful daughter is safe and free—
Sir Leoline greets thee thus through me!
He bids thee come without delay   505
With all thy numerous array
And take thy lovely daughter home:
And he will meet thee on the way
With all his numerous array
White with their panting palfreys' foam: 510
And, by mine honour! I will say,
That I repent me of the day
When I spake words of fierce disdain
To Roland de Vaux of Tryermaine!—
—For since that evil hour hath flown,   515
Many a summer's sun hath shone;
Yet ne'er found I a friend again
Like Roland de Vaux of Tryermaine.'

The lady fell, and clasped his knees,
Her face upraised, her eyes o'erflowing;   520
And Bracy replied, with faltering voice,
His gracious Hail on all bestowing!—
'Thy words, thou sire of Christabel,
Are sweeter than my harp can tell;
Yet might I gain a boon of thee,   525
This day my journey should not be,
So strange a dream hath come to me,
That I had vowed with music loud
To clear yon wood from thing unblest,
Warned by a vision in my rest!   530
For in my sleep I saw that dove,
That gentle bird, whom thou dost love,
And call'st by thy own daughter's name—
Sir Leoline! I saw the same
Fluttering, and uttering fearful moan,   535
Among the green herbs in the forest alone.
Which when I saw and when I heard,
I wonder'd what might ail the bird;

19 For besides being a vampire "Geraldine" is also a serpent-woman,
   and Christabel has been affected by contact with her.

For nothing near it could I see,   539
Save the grass and green herbs underneath the old tree.

'And in my dream methought I went
To search out what might there be found;
And what the sweet bird's trouble meant,
That thus lay fluttering on the ground.
I went and peered, and could descry   545
No cause for her distressful cry;
But yet for her dear lady's sake
I stooped, methought, the dove to take,
When lo! I saw a bright green snake
Coiled around its wings and neck.   550
Green as the herbs on which it couched,
Close by the dove's its head it crouched;
And with the dove it heaves and stirs,
Swelling its neck as she swelled hers!
I woke; it was the midnight hour,   555
The clock was echoing in the tower;
But though my slumber was gone by,
This dream it would not pass away—
It seems to live upon my eye!
And thence I vowed this self-same day   560
With music strong and saintly song
To wander through the forest bare,
Lest aught unholy loiter there.'

Thus Bracy said: the Baron, the while,
Half-listening heard him with a smile;   565
Then turned to Lady Geraldine,
His eyes made up of wonder and love;
And said in courtly accents fine,
'Sweet maid, Lord Roland's beauteous dove,
With arms more strong than harp or song,   570
Thy sire and I will crush the snake!'
He kissed her forehead as he spake,
And Geraldine in maiden wise
Casting down her large bright eyes,
With blushing cheek and courtesy fine   575
She turned her from Sir Leoline;
Softly gathering up her train,
That o'er her right arm fell again;
And folded her arms across her chest,
And couched her head upon her breast,[20]   580
And looked askance at Christabel—
Jesu, Maria, shield her well!

A snake's small eye blinks dull and shy;
And the lady's eyes they shrunk in her head,
Each shrunk up to a serpent's eye,   585
And with somewhat of malice, and more of dread,
At Christabel she looked askance!—

---

[20] Like a snake drawing back its head to strike.

One moment—and the sight was fled!
But Christabel in dizzy trance
Stumbling on the unsteady ground   590
Shuddered aloud, with a hissing sound;
And Geraldine again turned round,
And like a thing, that sought relief,
Full of wonder and full of grief,
She rolled her large bright eyes divine   595
Wildly on Sir Leoline.

The maid, alas! her thoughts are gone,
She nothing sees—no sight but one!
The maid, devoid of guile and sin,
I know not how, in fearful wise,   600
So deeply had she drunken in
That look, those shrunken serpent eyes,
That all her features were resigned
To this sole image in her mind:
And passively did imitate   605
That look of dull and treacherous hate!
And thus she stood, in dizzy trance,
Still picturing that look askance
With forced unconscious sympathy
Full before her father's view—   610
As far as such a look could be
In eyes so innocent and blue!

And when the trance was o'er, the maid
Paused awhile, and inly prayed:
Then falling at the Baron's feet,   615
'By my mother's soul do I entreat
That thou this woman send away!'
She said: and more she could not say:
For what she knew she could not tell,
O'er-mastered by the mighty spell.   620

Why is thy cheek so wan and wild,
Sir Leoline? Thy only child
Lies at thy feet, thy joy, thy pride,
So fair, so innocent, so mild;
The same, for whom thy lady died!   625
O by the pangs of her dear mother
Think thou no evil of thy child!
For her, and thee, and for no other,
She prayed the moment ere she died:
Prayed that the babe for whom she died,   630
Might prove her dear lord's joy and pride!
    That prayer her deadly pangs beguiled,
        Sir Leoline!
    And wouldst thou wrong thy only child,
        Her child and thine?   635

Within the Baron's heart and brain
If thoughts, like these, had any share,

They only swelled his rage and pain,
And did but work confusion there.
His heart was cleft with pain and rage, 640
His cheeks they quivered, his eyes were wild,
Dishonoured thus in his old age;
Dishonoured by his only child,
And all his hospitality
To the wronged daughter of his friend 645
By more than woman's jealousy
Brought thus to a disgraceful end—
He rolled his eye with stern regard
Upon the gentle minstrel bard,
And said in tones abrupt, austere— 650
'Why, Bracy! dost thou loiter here?
I bade thee hence!' The bard obeyed;
And turning from his own sweet maid,
The agèd knight, Sir Leoline,
Led forth the lady Geraldine! 655

The Conclusion to Part II

A little child, a limber elf,[21]
Singing, dancing to itself,
A fairy thing with red round cheeks,
That always finds, and never seeks,
Makes such a vision to the sight 660
As fills a father's eyes with light;
And pleasures flow in so thick and fast
Upon his heart, that he at last
Must needs express his love's excess
With words of unmeant bitterness. 665
Perhaps 'tis pretty to force together
Thoughts so all unlike each other;
To mutter and mock a broken charm,
To dally with wrong that does no harm.
Perhaps 'tis tender too and pretty 670
At each wild word to feel within
A sweet recoil of love and pity.
And what, if in a world of sin
(O sorrow and shame should this be true!)
Such giddiness of heart and brain 675
Comes seldom save from rage and pain,
So talks as it's most used to do.

FROST AT MIDNIGHT

Written and published in 1798, with "France" and
another, this quiet poem is at the opposite pole from
Christabel. Here, instead of imitation medievalism, are

domestic scene and reverie and a father's fervent wish
that a child may grow up in acceptance of man's heritage
of natural and spiritual beauty. Coleridge called this and
similar verses his "conversation poems"; they are comparable to the "conversation pieces" of the painters.

The Frost performs its secret ministry,
Unhelped by any wind. The owlet's cry
Came loud—and hark, again! loud as before.
The inmates of my cottage, all at rest,
Have left me to that solitude, which suits 5
Abstruser musings: save that at my side
My cradled infant[1] slumbers peacefully.
'Tis calm indeed! so calm, that it disturbs
And vexes meditation with its strange
And extreme silentness. Sea, hill, and wood, 10
This populous village! Sea, and hill, and wood,
With all the numberless goings-on of life,
Inaudible as dreams! the thin blue flame
Lies on my low-burnt fire, and quivers not;
Only that film,[2] which fluttered on the grate, 15
Still flutters there, the sole unquiet thing.
Methinks, its motion in this hush of nature
Gives it dim sympathies with me who live,
Making it a companionable form,
Whose puny flaps and freaks the idling Spirit 20
By its own moods interprets, every where
Echo or mirror seeking of itself,
And makes a toy of Thought.
⠀⠀⠀⠀⠀⠀⠀⠀⠀But O! how oft,
How oft, at school, with most believing mind,
Presageful, have I gazed upon the bars, 25
To watch that fluttering *stranger!* and as oft
With unclosed lids, already had I dreamt
Of my sweet birth-place, and the old church-tower,
Whose bells, the poor man's only music, rang
From morn to evening, all the hot Fair-day, 30
So sweetly, that they stirred and haunted me
With a wild pleasure, falling on mine ear
Most like articulate sounds of things to come!
So gazed I, till the soothing things, I dreamt,
Lulled me to sleep, and sleep prolonged my dreams! 35
And so I brooded all the following morn,
Awed by the stern preceptor's face, mine eye
Fixed with mock study on my swimming book:
Save if the door half opened, and I snatched
A hasty glance, and still my heart leaped up, 40
For still I hoped to see the *stranger's* face,
Townsman, or aunt, or sister more beloved,
My play-mate when we both were clothed alike!

---

21 We must suppose that the connection between this "conclusion"
and the Baron's impatience with his daughter would have been
made plainer if Coleridge had finished the poem.

1 Hartley Coleridge (1796–1849), the poet's eldest son.
2 Coleridge's note: ". . . these films are called *strangers* and supposed to portend the arrival of some absent friend."

Dear Babe, that sleepest cradled by my side,
Whose gentle breathings, heard in this deep calm,   45
Fill up the interspersèd vacancies
And momentary pauses of the thought!
My babe so beautiful! it thrills my heart
With tender gladness, thus to look at thee,
And think that thou shalt learn far other lore   50
And in far other scenes! For I was reared
In the great city, pent 'mid cloisters dim,
And saw nought lovely but the sky and stars.
But thou, my babe! shalt wander like a breeze
By lakes and sandy shores, beneath the crags   55
Of ancient mountain, and beneath the clouds,
Which image in their bulk both lakes and shores
And mountain crags: so shalt thou see and hear
The lovely shapes and sounds intelligible
Of that eternal language, which thy God   60
Utters, who from eternity doth teach
Himself in all, and all things in himself.
Great universal Teacher! he shall mould
Thy spirit, and by giving make it ask.

Therefore all seasons shall be sweet to thee,   65
Whether the summer clothe the general earth
With greenness, or the redbreast sit and sing
Betwixt the tufts of snow on the bare branch
Of mossy apple-tree, while the nigh thatch
Smokes in the sun-thaw; whether the eave-drops fall   70
Heard only in the trances of the blast,
Or if the secret ministry of frost
Shall hang them up in silent icicles,
Quietly shining to the quiet Moon.

FRANCE: AN ODE

Louis XVI was guillotined on January 21, 1793, and within
a few weeks England joined the European coalition
fighting the Revolutionary government. In the following
year the French armies took the offensive; conquest
followed conquest. Coleridge's ode attacks the invasion of
Switzerland early in 1798. The poem first appeared in the
London *Morning Post* of April 16 under the title "The
Recantation: an Ode," with an editorial note: "The
following excellent Ode will be in unison with the
feelings of every friend to Liberty and foe to Oppression;
of all who, admiring the French Revolution, detest and
deplore the conduct of France towards Switzerland. It is
very satisfactory to find so zealous and steady an advocate
for Freedom as Mr. Coleridge concur with us in condemning the conduct of France. . . . What we most
admire is the *avowal* of his sentiments, and public censure
of the unprincipled and atrocious conduct of France. The
Poem itself is written with great energy. [It contains]
some of the most vigorous lines we have ever read. . . ."

I

Ye Clouds! that far above me float and pause,
    Whose pathless march no mortal may controul!
    Ye Ocean-Waves! that, wheresoe'er ye roll,
Yield homage only to eternal laws!
Ye Woods! that listen to the night-birds singing,   5
    Midway the smooth and perilous slope reclined,
Save when your own imperious branches swinging,
    Have made a solemn music of the wind!
Where, like a man beloved of God,
Through glooms, which never woodman trod,   10
    How oft, pursuing fancies holy,
My moonlight way o'er flowering weeds I wound,
    Inspired, beyond the guess of folly,
By each rude shape and wild unconquerable sound!
O ye loud Waves! and O ye Forests high!   15
    And O ye Clouds that far above me soared!
Thou rising Sun! thou blue rejoicing Sky!
    Yea, every thing that is and will be free!
    Bear witness for me, wheresoe'er ye be,
With what deep worship I have still adored   20
    The spirit of divinest Liberty.

II

When France in wrath her giant-limbs upreared,
    And with that oath, which smote air, earth, and sea,
    Stamped her strong foot and said she would be free,
Bear witness for me, how I hoped and feared!   25
With what a joy my lofty gratulation
    Unawed I sang, amid a slavish band:
And when to whelm the disenchanted nation,
    Like fiends embattled by a wizard's wand,
        The Monarchs marched in evil day,   30
        And Britain joined the dire array;
    Though dear her shores and circling ocean,
Though many friendships, many youthful loves
    Had swoln the patriot emotion
And flung a magic light o'er all her hills and groves;   35
Yet still my voice, unaltered, sang defeat
    To all that braved the tyrant-quelling lance,
And shame too long delayed and vain retreat!
For ne'er, O Liberty! with partial aim
I dimmed thy light or damped thy holy flame;   40
    But blessed the paeans of delivered France,
And hung my head and wept at Britain's name.

III

'And what,' I said, 'though Blasphemy's loud scream[1]
    With that sweet music of deliverance strove!
    Though all the fierce and drunken passions wove   45
A dance more wild than e'er was maniac's dream!

----
[1] The Revolution officially renounced the Christian religion.

Ye storms, that round the dawning East assembled,
The Sun was rising, though yet hid his light!'
  And when, to soothe my soul, that hoped
      and trembled,
The dissonance ceased, and all seemed calm
      and bright;[2]   50
  When France her front[3] deep-scarr'd and gory
  Concealed with clustering wreaths of glory;
    When, insupportably advancing,
  Her arm made mockery of the warrior's ramp;[4]
    While timid looks of fury glancing,   55
  Domestic treason, crushed beneath her fatal stamp,
Writhed like a wounded dragon in his gore;
  Then I reproached my fears that would not flee;
'And soon,' I said, 'shall Wisdom teach her lore
In the low huts of them that toil and groan!   60
And, conquering by her happiness alone,
  Shall France compel the nations to be free,
Till Love and Joy look round, and call the
      Earth their own.'

IV

Forgive me, Freedom! O forgive those dreams!
  I hear thy voice, I hear thy loud lament,   65
  From bleak Helvetia's[5] icy caverns sent—
I hear thy groans upon her blood-stained streams!
  Heroes, that for your peaceful country perished,
  And ye that, fleeing, spot your mountain-snows
    With bleeding wounds; forgive me, that I
        cherished   70
One thought that ever blessed your cruel foes!
  To scatter rage, and traitorous guilt,
  Where Peace her jealous home had built;
    A patriot-race to disinherit
Of all that made their stormy wilds so dear;   75
    And with inexpiable spirit
To taint the bloodless freedom of the mountaineer—
O France, that mockest Heaven, adulterous, blind,
  And patriot only in pernicious toils!
Are these thy boasts, Champion of human kind?   80
  To mix with Kings in the low lust of sway,
Yell in the hunt, and share the murderous prey;
To insult the shrine of Liberty with spoils
  From freemen torn; to tempt and to betray?

V

  The Sensual and the Dark rebel in vain,   85
  Slaves by their own compulsion! In mad game
  They burst their manacles and wear the name

---

[2] After the Reign of Terror in Paris ended.
[3] Forehead.   [4] Menacing advance.   [5] Switzerland's.

Of Freedom, graven on a heavier chain![6]
  O Liberty! with profitless endeavour
Have I pursued thee, many a weary hour;   90
  But thou nor swell'st the victor's strain, nor ever
Didst breathe thy soul in forms of human power.
  Alike from all, howe'er they praise thee,
  (Nor prayer, nor boastful name delays thee)
    Alike from Priestcraft's harpy minions,   95
  And factious Blasphemy's obscener slaves,
    Thou speedest on thy subtle pinions,
The guide of homeless winds, and playmate of
      the waves!
And there I felt thee!—on that sea-cliff's verge, 99
  Whose pines, scarce travelled by the breeze above,
Had made one murmur with the distant surge!
Yes, while I stood and gazed, my temples bare,
And shot my being through earth, sea, and air,
  Possessing all things with intensest love,
    O Liberty! my spirit felt thee there.   105

DEJECTION: AN ODE

This poem went through several stages of revision. It was
originally composed at Keswick in the spring of 1802;
and there are manuscripts which show that, while it was
partially inspired by his love for Sara Hutchinson, the
Wordsworths were almost equally in Coleridge's mind.
The ode was first printed in the *Morning Post* on October 4, Wordsworth's wedding day, but with the directness
of the references to him reduced by changing *William*
to *Edmund*. Other allusions to him, to Dorothy, and to
Sara Hutchinson were left out entirely. Still later, as a
consequence of the estrangement, the references to
William and his poetry were reduced still further, and an
unnamed lady was substituted as the recipient of the
poet's good wishes.

These facts are of minor importance, since the poem is
mainly about Coleridge. It is himself he is thinking of,
far more than a brother poet or a beloved woman; he
is full of self-pity and of alarm about his future. By 1802
Coleridge was fast becoming the helpless victim of opium.
Behind these lines lurks the terrible conviction that his
creative powers are waning. The same burden of fear
has weighed heavily on many a stronger artist, often
without warrant. Coleridge's fear was well founded.

The poem has the following stanza as epigraph:

Late, late yestreen I saw the new Moon,
  With the old Moon in her arms;
And I fear, I fear, my Master dear!
  We shall have a deadly storm.
      Ballad of Sir Patrick Spence

---

[6] A note in a commonplace-book shows that Coleridge had read
or heard that in Genoa the word *Liberty* was inscribed on prison
doors and the chains of galley-slaves.

I

Well! If the Bard was weather-wise, who made
  The grand old ballad of Sir Patrick Spence,[1]
  This night, so tranquil now, will not go hence
Unroused by winds, that ply a busier trade
Than those which mould yon cloud in lazy flakes,   5
Or the dull sobbing draft, that moans and rakes
Upon the strings of this Aeolian lute,[2]
    Which better far were mute.
  For lo! the New-moon winter-bright!
  And overspread with phantom light,   10
  (With swimming phantom light o'erspread
  But rimmed and circled by a silver thread)
I see the old Moon in her lap, foretelling
  The coming-on of rain and squally blast.
And oh! that even now the gust were swelling,   15
  And the slant night-shower driving loud and fast!
Those sounds which oft have raised me, whilst
    they awed,
  And sent my soul abroad,
Might now perhaps their wonted impulse give,
Might startle this dull pain, and make it move
    and live!   20

II

A grief without a pang, void, dark, and drear,
  A stifled, drowsy, unimpassioned grief,
  Which finds no natural outlet, no relief,
    In word, or sigh, or tear—
O Lady![3] in this wan and heartless mood,   25
To other thoughts by yonder throstle woo'd,
  All this long eve, so balmy and serene,
Have I been gazing on the western sky,
  And its peculiar tint of yellow green:
And still I gaze—and with how blank an eye!   30
And those thin clouds above, in flakes and bars,
That give away their motion to the stars;
Those stars, that glide behind them or between,
Now sparkling, now bedimmed, but always seen:
Yon crescent Moon, as fixed as if it grew   35
In its own cloudless, starless lake of blue;
I see them all so excellently fair,
I see, not feel, how beautiful they are!

III

  My genial[4] spirits fail;
  And what can these avail   40

To lift the smothering weight from off my breast?
  It were a vain endeavour,
  Though I should gaze for ever
On that green light that lingers in the west:
I may not hope from outward forms to win   45
The passion and the life, whose fountains are within.

IV

O Lady! we receive but what we give,
And in our life alone does Nature live:
Ours is her wedding garment, ours her shroud!
  And would we aught behold, of higher worth,   50
Than that inanimate cold world allowed
To the poor loveless ever-anxious crowd,
  Ah! from the soul itself must issue forth
A light, a glory, a fair luminous cloud
    Enveloping the Earth—   55
And from the soul itself must there be sent
  A sweet and potent voice, of its own birth,
Of all sweet sounds the life and element![5]

V

O pure of heart! thou need'st not ask of me
What this strong music in the soul may be!   60
What, and wherein it doth exist,
This light, this glory, this fair luminous mist,
This beautiful and beauty-making power.
  Joy, virtuous Lady![6] Joy that ne'er was given,
Save to the pure, and in their purest hour,   65
Life, and Life's effluence,[7] cloud at once and shower,
Joy, Lady! is the spirit and the power,
Which wedding Nature to us gives in dower
  A new Earth and new Heaven,
Undreamt of by the sensual and the proud—   70
Joy is the sweet voice, Joy the luminous cloud—
    We in ourselves rejoice!
And thence flows all that charms or ear or sight,
  All melodies the echoes of that voice,
All colours a suffusion from that light.[8]   75

---

[1] Reprinted above, I, 196-7.
[2] The aeolian harp, popular in this period. It was a box with
  strings tuned in unison; when it was placed in the wind, its
  strings vibrated.
[3] Formerly *William*, not *Lady*. So also in lines 47, 67.
[4] Creative.

[5] I.e. (lines 47-63), the source of communion with nature and of
  creative power lies, not in external nature itself, but within the
  individual spirit. There was no difference between the views of
  Wordsworth and Coleridge on this important point.
[6] Formerly *blameless Poet*.   [7] Emanation, outflow.
[8] The following passage formerly came after line 75:
    "Calm, steadfast Spirit, guided from above,
    O Wordsworth! friend of my devoutest choice,
    Great son of genius! full of light and love
      Thus, thus dost thou rejoice.
    To thee do all things live from pole to pole,
    Their life the eddying of thy living soul.
    Brother and friend of my devoutest choice
    Thus may'st thou ever, evermore rejoice!"
  Compare the closing lines of the present version.

VI

There was a time when, though my path was rough,
  This joy within me dallied with distress,
And all misfortunes were but as the stuff
  Whence Fancy made me dreams of happiness:
For hope grew round me, like the twining vine,   80
And fruits, and foliage, not my own, seemed mine.
But now afflictions bow me down to earth:
Nor care I that they rob me of my mirth;
  But oh! each visitation
Suspends what nature gave me at my birth,   85
  My shaping spirit of Imagination.
For not to think of what I needs must feel,
  But to be still and patient, all I can;
And haply by abstruse research to steal
  From my own nature all the natural man—   90
  This was my sole resource, my only plan:
Till that which suits a part infects the whole,
And now is almost grown the habit of my soul.

VII

Hence, viper thoughts, that coil around my mind,
  Reality's dark dream!   95
I turn from you, and listen to the wind,
  Which long has raved unnoticed. What a scream
Of agony by torture lengthened out
That lute sent forth! Thou Wind, that rav'st without,
  Bare crag, or mountain-tairn,[9] or blasted tree,   100
Or pine-grove whither woodman never clomb,
Or lonely house, long held the witches' home,
  Methinks were fitter instruments for thee,
Mad Lutanist! who in this month of showers,
Of dark-brown gardens, and of peeping flowers,   105
Mak'st Devils' yule,[10] with worse than wintry song,
The blossoms, buds, and timorous leaves among.
  Thou Actor, perfect in all tragic sounds!
Thou mighty Poet, e'en to frenzy bold!
  What tell'st thou now about?   110
  'Tis of the rushing of an host in rout,
  With groans, of trampled men, with smarting
    wounds—
At once they groan with pain, and shudder with
    the cold!
But hush! there is a pause of deepest silence!
  And all that noise, as of a rushing crowd,   115
With groans, and tremulous shudderings—all is over—
  It tells another tale, with sounds less deep and loud!
  A tale of less affright,

---

[9] Pool.
[10] I.e., this wind would be more appropriate at Christmas time
  than in April.

And tempered with delight,
As[11] Otway's self[12] had framed the tender lay,—   120
  'Tis of a little child
  Upon a lonesome wild,
Not far from home, but she hath lost her way:
And now moans low in bitter grief and fear,
And now screams loud, and hopes to make her
    mother hear.   125

VIII

'Tis midnight, but small thoughts have I of sleep:
Full seldom may my friend such vigils keep!
Visit her,[13] gentle Sleep! with wings of healing,
  And may this storm be but a mountain-birth,
May all the stars hang bright above her dwelling,   130
  Silent as though they watched the sleeping Earth!
  With light heart may she rise,
  Gay fancy, cheerful eyes,
  Joy lift her spirit, joy attune her voice;
To her may all things live, from pole to pole,   135
Their life the eddying of her living soul!
  O simple spirit, guided from above,
Dear Lady![14] friend devoutest of my choice,
Thus mayest thou ever, evermore rejoice.

YOUTH AND AGE

Verse, a breeze mid blossoms straying,
Where Hope clung feeding, like a bee—
Both were mine! Life went a-maying
  With Nature, Hope, and Poesy,
    When I was young!   5

When I was young?—Ah, woful When!
Ah! for the change 'twixt Now and Then!
This breathing house not built with hands,
This body that does me grievous wrong,
O'er aery cliffs and glittering sands,   10
How lightly then it flashed along:—
Like those trim skiffs, unknown of yore,
On winding lakes and rivers wide,
That ask no aid of sail or oar,
That fear no spite of wind or tide!   15
Nought cared this body for wind or weather
When Youth and I lived in't together.

---

[11] As if.
[12] Formerly *thou thyself*. The following lines refer to Wordsworth's "Lucy Gray" (p. 51, above). Thomas Otway (see I,
  399), wrote the two best tragedies of the Restoration period;
  their appeal is chiefly to pity.
[13] This and the following feminine pronouns were formerly
  masculine.   [14] Formerly *Brother and*.

Flowers are lovely; Love is flower-like;
Friendship is a sheltering tree;
O! the joys, that came down shower-like,   20
Of Friendship, Love, and Liberty,
        Ere I was old!

Ere I was old? Ah, woful Ere,
Which tells me, Youth's no longer here!
O Youth! for years so many and sweet,   25
'Tis known, that Thou and I were one,
I'll think it but a fond conceit—[1]
It cannot be that Thou art gone!
Thy vesper-bell hath not yet toll'd:—
And thou wert aye a masker bold!   30
What strange disguise hast now put on,
To make believe, that thou art gone?
I see these locks in silvery slips,
This drooping gait, this altered size:
But Spring-tide blossoms on thy lips,   35
And tears take sunshine from thine eyes!
Life is but thought: so think I will
That Youth and I are house-mates still.

Dew-drops are the gems of morning,
But the tears of mournful eve!   40
Where no hope is, life's a warning
That only serves to make us grieve,
        When we are old:

That only serves to make us grieve
With oft and tedious taking-leave,
Like some poor nigh-related guest,
That may not rudely be dismist;
Yet hath outstay'd his welcome while,
And tells the jest without the smile.

WORK WITHOUT HOPE

LINES COMPOSED 21ST FEBRUARY 1825

All Nature seems at work. Slugs leave their lair—
The bees are stirring—birds are on the wing—
And Winter slumbering in the open air,
Wears on his smiling face a dream of Spring!
And I the while, the sole unbusy thing,   5
Nor honey make, nor pair, nor build, nor sing.

Yet well I ken the banks where amaranths[2] blow,
Have traced the fount whence streams of nectar flow.
Bloom, O ye amaranths! bloom for whom ye may,
For me ye bloom not! Glide, rich streams, away!   10
With lips unbrightened, wreathless brow, I stroll:
And would you learn the spells that drowse my soul?
Work without Hope draws nectar in a sieve,
And Hope without an object cannot live.

from BIOGRAPHIA LITERARIA

IN 1817, soon after its completion, appeared *Biographia
Literaria; or Biographical Sketches of My Literary Life and
Opinions.* An "immethodical miscellany," as Coleridge
acknowledged, it is his literary autobiography, an exposition of his philosophy of poetry, and one of the major
documents of Romantic theory. He had formerly accepted as adequately representative of his own views
Wordsworth's Preface to *Lyrical Ballads* (pp. 69 ff.,
above), with which the following pages should be compared. Since the appearance of the Preface, the but
partially healed breach in the poets' friendship had led
Coleridge to re-examine points of difference in their
theories, especially on the vital question of diction. Of
equal interest is his attempt to formulate his conception
of what poetry is. *Biographia Literaria* has been edited by   5
J. Shawcross (2 vols., 1907); it is also available in Everyman's Library.

from CHAPTER I

*The motives of the present work—Reception of the Author's
first publication—The discipline of his taste at school—The
effect of contemporary writers on youthful minds—Bowles's
sonnets—Comparison between the Poets before and since
Mr. Pope.*

IT HAS been my lot to have had my name introduced,
both in conversation, and in print, more frequently
than I find it easy to explain, whether I consider the
fewness, unimportance, and limited circulation of
my writings, or the retirement and distance in which   5
I have lived, both from the literary and political
world. Most often it has been connected with some
charge which I could not acknowledge, or some
principle which I had never entertained. Nevertheless, had I had no other motive or incitement, the   10

[1] Foolish notion.—Coleridge began this poem in 1823 but did not
complete it till 1832.

[2] Imaginary, unfading flowers.

SAMUEL TAYLOR COLERIDGE

Painted by Washington Allston, the American painter, in 1806, when Coleridge was about 34 years old. Allston, about 27 at this time, was studying abroad. The two remained friends and correspondents throughout their lives. (Washington Allston Trust)

CHARLES LAMB

In October, 1804, Lamb's sister Mary wrote, "William Hazlitt is painting my brother's picture, which has brought us acquainted with the whole family. I like William Hazlitt and his sister very much." This was the year in which Hazlitt's friendship with the Lambs began. Lamb was 29 years old, Hazlitt 26. A few years later Hazlitt gave up painting for writing. (National Portrait Gallery, London)

CHRIST'S HOSPITAL, LONDON

The Hall of the school attended by Coleridge, Lamb, and Leigh Hunt. The boys of the school wore blue tunics, white frills, and yellow stockings, whence the name Blue Coat School. The scene shows the annual ceremony of declamations by the "Grecians," the best students, who had won university scholarships. Engraving by T. Rowlandson and A. C. Pugin, *The Microcosm of London*, c. 1808. (Boston Public Library)

NEWSTEAD ABBEY

Once an Augustinian priory, this partially ruined edifice nea
Nottingham was inherited by Byron along with his title when
he was ten, and was his residence for a time after he left the
university. It had belonged to his family since 1539, and he
was intensely proud of it, but he was finally forced by his debt
to sell it.

GEORGE GORDON, LORD BYRON

From a miniature in the
Pierpont Morgan Library.

BYRON'S *WORKS*, VOLUME III

This title page from a collected edition of Byron's
poetry issued by his friend and publisher John
Murray in 1832 is typical of book design of the
Romantic Period. The artist, Clarkson Stanfield
(1793-1867), was particularly well known for his
marine paintings. Edward Finden, the engraver,
with his brother William, made a conspicuous success of engravings illustrating Byron's works.

reader would not have been troubled with this exculpation. What my additional purposes were, will be seen in the following pages. It will be found, that the least of what I have written concerns myself personally. I have used the narration chiefly for the purpose of giving a continuity to the work, in part for the sake of the miscellaneous reflections suggested to me by particular events, but still more as introductory to the statement of my principles in Politics, Religion, and Philosophy, and an application of the rules, deduced from philosophical principles, to poetry and criticism. But of the objects which I proposed to myself, it was not the least important to effect, as far as possible, a settlement of the long continued controversy concerning the true nature of poetic diction; and at the same time to define with the utmost impartiality the real *poetic* character of the poet,[1] by whose writings this controversy was first kindled, and has been since fuelled and fanned. . . .

At school I enjoyed the inestimable advantage of a very sensible, though at the same time a very severe master.[2] . . . I learnt from him, that Poetry, even that of the loftiest and, seemingly, that of the wildest odes, had a logic of its own, as severe as that of science; and more difficult, because more subtle, more complex, and dependent on more, and more fugitive causes. In the truly great poets, he would say, there is a reason assignable, not only for every word, but for the position of every word. . . .

In our own English compositions . . . he showed no mercy to phrase, metaphor, or image, unsupported by a sound sense, or where the same sense might have been conveyed with equal force and dignity in plainer words. Lute, harp, and lyre, muse, muses, and inspirations, Pegasus, Parnassus, and Hippocrene were all an abomination to him. In fancy I can almost hear him now, exclaiming "*Harp? Harp? Lyre? Pen and ink, boy, you mean! Muse, boy, Muse? Your Nurse's daughter, you mean! Pierian spring? Oh aye! the cloister-pump, I suppose!*" Nay, certain introductions, similes, and examples were placed by name on a list of interdiction. . . .

I had just entered on my seventeenth year, when the sonnets of Mr. Bowles,[3] twenty in number, and just then published in a quarto pamphlet, were first made known and presented to me. . . . My earliest acquaintances will not have forgotten the undisciplined eagerness and impetuous zeal, with which I laboured to make proselytes, not only of my companions, but of all with whom I conversed, of whatever rank, and in whatever place. As my school finances did not permit me to purchase copies, I made, within less than a year and a half, more than forty transcriptions, as the best presents I could offer to those, who had in any way won my regard. And with almost equal delight did I receive the three or four following publications of the same author.

Though I have seen and known enough of mankind to be well aware, that I shall perhaps stand alone in my creed, and that it will be well, if I subject myself to no worse charge than that of singularity; I am not therefore deterred from avowing, that I regard, and ever have regarded the obligations of intellect among the most sacred of the claims of gratitude. A valuable thought, or a particular train of thoughts, gives me additional pleasure, when I can safely refer and attribute it to the conversation or correspondence of another. My obligations to Mr. Bowles were indeed important, and for radical good. At a very premature age, even before my fifteenth year, I had bewildered myself in metaphysicks, and in theological controversy. Nothing else pleased me. History, and particular facts, lost all interest in my mind. Poetry (though for a school-boy of that age, I was above par in English versification, and had already produced two or three compositions which, I may venture to say, without reference to my age, were somewhat above mediocrity, and which had gained me more credit than the sound, good sense of my old master was at all pleased with,) poetry itself, yea, novels and romances, became insipid to me. In my friendless wanderings on our *leave-days*,[4] (for I was an orphan, and had scarcely any connections in London,) highly was I delighted, if any passenger, especially if he were drest in black, would enter into conversation with me. For I soon found the means of directing it to my favorite subjects

Of providence, fore-knowledge, will, and fate,
Fixed fate, free will, fore-knowledge absolute,
And found no end, in wandering mazes lost.[5]

This preposterous pursuit was, beyond doubt, injurious both to my natural powers, and to the progress of my education. It would perhaps have been destructive, had it been continued; but from this I was auspiciously withdrawn, partly indeed by an

---

[1] Wordsworth.
[2] The Rev. James Boyer, long headmaster of Christ's Hospital.
[3] The Rev. William Lisle Bowles (1762–1850); the actual merit of his poems scarcely justifies the youthful Coleridge's enthusiasm.

[4] Coleridge's note: "The Christ's Hospital phrase, not for holidays altogether, but for those on which the boys are permitted to go beyond the precincts of the school."
[5] *Paradise Lost*, II, 559–61.

accidental introduction to an amiable family,[6] chiefly however, by the genial influence of a style of poetry, so tender and yet so manly, so natural and real, and yet so dignified and harmonious, as the sonnets &c. of Mr. Bowles! Well were it for me, perhaps, had I never relapsed into the same mental disease; if I had continued to pluck the flower and reap the harvest from the cultivated surface, instead of delving in the unwholesome quicksilver mines of metaphysic depths. But if in after time I have sought a refuge from bodily pain and mismanaged sensibility in abstruse researches, which exercised the strength and subtlety of the understanding without awakening the feelings of the heart; still there was a long and blessed interval, during which my natural faculties were allowed to expand, and my original tendencies to develope themselves: my fancy, and the love of nature, and the sense of beauty in forms and sounds.

The second advantage, which I owe to my early perusal, and admiration of these poems, . . . bears more immediately on my present subject. Among those with whom I conversed, there were, of course, very many who had formed their taste, and their notions of poetry, from the writings of Mr. Pope and his followers: or to speak more generally, in that school of French poetry, condensed and invigorated by English understanding, which had predominated from the last century. I was not blind to the merits of this school, yet as from inexperience of the world, and consequent want of sympathy with the general subjects of these poems, they gave me little pleasure, I doubtless undervalued the *kind,* and with the presumption of youth withheld from its masters the legitimate name of poets. I saw that the excellence of this kind consisted in just and acute observations on men and manners in an artificial state of society, as its matter and substance: and in the logic of wit, conveyed in smooth and strong epigrammatic couplets, as its *form.* Even when the subject was addressed to the fancy, or the intellect, as in the Rape of the Lock, or the Essay on Man; nay, when it was a consecutive narration, as in that astonishing product of matchless talent and ingenuity, Pope's Translation of the Iliad; still a *point* was looked for at the end of each second line. . . . Meantime the matter and diction seemed to me characterized not so much by poetic thoughts, as by thoughts *translated* into the language of poetry. . . .

The controversies, occasioned by my unfeigned zeal for the honor of a favorite contemporary, then known to me only by his works,[7] were of great advantage in the formation and establishment of my taste and critical opinions. In my defence of the lines running into each other, instead of closing at each couplet, and of natural language, neither bookish, nor vulgar, neither redolent of the lamp, nor of the kennel, such as *I will remember thee;* instead of the same thought tricked up in the rag-fair finery of

——Thy image on her wing
Before my FANCY's eye shall MEMORY bring,

I had continually to adduce the metre and diction of the Greek Poets from Homer to Theocritus inclusive; and still more of our elder English poets from Chaucer to Milton. Nor was this all. But as it was my constant reply to authorities brought against me from later poets of great name, that no authority could avail in opposition to TRUTH, NATURE, LOGIC, and the LAWS of UNIVERSAL GRAMMAR; actuated too by my former passion for metaphysical investigations; I labored at a solid foundation, on which permanently to ground my opinions, in the component faculties of the human mind itself, and their comparative dignity and importance. According to the faculty or source, from which the pleasure given by any poem or passage was derived, I estimated the merit of such poem or passage. As the result of all my reading and meditation, I abstracted two critical aphorisms, deeming them to comprise the conditions and criteria of poetic style; first, that not the poem which we have *read,* but that to which we *return,* with the greatest pleasure, possesses the genuine power, and claims the name of *essential poetry.* Second, that whatever lines can be translated into other words of the same language, without diminution of their significance, either in sense, or association, or in any worthy feeling, are so far vicious in their diction. Be it however observed, that I excluded from the list of worthy feelings, the pleasure derived from mere novelty in the reader, and the desire of exciting wonderment at his powers in the author. . . . Our genuine admiration of a great poet is a continuous *under-current* of feeling; it is everywhere present, but seldom anywhere as a separate excitement. I was wont boldly to affirm, that it would be scarcely more difficult to push a stone out from the pyramids with the bare hand, than to alter a word, or the position of a word, in Milton or Shakespeare, (in their most important works at least,) without making the author say something else, or something worse, than he does say. One great distinction, I appeared to myself to

---

[6] Probably the family of Mary Evans, Coleridge's first love.

[7] Coleridge did not meet Bowles until 1797.

see plainly, between, even the characteristic faults of our elder poets, and the false beauty of the moderns. In the former, from DONNE to COWLEY, we find the most fantastic out-of-the-way thoughts, but in the most pure and genuine mother English; in the latter, the most obvious thoughts, in language the most fantastic and arbitrary. Our faulty elder poets sacrificed the passion and passionate flow of poetry, to the subtleties of intellect, and to the starts of wit; the moderns to the glare and glitter of a perpetual, yet broken and heterogeneous imagery, or rather to an amphibious something, made up, half of image, and half of abstract meaning. The one sacrificed the heart to the head; the other both heart and head to point and drapery.

The reader must make himself acquainted with the general style of composition that was at that time deemed poetry, in order to understand and account for the effect produced on me by the SONNETS, the MONODY at MATLOCK, and the HOPE, of Mr. Bowles; for it is peculiar to original genius to become less and less *striking,* in proportion to its success in improving the taste and judgement of its contemporaries. The poems of WEST,[8] indeed, had the merit of chaste and manly diction, but they were cold, and, if I may so express it, only *dead-coloured;* while in the best of Warton's[9] there is a stiffness, which too often gives them the appearance of imitations from the Greek. Whatever relation therefore of cause or impulse Percy's collection of Ballads[10] may bear to the most *popular* poems of the present day; yet in a more sustained and elevated style, of the then living poets, Bowles and Cowper were, to the best of my knowledge, the first who combined natural thoughts with natural diction; the first who reconciled the heart with the head. . . .

from CHAPTER IV

The lyrical ballads with the preface—Mr. Wordsworth's earlier poems—On fancy and imagination—The investigation of the distinction important to the fine arts.

. . . It will be sufficient for my purpose, if I have proved, that Mr. Southey's writings no more than my own furnished the original occasion to this fiction

of a *new school* of poetry, and to the clamors against its supposed founders and proselytes.[11]

As little do I believe that "Mr. WORDSWORTH's Lyrical Ballads" were in *themselves* the cause. I speak exclusively of the two volumes[12] so entitled. A careful and repeated examination of these confirms me in the belief, that the omission of less than an hundred lines would have precluded nine-tenths of the criticism on this work. I hazard this declaration, however, on the supposition, that the reader has taken it up, as he would have done any other collection of poems purporting to derive their subjects or interests from the incidents of domestic or ordinary life, intermingled with higher strains of meditation which the poet utters in his own person and character; with the proviso, that they were perused without knowledge of, or reference to, the author's peculiar opinions, and that the reader had not had his attention previously directed to those peculiarities. In these, as was actually the case with Mr. Southey's earlier works, the lines and passages which might have offended the general taste, would have been considered as mere inequalities, and attributed to inattention, not to perversity of judgement. The men of business who had passed their lives chiefly in cities, and who might therefore be expected to derive the highest pleasure from acute notices of men and manners conveyed in easy, yet correct and pointed language; and all those who, reading but little poetry, are most stimulated with that species of it, which seems most distant from prose, would probably have passed by the volume altogether. Others more catholic in their taste, and yet habituated to be most pleased when most excited, would have contented themselves with deciding, that the author had been successful in proportion to the elevation of his style and subject. Not a few, perhaps, might by their admiration of "the lines written near Tintern Abbey," those "left upon a Seat under a Yew Tree," the "old Cumberland Beggar," and "Ruth," have been gradually led to peruse with kindred feeling the "Brothers," the "Hart leap well," and whatever other poems in that collection may be described as holding a middle place between those written in the highest and those in the humblest style; as for instance between the "Tintern Abbey," and "the Thorn," or the "Simon Lee." Should their taste submit to no further change, and still remain unreconciled to the

---

8 Gilbert West (1703–56), imitator of Spenser and translator of Pindar and Euripides.

9 Thomas Warton (1728–90), miscellaneous writer and one of the few eighteenth-century authors of sonnets.

10 Bishop Percy's *Reliques of Ancient English Poetry* (1765).

11 In the preceding chapter Coleridge examines Southey's poetry with this aim in view.

12 The two volumes of the second edition, in which Wordsworth's Preface first appeared. The second volume contained poems by Wordsworth not included in the first edition.

colloquial phrases, or the imitations of them, that are, more or less, scattered through the class last mentioned; yet even from the small number of the latter, they would have deemed them but an inconsiderable subtraction from the merit of the whole work; or, what is sometimes not unpleasing in the publication of a new writer, as serving to ascertain the natural tendency, and consequently the proper direction of the author's genius.

In the critical remarks, therefore, prefixed and annexed to the "Lyrical Ballads," I believe that we may safely rest, as the true origin of the unexampled opposition which Mr. Wordsworth's writings have been since doomed to encounter. The humbler passages in the poems themselves were dwelt on and cited to justify the rejection of the theory. What in and for themselves would have been either forgotten or forgiven as imperfections, or at least comparative failures, provoked direct hostility when announced as intentional, as the result of choice after full deliberation. Thus the poems, admitted by *all* as excellent, joined with those which had pleased the far *greater* number, though they formed two-thirds of the whole work, instead of being deemed (as in all right they should have been, even if we take for granted that the reader judged aright) an atonement for the few exceptions, gave wind and fuel to the animosity against both the poems and the poet. . . .

That this conjecture is not wide from the mark, I am induced to believe from the noticeable fact, which I can state on my own knowledge, that the same general censure should have been grounded by almost every different person on some different poem. Among those, whose candour and judgement I estimate highly, I distinctly remember six who expressed their objections to the "Lyrical Ballads" almost in the same words, and altogether to the same purport, at the same time admitting, that several of the poems had given them great pleasure; and, strange as it might seem, the composition which one cited as execrable, another quoted as his favorite. . . . A friend whose *talents* I hold in the highest respect, but whose *judgement* and strong sound sense I have had almost continued occasion to *revere,* making the usual complaints to me concerning both the style and subjects of Mr. Wordsworth's minor poems; I admitted that there were some few of the tales and incidents, in which I could not myself find a sufficient cause for their having been recorded in metre. I mentioned the "Alice Fell" as an instance; "nay," replied my friend with more than usual quickness of manner, "I cannot agree with you *there*!—that, I own, *does* seem to me a remarkably pleasing poem."

In the "Lyrical Ballads" . . . I have heard at different times, and from different individuals every single poem *extolled* and *reprobated,* with the exception of those of loftier kind, which as was before observed, seem to have won universal praise. This fact of itself would have made me diffident in my censures, had not a still stronger ground been furnished by the strange contrast of the heat and long continuance of the opposition, with the nature of the faults stated as justifying it. The seductive faults, the dulcia vitia[13] of Cowley, Marini, or Darwin[14] might reasonably be thought capable of corrupting the public judgement for half a century, and require a twenty years' war, campaign after campaign, in order to dethrone the usurper and re-establish the legitimate taste. But that a downright simpleness, under the affectation of simplicity, prosaic words in feeble metre, silly thoughts in childish phrases, and a preference of mean, degrading, or at best trivial associations and characters, should succeed in forming a school of imitators, a company of almost *religious* admirers, and this too among young men of ardent minds, liberal education, and not

with academic laurels unbestowed;

and that this bare and bald *counterfeit* of poetry, which is characterized as *below* criticism, should for nearly twenty years have well-nigh *engrossed* criticism, as the main, if not the only, *butt* of review, magazine, pamphlet, poem, and paragraph;—this is indeed matter of wonder! Of yet greater is it, that the contest should still continue . . . undecided. . . .

During the last year of my residence at Cambridge, I became acquainted with Mr. Wordsworth's first[15] publication entitled "Descriptive Sketches"; and seldom, if ever, was the emergence of an original poetic genius above the literary horizon more evidently announced. In the form, style, and manner of the whole poem, and in the structure of the particular lines and periods, there is an harshness and acerbity connected and combined with words and images all a-glow, which might recall those products of the vegetable world, where gorgeous blossoms rise out of the hard and thorny rind and shell, within which the rich fruit was elaborating. The language was not

---

[13] This phrase repeats the sense of the preceding one.
[14] Coleridge intends these poets as examples of artificial language and far-fetched conceits. Giambattista Marini or Marino (1569–1625) was an Italian poet. Erasmus Darwin (1731–1802) is more favorably remembered today for his writings on biology than for his poems *The Loves of the Plants* and *The Botanic Garden.*
[15] Actually his second.

only peculiar[16] and strong, but at times knotty and contorted, as by its own impatient strength; while the novelty and struggling crowd of images, acting in conjunction with the difficulties of the style, demanded always a greater closeness of attention, than poetry, (at all events, than descriptive poetry) has a right to claim. It not seldom therefore justified the complaint of obscurity. . . .

The poetic PSYCHE, in its process to full development, undergoes as many changes as its Greek namesake, the butterfly.[17] And it is remarkable how soon genius clears and purifies itself from the faults and errors of its earliest products; faults which, in its earliest compositions, are the more obtrusive and confluent, because as heterogeneous elements, which had only a temporary use, they constitute the very *ferment,* by which themselves are carried off. Or we may compare them to some diseases, which must work on the humours, and be thrown out on the surface, in order to secure the patient from their future recurrence. I was in my twenty-fourth year, when I had the happiness of knowing Mr. Wordsworth personally, and while memory lasts, I shall hardly forget the sudden effect produced on my mind, by his recitation of a manuscript poem, which still remains unpublished, but of which the stanza and tone of style were the same as those of *The Female Vagrant,* as originally printed in the first volume of the "Lyrical Ballads." There was here no mark of strained thought, or forced diction, no crowd or turbulence of imagery; and, as the poet hath himself well described in his lines "on re-visiting the Wye,"[18] manly reflection, and human associations had given both variety, and an additional interest to natural objects, which in the passion and appetite of the first love they had seemed to him neither to need or permit. The occasional obscurities, which had risen from an imperfect controul over the resources of his native language, had almost wholly disappeared, together with that worse defect of arbitrary and illogical phrases, at once hackneyed, and fantastic, which hold so distinguished a place in the *technique* of ordinary poetry, and will, more or less, alloy the earlier poems of the truest genius, unless the attention has been specifically directed to their worthlessness and incongruity. I did not perceive anything particular in the mere style of the poem alluded to during its recitation, except indeed such difference as was not separable from the thought and manner; and the Spenserian stanza, which always, more or less, recalls to the reader's mind Spenser's own style, would doubtless have authorized, in my then opinion, a more frequent descent to the phrases of ordinary life, than could without an ill effect have been hazarded in the heroic couplet. It was not however the freedom from false taste, whether as to common defects, or to those more properly his own, which made so unusual an impression on my feelings immediately, and subsequently on my judgement. It was the union of deep feeling with profound thought; the fine balance of truth in observing, with the imaginative faculty in modifying the objects observed; and above all the original gift of spreading the tone, the *atmosphere,* and with it the depth and height of the ideal world around forms, incidents, and situations, of which, for the common view, custom had bedimmed all the lustre, had dried up the sparkle and the dew drops. "To find no contradiction in the union of old and new; to contemplate the ANCIENT of days and all his works with feelings as fresh, as if all had then sprang forth at the first creative fiat; characterizes the mind that feels the riddle of the world, and may help to unravel it. To carry on the feelings of childhood into the powers of manhood; to combine the child's sense of wonder and novelty with the appearances, which every day for perhaps forty years had rendered familiar;

> With sun and moon and stars throughout the year,
> And man and woman;

this is the character and privilege of genius, and one of the marks which distinguish genius from talents. And therefore is it the prime merit of genius and its most unequivocal mode of manifestation, so to represent familiar objects as to awaken in the minds of others a kindred feeling concerning them and that freshness of sensation which is the constant accompaniment of mental, no less than of bodily, convalescence. Who has not a thousand times seen snow fall on water? Who has not watched it with a new feeling, from the time that he has read Burns's comparison of sensual pleasure

> To snow that falls upon a river
> A moment white—then gone for ever![19]

In poems, equally as in philosophic disquisitions, genius produces the strongest impressions of novelty, while it rescues the most admitted truths from the

---

[16] Distinctive.
[17] Coleridge quotes (in a note) from "an unpublished poem" of his own ("The Butterfly"):
   "The butterfly the ancient Grecians made
   The soul's fair emblem, and its only name. . . ."
[18] "Tintern Abbey."

[19] Misquoted from "Tam o' Shanter," lines 61 f.

impotence caused by the very circumstance of their universal admission. Truths of all others the most awful and mysterious, yet being at the same time of universal interest, are too often considered as *so* true, that they lose all the life and efficiency of truth, and lie bed-ridden in the dormitory of the soul, side by side with the most despised and exploded errors." [20] . . .

CHAPTER XIV

Occasion of the Lyrical Ballads, and the objects originally proposed—Preface to the second edition—The ensuing controversy, its causes and acrimony—Philosophic definitions of a poem and poetry with scholia.

During the first year that Mr. Wordsworth and I were neighbours, our conversations turned frequently on the two cardinal points of poetry, the power of exciting the sympathy of the reader by a faithful adherence to the truth of nature, and the power of giving the interest of novelty by the modifying colors of imagination. The sudden charm, which accidents of light and shade, which moon-light or sun-set diffused over a known and familiar landscape, appeared to represent the practicability of combining both. These are the poetry of nature. The thought suggested itself (to which of us I do not recollect) that a series of poems might be composed of two sorts. In the one, the incidents and agents were to be, in part at least, supernatural; and the excellence aimed at was to consist in the interesting of the affections[21] by the dramatic truth of such emotions, as would naturally accompany such situations, supposing them real. And real in *this* sense they have been to every human being who, from whatever source of delusion, has at any time believed himself under supernatural agency. For the second class, subjects were to be chosen from ordinary life; the characters and incidents were to be such, as will be found in every village and its vicinity, where there is a meditative and feeling mind to seek after them, or to notice them, when they present themselves.

In this idea originated the plan of the "Lyrical Ballads"; in which it was agreed, that my endeavours should be directed to persons and characters supernatural, or at least romantic; yet so as to transfer from our inward nature a human interest and a semblance of truth sufficient to procure for these shadows of imagination that willing suspension of disbelief for the moment, which constitutes poetic faith. Mr. Wordsworth, on the other hand, was to propose to himself as his object, to give the charm of novelty to things of every day, and to excite a feeling analogous to the supernatural, by awakening the mind's attention to the lethargy of custom, and directing it to the loveliness and the wonders of the world before us; an inexhaustible treasure, but for which, in consequence of the film of familiarity and selfish solicitude, we have eyes, yet see not, ears that hear not, and hearts that neither feel nor understand.

With this view I wrote "The Ancient Mariner," and was preparing among other poems, "The Dark Ladie," and the "Christabel," in which I should have more nearly realized my ideal, than I had done in my first attempt. But Mr. Wordsworth's industry had proved so much more successful, and the number of his poems so much greater,[22] that my compositions, instead of forming a balance, appeared rather an interpolation of heterogeneous matter. Mr. Wordsworth added two or three poems written in his own character, in the impassioned, lofty, and sustained diction, which is characteristic of his genius. In this form the "Lyrical Ballads" were published; and were presented by him, as an *experiment,* whether subjects, which from their nature rejected the usual ornaments and extra-colloquial style of poems in general, might not be so managed in the language of ordinary life as to produce the pleasurable interest, which it is the peculiar business of poetry to impart. To the second edition he added a preface of considerable length; in which, notwithstanding some passages of apparently a contrary import, he was understood to contend for the extension of this style to poetry of all kinds, and to reject as vicious and indefensible all phrases and forms of style that were not included in what he (unfortunately, I think, adopting an equivocal expression) called the language of *real* life. From this preface, prefixed to poems in which it was impossible to deny the presence of original genius, however mistaken its direction might be deemed, arose the whole long-continued controversy. For from the conjunction of perceived power with supposed heresy I explain the inveteracy and in some instances, I grieve to say, the acrimonious passions, with which the controversy has been conducted by the assailants.

Had Mr. Wordsworth's poems been the silly, the childish things, which they were for a long time described as being: had they been really distinguished from the compositions of other poets merely by

---

[20] This long quotation is from an earlier work by Coleridge, *The Friend,* no. 5.   [21] Emotions.

[22] Only four of the twenty-three poems in the first edition were by Coleridge.

meanness of language and inanity of thought; had they indeed contained nothing more than what is found in the parodies and pretended imitations of them; they must have sunk at once, a dead weight, into the slough of oblivion, and have dragged the preface along with them. But year after year increased the number of Mr. Wordsworth's admirers. They were found too not in the lower classes of the reading public, but chiefly among young men of strong sensibility and meditative minds; and their admiration (inflamed perhaps in some degree by opposition) was distinguished by its intensity, I might almost say, by its *religious* fervour. These facts, and the intellectual energy of the author, which was more or less consciously felt, where it was outwardly and even boisterously denied, meeting with sentiments of aversion to his opinions, and of alarm at their consequences, produced an eddy of criticism, which would of itself have borne up the poems by the violence, with which it whirled them round and round. With many parts of this preface, in the sense attributed to them, and which the words undoubtedly seem to authorize, I never concurred; but on the contrary objected to them as erroneous in principle, and as contradictory (in appearance at least) both to other parts of the same preface, and to the author's own practice in the greater number of the poems themselves. Mr. Wordsworth in his recent collection has, I find, degraded this prefatory disquisition to the end of his second volume, to be read or not at the reader's choice. But he has not, as far as I can discover, announced any change in his poetic creed. At all events, considering it as the source of a controversy, in which I have been honoured more than I deserve by the frequent conjunction of my name with his, I think it expedient to declare once for all, in what points I coincide with his opinions, and in what points I altogether differ. But in order to render myself intelligible I must previously, in as few words as possible, explain my views, first, of a POEM; and secondly, of POETRY itself, in *kind,* and in *essence.*

The office of philosophical *disquisition* consists in just *distinction;* while it is the privilege of the philosopher to preserve himself constantly aware, that distinction is not division. In order to obtain adequate notions of any truth, we must intellectually separate its distinguishable parts; and this is the technical *process* of philosophy. But having so done, we must then restore them in our conceptions to the unity, in which they actually co-exist; and this is the *result* of philosophy. A poem contains the same elements as a prose composition; the difference therefore must consist in a different combination of them, in conse-

quence of a different object being proposed. According to the difference of the object will be the difference of the combination. It is possible, that the object may be merely to facilitate the recollection of any given facts or observations by artificial arrangement; and the composition will be a poem, merely because it is distinguished from prose by metre, or by rhyme, or by both conjointly. In this, the lowest sense, a man might attribute the name of a poem to the well-known enumeration of the days in the several months:

> Thirty days hath September,
> April, June, and November, &c.

and others of the same class and purpose. And as a particular pleasure is found in anticipating the recurrence of sounds and quantities, all compositions that have this charm super-added, whatever be their contents, *may* be entitled poems.

So much for the superficial *form.* A difference of object and contents supplies an additional ground of distinction. The immediate purpose may be the communication of truths; either of truth absolute and demonstrable, as in works of science; or of facts experienced and recorded, as in history. Pleasure, and that of the highest and most permanent kind, may *result* from the *attainment* of the end; but it is not itself the immediate end. In other works the communication of pleasure may be the immediate purpose; and though truth, either moral or intellectual, ought to be the *ultimate* end, yet this will distinguish the character of the author, not the class to which the work belongs. Blest indeed is that state of society, in which the immediate purpose would be baffled by the perversion of the proper ultimate end; in which no charm of diction or imagery could exempt the Bathyllus[23] even of an Anacreon, or the Alexis[24] of Virgil, from disgust and aversion!

But the communication of pleasure may be the immediate object of a work not metrically composed; and that object may have been in a high degree attained, as in novels and romances. Would then the mere superaddition of metre, with or without rhyme, entitle *these* to the name of poems? The answer is, that nothing can permanently please, which does not contain in itself the reason why it is so, and not otherwise. If metre be superadded, all other parts must be made consonant with it. They must be such, as to justify the perpetual and distinct

---

23 A youth of Samos loved by the tyrant Polycrates (sixth century B.C.) and mentioned by the Greek poet Anacreon (d. 488? B.C.).
24 A youth loved by a shepherd in the Second Eclogue of Vergil.

attention to each part, which an exact correspondent recurrence of accent and sound are calculated to excite. The final definition then, so deduced, may be thus worded. A poem is that species of composition, which is opposed to works of science, by proposing for its *immediate* object pleasure, not truth; and from all other species (having *this* object in common with it) it is discriminated by proposing to itself such delight from the *whole*, as is compatible with a distinct gratification from each component *part.*

Controversy is not seldom excited in consequence of the disputants attaching each a different meaning to the same word; and in few instances has this been more striking, than in disputes concerning the present subject. If a man chooses to call every composition a poem, which is rhyme, or measure, or both, I must leave his opinion uncontroverted. The distinction is at least competent to characterize the writer's intention. If it were subjoined, that the whole is likewise entertaining or affecting, as a tale, or as a series of interesting reflections, I of course admit this as another fit ingredient of a poem, and an additional merit. But if the definition sought for be that of a *legitimate* poem, I answer, it must be one, the parts of which mutually support and explain each other; all in their proportion harmonizing with, and supporting the purpose and known influences of metrical arrangement. The philosophic critics of all ages coincide with the ultimate judgement of all countries, in equally denying the praises of a just poem, on the one hand, to a series of striking lines or distiches,[25] each of which, absorbing the whole attention of the reader to itself, disjoins it from its context, and makes it a separate whole, instead of an harmonizing part; and on the other hand, to an unsustained composition, from which the reader collects rapidly the general result, unattracted by the component parts. The reader should be carried forward, not merely or chiefly by the mechanical impulse of curiosity, or by a restless desire to arrive at the final solution; but by the pleasureable activity of mind excited by the attractions of the journey itself. Like the motion of a serpent, which the Egyptians made the emblem of intellectual power; or like the path of sound through the air; at every step he pauses and half recedes, and from the retrogressive movement collects the force which again carries him onward. "Praecipitandus est *liber* spiritus,"[26] says Petronius Arbiter most happily. The epithet, *liber,* here balances the preceding verb;

and it is not easy to conceive more meaning condensed in fewer words.

But if this should be admitted as a satisfactory character of a poem, we have still to seek for a definition of poetry. The writings of PLATO, and Bishop TAYLOR,[27] and the "Theoria Sacra" of BURNET,[28] furnish undeniable proofs that poetry of the highest kind may exist without metre, and even without the contradistinguishing objects of a poem. The first chapter of Isaiah (indeed a very large portion of the whole book) is poetry in the most emphatic sense; yet it would be not less irrational than strange to assert, that pleasure, and not truth, was the immediate object of the prophet. In short, whatever *specific* import we attach to the word, poetry, there will be found involved in it, as a necessary consequence, that a poem of any length neither can be, or ought to be, all poetry. Yet if an harmonious whole is to be produced, the remaining parts must be preserved *in keeping* with the poetry; and this can be no otherwise effected than by such a studied selection and artificial arrangement, as will partake of *one*, though not a *peculiar* property of poetry. And this again can be no other than the property of exciting a more continuous and equal attention than the language of prose aims at, whether colloquial or written.

My own conclusions on the nature of poetry, in the strictest use of the word, have been in part anticipated in the preceding disquisition on the fancy and imagination.[29] What is poetry? is so nearly the same question with, what is a poet? that the answer to the one is involved in the solution of the other. For it is a distinction resulting from the poetic genius itself, which sustains and modifies the images, thoughts, and emotions of the poet's own mind.

The poet, described in *ideal* perfection, brings the whole soul of man into activity, with the subordination of its faculties to each other, according to their relative worth and dignity. He diffuses a tone and spirit of unity, that blends, and (as it were) *fuses,* each into each, by that synthetic and magical power, to which I would exclusively appropriate the name of imagination. This power, first put in action by the will and understanding, and retained under their irremissive,[30] though gentle and unnoticed, controul

25 Two-line units of verse.
26 A free spirit ought to be hurled along—i.e., if a poem is to seem inspired. (Petronius [1st century], *Satyricon,* chap. 118.)

27 Jeremy Taylor (1613–67), author of *The Liberty of Prophesying, Holy Living, Holy Dying,* etc.
28 The Rev. Thomas Burnet (d. 1715). His *Telluris Theoria Sacra* (in an English as well as a Latin text) propounded a fanciful theory of the origin of the earth.
29 In Chapter IV. Coleridge considered them "distinct and widely different faculties."
30 I.e., unremitting, incessant.

(*laxis effertur habenis*),[31] reveals itself in the balance or reconciliation of opposite or discordant qualities: of sameness, with difference; of the general, with the concrete; the idea, with the image; the individual, with the representative; the sense of novelty and freshness, with old and familiar objects; a more than usual state of emotion, with more than usual order; judgement ever awake and steady self-possession, with enthusiasm and feeling profound or vehement; and while it blends and harmonizes the natural and the artificial, still subordinates art to nature; the manner to the matter; and our admiration of the poet to our sympathy with the poetry. Doubtless, as Sir John Davies observes of the soul (and his words[32] may with slight alteration be applied, and even more appropriately, to the poetic IMAGINATION)

Doubtless this could not be, but that she turns
　Bodies to spirit by sublimation strange,
As fire converts to fire the things it burns,
　As we our food into our nature change.

From their gross matter she abstracts their forms,
　And draws a kind of quintessence from things;
Which to her proper[33] nature she transforms
　To bear them light on her celestial wings.

Thus does she, when from individual states
　She doth abstract the universal kinds;
Which then re-clothed in divers names and fates
　Steal access through our senses to our minds.

Finally, GOOD SENSE is the BODY of poetic genius, FANCY its DRAPERY, MOTION its LIFE, and IMAGINATION the SOUL that is everywhere, and in each; and forms all into one graceful and intelligent whole.

CHAPTER XV

The specific symptoms of poetic power elucidated in a critical analysis of Shakespeare's Venus and Adonis, and Lucrece.

In the application of these principles to purposes of practical criticism as employed in the appraisement of works more or less imperfect, I have endeavoured to discover what the qualities in a poem are, which may be deemed promises and specific symptoms of poetic power, as distinguished from general talent determined to poetic composition by accidental motives, by an act of the will, rather than by the inspiration of a genial and productive nature. In this investigation I could not, I thought, do better, than keep before me the earliest work of the greatest genius, that perhaps human nature has yet produced, our *myriad-minded* Shakespeare. I mean the "Venus and Adonis," and the "Lucrece";[34] works which give at once strong promises of the strength, and yet obvious proofs of the immaturity, of his genius. From these I abstracted the following marks, as characteristics of original poetic genius in general.

1. In the "Venus and Adonis," the first and most obvious excellence is the perfect sweetness of the versification; its adaptation to the subject; and the power displayed in varying the march of the words without passing into a loftier and more majestic rhythm than was demanded by the thoughts, or permitted by the propriety of preserving a sense of melody predominant. The delight in richness and sweetness of sound, even to a faulty excess, if it be evidently original, and not the result of an easily imitable mechanism, I regard as a highly favourable promise in the compositions of a young man. "The man that hath not music in his soul"[35] can indeed never be a genuine poet. Imagery (even taken from nature, much more when transplanted from books, as travels, voyages, and works of natural history); affecting incidents; just thoughts; interesting personal or domestic feelings; and with these the art of their combination or intertexture in the form of a poem; may all by incessant effort be acquired as a trade, by a man of talents and much reading, who, as I once before observed, has mistaken an intense desire of poetic reputation for a natural poetic genius; the love of the arbitrary end for a possession of the peculiar means. But the sense of musical delight, with the power of producing it, is a gift of imagination; and this together with the power of reducing multitude into unity of effect, and modifying a series of thoughts by some one predominant thought or feeling, may be cultivated and improved, but can never be learned. It is in these that "poeta nascitur non fit."[36]

2. A second promise of genius is the choice of subjects very remote from the private interests and circumstances of the writer himself. At least I have found, that where the subject is taken immediately from the author's personal sensations and experiences, the excellence of a particular poem is but an equivocal mark, and often a fallacious pledge, of genuine poetic power. We may perhaps remember

---

[31] Is carried along with loose reins. (Inaccurately quoted from Vergil, *Georgics*, II, 364.)
[32] Inaccurately quoted from Davies's "Of the Soul of Man," *Nosce Teipsum* (ed. Grosart, I, 43). 　　[33] Own.

[34] These poems were printed in 1593 and 1594.
[35] Cf. *The Merchant of Venice*, V, i, 83.
[36] A poet is born, not made.

the tale of the statuary,[37] who had acquired considerable reputation for the legs of his goddesses, though the rest of the statue accorded but indifferently with ideal beauty; till his wife, elated by her husband's praises, modestly acknowledged that she herself had been his constant model. In the "Venus and Adonis" this proof of poetic power exists even to excess. It is throughout as if a superior spirit more intuitive, more intimately conscious, even than the characters themselves, not only of every outward look and act, but of the flux and reflux of the mind in all its subtlest thoughts and feelings, were placing the whole before our view; himself meanwhile unparticipating in the passions, and actuated only by that pleasurable excitement, which had resulted from the energetic fervor of his own spirit in so vividly exhibiting what it had so accurately and profoundly contemplated. I think, I should have conjectured from these poems, that even then the great instinct, which impelled the poet to the drama, was secretly working in him, prompting him by a series and never broken chain of imagery, always vivid and, because unbroken, often minute; by the highest effort of the picturesque in words, of which words are capable, higher perhaps than was ever realized by any other poet, even Dante not excepted; to provide a substitute for that visual language, that constant intervention and running comment by tone, look and gesture, which in his dramatic works he was entitled to expect from the players. His Venus and Adonis seem at once the characters themselves and the whole representation of those characters by the most consummate actors. You seem to be told nothing, but to see and hear everything. Hence it is, that from the perpetual activity of attention required on the part of the reader; from the rapid flow, the quick change, and the playful nature of the thoughts and images; and above all from the alienation, and, if I may hazard such an expression, the utter *aloofness* of the poet's own feelings, from those of which he is at once the painter and the analyst; that though the very subject cannot but detract from the pleasure of a delicate mind, yet never was poem less dangerous on a moral account. Instead of doing as Ariosto,[38] and as, still more offensively, Wieland[39] has done, instead of degrading and deforming passion into appetite, the trials of love into the struggles of concupiscence; Shakespeare has

here represented the animal impulse itself, so as to preclude all sympathy with it, by dissipating the reader's notice among the thousand outward images, and now beautiful, now fanciful circumstances, which form its dresses and its scenery; or by diverting our attention from the main subject by those frequent witty or profound reflections, which the poet's ever active mind has deduced from, or connected with, the imagery and the incidents. The reader is forced into too much action to sympathize with the merely passive of our nature. As little can a mind thus roused and awakened be brooded on by mean and indistinct emotion, as the low, lazy mist can creep upon the surface of a lake, while a strong gale is driving it onward in waves and billows.

3. It has been before observed that images, however beautiful, though faithfully copied from nature, and as accurately represented in words, do not of themselves characterize the poet. They become proofs of original genius only as far as they are modified by a predominant passion; or by associated thoughts or images awakened by that passion; or when they have the effect of reducing multitude to unity, or succession to an instant; or lastly, when a human and intellectual life is transferred to them from the poet's own spirit,

Which shoots its being through earth, sea, and air.[40]

In the two following lines for instance, there is nothing objectionable, nothing which would preclude them from forming, in their proper place, part of a descriptive poem:

Behold yon row of pines, that shorn and bow'd
Bend from the sea-blast, seen at twilight eve.

But with a small alteration of rhythm, the same words would be equally in their place in a book of topography, or in a descriptive tour. The same image will rise into semblance of poetry if thus conveyed:

Yon row of bleak and visionary pines,
By twilight glimpse discerned, mark! how they flee
From the fierce sea-blast, all their tresses wild
Streaming before them.

I have given this as an illustration, by no means as an instance, of that particular excellence which I had in view, and in which Shakespeare even in his earliest, as in his latest, works surpasses all other poets. It is by this, that he still gives a dignity and a passion to the objects which he presents. Unaided by any previous

---

37 Sculptor.
38 The Renaissance Italian writer Ludovico Ariosto (1474–1533), author of the romantic epic *Orlando Furioso*.
39 Christoph Martin Wieland (1733–1813), German novelist and poet.

40 Cf. "France: An Ode," line 103 (p. 109, above).

excitement, they burst upon us at once in life and in power.

> Full many a glorious morning have I seen
> *Flatter* the mountain tops with sovereign eye.
> Shakespeare, Sonnet 33rd.

> Not mine own fears, nor the prophetic soul
> Of the wide world dreaming on things to come—
>
> *   *   *   *   *   *   *
> *   *   *   *   *   *   *
>
> The mortal moon hath her eclipse endur'd,
> And the sad augurs mock their own presage;
> Incertainties now crown themselves assur'd,
> And peace proclaims olives of endless age.
> Now with the drops of this most balmy time
> My Love looks fresh, and DEATH to me subscribes!
> Since spite of him, I'll live in this poor rhyme,
> While he insults o'er dull and speechless tribes.
> And thou in this shalt find thy monument,
> When tyrants' crests, and tombs of brass are spent.
> Sonnet 107.

As of higher worth, so doubtless still more characteristic of poetic genius does the imagery become, when it moulds and colors itself to the circumstances, passion, or character, present and foremost in the mind. For unrivalled instances of this excellence, the reader's own memory will refer him to the LEAR, OTHELLO, in short to which not of the *"great, ever living, dead man's"* dramatic works? "Inopem me copia fecit."[41] How true it is to nature, he has himself finely expressed in the instance of love in Sonnet 98.

> From you have I been absent in the spring,
> When proud pied April drest in all its trim
> Hath put a spirit of youth in every thing,
> That heavy Saturn laugh'd and leap'd with him.
> Yet nor the lays of birds, nor the sweet smell
> Of different flowers in odour and in hue,
> Could make me any summer's story tell,
> Or from their proud lap pluck them, where they grew:
> Nor did I wonder at the lilies white,
> Nor praise the deep vermilion in the rose;
> They were, tho' sweet, but figures of delight,
> Drawn after you, you pattern of all those.
> Yet seem'd it winter still, and, you away,
> *As with your shadow I with these did play!*

Scarcely less sure, or if a less valuable, not less indispensable mark

> Γονίμου μεν ποιητοῦ——
> ——ὅστις ῥῆμα γενναῖον λάκοι,[42]

will the imagery supply, when, with more than the power of the painter, the poet gives us the liveliest image of succession with the feeling of simultaneousness!

> With this, he breaketh from the sweet embrace
> Of those fair arms, that held him to her heart,
> And homeward through the dark lawns runs apace:
> *Look! how a bright star shooteth from the sky,*
> *So glides he in the night from Venus' eye.*[43]

4. The last character I shall mention, which would prove indeed but little, except as taken conjointly with the former; yet without which the former could scarce exist in a high degree, and (even if this were possible) would give promises only of transitory flashes and a meteoric power; is DEPTH, and ENERGY OF THOUGHT. No man was ever yet a great poet, without being at the same time a profound philosopher. For poetry is the blossom and the fragrancy of all human knowledge, human thoughts, human passions, emotions, language. In Shakespeare's *poems* the creative power and the intellectual energy wrestle as in a war embrace. Each in its excess of strength seems to threaten the extinction of the other. At length in the DRAMA they were reconciled, and fought each with its shield before the breast of the other. Or like two rapid streams that, at their first meeting within narrow and rocky banks, mutually strive to repel each other and intermix reluctantly and in tumult; but soon finding a wider channel and more yielding shores blend, and dilate, and flow on in one current and with one voice. The "Venus and Adonis" did not perhaps allow the display of the deeper passions. But the story of Lucretia seems to favor and even demand their intensest workings. And yet we find in *Shakespeare's* management of the tale neither pathos, nor any other *dramatic* quality. There is the same minute and faithful imagery as in the former poem, in the same vivid colors, inspirited by the same impetuous vigor of thought, and diverging and contracting with the same activity of the assimilative and of the modifying faculties; and with a yet larger display, a yet wider range of knowledge and reflection; and lastly, with the same perfect dominion, often *domination,* over the whole world of language. What then shall we say? even this; that Shakespeare, no mere child of nature; no automaton of genius; no passive vehicle of inspiration possessed by the spirit, not possessing it; first studied patiently, meditated deeply, understood minutely, till knowledge,

---

[41] I.e., the wealth of examples overwhelms me.
[42] Of a real poet, one who uttered a noble expression (adapted from Aristophanes, *The Frogs,* lines 96–7).

[43] *Venus and Adonis,* lines 811 ff. Coleridge omits the fourth line of the stanza.

become habitual and intuitive, wedded itself to his habitual feelings, and at length gave birth to that stupendous power, by which he stands alone, with no equal or second in his own class; to that power which seated him on one of the two glory-smitten summits of the poetic mountain, with Milton as his compeer, not rival. While the former darts himself forth, and passes into all the forms of human character and passion, the one Proteus of the fire and flood; the other attracts all forms and things to himself, into the unity of his own IDEAL. All things and modes of action shape themselves anew in the being of MILTON, while SHAKESPEARE becomes all things, yet for ever remaining himself. O what great men hast thou not produced, England! my country! truly indeed—

Must *we* be free or die, who speak the tongue,
Which SHAKESPEARE spake; the faith and morals hold,
Which MILTON held. In every thing we are sprung
Of earth's first blood, have titles manifold!
—WORDSWORTH[44]

Charles Lamb

1775–1834

THE FAMILIAR ESSAY differs from the Baconian by reason of its casual air, the intimacy with which the reader is addressed, and the author's appearance of having abandoned all reserve. Its wisdom may be as ripe as you will find in any kind of writing, but its tone is conversational, and the first personal pronoun is likely to be prominent. The best familiar essayists are pleasant egotists; the more they are encouraged by the public, the more egotistical they grow. What interests the essayist, he is confident, ought to interest everyone—even his merely personal experiences, the least of the incidents he has witnessed, the most trivial of his habits, tastes, and prejudices. This genre is therefore dependent on the personality of the writer. When you have read a man's familiar essays you feel that you know him. You will not keep on reading them unless you like him. Of all who have practiced this genre in England, Charles Lamb is the greatest and the best beloved. "Great" may seem too grand a word for these masterpieces of informality, but there is no escaping it.

Lamb was a Londoner through and through, the most infatuated with his subject of all who have written about London. He would not, he averred, exchange its dirtiest alley for the most imposing mountain in Cumberland. His view of the city was not the realist's nor the satirist's, but the romantic's; to the end of his life London was for Lamb a place of wonders. He was actually born within the precincts of an old London institution, the Inner Temple, where his father was a lawyer's clerk. He was seven when he entered another, the school of Christ's Hospital; Coleridge and Leigh Hunt were among his contemporaries there. One of Lamb's best-known essays is a description of "Christ's Hospital Five and Thirty Years Ago." The universities were not for him; he had no money, and a lifelong inability to conquer stammering barred his chances for a scholarship. He was not quite fifteen when he left school, and only seventeen when he entered the employ of the world's largest commercial enterprise, the East India Company, for which he worked as a bookkeeper at the East India House in Leadenhall Street for thirty-three years.

On the whole Lamb's essays appear to reflect a sunny life, and certainly he had out of life an immense amount of fun. Yet it was deeply clouded with tragedy. As a youth he was disappointed in love. For a time his mind was deranged, and he spent several weeks in an asylum. His recovery was complete and permanent; but about a year later, when he was in his twenty-second year, his sister Mary, then thirty-two, went insane. Before he could wrest the knife from her hand, she killed their invalid mother. On Mary's release from confinement Lamb abandoned all thought of marriage and assumed the burden of caring for her. The devoted pair are sometimes pictured bowed down by extreme poverty. Such was never the case, though they were obliged to live carefully; but whether poor or as in later years comfortably well off, Lamb was always the soul of generosity. He was not a borrower but a lender, and his habit when approached by a beggar was to thrust his hand into his pocket and bestow whatever coins came out with it. At first his responsibilities were heavy, despite the existence of an older brother who was a clerk at the South Sea House. Their father was in his dotage; he died in 1799. Mary had long and entirely lucid intervals; but she was subject to recurrent though brief attacks of madness. When Lamb saw the symptoms beginning he would lead her away to the asylum.

---

[44] From the sonnet beginning "It is not to be thought of," lines 11–14 (pp. 68 f., above).

Lamb's verse, both the early and the late, is of slender value. In his first important literary venture, a book for children, the popular *Tales from Shakespeare* (1807), Mary collaborated; she did the comedies and Charles the tragedies. The following year he edited *Specimens of English Dramatic Poets Who Lived about the Time of Shakespeare,* a book which became a major influence on the so-called Elizabethan Revival. Most of the old dramatists had been neglected during the eighteenth century. Lamb's anthology of short excerpts, with appreciative comments, brought them again into notice; moreover, it established his reputation as a critic.

He and Mary were now living, despite the shadow which always threatened, an uncommonly full life. They were voracious readers and playgoers and haunters of picture galleries. They were also great walkers, who thought nothing of a stroll of twenty or thirty miles. And they were rich in friends, by whom they were much visited. Coleridge and the Wordsworths headed the list, especially Coleridge, whom Lamb described as an "archangel, a little damaged," but also as the "touchstone of all my cogitations." Probably no other Englishman of the time had for intimates as many remarkable men as Lamb did. His circle also included Hazlitt, De Quincey, Southey, Leigh Hunt, the diarist Henry Crabb Robinson, the poet Tom Hood, the philosopher William Godwin, Thomas Barnes (first great editor of the London *Times*), the dramatist Sheridan Knowles, the lawyer and poet Bryan Waller Procter ("Barry Cornwall"), Vincent Novello (organist, composer, and founder of the great music-publishing house), the historical painter Benjamin Robert Haydon, the lawyer and dramatic poet Thomas Noon Talfourd, and a host of lesser lights. Not every name in the list is a great one; but these were all interesting men. In their company Lamb was as unpredictable as in his essays, capable in a drawing room of leapfrogging without advance notice over a fellow guest who happened to be stooping, or of infuriating a very minor but pretentious poet by introducing into his conversation scraps from his victim's poems as juvenile compositions of his own and capping the climax by quoting the opening lines of *Paradise Lost* as an excerpt from an early work by Charles Lamb.

Actually, his early work was undistinguished. He tried to supplement his income with prose fiction, drama, journalism, and children's books. One of his plays, a farce, was put on at Drury Lane; but it was damned on the opening night, and Lamb joined in the hisses lest he be taken for the author. Though he brought out a two-volume edition of his works in 1818, he did not really find himself as a writer till he was forty-five. Presumably the search had not been accelerated by his fondness for getting tipsy. It was in the pages of a new periodical, the *London Magazine,* that he made during the years 1820–1825 his permanent place in English literature with the essays signed "Elia." In them his whimsical personality, his delight in London and its oddities, his fund of human sympathy, and his quaint humor found a perfect medium of expression.

He was like his essays; that is attested by his letters, and by the innumerable anecdotes of his friends. And the charm of the essays arises principally from their being like their author. Once Lamb was asked whether he had ever heard Coleridge preach. He replied he had never heard him do anything else. His own aim is quite different. Unlike Bacon, Addison, Steele, and Johnson, he has no itch to improve his readers. What he wants is not to instruct but to share. It is a romantic aim, a poet's aim. Having found delight in certain things, whether common or out-of-the-way, he is anxious that we should not miss them. Thus in his own odd fashion he, too, is a kind of Ancient Mariner, not wishful of converting us to anything but eager to buttonhole us and open our eyes—not to abstract and universal truths, but to the presence all around us of all sorts of particular objects that can make life more interesting. His manner of accomplishing this is above all else whimsical; but Lamb goes beyond any predecessor in widening the range of the English essay.

In 1825 he retired from the East India House on a good pension; and, soon after, he and Mary moved to Enfield, a suburb ten miles out to the north. Their household included Emma Isola, an orphan they had adopted; shortly before Lamb's death she married the publisher Edward Moxon. In 1833 the Lambs moved for the last time, to Edmonton, one suburb closer to the city—the busses into London ran oftener, as Charles gleefully explains in a letter. His last years were saddened by the death of many a friend, and by the increasing frequency of Mary's attacks. He died in 1834, but she lived till 1847, on an annuity from the East India Company.

The standard edition of *The Works of Charles and Mary Lamb* (7 vols., 1903–5) was edited by E. V. Lucas. He also edited their letters (3 vols., 1935), some of which are fully as good as the famous essays. There are cheap reprints of the latter in Everyman's Library and The World's Classics, and Everyman also has two volumes of letters. The standard Life is by Lucas (revised ed., 2 vols., 1921). It is a charming account, rambling but helpfully indexed. A. Ainger's biography (1882) in the English Men of Letters series is more succinct. W. D. Howe's *Charles Lamb and His Friends* (1944) is a delightful and well-illustrated scrapbook.

Charles Lamb

THE OLD FAMILIAR FACES

Lamb's reputation is for his prose, but the following poem is characteristic and a great favorite. It was written and published in 1798, but the present text agrees with Lamb's revised version. Originally the poem contained, as lines 2-4, a stanza, subsequently and wisely canceled, referring to Lamb's mother and the "day of horrors" when his sister killed her. This is one of the few successful unrimed lyrics in English.

Where are they gone, the old familiar faces?

I have had playmates, I have had companions,
In my days of childhood, in my joyful school-days,
All, all are gone, the old familiar faces.

I have been laughing, I have been carousing,   5
Drinking late, sitting late, with my bosom cronies,
All, all are gone, the old familiar faces.

I loved a love[1] once, fairest among women;
Closed are her doors on me, I must not see her,
All, all are gone, the old familiar faces.   10

I have a friend,[2] a kinder friend has no man;
Like an ingrate, I left my friend abruptly;
Left him, to muse on the old familiar faces.

Ghost-like, I paced round the haunts of my childhood.
Earth seemed a desert I was bound to traverse,   15
Seeking to find the old familiar faces.

Friend of my bosom,[3] thou more than a brother,
Why wert not thou born in my father's dwelling?
So might we talk of the old familiar faces—

For some they have died, and some they have left me,
And some are taken from me;[4] all are departed;   21
All, all are gone, the old familiar faces.

ON THE TRAGEDIES OF SHAKSPEARE

CONSIDERED WITH REFERENCE TO THEIR FITNESS FOR STAGE REPRESENTATION

In this provocative essay Lamb argues that the presentation of a Shakespearean play is necessarily a reduction and distortion of the total experience which we receive from reading it. This is mainly due to the fact that Shakespeare's subtle analysis of the inner life, of individual thought and feeling, cannot be translated to the stage; in the theater it is sacrificed to a primary emphasis on action, or blurred by rough and conventional modes of depicting the passions. Though he overstates his case by failing to admit that a good actor, or that visual action and sound, may well reveal things in the text which a reader misses, Lamb is fundamentally right. The sensitive, educated mind will come closer to assimilating *Hamlet* by reading it than by seeing the best possible performance. But perhaps the main reason for this is not the one which Lamb emphasizes. It is the packed density of Shakespeare's writing, both structural and stylistic. Only slow, concentrated reading, with time to compare and contrast scenes widely separated in the play, can enable us to approach the whole meaning. (Lamb has this point in mind in the third paragraph, but he makes little of it.)

Historically, the essay shows the influence of Romanticism in the worship of Shakespeare as the inspired and original genius, the seizing on the internal workings of the mind as the point of primary interest (cf. Wordsworth's Preface to *Lyrical Ballads*, pp. 69 ff., above), and the admiration of great and heroic natures, even including criminals (cf. the Byronic hero with what Lamb says about Richard III).

Lamb contributed the essay to Leigh Hunt's *Reflector* (1811). The following text is based on the 1818 *Works*.

TAKING a turn the other day in the Abbey, I was struck with the affected attitude of a figure, which I do not remember to have seen before, and which upon examination proved to be a whole-length of the celebrated Mr. Garrick.[1] Though I would not go so far with some good Catholics abroad as to shut

---

[1] Her name was Anne Simmons.
[2] Perhaps Charles Lloyd, a friend of Coleridge. Lamb collaborated with him in the volume *Blank Verse* (1798), where this poem first appeared.
[3] Very likely Coleridge, to whose volume of 1796 Lamb had contributed a few verses.
[4] Probably a reference to his sister's removal to an asylum. These six words were italicized in the first version.

[1] This great actor had died in 1779.

players altogether out of consecrated ground, yet I own I was not a little scandalized at the introduction of theatrical airs and gestures into a place set apart to remind us of the saddest realities. Going nearer, I found inscribed under this harlequin figure the following lines:—

To paint fair Nature, by divine command,
Her magic pencil in his glowing hand,
A Shakspeare rose; then to expand his fame
Wide o'er this breathing world, a Garrick came.
Though sunk in death the forms the Poet drew,
The Actor's genius bade them breathe anew;
Though, like the bard himself, in night they lay,
Immortal Garrick call'd them back to day:
And till ETERNITY with power sublime
Shall mark the mortal hour of hoary TIME,
SHAKSPEARE and GARRICK like twin stars shall shine,
And earth irradiate with a beam divine.

It would be an insult to my readers' understanding to attempt anything like a criticism on this farrago of false thoughts and nonsense. But the reflection it led me into was a kind of wonder, how, from the days of the actor here celebrated to our own, it should have been the fashion to compliment every performer in his turn, that has had the luck to please the town in any of the great characters of Shakspeare, with the notion of possessing a *mind congenial with the poet's:* how people should come thus unaccountably to confound the power of originating poetical images and conceptions with the faculty of being able to read or recite the same when put into words;[2] or what connection that absolute mastery over the heart and soul of man, which a great dramatic poet possesses, has with those low tricks upon the eye and ear, which a player by observing a few general effects, which some common passion, as grief, anger, &c. usually has upon the gestures and exterior, can so easily compass. To know the internal workings and movements of a great mind, of an Othello or a Hamlet for instance, the *when* and the *why* and the *how far* they should be moved; to what pitch a passion is becoming; to give the reins and to pull in the curb exactly at the moment when the drawing in or the slackening is most graceful; seems to demand a reach of intellect of a vastly different

extent from that which is employed upon the bare imitation of the signs of these passions in the countenance or gesture, which signs are usually observed to be most lively and emphatic in the weaker sort of minds, and which signs can after all but indicate some passion, as I said before, anger, or grief, generally; but of the motives and grounds of the passion, wherein it differs from the same passion in low and vulgar natures, of these the actor can give no more idea by his face or gesture than the eye (without a metaphor) can speak, or the muscles utter intelligible sounds. But such is the instantaneous nature of the impressions which we take in at the eye and ear at a playhouse, compared with the slow apprehension oftentimes of the understanding in reading, that we are apt not only to sink the play-writer in the consideration which we pay to the actor, but even to identify in our minds, in a perverse manner, the actor with the character which he represents. It is difficult for a frequent playgoer to disembarrass the idea of Hamlet from the person and voice of Mr. K.[3] We speak of Lady Macbeth, while we are in reality thinking of Mrs. S. Nor is this confusion incidental alone to unlettered persons, who, not possessing the advantage of reading, are necessarily dependent upon the stage-player for all the pleasure which they can receive from the drama, and to whom the very idea of *what an author is* cannot be made comprehensible without some pain and perplexity of mind: the error is one from which persons otherwise not meanly lettered, find it almost impossible to extricate themselves.

Never let me be so ungrateful as to forget the very high degree of satisfaction which I received some years back from seeing for the first time a tragedy of Shakspeare performed, in which those two great performers sustained the principal parts. It seemed to embody and realize conceptions which had hitherto assumed no distinct shape. But dearly do we pay all our life after for this juvenile pleasure, this sense of distinctness. When the novelty is past, we find to our cost that instead of realizing an idea, we have only materialized and brought down a fine vision to the standard of flesh and blood. We have let go a dream, in quest of an unattainable substance.

How cruelly this operates upon the mind, to have its free conceptions thus crampt and pressed down to the measure of a strait-lacing actuality, may be judged from that delightful sensation of freshness, with which we turn to those plays of Shakspeare

---

2 Lamb's note: "It is observable that we fall into this confusion only in *dramatic* recitations. We never dream that the gentleman who reads Lucretius in public with great applause, is therefore a great poet and philosopher; nor do we find that Tom Davies, the bookseller, who is recorded to have recited the Paradise Lost better than any man in England in his day (though I cannot help thinking there must be some mistake in this tradition) was therefore, by his intimate friends, set upon a level with Milton."

3 John Philip Kemble (1757–1823). Mrs. S. in the next sentence is his sister, Sarah Kemble Siddons (1755–1831).

which have escaped being performed, and to those passages in the acting plays of the same writer which have happily been left out in performance. How far the very custom of hearing any thing *spouted,* withers and blows upon a fine passage, may be seen in those speeches from Henry the Fifth, etc., which are current in the mouths of school-boys from their being to be found in *Enfield Speakers,*[4] and such kind of books. I confess myself utterly unable to appreciate that celebrated soliloquy in Hamlet, beginning "To be or not to be,"[5] or to tell whether it be good, bad or indifferent, it has been so handled and pawed about by declamatory boys and men, and torn so inhumanly from its living place and principle of continuity in the play, till it is become to me a perfect dead member.

It may seem a paradox, but I cannot help being of opinion that the plays of Shakspeare are less calculated for performance on a stage, than those of almost any other dramatist whatever. Their distinguishing excellence is a reason that they should be so. There is so much in them, which comes not under the province of acting, with which eye, and tone, and gesture, have nothing to do.

The glory of the scenic art is to personate passion, and the turns of passion; and the more coarse and palpable the passion is, the more hold upon the eyes and ears of the spectators the performer obviously possesses. For this reason, scolding scenes, scenes where two persons talk themselves into a fit of fury, and then in a surprising manner talk themselves out of it again, have always been the most popular upon our stage. And the reason is plain, because the spectators are here most palpably appealed to, they are the proper judges in this war of words, they are the legitimate ring that should be formed round such "intellectual prize-fighters." Talking is the direct object of the imitation here. But in all the best dramas, and in Shakspeare above all, how obvious it is, that the form of *speaking,* whether it be in soliloquy or dialogue, is only a medium, and often a highly artificial one, for putting the reader or spectator into possession of that knowledge of the inner structure and workings of mind in a character, which he could otherwise never have arrived at *in that form of composition* by any gift short of intuition. We do here as we do with novels written in the *epistolary form.* How many improprieties, perfect solecisms in letter-writing, do we put up with in Clarissa[6] and other

books, for the sake of the delight which that form upon the whole gives us.

But the practice of stage representation reduces every thing to a controversy of elocution. Every character, from the boisterous blasphemings of Bajazet[7] to the shrinking timidity of womanhood, must play the orator. The love-dialogues of Romeo and Juliet, those silver-sweet sounds of lovers' tongues by night; the more intimate and sacred sweetness of nuptial colloquy between an Othello or a Posthumus[8] with their married wives, all those delicacies which are so delightful in the reading, as when we read of those youthful dalliances in Paradise—

> As beseem'd
> Fair couple link'd in happy nuptial league,
> Alone:[9]

by the inherent fault of stage representation, how are these things sullied and turned from their very nature by being exposed to a large assembly; when such speeches as Imogen addresses to her lord, come drawling out of the mouth of a hired actress, whose courtship, though nominally addressed to the personated Posthumus, is manifestly aimed at the spectators, who are to judge of her endearments and her returns of love.

The character of Hamlet is perhaps that by which, since the days of Betterton,[10] a succession of popular performers have had the greatest ambition to distinguish themselves. The length of the part may be one of their reasons. But for the character itself, we find it in a play, and therefore we judge it a fit subject of dramatic representation. The play itself abounds in maxims and reflections beyond any other, and therefore we consider it as a proper vehicle for conveying moral instruction. But Hamlet himself—what does he suffer meanwhile by being dragged forth as a public schoolmaster, to give lectures to the crowd! Why, nine parts in ten of what Hamlet does, are transactions between himself and his moral sense; they are the effusions of his solitary musings, which he retires to holes and corners and the most sequestered parts of the palace to pour forth; or rather, they are the silent meditations with which his bosom is bursting, reduced to *words* for the sake of the reader, who must else remain ignorant of what is passing there. These profound sorrows, these light-and-noise-abhorring ruminations, which the tongue scarce dares utter to deaf walls and chambers, how can they be represented by a gesticulating actor, who comes and

---

[4] A popular compilation of pieces for declamation, by the Rev. William Enfield.   [5] *Hamlet,* III, i, 56 ff.
[6] Samuel Richardson's masterpiece (1747-8).

[7] A character in Marlowe's *Tamburlaine.*
[8] In Shakespeare's *Cymbeline.*
[9] *Paradise Lost,* IV, 338-40.   [10] Died 1710.

mouths them out before an audience, making four hundred people his confidants at once? I say not that it is the fault of the actor so to do; he must pronounce them *ore rotundo*;[11] he must accompany them with his eye, he must insinuate them into his auditory by some trick of eye, tone, or gesture, or he fails. *He must be thinking all the while of his appearance, because he knows that all the while the spectators are judging of it.* And this is the way to represent the shy, negligent, retiring Hamlet.

It is true that there is no other mode of conveying a vast quantity of thought and feeling to a great portion of the audience, who otherwise would never earn it for themselves by reading, and the intellectual acquisition gained this way may, for aught I know, be inestimable; but I am not arguing that Hamlet should not be acted, but how much Hamlet is made another thing by being acted. I have heard much of the wonders which Garrick performed in this part; but as I never saw him, I must have leave to doubt whether the representation of such a character came within the province of his art. Those who tell me of him, speak of his eye, of the magic of his eye, and of his commanding voice: physical properties, vastly desirable in an actor, and without which he can never insinuate meaning into an auditory,—but what have they to do with Hamlet? what have they to do with intellect? In fact, the things aimed at in theatrical representation, are to arrest the spectator's eye upon the form and the gesture, and so to gain a more favourable hearing to what is spoken: it is not what the character is, but how he looks; not what he says, but how he speaks it. I see no reason to think that if the play of Hamlet were written over again by some such writer as Banks or Lillo,[12] retaining the process of the story, but totally omitting all the poetry of it, all the divine features of Shakspeare, his stupendous intellect; and only taking care to give us enough of passionate dialogue, which Banks or Lillo were never at a loss to furnish; I see not how the effect could be much different upon an audience, nor how the actor has it in his power to represent Shakspeare to us differently from his representation of Banks or Lillo. Hamlet would still be a youthful accomplished prince, and must be gracefully personated; he might be puzzled in his mind, wavering in his conduct, seemingly-cruel to Ophelia; he might see a ghost, and

start at it, and address it kindly when he found it to be his father; all this in the poorest and most homely language of the servilest creeper after nature that ever consulted the palate of an audience; without troubling Shakspeare for the matter: and I see not but there would be room for all the power which an actor has, to display itself. All the passions and changes of passion might remain: for those are much less difficult to write or act than is thought, it is a trick easy to be attained, it is but rising or falling a note or two in the voice, a whisper with a significant foreboding look to announce its approach, and so contagious the counterfeit appearance of any emotion is, that let the words be what they will, the look and tone shall carry it off and make it pass for deep skill in the passions.

It is common for people to talk of Shakspeare's plays being *so natural*; that every body can understand him. They are natural indeed, they are grounded deep in nature, so deep that the depth of them lies out of the reach of most of us. You shall hear the same persons say that George Barnwell is very natural, and Othello is very natural, that they are both very deep; and to them they are the same kind of thing. At the one they sit and shed tears, because a good sort of young man is tempted by a naughty woman to commit *a trifling peccadillo,* the murder of an uncle or so,[13] that is all, and so comes to an untimely end, which is *so moving;* and at the other, because a blacka-moor in a fit of jealousy kills his innocent white wife: and the odds are that ninety-nine out of a hundred would willingly behold the same catastrophe happen to both the heroes, and have thought the rope more due to Othello than to Barnwell. For of the texture of Othello's mind, the inward construction marvel-lously laid open with all its strengths and weaknesses, its heroic confidences and its human misgivings, its agonies of hate springing from the depths of love, they see no more than the spectators at a cheaper rate, who pay their pennies a-piece to look through the

13 Lamb's note: "If this note could hope to meet the eye of any of the Managers, I would entreat and beg of them, in the name of both the Galleries, that this insult upon the morality of the common people of London should cease to be eternally repeated in the holiday weeks. Why are the 'Prentices of this famous and well-governed city, instead of an amusement, to be treated over and over again with the nauseous sermon of George Barnwell? Why *at the end of their vistas* are we to place the *gallows?* Were I an uncle, I should not much like a nephew of mine to have such an example placed before his eyes. It is really making uncle-murder too trivial to exhibit it as done upon such slight motives —it is attributing too much to such characters as Millwood;—it is putting things into the heads of good young men, which they would never otherwise have dreamed of. Uncles that think any thing of their lives, should fairly petition the Chamberlain against it."

11 With well-rounded utterance (Horace, *Art of Poetry,* line 323).
12 John Banks (1652?–1706) wrote several inferior tragedies. George Lillo (1693–1739) is remembered as the author of a domestic tragedy, *The London Merchant, or The History of George Barnwell* (1731), which Lamb describes below.

man's telescope in Leicester-fields, see into the inward plot and topography of the moon. Some dim thing or other they see, they see an actor personating a passion, of grief, or anger, for instance, and they recognize it as a copy of the usual external effects of such passions; or at least as being true to *that symbol of the emotion which passes current at the theatre for it,* for it is often no more than that: but of the grounds of the passion, its correspondence to a great or heroic nature, which is the only worthy object of tragedy,—that common auditors know any thing of this, or can have any such notions dinned into them by the mere strength of an actor's lungs,—that apprehensions foreign to them should be thus infused into them by storm, I can neither believe, nor understand how it can be possible.

We talk of Shakspeare's admirable observation of life, when we should feel, that not from a petty inquisition into those cheap and every-day characters which surrounded him, as they surround us, but from his own mind, which was, to borrow a phrase of Ben Jonson's, the very "sphere of humanity," he fetched those images of virtue and of knowledge, of which every one of us recognizing a part, think we comprehend in our natures the whole; and oftentimes mistake the powers which he positively creates in us, for nothing more than indigenous faculties of our own minds, which only waited the application of corresponding virtues in him to return a full and clear echo of the same.

To return to Hamlet.—Among the distinguishing features of that wonderful character, one of the most interesting (yet painful) is that soreness of mind which makes him treat the intrusions of Polonius with harshness, and that asperity which he puts on in his interviews with Ophelia. These tokens of an unhinged mind (if they be not mixed in the latter case with a profound artifice of love, to alienate Ophelia by affected discourtesies, so to prepare her mind for the breaking off of that loving intercourse, which can no longer find a place amidst business so serious as that which he has to do) are parts of his character, which to reconcile with our admiration of Hamlet, the most patient consideration of his situation is no more than necessary; they are what we *forgive afterwards,* and explain by the whole of his character, but *at the time* they are harsh and unpleasant. Yet such is the actor's necessity of giving strong blows to the audience, that I have never seen a player in this character, who did not exaggerate and strain to the utmost these ambiguous features,—these temporary deformities in the character. They make him express a vulgar scorn at Polonius which utterly degrades his gentility, and which no explanation can render palatable; they make him shew contempt, and curl up the nose at Ophelia's father,—contempt in its very grossest and most hateful form; but they get applause by it: it is natural, people say; that is, the words are scornful, and the actor expresses scorn, and that they can judge of: but why so much scorn, and of that sort, they never think of asking.

So to Ophelia.—All the Hamlets that I have ever seen, rant and rave at her as if she had committed some great crime, and the audience are highly pleased, because the words of the part are satirical, and they are enforced by the strongest expression of satirical indignation of which the face and voice are capable. But then, whether Hamlet is likely to have put on such brutal appearances to a lady whom he loved so dearly, is never thought on. The truth is, that in all such deep affections as had subsisted between Hamlet and Ophelia, there is a stock of *supererogatory love* (if I may venture to use the expression), which in any great grief of heart, especially where that which preys upon the mind cannot be communicated, confers a kind of indulgence upon the grieved party to express itself, even to its heart's dearest object, in the language of a temporary alienation; but it is not alienation, it is a distraction purely, and so it always makes itself to be felt by that object: it is not anger, but grief assuming the appearance of anger,—love awkwardly counterfeiting hate, as sweet countenances when they try to frown: but such sternness and fierce disgust as Hamlet is made to shew, is no counterfeit, but the real face of absolute aversion,—of irreconcileable alienation. It may be said he puts on the madman; but then he should only so far put on this counterfeit lunacy as his own real distraction will give him leave; that is, incompletely, imperfectly; not in that confirmed, practised way, like a master of his art, or, as Dame Quickly would say, "like one of those harlotry players."[14]

I mean no disrespect to any actor, but the sort of pleasure which Shakspeare's plays give in the acting seems to me not at all to differ from that which the audience receive from those of other writers; and, *they being in themselves essentially so different from all others,* I must conclude that there is something in the nature of acting which levels all distinctions. And in fact, who does not speak indifferently[15] of the Gamester[16] and of Macbeth as fine stage performances, and praise the Mrs. Beverley in the same way

---

[14] *1 Henry IV,* II, iv, 437.
[15] I.e., making no distinction between them.
[16] A tragedy (1753) by Edward Moore (1712–57). Mrs. Beverley is a character in it.

as the Lady Macbeth of Mrs. S.? Belvidera, and Calista, and Isabella, and Euphrasia,[17] are they less liked than Imogen, or than Juliet, or than Desdemona? Are they not spoken of and remembered in the same way? Is not the female performer as great (as they call it) in one as in the other? Did not Garrick shine, and was he not ambitious of shining, in every drawling tragedy that his wretched day produced,— the productions of the Hooles and the Murphys and the Browns,[18]—and shall he have that honour to dwell in our minds for ever as an inseparable concomitant with Shakspeare? A kindred mind! O who can read that affecting sonnet of Shakspeare which alludes to his profession as a player:—

Oh for my sake do you with Fortune chide,
The guilty goddess of my harmless deeds,
That did not better for my life provide
Than public means which public custom breeds—
Thence comes it that my name receives a brand;
And almost thence my nature is subdued
To what it works in, like the dyer's hand.[19]

Or that other confession:—

Alas! 'tis true, I have gone here and there,
And made myself a motley to thy view,
Gored mine own thoughts, sold cheap what
    is most dear—[20]

Who can read these instances of jealous self-watchfulness in our sweet Shakspeare, and dream of any congeniality between him and one that, by every tradition of him, appears to have been as mere a player as ever existed; to have had his mind tainted with the lowest players' vices,—envy and jealousy, and miserable cravings after applause; one who in the exercise of his profession was jealous even of the women-performers that stood in his way; a manager full of managerial tricks and stratagems and finesse: that any resemblance should be dreamed of between him and Shakspeare,—Shakspeare who, in the plenitude and consciousness of his own powers, could with that noble modesty, which we can neither imitate nor appreciate, express himself thus of his own sense of his own defects:—

Wishing me like to one more rich in hope,
Featured like him, like him with friends possest;
Desiring *this man's art, and that man's scope.*[21]

I am almost disposed to deny to Garrick the merit of being an admirer of Shakspeare. A true lover of his excellencies he certainly was not; for would any true lover of them have admitted into his matchless scenes such ribald trash as Tate and Cibber,[22] and the rest of them, that

With their darkness durst affront his light,[23]

have foisted into the acting plays of Shakspeare? I believe it impossible that he could have had a proper reverence for Shakspeare, and have condescended to go through that interpolated scene in Richard the Third, in which Richard tries to break his wife's heart by telling her he loves another woman, and says, "if she survives this she is immortal." Yet I doubt not he delivered this vulgar stuff with as much anxiety of emphasis as any of the genuine parts; and for acting, it is as well calculated as any. But we have seen the part of Richard lately produce great fame to an actor by his manner of playing it, and it lets us into the secret of acting, and of popular judgements of Shakspeare derived from acting. Not one of the spectators who have witnessed Mr. C.'s[24] exertions in that part, but has come away with a proper conviction that Richard is a very wicked man, and kills little children in their beds, with something like the pleasure which the giants and ogres in children's books are represented to have taken in that practice; moreover, that he is very close and shrewd, and devilish cunning, for you could see that by his eye.

But is, in fact, this the impression we have in reading the Richard of Shakspeare? Do we feel any thing like disgust, as we do at that butcher-like representation of him that passes for him on the stage? A horror at his crimes blends with the effect which we feel, but how is it qualified, how is it carried off, by the rich intellect which he displays, his resources, his wit, his buoyant spirits, his vast knowledge and insight into characters, the poetry of his part,—not an atom of all which is made perceivable in Mr. C.'s way of acting it. Nothing but his crimes, his actions, is visible; they are prominent and staring; the murderer stands out, but where is the lofty genius,

---

17 Characters in, respectively, Thomas Otway's *Venice Preserved* (1682), Nicholas Rowe's *The Fair Penitent* (1703), Thomas Southerne's *The Fatal Marriage* (1694), and Arthur Murphy's *The Grecian Daughter* (1772).

18 John Hoole and the Rev. John Brown were very minor playwrights of Garrick's period. Arthur Murphy (1727–1805), author of a number of successful comedies and tragedies, also wrote a biography of Garrick (1801).

19 Sonnet III.   20 Sonnet 110.

21 Sonnet 29.

22 Lamb speaks further (below) of Colley Cibber's "improvement" of *Richard III* and Nahum Tate's of *King Lear*.

23 *Paradise Lost,* I, 391.

24 George Frederick Cooke (died 1811) first acted *Richard III* at Covent Garden on October 31, 1801.

the man of vast capacity—the profound, the witty, accomplished Richard?

The truth is, the Characters of Shakspeare are so much the objects of meditation rather than of interest or curiosity as to their actions, that while we are reading any of his great criminal characters,—Macbeth, Richard, even Iago,—we think not so much of the crimes which they commit, as of the ambition, the aspiring spirit, the intellectual activity, which prompts them to overleap those moral fences. Barnwell is a wretched murderer; there is a certain fitness between his neck and the rope; he is the legitimate heir to the gallows; nobody who thinks at all can think of any alleviating circumstances in his case to make him a fit object of mercy. Or to take an instance from the higher tragedy, what else but a mere assassin is Glenalvon![25] Do we think of anything but of the crime which he commits, and the rack which he deserves? That is all which we really think about him. Whereas in corresponding characters in Shakspeare, so little do the actions comparatively affect us, that while the impulses, the inner mind in all its perverted greatness, solely seems real and is exclusively attended to, the crime is comparatively nothing. But when we see these things represented, the acts which they do are comparatively every thing, their impulses nothing. The state of sublime emotion into which we are elevated by those images of night and horror which Macbeth is made to utter, that solemn prelude with which he entertains the time till the bell shall strike which is to call him to murder Duncan,—when we no longer read it in a book, when we have given up that vantage-ground of abstraction which reading possesses over seeing, and come to see a man in his bodily shape before our eyes actually preparing to commit a murder, if the acting be true and impressive, as I have witnessed it in Mr. K.'s performance of that part, the painful anxiety about the act, the natural longing to prevent it while it yet seems unperpetrated, the too close pressing semblance of reality, give a pain and an uneasiness which totally destroy all the delight which the words in the book convey, where the deed doing never presses upon us with the painful sense of presence: it rather seems to belong to history,—to something past and inevitable, if it has any thing to do with time at all. The sublime images, the poetry alone, is that which is present to our minds in the reading.

So to see Lear acted,—to see an old man tottering about the stage with a walking-stick, turned out of doors by his daughters in a rainy night, has nothing in it but what is painful and disgusting. We want to take him into shelter and relieve him. That is all the feeling which the acting of Lear ever produced in me. But the Lear of Shakspeare cannot be acted. The contemptible machinery by which they mimic the storm which he goes out in, is not more inadequate to represent the horror of the real elements, than any actor can be to represent Lear: they might more easily propose to personate the Satan of Milton upon a stage, or one of Michael Angelo's terrible figures. The greatness of Lear is not in corporal dimension, but in intellectual: the explosions of his passion are terrible as a volcano: they are storms turning up and disclosing to the bottom that sea, his mind, with all its vast riches. It is his mind which is laid bare. This case of flesh and blood seems too insignificant to be thought on; even as he himself neglects it. On the stage we see nothing but corporal infirmities and weakness, the impotence of rage; while we read it, we see not Lear, but we are Lear,—we are in his mind, we are sustained by a grandeur which baffles the malice of daughters and storms; in the aberrations of his reason, we discover a mighty irregular power of reasoning, immethodized from the ordinary purposes of life, but exerting its powers, as the wind blows where it listeth, at will upon the corruptions and abuses of mankind. What have looks, or tones, to do with that sublime identification of his age with that of the *heavens themselves,* when in his reproaches to them for conniving at the injustice of his children, he reminds them that "they themselves are old"?[26] What gesture shall we appropriate to this? What has the voice or the eye to do with such things? But the play is beyond all art, as the tamperings with it shew: it is too hard and stony; it must have love-scenes, and a happy ending. It is not enough that Cordelia is a daughter, she must shine as a lover too. Tate has put his hook in the nostrils of this Leviathan, for Garrick and his followers, the showmen of the scene, to draw the mighty beast about more easily. A happy ending!—as if the living martyrdom that Lear had gone through,—the flaying of his feelings alive, did not make a fair dismissal from the stage of life the only decorous thing for him. If he is to live and be happy after, if he could sustain this world's burden after, why all his pudder and preparation,—why torment us with all this unnecessary sympathy? As if the childish pleasure of getting his gilt robes and sceptre again could tempt him to act over again

[25] In John Home's *Douglas* (1756).

[26] *King Lear,* II, iv, 194.

his misused station—as if at his years, and with his experience, any thing was left but to die.

Lear is essentially impossible to be represented on a stage. But how many dramatic personages are there in Shakspeare, which though more tractable and feasible (if I may so speak) than Lear, yet from some circumstance, some adjunct to their character, are improper to be shewn to our bodily eye. Othello for instance. Nothing can be more soothing, more flattering to the nobler parts of our natures, than to read of a young Venetian lady of highest extraction, through the force of love and from a sense of merit in him whom she loved, laying aside every consideration of kindred, and country, and colour, and wedding with a *coal-black Moor*—(for such he is represented, in the imperfect state of knowledge respecting foreign countries in those days, compared with our own, or in compliance with popular notions, though the Moors are now well enough known to be by many shades less unworthy of a white woman's fancy)—it is the perfect triumph of virtue over accidents, of the imagination over the senses. She sees Othello's colour in his mind. But upon the stage, when the imagination is no longer the ruling faculty, but we are left to our poor unassisted senses, I appeal to every one that has seen Othello played, whether he did not, on the contrary, sink Othello's mind in his colour; whether he did not find something extremely revolting in the courtship and wedded caresses of Othello and Desdemona; and whether the actual sight of the thing did not overweigh all that beautiful compromise which we make in reading;—and the reason it should do so is obvious, because there is just so much reality presented to our senses as to give a perception of disagreement, with not enough of belief in the internal motives,—all that which is unseen,—to overpower and reconcile the first and obvious prejudices.[27] What we see upon a stage is body and bodily action; what we are conscious of in reading is almost exclusively the mind, and its movements: and this I think may sufficiently account for the very different sort of delight with which the same play so often affects us in the reading and the seeing.

It requires little reflection to perceive, that if those characters in Shakspeare which are within the precincts of nature, have yet something in them which appeals too exclusively to the imagination, to admit of their being made objects to the senses without suffering a change and a diminution,—that still stronger the objection must lie against representing another line of characters, which Shakspeare has introduced to give a wildness and a supernatural elevation to his scenes, as if to remove them still farther from that assimilation to common life in which their excellence is vulgarly supposed to consist. When we read the incantations of those terrible beings the Witches in Macbeth, though some of the ingredients of their hellish composition savour of the grotesque, yet is the effect upon us other than the most serious and appalling that can be imagined? Do we not feel spell-bound as Macbeth was? Can any mirth accompany a sense of their presence? We might as well laugh under a consciousness of the principle of Evil himself being truly and really present with us. But attempt to bring these things on to a stage, and you turn them instantly into so many old women, that men and children are to laugh at. Contrary to the old saying, that "seeing is believing," the sight actually destroys the faith; and the mirth in which we indulge at their expense, when we see these creatures upon a stage, seems to be a sort of indemnification which we make to ourselves for the terror which they put us in when reading made them an object of belief,—when we surrendered up our reason to the poet, as children to their nurses and their elders; and we laugh at our fears as children who thought they saw something in the dark, triumph when the bringing in of a candle discovers the vanity of their fears. For this exposure of supernatural agents upon a stage is truly bringing in a candle to expose their own delusiveness. It is the solitary taper and the book that generates a faith in these terrors: a ghost by chandelier light, and in good company, deceives no spectators,—a ghost that can be measured by the eye, and his human dimensions made out at leisure. The sight of a well-lighted house, and a well-dressed audience, shall arm the most nervous child against any apprehensions: as Tom Brown[28] says of the impenetrable skin of Achilles with his impenetrable armour over it, "Bully Dawson would have fought the devil with such advantages."

---

27 Lamb's note: "The error of supposing that because Othello's colour does not offend us in the reading, it should also not offend us in the seeing, is just such a fallacy as supposing that an Adam and Eve in a picture shall affect us just as they do in the poem. But in the poem we for a while have Paradisaical senses given us, which vanish when we see a man and his wife without clothes in the picture. The painters themselves feel this, as is apparent by the awkward shifts they have recourse to, to make them look not quite naked; by a sort of prophetic anachronism, antedating the invention of fig-leaves. So in the reading of the play, we see with Desdemona's eyes; in the seeing of it, we are forced to look with our own."

28 A miscellaneous writer (1663–1704), in *Observations on Vergil, Ovid, and Homer*. Bully Dawson was a notorious character of Restoration times.

Much has been said, and deservedly, in reprobation of the vile mixture which Dryden has thrown into the Tempest:[29] doubtless without some such vicious alloy, the impure ears of that age would never have sate out to hear so much innocence of love as is contained in the sweet courtship of Ferdinand and Miranda. But is the Tempest of Shakspeare at all a subject for stage representation? It is one thing to read of an enchanter, and to believe the wondrous tale while we are reading it; but to have a conjuror brought before us in his conjuring-gown, with his spirits about him, which none but himself and some hundred of favoured spectators before the curtain are supposed to see, involves such a quantity of the *hateful incredible,* that all our reverence for the author cannot hinder us from perceiving such gross attempts upon the senses to be in the highest degree childish and inefficient. Spirits and fairies cannot be represented, they cannot even be painted,—they can only be believed. But the elaborate and anxious provision of scenery, which the luxury of the age demands, in these cases works a quite contrary effect to what is intended. That which in comedy, or plays of familiar life, adds so much to the life of the imitation, in plays which appeal to the higher faculties positively destroys the illusion which it is introduced to aid. A parlour or a drawing-room,—a library opening into a garden,—a garden with an alcove in it,—a street, or the piazza of Covent-garden, does well enough in a scene; we are content to give as much credit to it as it demands; or rather, we think little about it,—it is little more than reading at the top of a page, "Scene, a Garden"; we do not imagine ourselves there, but we readily admit the imitation of familiar objects. But to think by the help of painted trees and caverns, which we know to be painted, to transport our minds to Prospero, and his island and his lonely cell;[30] or by the aid of a fiddle dexterously thrown in, in an interval of speaking, to make us believe that we hear those super-natural noises of which the isle was full:— the Orrery Lecturer at the Haymarket[31] might as well hope, by his musical glasses cleverly stationed out of sight behind his apparatus, to make us believe that we do indeed hear the chrystal spheres ring out that chime, which if it were to inwrap our fancy long, Milton thinks,

> Time would run back and fetch the age of gold,
> And speckled Vanity
> Would sicken soon and die,
> And leprous Sin would melt from earthly mould;
> Yea, Hell itself would pass away,
> And leave its dolorous mansions to the peering day.[32]

The garden of Eden, with our first parents in it, is not more impossible to be shown on a stage, than the Enchanted Isle, with its no less interesting and innocent first settlers.

The subject of Scenery is closely connected with that of the Dresses, which are so anxiously attended to on our stage. I remember the last time I saw Macbeth played, the discrepancy I felt at the changes of garment which he varied,—the shiftings and re-shiftings, like a Romish priest at mass. The luxury of stage-improvements, and the importunity of the public eye, require this. The coronation robe of the Scottish monarch was fairly a counterpart to that which our King wears when he goes to the Parliament-house,—just so full and cumbersome, and set out with ermine and pearls. And if things must be represented, I see not what to find fault with in this. But in reading, what robe are we conscious of? Some dim images of royalty—a crown and sceptre, may float before our eyes, but who shall describe the fashion of it? Do we see in our mind's eye what Webb[33] or any other robe-maker could pattern? This is the inevitable consequence of imitating every thing, to make all things natural. Whereas the reading of a tragedy is a fine abstraction. It presents to the fancy just so much of external appearances as to make us feel that we are among flesh and blood, while by far the greater and better part of our imagination is employed upon the thoughts and internal machinery of the character. But in acting, scenery, dress, the most contemptible things, call upon us to judge of their naturalness.

Perhaps it would be no bad similitude, to liken the pleasure which we take in seeing one of these fine plays acted, compared with that quiet delight which we find in the reading of it, to the different feelings with which a reviewer, and a man that is not a reviewer, reads a fine poem. The accursed critical habit,—the being called upon to judge and pronounce, must make it quite a different thing to the

---

[29] Dryden and D'avenant's adaptation.

[30] Lamb's note: "It will be said these things are done in pictures. But pictures and scenes are very different. Painting is a world of itself, but in scene-painting there is the attempt to deceive: and there is the discordancy, never to be got over, between painted scenes and real people."

[31] Astronomical lectures were given at the Theater Royal in the Haymarket.

[32] From Milton's ode "On the Morning of Christ's Nativity," lines 135–40.

[33] A maker of theatrical costumes.

former. In seeing these plays acted, we are affected just as judges. When Hamlet compares the two pictures of Gertrude's first and second husband, who wants to see the pictures? But in the acting, a miniature must be lugged out; which we know not to be the picture, but only to shew how finely a miniature may be represented. This showing of every thing levels all things: it makes tricks, bows, and curtesies, of importance. Mrs. S. never got more fame by any thing than by the manner in which she dismisses the guests in the banquet-scene in Macbeth: it is as much remembered as any of her thrilling tones or impressive looks. But does such a trifle as this enter into the imaginations of the readers of that wild and wonderful scene? Does not the mind dismiss the feasters as rapidly as it can? Does it care about the gracefulness of the doing it? But by acting, and judging of acting, all these non-essentials are raised into an importance, injurious to the main interest of the play.

I have confined my observations to the tragic parts of Shakspeare. It would be no very difficult task to extend the enquiry to his comedies; and to shew why Falstaff, Shallow, Sir Hugh Evans,[34] and the rest, are equally incompatible with stage representation. The length to which this Essay has run, will make it, I am afraid, sufficiently distasteful to the Amateurs of the Theatre, without going any deeper into the subject at present.

from ELIA

In 1823 was published in book form the remarkable series which, beginning in 1820, had appeared from time to time in the *London Magazine* over the signature "Elia." This pseudonym was the actual name of an old Italian clerk at the South Sea House, where Lamb had worked for a few months before he was employed by the East India Company. Only the more discriminating of the reviewers, among them Hazlitt and Leigh Hunt, recognized the rich humanity and humor in these essays. Though they have been repeatedly reprinted, a second edition was not called for in Lamb's lifetime; and his second collection, *The Last Essays of Elia* (1833), met at first with similar indifference. The first American edition of *Elia,* on the other hand, was an immediate success. Of the following selections the first three are from the volume of 1823, the remainder from *The Last Essays.* Their original appearance was during the years 1820–1825.

NEW YEAR'S EVE

Every man hath two birth-days: two days, at least, in every year, which set him upon revolving the lapse of time, as it affects his mortal duration. The one is that which in an especial manner he termeth *his.* In the gradual desuetude of old observances, this custom of solemnizing our proper birth-day hath nearly passed away, or is left to children, who reflect nothing at all about the matter, nor understand any thing in it beyond cake and orange. But the birth of a New Year is of an interest too wide to be pretermitted by king or cobbler. No one ever regarded the First of January with indifference. It is that from which all date their time, and count upon what is left. It is the nativity of our common Adam.

Of all sound of all bells—(bells, the music nighest bordering upon heaven)—most solemn and touching is the peal which rings out the Old Year. I never hear it without a gathering-up of my mind to a concentration of all the images that have been diffused over the past twelvemonth; all I have done or suffered, performed or neglected—in that regretted time. I begin to know its worth, as when a person dies. It takes a personal colour; nor was it a poetical flight in a contemporary, when he exclaimed

I saw the skirts of the departing Year.[1]

It is no more than what in sober sadness every one of us seems to be conscious of, in that awful leave-taking. I am sure I felt it, and all felt it with me, last night; though some of my companions affected rather to manifest an exhilaration at the birth of the coming year, than any very tender regrets for the decease of its predecessor. But I am none of those who—

Welcome the coming, speed the parting guest.[2]

I am naturally, beforehand, shy of novelties; new books, new faces, new years,—from some mental twist which makes it difficult in me to face the prospective. I have almost ceased to hope; and am sanguine only in the prospects of other (former) years.

---

34 All characters in *The Merry Wives of Windsor,* though Shakespeare's major portrayal of Falstaff is in *1 and 2 Henry IV* and *Henry V.*

1 Cf. Coleridge, *Ode to the Departing Year,* line 8.
2 Pope, translation of the *Odyssey,* XV, 84; translation of Horace, *Satires,* II, ii, 160.

I plunge into foregone visions and conclusions. I encounter pell-mell with past disappointments. I am armour-proof against old discouragements. I forgive, or overcome in fancy, old adversaries. I play over again *for love,* as the gamesters phrase it, games, for which I once paid so dear. I would scarce now have any of those untoward accidents and events of my life reversed. I would no more alter them than the incidents of some well-contrived novel. Methinks, it is better that I should have pined away seven of my goldenest years, when I was thrall to the fair hair, and fairer eyes, of Alice W——n,[3] than that so passionate a love-adventure should be lost. It was better that our family should have missed that legacy, which old Dorrell cheated us of, than that I should have at this moment two thousand pounds *in banco,* and be without the idea of that specious old rogue.

In a degree beneath manhood, it is my infirmity to look back upon those early days. Do I advance a paradox, when I say, that, skipping over the intervention of forty years, a man may have leave to love *himself,* without the imputation of self-love?

If I know aught of myself, no one whose mind is introspective—and mine is painfully so—can have a less respect for his present identity, than I have for the man Elia. I know him to be light, and vain, and humorsome; a notorious * * *; addicted to * * * *; averse from counsel, neither taking it, nor offering it; * * * besides; a stammering buffoon; what you will; lay it on, and spare not; I subscribe to it all, and much more, than thou canst be willing to lay at his door—but for the child Elia—that "other me," there, in the background—I must take leave to cherish the remembrance of that young master—with as little reference, I protest, to this stupid changeling of five-and-forty, as if it had been a child of some other house, and not of my parents. I can cry over its patient small-pox at five, and rougher medicaments. I can lay its poor fevered head upon the sick pillow at Christ's, and wake with it in surprise at the gentle posture of maternal tenderness hanging over it, that unknown had watched its sleep. I know how it shrank from any the least colour of falsehood.—God help thee, Elia, how art thou changed! Thou art sophisticated.—I know how honest, how courageous (for a weakling) it was—how religious, how imaginative, how hopeful! From what have I not fallen, if the child I remember was indeed myself,—and not some dissembling guardian, presenting a false identity, to

give the rule to my unpractised steps, and regulate the tone of my moral being!

That I am fond of indulging, beyond a hope of sympathy, in such retrospection, may be the symptom of some sickly idiosyncrasy. Or is it owing to another cause; simply, that being without wife or family, I have not learned to project myself enough out of myself; and having no offspring of my own to dally with, I turn back upon memory, and adopt my own early idea, as my heir and favourite? If these speculations seem fantastical to thee, reader—(a busy man perchance), if I tread out of the way of thy sympathy, and am singularly-conceited only, I retire, impenetrable to ridicule, under the phantom cloud of Elia.

The elders, with whom I was brought up, were of a character not likely to let slip the sacred observance of any old institution; and the ringing out of the Old Year was kept by them with circumstances of peculiar ceremony.—In those days the sound of those midnight chimes, though it seemed to raise hilarity in all around me, never failed to bring a train of pensive imagery into my fancy. Yet I then scarce conceived what it meant, or thought of it as a reckoning that concerned me. Not childhood alone, but the young man till thirty, never feels practically that he is mortal. He knows it indeed, and, if need were, he could preach a homily on the fragility of life; but he brings it not home to himself, any more than in a hot June we can appropriate to our imagination the freezing days of December. But now, shall I confess a truth?— I feel these audits but too powerfully. I begin to count the probabilities of my duration, and to grudge at the expenditure of moments and shortest periods, like misers' farthings. In proportion as the years both lessen and shorten, I set more count upon their periods, and would fain lay my ineffectual finger upon the spoke of the great wheel. I am not content to pass away "like a weaver's shuttle."[4] Those metaphors solace me not, nor sweeten the unpalatable draught of mortality. I care not to be carried with the tide, that smoothly bears human life to eternity; and reluct at[5] the inevitable course of destiny. I am in love with this green earth; the face of town and country; the unspeakable rural solitudes, and the sweet security of streets. I would set up my tabernacle here. I am content to stand still at the age to which I am arrived; I, and my friends: to be no younger, no richer, no handsomer. I do not want to be weaned by age; or drop, like mellow fruit, as they say, into the grave.—Any alteration, on this earth of mine, in

---

[3] Alice Winterton, identified with Anne Simmons; see "Dream Children," note 8 (p. 143, below).

[4] Job 7:6.   [5] Resist, rebel against.

diet or in lodging, puzzles and discomposes me. My household-gods plant a terrible fixed foot, and are not rooted up without blood. They do not willingly seek Lavinian shores.[6] A new state of being staggers me.

Sun, and sky, and breeze, and solitary walks, and summer holidays, and the greenness of fields, and the delicious juices of meats and fishes, and society, and the cheerful glass, and candle-light, and fire-side conversations, and innocent vanities, and jests, and *irony itself*—do these things go out with life?

Can a ghost laugh, or shake his gaunt sides, when you are pleasant with him?

And you, my midnight darlings, my Folios! must I part with the intense delight of having you (huge armfuls) in my embraces? Must knowledge come to me, if it come at all, by some awkward experiment of intuition, and no longer by this familiar process of reading?

Shall I enjoy friendships there, wanting the smiling indications which point me to them here—the recognisable face—the "sweet assurance of a look"[7]—?

In winter this intolerable disinclination to dying—to give it its mildest name—does more especially haunt and beset me. In a genial August noon, beneath a sweltering sky, death is almost problematic. At those times do such poor snakes as myself enjoy an immortality. Then we expand and burgeon. Then are we as strong again, as valiant again, as wise again, and a great deal taller. The blast that nips and shrinks me, puts me in thoughts of death. All things allied to the insubstantial, wait upon that master feeling; cold, numbness, dreams, perplexity; moonlight itself, with its shadowy and spectral appearances,—that cold ghost of the sun, or Phoebus' sickly sister, like that innutritious one denounced in the Canticles:[8]— I am none of her minions—I hold with the Persian.[9]

Whatsoever thwarts, or puts me out of my way, brings death into my mind. All partial evils, like humours, run into that capital plague-sore.—I have heard some profess an indifference to life. Such hail the end of their existence as a port of refuge; and speak of the grave as of some soft arms, in which they may slumber as on a pillow. Some have wooed death—but out upon thee, I say, thou foul, ugly phantom! I detest, abhor, execrate, and (with Friar John[10]) give thee to six-score thousand devils, as in

no instance to be excused or tolerated, but shunned as a universal viper; to be branded, proscribed, and spoken evil of! In no way can I be brought to digest thee, thou thin, melancholy *Privation*, or more frightful and confounding *Positive*!

Those antidotes, prescribed against the fear of thee, are altogether frigid and insulting, like thyself. For what satisfaction hath a man, that he shall "lie down with kings and emperors in death,"[11] who in his life-time never greatly coveted the society of such bed-fellows?—or, forsooth, that "so shall the fairest face appear"?[12]—why, to comfort me, must Alice W——n be a goblin? More than all, I conceive disgust at those impertinent and misbecoming familiarities, inscribed upon your ordinary tomb-stones. Every dead man must take upon himself to be lecturing me with his odious truism, that "such as he now is, I must shortly be." Not so shortly, friend, perhaps, as thou imaginest. In the meantime I am alive. I move about. I am worth twenty of thee. Know thy betters! Thy New Years' days are past. I survive, a jolly candidate for 1821. Another cup of wine—and while that turn-coat bell, that just now mournfully chanted the obsequies of 1820 departed, with changed notes lustily rings in a successor, let us attune to its peal the song made on a like occasion, by hearty, cheerful Mr. Cotton.—[13]

THE NEW YEAR.

Hark, the cock crows, and yon bright star
Tells us, the day himself's not far;
And see where, breaking from the night,
He gilds the western hills with light.
With him old Janus doth appear,
Peeping into the future year,
With such a look as seems to say,
The prospect is not good that way.
Thus do we rise ill sights to see,
And 'gainst ourselves to prophesy;
When the prophetic fear of things
A more tormenting mischief brings,
More full of soul-tormenting gall,
Than direst mischiefs can befall.
But stay! but stay! methinks my sight,
Better inform'd by clearer light,
Discerns sereneness in that brow,
That all contracted seem'd but now.
His revers'd face may show distaste,
And frown upon the ills are past;

---

6 An allusion to Aeneas, who after the fall of Troy finally settled in Italy ("Lavinian shores").
7 Misquoted from Matthew Roydon's elegy on Sir Philip Sidney.
8 See Song of Solomon 8:8.   9 I.e., I worship the sun.
10 A character in Rabelais.

11 Cf. Job 3:13–14 and Sir Thomas Browne, *Hydriotaphia,* Chapter V, "What time the persons of these ossuaries," etc.
12 From the eighteenth-century poet David Mallet's imitation ballad, *William and Margaret.*
13 Charles Cotton (1630–87), the friend of Izaak Walton.

But that which this way looks is clear,
And smiles upon the New-born Year.
He looks too from a place so high,
The year lies open to his eye;
And all the moments open are
To the exact discoverer.
Yet more and more he smiles upon
The happy revolution.
Why should we then suspect or fear
The influences of a year,
So smiles upon us the first morn,
And speaks us good so soon as born?
Plague on't! the last was ill enough,
This cannot but make better proof;
Or, at the worst, as we brush'd through
The last, why so we may this too;
And then the next in reason shou'd
Be superexcellently good:
For the worst ills (we daily see)
Have no more perpetuity
Than the best fortunes that do fall;
Which also bring us wherewithal
Longer their being to support,
Than those do of the other sort:
And who has one good year in three,
And yet repines a destiny,
Appears ungrateful in the case,
And merits not the good he has.
Then let us welcome the New Guest
With lusty brimmers of the best:
Mirth always should Good Fortune meet,
And renders e'en Disaster sweet:
And though the Princess turn her back,
Let us but line ourselves with sack,
We better shall by far hold out,
Till the next Year she face about.

How say you, reader—do not these verses smack
of the rough magnanimity of the old English vein?
Do they not fortify like a cordial; enlarging the heart,
and productive of sweet blood, and generous spirits,
in the concoction? Where be those puling fears of
death, just now expressed or affected?—Passed like a
cloud—absorbed in the purging sunlight of clear
poetry—clean washed away by a wave of genuine
Helicon,[14] your only Spa for these hypochondries.—
And now another cup of the generous! and a merry
New Year, and many of them, to you all, my masters!

---

[14] Helicon was a mountain, not a stream; but this confusion is a
frequent one.

MRS. BATTLE'S OPINIONS ON WHIST

"A CLEAR fire, a clean hearth,[1] and the rigour of the
game." This was the celebrated *wish* of old Sarah
Battle[2] (now with God) who, next to her devotions,
loved a good game at whist. She was none of your
lukewarm gamesters, your half and half players, who
have no objection to take a hand, if you want one to
make up a rubber; who affirm that they have no
pleasure in winning; that they like to win one game,
and lose another; that they can while away an hour
very agreeably at a card-table, but are indifferent
whether they play or no; and will desire an adversary, who has slipt a wrong card, to take it up and
play another. These insufferable triflers are the curse
of a table. One of these flies will spoil a whole pot.
Of such it may be said, that they do not play at cards,
but only play at playing at them.

Sarah Battle was none of that breed. She detested
them, as I do, from her heart and soul; and would
not, save upon a striking emergency, willingly seat
herself at the same table with them. She loved a
thorough-paced[3] partner, a determined enemy. She
took, and gave, no concessions. She hated favours.
She never made a revoke,[4] nor ever passed it over
in her adversary without exacting the utmost
forfeiture. She fought a good fight: cut and thrust.
She held not her good sword (her cards) "like a
dancer."[5] She sate bolt upright; and neither showed
you her cards, nor desired to see yours. All people
have their blind side—their superstitions; and I have
heard her declare, under the rose,[6] that Hearts was
her favourite suit.

I never in my life—and I knew Sarah Battle many
of the best years of it—saw her take out her snuff-box
when it was her turn to play; or snuff a candle in the
middle of a game; or ring for a servant, till it was
fairly over. She never introduced, or connived at,
miscellaneous conversation during its process. As she
emphatically observed, cards were cards: and if I
ever saw unmingled distaste in her fine last-century
countenance, it was at the airs of a young gentleman
of a literary turn, who had been with difficulty

---

[1] Lamb's note: "This was before the introduction of rugs, reader."
And he mentions the "crash" of the unswept cinders underfoot.

[2] The original of Mrs. Battle was probably Sarah Burney, wife of
Admiral James Burney (son of Dr. Johnson's friend, the historian
of music, and brother of the novelist Fanny Burney). Captain
Burney, as he was at this time, was a devotee of the game; his
wife was the leading member of the group Lamb played whist
with. This game was fundamentally the same as bridge, but there
was then no bidding for the privilege of naming trumps.

[3] Out and out.   [4] Renege, failure to follow suit.

[5] Shakespeare, *Antony and Cleopatra*, III, xi, 36.

[6] *Sub rosa*, confidentially.

persuaded to take a hand; and who, in his excess of candour, declared, that he thought there was no harm in unbending the mind now and then, after serious studies, in recreations of that kind! She could not bear to have her noble occupation, to which she wound up her faculties, considered in that light. It was her business, her duty, the thing she came into the world to do,—and she did it. She unbent her mind afterwards—over a book.

Pope was her favourite author: his Rape of the Lock her favourite work. She once did me the favour to play over with me (with the cards) his celebrated game of Ombre in that poem;[7] and to explain to me how far it agreed with, and in what points it would be found to differ from, tradrille.[8] Her illustrations were apposite and poignant; and I had the pleasure of sending the substance of them to Mr. Bowles:[9] but I suppose they came too late to be inserted among his ingenious notes upon that author.

Quadrille,[10] she has often told me, was her first love; but whist had engaged her maturer esteem. The former, she said, was showy and specious, and likely to allure young persons. The uncertainty and quick shifting of partners—a thing which the constancy of whist abhors;—the dazzling supremacy and regal investiture of Spadille[11]—absurd, as she justly observed, in the pure aristocracy of whist, where his crown and garter give him no proper power above his brother-nobility of the Aces;—the giddy vanity, so taking to the inexperienced, of playing alone:—above all, the overpowering attractions of a *Sans Prendre Vole*,[12]—to the triumph of which there is certainly nothing parallel or approaching, in the contingencies of whist;—all these, she would say, make quadrille a game of captivation to the young and enthusiastic. But whist was the *solider* game: that was her word. It was a long meal; not, like quadrille, a feast of snatches. One or two rubbers might co-extend in duration with an evening. They gave time to form rooted friendships, to cultivate steady enmities. She despised the chance-started, capricious, and ever fluctuating alliances of the other. The skirmishes of quadrille, she would say, reminded her of the petty ephemeral embroilments of the little Italian states, depicted by Machiavel: perpetually changing postures

and connexions; bitter foes to-day, sugared darlings to-morrow; kissing and scratching in a breath;—but the wars of whist were comparable to the long, steady, deep-rooted, rational antipathies of the great French and English nations.

A grave simplicity was what she chiefly admired in her favourite game. There was nothing silly in it, like the nob[13] in cribbage—nothing superfluous. No *flushes*—that most irrational of all pleas that a reasonable being can set up:—that any one should claim four by virtue of holding cards of the same mark and colour, without reference to the playing of the game, or the individual worth or pretensions of the cards themselves! She held this to be a solecism; as pitiful an ambition at cards as alliteration is in authorship. She despised superficiality, and looked deeper than the colours of things.—Suits were soldiers, she would say, and must have a uniformity of array to distinguish them: but what should we say to a foolish squire, who should claim a merit from dressing up his tenantry in red jackets, that never were to be marshalled—never to take the field?—She even wished that whist were more simple than it is; and, in my mind, would have stript it of some appendages, which, in the state of human frailty, may be venially, and even commendably allowed of. She saw no reason for the deciding of the trump by the turn of the card. Why not one suit always trumps?—Why two colours, when the mark of the suit would have sufficiently distinguished them without it?—

"But the eye, my dear Madam, is agreeably refreshed with the variety. Man is not a creature of pure reason—he must have his senses delightfully appealed to. We see it in Roman Catholic countries, where the music and the paintings draw in many to worship, whom your quaker spirit of unsensualising would have kept out.—You, yourself, have a pretty collection of paintings—but confess to me, whether, walking in your gallery at Sandham, among those clear Vandykes,[14] or among the Paul Potters in the ante-room, you ever felt your bosom glow with an elegant delight, at all comparable to *that* you have it in your power to experience most evenings over a well-arranged assortment of the court cards?—the pretty antic habits,[15] like heralds in a procession—the gay triumph-assuring scarlets—the contrasting

7 See I, 789–90, above.
8 A three-handed card game, somewhat like ombre.
9 The Rev. William Lisle Bowles (1762–1850), who inspired the youthful Coleridge (see pp. 113–15, above). He edited Pope in 1806.   10 Four-handed ombre.
11 The ace of spades.
12 A *vole* was a grand slam, taking all the tricks; *sans prendre* = without drawing cards.

13 True, the mere accident of holding the jack of the same suit as the card turned up adds in the scoring "one for his nob"; but Mrs. Battle maligns the best of all two-handed card games.
14 Sir Anthony Vandyke (1599–1641), a Fleming who became court painter to Charles I of England. Paul Potter (1625–54) was a Dutch painter, best known for pictures of animals.
15 Bizarre garments.

deadly-killing sables—the 'hoary majesty of spades'[16]—Pam in all his glory!—

"All these might be dispensed with; and, with their naked names upon the drab pasteboard, the game might go on very well, picture-less. But the *beauty* of cards would be extinguished for ever. Stripped of all that is imaginative in them, they must degenerate into mere gambling.—Imagine a dull deal board, or drum head, to spread them on, instead of that nice verdant carpet (next to nature's), fittest arena for those courtly combatants to play their gallant jousts and turneys in!—Exchange those delicately-turned ivory markers—(work of Chinese artist, unconscious of their symbol,—or as profanely slighting their true application as the arrantest Ephesian journeyman that turned out those little shrines for the goddess[17])—exchange them for little bits of leather (our ancestors' money), or chalk and a slate!"—

The old lady, with a smile, confessed the soundness of my logic; and to her approbation of my arguments on her favourite topic that evening, I have always fancied myself indebted for the legacy of a curious[18] cribbage board, made of the finest Sienna marble, which her maternal uncle (old Walter Plumer, whom I have elsewhere celebrated[19]) brought with him from Florence:—this, and a trifle of five hundred pounds, came to me at her death.

The former bequest (which I do not least value) I have kept with religious care; though she herself, to confess a truth, was never greatly taken with cribbage. It was an essentially vulgar game, I have heard her say,—disputing with her uncle, who was very partial to it. She could never heartily bring her mouth to pronounce "*go*"—or "*that's a go.*"[20] She called it an ungrammatical game. The pegging teased her.[21] I once knew her to forfeit a rubber (a five dollar stake), because she would not take advantage of the turn-up knave,[22] which would have given it her, but which she must have claimed by the disgraceful tenure of declaring "*two for his heels.*" There is something extremely genteel in this sort of self-denial. Sarah Battle was a gentlewoman born.

Piquet she held the best game at the cards for two persons, though she would ridicule the pedantry of the terms—such as pique repique[23]—the capot[24]—they savoured (she thought) of affectation. But games for two, or even three, she never greatly cared for. She loved the quadrate, or square. She would argue thus:—Cards are warfare: the ends are gain, with glory. But cards are war, in disguise of a sport: when single adversaries encounter, the ends proposed are too palpable. By themselves, it is too close[25] a fight: with spectators, it is not much bettered. No looker on can be interested, except for a bet, and then it is a mere affair of money; he cares not for your luck *sympathetically,* or for your play.—Three are still worse; a mere naked war of every man against every man, as in cribbage,[26] without league or alliance; or a rotation of petty and contradictory interests, a succession of heartless leagues, and not much more hearty infractions of them, as in tradrille. But in square[27] games (*she meant whist*) all that is possible to be attained in card-playing is accomplished. There are the incentives of profit with honour, common to every species—though the *latter* can be but very imperfectly enjoyed in those other games, where the spectator is only feebly a participator. But the parties in whist are spectators and principals too. They are a theatre to themselves, and a looker on is not wanted. He is rather worse than nothing, and an impertinence. Whist abhors neutrality, or interests beyond its sphere. You glory in some surprising stroke of skill or fortune, not because a cold—or even an interested —by-stander witnesses it, but because your *partner* sympathizes in the contingency. You win for two. You triumph for two. Two are exalted. Two again are mortified; which divides their disgrace, as the conjunction doubles (by taking off the invidiousness) your glories. Two losing to two are better reconciled, than one to one in that close butchery. The hostile feeling is weakened by multiplying the channels. War becomes a civil game.—By such reasonings as these the old lady was accustomed to defend her favourite pastime.

No inducement could ever prevail upon her to play at any game, where chance entered into the composition, *for nothing.* Chance, she would argue— and here again, admire the subtlety of her conclusion! —chance is nothing, but where something else depends upon it. It is obvious, that cannot be *glory.* What rational cause of exultation could it give to a man to turn up size ace[28] a hundred times together

---

16 Pope, *The Rape of the Lock,* III, 56.—*Pam* was the jack of clubs, the highest card in the old game of loo.

17 Diana. The craftsmen at Ephesus (Acts 19:23 ff.) who made them were afraid that St. Paul's preaching would ruin their trade.

18 Exquisite.   19 In an essay on "The South-Sea House."

20 If one player cannot play a card without bringing the total value of cards played above thirty-one, it is a "go," and his opponent scores one.

21 Scoring is marked by advancing pegs in the board.

22 Jack. It counts two for the person who turns it up after the cut.

23 Scoring sixty additional points for counting thirty in one's hand before one has led a card or his opponent has scored.

24 The taking of all the cards.   25 Private.

26 Which may be played by three instead of two.

27 I.e., four-handed.   28 I.e., throw seven at dice.

by himself? or before spectators, where no stake was depending?—Make a lottery of a hundred thousand tickets with but one fortunate number—and what possible principle of our nature, except stupid wonderment, could it gratify to gain that number as many times successively, without a prize?—Therefore she disliked the mixture of chance in backgammon, where it was not played for money. She called it foolish, and those people idiots, who were taken with a lucky hit under such circumstances. Games of pure skill were as little to her fancy. Played for a stake, they were a mere system of over-reaching. Played for glory, they were a mere setting of one man's wit—his memory, or combination-faculty rather—against another's; like a mock-engagement at a review, bloodless and profitless.—She could not conceive a *game* wanting the spritely infusion of chance,—the handsome excuses of good fortune. Two people playing at chess in a corner of a room whilst whist was stirring in the centre, would inspire her with insufferable horror and ennui. Those well-cut similitudes of Castles, and Knights, the *imagery* of the board, she would argue (and I think in this case justly) were entirely misplaced, and senseless. Those hard head-contests can in no instance ally with the fancy. They reject form and colour. A pencil and dry slate (she used to say) were the proper arena for such combatants.

To those puny objectors against cards, as nurturing the bad passions, she would retort, that man is a gaming animal. He must be always trying to get the better in something or other:—that this passion can scarcely be more safely expended than upon a game at cards: that cards are a temporary illusion; in truth, a mere drama; for we do but *play* at being mightily concerned, where a few idle shillings are at stake, yet, during the illusion, we *are* as mightily concerned as those whose stake is crowns and kingdoms. They are a sort of dream-fighting; much ado; great battling, and little bloodshed; mighty means for disproportioned ends: quite as diverting, and a great deal more innoxious,[29] than many of those more serious *games* of life, which men play, without esteeming them to be such.—

With great deference to the old lady's judgment in these matters, I think I have experienced some moments in my life, when playing at cards *for nothing* has even been agreeable. When I am in sickness, or not in the best spirits, I sometimes call for the cards, and play a game at piquet *for love* with my cousin Bridget—Bridget Elia.[30]

I grant there is something sneaking in it; but with a tooth-ache, or a sprained ankle,—when you are subdued and humble,—you are glad to put up with an inferior spring of action.

There is such a thing in nature, I am convinced, as *sick whist.*—

I grant it is not the highest style of man—I deprecate the manes[31] of Sarah Battle—she lives not, alas! to whom I should apologise.

At such times, those *terms* which my old friend objected to, come in as something admissible. I love to get a tierce or a quatorze,[32] though they mean nothing. I am subdued to an inferior interest. Those shadows of winning amuse me.

That last game I had with my sweet cousin (I capotted her)—(dare I tell thee, how foolish I am?)—I wished it might have lasted for ever, though we gained nothing, and lost nothing, though it was a mere shade of play: I would be content to go on in that idle folly for ever. The pipkin should be ever boiling, that was to prepare the gentle lenitive[33] to my foot, which Bridget was doomed to apply after the game was over: and, as I do not much relish appliances, there it should ever bubble. Bridget and I should be ever playing.

DREAM-CHILDREN

A REVERIE

Lamb's older brother, a clerk of the South Sea Company, had recently died. Chiefly to this loss, but also to his sister's tragedy, and perhaps to memories of a former sweetheart, Anne Simmons, the touching sentiment of this charming essay is due.

CHILDREN love to listen to stories about their elders, when *they* were children; to stretch their imagination to the conception of a traditionary great-uncle or grandame, whom they never saw. It was in this spirit that my little ones crept about me the other evening to hear about their great-grandmother Field, who lived in a great house in Norfolk[1] (a hundred times bigger than that in which they and papa lived) which had been the scene—so at least it was generally believed in that part of the country—of the tragic incidents which they had lately become familiar

---

[29] Harmless. [30] I.e., his sister, Mary Lamb.

[31] Shade, spirit.
[32] A *tierce* is a sequence of three cards in any suit, in piquet and other card games. A *quatorze* is four of a kind (tens or better); it counts fourteen in piquet. [33] Soothing application.
[1] The estate where Lamb's grandmother lived as housekeeper was actually in Hertfordshire. Norfolk, however, was the scene of the legendary Babes in the Wood.

with from the ballad of the Children in the Wood. Certain it is that the whole story of the children and their cruel uncle was to be seen fairly carved out in wood upon the chimney-piece of the great hall, the whole story down to the Robin Redbreasts,[2] till a foolish rich person pulled it down to set up a marble one of modern invention in its stead, with no story upon it. Here Alice put out one of her dear mother's looks, too tender to be called upbraiding. Then I went on to say, how religious and how good their great-grandmother Field was, how beloved and respected by every body, though she was not indeed the mistress of this great house, but had only the charge of it (and yet in some respects she might be said to be the mistress of it too) committed to her by the owner, who preferred living in a newer and more fashionable mansion which he had purchased somewhere in the adjoining county; but still she lived in it in a manner as if it had been her own, and kept up the dignity of the great house in a sort while she lived, which afterwards came to decay, and was nearly pulled down, and all its old ornaments stripped and carried away to the owner's other house, where they were set up, and looked as awkward as if some one were to carry away the old tombs they had seen lately at the Abbey,[3] and stick them up in Lady C.'s tawdry gilt drawing-room. Here John smiled, as much as to say, "that would be foolish indeed." And then I told how, when she came to die, her funeral was attended by a concourse of all the poor, and some of the gentry too, of the neighbourhood for many miles round, to show their respect for her memory, because she had been such a good and religious woman; so good indeed that she knew all the Psaltery[4] by heart, ay, and a great part of the Testament besides. Here little Alice spread her hands. Then I told what a tall, upright, graceful person their great-grandmother Field once was; and how in her youth she was esteemed the best dancer—here Alice's little right foot played an involuntary movement, till, upon my looking grave, it desisted—the best dancer, I was saying, in the county, till a cruel disease, called a cancer, came, and bowed her down with pain; but it could never bend her good spirits, or make them stoop, but they were still upright, because she was so good and religious. Then I told how she was used to sleep by herself in a lone chamber of the great lone house; and how she believed that an apparition of two infants was to be seen at midnight gliding up and down the great staircase near where she slept, but she said "those innocents would do her no harm"; and how frightened I used to be, though in those days I had my maid to sleep with me, because I was never half so good or religious as she—and yet I never saw the infants. Here John expanded all his eye-brows and tried to look courageous. Then I told how good she was to all her grand-children, having us to the great-house in the holydays, where I in particular used to spend many hours by myself, in gazing upon the old busts of the Twelve Caesars, that had been Emperors of Rome, till the old marble heads would seem to live again, or I to be turned into marble with them; how I never could be tired with roaming about that huge mansion, with its vast empty rooms, with their worn-out hangings, fluttering tapestry, and carved oaken panels, with the gilding almost rubbed out—sometimes in the spacious old-fashioned gardens, which I had almost to myself, unless when now and then a solitary gardening man would cross me—and how the nectarines and peaches hung upon the walls, without my ever offering[5] to pluck them, because they were forbidden fruit, unless now and then,—and because I had more pleasure in strolling about among the old melancholy-looking yew trees, or the firs, and picking up the red berries, and the fir apples,[6] which were good for nothing but to look at—or in lying about upon the fresh grass, with all the fine garden smells around me—or basking in the orangery, till I could almost fancy myself ripening too along with the oranges and the limes in that grateful warmth—or in watching the dace that darted to and fro in the fish-pond, at the bottom of the garden, with here and there a great sulky pike hanging midway down the water in silent state, as if it mocked at their impertinent friskings,—I had more pleasure in these busy-idle diversions than in all the sweet flavours of peaches, nectarines, oranges, and such like common baits of children. Here John slily deposited back upon the plate a bunch of grapes, which, not unobserved by Alice, he had meditated dividing with her, and both seemed willing to relinquish them for the present as irrelevant. Then in somewhat a more heightened tone, I told how, though their great-grandmother Field loved all her grand-children, yet in an especial manner she might be said to love their uncle, John L——,[7] because he was so handsome and spirited a youth, and a king to the rest of us; and, instead of moping about in solitary corners, like some of us, he would mount the most

---

[2] Who covered the children's bodies with leaves. The poem is reprinted in *The Oxford Book of Ballads*, pp. 854-9.
[3] Westminster.   [4] The Book of Psalms.

[5] Frying.   [6] I.e., cones.
[7] Lamb; see the headnote.

mettlesome horse he could get, when but an imp no bigger than themselves, and make it carry him half over the county in a morning, and join the hunters when there were any out—and yet he loved the old great house and gardens too, but had too much spirit to be always pent up within their boundaries—and how their uncle grew up to man's estate as brave as he was handsome, to the admiration of every body, but of their great-grandmother Field most especially; and how he used to carry me upon his back when I was a lame-footed boy—for he was a good bit older than me—many a mile when I could not walk for pain;—and how in after life he became lame-footed too, and I did not always (I fear) make allowances enough for him when he was impatient, and in pain, nor remember sufficiently how considerate he had been to me when I was lame-footed; and how when he died, though he had not been dead an hour, it seemed as if he had died a great while ago, such a distance there is betwixt life and death; and how I bore his death as I thought pretty well at first, but afterwards it haunted and haunted me; and though I did not cry or take it to heart as some do, and as I think he would have done if I had died, yet I missed him all day long, and knew not till then how much I had loved him. I missed his kindness, and I missed his crossness, and wished him to be alive again, to be quarreling with him (for we quarreled sometimes), rather than not have him again, and was as uneasy without him, as he their poor uncle must have been when the doctor took off his limb. Here the children fell a crying, and asked if their little mourning which they had on was not for uncle John, and they looked up, and prayed me not to go on about their uncle, but to tell them some stories about their pretty dead mother. Then I told how for seven long years, in hope sometimes, sometimes in despair, yet persisting ever, I courted the fair Alice W——n;[8] and, as much as children could understand, I explained to them what coyness, and difficulty, and denial meant in maidens—when suddenly, turning to Alice, the soul of the first Alice looked out at her eyes with such a reality of re-presentment, that I became in doubt which of them stood there before me, or whose that bright hair was; and while I stood gazing, both the children gradually grew fainter to my view, receding, and still receding till nothing at last but two

mournful features were seen in the uttermost distance, which, without speech, strangely impressed upon me the effects of speech; "We are not of Alice, nor of thee, nor are we children at all. The children of Alice call Bartrum father. We are nothing; less than nothing, and dreams. We are only what might have been, and must wait upon the tedious shores of Lethe millions of ages before we have existence, and a name"— and immediately awaking, I found myself quietly seated in my bachelor arm-chair, where I had fallen asleep, with the faithful Bridget unchanged by my side—but John L. (or James Elia) was gone forever.[9]

OLD CHINA

I HAVE an almost feminine partiality for old china. When I go to see any great house, I inquire for the china-closet, and next for the picture gallery. I cannot defend the order of preference, but by saying, that we have all some taste or other, of too ancient a date to admit of our remembering distinctly that it was an acquired one. I can call to mind the first play, and the first exhibition, that I was taken to; but I am not conscious of a time when china jars and saucers were introduced into my imagination.

I had no repugnance then—why should I now have?—to those little, lawless, azure-tinctured grotesques, that under the notion of men and women, float about, uncircumscribed by any element, in that world before perspective—a china tea-cup.

I like to see my old friends—whom distance cannot diminish—figuring up in the air (so they appear to our optics), yet on *terra firma* still—for so we must in courtesy interpret that speck of deeper blue, which the decorous artist, to prevent absurdity, had made to spring up beneath their sandals.

I love the men with women's faces, and the women, if possible, with still more womanish expressions.

Here is a young and courtly Mandarin, handing tea to a lady from a salver—two miles off. See how distance seems to set off respect! And here the same lady, or another—for likeness is identity on tea-cups—is stepping into a little fairy boat, moored on the hither side of this calm garden river, with a dainty mincing foot, which in a right angle of incidence (as angles go in our world) must infallibly land her in the midst of a flowery mead—a furlong off on the other side of the same strange stream!

8 Perhaps Anne Simmons, Lamb's youthful flame, for she married a pawnbroker named Bartram; but Alice, too, may be a dream and a regret, like the children. Two years before he wrote this essay, Lamb, then in his forty-fourth year, had proposed marriage to Fanny Kelly, a popular actress, who was twenty-nine. She rejected him, but they remained friends.

9 In another essay, "My Relations," the name for John Lamb is James Elia.

Farther on—if far or near can be predicated of their world—see horses, trees, pagodas, dancing the hays.[1]

Here—a cow and rabbit couchant, and co-extensive—so objects show, seen through the lucid atmosphere of fine Cathay.

I was pointing out to my cousin last evening, over our Hyson[2] (which we are old fashioned enough to drink unmixed still of an afternoon) some of these *speciosa miracula*[3] upon a set of extraordinary old blue china (a recent purchase) which we were now for the first time using; and could not help remarking, how favourable circumstances had been to us of late years, that we could afford to please the eye sometimes with trifles of this sort—when a passing sentiment seemed to over-shade the brows of my companion. I am quick at detecting these summer clouds in Bridget.[4]

"I wish the good old times would come again," she said, "when we were not quite so rich. I do not mean, that I want to be poor; but there was a middle state";—so she was pleased to ramble on,—"in which I am sure we were a great deal happier. A purchase is but a purchase, now that you have money enough and to spare. Formerly it used to be a triumph. When we coveted a cheap luxury (and, O! how much ado I had to get you to consent in those times!) we were used to have a debate two or three days before, and to weigh the *for* and *against,* and think what we might spare it out of, and what saving we could hit upon, that should be an equivalent. A thing was worth buying then, when we felt the money that we paid for it.

"Do you remember the brown suit, which you made to hang upon you, till all your friends cried shame upon you, it grew so thread-bare—and all because of that folio Beaumont and Fletcher,[5] which you dragged home late at night from Barker's in Covent-garden?[6] Do you remember how we eyed it for weeks before we could make up our minds to the purchase, and had not come to a determination till it was near ten o'clock of the Saturday night, when you set off from Islington,[7] fearing you should be too late—and when the old bookseller with some grumbling opened his shop, and by the twinkling taper (for he was setting bedwards) lighted out the relic from his dusty treasures—and when you lugged it

home, wishing it were twice as cumbersome—and when you presented it to me—and when we were exploring the perfectness of it[8] (*collating,* you called it)—and while I was repairing some of the loose leaves with paste, which your impatience would not suffer to be left till day-break—was there no pleasure in being a poor man? or can those neat black clothes which you wear now, and are so careful to keep brushed, since we have become rich and finical, give you half the honest vanity, with which you flaunted it about in that over-worn suit—your old corbeau[9]—for four or five weeks longer than you should have done, to pacify your conscience for the mighty sum of fifteen—or sixteen shillings was it?—a great affair we thought it then—which you had lavished on the old folio. Now you can afford to buy any book that pleases you, but I do not see that you ever bring me home any nice old purchases now.

"When you came home with twenty apologies for laying out a less number of shillings upon that print after Lionardo, which we christened the 'Lady Blanch';[10] when you looked at the purchase, and thought of the money—and thought of the money, and looked again at the picture—was there no pleasure in being a poor man? Now, you have nothing to do but to walk into Colnaghi's,[11] and buy a wilderness of Lionardos.[12] Yet do you?

"Then, do you remember our pleasant walks to Enfield, and Potter's Bar, and Waltham,[13] when we had a holyday—holydays, and all other fun, are gone, now we are rich—and the little hand-basket in which I used to deposit our day's fare of savory cold lamb and salad—and how you would pry about at noon-tide for some decent house, where we might go in, and produce our store—only paying for the ale that you must call for—and speculate upon the looks of the landlady, and whether she was likely to allow us a table-cloth—and wish for such another honest hostess, as Izaak Walton has described many a one on the pleasant banks of the Lea, when he went a fishing—and sometimes they would prove obliging enough, and sometimes they would look grudgingly upon us—but we had cheerful looks still for one another, and would eat our plain food savorily, scarcely grudging Piscator his Trout Hall?[14] Now,

---

1 Old English country-dances.
2 A kind of green tea from China.   3 Splendid marvels.
4 I.e., Lamb's sister Mary.
5 The famous Jacobean dramatists. The folios containing their plays are not only tall but thick books.
6 Barker's bookshop was on Russell Street in that vicinity.
7 For a time the Lambs lived near this northern suburb.

8 To see that no leaves were missing.
9 Raven, the trade name of the dark green, almost black cloth it was made of.
10 The "Modesty and Vanity" of Leonardo da Vinci (d. 1519).
11 A well-known print shop.
12 Cf. Shylock's "a wilderness of monkeys," *The Merchant of Venice,* III, i, 128.   13 All northern suburbs.
14 In Charles Cotton's continuation of Izaak Walton's *The Complete Angler.*

when we go out a day's pleasuring, which is seldom moreover, we *ride* part of the way—and go into a fine inn, and order the best of dinners, never debating the expense—which, after all, never has half the relish of those chance country snaps, when we were at the mercy of uncertain usage, and a precarious welcome.

"You are too proud to see a play anywhere now but in the pit. Do you remember where it was we used to sit, when we saw the battle of Hexham, and the surrender of Calais,[15] and Bannister[16] and Mrs. Bland[17] in the Children in the Wood[18]—when we squeezed out our shillings a-piece to sit three or four times in a season in the one-shilling gallery—where you felt all the time that you ought not to have brought me—and more strongly I felt obligation to you for having brought me—and the pleasure was the better for a little shame—and when the curtain drew up, what cared we for our place in the house, or what mattered it where we were sitting, when our thoughts were with Rosalind in Arden, or with Viola at the Court of Illyria?[19] You used to say, that the gallery was the best place of all for enjoying a play socially—that the relish of such exhibitions must be in proportion to the infrequency of going— that the company we met there, not being in general readers of plays, were obliged to attend the more, and did attend, to what was going on, on the stage— because a word lost would have been a chasm, which it was impossible for them to fill up. With such reflections we consoled our pride then—and I appeal to you, whether, as a woman, I met generally with less attention and accommodation, than I have done since in more expensive situations in the house? The getting in indeed, and the crowding up those inconvenient stair-cases, was bad enough,—but there was still a law of civility to woman recognised to quite as great an extent as we ever found in the other passages—and how a little difficulty overcome heightened the snug seat, and the play, afterwards! Now we can only pay our money, and walk in. You cannot see, you say, in the galleries now. I am sure we saw, and heard too, well enough then—but sight, and all, I think, is gone with our poverty.

"There was pleasure in eating strawberries, before they became quite common—in the first dish of peas, while they were yet dear—to have them for a nice supper, a treat. What treat can we have now?

If we were to treat ourselves now—that is, to have dainties a little above our means, it would be selfish and wicked. It is the very little more that we allow ourselves beyond what the actual poor can get at, that makes what I call a treat—when two people living together, as we have done, now and then indulge themselves in a cheap luxury, which both like; while each apologises, and is willing to take both halves of the blame to his single share. I see no harm in people making much of themselves in that sense of the word. It may give them a hint how to make much of others. But now—what I mean by the word —we never do make much of ourselves. None but the poor can do it. I do not mean the veriest poor of all, but persons as we were, just above poverty.

"I know what you were going to say, that it is mighty pleasant at the end of the year to make all meet—and much ado we used to have every Thirty-first Night of December to account for our exceedings—many a long face did you make over your puzzled accounts, and in contriving to make it out how we had spent so much—or that we had not spent so much—or that it was impossible we should spend so much next year—and still we found our slender capital decreasing—but then, betwixt ways, and projects, and compromises of one sort or another, and talk of curtailing this charge, and doing without that for the future—and the hope that youth brings, and laughing spirits (in which you were never poor till now,) we pocketed up our loss, and in conclusion, with 'lusty brimmers' (as you used to quote it out of *hearty cheerful Mr. Cotton*,[20] as you called him), we used to welcome in the 'coming guest.' Now we have no reckoning at all at the end of the old year— no flattering promises about the new year doing better for us."

Bridget is so sparing of her speech on most occasions, that when she gets into a rhetorical vein, I am careful how I interrupt it. I could not help, however, smiling at the phantom of wealth which her dear imagination had conjured up out of a clear income of poor — hundred pounds a year. "It is true we were happier when we were poorer, but we were also younger, my cousin. I am afraid we must put up with the excess, for if we were to shake the superflux[21] into the sea, we should not much mend ourselves. That we had much to struggle with, as we grew up together, we have reason to be most thankful. It strengthened, and knit our compact closer. We could

---

15 Both plays by George Colman the Younger (1762–1836).
16 John Bannister (1760–1836) was a leading comedian.
17 Maria Theresa Bland (1769–1838).
18 By Thomas Morton (1764–1838).
19 In Shakespeare's *As You Like It* and *Twelfth Night*.

20 In his poem "The New Year" (see pp. 137 f., above).
21 Distribute the surplus. The phrase is from Shakespeare's *King Lear*, III, iv, 35.

never have been what we have been to each other, if we had always had the sufficiency which you now complain of. The resisting power—those natural dilations of the youthful spirit, which circumstances cannot straiten—with us are long since passed away. Competence to age is supplementary youth; a sorry supplement indeed, but I fear the best that is to be had. We must ride, where we formerly walked: live better, and lie softer—and shall be wise to do so—than we had means to do in those good old days you speak of. Yet could those days return—could you and I once more walk our thirty miles a-day—could Bannister and Mrs. Bland again be young, and you and I be young to see them—could the good old one-shilling gallery days return—they are dreams, my cousin, now—but could you and I at this moment, instead of this quiet argument, by our well-carpeted fire-side, sitting on this luxurious sofa—be once more struggling up those inconvenient stair-cases, pushed about, and squeezed, and elbowed by the poorest rabble of poor gallery scramblers—could I once more hear those anxious shrieks of yours—and the delicious *Thank God, we are safe,* which always followed when the topmost stair, conquered, let in the first light of the whole cheerful theatre down beneath us—I know not the fathom line[22] that ever touched a descent so deep as I would be willing to bury more wealth in than Croesus[23] had, or the great Jew R——[24] is supposed to have, to purchase it. And now do just look at that merry little Chinese waiter holding an umbrella, big enough for a bed-tester,[25] over the head of that pretty insipid half-Madonna-ish chit of a lady in that very blue summer-house."

POOR RELATIONS

A POOR RELATION—is the most irrelevant thing in nature,—a piece of impertinent correspondency,—an odious approximation,—a haunting conscience,—a preposterous shadow, lengthening in the noontide of your prosperity,—an unwelcome remembrancer,—a perpetually recurring mortification,—a drain on your purse,—a more intolerable dun upon your pride,—a drawback upon success,—a rebuke to your rising,—a stain in your blood,—a blot on your scutcheon,—a rent in your garment,—a death's head[1]

at your banquet,—Agathocles' pot,[2]—a Mordecai[3] in your gate,—a Lazarus[4] at your door,—a lion in your path,—a frog in your chamber,—a fly in your ointment,[5]—a mote in your eye,[6]—a triumph to your enemy, an apology to your friends,—the one thing not needful,[7]—the hail in harvest,—the ounce of sour in a pound of sweet.

He is known by his knock. Your heart telleth you "That is Mr. ——." A rap, between familiarity and respect; that demands, and, at the same time, seems to despair of, entertainment. He entereth smiling and—embarrassed. He holdeth out his hand to you to shake, and—draweth it back again. He casually looketh in about dinner time—when the table is full. He offereth to go away, seeing you have company—but is induced to stay. He filleth a chair, and your visitor's two children are accommodated at a side table. He never cometh upon open days, when your wife says with some complacency, "My dear, perhaps Mr. —— will drop in to-day." He remembereth birth-days—and professeth he is fortunate to have stumbled upon one. He declareth against fish, the turbot being small—yet suffereth himself to be importuned into a slice against his first resolution. He sticketh by the port—yet will be prevailed upon to empty the remainder glass of claret, if a stranger press it upon him. He is a puzzle to the servants, who are fearful of being too obsequious, or not civil enough, to him. The guests think "they have seen him before." Everyone speculateth upon his condition; and the most part take him to be—a tide-waiter.[8] He calleth you by your Christian name, to imply that his other is the same with your own. He is too familiar by half, yet you wish he had less diffidence. With half the familiarity he might pass for a casual dependent; with more boldness he would be in no danger of being taken for what he is. He is too humble for a friend, yet taketh on him more state than befits a client.[9] He is a worse guest than a country tenant, inasmuch as he bringeth up no rent—yet 'tis odds, from his garb

---

[22] Cf. Shakespeare's *1 Henry IV,* I, iii, 204.

[23] King of Lydia in Asia Minor (d. 546 B.C.).

[24] Nathan Meyer Rothschild (1777–1836), founder of the English branch of the famous family of financiers.   [25] Canopy.

[1] Skull.

[2] This Sicilian king (d. 289 B.C.) is said to have disliked the sight of a pot, because it reminded him of his humble origin; he was a potter's son.

[3] Esther's foster father, who would not bow down to Haman but kept vigil at the palace gate to learn her fate; in the end Haman was hanged on the gallows prepared for Mordecai. See Esther 2, 3, 5:9–14, 6:10–12, and 7:9–10.

[4] The beggar who asked for the crumbs from the rich man's table (Luke 16:20 ff.).

[5] 1 Kings 13:24; Exodus 8:3, 6; Ecclesiastes 10:1.

[6] Matthew 7:3–5.   [7] Luke 10:42.

[8] A customs official; he went aboard ships as they came in on a full tide. Hence, one who is waiting for a favorable opportunity. I.e., as your fortunes improve, he is on hand.—*Condition* = status.

[9] Dependent.

and demeanour, that your guests take him for one. He is asked to make one at the whist table; refuseth on the score of poverty, and—resents being left out. When the company break up, he proffereth to go for a coach—and lets the servant go. He recollects your grandfather; and will thrust in some mean, and quite unimportant anecdote of—the family. He knew it when it was not quite so flourishing as "he is blest in seeing it now." He reviveth past situations to institute what he calleth—favourable comparisons. With a reflecting sort of congratulation, he will inquire the price of your furniture; and insults you with a special commendation of your window-curtains. He is of opinion that the urn is the more elegant shape, but, after all, there was something more comfortable about the old tea-kettle—which you must remember. He dare say you must find a great convenience in having a carriage of your own, and appealeth to your lady if it is not so. Inquireth if you have had your arms done on vellum yet; and did not know, till lately, that such-and-such had been the crest of the family. His memory is unseasonable; his compliments perverse; his talk a trouble; his stay pertinacious; and when he goeth away, you dismiss his chair into a corner, as precipitately as possible, and feel fairly rid of two nuisances.

There is a worse evil under the sun, and that is—a female Poor Relation. You may do something with the other; you may pass him off tolerably well; but your indigent she-relative is hopeless. "He is an old humourist,"[10] you may say, "and affects[11] to go threadbare. His circumstances are better than folks would take them to be. You are fond of having a Character at your table, and truly he is one." But in the indications of female poverty there can be no disguise. No woman dresses below herself from caprice. The truth must out without shuffling. "She is plainly related to the L—s; or what does she at their house?" She is, in all probability, your wife's cousin. Nine times out of ten, at least, this is the case. Her garb is something between a gentlewoman and a beggar, yet the former evidently predominates. She is most provokingly humble, and ostentatiously sensible to her inferiority. He may require to be repressed sometimes—*aliquando sufflaminandus erat*[12] —but there is no raising her. You send her soup at dinner, and she begs to be helped—after the gentle-

men. Mr. —— requests the honour of taking wine with her; she hesitates between Port and Madeira, and chooses the former—because he does. She calls the servant *Sir;* and insists on not troubling him to hold her plate. The housekeeper patronizes her. The children's governess takes upon her to correct her, when she has mistaken the piano for a harpsichord.

Richard Amlet, Esq., in the play,[13] is a notable instance of the disadvantages, to which this chimerical notion of *affinity constituting a claim to acquaintance,* may subject the spirit of a gentleman. A little foolish blood is all that is betwixt him and a lady of great estate. His stars are perpetually crossed by the malignant maternity of an old woman, who persists in calling him "her son Dick." But she has where-withal in the end to recompense his indignities, and float him again upon the brilliant surface, under which it had been her seeming business and pleasure all along to sink him. All men, besides, are not of Dick's temperament. I knew an Amlet in real life, who, wanting Dick's buoyancy, sank indeed. Poor W——[14] was of my own standing at Christ's,[15] a fine classic, and a youth of promise. If he had a blemish, it was too much pride; but its quality was inoffensive; it was not of that sort which hardens the heart, and serves to keep inferiors at a distance; it only sought to ward off derogation from itself. It was the principle of self-respect carried as far as it could go, without infringing upon that respect, which he would have every one else equally maintain for himself. He would have you to think alike with him on this topic. Many a quarrel have I had with him, when we were rather older boys, and our tallness[16] made us more obnoxious to observation in the blue clothes,[17] because I would not thread the alleys and blind ways of the town with him to elude notice, when we have been out together on a holiday in the streets of this sneering and prying metropolis. W—— went, sore with these notions, to Oxford, where the dignity and sweetness of a scholar's life, meeting with the alloy of a humble introduction, wrought in him a passionate devotion to the place, with a profound aversion from the society. The servitor's[18] gown (worse than his school array) clung to him with

---

10 Eccentric.   11 Chooses.
12 He sometimes had to be checked (from speaking). The remark of Augustus on the Roman senator and rhetorician Haterius. For Ben Jonson's application of it to Shakespeare, see I, 443, above.
13 *The Confederacy* by Sir John Vanbrugh, the Restoration dramatist and architect.
14 Elsewhere Lamb says this is his friend Joseph Favell, who "left Cambridge because he was asham'd of his father, who was a house-painter there."   15 Christ's Hospital.
16 Actually, Lamb was very small.
17 From the school uniform, the Christ's Hospital pupils were known as the Bluecoat boys.
18 Menial duties were formerly required of certain scholarship holders, called servitors at Oxford and sizars at Cambridge.

Nessian venom.[19] He thought himself ridiculous in a garb under which Latimer[20] must have walked erect; and in which Hooker,[21] in his young days, possibly flaunted in a vein of no discommendable vanity. In the depths of college shades, or in his lonely chamber, the poor student shrunk from observation. He found shelter among books, which insult not; and studies, that ask no questions of a youth's finances. He was lord of his library, and seldom cared for looking out beyond his domains. The healing influence of studious pursuits was upon him, to soothe and to abstract. He was almost a healthy man; when the waywardness of his fate broke out against him with a second and worse malignity. The father of W—— had hitherto exercised the humble profession of house-painter at N——, near Oxford. A supposed interest with some of the heads of the colleges had now induced him to take up his abode in that city, with the hope of being employed upon some public works which were talked of. From that moment I read in the countenance of the young man, the determination which at length tore him from academical pursuits for ever. To a person unacquainted with our Universities, the distance between the gownsmen and the townsmen, as they are called—the trading part of the latter especially—is carried to an excess that would appear harsh and incredible. The temperament of W——'s father was diametrically the reverse of his own. Old W—— was a little, busy, cringing tradesman, who, with his son upon his arm, would stand bowing and scraping, cap in hand, to any-thing that wore the semblance of a gown—insensible to the winks and opener remonstrances of the young man, to whose chamber-fellow, or equal in standing, perhaps, he was thus obsequiously and gratuitously ducking. Such a state of things could not last. W—— must change the air of Oxford or be suffocated. He chose the former; and let the sturdy moralist, who strains the point of the filial duties as high as they can bear, censure the dereliction; he cannot estimate the struggle. I stood with W——, the last afternoon I ever saw him, under the eaves of his paternal dwelling. It was in the fine lane leading from the High-street to the back of ***** college, where W—— kept his rooms. He seemed thoughtful, and more reconciled. I ventured to rally him—finding him in

a better mood—upon a representation of the Artist Evangelist,[22] which the old man, whose affairs were beginning to flourish, had caused to be set up in a splendid sort of frame over his really handsome shop, either as a token of prosperity, or badge of gratitude to his saint. W—— looked up at the Luke, and, like Satan, "knew his mounted sign—and fled."[23] A letter on his father's table the next morning, announced that he had accepted a commission in a regiment about to embark for Portugal. He was among the first who perished before the walls of St. Sebastian.[24]

I do not know how,[25] upon a subject which I began with treating half seriously, I should have fallen upon a recital so eminently painful; but this theme of poor relationship is replete with so much matter for tragic as well as comic associations, that it is difficult to keep the account distinct without blending. The earliest impressions which I received on this matter, are certainly not attended with anything painful, or very humiliating, in the recalling. At my father's table (no very splendid one) was to be found, every Saturday, the mysterious figure of an aged gentleman, clothed in neat black, of a sad yet comely appearance. His deportment was of the essence of gravity; his words few or none; and I was not to make a noise in his presence. I had little inclination to have done so—for my cue was to admire in silence. A particular elbow chair was appropriated to him, which was in no case to be violated. A peculiar sort of sweet pudding, which appeared on no other occasion, distinguished the days of his coming. I used to think him a prodigiously rich man. All I could make out of him was, that he and my father had been schoolfellows a world ago at Lincoln, and that he came from the Mint. The Mint I knew to be a place where all the money was coined—and I thought he was the owner of all that money. Awful ideas of the Tower[26] twined themselves about his presence. He seemed above human infirmities and passions. A sort of melancholy grandeur invested him. From some inexplicable doom I fancied him obliged to go about in an eternal suit of mourning; a captive—a stately being, let out

---

[19] Hercules killed himself on account of the pain caused by his wearing a shirt poisoned with the blood of the centaur Nessus, whom he had slain with a poisoned arrow.

[20] Bishop Hugh Latimer (d. 1555), Protestant martyr under Queen Mary Tudor, was a sizar at Cambridge.

[21] Richard Hooker (d. 1600), the celebrated theologian, was a servitor at Oxford.

[22] St. Luke was a physician and also, according to tradition, a painter.

[23] In *Paradise Lost*, IV, 1013–15, Satan sees a pair of scales in the heavens, with himself in the lighter one. Reading his fate in "his mounted scale," he flees.

[24] Thousands of British soldiers fell in Wellington's attack in 1813 on this seaport in northern Spain.

[25] A rambling structure is characteristic of the familiar essay—as well as of conversation. In his *Dictionary* Dr. Johnson defines the essay as "a loose sally of the mind."

[26] For the Mint stands on Tower Hill, near the Tower itself.

of the Tower on Saturdays. Often have I wondered at the temerity of my father, who, in spite of an habitual general respect which we all in common manifested towards him, would venture now and then to stand up against him in some argument, touching their youthful days. The houses of the ancient city of Lincoln are divided (as most of my readers know) between the dwellers on the hill, and in the valley. This marked distinction formed an obvious division between the boys who lived above (however brought together in a common school) and the boys whose paternal residence was on the plain; a sufficient cause of hostility in the code of these young Grotiuses.[27] My father had been a leading Mountaineer; and would still maintain the general superiority, in skill and hardihood, of the *Above Boys* (his own faction) over the *Below Boys* (so were they called), of which party his contemporary had been a chieftain. Many and hot were the skirmishes on this topic—the only one upon which the old gentleman was ever brought out—and bad blood bred; even sometimes almost to the recommencement (so I expected) of actual hostilities. But my father, who scorned to insist upon advantages, generally contrived to turn the conversation upon some adroit by-commendation of the old Minster; in the general preference of which, before all other cathedrals in the island, the dweller on the hill, and the plain-born, could meet on a conciliating level, and lay down their less important differences. Once only I saw the old gentleman really ruffled, and I remembered with anguish the thought that came over me: "Perhaps he will never come here again." He had been pressed to take another plate of the viand which I have already mentioned as the indispensable concomitant of his visits. He had refused, with a resistance amounting to rigour, when my aunt—an old Lincolnian, but who had something of this in common with my cousin Bridget,[28] that she would sometimes press civility out of season—uttered the following memorable application—"Do take another slice, Mr. Billet, for you do not get pudding every day." The old gentleman said nothing at the time—but he took occasion in the course of the evening, when some argument had intervened between them, to utter with an emphasis which chilled the company, and which chills me now as I write it—"Woman, you are superannuated!" John Billet did not survive long, after the digesting of this affront; but he survived long enough to assure me that peace was actually

restored! and if I remember aright, another pudding was discreetly substituted in the place of that which had occasioned the offence. He died at the Mint (Anno 1781) where he had long held, what he accounted, a comfortable independence; and with five pounds, fourteen shillings, and a penny, which were found in his escrutoire[29] after his decease, left the world, blessing God that he had enough to bury him, and that he had never been obliged to any man for a sixpence. This was—a Poor Relation.

THE SUPERANNUATED MAN

Sera tamen respexit Libertas.[1]

VIRGIL.

A Clerk I was in London gay.

O'KEEFE.[2]

IF peradventure, Reader, it has been thy lot to waste the golden years of thy life—thy shining youth—in the irksome confinement of an office; to have thy prison days prolonged through middle age down to decrepitude and silver hairs, without hope of release or respite; to have lived to forget that there are such things as holidays, or to remember them but as the prerogatives of childhood; then, and then only, will you be able to appreciate my deliverance.

It is now six and thirty years since I took my seat at the desk in Mincing-lane.[3] Melancholy was the transition at fourteen from the abundant play-time, and the frequently intervening vacations of school days, to the eight, nine, and sometimes ten hours' a-day attendance at a counting-house. But time partially reconciles us to anything. I gradually became content—doggedly contented, as wild animals in cages.

It is true I had my Sundays to myself; but Sundays, admirable as the institution of them is for purposes of worship, are for that very reason the very worst adapted for days of unbending and recreation. In particular, there is a gloom for me attendant upon a city Sunday, a weight in the air. I miss the cheerful cries of London, the music, and the ballad-singers—

---

27 Hugo Grotius (1583–1645), the great Dutch jurist, wrote a Latin treatise *On War and Peace.*   28 I.e., Mary Lamb.

29 Escritoire, desk.

1 Though late, Freedom nevertheless visited me. (Slightly misquoted from Vergil, *Eclogues,* I, 27.)—While Lamb is never literal in dealing with fact, this essay is essentially autobiographical.

2 John O'Keeffe (1747–1833), Irish actor and playwright, was not, however, the author of *Inkle and Yarico* (1787), from which this line of a song is quoted. It was a comic opera by George Colman the Younger (1762–1836).

3 The site of the East India House, near the Tower.

the buzz and stirring murmur of the streets. Those eternal bells depress me. The closed shops repel me. Prints, pictures, all the glittering and endless succession of knacks and gewgaws, and ostentatiously displayed wares of tradesmen, which make a week-day saunter through the less busy parts of the metropolis so delightful—are shut out. No book-stalls deliciously to idle over—no busy faces to recreate the idle man who contemplates them ever passing by—the very face of business a charm by contrast to his temporary relaxation from it. Nothing to be seen but unhappy countenances—or half-happy at best—of emancipated 'prentices and little tradesfolks, with here and there a servant maid that has got leave to go out, who, slaving all the week, with the habit has lost almost the capacity of enjoying a free hour; and livelily expressing the hollowness of a day's pleasuring. The very strollers in the fields on that day look anything but comfortable.

But besides Sundays I had a day at Easter, and a day at Christmas, with a full week in the summer to go and air myself in my native fields of Hertfordshire.[4] This last was a great indulgence; and the prospect of its recurrence, I believe, alone kept me up through the year, and made my durance tolerable. But when the week came round, did the glittering phantom of the distance keep touch with me? or rather was it not a series of seven uneasy days, spent in restless pursuit of pleasure, and a wearisome anxiety to find out how to make the most of them? Where was the quiet, where the promised rest? Before I had a taste of it, it was vanished. I was at the desk again, counting upon the fifty-one tedious weeks that must intervene before such another snatch would come. Still the prospect of its coming threw something of an illumination upon the darker side of my captivity. Without it, as I have said, I could scarcely have sustained my thraldom.

Independently of the rigours of attendance, I have ever been haunted with a sense (perhaps a mere caprice) of incapacity for business. This, during my latter years, had increased to such a degree, that it was visible in all the lines of my countenance. My health and my good spirits flagged. I had perpetually a dread of some crisis, to which I should be found unequal. Besides my daylight servitude, I served over again all night in my sleep, and would awake with terrors of imaginary false entries, errors in my accounts, and

the like. I was fifty years of age, and no prospect of emancipation presented itself. I had grown to my desk, as it were; and the wood had entered into my soul.

My fellows in the office would sometimes rally me upon the trouble legible in my countenance; but I did not know that it had raised the suspicions of any of my employers, when, on the 5th of last month, a day ever to be remembered by me, L——, the junior partner in the firm, calling me on one side, directly taxed me with my bad looks, and frankly inquired the cause of them. So taxed, I honestly made confession of my infirmity, and added that I was afraid I should eventually be obliged to resign his service. He spoke some words of course to hearten me, and there the matter rested. A whole week I remained labouring under the impression that I had acted imprudently in my disclosure; that I had foolishly given a handle against myself, and had been anticipating my own dismissal. A week passed in this manner, the most anxious one, I verily believe, in my whole life, when on the evening of the 12th of April, just as I was about quitting my desk to go home (it might be about eight o'clock) I received an awful summons to attend the presence of the whole assembled firm in the formidable back parlour. I thought, now my time is surely come, I have done for myself, I am going to be told that they have no longer occasion for me. L——, I could see, smiled at the terror I was in, which was a little relief to me,—when to my utter astonishment B——, the eldest partner, began a formal harangue to me on the length of my services, my very meritorious conduct during the whole of the time (the deuce, thought I, how did he find out that? I protest I never had the confidence to think as much). He went on to descant on the expediency of retiring at a certain time of life (how my heart panted!) and asking me a few questions as to the amount of my own property, of which I have a little, ended with a proposal, to which his three partners nodded a grave assent, that I should accept from the house, which I had served so well, a pension for life to the amount of two-thirds of my accustomed salary[5]—a magnificent offer! I do not know what I answered between surprise and gratitude, but it was understood that I accepted their proposal, and I was told that I was free from that hour to leave their service. I stammered out a bow, and at just ten minutes after eight I went home—for ever. This noble benefit—gratitude forbids me to conceal their names—I owe to the kindness of the most munificent

---

[4] Actually, Lamb was born in London. For his childhood days in Hertfordshire, his mother's and grandmother's county, see above, in "Dream-Children," and another of his essays, not here reprinted, "Mackery End."

[5] The pension was £450 a year.

firm in the world—the house of Boldero, Merry-weather, Bosanquet, and Lacy.[6]

Esto Perpetua![7]

For the first day or two I felt stunned, over-whelmed. I could only apprehend my felicity; I was too confused to taste it sincerely. I wandered about, thinking I was happy, and knowing that I was not. I was in the condition of a prisoner in the Old Bastile,[8] suddenly let loose after a forty years' confinement. I could scarce trust myself with myself. It was like passing out of Time into Eternity—for it is a sort of Eternity for a man to have his Time all to himself. It seemed to me that I had more time on my hands than I could ever manage. From a poor man, poor in Time, I was suddenly lifted up into a vast revenue; I could see no end of my possessions; I wanted some steward, or judicious bailiff, to manage my estates in Time for me. And here let me caution persons grown old in active business, not lightly, nor without weighing their own resources, to forego their cus-tomary employment all at once, for there may be danger in it. I feel it by myself, but I know that my resources are sufficient; and now that those first giddy raptures have subsided, I have a quiet home-feeling of the blessedness of my condition. I am in no hurry. Having all holidays, I am as though I had none. If Time hung heavy upon me, I could walk it away; but I do *not* walk all day long, as I used to do in those old transient holidays, thirty miles a day, to make the most of them. If Time were troublesome, I could read it away, but I do *not* read in that violent measure, with which, having no Time my own but candle-light Time, I used to weary out my head and eye-sight in by-gone winters. I walk, read or scribble (as now) just when the fit seizes me. I no longer hunt after pleasure; I let it come to me. I am like the man

—That's born, and has his years come to him,
In some green desart.[9]

"Years," you will say! "what is this superannuated simpleton calculating upon? He has already told us he is past fifty."

I have indeed lived nominally fifty years, but deduct out of them the hours which I have lived to other people, and not to myself, and you will find me still a young fellow. For *that* is the only true

Time, which a man can properly call his own, that which he has all to himself; the rest, though in some sense he may be said to live it, is other people's time, not his. The remnant of my poor days, long or short, is at least multiplied for me three-fold. My ten next years, if I stretch so far, will be as long as any preced-ing thirty. 'Tis a fair rule-of-three sum.

Among the strange fantasies which beset me at the commencement of my freedom, and of which all traces are not yet gone, one was, that a vast tract of time had intervened since I quitted the Counting House.[10] I could not conceive of it as an affair of yesterday. The partners, and the clerks, with whom I had for so many years, and for so many hours in each day of the year, been so closely associated—being suddenly removed from them—they seemed as dead to me. There is a fine passage, which may serve to illustrate this fancy, in a Tragedy[11] by Sir Robert Howard, speaking of a friend's death:

—'Twas but just now he went away;
I have not since had time to shed a tear;
And yet the distance does the same appear
As if he had been a thousand years from me.
Time takes no measure in Eternity.

To dissipate this awkward feeling, I have been fain to go among them once or twice since; to visit my old desk-fellows—my co-brethren of the quill—that I had left below in the state militant.[12] Not all the kindness with which they received me could quite restore to me that pleasant familiarity, which I had heretofore enjoyed among them. We cracked some of our old jokes, but methought they went off but faintly. My old desk; the peg where I hung my hat, were appropriated to another. I knew it must be, but I could not take it kindly. D——l take me, if I did not feel some remorse—beast, if I had not,—at quitting my old compeers, the faithful partners of my toils for six and thirty years, that smoothed for me with their jokes and conundrums the ruggedness of my professional road. Had it been so rugged then after all? or was I a coward simply? Well, it is too late to repent; and I also know, that these suggestions are a common fallacy of the mind on such occasions. But my heart smote me. I had violently broken the bands betwixt us. It was at least not courteous. I shall be some time before I get quite reconciled to the separation. Farewell, old cronies, yet not for long, for again and again I will come among ye, if I shall have your

---

[6] Fictitious names.   [7] May it be eternal.
[8] The prison in Paris that was demolished by the populace at the beginning of the French Revolution.
[9] Misquoted from *Hengist, King of Kent* (usually referred to by its subtitle, *The Mayor of Queenborough*), I, i, 133-4, by Thomas Middleton (d. 1627).

[10] Office. Lamb worked in the accountant's office.
[11] *The Vestal Virgin* (V, i) by this brother-in-law (1626-98) of Dryden.
[12] I.e., still actively engaged. Cf. "the Church militant" and "the Church triumphant."

leave. Farewell, Ch——,[13] dry, sarcastic, and friendly! Do——,[14] mild, slow to move, and gentlemanly! Pl——,[15] officious to do, and to volunteer, good services!—and thou, thou dreary pile, fit mansion for a Gresham[16] or a Whittington[17] of old, stately House of Merchants; with thy labyrinthine passages, and light-excluding, pent-up offices, where candles for one half the year supplied the place of the sun's light; unhealthy contributor to my weal, stern fosterer of my living, farewell! In thee remain, and not in the obscure collection of some wandering bookseller, my "works!"[18] There let them rest, as I do from my labours, piled on thy massy shelves, more MSS. in folio than ever Aquinas[19] left, and full as useful! My mantle I bequeath among ye.

A fortnight has passed since the date of my first communication.[20] At that period I was approaching to tranquillity, but had not reached it. I boasted of a calm indeed, but it was comparative only. Something of the first flutter was left; an unsettling sense of novelty; the dazzle to weak eyes of unaccustomed light. I missed my old chains, forsooth,[21] as if they had been some necessary part of my apparel. I was a poor Carthusian,[22] from strict cellular discipline suddenly by some revolution returned upon the world. I am now as if I had never been other than my own master. It is natural to me to go where I please, to do what I please. I find myself at eleven o'clock in the day in Bond-street,[23] and it seems to me that I have been sauntering there at that very hour for years past. I digress into Soho,[24] to explore a book-stall. Methinks I have been thirty years a collector. There is nothing strange nor new in it. I find myself before a fine picture in the morning. Was it ever otherwise? What is become of Fish-street Hill? Where is Fenchurch Street?[25] Stones of old Mincing-lane which I have worn with my daily pilgrimage for six and thirty years, to the footsteps of what toil-worn clerk are your everlasting flints now vocal? I indent the gayer flags of Pall Mall.[26] It is 'Change[27] time, and I am strangely among the Elgin marbles.[28] It was no hyperbole when I ventured to compare the change in my condition to a passing into another world. Time stands still in a manner to me. I have lost all distinction of season. I do not know the day of the week, or of the month. Each day used to be individually felt by me in its reference to the foreign post days; in its distance from, or propinquity to, the next Sunday. I had my Wednesday feelings, my Saturday nights' sensations. The genius of each day was upon me distinctly during the whole of it, affecting my appetite, spirits, &c. The phantom of the next day, with the dreary five to follow, sate as a load upon my poor Sabbath recreations. What charm has washed that Ethiop white? What is gone of Black Monday? All days are the same. Sunday itself—that unfortunate failure of a holyday as it too often proved, what with my sense of its fugitiveness, and over-care to get the greatest quantity of pleasure out of it—is melted down into a week day. I can spare to go to church now, without grudging the huge cantle[29] which it used to seem to cut out of the holyday. I have Time for everything. I can visit a sick friend. I can interrupt the man of much occupation when he is busiest. I can insult[30] over him with an invitation to take a day's pleasure with me to Windsor[31] this fine May-morning. It is Lucretian[32] pleasure to behold the poor drudges, whom I have left behind in the world, carking and caring;[33] like horses in a mill, drudging on in the same eternal round—and what is it all for? A man can never have too much Time to himself, nor too little to do. Had I a little son, I would christen him NOTHING-TO-DO; he should do nothing. Man, I verily believe, is out of his element, as long as he is operative. I am altogether for the life contemplative. Will no kindly

---

13 John Chambers (d. 1872).

14 Probably Henry Dodwell who, two years later, sent Lamb the appropriate gift of a sucking pig.

15 Presumably one W. D. Plumley.

16 Sir Thomas Gresham (d. 1579), financier, and founder of the Royal Exchange.

17 Richard Whittington (d. 1423), merchant, and lord mayor of London.

18 I.e., the ledgers kept by Lamb.

19 St. Thomas Aquinas (d. 1274), the Italian theologian. Lamb's gibe is not anti-Catholic; it merely reflects the prejudice against the scholastic philosophers.

20 This essay originally appeared in the *London Magazine* for May, 1825, in two parts, with one of the two quotations which now precede the essay heading each part. The second part began with this paragraph.   21 Indeed; i.e., believe it or not.

22 A member of a particularly strict order of monks founded in the eleventh century near Chartreuse, France.

23 A street in the West End, noted for its fashionable shops and art dealers' galleries.

24 A district on the edge of the West End, near the British Museum.

25 Both are near the East India House.

26 In the West End. Then a street (pronounced *pell-mell*) of fine residences and clubs.—*Everlasting flint* is in *Romeo and Juliet*, II, vi, 17.   27 Exchange, for mercantile transactions.

28 The great collection of sculptures in the British Museum, brought from Athens by the seventh Earl of Elgin in 1803–12.

29 Slice. See *1 Henry IV*, III, i, 100.   30 Exult.

31 A town about twenty miles up the Thames from London—the site of Windsor Castle.

32 The opening lines of Book II of *De Rerum Natura* (On the Nature of Things), by the Roman poet and Epicurean philosopher Lucretius (d. 55 B.C.), assert that we take pleasure in others' misfortunes.

33 Being full of worry and anxiety.

earthquake come and swallow up those accursed cotton mills? Take me that lumber of a desk there, and bowl it down

As low as to the fiends.[34]

I am no longer * * * * * *, clerk to the Firm of &c. I am Retired Leisure.[35] I am to be met with in trim gardens. I am already come to be known by my vacant face and careless gesture, perambulating at no fixed pace, nor with any settled purpose. I walk about; not to and from. They tell me, a certain *cum dignitate*[36] air, that has been buried so long with my other good parts, has begun to shoot forth in my person. I grow into gentility perceptibly. When I take up a newspaper it is to read the state of the opera. *Opus operatum est.*[37] I have done all that I came into this world to do. I have worked task work, and have the rest of the day to myself.

LETTERS

I. TO SAMUEL TAYLOR COLERIDGE

London, 27 SEPTEMBER, 1796

My dearest friend—White[1] or some of my friends or the public papers by this time may have informed you of the terrible calamities that have fallen on our family. I will only give you the outlines. My poor dear dearest sister in a fit of insanity has been the death of her own mother. I was at hand only time enough to snatch the knife out of her grasp. She is at present in a mad house, from whence I fear she must be moved to an hospital. God has preserved to me my senses,—I eat and drink and sleep, and have my judgment I believe very sound. My poor father was slightly wounded, and I am left to take care of him and my aunt. Mr. Norris of the Bluecoat school[2] has been very kind to us, and we have no other friend, but thank God I am very calm and composed, and able to do the best that remains to do. Write,—as religious a letter as possible—but no mention of what is gone and done with—with me the former things are passed away, and I have something more to do than[3] to feel——

God almighty
have us all in
his keeping.——

C. LAMB.

Mention nothing of poetry. I have destroyed every vestige of past vanities of that kind. Do as you please, but if you publish, publish mine (I give free leave) without name or initial, and never send me a book, I charge you, your[4] own judgment will convince you not to take notice of this yet to your dear wife.[5]— You look after your family,—I have my reason and strength left to take care of mine. I charge you don't think of coming to see me. Write. I will not see you if you come. God almighty love you and all of us——

II. TO WILLIAM WORDSWORTH

[JANUARY 30, 1801]

Thanks for your Letter and Present.[6] I had already borrowed your second volume. What most please me are, the Song of Lucy. . . .[7] *Simon's sickly daughter*[8] in the Sexton made me *cry*. Next to these are the description of the continuous Echoes in the story of Joanna's laugh,[9] where the mountains and all the scenery absolutely seem alive—and that fine Shaksperian character of the Happy Man, in the Brothers,

—that creeps about the fields,
Following his fancies by the hour, to bring
Tears down his cheek, or solitary smiles
Into his face, *until the Setting Sun
Write Fool upon his forehead.*[10]

I will mention one more: the delicate and curious feeling in the wish for the Cumberland Beggar, that he may have about him the melody of Birds, altho' he hear them not.[11] Here the mind knowingly passes

---

34 *Hamlet,* II, ii, 518-19.
35 These two words and "trim gardens" are from Milton's "Il Penseroso," lines 49-50.

1 James White, a friend since their school days at Christ's Hospital.
2 Richard Norris of Christ's Hospital. The Norrises were friends of the family.   3 Miswritten *that*.   4 Miswritten *you*.

36 From the Latin saying *Otium cum dignitate,* leisure with dignity.
37 The work is done.

5 Who was recovering from childbirth.
6 A copy of the second volume, just published, of *Lyrical Ballads.* —Lamb's letter is not dated, but the postmark is as above.
7 It is evident from the next letter, to Manning, that Lamb refers to "She dwelt among the untrodden ways." The four dots are in the original letter (now in the library of the University of Texas).   8 "To a Sexton," line 14.
9 In "Poems on the Naming of Places," no. II, "To Joanna."
10 "The Brothers," lines 108-12.
11 "The Old Cumberland Beggar," lines 184-5.

a fiction upon herself, first substituting her own feelings for the Beggar's, and, in the same breath detecting the fallacy, will not part with the wish.—The Poet's Epitaph is disfigured, to my taste by the vulgar satire upon parsons and lawyers in the beginning, and the coarse epithet of pin point[12] in the 6th stanza. All the rest is eminently good, and your own. I will just add that it appears to me a fault in the Beggar, that the instructions conveyed in it are too direct and like a lecture: they don't slide into the mind of the reader, while he is imagining no such matter. An intelligent reader finds a sort of insult in being told, I will teach you how to think upon this subject. This fault, if I am right, is in a ten-thousandth worse degree to be found in Sterne[13] and many many novelists & modern poets, who continually put a sign post up to shew where you are to feel. They set out with assuming their readers to be stupid. Very different from Robinson Crusoe, the Vicar of Wakefield, Roderick Random, and other beautiful bare narratives. There is implied an unwritten compact between Author and reader; I will tell you a story, and I suppose you will understand it. Modern novels "St. Leons"[14] and the like, are full of such flowers as these "Let not my reader suppose," "Imagine, if you can"—modest!—&c.—I will here have done with praise and blame. I have written so much, only that you may not think I have passed over your book without observation.—I am sorry that Coleridge has christened his Ancient Marinere[15] "a poet's Reverie"—it is as bad as Bottom the Weaver's declaration[16] that he is not a Lion but only the scenical representation of a Lion. What new idea is gained by this Title, but one subversive of all credit, which the tale should force upon us, of its truth? For me, I was never so affected with any human tale. After first reading it, I was totally possessed with it for many days—I dislike all the miraculous part of it, but the feelings of the man under the operation of such scenery dragged me along like Tom Piper's magic whistle. I totally differ from your idea that the Marinere should have had a character and profession. This is a beauty in Gulliver's Travels, where the mind

is kept in a placid state of little wonderments; but the Ancient Marinere undergoes such trials, as overwhelm and bury all individuality or memory of what he was, like the state of a man in a Bad dream, one terrible peculiarity of which is: that all consciousness of personality is gone. Your other observation is I think as well a little unfounded: the Marinere from being conversant in supernatural events *has* acquired a supernatural and strange cast of *phrase*, eye, appearance, &c. which frighten the wedding guest. You will excuse my remarks, because I am hurt and vexed that you should think it necessary, with a prose apology, to open the eyes of dead men that cannot see. To sum up a general opinion of the second vol.— I do not feel any one poem in it so forcibly as the Ancient Marinere, the Mad Mother,[17] and the Lines at Tintern Abbey in the first.—I could, too, have wished the Critical preface had appeared in a separate treatise. All its dogmas are true and just, and most of them new, *as* criticism. But they associate a *diminishing* idea with the Poems which follow, as having been written for *Experiment* on the public taste, more than having sprung (as they must have done) from living and daily circumstances.—I am prolix, because I am gratifyed in the opportunity of writing to you, and I don't well know when to leave off. I ought before this to have reply'd to your very kind invitation into Cumberland. With you and your sister I could gang[18] anywhere. But I am afraid whether I shall ever be able to afford so desperate a Journey. Separate from the pleasure of your company, I don't much care if I never see a mountain in my life. I have passed all my days in London, until I have formed as many and intense local attachments, as any of you mountaineers can have done with dead nature. The Lighted shops of the Strand and Fleet Street, the innumerable trades, tradesmen and customers, coaches, waggons, playhouses, all the bustle and wickedness round about Covent Garden, the very women of the town,[19] the Watchmen, drunken scenes, rattles,[20]—life awake, if you awake, at all hours of the night, the impossibility of being dull in Fleet Street, the crowds, the very dirt & mud, the Sun shining upon houses and pavements, the print shops, the old book stalls, parsons cheap'ning[21] books, coffee houses, steams of soups from kitchens, the pantomimes, London itself a pantomime and a masquerade,—all these things work themselves into my mind and feed me, without a power of satiating me. The wonder of these sights

---

[12] Wordsworth afterwards removed this expression from "A Poet's Epitaph."

[13] Described, along with the authors of the novels mentioned just below, in I, 683–4, above.

[14] William Godwin's *St. Leon* (1799).

[15] Spellings were more archaic in the first version of this poem.

[16] It is actually made by Snug, who plays the role (*A Midsummer Night's Dream*, V, i, 222–30); but the idea of reassuring the ladies originates with Snout, and Bottom elaborates it (III, i, 37 ff.).

[17] The poem beginning "Her eyes are wild."
[18] Go.   [19] Prostitutes, streetwalkers.
[20] Rackets, uproar.   [21] Cheapening, bargaining for.

impells me into night-walks about her crowded streets, and I often shed tears in the motley Strand from fulness of joy at so much Life.—All these emotions must be strange to you. So are your rural emotions to me. But consider, what must I have been doing all my life, not to have lent great portions of my heart with usury to such scenes?—

My attachments are all local, purely local. I have no passion (or have had none since I was in love, and then it was the spurious engendering of poetry & books) to groves and vallies. The rooms where I was born, the furniture which has been before my eyes all my life, a book case which has followed me about (like a faithful dog, only exceeding him in knowledge) wherever I have moved—old chairs, old tables, streets, squares, where I have sunned myself, my old school,—these are my mistresses. Have I not enough, without your mountains? I do not envy you. I should pity you, did I not know, that the Mind will make friends of any thing. Your sun & moon and skys and hills & lakes affect me no more, or scarcely come to me in more venerable characters, than as a gilded room with tapestry and tapers, where I might live with handsome visible objects. I consider the clouds above me but as a roof, beautifully painted but unable to satisfy the mind, and at last, like the pictures of the apartment of a connoisseur, unable to afford him any longer a pleasure. So fading upon me, from disuse, have been the Beauties of Nature, as they have been confinedly called; so ever fresh & green and warm are all the inventions of men and assemblies of men in this great city. I should certainly have laughed with dear Joanna.[22]

Give my kindest love, *and my sister's,* to D.[23] and yourself and a kiss from me to little Barbara Lewthwaite.[24]

C. LAMB.

Thanks for liking my Play!![25]

III. TO THOMAS MANNING[26]

FEB. 15, 1801.

I had need be cautious henceforward what opinion I give of the "Lyrical Ballads." All the North of England are in a turmoil. Cumberland and West-moreland have already declared a state of war. I lately received from Wordsworth a copy of the second volume, accompanied by an acknowledgment of having received from me many months since a copy of a certain Tragedy,[27] with excuses for not having made any acknowledgment sooner, it being owing to an "almost insurmountable aversion from Letter-writing." This letter I answered in due form and time, and enumerated several of the passages which had most affected me, adding, unfortunately, that no single piece had moved me so forcibly as the Ancient Mariner, The Mad Mother, or the Lines at Tintern Abbey. The Post did not sleep a moment. I received almost instantaneously a long letter of four sweating pages from my Reluctant Letter-Writer, the purport of which was, that he was sorry his 2d vol. had not given me more pleasure (Devil a hint did I give that it had *not pleased me*), and "was compelled to wish that my range of sensibility was more extended, being obliged to believe that I should receive large influxes of happiness and happy thoughts" (I suppose from the L.B.)—With a deal of stuff about a certain Union of Tenderness and Imagination, which in the sense he used Imagination was not the characteristic of Shakspeare, but which Milton possessed in a degree far exceeding other Poets: which Union, as the highest species of Poetry, and chiefly deserving that name, "He was most proud to aspire to"; then illustrating the said Union by two quotations from his own 2d vol. (which I had been so unfortunate as to miss). 1st Specimen.— a father addresses his son:

When thou
First camest into the World, as it befalls
To new-born Infants, thou didst sleep away
Two days: and Blessings from Thy father's Tongue
Then fell upon thee.[28]

The lines were thus undermarked, and then followed "This Passage, as combining in an extraordinary degree that Union of Imagination and Tenderness which I am speaking of, I consider as one of the Best I ever wrote!"

Second Specimen.—A youth, after years of absence, revisits his native place, and thinks (as most people do) that there has been strange alteration in his absence:—

And that the rocks
And everlasting Hills themselves were changed.[29]

---

22 See note 9, above, and the text to which it applies.
23 Dorothy Wordsworth.
24 Who appears in Wordsworth's poem "The Pet-Lamb."
25 *John Woodvil,* a manuscript of which Lamb had sent Wordsworth.
26 One of Lamb's closest friends (1772–1840), mathematician, traveler, and English pioneer in Chinese studies.

27 See note 25.
28 "Michael," lines 339–43, slightly misquoted.
29 "The Brothers," lines 98–9.

You see both these are good Poetry: but after one has been reading Shakspeare twenty of the best years of one's life, to have a fellow start up, and prate about some unknown quality, which Shakspeare possessed in a degree inferior to Milton and *somebody else!!* This was not to be *all* my castigation. Coleridge, who had not written to me some months before, starts up from his bed of sickness to reprove me for my hardy presumption: four long pages, equally sweaty and more tedious, came from him; assuring me that, when the works of a man of true genius such as W. undoubtedly was, do not please me at first sight, I should suspect the fault to lie "in me and not in them," etc., etc., etc., etc., etc. What am I to do with such people? I certainly shall write them a very merry Letter.[30] Writing to *you,* I may say that the 2d. vol. had no such pieces as the three I enumerated. It is full of original thinking and an observing mind, but it does not often make you laugh or cry.—It too artfully aims at simplicity of expression. And you sometimes doubt if Simplicity be not a cover for Poverty. The best Piece in it I will send you, being *short.* I have grievously offended my friends in the North by declaring my undue preference; but I need not fear you:—

She dwelt among the untrodden ways
  Beside the Springs of Dove,
A maid whom there were few to praise
  And very few to love.

A violet, by a mossy stone,
  Half hidden from the eye.
Fair as a star when only one
  Is shining in the sky.

She lived unknown; and few could know,
  When Lucy ceased to be.
But she is in the grave, and oh!
  The difference to me.[31]

This is choice and genuine, and so are many, many more. But one does not like to have 'em rammed down one's throat. "Pray, take it—it's very good—let me help you—eat faster."

At length George Dyer's[32] first volume is come to a birth. One volume of three—subscribers being allowed by the prospectus to pay for all at once (tho' it's very doubtful if the rest ever come to anything,

this having been already some years getting out). I paid two guineas for you and myself, which entitle us to the whole. I will send you your copy, if you are in a *great hurry.* Meantime you owe me a guinea.

George skipped about like a scorched pea at the receipt of so much cash. To give you a specimen of the beautiful absurdity of the notes, which defy imitation, take one: "Discrimination is not the *aim* of the present volume. It will be more strictly attended to in the next." One of the sonnets purports to have been written in Bedlam![33] This for a man to own![34]

The rest are addressed to Science, Genius, Melancholy—&c. &c.—two, to the river Cam[35]—an Ode to the Nightingale. Another to Howard,[36] beginning: "Spirit of meek Philanthropy!" One is entitled *The Madman*—"being collected by the author from several Madhouses." It begins: "Yes, yes,—'tis He!" A long poetical satire is addressed to "John Disney, D.D.[37]—his wife and daughter!!!"

Now to my own affairs. I have not taken that thing[38] to Colman, but I have proceeded one step in the business. I have enquired his address, and am promised it in a few days: Meantime three acts and a half are finished galopping, of a Play on a Persian story which I must father in April. But far, very far, from *Antonio*[39] in composition. O Jephtha, Judge of Israel,[40] what a fool I was!

C. LAMB.

IV. TO THOMAS MANNING

24th SEPT., 1802, *London.*

My dear Manning,

Since the date of my last letter I have been a traveller. A strong desire seized me of visiting remote regions. My first impulse was to go and see Paris.[41] It was a trivial objection to my aspiring mind, that I did not understand a word of the language, since I certainly intend some time in my life to see Paris, and equally certainly never intend to learn the language; therefore that could be no objection. However, I am very glad I did not go, because you had left Paris (I see) before I could have

---

30 If he did, it has apparently not survived.
31 Lamb misquotes slightly. For the true text, see p. 50, above.
32 Unitarian minister (1755–1841), minor poet, essayist, hack writer, eccentric, and friend of Lamb.

33 The insane asylum.   34 Admit.   35 At Cambridge.
36 John Howard (d. 1790), the prison reformer. Dyer's "Ode XVIII," in four quatrains, begins "Hard is the lot of meek philanthropy."
37 A Unitarian clergyman and writer (1746–1816).
38 Presumably his tragedy (note 25). George Colman the Younger was manager of the Haymarket Theater.
39 A tragedy by William Godwin; it had recently failed.
40 Cf. *Hamlet,* II, ii, 422.   41 He did, in 1822.

set out. I believe, Stoddart[42] promising to go with me another year prevented that plan. My next scheme, (for to my restless, ambitious mind London was become a bed of thorns) was to visit the far-famed Peak[43] in Derbyshire, where the Devil sits, they say, without breeches. *This* my purer mind rejected as indelicate. And my final resolve was, a tour to the Lakes. I set out with Mary to Keswick, without giving Coleridge any notice; for my time being precious did not admit of it. He received us with all the hospitality in the world, and gave up his time to show us all the wonders of the country. He dwells upon a small hill by the side of Keswick, in a comfortable house, quite enveloped on all sides by a net of mountains: great floundering bears and monsters they seemed, all couchant[44] and asleep. We got in in the evening, travelling in a post-chaise from Penrith,[45] in the midst of a gorgeous sunshine, which transmuted all the mountains into colours, purple, &c., &c. We thought we had got into Fairy Land. But that went off (as it never came again—while we stayed we had no more fine sunsets); and we entered Coleridge's comfortable study just in the dusk, when the mountains were all dark with clouds upon their heads. Such an impression I never received from objects of sight before, nor do I suppose I can ever again. Glorious creatures, fine old fellows, Skiddaw,[46] &c., I never shall forget ye, how ye lay about that night, like an intrenchment; gone to bed, as it seemed for the night, but promising that ye were to be seen in the morning. Coleridge had got a blazing fire in his study; which is a large, antique, ill-shaped room, with an old-fashioned organ, never played upon, big enough for a church, shelves of scattered folios, an Aeolian harp,[47] and an old sofa, half-bed, &c. And all looking out upon the last fading view of Skiddaw and his broad-breasted brethren: what a night! Here we stayed three full weeks, in which time I visited Wordsworth's cottage,[48] where we stayed a day or two with the Clarksons[49] (good people and most hospitable, at whose house we tarried one day and night,) and saw Lloyd.[50] The Wordsworths[51] were gone to Calais.

They have since been in London and past much time with us: he is now gone into Yorkshire to be married to a girl of small fortune, but he is in expectation of augmenting his own in consequence of the death of Lord Lonsdale,[52] who kept him out of his own in conformity with a plan my lord had taken up in early life of making everybody unhappy. So we have seen Keswick, Grasmere, Ambleside,[53] Ulswater (where the Clarksons live), and a place at the other end of Ulswater—I forget the name—to which we travelled on a very sultry day, over the middle of Helvellyn.[54] We have clambered up to the top of Skiddaw, and I have waded up the bed of Lodore.[55] In fine, I have satisfied myself, that there is such a thing as that which tourists call *romantic,* which I very much suspected before: they make such a spluttering about it, and toss their splendid epithets around them, till they give as dim a light as at four o'clock next morning the lamps do after an illumination. Mary was excessively tired, when she got about half-way up Skiddaw, but we came to a cold rill (than which nothing can be imagined more cold, running over cold stones), and with the reinforcement of a draught of cold water, she surmounted it most manfully. Oh, its fine black head, and the bleak air atop of it, with a prospect of mountains all about, and about, making you giddy; and then Scotland afar off, and the border countries so famous in song and ballad! It was a day that will stand out, like a mountain, I am sure, in my life. But I am returned (I have now been come home near three weeks—I was a month out), and you cannot conceive the degradation I felt at first, from being accustomed to wander free as air among mountains, and bathe in rivers without being controlled by any one, to come home and *work.* I felt very *little.* I had been dreaming I was a very great man. But that is going off, and I find I shall conform in time to that state of life to which it has pleased God to call me. Besides, after all, Fleet-street and the Strand are better places to live in for good and all than among Skiddaw. Still, I turn back to those great places where I wandered about, participating in their greatness. After all, I could not *live* in Skiddaw. I could spend a year—two, three years—among them, but I must have a prospect of seeing Fleet-street at the end of that time, or I should mope and pine away, I know. Still, Skiddaw is a fine creature. My habits are changing, I

---

[42] John Stoddart, a lawyer and friend, later knighted. His sister married William Hazlitt.   [43] A hill district.

[44] Lying down.

[45] In the northeastern part of the Lake District.

[46] A 3000-foot mountain near Keswick.

[47] A box with strings tuned in unison, to be played on by the wind.

[48] At Grasmere.

[49] Thomas Clarkson (1760–1846) led the crusade against the African slave trade.

[50] Charles Lloyd, minor man of letters, and friend of Coleridge, Lamb, and Manning.   [51] William and Dorothy.

[52] Whose estate Wordsworth's father had managed; the heir paid a debt long owed to the Wordsworths.

[53] A town near Lake Windermere.

[54] Third highest mountain of the Lake District.

[55] A brook famous for its fine waterfalls and cascades.

think: *i.e.*, from drunk to sober. Whether I shall be happier or not remains to be proved. I shall certainly be more happy in a morning; but whether I shall not sacrifice the fat, and the marrow, and the kidneys, *i.e.*, the night, glorious care-drowning night, that heals all our wrongs, pours wine into our mortifications, changes the scene from indifferent and flat to bright and brilliant!—O Manning, if I should have formed a diabolical resolution, by the time you come to England, of not admitting any spirituous liquors into my house, will you be my guest on such shameworthy terms? Is life, with such limitations, worth trying? The truth is, that my liquors bring a nest of friendly harpies about my house, who consume me. This is a pitiful tale to be read at St. Gothard;[56] but it is just now nearest my heart. Fenwick[57] is a ruined man. He is hiding himself from his creditors, and has sent his wife and children into the country. Fell,[58] my other drunken companion (that has been: nam hic caestus artemque repono[59]), is turned editor of

a "Naval Chronicle." Godwin (with a pitiful artificial wife) continues a steady friend, though the same facility does not remain of visiting him often. That Bitch[60] has detached Marshall[61] from his house, Marshall the man who went to sleep when the "Ancient Mariner" was reading: the old, steady, unalterable friend of the Professor. Holcroft[62] is not yet come to town. I expect to see him, and will deliver your message. How I hate *this part* of a letter. Things come crowding in to say, and no room for 'em. Some things are too little to be told, *i.e.* to have a preference; some are too big and circumstantial. Thanks for yours, which was most delicious. Would I had been with you, benighted, &c. I fear my head is turned with wandering. I shall never be the same acquiescent being. Farewell: write again quickly, for I shall not like to hazard a letter, not knowing where the fates have carried you. Farewell, my dear fellow.

C. LAMB.

William Hazlitt

1778–1830

NEXT in importance to Lamb as an essayist, and to Coleridge among the Romantic critics, stands William Hazlitt. The word *gusto* has become a commonplace in estimates of his style, and no better term has been found to describe its quality. To be sure, there are good writers, as there are good men, whose reserved and quiet manner is almost as if they whispered in your ear. By an ease approaching indifference, by understatement, by avoiding enthusiasm, by adopting an air of subtlety suggesting that a great deal more is meant than is said, they tease their readers into acquiescence and admiration. Such indirectness is no part of Hazlitt's method. He writes as a vehement, opinionated man talks; and there is a charm, sometimes a manlier charm, in that. He finds life irresistible—the poetry of Wordsworth—the clouds of metaphysics that rose round Coleridge—the raw, bloody knuckles

and smashed faces of the prize ring—the fierce bursts of passion Edmund Kean put into his furious acting of Shakespeare. About it all Hazlitt writes with fire and spirit, with zest and relish—in short, with gusto.

He was born in the county of Kent, where his father, a native of Ireland and a graduate of Glasgow, was a Unitarian minister. Hazlitt hardly does his father justice in the final essay of our selections. The Reverend William Hazlitt was no humdrum cleric but a republican and a friend of Benjamin Franklin, as well as the preacher of a liberal doctrine. In 1780 he went back to Ireland and took charge of a small congregation near Cork. His persistent intervention against the brutal treatment of American prisoners resulted in a court of inquiry; but it made him so unpopular that when young William was five the family left Ireland and began a four-year sojourn in America. A sympathizer with our Revolution, the elder

---

[56] The well-known pass over the Alps.

[57] John Fenwick, a friend. He was from time to time a journalist, and seems to have ordered his life on the principle that "money kept longer than three days stinks."

[58] R. Fell (his given name is unknown). Lamb met Fenwick and Fell through the philosopher and radical William Godwin.

[59] For here I lay aside the cestus and the profession (cf. Vergil, *Aeneid*, V, 484). The cestus was the Roman equivalent of a boxing glove, but it was loaded with iron or lead.

[60] Godwin's second wife; not Mary Wollstonecraft Godwin (d. 1797), mother of Shelley's second wife, Mary; but the former Mrs. Clairmont, mother of Claire Clairmont (Claire became Byron's mistress and mother of his daughter Allegra). Mrs. Godwin returned Lamb's dislike, but he wrote a number of children's books for her publishing business.

[61] Known only as a friend of "the Professor," i.e., Godwin.

[62] Thomas Holcroft (1749–1845), playwright, miscellaneous writer, and radical.

Hazlitt landed on our shores just after its close. He preached, as opportunity offered, from Maryland to Maine; but hostility to Unitarianism was then widespread. On his return to England he was offered a pulpit at Wem, a little Shropshire town near Shrewsbury. His youngest son was educated in a Unitarian seminary in London. He was twenty when he had the stimulating experience of a meeting with Coleridge, and not long afterward Coleridge introduced him to Wordsworth, by whom he was deeply impressed. He describes these meetings in his famous essay on "My First Acquaintance with Poets," most of which is reprinted below.

Hazlitt did not, however, become a poet, nor for some time a writer of any kind. He was principally attracted to philosophy and painting. For a while he worked under his brother, a pupil of Reynolds and a successful miniaturist. His own portrait of his father was accepted for the Exhibition of 1802. That fall he took advantage of the temporary peace with France to hurry over to Paris and study the pictures in the Louvre. For the French Revolution, and for Napoleon as its heir, Hazlitt conceived a lasting admiration. When the principles which nearly all the great Romantic writers originally professed were smothered by reaction, and men like Wordsworth, Coleridge, and Southey went over to the Tory camp, Hazlitt defied the world, the government, and his former friends. By the news of Bonaparte's ruin at Waterloo in 1815, says the painter Haydon, Hazlitt seemed for weeks "prostrated in mind and body, he walked about unwashed, unshaved, hardly sober by day, and always intoxicated by night . . . until at length, wakening up as it were from his stupor, he at once left off all stimulating liquors, and never touched them after." The account is overdramatic; at any rate it was not till 1817 that Hazlitt gave up drinking. But that he thought Waterloo a tragedy is true enough. He had called the Emperor's earlier withdrawal to Elba "the abdication of the human race in favour of the hereditary proprietors of the species."

To return to Hazlitt's early career. He did not long remain a painter. Though for several years he kept on with the brush, the conviction grew on him that he would never make a great painter. He began turning to his pen; his first subjects were philosophy, ethics, economics, and politics. In 1808 he married Sarah Stoddart, sister of a well-known lawyer and a friend of the Lambs. She was then thirty-three; Hazlitt was thirty. Miss Stoddart had, besides a small income, a house near Salisbury; for several years it was their home.

1812 was a decisive year, for Hazlitt came before the public with a course of lectures on philosophy and speedily won distinction as a lecturer and as a journalist. He was soon Parliamentary reporter, and afterwards dramatic critic, of the Morning Chronicle. Later he worked for other papers and contributed many essays and articles to Leigh Hunt's Examiner, the Edinburgh Review, and other periodicals; some were later published in book form. In the literary and political controversies of his time—they were conducted with a brutality which paralleled the bare-fisted matches of the prize fighters—Hazlitt battled with appropriate ferocity. His interests—this is one of the most attractive things about him—were uncommonly wide. He was a devoted rackets player, who in a moment of enthusiasm could say he would rather excel at that sport than be the best prose writer of the age; at the same time he was a connoisseur of painting. Above all, he had an unlimited capacity for experiencing life, for enjoying the experience, and for communicating his joy. He knew nearly all the leading writers; and as some of the following pages demonstrate, his were strong reactions concerning their merits and shortcomings.

As a more than merely journalistic critic, Hazlitt won his place in 1817 with a book on Characters of Shakespeare's Plays; he confirmed it by a rapid succession of lecture courses on The English Poets (delivered in 1818), The English Comic Writers (1818–19), and The Dramatic Literature of the Age of Elizabeth (1819). All were published soon after he gave them. The Spirit of the Age (1825) is a series of sketches of Hazlitt's contemporaries. A hard worker, he kept at his writing to the end. His last book, a Life of Napoleon, was completed and published only shortly before his death in 1830.

Some aspects of his personal life are not admirable. He was a quarrelsome fellow. Sooner or later he became estranged from nearly all his friends; Keats, the Lambs, and the dramatist Sheridan Knowles were exceptions. If he seems to brood over a persecution complex, complaining that "every man's hand is against me," he had some warrant. Particularly in the Quarterly Review and Blackwood's, he was subjected by the Tories to venomous, blackguardly attacks on his works, his person, and his character. He had a theory to explain this hostility: "I am not, in the ordinary acceptation of the word, a good-natured man—that is, many things annoy me besides what interferes with my own ease and interest. I hate a lie. A piece of injustice wounds me to the quick, though nothing but the report of it reach me. Therefore I have many enemies and few friends." Tarnished as he was in spots, he had heroic traits. Lamb, who did not share his political views, knew he had, and called him "in his natural and healthy state one of the wisest and finest spirits breathing. . . . I think I shall go to my grave without finding, or expecting to find, such another companion."

His relations with women failed to bring happiness. Having separated from his wife several years earlier, he became at the age of forty-four infatuated with the young daughter of a London tailor in whose house he had lodgings. He prevailed on his wife to divorce him, but was unable to induce the girl to marry him. His sensitiveness to the requirements, if not of propriety at any rate of common sense, was at the moment insufficient to keep him from publishing anonymously a transparent account of his unhappy passion in a little book purporting to be fiction called *Liber Amoris* (1823). Naturally, he cuts an absurd figure in it. The following year saw him married again, to a handsome widow with a comfortable income; she is said to have fallen in love with him for his writings. Much of the remainder of his life was spent abroad, in France and Italy. Several years after their marriage the second Mrs. Hazlitt left him; apparently his much-loved son by his first wife came between them. Yet although Hazlitt was afflicted by melancholy, he retained his zest to the end. According to his son his last words were, "I have had a happy life."

The *Complete Works* were edited by P. P. Howe (21 vols., 1930–34), a re-issue of the Waller-Glover edition with some expansion. Howe is also author of a good biography (1922). Everyman's Library and The World's Classics each includes several volumes of the best things; *Hazlitt on English Literature* (1913) is a good selection by J. Zeitlin; and *Selected Essays*, edited by G. Keynes (1930), gets 800 pages of Hazlitt into a single handy volume. There is a wordy and partisan but thorough and interesting Life by Catherine M. Maclean, *Born under Saturn* (1943).

William Hazlitt

from LECTURES ON THE ENGLISH POETS

HAZLITT delivered this series of eight lectures early in 1818 at the Surrey Institution, a foundation in London for the diffusion of knowledge to the general public. Among his auditors was John Keats. The course proved so successful that it was repeated in the spring. Beginning with a general lecture on poetry, Hazlitt dealt, mostly two at a time, with the leading poets from Chaucer and Spenser on. His treatment affords a good example of Romantic criticism, often penetrating, sometimes effusively rhapsodical, usually lively.

The Romantic critics are chiefly famous for their appreciation of the writers of the sixteenth and early seventeenth centuries, a number of whom they succeeded in rescuing from neglect. As a rule their criticism is impressionistic, and more notable for enthusiasm and taste than for knowledge or method. Shakespeare and his fellows are praised with a delightful warmth and eloquence, but too frequently for the wrong things or even for nonexistent things. Hazlitt on Shakespeare affords more heat than light. Accordingly, and because a tart contemporary's opinion of his betters always has a piquant interest, our sample of Hazlitt as a critic is from the somewhat acidulous concluding lecture of this series, where we may witness the application of a sensitive and confident mind to the difficult task of appraising the living poets. With respect to his comments on Byron, the reader should remember that the first two cantos of Byron's masterpiece, *Don Juan*, were not published till the year after this lecture was delivered. It is greatly to Hazlitt's credit that he was one of the few in England who at once perceived Wordsworth's greatness, although the tone of his general account of the Lake Poets is somewhat smart-alecky.

Cheap reprints of the *Lectures on the English Poets* are available in Everyman's Library and The World's Classics. In the following notes, "cf." before a reference gives warning that Hazlitt's quotation in the text is not exact.

from Lecture VIII

ON THE LIVING POETS

. . . IF MR. MOORE[1] has not suffered enough personally, Lord Byron (judging from the tone of his writings) might be thought to have suffered too much to be a truly great poet. If Mr. Moore lays himself too open to all the various impulses of things, the outward shews of earth and sky, to every breath that blows, to every stray sentiment that crosses his fancy; Lord Byron shuts himself up too much in the impenetrable gloom of his own thoughts, and buries the natural light of things in "nook monastic."[2] The Giaour, the Corsair, Childe Harold,[3] are all the same person, and they are apparently all himself. The everlasting repetition of one subject, the same dark

5

10

---

[1] Hazlitt's criticism of Thomas Moore immediately precedes our excerpt.   [2] *As You Like It*, III, ii, 442.
[3] The heroes (and titles) of three narrative poems by Byron.

ground of fiction, with the darker colours of the poet's mind spread over it, the unceasing accumulation of horrors on horror's head,[4] steels the mind against the sense of pain, as inevitably as the unwearied Siren sounds and luxurious monotony of Mr. Moore's poetry make it inaccessible to pleasure. Lord Byron's poetry is as morbid as Mr. Moore's is careless and dissipated. He has more depth of passion, more force and impetuosity, but the passion is always of the same unaccountable character, at once violent and sullen, fierce and gloomy. It is not the passion of a mind struggling with misfortune, or the hopelessness of its desires, but of a mind preying upon itself, and disgusted with, or indifferent to all other things. There is nothing less poetical than this sort of unaccommodating selfishness. There is nothing more repulsive than this sort of ideal absorption of all the interests of others, of the good and ills of life, in the ruling passion and moody abstraction of a single mind, as if it would make itself the centre of the universe, and there was nothing worth cherishing but its intellectual diseases. It is like a cancer, eating into the heart of poetry. But still there is power; and power rivets attention and forces admiration. "He hath a demon":[5] and that is the next thing to being full of the God. His brow collects the scattered gloom: his eye flashes livid fire that withers and consumes. But still we watch the progress of the scathing bolt with interest, and mark the ruin it leaves behind with awe. Within the contracted range of his imagination, he has great unity and truth of keeping. He chooses elements and agents congenial to his mind, the dark and glittering ocean, the frail bark hurrying before the storm, pirates and men that "house on the wild sea with wild usages."[6] He gives the tumultuous eagerness of action, and the fixed despair of thought. In vigour of style and force of conception, he in one sense surpasses every writer of the present day. His indignant apothegms are like oracles of misanthropy. He who wishes for "a curse to kill with,"[7] may find it in Lord Byron's writings. Yet he has beauty lurking underneath his strength, tenderness sometimes joined with the phrenzy of despair. A flash of golden light sometimes follows from a stroke of his pencil, like a falling meteor. The flowers that adorn his poetry bloom over charnel-houses and the grave! . . .

Walter Scott is the most popular of all the poets of the present day, and deservedly so. He describes that which is most easily and generally understood with more vivacity and effect than any body else. He has no excellences, either of a lofty or recondite kind, which lie beyond the reach of the most ordinary capacity to find out; but he has all the good qualities which all the world agree to understand. His style is clear, flowing, and transparent: his sentiments, of which his style is an easy and natural medium, are common to him with his readers. He has none of Mr. Wordsworth's idiosyncrasy. He differs from his readers only in a greater range of knowledge and facility of expression. His poetry belongs to the class of improvisatori[8] poetry. It has neither depth, height, nor breadth in it; neither uncommon strength, nor uncommon refinement of thought, sentiment, or language. It has no originality. But if this author has no research, no moving power in his own breast, he relies with the greater safety and success on the force of his subject. He selects a story such as is sure to please, full of incidents, characters, peculiar manners, costume, and scenery; and he tells it in a way that can offend no one. He never wearies or disappoints you. He is communicative and garrulous; but he is not his own hero. He never obtrudes himself on your notice to prevent your seeing the subject. What passes in the poem, passes much as it would have done in reality. The author has little or nothing to do with it. Mr. Scott has great intuitive power of fancy, great vividness of pencil in placing external objects and events before the eye. The force of his mind is picturesque, rather than *moral*. He gives more of the features of nature than the soul of passion. He conveys the distinct outlines and visible changes in outward objects, rather than "their mortal consequences."[9] He is very inferior to Lord Byron in intense passion, to Moore in delightful fancy, to Mr. Wordsworth in profound sentiment: but he has more picturesque power than any of them; that is, he places the objects themselves, about which *they* might feel and think, in a much more striking point of view, with greater variety of dress and attitude, and with more local truth of colouring. His imagery is Gothic[10] and grotesque. The manners and actions have the interest and curiosity belonging to a wild country and a distant period of time. Few descriptions have a more complete reality, a more striking appearance of life and motion, than that of the warriors in the Lady of the Lake, who start up at the command of Roderic Dhu, from their concealment

---

[4] *Othello*, III, iii, 370.   [5] Cf. John 10:20.
[6] From a play by Coleridge, *The Piccolomini*, I, iv, 117.
[7] Thomas Otway, *Venice Preserved*, II, ii, 57–8.

[8] I.e., composed or recited extemporaneously.
[9] *Macbeth*, V, iii, 5.   [10] Medieval and romantic.

under the fern, and disappear again in an instant.[11] The Lay of the Last Minstrel and Marmion are the first, and perhaps the best of his works. . . . The truth is, there is a modern air in the midst of the antiquarian research of Mr. Scott's poetry. It is history or tradition in masquerade. Not only the crust of old words and images is worn off with time,—the substance is grown comparatively light and worthless. The forms are old and uncouth; but the spirit is effeminate and frivolous. This is a deduction from the praise I have given to his pencil for extreme fidelity, though it has been no obstacle to its drawing-room success. He has just hit the town between the romantic and the fashionable; and between the two, secured all classes of readers on his side. In a word, I conceive that he is to the great poet, what an excellent mimic is to a great actor. There is no determinate impression left on the mind by reading his poetry. It has no results. The reader rises up from the perusal with new images and associations, but he remains the same man that he was before. A great mind is one that moulds the minds of others. Mr. Scott has put the Border Minstrelsy and scattered traditions of the country into easy, animated verse. But the Notes to his poems are just as entertaining as the poems themselves, and his poems are only entertaining.

Mr. Wordsworth is the most original poet now living. He is the reverse of Walter Scott in his defects and excellences. He has nearly all that the other wants, and wants all that the other possesses. His poetry is not external, but internal; it does not depend upon tradition, or story, or old song; he furnishes it from his own mind, and is his own subject. He is the poet of mere sentiment.[12] Of many of the Lyrical Ballads, it is not possible to speak in terms of too high praise, such as Hart-leap Well, the Banks of the Wye,[13] Poor Susan, parts of the Leech-gatherer, the lines to a Cuckoo, to a Daisy, the Complaint, several of the Sonnets, and a hundred others of inconceivable beauty, of perfect originality and pathos. They open a finer and deeper vein of thought and feeling than any poet in modern times has done, or attempted. He has produced a deeper impression, and on a smaller circle, than any other of his contemporaries. His powers have been mistaken by the age, nor does he exactly understand them himself. He cannot form a whole. He has not the constructive faculty. He can give only the fine tones of thought, drawn from his mind by accident or nature, like the sounds drawn from the Aeolian harp by the wandering gale.—He is totally deficient in all the machinery of poetry. His Excursion, taken as a whole, notwithstanding the noble materials thrown away in it, is a proof of this. The line labours, the sentiment moves slow, but the poem stands stock-still. The reader makes no way from the first line to the last. It is more than any thing in the world like Robinson Crusoe's boat, which would have been an excellent good boat, and would have carried him to the other side of the globe, but that he could not get it out of the sand where it stuck fast. I did what little I could to help to launch it at the time, but it would not do. I am not, however, one of those who laugh at the attempts or failures of men of genius. It is not my way to cry "Long life to the Conqueror." Success and desert are not with me synonymous terms; and the less Mr. Wordsworth's general merits have been understood, the more necessary is it to insist upon them. . . .

Mr. Wordsworth is at the head of that which has been denominated the Lake school of poetry; a school which, with all my respect for it, I do not think sacred from criticism or exempt from faults, of some of which faults I shall speak with becoming frankness; for I do not see that the liberty of the press ought to be shackled, or freedom of speech curtailed, to screen either its revolutionary or renegado extravagances. This school of poetry had its origin in the French revolution, or rather in those sentiments and opinions which produced that revolution; and which sentiments and opinions were indirectly imported into this country in translations from the German about that period. Our poetical literature had, towards the close of the last century, degenerated into the most trite, insipid, and mechanical of all things, in the hands of the followers of Pope and the old French school[14] of poetry. It wanted something to stir it up, and it found that something in the principles and events of the French revolution. From the impulse it thus received, it rose at once from the most servile imitation and tamest common-place, to the utmost pitch of singularity and paradox. The change in the belles-lettres was as complete, and to many persons as startling, as the change in politics, with which it went hand in hand. There was a mighty ferment in the heads of statesmen and poets, kings and people. According to the prevailing notions, all was to be natural and new. Nothing that was established was to be tolerated. All the common-

---

[11] Canto V, stanza ix.   [12] Sheer feeling.
[13] "Tintern Abbey." "The Leech-gatherer," mentioned just beyond, is "Resolution and Independence."

[14] Which conformed to the "Rules," formulated by the French neoclassical critics of the seventeenth and eighteenth centuries.

place figures of poetry, tropes,[15] allegories, personifications, with the whole heathen mythology, were instantly discarded; a classical allusion was considered as a piece of antiquated foppery; capital letters were no more allowed in print, than letters-patent of nobility were permitted in real life; kings and queens were dethroned from their rank and station in legitimate tragedy or epic poetry, as they were decapitated elsewhere; rhyme was looked upon as a relic of the feudal system, and regular metre was abolished along with regular government. Authority and fashion, elegance or arrangement, were hooted out of countenance, as pedantry and prejudice. Every one did that which was good in his own eyes. The object was to reduce all things to an absolute level; and a singularly affected and outrageous simplicity prevailed in dress and manners, in style and sentiment. A striking effect produced where it was least expected, something new and original, no matter whether good, bad, or indifferent, whether mean or lofty, extravagant or childish, was all that was aimed at, or considered as compatible with sound philosophy and an age of reason. The licentiousness grew extreme: Coryate's Crudities[16] were nothing to it. The world was to be turned topsy-turvy; and poetry, by the good will of our Adam-wits,[17] was to share its fate and begin de novo.[18] It was a time of promise, a renewal of the world and of letters; and the Deucalions,[19] who were to perform this feat of regeneration, were the present poet-laureat[20] and the two authors of the Lyrical Ballads. The Germans, who made heroes of robbers,[21] and honest women of cast-off mistresses, had already exhausted the extravagant and marvellous in sentiment and situation: our native writers adopted a wonderful simplicity of style and matter. The paradox they set out with was, that all things are by nature equally fit subjects for poetry; or that if there is any preference to be given, those that are the meanest and most unpromising are the best, as they leave the greatest scope for the unbounded stores of thought and fancy in the writer's own mind. Poetry had with them "neither buttress nor coigne of vantage to make its

pendant bed and procreant cradle."[22] It was not "born so high: its aiery buildeth in the cedar's top, and dallies with the wind, and scorns the sun."[23] It grew like a mushroom out of the ground; or was hidden in it like a truffle, which it required a particular sagacity and industry to find out and dig up. They founded the new school on a principle of sheer humanity, on pure nature void of art. It could not be said of these sweeping reformers and dictators in the republic of letters, that "in their train walked crowns and crownets; that realms and islands, like plates, dropt from their pockets":[24] but they were surrounded, in company with the Muses, by a mixed rabble of idle apprentices and Botany Bay[25] convicts, female vagrants, gipsies, meek daughters in the family of Christ,[26] of ideot boys[27] and mad mothers, and after them "owls and night-ravens flew."[28] They scorned "degrees, priority, and place, insisture, course, proportion, season, form, office, and custom in all line of order":[29]—the distinctions of birth, the vicissitudes of fortune, did not enter into their abstracted, lofty, and levelling calculation of human nature. He who was more than man, with them was none. They claimed kindred only with the commonest of the people: peasants, pedlars, and village-barbers were their oracles and bosom friends. Their poetry, in the extreme to which it professedly tended, and was in effect carried, levels all distinctions of nature and society; has "no figures nor no fantasies,"[30] which the prejudices of superstition or the customs of the world draw in the brains of men; "no trivial fond records"[31] of all that has existed in the history of past ages; it has no adventitious pride, pomp, or circumstance, to set it off; "the marshal's truncheon, nor the judge's robe";[32] neither traditions, reverence, nor ceremony, "that to great ones 'longs":[33] it breaks in pieces the golden images of poetry, and defaces its armorial bearings, to melt them down in the mould of common humanity or of its own upstart self-sufficiency. They took the

---

15 Figures of speech.

16 *Coryate's Crudities Hastily Gobbled Up* (1611) by the English traveler Thomas Coryate.

17 Original thinkers and writers.   18 Afresh.

19 In Greek mythology Deucalion and his wife were the only survivors of the Flood.   20 Southey.

21 A reference to Schiller's *Die Räuber* (The Robbers, 1781) and possibly to Goethe's *Götz von Berlichingen* (1773).—The next phrase doubtless refers to Lady Milford in Schiller's *Kabale und Liebe* (Intrigue and Love, 1784).

22 Cf. *Macbeth*, I, vi, 7–8.   23 Cf. *Richard III*, I, iii, 263–5.

24 Cf. *Antony and Cleopatra*, V, ii, 90–92.

25 The British convict settlement in Australia; Southey wrote several "Botany-Bay Eclogues."—"The Female Vagrant" was the original title of a portion of Wordsworth's poem later called "Guilt and Sorrow," and "Gipsies" is another of his poems.

26 A slight misquotation of line 53, addressed to Coleridge's wife, in his "The Aeolian Harp."

27 "The Idiot Boy" is one of Wordsworth's poems. "The Mad Mother" was an early title of another, now called "Her eyes are wild."   28 Unidentified.

29 Cf. Shakespeare's *Troilus and Cressida*, I, iii, 86–8. *Insisture* = steady motion onward.   30 *Julius Caesar*, II, i, 231.

31 *Hamlet*, I, v, 99. *Fond* = foolish, unimportant.

32 *Measure for Measure*, II, ii, 61.   33 *Ibid.*, line 59.

same method in their new-fangled "metre ballad-mongering"[34] scheme, which Rousseau did in his prose paradoxes—of exciting attention by reversing the established standards of opinion and estimation in the world. They were for bringing poetry back to its primitive simplicity and state of nature, as he was for bringing society back to the savage state: so that the only thing remarkable left in the world by this change, would be the persons who had produced it. A thorough adept[35] in this school of poetry and philanthropy is jealous of all excellence but his own. He does not even like to share his reputation with his subject; for he would have it all proceed from his own power and originality of mind. Such a one is slow to admire any thing that is admirable; feels no interest in what is most interesting to others, no grandeur in any thing grand, no beauty in any thing beautiful. He tolerates only what he himself creates; he sympathizes only with what can enter into no competition with him, with "the bare trees and mountains bare, and grass in the green field."[36] He sees nothing but himself and the universe. He hates all greatness and all pretensions to it, whether well or ill-founded. His egotism is in some respects a madness; for he scorns even the admiration of himself, thinking it a presumption in any one to suppose that he has taste or sense enough to understand him. He hates all science and all art; he hates chemistry, he hates conchology;[37] he hates Voltaire; he hates Sir Isaac Newton; he hates wisdom; he hates wit; he hates metaphysics, which he says are unintelligible, and yet he would be thought to understand them; he hates prose; he hates all poetry but his own; he hates the dialogues in Shakespeare; he hates music, dancing, and painting; he hates Rubens, he hates Rembrandt; he hates Raphael, he hates Titian; he hates Vandyke; he hates the antique; he hates the Apollo Belvidere;[38] he hates the Venus of Medicis. This is the reason that so few people take an interest in his writings, because he takes an interest in nothing that others do! . . .

It remains that I should say a few words of Mr. Coleridge; and there is no one who has a better right to say what he thinks of him than I have. "Is there here any dear friend of Caesar? To him I say, that Brutus's love to Caesar was no less than his."[39] But no matter.—His Ancient Mariner is his most remarkable performance, and the only one that I could point out to any one as giving an adequate idea of his great natural powers. It is high German, however, and in it he seems to "conceive of poetry but as a drunken dream, reckless, careless, and heedless, of past, present, and to come."[40] His tragedies (for he has written two) are not answerable[41] to it; they are, except a few poetical passages, drawling sentiment and metaphysical jargon. He has no genuine dramatic talent. There is one fine passage in his Christabel, that which contains the description of the quarrel between Sir Leoline and Sir Roland de Vaux of Tryermaine, who had been friends in youth. . . .[42] But I may say of him here, that he is the only person I ever knew who answered to the idea of a man of genius. He is the only person from whom I ever learnt any thing. There is only one thing he could learn from me in return, but *that* he has not. He was the first poet I ever knew. His genius at that time had angelic wings, and fed on manna. He talked on for ever; and you wished him to talk on for ever. His thoughts did not seem to come with labour and effort; but as if borne on the gusts of genius, and as if the wings of his imagination lifted him from off his feet. His voice rolled on the ear like the pealing organ, and its sound alone was the music of thought. His mind was clothed with wings; and raised on them, he lifted philosophy to heaven. In his descriptions, you then saw the progress of human happiness and liberty in bright and never-ending succession, like the steps of Jacob's ladder,[43] with airy shapes ascending and descending, and with the voice of God at the top of the ladder. And shall I, who heard him then, listen to him now? Not I! . . . .[44] That spell is broke; that time is gone for ever; that voice is heard no more: but still the recollection comes rushing by with thoughts of long-past years, and rings in my ears with never-dying sound. . . .

---

[34] Cf. *1 Henry IV*, III, i, 130.

[35] In the following passage Hazlitt is using journalistic materials he had published about a year before, with reference to Wordsworth. He afterwards repented, alleging that he wrote in fun, and maintaining (not very plausibly) that there was as little of malice as of truth in his statements.

[36] Wordsworth, "To My Sister," lines 7–8.

[37] That branch of zoology which deals with shells or mollusks.

[38] This statue of Apollo derived its second name from its gallery in the Vatican, as the one of Venus mentioned did from its once having stood in the Medici palace in Rome.—The passage omitted after the next sentence is a short paragraph on Southey.

[39] *Julius Caesar*, III, ii, 18–21 (slightly misquoted).

[40] Cf. *Measure for Measure*, IV, ii, 149–52.

[41] Commensurable, of corresponding value.

[42] Here Hazlitt quotes lines 408–30 (see p. 104, above). Doubtless, and doubtless rightly, he mentally applied them to Coleridge and himself.   [43] Genesis 28:12–15.

[44] Hazlitt's dots.

ON REASON AND IMAGINATION

THIS essay defines the central character of Romanticism, the revolt against eighteenth-century speculation and the demand for living experience. In the broadest terms this meant the rejection of thinking about life in favor of living it. In the area of knowledge it meant the recognition that the reason, the faculty which generalizes, could give us only abstract rules and definitions. It could *not* give us the living (or psychological) knowledge of things as they really exist in their concrete particularity, as they exist for the individual who sees them and feels them. For this we need the imagination, meaning the faculty of vivid and personal realization, as in the phrase "So-and-so or such-and-such struck my imagination." Hazlitt's discussion of ethics is simply the application of reason vs. imagination to the question of moral judgments. For Jeremy Bentham, whatever reason shows will produce more pleasure than pain for everyone concerned is a good or useful action. For Hazlitt, the right test is our immediate, emotional response. What shocks our feelings is instantly known to be evil. If the slave trade "haunts the imagination and lacerates the human heart," it is prejudged and self-condemned.

The essay is included in *Table-Talk; or, Original Essays* (1821–22). Inexpensive reprints of *Table-Talk* are available in Everyman's Library and The World's Classics.

I HATE people who have no notion of anything but generalities, and forms, and creeds, and naked propositions, even worse than I dislike those who cannot for the soul of them arrive at the comprehension of an abstract idea. There are those (even among philosophers) who, deeming that all truth is contained within certain outlines and common topics, if you proceed to add colour or relief from individuality, protest against the use of rhetoric as an illogical thing; and if you drop a hint of pleasure or pain as ever entering into "this breathing world,"[1] raise a prodigious outcry against all appeals to the passions.

It is, I confess, strange to me that men who pretend to more than usual accuracy in distinguishing and analysing, should insist that in treating of human nature, of moral good and evil, the nominal differences are alone of any value, or that in describing the feelings and motives of men, any thing that conveys the smallest idea of what those feelings are in any given circumstances, or can by parity of reason ever be in any others, is a deliberate attempt at artifice and delusion—as if a knowledge or representation of things as they really exist (rules and definitions apart) was a proportionable departure from the truth. They stick to the table of contents, and never open the volume of the mind. They are for having maps, not pictures of the world we live in: as much as to say that a bird's-eye view of things contains the truth, the whole truth, and nothing but the truth. If you want to look for the situation of a particular spot, they turn to a pasteboard globe, on which they fix their wandering gaze; and because you cannot find the object of your search in their bald "abridgements," tell you there is no such place, or that it is not worth inquiring after. They had better confine their studies to the celestial sphere and the signs of the zodiac; for there they will meet with no petty details to boggle at, or contradict their vague conclusions. Such persons would make excellent theologians, but are very indifferent philosophers.—To pursue this geographical reasoning a little farther. They may say that the map of a county or shire, for instance, is too large, and conveys a disproportionate idea of its relation to the whole. And we say that their map of the globe is too small, and conveys no idea of it at all.

—In the world's volume
Our Britain shows as of it, but not in it;
In a great pool a swan's nest:[2]

but is it really so? What! the county is bigger than the map at any rate: the representation falls short of the reality, by a million degrees, and you would omit it altogether in order to arrive at a balance of power in the non-entities of the understanding, and call this keeping within the bounds of sense and reason? and whatever does not come within those self-made limits is to be set aside as frivolous or monstrous. But "there are more things between heaven and earth than were ever dreamt of in this philosophy."[3] They cannot get them all in, *of the size of life,* and therefore they reduce them on a graduated scale, till they think they can. So be it, for certain necessary and general purposes, and in compliance with the infirmity of human intellect: but at other times, let us enlarge our conceptions to the dimensions of the original objects; nor let it be pretended that we have outraged truth and nature, because we have encroached on your diminutive mechanical standard. There is no language, no description that can strictly come up to the truth and force of reality: all we have to do is to

---

[1] Shakespeare, *Richard III*, I, i, 21.

[2] Cf. Shakespeare, *Cymbeline,* III, iv, 140–42.
[3] Cf. Shakespeare, *Hamlet,* I, v, 166–7.

guide our descriptions and conclusions by the reality. A certain proportion must be kept: we must not invert the rules of moral perspective. Logic should enrich and invigorate its decisions by the use of imagination; as rhetoric should be governed in its application, and guarded from abuse by the checks of the understanding. Neither, I apprehend, is sufficient alone. The mind can conceive only one or a few things in their integrity: if it proceeds to more, it must have recourse to artificial substitutes, and judge by comparison merely. In the former case, it may select the least worthy, and so distort the truth of things, by giving a hasty preference: in the latter, the danger is that it may refine and abstract so much as to attach no idea at all to them, corresponding with their practical value, or their influence on the minds of those concerned with them. Men act from individual impressions; and to know mankind, we should be acquainted with nature. Men act from passion; and we can only judge of passion by sympathy. Persons of the dry and husky class above spoken of, often seem to think even nature itself an interloper on their flimsy theories. They prefer the shadows in Plato's cave[4] to the actual objects without it. They consider men "as mice in an air-pump,"[5] fit only for their experiments; and do not consider the rest of the universe, or "all the mighty world of eye and ear,"[6] as worth any notice at all. This is making short, but not sure work. Truth does not lie *in vacuo*, any more than in a well. We must improve our concrete experience of persons and things into the contemplation of general rules and principles; but without being grounded in individual facts and feelings, we shall end as we began, in ignorance.

It is mentioned in a short account of the Last Moments of Mr. Fox,[7] that the conversation at the house of Lord Holland (where he died) turning upon Mr. Burke's style, that Noble Person objected to it as too gaudy and meretricious, and said that it was more profuse of flowers than fruit. On which Mr. Fox observed, that though this was a common objection, it appeared to him altogether an unfounded one; that on the contrary, the flowers often concealed the fruit beneath them, and the ornaments of style were rather an hindrance than an advantage to the sentiments they were meant to set off. In confirmation of this remark, he offered to take down the

book, and translate a page any where into his own plain, natural style; and by his doing so, Lord Holland was convinced that he had often missed the thought from having his attention drawn off to the dazzling imagery. Thus people continually find fault with the colours of style as incompatible with the truth of the reasoning, but without any foundation whatever. If it were a question about the figure of two triangles, and any person were to object that one triangle was green and the other yellow, and bring this to bear upon the acuteness or obtuseness of the angles, it would be obvious to remark that the colour had nothing to do with the question. But in a dispute whether two objects are coloured alike, the discovery, that one is green and the other yellow, is fatal. So with respect to moral truth (as distinct from mathematical), whether a thing is good or evil, depends on the quantity of passion, of feeling, of pleasure and pain connected with it, and with which we must be made acquainted in order to come to a sound conclusion, and not on the inquiry, whether it is round or square. Passion, in short, is the essence, the chief ingredient in moral truth; and the warmth of passion is sure to kindle the light of imagination on the objects around it. The "words that glow" are almost inseparable from the "thoughts that burn."[8] Hence logical reason and practical truth are *disparates*. It is easy to raise an outcry against violent invectives, to talk loud against extravagance and enthusiasm, to pick a quarrel with every thing but the most calm, candid, and qualified statement of facts: but there are enormities to which no words can do adequate justice. Are we then, in order to form a complete idea of them, to omit every circumstance of aggravation, or to suppress every feeling of impatience that arises out of the details, lest we should be accused of giving way to the influence of prejudice and passion? This would be to falsify the impression altogether, to misconstrue reason, and fly in the face of nature. Suppose, for instance, that in the discussions on the Slave-Trade, a description to the life was given of the horrors of the *Middle Passage*[9] (as it was termed), that you saw the manner in which thousands of wretches, year after year, were stowed together in the hold of a slave-ship, without air, without light, without food, without hope, so that what they suffered in reality was brought home to you in imagination, till you felt in sickness of heart as one of them, could it be said that this was a prejudging of the case, that your

---

4 *Republic*, Book VII.
5 Edmund Burke, "A Letter to a Noble Lord."
6 Wordsworth, "Tintern Abbey," lines 105–6.
7 The statesman Charles James Fox (1749–1806).

8 Cf. Thomas Gray, "The Progress of Poesy," line 110: "Thoughts that breathe, and words that burn."
9 The Atlantic voyage from Africa to the West Indies.

knowing the extent of the evil disqualified you from pronouncing sentence upon it, and that your disgust and abhorrence were the effects of a heated imagination? No. Those evils that inflame the imagination and make the heart sick, ought not to leave the head cool. This is the very test and measure of the degree of the enormity, that it involuntarily staggers and appals the mind. If it were a common iniquity, if it were slight and partial, or necessary, it would not have this effect; but it very properly carries away the feelings, and (if you will) overpowers the judgment, because it is a mass of evil so monstrous and unwarranted as not to be endured, even in thought. A man on the rack does not suffer the less, because the extremity of anguish takes away his command of feeling and attention to appearances. A pang inflicted on humanity is not the less real, because it stirs up sympathy in the breast of humanity. Would you tame down the glowing language of justifiable passion into that of cold indifference, of self-complacent, sceptical reasoning, and thus take out the sting of indignation from the mind of the spectator? Not, surely, till you have removed the nuisance by the levers that strong feeling alone can set at work, and have thus taken away the pang of suffering that caused it! Or say that the question were proposed to you, whether, on some occasion, you should thrust your hand into the flames, and were coolly told that you were not at all to consider the pain and anguish it might give you, nor suffer yourself to be led away by any such idle appeals to natural sensibility, but to refer the decision to some abstract, technical ground of propriety, would you not laugh in your adviser's face? Oh! no; where our own interests are concerned, or where we are sincere in our professions of regard, the pretended distinction between sound judgment and lively imagination is quickly done away with. But I would not wish a better or more philosophical standard of morality, than that we should think and feel towards others as we should, if it were our own case. If we look for a higher standard than this, we shall not find it; but shall lose the substance for the shadow! . . .

With respect to the atrocities committed in the Slave-Trade, it could not be set up as a doubtful plea in their favour, that the actual and intolerable sufferings inflicted on the individuals were compensated by certain advantages in a commercial and political point of view—in a moral sense they *cannot* be compensated. They hurt the public mind: they harden and sear the natural feelings. The evil is monstrous and palpable; the pretended good is remote and contingent. In morals, as in philosophy, *De non ap-*

parentibus et non existentibus eadem est ratio. What does not touch the heart, or come home to the feelings, goes comparatively for little or nothing. A benefit that exists merely in possibility, and is judged of only by the forced dictates of the understanding, is not a set-off against an evil (say of equal magnitude in itself) that strikes upon the senses, that haunts the imagination, and lacerates the human heart. A spectacle of deliberate cruelty, that shocks every one that sees and hears of it, is not to be justified by any calculations of cold-blooded self-interest—is not to be permitted in any case. It is prejudged and self-condemned. Necessity has been therefore justly called "the tyrant's plea."[10] It is no better with the mere doctrine of utility, which is the sophist's plea. Thus, for example, an infinite number of lumps of sugar put into Mr. Bentham's[11] artificial ethical scales would never weigh against the pounds of human flesh, or drops of human blood, that are sacrificed to produce them. The taste of the former on the palate is evanescent; but the others sit heavy on the soul. The one are an object to the imagination: the others only to the understanding. But man is an animal compounded both of imagination and understanding; and, in treating of what is good for man's nature, it is necessary to consider both. A calculation of the mere ultimate advantages, without regard to natural feelings and affections, may improve the external face and physical comforts of society, but will leave it heartless and worthless in itself. In a word, the sympathy of the individual with the consequences of his own act is to be attended to (no less than the consequences themselves) in every sound system of morality; and this must be determined by certain natural laws of the human mind, and not by rules of logic or arithmetic.

The aspect of a moral question is to be judged of very much like the face of a country, by the projecting points, by what is striking and memorable, by that which leaves traces of itself behind, or "casts its shadow before."[12] Millions of acres do not make a picture; nor the calculation of all the consequences in the world a sentiment. We must have some outstanding object for the mind, as well as the eye, to dwell on and recur to—something marked and decisive to give a tone and texture to the moral feelings. Not only is the attention thus roused and kept alive; but what is most important as to the principles of action, the desire of good or hatred of evil is

10 *Paradise Lost,* IV, 393–4.
11 On Jeremy Bentham see pp. 369 ff., below.
12 Cf. Thomas Campbell, "Lochiel's Warning," line 56.

powerfully excited. But all individual facts and history come under the head of what these people call *Imagination*. All full, true, and particular accounts they consider as romantic, ridiculous, vague, inflammatory. As a case in point, one of this school of thinkers[13] declares that he was qualified to write a better History of India from having never been there than if he had, as the last might lead to local distinctions or party-prejudices; that is to say, that he could describe a country better at second-hand than from original observation, or that from having seen no one object, place, or person, he could do ampler justice to the whole. It might be maintained, much on the same principle, that an artist would paint a better likeness of a person after he was dead, from description or different sketches of the face, than from having seen the individual living man. On the contrary, I humbly conceive that the seeing half a dozen wandering Lascars in the streets of London gives one a better idea of the soul of India, that cradle of the world, and (as it were) garden of the sun, than all the charts, records, and statistical reports that can be sent over, even under the classical administration of Mr. Canning. *Ex uno omnes*.[14] One Hindoo differs more from a citizen of London than he does from all other Hindoos; and by seeing the two first, man to man, you know comparatively and essentially what they are, nation to nation. By a very few specimens you fix the great leading differences, which are nearly the same throughout. Any one thing is a better representative of its kind, than all the words and definitions in the world can be. The sum total is indeed different from the particulars; but it is not easy to guess at any general result, without some previous induction of particulars and appeal to experience.

What can we reason, but from what we know?[15]

Again, it is quite wrong, instead of the most striking illustrations of human nature, to single out the stalest and tritest, as if they were most authentic and infallible; not considering that from the extremes you may infer the means, but you cannot from the means infer the extremes in any case. It may be said that the extreme and individual cases may be retorted upon us:—I deny it, unless it be with truth. The imagination is an *associating* principle; and has an instinctive perception when a thing belongs to a

system, or is only an exception to it. For instance, the excesses committed by the victorious besiegers of a town do not attach to the nation committing them, but to the nature of that sort of warfare, and are common to both sides. They may be struck off the score of national prejudices. The cruelties exercised upon slaves, on the other hand, grow out of the relation between master and slave; and the mind intuitively revolts at them as such. The cant about the horrors of the French Revolution is mere cant—every body knows it to be so: each party would have retaliated upon the other: it was a civil war, like that for a disputed succession: the general principle of the right or wrong of the change remains untouched. Neither would these horrors have taken place, except from Prussian manifestos, and treachery within: there were none in the American, and have been none in the Spanish Revolution. The massacre of St. Bartholomew arose out of the principles of that religion which exterminates with fire and sword, and keeps no faith with heretics.—If it be said that nicknames, party watch-words, bugbears, the cry of "No Popery," &c., are continually played off upon the imagination with the most mischievous effect, I answer that most of these bugbears and terms of vulgar abuse have arisen out of abstruse speculation or barbarous prejudice, and have seldom had their root in real facts or natural feelings. Besides, are not general topics, rules, exceptions, endlessly bandied to and fro, and balanced one against the other by the most learned disputants? Have not three-fourths of all the wars, schisms, heart-burnings in the world begun on mere points of controversy?—There are two classes whom I have found given to this kind of reasoning against the use of our senses and feelings in what concerns human nature, *viz.* knaves and fools. The last do it, because they think their own shallow dogmas settle all questions best without any farther appeal; and the first do it, because they know that the refinements of the head are more easily got rid of than the suggestions of the heart, and that a strong sense of injustice, excited by a particular case in all its aggravations, tells more against them than all the distinctions of the jurists. Facts, concrete existences, are stubborn things, and are not so soon tampered with or turned about to any point we please, as mere names and abstractions. Of these last it may be said,

A breath can *mar* them, as a breath has made:[16]

and they are liable to be puffed away by every wind

---

[13] The economist and philosopher James Mill (1773–1836), father of John Stuart Mill (see pp. 516 ff., below). He wrote a *History of British India* (1817–18).

[14] From one, all (adapted from Vergil's *Aeneid*, II, 65–6).

[15] Pope, *An Essay on Man*, I, 18.

[16] Cf. Goldsmith, *The Deserted Village*, line 54.

of doctrine, or baffled by every plea of convenience. I wonder that Rousseau gave in to this cant about the want of soundness in rhetorical and imaginative reasoning; and was so fond of this subject, as to make an abridgment of Plato's rhapsodies upon it, by which he was led to expel poets from his commonwealth. Thus two of the most flowery writers are those who have exacted the greatest severity of style from others. Rousseau was too ambitious of an exceedingly technical and scientific mode of reasoning, scarcely attainable in the mixed questions of human life, (as may be seen in his SOCIAL CONTRACT—a work of great ability, but extreme formality of structure) and it is probable he was led into this error in seeking to overcome his too great warmth of natural temperament and a tendency to indulge merely the impulses of passion. Burke, who was a man of fine imagination, had the good sense (without any of this false modesty) to defend the moral use of the imagination, and is himself one of the grossest instances of its abuse.

It is not merely the fashion among philosophers— the poets also have got into a way of scouting individuality as beneath the sublimity of their pretensions, and the universality of their genius. The philosophers have become mere logicians, and their rivals mere rhetoricians; for as these last must float on the surface, and are not allowed to be harsh and crabbed and recondite like the others, by leaving out the individual, they become common-place. They cannot reason, and they must declaim. Modern tragedy, in particular, is no longer like a vessel making the voyage of life, and tossed about by the winds and waves of passion, but is converted into a handsomely-constructed steamboat, that is moved by the sole expansive power of words. Lord Byron has launched several of these ventures lately[17] (if ventures they may be called) and may continue in the same strain as long as he pleases. We have not now a number of *dramatis personae* affected by particular incidents and speaking according to their feelings, or as the occasion suggests, but each mounting the rostrum, and delivering his opinion on fate, fortune, and the entire consummation of things. The individual is not of sufficient importance to occupy his own thoughts or the thoughts of others. The poet fills his page with *grandes pensées*. He covers the face of nature with the beauty of his sentiments and the brilliancy of his paradoxes. We have the subtleties of the head, instead of the workings of the heart, and

possible justifications instead of the actual motives of conduct. This all seems to proceed on a false estimate of individual nature and the value of human life. We have been so used to count by millions of late, that we think the units that compose them nothing, and are so prone to trace remote principles, that we neglect the immediate results. As an instance of the opposite style of dramatic dialogue, in which the persons speak for themselves, and to one another, I will give, by way of illustration, a passage from an old tragedy, in which a brother has just caused his sister to be put to a violent death.

Bosola. Fix your eye here.
Ferdinand. Constantly.
Bosola. Do you not weep?
Other sins only speak; murther shrieks out:
The element of water moistens the earth;
But blood flies upwards, and bedews the heavens.
  Ferdinand. Cover her face: mine eyes dazzle; she died
    young.
  Bosola. I think not so: her infelicity
Seem'd to have years too many.
  Ferdinand. She and I were twins:
And should I die this instant, I had lived
Her time to a minute.
            DUCHESS OF MALFY, Act IV. Scene 2.

How fine is the constancy with which he first fixes his eye on the dead body, with a forced courage, and then, as his resolution wavers, how natural is his turning his face away, and the reflection that strikes him on her youth and beauty and untimely death, and the thought that they were twins, and his measuring his life by hers up to the present period, as if all that was to come of it were nothing! Now, I would fain ask whether there is not in this contemplation of the interval that separates the beginning from the end of life, of a life too so varied from good to ill, and of the pitiable termination of which the person speaking has been the wilful and guilty cause, enough to "give the mind pause"?[18] Is not that revelation as it were of the whole extent of our being which is made by the flashes of passion and stroke of calamity, a subject sufficiently staggering to have place in legitimate tragedy? Are not the struggles of the will with untoward events and the adverse passions of others as interesting and instructive in the representation as reflections on the mutability of fortune or inevitableness of destiny, or on the passions of men in general? The tragic Muse does not merely utter muffled sounds: but we see the paleness on the

---

[17] On his plays see the introduction to Byron, pp. 211 ff., below.

[18] Cf. *Hamlet*, III, i, 68.

cheek, and the life-blood gushing from the heart! The interest we take in our own lives, in our successes or disappointments, and the *home* feelings that arise out of these, when well described, are the clearest and truest mirror in which we can see the image of human nature. For in this sense each man is a microcosm. What he is, the rest are—whatever his joys and sorrows are composed of, theirs are the same—no more, no less.

One touch of nature makes the whole world kin.[19]

But it must be the genuine touch of nature, not the outward flourishes and varnish of art. The spouting, oracular, didactic figure of the poet no more answers to the living man, than the lay-figure of the painter does. We may well say to such a one,

Thou hast no speculation in those eyes
That thou dost glare with: thy bones are marrowless,
Thy blood is cold![20]

Man is (so to speak) an endless and infinitely varied repetition: and if we know what one man feels, we so far know what a thousand feel in the sanctuary of their being. Our feeling of general humanity is at once an aggregate of a thousand different truths, and it is also the same truth a thousand times told. As is our perception of this original truth, the root of our imagination, so will the force and richness of the general impression proceeding from it be. The boundary of our sympathy is a circle which enlarges itself according to its propulsion from the centre—the heart. If we are imbued with a deep sense of individual weal or woe, we shall be awe-struck at the idea of humanity in general. If we know little of it but its abstract and common properties, without their particular application, their force or degrees, we shall care just as little as we know either about the whole or the individuals. If we understand the texture and vital feeling, we then can fill up the outline, but we cannot supply the former from having the latter given. Moral and poetical truth is like expression in a picture—the one is not to be attained by smearing over a large canvas, nor the other by bestriding a vague topic. In such matters, the most pompous sciolists are accordingly found to be the greatest contemners of human life. But I defy any great tragic writer to despise that nature which he understands, or that heart which he has probed, with all its rich bleeding materials of joy and sorrow. The subject may not be a source of much triumph to him, from its alternate light and shade, but it can never become one of supercilious indifference. He must feel a strong reflex interest in it, corresponding to that which he has depicted in the characters of others. Indeed, the object and end of playing, "both at the first and now, is to hold the mirror up to nature,"[21] to enable us to feel for others as for ourselves, or to embody a distinct interest out of ourselves by the force of imagination and passion. This is summed up in the wish of the poet—

To feel what others are, and know myself a man.[22]

If it does not do this, it loses both its dignity and its proper use.

ON GOING A JOURNEY

THE following essay first appeared in the *New Monthly Magazine* for January, 1822. It was reprinted in the second of the two volumes of *Table-Talk*. The present text incorporates Hazlitt's final revisions.

ONE of the pleasantest things in the world is going a journey; but I like to go by myself. I can enjoy society in a room; but out of doors, nature is company enough for me. I am then never less alone than when alone. "The fields his study, nature was his book."[1]

I cannot see the wit of walking and talking at the same time. When I am in the country, I wish to vegetate like the country. I am not for criticizing hedge-rows and black cattle. I go out of town in order to forget the town and all that is in it. There are those who for this purpose go to watering-places, and carry the metropolis with them. I like more elbow-room, and fewer incumbrances. I like solitude, when I give myself up to it, for the sake of solitude; nor do I ask for

—a friend in my retreat,
Whom I may whisper solitude is sweet.[2]

[19] Shakespeare, *Troilus and Cressida*, III, iii, 175.
[20] Cf. *Macbeth*, III, iv, 94–6.

[1] Robert Bloomfield, the shoemaker poet (1766–1823), *The Farmer's Boy*, "Spring," line 32.

[21] Cf. *Hamlet*, III, ii, 23–25.
[22] Cf. Thomas Gray, "Hymn to Adversity," line 48.

[2] William Cowper, *Retirement*, lines 741–2.

The soul of a journey is liberty, perfect liberty, to think, feel, do just as one pleases. We go a journey chiefly to be free of all impediments and of all inconveniences; to leave ourselves behind, much more to get rid of others. It is because I want a little breathing-space to muse on indifferent matters, where Contemplation

May plume her feathers and let grow her wings,
That in the various bustle of resort
Were all too ruffled, and sometimes impair'd,[3]

that I absent myself from the town for awhile, without feeling at a loss the moment I am left by myself. Instead of a friend in a post-chase or in a tilbury,[4] to exchange good things with, and vary the same stale topics over again, for once let me have a truce with impertinence. Give me the clear blue sky over my head, and the green turf beneath my feet, a winding road before me, and a three-hours' march to dinner—and then to thinking! It is hard if I cannot start some game on these lone heaths. I laugh, I run, I leap, I sing for joy. From the point of yonder rolling cloud, I plunge into my past being, and revel there, as the sun-burnt Indian plunges headlong into the wave that wafts him to his native shore. Then long-forgotten things, like "sunken wrack and sumless treasuries,"[5] burst upon my eager sight, and I begin to feel, think, and be myself again. Instead of an awkward silence, broken by attempts at wit or dull common-places, mine is that undisturbed silence of the heart which alone is perfect eloquence. No one likes puns, alliterations, antitheses, argument, and analysis better than I do; but I sometimes had rather be without them. "Leave, oh, leave me to my repose!"[6] I have just now other business in hand, which would seem idle to you, but is with me "the very stuff of the conscience."[7] Is not this wild rose sweet without a comment? Does not this daisy leap to my heart, set in its coat of emerald? Yet if I were to explain to you the circumstance that has so endeared it to me, you would only smile. Had I not better then keep it to myself, and let it serve me to brood over, from here to yonder craggy point, and from thence onward to the far-distant horizon? I should be but bad company all that way, and therefore prefer being alone. I have heard it said that you may, when the moody fit comes on, walk or ride on by yourself, and indulge your reveries. But this looks like a breach of manners, a neglect of others, and you are thinking all the time that you ought to rejoin your party. "Out upon such half-faced fellowship,"[8] say I. I like to be either entirely to myself, or entirely at the disposal of others; to talk or be silent, to walk or sit still, to be sociable or solitary. I was pleased with an observation of Mr. Cobbett's,[9] that "he thought it a bad French custom to drink our wine with our meals, and that an Englishman ought to do only one thing at a time." So I cannot talk and think, or indulge in melancholy musing and lively conversation by fits and starts. "Let me have a companion of my way," says Sterne,[10] "were it but to remark how the shadows lengthen as the sun goes down." It is beautifully said: but in my opinion, this continual comparing of notes interferes with the involuntary impression of things upon the mind, and hurts the sentiment. If you only hint what you feel in a kind of dumb show, it is insipid: if you have to explain it, it is making a toil of a pleasure. You cannot read the book of nature without being perpetually put to the trouble of translating it for the benefit of others. I am for the synthetical method on a journey, in preference to the analytical. I am content to lay in a stock of ideas then, and to examine and anatomise[11] them afterwards. I want to see my vague notions float like the down of the thistle before the breeze, and not to have them entangled in the briars and thorns of controversy. For once, I like to have it all my own way; and this is impossible unless you are alone, or in such company as I do not covet. I have no objection to argue a point with any one for twenty miles of measured road, but not for pleasure. If you remark the scent of a beanfield crossing the road, perhaps your fellow-traveller has no smell. If you point to a distant object, perhaps he is short-sighted, and has to take out his glass to look at it. There is a feeling in the air, a tone in the colour of a cloud, which hits your fancy, but the effect of which you are unable to account for. There is then no sympathy, but an uneasy craving after it, and a dissatisfaction which pursues you on the way, and in the end probably produces ill humor. Now I never quarrel with myself, and take all my own conclusions for granted till I find it necessary to defend them against objections. It is not merely that you may not be of accord on the objects and circumstances that present themselves before you—they may recall a number of

---

[3] Cf. Milton's *Comus*, lines 377–80.
[4] Gig, two-wheeled vehicle.
[5] Shakespeare, *Henry V*, I, ii, 165.
[6] Cf. Thomas Gray, "The Descent of Odin," line 50.
[7] Cf. *Othello*, I, ii, 2.

[8] Cf. *1 Henry IV*, I, iii, 208.
[9] William Cobbett (1763–1835), the radical politician and journalist.
[10] Cf. *Sermons of Mr. Yorick,* no. XVIII, by Laurence Sterne (1713–68), novelist and clergyman.   [11] Dissect, analyze.

ideas, and lead to associations too delicate and refined to be possibly communicated to others. Yet these I love to cherish, and sometimes still fondly clutch them, when I can escape from the throng to do so. To give way to our feelings before company, seems extravagance or affectation; on the other hand, to have to unravel this mystery of our being at every turn, and to make others take an equal interest in it (otherwise the end is not answered) is a task to which few are competent. We must "give it an understanding, but no tongue."[12] My old friend C——,[13] however, could do both. He could go on in the most delightful explanatory way over hill and dale, a summer's day, and convert a landscape into a didactic poem or a Pindaric ode. "He talked far above singing."[14] If I could so clothe my ideas in sounding and flowing words, I might perhaps wish to have some one with me to admire the swelling theme; or I could be more content, were it possible for me still to hear his echoing voice in the woods of All-Foxden.[15] They had "that fine madness in them which our first poets had";[16] and if they could have been caught by some rare instrument, would have breathed such strains as the following.

                    —Here be woods as green
As any, air likewise as fresh and sweet
As when smooth Zephyrus[17] plays on the fleet
Face of the curlèd stream, with flow'rs as many
As the young spring gives, and as choice as any;
Here be all new delights, cool streams and wells,
Arbours o'ergrown with woodbines, caves and dells:
Choose where thou wilt, while I sit by and sing,
Or gather rushes to make many a ring
For thy long fingers; tell thee tales of love,
How the pale Phoebe,[18] hunting in a grove,
First saw the boy Endymion, from whose eyes
She took eternal fire that never dies;
How she conveyed him softly in a sleep,
His temples bound with poppy, to the steep
Head of old, Latmos,[19] where she stoops each night,
Gilding the mountain with her brother's[20] light,
To kiss her sweetest.—[21]

Had I words and images at command like these, I would attempt to wake the thoughts that lie slumbering on golden ridges in the evening clouds: but at the sight of nature my fancy, poor as it is, droops and closes up its leaves, like flowers at sunset. I can make nothing out on the spot:—I must have time to collect myself.

In general, a good thing spoils out-of-door prospects:[22] it should be reserved for Table-talk. L——[23] is for this reason, I take it, the worst company in the world out of doors; because he is the best within. I grant, there is one subject on which it is pleasant to talk on a journey; and that is, what one shall have for supper when we get to our inn at night. The open air improves this sort of conversation or friendly altercation, by setting a keener edge on appetite. Every mile of the road heightens the flavour of the viands we expect at the end of it. How fine it is to enter some old town, walled and turreted, just at the approach of night-fall, or to come to some straggling village, with the lights streaming through the surrounding gloom; and then after inquiring for the best entertainment that the place affords, to "take one's ease at one's inn"![24] These eventful moments in our lives are in fact too precious, too full of solid, heartfelt happiness, to be frittered and dribbled away in imperfect sympathy. I would have them all to myself, and drain them to the last drop: they will do to talk of or to write about afterwards. What a delicate speculation it is, after drinking whole goblets of tea,

The cups that cheer, but not inebriate,[25]

and letting the fumes ascend into the brain, to sit considering what we shall have for supper—eggs and a rasher, a rabbit smothered in onions, or an excellent veal-cutlet! Sancho[26] in such a situation once fixed upon cow-heel;[27] and his choice, though he could not help it, is not to be disparaged. Then, in the intervals of pictured scenery and Shandean[28] contemplation, to catch the preparation and the stir in the kitchen—*Procul, O procul este profani!*[29] These hours are sacred to silence and to musing, to be treasured up in the memory, and to feed the source of smiling thoughts hereafter. I would not waste them in idle talk; or if I must have the integrity of fancy broken in upon, I would rather it were by a stranger than a friend. A stranger takes his hue and

---

[12] *Hamlet*, I, ii, 250.   [13] Coleridge.
[14] Beaumont and Fletcher, *Philaster*, V, v, 163–4.
[15] For Wordsworth's residence at Alfoxden, Somersetshire, and the talks with Coleridge which led to *Lyrical Ballads*, see pp. 44–45, above.
[16] Cf. Michael Drayton's "Elegy to Henry Reynolds," lines 109–10.
[17] The west wind.   [18] Diana.
[19] A mountain in Asia Minor.   [20] Apollo, the sun god.
[21] Cf. John Fletcher's *The Faithful Shepherdess*, I, iii, 26–43.

[22] Scenic views.   [23] Lamb.
[24] Cf. *1 Henry IV*, III, iii, 92–3.
[25] Cowper, *The Task*, IV, 39–40.
[26] The hero's peasant squire in the *Don Quixote* of Cervantes.
[27] I.e., foot, stewed so as to form a jelly.
[28] I.e., rambling, crotchety—in the vein of Laurence Sterne's *Tristram Shandy*.
[29] Stand off, off, ye vulgar (*Aeneid*, VI, 258).

character from the time and place; he is a part of the furniture and costume of an inn. If he is a Quaker, or from the West Riding[30] of Yorkshire, so much the better. I do not even try to sympathise with him, and he *breaks no squares*.[31] I associate nothing with my travelling companion but present objects and passing events. In his ignorance of me and my affairs, I in a manner forget myself. But a friend reminds one of other things, rips up old grievances, and destroys the abstraction of the scene. He comes in ungraciously between us and our imaginary character. Something is dropped in the course of conversation that gives a hint of your profession and pursuits; or from having some one with you that knows the less sublime portions of your history, it seems that other people do. You are no longer a citizen of the world: but your "unhousèd, free condition is put into circumscription and confine."[32] The *incognito* of an inn is one of its striking privileges —"lord of one's-self, uncumber'd with a name."[33] Oh! it is great to shake off the trammels of the world and of public opinion—to lose our importunate, tormenting, everlasting personal identity in the elements of nature, and become the creature of the moment, clear of all ties—to hold to the universe only by a dish of sweet-breads, and to owe nothing but the score[34] of the evening—and no longer seeking for applause and meeting with contempt, to be known by no other title than *the Gentleman in the parlour*! One may take one's choice of all characters in this romantic state of uncertainty as to one's real pretensions, and become indefinitely respectable and negatively right-worshipful. We baffle prejudice and disappoint conjecture; and from being so to others, begin to be objects of curiosity and wonder even to ourselves. We are no more those hackneyed common-places that we appear in the world: an inn restores us to the level of nature, and quits scores with society! I have certainly spent some enviable hours at inns—sometimes when I have been left entirely to myself, and have tried to solve some metaphysical problem, as once at Witham-common,[35] where I found out the proof that likeness is not a case of the association of ideas—at other times, when there have been pictures in the room, as at St. Neot's,[36]

(I think it was) where I first met with Gribelin's engravings of the Cartoons,[37] into which I entered at once; and at a little inn on the borders of Wales, where there happened to be hanging some of Westall's[38] drawings, which I compared triumphantly (for a theory that I had, not for the admired artist) with the figure of a girl who had ferried me over the Severn, standing up in a boat between me and the fading twilight—at other times I might mention luxuriating in books, with a peculiar interest in this way, as I remember sitting up half the night to read Paul and Virginia,[39] which I picked up at an inn at Bridgewater,[40] after being drenched in the rain all day; and at the same place I got through two volumes of Madame d'Arblay's Camilla.[41] It was on the tenth of April, 1798, that I sat down to a volume of the New Eloise,[42] at the inn at Llangollen,[43] over a bottle of sherry and a cold chicken. The letter I chose was that in which St. Preux describes his feelings as he first caught a glimpse from the heights of the Jura[44] of the Pays de Vaud, which I had brought with me as a *bonne bouche*[45] to crown the evening with. It was my birthday, and I had for the first time come from a place in the neighbourhood to visit this delightful spot. The road to Llangollen turns off between Chirk and Wrexham; and on passing a certain point, you come all at once upon the valley, which opens like an amphitheatre, broad, barren hills rising in majestic state on either side, with "green, upland swells that echo to the bleat of flocks"[46] below, and the river Dee babbling over its stony bed in the midst of them. The valley at this time "glittered green with sunny showers,"[47] and a budding ash-tree dipped its tender branches in the chiding stream. How proud, how glad I was to walk along the high road that commanded the delicious prospect, repeating the lines which I have just quoted from Mr. Coleridge's poems! But besides

30 One of the three administrative divisions of Yorkshire; i.e., remote, uncouth.   31 Does no harm.
32 Cf. *Othello*, I, ii, 26–7.
33 Cf. Dryden, "Epistle to My Honor'd Kinsman, John Driden," line 18.   34 Bill.
35 Though there is a Witham in Somersetshire, the reference is probably to a town in Essex about forty miles from London.
36 A town in Huntingdonshire about fifty miles from London.

37 I.e., Raphael's drawings, engraved by Simon Gribelin and published in 1707.
38 Richard Westall (1765–1836) was a well-known painter and book illustrator.
39 A widely read romance (1788) by Bernardin de St. Pierre.
40 In Somersetshire. This was when Hazlitt went to visit Coleridge at near-by Nether Stowey.
41 Fanny Burney (1752–1840) married a French refugee, General d'Arblay. She was the daughter of the musician and friend of Dr. Johnson, Dr. Charles Burney; the sister of Lamb's friend, Admiral James Burney; and author of several novels, including *Evelina* (1778) and *Camilla* (1796).
42 A novel (1761) in letter form by Jean Jacques Rousseau.
43 A town in Wales on the river Dee, thirty miles from Chester.
44 A mountain range between France and the Swiss canton of Vaud.
45 Choice morsel.
46 Cf. Coleridge, "Ode on the Departing Year," lines 125–6
47 Cf. *ibid.*, line 124.

the prospect which opened beneath my feet, another also opened to my inward sight, a heavenly vision, on which were written, in letters large as Hope could make them, these four words, LIBERTY, GENIUS, LOVE, VIRTUE; which have since faded into the light of common day,[48] or mock my idle gaze.

The beautiful is vanished, and returns not.[49]

Still I would return some time or other to this enchanted spot; but I would return to it alone. What other self could I find to share that influx of thoughts, of regret, and delight, the fragments of which I could hardly conjure up to myself, so much have they been broken and defaced! I could stand on some tall rock, and overlook the precipice of years that separates me from what I then was. I was at that time going shortly to visit the poet whom I have above named. Where is he now?[50] Not only I myself have changed; the world, which was then new to me, has become old and incorrigible. Yet will I turn to thee in thought, O silvan Dee,[51] as then thou wert, in joy, in youth and gladness; and thou shalt always be to me the river of Paradise, where I will drink of the waters of life freely![52]

There is hardly any thing that shows the short-sightedness or capriciousness of the imagination more than travelling does. With change of place we change our ideas; nay, our opinions and feelings. We can by an effort indeed transport ourselves to old and long-forgotten scenes, and then the picture of the mind revives again; but we forget those that we have just left. It seems that we can think but of one place at a time. The canvas of the fancy has only a certain extent, and if we paint one set of objects upon it, they immediately efface every other. We cannot enlarge our conceptions; we only shift our point of view. The landscape bares its bosom[53] to the enraptured eye; we take our fill of it; and seem as if we could form no other image of beauty or grandeur. We pass on, and think no more of it: the horizon that shuts it from our sight also blots it from our memory like a dream. In travelling through a wild barren country, I can form no idea of a woody and cultivated one. It appears to me that all the world must be barren, like what I see of it. In the country we forget the town, and in town we despise the country. "Beyond Hyde Park," says Sir Fopling Flutter,[54] "all is a desert." All that part of the map that we do not see before us is a blank. The world in our conceit of it is not much bigger than a nutshell. It is not one prospect expanded into another, county joined to county, kingdom to kingdom, lands to seas, making an image voluminous and vast;—the mind can form no larger idea of space than the eye can take in at a single glance. The rest is a name written on a map, a calculation of arithmetic. For instance, what is the true signification of that immense mass of territory and population, known by the name of China to us? An inch of paste-board on a wooden globe, of no more account than a China orange![55] Things near us are seen of the size of life: things at a distance are diminished to the size of the understanding. We measure the universe by ourselves, and even comprehend the texture of our own being only piece-meal. In this way, however, we remember an infinity of things and places. The mind is like a mechanical instrument that plays a great variety of tunes, but it must play them in succession. One idea recalls another, but it at the same time excludes all others. In trying to renew old recollections we cannot as it were unfold the whole web of our existence; we must pick out the single threads. So in coming to a place where we have formerly lived and with which we have intimate associations, every one must have found that the feeling grows more vivid the nearer we approach the spot, from the mere anticipation of the actual impression: we remember circumstances, feelings, persons, faces, names, that we had not thought of for years; but for the time all the rest of the world is forgotten!—To return to the question I have quitted above.

I have no objection to go to see ruins, aqueducts, pictures, in company with a friend or a party, but rather the contrary, for the former reason reversed. They are intelligible matters, and will bear talking about. The sentiment here is not tacit, but communicable and overt. Salisbury Plain is barren of criticism, but Stonehenge[56] will bear a discussion

---

[48] Cf. Wordsworth, "Ode: Intimations of Immortality," line 76. —Hazlitt is thinking of the young English radicals' chagrin when the French Revolution ended in the Napoleonic dictatorship and its principles failed of general adoption.

[49] Coleridge, translation of Schiller's *The Death of Wallenstein*, V, i, 68.

[50] Unlike Wordsworth and Coleridge, Hazlitt did not abandon his radical views.

[51] Cf. Wordsworth, "Tintern Abbey," lines 55–7.

[52] Cf. Revelation 22:17.

[53] Cf. Wordsworth's sonnet "The world is too much with us," line 5.

[54] Cf. Sir George Etherege's *The Man of Mode, or Sir Fopling Flutter*, V, ii, 151–2. (The remark is not made by Sir Fopling but by another character.)

[55] The sweet orange was originally brought from China.

[56] A mysterious group of large prehistoric hewn stones near Salisbury, Wiltshire (see the sketch in the upper right corner of the front end paper).

antiquarian, picturesque, and philosophical. In setting out on a party of pleasure, the first consideration always is where we shall go to: in taking a solitary ramble, the question is what we shall meet with by the way. The mind then is "its own place";[57] nor are we anxious to arrive at the end of our journey. I can myself do the honours indifferently[58] well to works of art and curiosity. I once took a party to Oxford[59] with no mean *éclat*—shewed them the seat of the Muses at a distance,

> With glistering spires and pinnacles adorn'd—[60]

descanted on the learned air that breathes from the grassy quadrangles and stone walls of halls and colleges—was at home in the Bodleian;[61] and at Blenheim[62] quite superseded the powdered Cicerone[63] that attended us, and that pointed in vain with his wand to common-place beauties in matchless pictures.—As another exception to the above reasoning, I should not feel confident in venturing on a journey in a foreign country without a companion. I should want at intervals to hear the sound of my own language. There is an involuntary antipathy in the mind of an Englishman to foreign manners and notions that requires the assistance of social sympathy to carry it off. As the distance from home increases, this relief, which was at first a luxury, becomes a passion and an appetite. A person would almost feel stifled to find himself in the deserts of Arabia without friends and countrymen: there must be allowed to be something in the view of Athens or old Rome that claims the utterance of speech; and I own that the Pyramids are too mighty for any single contemplation. In such situations, so opposite to all one's ordinary train of ideas, one seems a species by one's-self, a limb torn off from society, unless one can meet with instant fellowship and support.— Yet I did not feel this want or craving very pressing once, when I first set my foot on the laughing shores of France. Calais was peopled with novelty and delight. The confused, busy murmur of the place was like oil and wine poured into my ears; nor did the mariners' hymn, which was sung from the top of an old crazy vessel in the harbour, as the sun went down, send an alien sound into my soul. I breathed the air of general humanity. I walked over "the vine-covered hills and gay regions of France,"[64] erect and satisfied; for the image of man was not cast down and chained to the foot of arbitrary thrones. I was at no loss for language, for that of all the great schools of painting was open to me. The whole is vanished like a shade. Pictures, heroes, glory, freedom, all are fled: nothing remains but the Bourbons[65] and the French people!—There is undoubtedly a sensation in travelling into foreign parts that is to be had nowhere else: but it is more pleasing at the time than lasting. It is too remote from our habitual associations to be a common topic of discourse or reference, and, like a dream or another state of existence, does not piece into our daily modes of life. It is an animated but a momentary hallucination. It demands an effort to exchange our actual for our ideal identity; and to feel the pulse of our old transports revive very keenly, we must "jump"[66] all our present comforts and connexions. Our romantic and itinerant character is not to be domesticated. Dr. Johnson remarked[67] how little foreign travel added to the facilities of conversation in those who had been abroad. In fact, the time we have spent there is both delightful and in one sense instructive; but it appears to be cut out of our substantial, downright existence, and never to join kindly[68] on to it. We are not the same, but another, and perhaps more enviable individual, all the time we are out of our own country. We are lost to ourselves, as well as our friends. So the poet somewhat quaintly sings,

> Out of my country and myself I go.[69]

Those who wish to forget painful thoughts, do well to absent themselves for a while from the ties and objects that recall them; but we can be said only to fulfil our destiny in the place that gave us birth. I should on this account like well enough to spend the whole of my life in travelling abroad, if I could any where borrow another life to spend afterwards at home!

---

57 *Paradise Lost,* I, 254.
58 Fairly.   59 Charles and Mary Lamb, in the summer of 1810.
60 *Paradise Lost,* III, 550.   61 The university library.
62 A palace near Oxford, the nation's gift to the first Duke of Marlborough.
63 Sight-seers' guide. In this case, evidently a flunky in a powdered wig.
64 From a "Song . . . on the anniversary of the 14th of August, 1791," by the historian William Roscoe (1753–1831). This journey was in 1802.
65 The reactionary royal family restored by the Allies after the fall of Napoleon.   66 Risk. Cf. *Macbeth,* I, vii, 7.
67 In 1778 (Boswell's *Johnson,* ed. Hill, III, 352).
68 Naturally.   69 Unidentified.

from THE FIGHT

"THE FIGHT" was first published in the *New Monthly Magazine* for February, 1822. The contest took place on December 11, 1821, at Hungerford, Berkshire, between Tom Hickman, the Gas-Light Man (1785–1822), and Bill Neate, a butcher from Bristol, mother of champions. Neate was not a remarkable boxer, but he packed a terrific right-hand punch. This is the classic essay on prize fighting.

> ——The *fight,* the *fight's* the thing,
> Wherein I'll catch the conscience of the king.[1]

Where there's a will, there's a way.—I said so to myself, as I walked down Chancery-lane,[2] about half-past six o'clock on Monday the 10th of December, to inquire at Jack Randall's where the fight the next day was to be;[3] and I found "the proverb" nothing "musty"[4] in the present instance. I was determined to see this fight, come what would, and see it I did, in great style. It was my *first fight,* yet it more than answered my expectations. Ladies! it is to you I dedicate this description; nor let it seem out of character for the fair to notice the exploits of the brave. Courage and modesty are the old English virtues; and may they never look cold and askance on one another! Think, ye fairest of the fair, loveliest of the lovely kind, ye practisers of soft enchantment, how many more ye kill with poisoned baits than ever fell in the ring; and listen with subdued air and without shuddering, to a tale tragic only in appearance, and sacred to the FANCY![5]

I was going down Chancery-lane, thinking to ask at Jack Randall's where the fight was to be, when looking through the glass-door of the *Hole in the Wall,* I heard a gentleman asking the same question *at* Mrs. Randall, as the author of Waverley would express it.[6] Now Mrs. Randall stood answering the gentleman's question, with the authenticity of the lady of the Champion of the Light Weights. Thinks

I, I'll wait till this person comes out, and learn from him how it is. For to say a truth, I was not fond of going into this house of call for heroes and philosophers, ever since the owner of it (for Jack is no gentleman) threatened once upon a time to kick me out of doors for wanting a mutton-chop at his hospitable board, when the conqueror in thirteen battles was more full of *blue ruin*[7] than of good manners. . . .[8] I . . . was accommodated with a great coat, put up my umbrella to keep off a drizzling mist, and we began to cut through the air like an arrow. The mile-stones disappeared one after another, the rain kept off; Tom Turtle,[9] the trainer, sat before me on the coach-box, with whom I exchanged civilities as a gentleman going to the fight; the passion that had transported me an hour before was subdued to pensive regret and conjectural musing on the next day's battle; I was promised a place inside at Reading, and upon the whole, I thought myself a lucky fellow. Such is the force of imagination! On the outside of any other coach on the 10th of December, with a Scotch mist drizzling through the cloudy moonlight air, I should have been cold, comfortless, impatient, and, no doubt, wet through; but seated on the Royal mail, I felt warm and comfortable, the air did me good, the ride did me good, I was pleased with the progress we had made, and confident that all would go well through the journey. When I got inside at Reading, I found Turtle and a stout valetudinarian, whose costume bespoke him one of the FANCY, and who had risen from a three months' sick bed to get into the mail to see the fight. They were intimate, and we fell into a lively discourse. My friend the trainer was confined in his topics to fighting dogs and men, to bears and badgers; beyond this he was "quite chap-fallen,"[10] had not a word to throw at a dog, or indeed very wisely fell asleep, when any other game was started. The whole art of training (I, however, learnt from him) consists in two things, exercise and abstinence, abstinence and exercise, repeated alternately and without end. A yolk of an egg with a spoonful of rum in it is the

---

[1] Cf. *Hamlet,* II, ii, 633–4: "the play's the thing," etc.

[2] A London street running between High Holborn and the Strand. The prize fighter Jack Randall kept "The Hole in the Wall" there. It was not unusual for a successful pugilist to keep a "pub," that is, a tavern or saloon.

[3] In those days the location of matches was sometimes kept quiet till the last moment, to avoid interference. They were bloody affairs, fought without gloves, and with no limitation on the number of rounds.

[4] The discontented Hamlet (III, ii, 358–9) alludes to a "musty" proverb about how while the grass grows the steed starves.

[5] The fans and their heroes. All who are interested in a special sport, art, or pursuit.

[6] I.e., as a Scotsman would say.

[7] Cheap gin.

[8] Part of a long paragraph is here omitted. Hazlitt obtains his information, and after some difficulty secures a place on the top of a coach.

[9] According to Hazlitt's son this was John Thurtell (1794–1824), a well-known sporting man.

[10] Chopfallen, with jaw hanging. Hazlitt's quotation marks indicate that *Hamlet,* V, i, 212, is in his mind.

first thing in a morning, and then a walk of six miles till breakfast. This meal consists of a plentiful supply of tea and toast and beefsteaks. Then another six or seven miles till dinner-time, and another supply of solid beef or mutton with a pint of porter, and perhaps, at the utmost, a couple of glasses of sherry. Martin[11] trains on water, but this increases his infirmity on another very dangerous side. The Gas-man takes now and then a chirping[12] glass (under the rose[13]) to console him, during a six weeks' probation, for the absence of Mrs. Hickman—an agreeable woman, with (I understand) a pretty fortune of two hundred pounds. How matter presses on me! What stubborn things are facts! How inexhaustible is nature and art! "It is well," as I once heard Mr. Richmond[14] observe, "to see a variety." He was speaking of cock-fighting as an edifying spectacle. I cannot deny but that one learns more of what *is* (I do not say of what *ought to be*) in this desultory mode of practical study, than from reading the same book twice over, even though it should be a moral treatise. Where was I? I was sitting at dinner with the candidate for the honours of the ring, "where good digestion waits on appetite, and health on both."[15] Then follows an hour of social chat and native glee;[16] and afterwards, to another breathing over heathy hill or dale. Back to supper, and then to bed, and up by six again—Our hero

> Follows so the ever-running sun
> With profitable *ardour*—[17]

to the day that brings him victory or defeat in the green fairy circle.[18] Is not this life more sweet than mine?[19] I was going to say; but I will not libel any life by comparing it to mine, which is (at the date of these presents) bitter as coloquintida[20] and the dregs of aconitum! . . .[21]

Our present business was to get beds and a supper at an inn; but this was no easy task. The public-houses were full, and where you saw a light at a private house, and people poking their heads out of the casement to see what was going on, they instantly put them in and shut the window, the moment you seemed advancing with a suspicious overture for accommodation. Our guard and coachman thundered away at the outer gate of the Crown for some time without effect—such was the greater noise within;— and when the doors were unbarred, and we got admittance, we found a party assembled in the kitchen round a good hospitable fire, some sleeping, others drinking, others talking on politics and on the fight. A tall English yeoman (something like Matthews[22] in the face, and quite as great a wag)—

> A lusty man to ben an abbot able,—[23]

was making such a prodigious noise about rent and taxes, and the price of corn now and formerly, that he had prevented us from being heard at the gate. The first thing I heard him say was to a shuffling fellow who wanted to be off a bet for a shilling glass of brandy and water—"Confound it, man, don't be *insipid!*" Thinks I, that is a good phrase. It was a good omen. He kept it up so all night, nor flinched with the approach of morning. He was a fine fellow, with sense, wit, and spirit, a hearty body and a joyous mind, free-spoken, frank, convivial—one of that true English breed that went with Harry the Fifth to the siege of Harfleur—"standing like greyhounds in the slips,"[24] &c. We ordered tea and eggs (beds were soon found to be out of the question) and this fellow's conversation was *sauce piquante*. It did one's heart good to see him brandish his oaken towel[25] and to hear him talk. He made mince-meat of a drunken, stupid, red-face, quarrelsome, *frowsy* farmer, whose nose "he moralised into a thousand similes,"[26] making it out a firebrand like Bardolph's.[27] "I'll tell you what, my friend," says he, "the landlady has only to keep you here to save fire and candle. If one was to touch your nose, it would go off like a piece of charcoal." At this the other only grinned like an idiot, the sole variety in his purple face being his little peering grey eyes and yellow teeth; called for another glass, swore he would not stand it; and after many attempts to provoke his humorous antagonist to single combat, which the other turned off (after working him up to a ludicrous pitch of choler)

---

11 Jack Martin, the Baker. He had several epic fights with Jack Randall, who was known as the Prime Irish Lad.
12 Cheering.   13 *Sub rosa*, on the sly.
14 Bill Richmond, a colored boxer and instructor.
15 Cf. *Macbeth*, III, iv, 38–9.
16 Cf. Burns, "Address to the Unco Guid," line 33 (p. 35, above).
17 Cf. *Henry V*, IV, i, 293–4.
18 Circles of luxuriant grass used to be called fairy rings. Hazlitt is jocosely confusing them with the prize ring. Matches used to be fought out of doors, on the turf.
19 Cf. *As You Like It*, II, i, 2.
20 *Othello*, I, iii, 355–6. *Coloquintida*=the vine and fruit colocynth; *aconitum* is a poisonous herb.
21 A paragraph is here omitted, describing the rest of the journey, and Hazlitt's reunion with his friend "Joe Toms" (actually Joseph Parkes, a young lawyer), from whom he had become separated on the way.

22 Charles Mathews (1776–1835), a leading London comedian.
23 Cf. Chaucer, *The Canterbury Tales*, General Prologue, line 167.
24 Cf. *Henry V*, III, i, 31.   25 Staff.
26 Cf. *As You Like It*, II, i, 44–5.
27 Whose red face in *1* and *2 Henry IV*, *Henry V*, and *The Merry Wives of Windsor* is a stock theme for jesting.

with great adroitness, he fell quietly asleep with a glass of liquor in his hand, which he could not lift to his head. His laughing persecutor made a speech over him, and turning to the opposite side of the room, where they were all sleeping in the midst of this "loud and furious fun,"[28] said, "There's a scene, by G—d, for Hogarth[29] to paint. I think he and Shakespear were our two best men at copying life." This confirmed me in my good opinion of him. Hogarth, Shakespear, and Nature, were just enough for him (indeed for any man) to know. I said, "You read Cobbett,[30] don't you? At least," says I, "you talk just as well as he writes." He seemed to doubt this. But I said, "We have an hour to spare: if you'll get pen, ink, and paper, and keep on talking, I'll write down what you say; and if it doesn't make a capital Political Register,[31] I'll forfeit my head. You have kept me alive to-night, however. I don't know what I should have done without you." He did not dislike this view of the thing, nor my asking if he was not about the size of Jem Belcher; and told me soon afterwards, in the confidence of friendship, that "the circumstance which had given him nearly the greatest concern in his life, was Cribb's beating Jem[32] after he had lost his eye by racket-playing."—The morning dawns; that dim but yet clear light appears, which weighs like solid bars of metal on the sleepless eyelids; the guests drop down from their chambers one by one—but it was too late to think of going to bed now (the clock was on the stroke of seven), we had nothing for it but to find a barber's (the pole that glittered in the morning sun lighted us to his shop), and then a nine miles' march to Hungerford. The day was fine, the sky was blue, the mists were retiring from the marshy ground, the path was tolerably dry, the sitting-up all night had not done us much harm—at least the cause was good; we talked of this and that with amicable difference, roving and sipping of many subjects, but still invariably we returned to the fight. At length, a mile to the left of Hungerford, on a gentle eminence, we saw the ring surrounded by covered carts, gigs, and carriages, of which hundreds had passed us on the road; Toms[33] gave a youthful shout, and we hastened down a narrow lane to the scene of action.

Reader, have you ever seen a fight? If not, you have a pleasure to come, at least if it is a fight like that between the Gas-man and Bill Neate. The crowd was very great when we arrived on the spot; open carriages were coming up, with streamers flying and music playing, and the country-people were pouring in over hedge and ditch in all directions, to see their hero beat or be beaten. The odds were still on Gas, but only about five to four. Gully[34] had been down to try Neate, and had backed him considerably, which was a damper to the sanguine confidence of the adverse party. About two hundred thousand pounds were pending. The Gas says, he has lost 3000*l.* which were promised him by different gentlemen if he had won. He had presumed too much on himself, which had made others presume on him. This spirited and formidable young fellow seems to have taken for his motto the old maxim, that "there are three things necessary to success in life—*Impudence! Impudence! Impudence!*" It is so in matters of opinion, but not in the FANCY, which is the most practical of all things, though even here confidence is half the battle, but only half. Our friend had vapoured[35] and swaggered too much, as if he wanted to grin and bully his adversary out of the fight. "Alas! the Bristol man was not so tamed!"[36]— "This is *the grave-digger*" (would Tom Hickman exclaim in the moments of intoxication from gin and success, shewing his tremendous right hand), "this will send many of them to their long homes; I haven't done with them yet!" Why should he— though he had licked four of the best men within the hour, yet why should he threaten to inflict dishonorable chastisement on my old master Richmond,[37] a veteran going off the stage, and who has borne his sable honors meekly? Magnanimity, my dear Tom, and bravery, should be inseparable. Or why should he go up to his antagonist, the first time he ever saw him at the Fives[38] Court, and measuring him from head to foot with a glance of contempt, as Achilles surveyed Hector,[39] say to him, "What, are you Bill Neate? I'll knock more blood out of that great carcase of thine, this day fortnight, than you ever knock'd out of a bullock's!" It was not manly, 'twas not fighter-like. If he was sure of the victory (as he

[28] Perhaps reminiscent of Burn's "Tam o' Shanter," line 148 (p. 40, above).   [29] The eighteenth-century realist.

[30] See p. 171, note 9, above.

[31] Cobbett's weekly paper.

[32] In 1807 and 1809 the great champion Tom Cribb (1781–1848) beat James Belcher (1781–1811), whose career had been successful till he lost an eye in 1803.   [33] See note 21, above.

[34] John Gully (1783–1863), a retired prize fighter of great fame.

[35] Bragged.   [36] Cf. Cowper, *The Task,* II, 322.

[37] See note 14, above. Apparently Hazlitt had taken boxing lessons from him.

[38] A game similar to handball. The Fives Court was a building near Leicester Square devoted to sports, including boxing. Hazlitt used to play rackets there for hours on end.

[39] Cf. *Iliad,* XXII, 260 ff.

was not), the less said about it the better. Modesty should accompany the FANCY as its shadow. The best men were always the best behaved. Jem Belcher, the Game Chicken[40] (before whom the Gas-man could not have lived) were civil, silent men. So is Cribb, so is Tom Belcher,[41] the most elegant of sparrers, and not a man for every one to take by the nose. I enlarged on this topic in the mail (while Turtle was asleep), and said very wisely (as I thought) that impertinence was a part of no profession. A boxer was bound to beat his man, but not to thrust his fist, either actually or by implication, in every one's face. Even a highwayman, in the way of trade, may blow out your brains, but if he uses foul language at the same time, I should say he was no gentleman. A boxer, I would infer, need not be a blackguard or a coxcomb, more than another. Perhaps I press this point too much on a fallen man—Mr. Thomas Hickman has by this time learnt that first of all lessons, "That man was made to mourn."[42] He has lost nothing by the late fight but his presumption; and that every man may do as well without! By an over-display of this quality, however, the public had been prejudiced against him, and the knowing-ones were taken in. Few but those who had bet on him wished Gas to win. With my own prepossessions on the subject, the result of the 11th of December appeared to me as fine a piece of poetical justice as I had ever witnessed. The difference of weight between the two combatants (14 stone[43] to 12) was nothing to the sporting men. Great, heavy, clumsy, long-armed Bill Neate kicked the beam in the scale of the Gas-man's vanity. The amateurs were frightened at his big words, and thought that they would make up for the difference of six feet and five feet nine. Truly, the FANCY are not men of imagination. They judge of what has been, and cannot conceive of any thing that is to be. The Gas-man had won hitherto; therefore he must beat a man half as big again as himself—and that to a certainty. Besides, there are as many feuds, factions, prejudices, pedantic notions in the FANCY as in the state or in the schools. Mr. Gully is almost the only cool, sensible man among them, who exercises an unbiassed discretion, and is not a slave to his passions in these matters. But enough of reflections, and to our tale. The day,

as I have said, was fine for a December morning. The grass was wet, and the ground miry, and ploughed up with multitudinous feet, except that, within the ring itself, there was a spot of virgin-green closed in and unprofaned by vulgar tread, that shone with dazzling brightness in the mid-day sun. For it was now noon, and we had an hour to wait. This is the trying time. It is then the heart sickens, as you think what the two champions are about, and how short a time will determine their fate. After the first blow is struck, there is no opportunity for nervous apprehensions; you are swallowed up in the immediate interest of the scene—but

> Between the acting of a dreadful thing
> And the first motion, all the interim is
> Like a phantasma, or a hideous dream.[44]

I found it so as I felt the sun's rays clinging to my back, and saw the white wintry clouds sink below the verge of the horizon. "So," I thought, "my fairest hopes have faded from my sight!—so will the Gas-man's glory, or that of his adversary, vanish in an hour." The *swells* were parading in their white box-coats, the outer ring was cleared with some bruises on the heads and shins of the rustic assembly (for the *cockneys*[45] had been distanced by the sixty-six miles); the time drew near, I had got a good stand; a bustle, a buzz, ran through the crowd, and from the opposite side entered Neate, between his second and bottle-holder. He rolled along, swathed in his loose great coat, his knock-knees bending under his huge bulk; and, with a modest cheerful air, threw his hat into the ring. He then just looked round, and began quietly to undress; when from the other side there was a similar rush and an opening made, and the Gas-man came forward with a conscious air of anticipated triumph, too much like the cock-of-the-walk. He strutted about more than became a hero, sucked oranges with a supercilious air, and threw away the skin with a toss of his head, and went up and looked at Neate, which was an act of supererogation.[46] The only sensible thing he did was, as he strode away from the modern Ajax, to fling out his arms, as if he wanted to try whether they would do their work that day. By this time they had stripped, and presented a strong contrast in appearance. If Neate was like Ajax, "with Atlantean[47]

---

[40] Henry Pearce (1777–1809), a great fighter. He was a pupil of Jem Belcher, who came out of retirement for a match with him and was beaten.

[41] A brother of Jem Belcher and, though not his equal as a slugger, an accomplished boxer.

[42] The title of a poem by Burns.

[43] An English weight equal to 14 lbs.

[44] *Julius Caesar*, II, i, 63–5.

[45] Londoners. The rustics, who lived nearer, got there first.

[46] An unnecessary action.

[47] Strong; resembling Atlas, the Titan who held up the heavens. Hazlitt is quoting *Paradise Lost*, II, 306.

shoulders, fit to bear" the pugilistic reputation of all Bristol, Hickman might be compared to Diomed,[48] light, vigorous, elastic, and his back glistened in the sun, as he moved about, like a panther's hide. There was now a dead pause—attention was awe-struck. Who at that moment, big with a great event, did not draw his breath short—did not feel his heart throb? All was ready. They tossed up for the sun, and the Gas-man won. They were led up to the *scratch*—shook hands, and went at it.

In the first round every one thought it was all over. After making play a short time, the Gas-man flew at his adversary like a tiger, struck five blows in as many seconds, three first, and then following him as he staggered back, two more, right and left, and down he fell, a mighty ruin. There was a shout, and I said, "There is no standing this." Neate seemed like a lifeless lump of flesh and bone, round which the Gas-man's blows played with the rapidity of electricity or lightning, and you imagined he would only be lifted up to be knocked down again. It was as if Hickman held a sword or a fire in that right hand of his, and directed it against an unarmed body. They met again, and Neate seemed, not cowed, but particularly cautious. I saw his teeth clenched together and his brows knit close against the sun. He held out both his arms at full length straight before him, like two sledge-hammers, and raised his left an inch or two higher. The Gas-man could not get over this guard—they struck mutually and fell, but without advantage on either side. It was the same in the next round; but the balance of power was thus restored—the fate of the battle was suspended. No one could tell how it would end. This was the only moment in which opinion was divided; for, in the next, the Gas-man aiming a mortal blow at his adversary's neck, with his right hand, and failing from the length he had to reach, the other returned it with his left at full swing, planted a tremendous blow on his cheek-bone and eyebrow, and made a red ruin of that side of his face. The Gas-man went down, and there was another shout—a roar of triumph as the waves of fortune rolled tumultuously from side to side. This was a settler. Hickman got up, and "grinned horrible a ghastly smile,"[49] yet he was evidently dashed in his opinion of himself; it was the first time he had ever been so punished; all one side of his face was perfect scarlet, and his right eye was closed in dingy blackness, as he advanced to the fight,

less confident, but still determined. After one or two rounds, not receiving another such remembrancer, he rallied and went at it with his former impetuosity. But in vain. His strength had been weakened,—his blows could not tell at such a distance,—he was obliged to fling himself at his adversary, and could not strike from his feet; and almost as regularly as he flew at him with his right hand, Neate warded the blow, or drew back out of its reach, and felled him with the return of his left. There was little cautious sparring—no half-hits—no tapping and trifling, none of the *petitmaîtreship*[50] of the art—they were almost all knock-down blows:—the fight was a good stand up fight. The wonder was the half-minute time. If there had been a minute or more allowed between each round, it would have been intelligible how they should by degrees recover strength and resolution; but to see two men smashed to the ground, smeared with gore, stunned, senseless, the breath beaten out of their bodies; and then, before you recover from the shock, to see them rise up with new strength and courage, stand steady to inflict or receive mortal offence, and rush upon each other "like two clouds over the Caspian"[51]—this is the most astonishing thing of all:—this is the high and heroic state of man! From this time forward the event became more certain every round; and about the twelfth it seemed as if it must have been over. Hickman generally stood with his back to me; but in the scuffle, he had changed positions, and Neate just then made a tremendous lunge at him, and hit him full in the face. It was doubtful whether he would fall backwards or forwards; he hung suspended for a second or two, and then fell back, throwing his hands in the air, and with his face lifted up to the sky. I never saw any thing more terrific than his aspect just before he fell. All traces of life, of natural expression, were gone from him. His face was like a human skull, a death's head, spouting blood. The eyes were filled with blood, the nose streamed with blood, the mouth gaped blood. He was not like an actual man, but like a preternatural, spectral appearance, or like one of the figures in Dante's *Inferno*. Yet he fought on after this for several rounds, still striking the first desperate blow, and Neate standing on the defensive, and using the same cautious guard to the last, as if he had still all his work to do; and it was not till the Gas-man was so stunned in the seventeenth or eighteenth round, that his senses forsook him, and

---

[48] One of the Greek heroes in the *Iliad*.
[49] Cf. *Paradise Lost*, II, 846.

[50] Little-mastership, dandified mastery.
[51] Cf. *Paradise Lost*, II, 714–16.

he could not come to time, that the battle was declared over.[52] Ye who despise the FANCY, do something to shew as much *pluck,* or as much self-possession as this, before you assume a superiority which you have never given a single proof of by any one action in the whole course of your lives!—When the Gas-man came to himself, the first words he uttered were, "Where am I? What is the matter?" "Nothing is the matter, Tom,—you have lost the battle, but you are the bravest man alive." And Jackson[53] whispered to him, "I am collecting a purse for you, Tom."—Vain sounds, and unheard at that moment! Neate instantly went up and shook him cordially by the hand, and seeing some old acquaintance, began to flourish with his fists, calling out, "Ah, you always said I couldn't fight—What do you think now?" But all in good humour, and without any appearance of arrogance; only it was evident Bill Neate was pleased that he had won the fight. When it was over, I asked Cribb if he did not think it was a good one? He said, *"Pretty well!"* The carrier-pigeons now mounted into the air, and one of them flew with the news of her husband's victory to the bosom of Mrs. Neate. Alas, for Mrs. Hickman! . . .[54]

from MY FIRST ACQUAINTANCE WITH POETS

THIS essay appeared in the *Liberal* for April, 1823. "Immortal account" and "the finest essay in the English language" are among the praises admirers have showered on it.

MY FATHER was a Dissenting Minister at W—m[1] in Shropshire; and in the year 1798 (the figures that compose that date are to me like the "dreaded name of Demogorgon"[2]) Mr. Coleridge came to Shrewsbury, to succeed Mr. Rowe in the spiritual charge of a Unitarian congregation there. He did not come till late on the Saturday afternoon before he was to preach; and Mr. Rowe, who himself went down to the coach in a state of anxiety and expectation, to look for the arrival of his successor, could find no one at all answering the description but a round-faced man in a short black coat (like a shooting jacket) which hardly seemed to have been made for him, but who seemed to be talking at a great rate to his fellow-passengers. Mr. Rowe had scarce returned to give an account of his disappointment, when the round-faced man in black entered, and dissipated all doubts on the subject, by beginning to talk. He did not cease while he staid; nor has he since, that I know of. He held the good town of Shrewsbury in delightful suspense for three weeks that he remained there, "fluttering the *proud Salopians*[3] like an eagle in dove-cote";[4] and the Welsh mountains that skirt the horizon with their tempestuous confusion, agree to have heard no such mystic sounds since the days of

High-born Hoel's harp or soft Llewellyn's lay![5]

As we passed along between W—m and Shrewsbury, and I eyed their blue tops seen through the wintry branches, or the red rustling leaves of the sturdy oak-trees by the road-side, a sound was in my ears as of a Siren's song;[6] I was stunned, startled with it, as from deep sleep; but I had no notion then that I should ever be able to express my admiration to others in motley imagery or quaint allusion, till the light of his genius shone into my soul, like the sun's rays glittering in the puddles of the road. I was at that time dumb, inarticulate, helpless, like a worm by the way-side, crushed, bleeding, lifeless; but now, bursting from the deadly bands that bound them,

With Styx nine times round them,[7]

my ideas float on winged words, and as they expand their plumes, catch the golden light of other years.

---

52 Footnote by Hazlitt: "Scroggins said of the Gas-man, that he thought he was a man of that courage, that if his hands were cut off, he would still fight on with the stumps—like that of Widrington,—

'—In doleful dumps,
Who, when his legs were smitten off,
Still fought upon his stumps.' "

For the gallant squire Witherington, see the ballad "Chevy Chase," lines 93–104, 197–200 (I, 204–8, above). Jack Scroggins the Sailor (his real name was John Palmer) was another well-known prize fighter.

53 Presumably the retired prize fighter John ("Gentleman") Jackson (1769–1845), long the sporting world's leading figure. Byron took lessons from him.

1 Wem, a village about ten miles north of Shrewsbury. On Coleridge's candidacy for a pulpit at Shrewsbury, see p. 88, above.

2 *Paradise Lost,* II, 964–5. Demogorgon, a mysterious demon, was formerly credited with "a primordial creative power."

54 The remainder of the essay tells of the journey back to London.

3 *Salop* is another name for Shropshire.

4 Cf. Shakespeare's *Coriolanus,* V, vi, 115–16.

5 Gray, "The Bard," line 28.

6 In the *Odyssey,* Book XII, the sea nymphs known as the Sirens attempt by their singing to lure the sailors to destruction.

7 Cf. Pope, "Ode on St. Cecilia's Day," lines 90–91.

My soul has indeed remained in its original bondage, dark, obscure, with longings infinite and unsatisfied;[8] my heart, shut up in the prison-house of this rude clay, has never found, nor will it ever find, a heart to speak to; but that my understanding also did not remain dumb and brutish, or at length found a language to express itself, I owe to Coleridge. But this is not to my purpose.

My father lived ten miles from Shrewsbury, and was in the habit of exchanging visits with Mr. Rowe, and with Mr. Jenkins of Whitchurch (nine miles farther on) according to the custom of Dissenting Ministers in each other's neighbourhood. A line of communication is thus established, by which the flame of civil and religious liberty is kept alive, and nourishes its smouldering fire unquenchable, like the fires in the Agamemnon[9] of Aeschylus, placed at different stations, that waited for ten long years to announce with their blazing pyramids the destruction of Troy. Coleridge had agreed to come over to see my father, according to the courtesy of the country, as Mr. Rowe's probable successor; but in the meantime I had gone to hear him preach the Sunday after his arrival. A poet and a philosopher getting up into a Unitarian pulpit to preach the Gospel, was a romance in these degenerate days, a sort of revival of the primitive spirit of Christianity, which was not to be resisted.

It was in January, 1798, that I rose one morning before daylight, to walk ten miles in the mud, and went to hear this celebrated person preach. Never, the longest day I have to live, shall I have such another walk as this cold, raw, comfortless one, in the winter of the year 1798. *Il y a des impressions que ni le tems ni les circonstances peuvent effacer. Dusse-je vivre des siècles entiers, le doux tems de ma jeunesse ne peut renaître pour moi, ni s'effacer jamais dans ma mémoire.*[10] When I got there, the organ was playing the 100th psalm, and, when it was done, Mr. Coleridge rose and gave out his text, "And he went up into the mountain to pray, HIMSELF, ALONE."[11] As he gave out his text, his voice "rose like a steam of rich distilled perfumes,"[12] and when he came to the two last words, which he pronounced loud, deep, and distinct, it seemed to me, who was then young, as if

the sounds had echoed from the bottom of the human heart, and as if that prayer might have floated in solemn silence through the universe. The idea of St. John came into mind, "of one crying in the wilderness, who had his loins girt about, and whose food was locusts and wild honey."[13] The preacher then launched into his subject, like an eagle dallying with the wind. The sermon was upon peace and war; upon church and state—not their alliance, but their separation—on the spirit of the world and the spirit of Christianity, not as the same, but as opposed to one another. He talked of those who had "inscribed the cross of Christ on banners dripping with human gore." He made a poetical and pastoral excursion,— and to shew the fatal effects of war, drew a striking contrast between the simple shepherd boy, driving his team afield, or sitting under the hawthorn, piping to his flock, "as though he should never be old,"[14] and the same poor country-lad, crimped,[15] kidnapped, brought into town, made drunk at an alehouse, turned into a wretched drummer-boy, with his hair sticking on end with powder and pomatum,[16] a long cue at his back, and tricked out in the loathsome finery of the profession of blood.

Such were the notes our once-lov'd poet sung.[17]

And for myself, I could not have been more delighted if I had heard the music of the spheres.[18] Poetry and Philosophy had met together. Truth and Genius had embraced,[19] under the eye and with the sanction of Religion. This was even beyond my hopes. I returned home well satisfied. The sun that was still labouring pale and wan through the sky, obscured by thick mists, seemed an emblem of the *good cause;*[20] and the cold dank drops of dew that hung half melted on the beard of the thistle, had something genial and refreshing in them; for there was a spirit of hope and youth in all nature, that turned every thing into good. The face of nature had not then the brand of JUS DIVINUM[21] on it:

Like to that sanguine flower inscrib'd with woe.[22]

On the Tuesday following, the half-inspired[23] speaker came. I was called down into the room where

---

8 Cf. Wordsworth, "The Affliction of Margaret," line 63.

9 One of the greatest of the Greek tragedies (fifth century B.C.).

10 There are some impressions which neither time nor circumstances can efface. If I should live for whole centuries, the sweet time of my youth can not be reborn for me nor ever efface itself in my memory. (Misquoted from Rousseau's epistolary romance *Julie, ou La Nouvelle Héloïse* [1761], Part VI, letter 7.)

11 Cf. John 6:15.   12 Milton, *Comus,* line 556.

13 Cf. Matthew 3:3, 4.

14 From Sir Philip Sidney's *Arcadia,* Book I, chap. 2.

15 Trapped or lured into enlisting.   16 Pomade, hair grease.

17 Cf. Pope, "Epistle to Robert, Earl of Oxford," line 1.

18 The celestial spheres, which according to the Ptolemaic astronomy moved round the earth.   19 Cf. Psalms 85:10.

20 Of liberty and revolution.   21 Divine Right (of kings).

22 Milton, "Lycidas," line 106. The flower is the hyacinth, whose petals were supposed to be marked with the Greek exclamation of lament, *ai, ai.*   23 I.e., in part supernaturally motivated.

he was, and went half-hoping, half-afraid. He received me very graciously, and I listened for a long time without uttering a word. I did not suffer in his opinion by my silence. "For those two hours," he afterwards was pleased to say, "he was conversing with W. H.'s forehead!" His appearance was different from what I had anticipated from seeing him before. At a distance, and in the dim light of the chapel, there was to me a strange wildness in his aspect, a dusky obscurity, and I thought him pitted with the small-pox. His complexion was at that time clear, and even bright—

As are the children of yon azure sheen.[24]

His forehead was broad and high, light as if built of ivory, with large projecting eyebrows, and his eyes rolling beneath them like a sea with darkened lustre. "A certain tender bloom his face o'erspread,"[25] a purple tinge as we see it in the pale thoughtful complexions of the Spanish portrait-painters,[26] Murillo and Velasquez. His mouth was gross, voluptuous, open, eloquent; his chin good-humoured and round; but his nose, the rudder of the face, the index of the will, was small, feeble, nothing—like what he has done. It might seem that the genius of his face as from a height surveyed and projected him (with sufficient capacity and huge aspiration) into the world unknown of thought and imagination, with nothing to support or guide his veering purpose, as if Columbus had launched his adventurous course for the New World in a scallop,[27] without oars or compass. So at least I comment on it after the event. Coleridge in his person was rather above the common size, inclining to the corpulent, or like Lord Hamlet, "somewhat fat and pursy."[28] His hair (now, alas! grey) was then black and glossy as the raven's, and fell in smooth masses over his forehead. This long pendulous hair is peculiar to enthusiasts, to those whose minds tend heavenward; and is traditionally inseparable (though of a different colour) from the pictures of Christ. It ought to belong, as a character, to all who preach *Christ crucified*, and Coleridge was at that time one of those!

It was curious to observe the contrast between him and my father, who was a veteran in the cause, and then declining into the vale of years.[29] He had been a poor Irish lad, carefully brought up by his parents, and sent to the University of Glasgow (where he studied under Adam Smith[30]) to prepare him for his future destination. It was his mother's proudest wish to see her son a Dissenting Minister. So if we look back to past generations (as far as eye can reach) we see the same hopes, fears, wishes, followed by the same disappointments, throbbing in the human heart; and so we may see them (if we look forward) rising up for ever, and disappearing, like vapourish bubbles, in the human breast! After being tossed about from congregation to congregation in the heats of the Unitarian controversy, and squabbles about the American war, he had been relegated to an obscure village, where he was to spend the last thirty years of his life, far from the only converse that he loved, the talk about disputed texts of Scripture and the cause of civil and religious liberty. Here he passed his days, repining but resigned, in the study of the Bible, and the perusal of the Commentators,—huge folios, not easily got through, one of which would outlast a winter! Why did he pore on these from morn to night (with the exception of a walk in the fields or a turn in the garden to gather broccoli-plants or kidney-beans of his own rearing, with no small degree of pride and pleasure)? Here were "no figures nor no fantasies"[31]—neither poetry nor philosophy—nothing to dazzle, nothing to excite modern curiosity; but to his lack-lustre eyes there appeared, within the pages of the ponderous, unwieldy, neglected tomes, the sacred name of JEHOVAH in Hebrew capitals: pressed down by the weight of the style, worn to the last fading thinness of the understanding, there were glimpses, glimmering notions of the patriarchal wanderings, with palm-trees hovering in the horizon, and processions of camels at the distance of three thousand years; there was Moses with the Burning Bush,[32] the number of the Twelve Tribes, types, shadows, glosses on the law and the prophets; there were discussions (dull enough) on the age of Methuselah,[33] a mighty speculation! there were outlines, rude guesses at the shape of Noah's Ark and of the riches of Solomon's Temple; questions as to the date of the creation, predictions of the end of all things; the great lapses of time, the strange mutations of the globe were unfolded with the voluminous leaf, as it turned over; and though the soul might slumber with an hieroglyphic veil of inscrutable mysteries drawn over it, yet it was in a slumber ill-exchanged for all the sharpened realities of sense, wit, fancy, or reason.

24 Cf. James Thomson, *The Castle of Indolence*, II, xxxiii, 7.
25 Cf. *ibid.*, I, lvii, 3.   26 Of the seventeenth century.
27 *Shallop*, a kind of light, open boat.
28 Short-winded. Misquoted from *Hamlet*, V, ii, 298.
29 Cf. *Othello*, III, iii, 265–6.

30 The economist and philosopher (1723–90).
31 *Julius Caesar*, II, i, 231.   32 Exodus 3:1–6.
33 According to Genesis 5:27, he lived 969 years.

My father's life was comparatively a dream; but it was a dream of infinity and eternity, of death, the resurrection, and a judgment to come!

No two individuals were ever more unlike than were the host and his guest. A poet was to my father a sort of nondescript: yet whatever added grace to the Unitarian cause was to him welcome. He could hardly have been more surprised or pleased, if our visitor had worn wings. Indeed, his thoughts had wings; and as the silken sounds rustled round our little wainscoted parlour, my father threw back his spectacles over his forehead, his white hairs mixing with its sanguine hue; and a smile of delight beamed across his rugged cordial face, to think that Truth had found a new ally in Fancy.[34] Besides, Coleridge seemed to take considerable notice of me, and that of itself was enough. He talked very familiarly, but agreeably, and glanced over a variety of subjects. At dinner-time he grew more animated, and dilated in a very edifying manner on Mary Wolstonecraft[35] and Mackintosh.[36] The last, he said, he considered (on my father's speaking of his *Vindiciae Gallicae* as a capital performance) as a clever scholastic man—a master of the topics,—or as the ready warehouse-man of letters, who knew exactly where to lay his hand on what he wanted, though the goods were not his own. He thought him no match for Burke, either in style or matter. Burke was a metaphysician, Mackintosh a mere logician. Burke was an orator (almost a poet) who reasoned in figures, because he had an eye for nature: Mackintosh, on the other hand, was a rhetorician, who had only an eye to common-places. On this I ventured to say that I had always entertained a great opinion of Burke, and that (as far as I could find) the speaking of him with contempt might be made the test of a vulgar democratical mind. This was the first observation I ever made to Coleridge, and he said it was a very just and striking one. I remember the leg of Welsh mutton and the turnips on the table that day had the finest flavour imaginable. Coleridge added that Mackintosh and Tom Wedg-

wood[37] (of whom, however, he spoke highly) had expressed a very indifferent opinion of his friend Mr. Wordsworth, on which he remarked to them—"He strides on so far before you, that he dwindles in the distance!" Godwin had once boasted to him of having carried on an argument with Mackintosh for three hours with dubious success; Coleridge told him—"If there had been a man of genius in the room, he would have settled the question in five minutes." He asked me if I had ever seen Mary Wolstonecraft, and I said, I had once for a few moments, and that she seemed to me to turn off Godwin's objections to something she advanced with quite a playful, easy air. He replied, that "this was only one instance of the ascendancy which people of imagination exercised over those of mere intellect." He did not rate Godwin very high[38] (this was caprice or prejudice, real or affected) but he had a great idea of Mrs. Wolstonecraft's powers of conversation, none at all of her talent for book-making. We talked a little about Holcroft.[39] He had been asked if he was not much struck *with* him, and he said, he thought himself in more danger of being struck *by* him. I complained that he would not let me get on at all, for he required a definition of every the commonest word, explaining, "What do you mean by a *sensation*, Sir? What do you mean by an *idea*?" This, Coleridge said, was barricadoing the road to truth:—it was setting up a turnpike-gate at every step we took. I forget a great number of things, many more than I remember; but the day passed off pleasantly, and the next morning Mr. Coleridge was to return to Shrewsbury. When I came down to breakfast, I found that he had just received a letter from his friend T. Wedgwood, making him an offer of 150*l.* a-year if he chose to wave[40] his present pursuit, and devote himself entirely to the study of poetry and philosophy. Coleridge seemed to make up his mind to close with this proposal in the act of tying on one of his shoes. It threw an additional damp on his departure. It took the wayward enthusiast quite from us to cast him into Deva's winding vales,[41] or by the

<hr />

34 Hazlitt's note: "My father was one of those who mistook his talent after all. He used to be very much dissatisfied that I preferred his Letters to his Sermons. The last were forced and dry; the first came naturally from him. For ease, half-plays on words, and a supine, monkish, indolent pleasantry, I have never seen them equalled."

35 A well-known writer (1759–97), wife of William Godwin and mother of Shelley's second wife. The usual spelling is Wollstonecraft.

36 Sir James Mackintosh (1765–1832), the Scottish philosopher. He wrote in opposition to Burke, on behalf of the French Revolution.

37 Brother of the head of the great pottery firm. Their benefaction to Coleridge is mentioned in our introduction to that poet, and is described by Hazlitt a little farther on in this essay.

38 William Godwin (1756–1836), radical philosopher and novelist. Hazlitt's note: "He complained in particular of the presumption of attempting to establish the future immortality of man 'without' (as he said) 'knowing what Death was or what Life was'— and the tone in which he pronounced these two words seemed to convey a complete image of both."

39 Thomas Holcroft (1745–1809), radical dramatist.   40 Waive.

41 *Deva* = the river Dee, in Wales and Cheshire. Cf. Milton, "Lycidas," line 55: "Nor yet where Deva spreads her wizard stream." Hazlitt means that Coleridge decided to dedicate himself to poetry.

shores of old romance.[42] Instead of living at ten miles distance, of being the pastor of a Dissenting congregation at Shrewsbury, he was henceforth to inhabit the Hill of Parnassus,[43] to be a shepherd on the Delectable Mountains.[44] Alas! I knew not the way thither, and felt very little gratitude for Mr. Wedgwood's bounty. I was presently relieved from this dilemma; for Mr. Coleridge, asking for a pen and ink, and going to a table to write something on a bit of card, advanced towards me with undulating step, and giving me the precious document, said that that was his address, *Mr. Coleridge, Nether-Stowey, Somersetshire;* and that he should be glad to see me there in a few weeks' time, and, if I chose, would come half-way to meet me. I was not less surprised than the shepherd-boy (this simile is to be found in Cassandra[45]) when he sees a thunder-bolt fall close at his feet. I stammered out my acknowledgments and acceptance of this offer (I thought Mr. Wedgwood's annuity a trifle to it) as well as I could; and this mighty business being settled, the poet-preacher took leave, and I accompanied him six miles on the road. It was a fine morning in the middle of winter, and he talked the whole way. The scholar in Chaucer is described as going

—Sounding on his way.[46]

So Coleridge went on his. In digressing, in dilating, in passing from subject to subject, he appeared to me to float in air, to slide on ice. He told me in confidence (going along) that he should have preached two sermons before he accepted the situation at Shrewsbury, one on Infant Baptism, the other on the Lord's Supper, shewing that he could not administer either, which would have effectually disqualified him for the object in view. I observed that he continually crossed me on the way by shifting from one side of the foot-path to the other. This struck me as an odd movement; but I did not at that time connect it with any instability of purpose or involuntary change of principle, as I have done since. He seemed unable to keep on in a straight line. He spoke slightingly of Hume[47] (whose Essay on Miracles he said was stolen from an objection started in one of South's[48] sermons—*Credat*

Judaeus Apella![49]) I was not very much pleased at this account of Hume, for I had just been reading, with infinite relish, that completest of all metaphysical *choke-pears,*[50] his *Treatise on Human Nature,* to which the *Essays,* in point of scholastic subtlety and close reasoning, are mere elegant trifling, light summer-reading. Coleridge even denied the excellence of Hume's general style, which I think betrayed a want of taste or candour. He however made me amends by the manner in which he spoke of Berkeley.[51] He dwelt particularly on his *Essay on Vision* as a masterpiece of analytical reasoning. So it undoubtedly is. He was exceedingly angry with Dr. Johnson for striking the stone with his foot, in allusion to this author's Theory of Matter and Spirit, and saying, "Thus I confute him, Sir."[52] Coleridge drew a parallel (I don't know how he brought about the connection) between Bishop Berkeley and Tom Paine.[53] He said the one was an instance of a subtle, the other of an acute mind, than which no two things could be more distinct. The one was a shop-boy's quality, the other the characteristic of a philosopher. He considered Bishop Butler[54] as a true philosopher, a profound and conscientious thinker, a genuine reader of nature and of his own mind. He did not speak of his *Analogy,* but of his *Sermons at the Rolls' Chapel,* of which I had never heard. Coleridge somehow always contrived to prefer the *unknown* to the *known.* In this instance he was right. The *Analogy* is a tissue of sophistry, of wire-drawn, theological special-pleading; the *Sermons* (with the Preface to them) are in a fine vein of deep, matured reflection, a candid appeal to our observation of human nature, without pedantry and without bias. I told Coleridge I had written a few remarks, and was sometimes foolish enough to believe that I had made a discovery on the same subject (the *Natural Disinterestedness of the Human Mind*)—and I tried to explain my view of it to Coleridge, who listened with great willingness, but I did not succeed in making myself understood. I sat down to the task shortly afterwards for the twentieth time, got new pens and paper, determined to make clear work of it, wrote a few meagre sentences in the skeleton-style of a mathematical demonstration, stopped half-way down the second page; and, after trying in vain to pump up any words,

---

42 Wordsworth, "Poems on the Naming of Places," IV, 38.
43 I.e., devote himself to poetry.
44 In John Bunyan's *Pilgrim's Progress.*
45 In the romance *Cassandre* (1642–60) of the French novelist La Calprenède (Part II, Book 5).
46 Cf. Chaucer, *The Canterbury Tales,* General Prologue, line 307.
47 David Hume (1711–76), the historian and skeptical philosopher.
48 Robert South (1634–1716), a famous Anglican preacher.

49 Let the Jew Apella believe it—i.e., I shan't. (Horace, *Satires,* I, v, 100.)   50 The sourness of which constricts the throat.
51 For Bishop George Berkeley, the idealistic philosopher (1685–1753), and his verses on America, see I, 826, above.
52 Cf. Boswell's *Johnson,* ed. Hill, I, 471.
53 The revolutionist and Deist (1737–1809).
54 Joseph Butler (1692–1752), an Anglican theologian.

images, notions, apprehensions, facts, or observations, from that gulph of abstraction in which I had plunged myself for four or five years preceding, gave up the attempt as labour in vain, and shed tears of helpless despondency on the blank unfinished paper. I can write fast enough now. Am I better than I was then? Oh no! One truth discovered, one pang of regret at not being able to express it, is better than all the fluency and flippancy in the world. Would that I could go back to what I then was! Why can we not revive past times as we can revisit old places? If I had the quaint Muse of Sir Philip Sidney to assist me, I would write a *Sonnet to the Road between W—m and Shrewsbury,* and immortalise every step of it by some fond enigmatical conceit. I would swear that the very milestones had ears, and that Harmer-hill stooped with all its pines, to listen to a poet, as he passed! I remember but one other topic of discourse in this walk. He mentioned Paley,[55] praised the naturalness and clearness of his style, but condemned his sentiments, thought him a mere time-serving casuist, and said that "the fact of his work on Moral and Political Philosophy being made a text-book in our Universities was a disgrace to the national character." We parted at the six-mile stone; and I returned homeward pensive but much pleased. I had met with unexpected notice from a person, whom I believed to have been prejudiced against me. "Kind and affable to me had been his condescension, and should be honoured ever with suitable regard."[56] He was the first poet I had known, and he certainly answered to that inspired name. I had heard a great deal of his powers of conversation, and was not disappointed. In fact, I never met with any thing at all like them, either before or since. I could easily credit the accounts which were circulated of his holding forth to a large party of ladies and gentlemen, an evening or two before, on the Berkeleian Theory, when he made the whole material universe look like a transparency of fine words; and another story (which I believe he has somewhere told himself[57]) of his being asked to a party at Birmingham, of his smoking tobacco and going to sleep after dinner on a sofa, where the company found him to their no small surprise, which was increased to wonder when he started up of a sudden, and rubbing his eyes, looked about him, and launched into a three-hours' description of the third heaven, of which he had had a dream, very different from Mr. Southey's Vision of Judgment, and also from that other Vision of Judgment, which Mr. Murray, the Secretary of the Bridge-street Junto, has taken into his especial keeping![58]

On my way back, I had a sound in my ears, it was the voice of Fancy: I had a light before me, it was the face of Poetry. The one still lingers there, the other has not quitted my side! Coleridge in truth met me half-way on the ground of philosophy, or I should not have been won over to his imaginative creed. I had an uneasy, pleasurable sensation all the time, till I was to visit him. During those months the chill breath of winter gave me a welcoming; the vernal air was balm and inspiration to me. The golden sunsets, the silver star of evening, lighted me on my way to new hopes and prospects. *I was to visit Coleridge in the spring.* This circumstance was never absent from my thoughts, and mingled with all my feelings. I wrote to him at the time proposed, and received an answer postponing my intended visit for a week or two, but very cordially urging me to complete my promise then. This delay did not damp, but rather increased my ardour. In the meantime I went to Llangollen Vale,[59] by way of initiating myself in the mysteries of natural scenery; and I must say I was enchanted with it. I had been reading Coleridge's description of England, in his fine *Ode on the Departing Year,* and I applied it, *con amore,*[60] to the objects before me. That valley was to me (in a manner) the cradle of a new existence: in the river that winds through it, my spirit was baptised in the waters of Helicon![61]

I returned home, and soon after set out on my journey with unworn heart and untired feet. . . .[62]

The next day Wordsworth arrived from Bristol at Coleridge's cottage. I think I see him now. He answered in some degree to his friend's description of him, but was more gaunt and Don Quixote-like. He was quaintly dressed (according to the *costume* of that unconstrained period) in a brown fustian[63] jacket and striped pantaloons. There was something of a roll, a lounge in his gait, not unlike his own Peter

---

55 William Paley, author of the long-popular *Evidences of Christianity* (1794).   56 Cf. *Paradise Lost,* VIII, 648-50.
57 Part of this story appears in *Biographia Literaria,* chap. X.

58 Southey's poem describes the entrance of George III into heaven. Byron had written a satire on it. Charles Murray, a lawyer, was secretary of the Constitutional Association for Opposing Disloyal and Seditious Principles; its office was on New Bridge Street, in the Blackfriars district of London.
59 As he tells us in "On Going a Journey," pp. 173-4, above.
60 With love, zestfully.
61 The Greek mountain in Boeotia where Apollo and the Muses dwelt; to them its springs were sacred.
62 In a passage here omitted Hazlitt describes his walk to Nether Stowey and his reception by Coleridge.
63 A heavy cotton material similar to corduroy.

Bell.[64] There was a severe, worn pressure of thought about his temples, a fire in his eye (as if he saw something in objects more than the outward appearance), an intense high narrow forehead, a Roman nose, cheeks furrowed by strong purpose and feeling, and a convulsive inclination to laughter about the mouth, a good deal at variance with the solemn, stately expression of the rest of his face. Chantry's[65] bust wants the marking traits; but he was teazed into making it regular and heavy: Haydon's[66] head of him, introduced into the *Entrance of Christ into Jerusalem*, is the most like his drooping weight of thought and expression. He sat down and talked very naturally and freely, with a mixture of clear gushing accents in his voice, a deep guttural intonation, and a strong tincture of the northern *burr*, like the crust on wine. He instantly began to make havoc of the half of a Cheshire cheese on the table, and said triumphantly that "his marriage with experience had not been so unproductive as Mr. Southey's in teaching him a knowledge of the good things of this life." He had been to see the *Castle Spectre*, by Monk Lewis,[67] while at Bristol, and described it very well. He said "it fitted the taste of the audience like a glove." This *ad captandum*[68] merit was however by no means a recommendation of it, according to the severe principles of the new school, which reject rather than court popular effect. Wordsworth, looking out of the low, latticed window, said, "How beautifully the sun sets on that yellow bank!" I thought within myself, "With what eyes these poets see nature!" and ever after, when I saw the sun-set stream upon the objects facing it, conceived I had made a discovery, or thanked Mr. Wordsworth for having

made one for me! We went over to All-Foxden[69] again the day following, and Wordsworth read us the story of Peter Bell in the open air; and the comment made upon it by his face and voice was very different from that of some later critics! Whatever might be thought of the poem, "his face was a book where men might read strange matters,"[70] and he announced the fate of his hero in prophetic tones. There is a *chaunt* in the recitation both of Coleridge and Wordsworth, which acts as a spell upon the hearer, and disarms the judgment. Perhaps they have deceived themselves by making habitual use of this ambiguous accompaniment. Coleridge's manner is more full, animated, and varied; Wordsworth's more equable, sustained, and internal. The one might be termed more *dramatic*, the other more *lyrical*. Coleridge has told me that he himself liked to compose in walking over uneven ground, or breaking through the straggling branches of a copse-wood; whereas Wordsworth always wrote (if he could) walking up and down a straight gravel-walk, or in some spot where the continuity of his verse met with no collateral interruption. Returning that same evening, I got into a metaphysical argument with Wordsworth, while Coleridge was explaining the different notes of the nightingale to his sister, in which we neither of us succeeded in making ourselves perfectly clear and intelligible. Thus I passed three weeks at Nether Stowey and in the neighbourhood, generally devoting the afternoons to a delightful chat in an arbour made of bark by the poet's friend Tom Poole,[71] sitting under two fine elm-trees, and listening to the bees humming round us, while we quaffed our *flip*.[72] . . .

---

64 In the poem thus entitled.
65 Sir Francis L. Chantrey (d. 1841), a sculptor and painter.
66 Benjamin Robert Haydon (1786–1846), an historical painter. He also introduced a portrait of Keats into this picture.
67 Matthew Gregory Lewis (1775–1818), known as "Monk" from the title of one of his romances, wrote "Gothic" novels, plays, and poems; *The Castle Spectre* was a musical play.
68 *Ad captandum* [*vulgus*], for the sake of pleasing the crowd.

69 Coleridge had already taken Hazlitt to Alfoxden, but Wordsworth was away.   70 Cf. *Macbeth*, I, v, 63–4.
71 See above, p. 88.
72 Spiced ale.—Most of the remainder of the essay describes "a jaunt down the Bristol Channel, as far as Lynton," made by Coleridge, Hazlitt, and a certain John Chester before Hazlitt's return home.

Thomas De Quincey

1785-1859

THE second son of a well-to-do dry-goods merchant, De Quincey was born in Manchester in 1785. He was only seven when his father, whom tuberculosis had driven from the damp climate of England, came home to die. Though he was one of eight children, his temperament inclined him to solitude. At a tender age he took to books as to his native element; he was always reader and dreamer. He attended several undistinguished schools, the last at Manchester; from it, as he tells us in the *Confessions,* he ran away. He had inherited money from his father but could not get on with the five guardians who managed it. One of these was his mother, and her he went to see in the course of his flight. After much debate he was allowed to go his way, with a weekly allowance of one guinea, that is, five dollars, then worth in purchasing power between two and three times as much as now. That summer of 1802 he devoted to a walking trip in Wales, sleeping usually out of doors in a tiny tent of his own manufacture. Next, breaking communications with his family and abandoning the weekly guinea, he struck out for London, hoping he might talk some moneylender into an advance on his prospects as an heir. He found the moneylenders more cautious than helpful, and spent the winter in the dire poverty described in the first of our selections. He was then seventeen years old. A partial reconciliation with his guardians rescued him from life as a young derelict; they agreed to allow him £100 a year if he would enter Oxford.

This he did in 1803. He made no friends there: to him the interests of the average undergraduate seemed juvenile; and instead of exerting himself to seek out young men of comparable tastes and intelligence, he wrapped himself in a haughty cloak of intellectual pride. His studies were unusual and self-planned. He hired a German to teach him the elements of that language. Then he plunged, quite on his own, into the new German philosophy, against which in later years he turned because it conflicted with orthodox religion. De Quincey was a conservative in such matters, and in politics a lifelong Tory. His second main interest as a student was English literature, a subject then not seriously regarded at Oxford. He was among the warmest admirers of *Lyrical Ballads,* and succeeded in drawing Wordsworth into a correspondence.

On a visit to London in 1804 he made his first purchase of opium, to relieve neuralgic pains in his face; but he went on using the drug, which he took in the liquid form of laudanum, partly because he was frequently subject to depression. In 1808 he left Oxford, in the midst of his final examinations for the B. A. He had begun them well; but he seems to have worried over them too much, and he was irritated by the authorities' decision that replies during an oral examination in Greek should be made, not in Greek, which he spoke fluently, but in English. At that point De Quincey simply lost interest.

In the meantime his enthusiasms had centered in the North. He had recognized the genius of Wordsworth as soon as he read him. In 1807 he had made the acquaintance of Coleridge; and being now of age and in possession of his share of his father's estate, he had anonymously aided the great man with a present of £300. Later in the same year he had escorted Mrs. Coleridge and the children from Bristol to Keswick. On the way through Grasmere he met the Wordsworths, and stayed on to visit them. For years, till his marriage led to their estrangement, he was among their closest friends, as well as intimate with Coleridge; and when in 1809 the Wordsworths vacated Dove Cottage, De Quincey moved in. He was now in the midst of the Lake School, yet not of it. Opium and procrastination held him back from serious work. In 1817 he was married, beneath him as the Wordsworths thought, to Margaret Simpson, a farmer's daughter of the vicinity. She could neither read nor write; yet the marriage turned out well.

For several years De Quincey had been taking opium daily in appalling quantities; he was close to being a complete neurotic, broken in health, depressed in mind, paralyzed in will. His love affair with his future wife braced him up. But he never acquired more than intermittent control over the habit, and for a considerable period after the respite of 1816-17 he was in the dreadful state described below in "The Pains of Opium." His money had all been spent; and at last, desperate for means, he turned to his pen. In 1821, in two numbers of the *London Magazine,* appeared his *Confessions of an English Opium-Eater.* Still the most famous of his writings, it was an instantaneous success. For several years he was often in London, where Lamb, Hazlitt, and Thomas Hood became his friends. In 1830 he moved with his family—he had eight children—to Edinburgh, in or near which he made his home for the rest of his life. *Blackwood's Magazine,* to which he frequently contributed, was published there; and already he had a number of friends in the city, among them Thomas Carlyle and his wife.

Though there was a steady demand for his work, he was in financial difficulties most of the time—embroiled with (and frequently sued by) the tradesmen he patronized, the owners of the houses he rented, and the publishers with whom he dealt. Sometimes he lived with his family; but often when things got too thick for his tormented psyche, when the children were too noisy, or a process for debt was about to trap him, he would disappear to some secret lodging. From one to another he would dodge like a hunted creature of the woods. His agility in evading the creditors who repeatedly tried to send him to prison was astounding. Once, indeed, he was actually arrested; but the publisher of the *Encyclopaedia Britannica* happened to meet the melancholy procession jailward bound and, in return for the promise of a brace of articles on Shakespeare and Pope, paid the debt and set him free. His last few years, partly through his own earnings, partly from increased income after his mother's death, and partly because his daughters proved capable managers, were less harassed.

The important thing is that this man who coped with life so ineffectively and behaved so differently from the generality of sober citizens wrote a hundred and fifty magazine articles and in the process carved out a niche for himself in the history of English literature. Besides the autobiographical and critical work and the purely imaginative poems in prose from which our selections have been chosen, De Quincey wrote many sketches of poets past and present, and formal articles on history, philosophy, and economics. He spent his last decade chiefly in preparing, with much revision and often expansion, the collected edition of his works brought out at Boston in twenty-two volumes between 1851 and 1859. Among the most remarkable of the creative writings not represented below are *On Murder Considered as One of the Fine Arts* and *The English Mail-Coach;* some think the latter the best thing he ever did.

De Quincey is most admirable on his imaginative side, although his style is now outmoded. As a critic he does not take conspicuously high rank, except in the two examples given here: "On the Knocking at the Gate in *Macbeth*" and "Literature of Knowledge and Literature of Power." But even though no writer would think of employing a similar style today, anyone who is at all sensitive to the magical power of words is bound to respond, at least emotionally, to what De Quincey himself called his "impassioned prose." And although, like any journalist's, his work is uneven, there are many passages which reveal keen insight and many which touch the heart.

The standard edition, a poor one, is D. Masson's (14 vols., 1890). An excellent volume of selections was edited by P. V. D. Stern (*c.* 1937). The authoritative biography is by H. A. Eaton (1936).

Thomas De Quincey

from CONFESSIONS OF AN ENGLISH OPIUM-EATER

THE original version of this curious work—autobiographical, yet essay-like—appeared in the *London Magazine* for September and October, 1821, and was separately reprinted in the year following. Few have been able to resist the fascination of its style and the intimacy of the confession. As for its truth, the narrative is certainly based on fact; but the author did not scruple to heighten his effects: thirty-five years later, in rewriting and greatly enlarging the piece for his collected works, he toned down some of the episodes. He felt, however, that while "as a book of amusement" the revised form was an improvement, something had been lost of the original's "fugitive inspiration" and "extemporaneous excitement." Most critics have preferred the earlier and less discursive version, from which (with the omission of a few of De Quincey's footnotes) our selections are taken. It has been inadequately edited by R. Garnett (1885). The later version is given in Masson's edition of the *Works* (vol.

III); there are cheap reprints of it in Everyman's Library and The World's Classics.

PRELIMINARY CONFESSIONS

. . . I have often been asked how I came to be a regular opium-eater; and have suffered, very unjustly, in the opinion of my acquaintance, from being reputed to have brought upon myself all the sufferings which I shall have to record, by a long course of indulgence in this practice purely for the sake of creating an artificial state of pleasurable excitement. This, however, is a misrepresentation of my case. True it is, that for nearly ten years I did occasionally take opium for the sake of the exquisite pleasure it gave me: but, so long as I took it with this view, I was effectually protected from all material bad consequences, by the necessity of interposing long intervals between the several acts of indulgence, in order to renew the pleasurable sensations. It was not for the purpose of creating pleasure, but of mitigating pain in the severest degree, that I first began to use opium as an article of daily diet. In the twenty-eighth year of my age, a most painful affection of the stomach, which I had first experienced about ten years before, attacked me in great strength. This affection had originally been caused by extremities of hunger, suffered in my boyish days. During the season of hope and redundant happiness which succeeded (that is, from eighteen to twenty-four) it had slumbered: for the three following years it had revived at intervals; and now, under unfavourable circumstances, from depression of spirits, it attacked me with a violence that yielded to no remedies but opium. As the youthful sufferings, which first produced this derangement of the stomach, were interesting in themselves, and in the circumstances that attended them, I shall here briefly retrace them.

My father died when I was about seven years old, and left me to the care of four guardians. I was sent to various schools, great and small; and was very early distinguished for my classical attainments, especially for my knowledge of Greek. At thirteen, I wrote Greek with ease; and at fifteen my command of that language was so great, that I not only composed Greek verses in lyric metres, but could converse in Greek fluently and without embarrassment—an accomplishment which I have not since met with in any scholar of my times, and which, in my case, was owing to the practice of daily reading off the newspapers into the best Greek I could furnish *extempore:* for the necessity of ransacking my memory and invention, for all sorts and combinations of periphrastic expressions, as equivalents for modern ideas, images, relations of things, etc., gave me a compass of diction which would never have been called out by a dull translation of moral essays, etc. "That boy," said one of my masters, pointing the attention of a stranger to me, "that boy could harangue an Athenian mob, better than you or I could address an English one." He who honored me with this eulogy was a scholar, "and a ripe and good one"; and of all my tutors, was the only one whom I loved or reverenced. Unfortunately for me (and, as I afterwards learned, to this worthy man's great indignation), I was transferred to the care, first of a blockhead, who was in a perpetual panic, lest I should expose his ignorance; and finally, to that of a respectable scholar, at the head

of a great school on an ancient foundation.[1] This man had been appointed to his situation by ——[2] College, Oxford; and was a sound, well-built scholar, but (like most men, whom I have known from that college) coarse, clumsy, and inelegant. A miserable contrast he presented, in my eyes, to the Etonian brilliancy of my favourite master: and besides, he could not disguise from my hourly notice, the poverty and meagreness of his understanding. It is a bad thing for a boy to be, and to know himself, far beyond his tutors, whether in knowledge or in power of mind. This was the case, so far as regarded knowledge at least, not with myself only: for the two boys, who jointly with myself composed the first form, were better Grecians than the head-master, though not more elegant scholars, nor at all more accustomed to sacrifice to the graces. When I first entered, I remember that we read Sophocles; and it was a constant matter of triumph to us, the learned triumvirate of the first form, to see our "Archididascalus"[3] (as he loved to be called) conning our lessons before we went up, and laying a regular train, with lexicon and grammar, for blowing up and blasting (as it were) any difficulties he found in the choruses;[4] whilst *we* never condescended to open our books until the moment of going up, and were generally employed in writing epigrams upon his wig, or some such important matter. My two class-fellows were poor and dependent for their future prospects at the university, on the recommendation of the head-master; but I, who had a small patrimonial property, the income of which was sufficient to support me at college, wished to be sent thither immediately. I made earnest representations on the subject to my guardians, but all to no purpose. One, who was more reasonable, and had more knowledge of the world than the rest, lived at a distance: two of the other three resigned all their authority into the hands of the fourth; and this fourth, with whom I had to negotiate, was a worthy man, in his way, but haughty, obstinate, and intolerant of all opposition to his will. After a certain number of letters and personal interviews, I found that I had nothing to hope for, not even a compromise of the matter, from my guardian:

---

1 The names of these three teachers were, respectively, one Morgan (of the grammar school at Bath), the Rev. Edward Spencer (of a private school at Winkfield, Wiltshire), and one Lawson (of Manchester Grammar School).
2 Brasenose. From here on such blanks are filled in, when possible, from the final version or from notes.
3 Greek for *headmaster.*
4 The choruses in Greek tragedy sometimes contain difficult Greek.

unconditional submission was what he demanded: and I prepared myself, therefore, for other measures. Summer was now coming on with hasty steps, and my seventeenth birthday was fast approaching; after which day I had sworn within myself that I would no longer be numbered amongst school-boys. Money being what I chiefly wanted, I wrote to a woman of high rank,[5] who, though young herself, had known me from a child, and had latterly treated me with great distinction, requesting that she would "lend" me five guineas. For upwards of a week no answer came; and I was beginning to despond, when, at length, a servant put into my hands a double[6] letter, with a coronet on the seal. The letter was kind and obliging: the fair writer was on the sea-coast, and in that way the delay had arisen: she enclosed double of what I had asked, and good-naturedly hinted that if I should *never* repay her, it would not absolutely ruin her. Now then, I was prepared for my scheme: ten guineas, added to about two which I had remaining from my pocket money, seemed to me sufficient for an indefinite length of time: and at that happy age, if no *definite* boundary can be assigned to one's power, the spirit of hope and pleasure makes it virtually infinite.

It is a just remark of Dr. Johnson's[7] (and, what cannot often be said of his remarks, it is a very feeling one), that we never do anything consciously for the last time (of things, that is, which we have long been in the habit of doing) without sadness of heart. This truth I felt deeply, when I came to leave Manchester, a place which I did not love, and where I had not been happy. On the evening before I left Manchester for ever, I grieved when the ancient and lofty school-room resounded with the evening service, performed for the last time in my hearing; and at night, when the muster-roll of names was called over, and mine (as usual) was called first, I stepped forward, and, passing the head-master, who was standing by, I bowed to him, and looked earnestly in his face, thinking to myself, "He is old and infirm, and in this world I shall not see him again." I was right: I never *did* see him again, nor ever shall. He looked at me complacently, smiled good-naturedly, returned my salutation (or rather, my valediction), and we parted (though he knew it not) for ever. I could not reverence him intellectually: but he had been uniformly kind to me, and had allowed me many indulgences: and I grieved at the thought of the mortification I should inflict upon him.

The morning came which was to launch me into the world, and from which my whole succeeding life has, in many important points, taken its colouring. I lodged in the head-master's house, and had been allowed, from my first entrance, the indulgence of a private room, which I used both as a sleeping-room and as a study. At half after three I rose, and gazed with deep emotion at the ancient towers of the College Church, "drest in earliest light,"[8] and beginning to crimson with the radiant lustre of a cloudless July morning. I was firm and immovable in my purpose: but yet agitated by anticipation of uncertain danger and troubles; and, if I could have foreseen the hurricane and perfect hail-storm of affliction which soon fell upon me, well might I have been agitated. To this agitation the deep peace of the morning presented an affecting contrast, and in some degree a medicine. The silence was more profound than that of midnight: and to me the silence of a summer morning is more touching than all other silence, because, the light being broad and strong, as that of noon-day at other seasons of the year, it seems to differ from perfect day chiefly because man is not yet abroad; and thus, the peace of nature, and of the innocent creatures of God, seems to be secure and deep, only so long as the presence of man, and his restless and unquiet spirit, are not there to trouble its sanctity. I dressed myself, took my hat and gloves, and lingered a little in the room. For the last year and a half this room had been my "pensive citadel":[9] here I had read and studied through all the hours of night; and, though true it was that for the latter part of this time I, who was framed for love and gentle affections, had lost my gaiety and happiness, during the strife and fever of contention with my guardian; yet, on the other hand, as a boy so passionately fond of books, and dedicated to intellectual pursuits, I could not fail to have enjoyed many happy hours in the midst of general dejection. I wept as I looked round on the chair, hearth, writing-table, and other familiar objects, knowing too certainly that I looked upon them for the last time. Whilst I write this, it is eighteen[10] years ago; and yet, at this moment, I see distinctly, as if it were yesterday, the lineaments and expression of the object on which I fixed my parting gaze; it was a picture of the lovely ——, which hung over the mantel-piece; the eyes and mouth of which were so beautiful, and the whole countenance so radiant with benignity and divine tranquillity, that

5 Lady Carberry, an old friend, ten years older than De Quincey.
6 I.e., requiring twice the usual postage.   7 *Idler,* no. 103.
8 Unidentified.
9 Cf. "students with their pensive citadels," in Wordsworth's sonnet "Nuns fret not," line 3.
10 Corrected to *nineteen* in the final version.

I had a thousand times laid down my pen, or my book, to gather consolation from it, as a devotee from his patron saint. Whilst I was yet gazing upon it, the deep tones of Manchester clock proclaimed that it was four o'clock. I went up to the picture, kissed it, and then gently walked out, and closed the door for ever! . . .

Soon after this, I contrived, by means which I must omit for want of room, to transfer myself to London. And now began the latter and fiercer stage of my long sufferings; without using a disproportionate expression, I might say, of my agony. For I now suffered, for upwards of sixteen weeks, the physical anguish of hunger in various degrees of intensity; but as bitter, perhaps, as ever any human being can have suffered who has survived it. I would not needlessly harass my reader's feelings by a detail of all that I endured: for extremities such as these, under any circumstances of heaviest misconduct or guilt, cannot be contemplated even in description without a rueful pity that is painful to the natural goodness of the human heart. Let it suffice, at least on this occasion, to say, that a few fragments of bread from the breakfast-table of one individual (who supposed me to be ill, but did not know of my being in utter want), and these at uncertain intervals, constituted my whole support. During the former part of my sufferings (that is, generally in Wales, and always for the first two months in London), I was houseless, and very seldom slept under a roof. To this constant exposure to the open air I ascribe it mainly that I did not sink under my torments. Latterly, however, when colder and more inclement weather came on, and when, from the length of my sufferings, I had begun to sink into a more languishing condition, it was, no doubt, fortunate for me that the same person to whose breakfast-table I had access allowed me to sleep in a large unoccupied house, of which he was tenant. Unoccupied, I call it, for there was no household or establishment in it; nor any furniture indeed, except a table and a few chairs. But I found, on taking possession of my new quarters, that the house already contained one single inmate, a poor friendless child, apparently ten years old; but she seemed hunger-bitten; and sufferings of that sort often make children look older than they are. From this forlorn child I learned that she had slept and lived there alone for some time before I came: and great joy the poor creature expressed, when she found that I was in future, to be her companion through the hours of darkness. The house was large; and, from the want of furniture, the noise of the rats made a prodigious echoing on the spacious stair-case and hall; and,

amidst the real fleshly ills of cold, and, I fear, hunger, the forsaken child had found leisure to suffer still more (it appeared) from the self-created one of ghosts. I promised her protection against all ghosts whatsoever; but, alas! I could offer her no other assistance. We lay upon the floor, with a bundle of cursed law papers for a pillow: but with no other covering than a sort of large horseman's cloak: afterwards, however, we discovered, in a garret, an old sofa-cover, a small piece of rug, and some fragments of other articles, which added a little to our warmth. The poor child crept close to me for warmth, and for security against her ghostly enemies. When I was not more than usually ill, I took her into my arms, so that, in general, she was tolerably warm, and often slept when I could not: for, during the last two months of my sufferings, I slept much in the day-time, and was apt to fall into transient dozings at all hours. But my sleep distressed me more than my watching;[11] for, besides the tumultuousness of my dreams (which were only not so awful as those which I shall have to describe hereafter as produced by opium) my sleep was never more than what is called *dog-sleep;* so that I could hear myself moaning, and was often, as it seemed to me, wakened suddenly by my own voice; and, about this time, a hideous sensation began to haunt me as soon as I fell into a slumber, which has since returned upon me, at different periods of my life, viz. a sort of twitching (I know not where, but apparently about the region of the stomach), which compelled me violently to throw out my feet for the sake of relieving it. This sensation coming on as soon as I began to sleep, and the effort to relieve it constantly awaking me, at length I slept only from exhaustion; and from increasing weakness (as I said before), I was constantly falling asleep, and constantly awaking. Meantime, the master of the house sometimes came in upon us suddenly, and very early, sometimes not till ten o'clock, sometimes not at all. He was in constant fear of bailiffs: improving on the plan of Cromwell, every night he slept in a different quarter of London;[12] and I observed that he never failed to examine through a private window the appearance of those who knocked at the door, before he would allow it to be opened. He breakfasted alone: indeed, his tea equipage would hardly have admitted of his

---

11 Keeping awake.

12 According to the contemporary *History of the Rebellion* (Book XV) by Edward Hyde, first Earl of Clarendon, Cromwell frequently resorted to this precaution after he made himself dictator.

hazarding an invitation to a second person—any more than the quantity of esculent *matériel,* which, for the most part, was little more than a roll, or a few biscuits, which he had bought on his road from the place where he had slept. Or, if he *had* asked a party, as I once learnedly and facetiously observed to him— the several members of it must have *stood* in the relation to each other (not *sat* in any relation whatever) of succession, as the metaphysicians have it, and not of coexistence; in the relation of the parts of time, and not of the parts of space. During his breakfast, I generally contrived a reason for lounging in; and, with an air of as much indifference as I could assume, took up such fragments as he had left—sometimes, indeed, there were none at all. In doing this, I committed no robbery except upon the man himself, who was thus obliged (I believe), now and then, to send out at noon for an extra biscuit; for, as to the poor child, *she* was never admitted into his study (if I may give that name to his chief depository of parchments, law writings, etc.); that room was to her the Bluebeard room of the house, being regularly locked on his departure to dinner, about six o'clock, which usually was his final departure for the night. Whether this child was an illegitimate daughter of Mr. Brunell,[13] or only a servant, I could not ascertain; she did not herself know; but certainly she was treated altogether as a menial servant. No sooner did Mr. Brunell make his appearance, than she went below stairs, brushed his shoes, coat, etc.; and, except when she was summoned to run an errand, she never emerged from the dismal Tartarus[14] of the kitchens, etc. to the upper air, until my welcome knock at night called up her little trembling footsteps to the front door. Of her life during the day-time, however, I knew little but what I gathered from her own account at night; for, as soon as the hours of business commenced, I saw that my absence would be acceptable; and, in general, therefore, I went off and sat in the parks, or elsewhere, until night-fall. . . .

Meantime,[15] what had become of poor Ann?[16] For her I have reserved my concluding words: according to our agreement, I sought her daily, and waited for her every night, so long as I staid in London,
at the corner of Titchfield-street.[17] I inquired for her of every one who was likely to know her; and during the last hours of my stay in London I put into activity every means of tracing her that my knowledge of London suggested, and the limited extent of my power made possible. The street where she had lodged I knew, but not the house; and I remembered at last some account which she had given me of ill treatment from her landlord, which made it probable that she had quitted those lodgings before we parted. She had few acquaintance; most people, besides, thought that the earnestness of my inquiries arose from motives which moved their laughter, or their slight regard; and others, thinking I was in chase of a girl who had robbed me of some trifles, were naturally and excusably indisposed to give me any clue to her, if, indeed, they had any to give. Finally, as my despairing resource, on the day I left London I put into the hands of the only person who (I was sure) must know Ann by sight, from having been in company with us once or twice, an address to —— in —shire, at that time the residence of my family. But, to this hour, I have never heard a syllable about her. This, amongst such troubles as most men meet with in life, has been my heaviest affliction.—If she lived, doubtless we must have been sometimes in search of each other, at the very same moment, through the mighty labyrinths of London; perhaps even within a few feet of each other—a barrier no wider in a London street often amounting in the end to a separation for eternity! During some years, I hoped that she *did* live; and I suppose that, in the literal and unrhetorical use of the word *myriad,* I may say that on my different visits to London, I have looked into many, many myriads of female faces, in the hope of meeting her. I should know her again amongst a thousand, if I saw her for a moment; for, though not handsome, she had a sweet expression of countenance, and a peculiar and graceful carriage of the head.—I sought her, I have said, in hope. So it was for years; but now I should fear to see her; and her cough, which grieved me when I parted with her, is now my consolation. I now wish to see her no longer; but think of her, more gladly, as one long since laid in the grave; in the grave, I would hope, of a Magdalen;[18] taken away, before injuries and cruelty had blotted out and transfigured her ingenuous nature, or the brutalities of ruffians had completed the ruin they had begun.

---

13 Brunell, or Brown, was a shyster, to whom De Quincey had been referred by a moneylender. The house was in the Soho district, at the corner of Greek Street and Soho Square.

14 Infernal regions.

15 De Quincey, at length partially reconciled with his guardians, had been away from London for several months. He afterwards tried in vain to trace the child.

16 A young streetwalker whom he had met while a waif. She befriended him, and he felt a brother's affection for her.

17 I.e., the corner of Oxford and Great Titchfield streets, in the West End.

18 For Jesus's forgiveness of the repentant sinner Mary Magdalen, see Luke 7:36-50.

. . . If any man, poor or rich, were to say that he would tell us what had been the happiest day in his life, and the why, and the wherefore, I suppose that we should all cry out—Hear him! Hear him!—As to the happiest *day,* that must be very difficult for any wise man to name: because any event, that could occupy so distinguished a place in a man's retrospect of his life, or be entitled to have shed a special felicity on any one day, ought to be of such an enduring character, as that, accidents apart, it should have continued to shed the same felicity, or one not distinguishably less, on many years together. To the happiest *lustrum,*[20] however, or even to the happiest *year,* it may be allowed to any man to point without discountenance from[21] wisdom. This year, in my case, reader, was the one which we have now reached; though it stood, I confess, as a parenthesis between years of a gloomier character. It was a year of brilliant water (to speak after the manner of jewellers), set as it were, and insulated, in the gloom and cloudy melancholy of opium. Strange as it may sound, I had a little before this time descended suddenly, and without any considerable effort, from 320 grains of opium (*i. e.* eight thousand drops of laudanum) per day, to forty grains, or one eighth part. Instantaneously, and as if by magic, the cloud of profoundest melancholy which rested upon my brain, like some black vapours that I have seen roll away from the summits of mountains, drew off in one day (νυχθήμερον[22]); passed off with its murky banners as simultaneously as a ship that has been stranded, and is floated off by a springtide—

That moveth altogether, if it move at all.[23]

Now, then, I was again happy: I now took only 1000 drops of laudanum per day: and what was that? A latter spring had come to close up the season of youth: my brain performed its functions as healthily as ever before; I read Kant[24] again; and again I understood him, or fancied that I did. Again my feelings of pleasure expanded themselves to all around me: and if any man from Oxford or Cambridge, or from neither, had been announced to me in my

unpretending cottage,[25] I should have welcomed him with as sumptuous a reception as so poor a man could offer. Whatever else was wanting to a wise man's happiness,—of laudanum I would have given him as much as he wished, and in a golden cup. And, by the way, now that I speak of giving laudanum away, I remember, about this time, a little incident, which I mention, because, trifling as it was, the reader will soon meet it again in my dreams, which it influenced more fearfully than could be imagined. One day a Malay knocked at my door. What business a Malay could have to transact amongst English mountains, I cannot conjecture: but possibly he was on his road to a seaport about forty miles distant.[26]

The servant who opened the door to him was a young girl born and bred amongst the mountains, who had never seen an Asiatic dress of any sort: his turban, therefore, confounded her not a little; and, as it turned out, that his attainments in English were exactly of the same extent as hers in the Malay, there seemed to be an impassable gulf fixed between all communication of ideas, if either party had happened to possess any. In this dilemma, the girl, recollecting the reputed learning of her master (and, doubtless, giving me credit for a knowledge of all the languages of the earth, besides, perhaps, a few of the lunar ones), came and gave me to understand that there was a sort of demon below, whom she clearly imagined that my art could exorcise from the house. I did not immediately go down: but, when I did, the group which presented itself, arranged as it was by accident, though not very elaborate, took hold of my fancy and my eye in a way that none of the statuesque attitudes exhibited in the ballets at the Opera House, though so ostentatiously complex, had ever done. In a cottage kitchen, but panelled on the wall with dark wood that from age and rubbing resembled oak, and looking more like a rustic hall of entrance than a kitchen, stood the Malay—his turban and loose trowsers of dingy white relieved upon the dark panelling: he had placed himself nearer to the girl than she seemed to relish; though her native spirit of mountain intrepidity contended with the feeling of simple awe which her countenance expressed as she gazed upon the tiger-cat before her. And a more

---

[19] Preceding this section is one on "The Pleasures of Opium."
[20] Five-year period.
[21] Disapprobation by.   [22] A night and a day.
[23] Cf. Wordsworth, "Resolution and Independence," line 77 (p. 59, above).
[24] Immanuel Kant (1724–1804), the German transcendental philosopher.

[25] Dove Cottage, Grasmere. By 1813 opium was a daily habit with De Quincey. In 1817 he married; he had managed during the previous year to cut down his opium ration.
[26] De Quincey's note: "Between the seafaring populations on the coast of Lancashire and . . . of Cumberland . . . there was a slender current of interchange constantly going on . . . in part by sea, but in part also by land. . . ."

striking picture there could not be imagined, than the beautiful English face of the girl, and its exquisite fairness, together with her erect and independent attitude, contrasted with the sallow and bilious skin of the Malay, enamelled or veneered with mahogany, by marine air, his small, fierce, restless eyes, thin lips, slavish gestures and adorations. Half hidden by the ferocious-looking Malay, was a little child from a neighbouring cottage who had crept in after him, and was now in the act of reverting its head, and gazing upwards at the turban and the fiery eyes beneath it, whilst with one hand he caught at the dress of the young woman for protection. My knowledge of the Oriental tongues is not remarkably extensive, being indeed confined to two words —the Arabic word for barley, and the Turkish for opium (madjoon), which I have learned from Anastasius.[27] And, as I had neither a Malay dictionary, nor even Adelung's *Mithridates,*[28] which might have helped me to a few words, I addressed him in some lines from the Iliad; considering that, of such languages as I possessed, Greek, in point of longitude, came geographically nearest to an Oriental one. He worshipped me in a most devout manner, and replied in what I suppose was Malay. In this way I saved my reputation with my neighbours; for the Malay had no means of betraying the secret. He lay down upon the floor for about an hour, and then pursued his journey. On his departure, I presented him with a piece of opium. To him, as an Orientalist, I concluded that opium must be familiar: and the expression of his face convinced me that it was. Nevertheless, I was struck with some little consternation when I saw him suddenly raise his hand to his mouth, and (in the school-boy phrase) bolt the whole, divided into three pieces, at one mouthful. The quantity was enough to kill three dragoons and their horses: and I felt some alarm for the poor creature: but what could be done? I had given him the opium in compassion for his solitary life, on recollecting that if he had travelled on foot from London, it must be nearly three weeks since he could have exchanged a thought with any human being. I could not think of violating the laws of hospitality, by having him seized and drenched with an emetic, and thus frightening him into a notion that we were going to sacrifice him to some English idol. No: there was clearly

no help for it:—he took his leave: and for some days I felt anxious: but as I never heard of any Malay being found dead, I became convinced that he was used to opium: and that I must have done him the service I designed, by giving him one night of respite from the pains of wandering.

This incident I have digressed to mention, because this Malay (partly from the picturesque exhibition he assisted to frame, partly from the anxiety I connected with his image for some days) fastened afterwards upon my dreams, and brought other Malays with him worse than himself, that ran "a-muck" at me, and led me into a world of troubles.—But to quit this episode, and to return to my intercalary[29] year of happiness. I have said already, that on a subject so important to us all as happiness, we should listen with pleasure to any man's experience or experiments, even though he were but a plough-boy, who cannot be supposed to have ploughed very deep into such an intractable soil as that of human pains and pleasures, or to have conducted his researches upon any very enlightened principles. But I, who have taken happiness, both in a solid and a liquid shape, both boiled and unboiled, both East India and Turkey—who have conducted my experiments upon this very interesting subject with a sort of galvanic battery—and have, for the general benefit of the world, inoculated myself, as it were, with the poison of 8000 drops of laudanum per day (just for the same reason as a French surgeon inoculated himself lately with cancer—an English one, twenty years ago, with plague—and a third, I know not of what nation, with hydrophobia), *I,* it will be admitted, must surely know what happiness is, if any body does. And therefore I will here lay down an analysis of happiness; and as the most interesting mode of communicating it, I will give it, not didactically, but wrapt up and involved in a picture of one evening, as I spent every evening during the intercalary year when laudanum, though taken daily, was to me no more than the elixir of pleasure. This done, I shall quit the subject of happiness altogether, and pass to a very different one—the *pains of opium.*

Let there be a cottage, standing in a valley, eighteen miles from any town[30]—no spacious valley, but about two miles long by three quarters of a mile in average width; the benefit of which provision is,

---

27 A contemporary novel with an opium-eating Greek for hero.
28 The German philologist J. C. von Adelung (d. 1806) thus entitled a universal dictionary of languages (begun by him but completed by others), because Mithridates VI (d. 63 B.C.), king of Pontus, reputedly spoke twenty-two languages.

29 Inserted as an extra.
30 De Quincey's note in the revised edition of 1856: "The cottage and the valley concerned in this description were not imaginary: the valley was the lovely one, *in those days,* of Grasmere; and the cottage was occupied for more than twenty years by myself, as immediate successor, in the year 1809, to Wordsworth. . . ."

that all the families resident within its circuit will compose, as it were, one larger household personally familiar to your eye, and more or less interesting to your affections. Let the mountains be real mountains, between three and four thousand feet high; and the cottage a real cottage; not (as a witty author has it) "a cottage with a double coach-house":[31] let it be, in fact (for I must abide by the actual scene), a white cottage, embowered with flowering shrubs, so chosen as to unfold a succession of flowers upon the walls, and clustering around the windows, through all the months of spring, summer, and autumn—beginning, in fact, with May roses, and ending with jasmine. Let it, however, *not* be spring, nor summer, nor autumn—but winter, in his sternest shape. This is a most important point in the science of happiness. And I am surprised to see people overlook it, and think it matter of congratulation that winter is going; or, if coming, is not likely to be a severe one. On the contrary, I put up a petition annually for as much snow, hail, frost, or storm, of one kind or other, as the skies can possibly afford us. Surely every body is aware of the divine pleasures which attend a winter fire-side: candles at four o'clock, warm hearth-rugs, tea, a fair tea-maker, shutters closed, curtains flowing in ample draperies on the floor, whilst the wind and rain are raging audibly without,

> And at the doors and windows seem to call,
> As heav'n and earth they would together mell;[32]
> Yet the least entrance find they none at all;
> Whence sweeter grows our rest secure in massy hall.
> *Castle of Indolence.*[33]

All these are items in the description of a winter evening, which must surely be familiar to everybody born in a high latitude. And it is evident, that most of these delicacies, like ice-cream, require a very low temperature of the atmosphere to produce them: they are fruits which cannot be ripened without weather stormy or inclement, in some way or other. I am not *"particular,"* as people say, whether it be snow, or black frost, or wind so strong that (as Mr. Anti-slavery Clarkson[34] says) "you may lean your back against it like a post." I can put up even with rain, provided it rains cats and dogs: but something of the sort I must have: and, if I have it not, I think myself in a manner ill-used: for why am I called on to pay

so heavily for winter, in coals, and candles, and various privations that will occur even to gentlemen, if I am not to have the article good of its kind? No: a Canadian winter for my money: or a Russian one, where every man is but a co-proprietor with the north wind in the fee-simple[35] of his own ears. Indeed, so great an epicure am I in this matter, that I cannot relish a winter night fully, if it be much past St. Thomas's day,[36] and have degenerated into disgusting tendencies to vernal appearances: no: it must be divided by a thick wall of dark nights from all return of light and sunshine.—From the latter weeks of October to Christmas-eve, therefore, is the period during which happiness is in season, which, in my judgment, enters the room with the tea-tray; for tea, though ridiculed by those who are naturally of coarse nerves, or are become so from wine-drinking, and are not susceptible of influence from so refined a stimulant, will always be the favourite beverage of the intellectual: and, for my part, I would have joined Dr. Johnson in a *bellum internecinum*[37] against Jonas Hanway,[38] or any other impious person who should presume to disparage it.—But here, to save myself the trouble of too much verbal description, I will introduce a painter; and give him directions for the rest of the picture. Painters do not like white cottages, unless a good deal weather-stained: but as the reader now understands that it is a winter night, his services will not be required, except for the inside of the house.

Paint me, then, a room seventeen feet by twelve, and not more than seven and a half feet high. This, reader, is somewhat ambitiously styled, in my family, the drawing-room; but, being contrived "a double debt to pay,"[39] it is also, and more justly, termed the library; for it happens that books are the only article of property in which I am richer than my neighbours. Of these, I have about five thousand, collected gradually since my eighteenth year. Therefore, painter, put as many as you can into this room. Make it populous with books: and, furthermore, paint me a good fire; and furniture, plain and modest, befitting the unpretending cottage of a scholar. And, near the fire, paint me a tea-table; and (as it is clear that no creature can come to see one such a stormy night) place only two cups and saucers on the tea-tray; and,

[31] Coleridge, "The Devil's Thoughts," line 21.   [32] Mingle.
[33] By James Thomson. This passage is misquoted from Canto I, stanza 43.
[34] Thomas Clarkson (1760–1846) led the crusade in England against the African slave trade.

[35] Ownership.
[36] December 21.   [37] Mutually slaughterous war.
[38] A merchant (1712–86) said to have been "the first man who ventured to walk the streets of London with an umbrella over his head." His "Essay on Tea" aroused the ire of Dr. Johnson, a great tea-drinker; Johnson reviewed it, Hanway replied angrily, and Johnson answered the reply.
[39] Goldsmith, *The Deserted Village,* line 229.

if you know how to paint such a thing symbolically, or otherwise, paint me an eternal tea-pot—eternal *a parte ante,* and *a parte post;*[40] for I usually drink tea from eight o'clock at night to four o'clock in the morning. And, as it is very unpleasant to make tea, or to pour it out for ones-self, paint me a lovely young woman, sitting at the table. Paint her arms like Aurora's,[41] and her smiles like Hebe's:[42]—but no, dear M—,[43] not even in jest let me insinuate that thy power to illuminate my cottage rests upon a tenure so perishable as mere personal beauty; or that the witchcraft of angelic smiles lies within the empire of any earthly pencil. Pass, then, my good painter, to something more within its power: and the next article brought forward should naturally be myself—a picture of the Opium-eater, with his "little golden receptacle of the pernicious drug," lying beside him on the table. As to the opium, I have no objection to see a picture of *that,* though I would rather see the original: you may paint it, if you choose; but I apprize you that no "little" receptacle would, even in 1816, answer *my* purpose, who was at a distance from the "stately Pantheon,"[44] and all druggists (mortal or otherwise). No: you may as well paint the real receptacle, which was not of gold, but of glass, and as much like a wine-decanter as possible. Into this you may put a quart of ruby-colored laudanum: that, and a book of German metaphysics placed by its side, will sufficiently attest my being in the neighbourhood; but, as to myself,—there I demur. I admit that, naturally, I ought to occupy the foreground of the picture; that being the hero of the piece, or (if you choose) the criminal at the bar, my body should be had into court. This seems reasonable: but why should I confess, on this point, to a painter? or why confess at all? If the public (into whose private ear I am confidentially whispering my confessions, and not into any painter's) should chance to have framed some agreeable picture for itself, of the Opium-eater's exterior,—should have ascribed to him, romantically, an elegant person, or a handsome face, why should I barbarously tear from it so pleasing a delusion—pleasing both to the public and to me? No: paint me, if at all, according to your own

fancy; and, as a painter's fancy should teem with beautiful creations, I cannot fail, in that way, to be a gainer. And now, reader, we have run through all the ten categories of my condition, as it stood about 1816–1817: up to the middle of which latter year I judge myself to have been a happy man: and the elements of that happiness I have endeavoured to place before you, in the above sketch of the interior of a scholar's library, in a cottage among the mountains, on a stormy winter evening.

But now farewell—a long farewell to happiness—winter or summer! farewell to smiles and laughter! farewell to peace of mind! farewell to hope and to tranquil dreams, and to the blessed consolations of sleep! for more than three years and a half I am summoned away from these: I am now arrived at an Iliad of woes:[45] for I have now to record

THE PAINS OF OPIUM.

. . . I now pass[46] to what is the main subject of these latter confessions, to the history and journal of what took place in my dreams; for these were the immediate and proximate cause of my acutest suffering.

The first notice I had of any important change going on in this part of my physical economy was from the re-awakening of a state of eye generally incident to childhood, or exalted states of irritability. I know not whether my reader is aware that many children, perhaps most, have a power of painting, as it were, upon the darkness, all sorts of phantoms; in some, that power is simply a mechanic affection of the eye; others have a voluntary, or a semi-voluntary power to dismiss or to summon them; or, as a child once said to me when I questioned him on this matter, "I can tell them to go, and they go; but sometimes they come, when I don't tell them to come." Whereupon I told him that he had almost as unlimited command over apparitions as a Roman centurion[47] over his soldiers.—In the middle of 1817, I think it was, that this faculty became positively distressing to me: at night, when I lay awake in bed, vast processions passed along in mournful pomp; friezes of never-ending stories, that to my feelings were as sad and solemn as if they were stories drawn from times before Oedipus or Priam[48]—before

---

[40] Past and future.
[41] Goddess of the dawn; "rosy-fingered" is her epithet in Homer.
[42] Goddess of youth, and cupbearer to the gods.
[43] Margaret, De Quincey's wife.
[44] A concert hall and ballroom on Oxford Street. The druggist's where De Quincey made his first purchase of opium was near it. The quoted phrase is from Wordsworth's "Power of Music," line 3.

[45] The second line of the *Iliad* mentions the "innumerable woes" of the Greeks.
[46] After recounting how he suffered in his attempts to break the habit and how an "intellectual torpor" lasted four years.
[47] Captain; he commanded a "century," i.e., one hundred men.
[48] Figures in Greek legend and literature: Oedipus as king of Thebes, Priam as king of Troy.

Tyre—before Memphis.[49] And, at the same time, a corresponding change took place in my dreams; a theatre seemed suddenly opened and lighted up within my brain, which presented nightly spectacles of more than earthly splendour. And the four following facts may be mentioned, as noticeable at this time:

1. That, as the creative state of the eye increased, a sympathy seemed to arise between the waking and the dreaming states of the brain in one point—that whatsoever I happened to call up and to trace by a voluntary act upon the darkness was very apt to transfer itself to my dreams; so that I feared to exercise this faculty; for, as Midas turned all things to gold, that yet baffled his hopes and defrauded his human desires,[50] so whatsoever things capable of being visually represented I did but think of in the darkness, immediately shaped themselves into phantoms of the eye; and, by a process apparently no less inevitable, when thus once traced in faint and visionary colours, like writings in sympathetic ink,[51] they were drawn out by the fierce chemistry of my dreams, into insufferable splendour that fretted my heart.

2. For this, and all other changes in my dreams, were accompanied by deep-seated anxiety and gloomy melancholy, such as are wholly incommunicable by words. I seemed every night to descend, not metaphorically, but literally to descend, into chasms and sunless abysses, depths below depths, from which it seemed hopeless that I could ever reascend. Nor did I, by waking, feel that I *had* reascended. This I do not dwell upon; because the state of gloom which attended these gorgeous spectacles, amounting at least to utter darkness, as of some suicidal despondency, cannot be approached by words.

3. The sense of space, and in the end, the sense of time, were both powerfully affected. Buildings, landscapes, etc., were exhibited in proportions so vast as the bodily eye is not fitted to receive. Space swelled, and was amplified to an extent of unutterable infinity. This, however, did not disturb me so much as the vast expansion of time; I sometimes seemed to have lived for 70 or 100 years in one night; nay, sometimes had feelings representative of a millen-

nium, passed in that time, or, however, of a duration far beyond the limits of any human experience.

4. The minutest incidents of childhood, or forgotten scenes of later years, were often revived: I could not be said to recollect them; for if I had been told of them when waking, I should not have been able to acknowledge them as parts of my past experience. But placed as they were before me, in dreams like intuitions, and clothed in all their evanescent circumstances and accompanying feelings, I *recognised* them instantaneously. I was once told by a near relative of mine,[52] that having in her childhood fallen into a river, and being on the very verge of death but for the critical assistance which reached her, she saw in a moment her whole life, in its minutest incidents, arrayed before her simultaneously as in a mirror; and she had a faculty developed as suddenly for comprehending the whole and every part. This, from some opium experiences of mine, I can believe; I have, indeed, seen the same thing asserted twice in modern books, and accompanied by a remark which I am convinced is true; viz. that the dread book of account which the Scriptures speak of[53] is, in fact, the mind itself of each individual. Of this, at least, I feel assured, that there is no such thing as *forgetting* possible to the mind; a thousand accidents may and will interpose a veil between our present consciousness and the secret inscriptions on the mind; accidents of the same sort will also rend away this veil; but alike, whether veiled or unveiled, the inscription remains for ever; just as the stars seem to withdraw before the common light of day, whereas, in fact, we all know that it is the light which is drawn over them as a veil—and that they are waiting to be revealed, when the obscuring daylight shall have withdrawn.

Having noticed these four facts as memorably distinguishing my dreams from those of health, I shall now cite a case illustrative of the first fact; and shall then cite any others that I remember, either in their chronological order, or any other that may give them more effect as pictures to the reader.

I had been in youth, and even since, for occasional amusement, a great reader of Livy,[54] whom, I confess, that I prefer, both for style and matter, to any other of the Roman historians; and I had often felt as most solemn and appalling sounds, and most emphatically representative of the majesty of the Roman people, the two words so often occurring in Livy—*Consul Romanus;* especially when the consul is introduced in his military character. I mean to say, that

---

49 Tyre, in Lebanon, was in ancient times a Phoenician port; Memphis, now a village near Cairo, was the ancient capital of Egypt.

50 In Greek mythology this king of Phrygia was granted the faculty of turning everything he touched to gold. He soon asked the god to revoke the gift; for one thing, when he tried to eat, his food turned to gold.

51 Which is invisible till heat is applied.

52 His mother. 53 Revelation 20:12.
54 Author (59 B.C.–17 A.D.) of *The Annals of the Roman People*.

the words king—sultan—regent, &c. or any other titles of those who embody in their own persons the collective majesty of a great people, had less power over my reverential feelings. I had also, though no great reader of history, made myself minutely and critically familiar with one period of English history, namely, the period of the Parliamentary War,[55] having been attracted by the moral grandeur of some who figured in that day, and by the many interesting memoirs which survive those unquiet times. Both these parts of my lighter reading, having furnished me often with matter of reflection, now furnished me with matter for my dreams. Often I used to see, after painting upon the blank darkness a sort of rehearsal whilst waking, a crowd of ladies, and perhaps a festival, and dances. And I heard it said, or I said to myself, "These are English ladies from the unhappy times of Charles I. These are the wives and the daughters of those who met in peace, and sat at the same tables, and were allied by marriage or by blood; and yet, after a certain day in August, 1642, never smiled upon each other again, nor met but in the field of battle; and at Marston Moor, at Newbury, or at Naseby, cut asunder all ties of love by the cruel sabre, and washed away in blood the memory of ancient friendship."—The ladies danced, and looked as lovely as the court of George IV. Yet I knew, even in my dreams, that they had been in the grave for nearly two centuries.—This pageant would suddenly dissolve: and, at a clapping of hands, would be heard the heart-quaking sound of *Consul Romanus:* and immediately came "sweeping by,"[56] in gorgeous paludaments,[57] Paulus or Marius,[58] girt round by a company of centurions, with the crimson tunic hoisted on a spear,[59] and followed by the *alalagmos*[60] of the Roman legions.

Many years ago, when I was looking over Piranesi's[61] Antiquities of Rome, Mr. Coleridge, who was standing by, described to me a set of plates by that artist, called his *Dreams,* and which record the scenery of his own visions during the delirium of a fever: some of them (I describe only from memory of Mr. Coleridge's account) representing vast Gothic halls: on the floor of which stood all sorts of engines and machinery, wheels, cables, pulleys, levers, catapults, etc. etc., expressive of enormous power put forth, and resistance overcome. Creeping along the sides of the walls, you perceived a staircase; and upon it, groping his way upwards, was Piranesi himself: follow the stairs a little further, and you perceive it to come to a sudden, abrupt termination, without any balustrade, and allowing no step onwards to him who had reached the extremity, except into the depths below. Whatever is to become of poor Piranesi, you suppose, at least, that his labours must in some way terminate here. But raise your eyes, and behold a second flight of stairs still higher: on which again Piranesi is perceived, but this time standing on the very brink of the abyss. Again elevate your eye, and a still more aerial flight of stairs is beheld; and again is poor Piranesi busy on his aspiring labors: and so on, until the unfinished stairs and Piranesi both are lost in the upper gloom of the hall.—With the same power of endless growth and self-reproduction did my architecture proceed in dreams. In the early stage of my malady, the splendours of my dreams were indeed chiefly architectural: and I beheld such pomp of cities and palaces as was never yet beheld by the waking eye, unless in the clouds. . . . We hear it reported of Dryden, and of Fuseli[62] in modern times, that they thought proper to eat raw meat for the sake of obtaining splendid dreams: how much better, for such a purpose, to have eaten opium, which yet I do not remember that any poet is recorded to have done, except the dramatist Shadwell:[63] and in ancient days, Homer is, I think, rightly reputed to have known the virtues of opium.

To my architecture succeeded dreams of lakes and silvery expanses of water:—these haunted me so much, that I feared (though possibly it will appear ludicrous to a medical man) that some dropsical state or tendency of the brain might thus be making itself (to use a metaphysical word) *objective* and the sentient organ *project* itself as its own object.—For two months I suffered greatly in my head—a part of my bodily structure which had hitherto been so clear from all touch or taint of weakness (physically, I mean) that I used to say of it, as the last Lord Orford[64] said of

---

55 The Civil Wars of the mid-seventeenth century.

56 Milton, "Il Penseroso," line 98.

57 Latin *paludamenta,* military cloaks.

58 There were two Roman generals named Paulus. The first was killed fighting the Carthaginians at Cannae (216 B.C.); his son (d. 160 B.C.) defeated the last king of Macedonia. Marius (d. 86 B.C.) was the famous general and politician, victor against foreign foes and opponent of Sulla in the civil war of 88 B.C.

59 De Quincey's note: "The signal which announced a day of battle."

60 De Quincey's note: "A [Greek] word expressing collectively the gathering of the Roman war-cries—*Alála, Alála!*"

61 Giambattista Piranesi (1720–78), architect, painter, and engraver. His engravings influenced French and English architecture, in the latter case especially the style of Adam. There is no work by Piranesi entitled *Dreams,* but some of his architectural conceptions were not intended realistically.

62 Henry Fuseli (1741–1825), a Swiss painter who had his career in England.

63 Thomas Shadwell (d. 1692), the comic dramatist.

64 Horace Walpole (1717–97), the connoisseur and letter writer. —*Last* = late.

his stomach, that it seemed likely to survive the rest of my person.—Till now I had never felt a headache even, or any the slightest pain, except rheumatic pains caused by my own folly. However, I got over this attack, though it must have been verging on something very dangerous.

The waters now changed their character,—from translucent lakes, shining like mirrors, they now became seas and oceans. And now came a tremendous change, which, unfolding itself slowly like a scroll, through many months, promised an abiding torment; and, in fact, it never left me until the winding up of my case. Hitherto the human face had mixed often in my dreams, but not despotically, nor with any special power of tormenting. But now that which I have called the tyranny of the human face began to unfold itself. Perhaps some part of my London life might be answerable for this. Be that as it may, now it was that upon the rocking waters of the ocean the human face began to appear: the sea appeared paved with innumerable faces, upturned to the heavens: faces imploring, wrathful, despairing, surged upwards by thousands, by myriads, by generations, by centuries:—my agitation was infinite,—my mind tossed—and surged with the ocean.

May, 1818.

The Malay has been a fearful enemy for months. I have been every night, through his means, transported into Asiatic scenes. I know not whether others share in my feelings on this point; but I have often thought that if I were compelled to forego England, and to live in China, and among Chinese manners and modes of life and scenery, I should go mad. The causes of my horror lie deep; and some of them must be common to others. Southern Asia, in general, is the seat of awful images and associations. As the cradle of the human race, it would alone have a dim and reverential feeling connected with it. But there are other reasons. No man can pretend that the wild, barbarous, and capricious superstitions of Africa, or of savage tribes elsewhere, affect him in the way that he is affected by the ancient, monumental, cruel, and elaborate religions of Indostan,[65] etc. The mere antiquity of Asiatic things, of their institutions, histories, modes of faith, etc. is so impressive, that to me the vast age of the race and name overpowers the sense of youth in the individual. A young Chinese seems to me an antediluvian man renewed. Even Englishmen, though not bred in any knowledge of such institutions, cannot but shudder at the mystic sublimity of *castes* that have flowed apart, and refused to mix, through such immemorial tracts of time; nor can any man fail to be awed by the names of the Ganges, or the Euphrates. It contributes much to these feelings, that Southern Asia is, and has been for thousands of years, the part of the earth most swarming with human life, the great *officina gentium.*[66] Man is a weed in those regions. The vast empires also, into which the enormous population of Asia has always been cast, give a further sublimity to the feelings associated with all Oriental names or images. In China, over and above what it has in common with the rest of southern Asia, I am terrified by the modes of life, by the manners, and the barrier of utter abhorrence, and want of sympathy, placed between us by feelings deeper than I can analyze. I could sooner live with lunatics, or brute animals. All this, and much more than I can say, or have time to say, the reader must enter into, before he can comprehend the unimaginable horror which these dreams of Oriental imagery, and mythological tortures, impressed upon me. Under the connecting feeling of tropical heat and vertical sun-lights, I brought together all creatures, birds, beasts, reptiles, all trees and plants, usages and appearances, that are found in all tropical regions, and assembled them together in China or Indostan. From kindred feelings, I soon brought Egypt and all her gods under the same law. I was stared at, hooted at, grinned at, chattered at, by monkeys, by paroquets,[67] by cockatoos. I ran into pagodas: and was fixed, for centuries, at the summit, or in secret rooms; I was the idol; I was the priest; I was worshipped; I was sacrificed. I fled from the wrath of Brama through all the forests of Asia: Vishnu hated me; Seeva laid wait for me. I came suddenly upon Isis and Osiris:[68] I had done a deed, they said, which the ibis[69] and the crocodile trembled at. I was buried for a thousand years in stone coffins, with mummies and sphinxes, in narrow chambers at the heart of eternal pyramids. I was kissed, with cancerous kisses, by crocodiles; and laid, confounded with all unutterable slimy things, amongst reeds and Nilotic[70] mud.

---

65 Hindustan, India.

66 Factory of populations.
67 Parakeets, small parrots.
68 The Egyptian god of the underworld and judge of the dead. Isis, his sister and wife, was goddess of fertility.—The names mentioned just above are those of the great triad of gods in the Hindu religion: Brahma, the supreme spirit of the universe; Vishnu, "the Preserver"; Siva, god of destruction and of reproduction.
69 Like the crocodile, this bird was venerated by the ancient Egyptians.   70 Of the Nile.

I thus give the reader some slight abstraction of my Oriental dreams, which always filled me with such amazement at the monstrous scenery, that horror seemed absorbed, for a while, in sheer astonishment. Sooner or later, came a reflux of feeling that swallowed up the astonishment, and left me, not so much in terror, as in hatred and abomination of what I saw. Over every form, and threat, and punishment, and dim sightless incarceration, brooded a sense of eternity and infinity that drove me into an oppression as of madness. Into these dreams only, it was, with one or two slight exceptions, that any circumstances of physical horror entered. All before had been moral and spiritual terrors. But here the main agents were ugly birds, or snakes, or crocodiles; especially the last. The cursed crocodile became to me the object of more horror than almost all the rest. I was compelled to live with him; and (as was always the case almost in my dreams) for centuries. I escaped sometimes, and found myself in Chinese houses, with cane tables, etc. All the feet of the tables, sofas, etc., soon became instinct with life· the abominable head of the crocodile, and his leering eyes, looked out at me, multiplied into a thousand repetitions: and I stood loathing and fascinated. And so often did this hideous reptile haunt my dreams, that many times the very same dream was broken up in the very same way: I heard gentle voices speaking to me (I hear everything when I am sleeping); and instantly I awoke: it was broad noon; and my children were standing, hand in hand, at my bed-side; come to show me their coloured shoes, or new frocks, or to let me see them dressed for going out. I protest that so awful was the transition from the damned crocodile, and the other unutterable monsters and abortions of my dreams, to the sight of innocent *human* natures and of infancy, that, in the mighty and sudden revulsion of mind, I wept, and could not forbear it, as I kissed their faces.

. . . As a final specimen, I cite one of a different character, from 1820.

The dream commenced with a music which now I often heard in dreams—a music of preparation and of awakening suspense; a music like the opening of the Coronation Anthem, and which, like *that,* gave the feeling of a vast march—of infinite cavalcades filing off—and the tread of innumerable armies. The morning was come of a mighty day—a day of crisis and of final hope for human nature, then suffering some mysterious eclipse, and labouring in some dread extremity. Somewhere, I knew not where—somehow, I knew not how—by some beings, I knew not whom—a battle, a strife, an agony, was conducting,—was evolving like a great drama, or piece of music; with which my sympathy was the more insupportable from my confusion as to its place, its cause, its nature, and its possible issue. I, as is usual in dreams (where, of necessity, we make ourselves central to every movement), had the power, and yet had not the power, to decide it. I had the power, if I could raise myself, to will it; and yet again had not the power, for the weight of twenty Atlantics was upon me, or the oppression of inexpiable guilt. "Deeper than ever plummet sounded,"[71] I lay inactive. Then, like a chorus, the passion deepened. Some greater interest was at stake; some mightier cause than ever yet the sword had pleaded, or trumpet had proclaimed. Then came sudden alarms: hurryings to and fro: trepidations of innumerable fugitives, I knew not whether from the good cause or the bad: darkness and lights: tempest and human faces: and at last, with the sense that all was lost, female forms, and the features that were worth all the world to me, and but a moment allowed,—and clasped hands, and heart-breaking partings, and then—everlasting farewells! and, with a sigh, such as the caves of hell sighed when the incestuous mother uttered the abhorred name of death,[72] the sound was reverberated—everlasting farewells! and again, and yet again reverberated—everlasting farewells!

And I awoke in struggles, and cried aloud—"I will sleep no more!"[73] . . .

71 Cf. Shakespeare's *The Tempest,* V, i, 56.
72 See *Paradise Lost,* II, 746-67, 777-96.
73 The *Confessions* ends with five more paragraphs. De Quincey explains that he saw he would die if he continued the habit, and therefore determined to risk death in freeing himself. "I triumphed," he says, but he feels shattered though not dejected; the moral is "to fear and tremble," but his case "is at least a proof" that the habit can be conquered.

CRITICISM, like most matters worth the attention of a thoroughly alive mind, is worth little without imagination. In this famous essay (*London Magazine*, October, 1823) free rein is given to that impetuous faculty—some would say too free. If the neoclassical critics frequently equipped the bit with a pedantic curb, the Romantic critics rode with the lightest of snaffles and too often galloped over the hills and far away from the objective of the charge. One misses in the following paragraphs the firm hand and seat of a Dr. Johnson. Yet, however impressionistic and even rhapsodic this essay, there is wisdom here, the wisdom of vision rather than of precise knowledge. The passage under discussion is *Macbeth*, II, ii, 57-74.

FROM my boyish days I had always felt a great perplexity on one point in *Macbeth*. It was this:—the knocking at the gate which succeeds to the murder of Duncan produced to my feelings an effect for which I never could account. The effect was that it reflected back upon the murderer a peculiar awfulness and a depth of solemnity; yet, however obstinately I endeavoured with my understanding to comprehend this, for many years I never could see *why* it should produce such an effect.

Here I pause for one moment, to exhort the reader never to pay any attention to his understanding when it stands in opposition to any other faculty of his mind. The mere understanding, however useful and indispensable, is the meanest faculty in the human mind, and the most to be distrusted; and yet the great majority of people trust to nothing else,—which may do for ordinary life, but not for philosophical purposes. Of this out of ten thousand instances that I might produce I will cite one. Ask of any person whatsoever who is not previously prepared for the demand by a knowledge of perspective to draw in the rudest way the commonest appearance which depends upon the laws of that science,—as, for instance, to represent the effect of two walls standing at right angles to each other, or the appearance of the houses on each side of a street as seen by a person looking down the street from one extremity. Now, in all cases, unless the person has happened to observe in pictures how it is that artists produce these effects, he will be utterly unable to make the smallest approximation to it. Yet why? For he has actually seen the effect every day of his life. The reason is that he allows his understanding to overrule his eyes. His understanding, which includes no intuitive knowledge of the laws of vision, can furnish him with no

reason why a line which is known and can be proved to be a horizontal line should not *appear* a horizontal line: a line that made any angle with the perpendicular less than a right angle would seem to him to indicate that his houses were all tumbling down together. Accordingly, he makes the line of his houses a horizontal line, and fails, of course, to produce the effect demanded. Here, then, is one instance out of many in which not only the understanding is allowed to overrule the eyes, but where the understanding is positively allowed to obliterate the eyes, as it were; for not only does the man believe the evidence of his understanding in opposition to that of his eyes, but (what is monstrous) the idiot is not aware that his eyes ever gave such evidence. He does not know that he has seen (and therefore *quoad* his consciousness[1] has *not* seen) that which he *has* seen every day of his life.

But to return from this digression. My understanding could furnish no reason why the knocking at the gate in *Macbeth* should produce any effect, direct or reflected. In fact, my understanding said positively that it could *not* produce any effect. But I knew better; I felt that it did; and I waited and clung to the problem until further knowledge should enable me to solve it. At length, in 1812, Mr. Williams made his *début*[2] on the stage of Ratcliffe Highway,[3] and executed those unparalleled murders which have procured for him such a brilliant and undying reputation. On which murders, by the way, I must observe, that in one respect they have had an ill effect, by making the connoisseur in murder very fastidious in his taste, and dissatisfied by anything that has been since done in that line. All other murders look pale by the deep crimson of his; and, as an amateur once said to me in a querulous tone, "There has been absolutely nothing *doing* since his time, or nothing that's worth speaking of." But this is wrong, for it is unreasonable to expect all men to be great artists, and born with the genius of Mr. Williams. Now it will be remembered that in the first of these murders (that of the Marrs) the same incident (of a knocking

---

[1] As far as his consciousness is concerned.

[2] Beginning in 1827, De Quincey published (vol. XIII in Masson's ed.) several papers *On Murder Considered as One of the Fine Arts*. In a "Postscript" (added in 1854) he gives a detailed account of the murder of the Marr and Williamson families by John Williams, a sailor, in December, 1811.

[3] Now St. George Street, in the docks area.

at the door[4] soon after the work of extermination was complete) did actually occur which the genius of Shakespeare has invented; and all good judges, and the most eminent dilettanti,[5] acknowledged the felicity of Shakespeare's suggestion as soon as it was actually realized. Here, then, was a fresh proof that I had been right in relying on my own feeling, in opposition to my understanding; and again I set myself to study the problem. At length I solved it to my own satisfaction; and my solution is this:— Murder, in ordinary cases, where the sympathy is wholly directed to the case of the murdered person, is an incident of coarse and vulgar horror; and for this reason,—that it flings the interest exclusively upon the natural but ignoble instinct by which we cleave to life: an instinct which, as being indispensable to the primal law of self-preservation, is the same in kind (though different in degree) amongst all living creatures. This instinct, therefore, because it annihilates all distinctions, and degrades the greatest of men to the level of "the poor beetle that we tread on,"[6] exhibits human nature in its most abject and humiliating attitude. Such an attitude would little suit the purposes of the poet. What then must he do? He must throw the interest on the murderer. Our sympathy must be with *him* (of course I mean a sympathy of comprehension, a sympathy by which we enter into his feelings, and are made to understand them,—not a sympathy of pity or approbation).[7] In the murdered person, all strife of thought, all flux and reflux of passion and of purpose, are crushed by one overwhelming panic; the fear of instant death smites him "with its petrific[8] mace." But in the murderer, such a murderer as a poet will condescend to, there must be raging some great storm of passion,—jealousy, ambition, vengeance, hatred,—which will create a hell within him; and into this hell we are to look.

In *Macbeth*, for the sake of gratifying his own enormous and teeming faculty of creation, Shake-speare has introduced two murderers: and, as usual in his hands, they are remarkably discriminated: but,—though in Macbeth the strife of mind is greater than in his wife, the tiger spirit not so awake, and his feelings caught chiefly by contagion from her,— yet, as both were finally involved in the guilt of murder, the murderous mind of necessity is finally to be presumed in both. This was to be expressed; and, on its own account, as well as to make it a more proportionable antagonist to the unoffending nature of their victim, "the gracious Duncan,"[9] and adequately to expound "the deep damnation of his taking off,"[10] this was to be expressed with peculiar energy. We were to be made to feel that the human nature,—i.e. the divine nature of love and mercy, spread through the hearts of all creatures, and seldom utterly withdrawn from man,—was gone, vanished, extinct, and that the fiendish nature had taken its place. And, as this effect is marvellously accomplished in the *dialogues* and *soliloquies* themselves, so it is finally consummated by the expedient under consideration; and it is to this that I now solicit the reader's attention. If the reader has ever witnessed a wife, daughter, or sister in a fainting fit, he may chance to have observed that the most affecting moment in such a spectacle is *that* in which a sigh and a stirring announce the recommencement of suspended life. Or, if the reader has ever been present in a vast metropolis on the day when some great national idol was carried in funeral pomp to his grave, and, chancing to walk near the course through which it passed, has felt powerfully, in the silence and desertion of the streets, and in the stagnation of ordinary business, the deep interest which at that moment was possessing the heart of man,—if all at once he should hear the death-like stillness broken up by the sound of wheels rattling away from the scene, and making known that the transitory vision was dissolved, he will be aware that at no moment was his sense of the complete suspension and pause in ordinary human concerns so full and affecting as at that moment when the suspension ceases, and the goings-on of human life are suddenly resumed. All action in any direction is best expounded, measured, and made apprehensible, by reaction. Now, apply this to the case in *Macbeth*. Here, as I have said, the retiring of the human heart and the entrance of the fiendish heart was to be expressed and made sensible. Another world has stept in; and the murderers are taken out of the region of human things, human

---

4 By a maid-servant who had been sent out for some oysters.

5 Amateurs, fans. Cf. *amateur*, eleven lines earlier.

6 Cf. Shakespeare's *Measure for Measure*, III, i, 79.

7 De Quincey's note: "It seems almost ludicrous to guard and explain my use of a word in a situation where it would naturally explain itself. But it has become necessary to do so, in consequence of the unscholarlike use of the word *sympathy*, at present so general, by which, instead of taking it in its proper sense, as the act of reproducing in our minds the feelings of another, whether for hatred, indignation, love, pity, or approbation, it is made a mere synonym of the word *pity*; and hence, instead of saying 'sympathy *with* another,' many writers adopt the monstrous barbarism of 'sympathy *for* another.' "

8 Petrifying. Cf. *Paradise Lost*, X, 294.

9 *Macbeth*, III, i, 66.   10 *Macbeth*, I, vii, 20.

purposes, human desires. They are transfigured: Lady Macbeth is "unsexed";[11] Macbeth has forgot that he was born of woman; both are conformed to the image of devils; and the world of devils is suddenly revealed. But how shall this be conveyed and made palpable? In order that a new world may step in, this world must for a time disappear. The murderers and the murder must be insulated—cut off by an immeasurable gulf from the ordinary tide and succession of human affairs—locked up and sequestered in some deep recess; we must be made sensible that the world of ordinary life is suddenly arrested, laid asleep, tranced, racked into a dread armistice; time must be annihilated, relation to things without abolished; and all must pass self-withdrawn into a deep syncope and suspension of earthly passion. Hence it is that, when the deed is done, when the work of darkness is perfect, then the world of darkness passes away like a pageantry in the clouds:

the knocking at the gate is heard, and it makes known audibly that the reaction has commenced; the human has made its reflux upon the fiendish; the pulses of life are beginning to beat again; and the re-establishment of the goings-on of the world in which we live first makes us profoundly sensible of the awful parenthesis that has suspended them.

O mighty poet! Thy works are not as those of other men, simply and merely great works of art, but are also like the phenomena of nature, like the sun and the sea, the stars and the flowers, like frost and snow, rain and dew, hail-storm and thunder, which are to be studied with entire submission of our own faculties, and in the perfect faith that in them there can be no too much or too little, nothing useless or inert, but that, the farther we press in our discoveries, the more we shall see proofs of design and self-supporting arrangement where the careless eye had seen nothing but accident![12]

from SUSPIRIA DE PROFUNDIS

MORE than once in this book allusion has been made to the occasional existence of poetry in prose. To illustrate again: Shakespeare's "What a piece of work is a man! how noble in reason! how infinite in faculty!" etc. (*Hamlet*, II, ii, 316 ff.) is in content poetry though in form prose. With the growing recognition of this fact, we hear less nowadays of the term "prose-poetry," which used to be applied rather too freely to any sort of lush, imaginative prose, and sometimes to very bad writing. On the whole we are well rid of the term; yet it remains fairly applicable to such productions as those of Sir Thomas Browne in the seventeenth century (I, 543 ff., above) and to efforts like this of De Quincey's in the nineteenth, which some still consider the most remarkable thing he ever wrote. He began in 1845 a series of contributions to *Blackwood's* entitled *Suspiria de Profundis:*[1] *being a Sequel to the Confessions of an English Opium-Eater.* "Levana and Our Ladies of Sorrow" appeared in the June number with an explanatory note calling it a "dreamlegend." It is now a museum piece, by no means without beauty—indeed it has much beauty and a moving compassion—but certainly not a model either for a poet or for a writer who wishes to develop in our time an effective prose style. As "prose-poetry," the style is marked by its elaboration, by elevated diction, and by cadences so rhythmical that they can sometimes be scanned as verse. Impressive and imaginative as it all is, the pace seems too

deliberate; and we are tempted to exclaim, with the impatience of Hamlet's mother when she objects to the rhetoric of Polonius, "More matter, with less art!"

LEVANA AND OUR LADIES OF SORROW

OFTENTIMES at Oxford I saw Levana in my dreams. I knew her by her Roman symbols. Who is Levana? Reader, that do not pretend to have leisure for very much scholarship, you will not be angry with me for telling you. Levana was the Roman goddess that performed for the new-born infant the earliest office of ennobling kindness,—typical, by its mode, of that grandeur which belongs to man everywhere, and of that benignity in powers invisible which even in Pagan worlds sometimes descends to sustain it. At the very moment of birth, just as the infant tasted for the first time the atmosphere of our troubled planet, it was laid on the ground. *That* might bear

---

[11] Cf. *Macbeth*, I, v, 42.

[1] Sighs from the Depths.

[12] The soundness of the final paragraph is questionable, and the Romantic deification of Shakespeare is now generally rejected. He is still the "mighty poet" of that paragraph, perhaps of all the mightiest, but a fallible human being, too. De Quincey's main point is probably sound, but he does not touch on what is presumably the main purpose of the knocking, the intensification of the dramatic tension just after the crime and shortly before its discovery. The value of such effusions as De Quincey's lies less in their direct applicability to the play in question than in their stimulation of the reader's own imagination. They are, that is, more impressive as works of art themselves than as interpretations of Shakespeare.

different interpretations. But immediately, lest so grand a creature should grovel there for more than one instant, either the paternal hand, as proxy for the goddess Levana, or some near kinsman, as proxy for the father, raised it upright, bade it look erect as the king of all this world, and presented its forehead to the stars, saying, perhaps, in his heart, "Behold what is greater than yourselves!" This symbolic act represented the function of Levana. And that mysterious lady, who never revealed her face (except to me in dreams), but always acted by delegation, had her name from the Latin verb (as still it is the Italian verb) *levare,* to raise aloft.

This is the explanation of Levana. And hence it has arisen that some people have understood by Levana the tutelary power that controls the education of the nursery. She, that would not suffer at his birth even a prefigurative or mimic degradation for her awful ward, far less could be supposed to suffer the real degradation attaching to the non-development of his powers. She therefore watches over human education. Now, the word *edŭco,* with the penultimate[2] short, was derived (by a process often exemplified in the crystallisation of languages) from the word *edūco,* with the penultimate long. Whatsoever *educes,* or develops, *educates.* By the education of Levana, therefore, is meant,—not the poor machinery that moves by spelling-books and grammars, but that mighty system of central forces hidden in the deep bosom of human life, which by passion, by strife, by temptation, by the energies of resistance, works forever upon children,—resting not day or night, any more than the mighty wheel of day and night themselves, whose moments, like restless spokes, are glimmering[3] for ever as they revolve.

If, then, *these* are the ministries by which Levana works, how profoundly must she reverence the agencies of grief! But you, reader, think that children generally are not liable to grief such as mine. There are two senses in the word *generally,*—the sense of Euclid,[4] where it means *universally* (or in the whole extent of the *genus*[5]), and a foolish sense of this word, where it means *usually.* Now, I am far from saying that children universally are capable of grief like mine. But there are more than you ever heard of who die of grief in this island of ours. I will tell you a common case. The rules of Eton require that a boy on the *foundation*[6] should be there twelve years: he is superannuated at eighteen; consequently he must come at six. Children torn away from mothers and sisters at that age not unfrequently die. I speak of what I know. The complaint is not entered by the registrar as grief; but *that* it is. Grief of that sort, and at that age, has killed more than ever have been counted amongst its martyrs.

Therefore it is that Levana often communes with the powers that shake man's heart; therefore it is that she dotes upon grief. "These ladies," said I softly to myself, on seeing the ministers with whom Levana was conversing, "these are the Sorrows; and they are three in number: as the *Graces* are three, who dress man's life with beauty; the *Parcae*[7] are three, who weave the dark arras[8] of man's life in their mysterious loom always with colours sad in part, sometimes angry with tragic crimson and black; the *Furies* are three, who visit with retributions called from the other side of the grave offences that walk upon this; and once even the *Muses* were but three, who fit the harp, the trumpet, or the lute, to the great burdens[9] of man's impassioned creations. These are the Sorrows; all three of whom I know." The last words I say *now;* but in Oxford I said, "one of whom I know, and the others too surely I *shall* know." For already, in my fervent youth, I saw (dimly relieved upon the dark background of my dreams) the imperfect lineaments of the awful Sisters.

These sisters—by what name shall we call them? If I say simply "The Sorrows," there will be a chance of mistaking the term; it might be understood of individual sorrow,—separate cases of sorrow,—whereas I want a term expressing the mighty abstractions that incarnate themselves in all individual sufferings of man's heart, and I wish to have these abstractions presented as impersonations,—that is, as clothed with human attributes of life, and with functions pointing to flesh. Let us call them, therefore, *Our Ladies of Sorrow.*

---

2 Next to the last syllable.

3 De Quincey's note: "As I have never allowed myself to covet any man's ox nor his ass, nor anything that is his, still less would it become a philosopher to covet other people's images or metaphors. Here, therefore, I restore to Mr. Wordsworth this fine image of the revolving wheel and the glimmering spokes, as applied by him to the flying successions of day and night. I borrowed it for one moment in order to point my own sentence; which being done, the reader is witness that I now pay it back instantly by a note made for that sole purpose. On the same principle I often borrow their seals from young ladies, when closing my letters, because there is sure to be some tender sentiment upon them about 'memory,' or 'hope,' or 'roses,' or 'reunion,' and my correspondent must be a sad brute who is not touched by the eloquence of the seal, even if his taste is so bad that he remains deaf to mine." For the image, see Wordsworth's "Conclusion: To —" ("If these brief Records").

4 The Greek geometer who flourished about 300 B.C.

5 Class.   6 I.e., a scholarship holder.   7 Fates.

8 Tapestry.   9 Refrains, themes.

I know them thoroughly, and have walked in all their kingdoms. Three sisters they are, of one mysterious household; and their paths are wide apart; but of their dominion there is no end. Them I saw often conversing with Levana, and sometimes about myself. Do they talk, then? O no! Mighty phantoms like these disdain the infirmities of language. They may utter voices through the organs of man when they dwell in human hearts, but amongst themselves is no voice nor sound; eternal silence reigns in *their* kingdoms. They spoke not as they talked with Levana. They whispered not. They sang not. Though oftentimes methought they *might* have sung: for I upon earth had heard their mysteries oftentimes deciphered by harp and timbrel, by dulcimer and organ. Like God, whose servants they are, they utter their pleasure not by sounds that perish, or by words that go astray, but by signs in heaven, by changes on earth, by pulses in secret rivers, heraldries painted on darkness, and hieroglyphics written on the tablets of the brain. *They* wheeled in mazes; *I* spelled the steps. *They* telegraphed[10] from afar; *I* read the signals. *They* conspired together; and on the mirrors of darkness *my* eye traced the plots. *Theirs* were the symbols; *mine* are the words.

What is it the Sisters are? What is it that they do? Let me describe their form and their presence, if form it were that still fluctuated in its outline, or presence it were that for ever advanced to the front or for ever receded amongst shades.

The eldest of the three is named *Mater Lachrymarum,* Our Lady of Tears. She it is that night and day raves and moans, calling for vanished faces. She stood in Rama, where a voice was heard of lamentation,—Rachel weeping for her children, and refusing to be comforted.[11] She it was that stood in Bethlehem on the night when Herod's sword swept its nurseries of Innocents,[12] and the little feet were stiffened for ever which, heard at times as they trotted along floors overhead, woke pulses of love in household hearts that were not unmarked in heaven. Her eyes are sweet and subtle, wild and sleepy, by turns; oftentimes rising to the clouds, oftentimes challenging the heavens. She wears a diadem round her head. And I knew by childish memories that she could go abroad upon the winds, when she heard the sobbing of litanies, or the thundering of organs, and when she beheld the mustering of summer clouds. This Sister, the elder, it is that carries keys more than papal at her girdle, which open every cottage and every palace. She, to my knowledge, sat all last summer by the bedside of the blind beggar, him that so often and so gladly I talked with, whose pious daughter, eight years old, with the sunny countenance, resisted the temptations of play and village mirth, to travel all day long on dusty roads with her afflicted father. For this did God send her a great reward. In the spring time of the year, and whilst yet her own spring was budding, He recalled her to himself. But her blind father mourns for ever over *her;* still he dreams at midnight that the little guiding hand is locked within his own; and still he wakens to a darkness that is *now* within a second and a deeper darkness. This *Mater Lachrymarum* also has been sitting all this winter of 1844–5 within the bedchamber of the Czar,[13] bringing before his eyes a daughter (not less pious) that vanished to God not less suddenly, and left behind her a darkness not less profound. By the power of her keys it is that Our Lady of Tears glides, a ghostly intruder, into the chambers of sleepless men, sleepless women, sleepless children, from Ganges to the Nile, from Nile to Mississippi. And her, because she is the first-born of her house, and has the widest empire, let us honour with the title of "Madonna."

The second Sister is called *Mater Suspiriorum,* Our Lady of Sighs. She never scales the clouds, nor walks abroad upon the winds. She wears no diadem. And her eyes, if they were ever seen, would be neither sweet nor subtle; no man could read their story; they would be found filled with perishing dreams, and with wrecks of forgotten delirium. But she raises not her eyes; her head, on which sits a dilapidated turban, droops for ever, for ever fastens on the dust. She weeps not. She groans not. But she sighs inaudibly at intervals. Her sister, Madonna, is oftentimes stormy and frantic, raging in the highest against heaven, and demanding back her darlings. But Our Lady of Sighs never clamours, never defies, dreams not of rebellious aspirations. She is humble to abjectness. Hers is the meekness that belongs to the hopeless. Murmur she may, but it is in her sleep. Whisper she may, but it is to herself in the twilight. Mutter she does at times, but it is in solitary places that are desolate as she is desolate, in ruined cities, and when the sun has gone down to his rest. This Sister is the visitor of the Pariah,[14] of the Jew,[15] of the bondsman to the oar in Mediterranean galleys; of

---

[10] Signaled.
[11] Cf. Jeremiah 31:15 and Matthew 2:18.
[12] See Matthew 2:16.

[13] Nicholas I of Russia (1796–1855). His daughter Alexandra had died in the preceding summer.
[14] Member of a certain low caste in India.
[15] I.e., the persecuted Jew.

the English criminal in Norfolk Island,[16] blotted out from the books of remembrance in sweet far-off England; of the baffled penitent reverting his eyes for ever upon a solitary grave, which to him seems the altar overthrown of some past and bloody sacrifice, on which altar no oblations can now be availing, whether towards pardon that he might implore, or towards reparation that he might attempt. Every slave that at noonday looks up to the tropical sun with timid reproach, as he points with one hand to the earth, our general mother, but for *him* a stepmother, as he points with the other hand to the Bible, our general teacher, but against *him* sealed and sequestered;[17] every woman sitting in darkness, without love to shelter her head, or hope to illumine her solitude, because the heaven-born instincts kindling in her nature germs of holy affections, which God implanted in her womanly bosom, having been stifled by social necessities, now burn sullenly to waste, like sepulchral lamps amongst the ancients; every nun defrauded of her unreturning May-time by wicked kinsman, whom God will judge; every captive in every dungeon; all that are betrayed, and all that are rejected; outcasts by traditionary law, and children of *hereditary* disgrace: all these walk with Our Lady of Sighs. She also carries a key; but she needs it little. For her kingdom is chiefly amongst the tents of Shem,[18] and the houseless vagrant of every clime. Yet in the very highest ranks of man she finds chapels of her own; and even in glorious England there are some that, to the world, carry their heads as proudly as the reindeer, who yet secretly have received her mark upon their foreheads.

But the third Sister, who is also the youngest ——! Hush! whisper whilst we talk of *her!* Her kingdom is not large, or else no flesh should live; but within that kingdom all power is hers. Her head, turreted like that of Cybele,[19] rises almost beyond the reach of sight. She droops not; and her eyes, rising so high, *might* be hidden by distance. But, being what they are, they cannot be hidden: through the treble veil of crape which she wears the fierce light of a blazing misery, that rests not for matins or for vespers, for noon of day or noon of night, for ebbing or for flowing tide, may be read from the very ground. She is the defier of God. She also is the mother of lunacies, and the suggestress of suicides. Deep lie the roots of her power; but narrow is the nation that she rules. For she can approach only those in whom a profound nature has been upheaved by central convulsions; in whom the heart trembles and the brain rocks under conspiracies of tempest from without and tempest from within. Madonna moves with uncertain steps, fast or slow, but still with tragic grace. Our Lady of Sighs creeps timidly and stealthily. But this youngest Sister moves with incalculable motions, bounding, and with tiger's leaps. She carries no key; for, though coming rarely amongst men, she storms all doors at which she is permitted to enter at all. And *her* name is *Mater Tenebrarum,*—Our Lady of Darkness.

These were the *Semnai Theai,* or Sublime Goddesses, these were the *Eumenides*[20] or Gracious Ladies (so called by antiquity in shuddering propitiation) of my Oxford dreams. Madonna spoke. She spoke by her mysterious hand. Touching my head, she beckoned to Our Lady of Sighs; and *what* she spoke, translated out of the signs which (except in dreams) no man reads, was this:—

"Lo! here is he whom in childhood I dedicated to my altars. This is he that once I made my darling. Him I led astray, him I beguiled; and from heaven I stole away his young heart to mine. Through me did he become idolatrous; and through me it was, by languishing desires, that he worshipped the worm, and prayed to the wormy grave. Holy was the grave to him; lovely was its darkness; saintly its corruption. Him, this young idolater, I have seasoned for thee, dear gentle Sister of Sighs! Do thou take him now to *thy* heart, and season him for our dreadful sister. And thou,"—turning to the *Mater Tenebrarum,* she said—"wicked sister, that temptest and hatest, do thou take him from *her.* See that thy sceptre lie heavy on his head. Suffer not woman and her tenderness to sit near him in his darkness. Banish the frailties of hope; wither the relenting of love; scorch the fountains of tears; curse him as only *thou* canst curse. So shall he be accomplished in the furnace; so shall he see the things that ought *not* to be seen, sights that are abominable, and secrets that are unutterable. So shall he read elder truths, sad truths, grand truths, fearful truths. So shall he rise again *before* he dies. And so shall our commission be accomplished which from God we had,—to plague his heart until we had unfolded the capacities of his spirit."

---

[16] Between New Caledonia and New Zealand. It was once a penal settlement.

[17] De Quincey's note: "This, the reader will be aware, applies chiefly to the cotton and tobacco States of North America; but not to them only: on which account I have not scrupled to figure the sun which looks down upon slavery as *tropical*—no matter if strictly within the tropics, or simply so near to them as to produce a similar climate."

[18] Eldest son of Noah, and reputed ancestor of the nomadic tribes.

[19] A mother and earth goddess of Asia Minor, with whom the Greek Rhea became identified. Cybele, who was also worshipped in Rome, was represented wearing a turreted crown.

[20] A euphemistic name for the Furies of Greek mythology. Their business was vengeance, and driving their victims mad.

LITERATURE OF KNOWLEDGE AND LITERATURE OF POWER

In "Letters to a Young Man Whose Education Has Been Neglected" (*London Magazine,* 1823) De Quincey first expounded the central idea of the following selection, which for the sake of convenience editors have entitled "Literature of Knowledge and Literature of Power." A full comprehension of this distinction and its importance is likely to be a milestone in any reader's intellectual development; De Quincey acknowledges that it was enforced on him by his long association with Wordsworth. The passage constitutes less than one-seventh of a review of a new edition of Pope, in the *North British Review* for August, 1848. De Quincey reprinted the review as an essay in his collected works under the title "Alexander Pope." With one exception, his footnotes have been omitted from the present text.

... WHAT is it that we mean by *literature*? Popularly, and amongst the thoughtless, it is held to include everything that is printed in a book. Little logic is required to disturb *that* definition. The most thoughtless person is easily made aware that in the idea of *literature* one essential element is some relation to a general and common interest of man,—so that what applies only to a local, or professional, or merely personal interest, even though presenting itself in the shape of a book, will not belong to Literature. So far the definition is easily narrowed; and it is as easily expanded. For not only is much that takes a station in books not literature; but inversely, much that really *is* literature never reaches a station in books. The weekly sermons of Christendom, that vast pulpit literature which acts so extensively upon the popular mind—to warn, to uphold, to renew, to comfort, to alarm—does not attain the sanctuary of libraries in the ten-thousandth part of its extent. The Drama again,—as, for instance, the finest part of Shakspere's plays in England, and all leading Athenian plays in the noontide of the Attic[1] stage,— operated as a literature on the public mind, and were (according to the strictest letter of that term) *published* through the audiences that witnessed their representation some time before they were published as things to be read; and they were published in this scenical mode of publication with much more effect than they could have had as books during ages of costly copying or of costly printing.

Books, therefore, do not suggest an idea coextensive and interchangeable with the idea of Literature; since much literature, scenic, forensic,[2] or didactic (as from lecturers and public orators), may never come into books, and much that *does* come into books may connect itself with no literary interest. But a far more important correction, applicable to the common vague idea of literature, is to be sought not so much in a better definition of literature as in a sharper distinction of the two functions which it fulfils. In that great social organ which, collectively, we call literature, there may be distinguished two separate offices that may blend and often *do* so, but capable, severally, of a severe insulation, and naturally fitted for reciprocal repulsion. There is, first, the literature of *knowledge;* and, secondly, the literature of *power.* The function of the first is—to *teach;* the function of the second is—to *move:* the first is a rudder; the second, an oar or a sail. The first speaks to the *mere* discursive understanding; the second speaks ultimately, it may happen, to the higher understanding or reason, but always *through* affections[3] of pleasure and sympathy. Remotely, it may travel towards an object seated in what Lord Bacon calls *dry* light;[4] but, proximately, it does and must operate,—else it ceases to be a literature of *power,*— on and through that *humid* light which clothes itself in the mists and glittering *iris*[5] of human passions, desires, and genial emotions.

Men have so little reflected on the higher functions of literature as to find it a paradox if one should describe it as a mean or subordinate purpose of books to give information. But this is a paradox only in the sense which makes it honourable to be paradoxical. Whenever we talk in ordinary language of seeking information or gaining knowledge, we understand the words as connected with something of absolute novelty. But it is the grandeur of all truth which *can* occupy a very high place in human interests that it is never absolutely novel to the meanest of minds: it exists eternally by way of germ or latent principle in the lowest as in the highest, needing to be developed, but never to be planted. To be capable of transplantation is the immediate criterion of a truth that ranges on a lower scale. Besides which, there is a rarer thing than truth,—namely, *power,* or deep sympathy with truth. What is the effect, for instance,

---

[3] Feelings.
[4] "The light that a man receiveth by counsel from another is drier and purer than that which cometh from his own understanding and judgment; which is ever infused and drenched in his affections and customs" (Bacon's essay "Of Friendship"). See also above, I, 415, note 25 and the passage to which it refers.
[5] Rainbow.

---

[1] I.e., Athenian.   [2] Argumentative.

upon society, of children? By the pity, by the tenderness, and by the peculiar modes of admiration, which connect themselves with the helplessness, with the innocence, and with the simplicity of children, not only are the primal affections strengthened and continually renewed, but the qualities which are dearest in the sight of heaven,—the frailty, for instance, which appeals to forbearance, the innocence which symbolises the heavenly, and the simplicity which is most alien from the worldly,—are kept up in perpetual remembrance, and their ideals are continually refreshed. A purpose of the same nature is answered by the higher literature, viz. the literature of power. What do you learn from "Paradise Lost"? Nothing at all. What do you learn from a cookery-book? Something new, something that you did not know before, in every paragraph. But would you therefore put the wretched cookery-book on a higher level of estimation than the divine poem? What you owe to Milton is not any knowledge, of which a million separate items are still but a million of advancing steps on the same earthly level; what you owe is *power,*—that is, exercise and expansion to your own latent capacity of sympathy with the infinite, where every pulse and each separate influx is a step upwards, a step ascending as upon a Jacob's ladder[6] from earth to mysterious altitudes above the earth. *All* the steps of knowledge, from first to last, carry you further on the same plane, but could never raise you one foot above your ancient level of earth: whereas the very *first* step in power is a flight—is an ascending movement into another element where earth is forgotten.

Were it not that human sensibilities are ventilated and continually called out into exercise by the great phenomena of infancy, or of real life as it moves through chance and change, or of literature as it recombines these elements in the mimicries of poetry, romance, &c., it is certain that, like any animal power or muscular energy falling into disuse, all such sensibilities would gradually droop and dwindle. It is in relation to these great *moral* capacities of man that the literature of power, as contradistinguished from that of knowledge, lives and has its field of action. It is concerned with what is highest in man; for the Scriptures themselves never condescended to deal by suggestion or co-operation with the mere discursive understanding: when speaking of man in his intellectual capacity, the Scriptures speak not of the understanding, but of *"the understanding heart,"*[7]—

making the heart, i.e. the great *intuitive* (or non-discursive) organ, to be the interchangeable formula for man in his highest state of capacity for the infinite. Tragedy, romance, fairy tale, or epopee,[8] all alike restore to man's mind the ideals of justice, of hope, of truth, of mercy, of retribution, which else (left to the support of daily life in its realities) would languish for want of sufficient illustration.

What is meant, for instance, by *poetic justice?*—It does not mean a justice that differs by its object from the ordinary justice of human jurisprudence; for then it must be confessedly a very bad kind of justice; but it means a justice that differs from common forensic justice by the degree in which it *attains* its object, a justice that is more omnipotent over its own ends, as dealing—not with the refractory elements of earthly life, but with the elements of its own creation, and with materials flexible to its own purest preconceptions. It is certain that, were it not for the Literature of Power, these ideals would often remain amongst us as mere arid notional forms; whereas, by the creative forces of man put forth in literature, they gain a vernal life of restoration, and germinate into vital activities. The commonest novel, by moving in alliance with human fears and hopes, with human instincts of wrong and right, sustains and quickens those affections. Calling them into action, it rescues them from torpor. And hence the pre-eminency over all authors that merely *teach* of the meanest that *moves,* or that teaches, if at all, indirectly *by* moving. The very highest work that has ever existed in the Literature of Knowledge is but a *provisional* work: a book upon trial and sufferance, and *quamdiu bene se gesserit.*[9] Let its teaching be even partially revised, let it be but expanded,—nay, even let its teaching be but placed in a better order,—and instantly it is superseded. Whereas the feeblest works in the Literature of Power, surviving at all, survive as finished and unalterable amongst men. For instance, the *Principia* of Sir Isaac Newton[10] was a book *militant* on earth from the first. In all stages of its progress it would have to fight for its existence: 1st, as regards absolute truth; 2dly, when that combat was over, as regards its form or mode of presenting the truth. And as soon as a La Place,[11] or anybody else, builds higher upon the foundations laid by this book, effectually he throws it out of the sunshine into decay and darkness; by weapons won from this book he superannuates and destroys this book, so

---

[6] In a dream Jacob saw a ladder connecting earth and heaven (Genesis 28:12 ff.).   [7] 1 Kings 3:9, 12.

[8] Epic poem.   [9] As long as it behaves itself.
[10] In which (1687) he expounded his theory of gravitation.
[11] The Marquis Pierre Simon de Laplace (1749–1827), French astronomer and mathematician.

that soon the name of Newton remains as a mere *nominis umbra*,[12] but his book, as a living power, has transmigrated into other forms. Now, on the contrary, the Iliad, the Prometheus[13] of Aeschylus, the Othello or King Lear, the Hamlet or Macbeth, and the Paradise Lost, are not militant but triumphant[14] for ever, as long as the languages exist in which they speak or can be taught to speak. They never *can* transmigrate into new incarnations. To reproduce *these* in new forms, or variations, even if in some things they should be improved, would be to plagiarise. A good steam-engine is properly superseded by a better. But one lovely pastoral valley is not superseded by another, nor a statue of Praxiteles by a statue of Michael Angelo. These things are separated not by imparity but by disparity.[15] They are not thought of as unequal under the same standard, but as different in *kind,* and, if otherwise equal, as equal under a different standard. Human works of immortal beauty and works of nature in one respect stand on the same footing: they never absolutely repeat each other, never approach so near as not to differ; and they differ not as better and worse, or simply by more and less: they differ by undecipherable and incommunicable differences, that cannot be caught by mimicries, that cannot be reflected in the mirror of copies, that cannot become ponderable in the scales of vulgar comparison. . . .

At this hour, five hundred years since their creation, the tales of Chaucer, never equalled on this earth for their tenderness, and for life of picturesqueness, are read familiarly by many in the charming language of their natal day, and by others in the modernisations of Dryden, of Pope, and Wordsworth. At this hour, one thousand eight hundred years since their creation, the Pagan tales of Ovid, never equalled on this earth for the gaiety of their movement and the capricious graces of their narrative, are read by all Christendom.

This man's people and their monuments are dust; but *he* is alive: he has survived them, as he told us that he had it in his commission to do, by a thousand years; "and *shall* a thousand more."

All the literature of knowledge builds only ground-nests, that are swept away by floods, or confounded by the plough; but the literature of power builds nests in aerial altitudes of temples sacred from violation, or of forests inaccessible to fraud. *This* is a great prerogative of the *power* literature; and it is a greater which lies in the mode of its influence. The *knowledge* literature, like the fashion of this world, passeth away. An Encyclopaedia is its abstract; and, in this respect, it may be taken for its speaking symbol—that before one generation has passed an Encylopaedia is superannuated; for it speaks through the dead memory and unimpassioned understanding, which have not the repose of higher faculties, but are continually enlarging and varying their phylacteries.[16] But all literature properly so called—literature κατ' ἐξοχήν,[17] —for the very reason that it is so much more durable than the literature of knowledge, is (and by the very same proportion it is) more intense and electrically searching in its impressions. The directions in which the tragedy of this planet has trained our human feelings to play, and the combinations into which the poetry of this planet has thrown our human passions of love and hatred, of admiration and contempt, exercise a power for bad or good over human life that cannot be contemplated, when stretching through many generations, without a sentiment allied to awe.[18] And of this let every one be assured—that he owes to the impassioned books which he has read many a thousand more of emotions than he can consciously trace back to them. Dim by their origination, these emotions yet arise in him, and mould him through life, like forgotten incidents of his childhood. . . .

---

12 Shadow of a name.

13 One of the great Greek tragedies of the fifth century B.C.

14 Cf. the "Church militant" and "Church triumphant"; i.e., on earth, and eternal.

15 Not by being unequal but by being different.—Praxiteles (fourth century B.C.) and Michelangelo Buonarroti (d. 1564) were among the greatest of sculptors.

16 Small boxes containing certain passages from the Scriptures, worn by the Jews on the head and left arm during prayer.

17 Par excellence, i.e., pre-eminently such.

18 De Quincey's note: "The reason why the broad distinctions between the two literatures of power and knowledge so little fix the attention lies in the fact that a vast proportion of books,—history, biography, travels, miscellaneous essays, &c.,—lying in a middle zone, confound these distinctions, by interblending them. All that we call 'amusement' or 'entertainment' is a diluted form of the power belonging to passion, and also a mixed form; and, where threads of direct *instruction* intermingle in the texture with these threads of *power,* this absorption of the duality into one representative *nuance* neutralises the separate perception of either. Fused into a *tertium quid,* or neutral state, they disappear to the popular eye as the repelling forces which, in fact, they are."

George Gordon, Lord Byron

1788-1824

In ENGLAND Byron's literary reputation is still clouded by disapproval of his private life. There is in his case more excuse than usual for such confusion of relevancies and irrelevancies. With making his private life public he had himself a good deal to do. In him, along with genius, was a strong tendency to exhibitionism; and a poet who lends his poetry to the exposition of his own maladjustments has only himself to thank if notoriety as well as fame attaches to his memory. In forming judgments about an artist's contributions, an adult mind will discriminate between a man's personal lapses into falsity, insincerity, and bad taste, even if these weaknesses are occasionally reflected in his art, and the fidelity, truth, and integrity which mark his best work and must therefore, however latent or even distorted, form an element in his character. To deny this principle is to exalt theory above experience.

Whether Byron's most devastating troubles were beyond his control is a question for theologians and psychologists, since it involves the extent to which the will is or is not free. Certainly there were some wild characters among his forebears, and he had a bad bringing up. He was born in London in 1788. His father, who died when Byron was three, had been a captain in a Guards regiment. A dashing libertine, he had married two heiresses and spent their money. Byron's mother, deserted as soon as her fortune vanished, was a Scotch tartar. His guardian could not abide her, and saw as little as possible of her and the boy. Mrs. Byron, who drank more than was good for her, alternately caressed her son and taunted him with being a "lame brat." Precisely what was wrong with his foot or feet is uncertain. Whatever it was, it did not keep him from being an athlete—he boxed, fenced, and swam, and he was a dead shot; but he could not dance, and his walk was a running glide, almost on tiptoe. He suffered tortures at the hands of a clumsy quack who tried to cure him; but no one was able to correct the deformity.

Byron lived with his mother in shabby gentility at Aberdeen till he was ten, when the death of a great-uncle made him sixth Baron Byron. Educated at Harrow and Cambridge, he was still an undergraduate when he brought out his first volume, republished a few months later, revised and enlarged, under a new title, *Hours of Idleness* (1807). It was pounced on by the *Edinburgh Review* and cut up unmercifully. Byron was deeply offended, but not crushed. His retaliation, carefully prepared, was the sparkling satire *English Bards, and Scotch Reviewers,* which appeared in 1809.

In the same year Byron went abroad with a college friend for two years of travel. The war with Napoleon barred the customary Grand Tour; so they went to the Near East, by way of Portugal, Spain, Sardinia, and Malta. Byron visited a Turkish pasha in Albania, stayed in Athens, saw the ruins of Troy, swam the Dardanelles, and then went back to Greece alone. After a bout with a fever, he came home in 1811 looking and feeling thoroughly "Byronic"—the adjective has remained in circulation for one aspect of Romanticism. There were examples of the type before Byron; but in his actual life, in the pose he adopted, and in the first two cantos of *Childe Harold*—he had brought them back, along with some lyrics, from his Oriental adventuring—he fixed once and for all the Byronic image: a youthful hero of soaring spirit, intrepid but extravagantly moody, reckless, defiant of convention, equally capable of raptures and cynicism, sensitive, melancholy, pale, and "interesting." At a certain age, most talented young men go through a period of feeling that way or at least of hoping people will think they do. Maturity and common sense ordinarily put an end to the symptoms; but anyone who finds the mood or pose gratifying to his ego can, by giving way to it, allow it to become habitual. Byron coddled it, with disastrous results to himself and others.

His mother, whom he disliked, died a few weeks after his return. The publication in 1812 of *Childe Harold,* Cantos I and II, made him in a single day one of the most famous men in London. In three days the edition was sold out. Oddly enough, since he won his notoriety by flouting conventions, there was a substratum of neoclassicism in Byron's art. Instinctively he rejected the poetry of Wordsworth and Coleridge, praising Milton, Dryden, and Pope. Yet his own restlessness, as well as the temper of the times, drove him to Romanticism, despite his declaration in a letter to his publisher that "the more I think of it . . . *all* of us—Scott, Southey, Wordsworth, Moore, Campbell, I—are . . . upon a wrong revolutionary poetical system or systems, not worth a damn in itself."

Wrong or right, his literary glory was accompanied by an immense personal success. Eventually English high society turned savagely against him; but both before and after that revulsion, all he wrote was eagerly devoured. Young men of sensibility on the Continent and across the

Atlantic, as well as in Great Britain, aped the Byronic attitudes. As for women, they groveled at his feet. Byron was young; Byron was a lord; Byron was more than handsome, he was beautiful; Byron was masculine, yet equipped with a heart as responsive to feeling as any woman's—and he liked to put that heart on display, as if to demonstrate that a boundless capacity for suffering proved greatness of soul. He was partly the victim of a vogue as well as a co-founder. Before Byron was born, the hero of Goethe's novel *The Sorrows of Werther* had enchanted the public by going off into fits and spasms of delicious woe.

If Byron had resisted self-indulgence and stopped posing, his might have been a happier story. For at bottom he was a serious man. He had already taken his seat in the House of Lords and made several speeches. His maiden effort was against a bill imposing the death penalty on factory workers whose fear of losing their jobs had led to an epidemic of machine smashing. Byron was no Leveler; he was even a snob concerning the length of his pedigree. But he took the liberal-Whig side; and his second speech espoused another reform cause, Catholic Emancipation. Drury Lane, the principal London theater, was at the moment under management by a committee. Byron was elected to its membership and worked hard. None of these activities nor any of his dissipations was, however, allowed to divert him from his main business in the world. To poetry, amid many inconstancies, he remained throughout his life constant. While some would have it that, like a number of the neoclassicists he admired, Byron was merely an accomplished versifier, no one disputes that Byron has a large body of work to show for a life of only thirty-six years.

Drawing on his travels, he followed up his initial hit with some superficial but energetic Oriental poems which drove Scott from the field of narrative verse as decisively as Wellington and Blücher were soon to send Napoleon reeling from the field of Waterloo. 1813-14 saw the publication of *The Giaour, The Bride of Abydos, The Corsair,* and *Lara. Hebrew Melodies,* containing several of his best lyrics, appeared in 1815. The narrative poems sold enormously, but already a satanic saga was in whispered circulation about their author. There were rumors of amorous episodes, not all of which conformed to the pattern of Regency intrigue. No one was shocked that some were with ladies of very high position—a notable step upward from the harem of housemaids he had maintained, before he went traveling, at his decaying baronial seat of Newstead Abbey in Nottinghamshire. But full of danger, though certain public knowledge of it came long after Byron's death, was his incestuous passion for his half sister, Augusta Leigh, by whom he

probably had a daughter. Mrs. Leigh was four years older than her brother and unhappily married. Even this affair became known to some of his intimates; and Byron took a perverse delight in dropping hints of his abysmal wickedness, in conversation, letters, and poems. He was far too self-centered to be capable of experiencing the fullness of love; but Augusta came nearer than anyone else, or at any rate he thought she did, to being the love of his life. In spite of all his defiances, he was none the less haunted by a sense of guilt, which his early Calvinistic training no doubt intensified. Loving Augusta, he was embittered by the frustration imposed by the world's code. She was an easygoing, good-natured person without morals; but she saw that continued intimacy was likely to wreck them both. Accordingly, she urged him to marry and settle down.

He had already proposed, before his liaison with Augusta, to Anne Isabella Milbanke, and been disappointed. Two years later he renewed his proposal, immediately after rejection by another lady. The renewal was not because he was in love; he thought marriage the likeliest solution of his problem. When Miss Milbanke promptly accepted, he felt trapped. That maddening sensation accounts for the extreme mental cruelty he visited upon his unfortunate wife from the very day of their marriage, early in 1815. A serious girl, a student of mathematics, virtuous, proud, and firm of will, she was no mate for the wild Byron. Against her he held her failure to accept him the first time; had she done so, he told her, he would have been saved from a dreadful and irrevocable step. She was puzzled at first, but soon learned the truth. She was ready to ignore the past, but before long Augusta was under their roof and Lady Byron feared the worst. Early in 1816, after the birth of their daughter Ada, she had Byron medically examined and was informed that his actions could not be attributed to insanity. This report she accepted as confirmation of his essential wickedness; and having already returned with her baby to her parents' house, she declined to go back to her husband's.

Lady Byron did not make public her reasons, for one thing because she was and remained on friendly terms with Augusta and wished to avoid injuring her. Gossip ran riot; a storm of furious hostility broke round the poet. London society ostracized him. He had, besides, political enemies. His contempt for the loutish Prince Regent, soon to ascend the throne as George IV, had been openly expressed; by the Tories Byron was regarded as a subversive influence. To add to his troubles, he was tormented by the moneylenders from whom he had borrowed means for his extravagant mode of living. His properties, when he inherited them, were heavily encumbered; and for his early poems he refused to take any money. He was soon obliged to reverse that lofty stand, and to put Newstead Abbey on the market. About three months after his wife's departure, he consented to sign a separation agreement. A few days later he left England for ever. It was a corrosive experience, which he never got over. Even the print shops were doing a brisk business in caricatures depicting salient episodes of a life now held up to ridicule and condemnation. Byron did not see his wife and daughter again. The latter married the Earl of Lovelace; it was their son who in 1905, in the privately printed *Astarte,* finally set rumor at rest by publishing in justification of his grandmother the documents she and her advisers had left relating to Augusta and the separation.

Whether or not on account of the emotional pressures to which he had been subjected, the early months of Byron's life abroad witnessed a sudden growth in his poetic stature. He and his entourage made their way through the Low Countries and up the Rhine to Switzerland, where he encountered Shelley. This was prior to the suicide of Harriet, Shelley's first wife; he had eloped with Mary Wollstonecraft Godwin, whom he married as soon as he was free. In their household also resided Jane Clairmont, stepdaughter of Mary's father, William Godwin. Claire, as she preferred to be called, had insisted, before Byron left London, on becoming his mistress; she later bore him a daughter, Allegra.[1] The two poets saw much of each other and, being equally fond of boating, made together a complete circuit of the shores of Lake Geneva. It was now that Byron wrote "The Prisoner of Chillon," but of more importance is Canto III of *Childe Harold.* When Shelley returned to England with Mary and Claire, he took the manuscript with him and arranged for its publication. Byron later resumed his friendship with Shelley in Italy, till the latter's death intervened. Meanwhile he went from Switzerland to Venice, and thence to other Italian cities. Before the end of 1817 he had finished the fourth canto of *Childe Harold,* had written the drama *Manfred* with its enlargement of the Byronic hero, and in the satirical *Beppo* had begun to exploit a new vein. *Beppo* provides a slight foretaste of Byron's masterpiece, *Don Juan,* upon which he was at work by the autumn of 1818.

The year 1818 saw also the beginning of his final serious love affair. Unlike his others, this was begun in reasonable conformity with convention—the Italian convention which recognized, provided that all was dignified and without jealous scenes, the right of a young wife yoked with an elderly partner in a marriage of convenience to a *cavaliere servente* or lover-in-attendance. Still in her teens, the blonde Countess Teresa Guiccioli had a husband in his sixties. The wealthy Count acquiesced in an arrangement which society regarded as both inevitable and proper. Her love for Byron was unconcealed, and was accepted by her own family. For a while Byron came close with her to realizing the peace he had hoped his own marriage would bring. Eventually, however, Count Guiccioli took the lead in securing a Papal decree of separation. His motive was not so much resentment of his marital status—it was on his invitation that Byron was living in the Guiccioli palace at Ravenna —but alarm lest he become implicated in the revolutionary political schemes Byron was dabbling with. Nearly all of Italy was still under the Austrian heel, and the nationalistic aspirations of the aristocracy and intelligentsia enlisted the sympathy of liberals everywhere. At the Pope's insistence, Teresa returned in theory to her father Count Gamba; actually, her father soon came with her to live in Byron's establishment.

During the years from 1818 to 1823 the poetic power rose higher than ever. Aside from the incomparable *Don,* the best of the longer productions were the drama *Cain* and the brilliant satire *The Vision of Judgment* (both 1822). Byron also wrote, since it is by such means that an exile keeps his friends, some of the best letters ever penned. They scintillate with humor and wit; they are as nearly alive as it is possible for written words to be. But by 1823 he was thoroughly discontented again. Money was now plentiful, and he knew he was writing as well as ever; but he was bored with writing and even with existence, and he had quite mistakenly got into his head the notion that his day with the reading public was over. The bread of self-imposed exile can taste as bitter as any, and life has a way of neglecting to replenish cups drained too early. As for Teresa, Byron was honorably conscious of his obligations to her; but he no longer loved her—he had, in fact, opposed her severance from her husband. When at last he left her, it was not for another woman but for the cause of Greek independence.

The Greeks having risen against their Turkish masters, a committee to aid them had been formed in London. Byron's poetic reproaches of Greek submission had done more than anything else to arouse European sympathy. He was elected to membership on the committee and volunteered to serve as its agent in the field. Southern and western Greece were largely in the hands of the patriots; but the Turks were certain to renew the struggle, and meanwhile independence was jeopardized by

---

[1] Byron later had Allegra with him in Italy. When she was four, he entrusted her, wisely as it seemed, to the sisters of a convent. Claire was then in Italy, demanding to see her child; but Byron detested his former mistress, thought the "atheistic" Shelleyan and Godwinian background unsuitable for his daughter, and harshly refused even to correspond with her mother. The sequel was tragic. Allegra died at the convent in the spring of 1822 during a fever epidemic.

the Greeks' inability to unite and establish a government. Byron sailed from Genoa in midsummer, entertaining no illusions but "hoping to do some good " He spent the fall on the island of Cephalonia off the Gulfs of Patras and Corinth; rightly wary of the various factions' eagerness to see the color of his money, he was calmly sizing up the situation. In January, 1824, he went over to the mainland; and there, at the bug-infested, fever-ridden town of Missolonghi, he spent the last three months allotted him. Since the Turks held a number of fortresses, he began organizing an artillery brigade for their reduction. He also had five hundred Greek infantry-men who, though unwilling to serve under any native commander, were not averse to taking orders and pay from the rich English milord.

Though Byron was the general, it was not his fault that nothing was accomplished. His grasp of practical problems was more intelligent and less visionary than that of the professional soldier sent out as adviser by the London committee. There was no one, Greek, English, or German—the volunteers included several nationalities —on whom he could rely for both competence and loyalty to the cause. He was himself in bad health from anxiety and drinking, and the two young doctors on his staff were of little use. Friends urged him to withdraw and recuperate; but by then, as Mr. Nicolson says, Byron knew the only thing he could do for Greece was not to run away. That is why his death in April was heroic. He stuck to the post where he conceived his duty lay,

struggling with countless difficulties, military, financial, and political. Hope vanished, but he kept his nerve. When the town was threatened with assault he marched his brigade out as cool and steady as you please. The cause of his death was certified by his physicians as rheumatic fever induced by a chill caught while riding in a heavy downpour, but there is some reason to think it may have been typhoid or malaria. Contrary to his expressed wish, his body was shipped home to England instead of being buried in Greece.

Byron's publisher was John Murray II (1778-1843), whose father founded in 1768 the firm which still publishes the standard edition (13 vols., 1898-1904), the poetry (7 vols.) edited by E. H. Coleridge, the letters and journals (6 vols.) by R. E. Prothero [Lord Ernle]. There is a one-volume condensation of this edition of the poems. Two volumes of additional correspondence were later edited by Sir John Murray IV (1922). Selected editions of the poetry are numerous. Everyman's Library has the poems and plays in three volumes, and a volume of letters. In 1830 Byron's friend, the poet Thomas Moore, laid the foundations on which all subsequent biographies have been constructed. Three recent books comprise an excellent account of the life: P. Quennell's *Byron, The Years of Fame* (1935) and *Byron in Italy* (1941), and H. Nicolson's *Byron, The Last Journey* (1924). They do not entirely supersede Ethel C. Mayne's biography (revised ed., 2 vols., 1924). C. M. Fuess's *Lord Byron as a Satirist in Verse* (1912) is a useful study.

George Gordon, Lord Byron

from ENGLISH BARDS, AND SCOTCH REVIEWERS

BYRON was only nineteen when, in 1807, he was at work on a satire he intended to call *British Bards;* it was to be an attack on some contemporary poets. In January, 1808, the *Edinburgh Review* came out with a castigation of Byron's *Hours of Idleness* so severe that, as he afterwards acknowledged, it "knocked me down, but," he added, "I got up again." His method of regaining his feet and striking back was to make a careful revision and expansion of his satirical poem. It was published anonymously (though everyone knew it was Byron's) in March, 1809, and was an immediate success. Byron kept on adding and repolishing; an enlarged second edition appeared under his name in October. By 1812 a fifth was ready, extending to 1070 lines. Meanwhile Byron had returned from his adventures in the Levant, and was on friendly

terms with the Whig leaders Lord and Lady Holland, who are roughly handled in the poem as instigators of the *Edinburgh's* partisan reviewing. Byron suddenly ordered the whole fifth edition burned. Fortunately a few copies escaped, to form the basis of the standard text.

In time Byron repented a number of other rash judgments and expressions; but although the poem is uneven and he was to go far beyond it, he had written the best verse satire since Pope, whose *Dunciad* was its model. Wrong as he was (and when he was older knew he was) on Wordsworth and Coleridge, most of his victims deserved all they got. Quite aside from the chagrin of realizing too late that one has failed to discern great merit, there can be small satisfaction for a genius in the easy trouncing of mediocrity. "The greater part of this satire," Byron noted in 1816 in a copy of the fourth edition, "I most sincerely wish had never been written— not only on account of the injustice of much of the critical, and some of the personal part of it—but the tone and temper are such as I cannot approve." For all that, a good deal of the poem is still excellent fun; and Byron's regrets are not shared by his readers.

Still must I hear?—shall hoarse Fitzgerald[1] bawl
His creaking couplets in a tavern hall,
And I not sing, lest, haply, Scotch Reviews
Should dub me scribbler, and denounce my Muse?
Prepare for rhyme—I'll publish, right or wrong: 5
Fools are my theme; let Satire be my song. . . .

I, too, can scrawl, and once upon a time
I poured along the town a flood of rhyme,
A schoolboy freak, unworthy praise or blame;
I printed—older children do the same.   50
'Tis pleasant, sure, to see one's name in print;
A Book's a Book, altho' there's nothing in't. . . .

A man must serve his time to every trade
Save Censure[2]—Critics all are ready made.
Take hackneyed jokes from Miller,[3] got by rote,   65
With just enough of learning to misquote;
A mind well skilled to find, or forge, a fault;
A turn for punning—call it Attic salt;[4]
To Jeffrey[5] go, be silent and discreet,
His pay is just ten sterling pounds per sheet:[6]   70
Fear not to lie, 'twill seem a *sharper* hit;
Shrink not from blasphemy, 'twill pass for wit;
Care not for feeling—pass your proper jest,
And stand a Critic, hated yet caressed. . . .

Behold! in various throngs the scribbling crew,
For notice eager, pass in long review:
Each spurs his jaded Pegasus[7] apace,   145
And Rhyme and Blank maintain an equal race;
Sonnets on sonnets crowd, and ode on ode;
And Tales of Terror[8] jostle on the road;

Immeasurable measures[9] move along;
For simpering Folly loves a varied song,   150
To strange, mysterious Dulness still the friend,
Admires the strain she cannot comprehend.
Thus Lays of Minstrels[10]—may they be the last!—
On half-strung harps whine mournful to the blast.
While mountain spirits prate to river sprites,   155
That dames may listen to the sound at nights;
And goblin brats, of Gilpin Horner's[11] brood,
Decoy young Border-nobles through the wood,
And skip at every step, Lord knows how high,
And frighten foolish babes, the Lord knows why;   160
While high-born ladies in their magic cell,
Forbidding Knights to read who cannot spell,
Despatch a courier to a wizard's grave,
And fight with honest men to shield a knave.

Next view in state, proud prancing on his roan,   165
The golden-crested haughty Marmion,[12]
Now forging scrolls, now foremost in the fight,
Not quite a Felon, yet but half a Knight,
The gibbet or the field prepare to grace—
A mighty mixture of the great and base.   170
And think'st thou, Scott! by vain conceit perchance,
On public taste to foist thy stale romance,
Though Murray with his Miller[13] may combine
To yield thy muse just half-a-crown per line?
No! when the sons of song descend to trade,   175
Their bays[14] are sear, their former laurels fade.
Let such forgo the poet's sacred name,
Who rack their brains for lucre, not for fame:
Still for stern Mammon[15] may they toil in vain!
And sadly gaze on gold they cannot gain!   180
Such be their meed, such still the just reward
Of prostituted Muse and hireling bard!
For this we spurn Apollo's[16] venal son,
And bid a long "good night to Marmion."[17]

These are the themes that claim our plaudits now;   185
These are the Bards to whom the Muse must bow;

---

1 William Thomas Fitzgerald (c. 1759–1829), a poetaster who went about reciting his verses.   2 Criticism.
3 The name of Joe Miller (1684–1738), a low-comedian at Drury Lane, was without warrant attached to a collection of jokes compiled by John Mottley (1739). It had a long life.
4 Pungent wit.
5 Francis Jeffrey (1773–1850), founder and editor (1803–29) of the *Edinburgh Review;* subsequently a judge of Scotland's supreme court. He was hostile to the new poetry, and began his famous review of Wordsworth's *Excursion,* "This will never do."
6 Not of manuscript; the single piece of paper on which a number of pages are printed. In an octavo book there are sixteen pages to the sheet, eight on each side.
7 The winged horse, symbol of poetic inspiration.
8 The Gothic novelist, Matthew Gregory ("Monk") Lewis, brought out a collection thus entitled in 1799.

9 A hit at the varied meters used by the new poets.
10 Scott's first metrical romance, *The Lay of the Last Minstrel* (see p. 345, below).
11 Who figures in a border legend Scott had thought of using for a ballad before he decided to write another full-length romance.
12 See p. 345, below.
13 The Edinburgh publisher Constable paid Scott a thousand guineas for *Marmion.* Two London publishers, John Murray II and William Miller, bought quarter-shares from Constable.
14 Leaves of a kind of laurel, and hence a symbol of poetic distinction.
15 In the New Testament the demon of lust for riches.
16 God of poetry.   17 Canto VI, stanza xxviii, line 26.

While Milton, Dryden, Pope, alike forgot,
Resign their hallowed Bays to Walter Scott.[18]

The time has been, when yet the Muse was young,
When Homer swept the lyre, and Maro[19] sung,　　190
An Epic scarce ten centuries could claim,[20]
While awe-struck nations hailed the magic name:
The work of each immortal Bard appears
The single wonder of a thousand years.
Empires have mouldered from the face of earth,　　195
Tongues have expired with those who gave them birth,
Without the glory such a strain can give,
As even in ruin bids the language live.
Not so with us, though minor Bards content,
On one great work a life of labour spent:　　200
With eagle pinion soaring to the skies,
Behold the Ballad-monger Southey[21] rise!
To him let Camoëns, Milton, Tasso[22] yield,
Whose annual strains, like armies, take the field.
First in the ranks see Joan of Arc advance,　　205
The scourge of England and the boast of France!
Though burnt by wicked Bedford[23] for a witch,
Behold her statue placed in Glory's niche;
Her fetters burst, and just released from prison,
A virgin Phoenix[24] from her ashes risen.　　210
Next see tremendous Thalaba[25] come on,
Arabia's monstrous, wild, and wond'rous son;
Domdaniel's[26] dread destroyer, who o'erthrew
More mad magicians than the world e'er knew.
Immortal Hero! all thy foes o'ercome,　　215
For ever reign—the rival of Tom Thumb![27]
Since startled Metre fled before thy face,
Well wert thou doomed the last of all thy race!

Well might triumphant Genii bear thee hence,
Illustrious conqueror of common sense!　　220
Now, last and greatest, Madoc spreads his sails,
Cacique[28] in Mexico, and Prince in Wales;
Tells us strange tales, as other travellers do,
More old than Mandeville's,[29] and not so true.
Oh, Southey! Southey! cease thy varied song!　　225
A bard may chaunt too often and too long:
As thou art strong in verse, in mercy spare!
A fourth, alas! were more than we could bear.
But if, in spite of all the world can say,
Thou still wilt verseward plod thy weary way;[30]　　230
If still in Berkeley-Ballads most uncivil,
Thou wilt devote old women to the devil,[31]
The babe unborn thy dread intent may rue:
"God help thee,"[32] Southey, and thy readers too.

Next comes the dull disciple of thy school,　　235
That mild apostate from poetic rule,
The simple Wordsworth, framer of a lay
As soft as evening in his favourite May,
Who warns his friend "to shake off toil and trouble,
And quit his books, for fear of growing double";[33]　　240
Who, both by precept and example, shows
That prose is verse, and verse is merely prose;
Convincing all, by demonstration plain,
Poetic souls delight in prose insane;
And Christmas stories tortured into rhyme[34]　　245
Contain the essence of the true sublime.
Thus, when he tells the tale of Betty Foy,
The idiot mother of "an idiot Boy";
A moon-struck, silly lad, who lost his way,
And, like his bard, confounded night with day;[35]　　250
So close on each pathetic part he dwells,
And each adventure so sublimely tells,
That all who view the "idiot in his glory"[35]
Conceive the Bard the hero of the story.

Shall gentle Coleridge pass unnoticed here,　　255
To turgid ode and tumid stanza dear?
Though themes of innocence amuse him best,
Yet still Obscurity's a welcome guest.

[18] A dozen years later Byron wrote in his journal (Jan. 12, 1821): "Scott is certainly the most wonderful writer of the day. His novels are a new literature in themselves, and his poetry as good as any—if not better (only on an erroneous system). . . . I like him, too, for his manliness of character, for the extreme pleasantness of his conversation, and his good-nature to myself, personally. . . . I know no reading to which I fall with such alacrity as a work of W. Scott's."

[19] Vergil (Publius Vergilius Maro).

[20] Vergil (70–19 B.C.) lived at least nine centuries after Homer.

[21] For Robert Southey (1774–1843), not yet poet laureate, see pp. 354 ff., below. Southey wrote numerous ballads and epics.

[22] All justly famous epic poets. They lived, respectively, in sixteenth-century Portugal, seventeenth-century England, and sixteenth-century Italy.

[23] John of Lancaster (1389–1435), Duke of Bedford. He was an English general, uncle of Henry VI and regent; he delivered Joan to her executioners. Southey wrote an epic on her.

[24] The fabulous bird of Egyptian mythology.

[25] *Thalaba the Destroyer* and *Madoc* (line 221) were other epics by Southey.

[26] In Oriental story a magical meeting-place for wizards.

[27] Hero of Henry Fielding's famous burlesque, *The Tragedy of Tragedies, or The Life and Death of Tom Thumb the Great* (1730).

[28] Chief.

[29] Sir John Mandeville was the assumed name of an unknown compiler of a fourteenth-century book of travels.

[30] Cf. Gray's "Elegy," line 3, "The plowman homeward plods his weary way."

[31] In one of Southey's ballads, "The Old Woman of Berkeley," the Devil carries off the heroine.

[32] Southey, "The Soldier's Wife," line 3.

[33] Cf. the first stanza of "The Tables Turned," p. 47, above.—In his own copy of a later edition of his satire, Byron wrote "Unjust" in the margin of his lines on Wordsworth and Coleridge.

[34] See Wordsworth's "The Thorn."

[35] Cf. Wordsworth, "The Idiot Boy," line 452: "Thus answered Johnny in his glory."

If Inspiration should her aid refuse
To him who takes a Pixy for a muse,[36]
Yet none in lofty numbers can surpass
The bard who soars to elegize an ass:[37]
So well the subject suits his noble mind,
He brays, the Laureate of the long-eared kind. . . .

260

MAID OF ATHENS, ERE WE PART

Ζωή μου, σᾶς ἀγαπῶ

Maid of Athens,[1] ere we part,
Give, oh give me back my heart!
Or, since that has left my breast,
Keep it now, and take the rest!
Hear my vow before I go,
Ζωή μου, σᾶς ἀγαπῶ.[2]

5

By those tresses unconfined,
Wooed by each Aegean wind;
By those lids whose jetty fringe
Kiss thy soft cheeks' blooming tinge;
By those wild eyes like the roe,
Ζωή μου, σᾶς ἀγαπῶ.

10

By that lip I long to taste;
By that zone-encircled[3] waist;
By all the token-flowers that tell[4]
What words can never speak so well;
By Love's alternate joy and woe,
Ζωή μου, σᾶς ἀγαπῶ.

15

Maid of Athens! I am gone:
Think of me, sweet! when alone.
Though I fly to Istambol,
Athens holds my heart and soul:
Can I cease to love thee? No!
Ζωή μου, σᾶς ἀγαπῶ.

20

---

[36] Coleridge entitled an early ode "Songs of the Pixies."

[37] An early poem by Coleridge, not entirely successful but rather touching, is "To a Young Ass, Its Mother Being Tethered Near It."

[1] She is supposed to be Theresa Macri, eldest of the three daughters of the house where Byron lodged in Athens. She afterwards married an Englishman in the consular service.—Though inferior to Byron's best lyrics, this was long the most widely known. It was written in 1810.

[2] My life, I love you—"which," says Byron in a note, "sounds very prettily in all languages." Pronounce, in modern Greek (single *o* as in *stone*): Zó-ee moó, sahss áh-gah-pó.

[3] Girdled by belt or sash.   [4] In the "language of flowers."

from THE CORSAIR

The Corsair is the third of Byron's Oriental romances which in 1813–14 took London by storm. A large part of their fascination for the reading public sprang from the identification of the hero—who appears with only slightly varying lineaments in all—with Byron himself. The Byronic hero, whose preliminary portrait had been sketched in the first two cantos of *Childe Harold,* has literary antecedents, especially in the Gothic novels, but it was Byron who developed the figure in full detail, and highly influential it proved on innumerable heroes of poems, novels, and plays, not to mention young men, European and American, of taste and sensibility. The following excerpt from *The Corsair* is the description of the hero Conrad. For Byron's most mature handling of the type, the reader is advised to turn to two of his dramas, *Manfred* (1817) and *Cain* (1822), which are unfortunately too long to be reprinted here.

. . . That man of loneliness and mystery,
Scarce seen to smile and seldom heard to sigh;
Whose name appals the fiercest of his crew,
And tints each swarthy cheek with sallower hue;
Still sways their souls with that commanding art
That dazzles, leads, yet chills the vulgar heart.
What is that spell, that thus his lawless train
Confess and envy, yet oppose in vain?
What should it be that thus their faith can bind?
The power of Thought—the magic of the Mind!
Link'd with success, assumed and kept with skill,
That moulds another's weakness to its will;
Wields with their hands, but, still to these unknown,
Makes even their mightiest deeds appear his own.
Such hath it been—shall be—beneath the sun
The many still must labour for the one!
'Tis Nature's doom—but let the wretch who toils
Accuse not, hate not *him* who wears the spoils.
Oh! if he knew the weight of splendid chains,
How light the balance of his humbler pains!

175

180

185

190

Unlike the heroes of each ancient race,
Demons in act but Gods at least in face,
In Conrad's form seems little to admire,
Though his dark eyebrow shades a glance of fire;
Robust but not Herculean—to the sight
No giant frame sets forth his common height;
Yet, in the whole, who paused to look again,
Saw more than marks the crowd of vulgar men;
They gaze and marvel how—and still confess
That thus it is, but why they cannot guess.
Sunburnt his cheek, his forehead high and pale
The sable curls in wild profusion veil;
And oft perforce his rising lip reveals

195

200

205

The haughtier thought it curbs, but scarce conceals.
Though smooth his voice and calm his general mien,
Still seems there something he would not have seen:
His features' deepening lines and varying hue
At times attracted, yet perplex'd the view, 210
As if within that murkiness of mind
Work'd feelings fearful and yet undefined;
Such might it be—that none could truly tell—
Too close enquiry his stern glance would quell.
There breathe but few whose aspect might defy 215
The full encounter of his searching eye:
He had the skill, when Cunning's gaze would seek
To probe his heart and watch his changing cheek,
At once the observer's purpose to espy,
And on himself roll back his scrutiny, 220
Lest he to Conrad rather should betray
Some secret thought, than drag that chief's to day.
There was a laughing Devil in his sneer,
That raised emotions both of rage and fear;
And where his frown of hatred darkly fell, 225
Hope withering fled—and Mercy sigh'd farewell!

Slight are the outward signs of evil thought,
Within—within—'twas there the spirit wrought!
Love shows all changes—Hate, Ambition, Guile,
Betray no further than the bitter smile; 230
The lip's least curl, the lightest paleness thrown
Along the govern'd aspect, speak alone
Of deeper passions; and to judge their mien,
He, who would see, must be himself unseen.
Then—with the hurried tread, the upward eye, 235
The clenchèd hand, the pause of agony,
That listens, starting, lest the step too near
Approach intrusive on that mood of fear:
Then—with each feature working from the heart,
With feelings loosed to strengthen—not depart, 240
That rise—convulse—contend—that freeze or glow,
Flush in the cheek, or damp upon the brow;
Then—Stranger! if thou canst and tremblest not,
Behold his soul—the rest that soothes his lot!
Mark—how that lone and blighted bosom sears 245
The scathing thought of execrated years!
Behold—but who hath seen, or e'er shall see,
Man as himself—the secret spirit free?

Yet was not Conrad thus by Nature sent
To lead the guilty—guilt's worst instrument; 250
His soul was changed, before his deeds had driven
Him forth to war with man and forfeit heaven.
Warp'd by the world in Disappointment's school,
In words too wise, in conduct *there* a fool;
Too firm to yield, and far too proud to stoop, 255
Doom'd by his very virtues for a dupe,

He cursed those virtues as the cause of ill,
And not the traitors who betray'd him still;
Nor deem'd that gifts bestow'd on better men
Had left him joy, and means to give again. 260
Fear'd—shunn'd—belied—ere youth had lost her force,
He hated man too much to feel remorse
And thought the voice of wrath a sacred call,
To pay the injuries of some on all.
He knew himself a villain—but he deem'd 265
The rest no better than the thing he seem'd;
And scorn'd the best as hypocrites who hid
Those deeds the bolder spirit plainly did.
He knew himself detested, but he knew
The hearts that loathed him, crouch'd and dreaded too.
Lone, wild, and strange, he stood alike exempt 271
From all affection and from all contempt:
His name could sadden and his acts surprise,
But they that fear'd him dared not to despise.
Man spurns the worm, but pauses ere he wake 275
The slumbering venom of the folded snake:
The first may turn—but not avenge the blow;
The last expires—but leaves no living foe;
Fast to the doom'd offender's form it clings,
And he may crush—not conquer—still it stings! 280

None are all evil—quickening round his heart,
One softer feeling would not yet depart:
Oft could he sneer at others as beguiled
By passions worthy of a fool or child;
Yet 'gainst that passion vainly still he strove, 285
And even in him it asks the name of Love!
Yes, it was love—unchangeable—unchanged,
Felt but for one from whom he never ranged;
Though fairest captives daily met his eye,
He shunn'd, nor sought, but coldly pass'd them by; 290
Though many a beauty droop'd in prison'd bower,
None ever soothed his most unguarded hour.
Yes—it was love; if thoughts of tenderness,
Tried in temptation, strengthen'd by distress,
Unmoved by absence, firm in every clime, 295
And yet—Oh more than all!—untired by time;
Which nor defeated hope, nor baffled wile,
Could render sullen were she near to smile,
Nor rage could fire, nor sickness fret to vent
On her one murmur of his discontent; 300
Which still would meet with joy, with calmness part,
Lest that his look of grief should reach her heart:
Which nought removed, nor menaced to remove;—
If there be love in mortals—this was love!
He was a villain—ay—reproaches shower 305
On him—but not the passion, nor its power,
Which only proved, all other virtues gone,
Not guilt itself could quench this loveliest one! . . .

SHE WALKS IN BEAUTY

This beautiful lyric, and the piece which follows it, form part of a group called *Hebrew Melodies,* a title without any special application to some of the poems. Byron generously gave a number of his newest lyrics to a young composer, Isaac Nathan (1793–1864), who published them with settings adapted from old Jewish airs.

She walks in beauty,[5] like the night
   Of cloudless climes and starry skies;
And all that's best of dark and bright
   Meet in her aspect and her eyes:
Thus mellowed to that tender light   5
   Which heaven to gaudy day denies.

One shade the more, one ray the less,
   Had half impaired the nameless grace
Which waves in every raven tress,
   Or softly lightens o'er her face;   10
Where thoughts serenely sweet express,
   How pure, how dear their dwelling-place.

And on that cheek, and o'er that brow,
   So soft, so calm, yet eloquent,
The smiles that win, the tints that glow,   15
   But tell of days in goodness spent,
A mind at peace with all below,
   A heart whose love is innocent!

THE DESTRUCTION OF SENNACHERIB

The Assyrian[6] came down like the wolf on the fold,
And his cohorts were gleaming in purple and gold;
And the sheen of their spears was like stars on the sea,
When the blue wave rolls nightly on deep Galilee.

Like the leaves of the forest when Summer is green,   5
That host with their banners at sunset were seen:
Like the leaves of the forest when Autumn hath blown,
That host on the morrow lay withered and strown.

For the angel of Death spread his wings on the blast,
And breathed in the face of the foe as he passed;   10

And the eyes of the sleepers waxed deadly and chill,
And their hearts but once heaved—and for ever grew
   still!

And there lay the steed with his nostril all wide,
But through it there rolled not the breath of his pride;
And the foam of his gasping lay white on the turf,   15
And cold as the spray of the rock-beating surf.

And there lay the rider distorted and pale,
With the dew on his brow, and the rust on his mail;
And the tents were all silent—the banners alone—
The lances unlifted—the trumpet unblown.   20

And the widows of Ashur[7] are loud in their wail,
And the idols are broke in the temple of Baal;[8]
And the might of the Gentile, unsmote by the sword,
Hath melted like snow in the glance of the Lord!

WHEN WE TWO PARTED

Neither the date nor the occasion of this fine lyric is certain. It was first published in 1816.

When we two parted
   In silence and tears,
Half broken-hearted
   To sever for years,
Pale grew thy cheek and cold,   5
   Colder thy kiss;
Truly that hour foretold
   Sorrow to this.

The dew of the morning
   Sunk chill on my brow—   10
It felt like the warning
   Of what I feel now.
Thy vows are all broken,
   And light is thy fame:
I hear thy name spoken,   15
   And share in its shame.

They name thee before me,
   A knell to mine ear;
A shudder comes o'er me—
   Why wert thou so dear?   20
They know not I knew thee,
   Who knew thee too well:—
Long, long shall I rue thee,
   Too deeply to tell.

---

[5] Byron composed these lines the morning after seeing for the first time his second cousin's wife, the beautiful Mrs. Robert John Wilmot, at a party where she appeared in a mourning dress sewn with spangles.

[6] King Sennacherib of Assyria (d. 681 B.C.) conquered widely in the Middle East, and twice invaded Palestine (2 Kings 18:13 ff.). For the alleged destruction of his army by pestilence, see 2 Kings 19:35.

[7] Assyria.

[8] A favorite deity of various ancient peoples in the Middle East.

In secret we met— 25
   In silence I grieve,
That thy heart could forget,
   Thy spirit deceive.
If I should meet thee
   After long years, 30
How should I greet thee?—
   With silence and tears. *nile nepetether*

STANZAS FOR MUSIC

Byron wrote several poems with this title, but none of
the others equals this, which he composed in 1815. It
came out of a mood of melancholy inspired by his reflecting on how much less he was affected emotionally
than would once have been the case by the death of a
college friend, the Duke of Dorset, who was killed by a
fall from his horse while hunting.

There's not a joy the world can give like that it takes
   away,
When the glow of early thought declines in Feeling's
   dull decay;
'Tis not on Youth's smooth cheek the blush alone,
   which fades so fast,
But the tender bloom of heart is gone, ere Youth itself
   be past.

Then the few whose spirits float above the wreck of
   happiness 5
Are driven o'er the shoals of guilt or ocean of excess:
The magnet of their course is gone, or only points in
   vain
The shore to which their shivered sail shall never stretch
   again.

Then the mortal coldness of the soul like death itself
   comes down;
It cannot feel for others' woes, it dare not dream its
   own; 10
That heavy chill has frozen o'er the fountain of our
   tears,
And though the eye may sparkle still, 'tis where the ice
   appears.

Though wit may flash from fluent lips, and mirth
   distract the breast,
Through midnight hours that yield no more their
   former hope of rest;
'Tis but as ivy-leaves around the ruined turret wreath, 15
All green and wildly fresh without, but worn and gray
   beneath.

Oh, could I feel as I have felt,—or be what I have been,
Or weep as I could once have wept, o'er many a
   vanished scene;
As springs, in deserts found, seem sweet, all brackish
   though they be,
So, midst the withered waste of life, those tears would
   flow to me. 20

FARE THEE WELL

The occasion of these lines was the signing, in March,
1816, of the deed of separation by the poet and Lady
Byron. Byron's bad taste in publishing them is obvious.
At the head of the poem, which was published in the
same year, stood as a motto lines 408–13 and 419–26 of
Coleridge's *Christabel* (p. 104, above): "Alas! they had
been friends in youth," etc.

Fare thee well! and if for ever,
   Still for ever, fare *thee well*:
Even though unforgiving, never
   'Gainst thee shall my heart rebel.
Would that breast were bared before thee 5
   Where thy head so oft hath lain,
While that placid sleep came o'er thee
   Which thou ne'er canst know again:
Would that breast, by thee glanced over,
   Every inmost thought could show! 10
Then thou would'st at last discover
   'Twas not well to spurn it so.
Though the world for this commend thee—
   Though it smile upon the blow,
Even its praises must offend thee, 15
   Founded on another's woe:
Though my many faults defaced me,
   Could no other arm be found,
Than the one which once embraced me,
   To inflict a cureless wound? 20
Yet, oh yet, thyself deceive not—
   Love may sink by slow decay,
But by sudden wrench, believe not
   Hearts can thus be torn away:
Still thine own its life retaineth— 25
   Still must mine, though bleeding, beat;
And the undying thought which paineth
   Is—that we no more may meet.
These are words of deeper sorrow
   Than the wail above the dead; 30
Both shall live—but every morrow
   Wake us from a widowed bed.
And when thou would'st solace gather—

When our child's[9] first accents flow—
  Wilt thou teach her to say "Father!" *sweet* 35
    Though his care she must forgo?
When her little hands shall press thee—
  When her lip to thine is pressed—
Think of him whose prayer shall bless thee—
  Think of him thy love *had* blessed! 40
Should her lineaments resemble
  Those thou never more may'st see,
Then thy heart will softly tremble
  With a pulse yet true to me.
All my faults perchance thou knowest— 45
  All my madness—none can know;
All my hopes—where'er thou goest—
  Wither—yet with *thee* they go.
Every feeling hath been shaken;
  Pride—which not a world could bow— 50
Bows to thee—by thee forsaken,
  Even my soul forsakes me now:
But 'tis done—all words are idle—
  Words from me are vainer still;
But the thoughts we cannot bridle 55
  Force their way without the will.
Fare thee well! thus disunited—
  Torn from every nearer tie—
Seared in heart—and lone—and blighted—
  More than this I scarce can die. 60

THE PRISONER OF CHILLON

Chillon is a fortress at the east end of Lake Geneva near Montreux, Switzerland. In company with Shelley, Byron visited it in the summer of 1816; he composed the poem a few days later. François de Bonnivard was a patriot who took part in the resistance of the city of Geneva against the tyrannical attempts made by its bishop and by Charles III, Duke of Savoy, to destroy its self-government. Bonnivard was imprisoned at Chillon for six years, beginning in 1530. With the aid of Bern the Genevese established a Protestant republic in 1536. The castle of Chillon was captured, and Bonnivard was freed from the subterranean dungeon where he had spent the last four years of his imprisonment. In a prefatory note Byron confesses that when he wrote the poem he knew little of the historical facts; for example, the brothers are his own invention. "The Prisoner of Chillon" is hardly one of Byron's masterpieces, but its popularity continues: its theme is Liberty.

---

[9] Ada (1815–52), born shortly before her parents separated. Byron never saw her again. She was married in 1835; three years later her husband was created Earl of Lovelace. One of her three children married the poet, anti-imperialist, and Arabian-horse breeder Wilfrid Scawen Blunt.

Eternal Spirit of the chainless Mind!
  Brightest in dungeons, Liberty! thou art:
  For there thy habitation is the heart—
The heart which love of thee alone can bind;
And when thy sons to fetters are consigned— 5
  To fetters, and the damp vault's dayless gloom,
  Their country conquers with their martyrdom,
And Freedom's fame finds wings on every wind.
Chillon! thy prison is a holy place,
  And thy sad floor an altar—for 'twas trod, 10
Until his very steps have left a trace
  Worn, as if thy cold pavement were a sod,
By Bonnivard!—May none those marks efface!
  For they appeal from tyranny to God.

THE PRISONER OF CHILLON

I

My hair is gray, but not with years,
  Nor grew it white
  In a single night,
As men's have grown from sudden fears:
My limbs are bowed, though not with toil, 5
  But rusted with a vile repose,
For they have been a dungeon's spoil,
  And mine has been the fate of those
To whom the goodly earth and air
Are banned, and barred—forbidden fare; 10
But this was for my father's faith
I suffered chains and courted death;
That father perished at the stake
For tenets he would not forsake;
And for the same his lineal race 15
In darkness found a dwelling place;
We were seven—who now are one,
  Six in youth, and one in age,
Finished as they had begun,
  Proud of Persecution's rage; 20
One in fire, and two in field,
Their belief with blood have sealed,
Dying as their father died,
For the God their foes denied;—
Three were in a dungeon cast, 25
Of whom this wreck is left the last.

2

There are seven pillars of Gothic mould
In Chillon's dungeons deep and old,
There are seven columns, massy and grey,
Dim with a dull imprisoned ray, 30
A sunbeam which hath lost its way,

And through the crevice and the cleft
Of the thick wall is fallen and left;
Creeping o'er the floor so damp,
Like a marsh's meteor lamp:[1]   35
And in each pillar there is a ring,
   And in each ring there is a chain;
That iron is a cankering thing,
   For in these limbs its teeth remain,
With marks that will not wear away,   40
Till I have done with this new day,
Which now is painful to these eyes,
Which have not seen the sun so rise
For years—I cannot count them o'er,
I lost their long and heavy score   45
When my last brother drooped and died,
And I lay living by his side.

3

They chained us each to a column stone,
And we were three—yet, each alone;
We could not move a single pace,   50
We could not see each other's face,
But with that pale and livid light
That made us strangers in our sight:
And thus together—yet apart,
Fettered in hand, but joined in heart,   55
'T was still some solace in the dearth
Of the pure elements of earth,
To hearken to each other's speech,
And each turn comforter to each
With some new hope, or legend old,   60
Or song heroically bold;
But even these at length grew cold.
Our voices took a dreary tone,
An echo of the dungeon stone,
   A grating sound—not full and free   65
   As they of yore were wont to be;
   It might be fancy—but to me
They never sounded like our own.

4

I was the eldest of the three,
   And to uphold and cheer the rest   70
   I ought to do—and did my best—
And each did well in his degree.
   The youngest, whom my father loved,
Because our mother's brow was given
To him—with eyes as blue as heaven—   75
   For him my soul was sorely moved:
And truly might it be distressed
To see such bird in such a nest;

For he was beautiful as day—
   (When day was beautiful to me   80
   As to young eagles, being free)—
   A polar day, which will not see
A sunset till its summer's gone,
   Its sleepless summer of long light,
The snow-clad offspring of the sun: 85
   And thus he was as pure and bright,
And in his natural spirit gay,
With tears for naught but others' ills,
And then they flowed like mountain rills,
Unless he could assuage the woe   90
Which he abhorred to view below.

5

The other was as pure of mind,
But formed to combat with his kind;
Strong in his frame, and of a mood
Which 'gainst the world in war had[2] stood,   95
And perished in the foremost rank
   With joy:—but not in chains to pine:
His spirit withered with their clank,
   I saw it silently decline—
   And so perchance in sooth did mine: 100
But yet I forced it on to cheer
Those relics of a home so dear.
He was a hunter of the hills,
   Had followed there the deer and wolf;
   To him this dungeon was a gulf,   105
And fettered feet the worst of ills.

6

Lake Leman[3] lies by Chillon's walls:
A thousand feet in depth below
Its massy waters meet and flow;
Thus much the fathom-line was sent   110
From Chillon's snow-white battlement,
   Which round about the wave inthralls:
A double dungeon wall and wave
Have made—and like a living grave.
Below the surface of the lake   115
The dark vault lies wherein we lay:
We heard it ripple night and day;
   Sounding o'er our heads it knocked;
And I have felt the winter's spray
Wash through the bars when winds were high 120
And wanton in the happy sky;
   And then the very rock hath rocked,
   And I have felt it shake, unshocked,
Because I could have smiled to see
The death that would have set me free.   125

---

[1] I.e., a will-o'-the-wisp.

[2] Would have.
[3] Another name of Lake Geneva.

7

I said my nearer brother pined,
I said his mighty heart declined,
He loathed and put away his food;
It was not that 'twas coarse and rude,
For we were used to hunter's fare,   130
And for the like had little care:
The milk drawn from the mountain goat
Was changed for water from the moat,
Our bread was such as captives' tears
Have moistened many a thousand years,   135
Since man first pent his fellow men
Like brutes within an iron den;
But what were these to us or him?
These wasted not his heart or limb;
My brother's soul was of that mould   140
Which in a palace had grown cold,
Had his free breathing been denied
The range of the steep mountain's side;
But why delay the truth?—he died.
I saw, and could not hold his head,   145
Nor reach his dying hand—nor dead,—
Though hard I strove, but strove in vain,
To rend and gnash my bonds in twain.
He died—and they unlocked his chain,
And scooped for him a shallow grave   150
Even from the cold earth of our cave.
I begged them, as a boon, to lay
His corse in dust whereon the day
Might shine—it was a foolish thought,
But then within my brain it wrought,   155
That even in death his freeborn breast
In such a dungeon could not rest.
I might have spared my idle prayer—
They coldly laughed—and laid him there:
The flat and turfless earth above   160
The being we so much did love;
His empty chain above it leant,
Such Murder's fitting monument!

8

But he, the favorite and the flower,
Most cherished since his natal hour,   165
His mother's image in fair face,
The infant love of all his race,
His martyred father's dearest thought,
My latest care, for whom I sought
To hoard my life, that his might be   170
Less wretched now, and one day free;
He, too, who yet had held untired
A spirit natural or inspired—
He, too, was struck, and day by day
Was withered on the stalk away.   175

Oh, God! it is a fearful thing
To see the human soul take wing
In any shape, in any mood:
I've seen it rushing forth in blood,
I've seen it on the breaking ocean   180
Strive with a swoln convulsive motion,
I've seen the sick and ghastly bed
Of Sin delirious with its dread:
But these were horrors—this was woe
Unmixed with such—but sure and slow: 185
He faded, and so calm and meek,
So softly worn, so sweetly weak,
So tearless, yet so tender, kind,
And grieved for those he left behind;
With all the while a cheek whose bloom   190
Was as a mockery of the tomb,
Whose tints as gently sunk away
As a departing rainbow's ray;
An eye of most transparent light,
That almost made the dungeon bright,   195
And not a word of murmur—not
A groan o'er his untimely lot,—
A little talk of better days,
A little hope my own to raise,
For I was sunk in silence—lost   200
In this last loss, of all the most;
And then the sighs he would suppress
Of fainting Nature's feebleness,
More slowly drawn, grew less and less:
I listened, but I could not hear;   205
I called, for I was wild with fear;
I knew 't was hopeless, but my dread
Would not be thus admonishèd;
I called, and thought I heard a sound—
I burst my chain with one strong bound,   210
And rushed to him:—I found him not,
I only stirred in this black spot,
I only lived—*I* only drew
The accursèd breath of dungeon-dew;
The last, the sole, the dearest link   215
Between me and the eternal brink,
Which bound me to my failing race,
Was broken in this fatal place.
One on the earth, and one beneath—
My brothers—both had ceased to breathe!   220
I took that hand which lay so still,
Alas! my own was full as chill;
I had not strength to stir, or strive,
But felt that I was still alive—
A frantic feeling, when we know   225
That what we love shall ne'er be so.
    I know not why
    I could not die,

I had no earthly hope—but faith,
And that forbade a selfish death.   230

9

What next befell me then and there
   I know not well—I never knew—
First came the loss of light, and air,
   And then of darkness too:
I had no thought, no feeling—none—   235
Among the stones I stood a stone,
And was, scarce conscious what I wist,
As shrubless crags within the mist;
For all was blank, and bleak, and gray;
It was not night—it was not day,   240
It was not even the dungeon-light,
So hateful to my heavy sight,
But vacancy absorbing space,
And fixedness—without a place;
There were no stars—no earth—no time—   245
No check—no change—no good—no crime—
But silence, and a stirless breath
Which neither was of life nor death;
A sea of stagnant idleness,
Blind, boundless, mute, and motionless!   250

10

A light broke in upon my brain,—
   It was the carol of a bird;
It ceased, and then it came again,
   The sweetest song ear ever heard,
And mine was thankful till my eyes   255
Ran over with the glad surprise,
And they that moment could not see
I was the mate of misery;
But then by dull degrees came back
My senses to their wonted track;   260
I saw the dungeon walls and floor
Close slowly round me as before,
I saw the glimmer of the sun
Creeping as it before had done,
But through the crevice where it came   265
That bird was perched, as fond and tame,
   And tamer than upon the tree;
A lovely bird, with azure wings,
And song that said a thousand things,
   And seemed to say them all for me!   270
I never saw its like before,
I ne'er shall see its likeness more:
It seemed like me to want a mate,
But was not half so desolate,
And it was come to love me when   275
None lived to love me so again,
And cheering from my dungeon's brink,

Had brought me back to feel and think.
I know not if it late were free,
   Or broke its cage to perch on mine,   280
But knowing well captivity,
   Sweet bird! I could not wish for thine!
Or if it were, in wingèd guise,
A visitant from Paradise;
For—Heaven forgive that thought! the while   285
Which made me both to weep and smile—
I sometimes deemed that it might be
My brother's soul come down to me;
But then at last away it flew,
And then 't was mortal well I knew,   290
For he would never thus have flown—
And left me twice so doubly lone,—
Lone—as the corse within its shroud,
Lone—as a solitary cloud,
   A single cloud on a sunny day,   295
   While all the rest of heaven is clear,
   A frown upon the atmosphere,
   That hath no business to appear
     When skies are blue, and earth is gay.

11

A kind of change came in my fate,   300
My keepers grew compassionate;
I know not what had made them so,
They were inured to sights of woe,
But so it was:—my broken chain
With links unfastened did remain,   305
And it was liberty to stride
Along my cell from side to side,
And up and down, and then athwart,
And tread it over every part;
And round the pillars one by one,   310
Returning where my walk begun,
Avoiding only, as I trod,
My brothers' graves without a sod;
For if I thought with heedless tread
My step profaned their lowly bed,   315
My breath came gaspingly and thick,
And my crushed heart felt blind and sick.

12

I made a footing in the wall,
   It was not therefrom to escape,
For I had buried one and all,   320
   Who loved me in a human shape;
And the whole earth would henceforth be
A wider prison unto me:
No child—no sire—no kin had I,
No partner in my misery;   325
I thought of this, and I was glad,

For thought of them had made me mad;
But I was curious to ascend
To my barred windows, and to bend
Once more, upon the mountains high,   330
The quiet of a loving eye.

13

I saw them—and they were the same,
They were not changed like me in frame;
I saw their thousand years of snow
On high—their wide long lake below,   335
And the blue Rhone in fullest flow;
I heard the torrents leap and gush
O'er channelled rock and broken bush;
I saw the white-walled distant town,[4]
And whiter sails go skimming down;   340
And then there was a little isle,
Which in my very face did smile,
        The only one in view;
A small green isle, it seemed no more,
Scarce broader than my dungeon floor,   345
But in it there were three tall trees,
And o'er it blew the mountain breeze,
And by it there were waters flowing,
And on it there were young flowers growing,
        Of gentle breath and hue.   350
The fish swam by the castle wall,
And they seemed joyous each and all:
The eagle rode the rising blast,
Methought he never flew so fast
As then to me he seemed to fly;   355
And then new tears came in my eye,
And I felt troubled—and would fain
I had not left my recent chain;
And when I did descend again,

The darkness of my dim abode   360
Fell on me as a heavy load;
It was as is a new-dug grave,
Closing o'er one we sought to save,—
And yet my glance, too much opprest,
Had almost need of such a rest.   365

14

It might be months, or years, or days—
    I kept no count, I took no note—
I had no hope my eyes to raise,
    And clear them of their dreary mote;
At last men came to set me free;   370
    I asked not why, and recked not where;
It was at length the same to me,
Fettered or fetterless to be,
    I learned to love despair.
And thus when they appeared at last,   375
And all my bonds aside were cast,
These heavy walls to me had grown
A hermitage—and all my own!
And half I felt as they were come
To tear me from a second home: 380
With spiders I had friendship made,
And watched them in their sullen trade,
Had seen the mice by moonlight play,
And why should I feel less than they?
We were all inmates of one place,   385
And I, the monarch of each race,
Had power to kill—yet, strange to tell!
In quiet we had learned to dwell;
My very chains and I grew friends,
So much a long communion tends   390
To make us what we are:—even I
Regained my freedom with a sigh.

---

from CHILDE HAROLD'S PILGRIMAGE

BYRON began this poem in the fall of 1809, in Albania. The first canto was finished in Greece at the end of the year, the second in Turkey in March, 1810. On May 3 the poet swam the Dardanelles; midsummer found him back in Athens. His preface to Cantos I and II, published in 1812, alludes to their composition in the midst of the scenes described. "A fictitious character," he continues, "is introduced for the sake of giving some connection to the piece. . . . Harold is the child of imagination." Actually, of course, Harold is modeled on the poet himself —not the whole man, but Byron as he saw or tried to see himself in certain moods—despite his declaration in

a letter that "I would not be such a fellow as I have made my hero for all the world." As for the *Childe* of the title, we have already met this term in the medieval ballads; it signifies a youth of noble birth. Harold is more than a device for securing unity; the poem is essentially neither a book of travels nor a series of historical reflections. Byron is chiefly interested in himself, not the scenes—with the way he feels in the scene, his emotions as he recalls personal experience, the bearing on his own life of the meditations inspired by historic places. In other words, this is a highly subjective poem.

Canto III, reprinted in full below, is much superior; it was written in less than two months, soon after Byron signed the separation agreement and left England. He

[4] Villeneuve.

finished it in June, 1816, in Switzerland, after his journey through Belgium and along the Rhine. Eagerly awaited by the public, it was brought out in London that fall. The fourth canto was composed in Italy in the summer and autumn of 1817, and published the following spring. "Harold," not greatly in evidence in Canto III, is in this final canto frankly dropped in favor of the first personal pronoun. Several passages, including the closing lines, are given below.

Childe Harold is not a great poem, but it is an extraordinary accomplishment. Technical mastery is displayed in the handling of the Spenserian stanza, the poem is sprinkled with striking passages, and considering its length it is well sustained. If it does not offer the inescapability and cleansing power of great art, it nevertheless provides pleasant and sometimes stirring reading. In its own day it did more than that—Byron's eloquent assertion of his capacity for feeling provided a precedent and a widely adopted model, both in the writings and in the actual lives of many of his contemporaries.

CANTO III

Is thy face like thy mother's, my fair child!
Ada![1] sole daughter of my house and heart?
When last I saw thy young blue eyes they smiled,
And then we parted,—not as now we part,
But with a hope.[2]—
          Awaking with a start,   5
The waters heave around me; and on high
The winds lift up their voices: I depart,
Whither I know not; but the hour's gone by,
When Albion's[3] lessening shores could grieve or glad
mine eye.

Once more upon the waters! yet once more!   10
And the waves bound beneath me as a steed
That knows his rider. Welcome to their roar!
Swift be their guidance, wheresoe'er it lead!
Though the strained mast should quiver as a reed,
And the rent canvas fluttering strew the gale,   15
Still must I on; for I am as a weed,
Flung from the rock, on Ocean's foam to sail
Where'er the surge may sweep, the tempest's breath
    prevail.

In my youth's summer[4] I did sing of One,
The wandering outlaw of his own dark mind;   20

Again I seize the theme, then but begun,
And bear it with me, as the rushing wind
Bears the cloud onwards: in that Tale I find
The furrows of long thought, and dried-up tears,
Which, ebbing, leave a sterile track behind,   25
O'er which all heavily the journeying years
Plod the last sands of life,—where not a flower appears.

Since my young days of passion—joy or pain—
Perchance my heart and harp have lost a string—
And both may jar: it may be that in vain   30
I would essay, as I have sung, to sing:
Yet, though a dreary strain, to this I cling;
So that[5] it wean me from the weary dream
Of selfish grief or gladness—so it fling
Forgetfulness around me—it shall seem   35
To me, though to none else, a not ungrateful theme.

He, who grown agèd in this world of woe,
In deeds, not years, piercing the depths of life,
So that no wonder waits him—nor below
Can Love or Sorrow, Fame, Ambition, Strife,   40
Cut to his heart again with the keen knife
Of silent, sharp endurance—he can tell
Why Thought seeks refuge in lone caves, yet rife
With airy images, and shapes which dwell   44
Still unimpaired, though old, in the Soul's haunted cell.

'Tis to create, and in creating live
A being more intense, that we endow
With form our fancy, gaining as we give
The life we image, even as I do now—
What am I? Nothing: but not so art thou,   50
Soul of my thought! with whom I traverse earth,
Invisible but gazing, as I glow
Mixed with thy spirit, blended with thy birth,
And feeling still with thee in my crushed feelings' dearth.

Yet must I think less wildly:—I *have* thought   55
Too long and darkly, till my brain became
In its own eddy boiling and o'erwrought,
A whirling gulf of phantasy and flame;
And thus, untaught in youth my heart to tame,
My springs of life were poisoned. 'Tis too late!   60
Yet am I changed; though still enough the same
In strength to bear what Time can not abate,
And feed on bitter fruits without accusing Fate.

Something too much of this:[6]—but now 'tis past,
And the spell closes with its silent seal.[7]   65

---

1 See above, p. 221, note 9.
2 That he might see her again; it was slowly and reluctantly that he abandoned hope of a reconciliation with Lady Byron.
3 England's.
4 Byron was only twenty-one when he wrote Canto I of this poem.

5 Provided that, if.   6 *Hamlet,* III, ii, 79.
7 I.e., on the story ("spell") of my personal affairs is set the seal of silence. He will proceed with *Harold's* story.

Long absent Harold re-appears at last—
He of the breast which fain no more would feel,
Wrung with the wounds which kill not, but ne'er heal;
Yet Time, who changes all, had altered him
In soul and aspect as in age: years steal   70
Fire from the mind as vigour from the limb;
And Life's enchanted cup but sparkles near the brim.

His had been quaffed too quickly, and he found
The dregs were wormwood; but he filled again,
And from a purer fount, on holier ground,   75
And deemed its spring perpetual—but in vain!
Still round him clung invisibly a chain
Which galled forever, fettering though unseen,
And heavy though it clanked not; worn with pain,
Which pined although it spoke not, and grew keen,   80
Entering with every step he took through many a scene.

Secure in guarded coldness he had mixed
Again in fancied safety with his kind,
And deemed his spirit now so firmly fixed
And sheathed with an invulnerable mind,   85
That, if no joy, no sorrow lurked behind;
And he, as one, might 'midst the many stand
Unheeded, searching through the crowd to find
Fit speculation—such as in strange land   89
He found in wonder-works of God and Nature's hand.

But who can view the ripened rose, nor seek
To wear it? who can curiously behold
The smoothness and the sheen of Beauty's cheek,
Nor feel the heart can never all grow old?
Who can contémplate Fame through clouds unfold 95
The star which rises o'er her steep, nor climb?[8]
Harold, once more within the vortex, rolled
On with the giddy circle, chasing Time,
Yet with a nobler aim than in his Youth's fond prime.[9]

But soon he knew himself the most unfit   100
Of men to herd with Man, with whom he held
Little in common; untaught to submit
His thoughts to others, though his soul was quelled
In youth by his own thoughts: still uncompelled,
He would not yield dominion of his mind   105
To Spirits against whom his own rebelled,
Proud though in desolation—which could find
A life within itself, to breathe without mankind.

Where rose the mountains, there to him were friends;
Where rolled the Ocean, thereon was his home;   110

Where a blue sky, and glowing clime, extends,
He had the passion and the power to roam;
The desert, forest, cavern, breaker's foam,
Were unto him companionship; they spake
A mutual language, clearer than the tome   115
Of his land's tongue, which he would oft forsake
For Nature's pages glassed[10] by sunbeams on the lake.

Like the Chaldean[11] he could watch the stars,
Till he had peopled them with beings bright
As their own beams; and earth, and earthborn jars, 120
And human frailties, were forgotten quite:
Could he have kept his spirit to that flight
He had been happy; but this clay will sink
Its spark immortal, envying it the light
To which it mounts, as if to break the link   125
That keeps us from yon heaven which woos us to its
    brink.

But in Man's dwellings he became a thing
Restless and worn, and stern and wearisome,
Drooped as a wild-born falcon with clipt wing,
To whom the boundless air alone were home: 130
Then came his fit again,[12] which to o'ercome,
As eagerly the barred-up bird will beat
His breast and beak against his wiry dome
Till the blood tinge his plumage—so the heat
Of his impeded Soul would through his bosom eat. 135

Self-exiled Harold wanders forth again,
With nought of Hope left—but with less of gloom;
The very knowledge that he lived in vain,
That all was over on this side the tomb,
Had made Despair a smilingness assume,   140
Which, though 'twere wild,—as on the plundered
    wreck
When mariners would madly meet their doom
With draughts intemperate on the sinking deck,—
Did yet inspire a cheer, which he forbore to check.

Stop!—for thy tread is on an Empire's dust!   145
An Earthquake's spoil is sepulchered below!
Is the spot marked with no colossal bust?
Nor column trophied for triumphal show?
None;[13] but the *moral's truth*[14] tells simpler so.

---

8 I.e., without attempting to climb to the mountain peak where
  Fame resides.   9 Foolish spring.

10 Mirrored.
11 The Chaldeans of ancient Babylonia were famous astronomers
   and named a good many stars.   12 Cf. *Macbeth*, III, iv, 21.
13 Napoleon was finally defeated at Waterloo, near Brussels, on
   June 18, 1815, less than a year before Byron visited the field,
   over which he rode twice.
14 I.e., that the world reaped no advantage. Byron considered the
   battle a victory for the forces of reaction.

As the ground was before, thus let it be;— 150
How that red rain hath made the harvest grow!
And is this all the world has gained by thee,
Thou first and last of Fields! king-making[15] victory?

And Harold stands upon this place of skulls,
The grave of France, the deadly Waterloo! 155
How in an hour the Power which gave annuls
Its gifts, transferring fame as fleeting too!—
In "pride of place"[16] here last the Eagle[17] flew,
Then tore with bloody talon the rent plain,
Pierced by the shaft of banded nations through; 160
Ambition's life and labours all were vain—
He wears[18] the shattered links of the World's broken
    chain.

Fit retribution! Gaul[19] may champ the bit
And foam in fetters;—but is earth more free?
Did nations combat to make *One* submit? 165
Or league to teach all Kings true Sovereignty?
What! shall reviving Thraldom again be
The patched-up Idol[20] of enlightened days?
Shall we, who struck the Lion[21] down, shall we
Pay the Wolf[22] homage? proffering lowly gaze 170
And servile knees to Thrones? No; *prove*[23] before ye
    praise!

If not, o'er one fallen Despot boast no more!
In vain fair cheeks were furrowed with hot tears
For Europe's flowers long rooted up before
The trampler of her vineyards; in vain, years 175
Of death, depopulation, bondage, fears,
Have all been borne, and broken by the accord
Of roused-up millions: all that most endears
Glory, is when the myrtle wreathes a Sword
Such as Harmodius[24] drew on Athens' tyrant lord. 180

There was a sound of revelry by night,[25]
And Belgium's Capital had gathered then
Her Beauty and her Chivalry—and bright
The lamps shone o'er fair women and brave men;
A thousand hearts beat happily; and when 185
Music arose with its voluptuous swell,
Soft eyes looked love to eyes which spake again,
And all went merry as a marriage bell;
But hush! hark! a deep sound strikes like a rising knell!

Did ye not hear it?—No—'twas but the Wind, 190
Or the car rattling o'er the stony street;
On with the dance! let joy be unconfined;
No sleep till morn, when Youth and Pleasure meet
To chase the glowing Hours with flying feet—
But hark!—that heavy sound breaks in once more, 195
As if the clouds its echo would repeat;
And nearer—clearer—deadlier than before!
Arm! Arm! it is—it is—the cannon's opening roar!

Within a windowed niche of that high hall
Sate Brunswick's fated Chieftain;[26] he did hear 200
That sound the first amidst the festival,
And caught its tone with Death's prophetic ear;
And when they smiled because he deemed it near,
His heart more truly knew that peal too well
Which stretched his father on a bloody bier, 205
And roused the vengeance blood alone could quell;
He rushed into the field, and, foremost fighting, fell.

Ah! then and there was hurrying to and fro—
And gathering tears, and tremblings of distress,
And cheeks all pale, which but an hour ago 210
Blushed at the praise of their own loveliness;
And there were sudden partings, such as press
The life from out young hearts, and choking sighs
Which ne'er might be repeated; who could guess
If ever more should meet those mutual eyes, 215
Since upon night so sweet such awful morn could rise!

And there was mounting in hot haste—the steed,
The mustering squadron, and the clattering car,
Went pouring forward with impetuous speed,
And swiftly forming in the ranks of war— 220

---

[15] For the Emperor, whom some still considered the heir of the French Revolution, was beaten; the Bourbon, Louis XVIII, was king of France; and the other European monarchs could now feel secure on their thrones.
[16] The height of a bird's, especially a falcon's, flight. Quoted from *Macbeth*, II, iv, 12.   [17] Napoleon.
[18] Under guard, on his way to St. Helena.   [19] France.
[20] The so-called Holy Alliance made by the European monarchs. Though essentially meaningless, it became in the minds of liberals a symbol of the prevailing reaction.   [21] Napoleon.
[22] A dangerous but far from royal beast. The application is made in the clause which follows.
[23] Test the quality (of Europe's monarchs).
[24] In 514 B.C. the Athenian youths Harmodius and Aristogiton, concealing their weapons in myrtle branches, assassinated the tyrant Hipparchus.

[25] This famous passage refers to the ball (also described by Thackeray in *Vanity Fair*, chaps. 29–32) given by the Duchess of Richmond in Brussels the evening (June 15) before the Waterloo campaign opened with the Battle of Quatre Bras.
[26] Friedrich Wilhelm, Duke of Brunswick (1771–1815), nephew of George III, fell at Quatre Bras. His father, Duke Karl Wilhelm, was mortally wounded in 1806 at the Battle of Auerstedt, when the Prussian army under his command was defeated by Davout, one of Napoleon's marshals.

And the deep thunder peal on peal afar;
And near, the beat of the alarming drum
Roused up the soldier ere the Morning Star;
While thronged the citizens with terror dumb,
Or whispering, with white lips—"The foe! They come!
    They come!"   225

And wild and high the "Cameron's Gathering"[27] rose!
The war-note of Lochiel, which Albyn's[28] hills
Have heard, and heard, too, have her Saxon[29] foes:
How in the noon of night that pibroch[30] thrills,
Savage and shrill! But with the breath which fills   230
Their mountain-pipe, so fill the mountaineers
With the fierce native daring which instils
The stirring memory of a thousand years,
And Evan's—Donald's,[31] fame rings in each clansman's
    ears!

And Ardennes[32] waves above them her green leaves, 235
Dewy with Nature's tear-drops, as they pass—
Grieving, if aught inanimate e'er grieves,
Over the unreturning brave,—alas!
Ere evening to be trodden like the grass
Which *now* beneath them, but *above* shall grow   240
In its next verdure, when this fiery mass
Of living Valour, rolling on the foe
And burning with high Hope shall moulder cold and
    low.

Last noon beheld them full of lusty life;
Last eve in Beauty's circle proudly gay;   245
The Midnight brought the signal-sound of strife,
The morn the marshalling in arms,—the Day
Battle's magnificently-stern array!
The thunder-clouds close o'er it, which when rent
The earth is covered thick with other clay   250
Which her own clay shall cover, heaped and pent,[33]
Rider and horse,—friend,—foe—in one red burial blent!

---

27 The tune to which the Camerons gathered for war, played here
    as an assembly for the 92nd Highlanders. The chief of clan
    Cameron was called Lochiel, from his estate.
28 An old name of northern Scotland.
29 English and Lowland Scotch.
30 Martial music for the bagpipes.
31 Sir Evan Cameron of Lochiel (1629–1719) fought for the
    Stuarts in 1652, and raised his clan for them at Killiecrankie
    (1689) and again in the uprising of 1715. His grandson, Sir
    Donald, fought for Prince Charlie in 1745–6 and, escaping with
    a wound at Culloden, fled with him to France. Sir Evan's
    great-great-grandson, John Cameron, commanding the 92nd,
    was mortally wounded at Quatre Bras on June 16, 1815.
32 The forest in Belgium and northeastern France where the
    United States Army has also made history.   33 Confined.

Their praise is hymned by loftier harps than mine;
Yet one I would select from that proud throng,
Partly because they blend me with his line,   255
And partly that I did his Sire[34] some wrong,
And partly that bright names will hallow song;
And his was of the bravest, and when showered
The death-bolts deadliest the thinned files along,
Even where the thickest of War's tempest lowered, 260
They reached no nobler breast than thine, young,
    gallant Howard![35]

There have been tears and breaking hearts for thee,
And mine were nothing, had I such to give;
But when I stood beneath the fresh green tree,
Which living waves where thou didst cease to live, 265
And saw around me the wide field revive
With fruits and fertile promise, and the Spring
Come forth her work of gladness to contrive,
With all her reckless birds upon the wing,
I turned from all she brought to those she could not
    bring.   270

I turned to thee, to thousands, of whom each
And one as all a ghastly gap did make
In his own kind and kindred, whom to teach
Forgetfulness were mercy for their sake;
The Archangel's trump, not Glory's, must awake 275
Those whom they thirst for; though the sound of Fame
May for a moment soothe, it cannot slake
The fever of vain longing, and the name
So honoured but assumes a stronger, bitterer claim.

They mourn, but smile at length—and, smiling,
    mourn: 280
The tree will wither long before it fall;
The hull drives on, though mast and sail be torn;
The roof-tree sinks, but moulders on the hall
In massy hoariness; the ruined wall
Stands when its wind-worn battlements are gone; 285
The bars survive the captive they enthral;
The day drags through, though storms keep out the sun;
And thus the heart will break, yet brokenly live on:

Even as a broken Mirror, which the glass
In every fragment multiplies—and makes   290

---

34 Frederick Howard (1748–1825), fifth Earl of Carlisle, Byron's
    childhood guardian and his second cousin, whose writings he
    had insultingly characterized in *English Bards, and Scotch Re-
    viewers,* line 726.
35 Frederick Howard (1785–1815), the Earl's third son, fell at
    Waterloo late in the evening of the 18th, in the last cavalry
    charge against the left square of the French Guard. He was
    temporarily buried on the field, under three trees.

A thousand images of one that was
The same—and still the more, the more it breaks;
And thus the heart will do which not forsakes,
Living in shattered guise; and still, and cold,
And bloodless, with its sleepless sorrow aches,   295
Yet withers on till all without is old,
Showing no visible sign, for such things are untold.

There is a very life in our despair,
Vitality of poison,—a quick root
Which feeds these deadly branches; for it were   300
As nothing did we die; but Life will suit
Itself to Sorrow's most detested fruit,
Like to the apples[36] on the Dead Sea's shore,
All ashes to the taste: Did man compute
Existence by enjoyment, and count o'er   305
Such hours 'gainst years of life,—say, would he name
          threescore?

The Psalmist numbered out the years of man:
They are enough; and if thy tale be *true,*
Thou, who didst grudge him even that fleeting span,
More than enough, thou fatal Waterloo![37]   310
Millions of tongues record thee, and anew
Their children's lips shall echo them, and say—
"Here, where the sword united nations drew,
Our countrymen were warring on that day!"
And this is much—and all—which will not pass
          away.   315

There sunk the greatest nor the worst of men,[38]
Whose Spirit, antithetically mixed,
One moment of the mightiest, and again
On little objects with like firmness fixed;
Extreme in all things! hadst thou been betwixt,   320
Thy throne had still been thine, or never been;
For daring made thy rise as fall: thou seek'st
Even now to re-assume the imperial mien,[39]
And shake again the world, the Thunderer of the scene!

Conqueror and Captive of the Earth art thou!   325
She trembles at thee still, and thy wild name
Was ne'er more bruited in men's minds than now
That thou art nothing, save the jest of Fame,
Who wooed thee once, thy Vassal, and became

The flatterer of thy fierceness—till thou wert   330
A God unto thyself; nor less the same
To the astounded kingdoms all inert,
Who deemed thee for a time whate'er thou didst assert.

Oh, more or less than man—in high or low—
Battling with nations, flying from the field;   335
Now making monarchs' necks thy footstool, now
More than thy meanest soldier taught to yield;
An Empire thou could'st crush, command, rebuild,
But govern not thy pettiest passion, nor,
However deeply in men's spirits skilled,   340
Look through thine own, nor curb the lust of War,
Nor learn that tempted Fate will leave the loftiest Star.

Yet well thy soul hath brooked the turning tide
With that untaught innate philosophy,
Which, be it Wisdom, Coldness, or deep Pride,   345
Is gall and wormwood to an enemy.
When the whole host of hatred stood hard by,
To watch and mock thee shrinking, thou hast smiled
With a sedate and all-enduring eye;—
When Fortune fled her spoiled and favourite child,   350
He stood unbowed beneath the ills upon him piled.

Sager than in thy fortunes; for in them
Ambition steeled thee on too far to show
That just habitual scorn, which could contemn
Men and their thoughts; 'twas wise to feel, not so   355
To wear it ever on thy lip and brow,
And spurn the instruments thou wert to use
Till they were turned unto thine overthrow:
'Tis but a worthless world to win or lose;   359
So hath it proved to thee, and all such lot who choose.

If, like a tower upon a headlong rock,
Thou hadst been made to stand or fall alone,
Such scorn of man had helped to brave the shock;
But men's thoughts were the steps which paved thy
          throne,
Their admiration thy best weapon shone;   365
The part of Philip's son[40] was thine—not then
(Unless aside thy Purple[41] had been thrown)
Like stern Diogenes[42] to mock at men:
For sceptered cynics earth were far too wide a den.

But Quiet to quick bosoms is a Hell,   370
And *there* hath been thy bane; there is a fire
And motion of the Soul which will not dwell

---

[36] According to travelers, a fruit externally promising but worthless within.

[37] Since the men who fell there were young, whereas in Psalms 90:10 from seventy to eighty years are specified.

[38] Napoleon—neither the greatest nor the worst.

[39] He complained that, although his French suite continued to give him an emperor's honors, his British captors did not.

[40] Alexander the Great, son of Philip II of Macedon.
[41] Symbol of royalty.
[42] The Greek cynic philosopher (d. 323 B.C.), a contemporary of Alexander.

In its own narrow being, but aspire
Beyond the fitting medium of desire;
And, but once kindled, quenchless evermore,   375
Preys upon high adventure, nor can tire
Of aught but rest; a fever at the core,
Fatal to him who bears, to all who ever bore.

This makes the madmen who have made men mad
By their contagion; Conquerors and Kings,   380
Founders of sects and systems, to whom add
Sophists, Bards, Statesmen, all unquiet things
Which stir too strongly the soul's secret springs,
And are themselves the fools to those they fool;
Envied, yet how unenviable! what stings   385
Are theirs! One breast laid open were a school
Which would unteach Mankind the lust to shine or rule:

Their breath is agitation, and their life
A storm whereon they ride, to sink at last,
And yet so nursed and bigoted to strife,   390
That should their days, surviving perils past,
Melt to calm twilight, they feel overcast
With sorrow and supineness, and so die;
Even as a flame unfed, which runs to waste
With its own flickering, or a sword laid by,   395
Which eats into itself, and rusts ingloriously.

He who ascends to mountain tops shall find
The loftiest peaks most wrapt in clouds and snow;
He who surpasses or subdues mankind,
Must look down on the hate of those below.   400
Though high *above* the Sun of Glory glow,
And far *beneath* the Earth and Ocean spread,
Round him are icy rocks, and loudly blow
Contending tempests on his naked head,
And thus reward the toils which to those summits
            led.   405

Away with these! true Wisdom's world will be
Within its own creation, or in thine,
Maternal Nature! for who teems[43] like thee,
Thus on the banks of thy majestic Rhine?
There Harold gazes on a work divine,   410
A blending of all beauties; streams and dells,
Fruit, foliage, crag, wood, cornfield,[44] mountain, vine,
And chiefless castles breathing stern farewells
From gray but leafy walls, where Ruin greenly dwells.

And there they stand, as stands a lofty mind,   415
Worn, but unstooping to the baser crowd,

All tenantless, save to the crannying Wind,
Or holding dark communion with the Cloud.
There was a day when they were young and proud;
Banners on high, and battles[45] passed below;   420
But they who fought are in a bloody shroud,
And those which waved are shredless dust ere now,
And the bleak battlements shall bear no future blow.

Beneath these battlements, within those walls,
Power dwelt amidst her passions; in proud state   425
Each robber chief upheld his armèd halls,
Doing his evil will, nor less elate
Than mightier heroes of a longer date.
What want these outlaws[46] conquerors should have,
But History's purchased page to call them great?   430
A wider space—an ornamented grave?
Their hopes were not less warm, their souls were full as
            brave.

In their baronial feuds and single fields,
What deeds of prowess unrecorded died!
And Love, which lent a blazon[47] to their shields,   435
With emblems well devised by amorous pride,
Through all the mail of iron hearts would glide;
But still their flame was fierceness, and drew on
Keen contest and destruction near allied,
And many a tower for some fair mischief won,   440
Saw the discoloured Rhine beneath its ruin run.

But Thou, exulting and abounding river!
Making thy waves a blessing as they flow
Through banks whose beauty would endure forever
Could man but leave thy bright creation so,   445
Nor its fair promise from the surface mow
With the sharp scythe of conflict,—then to see
Thy valley of sweet waters, were to know
Earth paved like Heaven—and to seem such to me,
Even now what wants thy stream?—that it should
            Lethe[48] be.   450

A thousand battles have assailed thy banks,
But these and half their fame have passed away,
And Slaughter heaped on high his weltering ranks:
Their very graves are gone, and what are they?
Thy tide washed down the blood of yesterday,   455
And all was stainless, and on thy clear stream
Glassed, with its dancing light, the sunny ray;
But o'er the blackened Memory's blighting dream
Thy waves would vainly roll, all sweeping as they seem.

---

43 Breeds, is productive.—We have left Belgium, and are southward bound up the Rhine.   44 Grain field.
45 Battalions, forces.
46 What do these outlaws, i.e., the old German robber-barons, lack
which. . . .   47 A colorful heraldic device.
48 The river of forgetfulness.

Thus Harold inly said, and passed along,   460
Yet not insensible to all which here
Awoke the jocund birds to early song
In glens which might have made even exile dear:
Though on his brow were graven lines austere,
And tranquil sternness, which had ta'en the place   465
Of feelings fierier far but less severe—
Joy was not always absent from his face,
But o'er it in such scenes would steal with transient
    trace.

Nor was all love shut from him, though his days
Of Passion had consumed themselves to dust.   470
It is in vain that we would coldly gaze
On such as smile upon us; the heart must
Leap kindly back to kindness, though Disgust
Hath weaned it from all worldlings: thus he felt,
For there was soft Remembrance, and sweet Trust   475
In one fond breast,[49] to which his own would melt,
And in its tenderer hour on that his bosom dwelt.

And he had learned to love,—I know not why,
For this in such as him seems strange of mood,—
The helpless looks of blooming Infancy,   480
Even in its earliest nurture; what subdued,
To change like this, a mind so far imbued
With scorn of man, it little boots to know;
But thus it was; and though in solitude
Small power the nipped affections have to grow,   485
In him this glowed when all beside had ceased to glow.

And there was one soft breast, as hath been said,
Which unto his was bound by stronger ties
Than the church links withal;[50] and,—though unwed,
That love was pure—and, far above disguise,   490
Had stood the test of mortal enmities,
Still undivided, and cemented more
By peril, dreaded most in female eyes;
But this was firm, and from a foreign shore
Well to that heart might his these absent greetings
    pour!   495

1

The castled Crag of Drachenfels[51]
Frowns o'er the wide and winding Rhine,
Whose breast of waters broadly swells
Between the banks which bear the vine;
And hills all rich with blossomed trees,   500
And fields which promise corn and wine,
And scattered cities crowning these,

Whose far white walls along them shine,
Have strewed a scene, which I should see
With double joy wert *thou* with me.   505

2

And peasant girls, with deep blue eyes,
And hands which offer early flowers,
Walk smiling o'er this Paradise;
Above, the frequent feudal towers
Through green leaves lift their walls of gray;   510
And many a rock which steeply lowers,
And noble arch in proud decay,
Look o'er this vale of vintage-bowers;
But one thing want these banks of Rhine,—
Thy gentle hand to clasp in mine!   515

3

I send the lilies given to me—
Though long before thy hand they touch,
I know that they must withered be,
But yet reject them not as such;
For I have cherished them as dear,   520
Because they yet may meet thine eye,
And guide thy soul to mine even here,—
When thou behold'st them drooping nigh,
And know'st them gathered by the Rhine,
And offered from my heart to thine!   525

4

The river nobly foams and flows—
The charm of this enchanted ground,
And all its thousand turns disclose
Some fresher beauty varying round:
The haughtiest breast its wish might bound   530
Through life to dwell delighted here;
Nor could on earth a spot be found
To Nature and to me so dear—
Could thy dear eyes in following mine
Still sweeten more these banks of Rhine!   535

By Coblentz, on a rise of gentle ground,
There is a small and simple Pyramid
Crowning the summit of the verdant mound;
Beneath its base are Heroes' ashes hid—
Our enemy's—but let not that forbid   540
Honor to Marceau![52] o'er whose early tomb
Tears, big tears, gushed from the rough soldier's lid,
Lamenting and yet envying such a doom,
Falling for France, whose rights he battled to resume.

---

[49] Of his half sister, Augusta Leigh.   [50] With.
[51] The Dragon's Rock, on the Rhine near Bonn.

[52] François Séverin Marceau (1769–96), killed at Alterkirchen. As
    the inscription relates, he was a soldier at sixteen and a general
    at twenty-two.

Brief, brave, and glorious was his young career,— 545
His mourners were two hosts, his friends and foes;
And fitly may the stranger lingering here
Pray for his gallant Spirit's bright repose;—
For he was Freedom's Champion, one of those
The few in number, who had not o'erstept 550
The charter to chastise which she bestows
On such as wield her weapons; he had kept
The whiteness of his soul, and thus men o'er him wept.

Here Ehrenbreitstein,[53] with her shattered wall
Black with the miner's blast, upon her height 555
Yet shows of what she was, when shell and ball
Rebounding idly on her strength did light:—
A tower of Victory! from whence the flight
Of baffled foes was watched along the plain:
But Peace destroyed what War could never blight, 560
And laid those proud roofs bare to Summer's rain—
On which the iron shower for years had poured in vain.

Adieu to thee, fair Rhine! How long delighted
The stranger fain would linger on his way!
Thine is a scene alike where souls united 565
Or lonely Contemplation thus might stray;
And could the ceaseless vultures cease to prey
On self-condemning bosoms, it were here,
Where Nature, nor too somber nor too gay,
Wild but not rude, awful yet not austere, 570
Is to the mellow Earth as Autumn to the year.

Adieu to thee again! a vain adieu!
There can be no farewell to scene like thine;
The mind is coloured by thy every hue;
And if reluctantly the eyes resign 575
Their cherished gaze upon thee, lovely Rhine!
'Tis with the thankful glance of parting praise;
More mighty spots may rise—more glaring shine,
But none unite in one attaching maze,
The brilliant, fair, and soft,—the glories of old days, 580

The negligently grand, the fruitful bloom
Of coming ripeness, the white city's sheen,
The rolling stream, the precipice's gloom,
The forest's growth, and Gothic walls between,—
The wild rocks shaped, as they had turrets been, 585
In mockery of man's art; and these withal[54]
A race of faces happy as the scene,

Whose fertile bounties here extend to all,
Still springing o'er thy banks, though Empires near
  them fall.

But these recede. Above me are the Alps, 590
The Palaces of Nature, whose vast walls
Have pinnacled in clouds their snowy scalps,
And throned Eternity in icy halls
Of cold Sublimity, where forms and falls
The Avalanche—the thunderbolt of snow! 595
All that expands the spirit, yet appals,
Gather around these summits, as to show
How Earth may pierce to Heaven, yet leave vain man
  below.

But ere these matchless heights I dare to scan,
There is a spot should not be passed in vain,— 600
Morat![55] the proud, the patriot field! where man
May gaze on ghastly trophies of the slain,
Nor blush for those who conquered on that plain;
Here Burgundy bequeathed his tombless host,
A bony heap, through ages to remain, 605
Themselves their monument; the Stygian coast[56]
Unsepulchered they roamed, and shrieked each wander-
  ing ghost.

While Waterloo with Cannae's[57] carnage vies,
Morat and Marathon[58] twin names shall stand;
They were true Glory's stainless victories, 610
Won by the unambitious heart and hand
Of a proud, brotherly, and civic band,
All unbought champions in no princely cause
Of vice-entailed Corruption; they no land
Doomed to bewail the blasphemy of laws 615
Making Kings' rights divine, by some Draconic[59] clause.

By a lone wall a lonelier column rears
A gray and grief-worn aspect of old days;
'Tis the last remnant of the wreck of years,
And looks as with the wild-bewildered gaze 620
Of one to stone converted by amaze,

---

[55] Between Fribourg and Neuchâtel in Switzerland. At Morat in
    1476 the Swiss defeated Charles the Bold, Duke of Burgundy.
    The bones of the Burgundians were not permanently entombed
    till 1822.
[56] The bank of the mythological River Styx, on the border of
    Hades.
[57] In southeastern Italy. There in 216 B.C. Hannibal, in one of the
    most brilliant battles of history, defeated the Romans with
    great slaughter.
[58] The plain on the coast north of Athens, where in 490 B.C. the
    Persian invaders were crushed by the Greeks.
[59] Harsh. The Athenian legal code drawn up c. 621 B.C. by Draco
    was regarded as extremely severe.

---

[53] A famous fortress, opposite Coblentz; after a long siege, it was
    surrendered to the French in 1799, and soon after dismantled.
[54] Along with these.

Yet still with consciousness; and there it stands
Making a marvel that it not decays,
When the coeval[60] pride of human hands,   624
Leveled Aventicum,[61] hath strewed her subject lands.

And there—oh! sweet and sacred be the name!
Julia[62]—the daughter—the devoted—gave
Her youth to Heaven; her heart, beneath a claim
Nearest to Heaven's, broke o'er a father's grave.
Justice is sworn 'gainst tears, and hers would crave   630
The life she lived in—but the Judge was just—
And then she died on him she could not save.
Their tomb was simple, and without a bust,
And held within their urn one mind—one heart—one
    dust.

But these are deeds which should not pass away,   635
And names that must not wither, though the Earth
Forgets her empires with a just decay,
The enslavers and the enslaved—their death and birth;
The high, the mountain-majesty of Worth
Should be—and shall, survivor of its woe,   640
And from its immortality, look forth
In the Sun's face, like yonder Alpine snow,[63]
Imperishably pure beyond all things below.

Lake Leman[64] woos me with its crystal face,
The mirror where the stars and mountains view   645
The stillness of their aspect in each trace
Its clear depth yields of their far height and hue:
There is too much of Man here, to look through
With a fit mind the might which I behold;
But soon in me shall Loneliness renew   650
Thoughts hid, but not less cherished than of old,
Ere mingling with the herd had penned me in their fold.

To fly from, need not be to hate, mankind:
All are not fit with them to stir and toil,
Nor is it discontent to keep the mind   655
Deep in its fountain, lest it overboil
In the hot throng, where we become the spoil
Of our infection, till, too late and long,
We may deplore and struggle with the coil,[65]

In wretched interchange of wrong for wrong   660
Midst a contentious world, striving where none
    are strong.

There, in a moment, we may plunge our years
In fatal penitence, and in the blight
Of our own Soul turn all our blood to tears,
And colour things to come with hues of Night;   665
The race of life becomes a hopeless flight
To those that walk in darkness: on the sea
The boldest steer but where their ports invite—
But there are wanderers o'er eternity,
Whose bark drives on and on, and anchored ne'er
    shall be.   670

Is it not better, then, to be alone,   *nature*
And love Earth only for its earthly sake?
By the blue rushing of the arrowy Rhone,
Or the pure bosom of its nursing Lake,
Which feeds it as a mother who doth make   675
A fair but froward[66] infant her own care,
Kissing its cries away as these awake;—
Is it not better thus our lives to wear,
Than join the crushing crowd, doomed to inflict
    or bear?
                                                    *rather than hurt
                                                        or care*
I live not in myself, but I become   680
Portion of that around me; and to me
High mountains are a feeling, but the hum
Of human cities torture: I can see
Nothing to loathe in Nature, save to be
A link reluctant in a fleshly chain,   685
Classed among creatures, when the soul can flee,
And with the sky—the peak—the heaving plain
Of ocean, or the stars, mingle—and not in vain.

And thus I am absorbed, and this is life:—
I look upon the peopled desert past,   690
As on a place of agony and strife,
Where, for some sin, to Sorrow I was cast,
To act and suffer, but remount at last
With a fresh pinion; which I feel to spring,
Though young, yet waxing vigorous as the Blast   695
Which it would cope with, on delighted wing,
Spurning the clay-cold bonds which round our being
    cling.

And when, at length, the mind shall be all free
From what it hates in this degraded form,
Reft of its carnal life, save what shall be   700
Existent happier in the fly and worm,—

---

60 Contemporary.
61 The Roman capital of Helvetia (Switzerland), near Morat. The
    column was all that remained.
62 Julius Alpinus was executed by the Romans in 69 A.D. for re-
    bellion. An account of how his daughter, a young priestess, died
    after an attempt to save him seems to be a Renaissance forgery.
63 Mont Blanc.
64 Lake Geneva. On the southern shore, near the Shelleys, Byron
    had taken the Villa Diodati. "Too much of Man," etc. (lines
    648 ff.), doubtless refers to his anxiety to secure privacy from
    tourists who were attracted by his notoriety.
65 Tumult, trouble.

66 Willful.

When Elements to Elements conform,
And dust is as it should be, shall I not
Feel all I see, less dazzling, but more warm?
The bodiless thought? the Spirit of each spot?   705
Of which, even now, I share at times the immortal lot?

Are not the mountains, waves, and skies, a part
Of me and of my Soul, as I of them?
Is not the love of these deep in my heart
With a pure passion? should I not contemn   710
All objects, if compared with these? and stem
A tide of suffering, rather than forgo
Such feelings for the hard and worldly phlegm
Of those whose eyes are only turned below,
Gazing upon the ground, with thoughts which
      dare not glow?   715

But this is not my theme; and I return
To that which is immediate, and require
Those who find contemplation in the urn,
To look on One, whose dust was once all fire,—
A native of the land where I respire   720
The clear air for a while—a passing guest,
Where he became a being,—whose desire
Was to be glorious; 'twas a foolish quest,
The which to gain and keep, he sacrificed all rest.

Here the self-torturing sophist, wild Rousseau,   725
The apostle of Affliction, he who threw
Enchantment over Passion, and from Woe
Wrung overwhelming eloquence, first drew
The breath which made him wretched; yet he knew
How to make Madness beautiful, and cast   730
O'er erring deeds and thoughts a heavenly hue
Of words, like sunbeams, dazzling as they past
The eyes, which o'er them shed tears feelingly and fast.

His love was Passion's essence—as a tree
On fire by lightning; with ethereal flame   735
Kindled he was, and blasted; for to be
Thus and enamoured, were in him the same.
But his was not the love of living dame,
Nor of the dead who rise upon our dreams,
But of ideal Beauty, which became   740
In him existence, and o'erflowing teems
Along his burning page, distempered though it seems.

This breathed itself to life in Julie,[67] *this*
Invested her with all that's wild and sweet;

This hallowed, too, the memorable kiss   745
Which every morn his fevered lip would greet,
From hers, who but with friendship his would meet;[68]
But to that gentle touch, through brain and breast
Flashed the thrilled Spirit's love-devouring heat;
In that absorbing sigh perchance more blest   750
Than vulgar minds may be with all they seek possest.

His life was one long war with self-sought foes,
Or friends by him self-banished; for his mind
Had grown Suspicion's sanctuary, and chose,
For its own cruel sacrifice, the kind,   755
'Gainst whom he raged with fury strange and blind.
But he was phrensied,—wherefore, who may know?
Since cause might be which Skill could never find;
But he was phrensied by disease or woe,
To that worst pitch of all, which wears a reasoning
      show.   760

For then he was inspired, and from him came,
As from the Pythian's mystic cave[69] of yore,
Those oracles which set the world in flame,[70]
Nor ceased to burn till kingdoms were no more:
Did he not this for France? which lay, before,   765
Bowed to the inborn tyranny of years?
Broken and trembling to the yoke she bore,
Till by the voice of him and his compeers
Roused up to too much wrath, which follows
      o'ergrown fears?

They made themselves a fearful monument!   770
The wreck of old opinions—things which grew,
Breathed from the birth of Time: the veil they rent,
And what behind it lay, all earth shall view;
But good with ill they also overthrew,
Leaving but ruins, wherewith to rebuild   775
Upon the same foundation, and renew
Dungeons and thrones, which the same hour refilled,
As heretofore, because Ambition was self-willed.

But this will not endure, nor be endured!
Mankind have felt their strength, and made it felt.   780
They might have used it better, but, allured
By their new vigour, sternly have they dealt
On one another; Pity ceased to melt

---

[67] Heroine of *Julie, ou La Nouvelle Héloïse,* a romance by Jean
   Jacques Rousseau (1712–78).

[68] In his *Confessions* (II, 9) Rousseau describes the intensity (much
   admired by Byron) of his feelings when at the end of each
   morning's walk he exchanged the conventional kiss of greeting
   with the Comtesse d'Houdetot, who was another man's mistress.

[69] The site of Apollo's oracle at Delphi. His priestess, who uttered
   the prophecies in a state or appearance of frenzy, was known as
   the pythoness.

[70] I.e., he paved the way for the French Revolution.

With her once natural charities. But they,
Who in Oppression's darkness caved had dwelt,   785
They were not eagles, nourished with the day;
What marvel then, at times, if they mistook their prey?

What deep wounds ever closed without a scar?
The heart's bleed longest, and but heal to wear
That which disfigures it; and they who war   790
With their own hopes, and have been vanquished, bear
Silence, but not submission: in his lair
Fixed Passion holds his breath, until the hour
Which shall atone for years; none need despair:
It came—it cometh—and will come,—the power   795
To punish or forgive—in *one* we shall be slower.

Clear, placid Leman! thy contrasted lake,
With the wild world I dwelt in, is a thing
Which warns me, with its stillness, to forsake
Earth's troubled waters for a purer spring.   800
This quiet sail is as a noiseless wing
To waft me from distraction; once I loved
Torn Ocean's roar, but thy soft murmuring
Sounds sweet as if a Sister's voice reproved,
That I with stern delights should e'er have been so
    moved.   805

It is the hush of night, and all between
Thy margin and the mountains, dusk, yet clear,
Mellowed and mingling, yet distinctly seen,
Save darkened Jura,[71] whose capt heights appear
Precipitously steep; and drawing near,   810
There breathes a living fragrance from the shore,
Of flowers yet fresh with childhood; on the ear
Drops the light drip of the suspended oar,
Or chirps the grasshopper one good-night carol more.

He is an evening reveller who makes   815
His life an infancy, and sings his fill;
At intervals, some bird from out the brakes[72]
Starts into voice a moment, then is still.
There seems a floating whisper on the hill,
But that is fancy—for the Starlight dews   820
All silently their tears of Love instil,
Weeping themselves away, till they infuse
Deep into Nature's breast the spirit of her hues.

Ye Stars, which are the poetry of Heaven!
If in your bright leaves we would read the fate   825
Of men and empires,—'tis to be forgiven
That in our aspirations to be great,

Our destinies o'erleap their mortal state,
And claim a kindred with you; for ye are
A Beauty and a Mystery, and create   830
In us such love and reverence from afar,
That Fortune,—Fame,—Power,—Life, have named
    themselves a Star.

All Heaven and Earth are still though not in sleep,
But breathless, as we grow when feeling most;
And silent, as we stand in thoughts too deep:—   835
All Heaven and Earth are still. From the high host
Of stars to the lulled lake and mountain-coast,
All is concentered in a life intense,
Where not a beam, nor air, nor leaf is lost,
But hath a part of Being, and a sense   840
Of that which is of all Creator and Defence.

Then stirs the feeling infinite, so felt
In solitude, where we are *least* alone;
A truth, which through our being then doth melt,
And purifies from self; it is a tone,   845
The soul and source of Music, which makes known
Eternal harmony, and sheds a charm
Like to the fabled Cytherea's zone,[73]
Binding all things with beauty;—'twould disarm   849
The spectre Death, had he substantial power to harm.

Not vainly did the early Persian make
His altar the high places, and the peak
Of earth-o'ergazing mountains, and thus take
A fit and unwalled temple, there to seek
The Spirit, in whose honour shrines are weak,   855
Upreared of human hands. Come and compare
Columns and idol-dwellings—Goth or Greek—
With Nature's realms of worship, earth and air—
Nor fix on fond abodes to circumscribe thy prayer!

The sky is changed!—and such a change! Oh Night,   860
And Storm and Darkness, ye are wondrous strong,
Yet lovely in your strength, as is the light
Of a dark eye in Woman! Far along,
From peak to peak, the rattling crags among
Leaps the live thunder! Not from one lone cloud,   865
But every mountain now hath found a tongue,
And Jura answers, through her misty shroud,
Back to the joyous Alps, who call to her aloud!

And this is in the Night:—most glorious Night!
Thou wert not sent for slumber! let me be   870
A sharer in thy fierce and far delight,—
A portion of the tempest and of thee!

---

[71] A mountain range between Switzerland and France.
[72] Thickets.

[73] The belt or sash of Venus; worn by a mortal it attracted love.

How the lit lake shines, a phosphoric sea,
And the big rain comes dancing to the earth!
And now again 'tis black, and now, the glee   875
Of the loud hills shakes with its mountain-mirth,
As if they did rejoice o'er a young Earthquake's birth.

Now, where the swift Rhone cleaves his way between
Heights which appear as lovers who have parted
In hate, whose mining depths so intervene,   880
That they can meet no more, though broken-hearted:
Though in their souls, which thus each other thwarted,
Love was the very root of the fond rage
Which blighted their life's bloom, and then departed:—
Itself expired, but leaving them an age   885
Of years all winters,—war within themselves to wage:

Now, where the quick Rhone thus hath cleft his way,
The mightiest of the storms hath ta'en his stand:
For here, not one, but many, make their play
And fling their thunder-bolts from hand to hand,   890
Flashing and cast around: of all the band,
The brightest through these parted hills hath forked
His lightnings,—as if he did understand,
That in such gaps as Desolation worked,
There the hot shaft should blast whatever therein
    lurked.   895

Sky—Mountains—River—Winds—Lake—Lightnings! ye!
With night, and clouds, and thunder—and a Soul
To make these felt and feeling, well may be
Things that have made me watchful; the far roll
Of your departing voices, is the knoll[74]   900
Of what in me is sleepless,—if I rest.
But where of ye, O Tempests! is the goal?
Are ye like those within the human breast?
Or do ye find, at length, like eagles, some high nest?

Could I embody and unbosom now   905
That which is most within me,—could I wreak
My thoughts upon expression, and thus throw
Soul—heart—mind—passions—feelings—strong or
    weak—
All that I would have sought, and all I seek,
Bear, know, feel—and yet breathe—into *one* word,   910
And that one word were Lightning, I would speak;
But as it is, I live and die unheard,
With a most voiceless thought, sheathing it as a sword.

The Morn is up again, the dewy Morn,
With breath all incense, and with cheek all bloom—   915

Laughing the clouds away with playful scorn,
And living as if earth contained no tomb,—
And glowing into day: we may resume
The march of our existence: and thus I,
Still on thy shores, fair Leman! may find room   920
And food for meditation, nor pass by
Much, that may give us pause, if pondered fittingly.

Clarens![75] sweet Clarens, birthplace of deep Love!
Thine air is the young breath of passionate Thought;
Thy trees take root in Love; the snows above,   925
The very Glaciers have his colours caught,
And sun-set into rose-hues sees them wrought
By rays which sleep there lovingly: the rocks,
The permanent crags, tell here of Love, who sought
In them a refuge from the worldly shocks,   930
Which stir and sting the Soul with Hope that woos,
    then mocks.

Clarens! by heavenly feet thy paths are trod,—
Undying Love's, who here ascends a throne
To which the steps are mountains; where the God
Is a pervading Life and Light,—so shown   935
Not on those summits solely, nor alone
In the still cave and forest; o'er the flower
His eye is sparkling, and his breath hath blown,
His soft and summer breath, whose tender power
Passes the strength of storms in their most desolate
    hour.   940

All things are here of *Him;* from the black pines,
Which are his shade on high, and the loud roar
Of torrents, where he listeneth, to the vines
Which slope his green path downward to the shore,
Where the bowed Waters meet him, and adore,   945
Kissing his feet with murmurs; and the Wood,
The covert of old trees, with trunks all hoar,
But light leaves, young as joy, stands where it stood,
Offering to him, and his, a populous solitude.

A populous solitude of bees and birds,   950
And fairy-formed and many-coloured things,
Who worship him with notes more sweet than words,
And innocently open their glad wings,
Fearless and full of life: the gush of springs,
And fall of lofty fountains, and the bend   955
Of stirring branches, and the bud which brings
The swiftest thought of Beauty, here extend
Mingling—and made by Love—unto one mighty end.

---

[74] Knell.

[75] A village near Vevey on Lake Geneva. The reference is to the
    lovers in Rousseau's *La Nouvelle Héloïse.*

He who hath loved not, here would learn that lore,
And make his heart a spirit; he who knows   960
That tender mystery, will love the more;
For this is Love's recess, where vain men's woes,
And the world's waste, have driven him far from those,
For 'tis his nature to advance or die;
He stands not still, but or decays, or grows   965
Into a boundless blessing, which may vie
With the immortal lights, in its eternity!

'Twas not for fiction chose Rousseau this spot,
Peopling it with affections; but he found
It was the scene which Passion must allot   970
To the Mind's purified beings; 'twas the ground
Where early Love his Psyche's zone unbound,[76]
And hallowed it with loveliness: 'tis lone,
And wonderful, and deep, and hath a sound,
And sense, and sight of sweetness; here the Rhone   975
Hath spread himself a couch, the Alps have reared a
  throne.

Lausanne! and Ferney![77] ye have been the abodes
Of Names which unto you bequeathed a name;
Mortals, who sought and found, by dangerous roads,
A path to perpetuity of Fame: 980
They were gigantic minds, and their steep aim
Was, Titan-like, on daring doubts to pile
Thoughts which should call down thunder, and the
  flame
Of Heaven again assailed[78]— if Heaven, the while,
On man and man's research could deign do more than
  smile.   985

The one was fire and fickleness, a child
Most mutable in wishes, but in mind
A wit as various,—gay, grave, sage, or wild,—
Historian, bard, philosopher, combined;
He multiplied himself among mankind,   990
The Proteus[79] of their talents: But his own
Breathed most in ridicule,—which, as the wind,
Blew where it listed, laying all things prone,—
Now to o'erthrow a fool, and now to shake a throne.

The other, deep and slow, exhausting thought,   995
And hiving wisdom with each studious year,
In meditation dwelt—with learning wrought,
And shaped his weapon with an edge severe,
Sapping a solemn creed with solemn sneer;[80]
The lord of irony,—that master spell,   1000
Which stung his foes to wrath, which grew from fear,
And doomed him to the zealot's ready Hell,
Which answers to all doubts so eloquently well.

Yet, peace be with their ashes,—for by them,
If merited, the penalty is paid;   1005
It is not ours to judge,—far less condemn;
The hour must come when such things shall be made
Known unto all,—or hope and dread allayed
By slumber, on one pillow, in the dust,
Which, thus much we are sure, must lie decayed;   1010
And when it shall revive, as is our trust,
'Twill be to be forgiven—or suffer what is just.

But let me quit Man's works, again to read
His Maker's, spread around me, and suspend
This page, which from my reveries I feed,   1015
Until it seems prolonging without end.
The clouds above me to the white Alps tend,
And I must pierce them, and survey whate'er
May be permitted, as my steps I bend
To their most great and growing region, where   1020
The earth to her embrace compels the powers of air.

Italia, too! Italia! looking on thee,
Full flashes on the Soul the light of ages,
Since the fierce Carthaginian[81] almost won thee,
To the last halo of the Chiefs and Sages   1025
Who glorify thy consecrated pages;
Thou wert the throne and grave of empires—still,
The fount at which the panting Mind assuages
Her thirst of knowledge, quaffing there her fill,
Flows from the eternal source of Rome's imperial
  hill.   1030

Thus far have I proceeded in a theme
Renewed with no kind auspices:—to feel
We are not what we have been, and to deem
We are not what we should be,—and to steel
The heart against itself; and to conceal,   1035
With a proud caution, love, or hate, or aught,—
Passion or feeling, purpose, grief, or zeal,
Which is the tyrant Spirit of our thought,—
Is a stern task of soul:—No matter,—it is taught.

---

76 For Rousseau's growth in experience there, see his *Confessions*,
  I, 4.
77 At Ferney or Fernex (near Geneva) lived François Marie Arouet,
  called Voltaire (1694–1778), and at Lausanne (on the north
  shore of the Lake) the most famous of English historians,
  Edward Gibbon (1737–94).
78 As, in Greek mythology, the Titans attacked and were defeated
  by the Olympian gods.
79 A sea god who could assume varied forms.—The subject of this
  stanza is Voltaire; of the next, Gibbon, author of *The Decline
  and Fall of the Roman Empire*.

80 Gibbon is sometimes satirical at the expense of Christianity.
81 Hannibal (247–183 B.C.), who invaded Italy.

And for these words, thus woven into song,   1040
It may be that they are a harmless wile,—
The colouring of the scenes which fleet along,
Which I would seize, in passing, to beguile
My breast, or that of others, for a while.
Fame is the thirst of youth,—but I am not   1045
So young as to regard men's frown or smile,
As loss or guerdon of a glorious lot;—
I stood and stand alone,—remembered or forgot.

I have not loved the World, nor the World me;
I have not flattered its rank breath, nor bowed   1050
To its idolatries a patient knee,
Nor coined my cheek to smiles,—nor cried aloud
In worship of an echo: in the crowd
They could not deem me one of such—I stood
Among them, but not of them—in a shroud   1055
Of thoughts which were not their thoughts, and still
    could,
Had I not filed[82] my mind, which thus itself subdued.

I have not loved the World, nor the World me,—
But let us part fair foes; I do believe,
Though I have found them not, that there may be   1060
Words which are things,—hopes which will not deceive,
And Virtues which are merciful, nor weave
Snares for the failing: I would also deem
O'er others' griefs that some sincerely grieve—
That two, or one, are almost what they seem,—   1065
That Goodness is no name—and Happiness no dream.

My daughter! with thy name this song begun!
My daughter! with thy name thus much shall end!—
I see thee not—I hear thee not—but none
Can be so wrapt in thee; Thou art the Friend   1070
To whom the shadows of far years extend:
Albeit my brow thou never should'st behold,
My voice shall with thy future visions blend,
And reach into thy heart,—when mine is cold,
A token and a tone, even from thy father's mould.   1075

To aid thy mind's development,—to watch
Thy dawn of little joys,—to sit and see
Almost thy very growth,—to view thee catch
Knowledge of objects, wonders yet to thee!
To hold thee lightly on a gentle knee,   1080
And print on thy soft cheek a parent's kiss,—
This, it should seem, was not reserved for me—
Yet this was in my nature:—as it is,
I know not what is there, yet something like to this.

Yet, though dull Hate as duty should be taught,[83] 1085
I know that thou wilt love me,—though my name
Should be shut from thee, as a spell still fraught
With desolation, and a broken claim:
Though the grave closed between us,—'twere the
    same—
I know that thou wilt love me—though to drain   1090
My blood from out thy being were an aim,
And an attainment,—all would be in vain,—
Still thou would'st love me, still that more than life
    retain.

The child of Love, though born in bitterness,
And nurtured in Convulsion! Of thy sire   1095
These were the elements,—and thine no less.
As yet such are around thee,—but thy fire
Shall be more tempered, and thy hope far higher.
Sweet be thy cradled slumbers! O'er the sea
And from the mountains where I now respire,   1100
Fain would I waft such blessing upon thee,
As—with a sigh—I deem thou might'st have been to me!

from CANTO IV

I stood in Venice, on the "Bridge of Sighs";[1]
A Palace and a prison on each hand:
I saw from out the wave her structures rise
As from the stroke of the Enchanter's wand:
A thousand Years their cloudy wings expand   5
Around me, and a dying Glory smiles
O'er the far times, when many a subject land
Look'd to the wingèd Lion's[2] marble piles,
Where Venice sate in state, throned on her hundred
    isles!

She looks a sea Cybele,[3] fresh from Ocean,   10
Rising with her tiara of proud towers
At airy distance, with majestic motion,
A Ruler of the waters and their powers:
And such she was;—her daughters had their dowers
From spoils of nations, and the exhaustless East   15
Poured in her lap all gems in sparkling showers.
In purple was she robed, and of her feast
Monarchs partook, and deemed their dignity increased.

In Venice Tasso's echoes are no more,
And silent rows the songless gondolier;[4]   20

---

[82] Defiled (by admitting "their thoughts"). For *filed,* see *Macbeth,*
   III, i, 65.

[83] By Lady Byron.

[1] A covered bridge connecting the ducal palace with the prison.
[2] Symbol of Venice.
[3] I.e., a sea goddess corresponding to the great earth goddess; the
    latter was depicted wearing a turreted crown.
[4] The gondoliers used to sing stanzas from the epic *Jerusalem
    Delivered* of Torquato Tasso (1554–95).

Her palaces are crumbling to the shore,
And Music meets not always now the ear:
Those days are gone—but Beauty still is here.
States fall, arts fade—but Nature doth not die,
Nor yet forget how Venice once was dear,   25
The pleasant place of all festivity,
The Revel of the earth, the Masque of Italy!

But unto us she hath a spell beyond
Her name in story, and her long array
Of mighty shadows, whose dim forms despond   30
Above the Dogeless city's vanished sway;
Ours is a trophy which will not decay
With the Rialto;[5] Shylock and the Moor,[6]
And Pierre,[7] can not be swept or worn away—
The keystones of the Arch! though all were o'er, 35
For us repeopled were[8] the solitary shore.

The Beings of the Mind are not of clay:
Essentially immortal, they create
And multiply in us a brighter ray
And more beloved existence: that which Fate   40
Prohibits to dull life in this our state
Of mortal bondage, by these Spirits supplied,
First exiles, then replaces what we hate;
Watering the heart whose early flowers have died,
And with a fresher growth replenishing the void. . . . 45

Oh Rome! my Country! City of the Soul!
The orphans of the heart must turn to thee,   695
Lone Mother of dead Empires! and control
In their shut breasts their petty misery.
What are our woes and sufferance? Come and see
The cypress—hear the owl—and plod your way
O'er steps of broken thrones and temples—Ye!   700
Whose agonies are evils of a day—
A world is at our feet as fragile as our clay.

The Niobe[9] of nations! there she stands,
Childless and crownless, in her voiceless woe;
An empty urn within her wither'd hands,   705
Whose holy dust was scatter'd long ago;
The Scipios'[10] tomb contains no ashes now;

The very sepulchres lie tenantless
Of their heroic dwellers: dost thou flow,
Old Tiber![11] through a marble wilderness?   710
Rise, with thy yellow waves, and mantle her distress.

The Goth,[12] the Christian—Time—War—Flood, and
    Fire,
Have dealt upon the seven-hill'd City's pride;
She saw her glories star by star expire,
And up the steep barbarian Monarchs ride,   715
Where the car[13] climbed the Capitol;[14] far and wide
Temple and tower went down, nor left a site:
Chaos of ruins! who shall trace the void,
O'er the dim fragments cast a lunar light,
And say, "here was, or is," where all is doubly
    night? . . .   720

Can tyrants[15] but by tyrants[16] conquered be,
And Freedom find no Champion and no Child
Such as Columbia saw arise when she
Sprung forth a Pallas,[17] armed and undefiled?
Or must such minds be nourished in the wild,   860
Deep in the unpruned forest, 'midst the roar
Of cataracts, where nursing Nature smiled
On infant Washington? Has Earth no more
Such seeds within her breast, or Europe no such shore? . . .

Arches on arches! as it were that Rome,
Collecting the chief trophies of her line,   1145
Would build up all her triumphs in one dome,
Her Coliseum[18] stands; the moonbeams shine
As 'twere its natural torches—for divine
Should be the light which streams here,—to illume
This long-explored but still exhaustless mine   1150
Of Contemplation; and the azure gloom
Of an Italian night, where the deep skies assume

Hues which have words, and speak to ye of Heaven,
Floats o'er this vast and wondrous monument,
And shadows forth its glory. There is given   1155
Unto the things of earth, which Time hath bent,
A Spirit's feeling, and where he hath leant
His Hand, but broke his scythe, there is a power
And magic in the ruined battlement,
For which the Palace of the present hour   1160
Must yield its pomp, and wait till Ages are its dower.

5 The business district.
6 In *The Merchant of Venice* and *Othello*.
7 In the fine tragedy *Venice Preserved* (1682) by Thomas Otway.
8 Would be.
9 Her children were slain by the gods of classical mythology; and she, though turned by Zeus into stone, continued weeping for them.
10 The most famous members of this Roman family were: Scipio the Elder, who invaded Africa, thus forcing the Carthaginians to recall from Italy Hannibal, whom he crushed at Zama in 202 B.C.; and Scipio the Younger, who captured Carthage in 146 B.C.

11 The river which flows through Rome. It used periodically to flood parts of the city.
12 Rome was first sacked by the Goths in 410 A.D.   13 Chariot.
14 I.e., to the temple of Jupiter. It was on the Capitoline Hill.
15 I.e., the European monarchs.   16 Such as Napoleon.
17 Pallas Athena or Minerva, goddess of wisdom, who sprang full-armed from the head of Zeus or Jove.
18 The famous Colosseum, an amphitheater built *c.* 80 A.D.

Oh Time! the Beautifier of the dead,
Adorner of the ruin—Comforter
And only Healer when the heart hath bled;
Time! the Corrector where our judgments err,   1165
The test of Truth, Love—sole philosopher,
For all beside are sophists—from thy thrift,
Which never loses though it doth defer—
Time, the Avenger! unto thee I lift
My hands, and eyes, and heart, and crave of thee a
    gift: 1170

Amidst this wreck, where thou hast made a shrine
And temple more divinely desolate—
Among thy mightier offerings here are mine,
Ruins of years—though few, yet full of fate:—
If thou hast ever seen me too elate,   1175
Hear me not; but if calmly I have borne
Good, and reserved my pride against the hate
Which shall not whelm me, let me not have worn
This iron in my soul in vain—shall *they* not mourn?

And Thou, who never yet of human wrong   1180
Left the unbalanced scale, great Nemesis![19]
Here, where the ancient paid thee homage long—
Thou who didst call the Furies[20] from the abyss,
And round Orestes[21] bade them howl and hiss
For that unnatural retribution—just,   1185
Had it but been from hands less near—in this
Thy former realm, I call thee from the dust!
Dost thou not hear my heart?—Awake! thou shalt, and
    must.

It is not that I may not have incurred,
For my ancestral faults or mine, the wound   1190
I bleed withal; and, had it been conferred
With a just weapon, it had flowed unbound;
But now my blood shall not sink in the ground—
To thee I do devote it—*Thou* shalt take
The vengeance, which shall yet be sought and
    found—   1195
Which if *I* have not taken for the sake—
But let that pass—I sleep—but Thou shalt yet awake.

And if my voice break forth, 'tis not that now
I shrink from what is suffered: let him speak
Who hath beheld decline upon my brow,   1200
Or seen my mind's convulsion leave it weak;

But in this page a record will I seek.
Not in the air shall these my words disperse,
Though I be ashes; a far hour shall wreak
The deep prophetic fulness of this verse,   1205
And pile on human heads the mountain of my curse!

That curse shall be Forgiveness.—Have I not—
Hear me, my mother Earth! behold it, Heaven!—
Have I not had to wrestle with my lot?
Have I not suffered things to be forgiven?   1210
Have I not had my brain seared, my heart riven,
Hopes sapped, name blighted, Life's life lied away?
And only not to desperation driven,
Because not altogether of such clay
As rots into the souls of those whom I survey.   1215

From mighty wrongs to petty perfidy
Have I not seen what human things could do?
From the loud roar of foaming calumny
To the small whisper of the as paltry few—
And subtler venom of the reptile crew,   1220
The Janus[22] glance of whose significant eye,
Learning to lie with silence, would *seem* true,
And without utterance, save the shrug or sigh,
Deal round to happy fools its speechless obloquy.

But I have lived, and have not lived in vain: 1225
My mind may lose its force, my blood its fire,
And my frame perish even in conquering pain;
But there is that within me which shall tire
Torture and Time, and breathe when I expire;
Something unearthly, which they deem not of,   1230
Like the remembered tone of a mute lyre,
Shall on their softened spirits sink, and move
In hearts all rocky now the late remorse of Love.

The seal is set.—Now welcome, thou dread Power!
Nameless, yet thus omnipotent, which here   1235
Walk'st in the shadow of the midnight hour
With a deep awe, yet all distinct from fear;
Thy haunts are ever where the dead walls rear
Their ivy mantles, and the solemn scene
Derives from thee a sense so deep and clear   1240
That we become a part of what has been,
And grow upon the spot—all-seeing but unseen.

And here the buzz of eager nations ran,
In murmured pity, or loud-roared applause,
As man was slaughtered by his fellow man.   1245
And wherefore slaughtered? wherefore, but because

---

[19] The classical goddess of just retribution or vengeance.
[20] In Greek mythology three snake-haired spirits of vengeance.
[21] The son of Agamemnon; in Greek tragedy he avenges his
    father's murder by killing his mother and her lover.

[22] The Roman god of doors and beginnings, depicted with two
    faces looking opposite ways.

Such were the bloody Circus'[23] genial laws,
And the imperial pleasure.—Wherefore not?
What matters where we fall to fill the maws
Of worms—on battle-plains or listed spot?[24]   1250
Both are but theaters—where the chief actors rot.

I see before me the Gladiator[25] lie:
He leans upon his hand—his manly brow
Consents to death, but conquers agony,
And his drooped head sinks gradually low—   1255
And through his side the last drops, ebbing slow
From the red gash, fall heavy, one by one,
Like the first of a thunder-shower; and now
The arena swims around him—he is gone,
Ere ceased the inhuman shout which hailed the wretch
        who won.   1260

He heard it, but he heeded not—his eyes
Were with his heart—and that was far away;
He recked not of the life he lost nor prize,
But where his rude hut by the Danube lay,
There were his young barbarians all at play,   1265
There was their Dacian[26] mother—he, their sire,
Butchered to make a Roman holiday—
All this rushed with his blood—Shall he expire
And unavenged? Arise! ye Goths, and glut your ire!

But here, where Murder breathed her bloody steam;—
And here, where buzzing nations choked the ways, 1271
And roared or murmured like a mountain stream
Dashing or winding as its torrent strays;
Here, where the Roman million's blame or praise
Was death or life—the playthings of a crowd—   1275
My voice sounds much—and fall the stars' faint rays
On the arena void—seats crushed—walls bowed—
And galleries, where my steps seem echoes strangely
        loud.

A Ruin—yet what Ruin! from its mass
Walls—palaces—half-cities, have been reared;   1280
Yet oft the enormous skeleton ye pass,
And marvel where the spoil could have appeared.
Hath it indeed been plundered, or but cleared?
Alas! developed, opens the decay,
When the colossal fabric's form is neared: 1285

It will not bear the brightness of the day,
Which streams too much on all—years—man—have
        reft away.

But when the rising moon begins to climb
Its topmost arch, and gently pauses there—
When the stars twinkle through the loops[27] of Time,
And the low night-breeze waves along the air   1291
The garland-forest, which the gray walls wear,
Like laurels on the bald first Caesar's head—
When the light shines serene but doth not glare—
Then in this magic circle raise the dead;—[28]   1295
Heroes have trod this spot—'tis on their dust ye tread.

"While stands the Coliseum, Rome shall stand:
When falls the Coliseum, Rome shall fall;
And when Rome falls—the World." From our own
        land
Thus spake the pilgrims o'er this mighty wall   1300
In Saxon times, which we are wont to call
Ancient; and these three mortal things are still
On their foundations, and unaltered all—
Rome and her Ruin past Redemption's skill,
The World—the same wide den—of thieves, or what
        ye will. . . .   1305

Oh! that the Desert were my dwelling-place,   1585
With one fair Spirit for my minister,
That I might all forget the human race,
And, hating no one, love but only her!
Ye elements!—in whose ennobling stir
I feel myself exalted—Can ye not   1590
Accord me such a Being? Do I err
In deeming such inhabit many a spot?
Though with them to converse can rarely be our lot.

There is a pleasure in the pathless woods,
There is a rapture on the lonely shore,   1595
There is society, where none intrudes,
By the deep Sea, and Music in its roar:
I love not Man the less, but Nature more,
From these our interviews, in which I steal
From all I may be, or have been before,   1600
To mingle with the Universe, and feel
What I can ne'er express—yet cannot all conceal.

Roll on, thou deep and dark blue Ocean—roll!
Ten thousand fleets sweep over thee in vain;

---

[23] A large amphitheater, on whose arena the Romans' "games"
were held—especially the Circus Maximus.
[24] The area with its "list" or boundary.
[25] A famous statue, once thought to represent a dying gladiator.
[26] Dacia was a Roman province, conquered in 101–106 by the
emperor Trajan. It included parts of modern Hungary, Ro-
mania, and Bessarabia.

[27] Loopholes, windows.
[28] I.e., conjure them up, as the magicians did—within a charmed
circle.—Lines 1297-99 are from the Latin of the English historian the Venerable Bede (d. 735); quoted by Gibbon in The
Decline and Fall, where Byron found the saying. Gibbon thinks
Bede derived it from English pilgrims.

Man marks the earth with ruin—his control   1605
Stops with the shore;—upon the watery plain
The wrecks are all thy deed, nor doth remain
A shadow of man's ravage, save his own,
When, for a moment, like a drop of rain,
He sinks into thy depths with bubbling groan—   1610
Without a grave—unknelled, uncoffined, and unknown.

His steps are not upon thy paths,—thy fields
Are not a spoil for him,—thou dost arise
And shake him from thee; the vile strength he wields
For Earth's destruction thou dost all despise,   1615
Spurning him from thy bosom to the skies—
And send'st him, shivering in thy playful spray
And howling, to his Gods, where haply lies
His petty hope in some near port or bay,
And dashest him again to Earth:—there let him lay.[29]

The armaments which thunderstrike the walls   1621
Of rock-built cities, bidding nations quake,
And Monarchs tremble in their Capitals,
The oak Leviathans, whose huge ribs make
Their clay creator the vain title take   1625
Of Lord of thee, and Arbiter of War—
These are thy toys, and, as the snowy flake,
They melt into thy yeast of waves, which mar
Alike the Armada's pride or spoils of Trafalgar.[30]

Thy shores are empires, changed in all save thee—   1630
Assyria—Greece—Rome—Carthage—what are they?
Thy waters washed them power while they were free,
And many a tyrant since; their shores obey
The stranger, slave, or savage; their decay
Has dried up realms to deserts:—not so thou,   1635
Unchangeable, save to thy wild waves' play,
Time writes no wrinkle on thine azure brow—
Such as Creation's dawn beheld, thou rollest now.

Thou glorious mirror, where the Almighty's form
Glasses itself in tempests; in all time,   1640
Calm or convulsed—in breeze, or gale, or storm—
Icing the Pole, or in the torrid clime
Dark-heaving—boundless, endless, and sublime—
The image of Eternity—the throne
Of the Invisible; even from out thy slime   1645

The monsters of the deep are made—each Zone
Obeys thee—thou goest forth, dread, fathomless, alone.

And I have loved thee, Ocean! and my joy
Of youthful sports was on thy breast to be
Borne, like thy bubbles, onward: from a boy   1650
I wantoned with thy breakers—they to me
Were a delight; and if the freshening sea
Made them a terror—'twas a pleasing fear,
For I was as it were a Child of thee,
And trusted to thy billows far and near,   1655
And laid my hand upon thy mane—as I do here.

My task is done—my song hath ceased—my theme
Has died into an echo; it is fit
The spell should break of this protracted dream.
The torch shall be extinguished which hath lit   1660
My midnight lamp—and what is writ, is writ,—
Would it were worthier! but I am not now
That which I have been—and my visions flit
Less palpably before me—and the glow
Which in my Spirit dwelt is fluttering, faint, and low.

Farewell! a word that must be, and hath been—   1666
A sound which makes us linger;—yet—farewell!
Ye! who have traced the Pilgrim to the scene
Which is his last—if in your memories dwell
A thought which once was his—if on ye swell   1670
A single recollection—not in vain
He wore his sandal-shoon and scallop-shell;[31]
Farewell! with *him* alone may rest the pain,
If such there were—with *you*, the Moral of his Strain.

SO WE'LL GO NO MORE A-ROVING

This lightly tragic lyric, perhaps Byron's best, originally
formed, as did the verses "To Thomas Moore," parts of
letters written in 1817 to his old companion and brother
poet. Byron sent these letters from Italy on February 28
and July 10, adding in the latter that the first stanza of
"To Thomas Moore" had been written fifteen years
earlier, when he was leaving England. "So we'll go no
more a-roving" was composed in Lent, after a round of
dissipation and "up-all-nights" during the carnival at
Venice.

> So we'll go no more a-roving
>   So late into the night,
> Though the heart be still as loving,
>   And the moon be still as bright.

---

29 Lie. In the standard edition this grammatical lapse is explained
on the ground that the author was a lord, and wrote as well as
spoke with an appropriate "careless and negligent ease"!

30 After its defeat by the English many ships of the Spanish Armada
of 1588 were wrecked on the homeward voyage around Scotland and Ireland; and in 1805 the British lost in a storm a number
of the prizes captured in Nelson's victory at Trafalgar over the
French and Spanish fleets.

31 Worn on the hat by true pilgrims (from the Holy Land) as a
sign, like their sandals, of pilgrimage.

For the sword outwears its sheath, 5
  And the soul wears out the breast,
And the heart must pause to breathe,
  And Love itself have rest.

Though the night was made for loving,
  And the day returns too soon, 10
Yet we'll go no more a-roving
  By the light of the moon.

TO THOMAS MOORE

My boat is on the shore,
  And my bark is on the sea;
But, before I go, Tom Moore,
  Here's a double health to thee!

Here's a sigh to those who love me, 5
  And a smile to those who hate;
And, whatever sky's above me,
  Here's a heart for every fate.

Though the Ocean roar around me,
  Yet it still shall bear me on; 10
Though a desert shall surround me,
  It hath springs that may be won.

Were't the last drop in the well,
  As I gasped upon the brink,
Ere my fainting spirit fell, 15
  'Tis to thee that I would drink.

With that water, as this wine,
  The libation I would pour
Should be—peace with thine and mine,
  And a health to thee, Tom Moore. 20

from DON JUAN

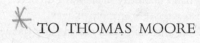

Don Juan is Byron's masterpiece, unfinished as he left it, and defiant as it is of classification. There is nothing else in literature quite like this poem, the range of which includes thrilling narrative, tender emotion, sharp satire, broad humor, sly wit, much mockery (sometimes in good taste, sometimes not), and occasionally the beauty of rapturous lyricism—most of Byron's best lyricism is here. Though parts of it still smack of the youthful, naughty Byron, it is a work of solidity and strength.

Byron began *Don Juan* in the autumn of 1818; the first two cantos were published the following summer. He wrote Cantos III and IV in the winter of 1819–20, and with the fifth they were brought out in August, 1821. He set to work on Canto VI in June of 1822; by the next March he had finished Canto XVI. Before he left for Greece in 1823 he had begun a seventeenth. Throughout these years, it is needless to remark, Byron might without exaggeration be called an industrious man. During the same period he wrote several other long poems, and all his plays except *Manfred*.

The *Don Juan* legend or saga took literary form in Spain, and was worked up in seventeenth-century Spanish and French dramas. In essence their hero is a libertine of such wickedness that he becomes more than merely amusing for his abnormal scope and energy. His defiance of morality, of human rights, of justice as well as decency, inspires by its sublime audacity a kind of tragic awe; and in the end he is most properly subjected to the fate of Dr. Faustus and dragged off to hell. The highest artistic treatment of the legend is Mozart's great opera *Don Giovanni* (1787).

Byron's hero (pronounce his name in English: *Don Joó-un*—not, as in Spanish, *Don Hwahn*) breaks with tradition. Yet the moral indignation which the poem originally encountered now seems odd. The first five cantos were actually printed without the name of either author or publisher, and the whole work was once regarded by some as calculated to corrupt any youthful reader who might circumvent his parents by getting hold of it. Juan is with Julia all innocence and inexperience, and with Haidée all love. Later on he becomes a reckless libertine, but without the slightest element of the Titan in rebellion against deity. He is certainly immoral, but he is no crusader against the moral code. On the contrary, it is the corruption of the current code that makes him what he is. He is human, he is humanity—as Byron, chiefly in and through himself, saw humanity. Byron liked privately to call him "Don Johnny," a sufficient indication that nothing satanic was intended. Juan's very weaknesses appeal to our instincts of toleration and regret for "the poor, damned human race"—because we know ourselves. That he lacks prudence and common sense is as obvious as his inability to control his passions. The great merits of the poem lie not in the narrative, admirably as Byron handles it, but in the vivacity, the rapid changes of mood, the variety, the wit, the humor, the satire, and the setting forth of the universal human comedy. *Don Juan* is not a treatise on ethics, either divine or diabolical (which is not to say that it is not rich in ethical implications); it is a reconstruction of human life on the plane of art. "A work of boundless genius," exclaims Goethe.

The stanzaic form is ottava rima, eight lines riming *ababab cc*. Part of the fun lies in the ingenuity with which the poet, sometimes comically forcing a rime, surprises us with rimed polysyllables, such as *intellectual* and *henpecked you all*.

from CANTO THE FIRST

I want a hero: an uncommon want,
  When every year and month sends forth a new one,
Till, after cloying the gazettes with cant,
  The age discovers he is not the true one;
Of such as these I should not care to vaunt,   5
  I'll therefore take our ancient friend Don Juan—
We all have seen him, in the pantomime,[1]
Sent to the devil somewhat ere his time. . . .

Brave men were living before Agamemnon[2]
  And since, exceeding valorous and sage,
A good deal like him too, though quite the same none;
  But then they shone not on the poet's page,   36
And so have been forgotten:—I condemn none,
  But can't find any in the present age
Fit for my poem (that is, for my new one);
So, as I said, I'll take my friend Don Juan.   40

Most epic poets plunge *"in medias res"*[3]
  (Horace makes this the heroic turnpike road),[4]
And then your hero tells, whene'er you please,
  What went before—by way of episode,
While seated after dinner at his ease,   45
  Beside his mistress in some soft abode,
Palace, or garden, paradise, or cavern,
Which serves the happy couple for a tavern.

That is the usual method, but not mine—
  My way is to begin with the beginning;   50
The regularity of my design
  Forbids all wandering as the worst of sinning,
And therefore I shall open with a line
  (Although it cost me half an hour in spinning)
Narrating somewhat of Don Juan's father,   55
  And also of his mother, if you'd rather.

In Seville was he born, a pleasant city,
  Famous for oranges and women,—he

Who has not seen it will be much to pity,
  So says the proverb—and I quite agree;   60
Of all the Spanish towns is none more pretty,
  Cadiz, perhaps—but that you soon may see;—
Don Juan's parents lived beside the river,
A noble stream, and called the Guadalquivir.

His father's name was Jóse—*Don,* of course,—   65
  A true Hidalgo,[5] free from every stain
Of Moor or Hebrew blood, he traced his source
  Through the most Gothic gentlemen of Spain;
A better cavalier ne'er mounted horse,
  Or, being mounted, e'er got down again,   70
Than Jóse, who begot our hero, who
Begot—but that's to come—Well, to renew: *humor*

His mother[6] was a learnèd lady, famed
  For every branch of every science known—
In every Christian language ever named,   75
  With virtues equalled by her wit alone:
She made the cleverest people quite ashamed,
  And even the good with inward envy groan,
Finding themselves so very much exceeded,
In their own way, by all the things that she did. . . .   80

Perfect she was, but as perfection is
  Insipid in this naughty world of ours,
Where our first parents never learned to kiss
  Till they were exiled from their earlier bowers,   140
Where all was peace, and innocence, and bliss,
  (I wonder how they got through the twelve hours),
Don Jóse, like a lineal son of Eve,
Went plucking various fruit without her leave.

He was a mortal of the careless kind,   145
  With no great love for learning, or the learned,
Who chose to go where'er he had a mind,
  And never dreamed his lady was concerned;
The world, as usual, wickedly inclined
  To see a kingdom or a house o'erturned,   150
Whispered he had a mistress, some said *two,*
But for domestic quarrels *one* will do.   *humor*

Now Donna Inez had, with all her merit,
  A great opinion of her own good qualities;
Neglect, indeed, requires a saint to bear it,   155
  And such, indeed, she was in her moralities;
But then she had a devil of a spirit,
  And sometimes mixed up fancies with realities,

---

[1] An adaptation of Thomas Shadwell's *The Libertine* (1675).
[2] The king who in Homer commands the Greek army against Troy. For the saying, see Horace, *Odes,* IV, ix, 25.
[3] Into the middle of things. Horace, *Ars Poetica,* line 148.
[4] I.e., Horace says that this is the best route to follow in writing a heroic poem.

[5] Nobleman (of the lower rank).
[6] This portrait, not fully reprinted here, is a caricature of Lady Byron.

And let few opportunities escape
Of getting her liege lord into a scrape.   160

This was an easy matter with a man
    Oft in the wrong, and never on his guard;
And even the wisest, do the best they can,
    Have moments, hours, and days, so unprepared,
That you might "brain them with their lady's fan";[7] 165
    And sometimes ladies hit exceeding hard,
And fans turn into falchions[8] in fair hands,
And why and wherefore no one understands.

'Tis pity learnèd virgins ever wed
    With persons of no sort of education,   170
Or gentlemen, who, though well born and bred,
    Grow tired of scientific conversation:
I don't choose to say much upon this head,
    I'm a plain man, and in a single station,
But—Oh! ye lords of ladies intellectual,   175
Inform us truly, have they not hen-pecked you all?

Don Jóse and his lady quarrelled—why,
    Not any of the many could divine,
Though several thousand people chose to try,
    'Twas surely no concern of theirs nor mine;   180
I loathe that low vice—curiosity;
    But if there's anything in which I shine,
'Tis in arranging all my friends' affairs,
Not having, of my own, domestic cares.

And so I interfered, and with the best   185
    Intentions, but their treatment was not kind;
I think the foolish people were possessed,
    For neither of them could I ever find,
Although their porter afterwards confessed—
    But that's no matter, and the worst's behind,   190
For little Juan o'er me threw, down stairs,
A pail of housemaid's water unawares.

A little curly-headed, good-for-nothing,
    And mischief-making monkey from his birth;
His parents ne'er agreed except in doting   195
    Upon the most unquiet imp on earth;
Instead of quarrelling, had they been but both in
    Their senses, they'd have sent young master forth
To school, or had him soundly whipped at home,
To teach him manners for the time to come.   200

Don Jóse and the Donna Inez led
    For some time an unhappy sort of life,
Wishing each other, not divorced, but dead;
    They lived respectably as man and wife,

Their conduct was exceedingly well-bred,   205
    And gave no outward signs of inward strife,
Until at length the smothered fire broke out,
And put the business past all kind of doubt.

For Inez called some druggists and physicians,
    And tried to prove her loving lord was *mad*,[9]   210
But as he had some lucid intermissions,
    She next decided he was only *bad*;
Yet when they asked her for her depositions,
    No sort of explanation could be had,
Save that her duty both to man and God   215
Required this conduct—which seemed very odd.

She kept a journal, where his faults were noted,
    And opened certain trunks of books and letters,
All which might, if occasion served, be quoted;
    And then she had all Seville for abettors,   220
Besides her good old grandmother (who doted);
    The hearers of her case became repeaters,
Then advocates, inquisitors, and judges,
Some for amusement, others for old grudges.

And then this best and meekest woman bore   225
    With such serenity her husband's woes,
Just as the Spartan ladies did of yore,
    Who saw their spouses killed, and nobly chose
Never to say a word about them more—
    Calmly she heard each calumny that rose,   230
And saw *his* agonies with such sublimity,
That all the world exclaimed, "What magnanimity!"

No doubt this patience, when the world is damning us,
    Is philosophic in our former friends;
'Tis also pleasant to be deem'd magnanimous,   235
    The more so in obtaining our own ends;
And what the lawyers call a "*malus animus*"[10]
    Conduct like this by no means comprehends:
Revenge in person's certainly no virtue,
But then 'tis not *my* fault, if *others* hurt you.   240

And if our quarrels should rip up old stories,
    And help them with a lie or two additional,
I'm not to blame, as you well know—no more is
    Any one else—they were become traditional;
Besides, their resurrection aids our glories   245
    By contrast, which is what we just were wishing all:
And Science profits by this resurrection—
Dead scandals form good subjects for dissection.

Their friends had tried at reconciliation,
    Then their relations, who made matters worse.   250

[7] Cf. *1 Henry IV*, II, iii, 27.   [8] Swords.

[9] Lady Byron sought medical opinion on her husband's sanity.
[10] Injurious spirit.

('Twere hard to tell upon a like occasion
  To whom it may be best to have recourse—
I can't say much for friend or yet relation):
  The lawyers did their utmost for divorce,
But scarce a fee was paid on either side   255
Before, unluckily, Don Jóse died. . . .

Dying intestate, Juan was sole heir
  To a chancery[11] suit, and messuages,[12] and lands,   290
Which, with a long minority and care,
  Promised to turn out well in proper hands:
Inez became sole guardian, which was fair,
  And answered but to Nature's just demands;
An only son left with an only mother   295
Is brought up much more wisely than another.

Sagest of women, even of widows, she
  Resolved that Juan should be quite a paragon,
And worthy of the noblest pedigree:
  (His Sire was of Castile, his Dam from Aragon):   300
Then, for accomplishments of chivalry,
  In case our Lord the King should go to war again,
He learned the arts of riding, fencing, gunnery,
And how to scale a fortress—or a nunnery.

But that which Donna Inez most desired,   305
  And saw into herself each day before all
The learnèd tutors whom for him she hired,
  Was, that his breeding should be strictly moral:
Much into all his studies she inquired,
  And so they were submitted first to her, all,   310
Arts, sciences, no branch was made a mystery
To Juan's eyes, excepting natural history.[13]

The languages, especially the dead,
  The sciences, and most of all the abstruse,
The arts, at least all such as could be said   315
  To be the most remote from common use,
In all these he was much and deeply read:
  But not a page of anything that's loose,
Or hints continuation of the species,
Was ever suffered, lest he should grow vicious. . . .   320

Young Juan waxed in goodliness and grace;   385
  At six a charming child, and at eleven
With all the promise of as fine a face
  As e'er to Man's maturer growth was given:
He studied steadily, and grew apace,
  And seemed, at least, in the right road to Heaven,   390
For half his days were passed at church, the other
Between his tutors, confessor, and mother.

At six, I said, he was a charming child,
  At twelve he was a fine, but quiet boy;
Although in infancy a little wild,   395
  They tamed him down amongst them: to destroy
His natural spirit not in vain they toiled,
  At least it seemed so; and his mother's joy
Was to declare how sage, and still, and steady,
Her young philosopher was grown already.   400

I had my doubts, perhaps I have them still,
  But what I say is neither here nor there:
I knew his father well, and have some skill
  In character—but it would not be fair
From sire to son to augur good or ill: 405
  He and his wife were an ill sorted pair—
But scandal's my aversion—I protest
Against all evil speaking, even in jest.

For my part I say nothing—nothing—but
  This I will say—my reasons are my own—   410
That if I had an only son to put
  To school (as God be praised that I have none),
'Tis not with Donna Inez I would shut
  Him up to learn his catechism alone,
No—no—I'd send him out betimes to college,   415
For there it was I picked up my own knowledge.

For there one learns—'tis not for me to boast,
  Though I acquired—but I pass over that,
As well as all the Greek I since have lost:
  I say that there's the place—but "Verbum sat,"[14]   420
I think I picked up too, as well as most,
  Knowledge of matters—but no matter what—
I never married—but, I think, I know
That sons should not be educated so.

Young Juan now was sixteen years of age,   425
  Tall, handsome, slender, but well knit: he seemed
Active, though not so sprightly, as a page;
  And everybody but his mother deemed
Him almost man; but she flew in a rage
  And bit her lips (for else she might have screamed)
If any said so—for to be precocious   431
Was in her eyes a thing the most atrocious.

Amongst her numerous acquaintance, all
  Selected for discretion and devotion,
There was the Donna Julia, whom to call   435
  Pretty were but to give a feeble notion
Of many charms in her as natural
  As sweetness to the flower, or salt to Ocean,

---

[11] Formerly the highest English court, and notorious for its delays.
[12] Dwellings and lands.   [13] I.e., biology.

[14] I.e., verbum sat sapienti est, a word to the wise is sufficient.

Her zone[15] to Venus, or his bow to Cupid,
(But this last simile is trite and stupid).   440

The darkness of her Oriental eye
  Accorded with her Moorish origin;
(Her blood was not all Spanish; by the by,
  In Spain, you know, this is a sort of sin;)
When proud Granada fell, and, forced to fly,   445
  Boabdil[16] wept: of Donna Julia's kin
Some went to Africa, some stayed in Spain—
Her great great grandmamma chose to remain. . . .

However this might be, the race went on   465
  Improving still through every generation,
Until it centred in an only son,
  Who left an only daughter; my narration
May have suggested that this single one
  Could be but Julia (whom on this occasion   470
I shall have much to speak about), and she
Was married, charming, chaste, and twenty-three.

Her eye (I'm very fond of handsome eyes)
  Was large and dark, suppressing half its fire
Until she spoke, then through its soft disguise   475
  Flashed an expression more of pride than ire,
And love than either; and there would arise
  A something in them which was not desire,
But would have been, perhaps, but for the soul
Which struggled through and chastened down the
    whole.   480

Her glossy hair was clustered o'er a brow
  Bright with intelligence, and fair, and smooth;
Her eyebrow's shape was like the aërial bow,
  Her cheek all purple with the beam of youth,
Mounting, at times, to a transparent glow,   485
  As if her veins ran lightning; she, in sooth,
Possessed an air and grace by no means common:
Her stature tall—I hate a dumpy woman.

Wedded she was some years, and to a man
  Of fifty, and such husbands are in plenty;   490
And yet, I think, instead of such a ONE
  'Twere better to have TWO of five-and-twenty,
Especially in countries near the sun:
  And now I think on 't, "*mi vien in mente*,"[17]
Ladies even of the most uneasy virtue   495
Prefer a spouse whose age is short of thirty.

'Tis a sad thing, I cannot choose but say,
  And all the fault of that indecent sun,
Who cannot leave alone our helpless clay,
  But will keep baking, broiling, burning on,   500
That howsoever people fast and pray,
  The flesh is frail, and so the soul undone:
What men call gallantry, and gods adultery,
Is much more common where the climate's sultry. . . .

Alfonso was the name of Julia's lord,
  A man well looking for his years, and who
Was neither much beloved nor yet abhorred: 515
  They lived together as most people do,
Suffering each other's foibles by accord,
  And not exactly either *one* or *two*;
Yet he was jealous, though he did not show it,
For Jealousy dislikes the world to know it. . . .   520

Juan she saw, and, as a pretty child,   545
  Caressed him often—such a thing might be
Quite innocently done, and harmless styled,
  When she had twenty years, and thirteen he;
But I am not so sure I should have smiled
  When he was sixteen, Julia twenty-three;   550
These few short years make wondrous alterations,
Particularly amongst sun-burnt nations.

Whate'er the cause might be, they had become
  Changed; for the dame grew distant, the youth shy,
Their looks cast down, their greetings almost dumb, 555
  And much embarrassment in either eye;
There surely will be little doubt with some
  That Donna Julia knew the reason why,
But as for Juan, he had no more notion
Than he who never saw the sea of Ocean.   560

Yet Julia's very coldness still was kind,
  And tremulously gentle her small hand
Withdrew itself from his, but left behind
  A little pressure, thrilling, and so bland
And slight, so very slight, that to the mind   565
  'Twas but a doubt; but ne'er magician's wand
Wrought change with all Armida's[18] fairy art
Like what this light touch left on Juan's heart.

And if she met him, though she smiled no more,
  She looked a sadness sweeter than her smile,   570
As if her heart had deeper thoughts in store
  She must not own, but cherished more the while
For that compression in its burning core;

---

[15] Belt or sash.
[16] Its last Moorish king, expelled in 1492 by Ferdinand and Isabella.
[17] It comes into my mind.

[18] A beautiful sorceress in the epic *Jerusalem Delivered* by Tasso.
She seduces the crusader Rinaldo.

Even Innocence itself has many a wile,
And will not dare to trust itself with truth,   575
And Love is taught hypocrisy from youth. . . .

Then there were sighs, the deeper for suppression,   585
    And stolen glances, sweeter for the theft,
And burning blushes, though for no transgression,
    Tremblings when met, and restlessness when left;
All these are little preludes to possession,
    Of which young Passion cannot be bereft,   590
And merely tend to show how greatly Love is
Embarrassed at first starting with a novice. . . .

She now determined that a virtuous woman
    Should rather face and overcome temptation,   610
That flight was base and dastardly, and no man
    Should ever give her heart the least sensation,
That is to say, a thought beyond the common
    Preference, that we must feel, upon occasion,
For people who are pleasanter than others,   615
But then they only seem so many brothers.

And even if by chance—and who can tell?
    The Devil's so very sly—she should discover
That all within was not so very well,
    And, if still free, that such or such a lover   620
Might please perhaps, a virtuous wife can quell
    Such thoughts, and be the better when they're over;
And if the man should ask, 'tis but denial:
I recommend young ladies to make trial.

And, then, there are such things as Love divine,   625
    Bright and immaculate, unmixed and pure,
Such as the angels think so very fine,
    And matrons, who would be no less secure,
Platonic, perfect, "just such love as mine";
    Thus Julia said—and thought so, to be sure;   630
And so I'd have her think, were I the man
On whom her reveries celestial ran.

Such love is innocent, and may exist
    Between young persons without any danger.
A hand may first, and then a lip be kissed;   635
    For my part, to such doings I'm a stranger,
But *hear* these freedoms form the utmost list
    Of all o'er which such love may be a ranger:
If people go beyond, 'tis quite a crime,
But not my fault—I tell them all in time.   640

Love, then, but Love within its proper limits,
    Was Julia's innocent determination
In young Don Juan's favour, and to him its
    Exertion might be useful on occasion;

And, lighted at too pure a shrine to dim its   645
    Ethereal lustre, with what sweet persuasion
He might be taught, by Love and her together—
I really don't know what, nor Julia either. . . .

So much for Julia! Now we'll turn to Juan.
    Poor little fellow! he had no idea
Of his own case, and never hit the true one;
    In feelings quick as Ovid's Miss Medea,[19]
He puzzled over what he found a new one,   685
    But not as yet imagined it could be a
Thing quite in course, and not at all alarming,
Which, with a little patience, might grow charming.

Silent and pensive, idle, restless, slow,
    His home deserted for the lonely wood,   690
Tormented with a wound he could not know,
    His, like all deep grief, plunged in solitude:
I'm fond myself of solitude or so,
    But then, I beg it may be understood,
By solitude I mean a Sultan's (not   695
A Hermit's) with a haram[20] for a grot. . . .

Young Juan wandered by the glassy brooks,
    Thinking unutterable things; he threw
Himself at length within the leafy nooks   715
    Where the wild branch of the cork forest grew;
There poets find materials for their books,
    And every now and then we read them through,
So that their plan and prosody[21] are eligible,
Unless, like Wordsworth, they prove unintelligible. 720

He, Juan (and not Wordsworth), so pursued
    His self-communion with his own high soul,
Until his mighty heart, in its great mood,
    Had mitigated part, though not the whole
Of its disease; he did the best he could   725
    With things not very subject to control,
And turned, without perceiving his condition,
Like Coleridge, into a metaphysician.

He thought about himself, and the whole earth,
    Of man the wonderful, and of the stars,   730
And how the deuce they ever could have birth;
    And then he thought of earthquakes, and of wars,
How many miles the moon might have in girth,
    Of air-balloons, and of the many bars

---

[19] The famous sorceress of classical legend who married Jason. She
is the heroine of the tragedy *Medea* by Euripides, but for the
present allusion see Ovid, *Metamorphoses*, VII, 9 ff.
[20] Harem, women's quarters.—*Grot* = cave.
[21] System of versification.

To perfect knowledge of the boundless skies;— 735
And then he thought of Donna Julia's eyes.

In thoughts like these true Wisdom may discern
  Longings sublime, and aspirations high,
Which some are born with, but the most part learn
  To plague themselves withal, they know not why: 740
'Twas strange that one so young should thus concern
  His brain about the action of the sky;
If *you* think 'twas Philosophy that this did,
I can't help thinking puberty assisted.

He pored upon the leaves, and on the flowers, 745
  And heard a voice in all the winds; and then
He thought of wood-nymphs and immortal bowers,
  And how the goddesses came down to men:
He missed the pathway, he forgot the hours,
  And when he looked upon his watch again, 750
He found how much old Time had been a winner—
He also found that he had lost his dinner. . . .

It was upon a day, a summer's day;—
  Summer's indeed a very dangerous season,
And so is spring about the end of May; 810
  The sun, no doubt, is the prevailing reason;
But whatsoe'er the cause is, one may say,
  And stand convicted of more truth than treason,
That there are months which nature grows more
    merry in,— 815
March has its hares, and May must have its heroine.

'Twas on a summer's day—the sixth of June:
  I like to be particular in dates,
Not only of the age, and year, but moon;
  They are a sort of post-house, where the Fates 820
Change horses, making History change its tune,
  Then spur away o'er empires and o'er states,
Leaving at last not much besides chronology,
Excepting the post-obits[22] of theology.

'Twas on the sixth of June, about the hour 825
  Of half-past six—perhaps still nearer seven—
When Julia sate within as pretty a bower
  As e'er held houri[23] in that heathenish heaven
Described by Mahomet, and Anacreon Moore,[24]

To whom the lyre and laurels have been given 830
With all the trophies of triumphant song—
He won them well, and may he wear them long!

She sate, but not alone; I know not well
  How this same interview had taken place,
And even if I knew, I should not tell— 835
  People should hold their tongues in any case;
No matter how or why the thing befell,
  But there were she and Juan, face to face—
When two such faces are so, 'twould be wise,
But very difficult, to shut their eyes. 840

How beautiful she looked! her conscious heart
  Glowed in her cheek, and yet she felt no wrong:
Oh Love! how perfect is thy mystic art,
  Strengthening the weak, and trampling on the strong!
How self-deceitful is the sagest part 845
  Of mortals whom thy lure hath led along!—
The precipice she stood on was immense,
So was her creed[25] in her own innocence.

She thought of her own strength, and Juan's youth,
  And of the folly of all prudish fears, 850
Victorious Virtue, and domestic Truth,
  And then of Don Alfonso's fifty years:
I wish these last had not occurred, in sooth,
  Because that number rarely much endears,
And through all climes, the snowy and the sunny, 855
Sounds ill in love, whate'er it may in money. . . .

Julia had honour, virtue, truth, and love 865
  For Don Alfonso; and she inly swore,
By all the vows below to Powers above,
  She never would disgrace the ring she wore,
Nor leave a wish which wisdom might reprove;
  And while she pondered this, besides much more, 870
One hand on Juan's carelessly was thrown,
Quite by mistake—she thought it was her own;

Unconsciously she leaned upon the other,
  Which played within the tangles of her hair;
And to contend with thoughts she could not smother
  She seemed, by the distraction of her air. 876
'Twas surely very wrong in Juan's mother
  To leave together this imprudent pair,
She who for many years had watched her son so—
I'm very certain *mine* would not have done so. 880

The hand which still held Juan's, by degrees
  Gently, but palpably confirmed its grasp,

---

22 I.e., post-obit bonds, payable after death. Cf. line 1000, below.
23 Nymph of the Mohammedan paradise.
24 The poet Thomas Moore (pp. 358 f., below), translator of *Odes of Anacreon* (1800). Anacreon (died 488? B.C.) survives in a handful of graceful lyrics, but his name became attached to a body of "Anacreontic" verse, much of it amorous. Moore is mentioned here on account of his Oriental poem *Lalla Rookh* (1817).

25 Belief.

As if it said, "Detain me, if you please";
    Yet there's no doubt she only meant to clasp
His fingers with a pure Platonic squeeze;   885
    She would have shrunk as from a toad, or asp,
Had she imagined such a thing could rouse
A feeling dangerous to a prudent spouse.

I cannot know what Juan thought of this,
    But what he did, is much what you would do;   890
His young lip thanked it with a grateful kiss,
    And then, abashed at its own joy, withdrew
In deep despair, lest he had done amiss,—
    Love is so very timid when 'tis new:
She blushed, and frowned not, but she strove to
        speak,   895
And held her tongue, her voice was grown so weak.

The sun set, and up rose the yellow moon:
    The Devil's in the moon for mischief; they
Who call'd her CHASTE, methinks, began too soon
    Their nomenclature; there is not a day,   900
The longest, not the twenty-first of June,
    Sees half the business in a wicked way,
On which three single hours of moonshine smile—
And then she looks so modest all the while!

There is a dangerous silence in that hour,   905
    A stillness, which leaves room for the full soul
To open all itself, without the power
    Of calling wholly back its self-control;
The silver light which, hallowing tree and tower,
    Sheds beauty and deep softness o'er the whole,   910
Breathes also to the heart, and o'er it throws
A loving languor, which is not repose.

And Julia sate with Juan, half embraced
    And half retiring from the glowing arm,
Which trembled like the bosom where 'twas placed; 915
    Yet still she must have thought there was no harm,
Or else 'twere easy to withdraw her waist;
    But then the situation had its charm,
And then—God knows what next—I can't go on;
I'm almost sorry that I e'er begun.   920

Oh Plato! Plato! you have paved the way,
    With your confounded fantasies, to more
Immoral conduct by the fancied sway
    Your system feigns o'er the controlless core
Of human hearts, than all the long array   925
    Of poets and romancers:—You're a bore,
A charlatan, a coxcomb—and have been,
At best, no better than a go-between.

And Julia's voice was lost, except in sighs,
    Until too late for useful conversation;   930
The tears were gushing from her gentle eyes,
    I wish, indeed, they had not had occasion;
But who, alas! can love, and then be wise?
    Not that Remorse did not oppose Temptation;
A little still she strove, and much repented,   935
And whispering "I will ne'er consent"—consented. . . .

Here my chaste Muse a liberty must take—
    Start not! still chaster reader—she'll be nice hence-
Forward, and there is no great cause to quake;   955
    This liberty is a poetic licence,
Which some irregularity may make
    In the design, and as I have a high sense
Of Aristotle and the Rules, 'tis fit
To beg his pardon when I err a bit.   960

This licence is to hope the reader will
    Suppose from June the sixth (the fatal day,
Without whose epoch my poetic skill
    For want of facts would all be thrown away),
But keeping Julia and Don Juan still   965
    In sight, that several months have passed; we'll say
'Twas in November, but I'm not so sure
About the day—the era's more obscure.

We'll talk of that anon.—'Tis sweet to hear
    At midnight on the blue and moonlit deep   970
The song and oar of Adria's[26] gondolier,
    By distance mellowed, o'er the waters sweep;
'Tis sweet to see the evening star appear;
    'Tis sweet to listen as the night-winds creep
From leaf to leaf; 'tis sweet to view on high   975
The rainbow, based on ocean, span the sky.

'Tis sweet to hear the watch-dog's honest bark
    Bay deep-mouthed welcome as we draw near home;
'Tis sweet to know there is an eye will mark
    Our coming, and look brighter when we come;   980
'Tis sweet to be awakened by the lark,
    Or lulled by falling waters; sweet the hum
Of bees, the voice of girls, the song of birds,
The lisp of children, and their earliest words.

Sweet is the vintage, when the showering grapes   985
    In Bacchanal profusion reel to earth,
Purple and gushing: sweet are our escapes
    From civic revelry to rural mirth;
Sweet to the miser are his glittering heaps,
    Sweet to the father is his first-born's birth,   990

---

26 The Adriatic's; i.e., in Venice.

Sweet is revenge—especially to women—
Pillage to soldiers, prize-money to seamen.

Sweet is a legacy, and passing sweet
    The unexpected death of some old lady,
Or gentleman of seventy years complete,   995
    Who've made "us youth"[27] wait too—too long
        already,
For an estate, or cash, or country seat,
    Still breaking, but with stamina so steady
That all the Israelites[28] are fit to mob its
Next owner for their double-damned post-obits.   1000

'Tis sweet to win, no matter how, one's laurels,
    By blood or ink; 'tis sweet to put an end
To strife; 'tis sometimes sweet to have our quarrels,
    Particularly with a tiresome friend:
Sweet is old wine in bottles, ale in barrels;   1005
    Dear is the helpless creature we defend
Against the world; and dear the schoolboy spot
We ne'er forget, though there we are forgot.

But sweeter still than this, than these, than all,
    Is first and passionate Love—it stands alone,   1010
Like Adam's recollection of his fall;
    The Tree of Knowledge has been plucked—all's
        known—
And Life yields nothing further to recall
    Worthy of this ambrosial sin, so shown,
No doubt in fable, as the unforgiven   1015
Fire which Prometheus[29] filched for us from Heaven. . . .

'Twas, as the watchmen say, a cloudy night;
    No moon, no stars, the wind was low or loud
By gusts, and many a sparkling hearth was bright   1075
    With the piled wood, round which the family crowd;
There's something cheerful in that sort of light,
    Even as a summer sky's without a cloud:
I'm fond of fire, and crickets, and all that,
A lobster salad, and champagne, and chat.   1080

'Twas midnight—Donna Julia was in bed,
    Sleeping, most probably,—when at her door
Arose a clatter might awake the dead,
    If they had never been awoke before,
And that they have been so we all have read,   1085
    And are to be so, at the least, once more;—

The door was fastened, but with voice and fist
First knocks were heard, then "Madam—Madam—hist!

"For God's sake, Madam—Madam—here's my master,
    With more than half the city at his back—   1090
Was ever heard of such a curst disaster!
    'Tis not my fault—I kept good watch—Alack!
Do pray undo the bolt a little faster—
    They're on the stair just now, and in a crack
Will all be here; perhaps he yet may fly—   1095
Surely the window's not so *very* high!"

By this time Don Alfonso was arrived,
    With torches, friends, and servants in great number;
The major part of them had long been wived,
    And therefore paused not to disturb the slumber   1100
Of any wicked woman, who contrived
    By stealth her husband's temples to encumber:[30]
Examples of this kind are so contagious,
Were *one* not punished, *all* would be outrageous.

I can't tell how, or why, or what suspicion   1105
    Could enter into Don Alfonso's head;
But for a cavalier of his condition[31]
    It surely was exceedingly ill-bred,
Without a word of previous admonition,
    To hold a levee round his lady's bed,   1110
And summon lackeys, armed with fire and sword,
To prove himself the thing he most abhorred.

Poor Donna Julia! starting as from sleep,
    (Mind—that I do not say—she had not slept),
Began at once to scream, and yawn, and weep;   1115
    Her maid, Antonia, who was an adept,
Contrived to fling the bed-clothes in a heap,
    As if she had just now from out them crept:
I can't tell why she should take all this trouble
To prove her mistress had been sleeping double.   1120

But Julia mistress, and Antonia maid,
    Appeared like two poor harmless women, who
Of goblins, but still more of men afraid,
    Had thought one man might be deterred by two,
And therefore side by side were gently laid,   1125
    Until the hours of absence should run through,
And truant husband should return, and say,
"My dear,—I was the first who came away."

Now Julia found at length a voice, and cried,
    "In heaven's name, Don Alfonso, what d'ye mean?

---

[27] As the elderly Falstaff describes himself and his associates in
1 Henry IV, II, ii, 89.   [28] I.e., Jewish moneylenders.
[29] In Greek myth the Titan who was punished by Zeus for stealing
fire and giving it to men.

[30] I.e., to make him by her infidelity a cuckold, in whose forehead
horns were supposed to grow, the badge of his dishonor.
[31] Rank.

Has madness seized you? would that I had died   1131
    Ere such a monster's victim I had been!
What may this midnight violence betide,
    A sudden fit of drunkenness or spleen?
Dare you suspect me, whom the thought would kill?
Search, then, the room!"—Alfonso said, "I will."   1136

He searched, *they* searched, and rummaged everywhere,
    Closet and clothes-press, chest and window-seat,
And found much linen, lace, and several pair
    Of stockings, slippers, brushes, combs, complete,   1140
With other articles of ladies fair,
    To keep them beautiful, or leave them neat:
Arras they pricked and curtains with their swords,
And wounded several shutters, and some boards.

Under the bed they searched, and there they found—
    No matter what—it was not that they sought;   1146
They opened windows, gazing if the ground
    Had signs or footmarks, but the earth said nought;
And then they stared each other's faces round:
    'Tis odd, not one of all these seekers thought,   1150
And seems to me almost a sort of blunder,
Of looking *in* the bed as well as under.

During this inquisition Julia's tongue
    Was not asleep—"Yes, search and search," she cried,
"Insult on insult heap, and wrong on wrong!   1155
    It was for this that I became a bride!
For this in silence I have suffered long
    A husband like Alfonso at my side;
But now I'll bear no more, nor here remain,
If there be law or lawyers in all Spain.   1160

"Yes, Don Alfonso! husband now no more,
    If ever you indeed deserved the name,
Is't worthy of your years?—you have three-score—
    Fifty, or sixty, it is all the same—
Is't wise or fitting, causeless to explore   1165
    For facts against a virtuous woman's fame?
Ungrateful, perjured, barbarous Don Alfonso,
How dare you think your lady would go on so? . . .

"Did not the Italian *Musico* Cazzani   1185
    Sing at my heart six months at least in vain?
Did not his countryman, Count Corniani,[32]
    Call me the only virtuous wife in Spain?
Were there not also Russians, English, many?
    The Count Strongstroganoff I put in pain,   1190

And Lord Mount Coffeehouse, the Irish peer,
Who killed himself for love (with wine) last year. . . .

"Was it for this you took your sudden journey,   1201
    Under pretence of business indispensable
With that sublime of rascals your attorney,
    Whom I see standing there, and looking sensible
Of having played the fool? though both I spurn, he
    Deserves the worst, his conduct's less defensible,   1206
Because, no doubt, 'twas for his dirty fee,
And not from any love to you nor me. . . .

"And now, Hidalgo! now that you have thrown   1225
    Doubt upon me, confusion over all,
Pray have the courtesy to make it known
    Who is the man you search for? how d'ye call
Him? what's his lineage? let him but be shown—
    I hope he's young and handsome—is he tall?   1230
Tell me—and be assured, that since you stain
Mine honour thus, it shall not be in vain.

"At least, perhaps, he has not sixty years,
    At that age he would be too old for slaughter,
Or for so young a husband's jealous fears—   1235
    (Antonia! let me have a glass of water.)
I am ashamed of having shed these tears,
    They are unworthy of my father's daughter;
My mother dreamed not in my natal hour,
That I should fall into a monster's power.   1240

"Perhaps 'tis of Antonia you are jealous,
    You saw that she was sleeping by my side,
When you broke in upon us with your fellows:
    Look where you please—we've nothing, sir, to hide;
Only another time, I trust, you'll tell us,   1245
    Or for the sake of decency abide
A moment at the door, that we may be
Dressed to receive so much good company. . . ."

But Don Alfonso stood with downcast looks,
    And, truth to say, he made a foolish figure;
When, after searching in five hundred nooks,
    And treating a young wife with so much rigour,
He gained no point, except some self-rebukes,   1285
    Added to those his lady with such vigour
Had poured upon him for the last half-hour,
Quick, thick, and heavy—as a thunder-shower. . . .

With him retired his "*posse comitatus*,"[33]   1305
    The attorney last, who lingered near the door

---

[32] The names of both Julia's Italian admirers are based by Byron on vulgar words.

[33] Properly, an armed force summoned by a sheriff to help preserve order.

Reluctantly, still tarrying there as late as
  Antonia let him—not a little sore
At this most strange and unexplain'd "*hiatus*"
  In Don Alfonso's facts, which just now wore   1310
An awkward look; as he revolved the case,
The door was fastened in his legal face.

No sooner was it bolted, than—Oh Shame!
  Oh Sin! Oh Sorrow! and Oh Womankind!
How can you do such things and keep your fame,   1315
  Unless this world, and t'other too, be blind?
Nothing so dear as an unfilched good name![34]
  But to proceed—for there is more behind:
With much heartfelt reluctance be it said,
Young Juan slipped, half-smothered, from the bed.   1320

He had been hid—I don't pretend to say
  How, nor can I indeed describe the where—
Young, slender, and packed easily, he lay,
  No doubt, in little compass, round or square;
But pity him I neither must nor may   1325
  His suffocation by that pretty pair;
'Twere better, sure, to die so, than be shut
With maudlin Clarence in his Malmsey[35] butt. . . .

What's to be done? Alfonso will be back   1345
  The moment he has sent his fools away.
Antonia's skill was put upon the rack,
  But no device could be brought into play—
And how to parry the renewed attack?
  Besides, it wanted but few hours of day: 1350
Antonia puzzled; Julia did not speak,
But pressed her bloodless lip to Juan's cheek.

He turned his lip to hers, and with his hand
  Call'd back the tangles of her wandering hair;
Even then their love they could not all command,   1355
  And half forgot their danger and despair:
Antonia's patience now was at a stand—
  "Come, come, 'tis no time now for fooling there,"
She whispered, in great wrath—"I must deposit
This pretty gentleman within the closet." . . .   1360

Now, Don Alfonso entering, but alone,
  Closed the oration of the trusty maid:
She loitered, and he told her to be gone,
  An order somewhat sullenly obeyed;   1380
However, present remedy was none,

---

[34] Cf. *Othello*, III, iii, 159.
[35] A kind of sweet wine. The execution in 1478 of the Duke of
  Clarence, brother of Edward IV and Richard III, was said to
  have been finished off by his being drowned in a cask of it.

And no great good seemed answered if she staid:
Regarding both with slow and sidelong view,
  She snuffed the candle, curtsied, and withdrew. . . .

Alfonso closed his speech, and begged her pardon,
  Which Julia half withheld, and then half granted,
And laid conditions he thought very hard on,   1435
  Denying several little things he wanted:
He stood like Adam lingering near his garden,
  With useless penitence perplexed and haunted,
Beseeching she no further would refuse,
When, lo! he stumbled o'er a pair of shoes.   1440

A pair of shoes!—what then? not much, if they
  Are such as fit with ladies' feet, but these
(No one can tell how much I grieve to say)
  Were masculine; to see them, and to seize,
Was but a moment's act.—Ah! well-a-day!   1445
  My teeth begin to chatter, my veins freeze!
Alfonso first examined well their fashion,
And then flew out into another passion.

He left the room for his relinquished sword,
  And Julia instant to the closet flew.   1450
"Fly, Juan, fly! for Heaven's sake—not a word—
  The door is open—you may yet slip through
The passage you so often have explored—
  Here is the garden-key—Fly—fly—Adieu!
Haste—haste! I hear Alfonso's hurrying feet—   1455
Day has not broke—there's no one in the street."

None can say that this was not good advice,
  The only mischief was, it came too late;
Of all experience 'tis the usual price,
  A sort of income-tax laid on by fate: 1460
Juan had reached the room-door in a trice,
  And might have done so by the garden-gate,
But met Alfonso in his dressing-gown,
Who threatened death—so Juan knocked him down.

Dire was the scuffle, and out went the light;   1465
  Antonia cried out "Rape!" and Julia "Fire!"
But not a servant stirred to aid the fight.
  Alfonso, pommelled to his heart's desire,
Swore lustily he'd be revenged this night;
  And Juan, too, blasphemed an octave higher;   1470
His blood was up: though young, he was a Tartar,
And not at all disposed to prove a martyr.

Alfonso's sword had dropped ere he could draw it,
  And they continued battling hand to hand,
For Juan very luckily ne'er saw it;   1475
  His temper not being under great command,

If at that moment he had chanced to claw it,
　Alfonso's days had not been in the land
Much longer.—Think of husbands', lovers' lives!
And how ye may be doubly widows—wives!　　　1480

Alfonso grappled to detain the foe,
　And Juan throttled him to get away,
And blood ('twas from the nose) began to flow;
　At last, as they more faintly wrestling lay,
Juan contrived to give an awkward blow,　　　1485
　And then his only garment quite gave way;
He fled, like Joseph,[36] leaving it; but there,
I doubt,[37] all likeness ends between the pair.

Lights came at length, and men, and maids, who found
　An awkward spectacle their eyes before;　　　1490
Antonia in hysterics, Julia swooned,
　Alfonso leaning, breathless, by the door;
Some half-torn drapery scattered on the ground,
　Some blood, and several footsteps, but no more:
Juan the gate gained, turned the key about,　　　1495
And liking not the inside, locked the out.

Here ends this canto.—Need I sing, or say,
　How Juan, naked, favoured by the night,
Who favours what she should not, found his way,
　And reached his home in an unseemly plight?　　　1500
The pleasant scandal which arose next day,
　The nine days' wonder which was brought to light,
And how Alfonso sued for a divorce,
Were in the English newspapers, of course. . . .

But Donna Inez, to divert the train
　Of one of the most circulating scandals
That had for centuries been known in Spain,　　　1515
　At least since the retirement of the Vandals,[38]
First vowed (and never had she vowed in vain)
　To Virgin Mary several pounds of candles;
And then, by the advice of some old ladies,
She sent her son to be shipped off from Cadiz.　　　1520

She had resolved that he should travel through
　All European climes, by land or sea,
To mend his former morals, and get new,
　Especially in France and Italy—
(At least this is the thing most people do).　　　1525
　Julia was sent into a convent—she
Grieved—but, perhaps, her feelings may be better
Shown in the following copy of her Letter:—

"They tell me 'tis decided you depart:
　'Tis wise—'tis well, but not the less a pain;　　　1530
I have no further claim on your young heart,
　Mine is the victim, and would be again:
To love too much has been the only art
　I used;—I write in haste, and if a stain
Be on this sheet, 'tis not what it appears;　　　1535
My eyeballs burn and throb, but have no tears. . . .

"Man's love is of Man's life a thing apart,　　　1545
　'Tis a Woman's whole existence; Man may range
The Court, Camp, Church, the Vessel, and the Mart;
　Sword, Gown, Gain, Glory, offer in exchange
Pride, Fame, Ambition, to fill up his heart,
　And few there are whom these cannot estrange;　　　1550
Men have all these resources, We but one,
To love again, and be again undone. . . ."

This was Don Juan's earliest scrape; but whether　　　1585
　I shall proceed with his adventures is
Dependent on the public altogether;
　We'll see, however, what they say to this:
Their favour in an author's cap's a feather,
　And no great mischief's done by their caprice;　　　1590
And if their approbation we experience,
Perhaps they'll have some more about a year hence.

My poem's epic, and is meant to be
　Divided in twelve books; each book containing,
With Love, and War, a heavy gale at sea,　　　1595
　A list of ships, and captains, and kings reigning,
New characters; the episodes are three:
　A panoramic view of Hell's in training,
After the style of Virgil and of Homer,
So that my name of Epic's no misnomer.　　　1600

All these things will be specified in time,
　With strict regard to Aristotle's rules,
The *Vade Mecum*[39] of the true sublime,
　Which makes so many poets, and some fools:
Prose poets like blank-verse, I'm fond of rhyme,　　　1605
　Good workmen never quarrel with their tools;
I've got new mythological machinery,
And very handsome supernatural scenery.

There's only one slight difference between
　Me and my epic brethren gone before,　　　1610
And here the advantage is my own, I ween
　(Not that I have not several merits more,
But this will more peculiarly be seen);
　They so embellish, that 'tis quite a bore

---

[36] See Genesis 39, especially verse 12.　　　[37] Suspect, fear.
[38] Who overran Gaul, Spain, North Africa, and Italy in the fourth
and fifth centuries. They migrated from Spain to Africa *c.* 428.

[39] Manual.

Their labyrinth of fables to thread through,   1615
Whereas this story's actually true.

If any person doubt it, I appeal
    To History, Tradition, and to Facts,
To newspapers, whose truth all know and feel,
    To plays in five, and operas in three acts;   1620
All these confirm my statement a good deal,
    But that which more completely faith exacts
Is, that myself, and several now in Seville,
Saw Juan's last elopement with the Devil.

If ever I should condescend to prose,   1625
    I'll write poetical commandments, which
Shall supersede beyond all doubt all those
    That went before; in these I shall enrich
My text with many things that no one knows,
    And carry precept to the highest pitch: 1630
I'll call the work "Longinus o'er a Bottle,
Or, Every Poet his *own* Aristotle."

Thou shalt believe in Milton, Dryden, Pope;
    Thou shalt not set up Wordsworth, Coleridge, Southey;
Because the first is crazed beyond all hope,   1635
    The second drunk, the third so quaint and mouthy:
With Crabbe[40] it may be difficult to cope,
    And Campbell's Hippocrene[41] is somewhat drouthy:
Thou shalt not steal from Samuel Rogers,[42] nor
Commit—flirtation with the muse of Moore.[43]   1640

Thou shalt not covet Mr. Sotheby's[44] Muse,
    His Pegasus,[45] nor anything that's his;
Thou shalt not bear false witness like "the Blues"[46]—
    (There's *one,* at least, is very fond of this);
Thou shalt not write, in short, but what I choose: 1645
    This is true criticism, and you may kiss—
Exactly as you please, or not,—the rod;
But if you don't, I'll lay it on, by G—d!

If any person should presume to assert
    This story is not moral, first, I pray,   1650
That they will not cry out before they're hurt,
    Then that they'll read it o'er again, and say

(But, doubtless, nobody will be so pert),
    That this is not a moral tale, though gay;
Besides, in Canto Twelfth, I mean to show   1655
The very place where wicked people go. . . .

But now at thirty years my hair is grey—
    (I wonder what it will be like at forty?
I thought of a peruke the other day—)
    My heart is not much greener; and, in short, I   1700
Have squandered my whole summer while 'twas May,
    And feel no more the spirit to retort; I
Have spent my life, both interest and principal,
And deem not, what I deemed—my soul invincible.

No more—no more—Oh! never more on me   1705
    The freshness of the heart can fall like dew,
Which out of all the lovely things we see
    Extracts emotions beautiful and new,
Hived in our bosoms like the bag o' the bee.
    Think'st thou the honey with those objects grew?
Alas! 'twas not in them, but in thy power   1711
To double even the sweetness of a flower.

No more—no more—Oh! never more, my heart,
    Canst thou be my sole world, my universe!
Once all in all, but now a thing apart,   1715
    Thou canst not be my blessing or my curse:
The illusion's gone for ever, and thou art
    Insensible, I trust, but none the worse,
And in thy stead I've got a deal of judgment,
Though Heaven knows how it ever found a lodgment.

My days of love are over; me no more   1721
    The charms of maid, wife, and still less of widow,
Can make the fool of which they made before,—
    In short, I must not lead the life I did do;
The credulous hope of mutual minds is o'er,   1725
    The copious use of claret is forbid too,
So for a good old-gentlemanly vice,
I think I must take up with avarice. . . .

But for the present, gentle reader! and
    Still gentler purchaser! the Bard—that's I—
Must, with permission, shake you by the hand,
    And so—"your humble servant, and Good-bye!"
We meet again, if we should understand   1765
    Each other; and if not, I shall not try
Your patience further than by this short sample—
'Twere well if others followed my example.

"Go, little Book, from this my solitude!
    I cast thee on the waters—go thy ways!   1770
And if, as I believe, thy vein be good,

---

40 George Crabbe (1754–1832), author of *The Village, The Parish Register, The Borough,* and other realistic poems.
41 Waters of a fountain on Mt. Helicon in Greece; i.e., poetic inspiration. On Thomas Campbell see p. 357, below.
42 Samuel Rogers (1763–1855) enjoyed a reputation far beyond his merit. He was offered the poet laureateship when Wordsworth died.   43 See above, note 24.
44 The poet and translator William Sotheby (1757–1833).
45 The winged horse of classical mythology; i.e., poetic inspiration.
46 Bluestockings, literary ladies.

The World will find thee after many days."[47]
When Southey's read, and Wordsworth understood,
   I can't help putting in my claim to praise—
The four first rhymes are Southey's every line: 1775
For God's sake, reader! take them not for mine.

from CANTO THE SECOND

Oh ye! who teach the ingenuous youth of nations,
   Holland, France, England, Germany, or Spain,
I pray ye flog them upon all occasions,
   It mends their morals, never mind the pain:
The best of mothers and of educations   5
   In Juan's case were but employed in vain,
Since, in a way that's rather of the oddest, he
Became divested of his native modesty.

Had he but been placed at a public school,[1]
   In the third form, or even in the fourth,   10
His daily task had kept his fancy cool,
   At least, had he been nurtured in the North.
Spain may prove an exception to the rule,
   But then exceptions always prove its worth—
A lad of sixteen causing a divorce   15
Puzzled his tutors very much, of course. . . .

Well—well; the World must turn upon its axis,   25
   And all Mankind turn with it, heads or tails,
And live and die, make love and pay our taxes,
   And as the veering wind shifts, shift our sails;
The King commands us, and the Doctor quacks us,
   The Priest instructs, and so our life exhales,   30
A little breath, love, wine, ambition, fame,
Fighting, devotion, dust,—perhaps a name. . . .

But to our tale: the Donna Inez sent
   Her son to Cadiz only to embark;
To stay there had not answered her intent,
   But why?—we leave the reader in the dark—   60
'Twas for a voyage the young man was meant,
   As if a Spanish ship were Noah's ark,
To wean him from the wickedness of earth,
And send him like a Dove of Promise forth.

Don Juan bade his valet pack his things   65
   According to direction, then received
A lecture and some money: for four springs
   He was to travel; and though Inez grieved

(As every kind of parting has its stings),
   She hoped he would improve—perhaps believed: 70
A letter, too, she gave (he never read it)
Of good advice—and two or three of credit. . . .

Juan embarked—the ship got under way,
   The wind was fair, the water passing rough;
A devil of a sea rolls in that bay,
   As I, who've crossed it oft, know well enough;
And, standing upon deck, the dashing spray   85
   Flies in one's face, and makes it weather-tough:
And there he stood to take, and take again,
His first—perhaps his last—farewell of Spain.

I can't but say it is an awkward sight
   To see one's native land receding through   90
The growing waters; it unmans one quite,
   Especially when life is rather new:
I recollect Great Britain's coast looks white,
   But almost every other country's blue,
When gazing on them, mystified by distance,   95
We enter on our nautical existence.

So Juan stood, bewildered on the deck:
   The wind sung, cordage strain'd, and sailors swore,
And the ship creaked, the town became a speck,
   From which away so fair and fast they bore.   100
The best of remedies is a beef-steak
   Against sea-sickness: try it, Sir, before
You sneer, and I assure you this is true,
For I have found it answer—so may you. . . .

And Juan wept, and much he sighed and thought,
   While his salt tears dropped into the salt sea,   130
"Sweets to the sweet"; (I like so much to quote;
   You must excuse this extract,—'tis where she,
The Queen of Denmark, for Ophelia brought
   Flowers to the grave;[2]) and, sobbing often, he
Reflected on his present situation,   135
And seriously resolved on reformation.

"Farewell, my Spain! a long farewell!" he cried,
   "Perhaps I may revisit thee no more,
But die, as many an exiled heart hath died,
   Of its own thirst to see again thy shore: 140
Farewell, where Guadalquivir's waters glide!
   Farewell, my mother! and, since all is o'er,
Farewell, too, dearest Julia!—(here he drew
Her letter out again, and read it through.)

---

[47] From the last stanza of the epilogue to Southey's "The Lay of the Laureate."

[1] I.e., a private school, like Eton, Harrow, etc.

[2] *Hamlet,* V, i, 266.

"And oh! if e'er I should forget, I swear— 145
    But that's impossible, and cannot be—
Sooner shall this blue Ocean melt to air,
    Sooner shall Earth resolve itself to sea,
Than I resign thine image, oh, my fair!
    Or think of anything, excepting thee; 150
A mind diseased no remedy can physic—
(Here the ship gave a lurch, and he grew sea-sick.)

"Sooner shall Heaven kiss earth—(here he fell sicker)
    Oh, Julia! what is every other woe?—
(For God's sake let me have a glass of liquor; 155
    Pedro, Battista, help me down below.)
Julia, my love—(you rascal, Pedro, quicker)—
    Oh, Julia!—(this curst vessel pitches so)—
Belovèd Julia, hear me still beseeching!"
(Here he grew inarticulate with retching.) 160

He felt that chilling heaviness of heart,
    Or rather stomach, which, alas! attends,
Beyond the best apothecary's art,
    The loss of Love, the treachery of friends,
Or death of those we dote on, when a part 165
    Of us dies with them as each fond hope ends:
No doubt he would have been much more pathetic,
But the sea acted as a strong emetic. . . .

His suite consisted of three servants and
    A tutor, the licentiate[3] Pedrillo,
Who several languages did understand, 195
    But now lay sick and speechless on his pillow
And, rocking in his hammock, longed for land,
    His headache being increased by every billow;
And the waves oozing through the port-hole made
His berth a little damp, and him afraid. 200

'Twas not without some reason, for the wind
    Increased at night, until it blew a gale;
And though 'twas not much to a naval mind,
    Some landsmen would have looked a little pale,
For sailors are, in fact, a different kind: 205
    At sunset they began to take in sail,
For the sky showed it would come on to blow,
And carry away, perhaps, a mast or so.

At one o'clock the wind with sudden shift
    Threw the ship right into the trough of the sea, 210
Which struck her aft, and made an awkward rift,
    Started the stern-post, also shattered the
Whole of her stern-frame, and, ere she could lift
    Herself from out her present jeopardy,

---

[3] Holder of a degree between bachelor and doctor.

The rudder tore away: 'twas time to sound 215
The pumps, and there were four feet water found. . . .

There she lay, motionless, and seem'd upset;
    The water left the hold, and washed the decks,
And made a scene men do not soon forget;
    For they remember battles, fires, and wrecks,
Or any other thing that brings regret, 245
    Or breaks their hopes, or hearts, or heads, or necks:
Thus drownings are much talked of by the divers,
And swimmers, who may chance to be survivors.

Immediately the masts were cut away,
    Both main and mizen; first the mizen went, 250
The main-mast followed: but the ship still lay
    Like a mere log, and baffled our intent.
Foremast and bowsprit were cut down, and they
    Eased her at last (although we never meant
To part with all till every hope was blighted), 255
And then with violence the old ship righted.

It may be easily supposed, while this
    Was going on, some people were unquiet,
That passengers would find it much amiss
    To lose their lives, as well as spoil their diet; 260
That even the able seaman, deeming his
    Days nearly o'er, might be disposed to riot,
As upon such occasions tars will ask
For grog, and sometimes drink rum from the cask.

There's nought, no doubt, so much the spirit calms 265
    As rum and true religion: thus it was,
Some plundered, some drank spirits, some sung psalms,
    The high wind made the treble, and as bass
The hoarse harsh waves kept time; fright cured the
        qualms
    Of all the luckless landsmen's sea-sick maws: 270
Strange sounds of wailing, blasphemy, devotion,
Clamoured in chorus to the roaring Ocean.

Perhaps more mischief had been done, but for
    Our Juan, who, with sense beyond his years,
Got to the spirit-room, and stood before 275
    It with a pair of pistols; and their fears,
As if Death were more dreadful by his door
    Of fire than water, spite of oaths and tears,
Kept still aloof the crew, who, ere they sunk,
Thought it would be becoming to die drunk. 280

"Give us more grog," they cried, "for it will be
    All one an hour hence." Juan answer'd, "No!
'Tis true that Death awaits both you and me,
    But let us die like men, not sink below

Like brutes":—and thus his dangerous post kept he, 285
  And none liked to anticipate the blow;
And even Pedrillo, his most reverend tutor,
Was for some rum a disappointed suitor. . . .

The ship was evidently settling now 345
  Fast by the head; and, all distinction gone,
Some went to prayers again, and made a vow
  Of candles to their saints—but there were none
To pay them with; and some looked o'er the bow;
  Some hoisted out the boats; and there was one 350
That begged Pedrillo for an absolution,
Who told him to be damned—in his confusion.

Some lashed them in their hammocks; some put on
  Their best clothes, as if going to a fair;
Some cursed the day on which they saw the Sun, 355
  And gnashed their teeth, and howling, tore their hair;
And others went on as they had begun,
  Getting the boats out, being well aware
That a tight boat will live in a rough sea,
Unless with breakers close beneath her lee. 360

The worst of all was, that in their condition,
  Having been several days in great distress,
'Twas difficult to get out such provision
  As now might render their long suffering less:
Men, even when dying, dislike inanition;[4] 365
  Their stock was damaged by the weather's stress:
Two casks of biscuit, and a keg of butter,
Were all that could be thrown into the cutter.

But in the long-boat they contrived to stow
  Some pounds of bread, though injured by the
    wet; 370
Water, a twenty-gallon cask or so;
  Six flasks of wine; and they contrived to get
A portion of their beef up from below,
  And with a piece of pork, moreover, met,
But scarce enough to serve them for a luncheon— 375
Then there was rum, eight gallons in a puncheon.

The other boats, the yawl and pinnace, had
  Been stove in the beginning of the gale;
And the long-boat's condition was but bad,
  As there were but two blankets for a sail, 380
And one oar for a mast, which a young lad
  Threw in by good luck over the ship's rail;
And two boats could not hold, far less be stored,
To save one half the people then on board.

'Twas twilight, and the sunless day went down 385
  Over the waste of waters; like a veil,
Which, if withdrawn, would but disclose the frown
  Of one whose hate is masked but to assail.
Thus to their hopeless eyes the night was shown,
  And grimly darkled o'er the faces pale, 390
And the dim desolate deep: twelve days had Fear
Been their familiar, and now Death was here.

Some trial had been making at a raft,
  With little hope in such a rolling sea,
A sort of thing at which one would have laughed, 395
  If any laughter at such times could be,
Unless with people who too much have quaffed,
  And have a kind of wild and horrid glee,
Half epileptical, and half hysterical:—
  Their preservation would have been a miracle. 400

At half-past eight o'clock, booms, hencoops, spars,
  And all things, for a chance, had been cast loose,
That still could keep afloat the struggling tars,
  For yet they strove, although of no great use:
There was no light in heaven but a few stars, 405
  The boats put off o'ercrowded with their crews;
She gave a heel, and then a lurch to port,
And, going down head foremost—sunk, in short.

Then rose from sea to sky the wild farewell—
  Then shrieked the timid, and stood still the brave—
Then some leaped overboard with dreadful yell, 411
  As[5] eager to anticipate their grave;
And the sea yawned around her like a hell,
  And down she sucked with her the whirling wave,
Like one who grapples with his enemy, 415
And strives to strangle him before he die.

And first one universal shriek there rushed,
  Louder than the loud Ocean, like a crash
Of echoing thunder; and then all was hushed,
  Save the wild wind and the remorseless dash 420
Of billows; but at intervals there gushed,
  Accompanied with a convulsive splash,
A solitary shriek, the bubbling cry
Of some strong swimmer in his agony.

The boats, as stated, had got off before, 425
  And in them crowded several of the crew;
And yet their present hope was hardly more
  Than what it had been, for so strong it blew
There was slight chance of reaching any shore;
  And then they were too many, though so few— 430

---

[4] Emptiness.

[5] As if.

Nine in the cutter, thirty in the boat,
Were counted in them when they got afloat. . . .

Juan got into the long-boat, and there
    Contrived to help Pedrillo to a place;
It seemed as if they had exchanged their care,
    For Juan wore the magisterial face
Which courage gives, while poor Pedrillo's pair   445
    Of eyes were crying for their owner's case:
Battista, though, (a name called shortly Tita),
Was lost by getting at some aqua-vita.[6]

Pedro, his valet, too, he tried to save,
    But the same cause, conducive to his loss,   450
Left him so drunk, he jumped into the wave,
    As o'er the cutter's edge he tried to cross,
And so he found a wine-and-watery grave;
    They could not rescue him although so close,
Because the sea ran higher every minute,   455
And for the boat—the crew kept crowding in it.

A small old spaniel,—which had been Don Jóse's,
    His father's, whom he loved, as ye may think,
For on such things the memory reposes
    With tenderness—stood howling on the brink,   460
Knowing, (dogs have such intellectual noses!)
    No doubt, the vessel was about to sink;
And Juan caught him up, and ere he stepped
Off threw him in, then after him he leaped.

He also stuffed his money where he could   465
    About his person, and Pedrillo's too,
Who let him do, in fact, whate'er he would,
    Not knowing what himself to say, or do,
As every rising wave his dread renewed;
    But Juan, trusting they might still get through,   470
And deeming there were remedies for any ill,
Thus re-embarked his tutor and his spaniel.

'Twas a rough night, and blew so stiffly yet,
    That the sail was becalmed between the seas,
Though on the wave's high top too much to set,   475
    They dared not take it in for all the breeze:
Each sea curled o'er the stern, and kept them wet,
    And made them bale without a moment's ease,
So that themselves as well as hopes were damped,
And the poor little cutter quickly swamped.   480

Nine souls more went in her: the long-boat still
    Kept above water, with an oar for mast,

Two blankets stitched together, answering ill
    Instead of sail, were to the oar made fast;
Though every wave rolled menacing to fill,   485
    And present peril all before surpassed,
They grieved for those who perished with the cutter,
And also for the biscuit-casks and butter. . . .

But man is a carnivorous production,
    And must have meals, at least one meal a day;   530
He cannot live, like woodcocks,[7] upon suction,
    But, like the shark and tiger, must have prey;
Although his anatomical construction
    Bears vegetables, in a grumbling way,
Your labouring people think beyond all question   535
Beef, veal, and mutton, better for digestion.

And thus it was with this our hapless crew;
    For on the third day there came on a calm,
And though at first their strength it might renew,
    And lying on their weariness like balm,   540
Lulled them like turtles sleeping on the blue
    Of Ocean, when they woke they felt a qualm,
And fell all ravenously on their provision,
Instead of hoarding it with due precision.

The consequence was easily foreseen—   545
    They ate up all they had, and drank their wine,
In spite of all remonstrances, and then
    On what, in fact, next day were they to dine?
They hoped the wind would rise, these foolish men!
    And carry them to shore; these hopes were fine,   550
But as they had but one oar, and that brittle,
It would have been more wise to save their victual.

The fourth day came, but not a breath of air,
    And Ocean slumbered like an unweaned child:
The fifth day, and their boat lay floating there,   555
    The sea and sky were blue, and clear, and mild—
With their one oar (I wish they had had a pair)
    What could they do? and Hunger's rage grew wild:
So Juan's spaniel, spite of his entreating,
Was killed, and portion'd out for present eating.   560

On the sixth day they fed upon his hide,
    And Juan, who had still refused, because
The creature was his father's dog that died,
    Now feeling all the vulture in his jaws,
With some remorse received (though first denied)   565
    As a great favour one of the fore-paws,
Which he divided with Pedrillo, who
Devoured it, longing for the other too.

6 Aqua vitae; brandy, etc.

7 This bird feeds chiefly at night. Like the duck it may appear to
live by "suction"; actually it depends on solid food.

The seventh day, and no wind—the burning sun
    Blistered and scorched, and, stagnant on the sea,   570
They lay like carcasses; and hope was none,
    Save in the breeze that came not: savagely
They glared upon each other—all was done,
    Water, and wine, and food,—and you might see
The longings of the cannibal arise   575
(Although they spoke not) in their wolfish eyes.

At length one whispered his companion, who
    Whispered another, and thus it went round,
And then into a hoarser murmur grew,
    An ominous, and wild, and desperate sound;   580
And when his comrade's thought each sufferer knew,
    'Twas but his own, suppressed till now, he found:
And out they spoke of lots for flesh and blood,
And who should die to be his fellow's food.

But ere they came to this, they that day shared   585
    Some leathern caps, and what remained of shoes;
And then they looked around them, and despaired,
    And none to be the sacrifice would choose;
At length the lots were torn up, and prepared,
    But of materials that must shock the Muse—   590
Having no paper, for the want of better,
They took by force from Juan Julia's letter.

Then lots were made, and marked, and mixed, and handed
    In silent horror, and their distribution
Lulled even the savage hunger which demanded,   595
    Like the Promethean vulture,[8] this pollution;
None in particular had sought or planned it,
    'Twas Nature gnawed them to this resolution,
By which none were permitted to be neuter—
And the lot fell on Juan's luckless tutor.   600

He but requested to be bled to death:
    The surgeon had his instruments, and bled
Pedrillo, and so gently ebbed his breath,
    You hardly could perceive when he was dead.
He died as born, a Catholic in faith,   605
    Like most in the belief in which they're bred,
And first a little crucifix he kissed,
And then held out his jugular and wrist.

The surgeon, as there was no other fee,
    Had his first choice of morsels for his pains;   610

But being thirstiest at the moment, he
    Preferred a draught from the fast-flowing veins:
Part was divided, part thrown in the sea,
    And such things as the entrails and the brains
Regaled two sharks, who followed o'er the billow—   615
The sailors ate the rest of poor Pedrillo.

The sailors ate him, all save three or four,
    Who were not quite so fond of animal food;
To these was added Juan, who, before
    Refusing his own spaniel, hardly could   620
Feel now his appetite increased much more;
    'Twas not to be expected that he should,
Even in extremity of their disaster,
Dine with them on his pastor and his master.[9]

'Twas better that he did not; for, in fact,   625
    The consequence was awful in the extreme;
For they, who were most ravenous in the act,
    Went raging mad—Lord! how they did blaspheme!
And foam, and roll, with strange convulsions racked,
    Drinking salt-water like a mountain-stream;   630
Tearing, and grinning, howling, screeching, swearing,
And, with hyaena-laughter, died despairing. . . .

And the same night there fell a shower of rain,   665
    For which their mouths gaped, like the cracks of earth
When dried to summer dust; till taught by pain,
    Men really know not what good water's worth;
If you had been in Turkey or in Spain,
    Or with a famished boat's-crew had your berth,   670
Or in the desert heard the camel's bell,
You'd wish yourself where Truth is—in a well.

It poured down torrents, but they were no richer
    Until they found a ragged piece of sheet,
Which served them as a sort of spongy pitcher,   675
    And when they deemed its moisture was complete,
They wrung it out, and though a thirsty ditcher[10]
    Might not have thought the scanty draught so sweet
As a full pot of porter, to their thinking
They ne'er till now had known the joys of drinking.   680

And their baked lips, with many a bloody crack,
    Sucked in the moisture, which like nectar streamed;
Their throats were ovens, their swoln tongues were black,
    As the rich man's[11] in Hell, who vainly screamed
To beg the beggar, who could not rain back   685
    A drop of dew, when every drop had seemed

---

8 One of the punishments devised by Zeus for the Titan Prometheus, who gave men the gift of fire by stealing it from heaven, was that a bird of prey should tear daily at his liver, which grew whole again by night.

9 I.e., his chaplain and his teacher.   10 Ditch digger.
11 Dives. See Luke 16:19 ff.

To taste of Heaven—If this be true, indeed,
Some Christians have a comfortable creed. . . .

As morning broke, the light wind died away,
   When he who had the watch sung out and swore, 770
If 'twas not land that rose with the Sun's ray,
   He wished that land he never might see more;
And the rest rubbed their eyes and saw a bay,
   Or thought they saw, and shaped their course for
      shore;
For shore it was, and gradually grew   775
Distinct, and high, and palpable to view.

And then of these some part burst into tears,
   And others, looking with a stupid stare,
Could not yet separate their hopes from fears,
   And seemed as if they had no further care;   780
While a few prayed—(the first time for some years)—
   And at the bottom of the boat three were
Asleep: they shook them by the hand and head,
And tried to awaken them, but found them dead. . . .

Meantime the current, with a rising gale,
   Still set them onwards to the welcome shore,
Like Charon's[12] bark of spectres, dull and pale:
   Their living freight was now reduced to four,
And three dead, whom their strength could not
      avail   805
   To heave into the deep with those before,
Though the two sharks still followed them, and dashed
The spray into their faces as they splashed.

Famine, despair, cold, thirst and heat, had done
   Their work on them by turns, and thinned them to
Such things a mother had not known her son   811
   Amidst the skeletons of that gaunt crew;
By night chilled, by day scorched, thus one by one
   They perished, until withered to these few,
But chiefly by a species of self-slaughter,   815
In washing down Pedrillo with salt water.

As they drew nigh the land, which now was seen
   Unequal in its aspect here and there,
They felt the freshness of its growing green,
   That waved in forest-tops, and smoothed the air, 820
And fell upon their glazed eyes like a screen
   From glistening waves, and skies so hot and bare—
Lovely seemed any object that should sweep
Away the vast—salt—dread—eternal Deep.

---

[12] In classical mythology, the ferryman who carries souls over the
River Styx.

The shore looked wild, without a trace of man,   825
   And girt by formidable waves; but they
Were mad for land, and thus their course they ran,
   Though right ahead the roaring breakers lay:
A reef between them also now began
   To show its boiling surf and bounding spray,   830
But finding no place for their landing better,
They ran the boat for shore,—and overset her.

But in his native stream, the Guadalquivir,
   Juan to lave his youthful limbs was wont;
And having learnt to swim in that sweet river,   835
   Had often turned the art to some account:
A better swimmer you could scarce see ever,
   He could, perhaps, have pass'd the Hellespont,
As once (a feat on which ourselves we prided)
Leander, Mr. Ekenhead, and I did.[13]   840

So here, though faint, emaciated, and stark,
   He buoyed his boyish limbs, and strove to ply
With the quick wave, and gain, ere it was dark,
   The beach which lay before him, high and dry:
The greatest danger here was from a shark,   845
   That carried off his neighbour by the thigh;
As for the other two, they could not swim,
So nobody arrived on shore but him.

Nor yet had he arrived but for the oar,
   Which, providentially for him, was washed   850
Just as his feeble arms could strike no more,
   And the hard wave o'erwhelm'd him as 'twas dashed
Within his grasp; he clung to it, and sore
   The waters beat while he thereto was lashed;
At last, with swimming, wading, scrambling, he   855
Rolled on the beach, half senseless, from the sea:

There, breathless, with his digging nails he clung
   Fast to the sand, lest the returning wave,
From whose reluctant roar his life he wrung,
   Should suck him back to her insatiate grave: 860
And there he lay, full length, where he was flung,
   Before the entrance of a cliff-worn cave,
With just enough of life to feel its pain,
And deem that it was saved, perhaps in vain. . . .

How long in his damp trance young Juan lay
   He knew not, for the earth was gone for him,
And Time had nothing more of night nor day
   For his congealing blood, and senses dim;

---

[13] Byron swam the Hellespont, or Dardanelles, on May 3, 1810.
Ekenhead was the naval lieutenant who made the swim with
him.

And how this heavy faintness passed away   885
  He knew not, till each painful pulse and limb,
And tingling vein, seemed throbbing back to life,
For Death, though vanquished, still retired with strife.

His eyes he opened, shut, again unclosed,
  For all was doubt and dizziness; he thought   890
He still was in the boat, and had but dozed,
  And felt again with his despair o'erwrought,
And wished it death in which he had reposed,
  And then once more his feelings back were brought,
And slowly by his swimming eyes was seen   895
A lovely female face of seventeen.

'Twas bending close o'er his, and the small mouth
  Seemed almost prying into his for breath;
And chafing him, the soft warm hand of youth
  Recalled his answering spirits back from Death;   900
And, bathing his chill temples, tried to soothe
  Each pulse to animation, till beneath
Its gentle touch and trembling care, a sigh
To these kind efforts made a low reply.

Then was the cordial poured, and mantle flung   905
  Around his scarce-clad limbs; and the fair arm
Raised higher the faint head which o'er it hung;
  And her transparent cheek, all pure and warm,
Pillowed his death-like forehead; then she wrung
  His dewy curls, long drenched by every storm;   910
And watched with eagerness each throb that drew
A sigh from his heaved bosom—and hers, too.

And lifting him with care into the cave,
  The gentle girl, and her attendant,—one
Young, yet her elder, and of brow less grave,   915
  And more robust of figure,—then begun
To kindle fire, and as the new flames gave
  Light to the rocks that roofed them, which the sun
Had never seen, the maid, or whatsoe'er
She was, appeared distinct, and tall, and fair. . . .   920

And these two tended him, and cheered him both
  With food and raiment, and those soft attentions,
Which are—as I must own—of female growth,
  And have ten thousand delicate inventions: 980
They made a most superior mess of broth,
  A thing which poesy but seldom mentions,
But the best dish that e'er was cooked since Homer's
Achilles order'd dinner for new comers.[14]

---

[14] *Iliad*, IX, 193 ff.

I'll tell you who they were, this female pair,   985
  Lest they should seem Princesses[15] in disguise;
Besides, I hate all mystery, and that air
  Of clap-trap, which your recent poets prize;
And so, in short, the girls they really were
  They shall appear before your curious eyes,   990
Mistress and maid; the first was only daughter
Of an old man, who lived upon the water.

A fisherman he had been in his youth,
  And still a sort of fisherman was he;
But other speculations were, in sooth,   995
  Added to his connection with the sea,
Perhaps not so respectable, in truth:
  A little smuggling, and some piracy,
Left him, at last, the sole of many masters
Of an ill-gotten million of piastres.[16]   1000

A fisher, therefore, was he,—though of men,[17]
  Like Peter the Apostle, and he fished
For wandering merchant-vessels, now and then,
  And sometimes caught as many as he wished;
The cargoes he confiscated,[18] and gain   1005
  He sought in the slave-market too, and dished
Full many a morsel for that Turkish trade,
By which, no doubt, a good deal may be made.

He was a Greek, and on his isle had built
  (One of the wild and smaller Cyclades[19])   1010
A very handsome house from out his guilt,
  And there he lived exceedingly at ease;
Heaven knows what cash he got, or blood he spilt,
  A sad[20] old fellow was he, if you please;
But this I know, it was a spacious building,   1015
Full of barbaric carving, paint, and gilding.

He had an only daughter, called Haidée,
  The greatest heiress of the Eastern Isles;
Besides, so very beautiful was she,
  Her dowry was as nothing to her smiles: 1020
Still in her teens, and like a lovely tree
  She grew to womanhood, and between whiles
Rejected several suitors, just to learn
How to accept a better in his turn.

And walking out upon the beach, below   1025
  The cliff, towards sunset, on that day she found,

---

[15] Accented in England on the second syllable.
[16] Coin of various Eastern countries, including Turkey.
[17] Cf. Matthew 4:19.
[18] Here accented (permissibly) on the second syllable.
[19] In the Aegean Sea.   [20] Shocking.

Insensible,—not dead, but nearly so,—
   Don Juan, almost famished, and half drowned;
But being naked, she was shocked, you know,
   Yet deemed herself in common pity bound,   1030
As far as in her lay, "to take him in,
A stranger"[21] dying—with so white a skin.

But taking him into her father's house
   Was not exactly the best way to save,
But like conveying to the cat the mouse,   1035
   Or people in a trance into their grave;
Because the good old man had so much "νους,"[22]
   Unlike the honest Arab thieves so brave,
He would have hospitably cured the stranger,
And sold him instantly when out of danger.   1040

And therefore, with her maid, she thought it best
   (A virgin always on her maid relies)
To place him in the cave for present rest:
   And when, at last, he opened his black eyes,
Their charity increased about their guest;   1045
   And their compassion grew to such a size,
It opened half the turnpike-gates to Heaven—
(St. Paul says,[23] 'tis the toll which must be given).

They made a fire,—but such a fire as they
   Upon the moment could contrive with such   1050
Materials as were cast up round the bay,—
   Some broken planks, and oars, that to the touch
Were nearly tinder, since so long they lay,
   A mast was almost crumbled to a crutch;
But, by God's grace, here wrecks were in such plenty,
That there was fuel to have furnished twenty.   1056

He had a bed of furs, and a pelisse,[24]
   For Haidée stripped her sables off to make
His couch; and, that he might be more at ease,
   And warm, in case by chance he should awake, 1060
They also gave a petticoat apiece,
   She and her maid,—and promised by daybreak
To pay him a fresh visit, with a dish
For breakfast, of eggs, coffee, bread, and fish.

And thus they left him to his lone repose: 1065
   Juan slept like a top, or like the dead,
Who sleep at last, perhaps (God only knows),
   Just for the present; and in his lulled head
Not even a vision of his former woes
   Throbbed in accursèd dreams, which sometimes
      spread   1070

Unwelcome visions of our former years,
Till the eye, cheated, opens thick with tears. . . .

And every day by daybreak—rather early
   For Juan, who was somewhat fond of rest—
She came into the cave, but it was merely
   To see her bird reposing in his nest;   1340
And she would softly stir his locks so curly,
   Without disturbing her yet slumbering guest,
Breathing all gently o'er his cheek and mouth,
As o'er a bed of roses the sweet South.[25] . . .

When Juan woke he found some good things ready,
   A bath, a breakfast, and the finest eyes
That ever made a youthful heart less steady,
   Besides her maid's, as pretty for their size;
But I have spoken of all this already—   1365
   And repetition's tiresome and unwise,—
Well—Juan, after bathing in the sea,
Came always back to coffee and Haidée.

Both were so young, and one so innocent,
   That bathing passed for nothing; Juan seemed 1370
To her, as 'twere, the kind of being sent,
   Of whom these two years she had nightly dreamed,
A something to be loved, a creature meant
   To be her happiness, and whom she deemed
To render happy: all who joy would win   1375
Must share it,—Happiness was born a Twin.

It was such pleasure to behold him, such
   Enlargement of existence to partake
Nature with him, to thrill beneath his touch,
   To watch him slumbering, and to see him wake: 1380
To live with him for ever were too much;
   But then the thought of parting made her quake;
He was her own, her ocean-treasure, cast
Like a rich wreck—her first love, and her last.

And thus a moon rolled on, and fair Haidée   1385
   Paid daily visits to her boy, and took
Such plentiful precautions, that still he
   Remained unknown within his craggy nook;
At last her father's prows put out to sea,
   For certain merchantmen upon the look,   1390
Not as of yore to carry off an Io,[26]
But three Ragusan vessels bound for Scio.[27]

---

[21] Cf. Matthew 25:35-36.   [22] Mind, good sense.
[23] See 1 Corinthians 13.   [24] Fur cloak.

[25] South wind. Cf. Shakespeare, *Twelfth Night*, I, i, 5-6, as emended by Pope and other editors (*south* for *sound*).
[26] A mortal maid, beloved by Zeus and persecuted by his wife. She wandered far, and among her adventures (as rationalized by Herodotus) was abduction by some Phoenician merchants.
[27] Another name for the Aegean island of Chios. Ragusa or Dubrovnik is a port on the eastern side of the Adriatic.

Then came her freedom, for she had no mother,
  So that, her father being at sea, she was
Free as a married woman, or such other 1395
  Female, as where she likes may freely pass,
Without even the encumbrance of a brother,
  The freest she that ever gazed on glass:
I speak of Christian lands in this comparison,
Where wives, at least, are seldom kept in garrison. 1400

Now she prolonged her visits and her talk
  (For they must talk), and he had learnt to say
So much as to propose to take a walk,—
  For little had he wandered since the day
On which, like a young flower snapped from the stalk,
  Drooping and dewy on the beach he lay,— 1406
And thus they walked out in the afternoon,
And saw the sun set opposite the moon.

It was a wild and breaker-beaten coast,
  With cliffs above, and a broad sandy shore, 1410
Guarded by shoals and rocks as by an host,
  With here and there a creek, whose aspect wore
A better welcome to the tempest-tost;
  And rarely ceased the haughty billow's roar,
Save on the dead long summer days, which make 1415
The outstretched Ocean glitter like a lake. . . .

The coast—I think it was the coast that I
  Was just describing—Yes, it *was* the coast—
Lay at this period quiet as the sky,
  The sands untumbled, the blue waves untossed,
And all was stillness, save the sea-bird's cry, 1445
  And dolphin's leap, and little billow crossed
By some low rock or shelve, that made it fret
Against the boundary it scarcely wet.

And forth they wandered, her sire being gone,
  As I have said, upon an expedition; 1450
And mother, brother, guardian, she had none,
  Save Zoe, who, although with due precision
She waited on her lady with the Sun,
  Thought daily service was her only mission,
Bringing warm water, wreathing her long tresses, 1455
And asking now and then for cast-off dresses.

It was the cooling hour, just when the rounded
  Red sun sinks down behind the azure hill,
Which then seems as if the whole earth it bounded,
  Circling all Nature, hushed, and dim, and still, 1460
With the far mountain-crescent half surrounded
  On one side, and the deep sea calm and chill
Upon the other, and the rosy sky
With one star sparkling through it like an eye.

And thus they wandered forth, and hand in hand, 1465
  Over the shining pebbles and the shells,
Glided along the smooth and hardened sand,
  And in the worn and wild receptacles
Worked by the storms, yet worked as it were plann'd
  In hollow halls, with sparry roofs and cells, 1470
They turned to rest; and, each clasped by an arm,
Yielded to the deep Twilight's purple charm.

They looked up to the sky, whose floating glow
  Spread like a rosy Ocean, vast and bright;
They gazed upon the glittering sea below, 1475
  Whence the broad Moon rose circling into sight;
They heard the waves splash, and the wind so low,
  And saw each other's dark eyes darting light
Into each other—and, beholding this,
Their lips drew near, and clung into a kiss; 1480

A long, long kiss, a kiss of Youth, and Love,
  And Beauty, all concéntrating like rays
Into one focus, kindled from above;
  Such kisses as belong to early days,
Where Heart, and Soul, and Sense, in concert move,
  And the blood's lava, and the pulse a blaze, 1486
Each kiss a heart-quake,—for a kiss's strength,
I think, it must be reckoned by its length.

By length I mean duration; theirs endured
  Heaven knows how long—no doubt they never
    reckoned; 1490
And if they had, they could not have secured
  The sum of their sensations to a second:
They had not spoken, but they felt allured,
  As if their souls and lips each other beckoned,
Which, being joined, like swarming bees they
    clung— 1495
Their hearts the flowers from whence the honey sprung.

They were alone, but not alone as they
  Who shut in chambers think it loneliness;
The silent Ocean, and the starlight bay,
  The twilight glow, which momently grew less, 1500
The voiceless sands, and dropping caves, that lay
  Around them, made them to each other press,
As if there were no life beneath the sky
Save theirs, and that their life could never die.

They feared no eyes nor ears on that lone beach; 1505
  They felt no terrors from the night; they were
All in all to each other: though their speech
  Was broken words, they *thought* a language there,—
And all the burning tongues the Passions teach
  Found in one sigh the best interpreter 1510

Of Nature's oracle—first love,—that all
Which Eve has left her daughters since her fall.

Haidée spoke not of scruples, asked no vows,
   Nor offered any; she had never heard
Of plight and promises to be a spouse,
   Or perils by a loving maid incurred;
She was all which pure Ignorance allows,
   And flew to her young mate like a young bird;
And, never having dreamt of falsehood, she
Had not one word to say of constancy.   1520

She loved, and was belovèd—she adored,
   And she was worshipped after Nature's fashion—
Their intense souls, into each other poured,
   If souls could die, had perished in that passion,—
But by degrees their senses were restored,   1525
   Again to be o'ercome, again to dash on;
And, beating 'gainst *his* bosom, Haidée's heart
Felt as if never more to beat apart.

Alas! they were so young, so beautiful,
   So lonely, loving, helpless, and the hour   1530
Was that in which the Heart is always full,
   And, having o'er itself no further power,
Prompts deeds Eternity can not annul,
   But pays off moments in an endless shower
Of hell-fire—all prepared for people giving   1535
Pleasure or pain to one another living.

Alas! for Juan and Haidée! they were
   So loving and so lovely—till then never,
Excepting our first parents, such a pair
   Had run the risk of being damned for ever;   1540
And Haidée, being devout as well as fair,
   Had, doubtless, heard about the Stygian river,
And Hell and Purgatory—but forgot
Just in the very crisis she should not.

They look upon each other, and their eyes   1545
   Gleam in the moonlight; and her white arm clasps
Round Juan's head, and his around her lies
   Half buried in the tresses which it grasps;
She sits upon his knee, and drinks his sighs,
   He hers, until they end in broken gasps;   1550
And thus they form a group that's quite antique,
Half naked, loving, natural, and Greek.

And when those deep and burning moments passed,
   And Juan sunk to sleep within her arms,
She slept not, but all tenderly, though fast,   1555
   Sustained his head upon her bosom's charms;

And now and then her eye to Heaven is cast,
   And then on the pale cheek her breast now warms,
Pillowed on her o'erflowing heart, which pants
With all it granted, and with all it grants.   1560

An infant when it gazes on a light,
   A child the moment when it drains the breast,
A devotee when soars the Host[28] in sight,
   An Arab with a stranger for a guest,
A sailor when the prize has struck[29] in fight,   1565
   A miser filling his most hoarded chest,
Feel rapture; but not such true joy are reaping
As they who watch o'er what they love while sleeping.

For there it lies so tranquil, so beloved,
   All that it hath of Life with us is living;   1570
So gentle, stirless, helpless, and unmoved,
   And all unconscious of the joy 'tis giving;
All it hath felt, inflicted, passed, and proved,
   Hushed into depths beyond the watcher's diving;
There lies the thing we love with all its errors   1575
And all its charms, like Death without its terrors.

The lady watched her lover—and that hour
   Of Love's, and Night's, and Ocean's solitude,
O'erflowed her soul with their united power;
   Amidst the barren sand and rocks so rude   1580
She and her wave-worn love had made their bower,
   Where nought upon their passion could intrude,
And all the stars that crowded the blue space
Saw nothing happier than her glowing face.

Alas! the love of Women! it is known   1585
   To be a lovely and a fearful thing;
For all of theirs upon that die is thrown,
   And if 'tis lost, Life hath no more to bring
To them but mockeries of the past alone,
   And their revenge is as the tiger's spring,   1590
Deadly, and quick, and crushing; yet, as real
Torture is theirs—what they inflict they feel.

They are right; for Man, to man so oft unjust,
   Is always so to Women: one sole bond
Awaits them—treachery is all their trust;   1595
   Taught to conceal their bursting hearts despond
Over their idol, till some wealthier lust
   Buys them in marriage—and what rests beyond?
A thankless husband—next a faithless lover—
Then dressing, nursing, praying—and all's over.   1600

---

28 The Eucharistic wafer or bread.
29 The captured ship has hauled down its flag.

Some take a lover, some take drams or prayers,
  Some mind their household, others dissipation,
Some run away, and but exchange their cares,
  Losing the advantage of a virtuous station;
Few changes e'er can better their affairs,   1605
  Theirs being an unnatural situation,
From the dull palace to the dirty hovel:
Some play the devil, and then write a novel.[30]

Haidée was Nature's bride, and knew not this;
  Haidée was Passion's child, born where the Sun   1610
Showers triple light, and scorches even the kiss
  Of his gazelle-eyed daughters; she was one
Made but to love, to feel that she was his
  Who was her chosen: what was said or done
Elsewhere was nothing. She had nought to fear,   1615
Hope, care, nor love beyond,—her heart beat *here*. . . .

from CANTO THE THIRD

Hail, Muse! *et cetera*.—We left Juan sleeping,
  Pillowed upon a fair and happy breast,
And watched by eyes that never yet knew weeping,
  And loved by a young heart, too deeply blest
To feel the poison through her spirit creeping,   5
  Or know who rested there, a foe to rest,
Had soiled the current of her sinless years,
And turned her pure heart's purest blood to tears!

Oh, Love! what is it in this world of ours
  Which makes it fatal to be loved? Ah, why   10
With cypress branches[1] hast thou wreathed thy
      bowers,
  And made thy best interpreter a sigh?
As those who dote on odours pluck the flowers,
  And place them on their breast—but place to die—
Thus the frail beings we would fondly cherish   15
Are laid within our bosoms but to perish.

In her first passion Woman loves her lover,
  In all the others all she loves is Love,
Which grows a habit she can ne'er get over,
  And fits her loosely—like an easy glove,   20
As you may find, whene'er you like to prove[2] her:
  One man alone at first her heart can move;

She then prefers him in the plural number,
Not finding that the additions much encumber. . . .

Haidée and Juan were not married, but
  The fault was theirs, not mine: it is not fair,   90
Chaste reader, then, in any way to put
  The blame on me, unless you wish they were;
Then if you'd have them wedded, please to shut
  The book which treats of this erroneous pair,
Before the consequences grow too awful;   95
'Tis dangerous to read of loves unlawful.

Yet they were happy,—happy in the illicit
  Indulgence of their innocent desires;
But more imprudent grown with every visit,
  Haidée forgot the island was her Sire's;   100
When we have what we like 'tis hard to miss it,
  At least in the beginning, ere one tires;
Thus she came often, not a moment losing,
Whilst her piratical papa was cruising.

Let not his mode of raising cash seem strange,   105
  Although he fleeced the flags of every nation,
For into a Prime Minister but change
  His title, and 'tis nothing but taxation;
But he, more modest, took an humbler range
  Of Life, and in an honester vocation   110
Pursued o'er the high seas his watery journey,
And merely practised as a sea-attorney.

The good old gentleman had been detained
  By winds and waves, and some important captures;
And, in the hope of more, at sea remained,   115
  Although a squall or two had damped his raptures,
By swamping one of the prizes; he had chained
  His prisoners, dividing them like chapters
In numbered lots; they all had cuffs and collars,   119
And averaged each from ten to a hundred dollars. . . .

Then, having settled his marine affairs,   145
  Despatching single cruisers here and there,
His vessel having need of some repairs,
  He shaped his course to where his daughter fair
Continued still her hospitable cares;
  But that part of the coast being shoal and bare, 150
And rough with reefs which ran out many a mile,
His port lay on the other side o' the isle. . . .

Lambro, our sea-solicitor,[3] who had
  Much less experience of dry land than Ocean,

---

[30] The eccentric Lady Caroline Lamb, having been (chiefly on her
own insistence) one of his mistresses during the Byron craze in
London, wrote *Glenarvon* (1816) after their affair was over; she
incorporated in it his farewell letter rejecting her.

[1] Emblem of sadness.   [2] Test.

[3] Sea lawyer; here = pirate (cf. line 112).

On seeing his own chimney-smoke, felt glad;
    But not knowing metaphysics, had no notion
Of the true reason of his not being sad,   205
    Or that of any other strong emotion;
He loved his child, and would have wept the loss of her,
But knew the cause no more than a philosopher.

He saw his white walls shining in the sun,
    His garden trees all shadowy and green;   210
He heard his rivulet's light bubbling run,
    The distant dog-bark; and perceived between
The umbrage of the wood, so cool and dun,
    The moving figures, and the sparkling sheen
Of arms (in the East all arm)—and various dyes   215
Of coloured garbs, as bright as butterflies.

And as the spot where they appear he nears,
    Surprised at these unwonted signs of idling,
He hears—alas! no music of the spheres,
    But an unhallowed, earthly sound of fiddling!   220
A melody which made him doubt his ears,
    The cause being past his guessing or unriddling;
A pipe, too, and a drum, and shortly after—
A most unoriental roar of laughter.

And still more nearly to the place advancing,   225
    Descending rather quickly the declivity,
Through the waved branches o'er the greensward
        glancing,
    'Midst other indications of festivity,
Seeing a troop of his domestics dancing
    Like Dervises,[4] who turn as on a pivot, he   230
Perceived it was the Pyrrhic dance[5] so martial,
To which the Levantines[6] are very partial.

And further on a troop of Grecian girls,
    The first and tallest her white kerchief waving,
Were strung together like a row of pearls,   235
    Linked hand in hand, and dancing; each too having
Down her white neck long floating auburn curls—
    (The least of which would set ten poets raving);
Their leader sang—and bounded to her song
With choral step and voice the virgin throng.   240

And here, assembled cross-legged round their trays,
    Small social parties just begun to dine;
Pilaus[7] and meats of all sorts met the gaze,
    And flasks of Samian and of Chian wine,[8]

And sherbet cooling in the porous vase;   245
    Above them their dessert grew on its vine;—
The orange and pomegranate nodding o'er,
Dropped in their laps, scarce plucked, their mellow
    store. . . .

Perhaps you think, in stumbling on this feast,
    He flew into a passion, and in fact
There was no mighty reason to be pleased;   315
    Perhaps you prophesy some sudden act,
The whip, the rack, or dungeon at the least,
    To teach his people to be more exact,
And that, proceeding at a very high rate,
He showed the royal penchants of a pirate.   320

You're wrong.—He was the mildest mannered man
    That ever scuttled ship or cut a throat;
With such true breeding of a gentleman,
    You never could divine his real thought;
No courtier could, and scarcely woman can   325
    Gird more deceit within a petticoat;
Pity he loved adventurous life's variety,
He was so great a loss to good society. . . .

Old Lambro passed unseen a private gate,
    And stood within his hall at eventide;
Meantime the lady and her lover sate
    At wassail in their beauty and their pride:
An ivory inlaid table spread with state   485
    Before them, and fair slaves on every side;
Gems, gold, and silver, formed the service mostly,
Mother of pearl and coral the less costly.

The dinner made about a hundred dishes;
    Lamb and pistachio nuts—in short, all meats,   490
And saffron soups, and sweetbreads; and the fishes
    Were of the finest that e'er flounced in nets,
Drest to a Sybarite's[9] most pampered wishes;
    The beverage was various sherbets
Of raisin, orange, and pomegranate juice,   495
Squeezed through the rind, which makes it best for use.

These were ranged round, each in its crystal ewer,
    And fruits, and date-bread loaves closed the repast,
And Mocha's berry, from Arabia pure,
    In small fine China cups, came in at last;   500
Gold cups of filigree, made to secure
    The hand from burning, underneath them placed;
Cloves, cinnamon, and saffron too were boiled
Up with the coffee, which (I think) they spoiled.

---

4 Dervishes, members of certain Mohammedan orders, famous
  for frenzied dances.   5 An ancient Greek martial dance.
6 Dwellers in the Levant or eastern Mediterranean countries.
7 Oriental dishes of rice with meat, chicken, or fish, and spices.
8 From the Aegean islands of Samos and Chios.

9 The people of the ancient Greek city of Sybaris in southern
  Italy were notorious for their luxury.

The hangings of the room were tapestry, made   505
    Of velvet panels, each of different hue,
And thick with damask flowers of silk inlaid;
    And round them ran a yellow border too;
The upper border, richly wrought, displayed,
    Embroidered delicately o'er with blue,   510
Soft Persian sentences, in lilac letters,
From poets, or the moralists their betters. . . .

Haidée and Juan carpeted their feet
    On crimson satin, bordered with pale blue;   530
Their sofa occupied three parts complete
    Of the apartment—and appeared quite new;
The velvet cushions (for a throne more meet)
    Were scarlet, from whose glowing center grew
A sun embossed in gold, whose rays of tissue,   535
Meridian-like, were seen all light to issue.

Crystal and marble, plate and porcelain,
    Had done their work of splendour; Indian mats
And Persian carpets, which the heart bled to stain,
    Over the floors were spread; gazelles and cats,   540
And dwarfs and blacks, and such like things, that gain
    Their bread as ministers and favourites (that's
To say, by degradation) mingled there
As plentiful as in a court, or fair.

There was no want of lofty mirrors, and   545
    The tables, most of ebony inlaid
With mother of pearl or ivory, stood at hand,
    Or were of tortoise-shell or rare woods made,
Fretted with gold or silver:—by command
    The greater part of these were ready spread   550
With viands and sherbets in ice—and wine—
Kept for all comers at all hours to dine.

Of all the dresses I select Haidée's:
    She wore two jelicks[10]—one was of pale yellow;
Of azure, pink, and white was her chemise—   555
    'Neath which her breast heaved like a little billow:
With buttons formed of pearls as large as peas,
    All gold and crimson shone her jelick's fellow,
And the striped white gauze baracan[11] that bound her,
Like fleecy clouds about the moon, flowed round her.

One large gold bracelet clasped each lovely arm,   561
    Lockless—so pliable from the pure gold
That the hand stretched and shut it without harm,
    The limb which it adorned its only mold;
So beautiful—its very shape would charm,   565
    And clinging, as if loath to lose its hold,

The purest ore enclosed the whitest skin
    That e'er by precious metal was held in.[12]

Around, as Princess of her father's land,
    A like gold bar above her instep rolled   570
Announced her rank;[13] twelve rings were on her hand;
    Her hair was starred with gems; her veil's fine fold
Below her breast was fastened with a band
    Of lavish pearls, whose worth could scarce be told;
Her orange silk full Turkish trousers furled   575
About the prettiest ankle in the world.

Her hair's long auburn waves down to her heel
    Flowed like an Alpine torrent which the sun
Dyes with his morning light,—and would conceal
    Her person if allowed at large to run,   580
And still they seemed resentfully to feel
    The silken fillet's curb, and sought to shun
Their bonds whene'er some Zephyr caught began
To offer his young pinion as her fan.

Round her she made an atmosphere of life,   585
    The very air seemed lighter from her eyes,
They were so soft and beautiful, and rife
    With all we can imagine of the skies,
And pure as Psyche ere she grew a wife—
    Too pure even for the purest human ties;   590
Her overpowering presence made you feel
It would not be idolatry to kneel.

Her eyelashes, though dark as night, were tinged
    (It is the country's custom, but in vain),
For those large black eyes were so blackly fringed,   595
    The glossy rebels mocked the jetty stain,
And in their native beauty stood avenged:
    Her nails were touched with henna; but, again
The power of Art was turned to nothing, for
They could not look more rosy than before.   600

The henna should be deeply dyed to make
    The skin relieved appear more fairly fair;
She had no need of this, day ne'er will break
    On mountain tops more heavenly white than her:
The eye might doubt if it were well awake,   605
    She was so like a vision; I might err,
But Shakespeare also says, 'tis very silly
"To gild refinèd gold, or paint the lily."[14]

---

[10] Vests or bodices.   [11] Barracan, a loose outer garment.

[12] Byron's note: "This dress is Moorish. . . . As the mother of
    Haidée was of Fez, her daughter wore the garb of the country."
[13] Byron's note: "A mark of sovereign rank in the women of the
    families of the Deys."
[14] Cf. Shakespeare, *King John,* IV, ii, 11.

Juan had on a shawl of black and gold,
 But a white baracan, and so transparent   610
The sparkling gems beneath you might behold,
 Like small stars through the milky way apparent;
His turban, furled in many a graceful fold,
 An emerald aigrette,[15] with Haidée's hair in 't,
Surmounted as its clasp—a glowing crescent,   615
Whose rays shone ever trembling, but incessant.

And now they were diverted by their suite,
 Dwarfs, dancing girls, black eunuchs, and a poet,
Which made their new establishment complete;
 The last was of great fame, and liked to show it; 620
His verses rarely wanted their due feet—
 And for his theme—he seldom sung below it,
He being paid to satirise or flatter,
As the Psalm says, "inditing a good matter."[16] . . .

He had travelled 'mongst the Arabs, Turks, and Franks,
 And knew the self-loves of the different nations; 666
And having lived with people of all ranks,
 Had something ready upon most occasions—
Which got him a few presents and some thanks.
 He varied with some skill his adulations;   670
To "do at Rome as Romans do," a piece
Of conduct was which *he* observed in Greece.

Thus, usually, when *he* was asked to sing,
 He gave the different nations something national;
'Twas all the same to him—"God save the King,"   675
 Or "Ça ira,"[17] according to the fashion all:
His Muse made increment of anything,
 From the high lyric down to the low rational:[18]
If Pindar sang horse-races,[19] what should hinder
Himself from being as pliable as Pindar?   680

In France, for instance, he would write a chanson;
 In England a six canto quarto tale,
In Spain he'd make a ballad or romance on
 The last war—much the same in Portugal;
In Germany, the Pegasus he'd prance on   685
 Would be old Goethe's—(see what says De Staël);[20]
In Italy he'd ape the "Trecentisti";[21]
In Greece, he'd sing some sort of hymn like this t' ye:

I

The Isles of Greece, the Isles of Greece!
 Where burning Sappho[22] loved and sung,   690
Where grew the arts of War and Peace,
 Where Delos rose, and Phoebus sprung![23]
Eternal summer gilds them yet,
But all, except their Sun, is set.

2

The Scian and the Teian Muse,[24]   695
 The Hero's harp, the Lover's lute,
Have found the fame your shores refuse:
 Their place of birth alone is mute
To sounds which echo further west
Than your Sires' "Islands of the Blest."[25]   700

3

The mountains look on Marathon—[26]
 And Marathon looks on the sea;
And musing there an hour alone,
 I dreamed that Greece might still be free;
For standing on the Persians' grave,   705
I could not deem myself a slave.

4

A King sate on the rocky brow
 Which looks o'er sea-born Salamis;[27]
And ships, by thousands, lay below,
 And men in nations;—all were his!   710
He counted them at break of day—
And, when the Sun set, where were they?

5

And where are they? and where art thou,
 My Country? On thy voiceless shore
The heroic lay is tuneless now—   715
 The heroic bosom beats no more!
And must thy Lyre, so long divine,
Degenerate into hands like mine?

6

'Tis something, in the dearth of Fame,
 Though linked among a fettered race,   720
To feel at least a patriot's shame,

---

[15] Plume.   [16] Psalms 45:1.
[17] A popular song of the French Revolution: "It will go on."
[18] Doubtless Byron is jeering at Southey, praised by Coleridge in
Biographia Literaria, chap. III, for having achieved success in
nearly every form of verse.
[19] I.e., in odes celebrating the Olympic victors. The games included chariot races.
[20] Mme. de Staël in *De l'Allemagne* (1810) praises Goethe extravagantly.
[21] Writers (or artists) of the fourteenth century; among them were
Dante, Petrarch, and Boccaccio.

[22] Perhaps the greatest of women poets. She flourished about
600 B.C., on the Aegean island of Lesbos.
[23] Phoebus Apollo, god of poetry, music, etc., was born on the
island of Delos, which rose from below the Aegean for the
express convenience of his mother.
[24] Homer, greatest of epic poets (hence, "the Hero's harp"), was
according to one account a native of the island of Scio (Chios).
Anacreon, who wrote love lyrics, was born (572? B.C.) at the
coastal city of Teos in Asia Minor.
[25] Which some of the ancients supposed to be in the Atlantic.
[26] Where in 490 B.C., on the coastal plain north of Athens, a small
army of Greeks defeated an invading horde of Persians.
[27] An island in the Gulf of Aegina, where in 480 B.C., while the
Persian King Xerxes looked on from shore, the Athenian fleet
won a decisive victory.

Even as I sing, suffuse my face;
For what is left the poet here?
For Greeks a blush—for Greece a tear.

7

Must *we* but weep o'er days more blest?   725
    Must *we* but blush?—Our fathers bled.
Earth! render back from out thy breast
    A remnant of our Spartan dead!
Of the three hundred grant but three,
To make a new Thermopylae![28]   730

8

What, silent still? and silent all?
    Ah! no;—the voices of the dead
Sound like a distant torrent's fall,
    And answer, "Let one living head,
But one arise,—we come, we come!"   735
'Tis but the living who are dumb.

9

In vain—in vain: strike other chords;
    Fill high the cup with Samian wine!
Leave battles to the Turkish hordes,
    And shed the blood of Scio's vine!   740
Hark! rising to the ignoble call—
How answers each bold Bacchanal!

10

You have the Pyrrhic dance as yet,
    Where is the Pyrrhic phalanx[29] gone?
Of two such lessons, why forget   745
    The nobler and the manlier one?
You have the letters Cadmus[30] gave—
Think ye he meant them for a slave?

11

Fill high the bowl with Samian wine!
    We will not think of themes like these!   750
It made Anacreon's song divine:
    He served—but served Polycrates[31]—
A Tyrant; but our masters then
Were still, at least, our countrymen.

12

The Tyrant of the Chersonese[32]   755
    Was Freedom's best and bravest friend;
That tyrant was Miltiades![33]
    Oh! that the present hour would lend
Another despot of the kind!
Such chains as his were sure to bind.   760

13

Fill high the bowl with Samian wine!
    On Suli's rock,[34] and Parga's shore,[35]
Exists the remnant of a line
    Such as the Doric[36] mothers bore;
And there, perhaps, some seed is sown,   765
The Heracleidan[37] blood might own.

14

Trust not for freedom to the Franks—[38]
    They have a king who buys and sells;
In native swords, and native ranks,
    The only hope of courage dwells;   770
But Turkish force, and Latin fraud,
Would break your shield, however broad.

15

Fill high the bowl with Samian wine!
    Our virgins dance beneath the shade—
I see their glorious black eyes shine;   775
    But gazing on each glowing maid,
My own the burning tear-drop laves,
To think such breasts must suckle slaves.

16

Place me on Sunium's marbled steep,[39]
    Where nothing, save the waves and I,   780
May hear our mutual murmurs sweep;
    There, swan-like, let me sing and die:
A land of slaves shall ne'er be mine—
Dash down yon cup of Samian wine!

Thus sung, or would, or could, or should have sung,
    The modern Greek, in tolerable verse;   786

---

[28] This pass in central Greece was held for three days in 480 B.C. by Leonidas I of Sparta, with only three hundred men, against the huge army of Xerxes. Though the Spartans learned that the Persians had found another route and would soon be in their rear, they all remained at their posts and died fighting.

[29] A formation of heavily armed infantry in close order, used effectively against the Romans by King Pyrrhus (d. 272 B.C.) of Epirus in northwestern Greece.

[30] Legendary founder of Thebes, in central Greece, and reputed introducer of the alphabet from Phoenicia.

[31] A tyrant of Samos in the sixth century B.C. Anacreon was one of his courtiers.

[32] The ancient name of Gallipoli Peninsula, on the north side of the Dardanelles.

[33] Who commanded the Athenian army at Marathon. He had formerly ruled the Chersonesus, whence he withdrew on account of Persian hostility.

[34] A mountainous region in Epirus (southern Albania). The Suliotes fought heroically against the Turks for Greek independence.   [35] A town near Suli.

[36] I.e., Spartan. The Dorians were one of the races which settled in Greece.

[37] The Heraclidae, or descendants of Hercules, were the legendary conquerors of the Peloponnesus, the southern part of Greece.

[38] I.e. (according to usage in the Levant), Europeans (but not including inhabitants of the Balkan countries).

[39] Now Cape Colonni, the southern tip of Attica, southeast of Athens. On it stood a temple to Athena.

If not like Orpheus[40] quite, when Greece was young,
   Yet in these times he might have done much worse:
His strain displayed some feeling—right or wrong;
   And feeling, in a poet, is the source   790
Of others' feeling; but they are such liars,
And take all colours—like the hands of dyers.

But words are things, and a small drop of ink,
   Falling like dew, upon a thought, produces
That which makes thousands, perhaps millions, think;
   'Tis strange, the shortest letter which man uses   796
Instead of speech, may form a lasting link
   Of ages; to what straits old Time reduces
Frail man, when paper—even a rag like this,
Survives himself, his tomb, and all that's his!   800

And when his bones are dust, his grave a blank,
   His station, generation, even his nation,
Become a thing, or nothing, save to rank
   In chronological commemoration,
Some dull MS.[41] oblivion long has sank,   805
   Or graven stone found in a barrack's station
In digging the foundation of a closet,[42]
May turn his name up, as a rare deposit.

And Glory long has made the sages smile;
   'Tis something, nothing, words, illusion, wind—   810
Depending more upon the historian's style
   Than on the name a person leaves behind:
Troy owes to Homer what whist owes to Hoyle:[43]
   The present century was growing blind
To the great Marlborough's skill in giving knocks,   815
Until his late Life by Archdeacon Coxe.[44]

Milton's the Prince of poets—so we say;
   A little heavy, but no less divine:
An independent being in his day—
   Learned, pious, temperate in love and wine;   820
But, his life falling into Johnson's way,[45]
   We're told this great High Priest of all the Nine[46]
Was whipped at college—a harsh sire—odd spouse,
For the first Mrs. Milton left his house.

All these are, *certes*, entertaining facts,   825
   Like Shakespeare's stealing deer, Lord Bacon's bribes;[47]
Like Titus' youth, and Caesar's earliest acts;[48]
   Like Burns (whom Doctor Currie[49] well describes);
Like Cromwell's pranks;[50]—but although Truth exacts
   These amiable descriptions from the scribes,   830
As most essential to their Hero's story,
They do not much contribute to his glory.

All are not moralists, like Southey, when
   He prated to the world of "Pantisocracy";[51]
Or Wordsworth unexcised,[52] unhired, who then   835
   Seasoned his pedlar[53] poems with democracy;
Or Coleridge, long before his flighty pen
   Let[54] to the *Morning Post* its aristocracy;[55]
When he and Southey, following the same path,
Espoused two partners (milliners of Bath).[56]   840

Such names at present cut a convict figure,
   The very Botany Bay[57] in moral geography;
Their loyal treason, renegado rigour,
   Are good manure for their more bare biography;
Wordsworth's last quarto, by the way, is bigger   845
   Than any since the birthday of typography;
A drowsy, frowzy poem, called the "Excursion,"
Writ in a manner which is my aversion.

He there builds up a formidable dyke
   Between his own and others' intellect;   850
But Wordsworth's poem, and his followers, like

---

[40] The Thracian poet and musician of Greek mythology.
[41] Pronounce, here, *em ess*.
[42] The meaning is a little clearer as the line stood in Byron's manuscript: "In digging drains for a new water-closet."
[43] Edmond Hoyle (1672–1769), the writer on card games, especially whist.
[44] William Coxe, an English historian and clergyman; his book on the first Duke of Marlborough (1650–1722), greatest of English soldiers, had appeared in 1818–19.
[45] It appears in Dr. Johnson's *Lives of the Poets*.
[46] Nine Muses.

[47] The tradition about Shakespeare has very slight foundations. The accusation that Bacon accepted bribes brought about his fall from political power.
[48] Both Julius Caesar (100–44 B.C.) and the emperor Titus (40?–81 A.D.) are accused of youthful wickedness by the second-century historian Suetonius.
[49] The general misunderstanding of Burns's character sprang from the misrepresentations of James Currie, a Scotch physician practicing in Liverpool, who in 1800 brought out a four-volume edition of Burns's poetry with a Life of the poet.
[50] After the Restoration, attempts were made to blacken Cromwell's character. He was charged, among other offenses, with having been a notorious robber of orchards in his childhood and a roisterer while a student at Cambridge.
[51] See above, introduction to Coleridge, p. 88.
[52] I.e., before he got his appointment as revenue-stamp distributor (p. 46, above).
[53] Doubtless a reference to Wordsworth's "Peter Bell." Moreover, the central figure of *The Excursion* is "the Wanderer," a philosophical peddler.   [54] Hired out.
[55] Byron means this ironically, of course. Coleridge had been a radical, and then recanted. For his connection with the *Morning Post* see, above, introduction to Coleridge, p. 89, and headnote to "France: an Ode," p. 108.
[56] This sneer is both snobbish and inaccurate. The older of the Fricker sisters—they were daughters of a bankrupt businessman—became seamstresses. Their home was in Bristol.
[57] The penal colony in Australia.

Joanna Southcote's[58] Shiloh and her sect,
Are things which in this century don't strike
    The public mind,—so few are the elect;
And the new births of both their stale Virginities   855
Have proved but Dropsies, taken for Divinities.

But let me to my story: I must own,
    If I have any fault, it is digression,
Leaving my people to proceed alone,
    While I soliloquize beyond expression: 860
But these are my addresses from the throne,[59]
    Which put off business to the ensuing session:
Forgetting each omission is a loss to
The world, not quite so great as Ariosto.[60]

I know that what our neighbours call "longueurs,"[61]   865
    (We've not so good a word, but have the thing,
In that complete perfection which insures
    An epic from Bob Southey every spring—)
Form not the true temptation which allures
    The reader; but 'twould not be hard to bring   870
Some fine examples of the Epopée,[62]
To prove its grand ingredient is Ennui.

We learn from Horace, "Homer sometimes sleeps";[63]
    We feel without him,—Wordsworth sometimes
        wakes,—
To show with what complacency he creeps,   875
    With his dear "Waggoners,"[64] around his lakes.
He wishes for "a boat" to sail the deeps—
    Of Ocean?—No, of air; and then he makes
Another outcry for "a little boat,"[65]
And drivels seas to set it well afloat.   880

If he must fain sweep o'er the ethereal plain,
    And Pegasus runs restive in his "Waggon,"
Could he not beg the loan of Charles's Wain?[66]
    Or pray Medea[67] for a single dragon?
Or if, too classic for his vulgar brain,   885

He feared his neck to venture such a nag on,
And he must needs mount nearer to the moon,
Could not the blockhead ask for a balloon?

"Pedlars," and "Boats," and "Waggons"! Oh! ye shades
    Of Pope and Dryden, are we come to this?   890
That trash of such sort not alone evades
    Contempt, but from the bathos' vast abyss
Floats scumlike uppermost, and these Jack Cades[68]
    Of sense and song above your graves may hiss—
The "little boatman" and his Peter Bell   895
Can sneer at him who drew "Achitophel"![69]

T' our tale.—The feast was over, the slaves gone,
    The dwarfs and dancing girls had all retired;
The Arab lore and Poet's song were done,
    And every sound of revelry expired;   900
The lady and her lover, left alone,
    The rosy flood of Twilight's sky admired;—
Ava Maria! o'er the earth and sea,
That heavenliest hour of Heaven is worthiest thee![70]

Ave Maria! blessèd be the hour!   905
    The time, the clime, the spot, where I so oft
Have felt that moment in its fullest power
    Sink o'er the earth—so beautiful and soft—
While swung the deep bell in the distant tower,
    Or the faint dying day-hymn stole aloft,   910
And not a breath crept through the rosy air,
And yet the forest leaves seemed stirred with prayer.

Ave Maria! 'tis the hour of prayer!
    Ave Maria! 'tis the hour of Love!
Ave Maria! may our spirits dare   915
    Look up to thine and to thy Son's above!
Ave Maria! oh that face so fair!
    Those downcast eyes beneath the Almighty Dove—
What though 'tis but a pictured image?—strike—
That painting is no idol,—'tis too like.   920

Some kinder casuists are pleased to say,
    In nameless print—that I have no devotion;
But set those persons down with me to pray,
    And you shall see who has the properest notion
Of getting into Heaven the shortest way;   925
    My altars are the mountains and the Ocean,

---

58 Joanna Southcott (1750–1814), a notorious religious fanatic, had
    a following of perhaps 100,000. She announced that she would
    give birth to Shiloh, a second Messiah, and even named the
    day. She died two months after the failure of her prophecy.
59 The British king opens every new session of Parliament with a
    speech "from the throne."
60 The Italian poet and dramatist (1474–1533). Though he left a
    comedy unfinished, the reference is doubtless to his eminence as
    an epic poet.
61 Literally, lengths; i.e. (here), tedious matters.   62 Epic.
63 Ars Poetica, line 359.   64 "The Waggoner" (1819).
65 See "Peter Bell" (1798).
66 Charles's Wagon or Wain, the constellation better known to us
    as the Big Dipper.
67 The sorceress wife of Jason, in classical myth, had a chariot
    drawn by dragons.

68 John Cade (d. 1450) led a popular uprising and held London
    for several days before being killed.
69 In a supplementary preface to the 1815 edition of his own
    poems, Wordsworth includes, besides an implied compliment,
    two or three strictures on Dryden.
70 The Blessed Virgin. Ave Maria = Hail, Mary!

Earth—air—stars,—all that springs from the great
    Whole,
Who hath produced, and will receive the Soul.

Sweet Hour of Twilight!—in the solitude
    Of the pine forest, and the silent shore   930
Which bounds Ravenna's immemorial wood,
    Rooted where once the Adrian[71] wave flowed o'er,
To where the last Caesarean fortress stood,
    Evergreen forest! which Boccaccio's lore
And Dryden's lay[72] made haunted ground to me,   935
How have I loved the twilight hour and thee!

The shrill cicalas,[73] people of the pine,
    Making their summer lives one ceaseless song,
Were the sole echoes, save my steed's and mine,
    And vesper bell's that rose the boughs along;   940
The spectre huntsman of Onesti's line,[74]
    His hell-dogs, and their chase, and the fair throng
Which learned from this example not to fly
From a true lover,—shadowed my mind's eye.

Oh, Hesperus![75] thou bringest all good things—   945
    Home to the weary, to the hungry cheer,
To the young bird the parent's brooding wings,
    The welcome stall to the o'erlaboured steer;
Whate'er of peace about our hearthstone clings,
    Whate'er our household gods protect of dear,   950
Are gathered round us by thy look of rest;
Thou bring'st the child, too, to the mother's breast.

Soft hour! which wakes the wish and melts the heart
    Of those who sail the seas, on the first day
When they from their sweet friends are torn apart;   955
    Or fills with love the pilgrim on his way
As the far bell of Vesper makes him start,
    Seeming to weep the dying day's decay;[76]
Is this a fancy which our reason scorns?   959
Ah! surely Nothing dies but Something mourns! . . .

---

71 Adriatic. Ravenna, on its Italian coast, was once a seaport; under
   the Byzantine Empire it became the capital of Italy, and "a
   lovely grove of pines covered the ground where the Roman
   fleet once rode at anchor" (Gibbon, *Decline and Fall*).
72 In the *Decameron* (V, 8) Boccaccio tells a romantic tale of the
   extraordinary manner in which a young man of Ravenna persuaded a disdainful young woman to marry him. Dryden retells
   the story in his *Fables* under the title "Theodore and Honoria."
73 Cicadas, often called locusts.
74 The huntsman of Boccaccio's tale (note 72) was a ghost, pursuing and killing (repeatedly) his cold mistress. The sight
   proved an object lesson to the mistress of the suitor, who was a
   member of the Onesti family.
75 The evening star. The first and last lines of this stanza are
   adapted from the surviving fragment of an exquisite lyric by
   Sappho.
76 A note by Byron credits the origin of the stanza, thus far, to
   Dante, *Purgatory*, VIII, 1–6.

from CANTO THE FOURTH

Nothing so difficult as a beginning
    In poesy, unless perhaps the end;
For oftentimes when Pegasus seems winning
    The race, he sprains a wing, and down we tend,
Like Lucifer when hurled from Heaven for sinning;   5
    Our sin the same, and hard as his to mend,
Being Pride, which leads the mind to soar too far,
Till our own weakness shows us what we are.

But Time, which brings all beings to their level,
    And sharp Adversity, will teach at last   10
Man,—and, as we would hope,—perhaps the Devil,
    That neither of their intellects are vast:
While Youth's hot wishes in our red veins revel,
    We know not this—the blood flows on too fast;
But as the torrent widens towards the Ocean,   15
We ponder deeply on each past emotion.

As boy, I thought myself a clever fellow,
    And wished that others held the same opinion;
They took it up when my days grew more mellow,
    And other minds acknowledged my dominion: 20
Now my sere Fancy "falls into the yellow
    Leaf,"[1] and Imagination droops her pinion,
And the sad truth which hovers o'er my desk
Turns what was once romantic to burlesque.

And if I laugh at any mortal thing,   25
    'Tis that I may not weep; and if I weep,
'Tis that our nature cannot always bring
    Itself to apathy, for we must steep
Our hearts first in the depths of Lethe's[2] spring,
    Ere what we least wish to behold will sleep: 30
Thetis baptized her mortal son in Styx;[3]
A mortal mother would on Lethe fix. . . .

Young Juan and his lady-love were left
    To their own hearts' most sweet society;
Even Time the pitiless in sorrow cleft
    With his rude scythe such gentle bosoms; he   60
Sighed to behold them of their hours bereft,
    Though foe to Love; and yet they could not be
Meant to grow old, but die in happy Spring,
Before one charm or hope had taken wing.

Their faces were not made for wrinkles, their   65
    Pure blood to stagnate, their great hearts to fail;

---

1 Cf. *Macbeth*, V, iii, 23.
2 The river of oblivion in Hades.
3 Another river of Hades. In it the nymph Thetis dipped her
   infant son Achilles to make him invulnerable.

The blank grey was not made to blast their hair,
But like the climes that know nor snow nor hail,
They were all summer; lightning might assail
And shiver them to ashes, but to trail   70
A long and snake-like life of dull decay
Was not for them—they had too little clay.

They were alone once more; for them to be
Thus was another Eden; they were never
Weary, unless when separate: the tree   75
Cut from its forest root of years—the river
Dammed from its fountain—the child from the knee
And breast maternal weaned at once for ever,—
Would wither less than these two torn apart;
Alas! there is no instinct like the Heart—   80

The heart—which may be broken: happy they!
Thrice fortunate! who of that fragile mould,
The precious porcelain of human clay,
Break with the first fall: they can ne'er behold
The long year linked with heavy day on day,   85
And all which must be borne, and never told;
While Life's strange principle will often lie
Deepest in those who long the most to die.

"Whom the gods love die young," was said of yore,
And many deaths do they escape by this: 90
The death of friends, and that which slays even more—
The death of Friendship, Love, Youth, all that is,
Except mere breath; and since the silent shore
Awaits at last even those who longest miss
The old Archer's shafts, perhaps the early grave   95
Which men weep over may be meant to save.

Haidée and Juan thought not of the dead—
The Heavens, and Earth, and Air, seemed made for
them:
They found no fault with Time, save that he fled;
They saw not in themselves aught to condemn: 100
Each was the other's mirror, and but read
Joy sparkling in their dark eyes like a gem,
And knew such brightness was but the reflection
Of their exchanging glances of affection.

The gentle pressure, and the thrilling touch,   105
The least glance better understood than words,
Which still said all, and ne'er could say too much;
A language, too, but like to that of birds,
Known but to them, at least appearing such
As but to lovers a true sense affords;   110
Sweet playful phrases, which would seem absurd
To those who have ceased to hear such, or ne'er
heard—

All these were theirs, for they were children still,
And children still they should have ever been;
They were not made in the real world to fill   115
A busy character in the dull scene,
But like two beings born from out a rill,
A Nymph and her belovèd, all unseen
To pass their lives in fountains and on flowers,
And never know the weight of human hours.   120

Moons changing had rolled on, and changeless found
Those their bright rise had lighted to such joys
As rarely they beheld throughout their round;
And these were not of the vain kind which cloys,
For theirs were buoyant spirits, never bound   125
By the mere senses; and that which destroys
Most love—possession—unto them appeared
A thing which each endearment more endeared.

Oh beautiful! and rare as beautiful!
But theirs was Love in which the Mind delights   130
To lose itself when the old world grows dull,
And we are sick of its hack sounds and sights,
Intrigues, adventures of the common school,
Its petty passions, marriages, and flights,
Where Hymen's torch[4] but brands one strumpet more,
Whose husband only knows her not a whore.   136

Hard words—harsh truth! a truth which many know.
Enough.—The faithful and the fairy pair,
Who never found a single hour too slow,
What was it made them thus exempt from care?   140
Young innate feelings all have felt below,
Which perish in the rest, but in them were
Inherent—what we mortals call romantic,
And always envy, though we deem it frantic.

This is in others a factitious[5] state,   145
An opium dream of too much youth and reading,
But was in them their nature or their fate:
No novels e'er had set their young hearts bleeding,
For Haidée's knowledge was by no means great,
And Juan was a boy of saintly breeding;   150
So that there was no reason for their loves
More than for those of nightingales or doves.

They gazed upon the sunset; 'tis an hour
Dear unto all, but dearest to *their* eyes,
For it had made them what they were: the power   155
Of Love had first o'erwhelmed them from such skies,

---

4 Symbol of marriage, Hymen being the classical god of marriage.
5 Artificial, sham.

When Happiness had been their only dower,
  And Twilight saw them linked in Passion's ties;
Charmed with each other, all things charmed that
    brought
The past still welcome as the present thought.   160

I know not why, but in that hour to-night,
  Even as they gazed, a sudden tremor came,
And swept, as 'twere, across their hearts' delight,
  Like the wind o'er a harp-string, or a flame,
When one is shook in sound, and one in sight;   165
  And thus some boding flashed through either frame,
And called from Juan's breast a faint low sigh,
While one new tear arose in Haidée's eye.

That large black prophet eye seemed to dilate
  And follow far the disappearing sun,   170
As if their last day of a happy date
  With his broad, bright, and dropping orb were gone;
Juan gazed on her as to ask his fate—
  He felt a grief, but knowing cause for none,
His glance inquired of hers for some excuse   175
For feelings causeless, or at least abstruse.

She turned to him, and smiled, but in that sort
  Which makes not others smile; then turned aside:
Whatever feeling shook her, it seemed short,
  And mastered by her wisdom or her pride;   180
When Juan spoke, too—it might be in sport—
  Of this their mutual feeling, she replied—
"If it should be so,—but—it cannot be—
Or I at least shall not survive to see."

Juan would question further, but she pressed   185
  His lip to hers, and silenced him with this,
And then dismissed the omen from her breast,
  Defying augury with that fond kiss;
And no doubt of all methods 'tis the best:
  Some people prefer wine—'tis not amiss;   190
I have tried both—so those who would a part take
May choose between the headache and the heartache.

One of the two, according to your choice,
  Woman or wine, you'll have to undergo;
Both maladies are taxes on our joys: 195
  But which to choose, I really hardly know;
And if I had to give a casting voice,[6]
  For both sides I could many reasons show,
And then decide, without great wrong to either,
It were much better to have both than neither.   200

---

[6] Deciding vote.

Juan and Haidée gazed upon each other
  With swimming looks of speechless tenderness,
Which mixed all feelings—friend, child, lover,
    brother—
  All that the best can mingle and express
When two pure hearts are poured in one another,   205
  And love too much, and yet can not love less;
But almost sanctify the sweet excess
By the immortal wish and power to bless.

Mixed in each other's arms, and heart in heart,
  Why did they not then die?—they had lived too   210
    long
Should an hour come to bid them breathe apart;
  Years could but bring them cruel things or wrong;
The World was not for them—nor the World's art
  For beings passionate as Sappho's song;
Love was born *with* them, *in* them, so intense, 215
It was their very Spirit—not a sense.

They should have lived together deep in woods,
  Unseen as sings the nightingale; they were
Unfit to mix in these thick solitudes
  Called social, haunts of Hate, and Vice, and Care: 220
How lonely every freeborn creature broods!
  The sweetest song-birds nestle in a pair;
The eagle soars alone; the gull and crow
Flock o'er their carrion, just like men below.

Now pillowed cheek to cheek, in loving sleep,   225
  Haidée and Juan their siesta took,
A gentle slumber, but it was not deep,
  For ever and anon a something shook
Juan, and shuddering o'er his frame would creep;
  And Haidée's sweet lips murmured like a brook   230
A wordless music, and her face so fair
Stirred with her dream, as rose-leaves with the air.

Or as the stirring of a deep clear stream
  Within an Alpine hollow, when the wind
Walks o'er it, was she shaken by the dream,   235
  The mystical Usurper of the mind—
O'erpowering us to be whate'er may seem
  Good to the soul which we no more can bind;
Strange state of being! (for 'tis still to be)
Senseless to feel, and with sealed eyes to see.   240

She dreamed of being alone on the sea-shore,
  Chained to a rock; she knew not how, but stir
She could not from the spot, and the loud roar
  Grew, and each wave rose roughly, threatening her;
And o'er her upper lip they seemed to pour,   245
  Until she sobbed for breath, and soon they were

Foaming o'er her lone head, so fierce and high—
Each broke to drown her, yet she could not die.

Anon—she was released, and then she strayed
  O'er the sharp shingles[7] with her bleeding feet,   250
And stumbled almost every step she made:
  And something rolled before her in a sheet,
Which she must still pursue howe'er afraid:
  'Twas white and indistinct, nor stopped to meet
Her glance nor grasp, for still she gazed and   255
    grasped,
And ran, but it escaped her as she clasped.

The dream changed:—in a cave she stood, its walls
  Were hung with marble icicles, the work
Of ages on its water-fretted halls,
  Where waves might wash, and seals might breed
    and lurk;   260
Her hair was dripping, and the very balls
  Of her black eyes seemed turned to tears, and mirk[8]
The sharp rocks looked below each drop they caught,
Which froze to marble as it fell,—she thought.

And wet, and cold, and lifeless at her feet,   265
  Pale as the foam that frothed on his dead brow,
Which she essayed in vain to clear, (how sweet
  Were once her cares, how idle seemed they now!)
Lay Juan, nor could aught renew the beat
  Of his quenched heart: and the sea dirges low   270
Rang in her sad ears like a Mermaid's song,
And that brief dream appeared a life too long.

And gazing on the dead, she thought his face
  Faded, or altered into something new—
Like to her Father's features, till each trace   275
  More like and like to Lambro's aspect grew—
With all his keen worn look and Grecian grace;
  And starting, she awoke, and what to view?
Oh! Powers of Heaven! what dark eye meets she there?
'Tis—'tis her father's—fixed upon the pair!   280

Then shrieking, she arose, and shrieking fell,
  With joy and sorrow, hope and fear, to see
Him whom she deemed a habitant where dwell
  The ocean-buried, risen from death, to be
Perchance the death of one she loved too well: 285
  Dear as her father had been to Haidée,
It was a moment of that awful kind—
I have seen such—but must not call to mind.

Up Juan sprang to Haidée's bitter shriek,
  And caught her falling, and from off the wall   290
Snatched down his sabre, in hot haste to wreak
  Vengeance on him who was the cause of all:
Then Lambro, who till now forbore to speak,
  Smiled scornfully, and said, "Within my call,
A thousand scimitars await the word;   295
Put up, young man, put up your silly sword."

And Haidée clung around him; "Juan, 'tis—
  'Tis Lambro—'tis my father! Kneel with me—
He will forgive us—yes—it must be—yes.
  Oh! dearest father, in this agony   300
Of pleasure and of pain—even while I kiss
  Thy garment's hem with transport, can it be
That doubt should mingle with my filial joy?
Deal with me as thou wilt, but spare this boy."

High and inscrutable the old man stood,   305
  Calm in his voice, and calm within his eye—
Not always signs with him of calmest mood:
  He looked upon her, but gave no reply;
Then turned to Juan, in whose cheek the blood
  Oft came and went, as there resolved to die;   310
In arms, at least, he stood, in act to spring
On the first foe whom Lambro's call might bring.

"Young man, your sword"; so Lambro once more said:
  Juan replied, "Not while this arm is free."
The old man's cheek grew pale, but not with dread,   315
  And drawing from his belt a pistol he
Replied, "Your blood be then on your own head."
  Then looked close at the flint, as if to see
'Twas fresh—for he had lately used the lock—
And next proceeded quietly to cock.   320

It has a strange quick jar upon the ear,
  That cocking of a pistol, when you know
A moment more will bring the sight to bear
  Upon your person, twelve yards off, or so;
A gentlemanly distance, not too near,   325
  If you have got a former friend for foe;
But after being fired at once or twice,
The ear becomes more Irish, and less nice.[9]

Lambro presented,[10] and one instant more
  Had stopped this Canto, and Don Juan's breath,   330
When Haidée threw herself her boy before;
  Stern as her sire: "On me," she cried, "let Death

---

7 Pebbles on a stony beach.   8 Murk, dark.

9 Delicate, finicky. Byron professes to think that constant listening
  to their own speech must accustom Irish ears to harshness.
10 Aimed.

Descend—the fault is mine; this fatal shore
　　He found—but sought not. I have pledged my faith;
I love him—I will die with him: I knew　　335
Your nature's firmness—know your daughter's too."

A minute past, and she had been all tears,
　　And tenderness, and infancy; but now
She stood as one who championed human fears—
　　Pale, statue-like, and stern, she wooed the blow;　340
And tall beyond her sex, and their compeers,
　　She drew up to her height, as if to show
A fairer mark; and with a fixed eye scanned
Her Father's face—but never stopped his hand.

He gazed on her, and she on him; 'twas strange　345
　　How like they looked! the expression was the same;
Serenely savage, with a little change
　　In the large dark eye's mutual-darted flame;
For she, too, was as one who could avenge,
　　If cause should be—a Lioness, though tame.　350
Her Father's blood before her Father's face
Boiled up, and proved her truly of his race.

I said they were alike, their features and
　　Their stature, differing but in sex and years;
Even to the delicacy of their hand　　355
　　There was resemblance, such as true blood wears;
And now to see them, thus divided, stand
　　In fixed ferocity, when joyous tears
And sweet sensations should have welcomed both,
Shows what the passions are in their full growth.　360

The father paused a moment, then withdrew
　　His weapon, and replaced it; but stood still,
And looking on her, as to look her through,
　　"Not I," he said, "have sought this stranger's ill;
Not I have made this desolation: few　　365
　　Would bear such outrage, and forbear to kill;
But I must do my duty—how thou hast
Done thine, the present vouches for the past.

"Let him disarm; or, by my father's head,
　　His own shall roll before you like a ball!"　370
He raised his whistle, as the word he said,
　　And blew; another answered to the call,
And rushing in disorderly, though led,
　　And armed from boot to turban, one and all,
Some twenty of his train came, rank on rank;　375
He gave the word,—"Arrest or slay the Frank."

Then, with a sudden movement, he withdrew
　　His daughter; while compressed within his clasp,
'Twixt her and Juan interposed the crew;
　　In vain she struggled in her father's grasp—　380

His arms were like a serpent's coil: then flew
　　Upon their prey, as darts an angry asp,
The file of pirates—save the foremost, who
　　Had fallen, with his right shoulder half cut through.

The second had his cheek laid open; but　385
　　The third, a wary, cool old sworder, took
The blows upon his cutlass, and then put
　　His own well in; so well, ere you could look,
His man was floored, and helpless at his foot,
　　With the blood running like a little brook　390
From two smart sabre gashes, deep and red—
One on the arm, the other on the head.

And then they bound him where he fell, and bore
　　Juan from the apartment: with a sign
Old Lambro bade them take him to the shore,　395
　　Where lay some ships which were to sail at nine.
They laid him in a boat, and plied the oar
　　Until they reached some galliots,[11] placed in line;
On board of one of these, and under hatches,
They stowed him, with strict orders to the watches.　400

The world is full of strange vicissitudes,
　　And here was one exceedingly unpleasant:
A gentleman so rich in the world's goods,
　　Handsome and young, enjoying all the present,
Just at the very time when he least broods　405
　　On such a thing, is suddenly to sea sent,
Wounded and chained so that he cannot move,
And all because a lady fell in love. . . .

The last sight which she saw was Juan's gore,
　　And he himself o'ermastered and cut down;
His blood was running on the very floor
　　Where late he trod, her beautiful, her own;　460
Thus much she viewed an instant and no more,—
　　Her struggles ceased with one convulsive groan;
On her Sire's arm, which until now scarce held
Her writhing, fell she like a cedar felled.

A vein had burst, and her sweet lips' pure dyes　465
　　Were dabbled with the deep blood which ran o'er;
And her head drooped, as when the lily lies
　　O'ercharged with rain: her summoned handmaids bore
Their lady to her couch with gushing eyes;
　　Of herbs and cordials they produced their store,　470
But she defied all means they could employ,
Like one Life could not hold, nor Death destroy.

Days lay she in that state unchanged, though chill—
　　With nothing livid, still her lips were red;

---

11 Small, swift galliots, propelled by oars and sails.

She had no pulse, but Death seemed absent still; 475
  No hideous sign proclaimed her surely dead;
Corruption came not in each mind to kill
  All hope; to look upon her sweet face bred
New thoughts of Life, for it seemed full of soul—
She had so much, Earth could not claim the whole. 480

The ruling passion, such as marble shows
  When exquisitely chiselled, still lay there,
But fixed as marble's unchanged aspect throws
  O'er the fair Venus,[12] but for ever fair;
O'er the Laocoön's all eternal throes,[13] 485
  And ever-dying Gladiator's[14] air,
Their energy like life forms all their fame,
Yet looks not life, for they are still the same.—

She woke at length, but not as sleepers wake,
  Rather the dead, for Life seemed something new, 490
A strange sensation which she must partake
  Perforce, since whatsoever met her view
Struck not on memory, though a heavy ache
  Lay at her heart, whose earliest beat still true
Brought back the sense of pain without the cause, 495
For, for a while, the Furies made a pause.

She looked on many a face with vacant eye,
  On many a token without knowing what:
She saw them watch her without asking why,
  And recked not who around her pillow sat; 500
Not speechless, though she spoke not—not a sigh
  Relieved her thoughts—dull silence and quick chat
Were tried in vain by those who served; she gave
No sign, save breath, of having left the grave.

Her handmaids tended, but she heeded not; 505
  Her Father watched, she turned her eyes away;
She recognized no being, and no spot,
  However dear or cherished in their day;
They changed from room to room—but all forgot—
  Gentle, but without memory she lay; 510
At length those eyes, which they would fain be weaning
Back to old thoughts, waxed full of fearful meaning.

And then a slave bethought her of a harp;
  The harper came, and tuned his instrument;

At the first notes, irregular and sharp, 515
  On him her flashing eyes a moment bent,
Then to the wall she turned as if to warp
  Her thoughts from sorrow through her heart re-sent;
And he began a long low island-song
Of ancient days, ere Tyranny grew strong. 520

Anon her thin wan fingers beat the wall
  In time to his old tune; he changed the theme,
And sung of Love; the fierce name struck through all
  Her recollection; on her flashed the dream
Of what she was, and is, if ye could call 525
  To be so being; in a gushing stream
The tears rushed forth from her o'erclouded brain,
Like mountain mists at length dissolved in rain.

Short solace, vain relief!—Thought came too quick,
  And whirled her brain to madness; she arose 530
As one who ne'er had dwelt among the sick,
  And flew at all she met, as on her foes;
But no one ever heard her speak or shriek,
  Although her paroxysm drew towards its close;—
Hers was a frenzy which disdained to rave, 535
Even when they smote her, in the hope to save.

Yet she betrayed at times a gleam of sense;
  Nothing could make her meet her Father's face,
Though on all other things with looks intense
  She gazed, but none she ever could retrace; 540
Food she refused, and raiment; no pretence
  Availed for either; neither change of place,
Nor time, nor skill, nor remedy, could give her
Senses to sleep—the power seemed gone for ever.

Twelve days and nights she withered thus; at last, 545
  Without a groan, or sigh, or glance, to show
A parting pang, the spirit from her passed:
  And they who watched her nearest could not know
The very instant, till the change that cast
  Her sweet face into shadow, dull and slow, 550
Glazed o'er her eyes—the beautiful, the black—
Oh! to possess such lustre—and then lack!

She died, but not alone; she held, within,
  A second principle of Life, which might
Have dawned a fair and sinless child of sin; 555
  But closed its little being without light,
And went down to the grave unborn, wherein
  Blossom and bough lie withered with one blight;
In vain the dews of Heaven descend above
The bleeding flower and blasted fruit of Love. 560

Thus lived—thus died she; never more on her
  Shall Sorrow light, or Shame. She was not made

---

[12] From references elsewhere it is clear that Byron means the Venus de' Medici at Florence.
[13] Another piece of classical sculpture, representing the legendary Trojan priest and his two sons being crushed by huge serpents sent by the goddess Athena to punish Laocoön for his skepticism over the wooden horse by means of which the Greeks got into the city.
[14] A famous statue once thought to represent a dying gladiator; cf. *Childe Harold*, IV, 1252 ff. (p. 242, above).

Through years or moons the inner weight to bear,
  Which colder hearts endure till they are laid
By age in earth: her days and pleasures were   565
  Brief, but delightful—such as had not staid
Long with her destiny; but she sleeps well
By the sea-shore, whereon she loved to dwell.

That isle is now all desolate and bare,
  Its dwellings down, its tenants passed away;   570
None but her own and Father's grave is there,
  And nothing outward tells of human clay;
Ye could not know where lies a thing so fair,
  No stone is there to show, no tongue to say,
What was; no dirge, except the hollow sea's,   575
Mourns o'er the beauty of the Cyclades.[15]

But many a Greek maid in a loving song
  Sighs o'er her name; and many an islander
With her Sire's story makes the night less long;
  Valour was his, and Beauty dwelt with her: 580
If she loved rashly, her life paid for wrong—
  A heavy price must all pay who thus err,
In some shape; let none think to fly the danger,
For soon or late Love is his own avenger. . . .

STANZAS WRITTEN ON THE ROAD BETWEEN FLORENCE AND PISA

Oh, talk not to me of a name great in story—
The days of our Youth are the days of our glory;
And the myrtle and ivy[1] of sweet two-and-twenty
Are worth all your laurels,[2] though ever so plenty.

What are garlands and crowns to the brow that is
    wrinkled?   5
'Tis but as a dead flower with May-dew besprinkled:
Then away with all such from the head that is hoary,
What care I for the wreaths that can *only* give glory?

Oh FAME!—if I e'er took delight in thy praises,
'Twas less for the sake of thy high-sounding phrases, 10
Than to see the bright eyes of the dear One discover,
She thought that I was not unworthy to love her.

There chiefly I sought thee, *there* only I found thee;
Her Glance was the best of the rays that surround thee;
When it sparkled o'er aught that was bright in my
    story,   15
I knew it was Love, and I felt it was Glory.

---

[15] The islands off southeastern Greece.

[1] Symbols of love and wine.—This lyric was written in 1821.
[2] All the laurels (i.e., fame and prizes) there are.

ON THIS DAY I COMPLETE MY THIRTY-SIXTH YEAR

'Tis time this heart should be unmoved,
  Since others it hath ceased to move:
Yet, though I cannot be beloved,
    Still let me love!

My days are in the yellow leaf;[3]   5
  The flowers and fruits of Love are gone;
The worm, the canker, and the grief
    Are mine alone!

The fire that on my bosom preys
  Is lone as some Volcanic isle;   10
No torch is kindled at its blaze—
    A funeral pile.

The hope, the fear, the jealous care,
  The exalted portion of the pain
And power of love, I cannot share,   15
    But wear the chain.

But 'tis not *thus*—and 'tis not *here*—
  Such thoughts should shake my soul, nor *now*,
Where Glory decks the hero's bier,
    Or binds his brow.   20

The Sword, the Banner, and the Field,
  Glory and Greece, around me see!
The Spartan, borne upon his shield,[4]
    Was not more free.

Awake! (not Greece—she *is* awake!)   25
  Awake, my spirit! Think through *whom*
Thy life-blood tracks its parent lake,
    And then strike home!

Tread those reviving passions down,
  Unworthy manhood!—unto thee   30
Indifferent should the smile or frown
    Of Beauty be.

If thou regret'st thy youth, *why live?*
  The land of honourable death
Is here:—up to the Field, and give   35
    Away thy breath!

Seek out—less often sought than found—
  A soldier's grave, for thee the best;
Then look around, and choose thy ground,
    And take thy Rest.   40

---

[3] Cf. *Macbeth*, V, iii, 23.—Byron wrote this poem at Missolonghi on Jan. 22, 1824, less than three months before he died.
[4] I.e., killed doing his duty, and carried home on his shield.

I. TO FRANÇIS HODGSON[1]

Lisbon, JULY 16, 1809.

Thus far have we pursued our route, and seen all sorts of marvellous sights, palaces, convents, etc.;—which, being to be heard in my friend Hobhouse's[2] forthcoming Book of Travels, I shall not anticipate by smuggling any account whatsoever to you in a private and clandestine manner. I must just observe that the village of Cintra in Estremadura[3] is the most beautiful, perhaps, in the world.

I am very happy here, because I loves oranges, and talks bad Latin to the monks, who understand it, as it is like their own,—and I goes into society (with my pocket-pistols), and I swims in the Tagus all across at once, and I rides on an ass or a mule, and swears Portuguese, and have got a diarrhoea and bites from the mosquitoes. But what of that? Comfort must not be expected by folks that go a pleasuring. . . .

Hodgson! send me the news, and the deaths and defeats and capital crimes and the misfortunes of one's friends; and let us hear of literary matters, and the controversies and the criticisms. All this will be pleasant—*Suave mari magno,*[4] etc. Talking of that, I have been sea-sick, and sick of the sea. Adieu.

Yours faithfully, etc.

II. TO HIS MOTHER

Prevesa,[5] NOVEMBER 12, 1809

My dear Mother,—

I have now been some time in Turkey: this place is on the coast, but I have traversed the interior of the province of Albania on a visit to the Pacha. I left Malta in the *Spider,* a brig of war, on the 21st of September, and arrived in eight days at Prevesa. I thence have been about 150 miles, as far as Tepaleen, his Highness's country palace, where I stayed three days. The name of the Pacha is *Ali,*[6] and he is considered a man of the first abilities: he governs the whole of Albania (the ancient Illyricum), Epirus, and part of Macedonia. His son, Vely Pacha, to whom he has given me letters, governs the Morea,[7] and has great influence in Egypt; in short, he is one of the most powerful men in the Ottoman empire. When I reached Yanina,[8] the capital, after a journey of three days over the mountains, through a country of the most picturesque beauty, I found that Ali Pacha was with his army in Illyricum, besieging Ibrahim Pacha in the castle of Berat.[9] He had heard that an Englishman of rank was in his dominions, and had left orders in Yanina with the commandant to provide a house, and supply me with every kind of necessary *gratis;* and, though I have been allowed to make presents to the slaves, etc., I have not been permitted to pay for a single article of household consumption.

I rode out on the vizier's[10] horses, and saw the palaces of himself and grandsons: they are splendid, but too much ornamented with silk and gold. I then went over the mountains through Zitza, a village with a Greek monastery (where I slept on my return), in the most beautiful situation (always excepting Cintra, in Portugal) I ever beheld. In nine days I reached Tepaleen.[11] Our journey was much prolonged by the torrents that had fallen from the mountains, and intersected the roads. I shall never forget the singular scene on entering Tepaleen at five in the afternoon, as the sun was going down. It brought to my mind (with some change of *dress,* however) Scott's description of Branksome Castle in his *Lay,*[12] and the feudal system. The Albanians, in their dresses (the most magnificent in the world, consisting of a long *white kilt,* gold-worked cloak, crimson velvet gold-laced jacket and waistcoat, silver-mounted pistols and daggers), the Tartars with their high caps, the Turks in their vast pelisses[13] and

---

[1] The following extracts are from R. E. Prothero's edition of the letters, with the kind permission of Charles Scribner's Sons, the American publishers of the standard edition of Byron.—Hodgson (1781–1852), a son-in-law of Byron's headmaster at Harrow, was a minor but prolific man of letters and one of the poet's best friends. In 1813, Byron enabled him to marry by presenting him with £1000. He was afterwards a country parson and eventually Provost of Eton.
[2] John Cam Hobhouse (1786–1869), Byron's traveling companion, lifelong friend, and executor. He afterwards held important ministerial posts in the British government.
[3] The Portuguese, not the Spanish, province.
[4] The opening words of Lucretius, *De Rerum Natura,* Book II: "It is sweet when on the great sea [the winds trouble the waters, to behold from the land the great hardship of someone else; not because there is pleasure to be had from anyone's being afflicted, but because it is sweet to see from what evils one is free]."
[5] In northwestern Greece, then a part of the Turkish Empire.

[6] Known as the Rob Roy of Albania, the tyrant Ali (1741–1822) was a brilliant soldier and administrator.
[7] Southern Greece, the peninsula of Peloponnesus.
[8] Ioannina, at the foot of the Pindus Mountains in northwestern Greece (Epirus).   [9] In central Albania.
[10] Ali was nominally the Turkish governor.
[11] Tepelini, in southern Albania, on the way to Berat.
[12] *The Lay of the Last Minstrel,* Canto I.   [13] Furred cloaks.

turbans, the soldiers and black slaves with the horses, the former in groups in an immense large open gallery in front of the palace, the latter placed in a kind of cloister below it, two hundred steeds ready caparisoned to move in a moment, couriers entering or passing out with the despatches, the kettle-drums beating, boys calling the hour from the minaret of the mosque, altogether, with the singular appearance of the building itself, formed a new and delightful spectacle to a stranger I was conducted to a very handsome apartment, and my health inquired after by the vizier's secretary, à-la-mode Turque![14]

The next day I was introduced to Ali Pacha. I was dressed in a full suit of staff uniform, with a very magnificent sabre, etc. The vizier received me in a large room paved with marble; a fountain was playing in the centre; the apartment was surrounded by scarlet ottomans.[15] He received me standing, a wonderful compliment from a Mussulman, and made me sit down on his right hand. I have a Greek interpreter for general use, but a physician of Ali's named Femlario, who understands Latin, acted for me on this occasion. His first question was, why, at so early an age, I left my country?—(the Turks have no idea of travelling for amusement). He then said, the English minister,[16] Captain Leake, had told him I was of a great family, and desired his respects to my mother; which I now, in the name of Ali Pacha, present to you. He said he was certain I was a man of birth, because I had small ears, curling hair, and little white hands, and expressed himself pleased with my appearance and garb. He told me to consider him as a father whilst I was in Turkey, and said he looked on me as his son. Indeed, he treated me like a child, sending me almonds and sugared sherbet, fruit and sweetmeats, twenty times a day. He begged me to visit him often, and at night, when he was at leisure. I then, after coffee and pipes, retired for the first time. I saw him thrice afterwards. It is singular that the Turks, who have no hereditary dignities, and few great families, except the Sultans, pay so much respect to birth; for I found my pedigree more regarded than my title.

To-day I saw the remains of the town of Actium,[17] near which Antony lost the world, in a small bay, where two frigates could hardly manoeuvre: a broken wall is the sole remnant. On another part of the gulf stand the ruins of Nicopolis, built by Augustus in honour of his victory. Last night I was at a Greek marriage; but this and a thousand things more I have neither time nor *space* to describe. . . .

I am going to-morrow, with a guard of fifty men, to Patras[18] in the Morea, and thence to Athens, where I shall winter. Two days ago I was nearly lost in a Turkish ship of war, owing to the ignorance of the captain and crew, though the storm was not violent. Fletcher[19] yelled after his wife, the Greeks called on all the saints, the Mussulmans on Alla; the captain burst into tears and ran below deck, telling us to call on God; the sails were split, the main-yard shivered, the wind blowing fresh, the night setting in, and all our chance was to make Corfu, which is in possession of the French, or (as Fletcher pathetically termed it) "a watery grave." I did what I could to console Fletcher, but finding him incorrigible, wrapped myself up in my Albanian capote (an immense cloak), and lay down on deck to wait the worst. I have learnt to philosophise in my travels; and if I had not, complaint was useless. Luckily the wind abated, and only drove us on the coast of Suli, on the main land, where we landed, and proceeded, by the help of the natives, to Prevesa again; but I shall not trust Turkish sailors in future, though the Pacha had ordered one of his own galliots[20] to take me to Patras. I am therefore going as far as Missolonghi by land, and there have only to cross a small gulf to get to Patras.

Fletcher's next epistle will be full of marvels. We were one night lost for nine hours in the mountains in a thunder-storm, and since nearly wrecked. In both cases Fletcher was sorely bewildered, from apprehensions of famine and banditti in the first, and drowning in the second instance. His eyes were a little hurt by the lightning, or crying (I don't know which), but are now recovered. When you write, address to me at Mr. Strané's, English consul, Patras, Morea.

I could tell you I know not how many incidents that I think would amuse you, but they crowd on my mind as much as they would swell my paper, and I can neither arrange them in the one, nor put them down on the other, except in the greatest confusion. I like the Albanians much; they are not all Turks; some tribes are Christians. But their religion makes little difference in their manner or conduct.

---

[14] In Turkish style. [15] Backless couches.
[16] An emissary of the British government, which aided Ali with munitions.
[17] Off which, in the famous battle of 31 B.C., Antony and Cleopatra were defeated by the fleet of Octavius, the future emperor Augustus.

[18] Near the entrance to the Gulf of Corinth.
[19] William Fletcher, Byron's valet; he was with Byron till the end came at Missolonghi.
[20] Small, swift galleys, using both sails and oars.

They are esteemed the best troops in the Turkish service. I lived on my route, two days at once, and three days again, in a barrack at Salora, and never found soldiers so tolerable, though I have been in the garrisons of Gibraltar and Malta, and seen Spanish, French, Sicilian, and British troops in abundance. I have had nothing stolen, and was always welcome to their provision and milk. Not a week ago an Albanian chief, (every village has its chief, who is called Primate), after helping us out of the Turkish galley in her distress, feeding us, and lodging my suite, consisting of Fletcher, a Greek, two Athenians, a Greek priest, and my companion, Mr. Hobhouse, refused any compensation but a written paper stating that I was well received; and when I pressed him to accept a few sequins,[21] "No," he replied; "I wish you to love me, not to pay me." These are his words. . . .

I am going to Athens, to study modern Greek, which differs much from the ancient, though radically similar. I have no desire to return to England, nor shall I, unless compelled by absolute want, and Hanson's[22] neglect; but I shall not enter into Asia for a year or two, as I have much to see in Greece, and I may perhaps cross into Africa, at least the Egyptian part. Fletcher, like all Englishmen, is very much dissatisfied, though a little reconciled to the Turks by a present of eighty piastres from the vizier, which, if you consider every thing, and the value of specie here, is nearly worth ten guineas English. He has suffered nothing but from cold, heat, and vermin, which those who lie in cottages and cross mountains in a cold country must undergo, and of which I have equally partaken with himself; but he is not valiant, and is afraid of robbers and tempests. I have no one to be remembered to in England, and wish to hear nothing from it, but that you are well, and a letter or two on business from Hanson, whom you may tell to write. I will write when I can, and beg you to believe me,

Your affectionate son,
BYRON.

III. TO THOMAS MOORE

Newstead Abbey, SEPT. 20, 1814.

Here's to her who long
    Hath waked the poet's sigh!
The girl who gave to song
    What gold could never buy.

My dear Moore,—I am going to be married—that is, I am accepted, and one usually hopes the rest will follow. My mother of the Gracchi[23] (that *are* to be) *you* think too strait-laced for me, although the paragon of only children, and invested with "golden opinions of all sorts of men,"[24] and full of "most blest conditions"[25] as Desdemona herself. Miss Milbanke is the lady, and I have her father's invitation to proceed there[26] in my elect capacity,—which, however, I cannot do till I have settled some business in London, and got a blue coat.

She is said to be an heiress, but of that I know nothing certainly, and shall not enquire. But I do know, that she has talents and excellent qualities; and you will not deny her judgment, after having refused six suitors and taken me.

Now, if you have any thing to say against this, pray do; my mind's made up, positively fixed, determined, and therefore I will listen to reason, because now it can do no harm. Things may occur to break it off, but I will hope not. In the mean time, I tell you (a *secret,* by the by,—at least, till I know she wishes it to be public) that I have proposed and am accepted. You need not be in a hurry to wish me joy, for one mayn't be married for months. I am going to town to-morrow: but expect to be here, on my way there, within a fortnight.

If this had not happened, I should have gone to Italy. In my way down,[27] perhaps, you will meet me at Nottingham, and come over with me here. I need not say that nothing will give me greater pleasure. I must, of course, reform thoroughly; and, seriously, if I can contribute to her happiness, I shall secure my own. She is so good a person, that—that—in short, I wish I was a better.

Ever, etc.

[23] "Cornelia, the Mother of the Gracchi" was the simple inscription on a statue to the memory of this Roman matron of the second century B.C., famous for her remark to a visiting lady who asked to see her jewels, "These are my jewels," as she presented her children. Her sons, Tiberius and Gaius Gracchus, lost their lives through political activities as democratic leaders.
[24] Cf. *Macbeth,* I, vii, 33.   [25] Cf. *Othello,* II, i, 255.
[26] To the Milbankes' house in the county of Durham. The proposal and acceptance were by letter.
[27] From London, i.e. (here), northward.

[21] A gold coin worth about $2.25.
[22] John Hanson, Byron's solicitor.

IV. TO THOMAS MOORE

Venice, JANUARY 28, 1817.

Your letter of the 8th is before me. The remedy for your plethora is simple—abstinence. I was obliged to have recourse to the like some years ago, I mean in point of *diet,* and, with the exception of some convivial weeks and days, (it might be months, now and then), have kept to Pythagoras[28] ever since. For all this, let me hear that you are better. You must not *indulge* in "filthy beer," nor in porter, nor eat *suppers*—the last are the devil to those who swallow dinner. . . .

I am truly sorry to hear of your father's misfortune—cruel at any time, but doubly cruel in advanced life.[29] However, you will, at least, have the satisfaction of doing your part by him, and, depend upon it, it will not be in vain. Fortune, to be sure, is a female, but not such a b—[30] as the rest (always excepting your wife and my sister from such sweeping terms); for she generally has some justice in the long run. I have no spite against her, though, between her and Nemesis, I have had some sore gauntlets to run—but then I have done my best to deserve no better. But to *you,* she is a good deal in arrear, and she will come round—mind if she don't: you have the vigour of life, of independence, of talent, spirit, and character all with you. What you can do for yourself, you have done and will do; and surely there are some others in the world who would not be sorry to be of use, if you would allow them to be useful, or at least attempt it.

I think of being in England in the spring. If there is a row, by the sceptre of King Ludd,[31] but I'll be one;[32] and if there is none, and only a continuance of "this meek,[33] piping time of peace," I will take a cottage a hundred yards to the south of your abode, and become your neighbour; and we will compose such canticles, and hold such dialogues, as shall be the terror of the *Times* (including the newspaper of that name), and the wonder, and honour, and praise of the *Morning Chronicle*[34] and posterity.

I rejoice to hear of your forthcoming[35] in February—though I tremble for the "magnificence," which you attribute to the new *Childe Harold.* I am glad you like it; it is a fine indistinct piece of poetical desolation, and my favourite. I was half mad during the time of its composition, between metaphysics, mountains, lakes, love unextinguishable, thoughts unutterable, and the nightmare of my own delinquencies. I should, many a good day, have blown my brains out, but for the recollection that it would have given pleasure to my mother-in-law; and, even *then,* if I could have been certain to haunt her—but I won't dwell upon these trifling family matters.

Venice is in the *estro*[36] of her carnival, and I have been up these last two nights at the ridotto[37] and the opera, and all that kind of thing. Now for an adventure. A few days ago a gondolier brought me a billet without a subscription,[38] intimating a wish on the part of the writer to meet me either in gondola, or at the island of San Lazaro, or at a third rendezvous, indicated in the note. "I know the country's disposition well"—in Venice "they do let Heaven see those tricks they dare not show,"[39] etc., etc.; so, for all response, I said that neither of the three places suited me; but that I would either be at home at ten at night *alone,* or be at the ridotto at midnight, where the writer might meet me masked. At ten o'clock I was at home and alone (Marianna[40] was gone with her husband to a conversazione[41]), when the door of my apartment opened, and in walked a well-looking and (for an Italian) *bionda*[42] girl of about nineteen, who informed me that she was married to the brother of my *amorosa,* and wished to have some conversation with me. I made a decent reply, and we had some talk in Italian and Romaic[43] (her mother being a Greek of Corfu), when, lo! in a very few minutes, in marches, to my very great astonishment, Marianna Segati, *in propria persona,*[44] and, after making a most polite courtesy to her sister-in-law and to me, without a single word seizes her said sister-in-law by the hair, and bestows upon her some sixteen slaps, which would have made your ear ache only to hear their echo. I need not describe the screaming which ensued. The luckless visitor took flight. I seized Marianna, who, after several vain efforts to get away in pursuit of the

---

28 To this Greek philosopher and mathematician of the sixth century B.C. was ascribed the doctrine that the end of earthly existence is purification of the soul.

29 The elder Moore, formerly a grocer and wine dealer, had been dismissed from his post as barrack-master at Dublin.

30 Thus the Prothero edition, without indicating whether the abbreviation is Byron's or an editor's.

31 A legendary king of ancient Britain.

32 Take part in it. The allusion is doubtless to the possibility that the widespread radical agitation might lead to violence.

33 Shakespeare wrote "weak" (*Richard III,* I, i, 24).

34 The *Times* was Tory, the *Chronicle* Whig.

35 The long-delayed publication of Moore's Oriental poem *Lalla Rookh,* though it was not for several months after this letter.

36 Ardor.   37 Masked ball.   38 Note without a signature.

39 *Othello,* III, iii, 201–3.

40 Marianna Segati, one of Byron's current mistresses. She was the vicious and avaricious wife of the tradesman in whose house he lodged.   41 I.e., social gathering.   42 Blonde.

43 Modern Greek.   44 In very person.

enemy, fairly went into fits in my arms; and, in spite of reasoning, eau de Cologne, vinegar, half a pint of water, and God knows what other waters beside, continued so till past midnight.

After damning my servants for letting people in without apprizing me, I found that Marianna in the morning had seen her sister-in-law's gondolier on the stairs, and, suspecting that his apparition boded her no good, had either returned of her own accord, or been followed by her maids or some other spy of her people to the conversazione, from whence she returned to perpetrate this piece of pugilism. I had seen fits before, and also some small scenery of the same genus in and out of our island: but this was not all. After about an hour, in comes—who? why, Signor Segati, her lord and husband, and finds me with his wife fainting upon a sofa, and all the apparatus of confusion, dishevelled hair, hats, handkerchiefs, salts, smelling bottles—and the lady as pale as ashes, without sense or motion. His first question was, "What is all this?" The lady could not reply—so I did. I told him the explanation was the easiest thing in the world; but, in the mean time, it would be as well to recover his wife—at least, her senses. This came about in due time of suspiration and respiration.

You need not be alarmed—jealousy is not the order of the day in Venice, and daggers are out of fashion; while duels, on love matters, are unknown —at least, with the husbands. But, for all this, it was an awkward affair; and though he must have known that I made love to Marianna, yet I believe he was not, till that evening, aware of the extent to which it had gone. It is very well known that almost all the married women have a lover; but it is usual to keep up the forms, as in other nations. I did not, therefore, know what the devil to say. I could not out with the truth, out of regard to her, and I did not choose to lie for my sake;—besides, the thing told itself. I thought the best way would be to let her explain it as she chose (a woman being never at a loss—the devil always sticks by them)—only determining to protect and carry her off, in case of any ferocity on the part of the Signor. I saw that he was quite calm. She went to bed, and next day—how they settled it, I know not, but settle it they did. Well—then I had to explain to Marianna about this never-to-be-sufficiently-confounded sister-in-law; which I did by swearing innocence, eternal constancy, etc., etc. ...[45] But the sister-in-law, very much discomposed with being treated in such wise, has (not having her own

shame before her eyes) told the affair to half Venice, and the servants (who were summoned by the fight and the fainting) to the other half. But, here, nobody minds such trifles, except to be amused by them. I don't know whether you will be so, but I have scrawled a long letter out of these follies.

Believe me ever, etc.

V. TO JOHN MURRAY

Venice, APRIL 6, 1819.

Dear Sir,—The Second Canto of *Don Juan* was sent, on Saturday last, by post, in 4 packets, two of 4, and two of three sheets each, containing in all two hundred and seventeen stanzas, octave measure. But I will permit no curtailments, except those mentioned about Castlereagh and the two *Bobs*[46] in the Introduction. You sha'n't make *Canticles* of my Cantos. The poem will please, if it is lively; if it is stupid, it will fail: but I will have none of your damned cutting and slashing. If you please, you may publish *anonymously*; it will perhaps be better; but I will battle my way against them all, like a Porcupine.

So you and Mr. Foscolo,[47] etc., want me to undertake what you call a "great work"? an Epic Poem, I suppose, or some such pyramid. I'll try no such thing; I hate tasks. And then "seven or eight years"! God send us all well this day three months, let alone years. If one's years can't be better employed than in sweating poesy, a man had better be a ditcher. And works, too!—is *Childe Harold* nothing? You have so many "*divine*" poems, is it nothing to have written a *Human* one? without any of your worn-out machinery. Why, man, I could have spun the thoughts of the four cantos of that poem into twenty, had I wanted to book-make, and its passion into as many modern tragedies. Since you want length, you shall have enough of *Juan,* for I'll make 50 cantos.

And Foscolo, too! Why does *he* not do something more than the *Letters of Ortis,*[48] and a tragedy, and

---

45 See note 30, above.

46 Robert Southey, the poet laureate, and Robert Stewart, better known as Viscount Castlereagh than by his subsequent title of Marquis of Londonderry. It was Castlereagh who sent Napoleon to St. Helena; he was foreign secretary and leader of the House of Commons from 1812 till his suicide in 1822.

47 This letter was in answer to one from Murray, Byron's publisher, on March 19. Ugo Foscolo (1778–1827), Italian writer, patriot, soldier in the Napoleonic armies, and professor at Padua, was now a refugee in England. Murray had written: "Here is Foscolo at my side, deploring that a man of your genius will not occupy some six or eight years in the composition of a work and subject worthy of you."

48 In which, in 1798, he expressed his disapproval of Napoleon's handing Venice over to Austria.

pamphlets? He has good fifteen years more at his command than I have: what has he done all that time?—proved his Genius, doubtless, but not fixed its fame, nor done his utmost.

Besides, I mean to write my best work in *Italian,* and it will take me nine years more thoroughly to master the language; and then if my fancy exists, and I exist too, I will try what I *can do really*. As to the Estimation of the English which you talk of,[49] let them calculate what it is worth, before they insult me with their insolent condescension.

I have not written for their pleasure. If they are pleased, it is that they chose to be so; I have never flattered their opinions, nor their pride; nor will I. Neither will I make "Ladies' books" *al dilettar le femine e la plebe*.[50] I have written from the fullness of my mind, from passion, from impulse, from many motives, but not for their "sweet voices."

I know the precise worth of popular applause, for few Scribblers have had more of it; and if I chose to swerve into their paths, I could retain it, or resume it, or increase it. But I neither love ye, nor fear ye; and though I buy with ye and sell with ye, and talk with ye, I will neither eat with ye, drink with ye, nor pray with ye.[51] They made me, without my search, a species of popular Idol; they, without reason or judgment, beyond the caprice of their good pleasure, threw down the Image from its pedestal; it was not broken with the fall, and they would, it seems, again replace it—but they shall not.

You ask about my health: about the beginning of the year I was in a state of great exhaustion, attended by such debility of Stomach that nothing remained upon it; and I was obliged to reform my "way of life," which was conducting me from the "yellow leaf"[52] to the Ground, with all deliberate speed. I am better in health and morals, and very much yours ever,

BN.

VI. TO THE COUNTESS GUICCIOLI

Bologna, AUGUST 25, 1819.

My dear Teresa,—

I have read this book[53] in your garden;—my love, you were absent, or else I could not have read it. It is a favourite book of yours, and the writer was a friend of mine. You will not understand these English words, and *others* will not understand them —which is the reason I have not scrawled them in Italian. But you will recognize the hand-writing of him who passionately loved you, and you will divine that, over a book which was yours, he could only think of love. In that word, beautiful in all languages, but most so in yours—*Amor mio*[54]—is comprised my existence here and hereafter. I feel I exist here, and I fear that I shall exist hereafter,—to *what* purpose you will decide; my destiny rests with you, and you are a woman, seventeen years of age, and two out of a convent. I wish that you had stayed there, with all my heart,—or, at least, that I had never met you in your married state.

But all this is too late. I love you, and you love me,—at least, you *say so,* and *act* as if you *did* so, which last is a great consolation in all events. But *I* more than love you, and cannot cease to love you.

Think of me, sometimes, when the Alps and the ocean divide us,—but they never will, unless you *wish* it.

BYRON.

VII. TO PERCY BYSSHE SHELLEY

Ravenna, APRIL 26, 1821.

The child[55] continues doing well, and the accounts are regular and favourable. It is gratifying to me that you and Mrs. Shelley do not disapprove of the step which I have taken, which is merely temporary.

I am very sorry to hear what you say of Keats— is it *actually* true? I did not think criticism had been so killing.[56] Though I differ from you essentially in your estimate of his performances, I so much abhor all unnecessary pain, that I would rather he had been seated on the highest peak of Parnassus than have perished in such a manner. Poor fellow! though with such inordinate self-love he would probably have not been very happy. I read the review of *Endymion* in the *Quarterly*. It was severe,—but surely not so severe as many reviews in that and other journals upon others.

I recollect the effect on me of the *Edinburgh* on my first poem; it was rage, and resistance, and redress—but not despondency nor despair. I grant that those are not amiable feelings; but, in this world of bustle and broil, and especially in the career of

---

[49] Murray had written that he wished Byron would allow himself "to be fully aware" of the "high estimation" in which he was held by his countrymen.

[50] To delight the women and the mob.   [51] Cf. *The Merchant of Venice,* I, iii, 36–9.   [52] Cf. *Macbeth,* V, iii, 22–3.

[53] This letter was written on the last page of Teresa's copy of *Corinne,* a novel (1807) by Mme. de Staël, whom Byron had met and liked in London and Switzerland.

[54] My love.

[55] Byron's daughter by Claire Clairmont. Allegra was now four, and Byron had placed her in a convent. See p. 213, note 1.

[56] Keats had died at Rome in February, 1821. Already the legend was circulating that a severe review in the *Quarterly* in 1818 had caused his fatal illness.

writing, a man should calculate upon his powers of *resistance* before he goes into the arena.

> Expect not life from pain nor danger free,
> Nor deem the doom of man reversed for thee.[57]

You know my opinion of *that second-hand* school of poetry. You also know my high opinion of your own poetry,—because it is of *no* school. I read *Cenci*[58]—but, besides that I think the *subject* essentially *un*dramatic, I am not an admirer of our old dramatists *as models*. I deny that the English have hitherto had a drama at all. Your *Cenci*, however, was a work of power, and poetry. As to *my* drama,[59] pray revenge yourself upon it, by being as free as I have been with yours.

I have not yet got your *Prometheus*,[60] which I long to see. I have heard nothing of mine, and do not know that it is yet published. I have published a pamphlet[61] on the Pope controversy, which you will not like. Had I known that Keats was dead—or that he was alive and so sensitive—I should have omitted some remarks[62] upon his poetry, to which I was provoked by his *attack* upon *Pope*,[63] and my disapprobation of *his own* style of writing.

You want me to undertake a great poem—I have not the inclination nor the power. As I grow older, the indifference—*not* to life, for we love it by instinct—but to the stimuli of life, increases. Besides, this late failure of the Italians[64] has latterly disappointed me for many reasons,—some public, some personal. My respects to Mrs. S.

Yours ever,
B.

P.S. Could not you and I contrive to meet this summer? Could not you take a run here *alone*?

VIII. TO JOHN MURRAY

Ravenna, SEPTEMBER 24th 1821.

Dear Murray—

I have been thinking over our late correspondence, and wish to propose to you the following articles for our future:—

1^{stly} That you shall write to me of yourself, of the health, wealth, and welfare of all friends; but of *me* (*quoad*[65] *me*) little or nothing.

2dly That you shall send me Soda powders, tooth-powder, tooth-brushes, or any such anti-odontalgic[66] or chemical articles, as heretofore, *ad libitum*,[67] upon being re-imbursed for the same.

3dly That you shall *not* send me any modern, or (as they are called) *new*, publications in *English whatsoever*, save and excepting any writing, prose or verse, of (or reasonably presumed to be of) Walter Scott, Crabbe,[68] Moore, Campbell,[69] Rogers,[70] Gifford,[71] Joanna Baillie,[72] Irving[73] (the American), Hogg,[74] Wilson (*Isle of Palms* man),[75] or *any* especial *single* work of fancy which is thought to be of considerable merit; *Voyages* and *travels*, provided that they are *neither in Greece, Spain, Asia Minor, Albania, nor Italy*, will be welcome. Having travelled the countries mentioned, I know that what is said of them can convey nothing farther which I desire to know about them. No other English works whatsoever.

4^{thly} That you send me *no periodical works* whatsoever—*no Edinburgh, Quarterly, Monthly*, nor any Review, Magazine, or Newspapers, English or foreign, of any description.

5^{thly} That you send me *no* opinions whatsoever, either *good, bad,* or *indifferent*, of yourself, or your friends, or others, concerning any work, or works, of mine, past, present, or to come.

6^{thly} That all negotiations in matters of business between you and me pass through the medium of the Honble Douglas Kinnaird,[76] my friend and trustee, or Mr. Hobhouse,[77] as *Alter Ego*,[78] and tantamount to myself during my absence, or presence.

Some of these propositions may at first seem strange, but they are founded. The quantity of trash I have received as books is incalculable, and neither amused nor instructed. Reviews and Magazines are

---

57 Cf. Dr. Johnson, *The Vanity of Human Wishes*, lines 155–6.
58 Shelley's tragedy *The Cenci* (1819).
59 Byron's historical tragedy *Marino Faliero, Doge of Venice;* it had in fact been published five days before, though Byron did not yet know that.
60 Shelley's "lyrical drama," *Prometheus Unbound* (1820).
61 *Letter . . . on the Rev. W. L. Bowles's Strictures on the Life and Writings of Pope* (March, 1821).
62 In *Observations upon "Observations." A Second Letter to John Murray* (written in March, 1821, but not published till 1835).
63 In Keats's "Sleep and Poetry," lines 193–206.
64 Risings by the Neapolitans and the Piedmontese had recently been crushed by the Austrians.

65 As far as.   66 Anti-toothache.   67 As you please.
68 The realistic poet George Crabbe (1754–1832), author of *The Village*, etc.
69 On Thomas Campbell see p. 357, below.
70 The poet Samuel Rogers (1763–1855), author of *The Pleasures of Memory*.
71 The critic and poet William Gifford (1756–1826), first editor (1809–24) of the *Quarterly Review*.
72 Scottish playwright and poet (1762–1851).
73 Washington Irving (1783–1859), whose romantic *The Sketch Book* had appeared in 1820.
74 James Hogg, the Scottish poet and miscellaneous writer (1770–1835), called "the Ettrick Shepherd."
75 The miscellaneous writer John Wilson ("Christopher North"—1785–1854); *The Isle of Palms* was his first volume of poetry.
76 A banker, member of the Drury Lane committee, and trustee for Lady Byron's marriage settlement.
77 See note 2 of this series.   78 Other self.

at the best but ephemeral and superficial reading: *who thinks* of the *grand article* of *last year* in any *given review?* In the next place, if they regard *myself,* they tend to increase *Egotism;* if favourable, I do not deny that the praise *elates,* and if unfavourable, that the abuse *irritates*—the latter may conduct me to inflict a species of Satire, which would neither do good to you nor to your friends: *they* may smile *now,* and so may *you;* but if I took you all in hand, it would not be difficult to cut you up like gourds. I did as much by as powerful people at nineteen years old, and I know little as yet in three-and-thirty, which should prevent me from making all your ribs Gridirons for your hearts, if such were my propensity. But it is *not.* Therefore let me hear none of your provocations. If any thing occurs so very *gross* as to require my notice, I shall hear of it from my personal friends. For the rest, I merely request to be left in ignorance.

The same applies to opinions, *good, bad,* or *indifferent,* of persons in conversation or correspondence: these do not *interrupt,* but they *soil* the *current* of my *Mind.* I am sensitive enough, but *not* till I am *touched;* and *here* I am beyond the touch of the short arms of literary England, except the few feelers of the Polypus that crawl over the Channel in the way of Extract.

All these precautions *in* England would be useless: the libeller or the flatterer would there reach me in spite of all; but in Italy we know little of literary England, and think less, except what reaches us through some garbled and brief extract in some miserable Gazette. For *two years* (excepting two or three articles cut out and sent to *you,* by the post) I never read a newspaper which was not forced upon me by some accident, and know, upon the whole, as little of England as you all do of Italy, and God knows *that* is little enough, with all your travels, etc., etc., etc. The English travellers *know Italy* as *you* know Guernsey: how much is *that?*

If any thing occurs so violently gross or personal as requires notice, Mr. D.ˢ Kinnaird will let me *know;* but of *praise* I desire to hear *nothing.*

You will say, "to what tends all this?" I will answer THAT;—to keep my mind *free and unbiassed* by all paltry and personal irritabilities of praise or censure;—to let my Genius take its natural direction, while my feelings are like the dead, who know nothing and feel nothing of all or aught that is said or done in their regard.

If you can observe these conditions, you will spare yourself and others some pain: let me not be worked upon to rise up; for if I do, it will not be for a little.

If you can *not* observe these conditions, we shall cease to be correspondents, but *not friends;* for I shall always be

Yours ever and truly,
BYRON.

P.S.—I have taken these resolutions not from any irritation against *you* or *yours,* but simply upon reflection that all reading, either praise or censure, of myself has done me harm. When I was in Switzerland and Greece, I was out of the way of hearing either, and *how I wrote there!* In Italy I am out of the way of it too; but latterly, partly through my fault, and partly through your kindness in wishing to send me the *newest* and most periodical publications, I have had a crowd of reviews, etc., thrust upon me, which have bored me with their jargon, of one kind or another, and taken off my attention from greater objects. You have also sent me a parcel of trash of poetry, for no reason that I can conceive, unless to provoke me to write a new *English Bards.* Now *this* I wish to avoid; for if ever I *do,* it will be a strong production; and I desire peace, as long as the fools will keep their nonsense out of my way.

IX. TO JOHN MURRAY

Pisa, AUGUST 3.ᵈ 1822.

Dear Sir,—

. . . I presume you have heard that Mr. Shelley and Capt. Williams[79] were lost on the 7.ᵗʰ Ul.ᵗᵒ[80] in their passage from Leghorn to Spezia in their own open boat. You may imagine the state of their families: I never saw such a scene, nor wish to see such another.

You were all brutally mistaken about Shelley, who was, without exception, the *best* and least selfish man I ever knew. I never knew one who was not a beast in comparison.

Yours ever,
N. B.[81]

[79] Edward Williams, a friend of Byron and Shelley, was lost on the final voyage of the latter's yacht.

[80] Ultimo, last; i.e., of last month.

[81] Lady Byron's uncle, Lord Wentworth, died in 1815, leaving a life interest in his property to her mother, Lady Milbanke, who then took the name Lady Noel. When his mother-in-law died early in 1822, Byron was a substantial beneficiary, since according to the terms of the separation his wife and he shared equally in the income from the property. He promptly added the surname Noel to his own.

Percy Bysshe Shelley

1792–1822

"A GREAT POET," observes the contemporary essayist H. W. Garrod, "is not an ordinary occurrence. We must not class the advent of great poetry with the daily delivery of the milk and the bread." Of England's great poets none was more the bringer of poetry's essence than Shelley. He was so dedicated a being, so intensely a poetic flame, that sentimentalists and popular biographers have said much of "Ariel" and presented us with a spirit rather than a man. Shelley was both. Like all artists of the first rank, he was tough and solid as well as tender and ethereal. A great deal of the poetry of this most poetic of poets was composed with a social purpose. Shelley's aim was nothing less than to reform the world; and for about twenty years after his death his *Queen Mab* was actually one of the edged tools of working-class propaganda. Shelley made us exquisite music; yet many of his poems came out of habitual hard thinking no less than from the raptures or the indignations of a nature extraordinarily sensitive to the world's beauty and the world's wrong. He also had vision; and for him, as for Plato, the great reality was the idea, not the thing. But to call this poet, as Matthew Arnold does, "a beautiful and ineffectual angel beating in the void his luminous wings in vain" is to take an extremely limited view. In vain? Only in the sense that all human endeavor may be called vain. In the void? Few commentators on politics have been able to hit harder or more accurately than Shelley does in some of his poems. Certainly it is true that his visionary and Platonic proclamations of an identical goodness and beauty beyond the unaided comprehension of ordinary citizens loom larger than any "practical" aspects of his work. If from time to time poets did not appear, to wear themselves out by harping on the existence now of better conceptions than most men are occupied with and on the possibility of better days than the invention of new gadgets or the stepping-up of airplanes' speed can reasonably promise, the world in which thoughtful people live would not be worth living in.

Shelley believed in progress and the perfectibility of man. If in some of his poems despair appears or self-pity, he did not falter—neither in vision nor in purpose. By the world he was neglected or condemned, but to the last he retained his consuming passion to do what he could to make it a better place. His benevolence was not merely formulated theoretically; it was also active and personal. Love in its highest and most comprehensive manifestations was, he believed, the surest guide to a better world. The injunction "Love thy neighbor as thyself" was for Shelley an immediate practical rule of conduct. He was not the kind of philanthropist who passes by on the other side when an individual need confronts him. In the presence of suffering Shelley was accustomed to move swiftly and directly. He was known to come home shoeless because he had met someone who needed shoes; and the number of those to whom his hand was extended and his purse opened was legion. When he was living in Italy a rumor reached him that a man had been sentenced to be burned alive for stealing a consecrated wafer. Shelley proposed to Byron that they organize a party of their friends to ride into the town and effect a rescue by force. Fortunately the man made his own escape before the poets went into action. That Shelley would cheerfully have given his life on this occasion there can be no question.

Shelley was born at Field Place, near Horsham, Sussex, the eldest child of a country squire, Timothy Shelley, and the eldest grandson of Sir Bysshe Shelley, a baronet who was both a holy terror and one of the wealthiest landowners of the county. Timothy Shelley had attended Oxford, taken the Grand Tour, and sat in the House of Commons; but though he was kindly and well-meaning, it cannot be said that his advantages had much expanded his mind. He was a Whig; but he was a conservative and staunchly conventional man:

> He always voted at his party's call,
> And he never thought of thinking for himself at all.

Like most respectable parents, he was alarmed when it began to appear that his elder son was brilliant, fearless, and contemptuous of accepted codes, religious, ethical, and political.

Shelley began his preparation at an academy near London, where he acquired a permanent taste for the physical sciences, especially chemistry and electricity. Then came six years at Eton. As superior lads often are, he was ill adjusted to the schoolboy milieu of sports, horseplay, and fighting. He was scribbling, of course, as well as reading voraciously; and at seventeen he published a worthless novel. A few months later appeared a volume of bad verse composed by him and one of his sisters. At Oxford, which was still characterized by the farcical indifference to education which had marked it in the eighteenth century, the slender, enthusiastic, almost girlishly sensitive youth, inclined to solitude, buried in reading of his own choice, his high-pitched voice raised in vehement argument against all ideas and institutions he considered inimical to freedom, was a puzzle to students and faculty; but he did find intellectual companionship with Thomas Jefferson Hogg (1792–1862), who became his lifelong friend. Having devoured Plato and also Godwin's *Political Justice,* Shelley was boiling over with ideas. He was only eighteen when his privately printed pamphlet, *The Necessity of Atheism,* based chiefly on the views of Locke and Hume, had the sole result of getting him and the devoted Hogg expelled from the university. The little treatise was anonymous; but Shelley was already viewed with suspicion, and the authorities charged him with its authorship. The friends refused point-blank to answer questions and were dismissed for contumacy. An ironical aspect of the affair is that Shelley was not really an atheist. His object was to establish the right to debate even the fundamentals of Christianity.

Understandably enough, this episode led to a row with his father. Instead of going home, Shelley went up to London, where he soon became interested in a boarding-school friend of his sisters'. Harriet Westbrook was the sixteen-year-old daughter of a rich retired tavern-keeper. Shelley was not in love with her, but as a college rebel he sympathized with her objections to school discipline. He thought he had found in her a convert to his views on society; she appealed to him for aid; and though he was in principle opposed to the institution of marriage, the upshot was a quixotic elopement that summer to Scotland. The union was not welcomed by either of the families; but funds were provided, and for a few months the newlyweds lived at Keswick near Southey, who was kind to them. Shelley never met Wordsworth, Coleridge, or De Quincey. Soon the couple were in Ireland, where from his efforts to aid the cause of freedom Shelley learned a good deal about the practical difficulties which can baffle political reformers—but not enough to call him to a halt. Much of the trouble he afterward encountered was the result of holding the highest principles, uncontaminated by compromise, and of acting on them immediately in particular cases without taking counsel of worldly prudence.

In 1813 Shelley came of age; and though for several years longer he was in financial straits, he was able now and then to raise a bit of money on his prospects as an heir. In the same year he published *Queen Mab,* a long philosophical poem mostly in blank verse—he later called it "trash"—setting forth his religious and social notions. They owed much to the radical thinker William Godwin, who held with Rousseau that the ills of modern society derive from the imperfections of its institutions and not from man himself, who is inherently good. It would, however, be a mistake to suppose that Shelley's social opinions were merely coincident with a vague urge to express utopian hopes. They were definite and,

as regards ways and means, carefully thought out. He saw then, as everyone does now, that Englishmen in the mass were at that stage of the Industrial Revolution subjected to a callous exploitation by the landed aristocracy and the new industrialists. Shelley did not advocate an armed popular uprising. His guiding star was "Love one another"; but he favored a capital levy and a constitutional reform which, by making political institutions more responsive to the people's will, would insure the country against a repetition of events in France.

In the spring of 1814 Shelley fell in love with Mary Wollstonecraft Godwin, William Godwin's daughter by his first marriage. Harriet, and still more her sister and confidante Eliza Westbrook, whom Shelley detested, would have liked to see him settle down comfortably in his appointed social station. Harriet was, moreover, increasingly unable to keep pace with her husband's mind. Shelley was unhappy; his estrangement from Harriet preceded his love for Mary. The latter had been reared in an atmosphere of unconventional principles; yet Godwin was the reverse of delighted when at seventeen his beautiful daughter eloped to France with Shelley. The lovers soon returned penniless to England. But in January, 1815, Shelley's grandfather died. By Harriet the poet had two children, and to her he assigned £200 of the £1000 annuity now settled on him. From her father Harriet also received £200 a year; money's purchasing power, it should be remembered, was then several times what it is now. Shelley sincerely believed, as other high-minded men and women have, that living with a woman he did not love was immoral; but he could not make Harriet see it. Of course the world thought him a scoundrel. Whatever its justification in terms of social stability, the world was, as Byron wrote soon after Shelley's death, "ill-naturedly, and ignorantly, and brutally mistaken" in its estimate of his character.

The year after the Battle of Waterloo brought Europe peace, and firmly seated reaction in the saddle to ride mankind, Shelley went abroad again with Mary. Byron's insistent mistress, Claire Clairmont, Godwin's step-daughter by his second marriage, tagged along. In Switzerland, in the spring of 1816, began Shelley's friendship with Byron; each of these great men deeply admired the other. Shelley had already published another long blank-verse poem, *Alastor* (1816); the subject is a poet of the ideal, who is punished for his self-centered withdrawal from society and sympathy with humanity. That fall he returned with Mary and Claire to England; and Shelley, to whom Byron had entrusted the manuscript, jacked up the publisher's price for the third canto of *Childe Harold* from $6,000 to $10,000.

Meanwhile, Harriet had been going rapidly downhill. Having sent her children away to board in the country, and possibly but not certainly sought consolation with some man whose identity is unknown, she had left her father's house and cut herself off so completely from Shelley that his efforts to locate and help her were unavailing. The landlady of the lodging house where she resided under an assumed name declared that she was pregnant, but Shelley's best biographer doubts that story. Harriet had, Professor White remarks, "entered Shelley's life with a threat of suicide if he did not return her love; she left it with the execution of her threat." Toward the end of 1816 she drowned herself. Shelley at once married Mary and attempted to secure custody of his children by Harriet. At the instigation of the Westbrooks, the high court of Chancery rejected his plea, on the ground that his conduct had made him unfit. Guardians were appointed, and Shelley never saw either child again. While Harriet was unquestionably an injured woman, the court's decision seems unjustified and brutal. It infuriated Shelley; and partly because of it, partly out of fear lest the court take from him his children by Mary, and partly for his health's sake, he spent the last four years of his life in Italy.

There he wrote his greatest poetry, especially during the years 1819–21. Save for an occasional denunciation of its allegedly diabolical sentiments, the journals (with honorable exceptions such as *Blackwood's*, the leading magazine of the day, and Leigh Hunt's *Examiner*) paid little attention to it. Few bought it. In addition to the poems, long or short, reprinted or mentioned below, Shelley composed other major works; perhaps the best of these is *The Cenci* (1819), a verse tragedy of incest and revenge. His prose works fill many pages; the masterpiece among them is *A Defence of Poetry*, reprinted in part below.

Two sons and a daughter were born to Shelley and his second wife. The elder son died at the age of three and the daughter in infancy; the younger son survived to inherit the baronetcy. From 1820 on, the Shelleys lived at Pisa; a circle of friends, English and Italian, was soon formed in the vicinity. Among the closest were Byron, the wild young Cornish adventurer Edward Trelawny, and Lieutenant Edward Williams (formerly of the East India Company's army) and his wife Jane.

The sad end of genius and creation came like a stroke of fate in Greek tragedy. Though clumsy with boats and no swimmer, Shelley loved the water, especially sailing. Despite the picture he gives of himself in some of his poems, he was not at all frail. He and Byron both had yachts built. Shelley's was the smaller, a twenty-four

footer, undecked. In May, 1822, he took a house near Lerici on the Gulf of Spezia. On July 8 he and Williams with a young sailor put out from Leghorn for a run back home along the coast. A violent squall came up, there appears to have been a collision with some boat never identified, and the *Don Juan* sank. There were no survivors. Several days elapsed before the bodies of Shelley and Williams were washed ashore. In one of the poet's pockets they found a volume of Sophocles, in another a volume of Keats. In the presence of Byron and other friends, Trelawny exhumed and cremated the mangled remains on the beaches where in compliance with Italian quarantine law they had been promptly buried. Shelley's ashes were placed in the Protestant cemetery at Rome, not far from the graves of his little son and Keats.

The Works in Verse and Prose were edited by H. B. Forman (8 vols., 1880), who also brought out a five-volume edition of the poems with a memoir (1892). The most elaborate edition of the collected writings is by R. Ingpen and W. E. Peck (10 vols., 1927–9). There is a handy little volume of selections from *Shelley's Literary and Philosophical Criticism*, edited by J. Shawcross (1909). G. E. Woodberry's edition of the *Complete Poetical Works* (4 vols., 1892) is good, and particularly useful is C. D. Locock's two-volume edition of the poems (1911). Among one-volume editions of the complete poems, T. Hutchinson's, with an introduction by B. P. Kurtz (Oxford Standard Authors, 1934), is pre-eminent. Cheap reprints of the poems are available in Everyman's Library (2 vols.) and The World's Classics (selections). The Modern Library gives Shelley and Keats together in a volume of its Giants series. An excellent and inexpensive selection is N. I. White's *The Best of Shelley* (1932).

Of the Lives, E. Dowden's (2 vols., revised ed., 1896), long the standard, has been superseded by N. I. White's (2 vols., 1940). Despite its unreliability, a fascinating book is E. J. Trelawny's *Recollections of the Last Days of Shelley and Byron* (1858). T. J. Hogg proved a disappointing biographer; but his incomplete Life (1858; reprinted jointly with Trelawny's *Recollections* and T. L. Peacock's *Memoirs of Shelley*, 2 vols., 1933) is valuable for Shelley at Oxford. Mrs. O. W. Campbell's *Shelley and the Unromantics* (2nd ed., 1924) is a violent but able study and biography. H. N. Brailsford's *Shelley, Godwin, and Their Circle* (Home University Library, no. 75) is helpful for the background of ideas; and in several books C. Grabo has emphasized Shelley's intellectuality and his knowledge of science.

Percy Bysshe Shelley

MUTABILITY

Shelley was about twenty-three when he felt and put
into the following terms the solemn truth that the great
fact of life is change.

We are as clouds that veil the midnight moon;
　How restlessly they speed, and gleam, and quiver,
Streaking the darkness radiantly!—yet soon
　Night closes round, and they are lost for ever:

Or like forgotten lyres, whose dissonant strings　　5
　Give various response to each varying blast,
To whose frail frame no second motion brings
　One mood or modulation like the last.

We rest.—A dream has power to poison sleep;
　We rise.—One wandering thought pollutes the day;
We feel, conceive or reason, laugh or weep;　　11
　Embrace fond woe, or cast our cares away:

It is the same!—For, be it joy or sorrow,
　The path of its departure still is free:
Man's yesterday may ne'er be like his morrow;　　15
　Naught may endure but Mutability.

HYMN TO INTELLECTUAL BEAUTY

According to his wife, the idea for this poem came to
Shelley when he was circumnavigating Lake Geneva
with Byron in the summer of 1816. These mystical
stanzas reflect his reading of Plato. By "intellectual"
Shelley here means *nonphysical* or *spiritual*. Plato argues
that the essential reality is not the material, impermanent
object but the eternal ideal, of which only fragmentary
aspects are embodied in things perceptible to our senses.
Above and beyond them, says Shelley, is the unifying
concept, Beauty, the Ideal, the One; it can be but imperfectly suggested by the beautiful objects we encounter
in a world of changing phenomena. Beauty itself we must
seek by contemplation. To this Platonic conclusion
Shelley adds that if we could perceive the Ideal, we
should attain a state of perfect love for all mankind.

The awful shadow of some unseen Power
　Floats though unseen among us,—visiting
　This various world with as inconstant wing
As summer winds that creep from flower to flower,—
Like moonbeams that behind some piny mountain
　　shower,　　5

It visits with inconstant glance
Each human heart and countenance;
Like hues and harmonies of evening,—
　Like clouds in starlight widely spread,—
　Like memory of music fled,—　　10
　Like aught that for its grace may be
Dear, and yet dearer for its mystery.

Spirit of BEAUTY, that dost consecrate
　With thine own hues all thou dost shine upon
　Of human thought or form,—where art thou gone?
Why dost thou pass away and leave our state,　　16
This dim vast vale of tears, vacant and desolate?
　Ask why the sunlight not for ever
　Weaves rainbows o'er yon mountain-river,
Why aught should fail and fade that once is shown,　　20
　Why fear and dream and death and birth
　Cast on the daylight of this earth
　Such gloom,—why man has such a scope
For love and hate, despondency and hope?

No voice from some sublimer world hath ever　　25
　To sage or poet these responses[1] given—
　Therefore the names of Demon,[2] Ghost, and Heaven,
Remain the records of their vain endeavour,
Frail spells—whose uttered charm might not avail to
　　sever,
　From all we hear and all we see,　　30
　Doubt, chance, and mutability.
Thy light alone—like mist o'er mountains driven,
　Or music by the night-wind sent
　Through strings of some still instrument,
　Or moonlight on a midnight stream,　　35
Gives grace and truth to life's unquiet dream.

Love, Hope, and Self-esteem, like clouds depart
　And come, for some uncertain moments lent.
　Man were immortal, and omnipotent,
Didst thou, unknown and awful as thou art,　　40
Keep with thy glorious train firm state within his heart.
　Thou messenger of sympathies,
　That wax and wane in lovers' eyes—
Thou—that to human thought art nourishment,
　Like darkness to a dying flame!　　45
　Depart not as thy shadow came,

---

[1] Answers to these questions.
[2] In this sense not an evil but an instructive spirit, which like a
ghost might provide man with knowledge of the unseen world.

Depart not—lest the grave should be,
Like life and fear, a dark reality.

While yet a boy I sought for ghosts, and sped
  Through many a listening chamber, cave and ruin, 50
  And starlight wood, with fearful steps pursuing
Hopes of high talk with the departed dead.
I called on poisonous names with which our youth is
      fed;
  I was not heard—I saw them not—
  When musing deeply on the lot   55
Of life, at that sweet time when winds are wooing
  All vital things that wake to bring
  News of birds and blossoming,—
  Sudden, thy shadow fell on me;
I shrieked, and clasped my hands in ecstasy! 60

I vowed that I would dedicate my powers
  To thee and thine—have I not kept the vow?
  With beating heart and streaming eyes, even now
I call the phantoms of a thousand hours
Each from his voiceless grave: they have in visioned
      bowers   65
  Of studious zeal or love's delight
  Outwatched with me the envious night—
They know that never joy illumed my brow
  Unlinked with hope that thou wouldst free
  This world from its dark slavery,   70
  That thou—O awful LOVELINESS,
Wouldst give whate'er these words cannot express.

The day becomes more solemn and serene
  When noon is past—there is a harmony
  In autumn, and a lustre in its sky,   75
Which through the summer is not heard or seen,
As if it could not be, as if it had not been!
  Thus let thy power, which like the truth
  Of nature on my passive youth
Descended, to my onward life supply   80
  Its calm—to one who worships thee,
  And every form containing thee,
  Whom, SPIRIT fair, thy spells did bind
To fear himself, and love all human kind.

OZYMANDIAS

Shelley wrote this irregular sonnet in 1817. Diodorus
Siculus, a Greek historian of the first century B.C., mentions the statue, which may still be seen. Shelley follows
him in using the Greek name of the Egyptian king,
Ramses II (1295–25 B.C.), the great builder.

I met a traveller from an antique land
Who said: Two vast and trunkless legs of stone
Stand in the desert. . . Near them, on the sand,
Half sunk, a shattered visage lies, whose frown,
And wrinkled lip, and sneer of cold command, 5
Tell that its sculptor well those passions read
Which yet survive, stamped on these lifeless things,
The hand that mocked them, and the heart that fed:[1]
And on the pedestal these words appear:
"My name is Ozymandias, king of kings: 10
Look on my works, ye Mighty, and despair!"
Nothing beside remains. Round the decay
Of that colossal wreck, boundless and bare
The lone and level sands stretch far away.

STANZAS

WRITTEN IN DEJECTION, NEAR NAPLES

The mood of desolation in this poem, composed late in
1818, was chiefly due to Shelley's ill health and to a
temporary estrangement from his wife which had
followed the death of their baby daughter Clara.

The sun is warm, the sky is clear,
  The waves are dancing fast and bright;
Blue isles and snowy mountains wear
  The purple noon's transparent might;
  The breath of the moist earth is light, 5
Around its unexpanded buds;
  Like many a voice of one delight,
  The winds, the birds, the ocean-floods,
The City's voice itself is soft, like Solitude's.

I see the Deep's untrampled floor   10
  With green and purple sea-weeds strown;
I see the waves upon the shore,
  Like light dissolved in star-showers, thrown:
  I sit upon the sands alone;
The lightning of the noontide ocean   15
  Is flashing round me, and a tone
Arises from its measured motion,
How sweet! did any heart now share in my emotion.

Alas! I have nor hope nor health,
  Nor peace within nor calm around,   20
Nor that content surpassing wealth
  The sage in meditation found,
  And walked with inward glory crowned;

---

[1] The *hand* is the sculptor's, who imitated or represented
("mocked") the monarch's passions; the *heart* is the king's—it
nourished those passions.

Nor fame, nor power, nor love, nor leisure.
　　Others I see whom these surround;　25
　Smiling they live, and call life pleasure;—
To me that cup has been dealt in another measure.

　Yet now despair itself is mild,
　　Even as the winds and waters are;
　I could lie down like a tired child,　30
　　And weep away the life of care
　Which I have borne and yet must bear,
　Till death like sleep might steal on me,
　　And I might feel in the warm air
　My cheek grow cold, and hear the sea　35
Breathe o'er my dying brain its last monotony.

　Some might lament that I were cold,
　　As I, when this sweet day is gone,
　Which my lost heart, too soon grown old,
　　Insults with this untimely moan;　40
　They might lament—for I am one
　Whom men love not,—and yet regret;
　　Unlike this day, which, when the sun
　Shall on its stainless glory set,
Will linger, though enjoyed, like joy in memory yet.　45

SONG TO
THE MEN OF ENGLAND

Shelley the radical, hopeful that a revolution is just
around the corner, speaks in the next three poems and
others, all composed in the fall of 1819 and inspired by
his hatred of England's reactionary government.

　Men of England, wherefore plough
　For the lords who lay ye low?
　Wherefore weave with toil and care
　The rich robes your tyrants wear?

　Wherefore feed, and clothe, and save,　5
　From the cradle to the grave,
　Those ungrateful drones who would
　Drain your sweat—nay, drink your blood?

　Wherefore, Bees of England, forge
　Many a weapon, chain, and scourge,　10
　That these stingless drones may spoil
　The forced produce of your toil?

　Have ye leisure, comfort, calm,
　Shelter, food, love's gentle balm?
　Or what is it ye buy so dear　15
　With your pain and with your fear?

　The seed ye sow, another reaps;
　The wealth ye find, another keeps;
　The robes ye weave, another wears;
　The arms ye forge, another bears.　20

　Sow seed,—but let no tyrant reap;
　Find wealth,—let no impostor heap;
　Weave robes,—let not the idle wear;
　Forge arms,—in your defence to bear.

　Shrink to your cellars, holes, and cells;　25
　In halls ye deck another dwells.
　Why shake the chains ye wrought? Ye see
　The steel ye tempered glance on ye.

　With plough and spade, and hoe and loom,
　Trace your grave, and build your tomb,　30
　And weave your winding-sheet, till fair
　England be your sepulchre.

ENGLAND IN 1819

An old, mad, blind, despised, and dying king,—[1]
Princes, the dregs of their dull race, who flow
Through public scorn—mud from a muddy spring;
Rulers, who neither see, nor feel, nor know,
But leech-like to their fainting country cling,　5
Till they drop, blind in blood, without a blow;
A people starved and stabbed in the untilled field,—
An army, which liberticide and prey
Makes as a two-edged sword to all who wield;
Golden and sanguine[2] laws which tempt and slay;　10
Religion Christless, Godless—a book sealed;
A Senate,—Time's worst statute[3] unrepealed,—
Are graves, from which a glorious Phantom may
Burst, to illumine our tempestuous day.

THE MASQUE OF ANARCHY

WRITTEN ON THE OCCASION OF THE
MASSACRE AT MANCHESTER

On a day in the summer of 1819 thousands of citizens
assembled at St. Peter's Field in Manchester in a mass
meeting called by the advocates of reform. The militia,
ordered to arrest the speaker, lost their heads and sabered
the workers. Several persons were killed and many
wounded. The national administration upheld the local

[1] George III (d. 1820).
[2] I.e., rooted in gold and blood.
[3] Imposing penalties on Catholics. It was mainly to advocate
Catholic Emancipation that Shelley went on his quixotic
mission to Ireland soon after his first marriage.

authorities. News of Peterloo, as the bloody affair was called in derisive contrast with the Army's victory at Waterloo, roused Shelley to a white heat of indignation, out of which was written the following powerful poem. Shelley sent it to Leigh Hunt for publication in the *Examiner;* but Hunt prudently withheld it till 1832, the year of the Reform Bill, when it was brought out in separate form.

As I lay asleep in Italy
There came a voice from over the Sea,
And with great power it forth led me
To walk in the visions of Poesy.

I met Murder on the way—   5
He had a mask like Castlereagh;[1]
Very smooth he looked, yet grim;
Seven bloodhounds followed him.

All were fat, and well they might
Be in admirable plight,   10
For one by one, and two by two,
He tossed them human hearts to chew,
Which from his wide cloak he drew.

Next came Fraud, and he had on,
Like Eldon,[2] an ermined gown;[3]   15
His big tears, for he wept well,
Turned to millstones as they fell,

And the little children, who
Round his feet played to and fro,
Thinking every tear a gem,   20
Had their brains knocked out by them.

Clothed with the Bible, as with light,
And the shadows of the night,
Like Sidmouth,[4] next, Hypocrisy
On a crocodile rode by.   25

And many more Destructions played
In this ghastly masquerade,

All disguised, even to the eyes,
Like Bishops, lawyers, peers, and spies.

Last came Anarchy: he rode   30
On a white Horse splashed with blood;
He was pale even to the lips,
Like Death in the Apocalypse.[5]

And he wore a kingly crown;
In his hand a sceptre shone;   35
On his brow this mark I saw—
"I AM GOD, AND KING, AND LAW!"

With a pace stately and fast,
Over English land he past,
Trampling to a mire of blood   40
The adoring multitude.

And a mighty troop around
With their trampling shook the ground,
Waving each a bloody sword
For the service of their Lord.   45

And, with glorious triumph, they
Rode through England, proud and gay,
Drunk as with intoxication
Of the wine of desolation.

O'er fields and towns, from sea to sea,   50
Past the pageant swift and free,
Tearing up, and trampling down,—
Till they came to London town.

And each dweller, panic-stricken,
Felt his heart with terror sicken   55
Hearing the tempestuous cry
Of the triumph of Anarchy.

For with pomp to meet him came,
Clothed in arms like blood and flame,
The hired Murderers, who did sing   60
"Thou art God, and Law, and King.

"We have waited, weak and lone,
For thy coming, Mighty One!
Our purses are empty, our swords are cold;
Give us glory, and blood, and gold."   65

Lawyers and priests, a motley crowd,
To the earth their pale brows bowed;
Like a bad prayer not over-loud,
Whispering—"Thou art Law and God."

---

[1] Robert Stewart (1769–1822), second Marquis of Londonderry, better known by his earlier title of Viscount Castlereagh, foreign secretary and leader of the House of Commons (1812–22). Three years after Shelley wrote his poem, Castlereagh gratified the liberals by cutting his own throat.

[2] John Scott (1751–1838), first Earl of Eldon, almost continuously lord chancellor from 1801 to 1827, and center of the government's resistance to reform. In his judicial capacity he had pronounced Shelley unfit to be the guardian of his children by his first wife, Harriet.   [3] Worn by judges.

[4] Henry Addington (1757–1844), first Viscount Sidmouth, was home secretary from 1812 to 1821. His policy of repression led directly to the outrage at Manchester.

[5] Revelation 6:8.

Then all cried with one accord,
"Thou art King, and God, and Lord;
Anarchy, to thee we bow,—
Be thy name made holy now!"

And Anarchy, the Skeleton,
Bowed and grinned to every one,
As well as if his education
Had cost ten millions to the Nation.

For he knew the Palaces
Of our Kings were rightly his;
His the sceptre, crown, and globe,
And the gold-inwoven robe.

So he sent his slaves before
To seize upon the Bank and Tower,[6]
And was proceeding with intent
To meet his pensioned parliament,

When one fled past, a Maniac maid,
And her name was Hope, she said:
But she looked more like Despair,
And she cried out in the air:

"My father Time is weak and grey
With waiting for a better day;
See how idiot-like he stands,
Fumbling with his palsied hands!

"He has had child after child,
And the dust of death is piled
Over every one but me—
Misery, oh, Misery!"

Then she lay down in the street,
Right before the horses' feet,
Expecting,[7] with a patient eye,
Murder, Fraud, and Anarchy;

When between her and her foes
A mist, a light, an image rose,—
Small at first, and weak, and frail
Like the vapour of a vale:

Till as clouds grow on the blast,
Like tower-crowned giants, striding fast,
And glare with lightnings as they fly,
And speak in thunder to the sky,

It grew—a Shape[8] arrayed in mail
Brighter than the viper's scale,
And upborne on wings whose grain[9]
Was as the light of sunny rain.

On its helm, seen far away,
A planet, like the Morning's, lay;
And those plumes its light rained through
Like a shower of crimson dew.

With step as soft as wind it past
O'er the heads of men—so fast
That they knew the presence there,
And looked,—and all was empty air.

As flowers beneath May's footstep waken,
As stars from Night's loose hair are shaken,
As waves arise when loud winds call,
Thoughts sprung where'er that step did fall.

And the prostrate multitude
Looked—and ankle-deep in blood,
Hope, that maiden most serene,
Was walking with a quiet mien:

And Anarchy, the ghastly birth,
Lay dead earth upon the earth;
The Horse of Death, tameless as wind,
Fled, and with his hoofs did grind
To dust the murderers thronged behind.

A rushing light of clouds and splendour,
A sense, awakening and yet tender,
Was heard and felt—and at its close
These words of joy and fear arose:

As if their own indignant Earth,
Which gave the Sons of England birth,
Had felt their blood upon her brow,
And shuddering with a mother's throe

Had turnèd every drop of blood
By which her face had been bedewed
To an accent unwithstood,—
As if her heart had cried aloud:

"Men of England, Heirs of Glory,
Heroes of unwritten story,
Nurslings of one mighty Mother,
Hopes of her, and one another;

70
75
80
85
90
95
100
105
110
115
120
125
130
135
140
145
150

---

[6] The Bank of England and the Tower of London.
[7] Awaiting.

[8] According to Hunt, Public Enlightenment. See line 125.
[9] Color.

"Rise like Lions after slumber,
In unvanquishable number;
Shake your chains to earth like dew
Which in sleep had fallen on you:—
Ye are many—they are few.   155

"What is Freedom?—ye can tell
That which slavery is, too well—
For its very name has grown
To an echo of your own.

"'Tis to work, and have such pay   160
As just keeps life from day to day
In your limbs,—as in a cell,
For the tyrants' use to dwell:

"So that ye for them are made
Loom, and plough, and sword, and spade,—   165
With or without your own will, bent
To their defence and nourishment.

"'Tis to see your children weak
With their mothers pine and peak,
When the winter winds are bleak:—   170
They are dying whilst I speak.

"'Tis to hunger for such diet
As the rich man in his riot[10]
Casts to the fat dogs that lie
Surfeiting beneath his eye.   175

"'Tis to let the Ghost of Gold[11]
Take from Toil a thousandfold
More than e'er its substance could
In the tyrannies of old:

"Paper coin—that forgery   180
Of the title-deeds which ye
Hold to something of the worth
Of the inheritance of Earth.

"'Tis to be a slave in soul
And to hold no strong controul   185
Over your own wills, but be
All that others make of ye.

"And, at length when ye complain
With a murmur weak and vain,
'Tis to see the Tyrant's crew   190
Ride over your wives and you:—
Blood is on the grass like dew!

"Then it is to feel revenge,
Fiercely thirsting to exchange
Blood for blood—and wrong for wrong:—   195
Do not thus when ye are strong!

"Birds find rest in narrow nest
When weary of their wingèd quest;
Beasts find fare in woody lair
When storm and snow are in the air.   200

"Horses, oxen, have a home,
When from daily toil they come;
Household dogs, when the wind roars,
Find a home within warm doors.

"Asses, swine, have litter spread   205
And with fitting food are fed;
All things have a home but one—
Thou, O Englishman, hast none!

"This is Slavery: savage men,
Or wild beasts within a den,   210
Would endure not as ye do:—
But such ills they never knew.

"What art thou, Freedom? Oh, could slaves
Answer from their living graves
This demand—tyrants would flee   215
Like a dream's dim imagery:

"Thou art not, as impostors say,
A shadow soon to pass away,
A superstition, and a name
Echoing from the cave of Fame.   220

"For the labourer thou art bread,
And a comely table spread,
From his daily labour come
In a neat and happy home.

"Thou art clothes, and fire, and food   225
For the trampled multitude:—
No—in countries that are free
Such starvation cannot be
As in England now we see.

"To the rich thou art a check;   230
When his foot is on the neck
Of his victim, thou dost make
That he treads upon a snake.

"Thou art Justice—ne'er for gold
May thy righteous laws be sold   235

[10] Revelry.   [11] I.e., paper, securities.

As laws are in England: thou
Shield'st alike the high and low.

"Thou art Wisdom—freemen never
Dream that God will damn forever
All who think those things untrue   240
Of which Priests make such ado.

"Thou art Peace—never by thee
Would blood and treasure wasted be
As tyrants wasted them, when all
Leagued to quench thy flame in Gaul.[12]   245

"What if English toil and blood
Was poured forth, even as a flood?
It availed, O Liberty!
To dim, but not extinguish thee.

"Thou art Love—the rich have kist   250
Thy feet, and like him following[13] Christ,
Give their substance to the free
And through the rough world follow thee:

"Or turn their wealth to arms, and make
War for thy belovèd sake   255
On wealth, and war, and fraud—whence they
Drew the power which is their prey.

"Science, Poetry and Thought
Are thy lamps; they make the lot
Of the dwellers in a cot   260
So serene, they curse it not.

"Spirit, patience, gentleness,
All that can adorn and bless,
Art thou. . . let deeds, not words, express
Thine exceeding loveliness.   265

"Let a great Assembly be
Of the fearless and the free,
On some spot of English ground
Where the plains stretch wide around.

"Let the blue sky overhead,   270
The green earth on which ye tread,
All that must eternal be,
Witness the solemnity.

"From the corners uttermost
Of the bounds of English coast;   275

From every hut, village and town
Where those who live and suffer, moan
For others' misery or their own;

"From the workhouse and the prison
Where, pale as corpses newly risen,   280
Woman, children, young and old,
Groan for pain, and weep for cold;

"From the haunts of daily life
Where is waged the daily strife
With common wants and common cares,   285
Which sows the human heart with tares,

"Lastly, from the palaces,
Where the murmur of distress
Echoes, like the distant sound
Of a wind alive around   290

"Those prison-halls of wealth and fashion,
Where some few feel such compassion,
For those who groan, and toil, and wail,
As must make their brethren pale;—

"Ye who suffer woes untold,   295
Or to feel or to behold
Your lost country bought and sold
With a price of blood and gold;—

"Let a vast Assembly be;
And with great solemnity   300
Declare with measured words that ye
Are, as God has made ye, free.

"Be your strong and simple words
Keen to wound as sharpened swords,
And wide as targes[14] let them be,   305
With their shade to cover ye.

"Let the tyrants pour around
With a quick and startling sound,
Like the loosening of a sea,
Troops of armed emblazonry.   310

"Let the charged artillery drive
Till the dead air seems alive
With the clash of clanging wheels,
And the tramp of horses' heels.

"Let the fixèd bayonet   315
Gleam with sharp desire to wet

---

[12] I.e., to suppress the French Revolution and Napoleon.
[13] Him who follows.

[14] Shields.

Its bright point in English blood,
Looking keen, as one for food.

"Let the horsemen's scimitars
Wheel and flash, like sphereless[15] stars   320
Thirsting to eclipse their burning
In a sea of death and mourning.

"Stand ye calm and resolute,
Like a forest, close and mute,
With folded arms, and looks which are   325
Weapons of unvanquished war;

"And let Panic, who outspeeds
The career of armèd steeds,
Pass, a disregarded shade,
Through your phalanx[16] undismayed.   330

"Let the Laws of your own land,
Good or ill, between ye stand,
Hand to hand, and foot to foot,
Arbiters of the dispute:—

"The old laws of England—they   335
Whose reverend heads with age are grey,
Children of a wiser day;
And whose solemn voice must be
Thine own echo—Liberty!

"On those who first should violate   340
Such sacred heralds in their state
Rest the blood that must ensue. . .
And it will not rest on you.

"And if then the tyrants dare,
Let them ride among you there,   345
Slash, and stab, and maim, and hew,—
What they like, that let them do.

"With folded arms and steady eyes,
And little fear, and less surprise,
Look upon them as they slay,   350
Till their rage has died away.

"Then they will return with shame
To the place from which they came,
And the blood thus shed will speak
In hot blushes on their cheek.   355

"Every woman in the land
Will point at them as they stand. . .
They will hardly dare to greet
Their acquaintance in the street,

"And the bold, true warriors   360
Who have hugged Danger in the wars,
Will turn to those who would be free,
Ashamed of such base company.

"And that slaughter to the Nation
Shall steam up like inspiration,   365
Eloquent, oracular;
A volcano heard afar.

"And these words shall then become
Like Oppression's thundered doom
Ringing through each heart and brain,   370
Heard again—again—again:—

"'Rise like Lions after slumber,
In unvanquishable number;
Shake your chains to earth, like dew
Which in sleep had fallen on you:—   375
Ye are many—they are few.'"

ODE TO THE WEST WIND

In that same fall of 1819 which saw Shelley writing fierce diatribes against the Tory politicians, he produced one of his most exquisite lyrics. But the "Ode to the West Wind" is not unrelated to the foregoing poems. Besides rare beauty, colored perhaps by the poem's having been written in a wood on the banks of the Arno near Florence, there is present (from the fourth strophe on) a passionate insistence that the poet's task goes beyond music making. Shelley would be bard and prophet, rousing mankind for the days he is sure will follow the autumn of decay and the winter of cessation—barren seasons, when the enemies of freedom succeed in coldly blocking humanity's forward march to a better world.

The basic meter of the "Ode" is an Italian one called *terza rima:* each tercet or set of three lines is laced to the next by rime, line 2 of each tercet riming with lines 1 and 3 of the following tercet (*aba bcb cdc,* etc.). Shelley makes a brilliant variation in this pattern by writing strophes of fourteen lines, each composed of four tercets plus a couplet which rimes with line 2 of the preceding tercet (*aba bcb cdc ded ee*).

I

O wild West Wind, thou breath of Autumn's being,
Thou, from whose unseen presence the leaves dead
Are driven, like ghosts from an enchanter fleeing,

Yellow, and black, and pale, and hectic red,
Pestilence-stricken multitudes: O thou,
Who chariotest to their dark wintry bed   5

The wingèd seeds, where they lie cold and low,
Each like a corpse within its grave, until
Thine azure sister[1] of the Spring shall blow

Her clarion o'er the dreaming earth, and fill   10
(Driving sweet buds like flocks to feed in air)
With living hues and odours plain and hill.

Wild Spirit, which art moving everywhere;
Destroyer and preserver; hear, oh, hear!

2

Thou on whose stream, 'mid the steep sky's
    commotion,   15
Loose clouds like Earth's decaying leaves are shed,
Shook from the tangled boughs of Heaven and Ocean,

Angels of rain and lightning: there are spread
On the blue surface of thine airy surge,
Like the bright hair uplifted from the head   20

Of some fierce Maenad,[2] even from the dim verge
Of the horizon to the zenith's height,
The locks of the approaching storm. Thou dirge

Of the dying Year, to which this closing[3] night
Will be the dome of a vast sepulchre,   25
Vaulted with all thy congregated might

Of vapours, from whose solid atmosphere
Black rain, and fire, and hail will burst: oh, hear!

3

Thou who didst waken from his summer dreams
The blue Mediterranean, where he lay,   30
Lulled by the coil of his crystalline streams,

Beside a pumice[4] isle in Baiae's[5] bay,
And saw in sleep old palaces and towers
Quivering within the wave's intenser day,

All overgrown with azure moss and flowers   35
So sweet, the sense faints picturing them! Thou
For whose path the Atlantic's level powers

Cleave themselves into chasms, while far below
The sea-blooms and the oozy woods which wear
The sapless foliage of the ocean know   40

Thy voice, and suddenly grow grey with fear,
And tremble and despoil themselves: oh, hear!

4

If I were a dead leaf thou mightest bear;
If I were a swift cloud to fly with thee;
A wave to pant beneath thy power, and share   45

The impulse of thy strength, only less free
Than thou, O uncontroulable! If even
I were as in my boyhood, and could be

The comrade of thy wanderings over Heaven,
As then, when to outstrip thy skiey speed   50
Scarce seemed a vision; I would ne'er have striven

As thus with thee in prayer in my sore need.
Oh! lift me as a wave, a leaf, a cloud!
I fall upon the thorns of life! I bleed!

A heavy weight of hours has chained and bowed   55
One too like thee: tameless, and swift, and proud.

5

Make me thy lyre, even as the forest is:
What if my leaves are falling like its own!
The tumult of thy mighty harmonies

Will take from both a deep, autumnal tone,   60
Sweet though in sadness. Be thou, Spirit fierce,
My spirit! Be thou me, impetuous one!

Drive my dead thoughts over the universe
Like withered leaves to quicken a new birth!
And, by the incantation of this verse,   65

Scatter, as from an unextinguished hearth
Ashes and sparks, my words among mankind!
Be through my lips to unawakened Earth

The trumpet of a prophecy! O Wind,
If Winter comes, can Spring be far behind?   70

---

[1] The south wind.   [2] Nymph attending Bacchus.
[3] I.e., closing down on the world.   [4] I.e., volcanic.
[5] A town near Naples.

THE INDIAN SERENADE

This lyric and the one following were written in 1819.

I arise from dreams of thee
  In the first sweet sleep of night,
When the winds are breathing low,
  And the stars are shining bright:
I arise from dreams of thee,   5
  And a spirit in my feet
Hath led me—who knows how?
  To thy chamber window, sweet!

The wandering airs they faint
  On the dark, the silent stream;   10
The Champak[1] odours fail
  Like sweet thoughts in a dream;
The nightingale's complaint,
  It dies upon her heart,
As I must die on thine,   15
  O belovèd as thou art!

Oh lift me from the grass!
  I die! I faint! I fail!
Let thy love in kisses rain
  On my lips and eyelids pale.   20
My cheek is cold and white, alas!
  My heart beats loud and fast,—
Oh! press it close to thine again,
  Where it will break at last.

LOVE'S PHILOSOPHY

The fountains mingle with the river,
  And the rivers with the ocean;
The winds of Heaven mix for ever
  With a sweet emotion;
Nothing in the world is single;   5
  All things by a law divine
In one another's being mingle;—
  Why not I with thine?

See the mountains kiss high Heaven,
  And the waves clasp one another;   10
No sister flower would be forgiven
  If it disdained its brother;
And the sunlight clasps the earth,
  And the moonbeams kiss the sea:
What is all this sweet work worth,   15
  If thou kiss not me?

---

[1] Or champac, an East Indian tree of the magnolia family.

SONGS *from* PROMETHEUS UNBOUND

This lyrical drama, in which Shelley's philosophy is embodied, was written in 1818–19 and published in 1820. The subject was suggested by the tragedy *Prometheus Bound* of Aeschylus. That play tells how the heroic Titan who stole fire from heaven and gave it to mankind was condemned by Zeus to be chained to Mt. Caucasus and tortured daily by a vulture preying on his liver, which constantly renewed itself. In the Greek myth, Zeus and Prometheus are eventually reconciled. In Shelley's conception the hero, Prometheus or the aspiring spirit of Man, whom the poet considers essentially good, is the bringer of civilization and, though Christlike in forgiving his enemy, remains also the defier of Zeus or Jupiter, whose overthrow, since he stands for the evil in Man's thought and especially for the tyranny of institutions and custom, is a prerequisite to Man's liberation. The first of the following lyrics is sung to end Act II by Asia, a nymph who loves Prometheus; she symbolizes love, nature, and the creative spirit. In Act III Jupiter is dethroned by Demogorgon, the principle of change, progress, and inevitability; and Prometheus is unbound. Act IV, which closes with Demogorgon's song "This is the day," is a rapturous hymn of hope for the newly delivered world.

MY SOUL IS AN ENCHANTED BOAT

My soul is an enchanted Boat,
  Which, like a sleeping swan, doth float
Upon the silver waves of thy sweet singing;[1]
  And thine doth like an Angel sit
  Beside the helm conducting it,   5
Whilst all the winds with melody are ringing.
  It seems to float ever, for ever,
  Upon that many-winding river,
  Between mountains, woods, abysses,
  A Paradise of wildernesses!   10
Till, like one in slumber bound,
Borne to the ocean, I float, down, around,
Into a sea profound, of ever-spreading sound:

  Meanwhile thy Spirit lifts its pinions
  In Music's most serene dominions;   15
Catching the winds that fan that happy Heaven.
  And we sail on, away, afar,
  Without a course, without a star,
But by the instinct of sweet music driven;
  Till through Elysian garden islets   20
  By thee, most beautiful of pilots,
  Where never mortal pinnace glided,
  The boat of my desire is guided:

---

[1] Asia has heard a spirit voice singing.

Realms where the air we breathe is Love,
Which in the winds and on the waves doth move,   25
Harmonizing this Earth with what we feel above.

  We have passed Age's icy caves,
  And Manhood's dark and tossing waves,
And Youth's smooth ocean, smiling to betray:
  Beyond the glassy gulphs we flee   30
  Of shadow-peopled Infancy,
Through Death and Birth, to a diviner day;
  A Paradise of vaulted bowers
  Lit by downward-gazing flowers,
  And watery paths that wind between   35
  Wildernesses calm and green,
Peopled by shapes too bright to see,
And rest, having beheld; somewhat like thee;
Which walk upon the sea, and chant melodiously!

THIS IS THE DAY

This is the Day, which down the void Abysm
At the Earth-born's spell yawns for Heaven's despotism,
  And Conquest is dragged captive through the deep;
Love, from its awful throne of patient power
In the wise heart, from the last giddy hour   5
  Of dread endurance, from the slippery, steep,
And narrow verge of crag-like agony, springs
And folds over the world its healing wings.

Gentleness, Virtue, Wisdom, and Endurance,—
These are the seals of that most firm assurance   10
  Which bars the pit over Destruction's strength;
And if, with infirm hand, Eternity,
Mother of many acts and hours, should free
  The serpent that would clasp her with his length,
These are the spells by which to re-assume   15
An empire o'er the disentangled Doom.

To suffer woes which Hope thinks infinite;
To forgive wrongs darker than death or night;
  To defy Power, which seems omnipotent;
To love, and bear; to hope till Hope creates   20
From its own wreck the thing it contemplates:
  Neither to change, nor falter, nor repent;
This, like thy glory, Titan, is to be
Good, great and joyous, beautiful and free;
This is alone Life, Joy, Empire, and Victory.   25

THE CLOUD

The date of this poem is uncertain; it was probably finished
in Italy in 1820, the year of its publication.

I bring fresh showers for the thirsting flowers,
  From the seas and the streams;
I bear light shade for the leaves when laid
  In their noonday dreams.
From my wings are shaken the dews that waken   5
  The sweet buds every one,
When rocked to rest on their mother's breast,
  As she dances about the sun.
I wield the flail of the lashing hail,
  And whiten the green plains under,   10
And then again I dissolve it in rain,
  And laugh as I pass in thunder.

I sift the snow on the mountains below,
  And their great pines groan aghast;
And all the night 'tis my pillow white,   15
  While I sleep in the arms of the blast.
Sublime on the towers of my skiey bowers,
  Lightning my pilot sits;
In a cavern under is fettered the thunder,—
  It struggles and howls at fits;   20
Over earth and ocean, with gentle motion,
  This pilot[1] is guiding me,
Lured by the love of the genii that move
  In the depths of the purple sea;
Over the rills, and the crags, and the hills,   25
  Over the lakes and the plains,
Wherever he dream under mountain or stream
  The Spirit he loves remains;
And I all the while bask in Heaven's blue smile,
  Whilst he is dissolving in rains.   30

The sanguine sunrise, with his meteor eyes,
  And his burning plumes outspread,
Leaps on the back of my sailing rack,[2]
  When the morning star shines dead:
As on the jag of a mountain crag,   35
  Which an earthquake rocks and swings,
An eagle alit one moment may sit
  In the light of its golden wings.
And when sunset may breathe, from the lit sea beneath,
  Its ardours of rest and of love,   40
And the crimson pall of eve may fall
  From the depth of Heaven above,
With wings folded I rest, on mine airy nest,
  As still as a brooding dove.

[1] Electricity.   [2] Mass of high, scudding cloud.

That orbèd maiden with white fire laden,   45
  Whom mortals call the moon,
Glides glimmering o'er my fleece-like floor,
  By the midnight breezes strewn;
And wherever the beat of her unseen feet,
  Which only the angels hear,   50
May have broken the woof of my tent's thin roof,
  The stars peep behind her and peer;
And I laugh to see them whirl and flee,
  Like a swarm of golden bees,
When I widen the rent in my wind-built tent,   55
  Till the calm rivers, lakes, and seas,
Like strips of the sky fallen through me on high,
  Are each paved with the moon and these.

I bind the sun's throne with a burning zone,[3]
  And the moon's with a girdle of pearl;   60
The volcanos are dim, and the stars reel and swim,
  When the whirlwinds my banner unfurl.
From cape to cape, with a bridge-like shape,
  Over a torrent sea,
Sunbeam-proof, I hang like a roof,—   65
  The mountains its columns be.
The triumphal arch through which I march
  With hurricane, fire, and snow,
When the Powers of the air are chained to my chair,
  Is the million-coloured bow;   70
The sphere-fire above its soft colours wove,
  While the moist Earth was laughing below.

I am the daughter of earth and water,
  And the nursling of the sky;
I pass through the pores of the ocean and shores; 75
  I change, but I cannot die.
For after the rain, when with never a stain
  The pavilion of Heaven is bare,
And the winds and sunbeams with their convex gleams,
  Build up the blue dome of air,   80
I silently laugh at my own cenotaph,[4]
  And out of the caverns of rain,
Like a child from the womb, like a ghost from the
    tomb,
  I arise and unbuild it again.

---

[3] Belt.
[4] An empty tomb built as a monument; i.e., the "blue dome" of
the sky.

TO A SKYLARK

This poem was written at Leghorn in the early summer of
1820.

Hail to thee, blithe Spirit!—
  Bird thou never wert!—
That from Heaven, or near it,
  Pourest thy full heart
In profuse strains of unpremeditated art.   5

Higher still and higher
  From the earth thou springest
Like a cloud of fire;
  The blue deep thou wingest,
And singing still dost soar, and soaring ever singest. 10

In the golden lightning
  Of the sunken sun,
O'er which clouds are bright'ning,
  Thou dost float and run;
Like an unbodied joy whose race is just begun.   15

The pale purple even
  Melts around thy flight;
Like a star of Heaven,
  In the broad daylight
Thou art unseen,—but yet I hear thy shrill delight, 20

Keen as are the arrows
  Of that silver sphere,
Whose intense lamp narrows
  In the white dawn clear
Until we hardly see—we feel that it is there: 25

All the earth and air
  With thy voice is loud,
As, when Night is bare,
  From one lonely cloud
The moon rains out her beams, and Heaven is
    overflowed.   30

What thou art we know not;
  What is most like thee?
From rainbow-clouds there flow not
  Drops so bright to see
As from thy presence showers a rain of melody.   35

Like a Poet hidden
  In the light of thought,
Singing hymns unbidden
  Till the world is wrought
To sympathy with hopes and fears it heeded not: 40

Like a high-born maiden
  In a palace-tower,
Soothing her love-laden
  Soul in secret hour
With music sweet as love, which overflows her
    bower: 45

Like a glow-worm golden
  In a dell of dew,
Scattering unbeholden[1]
  Its aërial hue
Among the flowers and grass which screen it from the
    view: 50

Like a rose embowered
  In its own green leaves,
By warm winds deflowered,
  Till the scent it gives
Makes faint with too much sweet those heavy wingèd
    thieves.   55

Sound of vernal showers
  On the twinkling grass;
Rain-awakened flowers,
  All that ever was
Joyous and clear and fresh, thy music doth surpass.   60

Teach us, Sprite[2] or Bird,
  What sweet thoughts are thine;
I have never heard
  Praise of love or wine
That panted forth a flood of rapture so divine: 65

Chorus hymeneal,[3]
  Or triumphal chaunt,
Matched with thine, would be all
  But an empty vaunt,
A thing wherein we feel there is some hidden want.   70

What objects are the fountains
  Of thy happy strain?
What fields or waves or mountains?
  What shapes of sky or plain?   74
What love of thine own kind? what ignorance of pain?

With thy clear keen joyance
  Languor cannot be:
Shadow of annoyance
  Never came near thee:
Thou lovest—but ne'er knew love's sad satiety.   80

Waking or asleep
  Thou of death must deem
Things more true and deep
  Than we mortals dream,   84
Or how could thy notes flow in such a crystal stream?

We look before and after,
  And pine for what is not:
Our sincerest laughter
  With some pain is fraught;
Our sweetest songs are those that tell of saddest
    thought.   90

Yet if we could scorn
  Hate and pride and fear;
If we were things born
  Not to shed a tear,
I know not how thy joy we ever should come near. 95

Better than all measures
  Of delightful sound—
Better than all treasures
  That in books are found,
Thy skill to poet were,[4] thou scorner of the ground! 100

Teach[5] me half the gladness
  That thy brain must know,
Such harmonious madness[6]
  From my lips would flow
The world should listen then—as I am listening now. 105

ADONAIS

AN ELEGY ON THE DEATH OF JOHN KEATS

AUTHOR OF ENDYMION, HYPERION, ETC.

This famous poem in Spenserian stanzas, written at Pisa
in the late spring of 1821, laments the death of Keats at
Rome several months earlier. The poets were not well
acquainted; it was some time after Keats's death that the
sad news reached Shelley. Had he known Keats better,
he could never have supposed that, as he states in a
preface here omitted, a savage review had killed him.

"Adonais," like "Lycidas," follows the ancient tradition of pastoral elegy; hence the name, another form of
Adonis, the unfortunate youth beloved by Venus and
celebrated by numerous poets and painters. No more
than Milton's "Lycidas" does Shelley's poem spring from
an outburst of sorrow for a personal loss. The subject is
the lot of the genius in general, and especially his liability
to misunderstanding and even persecution by the dull

---

[1] Unseen.   [2] Spirit.   [3] Marriage song.   [4] Would be.   [5] If thou wouldst teach.   [6] Inspired poetry.

and ignorant; as a whole the elegy is doubly moving because much of what Shelley says about Keats is applicable, intentionally so, to himself. The poem is very uneven. Parts of it fail to strike fire; but there are passages which blaze with light and power. Typically Shelleyan is the poetic statement of Platonic faith in the Ideal and in the individual spirit's capacity for reunion with it.

I weep for Adonais—he is dead!
Oh, weep for Adonais! though our tears
Thaw not the frost which binds so dear a head!
And thou, sad Hour, selected from all years
To mourn our loss, rouse thy obscure compeers,[1]
And teach them thine own sorrow; say, With me
Died Adonais; till the Future dares
Forget the Past, his fate and fame shall be
An echo and a light unto eternity!

Where wert thou, mighty Mother,[2] when he lay,   10
When thy Son lay, pierced by the shaft which flies
In darkness?[3] where was lorn Urania
When Adonais died? With veilèd eyes,
'Mid listening Echoes, in her Paradise
She sate, while one,[4] with soft enamoured breath,   15
Rekindled all the fading melodies,
With which, like flowers that mock the corse beneath,
He had adorned and hid the coming bulk of Death.

Oh, weep for Adonais—he is dead!
Wake, melancholy Mother, wake and weep!   20
Yet wherefore? Quench within their burning bed
Thy fiery tears, and let thy loud heart keep,
Like his, a mute and uncomplaining sleep;
For he is gone, where all things wise and fair
Descend;—oh, dream not that the amorous Deep   25
Will yet restore him to the vital air;
Death feeds on his mute voice, and laughs at our despair.

Most musical of mourners, weep again!
Lament anew, Urania!—He[5] died,
Who was the Sire of an immortal strain,   30
Blind, old, and lonely,—when his country's pride
The priest, the slave, and the liberticide
Trampled and mocked with many a loathèd rite
Of lust and blood; he went, unterrified,

Into the gulph of death; but his clear Sprite   35
Yet reigns o'er earth, the third[6] among the sons of light.

Most musical of mourners, weep anew!
Not all to that bright station dared to climb;
And happier they their happiness who knew,
Whose tapers yet burn through that night of time   40
In which suns perished; others more sublime,
Struck by the envious wrath of man or God,
Have sunk, extinct in their refulgent prime;
And some yet live, treading the thorny road,
Which leads, through toil and hate, to Fame's serene
    abode.   45

But now, thy youngest, dearest one has perished,
The nursling of thy widowhood, who grew,
Like a pale flower by some sad maiden cherished,
And fed with true-love tears, instead of dew;[7]
Most musical of mourners, weep anew!   50
Thy extreme hope, the loveliest and the last,
The bloom, whose petals, nipt before they blew,
Died on the promise of the fruit, is waste;
The broken lily lies—the storm is overpast.

To that high Capital,[8] where kingly Death   55
Keeps his pale court in beauty and decay,
He came; and bought, with price of purest breath,
A grave among the eternal.—Come away!
Haste, while the vault of blue Italian day
Is yet his fitting charnel-roof! while still   60
He lies, as if in dewy sleep he lay;
Awake him not! surely he takes his fill
Of deep and liquid rest, forgetful of all ill.

He will awake no more, oh, never more!—
Within the twilight chamber spreads apace   65
The shadow of white Death, and at the door
Invisible Corruption waits to trace
His extreme[9] way to her dim dwelling-place;
The eternal Hunger[10] sits, but pity and awe
Soothe her pale rage, nor dares she to deface   70
So fair a prey, till darkness, and the law
Of change, shall o'er his sleep the mortal curtain draw.

Oh, weep for Adonais!—The quick Dreams,[11]
The passion-wingèd Ministers of thought,
Who were his flocks, whom near the living streams

---

[1] Companions, hours still hidden ("obscure") because in the future.
[2] The Heavenly One (because she is the Muse of astronomy); but *Urania* is also one of the epithets for Aphrodite: the Uranian Venus was goddess of heavenly love, and thus of the Ideal or, in Shelley's phrase, "Intellectual Beauty."
[3] I.e., the arrow shot by an anonymous reviewer.
[4] Of the Echoes.   [5] Milton.

[6] It is evident from *A Defence of Poetry* that Shelley considered Homer and Dante Milton's two great predecessors as epic poets.
[7] An allusion to Keats's "Isabella."   [8] Rome.
[9] Adonais's last.
[10] Corruption, which consumes the body in the grave.
[11] Poems, poetic ideas.

Of his young spirit he fed, and whom he taught   76
The love which was its music, wander not,—
Wander no more, from kindling brain to brain,
But droop there, whence they sprung; and mourn
      their lot
Round the cold heart, where, after their sweet pain,[12]
They ne'er will gather strength, or find a home again. 81

And one with trembling hands clasps his cold head,
And fans him with her moonlight wings, and cries,
"Our love, our hope, our sorrow, is not dead;
See, on the silken fringe of his faint eyes,   85
Like dew upon a sleeping flower, there lies
A tear some Dream has loosened from his brain."
Lost Angel of a ruined Paradise![13]
She knew not 'twas her own,—as with no stain
She faded, like a cloud which had outwept its rain.   90

One from a lucid urn of starry dew
Washed his light limbs, as if embalming them;
Another clipt her profuse locks, and threw
The wreath upon him, like an anadem,[14]
Which frozen tears instead of pearls begem;   95
Another in her wilful grief would break
Her bow and wingèd reeds[15]—as if to stem
A greater loss with one which was more weak—
And dull the barbèd fire against his frozen cheek.

Another Splendour[16] on his mouth alit,   100
That mouth whence it was wont to draw the breath
Which gave it strength to pierce the guarded wit,[17]
And pass into the panting heart beneath
With lightning and with music: the damp death
Quenched its caress upon his icy lips;   105
And, as a dying meteor stains a wreath
Of moonlight vapour, which the cold night clips,[18]
It flushed through his pale limbs, and passed to its eclipse.

And others came . . . Desires and Adorations,
Wingèd Persuasions and veiled Destinies,   110
Splendours, and Glooms, and glimmering Incarnations
Of hopes and fears, and twilight Phantasies;
And Sorrow, with her family of Sighs,
And Pleasure, blind with tears, led by the gleam
Of her own dying smile instead of eyes,   115
Came in slow pomp;—the moving pomp might seem
Like pageantry of mist on an autumnal stream.

All he had loved, and moulded into thought,
From shape, and hue, and odour, and sweet sound,
Lamented Adonais. Morning sought   120
Her eastern watch-tower, and her hair unbound,
Wet with the tears which should adorn the ground,
Dimmed the aërial eyes that kindle day;
Afar the melancholy thunder moaned,
Pale Ocean in unquiet slumber lay,   125
And the wild winds flew round, sobbing in their dismay.

Lost Echo sits amid the voiceless mountains,
And feeds her grief with his remembered lay,
And will no more reply to winds or fountains,
Or amorous birds perched on the young green spray,
Or herdsman's horn, or bell at closing day;   131
Since she can mimic not his lips, more dear
Than those[19] for whose disdain she pined away
Into a shadow of all sounds:—a drear
Murmur, between their songs, is all the woodmen hear.

Grief made the young Spring wild, and she threw
      down   136
Her kindling buds, as if she Autumn were,
Or they dead leaves; since her delight is flown,
For whom should she have waked the sullen Year?
To Phoebus was not Hyacinth[20] so dear,   140
Nor to himself Narcissus, as to both
Thou, Adonais; wan they stand and sere
Amid the faint companions of their youth,
With dew all turned to tears; odour, to sighing ruth.

Thy spirit's sister, the lorn nightingale,   145
Mourns not her mate with such melodious pain;
Not so the eagle, who like thee could scale
Heaven, and could nourish in the sun's domain
Her mighty youth with morning, doth complain,
Soaring and screaming round her empty nest,   150
As Albion[21] wails for thee: the curse of Cain
Light on his head[22] who pierced thy innocent breast,
And scared the angel soul that was its earthly guest!

Ah woe is me! Winter is come and gone,
But grief returns with the revolving year;   155
The airs and streams renew their joyous tone;
The ants, the bees, the swallows reappear;
Fresh leaves and flowers deck the dead Seasons' bier;
The amorous birds now pair in every brake,

---

12 The pangs of the poet in giving them birth.
13 Adonais's mind.   14 Chaplet, garland.
15 Arrows by which the thoughts of Keats's poems were shot into
the "guarded wit" (see line 102).
16 I.e., "dream," poetic conception.
17 I.e., unresponsive minds.   18 Embraces.

19 Of Narcissus, the youth (enamored of himself) for whom, in the
myth, the nymph Echo pined away till she was only a voice.
20 The youth Hyacinthus, loved by Phoebus Apollo, who accidentally killed him. From his blood sprang the flower.
21 England.   22 The reviewer in the Quarterly.

And build their mossy homes in field and brere;[23] 160
And the green lizard, and the golden snake,
Like unimprisoned flames, out of their trance awake.

Through wood and stream and field and hill and
   Ocean
A quickening life from the Earth's heart has burst,
As it has ever done, with change and motion, 165
From the great morning of the world when first
God dawned on Chaos; in its steam immersed
The lamps of Heaven flash with a softer light;
All baser things pant with life's sacred thirst;
Diffuse themselves; and spend in love's delight, 170
The beauty and the joy of their renewèd might.

The leprous corpse touched by this spirit tender
Exhales itself in flowers of gentle breath;
Like incarnations of the stars, when splendour
Is changed to fragrance, they illumine death 175
And mock the merry worm that wakes beneath;
Nought we know, dies. Shall that alone which knows
Be as a sword consumed before the sheath
By sightless[24] lightning?—Th' intense atom glows
A moment, then is quenched in a most cold repose. 180

Alas! that all we loved of him should be,
But for our grief, as if it had not been,
And grief itself be mortal! Woe is me!
Whence are we, and why are we? of what scene
The actors or spectators? Great and mean 185
Meet massed in death, who lends what life must
   borrow.[25]
As long as skies are blue, and fields are green,
Evening must usher night, night urge the morrow,
Month follow month with woe, and year wake year to
   sorrow.

He will awake no more, oh, never more! 190
"Wake thou," cried Misery, "childless Mother! rise
Out of thy sleep, and slake in thy heart's core
A wound more fierce than his with tears and sighs."
And all the Dreams that watched Urania's eyes,
And all the Echoes whom their sister's song 195
Had held in holy silence, cried, "Arise!"
Swift as a Thought by the snake Memory stung,
From her ambrosial rest the fading Splendour sprung.

She rose like an autumnal Night, that springs
Out of the East, and follows wild and drear 200
The golden Day, which, on eternal wings,
Even as a ghost abandoning a bier,
Had left the Earth a corpse. Sorrow and fear
So struck, so roused, so rapt Urania;
So saddened round her like an atmosphere 205
Of stormy mist; so swept her on her way
Even to the mournful place where Adonais lay.

Out of her secret Paradise she sped,
Through camps and cities rough with stone, and steel,
And human hearts, which to her aery tread 210
Yielding not, wounded the invisible
Palms of her tender feet where'er they fell:
And barbèd tongues, and thoughts more sharp than
   they,
Rent the soft Form they never could repel,
Whose sacred blood, like the young tears of May, 215
Paved with eternal flowers that undeserving way.

In the death-chamber for a moment Death,
Shamed by the presence of that living Might,
Blushed to annihilation, and the breath
Revisited those lips, and life's pale light 220
Flashed through those limbs, so late her dear delight.
"Leave me not wild and drear and comfortless,
As silent lightning leaves the starless night!
Leave me not!" cried Urania: her distress
Roused Death: Death rose and smiled, and met her vain
   caress. 225

"Stay yet awhile! speak to me once again;
Kiss me, so long but as a kiss may live;
And in my heartless[26] breast and burning brain
That word, that kiss, shall all thoughts else survive,
With food of saddest memory kept alive, 230
Now thou art dead, as if it were a part
Of thee, my Adonais! I would give
All that I am to be as thou now art,
But I am chained to Time, and cannot thence depart!

"O gentle child, beautiful as thou wert, 235
Why didst thou leave the trodden paths of men
Too soon, and with weak hands though mighty heart
Dare the unpastured dragon[27] in his den?
Defenceless as thou wert, oh! where was then
Wisdom the mirrored shield,[28] or scorn the spear? 240

---

[23] Briar.
[24] Invisible. I.e. (line 177), everything of which we can have actual knowledge, i.e., all matter, is imperishable. How strange that the part of us which is conscious should perish, as if (lines 178–9) a bolt of lightning should destroy the sword (the mind) without destroying the sheath (the body).
[25] I.e., the great reality is not life but death.

[26] Because her heart was with Adonais.
[27] I.e., boldly seek out and expose yourself to the world's harshness, as Perseus in the Greek myth confronted Medusa, the snaky-haired Gorgon.
[28] The Gorgon's gaze could turn anyone to stone. Perseus looked at her reflection in his shield.

Or hadst thou waited the full cycle, when
Thy spirit should have filled its crescent sphere,
The monsters of life's waste had fled from thee like deer.

"The herded[29] wolves, bold only to pursue;
The obscene ravens, clamorous o'er the dead;   245
The vultures to the conqueror's banner true
Who feed where Desolation first has fed,
And whose wings rain contagion;—how they fled,
When, like Apollo, from his golden bow,
The Pythian[30] of the age one arrow sped   250
And smiled!—The spoilers tempt no second blow,—
They fawn on the proud feet that spurn them lying low.

"The sun comes forth, and many reptiles spawn;
He sets, and each ephemeral insect then
Is gathered into death without a dawn,   255
And the immortal stars awake again;
So it is in the world of living men:
A godlike mind soars forth, in its delight
Making earth bare and veiling Heaven,[31] and when
It sinks, the swarms that dimmed or shared its
      light   260
Leave to its kindred lamps[32] the spirit's awful night."

Thus ceased she: and the mountain shepherds came,
Their garlands sere, their magic mantles rent;
The Pilgrim of Eternity,[33] whose fame
Over his living head like Heaven is bent,   265
An early but enduring monument,
Came, veiling all the lightnings of his song
In sorrow; from her wilds Ierne sent
The sweetest lyrist of her saddest wrong,[34]
And love taught grief to fall like music from his
      tongue.   270

Midst others of less note, came one frail Form,[35]
A phantom among men; companionless
As the last cloud of an expiring storm
Whose thunder is its knell; he, as I guess,
Had gazed on Nature's naked loveliness,   275
Actaeon-like,[36] and now he fled astray

---

29 Running in pack; i.e., the critics.
30 Apollo was given this epithet for slaying the huge serpent known as the Python. The allusion is to Byron and his *English Bards, and Scotch Reviewers.*
31 Like the sun making the earth bright and unclouded, and the other heavenly bodies invisible.
32 The other heavenly bodies; i.e., other poets.
33 Byron, the Pilgrim of *Childe Harold.*
34 Ireland sent Tom Moore. Actually, however, he did not contribute a lamentation for Keats.   35 Shelley.
36 Actaeon, in Greek myth, saw Diana bathing. He was punished by being changed into a stag and hunted to his death by his own hounds.

With feeble steps o'er the world's wilderness,
And his own thoughts, along that rugged way,
Pursued, like raging hounds, their father and their prey.

A pardlike[37] Spirit beautiful and swift—   280
A Love in desolation masked;—a Power
Girt round with weakness;—it can scarce uplift
The weight of the superincumbent hour;
It is a dying lamp, a falling shower,
A breaking billow;—even whilst we speak   285
Is it not broken? On the withering flower
The killing sun smiles brightly: on a cheek
The life can burn in blood, even while the heart may
      break.

His head was bound with pansies[38] over-blown,
And faded violets, white, and pied, and blue;   290
And a light spear topped with a cypress cone,
Round whose rude shaft dark ivy-tresses grew
Yet dripping with the forest's noonday dew,
Vibrated, as the ever-beating heart   294
Shook the weak hand that grasped it; of that crew
He came the last, neglected and apart;
A herd-abandoned deer struck by the hunter's dart.

All stood aloof, and at his partial[39] moan
Smiled through their tears; well knew that gentle
      band
Who in another's fate now wept his own;   300
As in the accents of an unknown[40] land
He sung new sorrow; sad Urania scanned
The Stranger's mien, and murmured, "Who art
      thou?"
He answered not, but with a sudden hand
Made bare his branded and ensanguined brow,   305
Which was like Cain's or Christ's—oh! that it should
      be so!

What softer voice is hushed over the dead?
Athwart what brow is that dark mantle thrown?
What form leans sadly o'er the white death-bed,
In mockery of monumental stone,—   310
The heavy heart heaving without a moan?
If it be He,[41] who, gentlest of the wise,
Taught, soothed, loved, honoured the departed one,
Let me not vex, with inharmonious sighs,
The silence of that heart's accepted sacrifice.   315

---

37 Leopard-like.
38 Symbol of thought, as the violet is of modesty, the cypress of mourning, and the ivy of poets.
39 Sympathetic.   40 I.e., to Urania.
41 Leigh Hunt, one of Shelley's best friends. See pp. 360-61, below.

Our Adonais has drunk poison—oh,
What deaf and viperous murderer could crown
Life's early cup with such a draught of woe?
The nameless worm[42] would now itself disown:
It felt, yet could escape the magic tone   320
Whose prelude held all envy, hate, and wrong,
But what was howling in one breast alone,
Silent with expectation of the song,
Whose master's hand is cold, whose silver lyre unstrung.

Live thou, whose infamy is not thy fame!   325
Live! fear no heavier chastisement from me,
Thou noteless blot on a remembered name!
But be thyself, and know thyself to be!
And ever at thy season be thou free
To spill the venom when thy fangs o'erflow: 330
Remorse and Self-contempt shall cling to thee;
Hot Shame shall burn upon thy secret brow,
And like a beaten hound tremble thou shalt—as now.

Nor let us weep that our delight is fled[43]
Far from these carrion kites that scream below;   335
He wakes or sleeps with the enduring dead;
Thou canst not soar where he is sitting now.—
Dust to the dust! but the pure spirit shall flow
Back to the burning fountain whence it came,
A portion of the Eternal, which must glow   340
Through time and change, unquenchably the same,
Whilst thy cold embers[44] choke the sordid hearth of
   shame.

Peace, peace! he is not dead, he doth not sleep—
He hath awakened from the dream of life:
'Tis we, who, lost in stormy visions, keep   345
With phantoms an unprofitable strife,
And, in mad trance, strike with our spirit's knife
Invulnerable nothings.—We decay
Like corpses in a charnel;[45] fear and grief
Convulse us and consume us day by day,   350
And cold hopes swarm like worms within our living
   clay.

He has outsoared the shadow of our night;
Envy and calumny and hate and pain,
And that unrest which men miscall delight,
Can touch him not and torture not again;   355

From the contagion of the world's slow stain
He is secure, and now can never mourn
A heart grown cold, a head grown grey in vain;
Nor, when the spirit's self has ceased to burn,
With sparkless ashes load an unlamented urn.   360

He lives, he wakes—'tis Death is dead, not he;
Mourn not for Adonais.—Thou young Dawn,
Turn all thy dew to splendour, for from thee
The spirit thou lamentest is not gone;
Ye caverns and ye forests, cease to moan!   365
Cease, ye faint flowers and fountains, and thou Air,
Which like a mourning veil thy scarf hadst thrown
O'er the abandoned Earth, now leave it bare
Even to the joyous stars which smile on its despair!

He is made one with Nature: there is heard   370
His voice in all her music, from the moan
Of thunder to the song of night's sweet bird;
He is a presence to be felt and known
In darkness and in light, from[46] herb and stone,—
Spreading itself where'er that Power[47] may move   375
Which has withdrawn his being to its own;
Which wields the world with never-wearied love,
Sustains it from beneath, and kindles it above.

He is a portion of the loveliness
Which once he made more lovely: he doth bear   380
His part, while the one Spirit's plastic[48] stress
Sweeps through the dull dense world, compelling
   there
All new successions to the forms they wear;
Torturing th' unwilling dross that checks its flight
To its own likeness, as[49] each mass may bear.   385
And bursting in its beauty and its might
From trees and beasts and men into the Heaven's light.

The splendours of the firmament of time
May be eclipsed, but are extinguished not:
Like stars to their appointed height they climb,   390
And death is a low mist which cannot blot
The brightness it may veil. When lofty thought
Lifts a young heart above its mortal lair,
And love and life contend in it for what
Shall be its earthly doom, the dead live there[50]   395
And move like winds of light on dark and stormy air.

---

[42] Serpent; i.e., the anonymous reviewer in the *Quarterly* for April,
1818 (published in September). It was the Tory critic John
Wilson Croker (1780–1857), though Keats's friends suspected
another.
[43] With this stanza comes the "turn" of the poem; Shelley begins
soaring to a higher elevation.
[44] The reviewer's ashes.   [45] Charnel house, sepulcher.

[46] Emanating from.
[47] The Eternal, the burning fountain (line 339), the creative source
of all.   [48] Molding, creating.
[49] According as, to such extent as.
[50] In the young heart.

The inheritors of unfulfilled renown
Rose from their thrones, built beyond mortal thought,
Far in the Unapparent. Chatterton[51]
Rose pale,—his solemn agony had not   400
Yet faded from him; Sidney,[52] as he fought
And as he fell and as he lived and loved,
Sublimely mild, a Spirit without spot,
Arose; and Lucan,[53] by his death approved:
Oblivion as they rose shrank like a thing reproved.   405

And many more, whose names on Earth are dark,
But whose transmitted effluence cannot die
So long as fire outlives the parent spark,
Rose, robed in dazzling immortality.
"Thou art become as one of us," they cry,   410
"It was for thee yon kingless sphere has long
Swung blind[54] in unascended majesty,
Silent alone amid an Heaven of song.
Assume thy wingèd throne, thou Vesper[55] of our
    throng!"

Who mourns for Adonais? Oh come forth,   415
Fond wretch![56] and know thyself and him aright.
Clasp with thy panting soul the pendulous Earth;
As from a centre, dart thy spirit's light
Beyond all worlds, until its spacious might
Satiate the void circumference: then shrink   420
Even to a point within our day and night;
And keep thy heart light lest it make thee sink
When hope has kindled hope, and lured thee to the
    brink.[57]

Or go to Rome, which is the sepulchre,
Oh, not of him, but of our joy: 'tis nought   425
That ages, empires, and religions there
Lie buried in the ravage they have wrought;
For such as he can lend,—they borrow not
Glory[58] from those who made the world their prey;
And he is gathered to the kings of thought   430
Who waged contention with their time's decay,
And of the past are all that cannot pass away.

Go thou to Rome,—at once the Paradise,
The grave, the city, and the wilderness;
And where its wrecks like shattered mountains rise,
And flowering weeds, and fragrant copses dress   436

The bones of Desolation's nakedness,
Pass, till the Spirit of the spot shall lead
Thy footsteps to a slope of green access,[59]
Where, like an infant's smile, over the dead   440
A light of laughing flowers along the grass is spread;

And grey walls moulder round, on which dull Time
Feeds, like slow fire upon a hoary brand;
And one keen pyramid[60] with wedge sublime,
Pavilioning the dust of him who planned   445
This refuge for his memory, doth stand
Like flame transformed to marble; and beneath,
A field is spread, on which a newer band
Have pitched in Heaven's smile their camp of death,
Welcoming him we lose with scarce-extinguished
    breath.   450

Here pause: these graves are all too young as yet
To have outgrown the sorrow which consigned
Its charge to each; and if the seal is set,
Here, on one fountain of a mourning mind,[61]
Break it not thou! too surely shalt thou find   455
Thine own well full, if thou returnest home,
Of tears and gall. From the world's bitter wind
Seek shelter in the shadow of the tomb.
What Adonais is, why fear we to become?

The One[62] remains, the many change and pass;   460
Heaven's light forever shines, Earth's shadows fly;
Life, like a dome of many-coloured glass,
Stains[63] the white radiance of Eternity,
Until Death tramples it to fragments.—Die,
If thou wouldst be with that which thou dost seek![64]
Follow where all is fled!—Rome's azure sky,   466
Flowers, ruins, statues, music, words, are weak
The glory they transfuse with fitting truth to speak.

Why linger, why turn back, why shrink, my Heart?
Thy hopes are gone before: from all things here   470
They have departed; thou shouldst now depart!
A light is past from the revolving year,
And man, and woman; and what still is dear
Attracts to crush, repels to make thee wither.
The soft sky smiles,—the low wind whispers near: 475

---

51 In 1770, at the age of eighteen, this young poet killed himself.
52 Sir Philip Sidney (1554–86).
53 The Roman poet Lucan (39–65), author of the epic *Pharsalia*,
   killed himself after Nero had condemned him to death.
54 Without light.   55 Or Hesper, the evening star.
56 Presumably Shelley.   57 Of death.
58 I.e., by being buried there Keats confers distinction on Rome.

59 The Protestant cemetery. Shelley's ashes were soon buried
   there, too.
60 The tomb of Gaius Cestius, a Roman praetor and tribune.
61 Shelley's son William had been buried there in 1819. The graves
   are all "young" because the cemetery was new.
62 The Platonic Idea, the eternal and ultimate reality, as contrasted
   with "Earth's shadows," the impermanent and merely individual
   phenomena of life.
63 I.e., breaks up into individual and fragmentary colors.
64 The One (line 460).

'Tis Adonais calls! oh, hasten thither,—
No more let Life divide what Death can join together.

That Light whose smile kindles the Universe,
That Beauty in which all things work and move,
That Benediction which the eclipsing Curse   480
Of birth can quench not, that sustaining Love
Which, through the web of being, blindly wove
By man and beast and earth and air and sea,
Burns bright or dim, as each are mirrors of
The fire for which all thirst,—now beams on me,   485
Consuming the last clouds of cold mortality.

The breath[65] whose might I have invoked in song
Descends on me; my spirit's bark is driven,
Far from the shore, far from the trembling throng
Whose sails were never to the tempest given;   490
The massy earth and spherèd skies are riven!
I am borne darkly, fearfully, afar;
Whilst, burning through the inmost veil of Heaven,
The soul of Adonais, like a star,
Beacons from the abode where the Eternal are.   495

CHORUSES *from* HELLAS

Hellas, written at Pisa in the fall of 1821, is another of
Shelley's "lyrical dramas." He calls it "a series of lyric
pictures," but his aim was to help identify the Greek war
of independence with "the cause of civilisation and
social improvement. . . . We are all," he continues in his
preface, "Greeks. Our laws, our literature, our religion,
our arts, have their roots in Greece." The British government was still pro-Turk; but Shelley, rejoicing in the
success of a Spanish revolution, predicts that the peoples
of Greece, Italy, and Germany will yet rise triumphant
against the tyrants and their "bloody sceptres." It is, he
holds, Platonic idealism and the great thought of the past
that will eventually bring about a liberated world.

WORLDS ON WORLDS

Worlds on worlds are rolling ever
    From creation to decay,
Like the bubbles on a river,
    Sparkling, bursting, borne away.
But they are still immortal   5
    Who, through birth's orient portal
And death's dark chasm hurrying to and fro,
    Clothe their unceasing flight
    In the brief dust and light
Gathered around their chariots as they go;   10

[65] Of the spirit of the universe.

New shapes they still may weave,
    New gods, new laws receive;
Bright or dim are they, as the robes they last
    On Death's bare ribs had cast.

A power[1] from the unknown God,   15
    A Promethean[2] conqueror came;
Like a triumphal path he trod
    The thorns of death and shame.
    A mortal shape to him
    Was like the vapour dim   20
Which the orient planet animates with light;
    Hell, Sin, and Slavery came,
    Like bloodhounds mild and tame,
Nor preyed, until their Lord had taken flight;
    The moon of Mahomet   25
    Arose, and it shall set:
While blazoned as on Heaven's immortal noon
    The cross leads generations on.

Swift as the radiant shapes of sleep
    From one whose dreams are Paradise   30
Fly, when the fond wretch wakes to weep,
    And Day peers forth with her blank eyes;
    So fleet, so faint, so fair,
    The Powers of earth and air
Fled from the folding-star[3] of Bethlehem: 35
    Apollo, Pan, and Love,
    And even Olympian Jove,[4]
Grew weak, for killing Truth had glared on them;
    Our hills and seas and streams,
    Dispeopled of their dreams,   40
Their waters turned to blood, their dew to tears,
    Wailed for the golden years.[5]

THE WORLD'S GREAT AGE

The world's great age[6] begins anew,
    The golden years return,
The earth doth like a snake renew
    Her winter weeds[7] outworn:

[1] Jesus.
[2] I.e., like the civilizing Titan, Prometheus, who gave man fire.
[3] The evening star, at whose appearance the sheep are gathered
into the fold.
[4] I.e., the pagan gods of Greece and Rome: Apollo, of the sun,
poetry, and music; Pan, of flocks and herds, of woods and wild
life; Venus, of love and beauty; Jove or Zeus, dweller on Mt.
Olympus, home of the classical deities.
[5] In classical fable the age of primeval simplicity, before Jove
drove Saturn from the throne of heaven.
[6] See note 5, above.—This is the final chorus of the poem. Shelley
remarks in a note that it "is indistinct and obscure, as the event
of the living drama whose arrival it foretells."
[7] I.e., the garments or trappings of the long ages of evil.

Heaven smiles, and faiths and empires gleam   5
Like wrecks of a dissolving dream.

A brighter Hellas rears its mountains
  From waves serener far;
A new Peneus[8] rolls his fountains
  Against the morning-star.   10
Where fairer Tempes bloom, there sleep
Young Cyclads[9] on a sunnier deep.

A loftier Argo[10] cleaves the main,
  Fraught with a later prize;
Another Orpheus[11] sings again,   15
  And loves, and weeps, and dies.
A new Ulysses leaves once more
Calypso[12] for his native shore.

Oh, write no more the tale of Troy,
  If earth Death's scroll must be!   20
Nor mix with Laian[13] rage the joy
  Which dawns upon the free:
Although a subtler Sphinx renew
Riddles of death Thebes never knew.

Another Athens shall arise,
  And to remoter time   25
Bequeath, like sunset to the skies,
  The splendour of its prime;
And leave, if nought so bright may live,
All earth can take or Heaven can give.   30

Saturn and Love their long repose[14]
  Shall burst, more bright and good

---

8 Or Salambria, a river in Thessaly, Greece. It flows through the beautiful valley of Tempe.
9 The Cyclades, islands in the southwestern Aegean.
10 The ship in which Jason sailed to win the Golden Fleece.
11 The fabled Thracian poet and musician who journeyed to Hades and nearly succeeded in bringing back his wife Eurydice.
12 The nymph who tried to induce the Greek hero, homeward bound from the Trojan War, to remain on her island.
13 King Laius of Thebes was Oedipus's father. The misfortunes of this family are prominent among the subjects of Greek poetry and tragedy. It was Oedipus who solved the riddle of the Sphinx.
14 From Shelley's note: "Saturn and Love were among the deities of a real or imaginary state of innocence and happiness. *All those who fell,* or the Gods of Greece, Asia, and Egypt; the *One who rose,* or Jesus Christ, at whose appearance the idols of the Pagan World were amerced [punished by being deprived] of their worship; and *the many unsubdued,* or the monstrous objects of the idolatry of China, India, the Antarctic islands, and the native tribes of America, certainly have reigned over the understandings of men in conjunction or in succession, during periods in which all we know of evil has been in a state of portentous, and, until the revival of learning [the Renaissance], perpetually increasing, activity."

Than all who fell, than One who rose,
  Than many unsubdued:
Not gold, not blood, their altar dowers,   35
But votive tears and symbol flowers.

Oh, cease! must hate and death return?
  Cease! must men kill and die?
Cease! drain not to its dregs the urn
  Of bitter prophecy.   40
The world is weary of the past,—
Oh, might it die or rest at last!

TIME

During 1821 Shelley composed besides longer poems, among them "Adonais" and *Hellas,* a number of his finest short lyrics. From the work of that year come all our remaining selections except the last two, which were written in the closing months of the poet's life, in 1822.

Unfathomable Sea, whose waves are years;
  Ocean of Time, whose waters of deep woe
Are brackish with the salt of human tears!
  Thou shoreless flood, which in thy ebb and flow
Claspest the limits of mortality!   5
And sick of prey, yet howling on for more,
Vomitest thy wrecks on its inhospitable shore;
  Treacherous in calm, and terrible in storm,
  Who shall put forth on thee,
  Unfathomable Sea?   10

TO NIGHT

Swiftly walk o'er the western wave,
  Spirit of Night!
Out of the misty eastern cave,
Where, all the long and lone daylight,
Thou wovest dreams of joy and fear,   5
Which make thee terrible and dear,—
  Swift be thy flight!

Wrap thy form in a mantle grey,
  Star-inwrought!
Blind with thine hair the eyes of Day,   10
Kiss her until she be wearied out;
Then wander o'er city, and sea, and land,
Touching all with thine opiate wand—
  Come, long sought!

When I arose and saw the dawn,   15
  I sighed for thee;
When light rode high, and the dew was gone,
And noon lay heavy on flower and tree,

And the weary Day turned to his rest,
Lingering like an unloved guest,   20
    I sighed for thee.

Thy brother Death came, and cried,
    "Wouldst thou me?"
Thy sweet child Sleep, the filmy-eyed,
Murmured like a noontide bee,   25
"Shall I nestle near thy side?
Wouldst thou me?"—And I replied,
    "No, not thee!"

Death will come when thou art dead,
    Soon, too soon: 30
Sleep will come when thou art fled;
Of neither would I ask the boon
I ask of thee, belovèd Night,—
Swift be thine approaching flight,
    Come soon, soon!   35

SONG

Rarely, rarely, comest thou,
    Spirit of Delight!
Wherefore hast thou left me now
    Many a day and night?
Many a weary night and day   5
'Tis since thou art fled away.

How shall ever one like me
    Win thee back again?
With the joyous and the free
    Thou wilt scoff at pain.   10
Spirit false! thou hast forgot
All but those who need thee not.

As a lizard with the shade
    Of a trembling leaf,
Thou with sorrow art dismayed;   15
    Even the sighs of grief
Reproach thee, that thou art not near,
And reproach thou wilt not hear.

Let me set my mournful ditty
    To a merry measure;   20
Thou wilt never come for pity,
    Thou wilt come for pleasure;
Pity then will cut away
Those cruel wings, and thou wilt stay.

I love all that thou lovest,   25
    Spirit of Delight!

The fresh Earth in new leaves drest,
    And the starry night;
Autumn evening, and the morn
When the golden mists are born.   30

I love snow, and all the forms
    Of the radiant frost;
I love waves, and winds, and storms,—
    Everything almost
Which is Nature's, and may be   35
Untainted by man's misery.

I love tranquil solitude,
    And such society
As is quiet, wise, and good;
    Between thee and me   40
What difference? But thou dost possess
The things I seek, not love them less.

I love Love—though he has wings,
    And like light can flee;
But above all other things,   45
    Spirit, I love thee.
Thou art love and life! Oh come,
Make once more my heart thy home.

MUTABILITY

In company with a longer poem, *Epipsychidion*, this lyric and probably several of those that follow it appear to be inspired by Shelley's regret over the marriage of convenience in the fall of 1821 of Emilia Viviani, a beautiful Italian girl with whom he and his wife had become acquainted somewhat less than a year before. Emilia and the poet had not fallen in love, but were aware of an unusual spiritual sympathy for each other which Shelley, who was deeply moved, realized was unlikely to continue after her wedding.

The flower that smiles to-day
    To-morrow dies;
All that we wish to stay,
    Tempts and then flies;
What is this world's delight?   5
Lightning that mocks the night,
    Brief even as bright.

Virtue, how frail it is!
    Friendship how rare!
Love, how it sells poor bliss   10
    For proud despair!
But we, though soon they fall,
Survive their joy, and all
    Which ours we call.

Whilst skies are blue and bright,   15
          Whilst flowers are gay,
Whilst eyes that change ere night
          Make glad the day;
Whilst yet the calm hours creep,
Dream thou—and from thy sleep   20
          Then wake to weep.

A LAMENT

O world! O life! O time!
On whose last steps I climb
    Trembling at that where I had stood before;
When will return the glory of your prime?
          No more—oh, never more!   5

Out of the day and night
A joy has taken flight;
    Fresh Spring, and Summer, and Winter hoar,
Move my faint heart with grief,—but with delight
          No more—oh, never more!   10

TO ——

          Music, when soft voices die,
          Vibrates in the memory;
          Odours, when sweet violets sicken,
          Live within the sense they quicken.
          Rose-leaves, when the rose is dead,   5
          Are heaped for the belovèd's bed;
          And so thy thoughts, when thou art gone,
          Love itself shall slumber on.

SONNET: POLITICAL GREATNESS

Nor happiness, nor majesty, nor fame,
Nor peace, nor strength, nor skill in arms or arts,
Shepherd those herds whom Tyranny makes tame;
Verse echoes not one beating of their hearts,
History is but the shadow of their shame,   5
Art veils her glass, or from the pageant starts
As to oblivion their blind millions fleet,[1]
Staining that Heaven with obscene imagery
Of their own likeness. What are numbers knit
By force or custom? Man who man would be,   10
Must rule the empire of himself; in it
Must be supreme, establishing his throne
On vanquished will, quelling the anarchy
Of hopes and fears, being himself alone.

――――――

[1] Flit, hasten.

TO ——

One word is too often profaned
    For me to profane it,
One feeling too falsely disdained
    For thee to disdain it;
One hope is too like despair   5
    For prudence to smother,
And pity from thee more dear
    Than that from another.

I can give not what men call love,
    But wilt thou accept not   10
The worship the heart lifts above
    And the Heavens reject not;
The desire of the moth for the star,
    Of the night for the morrow,
The devotion to something afar   15
    From the sphere of our sorrow?

A DIRGE

Rough wind, that moanest loud
    Grief too sad for song;
Wild wind, when sullen cloud
    Knells all the night long;
Sad storm, whose tears are vain,   5
Bare woods, whose branches strain,
Deep caves and dreary main,
    Wail, for the world's wrong!

LINES: WHEN THE LAMP IS SHATTERED

          When the lamp is shattered,
          The light in the dust lies dead;
          When the cloud is scattered,
          The rainbow's glory is shed.
          When the lute is broken,   5
          Sweet tones are remembered not;
          When the lips have spoken,
          Loved accents are soon forgot.

          As music and splendour
          Survive not the lamp and the lute,   10
          The heart's echoes render
          No song when the spirit is mute:—
          No song but sad dirges,
          Like the wind in a ruined cell,
          Or the mournful surges   15
          That ring the dead seaman's knell.

When hearts have once mingled,
Love first leaves the well-built nest;
　The weak one is singled
To endure what it once possest.　20
　　O Love! who bewailest
The frailty of all things here,
　Why chose you the frailest
For your cradle, your home, and your bier?

　　　Its passions will rock thee,　25
As the storms rock the ravens on high:
　Bright reason will mock thee,
Like the sun from a wintry sky.
　　From thy nest every rafter
Will rot, and thine eagle home　30
　　Leave thee naked to laughter,
When leaves fall and cold winds come.

from A DEFENCE OF POETRY

THIS superb manifesto is one of the major expositions of the reasons why thoughtful men, whether artists or scientists, consider poetry and its functions of first-rate importance. Shelley intended to carry on the discussion in a second and a third Part; but he completed only Part I, about two-thirds of which is here reprinted. The occasion of the treatise was a whimsical attack on Romantic poetry by a gifted friend of Shelley's, Thomas Love Peacock (1785–1866), a minor poet, scholar, and miscellaneous writer, chiefly celebrated for his satirical novels. Peacock's *The Four Ages of Poetry* appeared in 1820. Shelley wrote his rejoinder in 1821; but on account of his death and the subsequent troubles of the Hunts, who were to publish it, the *Defence* remained in manuscript till 1840. The principal literary influences on its conceptions are Plato and Sir Philip Sidney's *The Defense of Poesy* (I, 259 ff., above).

The version printed in 1840, which is followed in our selections, was edited by Leigh Hunt's brother John and by Mary Shelley; they wisely removed a number of counterblasts to Peacock's remarks, in order to emphasize the essay's general application. The changes are discussed in the most useful edition: *Peacock's Four Ages of Poetry, Shelley's Defence of Poetry, Browning's Essay on Shelley,* edited by H. F. B. Brett-Smith (1921). Another good edition, confined to Shelley's essay, is A. S. Cook's (1891).

ACCORDING to one mode of regarding those two classes of mental action, which are called reason and imagination, the former may be considered as mind contemplating the relations borne by one thought to another, however produced; and the latter, as mind acting upon those thoughts so as to colour them with its own light, and composing from them, as from elements, other thoughts, each containing within itself the principle of its own integrity. The one is the τὸ ποιεῖν,[1] or the principle of synthesis, and has for its objects those forms which are common to universal nature and existence itself; the other is

the τὸ λογίζειν,[2] or principle of analysis, and its action regards the relations of things, simply as relations; considering thoughts, not in their integral unity, but as the algebraical representations which conduct to certain general results. Reason is the enumeration of quantities already known; imagination is the perception of the value of those quantities, both separately and as a whole. Reason respects the differences, and imagination the similitudes of things. Reason is to imagination as the instrument to the agent, as the body to the spirit, as the shadow to the substance.

Poetry, in a general sense, may be defined to be "the expression of the imagination"; and poetry is connate with the origin of man. Man is an instrument over which a series of external and internal impressions are driven, like the alternations of an ever-changing wind over an Aeolian lyre, which move it by their motion to ever-changing melody. But there is a principle within the human being, and perhaps within all sentient beings, which acts otherwise than in the lyre, and produces not melody alone, but harmony, by an internal adjustment of the sounds or motions thus excited to the impressions which excite them. It is as if the lyre could accommodate its chords to the motions of that which strikes them, in a determined proportion of sound; even as the musician can accommodate his voice to the sound of the lyre. A child at play by itself will express its delight by its voice and motions; and every inflexion of tone and every gesture will bear exact relation to a corresponding antitype in the pleasurable impressions which awakened it; it will be the reflected image of that impression; and as the lyre trembles and sounds after the wind has died away, so the child seeks, by prolonging in its voice and motions the duration of the effect, to prolong also a consciousness of the cause. In relation to the objects

---

[1] Making.

[2] Reasoning.

which delight a child, these expressions are what poetry is to higher objects. The savage (for the savage is to ages what the child is to years) expresses the emotions produced in him by surrounding objects in a similar manner; and language and gesture, together with plastic or pictorial imitation, become the image of the combined effect of those objects and his apprehension of them. Man in society, with all his passions and his pleasures, next becomes the object of the passions and pleasures of man; an additional class of emotions produces an augmented treasure of expression; and language, gesture, and the imitative arts, become at once the representation and the medium, the pencil and the picture, the chisel and the statue, the chord and the harmony. The social sympathies, or those laws from which as from its elements society results, begin to develop themselves from the moment that two human beings coexist; the future is contained within the present as the plant within the seed; and equality, diversity, unity, contrast, mutual dependence, become the principles alone capable of affording the motives according to which the will of a social being is determined to action, inasmuch as he is social; and constitute pleasure in sensation, virtue in sentiment, beauty in art, truth in reasoning, and love in the intercourse of kind. Hence men, even in the infancy of society, observe a certain order in their words and actions, distinct from that of the objects and the impressions represented by them, all expression being subject to the laws of that from which it proceeds. But let us dismiss those more general considerations which might involve an inquiry into the principles of society itself, and restrict our view to the manner in which the imagination is expressed upon its forms.

In the youth of the world, men dance and sing and imitate natural objects, observing in these actions, as in all others, a certain rhythm or order. And, although all men observe a similar, they observe not the same order, in the motions of the dance, in the melody of the song, in the combinations of language, in the series of their imitations of natural objects. For there is a certain order or rhythm belonging to each of these classes of mimetic representation, from which the hearer and the spectator receive an intenser and purer pleasure than from any other: the sense of an approximation to this order has been called taste by modern writers. Every man, in the infancy of art, observes an order which approximates more or less closely to that from which this highest delight results: but the diversity is not sufficiently marked, as that its gradations should be sensible, except in those instances where the predominance of this faculty of approximation to the beautiful (for so we may be permitted to name the relation between this highest pleasure and its cause) is very great. Those in whom it exists to excess are poets, in the most universal sense of the word; and the pleasure resulting from the manner in which they express the influence of society or nature upon their own minds, communicates itself to others, and gathers a sort of reduplication from the community. Their language is vitally metaphorical; that is, it marks the before unapprehended relations of things and perpetuates their apprehension, until words, which represent them, become, through time, signs for portions or classes of thought, instead of pictures of integral thoughts; and then, if no new poets should arise to create afresh the associations which have been thus disorganised, language will be dead to all the nobler purposes of human intercourse. These similitudes or relations are finely said by Lord Bacon to be "the same footsteps of nature impressed upon the various subjects of the world"[3]—and he considers the faculty which perceives them as the storehouse of axioms common to all knowledge. In the infancy of society every author is necessarily a poet, because language itself is poetry; and to be a poet is to apprehend the true and the beautiful, in a word, the good which exists in the relation subsisting, first between existence and perception, and secondly between perception and expression. Every original language near to its source is in itself the chaos of a cyclic poem; the copiousness of lexicography and the distinctions of grammar are the works of a later age, and are merely the catalogue and the forms of the creations of poetry.

But poets, or those who imagine and express this indestructible order, are not only the authors of language and of music, of the dance, and architecture, and statuary, and painting; they are the institutors of laws and the founders of civil society, and the inventors of the arts of life, and the teachers, who draw into a certain propinquity with the beautiful and the true that partial apprehension of the agencies of the invisible world which is called religion. Hence all original religions are allegorical, or susceptible of allegory, and, like Janus,[4] have a double face of false and true. Poets, according to the circumstances of the age and nation in which they appeared, were called, in the earlier epochs of the

---

[3] Cf. *The Advancement of Learning*, II, v, 3.

[4] The Roman god of doors, depicted with two faces looking in opposite directions.

world, legislators or prophets: a poet essentially comprises and unites both these characters. For he not only beholds intensely the present as it is, and discovers those laws according to which present things ought to be ordered, but he beholds the future in the present, and his thoughts are the germs of the flower and the fruit of latest time. Not that I assert poets to be prophets in the gross sense of the word, or that they can foretell the form as surely as they foreknow the spirit of events: such is the pretence of superstition, which would make poetry an attribute of prophecy, rather than prophecy an attribute of poetry. A poet participates in the eternal, the infinite, and the one; as far as relates to his conceptions, time and place and number are not. The grammatical forms which express the moods of time, and the difference of persons, and the distinction of place, are convertible with respect to the highest poetry without injuring it as poetry; and the choruses of Aeschylus, and the book of Job, and Dante's Paradise, would afford, more than any other writings, examples of this fact, if the limits of this essay did not forbid citation. The creations of sculpture, painting, and music, are illustrations still more decisive.

Language, colour, form, and religious and civil habits of action, are all the instruments and materials of poetry; they may be called poetry by that figure of speech which considers the effect as a synonyme of the cause. But poetry in a more restricted sense expresses those arrangements of language, and especially metrical language, which are created by that imperial faculty, whose throne is curtained within the invisible nature of man. And this springs from the nature itself of language, which is a more direct representation of the actions and passions of our internal being, and is susceptible of more various and delicate combinations, than colour, form, or motion, and is more plastic and obedient to the control of that faculty of which it is the creation. For language is arbitrarily produced by the imagination, and has relation to thoughts alone; but all other materials, instruments, and conditions of art, have relations among each other, which limit and interpose between conception and expression. The former is as a mirror which reflects, the latter as a cloud which enfeebles, the light of which both are mediums of communication. Hence the fame of sculptors, painters, and musicians, although the intrinsic powers of the great masters of these arts may yield in no degree to that of those who have employed language as the hieroglyphic of their thoughts, has never equalled that of poets in the restricted sense of the term; as two performers of equal skill will produce unequal effects from a guitar and a harp. The fame of legislators and founders of religions, so long as their institutions last, alone seems to exceed that of poets in the restricted sense; but it can scarcely be a question, whether, if we deduct the celebrity which their flattery of the gross opinions of the vulgar usually conciliates, together with that which belonged to them in their higher character of poets, any excess will remain.

We have thus circumscribed the word poetry within the limits of that art which is the most familiar and the most perfect expression of the faculty itself. It is necessary, however, to make the circle still narrower, and to determine the distinction between measured and unmeasured language; for the popular division into prose and verse is inadmissible in accurate philosophy.

Sounds as well as thoughts have relation both between each other and towards that which they represent, and a perception of the order of those relations has always been found connected with a perception of the order of the relations of thoughts. Hence the language of poets has ever affected a certain uniform and harmonious recurrence of sound, without which it were not poetry, and which is scarcely less indispensable to the communication of its actions, than the words themselves, without reference to that peculiar order. Hence the vanity of translation; it were as wise to cast a violet into a crucible that you might discover the formal principle of its colour and odour, as seek to transfuse from one language into another the creations of a poet. The plant must spring again from its seed, or it will bear no flower—and this is the burthen of the curse of Babel.

An observation of the regular mode of the recurrence of harmony in the language of poetical minds, together with its relation to music, produced metre, or a certain system of traditional forms of harmony and language. Yet it is by no means essential that a poet should accommodate his language to this traditional form, so that the harmony, which is its spirit, be observed. The practice is indeed convenient and popular, and to be preferred, especially in such composition as includes much action; but every great poet must inevitably innovate upon the example of his predecessors in the exact structure of his peculiar versification. The distinction between poets and prose writers is a vulgar error. The distinction between philosophers and poets has been anticipated. Plato was essentially a poet—the truth and splendour of his imagery, and the melody of his language, are the most intense that it is possible to conceive. He rejected the measure of the epic, dramatic, and lyrical forms, because he sought to kindle a harmony in thoughts divested of shape and action, and he forbore to invent any regular plan of rhythm which would include, under determinate forms, the varied pauses of his style. Cicero sought to imitate the cadence of his periods, but with little success. Lord Bacon was a poet. His language has a sweet and majestic rhythm, which satisfies the sense, no less than the almost superhuman wisdom of his philosophy satisfies the intellect; it is a strain which distends, and then bursts the circumference of the reader's mind, and pours itself forth together with it into the universal element with which it has perpetual sympathy. All the authors of revolutions in opinion are not only necessarily poets as they are inventors, nor even as their words unveil the permanent analogy of things by images which participate in the life of truth; but as their periods are harmonious and rhythmical, and contain in themselves the elements of verse; being the echo of the eternal music. Nor are those supreme poets, who have employed traditional forms of rhythm on account of the form and action of their subjects, less capable of perceiving and teaching the truth of things, than those who have omitted that form. Shakespeare, Dante, and Milton (to confine ourselves to modern writers) are philosophers of the very loftiest power.

A poem is the very image of life expressed in its eternal truth. There is this difference between a story and a poem,[5] that a story is a catalogue of detached facts, which have no other connexion than time, place, circumstance, cause, and effect; the other is the creation of actions according to the unchangeable forms of human nature, as existing in the mind of the Creator, which is itself the image of all other minds. The one is partial, and applies only to a definite period of time, and a certain combination of events which can never again recur; the other is universal, and contains within itself the germ of a relation to whatever motives or actions have place in the possible varieties of human nature. Time, which destroys the beauty and the use of the story of particular facts, stripped of the poetry which should invest them, augments that of poetry, and for ever develops new and wonderful applications of the eternal truth which it contains. Hence epitomes

have been called[6] the moths of just history; they eat out the poetry of it. A story of particular facts is as a mirror which obscures and distorts that which should be beautiful: poetry is a mirror which makes beautiful that which is distorted.

The parts of a composition may be poetical, without the composition as a whole being a poem. A single sentence may be considered as a whole, though it may be found in the midst of a series of unassimilated portions; a single word even may be a spark of inextinguishable thought. And thus all the great historians, Herodotus, Plutarch, Livy, were poets; and although the plan of these writers, especially that of Livy, restrained them from developing this faculty in its highest degree, they made copious and ample amends for their subjection, by filling all the interstices of their subjects with living images.

Having determined what is poetry, and who are poets, let us proceed to estimate its effects upon society.

Poetry is ever accompanied with pleasure: all spirits upon which it falls open themselves to receive the wisdom which is mingled with its delight. In the infancy of the world, neither poets themselves nor their auditors are fully aware of the excellence of poetry: for it acts in a divine and unapprehended manner, beyond and above consciousness; and it is reserved for future generations to contemplate and measure the mighty cause and effect in all the strength and splendour of their union. Even in modern times, no living poet ever arrived at the fullness of his fame; the jury which sits in judgement upon a poet, belonging as he does to all time, must be composed of his peers: it must be empanelled by time from the selectest of the wise of many generations. A poet is a nightingale, who sits in darkness and sings to cheer its own solitude with sweet sounds; his auditors are as men entranced by the melody of an unseen musician, who feel that they are moved and softened, yet know not whence or why. The poems of Homer and his contemporaries were the delight of infant Greece; they were the elements of that social system which is the column upon which all succeeding civilisation has reposed. Homer embodied the ideal perfection of his age in human character; nor can we doubt that those who read his verses were awakened to an ambition of becoming like to Achilles, Hector, and Ulysses: the truth and beauty of friendship, patriotism, and persevering devotion to an

---

[5] This distinction rests on Aristotle's assertion (*Poetics*, IX, 1–4) that poetry is more philosophical and serious than history, since the former deals with the general and the latter with the particular.

[6] By Bacon, *The Advancement of Learning*, II, ii, 4. *Epitomes* = abstracts, compendiums.

object, were unveiled to their depths in these immortal creations: the sentiments of the auditors must have been refined and enlarged by a sympathy with such great and lovely impersonations, until from admiring they imitated, and from imitation they identified themselves with the objects of their admiration. Nor let it be objected, that these characters are remote from moral perfection, and that they are by no means to be considered as edifying patterns for general imitation. Every epoch, under names more or less specious, has deified its peculiar errors; Revenge is the naked idol of the worship of a semi-barbarous age; and Self-deceit is the veiled image of unknown evil, before which luxury and satiety lie prostrate. But a poet considers the vices of his contemporaries as a temporary dress in which his creations must be arrayed, and which cover without concealing the eternal proportions of their beauty. An epic or dramatic personage is understood to wear them around his soul, as he may the ancient armour or the modern uniform around his body; whilst it is easy to conceive a dress more graceful than either. The beauty of the internal nature cannot be so far concealed by its accidental vesture, but that the spirit of its form shall communicate itself to the very disguise, and indicate the shape it hides from the manner in which it is worn. A majestic form and graceful motions will express themselves through the most barbarous and tasteless costume. Few poets of the highest class have chosen to exhibit the beauty of their conceptions in its naked truth and splendour; and it is doubtful whether the alloy of costume, habit, &c., be not necessary to temper this planetary music for mortal ears.[7]

The whole objection, however, of the immorality of poetry rests upon a misconception of the manner in which poetry acts to produce the moral improvement of man. Ethical science arranges the elements which poetry has created, and propounds schemes and proposes examples of civil and domestic life: nor is it for want of admirable doctrines that men hate, and despise, and censure, and deceive, and subjugate one another. But poetry acts in another and diviner manner. It awakens and enlarges the mind itself by rendering it the receptacle of a thousand unapprehended combinations of thought. Poetry lifts the veil from the hidden beauty of the world, and makes familiar objects be as if they were not familiar; it reproduces all that it represents, and the

impersonations clothed in its Elysian[8] light stand thenceforward in the minds of those who have once contemplated them, as memorials of that gentle and exalted content which extends itself over all thoughts and actions with which its coexists. The great secret of morals is love; or a going out of our own nature, and an identification of ourselves with the beautiful which exists in thought, action, or person, not our own. A man, to be greatly good, must imagine intensely and comprehensively; he must put himself in the place of another and of many others; the pains and pleasures of his species must become his own. The great instrument of moral good is the imagination; and poetry administers to the effect by acting upon the cause. Poetry enlarges the circumference of the imagination by replenishing it with thoughts of ever new delight, which have the power of attracting and assimilating to their own nature all other thoughts, and which form new intervals and interstices whose void for ever craves fresh food. Poetry strengthens the faculty which is the organ of the moral nature of man, in the same manner as exercise strengthens a limb. A poet therefore would do ill to embody his own conceptions of right and wrong, which are usually those of his place and time, in his poetical creations, which participate in neither. By this assumption of the inferior office of interpreting the effect, in which perhaps after all he might acquit himself but imperfectly, he would resign a glory in the participation in the cause. There was little danger that Homer, or any of the eternal poets, should have so far misunderstood themselves as to have abdicated this throne of their widest dominion. Those in whom the poetical faculty, though great, is less intense, as Euripides, Lucan,[9] Tasso, Spenser, have frequently affected[10] a moral aim, and the effect of their poetry is diminished in exact proportion to the degree in which they compel us to advert to this purpose. . . .[11]

But let us not be betrayed from a defence into a critical history of poetry and its influence on society. Be it enough to have pointed out the effects of poets, in the large and true sense of the word, upon their own and all succeeding times.

---

[7] A figurative allusion to the old belief that the "spheres," revolving around the earth, made music unheard by human beings.

[8] Blissful.

[9] For this Roman epic poet (d. 65 A.D.) Shelley had an exaggerated liking; hence his inappropriate mention here in company with the great author of Greek tragedy, the famous epic poet of the Italian Renaissance, and Spenser.   [10] Cultivated.

[11] The foregoing paragraphs constitute slightly less than the first third of the treatise. Shelley proceeds with a discussion of poetic drama and an historical survey of poetry and its bearing on civilization. The rest of our selection amounts to nearly the last third of the *Defence*.

But poets have been challenged[12] to resign the civic crown to reasoners and mechanists, on another plea. It is admitted that the exercise of the imagination is most delightful, but it is alleged that that of reason is more useful. Let us examine, as the grounds of this distinction, what is here meant by utility. Pleasure or good, in a general sense, is that which the consciousness of a sensitive and intelligent being seeks, and in which, when found, it acquiesces. There are two kinds of pleasure, one durable, universal and permanent; the other transitory and particular. Utility may either express the means of producing the former or the latter. In the former sense, whatever strengthens and purifies the affections, enlarges the imagination, and adds spirit to sense, is useful. But a narrower meaning may be assigned to the word utility, confining it to express that which banishes the importunity of the wants of our animal nature, the surrounding men with security of life, the dispersing the grosser delusions of superstition, and the conciliating such a degree of mutual forbearance among men as may consist with the motives of personal advantage.

Undoubtedly the promoters of utility, in this limited sense, have their appointed office in society. They follow the footsteps of poets, and copy the sketches of their creations into the book of common life. They make space, and give time. Their exertions are of the highest value, so long as they confine their administration of the concerns of the inferior powers of our nature within the limits due to the superior ones. But whilst the sceptic destroys gross superstitions, let him spare to deface, as some of the French writers have defaced, the eternal truths charactered upon the imaginations of men. Whilst the mechanist abridges, and the political economist combines, labour, let them beware that their speculations, for want of correspondence with those first principles which belong to the imagination, do not tend, as they have in modern England, to exasperate at once the extremes of luxury and want. They have exemplified the saying, "To him that hath, more shall be given; and from him that hath not, the little that he hath shall be taken away."[13] The rich have become richer, and the poor have become poorer; and the vessel of the state is driven between the Scylla and Charybdis[14] of anarchy and despotism. Such are the effects which must ever flow from an unmitigated exercise of the calculating faculty.

It is difficult to define pleasure in its highest sense; the definition involving a number of apparent paradoxes. For, from an inexplicable defect of harmony in the constitution of human nature, the pain of the inferior is frequently connected with the pleasures of the superior portions of our being. Sorrow, terror, anguish, despair itself, are often the chosen expressions of an approximation to the highest good. Our sympathy in tragic fiction depends on this principle; tragedy delights by affording a shadow of the pleasure which exists in pain. This is the source also of the melancholy which is inseparable from the sweetest melody. The pleasure that is in sorrow is sweeter than the pleasure of pleasure itself. And hence the saying, "It is better to go to the house of mourning than to the house of mirth."[15] Not that this highest species of pleasure is necessarily linked with pain. The delight of love and friendship, the ecstasy of the admiration of nature, the joy of the perception and still more of the creation of poetry, is often wholly unalloyed.

The production and assurance of pleasure in this highest sense is true utility. Those who produce and preserve this pleasure are poets or poetical philosophers.

The exertions of Locke, Hume, Gibbon, Voltaire, Rousseau,[16] and their disciples, in favour of oppressed and deluded humanity, are entitled to the gratitude of mankind. Yet it is easy to calculate the degree of moral and intellectual improvement which the world would have exhibited, had they never lived. A little more nonsense would have been talked for a century or two; and perhaps a few more men, women, and children burnt as heretics. We might not at this moment have been congratulating each other on the abolition[17] of the Inquisition in Spain. But it exceeds all imagination to conceive what would have been the moral condition of the world if neither Dante, Petrarch, Boccaccio, Chaucer, Shakespeare, Calderon,[18] Lord Bacon, nor Milton, had ever existed; if Raphael and Michael Angelo had never been born; if the Hebrew poetry had never been translated; if a revival of the study of Greek literature had never taken place; if no monuments of ancient sculpture had been handed down to us; and if the poetry of

---

[12] By Peacock, in the last four paragraphs of his attack.
[13] Cf. Mark 4:25.
[14] The famous rock and whirlpool which menaced navigation between Sicily and Italy.

[15] Cf. Ecclesiastes 7:2.
[16] Shelley's note: "Although Rousseau has been thus classed, he was essentially a poet. The others, even Voltaire, were mere reasoners."   [17] In the preceding year.
[18] The Spanish dramatist and poet Pedro Calderón de la Barca (1600–81).

the religion of the ancient world had been extinguished together with its belief. The human mind could never, except by the intervention of these excitements, have been awakened to the invention of the grosser sciences, and that application of analytical reasoning to the aberrations of society, which it is now attempted to exalt over the direct expression of the inventive and creative faculty itself.

We have more moral, political, and historical wisdom, than we know how to reduce into practice; we have more scientific and economical knowledge than can be accommodated to the just distribution of the produce which it multiplies. The poetry, in these systems of thought, is concealed by the accumulation of facts and calculating processes. There is no want of knowledge respecting what is wisest and best in morals, government, and political economy, or at least what is wiser and better than what men now practise and endure. But we let "*I dare not* wait upon *I would*, like the poor cat in the adage."[19] We want the creative faculty to imagine that which we know; we want the generous impulse to act that which we imagine; we want the poetry of life: our calculations have outrun conception; we have eaten more than we can digest. The cultivation of those sciences which have enlarged the limits of the empire of man over the external world, has, for want of the poetical faculty, proportionally circumscribed those of the internal world; and man, having enslaved the elements, remains himself a slave. To what but a cultivation of the mechanical arts in a degree disproportioned to the presence of the creative faculty, which is the basis of all knowledge, is to be attributed the abuse of all invention for abridging and combining labour, to the exasperation[20] of the inequality of mankind? From what other cause has it arisen that the discoveries which should have lightened, have added a weight to the curse imposed on Adam? Poetry, and the principle of Self, of which money is the visible incarnation, are the God and Mammon of the world.

The functions of the poetical faculty are twofold: by one it creates new materials of knowledge, and power, and pleasure; by the other it engenders in the mind a desire to reproduce and arrange them according to a certain rhythm and order, which may be called the beautiful and the good. The cultivation of poetry is never more to be desired than at periods when, from an excess of the selfish and calculating principle, the accumulation of the materials of ex-

ternal life exceed the quantity of the power of assimilating them to the internal laws of human nature. The body has then become too unwieldy for that which animates it.

Poetry is indeed something divine. It is at once the centre and circumference of knowledge; it is that which comprehends all science, and that to which all science must be referred. It is at the same time the root and blossom of all other systems of thought; it is that from which all spring, and that which adorns all; and that which, if blighted, denies the fruit and the seed, and withholds from the barren world the nourishment and the succession of the scions of the tree of life. It is the perfect and consummate surface and bloom of all things; it is as the odour and the colour of the rose to the texture of the elements which compose it, as the form and splendour of unfaded beauty to the secrets of anatomy and corruption. What were virtue, love, patriotism, friendship,—what were the scenery of this beautiful universe which we inhabit; what were our consolations on this side of the grave—and what were our aspirations beyond it, if poetry did not ascend to bring light and fire from those eternal regions where the owl-winged faculty of calculation dare not ever soar? Poetry is not like reasoning, a power to be exerted according to the determination of the will. A man cannot say, "I will compose poetry." The greatest poet even cannot say it; for the mind in creation is as a fading coal, which some invisible influence, like an inconstant wind, awakens to transitory brightness; this power arises from within, like the colour of a flower which fades and changes as it is developed, and the conscious portions of our nature are unprophetic either of its approach or its departure. Could this influence be durable in its original purity and force, it is impossible to predict the greatness of the results; but when composition begins, inspiration is already on the decline, and the most glorious poetry that has ever been communicated to the world is probably a feeble shadow of the original conceptions of the poet. I appeal to the greatest poets of the present day, whether it is not an error to assert that the finest passages of poetry are produced by labour and study. The toil and the delay recommended by critics can be justly interpreted to mean no more than a careful observation of the inspired moments, and an artificial connection of the spaces between their suggestions, by the intertexture of conventional expressions; a necessity only imposed by the limitedness of the poetical faculty itself: for Milton conceived the Paradise Lost as a whole before he executed it in portions. We have his own

---

[19] *Macbeth*, I, vii, 44–5.   [20] Intensification.

authority also for the Muse having "dictated" to him the "unpremeditated song."[21] And let this be an answer to those who would allege the fifty-six various readings of the first line of the Orlando Furioso.[22] Compositions so produced are to poetry what mosaic is to painting. This instinct and intuition of the poetical faculty is still more observable in the plastic and pictorial arts; a great statue or picture grows under the power of the artist as a child in the mother's womb; and the very mind which directs the hands in formation, is incapable of accounting to itself for the origin, the gradations, or the media of the process.

Poetry is the record of the best and happiest moments of the happiest and best minds. We are aware of evanescent visitations of thought and feeling, sometimes associated with place or person, sometimes regarding our own mind alone, and always arising unforeseen and departing unbidden, but elevating and delightful beyond all expression: so that even in the desire and the regret they leave, there cannot but be pleasure, participating as it does in the nature of its object. It is as it were the interpenetration of a diviner nature through our own; but its footsteps are like those of a wind over the sea, which the coming calm erases, and whose traces remain only, as on the wrinkled sand which paves it. These and corresponding conditions of being are experienced principally by those of the most delicate sensibility and the most enlarged imagination; and the state of mind produced by them is at war with every base desire. The enthusiasm of virtue, love, patriotism, and friendship, is essentially linked with such emotions; and whilst they last, self appears as what it is, an atom to a Universe. Poets are not only subject to these experiences as spirits of the most refined organisation, but they can colour all that they combine with the evanescent hues of this ethereal world; a word, a trait in the representation of a scene or a passion, will touch the enchanted chord, and reanimate, in those who have ever experienced these emotions, the sleeping, the cold, the buried image of the past. Poetry thus makes immortal all that is best and most beautiful in the world; it arrests the vanishing apparitions which haunt the interlunations[23] of life, and veiling them, or[24] in language or in form, sends them forth among mankind, bearing sweet news of kindred joy to those with whom their sisters abide—abide, because there is no portal of expression from the caverns of the spirit which they inhabit into the universe of things. Poetry redeems from decay the visitations of the divinity in man.

Poetry turns all things to loveliness; it exalts the beauty of that which is most beautiful, and it adds beauty to that which is most deformed; it marries exultation and horror, grief and pleasure, eternity and change; it subdues to union, under its light yoke, all irreconcilable things. It transmutes all that it touches, and every form moving within the radiance of its presence is changed by wondrous sympathy to an incarnation of the spirit which it breathes: its secret alchemy turns to potable gold the poisonous waters which flow from death through life; it strips the veil of familiarity from the world, and lays bare the naked and sleeping beauty, which is the spirit of its forms.

All things exist as they are perceived; at least in relation to the percipient. "The mind is its own place, and of itself can make a heaven of hell, a hell of heaven."[25] But poetry defeats the curse which binds us to be subjected to the accident of surrounding impressions. And whether it spreads its own figured curtain, or withdraws life's dark veil from before the scene of things, it equally creates for us a being within our being. It makes us the inhabitant of a world to which the familiar world is a chaos. It reproduces the common universe of which we are portions and percipients, and it purges from our inward sight the film of familiarity which obscures from us the wonder of our being. It compels us to feel that which we perceive, and to imagine that which we know. It creates anew the universe, after it has been annihilated in our minds by the recurrence of impressions blunted by reiteration. It justifies the bold and true word of Tasso: *Non merita nome di creatore, se non Iddio ed il Poeta.*[26]

A poet, as he is the author to others of the highest wisdom, pleasure, virtue and glory, so he ought personally to be the happiest, the best, the wisest, and the most illustrious of men. As to his glory, let time be challenged to declare whether the fame of any other institutor of human life be comparable to that of a poet. That he is the wisest, the happiest, and the best, inasmuch as he is a poet, is equally incontrovertible: the greatest poets have been men of the most spotless virtue, of the most consummate prudence, and, if we could look into the interior of

---

[21] Cf. *Paradise Lost*, IX, 20–24.
[22] The epic masterpiece of Lodovico Ariosto (1474–1533).
[23] I.e., dark intervals. [24] Either.

[25] *Paradise Lost*, I, 254–5.
[26] None deserves the name of creator save God and the poet.

their lives, the most fortunate of men: and the exceptions, as they regard those who possessed the poetic faculty in a high yet inferior degree, will be found on consideration to confine rather than destroy the rule. Let us for a moment stoop to the arbitration of popular breath, and usurping and uniting in our own persons the incompatible characters of accuser, witness, judge and executioner, let us decide without trial, testimony, or form, that certain motives of those who are "there sitting where we dare not soar,"[27] are reprehensible. Let us assume that Homer was a drunkard, that Virgil was a flatterer, that Horace was a coward, that Tasso was a madman, that Lord Bacon was a peculator, that Raphael was a libertine, that Spenser was a poet laureate. It is inconsistent with this division of our subject to cite living poets, but posterity has done ample justice to the great names now referred to. Their errors have been weighed and found to have been dust in the balance;[28] if their sins "were as scarlet, they are now white as snow":[29] they have been washed in the blood of the mediator and the redeemer,[30] time. Observe in what a ludicrous chaos the imputations of real or fictitious crime have been confused in the contemporary calumnies against poetry and poets; consider how little is, as it appears—or appears, as it is; look to your own motives, and judge not, lest ye be judged.[31]

Poetry, as has been said, differs in this respect from logic, that it is not subject to the control of the active powers of the mind, and that its birth and recurrence have no necessary connexion with the consciousness or will. It is presumptuous to determine that these are the necessary conditions of all mental causation, when mental effects are experienced insusceptible of being referred to them. The frequent recurrence of the poetical power, it is obvious to suppose, may produce in the mind a habit of order and harmony correlative with its own nature and with its effects upon other minds. But in the intervals of inspiration, and they may be frequent without being durable, a poet becomes a man, and is abandoned to the sudden reflux of the influences under which others habitually live. But as he is more delicately organized than other men, and sensible to pain and pleasure, both his own and that of others, in a degree unknown to them, he will avoid the one and pursue the other with an ardour

proportioned to this difference. And he renders himself obnoxious to calumny, when he neglects to observe the circumstances under which these objects of universal pursuit and flight have disguised themselves in one another's garments.

But there is nothing necessarily evil in this error, and thus cruelty, envy, revenge, avarice, and the passions purely evil, have never formed any portion of the popular imputations on the lives of poets.

I have thought it most favourable to the cause of truth to set down these remarks according to the order in which they were suggested to my mind, by a consideration of the subject itself, instead of observing the formality of a polemical reply;[32] but if the view which they contain be just, they will be found to involve a refutation of the arguers against poetry, so far at least as regards the first division of the subject. I can readily conjecture what should have moved the gall of some learned and intelligent writers who quarrel with certain versifiers; I, like them, confess myself unwilling to be stunned by the Theseids of the hoarse Codri of the day. Bavius and Maevius[33] undoubtedly are, as they ever were, insufferable persons. But it belongs to a philosophical critic to distinguish rather than confound.

The first part of these remarks has related to poetry in its elements and principles; and it has been shewn, as well as the narrow limits assigned them would permit, that what is called poetry, in a restricted sense, has a common source with all other forms of order and of beauty, according to which the materials of human life are susceptible of being arranged, and which is poetry in an universal sense.

The second part will have for its object an application of these principles to the present state of the cultivation of poetry, and a defence of the attempt to idealise the modern forms of manners and opinions, and compel them into a subordination to the imaginative and creative faculty. For the literature of England, an energetic development of which has ever preceded or accompanied a great and free development of the national will, has arisen as it were from a new birth. In spite of the low-thoughted envy which would undervalue contemporary merit, our own will be a memorable age in intellectual achievements, and we live among such philosophers and poets as surpass beyond comparison any who

---

27 Cf. *Paradise Lost,* IV, 829.
28 Cf. Daniel 5:27 and Isaiah 40:15.   29 Cf. Isaiah 1:18.
30 Cf. Revelation 7:14 and Hebrews 9:14-15, 12:24.
31 Matthew 7:1.

32 To Peacock's treatise.
33 A *Theseid* would be a poem on the subject of Theseus, the legendary ruler of Athens. Juvenal (*Satires,* I, 1–2) alludes to a bad one by "Codrus," possibly a fictitious name. Bavius and Maevius are mentioned as jealous poetasters by Vergil (*Eclogues,* III, 90) and Horace (*Epodes,* X).

have appeared since the last national struggle for civil and religious liberty.[34] The most unfailing herald, companion, and follower of the awakening of a great people to work a beneficial change in opinion or institution, is poetry. At such periods there is an accumulation of the power of communicating and receiving intense and impassioned conceptions respecting man and nature. The persons in whom this power resides, may often as far as regards many portions of their nature, have little apparent correspondence with that spirit of good of which they are the ministers. But even whilst they deny and abjure, they are yet compelled to serve, the power which is seated on the throne of their own soul. It is impossible to read the compositions of the most celebrated writers of the present day without being startled with the electric life which burns within their words. They measure the circumference and sound the depths of human nature with a comprehensive and all-penetrating spirit, and they are themselves perhaps the most sincerely astonished at its manifestations; for it is less their spirit than the spirit of the age. Poets are the hierophants[35] of an unapprehended inspiration; the mirrors of the gigantic shadows which futurity casts upon the present; the words which express what they understand not; the trumpets which sing to battle and feel not what they inspire; the influence which is moved not, but moves. Poets are the unacknowledged legislators of the world.

John Keats

1795–1821

THE last two lines of the "Ode on a Grecian Urn" sum up the life and works of John Keats. The life was for less than twenty-six years; the works are in volume the slenderest on which rests the reputation of any major English writer. Those lines, as famous as any in poetry, epitomize the devotion of a very great genius not only to the worship of beauty but also to understanding the significance of beauty. Keats was not a wide reader and persistent tough-minded thinker like Shelley; but like Shelley he was a dedicated spirit. That is still the chief point to be made about him, though it is true that until lately the intellectual element in his poetry was underestimated.

Keats was a Cockney, undistinguished by either birth or education. Born in London, where his father kept a livery stable, he and his younger brothers George and Thomas were sent to the suburban private school of John Clarke at Enfield. There, although when fully grown Keats measured barely over five feet, he was at first chiefly noted for his prowess in schoolboy fights. The Reverend Mr. Clarke was the father of Charles Cowden Clarke (1787–1877), who became a second-rate but influential reviewer and popularizer of Shakespeare studies. In his capacity as his father's assistant, he taught Keats to read and helped form his tastes. This, not his lectures nor his scholarship, is Cowden Clarke's best claim to remembrance. Fond of music and the theater as well as of literature, he joined the music-publishing house

of Novello, and married his partner's daughter. At school and afterwards, Clarke put his pupil-friend in touch with the world of art. Once he glimpsed it, Keats never lost sight of it, though life soon began conspiring against his ever entering it. His first profound impression seems to have been Clarke's introducing him to the poetry of Spenser; eventually, though he read many of the English poets, he was most responsive to Shakespeare and to the beauty of Greek literature and sculpture.

Keats was eight when his father was killed by falling from a horse. The year after, his mother married another stablekeeper; and the year after that (1806) she separated from her new husband and went with her four children —Keats had a younger sister as well as two brothers, all dearly loved—to live with her mother in the suburb of Edmonton. When Keats was fourteen she died of tuberculosis. The grandmother then made a will, leaving £8000 to be shared by her grandchildren on their coming of age. She died in 1814, but the estate was tied up in litigation and did not help solve the poet's problems. Meanwhile the two businessmen who had been appointed guardians took John out of school in 1811 and apprenticed him to a surgeon-apothecary at Edmonton. Four years later he was allowed to withdraw from the apprenticeship and pursue his medical studies at Guy's and St. Thomas's hospitals in London. He had already begun writing verse. By or soon after the summer of 1816, when he passed his examinations and received his

[34] In the seventeenth century.

[35] Priests, explainers of mysteries.

certificate for practice as an apothecary, he had met Leigh Hunt (who printed a sonnet of his in the *Examiner*), and through him Hazlitt, Lamb, Shelley, and the painter Haydon. Before 1816 was over, he had made his decision for poetry instead of medicine, and had composed the earliest of his great poems, "On First Looking into Chapman's Homer."

In 1817 appeared his maiden volume, *Poems*. Keats was living with his brothers at Hampstead, another of the northern suburbs. With characteristic generosity Shelley invited him to share his house; but Keats declined—he was always offish with Shelley, perhaps afraid that his independent line as a poet might be swerved by association. Much of Keats's energy that year went into *Endymion*, the longest of his poems. It runs to four "books," diffuse, experimental, and immature, but rich in splendid couplets.

Endymion was published the following spring. In 1817–18 *Blackwood's* ran a series of articles on "The Cockney School of Poetry"; the fourth (August, 1818) contained a cheap and scurrilous attack on Keats. As a protégé of the radical Hunt, he was bound to be pursued by the Tory journals. In September there was a savage onslaught in the *Quarterly*, the source of the baseless legend which was to arise later—Shelley and Byron believed it—that a hostile review had broken the poet's spirit and was the cause of his early death. Far from being crushed, he immediately began the second of his longer poems, *Hyperion*, which however he never completed. It is a blank-verse epic, more severe and Miltonic than *Endymion*. Keats was learning the necessity of poetic form, but the epic impulse flagged before he finished Book III, and he abandoned the project.[1]

He had spent the summer of 1818 on a walking tour in the North; illness forced him to abandon it. By the end of that year his brother Tom, whom he had nursed for months, was dead of consumption, the disease to which the poet himself was soon to fall victim. He was now in love with Fanny Brawne, a vivacious girl of eighteen, and they became engaged. The next year, 1819, saw the composition of the great odes and the sonnet "Bright Star"; but sickness, poverty, and a growing conviction that he and Fanny would never be able to marry were turning a life that had been reasonably happy, certainly not morbid, and uncommonly full of friendships, into a torment. Fanny has been accused of being a shallow, frivolous girl, incapable of understanding what she had in Keats; but recent studies and the publication of her letters put beyond question the fact that she loved him deeply. For his part he was wildly in love, so desperately that his emotions tore him to pieces. He was lacerated by a normal masculine jealousy, an unreserved abandonment of his entire being to love, worry over his health, and realization that insurmountable barriers lay between him and marriage. In a desperate effort to remove the financial barrier, he collaborated with his friend Charles Brown on a tragedy; but it is worthless.

In 1820 his third and last volume came out. Already his illness was acute; he was suffering repeated hemorrhages. Warned by his physician that he could not survive another English winter, Keats borrowed money and sailed for Italy in September with Joseph Severn, a painter friend. They were no sooner established in Rome than the poet suffered a severe relapse. In February, 1821, he died; and there, in the Protestant cemetery, he was buried. He had composed his epitaph: "Here lies one whose name was writ in water." Actually, he knew better. "I think," he had written in the previous October to his emigrant brother George in this country, "I shall be among the English Poets after my death." His development had been phenomenally rapid; nearly all his greatest poems were composed in a single spring, of 1819. The quality of his third book (1820) was in fact immediately recognized by a number of the leading critics. As for his influence, on most of the best Victorian poets it was to prove inescapable.

The best single volume for most readers is probably the inexpensive *Complete Poems and Selected Letters*, edited by C. D. Thorpe (1935). There is no full-length edition of the poems which can be called standard or entirely satisfactory. E. de Selincourt's (revised, 1926), H. W. Garrod's (1939), and H. B. Forman's (1908) all have their points, especially De Selincourt's. There is an excellent edition of the letters—as will be seen below, they are vital documents in human aspiration and suffering—by M. B. Forman (3rd ed., 1947). One of the Modern Library Giants gives the complete poems of Shelley and Keats in one volume; Keats's are also available in The World's Classics and Everyman's Library.

Probably no one who cares for poetry at all can resist Keats. Much has been written about him. Among the books worth reading are: S. Colvin's *John Keats* (1917, and subsequent editions; but on the whole his slim volume of 1887 in the English Men of Letters series is more serviceable); Amy Lowell's overlong, enthusiastic, but valuable *John Keats* (2 vols., 1925); and C. D. Thorpe's *The Mind of John Keats* (1926). H. W. Garrod's analytical but curiously limited *Keats* (1926) is a venomous and shallow performance, unworthy of the hand that penned his excellent study of Wordsworth.

---

[1] At the end of 1819 Keats made a fragmentary effort to reconstruct the poem as "The Fall of Hyperion." To it anyone who doubts that he was more than a mere sensuous dreamer should turn—for example, to Canto I, lines 145–210.

John Keats

ON FIRST LOOKING INTO CHAPMAN'S HOMER

Keats wrote the following lines in the fall of 1816, after sitting up all night with Cowden Clarke enchanted by his admission to the heroic world of Homer. George Chapman (1559?-1634), one of Shakespeare's leading contemporaries in tragedy and comedy, translated both the *Iliad* and the *Odyssey*.

Much have I travell'd in the realms of gold,[1]
  And many goodly states and kingdoms seen;
  Round many western islands[2] have I been
Which bards in fealty to Apollo[3] hold.
Oft of one wide expanse had I been told   5
  That deep-brow'd Homer ruled as his demesne;
  Yet did I never breathe its pure serene
Till I heard Chapman speak out loud and bold:
Then felt I like some watcher of the skies
  When a new planet swims into his ken;   10
Or like stout Cortez[4] when with eagle eyes
  He star'd at the Pacific—and all his men
Look'd at each other with a wild surmise—
  Silent, upon a peak in Darien.[5]

ON SEEING THE ELGIN MARBLES

It was another intense experience with art that produced the sense of magnitude which infuses this great sonnet, written (as was the next) in the spring of 1817. At the British Museum may still be seen the collection of Greek sculptures, especially from the Parthenon, brought back to London by the seventh Earl of Elgin and sold by him in 1816 to the British government for less than half their cost.

My spirit is too weak—mortality
  Weighs heavily on me like unwilling sleep,
  And each imagin'd pinnacle and steep
Of godlike hardship tells me I must die
Like a sick Eagle looking at the sky.
  Yet 'tis a gentle luxury to weep   5
  That I have not the cloudy winds to keep
Fresh for the opening of the morning's eye.

---

[1] I.e., literature.
[2] I.e., the modern literature of western Europe.
[3] The god of poetry.
[4] It was actually Balboa who made the discovery.
[5] The Isthmus of Panama.

Such dim-conceivèd glories of the brain
  Bring round the heart an undescribable feud;   10
So do these wonders a most dizzy pain,
  That mingles Grecian grandeur with the rude
Wasting of old Time—with a billowy main—
  A sun—a shadow of a magnitude.

ON THE SEA

It keeps eternal whisperings around
  Desolate shores, and with its mighty swell
  Gluts twice ten thousand caverns, till the spell
Of Hecate[6] leaves them their old shadowy sound.
Often 'tis in such gentle temper found,   5
  That scarcely will the very smallest shell
  Be moved for days from whence it sometime fell,
When last the winds of heaven were unbound.
Oh ye! who have your eye-balls vexed and tired,
  Feast them upon the wideness of the Sea;   10
  Oh ye! whose ears are dinn'd with uproar rude,
Or fed too much with cloying melody,—
  Sit ye near some old cavern's mouth, and brood
Until ye start, as if the sea-nymphs quired!

from ENDYMION

Keats's first long poem, *Endymion: A Poetic Romance*, written in 1817, retells the old myth of the mortal youth with whom the moon goddess fell in love. Book I begins as follows.

A thing of beauty is a joy for ever:
Its loveliness increases; it will never
Pass into nothingness; but still will keep
A bower quiet for us, and a sleep
Full of sweet dreams, and health, and quiet breathing.   5
Therefore, on every morrow, are we wreathing
A flowery band to bind us to the earth,
Spite of despondence, of the inhuman dearth
Of noble natures, of the gloomy days,
Of all the unhealthy and o'er-darkened ways   10
Made for our searching: yes, in spite of all,
Some shape of beauty moves away the pall
From our dark spirits. Such the sun, the moon,
Trees old, and young sprouting a shady boon
For simple sheep; and such are daffodils   15
With the green world they live in; and clear rills

---

[6] Goddess of magic.

That for themselves a cooling covert make
'Gainst the hot season; the mid forest brake,
Rich with a sprinkling of fair musk-rose blooms:
And such too is the grandeur of the dooms   20
We have imagined for the mighty dead;
All lovely tales that we have heard or read:
An endless fountain of immortal drink,
Pouring unto us from the heaven's brink.

Nor do we merely feel these essences   25
For one short hour; no, even as the trees
That whisper round a temple become soon
Dear as the temple's self, so does the moon,
The passion poesy, glories infinite,
Haunt us till they become a cheering light   30
Unto our souls, and bound to us so fast,
That, whether there be shine, or gloom o'ercast,
They always must be with us, or we die. . . .

ON SITTING DOWN TO READ
KING LEAR AGAIN

This poem and the three that follow were written in 1818.

O golden tongued Romance, with serene lute!
  Fair-plumèd Syren, Queen of far-away!
  Leave melodizing on this wintry day,
Shut up thine olden pages, and be mute:
Adieu! for, once again, the fierce dispute   5
  Betwixt damnation and impassion'd clay
  Must I burn through; once more humbly assay
The bitter-sweet of this Shakespearian fruit:
Chief Poet! and ye clouds of Albion,
  Begetters of our deep eternal theme!   10
When through the old oak Forest I am gone,
  Let me not wander in a barren dream,
But, when I am consumèd in the fire,
Give me new Phoenix wings to fly at my desire.

WHEN I HAVE FEARS

When I have fears that I may cease to be
  Before my pen has glean'd my teeming brain,
Before high-pilèd books, in charact'ry,[7]
  Hold like rich garners the full-ripen'd grain;
When I behold, upon the night's starr'd face,   5
  Huge cloudy symbols of a high romance,
And think that I may never live to trace
  Their shadows, with the magic hand of chance;

---

[7] Characters, letters, writing.

And when I feel, fair creature of an hour,
  That I shall never look upon thee more,   10
Never have relish in the faery power
  Of unreflecting love!—then on the shore
Of the wide world I stand alone, and think
Till love and fame to nothingness do sink.

LINES ON THE MERMAID TAVERN

Souls of poets dead and gone,
What Elysium[8] have ye known,
Happy field or mossy cavern,
Choicer than the Mermaid Tavern?[9]
Have ye tippled drink more fine   5
Than mine host's Canary wine?
Or are fruits of Paradise
Sweeter than those dainty pies
Of venison? O generous food!
Dressed as though bold Robin Hood   10
Would, with his maid Marian,
Sup and bowse[10] from horn and can.

I have heard that on a day
Mine host's sign-board flew away,
Nobody knew whither, till   15
An astrologer's old quill
To a sheepskin gave the story,—
Said he saw you in your glory,
Underneath a new-old sign
Sipping beverage divine,   20
And pledging with contented smack
The Mermaid in the Zodiac.[11]

Souls of Poets dead and gone,
What Elysium have ye known,
Happy field or mossy cavern,   25
Choicer than the Mermaid Tavern?

ODE

This poem was written on a blank page in Keats's copy
of the plays of Beaumont and Fletcher.

Bards of Passion and of Mirth,
Ye have left your souls on earth!
Have ye souls in heaven too,
Double-lived in regions new?

---

[8] The abode of the happy dead, in classical mythology.
[9] A famous London rendezvous of the Elizabethan and Jacobean
poets and dramatists.   [10] Drink, carouse.
[11] I.e., the poets have elevated the Mermaid to a place as a new sign
of the zodiac.

Yes, and those of heaven commune   5
With the spheres of sun and moon;
With the noise of fountains wond'rous,
And the parle[12] of voices thund'rous;
With the whisper of heaven's trees
And one another, in soft ease   10
Seated on Elysian lawns
Brows'd by none but Dian's fawns
Underneath large blue-bells tented,
Where the daisies are rose-scented,
And the rose herself has got   15
Perfume which on earth is not;
Where the nightingale doth sing
Not a senseless, trancèd thing,
But divine, melodious truth;
Philosophic numbers smooth;   20
Tales and golden histories
Of heaven and its mysteries.

Thus ye live on high, and then
On the earth ye live again;
And the souls ye left behind you   25
Teach us, here, the way to find you,
Where your other souls are joying
Never slumber'd, never cloying.
Here, your earth-born souls still speak
To mortals, of their little week;   30
Of their sorrows and delights;
Of their passions and their spites;
Of their glory and their shame;
What doth strengthen and what maim.
Thus ye teach us, every day,   35
Wisdom, though fled far away.

Bards of Passion and of Mirth,
Ye have left your souls on earth!
Ye have souls in heaven too,
Double-lived in regions new!   40

THE EVE OF ST. AGNES

All through the year 1819 Keats kept polishing and repolishing these Spenserian stanzas. The result is a work
of astounding craftsmanship, wrought with care for every
glowing piece in the mosaic of minute pictorial detail.
It falls within that department of the era's poetry which
includes the narrative verse of Scott and Coleridge's
Christabel, the department of imitative medieval romance; and it is excellent narrative, boldly executed in
swift sure strokes of suspense, till with the blessing of
every reader the happy lovers, heedless of how at last

---

12 Talk.

death will come for them as it now comes for Angela
and the Beadsman, steal softly out into the night and the
ages.

St. Agnes' Eve[1]—Ah, bitter chill it was!
The owl, for all his feathers, was a-cold;
The hare limp'd trembling through the frozen grass,
And silent was the flock in woolly fold:
Numb were the Beadsman's fingers, while he told[2]   5
His rosary, and while his frosted breath,
Like pious incense from a censer old,
Seem'd taking flight for heaven, without a death,
Past the sweet Virgin's picture, while his prayer he saith.

His prayer he saith, this patient, holy man;   10
Then takes his lamp, and riseth from his knees,
And back returneth, meagre, barefoot, wan,
Along the chapel aisle by slow degrees:
The sculptur'd dead, on each side, seem to freeze,
Emprison'd in black, purgatorial rails:[3]   15
Knights, ladies, praying in dumb orat'ries,[4]
He passeth by; and his weak spirit fails
To think how they may ache in icy hoods and mails.

Northward he turneth through a little door,
And scarce three steps, ere Music's golden tongue   20
Flatter'd to tears this agèd man and poor;
But no—already had his deathbell rung;
The joys of all his life were said and sung:
His was harsh penance on St. Agnes' Eve:
Another way he went, and soon among   25
Rough ashes sat he for his soul's reprieve,
And all night kept awake, for sinners' sake to grieve.

That ancient Beadsman heard the prelude soft;
And so it chanc'd, for many a door was wide,
From hurry to and fro. Soon, up aloft,   30
The silver, snarling trumpets 'gan to chide:
The level chambers, ready with their pride,
Were glowing to receive a thousand guests:
The carvèd angels, ever eager-eyed,
Star'd, where upon their heads the cornice rests,   35
With hair blown back, and wings put cross-wise on
their breasts.

At length burst in the argent[5] revelry,
With plume, tiara, and all rich array,

1 The night of January 20, supposed to be the year's coldest.
2 I.e., counted the beads as he repeated his Ave Marias. A beadsman is an inmate of an almshouse, required to pray for the soul
of its founder.
3 I.e., sculptured in garments ("rails") appropriate to purgatory.
4 Oratories, small chapels, "dumb" because tenanted by statues.
5 Silver, shining.

Numerous as shadows haunting fairily
The brain, new stuff'd, in youth, with triumphs gay 40
Of old romance. These let us wish away,
And turn, sole-thoughted, to one Lady there,
Whose heart had brooded, all that wintry day,
On love, and wing'd St. Agnes' saintly care,
As she had heard old dames full many times declare.   45

They told her how, upon St. Agnes' Eve,
Young virgins might have visions of delight,[6]
And soft adorings from their loves receive
Upon the honey'd middle of the night,
If ceremonies due they did aright;   50
As, supperless to bed they must retire,
And couch supine their beauties, lily white;
Nor look behind, nor sideways, but require[7]
Of Heaven with upward eyes for all that they desire.

Full of this whim was thoughtful Madeline: 55
The music, yearning like a God in pain,
She scarcely heard: her maiden eyes divine,
Fix'd on the floor, saw many a sweeping train[8]
Pass by—she heeded not at all: in vain
Came many a tiptoe, amorous cavalier,   60
And back retir'd; not cool'd by high disdain,
But she saw not: her heart was otherwhere:
She sigh'd for Agnes' dreams, the sweetest of the year.

She danc'd along with vague, regardless eyes,
Anxious her lips, her breathing quick and short: 65
The hallow'd hour was near at hand: she sighs
Amid the timbrels,[9] and the throng'd resort
Of whisperers in anger, or in sport;
'Mid looks of love, defiance, hate, and scorn,
Hoodwink'd[10] with faery fancy; all amort,[11]   70
Save to St. Agnes and her lambs[12] unshorn,
And all the bliss to be before to-morrow morn.

So, purposing each moment to retire,
She linger'd still. Meantime, across the moors,
Had come young Porphyro, with heart on fire   75
For Madeline. Beside the portal doors,
Buttress'd from moonlight, stands he, and implores
All saints to give him sight of Madeline,
But for one moment in the tedious hours,

That he might gaze and worship all unseen;   80
Perchance speak, kneel, touch, kiss—in sooth such
        things have been.

He ventures in: let no buzz'd whisper tell:
All eyes be muffled, or a hundred swords
Will storm his heart, Love's fev'rous citadel:
For him, those chambers held barbarian hordes,   85
Hyena foemen, and hot-blooded lords,
Whose very dogs would execrations howl
Against his lineage: not one breast affords
Him any mercy, in that mansion foul,
Save one old beldame, weak in body and in soul.   90

Ah, happy chance! the agèd creature came,
Shuffling along with ivory-headed wand,
To where he stood, hid from the torch's flame,
Behind a broad hall-pillar, far beyond
The sound of merriment and chorus bland: 95
He startled her; but soon she knew his face,
And grasp'd his fingers in her palsied hand,
Saying, "Mercy, Porphyro! hie thee from this place;
They are all here to-night, the whole blood-thirsty race!

"Get hence! get hence! there's dwarfish Hildebrand;
He had a fever late, and in the fit   101
He cursèd thee and thine, both house and land:
Then there's that old Lord Maurice, not a whit
More tame for his gray hairs—Alas me! flit!
Flit like a ghost away."—"Ah, Gossip[13] dear,   105
We're safe enough; here in this arm-chair sit,
And tell me how"—"Good Saints! not here, not here;
Follow me, child, or else these stones will be thy bier."

He followed through a lowly archèd way,
Brushing the cobwebs with his lofty plume,   110
And as she muttered "Well-a—well-a-day!"
He found him in a little moonlight room,
Pale, lattic'd, chill, and silent as a tomb.
"Now tell me where is Madeline," said he,
"O tell me, Angela, by the holy loom   115
Which none but secret sisterhood may see,
When they St. Agnes' wool are weaving piously."

"St. Agnes! Ah! it is St. Agnes' Eve—
Yet men will murder upon holy days:
Thou must hold water in a witch's sieve,   120
And be liege-lord of all the Elves and Fays,
To venture so: it fills me with amaze
To see thee, Porphyro!—St. Agnes' Eve!

---

6 I.e., a revelation of their future husbands, who will appear and
feast with them.   7 Ask.
8 Not, says Keats in a letter, "for 'concourse of passers by,' but
for 'skirts' sweeping along the floor."   9 Tambourines.
10 Blinded.   11 Lifeless, i.e., oblivious.
12 St. Agnes is regularly depicted with lambs. It was an annual
custom to bless two lambs and shear them; nuns then spun the
wool.

13 Godmother; here, elderly friend.

God's help! my lady fair the conjuror plays
This very night: good angels her deceive!   125
But let me laugh awhile, I've mickle[14] time to grieve."

Feebly she laugheth in the languid moon,
While Porphyro upon her face doth look,
Like puzzled urchin on an agèd crone
Who keepeth clos'd a wond'rous riddle-book,   130
As spectacled she sits in chimney nook.
But soon his eyes grew brilliant, when she told
His lady's purpose; and he scarce could brook[15]
Tears, at the thought of those enchantments cold
And Madeline asleep in lap of legends old.   135

Sudden a thought came like a full-blown rose,
Flushing his brow, and in his painèd heart
Made purple riot: then doth he propose
A stratagem, that makes the beldame start:
"A cruel man and impious thou art: 140
Sweet lady, let her pray, and sleep, and dream
Alone with her good angels, far apart
From wicked men like thee. Go, go! I deem
Thou canst not surely be the same that thou didst
         seem."

"I will not harm her, by all saints I swear,"   145
Quoth Porphyro: "O may I ne'er find grace
When my weak voice shall whisper its last prayer,
If one of her soft ringlets I displace,
Or look with ruffian passion in her face:
Good Angela, believe me by these tears;   150
Or I will, even in a moment's space,
Awake, with horrid shout, my foemen's ears,
And beard them, though they be more fang'd than
         wolves and bears."

"Ah! why wilt thou affright a feeble soul?
A poor, weak, palsy-stricken, churchyard thing,   155
Whose passing-bell may ere the midnight toll;
Whose prayers for thee, each morn and evening,
Were never miss'd."—Thus plaining, doth she bring
A gentler speech from burning Porphyro;
So woful, and of such deep sorrowing,   160
That Angela gives promise she will do
Whatever he shall wish, betide her weal or woe.

Which was, to lead him, in close secrecy,
Even to Madeline's chamber, and there hide
Him in a closet, of such privacy   165
That he might see her beauty unespied,

And win perhaps that night a peerless bride,
While legion'd faeries pac'd the coverlet,
And pale enchantment held her sleepy-eyed.
Never on such a night have lovers met,   170
Since Merlin paid his Demon all the monstrous debt.[16]

"It shall be as thou wishest," said the Dame:
"All cates[17] and dainties shall be storèd there
Quickly on this feast-night: by the tambour frame[18]
Her own lute thou wilt see: no time to spare,   175
For I am slow and feeble, and scarce dare
On such a catering trust my dizzy head.
Wait here, my child, with patience; kneel in prayer
The while: Ah! thou must needs the lady wed,
Or may I never leave my grave among the dead."   180

So saying, she hobbled off with busy fear.
The lover's endless minutes slowly pass'd;
The dame return'd, and whisper'd in his ear
To follow her; with agèd eyes aghast
From fright of dim espial. Safe at last,   185
Through many a dusky gallery, they gain
The maiden's chamber, silken, hush'd, and chaste;
Where Porphyro took covert, pleased amain.[19]
His poor guide hurried back with agues in her brain.

Her falt'ring hand upon the balustrade,   190
Old Angela was feeling for the stair,
When Madeline, St. Agnes' charmèd maid,
Rose, like a missioned spirit, unaware:
With silver taper's light, and pious care,
She turn'd, and down the agèd gossip led   195
To a safe level matting. Now prepare,
Young Porphyro, for gazing on that bed;
She comes, she comes again, like ring-dove fray'd[20] and
         fled.

Out went the taper as she hurried in;
Its little smoke, in pallid moonshine, died: 200
She clos'd the door, she panted, all akin
To spirits of the air, and visions wide:
No uttered syllable, or, woe betide!
But to her heart, her heart was voluble,
Paining with eloquence her balmy side;   205
As though a tongueless nightingale should swell
Her throat in vain, and die, heart-stifled, in her dell.

understand Shakspeare to his depths, and I have I am sure many friends, who, if I fail, will attribute any change in my Life and Temper to Humbleness rather than to Pride—to a cowering under the Wings of great Poets rather than to a Bitterness that I am not appreciated. I am anxious to get *Endymion* printed that I may forget it and proceed. I have coppied the 3rd Book and have begun the 4th. On running my Eye over the Proofs—I saw one Mistake —I will notice it presently and also any others if there be any. There should be no comma in "the raft branch down sweeping from a tall ash top."[22] I have besides made one or two alterations and also altered the 13 Line Page 32 to make sense of it as you will see. I will take care the Printer shall not trip up my Heels. There should be no dash after Dryope in this Line "Dryope's lone lulling of her child."[23] . . .

> Your sincere and oblig'd friend
> JOHN KEATS—

P. S. You shall have a short *Preface* in good time—

IV. TO BENJAMIN ROBERT HAYDON[24]

(MARCH 14, 1818)

Teignmouth SATURD. MORN

My dear Haydon—
. . . Here's some doggrel for you. . . .

> Where be ye going, you Devon Maid,
>   And what have ye there i' the Basket?
> Ye tight little fairy—just fresh from the dairy,
>   Will ye give me some cream if I ask it?
>
> I love your Meads and I love your flowers
>   And I love your junkets mainly;[25]
> But 'hind the door, I love kissing more,
>   O look not so disdainly!
>
> I love your Hills and I love your dales
>   And I love your flocks a-bleating—
> But O on the heather to lie together
>   With both our hearts a-beating.
>
> I'll put your Basket all safe in a nook
>   And your shawl I hang up on this willow,
> And we will sigh in the daisy's eye
>   And Kiss on a grass green pillow.

I know not if this rhyming fit has done anything— it will be safe with you if worthy to put among my Lyrics. . . . I think of seeing the Dart[26] and Plymouth —but I don't know. It has as yet been a Mystery to me how and when Wordsworth went. I can't help thinking he has returned to his Shell—with his beautiful Wife and his enchanting Sister. It is a great Pity that People should by associating themselves with the finest things, spoil them. Hunt has damned Hampstead[27] and Masks and Sonnets and Italian tales—Wordsworth has damned the lakes—Milman has damned the old drama[28]—West[29] has damned— wholesale—Peacock[30] has damned satire, Ollier[31] has damn'd Music—Hazlitt has damned the bigotted and the blue-stockined; how durst the Man?! he is your only good damner and if ever I am damn'd—damn me if I shouldn't like him to damn me. It will be not be long ere I see you, but I thought I would just give you a line out of Devon—

> Yours affectionately
> JOHN KEATS

Remember me to all we know

V. TO JOHN HAMILTON REYNOLDS

(MAY 3, 1818)

Teignmouth, MAY 3d.

My dear Reynolds.
. . . Were I to study physic or rather Medecine again, I feel it would not make the least difference in my Poetry; when the Mind is in its infancy a Bias is in reality a Bias, but when we have acquired more strength, a Bias becomes no Bias. Every department of Knowledge we see excellent and calculated towards a great whole. I am so convinced of this, that I am glad at not having given away my medical Books, which I shall again look over to keep alive the little I know thitherwards. . . . An extensive knowledge is needful to thinking people—it takes away the heat and fever; and helps, by widening speculation, to ease the Burden of the Mystery:[32] a

---

[22] *Endymion*, I, 334-5.   [23] *Ibid.*, I, 495.
[24] An historical painter (1786-1846).   [25] Extremely.
[26] A river in Devonshire.
[27] The London suburb where Keats lived.
[28] The poet and historian Henry Hart Milman (1791-1868). His verse drama *Fazio* had been produced in London on February 5.
[29] The American painter Benjamin West (1738-1820), established in London, had succeeded Reynolds as president of the Royal Academy.
[30] Thomas Love Peacock (1785-1866), Shelley's friend, author of miscellaneous works, especially novels.
[31] Charles Ollier (1788-1859), an amateur of the flute, was a member of the firm that had published Keats's first volume.
[32] Wordsworth, "Tintern Abbey," line 38.

thing I begin to understand a little, and which weighed upon you in the most gloomy and true sentence in your Letter. The difference of high Sensations with and without knowledge appears to me this—in the latter case we are falling continually ten thousand fathoms deep and being blown up again without wings and with all [the] horror of a bare shoulderd creature—in the former case, our shoulders are fledge, and we go thro' the same air and space without fear. . . .

You may be anxious to know for fact to what sentence in your Letter I allude. You say, "I fear there is little chance of any thing else in this life." You seem by that to have been going through with a more painful and acute zest the same labyrinth that I have—I have come to the same conclusion thus far. My Branchings out therefrom have been numerous: one of them is the consideration of Wordsworth's genius and as a help, in the manner of gold being the meridian Line of worldly wealth,—how he differs from Milton.—And here I have nothing but surmises, from an uncertainty whether Milton's apparently less anxiety for Humanity proceeds from his seeing further or no than Wordsworth: And whether Wordsworth has in truth epic passion, and martyrs himself to the human heart, the main region of his song. In regard to his genius alone—we find what he says true as far as we have experienced, and we can judge no further but by larger experience—for axioms in philosophy are not axioms until they are proved upon our pulses: We read fine things but never feel them to the full until we have gone the same steps as the Author.—I know this is not plain; you will know exactly my meaning when I say that now I shall relish Hamlet more than I ever have done—Or, better—You are sensible no Man can set down Venery as a bestial or joyless thing until he is sick of it and therefore all philosophizing on it would be mere wording. Until we are sick, we understand not;—in fine, as Byron says, "Knowledge is Sorrow";[33] and I go on to say that "Sorrow is Wisdom"—and further for aught we can know for certainty "Wisdom is folly"!—So you see how I have run away from Wordsworth, and Milton, and shall still run away from what was in my head, to observe, that some kind of letters are good squares, others handsome ovals, and other some orbicular, others spheroid—and why should not there be another species with two rough edges like a Rat-trap? I hope you will find all my long letters of that species, and all will be well; for by merely touching

the spring delicately and ethereally, the rough edged will fly immediately into a proper compactness; and thus you may make a good wholesome loaf, with your own leven in it, of my fragments—If you cannot find this said Rat-trap sufficiently tractable— alas for me, it being an impossibility in grain for my ink to stain otherwise: If I scribble long letters I must play my vagaries. I must be too heavy, or too light, for whole pages—I must be quaint and free of Tropes[34] and figures—I must play my draughts[35] as I please, and for my advantage and your erudition, crown a white with a black, or a black with a white, and move into black or white, far and near as I please—I must go from Hazlitt to Patmore,[36] and make Wordsworth and Coleman[37] play at leap-frog —or keep one of them down a whole half-holiday at fly the garter[38]—"from Gray to Gay, from Little to Shakespeare"[39]—Also, as a long cause requires two or more sittings of the Court, so a long letter will require two or more sittings of the Breech— wherefore I shall resume after dinner.—

Have you not seen a Gull, an orc,[40] a Sea Mew, or any thing to bring this Line to a proper length, and also fill up this clear part; that like the Gull I may dip[41]—I hope, not out of sight—and also, like a Gull, I hope to be lucky in a good sized fish—This crossing a letter is not without its association—for chequer work leads us naturally to a Milkmaid, a Milkmaid to Hogarth, Hogarth to Shakespeare, Shakespeare to Hazlitt, Hazlitt to Shakespeare—and thus by merely pulling an apron string we set a pretty peal of Chimes at work—Let them chime on while, with your patience, I will return to Wordsworth— whether or no he has an extended vision or a circumscribed grandeur—whether he is an eagle in his nest, or on the wing—And to be more explicit and to show you how tall I stand by the giant, I will put down a simile of human life as far as I now perceive it; that is, to the point to which I say we both have arrived at—Well—I compare human life to a large Mansion of Many Apartments, two of which I can only describe, the doors of the rest being as yet shut upon me. The first we step into we call the infant

[34] Figures of speech.   [35] Checkers.
[36] Peter George Patmore (1786–1855), a voluminous writer, and father of the Victorian poet Coventry Patmore.
[37] George Colman the Younger (1762–1836), a leading playwright.
[38] A variety of the game of leapfrog.
[39] Cf. Pope, Essay on Man, IV, 380: "From grave to gay, from lively to severe." "Little" was one of Tom Moore's pseudonyms.
[40] Grampus.
[41] Part of this letter was "crossed," i.e., written with lines running both horizontally and vertically. "Dip" was the first word to be obscured by this crisscross method.

[33] Cf. Manfred, I, i, 10.

or thoughtless Chamber, in which we remain as long as we do not think—We remain there a long while, and notwithstanding the doors of the second Chamber remain wide open, showing a bright appearance, we care not to hasten to it; but are at length imperceptibly impelled by the awakening of this thinking principle within us—we no sooner get into the second Chamber, which I shall call the Chamber of Maiden-Thought, than we become intoxicated with the light and the atmosphere, we see nothing but pleasant wonders, and think of delaying there for ever in delight: However among the effects this breathing is father of is that tremendous one of sharpening one's vision into the heart and nature of Man—of convincing one's nerves that the world is full of Misery and Heartbreak, Pain, Sickness, and oppression—whereby this Chamber of Maiden-Thought becomes gradually darken'd and at the same time on all sides of it many doors are set open—but all dark—all leading to dark passages —We see not the ballance of good and evil. We are in a Mist. *We* are now in that state—We feel the "burden of the Mystery." To this Point was Wordsworth come, as far as I can conceive, when he wrote "Tintern Abbey," and it seems to me that his Genius is explorative of those dark Passages. Now if we live, and go on thinking, we too shall explore them—he is a Genius and superior [to] us, in so far as he can, more than we, make discoveries, and shed a light in them—Here I must think Wordsworth is deeper than Milton—though I think it has depended more upon the general and gregarious advance of intellect, than individual greatness of Mind. . . . The Reformation produced such immediate and great benefits, that Protestantism was considered under the immediate eye of heaven, and its own remaining Dogmas and superstitions, then, as it were, regenerated, constituted those resting places and seeming sure points of Reasoning—from that I have mentioned, Milton, whatever he may have thought in the sequel, appears to have been content with these by his writings—He did not think into the human heart, as Wordsworth has done—Yet Milton as a Philosopher, had sure as great powers as Wordsworth—What is then to be inferr'd? O many things—It proves there is really a grand march of intellect—It proves that a mighty providence subdues the mightiest Minds to the service of the time being, whether it be in human Knowledge or Religion—I have often pitied a Tutor who has to hear "Nom:[42] Musa" so often dinn'd into his ears—I hope you may not have the same

pain in this scribbling—I may have read these things before, but I never had even a thus dim perception of them; and moreover I like to say my lesson to one who will endure my tediousness for my own sake—After all there is certainly something real in the World—Moore's present to Hazlitt[43] is real—I like that Moore, and am glad I saw him at the Theatre just before I left Town. Tom[44] has spit a leetle blood this afternoon, and that is rather a damper—but I know—the truth is there is something real in the World. Your third Chamber of Life shall be a lucky and a gentle one—stored with the wine of love—and the Bread of Friendship. When you see George[45] if he should not have received a letter from me tell him he will find one at home most likely—tell Bailey[46] I hope soon to see him—Remember me to all. The leaves have been out here, for mony a day—I have written to George for the first stanzas of my Isabel[47]—I shall have them soon and will copy the whole out for you.

Your affectionate friend
JOHN KEATS.

VI. TO FANNY KEATS (JULY 2–4, 1818)

Dumfries JULY 2nd

My dear Fanny,

I intended to have written to you from Kirkudbright[48] the town I shall be in to-morrow—but I will write now because my Knapsack has worn my coat in the Seams, my coat has gone to the Taylors and I have but one Coat to my back in these parts. I must tell you how I went to Liverpool with George and our new Sister and the Gentleman my fellow traveller through the Summer and Autumn—We had a tolerable journey to Liverpool—which I left the next morning before George was up for Lancaster—Then we set off from Lancaster on foot with our Knapsacks on, and have walked a Little zig zag through the mountains and Lakes of Cumberland and Westmoreland—We came from Carlisle yesterday to this place—We are employed in going up Mountains, looking at strange towns, prying into

---

[42] Nominative; i.e., has to hear students decline nouns, etc.

[43] Perhaps a presentation copy of Moore's *The Fudge Family in Paris,* which he had given Hazlitt in April.
[44] Keats's sick brother, who died toward the end of 1818.
[45] Keats's other brother.
[46] See note 1, above.   [47] "Isabella, or the Pot of Basil."
[48] Kirkcudbright (pronounced *Kirkoóbry*), in southwestern Scotland. Fanny Keats was John's sister. Their brother George with his bride was emigrating to the United States. Keats had said good-by at Liverpool and then set off on a northern tour with his friend Charles Armitage Brown (1786-1842), a writer for periodicals.

old ruins, and eating very hearty breakfasts. Here we are full in the Midst of broad Scotch "How is it a' wi' yoursel"—the Girls are walking about bare footed and in the worst cottages the Smoke finds its way out of the door. I shall come home full of news for you and for fear I should choak you by too great a dose at once I must make you used to it by a letter or two. We have been taken for travelling Jewellers, Razor sellers and Spectacle venders because friend Brown wears a pair—The first place we stopped at with our Knapsacks contained one Richard Bradshaw, a notorious tippler—He stood in the shape of a 5 and ballanced himself as well as he could saying with his nose right in Mr Brown's face "Do—yo—u sell Spect—ta—cles?" Mr Abbey[49] says we are Don Quixotes—tell him we are more generally taken for Pedlars. All I hope is that we may not be taken for excisemen in this whiskey country—We are generally up about 5 walking before breakfast and we complete our 20 Miles before dinner—Yesterday we visited Burns's Tomb and this morning the fine Ruins of Lincluden[50]—I had done thus far when my coat came back fortified at all points—so as we lose no time we set forth again through Galloway—all very pleasant and pretty with no fatigue when one is used to it—We are in the midst of Meg Merrilies' country of whom I suppose you have heard. . . .[51]

My dear Fanny I am ashamed of writing you such stuff, nor would I if it were not for being tired after my day's walking, and ready to tumble into bed so fatigued that when I am asleep you might sew my nose to my great toe and trundle me round the town like a Hoop, without waking me—Then I get so hungry—a Ham goes but a very little way and fowls are like Larks to me—A Batch of Bread I make no more ado with than a sheet of parliament;[52] and I can eat a Bull's head as easily as I used to do Bull's eyes[53]—I take a whole string of Pork Sausages down as easily as a Pen'orth of Lady's fingers—Oh dear I must soon be contented with an acre or two of oaten cake, a hogshead of Milk, and a Cloaths basket of Eggs morning noon and night when I get among the Highlanders—Before we see them we shall pass into Ireland and have a chat with the Paddies, and

look at the Giant's Cause-way which you must have heard of—I have not time to tell you particularly for I have to send a Journal to Tom of whom you shall hear all particulars or from me when I return. Since I began this we have walked sixty miles to Newton Stewart at which place I put in this Letter—to-night we sleep at Glenluce—tomorrow at Portpatrick and the next day we shall cross in the passage boat to Ireland—I hope Miss Abbey has quite recovered—Present my Respects to her and to Mr and Mrs Abbey—God bless you—

       Your affectionate Brother John—

Do write me a Letter directed to *Inverness,* Scotland—

VII. TO JAMES AUGUSTUS HESSEY[54]

(OCTOBER 9, 1818)

My dear Hessey,

You are very good in sending me the letter[55] from the Chronicle—and I am very bad in not acknowledging such a kindness sooner—pray forgive me.—It has so chanced that I have had that paper every day—I have seen to-day's. I cannot but feel indebted to those Gentlemen who have taken my part—As for the rest, I begin to get a little acquainted with my own strength and weakness.—Praise or blame has but a momentary effect on the man whose love of beauty in the abstract makes him a severe critic on his own Works. My own domestic criticism has given me pain without comparison beyond what Blackwood or the Quarterly could possibly inflict, and also when I feel I am right, no external praise can give me such a glow as my own solitary reperception & ratification of what is fine. J. S.[56] is perfectly right in regard to the slip-shod Endymion. That it is so is no fault of mine.—No!—though it may sound a little paradoxical. It is as good as I had power to make it—by myself. Had I been nervous about its being a perfect piece, & with that view asked advice, & trembled over every page, it would not have been written; for it is not in my nature to fumble—I will write independently.—I have written independently *without Judgment.*—I may write independently, & *with Judgment* hereafter. The Genius of Poetry must work out its own salvation in

---

49 Richard Abbey, who had been Keats's guardian. Fanny lived with the Abbeys.

50 A Benedictine abbey founded in the twelfth century near Dumfries.

51 Here Keats inserts a ballad on the gypsy and also some nonsense verses about his tour. He resumes his letter at Newton Steward on July 4.

52 Parliament-cake, gingerbread.

53 A kind of hard, round candy.

54 Taylor's junior partner in the publishing firm. See note 18, above.

55 On Oct. 3 and 8 two letters to the editor had appeared in the *Morning Chronicle* protesting against the *Quarterly's* attack on Keats. 56 The signature of the earlier of the letters.

a man. It cannot be matured by law and precept, but by sensation & watchfulness in itself. That which is creative must create itself—In Endymion, I leaped headlong into the Sea, and thereby have become better acquainted with the Soundings, the quicksands, & the rocks, than if I had stayed upon the green shore, and piped a silly pipe, and took tea & comfortable advice.—I was never afraid of failure; for I would sooner fail than not be among the greatest. But I am nigh getting into a rant. So, with remembrances to Taylor and Woodhouse[57] &c I am

Y^{rs} very sincerely

JOHN KEATS.

VIII. TO FANNY BRAWNE (JULY 8, 1819)

JULY 8th

My sweet Girl,

Your Letter gave me more delight than any thing in the world but yourself could do; indeed I am almost astonished that any absent one should have that luxurious power over my senses which I feel. Even when I am not thinking of you I receive your influence and a tenderer nature steeling upon me. All my thoughts, my unhappiest days and nights, have I find not at all cured me of my love of Beauty, but made it so intense that I am miserable that you are not with me: or rather breathe in that dull sort of patience that cannot be called Life. I never knew before, what such a love as you have made me feel, was; I did not believe in it; my Fancy was affraid of it, lest it should burn me up. But if you will fully love me, though there may be some fire, 'twill not be more than we can bear when moistened and bedewed with Pleasures. You mention "horrid people" and ask me whether it depend upon them, whether I see you again. Do understand me, my love, in this. I have so much of you in my heart that I must turn Mentor when I see a chance of harm befalling you. I would never see any thing but Pleasure in your eyes, love on your lips, and Happiness in your steps. I would wish to see you among those amusements suitable to your inclinations and spirits; so that our loves might be a delight in the midst of Pleasures agreeable enough, rather than a resource from vexations and cares. But I doubt much, in case of the worst, whether I shall be philosopher enough to follow my own Lessons: if I saw my resolution give you a pain I could not. Why may I not speak of your Beauty, since without that I could never have lov'd you? I cannot conceive any beginning of such love as I have for you but Beauty. There may be a sort of love for which, without the least sneer at it, I have the highest respect and can admire it in others: but it has not the richness, the bloom, the full form, the enchantment of love after my own heart. So let me speak of your Beauty, though to my own endangering; if you could be so cruel to me as to try elsewhere its Power. You say you are affraid I shall think you do not love me—in saying this you make me ache the more to be near you. I am at the diligent use of my faculties here,[58] I do not pass a day without sprawling some blank verse or tagging some rhymes; and here I must confess, that (since I am on that subject) I love you the more in that I believe you have liked me for my own sake and for nothing else. I have met with women whom I really think would like to be married to a Poem and to be given away by a Novel. I have seen your Comet,[59] and only wish it was a sign that poor Rice[60] would get well whose illness makes him rather a melancholy companion: and the more so as to conquer his feelings and hide them from me, with a forc'd Pun. I kiss'd your writing over in the hope you had indulg'd me by leaving a trace of honey—What was your dream? Tell it me and I will tell you the interpretation thereof.

Ever yours, my love!

JOHN KEATS.

Do not accuse me of delay—we have not here an opportunity of sending letters every day. Write speedily.

IX. TO FANNY BRAWNE (FEBRUARY, 1820?)

My dear Fanny,

Do not let your mother suppose that you hurt me by writing at night. For some reason or other your last night's note was not so treasureable as former ones. I would fain that you call me *Love* still. To see you happy and in high spirits is a great consolation to me—still let me believe that you are not half so happy as my restoration would make you. I am nervous, I own, and may think myself worse than I really am; if so you must indulge me, and pamper with that sort of tenderness you have manifested towards me in different Letters. My sweet creature

---

[57] Richard Woodhouse (1788–1834), a young lawyer, literary adviser to Taylor and Hessey, and an admirer of Keats.

[58] Keats is writing from Newport, Isle of Wight.
[59] One was visible early that July.
[60] Keats's friend James Rice, of whom not much is known.

when I look back upon the pains and torments I have suffer'd for you from the day I left you to go to the isle of Wight; the extasies in which I have pass'd some days and the miseries in their turn, I wonder the more at the Beauty which has kept up the spell so fervently. When I send this round I shall be in the front parlour watching to see you show yourself for a minute in the garden. How illness stands as a barrier betwixt me and you! Even if I was well—I must make myself as good a Philosopher as possible. Now I have had opportunities of passing nights anxious and awake I have found other thoughts intrude upon me. "If I should die," said I to myself, "I have left no immortal work behind me—nothing to make my friends proud of my memory—but I have lov'd the principle of beauty in all things, and if I had had time I would have made myself remember'd." Thoughts like these came very feebly whilst I was in health and every pulse beat for you— now you divide with this (may *I* say it?) "Last infirmity of noble minds"[61] all my reflection.

God bless you, Love.
J. KEATS.

X. TO CHARLES ARMITAGE BROWN[62]

(NOVEMBER 1–2, 1820)

Naples, 1 NOVEMBER.

My dear Brown,

Yesterday we were let out of Quarantine, during which my health suffered more from bad air and the stifled cabin than it had done the whole voyage. The fresh air revived me a little, and I hope I am well enough this morning to write to you a short calm letter;—if that can be called one, in which I am afraid to speak of what I would fainest dwell upon. As I have gone thus far into it, I must go on a little; —perhaps it may relieve the load of WRETCHED-NESS which presses upon me. The persuasion that I shall see her[63] no more will kill me. I cannot q— My dear Brown, I should have had her when I was in health, and I should have remained well. I can bear to die—I cannot bear to leave her. O, God! God! God! Everything I have in my trunks that reminds me of her goes through me like a spear. The silk lining she put in my travelling cap scalds my head. My imagination is horribly vivid about her—

I see her—I hear her. There is nothing in the world of sufficient interest to divert me from her a moment. This was the case when I was in England; I cannot recollect, without shuddering, the time that I was a prisoner at Hunt's, and used to keep my eyes fixed on Hampstead all day. Then there was a good hope of seeing her again—Now!—O that I could be buried near where she lives! I am afraid to write to her—to receive a letter from her—to see her handwriting would break my heart—even to hear of her anyhow, to see her name written, would be more than I can bear. My dear Brown, what am I to do? Where can I look for consolation or ease? If I had any chance of recovery, this passion would kill me. Indeed, through the whole of my illness, both at your house and at Kentish Town,[64] this fever has never ceased wearing me out. When you write to me, which you will do immediately, write to Rome (*poste restante*)[65]—if she is well and happy, put a mark thus +; if——

Remember me to all. I will endeavour to bear my miseries patiently. A person in my state of health should not have such miseries to bear. Write a short note to my sister, saying you have heard from me. Severn[66] is very well. If I were in better health I would urge your coming to Rome. I fear there is no one can give me any comfort. Is there any news of George? O, that something fortunate had ever happened to me or my brothers!—then I might hope,—but despair is forced upon me as a habit. My dear Brown, for my sake, be her advocate for ever. I cannot say a word about Naples; I do not feel at all concerned in the thousand novelties around me. I am afraid to write to her—I should like her to know that I do not forget her. Oh, Brown, I have coals of fire in my breast. It surprises me that the human heart is capable of containing and bearing so much misery. Was I born for this end? God bless her, and her mother, and my sister, and George, and his wife, and you, and all!

Your ever affectionate friend,
JOHN KEATS.

Thursday.—I was a day too early for the Courier. He sets out now. I have been more calm to-day, though in a half dread of not continuing so. . . . I must leave off. You bring my thoughts too near to Fanny. God bless you!

---

61 Cf. Milton, "Lycidas," line 71.   62 See note 48, above.
63 Fanny Brawne.

64 Then, like Hampstead, a northern suburb of London.
65 I.e., to be held till called for.
66 Joseph Severn (1793–1879), a painter and a friend of Keats, whom he had accompanied to Italy.

XI. TO CHARLES ARMITAGE BROWN

(NOVEMBER 30, 1820)

Rome, 30 NOVEMBER 1820.

My dear Brown,

'Tis the most difficult thing in the world to me to write a letter. My stomach continues so bad, that I feel it worse on opening any book,—yet I am much better than I was in quarantine. Then I am afraid to encounter the pro-ing and con-ing of anything interesting to me in England. I have an habitual feeling of my real life having passed, and that I am leading a posthumous existence. God knows how it would have been—but it appears to me—however, I will not speak of that subject. I must have been at Bedhampton nearly at the time you were writing to me from Chichester—how unfortunate—and to pass on the river too! There was my star predominant! I cannot answer anything in your letter, which followed me from Naples to Rome, because I am afraid to look it over again. I am so weak (in mind) that I cannot bear the sight of any handwriting of a friend I love so much as I do you. Yet I ride the little horse, and, at my worst, even in quarantine, summoned up more puns, in a sort of desperation, in one week than in any year of my life. There is one thought enough to kill me; I have been well, healthy, alert, &c., walking with her, and now—the knowledge of contrast, feeling for light and shade, all that information (primitive sense) necessary for a poem, are great enemies to the recovery of the stomach. There, you rogue, I put you to the torture; but you must bring your philosophy to bear, as I do mine, really, or how should I be able to live? Dr. Clark is very attentive to me; he says, there is very little the matter with my lungs, but my stomach, he says, is very bad. I am well disappointed in hearing good news from George, for it runs in my head we shall all die young.[67] I have not written to Reynolds yet, which he must think very neglectful; being anxious to send him a good account of my health, I have delayed it from week to week. If I recover, I will do all in my power to correct the mistakes made during sickness; and if I should not, all my faults will be forgiven. Severn is very well, though he leads so dull a life with me. Remember me to all friends, and tell Haslam[68] I should not have left London without taking leave of him, but from being so low in body and mind. Write to George as soon as you receive this, and tell him how I am, as far as you can guess; and also a note to my sister—who walks about my imagination like a ghost—she is so like Tom. I can scarcely bid you good-bye, even in a letter. I always made an awkward bow.

God bless you!

JOHN KEATS.

A Group of Lesser Romantics

Sir Walter Scott

1771-1832

SCOTT is the chief exponent of the antiquarian interest which was an important part of the Romantic Movement. Born in Edinburgh, he spent much of his childhood on his grandfather's farm of Sandyknowe in the valley of the Tweed. In that region of ruined castles and abbeys, where for centuries the Border raiders had harried and the tides of Anglo-Scottish war had ebbed and flowed, he stored his head with local history and legend, learning ballads by heart, and devouring romances. Later on, in Edinburgh, he found less exhilaration in his law books than in history, medieval literature, travel books, and Shakespeare's plays. He was particularly in love with the medieval—the "Gothic," which the neoclassicists had scorned. He delighted in his "raids," both along the Border and among the Highlands, into districts relatively little touched by modernity. He would talk with the oldest inhabitants, listening avidly to legend, folklore, and tales of Jacobite adventure.

His delight in the popular ballads bore early fruit in the most important collection since Percy's *Reliques* (1765): the three volumes of *Minstrelsy of the Scottish Border* (1802-3). A recitation of Coleridge's *Christabel* which he happened to hear impelled him to try his own hand at a metrical romance. In 1805 appeared *The Lay of the Last Minstrel,* the first of the long narrative poems which for a time gave Scott of all the living British poets first place in public esteem. *Marmion* was received with great acclaim in 1808, and two years later came the

---

67 George had settled in Louisville, Kentucky; he died there in 1841. Fanny Keats died in 1889, aged 86.
68 William Haslam (1795-1851), a businessman and Keats's devoted friend.

most popular of them all, *The Lady of the Lake*. With *Rokeby* (1812) sales began falling off, largely because of the sudden popularity of Byron's narrative poems; and several later titles made it clear that public taste for Scott's "stale romance," as the youthful Byron contemptuously termed it, had waned. Scott obediently abandoned the genre and turned to another, the historical novel. In it he more than duplicated his success as a poet.

His first novel, *Waverley*, was published anonymously in 1814. It was the first of a long series known as the Waverley Novels; for years Scott averaged two annually. Apparently out of sheer whimsy, he did not acknowledge his authorship till 1827; but it was an open secret long before then. Among the best of the earlier novels, in which he is more realistic than later, are *Guy Mannering*, *The Antiquary*, *Old Mortality*, *Rob Roy*, and *The Heart of Midlothian*, all published in 1815-18 and set in Scotland. To name only the best of the later, *Ivanhoe* (1819) hardly rises above the level of a good adventure yarn for boys, but Scott incorporates in it several thrilling scenes of England during the reign of Richard Lion-Heart; and *Kenilworth* (1821) takes us, with many historical inaccuracies, to the days of Queen Elizabeth. The France of Louis XI provides the setting of *Quentin Durward* (1823), while in *Redgauntlet* (1824) Scott returns to his native land.

These and many other books made a great deal of money, of which Scott determined at the outset to obtain a larger share than often falls to the lot of authors. Though he had no aptitude for commerce, he became a secret partner in a printing business, sold his copyrights for large sums, and obliged his publishers to employ his firm as printers. He had established himself on an estate called Abbotsford, on the banks of the Tweed near Melrose, in the Border country of southwestern Scotland. There rose an incredible dwelling, a baronial castle, which embodied the dream of a romantic boy who never entirely grew up. In this absurd structure—as absurd as the Gothic novels by which Scott's work was much influenced—he spent the larger part of the rest of his life, in as medieval an atmosphere as money could provide. There he played, in all sincerity, the hospitable role of the great gentleman. Abbotsford became a sinkhole of his fortune. With reckless folly he anticipated (that is, drew out and spent) the profits of books not yet written; and in 1826 his own firm and both its allied publishing houses failed. Scott's imprudence was not the only cause of the crash, but it was a major factor.

He might have tried for a fresh start by recourse to bankruptcy, but he thought that procedure unworthy of a gentleman. The creditors saw they stood to gain if they let him go on working—for them. Scott assumed his share of the debt, and drove his pen more furiously

than ever, at history and biography as well as more novels. In the next two years he earned $200,000; further profits accruing after his death paid his creditors in full. He managed to keep Abbotsford for his children. But his exertions killed him. Even after his first stroke of paralysis in 1830, he toiled doggedly on for another year. In 1832 he died.

Scott's eminence was and is due to a remarkable gift for storytelling; but he was a versatile man of letters, as well as a popular purveyor of romantic fiction. In addition to important labors as a ballad collector, he brought out monumental editions of Dryden (18 vols., 1808) and Swift (19 vols., 1814). A staunch and eventually quite irrational Tory, he helped in 1809 to launch the great *Quarterly Review* in London, to compete with the *Edinburgh Review*. In 1813 he declined the poet laureateship and recommended Southey. In 1820 he was made a baronet.

From his childhood a spinner of tales, Scott failed as an artist to provide either his poems or his novels with much of anything except sheer narrative and the physical detail of the background; and these have not proved sufficient to keep him prominently before the reading public. The following pages contain most of his real poetry. Despite its faults, the reader must be sluggish of heart who does not respond to the swoop and dash of "Lochinvar," the pathos of a young girl's death in "Proud Maisie," or the rattlety-bang swank and gallantry of "Bonny Dundee."

The novels are available in numerous reprints. A satisfactory edition of the *Poetical Works* is by J. L. Robertson in the Oxford Standard Authors series. The letters have been edited by H. J. C. Grierson (12 vols., 1932-37). Despite inaccuracies, the detailed Life by J. G. Lockhart, Scott's son-in-law, is one of the most famous biographies in English. There is a more recent Life by H. J. C. Grierson (1938). D. Carswell's *Scott and His Circle* (1930) is a lively though harshly flippant book.

LOCHINVAR

This "ballad" is sung by a lady at the Scottish court of James IV in *Marmion* (V, xii).

O, young Lochinvar is come out of the west,
Through all the wide Border[1] his steed was the best;
And save his good broadsword he weapons had none,
He rode all unarm'd, and he rode all alone.
So faithful in love, and so dauntless in war,   5
There never was knight like the young Lochinvar.

---

[1] The region of the frontier between Scotland and England.

He staid not for brake,[2] and he stopp'd not for stone,
He swam the Eske river where ford there was none;
But, ere he alighted at Netherby gate,
The bride had consented, the gallant came late: 10
For a laggard in love, and a dastard in war,
Was to wed the fair Ellen of brave Lochinvar.

So boldly he enter'd the Netherby Hall,
Among bride's-men, and kinsmen, and brothers, and all:
Then spoke the bride's father, his hand on his sword,   15
(For the poor craven bridegroom said never a word,)
"O come ye in peace here, or come ye in war,
Or to dance at our bridal, young Lord Lochinvar?"

"I long woo'd your daughter, my suit you denied;—
Love swells like the Solway, but ebbs like its tide;   20
And now am I come, with this lost love of mine,
To lead but one measure, drink one cup of wine.
There are maidens in Scotland more lovely by far,
That would gladly be bride to the young Lochinvar."

The bride kiss'd the goblet; the knight took it up,   25
He quaff'd off the wine, and he threw down the cup.
She look'd down to blush, and she look'd up to sigh,
With a smile on her lips, and a tear in her eye.
He took her soft hand, ere her mother could bar,—
"Now tread we a measure!" said young Lochinvar.   30

So stately his form, and so lovely her face,
That never a hall such a galliard[3] did grace:
While her mother did fret, and her father did fume,
And the bridegroom stood dangling his bonnet and
          plume;
And the bride-maidens whisper'd, "'Twere better by
          far   35
To have match'd our fair cousin with young Lochinvar."

One touch to her hand, and one word in her ear,
When they reach'd the hall-door, and the charger stood
          near;
So light to the croupe the fair lady he swung,
So light to the saddle before her he sprung!   40
"She is won! we are gone, over bank, bush, and scaur;[4]
They'll have fleet steeds that follow," quoth young
          Lochinvar.

There was mounting 'mong Graemes of the Netherby
          clan;
Forsters, Fenwicks, and Musgraves, they rode and they
          ran:

There was racing and chasing, on Cannobie Lee,   45
But the lost bride of Netherby ne'er did they see.
So daring in love, and so dauntless in war,
Have ye e'er heard of gallant like young Lochinvar?

HARP OF THE NORTH

These are the opening stanzas (note the Spenserian form)
of *The Lady of the Lake;* immediately after them the
narrative begins.

Harp of the North! that mouldering long hast hung
     On the witch-elm[5] that shades Saint Fillan's spring,
And down the fitful breeze thy numbers[6] flung,
     Till envious ivy did around thee cling,
Muffling with verdant ringlet every string,—   5
     O minstrel Harp, still must thine accents sleep?
'Mid rustling leaves and fountains murmuring,
     Still must thy sweeter sounds their silence keep,
Nor bid a warrior smile, nor teach a maid to weep?

Not thus, in ancient days of Caledon,[7]   10
     Was thy voice mute amid the festal crowd,
When lay of hopeless love, or glory won,
     Aroused the fearful, or subdued the proud.
At each according pause, was heard aloud
     Thine ardent symphony sublime and high!   15
Fair dames and crested chiefs attention bow'd;
     For still[8] the burden[9] of thy minstrelsy
Was Knighthood's dauntless deed, and Beauty's
          matchless eye.

O wake once more! how rude soe'er the hand
     That ventures o'er thy magic maze to stray;   20
O wake once more! though scarce my skill command
     Some feeble echoing of thine earlier lay:
Though harsh and faint, and soon to die away,
     And all unworthy of thy nobler strain,
Yet, if one heart throb higher at its sway,   25
     The wizard note has not been touch'd in vain.
Then silent be no more! Enchantress, wake again!

SOLDIER, REST

These stanzas form part of a song sung by the fair Ellen
in honor of the stranger knight in *The Lady of the Lake*
(I, xxxi).

          Soldier, rest! thy warfare o'er,
               Sleep the sleep that knows not breaking;

---

[2] Thicket.   [3] A lively old dance in the form of a five-step.
[4] Scar, rocky bank or hill.

[5] Wych-elm, Scotch elm.   [6] Measures, i. e., strains.
[7] Caledonia, Scotland.   [8] Ever.   [9] Theme.

Dream of battled fields no more,
  Days of danger, nights of waking.
In our isle's enchanted hall,   5
  Hands unseen thy couch are strewing,
Fairy strains of music fall,
  Every sense in slumber dewing.
Soldier, rest! thy warfare o'er,
Dream of fighting fields no more: 10
Sleep the sleep that knows not breaking,
Morn of toil, nor night of waking.

No rude sound shall reach thine ear,
  Armour's clang, or war-steed champing,
Trump nor pibroch[10] summon here   15
  Mustering clan, or squadron tramping.
Yet the lark's shrill fife may come,
  At the day-break from the fallow,[11]
And the bittern sound his drum,
  Blooming from the sedgy shallow.   20
Ruder sounds shall none be near,
Guards nor warders challenge here,
Here's no war-steed's neigh and champing,
Shouting clans or squadrons stamping.

CORONACH

The title means lamentation. The stanzas are sung, in *The
Lady of the Lake* (III, xvi), by mourners over the body of
the Highland chieftain Duncan.

He is gone on the mountain,
  He is lost to the forest,
Like a summer-dried fountain,
  When our need was the sorest.
The font,[12] reappearing,   5
  From the rain-drops shall borrow,
But to us comes no cheering,
  To Duncan no morrow!

The hand of the reaper
  Takes the ears that are hoary,   10
But the voice of the weeper
  Wails manhood in glory.
The autumn winds rushing
  Waft the leaves that are searest,
But our flower was in flushing,[13]   15
  When blighting was nearest.

Fleet foot on the correi,[14]
  Sage counsel in cumber,[15]
Red hand in the foray,
  How sound is thy slumber!   20
Like the dew on the mountain,
  Like the foam on the river,
Like the bubble on the fountain,
  Thou art gone, and for ever!

JOCK OF HAZELDEAN

Scott says the first stanza "is ancient"; he wrote the rest.
This poem and the next, both published in 1816, are not
parts of larger works.

"Why weep ye by the tide, ladie?
  Why weep ye by the tide?
I'll wed ye to my youngest son,
  And ye sall be his bride;
And ye sall be his bride, ladie,   5
  Sae comely to be seen"—
But aye she loot[16] the tears down fa'
  For Jock of Hazeldean.

"Now let this wilfu' grief be done,
  And dry that cheek so pale;   10
Young Frank is chief of Errington,
  And lord of Langley-dale;
His step is first in peaceful ha',
  His sword in battle keen"—
But aye she loot the tears down fa'   15
  For Jock of Hazeldean.

"A chain of gold ye sall not lack,
  Nor braid to bind your hair;
Nor mettled hound, nor managed[17] hawk,
  Nor palfrey fresh and fair;   20
And you, the foremost o' them a',
  Shall ride our forest queen"—
But aye she loot the tears down fa'
  For Jock of Hazeldean.

The kirk was deck'd at morning-tide,   25
  The tapers glimmer'd fair;
The priest and bridegroom wait the bride,
  And dame and knight are there.
They sought her baith by bower and ha';[18]
  The ladie was not seen!   30
She's o'er the Border, and awa'
  Wi' Jock of Hazeldean.

---

[10] Warlike music on the bagpipes.
[11] Plowed but unsowed field.   [12] Fountain, spring.
[13] Growth, vigor.

[14] Hillside hollow (where game may hide).   [15] Trouble.
[16] Let.   [17] Trained.   [18] Chamber and hall.

PIBROCH OF DONUIL DHU

Scott here elaborates the Gaelic words to "a very ancient pibroch belonging to Clan MacDonald," supposed to refer to a victory in 1431. *Pibroch* means war music on the bagpipes.

Pibroch of Donuil Dhu,[19]
  Pibroch of Donuil,
Wake thy wild voice anew,
  Summon Clan-Conuil.
Come away, come away,   5
  Hark to the summons!
Come in your war array,
  Gentles and commons.

Come from deep glen, and
  From mountain so rocky,   10
The war-pipe and pennon
  Are at Inverlochy.
Come every hill-plaid and
  True heart that wears one,
Come every steel blade, and   15
  Strong hand that bears one.

Leave untended the herd,
  The flock without shelter;
Leave the corpse uninterr'd,
  The bride at the altar;   20
Leave the deer, leave the steer,
  Leave nets and barges:
Come with your fighting gear,
  Broadswords and targes.[20]

Come as the winds come, when   25
  Forests are rended;
Come as the waves come, when
  Navies are stranded:
Faster come, faster come,
  Faster and faster,   30
Chief, vassal, page and groom,
  Tenant and master.

Fast they come, fast they come;
  See how they gather!
Wide waves the eagle plume,   35
  Blended with heather.
Cast your plaids,[21] draw your blades,
  Forward, each man, set!
Pibroch of Donuil Dhu,
  Knell for the onset!   40

---

[19] Donald the Black.   [20] Shields.
[21] The Highlanders' substitute for cloaks.

PROUD MAISIE

Sung by mad Madge Wildfire in Chapter 40 of *The Heart of Midlothian*, published in 1818.

Proud Maisie is in the wood,
  Walking so early.
Sweet Robin sits on the bush,
  Singing so rarely.

"Tell me, thou bonny bird,   5
  When shall I marry me?"
"When six braw[22] gentlemen
  Kirkward shall carry ye."

"Who makes the bridal bed,
  Birdie, say truly?"   10
"The grey-headed sexton
  That delves the grave duly.

"The glow-worm o'er grave and stone
  Shall light thee steady.
The owl from the steeple sing,   15
  'Welcome, proud lady.'"

BONNY DUNDEE

This spirited song is sung by the ranger Leonard in an unacted melodrama, *The Doom of Devorgoil* (II, ii), which Scott wrote in 1817–18 but did not publish till 1830.

To the Lords of Convention[1] 'twas Claver'se[2] who
  spoke,
"Ere the King's crown shall fall there are crowns to be
  broke;
So let each Cavalier who loves honour and me,
Come follow the bonnet of Bonny Dundee.

"Come fill up my cup, come fill up my can,   5
Come saddle your horses, and call up your men;
Come open the West Port,[3] and let me gang[4] free,
And it's room for the bonnets of Bonny Dundee!"

---

[22] Fine.

[1] William III summoned a convention of Scottish lords to pass on his and his wife's claim to the crown of Scotland; the convention declared it forfeited by James II, and offered it to William and Mary.
[2] John Graham of Claverhouse, first Viscount Dundee (1649?–1689), who had been conspicuous in persecuting the Covenanters or Presbyterians, withdrew to the Highlands and raised a force of three thousand clansmen. On July 27, 1689, as an army of William's Scottish troops was moving up the pass of Killiecrankie, Dundee charged it furiously, broke it, but fell mortally wounded in the moment of victory.
[3] Gate.   [4] Go.

Dundee he is mounted, he rides up the street,
The bells are rung backward,[5] the drums they are
    beat;   10
But the Provost,[6] douce[7] man, said, "Just e'en let him
    be,
The Gude Town is weel quit of that Deil of Dundee."
        Come fill up my cup, &c.

As he rode down the sanctified bends of the Bow,[8]
Ilk carline was flyting[9] and shaking her pow;[10]   15
But the young plants of grace[11] they look'd couthie and
    slee,[12]
Thinking, "Luck to thy bonnet, thou Bonny Dundee!"
        Come fill up my cup, &c.

With sour-featured Whigs the Grass-market[13] was
    cramm'd
As if half the West had set tryst to be hang'd;   20
There was spite in each look, there was fear in each e'e,
As they watch'd for the bonnets of Bonny Dundee.
        Come fill up my cup, &c.

These cowls of Kilmarnock[14] had spits and had spears,
And lang-hafted gullies[15] to kill Cavaliers;   25
But they shrunk to close-heads,[16] and the causeway was
    free,
At the toss of the bonnet of Bonny Dundee.
        Come fill up my cup, &c.

He spurr'd to the foot of the proud Castle rock,[17]
And with the gay Gordon[18] he gallantly spoke;   30
"Let Mons Meg[19] and her marrows[20] speak twa words
    or three,
For the love of the bonnet of Bonny Dundee."
        Come fill up my cup, &c.

The Gordon demands of him which way he goes—
"Where'er shall direct me the shade of Montrose![21]   35
Your Grace in short space shall hear tidings of me,
Or that low lies the bonnet of Bonny Dundee.
        Come fill up my cup, &c.

"There are hills beyond Pentland, and lands beyond
    Forth,[22]
If there's lords in the Lowlands, there's chiefs in the
    North;   40
There are wild Duniewassals,[23] three thousand times
    three,
Will cry *hoigh!* for the bonnet of Bonny Dundee.
        Come fill up my cup, &c.

"There's brass on the target[24] of barken'd[25] bull-hide;
There's steel in the scabbard that dangles beside;   45
The brass shall be burnish'd, the steel shall flash free,
At a toss of the bonnet of Bonny Dundee.
        Come fill up my cup, &c.

"Away to the hills, to the caves, to the rocks—
Ere I own an usurper, I'll couch with the fox;   50
And tremble, false Whigs, in the midst of your glee,
You have not seen the last of my bonnet and me!"
        Come fill up my cup, &c.

He waved his proud hand, and the trumpets were
    blown,
The kettle-drums clash'd, and the horsemen rode on,   55
Till on Ravelston's cliffs and on Clermiston's lee[26]
Died away the wild war-notes of Bonny Dundee.

    Come fill up my cup, come fill up my can,
    Come saddle the horses and call up the men,
    Come open your gates and let me gae free,   60
    For it's up with the bonnets of Bonny Dundee!

Walter Savage Landor
1775–1864

LANDOR was twenty-three, and his first book had been
out several years, when in 1798 Wordsworth and Coleridge published *Lyrical Ballads*. The last two poems in
the following selections appeared in 1863. Landor was

---

[5] I.e., the chimes are sounded in reverse, as an alarm signal.
[6] The chief magistrate or mayor of Edinburgh.
[7] Sober, cautious.
[8] The West Bow was a steep street which zigzagged from in
front of the Castle to the Grass-market; the Covenanters were
numerous there. They were called by the Cavaliers "the Bow-
head Saints," "the godly plants of the Bow," etc. The Bow got
its name from the arch ("bow") of a gate in the city's original
wall, which crossed the street.
[9] Every crone was scolding.   [10] Poll, head.
[11] I.e., the Puritan girls.   [12] Kindly and sly.
[13] Once the place of execution. See note 8, above.
[14] I.e., Presbyterians, Covenanters, or Puritans—wearing hoods
made at Kilmarnock in Ayrshire, instead of the Cavalier's or
Jacobite's jaunty bonnet.—*Spits* here = swords.
[15] Long-handled knives.
[16] Shrank back into the farther ends of alleys.
[17] Edinburgh Castle stands above the city on a great rock.
[18] George Gordon, first Duke of Gordon, was in command of the
Castle.
[19] A famous cannon of the Castle, supposed to have been cast at
Mons, Belgium.   [20] Mates.

[21] James Graham (1612–50), Marquis of Montrose, a famous
Covenanter who went over to the Stuart cause, invaded Scotland after the death of Charles I, and was captured and executed.
[22] The Pentland Hills are the nearest range to Edinburgh; north of
the city lies the Firth of Forth, beyond which are the Highlands.
[23] Highland gentlemen, but not chiefs.   [24] Shield.
[25] Tanned with bark.   [26] Lea, meadow.

then eighty-eight; Browning had already done most of his best work, Tennyson and Arnold a good deal of theirs. Landor's life thus spans two periods of literary history, but there is no doubt that he belongs to the earlier one. For all the firm, molding impress of classical form on his art and his unusual powers of condensation, one feels the Romantic warmth and drive behind the poetic impulse.

Landor's parents were wealthy; the knowledge that he was certain of a fortune no doubt encouraged the temperamental independence that appeared early in his character and marked it to the end. His career at school and at Oxford was distinguished by constant clashes with the authorities. His marriage in 1811 was the beginning of a long series of domestic difficulties. His attempt to establish an estate at Llanthony in South Wales involved him in quarrels with the local residents and in expensive litigation. Encumbered with debts, he fled in 1814 to France and thence to Italy, which was his home for most of the rest of his life. Even there his inability to control his hot temper continued to get him into quarrels; but he eventually formed many friendships—with Hazlitt, Browning, and Dickens, for example.

He had already published, among other things, a somewhat inflated epic, *Gebir* (1798), and a volume called *Simonidea* (1806). Probably soon after he went to live in Florence, in 1821, he began working on *Imaginary Conversations,* published in a succession of volumes from 1824 to 1846. They contain some of the most finished prose in English literature, but have never appealed widely to general readers; Landor's high place was won by his poems. In 1831 a collected edition of them appeared.

In 1835 Landor returned to England to live—alone, since his wife would not accompany him or permit any of their children to do so. His re-entrance on the London scene came when nearly all the great Romantic artists had died or were silent and while the great Victorians were still engaged in winning their spurs; and he was greatly lionized. In 1836 the most ambitious of his prose works was published, the philosophical *Pericles and Aspasia,* which some consider his masterpiece. This time the form is not conversation but letters. A collective edition of his works in 1846 was warmly welcomed. His *Hellenics* appeared in 1847, other volumes in 1853, 1858, and 1863.

In 1858 Landor went into exile again, once more as the result of a lawsuit. He went back to Italy. No real reconciliation with his family was possible, but he was befriended by Browning and several others, and his last years were not devoid of happiness. He died in 1864.

The standard edition is by T. E. Welby and S. Wheeler (16 vols., 1927–36). The latter has also issued a separate edition of the poems (3 vols., 1937). The World's Classics has a volume selected from *Imaginary Conversations;* the Everyman's Library volume is from the *Conversations* and the poems. The official biography is by J. Forster (1869); S. Colvin's (1881) is based on it. A fresher approach is offered by M. Elwin's *Savage Landor* (1941).

MOTHER, I CANNOT

An adaptation and expansion of a fragment by Sappho (*c.* 600 B.C.). This lyric and the next were published in 1806, in Landor's *Simonidea.* The title of this volume is from the name of Simonides of Ceos, another great Greek lyrist of about a century later than Sappho.

> Mother, I cannot mind my wheel;
>   My fingers ache, my lips are dry:
> Oh! if you felt the pain I feel!
>   But oh, who ever felt as I?
>
> No longer could I doubt him true;   5
>   All other men may use deceit:
> He always said my eyes were blue,
>   And often swore my lips were sweet.

AH WHAT AVAILS

Rose Aylmer (1779–1800) was the only daughter of the fourth Baron Aylmer. Landor met her at Swansea, Wales, when she was about seventeen. Not long afterwards she accompanied her aunt to Calcutta, where she died suddenly. In later reprints of the poem Landor made a few changes; the following text is that of 1846.

> Ah what avails the sceptred race,
>   Ah what the form divine!
> What every virtue, every grace!
>   Rose Aylmer, all were thine.
> Rose Aylmer, whom these wakeful eyes   5
>   May weep, but never see,
> A night of memories and of sighs
>   I consecrate to thee.

DIRCE

This poem and the next three were published in Landor's volume of 1831.

> Stand close around, ye Stygian set,
>   With Dirce in one boat conveyed!
> Or Charon,[1] seeing, may forget
>   That he is old and she a shade.

---

[1] In classical mythology old Charon ferried souls across the River Styx to Hades.—Landor takes his name for a lovely lady from a classical fable in which Dirce was the leading figure.

AWAY, MY VERSE

This lyric and the next two are from a section headed "Ianthe" in the 1831 volume. Others with that name were printed before and afterwards. Not all are necessarily to the same lady; but many of the "Ianthe" poems were addressed to an Irish girl, Sophia Jane Swift, who became Mrs. Godwin Swifte and subsequently the Countess de Molandé. Landor probably met her shortly before her first marriage, in 1803. As far as anyone was the love of his life, she was. That she became his mistress seems clear. He wanted her to leave her husband; but she evidently preferred a conventional Regency liaison to the scandal of a divorce and remarriage. Swifte died in 1814; meanwhile Landor had married. In 1816 she married her second husband, who died about 1827. When some two years later she visited Florence, a sentimental friendship with Landor sprang from the ashes of their old love and continued until her death in 1851.

Away, my verse; and never fear,
  As men before such beauty do;
On you she will not look severe,
  She will not turn her eyes from you.

Some happier graces could I lend
  That in her memory you should live,
Some little blemishes might blend . . .
  For it would please her to forgive.

PAST RUIN'D ILION

Past ruin'd Ilion[2] Helen lives,
  Alcestis[3] rises from the shades;
Verse calls them forth; 'tis verse that gives
  Immortal youth to mortal maids.

Soon shall Oblivion's deepening veil   5
  Hide all the peopled hills you see,
The gay, the proud, while lovers hail
  These many summers you and me.

The tear for fading beauty check,
  For passing glory cease to sigh;   10
One form shall rise above the wreck,
  One name, Ianthe, shall not die.

---

[2] Ilium, Troy.
[3] As famous in Greek legend for devotion to her husband as Helen was for the opposite reason.

WHEN HELEN FIRST

When Helen first saw wrinkles in her face
('Twas when some fifty long had settled there
And intermarried and brancht off awide)
She threw herself upon her couch, and wept:
On this side hung her head, and over that   5
Listlessly she let fall the faithless brass
That made the men as faithless.
                    But when you
Found them, or fancied them, and would not hear
That they were only vestiges of smiles,
Or the impression of some amorous hair   10
Astray from cloistered curls and roseat band,
Which had been lying there all night perhaps
Upon a skin so soft . . . *No, no,* you said,
Sure they are coming, yes, are come, are here . . .
Well, and what matters it . . . while you are too!   15

YES, I WRITE VERSES

This charming piece of light verse, presumably another "Ianthe" poem, was probably written in 1844. It was published in the two-volume *Works* of 1846.

Yes, I write verses now and then,
But blunt and flaccid is my pen,
No longer talkt of by young men
    As rather clever:
In the last quarter are my eyes,   5
You see it by their form and size;
Is it not time then to be wise?
    Or now or never.

Fairest that ever sprang from Eve!
While Time allows the short reprieve,   10
Just look at me! would you believe
    'Twas once a lover?
I cannot clear the five-bar gate,
But, trying first its timber's state,
Climb stiffly up, take breath, and wait   15
    To trundle over.

Thro' gallopade[4] I cannot swing
The entangling blooms of Beauty's spring:
I cannot say the tender thing,
    Be't true or false,   20
And am beginning to opine
Those girls are only half-divine
Whose waists yon wicked boys entwine
    In giddy waltz.

---

[4] A kind of lively dance.

I fear that arm above that shoulder,   25
I wish them wiser, graver, older,
Sedater, and no harm if colder
    And panting less.
Ah! people were not half so wild
In former days, when, starchly mild,   30
Upon her high-heel'd Essex[5] smiled
    The brave[6] Queen Bess.

TO BROWNING

This fine tribute appeared in the London *Morning Chronicle* for November 22, 1845.

There is delight in singing, though none hear
Beside the singer; and there is delight
In praising, though the praiser sit alone
And see the prais'd far off him, far above.
Shakespeare is not *our* poet, but the world's,   5
Therefore on him no speech; and brief for thee,
Browning! Since Chaucer was alive and hale,
No man hath walk'd along our roads with step
So active, so inquiring eye, or tongue
So varied in discourse. But warmer climes[7]   10
Give brighter plumage, stronger wing; the breeze
Of Alpine heights thou playest with, borne on
Beyond Sorrento[8] and Amalfi, where
The Siren waits thee, singing song for song.

IPHIGENEIA AND AGAMEMNON

One of the principal heroines of Greek legend and tragedy was this daughter of the leader of the campaign against Troy. He had offended Diana, and the vengeance of the goddess took the form of contrary winds which prevented the fleet from leaving Greece. Her wrath was placated by the sacrifice of Iphigeneia, and the ships sailed. This poem was published in 1846.

Iphigeneia,[9] when she heard her doom
At Aulis,[10] and when all beside the king
Had gone away, took his right-hand, and said,
"O father! I am young and very happy.

I do not think the pious Calchas[11] heard   5
Distinctly what the Goddess spake. Old age
Obscures the senses. If my nurse, who knew
My voice so well, sometimes misunderstood,
While I was resting on her knee both arms
And hitting it to make her mind my words,   10
And looking in her face, and she in mine,
Might not he also hear one word amiss,
Spoken from so far off, even from Olympus?"
The father placed his cheek upon her head,
And tears dropt down it, but the king of men   15
Replied not. Then the maiden spake once more.
"O father! sayst thou nothing? Hear'st thou not
Me, whom thou ever hast, until this hour,
Listen'd to fondly, and awaken'd me
To hear my voice amid the voice of birds,   20
When it was inarticulate as theirs,
And the down deadened it within the nest?"
He moved her gently from him, silent still,
And this, and this alone, brought tears from her,
Altho' she saw fate nearer: then with sighs,   25
"I thought to have laid down my hair before
Benignant Artemis,[12] and not have dimm'd
Her polisht altar with my virgin blood;
I thought to have selected the white flowers
To please the Nymphs, and to have askt of each   30
By name, and with no sorrowful regret,
Whether, since both my parents will'd the change,
I might at Hymen's[13] feet bend my clipt brow;
And (after these who mind us girls the most)
Adore our own Athena,[14] that she would   35
Regard me mildly with her azure eyes.
But father! to see you no more, and see
Your love, O father! go ere I am gone!"
Gently he moved her off, and drew her back,
Bending his lofty head far over hers,   40
And the dark depths of nature heaved and burst.
He turn'd away; not far, but silent still.
She now first shudder'd; for in him, so nigh,
So long a silence seem'd the approach of death,
And like it. Once again she rais'd her voice.   45
"O father! if the ships are now detain'd,
And all your vows move not the Gods above,
When the knife strikes me there will be one prayer
The less to them: and purer can there be

---

[5] Robert Devereux (1566–1601), second Earl of Essex, long Elizabeth's favorite courtier. [6] Fine, excellent.

[7] An invitation to Italy, where Browning did in fact go to live after his marriage in 1846.

[8] The home of the sea nymphs known as the Sirens came to be localized on certain islets near Naples and Sorrento. Amalfi is on the Gulf of Salerno near Naples.

[9] This is the Greek form; the usual English spelling is *Iphigenia*.

[10] A harbor of Boeotia in central Greece. It was the assembly port of the Greek fleet.

[11] The soothsayer who had reported the wish of the goddess. In another version Diana interposed and rescued Iphigeneia, who became one of her priestesses.

[12] The Greek name for Diana, goddess of virginity, to whom a sacrifice was due at marriage. [13] God of marriage.

[14] Landor's note: "Pallas Athena was patroness of Argos" in southern Greece. Agamemnon was a legendary king of the Argives.

Any, or more fervent than the daughter's prayer 50
For her dear father's safety and success?"
A groan that shook him shook not his resolve.
An agèd man now enter'd, and without
One word, stept slowly on, and took the wrist
Of the pale maiden. She lookt up and saw 55
The fillet of the priest and calm cold eyes.
Then turn'd she where her parent stood, and cried
"O father! grieve no more: the ships can sail."

TWENTY YEARS HENCE

Another of the "Ianthe" lyrics, published in 1846.

Twenty years hence my eyes may grow
If not quite dim, yet rather so,
Still yours from others they shall know
        Twenty years hence.

Twenty years hence tho' it may hap 5
That I be call'd to take a nap
In a cool cell where thunder-clap
        Was never heard,

There breathe but o'er my arch of grass
A not too sadly sigh'd *Alas,* 10
And I shall catch, ere you can pass,
        That wingèd word.

DYING SPEECH OF AN
OLD PHILOSOPHER

This quatrain appeared in 1849 in the *Examiner*. Landor wrote it on his seventy-fourth birthday.

I strove with none, for none was worth my strife:
    Nature I loved, and, next to Nature, Art:
I warm'd both hands before the fire of Life;
    It sinks; and I am ready to depart.

TO AGE

Originally printed in the *Examiner* for June 5, 1852.

Welcome, old friend! These many years
    Have we lived door by door:
The Fates have laid aside their shears[15]
    Perhaps for some few more.

---

[15] With which Atropos, one of the Fates of Greek myth, cuts the thread of life.

I was indocile at an age 5
    When better boys were taught,
But thou at length hast made me sage,
    If I am sage in aught.

Little I know from other men,
    Too little they from me, 10
But thou has pointed well the pen
    That writes these lines to thee.

Thanks for expelling Fear and Hope,
    One vile, the other vain;
One's scourge, the other's telescope, 15
    I shall not see again:

Rather what lies before my feet
    My notice shall engage . . .
He who hath brav'd Youth's dizzy heat
    Dreads not the frost of Age. 20

TO MY NINTH DECAD

Our last two selections were published in 1863. Both are "Ianthe" poems.

To my ninth decad I have tottered on,
    And no soft arm bends now my steps to steady;
She, who once led me where she would, is gone,
    So when he calls me, Death shall find me ready.

WELL I REMEMBER

Well I remember how you smiled
    To see me write your name upon
The soft sea-sand . . . "O! what a child!
    You think you're writing upon stone!"
I have since written what no tide 5
    Shall ever wash away, what men
Unborn shall read o'er ocean wide
    And find Ianthe's name again.

Robert Southey
1774–1843

IN our introductory sketch of Coleridge we have already seen how his brother-in-law studied at Oxford, planned and then withdrew from the Pantisocratic scheme for a utopian life in the United States, and finally settled down in the Lake country at Keswick. As with Coleridge and Wordsworth, his initial enthusiasm for the French Revolution turned into horror at the violence of its later stages, and he became a confirmed Tory. He supported his family, and largely Coleridge's, by his pen; volume succeeded volume. In good will and industry he was highly endowed, but he was seldom visited by inspiration. In 1813 Scott declined the poet laureateship and recommended Southey, who accepted. He was not a very good poet, though a few of his short poems are well known; some of his prose, especially his *Life of Nelson* (1813), is excellent. The story of "The Three Bears," inserted in a long miscellaneous prose work called *The Doctor,* may prove in the end his chief title to fame, though few who know the story know that Southey wrote it. Southey was an admirable man who meant well, worked hard, loved his neighbor, and occasionally wrote something worthwhile.

There is a Life in the English Men of Letters series by E. Dowden, who also edited a pocket-size volume of selections (1895) from the poetry. On a larger scale is M. H. Fitzgerald's selection from the poems (1909). Everyman's Library reprints the *Nelson,* The World's Classics a volume of the letters. W. Haller's *The Early Life* (1917) is the most careful biography.

THE BATTLE OF BLENHEIM

It was a summer evening,
　Old Kaspar's work was done,
And he before his cottage door
　Was sitting in the sun,
And by him sported on the green　　　　5
His little grandchild Wilhelmine.

She saw her brother Peterkin
　Roll something large and round,
Which he beside the rivulet
　In playing there had found;　　　　10
He came to ask what he had found,
That was so large, and smooth, and round.

Old Kaspar took it from the boy,
　Who stood expectant by;
And then the old man shook his head,　　　　15
　And with a natural sigh,
" 'Tis some poor fellow's skull," said he,
"Who fell in the great victory.[1]

"I find them in the garden,
　For there's many here about;　　　　20

---

[1] In 1704 at Blenheim in Bavaria, the great Duke of Marlborough and the Austrian general Prince Eugene of Savoy shattered a French and Bavarian army of Louis XIV, for whom this defeat was the beginning of the end of his dreams of conquest.—Southey's poem was written in 1798.

And often when I go to plough,
　The ploughshare turns them out!
For many thousand men," said he,
"Were slain in that great victory."

"Now tell us what 'twas all about,"　　　　25
　Young Peterkin, he cries;
And little Wilhelmine looks up
　With wonder-waiting eyes;
"Now tell us all about the war,
And what they fought each other for."　　　　30

"It was the English," Kaspar cried,
　"Who put the French to rout;
But what they fought each other for,
　I could not well make out;
But every body said," quoth he,　　　　35
"That 'twas a famous victory.

"My father lived at Blenheim then,
　Yon little stream hard by;
They burnt his dwelling to the ground,
　And he was forced to fly;　　　　40
So with his wife and child he fled,
Nor had he where to rest his head.

"With fire and sword the country round
　Was wasted far and wide,
And many a childing mother then,　　　　45
　And new-born baby died;
But things like that, you know, must be
At every famous victory.

"They say it was a shocking sight
　After the field was won;　　　　50
For many thousand bodies here
　Lay rotting in the sun;
But things like that, you know, must be
After a famous victory.

"Great praise the Duke of Marlbro' won,　　　　55
　And our good Prince Eugene."
"Why 'twas a very wicked thing!"
　Said little Wilhelmine.
"Nay . . . nay . . . my little girl," quoth he,
"It was a famous victory.　　　　60

"And every body praised the Duke,
　Who this great fight did win."
"But what good came of it at last?"
　Quoth little Peterkin.
"Why that I cannot tell," said he,　　　　65
"But 'twas a famous victory."

THE INCHCAPE ROCK[2]

No stir in the air, no stir in the sea,
The ship was still as she could be,
Her sails from heaven received no motion,
Her keel was steady in the ocean.

Without either sign or sound of their shock, 5
The waves flow'd over the Inchcape Rock;
So little they rose, so little they fell,
They did not move the Inchcape Bell.

The Abbot of Aberbrothok
Had placed that bell on the Inchcape Rock; 10
On a buoy in the storm it floated and swung,
And over the waves its warning rung.

When the Rock was hid by the surge's swell,
The mariners heard the warning bell;
And then they knew the perilous Rock, 15
And blest the Abbot of Aberbrothok.

The Sun in heaven was shining gay,
All things were joyful on that day;
The sea-birds scream'd as they wheel'd round,
And there was joyaunce in their sound. 20

The buoy of the Inchcape Bell was seen
A darker speck on the ocean green;
Sir Ralph the Rover walk'd his deck,
And he fixed his eye on the darker speck.

He felt the cheering power of spring, 25
It made him whistle, it made him sing;
His heart was mirthful to excess,
But the Rover's mirth was wickedness.

His eye was on the Inchcape float;
Quoth he, "My men, put out the boat, 30
And row me to the Inchcape Rock,
And I'll plague the Abbot of Aberbrothok."

The boat is lower'd, the boatmen row,
And to the Inchcape Rock they go;
Sir Ralph bent over from the boat, 35
And he cut the Bell from the Inchcape float.

Down sunk the Bell with a gurgling sound,
The bubbles rose and burst around;

Quoth Sir Ralph, "The next who comes to the
 Rock
Won't bless the Abbot of Aberbrothok." 40

Sir Ralph the Rover sail'd away,
He scour'd the seas for many a day;
And now grown rich with plunder'd store,
He steers his course for Scotland's shore.

So thick a haze o'erspreads the sky 45
They cannot see the Sun on high;
The wind hath blown a gale all day,
At evening it hath died away.

On the deck the Rover takes his stand,
So dark it is they see no land. 50
Quoth Sir Ralph, "It will be lighter soon,
For there is the dawn of the rising Moon."

"Canst hear," said one, "the breakers roar?
For methinks we should be near the shore."
"Now where we are I cannot tell, 55
But I wish I could hear the Inchcape Bell."

They hear no sound, the swell is strong;
Though the wind hath fallen they drift along,
Till the vessel strikes with a shivering shock,—
"Oh Christ! it is the Inchcape Rock!" 60

Sir Ralph the Rover tore his hair,
He curst himself in his despair;
The waves rushed in on every side,
The ship is sinking beneath the tide.

But even in his dying fear 65
One dreadful sound could the Rover hear,
A sound as if, with the Inchcape Bell,
The Devil below was ringing his knell.

MY DAYS AMONG THE DEAD

My days among the Dead[3] are passed;
 Around me I behold,
Where'er these casual eyes are cast,
 The mighty minds of old;
My never-failing friends are they, 5
With whom I converse day by day.

---

[2] Southey got his theme from a recorded legend about a reef off
the southeastern coast of Scotland.—The poem was written in
1802.

[3] I.e., with the books in his library.—Southey wrote this poem in
1818.

With them I take delight in weal,
　And seek relief in woe;
And while I understand and feel
　How much to them I owe,　　　　　10
My cheeks have often been bedew'd
With tears of thoughtful gratitude.

My thoughts are with the Dead, with them
　I live in long-past years,
Their virtues love, their faults condemn,　　15
　Partake their hopes and fears,
And from their lessons seek and find
Instruction with an humble mind.

My hopes are with the Dead, anon
　My place with them will be,　　　　20
And I with them shall travel on
　Through all Futurity;
Yet leaving here a name, I trust,
That will not perish in the dust.

Thomas Campbell
1777–1844

Two poets enjoyed during the Romantic ascendancy
reputations which now seem inexplicably inflated,
Samuel Rogers (1763–1855) and Thomas Campbell. The
former, though a remarkable conversationalist, is not
worth representation even in so modest a garner of
gleanings as this; the latter wrote several lyrics worth
knowing. Several of them, besides the spirited poem below, are still famous: "Lord Ullin's Daughter," "Hohen-
linden," and "Battle of the Baltic." Everyone knows one
of Campbell's lines (from *Gertrude of Wyoming*): "'Tis
distance lends enchantment to the view." Campbell was
born and educated in Glasgow. At twenty-one he made
his name as a poet with a dreary exercise in heroic
couplets, "The Pleasures of Hope." He soon moved to
London, where he lived till the year of his death as a
pensioner of the government. For ten years he edited
the *New Monthly Magazine*. His poems are available in
the Oxford Standard Authors and the Aldine series.

YE MARINERS OF ENGLAND

Ye Mariners of England
That guard our native seas,
Whose flag has braved, a thousand years,
The battle and the breeze—
Your glorious standard launch again　　5

To match another foe!
And sweep through the deep,
While the stormy winds do blow,—
While the battle rages loud and long,
And the stormy winds do blow.　　　　10

The spirits of your fathers
Shall start from every wave!
For the deck it was their field of fame,
And Ocean was their grave.
Where Blake[4] and mighty Nelson fell　　15
Your manly hearts shall glow,
As ye sweep through the deep,
While the stormy winds do blow,—
While the battle rages loud and long,
And the stormy winds do blow.　　　　20

Britannia needs no bulwarks,
No towers along the steep;
Her march is o'er the mountain waves,
Her home is on the deep.
With thunders from her native oak　　25
She quells the floods below,
As they roar on the shore
When the stormy winds do blow,—
When the battle rages loud and long,
And the stormy winds do blow.　　　　30

The meteor flag of England
Shall yet terrific burn,
Till danger's troubled night depart,
And the star of peace return.
Then, then, ye ocean warriors!　　　　35
Our song and feast shall flow
To the fame of your name,
When the storm has ceased to blow,—
When the fiery fight is heard no more,
And the storm has ceased to blow.　　　40

---

[4] This poem, published in the *Morning Chronicle* in 1801, reflects
England's confidence that her fleet would keep war and invasion
from her shores. Robert Blake (1599–1657) was the great admiral
of the Parliamentary party in the Civil Wars; subsequently he
destroyed, in four engagements, the naval supremacy of the
Dutch. Lord Nelson, after repeated victories over the French,
fell in the hour of triumph at Trafalgar in 1805; the reference
to him is a later insertion.

Thomas Moore

1779–1852

WE have already met Moore as a great friend of Byron. His is another Romantic reputation which time has diminished; but Tom Moore with all his facile sentiment had a true gift of song, and while no one now thinks him a great poet, everyone is fond of his best lyrics. The son of a grocer of Dublin, he was educated there at Trinity College. Then he went to London to study law, brought out some Anacreontic verse that attracted general attention, got an appointment at Bermuda, traveled in the United States, and on the commencement (after his return to England) of the publication (with music supplied by others) of his *Irish Melodies* (1808–34) scored a lasting success, both literary and social. His own singing of his lyrics was vastly enjoyed at social gatherings; he made a happy marriage with a penniless young actress in 1811; and life, if only he could increase his income a bit, seemed destined to be a bed of roses till in 1818 the dishonesty of his Bermudan deputy plunged him into debt and he had for several years to seek a refuge on the Continent. He was also to know keen domestic grief, for his three daughters all died in childhood, and his two sons at nineteen and twenty-nine. Moore was a versatile writer: besides lyrics he wrote stinging satirical verse against the Tories. He was a Whig, a Catholic, and an advocate of reform. His *Life of Byron* (1830) is important, but his fame today rests on his songs. The standard edition of his poems is by A. D. Godley (1910); a little volume of selections was edited by C. L. Falkiner (1903). Moore's *Memoirs, Journals, and Correspondence* was published in 1853–6 (8 vols.); a selection was edited as *Tom Moore's Diary* by J. B. Priestley (1925). There are several Lives; a good one is H. M. Jones's (1937).

THE HARP THAT ONCE THROUGH TARA'S HALLS

The harp that once through Tara's[5] halls
   The soul of music shed,
Now hangs as mute on Tara's walls
   As if that soul were fled.—
So sleeps the pride of former days,   5
   So glory's thrill is o'er,
And hearts, that once beat high for praise,
   Now feel that pulse no more.

No more to chiefs and ladies bright
   The harp of Tara swells;   10
The chord alone, that breaks at night,
   Its tale of ruin tells.
Thus Freedom now so seldom wakes,
   The only throb she gives,
Is when some heart indignant breaks,   15
   To show that still she lives.

BELIEVE ME, IF ALL THOSE ENDEARING YOUNG CHARMS

Believe me, if all those endearing young charms,
   Which I gaze on so fondly to-day,
Were to change by to-morrow, and fleet in my arms,
   Like fairy-gifts fading away,
Thou wouldst still be ador'd, as this moment thou art,   5
   Let thy loveliness fade as it will,
And around the dear ruin each wish of my heart
   Would entwine itself verdantly still.

It is not while beauty and youth are thine own,
   And thy cheeks unprofan'd by a tear,   10
That the fervour and faith of a soul can be known,
   To which time will but make thee more dear;
No, the heart that has truly lov'd never forgets,
   But as truly loves on to the close,
As the sun-flower turns on her god, when he sets,   15
   The same look which she turn'd when he rose.

THE TIME I'VE LOST IN WOOING

   The time I've lost in wooing,
   In watching and pursuing
     The light that lies
     In woman's eyes,
   Has been my heart's undoing.   5
   Though Wisdom oft has sought me,
   I scorn'd the lore she brought me,
     My only books
     Were woman's looks,
   And folly's all they've taught me.   10

   Her smile when Beauty granted,
   I hung with gaze enchanted,
     Like him, the sprite,[6]
     Whom maids by night
   Oft meet in glen that's haunted.   15

---

[5] In a hall on the hill of Tara the Irish kings, bards, and clergy used to deliberate on national affairs.—All but the last of our selections are from *Irish Melodies;* the exception is from *National Airs.* The first two poems were published in 1808, the others in 1815 and 1818.

[6] Moore notes that he means a kind of Irish fairy, who appears sometimes at dusk and as long as you keep your eyes on him remains in your power. If you glance away, he vanishes.

Like him, too, Beauty won me,
But while her eyes were on me;
    If once their ray
    Was turn'd away,
O! winds could not outrun me.   20

And are those follies going?
And is my proud heart growing
    Too cold or wise
    For brilliant eyes
Again to set it glowing?   25
No, vain, alas! th' endeavour
From bonds so sweet to sever;
    Poor Wisdom's chance
    Against a glance
Is now as weak as ever.   30

OFT, IN THE STILLY NIGHT

SCOTCH AIR

Oft, in the stilly night,
    Ere Slumber's chain has bound me,
Fond Memory brings the light
    Of other days around me;
        The smiles, the tears,   5
        Of boyhood's years,
    The words of love then spoken;
        The eyes that shone,
        Now dimm'd and gone,
    The cheerful hearts now broken!   10
Thus, in the stilly night,
    Ere Slumber's chain hath bound me,
Sad Memory brings the light
    Of other days around me.

When I remember all   15
    The friends, so link'd together,
I've seen around me fall,
    Like leaves in wintry weather;
        I feel like one
        Who treads alone   20
    Some banquet-hall deserted,
        Whose lights are fled,
        Whose garlands dead,
    And all but he departed!
Thus, in the stilly night,   25
    Ere Slumber's chain has bound me,
Sad Memory brings the light
    Of other days around me.

Ebenezer Elliott

1781–1849

THIS Yorkshire poet's father was known as Devil Elliott.
The boy worked for him in his iron foundry between
the ages of sixteen and twenty-three, at nominal wages.
When he married, Ebenezer invested his wife's small
capital in his father's business, which was in a bad way,
and lost it all. In 1821, on a little money raised by his
wife's relatives, he went into the iron trade for himself at
Sheffield. He retired in 1842. Elliott illustrates the connection between the Romantic Movement and the
Reform Movement. His earlier work (1818) would not
preserve his memory, but his *Corn Law Rhymes* (1831)
gave him his sobriquet of the "Corn-Law Rhymer."
Other notable volumes are *The Village Patriarch* (1829)
and *The Splendid Village* (1833–35). Elliott was a poet of
considerable strength, with a passion for social justice. A
good deal of his verse consists of uninspired though honest
neoclassical couplets, but he deserves to be better known.
His *Poetical Works* were edited by his son, Edwin Elliott
(revised ed., 2 vols., 1876), who does not tell us when
the following denunciation of child labor was written.
Preston is a Lancashire factory city.

PRESTON MILLS

The day was fair, the cannon roar'd,
    Cold blew the bracing north,
And Preston's Mills, by thousands, pour'd
    Their little captives forth.

All in their best they paced the street,   5
    All glad that they were free;
And sung a song with voices sweet—
    They sung of Liberty!

But from their lips the rose had fled,
    Like "death-in-life"[7] they smiled;   10
And still, as each pass'd by, I said,
    Alas! is that a child?

Flags waved, and men—a ghastly crew—
    March'd with them, side by side:
While, hand in hand, and two by two,   15
    They moved—a living tide.

Thousands and thousands—all so white!—
    With eyes so glazed and dull!

---

[7] See Coleridge, "The Ancient Mariner," line 193.

O God! it was indeed a sight
  Too sadly beautiful!   20

And, oh, the pang their voices gave
  Refuses to depart!
This is a wailing for the grave!
  I whisper'd to my heart.

It was as if, where roses blush'd,   25
  A sudden blasting gale
O'er fields of bloom had rudely rush'd,
  And turn'd the roses pale.

It was as if, in glen and grove,
  The wild birds sadly sung;   30
And every linnet mourn'd its love,
  And every thrush its young.

It was as if, in dungeon gloom,
  Where chain'd despair reclined,
A sound came from the living tomb,   35
  And hymn'd the passing wind.

And while they sang, and though they smiled,
  My soul groan'd heavily—
O who would be or have a child?
  A mother who would be?   40

Leigh Hunt

1784–1859

JAMES HENRY LEIGH HUNT was a friend of many of the
greatest literary men of his time, and as a liberal journalist
he fought a good fight, which got him two years in jail.
It is for his life more than for his works that he is now
respected, though he wrote copiously in verse and prose.
He was born at Southgate near London, and educated at
Christ's Hospital. In 1808 he and his brother John started
a liberal weekly, the *Examiner,* which ran fourteen years.
He drew his jail sentence for calling the Prince Regent "a
fat Adonis of fifty." He was permitted to have his family
with him, and to receive his friends; Byron gave a dinner party in his honor at the jail. In 1822 Shelley and
Byron brought Hunt and his family to Italy to found a
new magazine. Shelley was drowned a few days later,
and the project collapsed. Hunt had a large family; and
though he was aided by friends and eventually, after the
tide had turned to reform, by the government, he was
often in financial straits. On his return to London he tried
various journalistic ventures, wrote somewhat acidly of
Byron, edited several authors, composed an autobiog-

raphy, and went on with his verse and essays. His poems
were edited (not very well) by H. S. Melford for the
Oxford Standard Authors series. Two volumes of The
World's Classics are devoted to the *Autobiography* and
some of the *Essays and Sketches;* Everyman's Library has
a volume of *Selected Essays.* There is an unsatisfactory
Life by E. Blunden (1930).

ABOU BEN ADHEM[8]

Abou Ben Adhem (may his tribe increase!)
Awoke one night from a deep dream of peace,
And saw, within the moonlight in his room,
Making it rich, and like a lily in bloom,
An angel writing in a book of gold:—   5
Exceeding peace had made Ben Adhem bold,
And to the presence in the room he said,
"What writest thou?"—The vision raised its head,
And with a look made of all sweet accord,
Answered, "The names of those who love the Lord." 10
"And is mine one?" said Abou. "Nay, not so,"
Replied the angel. Abou spoke more low,
But cheerly still; and said, "I pray thee then,
Write me as one that loves his fellow-men."

  The angel wrote, and vanished. The next night   15
It came again with a great wakening light,
And showed the names whom love of God had blessed,
And lo! Ben Adhem's name led all the rest.

THE FISH, THE MAN, AND THE SPIRIT[9]

TO A FISH

You strange, astonished-looking, angle-faced,
  Dreary-mouthed, gaping wretches of the sea,
  Gulping salt-water everlastingly,
Cold-blooded, though with red your blood be graced,
And mute, though dwellers in the roaring waste;   5
  And you, all shapes beside, that fishy be,—
  Some round, some flat, some long, all devilry,
Legless, unloving, infamously chaste:—

O scaly, slippery, wet, swift, staring wights,
  What is't ye do? What life lead? eh, dull goggles?   10
How do ye vary your vile days and nights?
  How pass your Sundays? Are ye still but joggles
In ceaseless wash? Still nought but gapes and bites,
  And drinks, and stares, diversified with boggles?[10]

[8] Hunt's source for this poem (published in 1838) was the *Bib-
liothèque Orientale* of Barthélemy d'Herbelot, a seventeenth-
century French orientalist.
[9] This poem was published in 1836.   [10] Startled shyings away.

Amazing monster! that, for aught I know,   15
  With the first sight of thee didst make our race
  For ever stare! O flat and shocking face,
Grimly divided from the breast below!
Thou that on dry land horribly dost go
  With a split body and most ridiculous pace,   20
  Prong after prong, disgracer of all grace,
Long-useless-finned, haired, upright, unwet, slow!

O breather of the unbreathable, sword-sharp air,
  How canst exist? How bear thyself, thou dry
And dreary sloth? What particle canst share   25
  Of the only blessèd life, the watery?
I sometimes see of ye an actual *pair*
  Go by! linked fin by fin! most odiously.

THE FISH TURNS INTO A MAN, AND THEN INTO A SPIRIT, AND AGAIN SPEAKS

Indulge thy smiling scorn, if smiling still,
  O man! and loathe, but with a sort of love;   30
  For difference must its use by difference prove,
And, in sweet clang, the spheres with music fill.
One of the spirits am I, that at his will
  Live in what'er has life—fish, eagle, dove—
  No hate, no pride, beneath nought, nor above,   35
A visitor of the rounds of God's sweet skill.

Man's life is warm, glad, sad, 'twixt loves and graves,
  Boundless in hope, honoured with pangs austere,
Heaven-gazing; and his angel-wings he craves:—
  The fish is swift, small-needing, vague yet clear,   40
A cold, sweet, silver life, wrapped in round waves,
  Quickened with touches of transporting fear.

RONDEAU[11]

Jenny kissed me when we met,
  Jumping from the chair she sat in;
Time, you thief, who love to get
  Sweets into your list, put that in:
Say I'm weary, say I'm sad,   5
  Say that health and wealth have missed me,
Say I'm growing old, but add,
  Jenny kissed me.

---

[11] Despite its title, this delightful poem is not a rondeau, which is a complicated thirteen-line stanza invented by the French. Some think Jenny was Jane Carlyle; Hunt was a friend of the Carlyles. There are, however, other candidates, and it was *Nelly,* not *Jenny,* when the poem was first printed, in 1838.

Thomas Hood

1799–1845

LIKE Ebenezer Elliott, Hood is included here as a poet of social protest, though his poems range from comic pieces in a punning vein to romantic verse showing the influence of Keats. His writings appeared in a number of journals and miscellanies and were widely read. "The Song of the Shirt" was first printed in the Christmas number of *Punch* for 1843. W. Jerrold edited the *Poetical Works* (1906) and also wrote a biography of Hood (1907).

THE SONG OF THE SHIRT

With fingers weary and worn,
  With eyelids heavy and red,
A woman sat, in unwomanly rags,
  Plying her needle and thread—
Stitch! stitch! stitch!   5
  In poverty, hunger, and dirt,
And still with a voice of dolorous pitch
  She sang the "Song of the Shirt."

"Work! work! work!
  While the cock is crowing aloof!   10
And work—work—work,
  Till the stars shine through the roof!
It's Oh! to be a slave
  Along with the barbarous Turk,
Where woman has never a soul to save,   15
  If this is Christian work.

"Work—work—work,
  Till the brain begins to swim;
Work—work—work,
  Till the eyes are heavy and dim!   20
Seam, and gusset, and band,
  Band, and gusset, and seam,
Till over the buttons I fall asleep,
  And sew them on in a dream!

"Oh, men, with sisters dear!   25
  Oh, men, with mothers and wives!
It is not linen you're wearing out
  But human creatures' lives!
Stitch—stitch—stitch,
  In poverty, hunger, and dirt,   30
Sewing at once, with a double thread,
  A Shroud as well as a Shirt.

"But why do I talk of Death?
  That phantom of grisly bone,
I hardly fear its terrible shape,   35
  It seems so like my own—
It seems so like my own,
  Because of the fasts I keep;
Oh, God! that bread should be so dear,
  And flesh and blood so cheap!   40

"Work—work—work!
  My labor never flags;
And what are its wages? A bed of straw,
  A crust of bread—and rags.
That shattered roof—this naked floor— 45
  A table—a broken chair—
And a wall so blank, my shadow I thank
  For sometimes falling there!

"Work—work—work!
  From weary chime to chime,   50
Work—work—work,
  As prisoners work for crime!
Band, and gusset, and seam,
  Seam, and gusset, and band,
Till the heart is sick, and the brain benumbed,
  As well as the weary hand.   56

"Work—work—work,
  In the dull December light,
And work—work—work,
  When the weather is warm and bright— 60
While underneath the eaves
  The brooding swallows cling
As if to show me their sunny backs
  And twit me with the spring.

"Oh! but to breathe the breath   65
  Of the cowslip and primrose sweet—
With the sky above my head,
  And the grass beneath my feet;
For only one short hour
  To feel as I used to feel,   70
Before I knew the woes of want
  And the walk that costs a meal.

"Oh! but for one short hour!
  A respite however brief!
No blessèd leisure for love or hope,   75
  But only time for grief!
A little weeping would ease my heart,
  But in their briny bed
My tears must stop, for every drop
  Hinders needle and thread!"   80

Seam, and gusset, and band,
  Band, and gusset, and seam,
Work—work—work,
  Like the engine that works by steam!
A mere machine of iron and wood   85
  That toils for Mammon's sake,
Without a brain to ponder and craze
  Or a heart to feel—and break!

With fingers weary and worn,
  With eyelids heavy and red,   90
A woman sat, in unwomanly rags,
  Plying her needle and thread—
Stitch! stitch! stitch!
  In poverty, hunger, and dirt,
And still with a voice of dolorous pitch— 95
Would that its tone could reach the rich!—
  She sang this "Song of the Shirt!"

Thomas Lovell Beddoes

1803–1849

NONE of the minor Romantics has a more original or arresting voice than this poet, physiologist, and liberal, who might have felt more at home in the seventeenth than in the nineteenth century. There is in many of his poems a macabre quality reminiscent of John Webster. Beddoes was preoccupied with the thought of death, and he died by his own hand. The son of a well-known doctor, he was educated at the Charterhouse and Oxford and then went to Germany to study anatomy at Göttingen. He was still an undergraduate when his poetic drama *The Bride's Tragedy* was printed and enthusiastically reviewed. Most of his adult life was spent on the Continent, especially in Germany and Switzerland; not much is known about it in detail. He established connections with a number of revolutionary movements. Beddoes wrote voluminously, but aside from a few poems and articles he published only one play and one volume of poetry. He was, says his latest editor, "a poet of fragments." Often he could not make up his mind which of several versions was to be final. The *Works* have been edited by H. W. Donner (1935), who is also author of a *Life* (1935).

SONG[12]

How many times do I love thee, dear?
  Tell me how many thoughts there be

---

[12] This exquisite lyric is from the unfinished verse play *Torrismond*, written in 1824.

In the atmosphere
Of a new-fall'n year,
Whose white and sable hours appear 5
The latest flake of Eternity:—
So many times do I love thee, dear.

How many times do I love again?
Tell me how many beads there are
In a silver chain 10
Of evening rain,
Unravelled from the tumbling main,
And threading the eye of a yellow star:—
So many times do I love again.

THRENODY[13]

No sunny ray, no silver night,
Cruelly alight!
Glare of noontide, star of e'en,
Otherwhere descend!
No violet-eyed green, 5
Bare its daisies' yellow end,
The dewy debt receive of any eye!
It is a grave: and she doth lie
'Neath roses' root,
And the fawn's mossy foot, 10
Under the skylark's floor,
Whose graceful life held every day—
As lilies, dew—as dews, the starry ray—
More music, grace, delight than they.
When stars are few let light be here, 15
Of the softest, through the boughs
Berry-laden, sad and few;
And the wings of one small bird,
His form unseen, his voice unheard—

SONG[14]

Old Adam, the carrion crow,
The old crow of Cairo;
He sat in the shower, and let it flow
Under his tail and over his crest;
And through every feather 5
Leaked the wet weather;
And the bough swung under his nest;
For his beak it was heavy with marrow.
Is that the wind dying? O no;
It's only two devils, that blow 10

Through a murderer's bones, to and fro,
In the ghosts' moonshine.

Ho! Eve, my grey carrion wife,
When we have supped on king's marrow,
Where shall we drink and make merry our life?
Our nest it is queen Cleopatra's skull, 16
'Tis cloven and cracked,
And battered and hacked,
But with tears of blue eyes it is full:
Let us drink them, my raven of Cairo. 20
Is that the wind dying? O no;
It's only two devils, that blow
Through a murderer's bones, to and fro,
In the ghosts' moonshine.

DREAM-PEDLARY

If there were dreams to sell,
What would you buy?
Some cost a passing bell;[15]
Some a light sigh,
That shakes from Life's fresh crown 5
Only a roseleaf down.
If there were dreams to sell,
Merry and sad to tell,
And the crier rung the bell,
What would you buy? 10

A cottage lone and still,
With bowers nigh,
Shadowy, my woes to still,
Until I die.
Such pearls from Life's fresh crown 15
Fain would I shake me down.
Were dreams to have at will,
This would best heal my ill,
This would I buy.

But[16] there were dreams to sell 20
Ill didst thou buy;
Life is a dream, they tell,
Waking, to die.
Dreaming a dream to prize,
Is wishing ghosts to rise; 25
And if I had the spell
To call the buried, well,
Which one would I?

[13] Dirge. When this beautiful fragment was composed is uncertain; perhaps about 1825.
[14] From a version (1825–9) of the verse drama *Death's Jest-Book*.
[15] I.e., some dreams cost your life.—This is Beddoes's best-known poem. It was written between 1824 and 1844.
[16] Unless.

If there are ghosts to raise,
  What shall I call,   30
Out of hell's murky haze,
  Heaven's blue hall?
Raise my loved longlost boy
To lead me to his joy.
There are no ghosts to raise;   35
Out of death lead no ways;
  Vain is the call.

Know'st thou not ghosts to sue?
  No love thou hast.
Else lie, as I will do,   40
  And breathe thy last.
So out of Life's fresh crown
Fall like a rose-leaf down.
Thus are the ghosts to woo;
Thus are all dreams made true,   45
  Ever to last!

THE PHANTOM-WOOER[17]

A ghost, that loved a lady fair,
Ever in the starry air
  Of midnight at her pillow stood;
And, with a sweetness skies above
The luring words of human love,   5
  Her soul the phantom wooed.
Sweet and sweet is their poisoned note,
The little snakes of silver throat,
In mossy skulls that nest and lie,
Ever singing "die, oh! die."   10

Young soul put off your flesh, and come
With me into the quiet tomb,
  Our bed is lovely, dark, and sweet;
The earth will swing us, as she goes,
Beneath our coverlid of snows,   15
  And the warm leaden sheet.
Dear and dear is their poisoned note,
The little snakes of silver throat,
In mossy skulls that nest and lie,
Ever singing "die, oh! die."   20

A BEAUTIFUL NIGHT[18]

How lovely is the heaven of this night,
How deadly still its earth. The forest brute
Has crept into his cave, and laid himself
Where sleep has made him harmless like the lamb;
The horrid snake, his venom now forgot,   5
Is still and innocent as the honied flower
Under his head:—and man, in whom are met
Leopard and snake,—and all the gentleness
And beauty of the young lamb and the bud,
Has let his ghost out, put his thoughts aside   10
And lent his senses unto death himself;
Whereby the King and beggar all lie down
On straw or purple-tissue, are but bones
And air, and blood, equal to one another
And to the unborn and buried: so we go   15
Placing ourselves among the unconceived
And the old ghosts, wantonly, smilingly,
For sleep is fair and warm—

---

[17] Composed in 1844–48.

[18] This is a fragment from a later version of *Death's Jest-Book*, composed 1829–49.

The Victorian Period

THE VICTORIAN PERIOD

THE CHARACTER OF THE AGE

WHEN a writer in the *Edinburgh Review* for July, 1858, asked himself how best to describe "the remarkable period in which our own lot is cast," he did not call it the age of democracy or industry or science; still less, the age of moral earnestness and complacency. He seized on one characteristic which affirmed "a fact equally obvious and certain, . . . that we are living in *an age of transition;*—a period when changes, deeply and permanently affecting the whole condition of mankind, are occurring more rapidly, as well as [more] extensively, than at any prior time in human history." Other ages, of course, notably the Renaissance and the seventeenth century, have been periods of unusually rapid change and transition. What distinguishes the nineteenth century is the widespread consciousness of what was taking place. As Mill pointed out in his important essays of 1831 on *The Spirit of the Age* (the first of which, printed below, pp. 534 ff., is a fine introduction to the period), "The idea of comparing one's own age with former ages . . . had occurred to philosophers; but it never before was itself the dominant idea of any age." Never before had men been so acutely aware that their own times were "distinguished in a very remarkable manner from the times which preceded them." What did the Victorians mean by the times which preceded them? What did they think, by contrast, distinguished their own age?

In their minds the past was not the Romantic period and not even the eighteenth century. It was the Middle Ages. From their perspective it was the medieval tradition from which they had irrevocably broken—Christian orthodoxy under the rule of the Church, and civil government under the rule of king and nobility; the social structure of fixed classes, each with its recognized rights and duties; and the economic organization of village agriculture and town guilds. The breakup of this whole pattern of life and thought began with the Renaissance and Reformation, continued, quietly but steadily, through the next two centuries of philosophical rationalism and expanding business, and finally reached a point of conscious recognition when it "invaded outward objects." The French Revolution (1789), with its democratic appeal to the Rights of Man and its atheistical worship of the Goddess of Reason, was the first overt manifestation, in Mill's opinion, that Europe had entered into a state of transition. But in England the signs were not clearly recognized until the 1820's, at the threshold of the Victorian period.

Then it was that the rising agitation for an extension of the suffrage showed "that those were indeed new men, who insisted upon being governed in a new way." The new men were the captains of industry; and the new form of government which they demanded—and attained in 1832 with the passage of the Reform Bill—was a middle-class democracy. But the bloodless revolution which brought them to political power was simply the result of the more fundamental industrial and agrarian revolutions which gave them financial power. The crucial inventions—the steam engine, the spinning jenny, the water frame, the power loom, smelting by pit coal, and the application of the steam engine to blast furnaces—all date from the second half of the eighteenth century. In the following decades, the great improvement in the means of communication achieved by more canals, macadam roads, railways, and steamboats, hastened the growth of large-scale manufacturing by making possible a vast expansion of commerce. And just when the factories needed workmen in large numbers, the enclosure acts, as well as a sizable increase of population, provided the man power.

This industrial expansion radically altered the character of economic life:

In the towns the old theory of a "limited" and "well-regulated" trade, based on the local monopoly of a chartered few, subjecting themselves to a common set of rules about trade and apprenticeship, was . . . abandoned for the new principle of open world-competition wherein all traders who could muster the capital and enterprise were invited to buy in the cheapest market and sell in the dearest, and to hire their labour wherever they liked and on what conditions each could secure. The change, in town as well as country, caused a wide cleavage of sympathy and of interest between classes which had previously shared, each in its degree, the common advantages of a fixed system of life and work; now that everyone scrambled for himself, the rich became richer and the poor poorer. (G. M. Trevelyan)

Small wonder that in 1833 Bulwer-Lytton made the point that although "every age may be called an age of transition, . . . in our age the transition is *visible*." The first great change which sets off the Victorian era from the past was the arrival of big business and middle-class government.

The second is of a wholly different nature, though no less impressive and radical. It is the emergence, on a wide scale, of religious doubt, meaning either outright skepticism and the adoption of some purely secular and agnostic philosophy, or, more commonly, a state of hesitation and uncertainty, often half conscious, not merely between belief and unbelief in a supernatural reality, but also between conflicting forms of faith. If there is a supernatural reality, is its character revealed in Protestantism? (and if so, in which form of Protestantism?) or in Roman Catholicism? or simply in Theism? It is quite true that infidelity had been common among the eighteenth-century intellectuals, but it was not until the 1820's that the religious tradition began to lose its unquestioned authority in society as a whole, and that the doubt which once had hung, as Carlyle says, "in the background of our world," spread outward to the middle ground, and later to the foreground. By 1870, after the theory of evolution and Biblical criticism had added their dissolving influences, John Morley might well say that the age was "characteristically and cardinally an epoch of transition in the very foundations of belief and conduct."

The Victorian period was therefore conditioned, in its thinking, in its psychological atmosphere, in its moral and intellectual temper, by the two overwhelming facts which mark the difference between the nineteenth century and any previous period of modern history, bourgeois industrial society and the disintegration of Christian thought. Those crucial factors, which are everywhere reflected, directly or indirectly, in Victorian literature, are summed up in two pertinent descriptions of the time, the first by Herbert Spencer, the second by John Ruskin:

Throughout the civilized world, especially in England, and above all in America, social activity is almost wholly expended in material development. To subjugate Nature, and bring the powers of production and distribution to

their highest perfection, is the task of our age. . . . When the chief desideratum is industrial growth, honour is most conspicuously given to that which generally indicates the aiding of industrial growth. The English nation at present displays what we may call the commercial diathesis.

There never yet was a generation of men (savage or civilized) who, taken as a body, so wofully fulfilled the words "having no hope, and without God in the world," as the present civilized European race. . . . Nearly all our powerful men in this age of the world are unbelievers; the best of them in doubt and misery; the worst in reckless defiance; the plurality, in plodding hesitation, doing, as well as they can, what practical work lies ready to their hands. . . . Our earnest poets and deepest thinkers are doubtful and indignant (Tennyson, Carlyle).

Could not both quotations apply as well, almost, to our own period? We have a tendency to adopt a scornful or amused attitude toward the Victorians, as though we were quite different—and much superior. But the fact is that our social and religious situation is fundamentally the same; the age of transition still continues, and no social institutions nor any philosophy of life remotely so stable and widely accepted as those of the Middle Ages have yet emerged. That is why Victorian literature, especially its prose, is so alive today. It explores the very problems raised by the industrial and intellectual revolutions which are our problems too. Its analysis and criticism, both pro and con, of democracy and dictatorship, of free enterprise and socialism, and its various efforts to resolve the conflict of religion and science, speak to us directly. 1850 simply marks an earlier stage of the ideological conflicts of 1950. Their original shape and the various solutions which were proposed, first in the social area and then in the religious, are outlined in the sections that follow.

SOCIETY: THE PHILOSOPHY OF THE MIDDLE CLASS

On the strength of the Industrial Revolution, the new capitalists became the most powerful class in English society—potentially, but not yet actually. For they were excluded from the political life of the nation. The world of the 1820's was still the world of the old aristocracy in which a whole series of laws restrained the liberty of everyone who was not an aristocrat. Consider the humiliating position in the year 1825 of a successful Manchester businessman who happened to be a Presbyterian or a Congregationalist, a Baptist, a Quaker, or a Methodist, maybe a Jew or a Roman Catholic, in short anything except an Anglican (a member of the Church of

England). And he probably wasn't an Anglican, because the middle class since the seventeenth century had been very largely Puritan; it was the aristocracy that was solidly Anglican. This admirable citizen could not hold any office under the Crown, in the army, navy, or civil service; he could not sit on the Town Corporation, the governing board of his city; he could not graduate from either Oxford or Cambridge (the only universities in England at the time); he could not run his business efficiently because he was hampered by innumerable and now antiquated restrictions, especially a long series of Navigation Acts. Above all, he had no voice in the national government: he had no vote and, still worse, no representation in Parliament because the electoral districts had been drawn up centuries before, when Manchester and other industrial cities did not exist, and had never been revised. These are the circumstances in which Victorian liberalism was born. The middle class demanded freedom from the old aristocratic-Anglican restrictions. They wanted an extension of the franchise and the repeal of class legislation. This meant, theoretically, a democratic, or at any rate a partly democratic, form of government to replace the old constitution in which England had been ruled by the king and an oligarchy of landed nobility; and it meant, so far as power was concerned, that the government should be severely limited to the function of keeping public order, and should no longer interfere with the equal liberties of all citizens, regardless of creed or wealth. This is the liberal program which was carried to success between 1825 and 1835. The passage of the Reform Bill in 1832, which enfranchised half the middle class (the upper capitalist group) signalized its victory.

The political philosophy which expressed and formulated the concrete demands of the bourgeoisie had been worked out through the eighteenth century, notably by Locke and Rousseau, and been given embodiment in the French Rights of Man and in our own Declaration of Independence. For the Victorians, however, it was Jeremy Bentham and his disciples, known as the Utilitarians, who provided the middle class with their political theory. Bentham's starting point was the assumption that, whatever their pretensions, men are motivated, at bottom, by self-interest—that is to say, their real aim in life is to have as much pleasure and suffer as little pain as possible. It followed, therefore, that the purpose of government should be to promote "the greatest happiness of the greatest number." Whatever made for general happiness he called a useful law or a useful act of government. Whatever made for general

unhappiness was a useless law or a useless act of government. Hence the term Utilitarianism in its political application. On this premise Bentham based his argument for democracy. Would a monarchy promote the greatest good of the greatest number? By no means; it would promote the greatest good of the monarch. Would an oligarchy do it? Again no; it would promote its own good. Would a democracy do it? Yes, obviously, because then the government would be in the hands of the people, and the people would inevitably act for the greatest good of the people. Later in the century, John Stuart Mill put the liberal argument for democracy on firmer and wider grounds (see p. 518).

Finally, on the extent of state control, it is quite true that Bentham's first principle could have justified almost any amount of interference. If the purpose of government is to promote the general happiness, then it *may* do anything, and *should* do anything, that will achieve that end—even, in theory, the abolition of private property. And as a matter of fact, Benthamism had its influence, ironically enough, on the growth of English Socialism. Ironically, because no one would have been more horrified at such a result than the Benthamites. After all, their sympathies, conscious or otherwise, were strongly middle-class; and they staunchly believed in the utility of private property and the maximum amount of personal and business freedom. From their point of view, government would promote the general happiness by interfering just as little as possible. It *could* do anything, but it *would* do very little. And for two reasons, as stated by Bentham:

The motto, or watchword of government, . . . ought to be—*Be quiet.* For this quietism there are two main reasons:—1. Generally speaking, any interference . . . on the part of government is *needless.* . . . There is no one who knows what is for your interest, so well as yourself—no one who is disposed with so much ardor and constancy to pursue it. 2. Generally speaking, it is moreover likely to be pernicious . . . by the restraint or constraint imposed on the free agency of the individual. Pain is the general concomitant of the sense of such restraint, wherever it is experienced. . . . With few exceptions, and those not very considerable ones, the attainment of the maximum enjoyment will be most effectually secured by leaving each individual to pursue his own maximum of enjoyment.

Then Bentham adds a statement which at once reveals the connection of his theory with the economic desires of the middle class: "*Security* and *freedom* are all that industry requires. The request which agriculture, manufacturers, and commerce present to governments, is modest and reasonable as that which Diogenes made to Alexander: 'Stand out of my sunshine.' " In a word, the policy of the government should be *laissez faire*—hands off.

Especially with regard to business. The middle-class theory of political economy, which Bentham and the Utilitarians adopted, had been first formulated by Adam Smith in his famous and influential book on *The Wealth of Nations* (1776). He had argued that if the real value of the annual produce of a nation's land and labor was to be increased (as, of course, it should be), the government must limit itself to three duties: protecting the country from foreign invasion, protecting every citizen from the oppression of any other citizen, and erecting certain public institutions like law courts, post offices, and schools. Moreover, business was to be free not only from government interference but also from the whole system of local and guild regulation which, as we saw earlier, was breaking down in fact. If only all forms of preference and restraint were removed, and every man, worker or capitalist, "as long as he does not violate the laws of justice, is left perfectly free to pursue his own interest his own way, and to bring both his industry and capital into competition with those of any other man, or order of men," then the economic machine would function "naturally" and most efficiently—for the greatest good of the greatest number. Nothing is more characteristic of the liberal mind than this confidence in "free enterprise," this faith that unrestricted competition is at once the ideal means to develop the individual (the strongest survive, the weakest go down) and to give society the best products at the lowest prices.

The blessings of this liberal economy were not particularly apparent, however, to the millions of men, women, and children who, in the absence of any protection from either the state or effective trade unions, were exploited with a ruthlessness that has perhaps never been paralleled.

Official reports describe children of from six to eight working ten or twelve hours a day as stocking weavers, often fainting at their work, and slowly losing their eyesight. They describe needle-women who received 1½ pence for a shirt, and others who were paid 4½ pence a week for working sixteen hours a day on neckties. They speak of child labor in the mines, arsenic poisoning in the potteries, men fined for talking at their work, women in the last stages of pregnancy fined for sitting down. They record that one-fifth of the population of Liverpool lived in cellars, that 12,000 persons lived in 1400 houses in a London block four hundred yards square, that twenty persons could be found lying huddled on the floor of a single Glasgow room. This was the fruit of the industrial revolution.[1]

Efforts to relieve this situation by government action were few and feeble until late in the century, for the theory of *laissez faire*, which Adam Smith had applied to commerce, had been extended to industry by T. R. Malthus and David Ricardo. They were the creators of what Carlyle later called "the dismal science." "Dismal" is a masterly understatement for their theoretical argument against any alleviation of these appalling conditions, whether by government action or by private charity. The supposed "iron laws" of supply and demand made all interference useless. If wages were raised, population would increase, and the larger supply of labor would simply bring wages back to where they had been. Charity, public or private, not only encouraged idleness but tended to increase population and therefore to lower wages and intensify the struggle for survival. "To prevent the recurrence of misery, is, alas! beyond the power of man." The only possible alleviation was for the workers to limit the number of their children, and thus, by decreasing the supply of labor, to increase their wages.

Finally, implicit in the whole theory of liberalism, political and economic, is a new theory of society. It is no longer thought of in feudal terms as an organism or a partnership like a family, whose various members, each holding a fixed status in the hierarchy, were united by mutual obligations and loyalties. It is now considered a collection of individuals, each motivated by self-interest, each free to sell or purchase his labor in free competition at the best possible price. The bond between man and man is solely contractual, or, in Carlyle's famous phrase, "cash-nexus." But this is all to the good, because to do the best for yourself is to do the best for society. That is the very core of the liberal faith.

So much for the abstractions of philosophy. What is the concrete outlook of the middle class? Or to put it another way, what did it feel like to belong to a society dedicated to commercial expansion? Under what conditions would you have lived? By what characteristic goals, personal and national? By what moral ideals and intellectual standards of value? When those questions are explored, we can then answer for ourselves the more important question of

---

[1] Granville Hicks, *Figures in Transition*, p. 6. (Copyright 1939 by The Macmillan Company, and used with their permission.)

whether or not the temper of society today is very different.

In such a competitive system, business success, or even survival, demanded an economic struggle far beyond anything known before. And since new and ever more distant sources of supply were being opened up by the railroad and the steamship, there was the additional battle for new markets. Moreover, as the standard of living went up, the measure of sufficiency went up too; and the son fought for comforts which his father had had no incentive to strive for. Under these conditions the pressure of work was immensely increased. England became in literal fact the workshop of the world; and Englishmen, Emerson estimated, worked three times as hard as Europeans. In the professions, too, the immense competition for preferment made work and hard work "the only way now-a-days to rise." W. R. Greg's picture of English life in 1851 is hardly exaggerated:

The excessive toil required in nearly every occupation —the severity of the struggle for existence—the strain upon the powers of every man who runs the race of life in this land and age of high excitement, . . . is by no means confined to the lower orders. Throughout the whole community we are all called to labour too early and compelled to labour too severely and too long. We live sadly too fast. Our existence, in nearly all ranks, is a crush, a struggle, and a strife.

As Greg notices, the competition was not only stiff but fast. The tempo of business life had increased with its size:

Compare the magnitude and complexity of your business transactions, the rapidity, decision, and energy with which they have to be conducted, the incessant strain of thought and care which they involve, with the easy, methodical round of commerce in the days when the goods train, the ocean steamship, and the electric telegraph were unknown. (J. B. Brown in 1871)

These inventions, incidentally, stepped up the speed of life throughout the society; and though faster machines have been invented in our own times, the feeling of being rushed was every bit as great then as now. "That constant sense of being driven—not precisely like 'dumb' cattle, but cattle who must read, write, and talk more in twenty-four hours than twenty-four hours will permit, can never have been known to them." That sounds exactly like someone today talking of the Victorians. Actually it is Frances Cobbe in 1864 talking of the pre-Victorians.

The high pressure of business life was further intensified by the characteristic goals of a bourgeois society. When Spencer referred to England as being in the "commercial diathesis," he at once added, "and the undue admiration for wealth appears to be its concomitant—a relation still more conspicuous in the worship of 'the almighty dollar' by the Americans." But it was not so much wealth itself which motivated the economic struggle and won prestige as it was the social position which wealth could buy. The passion for money was complemented by the passion for social advancement. By 1840 Mill found the latter a major characteristic of English life:

In England, as well as in America, it appears to foreigners, and even to Englishmen recently returned from a foreign country, as if everybody had but one wish—to improve his condition, never to enjoy it; as if no Englishman cared to cultivate either the pleasures or the virtues corresponding to his station in society, but solely to get out of it as quickly as possible; or if that cannot be done, and until it is done, to seem to have got out of it.

It was the breakdown of class barriers, consequent upon the increasing wealth of the bourgeoisie and the declining wealth of the aristocracy, which made this ambition practical. "Now that a man may make money," said Ruskin, "and rise in the world, and associate himself, unreproached, with people once far above him, . . . it becomes a veritable shame to him to remain in the state he was born in, and everybody thinks it is his duty to try to be a 'gentleman.'" We must recognize the precision and importance, here, of the word "duty." The ambition to better one's position was rationalized by the liberal theory, mentioned above, that to do the best for yourself was to do the best for society. Beatrice Webb has described the creed of self-advancement as she knew it in her own middle-class home:

It was the bounden duty of every citizen to better his social status; to ignore those beneath him, and to aim steadily at the top rung of the social ladder. Only by this persistent pursuit by each individual of his own and his family's interest would the highest general level of civilisation be attained. . . . No one of the present generation realises with what sincerity and fervour these doctrines were held by the representative men and women of the mid-Victorian middle class.

However hard their conditions of life, their mood —and therefore the mood of the age—was highly optimistic. Individual success was part cause, part result of national success. England too was making money and advancing up the national ladder. Before Germany and the United States began to catch up late in the century, she had no rivals in industrial power, and from 1850 to 1914 was top nation of the world. Englishmen had good reason to view their achievement with pride and satisfaction, and natural, if not good, reason to view it, by moments, with a complacent and bumptious air of self-congratulation. Macaulay talked of his countrymen as "the greatest and most highly civilised people that ever the world saw," and boasted of their carrying "the means of locomotion and correspondence, every mechanical art, every manufacture, everything that promotes the convenience of life, to a perfection which our ancestors would have thought magical." (See also the salute to English science and commerce by Carlyle, pp. 427–29, below.)

We notice here the identification of civilization with material power; and it is true that Victorian pride was often founded on a childish admiration for mere size and quantity, for longer lines of railroads, more tons of coal, greater national income. (See Arnold's criticism, p. 761, below.) But not entirely. The worship of science and industry often sprang from a spontaneous admiration of the power of man to conquer nature, to discover her secrets and transform her material resources into productive usefulness. Why is Manchester at 5:30 a. m., with all the factory whistles blowing, a thrilling sight even to a man like Carlyle, so indignant at the condition of the workers and the Mammonism of the capitalists? Because it symbolizes "the triumph of man over matter" and bears victorious witness to his "manufacturing, commercial, economic *skill.*" It is the new sense of enormous technological and executive power, "the mastery, the achieve of the thing," quite as much as its actual "fruits," which won the glowing admiration of the Victorians and provoked much of their patriotic pride.

If they viewed the present with satisfaction, they looked to the future with unbounded hope. It was an age of great expectations. With so much already accomplished, and in so short a time, what wonders lie ahead! Macaulay's glamorous prophecy of the world of 1930—the population quadrupled, national income enormously expanded, "machines constructed on principles yet undiscovered" in every house, etc. (see pp. 460 f., below)—is a perfect index not only to the confident faith in progress but to its scientific basis and its predominantly material character. The law of Baconian philosophy, Macaulay said, is that "a point which yesterday was invisible is its goal today, and will be its starting-post tomorrow"; its end and aim, to increase the comforts and mitigate the pains of human life. After a hundred years of such progress, we are no longer so certain that it is the

summum bonum, or that Baconian science is the only philosophy we need. It is fair to add, however, that Macaulay and the middle class believed that scientific progress would mean moral progress as well. And to some extent they were right. Better health and better morals go together, as Kingsley and Dickens never tired of pointing out. Better conditions of living, consequent upon the cheaper cost of clothing and household supplies, make for a happier and more law-abiding population. But this line of thought was pushed to fantastic extremes. It was supposed (by Macaulay) that "every improvement of the means of locomotion . . . tends to remove national and provincial antipathies, and to bind together all the branches of the great human family," until—war would be a thing of the past! Nothing Victorian is more curious, and ironic, than the confident association of world peace with scientific progress, on the ground that international communication would replace the prejudice of insularity by friendly understanding and provide each nation with a ready market for its goods. Indeed, Herbert Spencer thought that the new industrial age *must* put an end to war by diffusing economic opportunities and benefits over the whole world, and making peace a requirement of prosperity. As capital became international and a thousand investments crossed every frontier, international peace would become a necessity. Great expectations indeed! And in Tennyson's "Locksley Hall" (p. 656) they even include "the Parliament of man, the Federation of the world." As a matter of fact, our own desire for world federation has its source in scientific progress, but of a kind the Victorians never conceived of. The age of optimism is long past.

Consonant with their conception of progress is the middle-class attitude toward intellectual culture. In lives so immersed in business, the test of value is utility conceived in terms of tangible and practical results. Thought is only useful, therefore, if it issues in better machinery, political, social, or mechanical. The investigation of truth as truth, the free play of the mind on subjects of "no practical account," is viewed with indifference and sometimes scorn. The man of action is exalted at the expense of the thinker and the artist; and the humanities, art, philosophy, literature, even history, are condemned as useless or patronized for "cultural"—that is, social—reasons. With heavy sarcasm, a writer in the Utilitarian *Westminster Review* asked to be informed how the "pursuit of literature and poetry . . . is to conduce towards cotton-spinning." The Society for the Diffusion of Useful Knowledge was founded in

1827, and the liberal reviews carried on a campaign to transform the old classical education into the study, primarily, of the natural and social sciences. Even a man like Charles Kingsley could tell the students of Wellington College that "only the knowledge which you get by observation" is power, and that the shrewd fellow who has an eye for facts and can turn them "to some particular use" will leave the man of book learning far behind in the race of life. The notion that books may so broaden and deepen one's knowledge of life, and so sharpen one's perceptions, that he can judge more intelligently and live more wisely, has dropped out of Kingsley's mind, and, to a large extent, out of the Victorian—in fact, the modern—mind. In bourgeois society the conception of utility became too narrow to include the great but intangible utility of the humanities, or to recognize the importance of what Arnold called "the whole life of the intelligence." This is not to imply that the age of Mill and Darwin did not make significant contributions to thought, or that there were not many Victorians who valued intellectual culture in theory and demonstrated it in practice—to the point in some cases, notably those of Newman and Arnold, of attacking the contemporary "preference of doing to thinking." But when we realize that "intellectuals" like Carlyle and Froude, Kingsley and Macaulay, were so infected by the bias of commercial life that they could support that preference (though for other reasons too, as we shall see), we have a measure of how deeply anti-intellectualism had permeated Victorian society.

But whatever its blindness to intellectual values, the middle class was keenly alive to moral values; and these are ultimately the more important. As Lecky pointed out, the Victorians owed their commercial success, personal and national, less to their intellect than to their character, specifically to their possession of what he significantly calls the "industrial virtues." "Temperance, industry, integrity, frugality, self-reliance, and self-restraint are the means by which the great masses of men rise from penury to comfort, and it is the nations in which these qualities are most diffused that in the long run are the most prosperous." These virtues had the further sanction of Puritanism, which had always been strong, and still was, among the middle class. The greatest, that is, the most compulsive, of them all was the second which Lecky mentions, industry. The duty to work (and conversely the sinfulness of not working) was at once a Puritan dogma and an economic necessity for social and financial success. Under that double pressure it was built into the Victorian temper so firmly that we

still feel its urgency today. The younger Thomas Arnold wrote of his father: "For all his children, the precept flowed steadily from his life, still more from his lips, 'Work.' Not, work at this or that—but, work." The Victorians could not understand what the Romantics meant by "wise passiveness." It was a contradiction in terms, and morally suspect. The only excuse for idleness was illness, even among the gentry. Sir Michael, in Mrs. Braddon's novel, *Lady Audley's Secret,* went "to his dressing-room to prepare for dinner after a day of lazy enjoyment, that is only legitimate for an invalid."

It is quite true, of course, that the ethical code was not always obeyed. There is plenty of evidence of immorality among the moral Victorians. Their ideal was too high for human nature: hence the discrepancy between their professions and their practice which we now call their hypocrisy. But on the whole, public and private life reached a higher level of moral probity than ever before or since. Certainly the Victorians would have been shocked by our moral skepticism, our bland uncertainty of what if any moral principles we should live by.

THE REACTION AGAINST POLITICAL LIBERALISM AND INDUSTRIAL SOCIETY

ALTHOUGH the middle-class philosophy of life we have been examining dominated the age, it did not go unchallenged. It was supported by Macaulay, Herbert Spencer, and Huxley (for the most part), but it was severely attacked by most of the Victorian "prophets." Dickens and Mrs. Gaskell, Kingsley and Disraeli in the novel, Tennyson and Mrs. Browning in verse, and in expository prose Carlyle and Ruskin, Newman and Mill, Arnold and Morris subjected its political liberalism, its worldly ambitions, its conception of man and society to searching criticism. Only Newman and Morris, however, ended with complete rejection. The others—and this is characteristic of the time—arrived at some compromise. At one point or another, they were in sympathy with the middle-class creed. Their aim was not to destroy it, but to check its inhuman tendencies and reintroduce the intellectual and spiritual ideals which it was forfeiting.

The attack on political-economic liberalism came from two directions, from the right and the left. In both cases it was fired by what Carlyle called "the Condition-of-England Question," the existence side by side of tremendous wealth and abject proverty. The suffering of the masses called for action; but so entrenched was the theory of *laissez faire* that the government would not act. Under these conditions it was inevitable that two opposing theories should have arisen: Tory Paternalism on the right and Socialism on the left.

The former, which first appears in the later work of Coleridge and Southey (for the latter, see p. 445, below), was the creed of Carlyle, Ruskin, and Disraeli. It emphasized the old feudal theory of a governing aristocracy which was responsible for the welfare of the whole nation. Democracy was a snare and a delusion. To entrust the country to the ignorant masses, without education or political experience, was not only absurd, it was dangerous. The majority might well vote the confiscation of private property: had they not done so once in France? The fear of democracy, which was felt even by liberals like Macaulay (see his "Letter on Democracy," p. 487, below) and by democrats like Mill, was natural enough at the time. No, the government should remain in the hands of an aristocracy, which usually meant the landed nobility, though Carlyle in middle life advocated the dictatorship of a Hero or else a new aristocracy of talent composed of the Captains of Industry. But in whatever form, this autocratic government was to carry out a program of labor legislation which would put an end at once to the appalling conditions of proletarian life. Factory acts and mine acts to limit the hours of work and make the conditions of work safer and more sanitary; free emigration to the colonies and a public works program to solve overpopulation and unemployment; a national system of free public schools; the establishment of semipermanent contracts so that laborers could not suddenly be thrown out of work—these are some of the remedies which were suggested (see, for example, the relevant chapter from *Past and Present,* pp. 438–41, below). Though they stop short of public ownership of industry, they point directly toward the collectivistic theory of the state which had grown up in England by the 80's and 90's, and which arrived in America with the Roosevelt New Deal. But the New Dealers were called "liberals." The change in the meaning of the term is significant. In the nineteenth century the liberals, as we have seen, were the businessmen who wished to free society from special aristocratic privileges and to establish equal social and economic freedom for all. We need not disparage their achievement if we recognize the truth of Carlyle's charge that this freedom meant, in fact, freedom for the "haves" and slavery for the "have-nots." The worker was free to refuse the job at the local factory at the local wage—but if he did, he starved. He was legally free but actually in chains. This explains why, in our sense of the term—

the freeing of the masses from coercion—the Tory Paternalists of the Victorian period were more liberal than the Liberals.

By the same token so were the Socialists. Socialism may be viewed as a parallel movement "from below," by the workers themselves, to gain the help of the state. It differs from Tory Paternalism by being democratic and by pushing beyond collectivism toward state ownership of utilities, land, and the major industries. In the Victorian period it first appeared in Robert Owen's scheme for cooperative communities; emerged as the radical wing of Chartism (the working-class movement of the 30's and 40's for universal manhood suffrage); won the guarded support of John Stuart Mill (who decided that even Communism was superior to the system of unreformed, *laissez-faire* capitalism, and advocated the nationalization of land); and finally arrived in the 1880's when the influence of Marx at last began to count and the Fabian Society (out of which the Labor Party grew) was founded. On the whole, however, Socialism was more of a threat than a living movement in the period. It added fear to the moral and humanitarian appeal of the Tory Paternalists, and thus contributed, indirectly, to the series of factory acts and mine acts which Tory pressure put through Parliament.

Consistently with their conception of government, the Paternalists denounced the Liberal theory of an atomic society in which each individual pursued his own interest, within the law, and the sole bond between man and man was "cash-nexus." Society, they asserted, was an organic whole like a family, and its guiding principle should be "one for all and all for one." The relationship of capital and labor, therefore, should be that of partners in a joint enterprise, animated by a spirit on the one side of humane consideration, and on the other of trust and obedience. Such a "philosophy" implies a much higher conception of human nature than that of the Utilitarians. Man is not a selfish animal motivated exclusively by self-interest. He is a child of God, blessed with a divine conscience and an innate capacity for human loyalty and pity. Not pleasure, therefore, but duty is the guide of life, and a man's true goal is not personal success, but the unselfish service of society as an end in itself. By this gospel Carlyle, the spokesman for Paternalism, hoped to preach the Captains of Industry out of their Mammonism and to turn the warfare of capital and labor into the peaceful cooperation of humane executives and loyal, obedient workers.

Though they might reject one or another part of this program, all of the great Victorian critics shared its central idealism. All of them felt, as Mill did, that an England whose celebrity had come to rest "upon her docks, her canals, her railroads" was "void of lofty aspirations." All of them agreed with Tennyson that "the inspiration of ideals" was badly needed to "combat the cynical indifference, the intellectual self-ishness, the sloth of will, the utilitarian materialism of a transition age"; and with Arnold that people needed a higher conception of progress and a sounder basis for national pride than bigger and faster machines and greater and greater wealth. Even at their best the qualities developed by commercial life seemed to the Victorian critics "not precisely those by which mankind raise themselves to the perfection of their nature," either moral or intellectual.

Bourgeois society was not, of course, lacking in moral emphasis, as we have seen; but its morality was both too narrowly identified with strict adherence to the letter of the law and too rigidly restricted to the efficient training of character for successful action (the industrial virtues like honesty, thrift, strenuous work are self-centered). Lecky found public opinion very severe in judging crimes of passion and drink, and very lenient in judging those "of ambition, cupidity, envy, malevolence, and callous selfishness," which lie beyond the reach of law. Mill noticed more than once the contrast between the greater technical virtue of the English and the higher ideals of the Continental nations, especially the French. The following passage is at once a brilliant analysis of "middle-class morality" and a plea for something higher:

One of the commonest types of character among us is that of a man all whose ambition is self-regarding; who has no higher purpose in life than to enrich or raise in the world himself and his family; who never dreams of making the good of his fellow-creatures or of his country an habitual object, further than giving away, annually or from time to time, certain sums in charity; but who has a conscience sincerely alive to whatever is generally considered wrong, and would scruple to use any very illegitimate means for attaining his self-interested objects. While it will often happen in other countries that men whose feelings and whose active energies point strongly in an unselfish direction, who have the love of their country, of human improvement, of human freedom, even of virtue, in great strength, and of whose thoughts and activity a large share is devoted to disinterested objects, will yet, in the pursuit of these or of any other objects that they strongly desire, permit themselves to do wrong things which the other man, though intrinsically, and taking the whole of his character, farther removed from what a human being ought to be, could not bring himself to commit. It is of no use to debate which of these two states of mind is the best, or rather the least bad. It is quite possible to cultivate the conscience and the sentiments too. Nothing hinders us from so training a man that he will not, even for a disinterested purpose, violate the moral law, and also feeding and encouraging those high feelings, on which we mainly rely for lifting men above low and sordid objects, and giving them a higher conception of what constitutes success in life.

How was this to be done? Partly by preaching a higher morality on the lines laid down by Carlyle, mentioned a moment ago, and adapted to Utilitarianism by Mill himself (see Mill's *Autobiography*, p. 527, below). Partly by the contemplation of "great characters in history, or even in fiction." Because the heroic image was the direct counterpoise to the "economic man," in theory and practice, it became the principal means by which the Victorian idealists tried to instill a nobler spirit into a commercial society.

The modern world says—"Mind your own business, and leave others to take care of theirs"; and whoever among us aspires to more than the negative abstaining from wrong, is left to his own guidance. There is no help for him, no instruction, no modern ideal which shall be to him what the heroes were to the young Greek or Roman, or the martyrs to the Middle-Age Christian. (J. A. Froude)

Further, the elevating effect on character so much needed might be achieved, as Mill also suggested, by the contemplation of beauty, both in nature and in art. Though it has no direct application to conduct, it lifts us out of our selfish concerns and helps to create a broad, sympathetic frame of mind. This third suggestion is best illustrated by Ruskin. His lifelong effort to quicken the appreciation of beauty in nature as well as in painting and architecture—and in both areas for its moral no less than its aesthetic values— was a one-man crusade to counteract the growing ugliness of urban and suburban England and the impoverishment of life when measured solely by utilitarian standards.

Finally, Newman and Arnold, as well as Mill, attacked the anti-intellectualism that is indigenous to the business mind. In Newman's *Idea of a University* and in Arnold's essays on "The Function of Criticism" and "Hellenism and Hebraism" the limitation of thought to practical ends and the Philistine notion that the liberal arts are useless are attacked with brilliant argument and satire. But the counterideal was not the "pure" intellectual or the academic scholar. What they wanted was the full development of all sides of human nature until modern man, whose mind and emotions are now divorced and whose faculties are narrowed to the demands of practical existence, shall again become an integrated human being.

THE RELIGIOUS SITUATION

As we can see from Carlyle's *Sartor Resartus* (completed in 1831), the second great factor which conditioned the thought and temper of the Victorians, the decline of religious faith, had already reached a crucial stage by 1830. The rise of the critical spirit at the Renaissance, reinforced by the new science of the seventeenth century, made it impossible for Christianity to stand any longer on ecclesiastical and traditional authority. It had either to be defended by reason, or abandoned for a rational religion of nature (Deism). In both cases the philosophers argued the existence of God from the need of a first cause or creator of the world, and from the belief that a universe which everywhere seemed so beautifully designed (from the stars in their courses to the intricate functioning of bodily organs) must have had an intelligent and beneficent architect. It was therefore reasonable to suppose that he intended a moral order based on moral laws as simple and clear as the physical laws of the natural order. And finally, since on earth the good were seldom rewarded and the evil often unpunished, it seemed equally reasonable to suppose a heaven and a hell where a just God would right the balance. To stop at this point was to be a Deist. The defenders of Christianity merely went on to argue that a wise and benevolent God would certainly have made a definite revelation through Jesus Christ of the great truths which all men needed to know for salvation; and they cited for proof the fact that such a revelation was foretold in the Old Testament by prophecies and confirmed in the New by miracles. This line of defense was developed in a long series of books called "Evidences of Christianity."

But by the nineteenth century it was sterile. The "Evidences" were useless, and even Deism was insecure. For this, David Hume is largely responsible. In his *Dialogues concerning Natural Religion* (1779) he turned the weapon of reason against reason itself. As to the argument from a first cause, how do we know, he asked, that the earth *was* created at a moment in time? Isn't it just as reasonable—or unreasonable—to assume that the universe was eternal and existed from the beginning as to assume a creator who is eternal and existed from the beginning? In like manner, how do we know that there ever was a chaos for a god to shape into order and design? Maybe design and order were the original form of nature. Because justice does not exist on earth, can we be sure it exists after death

—if there *is* any "after death"? In short, by submitting religion to the strict test of fact and reason, Hume decided that skepticism, in the sense of agnosticism (the belief that we cannot prove or disprove supernatural truths), was the only reasonable position. Such a conclusion, which was implicit in Gibbon's well-known account of Christianity in the *Decline and Fall of the Roman Empire* (chaps. 15, 16), made religious faith impossible. Impossible, that is, so long as one relied upon reason. But by demonstrating the dead end of the rational approach, Hume opened up, in effect, the possibility of a fresh approach through the imagination and the feelings. This important development and the various forms of religion it fathered will be discussed below.

While eighteenth-century religious thought was growing colder and weaker, the contemporary course of philosophy, under the same influence of scientific rationalism, was taking a more and more naturalistic, and even materialistic, direction. Starting from Bacon and Descartes, and developed by Locke and Hartley, Hume and Bentham, a series of axioms, in direct or indirect conflict with the religious tradition, had been built up. Nothing happens in nature except by physical causes: there is no supernatural interference, divine or demonic; and miracles, including the Incarnation, never occurred. All knowledge comes originally from experience—sensations are impressed upon a passive mind, likened to soft wax—and is then developed automatically by association (the fire-burn-pain association, for example, teaches the child that stoves are hot and dangerous). Consequently, men are the products of their environment in mind and character. What they do—or what they desire to do—is conditioned by the basic impulse of human nature, the avoidance of pain and the appetite for pleasure. They are therefore motivated by self-interest, and they act virtuously, so far as they do, out of fear of the law and public opinion.

This, of course, is no adequate summary of eighteenth-century philosophy. It simply isolates those ideas which, when combined with Hume's religious skepticism, undermined the entire Christian scheme of things, metaphysical and ethical—indeed, any religious view of life. The result was what Carlyle called "The Everlasting No," the denial of all the spiritual and moral beliefs of the past, until what was left was a universe "all void of Life, of Purpose, of Volition, even of Hostility: it was one huge, dead, immeasurable steam-engine, rolling on, in its dead indifference, to grind me limb from limb." That chapter (on pp. 392 ff., below) is eloquent testimony to the destructive impact of eighteenth-century rationalism in the opening decades of the nineteenth century. The Utilitarians, the economists, the fashionable world had no religious faith and no morality of any breadth and power.

But at this point the progress of disbelief was checked by a countermovement of religious faith, in one form or another, which held back the tide through the 30's and 40's, until a fresh wave of skepticism, resulting from Biblical criticism and the scientific theory of evolution, swept over England in the 50's and 60's and made doubt a characteristic of the whole society. Though the religious revival took various forms, its approach to the problem of faith was the same in all cases. Belief had to be based not on reason (Hume had disposed of that) but on "experience": on the intuitive apprehension of God in nature or in the conscience or in moments of high and noble feeling (which seem God-inspired); or on a "conversion" in which one feels the immediate presence of God; or on proving the truth of Christianity by actual trial, finding that it works. This approach is clearly indebted to the Romantic insistence on living experience in place of abstract speculation, and the complementary reliance on the inner authority of intuition or the "feelings of the heart" as guides to truth and conduct in place of reason.

It was altogether natural, therefore, that the religious revival among the Romantics took the form of belief in divine immanence, sometimes called Pantheism. In Wordsworth, Coleridge, and Shelley, in Goethe and Novalis in Germany (writers who influenced Carlyle), the aesthetic exaltation in the presence of natural beauty, especially in its more sublime forms (the star-lit sky, the ocean, mountain peaks) became a religious exaltation in which they felt the presence of a supernatural spirit. If to this awareness we add the emotions of wonder, awe, and reverence that go with it, and the moral effect of feeling purified of all that is selfish and evil, we have the Religion of Nature which became for Carlyle and Ruskin, and thousands of Victorians, a faith they could turn to, either in place of Christianity or as a reassuring support to Christian beliefs they could no longer accept on ecclesiastical or Biblical authority alone. (For Carlyle, see p. 397; for Ruskin, p. 578.)

This double function was also served by another form of natural (as opposed to revealed) religion which starts from personal experience. This is Theism. Here one finds God in the phenomenon of conscience. The inner voice, demanding moral action, insisting on the priority of duty over pleasure, is either interpreted directly as that of an all-powerful Judge and Governor (Newman), or is made the basis from which one deduces the existence of God and a moral universe (Kant, Fichte, and, under their influence, Carlyle). This "argument" could be used, as it was by Newman, to support Christianity. But many Victorians who could not accept the Christian revelation, especially those shaped by the Puritan tradition, found in Theism, with its strong moral urgency (ethically much stronger than Pantheism), an answer to their need. In fact, as the Romantic spirit waned, and the Puritan revival gained in force, the Religion of Nature was more and more displaced by this Religion of Conscience. It is characteristic of the time that the former is chiefly emphasized in *Sartor Resartus* (1833), while in *Past and Present* (1843) the latter stands almost alone—and Carlyle has emerged as perhaps the major Victorian prophet of Theism.

Meanwhile the subversive influence of eighteenth-century rationalism had been met by a powerful revival of Christianity which had taken three forms, Protestant, Liberal, and Anglo-Catholic. The Protestant revival, which is the earliest, had been initiated as far back as 1738 by John and Charles Wesley, the founders of the new Protestant sect of Methodism. In reaction against the optimistic and rational form of contemporary religion, the Wesleyans returned to the Puritan insistence on original sin and salvation by faith. By his own efforts man could not hope to live a virtuous life or to go to heaven. His whole nature had to be miraculously transformed by the grace of God. He had to be born again of the Spirit. But how? Certainly not by any external sacramental system administered by a church. Solely by the experience of "conversion." This was the tremendous moment when the sinner, in an access of repentance, cried out to Christ for mercy, and suddenly felt the inrush of divine grace. From that day forth he was a regenerate man, his heart filled with the love of God, his life a constant and spontaneous exercise of virtue, his soul saved. And his mind never in the slightest doubt. For his belief in God did not rest on any dubious argument, but on the very experience of the Divine Presence in the act of conversion.

This revival of Puritanism was not limited to the Methodists. It permeated the Church of England, where the disciples of Wesley who remained behind became the Low Church party, known as the "Evangelicals." They were famous for their ethical piety, their founding of foreign missions and Bible societies, and their philanthropic activities. William Wilberforce and Zachary Macaulay, father of

Thomas Babington, played important roles in the antislavery movement. But it was their moral fervor, one might say their Puritan conscience, which left the deepest mark on their age. The moral strictness, which in any case would have characterized a new industrial society, was strongly colored and intensified by Evangelicalism. It is the primary source of the Victorian sense of sin, which prohibited dancing, cardplaying, and the theater as things of the devil, made prudery and the maiden blush conventions of decency, forbade the reading of any literature which dealt with evil (even Charlotte Brontë thought one had better omit the comedies of Shakespeare), and turned Sunday into a day of gloom on which church services could be supplemented only by *Paradise Lost, Pilgrim's Progress,* or perhaps some pious story of Mrs. Sherwood's about "wicked girls who had gone to balls, dying immediately after of fever."

Although Evangelicalism penetrated into aristocratic and university circles, it was too fervid and emotional to capture the more highly educated or socially conservative classes. In these areas the Christian revival took other directions. Under the leadership of Thomas Arnold, the famous headmaster of Rugby and the father of Matthew, there grew up in the 1820's a school of Liberal Protestantism which later included F. D. Maurice and Charles Kingsley, Benjamin Jowett, the translator of Plato, Tennyson and Matthew Arnold. Thomas Arnold saw that the new spirit of the country, as represented by the Utilitarians, was at once secular and commercial. The crucial need of the time, therefore, was a strong state church "to Christianize the nation, and introduce the principles of Christianity into men's social and civil relations." But much of the nation belonged, not to the established Church of England, but to one or another of the Protestant sects. Hence Arnold's program to turn the Church of England into a truly national Protestant Church, a Broad Church. Why not? With the exception of Catholics and Unitarians, did not all Christians, he asked, "have a common ground in all that is essential in Christianity"? And this common ground was the worship of Jesus Christ, the Son of God, and the desire to live in holy and virtuous imitation of His life. True, this would mean that each sect would have to give up some of its special dogmas and the Church of England abandon its Thirty-nine Articles. But what matter? "Christian unity and the perfection of Christ's Church are independent of theological Articles of opinion; consisting in a certain moral state and moral and religious affections, which have existed in good Christians of all ages and all communions." This divorce of religion from theology, in which the former becomes a matter of feeling and conduct, and the latter a matter of opinion (to be believed or not, as the individual pleases), is highly characteristic of Victorian life. And even more so, perhaps, of Protestantism today. The fact is, of course, that theological dogmas—the Trinity, the Incarnation, the Atonement, the Redemption, to name only the most important—are miraculous. If they are subjected to the strict test of scientific fact and law, they are destroyed. And they had been destroyed, or had survived in name only, under the eighteenth-century examination of reason, to the point where Christianity, as we have seen, was in serious danger. But suppose the ground were shifted and the whole movement of theology, starting in St. John and St. Paul, continuing through the medieval schoolmen and the Protestant reformers, were seen as a huge monument to the subtlety and sophistication of the human intellect. Then one would turn back to the first three Gospels to find the true and simple "Religion of Christ"—namely, there is a God whose divine nature was revealed in Jesus Christ our Saviour, in the love and worship of whom is our moral strength and the promise of heavenly immortality. If you doubt it, try it; the practical results will prove the assumptions true. By this liberal faith Christianity might be saved in the modern world, and given so broad a basis that the union of all Protestants would be possible. Through one great national church, exerting its wide influence throughout society, the twin evils of the age, doubt and greed, might be destroyed.

But a group of men at Oxford, led by Newman, Keble, and Pusey, did not believe it. On the contrary they were convinced that Liberalism would "make shipwreck of Christian faith," and was, in fact, the "halfway house" to atheism. For where was the process of casting out dogma and miracle to stop? In an age of doubt another generation might find even Arnold's belief in the Incarnation incredible, and Christianity might disintegrate into Theism, which in turn might easily dissolve into some nonreligious form of ethical culture and humanitarian service. And these fears were not idle: the prophecy largely came to pass. The Oxford Movement, which Newman and Keble initiated in 1833 with a series of *Tracts for the Times,* was an attempt to save Christianity from its Liberal friends as well as its Utilitarian enemies, by insisting on its dogmatic and miraculous character. The great dogmas, they said, form a body of divinely revealed truth which it is sacrilege—and religious suicide—to submit to rational examination and human judgment. They are simply *given* on the supreme authority of God. The first principle of the Oxford Movement, as Newman said, was "the principle of dogma: my battle was with liberalism; by liberalism I meant the anti-dogmatic principle and its developments." (See Newman's "Note on Liberalism" printed below, especially the definition on p. 493 and the eighteen propositions at the end.)

The second principle was Catholicism, Anglo-Catholicism. When the Church of England cut its ties with Rome in the sixteenth century, it had attempted to steer a middle course, to retain *some* Catholic and adopt *some* Protestant doctrines and ceremonies. Although this rather ambiguous compromise satisfied the majority, it did not satisfy either the Puritans on the left, who wished to purify the Church from all Catholicism and make it entirely Protestant, or the Anglo-Catholics on the right, who felt that Protestantism had already gone too far and that the Catholic elements of the liturgy should be emphasized. In the minds of the latter, the English Church was not a new church set up at the Reformation, but a branch of the original Apostolic Church founded by Christ to be the guardian of dogma and the ark of salvation (by means of the sacraments administered by a priesthood possessing supernatural power). In course of time this Church of God had been corrupted by certain Roman Catholic errors like the doctrines of purgatory and transubstantiation. These had now been rightly rejected, along with the headship of the Pope. But unfortunately the Reformation had introduced new Protestant errors: salvation by faith alone; the denial that the sacraments were channels of grace, which had led in turn to denying the supernatural power of the priesthood; and worst of all, the shifting of supreme authority from the Church to the Bible, so that the individual reader became, in effect, the ultimate judge and interpreter of divine truth. Anglo-Catholicism was the attempt in the seventeenth century under Archbishop Laud to make the Church of England adopt a Catholic, though not quite a Roman Catholic, interpretation of Christianity. It had not succeeded, but its principles had been kept alive through the eighteenth century in various country parsonages, in one of which John Keble had been brought up.

The Oxford Movement was a revival of this Anglican tradition, a new attempt to make the Church of England Anglo-Catholic:

We were upholding that primitive Christianity which was delivered for all time by the early teachers of the Church, and which was registered and attested in the Anglican formularies and by the Anglican divines. That ancient religion had well nigh faded away out of the

land, through the political changes of the last 150 years, and it must be restored. It would be in fact a second Reformation:—a better reformation, for it would be a return not to the sixteenth century, but to the seventeenth. (Newman)

If it succeeded, the miraculous and dogmatic character of Christianity could be preserved and protected by the re-establishment of ecclesiastical authority; and Christianity could be saved not only from the misguided efforts of the Liberal Protestants but from the greater destructive force of modern skepticism.

For a while the movement won wide support, both among the clergy and also among many Victorians who found a welcome refuge from religious doubts and perplexities in Catholic authority. But the opposing forces were too strong. The Low Church party of the Evangelicals and the Broad Church party of the Liberals could unite with fighting conviction against such a High and Catholic conception of the Church. And both could appeal to the latent fear of Rome which is deeply ingrained in the English temper. When the showdown came, the English bishops reaffirmed the traditional Protestant interpretation of the liturgy and the Articles—and Newman turned to the only living Catholic church. His conversion to Rome in 1845 was a further blow to the movement he had led. But it remained alive; and the Anglo-Catholics today form a strong minority in the Church of England and the Episcopal Church of America.

The religious revival, in both the non-Christian and Christian forms we have examined, was sufficiently strong to check the influence of eighteenth-century rationalism and make it possible for most Victorians of the first generation (1830–1860) to maintain a supernatural faith. But not easily or firmly. The very existence of competing solutions, the clash of Theists and Christians, of Evangelicals and Liberals and Anglo-Catholics, and the inevitable raising of difficulties which otherwise would never have arisen, created an atmosphere which tended, ironically, to turn the very effort to dispel doubt into a fresh cause of doubt. ("Doubt" means primarily lack of firm convictions, beliefs only half believed, though the situation pushed some of the half-believers into becoming nonbelievers.) Another intangible but important source of doubt was the secular and naturalistic direction of contemporary life and thought. Where so much energy was being devoted, and so successfully, to the expansion of business and the increase of physical comfort, where the popular mind was fascinated by science, by its extraordinary inventions and its new knowledge of the universe no less than by its glamorous promises of far greater conquests to come, the religious point of view was difficult to maintain. "I am sometimes startled," said one Victorian, "to find to what a halt my old theological trains of thought and sentiment have come; I have never deliberately discarded them, but the scientific atmosphere seems to paralyse them." This must have been so in thousands of cases. Indeed, if Victorian science dealt religion a blow from which it has never recovered (and it is impossible to see how, even granting the vigorous life of many churches, one can call modern society religious), it was not so much by its shocking discoveries in evolution as by its silent attraction of the human mind away from a supernatural orientation.

But the discoveries carried weight. Through the eighteenth century and well into the nineteenth, the universe was still thought of as static. God had created the solar system at one moment in time, complete and perfect just as it was today and would always be till the end of the world. And everyone knew when this great event had occurred: it was in 4004 B. C.—according to one scholar, on October 23 at 9 a. m. The first dent in this static universe was made by a Frenchman named Laplace in 1799, when he advanced the nebular hypothesis. It taught that the solar system existed originally as a great gaseous nebula with a central kernel; as the mass cooled, the center condensed into the revolving sun, and the outer parts became revolving rings, which in turn condensed into the planets circling round the sun. With this hypothesis the idea of evolution was born. The next step was to explain the development of the earth from an incandescent state to its present condition. In the important work of James Hutton and especially Charles Lyell (*Principles of Geology,* 1830) the older theory of catastrophic changes by violent earthquakes or volcanic eruptions was replaced by the modern theory of uniformitarianism: all geological changes have occurred by the uniform operation of physical causes now in daily operation. Just as the surface of the globe is being changed today by the action of rain, rivers, the sea, and chemical decomposition, so it has always been changed. This meant that the date of the creation had to be radically revised, because only in terms of a tremendous period of time could one account by natural causes for the formation of so many layers of strata. Not 4004 B. C. but something closer to 1,000,000,000 B. C. was the truth.

The existence of strata from epochs separated by immense periods of time made the literal interpretation of Genesis no longer possible. All forms of animal life were plainly *not* created on the fifth and sixth days, but at widely separated periods. When the fossil remains of fish were found in the lower strata, reptiles in higher, birds and then mammals, including finally man, in the highest, the idea of *biological* evolution was inescapable. But it may be noticed that the first conception, which was widely established by 1850, was not what we would mean today by the term, and not what Darwin meant. The later meaning is that of an evolution of species, one from another, by natural means. The earlier concept still retained the notion of special creation, only not at one time. At widely separated intervals God created new species on what seemed to be an ascending scale, ending with the creation of man in His own image. This is all that most Victorians (and very likely Tennyson in *In Memoriam*) meant by evolution before Darwin. But once the principle of development by natural causes had been accepted in geology, it was very difficult to reject it in biology. The problem was to extend the principle of uniformitarianism to biological evolution (see Huxley's important remark on p. 620).

Though Darwin was not the first to do this (the Frenchman Lamarck had put forward a tentative theory in 1815), his *Origin of Species* (1859) was the epoch-making statement of evolution by natural causes. Taking over a suggestion by Malthus in his *Theory of Population* (1798)—that since population increases at a much higher rate than the supply of food, the poorest classes constantly live on the edge of starvation and only the strongest individuals survive in the struggle for existence—Darwin argued that in the jungle the same situation would produce a natural process of selection. Only those varieties best fitted to cope with their environment would survive to form new species, while those unequal to the struggle would die out. (For a detailed explanation of Darwin's theory, see Huxley's review of *The Origin of Species,* printed on pp. 610 ff., below). In itself this explanation did not go unchallenged, and there is a school of Neo-Lamarckians today. But the mass of evidence which Darwin brought forward was so impressive that the fact of a natural evolution, in one way or another, of all forms of life "from some one primordial form or sperm" gained wide and permanent acceptance.

One can vaguely imagine the explosion which this theory set off. In one terrible blow it seemed to destroy the traditional conceptions of man, of nature, and of the origin of religion and morality; and to substitute for each an interpretation that was deeply distressing. Man was reduced to an animal, the descendant of apes. Nature, which had been the witness of a divine and beneficent God and a source of moral elevation, became a battlefield in which individuals and species alike fought for their lives, and the victor was the best, not morally but physically, the toughest and the roughest and the quickest on the kill. If *this* nature was the creation of God, then God, as Tennyson put it, "is disease, murder and rapine." Or if not, then either there is no God and no immortality but only Nature, indifferent to all moral values, impelling all things to a life of instinctive cruelty ending in death; or else God and Nature are locked in an incredible and inexplicable strife. These terrible alternatives are all present, directly or by implication, in the famous passage of *In Memoriam* (see below, pp. 666–7, poems 54–56) where Tennyson expresses the profound doubts which the evolutionary view of nature had raised in the Victorian mind.

They were further increased when Darwin's principle of the struggle for survival was applied to the evolution of human society, and the origin of morals and religion was explained in purely naturalistic terms (see Huxley, pp. 631 ff.). The "tiger" instincts were first checked when animals combined, in the family or the pack, to fight together for better survival, and therefore tacitly agreed not to fight one another for the time being. Human society then made the important advance on wolf society of agreeing to use the force of the whole body against individuals who violated the truce and in favor of those who observed it. In this way, moral laws naturally developed, a conscience which demands their fulfillment was built into man through ages of tribal punishment and reward, and ideals of social service and self-sacrifice were created through ages of tribal praise, all in the cause of better personal survival by means of multiple and combined strength. Apparently it was not God who placed a conscience in man, and apparently virtuous conduct had nothing to do with His supposed will, or with an individual's supposed survival after death, but only with the will of the tribe, and the survival of the tribe (and the individual) here and now. As for high ideals, they were nothing at bottom but a disguised form of selfishness.

In this context it is easy to explain the origin and function of religion. It begins when primitive men imagine gods in the sun or the rain; and then, in the cause of survival from storms and droughts, the tribe institutes sacrifices and prayers to placate the gods and win their aid. Presently religion takes over the already existing moral code. Since no natural explanation of

moral laws is known, a supernatural one is assumed, and the laws of the tribe are called the laws of its tribal gods. This in turn gives those laws a more powerful sanction, since to violate them is now to evoke the wrath of the gods; and thus religion, because it helps so greatly to curb the centrifugal force of animal instincts and increase the cohesive power of morality, makes its natural contribution to tribal, and therefore individual, survival. In short, religion is not in the least an objective, supernatural reality which has been revealed by God to man, in the first century, by His only-begotten Son. It is a psychological superstition of such value in the struggle for existence that it has become a basic element of social life.

It was still possible, however, to be a Darwinian and at the same time to retain a belief in God as the creator of life. In claiming that "all living things . . . which have ever lived on this earth have descended from some one primordial form," Darwin had gone on at once to add, "into which life was first breathed by the Creator." And breathed, one could suppose, with full and purposive knowledge of the great process of development which He initiated, a development not only from lower to higher forms of life, but from the violence of tribal society up to the law-abiding civilization of nineteenth-century Europe. If evolution was the principle of the universe, it was a divine principle. Progress was God's providence. And if progress *on* earth, why not also, on the same terms of moral growth, progress *from* earth to heaven? This desperate attempt to seize the weapons of the enemy and use them in self-defense may be seen, along with the contrary implications of science, in Tennyson's *In Memoriam* (see poems 82, 118, and the end of the "Epilogue"). But aside from the fact that this religious reading of evolution was difficult to reconcile with "Nature red in tooth and claw," it was directly impugned by a fresh attack on human nature. The reduction of man to an animal was followed by his reduction to a machine.

Darwin might talk of God breathing life into the first sperm, but Huxley and other scientists would not believe that in the vast evolution of all things from some purely material beginning, like a spiral nebula, there was any moment of supernatural intervention. Why was not life itself a natural result of certain chemical elements uniting under exactly the right, fortuitous conditions? In his sensational essay "On the Physical Basis of Life" (1868), Huxley argued that the property of "life" or "vitality" was as much a product of the combination of oxygen, hydrogen, nitrogen, and carbon which forms the protoplasm that is common to all living beings, as the property of "aquosity" is the result of the combination of oxygen and hydrogen which forms water. If so, man has no spirit or soul independent of the body, but only a brain in which molecular changes, determined by external stimuli, give automatic rise to all our thoughts and all our actions. For Huxley, as for many physiologists and biologists today, man is simply a human automaton, a "physico-chemical organism, the lineal descendant of some bit of primordial slime; all his hopes and aspirations, . . . all his self-sacrifice and knowledge, are the result of the peculiar laws governing the chemical reactions that ultimately go to produce his behavior" (J. H. Randall). This extension of the realm of matter and law to a point where it includes human life itself is the Victorian nightmare:

> Science frees us in many ways . . . from the bodily terror which the savage feels. But she replaces that, in the minds of many, by a moral terror which is far more overwhelming. Am I—a man is driven to ask—am I, and all I love, the victims of an organized tyranny, from which there can be no escape—for there is not even a tyrant from whom I may perhaps beg mercy? Are we only helpless particles, at best separate parts of the wheels of a vast machine, which will use us till it has worn us away, and ground us to powder? Are our bodies—and if so, why not our souls?—the puppets, yea, the creatures of necessary circumstances, and all our strivings and sorrows only vain beatings against the wires of our cage? . . . Tell us not that the world is governed by universal law; the news is not comfortable, but simply horrible. . . . (Charles Kingsley)

What made the anti-Christian conclusions of modern science doubly disturbing was their direct conflict with the Bible. From the beginning Protestantism had substituted the Scriptures for the Church as the supreme source of authority. They were the Word of God, inspired by Him, and therefore worthy of unquestioning belief. The early Puritans and their Methodist-Evangelical descendants in the Victorian period preached, as Huxley says (p. 626), "the necessity, on pain of reprobation in this world and damnation in the next, of accepting, in the strict and literal sense, every statement contained in the Protestant Bible." Even Christians who did not go so far, and were ready to admit the propriety of mystical or allegorical interpretations, thought of the Bible as unlike any other book, a direct revelation of God's truth. That is why the anti-Biblical conclusions of modern science were far more shocking to the Victorians than they were, say, to Roman Catholics on the Continent. Science was not merely advancing antireligious theories; the theories threatened the sacred foundation of Christian faith. If a chapter here and a passage there were shown to be erroneous, where was the process going to stop? As Huxley put the ominous possibility, "if Scripture has been discovered 'not to be worthy of unquestioning belief,' faith 'in the supernatural itself' is, so far, undermined."

The destructive analysis of the Bible was not, however, the actual work of the scientists, nor were the new discoveries in science the only source of doubt about its reliability. In the late eighteenth century the so-called Higher Criticism had been inaugurated in Germany by literary and historical scholars. What they did was simply to treat the Bible like any other ancient book, and to extend the methods of scholarship from classical to Biblical studies. In doing so they followed three lines of criticism (as Huxley points out on p. 626, below): scientific historical criticism, centering on the separation of historical fact from fable and legend, and using comparative mythology to show that many supposed facts in the Bible, like Noah's flood, were common products of the mythopoetic faculty in all primitive peoples; scientific literary criticism, meaning the study of Biblical languages and literary forms, which showed that the Scriptures were written by many authors at widely different times and that certain dogmas had resulted from a literal reading of what was a conventional metaphor; and finally, scientific physical criticism, the testing of the Bible against modern scientific knowledge, with serious consequences not only for Genesis but for the miracles of the New Testament.

For a while the Higher Criticism reached only a few English thinkers—notably Thomas Arnold, who was its first, cautious exponent in England, and George Eliot, who was converted by it from Evangelical Christianity to agnosticism. But on the publication of *Essays and Reviews* in 1860 (written by seven English scholars and theologians), it broke over the public mind—and exactly one year after the explosive publication of *The Origin of Species*. Evolution and Biblical criticism converged in the 1860's until, as Matthew Arnold reported, there was "not a creed which is not shaken, not an accredited dogma which is not shown to be questionable, not a received tradition which does not threaten to dissolve." The doubt which through the early decades of the century had been checked or half buried now became a conscious and recognized fact of English life. By 1877 most Englishmen were either "deniers or doubters"; and our modern inheritance was complete. We were to live in a secular no less than an industrial society.

How did it feel to exist in this Victorian world of religious tension between the forces of renewed affirmation and of fresh denial? What effects did the total situation have on the temper of the time? What habits of thought, what moral attitudes should we attribute either to the revival of faith or to its radical decline?

As we have noticed in tracing the impact of evolution and Biblical criticism, the Victorians found religious doubt painful and disturbing to a degree which we can now hardly understand. If it is true, as Clifford Bax has claimed, that most people today do not bother their heads with "thoughts of 'God' or 'the soul' " and that "they behave, indeed, as though neither existed," nothing could be less Victorian. A hundred years ago men filled their books and magazines with endless discussions of God and the soul— indeed, you might say that *they* behaved as though *terrified* that neither existed. For we have Carlyle's word for it that the age was "at once destitute of faith and terrified at scepticism." Why the terror? Why could the Victorians not accept doubt or unbelief as indifferently as we do, or pretend to do?

Partly because it was new. Christian faith had for centuries been an assumption of European thought, and now suddenly in the nineteenth century, in the early manhood of men like Carlyle and Kingsley, Ruskin and Matthew Arnold, the foundation of the universe began to tremble. "Those who dwell in the tower of ancient faiths look about them," wrote John Morley, "in constant apprehension, misgiving, and wonder, with the hurried uneasy mien of people living amid earthquakes. The air seems full of missiles and all is doubt, hesitation, and shivering expectancy." We who have never been disinherited because we have never known religious certainty can only imagine the distress of the first sudden catastrophe. But the loss, or the threatened loss, of century-old beliefs was disturbing not only in itself but in its ominous implications. The Victorians imagined, or foresaw, that the decline of religion would have moral and social consequences of the direst kind. If men ceased to believe in God and a future life, the great sanctions of moral action would be gone; and once they were gone, the selfish passions of individuals and nations would be unleashed, and society would disintegrate into violence and war. Finally, and perhaps most immediately painful, was the sense of frustration which the loss of faith imposed on many sensitive minds. Men had so long lived and acted within a framework of Christian thought that gave their lives purpose and meaning, that its collapse could leave them at loose ends, their active energies

"paralysed . . . by enfeebling doubts." The closing stanzas of Arnold's "Scholar-Gipsy" (see pp. 736 f.) are an eloquent expression of "the sick fatigue" and the baffled wills of those "half-believers of our casual creeds" who "hesitate and falter life away." Under all their fine optimism, the Victorians at heart were filled with anxiety. So are we, but ours is political, while theirs was mainly religious.

Anxiety demands, and if possible compels, resolution. Because they found doubt so painful, the Victorians demanded something to believe in, or to think they believed in. The age, as Lord Acton acutely noted, was distracted between the difficulty of belief and the intense need of believing. Hence the paradoxical psychology of the period. On the one hand, the disintegration of traditional authority and the spread of the scientific attitude, emphasizing detached examination and empirical evidence, encouraged a spirit of critical inquiry. On the other, the pain of doubt dictated an almost frantic desire to welcome any new authority, any new philosophy of life, religious or naturalistic, with uncritical promptness.

It was not the acceptance of any single body of doctrine that distinguished the Victorian, but his insistent *attitude* of acceptance, his persistent belief in (but only rare examination of) the credentials of Authority, his innate desire to affirm and conform rather than to reject or to question. (A. C. Ward)

The crucial bearing of this psychology on Victorian literature, for writers and readers alike, will be considered below.

Finally, we may notice how various intellectual and moral attitudes already attributed to the influence of middle-class industrialism were equally indebted to the religious situation. The anti-intellectualism of business was reinforced by the fear of speculation. At a time when modern thought was undermining belief and men were terrified of skepticism, surely it was best to leave well enough alone and go about one's job. This was the conclusion not only of individuals like Carlyle and Kingsley, but also of public opinion. Religious thought that issued in any but orthodox conclusions was treated with the same weapons of social stigma and professional obstruction which are used today against similar freedom of political thought. (Mill's analysis of the situation and his fine defense of the free pursuit of truth are on pp. 545–48.) Furthermore, if the policy of "Don't think, work hard" was a protection against doubt, it was also a cure for those who caught the disease. "Let him who gropes painfully in darkness or uncertain light," says Carlyle, remember that " 'Doubt of any sort cannot be removed except by Action' " (p. 400). And he therefore closes his "Everlasting Yea" with a fervid injunction to "Produce! Produce! Were it but the pitifullest infinitesimal fraction of a Product, produce it, in God's name! . . . Work while it is called Today; for the Night cometh, wherein no man can work" (p. 400). Out of its context would anyone imagine that this was not the daily chant of the Captains of Industry? The Intellectual and Industrial Revolutions met together in the gospel of work, with the powerful encouragement of Puritan ethics. The child of business and doubt was an anti-intellectual.

He was also a man of the highest moral rectitude, at least in theory. If the revival of Puritanism strengthened the concern with morality natural in a bourgeois society, so did the decline of belief. When the old religious sanctions were losing their force, all the more need to stress the social obligations of virtuous conduct, and for agnostics to prove, by word and example, that moral living was not dependent on supernatural beliefs. On a famous occasion when George Eliot mentioned the three words which had so long been "inspiring trumpet-calls of men,—the words *God, Immortality, Duty,*—" she "pronounced, with terrible earnestness, how inconceivable was the *first,* how unbelievable was the *second,* and yet how peremptory and absolute the *third.*" It is because the first two words have lost their meaning that the third is given such passionate affirmation. In George Eliot's novels, as in the essays of other leading agnostics like Mill and Huxley, a Religion of Humanity is made a new basis for morals. The service of man displaces the service of God; a heaven on earth, not after death, becomes the goal of life; and the inspiration to share in the building of a finer humanity is made the sufficient source of ethical control and altruistic action. Closely related to this secular religion is another that centers on an ideal image, in this case not that of Man but of Men, the Religion of Hero-Worship. The preoccupation of Victorian literature with legendary heroes, Greek, medieval, and Teutonic, was partly motivated, as we have seen, by the need to supplant the commercial spirit by an heroic spirit; but partly also by the need to find a substitute for the old supernatural faith. In Carlyle's *Heroes and Hero-Worship* the heroic image has taken the place of the divine image, and the germ of Christianity, its living core in contrast to its dead theological forms, is said to be "hero-worship, heartfelt prostrate admiration, submission, burning, boundless, for a noblest godlike Form of Man." The same need to endow a natural object with spiritual values lies behind the complementary idealization of woman,

with its romantic-chivalric view of love (see the Brownings especially) and its sentimentalizing of the home and family life.

LITERATURE

IF we compare the literature of the Victorian age with the literature that preceded it or followed it, in the Romantic or the modern period, we are struck by its public character and its public importance. Of the great Romantic writers, only Byron and Scott were widely read, and essentially for entertainment. Wordsworth, Shelley, and Keats, Hazlitt and Lamb, had each a following of devotees but it was small. Moreover, although Romantic art sometimes dealt with contemporary political, economic, and religious problems, it did not center upon them nor did it handle them in a form likely to attract the general reader. If we add to these facts the antiartistic bias of both Utilitarianism and Evangelicalism, we can readily understand why the prestige of literature in 1830 had sunk to a low ebb. "A poet in our times," wrote Peacock a few years earlier,

is a semi-barbarian in a civilized community. He lives in the days that are past. His ideas, thoughts, feelings, associations, are all with barbarous manners, obsolete customs, and exploded superstitions. The march of his intellect is like that of a crab, backward. . . . In whatever degree poetry is cultivated, it must necessarily be to the neglect of some branch of useful study; and it is a lamentable spectacle to see minds capable of better things running to seed in the specious indolence of these empty, aimless mockeries of intellectual exertion.

On the whole, the situation today is very similar. Modern literature is a "thing apart"—too esoteric in content, too subtle and difficult in form, to reach any but a small audience of "intellectuals." The modern writer has no status. It is not to him but to specialists, or journalists, that people turn for answers to the pressing problems of our time. Only the novel on the level of entertainment commands a reading public of any size.

But between these two periods, for the fifty years from 1830 to 1880, literature was a living medium of culture. Because at its best it was in close touch with the general life of the time and spoke in a language that was simple without being flat or conventional, it commanded a wide audience. And the prestige of the writer was little short of amazing. If Carlyle's high claim (p. 407) that the Man of Letters was "our most important modern person," possessed of intuitive insight into "the True, Divine and Eternal," and therefore "the light of the world, . . . guiding it, like a sacred Pillar of Fire, in its dark pilgrimage" (a theory derived from the Romantic conception of the natural genius), if this was, at bottom, a counter-defiance hurled at Philistine indifference and a kind of self-sustaining boast, it came, none the less, to be widely acknowledged, not only by writers but by readers. According to Mill, Carlyle "made Artist the term for expressing the highest order of moral and intellectual greatness."

Mill's choice of adjectives is significant. The public nature and the public importance of Victorian literature rested precisely there, on its moral and intellectual character, and not on its imaginative recreation of life. The task of the writer, as Arnold put it, was "not to exhibit all the kingdoms of human life and the glory of them like Shakspeare, but to interpret human life afresh." It was his inevitable task in an age of radical transition, when the Church and the aristocracy had lost their traditional authority, when the most fundamental questions in politics and religion cried out for new answers, and all men were desperately in need of guidance and inspiration. Under such conditions his inevitable role, as we see plainly in Carlyle's lecture (p. 408), was that not of an artist but of a prophet. It was a platitude of Victorian criticism that authors were a modern priesthood whose duty was to "enlighten and encourage and purify public opinion." In short, the spirit of the age pulled literature away from its highest function of sensitive observation and imaginative insight, either completely, in expository prose, or partly, in poetry and fiction. But in doing so, and in forcing it to subserve the practical needs of contemporary life, it enabled the writer not only to turn the flank on Utilitarian-Evangelical hostility (literature *was* useful and it *was* moral), but to make his work a living influence on a society largely obtuse to artistic values.

The program of prophetic literature was most successfully carried out, because least disturbed by conflicting motives, in what is certainly the finest body of critical prose in English. Historically, this prose continued the tradition established by the eighteenth-century essayists, but with wider range and seriousness of content, greater length in form, and far more dogmatism in style. The differences are readily explained by the transitional character of the age. Walter Bagehot related the form in general to the same "democratic" audience for which Addison and Steele began to write, and its extension of length to the more complex problems that arose in the nineteenth century. The difference, he said, between ancient and modern writing of a philosophical kind was due to the fact that "we must instruct so many persons." So long as he wrote for a small group of educated men, the writer could be "systematic, suggesting all arguments, analyzing all difficulties, discussing all doubts"; but now that he must write for the multitude, "impatient of system, desirous of brevity, puzzled by formality," he had to give his ideas a simpler and shorter expression:

In this transition from ancient writing to modern, the review-like essay and the essay-like review fill a large space. Their small bulk, their slight pretension to systematic completeness,—their avowal, it might be said, of necessary incompleteness,—the facility of changing the subject, of selecting points to attack, of exposing only the best corner for defense, are great temptations . . . Unquestionably the *Spectator* and *Tatler,* and such like writings, had opened a similar vein; but their size was too small: they could only deal with small fragments or the extreme essence of a subject; they could not give a view of what was complicated, or analyze what was involved. The modern man must be told what to think; shortly, no doubt, but he *must* be told it. The essay-like criticism of modern times is about the length which he likes. The *Edinburgh Review,* which began the system, may be said to be, in this country, the commencement on large topics of suitable views for sensible persons.

The *Edinburgh Review* (Whig) was followed by the *Quarterly* (Tory), the *Westminster* (Utilitarian), and a score of others. The Victorian period is the golden age of the periodical at its highest level, where it is a vehicle for the best intelligence of the time. As that would suggest, much of the work of Macaulay and Arnold, Carlyle and Mill and Huxley, first appeared in the reviews. Some of their most famous books—Arnold's *Culture and Anarchy,* for example, and Huxley's *Science and the Christian Tradition*—were collections of essays reprinted from periodicals. Even whole books (*Past and Present* is a clear case) explore a range of loosely connected ideas in a series of essay-like chapters.

But the intellectual character of the age was as important as its democratic audience in making the essay a "natural" for the time. When there was no longer any accepted body of beliefs, and men were wrestling with a multitude of new facts and tentative theories, they saw truth in fragments—and wrote it in essays. Furthermore, the very limitation of length, which allowed the writer, as Bagehot says, to avoid "analyzing all difficulties, discussing all doubts," was entirely welcome to a public which wanted solutions and not deeper—and more confusing—analysis.

This last point bears directly on style. At a time when doubt was painful and the will to believe intense, what people craved above all was to be told

—and in no uncertain terms. They did not want balanced arguments in a cool and measured style. They wanted positive doctrine expressed with eloquent and dogmatic conviction. When Carlyle taught Froude a creed which saved him from atheism, "the lesson came from one who seemed 'to speak with authority and not as the Scribes,' as if what he said was absolute certainty beyond question or cavil." Had it not been so, Froude might not have been saved. One critic excused Ruskin's "arrogance and dogmatism" on the extraordinary ground that "even error, eloquently advocated with the honest conviction that it is truth, is better than truth coldly believed and languidly proclaimed"—extraordinary only if we forget that it was an age "at once destitute of faith and terrified at scepticism." For their part the prophets were not only willing to meet the public demand; they had their own good reasons for adopting the tone of authority. When each school of political or religious thought (often with its own periodical) was fighting its rivals, the sectarian spirit encouraged dogmatism. When the prestige of intuition that marked the Romantic reaction against eighteenth-century rationalism was at its height, and the artist was endowed with an almost mystical power of insight, the writer might well substitute authoritative statement for logical argument. What Spencer said of Carlyle could be applied to many, though not all, of the prose prophets: he "never set out from premises and reasoned his way to conclusions, but habitually dealt in intuitions and dogmatic assertions."

Between the prophetic literature of expository prose and that of poetry and fiction, one may make a rough distinction on the lines laid down by Carlyle (on p. 411). The former is intended to persuade, to affect public opinion; the latter to inspire, to affect the character. In the one case, doctrine is taught; in the other, "noble sentiments," either in the form of moral reflections or ideal images, usually both at once. George Eliot felt that the function of the novelist was "that of the *aesthetic,* not the doctrinal teacher,—the rousing of the nobler emotions, which make mankind desire the social right, not the prescribing of special measures." For Arnold, the function of poetry in an age when traditional religion was dying was "to interpret life for us, to console us, to sustain us."

This moral pressure on the artist first appeared in the 1830's, when a reaction against the verbal beauties of Shelley and Keats and the wild and passionate heroes of Byron called for a literature of "noble images and thoughts." Tennyson was forced to abandon his early romantic poetry of mood and impression to supply the age with moral reflections or heroic characters. Browning, whose natural gift was for detached observation, was induced by Elizabeth Barrett and the gospel of Carlyle to make his studies of men and women illustrations of moral aspiration. Though Arnold, with an eye on Clough and some of Tennyson, complained that verse had become "a channel for thinking aloud, instead of making anything," much of his own poetry is filled with moral reflection; or, when that is not the case, offers "some noble action of a heroic time" to inspire and sustain an anxious generation. And there is no doubt that the prophetic purpose was welcomed. In at least one Victorian home where the parents had been "emancipated" by reading Darwin and Huxley, and where no one mentioned the Bible or went to church, the children were brought up on the Greek pantheon and the Arthurian Round Table. In the living room hung a picture of Sir Galahad by Frederick Watts, with the quotation from Tennyson:

> My strength is as the strength of ten,
> Because my heart is pure.

On the library table was a finely bound copy of *The Poetical Works of Robert Browning* containing his modern version of chivalric love and his high doctrine of aspiration toward impossible goals:

> 'Tis not what man Does which exalts him, but
> what man Would do!

In literal fact the Victorian poets became, as Carlyle predicted, a modern priesthood.

It must not be supposed that in itself a didactic intention is fatal to a work of art, still less that poetry of noble images or moral reflection is bad poetry. Shakespeare and Milton may be cited at once to the contrary. The critical estimate depends on the treatment. The noble image must not be too noble; the hero must be a human being and not an idealized abstraction or a self-conscious preacher of his own virtues (like Galahad in the quotation from Tennyson just given). Moral reflections must be translated into music and image, not simply stated (as they might be in a treatise or a sermon, as they *are* in the line by Browning quoted above). They must be "experienced" by the sensibility of the artist, not merely "thought" by the mind. Or they must arise implicitly from the concrete presentation of character and action, instead of being explicitly injected. The Victorian record, in these respects, is varied. All one can say is that the strong demand of the age for high ideals and moral guidance made artistic success more difficult to achieve, though by no means impossible. Furthermore, these pressures were not always operative; and a considerable body of Victorian poetry is innocent of prophetic intention. By moments the poets turned away from the needs and problems of the time, and away from its "unpoetic" environment of dirt and smoke and cutthroat competition, to seek relief in some image of ideal beauty, of woods and flowers, of faraway places and olden times—ancient Greece or medieval England, the Orient or a land of lotos-eating. Side by side with the motive to instruct and inspire was the motive to escape. It is because the heroic image could satisfy both motives at once—and meet both desires in their readers—that the Victorian writers turned so often to the mythology of Greece and Scandinavia and the legends of a time when knighthood was in flower. It is highly significant that when Arnold told the poet to abandon thinking and writing about the problems of the age, he suggested that instead he ought "to delight himself with the contemplation of some noble action of a heroic time, and to enable others, through his representation of it, to delight in it also." You have your cake and eat it too—escape to the glamour of heroic adventure and feel the moral inspiration of a noble action. This double effect is produced by Arnold's "Sohrab and Rustum," Tennyson's *Idylls of the King*, Morris's *Earthly Paradise*—and in prose by Kingsley's *Heroes, or Greek Fairy Tales*.

But the positive and negative reactions to contemporary life could not always be fused. By moments they came into open conflict, and the poet found himself trying to express opposite and conflicting attitudes. This is particularly true of Tennyson. Though poems like "Ulysses," "The Palace of Art," "The Lotos-Eaters," and "Locksley Hall" contain fine passages and brilliant lines, they are not successful as works of art because they are incoherent. They try to combine an amoral image of escape with a moral call to virtuous action. In another and more subtle form the same unresolved tension is seen in Arnold's "Scholar-Gipsy."

To be a poet in the Victorian age was certainly difficult. Arnold saw the problem, and did his best to focus his imagination on the primary and elemental experiences of human life. But he was pulled away from that central line to the right or to the left, and induced, in spite of himself, either to offer his age some helpful advice in versified form, or to escape to some vision of peace and beauty. This is equally true of Tennyson, and partly of Browning. But however difficult they found it, all three succeeded by moments in keeping their imaginations fixed on important and living experience. Tennyson's "Vision of Sin," Browning's "Toccata of Galuppi's," Arnold's "Dover Beach," to take an example from each, are the record of direct and penetrating insights into Victorian life.

If the major poets did not invariably write like prophets, they all subscribed to the theory of prophetic literature. But starting in the 1850's a contrary tendency, in criticism and poetry, began to grow up which may be called the Aesthetic Movement. It included the Pre-Raphaelites (the Rossettis, Morris, to some extent Swinburne, as well as the painters Hunt, Millais, and Burne Jones), and the later Aesthetes and Decadents (Oscar Wilde and the early Yeats), with Walter Pater as chief critic-philosopher. Among these various men there was considerable diversity of opinion and practice, but they all agreed on one thing, that it was *not* the business of art to instruct or inspire, nor the function of an artist to be a prophet. Art, as the battle cry put it, was for art's sake, and an artist—was an artist. But what did this mean, in theory and in fact? There are various answers to that question all of which are implicit in Morris's lecture on Pre-Raphaelitism (see pp. 791 ff.).

The Aesthetic Movement began in 1848 when a new and radical group of painters, who called themselves Pre-Raphaelites, first exhibited their pictures. What was radical was their insistence that an artist should paint what he saw regardless of the traditional "rules" of painting. In technical terms they were Naturalists: they were imitating nature as they experienced it directly instead of nature as it had been portrayed by earlier painters; and they were painting "naturally," in forms and colors faithful to their experience, not in those which had come down in the art schools of Europe since the Renaissance as the "right" techniques. A passage from Ruskin describes the situation against which they were revolting, and incidentally explains the term "Pre-Raphaelitism":

It being required to produce a poet on canvas, what is our way of setting to work? We begin, in all probability, by telling the youth of fifteen or sixteen, that Nature is full of faults, and that he is to improve her; but that Raphael is perfection, and that the more he copies Raphael the better; that after much copying of Raphael, . . . he is to try to do something very clever, all out of his own head, but yet this clever something is to be properly subjected to Raphaelesque rules, is to have a principal light occupying one-seventh of its space, and a principal shadow occupying one-third of the same; that no two people's heads in the picture are to be turned the same way, and that all the personages represented are to possess ideal beauty of the highest order, which ideal beauty consists partly in a Greek outline of nose, partly in proportions expressible in decimal fractions between the lips and chin. . . . This I say is the kind of teaching which . . . we give to our young men. And we wonder we have no painters!

In short, Pre-Raphaelitism was a return, not to the form and style of early Italian painting, but to its freedom from the requirement of painting ideal figures according to the rules which Raphael had laid down. As Morris points out (p. 791), the same revolt had occurred fifty years earlier in literature when Wordsworth and Coleridge had led the reaction against neoclassical conventions in poetry and had set up the contrary aim of keeping the eye on the object, that is, imitating nature as they saw it—which explains why Ruskin can say that "the Pre-Raphaelite school was headed, in literary power, by Wordsworth." In origin, therefore, the Aesthetic Movement was not antididactic: it was antiacademic. But the primary insistence on fidelity to experience was, in effect, a rejection of the prophetic principle, and an extension to painting of the Romantic principle of Naturalism.

The Pre-Raphaelites, however, were neo-Romantic in a further sense which explains why, for all their talk about Naturalism, their art was realistic only in its sharply realized detail, and not in the least as an account of contemporary life. On the contrary, they deliberately turned away from the ugly, noisy world of industrial England, from the problems and doubts of an age of transition, to a far more beautiful and heroic past, ancient or medieval, secular or Christian. We may say "deliberately" because, though this tendency had appeared, as we have noticed, in Tennyson and Arnold, it was in direct contradiction to their prophetic creed and their normal practice. But the Pre-Raphaelites openly called themselves tellers of tales and "dreamers of dreams," whose only purpose was to provide the pleasure of escaping into a romantic world of the past. Indeed, in the "Apology" prefixed to *The Earthly Paradise* (see pp. 782 f.) Morris explicitly denied that he had any power to ease "the heavy trouble, the bewildering care that weighs us down" or any intention of setting "the crooked straight." He aimed only "to build a shadowy isle of bliss midmost the beating of the steely [Victorian] sea." In short, he was not a prophet but "the idle singer of an empty day."

In poetry this romantic withdrawal from contemporary life took two forms, both suggested in Morris's lecture. The first was narrative or dramatic verse, where the primary focus is on characters seen at a moment of emotional crisis (for example, Rossetti's "Troy-Town" or Morris's "Defence of Guenevere"). The indebtedness here to Browning is obvious, and was frankly acknowledged; but, as we should expect, Rossetti and Morris adopted only his dramatic technique and not his moralism, and they injected it into a form closer to the ballad than to the dramatic monologue.

The second kind of aesthetic poetry, which eventually displaced the first in importance, is indicated by Morris's reference to the ornamental and decorative side of the movement. It is a poetry of color and sound where imagery and rhythm are used, not to describe living characters or express human emotions, but to invoke a vague and intangible mood of beauty (see Morris's "Blue Closet" on the pictorial side, and Swinburne's "Garden of Proserpine" on the musical side). In terms of *literary* history, this decorative poetry abstracted the form of Romantic verse from its content, and combined the imagery of Keats with the lyrical rhythm of Shelley; and in doing so, it rejected all ideas, whether abstract or psychological. In fact, at its furthest development, in some of Swinburne, in the early Yeats, even concretely defined objects have disappeared and what is left is an "almost bodiless emotion." In terms of *intellectual* history, it marks the extreme withdrawal of the artist from the contemporary world into the Ivory Tower of the aesthetic imagination. There, and there only, could Yeats find a room where "tapestry, full of the blue and bronze of peacocks, fell over the doors, and shut out all history and activity untouched with beauty and peace." That room is symbol at once for the poetry and the poetic mind of the later Aesthetic Movement.

This was the dead end. In Hopkins and Hardy we see the start of that reaction against sensuous beauties of style and thinness, or preciousness, of experience which prepared the way for modern poetry. "My generation," said Yeats, in later life when he had outgrown his early theory and practice, threw over "poetical diction" and began the search "for hard positive subject-matter." But in the spirit of art and not prophecy. Modern poetry may be viewed as a profounder development, under the influence of the French Symbolists, of the principle of Art for Art's Sake.

GENERAL REFERENCES

For the political history of the period see G. M. Trevelyan, *British History in the Nineteenth Century* (1938); or, more briefly, J. A. Williamson, *The Evolution of England* (1931), chaps. 8–10.

For social and intellectual history the reader may consult J. H. Randall, Jr., *The Making of the Modern Mind* (1940 ed.), chaps. 11-15 on the important background of eighteenth-century thought, chaps. 16-22 on the nineteenth century; D. C. Somervell, *English Thought in the Nineteenth Century* (1929); G. M. Young, *Victorian England: Portrait of an Age* (1936); Esmé Wingfield-Stratford, *Those Earnest Victorians* (1930) and *The Victorian Sunset* (1932); H. V. Routh, *Money, Morals and Manners as Revealed in Modern Literature* (1935).

But the best social and intellectual history of the period is to be found in contemporary biography. Among the most revealing and representative are: A. P. Stanley, *The Life and Correspondence of Dr. Thomas Arnold* (1844); Edmund Gosse, *Father and Son* (1907); *Letters and Memorials of Charles Kingsley*, edited by his wife (abridged ed., 2 vols., 1877); John Stuart Mill, *Autobiography* (1873); John Morley, *Recollections* (2 vols., 1917), I, 3-144; and H. F. Brown, *John Addington Symonds, a Biography* (1894).

In addition, many Victorian novels throw significant light on the age. Dickens's *Hard Times* (1854), Disraeli's *Coningsby* (1844) and *Sybil: or, The Two Nations* (1845),

Mrs. Elizabeth Gaskell's *Mary Barton* (1848) and *North and South* (1855), and Kingsley's *Alton Locke* (1850) deal with political and economic problems. Religious and moral questions are central in Samuel Butler's *Way of All Flesh* (1903, but written about 1880), Kingsley's *Yeast* (1851), Trollope's *Barchester Towers* (1857), and Mrs. Humphry Ward's *Robert Elsmere* (1888).

There is no adequate account of Victorian literature as a whole. Oliver Elton, *A Survey of English Literature, 1780-1880* (4 vols., 1920), vols. III and IV, is the best general guide that exists. G. K. Chesterton's *The Victorian Age of Literature* (1913) is stimulating and breezy. The best secondary works deal with a few central figures: A. Cruse, *The Victorians and Their Reading* (1935); Graham Hough, *The Last Romantics* (1949), on Ruskin and the Aesthetic Movement; Vida Scudder, *Social Ideals in English Letters* (1923), part II, mainly on Carlyle, Ruskin, and Arnold; Basil Willey, *Nineteenth Century Studies* (1949), mainly on the prose critics from Coleridge to Matthew Arnold. The best account of poetry in the last decades of the century is in W. B. Yeats's *Autobiography* (1938 ed.).

Thomas Carlyle

1795-1881

THE THOUGHT and temper of the age is nowhere more fully revealed than in the work of Thomas Carlyle. Like so many Victorians, he started from traditional Christianity, passed through a period of doubt amounting for a while to outright disbelief in any supernatural order, and ended by the recovery of his faith in a new form, or new forms, of religion which seemed credible, as Christianity did not, in the light of modern thought. In politics his opposition to Benthamite liberalism, with its policy of *laissez faire*, and his plea for a strong central government to carry out a policy of labor legislation are characteristic not only of conservatives like Disraeli and Ruskin, but also of the "new" liberals in the sixties and seventies, Mill, Huxley, and Chamberlain. When we add to this pattern of thought his insistence upon the value of work and the importance of duty, his worship of heroes, and his ambivalent attitude toward commercial society (scorn for its low ideals but enthusiasm for its industrial achievements), we see that he reflects the very core of the Victorian temper.

Carlyle was born in Scotland in 1795, the son of humble parents who brought him up in the ethic and theology of Puritanism. In 1809 he entered Edinburgh University to prepare himself for the ministry, but his scientific and philosophical studies undermined his religious faith. After a period of schoolteaching he returned to Edinburgh

in 1818 to study law, but soon abandoned it for literature. The new religious philosophy which he had found in the contemporary German poets and philosophers he first discussed in a series of articles for the *Edinburgh Review* and presently embodied in the semiautobiographical *Sartor Resartus* (the tailor with a new suit of clothes), published in 1833. In the meanwhile he had married Jane Welsh in 1826; and after visiting London in 1831, where they met the leading writers of the day, especially John Stuart Mill, they settled permanently there in 1835. At the suggestion of Mill, who had been collecting materials on the subject which he handed over to his new friend, Carlyle now wrote his famous *History of the French Revolution* (1837). Henceforth history and biography were his major fields of work: his *Heroes and Hero-Worship* (1841) is a collection of biographies from Odin and Mohammed to Napoleon; *Past and Present* (1843) combines the history of a medieval monastery with essays on contemporary politics; in the *Letters and Speeches of Cromwell* (1845) and *The History of Frederick the Great* (1858-65) he fused history, biography, and political theory in the autocratic image of the hero. When he died in 1881, he seemed to most Victorians the great prophet of the age.

When Carlyle arrived at Edinburgh in 1809, he was shocked to find that most of his professors and fellow students treated Christianity, and to some extent even Deism, with cool acquiescence or outright ridicule. This was the fruit of eighteenth-century rationalism, stemming from Bacon and Descartes, Locke and Newton in the previous century, and developed by Hartley, Hume, and Bentham. (See the outline above in the General Introduction, pp. 376–377, which gives this essential background for understanding Carlyle.) In the work of these philosophers he found that all he had been taught to believe was denied, at least implicitly: there was no God immediately active in human life, or no God at all; man was not endowed with free will or with a God-given conscience, nor motivated by any unselfish sense of duty to God and society; and obviously, there was no original sin, no Incarnation or Atonement, and no Biblical miracles. This is the world into which Carlyle sank down from 1809 to 1818, and which he describes in the chapter from *Sartor Resartus* appropriately called "The Everlasting No." That chapter ends, however, with the start of his journey back to faith, the moment of sudden defiance, in August, 1822, when once for all he repudiated the whole conception of a "dead, steam-engine" universe without purpose or volition. *That* he would *not* believe in. But what *was* he to believe in? He found an answer in German Transcendentalism, notably in Kant, Fichte, and Goethe, where he met a view of man and nature at all points opposite to that of eighteenth-century rationalism. In this view the mind, far from being passive, is itself an active agent of knowledge (what we "know" is the product of both mind and experience, the former interpreting the latter); in addition to reason, there is a higher faculty of knowledge, an intuitive power of insight into the non-physical truths of religion, morality, and politics; matter is not the ultimate reality, but only an appearance in consciousness (the way the world appears to an organism which possesses a human mind and human senses); man is born with a moral will or conscience, able and free to choose between right and wrong; the highest goal of life is not pleasure but duty (meaning both the passive duty of accepting pain and suffering—what Carlyle calls "the worship of sorrow"—and the active duty of work); and finally, above all, there is a God immediately present in the universe: Nature is a symbol, manifestation, or "garment" of the divine spirit in the same way that a man's gestures or facial expressions may be said to manifest his personality. So fortified, Carlyle could again believe, not in Christianity, but in a religion which was part pantheism, part theism; and could thus answer "The Everlasting No" with "The Everlasting Yea."

But in the last analysis he did not rest his faith on the mystical-metaphysical idea of the universe as a symbolic manifestation of God. What he felt in nature, as we see in the first selection from *Heroes and Hero-Worship*, was not

so much the presence of a divine spirit as a sense of mystery, the profound mystery of human existence and the equally profound mystery beneath the facts of physical science. All our science is merely descriptive. It tells us that this object has these properties, that this law acts in that way, but *why* the properties or *why* the action is unknown. And since science permeated the Victorian mind, Carlyle's argument from mystery to God was bound to speak more persuasively than the mystical-metaphysical argument of German philosophy. What is mysterious, he said, is inexplicable (without natural explanation), and therefore supernatural, and therefore indirectly a witness to, or revelation of, a divine power:

Science has done much for us; but it is a poor science that would hide from us the great deep sacred infinitude of Nescience, whither we can never penetrate, on which all science swims as a mere superficial film. This world, after all our science and sciences, is still a miracle; wonderful, inscrutable, *magical* [i.e., supernatural] and more [i.e., divine], to whosoever will *think* of it.

It is not an accident that this passage appears in the opening paragraphs of *Heroes and Hero-Worship*, for the hero, as Carlyle conceived of him, was not only the man who found God behind the mystery of the universe, but was himself another finite revelation of the Infinite. He was literally inspired, a Seer or Prophet able to perceive intuitively what God wills or what he plans for mankind. "Really his utterances, are they not a kind of 'revelation'? . . . We must listen before all to him," as we no longer can listen to the Church or the Bible. Christ himself is reduced by Carlyle to "the greatest of all Heroes," and the germ of Christianity is said to be "hero-worship, heartfelt prostrate admiration, submission, burning, boundless, for a noblest godlike Form of Man." From there it is only a step to the secular cult of the hero and the Victorian effort to find in heroic legends or heroic lives the moral inspiration no longer supplied by religion.

That means, in effect, the substitution of the writer for the priest; and this too is explicit in Carlyle's book. His hero is not simply a political or military leader; he is also an intellectual leader. In "The Hero as Man of Letters," we see the Victorian conception of the writer as prophet, taking the place of the old Christian priesthood, providing a new religion, or at least the moral guidance and inspiration that men were ceasing to find in the Church.

This conception provides the best perspective for understanding Carlyle's peculiar—and at first baffling—style. Its essential character is prophetic. Like that of the Old Testament prophets, his method is not analysis, explanation, logical argument. It is passionate exhortation, confident statements on matters highly debatable, frequent imperatives ("Know it of a truth that . . ."), direct addresses to the reader in a charged and idiomatic speech (the prophet speaking to *you*), and a "shock" technique which startles one into attention by sudden, rapid shifts of form or by strange and often grotesque metaphors and illustrations. All this, with a minimum of logical argument, was exactly the right style for both the Victorian prophet and his disciples. However irritating it may be today, it was enormously popular with a generation longing to be told what to believe, and in no uncertain or debatable terms. And quite apart from this public demand, Carlyle's whole conception of the writer pointed in the same direction. If intuition rather than reason is his great faculty, then positive statement and not rational argument will be his natural technique.

The figure of the hero is closely linked with Carlyle's theory of history and his practice in historical writing. In theory he conceived of history too as a revelation of God: in the success and fate of nations we can see the hand of Providence rewarding virtue and punishing evil. But since history is made by great men, and not by impersonal economic forces, great men are "the inspired (speaking and acting) Texts of that divine Book of Revelation"— the texts on which the historian preaches. *The History of the French Revolution* (1837), which centers on Mirabeau and Danton, was written to show the manifest judgment of God upon the dissolute, luxury-loving court of Versailles. But it was also written simply to bring the men and the events vividly to life. For Carlyle often forgot his didactic theory, and under the influence of Scott made history a vivid recreation of the past. In this respect he belongs with Macaulay; though where Macaulay's art is narrative, Carlyle's is dramatic. He sees the past in a series of scenes, complete with dialogue and stage setting (see the selections from Book II of *Past and Present,* below). In one respect, however, these two historians are radically different. Because Carlyle saw the institutions of the past as so many efforts, successful then though now worn out, to embody the *permanent* spiritual goals of man (for religious faith, for political order, and so on), he could look at earlier times with a sympathy impossible for any liberal like Macaulay, who viewed his superstitious and autocratic ancestors with superior disdain. This explains why he inserted a sketch of medieval life, feudal and monastic, into a book on modern politics. *Past and Present* says, in effect, let us remember the living ideals of the past and give them new forms for the present: the ideal of religion in a new non-Catholic, non-Christian form; of work and service in a new secular, nonascetic form; of feudal authority in a new social organization where a natural aristocracy of talent shall take the place of the old landed aristocracy and again govern the country with a strong and paternal hand.

As this last "ideal" implies, *Past and Present* is a bitter arraignment of the Victorian liberal-business world. Carlyle cut under the worship of material success, the hurrahs for liberty and the blessings of competition, to expose the ugliness, physical and spiritual, of modern industrial society. Not that he was hostile to business as such. He was as ready as Macaulay to celebrate its industrial achievements; and under their spell as ready to turn anti-intellectual and exalt practical action at the expense of theoretical speculation (see pp. 427–29)—even readier, because for Carlyle work was not only an economic requirement, not only a Puritan command; it was a protection against the dangerous atheistical tendency of modern thought and a cure for modern doubt (see page 409). What Carlyle attacked was not business but the worldly and selfish spirit of the new industrialists, concerned only with their personal success, financial and social. And he attacked their political creed. He saw that their boasted policy of freedom (no government interference) meant, in fact, freedom for the capitalist but hardly for the laborer who had to take the job in the local factory at the local wage or go unemployed—and be free to starve. He saw that the liberal theory of society as a collection of free individuals, bound together only by a "cash-nexus," free from any personal obligations or responsibilities like those of feudal or family society, competing freely in an open market, might produce better goods at lower prices, but might also produce much worse human beings, devoid of charity, permeated by bitter and open hostility, especially between capital and labor.

The fundamental solution was a spiritual rebirth. No amount of tinkering with the machinery of government would produce a good society. That could only be done by producing good men through a powerful religious revival. If the Captains of Industry would recognize the reality of God and hear His voice in their conscience, commanding a life of duty and brotherly love—that is to say, if they would become heroic—they would cast out their Mammonism and treat their workers with justice and humanity; while the workers for their part would give their leaders the loyalty and devotion due to genuine heroes. But in the meanwhile, pending this utopia, something might be done to improve the appalling "condition-of-England" by a strong, paternalistic state that would carry through a program of labor legislation (see pp. 438–41); and by giving this political power not to the people (democracy seemed madness to Carlyle) but to a hero-dictator if possible, otherwise to a talented aristocracy—not the old, idle, pigeon-shooting, landed aristocracy, but a new aristocracy of brains and energy to be recruited from the Captains of Industry purged of their Mammonism and converted to Carlyle's religious and moral idealism.

The standard edition is *The Works of Thomas Carlyle*, ed. H. D. Traill (Centenary Edition, 30 vols., 1896–99). The best Life is by J. A. Froude (4 vols., 1882–84); though not always reliable, this is a brilliantly written biography, full of illuminating letters and journals. For critical interpretation, one may consult Louis Cazamian, *Thomas Carlyle* (1913; translated by E. K. Brown, 1932), and Emery Neff, *Carlyle and Mill* (1924; revised ed., 1926).

Thomas Carlyle

from SARTOR RESARTUS

Book II, Chapter 7
THE EVERLASTING NO[1] 390

UNDER the strange nebulous envelopment, wherein our Professor[2] has now shrouded himself, no doubt but his spiritual nature is nevertheless progressive, and growing: for how can the "Son of Time,"[3] in any case, stand still? We behold him, through those dim years, in a state of crisis, of transition: his mad Pilgrimings, and general solution into aimless Discontinuity, what is all this but a mad Fermentation; wherefrom, the fiercer it is, the clearer product will one day evolve itself?

Such transitions are ever full of pain: thus the Eagle when he molts is sickly; and, to attain his new beak, must harshly dash-off the old one upon rocks. What Stoicism soever our Wanderer, in his individual acts and motions, may affect, it is clear that there is a hot fever of anarchy and misery raging within; coruscations of which flash out: as, indeed, how could there be other? Have we not seen him disappointed, bemocked of Destiny, through long years? All that the young heart might desire and pray for has been denied; nay, as in the last worst instance,[4] offered and then snatched away. Ever an "excellent Passivity";[5] but of useful, reasonable Activity, essential to the

former as Food to Hunger, nothing granted: till at length, in this wild Pilgrimage, he must forcibly seize for himself an Activity, though useless, unreasonable. Alas, his cup of bitterness, which had been filling drop by drop, ever since that first "ruddy morning" in the Hinterschlag Gymnasium,[6] was at the very lip; and then with that poison-drop, of the Towgood-and-Blumine business, it runs over, and even hisses over in a deluge of foam.

He himself says once, with more justice than originality: "Man is, properly speaking, based upon Hope; he has no other possession but Hope; this world of his is emphatically the 'Place of Hope.'" What, then, was our Professor's possession? We see him, for the present, quite shut-out from Hope; looking not into the golden orient, but vaguely all round into a dim copper firmament, pregnant with earthquake and tornado.

Alas, shut-out from Hope, in a deeper sense than we yet dream of! For, as he wanders wearisomely through this world, he has now lost all tidings of another and higher. Full of religion, or at least of religiosity, as our Friend has since exhibited himself, he hides not that, in those days, he was wholly irreligious: "Doubt had darkened into Unbelief," says he; "shade after shade goes grimly over your soul, till you have the fixed, starless, Tartarean[7] black." To such readers as have reflected, what can be called reflecting, on man's life, and happily discovered, in contradiction to much Profit-and-Loss Philosophy,[8] speculative and practical, that Soul is *not* synonymous

---

[1] The title means the spirit of negation, denying any possible moral or spiritual values, positing instead a wholly materialistic universe, "all void of Life, of Purpose, of Volition, even of Hostility . . . one huge, dead, immeasurable Steam-engine, rolling on, in its dead indifference."

[2] Diogenes Teufelsdröckh, the hero of *Sartor Resartus* and the mouthpiece for Carlyle's ideas. The book purports to be his autobiography edited by Carlyle, who refers to himself as "the Editor." [3] Man.

[4] The loss of his lady-love, Blumine, to his friend Towgood, described in the previous chapter.

[5] Teufelsdröckh tells us he had early learned to "bear and forbear," and as a child had been held down by "a strait bond of Obedience." The resultant passivity, a combination of acceptance and renunciation, was excellent so far as it went, but it was negative inasmuch as it was not the product of active choice.

[6] It was a "red sunny Whitsuntide morning" when Teufelsdröckh went to school for the first time to the Strike-behind Academy.

[7] Tartarus was the lowest and darkest region of hell.

[8] The reference is to Utilitarianism with its doctrine that a good or virtuous action is one which produces a total balance of pleasure over pain; a bad or vicious action, one producing more pain than pleasure. One must, so to speak, calculate the Profit (pleasure) against the Loss (pain). To Carlyle this seemed an utterly sensual (stomach) philosophy. He opposes to it, in the next sentences, a "higher" one of service to God and man, regardless of pain. Not pleasure but duty is man's true goal.

with Stomach; who understand, therefore, in our Friend's words, "that, for man's well-being, Faith is properly the one thing needful; how, with it, Martyrs, otherwise weak, can cheerfully endure the shame and the cross; and without it, Worldlings puke-up their sick existence, by suicide, in the midst of luxury": to such, it will be clear that, for a pure moral nature, the loss of his religious Belief was the loss of everything. Unhappy young man! All wounds, the crush of long-continued Destitution, the stab of false Friendship, and of false Love, all wounds in thy so genial heart, would have healed again, had not its life-warmth been withdrawn. Well might he exclaim, in his wild way: "Is there no God, then; but at best an absentee God, sitting idle, ever since the first Sabbath, at the outside of his Universe, and *seeing* it go?[9] Has the word Duty no meaning; is what we call Duty no divine Messenger and Guide, but a false earthly Fantasm, made-up of Desire and Fear, of emanations from the Gallows and from Doctor Graham's Celestial Bed?[10] Happiness of an approving Conscience! Did not Paul of Tarsus, whom admiring men have since named Saint, feel that *he* was 'the chief of sinners,'[11] and Nero of Rome, jocund in spirit (*wohlgemuth*), spend much of his time in fiddling?[12] Foolish Wordmonger, and Motive-grinder, who in thy Logic-mill[13] hast an earthly mechanism for the Godlike itself, and wouldst fain grind me out Virtue from the husks of Pleasure,—I tell thee, Nay! To the unregenerate Prometheus Vinctus[14] of a man, it is ever the bitterest aggravation of his wretchedness that he is conscious of Virtue, that he feels himself the victim not of suffering only, but of injustice. What then? Is the heroic inspiration we name Virtue but some Passion; some bubble of the blood, bubbling in the direction others *profit* by? I know not: only this I know, If what thou namest Happiness be our true aim, then are we all astray. With Stupidity and sound digestion man may front much. But what, in these dull unimaginative days, are the terrors of Conscience to the diseases of the Liver! Not on Morality,

but on Cookery, let us build our stronghold: there brandishing our frying-pan, as censer, let us offer sweet incense to the Devil, and live at ease on the fat things *he* has provided for his Elect!"

Thus has the bewildered Wanderer to stand, as so many have done, shouting question after question into the Sibyl-cave[15] of Destiny, and receive no Answer but an Echo. It is all a grim Desert, this once-fair world of his; wherein is heard only the howling of wild-beasts, or the shrieks of despairing, hate-filled men; and no Pillar of Cloud by day, and no Pillar of Fire by night, any longer guides the Pilgrim.[16] To such length has the spirit of Inquiry carried him. "But what boots it (*was thut's*)?" cries he; "it is but the common lot in this era. Not having come to spiritual majority prior to the *Siècle de Louis Quinze*,[17] and not being born purely a Loghead (*Dummkopf*), thou hadst no other outlook. The whole world is, like thee, sold to Unbelief; their old Temples of the Godhead, which for long have not been rain-proof, crumble down; and men ask now: Where is the Godhead; our eyes never saw him?"

Pitiful enough were it, for all these wild utterances, to call our Diogenes wicked. Unprofitable servants as we all are,[18] perhaps at no era of his life was he more decisively the Servant of Goodness, the Servant of God, than even now when doubting God's existence. "One circumstance I note," says he: "after all the nameless woe that Inquiry, which for me, what it is not always, was genuine Love of Truth, had wrought me, I nevertheless still loved Truth, and would bate no jot[19] of my allegiance to her. 'Truth!' I cried, 'though the Heavens crush me for following her: no Falsehood! though a whole celestial Lubberland[20] were the price of Apostasy.' In conduct it was the same. Had a divine Messenger from the clouds, or miraculous Handwriting on the wall, convincingly proclaimed to me *This thou shalt do*, with what passionate readiness, as I often thought, would I have done it, had it been leaping into the infernal Fire. Thus, in spite of all Motive-grinders, and Mechanical Profit-and-Loss Philosophies, with the sick ophthalmia and hallucination they had brought on, was the Infinite nature of Duty still dimly present to me: living without God in the world,[21] of God's light I

---

[9] The eighteenth-century Deistic position, in which God was viewed as a mechanic or celestial clockmaker, who having created the world and set it going was then content to let it function without his participation or even his presence.

[10] Graham, an eighteenth-century quack, invented a bed said to cure sterility—a symbol here of the delusiveness of faith in materialism.   [11] I Timothy 1:15.

[12] By tradition Nero is supposed to have fiddled while Rome burned.

[13] A pun on the name of James Mill, one of the most ardent Utilitarians.

[14] Prometheus Bound represents a man of genius suffering under, but defying, an unjust fate.

[15] The Sibyl was reputed to know the innermost secrets of the universe.

[16] As happened to the Israelites in their flight from Egypt (Exodus 13:21-22).

[17] The century of Louis XV; i.e., the eighteenth century, known as one of rationalism and skepticism. See "The Hero as Man of Letters," pp. 414 ff., below.

[18] Luke 17:10.   [19] Abate not the smallest part.

[20] Land of luxurious ease.   [21] Ephesians 2:12.

was not utterly bereft; if my as yet sealed eyes, with their unspeakable longing, could nowhere see Him, nevertheless in my heart He was present, and His heaven-written Law still stood legible and sacred there."

Meanwhile, under all these tribulations, and temporal and spiritual destitutions, what must the Wanderer, in his silent soul, have endured! "The painfullest feeling," writes he, "is that of your own Feebleness (*Unkraft*); ever, as the English Milton says, to be weak is the true misery.[22] And yet of your Strength there is and can be no clear feeling, save by what you have prospered in, by what you have done. Between vague wavering Capability and fixed indubitable Performance, what a difference! A certain inarticulate Self-consciousness dwells dimly in us; which only our Works can render articulate and decisively discernible. Our Works are the mirror wherein the spirit first sees its natural lineaments. Hence, too, the folly of that impossible Precept, *Know thyself;* till it be translated into this partially possible one, *Know what thou canst work at.*

"But for me, so strangely unprosperous had I been, the net-result of my Workings amounted as yet simply to—Nothing. How then could I believe in my Strength, when there was as yet no mirror to see it in? Ever did this agitating, yet, as I now perceive, quite frivolous question, remain to me insoluble: Hast thou a certain Faculty, a certain Worth, such even as the most have not; or art thou the completest Dullard of these modern times? Alas! the fearful Unbelief is unbelief in yourself; and how could I believe? Had not my first, last Faith in myself, when even to me the Heavens seemed laid open, and I dared to love, been all-too cruelly belied? The speculative Mystery of Life grew ever more mysterious to me; neither in the practical Mystery[23] had I made the slightest progress, but been everywhere buffeted, foiled, and contemptuously cast out. A feeble unit in the middle of a threatening Infinitude, I seemed to have nothing given me but eyes, whereby to discern my own wretchedness. Invisible yet impenetrable walls, as of Enchantment, divided me from all living: was there, in the wide world, any true bosom I could press trustfully to mine? O Heaven, No, there was none! I kept a lock upon my lips: why should I speak much with that shifting variety of so-called Friends, in whose withered, vain and too-hungry souls, Friendship was but an incredible tradition? In such cases, your resource is to talk little, and that

little mostly from the Newspapers. Now when I look back, it was a strange isolation I then lived in. The men and women around me, even speaking with me, were but Figures: I had, practically, forgotten that they were alive, that they were not merely automatic. In the midst of their crowded streets, and assemblages, I walked solitary; and (except as it was my own heart, not another's, that I kept devouring) savage also, as the tiger in his jungle. Some comfort it would have been, could I, like a Faust,[24] have fancied myself tempted and tormented of the Devil; for a Hell, as I imagine, without Life, though only diabolic Life, were more frightful: but in our age of Down-pulling and Disbelief, the very Devil has been pulled down, you cannot so much as believe in a Devil. To me the Universe was all void of Life, of Purpose, of Volition, even of Hostility: it was one huge, dead, immeasurable Steam-engine, rolling on, in its dead indifference, to grind me limb from limb. O, the vast gloomy, solitary Golgotha,[25] and Mill of Death! Why was the Living banished thither companionless, conscious? Why, if there is no Devil; nay, unless the Devil is your God?"

A prey incessantly to such corrosions, might not, moreover, as the worst aggravation to them, the iron constitution even of a Teufelsdröckh threaten to fail? We conjecture that he has known sickness; and, in spite of his locomotive habits, perhaps sickness of the chronic sort. Hear this, for example: "How beautiful to die of broken-heart, on Paper! Quite another thing in practice; every window of your Feeling, even of your Intellect, as it were, begrimed and mud-bespattered, so that no pure ray can enter; a whole Drugshop in your inwards; the foredone soul drowning slowly in quagmires of Disgust!"

Putting all which external and internal miseries together, may we not find in the following sentences, quite in our Professor's still vein, significance enough? "From Suicide a certain aftershine (*Nachschein*) of Christianity withheld me: perhaps also a certain indolence of character; for, was not that a remedy I had at any time within reach? Often, however, was there a question present to me: Should some one now, at the turning of that corner, blow thee suddenly out of Space, into the other World, or other No-world, by pistol-shot,—how were it? On which ground, too, I have often, in sea-storms and sieged cities and other death-scenes, exhibited an imperturbability, which passed, falsely enough, for courage.

---

[22] *Paradise Lost*, I, 157.   [23] Occupation, profession.

[24] A medieval German scholar who sold his soul to the Devil in return for a life of hedonistic pleasure. Carlyle quotes below from Goethe's poem on the subject.
[25] The scene of Jesus's crucifixion; literally, place of skulls.

"So had it lasted," concludes the Wanderer, "so had it lasted, as in bitter protracted Death-agony, through long years. The heart within me, unvisited by any heavenly dewdrop, was smouldering in sulphurous, slow-consuming fire. Almost since earliest memory I had shed no tear; or once only when I, murmuring half-audibly, recited Faust's Deathsong, that wild *Selig der den er im Siegesglanze findet* (Happy whom he[26] finds in Battle's splendour), and thought that of this last Friend even I was not forsaken, that Destiny itself could not doom me not to die. Having no hope, neither had I any definite fear, were it of Man or of Devil: nay, I often felt as if it might be solacing, could the Arch-Devil himself, though in Tartarean terrors, but rise to me, that I might tell him a little of my mind. And yet, strangely enough, I lived in a continual, indefinite, pining fear; tremulous, pusillanimous, apprehensive of I knew not what: it seemed as if all things in the Heavens above and the Earth beneath would hurt me; as if the Heavens and the Earth were but boundless jaws of a devouring monster, wherein I, palpitating, waited to be devoured.

"Full of such humour, and perhaps the miserablest man in the whole French Capital or Suburbs, was I, one sultry Dog-day, after much perambulation, toiling along the dirty little *Rue Saint-Thomas de l'Enfer*,[27] among civic rubbish enough, in a close atmosphere, and over pavements hot as Nebuchadnezzar's Furnace;[28] whereby doubtless my spirits were little cheered; when, all at once, there rose a Thought in me, and I asked myself: 'What *art* thou afraid of? Wherefore, like a coward, dost thou forever pip and whimper, and go cowering and trembling? Despicable biped! what is the sum-total of the worst that lies before thee? Death? Well, Death; and say the pangs of Tophet[29] too, and all that the Devil and Man may, will, or can do against thee! Hast thou not a heart; canst thou not suffer whatsoever it be; and, as a Child of Freedom, though outcast, trample Tophet itself under thy feet, while it consumes thee? Let it come, then; I will meet it and defy it!' And as I so thought, there rushed like a stream of fire over my whole soul; and I shook base Fear away from me

forever. I was strong, of unknown strength; a spirit, almost a god. Ever from that time, the temper of my misery was changed: not Fear or whining Sorrow was it, but Indignation and grim fire-eyed Defiance.

"Thus had the EVERLASTING NO (*das ewige Nein*) pealed authoritatively through all the recesses of my Being, of my ME; and then was it that my whole ME stood up, in native God-created majesty, and with emphasis recorded its Protest. Such a Protest, the most important transaction in Life, may that same Indignation and Defiance, in a psychological point of view, be fitly called. The Everlasting No had said: 'Behold, thou art fatherless, outcast, and the Universe is mine (the Devil's)', to which my whole ME now made answer: '*I* am not thine, but Free, and forever hate thee!'[30]

"It is from this hour that I incline to date my Spiritual New-birth, or Baphometic[31] Fire-baptism; perhaps I directly thereupon began to be a Man."

Book II, Chapter 9

THE EVERLASTING YEA

"Temptations in the Wilderness!"[32] exclaims Teufelsdröckh: "Have we not all to be tried with such? Not so easily can the old Adam,[33] lodged in us by birth, be dispossessed. Our Life is compassed round with Necessity; yet is the meaning of Life itself no other than Freedom, than Voluntary Force; thus have we a warfare; in the beginning, especially, a hard-fought battle. For the God-given mandate, *Work thou in Welldoing*,[34] lies mysteriously written, in Promethean[35] Prophetic Characters, in our hearts; and leaves us no rest, night or day, till it be deciphered and obeyed; till it burn forth, in our conduct, a visible, acted Gospel of Freedom. And as the clay-given mandate, *Eat thou and be filled*,[36] at the same time persuasively proclaims itself through every

---

26 Death.
27 As the scene of Teufelsdröckh's experience Carlyle chose Paris because it typified all that was most skeptical and materialistic in French thought, and this particular street because of its infernal name.
28 The furnace prepared by the king of Babylon for the cremation of three Jews who would not worship a golden image (Daniel 3).
29 Hell.

30 See note 1, above. The importance of this experience lies in Teufelsdröckh's realization that he can protest against a wholly materialistic conception of the universe. His very "Indignation and grim fire-eyed Defiance" proved to him that there was something in his "whole Me," as distinct from the "mere Me" (the bodily part, belonging solely to the natural order), something which seemed not earth-created but God-created or of the spirit.
31 Baphomet was an idol whose rites included baptism by fire.
32 A reference to Christ's forty days in the wilderness. This section has repeated images from the gospel account (Matthew 4:1–11).
33 Original sin.
34 By the mouth of Paul: ". . . be not weary in well doing" (2 Thessalonians 3:13).
35 Fiery, from Prometheus's gift of fire to man. *Characters* = letters.
36 This, of course, was the Devil's suggestion to Christ in the wilderness, and the reader is meant to have the association in mind as he ponders this materialistic precept.

nerve,—must there not be a confusion, a contest, before the better Influence can become the upper?

"To me nothing seems more natural than that the Son of Man, when such God-given mandate first prophetically stirs within him, and the Clay must now be vanquished or vanquish,—should be carried of the spirit into grim Solitudes, and there fronting the Tempter do grimmest battle with him; defiantly setting him at naught, till he yield and fly. Name it as we choose: with or without visible Devil, whether in the natural Desert of rocks and sands, or in the populous moral Desert of selfishness and baseness,—to such Temptation are we all called. Unhappy if we are not! Unhappy if we are but Half-men, in whom that divine handwriting has never blazed forth, all-subduing, in true sun-splendour; but quivers dubiously amid meaner lights: or smoulders, in dull pain, in darkness, under earthly vapours!—Our Wilderness is the wide World in an Atheistic Century; our Forty Days are long years of suffering and fasting: nevertheless, to these also comes an end. Yes, to me also was given, if not Victory, yet the consciousness of Battle, and the resolve to persevere therein while life or faculty is left. To me also, entangled in the enchanted forests, demon-peopled, doleful of sight and of sound, it was given, after weariest wanderings, to work out my way into the higher sunlit slopes—of that Mountain[37] which has no summit, or whose summit is in Heaven only!"

He says elsewhere, under a less ambitious figure; as figures are, once for all, natural to him: "Has not thy Life been that of most sufficient men (tüchtigen Männer) thou hast known in this generation? An outflush of foolish young Enthusiasm, like the first fallow-crop,[38] wherein are as many weeds as valuable herbs: this all parched away, under the Droughts of practical and spiritual Unbelief, as Disappointment, in thought and act, often-repeated gave rise to Doubt, and Doubt gradually settled into Denial! If I have had a second-crop, and now see the perennial greensward, and sit under umbrageous cedars, which defy all Drought (and Doubt); herein too, be the Heavens praised, I am not without examples, and even exemplars."

So that, for Teufelsdröckh also, there has been a "glorious revolution":[39] these mad shadow-hunting and shadow-hunted Pilgrimings of his were but some purifying "Temptation in the Wilderness," before his apostolic work (such as it was) could begin; which Temptation is now happily over, and the Devil once more worsted! Was "that high moment in the Rue de l'Enfer," then, properly the turning-point of the battle; when the Fiend said, Worship me, or be torn in shreds; and was answered valiantly with an Apage Satana?[40]—Singular Teufelsdröckh, would thou hadst told thy singular story in plain words! But it is fruitless to look there, in those Paper-bags,[41] for such. Nothing but innuendoes, figurative crotchets: a typical Shadow, fitfully wavering, propheticosatiric; no clear logical Picture. "How paint to the sensual eye," asks he once, "what passes in the Holy-of-Holies of Man's Soul; in what words, known to these profane times, speak even afar-off of the unspeakable?" We ask in turn: Why perplex these times, profane as they are, with needless obscurity, by omission and by commission? Not mystical only is our Professor, but whimsical; and involves himself, now more than ever, in eye-bewildering chiaroscuro.[42] Successive glimpses, here faithfully imparted, our more gifted readers must endeavour to combine for their own behoof.

He says: "The hot Harmattan[43] wind had raged itself out; its howl went silent within me; and the long-deafened soul could now hear. I paused in my wild wanderings; and sat me down to wait, and consider; for it was as if the hour of change drew nigh. I seemed to surrender, to renounce utterly, and say: "Fly, then, false shadows of Hope; I will chase you no more, I will believe you no more. And ye too, haggard spectres of Fear, I care not for you; ye too are all shadows and a lie. Let me rest here: for I am way-weary and life-weary; I will rest here, were it but to die: to die or to live is alike to me; alike insignificant."—And again: "Here, then, as I lay in that CENTRE OF INDIFFERENCE;[44] cast, doubtless by benignant upper Influence, into a healing sleep, the heavy dreams rolled gradually away, and I awoke to a new Heaven and a new Earth. The first preliminary moral

---

[40] "Get thee hence, Satan."

[41] The manuscript of Teufelsdröckh's autobiography was found crammed into six paper bags.

[42] A pictorial term used here to mean alternations of clarity and obscurity.   [43] From the Sahara Desert.

[44] This is the title and the theme of the chapter between "The Everlasting No" and "The Everlasting Yea." After Teufelsdröckh had found himself able to defy the materialistic conception of the universe, he remained for a period in a state of indifference. Released from his previous "continual, indefinite, pining fear," he sought for the time being only rest and inactivity.

---

[37] Of insight or revelation.

[38] The first crop after a field has lain fallow.

[39] A purely verbal reference to the Revolution of 1688, which was known as "glorious" because it saved England both from absolutism and from Roman Catholicism.

Act, Annihilation of Self (*Selbsttödtung*),[45] had been happily accomplished; and my mind's eyes were now unsealed, and its hands ungyved."[46]

Might we not also conjecture that the following passage refers to his Locality, during this same "healing sleep"; that his Pilgrim-staff lies cast aside here, on "the high table-land"; and indeed that the repose is already taking wholesome effect on him? If it were not that the tone, in some parts, has more of riancy,[47] even of levity, than we could have expected! However, in Teufelsdröckh, there is always the strangest Dualism: light dancing, with guitar-music, will be going on in the forecourt, while by fits from within comes the faint whimpering of woe and wail. We transcribe the piece entire:

"Beautiful it was to sit there, as in my skyey Tent, musing and meditating; on the high table-land, in front of the Mountains; over me, as roof, the azure Dome, and around me, for walls, four azure-flowing curtains,—namely, of the Four azure Winds, on whose bottom-fringes also I have seen gilding. And then to fancy the fair Castles, that stood sheltered in these Mountain hollows; with their green flower-lawns, and white dames and damosels, lovely enough: or better still, the straw-roofed Cottages, wherein, stood many a Mother baking bread, with her children round her:—all hidden and protectingly folded-up in the valley-folds; yet there and alive, as sure as if I beheld them. Or to see, as well as fancy, the nine Towns and Villages, that lay round my mountain-seat, which, in still weather, were wont to speak to me (by their steeple-bells) with metal tongue; and, in almost all weather, proclaimed their vitality by repeated Smoke-clouds; whereon, as on a culinary horologue, I might read the hour of the day. For it was the smoke of cookery, as kind housewives at morning, midday, eventide, were boiling their husbands' kettles; and ever a blue pillar rose up into the air, successively or simultaneously, from each of the nine, saying, as plainly as smoke could say: Such and such a meal is getting ready here. Not uninteresting! For you have the whole Borough, with all its love-makings and scandal-mongeries, contentions and contentments, as in miniature, and could cover it all with your hat.—If, in my wide Wayfarings, I had learned to look into the business of the World in its details,

here perhaps was the place for combining it into general propositions, and deducing inferences therefrom.

"Often also could I see the black Tempest marching in anger through the distance: round some Schreckhorn,[48] as yet grim-blue, would the eddying vapour gather, and there tumultuously eddy, and flow down like a mad witch's hair; till, after a space, it vanished, and, in the clear sunbeam, your Schreckhorn stood smiling grim-white, for the vapour had held snow. How thou fermentest and elaboratest in thy great fermenting-vat and laboratory of an Atmosphere, of a World, O Nature!—Or what is Nature? Ha! why do I not name thee GOD? Art thou not the 'Living Garment of God'?[49] O Heavens, is it, in very deed, HE, then, that ever speaks through thee; that lives and loves in thee, that lives and loves in me?

"Fore-shadows, call them rather fore-splendours, of that Truth, and Beginning of Truths, fell mysteriously over my soul. Sweeter than Dayspring to the Shipwrecked in Nova Zembla;[50] ah, like the mother's voice to her little child that strays bewildered, weeping, in unknown tumults; like soft streamings of celestial music to my too-exasperated heart, came that Evangel. The Universe is not dead and demoniacal, a charnel-house with spectres; but godlike, and my Father's!

"With other eyes, too, could I now look upon my fellow man: with an infinite Love, an infinite Pity. Poor, wandering, wayward man! Art thou not tried, and beaten with stripes, even as I am? Ever, whether thou bear the royal mantle or the beggar's gabardine, art thou not so weary, so heavy-laden; and thy Bed of Rest is but a Grave. O my Brother, my Brother, why cannot I shelter thee in my bosom, and wipe away all tears from thy eyes!—Truly, the din of many-voiced Life, which, in this solitude, with the mind's organ, I could hear, was no longer a maddening discord, but a melting one; like inarticulate cries, and sobbings of a dumb creature, which in the ear of Heaven are prayers. The poor Earth, with her poor joys, was now my needy Mother, not my cruel Stepdame; Man, with his so mad Wants and so mean Endeavors, had become the dearer to me; and even for his sufferings and his sins, I now first named him Brother. Thus was

---

45 Once Teufelsdröckh had been able to reject materialism, he was no longer distracted by worries and fears about himself. Although this particular expression is taken from Novalis (1772–1801), a German poet and mystic much admired by Carlyle, the idea is the Christian one: Whoso loseth his life shall save it.
46 Unshackled.   47 Gaiety.

48 An Alpine peak.
49 It seems for a moment as if Teufelsdröckh was about to identify God and Nature, but it is important to notice the distinction he immediately establishes. Nature is not God, but the "God-written Apocalypse" or "the Garment thou seest Him by." See the introduction to Carlyle, p. 390.
50 Scene of a Dutch shipwreck in 1596.

I standing in the porch of that 'Sanctuary of Sorrow';[51] by strange, steep ways, had I too been guided thither; and ere long its sacred gates would open, and the 'Divine Depth of Sorrow'[52] lie disclosed to me."

The Professor says, he here first got eye on the Knot that had been strangling him, and straightway could unfasten it, and was free. "A vain interminable controversy," writes he, "touching what is at present called Origin of Evil, or some such thing, arises in every soul, since the beginning of the world; and in every soul, that would pass from idle Suffering into actual Endeavouring, must first be put an end to. The most, in our time, have to go content with a simple, incomplete enough Suppression of this controversy; to a few, some Solution of it is indispensable. In every new era, too, such Solution comes-out in different terms; and ever the Solution of the last era has become obsolete, and is found unserviceable. For it is man's nature to change his Dialect from century to century; he cannot help it though he would. The authentic *Church-Catechism* of our present century has not yet fallen into my hands: meanwhile, for my own private behoof, I attempt to elucidate the matter so. Man's Unhappiness, as I construe, comes of his Greatness; it is because there is an Infinite in him, which with all his cunning he cannot quite bury under the Finite. Will the whole Finance Ministers and Upholsterers and Confectioners of modern Europe undertake, in joint-stock company, to make one Shoeblack HAPPY? They cannot accomplish it, above an hour or two: for the Shoeblack also has a Soul quite other than his Stomach; and would require, if you consider it, for his permanent satisfaction and saturation, simply this allotment, no more, and no less: *God's infinite Universe altogether to himself*, therein to enjoy infinitely, and fill every wish as fast as it rose. Oceans of Hochheimer,[53] a Throat like that of Ophiuchus:[54] speak not of them; to the infinite Shoeblack they are as nothing. No sooner is your ocean filled, than he grumbles that it might have been of better vintage. Try him with half of a Universe, of an Omnipotence, he sets to quarrelling with the proprietor of the other half, and declares himself the most maltreated of men.—Always there is a black

spot in our sunshine: it is even, as I said, the *Shadow of Ourselves.*[55]

"But the whim we have of Happiness is somewhat thus. By certain valuations, and averages, of our own striking, we come upon some sort of average terrestrial lot; this we fancy belongs to us by nature, and of indefeasible right. It is simple payment of our wages, of our deserts; requires neither thanks nor complaint; only such *overplus* as there may be do we account Happiness; any *deficit* again is Misery. Now consider that we have the valuation of our own deserts ourselves, and what a fund of Self-conceit there is in each of us,—do you wonder that the balance should so often dip the wrong way, and many a Blockhead cry: See there, what a payment; was ever worthy gentleman so used!—I tell thee, Blockhead, it all comes of thy Vanity; of what thou *fanciest* those same deserts of thine to be. Fancy that thou deservest to be hanged (as is most likely), thou wilt feel it happiness to be only shot: fancy that thou deservest to be hanged in a hair-halter, it will be a luxury to die in hemp.[56]

"So true it is, what I then said, that *the Fraction of Life can be increased in value not so much by increasing your Numerator as by lessening your Denominator.* Nay, unless my Algebra deceive me, *Unity* itself divided by *Zero* will give *Infinity.* Make thy claim of wages a zero, then; thou hast the world under thy feet. Well did the Wisest of our time[57] write: 'It is only with Renunciation (*Entsagen*) that Life, properly speaking, can be said to begin.'

"I asked myself: What is this that, ever since earliest years, thou hast been fretting and fuming, and lamenting and self-tormenting, on account of? Say it in a word: is it not because thou art not HAPPY? Because the THOU (sweet gentleman) is not sufficiently honoured, nourished, soft-bedded, and lovingly cared-for? Foolish soul! What Act of Legislature was there that *thou* shouldst be Happy? A little while ago thou hadst no right to *be* at all. What if thou wert born and predestined not to be Happy, but to be Unhappy! Art thou nothing other than a Vulture, then, that fliest through the Universe seeking after somewhat to *eat*; and shrieking dolefully because

---

[51] An expression borrowed from Goethe, meaning here that Teufelsdröckh's heart is to become a sanctuary for the sorrows of mankind, which he now for the first time comprehends subjectively and with sympathy.

[52] The extent of God's understanding sorrow for man.

[53] A choice Rhenish wine.

[54] The figure of a man in a constellation which was particularly noteworthy for its large size.

[55] Man's sense of the infinite which will not allow him a definitive limit to his desires.

[56] It was more painful to be hanged with a rope made of hair than with a hempen rope.

[57] Johann Wolfgang von Goethe (1749-1832), the great German poet, dramatist, and prose writer, was Carlyle's particular hero. He wrote about Goethe at length and translated several of his works.

carrion enough is not given thee? Close thy *Byron;* open thy *Goethe.*"[58]

"*Es leuchtet mir ein,* I see a glimpse of it!" cries he elsewhere: "there is in man a HIGHER than Love of Happiness: he can do without Happiness, and instead thereof find Blessedness! Was it not to preach-forth this same HIGHER that sages and martyrs, the Poet and the Priest, in all times, have spoken and suffered; bearing testimony, through life and through death, of the Godlike that is in Man, and how in the God-like only has he Strength and Freedom? Which God-inspired Doctrine art thou also honoured to be taught; O Heavens! and broken with manifold merciful Afflictions, even till thou become contrite, and learn it! O, thank thy Destiny for these; thankfully bear what yet remain: thou hadst need of them; the Self in thee needed to be annihilated. By benignant fever-paroxysms is Life rooting out the deep-seated chronic Disease, and triumphs over Death. On the roaring billows of Time, thou art not engulfed, but borne aloft into the azure of Eternity. Love not Pleasure: love God. This is the EVERLASTING YEA, wherein all contradiction is solved: wherein whoso walks and works, it is well with him."

And again: "Small is it that thou canst trample the Earth with its injuries under thy feet, as old Greek Zeno[59] trained thee: thou canst love the Earth while it injures thee, and even because it injures thee; for this a Greater than Zeno was needed, and he too was sent. Knowest thou that '*Worship of Sorrow*'?[60] The Temple thereof, founded some eighteen centuries ago, now lies in ruins, overgrown with jungle, the habitation of doleful creatures: nevertheless, venture forward; in a low crypt, arched out of falling frag-ments, thou findest the Altar still there, and its sacred Lamp perennially burning."[61]

Without pretending to comment on which strange utterances, the Editor will only remark, that there lies beside them much of a still more questionable character; unsuited to the general apprehension; nay,

wherein he himself does not see his way. Nebulous disquisitions on Religion, yet not without bursts of splendour; on the "perennial continuance of Inspi-ration"; on Prophecy; that there are "true Priests, as well as Baal-Priests,[62] in our own day": with more of the like sort. We select some fractions, by way of finish to this farrago.

"Cease, my much-respected Herr von Voltaire,"[63] thus apostrophises the Professor: "shut thy sweet voice; for the task appointed thee seems finished. Sufficiently hast thou demonstrated this proposition, considerable or otherwise: That the Mythus of the Christian Religion looks not in the eighteenth century as it did in the eighth. Alas, were thy six-and-thirty quartos, and the six-and-thirty thousand other quartos and folios, and flying sheets or reams, printed before and since on the same subject, all needed to convince us of so little! But what next? Wilt thou help us to embody the divine Spirit of that Religion in a new Mythus, in a new vehicle and vesture, that our Souls, otherwise too like perishing, may live? What! thou hast no faculty in that kind? Only a torch for burning, no hammer for building? Take our thanks, then, and —thyself away.

"Meanwhile what are antiquated Mythuses to me? Or is the God present, felt in my own heart, a thing which Herr von Voltaire will dispute out of me; or dispute into me? To the '*Worship of Sorrow*' ascribe what origin and genesis thou pleasest, *has* not that Worship originated, and been generated; is it not *here*? Feel it in thy heart, and then say whether it is of God! This is Belief; all else is Opinion,—for which latter whoso will, let him worry and be worried."

"Neither," observes he elsewhere, "shall ye tear-out one another's eyes, struggling over 'Plenary Inspiration,'[64] and such-like: try rather to get a little even Partial Inspiration, each of you for yourself. One BIBLE I know,[65] of whose Plenary Inspiration doubt is not so much as possible; nay with my own eyes I saw the God's-Hand writing it: thereof all other Bibles are but Leaves,—say, in Picture-Writing to assist the weaker faculty."

Or to give the wearied reader relief, and, bring it to an end, let him take the following perhaps more intelligible passage:

---

[58] Teufelsdröckh hits at the contemporary adulation of the Byronic hero, driven like a vulture by a mad and despairing lust for power and self-indulgence. He offers instead the heroes of Goe-the, particularly Wilhelm Meister, men of moral integrity and spiritual insight.

[59] Stoic philosopher (flourished *c.* 300 B.C.) who taught men to despise the pleasures and injuries of life as of no consequence compared with the pursuit of virtue.

[60] Christ was greater than Zeno in that he taught men to love those who injured them and to love their very sorrows. See above, notes 51 and 52.

[61] I.e., in spite of the skepticism and materialism of the eighteenth century, the soul of Christianity is still burningly alive.

[62] Priests who served the pagan divinity Baal; i.e., priests of a false religion.

[63] Voltaire for Teufelsdröckh was the great antagonist of all positive, creative religious belief. He was purely destructive.

[64] The doctrine that every word of the Bible was inspired by God.

[65] Man's heart. Christianity has its verification, says Carlyle else-where, "in mysterious, ineffaceable characters . . . written in the purest nature of man."

"To me, in this our life," says the Professor, "which is an internecine warfare with the Time-spirit,[66] other warfare seems questionable. Hast thou in any way a Contention with thy brother, I advise thee, think well what the meaning thereof is. If thou gauge it to the bottom, it is simply this: 'Fellow, see! thou art taking more than thy share of Happiness in the world, something from *my* share: which, by the Heavens, thou shalt not; nay, I will fight thee rather.' —Alas, and the whole lot to be divided is such a beggarly matter, truly a 'feast of shells,' for the substance has been spilled out: not enough to quench one Appetite; and the collective human species clutching at them!—Can we not, in all such cases, rather say: 'Take it, thou too-ravenous individual; take that pitiful additional fraction of a share, which I reckoned mine, but which thou so wantest; take it with a blessing: would to Heaven I had enough for thee!'—If Fichte's *Wissenschaftslehre*[67] be, 'to a certain extent, Applied Christianity,' surely to a still greater extent, so is this. We have here not a Whole Duty of Man,[68] yet a Half Duty, namely, the Passive half: could we but do it, as we can demonstrate it!

"But indeed Conviction, were it never so excellent, is worthless till it convert itself into Conduct. Nay, properly Conviction is not possible till then; inasmuch as all Speculation is by nature endless, formless, a vortex amid vortices: only by a felt indubitable certainty of Experience does it find any centre to revolve round, and so fashion itself into a system. Most true is it, as a wise man teaches us,[69] that 'Doubt of any sort cannot be removed except by Action.' On which ground, too, let him who gropes painfully in darkness or uncertain light, and prays vehemently that the dawn may ripen into day, lay this other precept well to heart, which to me was of invaluable service: '*Do the Duty which lies nearest thee,*' which thou knowest to be a Duty! Thy second Duty will already have become clearer.

"May we not say, however, that the hour of Spiritual Enfranchisement is even this: When your Ideal World, wherein the whole man has been dimly struggling and inexpressibly languishing to work, becomes revealed and thrown open; and you discover, with amazement enough, like the Lothario in *Wilhelm Meister,* that your 'America[70] is here or nowhere'? The Situation that has not its Duty, its Ideal, was never yet occupied by man. Yes here, in this poor, miserable, hampered, despicable Actual, wherein thou even now standest, here or nowhere is thy Ideal: work it out therefrom; and working, believe, live, be free. Fool! the Ideal is in thyself, the impediment too is in thyself: thy Condition is but the stuff thou art to shape that same Ideal out of: what matters whether such stuff be of this sort or that, so the Form thou give it be heroic, be poetic? O thou that pinest in the imprisonment of the Actual, and criest bitterly to the gods for a kingdom wherein to rule and create, know this of a truth: the thing thou seekest is already with thee, 'here or nowhere,' couldst thou only see!

"But it is with man's Soul as it was with Nature: the beginning of Creation is—Light. Till the eye have vision, the whole members are in bonds. Divine moment, when over the tempest-tost Soul, as once over the wild-weltering Chaos, it is spoken: Let there be light! Ever to the greatest that has felt such moment, is it not miraculous and God-announcing; even as, under simpler figures, to the simplest and least. The mad primeval Discord is hushed; the rudely-jumbled conflicting elements bind themselves into separate Firmaments: deep silent rock-foundations are built beneath; and the skyey vault with its everlasting Luminaries above: instead of a dark wasteful Chaos, we have a blooming, fertile, Heaven-encompassed World.

"I too could now say to myself: Be no longer a Chaos, but a World, or even Worldkin. Produce! Produce! Were it but the pitifullest infinitesimal fraction of a Product, produce it, in God's name! 'Tis the utmost thou hast in thee: out with it, then. Up, up! Whatsoever thy hand findeth to do, do it with thy whole might. Work while it is called Today; for the Night cometh, wherein no man can work."[71]

[66] The constant struggle of man to survive despite the passing of time, which will in the end destroy him.
[67] The German philosopher Johann Gottlieb Fichte (1762–1814) taught that the highest wisdom lay in pursuing one's duty rather than one's happiness. This involves a renunciation which is akin to Christian teaching.
[68] A play upon the title of an anonymous devotional work, *The Whole Duty of Man,* widely read in the latter half of the seventeenth century.   [69] Goethe in *Wilhelm Meister.*

[70] Land of opportunity or ideal world.
[71] This paragraph is a famous epitome of Carlyle's doctrine of work. See also *Past and Present,* pp. 431, 432, below. The last lines are, of course, Biblical echoes (Ecclesiastes 9:10; John 9:4).

from ON HEROES, HERO-WORSHIP, AND THE HEROIC IN HISTORY[1]

from Lecture I

THE HERO AS DIVINITY[2]

Odin. Paganism: Scandinavian Mythology

WE have undertaken to discourse here for a little on Great Men, their manner of appearance in our world's business, how they have shaped themselves in the world's history, what ideas men formed of them, what work they did;—on Heroes, namely, and on their reception and performance; what I call Hero-worship and the Heroic in human affairs. Too evidently this is a large topic; deserving quite other treatment than we can expect to give it at present. A large topic; indeed, an illimitable one; wide as Universal History itself. For, as I take it, Universal History, the history of what man has accomplished in this world, is at bottom the History of the Great Men who have worked here. They were the leaders of men, these great ones; the modellers, patterns, and in a wide sense creators, of whatsoever the general mass of men contrived to do or to attain; all things that we see standing accomplished in the world are properly the outer material result, the practical realisation and embodiment, of Thoughts that dwelt in the Great Men sent into the world: the soul of the whole world's history, it may justly be considered, were the history of these. Too clearly it is a topic we shall do no justice to in this place!

One comfort is, that Great Men, taken up in any way, are profitable company. We cannot look, however imperfectly, upon a great man, without gaining something by him. He is the living light-fountain, which it is good and pleasant to be near. The light which enlightens, which has enlightened the darkness of the world; and this not as a kindled lamp only, but rather as a natural luminary shining by the gift of Heaven; a flowing light-fountain, as I say, of native original insight, of manhood and heroic nobleness;—in whose radiance all souls feel that it is well with them. On any terms whatsoever, you will not grudge to wander in such neighbourhood for a while. These Six classes of Heroes, chosen out of widely-distant countries and epochs, and in mere external figure differing altogether, ought, if we look faithfully at them, to illustrate several things for us. Could we see

them well, we should get some glimpses into the very marrow of the world's history. How happy, could I but, in any measure, in such times as these, make manifest to you the meanings of Heroism; the divine relation (for I may well call it such) which in all times unites a Great Man to other men;[3] and thus, as it were, not exhaust my subject, but so much as break ground on it! At all events, I must make the attempt.

It is well said, in every sense, that a man's religion is the chief fact with regard to him. A man's, or a nation of men's. By religion I do not mean here the church-creed which he professes, the articles of faith which he will sign and, in words or otherwise, assert; not this wholly, in many cases not this at all. We see men of all kinds of professed creeds attain to almost all degrees of worth or worthlessness under each or any of them. This is not what I call religion, this profession and assertion; which is often only a profession and assertion from the outworks of the man, from the mere argumentative region of him, if even so deep as that. But the thing a man does practically believe (and this is often enough *without* asserting it even to himself, much less to others); the thing a man does practically lay to heart, and know for certain, concerning his vital relations to this mysterious Universe, and his duty and destiny there, that is in all cases the primary thing for him, and creatively determines all the rest. That is his *religion;* or, it may be, his mere scepticism and *no-religion:* the manner it is in which he feels himself to be spiritually related to the Unseen World or No-World;[4] and I say, if you tell me what that is, you tell me to a very great extent what the man is, what the kind of things he will do is. Of a man or of a nation we inquire, therefore, first of all, What religion they had? Was it Heathenism,—plurality of gods, mere sensuous representation of this Mystery of Life, and for chief recognised element therein Physical Force? Was it Christianism; faith in an Invisible, not as real only, but as the only reality; Time, through every meanest moment of it, resting on Eternity;[5] Pagan empire of Force displaced by a

---

[3] The divine relation of the Great Man to other men lies in his being endowed by God with the qualities of leadership and heroism to which the generality must pay tribute of both worship and obedience.

[4] A world thought to contain no unseen reality.

[5] The belief that Time of itself does not exist, but is only a human mode of thought by which to relate events and experiences, a figment created by man to orient himself in Eternity. Carlyle was so fascinated by the nature of time that he even classed it as a religion.

---

[1] This is the title of the published lectures, originally delivered in London, May, 1840.

[2] Carlyle discussed the hero under six headings: as divinity, as prophet, as poet, as priest, as man of letters, and as king.

nobler supremacy, that of Holiness? Was it Scepticism, uncertainty and inquiry whether there was an Unseen World, any Mystery of Life except a mad one;—doubt as to all this, or perhaps unbelief and flat denial? Answering of this question is giving us the soul of the history of the man or nation. The thoughts they had were the parents of the actions they did; their feelings were parents of their thoughts: it was the unseen and spiritual in them that determined the outward and actual;—their religion, as I say, was the great fact about them. In these Discourses, limited as we are, it will be good to direct our survey chiefly to that religious phasis of the matter. That once known well, all is known. We have chosen as the first Hero in our series, Odin the central figure of Scandinavian Paganism; an emblem to us of a most extensive province of things. Let us look for a little at the Hero as Divinity, the oldest primary form of Heroism.

Surely it seems a very strange-looking thing this Paganism; almost inconceivable to us in these days. A bewildering, inextricable jungle of delusions, confusions, falsehoods, and absurdities, covering the whole field of Life! A thing that fills us with astonishment, almost, if it were possible, with incredulity,—for truly it is not easy to understand that sane men could ever calmly, with their eyes open, believe and live by such a set of doctrines. That men should have worshipped their poor fellow-man as a God, and not him only, but stocks[6] and stones, and all manner of animate and inanimate objects; and fashioned for themselves such a distracted chaos of hallucinations by way of Theory of the Universe: all this looks like an incredible fable. Nevertheless, it is a clear fact that they did it. Such hideous inextricable jungle of misworships, misbeliefs, men, made as we are, did actually hold by, and live at home in. This is strange. Yes, we may pause in sorrow and silence over the depths of darkness that are in man; if we rejoice in the heights of purer vision he has attained to. Such things were and are in man; in all men; in us too.

Some speculators have a short way of accounting for the Pagan religion: mere quackery, priestcraft, and dupery, say they; no sane man ever did believe it,—merely contrived to persuade other men, not worthy of the name of sane, to believe it! It will be often our duty to protest against this sort of hypothesis about men's doings and history; and I here, on the very threshold, protest against it in reference to Paganism, and to all other *isms* by which man has ever for a length of time striven to walk in this world.

They have all had a truth in them, or men would not have taken them up. Quackery and dupery do abound; in religions, above all in the more advanced decaying stages of religions, they have fearfully abounded; but quackery was never the originating influence in such things; it was not the health and life of such things, but their disease, the sure precursor of their being about to die! Let us never forget this. It seems to me a most mournful hypothesis, that of quackery giving birth to any faith even in savage men. Quackery gives birth to nothing; gives death to all things. We shall not see into the true heart of anything, if we look merely at the quackeries of it; if we do not reject the quackeries altogether; as mere diseases, corruptions, with which our and all men's sole duty is to have done with them, to sweep them out of our thoughts as out of our practice. Man everywhere is the born enemy of lies. . . .—We shall begin to have a chance of understanding Paganism, when we first admit that to its followers it was, at one time, earnestly true. Let us consider it very certain that men did believe in Paganism; men with open eyes, sound senses, men made altogether like ourselves; that we, had we been there, should have believed in it. Ask now, What Paganism could have been?

Another theory, somewhat more respectable, attributes such things to Allegory. It was a play of poetic minds, say these theorists; a shadowing-forth, in allegorical fable, in personification and visual form, of what such poetic minds had known and felt of this Universe. Which agrees, add they, with a primary law of human nature, still everywhere observably at work, though in less important things. That what a man feels intensely, he struggles to speak-out of him, to see represented before him in visual shape, and as if with a kind of life and historical reality in it. Now doubtless there is such a law, and it is one of the deepest in human nature; neither need we doubt that it did operate fundamentally in this business. The hypothesis which ascribes Paganism wholly or mostly to this agency, I call a little more respectable; but I cannot yet call it the true hypothesis. Think, would *we* believe, and take with us as our life-guidance, an allegory, a poetic sport? Not sport but earnest is what we should require. It is a most earnest thing to be alive in this world; to die is not sport for a man. Man's life never was a sport to him; it was a stern reality, altogether a serious matter to be alive!

I find, therefore, that though these Allegory theorists are on the way towards truth in this matter, they have not reached it either. Pagan Religion is indeed

---

[6] Images carved out of the stocks or trunks of trees.

an Allegory, a Symbol of what men felt and knew about the Universe; and all Religions are Symbols of that, altering always as that alters: but it seems to me a radical perversion, and even *in*version, of the business, to put that forward as the origin and moving cause, when it was rather the result and termination. To get beautiful allegories, a perfect poetic symbol, was not the want of men; but to know what they were to believe about this Universe, what course they were to steer in it; what, in this mysterious Life of theirs, they had to hope and to fear, to do and to forbear doing. The *Pilgrim's Progress* is an Allegory, and a beautiful, just and serious one: but consider whether Bunyan's Allegory could have *preceded* the Faith it symbolises! The Faith had to be already there, standing believed by everybody;—of which the Allegory could *then* become a shadow; and, with all its seriousness, we may say a *sportful* shadow, a mere play of the Fancy, in comparison with that awful Fact and scientific certainty which it poetically strives to emblem.[7] The Allegory is the product of the certainty, not the producer of it; not in Bunyan's nor in any other case. For Paganism, therefore, we have still to inquire, Whence came that scientific certainty, the parent of such a bewildered heap of allegories, errors and confusions? How was it, what was it?

Surely it were a foolish attempt to pretend "explaining," in this place, or in any place, such a phenomenon as that far-distant distracted cloudy imbroglio of Paganism,—more like a cloudfield than a distant continent of firm land and facts! It is no longer a reality, yet it was one. We ought to understand that this seeming cloudfield was once a reality; that not poetic allegory, least of all that dupery and deception was the origin of it. Men, I say, never did believe idle songs, never risked their soul's life on allegories: men in all times, especially in early earnest times, have had an instinct for detecting quacks, for detesting quacks. Let us try if, leaving out both the quack theory and the allegory one, and listening with affectionate attention to that far-off confused rumour of the Pagan ages, we cannot ascertain so much as this at least, That there was a kind of fact at the heart of them; that they too were not mendacious and distracted, but in their own poor way true and sane!

You remember that fancy of Plato's,[8] of a man who had grown to maturity in some dark distance, and was brought on a sudden into the upper air to see the sun rise. What would his wonder be, his rapt astonishment at the sight we daily witness with indifference! With the free open sense of a child, yet with the ripe faculty of a man, his whole heart would be kindled by that sight, he would discern it well to be Godlike, his soul would fall down in worship before it. Now, just such a childlike greatness was in the primitive nations. The first Pagan Thinker among rude men, the first man that began to think, was precisely this child-man of Plato's. Simple, open as a child, yet with the depth and strength of a man. Nature had as yet no name to him; he had not yet united under a name the infinite variety of sights, sounds, shapes and motions, which we now collectively name Universe, Nature, or the like,—and so with a name dismiss it from us. To the wild deep-hearted man all was yet new, not veiled under names or formulas; it stood naked, flashing-in on him there, beautiful, awful, unspeakable. Nature was to this man, what to the Thinker and Prophet it for ever is, *preter*natural. This green flowery rock-built earth, the trees, the mountains, rivers, many-sounding seas;—that great deep sea of azure that swims overhead; the winds sweeping through it; the black cloud fashioning itself together, now pouring out fire, now hail and rain; what *is* it? Ay, what? At bottom we do not yet know; we can never know at all. It is not by our superior insight that we escape the difficulty; it is by our superior levity, our inattention, our *want* of insight. It is by *not* thinking that we cease to wonder at it. Hardened round us, encasing wholly every notion we form, is a wrappage of traditions, hearsays, mere *words*. We call that fire of the black thundercloud "electricity," and lecture learnedly about it, and grind the like of it out of glass and silk: but *what* is it? What made it? Whence comes it? Whither goes it? Science has done much for us; but it is a poor science that would hide from us the great deep sacred infinitude of Nescience,[9] whither we can never penetrate, on which all science swims as a mere superficial film. This world, after all our science and sciences, is still a miracle; wonderful, inscrutable, *magical* and more, to whosoever will *think* of it.

---

[7] What the pagan religion strove to emblem was "what men felt and knew about the Universe." Carlyle's point is that pagan mythology was based upon real knowledge and sincere belief. "So much of truth, only under an ancient obsolete vesture, but the spirit of it still true, do I find in the Paganism of old nations. Nature is still divine; . . . the Hero is still worshipable: this, under poor cramped incipient forms, is what all Pagan religions have struggled, as they could, to set forth."

[8] In *The Republic,* Bk. VII.
[9] Sacred because in it lies the mystery of God.

That great mystery of TIME, were there no other; the illimitable, silent, never-resting thing called Time, rolling, rushing on, swift, silent, like an all-embracing ocean-tide, on which we and all the Universe swim like exhalations, like apparitions which *are,* and then *are not:* this is for ever very literally a miracle; a thing to strike us dumb,—for we have no word to speak about it. This Universe, ah me—what could the wild man know of it; what can we yet know? That it is a Force, and thousandfold Complexity of Forces; a Force which is *not we.* That is all; it is not we, it is altogether different from *us.* Force, Force, everywhere Force; we ourselves a mysterious Force in the centre of that. "There is not a leaf rotting on the highway but has Force in it: how else could it rot?" Nay surely, to the Atheistic Thinker, if such a one were possible, it must be a miracle too, this huge illimitable whirlwind of Force, which envelops us here; never-resting whirlwind, high as Immensity, old as Eternity. What is it? God's creation, the religious people answer; it is the Almighty God's! Atheistic science babbles poorly of it, with scientific nomenclatures, experiments and what-not, as if it were a poor dead thing, to be bottled-up in Leyden jars[10] and sold over counters: but the natural sense of man, in all times, if he will honestly apply his sense, proclaims it to be a living thing,—ah, an unspeakable, godlike thing; towards which the best attitude for us, after never so much science, is awe, devout prostration and humility of soul; worship if not in words, then in silence.

But now I remark farther: What in such a time as ours it requires a Prophet or Poet to teach us, namely, the stripping-off of those poor undevout wrappages, nomenclatures and scientific hearsays,—this, the ancient earnest soul, as yet unencumbered with these things, did for itself.[11] The world, which is now divine only to the gifted, was then divine to whosoever would turn his eye upon it. He stood bare before it face to face. "All was Godlike or God":— Jean Paul[12] still finds it so; the giant Jean Paul, who has power to escape out of hearsays; but there then were no hearsays. Canopus,[13] shining-down over the desert, with its blue diamond brightness (that wild blue spirit-like brightness, far brighter than we ever witness here), would pierce into the heart of the wild Ishmaelitish[14] man, whom it was guiding through the solitary waste there. To his wild heart, with all feelings in it, with no *speech* for any feeling, it might seem a little eye, that Canopus, glancing-out on him from the great deep Eternity; revealing the inner Splendour to him. Cannot we understand how these men *worshipped* Canopus; became what we call Sabeans,[15] worshipping the stars? Such is to me the secret of all forms of Paganism.

Worship is transcendent wonder; wonder for which there is now no limit or measure; that is worship. To these primeval men, all things and everything they saw exist beside them were an emblem of the Godlike, of some God.

And look what perennial fibre of truth was in that. To us also, through every star, through every blade of grass, is not a God made visible, if we will open our minds and eyes? We do not worship in that way now: but is it not reckoned still a merit, proof of what we call a "poetic nature," that we recognise how every object has a divine beauty in it; how every object still verily is "a window through which we may look into Infinitude itself"?[16] He that can discern the loveliness of things, we call him Poet, Painter, Man of Genius, gifted, lovable. These poor Sabeans did even what he does,—in their own fashion. That they did it, in what fashion soever, was a merit: better than what the entirely stupid man did, what the horse and camel did,—namely, nothing!

But now if all things whatsoever that we look upon are emblems to us of the Highest God, I add that more so than any of them is man such an emblem. You have heard of St. Chrysostom's celebrated saying in reference to the Shekinah,[17] or Ark of Testimony, visible Revelation of God, among the Hebrews: "The true Shekinah is Man!" Yes, it is even so: this is no vain phrase; it is veritably so. The essence of our being, the mystery in us that calls itself "I,"—ah, what words have we for such things?— is a breath of Heaven; the Highest Being reveals himself in man. This body, these faculties, this life

---

10 Special jars used in electrical experiments.

11 Actually this is an Irish bull: it would have been difficult for the ancient soul to strip off wrappages with which it was as yet unencumbered.

12 Johann Paul Richter (1763–1825) was a famous German humorist who, however, shared many of Carlyle's most serious and mystical ideas.

13 One of the brightest stars in the firmament.

14 Ishmael, the son of Abraham and Hagar, lived a solitary and wild life in the desert.

15 An Arab sect who worshiped the planets and the fixed stars.

16 The symbolic nature of the universe is one of Carlyle's favorite themes, and he is here quoting from his own *Sartor Resartus,* Bk. I, chap. II: "Rightly viewed no meanest object is insignificant; all objects are as windows, through which the philosophic eye looks into Infinitude itself. . . . All visible things are emblems. . . . Matter exists only spiritually, and to represent some Idea, and *body* it forth."

17 Chrysostom was a fourth-century patriarch of Constantinople. The Shekinah was the glory that appeared over the Ark, the manifestation of God.

of ours, is it not all as a vesture for that Unnamed? "There is but one Temple in the Universe," says the devout Novalis,[18] "and that is the Body of Man. Nothing is holier than that high form. Bending before men is a reverence done to this Revelation in the Flesh. We touch Heaven when we lay our hand on a human body!" This sounds much like a mere flourish of rhetoric; but it is not so. If well meditated, it will turn out to be a scientific fact; the expression, in such words as can be had, of the actual truth of the thing. *We* are the miracle of miracles,—the great inscrutable mystery of God. We cannot understand it, we know not how to speak of it, but we may feel and know, if we like, that it is verily so.

Well; these truths were once more readily felt than now. The young generations of the world, who had in them the freshness of young children, and yet the depth of earnest men, who did not think they had finished-off all things in Heaven and Earth by merely giving them scientific names, but had to gaze direct at them there, with awe and wonder: they felt better what of divinity is in man and Nature;—they, without being mad, could *worship* Nature, and man more than anything else in Nature. Worship, that is, as I said above, admire without limit: this, in the full use of their faculties, with all sincerity of heart, they could do. I consider Hero-worship to be the grand modifying element in that ancient system of thought. What I called the perplexed jungle of Paganism sprang, we may say, out of many roots: every admiration, adoration of a star or natural object, was a root or fibre of a root; but Hero-worship is the deepest root of all; the tap-root, from which in a great degree all the rest were nourished and grown.

And now if worship even of a star had some meaning in it, how much more might that of a Hero! Worship of a Hero is transcendent admiration of a Great Man. I say great men are still admirable! I say there is, at the bottom, nothing else admirable! No nobler feeling than this of admiration for one higher than himself dwells in the breast of man. It is to this hour, and at all hours, the vivifying influence in man's life. Religion I find stand upon it; not Paganism only, but far higher and truer religions,—all religion hitherto known. Hero-worship, heartfelt prostrate admiration, submission, burning, boundless, for a noblest godlike Form of Man,—is not that the germ of Christianity itself? The greatest of all Heroes in One—whom we do not name here! Let sacred silence meditate that sacred matter; you will find it

the ultimate perfection of a principle extant throughout man's whole history on earth.

Or coming into lower, less *un*speakable provinces, is not all Loyalty akin to religious Faith also? Faith is loyalty to some inspired Teacher, some spiritual Hero. And what therefore is loyalty proper, the life-breath of all society, but an effluence of Hero-worship, submissive admiration for the truly great? Society is founded on Hero-worship. All dignities of rank, on which human association rests, are what we may call a *Hero*-archy (Government of Heroes),—or a Hierarchy, for it is "sacred" enough withal! The Duke means *Dux*, Leader; King is *Kön-ning, Kanning,* Man that *knows* or *cans.*[19] Society everywhere is some representation, not *in*supportably inaccurate, of a graduated Worship of Heroes;—reverence and obedience done to men really great and wise. Not *in*supportably inaccurate, I say! They are all as banknotes, these social dignitaries, all representing gold;—and several of them, alas, always are *forged* notes. We can do with some forged false notes; with a good many even; but not with all, or the most of them forged! No: there have to come revolutions then; cries of Democracy, Liberty and Equality, and I know not what:—the notes being all false, and no gold to be had for *them,* people take to crying in their despair that there is no gold, that there never was any!—"Gold," Hero-worship, *is* nevertheless, as it was always and everywhere, and cannot cease till man himself ceases.

I am well aware that in these days Hero-worship, the thing I call Hero-worship, professes to have gone out, and finally ceased. This, for reasons which it will be worth while some time to inquire into, is an age that as it were denies the existence of great men; denies the desirableness of great men. Show our critics a great man, a Luther for example, they begin to what they call "account" for him; not to worship him, but take the dimensions of him,—and bring him out to be a little kind of man! He was the "creature of the Time," they say; the Time called him forth, the Time did everything, he nothing—but what we the little critic could have done too! This seems to me but melancholy work. The Time call forth? Alas, we have known Times *call* loudly enough for their great man; but not find him when they called! He was not there; Providence had not sent him; the Time, *calling* its loudest, had to go down to confusion and wreck because he would not come when called.

---

[18] See note 45 to *Sartor Resartus.*

[19] The etymology is mistaken (*king* actually derives from *cyning* or chief of race), but it fits perfectly with Carlyle's definition of a leader or hero as one who has the wisdom and the power to rule.

For if we will think of it, no Time need have gone to ruin, could it have *found* a man great enough, a man wise and good enough: wisdom to discern truly what the Time wanted, valour to lead it on the right road thither; these are the salvation of any Time. But I liken common languid Times, with their unbelief, distress, perplexity, with their languid doubting characters and embarrassed circumstances, impotently crumbling down into ever worse distress towards final ruin;—all this I liken to dry dead fuel, waiting for the lightning out of Heaven that shall kindle it. The great man, with his free force direct out of God's own hand, is the lightning. His word is the wise healing word which all can believe in. All blazes round him now, when he has once struck on it, into fire like his own. The dry mouldering sticks are thought to have called him forth. They did want him greatly; but as to calling him forth—!—Those are critics of small vision, I think, who cry: "See, is it not the sticks that made the fire?" No sadder proof can be given by a man of his own littleness than disbelief in great men. There is no sadder symptom of a generation than such general blindness to the spiritual lightning, with faith only in the heap of barren dead fuel. It is the last consummation of unbelief. In all epochs of the world's history, we shall find the Great Man to have been the indispensable saviour of his epoch;—the lightning, without which the fuel never would have burnt. The History of the World, I said already, was the Biography of Great Men.

Such small critics do what they can to promote unbelief and universal spiritual paralysis; but happily they cannot always completely succeed. In all times it is possible for a man to arise great enough to feel that they and their doctrines are chimeras and cobwebs. And what is notable, in no time whatever can they entirely eradicate out of living men's hearts a certain altogether peculiar reverence for Great Men; genuine admiration, loyalty, adoration, however dim and perverted it may be. Hero-worship endures forever while man endures. Boswell venerates his Johnson,[20] right truly even in the Eighteenth century. The unbelieving French believe in their Voltaire;[21] and burst-out round him into very curious Hero-worship, in that last act of his life when they "stifle

him under roses." It has always seemed to me extremely curious this of Voltaire. Truly, if Christianity be the highest instance of Hero-worship, then we may find here in Voltaireism one of the lowest! He whose life was that of a kind of Antichrist, does again on this side exhibit a curious contrast. No people ever were so little prone to admire at all as those French of Voltaire. *Persiflage* was the character of their whole mind; adoration had nowhere a place in it. Yet see! The old man of Ferney[22] comes up to Paris; an old, tottering, infirm man of eighty-four years. They feel that he too is a kind of Hero; that he has spent his life in opposing error and injustice, delivering Calases,[23] unmasking hypocrites in high places;—in short that *he* too, though in a strange way, has fought like a valiant man. They feel withal that, if *persiflage* be the great thing, there never was such a *persifleur*. He is the realised ideal of every one of them; the thing they are all wanting to be; of all Frenchmen the most French. *He* is properly their god,—such god as they are fit for.[24] Accordingly all persons, from the Queen Antoinette to the Douanier[25] at the Porte St. Denis, do they not worship him? People of quality disguise themselves as tavern-waiters. The Maître de Poste,[26] with a broad oath, orders his Postillion, "Va bon train; thou art driving M. de Voltaire." At Paris his carriage is "the nucleus of a comet, whose train fills whole streets." The ladies pluck a hair or two from his fur, to keep it as a sacred relic. There was nothing highest, beautifulest, noblest in all France, that did not feel this man to be higher, beautifuler, nobler.

Yes, from Norse Odin to English Samuel Johnson, from the divine Founder of Christianity to the withered Pontiff of Encyclopedism,[27] in all times and places, the Hero has been worshipped. It will ever be so. We all love great men; love, venerate and bow down submissive before great men: nay can we honestly bow down to anything else? Ah, does not every true man feel that he is himself made higher by

---

20 Carlyle discusses Johnson as an example of the Hero as Man of Letters in Lecture V.
21 The following passage is characteristic of Carlyle's ambivalent reaction to Voltaire. He both loathes him as an Antichrist and admires him as a champion of truth and justice. The scene of Voltaire's triumphant reception in Paris is one to which he frequently reverts. See *Sartor Resartus,* p. 399, above.

22 Voltaire's retreat during the last years of his life.
23 Voltaire had made great efforts in the middle of the eighteenth century on behalf of Jean Calas and his family, whom he felt to be unjustly persecuted.
24 A reflection of Carlyle's contempt for the French on grounds of their frivolity, an attitude widely shared by his countrymen.
25 Customs officer.
26 The postmaster, who was in charge of the horses and vehicles which carried the mail and, by accommodation, passengers. He tells the driver to make good speed.
27 Voltaire, who had been one of the contributors to the famous and, in Carlyle's opinion, scandalous *Encyclopédie* (1751–76). The work was an embodiment of the rationalism of the century and a thinly veiled attack on the established order in both church and state.

doing reverence to what is really above him? No nobler or more blessed feeling dwells in man's heart. And to me it is very cheering to consider that no sceptical logic, or general triviality, insincerity and aridity of any Time and its influences can destroy this noble inborn loyalty and worship that is in man. In times of unbelief, which soon have to become times of revolution, much down-rushing, sorrowful decay and ruin is visible to everybody. For myself, in these days, I seem to see in this indestructibility of Hero-worship the everlasting adamant[28] lower than which the confused wreck of revolutionary things cannot fall. The confused wreck of things crumbling and even crashing and tumbling all round us in these revolutionary ages, will get down so far; *no* farther. It is an eternal corner-stone, from which they can begin to build themselves up again. That man, in some sense or other, worships Heroes; that we all of us reverence and must ever reverence Great Men: this is, to me, the living rock amid all rushings-down whatsoever;—the one fixed point in modern revolutionary history, otherwise as if bottomless and shoreless. . . .

from Lecture V

THE HERO AS MAN OF LETTERS

Johnson, Rousseau, Burns[29]

HERO-GODS, Prophets, Poets, Priests are forms of Heroism that belong to the old ages, make their appearance in the remotest times; some of them have ceased to be possible long since, and cannot any more show themselves in this world. The Hero as *Man of Letters,* again, of which class we are to speak today, is altogether a product of these new ages; and so long as the wondrous art of *Writing,* or of Ready-writing which we call *Printing,* subsists, he may be expected to continue, as one of the main forms of Heroism for all future ages. He is, in various respects, a very singular phenomenon.

He is new, I say; he has hardly lasted above a century in the world yet. Never, till about a hundred years ago, was there seen any figure of a Great Soul living apart in that anomalous manner; endeavouring to speak-forth the inspiration that was in him by

Printed Books, and find place and subsistence by what the world would please to give him for doing that. Much had been sold and bought, and left to make its own bargain in the marketplace; but the inspired wisdom of a Heroic Soul never till then, in that naked manner. He, with his copyrights and copy-wrongs,[30] in his squalid garret, in his rusty coat; ruling (for this is what he does), from his grave, after death, whole nations and generations who would, or would not, give him bread while living,—is a rather curious spectacle! Few shapes of Heroism can be more unexpected.

Alas, the Hero from of old has had to cramp himself into strange shapes: the world knows not well at any time what to do with him, so foreign is his aspect in the world! It seemed absurd to us, that men, in their rude admiration, should take some wise great Odin for a god, and worship him as such; some wise great Mahomet for one god-inspired, and religiously follow his Law for twelve centuries: but that a wise great Johnson, a Burns, a Rousseau, should be taken for some idle nondescript, extant in the world to amuse idleness, and have a few coins and applauses thrown him, that he might live thereby; *this* perhaps, as before hinted, will one day seem a still absurder phasis of things!—Meanwhile, since it is the spiritual always that determines the material, this same Man-of-Letters Hero must be regarded as our most important modern person.[31] He, such as he may be, is the soul of all. What he teaches, the whole world will do and make. The world's manner of dealing with him is the most significant feature of the world's general position. Looking well at his life, we may get a glance, as deep as is readily possible for us, into the life of those singular centuries which have produced him, in which we ourselves live and work.

There are genuine Men of Letters, and not genuine; as in every kind there is a genuine and a spurious. If *Hero* be taken to mean genuine, then I say the Hero as Man of Letters will be found discharging a function for us which is ever honourable, ever the highest; and was once well known to be the highest. He is uttering-forth, in such way as he has, the inspired soul of him; all that a man, in any case, can do. I say *inspired;* for what we call "originality," "sincerity," "genius," the heroic quality we have no good name for, signifies that. The Hero is he who lives in the inward sphere

---

[28] Carlyle's use of the word as central core or foundation is probably peculiar to himself, but his meaning is clear.

[29] On Samuel Johnson see I, 851 ff.; on Robert Burns, pp. 23 ff., above. Jean-Jacques Rousseau (1712–78), French philosopher and writer, is generally considered rather loosely as the father of Romanticism and the French Revolution.

[30] Reference to the widespread piracy of books whereby the author lost all return for his work.

[31] This high estimate of the role of the man of letters was by no means peculiar to Carlyle. It was prevalent both in England and on the Continent, and the man of letters was often regarded in the light of a prophet. See the next paragraphs.

of things, in the True, Divine and Eternal, which exists always, unseen to most, under the Temporary, Trivial:[32] his being is in that; he declares that abroad, by act or speech as it may be, in declaring himself abroad. His life, as we said before, is a piece of the everlasting heart of Nature herself: all men's life is,—but the weak many know not the fact, and are untrue to it, in most times; the strong few are strong, heroic, perennial, because it cannot be hidden from them. The Man of Letters, like every Hero, is there to proclaim this in such sort as he can. Intrinsically it is the same function which the old generations named a man Prophet, Priest, Divinity for doing; which all manner of Heroes, by speech or by act, are sent into the world to do.

Fichte the German Philosopher[33] delivered, some forty years ago at Erlangen, a highly remarkable Course of Lectures on this subject: *Ueber das Wesen des Gelehrten,* On the Nature of the Literary Man." Fichte, in conformity with the Transcendental Philosophy, of which he was a distinguished teacher, declares first: That all things which we see or work with in this Earth, especially we ourselves and all persons, are as a kind of vesture or sensuous Appearance: that under all there lies, as the essence of them, what he calls the "Divine Idea of the World"; this is the Reality which "lies at the bottom of all Appearance." To the mass of men no such Divine Idea is recognisable in the world; they live merely, says Fichte, among the superficialities, practicalities and shows of the world, not dreaming that there is anything divine under them. But the Man of Letters is sent hither specially that he may discern for himself, and make manifest to us, this same Divine Idea; in every new generation it will manifest itself in a new dialect; and he is there for the purpose of doing that. Such is Fichte's phraseology; with which we need not quarrel. It is his way of naming what I here, by other words, am striving imperfectly to name; what there is at present no name for: The unspeakable Divine Significance, full of splendour, of wonder and terror, that lies in the being of every man, of every thing,—the Presence of the God who made every man and thing. Mahomet taught this in his dialect; Odin in his: it is the thing which all thinking hearts, in one dialect or another, are here to teach.

Fichte calls the Man of Letters, therefore, a Prophet, or as he prefers to phrase it, a Priest, continually un-

folding the Godlike to men: Men of Letters are a perpetual Priesthood, from age to age, teaching all men that a God is still present in their life; that all "Appearance," whatsoever we see in the world, is but as a vesture for the "Divine Idea of the World," for "that which lies at the bottom of Appearance." In the true Literary Man there is thus ever, acknowledged or not by the world, a sacredness: he is the light of the world; the world's Priest;—guiding it, like a sacred Pillar of Fire, in its dark pilgrimage through the waste of Time. Fichte discriminates with sharp zeal the *true* Literary Man, what we here call the *Hero* as Man of Letters, from multitudes of false unheroic. Whoever lives not wholly in this Divine Idea, or living partially in it, struggles not, as for the one good, to live wholly in it,—he is, let him live where else he like, in what pomps and prosperities he like, no Literary Man; he is, says Fichte, a "Bungler, *Stümper.*" Or at best, if he belong to the prosaic provinces, he may be a "Hodman";[34] Fichte even calls him elsewhere a "Nonentity," and has in short no mercy for him, no wish that *he* should continue happy among us! This is Fichte's notion of the Man of Letters. It means, in its own form, precisely what we here mean.

In this point of view, I consider that, for the last hundred years, by far the notablest of all Literary Men is Fichte's countryman, Goethe.[35] To that man too, in a strange way, there was given what we may call a life in the Divine Idea of the World; vision of the inward divine mystery: and strangely,[36] out of his Books, the world rises imaged once more as godlike, the workmanship and temple of a God. Illuminated all, not in fierce impure fire-splendour as of Mahomet,[37] but in mild celestial radiance;—really a Prophecy in these most unprophetic times; to my mind, by far the greatest, though one of the quietest, among all the great things that have come to pass in them. Our chosen specimen of the Hero as Literary Man would be this Goethe. And it were a very pleasant plan for me here to discourse of his heroism: for I consider him to be a true Hero; heroic in what he said and did, and perhaps still more in what he did not say and did not do; to me a noble spectacle: a great heroic ancient man, speaking and keeping silence as an ancient Hero, in the guise of a most modern, high-bred, high-cultivated Man of Letters!

---

[32] See just below the summary of Fichte's transcendental interpretation of the Nature of the Literary Man, of which this is an expression.
[33] See note 67 to *Sartor Resartus.*

[34] Here used to mean one who is capable only of unthinking manual labor.   [35] See note 57 to *Sartor Resartus.*
[36] Mysteriously, rather than unexpectedly.
[37] In "The Hero as Prophet," Carlyle speaks of Mahomet as "a fiery mass of Life . . . to *kindle* the world."

We have had no such spectacle; no man capable of affording such, for the last hundred-and-fifty years.

But at present, such is the general state of knowledge about Goethe, it were worse than useless to attempt speaking of him in this case. Speak as I might, Goethe, to the great majority of you, would remain problematic, vague; no impression but a false one could be realised. Him we must leave to future times. Johnson, Burns, Rousseau, three great figures from a prior time, from a far inferior state of circumstances, will suit us better here. Three men of the Eighteenth Century; the conditions of their life far more resemble what those of ours still are in England, than what Goethe's in Germany were. Alas, these men did not conquer like him; they fought bravely, and fell. They were not heroic bringers of the light, but heroic seekers of it. They lived under galling conditions; struggling as under mountains of impediment, and could not unfold themselves into clearness, or victorious interpretation of that "Divine Idea." It is rather the *Tombs* of three Literary Heroes that I have to show you. There are the monumental heaps, under which three spiritual giants lie buried. Very mournful, but also great and full of interest for us. We will linger by them for a while.

Complaint is often made, in these times, of what we call the disorganised condition of society: how ill many arranged forces of society fulfil their work; how many powerful forces are seen working in a wasteful, chaotic, altogether unarranged manner. It is too just a complaint, as we all know. But perhaps if we look at this of Books and the Writers of Books, we shall find here, as it were, the summary of all other disorganisation;—a sort of *heart*, from which, and to which, all other confusion circulates in the world! Considering what Book-writers do in the world, and what the world does with Book-writers, I should say, It is the most anomalous thing the world at present has to show.—We should get into a sea far beyond sounding, did we attempt to give account of this: but we must glance at it for the sake of our subject. The worst element in the life of these three Literary Heroes was, that they found their business and position such a chaos. On the beaten road there is tolerable travelling; but it is sore work, and many have to perish, fashioning a path through the impassable!

Our pious Fathers, feeling well what importance lay in the speaking of man to men, founded churches, made endowments, regulations; everywhere in the civilised world there is a Pulpit, environed with all manner of complex dignified appurtenances and furtherances, that therefrom a man with the tongue may, to best advantage, address his fellow-men. They felt that this was the most important thing; that without this there was no good thing. It is a right pious work, that of theirs; beautiful to behold! But now with the art of Writing, with the art of Printing, a total change has come over that business. The Writer of a Book, is not he a Preacher preaching not to this parish or that, on this day or that, but to all men in all times and places? Surely it is of the last importance that *he* do his work right, whoever do it wrong;—that the *eye* report not falsely, for then all the other members are astray! Well; how he may do his work, whether he do it right or wrong, or do it at all, is a point which no man in the world has taken the pains to think of. To a certain shopkeeper, trying to get some money for his books, if lucky, he is of some importance; to no other man of any. Whence he came, whither he is bound, by what ways he arrived, by what he might be furthered on his course, no one asks. He is an accident in society. He wanders like a wild Ishmaelite,[38] in a world of which he is as the spiritual light, either the guidance or the misguidance!

Certainly the Art of Writing is the most miraculous of all things man has devised. Odin's *Runes* were the first form of the work of a Hero;[39] *Books,* written words, are still miraculous *Runes,* the latest form! In Books lies the *soul* of the whole Past Time; the articulate audible voice of the Past, when the body and material substance of it has altogether vanished like a dream. Mighty fleets and armies, harbours and arsenals, vast cities, high-domed, many-engined,—they are precious, great: but what do they become? Agamemnon, the many Agamemnons, Pericleses, and their Greece;[40] all is gone now to some ruined fragments, dumb mournful wrecks and blocks: but the Books of Greece! There Greece, to every thinker, still very literally lives; can be called-up again into life. No magic *Rune* is stranger than a Book. All that Mankind has done, thought, gained or been: it is lying as in magic preservation in the pages of Books. They are the chosen possession of men.

---

38 See above, note 14. The Biblical image of the lonely Ishmael in the desert was a favorite with Carlyle.

39 In "The Hero as Divinity" Carlyle suggests that Odin was "the inventor of Letters" and defines runes as "the Scandinavian Alphabet."

40 Agamemnon was the legendary leader of the Greeks in the war against Troy, and Pericles was a great statesman and orator in Athens (fifth century B.C.). As men of action rather than men of letters, they left behind them, according to Carlyle, nothing but ruined fragments.

Do not Books still accomplish *miracles,* as *Runes* were fabled to do? They persuade men. Not the wretchedest circulating-library novel, which foolish girls thumb and con in remote villages, but will help to regulate the actual practical weddings and households of those foolish girls. So "Celia" felt, so "Clifford"[41] acted: the foolish Theorem of Life, stamped into those young brains, comes out as a solid Practice one day. Consider whether any *Rune* in the wildest imagination of Mythologist ever did such wonders as, on the actual firm Earth, some Books have done! What built St. Paul's Cathedral? Look at the heart of the matter, it was that divine Hebrew Book,—the word partly of the man Moses, an outlaw tending his Midianitish herds, four-thousand years ago, in the wildernesses of Sinai![42] It is the strangest of things, yet nothing is truer. With the art of Writing, of which Printing is a simple, an inevitable and comparatively insignificant corollary, the true reign of miracles for mankind commenced. It related, with a wondrous new contiguity and perpetual closeness, the Past and Distant with the Present in time and place; all times and all places with this our actual Here and Now. All things were altered for men; all modes of important work of men: teaching, preaching, governing, and all else.

To look at Teaching, for instance. Universities are a notable, respectable product of the modern ages. Their existence too is modified, to the very basis of it, by the existence of Books. Universities arose while there were yet no Books procurable; while a man, for a single Book, had to give an estate of land. That, in those circumstances, when a man had some knowledge to communicate, he should do it by gathering the learners round him, face to face, was a necessity for him. If you wanted to know what Abelard knew, you must go and listen to Abelard.[43] Thousands, as many as thirty-thousand, went to hear Abelard and that metaphysical theology of his. And now for any other teacher who had also something of his own to teach, there was a great convenience opened: so many thousands eager to learn were already assembled yonder; of all places the best place for him was that. For any third teacher it was better still; and grew ever the better, the more teachers there came. It only needed now that the King took notice of this new phenomenon; combined or agglomerated the various

schools into one school; gave it edifices, privileges, encouragements, and named it *Universitas,* or School of all Sciences: the University of Paris, in its essential characters, was there. The model of all subsequent Universities; which down even to these days, for six centuries now, have gone on to found themselves. Such, I conceive, was the origin of Universities.

It is clear, however, that with this simple circumstance, facility of getting Books, the whole conditions of the business from top to bottom were changed. Once invent Printing, you metamorphosed all Universities, or superseded them! The Teacher needed not now to gather men personally round him, that he might *speak* to them what he knew: print it in a Book, and all learners far and wide, for a trifle, had it each at his own fireside, much more effectually to learn it!—Doubtless there is still peculiar virtue in Speech; even writers of Books may still, in some circumstances, find it convenient to speak also,—witness our present meeting here! There is, one would say, and must ever remain while man has a tongue, a distinct province for Speech as well as for Writing and Printing. In regard to all things this must remain: to Universities among others. But the limits of the two have nowhere yet been pointed out, ascertained; much less put in practice: the University which would completely take-in that great new fact, of the existence of Printed Books, and stand on a clear footing for the Nineteenth Century as the Paris one did for the Thirteenth, has not yet come into existence. If we think of it, all that a University, or final highest School can do for us, is still but what the first School began doing,—teach us to *read.* We learn to *read,* in various languages, in various sciences; we learn the alphabet and letters of all manner of Books. But the place where we are to get knowledge, even theoretic knowledge, is the Books themselves! It depends on what we read, after all manner of Professors have done their best for us. The true University of these days is a Collection of Books.

But to the Church itself, as I hinted already, all is changed, in its preaching, in its working, by the introduction of Books. The Church is the working recognised Union of our Priests or Prophets, of those who by wise teaching guide the souls of men. While there was no Writing, even while there was no Easy-writing or *Printing,* the preaching of the voice was the natural sole method of performing this. But now with Books!—He that can write a true Book, to persuade England, is not he the Bishop and Archbishop, the Primate of England and of All England? I many a time say, the writers of Newspapers, Pamphlets, Poems, Books, these *are* the real working

---

41 Stock figures of the sentimental novel.
42 The word of Moses embodied in the Old Testament is part of the Christian religion, of which St. Paul's is a temple.
43 Peter Abelard (1079–1142), famous philosopher and teacher at the University of Paris.

effective Church of a modern country. Nay not only our preaching, but even our worship, is not it too accomplished by means of Printed Books? The noble sentiment which a gifted soul has clothed for us in melodious words, which brings melody into our hearts,—is not this essentially, if we will understand it, of the nature of worship? There are many, in all countries, who, in this confused time, have no other method of worship. He who, in any way, shows us better than we knew before that a lily of the fields is beautiful, does he not show it us as an effluence of the Fountain of all Beauty; as the *handwriting,* made visible there, of the great Maker of the Universe? He has sung for us, made us sing with him, a little verse of a sacred Psalm. Essentially so. How much more he who sings, who says, or in any way brings home to our heart the noble doings, feelings, darings and endurances of a brother man! He has verily touched our hearts as with a live coal *from the altar.* Perhaps there is no worship more authentic.

Literature, so far as it is Literature, is an "apocalypse of Nature," a revealing of the "open secret." It may well enough be named, in Fichte's style, a "continuous revelation" of the Godlike in the Terrestrial and Common. The Godlike does ever, in very truth, endure there; is brought out, now in this dialect, now in that, with various degrees of clearness: all true gifted Singers and Speakers are, consciously or unconsciously, doing so. The dark stormful indignation of a Byron, so wayward and perverse, may have touches of it; nay the withered mockery of a French sceptic,[44]—his mockery of the False, a love and worship of the True. How much more the sphere-harmony of a Shakspeare, of a Goethe; the cathedral-music of a Milton! They are something too, those humble genuine lark-notes of a Burns,— skylark, starting from the humble furrow,[45] far overhead into the blue depths, and singing to us so genuinely there! For all true singing is of the nature of worship; as indeed all true *working* may be said to be,[46]—whereof such *singing* is but the record, and fit melodious representation, to us. Fragments of a real "Church Liturgy" and "Body of Homilies," strangely disguised from the common eye, are to be found weltering in that huge froth-ocean of Printed Speech we loosely call Literature! Books are our Church too.

Or turning now to the Government of men. Witenagemote,[47] old Parliament, was a great thing. The affairs of the nation were there deliberated and decided; what we were to *do* as a nation. But does not, though the name Parliament subsists, the parliamentary debate go on now, everywhere and at all times, in a far more comprehensive way, *out* of Parliament altogether? Burke said there were Three Estates in Parliament; but, in the Reporters' Gallery yonder, there sat a *Fourth Estate* more important far than they all.[48] It is not a figure of speech, or a witty saying; it is a literal fact,—very momentous to us in these times. Literature is our Parliament too. Printing, which comes necessarily out of Writing, I say often, is equivalent to Democracy: invent Writing, Democracy is inevitable. Writing brings Printing; brings universal every-day extempore Printing, as we see at present. Whoever can speak, speaking now to the whole nation, becomes a power, a branch of government, with inalienable weight in law-making, in all acts of authority. It matters not what rank he has, what revenues or garnitures: the requisite thing is, that he have a tongue which others will listen to; this and nothing more is requisite. The nation is governed by all that has tongue in the nation: Democracy is virtually *there.* Add only, that whatsoever power exists will have itself, by and by, organised; working secretly under bandages, obscurations, obstructions, it will never rest till it get to work free, unencumbered, visible to all. Democracy virtually extant will insist on becoming palpably extant.—

On all sides, are we not driven to the conclusion that, of the things which man can do or make here below, by far the most momentous, wonderful and worthy are the things we call Books! Those poor bits of rag-paper with black ink on them;—from the Daily Newspaper to the sacred Hebrew Book, what have they not done, what are they not doing!—For indeed, whatever be the outward form of the thing (bits of paper, as we say, and black ink), is it not verily, at bottom, the highest act of man's faculty that produces a Book? It is the *Thought* of man; the true thaumaturgic virtue; by which man works all things whatsoever. All that he does, and brings to pass, is the vesture of a Thought. This London City, with all its houses, palaces, steam-engines, cathedrals, and huge immeasurable traffic and tumult, what is it but a Thought, but millions of Thoughts made into

---

44 A characteristic reference to Voltaire.

45 The image echoes that in Burns's poem "To a Mountain Daisy," lines 7–12 (p. 36, above).

46 Compare Carlyle's glorification of work at the close of "The Everlasting Yea."

47 The Anglo-Saxon Parliament.

48 The three estates were by tradition the nobility, the clergy, and the people. At the time of the French Revolution the press came to be known as "The Fourth Estate."

One;—a huge immeasurable Spirit of a THOUGHT, embodied in brick, in iron, smoke, dust, Palaces, Parliaments, Hackney Coaches, Katherine Docks, and the rest of it! Not a brick was made but some man had to *think* of the making of that brick.—The thing we called "bits of paper with traces of black ink," is the *purest* embodiment a Thought of man can have. No wonder it is, in all ways, the activest and noblest.

All this, of the importance and supreme importance of the Man of Letters in modern Society, and how the Press is to such a degree superseding the Pulpit, the Senate, the *Senatus Academicus*[49] and much else, has been admitted for a good while; and recognised often enough, in late times, with a sort of sentimental triumph and wonderment. It seems to me, the Sentimental by and by will have to give place to the Practical. If Men of Letters *are* so incalculably influential, actually performing such work for us from age to age, and even from day to day, then I think we may conclude that Men of Letters will not always wander like unrecognised unregulated Ishmaelites among us! Whatsoever thing, as I said above, has virtual unnoticed power will cast-off its wrappages, bandages, and step-forth one day with palpably articulated, universally visible power. That one man wear the clothes, and take the wages, of a function which is done by quite another:[50] there can be no profit in this; this is not right, it is wrong. And yet, alas, the *making* of it right,—what a business, for long times to come! Sure enough, this that we call Organisation of the Literary Guild is still a great way off, encumbered with all manner of complexities. If you asked me what were the best possible organisation for the Men of Letters in modern society; the arrangement of furtherance and regulation, grounded the most accurately on the actual facts of their position and of the world's position,—I should beg to say that the problem far exceeded my faculty! It is not one man's faculty; it is that of many successive men turned earnestly upon it, that will bring-out even an approximate solution. What the best arrangement were, none of us could say. But if you ask, Which is the worst? I answer: This which we now have, that Chaos should sit umpire in it;[51] this is the worst. To the best, or any good one, there is yet a long way.

One remark I must not omit, That royal or parliamentary grants of money are by no means the chief thing wanted! To give our Men of Letters stipends, endowments and all furtherance of cash, will do little towards the business. On the whole, one is weary of hearing about the omnipotence of money. I will say rather that, for a genuine man, it is no evil to be poor; that there ought to be Literary Men poor, —to show whether they are genuine or not! Mendicant Orders, bodies of good men doomed to *beg*, were instituted in the Christian Church; a most natural and even necessary development of the spirit of Christianity. It was itself founded on Poverty, on Sorrow, Contradiction, Crucifixion, every species of worldly Distress and Degradation. We may say, that he who has not known those things, and learned from them the priceless lessons they have to teach, has missed a good opportunity of schooling. To beg, and go barefoot, in coarse woollen cloak with a rope round your loins, and be despised of all the world, was no beautiful business;—nor an honourable one in any eye, till the nobleness of those who did so had made it honoured of some!

Begging is not in our course at the present time: but for the rest of it, who will say that a Johnson is not perhaps the better for being poor? It is needful for him, at all rates, to know that outward profit, that success of any kind is *not* the goal he has to aim at. Pride, vanity, ill-conditioned egoism of all sorts, are bred in his heart, as in every heart; need, above all, to be cast-out of his heart,—to be, with whatever pangs, torn-out of it, cast-forth from it, as a thing worthless. Byron, born rich and noble, made-out even less than Burns, poor and plebeian. Who knows but, in that same "best possible organisation" as yet far off, Poverty may still enter as an important element? What if our Men of Letters, men setting-up to be Spiritual Heroes, were still *then*, as they now are, a kind of "involuntary monastic order"; bound still to this same ugly Poverty,—till they had tried what was in it too, till they had learned to make it too do for them! Money, in truth, can do much, but it cannot do all. We must know the province of it, and confine it there; and even spurn it back, when it wishes to get farther.

Besides, were the money-furtherances, the proper season for them, the fit assigner of them, all settled,— how is the Burns to be recognized that merits these? He must pass through the ordeal, and prove himself. *This* ordeal; this wild welter of a chaos which is called Literary Life: this too is a kind of ordeal! There is clear truth in the idea that a struggle from the lower classes of society, towards the upper regions and

[49] The governing body of a university.
[50] A restatement of the earlier proposition that writers are now doing the work for which the clergy, the politicians, and the professors are receiving the credit and the remuneration.
[51] Cf. Milton's *Paradise Lost,* II, 907–8:
    "Chaos umpire sits
  And by decision more embroils the fray."

rewards of society, must ever continue. Strong men are born there, who ought to stand elsewhere than there. The manifold, inextricably complex, universal struggle of these constitutes, and must constitute, what is called the progress of society. For Men of Letters, as for all other sorts of men. How to regulate that struggle? There is the whole question. To leave it as it is, at the mercy of blind Chance; a whirl of distracted atoms, one cancelling the other; one of the thousand arriving saved, nine-hundred-and-ninety-nine lost by the way; your royal Johnson languishing inactive in garrets, or harnessed to the yoke of Printer Cave;[52] your Burns dying broken-hearted as a Gauger;[53] your Rousseau driven into mad exasperation, kindling French Revolutions by his paradoxes:[54] this, as we said, is clearly enough the *worst* regulation. The *best*, alas, is far from us!

And yet there can be no doubt but it is coming; advancing on us, as yet hidden in the bosom of centuries: this is a prophecy one can risk. For so soon as men get to discern the importance of a thing, they do infallibly set about arranging it, facilitating, forwarding it; and rest not till, in some approximate degree, they have accomplished that. I say, of all Priesthoods, Aristocracies, Governing Classes at present extant in the world, there is no class comparable for importance to that Priesthood of the Writers of Books. This is a fact which he who runs may read, —and draw inferences from. "Literature will take care of itself," answered Mr. Pitt,[55] when applied-to for some help for Burns. "Yes," adds Mr. Southey, "it will take care of itself; *and of you too*, if you do not look to it!"

The result to individual Men of Letters is not the momentous one; they are but individuals, an infinitesimal fraction of the great body; they can struggle on, and live or else die, as they have been wont. But it deeply concerns the whole society, whether it will set its *light* on high places, to walk thereby; or trample it under foot, and scatter it in all ways of wild waste (not without conflagration), as heretofore! Light is the one thing wanted for the world. Put wisdom in the head of the world, the world will fight its battle victoriously, and be the best world man can make it. I call this anomaly of a disorganic Literary Class the heart of all other anomalies, at once product and

parent; some good arrangement for that would be as the *punctum saliens*[56] of a new vitality and just arrangement for all. Already, in some European countries, in France, in Prussia, one traces some beginnings of an arrangement for the Literary Class; indicating the gradual possibility of such. I believe that it is possible; that it will have to be possible.

By far the most interesting fact I hear about the Chinese is one on which we cannot arrive at clearness, but which excites endless curiosity even in the dim state: this namely, that they do attempt to make their Men of Letters their Governors! It would be rash to say, one understood how this was done, or with what degree of success it was done. All such things must be very *unsuccessful*; yet a small degree of success is precious; the very attempt how precious! There does seem to be, all over China, a more or less active search everywhere to discover the men of talent that grow up in the young generation. Schools there are for every one: a foolish sort of training, yet still a sort. The youths who distinguish themselves in the lower school are promoted into favourable stations in the higher, that they may still more distinguish themselves,—forward and forward: it appears to be out of these that the Official Persons, and incipient Governors, are taken. These are they whom they *try* first, whether they can govern or not. And surely with the best hope: for they are the men that have already shown intellect. Try them: they have not governed or administered as yet; perhaps they cannot; but there is no doubt they *have* some Understanding,—without which no man can! Neither is Understanding a *tool*, as we are too apt to figure; "it is a *hand* which can handle any tool." Try these men: they are of all others the best worth trying.— Surely there is no kind of government, constitution, revolution, social apparatus or arrangement, that I know of in this world, so promising to one's scientific curiosity as this. The man of intellect at the top of affairs: this is the aim of all constitutions and revolutions, if they have any aim. For the man of true intellect, as I assert and believe always, is the noble-hearted man withal, the true, just, humane and valiant man. Get *him* for governor, all is got; fail to get him, though you had Constitutions plentiful as blackberries, and a Parliament in every village, there is nothing yet got!—

These things look strange, truly; and are not such as we commonly speculate upon. But we are fallen into strange times; these things will require to be speculated upon; to be rendered practicable, to be in

---

[52] Cave was the editor and owner of the *Gentleman's Magazine*, to which Johnson was a contributor during his early impoverished years in London.   [53] Excise officer.

[54] See above, note 29.

[55] The younger William Pitt, Prime Minister of England from 1783 to 1801 and from 1804 to 1806. On Southey, see pp. 354 ff., 444 f., above.

[56] A point from which to spring into action.

some way put in practice. These, and many others. On all hands of us, there is the announcement, audible enough, that the old Empire of Routine has ended; that to say a thing has long been, is no reason for its continuing to be. The things which have been are fallen into decay, are fallen into incompetence; large masses of mankind, in every society of our Europe, are no longer capable of living at all by the things which have been. When millions of men can no longer by their utmost exertion gain food for themselves, and "the third man for thirty-six weeks each year is short of third-rate potatoes,"[57] the things which have been must decidedly prepare to alter themselves!—I will now quit this of the organisation of Men of Letters.

Alas, the evil that pressed heaviest on those Literary Heroes of ours[58] was not the want of organisation for Men of Letters, but a far deeper one; out of which, indeed, this and so many other evils for the Literary Man, and for all men, had, as from their fountain, taken rise. That our Hero as Man of Letters had to travel without highway, companionless, through an inorganic chaos,—and to leave his own life and faculty lying there, as a partial contribution towards *pushing* some highway through it: this, had not his faculty itself been so perverted and paralysed, he might have put-up with, might have considered to be but the common lot of Heroes. His fatal misery was the *spiritual paralysis,* so we may name it, of the Age in which his life lay; whereby his life too, do what he might, was half-paralysed! The Eighteenth was a *Sceptical* Century; in which little word there is a whole Pandora's Box[59] of miseries. Scepticism means not intellectual Doubt alone, but moral Doubt; all sorts of *in*fidelity, insincerity, spiritual paralysis. Perhaps, in few centuries that one could specify since the world began, was a life of Heroism more difficult for a man. That was not an age of Faith,—an age of Heroes! The very possibility of Heroism had been, as it were, formally abnegated in the minds of all. Heroism was gone forever; Triviality, Formulism

and Common-place were come forever. The "age of miracles" had been, or perhaps had not been; but it was not any longer. An effete world; wherein Wonder, Greatness, Godhood could not now dwell;—in one word, a godless world!

How mean, dwarfish are their ways of thinking, in this time,—compared not with the Christian Shakspeares and Miltons, but with the old Pagan Skalds,[60] with any species of believing men! The living TREE Igdrasil,[61] with the melodious prophetic waving of its world-wide boughs, deep-rooted as Hela, has died-out into the clanking of a World-MACHINE. "Tree" and "Machine": contrast these two things. I, for my share, declare the world to be no machine! I say that it does *not* go by wheel-and-pinion "motives," self-interests, checks, balances; that there is something far other in it than the clank of spinning-jennies, and parliamentary majorities; and, on the whole, that it is not a machine at all!—The old Norse Heathen had a truer notion of God's-world than these poor Machine-Sceptics: the old Heathen Norse were *sincere*[62] men. But for these poor Sceptics there was no sincerity, no truth. Half-truth and hearsay was called truth. Truth, for most men, meant plausibility; to be measured by the number of votes you could get. They had lost any notion that sincerity was possible, or of what sincerity was. How many Plausibilities asking, with unaffected surprise and the air of offended virtue, What! am not I sincere? Spiritual Paralysis, I say, nothing left but a Mechanical life, was the characteristic of that century. For the common man, unless happily he stood *below* his century and belonged to another prior one, it was impossible to be a Believer, a Hero; he lay buried, unconscious, under these baleful influences. To the strongest man, only with infinite struggle and confusion was it possible to work himself half-loose; and lead as it were, in an enchanted, most tragical way, a spiritual death-in-life, and be a Half-Hero! Scepticism is the name we give to all this; as the chief symptom, as the chief origin of all this. Concerning which so much were to be said! It would take

---

[57] Carlyle is quoting from memory his own essay on "Chartism," chap. 4: "Ireland has near seven millions of working people, the third unit of whom . . . has not for thirty weeks each year as many third-rate potatoes as will suffice him."

[58] Carlyle switches here from consideration of men of letters in general to specific observations about the three writers he has chosen to discuss and the age in which they lived. The following paragraphs provide a summary of Carlyle's scornful reaction to the eighteenth century.

[59] A casket in Greek mythology, which when opened by Pandora released upon the world innumerable mental and physical ills.

[60] Ancient Scandinavian poets.

[61] The skalds sang of "the Ash-tree of Existence [which] has its roots deep-down in the kingdoms of Hela or Death; its trunk reaches up heaven-high, spreads its boughs over the whole Universe." ("The Hero as Divinity")

[62] Carlyle's use of this word tends to be personal. In general, he equates sincerity with belief and insincerity with skepticism. A sincere man is awed by "the great Fact of Existence. . . . Fly as he will, he cannot get out of the awful presence of this Reality. . . . Fearful and wonderful, real as Life, real as Death, is this Universe to him." ("The Hero as Prophet") Cf. "A world all sincere, a believing world." ("The Hero as Priest")

many Discourses, not a small fraction of one Discourse, to state what one feels about that Eighteenth Century and its ways. As indeed this, and the like of this, which we now call Scepticism, is precisely the black malady and life-foe, against which all teaching and discoursing since man's life began has directed itself: the battle of Belief against Unbelief is the never-ending battle! Neither is it in the way of crimination that one would wish to speak. Scepticism, for that century, we must consider as the decay of old ways of believing, the preparation afar off for new better and wider ways,—an inevitable thing. We will not blame men for it; we will lament their hard fate. We will understand that destruction of old *forms* is not destruction of everlasting *substances;* that Scepticism, as sorrowful and hateful as we see it, is not an end but a beginning.

The other day speaking, without prior purpose that way, of Bentham's theory of man and man's life,[63] I chanced to call it a more beggarly one than Mahomet's. I am bound to say, now when it is once uttered, that such is my deliberate opinion. Not that one would mean offence against the man Jeremy Bentham, or those who respect and believe him. Bentham himself, and even the creed of Bentham, seems to me comparatively worthy of praise. It is a determinate *being* what all the world, in a cowardly half-and-half manner, was tending to be. Let us have the crisis; we shall either have death or the cure. I call this gross, steam-engine Utilitarianism an approach towards new Faith. It was a laying-down of cant; a saying to oneself: "Well then, this world is a dead iron machine, the god of it Gravitation and selfish Hunger; let us see what, by checking and balancing, and good adjustment of tooth and pinion, can be made of it!" Benthamism has something complete, manful, in such fearless committal of itself to what it finds true; you may call it Heroic, though a Heroism with its *eyes* put out! It is the culminating point, and fearless ultimatum, of what lay in the half-and-half state, pervading man's whole existence in that Eighteenth Century. It seems to me, all deniers of Godhood, and all lip-believers of it, are bound to be Benthamites, if they have courage and honesty. Benthamism is an *eyeless* Heroism: the Human Species, like a hapless blinded Samson grinding in the Philistine Mill, clasps convulsively the pillars of

its Mill; brings huge ruin down, but ultimately deliverance withal.[64] Of Bentham I meant to say no harm.

But this I do say, and would wish all men to know and lay to heart, that he who discerns nothing but Mechanism in the Universe has in the fatalest way missed the secret of the Universe altogether. That all Godhood should vanish out of men's conception of this Universe seems to me precisely the most brutal error,—I will not disparage Heathenism by calling it a Heathen error,—that men could fall into. It is not true; it is false at the very heart of it. A man who thinks so will think *wrong* about all things in the world; this original sin will vitiate all other conclusions he can form. One might call it the most lamentable of Delusions,—not forgetting Witchcraft itself! Witchcraft worshipped at least a living Devil; but this worships a dead iron Devil; no God, not even a Devil!—Whatsoever is noble, divine, inspired, drops thereby out of life. There remains everywhere in life a despicable *caput-mortuum;*[65] the mechanical hull, all soul fled out of it. How can a man act heroically? The "Doctrine of Motives" will teach him that it is, under more or less disguise, nothing but a wretched love of Pleasure, fear of Pain; that Hunger, of applause, of cash, of whatsoever victual it may be, is the ultimate fact of man's life. Atheism, in brief;—which does indeed frightfully punish itself. The man, I say, is become spiritually a paralytic man; this godlike Universe a dead mechanical steam-engine, all working by motives, checks, balances, and I know not what; wherein, as in the detestable belly of some Phalaris'-Bull[66] of his own contriving, he the poor Phalaris sits miserably dying!

Belief I define to be the healthy act of a man's mind. It is a mysterious indescribable process, that of getting to believe;—indescribable, as all vital acts are. We have our mind given us, not that it may cavil and argue, but that it may see into something, give us clear belief and understanding about something, whereon we are then to proceed to act. Doubt, truly, is not itself a crime. Certainly we do not rush out, clutch-up the first thing we find, and straightway believe that! All manner of doubt, inquiry, σκέψις as it is named, about all manner of objects, dwells in every reasonable mind. It is the mystic working of the mind, on the object it is *getting* to know and

---

In his lecture on "The Hero as Prophet," where he delivered the following blast: "Benthamee Utility, virtue by Profit and Loss; reducing this God's-world to a dead brute Steam-engine, the infinite celestial Soul of Man to a kind of Hay-balance for weighing hay and thistles on, pleasures and pains on. . . ."

[64] Samson, blinded by the Philistines and set to grinding corn, seized the pillars of the temple and brought the building crashing to earth (Judges 16).—There is again a play upon the name of the Utilitarian thinker, James Mill.   [65] Skull.

[66] A brazen bull made for the Sicilian tyrant Phalaris (sixth century B.C.), in which he roasted his victims.

believe. Belief comes out of all this, above ground, like the tree from its hidden *roots*. But now if, even on common things, we require that a man keep his doubts *silent*, and not babble of them till they in some measure become affirmations or denials; how much more in regard to the highest things, impossible to speak-of in words at all! That a man parade his doubt, and get to imagine that debating and logic (which means at best only the manner of *telling* us your thought, your belief or disbelief, about a thing) is the triumph and true work of what intellect he has: alas, this is as if you should *overturn* the tree, and instead of green boughs, leaves and fruits, show us ugly taloned roots turned-up into the air,—and no growth, only death and misery going-on![67]

For the Scepticism, as I said, is not intellectual only; it is moral also; a chronic atrophy and disease of the whole soul. A man lives by believing something; not by debating and arguing about many things. A sad case for him when all that he can manage to believe is something he can button in his pocket, and with one or the other organ eat and digest! Lower than that he will not get. We call those ages in which he gets so low the mournfulest, sickest and meanest of all ages. The world's heart is palsied, sick: how can any limb of it be whole? Genuine Acting ceases in all departments of the world's work; dextrous Similitude of Acting begins. The world's wages are pocketed, the world's work is not done. Heroes have gone-out; Quacks have come-in. Accordingly, what Century, since the end of the Roman world, which also was a time of scepticism, simulacra and universal decadence, so abounds with Quacks as that Eighteenth? Consider them, with their tumid sentimental vapouring about virtue, benevolence,—the wretched Quack-squadron, Cagliostro[68] at the head of them! Few men were without quackery; they had got to consider it a necessary ingredient and amalgam for truth. Chatham,[69] our brave Chatham himself, comes down to the House, all wrapt and bandaged; he "has crawled out in great bodily suffering," and so on;—*forgets*, says Walpole, that he is acting the sick man; in the fire of debate, snatches his arm from the sling, and oratorically swings and brandishes it! Chatham himself lives the strangest mimetic life, half-hero, half-quack, all along. For indeed the world is full of

dupes; and you have to gain the *world's* suffrage! How the duties of the world will be done in that case, what quantities of error, which means failure, which means sorrow and misery, to some and to many, will gradually accumulate in all provinces of the world's business, we need not compute.

It seems to me, you lay your finger here on the heart of the world's maladies, when you call it a Sceptical World. An insincere world; a godless untruth of a world! It is out of this, as I consider, that the whole tribe of social pestilences, French Revolutions, Chartisms,[70] and what not, have derived their being,—their chief necessity to be. This must alter. Till this alter, nothing can beneficially alter. My one hope of the world, my inexpugnable consolation in looking at the miseries of the world, is that this is altering. Here and there one does now find a man who knows, as of old, that this world is a Truth, and no Plausibility and Falsity; that he himself is alive, not dead or paralytic; and that the world is alive, instinct with Godhood, beautiful and awful, even as in the beginning of days! One man once knowing this, many men, all men, must by and by come to know it. It lies there clear, for whosoever will take the *spectacles* off his eyes and honestly look, to know! For such a man the Unbelieving Century, with its unblessed Products, is already past: a new century is already come. The old unblessed Products and Performances, as solid as they look, are Phantasms, preparing speedily to vanish. To this and the other noisy, very great-looking Simulacrum with the whole world huzzahing at its heels, he can say, composedly stepping aside: Thou art not *true*; thou art not extant, only semblant; go thy way!—Yes, hollow Formulism, gross Benthamism, and other unheroic atheistic Insincerity is visibly and even rapidly declining. An unbelieving Eighteenth Century is but an exception,—such as now and then occurs. I prophesy that the world will once more become *sincere*; a believing world; with *many* Heroes in it, a heroic world! It will then be a victorious world; never till then.

Or indeed what of the world and its victories? Men speak too much about the world. Each one of us here, let the world go how it will, and be victorious or not victorious, has he not a Life of his own to lead?

67 On the anti-intellectual effect of doubt, cf. the General Introduction, p. 383, and *Sartor Resartus,* p. 400.
68 Count Cagliostro Palermo (1743–95), a notorious charlatan who pretended to sell eternal youth.
69 William Pitt the elder (1708–78). The incident is related by Horace Walpole (1717–97) in his *Memoirs of the Reign of George the Third.*
70 A movement which took its name from a charter drawn up by leaders of the workingmen embodying certain relatively moderate demands for popular rights. Carlyle discussed the movement at length and not unsympathetically in his tract "Chartism" in 1839. The agitation came to a climax in 1848, when the workers marched toward London to present a petition to Parliament but were repulsed by government troops and the leaders imprisoned or killed.

CHEYNE ROW, CHELSEA

In this London street stands Carlyle's house, where he worked in a soundproof room. (Paul Popper, Ltd.; photograph by Basil Collier)

THOMAS CARLYLE

From a photograph taken when Carlyle was 59 years old, ten years after the publication of *Past and Present* and at the time when he was at work on *Frederick the Great*. (Collection of J. R. Walden, Esq.)

BURY ST. EDMUNDS, SUFFOLK

The *Burg*, Bury, or 'Berry' as they call it, of St. Edmund is still a prosperous brisk Town . . . and on the eastern edge of it, still runs, long, black and massive, a range of monastic ruins. . . . See here the ancient massive Gateway. . . ." (Carlyle, *Past and Present*) St. Edmund died *c.* 870. The monastery was built in the eleventh century, the gateway shown here between 1327 and 1377. (Photograph by Arnold Kent, Norwich)

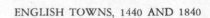

Catholic town in 1440.

ENGLISH TOWNS, 1440 AND 1840

"Not even Carlyle's account [in *Past and Present*] was s
eloquent and convincing an indictment of the present i
comparison with the past as the architect Pugin's *Contrast.*
. . . For if Carlyle's method was to let you read, Pugi
allowed you to see." (Wingfield-Stratford, *The Victoria*
Tragedy) The foreground of the imaginary 1840 town
largely occupied by a lunatic asylum, gas works, and a jai
(A. N. W. Pugin, *Contrasts; or Parallel between Edifice*
of the Middle Ages and Buildings of the Present Day, 1841

JOHN HENRY NEWMAN

From an engraving of the portrait made by Sir W. C.
Ross in 1847, when Newman was 46 years old, two years
after his conversion to Roman Catholicism. (British
Museum)

THOMAS HENRY HUXLEY

Pugin's contrast is largely parallel
by that between Newman, the a
firmer of traditional religious value
and Huxley, the apostle of the ne
science.

THE SAME TOWN IN 1840.

One Life; a little gleam of Time between two Eternities; no second chance to us for evermore! It were well for *us* to live not as fools and simulacra, but as wise and realities. The world's being saved will not save us; nor the world's being lost destroy us. We should look to ourselves: there is great merit here in the "duty of staying at home"! And, on the whole, to say truth, I never heard of "worlds" being "saved" in any other way. That mania of saving worlds is itself a piece of the Eighteenth Century with its windy sentimentalism. Let us not follow it too far. For the saving of the *world* I will trust confidently to the Maker of the world; and look a little to my own saving, which I am more competent to!—In brief, for the world's sake, and for our own, we will rejoice greatly that Scepticism, Insincerity, Mechanical Atheism, with all their poison-dews, are going, and as good as gone.—

Now it was under such conditions, in those times of Johnson, that our Men of Letters had to live. Times in which there was properly no truth in life. Old truths had fallen nigh dumb; the new lay yet hidden, not trying to speak. That Man's Life here below was a Sincerity and Fact, and would for ever continue such, no new intimation, in that dusk of the world, had yet dawned. No intimation; not even any

French Revolution,—which we define to be a Truth once more, though a Truth clad in hellfire! How different was the Luther's pilgrimage,[71] with its assured goal, from the Johnson's, girt with mere traditions, suppositions, grown now incredible, unintelligible! Mahomet's Formulas[72] were of "wood waxed and oiled," and could be *burnt* out of one's way: poor Johnson's were far more difficult to burn. —The strong man will ever find *work*, which means difficulty, pain, to the full measure of his strength. But to make-out a victory, in those circumstances of our poor Hero as Man of Letters, was perhaps more difficult than in any. Not obstruction, disorganisation, Bookseller Osborne and Fourpence-halfpenny a day;[73] not this alone; but the light of his own soul was taken from him. No landmark on the Earth; and, alas, what is that to having no loadstar in the Heaven! We need not wonder that none of those Three men rose to victory. That they fought truly is the highest praise. With a mournful sympathy we will contemplate, if not three living victorious Heroes, as I said, the Tombs of three fallen Heroes! They fell for us too; making a way for us. There are the mountains which they hurled abroad in their confused War of the Giants; under which, their strength and life spent, they now lie buried. . . .

from PAST AND PRESENT

Book II, Chapter 2

ST. EDMUNDSBURY[1]

THE *Burg,* Bury, or "Berry" as they call it, of St. Edmund is still a prosperous brisk Town; beautifully diversifying, with its clear brick houses, ancient clean streets, and twenty or fifteen thousand busy souls, the general grassy face of Suffolk; looking out right pleasantly, from its hill-slope, towards the rising Sun: and on the eastern edge of it, still runs, long, black and massive, a range of monastic ruins; into the wide internal spaces of which the stranger is admitted on payment of one shilling. Internal spaces laid out, at present, as a botanic garden. Here stranger or townsman, sauntering at his leisure amid these vast grim venerable ruins, may persuade himself that an Abbey of St. Edmundsbury did once exist; nay there is no

doubt of it: see here the ancient massive Gateway, of architecture interesting to the eye of Dilettantism;[2] and farther on, that other ancient Gateway, now about to tumble, unless Dilettantism, in these very months, can subscribe money to cramp it and prop it!

Here, sure enough, is an Abbey; beautiful in the eye of Dilettantism. Giant Pedantry also will step in,

[71] Because Luther lived in an age of faith. Luther was one of the heroes chosen by Carlyle in his lecture on "The Hero as Priest."

[72] The Formulas attacked by Mahomet were the contemporary idolatries. They could be "*burnt* out of one's way" because the originally sincere faith (now nothing but empty formulism) had been symbolized in wooden idols, rubbed with oil and wax.

[73] Dr. Johnson's restricted finances are constantly stressed by Boswell in his *Life,* where also is related Johnson's quarrel with Thomas Osborne, for whom he had prepared a *Catalogue of the Library of the Earl of Oxford.*

[2] One of the objects of Carlyle's attack in *Past and Present* is the lack of seriousness and responsibility on the part of the governing classes. "We must," he says, "exchange our dilettantisms for sincerities."

[1] The whole of Book II, entitled "The Ancient Monk," is devoted to an account of life in the monastery of St. Edmundsbury. For its significance, see the Introduction to Carlyle, p. 391.

with its huge *Dugdale* and other enormous *Monasticons*[3] under its arm, and cheerfully apprise you, That this was a very great Abbey, owner and indeed creator of St. Edmund's Town itself, owner of wide lands and revenues; nay that its lands were once a county of themselves; that indeed King Canute or Knut was very kind to it, and gave St. Edmund[4] his own gold crown off his head, on one occasion: for the rest, that the Monks were of such and such a genus, such and such a number; that they had so many carucates[5] of land in this hundred, and so many in that; and then farther that the large Tower or Belfry was built by such a one, and the smaller Belfry was built by &c., &c.—Till human nature can stand no more of it; till human nature desperately take refuge in forgetfulness, almost in flat disbelief of the whole business, Monks, Monastery, Belfries, Carucates and all! Alas, what mountains of dead ashes, wreck and burnt bones, does assiduous Pedantry dig up from the Past Time, and name it History, and Philosophy of History; till, as we say, the human soul sinks wearied and bewildered; till the Past Time seems all one infinite incredible grey void, without sun, stars, hearth-fires, or candle-light; dim offensive dust-whirlwinds filling universal Nature; and over your Historical Library, it is as if all the Titans had written for themselves: DRY RUBBISH SHOT[6] HERE!

And yet these grim old walls are not a dilettantism and dubiety; they are an earnest fact. It was a most real and serious purpose they were built for! Yes, another world it was, when these black ruins, white in their new mortar and fresh chiselling, first saw the sun as walls, long ago. Gauge not, with thy dilettante compasses, with that placid dilettante simper, the Heaven's-Watchtower of our Fathers, the fallen God's-Houses, the Golgotha[7] of true Souls departed!

Their architecture, belfries, land-carucates? Yes,—and that is but a small item of the matter. Does it never give thee pause, this other strange item of it, that men then had a *soul*,—not by hearsay alone, and as a figure of speech; but as a truth that they *knew*, and practically went upon! Verily it was another world then. Their Missals[8] have become incredible, a sheer platitude, sayest thou? Yes, a most poor platitude; and even, if thou wilt, an idolatry and blasphemy, should anyone persuade *thee* to believe them, to pretend praying by them. But yet it is pity we had lost tidings of our souls:—actually we shall have to go in quest of them again, or worse in all ways will befall! A certain degree of soul, as Ben Jonson[9] reminds us, is indispensable to keep the very body from destruction of the frightfullest sort; to "save us," says he, "the expense of *salt*."[10] Ben has known men who had soul enough to keep their body and five senses from becoming carrion, and save salt: —men, and also Nations. You may look in Manchester[11] Hunger-mobs and Corn-law Commons Houses, and various other quarters, and say whether either soul or else salt is not somewhat wanted at present!—

Another world, truly: and this present poor distressed world might get some profit by looking wisely into it, instead of foolishly. But at lowest, O dilettante friend, let us know always that it *was* a world, and not a void infinite of grey haze with phantasms swimming in it. These old St. Edmundsbury walls, I say, were not peopled with phantasms; but with men of flesh and blood, made altogether as we are. Had thou and I then been, who knows but we ourselves had taken refuge from an evil Time, and fled to dwell here, and meditate on an Eternity, in such fashion as we could? Alas, how like an old osseous fragment, a broken blackened shinbone of the old dead Ages, this black ruin looks out, not yet covered by the soil; still indicating what a once gigantic Life lies buried there! It is dead now, and dumb; but was alive once, and spake. For twenty generations, here was the earthly arena where painful[12] living men worked out their life-wrestle,—looked at by Earth, by Heaven and Hell. Bells tolled to prayers; and men, of many humours, various thoughts, chanted vespers, matins;—and round the little islet of their life rolled forever (as round ours still rolls, though we are blind and deaf) the illimitable Ocean, tinting all things with *its* eternal hues and reflexes; making strange prophetic music! How silent now; all departed, clean gone. The World-

---

[3] Sir William Dugdale, seventeenth-century English antiquarian, author of a history of British monasteries, *Monasticon Anglicanum*. Carlyle takes many a sly dig at antiquarian pedantry in these chapters.

[4] Edmund, king of East Anglia from 855 to 870, was the owner of the land on which the monastery was built in his memory. He was killed by invading Danes. Because he had been a just man and a good landlord he became venerated as a saint, according to Carlyle. He was far from being a contemporary of Canute, who ruled England from 1017 to 1035.

[5] Measure of land signifying as much as could be tilled by one plow in a year.   [6] Deposited.   [7] Cemetery.

[8] Literally the books containing the prayers and ritual of the Mass, but here representing religious belief.

[9] See above, I, 437 ff.

[10] If we are without souls, we are no better than dead carrion and, therefore, will need salt to keep us from rotting.

[11] Manchester was the scene of particular hardship and unrest among the workers.

[12] Painstaking; i.e., serious, as opposed to dilettante.

Dramaturgist has written: *Exeunt.*[13] The devouring Time-Demons have made away with it all: and in its stead, there is either nothing; or what is worse, offensive universal dust-clouds, and grey eclipse of Earth and Heaven, from "dry rubbish shot here!"—

Truly it is no easy matter to get across the chasm of Seven Centuries, filled with such material. But here, of all helps, is not a Boswell the welcomest; even a small Boswell?[14] Veracity, true simplicity of heart, how valuable are these always! He that speaks what *is* really in him, will find men to listen, though under never such impediments. Even gossip, springing free and cheery from a human heart, this too is a kind of veracity and *speech;*—much preferable to pedantry and inane grey haze! Jocelin is weak and garrulous, but he is human. Through the thin watery gossip of our Jocelin, we do get some glimpses of that deep-buried Time; discern veritably, though in a fitful intermittent manner, these antique figures and their life-method, face to face! Beautifully, in our earnest loving glance, the old centuries melt from opaque to partially translucent, transparent here and there; and the void black Night, one finds, is but the summing-up of innumerable peopled luminous *Days.* Not parchment Chartularies,[15] Doctrines of the Constitution, O Dryasdust; not altogether, my erudite friend!—

Readers who please to go along with us into this poor *Jocelini Chronica* shall wander inconveniently enough, as in wintry twilight, through some poor stripped hazel-grove, rustling with foolish noises, and perpetually hindering the eyesight; but across which, here and there, some real human figure is seen moving: very strange; whom we could hail if he would answer;—and we look into a pair of eyes deep as our own, *imaging* our own, but all unconscious of us; to whom we for the time are become as spirits and invisibles!

Book II, Chapter 4

ABBOT HUGO

It is true, all things have two faces, a light one and a dark. It is true, in three centuries much imperfection accumulates; many an Ideal, monastic or other, shooting forth into practice as it can, grows to a strange enough Reality; and we have to ask with amazement, Is this your Ideal! For, alas, the Ideal always has to grow in the Real, and to seek out its bed and board there, often in a very sorry way. No beautifullest Poet is a Bird-of-Paradise, living on perfumes; sleeping in the ether with outspread wings. The Heroic, *independent* of bed and board, is found in Drury-Lane Theatre[16] only; to avoid disappointments, let us bear this in mind.

By the law of Nature, too, all manner of Ideals have their fatal limits and lot; their appointed periods, of youth, of maturity or perfection, of decline, degradation, and final death and disappearance. There is nothing born but has to die. Ideal monasteries, once grown real, do seek bed and board in this world; do find it more and more successfully; do get at length too intent on finding it, exclusively intent on that. They are then like diseased corpulent bodies fallen idiotic, which merely eat and sleep; *ready* for "dissolution,"[17] by a Henry the Eighth or some other. Jocelin's St. Edmundsbury is still far from this last dreadful state: but here too the reader will prepare himself to see an Ideal not sleeping in the ether like a bird-of-paradise, but roosting as the common woodfowl do, in an imperfect, uncomfortable, more or less contemptible manner!—

Abbot Hugo, as Jocelin, breaking at once into the heart of the business, apprises us, had in those days grown old, grown rather blind, and his eyes were somewhat darkened, *aliquantulum caligaverunt oculi ejus.* He dwelt apart very much, in his *Talamus* or peculiar Chamber; got into the hands of flatterers, a set of mealy-mouthed persons who strove to make the passing hour easy for him,—for him easy, and for themselves profitable; accumulating in the distance mere mountains of confusion. Old Dominus Hugo sat inaccessible in this way, far in the interior, wrapped in his warm flannels and delusions; inaccessible to all voice of Fact; and bad grew ever worse with us. Not that our worthy old *Dominus Abbas* was inattentive to the divine offices, or to the maintenance of a devout spirit in us or in himself; but the Account-Books of the Convent fell into the frightfullest state, and Hugo's annual Budget grew yearly emptier, or filled with futile expectations, fatal deficit, wind and debts!

---

[13] Stage direction: "They go out."
[14] I.e., a chatty day-by-day account, like Boswell's in his *Life of Johnson.* Just such an account of life in St. Edmundsbury was the source of Carlyle's information about the monastery, "the 'Chronicle,' or private Boswellean Notebook, of Jocelin, a certain old St. Edmundsbury Monk." The *Chronicle* covers the years 1173–1202.   [15] Registers of charters.

[16] I.e., is a fiction, not a reality.
[17] Carlyle is playing upon the word, using it in its primary meaning in connection with his image as well as in its political meaning with reference to the drastic action of Henry VIII in the mid-sixteenth century in suppressing the monasteries.

His one worldly care was to raise ready money; sufficient for the day is the evil thereof. And how he raised it: From usurious insatiable Jews; every fresh Jew sticking on him like a fresh horseleech, sucking his and our life out; crying continually, Give, give! Take one example instead of scores. Our *Camera*[18] having fallen into ruin, William the Sacristan received charge to repair it; strict charge, but no money; Abbot Hugo would, and indeed could, give him no fraction of money. The *Camera* in ruins, and Hugo penniless and inaccessible, Willelmus Sacrista borrowed Forty Marcs (some Seven-and-twenty Pounds) of Benedict the Jew, and patched up our Camera again. But the means of repaying him? There were no means. Hardly could *Sacrista, Cellerarius,*[19] or any public officer, get ends to meet, on the indispensablest scale, with their shrunk allowances: ready money had vanished.

Benedict's Twenty-seven pounds grew rapidly at compound-interest; and at length, when it had amounted to a Hundred pounds, he, on a day of settlement, presents the account to Hugo himself. Hugo already owed him another Hundred of his own; and so here it has become Two Hundred! Hugo, in a fine frenzy, threatens to depose the Sacristan, to do this and do that; but, in the meanwhile, How to quiet your insatiable Jew? Hugo, for this couple of hundreds, grants the Jew his bond for Four hundred payable at the end of four years. At the end of four years there is, of course, still no money; and the Jew now gets a bond for Eight hundred and eighty pounds, to be paid by instalments, Fourscore pounds every year. Here was a way of doing business!

Neither yet is this insatiable Jew satisfied or settled with: he had papers against us of "small debts fourteen years old"; his modest claim amounts finally to "Twelve hundred pounds besides interest";—and one hopes he never got satisfied in this world; one almost hopes he was one of those beleaguered Jews who hanged themselves in York Castle shortly afterwards, and had his usances[20] and quittances and horseleech papers summarily set fire to! For approximate justice will strive to accomplish itself; if not in one way, then in another. Jews, and also Christians and Heathens, who accumulate in this manner, though furnished with never so many parchments, do, at times, "get their grinder-teeth successively pulled out of their head, each day a new grinder," till they consent to disgorge again. A sad fact,—worth reflecting on.

Jocelin, we see, is not without secularity: Our *Dominus Abbas* was intent enough on the divine offices; but then his Account-Books—?—One of the things that strike us most, throughout, in Jocelin's *Chronicle,* and indeed in Eadmer's[21] *Anselm,* and other old monastic Books, written evidently by pious men, is this, That there is almost no mention whatever of "personal religion" in them; that the whole gist of their thinking and speculation seems to be the "privileges of our order," "strict exaction of our dues," "God's honour" (meaning the honour of our Saint), and so forth. Is not this singular? A body of men, set apart for perfecting and purifying their own souls, do not seem disturbed about that in any measure: the "Ideal" says nothing about its idea; says much about finding bed and board for itself! How is this?

Why, for one thing, bed and board are a matter very apt to come to speech: it is much easier to *speak* of them than of ideas; and they are sometimes much more pressing with some! Nay, for another thing, may not this religious reticence, in these devout good souls, be perhaps a merit, and sign of health in them? Jocelin, Eadmer, and such religious men, have as yet nothing of "Methodism";[22] no Doubt or even root of Doubt. Religion is not a diseased self-introspection, an agonizing inquiry: their duties are clear to them, the way of supreme good plain, indisputable, and they are travelling on it. Religion lies over them like an all-embracing heavenly canopy, like an atmosphere and life-element, which is not spoken of, which in all things is presupposed without speech. Is not serene or complete Religion the highest aspect of human nature; as serene Cant, or complete No-religion, is the lowest and miserablest? Between which two, all manner of earnest Methodisms, introspections, agonizing inquiries, never so morbid, shall play their respective parts, not without approbation.

But let any reader fancy himself one of the Brethren in St. Edmundsbury Monastery under such circumstances! How can a Lord Abbot, all stuck over with horseleeches of this nature, front the world? He is fast losing his life-blood, and the Convent will be as one of Pharaoh's lean kine.[23] Old monks of experience draw their hoods deeper down; careful what

---

18 Council chamber.
19 Monk in charge of the wine cellar and other provisions.
20 Usurious documents.

21 Monk of Canterbury, intimate friend and biographer of Anselm, who was Archbishop of Canterbury from 1093 to 1109.
22 Carlyle distrusted Methodism as a morbid kind of egoism, "with its eye forever turned on its own navel; asking itself with torturing anxiety of Hope and Fear, 'Am I right? am I wrong? Shall I be saved? shall I not be damned?' "
23 The lean cattle seen by the king of Egypt in a dream, signifying seven years of poor harvests (Genesis, 41:27–30).

they say: the monk's first duty is obedience. Our Lord the King, hearing of such work, sends down his Almoner to make investigations: but what boots it? Abbot Hugo assembles us in Chapter; asks, "If there is any complaint?" Not a soul of us dare answer, "Yes, thousands!" but we all stand silent, and the Prior even says that things are in a very comfortable condition. Whereupon old Abbot Hugo, turning to the royal messenger, says, "You see!"—and the business terminates in that way. I, as a brisk-eyed, noticing youth and novice, could not help asking of the elders, asking of Magister Samson in particular: Why he, well-instructed and a knowing man, had not spoken out, and brought matters to a bearing?[24] Magister Samson was Teacher of the Novices, appointed to breed us up to the rules, and I loved him well. "*Fili mi,*" answered Samson, "the burnt child shuns the fire. Dost thou not know, our Lord the Abbot sent me once to Acre in Norfolk, to solitary confinement and bread and water, already? The Hinghams, Hugo and Robert, have just got home from banishment for speaking. This is the hour of darkness: the hour when flatterers rule and are believed. *Videat Dominus,* let the Lord see, and judge."

In very truth, what could poor old Abbot Hugo do? A frail old man; and the Philistines were upon him,—that is to say, the Hebrews. He had nothing for it but to shrink away from them; get back into his warm flannels, into his warm delusions again. Happily, before it was quite too late, he bethought him of pilgriming to St. Thomas of Canterbury. He set out, with a fit train, in the autumn days of the year 1180; near Rochester City, his mule threw him, dislocated his poor kneepan, raised incurable inflammatory fever; and the poor old man got his dismissal from the whole coil at once. St. Thomas à Becket, though in a circuitous way, had *brought* deliverance! Neither Jew usurers, nor grumbling monks, nor other importunate despicability of men or mud-elements afflicted Abbot Hugo any more; but he dropped his rosaries, closed his account-books, closed his old eyes, and lay down into the long sleep. Heavy-laden hoary old Dominus Hugo, fare thee well.

One thing we cannot mention without a due thrill of horror: namely, that, in the empty exchequer of Dominus Hugo, there was not found one penny to distribute to the Poor that they might pray for his soul! By a kind of godsend, Fifty shillings did, in the very nick of time, fall due, or seem to fall due, from one of his Farmers (the *Firmarius* de Palegrava), and he paid it, and the Poor had it; though, alas, this too only *seemed* to fall due, and we had it to pay again afterwards. Dominus Hugo's apartments were plundered by his servants, to the last portable stool, in a few minutes after the breath was out of his body. Forlorn old Hugo, fare thee well forever.

Book II, Chapter 8

THE ELECTION

ACCORDINGLY[25] our Prior assembles us in Chapter; and, we adjuring him before God to do justly, nominates, not by our selection, yet with our assent, Twelve Monks, moderately satisfactory. Of whom are Hugo Third-Prior, Brother Dennis a venerable man, Walter the *Medicus,* Samson *Subsacrista,* and other esteemed characters,—though Willelmus *Sacrista,* of the red nose,[26] too is one. These shall proceed straightway to Waltham;[27] and there elect the Abbot as they may and can. Monks are sworn to obedience; must not speak too loud, under penalty of footgyves, limbo, and bread and water: yet monks too would know what it is they are obeying. The St. Edmundsbury Community has no hustings,[28] ballot-box, indeed no open voting: yet by various vague manipulations, pulse-feelings, we struggle to ascertain what its virtual aim is, and succeed better or worse.

This question, however, rises; alas, a quite preliminary question: Will the *Dominus Rex* allow us to choose freely? It is to be hoped! Well, if so, we agree to choose one of our own Convent. If not, if the *Dominus Rex* will force a stranger on us, we decide on demurring, the Prior and his Twelve shall demur: we can appeal, plead, remonstrate; appeal even to the Pope, but trust it will not be necessary. Then there is this other question, raised by Brother Samson: What if the Thirteen should not themselves be able to agree? Brother Samson *Subsacrista,* one remarks, is ready oftenest with some question, some suggestion, that has wisdom in it. Though a servant of servants, and saying little, his words all tell, having sense in

---

[24] I.e., into the open.

[25] Electoral procedure, as indicated at the close of the preceding chapter, required an embassy of the prior and twelve other monks to the king, under whose supervision the election was to be made.

[26] Jocelin has previously complained of Willelmus's drinking.

[27] Waltham was the site of a famous abbey about twelve miles northeast of London. At this moment of crisis, King Henry II, who had the final say in the choice of a new abbot, was resident there.   [28] Temporary platform for political speakers.

them; it seems by his light mainly that we steer ourselves in this great dimness.

What if the Thirteen should not themselves be able to agree? Speak, Samson, and advise.—Could not, hints Samson, Six of our venerablest elders be chosen by us, a kind of electoral committee, here and now: of these, "with their hand on the Gospels, with their eye on the *Sacrosancta*," we take oath that they will do faithfully; let these, in secret and as before God, agree on Three whom they reckon fittest; write their names in a Paper, and deliver the same sealed, forthwith, to the Thirteen: one of those Three the Thirteen shall fix on, if permitted. If not permitted, that is to say, if the *Dominus Rex* force us to demur,—the Paper shall be brought back unopened, and publicly burned, that no man's secret bring him into trouble.

So Samson advises, so we act; wisely, in this and in other crises of the business. Our electoral committee, its eye on the *Sacrosancta,* is soon named, soon sworn; and we striking up the Fifth Psalm, "*Verba mea,*

> Give ear unto my words, O Lord,
> My meditation weigh,"

march out chanting, and leave the Six to their work in the Chapter here. Their work, before long, they announce as finished: they, with their eye on the Sacrosancta, imprecating the Lord to weigh and witness their meditation, have fixed on Three Names, and written them in this Sealed Paper. Let Samson Subsacrista, general servant of the party, take charge of it. On the morrow morning, our Prior and his Twelve will be ready to get under way.

This then is the ballot-box and electoral winnowing-machine they have at St. Edmundsbury: a mind fixed on the Thrice Holy, an appeal to God on high to witness their meditation: by far the best, and indeed the only good electoral winnowing-machine, —if men have souls in them. Totally worthless, it is true, and even hideous and poisonous, if men have no souls. But without soul, alas what winnowing-machine in human elections can be of avail? We cannot get along without soul; we stick fast, the mournfullest spectacle; and salt itself will not save us![29]

On the morrow morning, accordingly, our Thirteen set forth; or rather our Prior and Eleven; for Samson, as general servant of the party, has to linger, settling many things. At length he too gets upon the road; and, "carrying the sealed Paper in a leather pouch hung round his neck; and *froccum bajulans in ulnis*" (thanks to thee Bozzy Jocelin), "his frock-skirts looped over his elbow," showing substantial stern-works, tramps stoutly along. Away across the Heath, not yet of Newmarket[30] and horse-jockeying; across your Fleam-dike and Devil's-dike,[31] no longer useful as a Mercian East-Anglian boundary or bulwark: continually towards Waltham, and the Bishop of Winchester's House there, for his Majesty is in that. Brother Samson, as purse-bearer, has the reckoning always, when there is one, to pay; "delays are numerous," progress none of the swiftest.

But, in the solitude of the Convent, Destiny thus big and in her birthtime, what gossiping, what babbling, what dreaming of dreams! The secret of the Three our electoral elders alone know: some Abbot we shall have to govern us; but which Abbot, O which! One Monk discerns in a vision of the night-watches, that we shall get an Abbot of our own body, without needing to demur: a prophet appeared to him clad all in white, and said, "Ye shall have one of yours, and he will rage among you like a wolf, *saeviet ut lupus.*" Verily!—then which of ours? Another Monk now dreams: he has seen clearly which; a certain Figure taller by head and shoulders than the other two, dressed in alb and *pallium,*[32] and with the attitude of one about to fight;—which tall Figure a wise Editor would rather not name at this stage of the business! Enough that the vision is true: that Saint Edmund himself, pale and awful, seemed to rise from his Shrine, with naked feet, and say audibly, "He, *ille,* shall veil my feet"; which part of the vision also proves true. Such guessing, visioning, dim perscrutation of the momentous future: the very clothmakers, old women, all townsfolk speak of it, "and more than once it is reported in St. Edmundsbury, This one is elected; and then, This one and That other." Who knows?

But now, sure enough, at Waltham "on the Second Sunday of Quadragesima," which Dryasdust declares to mean the 22nd day of February, year 1182, Thirteen St. Edmundsbury Monks are, at last, seen processioning towards the Winchester Manorhouse; and in some high Presence-chamber, and Hall of State, get access to Henry II in all his glory. What a Hall,— not imaginary in the least, but entirely real and indisputable, though so extremely dim to us; sunk in the

---

[29] See note 10, above.

[30] Scene later of a celebrated race track.
[31] Channels of water, originally fortified boundaries between the low-lying lands of East Anglia and her neighbor to the west, Mercia.   [32] Ecclesiastical vestments.

deep distances of Night! The Winchester Manor-house has fled bodily, like a Dream of the old Night; not Dryasdust himself can show a wreck of it. House and people, royal and episcopal, lords and varlets, where are they? Why *there,* I say, Seven Centuries off; sunk *so* far in the Night, there they *are;* peep through the blankets of the old Night, and thou wilt see! King Henry himself is visibly there, a vivid, noble-looking man, with grizzled beard, in glittering uncertain costume; with earls round him, and bishops and dignitaries, in the like. The Hall is large, and has for one thing an altar near it,—chapel and altar adjoining it; but what gilt seats, carved tables, carpeting of rush-cloth, what arras-hangings,[33] and huge fire of logs:—alas, it has Human Life in it; and is not that the grand miracle, in what hangings or costume soever?—

The *Dominus Rex,* benignantly receiving our Thirteen with their obeisance, and graciously declaring that he will strive to act for God's honour, and the Church's good, commands, "by the Bishop of Winchester and Geoffrey the Chancellor,"—*Galfridus Cancellarius,* Henry's and the Fair Rosamond's authentic Son[34] present here!—commands, "That they, the said Thirteen, do now withdraw, and fix upon Three from their own Monastery." A work soon done; the Three hanging ready round Samson's neck, in that leather pouch of his. Breaking the seal, we find the names,—what think *ye* of it, ye higher dignitaries, thou indolent Prior, thou Willelmus *Sacrista* with the red bottle-nose?—the names, in this order: of Samson *Subsacrista,* of Roger the distressed Cellarer,[35] of Hugo *Tertius-Prior.*

The higher dignitaries, all omitted here, "flush suddenly red in the face"; but have nothing to say. One curious fact and question certainly is, How Hugo Third-Prior, who was of the electoral committee, came to nominate *himself* as one of the Three? A curious fact, which Hugo Third-Prior has never yet entirely explained, that I know of!—However, we return, and report to the King our Three names; merely altering the order; putting Samson last, as lowest of all. The King, at recitation of our Three, asks us: "Who are they? Were they born in my domain? Totally unknown to me! You must nominate three others." Whereupon Willelmus Sacrista says, "Our Prior must be named, *quia caput nostrum est,* being already our head." And the Prior responds,

"Willelmus Sacrista is a fit man, *bonus vir est,*"—for all his red nose. Tickle me, Toby, and I'll tickle thee![36] Venerable Dennis too is named; none in his conscience can say nay. There are now Six on our List. "Well," said the King, "they have done it swiftly, they! *Deus est cum eis.*"[37] The Monks withdraw again; and Majesty revolves, for a little, with his *Pares* and *Episcopi,*[38] Lords or "*Law-wards*"[39] and Soul-Overseers, the thoughts of the royal breast. The Monks wait silent in an outer room.

In short while, they are next ordered, To add yet another three; but not from their own Convent; from other Convents, "for the honour of my kingdom." Here,—what is to be done here? We will demur, if need be! We do name three, however, for the nonce: the Prior of St. Faith's, a good Monk of St. Neot's, a good Monk of St. Alban's; good men all; all made abbots and dignitaries since, at this hour. There are now Nine upon our List. What the thoughts of the Dominus Rex may be farther? The Dominus Rex, thanking graciously, sends out word that we shall now strike off three. The three strangers are instantly struck off. Willelmus Sacrista adds, that he will of his own accord decline,—a touch of grace and respect for the *Sacrosancta,* even in Willelmus! The King then orders us to strike off a couple more; then yet one more: Hugo Third-Prior goes, and Roger *Cellerarius,* and venerable Monk Dennis;—and now there remain on our List two only, Samson Subsacrista and the Prior.

Which of these two? It were hard to say,—by Monks who may get themselves foot-gyved and thrown into limbo, for speaking! We humbly request that the Bishop of Winchester and Geoffrey the Chancellor may again enter, and help us to decide. "Which do you want?" asks the Bishop. Venerable Dennis made a speech, "commending the persons of the Prior and Samson; but always in the corner of his discourse, *in angulo sui sermonis,* brought Samson in." "I see!" said the Bishop: "We are to understand that your Prior is somewhat remiss; that you want to have him you call Samson for Abbot." "Either of them is good," said venerable Dennis, almost trembling; "but we would have the better, if it pleased God." "Which of the two *do* you want?" inquires the Bishop pointedly. "Samson!" answered Dennis; "Samson!" echoed all of the rest that durst speak or echo anything: and Samson is reported to the King accordingly. His Majesty, advising of it for a moment,

---

[33] Tapestries.   [34] Henry's natural son.
[35] Distressed by his financial difficulties in providing for the monastery.

[36] Proverbial: say a good word for me, and I'll say one for you.
[37] God is with them.   [38] Peers and bishops.
[39] The etymology "guardians of the law" is strictly Carlyle's own.

orders that Samson be brought in with the other Twelve.

The King's Majesty, looking at us somewhat sternly, then says: "You present to me Samson; I do not know him: had it been your Prior, whom I do know, I should have accepted him: however, I will now do as you wish. But have a care of yourselves. By the true eyes of God, *per veros oculos Dei,* if you manage badly, I will be upon you!" Samson, therefore, steps forward, kisses the King's feet; but swiftly rises erect again, swiftly turns towards the altar, uplifting with the other Twelve, in clear tenor-note, the Fifty-first Psalm, *"Miserere mei Deus,*

> After thy loving-kindness, Lord,
> Have mercy upon *me*";

with firm voice, firm step and head, no change in his countenance whatever. "By God's eyes," said the King, "that one, I think, will govern the Abbey well." By the same oath (charged to your Majesty's account), I too am precisely of that opinion! It is some while since I fell in with a likelier man anywhere than this new Abbot Samson. Long life to him, and may the Lord *have* mercy on him as Abbot!

Thus, then, have the St. Edmundsbury Monks, without express ballot-box or other good winnowing-machine, contrived to accomplish the most important social feat a body of men can do, to winnow out the man that is to govern them: and truly one sees not that, by any winnowing-machine whatever, they could have done it better. O ye kind Heavens, there is in every Nation and Community *a fittest,* a wisest, bravest, best; whom could we find and make King over us, all were in very truth well;—the best that God and Nature had permitted *us* to make it![40] By what art discover him? Will the Heavens in their pity teach us no art; for our need of him is great!

Ballot-boxes, Reform Bills, winnowing-machines: all these are good, or are not so good;—alas, brethren, how *can* these, I say, be other than inadequate, be other than failures, melancholy to behold? Dim all souls of men to the divine, the high and awful meaning of Human Worth and Truth, we shall never, by

___

[40] Carlyle's ideal: the rule of the wise hero as king. This cannot be achieved, however, until men become serious rather than dilettante and believe again in the underlying spiritual reality of the universe. For the present "we have quietly closed our eyes to the eternal Substance of things, and opened them only to the Shows and Shams of things," and are therefore unable to recognize the true hero. The implication is that the monks of St. Edmundsbury were able to recognize the fittest, wisest, bravest, best among themselves, because in spite of their human weaknesses they were at heart believing men.

all the machinery in Birmingham, discover the True and Worthy. It is written, "if we are ourselves valets, there shall exist no hero for us; we shall not know the hero when we see him";—we shall take the quack for a hero; and cry, audibly through all ballot-boxes and machinery whatsoever, Thou art he; be thou King over us!

What boots it? Seek only deceitful Speciosity, money with gilt carriages, "fame" with newspaper-paragraphs, whatever name it bear, you will find only deceitful Speciosity; godlike Reality will be forever far from you. The Quack shall be legitimate inevitable King of you; no earthly machinery able to exclude the Quack. Ye shall be born thralls of the Quack, and suffer under him, till your hearts are near broken, and no French Revolution or Manchester Insurrection, or partial or universal volcanic combustions and explosions, never so many, can do more than "change the *figure* of your Quack"; the essence of him remaining, for a time and times.—"How long, O Prophet?" say some, with a rather melancholy sneer. Alas, ye *un*prophetic, ever till this come about: Till deep misery, if nothing softer will, have driven you out of your Speciosities *into* your Sincerities; and you find that there either is a Godlike in the world, or else ye are an unintelligible madness; that there is a God, as well as a Mammon and a Devil, and a Genius of Luxuries and canting Dilettantisms and Vain Shows! How long that will be, compute for yourselves. My unhappy brothers!—

Book III,[41] Chapter 2

GOSPEL OF MAMMONISM

READER, even Christian Reader as thy title goes, hast thou any notion of Heaven and Hell? I rather apprehend, not. Often as the words are on our tongue, they have got a fabulous or semi-fabulous character for most of us, and pass on like a kind of transient similitude, like a sound signifying little.

Yet it is well worth while for us to know, once and always, that they are not a similitude, nor a fable nor semi-fable; that they are an everlasting highest fact! "No Lake of Sicilian or other sulphur burns now anywhere in these ages," sayest thou? Well, and if there did not! Believe that there does not; believe it if thou wilt, nay hold by it as a real increase, a rise to higher stages, to wider horizons and empires. All this has vanished, or has not vanished; believe as thou wilt as to all this. But that an Infinite of Practical Impor-

___

[41] Book III is entitled "The Modern Worker."

tance,[42] speaking with strict arithmetical exactness, an *Infinite*, has vanished or can vanish from the Life of any Man: this thou shalt not believe! O brother, the Infinite of Terror, of Hope, of Pity, did it not at any moment disclose itself to thee, indubitable, unnameable? Came it never, like the gleam of *preternatural* Oceans, like the voice of old Eternities, far-sounding through thy heart of hearts? Never? Alas, it was not thy Liberalism then; it was thy Animalism! The Infinite is more sure than any other fact. But only men can discern it; mere building beavers, spinning arachnes, much more the predatory vulturous and vulpine species, do not discern it well!—

"The word Hell," says Sauerteig,[43] "is still frequently in use among the English People: but I could not without difficulty ascertain what they meant by it. Hell generally signifies the Infinite Terror, the thing a man *is* infinitely afraid of, and shudders and shrinks from, struggling with his whole soul to escape from it. There is a Hell therefore, if you will consider, which accompanies man, in all stages of his history, and religious or other development: but the Hells of men and Peoples differ notably. With Christians it is the infinite terror of being found guilty before the Just Judge. With old Romans, I conjecture, it was the terror not of Pluto,[44] for whom probably they cared little, but of doing unworthily, doing unvirtuously, which was their word for un*man*fully. And now what is it, if you pierce through his Cants, his oft-repeated Hearsays, what he calls his Worships and so forth,—what is it that the modern English soul does, in very truth, dread infinitely, and contemplate with entire despair? What *is* his Hell, after all these reputable, oft-repeated Hearsays, what is it? With hesitation, with astonishment, I pronounce it to be: The terror of 'Not succeeding'; of not making money, fame, or some other figure in the world,—chiefly of not making money! Is not that a somewhat singular Hell?"

Yes, O Sauerteig, it is very singular. If we do not "succeed," where is the use of us? We had better never have been born. "Tremble intensely," as our friend the Emperor of China says: *there* is the black Bottomless of Terror; what Sauerteig calls the "Hell of the English!"—But indeed this Hell belongs naturally to the Gospel of Mammonism, which also has its corresponding Heaven. For there *is* one Reality among so many Phantasms; about one thing we are

entirely in earnest: The making of money. Working Mammonism does divide the world with idle game-preserving Dilettantism:—thank Heaven that there is even a Mammonism, *any*thing we are in earnest about! Idleness is worst, Idleness alone is without hope: work earnestly at anything, you will by degrees learn to work at almost all things. There is endless hope in work, were it even work at making money.

True, it must be owned, we for the present, with our Mammon-Gospel, have come to strange conclusions. We call it a Society; and go about professing openly the totallest separation, isolation. Our life is not a mutual helpfulness; but rather, cloaked under due laws-of-war, named "fair competition" and so forth, it is a mutual hostility. We have profoundly forgotten everywhere that *Cash-payment* is not the sole relation of human beings; we think, nothing doubting, that *it* absolves and liquidates all engagements of man. "My starving workers?" answers the rich Millowner: "Did not I hire them fairly in the market? Did I not pay them, to the last sixpence, the sum covenanted for? What have I to do with them more?"—Verily Mammon-worship is a melancholy creed. When Cain, for his own behoof, had killed Abel, and was questioned, "Where is thy brother?" he too made answer, "Am I my brother's keeper?" Did I not pay my brother *his* wages, the thing he had merited from me?

O sumptuous Merchant-Prince, illustrious game-preserving Duke, is there no way of "killing" thy brother but Cain's rude way! "A good man by the very look of him, by his very presence with us as a fellow wayfarer in this Life-pilgrimage, *promises* so much": woe to him if he forget all such promises, if he never know that they are given! To a deadened soul, seared with the brute Idolatry of Sense, to whom going to Hell is equivalent to not making money, all "promises," and moral duties, that cannot be pleaded for in Courts of Request,[45] address themselves in vain. Money he can be ordered to pay, but nothing more. I have not heard in all Past History, and expect not to hear in all Future History, of any Society anywhere under God's Heaven supporting itself on such Philosophy. The Universe is not made so; it is made otherwise than so. The man or nation of men that thinks it is made so, marches forward nothing doubting, step after step; but marches—whither we know! In these last two centuries of Atheistic Government (near two centuries now, since the blessed restoration of his Sacred Majesty, and

---

[42] That can be demonstrated to have practical effect upon our lives.
[43] A mouthpiece for some of Carlyle's comments on the English. He is imagined as a "picturesque tourist" observing the English scene.   [44] Judge of the Underworld.

[45] Courts in which money disputes were heard.

Defender of the Faith, Charles Second), I reckon that we have pretty well exhausted what of "firm earth" there was for us to march on;—and are now, very ominously, shuddering, reeling, and let us hope trying to recoil, on the cliff's edge!—

For out of this that we call Atheism come so many other *isms* and falsities, each falsity with its misery at its heels!—A SOUL is not like wind (*spiritus,* or breath) contained within a capsule; the ALMIGHTY MAKER is not like a Clockmaker that once, in old immemorial ages, having *made* his Horologe of a Universe, sits ever since and sees it go![46] Not at all. Hence comes Atheism; come, as we say, many other *isms;* and as the sum of all, comes Valetism, the *reverse* of Heroism; sad root of all woes whatsoever. For indeed, as no man ever saw the above-said wind-element enclosed within its capsule, and finds it at bottom more deniable than conceivable; so too he finds, in spite of Bridgewater Bequests,[47] your Clockmaker Almighty an entirely questionable affair, a deniable affair;—and accordingly denies it, and along with it so much else. Alas, one knows not what and how much else! For the faith in an Invisible, Unnameable, Godlike, present everywhere in all that we see and work and suffer, is the essence of all faith whatsoever; and that once denied, or still worse, asserted with lips only, and out of bound prayerbooks only, what other thing remains believable? That Cant well-ordered is marketable Cant; that Heroism means gas-lighted Histrionism;[48] that seen with "clear eyes" (as they call Valet-eyes), no man is a Hero, or ever was a Hero, but all men are Valets and Varlets. The accursed practical quintessence of all sorts of Unbelief! For if there be now no Hero, and the Histrio himself begin to be seen into, what hope is there for the seed of Adam here below? We are the doomed everlasting prey of the Quack; who, now in this guise, now in that, is to filch us, to pluck and eat us, by such modes as are convenient for him. For the modes and guises I care little. The Quack once inevitable, let him come swiftly, let him pluck and eat me;—swiftly, that I may at least have done with him; for in his Quack-world I can have no wish to linger. Though he slay me, yet will I *not* trust in him. Though he conquer nations, and have all the Flunkeys of the Universe shouting at his heels, yet will I know well that *he* is an Inanity; that for him and his there is no continuance appointed, save only in Gehenna and the Pool.[49] Alas, the Atheist world, from its utmost summits of Heaven and Westminster Hall,[50] downwards through poor seven-feet Hats[51] and "Unveracities fallen hungry," down to the lowest cellars and neglected hunger-dens of it, is very wretched.

One of Dr. Alison's Scotch facts struck us much.[52] A poor Irish Widow, her husband having died in one of the Lanes of Edinburgh, went forth with her three children, bare of all resource, to solicit help from the Charitable Establishments of that City. At this Charitable Establishment and then at that she was refused; referred from one to the other, helped by none;—till she had exhausted them all; till her strength and heart failed her: she sank down in typhus-fever; died, and infected her Lane with fever, so that "seventeen other persons" died of fever there in consequence. The humane Physician asks thereupon, as with a heart too full for speaking, Would it not have been *economy* to help this poor Widow? She took typhus-fever, and killed seventeen of you! —Very curious. The forlorn Irish Widow applies to her fellow-creatures, as if saying, "Behold I am sinking, bare of help: ye must help me! I am your sister, bone of your bone; one God made us: ye must help me!" They answer, "No; impossible; thou art no sister of ours." But she proves her sisterhood; her typhus-fever kills *them:* they actually were her brothers, though denying it! Had human creature ever to go lower for a proof?

For, as indeed was very natural in such case, all government of the Poor by the Rich has long ago been given over to Supply-and-demand, Laissez-faire[53] and such like, and universally declared to be "impossible." "You are no sister of ours; what shadow of proof is there? Here are our parchments, our padlocks, proving indisputably our money-safes to be *ours,* and you to have no business with them. Depart! It is impossible!"—Nay, what wouldst thou thyself have us do? cry indignant readers. Nothing, my friends,—till you have got a soul for yourselves again. Till then all things are "impossible." Till then I cannot even bid you buy, as the old Spartans would have done, two-pence worth of powder and lead, and compendiously shoot to death this poor Irish

---

[46] See note 9 to *Sartor Resartus.*

[47] A sum of £8,000 left by the Earl of Bridgewater for the best treatise on God as the mechanistic creator of the universe.

[48] Play acting, i.e., sham.

[49] Hell.

[50] Westminster Hall or Parliament, as important in the eyes of atheists as any heaven they could conceive of.

[51] An advertising scheme described in Bk. II, chap. I, as a contemptible example of sham and dupery.

[52] Carlyle himself gives the reference to *Observations on the Management of the Poor in Scotland,* by William Pulteney Alison, M.D. (Edinburgh, 1840).

[53] See the introduction to Carlyle, p. 391.

Widow:[54] even that is "impossible" for you. Nothing is left but that she prove her sisterhood by dying, and infecting you with typhus. Seventeen of you lying dead will not deny such proof that she *was* flesh of your flesh; and perhaps some of the living may lay it to heart.

"Impossible": of a certain two-legged animal with feathers it is said, if you draw a distinct chalk-circle round him, he sits imprisoned, as if girt with the iron ring of Fate; and will die there, though within sight of victuals,—or sit in sick misery there, and be fatted to death. The name of this poor two legged animal is—Goose;[55] and they make of him, when well fattened, *Pâté de foie gras*,[56] much prized by some!

Book III, Chapter 5

THE ENGLISH

AND yet, with all thy theoretic platitudes, what a depth of practical sense in thee, great England! A depth of sense, of justice, and courage; in which, under all emergencies and world-bewilderments, and under this most complex of emergencies we now live in, there is still hope, there is still assurance!

The English are a dumb people. They can do great acts, but not describe them. Like the old Romans, and some few others, *their* Epic Poem is written on the Earth's surface: England her Mark! It is complained that they have no artists: one Shakespeare indeed; but for Raphael only a Reynolds; for Mozart nothing but a Mr. Bishop:[57] not a picture, not a song. And yet they did produce one Shakespeare: consider how the element of Shakespearean melody does lie imprisoned in their nature; reduced to unfold itself in mere Cottonmills, Constitutional Governments, and such like;—all the more interesting when it does become visible, as even in such unexpected shapes it succeeds in doing! Goethe spoke of the Horse, how impressive, almost affecting it was that an animal of such qualities should stand obstructed so; its speech nothing but an inarticulate neighing, its handiness mere *hoof*iness, the fingers all constricted, tied together, the finger-nails coagulated into a mere hoof, shod with iron. The more significant, thinks he, are those eye-lashings of the generous noble quadruped; those prancings, curvings of the neck clothed with thunder.

A Dog of Knowledge has free utterance; but the Warhorse is almost mute, very far from free! It is even so. Truly, your freest utterances are not by any means always the best: they are the worst rather; the feeblest, trivialest; their meaning prompt, but small, ephemeral. Commend me to the silent English, to the silent Romans. Nay, the silent Russians too I believe to be worth something: are they not even now drilling, under much obloquy, an immense semi-barbarous half-world from Finland to Kamtschatka, into rule, subordination, civilization,—really in an old Roman fashion; speaking no word about it; quietly hearing all manner of vituperative Able Editors speak! While your ever-talking, ever-gesticulating French, for example, what are they at this moment drilling?—Nay, of all animals, the freest of utterance, I should judge, is the genus *Simia*: go into the Indian woods, say all Travellers, and look what a brisk, adroit, unresting Ape-population it is!

The spoken Word, the written Poem, is said to be an epitome of the man; how much more the done Work. Whatsoever of morality and of intelligence; what of patience, perseverance, faithfulness, or method, insight, ingenuity, energy; in a word, whatsoever of Strength the man had in him will lie written in the Work he does. To work: why, it is to try himself against Nature, and her everlasting unerring Laws; these will tell a true verdict as to the man. So much of virtue and of faculty did *we* find in him; so much and no more! He had such capacity of harmonizing himself with *me* and my unalterable eververacious Laws; of co-operating and working as *I* bade him;—and has prospered, and has not prospered, as you see!—Working as great Nature bade him: does not that mean virtue of a kind; nay, of all kinds? Cotton can be spun and sold, Lancashire operatives can be got to spin it, and at length one has the woven webs and sells them, by following Nature's regulations in that matter: by not following Nature's regulations, you have them not. You have them not; —there is no Cotton-web to sell: Nature finds a bill against you; your "Strength" is not Strength, but Futility! Let faculty be honoured, so far as it is faculty. A man that can succeed in working is to me always a man.

---

54 The Spartans killed off their helots or slaves when they became too numerous.
55 In claiming that it is impossible to do anything about the deplorable condition of the poor, Englishmen are acting like geese.
56 A rich paste made of fatted goose livers. It is uncertain just what threat is contained in this allusion; most probably, revolution.
57 Raphael (1483–1520), an Italian and one of the world's greatest painters, in comparison with whom the English portrait-painter Sir Joshua Reynolds (1723–92) holds an inferior rank. The comparison in the realm of music is even more destructive of the prestige of England. The great Austrian composer Mozart (1756–91) is contrasted with a minor contemporary figure, Sir Henry Bishop (1786–1855).

How one loves to see the burly figure of him, this thick-skinned, seemingly opaque, perhaps sulky, almost stupid Man of Practice, pitted against some light adroit Man of Theory, all equipped with clear logic, and able anywhere to give you Why for Wherefore! The adroit Man of Theory, so light of movement, clear of utterance, with his bow full-bent and quiver full of arrow-arguments,—surely he will strike down the game, transfix everywhere the heart of the matter; triumph everywhere, as he proves that he shall and must do? To your astonishment, it turns out oftenest No. The cloudy-browed, thick-soled, opaque Practicality, with no logic utterance, in silence mainly, with here and there a low grunt or growl, has in him what transcends all logic-utterance: a Congruity with the Unuttered. The Speakable, which lies atop, as a superficial film, or outer skin, is his or is not his: but the Doable, which reaches down to the World's centre, you find him there!

The rugged Brindley[58] has little to say for himself; the rugged Brindley, when difficulties accumulate on him, retires silent, "generally to his bed"; retires "sometimes for three days together to his bed, that he may be in perfect privacy there," and ascertain in his rough head how the difficulties can be overcome. The ineloquent Brindley, behold he *has* chained seas together; his ships do visibly float over valleys, invisibly through the hearts of mountains; the Mersey and the Thames, the Humber and the Severn have shaken hands: Nature most audibly answers, Yea! The man of Theory twangs his full-bent bow: Nature's Fact ought to fall stricken, but does not: his logic-arrow glances from it as from a scaly dragon, and the obstinate Fact keeps walking its way. How singular! At bottom, you will have to grapple closer with the dragon; take it home to you, by real faculty, not by seeming faculty; try whether you are stronger or it is stronger. Close with it, wrestle it: sheer obstinate toughness of muscle; but much more, what we call toughness of heart, which will mean persistence hopeful and even desperate, unsubduable patience, composed candid openness, clearness of mind: all this shall be "strength" in wrestling your dragon; the whole man's real strength is in this work, we shall get the measure of him here.

Of all the Nations in the world at present the English are the stupidest in speech, the wisest in action. As good as a "dumb" Nation, I say, who cannot speak, and have never yet spoken,—spite of the Shakespeares and Miltons who show us what possibilities there are!—O Mr. Bull,[59] I look in that surly face of thine with a mixture of pity and laughter, yet also with wonder and veneration. Thou complainest not, my illustrious friend; and yet I believe the heart of thee is full of sorrow, of unspoken sadness, seriousness,—profound melancholy (as some have said) the basis of thy being. Unconsciously, for thou speakest of nothing, this great Universe is great to thee. Not by levity of floating, but by stubborn force of swimming, shalt thou make thy way. The Fates sing of thee that thou shalt many times be thought an ass and a dull ox, and shalt with a godlike indifference believe it. My friend,—and it is all untrue, nothing ever falser in point of fact! Thou art of those great ones whose greatness the small passer-by does not discern. Thy very stupidity is wiser than their wisdom. A grand *vis inertiae*[60] is in thee; how many grand qualities unknown to small men! Nature alone knows thee, acknowledges the bulk and strength of thee: thy Epic, unsung in words, is written in huge characters on the face of this Planet,—sea-moles, cotton-trades, railways, fleets and cities, Indian Empires, Americas, New-Hollands; legible throughout the Solar System!

But the dumb Russians too, as I said, they, drilling all wild Asia and wild Europe into military rank and file, a terrible yet hitherto a prospering enterprise, are still dumber. The old Romans also could not *speak,* for many centuries:—not till the world was theirs, and so many speaking Greekdoms, their logic-arrows all spent, had been absorbed and abolished. The logic-arrows, how they glanced futile from obdurate thick-skinned Facts; Facts to be wrestled down only by the real vigour of Roman thews!—As for me, I honour, in these loud-babbling days, all the Silent rather. A grand Silence that of Romans;—nay the grandest of all, is it not that of the gods! Even Triviality, Imbecility, that can sit silent, how respectable is it in comparison! The "talent of silence" is our fundamental one. Great honour to him whose Epic is a melodious hexameter Iliad; not a jingling Sham-Iliad, nothing true in it but the hexameters and forms merely. But still greater honour, if his Epic be a mighty Empire slowly built together, a mighty Series of Heroic Deeds,—a mighty Conquest over Chaos; *which* Epic the "Eternal Melodies" have, and must have, informed and dwelt in, as *it* sung itself! There is no mistaking that latter Epic. Deeds are greater than Words. Deeds have such a life, mute but

---

[58] James Brindley (1716–72), an engineer who constructed many aqueducts and canals.

[59] John Bull, the English equivalent of Uncle Sam.
[60] Inert strength.

undeniable, and grow as living trees and fruit-trees do; they people the vacuity of Time, and make it green and worthy. Why should the oak prove logically that it ought to grow, and will grow? Plant it, try it; what gifts of diligent judicious assimilation and secretion it has, of progress and resistance, of *force* to grow, will then declare themselves. My much-honoured, illustrious, extremely inarticulate Mr. Bull!—

Ask Bull his spoken opinion of any matter,—oftentimes the force of dullness can no farther go. You stand silent, incredulous, as over a platitude that borders on the Infinite. The man's Churchisms, Dissenterisms, Puseyisms, Benthamisms, College Philosophies, Fashionable Literatures, are unexampled in this world.[61] Fate's prophecy is fulfilled; you call the man an ox and an ass. But set him once to work, —respectable man! His spoken sense is next to nothing, nine-tenths of it palpable *non*sense: but his unspoken sense, his inner silent feeling of what is true, what does agree with fact, what is doable and what is not doable,—this seeks its fellow in the world. A terrible worker; irresistible against marshes, mountains, impediments, disorder, incivilization; everywhere vanquishing disorder, leaving it behind him as method and order. He "retires to his bed three days," and considers!

Nay withal, stupid as he is, our dear John,—ever, after infinite tumblings, and spoken platitudes innumerable from barrel-heads and parliament-benches, he does settle down somewhere about the just conclusion; you are certain that his jumblings and tumblings will end, after years or centuries, in the stable equilibrium. Stable equilibrium, I say; centre-of-gravity lowest;—not the unstable, with centre-of-gravity highest, as I have known it done by quicker people! For indeed, do but jumble and tumble sufficiently, you avoid that worse fault, of settling with your centre-of-gravity highest; your centre-of-gravity is certain to come lowest, and to stay there. If slowness, what we in our impatience call "stupidity," be the price of stable equilibrium over unstable, shall we grudge a little slowness? Not the least admirable quality of Bull is, after all, that of remaining insensible to logic; holding out for considerable periods, ten years or more, as in this of the Corn-Laws,[62] after all arguments and shadow of arguments

have faded away from him, till the very urchins on the street titter at the arguments he brings. Logic,— Λογική, the "Art of Speech,"—does indeed speak so and so; clear enough: nevertheless Bull still shakes his head; will see whether nothing else *illogical*, not yet "spoken," not yet able to be "spoken," do not lie in the business, as there so often does!—My firm belief is, that, finding himself now enchanted, hand-shackled, foot-shackled, in Poor-Law Bastilles[63] and elsewhere, he will retire three days to his bed, and *arrive* at a conclusion or two! His three-years "total stagnation of trade," alas, is not that a painful enough "lying in bed to consider himself"? Poor Bull!

Bull is a born Conservative; for this too I inexpressibly honour him. All great Peoples are conservative; slow to believe in novelties; patient of much error in actualities; deeply and for ever certain of the greatness that is in Law, in Custom once solemnly established, and now long recognized as just and final.—True, O Radical Reformer, there is no Custom that can, properly speaking, be final; none. And yet thou seest *Customs* which, in all civilized countries, are accounted final; nay, under the Old-Roman name of *Mores*, are accounted *Morality*, Virtue, Laws of God Himself. Such, I assure thee, not a few of them are; such almost all of them once were. And greatly do I respect the solid character,—a blockhead, thou wilt say; yes, but a well-conditioned blockhead, and the best-conditioned,—who esteems all "Customs once solemnly acknowledged" to be ultimate, divine, and the rule of a man to walk by, nothing doubting, not inquiring farther. What a time of it had we, were all men's life and trade still, in all parts of it, a problem, a hypothetic seeking, to be settled by painful Logics and Baconian Inductions![64] The Clerk in Eastcheap[65] cannot spend the day in verifying his Ready-Reckoner; he must take it as verified, true and indisputable; or his Bookkeeping by Double Entry will stand still. "Where is your Posted Ledger?" asks the Master at night.—"Sir," answers the other, "I was verifying my Ready-Reckoner, and find some errors. The Ledger is—!"—Fancy such a thing!

True, all turns on your Ready-Reckoner being moderately correct,—being *not* insupportably incorrect! A Ready-Reckoner which has led to distinct

<hr />

61 The English mind is muddled by all the contemporary controversies. Puseyism was the High Church movement.
62 The high tariffs on grain imported into England. They were repealed in 1846.
63 Workhouses. These were established by the Poor Law of 1834, and though they made for more efficient care of the poor, they were less "personal" than the earlier parish dole and seemed like prisons. Carlyle attacked them for dealing with people as so many objects rather than as individual human beings.
64 Scientific method established by Francis Bacon (1561–1626).
65 Financial district of London.

entries in your Ledger such as these: "*Creditor* an English People by fifteen hundred years of good Labour; and *Debtor* to lodging in enchanted Poor-Law Bastilles: *Creditor* by conquering the largest Empire the Sun ever saw; and *Debtor* to Donothing-ism and 'Impossible' written on all departments of the government thereof: *Creditor* by mountains of gold ingots earned; and *Debtor* to No Bread purchasable by them":—*such* Ready-Reckoner, methinks, is beginning to be suspect; nay is ceasing, and has ceased, to be suspect! Such Ready-Reckoner is a Solecism in Eastcheap; and must, whatever be the press of business, and will and shall be rectified a little. Business can go on no longer with *it*. The most Conservative English People, thickest-skinned, most patient of Peoples, is driven alike by its Logic and its Unlogic, by things "spoken," and by things not yet spoken or very speakable, but only felt and very unendurable, to be wholly a Reforming People. Their Life as it is has ceased to be longer possible for them.

Urge not this noble silent People: rouse not the Berserkir-rage[66] that lies in them! Do you know their Cromwells, Hampdens, their Pyms and Bradshaws?[67] Men very peaceable, but men that can be made very terrible! Men who, like their old Teutsch Fathers in Agrippa's days,[68] "have a soul that despises death"; to whom "death," compared with falsehoods and injustices, is light;—"in whom there is a rage unconquerable by the immortal gods!" Before this, the English People have taken very preternatural-looking Spectres by the beard; saying virtually: "And if thou *wert* 'preternatural'? Thou with thy 'divine-rights' grown diabolic wrongs? Thou,—not even 'natural'; decapitable; totally extinguishable!"—Yes, just so godlike as this People's patience was, even so godlike will and must its impatience be. Away, ye scandalous Practical Solecisms, children actually of the Prince of Darkness; ye have near broken our hearts; we can and will endure you no longer. Begone, we say; depart, while the play is good! By the Most High God, whose sons and born missionaries true men are, ye shall not continue here! You and we have become incompatible; can inhabit one house no longer. Either you must go, or we. Are ye ambitious to try *which* it shall be?

O my Conservative friends, who still specially name and struggle to approve yourselves "Con-

servative," would to Heaven I could persuade you of this world-old fact, than which Fate is not surer, That Truth and Justice alone are *capable* of being "conserved" and preserved! The thing which is unjust, which is *not* according to God's Law, will you, in a God's Universe, try to conserve that? It is so old, say you? Yes, and the hotter haste ought *you*, of all others, to be in to let it grow no older! If but the faintest whisper in your hearts intimate to you that it is not fair,—hasten, for the sake of Conservatism itself, to probe it rigorously, to cast it forth at once and for ever if guilty. How will or can you preserve *it*, the thing that is not fair? "Impossibility" a thousandfold is marked on that. And ye call yourselves Conservatives, Aristocracies:—ought not honour and nobleness of mind, if they had departed from all the Earth elsewhere, to find their last refuge with you? Ye unfortunate!

The bough that is dead shall be cut away, for the sake of the tree itself. Old? Yes, it is too old. Many a weary winter has it swung and creaked there, and gnawed and fretted, with its dead wood, the organic substance and still living fibre of this good tree; many a long summer has its ugly naked brown defaced the fair green umbrage; every day it has done mischief, and that only: off with it, for the tree's sake, if for nothing more; let the Conservatism that would preserve cut *it* away. Did no wood-forester apprise you that a dead bough with its dead root left sticking there is extraneous, poisonous; is as a dead iron spike, some horrid rusty ploughshare driven into the living substance;—nay is far worse; for in every windstorm ("commercial crisis" or the like), it frets and creaks, jolts itself to and fro, and cannot lie quiet as your dead iron spike would.

If I were the Conservative Party of England (which is another bold figure of speech), I would not for a hundred thousand pounds an hour allow those Corn-Laws to continue! Potosi and Golconda[69] put together would not purchase my assent to them. Do you count what treasuries of bitter indignation they are laying up for you in every just English heart? Do you know what questions, not as to Corn-prices and Sliding-scales alone, they are *forcing* every reflective Englishman to ask himself? Questions insoluble, or hitherto unsolved; deeper than any of our Logic-plummets hitherto will sound: questions deep enough,—which it were better that we did not name even in thought! You are forcing us to think of them, to begin uttering them. The utterance of them is begun; and where will it be ended, think you? When two millions of one's brother-men sit in Workhouses, and five

---

66 The berserk was in Norse folklore a warrior subject to fits of frenzy in battle.

67 Men who were roused by the evils of their time to become leaders of the Puritan Revolution in the middle of the seventeenth century.

68 Germanic tribes living in the time of Agrippa (63–12 B.C.).

69 Sites of fabulous treasure.

millions, as is insolently said, "rejoice in potatoes," there are various things that must be begun, let them end where they can.

Book III, Chapter 11
LABOUR[70]

FOR there is a perennial nobleness, and even sacredness, in Work. Were he never so benighted, forgetful of his high calling, there is always hope in a man that actually and earnestly works: in Idleness alone is there perpetual despair. Work, never so Mammonish, mean, *is* in communication with Nature; the real desire to get Work done will itself lead one more and more to truth, to Nature's appointments and regulations which are truth.

The latest Gospel in this world is, Know thy work and do it. "Know thyself": long enough has that poor "self" of thine tormented thee; thou wilt never get to "know" it, I believe! Think it not thy business, this of knowing thyself; thou art an unknowable individual: know what thou canst work at; and work at it, like a Hercules! That will be thy better plan.

It has been written, "an endless significance lies in Work"; a man perfects himself by working. Foul jungles are cleared away, fair seed-fields rise instead, and stately cities; and withal the man himself first ceases to be a jungle and foul unwholesome desert thereby. Consider how, even in the meanest sorts of Labour, the whole soul of a man is composed into a kind of real harmony, the instant he sets himself to work! Doubt, Desire, Sorrow, Remorse, Indignation, Despair itself, all these like helldogs lie beleaguering the soul of the poor dayworker, as of every man: but he bends himself with free valour against his task, and all these are stilled, all these shrink murmuring far off into their caves. The man is now a man. The blessed glow of Labour in him, is it not as purifying fire, wherein all poison is burnt up, and of sour smoke itself there is made bright blessed flame!

Destiny, on the whole, has no other way of cultivating us. A formless Chaos, once set it *revolving,* grows round and ever rounder; ranges itself, by mere force of gravity, into strata, spherical courses; is no longer a Chaos, but a round compacted World. What would become of the Earth, did she cease to revolve? In the poor old Earth, so long as she revolves, all inequalities, irregularities disperse themselves; all irregularities are incessantly becoming regular. Hast thou looked on the Potter's wheel,—one of the venerablest objects; old as the Prophet Ezekiel and far older? Rude lumps of clay, how they spin themselves up, by mere quick whirling, into beautiful circular dishes. And fancy the most assiduous Potter, but without his wheel; reduced to make dishes, or rather amorphous botches, by mere kneading and baking! Even such a Potter were Destiny, with a human soul that would rest and lie at ease, that would not work and spin! Of an idle unrevolving man the kindest Destiny, like the most assiduous Potter without wheel, can bake and knead nothing other than a botch; let her spend on him what expensive colouring, what gilding and enamelling she will, he is but a botch. Not a dish; no, a bulging, kneaded, crooked, shambling, squint-cornered, amorphous botch,—a mere enamelled vessel of dishonour! Let the idle think of this.

Blessed is he who has found his work; let him ask no other blessedness. He has a work, a life-purpose; he has found it, and will follow it! How, as a free-flowing channel, dug and torn by noble force through the sour mud-swamp of one's existence, like an ever-deepening river there, it runs and flows;—draining off the sour festering water, gradually from the root of the remotest grass-blade; making, instead of pestilential swamp, a green fruitful meadow with its clear-flowing stream. How blessed for the meadow itself, let the stream and *its* value be great or small! Labour is Life: from the inmost heart of the Worker rises his god-given Force, the sacred celestial Life-essence breathed into him by Almighty God; from his inmost heart awakens him to all nobleness,—to all knowledge, "self-knowledge" and much else, so soon as Work fitly begins. Knowledge? The knowledge that will hold good in working, cleave thou to that; for Nature herself accredits that, says Yea to that. Properly thou hast no other knowledge but what thou hast got by working: the rest is yet all a hypothesis of knowledge; a thing to be argued of in schools, a thing floating in the clouds, in endless logic-vortices, till we try it and fix it. "Doubt, of whatever kind, can be ended by Action alone."

And again, hast thou valued Patience, Courage, Perseverance, Openness to light; readiness to own thyself mistaken, to do better next time? All these, all virtues, in wrestling with the dim brute Powers of Fact, in ordering of thy fellows in such wrestle, there and elsewhere not at all, thou wilt continually learn. Set down a brave Sir Christopher[71] in the middle of

[70] This, of course, is one of the central themes of *Sartor Resartus.* See above, p. 400.

[71] Sir Christopher Wren (1632–1723), the architect of St. Paul's Cathedral, responsible for rebuilding large sections of London after the Great Fire (1666).

black ruined Stone-heaps, of foolish unarchitectural Bishops, redtape Officials, idle Nell-Gwyn Defenders of the Faith;[72] and see whether he will even raise a Paul's Cathedral out of all that, yea or no! Rough, rude, contradictory are all things and persons, from the mutinous masons and Irish hodmen, up to the idle Nell-Gwyn Defenders, to blustering redtape Officials, foolish unarchitectural Bishops. All these things and persons are there not for Christopher's sake and his Cathedral's; they are there for their own sake mainly! Christopher will have to conquer and constrain all these,—if he be able. All these are against him. Equitable Nature herself, who carries her mathematics and architectonics not on the face of her, but deep in the hidden heart of her,—Nature herself is but partially for him; will be wholly against him, if he constrain her not! His very money, where is it to come from? The pious munificence of England lies far-scattered, distant, unable to speak, and say, "I am here";—must be spoken to before it can speak. Pious munificence, and all help, is so silent, invisible like the gods; impediment, contradictions manifold are so loud and near! O brave Sir Christopher, trust thou in those, notwithstanding, and front all these;[73] understand all these; by valiant patience, noble effort, insight, by man's-strength, vanquish and compel all these,—and, on the whole, strike down victoriously the last topstone of that Paul's Edifice; thy monument for certain centuries, the stamp "Great Man" impressed very legibly on Portland stone there!—

Yes, all manner of help, and pious response from Men or Nature, is always what we call silent; cannot speak or come to light, till it be seen, till it be spoken to. Every noble work is at first "impossible." In very truth, for every noble work the possibilities will lie diffused through Immensity; inarticulate, undiscoverable except to faith. Like Gideon thou shalt spread out thy fleece at the door of thy tent; see whether under the wide arch of Heaven there be any bounteous moisture, or none. Thy heart and life-purpose shall be as a miraculous Gideon's fleece, spread out in silent appeal to Heaven; and from the kind Immensities, what from the poor unkind Localities and town and country Parishes there never could, blessed dew-moisture to suffice thee shall have fallen![74]

Work is of a religious nature:—work is of a *brave* nature; which it is the aim of all religion to be. All work of man is as the swimmer's: a waste ocean threatens to devour him; if he front it not bravely, it will keep its word. By incessant wise defiance of it, lusty rebuke and buffet of it, behold how it loyally supports him, bears him as its conqueror along. "It is so," says Goethe, "with all things that man undertakes in this world."

Brave Sea-captain, Norse Sea-king,—Columbus, my hero, royallest Sea-king of all! it is no friendly environment this of thine, in the waste deep waters; around thee mutinous discouraged souls, behind thee disgrace and ruin, before thee the unpenetrated veil of Night. Brother, these wild water-mountains, bounding from their deep bases (ten miles deep, I am told), are not entirely there on thy behalf! Meseems *they* have other work than floating thee forward:—and the huge Winds, that sweep from Ursa Major[75] to the Tropics and Equators, dancing their giant-waltz through the kingdoms of Chaos and Immensity, they care little about filling rightly or filling wrongly the small shoulder-of-mutton sails in this cockle-skiff of thine! Thou art not among articulate-speaking friends, my brother; thou art among immeasurable dumb monsters, tumbling, howling wide as the world here. Secret, far off, invisible to all hearts but thine, there lies a help in them: see how thou wilt get at that. Patiently thou wilt wait till the mad South-wester spend itself, saving thyself by dexterous science of defence, the while: valiantly, with swift decision, wilt thou strike in, when the favouring East, the Possible, springs up. Mutiny of men thou wilt sternly repress; weakness, despondency, thou wilt cheerily encourage: thou wilt swallow down complaint, unreason, weariness, weakness of others and thyself;—how much wilt thou swallow down! There shall be a depth of Silence in thee, deeper than this Sea, which is but ten miles deep: a Silence unsoundable; known to God only. Thou shalt be a Great Man. Yes, my World-Soldier, thou of the World Marine-service,—thou wilt have to be *greater* than this tumultuous unmeasured World here round thee is: thou, in thy strong soul, as with wrestler's arms, shalt embrace it, harness it down; and make it bear thee on,—to new Americas, or whither God wills!

---

72 Kings like Charles II. Part of his royal title was Defender of the Faith. Nell Gwyn, the actress, was his avowed mistress.

73 The antecedent of "those" is "pious munificence, and all help"; of "these," "impediment, contradictions manifold."

74 Gideon's fleece was found to be wet with dew while the ground around was dry (Judges 6:36–38).

75 The Great Bear or Big Dipper, a constellation which points to the north.

Book III, Chapter 13

DEMOCRACY

IF the Serene Highnesses and Majesties do not take note of that,[76] then, as I perceive, *that* will take note of itself! The time for levity, insincerity, and idle babble and play-acting, in all kinds, is gone by; it is a serious, grave time. Old long-vexed questions, not yet solved in logical words or parliamentary laws, are fast solving themselves in facts, somewhat unblessed to behold! This largest of questions, this question of Work and Wages, which ought, had we heeded Heaven's voice, to have begun two generations ago or more, cannot be delayed longer without hearing Earth's voice. "Labour" will verily need to be somewhat "organized," as they say,—God knows with what difficulty. Man will actually need to have his debts and earnings a little better paid by man; which, let Parliaments speak of them, or be silent of them, are eternally his due from man, and cannot, without penalty and at length not without death-penalty, be withheld. How much ought to cease among us straightway; how much ought to begin straightway, while the hours yet are!

Truly they are strange results to which this of leaving all to "Cash";[77] of quietly shutting up the God's Temple, and gradually opening wide-open the Mammon's Temple, with "Laissez-faire, and Every man for himself,"—have led us in these days! We have Upper, speaking Classes, who indeed do "speak" as never man spake before; the withered flimsiness, godless baseness and barrenness of whose Speech might of itself indicate what kind of Doing and practical Governing went on under it! For Speech is the gaseous element out of which most kinds of Practice and Performance, especially all kinds of moral Performance, condense themselves, and take shape; as the one is, so will the other be. Descending, accordingly, into the Dumb Class in its Stockport[78] Cellars and Poor-Law Bastilles, have we not to announce that they are hitherto unexampled in the History of Adam's Posterity?

Life was never a May-game for men: in all times the lot of the dumb millions born to toil was defaced with manifold sufferings, injustices, heavy burdens, avoidable and unavoidable; not play at all, but hard work that made the sinews sore and the heart sore. As bond-slaves, *villani, bordarii, sochemanni,* nay indeed as dukes, earls and kings, men were oftentimes made weary of their life; and had to say, in the sweat of their brow and of their soul, Behold, it is not sport, it is grim earnest, and our back can bear no more! Who knows not what massacrings and harryings there have been; grinding, long-continuing, unbearable injustices,—till the heart had to rise in madness, and some *"Eu Sachsen, nimith euer sachses,* You Saxons, out with your gully-knives, then!" You Saxons, some "arrestment," partial "arrestment of the Knaves and Dastards" has become indispensable! —The page of Dryasdust is heavy with such details.

And yet I will venture to believe that in no time, since the beginnings of Society, was the lot of those same dumb millions of toilers so entirely unbearable as it is even in the days now passing over us. It is not to die, or even to die of hunger, that makes a man wretched; many men have died; all men must die,— the last exit of us all is in a Fire-Chariot of Pain. But it is to live miserable we know not why; to work sore and yet gain nothing; to be heart-worn, weary, yet isolated, unrelated, girt-in with a cold universal Laissez-faire: it is to die slowly all our life long, imprisoned in a deaf, dead, Infinite Injustice, as in the accursed iron belly of a Phalaris' Bull![79] This is and remains for ever intolerable to all men whom God has made. Do we wonder at French Revolutions, Chartisms, Revolts of Three Days? The times, if we will consider them, are really unexampled.

Never before did I hear of an Irish Widow reduced to "prove her sisterhood by dying of typhus-fever and infecting seventeen persons,"—saying in such undeniable way, "You *see,* I was your sister!" Sisterhood, brotherhood, was often forgotten; but not till the rise of these ultimate Mammon and Shotbelt Gospels did I ever see it so expressly denied. If no pious Lord or *Law-ward* would remember it, always some pious Lady ("*Hlaf dig,*" Benefactress, "*Loaf-giveress,*" they say she is,—blessings on her beautiful heart!) was there, with mild mother-voice and hand, to remember it; some pious thoughtful *Elder,* what we now call "Prester," *Presbyter* or "Priest," was there to put all men in mind of it, in the name of the God who had made all.

[76] The antecedent of "that" is in the closing paragraph of the preceding chapter: "The proper Epic of this world . . . is now 'Tools and the Man.'" Carlyle means that the major problem of his time is industry and the worker.

[77] I.e., the theory that the only responsibility of the employer to his employee was that of wages.

[78] Used here as a symbol of the degraded living conditions of the workers. It was the site of a singularly grim crime committed because of poverty and starvation, which Carlyle related in Bk. I, Chap. 1.

[79] See note 66 to *Heroes and Hero-Worship.*

Not even in Black Dahomey[80] was it ever, I think, forgotten to the typhus-fever length. Mungo Park, resourceless, had sunk down to die under the Negro Village-Tree, a horrible White object in the eyes of all. But in the poor Black Woman, and her daughter who stood aghast at him, whose earthly wealth and funded capital consisted of one small calabash of rice, there lived a heart richer than "*Laissez-faire*": they, with a royal munificence, boiled their rice for him; they sang all night to him, spinning assiduous on their cotton distaffs, as he lay to sleep: "Let us pity the poor white man; no mother has he to fetch him milk, no sister to grind him corn!" Thou poor black Noble One,—thou *Lady* too: did not a God make thee too; was there not in thee too something of a God!—

Gurth, born thrall of Cedric the Saxon,[81] has been greatly pitied by Dryasdust and others. Gurth, with the brass collar round his neck, tending Cedric's pigs in the glades of the wood, is not what I call an exemplar of human felicity: but Gurth, with the sky above him, with the free air and tinted boscage and umbrage round him, and in him at least the certainty of supper and social lodging when he came home; Gurth to me seems happy, in comparison with many a Lancashire and Buckinghamshire man, of these days, not born thrall of anybody! Gurth's brass collar did not gall him: Cedric *deserved* to be his Master. The pigs were Cedric's, but Gurth too would get his parings of them. Gurth had the inexpressible satisfaction of feeling himself related indissolubly, though in a rude brass-collar way, to his fellow-mortals in this Earth. He had superiors, inferiors, equals.—Gurth is now "emancipated" long since; has what we call "Liberty." Liberty, I am told, is a Divine thing. Liberty when it becomes the "Liberty to die by starvation" is not so divine!

Liberty? The true liberty of a man, you would say, consisted in his finding out, or being forced to find out, the right path, and to walk thereon. To learn, or to be taught, what work he actually was able for; and then by permission, persuasion, and even compulsion, to set about doing of the same! That is his true blessedness, honour, "liberty" and maximum of wellbeing: if liberty be not that, I for one have small care about liberty. You do not allow a palpable madman to leap over precipices; you violate his liberty, you that are wise; and keep him, were it in strait-waistcoats, away from the precipices! Every stupid, every cowardly and foolish man is but a less palpable madman: his true liberty were that a wiser man, that any and every wiser man, could, by brass collars, or in whatever milder or sharper way, lay hold of him when he was going wrong, and order and compel him to go a little righter. O, if thou really art my *Senior*, Seigneur, my *Elder*, Presbyter or Priest,—if thou art in very deed my *Wiser*, may a beneficent instinct lead and impel thee to "conquer" me, to command me! If thou do know better than I what is good and right, I conjure thee in the name of God, force me to do it; were it by never such brass collars, whips and handcuffs, leave me not to walk over precipices! That I have been called, by all the Newspapers, a "free man" will avail me little, if my pilgrimage have ended in death and wreck. O that the Newspapers had called me slave, coward, fool, or what it pleased their sweet voices to name me, and I had attained not death, but life!—Liberty requires new definitions.

A conscious abhorrence and intolerance of Folly, of Baseness, Stupidity, Poltroonery and all that brood of things, dwells deep in some men: still deeper in others an *unconscious* abhorrence and intolerance, clothed moreover by the beneficent Supreme Powers in what stout appetites, energies, egoisms so-called, are suitable to it;—these latter are your Conquerors, Romans, Normans, Russians, Indo-English; Founders of what we call Aristocracies. Which indeed have they not the most "divine right" to found;—being themselves very truly Ἄριστοι, BRAVEST, BEST; and conquering generally a confused rabble of WORST, or at lowest, clearly enough, of WORSE? I think their divine right, tried, with affirmatory verdict, in the greatest Law-Court known to me, was good! A class of men who are dreadfully exclaimed against by Dryasdust; of whom nevertheless beneficent Nature has oftentimes had need; and may, alas, again have need.

When, across the hundredfold poor scepticisms, trivialisms, and constitutional cobwebberies of Dryasdust, you catch any glimpse of a William the Conqueror, a Tancred of Hauteville[82] or such like,—do you not discern veritably some rude outline of a true God-made King; whom not the Champion of England cased in tin,[83] but all Nature and the Universe were calling to the throne? It is absolutely necessary that he get thither. Nature does not mean her poor Saxon children to perish, of obesity, stupor or other malady, as yet: a stern Ruler and Line of

---

80 On the west coast of Africa, where the explorer Mungo Park (1771–1806) was once taken ill.
81 In Sir Walter Scott's *Ivanhoe*.

82 A Norman leader in the First Crusade.
83 A traditional impersonation of St. George, who appears in armor at the coronation ceremonies to guarantee the king's right to the throne.

Rulers therefore is called in,—a stern but most beneficent *perpetual House-Surgeon* is by Nature herself called in, and even the appropriate *fees* are provided for him! Dryasdust talks lamentably about Hereward and the Fen Counties; fate of Earl Waltheof;[84] Yorkshire and the North reduced to ashes; all of which is undoubtedly lamentable. But even Dryasdust apprises me of one fact: "A child, in this William's reign, might have carried a purse of gold from end to end of England." My erudite friend, it is a fact which outweighs a thousand! Sweep away thy constitutional, sentimental, and other cobwebberies; look eye to eye, if thou still have any eye, in the face of this big burly William Bastard: thou wilt see a fellow of most flashing discernment, of most strong lion-heart;—in whom, as it were, within a frame of oak and iron, the gods have planted the soul of "a man of genius"! Dost thou call that nothing? I call it an immense thing!—Rage enough was in this Willelmus Conquaestor, rage enough for his occasions;—and yet the essential element of him, as of all such men, is not scorching *fire*, but shining illuminative *light*. Fire and light are strangely interchangeable; nay, at bottom, I have found them different forms of the same most godlike "elementary substance" in our world: a thing worth stating in these days. The essential element of this Conquaestor is, first of all, the most sun-eyed perception of what *is* really what on this God's-Earth;—which, thou wilt find, does mean at bottom "Justice," and "Virtues" not a few: *Conformity* to what the Maker has seen good to make; that, I suppose, will mean Justice and a Virtue or two?—

Dost thou think Willelmus Conquaestor would have tolerated ten years' jargon, one hour's jargon, on the propriety of killing Cotton-manufactures by partridge Corn-Laws?[85] I fancy, this was not the man to knock out of his night's-rest with nothing but a noisy bedlamism in your mouth! "Assist us still better to bush the partridges; strangle Plugson who spins the shirts?"—"*Par la Splendeur de Dieu!*"—Dost thou think Willelmus Conquaestor, in this new time, with

Steam-engine Captains of Industry on one hand of him, and Joe-Manton Captains of Idleness on the other, would have doubted which *was* really the BEST; which did deserve strangling, and which not?

I have a certain indestructible regard for Willelmus Conquaestor. A resident House-Surgeon, provided by Nature for her beloved English People, and even furnished with the requisite fees, as I said; for he by no means felt himself doing Nature's work, this Willelmus, but his own work exclusively! And his own work withal it was; informed "*par la Splendeur de Dieu.*"—I say, it is necessary to get the work out of such a man, however harsh that be! When a world, not yet doomed for death, is rushing down to ever-deeper Baseness and Confusion, it is a dire necessity of Nature's to bring in her ARISTOCRACIES, her BEST, even by forcible methods. When their descendants or representatives cease entirely to *be* the Best, Nature's poor world will very soon rush down again to Baseness; and it becomes a dire necessity of Nature's to cast them out. Hence French Revolutions, Five-point Charters,[86] Democracies, and a mournful list of *Etceteras,* in these our afflicted times.

To what extent Democracy has now reached, how it advances irresistible with ominous, ever-increasing speed, he that will open his eyes on any province of human affairs may discern. Democracy is everywhere the inexorable demand of these ages, swiftly fulfilling itself. From the thunder of Napoleon battles, to the jabbering of Open-vestry in St. Mary Axe,[87] all things announce Democracy. A distinguished man, whom some of my readers will hear again with pleasure, thus writes to me what in these days he notes from the Wahngasse of Weissnichtwo, where our London fashions seem to be in full vogue. Let us hear the Herr Teufelsdröckh[88] again, were it but the smallest word!

"Democracy, which means despair of finding any Heroes to govern you, and contented putting up with the want of them,—alas, thou too, *mein Lieber,* seest well how close it is of kin to *Atheism,* and other sad *Isms:* he who discovers no God whatever, how shall he discover Heroes, the visible Temples of God?—Strange enough meanwhile it is, to observe with what thoughtlessness, here in our rigidly Conservative Country, men rush into Democracy with full cry. Beyond doubt, his Excellenz the Titular-Herr Ritter

[84] Two Anglo-Saxon heroes, famous for their resistance to William.
[85] Carlyle's point in this paragraph is that a strong and wise leader would have suppressed the privileges of the partridge-hunting aristocrats in favor of the manufacturers. He seems to forget for the moment that these industrialists are Mammon-worshipers and at least in part responsible for the "liberty to die by starvation"; his emphasis here is on the fact that they *do* work. Plugson is his symbolic figure of the manufacturer; Joe Manton was the fashionable gunsmith of the dilettante and idle aristocrats. "Par la splendeur de Dieu!" was a favorite oath of William the Conqueror.

[86] See note 70 to *Heroes and Hero-Worship.*
[87] An attempt to allow expression of the will of all tax-paying parishioners, considered a democratic innovation.
[88] See note 2 to *Sartor Resartus.* Teufelsdröckh is a professor at the University of Weissnichtwo (I-know-not-where). *Wahngasse* = Delusion Alley.

Kauderwälsch von Pferdefuss-Quacksalber, he our distinguished Conservative Premier himself,[89] and all but the thicker-headed of his Party, discern Democracy to be inevitable as death, and are even desperate of delaying it much!

"You cannot walk the streets without beholding Democracy announce itself: the very Tailor has become, if not properly Sansculottic, which to him would be ruinous,[90] yet a Tailor unconsciously symbolizing, and prophesying with his scissors, the reign of Equality. What now is our fashionable coat? A thing of superfinest texture, of deeply meditated cut; with Malines-lace cuffs; quilted with gold; so that a man can carry, without difficulty, an estate of land on his back? *Keineswegs,* By no manner of means! The Sumptuary Laws[91] have fallen into such a state of desuetude as was never before seen. Our fashionable coat is an amphibium between barn-sack and drayman's doublet. The cloth of it is studiously coarse; the colour a speckled soot-black or rust-brown grey;—the nearest approach to a Peasant's. And for shape,—thou shouldst see it! The last consummation of the year now passing over us is definable as Three Bags; a big bag for the body, two small bags for the arms, and by way of collar a hem! The first Antique Cheruscan[92] who, of felt-cloth or bear's-hide, with bone or metal needle, set about making himself a coat, before Tailors had yet awakened out of Nothing,—did not he make it even so? A loose wide poke for body, with two holes to let out the arms; this was his original coat: to which holes it was soon visible that two small loose pokes, or sleeves, easily appended, would be an improvement.

"Thus has the Tailor-art, so to speak, overset itself, like most other things; changed its centre-of-gravity; whirled suddenly over from zenith to nadir. Your Stulz,[93] with huge somerset, vaults from his high shopboard down to the depths of primal savagery,—carrying much along with him! For I will invite thee to reflect that the Tailor, as topmost ultimate froth of Human Society, is indeed swift-passing, evanescent, slippery to decipher; yet significant of much, nay of all. Topmost evanescent froth, he is churned up from the very lees, and from all intermediate regions of the liquor. The general outcome he, visible to the eye, of what men aimed to do, and were obliged and enabled to do, in this one public department of symbolizing themselves to each other by covering of their skins. A smack of all Human Life lies in the Tailor: its wild struggles towards beauty, dignity, freedom, victory; and how, hemmed in by Sedan and Huddersfield,[94] by Nescience, Dullness, ˙Prurience, and other sad necessities and laws of Nature, it has attained just to this: Grey savagery of Three Sacks with a hem!

"When the very Tailor verges towards Sansculottism, is it not ominous? The last Divinity of poor mankind dethroning himself; sinking *his* taper too, flame downmost, like the Genius of Sleep or of Death; admonitory that Tailor-time shall be no more!—For, little as one could advise Sumptuary Laws at the present epoch, yet nothing is clearer than that where ranks do actually exist, strict division of costumes will also be enforced; that if we ever have a new[95] Hierarchy and Aristocracy, acknowledged veritably as such, for which I daily pray Heaven, the Tailor will re-awaken; and be, by volunteering and appointment, consciously and unconsciously, a safeguard of that same."—Certain farther observations, from the same invaluable pen, on our never-ending changes of mode, our "perpetual nomadic and even ape-like appetite for change and mere change" in all the equipments of our existence, and the "fatal revolutionary character" thereby manifested, we suppress for the present. It may be admitted that Democracy, in all meanings of the word, is in full career; irresistible by any Ritter Kauderwälsch or other Son of Adam, as times go. "Liberty" is a thing men are determined to have.

But truly, as I had to remark in the meanwhile, "the liberty of not being oppressed by your fellow man" is an indispensable, yet one of the most insignificant fractional parts of Human Liberty. No man oppresses thee, can bid thee fetch or carry, come or go, without reason shown. True; from all men thou art emancipated: but from Thyself and from the Devil—? No man, wiser, unwiser, can make thee come or go: but thy own futilities, bewilderments,

89 This is a characteristically vituperative set of names for Sir Robert Peel, who was prime minister when *Past and Present* was being written. The general meaning is "one who talks nonsense."

90 The Sansculottes were a group of poor and extreme radicals active in the French Revolution. Inasmuch as such men could not afford culottes or knee breeches, it would be ruinous for the tailoring trade if they came to dominate the political scene.

91 Restrictions on expenditure for dress, furniture, etc.

92 Member of an early German tribe.

93 A fashionable London tailor.

94 Two cloth-manufacturing centers, one in France, the other in Yorkshire.

95 The word "new" is of vital importance; Carlyle is disgusted with the idle aristocracy of birth and inherited possessions, and looks for a *new* aristocracy, comprised of active, working Captains of Industry.

thy false appetites for Money, Windsor Georges[96] and such like? No man oppresses thee, O free and independent Franchiser: but does not this stupid Porter-pot oppress thee? No Son of Adam can bid thee come or go; but this absurd Pot of Heavy-wet,[97] this can and does! Thou art the thrall not of Cedric the Saxon, but of thy own brutal appetites, and this scoured dish of liquor. And thou pratest of thy "liberty"? Thou entire blockhead!

Heavy-wet and gin: alas, these are not the only kinds of thraldom. Thou who walkest in a vain show, looking out with ornamental dilettante sniff, and serene supremacy, at all Life and all Death; and amblest jauntily; perking up thy poor talk into crotchets, thy poor conduct into fatuous somnambulisms;—and *art* as an "enchanted Ape"[98] under God's sky, where thou mightest have been a man, had proper Schoolmasters and Conquerors, and Constables with cat-o'-nine tails, been vouchsafed thee: dost thou call that "liberty"? Or your unreposing Mammon-worshipper, again, driven, as if by Galvanisms, by Devils and Fixed-Ideas, who rises early and sits late, chasing the impossible; straining every faculty to "fill himself with the east wind,"—how merciful were it, could you, by mild persuasion or by the severest tyranny so-called, check him in his mad path, and turn him into a wiser one! All painful tyranny, in that case again, were but mild "surgery"; the pain of it cheap, as health and life, instead of galvanism and fixed-idea, are cheap at any price.

Sure enough, of all paths a man could strike into, there *is*, at any given moment, a *best path* for every man; a thing which, here and now, it were of all things *wisest* for him to do;—which could he be but led or driven to do, he were then doing "like a man," as we phrase it; all men and gods agreeing with him, the whole Universe virtually exclaiming Well-done to him! His success, in such case, were complete; his felicity a maximum. This path, to find this path and walk in it, is the one thing needful for him. Whatsoever forwards him in that, let it come to him even in the shape of blows and spurnings, is liberty: whatsoever hinders him, were it wardmotes, open-vestries, poll-booths, tremendous cheers, rivers of heavy-wet, is slavery.

The notion that a man's liberty consists in giving his vote at election-hustings, and saying, "Behold now I too have my twenty-thousandth part of a Talker in our National Palaver;[99] will not all the gods be good to me?"—is one of the pleasantest! Nature nevertheless is kind at present; and puts it into the heads of many, almost of all. The liberty especially which has to purchase itself by social isolation, and each man standing separate from the other, having "no business with him" but a cash-account: this is such a liberty as the Earth seldom saw;—as the Earth will not long put up with, recommend it how you may. This liberty turns out, before it have long continued in action, with all men flinging up their caps round it, to be, for the Working Millions, a liberty to die by want of food; for the Idle Thousands and Units, alas, a still more fatal liberty to live in want of work; to have no earnest duty to do in this God's-World any more. What becomes of a man in such predicament? Earth's Laws are silent; and Heaven's speak in a voice which is not heard. No work, and the ineradicable need of work, give rise to new very wondrous life-philosophies, new very wondrous life-practices! Dilettantism, Pococurantism,[1] Beau-Brummelism,[2] with perhaps an occasional, half-mad, protesting burst of Byronism, establish themselves: at the end of a certain period,—if you go back to "the Dead Sea," there is, say our Moslem friends, a very strange "Sabbath-day" transacting itself there![3] —Brethren, we know but imperfectly yet, after ages of Constitutional Government, what Liberty and Slavery are.

Democracy, the chase of Liberty in that direction, shall go its full course; unrestrained by him of Pferdefuss-Quacksalber, or any of *his* household. The Toiling Millions of Mankind, in most vital need and passionate instinctive desire of Guidance, shall cast away False-Guidance; and hope, for an hour, that No-Guidance will suffice them: but it can be for an hour only. The smallest item of human Slavery is the oppression of man by his Mock-Superiors; the palpablest, but I say at bottom the smallest. Let him shake off such oppression, trample it indignantly under his feet; I blame him not, I pity and commend him. But oppression by your Mock-Superiors well shaken off, the grand problem yet remains to solve: That of finding government by your Real-Superiors! Alas, how shall we ever learn the solution of that, benighted, bewildered, sniffing, sneering, god-forget-

---

[96] Orders of St. George were decorations bestowed by the king at Windsor. They symbolize here the urge for social climbing.

[97] Strong malt beverage.

[98] In Bk. III, chap. 3, Carlyle has described a race of men living by the Dead Sea who were changed by enchantment into chattering apes because they had made no use of their souls.

[99] Parliament.   [1] Indifferentism.

[2] Dandyism. Beau Brummell was the outstanding fop of the early nineteenth century.

[3] See note 98 on the enchanted apes. "Their worship on the Sabbath now is to roost there, with unmusical screeches, and half-remember that they had souls."

ting unfortunates as we are? It is a work for centuries; to be taught us by tribulations, confusions, insurrections, obstructions; who knows if not by conflagration and despair! It is a lesson inclusive of all other lessons; the hardest of all lessons to learn.

One thing I do know: Those Apes, chattering on the branches by the Dead Sea, never got it learned; but chatter there to this day. To them no Moses need come a second time;[4] a thousand Moseses would be but so many painted Phantasms, interesting Fellow-Apes of new strange aspect,—whom they would "invite to dinner," be glad to meet with in lion-soirées. To them the voice of Prophecy, of heavenly monition, is quite ended. They chatter there, all Heaven shut to them, to the end of the world. The unfortunates! Oh, what is dying of hunger, with honest tools in your hand, with a manful purpose in your heart, and much real labour lying round you done, in comparison? You honestly quit your tools; quit a most muddy confused coil of sore work, short rations, of sorrows, dispiritments and contradictions, having now honestly done with it all;—and await, not entirely in a distracted manner, what the Supreme Powers, and the Silences and the Eternities may have to say to you.

A second thing I know: This lesson will have to be learned,—under penalties! England will either learn it, or England also will cease to exist among Nations. England will either learn to reverence its Heroes, and discriminate them from its Sham-Heroes and Valets and gaslighted Histrios; and to prize them as the audible God's-voice, amid all inane jargons and temporary market-cries, and say to them with heart-loyalty, "Be ye King and Priest, and Gospel and Guidance for us": or else England will continue to worship new and ever-new forms of Quackhood,—and so, with what resiliences and reboundings matters little, go down to the Father of Quacks! Can I dread such things of England? Wretched, thick-eyed, gross-hearted mortals, why will ye worship lies, and "Stuffed Clothes-suits, created by the ninth-parts of men!"[5] It is not your purses that suffer; your farm-rents, your commerces, your mill-revenues, loud as ye lament over these; no, it is not these alone, but a far deeper than these: it is your souls that lie dead, crushed down under despicable Nightmares,

Atheisms, Brain-fumes; and are not souls at all, but mere succedanea[6] for *salt* to keep your bodies and their appetites from putrefying! Your cotton-spinning and thrice-miraculous mechanism, what is this too, by itself, but a larger kind of Animalism? Spiders can spin, Beavers can build and show contrivance: the Ant lays up accumulation of capital, and has, for aught I know, a Bank of Antland. If there is no soul in man higher than all that, did it reach to sailing on the cloud-rack and spinning sea-sand; then I say, man is but an animal, a more cunning kind of brute: he has no soul, but only a succedaneum for salt. Whereupon, seeing himself to be truly of the beasts that perish, he ought to admit it, I think;—and also straightway universally to kill himself; and so, in a manlike manner, at least, *end*, and wave these brute-worlds *his* dignified farewell!—

Book IV, Chapter 3

THE ONE INSTITUTION[7]

WHAT our Government can do in this grand Problem of the Working Classes of England? Yes, supposing the insane Corn-Laws totally abolished, all speech of them ended, and "from ten to twenty years of new possibility to live and find wages" conceded us in consequence: What the English Government might be expected to accomplish or attempt towards rendering the existence of our Labouring Millions somewhat less anomalous, somewhat less impossible, in the years that are to follow those "ten or twenty," if either "ten" or "twenty" there be? . . .

Of Time-Bill, Factory-Bill and other such Bills the present Editor has no authority to speak. He knows not, it is for others than he to know, in what specific ways it may be feasible to interfere, with Legislation, between the Workers and the Master-Workers;—knows only and sees, what all men are beginning to see, that Legislative interference, and interferences not a few are indispensable; that as a lawless anarchy of supply-and-demand, on market-wages alone, this province of things cannot longer be left. Nay interference has begun: there are already Factory Inspectors,—who seem to have no *lack* of work. Perhaps there might be Mine-Inspectors too: —might there not be Furrowfield Inspectors[8] withal, and ascertain for us how on seven-and-sixpence a week a human family does live! Interference has begun; it must continue, must extensively enlarge itself, deepen and sharpen itself. Such things cannot

---

4 The Dwellers by the Dead Sea might have escaped their fate if they had listened to Moses, who was sent to warn them, but they did not recognize the hero in him: rather they found him a humbug and a bore. See Bk. III, Chap. 3.

5 Old proverb: "Nine tailors make a man." The contemporary leaders of England seem to Carlyle to be tailors' dummies or quacks.

6 Substitutes.

7 The one orderly arrangement; here, of society.

8 Agricultural inspectors.

longer be idly lapped in darkness, and suffered to go on unseen: the Heavens do see them; the curse, not the blessing of the Heavens is on an Earth that refuses to see them.

Again, are not Sanitary Regulations possible for a Legislature? The old Romans had their Aediles;[9] who would, I think, in direct contravention to supply-and-demand, have rigorously seen rammed up into total abolition many a foul cellar in our Southwarks, Saint-Gileses, and dark poison-lanes; saying sternly, "Shall a Roman man dwell there?" The Legislature, at whatever cost of consequences, would have had to answer, "God forbid!"—The Legislature, even as it now is, could order all dingy Manufacturing Towns to cease from their soot and darkness; to let-in the blessed sunlight, the blue of Heaven, and become clear and clean; to burn their coal-smoke, namely, and make flame of it. Baths, free air, a wholesome temperature, ceilings twenty feet high, might be ordained, by Act of Parliament, in all establishments licensed as Mills. There are such Mills already extant; —honour to the builders of them![10] The Legislature can say to others: Go ye and do likewise; better if you can.

Every toiling Manchester, its smoke and soot all burnt, ought it not, among so many world-wide conquests, to have a hundred acres or so of free green-field, with trees on it, conquered, for its little children to disport in; for its all-conquering workers to take a breath of twilight air in? You would say so! A willing Legislature could say so with effect. A willing Legislature could say very many things! And to whatsoever "vested interest," or suchlike, stood up, gainsaying merely, "I shall lose profits,"—the willing Legislature would answer, "Yes, but my sons and daughters will gain health, and life, and a soul."— "What is to become of our Cotton-trade?" cried certain Spinners, when the Factory Bill[11] was proposed; "What is to become of our invaluable Cotton-trade?" The Humanity of England answered steadfastly: "Deliver me these rickety perishing souls of infants, and let your Cotton-trade take its chance. God Himself commands the one thing; not God especially the other. We cannot have prosperous Cotton-trades at the expense of keeping the Devil a partner in them!"—

Bills enough, were the Corn-Law Abrogation Bill once passed, and a Legislature willing! Nay this one Bill, which lies yet unenacted, a right Education Bill, is not this of itself the sure parent of innumerable wise Bills,—wise regulations, practical methods and proposals, gradually ripening towards the state of Bills? To irradiate with intelligence, that is to say, with order, arrangement and all blessedness, the Chaotic, Unintelligent: how, except by educating, *can* you accomplish this? That thought, reflection, articulate utterance and understanding be awakened in these individual million heads, which are the atoms of your Chaos: there is no other way of illuminating any Chaos! The sum-total of intelligence that is found in it, determines the extent of order that is possible for your Chaos,—the feasibility and rationality of what your Chaos will dimly demand from you, and will gladly obey when proposed by you! It is an exact equation; the one accurately measures the other.—If the whole English People, during these "twenty years of respite," be not educated, with at least schoolmaster's educating, a tremendous responsibility, before God and men, will rest somewhere! How dare any man, especially a man calling himself minister of God, stand up in any Parliament or place, under any pretext or delusion, and for a day or an hour forbid God's Light to come into the world, and bid the Devil's Darkness continue in it one hour more! For all light and science, under all shapes, in all degrees of perfection, is of God; all darkness, nescience, is of the Enemy of God. "The schoolmaster's creed is somewhat awry?" Yes, I have found few creeds entirely correct; few light-beams shining *white*, pure of admixture: but of all creeds and religions now or ever before known, was not that of thoughtless thriftless Animalism, of Distilled Gin, and Stupor and Despair, unspeakably the least orthodox? We will exchange *it* even with Paganism, with Fetishism; and, on the whole, must exchange it with something.

An effective "Teaching Service" I do consider that there must be; some Education Secretary, Captain-General of Teachers, who will actually contrive to get us *taught*. Then again, why should there not be an "Emigration Service," and Secretary, with adjuncts, with funds, forces, idle Navy-ships, and ever-increasing apparatus; in fine an *effective system* of Emigration; so that, at length, before our twenty years of respite ended, every honest willing Workman who found England too strait, and the "Organization of Labour" not yet sufficiently advanced, might find likewise a bridge built to carry him into new Western Lands, there to "organize" with more elbow-room some labour for himself? There to be a real blessing, raising new corn for us, purchasing new webs and hatchets from us; leaving us at least in peace; —instead of staying here to be a Physical-Force

---

9 Building inspectors.
10 Robert Owen and a few of his enlightened contemporaries.
11 The Factory Act of 1833, by which the working hours of women and children were restricted.

Chartist,[12] unblessed and no blessing! Is it not scandalous to consider that a Prime Minister could raise within the year, as I have seen it done, a Hundred and Twenty Millions Sterling to shoot the French;[13] and we are stopped short for want of the hundredth part of that to keep the English living? The bodies of the English living, and the souls of English living:—these two "Services," an Education Service and an Emigration Service, these with others will actually have to be organized!

A free bridge for Emigrants: why, we should then be on a par with America itself, the most favoured of all lands that have no government; and we should have, besides, so many traditions and mementoes of priceless things which America has cast away. We could proceed deliberately to "organize Labour," not doomed to perish unless we effected it within year and day;—every willing Worker that proved superfluous, finding a bridge ready for him. This verily will have to be done; the Time is big with this. Our little Isle is grown too narrow for us; but the world is wide enough yet for another Six Thousand Years. England's sure markets will be among new Colonies of Englishmen in all quarters of the Globe. All men trade with all men, when mutually convenient; and are even bound to do it by the Maker of men. Our friends of China, who guiltily refused to trade, in these circumstances,—had we not to argue with them, in cannon-shot at last, and convince them that they ought to trade![14] "Hostile Tariffs" will arise, to shut us out; and then again will fall, to let us in: but the Sons of England, speakers of the English language were it nothing more, will in all times have the ineradicable predisposition to trade with England. Mycale was the *Pan-Ionion*,[15] rendezvous of all the Tribes of Ion, for old Greece: why should not London long continue the *All-Saxon-home,* rendezvous of all the "Children of the Harz-Rock,"[16] arriving, in select samples, from the Antipodes and elsewhere, by steam and otherwise, to the "season" here!—What a Future; wide as the world, if we have the heart and heroism for it,—which, by Heaven's blessing, we shall:

Keep not standing fixed and rooted,
Briskly venture, briskly roam;
Head and hand, where'er thou foot it,
And stout heart are still at home.

In what land the sun does visit,
Brisk are we, whate'er betide:
To give space for wandering is it
That the world was made so wide.[17]

Fourteen hundred years ago, it was by a considerable "Emigration Service," never doubt it, by much enlistment, discussion and apparatus, that we ourselves arrived in this remarkable Island,—and got into our present difficulties among others!

It is true the English Legislature, like the English People, is of slow temper; essentially conservative. In our wildest periods of reform, in the Long Parliament[18] itself, you notice always the invincible instinct to hold fast by the Old; to admit the *minimum* of New; to expand, if it be possible, some old habit or method, already found fruitful, into new growth for the new need. It is an instinct worthy of all honour; akin to all strength and all wisdom. The Future hereby is not dissevered from the Past, but based continuously on it; grows with all the vitalities of the Past, and is rooted down deep into the beginnings of us. The English Legislature is entirely repugnant to believe in "new epochs." The English Legislature does not occupy itself with epochs; has, indeed, other business to do than looking at the Time-Horologe and hearing it tick! Nevertheless new epochs do actually come; and with them new imperious peremptory necessities; so that even an English Legislature has to look up, and admit, though with reluctance, that the hour has struck. The hour having struck, let us not say "impossible":—it will have to be possible! "Contrary to the habits of Parliament, the habits of Government"? Yes: but did any Parliament or Government ever sit in a Year Forty-three before? One of the most original, unexampled years and epochs; in several important respects, totally unlike any other! For Time, all-edacious and all-feracious, does run on: and the Seven Sleepers,[19] awakening hungry after a hundred years, find that it is not their old nurses who can now give them suck!

For the rest, let not any Parliament, Aristocracy, Millocracy, or Member of the Governing Class, con-

---

[12] Chartists were divided into two categories according to the methods they advocated for obtaining the Charter: Moral Force Chartists and Physical Force Chartists.

[13] To defeat Napoleon.

[14] The First Opium War, 1839–42, brought about by the desire of English traders to import opium into China.

[15] A shrine on the slope of Mt. Mycale in Asia Minor, the scene of a festival in which the twelve cities of the Ionian league periodically participated.

[16] A reference probably to the Germanic origin of the Saxons, the Harz Mountains being a range in Germany.

[17] Translated from Goethe's *Wilhelm Meister*.

[18] Sitting at the time of the English Civil Wars, 1640–49.

[19] Seven Christian youths who, according to legend, concealed themselves in a cave near Ephesus in the third century in order to escape pagan persecution and did not waken for two or three hundred years, by which time they found Christianity established.

demn with much triumph this small specimen of "remedial measures"; or ask again, with the least anger, of this Editor, What is to be done, How that alarming problem of the Working Classes is to be managed? Editors are not here, foremost of all, to say How. A certain Editor thanks the gods that nobody pays him three hundred thousand pounds a year, two hundred thousand, twenty thousand, or any similar sum of cash for saying How;—that his wages are very different, his work somewhat fitter for him. An Editor's stipulated work is to apprise *thee* that it must be done. The "way to do it,"—is to try it, knowing that thou shalt die if it be not done. There is the bare back, there is the web of cloth; thou shalt cut me a coat to cover the bare back, thou whose trade it is. "Impossible"? Hapless Fraction,[20] dost thou discern Fate there, half unveiling herself in the gloom of the future, with her gibbet-cords, her steel-whips, and very authentic Tailor's Hell; waiting to see whether it is "possible"? Out with thy scissors, and cut that cloth or thy own windpipe!

Book IV, Chapter 4

CAPTAINS OF INDUSTRY

If I believed that Mammonism with its adjuncts was to continue henceforth the one serious principle of our existence, I should reckon it idle to solicit remedial measures from any Government, the disease being insusceptible of remedy. Government can do much, but it can in no wise do all. Government, as the most conspicuous object in Society, is called upon to give signal of what shall be done; and, in many ways, to preside over, further, and command the doing of it. But the Government cannot do, by all its signalling and commanding, what the Society is radically indisposed to do. In the long-run every Government is the exact symbol of its People, with their wisdom and unwisdom; we have to say, Like People like Government.—The main substance of this immense Problem of Organizing Labour, and first of all of Managing the Working Classes, will, it is very clear, have to be solved by those who stand practically in the middle of it; by those who themselves work and preside over work. Of all that can be enacted by any Parliament in regard to it, the germs must already lie potentially extant in those two Classes, who are to obey such enactment. A Human Chaos *in* which there is no light, you vainly attempt

to irradiate by light shed *on* it: order never can arise there.

But it is my firm conviction that the "Hell of England" will *cease* to be that of "not making money"; that we shall get a nobler Hell and a nobler Heaven! I anticipate light *in* the Human Chaos, glimmering, shining more and more; under manifold true signals from without That light shall shine. Our deity no longer being Mammon,—O Heavens, each man will then say to himself: "Why such deadly haste to make money? I shall not go to Hell, even if I do not make money! There is another Hell, I am told!" Competition, at railway-speed, in all branches of commerce and work will then abate:—good felt-hats for the head, in every sense, instead of seven-feet lath-and-plaster hats on wheels,[21] will then be discoverable! Bubble-periods, with their panics and commercial crises, will again become infrequent; steady modest industry will take the place of gambling speculation. To be a noble Master, among noble Workers, will again be the first ambition with some few; to be a rich Master only the second. How the Inventive Genius of England, with the whirr of its bobbins and billy-rollers shoved somewhat into the backgrounds of the brain, will contrive and devise, not cheaper produce exclusively, but fairer distribution of the produce at its present cheapness! By degrees, we shall again have a Society with something of Heroism in it, something of Heaven's Blessing on it; we shall again have, as my German friend asserts, "instead of Mammon-Feudalism with unsold cotton-shirts and Preservation of the Game, noble just Industrialism and Government by the Wisest!"

It is with the hope of awakening here and there a British man to know himself for a man and divine soul, that a few words of parting admonition, to all persons to whom the Heavenly Powers have lent power of any kind in this land, may now be addressed. And first to those same Master-Workers, Leaders of Industry; who stand nearest, and in fact powerfullest, though not most prominent, being as yet in too many senses a Virtuality[22] rather than an Actuality.

The Leaders of Industry, if Industry is ever to be led, are virtually the Captains of the World; if there be no nobleness in them, there will never be an Aristocracy more. But let the Captains of Industry consider: once again, are they born of other clay than the old Captains of Slaughter; doomed for ever to be not Chivalry, but a mere gold-plated *Doggery*,—what the French well name *Canaille*, "Doggery" with

[20] Again a reference to the old proverb, "Nine tailors make a man."   [21] See above, p. 426, note 51.   [22] I.e., a potentiality.

more or less gold carrion at its disposal? Captains of Industry are the true Fighters, henceforth recognizable as the only true ones: Fighters against Chaos, Necessity and the Devils and Jötuns;[23] and lead on Mankind in that great, and alone true, and universal warfare; the stars in their courses fighting for them, and all Heaven and all Earth saying audibly, Well done! Let the Captains of Industry retire into their own hearts, and ask solemnly, If there is nothing but vulturous hunger for fine wines, valet reputation and gilt carriages, discoverable there? Of hearts made by the Almighty God I will not believe such a thing. Deep-hidden under wretchedest god-forgetting Cants, Epicurisms, Dead-Sea Apisms; forgotten as under foulest fat Lethe mud and weeds, there is yet, in all hearts born into this God's-World, a spark of the Godlike slumbering. Awake, O nightmare sleepers; awake, arise, or be for ever fallen! This is not playhouse poetry; it is sober fact. Our England, our world cannot live as it is. It will connect itself with a God again, or go down with nameless throes and fire-consummation to the Devils. Thou who feelest aught of such a Godlike stirring in thee, any faintest intimation of it as through heavy-laden dreams, follow *it*, I conjure thee. Arise, save thyself, be one of those that save thy country.

Bucaniers, Chactaw Indians, whose supreme aim in fighting is that they may get the scalps, the money, that they may amass scalps and money; out of such came no Chivalry, and never will! Out of such came only gore and wreck, infernal rage and misery; desperation quenched in annihilation. Behold it, I bid thee, behold there, and consider! What is it that thou have a hundred thousand-pound bills laid up in thy strong-room, a hundred scalps hung up in thy wigwam? I value not them or thee. Thy scalps and thy thousand-pound bills are as yet nothing, if no nobleness from within irradiate them; if no Chivalry, in action, or in embryo ever struggling towards birth and action, be there.

Love of men cannot be bought by cash-payment; and without love, men cannot endure to be together. You cannot lead a Fighting World without having it regimented, chivalried: the thing, in a day, becomes impossible; all men in it, the highest at first, the very lowest at last, discern consciously, or by a noble instinct, this necessity. And can you any more continue to lead a Working World unregimented, anarchic? I answer, and the Heavens and Earth are now answering, No! The thing becomes not "in a

day" impossible; but in some two generations it does. Yes, when fathers and mothers, in Stockport hunger-cellars, begin to eat their children, and Irish widows have to prove their relationship by dying of typhus-fever; and amid Governing "Corporations of the Best and Bravest," busy to preserve their game by "bushing," dark millions of God's human creatures start up in mad Chartisms, impracticable Sacred-Months,[24] and Manchester Insurrections;—and there is a virtual Industrial Aristocracy as yet only half-alive, spell-bound amid money-bags and ledgers; and an actual Idle Aristocracy seemingly near dead in somnolent delusions, in trespasses and double-barrels; "sliding," as on inclined-planes, which every new year they *soap* with new Hansard's-jargon[25] under God's sky, and so are "sliding" ever faster, towards a "scale"[26] and balance-scale whereon is written *Thou art found Wanting:*—in such days, after a generation or two, I say, it does become, even to the low and simple, very palpably impossible! No Working World, any more than a Fighting World, can be led on without a noble Chivalry of Work, and laws and fixed rules which follow out of that,—far nobler than any Chivalry of Fighting was. As an anarchic multitude on mere Supply-and-demand, it is becoming inevitable that we dwindle in horrid suicidal convulsion, and self-abrasion, frightful to the imagination, into *Chactaw* Workers. With wigwams and scalps,—with palaces and thousand-pound bills; with savagery, depopulation, chaotic desolation! Good Heavens, will not one French Revolution and Reign of Terror suffice us, but must there be two? There will be two if needed; there will be twenty if needed; there will be precisely as many as are needed. The Laws of Nature will have themselves fulfilled. That is a thing certain to me.

Your gallant battle-hosts and work-hosts, as the others did, will need to be made loyally yours; they must and will be regulated, methodically secured in their just share of conquest under you;—joined with you in veritable brotherhood, sonhood, by quite other and deeper ties than those of temporary day's wages! How would mere redcoated regiments, to say nothing of chivalries, fight for you, if you could discharge them on the evening of the battle, on payment of the stipulated shillings,—and they discharge you on the morning of it! Chelsea Hospitals,[27]

---

[23] Giants of Norse mythology.

[24] An allusion to the revolutionary calendar adopted in France in 1793; here, a symbol of the French Revolution itself.
[25] Discussion in Parliament. Journals of the debates were published by Hansard.
[26] Sliding scales or preferential tariffs were a particularly unpopular feature of the Corn Laws.   [27] For disabled soldiers.

pensions, promotions, rigorous lasting covenant on the one side and on the other, are indispensable even for a hired fighter. The Feudal Baron, much more,—how could he subsist with mere temporary mercenaries round him, at sixpence a day; ready to go over to the other side, if sevenpence were offered? He could not have subsisted;—and his noble instinct saved him from the necessity of even trying! The Feudal Baron had a Man's Soul in him; to which anarchy, mutiny, and the other fruits of temporary mercenaries, were intolerable: he had never been a Baron otherwise, but had continued a Chactaw and Bucanier. He felt it precious, and at last it became habitual, and his fruitful enlarged existence included it as a necessity, to have men round him who in heart loved him; whose life he watched over with rigour yet with love; who were prepared to give their life for him, if need came. It was beautiful; it was human! Man lives not otherwise, nor can live contented, anywhere or anywhen. Isolation is the sum-total of wretchedness to man. To be cut off, to be left solitary: to have a world alien, not your world; all a hostile camp for you; not a home at all, of hearts and faces who are yours, whose you are! It is the frightfullest enchantment; too truly a work of the Evil One. To have neither superior, nor inferior, nor equal, united manlike to you. Without father, without child, without brother. Man knows no sadder destiny. "How is each of us," exclaims Jean Paul,[28] "so lonely in the wide bosom of the All!" Encased each as in his transparent "ice-palace"; our brother visible in his, making signals and gesticulations to us; —visible, but for ever unattainable: on his bosom we shall never rest, nor he on ours. It was not a God that did this; no!

Awake, ye noble Workers, warriors in the one true war: all this must be remedied. It is you who are already half-alive, whom I will welcome into life; whom I will conjure in God's name to shake off your enchanted sleep, and live wholly! Cease to count scalps, gold-purses; not in these lies your or our salvation. Even these, if you count only these, will not be left. Let bucaniering be put far from you; alter, speedily abrogate all laws of the bucaniers, if you would gain any victory that shall endure. Let God's justice, let pity, nobleness and manly valour, with more gold-purses or with fewer, testify themselves in this your brief Life-transit to all the Eternities, the Gods and Silences. It is to you I call; for ye

are not dead, ye are already half-alive: there is in you a sleepless dauntless energy, the prime-matter of all nobleness in man. Honour to you in your kind. It is to you I call: ye know at least this, That the mandate of God to His creature man is: Work! The future Epic of the World rests not with those that are near dead, but with those that are alive, and those that are coming into life.

Look around you. Your world-hosts are all in mutiny, in confusion, destitution; on the eve of fiery wreck and madness! They will not march farther for you, on the sixpence a day and supply-and-demand principle: they will not; nor ought they, nor can they. Ye shall reduce them to order, begin reducing them. To order, to just subordination; noble loyalty in return for noble guidance. Their souls are driven nigh mad; let yours be sane and ever saner. Not as a bewildered bewildering mob; but as a firm regimented mass, with real captains over them, will these men march any more. All human interests, combined human endeavours, and social growths in this world, have, at a certain stage of their development, required organizing: and Work, the grandest of human interests, does now require it.

God knows, the task will be hard: but no noble task was ever easy. This task will wear away your lives, and the lives of your sons and grandsons: but for what purpose, if not for tasks like this, were lives given to men? Ye shall cease to count your thousand-pound scalps, the noble of you shall cease! Nay, the very scalps, as I say, will not long be left if you count on these. Ye shall cease wholly to be barbarous vulturous Chactaws, and become noble European Nineteenth-Century Men. Ye shall know that Mammon, in never such gigs and flunkey "respectabilities," is not the alone God; that of himself he is but a Devil, and even a Brute-god.

Difficult? Yes, it will be difficult. The short-fibre cotton; that too was difficult. The waste cotton-shrub, long useless, disobedient, as the thistle by the wayside,—have ye not conquered it; made it into beautiful bandana webs; white woven shirts for men; bright-tinted air-garments wherein flit goddesses? Ye have shivered mountains asunder, made the hard iron pliant to you as soft putty: the Forest-giants, Marsh-jötuns bear sheaves of golden grain; Aegir the Sea-demon himself stretches his back for a sleek highway to you, and on Firehorses and Windhorses ye career. Ye are most strong. Thor red-bearded, with his blue sun-eyes, with his cheery heart and strong thunder-hammer, he and you have prevailed. Ye are most strong, ye Sons of the icy North, of the far East,—far marching from your rugged Eastern

---

[28] Johann Paul Richter; see note 12 to *Heroes and Hero-Worship*.

Wildernesses, hitherward from the grey Dawn of Time! Ye are Sons of the *Jötun*-land; the land of Difficulties Conquered. Difficult? You must try this thing. Once try it with the understanding that it will and shall have to be done. Try it as ye try the paltrier thing, making of money! I will bet on you once more, against all Jötuns, Tailor-gods, Double-barrelled Law-wards,[29] and Denizens of Chaos whatsoever!

Thomas Babington Macaulay

1800–1859

WE noticed in the General Introduction that the Victorians thought of themselves as living in a changed world, a new outer world of big business and middle-class government, and a new inner world of religious doubt. Macaulay is a perfect index to the first of these two changes. He is the great spokesman of the middle class, or, more exactly, of the upper-middle class of businessmen who rose to power with the Industrial Revolution and who dominated the political and social order of the Victorian age. He gives us their philosophy of life in the broad sense that includes their ideals and attitudes as well as their specific beliefs.

Both by inheritance and by training Macaulay was well equipped to speak for the Captains of Industry. He was born in 1800, and thus reached maturity at exactly the time when the manufacturing system and the political agitation for extending the suffrage were first attracting wide attention. His father, Zachary Macaulay, was a wealthy London businessman, a leading Evangelical in religion, and a Tory in politics. The son was a precocious boy who formed the habit early in life of constant reading in both history and literature, and of writing, too. Before he was eight he had written a compendium of universal history and started two heroic poems in the manner of Scott. In 1818 he went to Cambridge, where he came under an influence exactly opposite to the Tory-Evangelical atmosphere of his home. This was Benthamism, which a brilliant group of young liberals was ardently preaching. They were crying out for a democratic form of government and the disestablishment of the Church of England. The crucial result of this influence on Macaulay was his adoption of a middle position. In religion he became a Broad Churchman, supporting the state church but eager to see it "liberalized" in doctrine, with major stress placed on Christian ethics. In politics he discarded his Toryism but refused to go to any democratic extremes. In short, he became a Whig Liberal, willing to reform the Church and eager to extend the suffrage to the middle class but no further.

When he left college in 1824, he had two great ambitions, to succeed in literature and in politics. He fulfilled both. In 1825 his essay on Milton, crammed with liberal doctrines, made him famous almost overnight; it was published, quite rightly, in the great Whig periodical, the *Edinburgh Review*. In the next five years he wrote a series of brilliant essays for the same magazine, striking at the Tories to the right and the Benthamites to the left, and urging a compromise that would "amend, conciliate, and preserve," precisely the position of the liberal Whigs of the 1820's. In 1830 he won a seat in the House of Commons, where his speeches in support of the 1832 Reform Bill marked the alliance of the Whigs with the middle-class industrialists.

In the years that followed, Macaulay was sent to India, to draw up the Indian penal code and reorganize Indian education on Western lines; continued, on his return, to follow his double career of literature and politics; and on his defeat for re-election in 1847, retired from public life to write his famous, and enormously popular, *History of England*. In 1857 he was raised to the peerage and became a Whig lord. In 1859, when he died, he was buried in Westminster Abbey, easily the most outstanding writer of the age in fame and popularity.

Such an amazing record of success must not blind us to his limitations. His mind was vigorous and sturdy, able to grasp broad principles and broad emotions, but insensitive to subtleties of thought and nuances of feeling. His command of ideas was inferior to his command of words: he was an orator rather than a thinker, and more of a debater than a seeker for truth. Above all, he had no capacity for growth. What he believed when he left Cambridge he always believed. He never re-examined his premises. This gave him a narrow strength. He knew where he stood and he stood there rigidly. And what he stood on was the Whig-Liberal creed, in politics and religion, which fitted the needs and desires of the middle-class capitalists.

In 1829 Robert Southey, the friend of Wordsworth and Coleridge, published a book called *Sir Thomas More: or,*

---

29 The idle aristocracy (lords) shooting partridges with double-barreled guns.

Colloquies on the Progress and Prospects of Society. Almost every page of it stated some opinion which outraged Macaulay's stolid convictions, so that his fighting review of it defines his political-economic position in black and white. Southey had once been a radical supporter of democracy and the French Revolution, but frightened by the Reign of Terror, the confiscation of property, and the attack on Switzerland in 1798, he swung violently in the other direction and became an extreme reactionary, opposed to all liberal reforms and advocating a strong autocratic government in the hands of the aristocracy and the Anglican Church. Against such blind reaction Macaulay's attack is welcome.

But there was another side of Southey's book much less ugly, and another side of Macaulay's review much less attractive. Southey was one of the first to recognize the terrible cost in human suffering of the factory system—the long hours and low wages, child labor, the slum conditions in the new industrial cities, the displacement of the old personal and human relationship of employer and employee in small factories and shops by the strictly business one of "cash-nexus," and above all the slavery of the worker in a system where, without the help of a union, he had to accept what he was offered or go unemployed. To this indictment Macaulay replies that there is less unemployment in the towns than in the country and that men now live longer in Manchester and Leeds than they used to! After which evasion, he pounces with devastating but empty rhetoric on the passage (pp. 447–8) where Southey seems to attack the factories on aesthetic grounds but in reality is using architecture as a symbol of moral conditions. (The force of "Mammon's temples" and "helotry" should be noted; and to make his real meaning clear to everyone except Macaulay, Southey ends by saying that these edifices are "as offensive to the eye *as to the mind*.") It is true that at one point Macaulay admits that the laboring classes in England suffer severe hardships, but he adds at once that they are no worse off than the same classes on the Continent. To which Southey might have replied, "Two wrongs do not make a right." In the first years of industrial achievement, it was hard to see the cost of the system, nor were the new capitalists eager to look the ugly facts in the face. Rhetorical sophistry was an easier way out.

Given their contrasting views of the factory system, their opposite political theories logically follow. Southey wants a strong aristocratic government which will enact a program of labor legislation—factory acts, an emigration service to the colonies to solve overpopulation, a great national works program to solve unemployment. If the state can vote millions for war, why not for war on poverty and destitution? But for the liberal Macaulay the duties of government are strictly limited to protecting the

persons and property of the people from attack. A strong state not only will crush individual freedom and initiative, but may well be a blundering, fumbling bureaucracy. Therefore, *laissez faire, laissez faire*! To which Southey answers, yes, government interference is bad, but to do nothing and let these appalling conditions continue is worse. Finally, in Macaulay's last paragraph we see the economic foundation of his political theory. If capital is "to find its most lucrative course," the government must keep hands off—and balance the budget.

On one thing, however, Southey and Macaulay saw eye to eye. They both hated democracy, Southey any democracy, Macaulay anything more than a middle-class democracy. The famous letter to Commodore Randall of the New York Yacht Club advances a prophetic and challenging thesis: that full democracy will lead either directly to communism and the end of civilization (the end, that is, of private property), or indirectly to dictatorship and the end of liberty—indirectly, because to ward off communism the middle class will be forced to back a dictatorship of the right. Many would agree with this analysis, though they might welcome one or the other alternative. Others will feel that the real danger of communism lies, not in democracy as such, but in the very system Macaulay is defending, a completely laissez-faire policy which does nothing to solve the explosive miseries and injustices of trade cycles, unemployment, large disparity of income. Certainly, Macaulay's letter is fair warning to any democracy which does not meet the economic problems of a capitalist economy.

The essay on Bacon is an exact complement to the essay on Southey. Both start from the same middle-class ideal of material progress; the difference is that in the Southey essay Macaulay has advocated the best *political* means of attaining that goal, and in the Bacon essay he advocates the best *intellectual* means or method of attaining it, namely, the application of science to industry and medicine. The important thing, however, in the "Bacon" is its revelation of the standard of values which the worship of science and industry produced. Macaulay assumes that in order to be valuable any action or study must be useful (it must issue in practical and tangible results) and it must be progressive (it must change and improve). The two are closely connected, since progress tends to be measured in terms of improved efficiency. These initial assumptions, especially utility, lead to the anti-intellectualism and the anti-idealism for which the essay is notorious. If practical results are exalted, theory and speculation, philosophy and art, as well as high ideals that cannot be achieved, will be considered useless; and the thinker (philosopher, theologian, artist) will seem of little account compared with the man of action, the scientist or businessman, who gets things done. Macaulay is so dominated by these attitudes that he can dismiss all the work of sixty generations of thinkers before Bacon as words, words, words; and can imagine that because the moral ideal of Stoicism was never achieved, it bore no "fruit" (as though no one had ever been better or happier for having tried, however unsuccessfully, to live like a Stoic). In the final paragraph we notice the substitution of psychiatry for moral philosophy (mental health and not moral character is a practical goal) and the divorce of religion from theology (religion is useful because it provides ethical restraints and the consoling promise of immortality; theology is not only useless but purely fanciful, since its "truths" cannot be scientifically demonstrated). In all these respects the essay is of central importance for revealing the effect on values, modern as well as Victorian, of a scientific, industrial society, and for showing us the resulting loss as well as the gain.

Macaulay's greatest work is his *History of England*. Although it covers only the reigns of James II and William and Mary, the plan was to deal with all the transactions, social life as well as political events, "which took place between the Revolution which brought the Crown into harmony with the Parliament [the Whig revolution of 1688], and the Revolution which brought the Parliament into harmony with the nation [the middle-class revolution of 1832]." Macaulay had two intentions. The first was to show the progress of liberty, as his plan suggests, and the progress of material wealth and power (so that the *History* complements the essays on Southey and Bacon); the second was to adapt the method of Scott to the writing of history and give "to truth those attractions which have been usurped by fiction":

To make the past present, to bring the distant near, to place us in the society of a great man or on the eminence which overlooks the field of a mighty battle, to invest with the reality of human flesh and blood beings whom we are too much inclined to consider as personified qualities in an allegory, to call up our ancestors before us with all their peculiarities of language, manners, and garb, to show us over their houses, to seat us at their tables, to rummage their old-fashioned wardrobes, to explain the uses of their ponderous furniture, these parts of the duty which properly belongs to the historian have been appropriated by the historical novelist.

Macaulay succeeded brilliantly in both intentions. His Whig view of history is still dominant, and his imaginative recreation of the past has never, except perhaps by Carlyle, been equaled.

The best edition of the *History of England* is that edited by C. H. Firth (6 vols., 1913–15). The standard biography is *The Life and Letters of Lord Macaulay* by G. O. Trevelyan (2 vols., 1876). Arthur Bryant's *Macaulay* (1932) is a competent modern study, which includes a bibliography. Mark Pattison's article in the eleventh edition of the *Encyclopaedia Britannica* is still the best short essay. For the study of Macaulay as a historian, his aims and methods, his virtues and limitations, C. H. Firth's *Commentary on Macaulay's History of England* (1938) is almost indispensable.

Thomas Babington Macaulay

from SOUTHEY'S COLLOQUIES[1]

... We now come to the conversations which pass between Mr. Southey and Sir Thomas More,[2] or rather between two Southeys, equally eloquent, equally angry, equally unreasonable, and equally given to talking about what they do not understand. Perhaps we could not select a better instance of the spirit which pervades the whole book than the passages in which Mr. Southey gives his opinion of the manufacturing system. There is nothing which he hates so bitterly. It is, according to him, a system more tyrannical than that of the feudal ages, a system of actual servitude, a system which destroys the bodies and degrades the minds of those who are engaged in it. He expresses a hope that the competition of other nations may drive us out of the field; that our foreign trade may decline; and that we may thus enjoy a restoration of national sanity and strength. But he seems to think that the extermination of the whole manufacturing population would be a blessing, if the evil could be removed in no other way.

Mr. Southey does not bring forward a single fact in support of these views; and, as it seems to us, there

1 This selection is from Macaulay's review of *Sir Thomas More: or, Colloquies on the Progress and Prospects of Society*, by Robert Southey, London, 1829. See the introduction to Macaulay, above.

2 Southey cast his book into the form of discussions between himself and the ghost of Sir Thomas More, the great humanist and statesman who was executed by order of Henry VIII because he would not disavow the supremacy of the Pope.

are facts which lead to a very different conclusion. In the first place, the poor-rate is very decidedly lower in the manufacturing than in the agricultural districts. If Mr. Southey will look over the Parliamentary returns on this subject, he will find that the amount of parochial relief required by the labourers in the different counties of England is almost exactly in inverse proportion to the degree in which the manufacturing system has been introduced into those counties. The returns for the years ending in March 1825, and in March 1828, are now before us. In the former year we find the poor-rate highest in Sussex, about twenty shillings to every inhabitant. Then come Buckinghamshire, Essex, Suffolk, Bedfordshire, Huntingdonshire, Kent, and Norfolk. In all these the rate is above fifteen shillings a head. We will not go through the whole. Even in Westmoreland and the North Riding of Yorkshire, the rate is at more than eight shillings. In Cumberland and Monmouthshire, the most fortunate of all the agricultural districts, it is at six shillings. But in the West Riding of Yorkshire, it is as low as five shillings: and when we come to Lancashire, we find it at four shillings, one-fifth of what it is in Sussex. The returns of the year ending in March 1828 are a little, and but a little, more unfavourable to the manufacturing districts. Lancashire, even in that season of distress, required a smaller poor-rate than any other district, and little more than one-fourth of the poor-rate raised in Sussex. Cumberland alone, of the agricultural districts, was as well off as the West Riding of Yorkshire. These facts seem to indicate that the manufacturer is both in a more comfortable and in a less dependent situation than the agricultural labourer.

As to the effect of the manufacturing system on the bodily health, we must beg leave to estimate it by a standard far too low and vulgar for a mind so imaginative as that of Mr. Southey, the proportion of births and deaths. We know that, during the growth of this atrocious system, this new misery, to use the phrases of Mr. Southey, this new enormity, this birth of a portentous age, this pest which no man can approve whose heart is not seared or whose understanding has not been darkened, there has been a great diminution of mortality, and that this diminution has been greater in the manufacturing towns than anywhere else. The mortality still is, as it always was, greater in towns than in the country. But the difference has diminished in an extraordinary degree. There is the best reason to believe that the annual mortality of Manchester, about the middle of the last century, was one in twenty-eight. It is now reckoned at one in forty-five. In Glasgow and Leeds a similar improvement has taken place. Nay, the rate of mortality in those three great capitals of the manufacturing districts is now considerably less than it was, fifty years ago, over England and Wales, taken together, open country and all. We might with some plausibility maintain that the people live longer because they are better fed, better lodged, better clothed, and better attended in sickness, and that these improvements are owing to that increase of national wealth which the manufacturing system has produced.

Much more might be said on this subject. But to what end? It is not from bills of mortality and statistical tables that Mr. Southey has learned his political creed. He cannot stoop to study the history of the system which he abuses, to strike the balance between the good and evil which it has produced, to compare district with district, or generation with generation. We will give his own reason for his opinion, the only reason which he gives for it, in his own words:—

We remained a while in silence looking upon the assemblage of dwellings below. Here, and in the adjoining hamlet of Millbeck, the effects of manufactures and of agriculture may be seen and compared. The old cottages are such as the poet and the painter equally delight in beholding. Substantially built of the native stone without mortar, dirtied with no white lime, and their long low roofs covered with slate, if they had been raised by the magic of some indigenous Amphion's music,[3] the materials could not have adjusted themselves more beautifully in accord with the surrounding scene; and time has still further harmonized them with weather stains, lichens, and moss, short grasses, and short fern, and stone-plants of various kinds. The ornamented chimneys, round or square, less adorned than those which, like little turrets, crest the houses of the Portuguese peasantry, and yet not less happily suited to their place; the hedge of clipt box beneath the windows, the rose-bushes beside the door, the little patch of flower-ground, with its tall hollyhocks in front; the garden beside, the bee-hives, and the orchard with its bank of daffodils and snow-drops, the earliest and the profusest in these parts, indicate in the owners some portion of ease and leisure, some regard to neatness and comfort, some sense of natural, and innocent, and healthful enjoyment. The new cottages of the manufacturers are upon the manufacturing pattern—naked, and in a row.

"How is it," said I, "that everything which is connected with manufactures presents such features of unqualified deformity? From the largest of Mammon's temples[4]

---

[3] An allusion to the legend that the walls of Thebes built themselves to the sound of Amphion's lyre.
[4] The temples of Mammon, god of greed, are the factories.

down to the poorest hovel in which his helotry are stalled, these edifices have all one character. Time will not mellow them; nature will neither clothe nor conceal them; and they will remain always as offensive to the eye as to the mind."

Here is wisdom. Here are the principles on which nations are to be governed. Rose-bushes and poor-rates, rather than steam-engines and independence. Mortality and cottages with weather-stains, rather than health and long life with edifices which time cannot mellow. We are told, that our age has invented atrocities beyond the imagination of our fathers; that society has been brought into a state compared with which extermination would be a blessing; and all because the dwellings of cotton-spinners are naked and rectangular. Mr. Southey has found out a way, he tells us, in which the effects of manufactures and agriculture may be compared. And what is this way? To stand on a hill, to look at a cottage and a factory, and to see which is the prettier. Does Mr. Southey think that the body of the English peasantry live, or ever lived, in substantial or orna-mented cottages, with box-hedges, flower-gardens, bee-hives, and orchards? If not, what is his parallel worth? We despise those mock philosophers, who think that they serve the cause of science by depreci-ating literature and the fine arts.[5] But if anything could excuse their narrowness of mind, it would be such a book as this. It is not strange that, when one enthusiast makes the picturesque the test of political good, another should feel inclined to proscribe al-together the pleasures of taste and imagination.

Thus it is that Mr. Southey reasons about matters with which he thinks himself perfectly conversant. We cannot, therefore, be surprised to find that he commits extraordinary blunders when he writes on points of which he acknowledges himself to be ignorant. He confesses that he is not versed in political economy, and that he has neither liking nor aptitude for it; and he then proceeds to read the public a lec-ture concerning it which fully bears out his confession.

"All wealth," says Sir Thomas More, "in former times was tangible. It consisted in land, money, or chattels, which were either of real or conventional value."

Montesinos,[6] as Mr. Southey somewhat affectedly calls himself, answers thus:—

[5] The Benthamite Utilitarians.
[6] The name of a chivalric hero in Spanish legend. Southey used it to point up his romantic Toryism.

"Jewels, for example, and pictures, as in Holland, where indeed at one time tulip bulbs answered the same purpose."

"That bubble," says Sir Thomas, "was one of those contagious insanities to which communities are sub-ject. All wealth was real, till the extent of commerce rendered a paper currency necessary; which differed from precious stones and pictures in this important point, that there was no limit to its production."

"We regard it," says Montesinos, "as the repre-sentative of real wealth; and, therefore, limited always to the amount of what it represents."

"Pursue that notion," answers the ghost, "and you will be in the dark presently. Your provincial bank-notes, which constitute almost wholly the circulating medium of certain districts, pass current to-day. To-morrow tidings may come that the house which issued them has stopt payment, and what do they represent then? You will find them the shadow of a shade."

We scarcely know at which end to begin to dis-entangle this knot of absurdities. We might ask, why it should be a greater proof of insanity in men to set a high value on rare tulips than on rare stones, which are neither more useful nor more beautiful? We might ask how it can be said that there is no limit to the production of paper money, when a man is hanged if he issues any in the name of another, and is forced to cash what he issues in his own? But Mr. Southey's error lies deeper still. "All wealth," says he, "was tangible and real till paper currency was intro-duced." Now, was there ever, since men emerged from a state of utter barbarism, an age in which there were no debts? Is not a debt, while the solvency of the debtor is undoubted, always reckoned as part of the wealth of the creditor? Yet is it tangible and real wealth? Does it cease to be wealth, because there is the security of a written acknowledgment for it? And what else is paper currency? Did Mr. Southey ever read a banknote? If he did, he would see that it is a written acknowledgment of a debt, and a promise to pay that debt. The promise may be violated: the debt may remain unpaid: those to whom it was due may suffer: but this is a risk not confined to cases of paper currency: it is a risk inseparable from the re-lation of debtor and creditor. Every man who sells goods for anything but ready money runs the risk of finding that what he considered as part of his wealth one day is nothing at all the next day. Mr. Southey refers to the picture-galleries of Holland. The pictures were undoubtedly real and tangible possessions. But surely it might happen that a burgomaster might owe a picture-dealer a thousand guilders for a Teniers.[7] What in this case corresponds to our paper money is not the picture, which is tangible, but the claim of the picture-dealer on his customer for the price of the picture; and this claim is not tangible. Now, would not the picture-dealer consider this claim as part of his wealth? Would not a tradesman who knew of the claim give credit to the picture-dealer the more readily on account of the claim? The burgomaster might be ruined. If so, would not those consequences follow which, as Mr. Southey tells us, were never heard of till paper money came into use? Yesterday this claim was worth a thousand guilders. To day what is it? The shadow of a shade.

It is true that, the more readily claims of this sort are transferred from hand to hand, the more extensive will be the injury produced by a single failure. The laws of all nations sanction, in certain cases, the transfer of rights not yet reduced into possession. Mr. Southey would scarcely wish, we should think, that all indorsements of bills and notes should be declared invalid. Yet even if this were done, the transfer of claims would imperceptibly take place, to a very great extent. When the baker trusts the butcher, for example, he is in fact, though not in form, trusting the butcher's customers. A man who owes large bills to tradesmen, and fails to pay them, almost always produces distress through a very wide circle of people with whom he never dealt.

In short, what Mr. Southey takes for a difference in kind is only a difference of form and degree. In every society men have claims on the property of others. In every society there is a possibility that some debtors may not be able to fulfil their obligations. In every society, therefore, there is wealth which is not tangible, and which may become the shadow of a shade.

Mr. Southey then proceeds to a dissertation on the national debt, which he considers in a new and most consolatory light, as a clear addition to the income of the country.

"You can understand," says Sir Thomas, "that it constitutes a great part of the national wealth."

"So large a part," answers Montesinos, "that the interest amounted, during the prosperous times of agriculture, to as much as the rental of all the land in Great Britain; and at present to the rental of all lands, all houses, and all other fixed property put together."

The Ghost and Laureate agree that it is very desirable that there should be so secure and advantageous a deposit for wealth as the funds afford. Sir Thomas then proceeds:—

"Another and far more momentous benefit must not be overlooked; the expenditure of an annual interest, equalling, as you have stated, the present rental of all fixed property."

"That expenditure," quoth Montesinos, "gives employment to half the industry in the kingdom, and feeds half the mouths. Take, indeed, the weight of the national debt from this great and complicated social machine, and the wheels must stop."

From this passage we should have been inclined to think that Mr. Southey supposes the dividends to be a free gift periodically sent down from heaven to the fundholders, as quails and manna were sent to the Israelites;[8] were it not that he has vouchsafed, in the following question and answer, to give the public some information which, we believe, was very little needed.

"Whence comes the interest?" says Sir Thomas.

"It is raised," answers Montesinos, "by taxation."

Now, has Mr. Southey ever considered what would be done with this sum if it were not paid as interest to the national creditor? If he would think over this matter for a short time, we suspect that the "momentous benefit" of which he talks would appear to him to shrink strangely in amount. A fundholder, we will suppose, spends dividends amounting to five hundred pounds a year; and his ten nearest neighbours pay fifty pounds each to the tax-gatherer, for the purpose of discharging the interest of the national debt. If the debt were wiped out, a measure, be it understood, which we by no means recommend, the fundholder would cease to spend his five hundred pounds a year. He would no longer give employment to industry, or put food into the mouths of labourers. This Mr. Southey thinks a fearful evil. But is there no mitigating circumstance? Each of the ten neighbours of our fundholder has fifty pounds a year more than formerly. Each of them will, as it seems to our feeble understandings, employ more industry and feed more mouths than formerly. The sum is exactly the same. It is in different hands. But on what grounds does Mr. Southey call upon us to believe that it is in the hands of men who will spend it less liberally or less judiciously? He seems to think that nobody but a fundholder can employ the poor; that, if a tax is remitted, those who formerly used to pay it proceed

---

[7] A painting by an artist named David Teniers, either the father (1582–1649) or the son (1610–90), both of whom had the same Christian name.

[8] As they were fleeing from Egypt.

immediately to dig holes in the earth, and to bury the sum which the Government had been accustomed to take; that no money can set industry in motion till such money has been taken by the tax-gatherer out of one man's pocket and put into another man's pocket. We really wish that Mr. Southey would try to prove this principle, which is indeed the foundation of his whole theory of finance: for we think it right to hint to him that our hard-hearted and unimaginative generation will expect some more satisfactory reason than the only one with which he has yet favoured it, namely, a similitude touching evaporation and dew.

Both the theory and the illustration, indeed, are old friends of ours. In every season of distress which we can remember, Mr. Southey has been proclaiming that it is not from economy, but from increased taxation, that the country must expect relief; and he still, we find, places the undoubting faith of a political Diafoirus, in his

> Resaignare, repurgare, et reclysterizare.[9]

"A people," he tells us, "may be too rich, but a government cannot be so."

"A state," says he, "cannot have more wealth at its command than may be employed for the general good, a liberal expenditure in national works being one of the surest means of promoting national prosperity; and the benefit being still more obvious, of an expenditure directed to the purposes of national improvement. But a people may be too rich."

We fully admit that a state cannot have at its command more wealth than may be employed for the general good. But neither can individuals, or bodies of individuals, have at their command more wealth than may be employed for the general good. If there be no limit to the sum which may be usefully laid out in public works and national improvement, then wealth, whether in the hands of private men or of the Government, may always, if the possessors choose to spend it usefully, be usefully spent. The only ground, therefore, on which Mr. Southey can possibly maintain that a government cannot be too rich, but that a people may be too rich, must be this, that governments are more likely to spend their money on good objects than private individuals.

But what is useful expenditure? "A liberal expenditure in national works," says Mr. Southey, "is one of

the surest means for promoting national prosperity." What does he mean by national prosperity? Does he mean the wealth of the State? If so, his reasoning runs thus: The more wealth a state has the better; for the more wealth a state has the more wealth it will have. This is surely something like that fallacy, which is ungallantly termed a lady's reason. If by national prosperity he means the wealth of the people, of how gross a contradiction is Mr. Southey guilty. A people, he tells us, may be too rich: a government cannot: for a government can employ its riches in making the people richer. The wealth of the people is to be taken from them, because they have too much, and laid out in works, which will yield them more.

We are really at a loss to determine whether Mr. Southey's reason for recommending large taxation is that it will make the people rich, or that it will make them poor. But we are sure that, if his object is to make them rich, he takes the wrong course. There are two or three principles respecting public works, which, as an experience of vast extent proves, may be trusted in almost every case.

It scarcely ever happens that any private man or body of men will invest property in a canal, a tunnel, or a bridge, but from an expectation that the outlay will be profitable to them. No work of this sort can be profitable to private speculators, unless the public be willing to pay for the use of it. The public will not pay of their own accord for what yields no profit or convenience to them. There is thus a direct and obvious connection between the motive which induces individuals to undertake such a work, and the utility of the work.

Can we find any such connection in the case of a public work executed by a government? If it is useful, are the individuals who rule the country richer? If it is useless, are they poorer? A public man may be solicitous for his credit. But is not he likely to gain more credit by an useless display of ostentatious architecture in a great town than by the best road or the best canal in some remote province? The fame of public works is a much less certain test of their utility than the amount of toll collected at them. In a corrupt age, there will be direct embezzlement. In the purest age, there will be abundance of jobbing. Never were the statesmen of any country more sensitive to public opinion, and more spotless in pecuniary transactions, than those who have of late governed England. Yet we have only to look at the buildings recently erected in London for a proof of our rule. In a bad age, the fate of the public is to be robbed outright. In a good age, it is merely to have the dearest and the worst of everything.

---

[9] Diafoirus is an ignorant quack in Molière's *Le Malade Imaginaire*. He tries to sound impressive by Latinizing the only remedies he has heard of: bleeding, purgation, and enema. By the like remedy of taxation, according to Macaulay, Southey would cure the people of too much money.

Buildings for State purposes the State must erect. And here we think that, in general, the State ought to stop. We firmly believe that five hundred thousand pounds subscribed by individuals for rail-roads or canals would produce more advantage to the public than five millions voted by Parliament for the same purpose. There are certain old saws about the master's eye and about everybody's business, in which we place very great faith.

There is, we have said, no consistency in Mr. Southey's political system. But if there be in his political system any leading principle, any one error which diverges more widely and variously than any other, it is that of which his theory about national works is a ramification. He conceives that the business of the magistrate is, not merely to see that the persons and property of the people are secure from attack, but that he ought to be a jack-of-all-trades, architect, engineer, schoolmaster, merchant, theologian, a Lady Bountiful in every parish, a Paul Pry in every house, spying, eaves-dropping, relieving, admonishing, spending our money for us, and choosing our opinions for us. His principle is, if we understand it rightly, that no man can do anything so well for himself as his rulers, be they who they may, can do it for him, and that a government approaches nearer and nearer to perfection, in proportion as it interferes more and more with the habits and notions of individuals.

He seems to be fully convinced that it is in the power of government to relieve all the distresses under which the lower orders labour. Nay, he considers doubt on this subject as impious. We cannot refrain from quoting his argument on this subject. It is a perfect jewel of logic:—

"Many thousands in your metropolis," says Sir Thomas More, "rise every morning without knowing how they are to subsist during the day; as many of them, where they are to lay their heads at night. All men, even the vicious themselves, know that wickedness leads to misery: but many, even among the good and the wise, have yet to learn that misery is almost as often the cause of wickedness."

"There are many," says Montesinos, "who know this, but believe that it is not in the power of human institutions to prevent this misery. They see the effect, but regard the causes as inseparable from the condition of human nature."

"As surely as God is good," replies Sir Thomas, "so surely there is no such thing as necessary evil. For, by the religious mind, sickness, and pain, and death, are not to be accounted evils."

Now if sickness, pain, and death, are not evils, we cannot understand why it should be an evil that thousands should rise without knowing how they are to subsist. The only evil of hunger is that it produces first pain, then sickness, and finally death. If it did not produce these, it would be no calamity. If these are not evils, it is no calamity. We will propose a very plain dilemma: either physical pain is an evil, or it is not an evil. If it is an evil, then there is necessary evil in the universe: if it is not, why should the poor be delivered from it?

Mr. Southey entertains as exaggerated a notion of the wisdom of governments as of their power. He speaks with the greatest disgust of the respect now paid to public opinion. That opinion is, according to him, to be distrusted and dreaded; its usurpation ought to be vigorously resisted; and the practice of yielding to it is likely to ruin the country. To maintain police is, according to him, only one of the ends of government. The duties of a ruler are patriarchal and paternal. He ought to consider the moral discipline of the people as his first object, to establish a religion, to train the whole community in that religion, and to consider all dissenters as his own enemies.

"Nothing," says Sir Thomas, "is more certain, than that religion is the basis upon which civil government rests; that from religion power derives its authority, laws their efficacy, and both their zeal and sanction; and it is necessary that this religion be established as for the security of the state, and for the welfare of the people, who would otherwise be moved to and fro with every wind of doctrine. A state is secure in proportion as the people are attached to its institutions; it is, therefore, the first and plainest rule of sound policy, that the people be trained up in the way they should go. The state that neglects this prepares its own destruction; and they who train them in any other way are undermining it. Nothing in abstract science can be more certain than these positions are."

"All of which," answers Montesinos, "are nevertheless denied by our professors of the arts Babblative and Scribblative: some in the audacity of evil designs, and others in the glorious assurance of impenetrable ignorance."

The greater part of the two volumes before us is merely an amplification of these paragraphs. What does Mr. Southey mean by saying that religion is demonstrably the basis of civil government? He cannot surely mean that men have no motives except those derived from religion for establishing and supporting civil government, that no temporal advantage is derived from civil government, that men would experience no temporal inconvenience from living in a state of anarchy? If he allows, as we think he must allow, that it is for the good of mankind in this world to have civil government, and that the great majority of mankind have always thought it for their good in this world to have civil government, we then have a basis for government quite distinct from religion. It is true that the Christian religion sanctions government, as it sanctions everything which promotes the happiness and virtue of our species. But we are at a loss to conceive in what sense religion can be said to be the basis of government, in which religion is not also the basis of the practices of eating, drinking, and lighting fires in cold weather. Nothing in history is more certain than that government has existed, has received some obedience, and has given some protection, in times in which it derived no support from religion, in times in which there was no religion that influenced the hearts and lives of men. It was not from dread of Tartarus, or from belief in the Elysian fields,[10] that an Athenian wished to have some institutions which might keep Orestes from filching his cloak, or Midias from breaking his head.[11] "It is from religion," says Mr. Southey, "that power derives its authority, and laws their efficacy." From what religion does our power over the Hindoos derive its authority, or the law in virtue of which we hang Brahmins[12] its efficacy? For thousands of years civil government has existed in almost every corner of the world, in ages of priestcraft, in ages of fanaticism, in ages of Epicurean indifference, in ages of enlightened piety. However pure or impure the faith of the people might be, whether they adored a beneficent or a malignant power, whether they thought the soul mortal or immortal, they have, as soon as they ceased to be absolute savages, found out their need of civil government, and instituted it accordingly. It is as universal as the practice of cookery. Yet, it is as certain, says Mr. Southey, as anything in abstract science, that government is founded on religion. We should like to know what notion Mr. Southey has of the demonstrations of abstract science. A very vague one, we suspect.

The proof proceeds. As religion is the basis of government, and as the State is secure in proportion as the people are attached to public institutions, it is therefore, says Mr. Southey, the first rule of policy, that the government should train the people in the way in which they should go; and it is plain that those who train them in any other way are undermining the State.

Now it does not appear to us to be the first object that people should always believe in the established religion and be attached to the established government. A religion may be false. A government may be oppressive. And whatever support government gives to false religions, or religion to oppressive governments, we consider as a clear evil.

The maxim, that governments ought to train the people in the way in which they should go, sounds well. But is there any reason for believing that a government is more likely to lead the people in the right way than the people to fall into the right way of themselves? Have there not been governments which were blind leaders of the blind? Are there not still such governments? Can it be laid down as a general rule that the movement of political and religious truth is rather downwards from the government to the people than upwards from the people to the government? These are questions which it is of importance to have clearly resolved. Mr. Southey declaims against public opinion, which is now, he tells us, usurping supreme power. Formerly, according to him, the laws governed; now public opinion governs. What are laws but expressions of the opinion of some class which has power over the rest of the community? By what was the world ever governed but by the opinion of some person or persons? By what else can it ever be governed? What are all systems, religious, political, or scientific, but opinions resting on evidence more or less satisfactory? The question is not between human opinion and some higher and more certain mode of arriving at truth, but between opinion and opinion, between the opinions of one man and another, or of one class and another, or of one generation and another. Public opinion is not infallible; but can Mr. Southey construct any institutions which shall secure to us the guidance of an infallible opinion? Can Mr. Southey select any family, any profession, any class, in short, distinguished by any plain badge from the rest of the community, whose opinion is more likely to be just than this much abused public opinion? Would he choose the peers, for example? Or the two hundred tallest men in the country? Or the poor Knights of Windsor?[13] Or children who are born with cauls? Or the seventh sons of seventh sons? We cannot suppose that he would recommend popular election; for that is

---

[10] Tartarus and the Elysian fields are respectively Hades and the land of the happy dead in Greek mythology.

[11] Orestes and Midias seem to be used merely as representative Greek names.

[12] The Hindus are a religious group in India, of which the Brahmins are a caste.

[13] An order of retired soldiers, with headquarters at Windsor.

merely an appeal to public opinion. And to say that society ought to be governed by the opinion of the wisest and best, though true, is useless. Whose opinion is to decide who are the wisest and best?

Mr. Southey and many other respectable people seem to think that, when they have once proved the moral and religious training of the people to be a most important object, it follows, of course, that it is an object which the government ought to pursue. They forget that we have to consider, not merely the goodness of the end, but also the fitness of the means. Neither in the natural nor in the political body have all members the same office. There is surely no contradiction in saying that a certain section of the community may be quite competent to protect the persons and property of the rest, yet quite unfit to direct our opinions, or to superintend our private habits.

So strong is the interest of a ruler to protect his subjects against all depredations and outrages except his own, so clear and simple are the means by which this end is to be effected, that men are probably better off under the worst governments in the world than they would be in a state of anarchy. Even when the appointment of magistrates has been left to chance, as in the Italian Republics, things have gone on far better than if there had been no magistrates at all, and if every man had done what seemed right in his own eyes. But we see no reason for thinking that the opinions of the magistrate on speculative questions are more likely to be right than those of any other man. None of the modes by which a magistrate is appointed, popular election, the accident of the lot, or the accident of birth, affords, as far as we can perceive, much security for his being wiser than any of his neighbours. The chance of his being wiser than all his neighbours together is still smaller. Now we cannot understand how it can be laid down that it is the duty and the right of one class to direct the opinions of another, unless it can be proved that the former class is more likely to form just opinions than the latter.

The duties of government would be, as Mr. Southey says that they are, paternal, if a government were necessarily as much superior in wisdom to a people as the most foolish father, for a time, is to the most intelligent child, and if a government loved a people as fathers generally love their children. But there is no reason to believe that a government will have either the paternal warmth of affection or the paternal superiority of intellect. Mr. Southey might as well say that the duties of the shoemaker are paternal, and that it is an usurpation in any man not

of the craft to say that his shoes are bad and to insist on having better. The division of labour would be no blessing, if those by whom a thing is done were to pay no attention to the opinion of those for whom it is done. The shoemaker, in the *Relapse*,[14] tells Lord Foppington that his Lordship is mistaken in supposing that his shoe pinches. "It does not pinch; it cannot pinch; I know my business; and I never made a better shoe." This is the way in which Mr. Southey would have a government treat a people who usurp the privilege of thinking. Nay, the shoemaker of Vanbrugh has the advantage in the comparison. He contented himself with regulating his customer's shoes, about which he had peculiar means of information, and did not presume to dictate about the coat and hat. But Mr. Southey would have the rulers of a country prescribe opinions to the people, not only about politics, but about matters concerning which a government has no peculiar sources of information, and concerning which any man in the streets may know as much and think as justly as the King, namely religion and morals.

Men are never so likely to settle a question rightly as when they discuss it freely. A government can interfere in discussion only by making it less free than it would otherwise be. Men are most likely to form just opinions when they have no other wish than to know the truth, and are exempt from all influence, either of hope or fear. Government, as government, can bring nothing but the influence of hopes and fears to support its doctrines. It carries on controversy, not with reasons, but with threats and bribes. If it employs reasons, it does so, not in virtue of any powers which belong to it as a government. Thus, instead of a contest between argument and argument, we have a contest between argument and force. Instead of a contest in which truth, from the natural constitution of the human mind, has a decided advantage over falsehood, we have a contest in which truth can be victorious only by accident.

And what, after all, is the security which this training gives to governments? Mr. Southey would scarcely propose that discussion should be more effectually shackled, that public opinion should be more strictly disciplined into conformity with established institutions, than in Spain and Italy. Yet we know that the restraints which exist in Spain and Italy have not prevented atheism from spreading among the educated classes, and especially among

---

[14] A comedy by the Restoration dramatist Sir John Vanbrugh (1666-1726).

those whose office it is to minister at the altars of God. All our readers know how, at the time of the French Revolution, priest after priest came forward to declare that his doctrine, his ministry, his whole life, had been a lie, a mummery during which he could scarcely compose his countenance sufficiently to carry on the imposture. This was the case of a false, or at least of a grossly corrupted religion. Let us take then the case of all others most favourable to Mr. Southey's argument. Let us take that form of religion which he holds to be the purest, the system of the Arminian[15] part of the Church of England. Let us take the form of government which he most admires and regrets, the government of England in the time of Charles the First. Would he wish to see a closer connection between Church and State than then existed? Would he wish for more powerful ecclesiastical tribunals? for a more zealous King? for a more active primate? Would he wish to see a more complete monopoly of public instruction given to the Established Church? Could any government do more to train the people in the way in which he would have them go? And in what did all this training end? The Report of the state of the Province of Canterbury, delivered by Laud[16] to his master at the close of 1639, represents the Church of England as in the highest and most palmy state. So effectually had the Government pursued that policy which Mr. Southey wishes to see revived that there was scarcely the least appearance of dissent. Most of the bishops stated that all was well among their flocks. Seven or eight persons in the diocese of Peterborough had seemed refractory to the Church, but had made ample submission. In Norfolk and Suffolk all whom there had been reason to suspect had made profession of conformity, and appeared to observe it strictly. It is confessed that there was a little difficulty in bringing some of the vulgar in Suffolk to take the sacrament at the rails in the chancel. This was the only open instance of nonconformity which the vigilant eye of Laud could detect in all the dioceses of his twenty-one suffragans, on the very eve of a revolution in which primate, and Church, and monarch, and monarchy were to perish together.

At which time would Mr. Southey pronounce the constitution more secure: in 1639, when Laud presented this Report to Charles; or now, when thousands of meetings openly collect millions of dissenters, when designs against the tithes[17] are openly avowed, when books attacking not only the Establishment, but the first principles of Christianity, are openly sold in the streets? The signs of discontent, he tells us, are stronger in England now than in France when the States-General[18] met: and hence he would have us infer that a revolution like that of France may be at hand. Does he not know that the danger of states is to be estimated, not by what breaks out of the public mind, but by what stays in it? Can he conceive anything more terrible than the situation of a government which rules without apprehension over a people of hypocrites, which is flattered by the press and cursed in the inner chambers, which exults in the attachment and obedience of its subjects, and knows not that those subjects are leagued against it in a freemasonry of hatred, the sign of which is every day conveyed in the glance of ten thousand eyes, the pressure of ten thousand hands, and the tone of ten thousand voices? Profound and ingenious policy! Instead of curing the disease, to remove those symptoms by which alone its nature can be known! To leave the serpent his deadly sting, and deprive him only of his warning rattle!

When the people whom Charles had so assiduously trained in the good way had rewarded his paternal care by cutting off his head, a new kind of training came into fashion. Another government arose[19] which, like the former, considered religion as its surest basis, and the religious discipline of the people as its first duty. Sanguinary laws were enacted against libertinism; profane pictures were burned; drapery was put on indecorous statues; the theatres were shut up; fast-days were numerous; and the Parliament resolved that no person should be admitted into any public employment, unless the House should be first satisfied of his vital godliness. We know what was the end of this training. We know that it ended in impiety, in filthy and heartless sensuality, in the dissolution of all ties of honour and morality. We know that at this very day scriptural phrases, scriptural names, perhaps some scriptural doctrines excite disgust and ridicule, solely because they are associated with the austerity of that period.

Thus has the experiment of training the people in established forms of religion been twice tried in

---

[15] The High Church party under Charles I, upholders of the divine right of kings and of strong ecclesiastical authority.

[16] William Laud (1573–1645) as Archbishop of Canterbury was one of Charles's outstanding supporters in attempting to defend the Church of England against Puritanism and the royal prerogative against the Commons. He was impeached by the Long Parliament and beheaded.

[17] Taxes established by the government for the support of the state Church, or Establishment.

[18] An assembly that met in Paris just before the outbreak of the French Revolution, so named from its being composed of members of the three estates, clergy, nobility, and people.

[19] The Commonwealth, 1649–60.

England on a large scale, once by Charles and Laud, and once by the Puritans. The High Tories of our time still entertain many of the feelings and opinions of Charles and Laud, though in a mitigated form; nor is it difficult to see that the heirs of the Puritans are still amongst us. It would be desirable that each of these parties should remember how little advantage or honour it formerly derived from the closest alliance with power, that it fell by the support of rulers and rose by their opposition, that of the two systems that in which the people were at any time drilled was always at that time the unpopular system, that the training of the High Church ended in the reign of the Puritans, and that the training of the Puritans ended in the reign of the harlots.[20]

This was quite natural. Nothing is so galling to a people not broken in from the birth as a paternal, or, in other words, a meddling government, a government which tells them what to read, and say, and eat, and drink, and wear. Our fathers could not bear it two hundred years ago; and we are not more patient than they. Mr. Southey thinks that the yoke of the Church is dropping off because it is loose. We feel convinced that it is borne only because it is easy, and that, in the instant in which an attempt is made to tighten it, it will be flung away. It will be neither the first nor the strongest yoke that has been broken asunder and trampled under foot in the day of the vengeance of England.

How far Mr. Southey would have the Government carry its measures for training the people in the doctrines of the Church, we are unable to discover. In one passage Sir Thomas More asks with great vehemence,

"Is it possible that your laws should suffer the unbelievers to exist as a party? Vetitum est adeo sceleris nihil?"[21]

Montesinos answers: "They avow themselves in defiance of the laws. The fashionable doctrine which the press at this time maintains is, that this is a matter in which the laws ought not to interfere, every man having a right, both to form what opinion he pleases upon religious subjects, and to promulgate that opinion."

It is clear, therefore, that Mr. Southey would not give full and perfect toleration to infidelity. In another passage, however, he observes with some truth, though too sweepingly, that "any degree of intolerance short of that full extent which the Papal Church exercises where it has the power, acts upon the opinions which it is intended to suppress, like pruning upon vigorous plants; they grow the stronger for it." These two passages, put together, would lead us to the conclusion that, in Mr. Southey's opinion, the utmost severity ever employed by the Roman Catholic Church in the days of its greatest power ought to be employed against unbelievers in England; in plain words, that Carlile and his shopmen ought to be burned in Smithfield,[22] and that every person who, when called upon, should decline to make a solemn profession of Christianity ought to suffer the same fate. We do not, however, believe that Mr. Southey would recommend such a course, though his language would, according to all the rules of logic, justify us in supposing this to be his meaning. His opinions form no system at all. He never sees, at one glance, more of a question than will furnish matter for one flowing and well-turned sentence; so that it would be the height of unfairness to charge him personally with holding a doctrine merely because that doctrine is deducible, though by the closest and most accurate reasoning, from the premises which he has laid down. We are, therefore, left completely in the dark as to Mr. Southey's opinions about toleration. Immediately after censuring the Government for not punishing infidels, he proceeds to discuss the question of the Catholic disabilities, now, thank God, removed, and defends them on the ground that the Catholic doctrines tend to persecution, and that the Catholics persecuted when they had power.

"They must persecute," says he, "if they believe their own creed, for conscience-sake; and if they do not believe it, they must persecute for policy; because it is only by intolerance that so corrupt and injurious a system can be upheld."

That unbelievers should not be persecuted is an instance of national depravity at which the glorified spirits stand aghast. Yet a sect of Christians is to be excluded from power, because those who formerly held the same opinions were guilty of persecution. We have said that we do not very well know what Mr. Southey's opinion about toleration is. But, on the whole, we take it to be this, that everybody is to tolerate him, and that he is to tolerate nobody.

We will not be deterred by any fear of misrepresentation from expressing our hearty approbation of the mild, wise, and eminently Christian manner in

---

[20] After the restoration of the monarchy in 1660 there was a period of marked licentiousness, doubtless a reaction against the repressions of the Puritan period.

[21] "Is nothing now forbidden to the wicked?"

[22] Scene of a cattle market in London where heretics were burned at the stake under Mary Tudor.

which the Church and the Government have lately acted with respect to blasphemous publications. We praise them for not having thought it necessary to encircle a religion pure, merciful, and philosophical, a religion to the evidence of which the highest intellects have yielded, with the defences of a false and bloody superstition. The ark of God was never taken till it was surrounded by the arms of earthly defenders.[23] In captivity, its sanctity was sufficient to vindicate it from insult, and to lay the hostile fiend prostrate on the threshold of his own temple. The real security of Christianity is to be found in its benevolent morality, in its exquisite adaptation to the human heart, in the facility with which its scheme accommodates itself to the capacity of every human intellect, in the consolation which it bears to the house of mourning, in the light with which it brightens the great mystery of the grave. To such a system it can bring no addition of dignity or of strength, that it is part and parcel of the common law. It is not now for the first time left to rely on the force of its own evidences and the attractions of its own beauty. Its sublime theology confounded the Grecian schools in the fair conflict of reason with reason. The bravest and wisest of the Caesars found their arms and their policy unavailing, when opposed to the weapons that were not carnal and the kingdom that was not of this world. The victory which Porphyry and Diocletian failed to gain[24] is not, to all appearance, reserved for any of those who have, in this age, directed their attacks against the last restraint of the powerful and the last hope of the wretched. The whole history of Christianity shows, that she is in far greater danger of being corrupted by the alliance of power, than of being crushed by its opposition. Those who thrust temporal sovereignty upon her treat her as their prototypes treated her author. They bow the knee, and spit upon her; they cry "Hail!" and smite her on the cheek; they put a sceptre in her hand, but it is a fragile reed; they crown her, but it is with thorns; they cover with purple the wounds which their own hands have inflicted on her; and inscribe magnificent titles over the cross on which they have fixed her to perish in ignominy and pain.

The general view which Mr. Southey takes of the prospects of society is very gloomy; but we comfort ourselves with the consideration that Mr. Southey is no prophet. He foretold, we remember, on the very eve of the abolition of the Test and Corporation Acts,[25] that these hateful laws were immortal, and that pious minds would long be gratified by seeing the most solemn religious rite of the Church profaned for the purpose of upholding her political supremacy. In the book before us, he says that Catholics cannot possibly be admitted into Parliament until those whom Johnson called "the bottomless Whigs"[26] come into power. While the book was in the press, the prophecy was falsified; and a Tory of the Tories,[27] Mr. Southey's own favourite hero, won and wore that noblest wreath, "Ob cives servatos."[28]

The signs of the times, Mr. Southey tells us, are very threatening. His fears for the country would decidedly preponderate over his hopes, but for a firm reliance on the mercy of God. Now, as we know that God has once suffered the civilised world to be overrun by savages, and the Christian religion to be corrupted by doctrines which made it, for some ages, almost as bad as Paganism, we cannot think it inconsistent with his attributes that similar calamities should again befall mankind.

We look, however, on the state of the world, and of this kingdom in particular, with much greater satisfaction and with better hopes. Mr. Southey speaks with contempt of those who think the savage state happier than the social. On this subject, he says, Rousseau[29] never imposed on him even in his youth. But he conceives that a community which has advanced a little way in civilisation is happier than one which has made greater progress. The Britons in the time of Caesar were happier, he suspects, than the English of the nineteenth century. On the whole, he selects the generation which preceded the Reformation as that in which the people of this country were better off than at any time before or since.

This opinion rests on nothing, as far as we can see, except his own individual associations. He is a man of

[23] Actually until the Israelites carried it into battle, hoping it would bring divine aid in defeating the Philistines.

[24] Porphyry, a Greek philosopher of the third century, attacked Christianity by argument; the Emperor Diocletian (245–313), by physical persecution.

[25] Both the Corporation Act (1661) and the Test Act (1673) forbade the holding of public office by anyone who would not receive communion according to the rites of the Church of England once a year. They were repealed in 1828.

[26] Dr. Johnson, Boswell relates, said of a friend, "Sir, he is a cursed Whig, a *bottomless* Whig, as they all are now." He meant that the Whigs lacked a core or bottom of sound principles.

[27] Catholic Emancipation was granted under the ministry of the Duke of Wellington, the last of the old Tories, in 1829, probably only to avert civil war, a concession that evidently took Southey by surprise.

[28] "On behalf of the delivered citizens."

[29] Jean Jacques Rousseau (1712–78), French philosopher who won wide acclaim by his attack on civilization and concomitant praise of a state of noble savagery.

letters; and a life destitute of literary pleasures seems insipid to him. He abhors the spirit of the present generation, the severity of its studies, the boldness of its inquiries, and the disdain with which it regards some old prejudices by which his own mind is held in bondage. He dislikes an utterly unenlightened age; he dislikes an investigating and reforming age. The first twenty years of the sixteenth century would have exactly suited him. They furnished just the quantity of intellectual excitement which he requires. The learned few read and wrote largely. A scholar was held in high estimation. But the rabble did not presume to think; and even the most inquiring and independent of the educated classes paid more reverence to authority, and less to reason, than is usual in our time. This is a state of things in which Mr. Southey would have found himself quite comfortable; and, accordingly, he pronounced it the happiest state of things ever known in the world.

The savages were wretched, says Mr. Southey; but the people in the time of Sir Thomas More were happier than either they or we. Now we think it quite certain that we have the advantage over the contemporaries of Sir Thomas More, in every point in which they had any advantage over savages.

Mr. Southey does not even pretend to maintain that the people in the sixteenth century were better lodged or clothed than at present. He seems to admit that in these respects there has been some little improvement. It is indeed a matter about which scarcely any doubt can exist in the most perverse mind that the improvements of machinery have lowered the price of manufactured articles, and have brought within the reach of the poorest some conveniences which Sir Thomas More or his master could not have obtained at any price.

The labouring classes, however, were, according to Mr. Southey, better fed three hundred years ago than at present. We believe that he is completely in error on this point. The condition of servants in noble and wealthy families, and of scholars at the Universities, must surely have been better in those times than that of day-labourers; and we are sure that it was not better than that of our workhouse paupers. From the household book of the Northumberland family, we find that in one of the greatest establishments of the kingdom the servants lived very much as common sailors live now. In the reign of Edward the Sixth the state of the students at Cambridge is described to us, on the very best authority, as most wretched. Many of them dined on pottage made of a farthing's worth of beef with a little salt and oatmeal, and literally nothing else. This account we have from a contemporary master of St. John's. Our parish poor now eat wheaten bread. In the sixteenth century the labourer was glad to get barley, and was often forced to content himself with poorer fare. In Harrison's introduction to Holinshed[30] we have an account of the state of our working population in the "golden days," as Mr. Southey calls them, "of good Queen Bess." "The gentilitie," says he, "commonly provide themselves sufficiently of wheat for their own tables, whylest their household and poore neighbours in some shires are inforced to content themselves with rye or barleie; yea, and in time of dearth, many with bread made eyther of beanes, peason, or otes, or of altogether, and some acornes among. I will not say that this extremity is oft so well to be seen in time of plentie as of dearth; but if I should I could easily bring my trial: for albeit there be much more grounde eared nowe almost in everye place then hathe beene of late yeares, yet such a price of corne continueth in eache towne and markete, without any just cause, that the artificer and poore labouring man is not able to reach unto it, but is driven to content himself with horse-corne." We should like to see what the effect would be of putting any parish in England now on allowance of "horse-corne." The helotry of Mammon[31] are not, in our day, so easily enforced to content themselves as the peasantry of that happy period, as Mr. Southey considers it, which elapsed between the fall of the feudal and the rise of the commercial tyranny.

"The people," says Mr. Southey, "are worse fed than when they were fishers." And yet in another place he complains that they will not eat fish. "They have contracted," says he, "I know not how, some obstinate prejudice against a kind of food at once wholesome and delicate, and everywhere to be obtained cheaply and in abundance, were the demand for it as general as it ought to be." It is true that the lower orders have an obstinate prejudice against fish. But hunger has no such obstinate prejudices. If what was formerly a common diet is now eaten only in times of severe pressure, the inference is plain. The people must be fed with what they at least think better food than that of their ancestors.

The advice and medicine which the poorest labourer can now obtain, in disease, or after an accident, is far superior to what Henry the Eighth could have commanded. Scarcely any part of the country is out of the reach of practitioners, who are probably not

[30] William Harrison (1534–93) wrote a "Description of England" which was published with Holinshed's *Chronicles* in 1577.
[31] The laborers.

so far inferior to Sir Henry Halford as they are superior to Dr. Butts.[32] That there has been a great improvement in this respect, Mr. Southey allows. Indeed he could not well have denied it. "But," says he, "the evils for which these sciences are the palliative, have increased since the time of the Druids, in a proportion that heavily overweighs the benefit of improved therapeutics." We know nothing either of the diseases or the remedies of the Druids. But we are quite sure that the improvement of medicine has far more than kept pace with the increase of disease during the last three centuries. This is proved by the best possible evidence. The term of human life is decidedly longer in England than in any former age, respecting which we possess any information on which we can rely. All the rants in the world about picturesque cottages and temples of Mammon will not shake this argument. No test of the physical well-being of society can be named so decisive as that which is furnished by bills of mortality. That the lives of the people of this country have been gradually lengthening during the course of several generations, is as certain as any fact in statistics; and that the lives of men should become longer and longer, while their bodily condition during life is becoming worse and worse, is utterly incredible.

Let our readers think over these circumstances. Let them take into the account the sweating sickness and the plague. Let them take into the account that fearful disease which first made its appearance in the generation to which Mr. Southey assigns the palm of felicity, and raged through Europe with a fury at which the physician stood aghast, and before which the people were swept away by myriads. Let them consider the state of the northern counties, constantly the scene of robberies, rapes, massacres, and conflagrations. Let them add to all this the fact that seventy-two thousand persons suffered death by the hands of the executioner during the reign of Henry the Eighth, and judge between the nineteenth and the sixteenth century.

We do not say that the lower orders in England do not suffer severe hardships. But, in spite of Mr. Southey's assertions, and in spite of the assertions of a class of politicians, who, differing from Mr. Southey in every other point, agree with him in this, we are inclined to doubt whether the labouring classes here really suffer greater physical distress than the labouring classes of the most flourishing countries of the Continent.

It will scarcely be maintained that the lazzaroni[33] who sleep under the porticoes of Naples, or the beggars who besiege the convents of Spain, are in a happier situation than the English commonalty. The distress which has lately been experienced in the northern part of Germany, one of the best governed and most prosperous regions of Europe, surpasses, if we have been correctly informed, anything which has of late years been known among us. In Norway and Sweden the peasantry are constantly compelled to mix bark with their bread; and even this expedient has not always preserved whole families and neighbourhoods from perishing together of famine. An experiment has lately been tried in the kingdom of the Netherlands, which has been cited to prove the possibility of establishing agricultural colonies on the waste lands of England, but which proves to our minds nothing so clearly as this, that the rate of subsistence to which the labouring classes are reduced in the Netherlands is miserably low, and very far inferior to that of the English paupers. No distress which the people here have endured for centuries approaches to that which has been felt by the French in our own time. The beginning of the year 1817 was a time of great distress in this island. But the state of the lowest classes here was luxury compared with that of the people of France. We find in Magendie's[34] *Journal de Physiologie Expérimentale* a paper on a point of physiology connected with the distress of that season. It appears that the inhabitants of six departments, Aix, Jura, Doubs, Haute Saone, Vosges, and Saone-et-Loire, were reduced first to oatmeal and potatoes, and at last to nettles, beanstalks, and other kinds of herbage fit only for cattle; that when the next harvest enabled them to eat barley-bread, many of them died from intemperate indulgence in what they thought an exquisite repast; and that a dropsy of a peculiar description was produced by the hard fare of the year. Dead bodies were found on the roads and in the fields. A single surgeon dissected six of these, and found the stomach shrunk, and filled with the unwholesome aliments which hunger had driven men to share with beasts. Such extremity of distress as this is never heard of in England, or even in Ireland. We are, on the whole, inclined to think, though we would speak with diffidence on a point on which it would be rash to pronounce a positive judgment without a much longer and closer investigation than we have bestowed upon it, that the labouring classes of this island, though they have their grievances and dis-

---

[32] The former was physician to George IV, William IV, and Victoria; the latter to Henry VIII.

[33] Beggars.
[34] François Magendie (1783–1855), French physiologist.

tresses, some produced by their own improvidence, some by the errors of their rulers, are on the whole better off as to physical comforts than the inhabitants of any equally extensive district of the old world. For this very reason, suffering is more acutely felt and more loudly bewailed here than elsewhere. We must take into the account the liberty of discussion, and the strong interest which the opponents of a ministry always have to exaggerate the extent of the public disasters. There are countries in which the people quietly endure distress that here would shake the foundations of the State, countries in which the inhabitants of a whole province turn out to eat grass with less clamour than one Spitalfields[35] weaver would make here, if the overseers were to put him on barley-bread. In those new commonwealths in which a civilised population has at its command a boundless extent of the richest soil, the condition of the labourer is probably happier than in any society which has lasted for many centuries. But in the old world we must confess ourselves unable to find any satisfactory record of any great nation, past or present, in which the working classes have been in a more comfortable situation than in England during the last thirty years. When this island was thinly peopled, it was barbarous: there was little capital; and that little was insecure. It is now the richest and most highly civilised spot in the world; but the population is dense. Thus we have never known that golden age which the lower orders in the United States are now enjoying. We have never known an age of liberty, of order, and of education, an age in which the mechanical sciences were carried to a great height, yet in which the people were not sufficiently numerous to cultivate even the most fertile valleys. But, when we compare our own condition with that of our ancestors, we think it clear that the advantages arising from the progress of civilisation have far more than counterbalanced the disadvantages arising from the progress of population. While our numbers have increased tenfold, our wealth has increased a hundredfold. Though there are so many more people to share the wealth now existing in the country than there were in the sixteenth century, it seems certain that a greater share falls to almost every individual than fell to the share of any of the corresponding class in the sixteenth century. The King keeps a more spendid court. The establishments of the nobles are more magnificent. The esquires are richer; the merchants are richer; the shopkeepers are richer. The serving-man,

the artisan, and the husbandman, have a more copious and palatable supply of food, better clothing, and better furniture. This is no reason for tolerating abuses, or for neglecting any means of ameliorating the condition of our poorer countrymen. But it is a reason against telling them, as some of our philosophers are constantly telling them, that they are the most wretched people who ever existed on the face of the earth.

We have already adverted to Mr. Southey's amusing doctrine about national wealth. A state, says he, cannot be too rich; but a people may be too rich. His reason for thinking this is extremely curious.

A people may be too rich, because it is the tendency of the commercial, and more especially of the manufacturing system, to collect wealth rather than to diffuse it. Where wealth is necessarily employed in any of the speculations of trade, its increase is in proportion to its amount. Great capitalists become like pikes in a fish-pond who devour the weaker fish; and it is but too certain, that the poverty of one part of the people seems to increase in the same ratio as the riches of another. There are examples of this in history. In Portugal, when the high tide of wealth flowed in from the conquests in Africa and the East, the effect of that great influx was not more visible in the augmented splendour of the court, and the luxury of the higher ranks, than in the distress of the people.

Mr. Southey's instance is not a very fortunate one. The wealth which did so little for the Portuguese was not the fruit either of manufactures or of commerce carried on by private individuals. It was the wealth, not of the people, but of the Government and its creatures, of those who, as Mr. Southey thinks, can never be too rich. The fact is, that Mr. Southey's proposition is opposed to all history, and to the phaenomena which surround us on every side. England is the richest country in Europe, the most commercial country, and the country in which manufactures flourish most. Russia and Poland are the poorest countries in Europe. They have scarcely any trade, and none but the rudest manufactures. Is wealth more diffused in Russia and Poland than in England? There are individuals in Russia and Poland whose incomes are probably equal to those of our richest countrymen. It may be doubted whether there are not, in those countries, as many fortunes of eighty thousand a year as here. But are there as many fortunes of two thousand a year, or of one thousand a year? There are parishes in England which contain more people of between three hundred and three thousand pounds a year than could be found in all the dominions of the

[35] A district in London largely given over to the weaving of silk.

Emperor Nicholas. The neat and commodious houses which have been built in London and its vicinity, for people of this class, within the last thirty years, would of themselves form a city larger than the capitals of some European kingdoms. And this is the state of society in which the great proprietors have devoured a smaller!

The cure which Mr. Southey thinks that he has discovered is worthy of the sagacity which he has shown in detecting the evil. The calamities arising from the collection of wealth in the hands of a few capitalists are to be remedied by collecting it in the hands of one great capitalist, who has no conceivable motive to use it better than other capitalists, the all-devouring State.

It is not strange that, differing so widely from Mr. Southey as to the past progress of society, we should differ from him also as to its probable destiny. He thinks, that to all outward appearance, the country is hastening to destruction; but he relies firmly on the goodness of God. We do not see either the piety or the rationality of thus confidently expecting that the Supreme Being will interfere to disturb the common succession of causes and effects. We, too, rely on his goodness, on his goodness as manifested, not in extraordinary interpositions, but in those general laws which it has pleased him to establish in the physical and in the moral world. We rely on the natural tendency of the human intellect to truth, and on the natural tendency of society to improvement. We know no well-authenticated instance of a people which has decidedly retrograded in civilisation and prosperity, except from the influence of violent and terrible calamities, such as those which laid the Roman Empire in ruins, or those which, about the beginning of the sixteenth century, desolated Italy. We know of no country which, at the end of fifty years of peace and tolerably good government, has been less prosperous than at the beginning of that period. The political importance of a state may decline, as the balance of power is disturbed by the introduction of new forces. Thus the influence of Holland and of Spain is much diminished. But are Holland and Spain poorer than formerly? We doubt it. Other countries have outrun them. But we suspect that they have been positively, though not relatively, advancing. We suspect that Holland is richer than when she sent her navies up the Thames,[36] that Spain is richer

than when a French king was brought captive to the footstool of Charles the Fifth.[37]

History is full of the signs of this natural progress of society. We see in almost every part of the annals of mankind how the industry of individuals, struggling up against wars, taxes, famines, conflagrations, mischievous prohibitions, and more mischievous protections, creates faster than governments can squander, and repairs whatever invaders can destroy. We see the wealth of nations increasing, and all the arts of life approaching nearer and nearer to perfection, in spite of the grossest corruption and the wildest profusion on the part of rulers.

The present moment is one of great distress.[38] But how small will that distress appear when we think over the history of the last forty years;[39] a war, compared with which all other wars sink into insignificance; taxation, such as the most heavily taxed people of former times could not have conceived; a debt larger than all the public debts that ever existed in the world added together; the food of the people studiously rendered dear; the currency imprudently debased, and imprudently restored. Yet is the country poorer than in 1790? We firmly believe that, in spite of all the misgovernment of her rulers, she has been almost constantly becoming richer and richer. Now and then there has been a stoppage, now and then a short retrogression; but as to the general tendency there can be no doubt. A single breaker may recede; but the tide is evidently coming in.

If we were to prophesy that in the year 1930 a population of fifty millions, better fed, clad, and lodged than the English of our time, will cover these islands, that Sussex and Huntingdonshire will be wealthier than the wealthiest parts of the West Riding of Yorkshire now are, that cultivation, rich as that of a flower-garden, will be carried up to the very tops of Ben Nevis and Helvellyn,[40] that machines constructed on principles yet undiscovered will be in every house, that there will be no highways but railroads, no travelling but by steam, that our debt,

---

36 Climax of the First Dutch War, 1665–67.

37 Francis I of France became a prisoner of Charles I of Spain (who as Holy Roman Emperor was Charles V) at the Battle of Pavia, 1525.

38 1830 was a year of agitation in England, leading up to the fall of Wellington and the installation of the Whig reformers under Lord Grey.

39 The last forty years had witnessed the French Revolution and the Napoleonic Wars, both of which had repercussions in England; and finally England had participated in the defeat of Bonaparte. Moreover, during those forty years the reactionary Tories had been, in Macaulay's opinion, "misgoverning."

40 Mountains in Scotland and the English Lake District, respectively, both in isolated and rugged terrain.

vast as it seems to us, will appear to our great-grandchildren a trifling encumbrance, which might easily be paid off in a year or two, many people would think us insane. We prophesy nothing; but this we say: If any person had told the Parliament which met in perplexity and terror after the crash in 1720 that in 1830 the wealth of England would surpass all their wildest dreams, that the annual revenue would equal the principal of that debt which they considered as an intolerable burden, that for one man of ten thousand pounds then living there would be five men of fifty thousand pounds, that London would be twice as large and twice as populous, and that nevertheless the rate of mortality would have diminished to one-half of what it then was, that the post-office would bring more into the exchequer than the excise and customs had brought in together under Charles the Second, that stage coaches would run from London to York in twenty-four hours, that men would be in the habit of sailing without wind, and would be beginning to ride without horses, our ancestors would have given as much credit to the prediction as they gave to *Gulliver's Travels*. Yet the prediction would have been true; and they would have perceived that it was not altogether absurd, if they had considered that the country was then raising every year a sum which would have purchased the fee-simple of the revenue of the Plantagenets,[41] ten times what supported the Government of Elizabeth, three times what, in the time of Cromwell, had been thought intolerably oppressive. To almost all men the state of things under which they have been used to live seems to be the necessary state of things. We have heard it said that five per cent. is the natural interest of money, that twelve is the natural number of a jury, that forty shillings is the natural qualification of a county voter. Hence it is that, though in every age everybody knows that up to his own time progressive improvement has been taking place, nobody seems to reckon on any improvement during the next generation.

We cannot absolutely prove that those are in error who tell us that society has reached a turning point, that we have seen our best days. But so said all who came before us, and with just as much apparent reason. "A million a year will beggar us," said the patriots of 1640. "Two millions a year will grind the country to powder," was the cry in 1660. "Six millions a year, and a debt of fifty millions!" exclaimed Swift, "the high allies have been the ruin of us."[42] "A hundred and forty millions of debt!" said Junius;[43] "well may we say that we owe Lord Chatham more than we shall ever pay, if we owe him such a load as this." "Two hundred and forty millions of debt!" cried all the statesmen of 1783 in chorus; "what abilities, or what economy on the part of a minister, can save a country so burdened?" We know that if, since 1783, no fresh debt had been incurred, the increased resources of the country would have enabled us to defray that debt at which Pitt, Fox, and Burke stood aghast, nay, to defray it over and over again, and that with much lighter taxation than what we have actually borne. On what principle is it that, when we see nothing but improvement behind us, we are to expect nothing but deterioration before us?

It is not by the intermeddling of Mr. Southey's idol, the omniscient and omnipotent State, but by the prudence and energy of the people, that England has hitherto been carried forward in civilisation; and it is to the same prudence and the same energy that we now look with comfort and good hope. Our rulers will best promote the improvement of the nation by strictly confining themselves to their own legitimate duties, by leaving capital to find its most lucrative course, commodities their fair price, industry and intelligence their natural reward, idleness and folly their natural punishment, by maintaining peace, by defending property, by diminishing the price of law, and by observing strict economy in every department of the State. Let the Government do this: the People will assuredly do the rest.

---

[41] Would have been sufficient to purchase absolute possession of the land which yielded the revenues of the Plantagenet family, England's rulers from 1154 to 1485.

[42] In the War of the Spanish Succession, 1701–12, when Holland and Austria fought as allies of England.

[43] Pseudonym of a Whig political writer, author of a series of letters, 1769–71, attacking Lord North, Chancellor of the Exchequer, and George III.

. . . THE chief peculiarity of Bacon's philosophy seems to us to have been this, that it aimed at things altogether different from those which his predecessors had proposed to themselves. This was his own opinion. "Finis scientiarum," says he, "a nemine adhuc bene positus est."[2] And again, "Omnium gravissimus error in deviatione ab ultimo doctrinarum fine consistit."[3] "Nec ipsa meta," says he elsewhere, "adhuc ulli, quod sciam, mortalium posita est et defixa."[4] The more carefully his works are examined, the more clearly, we think, it will appear that this is the real clue to his whole system, and that he used means different from those used by other philosophers, because he wished to arrive at an end altogether different from theirs.

What then was the end which Bacon proposed to himself? It was, to use his own emphatic expression, "fruit." It was the multiplying of human enjoyments and the mitigating of human sufferings. It was "the relief of man's estate." It was "commodis humanis inservire."[5] It was "efficaciter operari ad sublevanda vitae humanae incommoda."[6] It was "dotare vitam humanum novis inventis et copiis."[7] It was "genus humanam novis operibus et potestatibus continuo dotare."[8] This was the object of all his speculations in every department of science, in natural philosophy, in legislation, in politics, in morals.

Two words form the key of the Baconian doctrine, Utility and Progress. The ancient philosophy disdained to be useful, and was content to be stationary. It dealt largely in theories of moral perfection, which were so sublime that they never could be more than theories; in attempts to solve insoluble enigmas; in exhortations to the attainment of unattainable frames of mind. It could not condescend to the humble office of ministering to the comfort of human beings. All the schools contemned that office as degrading; some censured it as immoral. Once indeed Posidonius, a distinguished writer of the age of Cicero and Caesar, so far forgot himself as to enumerate, among the humbler blessings which mankind owed to philosophy, the discovery of the principle of the arch, and the introduction of the use of metals. This eulogy was considered as an affront, and was taken up with proper spirit. Seneca[9] vehemently disclaims these insulting compliments. Philosophy, according to him, has nothing to do with teaching men to rear arched roofs over their heads. The true philosopher does not care whether he has an arched roof or any roof. Philosophy has nothing to do with teaching men the uses of metals. She teaches us to be independent of all material substances, of all mechanical contrivances. The wise man lives according to nature. Instead of attempting to add to the physical comforts of his species, he regrets that his lot was not cast in that golden age when the human race had no protection against the cold but the skins of wild beasts, no screen from the sun but a cavern. To impute to such a man any share in the invention or improvement of a plough, a ship, or a mill is an insult. "In my own time," says Seneca, "there have been inventions of this sort, transparent windows, tubes for diffusing warmth equally through all parts of a building, shorthand, which has been carried to such a perfection that a writer can keep pace with the most rapid speaker. But the inventing of such things is drudgery for the lowest slaves; philosophy lies deeper. It is not her office to teach men how to use their hands. The object of her lessons is to form the soul. *Non est, inquam, instrumentorum ad usus necessarios opifex.*"[10] If the *non* were left out, this last sentence would be no bad description of the Baconian philosophy, and would, indeed, very much resemble several expressions in the *Novum Organum.*[11] "We shall next be told," exclaims Seneca, "that the first shoemaker was a philosopher." For our own part, if we are forced to make our choice between the first shoemaker and the author of the three books "On Anger,"[12] we pronounce for the shoemaker. It may be worse to be angry than to be wet. But shoes have kept millions

[1] From a review by Macaulay in the *Edinburgh Review* for July, 1837, of *The Works of Francis Bacon, Lord Chancellor of England,* edited by Basil Montagu, London, 1825–1834.

[2] "The goal of the sciences has not as yet been well defined by anyone." (*Novum Organum,* Lib. 1, aph. 81.) The title references in parentheses in this selection are Macaulay's.

[3] "The most serious error of all consists in deviation from the ultimate end of learning." (*De Augmentis,* Lib. 1.)

[4] "Nor has the limit itself been set and established up to now by any man, so far as I know." (*Cogitata et Visa.*)

[5] "To advance human comforts." (*De Augmentis,* Lib. 7, cap. 1.)

[6] "To work effectually to remove the discomforts of human life." (*De Augmentis,* Lib. 2, cap. 2.)

[7] "To endow human life with new discoveries and powers." (*Novum Organum,* Lib. 1, aph. 81.)

[8] "Ever anew to endow mankind with new achievements and powers." (*Cogitata et Visa.*)

[9] Seneca (*c.* 4 B.C.–65 A.D.), Roman Stoic philosopher, who was the tutor of the Emperor Nero.

[10] "She is not, I say, the maker of instruments for necessary purposes."   [11] One of Bacon's most important works.

[12] Seneca was the author of *De Ira.*

from being wet; and we doubt whether Seneca ever kept anybody from being angry.

It is very reluctantly that Seneca can be brought to confess that any philosopher had ever paid the smallest attention to anything that could possibly promote what vulgar people would consider as the well-being of mankind. He labours to clear Democritus[13] from the disgraceful imputation of having made the first arch, and Anacharsis[14] from the charge of having contrived the potter's wheel. He is forced to own that such a thing might happen; and it may also happen, he tells us, that a philosopher may be swift of foot. But it is not in his character of philosopher that he either wins a race or invents a machine. No, to be sure. The business of a philosopher was to declaim in praise of poverty with two millions sterling out at usury, to meditate epigrammatic conceits about the evils of luxury, in gardens which moved the envy of sovereigns, to rant about liberty, while fawning on the insolent and pampered freedmen of a tyrant, to celebrate the divine beauty of virtue with the same pen which had just before written a defence of the murder of a mother by a son.[15]

From the cant of this philosophy, a philosophy meanly proud of its own unprofitableness, it is delightful to turn to the lessons of the great English teacher. We can almost forgive all the faults of Bacon's life when we read that singularly graceful and dignified passage: "Ego certe, ut de me ipso, quod res est, loquar, et in iis quae nunc edo, et in iis quae in posterum meditor, dignitatem ingenii et nominis mei, si qua sit, saepius sciens et volens projicio, dum commodis humanis inserviam; quique architectus fortasse in philosophia et scientiis esse debeam, etiam operarius, et bajulus, et quidvis demum fio, cum haud pauca quae omnino fieri necesse sit, alii autem ob innatum superbiam subterfugiant, ipsi sustineam et exsequar."[16] This *philanthropia,* which, as he said

in one of the most remarkable of his early letters, "was so fixed in his mind, as it could not be removed," this majestic humility, this persuasion that nothing can be too insignificant for the attention of the wisest, which is not too insignificant to give pleasure or pain to the meanest, is the great characteristic distinction, the essential spirit of the Baconian philosophy. We trace it in all that Bacon has written on Physics, on Laws, on Morals. And we conceive that from this peculiarity all the other peculiarities of his system directly and almost necessarily sprang.

The spirit which appears in the passage of Seneca to which we have referred tainted the whole body of the ancient philosophy from the time of Socrates[17] downwards, and took possession of intellects with which that of Seneca cannot for a moment be compared. It pervades the dialogues of Plato. It may be distinctly traced in many parts of the works of Aristotle. Bacon has dropped hints from which it may be inferred that, in his opinion, the prevalence of this feeling was in a great measure to be attributed to the influence of Socrates. Our great countryman evidently did not consider the revolution which Socrates effected in philosophy as a happy event, and constantly maintained that the earlier Greek speculators, Democritus in particular, were, on the whole, superior to their more celebrated successors.

Assuredly if the tree which Socrates planted and Plato watered is to be judged of by its flowers and leaves, it is the noblest of trees. But if we take the homely test of Bacon, if we judge of the tree by its fruits, our opinion of it may perhaps be less favourable. When we sum up all the useful truths which we owe to that philosophy, to what do they amount? We find, indeed, abundant proofs that some of those who cultivated it were men of the first order of intellect. We find among their writings incomparable specimens both of dialectical and rhetorical art. We have no doubt that the ancient controversies were of use, in so far as they served to exercise the faculties of the disputants; for there is no controversy so idle that it may not be of use in this way. But, when we look for something more, for something which adds to the comforts or alleviates the calamities of the human race, we are forced to own ourselves disappointed. We are forced to say with Bacon that this celebrated philosophy ended in nothing but disputation, that it was neither a vineyard nor an olive-ground, but an intricate wood of briars and

---

[13] Greek philosopher (born *c.* 460 B.C.) whose learning and interests embraced other fields than pure philosophy, among which was mechanics.

[14] Anacharsis came to Athens from Scythia in the sixth century B.C. to study philosophy.

[15] This is evidently intended in part as a portrait of Seneca.

[16] "But I, certainly, to say how the matter stands with myself alone, both in respect to what I am now producing and in what I intend hereafter, often advisedly and deliberately throw aside the dignity of my name and wit, if such exist, in my endeavor to advance human comforts; and being one who should properly, perhaps, be an architect in philosophy and the sciences, I turn common laborer, hodman, anything that is wanted; taking upon myself the burden and execution of many things that must needs be done, and that others, through an inborn pride, shrink from and decline." (*De Augmentis,* Lib. 7, cap. 1.)

[17] Macaulay notes that prior to Socrates (470–399 B.C.) philosophers had been mainly occupied with the observation and explanation of physical phenomena, whereas after his time philosophy concerned itself with increasingly abstract questions.

thistles, from which those who lost themselves in it brought back many scratches and no food. . . . [18]

Words, and more words, and nothing but words, had been all the fruit of all the toil of all the most renowned sages of sixty generations. But the days of this sterile exuberance were numbered. . . . [19]

At this time Bacon appeared . . . . The philosophy which he taught was essentially new. It differed from that of the celebrated ancient teachers, not merely in method, but also in object. Its object was the good of mankind, in the sense in which the mass of mankind always have understood and always will understand the word good. "Meditor," said Bacon, "instaurationem philosophiae ejusmodi quae nihil inanis aut abstracti habeat, quaeque vitae humanae conditiones in melius provehat."[20]

The difference between the philosophy of Bacon and that of his predecessors cannot, we think, be better illustrated than by comparing his views on some important subjects with those of Plato. We select Plato, because we conceive that he did more than any other person towards giving to the minds of speculative men that bent which they retained till they received from Bacon a new impulse in a diametrically opposite direction.

It is curious to observe how differently these great men estimated the value of every kind of knowledge. Take Arithmetic for example. Plato, after speaking slightly of the convenience of being able to reckon and compute in the ordinary transactions of life, passes to what he considers as a far more important advantage. The study of the properties of numbers, he tells us, habituates the mind to the contemplation of pure truth, and raises us above the material universe. He would have his disciples apply themselves to this study, not that they may be able to buy or sell, not that they may qualify themselves to be shopkeepers or travelling merchants, but that they may learn to withdraw their minds from the ever-shifting spectacle of this visible and tangible world, and to fix them on the immutable essences of things.

Bacon, on the other hand, valued this branch of knowledge, only on account of its uses with reference to that visible and tangible world which Plato so much despised. He speaks with scorn of the mystical arithmetic of the later Platonists, and laments the propensity of mankind to employ, on mere matters of curiosity, powers the whole exertion of which is required for purposes of solid advantage. He advises arithmeticians to leave these trifles, and to employ themselves in framing convenient expressions, which may be of use in physical researches.

The same reasons which led Plato to recommend the study of arithmetic led him to recommend also the study of mathematics. The vulgar crowd of geometricians, he says, will not understand him. They have practice always in view. They do not know that the real use of the science is to lead men to the knowledge of abstract, essential, eternal truth. Indeed, if we are to believe Plutarch, Plato carried this feeling so far that he considered geometry as degraded by being applied to any purpose of vulgar utility. Archytas, it seems, had framed machines of extraordinary power on mathematical principles. Plato remonstrated with his friend, and declared that this was to degrade a noble intellectual exercise into a low craft, fit only for carpenters and wheelwrights. The office of geometry, he said, was to discipline the mind, not to minister to the base wants of the body. His interference was successful; and from that time, according to Plutarch, the science of mechanics was considered as unworthy of the attention of a philosopher.[21]

Archimedes[22] in a later age imitated and surpassed Archytas. But even Archimedes was not free from the prevailing notion that geometry was degraded by being employed to produce anything useful. It was with difficulty that he was induced to stoop from speculation to practice. He was half ashamed of those inventions which were the wonder of hostile nations, and always spoke of them slightingly as mere amusements, as trifles in which a mathematician might be suffered to relax his mind after intense application to the higher parts of his science.

The opinion of Bacon on this subject was diametrically opposed to that of the ancient philosophers. He valued geometry chiefly, if not solely, on account of those uses, which to Plato appeared so base. And it is remarkable that the longer Bacon lived the stronger this feeling became. When in 1605 he wrote the two books on the *Advancement of Learn-*

---

[18] In a passage here omitted, Macaulay gives further particulars as to the nature of the ancient philosophy and its continuing influence down to Bacon's day.

[19] In another omitted passage, Macaulay mentions the causes that "predisposed the public mind to a change"—principally the Reformation.

[20] "I contemplate a reorganization of philosophy which shall be neither empty nor abstract and which shall improve the conditions of human existence." (*Redargutio Philosophiarum.*)

[21] Plutarch was a famous Greek historian (46?–120?) best known as the author of the *Parallel Lives*. According to Macaulay's own note, the incident related about Archytas, philosopher, mathematician, and statesman of the fifth century B.C., is taken from Plutarch's *Symposiaca*, viii, and *Life of Marcellus*.

[22] Mathematician who lived at Syracuse in the third century B.C.

ing, he dwelt on the advantages which mankind derived from mixed mathematics; but he at the same time admitted that the beneficial effect produced by mathematical study on the intellect, though a collateral advantage, was "no less worthy than that which was principal and intended." But it is evident that his views underwent a change. When, near twenty years later, he published the *De Augmentis,* which is the *Treatise on the Advancement of Learning,* greatly expanded and carefully corrected, he made important alterations in the part which related to mathematics. He condemned with severity the high pretensions of the mathematicians, "delicias et fastum mathematicorum."[23] Assuming the well-being of the human race to be the end of knowledge, he pronounced that mathematical science could claim no higher rank than that of an appendage or auxiliary to other sciences. Mathematical science, he says, is the handmaid of natural philosophy; she ought to demean herself as such; and he declares that he cannot conceive by what ill chance it has happened that she presumes to claim precedence over her mistress. He predicts—a prediction which would have made Plato shudder—that as more and more discoveries are made in physics, there will be more and more branches of mixed mathematics. Of that collateral advantage the value of which, twenty years before, he rated so highly, he says not one word. This omission cannot have been the effect of mere inadvertence. His own treatise was before him. From that treatise he deliberately expunged whatever was favourable to the study of pure mathematics, and inserted several keen reflections on the ardent votaries of that study. This fact, in our opinion, admits of only one explanation. Bacon's love of those pursuits which directly tend to improve the condition of mankind, and his jealousy of all pursuits merely curious, had grown upon him, and had, it may be, become immoderate. He was afraid of using any expression which might have the effect of inducing any man of talents to employ in speculations, useful only to the mind of the speculator, a single hour which might be employed in extending the empire of man over matter. If Bacon erred here, we must acknowledge that we greatly prefer his error to the opposite error of Plato. We have no patience with a philosophy which, like those Roman matrons who swallowed abortives in order to preserve their shapes, takes pains to be barren for fear of being homely.

Let us pass to astronomy. This was one of the sciences which Plato exhorted his disciples to learn, but for reasons far removed from common habits of thinking. "Shall we set down astronomy," says Socrates,[24] "among the subjects of study?" "I think so," answers his young friend Glaucon: "to know something about the seasons, the months, and the years is of use for military purposes, as well as for agriculture and navigation." "It amuses me," says Socrates, "to see how afraid you are, lest the common herd of people should accuse you of recommending useless studies." He then proceeds, in that pure and magnificent diction which, as Cicero said, Jupiter would use if Jupiter spoke Greek, to explain, that the use of astronomy is not to add to the vulgar comforts of life, but to assist in raising the mind to the contemplation of things which are to be perceived by the pure intellect alone. The knowledge of the actual motions of the heavenly bodies Socrates considers as of little value. The appearances which make the sky beautiful at night are, he tells us, like the figures which a geometrician draws on the sand, mere examples, mere helps to feeble minds. We must get beyond them; we must neglect them; we must attain to an astronomy which is as independent of the actual stars as geometrical truth is independent of the lines of an ill-drawn diagram. This is, we imagine, very nearly, if not exactly, the astronomy which Bacon compared to the ox of Prometheus, a sleek, well-shaped hide, stuffed with rubbish, goodly to look at, but containing nothing to eat. He complained that astronomy had, to its great injury, been separated from natural philosophy, of which it was one of the noblest provinces, and annexed to the domain of mathematics. The world stood in need, he said, of a very different astronomy, of a living astronomy, of an astronomy which should set forth the nature, the motion, and the influences of the heavenly bodies, as they really are.

On the greatest and most useful of all human inventions, the invention of alphabetical writing, Plato did not look with much complacency. He seems to have thought that the use of letters had operated on the human mind as the use of the go-cart in learning to walk, or of corks in learning to swim, is said to operate on the human body. It was a support which, in his opinion, soon became indispensable to those who used it, which made vigorous exertion first unnecessary and then impossible. The powers of the intellect would, he conceived, have been more fully developed without this delusive aid. Men would

---

[23] "The daintiness and pride of mathematicians.."

[24] In Plato's *Republic,* Book VII.

have been compelled to exercise the understanding and the memory, and, by deep and assiduous meditation, to make truth thoroughly their own. Now, on the contrary, much knowledge is traced on paper, but little is engraved in the soul. A man is certain that he can find information at a moment's notice when he wants it. He therefore suffers it to fade from his mind. Such a man cannot in strictness be said to know anything. He has the show without the reality of wisdom. These opinions Plato has put into the mouth of an ancient king of Egypt.[25] But it is evident from the context that they were his own; and so they were understood to be by Quinctilian.[26] Indeed they are in perfect accordance with the whole Platonic system.

Bacon's views, as may easily be supposed, were widely different. The powers of the memory, he observes, without the help of writing, can do little towards the advancement of any useful science. He acknowledges that the memory may be disciplined to such a point as to be able to perform very extraordinary feats. But on such feats he sets little value. The habits of his mind, he tells us, are such that he is not disposed to rate highly any accomplishment, however rare, which is of no practical use to mankind. As to these prodigious achievements of the memory, he ranks them with the exhibitions of rope-dancers and tumblers. "These two performances," he says, "are much of the same sort. The one is an abuse of the powers of the body; the other is an abuse of the powers of the mind. Both may perhaps excite our wonder; but neither is entitled to our respect."

To Plato, the science of medicine appeared to be of very disputable advantages. He did not indeed object to quick cures for acute disorders, or for injuries produced by accidents. But the art which resists the slow sap of a chronic disease, which repairs frames enervated by lust, swollen by gluttony, or inflamed by wine, which encourages sensuality by mitigating the natural punishment of the sensualist, and prolongs existence when the intellect has ceased to retain its entire energy, had no share of his esteem. A life protracted by medical skill he pronounced to be a long death. The exercise of the art of medicine ought, he said, to be tolerated, so far as that art may serve to cure the occasional distempers of men whose constitutions are good. As to those who have bad constitutions, let them die; and the sooner the better. Such

men are unfit for war, for magistracy, for the management of their domestic affairs, for severe study and speculation. If they engage in any vigorous mental exercise, they are troubled with giddiness and fulness of the head, all which they lay to the account of philosophy. The best thing that can happen to such wretches is to have done with life at once. He quotes mythical authority in support of this doctrine; and reminds his disciples that the practice of the sons of Aesculapius,[27] as described by Homer, extended only to the cure of external injuries.

Far different was the philosophy of Bacon. Of all the sciences, that which he seems to have regarded with the greatest interest was the science which, in Plato's opinion, would not be tolerated in a well-regulated community. To make men perfect was no part of Bacon's plan. His humble aim was to make imperfect men comfortable. The beneficence of his philosophy resembled the beneficence of the common Father, whose sun rises on the evil and the good, whose rain descends for the just and the unjust. In Plato's opinion man was made for philosophy; in Bacon's opinion philosophy was made for man; it was a means to an end; and that end was to increase the pleasures and to mitigate the pains of millions who are not and cannot be philosophers. That a valetudinarian who took great pleasure in being wheeled along his terrace, who relished his boiled chicken and his weak wine and water, and who enjoyed a hearty laugh over the Queen of Navarre's tales,[28] should be treated as a *caput lupinum*[29] because he could not read the *Timaeus*[30] without a headache, was a notion which the humane spirit of the English school of wisdom altogether rejected. Bacon would not have thought it beneath the dignity of a philosopher to contrive an improved garden chair for such a valetudinarian, to devise some way of rendering his medicines more palatable, to invent repasts which he might enjoy, and pillows on which he might sleep soundly; and this though there might not be the smallest hope that the mind of the poor invalid would ever rise to the contemplation of the ideal beautiful and the ideal good. As Plato had cited the religious legends of Greece to justify his contempt for the more recondite parts of the art of healing, Bacon vindicated the dignity of that art by appealing to the

25 In his *Phaedrus*, 274–275.
26 Or Quintilian, famous Roman rhetorician (35?–100?).

27 Aesculapius, as portrayed by Homer in the *Iliad*, was the founder of medical art, and his sons were the doctors who accompanied the Greek army to Troy.
28 A collection of love stories, the *Heptameron*, made by Marguerite, Queen of Navarre (1492–1549).   29 An outlaw.
30 One of Plato's more difficult dialogues.

example of Christ, and reminded men that the great Physician of the soul did not disdain to be also the physician of the body.

When we pass from the science of medicine to that of legislation, we find the same difference between the systems of these two great men. Plato, at the commencement of the *Dialogue on Laws,* lays it down as a fundamental principle that the end of legislation is to make men virtuous. It is unnecessary to point out the extravagant conclusions to which such a proposition leads. Bacon well knew to how great an extent the happiness of every society must depend on the virtue of its members; and he also knew what legislators can and what they cannot do for the purpose of promoting virtue. The view which he has given of the end of legislation, and of the principal means for the attainment of that end, has always seemed to us eminently happy, even among the many happy passages of the same kind with which his works abound. "Finis et scopus quem leges intueri atque ad quem jussiones et sanctiones suas dirigere debent, non alius est quam ut cives feliciter degant. Id fiet si pietate et religione recte instituti, moribus honesti, armis adversus hostes externos tuti, legum auxilio adversus seditiones et privatas injurias muniti, imperio et magistratibus obsequentes, copiis et opibus locupletes et florentes fuerint."[31] The end is the well-being of the people. The means are the imparting of moral and religious education; the providing of everything necessary for defence against foreign enemies; the maintaining of internal order; the establishing of a judicial financial, and commercial system, under which wealth may be rapidly accumulated and securely enjoyed.

Even with respect to the form in which laws ought to be drawn, there is a remarkable difference of opinion between the Greek and the Englishman. Plato thought a preamble essential; Bacon thought it mischievous. Each was consistent with himself. Plato, considering the moral improvement of the people as the end of legislation, justly inferred that a law which commanded and threatened, but which neither convinced the reason, nor touched the heart, must be a most imperfect law. He was not content with deterring from theft a man who still continued to be a thief at heart, with restraining a son who hated his mother from beating his mother. The only obedience on which he set much value was the obedience which an enlightened understanding yields to reason, and which a virtuous disposition yields to precepts of virtue. He really seems to have believed that, by prefixing to every law an eloquent and pathetic exhortation, he should, to a great extent, render penal enactments superfluous. Bacon entertained no such romantic hopes; and he well knew the practical inconveniences of the course which Plato recommended. "Neque nobis," says he, "prologi legum qui inepti olim habiti sunt, et leges introducunt disputantes non jubentes, utique placerent, si priscos mores ferre possemus. . . . Quantum fieri potest prologi evitentur, et lex incipiat a jussione."[32]

Each of the great men whom we have compared intended to illustrate his system by a philosophical romance; and each left his romance imperfect. Had Plato lived to finish the *Critias,* a comparison between that noble fiction and the new *Atlantis*[33] would probably have furnished us with still more striking instances than any which we have given. It is amusing to think with what horror he would have seen such an institution as Solomon's House[34] rising in his republic: with what vehemence he would have ordered the brew-houses, the perfume-houses, and the dispensatories to be pulled down; and with what inexorable rigour he would have driven beyond the frontier all the Fellows of the College, Merchants of Light and Depredators, Lamps and Pioneers.

To sum up the whole, we should say that the aim of the Platonic philosophy was to exalt man into a god. The aim of the Baconian philosophy was to provide man with what he requires while he continues to be man. The aim of the Platonic philosophy was to raise us far above vulgar wants. The aim of the Baconian philosophy was to supply our vulgar wants. The former aim was noble; but the latter was attainable. Plato drew a good bow; but, like Acestes in Virgil, he aimed at the stars; and therefore, though there was no want of strength or skill, the shot was

---

[31] "The end and scope which laws should have in view, and to which they should direct their decrees and sanctions, is no other than the happiness of the citizens. And this will be effected if the citizens be rightly trained in piety and religion, sound in morality, protected by arms against foreign enemies, guarded by the shield of the laws against civil discords and private injuries, obedient to the government and the magistrates, and rich and flourishing in forces and wealth." (*De Augmentis,* Lib. 8, cap. 3, aph. 5.)

[32] "Nor do I approve the preambles to laws, which were formerly considered impertinent, and which present the laws as disputations rather than as commands so that they may be acceptable, if we could endure the ancient customs. As much as possible preambles should be avoided and the law should begin with its enactment." (*De Augmentis,* Lib. 8, cap. 3, aph. 69.)
[33] The *New Atlantis* by Bacon.
[34] The ideal college described in the *New Atlantis,* "dedicated to the study of the works and creatures of God," all with a strictly practical bias.

thrown away. His arrow was indeed followed by a track of dazzling radiance, but it struck nothing.

Volans liquidis in nubibus arsit arundo
Signavitque viam flammis, tenuisque recessit
Consumpta in ventos.[35]

Bacon fixed his eye on a mark which was placed on the earth, and within bow-shot, and hit it in the white. The philosophy of Plato began in words and ended in words, noble words indeed, words such as were to be expected from the finest of human intellects exercising boundless dominion over the finest of human languages. The philosophy of Bacon began in observations and ended in arts.

The boast of the ancient philosophers was that their doctrine formed the minds of men to a high degree of wisdom and virtue. This was indeed the only practical good which the most celebrated of those teachers even pretended to effect; and undoubtedly, if they had effected this, they would have deserved far higher praise than if they had discovered the most salutary medicines or constructed the most powerful machines. But the truth is that, in those very matters in which alone they professed to do any good to mankind, in those very matters for the sake of which they neglected all the vulgar interests of mankind, they did nothing, or worse than nothing. They promised what was impracticable; they despised what was practicable; they filled the world with long words and long beards; and they left it as wicked and as ignorant as they found it.

An acre in Middlesex is better than a principality in Utopia. The smallest actual good is better than the most magnificent promises of impossibilities. The wise man of the Stoics would, no doubt, be a grander object than a steam-engine. But there are steam-engines. And the wise man of the Stoics is yet to be born. A philosophy which should enable a man to feel perfectly happy while in agonies of pain would be better than a philosophy which assuages pain. But we know that there are remedies which will assuage pain; and we know that the ancient sages liked the toothache just as little as their neighbours. A philosophy which should extinguish cupidity would be better than a philosophy which should devise laws for the security of property. But it is possible to make laws which shall, to a very great extent, secure property. And we do not understand how any motives which the ancient philosophy furnished could extinguish cupidity. We know indeed that the philosophers were no better than other men. From the testimony of friends as well as of foes, from the confessions of Epictetus[36] and Seneca, as well as from the sneers of Lucian[37] and the fierce invectives of Juvenal,[38] it is plain that these teachers of virtue had all the vices of their neighbours, with the additional vice of hypocrisy. Some people may think the object of the Baconian philosophy a low object, but they cannot deny that, high or low, it has been attained. They cannot deny that every year makes an addition to what Bacon called "fruit." They cannot deny that mankind have made, and are making, great and constant progress in the road which he pointed out to them. Was there any such progressive movement among the ancient philosophers? After they had been declaiming eight hundred years, had they made the world better than when they began? Our belief is that, among the philosophers themselves, instead of a progressive improvement there was a progressive degeneracy. An abject superstition which Democritus or Anaxagoras[39] would have rejected with scorn, added the last disgrace to the long dotage of the Stoic and Platonic schools. Those unsuccessful attempts to articulate which are so delightful and interesting in a child shock and disgust in an aged paralytic; and in the same way, those wild and mythological fictions which charm us, when we hear them lisped by Greek poetry in its infancy, excite a mixed sensation of pity and loathing, when mumbled by Greek philosophy in its old age. We know that guns, cutlery, spyglasses, clocks, are better in our time than they were in the time of our fathers, and were better in the time of our fathers than they were in the time of our grandfathers. We might, therefore, be inclined to think that, when a philosophy which boasted that its object was the elevation and purification of the mind, and which for this object neglected the sordid office of ministering to the comforts of the body, had flourished in the highest honour during many hundreds of years, a vast moral amelioration must have taken

---

35 "For, as through cloud and rain the arrow was flying, it kindled, Marking its track with fire; then vanished from sight in the heavens, Wholly consumed." (Aeneid, V, 525–27. Conington's translation.)

36 Outstanding Stoic philosopher of the first century A.D.
37 Greek satirist (c. 120–180), who made mock of philosophers in general.
38 Roman poet and satirist (60?–140), who also disparaged philosophers.
39 Two early Greek philosophers, the first of whom propounded an atomic theory of the universe, while the latter believed in reason as a metaphysical principle. It is uncertain at just what specific "superstition" Macaulay is aiming, but he mentions almost immediately below some of the "late" philosophers, who are known to have dabbled in magic, divination, etc.

place. Was it so? Look at the schools of this wisdom four centuries before the Christian era and four centuries after that era. Compare the men whom those schools formed at those two periods. Compare Plato and Libanius.[40] Compare Pericles and Julian.[41] This philosophy confessed, nay boasted, that for every end but one it was useless. Had it attained that one end?

Suppose that Justinian, when he closed the schools of Athens,[42] had called on the last few sages who still haunted the Portico, and lingered round the ancient plane-trees, to show their title to public veneration: suppose that he had said: "A thousand years have elapsed since, in this famous city, Socrates posed Protagoras and Hippias;[43] during those thousand years a large proportion of the ablest men of every generation has been employed in constant efforts to bring to perfection the philosophy which you teach; that philosophy has been munificently patronised by the powerful; its professors have been held in the highest esteem by the public; it has drawn to itself almost all the sap and vigour of the human intellect: and what has it effected? What profitable truth has it taught us which we should not equally have known without it? What has it enabled us to do which we should not have been equally able to do without it?" Such questions, we suspect, would have puzzled Simplicius and Isidore.[44] Ask a follower of Bacon what the new philosophy, as it was called in the time of Charles the Second, has effected for mankind, and his answer is ready: "It has lengthened life; it has mitigated pain; it has extinguished diseases; it has increased the fertility of the soil; it has given new securities to the mariner; it has furnished new arms to the warrior; it has spanned great rivers and estuaries with bridges of form unknown to our fathers; it has guided the thunderbolt innocuously from heaven to earth; it has lighted up the night with the splendour of day; it has extended the range of the human vision; it has multiplied the power of the human muscles; it has accelerated motion; it has annihilated distance; it has facilitated intercourse, correspondence, all friendly offices, all despatch of business; it has enabled man to descend to the depths of the sea, to soar into the air, to penetrate securely into the noxious recesses of the earth, to traverse the land in cars which whirl along without horses, and the ocean in ships which run ten knots an hour against the wind. These are but a part of its fruits, and of its first fruits. For it is a philosophy which never rests, which has never attained, which is never perfect. Its law is progress. A point which yesterday was invisible is its goal to-day, and will be its starting-post to-morrow."

Great and various as the powers of Bacon were, he owes his wide and durable fame chiefly to this, that all those powers received their direction from common sense. His love of the vulgar useful, his strong sympathy with the popular notions of good and evil, and the openness with which he avowed that sympathy, are the secret of his influence. There was in his system no cant, no illusion. He had no anointing for broken bones, no fine theories de finibus,[45] no arguments to persuade men out of their senses. He knew that men, and philosophers as well as other men, do actually love life, health, comfort, honour, security, the society of friends, and do actually dislike death, sickness, pain, poverty, disgrace, danger, separation from those to whom they are attached. He knew that religion, though it often regulates and moderates these feelings, seldom eradicates them; nor did he think it desirable for mankind that they should be eradicated. The plan of eradicating them by conceits like those of Seneca, or syllogisms like those of Chrysippus,[46] was too preposterous to be for a moment entertained by a mind like his. He did not understand what wisdom there could be in changing names where it was impossible to change things; in denying that blindness, hunger, the gout, the rack, were evils, and calling them ἀποπροηγμένα;[47] in refusing to acknowledge that health, safety, plenty, were good things, and dubbing them by the name of ἀδιάφορα.[48] In his opinions on all these subjects, he was not a Stoic, nor an Epicurean, nor an Academic, but what would have been called by Stoics, Epicureans, and Academics a mere ἰδιώτης, a mere common man. And it was precisely because he was so that his name makes so great an era in the history of the world. It was because he dug deep that he was able to pile high. It was because, in order to lay his foundations, he

---

[40] Greek sophist and commentator (314–393), who was specifically charged with studying magic.

[41] Pericles was a leading Athenian statesman (fifth century B.C.) in the time of Greece's greatest intellectual vigor. Julian (331–363) was emperor of Rome in the days of its decadence; his devotion to classical philosophy was undercut by his belief in such superstitions as divination and sacrificial offerings.

[42] By an imperial edict in 529.

[43] Interlocutors in Plato's Protagoras.

[44] Among the last of the Neo-Platonists. Simplicius was actually teaching at the Academy when Justinian closed it.

[45] Concerning final ends or purposes.

[46] A leader of the Stoic school at Athens. He stated many of the Stoic ideas in the form of syllogisms.

[47] "Things relatively evil."   [48] "Things indifferent."

went down into those parts of human nature which lie low, but which are not liable to change, that the fabric which he reared has risen to so stately an elevation, and stands with such immovable strength.

We have sometimes thought that an amusing fiction might be written, in which a disciple of Epictetus and a disciple of Bacon should be introduced as fellow-travellers. They come to a village where the small-pox has just begun to rage, and find houses shut up, intercourse suspended, the sick abandoned, mothers weeping in terror over their children. The Stoic assures the dismayed population that there is nothing bad in the small-pox, and that to a wise man disease, deformity, death, the loss of friends, are not evils. The Baconian takes out a lancet and begins to vaccinate. They find a body of miners in great dismay. An explosion of noisome vapours has just killed many of those who were at work; and the survivors are afraid to venture into the cavern. The Stoic assures them that such an accident is nothing but a mere ἀποπροήγμενον.[49] The Baconian, who has no such fine word at his command, contents himself with devising a safety-lamp. They find a shipwrecked merchant wringing his hands on the shore. His vessel with an inestimable cargo has just gone down, and he is reduced in a moment from opulence to beggary. The Stoic exhorts him not to seek happiness in things which lie without himself, and repeats the whole chapter of Epictetus πρὸς τοὺς τὴν ἀπορίαν δεδοικότας.[50] The Baconian constructs a diving-bell, goes down in it, and returns with the most precious effects from the wreck. It would be easy to multiply illustrations of the difference between the philosophy of thorns and the philosophy of fruit, the philosophy of words and the philosophy of works.

Bacon has been accused of overrating the importance of those sciences which minister to the physical well-being of man, and of underrating the importance of moral philosophy; and it cannot be denied that persons who read the *Novum Organum* and the *De Augmentis*, without adverting to the circumstances under which those works were written, will find much that may seem to countenance the accusation. It is certain, however, that, though in practice he often went very wrong, and though, as his historical work and his essays prove, he did not hold, even in theory, very strict opinions on points of political morality, he was far too wise a man not to know how much our well-being depends on the regulation of our minds. The world for which he wished was not, as some people seem to imagine, a world of water-wheels, power-looms, steam-carriages, sensualists, and knaves. He would have been as ready as Zeno himself[51] to maintain that no bodily comforts which could be devised by the skill and labour of a hundred generations would give happiness to a man whose mind was under the tyranny of licentious appetite, of envy, of hatred, or of fear. If he sometimes appeared to ascribe importance too exclusively to the arts which increase the outward comforts of our species, the reason is plain. Those arts had been most unduly depreciated. They had been represented as unworthy of the attention of a man of liberal education . . . had undoubtedly caused many arts which were of the greatest utility, and which were susceptible of the greatest improvements, to be neglected by speculators, and abandoned to joiners, masons, smiths, weavers, apothecaries. It was necessary to assert the dignity of those arts, to bring them prominently forward, to proclaim that, as they have a most serious effect on human happiness, they are not unworthy of the attention of the highest human intellects. Again, it was by illustrations drawn from these arts that Bacon could most easily illustrate his principles. It was by improvements effected in these arts that the soundness of his principles could be most speedily and decisively brought to the test, and made manifest to common understandings. He acted like a wise commander who thins every other part of his line to strengthen a point where the enemy is attacking with peculiar fury, and on the fate of which the event of the battle seems likely to depend. In the *Novum Organum*, however, he distinctly and most truly declares that his philosophy is no less a Moral than a Natural Philosophy, that, though his illustrations are drawn from physical science, the principles which those illustrations are intended to explain are just as applicable to ethical and political inquiries as to inquiries into the nature of heat and vegetation. . . .

---

[49] "Relative evil."   [50] "To those who fear poverty."

[51] The founder of the Stoic school of philosophy. His teachings were roughly those outlined here by Macaulay.

from THE HISTORY OF ENGLAND
FROM THE ACCESSION OF JAMES THE SECOND

from CHAPTER I

I PURPOSE to write the history of England from the accession of King James the Second[1] down to a time which is within the memory of men still living. I shall recount the errors which, in a few months, alienated a loyal gentry and priesthood from the House of Stuart. I shall trace the course of that revolution which terminated the long struggle between our sovereigns and their parliaments, and bound up together the rights of the people and the title of the reigning dynasty. I shall relate how the new settlement was, during many troubled years, successfully defended against foreign and domestic enemies; how, under that settlement, the authority of law and the security of property were found to be compatible with a liberty of discussion and of individual action never before known; how, from the auspicious union of order and freedom, sprang a prosperity of which the annals of human affairs had furnished no example; how our country, from a state of ignominious vassalage, rapidly rose to the place of umpire among European powers; how her opulence and her martial glory grew together; how, by wise and resolute good faith, was gradually established a public credit fruitful of marvels which, to the statesmen of any former age, would have seemed incredible; how a gigantic commerce gave birth to a maritime power, compared with which every other maritime power, ancient or modern, sinks into insignificance; how Scotland, after ages of enmity, was at length united to England, not merely by legal bonds,[2] but by indissoluble ties of interest and affection; how, in America, the British colonies rapidly became far mightier and wealthier than the realms which Cortes and Pizarro[3] had added to the dominions of Charles the Fifth; how, in Asia, British adventurers founded an empire not less splendid, and more durable, than that of Alexander.[4]

Nor will it be less my duty faithfully to record disasters mingled with triumphs, and great national crimes and follies far more humiliating than any disaster. It will be seen that even what we justly account our chief blessings were not without alloy. It will be seen that the system which effectually secured our liberties against the encroachments of kingly power gave birth to a new class of abuses, from which absolute monarchies are exempt. It will be seen that, in consequence partly of unwise interference, and partly of unwise neglect, the increase of wealth and the extension of trade produced, together with immense good, some evils from which poor and rude societies are free. It will be seen how, in two important dependencies of the crown, wrong was followed by just retribution; how imprudence and obstinacy broke the ties which bound the North American colonies to the parent state; how Ireland, cursed by the domination of race over race, and of religion over religion, remained indeed a member of the empire, but a withered and distorted member, adding no strength to the body politic, and reproachfully pointed at by all who feared or envied the greatness of England.

Yet, unless I greatly deceive myself, the general effect of this chequered narrative will be to excite thankfulness in all religious minds, and hope in the breasts of all patriots. For the history of our country during the last hundred and sixty years is eminently the history of physical, of moral, and of intellectual improvement. Those who compare the age on which their lot has fallen with a golden age which exists only in their imagination, may talk of degeneracy and decay; but no man who is correctly informed as to the past will be disposed to take a morose or desponding view of the present.

I should very imperfectly execute the task which I have undertaken, if I were merely to treat of battles and sieges, of the rise and fall of administrations, of intrigues in the palace, and of debates in the parliament. It will be my endeavour to relate the history of the people as well as the history of the government; to trace the progress of useful and ornamental arts; to describe the rise of religious sects and the changes of literary taste; to portray the manners of successive generations; and not to pass by with neglect even the revolutions which have taken place in dress, furniture, repasts, and public amusements. I shall cheerfully bear the reproach of having descended below the

---

[1] 1685.—The selections from the *History* are so full of allusive material that it has seemed wise to provide annotation only where a clear reading of the meaning depends upon it.

[2] The union took place in 1707.

[3] Soldiers and explorers of the first half of the sixteenth century, subjects of Charles V of Spain; the former conquered Mexico and the latter Peru.

[4] While not to be compared with the Roman Empire, that of Alexander the Great in the fourth century B.C. was of tremendous power and extent.

dignity of history, if I can succeed in placing before the English of the nineteenth century a true picture of the life of their ancestors. . . .

from CHAPTER 3

I intend, in this chapter, to give a description of the state in which England was at the time when the crown passed from Charles the Second to his brother. Such a description, composed from scanty and dispersed materials, must necessarily be very imperfect. Yet it may perhaps correct some false notions which would make the subsequent narrative unintelligible or uninstructive.

If we would study with profit the history of our ancestors, we must be constantly on our guard against that delusion which the well-known names of families, places, and offices naturally produce, and must never forget that the country of which we read was a very different country from that in which we live. In every experimental science there is a tendency towards perfection. In every human being there is a wish to ameliorate his own condition. These two principles have often sufficed, even when counteracted by great public calamities and by bad institutions, to carry civilisation rapidly forward. No ordinary misfortune, no ordinary misgovernment, will do so much to make a nation wretched, as the constant progress of physical knowledge and the constant effort of every man to better himself will do to make a nation prosperous. It has often been found that profuse expenditure, heavy taxation, absurd commercial restrictions, corrupt tribunals, disastrous wars, seditions, persecutions, conflagrations, inundations, have not been able to destroy capital so fast as the exertions of private citizens have been able to create it. It can easily be proved that, in our own land, the national wealth has, during at least six centuries, been almost uninterruptedly increasing; that it was greater under the Tudors than under the Plantagenets; that it was greater under the Stuarts than under the Tudors; that, in spite of battles, sieges, and confiscations, it was greater on the day of the Restoration[5] than on the day when the Long Parliament met;[6] that, in spite of maladministration, of extravagance, of public bankruptcy, of two costly and unsuccessful wars, of the pestilence and of the fire,[7] it was greater on the day of the death of

Charles the Second than on the day of his Restoration.

This progress, having continued during many ages, became at length, about the middle of the eighteenth century, portentously rapid, and has proceeded, during the nineteenth century, with accelerated velocity. In consequence partly of our geographical and partly of our moral position, we have, during several generations, been exempt from evils which have elsewhere impeded the efforts and destroyed the fruits of industry. While every part of the Continent, from Moscow to Lisbon, has been the theatre of bloody and devastating wars, no hostile standard has been seen here but as a trophy. While revolutions have taken place all around us, our government has never once been subverted by violence. During more than a hundred years there has been in our island no tumult of sufficient importance to be called an insurrection; nor has the law been once borne down either by popular fury or by regal tyranny: public credit has been held sacred; the administration of justice has been pure: even in times which might by Englishmen be justly called evil times, we have enjoyed what almost every other nation in the world would have considered as an ample measure of civil and religious freedom. Every man has felt entire confidence that the state would protect him in the possession of what had been earned by his diligence and hoarded by his selfdenial. Under the benignant influence of peace and liberty, science has flourished, and has been applied to practical purposes on a scale never before known.

The consequence is that a change to which the history of the old world furnishes no parallel has taken place in our country. Could the England of 1685 be, by some magical process, set before our eyes, we should not know one landscape in a hundred or one building in ten thousand. The country gentleman would not recognise his own fields. The inhabitant of the town would not recognise his own street. Everything has been changed but the great features of nature and a few massive and durable works of human art. We might find out Snowdon and Windermere, the Cheddar Cliffs and Beachy Head. We might find out here and there a Norman minster, or a castle which witnessed the wars of the Roses. But, with such rare exceptions, everything would be strange to us. Many thousands of square miles which are now rich cornland and meadow, intersected by green hedgerows and dotted with villages and pleasant country seats, would appear as moors overgrown with furze, or fens abandoned to wild ducks. We should see straggling huts built of

---

[5] 1660.   [6] The Long Parliament sat from 1640 to 1649.
[7] The two Dutch Wars, the Great Plague in 1665, and the Great Fire of London in 1666.

wood and covered with thatch, where we now see manufacturing towns and seaports renowned to the farthest ends of the world. The capital itself would shrink to dimensions not much exceeding those of its present suburb on the south of the Thames. Not less strange to us would be the garb and manners of the people, the furniture and the equipages, the interior of the shops and dwellings. Such a change in the state of a nation seems to be at least as well entitled to the notice of a historian as any change of the dynasty or of the ministry. . . .

We may . . . with confidence pronounce that, when James the Second reigned, England contained between five million and five million five hundred thousand inhabitants. On the very highest supposition she then had less than one third of her present population, and less than three times the population which is now collected in her gigantic capital. . . .

We should be much mistaken if we pictured to ourselves the squires of the seventeenth century as men bearing a close resemblance to their descendants, the county members and chairmen of quarter sessions[8] with whom we are familiar. The modern country gentleman generally receives a liberal education, passes from a distinguished school to a distinguished college, and has ample opportunity to become an excellent scholar. He has generally seen something of foreign countries. A considerable part of his life has generally been passed in the capital; and the refinements of the capital follow him into the country. There is perhaps no class of dwellings so pleasing as the rural seats of the English gentry. In the parks and pleasure grounds, nature, dressed yet not disguised by art, wears her most alluring form. In the buildings, good sense and good taste combine to produce a happy union of the comfortable and the graceful. The pictures, the musical instruments, the library, would in any other country be considered as proving the owner to be an eminently polished and accomplished man. A country gentleman who witnessed the Revolution[9] was probably in receipt of about a fourth part of the rent which his acres now yield to his posterity. He was, therefore, as compared with his posterity, a poor man, and was generally under the necessity of residing, with little interruption, on his estate. To travel on the Continent, to maintain an establishment in London, or even to visit London frequently, were pleasures in which only the great proprietors could indulge. It may be confi-

dently affirmed that of the squires whose names were then in the Commissions of Peace and Lieutenancy,[10] not one in twenty went to town once in five years, or had ever in his life wandered so far as Paris. Many lords of manors had received an education differing little from that of their menial servants. The heir of an estate often passed his boyhood and youth at the seat of his family with no better tutors than grooms and gamekeepers, and scarce attained learning enough to sign his name to a Mittimus.[11] If he went to school and to college, he generally returned before he was twenty to the seclusion of the old hall, and there, unless his mind were very happily constituted by nature, soon forgot his academical pursuits in rural business and pleasures. His chief serious employment was the care of his property. He examined samples of grain, handled pigs, and, on market days, made bargains over a tankard with drovers and hop merchants. His chief pleasures were commonly derived from field sports and from an unrefined sensuality. His language and pronunciation were such as we should now expect to hear only from the most ignorant clowns. His oaths, coarse jests, and scurrilous terms of abuse, were uttered with the broadest accent of his province. It was easy to discern, from the first words which he spoke, whether he came from Somersetshire or Yorkshire. He troubled himself little about decorating his abode, and, if he attempted decoration, seldom produced anything but deformity. The litter of a farmyard gathered under the windows of his bedchamber, and the cabbages and gooseberry bushes grew close to his hall door. His table was loaded with coarse plenty, and guests were cordially welcomed to it. But, as the habit of drinking to excess was general in the class to which he belonged, and as his fortune did not enable him to intoxicate large assemblies daily with claret or canary, strong beer was the ordinary beverage. The quantity of beer consumed in those days was indeed enormous. For beer then was to the middle and lower classes, not only all that beer now is, but all that wine, tea, and ardent spirits now are. It was only at great houses, or on great occasions, that foreign drink was placed on the board. The ladies of the house, whose business it had commonly been to cook the repast, retired as soon as the dishes had been devoured, and left the gentlemen to their ale and tobacco. The coarse jollity of the afternoon was often prolonged till the revellers were laid under the table.

---

[8] Quarterly meetings of a court of justices of the peace held in the individual counties.   [9] The Glorious Revolution, 1688.

[10] Who held commissions as justices of the peace or as local representatives of the Crown in military matters.
[11] A writ or warrant.

It was very seldom that the country gentleman caught glimpses of the great world; and what he saw of it tended rather to confuse than to enlighten his understanding. His opinions respecting religion, government, foreign countries, and former times, having been derived, not from study, from observation, or from conversation with enlightened companions, but from such traditions as were current in his own small circle, were the opinions of a child. He adhered to them, however, with the obstinacy which is generally found in ignorant men accustomed to be fed with flattery. His animosities were numerous and bitter. He hated Frenchmen and Italians, Scotchmen and Irishmen, Papists and Presbyterians, Independents and Baptists, Quakers and Jews. Towards London and Londoners he felt an aversion which more than once produced important political effects. His wife and daughter were in tastes and acquirements below a housekeeper or a stillroom maid of the present day. They stitched and spun, brewed gooseberry wine, cured marigolds, and made the crust for the venison pasty.

From this description it might be supposed that the English esquire of the seventeenth century did not materially differ from a rustic miller or alehouse keeper of our time. There are, however, some important parts of his character still to be noted, which will greatly modify this estimate. Unlettered as he was and unpolished, he was still in some most important points a gentleman. He was a member of a proud and powerful aristocracy, and was distinguished by many both of the good and of the bad qualities which belong to aristocrats. His family pride was beyond that of a Talbot or a Howard. He knew the genealogies and coats of arms of all his neighbours, and could tell which of them had assumed supporters without any right, and which of them were so unfortunate as to be greatgrandsons of aldermen. He was a magistrate, and, as such, administered gratuitously to those who dwelt around him a rude patriarchal justice, which, in spite of innumerable blunders and of occasional acts of tyranny, was yet better than no justice at all. He was an officer of the trainbands;[12] and his military dignity, though it might move the mirth of gallants who had served a campaign in Flanders, raised his character in his own eyes and in the eyes of his neighbours . . . Thus the character of the English esquire of the seventeenth century was compounded of two elements which we seldom or never find united. His ignorance and uncouthness,

his low tastes and gross phrases, would, in our time, be considered as indicating a nature and a breeding thoroughly plebeian. Yet he was essentially a patrician, and had, in large measure, both the virtues and the vices which flourish among men set from their birth in high place, and used to respect themselves and to be respected by others. It is not easy for a generation accustomed to find chivalrous sentiments only in company with liberal studies and polished manners to image to itself a man with the deportment, the vocabulary, and the accent of a carter, yet punctilious on matters of genealogy and precedence, and ready to risk his life rather than see a stain cast on the honour of his house. It is however only by thus joining together things seldom or never found together in our own experience, that we can form a just idea of that rustic aristocracy which constituted the main strength of the armies of Charles the First, and which long supported, with strange fidelity, the interest of his descendants.

The gross, uneducated, untravelled country gentleman was commonly a Tory: but, though devotedly attached to hereditary monarchy, he had no partiality for courtiers and ministers. He thought, not without reason, that Whitehall was filled with the most corrupt of mankind, and that of the great sums which the House of Commons had voted to the crown since the Restoration part had been embezzled by cunning politicians, and part squandered on buffoons and foreign courtesans. His stout English heart swelled with indignation at the thought that the government of his country should be subject to French dictation.[13] Being himself generally an old Cavalier, or the son of an old Cavalier, he reflected with bitter resentment on the ingratitude with which the Stuarts had requited their best friends. Those who heard him grumble at the neglect with which he was treated, and at the profusion with which wealth was lavished on the bastards of Nell Gwynn and Madam Carwell,[14] would have supposed him ripe for rebellion. But all this ill humour lasted only till the throne was really in danger. It was precisely when those whom the sovereign had loaded with wealth and honours shrank from his side that the country gentlemen, so surly and mutinous in the season of his prosperity, rallied round him in a body. . . . There was one institution, and one only, which they prized even more than hereditary monarchy; and that institution was the

---

[12] Bands of trained citizens, who later developed into the militia.   [13] Charles II and James II received financial aid from Louis XIV of France in the hope of being independent of Parliament. In return, the French King had some say in the framing of England's foreign policy.   [14] Both mistresses of Charles II.

Church of England. Their love of the Church was not, indeed, the effect of study or meditation. Few among them could have given any reason, drawn from Scripture or ecclesiastical history, for adhering to her doctrines, her ritual, and her polity; nor were they, as a class, by any means strict observers of that code of morality which is common to all Christian sects. But the experience of many ages proves that men may be ready to fight to the death, and to persecute without pity, for a religion whose creed they do not understand, and whose precepts they habitually disobey.

The rural clergy were even more vehement in Toryism than the rural gentry, and were a class scarcely less important. It is to be observed, however, that the individual clergyman, as compared with the individual gentleman, then ranked much lower than in our days. The main support of the Church was derived from the tithe;[15] and the tithe bore to the rent a much smaller ratio than at present. King[16] estimated the whole income of the parochial and collegiate clergy at only four hundred and eighty thousand pounds a year; Davenant[17] at only five hundred and forty-four thousand a year. It is certainly now more than seven times as great as the larger of these two sums. The average rent of the land has not, according to any estimate, increased proportionally. It follows that the rectors and vicars must have been, as compared with the neighbouring knights and squires, much poorer in the seventeenth than in the nineteenth century.

The place of the clergyman in society had been completely changed by the Reformation. Before that event, ecclesiastics had formed the majority of the House of Lords, had, in wealth and splendour, equalled, and sometimes outshone, the greatest of the temporal barons, and had generally held the highest civil offices. Many of the Treasurers, and almost all the Chancellors of the Plantagenets were Bishops. The Lord Keeper of the Privy Seal and the Master of the Rolls[18] were ordinarily churchmen. Churchmen transacted the most important diplomatic business. Indeed, all that large portion of the administration which rude and warlike nobles were incompetent to conduct was considered as especially belonging to

divines. Men, therefore, who were averse to the life of camps, and who were, at the same time, desirous to rise in the state, commonly received the tonsure.[19] Among them were sons of all the most illustrious families, and near kinsmen of the throne, Scroops and Nevilles, Bourchiers, Staffords, and Poles. To the religious houses belonged the rents of immense domains, and all that large portion of the tithe which is now in the hands of laymen. Down to the middle of the reign of Henry the Eighth, therefore, no line of life was so attractive to ambitious and covetous natures as the priesthood. Then came a violent revolution. The abolition of the monasteries deprived the Church at once of the greater part of her wealth, and of her predominance in the Upper House of Parliament. There was no longer an Abbot of Glastonbury or an Abbot of Reading seated among the peers, and possessed of revenues equal to those of a powerful Earl. The princely splendour of William of Wykeham and of William of Waynflete had disappeared. The scarlet hat of the Cardinal, the silver cross of the Legate, were no more. The clergy had also lost the ascendency which is the natural reward of superior mental cultivation. Once the circumstance that a man could read had raised a presumption that he was in orders. But, in an age which produced such laymen as William Cecil and Nicholas Bacon, Roger Ascham and Thomas Smith, Walter Mildmay and Francis Walsingham, there was no reason for calling away prelates from their dioceses to negotiate treaties, to superintend the finances, or to administer justice. The spiritual character not only ceased to be a qualification for high civil office, but began to be regarded as a disqualification. Those worldly motives, therefore, which had formerly induced so many able, aspiring, and high born youths to assume the ecclesiastical habit, ceased to operate. Not one parish in two hundred then afforded what a man of family considered as a maintenance. There were still indeed prizes in the Church: but they were few; and even the highest were mean, when compared with the glory which had once surrounded the princes of the hierarchy. The state kept by Parker and Grindal[20] seemed beggarly to those who remembered the imperial pomp of Wolsey, his palaces, which had become the favourite abodes of royalty, Whitehall and Hampton Court, the three sumptuous tables daily spread in his refectory, the forty-four gorgeous copes in his chapel,

---

[15] Tax of the tenth part, in kind or in value, of the produce of the land, for the support of the clergy.

[16] Gregory King (1648–1712), author of *Natural and Political Observations and Conclusions upon the State and Condition of England* (1696).

[17] Charles Davenant (1656–1714), son of the dramatist, a political economist.   [18] Two of the highest offices in the state.

[19] The shaven patch on the crown of the head, the badge of the monastic and ecclesiastical professions.

[20] Two archbishops of Canterbury in the latter half of the sixteenth century. Wolsey had been the archbishop at the beginning of the century.

his running footmen in rich liveries, and his body guards with gilded poleaxes. Thus the sacerdotal office lost its attraction for the higher classes. During the century which followed the accession of Elizabeth, scarce a single person of noble descent took orders. At the close of the reign of Charles the Second, two sons of peers were Bishops; four or five sons of peers were priests, and held valuable preferment: but these rare exceptions did not take away the reproach which lay on the body. The clergy were regarded as, on the whole, a plebeian class. And, indeed, for one who made the figure of a gentleman, ten were mere menial servants. A large proportion of those divines who had no benefices, or whose benefices were too small to afford a comfortable revenue, lived in the houses of laymen. It had long been evident that this practice tended to degrade the priestly character. Laud[21] had exerted himself to effect a change; and Charles the First had repeatedly issued positive orders that none but men of high rank should presume to keep domestic chaplains. But these injunctions had become obsolete. Indeed, during the domination of the Puritans, many of the ejected ministers of the Church of England could obtain bread and shelter only by attaching themselves to the households of royalist gentlemen; and the habits which had been formed in those times of trouble continued long after the re-establishment of monarchy and episcopacy. In the mansions of men of liberal sentiments and cultivated understandings, the chaplain was doubtless treated with urbanity and kindness. His conversation, his literary assistance, his spiritual advice, were considered as an ample return for his food, his lodging, and his stipend. But this was not the general feeling of the country gentlemen. The coarse and ignorant squire, who thought that it belonged to his dignity to have grace said every day at his table by an ecclesiastic in full canonicals, found means to reconcile dignity with economy. A young Levite—such was the phrase then in use—might be had for his board, a small garret, and ten pounds a year, and might not only perform his own professional functions, might not only be the most patient of butts and of listeners, might not only be always ready in fine weather for bowls, and in rainy weather for shovel-board,[22] but might also save the expense of a gardener, or of a groom. Sometimes the reverend man nailed up the apricots; and sometimes he curried the coach horses. He cast up the farrier's bills. He walked ten miles with a message or a parcel. He was permitted to dine with the family; but he was expected to content himself with the plainest fare. He might fill himself with the corned beef and the carrots: but, as soon as the tarts and cheesecakes made their appearance, he quitted his seat, and stood aloof till he was summoned to return thanks for the repast, from a great part of which he had been excluded.

Perhaps, after some years of service, he was presented to a living sufficient to support him: but he often found it necessary to purchase his preferment by a species of Simony,[23] which furnished an inexhaustible subject of pleasantry to three or four generations of scoffers. With his cure he was expected to take a wife. The wife had ordinarily been in the patron's service; and it was well if she was not suspected of standing too high in the patron's favour. Indeed, the nature of the matrimonial connections which the clergymen of that age were in the habit of forming is the most certain indication of the place which the order held in the social system. An Oxonian, writing a few months after the death of Charles the Second, complained bitterly, not only that the country attorney and the country apothecary looked down with disdain on the country clergyman, but that one of the lessons most earnestly inculcated on every girl of honourable family was to give no encouragement to a lover in orders, and that, if any young lady forgot this precept, she was almost as much disgraced as by an illicit amour. Clarendon,[24] who assuredly bore no ill will to the priesthood, mentions it as a sign of the confusion of ranks which the great rebellion had produced, that some damsels of noble families had bestowed themselves on divines. A waiting woman was generally considered as the most suitable helpmate for a parson. Queen Elizabeth, as head of the Church, had given what seemed to be a formal sanction to this prejudice, by issuing special orders that no clergyman should presume to espouse a servant girl, without the consent of the master or mistress. During several generations accordingly the relation between divines and handmaidens was a theme for endless jest; nor would it be easy to find, in the comedy of the seventeenth century, a single instance of a clergyman who wins a spouse above the rank of a cook. Even so late as the time of George the Second, the keenest of all observers of life and manners, himself a priest,[25] remarked that, in a great

---

21 Archbishop of Canterbury under Charles I.
22 I.e., shuffleboard.

23 The purchase or sale of ecclesiastical office.
24 Lord Chancellor under Charles II and author of *The History of the Rebellion and Civil Wars in England.*
25 Jonathan Swift (1667–1745), famous English satirist and Dean of St. Patrick's Cathedral, Dublin, in his *Directions to Servants.*

household, the chaplain was the resource of a lady's maid whose character had been blown upon, and who was therefore forced to give up hopes of catching the steward.

In general the divine who quitted his chaplainship for a benefice and a wife found that he had only exchanged one class of vexations for another. Hardly one living in fifty enabled the incumbent to bring up a family comfortably. As children multiplied and grew, the household of the priest became more and more beggarly. Holes appeared more and more plainly in the thatch of his parsonage and in his single cassock. Often it was only by toiling on his glebe,[26] by feeding swine, and by loading dungcarts, that he could obtain daily bread; nor did his utmost exertions always prevent the bailiffs from taking his concordance and his inkstand in execution. It was a white day on which he was admitted into the kitchen of a great house, and regaled by the servants with cold meat and ale. His children were brought up like the children of the neighbouring peasantry. His boys followed the plough; and his girls went out to service. Study he found impossible: for the advowson[27] of his living would hardly have sold for a sum sufficient to purchase a good theological library; and he might be considered as unusually lucky if he had ten or twelve dog-eared volumes among the pots and pans on his shelves. Even a keen and strong intellect might be expected to rust in so unfavourable a situation.

Assuredly there was at that time no lack in the English Church of ministers distinguished by abilities and learning. But it is to be observed that these ministers were not scattered among the rural population. They were brought together at a few places where the means of acquiring knowledge were abundant, and where the opportunities of vigorous intellectual exercise were frequent. At such places were to be found divines qualified by parts, by eloquence, by wide knowledge of literature, of science, and of life, to defend their Church victoriously against heretics and sceptics, to command the attention of frivolous and worldly congregations, to guide the deliberations of senates, and to make religion respectable, even in the most dissolute of courts. Some laboured to fathom the abysses of metaphysical theology: some were deeply versed in biblical criticism; and some threw light on the darkest parts of ecclesiastical history. Some proved themselves consummate masters of logic. Some cultivated rhetoric with such assiduity and success that their discourses are still justly valued as models of style. These eminent men were to be found, with scarcely a single exception, at the Universities, at the great Cathedrals, or in the capital. . . .

Literature which could be carried by the post bag then formed the greater part of the intellectual nutriment ruminated by the country divines and country justices. The difficulty and expense of conveying large packets from place to place were so great that an extensive work was longer in making its way from Paternoster Row to Devonshire or Lancashire than it now is in reaching Kentucky. How scantily a rural parsonage was then furnished, even with books the most necessary to a theologian, has already been remarked. The houses of the gentry were not more plentifully supplied. Few knights of the shire had libraries so good as may now perpetually be found in a servants' hall or in the back parlour of a small shopkeeper. An esquire passed among his neighbours for a great scholar if *Hudibras* and *Baker's Chronicle, Tarlton's Jests,* and the *Seven Champions of Christendom* lay in his hall window among the fishing-rods and fowling-pieces. No circulating library, no book society then existed even in the capital; but in the capital those students who could not afford to purchase largely had a resource. The shops of the great booksellers, near St. Paul's Churchyard, were crowded every day and all day long with readers, and a known customer was often permitted to carry a volume home. In the country there was no such accommodation, and every man was under the necessity of buying whatever he wished to read.

As to the lady of the manor and her daughters, their literary stores generally consisted of a prayer book and a receipt book. But in truth they lost little by living in rural seclusion. For even in the highest ranks and in those situations which afforded the greatest facilities for mental improvement, the English women of that generation were decidedly worse educated than they have been at any other time since the Revival of Learning. At an earlier period, they had studied the masterpieces of ancient genius. In the present day, they seldom bestow much attention on the dead languages, but they are familiar with the tongue of Pascal and Molière, with the tongue of Dante and Tasso, with the tongue of Goethe and Schiller;[28] nor is there any purer or more graceful English than that which accomplished women now speak and write. But during the latter part of the seventeenth century, the culture of the female mind seems to have been almost entirely

---

[26] Cultivated plot of ground.   [27] Patronage.

[28] French, Italian, and German, respectively.

neglected. If a damsel had the least smattering of literature, she was regarded as a prodigy. Ladies highly born, highly bred, and naturally quick-witted were unable to write a line in their mother tongue without solecisms and faults of spelling such as a charity girl would now be ashamed to commit.

The explanation may easily be found. Extravagant licentiousness, the natural effect of extravagant austerity, was now the mode; and licentiousness had produced its ordinary effect, the moral and intellectual degradation of women. To their personal beauty it was the fashion to pay rude and impudent homage. But the admiration and desire which they inspired were seldom mingled with respect, with affection, or with any chivalrous sentiment. The qualities which fit them to be companions, advisers, confidential friends, rather repelled than attracted the libertines of Whitehall. In that court, a maid of honour, who dressed in such a manner as to do full justice to a white bosom, who ogled significantly, who danced voluptuously, who excelled in pert repartee, who was not ashamed to romp with lords of the bedchamber and captains of the guards, to sing sly verses with sly expression, or to put on a page's dress for a frolic, was more likely to be followed and admired, more likely to be honoured with royal attentions, more likely to win a rich and noble husband than Jane Grey or Lucy Hutchinson[29] would have been. In such circumstances the standard of female attainments was necessarily low; and it was more dangerous to be above that standard than to be beneath it. Extreme ignorance and frivolity were thought less unbecoming in a lady than the slightest tincture of pedantry. Of the too celebrated women whose faces we still admire on the walls of Hampton Court, few indeed were in the habit of reading anything more valuable than acrostics, lampoons, and translations of the *Clelia* and the *Grand Cyrus*.[30]

The literary acquirements, even of the accomplished gentlemen of that generation, seem to have been somewhat less solid and profound than at an earlier or a later period. Greek learning, at least, did not flourish among us in the days of Charles the Second as it had flourished before the Civil War, or as it again flourished long after the Revolution. There were undoubtedly scholars to whom the whole Greek literature from Homer to Photius[31] was familiar; but such scholars were to be found almost exclusively among the clergy resident at the Universities, and even at the Universities were few, and were not fully appreciated. At Cambridge it was not thought by any means necessary that a divine should be able to read the Gospels in the original. Nor was the standard at Oxford higher. When, in the reign of William the Third, Christ Church rose up as one man to defend the genuineness of the Epistles of Phalaris,[32] that great college, then considered as the first seat of philology in the kingdom, could not muster such a stock of Attic learning as is now possessed by several youths at every great public school. It may easily be supposed that a dead language, neglected at the Universities, was not much studied by men of the world. In a former age, the poetry and eloquence of Greece had been the delight of Raleigh and Falkland. In a later age, the poetry and eloquence of Greece were the delight of Pitt and Fox, of Windham and Grenville. But during the latter part of the seventeenth century there was in England scarcely one eminent statesman who could read with enjoyment a page of Sophocles or Plato.

Good Latin scholars were numerous. The language of Rome, indeed, had not altogether lost its imperial character, and was still, in many parts of Europe, almost indispensable to a traveller or a negotiator. To speak it well was therefore a much more common accomplishment than in our time; and neither Oxford nor Cambridge wanted poets who, on a great occasion, could lay at the foot of the throne happy imitations of the verses in which Virgil and Ovid had celebrated the greatness of Augustus.

Yet even the Latin was giving way to a younger rival. France united at that time almost every species of ascendency. Her military glory was at the height. She had vanquished mighty coalitions. She had dictated treaties. She had subjected great cities and provinces. She had forced the Castilian pride to yield her the precedence. She had summoned Italian princes to prostrate themselves at her footstool. Her authority was supreme in all matters of good breeding, from a duel to a minuet. She determined how a gentleman's coat must be cut, how long his peruke must be, whether his heels must be high or low, and whether the lace on his hat must be broad or narrow. In literature she gave law to the world. The fame of her

[29] Lady Jane Grey (1537–54) was a pupil of Roger Ascham and a distinguished student and humanist, while Lucy Hutchinson (b. 1620) was the loyal and esteemed wife of a distinguished Puritan leader, whose biography she wrote.

[30] Two immensely popular French heroic romances by Mademoiselle de Scudéry.

[31] A classical scholar of the ninth century.

[32] The controversy over the genuineness of these letters forms part of the background of Swift's *Battle of the Books*. Macaulay's point is that the scholars at Christ Church were not really equipped to certify the letters to be either genuine or spurious.

great writers filled Europe. No other country could produce a tragic poet equal to Racine, a comic poet equal to Molière, a trifler so agreeable as La Fontaine, a rhetorician so skillful as Bossuet. The literary glory of Italy and of Spain had set; that of Germany had not yet dawned. The genius, therefore, of the eminent men who adorned Paris shone forth with a splendour which was set off to full advantage by contrast. France, indeed, had at that time an empire over mankind, such as even the Roman Republic never attained. For when Rome was politically dominant, she was in arts and letters the humble pupil of Greece. France had, over the surrounding countries, at once the ascendency which Rome had over Greece, and the ascendency which Greece had over Rome. French was fast becoming the universal language, the language of fashionable society, the language of diplomacy. At several courts princes and nobles spoke it more accurately and politely than their mother tongue. In our island there was less of this servility than on the Continent. Neither our good nor our bad qualities were those of imitators. Yet even here homage was paid, awkwardly indeed and sullenly, to the literary supremacy of our neighbours. The melodious Tuscan,[33] so familiar to the gallants and ladies of the court of Elizabeth, sank into contempt. A gentleman who quoted Horace or Terence was considered in good company as a pompous pedant. But to garnish his conversation with scraps of French was the best proof which he could give of his parts and attainments. New canons of criticism, new models of style came into fashion. The quaint ingenuity which had deformed the verses of Donne and had been a blemish on those of Cowley[34] disappeared from our poetry. Our prose became less majestic, less artfully involved, less variously musical than that of an earlier age, but more lucid, more easy, and better fitted for controversy and narrative. In these changes it is impossible not to recognise the influence of French precept and of French example. Great masters of our language, in their most dignified compositions, affected to use French words when English words, quite as expressive and melodious, were at hand: and from France was imported the tragedy in rhyme, an exotic which, in our soil, drooped and speedily died.

It would have been well if our writers had also copied the decorum which their great French contemporaries, with few exceptions, preserved; for the profligacy of the English plays, satires, songs, and novels of that age is a deep blot on our national fame. The evil may easily be traced to its source. The wits and the Puritans had never been on friendly terms. There was no sympathy between the two classes. They looked on the whole system of human life from different points and in different lights. The earnest of each was the jest of the other. The pleasures of each were the torments of the other. To the stern precisian even the innocent sport of the fancy seemed a crime. To light and festive natures the solemnity of the zealous brethren furnished copious matter of ridicule. From the Reformation to the Civil War, almost every writer, gifted with a fine sense of the ludicrous, had taken some opportunity of assailing the straight-haired, snuffling, whining saints, who christened their children out of the Book of Nehemiah, who groaned in spirit at the sight of Jack in the Green,[35] and who thought it impious to taste plum porridge on Christmas Day. At length a time came when the laughers began to look grave in their turn. The rigid, ungainly zealots, after having furnished much good sport during two generations, rose up in arms, conquered, ruled, and, grimly smiling, trod down under their feet the whole crowd of mockers. The wounds inflicted by gay and petulant malice were retaliated with the gloomy and implacable malice peculiar to bigots who mistake their own rancour for virtue. The theatres were closed. The players were flogged. The press was put under the guardianship of austere licensers. The Muses were banished from their own favourite haunts, Cambridge and Oxford. Cowley, Crashaw, and Cleveland were ejected from their fellowships.[36] The young candidate for academical honours was no longer required to write Ovidian epistles or Virgilian pastorals, but was strictly interrogated by a synod of lowering Supralapsarians[37] as to the day and hour when he experienced the new birth. Such a system was of course fruitful of hypocrites. Under sober clothing and under visages composed to the expression of austerity lay hid during several years the intense desire of license and of revenge. At length that desire was gratified. The Restoration emancipated thousands of minds from a yoke

---

[33] The sonnets of Petrarch, written in the Tuscan dialect, had great vogue and influence in Elizabethan literary circles.
[34] On Donne, see I, 423 ff., above; on Cowley, I, 524 ff.

[35] A traditional figure, decked with boughs, at the May Day festivals.
[36] On Crashaw, see I, 500 ff., above. John Cleveland (1613-58) was a poet of considerable contemporary fame. All three were ejected because of their Royalist sympathies, and Crashaw was doubly suspect as a Roman Catholic.
[37] A particular group of Calvinists believing that the salvation of any particular individual was determined before the Fall of Man.

which had become insupportable. The old fight recommenced, but with an animosity altogether new. It was now not a sportive combat, but a war to the death. The Roundhead had no better quarter to expect from those whom he had persecuted than a cruel slave-driver can expect from insurgent slaves still bearing the marks of his collars and his scourges.

The war between wit and Puritanism soon became a war between wit and morality. The hostility excited by a grotesque caricature of virtue did not spare virtue herself. Whatever the canting Roundhead had regarded with reverence was insulted. Whatever he had proscribed was favoured. Because he had been scrupulous about trifles, all scruples were treated with derision. Because he had covered his failings with the mask of devotion, men were encouraged to obtrude with cynic impudence all their most scandalous vices on the public eye. Because he had punished illicit love with barbarous severity, virgin purity and conjugal fidelity were to be made a jest. To that sanctimonious jargon, which was his Shibboleth, was opposed another jargon not less absurd and much more odious. As he never opened his mouth except in scriptural phrase, the new breed of wits and fine gentlemen never opened their mouths without uttering ribaldry of which a porter would now be ashamed, and without calling on their Maker to curse them, sink them, confound them, blast them, and damn them.

It is not strange, therefore, that our polite literature, when it revived with the revival of the old civil and ecclesiastical polity, should have been profoundly immoral. A few eminent men, who belonged to an earlier and better age, were exempt from the general contagion. The verse of Waller[38] still breathed the sentiments which had animated a more chivalrous generation. Cowley, distinguished at once as a loyalist and as a man of letters, raised his voice courageously against the immorality which disgraced both letters and loyalty. A mightier spirit,[39] unsubdued by pain, danger, poverty, obloquy, and blindness, meditated, undisturbed by the obscene tumult which raged all around, a song so sublime and so holy that it would not have misbecome the lips of those ethereal Virtues whom he saw, with that inner eye which no calamity could darken, flinging down on the jasper pavement their crowns of amaranth and gold. The vigorous and fertile genius of Butler,[40] if it did not altogether escape the prevailing infection, took the disease in a mild form. But these were men whose minds had been trained in a world which had passed away. They gave place in no long time to a younger generation of poets, and of that generation, from Dryden down to Durfey,[41] the common characteristic was hard-hearted, shameless, swaggering licentiousness, at once inelegant and inhuman. The influence of these writers was doubtless noxious, yet less noxious than it would have been had they been less depraved. The poison which they administered was so strong that it was, in no long time, rejected with nausea. None of them understood the dangerous art of associating images of unlawful pleasure with all that is endearing and ennobling. None of them was aware that a certain decorum is essential even to voluptuousness, that drapery may be more alluring than exposure, and that the imagination may be far more powerfully moved by delicate hints which impel it to exert itself than by gross descriptions which it takes in passively.

The spirit of the Anti-Puritan reaction pervades almost the whole polite literature of the reign of Charles the Second. But the very quintessence of that spirit will be found in the comic drama. The playhouses, shut by the meddling fanatic in the day of his power, were again crowded. To their old attractions new and more powerful attractions had been added. Scenery, dresses, and decorations such as would now be thought mean and absurd, but such as would have been esteemed incredibly magnificent by those who, early in the seventeenth century, sat on the filthy benches of the Hope or under the thatched roof of the Rose,[42] dazzled the eyes of the multitude. The fascination of sex was called in to aid the fascination of art; and the young spectator saw, with emotions unknown to the contemporaries of Shakspeare and Jonson, tender and sprightly heroines personified by lovely women. From the day on which the theatres were reopened they became seminaries of vice, and the evil propagated itself. The profligacy of the representations soon drove away sober people. The frivolous and dissolute who remained required every year stronger and stronger stimulants. Thus the artists corrupted the spectators, and the spectators the artists,

38 Edmund Waller (see I, 517 ff., above), who managed to survive successfully the political changes of the seventeenth century.
39 Milton.

40 On Samuel Butler, see I, 519 ff. His mock-heroic satire on the Presbyterians and Independents, entitled *Hudibras,* was one of the books which might be found in the "hall window" of the country squire (p. 477, above).
41 Thomas D'Urfey (1653-1723), dramatist and song writer, attached to the courts of Charles II and James II.
42 Two popular theaters.

till the turpitude of the drama became such as must astonish all who are not aware that extreme relaxation is the natural effect of extreme restraint, and that an age of hypocrisy is, in the regular course of things, followed by an age of impudence.

Nothing is more characteristic of the times than the care with which the poets contrived to put all their loosest verses into the mouths of women. The compositions in which the greatest license was taken were the epilogues. They were almost always recited by favourite actresses, and nothing charmed the depraved audience so much as to hear lines grossly indecent repeated by a beautiful girl, who was supposed to have not yet lost her innocence.

Our theatre was indebted in that age for many plots and characters to Spain, to France, and to the old English masters; but whatever our dramatists touched they tainted. In their imitations the houses of Calderon's[43] stately and high spirited Castilian gentlemen became sties of vice, Shakspeare's Viola a procuress, Molière's misanthrope a ravisher, Molière's Agnes an adulteress. Nothing could be so pure or so heroic but that it became foul and ignoble by transfusion through those foul and ignoble minds.

Such was the state of the drama; and the drama was the department of light literature in which a poet had the best chance of obtaining a subsistence by his pen. The sale of books was so small that a man of the greatest name could expect only a pittance for the copyright of the best performance. There cannot be a stronger instance than the fate of Dryden's last production, the *Fables*. That volume was published when he was universally admitted to be the chief of living English poets. It contains about twelve thousand lines. The versification is admirable, the narratives and descriptions full of life. To this day *Palamon and Arcite, Cymon and Iphigenia, Theodore and Honoria* are the delight both of critics and of schoolboys. The collection includes *Alexander's Feast,* the noblest ode in our language. For the copyright Dryden received two hundred and fifty pounds, less than in our days has sometimes been paid for two articles in a review. Nor does the bargain seem to have been a hard one. For the book went off slowly, and a second edition was not required till the author had been ten years in his grave. By writing for the theatre it was possible to earn a much larger sum with much less trouble. Southern made seven hundred pounds by one play. Otway was raised from beggary to temporary afflu-

ence by the success of his *Don Carlos*. Shadwell cleared a hundred and thirty pounds by a single representation of the *Squire of Alsatia*. The consequence was that every man who had to live by his wit wrote plays whether he had any internal vocation to write plays or not. It was thus with Dryden. As a satirist he has rivaled Juvenal. As a didactic poet he perhaps might, with care and meditation, have rivalled Lucretius. Of lyric poets he is, if not the most sublime, the most brilliant and spirit-stirring. But nature, profuse to him of many rare gifts, had denied him the dramatic faculty. Nevertheless all the energies of his best years were wasted on dramatic composition. He had too much judgment not to be aware that in the power of exhibiting character by means of dialogue he was deficient. That deficiency he did his best to conceal, sometimes by surprising and amusing incidents, sometimes by stately declamation, sometimes by harmonious numbers, sometimes by ribaldry but too well suited to the taste of a profane and licentious pit. Yet he never obtained any theatrical success equal to that which rewarded the exertions of some men far inferior to him in general powers. He thought himself fortunate if he cleared a hundred guineas by a play; a scanty remuneration, yet apparently larger than he could have earned in any other way by the same quantity of labour.

The recompense which the wits of that age could obtain from the public was so small that they were under the necessity of eking out their incomes by levying contributions on the great. Every rich and good-natured lord was pestered by authors with a mendicancy so importunate, and a flattery so abject, as may in our time seem incredible. The patron to whom a work was inscribed was expected to reward the writer with a purse of gold. The fee paid for the dedication of a book was often much larger than the sum which any bookseller would give for the copyright. Books were therefore often printed merely that they might be dedicated. This traffic in praise completed the degradation of the literary character. Adulation pushed to the verge, sometimes of nonsense and sometimes of impiety, was not thought to disgrace a poet. Independence, veracity, self-respect, were things not expected by the world from him. In truth, he was in morals something between a pandar and a beggar.

To the other vices which degraded the literary character was added, toward the close of the reign of Charles the Second, the most savage intemperance of party spirit. The wits, as a class, had been impelled by their old hatred of Puritanism to take the side of the court, and had been found useful allies. Dryden,

---

[43] Celebrated Spanish poet and dramatist (1600–81).

in particular, had done good service to the government. His *Absalom and Achitophel,* the greatest satire of modern times, had amazed the town, had made its way with unprecedented rapidity even into rural districts, and had, wherever it appeared, bitterly annoyed the Exclusionists[44] and raised the courage of the Tories. But we must not, in the admiration which we naturally feel for noble diction and versification, forget the great distinctions of good and evil. The spirit by which Dryden and several of his compeers were at this time animated against the Whigs deserves to be called fiendish. The servile judges and sheriffs of those evil days could not shed blood so fast as the poets cried out for it. Calls for more victims, hideous jests on hanging, bitter taunts on those who, having stood by the king in the hour of danger, now advised him to deal mercifully and generously by his vanquished enemies, were publicly recited on the stage, and, that nothing might be wanting to the guilt and the shame, were recited by women, who, having long been taught to discard all modesty, were now taught to discard all compassion.

It is a remarkable fact that, while the lighter literature of England was thus becoming a nuisance and a national disgrace, the English genius was effecting in science a revolution which will, to the end of time, be reckoned among the highest achievements of the human intellect. Bacon had sown the good seed in a sluggish soil and an ungenial season. He had not expected an early crop, and in his last testament had solemnly bequeathed his fame to the next age. During a whole generation his philosophy had, amidst tumults, wars, and proscriptions, been slowly ripening in a few well-constituted minds. While factions were struggling for dominion over each other, a small body of sages had turned away with benevolent disdain from the conflict, and had devoted themselves to the nobler work of extending the dominion of man over matter. As soon as tranquillity was restored, these teachers easily found attentive audience. For the discipline through which the nation had passed had brought the public mind to a temper well fitted for the reception of the Verulamian[45] doctrine. The civil troubles had stimulated the faculties of the educated classes and had called forth a rest-

less activity and an insatiable curiosity such as had not before been known among us. Yet the effect of those troubles had been that schemes of political and religious reform were generally regarded with suspicion and contempt. During twenty years the chief employment of busy and ingenious men had been to frame constitutions with first magistrates, without first magistrates, with hereditary senates, with senates appointed by lot, with annual senates, with perpetual senates. In these plans nothing was omitted. All the detail, all the nomenclature, all the ceremonial of the imaginary government was fully set forth—Polemarchs and Phylarchs, Tribes and Galaxies, the Lord Archon and the Lord Strategus. Which ballot boxes were to be green and which red, which balls were to be of gold and which of silver, which magistrates were to wear hats and which black velvet caps with peaks, how the mace was to be carried and when the heralds were to uncover,—these and a hundred more such trifles were gravely considered and arranged by men of no common capacity and learning. But the time for these visions had gone by; and, if any steadfast republican still continued to amuse himself with them, fear of public derision and of a criminal information generally induced him to keep his fancies to himself. It was now unpopular and unsafe to mutter a word against the fundamental laws of the monarchy; but daring and ingenious men might indemnify themselves by treating with disdain what had lately been considered as the fundamental laws of nature. The torrent which had been dammed up in one channel rushed violently into another. The revolutionary spirit, ceasing to operate in politics, began to exert itself with unprecedented vigour and hardihood in every department of physics. The year 1660, the era of the restoration of the old constitution, is also the era from which dates the ascendency of the new philosophy. In that year the Royal Society,[46] destined to be a chief agent in a long series of glorious and salutary reforms, began to exist. In a few months experimental science became all the mode. The transfusion of blood, the ponderation of air, the fixation of mercury, succeeded to that place in the public mind which had been lately occupied by the controversies of the Rota.[47] Dreams of perfect forms of government made way for dreams of wings with which men were to fly from the Tower to the Abbey, and of double-keeled ships which were never to

---

[44] The poem attacks the Whig attempt by the Exclusion Bill and other means to exclude James, Duke of York, from succession to the English throne. Macaulay as a Whig was resentful of Dryden's "exposure" of the characters of the Whig leaders, the more so since if their measure had been adopted, the disastrous, if brief, reign of James II might have been avoided.
[45] Francis Bacon held the title of Lord Verulam.

[46] Founded to pursue the new philosophy of scientific induction outlined by Bacon. It included in its membership scientists, artists, men of letters, and churchmen.
[47] A political club of republican bent, founded in 1659.

founder in the fiercest storm. All classes were hurried along by the prevailing sentiment. Cavalier and Roundhead, Churchman and Puritan were for once allied. Divines, jurists, statesmen, nobles, princes swelled the triumph of the Baconian philosophy. Poets sang with emulous fervour the approach of the golden age. Cowley, in lines weighty with thought and resplendent with wit,[48] urged the chosen seed to take possession of the promised land flowing with milk and honey, that land which their great deliverer and lawgiver had seen as from the summit of Pisgah, but had not been permitted to enter. Dryden, with more zeal than knowledge, joined his voice to the general acclamation, and foretold things which neither he nor anybody else understood. The Royal Society, he predicted,[49] would soon lead us to the extreme verge of the globe, and there delight us with a better view of the moon. Two able and aspiring prelates, Ward, Bishop of Salisbury, and Wilkins, Bishop of Chester, were conspicuous among the leaders of the movement. Its history was eloquently written by a younger divine who was rising to high distinction in his profession, Thomas Sprat, afterwards Bishop of Rochester. Both Chief Justice Hale and Lord Keeper Guildford stole some hours from the business of their courts to write on hydrostatics. Indeed it was under the immediate directions of Guildford that the first barometers ever exposed to sale in London were constructed. Chemistry divided, for a time, with wine and love, with the stage and the gaming-table, with the intrigues of a courtier and the intrigues of a demagogue, the attention of the fickle Buckingham.[50] Rupert has the credit of having invented mezzotinto, and from him is named that curious bubble of glass which has long amused children and puzzled philosophers.[51] Charles himself had a laboratory at Whitehall, and was far more active and attentive there than at the council board. It was almost necessary to the character of a fine gentleman to have something to say about air-pumps and telescopes; and even fine ladies, now and then, thought it becoming to affect a taste for science, went in coaches and six to visit the Gresham curiosities,[52] and broke forth into cries of delight at finding that a magnet really attracted a needle, and that a microscope really made a fly look as large as a sparrow.

In this, as in every great stir of the human mind, there was doubtless something which might well move a smile. It is the universal law that whatever pursuit, whatever doctrine becomes fashionable shall lose a portion of that dignity which it had possessed while it was confined to a small but earnest minority, and was loved for its own sake alone. It is true that the follies of some persons who, without any real aptitude for science, professed a passion for it, furnished matter of contemptuous mirth to a few malignant satirists who belonged to the preceding generation, and were not disposed to unlearn the lore of their youth. But it is not less true that the great work of interpreting nature was performed by the English of that age as it had never before been performed in any age by any nation. The spirit of Francis Bacon was abroad, a spirit admirably compounded of audacity and sobriety. There was a strong persuasion that the whole world was full of secrets of high moment to the happiness of man, and that man had, by his Maker, been intrusted with the key which, rightly used, would give access to them. There was at the same time a conviction that in physics it was impossible to arrive at the knowledge of general laws except by the careful observation of particular facts. Deeply impressed with these great truths, the professors of the new philosophy applied themselves to their task, and before a quarter of a century had expired, they had given ample earnest of what has since been achieved. Already a reform of agriculture had been commenced. New vegetables were cultivated. New implements of husbandry were employed. New manures were applied to the soil. Evelyn had, under the formal sanction of the Royal Society, given instruction to his countrymen in planting.[53] Temple,[54] in his intervals of leisure, had tried many experiments in horticulture, and had proved that many delicate fruits, the natives of more favoured climates, might, with the help of art, be grown on English ground. Medicine, which in France was still in abject bondage and afforded an inexhaustible subject of just ridicule to Molière, had in England become an experimental and progressive

[48] In his "Ode to the Royal Society."
[49] In his poem entitled "Annus Mirabilis."
[50] Court favorite and member of the Cabal or personal cabinet of Charles II, notoriously licentious.
[51] Prince Rupert, Count Palatine and Duke of Bavaria (1619–82), invented a pear-shaped bubble made by dripping molten glass into water.
[52] Gresham College was the meeting place of the Royal Society, and there they also had a "repository" for their instruments and rarities.
[53] John Evelyn (1620–1706), chiefly remembered for his *Diary*, was an enthusiastic member of the Royal Society. His instruction in planting was embodied in his *Sylva*, which was widely read.
[54] Sir William Temple (1628–99), British diplomat and writer, also a devotee of gardening. He was one of the major figures in the controversy over the *Epistles of Phalaris* (p. 478, above).

science, and every day made some new advance, in defiance of Hippocrates and Galen.[55] The attention of speculative men had been, for the first time, directed to the important subject of sanitary police. The great plague of 1665 induced them to consider with care the defective architecture, draining, and ventilation of the capital. The great fire of 1666 afforded an opportunity for effecting extensive improvements. The whole matter was diligently examined by the Royal Society, and to the suggestions of that body must be partly attributed the changes which, though far short of what the public welfare required, yet made a wide difference between the new and the old London, and probably put a final close to the ravages of pestilence in our country. At the same time one of the founders of the society, Sir William Petty, created the science of political arithmetic, the humble but indispensable handmaid of political philosophy. To that period belonged the chemical discoveries of Boyle and the first botanical researches of Sloane. One after another, phantoms which had haunted the world through ages of darkness fled before the light. Astrology and alchemy became jests. Soon there was scarcely a county in which some of the quorum[56] did not smile contemptuously when an old woman was brought before them for riding on broomsticks or giving cattle the murrain. But it was in those noblest and most arduous departments of knowledge in which induction and mathematical demonstration cooperate for the discovery of truth that the English genius won in that age the most memorable triumphs. John Wallis placed the whole system of statics on a new foundation. Edmund Halley investigated the properties of the atmosphere, the ebb and flow of the sea, the laws of magnetism, and the course of the comets; nor did he shrink from toil, peril, and exile in the cause of science. While he, on the rock of St. Helena, mapped the constellations of the southern hemisphere, our national observatory was rising at Greenwich; and John Flamsteed, the first astronomer royal, was commencing that long series of observations which is never mentioned without respect and gratitude in any part of the globe. But the glory of these men, eminent as they were, is cast into the shade by the transcendent lustre of one immortal name. In Isaac Newton two kinds of intellectual power which have little in common and which are not often found together in a very high degree of vigour, but which

nevertheless are equally necessary in the most sublime departments of natural philosophy, were united as they have never been united before or since. There may have been minds as happily constituted as his for the cultivation of pure mathematical science; there may have been minds as happily constituted for the cultivation of science purely experimental; but in no other mind have the demonstrative faculty and the inductive faculty coexisted in such supreme excellence and perfect harmony. Perhaps in an age of Scotists and Thomists[57] even his intellect might have run to waste, as many intellects ran to waste which were inferior only to his. Happily the spirit of the age on which his lot was cast gave the right direction to his mind; and his mind reacted with tenfold force on the spirit of the age. In the year 1685 his fame, though splendid, was only dawning; but his genius was in the meridian. His great work, that work which effected a revolution in the most important provinces of natural philosophy, had been completed, but was not yet published, and was just about to be submitted to the consideration of the Royal Society.

It is not very easy to explain why the nation which was so far before its neighbours in science should in art have been far behind them all. Yet such was the fact. It is true that in architecture, an art which is half a science, an art in which none but a geometrician can excel, an art which has no standard of grace but what is directly or indirectly dependent on utility, an art of which the creations derive a part, at least, of their majesty from mere bulk, our country could boast of one truly great man, Christopher Wren; and the fire which laid London in ruins had given him an opportunity, unprecedented in modern history, of displaying his powers. The austere beauty of the Athenian portico, the gloomy sublimity of the Gothic arcade, he was, like almost all his contemporaries, incapable of emulating, and perhaps incapable of appreciating; but no man, born on our side of the Alps, has imitated with so much success the magnificence of the palace-like churches of Italy. Even the superb Louis[58] has left to posterity no work which can bear a comparison with Saint Paul's. But at the close of the reign of Charles the Second there was not a single English painter or statuary whose name is now remembered. This sterility is somewhat mysterious, for painters and statuaries were by no means a

---

55 The revered authorities of traditional medicine.
56 Justices of the peace sitting in quarter sessions.

57 The followers respectively of Duns Scotus and Thomas Aquinas, medieval philosophers who seemed to advocates of science like Bacon, Newton, and Macaulay to be wasting their time on fanciful and useless abstractions.
58 Louis XIV of France.

despised or an ill-paid class. Their social position was at least as high as at present. Their gains, when compared with the wealth of the nation and with the remuneration of other descriptions of intellectual labour, were even larger than at present. Indeed, the munificent patronage which was extended to artists drew them to our shores in multitudes. Lely,[59] who has preserved to us the rich curls, the full lips, and the languishing eyes of the frail beauties celebrated by Hamilton,[60] was a Westphalian. He had died in 1680, having long lived splendidly, having received the honour of knighthood, and having accumulated a good estate out of the fruits of his skill. His noble collection of drawings and pictures was, after his decease, exhibited by the royal permission in the Banqueting House at Whitehall, and sold by auction for the almost incredible sum of twenty-six thousand pounds, a sum which bore a greater proportion to the fortunes of the rich men of that day than a hundred thousand pounds would bear to the fortunes of the rich men of our time. Lely was succeeded by his countryman Godfrey Kneller, who was made first a knight and then a baronet, and who, after keeping up a sumptuous establishment, and after losing much money by unlucky speculations, was still able to bequeath a large fortune to his family. The two Vandeveldes, natives of Holland, had been induced by English liberality to settle here, and had produced for the king and his nobles some of the finest sea-pieces in the world. Another Dutchman, Simon Varelst, painted glorious sunflowers and tulips for prices such as had never before been known. Verrio, a Neapolitan, covered ceilings and staircases with Gorgons and Muses, Nymphs and Satyrs, Virtues and Vices, Gods quaffing nectar, and laurelled princes riding in triumph. The income which he derived from his performances enabled him to keep one of the most expensive tables in England. For his pieces at Windsor alone he received seven thousand pounds, a sum then sufficient to make a gentleman of moderate wishes perfectly easy for life, a sum greatly exceeding all that Dryden, during a literary life of forty years, obtained from the booksellers. Verrio's chief assistant and successor, Lewis Laguerre, came from France. The two most celebrated sculptors of that day were also foreigners. Cibber, whose pathetic emblems of Fury and Melancholy still adorn Bedlam,

was a Dane. Gibbons, to whose graceful fancy and delicate touch many of our palaces, colleges, and churches owe their finest decorations, was a Dutchman. Even the designs for the coin were made by French artists. Indeed, it was not till the reign of George the Second that our country could glory in a great painter; and George the Third was on the throne before she had reason to be proud of any of her sculptors.

It is time that this description of the England which Charles the Second governed should draw to a close. Yet one subject of the highest moment still remains untouched. Nothing has yet been said of the great body of the people, of those who held the ploughs, who tended the oxen, who toiled at the looms of Norwich, and squared the Portland stone for St. Paul's. Nor can very much be said. The most numerous class is precisely the class respecting which we have the most meagre information. In those times philanthropists did not yet regard it as a sacred duty, nor had demagogues yet found it a lucrative trade, to talk and write about the distress of the labourer. History was too much occupied with courts and camps to spare a line for the hut of the peasant or the garret of the mechanic. The press now often sends forth in a day a greater quantity of discussion and declamation about the condition of the working man than was published during the twenty-eight years which elapsed between the Restoration and the Revolution. But it would be a great error to infer from the increase of complaint that there has been any increase of misery. . . .

In one respect it must be admitted that the progress of civilisation has diminished the physical comforts of a portion of the poorest class. It has already been mentioned that, before the Revolution, many thousands of square miles, now enclosed and cultivated, were marsh, forest, and heath. Of this wild land much was, by law, common, and much of what was not common by law was worth so little that the proprietors suffered it to be common in fact. In such a tract, squatters and trespassers were tolerated to an extent now unknown. The peasant who dwelt there could, at little or no charge, procure occasionally some palatable addition to his hard fare, and provide himself with fuel for the winter. He kept a flock of geese on what is now an orchard rich with apple blossoms. He snared wild fowl on the fen which has long since been drained and divided into corn fields and turnip fields. He cut turf among the furze bushes on the moor which is now a meadow bright with clover and renowned for butter and cheese. The progress of agriculture and the increase in population

[59] Sir Peter Lely (1618-80), Dutch-English court painter to Charles II.
[60] Anthony Hamilton (1646-1720) wrote the memoirs of the Count de Gramont, his brother-in-law, the second part of which deals with the English court.

necessarily deprived him of these privileges. But against this disadvantage a long list of advantages is to be set off. Of the blessings which civilisation and philosophy bring with them a large proportion is common to all ranks, and would, if withdrawn, be missed as painfully by the labourer as by the peer. The market-place which the rustic can now reach with his cart in an hour was, 160 years ago, a day's journey from him. The street which now affords to the artisan, during the whole night, a secure, a convenient, and a brilliantly lighted walk was, 160 years ago, so dark after sunset that he would not have been able to see his hand, so ill paved that he would have run constant risk of breaking his neck, and so ill watched that he would have been in imminent danger of being knocked down and plundered of his small earnings. . . . Some frightful diseases have been extirpated by science; and some have been banished by police. The term of human life has been lengthened over the whole kingdom, and especially in the towns. . . .

Still more important is the benefit which all orders of society, and especially the lower orders, have derived from the mollifying influence of civilisation on the national character. The groundwork of that character has indeed been the same through many generations, in the sense in which the groundwork of the character of an individual may be said to be the same when he is a rude and thoughtless schoolboy and when he is a refined and accomplished man. It is pleasing to reflect that the public mind of England has softened while it has ripened, and that we have, in the course of ages, become not only a wiser, but also a kinder people. There is scarcely a page of the history or lighter literature of the seventeenth century which does not contain some proof that our ancestors were less humane than their posterity. The discipline of workshops, of schools, of private families, though not more efficient than at present, was infinitely harsher. Masters, well born and bred, were in the habit of beating their servants. Pedagogues knew no way of imparting knowledge but by beating their pupils. Husbands, of decent station, were not ashamed to beat their wives. The implacability of hostile factions was such as we can scarcely conceive. Whigs were disposed to murmur because Stafford was suffered to die without seeing his bowels burned before his face. Tories reviled and insulted Russell as his coach passed from the Tower to the scaffold in Lincoln's Inn Fields. As little mercy was shown by the populace to sufferers of an humbler rank. If an offender was put into the pillory, it was well if he escaped with life from the shower of brick-

bats and paving stones. If he was tied to the cart's tail, the crowd pressed round him, imploring the hangman to give it to the fellow well, and to make him howl. Gentlemen arranged parties of pleasure to Bridewell[61] on court days, for the purpose of seeing the wretched women who beat hemp there whipped. A man pressed to death for refusing to plead, a woman burned for coining excited less sympathy than is now felt for a galled horse or an over-driven ox. Fights, compared with which a boxing match is a refined and humane spectacle, were among the favourite diversions of a large part of the town. Multitudes assembled to see gladiators hack each other to pieces with deadly weapons, and shouted with delight when one of the combatants lost a finger or an eye. The prisons were hells on earth, seminaries of every crime and of every disease. At the assizes[62] the lean and yellow culprits brought with them from their cells to the dock an atmosphere of stench and pestilence which sometimes avenged them signally on bench, bar, and jury. But on all this misery society looked with profound indifference. Nowhere could be found that sensitive and restless compassion which has, in our time, extended a powerful protection to the factory child, to the Hindoo widow, to the negro slave, which pries into the stores and water-casks of every emigrant ship, which winces at every lash laid on the back of a drunken soldier, which will not suffer the thief in the hulks to be ill fed or over-worked, and which has repeatedly endeavoured to save the life even of the murderer. It is true that compassion ought, like all other feelings, to be under the government of reason, and has, for want of such government, produced some ridiculous and some deplorable effects. But the more we study the annals of the past, the more shall we rejoice that we live in a merciful age, in an age in which cruelty is abhorred, and in which pain, even when deserved, is inflicted reluctantly and from a sense of duty. Every class doubtless has gained largely by this great moral change; but the class which has gained most is the poorest, the most dependent, and the most defence-less.[63]

The general effect of the evidence which has been submitted to the reader seems hardly to admit of doubt. Yet, in spite of evidence, many will still image to themselves the England of the Stuarts as a more pleasant country than the England in which we

---

[61] House of correction.
[62] Periodical sessions of the court.
[63] Compare this with a similar passage in Macaulay's review of Southey's *Colloquies*, pp. 457 ff., above.

live. It may at first sight seem strange that society, while constantly moving forward with eager speed, should be constantly looking backward with tender regret. But these two propensities, inconsistent as they may appear, can easily be resolved into the same principle. Both spring from our impatience of the state in which we actually are. That impatience, while it stimulates us to surpass preceding generations, disposes us to overrate their happiness. It is, in some sense, unreasonable and ungrateful in us to be constantly discontented with a condition which is constantly improving. But, in truth, there is constant improvement precisely because there is constant discontent. If we were perfectly satisfied with the present, we should cease to contrive, to labour, and to save with a view to the future. And it is natural that, being dissatisfied with the present, we should form a too favourable estimate of the past.

In truth we are under a deception similar to that which misleads the traveller in the Arabian desert. Beneath the caravan all is dry and bare; but far in advance and far in the rear is the semblance of refreshing waters. The pilgrims hasten forward and find nothing but sand where, an hour before, they had seen a lake. They turn their eyes and see a lake where, an hour before, they were toiling through sand. A similar illusion seems to haunt nations through every stage of the long progress from poverty and barbarism to the highest degrees of opulence and civilisation. But if we resolutely chase the mirage backward, we shall find it recede before us into the regions of fabulous antiquity. It is now the fashion to place the golden age of England in times when noblemen were destitute of comforts the want of which would be intolerable to a modern footman, when farmers and shopkeepers breakfasted on loaves the very sight of which would raise a riot in a modern workhouse, when men died faster in the purest country air than they now die in the most pestilential lanes of our towns, and when men died faster in the lanes of our towns than they now die on the coast of Guiana. We too shall, in our turn, be outstripped, and in our turn be envied. It may well be, in the twentieth century, that the peasant of Dorsetshire may think himself miserably paid with fifteen shillings a week; that the carpenter at Greenwich may receive ten shillings a day; that labouring men may be as little used to dine without meat as they now are to eat ryebread; that sanitary police and medical discoveries may have added several more years to the average length of human life; that numerous comforts and luxuries which are now unknown, or confined to a few, may be within the reach of every diligent and thrifty working man. And yet it may then be the mode to assert that the increase of wealth and the progress of science have benefited the few at the expense of the many, and to talk of the reign of Queen Victoria as the time when England was truly merry England, when all classes were bound together by brotherly sympathy, when the rich did not grind the faces of the poor, and when the poor did not envy the splendour of the rich.

LETTER ON DEMOCRACY[1]

Holly Lodge, Kensington, London,

MAY 23, 1857

Dear Sir:

You are surprised to learn that I have not a high opinion of Mr. Jefferson,[2] and I am surprised at your surprise. I am certain that I never wrote a line, and that I never in Parliament—a place where it is the fashion to court the populace—uttered a word, indicating an opinion that the Supreme authority in a State ought to be trusted to the majority of citizens told by the head;[3] in other words to the poorest and most ignorant part of society. I have long been convinced that institutions purely democratic must, sooner or later destroy liberty or civilization, or both. In Europe, where the population is dense, the effect of such institutions would be instantaneous.

What happened lately in France is an example. In 1848 a pure democracy was established there.[4] During a short time there was reason to expect a general

[1] Addressed to Commodore H. S. Randall of the New York Yacht Club, and reprinted from the *Review of Reviews and World's Work,* XC (July, 1934), 38–39.

[2] Thomas Jefferson (1743–1826), drafter of the American Declaration of Independence and third president of the United States.

[3] Counted by individuals; i.e., universal manhood suffrage.

[4] The Second French Republic, set up on February 24, 1848, provided for universal suffrage and instituted various socialistic measures, but, lacking strong and experienced leadership, it quickly succumbed to the political intrigues of Louis-Napoleon, first as president and then as emperor.

spoliation, a national bankruptcy, a new partition of the soil, a maximum of prices, a ruinous load of taxation laid on the rich for the purpose of supporting the poor in idleness. Such a system would, in twenty years, have made France as poor and barbarous as the France of the Carlovingians. Happily, the danger was averted; and now there is a despotism, a silent tribune, an enslaved press. Liberty is gone but civilization has been saved.

I have not the smallest doubt that, if we had a purely democratic Government here, the effect would be the same. Either the poor would plunder the rich and civilization would perish, or order and prosperity would be saved by a strong military government, and liberty would perish.

You may think that your country enjoys an exemption from these evils; I will frankly own to you that I am of a very different opinion. Your fate I believe to be certain, though it is deferred by a physical cause. As long as you have a boundless extent of fertile and unoccupied land, your laboring population will be far more at ease than the laboring population of the old world; and while that is the case the Jefferson politics may continue to exist without causing any fatal calamity. But the time will come when New England will be as thickly settled as Old England. Wages will be as low, and will fluctuate as much with you as with us. You will have your Manchesters and Birminghams. And in those Manchesters and Birminghams hundreds and thousands of artisans will sometimes be out of work. Then your institutions will be fairly brought to the test. Distress everywhere makes the labourer mutinous and discontented, and inclines him to listen with eagerness to agitators, who tell him that it is a monstrous iniquity that one man should have a million while another cannot get a full meal.

In bad years there is plenty of grumbling here, and sometimes a little rioting; but it matters little, for here the sufferers are not the rulers. The supreme power is in the hands of a class numerous indeed, but select— of an educated class—of a class which is and knows itself to be, deeply interested in the security of property and the maintenance of order. Accordingly, the malcontents are gently but firmly restrained. The bad time is got over without robbing the wealthy to relieve the indigent. The springs of national prosperity soon begin to flow again; work is plentiful, wages rise and all is tranquillity and cheerfulness. I have seen England pass, three or four times, through such critical seasons as I have described.

Through such seasons the United States will have to pass in the course of the next century, if not of this. How will you pass through them? I heartily wish you good deliverance. But my reason is quite plain that your Government will never be able to restrain a distressed and discontented majority. For, with you the majority is the government, and has the rich, who are always the minority, absolutely at its mercy. The day will come when in the State of New York, a multitude of people, none of whom has had more than half a breakfast, or expects to have more than half a dinner, will choose a Legislature. Is it possible to doubt what sort of Legislature will be chosen? On one side is a statesman preaching patience, respect for vested rights, strict observance of public faith; on the other is a demagogue, ranting about the tyranny of the capitalists and usurers, and asking why anybody should be permitted to drink champagne and to ride in a carriage while thousands of honest folks are in want of necessaries. Which of the two candidates is likely to be preferred by a workman who hears his children cry for bread?

I seriously apprehend you will, in some season of adversity as I have described, do things that will prevent prosperity from returning; that you will act like people who should, in a season of scarcity, partake of absolute famine. There will be, I fear, spoliation. The spoliation will increase the distress. The distress will produce fresh spoliation. There is nothing to stop you. Your Constitution is all sail and no anchor.

As I said before, when a society has entered on its downward progress either civilization or liberty must perish. Either some Caesar or Napoleon will seize the rein of Government with a strong hand or your republic will be as fearfully plundered and laid waste by barbarians in the Twentieth Century as the Roman Empire was in the Fifth—with this difference that the Huns and Vandals who ravaged the Roman Empire came from without, and that your Huns and Vandals have been engendered within your country by your own institutions.

Thinking this, of course, I cannot reckon Jefferson among the benefactors of mankind.

Yours respectfully,

Thomas Babington Macaulay.

John Henry Newman

1801–1890

JOHN HENRY NEWMAN was the most highly gifted of all the Victorians. He possessed both a subtle mind and a sensitive imagination. He was at once a thinker and an artist. He could use language to record the most inward "modes of being," whether his own or other men's, and he could use it with superb rhetorical force to move and persuade. He was a great man and a great writer.

Newman was born at London in 1801, the son of a rather worldly banker and a rather pious mother. In early life he had various mystical or quasi-mystical experiences. He sometimes "thought life might be a dream, or I an Angel, and all this world a deception, my fellow-angels by a playful device . . . deceiving me with the semblance of a material world." In the beauty of nature he found a reflection or symbol of divine beauty. In the voice of conscience he felt the presence "of a Supreme Governor, a Judge, holy, just, powerful, all-seeing, retributive." But though his mother had taught him his catechism and taken him to the Church of England on Sundays, this religious awareness was unconnected with any definite creed; and indeed it did not hold a central place in his mind or heart. Then in 1816 occurred the major event of his life, an event which changed him so radically that he found it difficult, he said, to recognize the identity of the boy before it and after it. Under the influence of the Reverend Walter Mayers, a devout Evangelical who was one of his teachers at the boarding school to which he had been sent in 1808, Newman experienced an "inward conversion" which brought him two new and everlasting convictions: the absolute certainty of two "supreme and luminously self-evident beings, myself [i.e., his immortal soul] and my Creator," and the truth of the central dogmas of Christianity, revealed by God through Christ— Original Sin, the Trinity, the Incarnation, the Atonement, Redemption, and the Resurrection. From this time to his death seventy-four years later, Newman believed unwaveringly in the reality of God and personal immortality, and in the miraculous and dogmatic character of Christianity. His later changes, from Evangelicalism to Anglo-Catholicism to Roman Catholicism, resulted from changing conceptions of the importance and meaning of various dogmas and subsidiary doctrines, especially the doctrine of the Church.

In 1817 he went to Oxford, where he became a brilliant student, and though he blew up in the final examinations and failed to receive high honors, he was elected in 1822 a fellow of Oriel College, at that time the outstanding college in the university. So opened a new chapter in his life, for not one of his new companions was an Evangelical. John Keble was an Anglo-Catholic; the rest were liberal Protestants.

At first Newman was drawn toward the liberals, but when he recognized the antidogmatic tendency of their thinking, he not only turned *away* from religious liberalism, he turned *against* it, convinced that if Christianity were to survive in the modern world, liberalism would have to be crushed. Years later, in a speech at Rome when he was made a cardinal (1879), he said, "For thirty, forty, fifty years [i.e., since 1829] I have resisted to the best of my powers the spirit of Liberalism in religion. Never did Holy Church need champions against it more sorely than now, when, alas! it is an error overspreading, as a snare, the whole earth." This is the central clue, not only to Newman's life, but to the Oxford Movement which he and his friends initiated. Its first principle was "the principle of dogma: my battle was with liberalism; by liberalism I meant the anti-dogmatic principle and its developments." Its second principle was Catholicism, Anglo-Catholicism. The connection is of the highest importance. Newman became a Catholic partly because Catholicism offered him a position from which, better than any other in his time, he could fight liberalism.

But what exactly did he mean by liberalism in religion? and why did he think it would make shipwreck of Christianity? He wrote the famous "Note on Liberalism" in answer to those questions. Liberalism meant, in the first place, the refusal to accept anything on authority, whether of the Bible or the creeds or the church. Belief was a matter of private judgment. One had to decide for himself what was true; he had to satisfy his own reason (see Propositions 1 and 9 at the end of the "Note"). This meant, in effect, the denial of any definite body of revealed truth to be accepted on faith. But to Newman the great dogmas of Christianity were a revelation of God, given on His supreme authority, and embodied at scattered places in the New Testament and in summary form in the three creeds. If they were subjected to reason and private judgment, one person accepting some, another accepting others, the whole dogmatic structure would disintegrate. Religion would no longer rest on any objective body of truth. Dogmas would be simply matters of opinion which this person or that church happened to believe (see Proposition 3). And Christianity would become a mixture of pious feeling and Christian ethics.

Newman was right. The simple "Religion of Christ" (defined in the General Introduction, p. 378) has become the religion of most Protestants today.

What is "wrong" with it? It is unstable. It tends to disintegrate, actually if not consciously, into ethical culture and moral humanitarianism. All religious people have periods of spiritual dryness when they lose the immediate sense of God. When that happens to a liberal, he has nothing to fall back upon, no structure of belief, no ecclesiastical life, to which his religious emotions have become attached, and which can sustain him and hold him until—partly through these very objects—he can recover the central experience of divine reality. And if at the same time he is living in a world where atheism and agnosticism are all around him, where the secular and scientific atmosphere is thick, the chances are a hundred to one that he will lose the supernatural life of his religion altogether and drift downward into a naturalistic religion of humanity and social service. That is why Newman called liberalism the halfway house to atheism. That is why he hated it, not merely because he was a Catholic, not merely because he believed in dogmatic Christianity, but because he was fighting to save religion in the modern world. It is a measure of his extraordinary insight that he saw, far more clearly than they did, where the Oriel liberals were going, and saw the necessity of defending revelation from the destructive force of reason if religion were to survive.

No wonder, at this crucial moment, that John Keble and his younger friend, Hurrell Froude, both Anglo-Catholics, came to exert a determining influence on Newman's personal life and public career. Anglo-Catholicism offered him the idea of a visible church founded by Christ to be the ark of salvation, through the power of the sacraments, and the guardian of dogma. This idea had been embodied in the theology, the polity, and the ritual of the Church of the fourth and fifth centuries. That original Catholic and Apostolic Church was therefore the right and true model of what the Church of England ought to be, but unfortunately was not, because it had been corrupted at the Reformation by various Protestant errors, like belief in salvation by faith alone, assertion of the supreme authority of the Bible, and denial of the supernatural power of the priesthood. The Oxford Movement was the attempt to reform the Church of England on Catholic lines, Catholic but not Roman Catholic, since the Anglo-Catholics deny the headship of the Pope and various Roman dogmas relating to the sacraments, purgatory, the Virgin, etc., which they consider medieval corruptions of primitive doctrine. (Cf. a somewhat different account of Anglo-Catholicism in the General Introduction, p. 379, which brings out its seventeenth-century antecedents.)

Beginning in 1833 Newman and his friends published a series of *Tracts for the Times,* pleading for a Catholic interpretation of the Church. The movement won wide support among the clergy; but when it failed to win the official approval of the bishops, who insisted on the traditional Protestant interpretation, Newman had no recourse, he felt, but to secede and join the Roman Church. His "shocking" conversion, which he later explained in his superb autobiography, *Apologia pro Vita Sua* (1864), occurred in 1845.

Newman's life and thought were informed by two great objects: religion and education, Christianity and the Liberal Arts. In the Oxford years the former had dominated his mind; when he became a Roman Catholic and was asked to be the rector of a Catholic university to be founded at Dublin, he turned much of his attention to the latter. In 1852 he delivered the famous lectures on *The Scope and Nature of University Education,* to which he later added ten more essays on *University Subjects;* the two series were published together in 1873 as *The Idea of a University.* This book is Newman's apologia for a liberal education, complementing the *Apologia* for his Catholic Christianity.

In the 1852 lectures Newman had to defend his position against two quite different enemies: on the one hand, against the utilitarians, who could see no "use" in such an impractical education; and on the other, against the Catholics in Ireland, and elsewhere, who could only view with alarm the study of modern subjects like natural science and philosophy as a dangerous threat to Catholic orthodoxy. It is because both enemies, especially the first, are still with us that Newman's fine defense of a liberal education is as relevant today as it was a century ago.

What is the function of a liberal arts college? Should it try to prepare men and women for professional and business careers? Certainly not. That is the job of vocational schools of law and medicine, business and engineering. Should it aim to train character, to quicken the moral and religious side of human nature? Again no. That is the function of the family and the church. The right and sole end of higher education is the cultivation of the intellect. "It contemplates neither moral impression nor mechanical production; it professes to exercise the mind neither in art [professional skills] nor in duty; its function is intellectual culture." Why?

First, because knowledge is capable of being its own end, though it may and does have further ends. Human beings seek perfection. They admire and enjoy the beauty of trees irrespective of any fruit they bear, the beauty of moral character irrespective of particular action. "In like manner there is a beauty, there is a perfection, of the intellect" irrespective of anything it may accomplish. But in what does it consist? What *is* a perfectly cultivated mind? Certainly it is not a mind that is merely stored with knowledge; and the educated man is not the student who has taken courses in a wide range of subjects and who can "talk about" Egyptian art and feudalism and Wordsworth's theory of poetry and family life in American society. This is mere knowledge, cultural veneer. The mind is stocked but unchanged. Education means the enlightenment or enlargement of the mind.

The enlargement consists, not merely in the passive reception into the mind of a number of ideas hitherto unknown to it, but in the mind's energetic and simultaneous action upon and towards and among those new ideas, which are rushing in upon it. . . . It is a making the objects of our knowledge subjectively our own, or, to use a familiar word, it is a digestion of what we receive, into the substance of our previous state of thought; and without this no enlargement is said to follow. There is no enlargement, unless there be a comparison of ideas one with another, as they come before the mind, and a systematizing of them. We feel our minds to be growing and expanding *then*, when we not only learn, but refer what we learn to what we know already.

That is the very heart of the matter—and the very thing most often neglected. The tragedy of education is that most students, and many teachers, spend hundreds of hours in learning new ideas without stopping to bring them into contact with their old assumptions, or ever asking what their value and meaning is *now to them*. Most B. A.'s are therefore "only possessed by their knowledge, not possessed of it."

But even when it "works," is a liberal education really valuable? The perfection of the intellect may be a legitimate end in its own right, but if it has no other, is it worth the time and expense of four years in college?

Perhaps we should do better to study practical subjects which would prepare us for practical life. This vocational pressure began in the nineteenth century. It reflects both the democratic extension of education, once confined to men of leisure, to the middle and lower classes, and the modern commercial environment that grew up after the Industrial Revolution. But at bottom it rests on ignorance of the larger and intangible utility of a liberal education. Newman calls attention to the value of the latter in training men to think and reason, to compare and discriminate and analyze. The educated man is likely to be a better lawyer or doctor or broker. This at least is recognized in theory. What is almost totally overlooked is that the educated man is likely to be a better *man*, not morally but intellectually, a more intelligent human being; and therefore able, a little more wisely, to make the judgments and decisions everyone is called on constantly to make. The process of assimilating knowledge, of comparing what we learn with what we know, issues in "an acquired faculty of judgment, of clear-sightedness, of sagacity, of wisdom, of philosophical reach of mind, and of intellectual self-possession and repose." Is anything short of moral and spiritual power *more* useful?

The collected works of Newman have been published in 41 volumes by Longmans, Green and Co. The *Apologia pro Vita Sua* and *The Idea of a University* are both reprinted in Everyman's Library. The standard biography is by Wilfred Ward (2 vols., 1912), but it deals almost entirely with the Roman Catholic half of Newman's life. For the early years, see Maisie Ward, *Young Mr. Newman* (1948). R. H. Hutton, *Cardinal Newman* (1905), is a good short biography. C. F. Harrold, *John Henry Newman: An Expository and Critical Study of His Mind, Thought, and Art* (1945), is the best work of criticism in English on Newman.

John Henry Newman

from APOLOGIA PRO VITA SUA

Note A

LIBERALISM

I HAVE been asked to explain more fully what it is I mean by "Liberalism," because merely to call it the Anti-dogmatic Principle is to tell very little about it. An explanation is the more necessary, because such good Catholics and distinguished writers as Count Montalembert[1] and Father Lacordaire[2] use the word in a favourable sense, and claim to be Liberals themselves. "The only singularity," says the former of the two in describing his friend, "was his Liberalism. By a phenomenon, at that time unheard of, this convert,[3] this seminarist, this confessor of nuns, was just as stubborn a liberal, as in the days when he was a student and a barrister."—Life (transl.), p. 19.

I do not believe that it is possible for me to differ in any important matter from two men whom I so highly admire. In their general line of thought and conduct I enthusiastically concur, and consider them to be before their age. And it would be strange indeed if I did not read with a special interest, in M. de Montalembert's beautiful volume, of the unselfish aims, the thwarted projects, the unrequited toils, the grand and tender resignation of Lacordaire. If I hesitate to adopt their language about Liberalism, I impute the necessity of such hesitation to some differences between us in the use of words or in the circumstances of country; and thus I reconcile myself to remaining faithful to my own conception of it, though I cannot have their voices to give force to mine. Speaking then in my own way, I proceed to explain what I meant as a Protestant by Liberalism, and to do so in connexion with the circumstances under which that system of opinion came before me at Oxford.

If I might presume to contrast Lacordaire and myself, I should say, that we had been both of us inconsistent,—he, a Catholic, in calling himself a Liberal; I, a Protestant, in being an Anti-liberal; and moreover, that the cause of this inconsistency had been in both cases one and the same. That is, we were both of us such good conservatives, as to take up with what we happened to find established in our respective countries, at the time when we came into active life. Toryism was the creed of Oxford; he inherited, and made the best of, the French Revolution.

When, in the beginning of the present century, not very long before my own time, after many years of moral and intellectual declension, the University of Oxford woke up to a sense of its duties, and began to reform itself,[4] the first instruments of this change, to whose zeal and courage we all owe so much, were naturally thrown together for mutual support, against the numerous obstacles which lay in their path, and stood out in relief from the body of residents, who, though many of them men of talent themselves, cared little for the object which the others had at heart. These Reformers, as they may be called, were for some years members of scarcely more than three or four Colleges; and their own Colleges, as being under their direct influence, of course had the benefit of those stricter views of discipline and teaching, which they themselves were urging on the University. They had, in no long time, enough of real progress in their several spheres of exertion, and enough of reputation out of doors, to warrant them in considering themselves the *élite* of the place; and it is not wonderful if they were in consequence led to look down upon the majority of Colleges, which had not kept pace with the reform, or which had been hostile to it. And, when those rivalries of one man with another arose, whether personal or collegiate, which befall literary and scientific societies, such disturbances did but tend to raise in their eyes the value which they had already set upon academical distinction, and increase their zeal in pursuing it. Thus was formed an intellectual circle or class in the University,—men, who felt they

---

[1] Comte Charles René de Montalembert (1810–70) was a Roman Catholic politician and historian whose liberal ideas with regard to education, ecclesiastical jurisdiction, etc. irritated the more conservative elements in his church, but who raised no questions of dogma.

[2] Père Lacordaire (1802–61) was a more pronounced radical, advocating separation of church and state, the freeing of education from both state and church domination, popular sovereignty in civil affairs, etc. He too was a liberal in ecclesiastical politics but not in theology.

[3] Before becoming a priest, Lacordaire had been accepted at the bar and had been a professed disciple of Voltaire.

[4] It was only awakened by attacks from Adam Smith in *The Wealth of Nations* and in a series of articles in the *Edinburgh Review*, pointing out its wealth and privilege and its antiquated and perfunctory educational system.

had a career before them, as soon as the pupils, whom they were forming, came into public life; men, whom non-residents, whether country parsons or preachers of the Low Church, on coming up from time to time to the old place, would look at, partly with admiration, partly with suspicion, as being an honour indeed to Oxford, but withal exposed to the temptation of ambitious views, and to the spiritual evils signified in what is called the "pride of reason."

Nor was this imputation altogether unjust; for, as they were following out the proper idea of a University, of course they suffered more or less from the moral malady incident to such a pursuit. The very object of such great institutions lies in the cultivation of the mind and the spread of knowledge; if this object, as all human objects, has its dangers at all times, much more would these exist in the case of men, who were engaged in a work of reformation, and had the opportunity of measuring themselves, not only with those who were their equals in intellect, but with the many, who were below them. In this select circle or class of men, in various Colleges, the direct instruments and the choice fruit of real University Reform, we see the rudiments of the Liberal party.

Whenever men are able to act at all, there is the chance of extreme and intemperate action; and therefore, when there is exercise of mind, there is the chance of wayward or mistaken exercise. Liberty of thought is in itself a good; but it gives an opening to false liberty. Now by Liberalism I mean false liberty of thought, or the exercise of thought upon matters, in which, from the constitution of the human mind, thought cannot be brought to any successful issue, and therefore is out of place. Among such matters are first principles of whatever kind; and of these the most sacred and momentous are especially to be reckoned the truths of Revelation. Liberalism then is the mistake of subjecting to human judgment those revealed doctrines which are in their nature beyond and independent of it, and of claiming to determine on intrinsic grounds the truth and value of propositions which rest for their reception simply on the external authority of the Divine Word.

Now certainly the party of whom I have been speaking, taken as a whole, were of a character of mind out of which Liberalism might easily grow up, as in fact it did; certainly they breathed around an influence which made men of religious seriousness shrink into themselves. But, while I say as much as this, I have no intention whatever of implying that the talent of the University, in the years before and after 1820, was liberal in its theology, in the sense in which the bulk of the educated classes through the country are liberal now. I would not for the world be supposed to detract from the Christian earnestness, and the activity in religious works, above the average of men, of many of the persons in question. They would have protested against their being supposed to place reason before faith, or knowledge before devotion; yet I do consider that they unconsciously encouraged and successfully introduced into Oxford a licence of opinion which went far beyond them. In their day they did little more than take credit to themselves for enlightened views, largeness of mind, liberality of sentiment, without drawing the line between what was just and what was inadmissible in speculation, and without seeing the tendency of their own principles; and engrossing, as they did, the mental energy of the University, they met for a time with no effectual hindrance to the spread of their influence, except (what indeed at the moment was most effectual, but not of an intellectual character) the thorough-going Toryism and traditionary Church-of-Englandism of the great body of the Colleges and Convocation.[5]

Now and then a man of note appeared in the Pulpit or Lecture Rooms of the University, who was a worthy representative of the more religious and devout Anglicans. These belonged chiefly to the High-Church party; for the party called Evangelical[6] never has been able to breathe freely in the atmosphere of Oxford, and at no time has been conspicuous, as a party, for talent or learning. But of the old High Churchmen several exerted some sort of Antiliberal influence in the place, at least from time to time, and that influence of an intellectual nature. Among these especially may be mentioned Mr. John Miller, of Worcester College, who preached the Bampton Lecture in the year 1817. But, as far as I know, he who turned the tide, and brought the talent of the University round to the side of the old theology, and against what was familiarly called "march-of-mind," was Mr. Keble.[7] In and from Keble the mental activity of Oxford took that contrary direction which issued in what was called Tractarianism.[8]

---

[5] The assembly of all the masters of art and doctors of the higher faculties which has final control of university affairs.

[6] See General Introduction, p. 377.

[7] John Keble (1792–1866), by whom Newman was profoundly influenced. Together with Newman and Hurrell Froude, he originated the Oxford Movement.

[8] I.e., the Oxford Movement. The term was derived from *Tracts for the Times;* see p. 490.

Keble was young in years, when he became a University celebrity, and younger in mind. He had the purity and simplicity of a child. He had few sympathies with the intellectual party, who sincerely welcomed him as a brilliant specimen of young Oxford. He instinctively shut up before literary display, and pomp and donnishness of manner, faults which always will beset academical notabilities. He did not respond to their advances. His collision with them (if it may be so called) was thus described by Hurrell Froude[9] in his own way. "Poor Keble!" he used gravely to say, "he was asked to join the aristocracy of talent, but he soon found his level." He went into the country, but his instance serves to prove that men need not, in the event, lose that influence which is rightly theirs, because they happen to be thwarted in the use of the channels natural and proper to its exercise. He did not lose his place in the minds of men because he was out of their sight.

Keble was a man who guided himself and formed his judgments, not by processes of reason, by inquiry or by argument, but, to use the word in a broad sense, by authority. Conscience is an authority; the Bible is an authority; such is the Church; such is Antiquity; such are the words of the wise; such are hereditary lessons; such are ethical truths; such are historical memories, such are legal saws and state maxims; such are proverbs; such are sentiments, presages, and prepossessions. It seemed to me as if he ever felt happier, when he could speak or act under some such primary or external sanction; and could use argument mainly as a means of recommending or explaining what had claims on his reception prior to proof. He even felt a tenderness, I think, in spite of Bacon, for the Idols of the Tribe and the Den, of the Market and the Theatre.[10] What he hated instinctively was heresy, insubordination, resistance to things established, claims of independence, disloyalty, innovation, a critical, censorious spirit. And such was the main principle of the school which in the course of years was formed around him; nor is it easy to set limits to its influence in its day; for multitudes of men, who did not profess its teaching, or accept its peculiar doctrines, were willing nevertheless, or found it to their purpose, to act in company with it.

Indeed for a time it was practically the champion and advocate of the political doctrines of the great clerical interest through the country,[11] who found in Mr. Keble and his friends an intellectual, as well as moral support to their cause, which they looked for in vain elsewhere. His weak point, in their eyes, was his consistency; for he carried his love of authority and old times so far, as to be more than gentle towards the Catholic Religion, with which the Toryism of Oxford and of the Church of England had no sympathy. Accordingly, if my memory be correct, he never could get himself to throw his heart into the opposition made to Catholic Emancipation,[12] strongly as he revolted from the politics and the instruments by means of which that Emancipation was won. I fancy he would have had no difficulty in accepting Dr. Johnson's saying about "the first Whig";[13] and it grieved and offended him that the "Via prima salutis"[14] should be opened to the Catholic body from the Whig quarter. In spite of his reverence for the Old Religion, I conceive that on the whole he would rather have kept its professors beyond the pale of the Constitution with the Tories, than admit them on the principles of the Whigs. Moreover, if the Revolution of 1688[15] was too lax in principle for him and his friends, much less, as is very plain, could they endure to subscribe to the revolutionary doctrines of 1776 and 1789,[16] which they felt to be absolutely and entirely out of keeping with theological truth.

The Old Tory or Conservative party in Oxford had in it no principle or power of development, and that from its very nature and constitution: it was otherwise with the Liberals. They represented a new idea, which was but gradually learning to recognise itself, to ascertain its characteristics and external relations, and to exert an influence upon the University. The party grew, all the time that I was in Oxford, even in numbers, certainly in breadth and definiteness of doctrine, and in power. And, what was a far higher consideration, by the accession of Dr.

---

[11] At this period there was threat of "disestablishment," i.e., of withdrawing both the prestige and the financial support which accrued to the Church of England as the official established church of the country.

[12] Movement to restore to Roman Catholics their civil and personal equality with Protestants. A bill to this effect was passed in 1829.

[13] Boswell reports in his *Life of Dr. Johnson* that Johnson claimed the first Whig was the Devil.

[14] The first way or step of salvation.

[15] The Whig Revolution which forced James II off the throne and transferred power from the king to Parliament.

[16] The American Declaration of Independence and the French Rights of Man. Cf. Proposition 17, p. 496, below.

---

[9] A fellow of Oriel and an intimate friend of Newman, deeply Anglo-Catholic in his thought.

[10] As defined by Sir Francis Bacon, these are false notions which arise from the limitations of human nature, from the constitution of the individual, from the association of men, and from unfounded philosophical systems, respectively.

Arnold's pupils,[17] it was invested with an elevation of character which claimed the respect even of its opponents. On the other hand, in proportion as it became more earnest and less self-applauding, it became more free-spoken; and members of it might be found who, from the mere circumstance of remaining firm to their original professions, would in the judgment of the world, as to their public acts, seem to have left it for the Conservative camp. Thus, neither in its component parts nor in its policy, was it the same in 1832, 1836, and 1841, as it was in 1845.

These last remarks will serve to throw light upon a matter personal to myself, which I have introduced into my Narrative, and to which my attention has been pointedly called, now that my Volume is coming to a second edition.

It has been strongly urged upon me to re-consider the following passages which occur in it: "The men who had driven me from Oxford were distinctly the Liberals, it was they who had opened the attack upon Tract 90," vol. ii. p. 63, and "I found no fault with the Liberals; they had beaten me in a fair field," vol. ii. p. 74.

I am very unwilling to seem ungracious, or to cause pain in any quarter; still I am sorry to say I cannot modify these statements. It is surely a matter of historical fact that I left Oxford upon the University proceedings of 1841;[18] and in those proceedings, whether we look to the Heads of Houses or the resident Masters, the leaders, if intellect and influence make men such, were members of the Liberal party. Those who did not lead, concurred or acquiesced in them,—I may say, felt a satisfaction. I do not recollect any Liberal who was on my side on that occasion. Excepting the Liberal, no other party as a party, acted against me. I am not complaining of them; I deserved nothing else at their hands. They could not undo in 1845,[19] even had they wished it (and there is no proof they did), what they had done in 1841. In 1845, when I had already given up the contest for four years, and my part in it had passed into the hands of others, then some of those who were prominent against me in 1841, feeling (what they had not felt in 1841) the danger of driving a number of my followers to Rome, and joined by younger friends who had come into University importance since 1841 and felt kindly towards me, adopted a course more consistent with their principles, and proceeded to shield from the zeal of the Hebdomadal Board,[20] not me, but professedly, all parties through the country,—Tractarians, Evangelicals, Liberals in general,—who had to subscribe to the Anglican formularies,[21] on the ground that those formularies, rigidly taken, were, on some point or other, a difficulty to all parties alike. . . .

I conclude this notice of Liberalism in Oxford, and the party which was antagonistic to it, with some propositions in detail, which, as a member of the latter, and together with the High Church, I earnestly denounced and abjured.

1. No religious tenet is important, unless reason shows it to be so.

Therefore, e.g. the doctrine of the Athanasian Creed[22] is not to be insisted on, unless it tends to convert the soul; and the doctrine of the Atonement is to be insisted on, if it does convert the soul.

2. No one can believe what he does not understand.

Therefore, e.g. there are no mysteries in true religion.

3. No theological doctrine is any thing more than an opinion which happens to be held by bodies of men.

Therefore, e.g. no creed, as such, is necessary for salvation.

4. It is dishonest in a man to make an act of faith in what he has not had brought home to him by actual proof.

Therefore, e.g. the mass of men ought not absolutely to believe in the divine authority of the Bible.

5. It is immoral in a man to believe more than he can spontaneously receive as being congenial to his moral and mental nature.

Therefore, e.g. a given individual is not bound to believe in eternal punishment.

6. No revealed doctrines or precepts may reasonably stand in the way of scientific conclusions.

Therefore, e.g. Political Economy may reverse our Lord's declarations about poverty and riches, or a system of Ethics may teach that the highest condition

---

[17] From Rugby, where Thomas Arnold, the father of Matthew, was headmaster. His liberal views on theology and church reform were deeply impressed upon his students.

[18] The bitter attack by the Heads of the Oxford Colleges upon Newman's interpretation, in Tract 90, of the Thirty-nine Articles, which define the basic beliefs of the Church of England. He had attempted to show that they did not preclude the doctrines of Anglo-Catholicism.

[19] The year in which Newman became a Roman Catholic.

[20] A board of seven set up to initiate and canvass matters that were to be submitted to Convocation.

[21] The Thirty-nine Articles.

[22] As distinct from the Apostles' Creed, the Athanasian stresses the one substance of God and Christ, which might well present a stumbling block to one whose faith was founded on reason alone.

of body is ordinarily essential to the highest state of mind.

7. Christianity is necessarily modified by the growth of civilization, and the exigencies of times.

Therefore, *e.g.* the Catholic priesthood, though necessary in the Middle Ages, may be superseded now.

8. There is a system of religion more simply true than Christianity as it has ever been received.

Therefore, *e.g.* we may advance that Christianity is the "corn of wheat" which has been dead for 1800 years, but at length will bear fruit; and that Mahometanism is the manly religion, and existing Christianity the womanish.

9. There is a right of Private Judgment: that is, there is no existing authority on earth competent to interfere with the liberty of individuals in reasoning and judging for themselves about the Bible and its contents, as they severally please.

Therefore, *e.g.* religious establishments requiring subscription are Anti-christian.

10. There are rights of conscience such, that every one may lawfully advance a claim to profess and teach what is false and wrong in matters, religious, social, and moral, provided that to his private conscience it seems absolutely true and right.

Therefore, *e.g.* individuals have a right to preach and practise fornication and polygamy.

11. There is no such thing as a national or state conscience.

Therefore, *e.g.* no judgments can fall upon a sinful or infidel nation.

12. The civil power has no positive duty, in a normal state of things, to maintain religious truth.

Therefore, *e.g.* blasphemy and sabbath-breaking are not rightly punishable by law.

13. Utility and expedience are the measure of political duty.

Therefore, *e.g.* no punishment may be enacted, on the ground that God commands it: *e.g.* on the text,

"Whoso sheddeth man's blood, by man shall his blood be shed."

14. The Civil Power may dispose of Church property without sacrilege.

Therefore, *e.g.* Henry VIII. committed no sin in his spoliations.[23]

15. The Civil Power has the right of ecclesiastical jurisdiction and administration.

Therefore, *e.g.* Parliament may impose articles of faith on the Church or suppress Dioceses.

16. It is lawful to rise in arms against legitimate princes.

Therefore, *e.g.* the Puritans in the seventeenth century, and the French in the eighteenth, were justified in their Rebellion and Revolution respectively.

17. The people are the legitimate source of power.

Therefore, *e.g.* Universal Suffrage is among the natural rights of man.

18. Virtue is the child of knowledge, and vice of ignorance.

Therefore, *e.g.* education, periodical literature, railroad travelling, ventilation, drainage, and the arts of life, when fully carried out, serve to make a population moral and happy.

All of these propositions, and many others too, were familiar to me thirty years ago,[24] as in the number of the tenets of Liberalism, and, while I gave in to none of them except No. 12, and perhaps No. 11, and partly No. 1, before I began to publish, so afterwards I wrote against most of them in some part or other of my Anglican works. . . .

I need hardly say that the above Note is mainly historical. How far the Liberal party of 1830–40 really held the above eighteen Theses, which I attributed to them, and how far and in what sense I should oppose those Theses now, could scarcely be explained without a separate Dissertation.

---

from THE IDEA OF A UNIVERSITY

from Discourse V

KNOWLEDGE ITS OWN END

A UNIVERSITY may be considered with reference either to its Students or to its Studies; and the principle, that all Knowledge is a whole and the separate Sciences[1] parts of one, which I have hitherto been using in behalf of its studies, is equally important when we direct our attention to its students. Now then I turn to the students, and shall consider the education which, by virtue of this principle, a University will give them; and thus I shall be introduced, Gentlemen, to the second question, which I proposed to discuss, viz. whether and in what sense its teaching,

---

[1] I.e., the separate branches or fields of knowledge.

[23] His dissolution of the monasteries and appropriation of their property. [24] He is writing in 1864.

viewed relatively to the taught, carries the attribute of Utility[2] along with it.

I

I have said that all branches of knowledge are connected together, because the subject-matter of knowledge is intimately united in itself, as being the acts and the work of the Creator. Hence it is that the Sciences, into which our knowledge may be said to be cast, have multiplied bearings one on another, and an internal sympathy, and admit, or rather demand, comparison and adjustment. They complete, correct, balance each other. This consideration, if well-founded, must be taken into account, not only as regards the attainment of truth, which is their common end, but as regards the influence which they exercise upon those whose education consists in the study of them. I have said already, that to give undue prominence to one is to be unjust to another; to neglect or supersede these is to divert those from their proper object. It is to unsettle the boundary lines between science and science, to disturb their action, to destroy the harmony which binds them together. Such a proceeding will have a corresponding effect when introduced into a place of education. There is no science but tells a different tale, when viewed as a portion of a whole, from what it is likely to suggest when taken by itself, without the safeguard, as I may call it, of others.

Let me make use of an illustration. In the combination of colours, very different effects are produced by a difference in their selection and juxtaposition; red, green, and white change their shades, according to the contrast to which they are submitted. And, in like manner, the drift and meaning of a branch of knowledge varies with the company in which it is introduced to the student. If his reading is confined simply to one subject, however such division of labour may favour the advancement of a particular pursuit, a point into which I do not here enter, certainly it has a tendency to contract his mind. If it is incorporated with others, it depends on those others as to the kind of influence which it exerts upon him. Thus the Classics, which in England are the means of

refining the taste, have in France subserved the spread of revolutionary and deistical doctrines. In Metaphysics, again, Butler's[3] *Analogy of Religion,* which has had so much to do with the conversion to the Catholic faith of members of the University of Oxford, appeared to Pitt and others, who had received a different training, to operate only in the direction of infidelity. And so again, Watson, Bishop of Llandaff, as I think he tells us in the narrative of his life, felt the science of Mathematics to indispose the mind to religious belief, while others see in its investigations the best parallel, and thereby defence, of the Christian Mysteries. In like manner, I suppose, Arcesilaus would not have handled logic as Aristotle, nor Aristotle have criticized poets as Plato; yet reasoning and poetry are subject to scientific rules.

It is a great point then to enlarge the range of studies which a University professes, even for the sake of the students; and, though they cannot pursue every subject which is open to them, they will be the gainers by living among those and under those who represent the whole circle. This I conceive to be the advantage of a seat of universal learning, considered as a place of education. An assemblage of learned men, zealous for their own sciences, and rivals of each other, are brought, by familiar intercourse and for the sake of intellectual peace, to adjust together the claims and relations of their respective subjects of investigation. They learn to respect, to consult, to aid each other. Thus is created a pure and clear atmosphere of thought, which the student also breathes, though in his own case he only pursues a few sciences out of the multitude. He profits by an intellectual tradition, which is independent of particular teachers, which guides him in his choice of subjects, and duly interprets for him those which he chooses. He apprehends the great outlines of knowledge, the principles on which it rests, the scale of its parts, its lights and its shades, its great points and its little, as he otherwise cannot apprehend them. Hence it is that his education is called "Liberal."[4] A habit of mind is formed which lasts through life, of which the attributes are, freedom, equitableness, calmness, moderation, and wisdom; or what in a former Discourse I have ventured to call a philosophical habit. This then I would assign as the special fruit of the education furnished at a University, as

---

[2] This discourse is a reply to those who charged liberal or humane studies with "remoteness from the occupations and duties of life, to which they are the formal introduction." It should be compared with Macaulay's description and advocacy of Baconian philosophy, whose aim "was to supply our vulgar wants." Newman had Bacon and Macaulay's essay on him specifically in view, as well as a series of articles at the beginning of the century in the *Edinburgh Review,* attacking classical education at Oxford.

[3] Joseph Butler (1692–1752). The *Analogy,* as Newman tells us in the *Apologia,* had a profound effect upon his thinking, but it was probably only through his admiration and interpretation that it had anything like the influence attributed to it here.

[4] As distinguished from a professional or vocational education.

contrasted with other places of teaching or modes of teaching. This is the main purpose of a University in its treatment of its students.

And now the question is asked me, What is the use of it? and my answer will constitute the main subject of the Discourses which are to follow.

2

Cautious and practical thinkers, I say, will ask of me, what, after all, is the gain of this Philosophy, of which I make such account, and from which I promise so much. Even supposing it to enable us to exercise the degree of trust exactly due to every science respectively, and to estimate precisely the value of every truth which is anywhere to be found, how are we better for this master view of things, which I have been extolling? Does it not reverse the principle of the division of labour? will practical objects be obtained better or worse by its cultivation? to what then does it lead? where does it end? what does it do? how does it profit? what does it promise? Particular sciences are respectively the basis of definite arts, which carry on to results tangible and beneficial the truths which are the subjects of the knowledge attained; what is the Art of this science of sciences? what is the fruit of such a Philosophy? what are we proposing to effect, what inducements do we hold out to the Catholic community, when we set about the enterprise of founding a University?

I am asked what is the end of University Education, and of the Liberal or Philosophical Knowledge which I conceive it to impart: I answer, that what I have already said has been sufficient to show that it has a very tangible, real, and sufficient end, though the end cannot be divided from that knowledge itself. Knowledge is capable of being its own end. Such is the constitution of the human mind, that any kind of knowledge, if it be really such, is its own reward. And if this is true of all knowledge, it is true also of that special Philosophy, which I have made to consist in a comprehensive view of truth in all its branches, of the relations of science to science, of their mutual bearings, and their respective values. What the worth of such an acquirement is, compared with other objects which we seek,—wealth or power or honour or the conveniences and comforts of life, I do not profess here to discuss; but I would maintain, and mean to show, that it is an object, in its own nature so really and undeniably good, as to be the compensation of a great deal of thought in the compassing, and a great deal of trouble in the attaining.

Now, when I say that Knowledge is, not merely a means to something beyond it, or the preliminary of

certain arts into which it naturally resolves, but an end sufficient to rest in and to pursue for its own sake, surely I am uttering no paradox, for I am stating what is both intelligible in itself, and has ever been the common judgment of philosophers and the ordinary feeling of mankind. I am saying what at least the public opinion of this day ought to be slow to deny, considering how much we have heard of late years, in opposition to Religion, of entertaining, curious, and various knowledge. I am but saying what whole volumes have been written to illustrate, viz. by a "selection from the records of Philosophy, Literature, and Art, in all ages and countries, of a body of examples, to show how the most unpropitious circumstances have been unable to conquer an ardent desire for the acquisition of knowledge."[5] That further advantages accrue to us and redound to others by its possession, over and above what it is in itself, I am very far indeed from denying; but, independent of these, we are satisfying a direct need of our nature in its very acquisition; and, whereas our nature, unlike that of the inferior creation, does not at once reach its perfection, but depends, in order to it, on a number of external aids and appliances, Knowledge, as one of the principal of these, is valuable for what its very presence in us does for us after the manner of a habit, even though it be turned to no further account, nor subserve any direct end.

3

Hence it is that Cicero, in enumerating the various heads of mental excellence, lays down the pursuit of Knowledge for its own sake, as the first of them. "This pertains most of all to human nature," he says, "for we are all of us drawn to the pursuit of Knowledge; in which to excel we consider excellent, whereas to mistake, to err, to be ignorant, to be deceived, is both an evil and a disgrace."[6] And he considers Knowledge the very first object to which we are attracted, after the supply of our physical wants. After the calls and duties of our animal existence, as they may be termed, as regards ourselves, our family, and our neighbours, follows, he tells us, "the search after truth. Accordingly, as soon as we escape from the pressure of necessary cares, forthwith we desire to see, to hear, and to learn; and consider the knowledge of what is hidden or is wonderful a condition of our happiness."

[5] The quotation is from the Introduction to *Pursuit of Knowledge under Difficulties* by George Craik.
[6] At the beginning of his *De Officiis*.

This passage, though it is but one of many similar passages in a multitude of authors, I take for the very reason that it is so familiarly known to us; and I wish you to observe, Gentlemen, how distinctly it separates the pursuit of Knowledge from those ulterior objects to which certainly it can be made to conduce, and which are, I suppose, solely contemplated by the persons who would ask of me the use of a University or Liberal Education. So far from dreaming of the cultivation of Knowledge directly and mainly in order to our physical comfort and enjoyment, for the sake of life and person, of health, of the conjugal and family union, of the social tie and civil security, the great Orator implies, that it is only after our physical and political needs are supplied, and when we are "free from necessary duties and cares," that we are in a condition for "desiring to see, to hear, and to learn." Nor does he contemplate in the least degree the reflex or subsequent action of Knowledge, when acquired, upon those material goods which we set out by securing before we seek it; on the contrary, he expressly denies its bearing upon social life altogether, strange as such a procedure is to those who live after the rise of the Baconian philosophy,[7] and he cautions us against such a cultivation of it as will interfere with our duties to our fellow-creatures. "All these methods," he says, "are engaged in the investigation of truth; by the pursuit of which to be carried off from public occupations is a transgression of duty. For the praise of virtue lies altogether in action; yet intermissions often occur, and then we recur to such pursuits; not to say that the incessant activity of the mind is vigorous enough to carry us on in the pursuit of knowledge, even without any exertion of our own." The idea of benefiting society by means of "the pursuit of science and knowledge," did not enter at all into the motives which he would assign for their cultivation.

This was the ground of the opposition which the elder Cato made to the introduction of Greek Philosophy among his countrymen, when Carneades[8] and his companions, on occasion of their embassy, were charming the Roman youth with their eloquent expositions of it. The fit representative of a practical people, Cato estimated everything by what it produced; whereas the Pursuit of Knowledge promised

nothing beyond Knowledge itself. He despised that refinement or enlargement of mind of which he had no experience.

4

Things, which can bear to be cut off from everything else and yet persist in living, must have life in themselves; pursuits, which issue in nothing, and still maintain their ground for ages, which are regarded as admirable, though they have not as yet proved themselves to be useful, must have their sufficient end in themselves, whatever it turn out to be. And we are brought to the same conclusion by considering the force of the epithet, by which the knowledge under consideration is popularly designated. It is common to speak of "*liberal* knowledge," of the "*liberal* arts and studies," and of a "*liberal* education," as the especial characteristic or property of a University and of a gentleman; what is really meant by the word? Now, first, in its grammatical sense it is opposed to *servile;* and by "servile work" is understood, as our catechisms inform us, bodily labour, mechanical employment, and the like, in which the mind has little or no part. Parallel to such servile works are those arts, if they deserve the name, of which the poet speaks,[9] which owe their origin and their method to hazard, not to skill; as, for instance, the practice and operations of an empiric. As far as this contrast may be considered as a guide into the meaning of the word, liberal education and liberal pursuits are exercises of mind, of reason, of reflection.

But we want something more for its explanation, for there are bodily exercises which are liberal, and mental exercises which are not so. For instance, in ancient times the practitioners in medicine were commonly slaves; yet it was an art as intellectual in its nature, in spite of the pretence, fraud, and quackery with which it might then, as now, be debased, as it was heavenly in its aim. And so in like manner, we contrast a liberal education with a commercial education or a professional; yet no one can deny that commerce and the professions afford scope for the highest and most diversified powers of mind. There is then a great variety of intellectual exercises, which are not technically called "liberal"; on the other hand, I say, there are exercises of the body which do receive that appellation. Such, for instance, was the palaestra,[10] in ancient times; such the Olympic games, in which strength and dexterity of body as well as of mind gained the prize. In Xenophon[11] we

7 To Bacon practical usefulness was the justification of knowledge. See Macaulay's essay on Bacon, above.
8 A Greek skeptic philosopher who so alarmed the Roman statesman Cato (234–149 B.C.) by the charm his eloquent sophistries were exerting in Rome that he was sent back to Athens.
9 Agathon (fifth century B.C.) as quoted by Aristotle in the *Nicomachean Ethics,* VI, according to Newman's own note.
10 Wrestling.   11 Greek historian of the fifth century B.C.

read of the young Persian nobility being taught to ride on horseback and to speak the truth; both being among the accomplishments of a gentleman. War, too, however rough a profession, has ever been accounted liberal, unless in cases when it becomes heroic, which would introduce us to another subject.

Now comparing these instances together, we shall have no difficulty in determining the principle of this apparent variation in the application of the term which I am examining. Manly games, or games of skill, or military prowess, though bodily, are, it seems, accounted liberal; on the other hand, what is merely professional, though highly intellectual, nay, though liberal in comparison of trade and manual labour, is not simply called liberal, and mercantile occupations are not liberal at all. Why this distinction? because that alone is liberal knowledge, which stands on its own pretensions, which is independent of sequel, expects no complement, refuses to be *informed* (as it is called) by any end, or absorbed into any art, in order duly to present itself to our contemplation. The most ordinary pursuits have this specific character, if they are self-sufficient and complete; the highest lose it, when they minister to something beyond them. It is absurd to balance, in point of worth and importance, a treatise on reducing fractures with a game of cricket or a fox-chase; yet of the two the bodily exercise has that quality which we call "liberal," and the intellectual has not. And so of the learned professions altogether, considered merely as professions; although one of them be the most popularly beneficial, and another the most politically important, and the third the most intimately divine of all human pursuits, yet the very greatness of their end, the health of the body, or of the commonwealth, or of the soul, diminishes, not increases, their claim to the appellation "liberal," and that still more, if they are cut down to the strict exigencies of that end. If, for instance, Theology instead of being cultivated as a contemplation, be limited to the purposes of the pulpit or be represented by the catechism, it loses—not its usefulness, not its divine character, not its meritoriousness, (rather it gains a claim upon these titles by such charitable condescension),—but it does lose the particular attribute which I am illustrating; just as a face worn by tears and fasting loses its beauty, or a labourer's hand loses its delicateness;—for Theology thus exercised is not simple knowledge, but rather is an art or a business making use of Theology. And thus it appears that even what is supernatural need not be liberal, nor need a hero be a gentleman, for the plain reason that one idea is not another idea. And in like

manner the Baconian Philosophy, by using its physical sciences in the service of man, does thereby transfer them from the order of Liberal Pursuits to, I do not say the inferior, but the distinct class of the Useful. And, to take a different instance, hence again, as is evident, whenever personal gain is the motive, still more distinctive an effect has it upon the character of a given pursuit; thus racing, which was a liberal exercise in Greece, forfeits its rank in times like these, so far as it is made the occasion of gambling.

All that I have been now saying is summed up in a few characteristic words of the great Philosopher.[12] "Of possessions," he says, "those rather are useful, which bear fruit; those *liberal, which tend to enjoyment*. By fruitful, I mean, which yield revenue; by enjoyable, where *nothing accrues of consequence beyond the using*." . . .

6

Now bear with me, Gentlemen, if what I am about to say, has at first sight a fanciful appearance. Philosophy, then, or Science, is related to Knowledge in this way:—Knowledge is called by the name of Science or Philosophy, when it is acted upon, informed, or if I may use a strong figure, impregnated by Reason. Reason is the principle of that intrinsic fecundity of Knowledge, which, to those who possess it, is its especial value, and which dispenses with the necessity of their looking abroad for any end to rest upon external to itself. Knowledge, indeed, when thus exalted into a scientific form, is also power; not only is it excellent in itself, but whatever such excellence may be, it is something more, it has a result beyond itself. Doubtless; but that is a further consideration, with which I am not concerned. I only say that, prior to its being a power, it is a good; that it is, not only an instrument, but an end. I know well it may resolve itself into an art, and terminate in a mechanical process, and in tangible fruit; but it also may fall back upon that Reason which informs it, and resolve itself into Philosophy. In one case it is called Useful Knowledge, in the other Liberal. The same person may cultivate it in both ways at once; but this again is a matter foreign to my subject; here I do but say that there are two ways of using Knowledge, and in matter of fact those who use it in one way are not likely to use it in the other, or at least in a very limited measure. You see, then, here are two methods of Education; the end of the one is to be

---

12 Aristotle. The quotation, according to Newman, is taken from the *Rhetoric*, I, 5.

philosophical, of the other to be mechanical; the one rises towards general ideas, the other is exhausted upon what is particular and external. Let me not be thought to deny the necessity, or to decry the benefit, of such attention to what is particular and practical, as belongs to the useful or mechanical arts; life could not go on without them; we owe our daily welfare to them; their exercise is the duty of the many, and we owe to the many a debt of gratitude for fulfilling that duty. I only say that Knowledge, in proportion as it tends more and more to be particular, ceases to be Knowledge. It is a question whether Knowledge can in any proper sense be predicated of the brute creation; without pretending to metaphysical exactness of phraseology, which would be unsuitable to an occasion like this, I say, it seems to me improper to call that passive sensation, or perception of things, which brutes seem to possess, by the name of Knowledge. When I speak of Knowledge, I mean something intellectual, something which grasps what it perceives through the senses; something which takes a view of things; which sees more than the senses convey; which reasons upon what it sees, and while it sees; which invests it with an idea. It expresses itself, not in a mere enunciation, but by an enthymeme:[13] it is of the nature of science from the first, and in this consists its dignity. The principle of real dignity in Knowledge, its worth, its desirableness, considered irrespectively of its results, is this germ within it of a scientific or a philosophical process. This is how it comes to be an end in itself; this is why it admits of being called Liberal. Not to know the relative disposition of things is the state of slaves or children; to have mapped out the Universe is the boast, or at least the ambition, of Philosophy.

Moreover, such knowledge is not a mere extrinsic or accidental advantage, which is ours to-day and another's to-morrow, which may be got up from a book, and easily forgotten again, which we can command or communicate at our pleasure, which we can borrow for the occasion, carry about in our hand, and take into the market; it is an acquired illumination, it is a habit, a personal possession, and an inward endowment. And this is the reason, why it is more correct, as well as more usual, to speak of a University as a place of education, than of instruction, though, when knowledge is concerned, instruction would at first sight have seemed the more appropriate word. We are instructed, for instance, in manual exercises, in the fine and useful arts, in trades, and in ways of

---

[13] A form of reasoning in which one premise is understood but not expressed.

business; for these are methods, which have little or no effect upon the mind itself, are contained in rules committed to memory, to tradition, or to use, and bear upon an end external to themselves. But education is a higher word; it implies an action upon our mental nature, and the formation of a character; it is something individual and permanent, and is commonly spoken of in connexion with religion and virtue. When, then, we speak of the communication of Knowledge as being Education, we thereby really imply that that Knowledge is a state or condition of mind; and since cultivation of mind is surely worth seeking for its own sake, we are thus brought once more to the conclusion, which the word "Liberal" and the word "Philosophy" have already suggested, that there is a Knowledge, which is desirable, though nothing come of it, as being of itself a treasure, and a sufficient remuneration of years of labour.

7

This, then, is the answer which I am prepared to give to the question with which I opened this Discourse. Before going on to speak of the object of the Church in taking up Philosophy, and the uses to which she puts it, I am prepared to maintain that Philosophy is its own end, and, as I conceive, I have now begun the proof of it. I am prepared to maintain that there is a knowledge worth possessing for what it is, and not merely for what it does; and what minutes remain to me today I shall devote to the removal of some portion of the indistinctness and confusion with which the subject may in some minds be surrounded.

It may be objected then, that, when we profess to seek Knowledge for some end or other beyond itself, whatever it be, we speak intelligibly; but that, whatever men may have said, however obstinately the idea may have kept its ground from age to age, still it is simply unmeaning to say that we seek Knowledge for its own sake, and for nothing else; for that it ever leads to something beyond itself, which therefore is its end, and the cause why it is desirable;—moreover, that this end is twofold, either of this world or of the next; that all knowledge is cultivated either for secular objects or for eternal; that if it is directed to secular objects, it is called Useful Knowledge, if to eternal, Religious or Christian Knowledge;—in consequence, that if, as I have allowed, this Liberal Knowledge does not benefit the body or estate, it ought to benefit the soul; but if the fact be really so, that it is neither a physical or a secular good on the one hand, nor a moral good on the other, it cannot be a good at all, and is not worth the trouble which is necessary for its acquisition.

And then I may be reminded that the professors of this Liberal or Philosophical Knowledge have themselves, in every age, recognized this exposition of the matter, and have submitted to the issue in which it terminates; for they have ever been attempting to make men virtuous; or, if not, at least have assumed that refinement of mind was virtue, and that they themselves were the virtuous portion of mankind. This they have professed on the one hand; and on the other, they have utterly failed in their professions, so as ever to make themselves a proverb among men, and a laughing-stock both to the grave and the dissipated portion of mankind, in consequence of them. Thus they have furnished against themselves both the ground and the means of their own exposure, without any trouble at all to anyone else. In a word, from the time that Athens was the University of the world, what has Philosophy taught men, but to promise without practising, and to aspire without attaining? What has the deep and lofty thought of its disciples ended in but eloquent words?[14] Nay, what has its teaching ever meditated, when it was boldest in its remedies for human ill, beyond charming us to sleep by its lessons, that we might feel nothing at all? like some melodious air, or rather like those strong and transporting perfumes, which at first spread their sweetness over everything they touch, but in a little while do but offend in proportion as they once pleased us. Did Philosophy support Cicero under the disfavour of the fickle populace,[15] or nerve Seneca to oppose an imperial tyrant?[16] It abandoned Brutus,[17] as he sorrowfully confessed, in his greatest need, and it forced Cato, as his panegyrist strangely boasts, into the false position of defying heaven.[18] How few can be counted among its professors, who, like Polemon,[19] were thereby converted from a profligate

course, or like Anaxagoras,[20] thought the world well lost in exchange for its possession? The philosopher in *Rasselas*[21] taught a superhuman doctrine, and then succumbed without an effort to a trial of human affection.

"He discoursed," we are told, "with great energy on the government of the passions. His look was venerable, his action graceful, his pronunciation clear, and his diction elegant. He showed, with great strength of sentiment and variety of illustration, that human nature is degraded and debased, when the lower faculties predominate over the higher. He communicated the various precepts given, from time to time, for the conquest of passion, and displayed the happiness of those who had obtained the important victory, after which man is no longer the slave of fear, nor the fool of hope. . . . He enumerated many examples of heroes immovable by pain or pleasure, who looked with indifference on those modes or accidents to which the vulgar give the names of good and evil."

Rasselas in a few days found the philosopher in a room half darkened, with his eyes misty, and his face pale. "Sir," said he, "you have come at a time when all human friendship is useless; what I suffer cannot be remedied, what I have lost cannot be supplied. My daughter, my only daughter, from whose tenderness I expected all the comforts of my age, died last night of a fever." "Sir," said the prince, "mortality is an event by which a wise man can never be surprised; we know that death is always near, and it should therefore always be expected." "Young man," answered the philosopher, "you speak like one who has never felt the pangs of separation." "Have you, then, forgot the precept," said Rasselas, "which you so powerfully enforced? . . . consider that external things are naturally variable, but truth and reason are always the same." "What comfort," said the mourner, "can truth and reason afford me? Of what effect are they now, but to tell me that my daughter will not be restored?"

8

Better, far better, to make no professions, you will say, than to cheat others with what we are not, and to scandalize them with what we are. The sensualist, or the man of the world, at any rate, is not the victim of fine words, but pursues a reality and gains it. The Philosophy of Utility, you will say, Gentlemen, has at least done its work; and I grant it,—it aimed low,

---

[14] Compare Bacon's view as set forth in Macaulay's essay, above, even to the verbal echo: "The philosophy of Plato began in words and ended in words" (p. 468).

[15] Plutarch describes in detail how low-spirited Cicero became in exile, so dejected "as none could have expected in a man who had devoted so much of his life to study and learning."

[16] Instead of opposing Nero, for whom he had been both tutor and virtual regent, Seneca tried to retire from public affairs.

[17] On the eve of their final battle with Antony, Brutus, according to Plutarch, confessed to Cassius that his philosophy was insufficient to enable him to accept the fate of defeat, and that if the issue were against them he would kill himself, which he did.

[18] Cato the Younger, in Plutarch's account, defied heaven by declaring that he was master of his own life or death and committing suicide.

[19] A profligate Athenian youth who accidentally heard a philosopher discourse on temperance and was induced thereby to become abstemious. He later became head of the Platonic school in Athens.

[20] A Greek philosopher of the fifth century B.C. who sold all his worldly goods in order to devote himself to philosophy.

[21] A novel by Samuel Johnson (see I, 864-5, above).

but it has fulfilled its aim.[22] If that man of great intellect who has been its Prophet in the conduct of life played false to his own professions,[23] he was not bound by his philosophy to be true to his friend or faithful in his trust. Moral virtue was not the line in which he undertook to instruct men; and though, as the poet calls him, he were the "meanest" of mankind,[24] he was so in what may be called his private capacity and without any prejudice to the theory of induction. He had a right to be so, if he chose, for anything that the Idols of the den or the theatre[25] had to say to the contrary. His mission was the increase of physical enjoyment and social comfort;[26] and most wonderfully, most awfully has he fulfilled his conception and his design. Almost day by day have we fresh and fresh shoots, and buds, and blossoms, which are to ripen into fruit, on that magical tree of Knowledge which he planted, and to which none of us perhaps, except the very poor, but owes, if not his present life, at least his daily food, his health, and general well-being. He was the divinely provided minister of temporal benefits to all of us so great, that, whatever I am forced to think of him as a man, I have not the heart, from mere gratitude, to speak of him severely. And, in spite of the tendencies of his philosophy, which are, as we see at this day, to depreciate, or to trample on Theology, he has himself, in his writings, gone out of his way, as if with a prophetic misgiving of those tendencies, to insist on it as the instrument of that beneficent Father, who, when He came on earth in visible form, took on Him first and most prominently the office of assuaging the bodily wounds of human nature.[27] And truly, like the old mediciner in the tale, "he sat diligently at his work, and hummed, with cheerful countenance, a pious song"; and then in turn "went out singing into the meadows so gaily, that those who had seen him from afar might well have thought it was a youth gathering flowers for his beloved, instead of an old physician gathering healing herbs in the morning dew."[28]

22 Direct allusion to Macaulay's essay: "Some people may think the object of the Baconian philosophy a low object, but they cannot deny that, high or low, it has been attained." Above, p. 468.

23 Bacon as Lord Chancellor was charged with bribery, and, indeed, admitted corruption and neglect.

24 Pope in his *Essay on Man* termed Bacon "the wisest, brightest, meanest of mankind."

25 See above, p. 494, note 10.

26 "It will be seen that on the whole I agree with Lord Macaulay in his Essay on Bacon's Philosophy. I do not know whether he would agree with me." (Newman)

27 "*De Augment.* IV, 2, vid. Macaulay's Essay." (Newman) See above, pp. 466-7.

28 "Fouqué's *Unknown Patient*." (Newman) The parallel is between the "old mediciner" and the Deity.

Alas, that men, in the action of life or in their heart of hearts, are not what they seem to be in their moments of excitement, or in their trances or intoxications of genius,—so good, so noble, so serene! Alas, that Bacon too in his own way should after all be but the fellow of those heathen philosophers who in their disadvantages had some excuse for their inconsistency, and who surprise us rather in what they did say than in what they did not do! Alas, that he too, like Socrates or Seneca, must be stripped of his holyday coat, which looks so fair, and should be but a mockery amid his most majestic gravity of phrase; and, for all his vast abilities, should, in the littleness of his own moral being, but typify the intellectual narrowness of his school! However, granting all this, heroism after all was not his philosophy:—I cannot deny he has abundantly achieved what he proposed. His is simply a Method whereby bodily discomforts and temporal wants are to be most effectually removed from the greatest number; and already, before it has shown any signs of exhaustion, the gifts of nature, in their most artificial shapes and luxurious profusion and diversity, from all quarters of the earth, are, it is undeniable, by its means brought even to our doors, and we rejoice in them.

9

Useful Knowledge then, I grant, has done its work; and Liberal Knowledge as certainly has not done its work,—that is, supposing, as the objectors assume, its direct end, like Religious Knowledge, is to make men better; but this, I will not for an instant allow, and, unless I allow it, those objectors have said nothing to the purpose. I admit, rather I maintain, what they have been urging, for I consider Knowledge to have its end in itself. For all its friends, or its enemies, may say, I insist upon it, that it is as real a mistake to burden it with virtue or religion as with the mechanical arts. Its direct business is not to steel the soul against temptation or to console it in affliction, any more than to set the loom in motion, or to direct the steam carriage; be it ever so much the means or the condition of both material and moral advancement, still, taken by and in itself, it as little mends our hearts as it improves our temporal circumstances. And if its eulogists claim for it such a power, they commit the very same kind of encroachment on a province not their own as the political economist who should maintain that his science educated him for casuistry or diplomacy. Knowledge is one thing, virtue is another; good sense is not conscience, refinement is not humility, nor is largeness and justness of view faith. Philosophy, however enlightened, however profound, gives no command over the passions, no influential motives, no vivifying principles. Liberal Education makes not the Christian, not the Catholic, but the gentleman. It is well to be a gentleman, it is well to have a cultivated intellect, a delicate taste, a candid, equitable, dispassionate mind, a noble and courteous bearing in the conduct of life;—these are the connatural qualities of a large knowledge; they are the objects of a University; I am advocating, I shall illustrate and insist upon them; but still, I repeat, they are no guarantee for sanctity or even for conscientiousness, they may attach to the man of the world, to the profligate, to the heartless, —pleasant, alas, and attractive as he shows when decked out in them. Taken by themselves, they do but seem to be what they are not; they look like virtue at a distance, but they are detected by close observers, and on the long run; and hence it is that they are popularly accused of pretence and hypocrisy, not, I repeat, from their own fault, but because their professors and their admirers persist in taking them for what they are not, and are officious in arrogating for them a praise to which they have no claim. Quarry the granite rock with razors, or moor the vessel with a thread of silk; then may you hope with such keen and delicate instruments as human knowledge and human reason to contend against those giants, the passion and the pride of man.

Surely we are not driven to theories of this kind, in order to vindicate the value and dignity of Liberal Knowledge. Surely the real grounds on which its pretensions rest are not so very subtle or abstruse, so very strange or improbable. Surely it is very intelligible to say, and that is what I say here, that Liberal Education, viewed in itself, is simply the cultivation of the intellect, as such, and its object is nothing more or less than intellectual excellence. Everything has its own perfection, be it higher or lower in the scale of things; and the perfection of one is not the perfection of another. Things animate, inanimate, visible, invisible, all are good in their kind, and have a *best* of themselves, which is an object of pursuit. Why do you take such pains with your garden or your park? You see to your walks and turf and shrubberies; to your trees and drives; not as if you meant to make an orchard of the one, or corn or pasture land of the other, but because there is a special beauty in all that is goodly in wood, water, plain, and slope, brought all together by art into one shape, and grouped into one whole. Your cities are beautiful, your palaces, your public buildings, your territorial mansions, your churches; and their beauty leads to nothing beyond itself. There is a physical beauty and a moral; there is a beauty of person, there is a beauty of our moral being, which is natural virtue; and in like manner there is a beauty, there is a perfection, of the intellect. There is an ideal perfection in these various subject-matters, towards which individual instances are seen to rise, and which are the standards for all instances whatever. The Greek divinities and demigods, as the statuary has moulded them, with their symmetry of figure and their high forehead and their regular features, are the perfection of physical beauty. The heroes, of whom history tells, Alexander, or Caesar, or Scipio, or Saladin, are the representatives of that magnanimity or self-mastery which is the greatness of human nature. Christianity too has its heroes, and in the supernatural order, and we call them Saints. The artist puts before him beauty of feature and form; the poet, beauty of mind; the preacher, the beauty of grace: then intellect too, I repeat, has its beauty, and it has those who aim at it. To open the mind, to correct it, to refine it, to enable it to know, and to digest, master, rule, and use its knowledge, to give it power over its own faculties, application, flexibility, method, critical exactness, sagacity, resource, address, eloquent expression, is an object as intelligible (for here we are inquiring, not what the object of a Liberal Education is worth, nor what use the Church makes of it, but what it is in itself), I say, an object as intelligible as the cultivation of virtue, while, at the same time, it is absolutely distinct from it.

10

This indeed is but a temporal object, and a transitory possession: but so are other things in themselves which we make much of and pursue. The moralist will tell us that man, in all his functions, is but a flower which blossoms and fades, except so far as a higher principle breathes upon him, and makes him and what he is immortal. Body and mind are carried on into an eternal state of being by the gifts of Divine Munificence; but at first they do but fail in a failing world; and if the powers of intellect decay, the powers of the body have decayed before them, and, as an Hospital or an Almshouse, though its end be ephemeral, may be sanctified to the service of religion, so surely may a University, even were it nothing more than I have as yet described it. We attain to heaven by using this world well, though it is to pass away; we perfect our nature, not by undoing it, but by adding to it what is more than nature, and directing it towards aims higher than its own.

from Discourse VI

KNOWLEDGE VIEWED IN RELATION TO LEARNING

1

It were well if the English, like the Greek language, possessed some definite word to express, simply and generally, intellectual proficiency or perfection, such as "health," as used with reference to the animal frame, and "virtue," with reference to our moral nature. . . .

In default of a recognized term, I have called the perfection or virtue of the intellect by the name of philosophy, philosophical knowledge, enlargement of mind, or illumination; terms which are not uncommonly given to it by writers of this day; but, whatever name we bestow on it, it is, I believe, as a matter of history, the business of a University to make this intellectual culture its direct scope, or to employ itself in the education of the intellect,—just as the work of a Hospital lies in healing the sick or wounded, of a Riding or Fencing School, or of a Gymnasium, in exercising the limbs, of an Almshouse, in aiding and solacing the old, of an Orphanage, in protecting innocence, of a Penitentiary, in restoring the guilty. I say, a University, taken in its bare idea, and before we view it as an instrument of the Church, has this object and this mission; it contemplates neither moral impression nor mechanical production; it professes to exercise the mind neither in art[29] nor in duty; its function is intellectual culture; here it may leave its scholars, and it has done its work when it has done as much as this. It educates the intellect to reason well in all matters, to reach out towards truth, and to grasp it.

2

. . . I have then to investigate, in the Discourses which follow, those qualities and characteristics of the intellect in which its cultivation issues or rather consists; and, with a view of assisting myself in this undertaking, I shall recur to certain questions which have already been touched upon. These questions are three: viz. the relation of intellectual culture, first, to *mere* knowledge; secondly, to *professional* knowledge; and thirdly, to *religious* knowledge. In other words, are *acquirements* and *attainments* the scope of a University Education? or *expertness in particular arts and pursuits*? or *moral and religious proficiency*? or something besides these three? These questions I shall examine in succession, with the purpose I have mentioned; and I

hope to be excused, if, in this anxious undertaking, I am led to repeat what, either in these Discourses or elsewhere, I have already put upon paper. And first, of *Mere Knowledge,* or Learning, and its connexion with intellectual illumination or Philosophy.

3

I suppose the *primâ-facie* view which the public at large would take of a University, considering it as a place of Education, is nothing more or less than a place for acquiring a great deal of knowledge on a great many subjects. Memory is one of the first developed of the mental faculties; a boy's business when he goes to school is to learn, that is, to store up things in his memory. For some years his intellect is little more than an instrument for taking in facts, or a receptacle for storing them; he welcomes them as fast as they come to him; he lives on what is without; he has his eyes ever about him; he has a lively susceptibility of impressions; he imbibes information of every kind; and little does he make his own in a true sense of the word, living rather upon his neighbours all around him. He has opinions, religious, political, and literary, and, for a boy, is very positive in them and sure about them; but he gets them from his schoolfellows, or his masters, or his parents, as the case may be. Such as he is in his other relations, such also is he in his school exercises; his mind is observant, sharp, ready, retentive; he is almost passive in the acquisition of knowledge. I say this in no disparagement of the idea of a clever boy. Geography, chronology, history, language, natural history, he heaps up the matter of these studies as treasures for a future day. It is the seven years of plenty with him: he gathers in by handfuls, like the Egyptians, without counting;[30] and though, as time goes on, there is exercise for his argumentative powers in the Elements of Mathematics, and for his taste in the Poets and Orators, still, while at school, or at least, till quite the last years of his time, he acquires, and little more; and when he is leaving for the University, he is mainly the creature of foreign influences and circumstances, and made up of accidents, homogeneous or not, as the case may be. Moreover, the moral habits, which are a boy's praise, encourage and assist this result; that is, diligence, assiduity, regularity, despatch, persevering application; for these are the direct conditions of acquisition, and naturally lead to it. Acquirements, again, are emphatically producible,

---

[29] Used here in the sense of a mechanical or vocational skill.

[30] Under the direction of Joseph in the seven years of plenty as provision against the seven years of famine which were to follow (Genesis, 41:49).

and at a moment; they are a something to show, both for master and scholar; an audience, even though ignorant themselves of the subjects of an examination, can comprehend when questions are answered and when they are not. Here again is a reason why mental culture is in the minds of men identified with the acquisition of knowledge.

The same notion possesses the public mind, when it passes on from the thought of a school to that of a University: and with the best of reasons so far as this, that there is no true culture without acquirements, and that philosophy presupposes knowledge. It requires a great deal of reading, or a wide range of information, to warrant us in putting forth our opinions on any serious subject; and without such learning the most original mind may be able indeed to dazzle, to amuse, to refute, to perplex, but not to come to any useful result or any trustworthy conclusion. There are indeed persons who profess a different view of the matter, and even act upon it. Every now and then you will find a person of vigorous or fertile mind, who relies upon his own resources, despises all former authors, and gives the world, with the utmost fearlessness, his views upon religion, or history, or any other popular subject. And his works may sell for a while; he may get a name in his day; but this will be all. His readers are sure to find in the long run that his doctrines are mere theories, and not the expression of facts, that they are chaff instead of bread, and then his popularity drops as suddenly as it rose.

Knowledge, then, is the indispensable condition of expansion of mind, and the instrument of attaining to it; this cannot be denied, it is ever to be insisted on; I begin with it as a first principle; however, the very truth of it carries men too far, and confirms to them the notion that it is the whole of the matter. A narrow mind is thought to be that which contains little knowledge; and an enlarged mind, that which holds a great deal; and what seems to put the matter beyond dispute is, the fact of the great number of studies which are pursued in a University, by its very profession. Lectures are given on every kind of subject; examinations are held; prizes awarded. There are moral, metaphysical, physical Professors; Professors of languages, of history, of mathematics, of experimental science. Lists of questions are published, wonderful for their range and depth, variety and difficulty; treatises are written, which carry upon their very face the evidence of extensive reading or multifarious information; what then is wanting for mental culture to a person of large reading and scientific attainments? what is grasp of mind but acquirement? where shall philosophical repose be found, but in the consciousness and enjoyment of large intellectual possessions?

And yet this notion is, I conceive, a mistake, and my present business is to show that it is one, and that the end of a Liberal Education is not mere knowledge, or knowledge considered in its *matter*; and I shall best attain my object, by actually setting down some cases, which will be generally granted to be instances of the process of enlightenment or enlargement of mind, and others which are not, and thus, by the comparison, you will be able to judge for yourselves, Gentlemen, whether Knowledge, that is, acquirement, is after all the real principle of the enlargement, or whether that principle is not rather something beyond it.

For instance,[31] let a person, whose experience has hitherto been confined to the more calm and unpretending scenery of these islands, whether here or in England, go for the first time into parts where physical nature puts on her wilder and more awful forms, whether at home or abroad, as into mountainous districts; or let one, who has ever lived in a quiet village, go for the first time to a great metropolis,— then I suppose he will have a sensation which perhaps he never had before. He has a feeling not in addition or increase of former feelings, but of something different in its nature. He will perhaps be borne forward, and find for a time that he has lost his bearings. He has made a certain progress, and he has a consciousness of mental enlargement; he does not stand where he did, he has a new centre, and a range of thoughts to which he was before a stranger.

Again, the view of the heavens which the telescope opens upon us, if allowed to fill and possess the mind, may almost whirl it round and make it dizzy. It brings in a flood of ideas, and is rightly called an intellectual enlargement, whatever is meant by the term.

And so again, the sight of beasts of prey and other foreign animals, their strangeness, the originality (if I may use the term) of their forms and gestures and habits and their variety and independence of each other, throw us out of ourselves into another creation, and as if under another Creator, if I may so express the temptation which may come on the mind. We seem to have new faculties, or a new exercise for our

---

31 "The pages which follow are taken almost *verbatim* from the author's 14th (Oxford) University Sermon, which, at the time of writing this Discourse, he did not expect ever to reprint." (Newman)

faculties, by this addition to our knowledge; like a prisoner, who, having been accustomed to wear manacles or fetters, suddenly finds his arms and legs free.

Hence Physical Science generally, in all its departments, as bringing before us the exuberant riches and resources, yet the orderly course, of the Universe, elevates and excites the student, and at first, I may say, almost takes away his breath, while in time it exercises a tranquilizing influence upon him.

Again, the study of history is said to enlarge and enlighten the mind, and why? because, as I conceive, it gives it a power of judging of passing events, and of all events, and a conscious superiority over them, which before it did not possess.

And in like manner, what is called seeing the world, entering into active life, going into society, travelling, gaining acquaintance with the various classes of the community, coming into contact with the principles and modes of thought of various parties, interests, and races, their views, aims, habits and manners, their religious creeds and forms of worship,—gaining experience how various yet how alike men are, how low-minded, how bad, how opposed, yet how confident in their opinions; all this exerts a perceptible influence upon the mind, which it is impossible to mistake, be it good or be it bad, and is popularly called its enlargement.

And then again, the first time the mind comes across the arguments and speculations of unbelievers, and feels what a novel light they cast upon what he has hitherto accounted sacred; and still more, if it gives in to them and embraces them, and throws off as so much prejudice what it has hitherto held, and, as if waking from a dream, begins to realize to its imagination that there is now no such thing as law and the transgression of law, that sin is a phantom, and punishment a bugbear, that it is free to sin, free to enjoy the world and the flesh; and still further, when it does enjoy them, and reflects that it may think and hold just what it will, that "the world is all before it where to choose," and what system to build up as its own private persuasion; when this torrent of wilful thoughts rushes over and inundates it, who will deny that the fruit of the tree of knowledge, or what the mind takes for knowledge, has made it one of the gods, with a sense of expansion and elevation, —an intoxication in reality, still, so far as the subjective state of the mind goes, an illumination? Hence the fanaticism of individuals or nations, who suddenly cast off their Maker. Their eyes are opened; and, like the judgment-stricken king in the Tragedy,[32] they see two suns, and a magic universe, out of which they look back upon their former state of faith and innocence with a sort of contempt and indignation, as if they were then but fools, and the dupes of imposture.

On the other hand, Religion has its own enlargement, and an enlargement, not of tumult, but of peace. It is often remarked of uneducated persons, who have hitherto thought little of the unseen world, that, on their turning to God, looking into themselves, regulating their hearts, reforming their conduct, and meditating on death and judgment, heaven and hell, they seem to become, in point of intellect, different beings from what they were. Before, they took things as they came, and thought no more of one thing than another. But now every event has a meaning; they have their own estimate of whatever happens to them; they are mindful of times and seasons, and compare the present with the past; and the world, no longer dull, monotonous, unprofitable, and hopeless, is a various and complicated drama, with parts and an object, and an awful moral.

Now from these instances, to which many more might be added, it is plain, first, that the communication of knowledge certainly is either a condition or the means of that sense of enlargement or enlightenment, of which at this day we hear so much in certain quarters: this cannot be denied; but next, it is equally plain, that such communication is not the whole of the process. The enlargement consists, not merely in the passive reception into the mind of a number of ideas hitherto unknown to it, but in the mind's energetic and simultaneous action upon and towards and among those new ideas, which are rushing in upon it. It is the action of a formative power, reducing to order and meaning the matter of our acquirements; it is a making the objects of our knowledge subjectively our own, or, to use a familiar word, it is a digestion of what we receive, into the substance of our previous state of thought; and without this no enlargement is said to follow. There is no enlargement, unless there be a comparison of ideas one with another, as they come before the mind, and a systematizing of them. We feel our minds to be growing and expanding *then,* when we not only learn, but refer what we learn to what we know already. It is not the mere addition to our knowledge that is the illumination; but the locomotion, the movement onwards, of that mental centre, to which both what we know, and what we are learning, the accumulating mass of our acquirements, gravitates. And therefore a truly great intellect, and recognized

[32] The king of Thebes in the *Bacchae* of Euripides.

to be such by the common opinion of mankind, such as the intellect of Aristotle, or of St. Thomas, or of Newton, or of Goethe, (I purposely take instances within and without the Catholic pale, when I would speak of the intellect as such,) is one which takes a connected view of old and new, past and present, far and near, and which has an insight into the influence of all these one on another; without which there is no whole, and no centre. It possesses the knowledge, not only of things, but also of their mutual and true relations; knowledge, not merely considered as acquirement, but as philosophy.

Accordingly, when this analytical, distributive, harmonizing process is away, the mind experiences no enlargement, and is not reckoned as enlightened or comprehensive, whatever it may add to its knowledge. For instance, a great memory, as I have already said, does not make a philosopher, any more than a dictionary can be called a grammar. There are men who embrace in their minds a vast multitude of ideas, but with little sensibility about their real relations towards each other. These may be antiquarians, annalists, naturalists; they may be learned in the law; they may be versed in statistics; they are most useful in their own place; I should shrink from speaking disrespectfully of them; still, there is nothing in such attainments to guarantee the absence of narrowness of mind. If they are nothing more than well-read men, or men of information, they have not what specially deserves the name of culture of mind, or fulfils the type of Liberal Education.

In like manner, we sometimes fall in with persons who have seen much of the world, and of the men who, in their day, have played a conspicuous part in it, but who generalize nothing, and have no observation, in the true sense of the word. They abound in information in detail, curious and entertaining, about men and things; and, having lived under the influence of no very clear or settled principles, religious or political, they speak of every one and every thing, only as so many phenomena, which are complete in themselves, and lead to nothing, not discussing them, or teaching any truth, or instructing the hearer, but simply talking. No one would say that these persons, well informed as they are, had attained to any great culture of intellect or to philosophy.

The case is the same still more strikingly where the persons in question are beyond dispute men of inferior powers and deficient education. Perhaps they have been much in foreign countries, and they receive, in a passive, otiose, unfruitful way, the various facts which are forced upon them there. Seafaring men,

for example, range from one end of the earth to the other; but the multiplicity of external objects, which they have encountered, forms no symmetrical and consistent picture upon their imagination; they see the tapestry of human life, as it were, on the wrong side, and it tells no story. They sleep, and they rise up, and they find themselves, now in Europe, now in Asia; they see visions of great cities and wild regions; they are in the marts of commerce, or amid the islands of the South; they gaze on Pompey's Pillar,[33] or on the Andes; and nothing which meets them carries them forward or backward, to any idea beyond itself. Nothing has a drift or relation; nothing has a history or a promise. Every thing stands by itself, and comes and goes in its turn, like the shifting scenes of a show, which leave the spectator where he was. Perhaps you are near such a man on a particular occasion, and expect him to be shocked or perplexed at something which occurs; but one thing is much the same to him as another, or, if he is perplexed, it is as not knowing what to say, whether it is right to admire, or to ridicule, or to disapprove, while conscious that some expression of opinion is expected from him; for in fact he has no standard of judgment at all, and no landmarks to guide him to a conclusion. Such is mere acquisition, and, I repeat, no one would dream of calling it philosophy.

Instances, such as these, confirm, by the contrast, the conclusion I have already drawn from those which preceded them. That only is true enlargement of mind which is the power of viewing many things at once as one whole, of referring them severally to their true place in the universal system, of understanding their respective values, and determining their mutual dependence. Thus is that form of Universal Knowledge, of which I have on a former occasion spoken, set up in the individual intellect, and constitutes its perfection. Possessed of this real illumination, the mind never views any part of the extended subject-matter of Knowledge without recollecting that it is but a part, or without the associations which spring from this recollection. It makes every thing in some sort lead to every thing else; it would communicate the image of the whole to every separate portion, till that whole becomes in imagination like a spirit, every where pervading and penetrating its component parts, and giving them one definite meaning. Just as our bodily organs, when

_____
[33] At Alexandria.

mentioned, recall their function in the body, as the word "creation" suggests the Creator, and "subjects" a sovereign, so, in the mind of the Philosopher, as we are abstractedly conceiving of him, the elements of the physical and moral world, sciences, arts, pursuits, ranks, offices, events, opinions, individualities, are all viewed as one, with correlative functions and as gradually by successive combinations converging, one and all, to the true centre.

To have even a portion of this illuminative reason and true philosophy is the highest state to which nature can aspire, in the way of intellect; it puts the mind above the influences of chance and necessity, above anxiety, suspense, unsettlement, and superstition, which is the lot of the many. Men, whose minds are possessed with some one object, take exaggerated views of its importance, are feverish in the pursuit of it, make it the measure of things which are utterly foreign to it, and are startled and despond if it happens to fail them. They are ever in alarm or in transport. Those, on the other hand, who have no object or principle whatever to hold by, lose their way, every step they take. They are thrown out, and do not know what to think or say, at every fresh juncture; they have no view of persons, or occurrences, or facts, which come suddenly upon them, and they hang upon the opinion of others, for want of internal resources. But the intellect, which has been disciplined to the perfection of its powers, which knows, and thinks while it knows, which has learned to leaven the dense mass of facts and events with the elastic force of reason, such an intellect cannot be partial, cannot be exclusive, cannot be impetuous, cannot be at a loss, cannot but be patient, collected, and majestically calm, because it discerns the end in every beginning, the origin in every end, the law in every interruption, the limit in each delay; because it ever knows where it stands, and how its path lies from one point to another. It is the τετρά-γωνος[34] of the Peripatetic,[35] and has the "nil admirari" of the Stoic,—[36]

> Felix qui potuit rerum cognoscere causas,
> Atque metus omnes, inexorabile fatum
> Subjecit pedibus, strepitumque Acherontis avari.[37]

---

[34] Square or symbol of perfect development.
[35] The disciples of Aristotle were called Peripatetics because of the master's habit of walking about as he taught them.
[36] The phrase, meaning "be moved by nothing," is often cited as the keystone of the Stoic philosophy, which taught indifference to both pleasure and pain.
[37] From Vergil's *Georgics,* II, 490–493: "Happy is he who could know the causes of things and put under his feet all fears and inexorable fate and the roar of greedy Acheron."

There are men who, when in difficulties, originate at the moment vast ideas or dazzling projects; who, under the influence of excitement, are able to cast a light, almost as if from inspiration, on a subject or course of action which comes before them; who have a sudden presence of mind equal to any emergency, rising with the occasion, and an undaunted magnanimous bearing, and an energy and keenness which is but made intense by opposition. This is genius, this is heroism; it is the exhibition of a natural gift, which no culture can teach, at which no Institution can aim; here, on the contrary, we are concerned, not with mere nature, but with training and teaching. That perfection of the Intellect, which is the result of Education, and its *beau idéal,* to be imparted to individuals in their respective measures, is the clear, calm, accurate vision and comprehension of all things, as far as the finite mind can embrace them, each in its place, and with its own characteristics upon it. It is almost prophetic from its knowledge of history; it is almost heart-searching from its knowledge of human nature; it has almost supernatural charity from its freedom from littleness and prejudice; it has almost the repose of faith, because nothing can startle it; it has almost the beauty and harmony of heavenly contemplation, so intimate is it with the eternal order of things and the music of the spheres.

7

And now, if I may take for granted that the true and adequate end of intellectual training and of a University is not Learning or Acquirement, but rather, is Thought or Reason exercised upon Knowledge, or what may be called Philosophy, I shall be in a position to explain the various mistakes which at the present day beset the subject of University Education.

I say then, if we would improve the intellect, first of all, we must ascend; we cannot gain real knowledge on a level; we must generalize, we must reduce to method, we must have a grasp of principles, and group and shape our acquisitions by means of them. It matters not whether our field of operation be wide or limited; in every case, to command it, is to mount above it. Who has not felt the irritation of mind and impatience created by a deep, rich country, visited for the first time, with winding lanes, and high hedges, and green steeps, and tangled woods, and every thing smiling indeed, but in a maze? The same feeling comes upon us in a strange city, when we have no map of its streets. Hence you hear of practised travellers, when they first come into a place, mounting some high hill or church tower, by way of reconnoitring its neighbourhood. In like manner, you must be above your knowledge, not under it, or it will oppress you; and the more you have of it, the greater will be the load. The learning of a Salmasius[38] or a Burman,[39] unless you are its master, will be your tyrant. "Imperat aut servit";[40] if you can wield it with a strong arm, it is a great weapon; otherwise,

Vis consili expers
Mole ruit suâ.[41]

You will be overwhelmed, like Tarpeia,[42] by the heavy wealth which you have exacted from tributary generations. . . .

8

. . . I will tell you, Gentlemen, what has been the practical error of the last twenty years—not to load the memory of the student with a mass of undigested knowledge, but to force upon him so much that he has rejected all. It has been the error of distracting and enfeebling the mind by an unmeaning profusion of subjects; of implying that a smattering in a dozen branches of study is not shallowness, which it really is, but enlargement, which it is not; of considering an acquaintance with the learned names of things and persons, and the possession of clever duodecimos, and attendance on eloquent lecturers, and membership with scientific institutions, and the sight of the experiments of a platform and the specimens of a museum, that all this was not dissipation of mind, but progress. All things now are to be learned at once, not first one thing, then another, not one well, but many badly. Learning is to be without exertion, without attention, without toil; without grounding, without advance, without finishing. There is to be nothing individual in it; and this, forsooth, is the wonder of the age. What the steam engine does with matter, the printing press is to do with mind; it is to act mechanically, and the population is to be passively, almost unconsciously enlightened, by the mere multiplication and dissemination of volumes. Whether it be the school boy, or the school girl, or the youth at college, or the mechanic in the town, or the politician in the senate, all have been the victims in one way or other of this most preposterous and

pernicious of delusions. Wise men have lifted up their voices in vain; and at length, lest their own institutions should be outshone and should disappear in the folly of the hour, they have been obliged, as far as they could with a good conscience, to humour a spirit which they could not withstand, and make temporizing concessions at which they could not but inwardly smile.

It must not be supposed that, because I so speak, therefore I have some sort of fear of the education of the people: on the contrary, the more education they have, the better, so that it is really education. Nor am I an enemy to the cheap publication of scientific and literary works, which is now in vogue: on the contrary, I consider it a great advantage, convenience, and gain; that is, to those to whom education has given a capacity for using them. Further, I consider such innocent recreations as science and literature are able to furnish will be a very fit occupation of the thoughts and the leisure of young persons, and may be made the means of keeping them from bad employments and bad companions. Moreover, as to that superficial acquaintance with chemistry, and geology, and astronomy, and political economy, and modern history, and biography, and other branches of knowledge, which periodical literature and occasional lectures and scientific institutions diffuse through the community, I think it a graceful accomplishment, and a suitable, nay, in this day a necessary accomplishment, in the case of educated men. Nor, lastly, am I disparaging or discouraging the thorough acquisition of any one of these studies, or denying that, as far as it goes, such thorough acquisition is a real education of the mind. All I say is, call things by their right names, and do not confuse together ideas which are essentially different. A thorough knowledge of one science and a superficial acquaintance with many, are not the same thing; a smattering of a hundred things or a memory for detail, is not a philosophical or comprehensive view. Recreations are not education; accomplishments are not education. Do not say, the people must be educated, when, after all, you only mean, amused, refreshed, soothed, put into good spirits and good humour, or kept from vicious excesses. I do not say that such amusements, such occupations of mind, are not a great gain; but they are not education. You may as well call drawing and fencing education, as a general knowledge of botany or conchology. Stuffing birds or playing stringed instruments is an elegant pastime, and a resource to the idle, but it is not education; it does not form or cultivate the intellect. Education is a high word; it is the preparation for knowledge,

---

[38] Very learned French scholar of the first half of the seventeenth century.

[39] Either one of two eminent Dutch classical scholars having identical names in the seventeenth and eighteenth centuries.

[40] "It rules or it serves."

[41] "Strength deprived of wisdom is destroyed by its own weight" (Horace, *Odes*, III, iv, 65).

[42] A Roman maiden who betrayed her city to the Sabines and was then crushed by the invaders under their shields.

and it is the imparting of knowledge in proportion to that preparation. We require intellectual eyes to know withal, as bodily eyes for sight. We need both objects and organs intellectual; we cannot gain them without setting about it; we cannot gain them in our sleep, or by hap-hazard. The best telescope does not dispense with eyes; the printing press or the lecture room will assist us greatly, but we must be true to ourselves, we must be parties in the work. A University is, according to the usual designation, an Alma Mater, knowing her children one by one, not a foundry, or a mint, or a treadmill.

9

I protest to you, Gentlemen, that if I had to choose between a so-called University, which dispensed with residence and tutorial superintendence, and gave its degrees to any person who passed an examination in a wide range of subjects, and a University which had no professors or examinations at all, but merely brought a number of young men together for three or four years, and then sent them away as the University of Oxford is said to have done some sixty years since, if I were asked which of these two methods was the better discipline of the intellect,—mind, I do not say which is *morally* the better, for it is plain that compulsory study must be a good and idleness an intolerable mischief,—but if I must determine which of the two courses was the more successful in training, moulding, enlarging the mind, which sent out men the more fitted for their secular duties, which produced better public men, men of the world, men whose names would descend to posterity, I have no hesitation in giving the preference to that University which did nothing, over that which exacted of its members an acquaintance with every science under the sun. And, paradox as this may seem, still if results be the test of systems, the influence of the public schools and colleges of England, in the course of the last century, at least will bear out one side of the contrast as I have drawn it. What would come, on the other hand, of the ideal systems of education which have fascinated the imagination of this age, could they ever take effect, and whether they would not produce a generation frivolous, narrow-minded, and resourceless, intellectually considered, is a fair subject for debate; but so far is certain, that the Universities and scholastic establishments, to which I refer, and which did little more than bring together first boys and then youths in large numbers, these institutions, with miserable deformities on the side of morals, with a hollow profession of Christianity, and a heathen code of ethics,—I say, at least

they can boast of a succession of heroes and statesmen, of literary men and philosophers, of men conspicuous for great natural virtues, for habits of business, for knowledge of life, for practical judgment, for cultivated tastes, for accomplishments, who have made England what it is,—able to subdue the earth, able to domineer over Catholics.

How is this to be explained? I suppose as follows: When a multitude of young men, keen, open-hearted, sympathetic, and observant, as young men are, come together and freely mix with each other, they are sure to learn one from another, even if there be no one to teach them; the conversation of all is a series of lectures to each, and they gain for themselves new ideas and views, fresh matter of thought, and distinct principles for judging and acting, day by day. An infant has to learn the meaning of the information which its senses convey to it, and this seems to be its employment. It fancies all that the eye presents to it to be close to it, till it actually learns the contrary, and thus by practice does it ascertain the relations and uses of those first elements of knowledge which are necessary for its animal existence. A parallel teaching is necessary for our social being, and it is secured by a large school or a college; and this effect may be fairly called in its own department an enlargement of mind. It is seeing the world on a small field with little trouble; for the pupils or students come from very different places, and with widely different notions, and there is much to generalize, much to adjust, much to eliminate, there are inter-relations to be defined, and conventional rules to be established, in the process, by which the whole assemblage is moulded together, and gains one tone and one character.

Let it be clearly understood, I repeat it, that I am not taking into account moral or religious considerations; I am but saying that that youthful community will constitute a whole, it will embody a specific idea, it will represent a doctrine, it will administer a code of conduct, and it will furnish principles of thought and action. It will give birth to a living teaching, which in course of time will take the shape of a self-perpetuating tradition, or a *genius loci*,[43] as it is sometimes called; which haunts the home where it has been born, and which imbues and forms, more or less, and one by one, every individual who is successively brought under its shadow. Thus it is that, independent of direct instruction on the part of Superiors, there is a sort of self-education in the aca-

---

[43] Spirit or atmosphere of the place.

demic institutions of Protestant England; a characteristic tone of thought, a recognized standard of judgment is found in them, which, as developed in the individual who is submitted to it, becomes a twofold source of strength to him, both from the distinct stamp it impresses on his mind, and from the bond of union which it creates between him and others,—effects which are shared by the authorities of the place, for they themselves have been educated in it, and at all times are exposed to the influence of its ethical atmosphere. Here then is a real teaching, whatever be its standards and principles, true or false; and it at least tends towards cultivation of the intellect; it at least recognizes that knowledge is something more than a sort of passive reception of scraps and details; it is a something, and it does a something, which never will issue from the most strenuous efforts of a set of teachers, with no mutual sympathies and no inter-communion, of a set of examiners with no opinions which they dare profess, and with no common principles, who are teaching or questioning a set of youths who do not know them, and do not know each other, on a large number of subjects, different in kind, and connected by no wide philosophy, three times a week, or three times a year, or once in three years, in chill lecture-rooms or on a pompous anniversary.

10

Nay, self-education in any shape, in the most restricted sense, is preferable to a system of teaching which, professing so much, really does so little for the mind. Shut your College gates against the votary of knowledge, throw him back upon the searchings and the efforts of his own mind; he will gain by being spared an entrance into your Babel. Few, indeed, there are who can dispense with the stimulus and support of instructors, or will do any thing at all, if left to themselves. And fewer still (though such great minds are to be found), who will not, from such unassisted attempts, contract a self-reliance and a self-esteem, which are not only moral evils, but serious hindrances to the attainment of truth. And next to none, perhaps, or none, who will not be reminded from time to time of the disadvantage under which they lie, by their imperfect grounding, by the breaks, deficiencies, and irregularities of their knowledge, by the eccentricity of opinion and the confusion of principle which they exhibit. They will be too often ignorant of what every one knows and takes for granted, of that multitude of small truths which fall upon the mind like dust, impalpable and ever accumulating; they may be unable to converse,

they may argue perversely, they may pride themselves on their worst paradoxes or their grossest truisms, they may be full of their own mode of viewing things, unwilling to be put out of their way, slow to enter into the minds of others;—but, with these and whatever other liabilities upon their heads, they are likely to have more thought, more mind, more philosophy, more true enlargement, than those earnest but ill-used persons, who are forced to load their minds with a score of subjects against an examination, who have too much on their hands to indulge themselves in thinking or investigation, who devour premiss and conclusion together with indiscriminate greediness, who hold whole sciences on faith, and commit demonstrations to memory, and who too often, as might be expected, when their period of education is passed, throw up all they have learned in disgust, having gained nothing really by their anxious labours, except perhaps the habit of application.

Yet such is the better specimen of the fruit of that ambitious system which has of late years been making way among us: for its result on ordinary minds, and on the common run of students, is less satisfactory still; they leave their place of education simply dissipated and relaxed by the multiplicity of subjects, which they have never really mastered, and so shallow as not even to know their shallowness. How much better, I say, is it for the active and thoughtful intellect, where such is to be found, to eschew the College and the University altogether, than to submit to drudgery so ignoble, a mockery so contumelious! How much more profitable for the independent mind, after the mere rudiments of education, to range through a library at random, taking down books as they meet him, and pursuing the trains of thought which his mother wit suggests! How much healthier to wander into the fields, and there with the exiled Prince to find "tongues in the trees, books in the running brooks"![44] How much more genuine an education is that of the poor boy in the Poem[45]—a Poem, whether in conception or in execution, one of the most touching in our language—who, not in the wide world, but ranging day by day around his

---

44 Shakespeare's *As You Like It*, II, 1, 16.
45 "Crabbe's *Tales of the Hall*. This Poem, let me say, I read on its first publication, above thirty years ago, with extreme delight, and have never lost my love of it; and on taking it up lately, found I was even more touched by it than heretofore. A work which can please in youth and age, seems to fulfil (in logical language) the *accidental definition* of a Classic. [A further course of twenty years has past, and I bear the same witness in favour of this Poem.]" (Newman)

widowed mother's home, "a dexterous gleaner" in a narrow field, and with only such slender outfit

> as the village school and books a few
> Supplied,

contrived from the beach, and the quay, and the fisher's boat, and the inn's fireside, and the trades-man's shop, and the shepherd's walk, and the smug-gler's hut, and the mossy moor, and the screaming gulls, and the restless waves, to fashion for himself a philosophy and a poetry of his own!

But in a large subject, I am exceeding my necessary limits. Gentlemen, I must conclude abruptly; and postpone any summing up of my argument, should that be necessary, to another day.

from Discourse VII

KNOWLEDGE VIEWED IN RELATION TO PROFESSIONAL SKILL

I

I HAVE been insisting, in my two preceding Discourses, first, on the cultivation of the intellect, as an end which may reasonably be pursued for its own sake; and next, on the nature of that cultivation, or what that cultivation consists in. Truth of whatever kind is the proper object of the intellect; its culti-vation then lies in fitting it to apprehend and contem-plate truth. Now the intellect in its present state, with exceptions which need not here be specified, does not discern truth intuitively, or as a whole. We know, not by a direct and simple vision, not at a glance, but, as it were, by piecemeal and accumu-lation, by a mental process, by going round an object, by the comparison, the combination, the mutual correction, the continual adaptation, of many partial notions, by the employment, concentration, and joint action of many faculties and exercises of mind. Such a union and concert of the intellectual powers, such an enlargement and development, such a comprehensiveness, is necessarily a matter of train-ing. And again, such a training is a matter of rule; it is not mere application, however exemplary, which introduces the mind to truth, nor the reading many books, nor the getting up many subjects, nor the witnessing many experiments, nor the attending many lectures. All this is short of enough; a man may have done it all, yet be lingering in the vestibule of knowledge:—he may not realize what his mouth

utters; he may not see with his mental eye what confronts him; he may have no grasp of things as they are; or at least he may have no power at all of advancing one step forward of himself, in conse-quence of what he has already acquired, no power of discriminating between truth and falsehood, of sifting out the grains of truth from the mass, of arranging things according to their real value, and, if I may use the phrase, of building up ideas. Such a power is the result of a scientific formation of mind; it is an acquired faculty of judgment, of clear-sightedness, of sagacity, of wisdom, of philosophical reach of mind, and of intellectual self-possession and repose,—quali-ties which do not come of mere acquirement. The bodily eye, the organ for apprehending material ob-jects, is provided by nature; the eye of the mind, of which the object is truth, is the work of discipline and habit.

This process of training, by which the intellect, instead of being formed or sacrificed to some par-ticular or accidental purpose, some specific trade or profession, or study or science, is disciplined for its own sake, for the perception of its own proper object, and for its own highest culture, is called Liberal Edu-cation; and though there is no one in whom it is carried as far as is conceivable, or whose intellect would be a pattern of what intellects should be made, yet there is scarcely any one but may gain an idea of what real training is, and at least look towards it, and make its true scope and result, not something else, his standard of excellence; and numbers there are who may submit themselves to it, and secure it to themselves in good measure. And to set forth the right standard, and to train according to it, and to help forward all students towards it according to their various capacities, this I conceive to be the business of a University.

2

Now this is what some great men are very slow to allow; they insist that Education should be confined to some particular and narrow end, and should issue in some definite work, which can be weighed and measured. They argue as if everything, as well as every person, had its price; and that where there has been a great outlay, they have a right to expect a return in kind. This they call making Education and Instruction "useful," and "Utility" becomes their watchword. With a fundamental principle of this nature, they very naturally go on to ask, what there is to show for the expense of a University; what is the real worth in the market of the article called "a Liberal Education," on the supposition that it does not teach us definitely how to advance our manufactures, or to improve our lands, or to better our civil economy; or again, if it does not at once make this man a lawyer, that an engineer, and that a surgeon; or at least if it does not lead to discoveries in chemistry, astronomy, geology, magnetism, and science of every kind.

This question, as might have been expected, has been keenly debated in the present age, and formed one main subject of the controversy, to which I referred in the Introduction to the present Discourses, as having been sustained in the first decade of this century by a celebrated Northern Review on the one hand, and defenders of the University of Oxford on the other.[46] Hardly had the authorities of that ancient seat of learning, waking from their long neglect, set on foot a plan for the education of the youth committed to them, than the representatives of science and literature in the city, which has sometimes been called the Northern Athens,[47] remonstrated, with their gravest arguments and their most brilliant satire, against the direction and shape which the reform was taking. Nothing would content them, but that the University should be set to rights on the basis of the philosophy of Utility; a philosophy, as they seem to have thought, which needed but to be proclaimed in order to be embraced. In truth, they were little aware of the depth and force of the principles on which the academical authorities were proceeding, and, this being so, it was not to be expected that they would be allowed to walk at leisure over the field of controversy which they had selected. Accordingly they were encountered in behalf of the University by two men of great name and influence in their day,[48] of very different minds, but united, as by Collegiate ties, so in the clear-sighted and large view which they took of the whole subject of Liberal Education; and the defence thus provided for the Oxford studies has kept its ground to this day. . . .

5

. . . Let us take "useful," as Locke[49] takes it, in its proper and popular sense, and then we enter upon a large field of thought, to which I cannot do justice in one Discourse, though to-day's is all the space that I can give to it. I say, let us take "useful" to mean, not what is simply good, but what *tends* to good, or is the *instrument* of good; and in this sense also, Gentlemen, I will show you how a liberal education is truly and fully a useful, though it be not a professional, education. "Good" indeed means one thing, and "useful" means another; but I lay it down as a principle, which will save us a great deal of anxiety, that, though the useful is not always good, the good is always useful. Good is not only good, but reproductive of good; this is one of its attributes; nothing is excellent, beautiful, perfect, desirable for its own sake, but it overflows, and spreads the likeness of itself all around it. Good is prolific; it is not only good to the eye, but to the taste; it not only attracts us, but it communicates itself; it excites first our admiration and love, then our desire and our gratitude, and that, in proportion to its intenseness and fulness in particular instances. A great good will impart great good. If then the intellect is so excellent a portion of us, and its cultivation so excellent, it is not only beautiful, perfect, admirable, and noble in itself, but in a true and high sense it must be useful to the possessor and to all around him; not useful in any low, mechanical, mercantile sense, but as diffusing good, or as a blessing, or a gift, or power, or a treasure, first to the owner, then through him to the world. I say then, if a liberal education be good, it must necessarily be useful too.

6

You will see what I mean by the parallel of bodily health. Health is a good in itself, though nothing came of it, and is especially worth seeking and cherishing; yet, after all, the blessings which attend its presence are so great, while they are so close to it and so redound back upon it and encircle it, that we never think of it except as useful as well as good, and praise and prize it for what it does, as well as for what it is, though at the same time we cannot point out any definite and distinct work or production which it can be said to effect. And so as regards intellectual culture, I am far from denying utility in this large sense as

---

[46] The impractical nature of Oxford education was attacked in the *Edinburgh Review*, 1808–1810. The University was defended in the first instance by its Professor of Poetry, Edward Copleston, seconded by John Davison, Fellow of Oriel College. That the attack did, however, pave the way for certain needed reforms is pointed out by Newman in his "Note on Liberalism," above, p. 492.   [47] Edinburgh.   [48] Copleston and Davison.

[49] In the passage that has been omitted at the beginning of this section, Newman cites the celebrated seventeenth-century philosopher John Locke and his nineteenth-century disciples as "condemning the ordinary subjects in which boys are instructed at school, on the ground that they are not needed by them in after life." The authors of the articles in the *Edinburgh Review* (see note 46) are identified with Locke in asking the question which Newman here proposes to answer: "What other measure of dignity in intellectual labour is there but usefulness?"

the end of Education, when I lay it down, that the culture of the intellect is a good in itself and its own end; I do not exclude from the idea of intellectual culture what it cannot but be, from the very nature of things; I only deny that we must be able to point out, before we have any right to call it useful, some art, or business, or profession, or trade, or work, as resulting from it, and as its real and complete end. The parallel is exact:—As the body may be sacrificed to some manual or other toil, whether moderate or oppressive, so may the intellect be devoted to some specific profession; and I do not call *this* the culture of the intellect. Again, as some member or organ of the body may be inordinately used and developed, so may memory, or imagination, or the reasoning faculty; and *this* again is not intellectual culture. On the other hand, as the body may be tended, cherished, and exercised with a simple view to its general health, so may the intellect also be generally exercised in order to its perfect state; and this *is* its cultivation.

Again, as health ought to precede labour of the body, and as a man in health can do what an unhealthy man cannot do, and as of his health the properties are strength, energy, agility, graceful carriage and action, manual dexterity, and endurance of fatigue, so in like manner general culture of mind is the best aid to professional and scientific study, and educated men can do what illiterate cannot; and the man who has learned to think and to reason and to compare and to discriminate and to analyse, who has refined his taste, and formed his judgment, and sharpened his mental vision, will not indeed at once be a lawyer, or a pleader, or an orator, or a statesman, or a physician, or a good landlord, or a man of business, or a soldier, or an engineer, or a chemist, or a geologist, or an antiquarian, but he will be placed in that state of intellect in which he can take up any one of the sciences or callings I have referred to, or any other for which he has a taste or special talent, with an ease, a grace, a versatility, and a success, to which another is a stranger. In this sense then, and as yet I have said but a very few words on a large subject, mental culture is emphatically *useful*.

If then I am arguing, and shall argue, against Professional or Scientific knowledge as the sufficient end of a University Education, let me not be supposed, Gentlemen, to be disrespectful towards particular studies, or arts, or vocations, and those who are engaged in them. In saying that Law or Medicine is not the end of a University course, I do not mean to imply that the University does not teach Law or Medicine. What indeed can it teach at all, if it does not teach something particular? It teaches *all* knowl-

edge by teaching all *branches* of knowledge, and in no other way. I do but say that there will be this distinction as regards a Professor of Law, or of Medicine, or of Geology, or of Political Economy, in a University and out of it, that out of a University he is in danger of being absorbed and narrowed by his pursuit, and of giving Lectures which are the Lectures of nothing more than a lawyer, physician, geologist, or political economist; whereas in a University he will just know where he and his science stand, he has come to it, as it were, from a height, he has taken a survey of all knowledge, he is kept from extravagance by the very rivalry of other studies, he has gained from them a special illumination and largeness of mind and freedom and self-possession, and he treats his own in consequence with a philosophy and a resource, which belongs not to the study itself, but to his liberal education.

This then is how I should solve the fallacy, for so I must call it, by which Locke and his disciples would frighten us from cultivating the intellect, under the notion that no education is useful which does not teach us some temporal calling, or some mechanical art, or some physical secret. I say that a cultivated intellect, because it is a good in itself, brings with it a power and a grace to every work and occupation which it undertakes, and enables us to be more useful, and to a greater number. There is a duty we owe to human society as such, to the state to which we belong, to the sphere in which we move, to the individuals towards whom we are variously related, and whom we successively encounter in life; and that philosophical or liberal education, as I have called it, which is the proper function of a University, if it refuses the foremost place to professional interests, does but postpone them to the formation of the citizen, and, while it subserves the larger interests of philanthropy, prepares also for the successful prosecution of those merely personal objects, which at first sight it seems to disparage. . . .

10

. . . Today I have confined myself to saying that that training of the intellect, which is best for the individual himself, best enables him to discharge his duties to society. The Philosopher, indeed, and the man of the world differ in their very notion, but the methods, by which they are respectively formed, are pretty much the same. The Philosopher has the same command of matters of thought, which the true citizen and gentleman has of matters of business and conduct. If then a practical end must be assigned to a University course, I say it is that of training good members of society. Its art is the art of social life, and its end is fitness for the world. It neither confines its views to particular professions on the one hand, nor creates heroes or inspires genius on the other. Works indeed of genius fall under no art; heroic minds come under no rule; a University is not a birthplace of poets or of immortal authors, of founders of schools, leaders of colonies, or conquerors of nations. It does not promise a generation of Aristotles or Newtons, of Napoleons or Washingtons, of Raphaels or Shakespeares, though such miracles of nature it has before now contained within its precincts. Nor is it content on the other hand with forming the critic or the experimentalist, the economist or the engineer, though such too it includes within its scope. But a University training is the great ordinary means to a great but ordinary end; it aims at raising the intellectual tone of society, at cultivating the public mind, at purifying the national taste, at supplying true principles to popular enthusiasm and fixed aims to popular aspiration, at giving enlargement and sobriety to the ideas of the age, at facilitating the exercise of political power, and refining the intercourse of private life. It is the education which gives a man a clear conscious view of his own opinions and judgments, a truth in developing them, an eloquence in expressing them, and a force in urging them. It teaches him to see things as they are, to go right to the point, to disentangle a skein of thought, to detect what is sophistical, and to discard what is irrelevant. It prepares him to fill any post with credit, and to master any subject with facility. It shows him how to accommodate himself to others, how to throw himself into their state of mind, how to bring before them his own, how to influence them, how to come to an understanding with them, how to bear with them. He is at home in any society, he has common ground with every class; he knows when to speak and when to be silent; he is able to converse, he is able to listen; he can ask a question pertinently, and gain a lesson seasonably, when he has nothing to impart himself; he is ever ready, yet never in the way; he is a pleasant companion, and a comrade you can depend upon; he knows when to be serious and when to trifle, and he has a sure tact which enables him to trifle with gracefulness and to be serious with effect. He has the repose of a mind which lives in itself, while it lives in the world, and which has resources for its happiness at home when it cannot go abroad. He has a gift which serves him in public, and supports him in retirement, without which good fortune is but vulgar, and with which failure and disappointment have a charm. The art which tends to make a man all this, is in the object which it pursues as useful as the art of wealth or the art of health, though it is less susceptible of method, and less tangible, less certain, less complete in its result.

John Stuart Mill

1806–1873

STRICTLY speaking, John Stuart Mill is not a literary figure. He had little ability to communicate living experience or to bring ideas to life through metaphor and imagery, so that they could be felt and seen as well as understood. He could write clearly, forcefully, and with an impressive sincerity and conviction, but he could not write graphically in a language capable of revealing the color and emotional quality of his thought. Its range and significance, however, is so great that no one who wishes to understand the Victorian period can afford to neglect him.

He was born in 1806, the eldest son of James Mill, the ardent disciple and personal friend of Bentham. From his birth, therefore, Mill was dedicated to the cause of Utilitarianism. To that end he was subjected to a rigorous and thorough education, with his father as teacher. He began the study of Greek at the age of three and Latin at eight, covered much of ancient and modern history and philosophy before he was thirteen, did considerable work in physical science and mathematics, and then completed his education at sixteen with a close study of Bentham and the political economists whom Bentham admired, Adam Smith, Ricardo, and Malthus, all of whom advocated a policy of *laissez faire*. In method this education was almost entirely intellectual. Mill's mind was so well trained in logical analysis and his sensibility so well starved (literature and art were of small account in Utilitarian theory) that he became, as he confesses, a reasoning machine. As for religious and moral training, the former did not exist (James Mill was an agnostic, and his son, therefore, was "one of the very few examples, in this country, of one who has, not thrown off religious belief, but never had it"); while the latter was Utilitarian in principle and method. Starting from the assumption that men are motivated almost entirely by the desire for pleasure, Bentham's plan was to make the social—that is, the moral—action pleasurable and the antisocial, antimoral action painful. This was already being done, to some extent, by law and public opinion, but far better results might be achieved by a rigorous discipline in early life. Whenever a child did a social act or adopted a social attitude, he was to be praised or given a tangible reward; whenever the reverse, he was to be blamed or punished. In this way unbreakable associations would supposedly be built up between social good and personal pleasure, between social harm and personal pain, until ultimately the grown man would "instinctively" do the unselfish thing, though his motivation, of course, would be selfish. This was the system tried out on young Mill; but with the additional twist of teaching him to associate his own greatest happiness with a life of positive service to society. By day he was to earn his living at the East India Company (where he started as a clerk in 1823 and rose to the second highest office before the Company was taken over by the state in 1858 and Mill retired from business). But by night, and on week ends and vacations, he was to reform society on Utilitarian lines. He was to persuade people of the value of democracy, of an enlightened self-interest, of an education wider than the classics which would include modern science and political economy, and all other projects which Bentham and James Mill were advocating (see p. 522 for a summary). The main vehicle for this propaganda was the *Westminster Review,* founded in 1824 as an organ of Utilitarianism to rival the Tory *Quarterly Review* and the Whig *Edinburgh Review.*

Then in 1826, when Mill was twenty, occurred the event which changed his life and widened his thinking far beyond the bounds of Benthamism. This was a severe nervous breakdown which brought him to the edge of suicide. As a modern scholar has recently shown, its real cause, unknown to Mill, lay in a repressed desire for the death of his father (which is the explanation for the sense of guilt Mill recognized but could not explain: see p. 524). This was the result partly of long years of fear and hatred, bred by James Mill's irritable temper and his severe discipline, unmitigated by any tenderness of feeling; and partly of the frustrated wish to escape from a parental domination so strong that the boy could not call his soul his own or stand on his own feet. No wonder, therefore, that his reading of Marmontel's passage (see p. 526, below) relating the death of a father and the delighted assumption of his place by the son, started the process of recovery (Mill being able in this substituted form to rejoice in what he secretly and guiltily desired for himself, and thus to rid himself partially of his repressed emotions).

But in that pre-Freudian age, he had no conscious inkling of the real facts. He, therefore, explained his breakdown in another way, of no significance as explanation, but of great significance for the development of his thought.

In the early weeks of depression, he had asked himself how he would feel if all his dreams for social improvement were fulfilled. The answer should have been "Superlatively happy," since he had been taught to identify his own happiness with that of society; but the answer was "Miserable." Plainly, something was wrong with his Benthamite education. In a highly important but difficult passage (pp. 525–6), he concludes that the theory of association was sound enough, but that the linkage between personal happiness and social good must have been too weak and too much exposed to dissolution. In all such associations there must be "something artificial and casual." Why *should* my own pleasure be tied up with social good rather than with personal achievement or anything else? The linkage is arbitrarily made by the parent; and in Mill's case had been made entirely by the instruments of "praise and blame, reward and punishment." But logical analysis, in which he had been almost exclusively trained, is exactly the faculty best calculated to "separate ideas which have only casually clung together." This, clearly, was what had happened. How could it have been prevented, and be prevented in the future? First, through making the associations stronger and more intense by presenting social action as something thrilling and exciting on its own account, an heroic crusade for humanity, and not merely something which can win the reformer praise and reward. Then his personal feelings would be far more intimately attached to humanitarian goals, and would less readily yield to analysis. And perhaps they would not yield at all if, second, analytical training were supplemented, and its dominance checked, by a training of the feelings and the imagination.

This rationale of his breakdown led Mill to two radical changes in his intellectual outlook. He decided that although happiness was the aim of life, it was only to be attained, as a by-product, from the pursuit of some other object, the happiness of others or the improvement of mankind, "followed not as a means, but as itself an ideal end." The other crucial change lay in the method by which he thought a good society might be attained. The great need, he decided, was not for better public opinion and better institutions, political and educational; it was for better men. Social progress depended at bottom on "the internal culture of the individual," of the whole individual, of his feelings no less than his intellect. And by the cultivation of the feelings, Mill meant the development of the moral as well as the aesthetic sensibility. What he wanted, therefore, and what almost all of his work was intended to forward, directly or indirectly, was self-development, sometimes meaning the development of one's individual personality (following one's own genius), sometimes meaning the development of all one's potentialities of mind and character and imagination.

It is obvious that these two changes in the foundations of Mill's philosophy, presently confirmed by his reading of Wordsworth, carried him at once outside Benthamism. Indeed, they were cardinal doctrines of the anti-Benthamite school of Wordsworth, Coleridge, and Carlyle, and of the German philosophers and poets they admired. Mill himself noticed the parallel of the first with Carlyle's "anti-self-consciousness theory" (see "The Everlasting Yea") and remarked of the second that the Germano-Coleridgean philosophers looked on "the culture of the inward man as the problem of problems" (cf. Carlyle's focus on individual regeneration, and his reference to external social reforms as Morison's pills). In short, Mill's breakdown proved a blessing in disguise. It widened his personal friendships to include not only Carlyle, with whom he was on intimate terms for many years, but also the Coleridgeans F. D. Maurice and John Sterling. It widened his reading to include Kant, Fichte, Goethe, along with the French romantic historians Guizot and Michelet and the French philosophers Saint-Simon and Comte, who were challenging laissez-faire capitalism and propounding a theory of history in which organic periods of belief like the Middle Ages were succeeded by critical periods of doubt and transition like the present (see p. 531, and the chapter from Mill's *Spirit of the Age*). It led to his conviction that no creed ever contained more than half of the truth and that the whole truth lay in a synthesis of opposing views (of which his own later work was to be an example). It inspired that fine, and very un-Victorian, plea "to consider one's opponents as one's allies, as people climbing the hill on the other side."

So long as Mill was a Benthamite, he had thought of liberty as something essentially negative. It meant freedom *from* interference; and the function of government was solely to maintain law and order. This was the cornerstone of early Victorian liberalism; it is perfectly exemplified in Macaulay's essay on Southey. But Mill now came to think of liberty as something positive. It meant freedom *to* develop and grow to one's full capacity. As a result, his evaluation of democracy changed and deepened (see his *Representative Government*, 1861). Once, under the influence of Bentham and James Mill, he had advocated democracy because only when government was in the hands of the people would it act for the greatest good of the people—and not for the greatest good of a monarch or an oligarchy. Now he saw that it was also valuable because, if the people had to manage their own government, national and local, they would gain in self-reliance

and self-dependence: their active faculties would be developed and their social feelings stimulated. In theory the Benthamites would have accepted a dictator provided he governed for the greatest good of society. But not Mill, because from his point of view dictatorship, however benevolent, promotes dependence and passive obedience. It curbs the very development of individuality which democracy encourages. In one other particular Mill extended democratic theory. The Benthamites never went beyond manhood suffrage. Mill argued for universal suffrage on the grounds that women too must be represented if *their* greatest good was not to be overlooked, and that they too needed the stimulus of self-development that democracy provides.

If a free society is one in which all individuals have the maximum opportunity to grow to their full capacity, moral and intellectual, is this best attained under laissez-faire capitalism? Mill had thought so once, but when he saw the suffering of the laboring classes in the 1840's and read *Past and Present*, he became convinced that a majority of the nation had no such opportunity under the existing system. "The generality of labourers in this and most other countries," he wrote in his *Principles of Political Economy* (1848), "have as little choice of occupation or freedom of locomotion, are practically as dependent on fixed rules and on the will of others, as they could be on any system short of actual slavery." And then he spoke those astonishing words, at once the measure of his own capacity for growth and of his remarkable open-mindedness, "The restraints of Communism would be freedom in comparison with the present condition of the majority of the human race." So it was that Mill, the liberal, in the cause of gaining greater freedom for the have-nots, came to advocate a greater and greater extension of government action—high inheritance taxes, state control of public utilities, the nationalization of land—until finally he called himself a socialist and talked of a time when all men would be required to work and the division of labor would be made on an acknowledged principle of justice. But he saw the dilemma. If the creation of a society where all should have an equal freedom to grow meant the erection of an all-powerful state, the very freedom he was seeking would be destroyed, and individual liberty would be crushed beneath an omnipotent regimentation. How, he asked, can we unite "the greatest individual liberty of action, with a common ownership in the raw material of the globe, and an equal participation of all in the benefits of combined labour"? That was "the social problem of the future"—and it still is.

This gives us the right perspective on the famous essay *On Liberty* (1859), which has been called the finest expression of Victorian, and modern, liberalism. If a large measure of social control was a necessity to insure equal freedom for all, it was equally necessary to define a limit to political and social power if individuality was to be preserved. That limit was self-protection. "The only purpose for which power can be rightfully exercised over any member of a civilised community, against his will, is to prevent harm to others. . . . Over himself, over his own body and mind, the individual is sovereign" (p. 540).

The danger at the time was not the tyranny of the state but that of public opinion—the tendency of Victorian society, as of all societies, "to fetter the development, and, if possible, prevent the formation, of any individuality not in harmony with its ways," by using the weapons of social stigma and ostracism. In Chapter 2 Mill attacks the effort to curb freedom of thought and speech, in Chapter 3 the effort to curb freedom of action and character. The former is a fine exposure of the Victorian attempt to suppress speculation for fear it might undermine religious belief and consequently moral order. As Mill points out, in an age terrified of skepticism it was wholly natural to defend traditional doctrines because they were useful, and to stigmatize anyone who questioned them in the name of truth (p. 542). In such an atmosphere not only was speculation *discouraged*, but hypocrisy was *encouraged*, outward conformity to the accepted beliefs but inward dissent. That important connection between Victorian anti-intellectualism and Victorian hypocrisy is brought out in the last paragraphs of the selection. "The ban placed on all inquiry which does not end in the orthodox conclusions" thwarted the development of great minds either by turning them away from the pursuit of truth altogether, or by forcing them into timid and sophistical efforts to fit "their own conclusions to premises which they have internally renounced."

In Chapter 3 it is the development of character, meaning both a person's individual bent and all his capacities, which Mill finds jeopardized, unconsciously by modern democratic civilization, and consciously by public opinion. He recognized—what is even truer today—that people were living more and more in the same world—hearing the same things, going to the same places, sharing the same ambitions—as class lines were breaking down and science was providing better and faster means of communication. As a result, one of the two prerequi-

sites for promoting individuality, variety of situations, was steadily disappearing (see p. 556). This lay beyond control, but the other prerequisite, freedom from social pressure, might and should be demanded in opposition to democratic and Puritan public opinion. In any democracy the "average" or "typical" citizen may readily be made the standard to which all must conform on pain of being criticized as "different"; and if that society is also strongly Puritan, the slightest deviation from a rigid and severe moral code will be sufficient to incite public ostracism (see especially p. 554). Moreover, since Puritanism exalted the Christian doctrine of self-denial, and viewed the passions and the intellect as dangerous faculties to be kept severely in check, it was naturally a force in Victorian society running counter to Mill's deepest convictions. " 'Pagan self-assertion,' " he insists, "is one of the elements of human worth, as well as 'Christian self-denial.' There is a Greek ideal of self-development, which the Platonic and Christian ideal of self-government blends with, but does not supersede." This is the core of Matthew Arnold's famous essay on "Hebraism and Hellenism"; for Arnold, with his plea for the intellectual life and the rounded development of human nature, is the follower of Mill.

There is no standard edition of Mill's work. The *Autobiography*, edited by Harold Laski, is in The World's Classics; *Utilitarianism, On Liberty,* and *Representative Government* share a volume in Everyman's Library. Mill's major essays have been collected as *Dissertations and Discussions* (4 or 5 volumes, depending on the edition): see especially "Civilization," "Bentham," and "Coleridge." *The Spirit of the Age* has been edited by F. von Hayek (1942). There is no good study of Mill. Alexander Bain's *John Stuart Mill* (1882) is an adequate biography; Leslie Stephen's *The English Utilitarians* (1900), Vol. III, is a survey of his books. Charles L. Street's *Individualism and Individuality in the Philosophy of John Stuart Mill* (1926) is an able study of the central strand of his thought. James Bonar's essay in his *Philosophy and Political Economy* (1893) is still a useful summary of Mill's intellectual development. The new interpretation of Mill's nervous breakdown, referred to above, is by A. W. Levi, "The Mental Crisis of John Stuart Mill," *Psycho-Analytical Review*, XXXII (1945), 88-101.

John Stuart Mill

from AUTOBIOGRAPHY

from Chapter 4

YOUTHFUL PROPAGANDISM. THE *West-*
minster Review

. . . AT this period,[1] when Liberalism seemed to be becoming the tone of the time, when improvement of institutions was preached from the highest places, and a complete change of the constitution of Parliament was loudly demanded in the lowest, it is not strange that attention should have been roused by the regular appearance in controversy of what seemed a new school of writers, claiming to be the legislators and theorists of this new tendency. The air of strong conviction with which they wrote, when scarcely any one else seemed to have an equally strong faith in as definite a creed; the boldness with which they tilted against the very front of both the existing political parties; their uncompromising profession of opposition to many of the generally received opinions, and the suspicion they lay under of holding others still more heterodox than they professed; the talent and verve of at least my father's articles, and the appearance of a corps behind him sufficient to carry on a Review;[2] and finally, the fact that the Review was bought and read, made the so-called Bentham school in philosophy and politics fill a greater place in the public mind than it had held before, or has ever again held since other equally earnest schools of thought have arisen in England. As I was in the headquarters of it, knew of what it was composed, and as one of the most active of its very small number, might say without undue assumption, *quorum pars magna fui,*[3] it belongs to me more than to most others, to give some account of it.

This supposed school, then, had no other existence than what was constituted by the fact, that my father's writings and conversation drew round him a certain number of young men who had already imbibed, or who imbibed from him, a greater or smaller portion of his very decided political and philosophical opinions. The notion that Bentham was surrounded by a band of disciples who received their opinions from his lips, is a fable to which my father did justice in his "Fragment on Mackintosh,"[4] and which, to all who knew Mr. Bentham's habits of life and manner of conversation, is simply ridiculous. The influence which Bentham exercised was by his writings. Through them he has produced, and is producing, effects on the condition of mankind, wider and deeper, no doubt, than any which can be attributed to my father. He is a much greater name in history. But my father exercised a far greater personal ascendancy. He *was* sought for the vigour and instructiveness of his conversation, and did use it largely as an instrument for the diffusion of his opinions. I have never known any man who could do such ample justice to his best thoughts in colloquial discussion. His perfect command over his great mental resources, the terseness and expressiveness of his language and the moral earnestness as well as intellectual force of his delivery, made him one of the most striking of all argumentative conversers: and he was full of anecdote, a hearty laugher, and, when with people whom he liked, a most lively and amusing companion. It was not solely, or even chiefly, in diffusing his merely intellectual convictions that his power showed itself: it was still more through the influence of a quality, of which I have only since learnt to appreciate the extreme rarity: that exalted public spirit, and regard above all things to the good of the whole, which warmed into life and activity every germ of similar virtue that existed in the minds he came in contact with: the desire he made them feel for his approbation, the shame at his disapproval; the moral support which his conversation and his very existence gave to those who were aiming at the same objects, and the encouragement he afforded to the fainthearted or desponding among them, by the firm confidence which (though the reverse of sanguine as to the results to be expected in any one particular case) he always felt in the power of reason, the general progress of improvement, and the good which individuals could do by judicious effort.

It was my father's opinions which gave the distinguishing character to the Benthamic or utilitarian

---

[1] The 1820's.—The *Autobiography* on which Mill worked at intervals during the last twenty years of his life, was published in 1873, shortly after his death.

[2] The *Westminster Review,* the organ of the Utilitarians or Benthamites.

[3] I was a great part of it.

[4] Sir James Mackintosh (1765–1832) was a Scottish philosopher.

propagandism of that time. They fell singly, scattered from him, in many directions, but they flowed from him in a continued stream principally in three channels. One was through me, the only mind directly formed by his instructions, and through whom considerable influence was exercised over various young men, who became in their turn, propagandists. A second was through some of the Cambridge contemporaries of Charles Austin,[5] who, either initiated by him or under the general mental impulse which he gave, had adopted many opinions allied to those of my father, and some of the more considerable of whom afterwards sought my father's acquaintance and frequented his house. Among these may be mentioned Strutt, afterwards Lord Belper, and the present Lord Romilly, with whose eminent father, Sir Samuel, my father had of old been on terms of friendship. The third channel was that of a younger generation of Cambridge undergraduates, contemporary, not with Austin, but with Eyton Tooke,[6] who were drawn to that estimable person by affinity of opinions, and introduced by him to my father: the most notable of these was Charles Buller.[7] Various other persons individually received and transmitted a considerable amount of my father's influence: for example, Black[8] (as before mentioned) and Fonblanque:[9] most of these, however, we accounted only partial allies; Fonblanque, for instance, was always divergent from us on many important points. But indeed there was by no means complete unanimity among any portion of us, nor had any of us adopted implicitly all my father's opinions. For example, although his Essay on Government was regarded probably by all of us as a masterpiece of political wisdom, our adhesion by no means extended to the paragraph of it, in which he maintains that women may consistently with good government, be excluded from the suffrage, because their interest is the same with that of men. From this doctrine, I, and all those who formed my chosen associates, most positively dissented. It is due to my father to say that he denied having intended to affirm that women *should* be excluded, any more than men under the age of forty, concerning whom he maintained, in the very next paragraph, an exactly similar thesis. He was, as he truly said, not discussing whether the suffrage had better be restricted, but only (assuming that it is to be restricted) what is the utmost limit of restriction, which does not necessarily involve a sacrifice of the securities for good government. But I thought then, as I have always thought since, that the opinion which he acknowledged, no less than that which he disclaimed, is as great an error as any of those against which the Essay was directed; that the interest of women is included in that of men exactly as much and no more, as the interest of subjects is included in that of kings; and that every reason which exists for giving the suffrage to anybody, demands that it should not be withheld from women. This was also the general opinion of the younger proselytes; and it is pleasant to be able to say that Mr. Bentham, on this important point, was wholly on our side.

But though none of us, probably, agreed in every respect with my father, his opinions, as I said before, were the principal element which gave its colour and character to the little group of young men who were the first propagators of what was afterwards called "Philosophic Radicalism." Their mode of thinking was not characterized by Benthamism in any sense which has relation to Bentham as a chief or guide, but rather by a combination of Bentham's point of view with that of the modern political economy, and with the Hartleian[10] metaphysics. Malthus's population principle[11] was quite as much a banner, and point of union among us, as any opinion specially belonging to Bentham. This great doctrine, originally brought forward as an argument against the indefinite improvability of human affairs, we took up with ardent zeal in the contrary sense, as indicating the sole means of realizing that improvability by securing full

[5] A slightly older contemporary of Mill, who had been much influenced by James Mill. Earlier in the *Autobiography* Mill says: "It is my belief that much of the notion popularly entertained of the tenets and sentiments of what are called Benthamites or Utilitarians had its origin in paradoxes thrown out by Charles Austin."

[6] A member of the early Utilitarian Society, a group planned by Mill, as he tells us earlier, in the winter of 1822–23, "to be composed of young men agreeing in fundamental principles—acknowledging Utility as their standard in ethics and politics. . . . The number never, I think, reached ten, and the society was broken up in 1826." He mentions Tooke as one of the members who became his intimate companions.

[7] English statesman (1806–48), who had a considerable share, aided by Mill himself, in drawing up the famous Durham report on North America, which first laid down the general principles of the British Commonwealth of Nations.

[8] John Black (1783–1855), the editor of the *Morning Chronicle,* under whose aegis the paper "became to a considerable extent a vehicle of the opinions of the Utilitarian Radicals." (Mill)

[9] Albany Fonblanque (1793–1872), one of the principal contributors to the *Morning Chronicle.*

[10] Of David Hartley (c. 1705–57), materialist philosopher and founder of English associational psychology.

[11] That since population increases in a geometrical and means of subsistence only in an arithmetical ratio, mankind was constantly and inevitably subject to crime, disease, and war.

employment at high wages to the whole labouring population through a voluntary restriction of the increase of their numbers. The other leading characteristics of the creed, which we held in common with my father, may be stated as follows:

In politics, an almost unbounded confidence in the efficacy of two things: representative government, and complete freedom of discussion. So complete was my father's reliance on the influence of reason over the minds of mankind, whenever it is allowed to reach them, that he felt as if all would be gained if the whole population were taught to read, if all sorts of opinions were allowed to be addressed to them by word and in writing, and if by means of the suffrage they could nominate a legislature to give effect to the opinions they adopted. He thought that when the legislature no longer represented a class interest, it would aim at the general interest, honestly and with adequate wisdom; since the people would be sufficiently under the guidance of educated intelligence, to make in general a good choice of persons to represent them, and having done so, to leave to those whom they had chosen a liberal discretion. Accordingly aristocratic rule, the government of the Few in any of its shapes, being in his eyes the only thing which stood between mankind and an administration of their affairs by the best wisdom to be found among them, was the object of his sternest disapprobation, and a democratic suffrage the principal article of his political creed, not on the ground of liberty, Rights of Man, or any of the phrases, more or less significant, by which, up to that time, democracy had usually been defended, but as the most essential of "securities for good government." In this, too, he held fast only to what he deemed essentials; he was comparatively indifferent to monarchical or republican forms—far more so than Bentham, to whom a king, in the character of "corrupter-general," appeared necessarily very noxious. Next to aristocracy, an established church, or corporation of priests, as being by position the great depravers of religion, and interested in opposing the progress of the human mind, was the object of his greatest detestation; though he disliked no clergyman personally who did not deserve it, and was on terms of sincere friendship with several. In ethics, his moral feelings were energetic and rigid on all points which he deemed important to human well being, while he was supremely indifferent in opinion (though his indifference did not show itself in personal conduct) to all those doctrines of the common morality, which he thought had no foundation but in asceticism and priestcraft. He looked forward, for example, to a considerable increase of freedom in the relations between the sexes, though without pretending to define exactly what would be, or ought to be, the precise conditions of that freedom. This opinion was connected in him with no sensuality either of a theoretical or of a practical kind. He anticipated, on the contrary, as one of the beneficial effects of increased freedom, that the imagination would no longer dwell upon the physical relation and its adjuncts, and swell this into one of the principal objects of life; a perversion of the imagination and feelings, which he regarded as one of the deepest seated and most pervading evils in the human mind. In psychology, his fundamental doctrine was the formation of all human character by circumstances, through the universal Principle of Association, and the consequent unlimited possibility of improving the moral and intellectual condition of mankind by education. Of all his doctrines none was more important than this, or needs more to be insisted on: unfortunately there is none which is more contradictory to the prevailing tendencies of speculation, both in his time and since.

These various opinions were seized on with youthful fanaticism by the little knot of young men of whom I was one: and we put into them a sectarian spirit, from which, in intention at least, my father was wholly free. What we (or rather a phantom substituted in the place of us) were sometimes, by a ridiculous exaggeration, called by others, namely a "school," some of us for a time really hoped and aspired to be. The French *philosophes*[12] of the eighteenth century were the example we sought to imitate, and we hoped to accomplish no less results. No one of the set went to so great excesses in this boyish ambition as I did; which might be shown by many particulars, were it not an useless waste of space and time.

All this, however, is properly only the outside of our existence; or, at least, the intellectual part alone, and no more than one side of that. In attempting to penetrate inward, and give any indication of what we were as human beings, I must be understood as speaking only of myself, of whom alone I can speak from sufficient knowledge; and I do not believe that the picture would suit any of my companions without many and great modifications.

---

12 A name given to a group of writers, most of whom were French, who were skeptics in religion, materialists in philosophy, and hedonists in ethics. Principal representatives included Diderot, D'Alembert, Helvetius, and Condorcet.

I conceive that the description so often given of a Benthamite, as a mere reasoning machine, though extremely inapplicable to most of those who have been designated by that title, was during two or three years of my life not altogether untrue of me. It was perhaps as applicable to me as it can well be to any one just entering into life, to whom the common objects of desire must in general have at least the attraction of novelty. There is nothing very extraordinary in this fact: no youth of the age I then was, can be expected to be more than one thing, and this was the thing I happened to be. Ambition and desire of distinction, I had in abundance, and zeal for what I thought the good of mankind was my strongest sentiment, mixing with and colouring all others. But my zeal was as yet little else, at that period of my life, than zeal for speculative opinions. It had not its root in genuine benevolence, or sympathy with mankind; though these qualities held their due place in my ethical standard. Nor was it connected with any high enthusiasm for ideal nobleness. Yet of this feeling I was imaginatively very susceptible; but there was at that time an intermission of its natural aliment, poetical culture, while there was a superabundance of the discipline antagonistic to it, that of mere logic and analysis. Add to this that, as already mentioned, my father's teachings tended to the undervaluing of feeling. It was not that he was himself cold-hearted or insensible; I believe it was rather from the contrary quality; he thought that feeling could take care of itself; that there was sure to be enough of it if actions were properly cared about. Offended by the frequency with which, in ethical and philosophical controversy, feeling is made the ultimate reason and justification of conduct, instead of being itself called on for a justification, while, in practice, actions the effect of which on human happiness is mischievous, are defended as being required by feeling, and the character of a person of feeling obtains a credit for desert, which he thought only due to actions, he had a real impatience of attributing praise to feeling, or of any but the most sparing reference to it, either in the estimation of persons or in the discussion of things. In addition to the influence which this characteristic in him, had on me and others, we found all the opinions to which we attached most importance, constantly attacked on the ground of feeling. Utility was denounced as cold calculation; political economy as hard-hearted; anti-population doctrines as repulsive to the natural feelings of mankind. We retorted by the word "sentimentality," which, along with "declamation" and "vague generalities," served us as common terms of opprobrium. Although we were generally in the right, as against those who were opposed to us, the effect was that the cultivation of feeling (except the feelings of public and private duty), was not in much esteem among us, and had very little place in the thoughts of most of us, myself in particular. What we principally thought of, was to alter people's opinions; to make them believe according to evidence, and know what was their real interest, which when they once knew, they would, we thought, by the instrument of opinion, enforce a regard to it upon one another. While fully recognising the superior excellence of unselfish benevolence and love of justice, we did not expect the regeneration of mankind from any direct action on those sentiments, but from the effect of educated intellect, enlightening the selfish feelings. Although this last is prodigiously important as a means of improvement in the hands of those who are themselves impelled by nobler principles of action, I do not believe that any one of the survivors of the Benthamites or Utilitarians of that day, now relies mainly upon it for the general amendment of human conduct.

From this neglect both in theory and in practice of the cultivation of feeling, naturally resulted, among other things, an undervaluing of poetry, and of Imagination generally, as an element of human nature. It is, or was, part of the popular notion of Benthamites, that they are enemies of poetry: this was partly true of Bentham himself; he used to say that "all poetry is misrepresentation": but in the sense in which he said it, the same might have been said of all impressive speech; of all representation or inculcation more oratorical in its character than a sum in arithmetic. An article of Bingham's[13] in the first number of the Westminster Review, in which he offered as an explanation of something which he disliked in Moore,[14] that "Mr. Moore *is* a poet, and therefore is *not* a reasoner," did a good deal to attach the notion of hating poetry to the writers in the Review. But the truth was that many of us were great readers of poetry; Bingham himself had been a writer of it, while as regards me (and the same thing might be said of my father), the correct statement would be, not that I disliked poetry, but that I was theoretically indifferent to it. I disliked any sentiments in poetry which I should have disliked in prose; and that included a great deal. And I was wholly

---

13 Peregrine Bingham (1788–1864), a frequent contributor in the early days of the *Westminster Review*. "The literary and artistic department [of the first number] had rested chiefly on Mr. Bingham." (Mill)
14 On Thomas Moore see pp. 358–9, above.

blind to its place in human culture, as a means of educating the feelings. But I was always personally very susceptible to some kinds of it. In the most sectarian period of my Benthamism, I happened to look into Pope's Essay on Man, and though every opinion in it was contrary to mine, I well remember how powerfully it acted on my imagination. Perhaps at that time poetical composition of any higher type than eloquent discussion in verse, might not have produced a similar effect on me: at all events I seldom gave it an opportunity. This, however, was a mere passive state. Long before I had enlarged in any considerable degree, the basis of my intellectual creed, I had obtained in the natural course of my mental progress, poetic culture of the most valuable kind, by means of reverential admiration for the lives and characters of heroic persons; especially the heroes of philosophy.[15] The same inspiring effect which so many of the benefactors of mankind have left on record that they had experienced from Plutarch's Lives,[16] was produced on me by Plato's pictures of Socrates,[17] and by some modern biographies, above all by Condorcet's Life of Turgot;[18] a book well calculated to rouse the best sort of enthusiasm, since it contains one of the wisest and noblest of lives, delineated by one of the wisest and noblest of men. The heroic virtue of these glorious representatives of the opinions with which I sympathized, deeply affected me, and I perpetually recurred to them as others do to a favourite poet, when needing to be carried up into the more elevated regions of feeling and thought. I may observe by the way that this book cured me of my sectarian follies. The two or three pages beginning "Il regardait toute secte comme nuisible,"[19] and explaining why Turgot always kept himself perfectly distinct from the Encyclopedists,[20] sank deeply into my mind. I left off designating myself and others as Utilitarians, and by the pronoun "we" or any other collective designation, I ceased to *afficher*[21] sectarianism. My real inward sectarianism I did not get rid of till later, and much more gradually. . . .

---

[15] For Mill's identification of "poetic culture" with the cultivation of the moral sensibility, see below, p. 527.

[16] Plutarch wrote the *Lives* to provide inspiring examples of wise and heroic conduct.   [17] In *The Republic*.

[18] Turgot was an eighteenth-century French statesman who endeavored to effect liberal reforms until his dismissal by Louis XVI. Such a figure naturally appealed to Mill, as it had to the liberal *philosophe* Condorcet.

[19] He considered all sects or schools as harmful.

[20] Another name for the French *philosophes,* applied because they published their "subversive" ideas in the form of a harmless-looking encyclopedia.

[21] Literally, to advertise by placards; here, to proclaim publicly.

from Chapter 5

A CRISIS IN MY MENTAL HISTORY. ONE STAGE ONWARD

For some years after this time[22] I wrote very little, and nothing regularly, for publication: and great were the advantages which I derived from the intermission. It was of no common importance to me, at this period, to be able to digest and mature my thoughts for my own mind only, without any immediate call for giving them out in print. Had I gone on writing, it would have much disturbed the important transformation in my opinions and character, which took place during those years. The origin of this transformation, or at least the process by which I was prepared for it, can only be explained by turning some distance back.

From the winter of 1821, when I first read Bentham, and especially from the commencement of the Westminster Review, I had what might truly be called an object in life; to be a reformer of the world. My conception of my own happiness was entirely identified with this object. The personal sympathies I wished for were those of fellow labourers in this enterprise. I endeavoured to pick up as many flowers as I could by the way; but as a serious and permanent personal satisfaction to rest upon, my whole reliance was placed on this; and I was accustomed to felicitate myself on the certainty of a happy life which I enjoyed, through placing my happiness in something durable and distant, in which some progress might be always making, while it could never be exhausted by complete attainment. This did very well for several years, during which the general improvement going on in the world and the idea of myself as engaged with others in struggling to promote it, seemed enough to fill up an interesting and animated existence. But the time came when I awakened from this as from a dream. It was in the autumn of 1826. I was in a dull state of nerves, such as everybody is occasionally liable to; unsusceptible to enjoyment or pleasurable excitement; one of those moods when what is pleasure at other times, becomes insipid or indifferent; the state, I should think, in which converts to Methodism usually are, when smitten by their first "conviction of sin." In this frame of mind it occurred to me to put the question directly to myself: "Suppose that all your objects in life were realized; that all the changes in institutions and opinions which you are looking forward to, could be completely

[22] 1828.

effected at this very instant: would this be a great joy and happiness to you?" And an irrepressible self-consciousness distinctly answered, "No!" At this my heart sank within me: the whole foundation on which my life was constructed fell down. All my happiness was to have been found in the continual pursuit of this end. The end had ceased to charm, and how could there ever again be any interest in the means? I seemed to have nothing left to live for.

At first I hoped that the cloud would pass away of itself; but it did not. A night's sleep, the sovereign remedy for the smaller vexations of life, had no effect on it. I awoke to a renewed consciousness of the woful fact. I carried it with me into all companies, into all occupations. Hardly anything had power to cause me even a few minutes' oblivion of it. For some months the cloud seemed to grow thicker and thicker. The lines in Coleridge's "Dejection"—I was not then acquainted with them—exactly describe my case:

A grief without a pang, void, dark and drear,
A drowsy, stifled, unimpassioned grief,
Which finds no natural outlet or relief
In word, or sigh, or tear.

In vain I sought relief from my favourite books; those memorials of past nobleness and greatness from which I had always hitherto drawn strength and animation. I read them now without feeling, or with the accustomed feeling *minus* all its charm; and I became persuaded, that my love of mankind, and of excellence for its own sake, had worn itself out. I sought no comfort by speaking to others of what I felt. If I had loved any one sufficiently to make confiding my griefs a necessity, I should not have been in the condition I was. I felt, too, that mine was not an interesting, or in any way respectable distress. There was nothing in it to attract sympathy. Advice, if I had known where to seek it, would have been most precious. The words of Macbeth to the physician[23] often occurred to my thoughts. But there was no one on whom I could build the faintest hope of such assistance. My father, to whom it would have been natural to me to have recourse in any practical difficulties, was the last person to whom, in such a case as this, I looked for help. Everything convinced me that he had no knowledge of any such mental state as I was suffering from, and that even if he could

be made to understand it, he was not the physician who could heal it. My education, which was wholly his work, had been conducted without any regard to the possibility of its ending in this result; and I saw no use in giving him the pain of thinking that his plans had failed, when the failure was probably irremediable, and, at all events, beyond the power of *his* remedies. Of other friends, I had at that time none to whom I had any hope of making my condition intelligible. It was however abundantly intelligible to myself; and the more I dwelt upon it, the more hopeless it appeared.

My course of study had led me to believe, that all mental and moral feelings and qualities, whether of a good or of a bad kind, were the results of association; that we love one thing, and hate another, take pleasure in one sort of action or contemplation, and pain in another sort, through the clinging of pleasurable or painful ideas to those things, from the effect of education or of experience. As a corollary from this, I had always heard it maintained by my father, and was myself convinced, that the object of education should be to form the strongest possible associations of the salutary class; associations of pleasure with all things beneficial to the great whole, and of pain with all things hurtful to it. This doctrine appeared inexpugnable; but it now seemed to me, on retrospect, that my teachers had occupied themselves but superficially with the means of forming and keeping up these salutary associations. They seemed to have trusted altogether to the old familiar instruments, praise and blame, reward and punishment. Now, I did not doubt that by these means, begun early, and applied unremittingly, intense associations of pain and pleasure, especially of pain, might be created, and might produce desires and aversions capable of lasting undiminished to the end of life. But there must always be something artificial and casual in associations thus produced. The pains and pleasures thus forcibly associated with things, are not connected with them by any natural tie; and it is therefore, I thought, essential to the durability of these associations, that they should have become so intense and inveterate as to be practically indissoluble, before the habitual exercise of the power of analysis had commenced. For I now saw, or thought I saw, what I had always before received with incredulity—that the habit of analysis has a tendency to wear away the feelings: as indeed it has, when no other mental habit is cultivated, and the analysing spirit remains without its natural complements and correctives. The very excellence of analysis (I argued) is that it tends to weaken and undermine whatever is the result of prejudice;

---

[23] "Canst thou not minister to a mind diseas'd,
  Pluck from the memory a rooted sorrow,
  Raze out the written troubles of the brain,
  And with some sweet oblivious antidote
  Cleanse the stuff'd bosom of that perilous stuff
  Which weighs upon the heart?" (*Macbeth*, V, iii, 40–45)

that it enables us mentally to separate ideas which have only casually clung together: and no associations whatever could ultimately resist this dissolving force, were it not that we owe to analysis our clearest knowledge of the permanent sequences in nature; the real connexions between Things, not dependent on our will and feelings; natural laws, by virtue of which, in many cases, one thing is inseparable from another in fact; which laws, in proportion as they are clearly perceived and imaginatively realized, cause our ideas of things which are always joined together in Nature, to cohere more and more closely in our thoughts. Analytic habits may thus even strengthen the associations between causes and effects, means and ends, but tend altogether to weaken those which are, to speak familiarly, a *mere* matter of feeling. They are therefore (I thought) favourable to prudence and clear-sightedness, but a perpetual worm at the root both of the passions and of the virtues; and, above all, fearfully undermine all desires, and all pleasures, which are the effects of association, that is, according to the theory I held, all except the purely physical and organic; of the entire insufficiency of which to make life desirable, no one had a stronger conviction than I had. These were the laws of human nature, by which, as it seemed to me, I had been brought to my present state. All those to whom I looked up, were of opinion that the pleasure of sympathy with human beings, and the feelings which made the good of others, and especially of mankind on a large scale, the object of existence, were the greatest and surest sources of happiness. Of the truth of this I was convinced, but to know that a feeling would make me happy if I had it, did not give me the feeling. My education, I thought, had failed to create these feelings in sufficient strength to resist the dissolving influence of analysis, while the whole course of my intellectual cultivation had made precocious and premature analysis the inveterate habit of my mind. I was thus, as I said to myself, left stranded at the commencement of my voyage, with a well-equipped ship and a rudder, but no sail; without any real desire for the ends which I had been so carefully fitted out to work for: no delight in virtue, or the general good, but also just as little in anything else. The fountains of vanity and ambition seemed to have dried up within me, as completely as those of benevolence. I had had (as I reflected) some gratification of vanity at too early an age: I had obtained some distinction, and felt myself of some importance, before the desire of distinction and of importance had grown into a passion: and little as it was which I had attained, yet having been attained too early, like all pleasures

enjoyed too soon, it had made me *blasé* and indifferent to the pursuit. Thus neither selfish nor unselfish pleasures were pleasures to me. And there seemed no power in nature sufficient to begin the formation of my character anew, and create in a mind now irretrievably analytic, fresh associations of pleasure with any of the objects of human desire.

These were the thoughts which mingled with the dry heavy dejection of the melancholy winter of 1826-7. During this time I was not incapable of my usual occupations. I went on with them mechanically, by the mere force of habit. I had been so drilled in a certain sort of mental exercise, that I could still carry it on when all the spirit had gone out of it. I even composed and spoke several speeches at the debating society, how, or with what degree of success, I know not. Of four years continual speaking at that society, this is the only year of which I remember next to nothing. Two lines of Coleridge, in whom alone of all writers I have found a true description of what I felt, were often in my thoughts, not at this time (for I had never read them), but in a later period of the same mental malady:

> Work without hope draws nectar in a sieve,
> And hope without an object cannot live.[24]

In all probability my case was by no means so peculiar as I fancied it, and I doubt not that many others have passed through a similar state; but the idiosyncrasies of my education had given to the general phenomenon a special character, which made it seem the natural effect of causes that it was hardly possible for time to remove. I frequently asked myself, if I could, or if I was bound to go on living, when life must be passed in this manner. I generally answered to myself, that I did not think I could possibly bear it beyond a year. When, however, not more than half that duration of time had elapsed, a small ray of light broke in upon my gloom. I was reading, accidentally, Marmontel's "Memoires,"[25] and came to the passage which relates his father's death, the distressed position of the family, and the sudden inspiration by which he, then a mere boy, felt and made them feel that he would be everything to them—would supply the place of all that they had lost. A vivid conception of the scene and its feelings came over me, and I was moved to tears. From this moment my burden grew lighter. The oppression of the thought that all feeling was dead within me, was gone. I was no longer hopeless: I was not a stock or a stone. I had still, it

24 The last lines of *Work without Hope* (p. 112, above).
25 *Mémoires d'un père* (1804) by Jean François Marmontel.

seemed, some of the material out of which all worth of character, and all capacity for happiness, are made. Relieved from my ever present sense of irremediable wretchedness, I gradually found that the ordinary incidents of life could again give me some pleasure; that I could again find enjoyment, not intense, but sufficient for cheerfulness, in sunshine and sky, in books, in conversation, in public affairs; and that there was, once more, excitement, though of a moderate kind, in exerting myself for my opinions, and for the public good. Thus the cloud gradually drew off, and I again enjoyed life: and though I had several relapses, some of which lasted many months, I never again was as miserable as I had been.

The experiences of this period had two very marked effects on my opinions and character. In the first place, they led me to adopt a theory of life, very unlike that on which I had before acted, and having much in common with what at that time I certainly had never heard of, the anti-self-consciousness theory of Carlyle.[26] I never, indeed, wavered in the conviction that happiness is the test of all rules of conduct, and the end of life. But I now thought that this end was only to be attained by not making it the direct end. Those only are happy (I thought) who have their minds fixed on some object other than their own happiness; on the happiness of others, on the improvement of mankind, even on some art or pursuit, followed not as a means, but as itself an ideal end. Aiming thus at something else, they find happiness by the way. The enjoyments of life (such was now my theory) are sufficient to make it a pleasant thing, when they are taken *en passant*, without being made a principal object. Once make them so, and they are immediately felt to be insufficient. They will not bear a scrutinizing examination. Ask yourself whether you are happy, and you cease to be so. The only chance is to treat, not happiness, but some end external to it, as the purpose of life. Let your self-consciousness, your scrutiny, your self-interrogation, exhaust themselves on that; and if otherwise fortunately circumstanced you will inhale happiness with the air you breathe, without dwelling on it or thinking about it, without either forestalling it in imagination, or putting it to flight by fatal questioning. This theory now became the basis of my philosophy of life. And I still hold to it as the best theory for all those who have but a moderate degree

of sensibility and of capacity for enjoyment, that is, for the great majority of mankind.

The other important change which my opinions at this time underwent, was that I, for the first time, gave its proper place, among the prime necessities of human well-being, to the internal culture of the individual. I ceased to attach almost exclusive importance to the ordering of outward circumstances, and the training of the human being for speculation and for action.

I had now learnt by experience that the passive susceptibilities needed to be cultivated as well as the active capacities, and required to be nourished and enriched as well as guided. I did not, for an instant, lose sight of, or undervalue, that part of the truth which I had seen before; I never turned recreant to intellectual culture, or ceased to consider the power and practice of analysis as an essential condition both of individual and of social improvement. But I thought that it had consequences which required to be corrected, by joining other kinds of cultivation with it. The maintenance of a due balance among the faculties, now seemed to me of primary importance. The cultivation of the feelings became one of the cardinal points in my ethical and philosophical creed.[27] And my thoughts and inclinations turned in an increasing degree towards whatever seemed capable of being instrumental to that object.

I now began to find meaning in the things which I had read or heard about the importance of poetry and art as instruments of human culture. But it was some time longer before I began to know this by personal experience. The only one of the imaginative arts in which I had from childhood taken great pleasure, was music; the best effect of which (and in this it surpasses perhaps every other art) consists in exciting enthusiasm; in winding up to a high pitch those feelings of an elevated kind which are already in the character, but to which this excitement gives a glow and a fervour, which, though transitory at its utmost height, is precious for sustaining them at other times. This effect of music I had often experienced; but like all my pleasurable susceptibilities it was suspended during the gloomy period. I had sought relief again and again from this quarter, but found none. After the tide had turned, and I was in process of recovery, I had been helped forward by music, but in a much less elevated manner. I at this time first became acquainted with Weber's Oberon,[28] and the extreme

---

[26] The theory that to seek consciously for happiness is to miss it, a conclusion which Mill now draws for himself. For Carlyle, see above, p. 398.

[27] It should be noticed that Mill means to include, and with primary emphasis, the *moral* feelings. Cf. the next paragraph.

[28] An English romantic opera by Carl Maria von Weber, first produced in London in 1826.

pleasure which I drew from its delicious melodies did me good, by showing me a source of pleasure to which I was as susceptible as ever. The good, however, was much impaired by the thought, that the pleasure of music (as is quite true of such pleasure as this was, that of mere tune) fades with familiarity, and requires either to be revived by intermittence, or fed by continual novelty. And it is very characteristic both of my then state, and of the general tone of my mind at this period of my life, that I was seriously tormented by the thought of the exhaustibility of musical combinations. The octave consists only of five tones and two semitones, which can be put together in only a limited number of ways, of which but a small proportion are beautiful: most of these, it seemed to me, must have been already discovered, and there could not be room for a long succession of Mozarts and Webers, to strike out, as these had done, entirely new and surpassingly rich veins of musical beauty. This source of anxiety may, perhaps, be thought to resemble that of the philosophers of Laputa,[29] who feared lest the sun should be burnt out. It was, however, connected with the best feature in my character, and the only good point to be found in my very unromantic and in no way honourable distress. For though my dejection, honestly looked at, could not be called other than egotistical, produced by the ruin, as I thought, of my fabric of happiness, yet the destiny of mankind in general was ever in my thoughts, and could not be separated from my own. I felt that the flaw in my life, must be a flaw in life itself; that the question was, whether, if the reformers of society and government could succeed in their objects, and every person in the community were free and in a state of physical comfort, the pleasures of life, being no longer kept up by struggle and privation, would cease to be pleasures. And I felt that unless I could see my way to some better hope than this for human happiness in general, my dejection must continue; but that if I could see such an outlet, I should then look on the world with pleasure; content as far as I was myself concerned, with any fair share of the general lot.

This state of my thoughts and feelings made the fact of my reading Wordsworth for the first time (in the autumn of 1828), an important event in my life. I took up the collection of his poems from curiosity, with no expectation of mental relief from it, though I had before resorted to poetry with that hope. In the worst period of my depression, I had read through the whole of Byron (then new to me), to try whether a poet, whose peculiar department was supposed to be that of the intenser feelings, could rouse any feeling in me. As might be expected, I got no good from this reading, but the reverse. The poet's state of mind was too like my own. His was the lament of a man who had worn out all pleasures, and who seemed to think that life, to all who possess the good things of it, must necessarily be the vapid, uninteresting thing which I found it. His Harold and Manfred had the same burden on them which I had; and I was not in a frame of mind to desire any comfort from the vehement sensual passion of his Giaours, or the sullenness of his Laras. But while Byron was exactly what did not suit my condition, Wordsworth was exactly what did. I had looked into the Excursion two or three years before, and found little in it; and I should probably have found as little, had I read it at this time. But the miscellaneous poems, in the two-volume edition of 1815 (to which little of value was added in the latter part of the author's life), proved to be the precise thing for my mental wants at that particular juncture.

In the first place, these poems addressed themselves powerfully to one of the strongest of my pleasurable susceptibilities, the love of rural objects and natural scenery; to which I had been indebted not only for much of the pleasure of my life, but quite recently for relief from one of my longest relapses into depression. In this power of rural beauty over me, there was a foundation laid for taking pleasure in Wordsworth's poetry; the more so, as his scenery lies mostly among mountains, which, owing to my early Pyrenean excursion,[30] were my ideal of natural beauty. But Wordsworth would never have had any great effect on me, if he had merely placed before me beautiful pictures of natural scenery. Scott does this still better than Wordsworth, and a very second-rate landscape does it more effectually than any poet. What made Wordsworth's poems a medicine for my state of mind, was that they expressed, not mere outward beauty, but states of feeling, and of thought coloured by feeling, under the excitement of beauty. They seemed to be the very culture of the feelings, which I was in quest of. In them I seemed to draw from a source of inward joy, of sympathetic and imaginative pleasure, which could be shared in by all human beings; which had no connexion with struggle or imperfection, but would be made richer by every improvement in the physical

---

[29] In *Gulliver's Travels,* Part III, which satirizes the absurdities and impracticalities into which abstract philosophers, mathematicians, etc., may fall.

[30] Made with family friends in 1820.

or social condition of mankind. From them I seemed to learn what would be the perennial sources of happiness, when all the greater evils of life shall have been removed. And I felt myself at once better and happier as I came under their influence. There have certainly been, even in our own age, greater poets than Wordsworth; but poetry of deeper and loftier feeling could not have done for me at that time what his did. I needed to be made to feel that there was real, permanent happiness in tranquil contemplation. Wordsworth taught me this, not only without turning away from, but with a greatly increased interest in the common feelings and common destiny of human beings. And the delight which these poems gave me, proved that with culture of this sort, there was nothing to dread from the most confirmed habit of analysis. At the conclusion of the Poems came the famous Ode, falsely called Platonic,[31] "Intimations of Immortality": in which, along with more than his usual sweetness of melody and rhythm, and along with the two passages of grand imagery but bad philosophy so often quoted, I found that he too had had similar experience to mine; that he also had felt that the first freshness of youthful enjoyment of life was not lasting; but that he had sought for compensation, and found it, in the way in which he was now teaching me to find it. The result was that I gradually, but completely, emerged from my habitual depression and was never again subject to it. I long continued to value Wordsworth less according to his intrinsic merits, than by the measure of what he had done for me. Compared with the greatest poets, he may be said to be the poet of unpoetical natures, possessed of quiet and contemplative tastes. But unpoetical natures are precisely those which require poetic cultivation. This cultivation Wordsworth is much more fitted to give, than poets who are intrinsically far more poets than he.

It so fell out that the merits of Wordsworth were the occasion of my first public declaration of my new way of thinking, and separation from those of my habitual companions who had not undergone a similar change. The person with whom at that time I was most in the habit of comparing notes on such subjects was Roebuck,[32] and I induced him to read Wordsworth, in whom he also at first seemed to find much to admire: but I, like most Wordsworth-ians, threw myself into strong antagonism to Byron, both as a poet and as to his influence on the character. Roebuck, all whose instincts were those of action and struggle, had, on the contrary, a strong relish and great admiration of Byron, whose writings he regarded as the poetry of human life, while Wordsworth's, according to him, was that of flowers and butterflies. We agreed to have the fight out at our Debating Society,[33] where we accordingly discussed for two evenings the comparative merits of Byron and Wordsworth, propounding and illustrating by long recitations our respective theories of poetry: Sterling[34] also, in a brilliant speech, putting forward his particular theory. This was the first debate on any weighty subject in which Roebuck and I had been on opposite sides. The schism between us widened from this time more and more, though we continued for some years longer to be companions. In the beginning, our chief divergence related to the cultivation of the feelings. Roebuck was in many respects very different from the vulgar notion of a Benthamite or Utilitarian. He was a lover of poetry and of most of the fine arts. He took great pleasure in music, in dramatic performances, especially in painting, and himself drew and designed landscapes with great facility and beauty. But he never could be made to see that these things have any value as aids in the formation of character. Personally, instead of being, as Benthamites are supposed to be, void of feeling, he had very quick and strong sensibilities. But, like most Englishmen who have feelings, he found his feelings stand very much in his way. He was much more susceptible to the painful sympathies than to the pleasurable, and looking for his happiness elsewhere, he wished that his feelings should be deadened rather than quickened. And, in truth, the English character, and English social circumstances, make it so seldom possible to derive happiness from the exercise of the sympathies, that it is not wonderful if they count for little in an Englishman's scheme of life. In most other countries the paramount importance of the sympathies as a constituent of individual happiness is an axiom, taken for granted rather than needing any formal statement; but most English thinkers almost seem to regard them as necessary evils, required for keeping men's actions benevolent and compassionate. Roebuck was, or appeared to be, this kind of Englishman. He saw little good in any cultivation of the

---

[31] Wordsworth himself protested that the ode was not an expression of Platonic philosophy.
[32] John Arthur Roebuck (1801–79), a member of Mill's early Utilitarian Society, 1823–26, who later became a politician and reformer.

[33] The London Debating Society, organized (1825) and originally supported mainly by Mill and Roebuck.
[34] John Sterling (1806–44), man of letters, friend of Coleridge, Wordsworth, and Carlyle, the last of whom wrote his Life.

feelings, and none at all in cultivating them through the imagination, which he thought was only cultivating illusions. It was in vain I urged on him that the imaginative emotion which an idea, when vividly conceived, excites in us, is not an illusion but a fact, as real as any of the other qualities of objects; and far from implying anything erroneous and delusive in our mental apprehension of the object, is quite consistent with the most accurate knowledge and most perfect practical recognition of all its physical and intellectual laws and relations. The intensest feeling of the beauty of a cloud lighted by the setting sun, is no hindrance to my knowing that the cloud is vapour of water, subject to all the laws of vapours in a state of suspension; and I am just as likely to allow for, and act on, these physical laws whenever there is occasion to do so, as if I had been incapable of perceiving any distinction between beauty and ugliness.

While my intimacy with Roebuck diminished, I fell more and more into friendly intercourse with our Coleridgian adversaries in the Society, Frederick Maurice[35] and John Sterling, both subsequently so well known, the former by his writings, the latter through the biographies by Hare[36] and Carlyle. Of these two friends, Maurice was the thinker, Sterling the orator, and impassioned expositor of thoughts which, at this period, were almost entirely formed for him by Maurice.

With Maurice I had for some time been acquainted through Eyton Tooke, who had known him at Cambridge, and although my discussions with him were almost always disputes, I had carried away from them much that helped to build up my new fabric of thought, in the same way as I was deriving much from Coleridge, and from the writings of Goethe and other German authors which I read during these years. . . . I found the fabric of my old and taught opinions giving way in many fresh places, and I never allowed it to fall to pieces, but was incessantly occupied in weaving it anew. I never, in the course of my transition, was content to remain, for ever so short a time, confused and unsettled. When I had taken in any new idea, I could not rest till I had adjusted its relation to my old opinions, and ascertained exactly how far its effect ought to extend in modifying or superseding them. . . .

---

[35] Frederick Denison Maurice (1805–72), clergyman, leader of the Broad Church and the Christian Socialist movements.
[36] Julius Hare (1795–1855), editor of Sterling's *Essays and Tales* and author of a life of Sterling.

If I am asked, what system of political philosophy I substituted for that which, as a philosophy, I had abandoned, I answer, No system: only a conviction that the true system was something much more complex and many-sided than I had previously had any idea of, and that its office was to supply, not a set of model institutions, but principles from which the institutions suitable to any given circumstances might be deduced. The influences of European, that is to say, Continental, thought, and especially those of the reaction of the nineteenth century against the eighteenth, were now streaming in upon me. They came from various quarters: from the writings of Coleridge, which I had begun to read with interest even before the change in my opinions; from the Coleridgians with whom I was in personal intercourse; from what I had read of Goethe; from Carlyle's early articles in the Edinburgh and Foreign Reviews, though for a long time I saw nothing in these (as my father saw nothing in them to the last) but insane rhapsody. From these sources, and from the acquaintance I kept up with the French literature of the time, I derived, among other ideas which the general turning upside down of the opinions of European thinkers had brought uppermost, these in particular: That the human mind has a certain order of possible progress, in which some things must precede others, an order which governments and public instructors can modify to some, but not to an unlimited extent: that all questions of political institutions are relative, not absolute, and that different stages of human progress not only *will* have, but *ought* to have, different institutions: that government is always either in the hands, or passing into the hands, of whatever is the strongest power in society, and that what this power is, does not depend on institutions, but institutions on it: that any general theory or philosophy of politics supposes a previous theory of human progress, and that this is the same thing with a philosophy of history. These opinions, true in the main, were held in an exaggerated and violent manner by the thinkers with whom I was now most accustomed to compare notes, and who, as usual with a reaction, ignored that half of the truth which the thinkers of the eighteenth century saw. But though, at one period of my progress, I for some time undervalued that great century, I never joined in the reaction against it, but kept as firm hold of one side of the truth as I took of the other. The fight between the nineteenth century and the eighteenth always reminded me of the battle about the shield, one side of which was white and the other black. I marvelled at the blind rage with which the combatants rushed against one another. I applied to them, and to Coleridge himself, many of Coleridge's sayings about half truths;[37] and Goethe's device, "many-sidedness,"[38] was one which I would most willingly, at this period, have taken for mine.

The writers by whom, more than by any others, a new mode of political thinking was brought home to me, were those of the St. Simonian school[39] in France. In 1829 and 1830 I became acquainted with some of their writings. They were then only in the earlier stages of their speculations. They had not yet dressed out their philosophy as a religion, nor had they organized their scheme of Socialism. They were just beginning to question the principle of hereditary property. I was by no means prepared to go with them even this length; but I was greatly struck with the connected view which they for the first time presented to me, of the natural order of human progress; and especially with their division of all history into organic periods and critical periods. During the organic periods (they said) mankind accept with firm conviction some positive creed, claiming jurisdiction over all their actions, and containing more or less of truth and adaptation to the needs of humanity. Under its influence they make all the progress compatible with the creed, and finally outgrow it; when a period follows of criticism and negation, in which mankind lose their old convictions without acquiring any new ones, of a general or authoritative character, except the conviction that the old are false. The period of Greek and Roman polytheism, so long as really believed in by instructed Greeks and Romans, was an organic period, succeeded by the critical or sceptical period of the Greek philosophers. Another organic period came in with Christianity. The corresponding critical period began with the Reformation, has lasted ever since, still lasts, and cannot altogether cease until a new organic period has been inaugurated by the triumph of a yet more advanced creed. These ideas, I knew, were not peculiar to the St. Simonians; on the contrary, they were the general property of Europe, or at least of Germany and France, but they had never, to my knowledge, been so completely systematized as by these writers, nor the distinguishing characteristics of a critical period so powerfully set forth; for I was not then acquainted with Fichte's Lectures on "The Characteristics of the Present Age."[40] In Carlyle, indeed, I found bitter denunciations of an "age of unbelief," and of the present age as such, which I, like most people at that time, supposed to be passionate protests in favour of the old modes of belief. But all that was true in these denunciations, I thought that I found more calmly and philosophically stated by the St. Simonians. Among their publications, too, there was one which seemed to me far superior to the rest; in which the general idea was matured into something much more definite and instructive. This was an early work of Auguste Comte,[41] who then called himself, and even announced himself in the title-page as, a pupil of Saint Simon. In this tract M. Comte first put forth the doctrine, which he afterwards so copiously illustrated, of the natural succession of three stages in every department of human knowledge: first, the theological, next the metaphysical, and lastly, the positive stage; and contended, that social science must be subject to the same law; that the feudal and Catholic system was the concluding phasis of the theological state of the social science, Protestantism the commencement, and the doctrines of the French Revolution the consummation, of the metaphysical; and that its positive state was yet to come. This doctrine harmonized well with my existing notions, to which it seemed to give a scientific shape. I already regarded the methods of physical science as the proper models for political. But the chief benefit which I derived at this time from the trains of thought suggested by the St. Simonians and by Comte, was, that I obtained a clearer conception than ever before of the peculiarities of an era of transition in opinion, and ceased to mistake the moral and intellectual characteristics of such an era, for the normal attributes of humanity. I looked forward, through the present age of loud disputes but generally weak convictions, to a future which shall unite the best qualities of the critical with the best qualities of the organic periods; un-

---

[37] In Mill's essay on Coleridge, quoting from the latter's *Literary Remains,* iii, 145, he says: "Almost all errors he holds to be 'truths misunderstood,' 'half-truths taken as the whole,' though not the less, but the more dangerous on that account." See below, "The Spirit of the Age," pp. 537-8.

[38] One of Goethe's maxims (no. 1337): "Let us then be many-sided."

[39] Considered the founders of French Socialism, in which the state would own all property and the worker would be rewarded according to the quality and quantity of his work.

[40] In these lectures the German philosopher Johann Gottlieb Fichte (1762–1814) brilliantly arraigned the eighteenth century as an age of skepticism.

[41] Auguste Comte (1798–1857), founder of the positivist philosophy, in which only positive facts and observable phenomena, with the objective relations of these and the laws which determine them, are recognized, all inquiry into causes or ultimate origins being abandoned. Furthermore, it postulates a "positive stage" of human development in which the laws of science become the proper models for the structure of society.

checked liberty of thought, unbounded freedom of individual action in all modes not hurtful to others; but also, convictions as to what is right and wrong, useful and pernicious, deeply engraven on the feelings by early education and general unanimity of sentiment, and so firmly grounded in reason and in the true exigencies of life, that they shall not, like all former and present creeds, religious, ethical, and political, require to be periodically thrown off and replaced by others.

M. Comte soon left the St. Simonians, and I lost sight of him and his writings for a number of years. But the St. Simonians I continued to cultivate. I was kept *au courant* of[42] their progress by one of their most enthusiastic disciples, M. Gustave d'Eichthal, who about that time passed a considerable interval in England. I was introduced to their chiefs, Bazard and Enfantin, in 1830; and as long as their public teachings and proselytism continued, I read nearly everything they wrote. Their criticisms on the common doctrines of Liberalism seemed to me full of important truth; and it was partly by their writings that my eyes were opened to the very limited and temporary value of the old political economy, which assumes private property and inheritance as indefeasible facts, and freedom of production and exchange as the *dernier mot*[43] of social improvement. The scheme gradually unfolded by the St. Simonians, under which the labour and capital of society would be managed for the general account of the community, every individual being required to take a share of labour, either as thinker, teacher, artist, or producer, all being classed according to their capacity, and remunerated according to their work, appeared to me a far superior description of Socialism to Owen's.[44] Their aim seemed to me desirable and rational, however their means might be inefficacious; and though I neither believed in the practicability, nor in the beneficial operation of their social machinery, I felt that the proclamation of such an ideal of human society could not but tend to give a beneficial direction to the efforts of others to bring society, as at present constituted, nearer to some ideal standard. I honoured them most of all for what they have been most cried down for—the boldness and freedom from prejudice with which they treated the subject of family, the most important of any, and needing more fundamental alterations than remain to be made in any other great social institution, but on which scarcely any reformer has the courage to touch. In proclaiming the perfect equality of men and women, and an entirely new order of things in regard to their relations with one another, the St. Simonians, in common with Owen and Fourier,[45] have entitled themselves to the grateful remembrance of future generations.

In giving an account of this period of my life, I have only specified such of my new impressions as appeared to me, both at the time and since, to be a kind of turning points, marking a definite progress in my mode of thought. But these few selected points give a very insufficient idea of the quantity of thinking which I carried on respecting a host of subjects during these years of transition. Much of this, it is true, consisted in rediscovering things known to all the world, which I had previously disbelieved, or disregarded. But the rediscovery was to me a discovery, giving me plenary possession of the truths, not as traditional platitudes, but fresh from their source: and it seldom failed to place them in some new light, by which they were reconciled with, and seemed to confirm while they modified, the truths less generally known which lay in my early opinions, and in no essential part of which I at any time wavered. All my new thinking only laid the foundation of these more deeply and strongly, while it often removed misapprehension and confusion of ideas which had perverted their effect. For example, during the later returns of my dejection, the doctrine of what is called Philosophical Necessity weighed on my existence like an incubus. I felt as if I was scientifically proved to be the helpless slave of antecedent circumstances; as if my character and that of all others had been formed for us by agencies beyond our control, and was wholly out of our own power. I often said to myself, what a relief it would be if I could disbelieve the doctrine of the formation of character by circumstances; and remembering the wish of Fox[46] respecting the doctrine of resistance to governments, that it might never be forgotten by kings, nor remembered by subjects, I said that it would be a blessing if the doctrine of necessity could be believed by all *quoad*[47] the characters of others,

---

[42] In touch with.　　　[43] Last word.
[44] Because in the theory of Robert Owen (1771–1858), wealthy mill-owner and founder of several socialist communities, there was to be no distinction in remuneration according to the work done. All men were to receive "from the general store of the community" what they required.

[45] Charles Fourier (1772–1837) was one of the earliest French communists.
[46] Charles James Fox (1749–1806), liberal and humanitarian statesman, distinguished by his opposition to George III and the ultraconservative Tories in the government.
[47] As to, in regard to.

and disbelieved in regard to their own. I pondered painfully on the subject, till gradually I saw light through it. I perceived, that the word Necessity, as a name for the doctrine of Cause and Effect applied to human action, carried with it a misleading association; and that this association was the operative force in the depressing and paralysing influence which I had experienced: I saw that though our character is formed by circumstances, our own desires can do much to shape those circumstances; and that what is really inspiriting and ennobling in the doctrine of freewill, is the conviction that we have real power over the formation of our own character; that our will, by influencing some of our circumstances, can modify our future habits or capabilities of willing. All this was entirely consistent with the doctrine of circumstances, or rather, was that doctrine itself, properly understood. From that time I drew in my own mind, a clear distinction between the doctrine of circumstances, and Fatalism; discarding altogether the misleading word Necessity. The theory, which I now for the first time rightly apprehended, ceased altogether to be discouraging, and besides the relief to my spirits, I no longer suffered under the burden, so heavy to one who aims at being a reformer in opinions, of thinking one doctrine true, and the contrary doctrine morally beneficial. The train of thought which had extricated me from this dilemma, seemed to me, in after years, fitted to render a similar service to others; and it now forms the chapter on Liberty and Necessity in the concluding Book of my system of Logic.

Again, in politics, though I no longer accepted the doctrine of the Essay on Government[48] as a scientific theory; though I ceased to consider representative democracy as an absolute principle, and regarded it as a question of time, place, and circumstance; though I now looked upon the choice of political institutions as a moral and educational question more than one of material interests, thinking that it ought to be decided mainly by the consideration, what great improvement in life and culture stands next in order for the people concerned, as the condition of their further progress, and what institutions are most likely to promote that; nevertheless, this change in the premises of my political philosophy did not alter my practical political creed as to the requirements of my own time and country. I was as much as ever a Radical and Democrat for Europe, and especially for England. I

---

[48] By his father, James Mill.

thought the predominance of the aristocratic classes, the noble and the rich, in the English constitution, an evil worth any struggle to get rid of; not on account of taxes, or any such comparatively small inconvenience, but as the great demoralizing agency in the country. Demoralizing, first, because it made the conduct of the Government an example of gross public immorality, through the predominance of private over public interests in the State, and the abuse of the powers of legislation for the advantage of classes. Secondly, and in a still greater degree, because the respect of the multitude always attaching itself principally to that which, in the existing state of society, is the chief passport to power; and under English institutions, riches, hereditary or acquired, being the almost exclusive source of political importance; riches, and the signs of riches, were almost the only things really respected, and the life of the people was mainly devoted to the pursuit of them. I thought, that while the higher and richer classes held the power of government, the instruction and improvement of the mass of the people were contrary to the self-interest of those classes, because tending to render the people more powerful for throwing off the yoke: but if the democracy obtained a large, and perhaps the principal share, in the governing power, it would become the interest of the opulent classes to promote their education, in order to ward off really mischievous errors, and especially those which would lead to unjust violations of property. On these grounds I was not only as ardent as ever for democratic institutions, but earnestly hoped that Owenite, St. Simonian, and all other anti-property doctrines might spread widely among the poorer classes; not that I thought those doctrines true, or desired that they should be acted on, but in order that the higher classes might be made to see that they had more to fear from the poor when uneducated, than when educated. . . .

I have already mentioned Carlyle's earlier writings as one of the channels through which I received the influences which enlarged my early narrow creed; but I do not think that those writings, by themselves, would ever have had any effect on my opinions. What truths they contained, though of the very kind which I was already receiving from other quarters, were presented in a form and vesture less suited than any other to give them access to a mind trained as mine had been. They seemed a haze of poetry and German metaphysics, in which almost the only clear thing was a strong animosity to most of the opinions which were the basis of my mode of thought; religious scepticism, utilitarianism, the doctrine of circumstances, and the attaching any importance to democracy, logic, or political economy. Instead of my having been taught anything, in the first instance, by Carlyle, it was only in proportion as I came to see the same truths through media more suited to my mental constitution, that I recognised them in his writings. Then, indeed, the wonderful power with which he put them forth made a deep impression upon me, and I was during a long period one of his most fervent admirers; but the good his writings did me, was not as philosophy to instruct, but as poetry to animate. Even at the time when our acquaintance commenced, I was not sufficiently advanced in my new modes of thought, to appreciate him fully; a proof of which is, that on his showing me the manuscript of Sartor Resartus, his best and greatest work, which he had just then finished, I made little of it; though when it came out about two years afterwards in Fraser's Magazine I read it with enthusiastic admiration and the keenest delight. I did not seek and cultivate Carlyle less on account of the fundamental differences in our philosophy. He soon found out that I was not "another mystic," and when for the sake of my own integrity I wrote to him a distinct

profession of all those of my opinions which I knew he most disliked, he replied that the chief difference between us was that I "was as yet consciously nothing of a mystic." I do not know at what period he gave up the expectation that I was destined to become one; but though both his and my opinions underwent in subsequent years considerable changes, we never approached much nearer to each other's modes of thought than we were in the first years of our acquaintance. I did not, however, deem myself a competent judge of Carlyle. I felt that he was a poet, and that I was not; that he was a man of intuition, which I was not; and that as such, he not only saw many things long before me, which I could only when they were pointed out to me, hobble after and prove, but that it was highly probable he could see many things which were not visible to me even after they were pointed out. I knew that I could not see round him, and could never be certain that I saw over him; and I never presumed to judge him with any definiteness, until he was interpreted to me by one greatly the superior of us both—who was more a poet than he, and more a thinker than I—whose own mind and nature included his, and infinitely more. . . . [49]

THE SPIRIT OF THE AGE,[1] NO. I

THE "spirit of the age" is in some measure a novel expression. I do not believe that it is to be met with in any work exceeding fifty years in antiquity. The idea of comparing one's own age with former ages, or with our notion of those which are yet to come, had occurred to philosophers; but it never before was itself the dominant idea of any age.

It is an idea essentially belonging to an age of change. Before men begin to think much and long on the peculiarities of their own times, they must have begun to think that those times are, or are destined to be, distinguished in a very remarkable manner from the times which preceded them. Mankind are then divided, into those who are still what they were, and those who have changed: into the men of the present

age, and the men of the past. To the former, the spirit of the age is a subject of exultation; to the latter, of terror; to both, of eager and anxious interest. The wisdom of ancestors, and the march of intellect, are bandied from mouth to mouth; each phrase originally an expression of respect and homage, each ultimately usurped by the partisans of the opposite catch-word, and in the bitterness of their spirit, turned into the sarcastic jibe of hatred and insult.

The present times possess this character. A change has taken place in the human mind; a change which, being effected by insensible gradations, and without noise, had already proceeded far before it was generally perceived. When the fact disclosed itself, thousands awoke as from a dream. They knew not what processes had been going on in the minds of others, or even in their own, until the change began to invade outward objects; and it became clear that those were indeed new men, who insisted upon being governed in a new way.

[1] "I attempted," says Mill, "in the beginning of 1831, to embody in a series of articles, headed 'The Spirit of the Age,' some of my new opinions, and especially to point out in the character of the present age, the anomalies and evils characteristic of the transition from a system of opinions which had worn out, to another only in process of being formed." The articles appeared in the Examiner, a radical weekly, from January through May, and were signed merely "A. B." Only the first article is reprinted here.

[49] The subject of this extraordinary eulogy is Mrs. Harriet Taylor, with whom Mill fell violently in love, and whom he subsequently married.

But mankind are now conscious of their new position. The conviction is already not far from being universal, that the times are pregnant with change; and that the nineteenth century will be known to posterity as the era of one of the greatest revolutions of which history has preserved the remembrance, in the human mind, and in the whole constitution of human society. Even the religious world teems with new interpretations of the Prophecies, foreboding mighty changes near at hand. It is felt that men are henceforth to be held together by new ties, and separated by new barriers; for the ancient bonds will now no longer unite, nor the ancient boundaries confine. Those men who carry their eyes in the back of their heads and can see no other portion of the destined track of humanity than that which it has already travelled, imagine that because the old ties are severed mankind henceforth are not to be connected by any ties at all; and hence their affliction, and their awful warnings. For proof of this assertion, I may refer to the gloomiest book ever written by a cheerful man—Southey's "Colloquies on the Progress and Prospects of Society";[2] a very curious and not uninstructive exhibition of one of the points of view from which the spirit of the age may be contemplated. They who prefer the ravings of a party politician to the musings of a recluse, may consult a late article in Blackwood's Magazine,[3] under the same title which I have prefixed to this paper. For the reverse of the picture, we have only to look into any popular newspaper or review.

Amidst all this indiscriminate eulogy and abuse, these undistinguishing hopes and fears, it seems to be a very fit subject for philosophical inquiry, what the spirit of the age really is; and how or wherein it differs from the spirit of any other age. The subject is deeply important: for, whatever we may think or affect to think of the present age, we cannot get out of it; we must suffer with its sufferings, and enjoy with its enjoyments; we must share in its lot, and, to be either useful or at ease, we must even partake its character. No man whose good qualities were mainly those of another age, ever had much influence on his own. And since every age contains in itself the germ of all future ages as surely as the acorn contains the future forest, a knowledge of our own age is the fountain of prophecy—the only key to the history of posterity. It is only in the present that we can know

the future; it is only through the present that it is in our power to influence that which is to come.

Yet, because our own age is *familiar* to us, we are presumed, if I may judge from appearances, to know it by nature. A statesman, for example, if it be required of him to have studied any thing at all (which, however, is more than I would venture to affirm) is supposed to have studied history—which is at best the spirit of ages long past, and more often the mere inanimate carcass without the spirit: but is it ever asked (or to whom does the question ever occur?) whether he understands his own age? Yet that also is history, and the most important part of history, and the only part which a man may know and understand, with absolute certainty, by using the proper means. He may learn in a morning's walk through London more of the history of England during the nineteenth century, than all the professed English histories in existence will tell him concerning the other eighteen: for, the obvious and universal facts, which every one sees and no one is astonished at, it seldom occurs to any one to place upon record; and posterity, if it learn the rule, learns it, generally, from the notice bestowed by contemporaries on some accidental exception. Yet are politicians and philosophers perpetually exhorted to judge of the present by the past, when the present alone affords a fund of materials for judging, richer than the whole stores of the past, and far more accessible.

But it is unadvisable to dwell longer on this topic, lest we should be deemed studiously to exaggerate that want, which we desire that the reader should think ourselves qualified to supply. It were better, without further preamble, to enter upon the subject, and be tried by our ideas themselves, rather than by the need of them.

The first of the leading peculiarities of the present age is, that it is an age of transition. Mankind have outgrown old institutions and old doctrines, and have not yet acquired new ones. When we say outgrown, we intend to prejudge nothing. A man may not be either better or happier at six-and-twenty, than he was at six years of age: but the same jacket which fitted him then, will not fit him now.

The prominent trait just indicated in the character of the present age, was obvious a few years ago only to the more discerning: at present it forces itself upon the most inobservant. Much might be said, and shall be said on a fitting occasion, of the mode in which the old order of things has become unsuited to the state of society and of the human mind. But when almost every nation on the continent of Europe has achieved, or is in the course of rapidly achieving, a change in

---

[2] See Macaulay's review of the book, pp. 446 ff., above.
[3] In the issue of December, 1830. Unsigned.

its form of government; when our own country, at all former times the most attached in Europe to its old institutions, proclaims almost with one voice that they are vicious both in the outline and in the details, and that they *shall* be renovated, and purified, and made fit for civilized man, we may assume that a part of the effects of the cause just now pointed out, speak sufficiently loudly for themselves. To him who can reflect, even these are but indications which tell of a more vital and radical change. Not only, in the conviction of almost all men, things as they are, are wrong—but, according to that same conviction, it is not by remaining in the old ways that they can be set right. Society demands, and anticipates, not merely a new machine, but a machine constructed in another manner. Mankind will not be led by their old maxims, nor by their old guides; and they will not choose either their opinions or their guides as they have done heretofore. The ancient constitutional texts were formerly spells which would call forth or allay the spirit of the English people at pleasure: what has become of the charm? Who can hope to sway the minds of the public by the old maxims of law, or commerce, or foreign policy, or ecclesiastical policy? Whose feelings are now roused by the mottoes and watch-words of Whig and Tory? And what Whig or Tory could command ten followers in the warfare of politics by the weight of his own personal authority? Nay, what landlord could call forth his tenants, or what manufacturer his men? Do the poor respect the rich, or adopt their sentiments? Do the young respect the old, or adopt their sentiments? Of the feelings of our ancestors it may almost be said that we retain only such as are the natural and necessary growth of a state of human society, however constituted; and I only adopt the energetic expression of a member of the House of Commons, less than two years ago, in saying of the young men, even of that rank in society, that they are ready to advertise for opinions.

Since the facts are so manifest, there is the more chance that a few reflections on their causes, and on their probable consequences, will receive whatever portion of the reader's attention they may happen to deserve.

With respect, then, to the discredit into which old institutions and old doctrines have fallen, I may premise, that this discredit is, in my opinion, perfectly deserved. Having said this, I may perhaps hope, that no perverse interpretation will be put upon the remainder of my observations, in case some of them should not be quite so conformable to the sentiments of the day as my commencement might give reason to expect. The best guide is not he who, when people

are in the right path, merely praises it, but he who shows them the pitfalls and the precipices by which it is endangered; and of which, as long as they were in the wrong road, it was not so necessary that they should be warned.

There is one very easy, and very pleasant way of accounting for this general departure from the modes of thinking of our ancestors: so easy, indeed, and so pleasant, especially to the hearer, as to be very convenient to such writers for hire or for applause, as address themselves not to the men of the age that is gone by, but to the men of the age which has commenced. This explanation is that which ascribes the altered state of opinion and feeling to the growth of the human understanding. According to this doctrine, we reject the sophisms and prejudices which misled the uncultivated minds of our ancestors, because we have learnt too much, and have become too wise, to be imposed upon by such sophisms and such prejudices. It is our knowledge and our sagacity which keep us free from these gross errors. We have now risen to the capacity of perceiving our true interests; and it is no longer in the power of impostors and charlatans to deceive us.

I am unable to adopt this theory. Though a firm believer in the improvement of the age, I do not believe that its improvement has been of this kind. The grand achievement of the present age is the *diffusion* of *superficial* knowledge; and that surely is no trifle, to have been accomplished by a single generation. The persons who are in possession of knowledge adequate to the formation of sound opinions by their own lights, form also a constantly increasing number, but hitherto at all times a small one. It would be carrying the notion of the march of intellect too far, to suppose that an average man of the present day is superior to the greatest men of the beginning of the eighteenth century; yet they *held* many opinions which we are fast renouncing. The intellect of the age, therefore, is not the cause which we are in search of. I do not perceive that, in the mental training which has been received by the immense majority of the reading and thinking part of my countrymen, or in the kind of knowledge and other intellectual aliment which has been supplied to them, there is any thing likely to render them much less accessible to the influence of imposture and charlatanerie than there ever was. . . . Neither do I see, in such observations as I am able to make upon my cotemporaries, evidence that they have any principle within them which renders them much less liable now than at any former period to be misled by sophisms and prejudices. All I see is, that the opinions which have been transmitted to them from their ancestors, are not the kind of sophisms and prejudices which are fitted to possess any considerable ascendancy in their altered frame of mind. And I am rather inclined to account for this fact in a manner not reflecting such extraordinarily great honour upon the times we live in, as would result from the theory by which all is ascribed to the superior expansion of our understandings.

The intellectual tendencies of the age, considered both on the favourable and on the unfavourable side, it will be necessary, in the prosecution of the present design, to review and analyse in some detail. For the present it may be enough to remark, that it is seldom safe to ground a positive estimate of a character upon mere negatives: and that the faults or the prejudices, which a person, or an age, or a nation *has not,* go but a very little way with a wise man towards forming a high opinion of them. A person may be without a single prejudice, and yet utterly unfit for every purpose in nature. To have erroneous convictions is one evil; but to have no strong or deep-rooted convictions at all, is an enormous one. Before I compliment either a man or a generation upon having got rid of their prejudices, I require to know what they have substituted in lieu of them.

Now, it is self-evident that no fixed opinions have yet generally established themselves in the place of those which we have abandoned; that no new doctrines, philosophical or social, as yet command, or appear likely soon to command, an assent at all comparable in unanimity to that which the ancient doctrines could boast of while they continued in vogue. So long as this intellectual anarchy shall endure, we may be warranted in believing that we are in a fair way to become wiser than our forefathers; but it would be premature to affirm that we are already wiser. We have not yet advanced beyond the unsettled state, in which the mind is, when it has recently found itself out in a grievous error, and has not yet satisfied itself of the truth. The men of the present day rather incline to an opinion than embrace it; few, except the very penetrating, or the very presumptuous, have full confidence in their own convictions. This is not a state of health, but, at the best, of convalescence. It is a necessary stage in the progress of civilization, but it is attended with numerous evils; as one part of a road may be rougher or more dangerous than another, although every step brings the traveller nearer to his desired end.

Not increase of wisdom, but a cause of the reality of which we are better assured, may serve to account for the decay of prejudices; and this is, increase of discussion. Men may not reason better, concerning the great questions in which human nature is interested, but they reason more. Large subjects are discussed more, and longer, and by more minds. Discussion has penetrated deeper into society; and if no greater numbers than before have attained the higher degrees of intelligence, fewer grovel in that state of abject stupidity, which can only co-exist with utter apathy and sluggishness.

The progress which we have made, is precisely that sort of progress which increase of discussion suffices to produce, whether it be attended with increase of wisdom or no. To discuss, and to question established opinions, are merely two phrases for the same thing. When all opinions are questioned, it is in time found out what are those which will not bear a close examination. Ancient doctrines are then put upon their proofs; and those which were originally errors, or have become so by change of circumstances, are thrown aside. Discussion does this. It is by discussion, also, that true opinions are discovered and diffused. But this is not so certain a consequence of it as the weakening of error. To be rationally assured that a given doctrine is *true*, it is often necessary to examine and weigh an immense variety of facts. One single well-established fact, clearly irreconcilable with a doctrine, is sufficient to prove that it is *false*. Nay, opinions often upset themselves by their own incoherence; and the impossibility of their being well-founded may admit of being brought home to a mind not possessed of so much as one positive truth. All the inconsistencies of an opinion with itself, with obvious facts, or even with other prejudices, discussion evolves and makes manifest: and indeed this mode of refutation, requiring less study and less real knowledge than any other, is better suited to the inclination of most disputants. But the moment, and the mood of mind, in which men break loose from an error, is not, except in natures very happily constituted, the most favourable to those mental processes which are necessary to the investigation of truth. What led them wrong at first, was generally nothing else but the incapacity of seeing more than one thing at a time; and that incapacity is apt to stick to them when they have turned their eyes in an altered direction. They usually resolve that the new light which has broken in upon them shall be the sole light; and they wilfully and passionately blew out the ancient lamp, which, though it did not show them what they now see, served very well to enlighten the objects in its immediate neighbourhood. Whether men adhere to old opinions or adopt new ones, they have in general an invincible propensity to split the truth, and take half, or less than half of it; and a habit of erecting their quills and bristling up like a porcupine against any one who brings them the other half, as if he were attempting to deprive them of the portion which they have.

I am far from denying, that, besides getting rid of error, we are also continually enlarging the stock of positive truth. In physical science and art, this is too manifest to be called in question; and in the moral and social sciences, I believe it to be as undeniably true. The wisest men in every age generally surpass in wisdom the wisest of any preceding age, because the wisest men possess and profit by the constantly increasing accumulation of the ideas of all ages: but the multitude (by which I mean the majority of all ranks) have the ideas of their own age, and no others: and if the multitude of one age are nearer to the truth than the multitude of another, it is only in so far as they are guided and influenced by the authority of the wisest among them. . . .

from ON LIBERTY

from Chapter 1

INTRODUCTORY

THE subject of this Essay is not the so-called Liberty of the Will, so unfortunately opposed to the misnamed doctrine of Philosophical Necessity;[1] but Civil, or Social Liberty: the nature and limits of the power which can be legitimately exercised by society over the individual. A question seldom stated, and hardly ever discussed, in general terms, but which profoundly influences the practical controversies of the age by its latent presence, and is likely soon to make itself recognized as the vital question of the future. It is so far from being new, that, in a certain sense, it has divided mankind, almost from the remotest ages; but in the stage of progress into which the more civilized portions of the species have now entered, it presents itself under new conditions, and requires a different and more fundamental treatment.

The struggle between Liberty and Authority is the most conspicuous feature in the portions of history with which we are earliest familiar, particularly in that of Greece, Rome, and England. But in old times this contest was between subjects, or some classes of subjects, and the Government. By liberty, was meant protection against the tyranny of the political rulers. The rulers were conceived (except in some of the popular governments of Greece) as in a necessarily antagonistic position to the people whom they ruled. They consisted of a governing One, or a governing tribe or caste, who derived their authority from inheritance or conquest, who, at all events, did not hold it at the pleasure of the governed, and whose supremacy men did not venture, perhaps did not desire, to contest, whatever precautions might be taken against its oppressive exercise. Their power was regarded as necessary, but also as highly dangerous; as a weapon which they would attempt to use against their subjects, no less than against external enemies. To prevent the weaker members of the community from being preyed upon by innumerable vultures, it was needful that there should be an animal of prey stronger than the rest, commissioned to keep them down. But as the king of the vultures would be no less bent upon preying on the flock than any of the minor harpies, it was indispensable to be in a perpetual attitude of defence against his beak and claws. The aim, therefore, of patriots was to set limits to the power which the ruler should be suffered to exercise over the community; and this limitation was what they meant by liberty. It was attempted in two ways. First, by obtaining a recognition of certain immunities, called political liberties or rights, which it was to be regarded as a breach of duty in the ruler to infringe, and which, if he did infringe, specific resistance, or general rebellion, was held to be justifiable. A second, and generally a later expedient, was the establishment of constitutional checks, by which the consent of the community, or of a body of some sort, supposed to represent its interests, was made a necessary condition to some of the more important acts of the governing power. To the first of these modes of limitation, the ruling power, in most European countries, was compelled, more or less, to submit. It was not so with the second; and, to attain this, or when already in some degree possessed, to attain it more completely, became everywhere the principal object of the lovers of liberty. And so long as mankind were content to combat one enemy by

---

[1] The reference is to the issue between the belief that man is free to choose what he will do and the opposed doctrine that his every action is determined ultimately by external factors.

another, and to be ruled by a master, on condition of being guaranteed more or less efficaciously against his tyranny, they did not carry their aspirations beyond this point.

A time, however, came, in the progress of human affairs, when men ceased to think it a necessity of nature that their governors should be an independent power, opposed in interest to themselves. It appeared to them much better that the various magistrates of the State should be their tenants or delegates, revocable at their pleasure. In that way alone, it seemed, could they have complete security that the powers of government would never be abused to their disadvantage. By degrees this new demand for elective and temporary rulers became the prominent object of the exertions of the popular party, wherever any such party existed; and superseded, to a considerable extent, the previous efforts to limit the power of rulers. As the struggle proceeded for making the ruling power emanate from the periodical choice of the ruled, some persons began to think that too much importance had been attached to the limitation of the power itself. *That* (it might seem) was a resource against rulers whose interests were habitually opposed to those of the people. What was now wanted was, that the rulers should be identified with the people; that their interest and will should be the interest and will of the nation. The nation did not need to be protected against its own will. There was no fear of its tyrannizing over itself. Let the rulers be effectually responsible to it, promptly removable by it, and it could afford to trust them with power of which it could itself dictate the use to be made. Their power was but the nation's own power, concentrated, and in a form convenient for exercise. This mode of thought, or rather perhaps of feeling, was common among the last generation of European liberalism, in the Continental section of which it still apparently predominates. Those who admit any limit to what a government may do, except in the case of such governments as they think ought not to exist, stand out as brilliant exceptions among the political thinkers of the Continent. A similar tone of sentiment might by this time have been prevalent in our own country, if the circumstances which for a time encouraged it, had continued unaltered.

But, in political and philosophical theories, as well as in persons, success discloses faults and infirmities which failure might have concealed from observation. The notion, that the people have no need to limit their power over themselves, might seem axiomatic, when popular government was a thing only dreamed about, or read of as having existed at some distant period of the past. Neither was that notion necessarily disturbed by such temporary aberrations as those of the French Revolution, the worst of which were the work of an usurping few, and which, in any case, belonged, not to the permanent working of popular institutions, but to a sudden and convulsive outbreak against monarchical and aristocratic despotism. In time, however, a democratic republic came to occupy a large portion of the earth's surface, and made itself felt as one of the most powerful members of the community of nations; and elective and responsible government became subject to the observations and criticisms which wait upon a great existing fact. It was now perceived that such phrases as "self-government," and "the power of the people over themselves," do not express the true state of the case. The "people" who exercise the power are not always the same people with those over whom it is exercised; and the "self-government" spoken of is not the government of each by himself, but of each by all the rest. The will of the people, moreover, practically means the will of the most numerous or the most active *part* of the people; the majority, or those who succeed in making themselves accepted as the majority; the people, consequently, *may* desire to oppress a part of their number; and precautions are as much needed against this as against any other abuse of power. The limitation, therefore, of the power of government over individuals loses none of its importance when the holders of power are regularly accountable to the community, that is, to the strongest party therein. This view of things, recommending itself equally to the intelligence of thinkers and to the inclination of those important classes in European society to whose real or supposed interests democracy is adverse, has had no difficulty in establishing itself; and in political speculations "the tyranny of the majority" is now generally included among the evils against which society requires to be on its guard.

Like other tyrannies, the tyranny of the majority was at first, and is still vulgarly, held in dread, chiefly as operating through the acts of the public authorities. But reflecting persons perceived that when society is itself the tyrant—society collectively, over the separate individuals who compose it—its means of tyrannizing are not restricted to the acts which it may do by the hands of its political functionaries. Society can and does execute its own mandates: and if it issues wrong mandates instead of right, or any mandates at all in things with which it ought not to meddle, it practises a social tyranny more formidable than many kinds of political oppression, since, though not usually upheld by such extreme penalties, it leaves fewer part of the public can be made to feel its value—to see that it is good there should be differences, even though not for the better, even though, as it may appear to them, some should be for the worse. If the claims of Individuality are ever to be asserted, the time is now, while much is still wanting to complete the enforced assimilation. It is only in the earlier stages that any stand can be successfully made against the encroachment. The demand that all other people shall resemble ourselves, grows by what it feeds on. If resistance waits till life is reduced *nearly* to one uniform type, all deviations from that type will come to be considered impious, immoral, even monstrous and contrary to nature. Mankind speedily become unable to conceive diversity, when they have been for some time unaccustomed to see it.

John Ruskin

1819–1900

Ruskin was born at London in 1819, the only child of a wealthy merchant with artistic and literary interests, and a mother who was a devout Evangelical. This double influence, aesthetic and moral, colored the whole of Ruskin's life and work. Most of his formal education before he went to Oxford in 1837 consisted of a rigid course in the Bible, given by his mother in the mornings, and another, less rigid, in English literature, which his father read aloud in the evenings or the boy pursued in the family library during the afternoons. But observation was as important as books, ultimately more so, in the development of his taste and sensibility. Since he was not allowed to play with toys or with boys (his mother was afraid he might get hurt, physically or morally), he was forced to spend long hours "tracing the squares and comparing the colors of my carpet, . . . or counting the bricks in the opposite houses," with the important result that his eye was trained to sharp and accurate perception. After carpets and bricks, he began to observe nature, first in his garden at Herne Hill, and then with increasing delight on summer travels with his parents, when he discovered the English landscape, the ocean at Dover, the lakes and mountains of Westmorland, and finally the splendors of the Alps. But his response to nature was scientific as well as aesthetic. He looked at the strata of the Alps as well as at their beauty; and brought home from his summer trips specimens of rocks and flowers which he examined closely and described in detail for the catalogue he wrote of his own museum. As a matter of fact, his first published work appeared in a magazine of natural history, and his scientific studies had an important influence later on his theory of art.

But the romantic interest in nature predominated. It led him presently to sketching trees and mountains, and to spending hours in art shops and museums looking at landscapes. Then in 1833 the discovery of Turner's engravings of the Italian lakes "determined," he says, "the main tenor of my life," that is, made him a critic of art. For when his hero was viciously attacked in the reviews, Ruskin leapt to his defense (and that of other modern painters of landscape) and published, at the age of twenty-four, a remarkable book called *Modern Painters* (1843). To some extent it advanced a theory of aesthetics, which we shall consider in a moment, but for the most part it was filled with striking descriptions of nature drawn from his own experience, and set down to prove that Turner's landscapes, contrary to the charge that they were fantastic, were true to life. As he says himself, in a revealing passage, it was not his knowledge or his love of art (both of which were relatively slight in 1843) but of mountains and the sea which made him feel he could judge more justly of Turner than others could.

The aesthetic development here outlined did not take place, however, without the counterinfluence of Ruskin's Evangelical training. Because the Puritan tradition had always been suspicious of sensuous pleasures, like those of natural beauty and the arts in general, it was impossible for the boy to enjoy either nature or painting "straight" without a feeling of guilt. His first ecstatic glimpse of mountain scenery was dashed by an "alarmed sense of the sin of being so happy among the hills," so that he felt a profane and rebellious character, compared to his mother.[1] No wonder he spoke later of nature as coming to him "often in the form of a temptation." But also, by great good luck, it came to him in another form, as a "safeguard," he calls it (the choice of the word is revealing). "It was . . . inconsistent with every evil feeling, with spite, anger, covetousness, discontent, and every

---

[1] To be sure, this reaction occurred on a Sunday, but it would have been only less in degree, not different in kind, on a weekday.

other hateful passion"; and though it did not strengthen his character, it had much power in molding it. Furthermore, he felt a "Sanctity in the whole of nature," and interpreted the joy he experienced as the satisfaction "of a sort of heart-hunger" by "the presence of a Great and Holy Spirit." These experiences, recounted in the important chapter on "The Moral of Landscape" (printed below), remind us at once of Wordsworth and Carlyle, to whom, Ruskin later said, he owed much; and certainly the religio-moral view of nature, which conditioned his earliest reactions, was an inheritance from the Romantics. It thus provided the saving reconciliation of aesthetics and ethics, of father and mother, which he so badly needed. For if the sky was "fitted in all its functions for the perpetual comfort and exalting of the heart, for soothing it and purifying it from its dross and dust," why not also a painting of the sky? And if so, the art of landscape—maybe all great art rightly looked at—was not a sinful or an idle form of amusement. It was something of the greatest importance to society. In 1844 Ruskin wrote his *apologia* in a letter which might have been addressed to his mother —or to his own conscience:

Now observe—I am not engaged in selfish cultivation of critical acumen, but in ardent endeavour to spread the love and knowledge of art among all classes, . . . and [in] directing the public to expect and the artist to intend—an earnest and elevating *moral* influence in all that they admire and achieve.

The theory of art which Ruskin developed in the successive volumes of *Modern Painters* (from volume I in 1843 to volume V in 1860) was founded squarely on his personal experience. He read the standard works on aesthetics (by Burke, Reynolds, Coleridge, and Hazlitt), but it was his own reactions to nature, romantic, scientific, and Evangelical, which determined his critical principles.

The first of these may be called Naturalism. This was the doctrine, first asserted for literature by the Romantics and for painting by Ruskin (though there are anticipations in Hazlitt), that the artist should describe nature as he saw it, and not, as the neoclassicists had maintained, "nature to advantage dressed"; and that he should do so in whatever form naturally fitted his materials regardless of the "rules" or conventions of art laid down in neoclassical criticism. (See the General Introduction, p. 387, and the important quotation there from Ruskin.) Furthermore, "nature as he saw it" meant the concrete object in all of its detailed particularity, and not the general type which had been the focus of eighteenth-century art. But between the Naturalism of the Romantics and that of Ruskin there is an important difference. Ruskin took the element of realism in Romantic poetry (which he noticed in the

imagery of Wordsworth, Byron, and Keats) and made it central. His dictum that art must produce on the beholder's mind "precisely the impression which the reality would have produced" has no parallel in Romantic criticism. It came from the influence of his scientific studies (he pointed out that natural science had rendered our knowledge of nature "fruitful in accumulation and exquisite in accuracy"), and from his desire that a landscape should give him as nearly as possible the same experience he loved at first-hand and took in through a pair of very sharp eyes. The boy who stared at the pattern of carpets and studied the formation of strata became the critic who said, "He who is closest to Nature is best. . . . The more facts you give, the greater you are."

Not that Ruskin thought art should be merely photographic. He made room for an element of selection and arrangement even in what he called "imitative realism" (in the engraving of famous churches and lakes, or the painting of the Dutch School). And still further, he always maintained that the highest form of art was "imaginative realism." (See p. 574, where the two forms are contrasted, and there called Historical and Poetical painting.) The great artist does not give the facts as such, but the impression they made on his mind, the essential character or quality of his experience. Indeed, Ruskin's insistence that "the virtue of the Imagination is its reaching, by intuition and intensity of gaze (not by reasoning, but by its authoritative opening and revealing power), a more essential truth than is seen at the surface of things" was a valuable protest (and still is today) against the mistaken notion, engendered by science, that reason alone is a valid instrument of truth and that the poetic imagination dreams up charming and quite unreal pictures of life. Ruskin saw that the "truth of impression" grasped by the imagination of a great artist deepens and sharpens our perceptions of human experience. But this "impression" was to be painted realistically, in clear outline and finished detail. Ruskin hated Impressionism because his own impressions were always realistic. His theory of Naturalism, therefore, applies to the painting of the Pre-Raphaelites (whom he both influenced and defended), and to the literature of realism, in the poetry of Browning and the novels of the mid-Victorians, but not to the later work of the Symbolists and Impressionists.

Furthermore, we have to recognize that Ruskin hated or disparaged even realism in certain forms. He looks at a realistic picture by Teniers, the Flemish painter, of sots quarreling over their dice and calls it "an entirely base and evil picture. It is an expression of delight in . . . a vile thing." He looks at a Dutch painting of taverns and interiors with its clarity and detail and finds it trivial because the subjects are trivial. In both cases the two things that are lacking —and his insistence on which qualifies his realistic naturalism and completes his theory of art—are beauty and nobility. Great art must be beautiful, though not at the expense of truth. The beauty must not be achieved by removing everything ugly, nor by making the object an idealization of life. "Great art accepts Nature as she is"; it admits, in subordinate place, what is ugly or evil, and it then "directs the eyes and thoughts to what is most perfect in her," that is, to a beauty of face or form, mountain or tree, which *does* exist, however rare and uncommon it may be. Finally, in the doctrine of nobility we hear the voice of the Victorian prophet, brought up an Evangelical and molded by the moral idealism of the age, defining poetry, whether in verse or paint, as "the suggestion, by the imagination, of noble grounds for the noble emotions," and setting up as the greatest subject of art the heroic image, "the acts or meditations of great men." Ruskin's theory of art, taken as a whole, owed its enormous vogue to its combination of the realistic-scientific taste that was new to the age with the reassertion of those aesthetic and moral values of the past which modern civilization threatened to destroy.

Broadly speaking, a work of art may be looked at in two ways, directly as the expression of experience, or indirectly as a revelation of the artist and his time. The first approach is critical, the second biographical and historical. In Ruskin's earliest work (volumes I and II of *Modern Painters*) the first point of view is predominant; but when he turned from painting to architecture (where the relationship between art and society is always conspicuous) and wrote *The Seven Lamps of Architecture* (1849) and *The Stones of Venice* (1851 and 1853), he became more and more preoccupied with the character of the age which built the buildings or painted the pictures under examination, whether ancient or modern. But his point of view was not what we would call "scientific" or "scholarly." It was not open or detached. Though he ceased to be an Evangelical under the skeptical influences of the time, he never ceased to be a moralist. We have just seen how this affected his critical theory, and we could predict that it would make his historical search for the character of the artist or the society behind the art a search for its *moral* character.

But moral in a wide sense of the term that includes political and economic life. Under the influence of *Past and Present*, Ruskin became increasingly concerned with the evils of industrialism—the greed and selfishness of the new capitalists, the suffering of the workers under laissez-faire liberalism, and in particular the reduction of men to machines by the assembly-line methods of the modern factory. "For my own part," he cries out, "I will put up with this state of things, passively, not an hour longer. . . . I simply cannot paint, nor read, nor look at minerals, nor do anything else that I like, and the very

light of the morning sky, when there is any—which is seldom, nowadays, near London [or Bradford, where he gave the lecture on "Traffic"]—has become hateful to me, because of the misery that I know of, and see signs of, where I know it not, which no imagination can interpret too bitterly. Therefore, . . . I will endure it no longer quietly; but henceforward, with any few or many who will help, do my poor best to abate this misery." This was the state of mind which filled his architectural works with bitter arraignments of industrial civilization as he saw it reflected directly in modern, or indirectly, by contrast, in Greek or Gothic, building (see "The Nature of Gothic," printed below); and which eventually led him to abandon art-criticism altogether, in later life, and write a series of political and economic tracts for the times, most notably *Unto This Last* (1862), *The Crown of Wild Olive* (1866), in which the brilliant lecture on "Traffic" appeared, and the letters addressed to workingmen called *Fors Clavigera* (1871–84).

On the positive side, what did Ruskin have to propose? First, that so far as possible men should abandon the machines which were degrading workers into human automatons and robbing work of any incentive but money, and return, for the most part, to the old system of handicrafts where a man might use his creative imagination and find pride and pleasure in making a table or a pair of shoes. No doubt this proposal (though Morris took it quite seriously) was a futile effort to sweep back the tide with a broom. But what Ruskin says, in "The Nature of Gothic," about the destructive effect of machines on human nature is profoundly true. He may even be right about the source of the angry discontent of the proletariat that is promoting the rise of communism, namely, not low wages or envy of the rich, but bitter revulsion, however unconscious, against the degradation of life which their mechanical work is forcing upon them. But needless to say, Ruskin had little hope of setting back the clock. His more practical suggestions follow, in general, the Tory Paternalism he learned from Scott and his early travels (see p. 561), and from Carlyle. This meant, on the political side, the rejection of democracy in favor of a strong central government which would carry interference even farther than Carlyle had thought of, to the point of establishing old-age pensions, providing work for the unemployed, and regulating wages and prices—in short, a highly controlled capitalist economy. It is not surprising that Ruskin has been called one of the fathers of English Socialism. But political reformation would not be enough —indeed, it would only touch the surface. At bottom, the great need was for moral regeneration. Though the lecture on "Traffic" is mainly a superb attack on the worldliness and irresponsibility of the big businessmen who sat listening, it included Ruskin's plea for a heroism of trade.

Why should not a merchant conceive of his function as a soldier does of his, as that of serving his country rather than serving himself? of being a captain with men to lead and be responsible for? of being capable, if necessary, of the courage and self-sacrifice of a hero? In short, the heroic manufacturer would produce the best quality of goods at a small profit, constantly consider the welfare of his workmen, and stand ready to accept the fortunes of war, however destructive of his own prosperity. But the achievement of such an ideal was not very likely in a society where both the Christian and the feudal traditions were dying or dead. The trouble with Victorian idealism is not that it was too idealistic (so is Christian morality, and its influence has been tremendous) but that it had nothing to build on, no philosophy of life widely and firmly established which could support and sustain it. The Bradford millionaires who heard "Traffic" could not

have shrugged it off, as they undoubtedly did, had they had any real belief in the Gospels, or any living sense of a society where classes were bound together by mutual responsibilities. And Ruskin is really aware of this. He knows what goddess they adore, and how empty of heroism her followers must be. His phrasing admits it. "If one could contrive to attach the notion of conquest to them [feeding and clothing a population] anyhow!" No wonder his plea for idealism is so wistful beside the anger of his incisive attack on the worship of "Getting-on."

The standard edition, filled with reproductions of Ruskin's own drawings to illustrate the text, is that edited by E. T. Cook and A. Wedderburn (39 vols., 1903–12). The best Life is Ruskin's own autobiography called *Praeterita*. A good study, which combines biography with critical exposition, is *John Ruskin* (1933) by R. H. Wilenski.

John Ruskin

from PRAETERITA[1]

from Chapter 1

THE SPRINGS OF WANDEL[2]

I AM, and my father was before me, a violent Tory of the old school;—Walter Scott's school, that is to say, and Homer's.[3] I name these two out of the numberless great Tory writers, because they were my own two masters. I had Walter Scott's novels, and the *Iliad* (Pope's translation), for constant reading when I was a child, on week-days: on Sundays their effect was tempered by *Robinson Crusoe* and the *Pilgrim's Progress;* my mother having it deeply in her heart to make an evangelical clergyman of me. Fortunately, I had an aunt more evangelical than my mother; and my aunt gave me cold mutton for Sunday's dinner,[4] which—as I much

preferred it hot—greatly diminished the influence of the *Pilgrim's Progress;* and the end of the matter was, that I got all the noble imaginative teaching of Defoe and Bunyan, and yet—am not an evangelical clergyman. 5

I had, however, still better teaching than theirs, and that compulsorily, and every day of the week.

Walter Scott and Pope's Homer were reading of my own election, and my mother forced me, by steady daily toil, to learn long chapters of the Bible 10 by heart; as well as to read it every syllable through, aloud, hard names and all, from Genesis to the Apocalypse, about once a year: and to that discipline—patient, accurate, and resolute—I owe, not only a knowledge of the book, which I find occasionally 15 serviceable, but much of my general power of taking pains, and the best part of my taste in literature. From Walter Scott's novels I might easily, as I grew older, have fallen to other people's novels; and Pope might, perhaps, have led me to take Johnson's 20 English, or Gibbon's, as types of language;[5] but, once knowing the 32d of Deuteronomy, the 119th Psalm, the 15th of 1st Corinthians, the Sermon on the Mount, and most of the Apocalypse, every syllable

---

[1] This is the title, meaning "Things Past," that Ruskin gave to his autobiography, written between 1885 and 1889.
[2] The sources of a small stream near which Ruskin played as a child.
[3] A little below, Ruskin defines the Toryism of Scott and Homer as "a most sincere love of kings, and dislike of everybody who attempted to disobey them."
[4] The Evangelicals were strict observers of the Sabbath, and Ruskin's aunt would not allow a hot meal to be prepared on Sunday.

[5] Ruskin has in mind the rather formalized styles of Dr. Johnson and of the historian Edward Gibbon.

by heart, and having always a way of thinking with myself what words meant, it was not possible for me, even in the foolishest times of youth, to write entirely superficial or formal English; and the affectation of trying to write like Hooker and George Herbert[6] was the most innocent I could have fallen into.

From my own chosen masters, then, Scott and Homer, I learned the Toryism which my best afterthought has only served to confirm.

That is to say, a most sincere love of kings, and dislike of everybody who attempted to disobey them. Only, both by Homer and Scott, I was taught strange ideas about kings, which I find for the present much obsolete; for, I perceived that both the author of the *Iliad* and the author of *Waverley* made their kings, or king-loving persons, do harder work than anybody else. Tydides or Idomeneus always killed twenty Trojans to other people's one, and Redgauntlet speared more salmon than any of the Solway fishermen; and—which was particularly a subject of admiration to me—I observed that they not only did more, but in proportion to their doings *got* less than other people—nay, that the best of them were even ready to govern for nothing! and let their followers divide any quantity of spoil or profit. Of late it has seemed to me that the idea of a king has become exactly the contrary of this, and that it has been supposed the duty of superior persons generally to govern less, and get more, than anybody else. So that it was, perhaps, quite as well that in those early days my contemplation of existent kingship was a very distant one.[7]

The aunt who gave me cold mutton on Sundays was my father's sister: she lived at Bridge-end, in the town of Perth, and had a garden full of gooseberry-bushes, sloping down to the Tay, with a door opening to the water, which ran past it, clear-brown over the pebbles three or four feet deep; swift-eddying,—an infinite thing for a child to look down into.

My father began business as a wine-merchant, with no capital, and a considerable amount of debts bequeathed him by my grandfather. He accepted the bequest, and paid them all before he began to lay by anything for himself,—for which his best friends called him a fool, and I, without expressing any opinion as to his wisdom, which I knew in such matters to be at least equal to mine, have written on the granite slab over his grave that he was "an entirely honest merchant." As days went on he was able to take a house in Hunter Street, Brunswick Square, No. 54, (the windows of it, fortunately for me, commanded a view of a marvellous iron post, out of which the water-carts were filled through beautiful little trap-doors, by pipes like boa-constrictors; and I was never weary of contemplating that mystery, and the delicious dripping consequent); and as years went on, and I came to be four or five years old, he could command a postchaise and pair for two months in the summer, by help of which, with my mother and me, he went the round of his country customers (who liked to see the principal of the house his own traveller); so that, at a jog-trot pace, and through the panoramic opening of the four windows of a post-chaise, made more panoramic still to me because my seat was a little bracket in front, (for we used to hire the chaise regularly for the two months out of Long Acre, and so could have it bracketed and pocketed as we liked,) I saw all the high-roads, and most of the cross ones, of England and Wales; and great part of lowland Scotland, as far as Perth, where every other year we spent the whole summer; and I used to read the *Abbot* at Kinross, and the *Monastery* in Glen Farg, which I confused with "Glendearg," and thought that the White Lady had as certainly lived by the streamlet in that glen of the Ochils, as the Queen of Scots in the island of Loch Leven.[8]

To my farther great benefit, as I grew older, I thus saw nearly all the noblemen's houses in England; in reverent and healthy delight of uncovetous admiration,—perceiving, as soon as I could perceive any political truth at all, that it was probably much happier to live in a small house, and have Warwick Castle to be astonished at, than to live in Warwick Castle and have nothing to be astonished at; but that, at all events, it would not make Brunswick Square in the least more pleasantly habitable, to pull Warwick Castle down. And at this day, though I have kind invitations enough to visit America, I could not, even for a couple of months, live in a country so miserable as to possess no castles.

Nevertheless, having formed my notion of kinghood chiefly from the FitzJames of the *Lady of the Lake,* and of noblesse from the Douglas there, and the Douglas in *Marmion,*[9] a painful wonder soon

---

[6] Richard Hooker and George Herbert were also formal stylists, of the seventeenth century, but their language was closer to that of the King James version of the Bible.

[7] Ruskin is referring to the unedifying manners and morals at the English court under George IV (1820–30).

[8] *The Abbot* and *The Monastery* are both novels by Scott. Mary Queen of Scots appears in the former and the White Lady in the latter.

[9] That is, from Scott, who was the author of these two narrative poems.

arose in my child-mind, why the castles should now be always empty. Tantallon was there; but no Archibald of Angus:—Stirling, but no Knight of Snowdoun. The galleries and gardens of England were beautiful to see—but his Lordship and her Ladyship were always in town, said the housekeepers and gardeners. Deep yearning took hold of me for a kind of "Restoration," which I began slowly to feel that Charles the Second had not altogether effected, though I always wore a gilded oak-apple very piously in my button-hole on the 29th of May.[10] It seemed to me that Charles the Second's Restoration had been, as compared with the Restoration I wanted, much as that gilded oak-apple to a real apple. And as I grew wiser, the desire for sweet pippins instead of bitter ones, and Living Kings instead of dead ones, appeared to me rational as well as romantic; and gradually it has become the main purpose of my life to grow pippins, and its chief hope, to see Kings.[11] . . .

Nor did I painfully wish, what I was never permitted for an instant to hope, or even imagine, the possession of such things as one saw in toy-shops. I had a bunch of keys to play with, as long as I was capable only of pleasure in what glittered and jingled; as I grew older, I had a cart, and a ball; and when I was five or six years old, two boxes of well-cut wooden bricks. With these modest, but, I still think, entirely sufficient possessions, and being always summarily whipped if I cried, did not do as I was bid, or tumbled on the stairs, I soon attained serene and secure methods of life and motion; and could pass my days contentedly in tracing the squares and comparing the colours of my carpet;—examining the knots in the wood of the floor, or counting the bricks in the opposite houses; with rapturous intervals of excitement during the filling of the water-cart, through its leathern pipe, from the dripping iron post at the pavement edge; or the still more admirable proceedings of the turncock, when he turned and turned till a fountain sprang up in the middle of the street. But the carpet, and what patterns I could find in bed-covers, dresses, or wall-papers to be examined, were my chief resources, and my attention to the particulars in these was soon so accurate, that when at three and a half I was taken to have my portrait painted by

Mr. Northcote,[12] I had not been ten minutes alone with him before I asked him why there were holes in his carpet. The portrait in question represents a very pretty child with yellow hair, dressed in a white frock like a girl, with a broad light-blue sash and blue shoes to match; the feet of the child wholesomely large in proportion to its body; and the shoes still more wholesomely large in proportion to the feet. . . .

My mother had, as she afterward told me, solemnly "devoted me to God" before I was born; in imitation of Hannah.[13]

Very good women are remarkably apt to make away with their children prematurely, in this manner: the real meaning of the pious act being, that, as the sons of Zebedee are not (or at least they hope not), to sit on the right and left of Christ, in His kingdom, their own sons may perhaps, they think, in time be advanced to that respectable position in eternal life; especially if they ask Christ very humbly for it every day: and they always forget in the most naïve way that the position is not His to give![14]

"Devoting me to God," meant, as far as my mother knew herself what she meant, that she would try to send me to college, and make a clergyman of me: and I was accordingly bred for "the Church." My father, who—rest be to his soul—had the exceedingly bad habit of yielding to my mother in large things and taking his own way in little ones, allowed me, without saying a word, to be thus withdrawn from the sherry trade as an unclean thing; not without some pardonable participation in my mother's ultimate views for me. For, many and many a year afterward, I remember, while he was speaking to one of our artist friends, who admired Raphael, and greatly regretted my endeavors to interfere with that popular taste,[15]—while my father and he were condoling with each other on my having been impudent enough to think I could tell the public about Turner[16] and

---

[10] Anniversary of the restoration of Charles II in 1660.

[11] "The St. George's Company was founded [by Ruskin] for the promotion of agricultural instead of town life: and my only hope of prosperity for England, or any other country, in whatever life they lead, is in their discovering and obeying men capable of Kinghood." (Ruskin)

[12] James Northcote, a disciple of Sir Joshua Reynolds, and a distinguished portrait and historical painter.

[13] The mother of Samuel, who dedicated him to the service of the Lord (1 Samuel 1).

[14] The wife of Zebedee asked that her sons James and John might sit in these positions, and Jesus replied that not he but God would make the decision (Matthew 20:20–23).

[15] Ruskin had originally greatly admired Raphael, but on a visit to Rome in 1840 he began to have reservations; he continued to admire the earlier work of the artist but felt that his later work embodied false ideals and conventions which finally made him "the ruin of art." Ruskin's reaction is, of course, closely akin to that of the Pre-Raphaelites. See p. 388.

[16] J. M. W. Turner (1775–1851), English landscape painter. Ruskin's admiration for him determined in large part his career as art critic.

Raphael,—instead of contenting myself, as I ought, with explaining the way of their souls' salvation to them—and what an amiable clergyman was lost in me,—"Yes," said my father, with tears in his eyes—(true and tender tears, as ever father shed,) "he would have been a Bishop."

Luckily for me, my mother, under these distinct impressions of her own duty, and with such latent hopes of my future eminence, took me very early to church;—where, in spite of my quiet habits, and my mother's golden vinaigrette, always indulged to me there, and there only, with its lid unclasped that I might see the wreathed open pattern above the sponge, I found the bottom of the pew so extremely dull a place to keep quiet in, (my best story-books being also taken away from me in the morning,) that, as I have somewhere said before, the horror of Sunday used even to cast its prescient gloom as far back in the week as Friday—and all the glory of Monday, with church seven days removed again, was no equivalent for it.

Notwithstanding, I arrived at some abstract in my own mind of the Rev. Mr. Howell's sermons; and occasionally, in imitation of him, preached a sermon at home over the red sofa cushions;—this performance being always called for by my mother's dearest friends, as the great accomplishment of my childhood. The sermon was, I believe, some eleven words long;—very exemplary, it seems to me, in that respect—and I still think must have been the purest gospel, for I know it began with, "People, be good." ...

from Chapter 2

HERNE-HILL ALMOND BLOSSOMS

When I was about four years old my father found himself able to buy the lease of a house on Herne Hill, a rustic eminence four miles south of the "Standard in Cornhill";[17] of which the leafy seclusion remains, in all essential points of character, unchanged to this day: certain Gothic splendors, lately indulged in by our wealthier neighbors, being the only serious innovations; and these are so graciously concealed by the fine trees of their grounds, that the passing viator remains unappalled by them; and I can still walk up and down the piece of road between the Fox tavern and the Herne Hill station, imagining myself four years old.

---

[17] A water tower in the central part of London, from which outlying distances were commonly measured.

Our house was the northernmost of a group which stand accurately on the top or dome of the hill, where the ground is for a small space level, as the snows are, (I understand,) on the dome of Mont Blanc; presently falling, however, in what may be, in the London clay formation, considered a precipitous slope, to our valley of Chamouni (or of Dulwich) on the east; and with a softer descent into Cold Harbour-lane on the west: on the south, no less beautifully declining to the dale of the Effra, (doubtless shortened from Effrena, signifying the "Unbridled" river; recently, I regret to say, bricked over for the convenience of Mr. Biffin, chemist, and others); while on the north, prolonged indeed with slight depression some half mile or so, and receiving, in the parish of Lambeth, the chivalric title of "Champion Hill," it plunges down at last to efface itself in the plains of Peckham, and the rural barbarism of Goose Green.

The group, of which our house was the quarter, consisted of two precisely similar partner-couples of houses, gardens and all to match; still the two highest blocks of buildings seen from Norwood on the crest of the ridge; so that the house itself, three-storied, with garrets above, commanded, in those comparatively smokeless days, a very notable view from its garret windows, of the Norwood hills on one side, and the winter sunrise over them; and of the valley of the Thames on the other, with Windsor telescopically clear in the distance, and Harrow, conspicuous always in fine weather to open vision against the summer sunset. It had front and back garden in sufficient proportion to its size; the front, richly set with old evergreens, and well-grown lilac and laburnum; the back, seventy yards long by twenty wide, renowned over all the hill for its pears and apples, which had been chosen with extreme care by our predecessor, (shame on me to forget the name of a man to whom I owe so much!)—and possessing also a strong old mulberry tree, a tall white-heart cherry tree, a black Kentish one, and an almost unbroken hedge, all round, of alternate gooseberry and currant bush; decked, in due season, (for the ground was wholly beneficent,) with magical splendor of abundant fruit: fresh green, soft amber, and rough-bristled crimson bending the spinous branches; clustered pearl and pendant ruby joyfully discoverable under the large leaves that looked like vine.

The differences of primal importance which I observed between the nature of this garden, and that of Eden, as I had imagined it, were, that, in this one, *all* the fruit was forbidden; and there were no companionable beasts: in other respects the little domain answered every purpose of Paradise to me; and the climate, in that cycle of our years, allowed me to pass most of my life in it. My mother never gave me more to learn than she knew I could easily get learnt, if I set myself honestly to work, by twelve o'clock. She never allowed anything to disturb me when my task was set; if it was not said rightly by twelve o'clock, I was kept in till I knew it, and in general, even when Latin Grammar came to supplement the Psalms, I was my own master for at least an hour before half-past one dinner, and for the rest of the afternoon.

My mother, herself finding her chief personal pleasure in her flowers, was often planting or pruning beside me, at least if I chose to stay beside *her*. I never thought of doing anything behind her back which I would not have done before her face; and her presence was therefore no restraint to me; but, also, no particular pleasure, for, from having always been left so much alone, I had generally my own little affairs to see after; and, on the whole, by the time I was seven years old, was already getting too independent, mentally, even of my father and mother; and, having nobody else to be dependent upon, began to lead a very small, perky, contented, conceited, Cock-Robinson-Crusoe sort of life, in the central point which it appeared to me, (as it must naturally appear to geometrical animals,) that I occupied in the universe.

This was partly the fault of my father's modesty; and partly of his pride. He had so much more confidence in my mother's judgment as to such matters than in his own, that he never ventured even to help, much less to cross her, in the conduct of my education; on the other hand, in the fixed purpose of making an ecclesiastical gentleman of me, with the superfinest of manners, and access to the highest circles of fleshly and spiritual society, the visits to Croydon, where I entirely loved my aunt, and young baker-cousins, became rarer and more rare: the society of our neighbors on the hill could not be had without breaking up our regular and sweetly selfish manner of living; and on the whole, I had nothing animate to care for, in a childish way, but myself, some nests of ants, which the gardener would never leave undisturbed for me, and a sociable bird or two; though I never had the sense or perseverance to make one really tame. But that was partly because, if ever I managed to bring one to be the least trustful of me, the cats got it.

Under these circumstances, what powers of imagination I possessed, either fastened themselves on inanimate things—the sky, the leaves, and pebbles,

observable within the walls of Eden,—or caught at any opportunity of flight into regions of romance, compatible with the objective realities of existence in the nineteenth century, within a mile and a quarter of Camberwell Green.

Herein my father, happily, though with no definite intention other than of pleasing me, when he found he could do so without infringing any of my mother's rules, became my guide. I was particularly fond of watching him shave; and was always allowed to come into his room in the morning (under the one in which I am now writing), to be the motionless witness of that operation. Over his dressing-table hung one of his own water-colour drawings, made under the teaching of the elder Nasmyth;[18] I believe, at the High School of Edinburgh. It was done in the early manner of tinting, which, just about the time when my father was at the High School, Dr. Monro[19] was teaching Turner; namely, in grey under-tints of Prussian blue and British ink, washed with warm colour afterward on the lights. It represented Conway Castle, with its Frith,[20] and, in the foreground, a cottage, a fisherman, and a boat at the water's edge.

When my father had finished shaving, he always told me a story about this picture. The custom began without any initial purpose of his, in consequence of my troublesome curiosity whether the fisherman lived in the cottage, and where he was going to in the boat. It being settled, for peace' sake, that he *did* live in the cottage, and was going in the boat to fish near the castle, the plot of the drama afterward gradually thickened; and became, I believe, involved with that of the tragedy of *Douglas,* and of the *Castle Spectre,*[21] in both of which pieces my father had performed in private theatricals, before my mother, and a select Edinburgh audience, when he was a boy of sixteen, and she, at grave twenty, a model housekeeper, and very scornful and religiously suspicious of theatricals. But she was never weary of telling me, in later years, how beautiful my father looked in his Highland dress, with the high black feathers.

In the afternoons, when my father returned (always punctually) from his business, he dined, at half-past four, in the front parlor, my mother sitting beside him to hear the events of the day, and give counsel and encouragement with respect to the same;—

---

18 Scottish portrait and landscape painter.
19 Physician and art patron, from whom, according to Ruskin, Turner got "some practical teaching."
20 Either a wooded park or an estuary.
21 Two late eighteenth-century dramas, the first by John Home, the second by M. G. Lewis.

chiefly the last, for my father was apt to be vexed if orders for sherry fell the least short of their due standard, even for a day or two. I was never present at this time, however, and only avouch what I relate by hearsay and probable conjecture; for between four and six it would have been a grave misdemeanor in me if I so much as approached the parlor door. After that, in summer time, we were all in the garden as long as the day lasted; tea under the white-heart cherry tree; or in winter and rough weather, at six o'clock in the drawing-room,—I having my cup of milk, and slice of bread-and-butter, in a little recess, with a table in front of it, wholly sacred to me; and in which I remained in the evenings as an Idol in a niche, while my mother knitted, and my father read to her,—and to me, so far as I chose to listen.

The series of the Waverley novels, then drawing toward its close, was still the chief source of delight in all households caring for literature; and I can no more recollect the time when I did not know them than when I did not know the Bible; but I have still a vivid remembrance of my father's intense expression of sorrow mixed with scorn, as he threw down *Count Robert of Paris,*[22] after reading three or four pages; and knew that the life of Scott was ended: the scorn being a very complex and bitter feeling in him, —partly, indeed, of the book itself, but chiefly of the wretches who were tormenting and selling the wrecked intellect, and not a little, deep down, of the subtle dishonesty which had essentially caused the ruin. My father never could forgive Scott his concealment of the Ballantyne partnership.

Such being the salutary pleasures of Herne Hill, I have next with deeper gratitude to chronicle what I owe to my mother for the resolutely consistent lessons which so exercised me in the Scriptures as to make every word of them familiar to my ear in habitual music,—yet in that familiarity reverenced, as transcending all thought, and ordaining all conduct.

This she effected, not by her own sayings or personal authority; but simply by compelling me to read the book thoroughly, for myself. As soon as I was able to read with fluency, she began a course of Bible work with me, which never ceased till I went to Oxford. She read alternate verses with me, watching, at first, every intonation of my voice, and correcting the false ones, till she made me understand the verse, if within my reach, rightly, and energetically. It might be beyond me altogether; that she did not care about; but she made sure that as soon as I got hold of it at all, I should get hold of it by the right end.

In this way she began with the first verse of Genesis, and went straight through, to the last verse of the Apocalypse; hard names, numbers, Levitical law, and all; and began again at Genesis the next day. If a name was hard, the better the exercise in pronunciation,—if a chapter was tiresome, the better lesson in patience,—if loathsome, the better lesson in faith that there was some use in its being so outspoken. After our chapters, (from two to three a day, according to their length, the first thing after breakfast, and no interruption from servants allowed,—none from visitors, who either joined in the reading or had to stay upstairs,—and none from any visitings or excursions, except real travelling,) I had to learn a few verses by heart, or repeat, to make sure I had not lost, something of what was already known; and, with the chapters thus gradually possessed from the first word to the last, I had to learn the whole body of the fine old Scottish paraphrases,[23] which are good, melodious, and forceful verse; and to which, together with the Bible itself, I owe the first cultivation of my ear in sound.

It is strange that of all the pieces of the Bible which my mother thus taught me, that which cost me most to learn, and which was, to my child's mind, chiefly repulsive—the 119th Psalm—has now become of all the most precious to me, in its overflowing and glorious passion of love for the Law of God, in opposition to the abuse of it by modern preachers of what they imagine to be His gospel.

But it is only by deliberate effort that I recall the long morning hours of toil, as regular as sunrise,— toil on both sides equal—by which, year after year, my mother forced me to learn these paraphrases, and chapters, (the eighth of 1st Kings being one—try it, good reader, in a leisure hour!) allowing not so much as a syllable to be missed or misplaced; while every sentence was required to be said over and over again till she was satisfied with the accent of it. I recollect a struggle between us of about three weeks, concerning the accent of the "of" in the lines

"Shall any following spring revive
The ashes of the urn?"—

---

22 Scott was a very ill man when he wrote this, his next to last novel. He was actually writing himself to death in an endeavor to pay off his share of the debt incurred by the failure of his publisher, with whom he had been a business partner. Although the partnership was concealed, there does not seem to have been any dishonest intention. (See above, p. 346.)

23 *Translations and Paraphrases in Verse collected and prepared by . . . the Church of Scotland, in order to be sung in Churches.* The quotation below is from this collection.

I insisting, partly in childish obstinacy, and partly in true instinct for rhythm, (being wholly careless on the subject both of urns and their contents,) on reciting it with an accented *of*. It was not, I say, till after three weeks' labor, that my mother got the accent lightened on the "of" and laid on the ashes, to her mind. But had it taken three years she would have done it, having once undertaken to do it. And, assuredly, had she not done it,—well, there's no knowing what would have happened; but I am very thankful she *did*.

I have just opened my oldest (in use) Bible,—a small, closely, and very neatly printed volume it is, printed in Edinburgh by Sir D. Hunter Blair and J. Bruce, Printers to the King's Most Excellent Majesty, in 1816. Yellow, now, with age; and flexible, but not unclean, with much use; except that the lower corners of the pages at 8th of 1st Kings, and 32d Deuteronomy, are worn somewhat thin and dark, the learning of these two chapters having cost me much pains. My mother's list of the chapters with which, thus learned, she established my soul in life,[24] has just fallen out of it. I will take what indulgence the incurious reader can give me, for printing the list thus accidentally occurrent:

Exodus	chapters	15th and 20th.
2 Samuel	"	1st, from 17th verse to the end.
1 Kings	"	8th.
Psalms	"	23rd, 32nd, 90th, 91st, 103rd, 112th, 119th, 139th.
Proverbs	"	2nd, 3rd, 8th, 12th.
Isaiah	"	58th.
Matthew	"	5th, 6th, 7th.
Acts	"	26th.
1 Corinthians	"	13th, 15th.
James	"	4th.
Revelation	"	5th, 6th.

And truly, though I have picked up the elements of a little further knowledge—in mathematics, meteorology, and the like, in after life,—and owe not a little to the teaching of many people, this maternal installation of my mind in that property of chapters, I count very confidently the most precious, and, on the whole, the one *essential* part of all my education.

And it is perhaps already time to mark what advantage and mischief, by the chances of life up to seven years old, had been irrevocably determined for me.

I will first count my blessings (as a not unwise friend once recommended me to do, continually; whereas I have a bad trick of always numbering the thorns in my fingers and not the bones in them).

And for best and truest beginning of all blessings, I had been taught the perfect meaning of Peace, in thought, act, and word.

I never had heard my father's or mother's voice once raised in any question with each other; nor seen an angry, or even slightly hurt or offended, glance in the eyes of either. I had never heard a servant scolded; nor even suddenly, passionately, or in any severe manner, blamed. I had never seen a moment's trouble or disorder in any household matter; nor anything whatever either done in a hurry, or undone in due time. I had no conception of such a feeling as anxiety; my father's occasional vexation in the afternoons, when he had only got an order for twelve butts after expecting one for fifteen, as I have just stated, was never manifested to *me*; and itself related only to the question whether his name would be a step higher or lower in the year's list of sherry exporters; for he never spent more than half his income, and therefore found himself little incommoded by occasional variations in the total of it. I had never done any wrong that I knew of—beyond occasionally delaying the commitment to heart of some improving sentence, that I might watch a wasp on the window-pane, or a bird in the cherry tree; and I had never seen any grief.

Next to this quite priceless gift of Peace, I had received the perfect understanding of the natures of Obedience and Faith. I obeyed word, or lifted finger, of father or mother, simply as a ship her helm; not only without idea of resistance, but receiving the direction as a part of my own life and force, and helpful law, as necessary to me in every moral action as the law of gravity in leaping. And my practice in Faith was soon complete: nothing was ever promised me that was not given; nothing ever threatened me that was not inflicted, and nothing ever told me that was not true.

Peace, obedience, faith; these three for chief good; next to these, the habit of fixed attention with both eyes and mind—on which I will not further enlarge at this moment, this being the main practical faculty of my life, causing Mazzini[25] to say of me, in conversation authentically reported, a year or two before his death, that I had "the most analytic mind in Europe." An opinion in which, so far as I am acquainted with Europe, I am myself entirely disposed to concur.

---

24 "This expression . . . has naturally been supposed by some readers to mean that my mother at this time made me vitally and evangelically religious. The fact was far otherwise. I meant only that she gave me secure *ground* for all future life, practical or spiritual. See the paragraph next following." (Ruskin)

25 The famous Italian patriot, for whom Ruskin had great admiration.

Lastly, an extreme perfection in palate and all other bodily senses, given by the utter prohibition of cake, wine, comfits, or, except in carefullest restriction, fruit; and by fine preparation of what food was given me. Such I esteem the main blessings of my childhood;—next, let me count the equally dominant calamities.

First, that I had nothing to love.

My parents were—in a sort—visible powers of nature to me, no more loved than the sun and the moon: only I should have been annoyed and puzzled if either of them had gone out; (how much, now, when both are darkened!)—still less did I love God; not that I had any quarrel with Him, or fear of Him; but simply found what people told me was His service, disagreeable; and what people told me was His book, not entertaining. I had no companions to quarrel with, neither; nobody to assist, and nobody to thank. Not a servant was ever allowed to do anything for me, but what it was their duty to do; and why should I have been grateful to the cook for cooking, or the gardener for gardening,—when the one dared not give me a baked potato without asking leave, and the other would not let my ants' nest alone, because they made the walks untidy? The evil consequence of all this was not, however, what might perhaps have been expected, that I grew up selfish or unaffectionate; but that, when affection did come, it came with violence utterly rampant and unmanageable, at least by me, who never before had anything to manage.

For (second of chief calamities) I had nothing to endure. Danger or pain of any kind I knew not: my strength was never exercised, my patience never tried, and my courage never fortified. Not that I was ever afraid of anything,—either ghosts, thunder, or beasts; and one of the nearest approaches to insubordination which I was ever tempted into as a child, was in passionate effort to get leave to play with the lion's cubs in Wombwell's menagerie.

Thirdly. I was taught no precision nor etiquette of manners; it was enough if, in the little society we saw, I remained unobtrusive, and replied to a question without shyness: but the shyness came later, and increased as I grew conscious of the rudeness arising from the want of social discipline, and found it impossible to acquire, in advanced life, dexterity in any bodily exercise, skill in any pleasing accomplishment, or ease and tact in ordinary behavior.

Lastly, and chief of evils. My judgment of right and wrong, and powers of independent action, were left entirely undeveloped; because the bridle and blinkers were never taken off me. Children should have their times of being off duty, like soldiers; and when once the obedience, if required, is certain, the little creature should be very early put for periods of practice in complete command of itself; set on the bare-backed horse of its own will, and left to break it by its own strength. But the ceaseless authority exercised over my youth left me, when cast out at last into the world, unable for some time to do more than drift with its vortices.

My present verdict, therefore, on the general tenor of my education at that time, must be, that it was at once too formal and too luxurious; leaving my character, at the most important moment for its construction, cramped indeed, but not disciplined; and only by protection innocent, instead of by practice virtuous.

from MODERN PAINTERS, VOLUME III

from Chapter I

OF THE RECEIVED OPINIONS TOUCHING THE "GRAND STYLE"[1]

. . . IT seems to me, and may seem to the reader, strange that we should need to ask the question, "What is poetry?" Here is a word we have been using all our lives, and, I suppose, with a very distinct idea attached to it; and when I am now called upon to give a definition of this idea, I find myself at a pause. What is more singular, I do not at present recollect hearing the question often asked, though surely it is a very natural one; and I never recollect hearing it answered, or even attempted to be answered. In general, people shelter themselves under metaphors, and while we hear poetry described as an utterance of the soul, an effusion of Divinity, or

---

[1] The word "style" is used in a wide sense, which covers content as well as form. The "Grand Style" may be paraphrased as "Great Art." In this chapter Ruskin begins his discussion of what determines greatness in art by examining some of Sir Joshua Reynolds' theories, in the course of which he is led to the definition of poetry which follows. Note that he uses "poetry" to mean the artistic use of either colors or language, so that the definition amounts to a definition of art.

voice of nature, or in other terms equally elevated and obscure, we never attain anything like a definite explanation of the character which actually distinguishes it from prose.

I come, after some embarrassment, to the conclusion, that poetry "is the suggestion, by the imagination, of noble grounds for the noble emotions." I mean, by the noble emotions, those four principal sacred passions—Love, Veneration, Admiration, and Joy (this latter especially, if unselfish); and their opposites—Hatred, Indignation (or Scorn), Horror, and Grief,—this last, when unselfish, becoming Compassion. These passions in their various combinations constitute what is called "poetical feeling," when they are felt on noble grounds, that is, on great and true grounds. Indignation, for instance, is a poetical feeling, if excited by serious injury; but it is not a poetical feeling if entertained on being cheated out of a small sum of money. It is very possible the manner of the cheat may have been such as to justify considerable indignation; but the feeling is nevertheless not poetical unless the grounds of it be large as well as just. In like manner, energetic admiration may be excited in certain minds by a display of fireworks, or a street of handsome shops; but the feeling is not poetical, because the grounds of it are false, and therefore ignoble. There is in reality nothing to deserve admiration either in the firing of packets of gunpowder, or in the display of the stocks of warehouses. But admiration excited by the budding of a flower is a poetical feeling, because it is impossible that this manifestation of spiritual power and vital beauty can ever be enough admired.

Farther, it is necessary to the existence of poetry that the grounds of these feelings should be *furnished by the imagination.* Poetical feeling, that is to say, mere noble emotion, is not poetry. It is happily inherent in all human nature deserving the name, and is found often to be purest in the least sophisticated. But the power of assembling, by *the help of the imagination,* such images as will excite these feelings, is the power of the poet or literally of the "Maker."

Now this power of exciting the emotions depends of course on the richness of the imagination, and on its choice of those images which, in combination, will be most effective, or, for the particular work to be done, most fit. And it is altogether impossible for a writer not endowed with invention to conceive what tools a true poet will make use of, or in what way he will apply them, or what unexpected results he will bring out by them; so that it is vain to say that the details of poetry ought to possess, or ever do possess, any *definite* character. Generally speaking, poetry runs into finer and more delicate details than prose; but the details are not poetical because they are more delicate, but because they are employed so as to bring out an affecting result. For instance, no one but a true poet would have thought of exciting our pity for a bereaved father by describing his way of locking the door of his house:

> Perhaps to himself at that moment he said,
> "The key I must take, for my Ellen is dead."
> But of this in my ears not a word did he speak;
> And he went to the chase with a tear on his cheek.[2]

In like manner, in painting, it is altogether impossible to say beforehand what details a great painter may make poetical by his use of them to excite noble emotions: and we shall, therefore, find presently that a painting is to be classed in the great or inferior schools, not according to the kind of details which it represents, but according to the uses for which it employs them.

It is only farther to be noticed, that infinite confusion has been introduced into this subject by the careless and illogical custom of opposing painting to poetry, instead of regarding poetry as consisting in a noble use, whether of colours or words. Painting is properly to be opposed to *speaking* or *writing,* but not to *poetry.* Both painting and speaking are methods of expression. Poetry is the employment of either for the noblest purposes. . . .

from Chapter 3

OF THE REAL NATURE OF GREATNESS OF STYLE

. . . The best way will be, therefore, I think, to sketch out at once in this chapter, the different characters which really constitute "greatness" of style,[3] and to indicate the principal directions of the outbranching misapprehensions of them; then, in the succeeding chapters, to take up in succession those which need more talk about them, and follow out at leisure whatever inquiries they may suggest.

I. CHOICE OF NOBLE SUBJECT.—Greatness of style consists, then: first, in the habitual choice of subjects of thought which involve wide interests and profound passions, as opposed to those which involve narrow interests and slight passions. The style is

---

[2] The last stanza of "The Childless Father" by Wordsworth.

[3] In the passage omitted at the beginning of this chapter Ruskin points out that "we have at all times some instinctive sense that the function of one painter is greater than that of another" and that our problem is to determine a true measure of this greatness.

greater or less in exact proportion to the nobleness of the interests and passions involved in the subject. The habitual choice of sacred subjects, such as the Nativity, Transfiguration, Crucifixion (if the choice be sincere), implies that the painter has a natural disposition to dwell on the highest thoughts of which humanity is capable; it constitutes him so far forth a painter of the highest order, as, for instance, Leonardo,[4] in his painting of the Last Supper: he who delights in representing the acts or meditations of great men, as, for instance, Raphael painting the School of Athens, is, so far forth, a painter of the second order: he who represents the passions and events of ordinary life, of the third. And in this ordinary life, he who represents deep thoughts and sorrows, as, for instance, Hunt,[5] in his Claudio and Isabella, and such other works, is of the highest rank in his sphere: and he who represents the slight malignities and passions of the drawing-room, as, for instance, Leslie,[6] of the second rank; he who represents the sports of boys, or simplicities of clowns, as Webster[7] or Teniers,[8] of the third rank; and he who represents brutalities and vices (for delight in them, and not for rebuke of them), of no rank at all, or rather of a negative rank, holding a certain order in the abyss.

The reader will, I hope, understand how much importance is to be attached to the sentence in the first parenthesis, "if the choice be sincere"; for choice of subject is, of course, only available as a criterion of the rank of the painter, when it is made from the heart. Indeed, in the lower orders of painting, the choice is always made from such heart as the painter has; for his selection of the brawls of peasants or sports of children can, of course, proceed only from the fact that he has more sympathy with such brawls or pastimes than with nobler subjects. But the choice of the higher kind of subjects is often insincere; and may, therefore, afford no real criterion of the painter's rank. The greater number of men who have lately painted religious or heroic subjects have done so in mere ambition, because they had been taught that it

was a good thing to be a "high-art"[9] painter; and the fact is that, in nine cases out of ten, the so-called historical or "high-art" painter is a person infinitely inferior to the painter of flowers or still life. He is, in modern times, nearly always a man who has great vanity without pictorial capacity, and differs from the landscape or fruit painter merely in misunderstanding and overestimating his own powers. He mistakes his vanity for inspiration, his ambition for greatness of soul, and takes pleasure in what he calls "the ideal," merely because he has neither humility nor capacity enough to comprehend the real.

But also observe, it is not enough even that the choice be sincere. It must also be wise. It happens very often that a man of weak intellect, sincerely desiring to do what is good and useful, will devote himself to high art subjects because he thinks them the only ones on which time and toil can be usefully spent, or, sometimes, because they are really the only ones he has pleasure in contemplating. But not having intellect enough to enter into the minds of truly great men, or to imagine great events as they really happened, he cannot become a great painter; he degrades the subjects he intended to honour, and his work is more utterly thrown away, and his rank as an artist in reality lower, than if he had devoted himself to the imitation of the simplest objects of natural history. The works of Overbeck[10] are a most notable instance of this form of error.

It must also be remembered, that in nearly all the great periods of art the choice of subject has not been left to the painter. His employer,—abbot, baron, or monarch,—determined for him whether he should earn his bread by making cloisters bright with choirs of saints, painting coats of arms on leaves of romances, or decorating presence-chambers with complimentary mythology; and his own personal feelings are ascertainable only by watching, in the themes assigned to him, what are the points in which he seems to take most pleasure. Thus, in the prolonged ranges of varied subjects with which Benozzo Gozzoli decorated the cloisters of Pisa, it is easy to see that love of simple domestic incident, sweet landscape, and glittering ornament, prevails slightly

---

4 Leonardo da Vinci (1452–1519).

5 Holman Hunt (1827–1910) was a leader in the Pre-Raphaelite movement. His "Claudio and Isabella," exhibited at the Royal Academy in 1853, was much admired by Ruskin.

6 Charles Robert Leslie (1794–1859), American-born English painter of fashionable life.

7 Thomas Webster, minor painter of the nineteenth century whose interests lay in school and village scenes.

8 There were two Dutch painters of this name, in the sixteenth and seventeenth centuries respectively, both of them of the realistic school.

9 In Chapter 1 of this volume Ruskin says that for the last hundred and fifty years critics have used the terms " 'High Art,' 'Great or Ideal Style,' and other such, as descriptive of a certain noble manner of painting," and have characterized "as 'vulgar,' or 'low,' or 'realist,' another manner of painting and conceiving." The distinction includes, of course, the subject-matter.

10 Nineteenth-century German painter who, upon his conversion to Roman Catholicism, devoted himself entirely to sacred subjects. His pictures were full of devout feeling but hard in color and outline.

over the solemn elements of religious feeling, which, nevertheless, the spirit of the age instilled into him in such measure as to form a very lovely and noble mind, though still one of the second order. In the work of Orcagna, an intense solemnity and energy in the sublimest groups of his figures, fading away as he touches inferior subjects, indicates that his home was among the archangels, and his rank among the first of the sons of men: while Correggio,[11] in the sidelong grace, artificial smiles, and purple languors of his saints, indicates the inferior instinct which would have guided his choice in quite other directions, had it not been for the fashion of the age, and the need of the day.

It will follow, of course, from the above considerations, that the choice which characterizes the school of high art is seen as much in the treatment of a subject as in its selection, and that the expression of the thoughts of the persons represented will always be the first thing considered by the painter who worthily enters that highest school. For the artist who sincerely chooses the noblest subject will also choose chiefly to represent what makes that subject noble, namely, the various heroism or other noble emotions of the persons represented. If, instead of this, the artist seeks only to make his picture agreeable by the composition of its masses and colours, or by any other merely pictorial merit, as fine drawing of limbs, it is evident, not only that any other subject would have answered his purpose as well, but that he is unfit to approach the subject he has chosen, because he cannot enter into its deepest meaning, and therefore cannot in reality have chosen it for that meaning. Nevertheless, while the expression is always to be the first thing considered, all other merits must be added to the utmost of the painter's power; for until he can both colour and draw beautifully he has no business to consider himself a painter at all,[12] far less to attempt the noblest subjects of painting; and, when he has once possessed himself of these powers, he will naturally and fitly employ them to deepen and perfect the impression made by the sentiment of his subject.

The perfect unison of expression, as the painter's main purpose, with the full and natural exertion of his pictorial power in the details of the work, is found only in the old Pre-Raphaelite periods, and in the modern Pre-Raphaelite school.[13] In the works of Giotto, Angelico, Orcagna, John Bellini, and one or two more, these two conditions of high art are entirely fulfilled, so far as the knowledge of those days enable them to be fulfilled; and in the modern Pre-Raphaelite school they are fulfilled nearly to the uttermost. Hunt's Light of the World is, I believe, the most perfect instance of expressional purpose with technical power, which the world has yet produced.

Now in the Post-Raphaelite period of ancient art, and in the spurious high art of modern times, two broad forms of error divide the schools; the one consisting in (A) the superseding of expression by technical excellence, and the other in (B) the superseding of technical excellence by expression.

(A). Superseding expression by technical excellence.—This takes place most frankly, and therefore most innocently, in the work of the Venetians.[14] They very nearly ignore expression altogether, directing their aim exclusively to the rendering of external truths of colour and form. Paul Veronese will make the Magdalene wash the feet of Christ with a countenance as absolutely unmoved as that of any ordinary servant bringing a ewer to her master, and will introduce the supper at Emmaus[15] as a background to the portraits of two children playing with a dog. Of the wrongness or rightness of such a proceeding we shall reason in another place; at present we have to note it merely as displacing the Venetian work from the highest or expressional rank of art. But the error is generally made in a more subtle and dangerous way. The artist deceives himself into the idea that he is doing all he can to elevate his subject by treating it under rules of art, introducing into it accurate science, and collecting for it the beauties of (so-called) ideal form; whereas he may, in reality, be all the while sacrificing his subject to his own vanity or pleasure, and losing truth, nobleness, and impressiveness for the sake of delightful lines or creditable pedantries.

(B). Superseding technical excellence by expression.—This is usually done under the influence of another kind of vanity. The artist desires that men should think he has an elevated soul, affects to despise the ordinary excellence of art, contemplates with

---

[11] All three of the painters here described belonged to the Italian Renaissance.

[12] The stress which Ruskin laid upon subject matter or content sometimes tends to obscure his insistence upon, and assumption of, technical skill as an indispensable prerequisite to any artistic excellence.

[13] The old periods, of course, were those actually before the time of Raphael (1483–1520). The modern school, of which Ruskin was an ardent champion, is described in the General Introduction, p. 387.

[14] Chief among the great Venetian painters were Titian, Giorgione, Tintoretto, and Veronese.

[15] The meal that Jesus ate with two of his disciples at a village outside Jerusalem after his resurrection (Luke 24:13–35).

separated egotism[16] the course of his own imaginations or sensations, and refuses to look at the real facts round about him, in order that he may adore at leisure the shadow of himself. He lives in an element of what he calls tender emotions and lofty aspirations; which are, in fact, nothing more than very ordinary weaknesses or instincts, contemplated through a mist of pride. A large range of modern German art comes under this head.

A more interesting and respectable form of this error is fallen into by some truly earnest men, who, finding their powers not adequate to the attainment of great artistical excellence, but adequate to rendering, up to a certain point, the expression of the human countenance, devote themselves to that object alone, abandoning effort in other directions, and executing the accessories of their pictures feebly or carelessly. With these are associated another group of philosophical painters, who suppose the artistical merits of other parts *adverse* to the expression, as drawing the spectator's attention away from it, and who paint in grey colour, and imperfect light and shade, by way of enforcing the purity of their conceptions. Both these classes of conscientious but narrow-minded artists labour under the same grievous mistake of imagining that wilful fallacy can ever be either pardonable or helpful. They forget that colour, if used at all, must be either true or false, and that what *they* call chastity, dignity, and reserve, is, to the eye of any person accustomed to nature, pure, bold, and impertinent falsehood. It does not, in the eyes of any soundly minded man, exalt the expression of a female face that the cheeks should be painted of the colour of clay, nor does it in the least enhance his reverence for a saint to find the scenery around him deprived, by his presence, of sunshine.[17] It is an important consolation, however, to reflect that no artist ever fell into any of these last three errors (under head B.) who had really the capacity of becoming a great painter. No man ever despised colour who could produce it; and the error of these sentimentalists and philosophers is not so much in the choice of their manner of painting, as in supposing themselves capable of painting at all. Some of them might have made efficient sculptors, but the greater number had their mission in some other sphere than that of art, and would have found, in works of practical charity, better employment for their gentleness and sentimentalism, than in

denying to human beauty its colour, and to natural scenery its light; in depriving heaven of its blue, and earth of its bloom, valour of its glow, and modesty of its blush.

II. Love of Beauty.—The second characteristic of the great school of art is, that it introduces in the conception of its subject as much beauty as is possible, consistently with truth.[18]

[18] "As here, for the first time, I am obliged to use the terms Truth and Beauty in a kind of opposition, I must therefore stop for a moment to state clearly the relation of these two qualities of art; and to protest against the vulgar and foolish habit of confusing truth and beauty with each other. People with shallow powers of thought, desiring to flatter themselves with the sensation of having attained profundity, are continually doing the most serious mischief by introducing confusion into plain matters, and then valuing themselves on being confounded. Nothing is more common than to hear people who desire to be thought philosophical, declare that 'beauty is truth,' and 'truth is beauty.' I would most earnestly beg every sensible person who hears such an assertion made to nip the germinating philosopher in his ambiguous bud; and beg him, if he really believes his own assertion, never thenceforward to use two words for the same thing. The fact is, truth and beauty are entirely distinct, though often related, things. One is a property of statements, the other of objects. The statement that 'two and two make four' is true, but it is neither beautiful nor ugly, for it is invisible; a rose is lovely, but it is neither true nor false, for it is silent. That which shows nothing cannot be fair, and that which asserts nothing cannot be false. Even the ordinary use of the words false and true as applied to artificial and real things, is inaccurate. An artificial rose is not a 'false' rose, it is not a rose at all. The falseness is in the person who states, or induces the belief, that it *is* a rose.

"Now, therefore, in things concerning art, the words true and false are only to be rightly used while the picture is considered as a statement of facts. The painter asserts that this which he has painted is the form of a dog, a man, or a tree. If it be *not* the form of a dog, a man, or a tree, the painter's statement is false; and therefore we justly speak of a false line, or false colour; not that any line or colour can in themselves be false, but they become so when they convey a statement that they resemble something which they do *not* resemble. But the beauty of the lines or colours is wholly independent of any such statement. They may be beautiful lines, though quite inaccurate, and ugly lines, though quite faithful. A picture may be frightfully ugly, which represents with fidelity some base circumstance of daily life; and a painted window may be exquisitely beautiful, which represents men with eagles' faces, and dogs with blue heads and crimson tails (though, by the way, this is not in the strict sense *false* art, as we shall see hereafter, inasmuch as it means no assertion that men ever *had* eagles' faces). If this were not so, it would be impossible to sacrifice truth to beauty; for to attain the one would always be to attain the other. But, unfortunately, this sacrifice is exceedingly possible, and it is chiefly this which characterises the false schools of high art, so far as high art consists in the pursuit of beauty. For although truth and beauty are independent of each other, it does not follow that we are at liberty to pursue whichever we please. They are indeed separable, but it is wrong to separate them; they are to be sought together in the order of their worthiness; that is to say, truth first, and beauty afterwards. High art differs from low art in possessing an excess of beauty in addition to its truth, not in possessing an excess of beauty inconsistent with truth." (Ruskin)

---

[16] An egotism that has separated him from the ordinary artist.
[17] Ruskin has mainly in view here the academic painting of the period, against which the Pre-Raphaelites rebelled. That he was also thinking of Rembrandt is clear from section III.

For instance, in any subject consisting of a number of figures, it will make as many of those figures beautiful as the faithful representation of humanity will admit. It will not deny the facts of ugliness or decrepitude, or relative inferiority and superiority of feature as necessarily manifested in a crowd, but it will, so far as it is in its power, seek for and dwell upon the fairest forms, and in all things insist on the beauty that is in them, not on the ugliness. In this respect, schools of art become higher in exact proportion to the degree in which they apprehend and love the beautiful. Thus, Angelico, intensely loving all spiritual beauty, will be of the highest rank; and Paul Veronese and Correggio, intensely loving physical and corporeal beauty, of the second rank; and Albert Dürer, Rubens, and in general the Northern artists, apparently insensible to beauty, and caring only for truth, whether shapely or not, of the third rank; and Teniers and Salvator, Caravaggio, and other such worshippers of the depraved, of no rank, or, as we said before, of a certain order in the abyss.

The corruptions of the schools of high art, so far as this particular quality is concerned, consists in the sacrifice of truth to beauty. Great art dwells on all that is beautiful; but false art omits or changes all that is ugly. Great art accepts Nature as she is, but directs the eyes and thoughts to what is most perfect in her; false art saves itself the trouble of direction by removing or altering whatever it thinks objectionable. The evil results of which proceeding are twofold.

First.[19] That beauty deprived of its proper foils and adjuncts ceases to be enjoyed as beauty, just as light deprived of all shadow ceases to be enjoyed as light. A white canvas cannot produce an effect of sunshine; the painter must darken it in some places before he can make it look luminous in others; nor can an uninterrupted succession of beauty produce the true effect of beauty; it must be foiled by inferiority before its own power can be developed. Nature has for the most part mingled her inferior and nobler elements as she mingles sunshine with shade, giving due use and influence to both, and the painter who chooses to remove the shadow, perishes in the burning desert he has created. The truly high and beautiful art of Angelico is continually refreshed and strengthened by his frank portraiture of the most ordinary features of his brother monks, and of the recorded peculiarities of ungainly sanctity; but the modern German and Raphaelesque schools lose all honour and nobleness in barber-like admiration of handsome faces, and have, in fact, no real faith except in straight noses and curled hair. Paul Veronese opposes the dwarf to the soldier, and the negress to the queen;[20] Shakspeare places Caliban beside Miranda, and Autolycus beside Perdita;[21] but the vulgar idealist withdraws his beauty to the safety of the saloon,[22] and his innocence to the seclusion of the cloister; he pretends that he does this in delicacy of choice and purity of sentiment, while in truth he has neither courage to front the monster, nor wit enough to furnish the knave.

It[23] is only by the habit of representing faithfully all things, that we can truly learn what is beautiful, and what is not. The ugliest objects contain some element of beauty; and in all, it is an element peculiar to themselves, which cannot be separated from their ugliness, but must either be enjoyed together with it, or not at all. The more a painter accepts nature as he finds it, the more unexpected beauty he discovers in what he at first despised; but once let him arrogate the right of rejection, and he will gradually contract his circle of enjoyment, until what he supposed to be nobleness of selection ends in narrowness of perception. Dwelling perpetually upon one class of ideas, his art becomes at once monstrous and morbid; until at last he cannot faithfully represent even what he chooses to retain; his discrimination contracts into darkness, and his fastidiousness fades into fatuity.

High art, therefore, consists neither in altering, nor in improving nature; but in seeking throughout nature for "whatsoever things are lovely, and whatsoever things are pure",[24] in loving these, in displaying to the utmost of the painter's power such loveliness as is in them, and directing the thoughts of others to them by winning art, or gentle emphasis. Of the degree in which this can be done, and in which it may be permitted to gather together, without falsifying, the finest forms or thoughts, so as to create a sort of perfect vision, we shall have to speak hereafter: at present, it is enough to remember that art (caeteris paribus)[25] is great in exact proportion to the love of beauty shown by the painter, provided that love of beauty forfeit no atom of truth.

---

19 "Evil first, that we lose the true *force* of beauty." (Ruskin, marginal summary)

20 In his pictures "Alexander and the Family of Darius" and "The Queen of Sheba," respectively.

21 In *The Tempest* and *The Winter's Tale,* respectively.

22 The English equivalent of the French salon, meaning a large room for social purposes or for the exhibition of works of art,

23 "Evil second,—we lose the true *quantity* of beauty." (Ruskin, marginal summary)   24 Philippians 4:8.

25 Other things being equal.

III. SINCERITY.—The next[26] characteristic of great art is that it includes the largest possible quantity of Truth in the most perfect possible harmony. If it were possible for art to give all the truths of nature, it ought to do it. But this is not possible. Choice must always be made of some facts which *can* be represented, from among others which must be passed by in silence, or even, in some respects, misrepresented. The inferior artist chooses unimportant and scattered truths; the great artist chooses the most necessary first, and afterwards the most consistent with these, so as to obtain the greatest possible and most harmonious *sum*. For instance, Rembrandt always chooses to represent the exact force with which the light on the most illumined part of an object is opposed to its obscurer portions. In order to obtain this, in most cases, not very important truth, he sacrifices the light and colour of five sixths of his picture; and the expression of every character of objects which depends on tenderness of shape or tint. But he obtains his single truth, and what picturesque and forcible expression is dependent upon it, with magnificent skill and subtlety. Veronese, on the contrary, chooses to represent the great relations of visible things to each other, to the heaven above, and to the earth beneath them. He holds it more important to show how a figure stands relieved from delicate air, or marble wall; how as a red, or purple, or white figure, it separates itself, in clear discernibility, from things not red, nor purple, nor white; how infinite daylight shines round it; how innumerable veils of faint shadow invest it; how its blackness and darkness are, in the excess of their nature, just as limited and local as its intensity of light: all this, I say, he feels to be more important than showing merely the exact *measure* of the spark of sunshine that gleams on a dagger-hilt, or glows on a jewel. All this, moreover, he feels to be harmonious,—capable of being joined in one great system of spacious truth. And with inevitable watchfulness, inestimable subtlety, he unites all this in tenderest balance, noting in each hair's-breadth of colour, not merely what its rightness or wrongness is in itself, but what its relation is to every other on his canvas; restraining, for truth's sake, his exhaustless energy; reining back, for truth's sake, his fiery strength; veiling, before truth, the vanity of brightness; penetrating, for truth, the discouragement of gloom; ruling his restless invention with a rod of iron; pardoning no error, no thoughtlessness, no forgetfulness; and subduing all his powers, impulses, and imaginations, to the arbitrament of a merciless justice, and the obedience of an incorruptible verity.

I give this instance with respect to colour and shade; but, in the whole field of art, the difference between the great and inferior artists is of the same kind, and may be determined at once by the question, which of them conveys the largest sum of truth?

It follows from this principle,[27] that in general all *great* drawing is *distinct* drawing; for truths which are rendered indistinctly might, for the most part, as well not be rendered at all. There are, indeed, certain facts of mystery, and facts of indistinctness, in all objects, which must have their proper place in the general harmony, and the reader will presently find me, when we come to that part of our investigation, telling him that all good drawing must in some sort be *in*distinct. We may, however, understand this apparent contradiction, by reflecting that the highest knowledge always involves a more advanced perception of the fields of the unknown; and, therefore, it may most truly be said, that to know anything well involves a profound sensation of ignorance, while yet it is equally true that good and noble knowledge is distinguished from vain and useless knowledge chiefly by its clearness and distinctness, and by the vigorous consciousness of what is known and what is not.

So in art. The best drawing involves a wonderful perception and expression of indistinctness; and yet all noble drawing is separated from the ignoble by its distinctness, by its fine expression and firm assertion of *Something*; whereas the bad drawing, without either firmness or fineness, expresses and asserts *Nothing*. The first thing, therefore, to be looked for as a sign of noble art, is a clear consciousness of what is drawn and what is not; the bold statement, and frank confession—"*This* I know," "*that* I know not"; and, generally speaking, all haste, slurring, obscurity, indecision, are signs of low art, and all calmness, distinctness, luminousness, and positiveness, of high art.

It follows, secondly, from this principle,[28] that as the great painter is always attending to the sum and harmony of his truths rather than to one or the other of any group, a quality of Grasp is visible in his work, like the power of a great reasoner over his subject, or a great poet over his conception, manifesting itself

---

[26] "I name them in order of *increasing*, not decreasing importance." (Ruskin)

[27] "Corollary 1st: Great art is generally distinct." (Ruskin, marginal summary)

[28] "Corollary 2nd: Great art is generally large in masses and in scale." (Ruskin, marginal summary)

very often in missing out certain details or less truths (which, though good in themselves, he finds are in the way of others), and in a sweeping manner of getting the beginnings and ends of things shown at once, and the squares and depths rather than the surfaces: hence, on the whole, a habit of looking at large masses rather than small ones; and even a physical largeness of handling, and love of working, if possible, on a large scale; and various other qualities, more or less imperfectly expressed by such technical terms as breadth, massing, unity, boldness, &c., all of which are, indeed, great qualities when they mean breadth of truth, weight of truth, unity of truth, and courageous assertion of truth; but which have all their correlative errors and mockeries, almost universally mistaken for them,—the breadth which has no contents, the weight which has no value, the unity which plots deception, and the boldness which faces out fallacy.

And it is to be noted especially respecting largeness of scale, that though for the most part it is characteristic of the more powerful masters, they having both more invention wherewith to fill space (as Ghirlandajo wished that he might paint all the walls of Florence),[29] and, often, an impetuosity of mind which makes them like free play for hand and arm (besides that they usually desire to paint everything in the foreground of their picture of the natural size), yet, as this largeness of scale involves the placing of the picture at a considerable distance from the eye, and this distance involves the loss of many delicate details, and especially of the subtle lines of expression in features, it follows that the masters of refined detail and human expression are apt to prefer a small scale to work upon; so that the chief masterpieces of expression which the world possesses are small pictures by Angelico, in which the figures are rarely more than six or seven inches high; in the best works of Raphael and Leonardo the figures are almost always less than life; and the best works of Turner do not exceed the size of 18 inches by 12.

As its greatness depends on the sum of truth, and this sum of truth can always be increased by delicacy of handling, it follows that all great art must have this delicacy to the utmost possible degree.[30] This rule is infallible and inflexible. All coarse work is the sign of low art. Only, it is to be remembered, that coarseness must be estimated by the distance from the eye; it being necessary to consult this distance, when great, by laying on touches which appear coarse when seen near; but which, so far from being coarse, are, in reality, more delicate in a master's work than the finest close handling, for they involve a calculation of result, and are laid on with a subtlety of sense precisely correspondent to that with which a good archer draws his bow; the spectator seeing in the action nothing but the strain of the strong arm, while there is, in reality, in the finger and eye, an ineffably delicate estimate of distance, and touch on the arrow plume. And, indeed, this delicacy is generally quite perceptible to those who know what the truth is, for strokes by Tintoret or Paul Veronese, which were done in an instant, and look to an ignorant spectator merely like a violent dash of loaded colour (and are, as such, imitated by blundering artists), are, in fact, modulated by the brush and finger to that degree of delicacy that no single grain of the colour could be taken from the touch without injury; and little golden particles of it, not the size of a gnat's head, have important share and function in the balances of light in a picture perhaps fifty feet long. Nearly *every* other rule applicable to art has some exception but this. This has absolutely none. All great art is delicate art, and all coarse art is bad art. Nay, even to a certain extent, all *bold* art is bad art; for boldness is not the proper word to apply to the courage and swiftness of a great master, based on knowledge, and coupled with fear and love. There is as much difference between the boldness of the true and the false masters, as there is between the courage of a pure woman and the shamelessness of a lost one.

IV. INVENTION.—The last characteristic of great art is that it must be inventive, that is, be produced by the imagination. In this respect, it must precisely fulfil the definition already given of poetry; and not only present grounds for noble emotion, but furnish these grounds by *imaginative power*. Hence there is at once a great bar fixed between the two schools of Lower and Higher Art. The lower merely copies what is set before it, whether in portrait, landscape, or still-life; the higher either entirely imagines its subject, or arranges the materials presented to it, so as to manifest the imaginative power in all the three phases which have been already explained in the second volume.

And this was the truth which was confusedly present in Reynolds's mind when he spoke, as above quoted, of the difference between Historical and

---

[29] This great fifteenth-century master of fresco is reported by Vasari to have complained, "Now that I have begun to get into the spirit and comprehend the method of this art, I grudge that they do not commission me to paint the whole circuit of the walls of Florence with stories."

[30] "Corollary 3rd: Great art is always delicate." (Ruskin, marginal summary)

Poetical painting.[31] *Every relation of the plain facts which the painter saw* is proper *historical* painting. If those facts are unimportant (as that he saw a gambler quarrel with another gambler, or a sot enjoying himself with another sot), then the history is trivial; if the facts are important (as that he saw such and such a great man look thus, or act thus, at such a time), then the history is noble: in each case perfect truth of narrative being supposed, otherwise the whole thing is worthless, being neither history nor poetry, but plain falsehood. And farther, as greater or less elegance and precision are manifested in the relation or painting of the incidents, the merit of the work varies; so that, what with difference of subject, and what with difference of treatment, historical painting falls or rises in changeful eminence, from Dutch trivialities[32] to a Velasquez[33] portrait, just as historical talking or writing varies in eminence, from an old woman's story-telling up to Herodotus.[34] Besides which, certain operations of the imagination come into play inevitably, here and there, so as to touch the history with some light of poetry, that is, with some light shot forth of the narrator's mind, or brought out by the way he has put the accidents together: and wherever the imagination has thus had anything to do with the matter at all (and it must be somewhat cold work where it has not), then, the confines of the lower and higher schools touching each other, the work is coloured by both; but there is no reason why, therefore, we should in the least confuse the historical and poetical characters, any more than that we should confuse blue with crimson, because they may overlap each other, and produce purple.

Now, historical or simply narrative art is very precious in its proper place and way, but it is never *great* art until the poetical or imaginative power touches it; and in proportion to the stronger manifestation of this power, it becomes greater and greater, while the highest art is purely imaginative, all its materials being wrought into their form by invention. . . .

Farther, imaginative art always *includes* historical art; so that, strictly speaking, according to the analogy

above used, we meet with the pure blue, and with the crimson ruling the blue and changing it into kingly purple, but not with the pure crimson: for all imagination must deal with the knowledge it has before accumulated; it never produces anything but by combination or contemplation. Creation, in the full sense, is impossible to it. And the mode in which the historical faculties are included by it is often quite simple, and easily seen. Thus, in Hunt's great poetical picture of the Light of the World, the whole thought and arrangement of the picture being imaginative, the several details of it are wrought out with simple portraiture; the ivy, the jewels, the creeping plants, and the moonlight being calmly studied or remembered from the things themselves. But of all these special ways in which the invention works with plain facts, we shall have to treat farther afterwards.

And now, finally, since this poetical power includes the historical, if we glance back to the other qualities required in great art, and put all together, we find that the sum of them is simply the sum of all the powers of man. For as (1) the choice of the high subject involves all conditions of right moral choice, and as (2) the love of beauty involves all conditions of right admiration, and as (3) the grasp of truth involves all strength of sense, evenness of judgment, and honesty of purpose, and as (4) the poetical power involves all swiftness of invention, and accuracy of historical memory, the sum of all these powers is the sum of the human soul. Hence we see why the word "Great" is used of this art. It is literally great. It compasses and calls forth the entire human spirit, whereas any other kind of art, being more or less small or narrow, compasses and calls forth only *part* of the human spirit. Hence the idea of its magnitude is a literal and just one, the art being simply less or greater in proportion to the number of faculties it exercises and addresses. And this is the ultimate meaning of the definition I gave of it long ago,[35] as containing the "greatest number of the greatest ideas."

Such, then, being the characters required in order to constitute high art, if the reader will think over them a little, and over the various ways in which they may be falsely assumed, he will easily perceive how spacious and dangerous a field of discussion they open to the ambitious critic, and of error to the ambitious artist; he will see how difficult it must be, either to distinguish what is truly great art from the mockeries of it, or to rank the real artists in anything like a progressive system of greater and less. For it will have been observed that the various qualities

---

[31] Ruskin in Chapter 1 sums up Reynolds's distinction: painting is historical when it attends "to literal truth and 'minute exactness in the details of nature modified by accident'" and poetical when it attends only "to the invariable."

[32] Ruskin is thinking of the domestic and familiar scenes favored by the Dutch painters.

[33] Perhaps the greatest of Spanish painters, noted particularly for his portraits.

[34] Greek historian of the fifth century B.C., known as "the father of history."

[35] In the first volume of *Modern Painters,* 1843.

which form greatness are partly inconsistent with each other (as some virtues are, docility and firmness for instance), and partly independent of each other; and the fact is, that artists differ not more by mere capacity, than by the component *elements* of their capacity, each possessing in very different proportions the several attributes of greatness; so that, classed by one kind of merit, as, for instance, purity of expression, Angelico will stand highest; classed by another, sincerity of manner, Veronese will stand highest; classed by another, love of beauty, Leonardo will stand highest, and so on: hence arise continual disputes and misunderstandings among those who think that high art must always be one and the same, and that great artists ought to unite all great attributes in an equal degree.

In one of the exquisitely finished tales of Marmontel, a company of critics are received at dinner by the hero of the story, an old gentleman, somewhat vain of his *acquired* taste, and his niece, by whose incorrigible *natural* taste he is seriously disturbed and tormented. During the entertainment, "On parcourut tous les genres de littérature, et pour donner plus d'essor à l'érudition et à la critique, on mit sur le tapis cette question toute neuve, sçavoir, lequel méritoit la préférence de Corneille ou de Racine. L'on disoit même là-dessus les plus belles choses du monde, lorsque la petite nièce, qui n'avoit pas dit un mot, s'avisa de demander naïvement lequel des deux fruits, de l'orange ou de la pêche, avoit le goût le plus exquis et méritoit le plus d'éloges. Son oncle rougit de sa simplicité, et les convives baissèrent tous les yeux sans daigner répondre à cette bêtise. Ma nièce, dit Fintac, à votre âge, il faut sçavoir écouter, et se taire."[36]

I cannot close this chapter with shorter or better advice to the reader, than merely, whenever he hears discussions about the relative merits of great masters, to remember the young lady's question. It is, indeed, true that there *is* a relative merit, that a peach is nobler than a hawthorn berry, and still more a hawthorn

berry than a bead of the nightshade; but in each rank of fruits, as in each rank of masters, one is endowed with one virtue, and another with another; their glory is their dissimilarity, and they who propose to themselves in the training of an artist that he should unite the colouring of Tintoret, the finish of Albert Dürer, and the tenderness of Correggio, are no wiser than a horticulturist would be, who made it the object of his labour to produce a fruit which should unite in itself the lusciousness of the grape, the crispness of the nut, and the fragrance of the pine.

And from these considerations one most important practical corollary is to be deduced, with the good help of Mademoiselle Agathe's[37] simile, namely, that the greatness or smallness of a man is, in the most conclusive sense, determined for him at his birth, as strictly as it is determined for a fruit whether it is to be a currant or an apricot. Education, favourable circumstances, resolution, and industry can do much; in a certain sense they do *everything*; that is to say, they determine whether the poor apricot shall fall in the form of a green bead, blighted by the east wind, and be trodden under foot, or whether it shall expand into tender pride, and sweet brightness of golden velvet. But apricot out of currant,—great man out of small,—did never yet art or effort make; and, in a general way, men have their excellence nearly fixed for them when they are born; a little cramped and frost-bitten on one side, a little sun-burnt and fortune-spotted on the other, they reach, between good and evil chances, such size and taste as generally belong to the men of their calibre, and, the small in their serviceable bunches, the great in their golden isolation, have, these no cause for regret, nor those for disdain.

Therefore it is, that every system of teaching is false which holds forth "great art" as in any wise to be taught to students, or even to be aimed at by them. Great art is precisely that which never was, nor will be taught, it is preeminently and finally the expression of the spirits of great men; so that the only wholesome teaching is that which simply endeavours to fix those characters of nobleness in the pupil's mind, of which it seems easily susceptible; and without holding out to him, as a possible or even probable result, that he should ever paint like Titian, or carve like Michael Angelo, enforces upon him the manifest possibility, and assured duty, of endeavouring to draw in a manner at least honest and intelligible; and cultivates in him those general charities of heart, sincerities of

---

[36] "Le Connoisseur" in his *Contes moraux*. The quoted passage may be translated: "They discussed all kinds of literature and, to allow greater flights of erudition and criticism, they proposed this entirely original question, namely, which was to be preferred, Corneille or Racine. They were just saying the finest things in the world, when the little niece, who had not said a word, took it into her head to ask naïvely which of the two fruits, oranges or pears, had the more delicious taste and deserved the greater praise. Her uncle blushed for her simplicity and the guests lowered their eyes without condescending to reply to this stupidity. 'My niece,' said Fintac, 'at your age you should know how to listen and keep quiet.'"

[37] The niece in Marmontel's tale.

thought, and graces of habit which are likely to lead him, throughout life, to prefer openness to affectation, realities to shadows, and beauty to corruption.

from Chapter 17

THE MORAL OF LANDSCAPE[38]

. . . The first thing which I remember, as an event in life,[39] was being taken by my nurse to the brow of Friar's Crag on Derwentwater; the intense joy, mingled with awe, that I had in looking through the hollows in the mossy roots, over the crag, into the dark lake, has associated itself more or less with all twining roots of trees ever since. Two other things I remember, as, in a sort, beginnings of life;—crossing Shapfells (being let out of the chaise to run up the hills), and going through Glenfarg, near Kinross, in a winter's morning, when the rocks were hung with icicles; these being culminating points in an early life of more travelling than is usually indulged to a child.[40] In such journeyings, whenever they brought me near hills, and in all mountain ground and scenery, I had a pleasure, as early as I can remember, and continuing till I was eighteen or twenty, infinitely greater than any which has been since possible to me in anything; comparable for intensity only to the joy of a lover in being near a noble and kind mistress, but no more explicable or definable than that feeling of love itself. Only thus much I can remember, respecting it, which is important to our present subject.

First: it was never independent of associated thought. Almost as soon as I could see or hear, I had got reading enough to give me associations with all kinds of scenery; and mountains, in particular, were always partly confused with those of my favourite book, Scott's *Monastery;* so that Glenfarg and all other glens were more or less enchanted to me, filled with forms of hesitating creed about Christie of the Clint Hill, and the monk Eustace; and with a general presence of White Lady[41] everywhere. I also generally knew, or was told by my father and mother, such

simple facts of history as were necessary to give more definite and justifiable association to other scenes which chiefly interested me, such as the ruins of Lochleven and Kenilworth; and thus my pleasure in mountains or ruins was never, even in earliest childhood, free from a certain awe and melancholy, and general sense of the meaning of death, though, in its principal influence, entirely exhilarating and gladdening.

Secondly: it was partly dependent on contrast with a very simple and unamused mode of general life: I was born in London, and accustomed, for two or three years, to no other prospect than that of the brick walls over the way; had no brothers nor sisters, nor companions; and though I could always make myself happy in a quiet way, the beauty of the mountains had an additional charm of change and adventure which a country-bred child would not have felt.

Thirdly: there was no definite religious feeling mingled with it. I partly believed in ghosts and fairies; but supposed that angels belonged entirely to the Mosaic dispensation, and cannot remember any single thought or feeling connected with them. I believed that God was in heaven, and could hear me and see me; but this gave me neither pleasure nor pain, and I seldom thought of it at all. I never thought of nature as God's work, but as a separate fact or existence.

Fourthly: it was entirely unaccompanied by powers of reflection or invention. Every fancy that I had about nature was put into my head by some book; and I never reflected about anything till I grew older; and then, the more I reflected, the less nature was precious to me: I could then make myself happy, by thinking, in the dark, or in the dullest scenery; and the beautiful scenery became less essential to my pleasure.

Fifthly: it was, according to its strength, inconsistent with every evil feeling, with spite, anger, covetousness, discontent, and every other hateful passion; but would associate itself deeply with every just and noble sorrow, joy, or affection. It had not, however, always the power to repress what was inconsistent with it; and, though only after stout contention, might at last be crushed by what it had partly repressed. And as it only acted by setting one impulse against another, though it had much power in moulding the character, it had hardly any in strengthening it; it formed temperament, but never instilled principle; it kept me generally good-humoured and kindly, but could not teach me perseverance or self-denial: what firmness or principle I had was quite

---

[38] Ruskin proposes to discuss in this chapter what are the probable or usual effects of taking pleasure in nature or landscape. Are they good or bad? And he feels that in the case of no one else can he judge these effects so well as in his own, particularly in earliest youth.

[39] I.e., the first event in the history of his pleasure in nature.

[40] For Ruskin's description of his early travels with his parents, see above, p. 561.

[41] All these characters are to be found in *The Monastery.*

independent of it; and it came itself nearly as often in the form of a temptation as of a safeguard, leading me to ramble over hills when I should have been learning lessons, and lose days in reveries which I might have spent in doing kindnesses.

Lastly: although there was no definite religious sentiment mingled with it, there was a continual perception of Sanctity in the whole of nature, from the slightest thing to the vastest;—an instinctive awe, mixed with delight; an indefinable thrill, such as we sometimes imagine to indicate the presence of a disembodied spirit. I could only feel this perfectly when I was alone; and then it would often make me shiver from head to foot with the joy and fear of it, when after being some time away from hills, I first got to the shore of a mountain river, where the brown water circled among the pebbles, or when I saw the first swell of distant land against the sunset, or the first low broken wall, covered with mountain moss. I cannot in the least *describe* the feeling; but I do not think this is my fault, nor that of the English language, for, I am afraid, no feeling *is* describable. If we had to explain even the sense of bodily hunger to a person who had never felt it, we should be hard put to it for words; and this joy in nature seemed to me to come of a sort of heart-hunger, satisfied

with the presence of a Great and Holy Spirit. These feelings remained in their full intensity till I was eighteen or twenty, and then, as the reflective and practical power increased, and the "cares of this world" gained upon me, faded gradually away, in the manner described by Wordsworth in his *Intimations of Immortality.*

I cannot, of course, tell how far I am justified in supposing that these sensations may be reasoned upon as common to children in general. In the same degree they are not of course common, otherwise children would be, most of them, very different from what they are in their choice of pleasures. But, as far as such feelings exist, I apprehend they are more or less similar in their nature and influence; only producing different characters according to the elements with which they are mingled. Thus, a very religious child may give up many pleasures to which its instincts lead it, for the sake of irksome duties; and an inventive child would mingle its love of nature with watchfulness of human sayings and doings: but I believe the feelings I have endeavoured to describe are the pure landscape-instinct; and the likelihoods of good or evil resulting from them may be reasoned upon as generally indicating the usefulness or danger of the modern love and study of landscape. . . .

from THE STONES OF VENICE, VOLUME II

from Chapter 6

THE NATURE OF GOTHIC [1]

. . . I SHALL endeavour . . . to give the reader in this chapter an idea, at once broad and definite, of the true nature of *Gothic* architecture, properly so called. . . .

. . . We shall find that Gothic architecture has external forms and internal elements. Its elements are certain mental tendencies of the builders, legibly expressed in it; as fancifulness, love of variety, love of richness, and such others. Its external forms are pointed arches, vaulted roofs, etc. And unless both the elements and the forms are there, we have no right to call the style Gothic. It is not enough that it has the Form, if it have not also the power and life. It is not enough that it has the Power, if it have not

the form. We must therefore inquire into each of these characters successively; and determine first, what is the Mental Expression, and secondly, what the Material Form of Gothic architecture, properly so called.

Mental Power or Expression. What characters, we have to discover, did the Gothic builders love, or instinctively express in their work, as distinguished from all other builders?

. . . I believe . . . that the characteristic or moral elements of Gothic are the following, placed in the order of their importance:

1. Savageness.
2. Changefulness.
3. Naturalism.
4. Grotesqueness.
5. Rigidity.
6. Redundance.

These characters are here expressed as belonging to the building; as belonging to the builder, they would be expressed thus:—1. Savageness or Rudeness. 2. Love of Change. 3. Love of Nature. 4. Dis-

---

[1] The rough, general definition of Gothic is that style of architecture prevalent in Western Europe from the twelfth to the fifteenth century, of which the chief characteristic is the pointed arch.

turbed Imagination. 5. Obstinacy. 6. Generosity. . . .
I shall proceed to examine them in their order.

1. SAVAGENESS.—I am not sure when the word
"Gothic" was first generically applied to the architecture of the North; but I presume that, whatever
the date of its original usage, it was intended to imply
reproach, and express the barbaric character of the
nations among whom that architecture arose. It
never implied that they were literally of Gothic
lineage, far less that their architecture had been
originally invented by the Goths themselves; but it
did imply that they and their buildings together
exhibited a degree of sternness and rudeness, which,
in contradistinction to the character of Southern and
Eastern nations, appeared like a perpetual reflection
of the contrast between the Goth and the Roman in
their first encounter. And when that fallen Roman,
in the utmost impotence of his luxury, and insolence
of his guilt, became the model for the imitation of
civilized Europe, at the close of the so-called Dark
ages,[2] the word Gothic became a term of unmitigated contempt, not unmixed with aversion. From
that contempt, by the exertion of the antiquaries and
architects of this century, Gothic architecture has
been sufficiently vindicated; and perhaps some among
us, in our admiration of the magnificent science of its
structure, and sacredness of its expression, might
desire that the term of ancient reproach should be
withdrawn, and some other, of more apparent
honourableness, adopted in its place. There is no
chance, as there is no need, of such a substitution. As
far as the epithet was used scornfully, it was used
falsely; but there is no reproach in the word, rightly
understood; on the contrary, there is a profound
truth, which the instinct of mankind almost unconsciously recognizes. It is true, greatly and deeply
true, that the architecture of the North is rude and
wild; but it is not true, that, for this reason, we are
to condemn it, or despise. Far otherwise: I believe it
is in this very character that it deserves our profoundest reverence.

The charts of the world which have been drawn
up by modern science have thrown into a narrow
space the expression of a vast amount of knowledge,
but I have never yet seen any one pictorial enough to
enable the spectator to imagine the kind of contrast
in physical character which exists between Northern
and Southern countries. We know the differences in
detail, but we have not that broad glance and grasp
which would enable us to feel them in their fulness.
We know that gentians grow on the Alps, and olives
on the Apennines; but we do not enough conceive
for ourselves that variegated mosaic of the world's
surface which a bird sees in its migration, that difference between the district of the gentian and of the
olive which the stork and the swallow see far off, as
they lean upon the sirocco[3] wind. Let us, for a
moment, try to raise ourselves even above the level
of their flight, and imagine the Mediterranean lying
beneath us like an irregular lake, and all its ancient
promontories sleeping in the sun: here and there an
angry spot of thunder, a gray stain of storm, moving
upon the burning field; and here and there a fixed
wreath of white volcano smoke, surrounded by its
circle of ashes; but for the most part a great peacefulness of light, Syria and Greece, Italy and Spain, laid
like pieces of a golden pavement into the sea-blue,
chased, as we stoop nearer to them, with bossy
beaten work of mountain chains, and glowing softly
with terraced gardens, and flowers heavy with frankincense, mixed among masses of laurel, and orange,
and plumy palm, that abate with their gray-green
shadows the burning of the marble rocks, and of the
ledges of porphyry sloping under lucent sand. Then
let us pass farther toward the north, until we see the
orient colors change gradually into a vast belt of
rainy green, where the pastures of Switzerland, and
poplar valleys of France, and dark forests of the Danube and Carpathians stretch from the mouths of the
Loire to those of the Volga, seen through clefts in
gray swirls of rain-cloud and flaky veils of the mist
of the brooks, spreading low along the pasture lands:
and then, farther north still, to see the earth heave
into mighty masses of leaden rock and heathy moor,
bordering with a broad waste of gloomy purple that
belt of field and wood, and splintering into irregular
and grisly islands amidst the northern seas, beaten by
storm, and chilled by ice-drift, and tormented by
furious pulses of contending tide, until the roots of the
last forests fail from among the hill ravines, and the
hunger of the north wind bites their peaks into
barrenness; and, at last, the wall of ice, durable like
iron, sets, deathlike, its white teeth against us out of
the polar twilight. And, having once traversed in
thought this gradation of the zoned iris[4] of the earth

[2] Roughly the period from 400 to 1400. The Middle or Dark
Ages came to a close with the beginnings of the Italian Renaissance, at which time the example of all excellence was deemed
to be in Greek and Roman antiquity.

[3] A hot wind blowing northward from Africa across the southern
Mediterranean countries.
[4] Ruskin imagines the different zones on the curving surface of
the earth to appear like the bands of color in a rainbow when
viewed from the great height he has stipulated. Iris, in Greek
myth, was the personification of the rainbow.

in all its material vastness, let us go down nearer to it, and watch the parallel change in the belt of animal life; the multitudes of swift and brilliant creatures that glance in the air and sea, or tread the sands of the southern zone; striped zebras and spotted leopards, glistening serpents, and birds arrayed in purple and scarlet. Let us contrast their delicacy and brilliancy of color, and swiftness of motion, with the frost-cramped strength, and shaggy covering, and dusky plumage of the northern tribes; contrast the Arabian horse with the Shetland, the tiger and leopard with the wolf and bear, the antelope with the elk, the bird of paradise with the osprey; and then, submissively acknowledging the great laws by which the earth and all that it bears are ruled throughout their being, let us not condemn, but rejoice in the expression by man of his own rest in the statutes of the lands that gave him birth.[5] Let us watch him with reverence as he sets side by side the burning gems, and smooths with soft sculpture the jasper pillars, that are to reflect a ceaseless sunshine, and rise into a cloudless sky: but not with less reverence let us stand by him, when, with rough strength and hurried stroke, he smites an uncouth animation out of the rocks which he has torn from among the moss of the moorland, and heaves into the darkened air the pile of iron buttress and rugged wall, instinct with work of an imagination as wild and wayward as the northern sea; creatures of ungainly shape and rigid limb, but full of wolfish life; fierce as the winds that beat, and changeful as the clouds that shade them.

There is, I repeat, no degradation, no reproach in this, but all dignity and honourableness: and we should err grievously in refusing either to recognize as an essential character of the existing architecture of the North, or to admit as a desirable character in that which it yet may be, this wildness of thought, and roughness of work; this look of mountain brotherhood between the cathedral and the Alp; this magnificence of sturdy power, put forth only the more energetically because the fine finger-touch was chilled away by the frosty wind, and the eye dimmed by the moor-mist, or blinded by the hail; this outspeaking of the strong spirit of men who may not gather redundant fruitage from the earth, nor bask in dreamy benignity of sunshine, but must break the rock for bread, and cleave the forest for fire, and show, even in what they did for their delight, some of the hard

---

[5] Let us admire man's acceptance of the geographical conditions under which he must live and the fact that his artistic efforts or expressions are suited to these conditions.

habits of the arm and heart that grew on them as they swung the ax or pressed the plough.

If, however, the savageness of Gothic architecture, merely as an expression of its origin among Northern nations, may be considered, in some sort, a noble character, it possesses a higher nobility still, when considered as an index, not of climate, but of religious principle.

In the 13th and 14th paragraphs of Chapter XXI of the first volume of this work, it was noticed that the systems of architectural ornament, properly so called, might be divided into three:—1. Servile ornament, in which the execution or power of the inferior workman is entirely subjected to the intellect of the higher;—2. Constitutional ornament, in which the executive inferior power is, to a certain point, emancipated and independent, having a will of its own, yet confessing its inferiority and rendering obedience to higher powers;—and 3. Revolutionary ornament, in which no executive inferiority is admitted at all. I must here explain the nature of these divisions at somewhat greater length.

Of Servile ornament, the principal schools are the Greek, Ninevite, and Egyptian; but their servility is of different kinds. The Greek master-workman was far advanced in knowledge and power above the Assyrian or Egyptian. Neither he nor those for whom he worked could endure the appearance of imperfection in anything; and, therefore, what ornament he appointed to be done by those beneath him was composed of mere geometrical forms,—balls, ridges, and perfectly symmetrical foliage,—which could be executed with absolute precision by line and rule, and were as perfect in their way, when completed, as his own figure sculpture. The Assyrian and Egyptian, on the contrary, less cognizant of accurate form in anything, were content to allow their figure sculpture to be executed by inferior workmen, but lowered the method of its treatment to a standard which every workman could reach, and then trained him by discipline so rigid, that there was no chance of his falling beneath the standard appointed. The Greek gave to the lower workman no subject which he could not perfectly execute. The Assyrian gave him subjects which he could only execute imperfectly, but fixed a legal standard for his imperfection. The workman was, in both systems, a slave.

But in the mediaeval, or especially Christian, system of ornament, this slavery is done away with altogether; Christianity having recognized, in small things as well as great, the individual value of every soul. But it not only recognizes its value; it confesses its imperfection, in only bestowing dignity upon the acknowledgment of unworthiness. That admission of lost power and fallen nature, which the Greek or Ninevite felt to be intensely painful, and, as far as might be, altogether refused, the Christian makes daily and hourly, contemplating the fact of it without fear, as tending, in the end, to God's greater glory. Therefore, to every spirit which Christianity summons to her service, her exhortation is: Do what you can, and confess frankly what you are unable to do; neither let your effort be shortened for fear of failure, nor your confession silenced for fear of shame. And it is, perhaps, the principal admirableness of the Gothic schools of architecture, that they thus receive the results of the labor of inferior minds; and out of fragments full of imperfection, and betraying that imperfection in every touch, indulgently raise up a stately and unaccusable whole.

But the modern English mind has this much in common with that of the Greek, that it intensely desires, in all things, the utmost completion or perfection compatible with their nature. This is a noble character in the abstract, but becomes ignoble when it causes us to forget the relative dignities of that nature itself, and to prefer the perfectness of the lower nature to the imperfection of the higher; not considering that as, judged by such a rule, all the brute animals would be preferable to man, because more perfect in their functions and kind, and yet are always held inferior to him, so also in the works of man, those which are more perfect in their kind are always inferior to those which are, in their nature, liable to more faults and shortcomings. For the finer the nature, the more flaws it will show through the clearness of it; and it is a law of this universe, that the best things shall be seldomest seen in their best form. The wild grass grows well and strongly, one year with another; but the wheat is, according to the greater nobleness of its nature, liable to the bitterer blight. And therefore, while in all things that we see or do, we are to desire perfection, and strive for it, we are nevertheless not to set the meaner thing, in its narrow accomplishment, above the nobler thing, in its mighty progress; not to esteem smooth minuteness above shattered majesty; not to prefer mean victory to honorable defeat; not to lower the level of our aim, that we may the more surely enjoy the complacency of success. But, above all, in our dealings with the souls of other men, we are to take care how we check, by severe requirement or narrow caution, efforts which might otherwise lead to a noble issue; and, still more, how we withhold our admiration from great excellencies, because they are mingled with rough faults. Now, in the make and nature of

every man, however rude or simple, whom we employ in manual labor, there are some powers for better things; some tardy imagination, torpid capacity of emotion, tottering steps of thought, there are, even at the worst; and in most cases it is all our own fault that they *are* tardy or torpid. But they cannot be strengthened, unless we are content to take them in their feebleness, and unless we prize and honor them in their imperfection above the best and most perfect manual skill. And this is what we have to do with all our labourers; to look for the *thoughtful* part of them, and get that out of them, whatever we lose for it, whatever faults and errors we are obliged to take with it. For the best that is in them cannot manifest itself, but in company with much error. Understand this clearly: You can teach a man to draw a straight line, and to cut one; to strike a curved line, and to carve it; and to copy and carve any number of given lines or forms, with admirable speed and perfect precision; and you find his work perfect of its kind: but if you ask him to think about any of those forms, to consider if he cannot find any better in his own head, he stops; his execution becomes hesitating; he thinks, and ten to one he thinks wrong; ten to one he makes a mistake in the first touch he gives to his work as a thinking being. But you have made a man of him for all that. He was only a machine before, an animated tool.

And observe, you are put to stern choice in this matter. You must either make a tool of the creature, or a man of him. You cannot make both. Men were not intended to work with the accuracy of tools, to be precise and perfect in all their actions. If you will have that precision out of them, and make their fingers measure degrees like cogwheels, and their arms strike curves like compasses, you must unhumanize them. All the energy of their spirits must be given to make cogs and compasses of themselves. All their attention and strength must go to the accomplishment of the mean act. The eye of the soul must be bent upon the finger-point, and the soul's force must fill all the invisible nerves that guide it, ten hours a day, that it may not err from its steely precision, and so soul and sight be worn away, and the whole human being be lost at last—a heap of sawdust, so far as its intellectual work in this world is concerned: saved only by its Heart, which cannot go into the form of cogs and compasses, but expands, after the ten hours are over, into fireside humanity. On the other hand, if you will make a man of the working creature, you cannot make a tool. Let him but begin to imagine, to think, to try to do anything worth doing; and the engine-turned precision is lost at once. Out come all his roughness, all his dulness, all his incapability; shame upon shame, failure upon failure, pause after pause: but out comes the whole majesty of him also; and we know the height of it only when we see the clouds settling upon him. And, whether the clouds be bright or dark, there will be transfiguration behind and within them.

And now, reader, look round this English room of yours, about which you have been proud so often, because the work of it was so good and strong, and the ornaments of it so finished. Examine again all those accurate mouldings, and perfect polishings, and unerring adjustments of the seasoned wood and tempered steel. Many a time you have exulted over them, and thought how great England was, because her slightest work was done so thoroughly. Alas! if read rightly, these perfectnesses are signs of a slavery in our England a thousand times more bitter and more degrading than that of the scourged African, or helot Greek. Men may be beaten, chained, tormented, yoked like cattle, slaughtered like summer flies, and yet remain in one sense, and the best sense, free. But to smother their souls with them, to blight and hew into rotting pollards the suckling branches of their human intelligence, to make the flesh and skin which, after the worm's work on it, is to see God, into leathern thongs to yoke machinery with,—this it is to be slave-masters indeed; and there might be more freedom in England, though her feudal lords' lightest words were worth men's lives, and though the blood of the vexed husbandman dropped in the furrows of her fields, than there is while the animation of her multitudes is sent like fuel to feed the factory smoke, and the strength of them is given daily to be wasted into the fineness of a web, or racked into the exactness of a line.

And, on the other hand, go forth again to gaze upon the old cathedral front, where you have smiled so often at the fantastic ignorance of the old sculptors: examine once more those ugly goblins, and formless monsters, and stern statues, anatomiless and rigid; but do not mock at them, for they are signs of the life and liberty of every workman who struck the stone; a freedom of thought, and rank in scale of being, such as no laws, no charters, no charities can secure; but which it must be the first aim of all Europe at this day to regain for her children.

Let me not be thought to speak wildly or extravagantly. It is verily this degradation of the operative into a machine, which, more than any other evil of the times, is leading the mass of the nations everywhere into vain, incoherent, destructive struggling for a freedom of which they cannot explain the nature to themselves. Their universal outcry against wealth, and against nobility, is not forced from them either by the pressure of famine, or the sting of mortified pride. These do much, and have done much in all ages; but the foundations of society were never yet shaken as they are at this day. It is not that men are ill fed, but that they have no pleasure in the work by which they make their bread, and therefore look to wealth as the only means of pleasure. It is not that men are pained by the scorn of the upper classes, but they cannot endure their own; for they feel that the kind of labor to which they are condemned is verily a degrading one, and makes them less than men. Never had the upper classes so much sympathy with the lower, or charity for them, as they have at this day, and yet never were they so much hated by them: for, of old, the separation between the noble and the poor was merely a wall built by law; now it is a veritable difference in level of standing, a precipice between upper and lower grounds in the field of humanity, and there is pestilential air at the bottom of it. I know not if a day is ever to come when the nature of right freedom will be understood, and when men will see that to obey another man, to labor for him, yield reverence to him or to his place, is not slavery. It is often the best kind of liberty,— liberty from care. The man who says to one, Go, and he goeth, and to another, Come, and he cometh, has, in most cases, more sense of restraint and difficulty than the man who obeys him. The movements of the one are hindered by the burden on his shoulder; of the other, by the bridle on his lips: there is no way by which the burden may be lightened; but we need not suffer from the bridle if we do not champ at it. To yield reverence to another, to hold ourselves and our lives at his disposal, is not slavery; often it is the noblest state in which a man can live in this world. There is, indeed, a reverence which is servile, that is to say, irrational or selfish: but there is also noble reverence, that is to say, reasonable and loving; and a man is never so noble as when he is reverent in this kind; nay, even if the feeling pass the bounds of mere reason, so that it be loving, a man is raised by it. Which had, in reality, most of the serf nature in him,—the Irish peasant who was lying in wait yesterday for his landlord, with his musket muzzle thrust through the ragged hedge;[6] or that old mountain servant, who 200 years ago, at Inverkeithing, gave up his own life and the lives of his seven

---

[6] At the time Ruskin was writing, agrarian discontent was running high in Ireland and several landlords had been murdered by discontented tenants.

sons for his chief?—as each fell, calling forth his brother to the death, "Another for Hector!"[7] And therefore, in all ages and all countries, reverence has been paid and sacrifice made by men to each other, not only without complaint, but rejoicingly; and famine, and peril, and sword, and all evil, and all shame, have been borne willingly in the causes of masters and kings; for all these gifts of the heart ennobled the men who gave, not less than the men who received them, and nature prompted, and God rewarded the sacrifice. But to feel their souls withering within them, unthanked, to find their whole being sunk into an unrecognized abyss, to be counted off into a heap of mechanism, numbered with its wheels, and weighed with its hammer strokes,—this, nature bade not,—this, God blesses not,—this, humanity for no long time is able to endure.

We have much studied and much perfected, of late, the great civilized invention of the division of labor; only we give it a false name. It is not, truly speaking, the labor that is divided; but the men:— Divided into mere segments of men—broken into small fragments and crumbs of life; so that all the little piece of intelligence that is left in a man is not enough to make a pin, or a nail, but exhausts itself in making the point of a pin or the head of a nail. Now it is a good and desirable thing, truly, to make many pins in a day; but if we could only see with what crystal sand their points were polished,—sand of human soul, much to be magnified before it can be discerned for what it is—we should think there might be some loss in it also. And the great cry that rises from all our manufacturing cities, louder than their furnace blast, is all in very deed for this,—that we manufacture everything there except men; we blanch cotton, and strengthen steel, and refine sugar, and shape pottery; but to brighten, to strengthen, to refine, or to form a single living spirit, never enters into our estimate of advantages. And all the evil to which that cry is urging our myriads can be met only in one way: not by teaching nor preaching, for to teach them is but to show them their misery, and to preach to them, if we do nothing more than preach, is to mock at it. It can be met only by a right understanding, on the part of all classes, of what kinds of labour are good for men, raising them, and making them happy; by a determined sacrifice of such convenience, or beauty, or cheapness as is to be got only by the degradation of the workman; and by

equally determined demand for the products and results of healthy and ennobling labor.

And how, it will be asked, are these products to be recognized, and this demand to be regulated? Easily: by the observance of three broad and simple rules:

1. Never encourage the manufacture of any article not absolutely necessary, in the production of which *Invention* has no share.

2. Never demand an exact finish for its own sake, but only for some practical or noble end.

3. Never encourage imitation or copying of any kind, except for the sake of preserving record of great works.

The second of these principles is the only one which directly rises out of the consideration of our immediate subject; but I shall briefly explain the meaning and extent of the first also, reserving the enforcement of the third for another place.

1. Never encourage the manufacture of anything not necessary, in the production of which invention has no share.

For instance. Glass beads are utterly unnecessary, and there is no design or thought employed in their manufacture. They are formed by first drawing out the glass into rods; these rods are chopped up into fragments of the size of beads by the human hand, and the fragments are then rounded in the furnace. The men who chop up the rods sit at their work all day, their hands vibrating with a perpetual and exquisitely timed palsy, and the beads dropping beneath their vibration like hail. Neither they, nor the men who draw out the rods or fuse the fragments, have the smallest occasion for the use of any single human faculty; and every young lady, therefore, who buys glass beads is engaged in the slave-trade, and in a much more cruel one than that which we have so long been endeavouring to put down.[8]

But glass cups and vessels may become the subjects of exquisite invention; and if in buying these we pay for the invention, that is to say, for the beautiful form, or color, or engraving, and not for mere finish of execution, we are doing good to humanity.

So, again, the cutting of precious stones, in all ordinary cases, requires little exertion of any mental faculty; some tact and judgment in avoiding flaws, and so on, but nothing to bring out the whole mind. Every person who wears cut jewels merely for the sake of their value is, therefore, a slave-driver.

---

7 The incident is recounted in the preface to Scott's *The Fair Maid of Perth*, according to Ruskin.

8 Slavery had been abolished in British colonies in 1833; the effort at the time Ruskin was writing was to suppress it throughout the world, particularly in America.

But the working of the goldsmith, and the various designing of grouped jewellery and enamel-work, may become the subject of the most noble human intelligence. Therefore, money spent in the purchase of well-designed plate, of precious engraved vases, cameos, or enamels, does good to humanity; and, in work of this kind, jewels may be employed to heighten its splendor; and their cutting is then a price paid for the attainment of a noble end, and thus perfectly allowable.

I shall perhaps press this law farther elsewhere, but our immediate concern is chiefly with the second, namely, never to demand an exact finish, when it does not lead to a noble end. For observe, I have only dwelt upon the rudeness of Gothic, or any other kind of imperfectness, as admirable, where it was impossible to get design or thought without it. If you are to have the thought of a rough and untaught man, you must have it in a rough and untaught way; but from an educated man, who can without effort express his thoughts in an educated way, take the graceful expression, and be thankful. Only get the thought, and do not silence the peasant because he cannot speak good grammar, or until you have taught him his grammar. Grammar and refinement are good things, both, only be sure of the better thing first. And thus in art, delicate finish is desirable from the greatest masters, and is always given by them. In some places Michael Angelo, Leonardo, Phidias, Perugino, Turner, all finished with the most exquisite care; and the finish they give always leads to the fuller accomplishment of their noble purposes. But lower men than these cannot finish, for it requires consummate knowledge to finish consummately, and then we must take their thoughts as they are able to give them. So the rule is simple: Always look for invention first, and after that, for such execution as will help the invention, and as the inventor is capable of without painful effort, and no more. Above all, demand no refinement of execution where there is no thought, for that is slaves' work, unredeemed. Rather choose rough work than smooth work, so only that the practical purpose be answered, and never imagine there is reason to be proud of anything that may be accomplished by patience and sand-paper.

I shall only give one example, which however will show the reader what I mean, from the manufacture already alluded to, that of glass. Our modern glass is exquisitely clear in its substance, true in its form, accurate in its cutting. We are proud of this. We ought to be ashamed of it. The old Venice glass was muddy, inaccurate in all its forms, and clumsily cut, if at all. And the old Venetian was justly proud of it. For there is this difference between the English and Venetian workman, that the former thinks only of accurately matching his patterns, and getting his curves perfectly true and his edges perfectly sharp, and becomes a mere machine for rounding curves and sharpening edges; while the old Venetian cared not a whit whether his edges were sharp or not, but he invented a new design for every glass that he made, and never moulded a handle or a lip without a new fancy in it. And therefore, though some Venetian glass is ugly and clumsy enough when made by clumsy and uninventive workmen, other Venetian glass is so lovely in its forms that no price is too great for it; and we never see the same form in it twice. Now you cannot have the finish and the varied form too. If the workman is thinking about his edges, he cannot be thinking of his design; if of his design, he cannot think of his edges. Choose whether you will pay for the lovely form or the perfect finish, and choose at the same moment whether you will make the worker a man or a grindstone.

Nay, but the reader interrupts me,—"If the workman can design beautifully, I would not have him kept at the furnace. Let him be taken away and made a gentleman, and have a studio, and design his glass there, and I will have it blown and cut for him by common workmen, and so I will have my design and my finish too."

All ideas of this kind are founded upon two mistaken suppositions: the first, that one man's thoughts can be, or ought to be, executed by another man's hands; the second, that manual labour is a degradation, when it is governed by intellect.

On a large scale, and in work determinable by line and rule, it is indeed both possible and necessary that the thoughts of one man should be carried out by the labour of others; in this sense I have already defined the best architecture to be the expression of the mind of manhood by the hands of childhood. But on a smaller scale, and in a design which cannot be mathematically defined, one man's thoughts can never be expressed by another: and the difference between the spirit of touch of the man who is inventing, and of the man who is obeying directions, is often all the difference between a great and a common work of art. How wide the separation is between original and second-hand execution, I shall endeavour to show elsewhere; it is not so much to our purpose here as to mark the other and more fatal error of despising manual labor when governed by intellect; for it is no less fatal an error to despise it when thus regulated by intellect, than to value it for its own sake. We are always in these days endeavouring to separate the two; we want one man to be always thinking, and another to be always working, and we call one a gentleman, and the other an operative; whereas the workman ought often to be thinking, and the thinker often to be working, and both should be gentlemen, in the best sense. As it is, we make both ungentle, the one envying, the other despising, his brother; and the mass of society is made up of morbid thinkers, and miserable workers. Now it is only by labour that thought can be made healthy, and only by thought that labour can be made happy, and the two cannot be separated with impunity. It would be well if all of us were good handicraftsmen in some kind, and the dishonor of manual labour done away with altogether; so that though there should still be a trenchant distinction of race between nobles and commoners, there should not, among the latter, be a trenchant distinction of employment, as between idle and working men, or between men of liberal and illiberal professions. All professions should be liberal, and there should be less pride felt in peculiarity of employment, and more in excellence of achievement. And yet more, in each several profession, no master should be too proud to do its hardest work. The painter should grind his own colors; the architect work in the mason's yard with his men; the master-manufacturer be himself a more skilful operative than any man in his mills; and the distinction between one man and another be only in experience and skill, and the authority and wealth which these must naturally and justly obtain.

I should be led far from the matter in hand, if I were to pursue this interesting subject. Enough, I trust, has been said to show the reader that the rudeness or imperfection which at first rendered the term "Gothic" one of reproach is indeed, when rightly understood, one of the most noble characters of Christian architecture, and not only a noble but an *essential* one. It seems a fantastic paradox, but it is nevertheless a most important truth, that no architecture can be truly noble which is *not* imperfect. And this is easily demonstrable. For since the architect, whom we will suppose capable of doing all in perfection, cannot execute the whole with his own hands, he must either make slaves of his workmen in the old Greek, and present English fashion, and level his work to a slave's capacities, which is to degrade it; or else he must take his workmen as he finds them, and let them show their weaknesses together with their strength, which will involve the Gothic imperfection, but render the whole work as noble as the intellect of the age can make it.

But the principle may be stated more broadly still. I have confined the illustration of it to architecture, but I must not leave it as if true of architecture only. Hitherto I have used the words imperfect and perfect merely to distinguish between work grossly unskilful, and work executed with average precision and science; and I have been pleading that any degree of unskilfulness should be admitted, so only that the labourer's mind had room for expression. But, accurately speaking, no good work whatever can be perfect, and *the demand for perfection is always a sign of a misunderstanding of the ends of art.*

This for two reasons, both based on everlasting laws. The first, that no great man ever stops working till he has reached his point of failure: that is to say, his mind is always far in advance of his powers of execution, and the latter will now and then give way in trying to follow it; besides that he will always give to the inferior portions of his work only such inferior attention as they require; and according to his greatness he becomes so accustomed to the feeling of dissatisfaction with the best he can do, that in moments of lassitude or anger with himself he will not care though the beholder be dissatisfied also. I believe there has only been one man who would not acknowledge this necessity, and strove always to reach perfection, Leonardo; the end of his vain effort being merely that he would take ten years to a picture and leave it unfinished. And therefore, if we are to have great men working at all, or less men doing their best, the work will be imperfect, however beautiful. Of human work none but what is bad can be perfect, in its own bad way.[9]

The second reason is, that imperfection is in some sort essential to all that we know of life. It is the sign of life in a mortal body, that is to say, of a state of progress and change. Nothing that lives is, or can be, rigidly perfect; part of it is decaying, part nascent. The foxglove blossom,—a third part bud, a third part past, a third part in full bloom,—is a type of the life of this world. And in all things that live there are certain irregularities and deficiencies which are not only signs of life, but sources of beauty. No human face is exactly the same in its lines on each side, no leaf perfect in its lobes, no branch in its symmetry. All admit irregularity as they imply change; and to banish imperfection is to destroy expression, to check

---

9 "The Elgin marbles are supposed by many persons to be 'perfect.' In the most important portions they indeed approach perfection, but only there. The draperies are unfinished, the hair and wool of the animals are unfinished, and the entire bas-reliefs of the frieze are roughly cut." (Ruskin)

exertion, to paralyze vitality. All things are literally better, lovelier, and more beloved for the imperfections which have been divinely appointed, that the law of human life may be Effort, and the law of human judgment, Mercy.

Accept this then for a universal law, that neither architecture nor any other noble work of man can be good unless it be imperfect; and let us be prepared for the otherwise strange fact, which we shall discern clearly as we approach the period of the Renais-[10]sance, that the first cause of the fall of the arts of Europe was a relentless requirement of perfection, incapable alike either of being silenced by veneration for greatness, or softened into forgiveness of simplicity.[5]

Thus far then of the Rudeness or Savageness, which is the first mental element of Gothic architecture. It is an element in many other healthy architectures also, as in Byzantine and Romanesque;[10] but true Gothic cannot exist without it. . . .[10]

from THE CROWN OF WILD OLIVE[1]

Lecture II

TRAFFIC[2]

MY good Yorkshire friends, you asked me down here among your hills that I might talk to you about this Exchange you are going to build; but, earnestly and seriously asking you to pardon me, I am going to do nothing of the kind. I cannot talk, or at least can say very little, about this same Exchange. I must talk of[10] quite other things, though not willingly;—I could not deserve your pardon, if, when you invited me to speak on one subject, I *wilfully* spoke on another. But I cannot speak, to purpose, of anything about which I do not care; and most simply and sorrowfully I[15] have to tell you, in the outset, that I do *not* care about this Exchange of yours.

If, however, when you sent me your invitation, I had answered, "I won't come, I don't care about the Exchange of Bradford," you would have been justly[20] offended with me, not knowing the reason of so blunt a carelessness. So I have come down, hoping that you will patiently let me tell you why, on this, and many other such occasions, I now remain silent, when formerly I should have caught at the oppor-[25]tunity of speaking to a gracious audience.

In a word, then, I do not care about this Exchange —because *you* don't; and because you know perfectly well I cannot make you. Look at the essential conditions of the case, which you, as business men, know[30] perfectly well, though perhaps you think I forget them. You are going to spend £30,000, which to you, collectively, is nothing; the buying a new coat is, as to the cost of it, a much more important matter of consideration to me, than building a new Exchange is to you. But you think you may as well have the[5] right thing for your money. You know there are a great many odd styles of architecture about; you don't want to do anything ridiculous; you hear of me, among others, as a respectable architectural man-milliner; and you send for me, that I may tell you[10] the leading fashion; and what is, in our shops, for the moment, the newest and sweetest thing in pinnacles.

Now, pardon me for telling you frankly, you cannot have good architecture merely by asking people's advice on occasion. All good architecture is the ex-[15]pression of national life and character, and it is produced by a prevalent and eager national taste, or desire for beauty. And I want you to think a little of the deep significance of this word "taste"; for no statement of mine has been more earnestly or oftener[20] controverted than that good taste is essentially a moral quality. "No," say many of my antagonists, "taste is one thing, morality is another. Tell us what is pretty: we shall be glad to know that; but we need no sermons—even were you able to preach them,[25] which may be doubted."

Permit me, therefore, to fortify this old dogma of mine somewhat. Taste is not only a part and an index of morality;—it is the ONLY morality. The first, and last, and closest trial question to any living creature[30] is, "What do you like?" Tell me what you like, and I'll tell you what you are. Go out into the street, and ask the first man or woman you meet, what their

---

[1] The victor at the ancient Olympic Games was rewarded simply with a wreath made of the leaves of the wild olive. Ruskin's title is intended to suggest that honor alone, rather than riches, should be our goal.

[2] Delivered at the Town Hall, Bradford, April 21, 1864. *Traffic* means trade.

[10] The former flourished in the Byzantine Empire in the fifth and sixth centuries, the latter in the countries of southern Europe that had come under Roman domination, roughly from the fifth to the twelfth century.

"taste" is; and if they answer candidly, you know them, body and soul. "You, my friend in the rags, with the unsteady gait, what do *you* like?" "A pipe and a quartern of gin." I know you. "You, good woman, with the quick step and tidy bonnet, what do you like?" "A swept hearth, and a clean tea-table; and my husband opposite me, and a baby at my breast." Good, I know you also. "You, little girl with the golden hair and the soft eyes, what do you like?" "My canary, and a run among the wood hyacinths." "You, little boy with the dirty hands, and the low forehead, what do you like?" "A shy at the sparrows, and a game at pitch farthing." Good; we know them all now. What more need we ask?

"Nay," perhaps you answer; "we need rather to ask what these people and children do, than what they like. If they *do* right, it is no matter that they like what is wrong; and if they *do* wrong, it is no matter that they like what is right. Doing is the great thing; and it does not matter that the man likes drinking, so that he does not drink; nor that the little girl likes to be kind to her canary, if she will not learn her lessons; nor that the little boy likes throwing stones at the sparrows, if he goes to the Sunday school." Indeed, for a short time, and in a provisional sense, this is true. For if, resolutely, people do what is right, in time to come they like doing it. But they only are in a right moral state when they *have* come to like doing it; and as long as they don't like it, they are still in a vicious state. The man is not in health of body who is always thinking of the bottle in the cupboard, though he bravely bears his thirst; but the man who heartily enjoys water in the morning, and wine in the evening, each in its proper quantity and time. And the entire object of true education is to make people not merely *do* the right things, but *enjoy* the right things:—not merely industrious, but to love industry—not merely learned, but to love knowledge—not merely pure, but to love purity—not merely just, but to hunger and thirst after justice.

But you may answer or think, "Is the liking for outside ornaments,—for pictures, or statues, or furniture, or architecture, a moral quality?" Yes, most surely, if a rightly set liking. Taste for *any* pictures or statues is not a moral quality, but taste for good ones is. Only here again we have to define the word "good." I don't mean by "good," clever—or learned—or difficult in the doing. Take a picture by Teniers, of sots quarrelling over their dice;[3] it is an entirely clever picture; so clever that nothing in its kind has ever been done equal to it; but it is also an entirely base and evil picture. It is an expression of delight in the prolonged contemplation of a vile thing, and delight in that is an "unmannered," or "immoral" quality. It is "bad taste" in the profoundest sense—it is the taste of the devils. On the other hand, a picture of Titian's, or a Greek statue, or a Greek coin, or a Turner landscape, expresses delight in the perpetual contemplation of a good and perfect thing. That is an entirely moral quality—it is the taste of the angels. And all delight in fine art, and all love of it, resolve themselves into simple love of that which deserves love. That deserving is the quality which we call "loveliness"—(we ought to have an opposite word, hateliness, to be said of the things which deserve to be hated); and it is not an indifferent nor optional thing whether we love this or that; but it is just the vital function of all our being. What we *like* determines what we *are*, and is the sign of what we are; and to teach taste is inevitably to form character.

As I was thinking over this, in walking up Fleet Street the other day, my eye caught the title of a book standing open in a bookseller's window. It was—"On the necessity of the diffusion of taste among all classes." "Ah," I thought to myself, "my classifying friend, when you have diffused your taste, where will your classes be? The man who likes what you like, belongs to the same class with you, I think. Inevitably so. You may put him to other work if you choose; but, by the condition you have brought him into, he will dislike the work as much as you would yourself. You get hold of a scavenger or a costermonger, who enjoyed the Newgate Calendar[4] for literature, and 'Pop goes the Weasel' for music. You think you can make him like Dante and Beethoven? I wish you joy of your lessons; but if you do, you have made a gentleman of him:—he won't like to go back to his costermongering."

And so completely and unexceptionally is this so, that, if I had time tonight, I could show you that a nation cannot be affected by any vice, or weakness, without expressing it, legibly, and for ever, either in bad art, or by want of art; and that there is no national virtue, small or great, which is not manifestly expressed in all the art which circumstances enable the people possessing that virtue to produce. Take, for instance, your great English virtue of enduring and patient courage. You have at present in England only

---

[3] Probably the picture "Flemish Tap-Room" by the younger Teniers (1610–90).

[4] An account of the crimes committed by the inmates of Newgate Prison which used to be published at regular intervals.

one art of any consequence—that is, iron-working. You know thoroughly well how to cast and hammer iron. Now, do you think, in those masses of lava which you build volcanic cones to melt, and which you forge at the mouths of the Infernos you have created; do you think on those iron plates, your courage and endurance are not written for ever,—not merely with an iron pen, but on iron parchment? And take also your great English vice—European vice—vice of all the world—vice of all other worlds that roll or shine in heaven, bearing with them yet the atmosphere of hell—the vice of jealousy, which brings competition into your commerce, treachery into your councils, and dishonour into your wars— that vice which has rendered for you, and for your next neighbouring nation, the daily occupations of existence no longer possible, but with the mail upon your breasts and the sword loose in its sheath;[5] so that at last, you have realised for all the multitudes of the two great peoples who lead the so-called civilisation of the earth,—you have realised for them all, I say. in person and in policy, what was once true only of the rough Border riders of your Cheviot hills—

> They carved at the meal
> With gloves of steel,
> And they drank the red wine through the
> helmet barr'd;[6]—

do you think that this national shame and dastardliness of heart are not written as legibly on every rivet of your iron armour as the strength of the right hands that forged it?

Friends, I know not whether this thing be the more ludicrous or the more melancholy. It is quite unspeakably both. Suppose, instead of being now sent for by you, I had been sent for by some private gentleman, living in a suburban house, with his garden separated only by a fruit wall from his next door neighbour's; and he had called me to consult with him on the furnishing of his drawing-room. I begin looking about me, and find the walls rather bare; I think such and such a paper might be desirable —perhaps a little fresco here and there on the ceiling —a damask curtain or so at the windows. "Ah," says my employer, "damask curtains, indeed! That's all very fine, but you know I can't afford that kind of thing just now!" "Yet the world credits you with a splendid income!" "Ah, yes," says my friend, "but do you know, at present I am obliged to spend it nearly all in steel-traps?" "Steel-traps! for whom?" "Why, for that fellow on the other side the wall, you know; we're very good friends, capital friends; but we are obliged to keep our traps set on both sides of the wall; we could not possibly keep on friendly terms without them, and our spring guns. The worst of it is, we are both clever fellows enough; and there's never a day passes that we don't find out a new trap, or a new gun-barrel, or something; we spend about fifteen millions a year each in our traps, take it altogether; and I don't see how we're to do with less." A highly comic state of life for two private gentlemen! but for two nations, it seems to me, not wholly comic. Bedlam would be comic, perhaps, if there were only one madman in it; and your Christmas pantomime is comic, when there is only one clown in it; but when the whole world turns clown, and paints itself red with its own heart's blood instead of vermilion, it is something else than comic, I think.

Mind, I know a great deal of this is play, and willingly allow for that. You don't know what to do with yourselves for a sensation: fox-hunting and cricketing will not carry you through the whole of this unendurably long mortal life: you liked popguns when you were schoolboys, and rifles and Armstrongs are only the same things better made: but then the worst of it is, that what was play to you when boys, was not play to the sparrows; and what is play to you now, is not play to the small birds of State neither; and for the black eagles, you are somewhat shy of taking shots at them, if I mistake not.[7]

I must get back to the matter in hand, however. Believe me, without farther instance, I could show you, in all time, that every nation's vice, or virtue, was written in its art: the soldiership of early Greece; the sensuality of late Italy; the visionary religion of Tuscany; the splendid human energy of Venice. I have no time to do this tonight (I have done it elsewhere before now); but I proceed to apply the principle to ourselves in a more searching manner.

I notice that among all the new buildings which cover your once wild hills, churches and schools are mixed in due, that is to say, in large proportion, with

---

[5] Ruskin is here inveighing against the foreign policy of England, particularly during the second term of Palmerston as Prime Minister, and deploring the mutually suspicious attitudes of France and England. The English were frightened at the renewed threat of invasion by France under Louis Napoleon.

[6] Scott's *Lay of the Last Minstrel*, Canto I, stanza 4.

[7] The small birds of state were Poland and Denmark; the former made a bid for freedom from Russia which Palmerston's cabinet would not support, and the latter was attacked by Prussia and Austria, again without intervention from England. The black eagle was the Austrian insignia, and the Order of the Black Eagle was a Prussian military decoration.

your mills and mansions; and I notice also that the churches and schools are almost always Gothic, and the mansions and mills are never Gothic. May I ask the meaning of this? for, remember, it is peculiarly a modern phenomenon. When Gothic was invented, houses were Gothic as well as churches; and when the Italian style superseded the Gothic, churches were Italian as well as houses. If there is a Gothic spire to the Cathedral of Antwerp, there is a Gothic belfry to the Hôtel de Ville at Brussels; if Inigo Jones builds an Italian Whitehall, Sir Christopher Wren[8] builds an Italian St. Paul's. But now you live under one school of architecture, and worship under another. What do you mean by doing this? Am I to understand that you are thinking of changing your architecture back to Gothic; and that you treat your churches experimentally, because it does not matter what mistakes you make in a church? Or am I to understand that you consider Gothic a pre-eminently sacred and beautiful mode of building, which you think, like the fine frankincense, should be mixed for the tabernacle only, and reserved for your religious services? For if this be the feeling, though it may seem at first as if it were graceful and reverent, at the root of the matter, it signifies neither more nor less than that you have separated your religion from your life.

For consider what a wide significance this fact has: and remember that it is not you only, but all the people of England, who are behaving thus, just now.

You have all got into the habit of calling the church "the house of God." I have seen, over the doors of many churches, the legend actually carved, "*This is the house of God and this is the gate of heaven.*" Now, note where that legend comes from, and of what place it was first spoken.[9] A boy leaves his father's house to go on a long journey on foot, to visit his uncle: he has to cross a wild hill-desert; just as if one of your own boys had to cross the wolds to visit an uncle at Carlisle. The second or third day your boy finds himself somewhere between Hawes and Brough, in the midst of the moors, at sunset. It is stony ground, and boggy; he cannot go one foot farther that night. Down he lies, to sleep, on Wharnside, where best he may, gathering a few of the stones together to put under his head;—so wild the place is, he cannot get anything but stones. And there, lying under the broad night, he has a dream; and he sees

a ladder set up on the earth, and the top of it reaches to heaven, and the angels of God are seen ascending and descending upon it. And when he wakes out of his sleep, he says, "How dreadful is this place; surely this is none other than the house of God, and this is the gate of heaven." This PLACE, observe; not this church; not this city; not this stone, even, which he puts up for a memorial—the piece of flint on which his head was lain. But this *place;* this windy slope of Wharnside; this moorland hollow, torrent-bitten, snow-blighted; this *any* place where God lets down the ladder. And how are you to know where that will be? or how are you to determine where it may be, but by being ready for it always? Do you know where the lightning is to fall next? You *do* know that, partly; you can guide the lightning; but you cannot guide the going forth of the Spirit, which is as that lightning when it shines from the east to the west.

But the perpetual and insolent warping of that strong verse to serve a merely ecclesiastical purpose,[10] is only one of the thousand instances in which we sink back into gross Judaism. We call our churches "temples." Now, you know perfectly well they are *not* temples. They have never had, never can have, anything whatever to do with temples. They are "synagogues"—"gathering places"—where you gather yourselves together as an assembly; and by not calling them so, you again miss the force of another mighty text—"Thou, when thou prayest, shalt not be as the hypocrites are; for they love to pray standing in the *churches*" [we should translate it], "that they may be seen of men. But thou, when thou prayest, enter into thy closet, and when thou hast shut thy door, pray to thy Father,"—which is, not in chancel nor in aisle, but "in secret."[11]

Now, you feel, as I say this to you—I know you feel—as if I were trying to take away the honour of your churches. Not so; I am trying to prove to you the honour of your houses and your hills; not that the Church is not sacred—but that the whole Earth is. I would have you feel what careless, what constant, what infectious sin there is in all modes of thought, whereby, in calling your churches only "holy," you call your hearths and homes "profane"; and have separated yourselves from the heathen by casting all

---

8 Two seventeenth-century English architects, exponents of the classic style. The former designed the banqueting hall for the news palace of Whitehall.

9 See Genesis 28 for the story of Jacob's journey and his dream of the ladder let down from heaven.

10 As a Protestant and an Evangelical, Ruskin attacks in these two paragraphs the stress laid by Roman and Anglo Catholics upon church and temple as the house of God and gate to heaven. To him worship and salvation were respectively the function and the reward of the heart alone, independent of any ecclesiastical building or priesthood. It was precisely this emphasis upon the external forms of worship that led Thomas Arnold, as well as Ruskin, to say that the spirit behind the Oxford Movement was Judaism. 11 Cf. Matthew 6:5, 6.

your household gods to the ground, instead of recognising, in the places of their many and feeble Lares,[12] the presence of your One and Mighty Lord and Lar.

"But what has all this to do with our Exchange?" you ask me, impatiently. My dear friends, it has just everything to do with it; on these inner and great questions depend all the outer and little ones; and if you have asked me down here to speak to you, because you had before been interested in anything I have written, you must know that all I have yet said about architecture was to show this. The book I called *The Seven Lamps* was to show that certain right states of temper and moral feeling were the magic powers by which all good architecture, without exception, had been produced. *The Stones of Venice* had, from beginning to end, no other aim than to show that the Gothic architecture of Venice had risen out of, and indicated in all its features, a state of pure national faith, and of domestic virtue; and that its Renaissance architecture had arisen out of, and in all its features indicated, a state of concealed national infidelity, and of domestic corruption. And now, you ask me what style is best to build in, and how can I answer, knowing the meaning of the two styles, but by another question—do you mean to build as Christians or as Infidels? And still more—do you mean to build as honest Christians or as honest Infidels? as thoroughly and confessedly either one or the other? You don't like to be asked such rude questions. I cannot help it; they are of much more importance than this Exchange business; and if they can be at once answered, the Exchange business settles itself in a moment. But before I press them farther, I must ask leave to explain one point clearly.

In all my past work, my endeavour has been to show that good architecture is essentially religious—the production of a faithful and virtuous, not of an infidel and corrupted people. But in the course of doing this, I have had also to show that good architecture is not *ecclesiastical*. People are so apt to look upon religion as the business of the clergy, not their own, that the moment they hear of anything depending on "religion," they think it must also have depended on the priesthood; and I have had to take what place was to be occupied between these two errors, and fight both, often with seeming contradiction. Good architecture is the work of good and believing men; therefore, you say, at least some people say, "Good architecture must essentially have been the work of the clergy, not of the laity." No

—a thousand times no; good architecture[13] has always been the work of the commonalty, *not* of the clergy. "What," you say, "those glorious cathedrals —the pride of Europe—did their builders not form Gothic architecture?" No; they corrupted Gothic architecture. Gothic was formed in the baron's castle, and the burgher's street. It was formed by the thoughts, and hands, and powers of labouring citizens and warrior kings. By the monk it was used as an instrument for the aid of his superstition; when that superstition became a beautiful madness, and the best hearts of Europe vainly dreamed and pined in the cloister, and vainly raged and perished in the crusade,—through that fury of perverted faith and wasted war, the Gothic rose also to its loveliest, most fantastic, and, finally, most foolish dreams; and in those dreams was lost.

I hope, now, that there is no risk of your misunderstanding me when I come to the gist of what I want to say tonight;—when I repeat, that every great national architecture has been the result and exponent of a great national religion. You can't have bits of it here, bits there—you must have it everywhere or nowhere. It is not the monopoly of a clerical company—it is not the exponent of a theological dogma —it is not the hieroglyphic writing of an initiated priesthood; it is the manly language of a people inspired by resolute and common purpose, and rendering resolute and common fidelity to the legible laws of an undoubted God.

Now there have as yet been three distinct schools of European architecture. I say, European, because Asiatic and African architectures belong so entirely to other races and climates, that there is no question of them here; only, in passing, I will simply assure you that whatever is good or great in Egypt, and Syria, and India, is just as good or great for the same reasons as the buildings on our side of the Bosphorus. We Europeans, then, have had three great religions: the Greek, which was the worship of the God of Wisdom and Power; the Mediaeval, which was the worship of the God of Judgment and Consolation; the Renaissance, which was the worship of the God of Pride and Beauty; these three we have had—they are past,—and now, at last, we English have got a fourth religion, and a God of our own, about which I want to ask you. But I must explain these three old ones first.

I repeat, first, the Greeks essentially worshipped the God of Wisdom; so that whatever contended against

---

12 The Roman divinities of the household.

13 "And all other arts, for the most part; even of incredulous and secularly-minded commonalties." (Ruskin, 1873)

their religion,—to the Jews a stumbling-block,—was, to the Greeks—*Foolishness*.[14]

The first Greek idea of deity was that expressed in the word, of which we keep the remnant in our words "*Di*-urnal" and "*Di*-vine"—the god of *Day*, Jupiter the revealer. Athena is his daughter, but especially daughter of the Intellect, springing armed from the head. We are only with the help of recent investigation beginning to penetrate the depth of meaning couched under the Athenaic symbols: but I may note rapidly, that her aegis, the mantle with the serpent fringes, in which she often, in the best statues, is represented as folding up her left hand, for better guard; and the Gorgon,[15] on her shield, are both representative mainly of the chilling horror and sadness (turning men to stone, as it were) of the outmost and superficial spheres of knowledge—that knowledge which separates, in bitterness, hardness, and sorrow, the heart of the full-grown man from the heart of the child. For out of imperfect knowledge spring terror, dissension, danger, and disdain; but from perfect knowledge, given by the full-revealed Athena, strength and peace, in sign of which she is crowned with the olive spray, and bears the resistless spear.

This, then, was the Greek conception of purest Deity; and every habit of life, and every form of his art developed themselves from the seeking this bright, serene, resistless wisdom; and setting himself, as a man, to do things evermore rightly and strongly;[16] not with any ardent affection or ultimate hope; but with a resolute and continent energy of will, as knowing that for failure there was no consolation, and for sin there was no remission. And the Greek architecture rose unerring, bright, clearly defined, and self-contained.

Next followed in Europe the great Christian faith, which was essentially the religion of Comfort. Its great doctrine is the remission of sins; for which cause, it happens, too often, in certain phases of Christianity, that sin and sickness themselves are partly glorified, as if, the more you had to be healed of, the more divine was the healing. The practical result of this doctrine, in art, is a continual contemplation of sin and disease, and of imaginary states of purification from them; thus we have an architecture conceived in a mingled sentiment of melancholy and aspiration, partly severe, partly luxuriant, which will bend itself to every one of our needs, and every one of our fancies, and be strong or weak with us, as we are strong or weak ourselves. It is, of all architecture, the basest, when base people build it—of all, the noblest, when built by the noble.

And now note that both these religions—Greek and Mediaeval—perished by falsehood in their own main purpose. The Greek religion of Wisdom perished in a false philosophy—"Oppositions of science, falsely so called."[17] The Mediaeval religion of Consolation perished in false comfort; in remission of sins given lyingly. It was the selling of absolution that ended the Mediaeval faith;[18] and I can tell you more, it is the selling of absolution which, to the end of time, will mark false Christianity. Pure Christianity gives her remission of sins only by *ending* them; but false Christianity gets her remission of sins by *compounding for* them. And there are many ways of compounding for them. We English have beautiful little quiet ways of buying absolution, whether in low Church or high, far more cunning than any of Tetzel's trading.[19]

Then, thirdly, there followed the religion of Pleasure, in which all Europe gave itself to luxury, ending in death. First, *bals masqués* in every saloon,[20] and then guillotines in every square. And all these three worships issue in vast temple building. Your Greek worshipped Wisdom, and built you the Parthenon[21]—the Virgin's temple. The Mediaeval

---

[14] The reference is to 1 Corinthians 1:23: "But we preach Christ crucified, unto the Jews a stumblingblock, and unto the Greeks foolishness."

[15] In Greek mythology Athena lent her shield to Perseus for the slaying of the Gorgon Medusa, one glance at whose face would have turned him into stone. In gratitude he placed the Gorgon's head, with its fatal power still inherent, upon the shield before returning it to the goddess.

[16] "It is an error to suppose that the Greek worship, or seeking, was chiefly of Beauty. It was essentially of rightness and strength, founded on Forethought; the principal character of Greek art is not beauty, but design: and the Dorian Apollo-worship and Athenian Virgin-worship are both expressions of adoration of divine wisdom and purity. Next to these great deities, rank, in power over the national mind, Dionysus and Ceres, the givers of human strength and life; then, for heroic example, Hercules. There is no Venus-worship among the Greeks in the great times: and the Muses are essentially teachers of Truth, and of its harmonies." (Ruskin)

[17] This is probably a reference to the destructive effect of the questionings of the Sophists, who undermined faith in the early Olympian deities and the moral and intellectual ideals associated with them. It was a later manifestation of the same skeptical tendency that Paul warned Timothy against: "O Timothy, keep that which is committed to thy trust, avoiding profane and vain babblings, and oppositions of science falsely so called" (1 Timothy 6:20).

[18] It was one of the abuses attacked by Luther in his demands for a reformation within the Catholic church, demands which produced in the end the establishment of the various Reformed or Protestant churches of central and northwestern Europe.

[19] Tetzel was the papal agent by whose sale of indulgences or absolution Luther's remonstrances were specifically evoked.

[20] Masked balls in every drawing room.

[21] Temple of Athena built on an eminence overlooking Athens, the Acropolis.

worshipped Consolation, and built you Virgin temples also—but to our Lady of Salvation. Then the Revivalist[22] worshipped beauty, of a sort, and built you Versailles and the Vatican.[23] Now, lastly, will you tell me what *we* worship, and what *we* build?

You know we are speaking always of the real, active, continual, national worship; that by which men act, while they live; not that which they talk of, when they die. Now, we have, indeed, a nominal religion, to which we pay tithes of property and sevenths of time;[24] but we have also a practical and earnest religion, to which we devote nine-tenths of our property and six-sevenths of our time. And we dispute a great deal about the nominal religion: but we are all unanimous about this practical one; of which I think you will admit that the ruling goddess may be best generally described as the "Goddess of Getting-on," or "Britannia of the Market." The Athenians had an "Athena Agoraia," or Athena of the Market; but she was a subordinate type of their goddess, while our Britannia Agoraia is the principal type of ours. And all your great architectural works are, of course, built to her. It is long since you built a great cathedral; and how you would laugh at me if I proposed building a cathedral on the top of one of these hills of yours, to make it an Acropolis! But your railroad mounds, vaster than the walls of Babylon; your railroad stations, vaster than the temple of Ephesus, and innumerable; your chimneys, how much more mighty and costly than cathedral spires! your harbour-piers; your warehouses; your exchanges!—all these are built to your great Goddess of "Getting-on"; and she has formed, and will continue to form, your architecture, as long as you worship her; and it is quite vain to ask me to tell you how to build to *her*; you know far better than I.

There might, indeed, on some theories, be a conceivably good architecture for Exchanges—that is to say, if there were any heroism in the fact or deed of exchange which might be typically carved on the outside of your building. For, you know, all beautiful architecture must be adorned with sculpture or painting; and for sculpture or painting, you must have a subject. And hitherto it has been a received opinion among the nations of the world that the only right subjects for either, were *heroisms* of some sort. Even on his pots and his flagons, the Greek put a Hercules slaying lions, or an Apollo slaying serpents, or Bacchus slaying melancholy giants, and earthborn despondencies. On his temples, the Greek put contests of great warriors in founding states, or of gods with evil spirits. On his houses and temples alike, the Christian put carvings of angels conquering devils; or of hero-martyrs exchanging this world for another; subject inappropriate, I think, to our direction of exchange here. And the Master of Christians not only left His followers without any orders as to the sculpture of affairs of exchange on the outside of buildings, but gave some strong evidence of His dislike of affairs of exchange within them.[25] And yet there might surely be a heroism in such affairs; and all commerce become a kind of selling of doves, not impious. The wonder has always been great to me, that heroism has never been supposed to be in any wise consistent with the practice of supplying people with food, or clothes; but rather with that of quartering one's self upon them for food, and stripping them of their clothes. Spoiling of armour is an heroic deed in all ages; but the selling of clothes, old or new, has never taken any colour of magnanimity. Yet one does not see why feeding the hungry and clothing the naked should ever become base businesses, even when engaged in on a large scale. If one could contrive to attach the notion of conquest to them anyhow! so that, supposing there were anywhere an obstinate race, who refused to be comforted, one might take some pride in giving them compulsory comfort![26] and, as it were, "*occupying* a country" with one's gifts, instead of one's armies? If one could only consider it as much a victory to get a barren field sown, as to get an eared field stripped; and contend who should build villages, instead of who should "carry" them! Are not all forms of heroism conceivable in doing these serviceable deeds? You doubt who is strongest? It might be ascertained by push of spade, as well as push of sword. Who is wisest? There are witty things to be thought of in planning other business than campaigns. Who is bravest? There are always the elements to fight with, stronger than men; and nearly as merciless.

The only absolutely and unapproachably heroic element in the soldier's work seems to be—that he is paid little for it—and regularly: while you traffickers, and exchangers, and others occupied in presumably benevolent business, like to be paid much for it—and by chance. I never can make out how it is that a *knight*-errant does not expect to be paid for his trouble, but a *pedlar*-errant always does;—that people

[22] Those who wished to revive classical antiquity.
[23] The palaces of the French kings and of the Pope, respectively.
[24] One-tenth of our income and one day of our week.

[25] When he drove the money-changers from the temple.
[26] "Quite serious, all this, though it reads like jest." (Ruskin, 1873)

JOHN RUSKIN

Painted by the Pre-Raphaelite artist Sir
John Millais. Ruskin and Millais, who became acquainted in 1851, traveled together
in Scotland in 1853, about the time this
portrait was painted. In 1855 Millais married Mrs. Ruskin, whose first marriage had
been annulled.

ENGRAVING OF DOVER
BY J. M. W. TURNER

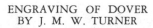

Ruskin wrote the first volume of *Modern
Painters* (1843) largely to defend Turner
(1775-1851) against the charge that his
highly imaginative paintings, especially
his landscapes, were not true to life. The
statement of his aesthetic principles which
Ruskin had originally designed as a "short
pamphlet" eventually ran to five volumes,
the last published in 1860.

UNIVERSITY MUSEUM, OXFORD

The museum, built 1855-60, shows the use of iron for architectural purposes. At the suggestion of Ruskin, however, the iron was partly concealed by Italian Gothic masonry. (National Buildings Record)

OXFORD FROM THE AIR

The quadrangle of Balliol College (the college of John Wyclif, John Evelyn, Adam Smith, Robert Southey, A. H. Clough, Matthew Arnold, and A. C. Swinburne) is in the immediate foreground, center. The spire center, is that of St. Mary's Church, built about 1480, where Archbishop Cranmer was tried in 1555 and Newman was vicar from 1828 to 1843. Left and beyond the spire University College, which Shelley attended in 1810. (Aero Pictorial Ltd.)

are willing to take hard knocks for nothing, but never to sell ribands cheap; that they are ready to go on fervent crusades, to recover the tomb of a buried God, but never on any travels to fulfil the orders of a living one;—that they will go anywhere barefoot to preach their faith, but must be well bribed to practise it, and are perfectly ready to give the Gospel gratis, but never the loaves and fishes.[27]

If you chose to take the matter up on any such soldierly principle; to do your commerce, and your feeding of nations, for fixed salaries; and to be as particular about giving people the best food, and the best cloth, as soldiers are about giving them the best gunpowder, I could carve something for you on your exchange worth looking at. But I can only at present suggest decorating its frieze with pendant purses; and making its pillars broad at the base, for the sticking of bills. And in the innermost chambers of it there might be a statue of Britannia of the Market, who may have, perhaps advisably, a partridge for her crest, typical at once of her courage in fighting for noble ideas, and of her interest in game; and round its neck, the inscription in golden letters, "Perdix fovit quae non peperit."[28] Then, for her spear, she might have a weaver's beam; and on her shield, instead of St. George's Cross, the Milanese boar, semi-fleeced, with the town of Gennesaret proper, in the field;[29] and the legend, "In the best market,"[30] and her corslet, of leather, folded over her heart in the shape of a purse, with thirty slits in

it, for a piece of money to go in at, on each day of the month. And I doubt not but that people would come to see your exchange, and its goddess, with applause.

Nevertheless, I want to point out to you certain strange characters in this goddess of yours. She differs from the great Greek and Mediaeval deities essentially in two things—first, as to the continuance of her presumed power; secondly, as to the extent of it.

First, as to the Continuance.

The Greek Goddess of Wisdom gave continual increase of wisdom, as the Christian Spirit of Comfort (or Comforter) continual increase of comfort. There was no question, with these, of any limit or cessation of function. But with your Agora Goddess, that is just the most important question. Getting on—but where to? Gathering together—but how much? Do you mean to gather always—never to spend? If so, I wish you joy of your goddess, for I am just as well off as you, without the trouble of worshipping her at all. But if you do not spend, somebody else will—somebody else must. And it is because of this (among many other such errors) that I have fearlessly declared your so-called science of Political Economy to be no science; because, namely, it has omitted the study of exactly the most important branch of the business—the study of *spending*. For spend you must, and as much as you make, ultimately. You gather corn:—will you bury England under a heap of grain; or will you, when you have gathered, finally eat? You gather gold:—will you make your house-roofs of it, or pave your streets with it? That is still one way of spending it. But if you keep it, that you may get more, I'll give you more; I'll give you all the gold you want—all you can imagine—if you can tell me what you'll do with it. You shall have thousands of gold pieces;—thousands of thousands—millions—mountains, of gold: where will you keep them? Will you put an Olympus of silver upon a golden Pelion—make Ossa like a wart?[31] Do you think the rain and dew would then come down to you, in the streams from such mountains, more blessedly than they will down the mountains which God has made for you, of moss and whinstone? But it is not gold that you want to gather! What is it? greenbacks? No; not those neither. What is it then—is it ciphers after a capital I? Cannot you practise writing ciphers, and write as many as you want! Write ciphers for an hour every morning, in a big book, and say every evening, I am worth all those naughts more than I was yesterday. Won't that do? Well, what in the name of

27 "Please think over this paragraph, too briefly and antithetically put, but one of those which I am happiest in having written." (Ruskin, 1873) The loaves and fishes, of course, are an allusion to Christ's feeding of the multitude.

28 "*Jeremiah*, XVII, 11 (best in Septuagint and Vulgate). 'As the partridge, fostering what she brought not forth, so he that getteth riches, not by right, shall leave them in the midst of his days, and at his end shall be a fool.'" (Ruskin)

29 The substitution of the Milanese boar for the Cross of St. George which was usually portrayed on Britannia's shield is intended to symbolize England's turning away from the ideals of chivalry exemplified by St. George, her patron saint, to greed and reliance on guns and armor plate (which Ruskin has stigmatized above), since the Milanese had been particularly noted as armorers. By association Ruskin apparently moved from the boar (wild swine) to the Biblical story of the Gadarene (or, Matthew 8:28, "Gergesene") swine who became possessed of demons. On two other occasions when he referred to this miracle (in *Fors Clavigera*, letter 61), Ruskin also located the scene at Gennesaret instead of Gadara on Gergesa, on what authority has not been ascertained. What particular modern industrial city Ruskin had in mind is uncertain and immaterial, but conceivably it was Bradford itself.

30 Allusion to the slogan of laissez-faire capitalism, "Buy in the cheapest and sell in the dearest market." See the General Introduction, above, p. 370. Ruskin in 1873 made the following annotation: "Meaning, fully, 'We have brought our pigs to it.'"

31 In Greek mythology, the giants in attempting to reach Mount Olympus (or heaven) piled the mountains Pelion and Ossa one upon the other.

Plutus[32] is it you want? Not gold, not greenbacks, not ciphers after a capital I? You will have to answer, after all, "No; we want, somehow or other, money's *worth*." Well, what is that? Let your Goddess of Getting-on discover it, and let her learn to stay therein.

Second. But there is yet another question to be asked respecting this Goddess of Getting-on. The first was of the continuance of her power; the second is of its extent.

Pallas[33] and the Madonna were supposed to be all the world's Pallas, and all the world's Madonna. They could teach all men, and they could comfort all men. But, look strictly into the nature of the power of your Goddess of Getting-on; and you will find she is the Goddess—not of everybody's getting on—but only of somebody's getting on. This is a vital, or rather deathful, distinction. Examine it in your own ideal of the state of national life which this Goddess is to evoke and maintain. I asked you what it was, when I was last here;[34]—you have never told me. Now, shall I try to tell you?

Your ideal of human life then is, I think, that it should be passed in a pleasant undulating world, with iron and coal everywhere underneath it. On each pleasant bank of this world is to be a beautiful mansion, with two wings; and stables, and coach-houses; a moderately-sized park; a large garden and hot-houses; and pleasant carriage drives through the shrubberies. In this mansion are to live the favoured votaries of the Goddess; the English gentleman, with his gracious wife, and his beautiful family; always able to have the boudoir and the jewels for the wife, and the beautiful ball dresses for the daughters, and hunters for the sons, and a shooting in the Highlands for himself. At the bottom of the bank, is to be the mill; not less than a quarter of a mile long, with one steam engine at each end, and two in the middle, and a chimney three hundred feet high. In this mill are to be in constant employment from eight hundred to a thousand workers, who never drink, never strike, always go to church on Sunday, and always express themselves in respectful language.

Is not that, broadly, and in the main features, the kind of thing you propose to yourselves? It is very pretty indeed, seen from above; not at all so pretty, seen from below. For, observe, while to one family this deity is indeed the Goddess of Getting-on, to a thousand families she is the Goddess of *not* Getting-on. "Nay," you say, "they have all their chance." Yes, so has every one in a lottery, but there must always be the same number of blanks. "Ah! but in a lottery it is not skill and intelligence which take the lead, but blind chance." What then! do you think the old practice, that "they should take who have the power, and they should keep who can," is less iniquitous, when the power has become power of brains instead of fist? and that, though we may not take advantage of a child's or a woman's weakness, we may of a man's foolishness? "Nay, but finally, work must be done, and some one must be at the top, some one at the bottom." Granted, my friends. Work must always be, and captains of work must always be; and if you in the least remember the tone of any of my writings, you must know that they are thought unfit for this age, because they are always insisting on need of government, and speaking with scorn of liberty. But I beg you to observe that there is a wide difference between being captains or governors of work, and taking the profits of it. It does not follow, because you are general of an army, that you are to take all the treasure, or land, it wins (if it fight for treasure or land); neither, because you are king of a nation, that you are to consume all the profits of the nation's work. Real kings, on the contrary, are known invariably by their doing quite the reverse of this—by their taking the least possible quantity of the nation's work for themselves. There is no test of real kinghood so infallible as that. Does the crowned creature live simply, bravely, unostentatiously? probably he *is* a King. Does he cover his body with jewels, and his table with delicates? in all probability he is *not* a King. It is possible he may be, as Solomon was; but that is when the nation shares his splendour with him. Solomon made gold, not only to be in his own palace as stones, but to be in Jerusalem as stones. But, even so, for the most part, these splendid king-hoods expire in ruin, and only the true kinghoods live, which are of royal labourers governing loyal labourers; who, both leading rough lives, establish the true dynasties. Conclusively you will find that because you are king of a nation, it does not follow that you are to gather for yourself all the wealth of that nation; neither, because you are king of a small part of the nation, and lord over the means of its maintenance—over field, or mill, or mine,—are you to take all the produce of that piece of the foundation of national existence for yourself.

You will tell me I need not preach against these things, for I cannot mend them. No, good friends, I cannot; but you can, and you will; or something else

---

[32] God of riches.

[33] Pallas Athena, goddess of wisdom.

[34] Ruskin had delivered a previous lecture at Bradford in 1859 at the inauguration of the Bradford School of Design.

can and will. Even good things have no abiding power—and shall these evil things persist in victorious evil? All history shows, on the contrary, that to be the exact thing they never can do. Change *must* come; but it is ours to determine whether change of growth, or change of death. Shall the Parthenon be in ruins on its rock, and Bolton priory[35] in its meadow, but these mills of yours be the consummation of the buildings of the earth, and their wheels be as the wheels of eternity? Think you that "men may come, and men may go," but—mills—go on for ever?[36] Not so; out of these, better or worse shall come; and it is for you to choose which.

I know that none of this wrong is done with deliberate purpose. I know, on the contrary, that you wish your workmen well; that you do much for them, and that you desire to do more for them, if you saw your way to such benevolence safely. I know that even all this wrong and misery are brought about by a warped sense of duty, each of you striving to do his best; but, unhappily, not knowing for whom this best should be done. And all our hearts have been betrayed by the plausible impiety of the modern economist,[37] telling us that, "To do the best for ourselves, is finally to do the best for others." Friends, our great Master said not so; and most absolutely we shall find this world is not made so. Indeed, to do the best for others, is finally to do the best for ourselves; but it will not do to have our eyes fixed on that issue. The Pagans had got beyond that. Hear what a Pagan says of this matter; hear what were, perhaps, the last written words of Plato,—if not the last actually written (for this we cannot know), yet assuredly in fact and power his parting words—in which, endeavouring to give full crowning and harmonious close to all his thoughts, and to speak the sum of them by imagined sentence of the Great Spirit, his strength and his heart fail him, and the words cease, broken off for ever.

They are at the close of the dialogue called *Critias,* in which he describes, partly from real tradition, partly in ideal dream, the early state of Athens; and the genesis, and order, and religion, of the fabled isle of Atlantis; in which genesis he conceives the same first perfection and final degeneracy of man, which in our own Scriptural tradition is expressed by saying that the Sons of God inter-married with the daughters of men, for he supposes the earliest race to have been indeed the children of God; and to have corrupted themselves, until "their spot was not the spot of his children." And this, he says, was the end; that indeed "through many generations, so long as the God's nature in them yet was full, they were submissive to the sacred laws, and carried themselves lovingly to all that had kindred with them in divineness; for their uttermost spirit was faithful and true, and in every wise great; so that, in *all meekness of wisdom, they dealt with each other,* and took all the chances of life; and despising all things except virtue, they cared little what happened day by day, and *bore lightly the burden* of gold and of possessions; for they saw that, if *only their common love and virtue increased, all these things would be increased together with them;* but to set their esteem and ardent pursuit upon material possession would be to lose that first, and their virtue and affection together with it. And by such reasoning, and what of the divine nature remained in them, they gained all this greatness of which we have already told; but when the God's part of them faded and became extinct, being mixed again and again, and effaced by the prevalent mortality; and the human nature at last exceeded, they then became unable to endure the courses of fortune; and fell into shapelessness of life, and baseness in the sight of him who could see, having lost everything that was fairest of their honour; while to the blind hearts which could not discern the true life, tending to happiness, it seemed that they were then chiefly noble and happy, being filled with all iniquity of inordinate possession and power. Whereupon, the God of Gods, whose Kinghood is in laws, beholding a once just nation thus cast into misery, and desiring to lay such punishment upon them as might make them repent into restraining, gathered together all the gods into his dwelling place, which from heaven's centre overlooks whatever has part in creation; and having assembled them, he said"—

The rest is silence.[38] Last words of the chief wisdom of the heathen, spoken of this idol of riches; this idol of yours; this golden image, high by measureless cubits, set up where your green fields of England are furnace-burnt into the likeness of the plain of Dura:[39] this idol, forbidden to us, first of all idols, by our own Master and faith; forbidden to us

---

[35] Ruins of a beautiful abbey in Yorkshire.
[36] Cf. Tennyson's *The Brook:* "Men may come, and men may go, but I go on for ever."
[37] The liberals. See General Introduction, p. 371.

[38] Hamlet's last words. Ruskin means that the *Critias* was broken off at this point.
[39] Plain in the province of Babylon where Nebuchadnezzar set up the golden idol. Almost certainly the word "furnace-burnt" is intended to recall the fiery furnace into which Shadrach, Meshach, and Abednego were cast for refusing to worship the idol (Daniel 3).

also by every human lip that has ever, in any age or people, been accounted of as able to speak according to the purposes of God. Continue to make that forbidden deity your principal one, and soon no more art, no more science, no more pleasure will be possible. Catastrophe will come; or, worse than catastrophe, slow mouldering and withering into Hades. But if you can fix some conception of a true human state of life to be striven for—life, good for all men, as for yourselves; if you can determine some honest and simple order of existence; following those trodden ways of wisdom which are pleasantness, and seeking her quiet and withdrawn paths, which are peace;—then, and so sanctifying wealth into "common-wealth," all your art, your literature, your daily labours, your domestic affection, and citizen's duty, will join and increase into one magnificent harmony. You will know then how to build, well enough; you will build with stone well, but with flesh better; temples not made with hands, but riveted of hearts; and that kind of marble, crimson-veined, is indeed eternal.

Thomas Henry Huxley

1825–1895

In his *Notebooks* Samuel Butler has an entry headed "Personified Science":

Science is being daily more and more personified and anthropomorphised into a god. By and by they will say that science took our nature upon him, and sent down his only begotten son, Charles Darwin, or Huxley, into the world so that those who believe in him, etc.

This indicates the real significance of Huxley (far more than of Darwin) in the history of Victorian thought.[1] He was *the prophet of science*. What was he sent down to reveal? First, the revolutionary discoveries of the age in geology and biology. With wonderful clarity and illustrative power, in a long series of popular lectures and articles, he explained to the Victorians the theories of evolution which had been put forward in technical language by men like Lyell and Darwin. But he was more than a brilliant popularizer. He was a philosopher who thought science the key to all truth and who wanted to extend the application of scientific theory and method to all fields of knowledge. This meant testing the validity of traditional beliefs, especially religious beliefs as expressed in the Bible, by a scientific standard of proof. It meant asking, What does science tell us about the universe in which we live? the origin and nature of man? the source and sanction of morality? the beginnings of religion? the forces of cohesion and disruption in society? In short, Huxley aimed at nothing less than a complete reconstruction of thought in the light of science. The range of his writing, therefore, goes far beyond science itself to include philosophy, ethics, religion, political theory, and education. "To promote the increase of natural knowledge and to forward the application of scientific methods of investigation to all the problems of life" were the two great objects he had in view.

But the pursuit of these goals involved him in two other causes, both of which are reflected, and their importance emphasized, by the fact that Huxley's enthusiastic reception in America in 1876 was given not so much to "the preacher of new doctrines" as to the champion "of *freedom* and *sincerity*." These additional roles were forced upon him by the religious situation. Alarmed by the skeptical implications of science, the churches appealed to the authority of the Bible, every statement of which was still widely considered to be the word of God and therefore to be accepted without question. If science came to different conclusions, it was wrong; if scientists, relying on "carnal reason," denied any of its truths, they were morally reprehensible (see p. 625). No wonder Huxley waved the liberal banner and demanded the right of free thought and free speech even when they were anti-Christian or antireligious, and the right to follow reason even when it ran counter to religious authority. How important this role was, in his own mind, can be seen at the end of his "Autobiography," where he thinks his worldly honors of small account compared with his contribution to "the New Reformation" (see p. 603 and the note).

Finally, Huxley became something like an apostle of veracity to a generation which found itself caught between belief and unbelief, and often forced, by social pressures or psychological fears, into professing to believe what in fact it only half-believed or gravely doubted. Against such insincerities and evasions, however natural at the time, he struck with telling force, and his demand that men "rest

---

[1] For the factual details of Huxley's life, see his own "Autobiography," printed below.

in no lie" gave many later Victorians the courage to express their doubts or their outright disbelief.

The essay on "Science and Culture" is a plea for the study of science against the opposition of both the businessmen, who were slow to perceive its practical possibilities, and the scholars and schoolmasters, who clung to the old classical education. The argument, therefore, stresses the contribution of scientific education to industrial progress, on the one hand; and on the other, to culture—that is, to our understanding of human life. The battle to get science into the curriculum has long since been won, but its vocational value has almost submerged its cultural value, until today it is rarely taught as a liberal subject. Huxley would hardly approve of a science curriculum exclusively devoted to training chemists and engineers. He would insist that it contain historical courses which would explore the successive impacts of scientific discoveries upon man's moral, religious, and philosophical outlook.

On the other hand, the essay also reveals how seriously the cult of science could undermine the cultural values of the humanities. Though Huxley professes to recognize that unless the study of science is combined with the study of literature (in the wide sense that includes philosophy and history) the result will be a lopsided man, in point of fact he exalts science at the expense of literature. He is willing to say that men preparing for a career in medicine, business, or science need not bother with a literary education. He is willing to accept Sir Josiah Mason's College as providing "a fairly complete culture" because instruction in the English, French, and German *languages* is to be offered. He calls "literary or artistic culture a never-failing source of pleasures" which are morally wholesome, without pointing out that their real value lies in their power to extend our knowledge and quicken our perceptions of life. He can even claim that "the free employment of reason, in accordance with scientific method, is the sole method of reaching truth," which is at once to question the validity of much of our intellectual inheritance; for it is not to logic but to intuition that we owe the most important insights men have had into moral and religious life. In short, Huxley is right in insisting on the values of science, but his overinsistence upon them, with the consequent disparagement of the humanities, reveals the destructive influence of the scientific mind upon our cultural tradition.

Even more serious has been its similar effect on the religious tradition. The antireligious implications of nineteenth-century science (described at length in the General Introduction) may be summarized here in a series of propositions, all of which Huxley maintained. The universe, to all intents and purposes, is infinite in space and infinite in time. It is not static but dynamic, in a continuous process of evolution which started from some "primordial molecular arrangement" and has been going on ever since by scientific laws. Organic life began when hydrogen, oxygen, nitrogen, and carbon came together in a complex relationship under just the right climatic conditions. Its origin, therefore, was completely material. From this original sperm all later life has naturally descended: man is an animal, and animals are merely physical automata. All of man's actions and thoughts are determined by molecular changes in the brain, which are determined by external stimuli, which in turn are simply parts of the great mechanism of cause and effect which "composes the sum of existence." Consequently, man has no immaterial soul or spirit, and no moral will that is free to control his thinking or his conduct. He is simply a human automaton. This is the scientific picture of the universe which had emerged by 1870, and which Huxley did so much to publicize. And yet, in the very teeth of these propositions, he could turn around and say that in a world so full of misery and ignorance, it is "the plain duty of each and all of us to try to make the little corner he can influence somewhat less miserable and somewhat less ignorant than it was before he entered it." The automaton can choose to make the world a better place! The fact is that Huxley was not only a scientist, he was also a humanist and a humanitarian; and the first self was always arriving at conclusions which the second could not endure. He therefore tried, with dubious success, to sit on two stools at once. So did Tennyson and many other Victorians unable to deny either the logic of mechanistic science or the inner assurance of free will. The situation still exists, as Whitehead has pointed out:

A scientific realism, based on mechanism, is conjoined with an unwavering belief in the world of men and of the higher animals as being composed of self-determining organisms. This radical inconsistency at the basis of modern thought accounts for much that is half-hearted and wavering in our civilisation.

The same tension can be seen in Huxley's ethics. On the one hand, he derived the moral will and moral laws from the automatic working of Darwin's principle of natural selection. In the cause of better survival, men banded together into tribes, which meant that they had to establish certain moral laws so that they could work together. These were enforced by tribal punishments on all who disobeyed them, with the result that out of fear (but ultimately for the sake of personal survival) a conscience was gradually instilled into primitive man. At the same time, social ideals were set up which exalted duty and self-sacrifice because they could add further weight to the force of conscience in giving the tribe greater cohesive strength—and the individual a greater chance of survival. Altruism, therefore, was simply a disguised form of selfishness.

These are the beliefs of Huxley the scientist (see pp. 631 ff.). But Huxley the humanist can talk of an "innate sense of moral beauty and ugliness" which is possessed by a few "men of moral genius, to whom we owe ideals of duty and visions of moral perfection" unattainable by ordinary persons, and from whom the latter derive an inspiration to spend their lives trying to embody these ideals in the actual world. One of the essays ends with an appeal to all of us to strive upward "towards those high peaks, where, resting in eternal calm, reason [ethical reason or moral intuition] discerns the undefined but bright ideal of the highest Good." This is the language of moral idealism. It is the language of Plato. And it never appeared in any natural history of morality. The logic of science was always leading Huxley to a position which his humanism repudiated. But he could not let go his hold of either.

Both sides of his mind can be seen again in the two volumes which he devoted directly to the subject of religion (*Science and Hebrew Tradition* and *Science and Christian Tradition,* to both of which the "Prologue" printed below, pp. 623 ff., was a general preface). On the one hand, he applied the new scientific criticism (historical, literary, and physical) to the Bible, with the intention of disproving or rationalizing the entire body of supernatural dogma and miracle. When he finished, the Bible had been reduced to a typical primitive document full of superstition and myth. But his liberal opponents insisted that no amount of Biblical criticism could disprove the core of religion, the belief in God and immortality. Huxley, forced reluctantly to agree, added a corollary. He said, "Right, there is no *disproof* of those beliefs, but don't forget, there is no *proof* of them either"; and by proof he meant objective evidence capable of public verification. This is the agnostic position, standing between faith and atheism; not denial of belief but denial that we have sufficient reason to believe. Huxley himself coined the term *agnosticism* (literally, "no knowledge") in 1869 to describe, with proper caution, the conclusions of the scientific mind. But we must remember that there is the genuine agnostic, honestly in doubt, earnestly trying to discover whether or not there is a supernatural order; and there is the polemical agnostic, at heart an atheist, but too smart to claim that there is no supernatural order, though ready enough to propagate his conviction by insinuation and aspersion. Huxley was a polemical agnostic (see his real belief in the note on p. 628, but his official agnosticism in the text above; and notice the brilliant anti-religious rhetoric on p. 625, where he stacks all the cards on the side of naturalism). Nevertheless, Huxley the humanist was only too eager to "save" both the Bible and the Church. Both had to be purged of their supernatural and theological elements, but when that was done, the residue would be sound morality. The function of both, he thought, ought to be "the setting before men's minds of an ideal of true, just, and pure living." This Victorian reduction of religion and the Sunday service to moral and humanitarian inspiration has largely captured the Protestant churches. But one may wonder if the inspiration can have much compulsion when it is divorced from the faith which once gave it meaning and power.

The standard biography is the *Life and Letters of Thomas Henry Huxley,* by his son, Leonard Huxley (2 vols., London, 1900, or New York, 1901). On his thought, there is a good essay in Robert Shafer's *Christianity and Naturalism* (1926); on his style, see Aldous Huxley, "T. H. Huxley as a Man of Letters" in *Huxley Memorial Lectures at the Imperial College of Science and Technology* (London, 1932), and Walter E. Houghton, "The Rhetoric of T. H. Huxley," *University of Toronto Quarterly,* XVIII (1948–49), 159–175.

Thomas Henry Huxley

AUTOBIOGRAPHY

And when I consider, in one view, the many things . . . which I have upon my hands, I feel the burlesque of being employed in this manner at my time of life. But, in another view, and taking in all circumstances, these things, as trifling as they may appear, no less than things of greater importance, seem to be put upon me to do. . . .
—BISHOP BUTLER[1] *to the* DUCHESS OF SOMERSET.

THE "many things" to which the Duchess's correspondent here refers are the repairs and improvements of the episcopal seat at Auckland. I doubt if the great apologist, greater in nothing than in the simple dignity of his character, would have considered the writing an account of himself as a thing which could be put upon him to do, whatever circumstances might be taken in. But the good bishop lived in an age when a man might write books and yet be permitted to keep his private existence to himself; in the pre-Boswellian epoch, when the germ of the photographer lay in the womb of the distant future, and the interviewer who pervades our age was an unforeseen, indeed unimaginable, birth of time.

At present, the most convinced believer in the aphorism "*Bene qui latuit, bene vixit,*"[2] is not always able to act up to it. An importunate person informs him that his portrait is about to be published and will be accompanied by a biography which the importunate person proposes to write. The sufferer knows what that means; either he undertakes to revise the "biography" or he does not. In the former case, he makes himself responsible; in the latter, he allows the publication of a mass of more or less fulsome inaccuracies for which he will be held responsible by those who are familiar with the prevalent art of self-advertisement. On the whole, it may be better to get over the "burlesque of being employed in this manner" and do the thing himself.

It was by reflections of this kind that, some years ago, I was led to write and permit the publication of the subjoined sketch.

I was born about eight o'clock in the morning on the 4th of May, 1825, at Ealing, which was, at that time, as quiet a little country village as could be found within half-a-dozen miles of Hyde Park Corner. Now it is a suburb of London with, I believe, 30,000 inhabitants. My father was one of the masters in a large semipublic school which at one time had a high reputation. I am not aware that any portents preceded my arrival in this world, but, in my childhood, I remember hearing a traditional account of the manner in which I lost the chance of an endowment of great practical value. The windows of my mother's room were open, in consequence of the unusual warmth of the weather. For the same reason, probably, a neighboring beehive had swarmed, and the new colony, pitching on the window-sill, was making its way into the room when the horrified nurse shut down the sash. If that well-meaning woman had only abstained from her ill-timed interference, the swarm might have settled on my lips, and I should have been endowed with that mellifluous eloquence which, in this country, leads far more surely than worth, capacity, or honest work, to the highest places in Church and State. But the opportunity was lost, and I have been obliged to content myself through life with saying what I mean in the plainest of plain language, than which, I suppose, there is no habit more ruinous to a man's prospects of advancement.

Why I was christened Thomas Henry I do not know; but it is a curious chance that my parents should have fixed for my usual denomination upon the name of that particular Apostle with whom I have always felt most sympathy. Physically and mentally I am the son of my mother so completely—even down to peculiar movements of the hands, which made their appearance in me as I reached the age she had when I noticed them—that I can hardly find any trace of my father in myself, except an inborn faculty for drawing, which unfortunately, in my case, has never been cultivated, a hot temper, and that amount of tenacity of purpose which unfriendly observers sometimes call obstinacy.

My mother was a slender brunette, of an emotional and energetic temperament, and possessed of the most piercing black eyes I ever saw in a woman's head. With no more education than other women of the middle classes in her day, she had an excellent mental capacity. Her most distinguishing characteristic, however, was rapidity of thought. If one ventured to

---

[1] Bishop Joseph Butler (1692–1752), author of the widely read *Analogy of Religion*.
[2] "He who has lived inconspicuously has lived well." (Ovid, *Tristia*, III, iv, 25.)

suggest she had not taken much time to arrive at any conclusion, she would say, "I cannot help it, things flash across me." That peculiarity has been passed on to me in full strength; it has often stood me in good stead; it has sometimes played me sad tricks, and it has always been a danger. But, after all, if my time were to come over again, there is nothing I would less willingly part with than my inheritance of mother wit.

I have next to nothing to say about my childhood. In later years my mother, looking at me almost reproachfully, would sometimes say, "Ah! you were such a pretty boy!" whence I had no difficulty in concluding that I had not fulfilled my early promise in the matter of looks. In fact, I have a distinct recollection of certain curls of which I was vain, and of a conviction that I closely resembled that handsome, courtly gentleman, Sir Herbert Oakley, who was vicar of our parish, and who was as a god to us country folk, because he was occasionally visited by the then Prince George of Cambridge. I remember turning my pinafore wrong side forwards in order to represent a surplice, and preaching to my mother's maids in the kitchen as nearly as possible in Sir Herbert's manner one Sunday morning when the rest of the family were at church. That is the earliest indication I can call to mind of the strong clerical affinities which my friend Mr. Herbert Spencer has always ascribed to me, though I fancy they have for the most part remained in a latent state.

My regular school training was of the briefest, perhaps fortunately, for though my way of life has made me acquainted with all sorts and conditions of men, from the highest to the lowest, I deliberately affirm that the society I fell into at school was the worst I have ever known. We boys were average lads, with much the same inherent capacity for good and evil as any others; but the people who were set over us cared about as much for our intellectual and moral welfare as if they were baby-farmers. We were left to the operation of the struggle for existence among ourselves, and bullying was the least of the ill practices current among us. Almost the only cheerful reminiscence in connection with the place which arises in my mind is that of a battle I had with one of my classmates, who had bullied me until I could stand it no longer. I was a very slight lad, but there was a wildcat element in me which, when roused, made up for lack of weight, and I licked my adversary effectually. However, one of my first experiences of the extremely rough-and-ready nature of justice, as exhibited by the course of things in general, arose out of the fact that I—the victor—had a black eye, while he—the vanquished—had none, so that I got into disgrace and he did not. We made it up, and thereafter I was unmolested. One of the greatest shocks I ever received in my life was to be told a dozen years afterwards by the groom who brought me my horse in a stable-yard in Sydney that he was my quondam antagonist. He had a long story of family misfortune to account for his position, but at that time it was necessary to deal very cautiously with mysterious strangers in New South Wales, and on inquiry I found that the unfortunate young man had not only been "sent out," but had undergone more than one colonial conviction.

As I grew older, my great desire was to be a mechanical engineer, but the fates were against this and, while very young, I commenced the study of medicine under a medical brother-in-law. But, though the Institute of Mechanical Engineers would certainly not own me, I am not sure that I have not all along been a sort of mechanical engineer *in partibus infidelium*.[3] I am now occasionally horrified to think how very little I ever knew or cared about medicine as the art of healing. The only part of my professional course which really and deeply interested me was physiology, which is the mechanical engineering of living machines; and, notwithstanding that natural science has been my proper business, I am afraid there is very little of the genuine naturalist in me. I never collected anything, and species work was always a burden to me; what I cared for was the architectural and engineering part of the business, the working out the wonderful unity of plan in the thousands and thousands of diverse living constructions, and the modifications of similar apparatuses to serve diverse ends. The extraordinary attraction I felt towards the study of the intricacies of living structure nearly proved fatal to me at the outset. I was a mere boy—I think between thirteen and fourteen years of age—when I was taken by some older student friends of mine to the first post-mortem examination I ever attended. All my life I have been most unfortunately sensitive to the disagreeables which attend anatomical pursuits, but on this occasion my curiosity overpowered all other feelings, and I spent two or three hours in gratifying it. I did not cut myself, and none of the ordinary symptoms of dissection-poison supervened, but poisoned I was somehow, and I remember sinking into a strange state of apathy. By way of a last chance, I was sent to the care of some good, kind people, friends of my

---

3 "In heathen or foreign parts." Huxley is here thinking of himself as a mechanical engineer in the "foreign" field of physiology.

father's, who lived in a farmhouse in the heart of Warwickshire. I remember staggering from my bed to the window on the bright spring morning after my arrival, and throwing open the casement. Life seemed to come back on the wings of the breeze, and to this day the faint odor of wood-smoke, like that which floated across the farmyard in the early morning, is as good to me as the "sweet south upon a bed of violets." I soon recovered, but for years I suffered from occasional paroxysms of internal pain, and from that time my constant friend, hypochondriacal dyspepsia, commenced his half century of co-tenancy of my fleshly tabernacle.

Looking back on my *Lehrjahre*,[4] I am sorry to say that I do not think that any account of my doings as a student would tend to edification. In fact, I should distinctly warn ingenuous youth to avoid imitating my example. I worked extremely hard when it pleased me, and when it did not—which was a very frequent case—I was extremely idle (unless making caricatures of one's pastors and masters is to be called a branch of industry), or else wasted my energies in wrong directions. I read everything I could lay hands upon, including novels, and took up all sorts of pursuits to drop them again quite as speedily. No doubt it was very largely my own fault, but the only instruction from which I ever obtained the proper effect of education was that which I received from Mr. Wharton Jones, who was the lecturer on physiology at the Charing Cross School of Medicine. The extent and precision of his knowledge impressed me greatly, and the severe exactness of his method of lecturing was quite to my taste. I do not know that I have ever felt so much respect for anybody as a teacher before or since. I worked hard to obtain his approbation, and he was extremely kind and helpful to the youngster who, I am afraid, took up more of his time than he had any right to do. It was he who suggested the publication of my first scientific paper —a very little one—in the *Medical Gazette* of 1845, and most kindly corrected the literary faults which abounded in it, short as it was; for at that time, and for many years afterwards, I detested the trouble of writing, and would take no pains over it.

It was in the early spring of 1846, that, having finished my obligatory medical studies and passed the first M.B. examination at the London University— though I was still too young to qualify at the College of Surgeons—I was talking to a fellow student (the present eminent physician, Sir Joseph Fayrer), and wondering what I should do to meet the imperative

necessity for earning my own bread, when my friend suggested that I should write to Sir William Burnett, at that time Director-General for the Medical Service of the Navy, for an appointment. I thought this rather a strong thing to do, as Sir William was personally unknown to me, but my cheery friend would not listen to my scruples, so I went to my lodgings and wrote the best letter I could devise. A few days afterwards I received the usual official circular of acknowledgement, but at the bottom there was written an instruction to call at Somerset House on such a day. I thought that looked like business, so at the appointed time I called and sent in my card, while I waited in Sir William's anteroom. He was a tall, shrewd-looking old gentleman, with a broad Scotch accent— and I think I see him now as he entered with my card in his hand. The first thing he did was to return it, with the frugal reminder that I should probably find it useful on some other occasion. The second was to ask whether I was an Irishman. I suppose the air of modesty about my appeal must have struck him. I satisfied the Director-General that I was English to the backbone, and he made some inquiries as to my student career, finally desiring me to hold myself ready for examination. Having passed this, I was in Her Majesty's Service, and entered on the books of Nelson's old ship, the *Victory*, for duty at Haslar Hospital, about a couple of months after I made my application.

My official chief at Haslar was a very remarkable person, the late Sir John Richardson, an excellent naturalist, and far-famed as an indomitable Arctic traveler. He was a silent, reserved man, outside the circle of his family and intimates; and, having a full share of youthful vanity, I was extremely disgusted to find that "Old John," as we irreverent youngsters called him, took not the slightest notice of my worshipful self either the first time I attended him, as it was my duty to do, or for some weeks afterwards. I am afraid to think of the lengths to which my tongue may have run on the subject of the churlishness of the chief, who was, in truth, one of the kindest-hearted and most considerate of men. But one day, as I was crossing the hospital square, Sir John stopped me, and heaped coals of fire on my head by telling me that he had tried to get me one of the resident appointments, much coveted by the assistant surgeons, but that the Admiralty had put in another man. "However," said he, "I mean to keep you here till I can get you something you will like," and turned upon his heel without waiting for the thanks I stammered out. That explained how it was I had not been packed off to the West Coast of Africa like some

---

[4] Student years.

of my juniors, and why, eventually, I remained altogether seven months at Haslar.

After a long interval, during which "Old John" ignored my existence almost as completely as before, he stopped me again as we met in a casual way, and describing the service on which the *Rattlesnake* was likely to be employed, said that Captain Owen Stanley, who was to command the ship, had asked him to recommend an assistant surgeon who knew something of science; would I like that? Of course I jumped at the offer. "Very well, I give you leave; go to London at once and see Captain Stanley." I went, saw my future commander, who was very civil to me, and promised to ask that I should be appointed to his ship, as in due time I was. It is a singular thing that, during the few months of my stay at Haslar, I had among my messmates two future Directors-General of the Medical Service of the Navy (Sir Alexander Armstrong and Sir John Watt-Reid), with the present President of the College of Physicians and my kindest of doctors, Sir Andrew Clark.

Life on board Her Majesty's ships in those days was a very different affair from what it is now, and ours was exceptionally rough, as we were often many months without receiving letters or seeing any civilized people but ourselves. In exchange, we had the interest of being about the last voyagers, I suppose, to whom it could be possible to meet with people who knew nothing of firearms—as we did on the south coast of New Guinea—and of making acquaintance with a variety of interesting savage and semicivilized people. But, apart from experience of this kind and the opportunities offered for scientific work, to me, personally, the cruise was extremely valuable. It was good for me to live under sharp discipline; to be down on the realities of existence by living on bare necessaries; to find out how extremely well worth living life seemed to be when one woke up from a night's rest on a soft plank, with the sky for canopy and cocoa and weevily biscuit the sole prospect for breakfast; and, more especially, to learn to work for the sake of what I got for myself out of it, even if it all went to the bottom and I along with it. My brother officers were as good fellows as sailors ought to be and generally are, but, naturally, they neither knew nor cared anything about my pursuits, nor understood why I should be so zealous in pursuit of the objects which my friends, the middies, christened "Buffons," after the title conspicuous on a volume of the *Suites à Buffon*,[5] which stood on my shelf in the chart room.

During the four years of our absence, I sent home communication after communication to the "Linnean Society,"[6] with the same result as that obtained by Noah when he sent the raven out of his ark. Tired at last of hearing nothing about them, I determined to do or die, and in 1849 I drew up a more elaborate paper and forwarded it to the Royal Society.[7] This was my dove, if I had only known it. But owing to the movements of the ship, I heard nothing of that either until my return to England in the latter end of the year 1850, when I found that it was printed and published, and that a huge packet of separate copies awaited me. When I hear some of my young friends complain of want of sympathy and encouragement, I am inclined to think that my naval life was not the least valuable part of my education.

Three years after my return were occupied by a battle between my scientific friends on the one hand and the Admiralty on the other, as to whether the latter ought, or ought not, to act up to the spirit of a pledge they had given to encourage officers who had done scientific work by contributing to the expense of publishing mine. At last the Admiralty, getting tired, I suppose, cut short the discussion by ordering me to join a ship, which thing I declined to do, and as Rastignac, in the *Père Goriot,* says to Paris, I said to London, "*à nous deux*."[8] I desired to obtain a Professorship of either Physiology or Comparative Anatomy, and as vacancies occurred I applied, but in vain. My friend, Professor Tyndall, and I were candidates at the same time, he for the Chair of Physics and I for that of Natural History in the University of Toronto, which, fortunately, as it turned out, would not look at either of us. I say fortunately, not from any lack of respect for Toronto, but because I soon made up my mind that London was the place for me, and hence I have steadily declined the inducements to leave it, which have at various times been offered. At last, in 1854, on the translation of my warm friend Edward Forbes, to Edinburgh, Sir Henry De la Beche, the Director-General of the Geological Survey, offered me the post Forbes vacated of Paleontologist and Lecturer on Natural History. I refused the former point-blank, and accepted the latter only provisionally, telling Sir Henry that I did not care for fossils, and that I should give

---

6 Founded in 1788 for the promotion of zoology and botany and named for the Swedish botanist Carl von Linné.

7 The Royal Society was the oldest scientific society in England. For a description of its early activities, see Macaulay, *History of England,* Chapter III, above, pp. 482–3.

8 *Le Père Goriot* is a novel by Honoré de Balzac (1799–1850). The French phrase means, "Now the issue is squarely between the two of us."

---

5 Supplements to the *Histoire Naturelle,* written by the great French naturalist Georges Buffon (1707–88).

up Natural History as soon as I could get a physiological post. But I held the office for thirty-one years, and a large part of my work has been paleontological.

At that time I disliked public speaking, and had a firm conviction that I should break down every time I opened my mouth. I believe I had every fault a speaker could have (except talking at random or indulging in rhetoric), when I spoke to the first important audience I ever addressed, on a Friday evening at the Royal Institution,[9] in 1852. Yet, I must confess to having been guilty, *malgré moi*,[10] of as much public speaking as most of my contemporaries, and for the last ten years it ceased to be so much of a bugbear to me. I used to pity myself for having to go through this training, but I am now more disposed to compassionate the unfortunate audiences, especially my ever-friendly hearers at the Royal Institution, who were the subjects of my oratorical experiments.

The last thing that it would be proper for me to do would be to speak of the work of my life, or to say at the end of the day whether I think I have earned my wages or not. Men are said to be partial judges of themselves. Young men may be—I doubt if old men are. Life seems terribly foreshortened as they look back, and the mountain they set themselves to climb in youth turns out to be a mere spur of immeasurably higher ranges when, with failing breath, they reached the top. But if I may speak of the objects I have had more or less definitely in view since I began the ascent of my hillock, they are briefly these: To promote the increase of natural knowledge and to forward the application of scientific methods of investigation to all the problems of life to the best of my ability, in the conviction, which has grown with my growth and strengthened with my strength, that there is no alleviation for the sufferings of mankind except veracity of thought and of action, and the resolute facing of the world as it is when the garment of make-believe by which pious hands have hidden its uglier features is stripped off.

It is with this intent that I have subordinated any reasonable, or unreasonable, ambition for scientific fame which I may have permitted myself to entertain to other ends: to the popularization of science; to the development and organization of scientific education; to the endless series of battles and skirmishes over evolution; and to untiring opposition to that ecclesiastical spirit, that clericalism, which in England, as everywhere else, and to whatever denomination it may belong, is the deadly enemy of science.

In striving for the attainment of these objects, I have been but one among many, and I shall be well content to be remembered, or even not remembered, as such. Circumstances, among which I am proud to reckon the devoted kindness of many friends, have led to my occupation of various prominent positions, among which the Presidency of the Royal Society is the highest. It would be mock modesty on my part, with these and other scientific honors which have been bestowed upon me, to pretend that I have not succeeded in the career which I have followed, rather because I was driven into it than of my own free will; but I am afraid I should not count even these things as marks of success if I could not hope that I had somewhat helped that movement of opinion which has been called the New Reformation.[11]

SCIENCE AND CULTURE[1]

Six years ago, as some of my present hearers may remember, I had the privilege of addressing a large assemblage of the inhabitants of this city, who had gathered together to do honor to the memory of their famous townsman, Joseph Priestley;[2] and, if any satisfaction attaches to posthumous glory, we may hope that the *manes*[3] of the burnt-out philosopher were then finally appeased.

No man, however, who is endowed with a fair share of common sense, and not more than a fair share of vanity, will identify either contemporary or

---

[9] A scientific society.   [10] In spite of myself.

[1] This essay was originally delivered on October 1, 1880, as a lecture at the opening of the new Science College founded by Sir Josiah Mason at Birmingham.

[2] A distinguished scientist and political economist as well as a Unitarian clergyman (1733–1804). Because of his liberal sympathies and the panic engendered by the French Revolution, his house was attacked and burned by a mob in 1791. Both his scientific instruments and his manuscripts were destroyed.

[11] Cf. Huxley's letter to his wife in 1873: "The part I have to play is not to found a new school of thought or to reconcile the antagonisms of the old schools. We are in the midst of a gigantic movement greater than that which preceded and produced the Reformation, and really only the continuation of that movement. But there is nothing new in the ideas which lie at the bottom of the movement, nor is any reconcilement possible between free thought and traditional authority."

[3] Ancestral spirits.

posthumous fame with the highest good; and Priestley's life leaves no doubt that he, at any rate, set a much higher value upon the advancement of knowledge, and the promotion of that freedom of thought which is at once the cause and the consequence of intellectual progress.

Hence I am disposed to think that, if Priestley could be amongst us today, the occasion of our meeting would afford him even greater pleasure than the proceedings which celebrated the centenary of his chief discovery.[4] The kindly heart would be moved, the high sense of social duty would be satisfied, by the spectacle of well-earned wealth neither squandered in tawdry luxury and vainglorious show, nor scattered with the careless charity which blesses neither him that gives nor him that takes, but expended in the execution of a well-considered plan for the aid of present and future generations of those who are willing to help themselves.

We shall all be of one mind thus far. But it is needful to share Priestley's keen interest in physical science; and to have learned, as he had learned, the value of scientific training in fields of inquiry apparently far remote from physical science; in order to appreciate, as he would have appreciated, the value of the noble gift which Sir Josiah Mason has bestowed upon the inhabitants of the Midland district.

For us children of the nineteenth century, however, the establishment of a college under the conditions of Sir Josiah Mason's Trust, has a significance apart from any which it could have possessed a hundred years ago. It appears to be an indication that we are reaching the crisis of the battle, or rather of the long series of battles, which have been fought over education in a campaign which began long before Priestley's time, and will probably not be finished just yet.

In the last century, the combatants were the champions of ancient literature on the one side, and those of modern literature on the other; but, some thirty years ago, the contest became complicated by the appearance of a third army, ranged round the banner of physical science.

I am not aware that anyone has authority to speak in the name of this new host. For it must be admitted to be somewhat of a guerilla force, composed largely of irregulars, each of whom fights pretty much for his own hand. But the impressions of a full private, who has seen a good deal of service in the ranks, respecting the present position of affairs and the conditions of a permanent peace, may not be devoid of interest; and I do not know that I could make a better use of the present opportunity than by laying them before you.

From the time that the first suggestion to introduce physical science into ordinary education was timidly whispered, until now, the advocates of scientific education have met with opposition of two kinds. On the one hand, they have been pooh-poohed by the men of business who pride themselves on being the representatives of practicality; while, on the other hand, they have been excommunicated by the classical scholars, in their capacity of Levites in charge of the ark of culture and monopolists of liberal education.[5]

The practical men believed that the idol whom they worship—rule of thumb—has been the source of the past prosperity, and will suffice for the future welfare of the arts and manufactures. They were of opinion that science is speculative rubbish; that theory and practice have nothing to do with one another; and that the scientific habit of mind is an impediment, rather than an aid, in the conduct of ordinary affairs.

I have used the past tense in speaking of the practical men—for although they were very formidable thirty years ago, I am not sure that the pure species has not been extirpated. In fact, so far as mere argument goes, they have been subjected to such a *feu d'enfer*[6] that it is a miracle if any have escaped. But I have remarked that your typical practical man has an unexpected resemblance to one of Milton's angels. His spiritual wounds, such as are inflicted by logical weapons, may be as deep as a well and as wide as a church door, but beyond shedding a few drops of ichor, celestial or otherwise, he is no whit the worse. So, if any of these opponents be left, I will not waste time in vain repetition of the demonstrative evidence of the practical value of science; but knowing that a parable will sometimes penetrate where syllogisms fail to effect an entrance, I will offer a story for their consideration.

Once upon a time, a boy,[7] with nothing to depend upon but his own vigorous nature, was thrown into the thick of the struggle for existence in the midst of a great manufacturing population. He seems to have had a hard fight, inasmuch as, by the time he was thirty years of age, his total disposable funds

---

4 That of oxygen.

5 Using the Biblical designation of those appointed to guard the Ark of the Lord, Huxley implies that the classical scholars, i.e., the universities, are endowing their particular culture with an aura of sanctity that may well be founded on mere tradition.
6 Barrage (literally, hell-fire).
7 Sir Josiah Mason.

amounted to twenty pounds. Nevertheless, middle life found him giving proof of his comprehension of the practical problems he had been roughly called upon to solve, by a career of remarkable prosperity.

Finally, having reached old age with its well-earned surroundings of "honor, troops of friends," the hero of my story bethought himself of those who were making a like start in life, and how he could stretch out a helping hand to them.

After long and anxious reflection this successful practical man of business could devise nothing better than to provide them with the means of obtaining "sound, extensive, and practical scientific knowledge." And he devoted a large part of his wealth and five years of incessant work to this end.

I need not point the moral of a tale which, as the solid and spacious fabric of the Scientific College assures us, is no fable, nor can anything which I could say intensify the force of this practical answer to practical objections.

We may take it for granted then, that, in the opinion of those best qualified to judge, the diffusion of thorough scientific education is an absolutely essential condition of industrial progress; and that the college which has been opened today will confer an inestimable boon upon those whose livelihood is to be gained by the practice of the arts and manufactures of the district.

The only question worth discussion is, whether the conditions, under which the work of the college is to be carried out, are such as to give it the best possible chance of achieving permanent success.

Sir Josiah Mason, without doubt most wisely, has left very large freedom of action to the trustees, to whom he proposes ultimately to commit the administration of the college, so that they may be able to adjust its arrangements in accordance with the changing conditions of the future. But, with respect to three points, he has laid most explicit injunctions upon both administrators and teachers.

Party politics are forbidden to enter into the minds of either, so far as the work of the college is concerned; theology is as sternly banished from its precincts; and finally, it is especially declared that the college shall make no provision for "mere literary instruction and education."

It does not concern me at present to dwell upon the first two injunctions any longer than may be needful to express my full conviction of their wisdom. But the third prohibition brings us face to face with those other opponents of scientific education, who are by no means in the moribund condition of the practical man, but alive, alert, and formidable.

It is not impossible that we shall hear this express exclusion of "literary instruction and education" from a college which, nevertheless, professes to give a high and efficient education, sharply criticized. Certainly the time was that the Levites of culture would have sounded their trumpets against its walls as against an educational Jericho.[8]

How often have we not been told that the study of physical science is incompetent to confer culture; that it touches none of the higher problems of life; and, what is worse, that the continual devotion to scientific studies tends to generate a narrow and bigoted belief in the applicability of scientific methods to the search after truth of all kinds? How frequently one has reason to observe that no reply to a troublesome argument tells so well as calling its author a "mere scientific specialist." And, as I am afraid it is not permissible to speak of this form of opposition to scientific education in the past tense, may we not expect to be told that this, not only omission, but prohibition, of "mere literary instruction and education" is a patent example of scientific narrow-mindedness?

I am not acquainted with Sir Josiah Mason's reasons for the action which he has taken; but if, as I apprehend is the case, he refers to the ordinary classical course of our schools and universities by the name of "mere literary instruction and education," I venture to offer sundry reasons of my own in support of that action.

For I hold very strongly by two convictions. The first is that neither the discipline nor the subject-matter of classical education is of such direct value to the student of physical science as to justify the expenditure of valuable time upon either; and the second is, that for the purpose of attaining real culture, an exclusively scientific education is at least as effectual as an exclusively literary education.

I need hardly point out to you that these opinions, especially the latter, are diametrically opposed to those of the great majority of educated Englishmen, influenced as they are by school and university traditions. In their belief, culture is obtainable only by a liberal education; and a liberal education is synonymous, not merely with education and instruction in literature, but in one particular form of literature, namely, that of Greek and Roman antiquity. They hold that the man who has learned

---

8 As the walls of Jericho in the Bible story were destroyed by the blowing of the Levites' trumpets (Joshua 6), so the proponents of classical culture would once have tried to destroy the College by a loud noise of protest.

Latin and Greek, however little, is educated; while he who is versed in other branches of knowledge, however deeply, is a more or less respectable specialist, not admissible into the cultured caste. The stamp of the educated man, the university degree, is not for him.

I am too well acquainted with the generous catholicity of spirit, the true sympathy with scientific thought, which pervades the writings of our chief apostle of culture[9] to identify him with these opinions; and yet one may cull from one and another of those epistles to the Philistines, which so much delight all who do not answer to that name, sentences which lend them some support.

Mr. Arnold tells us that the meaning of culture is "to know the best that has been thought and said in the world."[10] It is the criticism of life contained in literature. That criticism regards "Europe as being, for intellectual and spiritual purposes, one great confederation, bound to a joint action and working to a common result; and whose members have, for their common outfit, a knowledge of Greek, Roman, and Eastern antiquity, and of one another. Special, local, and temporary advantages being put out of account, that modern nation will in the intellectual and spiritual sphere make most progress, which most thoroughly carries out this program. And what is that but saying that we too, all of us, as individuals, the more thoroughly we carry it out, shall make the more progress?"

We have here to deal with two distinct propositions. The first, that a criticism of life is the essence of culture; the second, that literature contains the materials which suffice for the construction of such criticism.

I think that we must all assent to the first proposition. For culture certainly means something quite different from learning or technical skill. It implies the possession of an ideal, and the habit of critically estimating the value of things by comparison with a theoretic standard. Perfect culture should supply a complete theory of life, based upon a clear knowledge alike of its possibilities and of its limitations.

But we may agree to all this, and yet strongly dissent from the assumption that literature alone is competent to supply this knowledge. After having learned all that Greek, Roman, and Eastern antiquity have thought and said, and all that modern literatures have to tell us, it is not self-evident that we have laid a sufficiently broad and deep foundation for that criticism of life which constitutes culture.

Indeed, to anyone acquainted with the scope of physical science, it is not at all evident. Considering progress only in the "intellectual and spiritual sphere," I find myself wholly unable to admit that either nations or individuals will really advance, if their common outfit draws nothing from the stores of physical science. I should say that an army, without weapons of precision and with no particular base of operations, might more hopefully enter upon a campaign on the Rhine, than a man, devoid of a knowledge of what physical science has done in the last century, upon a criticism of life.

When a biologist meets with an anomaly, he instinctively turns to the study of development to clear it up. The rationale of contradictory opinions may with equal confidence be sought in history.

It is, happily, no new thing that Englishmen should employ their wealth in building and endowing institutions for educational purposes. But, five or six hundred years ago, deeds of foundation expressed or implied conditions as nearly as possible contrary to those which have been thought expedient by Sir Josiah Mason. That is to say, physical science was practically ignored, while a certain literary training was enjoined as a means to the acquirement of knowledge which was essentially theological.

The reason of this singular contradiction between the actions of men alike animated by a strong and disinterested desire to promote the welfare of their fellows, is easily discovered.

At that time, in fact, if anyone desired knowledge beyond such as could be obtained by his own observation, or by common conversation, his first necessity was to learn the Latin language, inasmuch as all the higher knowledge of the western world was contained in works written in that language. Hence, Latin grammar, with logic and rhetoric, studied through Latin, were the fundamentals of education. With respect to the substance of the knowledge imparted through this channel, the Jewish and Christian Scriptures, as interpreted and supplemented by the Romish Church, were held to contain a complete and infallibly true body of information.

Theological dicta were, to the thinkers of those days, that which the axioms and definitions of Euclid

---

9 It is, of course, Matthew Arnold that is envisaged here. Huxley refers to Arnold's essays as "epistles to the Philistines" because Arnold, using the parallel of the Biblical account of the struggle of the Hebrews, the chosen of God, with their enemies, had termed the enemies of culture—and in this category he included the whole English middle class—"Philistines."

10 The two quotations from Arnold in this paragraph are from his essay "The Function of Criticism at the Present Time" reprinted below, pp. 748 ff.).

are to the geometers of these. The business of the philosophers of the Middle Ages was to deduce from the data furnished by the theologians, conclusions in accordance with ecclesiastical decrees. They were allowed the high privilege of showing, by logical process, how and why that which the Church said was true, must be true. And if their demonstrations fell short of or exceeded this limit, the Church was maternally ready to check their aberrations; if need were by the help of the secular arm.

Between the two, our ancestors were furnished with a compact and complete criticism of life. They were told how the world began and how it would end; they learned that all material existence was but a base and insignificant blot upon the fair face of the spiritual world, and that nature was, to all intents and purposes, the playground of the devil; they learned that the earth is the center of the visible universe, and that man is the cynosure of things terrestrial; and more especially was it inculcated that the course of nature had no fixed order, but that it could be, and constantly was, altered by the agency of innumerable spiritual beings, good and bad, according as they were moved by the deeds and prayers of men. The sum and substance of the whole doctrine was to produce the conviction that the only thing really worth knowing in this world was how to secure that place in a better which, under certain conditions, the Church promised.

Our ancestors had a living belief in this theory of life, and acted upon it in their dealings with education, as in all other matters. Culture meant saintliness— after the fashion of the saints of those days; the education that led to it was, of necessity, theological; and the way to theology lay through Latin.

That the study of nature—further than was requisite for the satisfaction of everyday wants—should have any bearing on human life was far from the thoughts of men thus trained. Indeed, as nature had been cursed for man's sake, it was an obvious conclusion that those who meddled with nature were likely to come into pretty close contact with Satan. And, if any born scientific investigator followed his instincts, he might safely reckon upon earning the reputation, and probably upon suffering the fate, of a sorcerer.

Had the western world been left to itself in Chinese isolation, there is no saying how long this state of things might have endured. But, happily, it was not left to itself. Even earlier than the thirteenth century, the development of Moorish civilization in Spain and the great movement of the Crusades had introduced the leaven which, from that day to this, has never ceased to work. At first, through the intermediation of Arabic translations, afterwards by the study of the originals, the western nations of Europe became acquainted with the writings of the ancient philosophers and poets, and, in time, with the whole of the vast literature of antiquity.

Whatever there was of high intellectual aspiration or dominant capacity in Italy, France, Germany, and England, spent itself for centuries in taking possession of the rich inheritance left by the dead civilizations of Greece and Rome. Marvelously aided by the invention of printing, classical learning spread and flourished. Those who possessed it prided themselves on having attained the highest culture then within the reach of mankind.

And justly. For, saving Dante on his solitary pinnacle, there was no figure in modern literature at the time of the Renascence to compare with the men of antiquity; there was no art to compete with their sculpture; there was no physical science but that which Greece had created. Above all, there was no other example of perfect intellectual freedom—of the unhesitating acceptance of reason as the sole guide to truth and the supreme arbiter of conduct.

The new learning necessarily soon exerted a profound influence upon education. The language of the monks and schoolmen seemed little better than gibberish to scholars fresh from Virgil and Cicero, and the study of Latin was placed upon a new foundation. Moreover, Latin itself ceased to afford the sole key to knowledge. The student who sought the highest thought of antiquity, found only a second-hand reflection of it in Roman literature, and turned his face to the full light of the Greeks. And after a battle, not altogether dissimilar to that which is at present being fought over the teaching of physical science, the study of Greek was recognized as an essential element of all higher education.

Thus the Humanists, as they were called, won the day; and the great reform which they effected was of incalculable service to mankind. But the Nemesis[11] of all reformers is finality; and the reformers of education, like those of religion, fell into the profound, however common, error of mistaking the beginning for the end of the work of reformation.

The representatives of the Humanists, in the nineteenth century, take their stand upon classical education as the sole avenue to culture, as firmly as if we were still in the age of Renascence. Yet, surely, the

---

11 Ancient goddess of retributive justice, whose name is used to mean "undoing."

present intellectual relations of the modern and the ancient worlds are profoundly different from those which obtained three centuries ago. Leaving aside the existence of a great and characteristically modern literature, of modern painting, and, especially, of modern music, there is one feature of the present state of the civilized world which separates it more widely from the Renascence than the Renascence was separated from the Middle Ages.

This distinctive character of our own times lies in the vast and constantly increasing part which is played by natural knowledge. Not only is our daily life shaped by it, not only does the prosperity of millions of men depend upon it, but our whole theory of life has long been influenced, consciously or unconsciously, by the general conceptions of the universe which have been forced upon us by physical science.

In fact, the most elementary acquaintance with the results of scientific investigation shows us that they offer a broad and striking contradiction to the opinion so implicitly credited and taught in the Middle Ages.

The notions of the beginning and the end of the world entertained by our forefathers are no longer credible. It is very certain that the earth is not the chief body in the material universe, and that the world is not subordinated to man's use. It is even more certain that nature is the expression of a definite order with which nothing interferes, and that the chief business of mankind is to learn that order and govern themselves accordingly. Moreover this scientific "criticism of life" presents itself to us with different credentials from any other. It appeals not to authority, nor to what anybody may have thought or said, but to nature. It admits that all our interpretations of natural fact are more or less imperfect and symbolic, and bids the learner seek for truth not among words but among things. It warns us that the assertion which outstrips evidence is not only a blunder but a crime.

The purely classical education advocated by the representatives of the Humanists in our day, gives no inkling of all this. A man may be a better scholar than Erasmus,[12] and know no more of the chief causes of the present intellectual fermentation than Erasmus did. Scholarly and pious persons, worthy of all respect, favor us with allocutions upon the sadness of the antagonism of science to their medieval way of thinking, which betray an ignorance of the first principles of scientific investigation, an incapacity for understanding what a man of science means by ve-

racity, and an unconsciousness of the weight of established scientific truths, which is almost comical.

There is no great force in the *tu quoque*[13] argument, or else the advocates of scientific education might fairly enough retort upon the modern Humanists that they may be learned specialists, but that they possess no such sound foundation for a criticism of life as deserves the name of culture. And, indeed, if we were disposed to be cruel, we might urge that the Humanists have brought this reproach upon themselves, not because they are too full of the spirit of the ancient Greek, but because they lack it.

The period of the Renascence is commonly called that of the "Revival of Letters," as if the influences then brought to bear upon the mind of Western Europe had been wholly exhausted in the field of literature. I think it is very commonly forgotten that the revival of science, effected by the same agency, although less conspicuous, was not less momentous.

In fact, the few and scattered students of nature of that day picked up the clue to her secrets exactly as it fell from the hands of the Greeks a thousand years before. The foundations of mathematics were so well laid by them, that our children learn their geometry from a book written for the schools of Alexandria two thousand years ago.[14] Modern astronomy is the natural continuation and development of the work of Hipparchus and of Ptolemy; modern physics of that of Democritus and of Archimedes; it was long before modern biological science outgrew the knowledge bequeathed to us by Aristotle, by Theophrastus, and by Galen.

We cannot know all the best thoughts and sayings of the Greeks unless we know what they thought about natural phenomena. We cannot fully apprehend their criticism of life unless we understand the extent to which that criticism was affected by scientific conceptions. We falsely pretend to be the inheritors of their culture, unless we are penetrated, as the best minds among them were, with an unhesitating faith that the free employment of reason, in accordance with scientific method, is the sole method of reaching truth.

Thus I venture to think that the pretensions of our modern Humanists to the possession of the monopoly of culture and to the exclusive inheritance of the spirit of antiquity must be abated, if not abandoned. But I should be very sorry that anything I have said should be taken to imply a desire on my part to depreciate the value of classical education, as it might

---

12 The Dutch classical scholar (1466–1536) was reputed to be the most learned man of his time.

13 "You, too." If it's true of me, it's just as true of you.
14 By Euclid.

be and as it sometimes is. The native capacities of mankind vary no less than their opportunities; and while culture is one, the road by which one man may best reach it is widely different from that which is most advantageous to another. Again, while scientific education is yet inchoate and tentative, classical education is thoroughly well organized upon the practical experience of generations of teachers. So that, given ample time for learning and estimation for ordinary life, or for a literary career, I do not think that a young Englishman in search of culture can do better than follow the course usually marked out for him, supplementing its deficiencies by his own efforts.

But for those who mean to make science their serious occupation; or who intend to follow the profession of medicine; or who have to enter early upon the business of life; for all these, in my opinion, classical education is a mistake; and it is for this reason that I am glad to see "mere literary education and instruction" shut out from the curriculum of Sir Josiah Mason's College, seeing that its inclusion would probably lead to the introduction of the ordinary smattering of Latin and Greek.

Nevertheless, I am the last person to question the importance of genuine literary education, or to suppose that intellectual culture can be complete without it. An exclusively scientific training will bring about a mental twist as surely as an exclusively literary training. The value of the cargo does not compensate for a ship's being out of trim; and I should be very sorry to think that the Scientific College would turn out none but lopsided men.

There is no need, however, that such a catastrophe should happen. Instruction in English, French, and German is provided, and thus the three greatest literatures of the modern world are made accessible to the student.

French and German, and especially the latter language, are absolutely indispensable to those who desire full knowledge in any department of science. But even supposing that the knowledge of these languages acquired is not more than sufficient for purely scientific purposes, every Englishman has, in his native tongue, an almost perfect instrument of literary expression; and, in his own literature, models of every kind of literary excellence. If an Englishman cannot get literary culture out of his Bible, his Shakespeare, his Milton, neither, in my belief, will the profoundest study of Homer and Sophocles, Virgil and Horace, give it to him.

Thus, since the constitution of the college makes sufficient provision for literary as well as for scientific education, and since artistic instruction is also contemplated, it seems to me that a fairly complete culture is offered to all who are willing to take advantage of it.

But I am not sure that at this point the "practical" man, scotched[15] but not slain, may ask what all this talk about culture has to do with an institution, the object of which is defined to be "to promote the prosperity of the manufactures and the industry of the country." He may suggest that what is wanted for this end is not culture, nor even a purely scientific discipline, but simply a knowledge of applied science.

I often wish that this phrase, "applied science," had never been invented. For it suggests that there is a sort of scientific knowledge of direct practical use, which can be studied apart from another sort of scientific knowledge, which is of no practical utility, and which is termed "pure science." But there is no more complete fallacy than this. What people call applied science is nothing but the application of pure science to particular classes of problems. It consists of deductions from those general principles, established by reasoning and observation, which constitute pure science. No one can safely make these deductions until he has a firm grasp of the principles; and he can obtain that grasp only by personal experience of the operations of observation and of reasoning on which they are founded.

Almost all the processes employed in the arts and manufactures fall within the range either of physics or of chemistry. In order to improve them, one must thoroughly understand them; and no one has a chance of really understanding them, unless he has obtained that mastery of principles and that habit of dealing with facts, which is given by long-continued and well-directed purely scientific training in the physical and the chemical laboratory. So that there really is no question as to the necessity of purely scientific discipline, even if the work of the college were limited by the narrowest interpretation of its stated aims.

And, as to the desirableness of a wider culture than that yielded by science alone, it is to be recollected that the improvement of manufacturing processes is only one of the conditions which contribute to the prosperity of industry. Industry is a means and not an end; and mankind work only to get something which they want. What that something is depends partly on their innate, and partly on their acquired, desires.

If the wealth resulting from prosperous industry is to be spent upon the gratification of unworthy desires, if the increasing perfection of manufacturing processes is to be accompanied by an increasing

---

15 Gashed. Cf. *Macbeth*, III, ii. 13.

debasement of those who carry them on, I do not see the good of industry and prosperity.

Now it is perfectly true that men's views of what is desirable depend upon their characters; and that the innate proclivities to which we give that name are not touched by any amount of instruction. But it does not follow that even mere intellectual education may not, to an indefinite extent, modify the practical manifestation of the characters of men in their actions, by supplying them with motives unknown to the ignorant. A pleasure-loving character will have pleasure of some sort; but, if you give him the choice, he may prefer pleasures which do not degrade him to those which do. And this choice is offered to every man, who possesses in literary or artistic culture a never-failing source of pleasures, which are neither withered by age, nor staled by custom, nor embittered in the recollection by the pangs of self-reproach.

If the institution opened today fulfills the intention of its founder, the picked intelligences among all classes of the population of this district will pass through it. No child born in Birmingham, henceforward, if he have the capacity to profit by the opportunities offered to him, first in the primary and other schools, and afterwards in the Scientific College, need fail to obtain, not merely the instruction, but the culture most appropriate to the conditions of his life.

Within these walls, the future employer and the future artisan may sojourn together for a while, and carry, through all their lives, the stamp of the influences then brought to bear upon them. Hence, it is not beside the mark to remind you, that the prosperity of industry depends not merely upon the improvement of manufacturing processes, not merely upon the ennobling of the individual character, but upon a third condition, namely, a clear understanding of the conditions of social life, on the part of both the capitalist and the operative, and their agreement upon common principles of social action. They must learn that social phenomena are as much the expression of natural laws as any others; that no social arrangements can be permanent unless they harmonize with the requirements of social statics and dynamics;[16] and that, in the nature of things, there is an arbiter whose decisions execute themselves.

But this knowledge is only to be obtained by the application of the methods of investigation adopted in physical researches to the investigation of the phenomena of society. Hence, I confess, I should like to see one addition made to the excellent scheme of education propounded for the college, in the shape of provision for the teaching of sociology. For though we are all agreed that party politics are to have no place in the instruction of the college; yet in this country, practically governed as it is now by universal suffrage, every man who does his duty must exercise political functions. And, if the evils which are inseparable from the good of political liberty are to be checked, if the perpetual oscillation of nations between anarchy and despotism is to be replaced by the steady march of self-restraining freedom; it will be because men will gradually bring themselves to deal with political, as they now deal with scientific questions; to be as ashamed of undue haste and partisan prejudice in the one case as in the other; and to believe that the machinery of society is at least as delicate as that of a spinning-jenny, and as little likely to be improved by the meddling of those who have not taken the trouble to master the principles of its action.

In conclusion, I am sure that I make myself the mouthpiece of all present in offering to the venerable founder of the institution, which now commences its beneficent career, our congratulations on the completion of his work; and in expressing the conviction, that the remotest posterity will point to it as a crucial instance of the wisdom which natural piety leads all men to ascribe to their ancestors.

from DARWINIANA[1]

from THE ORIGIN OF SPECIES

MR. DARWIN's long-standing and well-earned scientific eminence probably renders him indifferent to that social notoriety which passes by the name of success; but if the calm spirit of the philosopher have not yet wholly superseded the ambition and the vanity of the carnal man within him, he must be well satisfied with the results of his venture in publishing the "Origin of Species." Overflowing the narrow bounds of purely scientific circles, the "species question" divides with Italy and the Volunteers the

---

[16] The laws of society, as they affect either its successive states or its development from one state to the next.

[1] In *Darwiniana* (1893) Huxley collected his most important essays and lectures on evolution. The present essay was a review (1860) of Darwin's *The Origin of Species by Means of Natural Selection, or The Preservation of Favored Races in the Struggle for Life* (1859).

attention of general society.[2] Everybody has read Mr. Darwin's book, or, at least, has given an opinion upon its merits or demerits; pietists, whether lay or ecclesiastic, decry it with the mild railing which sounds so charitable; bigots denounce it with ignorant invective; old ladies of both sexes consider it a decidedly dangerous book; and even savants, who have no better mud to throw, quote antiquated writers to show that its author is no better than an ape himself; while every philosophical thinker hails it as a veritable Whitworth gun[3] in the armoury of liberalism; and all competent naturalists and physiologists, whatever their opinions as to the ultimate fate of the doctrines put forth, acknowledge that the work in which they are embodied is a solid contribution to knowledge and inaugurates a new epoch in natural history.

Nor has the discussion of the subject been restrained within the limits of conversation. When the public is eager and interested, reviewers must minister to its wants; and the genuine *littérateur*[4] is too much in the habit of acquiring his knowledge from the book he judges—as the Abyssinian is said to provide himself with steaks from the ox which carries him—to be withheld from criticism of a profound scientific work by the mere want of the requisite preliminary scientific acquirement; while, on the other hand, the men of science who wish well to the new views, no less than those who dispute their validity, have naturally sought opportunities of expressing their opinions. Hence it is not surprising that almost all the critical journals have noticed Mr. Darwin's work at greater or less length; and so many disquisitions, of every degree of excellence, from the poor product of ignorance, too often stimulated by prejudice, to the fair and thoughtful essay of the candid student of Nature, have appeared, that it seems an almost hopeless task to attempt to say anything new upon the question.

But it may be doubted if the knowledge and acumen of prejudged scientific opponents, and the subtlety of orthodox special pleaders, have yet exerted their full force in mystifying the real issues of the great controversy which has been set afoot, and whose end is hardly likely to be seen by this generation; so that, at this eleventh hour, and even failing anything new, it may be useful to state afresh that which is true, and to put the fundamental positions

advocated by Mr. Darwin in such a form that they may be grasped by those whose special studies lie in other directions. And the adoption of this course may be the more advisable, because, notwithstanding its great deserts, and indeed partly on account of them, the "Origin of Species" is by no means an easy book to read—if by reading is implied the full comprehension of an author's meaning. . . .

Thus while it may be doubted if, for some years, any one is likely to be competent to pronounce judgment on all the issues raised by Mr. Darwin, there is assuredly abundant room for him, who, assuming the humbler, though perhaps as useful, office of an interpreter between the "Origin of Species" and the public, contents himself with endeavouring to point out the nature of the problems which it discusses; to distinguish between the ascertained facts and the theoretical views which it contains; and finally, to show the extent to which the explanation it offers satisfies the requirements of scientific logic. At any rate, it is this office which we purpose to undertake in the following pages.

It may be safely assumed that our readers have a general conception of the nature of the objects to which the word "species" is applied; but it has, perhaps, occurred to a few, even to those who are naturalists *ex professo*,[5] to reflect, that, as commonly employed, the term has a double sense and denotes two very different orders of relations. When we call a group of animals, or of plants, a species, we may imply thereby, either that all these animals or plants have some common peculiarity of form or structure; or, we may mean that they possess some common functional character. That part of biological science which deals with form and structure is called Morphology—that which concerns itself with function, Physiology—so that we may conveniently speak of these two senses, or aspects, of "species"—the one as morphological, the other as physiological. Regarded from the former point of view, a species is nothing more than a kind of animal or plant, which is distinctly definable from all others, by certain constant, and not merely sexual, morphological peculiarities. Thus horses form a species, because the group of animals to which that name is applied is distinguished from all others in the world by the following constantly associated characters. They have—1, A vertebral column; 2, Mammae; 3, A placental embryo; 4, Four legs; 5, A single well-developed toe in each foot provided with a hoof; 6, A bushy tail; and 7, Callosities on the inner sides of both the fore

[2] 1859–61 were the years of Garibaldi's attempt to drive the Austrians out of Italy. The events were followed with great interest in England. In 1859, fear of the ambitions of Napoleon III resulted in the formation of a Volunteer Corps.

[3] A gun with the latest improvements.

[4] Professional man of letters.

[5] By profession.

and the hind legs. The asses, again, form a distinct species, because, with the same characters, as far as the fifth in the above list, all asses have tufted tails, and have callosities only on the inner side of the fore-legs. If animals were discovered having the general characters of the horse, but sometimes with cal-losities only on the fore-legs, and more or less tufted tails; or animals having the general characters of the ass, but with more or less bushy tails, and sometimes with callosities on both pairs of legs, besides being intermediate in other respects—the two species would have to be merged into one. They could no longer be regarded as morphologically distinct species, for they would not be distinctly definable one from the other. . . .

The student of Nature wonders the more and is astonished the less, the more conversant he becomes with her operations; but of all the perennial miracles she offers to his inspection, perhaps the most worthy of admiration is the development of a plant or of an animal from its embryo. Examine the recently laid egg of some common animal, such as a salamander or newt. It is a minute spheroid in which the best microscope will reveal nothing but a structureless sac, enclosing a glairy[6] fluid, holding granules in suspension. But strange possibilities lie dormant in that semi-fluid globule. Let a moderate supply of warmth reach its watery cradle, and the plastic matter undergoes changes so rapid, yet so steady and purposelike in their succession, that one can only compare them to those operated by a skilled modeller upon a formless lump of clay. As with an invisible trowel, the mass is divided and subdivided into smaller and smaller portions, until it is reduced to an aggregation of granules not too large to build withal the finest fabrics of the nascent organism. And, then, it is as if a delicate finger traced out the line to be occupied by the spinal column, and moulded the contour of the body; pinching up the head at one end, the tail at the other, and fashioning flank and limb into due salamandrine proportions, in so artistic a way, that, after watching the process hour by hour, one is almost involuntarily possessed by the notion, that some more subtle aid to vision than an achro-matic,[7] would show the hidden artist, with his plan before him, striving with skilful manipulation to perfect his work.

As life advances, and the young amphibian ranges the waters, the terror of his insect contemporaries, not only are the nutritious particles supplied by its prey, by the addition of which to its frame, growth takes place, laid down, each in its proper spot, and in such due proportion to the rest, as to reproduce the form, the colour, and the size, characteristic of the parental stock; but even the wonderful powers of reproducing lost parts possessed by these animals are controlled by the same governing tendency. Cut off the legs, the tail, the jaws, separately or all together, and, as Spallanzani showed long ago, these parts not only grow again, but the redintegrated limb is formed on the same type as those which were lost. The new jaw, or leg, is a newt's, and never by any accident more like that of a frog. What is true of the newt is true of every animal and of every plant; the acorn tends to build itself up again into a woodland giant such as that from whose twig it fell; the spore of the humblest lichen reproduces the green or brown incrustation which gave it birth; and at the other end of the scale of life, the child that resembled neither the paternal nor the maternal side of the house would be regarded as a kind of monster.

So that the one end to which, in all living beings, the formative impulse is tending—the one scheme which the Archaeus[8] of the old speculators strives to carry out, seems to be to mould the offspring into the likeness of the parent. It is the first great law of reproduction, that the offspring tends to resemble its parent or parents, more closely than anything else.

Science will some day show us how this law is a necessary consequence of the more general laws which govern matter; but, for the present, more can hardly be said than that it appears to be in harmony with them. We know that the phaenomena of vitality are not something apart from other physical phaenomena, but one with them; and matter and force are the two names of the one artist who fashions the living as well as the lifeless. Hence living bodies should obey the same great laws as other matter—nor, throughout Nature, is there a law of wider application than this, that a body impelled by two forces takes the direction of their resultant. But living bodies may be regarded as nothing but ex-tremely complex bundles of forces held in a mass of matter, as the complex forces of a magnet are held in the steel by its coercive force; and, since the differ-ences of sex are comparatively slight, or, in other words, the sum of the forces in each has a very similar tendency, their resultant, the offspring, may reason-ably be expected to deviate but little from a course parallel to either, or to both.

---

[6] Resembling white of egg. [7] Special type of microscope. [8] A kind of indwelling spirit posited by early medical research.

Represent the reason of the law to ourselves by what physical metaphor or analogy we will, however, the great matter is to apprehend its existence and the importance of the consequences deducible from it. For things which are like to the same are like to one another; and if, in a great series of generations, every offspring is like its parent, it follows that all the offspring and all the parents must be like one another; and that, given an original parental stock, with the opportunity of undisturbed multiplication, the law in question necessitates the production, in course of time, of an indefinitely large group, the whole of the members of which are at once very similar and are blood relations, having descended from the same parent, or pair of parents. The proof that all the members of any given group of animals, or plants, had thus descended, would be ordinarily considered sufficient to entitle them to the rank of physiological species, for most physiologists consider species to be definable as "the offspring of a single primitive stock."

But though it is quite true that all those groups we call species *may*, according to the known laws of reproduction, have descended from a single stock, and though it is very likely they really have done so, yet this conclusion rests on deduction and can hardly hope to establish itself upon a basis of observation. And the primitiveness of the supposed single stock, which, after all, is the essential part of the matter, is not only a hypothesis, but one which has not a shadow of foundation, if by "primitive" be meant "independent of any other living being." A scientific definition, of which an unwarrantable hypothesis forms an essential part, carries its condemnation within itself; but, even supposing such a definition were, in form, tenable, the physiologist who should attempt to apply it in Nature would soon find himself involved in great, if not inextricable, difficulties. As we have said, it is indubitable that offspring *tend* to resemble the parental organism, but it is equally true that the similarity attained never amounts to identity either in form or in structure. There is always a certain amount of deviation, not only from the precise characters of a single parent, but when, as in most animals and many plants, the sexes are lodged in distinct individuals, from an exact mean between the two parents. And indeed, on general principles, this slight deviation seems as intelligible as the general similarity, if we reflect how complex the co-operating "bundles of forces" are, and how improbable it is that, in any case, their true resultant shall coincide with any mean between the more obvious characters of the two parents. Whatever be its cause, however,

the co-existence of this tendency to minor variation with the tendency to general similarity, is of vast importance in its bearing on the question of the origin of species.

As a general rule, the extent to which an offspring differs from its parent is slight enough; but, occasionally, the amount of difference is much more strongly marked, and then the divergent offspring receives the name of a Variety. Multitudes, of what there is every reason to believe are such varieties, are known, but the origin of very few has been accurately recorded, and of these we will select two as more especially illustrative of the main features of variation. The first of them is that of the "Ancon" or "Otter" sheep, of which a careful account is given by Colonel David Humphreys, F.R.S., in a letter to Sir Joseph Banks, published in the "Philosophical Transactions" for 1813. It appears that one Seth Wright, the proprietor of a farm on the banks of the Charles River, in Massachusetts, possessed a flock of fifteen ewes and a ram of the ordinary kind. In the year 1791, one of the ewes presented her owner with a male lamb, differing, for no assignable reason, from its parents by a proportionally long body and short bandy legs, whence it was unable to emulate its relatives in those sportive leaps over the neighbours' fences, in which they were in the habit of indulging, much to the good farmer's vexation.

The second case is that detailed by a no less unexceptionable authority than Réaumur, in his "Art de faire éclore les Poulets."[9] A Maltese couple, named Kelleia, whose hands and feet were constructed upon the ordinary human model, had born to them a son, Gratio, who possessed six perfectly movable fingers on each hand, and six toes, not quite so well formed, on each foot. No cause could be assigned for the appearance of this unusual variety of the human species.

Two circumstances are well worthy of remark in both these cases. In each, the variety appears to have arisen in full force, and, as it were, *per saltum*;[10] a wide and definite difference appearing, at once, between the Ancon ram and the ordinary sheep; between the six-fingered and six-toed Gratio Kelleia and ordinary men. In neither case is it possible to point out any obvious reason for the appearance of the variety. Doubtless there were determining causes for these as for all other phaenomena; but they do not appear, and we can be tolerably certain that what are

---

9 "How to Hatch Chickens." Réaumur (1683-1757) was a French scientist and inventor.
10 Literally, at a leap; all at once.

ordinarily understood as changes in physical conditions, as in climate, in food, or the like, did not take place and had nothing to do with the matter. It was no case of what is commonly called adaptation to circumstances; but, to use a conveniently erroneous phrase, the variations arose spontaneously. The fruitless search after final causes leads their pursuers a long way; but even those hardy teleologists, who are ready to break through all the laws of physics in chase of their favourite will-o'-the-wisp, may be puzzled to discover what purpose could be attained by the stunted legs of Seth Wright's ram or the hexadactyle members of Gratio Kelleia.

Varieties then arise we know not why; and it is more than probable that the majority of varieties have arisen in this "spontaneous" manner, though we are, of course, far from denying that they may be traced, in some cases, to distinct external influences; which are assuredly competent to alter the character of the tegumentary covering, to change colour, to increase or diminish the size of muscles, to modify constitution, and, among plants, to give rise to the metamorphosis of stamens into petals, and so forth. But however they may have arisen, what especially interests us at present is, to remark that, once in existence, many varieties obey the fundamental law of reproduction that like tends to produce like; and their offspring exemplify it by tending to exhibit the same deviation from the parental stock as themselves. Indeed, there seems to be, in many instances, a prepotent influence about a newly-arisen variety which gives it what one may call an unfair advantage over the normal descendants from the same stock. This is strikingly exemplified by the case of Gratio Kelleia, who married a woman with the ordinary pentadactyle extremities, and had by her four children, Salvator, George, André, and Marie. Of these children Salvator, the eldest boy, had six fingers and six toes, like his father; the second and third, also boys, had five fingers and five toes, like their mother, though the hands and feet of George were slightly deformed. The last, a girl, had five fingers and five toes, but the thumbs were slightly deformed. The variety thus reproduced itself purely in the eldest, while the normal type reproduced itself purely in the third, and almost purely in the second and last: so that it would seem, at first, as if the normal type were more powerful than the variety. But all these children grew up and intermarried with normal wives and husband, and then, note what took place: Salvator had four children, three of whom exhibited the hexadactyle members of their grandfather and father, while the youngest had the pentadactyle limbs of the mother and grandmother; so that here, notwithstanding a double pentadactyle dilution of the blood, the hexadactyle variety had the best of it. The same pre-potency of the variety was still more markedly exemplified in the progeny of two of the other children, Marie and George. Marie (whose thumbs only were deformed) gave birth to a boy with six toes, and three other normally formed children; but George, who was not quite so pure a pentadactyle, begot, first, two girls, each of whom had six fingers and toes; then a girl with six fingers on each hand and six toes on the right foot, but only five toes on the left; and lastly, a boy with only five fingers and toes. In these instances, therefore, the variety, as it were, leaped over one generation to reproduce itself in full force in the next. Finally, the purely pentadactyle André was the father of many children, not one of whom departed from the normal parental type.

If a variation which approaches the nature of a monstrosity can strive thus forcibly to reproduce itself, it is not wonderful that less aberrant modifications should tend to be preserved even more strongly; and the history of the Ancon sheep is, in this respect, particularly instructive. With the "'cuteness" characteristic of their nation, the neighbours of the Massachusetts farmer imagined it would be an excellent thing if all his sheep were imbued with the stay-at-home tendencies enforced by Nature upon the newly-arrived ram; and they advised Wright to kill the old patriarch of his fold, and install the Ancon ram in his place. The result justified their sagacious anticipations, and coincided very nearly with what occurred to the progeny of Gratio Kelleia. The young lambs were almost always either pure Ancons, or pure ordinary sheep. But when sufficient Ancon sheep were obtained to interbreed with one another, it was found that the offspring was always pure Ancon. Colonel Humphreys, in fact, states that he was acquainted with only "one questionable case of a contrary nature." Here, then, is a remarkable and well-established instance, not only of a very distinct race being established *per saltum,* but of that race breeding "true" at once, and showing no mixed forms, even when crossed with another breed.

By taking care to select Ancons of both sexes, for breeding from, it thus became easy to establish an extremely well-marked race; so peculiar that, even when herded with other sheep, it was noted that the Ancons kept together. And there is every reason to believe that the existence of this breed might have been indefinitely protracted; but the introduction of the Merino sheep, which were not only very superior to the Ancons in wool and meat, but quite as quiet and orderly, led to the complete neglect of the new breed, so that, in 1813, Colonel Humphreys found it difficult to obtain the specimen, the skeleton of which was presented to Sir Joseph Banks. We believe that, for many years, no remnant of it has existed in the United States.

Gratio Kelleia was not the progenitor of a race of six-fingered men, as Seth Wright's ram became a nation of Ancon sheep, though the tendency of the variety to perpetuate itself appears to have been fully as strong in the one case as in the other. And the reason of the difference is not far to seek. Seth Wright took care not to weaken the Ancon blood by matching his Ancon ewes with any but males of the same variety, while Gratio Kelleia's sons were too far removed from the patriarchal times to intermarry with their sisters; and his grand-children seem not to have been attracted by their six-fingered cousins. In other words, in the one example a race was produced, because, for several generations, care was taken to *select* both parents of the breeding stock from animals exhibiting a tendency to vary in the same direction; while, in the other, no race was evolved, because no such selection was exercised. A race is a propagated variety; and as, by the laws of reproduction, offspring tend to assume the parental forms, they will be more likely to propagate a variation exhibited by both parents than that possessed by only one.

There is no organ of the body of an animal which may not, and does not, occasionally, vary more or less from the normal type; and there is no variation which may not be transmitted and which, if selectively transmitted, may not become the foundation of a race. This great truth, sometimes forgotten by philosophers, has long been familiar to practical agriculturists and breeders; and upon it rest all the methods of improving the breeds of domestic animals, which, for the last century, have been followed with so much success in England. Colour, form, size, texture of hair or wool, proportions of various parts, strength or weakness of constitution, tendency to fatten or to remain lean, to give much or little milk, speed, strength, temper, intelligence, special instincts; there is not one of these characters the transmission of which is not an every-day occurrence within the experience of cattle-breeders, stock-farmers, horse-dealers, and dog and poultry fanciers. Nay, it is only the other day that an eminent physiologist, Dr. Brown-Séquard, communicated to the Royal Society his discovery that epilepsy, artificially produced in guinea-pigs, by a means which he has discovered, is transmitted to their offspring.

But a race, once produced, is no more a fixed and immutable entity than the stock whence it sprang; variations arise among its members, and as these variations are transmitted like any others, new races may be developed out of the pre-existing one *ad infinitum,* or, at least, within any limit at present determined. Given sufficient time and sufficiently careful selection, and the multitude of races which may arise from a common stock is as astonishing as are the extreme structural differences which they may present. A remarkable example of this is to be found in the rock-pigeon, which Mr. Darwin has, in our opinion, satisfactorily demonstrated to be the progenitor of all our domestic pigeons, of which there are certainly more than a hundred well-marked races. The most noteworthy of these races are, the four great stocks known to the "fancy" as tumblers, pouters, carriers, and fantails; birds which not only differ most singularly in size, colour, and habits, but in the form of the beak and of the skull: in the proportions of the beak to the skull; in the number of tail-feathers; in the absolute and relative size of the feet; in the presence or absence of the uropygial gland; in the number of vertebrae in the back; in short, in precisely those characters in which the genera and species of birds differ from one another.

And it is most remarkable and instructive to observe, that none of these races can be shown to have been originated by the action of changes in what are commonly called external circumstances, upon the wild rock-pigeon. On the contrary, from time immemorial pigeon-fanciers have had essentially similar methods of treating their pets, which have been housed, fed, protected and cared for in much the same way in all pigeonries. In fact, there is no case better adapted than that of the pigeons to refute the doctrine which one sees put forth on high authority, that "no other characters than those founded on the development of bone for the attachment of muscles" are capable of variation. In precise contradiction of this hasty assertion, Mr. Darwin's researches prove that the skeleton of the wings in domestic pigeons has hardly varied at all from that of the wild type; while, on the other hand, it is in exactly those respects, such as the relative length of the beak and skull, the number of the vertebrae, and the number of the tail-feathers, in which muscular exertion can have no important influence, that the utmost amount of variation has taken place.

We have said that the following out of the properties exhibited by physiological species would lead us into difficulties, and at this point they begin to be obvious; for if, as the result of spontaneous variation and of selective breeding, the progeny of a common stock may become separated into groups distinguished from one another by constant, not sexual, morphological characters, it is clear that the physiological definition of species is likely to clash with the morphological definition. No one would hesitate to describe the pouter and the tumbler as distinct species, if they were found fossil, or if their skins and skeletons were imported, as those of exotic wild birds commonly are—and without doubt, if considered alone, they are good and distinct morphological species. On the other hand, they are not physiological species, for they are descended from a common stock, the rock-pigeon.

Under these circumstances, as it is admitted on all sides that races occur in Nature, how are we to know whether any apparently distinct animals are really of different physiological species, or not, seeing that the amount of morphological difference is no safe guide? Is there any test of a physiological species? The usual answer of physiologists is in the affirmative. It is said that such a test is to be found in the phaenomena of hybridisation—in the results of crossing races, as compared with the results of crossing species.

So far as the evidence goes at present, individuals, of what are certainly known to be mere races produced by selection, however distinct they may appear to be, not only breed freely together, but the offspring of such crossed races are perfectly fertile with one another. Thus, the spaniel and the greyhound, the dray-horse and the Arab, the pouter and the tumbler, breed together with perfect freedom, and their mongrels, if matched with other mongrels of the same kind, are equally fertile.

On the other hand, there can be no doubt that the individuals of many natural species are either absolutely infertile if crossed with individuals of other species, or, if they give rise to hybrid offspring, the hybrids so produced are infertile when paired together. The horse and the ass, for instance, if so crossed, give rise to the mule, and there is no certain evidence of offspring ever having been produced by a male and female mule. The unions of the rock-pigeon and the ring-pigeon appear to be equally barren of result. Here, then, says the physiologist, we have a means of distinguishing any two true species from any two varieties. If a male and a female, selected from each group, produce offspring, and that offspring is fertile with others produced in the same way, the groups are races and not species. If, on the other hand, no result ensues, or if the offspring are infertile with others produced in the same way, they are true

physiological species. The test would be an admirable one, if, in the first place, it were always practicable to apply it, and if, in the second, it always yielded results susceptible of a definite interpretation. . . .

Up to this point, we have been dealing with matters of fact, and the statements which we have laid before the reader would, to the best of our knowledge, be admitted to contain a fair exposition of what is at present known respecting the essential properties of species, by all who have studied the question. And whatever may be his theoretical views, no naturalist will probably be disposed to demur to the following summary of that exposition:—

Living beings, whether animals or plants, are divisible into multitudes of distinctly definable kinds, which are morphological species. They are also divisible into groups of individuals, which breed freely together, tending to reproduce their like, and are physiological species. Normally resembling their parents, the offspring of members of these species are still liable to vary; and the variation may be perpetuated by selection, as a race, which race, in many cases, presents all the characteristics of a morphological species. But it is not as yet proved that a race ever exhibits, when crossed with another race of the same species, those phaenomena of hybridisation which are exhibited by many species when crossed with other species. On the other hand, not only is it not proved that all species give rise to hybrids infertile *inter se,* but there is much reason to believe that, in crossing, species exhibit every gradation from perfect sterility to perfect fertility.

Such are the most essential characteristics of species. Even were man not one of them—a member of the same system and subject to the same laws—the question of their origin, their causal connexion, that is, with the other phaenomena of the universe, must have attracted his attention, as soon as his intelligence had raised itself above the level of his daily wants.

Indeed history relates that such was the case, and has embalmed for us the speculations upon the origin of living beings, which were among the earliest products of the dawning intellectual activity of man. In those early days positive knowledge was not to be had, but the craving after it needed, at all hazards, to be satisfied, and according to the country, or the turn of thought, of the speculator, the suggestion that all living things arose from the mud of the Nile, from a primeval egg, or from some more anthropomorphic agency, afforded a sufficient resting-place for his curiosity. The myths of Paganism are as dead as Osiris or Zeus, and the man who should revive them, in opposition to the knowledge of our time, would be justly laughed to scorn; but the coeval imaginations current among the rude inhabitants of Palestine, recorded by writers whose very name and age are admitted by every scholar to be unknown, have unfortunately not yet shared their fate, but, even at this day, are regarded by nine-tenths of the civilised world as the authoritative standard of fact and the criterion of the justice of scientific conclusions, in all that relates to the origin of things, and, among them, of species. In this nineteenth century, as at the dawn of modern physical science, the cosmogony of the semi-barbarous Hebrew is the incubus of the philosopher and the opprobrium of the orthodox. Who shall number the patient and earnest seekers after truth, from the days of Galileo until now, whose lives have been embittered and their good name blasted by the mistaken zeal of Bibliolaters? Who shall count the host of weaker men whose sense of truth has been destroyed in the effort to harmonise impossibilities—whose life has been wasted in the attempt to force the generous new wine of Science into the old bottles of Judaism, compelled by the outcry of the same strong party?

It is true that if philosophers have suffered, their cause has been amply avenged. Extinguished theologians lie about the cradle of every science as the strangled snakes beside that of Hercules; and history records that whenever science and orthodoxy have been fairly opposed, the latter has been forced to retire from the lists, bleeding and crushed if not annihilated; scotched, if not slain. But orthodoxy is the Bourbon[11] of the world of thought. It learns not, neither can it forget; and though, at present, bewildered and afraid to move, it is as willing as ever to insist that the first chapter of Genesis contains the beginning and the end of sound science; and to visit, with such petty thunderbolts as its half-paralysed hands can hurl, those who refuse to degrade Nature to the level of primitive Judaism.

Philosophers, on the other hand, have no such aggressive tendencies. With eyes fixed on the noble goal to which "per aspera et ardua"[12] they tend, they may, now and then, be stirred to momentary wrath by the unnecessary obstacles with which the ignorant, or the malicious, encumber, if they cannot bar, the difficult path; but why should their souls be deeply vexed? The majesty of Fact is on their side, and the elemental forces of Nature are working for them.

Not a star comes to the meridian at its calculated time but testifies to the justice of their methods—their beliefs are "one with the falling rain and with the growing corn." By doubt[13] they are established, and open inquiry is their bosom friend. Such men have no fear of traditions however venerable, and no respect for them when they become mischievous and obstructive; but they have better than mere antiquarian business in hand, and if dogmas, which ought to be fossil but are not, are not forced upon their notice, they are too happy to treat them as non-existent.

The hypotheses respecting the origin of species which profess to stand upon a scientific basis, and, as such, alone demand serious attention, are of two kinds. The one, the "special creation" hypothesis, presumes every species to have originated from one or more stocks, these not being the result of the modification of any other form of living matter—or arising by natural agencies—but being produced, as such, by a supernatural creative act.

The other, the so-called "transmutation" hypothesis, considers that all existing species are the result of the modification of pre-existing species, and those of their predecessors, by agencies similar to those which at the present day produce varieties and races, and therefore in an altogether natural way; and it is a probable, though not a necessary consequence of this hypothesis, that all living beings have arisen from a single stock. With respect to the origin of this primitive stock, or stocks, the doctrine of the origin of species is obviously not necessarily concerned. The transmutation hypothesis, for example, is perfectly consistent either with the conception of a special creation of the primitive germ, or with the supposition of its having arisen, as a modification of inorganic matter, by natural causes.

The doctrine of special creation owes its existence very largely to the supposed necessity of making science accord with the Hebrew cosmogony; but it is curious to observe that, as the doctrine is at present maintained by men of science, it is as hopelessly inconsistent with the Hebrew view as any other hypothesis.

If there be any result which has come more clearly out of geological investigation than another, it is, that the vast series of extinct animals and plants is not divisible, as it was once supposed to be, into distinct groups, separated by sharply-marked boundaries. There are no great gulfs between epochs and formations—no successive periods marked by the ap-

---

[11] The Bourbons were the ruling family of France, whose inability to change with the times eventually cost them the throne.
[12] Through bitterness and difficulty.

[13] I.e., their role is to question.

pearance of plants, of water animals, and of land animals, *en masse*. Every year adds to the list of links between what the older geologists supposed to be widely separated epochs: witness the crags linking the drift with older tertiaries; the Maestricht beds linking the tertiaries with the chalk; the St. Cassian beds exhibiting an abundant fauna of mixed mesozoic and palaeozoic types, in rocks of an epoch once supposed to be eminently poor in life; witness, lastly, the incessant disputes as to whether a given stratum shall be reckoned devonian or carboniferous, silurian or devonian, cambrian or silurian.

This truth is further illustrated in a most interesting manner by the impartial and highly competent testimony of M. Pictet, from whose calculations of what percentage of the genera of animals, existing in any formation, lived during the preceding formation, it results that in no case is the proportion less than *one-third,* or 33 per cent. It is the triassic formation, or the commencement of the mesozoic epoch, which has received the smallest inheritance from preceding ages. The other formations not uncommonly exhibit 60, 80, or even 94 per cent. of genera in common with those whose remains are imbedded in their predecessor. Not only is this true, but the subdivisions of each formation exhibit new species characteristic of, and found only in, them; and, in many cases, as in the lias for example, the separate beds of these subdivisions are distinguished by well-marked and peculiar forms of life. A section, a hundred feet thick, will exhibit, at different heights, a dozen species of ammonite, none of which passes beyond its particular zone of limestone, or clay, into the zone below it or into that above it; so that those who adopt the doctrine of special creation must be prepared to admit, that at intervals of time, corresponding with the thickness of these beds, the Creator thought fit to interfere with the natural course of events for the purpose of making a new ammonite. It is not easy to transplant oneself into the frame of mind of those who can accept such a conclusion as this, on any evidence short of absolute demonstration; and it is difficult to see what is to be gained by so doing, since, as we have said, it is obvious that such a view of the origin of living beings is utterly opposed to the Hebrew cosmogony. Deserving no aid from the powerful arm of Bibliolatry, then, does the received form of the hypothesis of special creation derive any support from science or sound logic? Assuredly not much. The arguments brought forward in its favour all take one form: If species were not supernaturally created, we cannot understand the facts *x,* or *y,* or *z;* we cannot understand the structure of animals or plants, unless we suppose they were contrived for special ends; we cannot understand the structure of the eye, except by supposing it to have been made to see with; we cannot understand instincts, unless we suppose animals to have been miraculously endowed with them.

As a question of dialectics, it must be admitted that this sort of reasoning is not very formidable to those who are not to be frightened by consequences. It is an *argumentum ad ignorantiam*—take this explanation or be ignorant. But suppose we prefer to admit our ignorance rather than adopt a hypothesis at variance with all the teachings of Nature? Or, suppose for a moment we admit the explanation, and then seriously ask ourselves how much the wiser are we; what does the explanation explain? Is it any more than a grandiloquent way of announcing the fact, that we really know nothing about the matter? A phaenomenon is explained when it is shown to be a case of some general law of Nature; but the supernatural interposition of the Creator can, by the nature of the case, exemplify no law, and if species have really arisen in this way, it is absurd to attempt to discuss their origin.

Or, lastly, let us ask ourselves whether any amount of evidence which the nature of our faculties permits us to attain, can justify us in asserting that any phaenomenon is out of the reach of natural causation. To this end it is obviously necessary that we should know all the consequences to which all possible combinations, continued through unlimited time, can give rise. If we knew these, and found none competent to originate species, we should have good ground for denying their origin by natural causation. Till we know them, any hypothesis is better than one which involves us in such miserable presumption.

But the hypothesis of special creation is not only a mere specious mask for our ignorance; its existence in Biology marks the youth and imperfection of the science. For what is the history of every science but the history of the elimination of the notion of creative, or other interferences, with the natural order of the phaenomena which are the subject-matter of that science? When Astronomy was young "the morning stars sang together for joy," and the planets were guided in their courses by celestial hands. Now, the harmony of the stars has resolved itself into gravitation according to the inverse squares of the distances, and the orbits of the planets are deducible from the laws of the forces which allow a schoolboy's stone to break a window. The lightning was the angel of the Lord; but it has pleased Providence, in these modern times, that science should make it the humble messenger of man, and we know that every flash that shimmers about the horizon on a summer's evening is determined by ascertainable conditions, and that its direction and brightness might, if our knowledge of these were great enough, have been calculated.

The solvency of great mercantile companies rests on the validity of the laws which have been ascertained to govern the seeming irregularity of that human life which the moralist bewails as the most uncertain of things; plague, pestilence, and famine are admitted, by all but fools, to be the natural result of causes for the most part fully within human control, and not the unavoidable tortures inflicted by wrathful Omnipotence upon His helpless handiwork.

Harmonious order governing eternally continuous progress—the web and woof of matter and force interweaving by slow degrees, without a broken thread, that veil which lies between us and the Infinite—that universe which alone we know or can know; such is the picture which science draws of the world, and in proportion as any part of that picture is in unison with the rest, so may we feel sure that it is rightly painted. Shall Biology alone remain out of harmony with her sister sciences?

Such arguments against the hypothesis of the direct creation of species as these are plainly enough deducible from general considerations; but there are, in addition, phaenomena exhibited by species themselves, and yet not so much a part of their very essence as to have required earlier mention, which are in the highest degree perplexing, if we adopt the popularly accepted hypothesis. Such are the facts of distribution in space and in time; the singular phaenomena brought to light by the study of development; the structural relations of species upon which our systems of classification are founded; the great doctrines of philosophical anatomy, such as that of homology, or of the community of structural plan exhibited by large groups of species differing very widely in their habits and functions.

The species of animals which inhabit the sea on opposite sides of the isthmus of Panama are wholly distinct;[14] the animals and plants which inhabit islands are commonly distinct from those of the neighbouring mainlands, and yet have a similarity of aspect. The mammals of the latest tertiary epoch in the Old and New Worlds belong to the same genera, or family groups, as those which now inhabit the same great geographical area. The crocodilian reptiles which existed in the earliest secondary epoch were similar in general structure to those now living, but exhibit slight differences in their vertebrae, nasal passages, and one or two other points. The guineapig has teeth which are shed before it is born, and hence can never subserve the masticatory purpose for which they seem contrived, and, in like manner, the female dugong has tusks which never cut the gum. All the members of the same great group run through similar conditions in their development, and all their parts, in the adult state, are arranged according to the same plan. Man is more like a gorilla than a gorilla is like a lemur. Such are a few, taken at random, among the multitudes of similar facts which modern research has established; but when the student seeks for an explanation of them from the supporters of the received hypothesis of the origin of species, the reply he receives is, in substance, of Oriental simplicity and brevity—"Mashallah! it so pleases God!" There are different species on opposite sides of the isthmus of Panama, because they were created different on the two sides. The pliocene mammals are like the existing ones, because such was the plan of creation; and we find rudimental organs and similarity of plan, because it has pleased the Creator to set before Himself a "divine exemplar or archetype," and to copy it in His works; and somewhat ill, those who hold this view imply, in some of them. That such verbal hocus-pocus should be received as science will one day be regarded as evidence of the low state of intelligence in the nineteenth century, just as we amuse ourselves with the phraseology about Nature's abhorrence of a vacuum, wherewith Torricelli's[15] compatriots were satisfied to explain the rise of water in a pump. And be it recollected that this sort of satisfaction works not only negative but positive ill, by discouraging inquiry, and so depriving man of the usufruct of one of the most fertile fields of his great patrimony, Nature.

The objections to the doctrine of the origin of species by special creation which have been detailed, must have occurred, with more or less force, to the mind of every one who has seriously and independently considered the subject. It is therefore no wonder that, from time to time, this hypothesis should have been met by counter hypotheses, all as well, and some better founded than itself; and it is curious to remark that the inventors of the opposing views seem to have been led into them as much by their knowledge of geology, as by their acquaintance

14 "Recent investigations tend to show that this statement is not strictly accurate." (Huxley, 1870)

15 Italian physicist (1608–47) who discovered the principle of the barometer.

with biology. In fact, when the mind has once admitted the conception of the gradual production of the present physical state of our globe, by natural causes operating through long ages of time, it will be little disposed to allow that living beings have made their appearance in another way. . . .

Impelled towards the hypothesis of the transmutation of species, partly by his general cosmological and geological views; partly by the conception of a graduated, though irregularly branching, scale of being, which had arisen out of his profound study of plants and of the lower forms of animal life, Lamarck,[16] whose general line of thought often closely resembles that of De Maillet,[17] made a great advance upon the crude and merely speculative manner in which that writer deals with the question of the origin of living beings, by endeavouring to find physical causes competent to effect that change of one species into another, which De Maillet had only supposed to occur. And Lamarck conceived that he had found in Nature such causes, amply sufficient for the purpose in view. It is a physiological fact, he says, that organs are increased in size by action, atrophied by inaction; it is another physiological fact that modifications produced are transmissible to offspring. Change the actions of an animal, therefore, and you will change its structure, by increasing the development of the parts newly brought into use and by the diminution of those less used; but by altering the circumstances which surround it you will alter its actions, and hence, in the long run, change of circumstance must produce change of organisation. All the species of animals, therefore, are, in Lamarck's view, the result of the indirect action of changes of circumstance, upon those primitive germs which he considered to have originally arisen, by spontaneous generation, within the waters of the globe. It is curious, however, that Lamarck should insist so strongly as he has done, that circumstances never in any degree directly modify the form or the organisation of animals, but only operate by changing their wants and consequently their actions; for he thereby brings upon himself the obvious question, How, then, do plants, which cannot be said to have wants or actions, become modified? To this he replies, that they are modified by the changes in their nutritive processes, which are effected by changing circumstances; and it does not seem to have occurred to him that such changes might be as well supposed to take place among animals.

When we have said that Lamarck felt that mere speculation was not the way to arrive at the origin of species, but that it was necessary, in order to the establishment of any sound theory on the subject, to discover by observation or otherwise, some *vera causa*,[18] competent to give rise to them; that he affirmed the true order of classification to coincide with the order of their development one from another; that he insisted on the necessity of allowing sufficient time, very strongly; and that all the varieties of instinct and reason were traced back by him to the same cause as that which has given rise to species, we have enumerated his chief contributions to the advance of the question. On the other hand, from his ignorance of any power in Nature competent to modify the structure of animals, except the development of parts, or atrophy of them, in consequence of a change of needs, Lamarck was led to attach infinitely greater weight than it deserves to this agency, and the absurdities into which he was led have met with deserved condemnation. Of the struggle for existence, on which, as we shall see, Mr. Darwin lays such great stress, he had no conception; indeed, he doubts whether there really are such things as extinct species, unless they be such large animals as may have met their death at the hands of man; and so little does he dream of there being any other destructive causes at work, that, in discussing the possible existence of fossil shells, he asks, "Pourquoi d'ailleurs seroient-ils perdues dès que l'homme n'a pu opérer leur destruction?"[19] ("Phil. Zool.," vol. i. p. 77.) Of the influence of selection Lamarck has as little notion, and he makes no use of the wonderful phaenomena which are exhibited by domesticated animals, and illustrate its powers. The vast influence of Cuvier[20] was employed against the Lamarckian views, and, as the untenability of some of his conclusions was easily shown, his doctrines sank under the opprobrium of scientific, as well as of theological, heterodoxy. Nor have the efforts made of late years to revive them tended to re-establish their credit in the minds of sound thinkers acquainted with the facts of the case; indeed it may be doubted whether Lamarck has not suffered more from his friends than from his foes.

Two years ago, in fact, though we venture to question if even the strongest supporters of the

---

16 Jean Baptiste Lamarck (1744–1829), celebrated French naturalist, one of the founders of the doctrine of biological evolution.

17 Benoît de Maillet, French consul-general in Egypt, whose speculations on the origin of the earth and its inhabitants were published anonymously in 1748.

18 True cause.

19 "Besides, why should they have been lost since man could not have brought about their destruction?"

20 Georges Cuvier (1769–1832), French naturalist, founder of the science of comparative anatomy.

special creation hypothesis had not, now and then, an uneasy consciousness that all was not right, their position seemed more impregnable than ever, if not by its own inherent strength, at any rate by the obvious failure of all the attempts which had been made to carry it. On the other hand, however much the few, who thought deeply on the question of species, might be repelled by the generally received dogmas, they saw no way of escaping from them save by the adoption of suppositions so little justified by experiment or by observation as to be at least equally distasteful.

The choice lay between two absurdities and a middle condition of uneasy scepticism; which last, however unpleasant and unsatisfactory, was obviously the only justifiable state of mind under the circumstances.

Such being the general ferment in the minds of naturalists, it is no wonder that they mustered strong in the rooms of the Linnaean Society, on the 1st of July of the year 1858,[21] to hear two papers by authors living on opposite sides of the globe, working out their results independently, and yet professing to have discovered one and the same solution of all the problems connected with species. The one of these authors was an able naturalist, Mr. Wallace,[22] who had been employed for some years in studying the productions of the islands of the Indian Archipelago, and who had forwarded a memoir embodying his views to Mr. Darwin, for communication to the Linnaean Society. On perusing the essay, Mr. Darwin was not a little surprised to find that it embodied some of the leading ideas of a great work which he had been preparing for twenty years, and parts of which, containing a development of the very same views, had been perused by his private friends fifteen or sixteen years before. Perplexed in what manner to do full justice both to his friend and to himself, Mr. Darwin placed the matter in the hands of Dr. Hooker and Sir Charles Lyell, by whose advice he communicated a brief abstract of his own views to the Linnaean Society, at the same time that Mr. Wallace's paper was read. Of that abstract, the work on the "Origin of Species" is an enlargement; but a complete statement of Mr. Darwin's doctrine is looked for in the large and well-illustrated work which he is said to be preparing for publication.

The Darwinian hypothesis has the merit of being eminently simple and comprehensible in principle, and its essential positions may be stated in a very few words: all species have been produced by the development of varieties from common stocks; by the conversion of these, first into permanent races and then into new species, by the process of *natural selection*, which process is essentially identical with that artificial selection by which man has originated the races of domestic animals—the *struggle for existence* taking the place of man, and exerting, in the case of natural selection, that selective action which he performs in artificial selection.

The evidence brought forward by Mr. Darwin in support of his hypothesis is of three kinds. First, he endeavours to prove that species may be originated by selection; secondly, he attempts to show that natural causes are competent to exert selection; and thirdly, he tries to prove that the most remarkable and apparently anomalous phaenomena exhibited by the distribution, development, and mutual relations of species, can be shown to be deducible from the general doctrine of their origin, which he propounds, combined with the known facts of geological change; and that, even if all these phaenomena are not at present explicable by it, none are necessarily inconsistent with it.

There cannot be a doubt that the method of inquiry which Mr. Darwin has adopted is not only rigorously in accordance with the canons of scientific logic, but that it is the only adequate method. Critics exclusively trained in classics or in mathematics, who have never determined a scientific fact in their lives by induction from experiment or observation, prate learnedly about Mr. Darwin's method, which is not inductive enough, not Baconian enough, forsooth, for them. But even if practical acquaintance with the process of scientific investigation is denied them, they may learn, by the perusal of Mr. Mill's admirable chapter "On the Deductive Method,"[23] that there are multitudes of scientific inquiries in which the method of pure induction helps the investigator but a very little way.

"The mode of investigation," says Mr. Mill, "which, from the proved inapplicability of direct methods of observation and experiment, remains to us as the main source of the knowledge we possess, or can acquire, respecting the conditions and laws of recurrence of the more complex phaenomena, is called, in its most general expression, the deductive method, and consists of three operations: the first, one of direct induction; the second, of ratiocination; and the third, of verification."

Now, the conditions which have determined the existence of species are not only exceedingly complex, but, so far as the great majority of them are

---

[21] See p. 602, note 6.
[22] Alfred Russell Wallace (1823–1913).

[23] In John Stuart Mill's *System of Logic* (1843).

concerned, are necessarily beyond our cognisance. But what Mr. Darwin has attempted to do is in exact accordance with the rule laid down by Mr. Mill; he has endeavoured to determine certain great facts inductively, by observation and experiment; he has then reasoned from the data thus furnished; and lastly, he has tested the validity of his ratiocination by comparing his deductions with the observed facts of Nature. Inductively, Mr. Darwin endeavours to prove that species arise in a given way. Deductively, he desires to show that, if they arise in that way, the facts of distribution, development, classification, &c., may be accounted for, *i.e.* may be deduced from their mode of origin, combined with admitted changes in physical geography and climate, during an indefinite period. And this explanation, or coincidence of observed with deduced facts, is, so far as it extends, a verification of the Darwinian view.

There is no fault to be found with Mr. Darwin's method, then; but it is another question whether he has fulfilled all the conditions imposed by that method. Is it satisfactorily proved, in fact, that species may be originated by selection? that there is such a thing as natural selection? that none of the phaenomena exhibited by species are inconsistent with the origin of species in this way? If these questions can be answered in the affirmative, Mr. Darwin's view steps out of the rank of hypotheses into those of proved theories; but, so long as the evidence at present adduced falls short of enforcing that affirmation, so long, to our minds, must the new doctrine be content to remain among the former—an extremely valuable, and in the highest degree probable, doctrine, indeed the only extant hypothesis which is worth anything in a scientific point of view; but still a hypothesis, and not yet the theory of species.

After much consideration, and with assuredly no bias against Mr. Darwin's views, it is our clear conviction that, as the evidence stands, it is not absolutely proven that a group of animals, having all the characters exhibited by species in Nature, has ever been originated by selection, whether artificial or natural. Groups having the morphological character of species—distinct and permanent races in fact— have been so produced over and over again; but there is no positive evidence, at present, that any group of animals has, by variation and selective breeding, given rise to another group which was, even in the least degree, infertile with the first. Mr. Darwin is perfectly aware of this weak point, and brings forward a multitude of ingenious and important arguments to diminish the force of the objection. We admit the value of these arguments to

their fullest extent; nay, we will go so far as to express our belief that experiments, conducted by a skilful physiologist, would very probably obtain the desired production of mutually more or less infertile breeds from a common stock, in a comparatively few years; but still, as the case stands at present, this "little rift within the lute"[24] is not to be disguised nor overlooked.

In the remainder of Mr. Darwin's argument our own private ingenuity has not hitherto enabled us to pick holes of any great importance; and judging by what we hear and read, other adventurers in the same field do not seem to have been much more fortunate. It has been urged, for instance, that in his chapters on the struggle for existence and on natural selection, Mr. Darwin does not so much prove that natural selection does occur, as that it must occur; but, in fact, no other sort of demonstration is attainable. A race does not attract our attention in Nature until it has, in all probability, existed for a considerable time, and then it is too late to inquire into the conditions of its origin. Again, it is said that there is no real analogy between the selection which takes place under domestication, by human influence, and any operation which can be effected by Nature, for man interferes intelligently. Reduced to its elements, this argument implies that an effect produced with trouble by an intelligent agent must, *a fortiori*,[25] be more troublesome, if not impossible, to an unintelligent agent. Even putting aside the question whether Nature, acting as she does according to definite and invariable laws, can be rightly called an unintelligent agent, such a position as this is wholly untenable. Mix salt and sand, and it shall puzzle the wisest of men, with his mere natural appliances, to separate all the grains of sand from all the grains of salt; but a shower of rain will effect the same object in ten minutes. And so, while man may find it tax all his intelligence to separate any variety which arises, and to breed selectively from it, the destructive agencies incessantly at work in Nature, if they find one variety to be more soluble in circumstances than the other, will inevitably, in the long run, eliminate it.

A frequent and a just objection to the Lamarckian hypothesis of the transmutation of species is based upon the absence of transitional forms between many species. But against the Darwinian hypothesis this argument has no force. Indeed, one of the most valuable and suggestive parts of Mr. Darwin's work

---

24 I.e., flaw in the argument.
25 With stronger reason.

is that in which he proves, that the frequent absence of transitions is a necessary consequence of his doctrine, and that the stock whence two or more species have sprung, need in no respect be intermediate between these species. If any two species have arisen from a common stock in the same way as the carrier and the pouter, say, have arisen from the rock-pigeon, then the common stock of these two species need be no more intermediate between the two than the rock-pigeon is between the carrier and pouter. Clearly appreciate the force of this analogy, and all the arguments against the origin of species by selection, based on the absence of transitional forms, fall to the ground. And Mr. Darwin's position might, we think, have been even stronger than it is if he had not embarrassed himself with the aphorism, "*Natura non facit saltum*,"[26] which turns up so often in his pages. We believe, as we have said above, that Nature does make jumps now and then, and a recognition of the fact is of no small importance in disposing of many minor objections to the doctrine of transmutation.

But we must pause. The discussion of Mr. Darwin's arguments in detail would lead us far beyond the limits within which we proposed, at starting, to confine this article. Our object has been attained if we have given an intelligible, however brief, account of the established facts connected with species, and of the relation of the explanation of those facts offered by Mr. Darwin to the theoretical views held by his predecessors and his contemporaries, and, above all, to the requirements of scientific logic. We have ventured to point out that it does not, as yet, satisfy all those requirements; but we do not hesitate to assert that it is as superior to any preceding or contemporary hypothesis, in the extent of observational and experimental basis on which it rests, in its rigorously scientific method, and in its power of explaining biological phaenomena, as was the hypothesis of Copernicus to the speculations of Ptolemy.[27] But the planetary orbits turned out to be not quite circular after all, and, grand as was the service Copernicus rendered to science, Kepler and Newton had to come after him. What if the orbit of Darwinism should be a little too circular? What if species should offer residual phaenomena, here and there, not explicable by natural selection? Twenty years hence naturalists may be in a position to say whether this is, or is not, the case; but in either event they will owe the author of "The Origin of Species" an immense debt of gratitude. We should leave a very wrong impression on the reader's mind if we permitted him to suppose that the value of that work depends wholly on the ultimate justification of the theoretical views which it contains. On the contrary, if they were disproved to-morrow, the book would still be the best of its kind—the most compendious statement of well-sifted facts bearing on the doctrine of species that has ever appeared. The chapters on Variation, on the Struggle for Existence, on Instinct, on Hybridism, on the Imperfection of the Geological Record, on Geographical Distribution, have not only no equals, but, so far as our knowledge goes, no competitors, within the range of biological literature. And viewed as a whole, we do not believe that, since the publication of Von Baer's "Researches on Development," thirty years ago, any work has appeared calculated to exert so large an influence, not only on the future of Biology, but in extending the domination of Science over regions of thought into which she has, as yet, hardly penetrated.

from ESSAYS UPON SOME CONTROVERTED QUESTIONS[1]

PROLOGUE

Le plus grand service qu'on puisse rendre à la science est d'y faire place nette avant d'y rien construire.—CUVIER.[2]

MOST of the Essays comprised in the present volume have been written during the last six or seven years, without premeditated purpose or intentional connection, in reply to attacks upon doctrines which I hold to be well founded; or in refutation of allegations respecting matters lying within the province of natural knowledge, which I believe to be erroneous; and they bear the mark of their origin in the controversial tone which pervades them.

[26] Nature does not make jumps. See above, pp. 613–14.

[27] A tremendous step forward was taken when Copernicus proved (1543) that Ptolemy was mistaken in thinking that the earth was the center of the universe.

[1] This volume (1892) was later expanded into two books, *Science and Hebrew Tradition* and *Science and Christian Tradition*. The "Prologue" was then reprinted in the latter.

[2] "The greatest service one can render to knowledge is to clear the ground before starting to build anything." On Cuvier see p. 620, note 20, above.

Of polemical writing, as of other kinds of warfare, I think it may be said, that it is often useful, sometimes necessary, and always more or less of an evil. It is useful, when it attracts attention to topics which might otherwise be neglected; and when, as does sometimes happen, those who come to see a contest remain to think. It is necessary, when the interests of truth and of justice are at stake. It is an evil, in so far as controversy always tends to degenerate into quarrelling, to swerve from the great issue of what is right and what is wrong to the very small question of who is right and who is wrong. I venture to hope that the useful and the necessary were more conspicuous than the evil attributes of literary militancy, when these papers were first published; but I have had some hesitation about reprinting them. If I may judge by my own taste, few literary dishes are less appetising than cold controversy; moreover, there is an air of unfairness about the presentation of only one side of a discussion, and a flavour of unkindness in the reproduction of "winged words," which, however appropriate at the time of their utterance, would find a still more appropriate place in oblivion. Yet, since I could hardly ask those who have honoured me by their polemical attentions to confer lustre on this collection, by permitting me to present their lucubrations along with my own; and since it would be a manifest wrong to them to deprive their, by no means rare, vivacities of language of such justification as they may derive from similar freedoms on my part; I came to the conclusion that my best course was to leave the essays just as they were written; assuring my honourable adversaries that any heat of which signs may remain was generated, in accordance with the law of the conservation of energy, by the force of their own blows, and has long since been dissipated into space.

But, however the polemical concomitants of these discussions may be regarded—or better, disregarded —there is no doubt either about the importance of the topics of which they treat, or as to the public interest in the "Controverted Questions" with which they deal. Or rather, the Controverted Question; for disconnected as these pieces may, perhaps, appear to be, they are, in fact, concerned only with different aspects of a single problem, with which thinking men have been occupied, ever since they began seriously to consider the wonderful frame of things in which their lives are set, and to seek for trustworthy guidance among its intricacies.

Experience speedily taught them that the shifting scenes of the world's stage have a permanent background; that there is order amidst the seeming con-fusion, and that many events take place according to unchanging rules. To this region of familiar steadiness and customary regularity they gave the name of Nature. But, at the same time, their infantile and untutored reason, little more, as yet, than the play-fellow of the imagination, led them to believe that this tangible, commonplace, orderly world of Nature was surrounded and interpenetrated by another intangible and mysterious world, no more bound by fixed rules than, as they fancied, were the thoughts and passions which coursed through their minds and seemed to exercise an intermittent and capricious rule over their bodies. They attributed to the entities, with which they peopled this dim and dreadful region, an unlimited amount of that power of modifying the course of events of which they themselves possessed a small share, and thus came to regard them as not merely beyond, but above, Nature.

Hence arose the conception of a "Supernature" antithetic to "Nature"—the primitive dualism of a natural world "fixed in fate" and a supernatural, left to the free play of volition—which has pervaded all later speculation and, for thousands of years, has exercised a profound influence on practice. For it is obvious that, on this theory of the Universe, the successful conduct of life must demand careful attention to both worlds; and, if either is to be neglected, it may be safer that it should be Nature. In any given contingency, it must doubtless be desirable to know what may be expected to happen in the ordinary course of things; but it must be quite as necessary to have some inkling of the line likely to be taken by supernatural agencies able, and possibly willing, to suspend or reverse that course. Indeed, logically developed, the dualistic theory must needs end in almost exclusive attention to Supernature, and in trust that its over-ruling strength will be exerted in favour of those who stand well with its denizens. On the other hand, the lessons of the great schoolmaster, experience, have hardly seemed to accord with this conclusion. They have taught, with considerable emphasis, that it does not answer to neglect Nature; and that, on the whole, the more attention paid to her dictates the better men fare.

Thus the theoretical antithesis brought about a practical antagonism. From the earliest times of which we have any knowledge, Naturalism and Supernaturalism have consciously, or unconsciously, competed and struggled with one another; and the varying fortunes of the contest are written in the records of the course of civilisation, from those of Egypt and Babylonia, six thousand years ago, down to those of our own time and people.

OLIVER TWIST

This enormously popular novel appeared in 1837-38, when Dickens was in his middle twenties. It was liberally illustrated by George Cruikshank, the most famous contemporary book-illustrator. Cruikshank (1792-1878), gifted as a humorist and caricaturist, was also a serious interpreter of the degradation of the London slums. The frontispiece shown to the right portrays the famous episode in which Bill Sikes meets his death. (Harvard College Library)

OLIVER TWIST;

OR, THE

PARISH BOY'S PROGRESS.

BY "BOZ."

IN THREE VOLUMES.

VOL. III.

LONDON:
RICHARD BENTLEY, NEW BURLINGTON STREET
1838.

THE OPENING OF THE GREAT INDUSTRIAL EXHIBITION OF ALL NATIONS.
BY HER MOST GRACIOUS MAJESTY QUEEN VICTORIA AND HIS ROYAL HIGHNESS PRINCE ALBERT, ON THE 1ST OF MAY, 1851.

THE EXHIBITION OF 1851

Cruikshank's engraving of the scene in the Crystal Palace when the Industrial Exhibition was opened by Queen Victoria and Prince Albert. The display of England's industrial achievement made an immense impression on the 6,039,195 persons who visited the fair. Here "the Archbishop is offering up a Prayer for the Divine blessing upon the objects of this Great Exhibition." (Boston Public Library)

Duke Street

Feet 100 50 0 100

Woodstock Road

Feet 100 50 0 100

WORKERS' HOUSING IN LIVERPOOL

When population figures began to soar in this industrial city at the end of the eighteenth century, many landlords increased their revenue by cramming their back yards with cabins, leaving only narrow courts for access (right, figure 1); and this back-to-back arrangement served as the model for many new tenements (figure 2). By 1840, a fifth of the city's population of 300,000 lived in such dark, insanitary blocks. A start toward improvement was made in 1842 with an Act which stipulated that the court must be at least 15 feet wide, though the entrance might be as narrow as 5 feet (figure 3). Above, a photograph made in 1924 shows a Victorian slum still standing. (Director of Housing, Liverpool)

Graveyard

St Augustine Street

Blenheim Street   Ashfield Street

Ft. 100 50 0 100

MILLWORKERS' DWELLINGS IN BURNLEY, LANCASHIRE

By the end of the century considerable improvement had been made in industrial housing, but even today monotony and crowding continue to dominate many populous areas. (Aero Pictorial Ltd.)

These records inform us that, so far as men have paid attention to Nature, they have been rewarded for their pains. They have developed the Arts which have furnished the conditions of civilised existence; and the Sciences, which have been a progressive revelation of reality and have afforded the best discipline of the mind in the methods of discovering truth. They have accumulated a vast body of universally accepted knowledge; and the conceptions of man and of society, of morals and of law, based upon that knowledge, are every day more and more, either openly or tacitly, acknowledged to be the foundations of right action.

History also tells us that the field of the supernatural has rewarded its cultivators with a harvest, perhaps not less luxuriant, but of a different character. It has produced an almost infinite diversity of Religions. These, if we set aside the ethical concomitants upon which natural knowledge also has a claim, are composed of information about Supernature; they tell us of the attributes of supernatural beings, of their relations with Nature, and of the operations by which their interference with the ordinary course of events can be secured or averted. It does not appear, however, that supernaturalists have attained to any agreement about these matters, or that history indicates a widening of the influence of supernaturalism on practice, with the onward flow of time. On the contrary, the various religions are, to a great extent, mutually exclusive; and their adherents delight in charging each other, not merely with error, but with criminality, deserving and ensuing[3] punishment of infinite severity. In singular contrast with natural knowledge, again, the acquaintance of mankind with the supernatural appears the more extensive and the more exact, and the influence of supernatural doctrines upon conduct the greater, the further back we go in time and the lower the stage of civilisation submitted to investigation. Historically, indeed, there would seem to be an inverse relation between supernatural and natural knowledge. As the latter has widened, gained in precision and in trustworthiness, so has the former shrunk, grown vague and questionable; as the one has more and more filled the sphere of action, so has the other retreated into the region of meditation, or vanished behind the screen of mere verbal recognition.

Whether this difference of the fortunes of Naturalism and of Supernaturalism is an indication of the progress, or of the regress, of humanity; of a fall from, or an advance towards, the higher life; is a matter of opinion. The point to which I wish to direct attention is that the difference exists and is making itself felt. Men are growing to be seriously alive to the fact that the historical evolution of humanity, which is generally, and I venture to think not unreasonably, regarded as progress, has been, and is being, accompanied by a co-ordinate elimination of the supernatural from its originally large occupation of men's thoughts. The question—How far is this process to go?—is, in my apprehension, the Controverted Question of our time. . . .[4]

My memory, unfortunately, carries me back to the fourth decade of the nineteenth century, when the evangelical flood had a little abated and the tops of certain mountains were soon to appear, chiefly in the neighbourhood of Oxford; but when nevertheless, bibliolatry was rampant; when church and chapel alike proclaimed, as the oracles of God, the crude assumptions of the worst informed and, in natural sequence, the most presumptuously bigoted, of all theological schools.

In accordance with promises made on my behalf, but certainly without my authorisation, I was very early taken to hear "sermons in the vulgar tongue." And vulgar enough often was the tongue in which some preacher, ignorant alike of literature, of history, of science, and even of theology, outside that patronised by his own narrow school, poured forth, from the safe entrenchment of the pulpit, invectives against those who deviated from his notion of orthodoxy. From dark allusions to "sceptics" and "infidels," I became aware of the existence of people who trusted in carnal reason; who audaciously doubted that the world was made in six natural days, or that the deluge was universal; perhaps even went so far as to question the literal accuracy of the story of Eve's temptation, or of Balaam's ass; and, from the horror of the tones in which they were mentioned, I should have been justified in drawing the conclusion that these rash men belonged to the criminal classes. At the same time, those who were more directly responsible for providing me with the knowledge essential to the right guidance of life (and who sincerely desired to do so), imagined they were discharging that most sacred duty by impressing upon my childish mind

---

[3] Bringing about as a consequence.

[4] The passage which has been omitted here gives a summary historical account of the various manifestations of belief in the supernatural, culminating in the Methodist and Evangelical movements of the late eighteenth century.

the necessity, on pain of reprobation in this world and damnation in the next, of accepting, in the strict and literal sense, every statement contained in the Protestant Bible. I was told to believe, and I did believe, that doubt about any of them was a sin, not less reprehensible than a moral delict. I suppose that, out of a thousand of my contemporaries, nine hundred, at least, had their minds systematically warped and poisoned, in the name of the God of truth, by like discipline. I am sure that, even a score of years later, those who ventured to question the exact historical accuracy of any part of the Old Testament and *a fortiori*[5] of the Gospels, had to expect a pitiless shower of verbal missiles, to say nothing of the other disagreeable consequences which visit those who, in any way, run counter to that chaos of prejudices called public opinion. . . .

Among the watchers of the course of the world of thought, some view with delight and some with horror, the recrudescence of Supernaturalism which manifests itself among us, in shapes ranged along the whole flight of steps, which, in this case, separates the sublime from the ridiculous—from Neo-Catholicism and Inner-light mysticism,[6] at the top, to unclean things, not worthy of mention in the same breath, at the bottom. In my poor opinion, the importance of these manifestations is often greatly over-estimated. The extant forms of Supernaturalism have deep roots in human nature, and will undoubtedly die hard; but, in these latter days, they have to cope with an enemy whose full strength is only just beginning to be put out, and whose forces, gathering strength year by year, are hemming them round on every side. This enemy is Science, in the acceptation of systematised natural knowledge, which, during the last two centuries, has extended those methods of investigation, the worth of which is confirmed by daily appeal to Nature, to every region in which the Supernatural has hitherto been recognised.

When scientific historical criticism reduced the annals of heroic Greece and of regal Rome to the level of fables; when the unity of authorship of the *Iliad* was successfully assailed by scientific literary criticism; when scientific physical criticism, after exploding the geocentric theory of the universe and reducing the solar system itself to one of millions of groups of like cosmic specks, circling, at unimaginable distances from one another through infinite space, showed the supernaturalistic theories of the duration of the earth and of life upon it, to be as inadequate as those of its relative dimensions and importance had been; it needed no prophetic gift to see that, sooner or later, the Jewish and the early Christian records would be treated in the same manner; that the authorship of the Hexateuch[7] and of the Gospels would be as severely tested; and that the evidence in favour of the veracity of many of the statements found in the Scriptures would have to be strong indeed, if they were to be opposed to the conclusions of physical science. In point of fact, so far as I can discover, no one competent to judge of the evidential strength of these conclusions, ventures now to say that the biblical accounts of the creation and of the deluge are true in the natural sense of the words of the narratives. The most modern Reconcilers venture upon is to affirm, that some quite different sense may be put upon the words; and that this non-natural sense may, with a little trouble, be manipulated into some sort of non-contradiction of scientific truth.

My purpose, in the essay (XVI.) which treats of the narrative of the Deluge, was to prove, by physical criticism, that no such event as that described ever took place; to exhibit the untrustworthy character of the narrative demonstrated by literary criticism; and, finally, to account for its origin, by producing a form of those ancient legends of pagan Chaldaea, from which the biblical compilation is manifestly derived. I have yet to learn that the main propositions of this essay can be seriously challenged.

In the essays (II., III.) on the narrative of the Creation, I have endeavoured to controvert the assertion that modern science supports, either the interpretation put upon it by Mr. Gladstone,[8] or any interpretation which is compatible with the general sense of the narrative, quite apart from particular details. The first chapter of Genesis teaches the supernatural creation of the present forms of life; modern science teaches that they have come about by evolution. The first chapter of Genesis teaches the successive origin—firstly, of all the plants, secondly, of all the aquatic and aerial animals, thirdly, of all the terrestrial animals,

---

[5] Even more so.

[6] Neo-Catholicism was the movement inaugurated by Newman towards repudiating the Protestant Reformation and stressing instead the affinity of the English Church with that of Rome. Huxley discusses the movement in the passage which has been omitted just above. Inner-light mysticism was the position of such extreme Protestant sects as the Quakers, who rejected the authority of both the Bible and the Church in favor of guidance by divine inspiration.

[7] The first six books of the Bible.

[8] The great political leader of the liberal party in Victorian England. In 1885 he attempted to prove that the order of creation given in Genesis is supported by the evidence of science.

which now exist—during distinct intervals of time; modern science teaches that, throughout all the duration of an immensely long past, so far as we have any adequate knowledge of it (that is as far back as the Silurian epoch), plants, aquatic, aerial, and terrestrial animals have co-existed; that the earliest known are unlike those which at present exist; and that the modern species have come into existence as the last terms of a series, the members of which have appeared one after another. Thus, far from confirming the account in Genesis, the results of modern science, so far as they go, are in principle, as in detail, hopelessly discordant with it.

Yet, if the pretensions to infallibility set up, not by the ancient Hebrew writings themselves, but by the ecclesiastical champions and friends from whom they may well pray to be delivered, thus shatter themselves against the rock of natural knowledge, in respect of the two most important of all events, the origin of things and the palingenesis of terrestrial life,[9] what historical credit dare any serious thinker attach to the narratives of the fabrication of Eve, of the Fall, of the commerce between the *Bene Elohim*[10] and the daughters of men, which lie between the creational and the diluvial legends? And, if these are to lose all historical worth, what becomes of the infallibility of those who, according to the later scriptures, have accepted them, argued from them, and staked far-reaching dogmatic conclusions upon their historical accuracy?

It is the merest ostrich policy for contemporary ecclesiasticism to try to hide its Hexateuchal head—in the hope that the inseparable connection of its body with pre-Abrahamic legends may be overlooked. The question will still be asked, if the first nine chapters of the Pentateuch[11] are unhistorical, how is the historical accuracy of the remainder to be guaranteed? What more intrinsic claim has the story of the Exodus than that of the Deluge, to belief? If God did not walk in the Garden of Eden, how can we be assured that he spoke from Sinai?

In some other of the following essays (IX., X., XI., XII., XIV., XV.) I have endeavoured to show that sober and well-founded physical and literary criticism plays no less havoc with the doctrine that the canonical scriptures of the New Testament "declare incontrovertibly the actual historical truth in all records." We are told that the Gospels contain a true revelation of the spiritual world—a proposition which, in one sense of the word "spiritual," I should not think it necessary to dispute. But, when it is taken to signify that everything we are told about the world of spirits in these books is infallibly true; that we are bound to accept the demonology which constitutes an inseparable part of their teaching; and to profess belief in a Supernaturalism as gross as that of any primitive people—it is at any rate permissible to ask why? Science may be unable to define the limits of possibility, but it cannot escape from the moral obligation to weigh the evidence in favour of any alleged wonderful occurrence; and I have endeavoured to show that the evidence for the Gadarene miracle[12] is altogether worthless. We have simply three, partially discrepant, versions of a story, about the primitive form, the origin, and the authority for which we know absolutely nothing. But the evidence in favour of the Gadarene miracle is as good as that for any other.

Elsewhere, I have pointed out that it is utterly beside the mark to declaim against these conclusions on the ground of their asserted tendency to deprive mankind of the consolations of the Christian faith, and to destroy the foundations of morality; still less to brand them with the question-begging vituperative appellation of "infidelity." The point is not whether they are wicked; but, whether, from the point of view of scientific method, they are irrefragably true. If they are, they will be accepted in time, whether they are wicked, or not wicked. Nature, so far as we have been able to attain to any insight into her ways, recks little about consolation and makes for righteousness by very round-about paths. And, at any rate, whatever may be possible for other people, it is becoming less and less possible for the man who puts his faith in scientific methods of ascertaining truth, and is accustomed to have that faith justified by daily experience, to be consciously false to his principle in any matter. But the number of such men, driven into the use of scientific methods of inquiry and taught to trust them, by their education, their daily professional and business needs, is increasing and will continually increase. The phraseology of Supernaturalism may remain on men's lips, but in practice they are Naturalists. The magistrate who listens with devout attention to the precept "Thou shalt not suffer a witch to live" on Sunday, on Monday dismisses, as intrinsically absurd, a charge of bewitching a cow brought against some old woman; the superintendent

---

[9] The belief that the present forms of life reproduce exactly the ancestral forms.   [10] Sons of God (see Genesis 6:2).
[11] The first five books of the Bible.

[12] By which Jesus cast out the devils from a madman into a herd of swine (Mark 5:1–20; cf. Matthew 8:28–34, Luke 8:26–40).

of a lunatic asylum who substituted exorcism for rational modes of treatment would have but a short tenure of office; even parish clerks doubt the utility of prayers for rain, so long as the wind is in the east; and an outbreak of pestilence sends men, not to the churches, but to the drains. In spite of prayers for the success of our arms and *Te Deums* for victory, our real faith is in big battalions and keeping our powder dry; in knowledge of the science of warfare; in energy, courage, and discipline. In these, as in all other practical affairs, we act on the aphorism "*Laborare est orare*";[13] we admit that intelligent work is the only acceptable worship; and that, whether there be a Supernature or not, our business is with Nature.

It is important to note that the principle of the scientific Naturalism of the latter half of the nineteenth century, in which the intellectual movement of the Renascence has culminated, and which was first clearly formulated by Descartes,[14] leads not to the denial of the existence of any Supernature;[15] but simply to the denial of the validity of the evidence adduced in favour of this, or of that, extant form of Supernaturalism.

Looking at the matter from the most rigidly scientific point of view, the assumption that, amidst the myriads of worlds scattered through endless space, there can be no intelligence, as much greater than man's as his is greater than a blackbeetle's; no being endowed with powers of influencing the course of nature as much greater than his, as his is greater than a snail's, seems to me not merely baseless, but impertinent. Without stepping beyond the analogy of that which is known, it is easy to people the cosmos with entities, in ascending scale, until we reach something practically indistinguishable from omnipotence, omnipresence, and omniscience. If our intelligence can, in some matters, surely reproduce the past of thousands of years ago and anticipate the future, thousands of years hence, it is clearly within the limits of possibility that some greater intellect, even

of the same order, may be able to mirror the whole past and the whole future; if the universe is penetrated by a medium of such a nature that a magnetic needle on the earth answers to a commotion in the sun, an omnipresent agent is also conceivable; if our insignificant knowledge gives us some influence over events, practical omniscience may confer indefinably greater power. Finally, if evidence that a thing may be, were equivalent to proof that it is, analogy might justify the construction of a naturalistic theology and demonology not less wonderful than the current supernatural; just as it might justify the peopling of Mars, or of Jupiter, with living forms to which terrestrial biology offers no parallel. Until human life is longer and the duties of the present press less heavily, I do not think that wise men will occupy themselves with Jovian, or Martian, natural history; and they will probably agree to a verdict of "not proven" in respect of naturalistic theology, taking refuge in that agnostic confession, which appears to me to be the only position for people who object to say that they know what they are quite aware they do not know. As to the interests of morality, I am disposed to think that if mankind could be got to act up to this last principle in every relation of life, a reformation would be effected such as the world has not yet seen; an approximation to the millennium, such as no supernaturalistic religion has ever yet succeeded, or seems likely ever to succeed, in effecting.

I have hitherto dwelt upon scientific Naturalism chiefly in its critical and destructive aspect. But the present incarnation of the spirit of the Renascence differs from its predecessor in the eighteenth century, in that it builds up, as well as pulls down.

That of which it has laid the foundation, of which it is already raising the superstructure, is the doctrine of evolution. But so many strange misconceptions are current about this doctrine—it is attacked on such false grounds by its enemies, and made to cover so much that is disputable by some of its friends, that I think it well to define as clearly as I can, what I do not and what I do understand by the doctrine.

I have nothing to say to any "Philosophy of Evolution." Attempts to construct such a philosophy may be as useful, nay, even as admirable, as was the attempt of Descartes to get at a theory of the universe by the same *a priori* road;[16] but, in my judgment, they are as premature. Nor, for this purpose, have I to do with any theory of the "Origin of Species,"

[13] "To work is to pray."

[14] René Descartes (1596–1650) rejected traditional authority of every sort, founding his philosophy on "clear and distinct ideas." He concluded that he had such an idea of the deity.

[15] "I employ the words 'Supernature' and 'Supernatural' in their popular senses. For myself, I am bound to say that the term 'Nature' covers the totality of that which is. The world of psychical phenomena appears to me to be as much part of 'Nature' as the world of physical phenomena; and I am unable to perceive any justification for cutting the Universe into two halves, one natural and one supernatural." (Huxley)

[16] By deductive logic, without reference to observed facts.

much as I value that which is known as the Darwinian theory. That the doctrine of natural selection presupposes evolution is quite true; but it is not true that evolution necessarily implies natural selection. In fact, evolution might conceivably have taken place without the development of groups possessing the characters of species.

For me, the doctrine of evolution is no speculation, but a generalisation of certain facts, which may be observed by any one who will take the necessary trouble. These facts are those which are classed by biologists under the heads of Embryology and of Palaeontology. Embryology proves that every higher form of individual life becomes what it is by a process of gradual differentiation from an extremely low form; palaeontology proves, in some cases, and renders probable in all, that the oldest types of a group are the lowest; and that they have been followed by a gradual succession of more and more differentiated forms. It is simply a fact, that evolution of the individual animal and plant is taking place, as a natural process, in millions and millions of cases every day; it is a fact, that the species which have succeeded one another in the past, do, in many cases, present just those morphological relations, which they must possess, if they had proceeded, one from the other, by an analogous process of evolution.

The alternative presented, therefore, is: either the forms of one and the same type—say, *e.g.*, that of the Horse tribe—arose successively but independently of one another, at intervals, during myriads of years; or, the later forms are modified descendants of the earlier. And the latter supposition is so vastly more probable than the former, that rational men will adopt it, unless satisfactory evidence to the contrary can be produced. The objection sometimes put forward, that no one yet professes to have seen one species pass into another, comes oddly from those who believe that mankind are all descended from Adam. Has any one then yet seen the production of negroes from a white stock, or *vice versâ*? Moreover, is it absolutely necessary to have watched every step of the progress of a planet, to be justified in concluding that it really does go round the sun? If so, astronomy is in a bad way.

I do not, for a moment, presume to suggest that some one, far better acquainted than I am with astronomy and physics; or that a master of the new chemistry, with its extraordinary revelations; or that a student of the development of human society, of language, and of religions, may not find a sufficient foundation for the doctrine of evolution in these several regions. On the contrary, I rejoice to see that

scientific investigation, in all directions, is tending to the same result. And it may well be, that it is only my long occupation with biological matters that leads me to feel safer among them than anywhere else. Be that as it may, I take my stand on the facts of embryology and of palaeontology; and I hold that our present knowledge of these facts is sufficiently thorough and extensive to justify the assertion that all future philosophical and theological speculations will have to accommodate themselves to some such common body of established truths as the following:—

1. Plants and animals have existed on our planet for many hundred thousand, probably millions, of years. During this time, their forms, or species, have undergone a succession of changes, which eventually gave rise to the species which constitute the present living population of the earth. There is no evidence, nor any reason to suspect, that this secular process of evolution is other than a part of the ordinary course of nature; there is no more ground for imagining the occurrence of supernatural intervention, at any moment in the development of species in the past, than there is for supposing such intervention to take place, at any moment in the development of an individual animal or plant, at the present day.

2. At present, every individual animal or plant commences its existence as an organism of extremely simple anatomical structure; and it acquires all the complexity it ultimately possesses by gradual differentiation into parts of various structure and function. When a series of specific forms of the same type, extending over a long period of past time, is examined, the relation between the earlier and the later forms is analogous to that between earlier and later stages of individual development. Therefore, it is a probable conclusion that, if we could follow living beings back to their earlier states, we should find them to present forms similar to those of the individual germ, or, what comes to the same thing, of those lowest known organisms which stand upon the boundary line between plants and animals. At present, our knowledge of the ancient living world stops very far short of this point.

3. It is generally agreed, and there is certainly no evidence to the contrary, that all plants are devoid of consciousness; that they neither feel, desire, nor think. It is conceivable that the evolution of the primordial living substance should have taken place only along the plant line. In that case, the result might have been a wealth of vegetable life, as great, perhaps as varied, as at present, though certainly widely different from the present flora, in the evolution of which animals have played so great a part. But the living world thus

constituted would be simply an admirable piece of unconscious machinery, the working out of which lay potentially in its primitive composition; pleasure and pain would have no place in it; it would be a veritable Garden of Eden without any tree of the knowledge of good and evil. The question of the moral government of such a world could no more be asked, than we could reasonably seek for a moral purpose in a kaleidoscope.

4. How far down the scale of animal life the phenomena of consciousness are manifested, it is impossible to say. No one doubts their presence in his fellow-men; and, unless any strict Cartesians are left, no one doubts that mammals and birds are to be reckoned creatures that have feelings analogous to our smell, taste, sight, hearing, touch, pleasure, and pain. For my own part, I should be disposed to extend this analogical judgment a good deal further. On the other hand, if the lowest forms of plants are to be denied consciousness, I do not see on what ground it is to be ascribed to the lowest animals. I find it hard to believe that an infusory animalcule, a foraminifer, or a fresh-water polype is capable of feeling; and, in spite of Shakspere, I have doubts about the great sensitiveness of the "poor beetle that we tread upon." The question is equally perplexing when we turn to the stages of development of the individual. Granted a fowl feels; that the chick just hatched feels; that the chick when it chirps within the egg may possibly feel; what is to be said of it on the fifth day, when the bird is there, but with all its tissues nascent? Still more, on the first day, when it is nothing but a flat cellular disk? I certainly cannot bring myself to believe that this disk feels. Yet if it does not, there must be some time in the three weeks, between the first day and the day of hatching, when, as a concomitant, or a consequence, of the attainment by the brain of the chick of a certain stage of structural evolution, consciousness makes its appearance. I have frequently expressed my incapacity to understand the nature of the relation between consciousness and a certain anatomical tissue, which is thus established by observation. But the fact remains that, so far as observation and experiment go, they teach us that the psychical phenomena are dependent on the physical.

In like manner, if fishes, insects, scorpions, and such animals as the pearly nautilus, possess feeling, then undoubtedly consciousness was present in the world as far back as the Silurian epoch. But, if the earliest animals were similar to our rhizopods and monads, there must have been some time, between the much earlier epoch in which they constituted the whole animal population and the Silurian, in which feeling dawned, in consequence of the organism having reached the stage of evolution on which it depends.

5. Consciousness has various forms, which may be manifested independently of one another. The feelings of light and colour, of sound, of touch, though so often associated with those of pleasure and pain, are, by nature, as entirely independent of them as is thinking. An animal devoid of the feelings of pleasure and of pain, may nevertheless exhibit all the effects of sensation and purposive action. Therefore, it would be a justifiable hypothesis that, long after organic evolution had attained to consciousness, pleasure and pain were still absent. Such a world would be without either happiness or misery; no act could be punished and none could be rewarded; and it could have no moral purpose.

6. Suppose, for argument's sake, that all mammals and birds are subjects of pleasure and pain. Then we may be certain that these forms of consciousness were in existence at the beginning of the Mesozoic epoch. From that time forth, pleasure has been distributed without reference to merit, and pain inflicted without reference to demerit, throughout all but a mere fraction of the higher animals. Moreover, the amount and the severity of the pain, no less than the variety and acuteness of the pleasure, have increased with every advance in the scale of evolution. As suffering came into the world, not in consequence of a fall, but of a rise, in the scale of being, so every further rise has brought more suffering. As the evidence stands, it would appear that the sort of brain which characterises the highest mammals and which, so far as we know, is the indispensable condition of the highest sensibility, did not come into existence before the Tertiary epoch. The primordial anthropoid was probably, in this respect, on much the same footing as his pithecoid kin.[17] Like them he stood upon his "natural rights," gratified all his desires to the best of his ability, and was as incapable of either right or wrong doing as they. It would be as absurd as in their case, to regard his pleasures, any more than theirs, as moral rewards, and his pains, any more than theirs, as moral punishments.

7. From the remotest ages of which we have any cognizance, death has been the natural and, apparently, the necessary concomitant of life. In our hypothetical world (3),[18] inhabited by nothing but plants, death must have very early resulted from the

---

17 The manlike ape was on much the same footing as the apelike man.　　18 As described in the paragraph above numbered 3.

struggle for existence: many of the crowd must have jostled one another out of the conditions on which life depends. The occurrence of death, as far back as we have any fossil record of life, however, needs not to be proved by such arguments; for, if there had been no death there would have been no fossil remains, such as the great majority of those we met with. Not only was there death in the world, as far as the record of life takes us; but, ever since mammals and birds have been preyed upon by carnivorous animals, there has been painful death, inflicted by mechanisms specially adapted for inflicting it.

8. Those who are acquainted with the closeness of the structural relations between the human organisation and that of the mammals which come nearest to him, on the one hand; and with the palaeontological history of such animals as horses and dogs, on the other; will not be disposed to question the origin of man from forms which stand in the same sort of relation to *Homo sapiens,* as *Hipparion* does to *Equus.* I think it a conclusion, fully justified by analogy, that, sooner or later, we shall discover the remains of our less specialised primatic ancestors in the strata which have yielded the less specialised equine and canine quadrupeds. At present, fossil remains of men do not take us back further than the later part of the Quaternary epoch; and, as was to be expected, they do not differ more from existing men, than Quaternary horses differ from existing horses. Still earlier we find traces of man, in implements such as are used by the ruder savages at the present day. Later, the remains of the palaeolithic and neolithic[19] conditions take us gradually from the savage state to the civilisations of Egypt and of Mycenae; though the true chronological order of the remains actually discovered may be uncertain.

9. Much has yet to be learned, but, at present, natural knowledge affords no support to the notion that men have fallen from a higher to a lower state. On the contrary, everything points to a slow natural evolution; which, favoured by the surrounding conditions in such localities as the valleys of the Yang-tse-kang, the Euphrates, and the Nile, reached a relatively high pitch, five or six thousand years ago; while, in many other regions, the savage condition has persisted down to our day. In all this vast lapse of time there is not a trace of the occurrence of any general destruction of the human race; not the smallest indication that man has been treated on any other principles than the rest of the animal world.

_____

[19] Of the early and later stone ages, respectively.

10. The results of the process of evolution in the case of man, and in that of his more nearly allied contemporaries, have been marvellously different. Yet it is easy to see that small primitive differences of a certain order, must, in the long run, bring about a wide divergence of the human stock from the others. It is a reasonable supposition that, in the earliest human organisms, an improved brain, a voice more capable of modulation and articulation, limbs which lent themselves better to gesture, a more perfect hand, capable among other things of imitating form in plastic or other material, were combined with the curiosity, the mimetic tendency, the strong family affection of the next lower group; and that they were accompanied by exceptional length of life and a prolonged minority. The last two peculiarities are obviously calculated to strengthen the family organisation, and to give great weight to its educative influences. The potentiality of language, as the vocal symbol of thought, lay in the faculty of modulating and articulating the voice. The potentiality of writing, as the visual symbol of thought, lay in the hand that could draw; and in the mimetic tendency, which, as we know, was gratified by drawing, as far back as the days of Quaternary man. With speech as the record, in tradition, of the experience of more than one generation; with writing as the record of that of any number of generations; the experience of the race, tested and corrected generation after generation, could be stored up and made the starting point for fresh progress. Having these perfectly natural factors of the evolutionary process in man before us, it seems unnecessary to go further a-field in search of others.

11. That the doctrine of evolution implies a former state of innocence of mankind is quite true; but, as I have remarked, it is the innocence of the ape and of the tiger, whose acts, however they may run counter to the principles of morality, it would be absurd to blame. The lust of the one and the ferocity of the other are as much provided for in their organisation, are as clear evidences of design, as any other features that can be named.

Observation and experiment upon the phenomena of society soon taught men that, in order to obtain the advantages of social existence, certain rules must be observed. Morality commenced with society. Society is possible only upon the condition that the members of it shall surrender more or less of their individual freedom of action. In primitive societies, individual selfishness is a centrifugal force of such intensity that it is constantly bringing the social organisation to the verge of destruction. Hence the prominence of the positive rules of obedience to the elders; of standing by the family or the tribe in all emergencies; of fulfilling the religious rites, non-observance of which is conceived to damage it with the supernatural powers, belief in whose existence is one of the earliest products of human thought; and of the negative rules, which restrain each from meddling with the life or property of another.

12. The highest conceivable form of human society is that in which the desire to do what is best for the whole, dominates and limits the action of every member of that society. The more complex the social organisation the greater the number of acts from which each man must abstain, if he desires to do that which is best for all. Thus the progressive evolution of society means increasing restriction of individual freedom in certain directions.

With the advance of civilisation, and the growth of cities and of nations by the coalescence of families and of tribes, the rules which constitute the common foundation of morality and of law became more numerous and complicated, and the temptations to break or evade many of them stronger. In the absence of a clear apprehension of the natural sanctions of these rules, a supernatural sanction was assumed; and imagination supplied the motives which reason was supposed to be incompetent to furnish. Religion, at first independent of morality, gradually took morality under its protection; and the supernaturalists have ever since tried to persuade mankind that the existence of ethics is bound up with that of supernaturalism.

I am not of that opinion. But, whether it is correct or otherwise, it is very clear to me that, as Beelzebub is not to be cast out by the aid of Beelzebub, so morality is not to be established by immorality. It is, we are told, the special peculiarity of the devil that he was a liar from the beginning. If we set out in life with pretending to know that which we do not know; with professing to accept for proof evidence which we are well aware is inadequate; with wilfully shutting our eyes and our ears to facts which militate against this or that comfortable hypothesis; we are assuredly doing our best to deserve the same character.

I have not the presumption to imagine that, in spite of all my efforts, errors may not have crept into these propositions. But I am tolerably confident that time will prove them to be substantially correct. And if they are so, I confess I do not see how any extant supernaturalistic system can also claim exactness. That they are irreconcilable with the biblical cosmogony, anthropology, and theodicy is obvious; but

they are no less inconsistent with the sentimental Deism of the "Vicaire Savoyard"[20] and his numerous modern progeny. It is as impossible, to my mind, to suppose that the evolutionary process was set going with full foreknowledge of the result and yet with what we should understand by a purely benevolent intention, as it is to imagine that the intention was purely malevolent. And the prevalence of dualistic theories from the earliest times to the present day— whether in the shape of the doctrine of the inherently evil nature of matter; of an Ahriman;[21] of a hard and cruel Demiurge;[22] of a diabolical "prince of this world," show how widely this difficulty has been felt.

Many seem to think that, when it is admitted that the ancient literature, contained in our Bibles, has no more claim to infallibility than any other ancient literature; when it is proved that the Israelites and their Christian successors accepted a great many supernaturalistic theories and legends which have no better foundation than those of heathenism, nothing remains to be done but to throw the Bible aside as so much waste paper.

I have always opposed this opinion. It appears to me that if there is anybody more objectionable than the orthodox Bibliolater it is the heterodox Philistine, who can discover in a literature which, in some respects, has no superior, nothing but a subject for scoffing and an occasion for the display of his conceited ignorance of the debt he owes to former generations.

Twenty-two years ago I pleaded for the use of the Bible as an instrument of popular education, and I venture to repeat what I then said:

"Consider the great historical fact that, for three centuries, this book has been woven into the life of all that is best and noblest in English history; that it has become the national Epic of Britain and is as familiar to gentle and simple,[23] from John o' Groat's House to Land's End,[24] as Dante and Tasso once were to the Italians; that it is written in the noblest and purest English and abounds in exquisite beauties of mere literary form; and, finally, that it forbids the veriest hind, who never left his village, to be ignorant of the existence of other countries and other civilisations and of a great past, stretching back to the furthest limits of the oldest nations in the world. By the study of what other book could children be so

---

20 A mouthpiece for Jean Jacques Rousseau in *Émile*.
21 The principle of evil in the Zoroastrian system.
22 Creator of the world in the Platonic philosophy.
23 To gentleman and simple peasant.
24 The extreme northern and extreme southern points of England, respectively.

much humanised and made to feel that each figure in that vast historical procession fills, like themselves, but a momentary space in the interval between the Eternities; and earns the blessings or the curses of all time, according to its effort to do good and hate evil, even as they also are earning their payment for their work?"

At the same time, I laid stress upon the necessity of placing such instruction in lay hands; in the hope and belief, that it would thus gradually accommodate itself to the coming changes of opinion; that the theology and the legend would drop more and more out of sight, while the perennially interesting historical, literary, and ethical contents would come more and more into view.

I may add yet another claim of the Bible to the respect and the attention of a democratic age. Throughout the history of the western world, the Scriptures, Jewish and Christian, have been the great instigators of revolt against the worst forms of clerical and political despotism. The Bible has been the *Magna Charta* of the poor and of the oppressed; down to modern times, no State has had a constitution in which the interests of the people are so largely taken into account, in which the duties, so much more than the privileges, of rulers are insisted upon, as that drawn up for Israel in Deuteronomy and in Leviticus; nowhere is the fundamental truth that the welfare of the State, in the long run, depends on the uprightness of the citizen so strongly laid down. Assuredly, the Bible talks no trash about the rights of man; but it insists on the equality of duties, on the liberty to bring about that righteousness which is somewhat different from struggling for "rights"; on the fraternity of taking thought for one's neighbour as for one's self.

So far as such equality, liberty, and fraternity are included under the democratic principles which assume the same names, the Bible is the most democratic book in the world. As such it began, through the heretical sects, to undermine the clerico-political despotism of the middle ages, almost as soon as it was formed, in the eleventh century; Pope and King had as much as they could do to put down the Albigenses and the Waldenses in the twelfth and thirteenth centuries; the Lollards and the Hussites gave them still more trouble in the fourteenth and fifteenth; from the sixteenth century onward, the Protestant sects have favoured political freedom in proportion to the degree in which they have refused to acknowledge any ultimate authority save that of the Bible.

But the enormous influence which has thus been exerted by the Jewish and Christian Scriptures has had no necessary connection with cosmogonies, demonologies, and miraculous interferences. Their strength lies in their appeals, not to the reason, but to the ethical sense. I do not say that even the highest biblical ideal is exclusive of others or needs no supplement. But I do believe that the human race is not yet, possibly may never be, in a position to dispense with it.

Alfred Lord Tennyson

1809–1892

TENNYSON'S appointment as poet laureate in 1850 was altogether fitting, for more than anyone else he expressed in verse the dominant ideas and attitudes of the period: the passionate belief in progress, the conservative pride in English freedom, the religious doubts but the triumph of faith (and a broad, liberal faith outside creeds and ecclesiastical forms), and, above all, the moral earnestness and the moral idealism which exalted Duty, Love, and the Home. Today, much of this poetry is dated, but Tennyson still commands a living interest for three reasons. His lyrics are among the finest in the language. His development from a late Romantic into a Victorian poet has great historical significance. And, thirdly, his poetry contains a strain of anti-Victorianism, unnoticed or explained away by the Victorians, which demands a fresh critical and psychological approach.

Tennyson was born in 1809 at Somersby in Lincolnshire, not far from the North Sea. His father was the rector of the parish church, a man of literary and artistic tastes, and of bitter and irritable temper. In this environment Alfred started early to write verse, and to develop the somber and melancholy spirit that colors much of his work. Hallam Tennyson reported that "More than once Alfred, scared by his father's fits of despondency, went out through the black night, and threw himself on a grave in the churchyard, praying to be beneath the sod himself." No doubt there is an element here of youthful romantic posturing, but it is probably true, as W. H. Auden has claimed, that Tennyson's most genuine and personal feelings were almost entirely those of loneliness, depression, and the desire for death. Certainly those are the dominant notes in the poems which he contributed to a joint volume, with his brothers Charles and Frederick, in 1827, and they inform the "Song," "Mariana," and "Tithonus," the first selections below.

After being educated largely at home by his father, Tennyson entered Cambridge in 1828, where he came under a new and important influence. This was a group of young intellectuals called the Apostles, one of whom, Arthur Henry Hallam, became his closest friend. The Apostles were great admirers, not only of Wordsworth, but of two obscure modern poets named Shelley and Keats; indeed, in 1829 they published the first English edition of Shelley's *Adonais,* his elegy on the death of Keats. The double effect of these new literary idols is apparent in Tennyson's second volume, *Poems, Chiefly Lyrical* (1830). They suggested, on the one hand, the possibility of combining the pictorial imagery of Keats with the musical rhythms of Shelley and thus creating an aesthetic poetry of mood and atmosphere; and on the other, they suggested (Shelley in particular) a poetry almost the reverse of this, of philosophical and political ideas.

The first genre, which was to reappear later in the work of the Pre-Raphaelites and the young Yeats, is to be clearly distinguished from Romantic poetry, however much it may be derived from it. If we compare Keats's "To Autumn" (p. 336, above) with Tennyson's "Song" on the same subject (p. 636), we see at once that where Keats describes an object, Tennyson invokes a mood. In the one case, the reader "sees" autumn; in the other, he doesn't "see" anything, he simply feels a mixture of emotions (depression, dejection, weariness, fatigue, the sense of decay and death) which combine to create an intangible but none the less vivid impression. In short, Tennyson's poem is not about autumn at all; autumn simply provided the set of images which he needed to communicate a particular mood. In the same way, "Mariana" is not about a woman who has lost her lover: the woman and the refrain are merely the principal images which combine with those of lonely remoteness and dilapidation to evoke a similar mood of melancholia. ("Tithonus," by contrast, *does* center on a human situation, which in this case, as in Romantic poetry in general as distinct from aesthetic poetry, is the source of the emotions of fatigue and weariness.) In "The Sea-Fairies" rhythm replaces imagery as the dominant technique for evoking an impression of bright and rapid motion. It is perhaps the finest piece of music in English verse before Swinburne.

If this was Tennyson's starting-point, why did he shift, or try to shift, his theory and practice of poetry from Romantic aestheticism to Victorian didacticism, in the large sense that covers lofty sentiments and ideals? The first and immediate answer is the Apostles. They *were* apostles because they felt commissioned to "preach to the sons of men dwelling in outer darkness new truths in regard to literature and religion, the cultivation of a loftier philosophy, a purer poetry, higher ideals in life and letters." Judged by this aim, they could only feel that Tennyson was misdirecting his poetic gift. Trench took him aside and said, "Tennyson, we cannot live in art." Venables told him his verse was too largely imbued with magic to appeal to popular taste, and urged him to base his poetry more on the "broad and common interests of the time," of which he ought to be the artistic exponent and unifier. Tennyson "pondered all that had been said," and presently began to write "with a deeper and a fuller insight into the requirements of the age." Of the age, because the program of the Apostles simply reflected the need of the period, not only for new truths—new liberal truths—in religion and politics, but also loftier ideals in life, philosophy, and poetry to counteract the "low" view of man and society for which the three B's were responsible—Byron, Business, and Benthamism. (See the General Introduction, pp. 371-2, 374-5.)

This new conception of his role, which had behind it the further authority of both Wordsworth and Shelley, is announced by Tennyson in "The Poet" (where the influence of the "Ode to the West Wind" is apparent), and reflected in the two poems that follow, "You Ask Me, Why" and "Sir Galahad." But Tennyson's conversion was far from wholehearted. "Alas for me!" he wrote to Hallam, "I have more of the beautiful than the good!" This explains the conflict of intentions which spoils both "The Palace of Art" and "Oenone." Although the former was written to support Trench's warning that "we cannot live in art," and to preach the moral lessons announced in the introductory poem "To ——" (probably Trench), the fact is that Tennyson is so concerned with his lengthy description of the palace and its paintings, and so vague about the soul's pilgrimage at the end, that the poem falls between two stools. In "Oenone," heartbroken grief, pictorial beauties (which Oenone stops at every moment to phrase with conscious artistry), and a Victorian sermon from Athene compete together for the distracted reader's attention.

The second aspect of Tennyson's development from 1830 to 1842, in addition to the shift in his theory of poetry, was the increase of his early melancholia and a growing distaste for Victorian society. The 1832 volume was severely criticized in contemporary reviews by Lockhart and Croker; in 1833 Arthur Hallam suddenly died, leaving Tennyson not only stricken with grief but filled with profoundly distressing doubts about the beneficence of a God who could sanction the death of so remarkable a man as Hallam on the very threshold of a great career; in 1836 he fell in love with Emily Sellwood, but their engagement was broken off a few years later, and a long period of trying and uncertain relationship followed before they were eventually married in 1850; and finally, Tennyson was beset with financial difficulties, first when his father died in 1836, and then when he took what money he had and invested it in Dr. Allen's wood-carving machine, only to lose every penny, and to fall into "so severe a hypochondria . . . that his friends despaired of his life." But in 1842 the tide began to turn. His new volume of poems, published in that year, was well received. In 1845 he was given a government pension. *The Princess* (1847), on the emancipation of women, was followed in 1850 by the famous *In Memoriam* and the poet-laureateship; and though *Maud* (1855) was not a popular success, the first four *Idylls of the King* (1859) established him firmly as the great poet of the age and the major exponent of Victorian ideals. When he died in 1892, he was buried, of course, in Westminster Abbey.

Five years later the official biography by his son Hallam was the life of Tennyson the Victorian prophet—and yet, here and there, like curious excrescences, the text was punctuated by some very un-Victorian, even sometimes anti-Victorian, remarks. The poet laureate had once laughed at a tremendous "duty-woman," had claimed it was right to enjoy leisure, had thought a glacier covered with debris looked "as if a thousand London seasons had passed over it," had spoken of "a mighty wave of evil passing over the world," and had called the Victorian period "an age of lies, and also an age of stinks."

This bitter strain of reaction, reinforced by his own misfortunes, brought into his poetry a hostile element, in the form either of escape or criticism, and one which often clashes with the "correct" expression of Victorian ideals. An unresolved tension, which is analogous to that mentioned above between the aesthetic and the moral, is seen in "Ulysses," where the attraction of abandoning the responsibilities of daily life and setting sail on a romantic voyage of endless experience (drinking life to the lees) is followed by the moral appeal to strive, to conquer, and not to yield; in "The Lotos-Eaters," where the final stanza (in the revised version of 1842) introduces a moral condemnation of the life of sensual pleasure which the previous stanzas have presented sympathetically; in "Locksley Hall," which Tennyson attempted to make a coherent eulogy of social and scientific progress by writing off the accompanying hostile attitude (expressed directly in the attack on greed, indirectly in the retreat to an Oriental Eden far from railroads and "march of mind"

and cramped passions) as that of a "jaundiced eye," but where, in fact, the latter attitude, in both forms, is expressed as firmly and sanely as the former. Only in "The Vision of Sin" (and in parts of *Maud*) did he succeed in giving direct and coherent expression to his deep distaste for the age; and then only because the protagonist was a man of "ruin'd blood," whose powerful exposure of hypocrisy and vacillation could pass for the ravings of madness. Tennyson would have been a greater poet—though far less of a Victorian poet—if he could have allowed his keen sense of evil and stupidity a free expression, unchecked by the pressure to affirm the social and moral ideals of the time, and unsublimated in any image of escape.

In their final form the *Idylls of the King* were intended to show the disastrous consequences that followed from the initial sin of Lancelot and Guinevere: the spread of evil through the community, which breeds loss of pure faith in God and the Moral Law, which then turns religion from "practical goodness and holiness to superstition," that is, to selfish searching for visions of the Holy Grail (the reference is to the ascetic and ecclesiastical emphasis of the Oxford Movement). This "moral" was then supplemented by heroic or ideal images of courage and love. But no one can read the *Idylls* without feeling Tennyson's delight in the beauty and glamour of days when knighthood and not Victorianism was in flower. In descriptions of armor and Gothic towers, in tales of magic and adventure, the aesthetic-escapist sensibility found renewed expression. But here and there, most noticeably in the earlier *Idylls,* Tennyson's insight into the darker sides of human experience is released. If "Lancelot and Elaine" contains an ideal picture of pure and innocent love, it also contains, and centrally, a picture of burnt-out and disillusioned love, where a man and woman are held together out of habit and waning sexual attraction in a relationship they have not power to break. This is Tennyson's finest study in human psychology. It is, like "The Vision of Sin," a moral but not a moralistic poem.

The philosophical *In Memoriam* complements the "epic" *Idylls of the King.* Under the liberal influence of the Apostles, Tennyson had sloughed off much of Christian theology until his religion was reduced, as it was for many Victorians, to a simple faith in God, in a divine moral law speaking through conscience, and in the immortality of the soul. But the new science of evolution threatened to destroy all religious belief whatever. What Tennyson did, and what made the poem so significant at the time, was to admit the arguments of "atheistical science" and then answer them by showing that evolution might be given a moral and religious interpretation (see the General Introduction, pp. 380–82, where there are various references to *In Memoriam*). But at bottom Tennyson's answer was not logical but emotional. He simply refused to believe that man was merely a product of nature dying a natural death in a universe of mechanical force. To do so would be to deny everything which makes life worth living, to deny our innermost feelings of freedom and dignity. I will *not* believe it! (See No. 120 and No. 123.) And then, once a godless universe is defied and repudiated, the way back to faith is opened up (cf. Carlyle's progress from "The Everlasting No" to "The Everlasting Yea"). From various experiences Tennyson reached, or thought he reached, an intuitive sense of God: from what he called the miraculous fact of free will, "apparently an act of self-limitation by the Infinite, and yet a revelation by Himself of Himself"; from the capacity of man, at times, for exalted, unselfish love, which seemed to attest a "higher" nature made in God's image; and from moments of fear and doubt when he felt a childlike sense that his Father was near (see No. 124). Though we may not be able to follow him to his religious conclusion, we dare not question his emotional repudiation of the scientific picture. The whole drift of *our* thinking leads to exactly the same view of a meaningless universe of nature, and yet something inside *us* rebels, if not so violently and consciously as in Tennyson. We talk materialism but we do not believe it.

How successful was Tennyson's double effort, logical and intuitive, to answer religious doubts? Did he recover a firm belief? The answer is "yes" if one reads the Prologue or the Epilogue, or a poem like No. 124. But it is "no" when one finishes the group from No. 54 to No. 56. The truth lies, I think, in between. Tennyson's faith was not strong and firm, not really faith at all. It was a hope, a guess, a trust that the religious reading of life was true; and it is no accident that the word "trust" in particular echoes all through the poem. *In Memoriam* is not a poem of faith nor a poem of doubt. It is a poem of trust.

Tennyson's *Works*, with his own notes, have been edited by Hallam Tennyson in six volumes (1908) and in one volume (1913). Charles Tennyson's *Alfred Tennyson* (1949) has not displaced Hallam Tennyson's *Alfred Lord Tennyson: A Memoir* (2 vols., 1897) as the standard biography. In spite of its solemn consecration of the Victorian poet laureate, the latter is indispensable for the letters and conversations and the large amount of contemporary comment by men like Jowett, Sidgwick, and Spedding which it reprints. The best critical book is Harold Nicolson's *Tennyson: Aspects of His Life, Character, and Poetry* (1923). W. H. Auden has written an introduction to *A Selection from the Poems of Alfred Lord Tennyson* (1944) which emphasizes the anti-Victorian segment of his personality.

Alfred Lord Tennyson

SONG

I

A spirit haunts the year's last hours
Dwelling amid these yellowing bowers:
   To himself he talks;
For at eventide, listening earnestly,
At his work you may hear him sob and sigh   5
   In the walks;
Earthward he boweth the heavy stalks
Of the mouldering flowers.
Heavily hangs the broad sunflower
   Over its grave i' the earth so chilly;   10
Heavily hangs the hollyhock,
   Heavily hangs the tiger-lily.

II

The air is damp, and hushed, and close,
As a sick man's room when he taketh repose
   An hour before death;   15

My very heart faints and my whole soul grieves
At the moist rich smell of the rotting leaves,
   And the breath
Of the fading edges of box beneath,
And the year's last rose.   20
Heavily hangs the broad sunflower
   Over its grave i' the earth so chilly;
Heavily hangs the hollyhock,
   Heavily hangs the tiger-lily.

MARIANA

"Mariana in the moated grange."
            Measure for Measure

With blackest moss the flower-plots
   Were thickly crusted, one and all;
The rusted nails fell from the knots
   That held the pear to the gable-wall.
The broken sheds looked sad and strange: 5

Uplifted was the clinking latch;
Weeded and worn the ancient thatch
Upon the lonely moated grange.
　　She only said, "My life is dreary,
　　　He cometh not," she said;
　　She said, "I am aweary, aweary,
　　　I would that I were dead!"　　　　10

Her tears fell with the dews at even;
　Her tears fell ere the dews were dried;
She could not look on the sweet heaven,　　15
　Either at morn or eventide.
After the flitting of the bats,
　When thickest dark did trance the sky,
She drew her casement-curtain by,
　And glanced athwart the glooming flats.　　20
　　She only said, "The night is dreary,
　　　He cometh not," she said;
　　She said, "I am aweary, aweary,
　　　I would that I were dead!"

Upon the middle of the night,　　　　25
　Waking she heard the night-fowl crow;
The cock sung out an hour ere light;
　From the dark fen the oxen's low
Came to her; without hope of change,
　In sleep she seemed to walk forlorn,　　30
Till cold winds woke the gray-eyed morn
About the lonely moated grange.
　　She only said, "The day is dreary,
　　　He cometh not," she said;
　　She said, "I am aweary, aweary,　　35
　　　I would that I were dead!"

About a stone-cast from the wall
　A sluice with blackened waters slept,
And o'er it many, round and small,
　The clustered marish-mosses crept.　　40
Hard by a poplar shook alway,
　All silver-green with gnarlèd bark:
For leagues no other tree did mark
　The level waste, the rounding gray.
　　She only said, "My life is dreary,　　45
　　　He cometh not," she said;
　　She said, "I am aweary, aweary,
　　　I would that I were dead!"

And ever when the moon was low,
　And the shrill winds were up and away,　　50
In the white curtain, to and fro,
　She saw the gusty shadow sway.
But when the moon was very low,
　And wild winds bound within their cell,

The shadow of the poplar fell　　　　55
　Upon her bed, across her brow.
　　She only said, "The night is dreary,
　　　He cometh not," she said;
　　She said, "I am aweary, aweary,
　　　I would that I were dead!"　　　　60

All day within the dreamy house,
　The doors upon their hinges creaked;
The blue fly sung in the pane; the mouse
　Behind the mouldering wainscot shrieked,
Or from the crevice peered about.　　65
　Old faces glimmered through the doors,
　Old footsteps trod the upper floors,
Old voices called her from without.
　　She only said, "My life is dreary,
　　　He cometh not," she said;　　70
　　She said, "I am aweary, aweary,
　　　I would that I were dead!"

The sparrow's chirrup on the roof,
　The slow clock ticking, and the sound
Which to the wooing wind aloof　　75
　The poplar made, did all confound
Her sense; but most she loathed the hour
　When the thick-moted sunbeam lay
Athwart the chambers, and the day
Was sloping toward his western bower.　　80
　　Then said she, "I am very dreary,
　　　He will not come," she said;
　　She said, "I am aweary, aweary,
　　　O God, that I were dead!"

TITHONUS[1]

The woods decay, the woods decay and fall,
The vapors weep their burthen to the ground,
Man comes and tills the field and lies beneath,
And after many a summer dies the swan.
Me only cruel immortality
Consumes: I wither slowly in thine arms,　　5

---

[1] Aurora (or Eos), goddess of the dawn, loved Tithonus and
secured for him from Zeus eternal life; but, since she had failed
to ask for immortal youth, he gradually grew older and feebler
until at last he begged to be allowed to die. According to the
myth, he was finally changed into a grasshopper.
　"The basic conflicts of the poem are those between light and
dark, warmth and cold, beauty and ugliness, youth and age.
But the ultimate mood and attitude of the poem go beyond its
dramatic situation, the problem of love between Tithonus and
Eos, . . . to express a more profound contrast, a revulsion from
the terms of all life and health and a yearning for death." (Mary
Donahue Ellmann)

Here at the quiet limit of the world,
A white-haired shadow roaming like a dream
The ever-silent spaces of the East,
Far-folded mists, and gleaming halls of morn.   10

Alas! for this gray shadow, once a man—
So glorious in his beauty and thy choice,
Who madest him thy chosen, that he seemed
To his great heart none other than a God!
I asked thee, "Give me immortality."   15
Then didst thou grant mine asking with a smile,
Like wealthy men who care not how they give.
But thy strong Hours indignant worked their wills,
And beat me down and marred and wasted me,
And though they could not end me, left me maimed   20
To dwell in presence of immortal youth,
Immortal age beside immortal youth,
And all I was, in ashes. Can thy love,
Thy beauty, make amends, though even now,
Close over us, the silver star,[2] thy guide,   25
Shines in those tremulous eyes that fill with tears
To hear me? Let me go: take back thy gift:
Why should a man desire in any way
To vary from the kindly race of men,
Or pass beyond the goal of ordinance   30
Where all should pause, as is most meet for all?

A soft air fans the cloud apart; there comes
A glimpse of that dark world where I was born.
Once more the old mysterious glimmer steals
From thy pure brows, and from thy shoulders pure,   35
And bosom beating with a heart renewed.
Thy cheek begins to redden through the gloom,
Thy sweet eyes brighten slowly close to mine,
Ere yet they blind the stars, and the wild team[3]
Which love thee, yearning for thy yoke, arise,   40
And shake the darkness from their loosened manes,
And beat the twilight into flakes of fire.

Lo! ever thus thou growest beautiful
In silence, then before thine answer given
Departest, and thy tears are on my cheek.   45

Why wilt thou ever scare me with thy tears,
And make me tremble lest a saying learnt,
In days far-off, on that dark earth, be true?
"The Gods themselves cannot recall their gifts."

Ay me! ay me! with what another heart   50
In days far-off, and with what other eyes

I used to watch—if I be he that watched—
The lucid outline forming round thee; saw
The dim curls kindle into sunny rings;
Changed with thy mystic change, and felt my blood   55
Glow with the glow that slowly crimsoned all
Thy presence and thy portals, while I lay,
Mouth, forehead, eyelids, growing dewy-warm
With kisses balmier than half-opening buds
Of April, and could hear the lips that kissed   60
Whispering I knew not what of wild and sweet,
Like that strange song I heard Apollo sing,
While Ilion like a mist rose into towers.[4]

Yet hold me not for ever in thine East:
How can my nature longer mix with thine?   65
Coldly thy rosy shadows bathe me, cold
Are all thy lights, and cold my wrinkled feet
Upon thy glimmering thresholds, when the steam
Floats up from those dim fields about the homes
Of happy men that have the power to die,   70
And grassy barrows of the happier dead.
Release me, and restore me to the ground;
Thou seëst all things, thou wilt see my grave:
Thou wilt renew thy beauty morn by morn;
I earth in earth forget these empty courts,   75
And thee returning on thy silver wheels.

THE SEA-FAIRIES[1]

Slow sailed the weary mariners and saw,
Betwixt the green brink and the running foam,
Sweet faces, rounded arms, and bosoms pressed
To little harps of gold; and while they mused
Whispering to each other half in fear,   5
Shrill music reached them on the middle sea.

Whither away, whither away, whither away? fly no
      more.
Whither away from the high green field, and the happy
      blossoming shore?
Day and night to the billow the fountain calls;
Down shower the gambolling waterfalls   10
From wandering over the lea;
Out of the live-green heart of the dells
They freshen the silvery-crimson shells,
And thick with white bells the clover-hill swells
High over the full-toned sea.   15
O, hither, come hither and furl your sails,

---

[2] The morning star.
[3] The horses which drew the chariot of dawn.

[4] The walls of Troy were said to have risen to the music of Apollo.

[1] The sirens who tempted Odysseus and his mariners on their way home from Troy.

Come hither to me and to me;
Hither, come hither and frolic and play;
Here it is only the mew that wails;
We will sing to you all the day.   20
Mariner, mariner, furl your sails,
For here are the blissful downs and dales,
And merrily, merrily carol the gales,
And the spangle dances in bight and bay,
And the rainbow forms and flies on the land   25
Over the islands free;
And the rainbow lives in the curve of the sand;
Hither, come hither and see;
And the rainbow hangs on the poising wave,
And sweet is the color of cove and cave,   30
And sweet shall your welcome be.
O, hither, come hither, and be our lords,
For merry brides are we:
We will kiss sweet kisses, and speak sweet words;
O, listen, listen, your eyes shall glisten   35
With pleasure and love and jubilee:
O, listen, listen, your eyes shall glisten
When the sharp clear twang of the golden chords
Runs up the ridgèd sea.
Who can light on as happy a shore   40
All the world o'er, all the world o'er?
Whither away? listen and stay; mariner, mariner, fly
    no more.

THE LADY OF SHALOTT

PART I

On either side the river lie
Long fields of barley and of rye,
That clothe the wold and meet the sky;
And through the field the road runs by
    To many-towered Camelot;[1]   5
And up and down the people go,
Gazing where the lilies blow
Round an island there below,
    The island of Shalott.

Willows whiten,[2] aspens quiver,   10
Little breezes dusk and shiver
Through the wave that runs for ever
By the island in the river
    Flowing down to Camelot.
Four gray walls, and four gray towers,   15
Overlook a space of flowers,

[1] The seat of King Arthur's court.
[2] The wind turns up the white underside of the leaves.

And the silent isle imbowers
    The Lady of Shalott.

By the margin, willow-veiled,
Slide the heavy barges trailed   20
By slow horses; and unhailed
The shallop flitteth silken-sailed
    Skimming down to Camelot:
But who hath seen her wave her hand?
Or at the casement seen her stand?
Or is she known in all the land,
    The Lady of Shalott?

Only reapers, reaping early
In among the bearded barley,
Hear a song that echoes cheerly   30
From the river winding clearly,
    Down to towered Camelot;
And by the moon the reaper weary,
Piling sheaves in uplands airy,
Listening, whispers " 'Tis the fairy   35
    Lady of Shalott."

PART 2

There she weaves by night and day
A magic web with colors gay.
She has heard a whisper say,
A curse is on her if she stay   40
    To look down to Camelot.
She knows not what the curse may be,
And so she weaveth steadily,
And little other care hath she,
    The Lady of Shalott.   45

And moving through a mirror clear
That hangs before her all the year,
Shadows of the world appear.
There she sees the highway near
    Winding down to Camelot;   50
There the river eddy whirls,
And there the surly village-churls,
And the red cloaks of market girls,
    Pass onward from Shalott.

Sometimes a troop of damsels glad,   55
An abbot on an ambling pad,[3]
Sometimes a curly shepherd-lad,
Or long-haired page in crimson clad,
    Goes by to towered Camelot;
And sometimes through the mirror blue   60

[3] An easy-gaited horse.

The knights come riding two and two;
She hath no loyal knight and true,
    The Lady of Shalott.

But in her web she still delights
To weave the mirror's magic sights,   65
For often through the silent nights
A funeral, with plumes and lights
    And music, went to Camelot;
Or when the moon was overhead,
Came two young lovers lately wed;   70
"I am half sick of shadows," said
    The Lady of Shalott.

PART 3

A bow-shot from her bower-eaves,
He rode between the barley-sheaves,
The sun came dazzling through the leaves,   75
And flamed upon the brazen greaves
    Of bold Sir Lancelot.
A red-cross knight forever kneeled
To a lady in his shield,
That sparkled on the yellow field,   80
    Beside remote Shalott.

The gemmy bridle glittered free,
Like to some branch of stars we see
Hung in the golden Galaxy.[4]
The bridle bells rang merrily   85
    As he rode down to Camelot;
And from his blazoned baldric slung
A mighty silver bugle hung,
And as he rode his armor rung,
    Beside remote Shalott.   90

All in the blue unclouded weather
Thick-jeweled shone the saddle-leather,
The helmet and the helmet-feather
Burned like one burning flame together,
    As he rode down to Camelot;   95
As often through the purple night,
Below the starry clusters bright,
Some bearded meteor, trailing light,
    Moves over still Shalott.

His broad clear brow in sunlight glowed;   100
On burnished hooves his war-horse trode;
From underneath his helmet flowed
His coal-black curls as on he rode,
    As he rode down to Camelot.

---

[4] The Milky Way.

From the bank and from the river   105
He flashed into the crystal mirror,
"Tirra lirra," by the river
    Sang Sir Lancelot.

She left the web, she left the loom,
She made three paces through the room,   110
She saw the water lily bloom,
She saw the helmet and the plume,
    She looked down to Camelot.
Out flew the web and floated wide;
The mirror cracked from side to side;   115
"The curse is come upon me," cried
    The Lady of Shalott.

PART 4

In the stormy east-wind straining,
The pale yellow woods were waning,
The broad stream in his banks complaining,   120
Heavily the low sky raining
    Over towered Camelot;
Down she came and found a boat
Beneath a willow left afloat,
And round about the prow she wrote   125
    The Lady of Shalott.

And down the river's dim expanse
Like some bold seër in a trance,
Seeing all his own mischance—
With a glassy countenance   130
    Did she look to Camelot.
And at the closing of the day
She loosed the chain, and down she lay;
The broad stream bore her far away,
    The Lady of Shalott.   135

Lying, robed in snowy white
That loosely flew to left and right—
The leaves upon her falling light—
Through the noises of the night
    She floated down to Camelot;   140
And as the boat-head wound along
The willowy hills and fields among,
They heard her singing her last song,
    The Lady of Shalott.

Heard a carol, mournful, holy,   145
Chanted loudly, chanted lowly,
Till her blood was frozen slowly,
And her eyes were darkened wholly,
    Turned to towered Camelot.
For ere she reached upon the tide   150

The first house by the water-side,
  Singing in her song she died,
    The Lady of Shalott.

Under tower and balcony,
By garden-wall and gallery,
A gleaming shape she floated by,
Dead-pale between the houses high,   155
  Silent into Camelot.
Out upon the wharfs they came,
Knight and burgher, lord and dame,   160
And round the prow they read her name,
  The Lady of Shalott.

Who is this? And what is here?
And in the lighted palace near
Died the sound of royal cheer;   165
And they crossed themselves for fear,
  All the knights at Camelot.
But Lancelot mused a little space;
He said, "She has a lovely face;
God in his mercy lend her grace,   170
  The Lady of Shalott."

THE POET

The poet in a golden clime was born,
  With golden stars above;
Dowered with the hate of hate, the scorn of scorn,
    The love of love.

He saw through life and death, through good and ill, 5
  He saw through his own soul.
The marvel of the everlasting will,
    An open scroll,

Before him lay; with echoing feet he threaded
  The secretest walks of fame: 10
The viewless arrows of his thoughts were headed
    And winged with flame,

Like Indian reeds[1] blown from his silver tongue,
  And of so fierce a flight,
From Calpe unto Caucasus[2] they sung,   15
    Filling with light

And vagrant melodies the winds which bore
  Them earthward till they lit;

Then, like the arrow-seeds of the field flower,[3]
    The fruitful wit   20

Cleaving, took root, and springing forth anew
  Where'er they fell, behold,
Like to the mother plant in semblance, grew
    A flower all gold,

And bravely furnished all abroad to fling   25
  The wingèd shafts of truth,
To throng with stately blooms the breathing spring
    Of Hope and Youth.

So many minds did gird their orbs with beams,
  Though one did fling the fire.   30
Heaven flowed upon the soul in many dreams
    Of high desire.

Thus truth was multiplied on truth, the world
  Like one great garden showed,
And through the wreaths of floating dark upcurled, 35
    Rare sunrise flowed.

And Freedom reared in that august sunrise
  Her beautiful bold brow,
When rites and forms[4] before his burning eyes
    Melted like snow.   40

There was no blood upon her maiden robes
  Sunned by those orient skies;
But round about the circles of the globes
    Of her keen eyes[5]

And in her raiment's hem was traced in flame   45
  WISDOM, a name to shake
All evil dreams of power—a sacred name.
    And when she spake,

Her words did gather thunder as they ran,
  And as the lightning to the thunder   50
Which follows it, riving the spirit of man,
    Making earth wonder,

So was their meaning to her words. No sword
  Of wrath her right arm whirled,
But one poor poet's scroll, and with *his* word   55
  She shook the world.

---

[1] Arrows blown from a blowpipe.
[2] From Gibraltar to the Caucasus Mountains, that is, through Europe from its western to its eastern limits.

[3] The dandelion.
[4] The old tyrannical forms of monarchy and the church.
[5] The word "wisdom" (see the next lines) is reflected in her eyes.

YOU ASK ME, WHY, THOUGH ILL AT EASE

You ask me, why, though ill at ease,
  Within this region I subsist,
  Whose spirits falter in the mist,
And languish for the purple seas.

It is the land that freemen till,   5
  That sober-suited Freedom chose,
  The land, where girt with friends or foes
A man may speak the thing he will;

A land of settled government,
  A land of just and old renown,   10
  Where Freedom slowly broadens down
From precedent to precedent;

Where faction seldom gathers head,
  But by degrees to fullness wrought,
  The strength of some diffusive thought   15
Hath time and space to work and spread.

Should banded unions persecute
  Opinion, and induce a time
  When single thought is civil crime,
And individual freedom mute;   20

Though Power should make from land to land
  The name of Britain trebly great—
  Though every channel of the State
Should fill and choke with golden sand—

Yet waft me from the harbor-mouth,   25
  Wild wind! I seek a warmer sky,
  And I will see before I die
The palms and temples of the South.

SIR GALAHAD

My good blade carves the casques[1] of men,
  My tough lance thrusteth sure,
My strength is as the strength of ten,
  Because my heart is pure.
The shattering trumpet shrilleth high,   5
  The hard brands shiver on the steel,
The splintered spear-shafts crack and fly,
  The horse and rider reel:
They reel, they roll in clanging lists,
  And when the tide of combat stands,   10

Perfume and flowers fall in showers,
  That lightly rain from ladies' hands.

How sweet are looks that ladies bend
  On whom their favors fall!
For them I battle till the end,   15
  To save from shame and thrall:
But all my heart is drawn above,
  My knees are bowed in crypt and shrine:
I never felt the kiss of love,
  Nor maiden's hand in mine.   20
More bounteous aspects on me beam,
  Me mightier transports move and thrill;
So keep I fair through faith and prayer
  A virgin heart in work and will.

When down the stormy crescent[2] goes,   25
  A light before me swims,
Between dark stems the forest glows,
  I hear a noise of hymns.
Then by some secret shrine I ride;
  I hear a voice but none are there;   30
The stalls are void, the doors are wide,
  The tapers burning fair.
Fair gleams the snowy altar-cloth,
  The silver vessels sparkle clean,
The shrill bell rings, the censer swings,   35
  And solemn chaunts resound between.

Sometimes on lonely mountain-meres
  I find a magic bark;
I leap on board; no helmsman steers;
  I float till all is dark.   40
A gentle sound, an awful light!
  Three angels bear the holy Grail;[3]
With folded feet, in stoles of white,
  On sleeping wings they sail.
Ah, blessed vision! blood of God!   45
  My spirit beats her mortal bars,
As down dark tides the glory slides,
  And star-like mingles with the stars.

When on my goodly charger borne
  Through dreaming towns I go,   50
The cock crows ere the Christmas morn,
  The streets are dumb with snow.
The tempest crackles on the leads,[4]
  And, ringing, springs from brand and mail;

---

[1] Helmets.

[2] The new moon.
[3] The cup in which Joseph of Arimathea was said to have caught the drops of blood that fell from Christ on the cross, and which supposedly he had brought to England.
[4] Leaded roofs.

But o'er the dark a glory spreads,
  And gilds the driving hail.
I leave the plain, I climb the height;
  No branchy thicket shelter yields;
But blessèd forms in whistling storms
  Fly o'er waste fens and windy fields.   60

A maiden knight—to me is given
  Such hope, I know not fear;
I yearn to breathe the airs of heaven
  That often meet me here.
I muse on joy that will not cease,   65
  Pure spaces clothed in living beams,
Pure lilies of eternal peace,
  Whose odors haunt my dreams;
And, stricken by an angel's hand,
  This mortal armor that I wear,   70
This weight and size, this heart and eyes,
  Are touched, are turned to finest air.

The clouds are broken in the sky,
  And through the mountain-walls
A rolling organ-harmony   75
  Swells up and shakes and falls.
Then move the trees, the copses nod,
  Wings flutter, voices hover clear:
"O just and faithful knight of God!
  Ride on! the prize is near."   80
So pass I hostel, hall, and grange;
  By bridge and ford, by park and pale,
All-armed I ride, whate'er betide,
  Until I find the holy Grail.

TO ———

WITH THE FOLLOWING POEM[1]

I send you here a sort of allegory,
(For you will understand it) of a soul,
A sinful soul possessed of many gifts,
A spacious garden full of flowering weeds,
A glorious Devil, large in heart and brain,   5
That did love Beauty only (Beauty seen
In all varieties of mould and mind),
And Knowledge for its beauty; or if Good,
Good only for its beauty, seeing not
That Beauty, Good, and Knowledge, are three sisters 10
That dote upon each other, friends to man,

---

[1] The dedication is probably to R. C. Trench, one of the Apostles, who took Tennyson aside and warned him that "we cannot live in art." That remark, according to Tennyson, was the "inspiration" for "The Palace of Art," which follows.

Living together under the same roof,
And never can be sundered without tears.
And he that shuts Love out, in turn shall be
Shut out from Love, and on her threshold lie   15
Howling in outer darkness. Not for this
Was common clay ta'en from the common earth
Moulded by God, and tempered with the tears
Of angels to the perfect shape of man.

THE PALACE OF ART

I built my soul a lordly pleasure-house,
  Wherein at ease for aye to dwell.
I said, "O Soul, make merry and carouse,
  Dear soul, for all is well."

A huge crag-platform, smooth as burnished brass,   5
  I chose. The rangèd ramparts bright
From level meadow-bases of deep grass
  Suddenly scaled the light.

Thereon I built it firm. Of ledge or shelf
  The rock rose clear, or winding stair.   10
My soul would live alone unto herself
  In her high palace there.

And "while the world runs round and round," I said,
  "Reign thou apart, a quiet king,
Still as, while Saturn whirls, his steadfast shade   15
  Sleeps on his luminous ring."[2]

To which my soul made answer readily:
  "Trust me, in bliss I shall abide
In this great mansion, that is built for me,
  So royal-rich and wide."   20

    * * * * *

Four courts I made, East, West, and South and North,
  In each a squarèd lawn, wherefrom
The golden gorge of dragons spouted forth
  A flood of fountain-foam.

And round the cool green courts there ran a row   25
  Of cloisters, branched like mighty woods,
Echoing all night to that sonorous flow
  Of spouted fountain-floods;

And round the roofs a gilded gallery
  That lent broad verge to distant lands,   30
Far as the wild swan wings, to where the sky
  Dipped down to sea and sands.

---

[2] The shadow of whirling Saturn cast on the luminous ring that surrounds the planet appears to be motionless.

From those four jets four currents in one swell
    Across the mountain streamed below
In misty folds, that floating as they fell   35
    Lit up a torrent-bow.

And high on every peak a statue seemed
    To hang on tiptoe, tossing up
A cloud of incense of all odor steamed
    From out a golden cup.   40

So that she thought, "And who shall gaze upon
    My palace with unblinded eyes,
While this great bow will waver in the sun,
    And that sweet incense rise?"

For that sweet incense rose and never failed,   45
    And, while day sank or mounted higher,
The light aërial gallery, golden-railed,
    Burnt like a fringe of fire.

Likewise the deep-set windows, stained and traced,
    Would seem slow-flaming crimson fires   50
From shadowed grots of arches interlaced,
    And tipped with frost-like spires.

* * * * *

Full of long-sounding corridors it was,
    That over-vaulted grateful gloom,
Through which the livelong day my soul did pass,   55
    Well-pleased, from room to room.

Full of great rooms and small the palace stood,
    All various, each a perfect whole
From living Nature, fit for every mood
    And change of my still soul.   60

For some were hung with arras green and blue,
    Showing a gaudy summer-morn,
Where with puffed cheek the belted hunter blew
    His wreathèd bugle-horn.

One seemed all dark and red—a tract of sand,   65
    And some one pacing there alone,
Who paced for ever in a glimmering land,
    Lit with a low large moon.

One showed an iron coast and angry waves.
    You seemed to hear them climb and fall   70
And roar rock-thwarted under bellowing caves
    Beneath the windy wall.

And one, a full-fed river winding slow
    By herds upon an endless plain,

The ragged rims of thunder brooding low,   75
    With shadow-streaks of rain.

And one, the reapers at their sultry toil.
    In front they bound the sheaves. Behind
Were realms of upland, prodigal in oil,
    And hoary to the wind.[3]   80

And one a foreground black with stones and slags,
    Beyond, a line of heights, and higher
All barred with long white cloud the scornful crags,
    And highest, snow and fire.

And one, an English home—gray twilight poured   85
    On dewy pastures, dewy trees,
Softer than sleep—all things in order stored,
    A haunt of ancient Peace.

Nor these alone, but every landscape fair,
    As fit for every mood of mind,   90
Or gay, or grave, or sweet, or stern, was there
    Not less than truth designed.

* * * * *

Or the maid-mother by a crucifix,
    In tracts of pasture sunny-warm,
Beneath branch-work of costly sardonyx   95
    Sat smiling, babe in arm.

Or in a clear-walled city on the sea,
    Near gilded organ-pipes, her hair
Wound with white roses, slept Saint Cecily;[4]
    An angel looked at her.   100

Or thronging all one porch of Paradise
    A group of Houris[5] bowed to see
The dying Islamite,[6] with hands and eyes
    That said, We wait for thee.

Or mythic Uther's deeply-wounded son[7]   105
    In some fair space of sloping greens
Lay, dozing in the vale of Avalon,[8]
    And watched by weeping queens.

Or hollowing one hand against his ear,
    To list a foot-fall, ere he saw   110

---

[3] Cf. p. 639, note 2, above.
[4] Patron saint of music.
[5] Maidens who lived in the Mohammedan paradise.
[6] Mohammedan.
[7] King Arthur.
[8] Earthly paradise to which Arthur was borne by the queens referred to in the next line.

The wood-nymph, stayed the Ausonian king to hear
　Of wisdom and of law.[9]

Or over hills with peaky tops engrailed,[10]
　And many a tract of palm and rice,
The throne of Indian Cama[11] slowly sailed　　115
　A summer fanned with spice.

Or sweet Europa's mantle blew unclasped,
　From off her shoulder backward borne;
From one hand drooped a crocus; one hand grasped
　The mild bull's golden horn.[12]　　120

Or else flushed Ganymede,[13] his rosy thigh
　Half-buried in the eagle's down,
Sole as a flying star shot through the sky
　Above the pillared town.

Nor these alone; but every legend fair　　125
　Which the supreme Caucasian mind[14]
Carved out of Nature for itself, was there,
　Not less than life, designed.

* * * * *

Then in the towers I placed great bells that swung,
　Moved of themselves, with silver sound;　　130
And with choice paintings of wise men I hung
　The royal dais round.

For there was Milton like a seraph strong,
　Beside him Shakespeare bland and mild;
And there the world-worn Dante grasped his song,　　135
　And somewhat grimly smiled.

And there the Ionian father of the rest;[15]
　A million wrinkles carved his skin;
A hundred winters snowed upon his breast,
　From cheek and throat and chin.　　140

Above, the fair hall-ceiling stately-set
　Many an arch high up did lift,
And angels rising and descending met
　With interchange of gift.

Below was all mosaic choicely planned　　145
　With cycles of the human tale

Of this wide world, the times of every land
　So wrought, they will not fail.

The people here, a beast of burden slow,
　Toiled onward, pricked with goads and stings;　　150
Here played a tiger, rolling to and fro
　The heads and crowns of kings;

Here rose an athlete, strong to break or bind
　All force in bonds that might endure,
And here once more like some sick man declined,　　155
　And trusted any cure.

But over these she trod; and those great bells
　Began to chime. She took her throne;
She sat betwixt the shining oriels,
　To sing her songs alone.　　160

And through the topmost oriels' colored flame
　Two god-like faces gazed below.
Plato the wise, and large-browed Verulam,[16]
　The first of those who know.

And all those names that in their motion were　　165
　Full-welling fountain-heads of change,
Betwixt the slender shafts were blazoned fair
　In diverse raiment strange;

Through which the lights, rose, amber, emerald, blue,
　Flushed in her temples and her eyes,　　170
And from her lips, as morn from Memnon,[17] drew
　Rivers of melodies.

No nightingale delighteth to prolong
　Her low preamble all alone,
More than my soul to hear her echoed song　　175
　Throb through the ribbèd stone;

Singing and murmuring in her feastful mirth,
　Joying to feel herself alive,
Lord over Nature, lord of the visible earth,
　Lord of the senses five;　　180

Communing with herself: "All these are mine,
　And let the world have peace or wars,
'Tis one to me." She—when young night divine
　Crowned dying day with stars,

Making sweet close of his delicious toils—　　185
　Lit light in wreaths and anadems,[18]

---

[9] Numa, early Roman king (*Ausonian* = Italian), was counseled by the nymph Egeria.　　[10] Indented.
[11] God of love in Hindu mythology.
[12] Europa, princess of Phoenicia, was courted by Zeus in the disguise of a white bull.
[13] Trojan boy whom Zeus, in the form of an eagle, carried off to Olympus and made the cupbearer of the gods.
[14] Race.　　[15] Homer.

[16] Francis Bacon.
[17] A statue near Thebes in Egypt supposed to respond with music to the first rays of the sun.　　[18] Garlands.

And pure quintessences of precious oils
    In hollowed moons of gems,

To mimic heaven; and clapped her hands and cried,
    "I marvel if my still delight   190
In this great house so royal-rich, and wide,
    Be flattered to the height.

"O all things fair to sate my various eyes!
    O shapes and hues that please me well!
O silent faces of the Great and Wise,   195
    My Gods, with whom I dwell!

"O god-like isolation which art mine,
    I can but count thee perfect gain,
What time I watch the darkening droves of swine
    That range on yonder plain.   200

"In filthy sloughs they roll a prurient skin,
    They graze and wallow, breed and sleep;
And oft some brainless devil enters in,
    And drives them to the deep."

Then of the moral instinct would she prate   205
    And of the rising from the dead,
As hers by right of full-accomplished Fate;
    And at the last she said:

"I take possession of man's mind and deed.
    I care not what the sects may brawl.   210
I sit as God holding no form of creed,
    But contemplating all."

        *   *   *   *   *   *

Full oft the riddle of the painful earth
    Flashed through her as she sat alone,
Yet not the less held she her solemn mirth,   215
    And intellectual throne.

And so she throve and prospered; so three years
    She prospered; on the fourth she fell,
Like Herod, when the shout was in his ears,[19]
    Struck through with pangs of hell.   220

Lest she should fail and perish utterly,
    God, before whom ever lie bare
The abysmal deeps of Personality,
    Plagued her with sore despair.   224

When she would think, where'er she turned her sight
    The airy hand confusion wrought,

Wrote, "Mene, mene,"[20] and divided quite
    The kingdom of her thought.

Deep dread and loathing of her solitude
    Fell on her, from which mood was born   230
Scorn of herself; again, from out that mood
    Laughter at her self-scorn.

"What! is not this my place of strength," she said,
    "My spacious mansion built for me,
Whereof the strong foundation-stones were laid   235
    Since my first memory?"

But in dark corners of her palace stood
    Uncertain shapes; and unawares
On white-eyed phantasms weeping tears of blood,
    And horrible nightmares,   240

And hollow shades enclosing hearts of flame,
    And, with dim fretted foreheads all,
On corpses three-months-old at noon she came,
    That stood against the wall.

A spot of dull stagnation, without light   245
    Or power of movement, seemed my soul,
'Mid onward-sloping motions infinite
    Making for one sure goal.

A still salt pool, locked in with bars of sand,
    Left on the shore; that hears all night   250
The plunging seas draw backward from the land
    Their moon-led waters white.

A star that with the choral starry dance
    Joined not, but stood, and standing saw
The hollow orb of moving Circumstance   255
    Rolled round by one fixed law.

Back on herself her serpent pride had curled.
    "No voice," she shrieked in that lone hall,
"No voice breaks through the stillness of this world;
    One deep, deep silence all!"   260

She, moldering with the dull earth's moldering sod,
    Inwrapt tenfold in slothful shame,
Lay there exilèd from eternal God,
    Lost to her place and name;

And death and life she hated equally,   265
    And nothing saw, for her despair,

---

[19] As the people shouted their praise of him as a god, Herod was struck down by the angel of the Lord "because he gave not God the glory." (Acts 12:21–23)

[20] One of the words of warning written on the wall of Belshazzar's palace which Daniel interpreted as meaning, "God hath numbered thy kingdom, and finished it" (Daniel 5:17–31).

But dreadful time, dreadful eternity,
   No comfort anywhere;

Remaining utterly confused with fears,
   And ever worse with growing time,   270
And ever unrelieved by dismal tears,
   And all alone in crime:

Shut up as in a crumbling tomb, girt round
   With blackness as a solid wall,
Far off she seemed to hear the dully sound   275
   Of human footsteps fall:

As in strange lands a traveler walking slow,
   In doubt and great perplexity,
A little before moon-rise hears the low
   Moan of an unknown sea;   280

And knows not if it be thunder, or a sound
   Of rocks thrown down, or one deep cry
Of great wild beasts; then thinketh, "I have found
   A new land, but I die."

She howled aloud, "I am on fire within.   285
   There comes no murmur of reply.
What is it that will take away my sin,
   And save me lest I die?"

So when four years were wholly finishèd,
   She threw her royal robes away.   290
"Make me a cottage in the vale," she said,
   "Where I may mourn and pray.

"Yet pull not down my palace towers, that are
   So lightly, beautifully built;
Perchance I may return with others there   295
   When I have purged my guilt."

OENONE[1]

There lies a vale in Ida, lovelier
Than all the valleys of Ionian hills.
The swimming vapor slopes athwart the glen,
Puts forth an arm, and creeps from pine to pine,
And loiters, slowly drawn. On either hand   5
The lawns and meadow-ledges midway down
Hang rich in flowers, and far below them roars

[1] A nymph, daughter of Mt. Ida and the river Simois, both near Troy, who was beloved by Paris until the fatal day when he awarded the apple engraved "for the fairest" to Aphrodite. Aphrodite gave him Helen of Troy in return—and Oenone was deserted.

The long brook falling through the cloven ravine
In cataract after cataract to the sea.
Behind the valley topmost Gargarus[2]   10
Stands up and takes the morning; but in front
The gorges, opening wide apart, reveal
Troas and Ilion's columned citadel,[3]
The crown of Troas.
               Hither came at noon
Mournful Oenone, wandering forlorn   15
Of Paris, once her playmate on the hills.
Her cheek had lost the rose, and round her neck
Floated her hair or seemed to float in rest.
She, leaning on a fragment twined with vine,
Sang to the stillness, till the mountain-shade   20
Sloped downward to her seat from the upper cliff.

   "O mother Ida, many-fountained Ida,
Dear mother Ida, harken ere I die.
For now the noonday quiet holds the hill;
The grasshopper is silent in the grass;   25
The lizard, with his shadow on the stone,
Rests like a shadow, and the winds are dead.
The purple flowers droop, the golden bee
Is lily-cradled; I alone awake.
My eyes are full of tears, my heart of love,   30
My heart is breaking, and my eyes are dim,
And I am all aweary of my life.

   "O mother Ida, many-fountained Ida,
Dear mother Ida, harken ere I die.
Hear me, O Earth, hear me, O Hills, O Caves   35
That house the cold crowned snake! O mountain brooks,
I am the daughter of a River-God,
Hear me, for I will speak, and build up all
My sorrow with my song, as yonder walls
Rose slowly to a music slowly breathed,[4]   40
A cloud that gathered shape: for it may be
That, while I speak of it, a little while
My heart may wander from its deeper woe.

   "O mother Ida, many-fountained Ida,
Dear mother Ida, harken ere I die.   45
I waited underneath the dawning hills,
Aloft the mountain lawn was dewy-dark,
And dewy-dark aloft the mountain pine:
Beautiful Paris, evil-hearted Paris,
Leading a jet-black goat white-horned, white-
     hooved,   50
Came up from reedy Simois all alone.

[2] Highest peak of Mt. Ida.
[3] The region surrounding Troy, and Troy itself.
[4] See "Tithonus," note 4.

"O mother Ida, harken ere I die.
Far-off the torrent called me from the cleft;
Far up the solitary morning smote
The streaks of virgin snow. With down-dropt eyes   55
I sat alone; white-breasted like a star
Fronting the dawn he moved; a leopard skin
Drooped from his shoulder, but his sunny hair
Clustered about his temples like a God's;
And his cheek brightened as the foam-bow brightens   60
When the wind blows the foam, and all my heart
Went forth to embrace him coming ere he came.

"Dear mother Ida, harken ere I die.
He smiled, and opening out his milk-white palm
Disclosed a fruit of pure Hesperian gold,   65
That smelt ambrosially,[5] and while I looked
And listened, the full-flowing river of speech
Came down upon my heart.
                                 " 'My own Oenone,
Beautiful-browed Oenone, my own soul,
Behold this fruit, whose gleaming rind ingraven   70
"For the most fair," would seem to award it thine,
As lovelier than whatever Oread haunt
The knolls of Ida, loveliest in all grace
Of movement, and the charm of married brows.'

"Dear mother Ida, harken ere I die.   75
He prest the blossom of his lips to mine,
And added, 'This was cast upon the board,
When all the full-faced presence of the Gods
Ranged in the halls of Peleus;[6] whereupon
Rose feud, with question unto whom 'twere due;   80
But light-foot Iris[7] brought it yester-eve,
Delivering, that to me, by common voice
Elected umpire, Herè comes to-day,
Pallas and Aphroditè, claiming each
This meed of fairest.[8] Thou, within the cave   85
Behind yon whispering tuft of oldest pine,
Mayst well behold them unbeheld, unheard
Hear all, and see thy Paris judge of Gods.'

"Dear mother Ida, harken ere I die.
It was the deep midnoon; one silvery cloud   90
Had lost his way between the piney sides
Of this long glen. Then to the bower they came,

Naked they came to that smooth-swarded bower,
And at their feet the crocus brake like fire,
Violet, amaracus, and asphodel,   95
Lotos and lilies; and a wind arose,
And overhead the wandering ivy and vine,
This way and that, in many a wild festoon
Ran riot, garland in the gnarlèd boughs
With bunch and berry and flower through and
    through.   100

"O mother Ida, harken ere I die.
On the tree-tops, a crested peacock lit,[9]
And o'er him flowed a golden cloud, and leaned
Upon him, slowly dropping fragrant dew.
Then first I heard the voice of her, to whom   105
Coming through Heaven, like a light that grows
Larger and clearer, with one mind the Gods
Rise up for reverence. She to Paris made
Proffer of royal power, ample rule
Unquestioned, overflowing revenue   110
Wherewith to embellish state, 'from many a vale
And river-sundered champaign clothed with corn,
Or labored mines undrainable of ore.
Honor,' she said, 'and homage, tax and toll,
From many an inland town and haven large,   115
Mast-thronged beneath her shadowing citadel
In glassy bays among her tallest towers.'

"O mother Ida, harken ere I die.
Still she spake on and still she spake of power,
'Which in all action is the end of all;   120
Power fitted to the season; wisdom-bred
And throned of wisdom—from all neighbor crowns
Alliance and allegiance, till thy hand
Fail from the sceptre-staff. Such boon from me,
From me, Heaven's Queen, Paris, to thee king-born,   125
A shepherd all thy life but yet king-born,
Should come most welcome, seeing men, in power
Only, are likest gods, who have attained
Rest in a happy place and quiet seats
Above the thunder, with undying bliss   130
In knowledge of their own supremacy.'

"Dear mother Ida, harken ere I die.
She ceased, and Paris held the costly fruit
Out at arm's-length, so much the thought of power
Flattered his spirit; but Pallas where she stood   135
Somewhat apart, her clean and barèd limbs
O'erthwarted with the brazen-headed spear
Upon her pearly shoulder leaning cold,

---

[5] A fruit like the golden apples guarded by the Hesperides which smells like ambrosia, the food of the gods.
[6] At the wedding feast of Thetis and Peleus.
[7] Messenger of the gods.
[8] Herè is Juno, the wife of Jupiter; Pallas Athena, or Minerva, is the goddess of wisdom; Aphroditè is Venus, goddess of love and beauty.

[9] Bird sacred to Herè.

The while, above, her full and earnest eye
Over her snow-cold breast and angry cheek   140
Kept watch, waiting decision, made reply.

   " 'Self-reverence, self-knowledge, self-control,
These three alone lead life to sovereign power.
Yet not for power (power of herself
Would come uncalled for) but to live by law,   145
Acting the law we live by without fear;
And, because right is right, to follow right
Were wisdom in the scorn of consequence.'

   "Dear mother Ida, harken ere I die.
Again she said: 'I woo thee not with gifts.   150
Sequel of guerdon[10] could not alter me
To fairer. Judge thou me by what I am,
So shalt thou find me fairest.
                              " 'Yet, indeed,
If gazing on divinity disrobed
Thy mortal eyes are frail to judge of fair,   155
Unbiassed by self-profit, oh! rest thee sure
That I shall love thee well and cleave to thee,
So that my vigor, wedded to thy blood,
Shall strike within thy pulses, like a God's,
To push thee forward through a life of shocks,   160
Dangers, and deeds, until endurance grow
Sinewed with action, and the full-grown will,
Circled through all experiences, pure law,
Commeasure perfect freedom.'
                              "Here she ceased,
And Paris pondered, and I cried, 'O Paris,   165
Give it to Pallas!' but he heard me not,
Or hearing would not hear me, woe is me!

   "O mother Ida, many-fountained Ida,
Dear mother Ida, harken ere I die.
Idalian Aphroditè beautiful,   170
Fresh as the foam, new-bathed in Paphian wells,[11]
With rosy slender fingers backward drew
From her warm brows and bosom her deep hair
Ambrosial, golden round her lucid throat
And shoulder; from the violets her light foot   175
Shone rosy-white, and o'er her rounded form
Between the shadows of the vine-bunches
Floated the glowing sunlights, as she moved.

   "Dear mother Ida, harken ere I die.
She with a subtle smile in her mild eyes,   180

The herald of her triumph, drawing nigh
Half-whispered in his ear, 'I promise thee
The fairest and most loving wife in Greece.'
She spoke and laughed; I shut my sight for fear:
But when I looked, Paris had raised his arm,   185
And I beheld great Herè's angry eyes,
As she withdrew into the golden cloud,
And I was left alone within the bower;
And from that time to this I am alone,
And I shall be alone until I die.   190

   "Yet, mother Ida, harken ere I die.
Fairest—why fairest wife? am I not fair?
My love hath told me so a thousand times.
Methinks I must be fair, for yesterday,
When I past by, a wild and wanton pard,[12]   195
Eyed like the evening star, with playful tail
Crouched fawning in the weed. Most loving is she?
Ah me, my mountain shepherd, that my arms
Were wound about thee, and my hot lips prest
Close, close to thine in that quick-falling dew   200
Of fruitful kisses, thick as Autumn rains
Flash in the pools of whirling Simois.

   "O mother, hear me yet before I die.
They came, they cut away my tallest pines,[13]
My dark tall pines, that plumed the craggy ledge   205
High over the blue gorge, and all between
The snowy peak and snow-white cataract
Fostered the callow eaglet—from beneath
Whose thick mysterious boughs in the dark morn
The panther's roar came muffled, while I sat   210
Low in the valley. Never, never more
Shall lone Oenone see the morning mist
Sweep thro' them; never see them overlaid
With narrow moon-lit slips of silver cloud,
Between the loud stream and the trembling stars.   215

   "O mother, hear me yet before I die.
I wish that somewhere in the ruined folds,
Among the fragments tumbled from the glens,
Of the dry thickets, I could meet with her
The Abominable,[14] that uninvited came   220
Into the fair Peleïan banquet-hall,
And cast the golden fruit upon the board,
And bred this change; that I might speak my mind,
And tell her to her face how much I hate
Her presence, hated both of Gods and men.   225

_____

[10] The reward which will follow if he gives her the apple.
[11] Idalium and Paphos were towns where Aphroditè was worshiped.
    She was said to have landed at Paphos after her birth in the sea.

[12] Leopard.
[13] To build ships with which to sail across the Aegean Sea to
    Greece, where Helen was living.
[14] Eris, goddess of discord.

"O mother, hear me yet before I die.
Hath he not sworn his love a thousand times,
In this green valley, under this green hill,
Ev'n on this hand, and sitting on this stone?
Sealed it with kisses? watered it with tears?
O happy tears, and how unlike to these!
O happy Heaven, how canst thou see my face?
O happy earth, how canst thou bear my weight?
O death, death, death, thou ever-floating cloud,
There are enough unhappy on this earth,   235
Pass by the happy souls, that love to live;
I pray thee, pass before my light of life,
And shadow all my soul, that I may die.
Thou weighest heavy on the heart within,
Weigh heavy on my eyelids; let me die.   240

"O mother, hear me yet before I die.
I will not die alone, for fiery thoughts
Do shape themselves within me, more and more,
Whereof I catch the issue, as I hear
Dead sounds at night come from the inmost hills,   245
Like footsteps upon wool. I dimly see
My far-off doubtful purpose,[15] as a mother
Conjectures of the features of her child
Ere it is born: her child!—a shudder comes
Across me: never child be born of me,   250
Unblest, to vex me with his father's eyes!

"O mother, hear me yet before I die.
Hear me, O earth. I will not die alone,
Lest their shrill happy laughter come to me
Walking the cold and starless road of Death   255
Uncomforted, leaving my ancient love
With the Greek woman. I will rise and go
Down into Troy, and ere the stars come forth
Talk with the wild Cassandra,[16] for she says
A fire dances before her, and a sound   260
Rings ever in her ears of armèd men.
What this may be I know not, but I know
That, wheresoe'er I am by night and day,
All earth and air seem only burning fire."

---

15 To refuse Paris's request that she heal the wound which she
foresees he will receive in the Trojan War, and thus to gain her
revenge. This explains her statement (line 242) that she will not
die alone.
16 Daughter of Priam, gifted with the power of prophecy. She
foretold the Trojan War.

ULYSSES

It little profits that an idle king,
By this still hearth, among these barren crags,[1]
Matched with an aged wife, I mete and dole
Unequal laws unto a savage race,
That hoard, and sleep, and feed, and know not me.   5

I cannot rest from travel; I will drink
Life to the lees: all times I have enjoyed
Greatly, have suffered greatly, both with those
That loved me, and alone; on shore, and when
Through scudding drifts the rainy Hyades[2]   10
Vexed the dim sea: I am become a name;
For always roaming with a hungry heart
Much have I seen and known: cities of men
And manners, climates, councils, governments,
Myself not least, but honored of them all;   15
And drunk delight of battle with my peers,
Far on the ringing plains of windy Troy.
I am a part of all that I have met;
Yet all experience is an arch wherethrough
Gleams that untraveled world, whose margin fades   20
For ever and for ever when I move.
How dull it is to pause, to make an end,
To rust unburnished, not to shine in use!
As though to breathe were life. Life piled on life
Were all too little, and of one to me   25
Little remains; but every hour is saved
From that eternal silence, something more,[3]
A bringer of new things; and vile it were
For some three suns to store and hoard myself,
And this gray spirit yearning in desire   30
To follow knowledge like a sinking star,
Beyond the utmost bound of human thought.

This is my son, mine own Telemachus,
To whom I leave the scepter and the isle—
Well-loved of me, discerning to fulfill   35
This labor, by slow prudence to make mild
A rugged people, and through soft degrees
Subdue them to the useful and the good.
Most blameless is he, centered in the sphere
Of common duties, decent not to fail   40
In offices of tenderness, and pay
Meet adoration to my household gods,
When I am gone. He works his work, I mine.

---

1 Of the island of Ithaca, off the west coast of Greece, the home
of Ulysses, to which he had returned, after ten years of wandering, from Troy.
2 A group of stars associated with the rainy season.
3 I.e., may be something more than just another hour.

650   THE VICTORIAN PERIOD

There lies the port; the vessel puffs her sail;
There gloom the dark broad seas. My mariners,   45
Souls that have toiled, and wrought, and thought with
    me—
That ever with a frolic welcome took
The thunder and the sunshine, and opposed
Free hearts, free foreheads—you and I are old;
Old age hath yet his honor and his toil;   50
Death closes all; but something ere the end,
Some work of noble note, may yet be done,
Not unbecoming men that strove with Gods.
The lights begin to twinkle from the rocks;
The long day wanes; the slow moon climbs; the deep   55
Moans round with many voices. Come, my friends,
'Tis not too late to seek a newer world.
Push off, and sitting well in order smite
The sounding furrows; for my purpose holds
To sail beyond the sunset, and the baths   60
Of all the western stars, until I die.
It may be that the gulfs will wash us down;
It may be we shall touch the Happy Isles,[4]
And see the great Achilles, whom we knew.
Though much is taken, much abides; and though   65
We are not now that strength which in old days
Moved earth and heaven, that which we are, we are;
One equal temper of heroic hearts,
Made weak by time and fate, but strong in will
To strive, to seek, to find, and not to yield.[5]   70

THE LOTOS-EATERS

"Courage!" he said,[1] and pointed toward the land,
"This mounting wave will roll us shoreward soon."
In the afternoon they came unto a land
In which it seemèd always afternoon.
All round the coast the languid air did swoon,   5
Breathing like one that hath a weary dream.
Full-faced above the valley stood the moon;
And like a downward smoke, the slender stream
Along the cliff to fall and pause and fall did seem.

A land of streams! some, like a downward smoke,   10
Slow-dropping veils of thinnest lawn, did go;
And some through wavering lights and shadows broke,

[4] The abode of the Greek heroes after death.
[5] Tennyson told his son that the poem was written shortly after
Arthur Hallam's death, "and gave my feeling about the need
of going forward, and braving the struggle of life." But it also
gives his feeling of escaping the struggle of life by the distraction
of endless experience for its own sake.

[1] Ulysses speaking to his men on their way back from Troy to
Ithaca.

Rolling a slumbrous sheet of foam below.
They saw the gleaming river seaward flow
From the inner land; far off, three mountain-tops,   15
Three silent pinnacles of aged snow,
Stood sunset-flushed; and, dewed with showery drops,
Up-clomb the shadowy pine above the woven copse.

The charmèd sunset lingered low adown
In the red West; through mountain clefts the dale   20
Was seen far inland, and the yellow down
Bordered with palm, and many a winding vale
And meadow, set with slender galingale;[2]
A land where all things always seemed the same!
And round about the keel with faces pale,   25
Dark faces pale against that rosy flame,
The mild-eyed melancholy Lotos-eaters came.

Branches they bore of that enchanted stem,
Laden with flower and fruit, whereof they gave
To each, but whoso did receive of them,   30
And taste, to him the gushing of the wave
Far far away did seem to mourn and rave
On alien shores; and if his fellow spake,
His voice was thin, as voices from the grave;
And deep-asleep he seemed, yet all awake,   35
And music in his ears his beating heart did make.

They sat them down upon the yellow sand
Between the sun and moon upon the shore;
And sweet it was to dream of Fatherland,
Of child, and wife, and slave; but evermore   40
Most weary seemed the sea, weary the oar,
Weary the wandering fields of barren foam.
Then someone said, "We will return no more";
And all at once they sang, "Our island home
Is far beyond the wave; we will no longer roam."   45

CHORIC SONG

There is sweet music here that softer falls
Than petals from blown roses on the grass,
Or night-dews on still waters between walls
Of shadowy granite, in a gleaming pass;
Music that gentlier on the spirit lies,   50
Than tired eyelids upon tired eyes;
Music that brings sweet sleep down from the blissful
    skies.
Here are cool mosses deep,
And through the moss the ivies creep,
And in the stream the long-leaved flowers weep,   55
And from the craggy ledge the poppy hangs in sleep.

[2] A kind of grass.

Why are we weighed upon with heaviness,
And utterly consumed with sharp distress,
While all things else have rest from weariness?
All things have rest; why should we toil alone,   60
We only toil, who are the first of things,
And make perpetual moan,
Still from one sorrow to another thrown;
Nor ever fold our wings,
And cease from wanderings,   65
Nor steep our brows in slumber's holy balm;
Nor harken what the inner spirit sings,
"There is no joy but calm!"
Why should we only toil, the roof and crown of
          things?

Lo! in the middle of the wood,   70
The folded leaf is wooed from out the bud
With winds upon the branch, and there
Grows green and broad, and takes no care,
Sun-steeped at noon, and in the moon
Nightly dew-fed; and turning yellow   75
Falls, and floats adown the air.
Lo! sweetened with the summer light,
The full-juiced apple, waxing over-mellow,
Drops in a silent autumn night.
All its allotted length of days,   80
The flower ripens in its place,
Ripens and fades, and falls, and hath no toil,
Fast-rooted in the fruitful soil.

Hateful is the dark-blue sky,
Vaulted o'er the dark-blue sea.   85
Death is the end of life; ah, why
Should life all labor be?
Let us alone. Time driveth onward fast,
And in a little while our lips are dumb.
Let us alone. What is it that will last?   90
All things are taken from us, and become
Portions and parcels of the dreadful Past.
Let us alone. What pleasure can we have
To war with evil? Is there any peace
In ever climbing up the climbing wave?   95
All things have rest, and ripen toward the grave
In silence; ripen, fall and cease;
Give us long rest or death, dark death, or dreamful ease.

How sweet it were, hearing the downward stream,
With half-shut eyes ever to seem   100
Falling asleep in a half-dream!
To dream and dream, like yonder amber light,
Which will not leave the myrrh-bush on the height;
To hear each other's whispered speech;
Eating the Lotos day by day,   105

To watch the crisping ripples on the beach,
And tender curving lines of creamy spray;
To lend our hearts and spirits wholly
To the influence of mild-minded melancholy;
To muse and brood and live again in memory,   110
With those old faces of our infancy
Heaped over with a mound of grass,
Two handfuls of white dust, shut in an urn of brass!

Dear is the memory of our wedded lives,
And dear the last embraces of our wives   115
And their warm tears; but all hath suffered change:
For surely now our household hearths are cold;
Our sons inherit us; our looks are strange;
And we should come like ghosts to trouble joy.
Or else the island princes over-bold   120
Have eat our substance, and the minstrel sings
Before them of the ten years' war in Troy,
And our great deeds, as half-forgotten things.
Is there confusion in the little isle?
Let what is broken so remain.   125
The gods are hard to reconcile;
'Tis hard to settle order once again.
There is confusion worse than death,
Trouble on trouble, pain on pain,
Long labor unto aged breath,   130
Sore task to hearts worn out by many wars
And eyes grown dim with gazing on the pilot-stars.

But, propped on beds of amaranth[3] and moly,[4]
How sweet (while warm airs lull us, blowing lowly)
With half-dropped eyelid still,   135
Beneath a heaven dark and holy,
To watch the long bright river drawing slowly
His waters from the purple hill—
To hear the dewy echoes calling
From cave to cave through the thick-twinèd vine—   140
To watch the emerald-colored water falling
Through many a wov'n acanthus-wreath divine![5]
Only to hear and see the far-off sparkling brine,
Only to hear were sweet, stretched out beneath the pine.

The Lotos blooms below the barren peak;   145
The Lotos blows by every winding creek;
All day the wind breathes low with mellower tone;
Through every hollow cave and alley lone
Round and round the spicy downs the yellow Lotos-
          dust is blown.
We have had enough of action, and of motion we,   150

---

[3] A flower that could not fade.   [4] An herb of magical power.
[5] Acanthus was a plant sacred to the gods.

Rolled to starboard, rolled to larboard, when the surge
    was seething free,
Where the wallowing monster spouted his foam-
    fountains in the sea.
Let us swear an oath, and keep it with an equal mind,
In the hollow Lotos-land to live and lie reclined
On the hills like Gods together, careless of mankind. 155
For they lie beside their nectar, and the bolts are hurled
Far below them in the valleys, and the clouds are
    lightly curled
Round their golden houses, girdled with the gleaming
    world;
Where they smile in secret, looking over wasted lands,
Blight and famine, plague and earthquake, roaring
    deeps and fiery sands,   160
Clanging fights, and flaming towns, and sinking ships,
    and praying hands.
But they smile, they find a music centered in a doleful
    song
Steaming up, a lamentation and an ancient tale of wrong,
Like a tale of little meaning though the words are strong;
Chanted from an ill-used race of men that cleave the
    soil,   165
Sow the seed, and reap the harvest with enduring toil,
Storing yearly little dues of wheat, and wine and oil;
Till they perish and they suffer—some, 'tis whispered—
    down in hell
Suffer endless anguish, others in Elysian valleys dwell,[6]
Resting weary limbs at last on beds of asphodel.   170
Surely, surely, slumber is more sweet than toil, the shore
Than labor in the deep mid-ocean, wind and wave
    and oar;
O rest ye, brother mariners, we will not wander more.[7]

LOCKSLEY HALL

Comrades, leave me here a little, while as yet 'tis early
    morn;
Leave me here, and when you want me, sound upon
    the bugle horn.

'Tis the place, and all around it, as of old, the curlews[1] call,

---

[6] The Elysian fields were the paradise of the Greeks.
[7] By introducing into the second version of the poem this comparison of the lotos-eaters to the Lucretian gods, aloof "from
all human interests and elevated action," living in "an Epicurean and therefore hard-hearted repose, sweetened not troubled
by the endless wail from the earth" (Memoir, I, 504), Tennyson
injected a moral-religious judgment into an amoral poem, and
suddenly asked the reader to condemn what had earlier been
presented as entirely attractive and desirable. Did he try to
"save" a poem of escape by tacking on a moral?

[1] Seashore birds with long bills.

Dreary gleams about the moorland flying over Locksley
    Hall;[2]

Locksley Hall, that in the distance overlooks the sandy
    tracts,   5
And the hollow ocean-ridges roaring into cataracts.

Many a night from yonder ivied casement, ere I went
    to rest,
Did I look on great Orion sloping slowly to the west.

Many a night I saw the Pleiads, rising through the
    mellow shade,
Glitter like a swarm of fire-flies tangled in a silver
    braid.   10

Here about the beach I wandered, nourishing a youth
    sublime
With the fairy tales of science, and the long result of
    Time;

When the centuries behind me like a fruitful land
    reposed;
When I clung to all the present for the promise that
    it closed;

When I dipped into the future far as human eye
    could see;   15
Saw the Vision of the world, and all the wonder that
    would be.—

In the spring a fuller crimson comes upon the robin's
    breast;
In the spring the wanton lapwing gets himself another
    crest;

In the spring a livelier iris changes on the burnished
    dove;[3]
In the spring a young man's fancy lightly turns to
    thoughts of love.   20

Then her cheek was pale and thinner than should be
    for one so young,
And her eyes on all my motions with a mute observance
    hung.

And I said, "My cousin Amy, speak and speak the
    truth to me,

---

[2] Tennyson said he meant "to express the flying gleams of light
across a dreary moorland."
[3] The rainbow colors on the dove's neck become brighter during
the mating season.

Trust me, cousin, all the current of my being sets to
    thee."

On her pallid cheek and forehead came a color and
    a light,   25
As I have seen the rosy red flushing in the northern
    night.

And she turned—her bosom shaken with a sudden
    storm of sighs—
All the spirit deeply dawning in the dark of hazel eyes—

Saying, "I have hid my feelings, fearing they should
    do me wrong";
Saying, "Dost thou love me, cousin?" weeping, "I
    have loved thee long."   30

Love took up the glass of Time, and turned it in his
    glowing hands;
Every moment, lightly shaken, ran itself in golden sands.

Love took up the harp of Life, and smote on all the
    chords with might;
Smote the chord of Self, that, trembling, passed in
    music out of sight.

Many a morning on the moorland did we hear the
    copses ring,   35
And her whisper thronged my pulses with the fullness
    of the spring.

Many an evening by the waters did we watch the
    stately ships,
And our spirits rushed together at the touching of the lips.

O my cousin, shallow-hearted! O my Amy, mine no
    more!
O the dreary, dreary moorland! O the barren, barren
    shore!   40

Falser than all fancy fathoms, falser than all songs have
    sung,
Puppet to a father's threat, and servile to a shrewish
    tongue![4]

Is it well to wish thee happy?—having known me—
    to decline
On a range of lower feelings and a narrower heart
    than mine!

[4] I.e., she weakly yielded to her parents' desire that she marry
another man, of more wealth and social position.

Yet it shall be; thou shalt lower to his level day by day,
What is fine within thee growing coarse to sympathize
    with clay.   46

As the husband is, the wife is; thou are mated with a
    clown,
And the grossness of his nature will have weight to
    drag thee down.

He will hold thee, when his passion shall have spent its
    novel force,
Something better than his dog, a little dearer than his
    horse.   50

What is this? his eyes are heavy; think not they are
    glazed with wine.
Go to him; it is thy duty; kiss him; take his hand in thine.

It may be my lord is weary, that his brain is overwrought;
Soothe him with thy finer fancies, touch him with thy
    lighter thought.

He will answer to the purpose, easy things to
    understand—   55
Better thou wert dead before me, though I slew thee
    with my hand!

Better thou and I were lying, hidden from the heart's
    disgrace,
Rolled in one another's arms, and silent in a last embrace.

Cursèd be the social wants that sin against the strength
    of youth!
Cursèd be the social lies that warp us from the living
    truth!   60

Cursèd be the sickly forms that err from honest Nature's
    rule!
Cursèd be the gold that gilds the straitened forehead of
    the fool!

Well—'tis well that I should bluster!—Hadst thou less
    unworthy proved—
Would to God—for I had loved thee more than ever
    wife was loved.

Am I mad, that I should cherish that which bears but
    bitter fruit?   65
I will pluck it from my bosom, though my heart be
    at the root.

Never, though my mortal summers to such length of
    years should come

As the many-wintered crow that leads the clanging
    rookery home.

Where is comfort? in division of the records of the
    mind?
Can I part her from herself, and love her, as I knew
    her, kind?   70

I remember one that perished; sweetly did she speak
    and move;
Such a one do I remember, whom to look at was to love.

Can I think of her as dead, and love her for the love
    she bore?
No—she never loved me truly; love is love for
    evermore.

Comfort? comfort scorned of devils! this is truth the
    poet sings,[5]   75
That a sorrow's crown of sorrow is remembering
    happier things.

Drug thy memories, lest thou learn it, lest thy heart be
    put to proof,
In the dead unhappy night, and when the rain is on
    the roof.

Like a dog, he[6] hunts in dreams, and thou art staring
    at the wall,
Where the dying night-lamp flickers, and the shadows
    rise and fall.   80

Then a hand shall pass before thee, pointing to his
    drunken sleep,
To thy widowed marriage-pillows, to the tears that
    thou wilt weep.

Thou shalt hear the "Never, never," whispered by the
    phantom years,
And a song from out the distance in the ringing of
    thine ears;

And an eye shall vex thee looking ancient kindness on
    thy pain.   85
Turn thee, turn thee on thy pillow; get thee to thy
    rest again.

Nay, but Nature brings thee solace; for a tender voice
    will cry.
'Tis a purer life than thine; a lip to drain thy trouble dry.

Baby lips will laugh me down; my latest rival brings
    thee rest.
Baby fingers, waxen touches, press me from the
    mother's breast.   90

Oh, the child too clothes the father with a dearness
    not his due.
Half is thine and half is his; it will be worthy of the two.

Oh, I see thee old and formal, fitted to thy petty part,
With a little hoard of maxims preaching down a
    daughter's heart.

"They were dangerous guides, the feelings—she herself
    was not exempt—   95
Truly, she herself had suffered"—Perish in thy
    self-contempt!

Overlive it—lower yet—be happy! wherefore should
    I care?
I myself must mix with action, lest I wither by despair.

What is that which I should turn to, lighting upon days
    like these?
Every door is barred with gold, and opens but to
    golden keys.   100

Every gate is thronged with suitors, all the markets
    overflow.
I have but an angry fancy; what is that which I should
    do?

I had been content to perish, falling on the foeman's
    ground,
When the ranks are rolled in vapor, and the winds are
    laid with sound.

But the jingling of the guinea helps the hurt that
    Honor feels,   105
And the nations do but murmur, snarling at each
    other's heels.

Can I but relive in sadness? I will turn that earlier page.
Hide me from my deep emotion, O thou wondrous
    Mother-Age!

Make me feel the wild pulsation that I felt before the
    strife,
When I heard my days before me, and the tumult of
    my life;

---

[5] Dante in the *Inferno*, V, 121.   [6] Amy's husband.

Yearning for the large excitement that the coming
    years would yield,
Eager-hearted as a boy when first he leaves his father's
    field,

And at night along the dusky highway near and nearer
    drawn,
Sees in heaven the light of London flaring like a dreary
    dawn;

And his spirit leaps within him to be gone before
    him then,   115
Underneath the light he looks at, in among the throngs
    of men;

Men, my brothers, men the workers, ever reaping
    something new;
That which they have done but earnest of the things
    that they shall do:

For I dipped into the future, far as human eye could
    see,
Saw the Vision of the world, and all the wonder that
    would be;   120

Saw the heavens fill with commerce, argosies of
    magic sails,
Pilots of the purple twilight, dropping down with
    costly bales;

Heard the heavens fill with shouting, and there rained
    a ghastly dew
From the nations' airy navies grappling in the central
    blue;

Far along the world-wide whisper of the south-wind
    rushing warm,   125
With the standards of the peoples plunging through the
    thunder-storm;

Till the war-drum throbbed no longer, and the battle-
    flags were furled
In the Parliament of man, the Federation of the world.

There the common sense of most shall hold a fretful
    realm in awe,
And the kindly earth shall slumber, lapped in universal
    law.   130

So I triumphed ere my passion sweeping through me
    left me dry,
Left me with the palsied heart, and left me with the
    jaundiced eye;

Eye, to which all order festers, all things here are out
    of joint:
Science moves, but slowly slowly, creeping on from
    point to point;

Slowly comes a hungry people, as a lion, creeping
    nigher,   135
Glares at one that nods and winks behind a slowly
    dying fire.

Yet I doubt not through the ages one increasing purpose
    runs,
And the thoughts of men are widened with the process
    of the suns.[7]

What is that to him that reaps not harvest of his
    youthful joys,
Though the deep heart of existence beat forever like
    a boy's?   140

Knowledge comes, but wisdom lingers, and I linger
    on the shore,
And the individual withers, and the world is more
    and more.[8]

Knowledge comes, but wisdom lingers, and he bears
    a laden breast,
Full of sad experience, moving toward the stillness of
    his rest.

Hark, my merry comrades call me, sounding on the
    bugle-horn,   145
They to whom my foolish passion were a target for
    their scorn.

Shall it not be scorn to me to harp on such a moldered
    string?
I am shamed through all my nature to have loved so
    slight a thing.

Weakness to be wroth with weakness! woman's pleasure,
    woman's pain—
Nature made them blinder motions bounded in a
    shallower brain.   150

Woman is the lesser man, and all thy passions, matched
    with mine,
Are as moonlight unto sunlight, and as water unto wine—

---

7 The passage of the years.

8 Many Victorians, notably Mill and Arnold, felt that the advance of democracy was forcing people to become more and
more alike, that is, more and more like "the average man."

Here at least, where nature sickens, nothing. Ah, for
 some retreat
Deep in yonder shining Orient, where my life began
 to beat;

Where in wild Mahratta-battle[9] fell my father evil-
 starred;—   155
I was left a trampled orphan, and a selfish uncle's ward.

Or to burst all links of habit—there to wander far
 away,
On from island unto island at the gateways of the day.

Larger constellations burning, mellow moons and
 happy skies,
Breadths of tropic shade and palms in cluster, knots
 of Paradise.   160

Never comes the trader, never floats an European flag,
Slides the bird o'er lustrous woodland, swings the
 trailer[10] from the crag;

Droops the heavy-blossomed bower, hangs the heavy-
 fruited tree—
Summer isles of Eden lying in dark-purple spheres of sea.

There methinks would be enjoyment more than in this
 march of mind,   165
In the steamship, in the railway, in the thoughts that
 shake mankind.

There the passions cramped no longer shall have scope
 and breathing space;
I will take some savage woman, she shall rear my
 dusky race.

Iron jointed, supple-sinewed, they shall dive, and they
 shall run,
Catch the wild goat by the hair, and hurl their lances
 in the sun;   170

Whistle back the parrot's call, and leap the rainbows
 of the brooks,
Not with blinded eyesight poring over miserable books—

Fool, again the dream, the fancy! but I *know* my words
 are wild,
But I count the gray barbarian lower than the Christian
 child.

I, to herd with narrow foreheads, vacant of our glorious
 gains,   175
Like a beast with lower pleasures, like a beast with
 lower pains!

Mated with a squalid savage—what to me were sun
 or clime?
I the heir of all the ages, in the foremost files of time—

I that rather held it better men should perish one by one,
Than that earth should stand at gaze like Joshua's
 moon in Ajalon![11]   180

Not in vain the distance beacons. Forward, forward
 let us range,
Let the great world spin forever down the ringing
 grooves of change.

Through the shadow of the globe we sweep into the
 younger day;
Better fifty years of Europe than a cycle of Cathay.

Mother-Age (for mine I knew not) help me as when
 life begun;   185
Rift the hills, and roll the waters, flash the lightnings,
 weigh the Sun.

Oh, I see the crescent promise of my spirit hath not set.
Ancient founts of inspiration well through all my
 fancy yet.

Howsoever these things be, a long farewell to Locksley
 Hall!
Now for me the woods may wither, now for me the
 roof-tree fall.   190

Comes a vapor from the margin, blackening over heath
 and holt,
Cramming all the blast before it, in its breast a
 thunderbolt.

Let it fall on Locksley Hall, with rain or hail, or fire
 or snow;
For the mighty wind arises, roaring seaward, and I go.

----

[9] In a battle in India against the tribe of the Mahrattas.
[10] A trailing vine.

[11] Joshua commanded the moon to stand still in the valley of
 Ajalon (Joshua 10: 12–13).

THE VISION OF SIN

I

I had a vision when the night was late:
A youth came riding toward a palace-gate.
He rode a horse with wings, that would have flown,
But that his heavy rider kept him down.[1]
And from the palace came a child of sin,   5
And took him by the curls, and led him in,
Where sat a company with heated eyes,
Expecting when a fountain should arise:
A sleepy light upon their brows and lips—
As when the sun, a crescent of eclipse,   10
Dreams over lake and lawn, and isles and capes—
Suffused them, sitting, lying, languid shapes,
By heaps of gourds, and skins of wine, and piles of grapes.

II

Then methought I heard a mellow sound,
Gathering up from all the lower ground;   15
Narrowing in to where they sat assembled
Low voluptuous music winding trembled,
Woven in circles. They that heard it sighed,
Panted hand-in-hand with faces pale,
Swung themselves, and in low tones replied;   20
Till the fountain spouted, showering wide
Sleet of diamond-drift and pearly hail;
Then the music touched the gates and died;
Rose again from where it seemed to fail,
Stormed in orbs of song, a growing gale;   25
Till thronging in and in, to where they waited,
As 't were a hundred-throated nightingale,
The strong tempestuous treble throbbed and palpitated;
Ran into its giddiest whirl of sound,
Caught the sparkles, and in circles,   30
Purple gauzes, golden hazes, liquid mazes,
Flung the torrent rainbow round:[2]
Then they started from their places,
Moved with violence, changed in hue,
Caught each other with wild grimaces,   35
Half-invisible to the view,
Wheeling with precipitate paces

To the melody, till they flew,
Hair, and eyes, and limbs, and faces,
Twisted hard in fierce embraces,   40
Like to Furies, like to Graces,
Dashed together in blinding dew;[3]
Till, killed with some luxurious agony,
The nerve-dissolving melody
Fluttered headlong from the sky.   45

III

And then I looked up toward a mountain-tract,
That girt the region with high cliff and lawn:
I saw that every morning, far withdrawn
Beyond the darkness and the cataract,
God made Himself an awful rose of dawn,   50
Unheeded; and detaching, fold by fold,
From those still heights, and, slowly drawing near,
A vapor heavy, hueless, formless, cold,
Came floating on for many a month and year,
Unheeded;[4] and I thought I would have spoken,   55
And warned that madman ere it grew too late:
But, as in dreams, I could not. Mine was broken,
When that cold vapor touched the palace gate,
And linked again.[5] I saw within my head
A gray and gap-toothed man as lean as death,   60
Who slowly rode across a withered heath,
And lighted at a ruined inn, and said:

IV

"Wrinkled ostler, grim and thin!
    Here is custom come your way;
Take my brute, and lead him in,   65
    Stuff his ribs with mouldy hay.

"Bitter barmaid, waning fast!
    See that sheets are on my bed;[6]
What! the flower of life is past;
    It is long before you wed.   70

---

[1] Tennyson is drawing an analogy between this youth and Bellerophon, who tried to fly to heaven on the winged horse Pegasus, but fell. For the full meaning cf. Tennyson's remark (*Memoir*, II, 337), "The higher moral imagination enslaved to sense is like an eagle caught by the feet in a snare, baited with carrion, so that it cannot use its wings to soar."

[2] The fountain rising from below (doubtless Tennyson means to suggest from hell) is probably a fountain of music, and the succeeding images of water and wind represent the "river" and "storm" of Bacchanalian song. The impressionistic technique is striking.

[3] Another fine piece of impressionism. Dew means mist. The Graces and the Furies suggest the combination of sensuous beauty and sadistic passion.

[4] According to Tennyson, the "mists of satiety," which come down from the heights because they are the threatened punishment of God upon a life of sensuality. But both God and the approaching punishment are unheeded by the youth. The metaphor of a stream of vapor with its epithets (heavy, hueless, formless, cold) is chosen for contrast with the music imagery above, to underscore the difference between satiety and the first excited indulgence.

[5] My dream was broken, and then linked up again with a new image of the madman years later.

[6] An invitation, which the barmaid refuses (see the next two lines).

"Slipshod waiter, lank and sour,
　　At the Dragon[7] on the heath!
Let us have a quiet hour,
　　Let us hob-and-nob with Death.

"I am old, but let me drink;　　75
　　Bring me spices, bring me wine;
I remember, when I think,
　　That my youth was half divine.[8]

"Wine is good for shriveled lips,
　　When a blanket wraps the day,　　80
When the rotten woodland drips,
　　And the leaf is stamped in clay.

"Sit thee down, and have no shame,
　　Cheek by jowl, and knee by knee;
What care I for any name?　　85
　　What for order or degree?

"Let me screw thee up a peg;[9]
　　Let me loose thy tongue with wine;
Callest thou that thing a leg?
　　Which is thinnest? thine or mine?　　90

"Thou shalt not be saved by works;
　　Thou hast been a sinner too;
Ruined trunks on withered forks,
　　Empty scarecrows, I and you!

"Fill the cup and fill the can:　　95
　　Have a rouse[10] before the morn:
Every moment dies a man,
　　Every moment one is born.[11]

"We are men of ruined blood;
　　Therefore comes it we are wise.　　100
Fish are we that love the mud,
　　Rising to no fancy-flies.[12]

"Name and fame! to fly sublime
　　Through the courts, the camps, the schools,
Is to be the ball of Time,　　105
　　Bandied by the hands of fools.[13]

"Friendship!—to be two in one—
　　Let the canting liar pack!
Well I know, when I am gone,
　　How she mouths behind my back.[14]　　110

"Virtue!—to be good and just—
　　Every heart, when sifted well,
Is a clot of warmer dust,
　　Mixed with cunning sparks of hell.

"O, we two as well can look　　115
　　Whited thought and cleanly life[15]
As the priest, above his book
　　Leering at his neighbor's wife.

"Fill the cup and fill the can:
　　Have a rouse before the morn:　　120
Every moment dies a man,
　　Every moment one is born.

"Drink, and let the parties[16] rave;
　　They are filled with idle spleen;
Rising, falling, like a wave,　　125
　　For they know not what they mean.

"He that roars for liberty
　　Faster binds a tyrant's power;[17]
And the tyrant's cruel glee
　　Forces on the freer hour.　　130

"Fill the can, and fill the cup:
　　All the windy ways of men
Are but dust that rises up,
　　And is lightly laid again.

"Greet her with applausive breath,　　135
　　Freedom, gaily doth she tread;
In her right a civic wreath,
　　In her left a human head.

---

7 The name of the inn.　　8 Cf. line 3.
9 A notch or degree (cf. previous line). Let me raise you up with a drink so that you'll feel my equal (which he is in the sense brought out in the next stanza).　　10 Carouse.
11 Human life is just an endless round of birth and death, death and birth. Hence the emotional attitude of weary futility which the lines express.
12 This is the key stanza. The "hero" is by no means merely a debauched sinner and the poem is not a moralistic sermon on the results of sin. From living in the mud, the sinner has become wise to the illusions of life. He has learned, for one thing, to penetrate below fair exteriors to the ugliness that often lies beneath. Lines 103–118 give three examples of "fancy-flies": name and fame, friendship, and virtue.

13 I.e., is to be at the beck and call of fools.
14 How the professed friend runs me down behind my back.
15 You and I (the waiter) can as well put on the pretense of virtue.
16 The political parties. Lines 123–150 describe the futile course of politics, action and reaction. Cf. Tennyson (Memoir, II, 339): "Action and Reaction is the miserable see-saw of our child-world."
17 Cf. Tennyson (Memoir, II, 338): "Violent, selfish, unreasoning democracy would bring . . . the iron rule of a Cromwell"—as it had brought the iron rule of Napoleon.

"No, I love not what is new;
    She is of an ancient house:
And I think we know the hue
    Of that cap upon her brows.[18]   140

"Let her go! her thirst she slakes
    Where the bloody conduit runs,
Then her sweetest meal she makes   145
    On the first-born of her sons.

"Drink to lofty hopes that cool—
    Visions of a perfect State;
Drink we, last, the public fool,
    Frantic love and frantic hate.   150

"Chant me now some wicked stave,[19]
    Till thy drooping courage rise,
And the glow-worm of the grave
    Glimmer in thy rheumy eyes.

"Fear not thou to loose thy tongue;   155
    Set thy hoary fancies free;
What is loathsome to the young
    Savors well to thee and me.

"Change, reverting to the years,[20]
    When thy nerves could understand   160
What there is in loving tears,
    And the warmth of hand in hand.

"Tell me tales of thy first love—
    April hopes, the fools of chance;
Till the graves begin to move,   165
    And the dead begin to dance.[21]

"Fill the can, and fill the cup:
    All the windy ways of men
Are but dust that rises up,
    And is lightly laid again.   170

"Trooping from their mouldy dens
    The chap-fallen[22] circle spreads:
Welcome, fellow-citizens,
    Hollow hearts and empty heads![23]

"You are bones, and what of that?   175
    Every face, however full,
Padded round with flesh and fat,
    Is but modeled on a skull.

"Death is king, and Vivat Rex![24]
    Tread a measure on the stones,   180
Madam—if I know your sex,
    From the fashion of your bones.

"No, I cannot praise the fire
    In your eye—nor yet your lip;
All the more do I admire   185
    Joints of cunning workmanship.

"Lo! God's likeness—the ground-plan—
    Neither modeled, glazed, nor framed;
Buss[25] me, thou rough sketch of man,
    Far too naked to be shamed!   190

"Drink to Fortune, drink to Chance,[26]
    While we keep a little breath!
Drink to heavy Ignorance![27]
    Hob-and-nob with brother Death!

"Thou art mazed,[28] the night is long,   195
    And the longer night is near:
What! I am not all as wrong
    As a bitter jest is dear.[29]

"Youthful hopes, by scores, to all,
    When the locks are crisp and curled;[30]   200
Unto me my maudlin gall
    And my mockeries of the world.

"Fill the cup, and fill the can:
    Mingle madness, mingle scorn!
Dregs of life, and lees of man;   205
    Yet we will not die forlorn."[31]

v

The voice grew faint; there came a further change;
Once more uprose the mystic mountain-range;

---

[18] The red cap of the French revolutionists.
[19] Some bawdy song.
[20] No, change that and sing instead of the years of youth.
[21] The ghosts of those you loved.
[22] Jaw-fallen. The image is that of a gaping skeleton.
[23] Cf. line 94. Here and in the next stanzas the process of stripping off the illusions of life is extended from the moral and political orders to man himself. Under life, so to speak, is death. Death is king.

[24] Long live the king.   [25] Kiss.
[26] The irony is sardonic.
[27] Of both the past (cf. lines 75-78, 163-164) and the future (the actual fact of death).   [28] Drunk.
[29] What! You question my interpretation of life? I am not as far from being wrong as a bitter jest, like my interpretation, is from being dear (appreciated). Or, in looser paraphrase, my bitter jests are more true than welcome.
[30] Cf. lines 6 and 164.
[31] Hopeless and abandoned. The prophecy is fulfilled in the next stanza.

Below were men and horses pierced with worms,
And slowly quickening into lower forms;   210
By shards[32] and scurf[33] of salt, and scum of dross,
Old plash[34] of rains, and refuse patched with moss.
Then some one spake: "Behold! it was a crime
Of sense avenged by sense that wore with time."[35]
Another said: "The crime of sense became   215
The crime of malice,[36] and is equal blame."
And one: "He had not wholly quenched his power;
A little grain of conscience made him sour."[37]
At last I heard a voice upon the slope
Cry to the summit, "Is there any hope?"   220
To which an answer pealed from that high land,
But in a tongue no man could understand;
And on the glimmering limit far withdrawn
God made Himself an awful rose of dawn.

BREAK, BREAK, BREAK

Break, break, break,
　　On thy cold gray stones, O Sea!
And I would that my tongue could utter
　　The thoughts that arise in me.

O well for the fisherman's boy,   5
　　That he shouts with his sister at play!
O well for the sailor lad,
　　That he sings in his boat on the bay!

And the stately ships go on
　　To their haven under the hill;   10
But O for the touch of a vanished hand,
　　And the sound of a voice that is still!

Break, break, break,
　　At the foot of thy crags, O Sea!
But the tender grace of a day that is dead   15
　　Will never come back to me.

---

[32] Broken chinaware.　　[33] Scaly incrustation.
[34] Puddles.
[35] "The sensualist becomes worn out by his senses" (Tennyson's
note), as predicted in lines 51–55.
[36] Sensuality led to a malicious attack on life.
[37] The first two judgments are not wrong, but they leave out the
all-important fact, demonstrated in section IV, that the man
still had power (the power of insight) and a conscience which
made him sour. Only a bitter moralist could attack the febrile
and hypocritical character of human life as he does in the
stanzas on the moral and political orders. As a result (see the
last lines) God holds out the bright promise of salvation.

SWEET AND LOW[1]

Sweet and low, sweet and low,
　　Wind of the western sea,
Low, low, breathe and blow,
　　Wind of the western sea!
Over the rolling waters go,   5
Come from the dying moon, and blow,
　　Blow him again to me;
While my little one, while my pretty one, sleeps.

Sleep and rest, sleep and rest,
　　Father will come to thee soon;   10
Rest, rest, on mother's breast,
　　Father will come to thee soon;
Father will come to his babe in the nest,
Silver sails all out of the west
　　Under the silver moon;   15
Sleep, my little one, sleep, my pretty one, sleep.

THE SPLENDOR FALLS
ON CASTLE WALLS

The splendor falls on castle walls
　　And snowy summits old in story;
The long light shakes across the lakes,
　　And the wild cataract leaps in glory.
Blow, bugle, blow, set the wild echoes flying,   5
Blow, bugle; answer, echoes, dying, dying, dying.

　　O hark, O hear! how thin and clear,
　　　　And thinner, clearer, farther going!
　　O sweet and far from cliff and scar
　　　　The horns of Elfland faintly blowing!   10
Blow, let us hear the purple glens replying:
Blow, bugle; answer, echoes, dying, dying, dying.

　　O love, they die in yon rich sky,
　　　　They faint on hill or field or river;
　　Our echoes roll from soul to soul,   15
　　　　And grow for ever and for ever.
Blow, bugle, blow, set the wild echoes flying,
And answer, echoes, answer, dying, dying, dying.

TEARS, IDLE TEARS

Tears, idle tears, I know not what they mean,
Tears from the depth of some divine despair
Rise in the heart, and gather to the eyes,

---

[1] This lyric and the next six are from The Princess (1847; 2nd ed.,
1850).

In looking on the happy Autumn-fields,
And thinking of the days that are no more.   5

Fresh as the first beam glittering on a sail,
That brings our friends up from the underworld,
Sad as the last which reddens over one
That sinks with all we love below the verge;
So sad, so fresh, the days that are no more.   10

Ah, sad and strange as in dark summer dawns
The earliest pipe of half-awakened birds
To dying ears, when unto dying eyes
The casement slowly grows a glimmering square;
So sad, so strange, the days that are no more.   15

Dear as remembered kisses after death,
And sweet as those by hopeless fancy feigned
On lips that are for others; deep as love,
Deep as first love, and wild with all regret;
O Death in Life, the days that are no more.   20

HOME THEY BROUGHT
HER WARRIOR DEAD

Home they brought her warrior dead:
   She nor swooned nor uttered cry:
All her maidens, watching, said,
   "She must weep or she will die."

Then they praised him, soft and low,   5
   Called him worthy to be loved,
Truest friend and noblest foe;
   Yet she neither spoke nor moved.

Stole a maiden from her place,
   Lightly to the warrior stepped,   10
Took the face-cloth from the face;
   Yet she neither moved nor wept.

Rose a nurse of ninety years,
   Set his child upon her knee—
Like summer tempest came her tears—   15
   "Sweet my child, I live for thee."

ASK ME NO MORE

Ask me no more: the moon may draw the sea;
   The cloud may stoop from heaven and take
     the shape,
   With fold to fold, of mountain or of cape;
But O too fond, when have I answered thee?
       Ask me no more.   5

Ask me no more: what answer should I give?
   I love not hollow cheek or faded eye;
   Yet, O my friend, I will not have thee die!
Ask me no more, lest I should bid thee live;
       Ask me no more.   10

Ask me no more: thy fate and mine are sealed;
   I strove against the stream and all in vain;
   Let the great river take me to the main.
No more, dear love, for at a touch I yield;
       Ask me no more.   15

NOW SLEEPS THE CRIMSON PETAL

Now sleeps the crimson petal, now the white;
Nor waves the cypress in the palace walk;
Nor winks the gold fin in the porphyry font:
The fire-fly wakens; waken thou with me.

Now droops the milkwhite peacock like a ghost,   5
And like a ghost she glimmers on to me.

Now lies the Earth all Danaë[2] to the stars,
And all thy heart lies open unto me.

Now slides the silent meteor on, and leaves
A shining furrow, as thy thoughts in me.   10

Now folds the lily all her sweetness up,
And slips into the bosom of the lake:
So fold thyself, my dearest, thou, and slip
Into my bosom and be lost in me.

COME DOWN, O MAID

Come down, O maid, from yonder mountain height:
What pleasure lives in height (the shepherd sang),
In height and cold, the splendor of the hills?
But cease to move so near the Heavens, and cease
To glide a sunbeam by the blasted Pine,   5
To sit a star upon the sparkling spire;
And come, for Love is of the valley, come,
For Love is of the valley, come thou down
And find him; by the happy threshold, he,
Or hand in hand with Plenty in the maize,   10
Or red with spirted purple of the vats,
Or foxlike in the vine;[3] nor cares to walk

---

[2] Princess to whom Zeus descended in the form of a golden shower.

[3] Like the foxes who lurked in the vines of tender grapes (Song of Solomon 2:15).

With Death and Morning on the silver horns,[4]
Nor wilt thou snare him in the white ravine,
Nor find him dropped upon the firths of ice,[5]   15
That huddling slant in furrow-cloven falls
To roll the torrent out of dusky doors:
But follow; let the torrent dance thee down
To find him in the valley; let the wild
Lean-headed eagles yelp alone, and leave   20
The monstrous ledges there to slope, and spill
Their thousand wreaths of dangling water-smoke,
That like a broken purpose waste in air:
So waste not thou; but come; for all the vales
Await thee; azure pillars of the hearth[6]   25
Arise to thee; the children call, and I
Thy shepherd pipe, and sweet is every sound,
Sweeter thy voice, but every sound is sweet;

Myriads of rivulets hurrying through the lawn,
The moan of doves in immemorial elms,   30
And murmuring of innumerable bees.

THE EAGLE

FRAGMENT

He clasps the crag with crooked hands;
Close to the sun in lonely lands,
Ringed with the azure world, he stands.

The wrinkled sea beneath him crawls;
He watches from his mountain walls,   5
And like a thunderbolt he falls.

from IN MEMORIAM A. H. H.[1]

OBIIT 1833

PROLOGUE

Strong Son of God, immortal Love,
　Whom we, that have not seen thy face,
　By faith, and faith alone, embrace,
Believing where we cannot prove;

Thine are these orbs of light and shade;[2]   5
　Thou madest Life in man and brute;
　Thou madest Death; and lo, thy foot
Is on the skull which thou hast made.

Thou wilt not leave us in the dust:
　Thou madest man, he knows not why,   10
　He thinks he was not made to die;
And thou hast made him; thou art just.

Thou seemest human and divine,
　The highest, holiest manhood, thou;
　Our wills are ours, we know not how;   15
Our wills are ours, to make them thine.

Our little systems[3] have their day;
　They have their day and cease to be;

They are but broken lights of thee,
And thou, O Lord, art more than they.   20

We have but faith; we cannot know;
　For knowledge is of things we see;
　And yet we trust it comes from thee,
A beam in darkness; let it grow.

Let knowledge grow from more to more,   25
　But more of reverence in us dwell;
　That mind and soul, according well,
May make one music as before,[4]

But vaster. We are fools and slight;
　We mock thee when we do not fear;   30
　But help thy foolish ones to bear;
Help thy vain worlds to bear thy light.

Forgive what seemed my sin in me;
　What seemed my worth since I began;
　For merit lives from man to man,   35
And not from man, O Lord, to thee.

Forgive my grief for one removed,
　Thy creature, whom I found so fair.
　I trust he lives in thee, and there
I find him worthier to be loved.   40

---

[4] Peaks in the Alps.   [5] Glaciers.   [6] Columns of smoke.

[1] Tennyson's close friend, Arthur Henry Hallam, whom he met at Cambridge, and who died at Vienna at the age of twenty-two.
[2] Literally, the planets, partly in the light of the sun, partly in the shade; but Tennyson means to suggest the light of life and the shadow of death.   [3] Of theology and philosophy.

[4] Before the separation effected by modern science, which has driven the mind to deny what the soul feels or longs for.

ALFRED LORD TENNYSON   663

Forgive these wild and wandering cries,[5]
    Confusions of a wasted youth;
    Forgive them where they fail in truth,
And in thy wisdom make me wise.

3

O Sorrow, cruel fellowship,
    O Priestess in the vaults of Death,
    O sweet and bitter in a breath,
What whispers from thy lying lip?

"The stars," she whispers, "blindly run;   5
    A web is woven across the sky;
    From out waste places comes a cry,
And murmurs from the dying sun;[6]

"And all the phantom, Nature, stands—
    With all her music in her tone,
    A hollow echo of my own,—[7]   10
A hollow form with empty hands."

And shall I take a thing so blind,[8]
    Embrace her as my natural good;
    Or crush her, like a vice of blood,   15
Upon the threshold of the mind?

4

To Sleep I give my powers away;
    My will is bondsman to the dark;
    I sit within a helmless bark,
And with my heart I muse and say:

O heart, how fares it with thee now,   5
    That thou shouldst fail from thy desire,
    Who scarcely darest to inquire,
"What is it makes me beat so low?"

Something it is which thou hast lost,
    Some pleasure from thine early years.   10
    Break, thou deep vase of chilling tears,
That grief hath shaken into frost!

Such clouds of nameless trouble cross
    All night below the darkened eyes;

---

[5] The 131 short lyrics, written at various times between 1833 and
1850, which comprise the poem.
[6] Because his sorrow lacks the resolution of firm faith, it calls up
the vision of a mechanical universe, from which (lines 6–7) man
has evolved. The sun is dying because it will some day lose its
heat.
[7] That is, of Sorrow's own despairing tone.
[8] As this sorrow and its reading of the universe.

With morning wakes the will, and cries,   15
"Thou shalt not be the fool of loss."

5

I sometimes hold it half a sin
    To put in words the grief I feel;
    For words, like Nature, half reveal
And half conceal the Soul within.

But, for the unquiet heart and brain,   5
    A use in measured language lies;
    The sad mechanic exercise,
Like dull narcotics, numbing pain.

In words, like weeds,[9] I'll wrap me o'er,
    Like coarsest clothes against the cold;   10
    But that large grief which these enfold
Is given in outline and no more.

6

One writes, that "other friends remain,"
    That "loss is common to the race"—
    And common is the commonplace,
And vacant chaff well meant for grain.

That loss is common would not make   5
    My own less bitter, rather more.
    Too common! Never morning wore
To evening, but some heart did break.

O father, wheresoe'er thou be,
    That pledgest now thy gallant son;   10
    A shot, ere half thy draught be done,
Hath stilled the life that beat from thee.

O mother, praying God will save
    Thy sailor,—while thy head is bowed,
    His heavy-shotted hammock-shroud   15
Drops in his vast and wandering grave.

Ye know no more than I who wrought
    At that last hour to please him well;
    Who mused on all I had to tell,
And something written, something thought;   20

Expecting still his advent home;
    And ever met him on his way
    With wishes, thinking, "here to-day,"
Or, "here to-morrow will he come."

---

[9] Garments.

O somewhere, meek, unconscious dove,   25
    That sittest ranging[10] golden hair;
    And glad to find thyself so fair,
Poor child, that waitest for thy love!

For now her father's chimney glows
    In expectation of a guest;   30
    And thinking "this will please him best,"
She takes a riband or a rose;

For he will see them on to-night;
    And with the thought her color burns;
    And, having left the glass, she turns   35
Once more to set a ringlet right;

And, even when she turned, the curse
    Had fallen, and her future Lord
    Was drowned in passing thro' the ford,
Or killed in falling from his horse.   40

O, what to her shall be the end?
    And what to me remains of good?
    To her, perpetual maidenhood,
And unto me, no second friend.

7

Dark house,[11] by which once more I stand
    Here in the long unlovely street,
    Doors, where my heart was used to beat
So quickly, waiting for a hand,

A hand that can be clasped no more—   5
    Behold me, for I cannot sleep,
    And like a guilty thing I creep
At earliest morning to the door.

He is not here; but far away
    The noise of life begins again,   10
    And ghastly through the drizzling rain
On the bald street breaks the blank day.

11

Calm is the morn without a sound,
    Calm as to suit a calmer grief,
    And only through the faded leaf
The chestnut pattering to the ground;

Calm and deep peace on this high wold,   5
    And on these dews that drench the furze,

And all the silvery gossamers
That twinkle into green and gold;

Calm and still light on yon great plain
    That sweeps with all its autumn bowers,   10
    And crowded farms and lessening towers,
To mingle with the bounding main;

Calm and deep peace in this wide air,
    These leaves that redden to the fall;
    And in my heart, if calm at all,   15
If any calm, a calm despair;

Calm on the seas, and silver sleep,
    And waves that sway themselves in rest,
    And dead calm in that noble breast
Which heaves but with the heaving deep.[12]   20

27

I envy not in any moods
    The captive void of noble rage,
    The linnet born within the cage,
That never knew the summer woods;

I envy not the beast that takes   5
    His license in the field of time,
    Unfettered by the sense of crime,
To whom a conscience never wakes;

Nor, what may count itself as blest,
    The heart that never plighted troth   10
    But stagnates in the weeds of sloth;
Nor any want-begotten rest.[13]

I hold it true, whate'er befall;
    I feel it, when I sorrow most;
    'Tis better to have loved and lost   15
Than never to have loved at all.

28

The time draws near the birth of Christ:[14]
    The moon is hid; the night is still;
    The Christmas bells from hill to hill
Answer each other in the mist.

Four voices of four hamlets round,   5
    From far and near, on mead and moor,

---

[10] Arranging.   [11] Where Hallam had lived.

[12] The body of Hallam is being brought home by ship to England.
[13] Nor any peace of mind purchased by the lack of some valuable quality or experience.
[14] Christmas of 1833, the year of Hallam's death.

Swell out and fail, as if a door
　　Were shut between me and the sound;

Each voice four changes[15] on the wind,
　　That now dilate, and now decrease,
　　Peace and goodwill, goodwill and peace,
Peace and goodwill, to all mankind.

This year I slept and woke with pain,
　　I almost wished no more to wake,
　　And that my hold on life would break　15
Before I heard those bells again;

But they my troubled spirit rule,
　　For they controlled me when a boy;
　　They bring me sorrow touched with joy,
The merry, merry bells of Yule.　　20

30

With trembling fingers did we weave
　　The holly round the Christmas hearth;
　　A rainy cloud possessed the earth,
And sadly fell our Christmas-eve.

At our old pastimes in the hall　　5
　　We gamboled, making vain pretense
　　Of gladness, with an awful sense
Of one mute Shadow watching all.

We paused: the winds were in the beech;
　　We heard them sweep the winter land;　10
　　And in a circle hand-in-hand
Sat silent, looking each at each.

Then echo-like our voices rang;
　　We sung, though every eye was dim,
　　A merry song we sang with him　15
Last year; impetuously we sang;

We ceased; a gentler feeling crept
　　Upon us; surely rest is meet:
　　"They rest," we said, "their sleep is sweet,"
And silence followed, and we wept.　　20

Our voices took a higher range;
　　Once more we sang: "They do not die
　　Nor lose their mortal sympathy,
Nor change to us, although they change;

---

15 Sequences in which a peal of bells is rung.

"Rapt from the fickle and the frail　　25
　　With gathered power, yet the same,
　　Pierces the keen seraphic flame
From orb to orb, from veil to veil."[16]

Rise, happy morn, rise, holy morn,
　　Draw forth the cheerful day from night;　30
　　O Father, touch the east, and light
The light that shone when Hope was born.[17]

50

Be near me when my light is low,
　　When the blood creeps, and the nerves prick
　　And tingle; and the heart is sick,
And all the wheels of Being slow.

Be near me when the sensuous frame　　5
　　Is racked with pangs that conquer trust;
　　And Time, a maniac scattering dust,
And Life, a Fury slinging flame.

Be near me when my faith is dry,
　　And men[18] the flies of latter spring,　10
　　That lay their eggs, and sting and sing
And weave their petty cells and die.

Be near me when I fade away,
　　To point the term of human strife,[19]
　　And on the low dark verge of life　15
The twilight of eternal day.

54

O yet we trust that somehow good
　　Will be the final goal of ill,
　　To pangs of nature, sins of will,
Defects of doubt, and taints of blood;

That nothing walks with aimless feet;　5
　　That not one life shall be destroyed,
　　Or cast as rubbish to the void,
When God hath made the pile complete;

That not a worm is cloven in vain;
　　That not a moth with vain desire　10
　　Is shriveled in a fruitless fire,
Or but subserves another's gain.[20]

---

16 The soul, freed from the flesh but its essence unchanged, passes from world to world in successively higher embodiments.
17 With Christ, who brought the hope of immortality.
18 And men seem.
19 To point to the end of human life (stated in line 16).
20 In the struggle for survival.

Behold, we know not anything;
    I can but trust that good shall fall
    At last—far off—at last, to all,
And every winter change to spring.   15

So runs my dream; but what am I?
    An infant crying in the night;
    An infant crying for the light;
And with no language but a cry.   20

55

The wish, that of the living whole
    No life may fail beyond the grave,
    Derives it not from what we have
The likest God within the soul?[21]

Are God and Nature then at strife,
    That Nature lends such evil dreams?
    So careful of the type[22] she seems,
So careless of the single life;   5

That I, considering everywhere
    Her secret meaning in her deeds,
    And finding that of fifty seeds
She often brings but one to bear,   10

I falter where I firmly trod,
    And falling with my weight of cares
    Upon the great world's altar-stairs
That slope through darkness up to God,   15

I stretch lame hands of faith, and grope,
    And gather dust and chaff, and call
    To what I feel is Lord of all,
And faintly trust the larger hope.[23]   20

56

"So careful of the type?" but no.
    From scarpèd cliff and quarried stone
    She cries, "A thousand types are gone;
I care for nothing, all shall go.[24]

"Thou makest thine appeal to me;
    I bring to life, I bring to death;   5

The spirit does but mean the breath;
I know no more." And he, shall he,

Man, her last work, who seemed so fair,
    Such splendid purpose in his eyes,   10
    Who rolled the psalm to wintry skies,
Who built him fanes of fruitless prayer,

Who trusted God was love indeed
    And love Creation's final law—
    Though Nature, red in tooth and claw   15
With ravine, shrieked against his creed—

Who loved, who suffered countless ills,
    Who battled for the True, the Just,
    Be blown about the desert dust,
Or sealed within the iron hills?   20

No more? A monster then, a dream,
    A discord.[25] Dragons of the prime,
    That tare each other in their slime,
Were mellow music matched with him.[26]

O life as futile, then, as frail!   25
    O for thy voice[27] to soothe and bless!
    What hope of answer, or redress?
Behind the veil, behind the veil.

78

Again at Christmas did we weave
    The holly round the Christmas hearth;
    The silent snow possessed the earth,
And calmly fell our Christmas-eve:

The yule-clog[28] sparkled keen with frost,   5
    No wing of wind the region swept,
    But over all things brooding slept
The quiet sense of something lost.

As in the winters left behind,
    Again our ancient games had place,   10
    The mimic picture's breathing grace,[29]
And dance and song and hoodman-blind.

21 That is, from Love, which makes us long for the survival of
    every life after death.
22 The species.
23 Expressed in lines 1-2.
24 Nature is as careless of the species as of the individual, as we
    can see from the fossil remains of dead species discovered in
    quarried stone and scarped cliff (a cliff cut away perpendicularly,
    so that the strata in which fossils are embedded are exposed).

25 Is that the whole story? Then man is a monster (a beast in
    human shape), a dream that vanishes (since he has no immortal
    soul), a discord (when his hopes and traditions clash so violently
    with what appear to be the facts: cf. Prologue, lines 27-28,
    and note 4).
26 Because they at least had no delusions of spiritual life and sur-
    vival, and were therefore more harmoniously adjusted to
    existence than man.   27 Hallam's.
28 Log.—This is the second Christmas after Hallam's death.
29 Tableaux of famous paintings.

Who showed a token of distress?
       No single tear, no mark of pain:
       O sorrow, then can sorrow wane?   15
O grief, can grief be changed to less?

O last regret, regret can die!
       No—mixed with all this mystic frame,
       Her deep relations are the same,
But with long use her tears are dry.   20

82

I wage not any feud with Death
       For changes wrought on form and face;
       No lower life that earth's embrace
May breed with him, can fright my faith.

Eternal process moving on,
       From state to state the spirit walks;[30]
       And these are but the shattered stalks,
Or ruined chrysalis of one.[31]

Nor blame I Death, because he bare[32]
       The use of virtue[33] out of earth;   10
       I know transplanted human worth
Will bloom to profit, otherwhere.

For this alone on Death I wreak
       The wrath that garners in my heart:
       He put our lives so far apart   15
We cannot hear each other speak.

96

You[34] say, but with no touch of scorn,
       Sweet-hearted, you, whose light-blue eyes
       Are tender over drowning flies,
You tell me, doubt is Devil-born.

I know not; one[35] indeed I knew   5
       In many a subtle question versed,
       Who touched a jarring lyre at first,
But ever strove to make it true;

Perplexed in faith, but pure in deeds,
       At last he beat his music out.   10

There lives more faith in honest doubt,
Believe me, than in half the creeds.[36]

He fought his doubts and gathered strength,
       He would not make his judgment blind,
       He faced the specters of the mind   15
And laid them; thus he came at length

To find a stronger faith his own;
       And Power was with him in the night,
       Which makes the darkness and the light,
And dwells not in the light alone,   20

But in the darkness and the cloud,
       As over Sinaï's peaks of old,
       While Israel made their gods of gold,[37]
Although the trumpet blew so loud.

104

The time draws near the birth of Christ;[38]
       The moon is hid, the night is still;
       A single church below the hill
Is pealing, folded in the mist.

A single peal of bells below,   5
       That wakens at this hour of rest
       A single murmur in the breast,
That these are not the bells I know.

Like strangers' voices here they sound,
       In lands where not a memory strays,   10
       Nor landmark breathes of other days,
But all is new unhallowed ground.

105

Tonight ungathered let us leave
       This laurel, let this holly stand;
       We live within the stranger's land,
And strangely falls our Christmas-eve.

[30] As the body passes into lower forms of life, the spirit moves upward into higher states (cf. No. 30 above).
[31] "These" seems to refer to line 2. The general meaning is that the dead body is but the shattered support or ruined chrysalis of one state of the spirit.   [32] Bore.
[33] The practice of virtue by Hallam, or in other words, the virtuous Hallam.
[34] Some woman of simple faith.   [35] Hallam.

[36] These lines must be read with what follows. In doubt that is honestly, i.e., openly and squarely, faced and fought, there lies, potentially, a much stronger because firmer faith than that of half the people who claim to be orthodox believers (and often scorn the doubters as sinners: cf. line 4) but whose faith is really weak because they have purchased it dishonestly by refusing to face any arguments to the contrary (by making their judgment blind).
[37] God dwells in the darkness of doubt just as he dwelt in the darkness over Mt. Sinai when he was hidden in a storm cloud. Below, the Israelites were worshiping the golden calf (which may be an allusion to the Victorians whose doors are barred with gold, and open but to golden keys: see "Locksley Hall," line 100, above).
[38] The Christmas of 1837. The family had moved from Somersby to Epping Forest.

Our father's dust is left alone 5
 And silent under other snows;
 There in due time the woodbine blows,
The violet comes, but we are gone.

No more shall wayward grief abuse
 The genial hour with mask and mime; 10
 For change of place, like growth of time,
Has broke the bond of dying use.

Let cares that petty shadows cast,
 By which our lives are chiefly proved,
 A little spare the night I loved, 15
And hold it solemn to the past.

But let no footstep beat the floor,
 Nor bowl of wassail mantle[39] warm;
 For who would keep an ancient form
Through which the spirit breathes no more? 20

Be neither song, nor game, nor feast;
 Nor harp be touched, nor flute be blown;
 No dance, no motion, save alone
What lightens in the lucid east

Of rising worlds[40] by yonder wood. 25
 Long sleeps the summer in the seed;
 Run out your measured arcs, and lead
The closing cycle rich in good.[41]

106

Ring out, wild bells, to the wild sky,
 The flying cloud, the frosty light;
 The year is dying in the night;
Ring out, wild bells, and let him die.

Ring out the old, ring in the new, 5
 Ring, happy bells, across the snow;
 The year is going, let him go;
Ring out the false, ring in the true.

Ring out the grief that saps the mind,
 For those that here we see no more; 10
 Ring out the feud of rich and poor,
Ring in redress to all mankind.

Ring out a slowly dying cause,
 And ancient forms of party strife;

Ring in the nobler modes of life, 15
With sweeter manners, purer laws.

Ring out the want, the care, the sin,
 The faithless coldness of the times;
 Ring out, ring out my mournful rhymes,
But ring the fuller minstrel in. 20

Ring out false pride in place and blood,
 The civic slander and the spite;
 Ring in the love of truth and right,
Ring in the common love of good.

Ring out old shapes of foul disease; 25
 Ring out the narrowing lust of gold;
 Ring out the thousand wars of old,
Ring in the thousand years of peace.

Ring in the valiant man and free,
 The larger heart, the kindlier hand; 30
 Ring out the darkness of the land,
Ring in the Christ that is to be.[42]

116

Is it, then, regret for buried time
 That keenlier in sweet April wakes,
 And meets the year, and gives and takes
The colors of the crescent prime?

Not all: the songs, the stirring air, 5
 The life re-orient out of dust,
 Cry through the sense to hearten trust
In that which made the world so fair.

Not all regret: the face will shine
 Upon me, while I muse alone; 10
 And that dear voice, I once have known,
Still speak to me of me and mine;

Yet less of sorrow lives in me
 For days of happy commune dead;
 Less yearning for the friendship fled, 15
Than some strong bond which is to be.

118

Contemplate all this work of Time,
 The giant laboring in his youth;

---

39 Wine with a cover of froth.   40 Stars.
41 The final period of perfection: cf. the next poem and the very
 last stanza of *In Memoriam*.

42 According to his son (*Memoir*, I, 326), Tennyson thought "that
the forms of Christian religion would alter; but that the spirit
of Christ would still grow from more to more"; and he looked
forward to a time "when the controversies of creeds shall have
vanished."

Nor dream of human love and truth,
As dying Nature's earth and lime;[43]

But trust that those we call the dead   5
  Are breathers of an ampler day
  For[44] ever nobler ends. They[45] say,
The solid earth whereon we tread

In tracts of fluent heat began,[46]
  And grew to seeming-random forms,   10
  The seeming prey of cyclic storms,[47]
Till at the last arose the man;[48]

Who throve and branched from clime to clime,
  The herald of a higher race,[49]
  And of himself in higher place,[50]   15
If so he type this work of time

Within himself, from more to more;[51]
  Or,[52] crowned with attributes of woe
  Like glories, move his course, and show
That life is not as idle ore,   20

But iron dug from central gloom,
  And heated hot with burning fears,
  And dipt in baths of hissing tears,
And battered with the shocks of doom

To shape and use. Arise and fly   25
  The reeling Faun, the sensual feast;
  Move upward, working out the beast
And let the ape and tiger die.

120

I trust I have not wasted breath:[53]
  I think we are not wholly brain,

---

[43] Do not dream that the human spirit dies with the natural body made of earth and lime.
[44] For the purpose of.
[45] The astronomers and the geologists.
[46] A reference to the nebular hypothesis. See the General Introduction, p. 380.
[47] Periodic cataclysms. The line refers to the older theory of geological change which Lyell attacked. See the General Introduction, p. 380.
[48] From lower forms of life? By special creation of God? Either may be the reading, and Tennyson may have intended the ambiguity.   [49] Of men on earth.
[50] Than on the earth.
[51] Provided he imitate the progressive work of time in his own moral life (cf. the last stanza).
[52] Or (see the next lines) provided he make pain and suffering the instruments of moral growth.
[53] Breath that wastes away till it ceases at death. I trust I am not merely mortal.

Magnetic mockeries;[54] not in vain,
Like Paul with beasts, I fought with Death;[55]

Not only[56] cunning casts in clay: 5
  Let Science prove we are, and then
  What matters Science unto men,
At least to me? I would not stay.

Let him, the wiser man[57] who springs
  Hereafter, up from childhood shape   10
  His action like the greater ape,
But I was *born* to other things.

123

There rolls the deep where grew the tree.
  O earth, what changes hast thou seen!
  There where the long street roars hath been
The stillness of the central sea.

The hills are shadows, and they flow   5
  From form to form, and nothing stands;
  They melt like mist, the solid lands,
Like clouds they shape themselves and go.

But in my spirit will I dwell,[58]
  And dream my dream, and hold it true;   10
  For though my lips may breathe adieu,
I cannot think the thing farewell.

124

That which we dare invoke to bless;
  Our dearest faith; our ghastliest doubt;[59]
  He, They, One, All;[60] within, without;
The Power in darkness whom we guess;

I found Him not in world or sun,   5
  Or eagle's wing, or insect's eye;
  Nor through the questions men may try,
The petty cobwebs we have spun;[61]

---

[54] Human automatons controlled by magnetic force: cf. the General Introduction, pp. 381-2.
[55] I fought against the view of human life as ending in death, as Paul did also, who likened the fight to a battle with beasts (1 Corinthians 15:32).   [56] We are not merely.
[57] Made wiser by science. The tone is ironic.
[58] Not in my senses, which would lead me to think that nothing whatever was permanent or lasting (not even a soul), and that everything is part of a meaningless process of change.
[59] The subject or object of both faith and doubt.
[60] However we may think of this object, as God or the gods, or as an impersonal "unity in all things or all things together" (Bradley).
[61] He did not deduce the existence of God in eighteenth-century fashion by claiming that design in nature pointed to a designer, nor from any rational arguments.

If e'er when faith had fallen asleep,
    I heard a voice, "Believe no more,"   10
    And heard an ever-breaking shore
That tumbled in the Godless deep;[62]

A warmth within the breast would melt
    The freezing reason's colder part,
    And like a man in wrath the heart   15
Stood up and answered, "I have felt."[63]

No, like a child in doubt and fear:
    But that blind clamor made me wise;
    Then was I as a child that cries,
But, crying, knows his father near;[64]   20

And what I am[65] beheld again
    What is,[66] and no man understands;
    And out of darkness came the hands
That reach through nature, moulding men.[67]

130

Thy voice is on the rolling air;
    I hear thee where the waters run;
    Thou standest in the rising sun,
And in the setting thou art fair.

What art thou then? I cannot guess;   5
    But though I seem in star and flower
    To feel thee some diffusive power,
I do not therefore love thee less:

My love involves the love before;
    My love is vaster passion now;   10
    Though mixed with God and Nature thou,
I seem to love thee more and more.

Far off thou art, but ever nigh;
    I have thee still, and I rejoice;
    I prosper, circled with thy voice;   15
I shall not lose thee though I die.

131

O living will[68] that shalt endure
    When all that seems[69] shall suffer shock,
    Rise in the spiritual rock,
Flow through our deeds and make them pure,[70]

That we may lift from out of dust   5
    A voice as unto him that hears,
    A cry above the conquered years
To one that with us works, and trust,

With faith that comes of self-control,
    The truths that never can be proved   10
    Until we close with all we loved,
And all we flow from, soul in soul.

from EPILOGUE

. . . A soul shall draw from out the vast[71]
And strike his being into bounds,[72]

And, moved through life of lower phase,[73]   125
    Result in man, be born and think,
    And act and love, a closer link
Betwixt us and the crowning race

Of those that, eye to eye, shall look
    On knowledge; under whose command   130
    Is Earth and Earth's, and in their hand
Is Nature like an open book;

No longer half-akin to brute,
    For all we thought and loved and did,
    And hoped, and suffered, is but seed   135
Of what in them is flower and fruit;

Whereof the man, that with me trod
    This planet, was a noble type
    Appearing ere the times were ripe,
That friend of mine who lives in God,   140

That God, which ever lives and loves,
    One God, one law, one element,
    And one far-off divine event,
To which the whole creation moves.

---

[62] That is, felt the atheistical implications of No. 123, lines 1–8.

[63] Known spiritual reality from experience. But that is a boast. Tennyson at once corrects himself and gives the real facts in the next stanza.

[64] When he cried out like a child in doubt and fear, that blind clamor brought him wisdom because he felt the immediate sense of a father (i.e., a divine Father) close by. The lines describe a religious-mystical experience by analogy with a psychological experience in childhood.

[65] My spirit or soul.   [66] Spiritual reality.

[67] Contrast this high moment of faith with the end of No. 55.

[68] According to Tennyson, he meant the moral will in man.

[69] All that seems so lasting.

[70] In 1 Corinthians 10:4, Christ is called a spiritual rock. May the moral will of man, inspired by the love or example of Christ, flow through our deeds.

[71] The child of Edmund Lushington and Tennyson's sister Cecilia, whose marriage is celebrated in the "Epilogue."

[72] The womb.

[73] The embryonic development roughly parallels the successive stages of animal evolution.

from IDYLLS OF THE KING

DEDICATION

These to His Memory[1]—since he held them dear,
Perchance as finding there unconsciously
Some image of himself—I dedicate,
I dedicate, I consecrate with tears—
These Idylls.

       And indeed He seems to me   5
Scarce other than my king's ideal knight,
"Who reverenced his conscience as his king;
Whose glory was, redressing human wrong;
Who spake no slander, no, nor listened to it;
Who loved one only and who clave to her—"[2]   10
Her—over all whose realms to their last isle,
Commingled with the gloom of imminent war,
The shadow of His loss drew like eclipse,
Darkening the world. We have lost him: he is gone:
We know him now: all narrow jealousies   15
Are silent; and we see him as he moved,
How modest, kindly, all-accomplished, wise,
With what sublime repression of himself,
And in what limits, and how tenderly;
Not swaying to this faction or to that;   20
Not making his high place the lawless perch
Of winged ambitions, nor a vantage-ground
For pleasure; but thro' all this tract of years
Wearing the white flower of a blameless life,
Before a thousand peering littlenesses,   25
In that fierce light which beats upon a throne,
And blackens every blot: for where is he,
Who dares foreshadow for an only son
A lovelier life, a more unstained, than his?
Or how should England dreaming of *his* sons   30
Hope more for these than some inheritance
Of such a life, a heart, a mind as thine,
Thou noble Father of her Kings to be,
Laborious for her people and her poor—
Voice in the rich dawn of an ampler day—   35
Far-sighted summoner of War and Waste
To fruitful strifes and rivalries of peace—
Sweet nature gilded by the gracious gleam
Of letters, dear to Science, dear to Art,
Dear to thy land[3] and ours, a Prince indeed,   40
Beyond all titles, and a household name,
Hereafter, thro' all times, Albert the Good.

---

[1] Prince Albert, consort of Queen Victoria. He died in 1861.
[2] A paraphrase of King Arthur's speech in "Guinevere," one of the *Idylls,* where he summarizes the code of the Round Table.
[3] Saxe-Coburg-Gotha in Germany, the Prince's native land.

Break not, O woman's-heart, but still endure;
Break not, for thou art Royal, but endure,
Remembering all the beauty of that star   45
Which shone so close beside Thee that ye made
One light together, but has past and leaves
The Crown a lonely splendour.

               May all love,
His love, unseen but felt, o'ershadow Thee,
The love of all Thy sons encompass Thee,   50
The love of all Thy daughters cherish Thee,
The love of all Thy people comfort Thee,
Till God's love set Thee at his side again!

LANCELOT AND ELAINE

Elaine the fair, Elaine the lovable,
Elaine, the lily maid of Astolat,
High in her chamber up a tower to the east
Guarded the sacred shield of Lancelot;
Which first she placed where morning's earliest ray   5
Might strike it, and awake her with the gleam;
Then fearing rust or soilure fashioned for it
A case of silk, and braided thereupon
All the devices blazoned on the shield
In their own tinct, and added, of her wit,   10
A border fantasy of branch and flower,
And yellow-throated nestling in the nest.
Nor rested thus content, but day by day,
Leaving her household and good father, climbed
That eastern tower, and entering barred her door,   15
Stript off the case, and read the naked shield,
Now guessed a hidden meaning in his arms,
Now made a pretty history to herself
Of every dint a sword had beaten in it,
And every scratch a lance had made upon it,   20
Conjecturing when and where: this cut is fresh;
That ten years back; this dealt him at Caerlyle;
That at Caerleon; this at Camelot:
And ah God's mercy, what a stroke was there!
And here a thrust that might have killed, but God   25
Broke the strong lance, and rolled his enemy down,
And saved him: so she lived in fantasy.

   How came the lily maid by that good shield
Of Lancelot, she that knew not ev'n his name?
He left it with her, when he rode to tilt   30
For the great diamond in the diamond jousts,
Which Arthur had ordained, and by that name
Had named them, since a diamond was the prize.

For Arthur, long before they crowned him King,
Roving the trackless realms of Lyonnesse,   35
Had found a glen, gray boulder and black tarn.[4]
A horror lived about the tarn, and clave
Like its own mists to all the mountain side:
For here two brothers, one a king, had met
And fought together; but their names were lost;   40
And each had slain his brother at a blow;
And down they fell and made the glen abhorred:
And there they lay till all their bones were bleached,
And lichened into color with the crags:
And he, that once was king, had on a crown   45
Of diamonds, one in front, and four aside.
And Arthur came, and laboring up the pass,
All in a misty moonshine, unawares
Had trodden that crowned skeleton, and the skull
Brake from the nape, and from the skull the crown   50
Rolled into light, and turning on its rims
Fled like a glittering rivulet to the tarn:
And down the shingly scaur[5] he plunged, and caught,
And set it on his head, and in his heart
Heard murmurs, "Lo, thou likewise shalt be King."   55

    Thereafter, when a King, he had the gems
Plucked from the crown, and showed them to his knights,
Saying, "These jewels, whereupon I chanced
Divinely,[6] are the kingdom's, not the King's—
For public use: henceforward let there be,   60
Once every year, a joust for one of these:
For so by nine years' proof we needs must learn
Which is our mightiest, and ourselves shall grow
In use of arms and manhood, till we drive
The heathen,[7] who, some say, shall rule the land   65
Hereafter, which God hinder." Thus he spoke:
And eight years past, eight jousts had been, and still
Had Lancelot won the diamond of the year,
With purpose to present them to the Queen,
When all were won; but meaning all at once   70
To snare her royal fancy with a boon
Worth half her realm, had never spoken word.

    Now for the central diamond and the last
And largest, Arthur, holding then his court
Hard on the river nigh the place which now   75
Is this world's hugest,[8] let proclaim a joust
At Camelot, and when the time drew nigh
Spake (for she had been sick) to Guinevere,
"Are you so sick, my Queen, you cannot move

To these fair jousts?" "Yea, lord," she said, "ye know
    it."   80
"Then will ye miss," he answered, "the great deeds
Of Lancelot, and his prowess in the lists,
A sight ye love to look on." And the Queen
Lifted her eyes, and they dwelt languidly
On Lancelot, where he stood beside the King.   85
He, thinking that he read her meaning there,
"Stay with me, I am sick; my love is more
Than many diamonds," yielded; and a heart
Love-loyal to the least wish of the Queen
(However much he yearned to make complete   90
The tale of diamonds for his destined boon)
Urged him to speak against the truth, and say,
"Sir King, mine ancient wound is hardly whole,
And lets me from the saddle"; and the King
Glanced first at him, then her, and went his way.   95
No sooner gone than suddenly she began:

    "To blame, my lord Sir Lancelot, much to blame!
Why go ye not to these fair jousts? the knights
Are half of them our enemies, and the crowd
Will murmur, 'Lo the shameless ones, who take   100
Their pastime now the trustful King is gone!'"
Then Lancelot vext at having lied in vain:
"Are ye so wise? ye were not once so wise,
My Queen, that summer, when ye loved me first.
Then of the crowd ye took no more account   105
Than of the myriad cricket of the mead,
When its own voice clings to each blade of grass,
And every voice is nothing. As to knights,
Them surely can I silence with all ease.
But now my loyal worship is allowed   110
Of all men: many a bard, without offence,
Has linked our names together in his lay,
Lancelot, the flower of bravery, Guinevere,
The pearl of beauty: and our knights at feast
Have pledged us in this union, while the King   115
Would listen smiling. How then? is there more?
Has Arthur spoken aught? or would yourself,
Now weary of my service and devoir,
Henceforth be truer to your faultless lord?"[9]

    She broke into a little scornful laugh: 120
"Arthur, my lord, Arthur, the faultless King,
That passionate perfection, my good lord—
But who can gaze upon the Sun in heaven?
He never spake word of reproach to me,
He never had a glimpse of mine untruth,   125

---

[4] Mountain lake.   [5] Steep bank covered with loose gravel.
[6] By divine guidance.   [7] The Angles, Saxons, and Jutes.
[8] London.

[9] The captious and weary tone of this speech, so lacking in any
feeling of love, indicates at once the burnt-out character of the
love affair.

He cares not for me: only here to-day
There gleamed a vague suspicion in his eyes:
Some meddling rogue has tampered with him—else
Rapt in this fancy of his Table Round,
And swearing men to vows impossible,   130
To make them like himself: but, friend, to me
He is all fault who hath no fault at all:
For who loves me must have a touch of earth;
The low sun makes the color:[10] I am yours,
Not Arthur's, as ye know, save by the bond.[11] 135
And therefore hear my words: go to the jousts:
The tiny-trumpeting gnat can break our dream
When sweetest; and the vermin voices here
May buzz so loud—we scorn them, but they sting."

Then answered Lancelot, the chief of knights: 140
"And with what face, after my pretext made,
Shall I appear, O Queen, at Camelot, I
Before a King who honors his own word,
As if it were his God's?"

                          "Yea," said the Queen,
"A moral child without the craft to rule,   145
Else had he not lost me: but listen to me,
If I must find you wit: we hear it said
That men go down before your spear at a touch,
But knowing you are Lancelot; your great name,
This conquers: hide it therefore; go unknown: 150
Win! by this kiss you will:[12] and our true King
Will then allow your pretext, O my knight,
As all for glory; for to speak him true,
Ye know right well, how meek soe'er he seem,
No keener hunter after glory breathes.   155
He loves it in his knights more than himself:
They prove to him his work: win and return."

Then got Sir Lancelot suddenly to horse,
Wroth at himself. Not willing to be known,
He left the barren-beaten thoroughfare,   160
Chose the green path that showed the rarer foot,
And there among the solitary downs,
Full often lost in fancy, lost his way;
Till as he traced a faintly-shadowed track,
That all in loops and links among the dales   165
Ran to the Castle of Astolat, he saw
Fired from the west, far on a hill, the towers.
Thither he made, and blew the gateway horn.
Then came an old, dumb, myriad-wrinkled man,
Who let him into lodging and disarmed.   170
And Lancelot marvelled at the wordless man;

And issuing found the Lord of Astolat
With two strong sons, Sir Torre and Sir Lavaine,
Moving to meet him in the castle court;
And close behind them stept the lily maid   175
Elaine, his daughter: mother of the house
There was not: some light jest among them rose
With laughter dying down as the great knight
Approached them: then the Lord of Astolat:
"Whence comest thou, my guest, and by what name 180
Livest between the lips? for by thy state
And presence I might guess thee chief of those,
After the King, who eat in Arthur's halls.
Him have I seen: the rest, his Table Round,
Known as they are, to me they are unknown."   185

Then answered Lancelot, the chief of knights:
"Known am I, and of Arthur's hall, and known,
What I by mere mischance have brought, my shield.
But since I go to joust as one unknown
At Camelot for the diamond, ask me not,   190
Hereafter ye shall know me—and the shield—
I pray you lend me one, if such you have,
Blank, or at least with some device not mine."

Then said the Lord of Astolat, "Here is Torre's:
Hurt in his first tilt was my son, Sir Torre.   195
And so, God wot, his shield is blank enough.
His ye can have." Then added plain Sir Torre,
"Yea, since I cannot use it, ye may have it."
Here laughed the father saying, "Fie, Sir Churl,
Is that an answer for a noble knight?   200
Allow him![13] but Lavaine, my younger here,
He is so full of lustihood, he will ride,
Joust for it, and win, and bring it in an hour,
And set it in this damsel's golden hair,
To make her thrice as wilful as before."   205

"Nay, father, nay good father, shame me not
Before this noble knight," said young Lavaine,
"For nothing. Surely I but played on Torre:
He seemed so sullen, vext he could not go:
A jest, no more! for, knight, the maiden dreamt 210
That some one put this diamond in her hand,
And that it was too slippery to be held,
And slipt and fell into some pool or stream,
The castle-well, belike; and then I said
That *if* I went and *if* I fought and won it   215
(But all was jest and joke among ourselves)
Then must she keep it safelier. All was jest."[14]

---

[10] Contrast line 123. The clouds are bright with attractive color
only when the sun is low, near the earth, at rising or setting.
[11] The matter-of-fact tone reinforces the implications mentioned
in note 9.   [12] A very casual kiss.

[13] Forgive him.
[14] But not entirely, one suspects. The truth lies somewhere between the father's account of the incident, which puts the worst
interpretation upon it (the Lord of Astolat manages to take a
crack at all three of his children), and Lavaine's, which puts
it in the best light.

But, father, give me leave, an if he will,
To ride to Camelot with this noble knight:
Win shall I not, but do my best to win: 220
Young as I am, yet would I do my best."

    "So ye will grace me," answered Lancelot,
Smiling a moment, "with your fellowship
O'er these waste downs whereon I lost myself,
Then were I glad of you as guide and friend: 225
And you shall win this diamond,—as I hear
It is a fair large diamond,—if ye may,
And yield it to this maiden, if ye will."
"A fair large diamond," added plain Sir Torre,
"Such be for queens, and not for simple maids."   230
Then she, who held her eyes upon the ground,
Elaine, and heard her name so tost about,
Flushed slightly at the slight disparagement
Before the stranger knight, who, looking at her,
Full courtly, yet not falsely, thus returned: 235
"If what is fair be but for what is fair,
And only queens are to be counted so,
Rash were my judgment then, who deem this maid
Might wear as fair a jewel as is on earth,
Not violating the bond of like to like."   240

    He spoke and ceased: the lily maid Elaine,
Won by the mellow voice before she looked,
Lifted her eyes, and read his lineaments.
The great and guilty love he bare the Queen,
In battle with the love he bare his lord,   245
Had marred his face, and marked it ere his time.
Another sinning on such heights with one,
The flower of all the west and all the world,
Had been the sleeker for it: but in him
His mood was often like a fiend, and rose   250
And drove him into wastes and solitudes
For agony, who was yet a living soul.[15]
Marred as he was, he seemed the goodliest man
That ever among ladies ate in hall,
And noblest, when she lifted up her eyes.   255
However marred, of more than twice her years,
Seamed with an ancient swordcut on the cheek,
And bruised and bronzed, she lifted up her eyes
And loved him, with that love which was her doom.

    Then the great knight, the darling of the court,   260
Loved of the loveliest, into that rude hall
Stept with all grace, and not with half disdain

Hid under grace, as in a smaller time,[16]
But kindly man moving among his kind:
Whom they with meats and vintage of their best   265
And talk and minstrel melody entertained.
And much they asked of court and Table Round,
And ever well and readily answered he;
But Lancelot, when they glanced at Guinevere,
Suddenly speaking of the wordless man,   270
Heard from the Baron that, ten years before,
The heathen caught and reft him of his tongue.
"He learnt and warned me of their fierce design
Against my house, and him they caught and maimed;
But I, my sons, and little daughter fled   275
From bonds or death, and dwelt among the woods
By the great river in a boatman's hut.
Dull days were those, till our good Arthur broke
The Pagan yet once more on Badon hill."

    "O there, great lord, doubtless," Lavaine said, rapt   280
By all the sweet and sudden passion of youth
Toward greatness in its elder, "you have fought.
O tell us—for we live apart—you know
Of Arthur's glorious wars." And Lancelot spoke
And answered him at full, as having been   285
With Arthur in the fight which all day long
Rang by the white mouth of the violent Glem;
And in the four loud battles by the shore
Of Duglas; that on Bassa; then the war
That thundered in and out the gloomy skirts   290
Of Celidon the forest; and again
By Castle Gurnion, where the glorious King
Had on his cuirass worn our Lady's Head,
Carved of one emerald centered in a sun
Of silver rays, that lightened as he breathed;   295
And at Caerleon had he helped his lord,
When the strong neighings of the wild white Horse
Set every gilded parapet shuddering;
And up in Agned-Cathregonion too,
And down the waste sand-shores of Trath Treroit,   300
Where many a heathen fell; "and on the mount
Of Badon I myself beheld the King
Charge at the head of all his Table Round,
And all his legions crying Christ and him,
And break them; and I saw him, after, stand   305
High on a heap of slain, from spur to plume
Red as the rising sun with heathen blood,
And seeing me, with a great voice he cried,
'They are broken, they are broken!' for the King,
However mild he seems at home, nor cares   310
For triumph in our mimic wars, the jousts—
For if his own knight cast him down, he laughs
Saying, his knights are better men than he—

---

[15] Whose soul was still alive, not deadened by sin. But the poem
suggests that Lancelot's "agony" was as much disgust at himself and the whole weary "situation" which he cannot break
with as it was a sense of guilt. See lines 1230–31 and his final
speech at the end.

[16] A lesser age.

Yet in this heathen war the fire of God
Fills him: I never saw his like: there lives   315
No greater leader."
                    While he uttered this,
Low to her own heart said the lily maid,
"Save your great self, fair lord"; and when he fell
From talk of war to traits of pleasantry—
Being mirthful he, but in a stately kind—   320
She still took note that when the living smile
Died from his lips, across him came a cloud
Of melancholy severe, from which again,
Whenever in her hovering to and fro
The lily maid had striven to make him cheer,   325
There brake a sudden-beaming tenderness
Of manners and of nature: and she thought
That all was nature,[17] all, perchance, for her.
And all night long his face before her lived,
As when a painter, poring on a face,   330
Divinely thro' all hindrance finds the man
Behind it, and so paints him that his face,
The shape and color of a mind and life,
Lives for his children, ever at its best
And fullest; so the face before her lived,   335
Dark-splendid, speaking in the silence, full
Of noble things, and held her from her sleep.
Till rathe[18] she rose, half-cheated in the thought
She needs must bid farewell to sweet Lavaine.
First as in fear, step after step, she stole   340
Down the long tower-stairs, hesitating:
Anon, she heard Sir Lancelot cry in the court,
"This shield, my friend, where is it?" and Lavaine
Past inward, as she came from out the tower.
There to his proud horse Lancelot turned, and
    smoothed   345
The glossy shoulder, humming to himself.
Half-envious of the flattering hand, she drew
Nearer and stood. He looked, and more amazed
Than if seven men had set upon him, saw
The maiden standing in the dewy light.   350
He had not dreamed she was so beautiful.
Then came on him a sort of sacred fear,
For silent, tho' he greeted her, she stood
Rapt on his face as if it were a God's.
Suddenly flashed on her a wild desire,   355
That he should wear her favor at the tilt.
She braved a riotous heart in asking for it.
"Fair lord, whose name I know not—noble it is,
I well believe, the noblest—will you wear
My favor at this tourney?" "Nay," said he,   360

"Fair lady, since I never yet have worn
Favor of any lady in the lists.
Such is my wont, as those, who know me, know."
"Yea, so," she answered; "then in wearing mine
Needs must be lesser likelihood, noble lord,   365
That those who know should know you." And he turned
Her counsel up and down within his mind,
And found it true, and answered, "True, my child.
Well, I will wear it:[19] fetch it out to me:
What is it?" and she told him, "A red sleeve   370
Broidered with pearls," and brought it: then he bound
Her token on his helmet, with a smile
Saying, "I never yet have done so much
For any maiden living," and the blood
Sprang to her face and filled her with delight;   375
But left her all the paler, when Lavaine
Returning brought the yet-unblazoned shield,
His brother's; which he gave to Lancelot,
Who parted with his own to fair Elaine:
"Do me this grace, my child, to have my shield   380
In keeping till I come." "A grace to me,"
She answered, "twice to-day. I am your squire!"
Whereat Lavaine said, laughing, "Lily maid,
For fear our people call you lily maid
In earnest, let me bring your color back;   385
Once, twice, and thrice: now get you hence to bed":
So kissed her, and Sir Lancelot his own hand,[20]
And thus they moved away: she stayed a minute,
Then made a sudden step to the gate, and there—
Her bright hair blown about the serious face   390
Yet rosy-kindled with her brother's kiss—
Paused by the gateway, standing near the shield
In silence, while she watched their arms far-off
Sparkle, until they dipt below the downs.
Then to her tower she climbed, and took the shield, 395
There kept it, and so lived in fantasy.

Meanwhile the new companions past away
Far o'er the long backs of the bushless downs,
To where Sir Lancelot knew there lived a knight
Not far from Camelot, now for forty years   400
A hermit, who had prayed, labored and prayed,
And ever laboring had scooped himself
In the white rock a chapel and a hall
Of massive columns, like a shorecliff cave,
And cells and chambers: all were fair and dry;   405
The green light from the meadows underneath
Struck up and lived along the milky roofs;
And in the meadows tremulous aspen-trees

---

[17] Natural, spontaneous.   [18] Early.

[19] Because of her argument? her beauty? her flattery?
[20] Kissed his hand to her.

And poplars made a noise of falling showers.
And thither wending there that night they bode.   410

    But when the next day broke from underground,
And shot red fire and shadows thro' the cave,
They rose, heard mass, broke fast, and rode away:
Then Lancelot saying, "Hear, but hold my name
Hidden, you ride with Lancelot of the Lake,"   415
Abashed Lavaine, whose instant reverence,
Dearer to true young hearts than their own praise,
But left him leave to stammer, "Is it indeed?"
And after muttering "The great Lancelot,"
At last he got his breath and answered, "One,   420
One have I seen—that other, our liege lord,
The dread Pendragon, Britain's King of kings,
Of whom the people talk mysteriously,
He will be there—then were I stricken blind
That minute, I might say that I had seen."   425

    So spake Lavaine, and when they reached the lists
By Camelot in the meadow, let his eyes
Run thro' the peopled gallery which half round
Lay like a rainbow fall'n upon the grass,
Until they found the clear-faced King, who sat   430
Robed in red samite, easily to be known,
Since to his crown the golden dragon clung,
And down his robe the dragon writhed in gold,
And from the carven-work behind him crept
Two dragons gilded, sloping down to make   435
Arms for his chair, while all the rest of them
Thro' knots and loops and folds innumerable
Fled ever thro' the woodwork, till they found
The new design wherein they lost themselves,
Yet with all ease, so tender was the work: 440
And, in the costly canopy o'er him set,
Blazed the last diamond of the nameless king.

    Then Lancelot answered young Lavaine and said,
"Me you call great: mine is the firmer seat,
The truer lance: but there is many a youth   445
Now crescent,[21] who will come to all I am
And overcome it; and in me there dwells
No greatness, save it be some far-off touch
Of greatness to know well I am not great:
There is the man." And Lavaine gaped upon him   450
As on a thing miraculous, and anon
The trumpets blew; and then did either side,
They that assailed, and they that held the lists,
Set lance in rest, strike spur, suddenly move,
Meet in the midst, and there so furiously   455

---

[21] Growing up.

Shock, that a man far-off might well perceive,
If any man that day were left afield,
The hard earth shake, and a low thunder of arms.
And Lancelot bode a little, till he saw
Which were the weaker; then he hurled into it   460
Against the stronger: little need to speak
Of Lancelot in his glory! King, duke, earl,
Count, baron—whom he smote, he overthrew.

    But in the field were Lancelot's kith and kin,
Ranged with the Table Round that held the lists,   465
Strong men, and wrathful that a stranger knight
Should do and almost overdo the deeds
Of Lancelot; and one said to the other, "Lo!
What is he? I do not mean the force alone—
The grace and versatility of the man!   470
Is it not Lancelot?" "When has Lancelot worn
Favor of any lady in the lists?
Not such his wont, as we, that know him, know."
"How then? who then?" a fury seized them all,
A fiery family passion for the name   475
Of Lancelot, and a glory one with theirs.
They couched their spears and pricked their steeds, and
    thus,
Their plumes driv'n backward by the wind they made
In moving, all together down upon him
Bare, as a wild wave in the wide North-sea,   480
Green-glimmering toward the summit, bears, with all
Its stormy crests that smoke against the skies,
Down on a bark, and overbears the bark,
And him that helms it, so they overbore
Sir Lancelot and his charger, and a spear   485
Down-glancing lamed the charger, and a spear
Pricked sharply his own cuirass, and the head
Pierced thro' his side, and there snapt, and remained.

    Then Sir Lavaine did well and worshipfully;
He bore a knight of old repute to the earth,   490
And brought his horse to Lancelot where he lay.
He up the side, sweating with agony, got,
But thought to do while he might yet endure,
And being lustily holpen by the rest,
His party,—tho' it seemed half-miracle   495
To those he fought with,—drave his kith and kin,
And all the Table Round that held the lists,
Back to the barrier; then the trumpets blew
Proclaiming his the prize, who wore the sleeve
Of scarlet, and the pearls; and all the knights,   500
His party, cried "Advance and take thy prize
The diamond"; but he answered, "Diamond me
No diamonds! for God's love, a little air!
Prize me no prizes, for my prize is death!
Hence will I, and I charge you, follow me not."   505

He spoke, and vanished suddenly from the field
With young Lavaine into the poplar grove.
There from his charger down he slid, and sat,
Gasping to Sir Lavaine, "Draw the lance-head":
"Ah my sweet lord Sir Lancelot," said Lavaine,   510
"I dread me, if I draw it, you will die."
But he, "I die already with it: draw—
Draw,"—and Lavaine drew, and Sir Lancelot gave
A marvellous great shriek and ghastly groan,
And half his blood burst forth, and down he sank   515
For the pure pain, and wholly swooned away.
Then came the hermit out and bare him in,
There stanched his wound; and there, in daily doubt
Whether to live or die, for many a week
Hid from the wild world's rumor by the grove   520
Of poplars with their noise of falling showers,
And ever-tremulous aspen-trees, he lay.

But on that day when Lancelot fled the lists,
His party, knights of utmost North and West,
Lords of waste marches, kings of desolate isles,   525
Came round their great Pendragon, saying to him,
"Lo, Sire, our knight, thro' whom we won the day,
Hath gone sore wounded, and hath left his prize
Untaken, crying that his prize is death."
"Heaven hinder," said the King, "that such an one,   530
So great a knight as we have seen to-day—
He seemed to me another Lancelot—
Yea, twenty times I thought him Lancelot—
He must not pass uncared for. Wherefore, rise,
O Gawain, and ride forth and find the knight.   535
Wounded and wearied needs must he be near.
I charge you that you get at once to horse.
And, knights and kings, there breathes not one of you
Will deem this prize of ours is rashly given:
His prowess was too wondrous. We will do him   540
No customary honor: since the knight
Came not to us, of us to claim the prize,
Ourselves will send it after. Rise and take
This diamond, and deliver it, and return,
And bring us where he is, and how he fares,   545
And cease not from your quest until ye find."

So saying, from the carven flower above,
To which it made a restless heart, he took,
And gave, the diamond: then from where he sat
At Arthur's right, with smiling face arose,   550
With smiling face and frowning heart, a Prince
In the mid might and flourish of his May,
Gawain, surnamed The Courteous, fair and strong,
And after Lancelot, Tristram, and Geraint
And Gareth, a good knight, but therewithal   555
Sir Modred's brother, and the child of Lot,[22]

Nor often loyal to his word, and now
Wroth that the King's command to sally forth
In quest of whom he knew not, made him leave
The banquet, and concourse of knights and kings.   560

So all in wrath he got to horse and went;
While Arthur to the banquet, dark in mood,
Past, thinking "Is it Lancelot who hath come
Despite the wound he spake of, all for gain
Of glory, and hath added wound to wound,   565
And ridd'n away to die?" So feared the King,
And, after two days' tarriance there, returned.
Then when he saw the Queen, embracing asked,
"Love, are you yet so sick?" "Nay, lord," she said.
"And where is Lancelot?" Then the Queen amazed,   570
"Was he not with you? won he not your prize?"
"Nay, but one like him." "Why that like was he."
And when the King demanded how she knew,
Said, "Lord, no sooner had ye parted from us,
Than Lancelot told me of a common talk   575
That men went down before his spear at a touch,
But knowing he was Lancelot; his great name
Conquered; and therefore would he hide his name
From all men, ev'n the King, and to this end
Had made the pretext of a hindering wound,   580
That he might joust unknown of all, and learn
If his old prowess were in aught decayed;
And added, 'Our true Arthur, when he learns,
Will well allow my pretext, as for gain
Of purer glory.' "
             Then replied the King: 585
"Far lovelier in our Lancelot had it been,
In lieu of idly dallying with the truth,
To have trusted me as he hath trusted thee.
Surely his King and most familiar friend
Might well have kept his secret. True, indeed,   590
Albeit I know my knights fantastical,
So fine a fear in our large Lancelot
Must needs have moved my laughter: now remains
But little cause for laughter: his own kin—
Ill news, my Queen, for all who love him, this!—   595
His kith and kin, not knowing, set upon him;
So that he went sore wounded from the field:
Yet good news too: for goodly hopes are mine
That Lancelot is no more a lonely heart.[23]
He wore, against his wont, upon his helm   600
A sleeve of scarlet, broidered with great pearls,
Some gentle maiden's gift."
                 "Yea, lord," she said,

---

22 Brother of a traitor and child of another.
23 Are the final words ironic? If so, line 595, just above, is pointed.

"Thy hopes are mine," and saying that, she choked,
And sharply turned about to hide her face,
Past to her chamber, and there flung herself   605
Down on the great King's couch, and writhed upon it,
And clenched her fingers till they bit the palm,
And shrieked out "Traitor" to the unhearing wall,
Then flashed into wild tears, and rose again,
And moved about her palace, proud and pale.   610

Gawain the while thro' all the region round
Rode with his diamond, wearied of the quest,
Touched at all points, except the poplar grove,
And came at last, tho' late, to Astolat:
Whom glittering in enamelled arms the maid   615
Glanced at, and cried, "What news from Camelot, lord?
What of the knight with the red sleeve?" "He won."
"I knew it," she said. "But parted from the jousts
Hurt in the side," whereat she caught her breath;
Thro' her own side she felt the sharp lance go;   620
Thereon she smote her hand: wellnigh she swooned:
And, while he gazed wonderingly at her, came
The Lord of Astolat out, to whom the Prince
Reported who he was, and on what quest
Sent, that he bore the prize and could not find   625
The victor, but had ridd'n a random round
To seek him, and had wearied of the search.
To whom the Lord of Astolat, "Bide with us,
And ride no more at random, noble Prince!
Here was the knight, and here he left a shield;   630
This will he send or come for: furthermore
Our son is with him; we shall hear anon,
Needs must we hear." To this the courteous Prince
Accorded with his wonted courtesy,
Courtesy with a touch of traitor in it,   635
And stayed; and cast his eyes on fair Elaine:
Where could be found face daintier? then her shape
From forehead down to foot, perfect—again
From foot to forehead exquisitely turned:[24]
"Well—if I bide, lo! this wild flower for me!"   640
And oft they met among the garden yews,
And there he set himself to play upon her
With sallying wit, free flashes from a height
Above her, graces of the court, and songs,
Sighs, and slow smiles, and golden eloquence   645
And amorous adulation, till the maid
Rebelled against it, saying to him, "Prince,
O loyal nephew of our noble King,
Why ask you not to see the shield he left,

Whence you might learn his name? Why slight your
          King,   650
And lose the quest he sent you on, and prove
No surer than our falcon yesterday,
Who lost the hern we slipt her at, and went
To all the winds?" "Nay, by mine head," said he,
"I lose it, as we lose the lark in heaven,   655
O damsel, in the light of your blue eyes;
But an ye will it let me see the shield."
And when the shield was brought, and Gawain saw
Sir Lancelot's azure lions, crowned with gold,
Ramp in the field, he smote his thigh, and mocked: 660
"Right was the King! our Lancelot! that true man!"
"And right was I," she answered merrily, "I,
Who dreamed my knight the greatest knight of all."
"And if I dreamed," said Gawain, "that you love
This greatest knight, your pardon! lo, ye know it![25]   665
Speak therefore: shall I waste myself in vain?"
Full simple was her answer, "What know I?
My brethren have been all my fellowship;
And I, when often they have talked of love,
Wished it had been my mother, for they talked,   670
Meseemed, of what they knew not; so myself—
I know not if I know what true love is,
But if I know, then, if I love not him,
I know there is none other I can love."
"Yea, by God's death," said he, "ye love him well,   675
But would not, knew ye what all others know,
And whom he loves." "So be it," cried Elaine,
And lifted her fair face and moved away:
But he pursued her, calling, "Stay a little!
One golden minute's grace! he wore your sleeve: 680
Would he break faith with one I may not name?
Must our true man change like a leaf at last?
Nay—like enow: why then, far be it from me
To cross our mighty Lancelot in his loves!
And, damsel, for I deem you know full well   685
Where your great knight is hidden, let me leave
My quest with you; the diamond also: here!
For if you love, it will be sweet to give it;
And if he love, it will be sweet to have it
From your own hand; and whether he love or not,   690
A diamond is a diamond.[26] Fare you well
A thousand times!—a thousand times farewell!
Yet, if he love, and his love hold, we two
May meet at court hereafter: there, I think,
So ye will learn the courtesies of the court,   695
We two shall know each other."

[24] What Gawain saw when he looked at Elaine, or more exactly, the way he looked at Elaine, is intended to contrast with Lancelot's view of her at lines 348–351.

[25] The elliptical phrasing seems to mean, "If I've made love to you when you love another, I shall ask your pardon, as you know I would."

[26] A fine summary of Gawain's philosophy.

                    Then he gave,
And slightly kissed the hand to which he gave,
The diamond, and all wearied of the quest
Leapt on his horse, and carolling as he went
A true-love ballad, lightly rode away.   700

    Thence to the court he past; there told the King
What the King knew, "Sir Lancelot is the knight."
And added, "Sire, my liege, so much I learnt;
But failed to find him, tho' I rode all round
The region: but I lighted on the maid   705
Whose sleeve he wore; she loves him; and to her,
Deeming our courtesy is the truest law,
I gave the diamond: she will render it;
For by mine head she knows his hiding-place."

    The seldom-frowning King frowned, and replied, 710
"Too courteous truly! ye shall go no more
On quest of mine, seeing that ye forget
Obedience is the courtesy due to kings."

    He spake and parted. Wroth, but all in awe,
For twenty strokes of the blood, without a word,   715
Lingered that other, staring after him;
Then shook his hair, strode off, and buzzed abroad
About the maid of Astolat, and her love.
All ears were pricked at once, all tongues were loosed:
"The maid of Astolat loves Sir Lancelot,   720
Sir Lancelot loves the maid of Astolat."
Some read the King's face, some the Queen's, and all
Had marvel what the maid might be, but most
Predoomed her as unworthy. One old dame
Came suddenly on the Queen with the sharp news. 725
She, that had heard the noise of it before,
But sorrowing Lancelot should have stooped so low,[27]
Marred her friend's aim with pale tranquillity.
So ran the tale like fire about the court,
Fire in dry stubble a nine-days' wonder flared: 730
Till even the knights at banquet twice or thrice
Forgot to drink to Lancelot and the Queen,
And pledging Lancelot and the lily maid
Smiled at each other, while the Queen, who sat
With lips severely placid, felt the knot   735
Climb in her throat, and with her feet unseen
Crushed the wild passion out against the floor
Beneath the banquet, where the meats became
As wormwood, and she hated all who pledged.

    But far away the maid in Astolat,   740
Her guiltless rival, she that ever kept
The one-day-seen Sir Lancelot in her heart,

_____

[27] The lines are her reply to the old dame, in indirect discourse.

Crept to her father, while he mused alone,
Sat on his knee, stroked his gray face and said,
"Father, you call me wilful, and the fault   745
Is yours who let me have my will, and now,
Sweet father, will you let me lose my wits?"
"Nay," said he, "surely." "Wherefore, let me hence,"
She answered, "and find out our dear Lavaine."
"Ye will not lose your wits for dear Lavaine: 750
Bide," answered he: "we needs must hear anon
Of him, and of that other." "Ay," she said,
"And of that other, for I needs must hence
And find that other, wheresoe'er he be,
And with mine own hand give his diamond to him, 755
Lest I be found as faithless in the quest
As yon proud Prince who left the quest to me.
Sweet father, I behold him in my dreams
Gaunt as it were the skeleton of himself,
Death-pale, for lack of gentle maiden's aid.   760
The gentler-born the maiden, the more bound,
My father, to be sweet and serviceable
To noble knights in sickness, as ye know,
When these have worn their tokens: let me hence,
I pray you." Then her father nodding said,   765
"Ay, ay, the diamond: wit ye well, my child,
Right fain were I to learn this knight were whole,
Being our greatest: yea, and you must give it—
And sure I think this fruit is hung too high
For any mouth to gape for save a queen's—   770
Nay, I mean nothing: so then, get you gone,
Being so very wilful you must go."

    Lightly, her suit allowed, she slipt away,
And while she made her ready for her ride,
Her father's latest word hummed in her ear,   775
"Being so very wilful you must go,"
And changed itself and echoed in her heart,
"Being so very wilful you must die."
But she was happy enough and shook it off,
As we shake off the bee that buzzes at us;   780
And in her heart she answered it and said,
"What matter, so I help him back to life?"
Then far away with good Sir Torre for guide
Rode o'er the long backs of the bushless downs
To Camelot, and before the city-gates   785
Came on her brother with a happy face
Making a roan horse caper and curvet
For pleasure all about a field of flowers:
Whom when she saw, "Lavaine," she cried, "Lavaine,
How fares my lord Sir Lancelot?" He amazed,   790
"Torre and Elaine! why here? Sir Lancelot!
How know ye my lord's name is Lancelot?"
But when the maid had told him all her tale,
Then turned Sir Torre, and being in his moods

Left them, and under the strange-statued gate, 795
Where Arthur's wars were rendered mystically,
Past up the still rich city to his kin,
His own far blood, which dwelt at Camelot;
And her, Lavaine across the poplar grove
Led to the caves: there first she saw the casque 800
Of Lancelot on the wall: her scarlet sleeve,
Tho' carved and cut, and half the pearls away,
Streamed from it still; and in her heart she laughed,
Because he had not loosed it from his helm,
But meant once more perchance to tourney in it. 805
And when they gained the cell wherein he slept,
His battle-writhen arms and mighty hands
Lay naked on the wolfskin, and a dream
Of dragging down his enemy made them move.
Then she that saw him lying unsleek, unshorn, 810
Gaunt as it were the skeleton of himself,
Uttered a little tender dolorous cry.
The sound not wonted in a place so still
Woke the sick knight, and while he rolled his eyes
Yet blank from sleep, she started to him, saying, 815
"Your prize the diamond sent you by the King":
His eyes glistened: she fancied "Is it for me?"
And when the maid had told him all the tale
Of King and Prince, the diamond sent, the quest
Assigned to her not worthy of it, she knelt 820
Full lowly by the corners of his bed,
And laid the diamond in his open hand.
Her face was near, and as we kiss the child
That does the task assigned, he kissed her face.
At once she slipt like water to the floor. 825
"Alas," he said, "your ride hath wearied you.
Rest must you have." "No rest for me," she said;
"Nay, for near you, fair lord, I am at rest."
What might she mean by that? his large black eyes,
Yet larger thro' his leanness, dwelt upon her, 830
Till all her heart's sad secret blazed itself
In the heart's colors on her simple face;
And Lancelot looked and was perplext in mind,
And being weak in body said no more;
But did not love the color; woman's love, 835
Save one, he not regarded, and so turned
Sighing, and feigned a sleep until he slept.

Then rose Elaine and glided thro' the fields,
And past beneath the weirdly-sculptured gates
Far up the dim rich city to her kin; 840
There bode the night: but woke with dawn, and past
Down thro' the dim rich city to the fields,
Thence to the cave: so day by day she past
In either twilight ghost-like to and fro
Gliding, and every day she tended him, 845
And likewise many a night: and Lancelot

Would, tho' he called his wound a little hurt
Whereof he should be quickly whole, at times
Brain-feverous in his heat and agony, seem
Uncourteous, even he: but the meek maid 850
Sweetly forbore him ever, being to him
Meeker than any child to a rough nurse,
Milder than any mother to a sick child,
And never woman yet, since man's first fall,
Did kindlier unto man, but her deep love 855
Upbore her; till the hermit, skilled in all
The simples and the science of that time,
Told him that her fine care had saved his life.
And the sick man forgot her simple blush,
Would call her friend and sister, sweet Elaine, 860
Would listen for her coming and regret
Her parting step, and held her tenderly,
And loved her with all love except the love
Of man and woman when they love their best,
Closest and sweetest, and had died the death 865
In any knightly fashion for her sake.
And peradventure had he seen her first
She might have made this and that other world
Another world for the sick man; but now
The shackles of an old love straitened him, 870
His honor rooted in dishonor stood,
And faith unfaithful kept him falsely true.[28]

Yet the great knight in his mid-sickness made
Full many a holy vow and pure resolve.
These, as but born of sickness, could not live: 875
For when the blood ran lustier in him again,
Full often the bright image of one face,
Making a treacherous quiet in his heart,
Dispersed his resolution like a cloud.
Then if the maiden, while that ghostly grace[29] 880
Beamed on his fancy, spoke, he answered not,
Or short and coldly, and she knew right well
What the rough sickness meant, but what this meant
She knew not, and the sorrow dimmed her sight,
And drave her ere her time across the fields 885
Far into the rich city, where alone
She murmured, "Vain, in vain: it cannot be.
He will not love me: how then? must I die?"
Then as a little helpless innocent bird,
That has but one plain passage of few notes, 890
Will sing the simple passage o'er and o'er
For all an April morning, till the ear
Wearies to hear it, so the simple maid
Went half the night repeating, "Must I die?"

---

[28] His faith to Guinevere, which was unfaithfulness to her husband
and his king, Arthur, kept him true to her and false to him.
[29] The image of Guinevere.

And now to right she turned, and now to left,   895
And found no ease in turning or in rest;
And "Him or death," she muttered, "death or him,"
Again and like a burthen,[30] "Him or death."

But when Sir Lancelot's deadly hurt was whole,
To Astolat returning rode the three.   900
There morn by morn, arraying her sweet self
In that wherein she deemed she looked her best,
She came before Sir Lancelot, for she thought,
"If I be loved, these are my festal robes,
If not, the victim's flowers before he fall."[31]   905
And Lancelot ever prest upon the maid
That she should ask some goodly gift of him
For her own self or hers; "and do not shun
To speak the wish most near to your true heart;
Such service have ye done me, that I make   910
My will of yours, and Prince and Lord am I
In mine own land, and what I will I can."
Then like a ghost she lifted up her face,
But like a ghost without the power to speak.
And Lancelot saw that she withheld her wish,   915
And bode among them yet a little space
Till he should learn it; and one morn it chanced
He found her in among the garden yews,
And said, "Delay no longer, speak your wish,
Seeing I go to-day": then out she brake: 920
"Going? and we shall never see you more.
And I must die for want of one bold word."
"Speak: that I live to hear," he said, "is yours."
Then suddenly and passionately she spoke:
"I have gone mad. I love you: let me die."   925
"Ah, sister," answered Lancelot, "what is this?"
And innocently extending her white arms,
"Your love," she said, "your love—to be your wife."
And Lancelot answered, "Had I chosen to wed,
I had been wedded earlier, sweet Elaine: 930
But now there never will be wife of mine."
"No, no," she cried, "I care not to be wife,
But to be with you still, to see your face,
To serve you, and to follow you thro' the world."
And Lancelot answered, "Nay, the world, the world,   935
All ear and eye, with such a stupid heart
To interpret ear and eye, and such a tongue
To blare its own interpretation—nay,
Full ill then should I quit your brother's love,
And your good father's kindness." And she said,   940
"Not to be with you, not to see your face—
Alas for me then, my good days are done."

"Nay, noble maid," he answered, "ten times nay!
This is not love: but love's first flash in youth,
Most common: yea, I know it of mine own self: 945
And you yourself will smile at your own self
Hereafter, when you yield your flower of life
To one more fitly yours, not thrice your age:[32]
And then will I, for true you are and sweet
Beyond mine old belief in womanhood,   950
More specially should your good knight be poor,
Endow you with broad land and territory
Even to the half my realm beyond the seas,[33]
So that would make you happy: furthermore,
Ev'n to the death, as tho' ye were my blood,   955
In all your quarrels will I be your knight.
This will I do, dear damsel, for your sake,
And more than this I cannot."
                                         While he spoke
She neither blushed nor shook, but deathly-pale
Stood grasping what was nearest, then replied: 960
"Of all this will I nothing"; and so fell,
And thus they bore her swooning to her tower.

Then spake, to whom thro' those black walls of yew
Their talk had pierced, her father: "Ay, a flash,
I fear me, that will strike my blossom dead.   965
Too courteous are ye, fair Lord Lancelot.
I pray you, use some rough discourtesy
To blunt or break her passion."
                                         Lancelot said,
"That were against me: what I can I will";
And there that day remained, and toward even   970
Sent for his shield: full meekly rose the maid,
Stript off the case, and gave the naked shield;
Then, when she heard his horse upon the stones,
Unclasping flung the casement back, and looked
Down on his helm, from which her sleeve had gone. 975
And Lancelot knew the little clinking sound;
And she by tact of love was well aware
That Lancelot knew that she was looking at him.
And yet he glanced not up, nor waved his hand,
Nor bade farewell, but sadly rode away.   980
This was the one discourtesy that he used.

So in her tower alone the maiden sat:
His very shield was gone; only the case,
Her own poor work, her empty labor, left.
But still she heard him, still his picture formed   985
And grew between her and the pictured wall.
Then came her father, saying in low tones,

---

[30] Refrain.
[31] Sacrificial animals were decorated with flowers.

[32] The exaggeration is deliberate. He is only a little more than
twice her age (see line 256).
[33] His ancestral estates were in Brittany.

"Have comfort," whom she greeted quietly.
Then came her brethren saying, "Peace to thee,
Sweet sister," whom she answered with all calm.   990
But when they left her to herself again,
Death, like a friend's voice from a distant field
Approaching thro' the darkness, called; the owls
Wailing had power upon her, and she mixt
Her fancies with the sallow-rifted glooms   995
Of evening, and the moanings of the wind.

And in those days she made a little song,
And called her song "The Song of Love and Death,"
And sang it: sweetly could she make and sing.

"Sweet is true love tho' given in vain, in vain;   1000
And sweet is death who puts an end to pain:
I know not which is sweeter, no, not I.

"Love, art thou sweet? then bitter death must be:
Love, thou art bitter; sweet is death to me.
O Love, if death be sweeter, let me die.   1005

"Sweet love, that seems not made to fade away,
Sweet death, that seems to make us loveless clay,
I know not which is sweeter, no, not I.

"I fain would follow love, if that could be;
I needs must follow death, who calls for me;   1010
Call and I follow, I follow! let me die."

High with the last line scaled her voice, and this,
All in a fiery dawning wild with wind
That shook her tower, the brothers heard, and thought
With shuddering, "Hark the Phantom of the house   1015

That ever shrieks before a death," and called
The father, and all three in hurry and fear
Ran to her, and lo! the blood-red light of dawn
Flared on her face, she shrilling, "Let me die!"

As when we dwell upon a word we know,   1020
Repeating, till the word we know so well
Becomes a wonder, and we know not why,
So dwelt the father on her face, and thought
"Is this Elaine?" till back the maiden fell,
Then gave a languid hand to each, and lay,   1025
Speaking a still good-morrow with her eyes.
At last she said, "Sweet brothers, yesternight
I seemed a curious little maid again,
As happy as when we dwelt among the woods,
And when ye used to take me with the flood   1030
Up the great river in the boatman's boat.
Only ye would not pass beyond the cape
That has the poplar on it: there ye fixt
Your limit, oft returning with the tide.
And yet I cried because ye would not pass   1035
Beyond it, and far up the shining flood
Until we found the palace of the King.
And yet ye would not; but this night I dreamed
That I was all alone upon the flood,
And then I said, 'Now shall I have my will':   1040
And there I woke, but still the wish remained.
So let me hence that I may pass at last
Beyond the poplar and far up the flood,
Until I find the palace of the King.
There will I enter in among them all,   1045
And no man there will dare to mock at me;
But there the fine Gawain will wonder at me,
And there the great Sir Lancelot muse at me;
Gawain, who bade a thousand farewells to me,
Lancelot, who coldly went, nor bade me one: 1050
And there the King will know me and my love,
And there the Queen herself will pity me,
And all the gentle court will welcome me,
And after my long voyage I shall rest!"

"Peace," said her father, "O my child, ye seem   1055
Light-headed, for what force is yours to go
So far, being sick? and wherefore would ye look
On this proud fellow again, who scorns us all?"

Then the rough Torre began to heave and move,
And bluster into stormy sobs and say,   1060
"I never loved him: an I meet with him,
I care not howsoever great he be,
Then will I strike at him and strike him down,
Give me good fortune, I will strike him dead,
For this discomfort he hath done the house."   1065

To whom the gentle sister made reply,
"Fret not yourself, dear brother, nor be wroth,
Seeing it is no more Sir Lancelot's fault
Not to love me, than it is mine to love
Him of all men who seems to me the highest."   1070

"Highest?" the father answered, echoing "highest?"
(He meant to break the passion in her) "nay,
Daughter, I know not what you call the highest;
But this I know, for all the people know it,
He loves the Queen, and in an open shame: 1075
And she returns his love in open shame;
If this be high, what is it to be low?"

Then spake the lily maid of Astolat:
"Sweet father, all too faint and sick am I
For anger: these are slanders: never yet   1080

Was noble man but made ignoble talk.
He makes no friend who never made a foe.
But now it is my glory to have loved
One peerless, without stain: so let me pass,
My father, howsoe'er I seem to you,   1085
Not all unhappy, having loved God's best
And greatest, tho' my love had no return:
Yet, seeing you desire your child to live,
Thanks, but you work against your own desire;
For if I could believe the things you say   1090
I should but die the sooner; wherefore cease,
Sweet father, and bid call the ghostly man
Hither, and let me shrive me clean,[34] and die."

So when the ghostly man had come and gone,
She with a face, bright as for sin forgiven,   1095
Besought Lavaine to write as she devised
A letter, word for word; and when he asked
"Is it for Lancelot, is it for my dear lord?
Then will I bear it gladly"; she replied,
"For Lancelot and the Queen and all the world,   1100
But I myself must bear it." Then he wrote
The letter she devised; which being writ
And folded, "O sweet father, tender and true,
Deny me not," she said—"ye never yet
Denied my fancies—this, however strange,   1105
My latest: lay the letter in my hand
A little ere I die, and close the hand
Upon it; I shall guard it even in death.
And when the heat is gone from out my heart,
Then take the little bed on which I died   1110
For Lancelot's love, and deck it like the Queen's
For richness, and me also like the Queen
In all I have of rich, and lay me on it.
And let there be prepared a chariot-bier
To take me to the river, and a barge   1115
Be ready on the river, clothed in black.
I go in state to court, to meet the Queen.
There surely I shall speak for mine own self,
And none of you can speak for me so well.
And therefore let our dumb old man alone   1120
Go with me, he can steer and row, and he
Will guide me to that palace, to the doors."

She ceased: her father promised; whereupon
She grew so cheerful that they deemed her death
Was rather in the fantasy than the blood.   1125
But ten slow mornings past, and on the eleventh
Her father laid the letter in her hand,

And closed the hand upon it, and she died.
So that day there was dole in Astolat.

But when the next sun brake from underground,   1130
Then, those two brethren slowly with bent brows
Accompanying, the sad chariot-bier
Past like a shadow thro' the field, that shone
Full-summer, to that stream whereon the barge,
Palled all its length in blackest samite, lay.   1135
There sat the lifelong creature of the house,
Loyal, the dumb old servitor, on deck,
Winking his eyes, and twisted all his face.
So those two brethren from the chariot took
And on the black decks laid her in her bed,   1140
Set in her hand a lily, o'er her hung
The silken case with braided blazonings,
And kissed her quiet brows, and saying to her
"Sister, farewell for ever," and again
"Farewell, sweet sister," parted all in tears.   1145
Then rose the dumb old servitor, and the dead,
Oared by the dumb, went upward with the flood—
In her right hand the lily, in her left
The letter—all her bright hair streaming down—
And all the coverlid was cloth of gold   1150
Drawn to her waist, and she herself in white
All but her face, and that clear-featured face
Was lovely, for she did not seem as dead,
But fast asleep, and lay as tho' she smiled.

That day Sir Lancelot at the palace craved   1155
Audience of Guinevere, to give at last
The price of half a realm, his costly gift,
Hard-won and hardly won with bruise and blow,
With deaths of others, and almost his own,
The nine-years-fought-for diamonds: for he saw   1160
One of her house, and sent him to the Queen
Bearing his wish, whereto the Queen agreed
With such and so unmoved a majesty
She might have seemed her statue, but that he,
Low-drooping till he wellnigh kissed her feet   1165
For loyal awe, saw with a sidelong eye
The shadow of some piece of pointed lace,
In the Queen's shadow, vibrate on the walls,[35]
And parted, laughing in his courtly heart.

All in an oriel on the summer side,   1170
Vine-clad, of Arthur's palace toward the stream,
They met, and Lancelot kneeling uttered, "Queen,
Lady, my liege, in whom I have my joy,
Take, what I had not won except for you,
These jewels, and make me happy, making them   1175

---

[34] Call the priest to give me absolution, so that I may be cleansed of sin.

[35] That is, saw that she was trembling (with jealous anger).

An armlet for the roundest arm on earth,
Or necklace for a neck to which the swan's
Is tawnier than her cygnet's:[36] these are words:
Your beauty is your beauty, and I sin
In speaking, yet O grant my worship of it   1180
Words, as we grant grief tears. Such sin in words
Perchance, we both can pardon:[37] but, my Queen,
I hear of rumors flying thro' your court.
Our bond, as not the bond of man and wife,
Should have in it an absoluter trust   1185
To make up that defect: let rumors be:
When did not rumors fly? these, as I trust
That you trust me in your own nobleness,
I may not well believe that you believe."

While thus he spoke, half turned away, the Queen 1190
Brake from the vast oriel-embowering vine
Leaf after leaf, and tore, and cast them off,
Till all the place whereon she stood was green;
Then, when he ceased, in one cold passive hand
Received at once and laid aside the gems   1195
There on a table near her, and replied:

"It may be, I am quicker of belief
Than you believe me, Lancelot of the Lake.
Our bond is not the bond of man and wife.
This good is in it, whatsoe'er of ill,   1200
It can be broken easier. I for you
This many a year have done despite and wrong
To one whom ever in my heart of hearts
I did acknowledge nobler. What are these?
Diamonds for me! they had been thrice their worth 1205
Being your gift, had you not lost your own.
To loyal hearts the value of all gifts
Must vary as the giver's. Not for me!
For her! for your new fancy. Only this
Grant me, I pray you: have your joys apart.   1210
I doubt not that however changed, you keep
So much of what is graceful: and myself
Would shun to break those bounds of courtesy
In which as Arthur's Queen I move and rule:
So cannot speak my mind. An end to this!   1215
A strange one! yet I take it with Amen.
So pray you, add my diamonds to her pearls;
Deck her with these; tell her, she shines me down:
An armlet for an arm to which the Queen's
Is haggard, or a necklace for a neck   1220
O as much fairer—as a faith once fair

Was richer than these diamonds—hers not mine—
Nay, by the mother of our Lord himself,
Or hers or mine, mine now to work my will—
She shall not have them."

Saying which she seized, 1225
And, thro' the casement standing wide for heat,
Flung them, and down they flashed, and smote the stream.
Then from the smitten surface flashed, as it were,
Diamonds to meet them, and they past away.
Then while Sir Lancelot leant, in half disdain   1230
At love, life, all things, on the window ledge,
Close underneath his eyes, and right across
Where these had fallen, slowly past the barge
Whereon the lily maid of Astolat
Lay smiling, like a star in blackest night.   1235

But the wild Queen, who saw not, burst away
To weep and wail in secret; and the barge,
On to the palace-doorway sliding, paused.
There two stood armed, and kept the door; to whom,
All up the marble stair, tier over tier,   1240
Were added mouths that gaped, and eyes that asked
"What is it?" but that oarsman's haggard face,
As hard and still as is the face that men
Shape to their fancy's eye from broken rocks
On some cliff-side, appalled them, and they said, 1245
"He is enchanted, cannot speak—and she,
Look how she sleeps—the Fairy Queen, so fair!
Yea, but how pale! what are they? flesh and blood?
Or come to take the King to Fairyland?
For some do hold our Arthur cannot die,   1250
But that he passes into Fairyland."

While thus they babbled of the King, the King
Came girt with knights: then turned the tongueless man
From the half-face to the full eye, and rose
And pointed to the damsel, and the doors.   1255
So Arthur bade the meek Sir Percivale
And pure Sir Galahad to uplift the maid;
And reverently they bore her into hall.
Then came the fine Gawain and wondered at her,
And Lancelot later came and mused at her,   1260
And last the Queen herself, and pitied her:
But Arthur spied the letter in her hand,
Stoopt, took, brake seal, and read it; this was all:

"Most noble lord, Sir Lancelot of the Lake,
I, sometime called the maid of Astolat,   1265
Come, for you left me taking no farewell,
Hither, to take my last farewell of you.
I loved you, and my love had no return,
And therefore my true love has been my death.
And therefore to our Lady Guinevere,   1270

[36] The neck of the young swan, or cygnet, is tawny or yellowish.
     Compared with yours even the swan's white neck is tawnier
     than a cygnet's.
[37] To this point the speech is completely formal and courtly.

ALFRED LORD TENNYSON   685

And to all other ladies, I make moan:
Pray for my soul, and yield me burial.
Pray for my soul thou too, Sir Lancelot,
As thou art a knight peerless."

     Thus he read;
And ever in the reading, lords and dames 1275
Wept, looking often from his face who read
To hers which lay so silent, and at times,
So touched were they, half-thinking that her lips,
Who had devised the letter, moved again.

  Then freely spoke Sir Lancelot to them all: 1280
"My lord liege Arthur, and all ye that hear,
Know that for this most gentle maiden's death
Right heavy am I; for good she was and true,
But loved me with a love beyond all love
In women, whomsoever I have known.   1285
Yet to be loved makes not to love again;
Not at my years, however it hold in youth.
I swear by truth and knighthood that I gave
No cause, not willingly, for such a love:
To this I call my friends in testimony, 1290
Her brethren, and her father, who himself
Besought me to be plain and blunt, and use,
To break her passion, some discourtesy
Against my nature: what I could, I did.
I left her and I bade her no farewell; 1295
Tho', had I dreamt the damsel would have died,
I might have put my wits to some rough use,
And helped her from herself."

     Then said the Queen
(Sea was her wrath, yet working after storm),
"Ye might at least have done her so much grace, 1300
Fair lord, as would have helped her from her death."[38]
He raised his head, their eyes met and hers fell,
He adding:

    "Queen, she would not be content
Save that I wedded her, which could not be.
Then might she follow me thro' the world, she asked;
It could not be. I told her that her love 1306
Was but the flash of youth, would darken down
To rise hereafter in a stiller flame
Toward one more worthy of her—then would I,
More specially were he, she wedded, poor, 1310
Estate them with large land and territory
In mine own realm beyond the narrow seas,
To keep them in all joyance: more than this
I could not; this she would not, and she died."

  He pausing, Arthur answered, "O my knight, 1315
It will be to thy worship,[39] as my knight,

And mine, as head of all our Table Round,
To see that she be buried worshipfully."[40]

  So toward that shrine which then in all the realm
Was richest, Arthur leading, slowly went 1320
The marshalled Order of their Table Round,
And Lancelot sad beyond his wont, to see
The maiden buried, not as one unknown,
Nor meanly, but with gorgeous obsequies,
And mass, and rolling music, like a queen. 1325
And when the knights had laid her comely head
Low in the dust of half-forgotten kings,
Then Arthur spake among them, "Let her tomb
Be costly, and her image thereupon,
And let the shield of Lancelot at her feet 1330
Be carven, and her lily in her hand.
And let the story of her dolorous voyage
For all true hearts be blazoned on her tomb
In letters gold and azure!" which was wrought
Thereafter; but when now the lords and dames 1335
And people, from the high door streaming, brake
Disorderly, as homeward each, the Queen,
Who marked Sir Lancelot where he moved apart,
Drew near, and sighed in passing, "Lancelot,
Forgive me; mine was jealousy in love." 1340
He answered with his eyes upon the ground,
"That is love's curse; pass on, my Queen, forgiven."
But Arthur, who beheld his cloudy brows,
Approached him, and with full affection said,

  "Lancelot, my Lancelot, thou in whom I have 1345
Most joy and most affiance,[41] for I know
What thou hast been in battle by my side,
And many a time have watched thee at the tilt
Strike down the lusty and long practised knight,
And let the younger and unskilled go by 1350
To win his honor and to make his name,
And loved thy courtesies and thee, a man
Made to be loved; but now I would to God,
Seeing the homeless trouble in thine eyes,
Thou couldst have loved this maiden, shaped, it seems,
By God for thee alone, and from her face, 1356
If one may judge the living by the dead,
Delicately pure and marvellously fair,
Who might have brought thee, now a lonely man
Wifeless and heirless, noble issue, sons 1360
Born to the glory of thy name and fame,
My knight, the great Sir Lancelot of the Lake."

  Then answered Lancelot: "Fair she was, my King,
Pure, as you ever wish your knights to be.

---

[38] Have prevented her death. [39] Honor.

[40] Honorably. [41] Reliance.

To doubt her fairness were to want an eye, 1365
To doubt her pureness were to want a heart—
Yea, to be loved, if what is worthy love
Could bind him, but free love will not be bound."

"Free love, so bound, were freëst," said the King.
"Let love be free; free love is for the best: 1370
And, after heaven, on our dull side of death,
What should be best, if not so pure a love
Clothed in so pure a loveliness? yet thee
She failed to bind, tho' being, as I think,
Unbound as yet, and gentle, as I know." 1375

And Lancelot answered nothing, but he went,
And at the inrunning of a little brook
Sat by the river in a cove, and watched
The high reed wave, and lifted up his eyes
And saw the barge that brought her moving down, 1380
Far-off, a blot upon the stream, and said
Low in himself, "Ah simple heart and sweet,
Ye loved me, damsel, surely with a love
Far tenderer than my Queen's. Pray for thy soul?
Ay, that will I. Farewell too—now at last— 1385
Farewell, fair lily. 'Jealousy in love?'
Not rather[42] dead love's harsh heir, jealous pride?
Queen, if I grant the jealousy as of love,
May not your crescent[43] fear for name and fame
Speak, as it waxes, of a love that wanes? 1390
Why did the King dwell on my name to me?
Mine own name shames me, seeming a reproach,
Lancelot, whom the Lady of the Lake
Caught from his mother's arms—the wondrous one
Who passes thro' the vision of the night— 1395
She chanted snatches of mysterious hymns
Heard on the winding waters, eve and morn
She kissed me saying, 'Thou art fair, my child,
As a king's son,' and often in her arms
She bare me, pacing on the dusky mere. 1400
Would she had drowned me in it, where'er it be!
For what am I? what profits me my name

Of greatest knight? I fought for it, and have it:
Pleasure to have it, none; to lose it, pain;
Now grown a part of me: but what use in it? 1405
To make men worse by making my sin known?
Or sin seem less, the sinner seeming great?
Alas for Arthur's greatest knight, a man
Not after Arthur's heart! I needs must break
These bonds that so defame me: not without 1410
She wills it: would I, if she willed it? nay,
Who knows? but if I would not, then may God,
I pray him, send a sudden Angel down
To seize me by the hair and bear me far,
And fling me deep in that forgotten mere, 1415
Among the tumbled fragments of the hills."

So groaned Sir Lancelot in remorseful pain,
Not knowing he should die a holy man.

CROSSING THE BAR

Sunset and evening star,
   And one clear call for me!
And may there be no moaning of the bar,
   When I put out to sea,

But such a tide as moving seems asleep, 5
   Too full for sound and foam,
When that which drew from out the boundless deep
   Turns again home.

Twilight and evening bell,
   And after that the dark! 10
And may there be no sadness of farewell,
   When I embark;

For though from out our bourne of Time and Place
   The flood may bear me far,
I hope to see my Pilot face to face 15
   When I have crossed the bar.

---

[42] Was it not rather.   [43] Growing.

Robert Browning

1812–1889

BROWNING was born in 1812 at Camberwell, a suburb of London. His father, like Ruskin's, was a wealthy business-man with well developed tastes for history, art, and music; his mother, like Ruskin's, was a devout Puritan, though with a sunnier disposition, which the boy inherited. And like Ruskin again, he was largely educated at home, where he read widely in his father's library, finding most delight in history and in modern poetry (Scott, Byron, and especially Shelley, his great idol). So nourished, he assimilated much of the Romantic temper, the thirst for knowledge and experience, an ardent longing for the Ideal, and a marked self-consciousness. All these charac-teristics are reflected in his first long poem, *Pauline* (1833), which Browning later described in two passages that throw important light on his development as a poet:

The following Poem was written in pursuance of a foolish plan which occupied me mightily for a time, and which had for its object the enabling me to assume & realize I know not how many different characters;— meanwhile the world was never to guess that "Brown, Smith, Jones & Robinson" (as the spelling books have it) the respective authors of this poem, the other novel, such an opera, such a speech, etc. etc. were no other than one and the same individual. The present abortion was the first work of the *Poet* of the batch, who would have been more legitimately *myself* than most of the others; but I surrounded him with all manner of (to my then notion) poetical accessories, and had planned quite a delightful life for him. (1837)

The thing was my earliest attempt at "poetry always dramatic in principle, and so many utterances of so many imaginary persons, not mine," which I have since written according to a scheme less extravagant and scale less impracticable than were ventured upon in this crude preliminary sketch. (1867)

The words in quotation marks in the second statement (Browning is quoting himself) define the central principle of his aesthetics, on which he wrote the long series of dramatic monologues which began to appear in the 1840's and comprise his two main volumes, appropriately called *Men and Women* (1855) and *Dramatis Personae* (1864). But in 1832, as the first statement reveals, Brown-ing's temperament was entirely too subjective to make the plan anything other than a slightly disguised series of personal confessions in the Romantic tradition. Or to put the same thing differently, he was too much under the influence of Byron (all of whose heroes are Byron)

and of Shelley (whose record of his own poetic sensibility in *Alastor* was the immediate model for *Pauline*) to write dramatic poetry. Consequently, in despite of his plan, his first poem was really an account of his own youthful soul, which he imagined he had concealed under a dra-matic framework.

But he was quickly disabused. In a review written by John Stuart Mill, the author was credited with "con-siderable poetic powers" but with "a more intense and morbid self-consciousness" than Mill had ever known in any sane human being. The world *had* guessed—and easily—that the protagonist was the poet. Browning was humiliated—and *Pauline* was promptly called an "abor-tion." His next poems, *Paracelsus* (1835) and *Sordello* (1840), were more explicitly dramatic, but the protago-nists of both were still romantic characters in search of a philosophy, and still very like Robert Browning. Years later he is reported to have said that "his early poems were so transparent in their [personal] meaning as to draw down upon him the ridicule of the critics, and that, boy as he was, this ridicule and censure stung him into quite another style of writing"—that is to say, into a style that was in fact, and not in pretense, "dramatic in principle."

But no amount of criticism would have produced this transformation if Browning had been merely a Victorian Shelley. The truth was, however, that in addition to ardent idealism, he possessed a sharp eye for psychological realities and a considerable gift for detached observation of human nature. This side of his temperament was exercised and developed by ten years of playwriting (1837–47), during which Shakespeare took the place of Shelley as his poetic model. His plays were not successful. The action was constantly impeded by long speeches in which the characters analyzed their emotions or justified their conduct. But what was a liability on the stage might be a virtue in poetry if the method of self-analysis were transferred to short character sketches in the form of dramatic speeches.

Exactly when and how Browning made that all-important discovery and thus found his true bent is unknown, but it was certainly affected by three things. One was Shakespeare's soliloquies. The second was the poetry of John Donne, so frequently quoted in the letters to Elizabeth Barrett (1845–46). In Donne's "Elegies" he found realistic studies of men and women, and in the "Songs and Sonnets" a series of dramatic monologues, idiomatic in diction and rhythm, psychological in focus, and emotionally intense (the poem often beginning with a passionate outburst at a moment of crisis). Finally, the old plan of a group of long biographical poems like *Pauline,* written in a romantic style, in which he would assume "many different characters," lay in the back of his mind, ready to be transformed, under the combined influences of the theater, Shakespeare, and Donne, into a series of short, dramatic monologues where the several protagonists would reveal their own characters in a medium of natural speech.

The affinity with Donne not only suggests that in many ways Browning is the most modern of the Victorian poets, with the exception perhaps of Hopkins; it gives the right clue to his contemporary reputation. For Donne made the same appeal to the younger generation of Jacobeans that Browning did to the younger generation of Rossetti and Morris, Morley and Pater. To any Jacobean tired of the "literary" verse of Spenser and Sidney, of pastorals and allegories and Petrarchan conceits, Donne offered a poetry at once more passionately alive and more psychologically profound. In the same way the younger Victorians were delighted to find in Browning a range and intensity of experience quite lacking in contemporary verse. Morley's reaction in 1869 is revealing:

The truth is, we have for long been so debilitated by pastorals, by graceful presentation of the Arthurian legend for drawing-rooms, by idylls, . . . by verse directly didactic, that a rude blast of air from the outside welter of human realities is apt to give a shock, that might well show in what simpleton's paradise we have been living. The ethics of the rectory parlour set to sweet music, the respectable aspirations of the sentimental curate married to exquisite verse, the everlasting glorification of domestic sentiment, . . . all this might seem to be making valetudinarians of us all. . . .

[From Browning] there comes out a long procession of human figures, infinitely various in form and thought, in character and act; a group of men and women, eager, passionate, indifferent; tender and ravenous, mean and noble, humorous and profound. . . . And they all come out with a certain Shakespearian fulness, vividness, directness. Above all, they are every one of them men and women, with free play of human life in limb and feature, as in an antique sculpture. So much of modern art, in poetry as in painting, runs to mere drapery.

That might have been said by a Jacobean in the early 1600's with Spenser and Donne in his mind. In the same vein Walter Pater not only praised Browning for renouncing the "selfish serenities of wild-wood and dream-palace" to observe the acts of living men, but found that his concern with psychological analysis made him "the most modern, to modern people the most important, of poets." It is because the point of view reflected in these passages, both negatively in the reaction against didactic and aesthetic verse, and positively in the taste for psychological realism, became widespread by 1920 that Browning is far more of a modern poet today than either Tennyson or Arnold.

Even his obscurity is modern: the touch-and-go allusions which demand extensive knowledge on the reader's part; the plunging *in medias res* without explanation of who is speaking or where and when; above all, the elliptical syntax and the sudden jump from thought to thought without benefit of connecting links. With reference to the last, Julia Wedgwood once protested to Browning, in terms often echoed later by readers of Eliot and Auden, against his use of "hieroglyphics." "You must treat us respectfully," she said, "and not fling us torn scraps of meaning, leaving us to supply the gaps." And the explanation, in both cases, is the same. "I have observed," wrote Elizabeth Barrett, ". . . that a good deal of what is called obscurity in you, arises from a habit of very subtle association; so subtle, that you are probably unconscious of it, . . . the effect of which is to throw together on the same level and in the same light, things of likeness and unlikeness—till the reader grows confused as I did." But Browning was no more unconscious of it than Eliot. When Ruskin complained of his obscurity, he answered, "You ought, I think, to keep pace with the thought tripping from ledge to ledge of my 'glaciers,' as you call them, not stand poking your alpen stock into the holes, and demonstrating that no foot could have stood there;—suppose it sprang over there?" And a moment later, apropos of a particular jump, he adds the revealing remark, "The whole is all but a simultaneous feeling with me." In modern verse the same effort to reflect the very movement of the mind, and therefore to discard the logical and grammatical connections which falsify the immediacy of experience, is carried much further. No reader of Eliot will find Browning's obscurity difficult, or fail to understand its main function. And in any event, it is only a matter of the line. His poems as a whole are far longer, far more discursive, than modern work. But to the Victorians, as Elizabeth Barrett says, his condensed phrasing was all very new and confusing.

So was another characteristic of his poetry which is modern. This is his willingness to present "bad" characters without the moral condemnation his mid-Victorian readers expected. At times he could adopt an almost clinical view of a criminal (the lover of Porphyria or the woman in "The Laboratory"), or still worse, he could treat with sympathy what obviously called for instant reproof (the life of Lippo Lippi and the lovers in "Respectability"). On one occasion Browning criticized his wife for being without a "scientific interest in evil"; and on another claimed that "all morbidness of the soul is worth the soul's study." Related to this suspension of judgment is his habit of implying opposite judgments, so that the reader must balance the good with the evil and arrive at his own conclusion, somewhere between the warm approval or the righteous condemnation which Victorian morality demanded. As one critic has recently said, "The Duke of Ferrara may not be all bad even though he seems to have had his last wife murdered; and his Duchess may not be all saint, even though she smiled sweetly at everyone." The Bishop who orders his tomb "alternately shocks and delights, in a poem which is neither an indictment of the Italian Renaissance nor a panegyric." I suspect, however, that the earnest Victorians failed to realize that Browning's own attitude was ambivalent. They condemned Duke and Bishop outright. And unfortunately this one-sided reading has been carried down into modern textbooks and anthologies, where we may be told, for example, that the Friar in the Spanish Cloister is filled with the passion of hate, or that Andrea del Sarto is "the kind of man Browning considers most contemptible (worse than an energetic criminal)."

But even so, even though the Victorians *could* find a "moral" in Browning's neutral or balanced studies of dubious characters, the lesson was obviously blurred and weakened by his dramatic detachment. As one critic pointed out to him in 1846, it was not "by the dramatic medium that poets teach most impressively. . . . It is too difficult for the common reader to analyse, and to discern between the vivid and the earnest." Consequently, as that implies, the critic begged him "to speak yourself out of that personality which God made, and with the voice which He tuned"; and, because he had thought so deeply on life and its ends, to teach others what he had learned "in the directest and most impressive way, the mask thrown off."

What made this comment so important for Browning's development was that the critic was Elizabeth Barrett. The famous love affair is too well known to need retelling. They were married in 1846 and lived in Italy until Mrs. Browning's death in 1861. After that Browning returned to London to become a popular guest at dinner parties, and to write, for the most part, a series of long poems, most notably *The Ring and the Book* (1869).

In the meanwhile, though his form continued to be dramatic, his intention, under his wife's influence and the pressure of the time, became more and more prophetic. The purpose of the artist defined in "Fra Lippo Lippi" (at lines 282 ff.), to paint the shapes of things just as they are so that men may become more aware of the world, is crossed and to some extent displaced by the purpose "to rule—by thought insight to deed." It is this didactic strain, and still more the particular nature of the thought that Browning came to teach, which make him a Victo-

rian poet, and which are so foreign to contemporary taste that, for all his modern characteristics, he has not been a living poet for the twentieth century. That is why the critics who have admired John Donne have neglected or disparaged his nineteenth-century disciple.

In itself Browning's ethical philosophy, partly Puritan, partly Romantic, in which life is conceived of as a moral testing ground—those who strive for high goals are spiritually successful, while those who succeed in attaining low aims really fail—can still carry weight. But it is harder to accept his glorification of the moral struggle as an heroic battle in which "good" is certain of victory, and the gallant warrior certain of a heaven where his goal will be reached. Browning's poetry, though filled with tragedy, is never tragic. The relative ease of his own life and the complacent optimism in his environment blinded him, for all his psychological insight, to the deepest levels of experience. The objection may be put in another form. He was so ready to exalt the life of aspiration—what matter the failure, fight on, strive ever, there as here—that he could be horribly oblivious to the pain involved. Is there any other body of poetry so filled with defeat and frustration and so lacking in suffering? That is why a poem like "The Last Ride Together" seems shallow: it is romantic in the derogatory sense. And the criticism bites hard in a period like ours, so acutely aware of suffering and so suspicious of romantic idealizations.

Browning's philosophy of love is equally vulnerable today. The theory of "elective affinities," of two people and two only made for each other; the idea of the "critical moment" when the great lover goes forward regardless of obstacles and continues to love regardless of the outcome, while the little lover draws back out of selfish or worldly considerations; and above all, as these doctrines imply, the idealization of romantic love into what he calls the "summum bonum," the highest of all goals of aspiration—these attitudes, for better or worse, are now more likely to stir ridicule than inspiration.

But in the 1880's, when the Browning Societies were being founded all over England and America, his philosophy of life and love was not only alive, it was the conservative leaven which gave his poetry a range of appeal that no other poet of the time could command. For here was psychological realism and full-blooded life combined with all the moral idealism one could ask for, not only in an ethic of aspiration, but best of all in a conception of love which recognized human passion and yet made it a spiritual inspiration. Here, indeed, was the perfect poet-prophet for the later Victorians who wanted to open the door wide enough to let in a good blast of fresh air, but who did not want to leave the Victorian home. In the next generation the exodus made Browning's philosophy a liability. Fortunately it does not appear in many of his best poems, and where it does, it is sometimes conceived dramatically (as in "Andrea del Sarto"), so that whatever may be our personal disagreement, we recognize its psychological rightness in the mouth of the speaker.

The best text is *The Works of Robert Browning* (Centenary Edition), edited by F. G. Kenyon (10 vols., 1912). A good selection with a useful introduction and notes is *Browning: Pippa Passes and Shorter Poems*, edited by J. E. Baker (1947). The standard Life is by H. W. Griffin and H. C. Minchin (2nd ed. revised, 1938). Edward Berdoe's

Browning Cyclopaedia (1891, and later editions) contains extensive discussions of all the poems, but it must be used with caution. W. C. De Vane's *Browning Handbook* (1935) supplies valuable information about dates of writing, publication, sources, etc. There is no good critical book. Some valuable essays are those by Walter Bagehot, "Wordsworth, Tennyson, and Browning," in his *Literary Studies* (1879); Paul Elmer More, "Why Is Browning Popular?", in *Shelburne Essays, Third Series* (1905); and Douglas Bush, "Browning," in *Mythology and the Romantic Tradition in English Poetry* (1937).

Robert Browning

MY LAST DUCHESS

FERRARA[1]

That 's my last Duchess painted on the wall,
Looking as if she were alive. I call
That piece a wonder, now: Frà Pandolf's[2] hands
Worked busily a day, and there she stands.
Will 't please you sit and look at her? I said
"Frà Pandolf" by design, for never read
Strangers like you that pictured countenance,
The depth and passion of its earnest glance,
But to myself they turned (since none puts by
The curtain I have drawn for you, but I)   10
And seemed as they would ask me, if they durst,
How such a glance came there; so, not the first
Are you to turn and ask thus. Sir, 't was not
Her husband's presence only, called that spot
Of joy into the Duchess' cheek: perhaps   15
Frà Pandolf chanced to say "Her mantle laps
Over my lady's wrist too much," or "Paint
Must never hope to reproduce the faint
Half-flush that dies along her throat"; such stuff
Was courtesy, she thought, and cause enough   20
For calling up that spot of joy. She had
A heart—how shall I say?—too soon made glad,
Too easily impressed; she liked whate'er
She looked on, and her looks went everywhere.
Sir, 't was all one! My favour at her breast,   25
The dropping of the daylight in the West,

The bough of cherries some officious fool
Broke in the orchard for her, the white mule
She rode with round the terrace—all and each
Would draw from her alike the approving speech,   30
Or blush, at least. She thanked men,—good! but thanked
Somehow—I know not how—as if she ranked
My gift of a nine-hundred-years-old name
With anybody's gift. Who 'd stoop to blame
This sort of trifling? Even had you skill   35
In speech—(which I have not)—to make your will
Quite clear to such an one, and say, "Just this
Or that in you disgusts me; here you miss,
Or there exceed the mark"—and if she let
Herself be lessoned so, nor plainly set   40
Her wits to yours, forsooth, and made excuse,
—E'en then would be some stooping; and I choose
Never to stoop. Oh, sir, she smiled, no doubt,
Whene'er I passed her; but who passed without
Much the same smile? This grew; I gave commands;   45
Then all smiles stopped together.[3] There she stands
As if alive. Will 't please you rise? We'll meet
The company below, then. I repeat,
The Count your master's known munificence
Is ample warrant that no just pretence   50
Of mine for dowry will be disallowed;
Though his fair daughter's self, as I avowed
At starting, is my object. Nay, we'll go
Together down, sir! Notice Neptune, though,
Taming a sea-horse, thought a rarity,   55
Which Claus of Innsbruck[4] cast in bronze for me!

---

[1] Place, the Italian town of Ferrara; time, the Renaissance. The Duke of Ferrara speaks to the Count's envoy.
[2] Brother Pandolf, an imaginary painter.

[3] Browning explained that "the commands were that she should be put to death, or he might have had her shut up in a convent."
[4] An imaginary sculptor.

COUNT GISMOND

Christ God who savest man, save most
   Of men Count Gismond who saved me!
Count Gauthier, when he chose his post,
   Chose time and place and company
To suit it; when he struck at length   5
My honor, 'twas with all his strength.

And doubtlessly ere he could draw
   All points to one, he must have schemed!
That miserable morning saw
   Few half so happy as I seemed,   10
While being dressed in queen's array
To give our tourney prize away.

I thought they loved me, did me grace
   To please themselves; 'twas all their deed;
God makes, or fair or foul, our face;   15
   If showing mine so caused to bleed
My cousins' hearts, they should have dropped
A word, and straight the play had stopped.

They, too, so beauteous! Each a queen
   By virtue of her brow and breast;   20
Not needing to be crowned, I mean,
   As I do. E'en when I was dressed,
Had either of them spoke, instead
Of glancing sideways with still head!

But no: they let me laugh, and sing   25
   My birthday song quite through, adjust
The last rose in my garland, fling
   A last look on the mirror, trust
My arms to each an arm of theirs,
And so descend the castle-stairs—   30

And come out on the morning-troop
   Of merry friends who kissed my cheek,
And called me queen, and made me stoop
   Under the canopy—(a streak
That pierced it, of the outside sun,   35
Powdered with gold its gloom's soft dun)—

And they could let me take my state
   And foolish throne amid applause

Of all come there to celebrate
   My queen's-day—Oh I think the cause   40
Of much was, they forgot no crowd
Makes up for parents in their shroud!

However that be, all eyes were bent
   Upon me, when my cousins cast
Theirs down; 'twas time I should present   45
   The victor's crown, but . . . there, 'twill last
No long time . . . the old mist again
Blinds me as then it did.[2] How vain!

See! Gismond's at the gate, in talk
   With his two boys: I can proceed.   50
Well, at that moment, who should stalk
   Forth boldly—to my face, indeed—
But Gauthier, and he thundered "Stay!"
And all stayed. "Bring no crowns, I say!

"Bring torches! Wind the penance-sheet   55
   About her! Let her shun the chaste,
Or lay herself before their feet!
   Shall she whose body I embraced
A night long, queen it in the day?
For honor's sake no crowns, I say!"   60

I? What I answered? As I live,
   I never fancied such a thing
As answer possible to give.
   What says the body where they spring
Some monstrous torture-engine's whole   65
Strength on it? No more says the soul.

Till out strode Gismond; then I knew
   That I was saved. I never met
His face before, but, at first view,
   I felt quite sure that God had set   70
Himself to Satan; who would spend
A minute's mistrust on the end?

He strode to Gauthier, in his throat
   Gave him the lie, then struck his mouth
With one back-handed blow that wrote   75
   In blood men's verdict there. North, South,
East, West, I looked. The lie was dead,
And damned, and truth stood up instead.

This glads me most, that I enjoyed
   The heart of the joy, with my content   80
In watching Gismond unalloyed

---

[1] Place, the town of Aix in Provence, a section of southern France; time, the Middle Ages. The wife of Count Gismond speaks to a friend of hers named Adela. The poem was originally grouped with "My Last Duchess," and the two together were called *Italy and France*.

[2] At the memory of that moment, everything goes blank again, as it did originally.

By any doubt of the event:
God took that on him—I was bid
Watch Gismond for my part: I did.

Did I not watch him while he let   85
    His armorer just brace his greaves,
Rivet his hauberk, on the fret
    The while! His foot . . . my memory leaves
No least stamp out, nor how anon
He pulled his ringing gauntlets on.

And e'en before the trumpet's sound
    Was finished, prone lay the false knight,
Prone as his lie, upon the ground:
    Gismond flew at him, used no sleight
O' the sword, but open-breasted drove,   95
Cleaving till out the truth he clove.

Which done, he dragged him to my feet
    And said, "Here die, but end thy breath
In full confession, lest thou fleet
    From my first, to God's second death![3]   100
Say, hast thou lied?" And, "I have lied
To God and her," he said, and died.[4]

Then Gismond, kneeling to me, asked
    —What safe my heart holds, though no word
Could I repeat now, if I tasked   105
    My powers for ever, to a third
Dear even as you are. Pass the rest
Until I sank upon his breast.

Over my head his arm he flung
    Against the world; and scarce I felt   110
His sword (that dripped by me and swung)
    A little shifted in its belt:
For he began to say the while
How South our home lay many a mile.

So 'mid the shouting multitude   115
    We two walked forth to never more
Return. My cousins have pursued
    Their life, untroubled as before
I vexed them. Gauthier's dwelling-place
God lighten! May his soul find grace!   120

Our elder boy has got the clear
    Great brow;[5] though when his brother's black
Full eye shows scorn, it[6] . . . Gismond here?
    And have you brought my tercel[7] back?
I just was telling Adela   125
How many birds it struck since May.

SOLILOQUY OF THE SPANISH CLOISTER

Gr-r-r—there go, my heart's abhorrence!
    Water your damned flower-pots, do!
If hate killed men, Brother Lawrence,
    God's blood, would not mine kill you!
What? your myrtle-bush wants trimming?   5
    Oh, that rose has prior claims—
Needs its leaden vase filled brimming?
    Hell dry you up with its flames!

At the meal we sit together:
    Salve tibi![1] I must hear   10
Wise talk of the kind of weather,
    Sort of season, time of year:
Not a plenteous cork-crop: scarcely
    Dare we hope oak-galls,[2] *I doubt:*
What's the Latin name for "parsley"?   15
    What's the Greek name for Swine's Snout?

Whew! We'll have our platter burnished,
    Laid with care on our own shelf!
With a fire-new spoon we're furnished,
    And a goblet for ourself,   20
Rinsed like something sacrificial
    Ere 'tis fit to touch our chaps—
Marked with L for our initial!
    (He-he! There his lily snaps!)

Saint, forsooth! While brown Dolores   25
    Squats outside the Convent bank
With Sanchicha, telling stories,
    Steeping tresses in the tank,
Blue-black, lustrous, thick like horsehairs,
    —Can't I see his dead eye glow,   30
Bright as 'twere a Barbary corsair's?[3]
    (That is, if he'd let it show!)

---

[3] In hell.
[4] The temptation to suspect that Gauthier was a rejected lover who knew whereof he spoke has to be put aside because the poem upholds the medieval confidence in the ordeal by duel (see again lines 70–72, 83). Was he the instrument of a plot devised by the envious cousins to ruin the speaker's character? (See lines 117–119 as well as the opening stanzas.)

[5] Of his father.   [6] It too resembles his father's eye.
[7] Male falcon used in hunting.

[1] "Hail to thee." The italics here and in lines 13–15 are used to indicate remarks of Brother Lawrence's which the friar is quoting.
[2] Oak apples produced on the leaves of the oak, valuable for their tannic acid.   [3] Pirate from the coast of north Africa.

When he finishes refection,[4]
 Knife and fork he never lays
Cross-wise, to my recollection, 35
 As do I, in Jesu's praise.
I the Trinity illustrate,
 Drinking watered orange-pulp—
In three sips the Arian[5] frustrate;
 While he drains his at one gulp. 40

Oh, those melons! If he's able
 We're to have a feast! so nice!
One goes to the Abbot's table,
 All of us get each a slice.
How go on your flowers? None double? 45
 Not one fruit-sort can you spy?
Strange!—And I, too, at such trouble
 Keep them close-nipped on the sly!

There's a great text in Galatians,[6]
 Once you trip on it, entails 50
Twenty-nine distinct damnations,
 One sure, if another fails:
If I trip him just a-dying,
 Sure of heaven as sure can be,
Spin him round and send him flying 55
 Off to hell, a Manichee?[7]

Or, my scrofulous French novel
 On gray paper with blunt type!
Simply glance at it, you grovel
 Hand and foot in Belial's gripe: 60
If I double down its pages
 At the woeful sixteenth print,
When he gathers his greengages,
 Ope a sieve and slip it in't?

Or, there's Satan!—one might venture 65
 Pledge one's soul to him, yet leave
Such a flaw in the indenture
 As he'd miss till, past retrieve,
Blasted lay that rose-acacia
 We're so proud of![8] *Hy, Zy, Hine*[9] . . . 70

'St, there's Vespers! *Plena gratiâ,*
 Ave, Virgo![10] Gr-r-r—you swine![11]

PORPHYRIA'S LOVER[1]

The rain set early in to-night,
 The sullen wind was soon awake,
It tore the elm-tops down for spite,
 And did its worst to vex the lake:
 I listened with heart fit to break. 5
When glided in Porphyria; straight
 She shut the cold out and the storm,
And kneeled and made the cheerless grate
 Blaze up, and all the cottage warm;
 Which done, she rose, and from her form 10
Withdrew the dripping cloak and shawl,
 And laid her soiled gloves by, untied
Her hat and let the damp hair fall,
 And, last, she sat down by my side
 And called me. When no voice replied, 15
She put my arm about her waist,
 And made her smooth white shoulder bare,
And all her yellow hair displaced,
 And, stooping, made my cheek lie there,
 And spread, o'er all, her yellow hair, 20
Murmuring how she loved me—she
 Too weak, for all her heart's endeavor,
To set its struggling passion free
 From pride, and vainer ties dissever,
 And give herself to me forever.[2] 25
But passion sometimes would prevail,
 Nor could to-night's gay feast restrain
A sudden thought of one so pale
 For love of her, and all in vain:
 So, she was come through wind and rain. 30
Be sure I looked up at her eyes
 Happy and proud; at last I knew
Porphyria worshipped me;[3] surprise
 Made my heart swell, and still it grew
 While I debated what to do. 35
That moment she was mine, mine, fair,
 Perfectly pure and good: I found
A thing to do, and all her hair

---

[4] Dinner.
[5] Follower of Arius, the fourth-century heretic who denied the dogma of the Trinity. [6] Perhaps Galatians 3:10 or 5:19–21.
[7] If I can trip him into some Manichean heresy (into saying, for example, that both Good and Evil are in eternal opposition, when the orthodox Christian view is that God, the Good, is alone eternal), I can send him to hell.
[8] Or I might make a bargain with Satan to give him my soul if he guaranteed to take Brother Lawrence's to hell, but with a flaw in the contract which would allow me to escape.
[9] Possibly the sounds of the vesper bells.

[10] "Hail, Virgin, full of grace."
[11] It is customary to assume that the poem is "a brilliant analysis of the passion of hate," but is "hate" the right word for the petty spite of lines 45–48 and the ingenious, half-amused play of fancy in lines 49–70? The speaker is mean and malicious, certainly, but Brother Lawrence was a great big bore.

[1] Printed originally with another study in abnormal psychology ("Johannes Agricola"), under the over-all title *Madhouse Cells.*
[2] Perhaps, but perhaps this is his own interpretation.
[3] Perhaps, but lines 16–21 do not suggest worship; and cf. line 26.

In one long yellow string I wound
Three times her little throat around,   40
And strangled her. No pain felt she;
I am quite sure she felt no pain.
As a shut bud that holds a bee,
I warily oped her lids: again
Laughed the blue eyes without a stain.   45
And I untightened next the tress
About her neck; her cheek once more
Blushed bright beneath my burning kiss:
I propped her head up as before,
Only, this time my shoulder bore   50
Her head, which droops upon it still:
The smiling rosy little head,
So glad it has its utmost will,
That all it scorned at once is fled,
And I, its love, am gained instead!   55
Porphyria's love: she guessed not how
Her darling one wish would be heard.[4]
And thus we sit together now,
And all night long we have not stirred,
And yet God has not said a word![5]   60

"HOW THEY BROUGHT THE GOOD NEWS FROM GHENT TO AIX"[1]

[16—]

I sprang to the stirrup, and Joris, and he;
I galloped, Dirck galloped, we galloped all three;
"Good speed!" cried the watch, as the gate-bolts undrew;
"Speed!" echoed the wall to us galloping through;
Behind shut the postern,[2] the lights sank to rest,   5
And into the midnight we galloped abreast.

Not a word to each other; we kept the great pace
Neck by neck, stride by stride, never changing our place;
I turned in my saddle and made its girths tight,
Then shortened each stirrup, and set the pique[3] right, 10
Rebuckled the cheek-strap, chained slacker the bit,
Nor galloped less steadily Roland a whit.

'Twas moonset at starting; but while we drew near
Lokeren, the cocks crew and twilight dawned clear;

At Boom, a great yellow star came out to see;   15
At Duffeld, 'twas morning as plain as could be;
And from Mecheln church-steeple we heard the half-
        chime,
So Joris broke silence with, "Yet there is time!"

At Aershot, up leaped of a sudden the sun,
And against him the cattle stood black every one,   20
To stare through the mist at us galloping past,
And I saw my stout galloper Roland at last,
With resolute shoulders, each butting away
The haze, as some bluff river headland its spray:

And his low head and crest, just one sharp ear bent
        back   25
For my voice, and the other pricked out on his track;
And one eye's black intelligence,—ever that glance
O'er its white edge at me, his own master, askance!
And the thick heavy spume-flakes which aye and anon
His fierce lips shook upwards in galloping on.   30

By Hasselt, Dirck groaned; and cried Joris, "Stay spur!
Your Roos galloped bravely, the fault's not in her,
We'll remember at Aix"—for one heard the quick
        wheeze
Of her chest, saw the stretched neck and staggering
        knees,
And sunk tail, and horrible heave of the flank,   35
As down on her haunches she shuddered and sank.

So, we were left galloping, Joris and I,
Past Looz and past Tongres, no cloud in the sky;
The broad sun above laughed a pitiless laugh,
'Neath our feet broke the brittle bright stubble like
        chaff;   40
Till over by Dalhem a dome-spire sprang white,
And "Gallop," gasped Joris, "for Aix is in sight!"

"How they'll greet us!"—and all in a moment his roan
Rolled neck and croup over, lay dead as a stone;
And there was my Roland to bear the whole weight   45
Of the news which alone could save Aix from her fate,
With his nostrils like pits full of blood to the brim,
And with circles of red for his eye-sockets' rim.

Then I cast loose my buffcoat, each holster let fall,
Shook off both my jack-boots, let go belt and all,   50
Stood up in the stirrup, leaned, patted his ear,
Called my Roland his pet-name, my horse without
        peer;
Clapped my hands, laughed and sang, any noise,
        bad or good,
Till at length into Aix Roland galloped and stood.

---

[4] Was there ever a more amazing piece of rationalization than we get in lines 36–57?
[5] Of course not! How *could* God punish a man like me for rescuing a woman from all she scorned and ending her life at her highest moment!
[1] From Ghent in Belgium to Aix-la-Chapelle in West Prussia, a hundred miles away. The towns mentioned lie on the road between the two. Browning said that the incident was imaginary.
[2] The gate of the walled city of Ghent.
[3] Pommel of the saddle.

And all I remember is—friends flocking round   55
As I sat with his head 'twixt my knees on the ground;
And no voice but was praising this Roland of mine,
As I poured down his throat our last measure of wine,
Which (the burgesses voted by common consent)
Was no more than his due who brought good news
       from Ghent.   60

HOME-THOUGHTS, FROM ABROAD

Oh, to be in England
Now that April's there,
And whoever wakes in England
Sees, some morning, unaware,
That the lowest boughs and the brush-wood sheaf   5
Round the elm-tree bole are in tiny leaf,
While the chaffinch sings on the orchard bough
In England—now!

And after April, when May follows,
And the white-throat builds, and all the swallows!   10
Hark, where my blossomed pear-tree in the hedge
Leans to the field and scatters on the clover
Blossoms and dewdrops—at the bent spray's edge—
That's the wise thrush; he sings each song twice over,
Lest you should think he never could recapture   15
The first fine careless rapture!
And though the fields look rough with hoary dew,
All will be gay when noontide wakes anew
The buttercups, the little children's dower
—Far brighter than this gaudy melon-flower!   20

HOME-THOUGHTS, FROM THE SEA

Nobly, nobly Cape Saint Vincent[1] to the Northwest
       died away;
Sunset ran, one glorious blood-red, reeking into Cadiz
       Bay;
Bluish 'mid the burning water, full in face Trafalgar[2]
       lay;
In the dimmest Northeast distance dawned Gibraltar
       grand and gray;
"Here and here did England help me: how can I help
       England?"—say,   5
Whoso turns as I, this evening, turn to God to praise
       and pray,
While Jove's planet rises yonder, silent over Africa.

---

1 At the southwestern tip of Portugal, where Nelson defeated the
   Spanish fleet in 1797.
2 The cape, east of Cadiz Bay on the southern coast of Spain,
   where Nelson won his famous victory (1805) over the French
   and Spanish.

THE BISHOP ORDERS HIS TOMB AT SAINT PRAXED'S CHURCH[1]

ROME, 15—

Vanity, saith the preacher, vanity![2]
Draw round my bed: is Anselm keeping back?
Nephews[3]—sons mine . . . ah God, I know not![4] Well—
She, men would have to be your mother once,
Old Gandolf[5] envied me, so fair she was!   5
What 's done is done, and she is dead beside,
Dead long ago, and I am Bishop since,
And as she died so must we die ourselves,
And thence ye may perceive the world 's a dream.
Life, how and what is it? As here I lie   10
In this state-chamber, dying by degrees,
Hours and long hours in the dead night, I ask
"Do I live, am I dead?" Peace, peace seems all.
Saint Praxed's ever was the church for peace;
And so, about this tomb of mine. I fought   15
With tooth and nail to save my niche, ye know:
—Old Gandolf cozened me, despite my care;
Shrewd was that snatch from out the corner South
He graced his carrion with, God curse the same!
Yet still my niche is not so cramped but thence   20
One sees the pulpit o' the epistle-side,[6]
And somewhat of the choir, those silent seats,
And up into the aery dome where live
The angels, and a sunbeam 's sure to lurk:
And I shall fill my slab of basalt there,   25
And 'neath my tabernacle[7] take my rest,
With those nine columns round me, two and two,
The odd one at my feet where Anselm stands:
Peach-blossom marble all, the rare, the ripe
As fresh-poured red wine of a mighty pulse.   30
—Old Gandolf with his paltry onion-stone,[8]
Put me where I may look at him! True peach,
Rosy and flawless: how I earned the prize!
Draw close: that conflagration of my church

---

1 Ruskin said he knew "of no other piece of modern English,
   prose or poetry, in which there is so much told, as in these
   lines, of the Renaissance spirit,—its worldliness, inconsistency,
   pride, hypocrisy, ignorance of itself, love of art, of luxury, and
   of good Latin." This may be true, but the poem is not about a
   period but a man, a human being first, and second, a bishop
   who lived in the Renaissance.
2 Cf. Ecclesiastes 1:2. Does the Bishop speak this line perfuncto-
   rily? Or genuinely, as a comment on human life and his own in
   particular? Cf. similar remarks throughout the poem.
3 A euphemism for illegitimate sons.
4 The repetition of this phrase at line 39 shows that it does not
   here express doubt as to whether or not the sons are his. It seems
   to mean, I know not whether I am damned or saved; or (cf.
   line 10), I know not how or what life is; or (cf. lines 13 and 113),
   "Do I live, am I dead?" Probably all these alternatives are
   vaguely present in his mind at once.   5 His predecessor.
6 The right-hand side as one faces the altar.   7 The canopy.
8 Inferior grade of marble that peels off in layers.

—What then? So much was saved if aught were
    missed![9]   35
My sons, ye would not be my death? Go dig
The white-grape vineyard where the oil-press stood,
Drop water gently till the surface sink,
And if ye find . . . Ah, God I know not, I! . . .
Bedded in store of rotten figleaves soft,   40
And corded up in a tight olive-frail,[10]
Some lump, ah God, of *lapis lazuli*,
Big as a Jew's head cut off at the nape,
Blue as a vein o'er the Madonna's breast . . .
Sons, all have I bequeathed you, villas, all,   45
That brave Frascati villa with its bath,
So, let the blue lump poise between my knees,
Like God the Father's globe on both his hands
Ye worship in the Jesu Church[11] so gay,
For Gandolf shall not choose but see and burst! 50
Swift as a weaver's shuttle fleet our years:[12]
Man goeth to the grave, and where is he?
Did I say basalt for my slab, sons? Black—
'T was ever antique-black[13] I meant! How else
Shall ye contrast my frieze to come beneath? 55
The bas-relief in bronze ye promised me,
Those Pans and Nymphs ye wot of, and perchance
Some tripod, thyrsus,[14] with a vase or so,
The Saviour at his sermon on the mount,
Saint Praxed in a glory,[15] and one Pan   60
Ready to twitch the Nymph's last garment off,
And Moses with the tables . . . but I know
Ye mark me not! What do they whisper thee,
Child of my bowels, Anselm? Ah, ye hope
To revel down my villas while I gasp   65
Bricked o'er with beggar's mouldy travertine[16]
Which Gandolf from his tomb-top[17] chuckles at!
Nay, boys, ye love me—all of jasper, then!
'T is jasper ye stand pledged to, lest I grieve.
My bath must needs be left behind, alas!   70
One block, pure green as a pistachio-nut,
There's plenty jasper somewhere in the world—
And have I not Saint Praxed's ear to pray
Horses for ye, and brown Greek manuscripts,
And mistresses with great smooth marbly limbs? 75

—That 's if ye carve my epitaph aright,
Choice Latin, picked phrase, Tully's every word,
No gaudy ware like Gandolf's second line—
Tully, my masters? Ulpian serves his need![18]
And then how I shall lie through centuries,   80
And hear the blessèd mutter of the mass,
And see God made and eaten all day long,[19]
And feel the steady candle-flame, and taste
Good strong thick stupefying incense-smoke!
For as I lie here, hours of the dead night,   85
Dying in state and by such slow degrees,
I fold my arms as if they clasped a crook,
And stretch my feet forth straight as stone can point,
And let the bedclothes, for a mortcloth,[20] drop
Into great laps and folds of sculptor's-work: 90
And as yon tapers dwindle, and strange thoughts
Grow, with a certain humming in my ears,
About the life before I lived this life,
And this life too, popes, cardinals and priests,
Saint Praxed at his sermon on the mount,[21]   95
Your tall pale mother with her talking eyes,
And new-found agate urns as fresh as day,
And marble's language, Latin pure, discreet,
—Aha, ELUCESCEBAT[22] quoth our friend?
No Tully, said I, Ulpian at the best!   100
Evil and brief hath been my pilgrimage.
All *lapis*, all, sons! Else I give the Pope
My villas! Will ye ever eat my heart?
Ever your eyes were as a lizard's quick,
They glitter like your mother's for my soul,   105
Or ye would heighten my impoverished frieze,
Piece out its starved design, and fill my vase
With grapes, and add a vizor and a Term,[23]
And to the tripod ye would tie a lynx
That in his struggle throws the thyrsus down,   110
To comfort me on my entablature
Whereon I am to lie till I must ask
"Do I live, am I dead?" There, leave me, there!
For ye have stabbed me with ingratitude
To death—ye wish it—God, ye wish it! Stone—   115
Gritstone,[24] a-crumble! Clammy squares which sweat
As if the corpse they keep were oozing through—
And no more *lapis* to delight the world!
Well, go! I bless ye. Fewer tapers there,
But in a row: and, going, turn your backs   120

[9] If the lapis lazuli had been missed after the fire, he would have said he saved it. But fortunately it was not, and he buried it for later—and personal—use. This is a nice observation of where a conscience may draw the line.   [10] Olive basket.
[11] Church of Il Jesu in Rome.
[12] Cf. Job 7:6: "My days are swifter than a weaver's shuttle. . . ."
[13] A black marble, more beautiful than basalt.
[14] Designs for the frieze: a stool like that on which the priestess of Apollo sat when she spoke oracular prophecies at Delphi, or the staff carried by the followers of Bacchus, the god of wine.
[15] With a halo.   [16] Cheap limestone.
[17] The effigy of Gandolf sculptured on top of his tomb.

[18] The decadent Latin of Domitius Ulpianus, a Roman jurist of the third century, far inferior to that of Cicero.
[19] A reference to the doctrine of transubstantiation.
[20] Funeral pall.
[21] The confusion of St. Praxed (a woman) with Christ shows that his mind is wandering. Cf. their juxtaposition in lines 59–60.
[22] "He was famous," a word in the inscription on Gandolf's tomb. This at best is Ulpian Latin. The pure, Ciceronian form would have been *elucebat*.
[23] A mask and a bust on a pedestal.   [24] Coarse sandstone.

—Ay, like departing altar-ministrants,
And leave me in my church, the church for peace,
That I may watch at leisure if he leers—
Old Gandolf—at me, from his onion-stone,
As still he envied me, so fair she was!   125

THE LABORATORY
ANCIEN RÉGIME[1]

Now that I, tying thy glass mask[2] tightly,
May gaze through these faint smokes curling whitely,
As thou pliest thy trade in this devil's-smithy—
Which is the poison to poison her, prithee?

He is with her, and they know that I know   5
Where they are, what they do: they believe my tears flow
While they laugh, laugh at me, at me fled to the drear
Empty church, to pray God in, for them!—I am here.

Grind away, moisten and mash up thy paste,
Pound at thy powder,—I am not in haste!   10
Better sit thus, and observe thy strange things,
Than go where men wait me and dance at the King's.

That in the mortar—you call it a gum?
Ah, the brave tree whence such gold oozings come!
And yonder soft phial, the exquisite blue,   15
Sure to taste sweetly,—is that poison too?

Had I but all of them, thee and thy treasures,
What a wild crowd of invisible pleasures!
To carry pure death in an ear-ring, a casket,
A signet, a fan-mount, a filigree basket!   20

Soon, at the King's, a mere lozenge to give,
And Pauline should have just thirty minutes to live!
But to light a pastile,[3] and Elise, with her head
And her breast and her arms and her hands, should drop
    dead![4]

Quick—is it finished? The colour's too grim!   25
Why not soft like the phial's, enticing and dim?
Let it brighten her drink, let her turn it and stir,
And try it and taste, ere she fix and prefer![5]

---

[1] The "Old Order" of aristocratic life in France before the
Revolution. Lines 19–20 suggest that the time is the Renaissance.
[2] A mask worn to protect the face against radiant heat, originally
in glassworks.
[3] A cone of paste burned as a perfume, in this case poisonous
perfume.
[4] Pauline and Elise are two other women she would be happy to
see poisoned.   [5] Ere she decides exactly how she prefers it.

What a drop! She's not little, no minion[6] like me!
That's why she ensnared him: this never will free   30
The soul from those masculine eyes,—say "no!"
To that pulse's magnificent come-and-go.

For only last night, as they whispered, I brought
My own eyes to bear on her so, that I thought
Could I keep them one half minute fixed, she would
    fall   35
Shrivelled; she fell not; yet this does it all!

Not that I bid you spare her the pain;
Let death be felt and the proof remain:
Brand, burn up, bite into its grace—
He is sure to remember her dying face!   40

Is it done? Take my mask off! Nay, be not morose;
It kills her, and this prevents seeing it close:
The delicate droplet, my whole fortune's fee!
If it hurts her, beside, can it ever hurt me?

Now, take all my jewels, gorge gold to your fill,   45
You may kiss me, old man, on my mouth if you will!
But brush this dust off me, lest horror it brings
Ere I know it—next moment I dance at the King's!

MEETING AT NIGHT

The gray sea and the long black land;
And the yellow half-moon large and low;
And the startled little waves that leap
In fiery ringlets from their sleep,
As I gain the cove with pushing prow,   5
And quench its speed i' the slushy sand.

Then a mile of warm sea-scented beach;
Three fields to cross till a farm appears;
A tap at the pane, the quick sharp scratch
And blue spurt of a lighted match,   10
And a voice less loud, through its joys and fears,
Than the two hearts beating each to each!

PARTING AT MORNING

Round the cape of a sudden came the sea,
And the sun looked over the mountain's rim:
And straight was a path of gold for him,[7]
And the need of a world of men for me.[8]

---

[6] A small, delicate person.   [7] The sun.
[8] Browning said of the two poems taken together, "It is his
confession of how fleeting is the belief (implied in the first part)
that such raptures are self-sufficient and enduring—as for a time
they appear."

LOVE AMONG THE RUINS

Where the quiet-coloured end of evening smiles
    Miles and miles
On the solitary pastures where our sheep
    Half-asleep
Tinkle homeward through the twilight, stray or stop   5
    As they crop—
Was the site once of a city great and gay,
    (So they say)
Of our country's very capital, its prince
    Ages since   10
Held his court in, gathered councils, wielding far
    Peace or war.

Now,—the country does not even boast a tree,
    As you see,
To distinguish slopes of verdure, certain rills   15
    From the hills
Intersect and give a name to, (else they run
    Into one)
Where the domed and daring palace shot its spires
    Up like fires   20
O'er the hundred-gated circuit of a wall
    Bounding all,
Made of marble, men might march on nor be pressed,
    Twelve abreast.

And such plenty and perfection, see, of grass   25
    Never was!
Such a carpet as, this summer-time, o'er-spreads
    And embeds
Every vestige of the city, guessed alone,
    Stock or stone—   30
Where a multitude of men breathed joy and woe
    Long ago;
Lust of glory pricked their hearts up, dread of shame
    Struck them tame;
And that glory and that shame alike, the gold   35
    Bought and sold.

Now,—the single little turret that remains
    On the plains,
By the caper[1] overrooted, by the gourd
    Overscored,   40
While the patching houseleek's[2] head of blossom winks
    Through the chinks—
Marks the basement whence a tower in ancient time
    Sprang sublime,
And a burning ring, all round, the chariots traced   45
    As they raced,

And the monarch and his minions and his dames
    Viewed the games.

And I know, while thus the quiet-coloured eve
    Smiles to leave   50
To their folding, all our many-tinkling fleece
    In such peace,
And the slopes and rills in undistinguished gray
    Melt away—
That a girl with eager eyes and yellow hair   55
    Waits me there
In the turret whence the charioteers caught soul
    For the goal,
When the king looked, where she looks now, breathless,
    dumb
    Till I come.   60

But he looked upon the city, every side,
    Far and wide,
All the mountains topped with temples, all the glades'
    Colonnades,
All the causeys,[3] bridges, aqueducts,—and then,   65
    All the men!
When I do come, she will speak not, she will stand,
    Either hand
On my shoulder, give her eyes the first embrace
    Of my face,   70
Ere we rush, ere we extinguish sight and speech
    Each on each.

In one year they sent a million fighters forth
    South and North,
And they built their gods a brazen pillar high   75
    As the sky,
Yet reserved a thousand chariots in full force—
    Gold, of course.
Oh heart! oh blood that freezes, blood that burns!
    Earth's returns   80
For whole centuries of folly, noise and sin!
    Shut them in,
With their triumphs and their glories and the rest!
    Love is best.

UP AT A VILLA—DOWN IN THE CITY

(AS DISTINGUISHED BY AN ITALIAN PERSON OF QUALITY)

Had I but plenty of money, money enough and to spare,
The house for me, no doubt, were a house in the city-
    square;
Ah, such a life, such a life, as one leads at the window
    there!

---

[1] A brambly bush.   [2] Small plant with clustered petals.

[3] Causeways, i.e., raised roads across low ground.

Something to see, by Bacchus,[4] something to hear, at least!

There, the whole day long, one's life is a perfect feast;   5

While up at a villa one lives, I maintain it, no more than a beast.

Well now, look at our villa! stuck like the horn of a bull

Just on a mountain-edge as bare as the creature's skull,

Save a mere shag of a bush with hardly a leaf to pull!

—I scratch my own,[5] sometimes, to see if the hair's turned wool.   10

But the city, oh the city—the square with the houses! Why?

They are stone-faced, white as a curd, there's something to take the eye!

Houses in four straight lines, not a single front awry;

You watch who crosses and gossips, who saunters, who hurries by;

Green blinds, as a matter of course, to draw when the sun gets high;   15

And the shops with fanciful signs which are painted properly.

What of a villa? Though winter be over in March by rights,

'Tis May perhaps ere the snow shall have withered well off the heights:

You've the brown ploughed land before, where the oxen steam and wheeze,

And the hills over-smoked behind by the faint gray olive-trees.   20

Is it better in May, I ask you? You've summer all at once;

In a day he leaps complete with a few strong April suns.

'Mid the sharp short emerald wheat, scarce risen three fingers well,

The wild tulip, at end of its tube, blows out its great red bell

Like a thin clear bubble of blood, for the children to pick and sell.   25

Is it ever hot in the square? There's a fountain to spout and splash!

In the shade it sings and springs; in the shine such foam-bows flash

On the horses with curling fish-tails, that prance and paddle and pash

Round the lady atop in her conch[6]—fifty gazers do not abash,

Though all that she wears is some weeds round her waist in a sort of sash.   30

All the year long at the villa, nothing to see though you linger!

Except yon cypress that points like death's lean lifted forefinger.

Some think fireflies pretty, when they mix i' the corn and mingle,

Or thrid[7] the stinking hemp till the stalks of it seem a-tingle.

Late August or early September, the stunning cicala is shrill,   35

And the bees keep their tiresome whine round the resinous firs on the hill.

Enough of the seasons,—I spare you the months of the fever and chill.

Ere you open your eyes in the city, the blessed church-bells begin:

No sooner the bells leave off than the diligence rattles in:

You get the pick of the news, and it costs you never a pin.   40

By and by there's the travelling doctor gives pills, lets blood, draws teeth;

Or the Pulcinello-trumpet[8] breaks up the market beneath.

At the post-office such a scene-picture[9]—the new play, piping hot!

And a notice how, only this morning, three liberal thieves[10] were shot.

Above it, behold the Archbishop's most fatherly of rebukes,   45

And beneath, with his crown and his lion, some little new law of the Duke's!

Or a sonnet with flowery marge,[11] to the Reverend Don So-and-so,

Who is Dante, Boccaccio, Petrarca, Saint Jerome, and Cicero,[12]

"And moreover," (the sonnet goes rhyming,) "the skirts of Saint Paul has reached,

Having preached us those six Lent-lectures more unctuous than ever he preached."   50

---

6 Shell.   7 Thread.

8 Trumpet announcing the puppet show, in which Pulcinello was the clown.   9 Picture advertising the new play.

10 Members of the revolutionary party fighting to free Italy from Austrian control. The word "thieves" may be the aristocrat's term for "patriots."

11 Decorated in the margin with flowers.

12 Who is, according to the flattering poet, the equal of Dante, etc.

---

4 Mild Italian oath.   5 My own skull.

Noon strikes,—here sweeps the procession! our Lady
    borne smiling and smart
With a pink gauze gown all spangles, and seven swords
    stuck in her heart![13]
Bang-whang-whang goes the drum, *tootle-te-tootle* the fife;
No keeping one's haunches still: it's the greatest pleasure
    in life.

But bless you, it's dear—it's dear! fowls, wine, at
    double the rate.   55
They have clapped a new tax upon salt, and what oil
    pays passing the gate
It's a horror to think of. And so, the villa for me, not
    the city!
Beggars can scarcely be choosers: but still—ah, the pity,
    the pity!
Look, two and two go the priests, then the monks with
    cowls and sandals,
And the penitents dressed in white shirts, a-holding the
    yellow candles;   60
One, he carries a flag up straight, and another a cross
    with handles,
And the Duke's guard brings up the rear, for the better
    prevention of scandals:
Bang-whang-whang goes the drum, *tootle-te-tootle* the fife.
Oh, a day in the city-square, there is no such pleasure
    in life!

FRA LIPPO LIPPI[1]

I am poor brother Lippo, by your leave!
You need not clap your torches to my face.
Zooks,[2] what's to blame? you think you see a monk!
What, 'tis past midnight, and you go the rounds,
And here you catch me at an alley's end   5
Where sportive ladies leave their doors ajar?
The Carmine's my cloister: hunt it up,
Do,—harry out, if you must show your zeal,
Whatever rat, there, haps on his wrong hole,
And nip each softling of a wee white mouse,   10
Weke, weke, that's crept to keep him company!
Aha, you know your betters! Then, you'll take
Your hand away that's fiddling on my throat,
And please to know me likewise. Who am I?
Why, one, sir, who is lodging with a friend   15
Three streets off—he's a certain . . . how d'ye call?

Master—a . . . Cosimo of the Medici,[3]
I' the house that caps the corner. Boh! you were best![4]
Remember and tell me, the day you're hanged,
How you affected such a gullet's-gripe!   20
But you, sir, it concerns you that your knaves
Pick up a manner nor discredit you:
Zooks, are we pilchards,[5] that they sweep the streets
And count fair prize what comes into their net?
He's Judas to a tittle, that man is![6]   25
Just such a face! Why, sir, you make amends.
Lord, I'm not angry! Bid your hangdogs go
Drink out this quarter-florin to the health
Of the munificent House that harbors me
(And many more beside, lads! more beside!)   30
And all's come square again. I'd like his face—
His, elbowing on his comrade in the door
With the pike and lantern,—for the slave[7] that holds
John Baptist's head a-dangle by the hair
With one hand ("Look you, now," as who should say)   35
And his weapon in the other, yet unwiped!
It's not your chance to have a bit of chalk,
A wood-coal or the like? or you should see!
Yes, I'm the painter, since you style me so.
What, brother Lippo's doings, up and down,   40
You know them and they take you? like enough!
I saw the proper twinkle in your eye—
'Tell you, I liked your looks at very first.
Let's sit and set things straight now, hip to haunch.
Here's spring come, and the nights one makes up bands   45
To roam the town and sing out carnival,
And I've been three weeks shut within my mew,[8]
A-painting for the great man, saints and saints
And saints again. I could not paint all night—
Ouf! I leaned out of window for fresh air.   50
There came a hurry of feet and little feet,
A sweep of lute-strings, laughs, and whifts of song,—
Flower o' the broom,
Take away love, and our earth is a tomb!
Flower o' the quince,   55
I let Lisa go, and what good in life since?
Flower o' the thyme—and so on. Round they went.
Scarce had they turned the corner when a titter

---

[13] The seven swords symbolize the seven great sorrows endured by the Virgin.

[1] Filippo Lippi, a Carmelite friar and painter, who lived at Florence in the fifteenth century.   [2] Gadzooks (an oath).

[3] Banker and patron of the arts (1389–1464), the real ruler of Florence.
[4] "You do well to take your hand off my throat," which the guard does instantly on hearing the name of Cosimo. The "you" in line 21 is the captain of the group.
[5] A kind of cheap fish.
[6] One of the guard whom Lippo, with the sharp eye of a painter, has just noticed.
[7] That is, as a model for the slave in the picture he goes on to describe. On John the Baptist's death see Mark 6:17–28.
[8] Coop or pen.

Like the skipping of rabbits by moonlight,—three slim
    shapes,
And a face that looked up . . . zooks, sir, flesh and
    blood,   60
That's all I'm made of! Into shreds it went,
Curtain and counterpane and coverlet,
All the bed-furniture—a dozen knots,
There was a ladder! Down I let myself,
Hands and feet, scrambling somehow, and so dropped, 65
And after them. I came up with the fun
Hard by Saint Laurence,[9] hail fellow, well met,—
Flower o' the rose,
If I've been merry, what matter who knows?
And so as I was stealing back again   70
To get to bed and have a bit of sleep
Ere I rise up to-morrow and go work
On Jerome knocking at his poor old breast
With his great round stone to subdue the flesh,[10]
You snap me of the sudden. Ah, I see!   75
Though your eye twinkles still, you shake your head—
Mine's shaved—a monk, you say—the sting's in that!
If Master Cosimo announced himself,
Mum's the word naturally; but a monk!
Come, what am I a beast for? tell us, now!   80
I was a baby when my mother died
And father died and left me in the street.
I starved there, God knows how, a year or two
On fig-skins, melon-parings, rinds and shucks,
Refuse and rubbish. One fine frosty day,   85
My stomach being empty as your hat,
The wind doubled me up and down I went.
Old Aunt Lapaccia trussed me[11] with one hand,
(Its fellow was a stinger as I knew)
And so along the wall, over the bridge,   90
By the straight cut to the convent. Six words there,
While I stood munching my first bread that month:
"So boy, you're minded," quoth the good fat father
Wiping his own mouth, 'twas refection-time,—
"To quit this very miserable world?   95
Will you renounce" . . . "the mouthful of bread?"
    thought I;
By no means! Brief, they made a monk of me;
I did renounce the world, its pride and greed,
Palace, farm, villa, shop, and banking-house,
Trash, such as these poor devils of Medici   100
Have given their hearts to—all at eight years old.
Well, sir, I found in time, you may be sure,
'Twas not for nothing—the good bellyful,

The warm serge and the rope that goes all round,
And day-long blessed idleness beside!   105
"Let's see what the urchin's fit for"—that came next.
Not overmuch their way, I must confess.
Such a to-do! They tried me with their books;
Lord, they'd have taught me Latin in pure waste!
Flower o' the clove,   110
All the Latin I construe is, "amo" I love!
But, mind you, when a boy starves in the streets
Eight years together, as my fortune was,
Watching folk's faces to know who will fling
The bit of half-stripped grape-bunch he desires,   115
And who will curse or kick him for his pains,—
Which gentleman processional[12] and fine,
Holding a candle to the Sacrament,
Will wink and let him lift a plate and catch
The droppings of the wax to sell again,   120
Or holla for the Eight[13] and have him whipped,—
How say I?—nay, which dog bites, which lets drop
His bone from the heap of offal in the street,—
Why, soul and sense of him grow sharp alike,
He learns the look of things, and none the less   125
For admonition from the hunger-pinch.
I had a store of such remarks, be sure,
Which, after I found leisure, turned to use.
I drew men's faces on my copy-books,
Scrawled them within the antiphonary's[14] marge,   130
Joined legs and arms to the long music-notes,
Found eyes and nose and chin for A's and B's,
And made a string of pictures of the world
Betwixt the ins and outs of verb and noun,
On the wall, the bench, the door. The monks looked
    black.   135
"Nay," quoth the Prior, "turn him out, d'ye say?
In no wise. Lose a crow and catch a lark.
What if at last we get our man of parts,
We Carmelites, like those Camaldolese
And Preaching Friars,[15] to do our church up fine   140
And put the front on it that ought to be!"
And hereupon he bade me daub away.
Thank you! my head being crammed, the walls a blank,
Never was such prompt disemburdening.
First, every sort of monk, the black and white,   145
I drew them, fat and lean: then, folk at church,
From good old gossips waiting to confess
Their cribs[16] of barrel-droppings, candle-ends,—
To the breathless fellow at the altar-foot,
Fresh from his murder, safe[17] and sitting there   150
With the little children round him in a row

---

[9] The church of San Lorenzo.
[10] Picture of St. Jerome (340–420) on which Lippo is working,
invented by Browning to set up an ironic contrast with the
character and habits of the painter.   [11] Held me up firmly.

[12] Gentleman walking in a religious procession.
[13] The magistrates of Florence.   [14] Choir-book's.
[15] Two rival religious orders.
[16] Thefts.   [17] Because he cannot be arrested in the church.

Of admiration, half for his beard and half
For that white anger of his victim's son
Shaking a fist at him with one fierce arm,
Signing himself with the other because of Christ   155
(Whose sad face on the cross sees only this
After the passion of a thousand years)
Till some poor girl, her apron o'er her head,
(Which the intense eyes looked through) came at eve
On tiptoe, said a word, dropped in a loaf,   160
Her pair of earrings and a bunch of flowers
(The brute took growling), prayed, and so was gone.
I painted all, then cried " 'Tis ask and have;
Choose, for more's ready!"—laid the ladder flat,
And showed my covered bit of cloister-wall.   165
The monks closed in a circle and praised loud
Till checked, taught what to see and not to see,
Being simple bodies,—"That's the very man!
Look at the boy who stoops to pat the dog!
That woman's like the Prior's niece who comes   170
To care about his asthma: it's the life!"
But there my triumph's straw-fire flared and funked;
Their betters took their turn to see and say:
The Prior and the learned pulled a face
And stopped all that in no time. "How? what's here?
Quite from the mark of painting, bless us all!   176
Faces, arms, legs, and bodies like the true
As much as pea and pea! it's devil's-game!
Your business is not to catch men with show,
With homage to the perishable clay,   180
But lift them over it, ignore it all,
Make them forget there's such a thing as flesh.
Your business is to paint the souls of men—
Man's soul, and it's a fire, smoke . . . no, it's not . . .
It's vapor done up like a new-born babe—   185
(In that shape when you die it leaves your mouth)
It's . . . well, what matters talking, it's the soul!
Give us no more of body than shows soul!
Here's Giotto with his Saint a-praising God,
That sets us praising,—why not stop with him?[18]   190
Why put all thoughts of praise out of our head
With wonder at lines, colors, and what not?
Paint the soul, never mind the legs and arms!
Rub all out, try at it a second time.
Oh, that white smallish female with the breasts,   195
She's just my niece . . . Herodias, I would say,—
Who went and danced and got men's heads cut off![19]

Have it all out!" Now, is this sense, I ask?
A fine way to paint soul, by painting body
So ill, the eye can't stop there, must go further   200
And can't fare worse! Thus, yellow does for white
When what you put for yellow's simply black,
And any sort of meaning looks intense
When all beside itself means and looks naught.
Why can't a painter lift each foot in turn,   205
Left foot and right foot, go a double step,
Make his flesh liker and his soul more like,
Both in their order? Take the prettiest face,
The Prior's niece . . . patron-saint—is it so pretty
You can't discover if it means hope, fear,   210
Sorrow or joy? won't beauty go with these?
Suppose I've made her eyes all right and blue,
Can't I take breath and try to add life's flash,
And then add soul and heighten them three-fold?
Or say there's beauty with no soul at all—   215
(I never saw it—put the case the same—)
If you get simple beauty and naught else,
You get about the best thing God invents:
That's somewhat: and you'll find the soul you have
        missed,
Within yourself, when you return him thanks.   220
"Rub all out!" Well, well, there's my life, in short,
And so the thing has gone on ever since.
I'm grown a man no doubt, I've broken bounds:
You should not take a fellow eight years old
And make him swear to never kiss the girls.   225
I'm my own master, paint now as I please—
Having a friend, you see, in the Corner-house!
Lord, it's fast holding by the rings in front[20]—
Those great rings serve more purposes than just
To plant a flag in, or tie up a horse!   230
And yet the old schooling sticks, the old grave eyes
Are peeping o'er my shoulder as I work,
The heads shake still—"It's art's decline, my son!
You're not of the true painters, great and old;
Brother Angelico's the man, you'll find;   235
Brother Lorenzo stands his single peer:[21]
Fag on at flesh, you'll never make the third!"
Flower o' the pine,
You keep your mistr . . . manners, and I'll stick to mine!
I'm not the third, then: bless us, they must know!   240
Don't you think they're the likeliest to know,
They with their Latin? So, I swallow my rage,
Clench my teeth, suck my lips in tight, and paint
To please them—sometimes do and sometimes don't;

---

[18] That is, why not continue to follow the medieval conception of
painting exemplified by Giotto (1276–1337)? Lippo and Masaccio
(line 276) led the reaction that introduced realism.
[19] It was not Herodias but her daughter Salome who at Herodias's
instigation asked Herod to reward her dancing by giving her
John the Baptist's head on a platter (cf. lines 33–34 and note 7,
above).

[20] The iron rings on the front of the palace give Lippo something
to hold fast by, which makes them symbols for the protection
and patronage of Cosimo.
[21] Fra Angelico and Lorenzo Monaco were painters who worked
in the medieval tradition against which Lippo was revolting.

For, doing most, there's pretty sure to come 245
A turn, some warm eve finds me at my saints—
A laugh, a cry, the business of the world—
(*Flower o' the peach,*
Death for us all, and his own life for each!)
And my whole soul revolves, the cup runs over, 250
The world and life's too big to pass for a dream,
And I do these wild things in sheer despite,
And play the fooleries you catch me at,
In pure rage! The old mill-horse, out at grass
After hard years, throws up his stiff heels so, 255
Although the miller does not preach to him
The only good of grass is to make chaff.
What would men have? Do they like grass or no—
May they or mayn't they? all I want's the thing
Settled for ever one way. As it is, 260
You tell too many lies and hurt yourself:
You don't like what you only like too much,
You do like what, if given you at your word,
You find abundantly detestable.
For me, I think I speak as I was taught; 265
I always see the garden and God there
A-making man's wife: and, my lesson learned,
The value and significance of flesh,
I can't unlearn ten minutes afterwards.

You understand me: I'm a beast, I know. 270
But see, now—why, I see as certainly
As that the morning-star's about to shine,
What will hap some day. We've a youngster here
Comes to our convent, studies what I do,
Slouches and stares and lets no atom drop: 275
His name is Guidi—he'll not mind the monks—
They call him Hulking Tom, he lets them talk—
He picks my practice up[22]—he'll paint apace,
I hope so—though I never live so long,
I know what's sure to follow. You be judge! 280
You speak no Latin more than I, belike;
However, you're my man, you've seen the world
—The beauty and the wonder and the power,
The shapes of things, their colors, lights and shades,
Changes, surprises,—and God made it all! 285
—For what? Do you feel thankful, ay or no,
For this fair town's face, yonder river's line,
The mountain round it and the sky above,
Much more the figures of man, woman, child,
These are the frame to? What's it all about? 290
To be passed over, despised? or dwelt upon,
Wondered at? oh, this last of course!—you say.

But why not do as well as say,—paint these
Just as they are, careless what comes of it?
God's works—paint any one, and count it crime 295
To let a truth slip. Don't object, "His works
Are here already; nature is complete:
Suppose you reproduce her—(which you can't)
There's no advantage! you must beat her, then."
For, don't you mark? we're made so that we love 300
First when we see them painted, things we have passed
Perhaps a hundred times nor cared to see;
And so they are better, painted—better to us,
Which is the same thing. Art was given for that;
God uses us to help each other so, 305
Lending our minds out. Have you noticed, now,
Your cullion's[23] hanging face? A bit of chalk,
And trust me but you should, though! How much
       more,
If I drew higher things with the same truth!
That were to take the Prior's pulpit-place, 310
Interpret God to all of you! Oh, oh,
It makes me mad to see what men shall do
And we in our graves! This world's no blot for us,
Nor blank; it means intensely, and means good:
To find its meaning is my meat and drink. 315
"Ay, but you don't so instigate to prayer!"
Strikes in the Prior: "when your meaning's plain
It does not say to folk—remember matins,
Or, mind you fast next Friday!" Why, for this
What need of art at all? A skull and bones, 320
Two bits of stick nailed crosswise, or, what's best,
A bell to chime the hour with, does as well.
I painted a Saint Laurence six months since
At Prato, splashed the fresco in fine style:
"How looks my painting, now the scaffold's
       down?" 325
I ask a brother: "Hugely," he returns—
"Already not one phiz of your three slaves
Who turn the Deacon off his toasted side,
But's scratched and prodded to our heart's content,
The pious people have so eased their own 330
With coming to say prayers there in a rage:
We get on fast to see the bricks beneath.[24]
Expect another job this time next year,
For pity and religion grow i' the crowd—
Your painting serves its purpose!" Hang the fools![25] 335

---

22 Tommaso Guidi, more commonly known as Masaccio, was
more probably Lippo's master than his pupil, but both shared
the same theory.

23 Rascal's.
24 Lippo's mural of St. Lawrence, showing him being turned over
on the gridiron so that his other side may be broiled, was so
realistic that people have scratched at the three torturers until
the paint has almost been worn off, exposing the bricks beneath.
Prato is a town near Florence.
25 Since it was hardly Lippo's purpose to promote religion in this
way.

—That is—you'll not mistake an idle word
Spoke in a huff by a poor monk, God wot,
Tasting the air this spicy night which turns
The unaccustomed head like Chianti wine!
Oh, the church knows! don't misreport me, now!   340
It's natural a poor monk out of bounds
Should have his apt word to excuse himself:
And hearken how I plot to make amends.
I have bethought me: I shall paint a piece
. . . There's for you! Give me six months, then go,
   see   345
Something in Sant' Ambrogio's![26] Bless the nuns!
They want a cast o' my office.[27] I shall paint
God in the midst, Madonna and her babe,
Ringed by a bowery flowery angel-brood,
Lilies and vestments and white faces, sweet   350
As puff on puff of grated orris-root
When ladies crowd to Church at midsummer.
And then i' the front, of course a saint or two—
Saint John, because he saves the Florentines,[28]
Saint Ambrose, who puts down in black and white   355
The convent's friends and gives them a long day,
And Job, I must have him there past mistake,
The man of Uz (and Us without the z,
Painters who need his patience). Well, all these
Secured at their devotion, up shall come   360
Out of a corner[29] when you least expect,
As one by a dark stair into a great light,
Music and talking, who but Lippo! I!—
Mazed, motionless, and moonstruck—I'm the man!
Back I shrink—what is this I see and hear?   365
I, caught up with my monk's-things by mistake,
My old serge gown and rope that goes all round,
I, in this presence, this pure company!
Where's a hole, where's a corner for escape?
Then steps a sweet angelic slip of a thing   370
Forward, puts out a soft palm—"Not so fast!"
—Addresses the celestial presence, "nay—
He made you and devised you, after all,
Though he's none of you! Could Saint John there
   draw—
His camel-hair make up a painting-brush?   375
We come to brother Lippo for all that,
Iste perfecit opus!"[30] So, all smile—
I shuffle sideways with my blushing face
Under the cover of a hundred wings

---

[26] In the convent in Florence, whose patron saint is St. Ambrose; there Lippo painted "The Coronation of the Virgin," which he goes on to describe.   [27] An example of my art.
[28] John the Baptist, patron saint of Florence.
[29] Of the picture.
[30] "This man made the work," words which appear in the painting near Lippo, who is in the lower right-hand corner.

Thrown like a spread of kirtles when you're gay   380
And play hot cockles,[31] all the doors being shut,
Till, wholly unexpected, in there pops
The hothead husband! Thus I scuttle off
To some safe bench behind, not letting go
The palm of her, the little lily thing   385
That spoke the good word for me in the nick,
Like the Prior's niece . . . Saint Lucy, I would say.[32]
And so all's saved for me, and for the church
A pretty picture gained. Go, six months hence!
Your hand, sir, and good-by: no lights, no lights!   390
The street's hushed, and I know my own way back,
Don't fear me! There's the grey beginning. Zooks!

A TOCCATA OF GALUPPI'S[1]

O Galuppi, Baldassaro, this is very sad to find!
I can hardly misconceive you; it would prove me deaf
   and blind;
But although I take your meaning, 'tis with such a
   heavy mind!

Here you come with your old music, and here's all the
   good it brings.[2]
What, they lived once thus at Venice where the
   merchants were the kings,   5
Where St. Mark's is, where the Doges used to wed the
   sea with rings?[3]

Aye, because the sea's the street there; and 'tis arched
   by . . . what you call . . .
Shylock's bridge with houses on it,[4] where they kept
   the carnival:
I was never out of England—it's as if I saw it all.

Did young people take their pleasure when the sea was
   warm in May?   10

---

[31] A game.
[32] The "sweet angelic slip of a thing" who steps forward to defend him in the picture is St. Lucy, for whom the Prior's niece has again served as model (cf. lines 170, 195–6, 208–9).

[1] Baldassare Galuppi was a Venetian composer of the eighteenth century, "good alike at grave and gay" music (see line 26). In the poem the speaker is playing one of his toccatas, a casual piece, light in tone and free in movement. But the poem is not about Galuppi nor about music, nor even, strictly speaking, about the Venetians whom Galuppi and the toccata call up in the speaker's mind as he listens. It is about the speaker himself.
[2] These first four lines must be reread at the end of the poem. They are the speaker's final comment on the second strand of thought which the music suggests, in lines 31–45.
[3] The Doge, who was the chief magistrate of Venice, threw a ring into the Adriatic once a year to symbolize the "marriage" of Venice, a great commercial power, with the sea.
[4] The Rialto, a bridge over the Grand Canal.

Balls and masks begun at midnight, burning ever to
  mid-day,
When they made up fresh adventures for the morrow,
  do you say?

Was a lady such a lady, cheeks so round and lips so
  red,—
On her neck the small face buoyant, like a bell-flower
  on its bed,
O'er the breast's superb abundance where a man might
  base his head?   15

Well, and it was graceful of them—they'd break talk
  off and afford—
She, to bite her mask's black velvet—he, to finger on
  his sword,
While you sat and played Toccatas, stately at the
  clavichord?

What? Those lesser thirds so plaintive, sixths diminished,
  sigh on sigh,
Told them something? Those suspensions, those
  solutions—"Must we die?"[5]   20
Those commiserating sevenths—"Life might last! we
  can but try!"[6]

"Were you happy?"—"Yes."—"And are you still as
  happy?"—"Yes. And you?"
—"Then, more kisses!"—"Did I stop them, when a
  million seemed so few?"
Hark, the dominant's persistence till it must be
  answered to!

So, an octave struck the answer.[7] Oh, they praised you,
  I dare say!   25
"Brave Galuppi! that was music! good alike at grave
  and gay!
I can always leave off talking when I hear a master
  play!"

Then they left you for their pleasure; till in due time,
  one by one,
Some with lives that came to nothing, some with deeds
  as well undone,

Death stepped tacitly and took them where they never
  see the sun.[8]   30

But when I sit down to reason, think to take my stand
  nor swerve,
While I triumph o'er a secret wrung from nature's close
  reserve,
In you come with your cold music till I creep through
  every nerve.[9]

Yes, you, like a ghostly cricket, creaking where a house
  was burned:
"Dust and ashes, dead and done with, Venice spent
  what Venice earned.   35
The soul, doubtless, is immortal—where a soul can be
  discerned.

"Yours for instance: you know physics, something of ·
  geology,
Mathematics are your pastime; souls shall rise in their
  degree;
Butterflies may dread extinction—you'll not die, it
  cannot be!

"As for Venice and her people, merely born to bloom
  and drop,   40
Here on earth they bore their fruitage, mirth and folly
  were the crop;
What of soul was left, I wonder, when the kissing had
  to stop?

"Dust and ashes!" So you creak it, and I want the heart
  to scold.[10]
Dear dead women, with such hair, too—what's become
  of all the gold
Used to hang and brush their bosoms? I feel chilly
  and grown old.[11]   45

---

[8] Into their graves. Only the virtuous gain the reward of immortality (cf. lines 38–43).

[9] Suddenly the taunting tone of the music, which has been reflecting the speaker's moral judgment on the pleasure-loving
Venetians, seems to be turned upon his own complacent superiority—explicitly on his belief in immortality, which he thought
he had triumphantly maintained in the face of his scientific
investigations. The irony in lines 36–39 is emphatic.

[10] Not Galuppi, but the Venetians he has been rapping for their
"mirth and folly," but no longer has the heart to scold now
that his capacity to feel different and superior has been undermined (by recognizing that he too may be as mortal as they).

[11] This second reversal of attitude follows from the first. Once his
moral-religious complacency is gone, he can see the charm and
beauty of Venetian life—and now, by contrast, no longer feel
self-righteous, but "chilly and grown old." The poem is a
remarkable study of a moment of self-criticism, in which one's
egotistic pretensions are suddenly pricked.

---

[5] The musical terms refer to dissonant effects which suggest the
idea of death to the listening dancers.

[6] The "sevenths" give a more pleasing effect which awakens a
more hopeful idea.

[7] The dominant is answered in the tonic, an octave above the
first presentation of the theme. Although with the "commiserating sevenths" life seemed possible, in a kind of pleasing melancholy, the inevitable solution reinforces the idea of death. (This
note is adapted from one by Prof. J. E. Baker.)

MY STAR

All that I know
  Of a certain star
Is, it can throw
  (Like the angled spar[1])
Now a dart of red,   5
  Now a dart of blue;
Till my friends have said
  They would fain see, too,
My star that dartles the red and the blue!
Then it stops like a bird; like a flower, hangs furled: 10
  They must solace themselves with the Saturn above it.
What matter to me if their star is a world?
  Mine has opened its soul to me; therefore I love it.

RESPECTABILITY

Dear, had the world in its caprice
  Deigned to proclaim "I know you both,
  Have recognized your plighted troth,
Am sponsor for you: live in peace!"[2]—
How many precious months and years   5
  Of youth had passed, that speed so fast,
  Before we found it out at last,
The world, and what it fears?[3]

How much of priceless life were spent[4]
  With men that every virtue decks,   10
  And women models of their sex,
Society's true ornament,—
Ere we dared wander, nights like this,
  Through wind and rain,[5] and watch the Seine,
  And feel the Boulevard break again   15
To warmth and light and bliss?

I know! the world proscribes not love;
  Allows my finger to caress
  Your lips' contour and downiness,
Provided it supply a glove.[6]   20
The world's good word!—the Institute![7]

---

[1] Iceland spar which acts like a prism, breaking the light into different colors.
[2] That is, "You may live together as lovers."
[3] Before we discovered that what the world fears and condemns is any violation of its respectable conventions.
[4] How much of priceless freedom to live our own lives would have been spent. . . .
[5] Symbolic of freedom to do the unconventional.
[6] Provided we wear the gloves of respectability it supplies to cover the naked fact of love—i.e., provided we get married.
[7] The Institute of France on the left bank of the Seine, which they are just passing.

Guizot receives Montalembert![8]
Eh? Down the court three lampions[9] flare:
Put forward your best foot![10]

THE LAST RIDE TOGETHER

I said—Then, dearest, since 'tis so,
Since now at length my fate I know,
Since nothing all my love avails,
Since all, my life seemed meant for, fails,
  Since this was written and needs must be—   5
My whole heart rises up to bless
Your name in pride and thankfulness!
Take back the hope you gave,—I claim
Only a memory of the same,
  —And this beside, if you will not blame,   10
  Your leave for one more last ride with me.

My mistress bent that brow of hers;
Those deep dark eyes where pride demurs
When pity would be softening through,
Fixed me a breathing-while or two   15
  With life or death in the balance: right!
The blood replenished me again;
My last thought was at least not vain:
I and my mistress, side by side,
Shall be together, breathe and ride,   20
So, one day more am I deified.
  Who knows but the world may end tonight?

Hush! if you saw some western cloud
All billowy-bosomed, over-bowed
By many benedictions—sun's   25
And moon's and evening-star's at once—
  And so, you, looking and loving best,
Conscious grew, your passion drew
Cloud, sunset, moonrise, star-shine too,
Down on you, near and yet more near,   30
Till flesh must fade for heaven was here!—
Thus leant she and lingered—joy and fear!
  Thus lay she a moment on my breast.

Then we began to ride. My soul
Smoothed itself out, a long-cramped scroll   35
Freshening and fluttering in the wind.
Past hopes already lay behind.

---

[8] Guizot, the constitutional royalist, welcomes the liberal Montalembert, whom he really hated as a political enemy, into the French Academy (which met in the Institute). The world's good word countenances even hypocrisy in the cause of propriety.
[9] Elaborate lamps in the courtyard of the Institute.
[10] Be respectable now for ten yards!

What need to strive with a life awry?
Had I said that, had I done this,
So might I gain, so might I miss. 40
Might she have loved me? just as well
She might have hated, who can tell!
Where had I been now if the worst befell?
    And here we are riding, she and I.

Fail I alone, in words and deeds? 45
Why, all men strive and who succeeds?
We rode; it seemed my spirit flew,
Saw other regions, cities new,
    As the world rushed by on either side.
I thought,—All labor, yet no less 50
Bear up beneath their unsuccess.
Look at the end of work, contrast
The petty done, the undone vast,
This present of theirs with the hopeful past!
    I hoped she would love me; here we ride. 55

What hand and brain went ever paired?
What heart alike conceived and dared?
What act proved all its thought had been?
What will but felt the fleshly screen?
    We ride and I see her bosom heave. 60
There's many a crown for who can reach.[1]
Ten lines, a statesman's life in each![2]
The flag stuck on a heap of bones,
A soldier's doing! what atones?
They scratch his name on the Abbey stones.[3] 65
    My riding is better, by their leave.

What does it all mean, poet? Well,
Your brains beat into rhythm, you tell
What we felt only; you expressed
You hold things beautiful the best,
    And pace them in rhyme so, side by side. 70
'Tis something, nay 'tis much: but then,
Have you yourself what's best for men?
Are you—poor, sick, old ere your time—
Nearer one whit your own sublime 75
Than we who never have turned a rhyme?
    Sing, riding's a joy! For me, I ride.

And you, great sculptor—so, you gave
A score of years to Art, her slave,
And that's your Venus, whence we turn 80
To yonder girl that fords the burn![4]
    You acquiesce, and shall I repine?

What, man of music, you grown gray
With notes and nothing else to say,
Is this your sole praise from a friend, 85
"Greatly his opera's strains intend,
But in music we know how fashions end!"
    I gave my youth; but we ride, in fine.

Who knows what's fit for us? Had fate
Proposed bliss here should sublimate[5] 90
My being—had I signed the bond—
Still one must lead some life beyond,
    Have a bliss to die with, dim-descried.
This foot once planted on the goal,
This glory-garland round my soul, 95
Could I descry such? Try and test!
I sink back shuddering from the quest.
Earth being so good, would heaven seem best?
    Now, heaven and she are beyond this ride.

And yet—she has not spoke so long! 100
What if heaven be that, fair and strong
At life's best, with our eyes upturned
Whither life's flower is first discerned,
    We, fixed so, ever should so abide?
What if we still ride on, we two, 105
With life forever old yet new,
Changed not in kind but in degree,
The instant made eternity,—
And heaven just prove that I and she
    Ride, ride together, forever ride? 110

ANDREA DEL SARTO

CALLED "THE FAULTLESS PAINTER"[1]

But do not let us quarrel any more,
No, my Lucrezia; bear with me for once:
Sit down and all shall happen as you wish.
You turn your face, but does it bring your heart?
I'll work then for your friend's friend, never fear, 5
Treat his own subject after his own way,

[5] Exalt to its highest pitch.

[1] Florentine painter (1486–1531), famous for his technical skill but also for his lack of "grandeur, richness, and force," and therefore a perfect example of Browning's philosophy of "failure in success," complementing the "success in failure" of the lover in "The Last Ride Together." But the poem is not the exemplum for a moral; it is a study in character. In Vasari's account of Andrea (see note 9), which is the main source of the poem, Browning's imagination seized primarily, not on the "faultless" idea, but on the statement that "there was a certain timidity of mind, a sort of diffidence and want of force in his nature." Consequently, he wrote an analysis of the kind of person we call pathetically weak. All of Andrea's various attitudes may be traced to this central characteristic.

[1] Many a crown for those who aim only at objects they can reach.
[2] Ten lines of eulogy in the history books.
[3] On his tombstone in Westminster Abbey.   [4] Brook.

Fix his own time, accept too his own price,
And shut the money into this small hand
When next it takes mine. Will it? tenderly?
Oh, I'll content him,—but to-morrow, Love!   10
I often am much wearier than you think,
This evening more than usual, and it seems
As if—forgive now—should you let me sit
Here by the window with your hand in mine
And look a half-hour forth on Fiesole,[2]   15
Both of one mind, as married people use,[3]
Quietly, quietly the evening through,
I might get up to-morrow to my work
Cheerful and fresh as ever. Let us try.
To-morrow, how you shall be glad for this!   20
Your soft hand is a woman of itself,
And mine the man's bared breast she curls inside.
Don't count the time lost, neither; you must serve
For each of the five pictures we require:
It saves a model. So! keep looking so—   25
My serpentining beauty, rounds on rounds!
—How could you ever prick those perfect ears,
Even to put the pearl there! oh, so sweet—
My face, my moon, my everybody's moon,
Which everybody looks on and calls his,   30
And, I suppose, is looked on by in turn,
While she looks—no one's: very dear, no less.
You smile? why, there's my picture ready made,
There's what we painters call our harmony!
A common greyness silvers everything,—   35
All in a twilight, you and I alike
—You, at the point of your first pride in me
(That's gone you know),—but I, at every point;
My youth, my hope, my art, being all toned down
To yonder sober pleasant Fiesole.   40
There's the bell clinking from the chapel-top;
That length of convent-wall across the way
Holds the trees safer, huddled more inside;
The last monk leaves the garden; days decrease,
And autumn grows, autumn in everything.   45
Eh? the whole seems to fall into a shape
As if I saw alike my work and self
And all that I was born to be and do,
A twilight-piece. Love, we are in God's hand.
How strange now, looks the life he makes us lead; 50
So free we seem, so fettered fast we are!
I feel He laid the fetter: let it lie!
This chamber for example—turn your head—
All that's behind us! you don't understand
Nor care to understand about my art,   55
But you can hear at least when people speak;

And that cartoon,[4] the second from the door
—It is the thing, Love! so such things should be—
Behold Madonna!—I am bold to say.
I can do with my pencil what I know,   60
What I see, what at bottom of my heart
I wish for, if I ever wish so deep—
Do easily, too—when I say, perfectly,
I do not boast, perhaps: yourself are judge,
Who listened to the Legate's[5] talk last week,   65
And just as much they used to say in France.
At any rate 'tis easy, all of it!
No sketches first, no studies, that's long past:
I do what many dream of all their lives,
—Dream? strive to do, and agonise to do,   70
And fail in doing. I could count twenty such
On twice your fingers, and not leave this town,
Who strive—you don't know how the others strive
To paint a little thing like that you smeared
Carelessly passing with your robes afloat,—   75
Yet do much less, so much less, Someone says,[6]
(I know his name, no matter)—so much less!
Well, less is more, Lucrezia: I am judged.
There burns a truer light of God in them,
In their vexed beating stuffed and stopped-up brain, 80
Heart, or whate'er else, than goes on to prompt
This low-pulsed forthright craftsman's hand of mine.
Their works drop groundward, but themselves, I know,
Reach many a time a heaven that's shut to me,
Enter and take their place there sure enough,   85
Though they come back and cannot tell the world.
My works are nearer heaven, but I sit here.
The sudden blood of these men! at a word—
Praise them, it boils, or blame them, it boils too.
I, painting from myself and to myself,   90
Know what I do, am unmoved by men's blame
Or their praise either. Somebody remarks
Morello's[7] outline there is wrongly traced,
His hue mistaken; what of that? or else,
Rightly traced and well ordered; what of that?   95
Speak as they please, what does the mountain care?
Ah, but a man's reach should exceed his grasp,
Or what's a heaven for? all is silver-grey
Placid and perfect with my art: the worse!
I know both what I want and what might gain,   100
And yet how profitless to know, to sigh
"Had I been two, another and myself,
Our head would have o'erlooked the world!" No doubt.
Yonder's a work now, of that famous youth
The Urbinate[8] who died five years ago.   105

---

[2] Suburb of Florence.   [3] Are accustomed to do.

[4] Preliminary drawing for a painting.   [5] The Pope's envoy.
[6] Michelangelo (see lines 184 and 199).
[7] Mountain north of Florence.
[8] Raphael (1483-1520), who was born at Urbino.

('Tis copied, George Vasari[9] sent it me.)
Well, I can fancy how he did it all,
Pouring his soul, with kings and popes to see,
Reaching, that heaven might so replenish him,
Above and through his art—for it gives way;   110
That arm is wrongly put—and there again—
A fault to pardon in the drawing's lines,
Its body, so to speak: its soul is right,
He means right—that, a child may understand.
Still, what an arm! and I could alter it.   115
But all the play, the insight and the stretch—
Out of me, out of me! And wherefore out?
Had you enjoined them on me, given me soul,
We might have risen to Rafael, I and you!
Nay, Love, you did give all I asked, I think—   120
More than I merit, yes, by many times.
But had you—oh, with the same perfect brow,
And perfect eyes, and more than perfect mouth,
And the low voice my soul hears, as a bird
The fowler's pipe, and follows to the snare—   125
Had you, with these the same, but brought a mind!
Some women do so. Had the mouth there urged
"God and the glory! never care for gain.
The present by the future, what is that?
Live for fame, side by side with Agnolo![10]   130
Rafael is waiting: up to God, all three!"
I might have done it for you. So it seems:
Perhaps not. All is as God over-rules.
Beside, incentives come from the soul's self;
The rest avail not. Why do I need you?   135
What wife had Rafael, or has Agnolo?
In this world, who can do a thing, will not;
And who would do it, cannot, I perceive:
Yet the will's somewhat—somewhat, too, the power—
And thus we half-men struggle. At the end,   140
God, I conclude, compensates, punishes.
'Tis safer for me, if the award be strict,
That I am something underrated here,
Poor this long while, despised, to speak the truth.
I dared not, do you know, leave home all day,   145
For fear of chancing on the Paris lords.
The best is when they pass and look aside;
But they speak sometimes; I must bear it all.
Well may they speak! That Francis, that first time,
And that long festal year at Fontainebleau![11]   150
I surely then could sometimes leave the ground,
Put on the glory, Rafael's daily wear,

In that humane great monarch's golden look,—
One finger in his beard or twisted curl
Over his mouth's good mark that made the smile,   155
One arm about my shoulder, round my neck,
The jingle of his gold chain in my ear,
I painting proudly with his breath on me,
All his court round him, seeing with his eyes,
Such frank French eyes, and such a fire of souls   160
Profuse, my hand kept plying by those hearts,—
And, best of all, this, this, this face beyond,
This in the background, waiting on my work,
To crown the issue with a last reward!
A good time, was it not, my kingly days?   165
And had you not grown restless . . . but I know—
'Tis done and past; 'twas right, my instinct said;
Too live the life grew, golden and not grey,
And I'm the weak-eyed bat no sun should tempt
Out of his grange whose four walls make his world.   170
How could it end in any other way?
You called me, and I came home to your heart.
The triumph was—to reach and stay there; since
I reached it ere the triumph, what is lost?
Let my hands frame your face in your hair's gold,   175
You beautiful Lucrezia that are mine!
"Rafael did this, Andrea painted that;
The Roman's[12] is the better when you pray,
But still the other's Virgin was his wife—"
Men will excuse me. I am glad to judge   180
Both pictures in your presence; clearer grows
My better fortune, I resolve to think.
For, do you know, Lucrezia, as God lives,
Said one day Agnolo, his very self,
To Rafael . . . I have known it all these years . . .   185
(When the young man was flaming out his thoughts
Upon a palace-wall for Rome to see,
Too lifted up in heart because of it)
"Friend, there's a certain sorry little scrub
Goes up and down our Florence, none cares how,   190
Who, were he set to plan and execute
As you are, pricked on by your popes and kings,
Would bring the sweat into that brow of yours!"
To Rafael's!—And indeed the arm is wrong.
I hardly dare . . . yet, only you to see,   195
Give the chalk here—quick, thus the line should go!
Ay, but the soul! he's Rafael! rub it out!
Still, all I care for, if he spoke the truth
(What he? why, who but Michel Agnolo?
Do you forget already words like those?)   200
If really there was such a chance, so lost,—
Is, whether you're—not grateful—but more pleased.
Well, let me think so. And you smile indeed!
This hour has been an hour! Another smile?

---

[9] The pupil of Andrea and the author of *The Lives of the Most
Eminent Painters, Sculptors, and Architects.*   [10] Michelangelo.

[11] In 1518 Andrea was invited by King Francis I of France to
decorate his palace at Fontainebleau. When he was sent back to
Florence to buy paintings for the King, he used the money to
build a house for himself and Lucrezia (which explains his fear
of meeting any Paris lords who might recognize him).

[12] Raphael's.

If you would sit thus by me every night   205
I should work better, do you comprehend?
I mean that I should earn more, give you more.
See, it is settled dusk now; there's a star;
Morello's gone, the watch-lights show the wall,
The cue-owls speak the name we call them by.   210
Come from the window, love,—come in, at last,
Inside the melancholy little house
We built to be so gay with. God is just.
King Francis may forgive me; oft at nights
When I look up from painting, eyes tired out,   215
The walls become illumined, brick from brick
Distinct, instead of mortar, fierce bright gold,
That gold of his I did cement them with!
Let us but love each other. Must you go?
That Cousin[13] here again? he waits outside?   220
Must see you—you, and not with me? Those loans?
More gaming debts to pay? you smiled for that?
Well, let smiles buy me! have you more to spend?
While hand and eye and something of a heart
Are left me, work's my ware, and what's it worth? 225
I'll pay my fancy. Only let me sit
The grey remainder of the evening out,
Idle, you call it, and muse perfectly
How I could paint, were I but back in France,
One picture, just one more —the Virgin's face,   230
Not yours this time! I want you at my side
To hear them—that is, Michel Agnolo—
Judge all I do and tell you of its worth.
Will you? To-morrow, satisfy your friend.
I take the subjects for his corridor,   235
Finish the portrait out of hand—there, there,
And throw him in another thing or two
If he demurs; the whole should prove enough
To pay for this same Cousin's freak. Beside,
What's better and what's all I care about,   240
Get you the thirteen scudi[14] for the ruff!
Love, does that please you? Ah, but what does he,
The Cousin! what does he to please you more?

    I am grown peaceful as old age to-night.
I regret little, I would change still less.   245
Since there my past life lies, why alter it?
The very wrong to Francis!—it is true
I took his coin, was tempted and complied,
And built this house and sinned, and all is said.
My father and my mother died of want.   250
Well, had I riches of my own? you see
How one gets rich! Let each one bear his lot.
They were born poor, lived poor, and poor they died:

And I have labored somewhat in my time
And not been paid profusely. Some good son   255
Paint my two hundred pictures—let him try!
No doubt, there's something strikes a balance. Yes,
You loved me quite enough, it seems tonight.
This must suffice me here. What would one have?
In heaven, perhaps, new chances, one more chance— 260
Four great walls in the New Jerusalem,[15]
Meted on each side by the angel's reed,
For Leonard,[16] Rafael, Agnolo and me
To cover—the three first without a wife,
While I have mine! So—still they overcome   265
Because there's still Lucrezia,—as I choose.

    Again the Cousin's whistle! Go, my Love.

MEMORABILIA

Ah, did you once see Shelley plain,
    And did he stop and speak to you
And did you speak to him again?
    How strange it seems and new!

But you were living before that,   5
    And also you are living after;
And the memory I started at—
    My starting moves your laughter.

I crossed a moor, with a name of its own
    And a certain use in the world no doubt,   10
Yet a hand's-breadth of it shines alone
    'Mid the blank miles round about:

For there I picked up on the heather
    And there I put inside my breast
A molted feather, an eagle feather!   15
    Well, I forget the rest.

TWO IN THE CAMPAGNA[1]

I wonder do you feel to-day
    As I have felt since, hand in hand,
We sat down on the grass, to stray
    In spirit better through the land,
This morn of Rome and May?   5

For me, I touched a thought, I know,
    Has tantalized me many times,

---

[15] Heaven (see Revelation 21:10-21).   [16] Leonardo da Vinci.

[1] The Campagna is a large open plain outside Rome which is
dotted with ancient ruins (hence the metaphor of "Rome's
ghost" in line 25).

---

[13] Euphemism for lover.   [14] Italian coins.

(Like turns of thread the spiders throw
  Mocking across our path) for rhymes
To catch at and let go.[2]   10

Help me to hold it! First it left
  The yellowing fennel, run to seed
There, branching from the brickwork's cleft,
  Some old tomb's ruin: yonder weed
Took up the floating weft,[3]   15

Where one small orange cup amassed
  Five beetles,—blind and green they grope
Among the honey-meal: and last,
  Everywhere on the grassy slope
I traced it. Hold it fast!   20

The champaign[4] with its endless fleece
  Of feathery grasses everywhere!
Silence and passion, joy and peace,
  An everlasting wash of air—
Rome's ghost since her decease.   25

Such life here, through such lengths of hours,
  Such miracles performed in play,
Such primal naked forms of flowers,
  Such letting nature have her way
While heaven looks from its towers!   30

How say you? Let us, O my dove,
  Let us be unashamed of soul,
As earth lies bare to heaven above!
  How is it under our control
To love or not to love?   35

I would that you were all to me,
  You that are just so much, no more.[5]
Nor yours nor mine, nor slave nor free!
  Where does the fault lie? What the core
O' the wound, since wound must be?   40

I would I could adopt your will,
  See with your eyes, and set my heart
Beating by yours, and drink my fill
  At your soul's springs,—your part my part
In life, for good and ill.   45

No. I yearn upward, touch you close,
  Then stand away. I kiss your cheek,
Catch your soul's warmth,—I pluck the rose
  And love it more than tongue can speak—
Then the good minute goes.[6]   50

Already how am I so far
  Out of that minute? Must I go
Still like the thistle-ball, no bar,
  Onward, whenever light winds blow,
Fixed by no friendly star?[7]   55

Just when I seemed about to learn![8]
  Where is the thread now? Off again!
The old trick! Only I discern—
  Infinite passion, and the pain
Of finite hearts that yearn.[9]   60

A GRAMMARIAN'S FUNERAL

SHORTLY AFTER THE REVIVAL OF LEARNING IN EUROPE

Let us begin and carry up this corpse,
  Singing together.
Leave we the common crofts, the vulgar thorpes[1]
  Each in its tether
Sleeping safe on the bosom of the plain,   5
  Cared-for till cock-crow:
Look out if yonder be not day again
  Rimming the rock-row![2]
That's the appropriate country; there, man's thought,
  Rarer, intenser,   10
Self-gathered for an outbreak, as it ought,
  Chafes in the censer.
Leave we the unlettered plain its herd and crop;
  Seek we sepulture
On a tall mountain, citied to the top,   15
  Crowded with culture!

---

[2] The thread of thought that he has never been able to express in rimes is like the thread which a spider throws across a path, attaching it to a branch, letting go, then swinging down to attach it to a stone (these objects being similes for the rimes).

[3] Cross-thread (a weaving term) of my thought.

[4] The Campagna.

[5] The obvious meaning (that I am only half in love with you) is rendered very doubtful by the next three stanzas.

[6] Since this stanza implies that they share the fullness of love, what they lack is simply the complete sense of oneness and identity of will described in lines 41–45. The correct reading of lines 34–38 is thus made clear. The lovers have this oneness only by moments, after which they again feel their individual identities and know the sense of separation.

[7] Must I always lack the steady and overpowering influence of one star? Cf. lines 41–45.

[8] To learn the answers to the questions in lines 39–40, and follow the thread of his thought to a satisfactory conclusion.

[9] Though why this should be so, what is the core of the wound, I cannot discern. If lines 11–30 are now reread, their general purpose becomes clear. In the Campagna Browning feels the joy and peace of complete fulfillment. But that is in nature; human nature is different. There finite hearts feel an infinite passion and know the pain of its frustration.

[1] The enclosed fields and the small villages (in the valley).

[2] The morning sun is just striking the rocky top of the mountain.

All the peaks soar, but one the rest excels;
    Clouds overcome it;
No! yonder sparkle is the citadel's
    Circling its summit.   20
Thither our path lies; wind we up the heights;
    Wait ye the warning?
Our low life was the level's and the night's;
    He's for the morning.
Step to a tune, square chests, erect each head,   25
    'Ware the beholders!
This is our master, famous, calm and dead,
    Borne on our shoulders.

Sleep, crop and herd! sleep, darkling thorpe and croft,
    Safe from the weather!   30
He, whom we convoy to his grave aloft,
    Singing together,
He was a man born with thy face and throat,
    Lyric Apollo!
Long he lived nameless: how should Spring take note 35
    Winter would follow?
Till lo, the little touch, and youth was gone!
    Cramped and diminished,
Moaned he, "New measures, other feet anon!
    My dance is finished"?   40
No, that's the world's way: (keep the mountain-side,
    Make for the city!)
He knew the signal, and stepped on with pride
    Over men's pity;
Left play for work, and grappled with the world   45
    Bent on escaping:[3]
"What's in the scroll," quoth he, "thou keepest furled?
    Show me their shaping,
Theirs who most studied man, the bard and sage,[4]—
    Give!"—So, he gowned him,[5]   50
Straight got by heart that book to its last page:
    Learnèd, we found him.
Yea, but we found him bald too, eyes like lead,
    Accents uncertain:
"Time to taste life," another would have said,   55
    "Up with the curtain!"
This man said rather, "Actual life comes next?
    Patience a moment!
Grant I have mastered learning's crabbèd text,
    Still there's the comment.   60
Let me know all! Prate not of most or least,
    Painful or easy!

Even to the crumbs I'd fain eat up the feast,
    Ay, nor feel queasy."
Oh, such a life as he resolved to live,   65
    When he had learned it,
When he had gathered all books had to give!
    Sooner, he spurned it.
Image the whole, then execute the parts—
    Fancy the fabric   70
Quite, ere you build, ere steel strike fire from quartz,
    Ere mortar dab brick!

(Here's the town-gate reached: there's the market-place
    Gaping before us.)
Yea, this in him was the peculiar grace   75
    (Hearten our chorus!)
That before living he'd learn how to live—
    No end to learning:
Earn the means first—God surely will contrive
    Use for our earning.   80
Others mistrust and say, "But time escapes:
    Live now or never!"
He said, "What's time? Leave Now for dogs and apes!
    Man has Forever."
Back to his book then: deeper drooped his head: 85
    Calculus[6] racked him:
Leaden before, his eyes grew dross of lead:
    Tussis[7] attacked him.
"Now, master, take a little rest!"—not he!
    (Caution redoubled,   90
Step two abreast, the way winds narrowly!)
    Not a whit troubled
Back to his studies, fresher than at first,
    Fierce as a dragon
He (soul-hydroptic[8] with a sacred thirst)   95
    Sucked at the flagon.
Oh, if we draw a circle premature,
    Heedless of far gain,
Greedy for quick returns of profit, sure
    Bad is our bargain!   100
Was it not great? did not he throw on God,
    (He loves the burthen)—
God's task to make the heavenly period
    Perfect the earthen?
Did not he magnify the mind, show clear   105
    Just what it all meant?
He would not discount life, as fools do here,
    Paid by instalment.
He ventured neck or nothing—heaven's success
    Found, or earth's failure: 110

---

[3] Grappled with the meaning of life, which seems bent on escaping our understanding.
[4] "Their shaping" means either what manner of men they were or what their creative interpretation of life was.
[5] Put on a scholar's gown.

[6] The disease called the stone.
[7] A bronchial cough.   [8] Soul-thirsty.

"Wilt thou trust death or not?" He answered "Yes:
    Hence with life's pale lure!"
That low man seeks a little thing to do,
    Sees it and does it:
This high man, with a great thing to pursue,   115
    Dies ere he knows it.
That low man goes on adding one to one,
    His hundred's soon hit:
This high man, aiming at a million,
    Misses an unit.   120
That, has the world here—should he need the next,
    Let the world mind him!
This, throws himself on God, and unperplexed
    Seeking shall find him.
So, with the throttling hands of death at strife,   125
    Ground he at grammar;
Still, through the rattle,[9] parts of speech were rife;
    While he could stammer
He settled *Hoti's* business—let it be!—
    Properly based *Oun*—   130
Gave us the doctrine of the enclitic *De*,[10]
    Dead from the waist down.
Well, here's the platform, here's the proper place:
    Hail to your purlieus,
All ye highfliers of the feathered race,   135
    Swallows and curlews!
Here's the top-peak; the multitude below
    Live, for they can, there:
This man decided not to Live but Know—
    Bury this man there?   140
Here—here's his place, where meteors shoot, clouds
      form,
    Lightnings are loosened,
Stars come and go! Let joy break with the storm,
    Peace let the dew send!
Lofty designs must close in like effects: 145
    Loftily lying,
Leave him—still loftier than the world suspects,
    Living and dying.[11]

---

[9] Death rattle in his throat.

[10] The italicized words are Greek particles which were discussed by the Renaissance philologists.

[11] The modern reader may be tempted to interpret this poem as a portrayal of compulsive psychology: the grammarian turns away from life (lines 55–58, 65–68), buries himself in feverish work—and without regard, eventually, to its value, when the humanist studying how to live (see lines 75–77) becomes the pedant pursuing the most trivial grammatical distinctions (lines 125–132)—and drives himself literally to death. But the meaning of the poem is controlled, if not with entire success, by the central statement (lines 101–124) of Browning's religious philosophy of aspiration. The grammarian, with sublime disregard of the ills and the brevity of human existence (such a man "has Forever"), pursues with his whole soul the *complete* fulfillment of "a great thing," namely, absolute mastery of ancient literature, which rightly includes the subtlest points of grammar.

PROSPICE[1]

Fear death?—to feel the fog in my throat,
    The mist in my face,
When the snows begin, and the blasts denote
    I am nearing the place,
The power of the night, the press of the storm,   5
    The post of the foe;
Where he stands, the Arch Fear in a visible form,
    Yet the strong man must go:
For the journey is done and the summit attained,
    And the barriers fall,   10
Though a battle's to fight ere the guerdon be gained,
    The reward of it all.
I was ever a fighter, so—one fight more,
    The best and the last!
I would hate that death bandaged my eyes, and
      forbore,   15
    And bade me creep past.
No! let me taste the whole of it, fare like my peers
    The heroes of old,
Bear the brunt, in a minute pay glad life's arrears
    Of pain, darkness and cold.   20
For sudden the worst turns the best to the brave,
    The black minute's at end,
And the elements' rage, the fiend-voices that rave,
    Shall dwindle, shall blend,
Shall change, shall become first a peace out of pain,   25
    Then a light, then thy breast,
O thou soul of my soul! I shall clasp thee again,
    And with God be the rest!

ADAM, LILITH, AND EVE

One day it thundered and lightened.
Two women, fairly frightened,
Sank to their knees, transformed, transfixed,
At the feet of the man who sat betwixt;
And "Mercy!" cried each—"if I tell the truth   5
Of a passage in my youth!"

Said This:[2] "Do you mind the morning
I met your love with scorning?
As the worst of the venom left my lips,
I thought, 'If, despite this lie, he strips   10
The mask from my soul with a kiss—I crawl
His slave,—soul, body and all!' "

---

[1] "Look forward." The poem was probably written soon after Mrs. Browning's death in 1861.

[2] Lilith, Adam's mate before he married Eve.

Said That:[3] "We stood to be married;
The priest, or someone, tarried;
'If Paradise-door prove locked?' smiled you.   15
I thought, as I nodded, smiling too,
'Did one, that's away, arrive—nor late
Nor soon should unlock Hell's gate!' "[4]

It ceased to lighten and thunder.
Up started both in wonder,   20
Looked round and saw that the sky was clear,
Then laughed, "Confess you believed us, dear!"
"I saw through the joke!" the man replied.[5]
They re-seated themselves beside.[6]

EPILOGUE
TO *ASOLANDO*[7]

At the midnight in the silence of the sleep-time,
    When you set your fancies free,
Will they pass to where—by death, fools think,
    imprisoned—

Low he lies who once so loved you, whom you loved
    so,
    —Pity me?   5

Oh to love so, be so loved, yet so mistaken!
    What had I on earth to do
With the slothful, with the mawkish, the unmanly?
Like the aimless, helpless, hopeless, did I drivel—
    Being—who?   10

One who never turned his back but marched breast
    forward,
    Never doubted clouds would break,
Never dreamed, though right were worsted, wrong
    would triumph,
Held we fall to rise, are baffled to fight better,
    Sleep to wake.   15

No, at noonday in the bustle of man's work-time
    Greet the unseen with a cheer!
Bid him forward, breast and back as either should be,
"Strive and thrive!" cry "Speed,—fight on, fare ever
    There as here!"   20

Matthew Arnold

1822–1888

ARNOLD was the famous son of a famous father. Thomas Arnold was the headmaster of Rugby, a leader of the Broad Church school of Liberal Protestantism (see the General Introduction, p. 378, where his religious position is described), and a very earnest Victorian who summoned his boys to a life of moral warfare and strenuous work. The son was something of a black sheep. Partly in reaction against his father, he cultivated the elegant airs of a dandy. At Oxford, where he matriculated in 1841 after a school education at Winchester and Rugby,

he went fishing when he should have been studying, wore wondrous waistcoats in the latest French fashion, and entertained his friends with practical jokes and "a genial amount of ribaldry." But there was nothing light or gay about the poems which he published in 1849. Even his sister, to say nothing of his Oxford associates, found the volume "almost like a new Introduction to him. . . . I felt there was so much more of . . . practical questioning in Matt's book than I was at all prepared for; in fact that it showed a knowledge of life and conflict which was strangely like experience if it was not the thing itself; and this . . . I should not have looked for."

The key words here are "questioning" and "conflict." The fact is that Arnold's dandyism was largely a mask, either adopted deliberately to hide an inner distress of mind he did not want to discuss, or assumed instinctively as a kind of laughing that he might not weep. For he was suffering from the disease of the nineteenth century, the collapse of traditional beliefs, especially in religion, as the waves of modern thought—science and Utilitarianism and Biblical criticism—broke over his head at Oxford, to leave him, as they left his friend Clough, without compass or stars, in a painful darkness of indecision and

---

[3] Eve.

[4] If only the man I really love would arrive, I wouldn't unlock hell's gate by marrying you.

[5] The remark is double-edged. To them it means (or rather, they are willing to assume that it means), "Yes, I saw that you were only joking"; but to himself and to the reader it means, "I saw through the whole wretched joke, your false pretensions of a lifetime, and your latest attempt to make me think your true confessions were only a joke."

[6] As if nothing had happened. The poem is a wonderfully wry comment on the masks (of scorn, of love, of ignorance) which people put on in order to live together with some show of peace and stability, and continue to wear even when they have been seen through. Cf. Guizot's mask in "Respectability," p. 707, above.   [7] The last poem in Browning's last book, *Asolando*.

doubt (see, below, the description of the Victorians in "The Scholar-Gipsy," lines 161–230). He felt himself "wandering between two worlds, one dead, the other powerless to be born, with nowhere yet to rest my head."

As this statement implies, Arnold's melancholy is shot through with a sense of loneliness. The old relationship between man and God, and between man and nature (cf. Wordsworth), is broken, leaving man alone in an indifferent universe of mechanical law. The decay of the old social structure, under industrial and democratic pressure, and the rise of the large impersonal city have put an end to the binding associations of fixed classes and small communities. The individual is thus thrown back upon himself in painful isolation, both cosmic and social. (See especially the two poems to Marguerite.)

Though by moments Arnold sought release from his melancholia by escaping to the peace and beauty of nature, as in "The Scholar-Gipsy," his normal—and very mid-Victorian—attitude was a resolve "to make a habitual war on depression and low spirits," and a conviction that "nothing can absolve us from the duty of doing all we can to keep alive our courage and activity." But how? What philosophy could take the place of his lost Christianity and give him, and his age, renewed strength and inspiration? The question led Arnold to different answers, with the result, as he said himself, that his poems cannot be made to square in all their parts. They are fragments, because "I am fragments." And no one should plague himself "to find a consistent meaning."

One answer to be found is the Stoicism of Epictetus and Marcus Aurelius, with its doctrines of self-reliance and the imitation of nature. So long as men depend on external things for their happiness, on the attainment of wealth or fame or love, they are doomed to disappointment and frustration. Only by achieving *self*-dependence through mastering their possessive passions and adopting an attitude of Stoic detachment can they gain inner calm and peace of mind. This did not mean, however, that man was to turn away from active life in the world. Since his goal was to "live according to nature," and all things had a "natural" function to pursue—the vine to bear grapes, the sun to shine—man was to serve society in whatever role "naturally" fitted his temper and abilities. This is what Arnold means by "quiet work," in the world but not of it, as contrasted with the battling, noisy work which is motivated by personal and worldly ambitions. In one respect, however, Arnold found Stoicism unsatisfactory. "The burden [it] laid upon man is well-nigh greater than he can bear." It said, Renounce your natural desires, grit your teeth, and you will be serene. But most men, Arnold felt, including himself, needed something more hopeful and inspiring "to make moral action perfect." This something was religion,

whose paramount virtue is that "it has *lighted up* morality; that it has supplied the emotion and inspiration needful for carrying the sage along the narrow way perfectly, for carrying the ordinary man along it at all"; and more than any other religion Christianity has manifested this virtue "with unexampled splendour." What he had in mind, however, was not the Christian faith but the Christian ethic, and in particular the Puritan-Christian ethic which lays major emphasis on moral struggle and aspiration rather than on forgiveness and humility—on warring against evil, within and without, and on living a strenuous life of hard labor in the service of God by serving society. There is much which harmonizes here with the ethic of Stoicism, but there is a clear distinction between "quiet work" and "strenuous work," between emphasizing detachment and emphasizing active effort. (Cf. "Quiet Work" and "Self-Dependence" with "The Better Part" and "Morality." The contrast is explicit in "In Harmony with Nature.") Finally, the search for a constructive philosophy led Arnold to a third answer, one which is indebted both to his sympathy with aristocracy and his admiration for dynamic personality—that is, for the decisive force he so badly lacked himself and which he recognized in his father. This is the hero-worship which is seen in "Sohrab and Rustum," the inspiring image of a great man, great in courage and energy, still greater in moral character; and if not noble by birth, always noble in spirit. "I am glad you like the Gipsy Scholar," he wrote to his friend Clough, "but what does it *do* for you? Homer *animates*—Shakespeare *animates*—in its poor way I think Sohrab and Rustum *animates*—the Gipsy Scholar at best awakens a pleasing melancholy. But this is not what we want. 'The complaining millions of men Darken in labour and pain'— what they want is something to *animate* and *ennoble* them."

If Arnold's poetry reveals, primarily, a series of tentative answers to the Victorian question of how to live in an age of transition, it also reveals a series of inner conflicts within the man himself. When he asked, what am I—what is my true nature? and what should I be or do? he came to various and opposing conclusions. Should he be a critic and thinker or a poet? Should he try to "solve the Universe," as Clough was trying to do, or should he be a sensitive observer of life, especially of natural beauty? If the latter is the unhesitating choice of "The Scholar-Gipsy," the two are nearly balanced in the juxtaposition of Goethe and Wordsworth in "Memorial Verses." Sometimes the conflict is between a life of action and achievement in the world (Arnold became private secretary to Lord Lansdowne in 1847 and was strongly attracted toward a social and political career), and on the other hand the rejection of personal ambition for the contemplative existence of a poet or the detached resignation of a Stoic. Finally, there is the "pagan" desire for passionate and sensuous experience, and at the same time the "Christian" desire for moral control and moral aspiration. Though the former is given positive approval in the Byron of "Memorial Verses" and the latter in "The Better Part" and "In Harmony with Nature," the conflict of the two appears in "Morality" and is suggested in "The Forsaken Merman."

In the face of these tensions, the insistent desire of Arnold's early years was to discover what he calls his "buried life," his "genuine self." Which of these attitudes was his own "line"? And in particular, if his vocation was to be an inspector of schools (which he became in 1851) and an official observer of education in France and Germany, should his avocation be poetry or criticism? In the event, he decided—or was forced by the pressure of the time and the influence of his father to decide—in favor of criticism. After publishing three volumes of verse between 1849 and 1853, he ceased to write poetry, except occasionally; and in 1857, when he was elected Professor of Poetry at Oxford, he began his career as Victorian critic, not only of literature (in two volumes of *Essays in Criticism,* 1865 and 1888) but also of society and politics (in *Culture and Anarchy,* 1869) and of religion (in *Literature and Dogma,* 1873). But the dividing lines are loose and the divisions somewhat arbitrary, because almost everywhere Arnold's attention is centered on the contemporary situation. What is wrong with Victorian life? and what can be done about it?

This focus is apparent in his theory, as well as in his practice, of poetry. It is true that the principles laid down in the preface to the 1853 *Poems* are classical: the insistence on organic structure and the subordination of the parts to the whole, the rejection of subjective analysis for an objective story, and the choice of ancient rather than of modern subjects. But to think of the essay as a classical protest against Romanticism is to pick it up by the wrong handle. Its basic motivation was the desire to provide an age of "spiritual discomfort" with a poetry that would "inspirit and rejoice"; and to *that* end modern subjects and introspective analyses, both of which could only increase one's depression, are rejected, and the right focus of poetry is said to be "some noble action of a heroic time" in which no incidental beauties of imagery will distract the reader's attention and so "impair the grandiose effect of the whole." This is the theory on which "Sohrab and Rustum" was conceived and written. But most of Arnold's poems are more representative of his later critical position, which found that poetry interpreted life in two ways—"by expressing with magical felicity the physiognomy and movement of the outward world [of nature], and . . . by expressing, with inspired conviction, the ideas and laws of the inward

world of man's moral and spiritual nature." In both ways, he says, "it *reconciles* him [man] with himself and the universe." In the former it does so through the calming effect of natural beauty (cf. "The Scholar-Gipsy"); in the latter by the inspiration not only of heroic action but also of moral statement or injunction (cf. such poems as "Quiet Work" and "Self-Dependence").

For the most part, however, Arnold's criticism is social rather than literary. As he studied the men he met in London society and provincial towns, he felt the narrow and limited character of their humanity. They were "incomplete and mutilated men." They had developed one side of human nature, "the obligation of duty, self-control, and work," at the expense of a rounded development which would find room for the aesthetic and especially the intellectual sides of human nature. He traced this fragmentary emphasis to the practical bias of the English temper, to the political spirit of an age of reform driving too quickly at immediate action and adopting too rigidly a particular program, to the tendency of a commercial society to measure value in terms of utility (and therefore to disparage philosophy and literature as useless), and above all to the Puritan tradition, strong in the middle class, and requickened by Evangelicalism, with its suspicion of the arts and its paramount stress on moral conduct. As a result he found a widespread indifference to ideas as such, to what he called "the whole life of intelligence"; and a serious lack of critical minds sufficiently balanced and flexible to explore all sides of a problem, and sufficiently educated to bring to bear on it the wisdom of the past. Furthermore, Arnold was disturbed by the absence of any intellectual authority. Indeed, the very conception of intellectual standards of value had almost disappeared in an age that carried the worship of liberty and individuality to the point of saying that everyone should be free to believe whatever he thought best. As Newman put it, sarcastically, "free discussion and fallible judgment are prized as the birthright of each individual."

Implicit in this analysis of what was wrong with Victorian life is Arnold's counterplea for Culture. He uses the term broadly, and somewhat loosely, to cover the three things he felt that his time, and the middle class in particular, most needed. One was the harmonious development of human nature so that "beauty and intelligence" would find their rightful place side by side with the moral will. Since the latter, though the most important, was now so exclusively cultivated (Carlyle, he said, was bringing coals to Newcastle), Arnold called for Sweetness and Light. Especially Light. The pursuit of Culture also means, in the second place, the pursuit of intelligence, for which he coined another famous epithet, Hellenism, the better to oppose it to the sole concern of

Hebraism with morality. The intelligent mind, that is, the critical mind or the cultured mind, has all the intellectual virtues so lacking in Victorian society: detachment, flexibility, openness, patience. And it has available, for comparison and contrast with any one idea it is examining, the best that has been thought and known about all the great questions of human knowledge. It is the liberal mind liberally educated.

Finally, such a mind, whether judging books as a critic or judging what is best and wisest to believe or to do as a man, has before it "a high and perfect ideal," a standard of perfection far higher and more authoritative than private judgment. But what standard? And how is it discovered? The standard, as Arnold keeps repeating, is "things as they are": the critic must "see the object as in itself it really is"; the man of culture must "see things as they really are." Arnold did not mean by this, except occasionally, what a scientist would mean or a historian. He did not mean anything which could be observed. On the contrary he meant "a knowledge of the universal order which seems to be intended and aimed at in the world"; and not a natural but a supranatural order. Things as they are means as they are in the Platonic world of ideas (the phrase, indeed, is a quotation from Plato); or it means, in Christian terms, as they are in the mind of God ("to see things as they are," Arnold says, is to learn "the will of God"). It was Arnold's faith not only that such a higher order was real, but that the cultured mind could perceive it by the power of what he calls Right Reason, or sometimes Imaginative Reason. This, of course, was not the reason of the scientist or the logician, but neither was it the intuition of a mystic. It was available to all men of wide observation and learning who practiced the intellectual virtues. It was simply the insight of an educated mind, able to do on a higher and more complex level what a sailor, for example, from long experience on the sea can do on a lower level. Where the common sense of the latter can judge the weather with remarkable accuracy, so the Imaginative Reason of the former can judge the wisest course of action for men to follow at a particular time, and even beyond that, in any time. One does not have to accept the ontological, or objective, validity of a higher universal order to agree with Arnold that the more intelligent a man is, the more clearly he "sees" and the more wisely, other things being equal, he acts. Arnold belongs, in this respect, with Mill and Newman. In their several ways those three men were the great champions of "the whole life of intelligence" in an age too dominated by the contrary forces of business and Puritanism.

A collected edition of Arnold's work has been published in 15 vols. (1903–1904). C. B. Tinker and H. F. Lowry have edited the definitive text of the *Poetical Works* (1950). There is a good selection of both the poetry and prose, edited by Lionel Trilling, in The Portable Library (Viking Press, 1949). The best critical study is Trilling's *Matthew Arnold* (1939). *The Poetry of Matthew Arnold. A Commentary* by Tinker and Lowry (1940) is a valuable handbook.

Matthew Arnold

QUIET WORK

One lesson, Nature, let me learn of thee,
One lesson that in every wind is blown,
One lesson of two duties kept at one,
Though the loud world proclaim their enmity—

Of toil unsevered from tranquillity!   5
Of labor, that in lasting fruit outgrows
Far noisier schemes, accomplished in repose,
Too great for haste, too high for rivalry!

Yes, while on earth a thousand discords ring,
Man's fitful uproar mingling with his toil,   10
Still do thy sleepless ministers move on,

Their glorious tasks in silence perfecting;
Still working, blaming still our vain turmoil,
Laborers that shall not fail, when man is gone.

TO A FRIEND[1]

Who prop, thou ask'st, in these bad days, my mind?—
He much, the old man,[2] who, clearest-souled of men,
Saw The Wide Prospect,[3] and the Asian Fen,[4]
And Tmolus hill, and Smyrna bay,[5] though blind.

Much he,[6] whose friendship I not long since won,   5
That halting slave, who in Nicopolis

---

[1] Probably Clough.
[2] Homer.
[3] Arnold explains that this phrase is a literal translation of the Greek word Europe, and suggests that it described the appearance of the European coast as seen by the Greeks from Asia Minor.
[4] "The name Asia, again, comes, it has been thought, from the muddy fens of the rivers of Asia Minor." (Arnold)
[5] A mountain and a seaport in Asia Minor.
[6] Epictetus, the Stoic philosopher (60?–140?).

Taught Arrian, when Vespasian's brutal son
Cleared Rome of what most shamed him.[7] But be his[8]

My special thanks, whose even-balanced soul,
From first youth tested up to extreme old age,   10
Business could not make dull, nor passion wild;

Who saw life steadily, and saw it whole;[9]
The mellow glory of the Attic stage,
Singer of sweet Colonus,[10] and its child.[11]

SHAKESPEARE

Others abide our question. Thou art free.
We ask and ask—Thou smilest and art still,
Out-topping knowledge. For the loftiest hill,
Who to the stars uncrowns his majesty,

Planting his steadfast footsteps in the sea,   5
Making the heaven of heavens his dwelling-place,
Spares but the cloudy border of his base
To the foiled searching of mortality;

And thou, who didst the stars and sunbeams know,
Self-schooled, self-scanned, self-honored, self-secure,   10
Didst tread on earth unguessed at.—Better so!

All pains the immortal spirit must endure,
All weakness which impairs, all griefs which bow,
Find their sole speech in that victorious brow.

IN HARMONY WITH NATURE

TO A PREACHER

"In harmony with Nature"? Restless fool,
Who with such heat dost preach what were to thee,
When true, the last impossibility—
To be like Nature strong, like Nature cool!

Know, man hath all which Nature hath, but more,   5
And in that *more* lie all his hopes of good.
Nature is cruel, man is sick of blood;
Nature is stubborn, man would fain adore;

Nature is fickle, man hath need of rest;
Nature forgives no debt, and fears no grave;[12]   10
Man would be mild, and with safe conscience blest.

Man must begin, know this, where Nature ends;
Nature and man can never be fast friends.
Fool, if thou canst not pass her, rest her slave!

THE FORSAKEN MERMAN

Come, dear children, let us away;
Down and away below!
Now my brothers call from the bay,
Now the great winds shoreward blow,
Now the salt tides seaward flow;
Now the wild white horses play,
Champ and chafe and toss in the spray.
Children dear, let us away!
This way, this way!

Call her once before you go—   10
Call once yet!
In a voice that she will know:
"Margaret! Margaret!"
Children's voices should be dear
(Call once more) to a mother's ear;   15
Children's voices, wild with pain—
Surely she will come again!
Call her once and come away;
This way, this way!
"Mother dear, we cannot stay!   20
The wild white horses foam and fret."
Margaret! Margaret!

Come, dear children, come away down;
Call no more!
One last look at the white-walled town,   25
And the little grey church on the windy shore;
Then come down!
She will not come though you call all day;
Come away, come away!

Children dear, was it yesterday   30
We heard the sweet bells over the bay?
In the caverns where we lay,
Through the surf and through the swell,
The far-off sound of a silver bell?
Sand-strewn caverns, cool and deep,   35
Where the winds are all asleep;

----

7 Who taught Arrian, the Greek historian, in Nicopolis in Greece
after the Emperor Domitian, shamed by philosophy, drove
Epictetus out of Rome.   8 Sophocles.
9 As a whole, coherently, not in fragments.
10 In his *Oedipus at Colonus*.
11 He was born at Colonus near Athens.

12 Cf. lines 7–10 with Nature in Tennyson's *In Memoriam*, No. 56,
p. 667, above.

Where the spent lights quiver and gleam,
Where the salt weed sways in the stream,
Where the sea-beasts, ranged all round,
Feed in the ooze of their pasture-ground; 40
Where the sea-snakes coil and twine,
Dry their mail and bask in the brine;
Where great whales come sailing by,
Sail and sail, with unshut eye,
Round the world for ever and aye? 45
When did music come this way?
Children dear, was it yesterday?

Children dear, was it yesterday
(Call yet once) that she went away?
Once she sate with you and me, 50
On a red gold throne in the heart of the sea,
And the youngest sate on her knee.
She combed its bright hair, and she tended it well,
When down swung the sound of a far-off bell.
She sighed, she looked up through the clear green sea; 55
She said: "I must go, for my kinsfolk pray
In the little grey church on the shore to-day.
'Twill be Easter-time in the world—ah me!
And I lose my poor soul, Merman, here with thee."
I said: "Go up, dear heart, through the waves; 60
Say thy prayer, and come back to the kind sea-caves."
She smiled, she went up through the surf in the bay.
Children dear, was it yesterday?

Children dear, were we long alone?
"The sea grows stormy, the little ones moan; 65
Long prayers," I said, "in the world they say;
Come!" I said; and we rose through the surf in the bay.
We went up the beach, by the sandy down
Where the sea-stocks bloom, to the white-walled town;
Through the narrow paved streets, where all was still, 70
To the little grey church on the windy hill.
From the church came a murmur of folk at their
    prayers,
But we stood without in the cold blowing airs.
We climbed on the graves, on the stones worn with
    rains,
And we gazed up the aisle through the small leaded
    panes. 75
She sate by the pillar; we saw her clear:
"Margaret, hist! come quick, we are here!
Dear heart," I said, "we are long alone;
The sea grows stormy, the little ones moan."
But, ah, she gave me never a look, 80
For her eyes were sealed to the holy book!
Loud prays the priest; shut stands the door.
Come away, children, call no more!
Come away, come down, call no more!

Down, down, down! 85
Down to the depths of the sea!
She sits at her wheel in the humming town,
Singing most joyfully.
Hark, what she sings: "O joy, O joy,
For the humming street, and the child with its toy! 90
For the priest, and the bell,[1] and the holy well;[2]
For the wheel where I spun,
And the blessed light of the sun!"
And so she sings her fill,
Singing most joyfully, 95
Till the spindle drops from her hand,
And the whizzing wheel stands still.
She steals to the window, and looks at the sand,
And over the sand at the sea;
And her eyes are set in a stare; 100
And anon there breaks a sigh,
And anon there drops a tear,
From a sorrow-clouded eye,
And a heart sorrow-laden,
A long, long sigh; 105
For the cold strange eyes of a little Mermaiden
And the gleam of her golden hair.

Come away, away children;
Come children, come down!
The hoarse wind blows coldly; 110
Lights shine in the town.
She will start from her slumber
When gusts shake the door;
She will hear the winds howling,
Will hear the waves roar. 115
We shall see, while above us
The waves roar and whirl,
A ceiling of amber,
A pavement of pearl.
Singing, "Here came a mortal, 120
But faithless was she!
And alone dwell for ever
The kings of the sea."

But, children, at midnight,
When soft the winds blow, 125
When clear falls the moonlight,
When spring-tides are low;
When sweet airs come seaward
From heaths starred with broom,
And high rocks throw mildly 130
On the blanched sands a gloom;
Up the still, glistening beaches,

---

[1] The bell that is rung at the consecration of the bread and the wine in the Mass.   [2] The font where holy water is kept.

Up the creeks we will hie,
Over banks of bright seaweed
The ebb-tide leaves dry.   135
We will gaze, from the sand-hills,
At the white, sleeping town;
At the church on the hill-side—
And then come back down.
Singing, "There dwells a loved one,   140
But cruel is she!
She left lonely for ever
The kings of the sea."[3]

MEMORIAL VERSES

APRIL, 1850

Goethe in Weimar sleeps, and Greece,
Long since, saw Byron's struggle cease.[4]
But one such death remained to come;
The last poetic voice is dumb—
We stand today by Wordsworth's tomb.   5

When Byron's eyes were shut in death,
We bowed our head and held our breath.
He taught us little; but our soul
Had *felt* him like the thunder's roll.
With shivering heart the strife we saw   10
Of passion with eternal law;
And yet with reverential awe
We watched the fount of fiery life
Which served for that Titanic strife.

When Goethe's death was told, we said: 15
Sunk, then, is Europe's sagest head.
Physician of the iron age,[5]
Goethe has done his pilgrimage.
He took the suffering human race,
He read each wound, each weakness clear,   20
And struck his finger on the place,
And said: *Thou ailest here, and here!*
He looked on Europe's dying hour[6]

Of fitful dream and feverish power;
His eye plunged down the weltering strife,   25
The turmoil of expiring life—
He said: *The end is everywhere;*
Art still has truth, take refuge there!
And he was happy, if to know
Causes of things, and far below   30
His feet to see the lurid flow
Of terror, and insane distress,
And headlong fate, be happiness.[7]

And Wordsworth!—Ah, pale ghosts, rejoice!
For never has such soothing voice   35
Been to your shadowy world conveyed,
Since erst, at morn, some wandering shade
Heard the clear song of Orpheus come
Through Hades, and the mournful gloom.[8]
Wordsworth has gone from us—and ye,   40
Ah, may ye feel his voice as we!
He too upon a wintry clime
Had fallen—on this iron time
Of doubts, disputes, distractions, fears.
He found us when the age had bound   45
Our souls in its benumbing round;
He spoke, and loosed our heart in tears.
He laid us as we lay at birth
On the cool flowery lap of earth,
Smiles broke from us and we had ease;   50
The hills were round us, and the breeze
Went o'er the sun-lit fields again;
Our foreheads felt the wind and rain.
Our youth returned; for there was shed
On spirits that had long been dead,   55
Spirits dried up and closely furled,
The freshness of the early world.

Ah! since dark days still bring to light
Man's prudence and man's fiery might,
Time may restore us in his course   60
Goethe's sage mind and Byron's force;
But where will Europe's latter hour
Again find Wordsworth's healing power?

---

[3] Is this poem an allegory of Protestantism and the disciplined life of work (in plain whites and grays) vs. Paganism and the sensuous life of nature (in reds and golds)? If it is, it is also a supernatural poem on Coleridge's formula (see p. 118), where just enough reality is injected into a world of faery fantasy to procure our "willing suspension of disbelief." For the reality, cf. the two poems to Marguerite, p. 740, below.

[4] Goethe died at Weimar in 1832, Byron in Greece in 1824.

[5] The age of war and revolution, political and intellectual (1789–1832). Cf. the further definition of iron time in lines 43–44. Both Arnold and Carlyle viewed Goethe as the perfect type of the artist as prophet (hence, "physician").

[6] Cf. the General Introduction, p. 367.

[7] These lines are a paraphrase of Vergil (*Georgics*, II, 490 ff.). Arnold expects the reader not only to recognize them as such but to remember the context, where the poet "who hath availed to know the causes of things, and hath laid all fears and immitigable Fate and the roar of hungry Acheron under his feet" is contrasted with the poet who turns away from the problems and discords of society to live content by "stream and woodland" (Mackail's translation). Since the latter is clearly the poet (Wordsworth) of the next verse paragraph, the lines carry an extra suggestion which makes them transitional.

[8] On the occasion when Orpheus sang for Pluto, god of the underworld, in return for which Pluto agreed to give him back his wife, Eurydice.

Others will teach us how to dare,
And against fear our breast to steel; 65
Others will strengthen us to bear—
But who, ah! who, will make us feel?
The cloud of mortal destiny,
Others will front it fearlessly—
But who, like him, will put it by? 70

Keep fresh the grass upon his grave,
O Rotha,[9] with thy living wave!
Sing him thy best! for few or none
Hears thy voice right, now he is gone.

SELF-DEPENDENCE

Weary of myself, and sick of asking
What I am, and what I ought to be,
At this vessel's prow I stand, which bears me
Forwards, forwards, o'er the starlit sea.

And a look of passionate desire
O'er the sea and to the stars I send: 5
"Ye who from my childhood up have calmed me,
Calm me, ah, compose me to the end!

"Ah, once more," I cried, "ye stars, ye waters,
On my heart your mighty charm renew; 10
Still, still let me, as I gaze upon you,
Feel my soul becoming vast like you!"

From the intense, clear, star-sown vault of heaven,
Over the lit sea's unquiet way,
In the rustling night-air came the answer: 15
"Wouldst thou be as these are? Live as they.[10]

"Unaffrighted by the silence round them,
Undistracted by the sights they see,
These demand not that the things without them
Yield them love, amusement, sympathy. 20

"And with joy the stars perform their shining,
And the sea its long moon-silvered roll;
For self-poised they live, nor pine with noting
All the fever of some differing soul.

"Bounded by themselves, and unregardful 25
In what state God's other works may be,

---

[9] Stream near Grasmere, where Wordsworth was buried.
[10] This line is a criticism of Arnold's previous attitude (in lines 9–12), where his appreciation of the stars was merely aesthetic, for their sublime beauty alone, without regard to their moral lesson of how to live.

In their own tasks all their powers pouring,
These attain the mighty life you see."

O air-born voice! long since, severely clear,
A cry like thine in mine own heart I hear: 30
"Resolve to be thyself; and know, that he,
Who finds himself, loses his misery!"

A SUMMER NIGHT

In the deserted moon-blanched street,
How lonely rings the echo of my feet!
Those windows, which I gaze at, frown,
Silent and white, unopening down,
Repellent as the world;—but see, 5
A break between the housetops shows
The moon! and, lost behind her, fading dim
Into the dewy dark obscurity
Down at the far horizon's rim,
Doth a whole tract of heaven disclose! 10

And to my mind the thought
Is on a sudden brought
Of a past night, and a far different scene.
Headlands stood out into the moon-lit deep
As clearly as at noon; 15
The spring-tide's brimming flow
Heaved dazzlingly between;
Houses, with long white sweep,
Girdled the glistening bay;
Behind, through the soft air, 20
The blue haze-cradled mountains spread away.
That night was far more fair—
But the same restless pacings to and fro,
And the same vainly throbbing heart was there,
And the same bright, calm moon. 25

And the calm moonlight seems to say:
Hast thou then still the old unquiet breast,
That neither deadens into rest,
Nor ever feels the fiery glow
That whirls the spirit from itself away, 30
But fluctuates to and fro,
Never by passion quite possessed,
And never quite benumbed by the world's sway?—
And I, I know not if to pray
Still to be what I am, or yield and be 35
Like all the other men I see.

For most men in a brazen prison live,
Where, in the sun's hot eye,
With heads bent o'er their toil, they languidly
Their lives to some unmeaning taskwork give, 40

Dreaming of nought beyond their prison-wall.
And as, year after year,
Fresh products of their barren labour fall
From their tired hands, and rest
Never yet comes more near,   45
Gloom settles slowly down over their breast;
And while they try to stem
The waves of mournful thought by which they are prest,
Death in their prison reaches them,
Unfreed, having seen nothing, still unblest.   50

And the rest, a few,
Escape their prison and depart
On the wide ocean of life anew.
There the freed prisoner, where'er his heart
Listeth, will sail;   55
Nor does he know how there prevail,
Despotic on that sea,
Trade-winds which cross it from eternity.[1]
Awhile he holds some false way, undebarred
By thwarting signs, and braves   60
The freshening wind and blackening waves.
And then the tempest strikes him; and between
The lightning-bursts is seen
Only a driving wreck,
And the pale master on his spar-strewn deck   65
With anguished face and flying hair
Grasping the rudder hard,
Still bent to make some port he knows not where,
Still standing for some false, impossible shore.
And sterner comes the roar   70
Of sea and wind, and through the deepening gloom
Fainter and fainter wreck and helmsman loom,
And he too disappears, and comes no more.

Is there no life, but these alone?
Madman or slave, must man be one?[2]   75

Plainness and clearness without shadow of stain!
Clearness divine!
Ye heavens, whose pure dark regions have no sign
Of languor, though so calm, and, though so great,
Are yet untroubled and unpassionate;   80
Who, though so noble, share in the world's toil,
And, though so tasked, keep free from dust and soil![3]
I will not say that your mild deeps retain
A tinge, it may be, of their silent pain

Who have longed deeply once, and longed in vain—[4]   85
But I will rather say that you remain
A world above man's head, to let him see
How boundless might his soul's horizons be,
How vast, yet of what clear transparency!
How it were good to abide there, and breathe free;   90
How fair a lot to fill
Is left to each man still!

THE BURIED LIFE

Light flows our war of mocking words, and yet,
Behold, with tears mine eyes are wet!
I feel a nameless sadness o'er me roll.
Yes, yes, we know that we can jest,
We know, we know that we can smile!   5
But there's a something in this breast,
To which thy light words bring no rest,
And thy gay smiles no anodyne.
Give me thy hand, and hush awhile,
And turn those limpid eyes on mine,   10
And let me read there, love! thy inmost soul.

Alas! is even love too weak
To unlock the heart, and let it speak?
Are even lovers powerless to reveal
To one another what indeed they feel?   15
I knew the mass of men concealed
Their thoughts, for fear that if revealed
They would by other men be met
With blank indifference, or with blame reproved;
I knew they lived and moved   20
Tricked in disguises, alien to the rest
Of men, and alien to themselves—and yet
The same heart beats in every human breast!

But we, my love!—doth a like spell benumb
Our hearts, our voices?—must we too be dumb?   25

Ah, well for us, if even we,
Even for a moment, can get free
Our heart, and have our lips unchained;
For that which seals them hath been deep-ordained!

Fate, which foresaw   30
How frivolous a baby man would be—
By what distractions he would be possessed,
How he would pour himself in every strife,
And well-nigh change his own identity—

[1] Moral laws which he ignores at his peril.
[2] The slave of lines 37–50 or the madman of lines 51–73.
[3] Cf. the last two stanzas of "Self-Dependence." Each passage helps to illuminate the other.

[4] This is an aside. What Arnold wants to say follows in lines 86–92. But he feels, from his own experience, that the stoical attitude of the stars is partly a refuge from disappointed hopes.

That it might keep from his capricious play   35
His genuine self, and force him to obey
Even in his own despite his being's law,
Bade through the deep recesses of our breast
The unregarded river of our life
Pursue with indiscernible flow its way;   40
And that we should not see
The buried stream, and seem to be
Eddying at large in blind uncertainty,
Though driving on with it eternally.

But often, in the world's most crowded streets,   45
But often, in the din of strife,
There rises an unspeakable desire
After the knowledge of our buried life;
A thirst to spend our fire and restless force
In tracking out our true, original course;   50
A longing to inquire
Into the mystery of this heart which beats
So wild, so deep in us—to know
Whence our lives come and where they go.
And many a man in his own breast then delves,   55
But deep enough, alas! none ever mines.
And we have been on many thousand lines,
And we have shown, on each, spirit and power;
But hardly have we, for one little hour,
Been on our own line, have we been ourselves—[5]   60
Hardly had skill to utter one of all
The nameless feelings that course through our breast,
But they course on for ever unexpressed.
And long we try in vain to speak and act
Our hidden self, and what we say and do   65
Is eloquent, is well—but 'tis not true!
And then we will no more be racked
With inward striving, and demand
Of all the thousand nothings of the hour
Their stupefying power;[6]   70
Ah yes, and they benumb us at our call!
Yet still, from time to time, vague and forlorn,
From the soul's subterranean depth upborne
As from an infinitely distant land,
Come airs, and floating echoes, and convey   75
A melancholy into all our day.

Only—but this is rare—
When a belovèd hand is laid in ours,
When, jaded with the rush and glare
Of the interminable hours,   80
Our eyes can in another's eyes read clear,

When our world-deafened ear
Is by the tones of a loved voice caressed—
A bolt is shot back somewhere in our breast,
And a lost pulse of feeling stirs again.   85
The eye sinks inward, and the heart lies plain,
And what we mean, we say, and what we would, we
    know.
A man becomes aware of his life's flow,
And hears its winding murmur; and he sees
The meadows where it glides, the sun, the breeze.   90

And there arrives a lull in the hot race
Wherein he doth for ever chase
That flying and elusive shadow, rest.
An air of coolness plays upon his face,
And an unwonted calm pervades his breast.   95
And then he thinks he knows
The hills where his life rose,
And the sea where it goes.

MORALITY

We cannot kindle when we will
The fire which in the heart resides;
The spirit bloweth and is still,
In mystery our soul abides.
    But tasks in hours of insight willed,   5
    Can be through hours of gloom fulfilled.

With aching hands and bleeding feet
We dig and heap, lay stone on stone;
We bear the burden and the heat
Of the long day, and wish 'twere done.   10
    Not till the hours of light return,
    All we have built do we discern.

Then, when the clouds are off the soul,
When thou dost bask in Nature's eye,
Ask, how *she* viewed thy self-control,   15
Thy struggling, tasked morality—
    Nature, whose free, light, cheerful air,
    Oft made thee, in thy gloom, despair.

And she, whose censure thou dost dread,
Whose eyes thou wast afraid to seek,   20
See, on her face a glow is spread,
A strong emotion on her cheek!
    "Ah, child," she cries, "that strife divine,
    Whence was it, for it is not mine?

"There is no effort on *my* brow—   25
I do not strive, I do not weep:

---

[5] Cf. the last lines of "Self-Dependence."
[6] Their power to deaden or numb the pain of "inward striving."

I rush with the swift spheres and glow
In joy, and when I will, I sleep.[7]
    Yet that severe, that earnest air,
    I saw, I felt it once—but where?   30

"I knew not yet the gauge of time,
Nor wore the manacles of space;
I felt it in some other clime,
I saw it in some other place.
    'Twas when the heavenly house I trod,   35
    And lay upon the breast of God."[8]

SOHRAB AND RUSTUM

AN EPISODE

And the first gray of morning filled the east,
And the fog rose out of the Oxus stream.[1]
But all the Tartar camp along the stream
Was hushed, and still the men were plunged in sleep;
Sohrab alone, he slept not:[2] all night long   5
He had lain wakeful, tossing on his bed;
But when the gray dawn stole into his tent,
He rose, and clad himself, and girt his sword,
And took his horseman's cloak, and left his tent,
And went abroad into the cold wet fog,   10
Through the dim camp to Peran-Wisa's[3] tent.

    Through the black Tartar tents he passed, which stood
Clustering like bee-hives on the low flat strand
Of Oxus, where the summer-floods o'erflow
When the sun melts the snows in high Pamere:[4]   15
Through the black tents he passed, o'er that low strand,
And to a hillock came, a little back
From the stream's brink—the spot where first a boat,
Crossing the stream in summer, scrapes the land.
The men of former times had crowned the top   20
With a clay fort; but that was fall'n, and now
The Tartars built there Peran-Wisa's tent,
A dome of laths, and o'er it felts were spread.

And Sohrab came there, and went in, and stood
Upon the thick piled[5] carpets in the tent,   25
And found the old man sleeping on his bed
Of rugs and felts, and near him lay his arms.
And Peran-Wisa heard him, though the step
Was dulled; for he slept light, an old man's sleep;
And he rose quickly on one arm, and said:—   30
    "Who art thou? for it is not yet clear dawn.
Speak! is there news, or any night alarm?"
    But Sohrab came to the bedside, and said:—
"Thou know'st me, Peran-Wisa! it is I.
The sun is not yet risen, and the foe   35
Sleep; but I sleep not; all night long I lie
Tossing and wakeful, and I come to thee.
For so did King Afrasiab bid me seek
Thy counsel, and to heed thee as thy son,
In Samarcand, before the army marched;   40
And I will tell thee what my heart desires.
Thou know'st if, since from Ader-baijan[6] first
I came among the Tartars and bore arms,
I have still served Afrasiab well, and shown,
At my boy's years, the courage of a man.   45
This too thou know'st, that, while I still bear on
The conquering Tartar ensigns through the world,
And beat the Persians back on every field,
I seek one man, one man, and one alone—
Rustum, my father; who I hoped should greet,   50
Should one day greet, upon some well-fought field
His not unworthy, not inglorious son.
So I long hoped, but him I never find.
Come then, hear now, and grant me what I ask.
Let the two armies rest to-day: but I   55
Will challenge forth the bravest Persian lords
To meet me, man to man: if I prevail,
Rustum will surely hear it; if I fall—
Old man, the dead need no one, claim no kin.
Dim is the rumor of a common fight,   60
Where host meets host, and many names are sunk;
But of a single combat fame speaks clear."
    He spoke; and Peran-Wisa took the hand
Of the young man in his, and sighed, and said:—
    "O Sohrab, an unquiet heart is thine!   65
Canst thou not rest among the Tartar chiefs,
And share the battle's common chance with us
Who love thee, but must press for ever first,
In single fight incurring single risk,
To find a father thou hast never seen?   70
That were far best, my son, to stay with us
Unmurmuring; in our tents, while it is war,
And when 'tis truce, then in Afrasiab's towns.

---

[7] Nature symbolizes a nonmoral life of rich and varied experience, free from the struggle to discipline the moral will to a life of concentrated work. (Cf. the life of the poet which Arnold once set out to live and his life as an inspector of schools, fulfilled in many hours of gloom, though the latter came later, after the poem was written.)

[8] Before the creation (hence lines 31–32). Nature as well as Morality is divine in origin, but the moral life is the higher, closer to God. The poem brings out the cost involved (both the joy lost, and the pain endured) of choosing the latter.

[1] A great river in central Asia.

[2] Although a Persian by birth, Sohrab has taken service under Afrasiab, king of the Tartars.

[3] The general of the Tartar army.

[4] Plateau in central Asia.

[5] Heavy-napped.

[6] Province in northwestern Persia where Sohrab's mother lived (cf. line 590).

But, if this one desire indeed rules all,
To seek out Rustum—seek him not through fight!   75
Seek him in peace, and carry to his arms,
O Sohrab, carry an unwounded son!
But far hence seek him, for he is not here.
For now it is not as when I was young,
When Rustum was in front of every fray;   80
But now he keeps apart, and sits at home,
In Seistan,[7] with Zal, his father old.
Whether that his own mighty strength at last
Feels the abhorred approaches of old age,
Or in some quarrel with the Persian King.   85
There go!—Thou wilt not? Yet my heart forebodes
Danger or death awaits thee on this field.
Fain would I know thee safe and well, though lost
To us; fain therefore send thee hence, in peace
To seek thy father, not seek single fights   90
In vain:—but who can keep the lion's cub
From ravening, and who govern Rustum's son?
Go, I will grant thee what thy heart desires."

So said he, and dropped Sohrab's hand, and left
His bed, and the warm rugs whereon he lay;   95
And o'er his chilly limbs his woollen coat
He passed, and tied his sandals on his feet,
And threw a white cloak round him, and he took
In his right hand a ruler's staff, no sword;
And on his head he set his sheep-skin cap,   100
Black, glossy, curled, the fleece of Kara-Kul;[8]
And raised the curtain of his tent, and called
His herald to his side, and went abroad.

The sun by this had risen, and cleared the fog
From the broad Oxus and the glittering sands.   105
And from their tents the Tartar horsemen filed
Into the open plain; so Haman bade—
Haman, who next to Peran-Wisa ruled
The host, and still was in his lusty prime.
From their black tents, long files of horse, they
          streamed: 110
As when some gray November morn the files,
In marching order spread, of long-necked cranes
Stream over Casbin and the southern slopes
Of Elburz, from the Aralian estuaries,
Or some frore[9] Caspian reed-bed, southward bound   115
For the warm Persian sea-board—so they streamed.
The Tartars of the Oxus, the King's guard,
First, with black sheep-skin caps and with long spears;
Large men, large steeds; who from Bokhara come
And Khiva, and ferment the milk of mares.   120
Next the more temperate Toorkmuns of the south,

The Tukas, and the lances of Salore,
And those from Attruck and the Caspian sands;
Light men and on light steeds, who only drink
The acrid milk of camels, and their wells.   125
And then a swarm of wandering horse, who came
From far, and a more doubtful service owned;
The Tartars of Ferghana, from the banks
Of the Jaxartes, men with scanty beards
And close-set skull-caps; and those wilder hordes   130
Who roam o'er Kipchak and the northern waste,
Kalmucks and unkempt Kuzzaks, tribes who stray
Nearest the Pole, and wandering Kirghizzes,
Who come on shaggy ponies from Pamere;
These all filed out from camp into the plain.   135
And on the other side the Persians formed:
First a light cloud of horse, Tartars they seemed,
The Ilyats of Khorassan: and behind,
The royal troops of Persia, horse and foot,
Marshalled battalions bright in burnished steel.   140
But Peran-Wisa with his herald came,
Threading the Tartar squadrons to the front,
And with his staff kept back the foremost ranks.
And when Ferood, who led the Persians, saw
That Peran-Wisa kept the Tartars back,   145
He took his spear, and to the front he came,
And checked his ranks, and fixed them where they stood.
And the old Tartar came upon the sand
Betwixt the silent hosts, and spake, and said:—

"Ferood, and ye, Persians and Tartars, hear!   150
Let there be truce between the hosts to-day.
But choose a champion from the Persian lords
To fight our champion Sohrab, man to man."

As, in the country, on a morn in June,
When the dew glistens on the pearlèd ears,   155
A shiver runs through the deep corn for joy—
So, when they heard what Peran-Wisa said,
A thrill through all the Tartar squadrons ran
Of pride and hope for Sohrab, whom they loved.

But as a troop of pedlars, from Cabool,   160
Cross underneath the Indian Caucasus,
That vast sky-neighboring mountain of milk snow;
Crossing so high, that, as they mount, they pass
Long flocks of travelling birds dead on the snow,
Choked by the air, and scarce can they themselves   165
Slake their parched throats with sugared mulberries—
In single file they move, and stop their breath,
For fear they should dislodge the o'er-hanging snows—
So the pale Persians held their breath with fear.

And to Ferood his brother chiefs came up   170
To counsel: Gudurz and Zoarrah came,
And Feraburz, who ruled the Persian host
Second, and was the uncle of the King;
These came and counselled, and then Gudurz said:—

---

[7] Region bordering on eastern Persia.
[8] Of karakul sheep, from the province of Bokhara.
[9] Frozen.

"Ferood, shame bids us take their challenge up, 175
Yet champion have we none to match this youth.
He has the wild stag's foot, the lion's heart.
But Rustum came last night; aloof he sits
And sullen, and has pitched his tents apart.
Him will I seek, and carry to his ear 180
The Tartar challenge, and this young man's name.
Haply he will forget his wrath, and fight.
Stand forth the while, and take their challenge up."

  So spake he; and Ferood stood forth and cried:—
"Old man, be it agreed as thou hast said! 185
Let Sohrab arm, and we will find a man."

  He spake; and Peran-Wisa turned, and strode
Back through the opening squadrons to his tent.
But through the anxious Persians Gudurz ran,
And crossed the camp which lay behind, and reached, 190
Out on the sands beyond it, Rustum's tents.
Of scarlet cloth they were, and glittering gay,
Just pitched: the high pavilion in the midst
Was Rustum's, and his men lay camped around.
And Gudurz entered Rustum's tent, and found 195
Rustum; his morning meal was done, but still
The table stood before him, charged with food—
A side of roasted sheep, and cakes of bread,
And dark green melons; and there Rustum sate
Listless, and held a falcon on his wrist, 200
And played with it; but Gudurz came and stood
Before him; and he looked, and saw him stand,
And with a cry sprang up, and dropped the bird,
And greeted Gudurz with both hands, and said:—

  "Welcome! these eyes could see no better sight. 205
What news? but sit down first, and eat and drink."

  But Gudurz stood in the tent-door, and said:—
"Not now! a time will come to eat and drink,
But not to-day; to-day has other needs.
The armies are drawn out, and stand at gaze; 210
For from the Tartars is a challenge brought
To pick a champion from the Persian lords
To fight their champion—and thou know'st his name—
Sohrab men call him, but his birth is hid.
O Rustum, like thy might is this young man's! 215
He has the wild stag's foot, the lion's heart;
And he is young, and Iran's[10] chiefs are old,
Or else too weak; and all eyes turn to thee.
Come down and help us, Rustum, or we lose!"

  He spoke: but Rustum answered with a smile:— 220
"Go to! if Iran's chiefs are old, then I
Am older; if the young are weak, the King
Errs strangely; for the King, for Kai-Khosroo,
Himself is young, and honors younger men,

_____
[10] Persia's.

And lets the agèd moulder to their graves. 225
Rustum he loves no more, but loves the young—
The young may rise at Sohrab's vaunts, not I.
For what care I, though all speak Sohrab's fame?
For would that I myself had such a son,
And not that one slight helpless girl I have— 230
A son so famed, so brave, to send to war,
And I to tarry with the snow-haired Zal,
My father, whom the robber Afghans vex,
And clip his borders short, and drive his herds,
And he has none to guard his weak old age. 235
There would I go, and hang my armor up,
And with my great name fence that weak old man,
And spend the goodly treasures I have got,
And rest my age, and hear of Sohrab's fame,
And leave to death the hosts of thankless kings, 240
And with these slaughterous hands draw sword no more."

  He spoke, and smiled; and Gudurz made reply:—
"What then, O Rustum, will men say to this,
When Sohrab dares our bravest forth, and seeks
Thee most of all, and thou, whom most he seeks, 245
Hidest thy face? Take heed, lest men should say:
'Like some old miser, Rustum hoards his fame,
And shuns to peril it with younger men.'"

  And, greatly moved, then Rustum made reply:—
"O Gudurz, wherefore dost thou say such words? 250
Thou knowest better words than this to say.
What is one more, one less, obscure or famed,
Valiant or craven, young or old, to me?
Are not they mortal, am not I myself?
But who for men of nought would do great deeds? 255
Come, thou shalt see how Rustum hoards his fame!
But I will fight unknown, and in plain arms;[11]
Let not men say of Rustum, he was matched
In single fight with any mortal man."

  He spoke, and frowned; and Gudurz turned, and
    ran 260
Back quickly through the camp in fear and joy—
Fear at his wrath, but joy that Rustum came.
But Rustum strode to his tent door, and called
His followers in, and bade them bring his arms,
And clad himself in steel: the arms he chose 265
Were plain, and on his shield was no device,
Only his helm was rich, inlaid with gold,
And from the fluted spine atop, a plume
Of horsehair waved, a scarlet horsehair plume.
So armed, he issued forth; and Ruksh, his horse, 270
Followed him like a faithful hound at heel—
Ruksh, whose renown was noised through all the earth,
The horse whom Rustum on a foray once
Did in Bokhara by the river find

_____
[11] Without the markings which would reveal his identity.

A colt beneath its dam, and drove him home,   275
And reared him; a bright bay, with lofty crest,
Dight[12] with a saddle-cloth of broidered green
Crusted with gold, and on the ground were worked
All beasts of chase, all beasts which hunters know.
So followed, Rustum left his tents, and crossed   280
The camp, and to the Persian host appeared.
And all the Persians knew him, and with shouts
Hailed; but the Tartars knew not who he was.
And dear as the wet diver to the eyes
Of his pale wife who waits and weeps on shore,   285
By sandy Bahrein, in the Persian Gulf,
Plunging all day into the blue waves, at night,
Having made up his tale of precious pearls,
Rejoins her in their hut upon the sands—
So dear to the pale Persians Rustum came.   290

  And Rustum to the Persian front advanced,
And Sohrab armed in Haman's tent, and came.
And as afield the reapers cut a swath
Down through the middle of a rich man's corn,
And on each side are squares of standing corn,   295
And in the midst a stubble, short and bare—
So on each side were squares of men, with spears
Bristling, and in the midst, the open sand.
And Rustum came upon the sand, and cast
His eyes toward the Tartar tents, and saw   300
Sohrab come forth, and eyed him as he came.

  As some rich woman, on a winter's morn,
Eyes through her silken curtains the poor drudge
Who with numb blackened fingers makes her fire—
At cock-crow, on a starlit winter's morn,   305
When the frost flowers the whitened window-panes—
And wonders how she lives, and what the thoughts
Of that poor drudge may be; so Rustum eyed
The unknown adventurous youth, who from afar
Came seeking Rustum, and defying forth   310
All the most valiant chiefs: long he perused
His spirited air, and wondered who he was.
For very young he seemed, tenderly reared;
Like some young cypress, tall, and dark, and straight,
Which in a queen's secluded garden throws   315
Its slight dark shadow on the moonlit turf,
By midnight, to a bubbling fountain's sound—
So slender Sohrab seemed, so softly reared.
And a deep pity entered Rustum's soul
As he beheld him coming; and he stood,   320
And beckoned to him with his hand, and said:—

  "O thou young man, the air of Heaven is soft,
And warm, and pleasant; but the grave is cold!
Heaven's air is better than the cold dead grave.

---

[12] Caparisoned.

Behold me! I am vast, and clad in iron,   325
And tried; and I have stood on many a field
Of blood, and I have fought with many a foe—
Never was that field lost, or that foe saved.
O Sohrab, wherefore wilt thou rush on death?
Be governed! quit the Tartar host, and come   330
To Iran, and be as my son to me,
And fight beneath my banner till I die!
There are no youths in Iran brave as thou."

  So he spake, mildly: Sohrab heard his voice,
The mighty voice of Rustum, and he saw   335
His giant figure planted on the sand,
Sole, like some single tower, which a chief
Has builded on the waste in former years
Against the robbers; and he saw that head,
Streaked with its first gray hairs;—hope filled his
                soul,   340
And he ran forward and embraced his knees,
And clasped his hand within his own, and said:—
  "O, by thy father's head! by thine own soul!
Art thou not Rustum? speak! art thou not he?"

  But Rustum eyed askance the kneeling youth,   345
And turned away, and spake to his own soul:—
  "Ah me, I muse what this young fox may mean!
False, wily, boastful, are these Tartar boys.
For if I now confess this thing he asks,
And hide it not, but say: Rustum is here!   350
He will not yield indeed, nor quit our foes,
But he will find some pretext not to fight,
And praise my fame, and proffer courteous gifts,
A belt or sword perhaps, and go his way.
And on a feast-tide, in Afrasiab's hall,   355
In Samarcand, he will arise and cry:
'I challenged once, when the two armies camped
Beside the Oxus, all the Persian lords
To cope with me in single fight; but they
Shrank, only Rustum dared; then he and I   360
Changed gifts, and went on equal terms away.'
So will he speak, perhaps, while men applaud;
Then were the chiefs of Iran shamed through me."

  And then he turned, and sternly spake aloud:—
"Rise! wherefore dost thou vainly question thus   365
Of Rustum? I am here, whom thou hast called
By challenge forth: make good thy vaunt, or yield!
Is it with Rustum only thou wouldst fight?
Rash boy, men look on Rustum's face and flee!
For well I know, that did great Rustum stand   370
Before thy face this day, and were revealed,
There would be then no talk of fighting more.
But being what I am, I tell thee this—
Do thou record it in thine inmost soul:
Either thou shalt renounce thy vaunt and yield,   375
Or else thy bones shall strew this sand, till winds

Bleach them, or Oxus with his summer-floods,
Oxus in summer wash them all away."
   He spoke: and Sohrab answered, on his feet:—
"Art thou so fierce? Thou wilt not fright me so!   380
I am no girl, to be made pale by words.
Yet this thou hast said well, did Rustum stand
Here on this field, there were no fighting then.
But Rustum is far hence, and we stand here.
Begin! thou art more vast, more dread than I,   385
And thou art proved, I know, and I am young—
But yet success sways with the breath of Heaven.
And though thou thinkest that thou knowest sure
Thy victory, yet thou canst not surely know.
For we are all, like swimmers in the sea,   390
Poised on the top of a huge wave of fate,
Which hangs uncertain to which side to fall.
And whether it will heave us up to land,
Or whether it will roll us out to sea,
Back out to sea, to the deep waves of death,   395
We know not, and no search will make us know;
Only the event will teach us in its hour."
   He spoke, and Rustum answered not, but hurled
His spear; down from the shoulder, down it came,
As on some partridge in the corn a hawk,   400
That long has towered in the airy clouds,
Drops like a plummet; Sohrab saw it come,
And sprang aside, quick as a flash: the spear
Hissed, and went quivering down into the sand,
Which it sent flying wide;—then Sohrab threw   405
In turn, and full struck Rustum's shield; sharp rang,
The iron plates rang sharp, but turned the spear.
And Rustum seized his club, which none but he
Could wield: an unlopped trunk it was, and huge,
Still rough—like those which men in treeless plains   410
To build them boats fish from the flooded rivers,
Hyphasis or Hydaspes, when, high up
By their dark springs, the wind in winter-time
Has made in Himalayan forests wrack,
And strewn the channels with torn boughs—so huge   415
The club which Rustum lifted now, and struck
One stroke; but again Sohrab sprang aside,
Lithe as the glancing snake, and the club came
Thundering to earth, and leaped from Rustum's hand.
And Rustum followed his own blow, and fell   420
To his knees, and with his fingers clutched the sand.
And now might Sohrab have unsheathed his sword,
And pierced the mighty Rustum while he lay
Dizzy, and on his knees, and choked with sand;
But he looked on, and smiled, nor bared his sword,   425
But courteously drew back, and spoke, and said:—
   "Thou strik'st too hard! that club of thine will float
Upon the summer-floods, and not my bones.
But rise, and be not wroth! not wroth am I;

No, when I see thee, wrath forsakes my soul.   430
Thou say'st, thou art not Rustum: be it so!
Who art thou then, that canst so touch my soul?
Boy as I am, I have seen battles too—
Have waded foremost in their bloody waves,
And heard their hollow roar of dying men;   435
But never was my heart thus touched before.
Are they from Heaven, these softenings of the heart?
O thou old warrior, let us yield to Heaven!
Come, plant we here in earth our angry spears,
And make a truce, and sit upon this sand,   440
And pledge each other in red wine, like friends,
And thou shalt talk to me of Rustum's deeds.
There are enough foes in the Persian host,
Whom I may meet, and strike, and feel no pang;
Champions enough Afrasiab has, whom thou   445
Mayst fight; fight *them,* when they confront thy spear!
But oh, let there be peace 'twixt thee and me!"
   He ceased, but while he spake, Rustum had risen,
And stood erect, trembling with rage: his club
He left to lie, but had regained his spear,   450
Whose fiery point now in his mailed right-hand
Blazed bright and baleful, like that autumn-star,[13]
The baleful sign of fevers: dust had soiled
His stately crest, and dimmed his glittering arms.
His breast heaved, his lips foamed, and twice his
   voice   455
Was choked with rage: at last these words broke way:—
   "Girl! nimble with thy feet, not with thy hands!
Curled minion, dancer, coiner of sweet words!
Fight, let me hear thy hateful voice no more!
Thou art not in Afrasiab's gardens now   460
With Tartar girls, with whom thou art wont to dance;
But on the Oxus-sands, and in the dance
Of battle, and with me, who make no play
Of war; I fight it out, and hand to hand.
Speak not to me of truce, and pledge, and wine!   465
Remember all thy valor: try thy feints
And cunning! all the pity I had is gone;
Because thou hast shamed me before both the hosts
With thy light skipping tricks, and thy girl's wiles."
   He spoke, and Sohrab kindled at his taunts,   470
And he too drew his sword: at once they rushed
Together, as two eagles on one prey
Come rushing down together from the clouds,
One from the east, one from the west; their shields
Dashed with a clang together, and a din   475
Rose, such as that the sinewy woodcutters
Make often in the forest's heart at morn,
Of hewing axes, crashing trees—such blows
Rustum and Sohrab on each other hailed.

[13] Sirius, the Dog Star.

And you would say that sun and stars took part   480
In that unnatural conflict; for a cloud
Grew suddenly in Heaven, and darked the sun
Over the fighters' heads; and a wind rose
Under their feet, and moaning swept the plain,
And in a sandy whirlwind wrapped the pair.   485
In gloom they twain were wrapped, and they alone;
For both the on-looking hosts on either hand
Stood in broad daylight, and the sky was pure,
And the sun sparkled on the Oxus stream.
But in the gloom they fought, with bloodshot eyes   490
And laboring breath; first Rustum struck the shield
Which Sohrab held stiff out; the steel-spiked spear
Rent the tough plates, but failed to reach the skin,
And Rustum plucked it back with angry groan.
Then Sohrab with his sword smote Rustum's helm,   495
Nor clove its steel quite through; but all the crest
He shore away, and that proud horse-hair plume,
Never till now defiled, sank to the dust;
And Rustum bowed his head; but then the gloom
Grew blacker, thunder rumbled in the air,   500
And lightnings rent the cloud; and Ruksh, the horse,
Who stood at hand, uttered a dreadful cry;—
No horse's cry was that, most like the roar
Of some pained desert lion, who all day
Hath trailed the hunter's javelin in his side,   505
And comes at night to die upon the sand.
The two hosts heard that cry, and quaked for fear,
And Oxus curdled as it crossed his stream.
But Sohrab heard, and quailed not, but rushed on,
And struck again; and again Rustum bowed   510
His head; but this time all the blade, like glass,
Sprang in a thousand shivers on the helm,
And in his hand the hilt remained alone.
Then Rustum raised his head; his dreadful eyes
Glared, and he shook on high his menacing spear,   515
And shouted: *Rustum!*—Sohrab heard that shout,
And shrank amazed: back he recoiled one step,
And scanned with blinking eyes the advancing form;
And then he stood bewildered; and he dropped
His covering shield, and the spear pierced his side.   520
He reeled, and staggering back, sank to the ground;
And then the gloom dispersed, and the wind fell,
And the bright sun broke forth, and melted all
The cloud; and the two armies saw the pair—
Saw Rustum standing, safe upon his feet,   525
And Sohrab, wounded, on the bloody sand.
    Then with a bitter smile, Rustum began:—
"Sohrab, thou thoughtest in thy mind to kill
A Persian lord this day, and strip his corpse,
And bear thy trophies to Afrasiab's tent.   530
Or else that the great Rustum would come down
Himself to fight, and that thy wiles would move

His heart to take a gift, and let thee go.
And then that all the Tartar host would praise
Thy courage or thy craft, and spread thy fame,   535
To glad thy father in his weak old age.
Fool, thou art slain, and by an unknown man!
Dearer to the red jackals shalt thou be
Than to thy friends, and to thy father old."
    And, with a fearless mien, Sohrab replied:—   540
"Unknown thou art; yet thy fierce vaunt is vain.
Thou dost not slay me, proud and boastful man!
No! Rustum slays me, and this filial heart.
For were I matched with ten such men as thee,
And I were that which till to-day I was,   545
They should be lying here, I standing there.
But that belovèd name unnerved my arm—
That name, and something, I confess, in thee,
Which troubles all my heart, and made my shield
Fall; and thy spear transfixed an unarmed foe.   550
And now thou boastest, and insult'st my fate.
But hear thou this, fierce man, tremble to hear:
The mighty Rustum shall avenge my death!
My father, whom I seek through all the world,
He shall avenge my death, and punish thee!"   555
    As when some hunter in the spring hath found
A breeding eagle sitting on her nest,
Upon the craggy isle of a hill-lake,
And pierced her with an arrow as she rose,
And followed her to find her where she fell   560
Far off;—anon her mate comes winging back
From hunting, and a great way off descries
His huddling young left sole; at that, he checks
His pinion, and with short uneasy sweeps
Circles above his eyry, with loud screams   565
Chiding his mate back to her nest; but she
Lies dying, with the arrow in her side,
In some far stony gorge out of his ken,
A heap of fluttering feathers—never more
Shall the lake glass her, flying over it;   570
Never the black and dripping precipices
Echo her stormy scream as she sails by:—
As that poor bird flies home, nor knows his loss,
So Rustum knew not his own loss, but stood
Over his dying son, and knew him not.   575
    But, with a cold incredulous voice, he said:—
"What prate is this of fathers and revenge?
The mighty Rustum never had a son."
    And, with a failing voice, Sohrab replied:—
"Ah! yes, he had! and that lost son am I.   580
Surely the news will one day reach his ear,
Reach Rustum, where he sits, and tarries long,
Somewhere, I know not where, but far from here,
And pierce him like a stab, and make him leap
To arms, and cry for vengeance upon thee.   585

Fierce man, bethink thee, for an only son!
What will that grief, what will that vengeance be?
Oh, could I live, till I that grief had seen!
Yet him I pity not so much, but her,
My mother, who in Ader-baijan dwells   590
With that old king, her father, who grows gray
With age, and rules over the valiant Koords.
Her most I pity, who no more will see
Sohrab returning from the Tartar camp,
With spoils and honor, when the war is done.   595
But a dark rumor will be bruited up,
From tribe to tribe, until it reach her ear;
And then will that defenceless woman learn
That Sohrab will rejoice her sight no more,
But that in battle with a nameless foe,   600
By the far-distant Oxus, he is slain."

  He spoke; and as he ceased, he wept aloud,
Thinking of her he left, and his own death.
He spoke; but Rustum listened, plunged in thought.
Nor did he yet believe it was his son   605
Who spoke, although he called back names he knew;
For he had had sure tidings that the babe,
Which was in Ader-baijan born to him,
Had been a puny girl, no boy at all—
So that sad mother sent him word, for fear   610
Rustum should take the boy, to train in arms.
And so he deemed that either Sohrab took,
By a false boast, the style of Rustum's son;
Or that men gave it him, to swell his fame.
So deemed he; yet he listened, plunged in thought 615
And his soul set to grief, as the vast tide
Of the bright rocking Ocean sets to shore
At the full moon: tears gathered in his eyes;
For he remembered his own early youth,
And all its bounding rapture; as, at dawn,   620
The shepherd from his mountain-lodge descries
A far, bright city, smitten by the sun,
Through many rolling clouds—so Rustum saw
His youth; saw Sohrab's mother, in her bloom;
And that old king, her father, who loved well   625
His wandering guest, and gave him his fair child
With joy; and all the pleasant life they led,
They three, in that long-distant summer-time—
The castle, and the dewy woods, and hunt
And hound, and morn on those delightful hills   630
In Ader-baijan. And he saw that youth,
Of age and looks to be his own dear son,
Piteous and lovely, lying on the sand,
Like some rich hyacinth which by the scythe
Of an unskilful gardener has been cut,   635
Mowing the garden grass-plots near its bed,
And lies, a fragrant tower of purple bloom,
On the mown, dying grass—so Sohrab lay,

Lovely in death, upon the common sand.
And Rustum gazed on him with grief, and said:—   640
  "O Sohrab, thou indeed art such a son
Whom Rustum, wert thou his, might well have loved.
Yet here thou errest, Sohrab, or else men
Have told thee false—thou art not Rustum's son.
For Rustum had no son: one child he had—   645
But one—a girl; who with her mother now
Plies some light female task, nor dreams of us—
Of us she dreams not, nor of wounds, nor war."

  But Sohrab answered him in wrath; for now
The anguish of the deep-fixed spear grew fierce,   650
And he desirèd to draw forth the steel,
And let the blood flow free, and so to die—
But first he would convince his stubborn foe;
And, rising sternly on one arm, he said:—

  "Man, who art thou who dost deny my words?   655
Truth sits upon the lips of dying men,
And falsehood, while I lived, was far from mine.
I tell thee, pricked upon this arm I bear
That seal which Rustum to my mother gave,
That she might prick it on the babe she bore."   660

  He spoke; and all the blood left Rustum's cheeks,
And his knees tottered, and he smote his hand
Against his breast, his heavy mailèd hand,
That the hard iron corslet clanked aloud;
And to his heart he pressed the other hand,   665
And in a hollow voice he spake, and said:—

  "Sohrab, that were a proof which could not lie!
If thou show this, then art thou Rustum's son."

  Then, with weak hasty fingers, Sohrab loosed
His belt, and near the shoulder bared his arm,   670
And showed a sign in faint vermilion points
Pricked; as a cunning workman, in Pekin,
Pricks with vermilion some clear porcelain vase,
An emperor's gift—at early morn he paints,
And all day long, and, when night comes, the lamp 675
Lights up his studious forehead and thin hands—
So delicately pricked the sign appeared
On Sohrab's arm, the sign of Rustum's seal.
It was that griffin, which of old reared Zal,
Rustum's great father, whom they left to die,   680
A helpless babe, among the mountain rocks;
Him that kind creature found, and reared, and loved—
Then Rustum took it for his glorious sign.
And Sohrab bared that image on his arm,
And himself scanned it long with mournful eyes,   685
And then he touched it with his hand and said:—

  "How say'st thou? Is that sign the proper sign
Of Rustum's son, or of some other man's?"

  He spoke: but Rustum gazed, and gazed, and stood
Speechless; and then he uttered one sharp cry: 690
"O boy—thy father!"—and his voice choked there.

And then a dark cloud passed before his eyes,
And his head swam, and he sank down to earth.
But Sohrab crawled to where he lay, and cast
His arms about his neck, and kissed his lips,   695
And with fond faltering fingers stroked his cheeks,
Trying to call him back to life; and life
Came back to Rustum, and he oped his eyes,
And they stood wide with horror; and he seized
In both his hands the dust which lay around,   700
And threw it on his head, and smirched his hair,—
His hair, and face, and beard, and glittering arms;
And strong convulsive groanings shook his breast,
And his sobs choked him; and he clutched his sword,
To draw it, and forever let life out.   725
But Sohrab saw his thought, and held his hands,
And with a soothing voice he spake, and said:—
    "Father, forbear! for I but meet to-day
The doom that at my birth was written down
In Heaven, and thou art Heaven's unconscious hand. 710
Surely my heart cried out that it was thou,
When first I saw thee; and thy heart spoke too,
I know it! but fate trod those promptings down
Under its iron heel; fate, fate engaged
The strife, and hurled me on my father's spear.   715
But let us speak no more of this! I find
My father; let me feel that I have found!
Come, sit beside me on this sand, and take
My head betwixt thy hands, and kiss my cheeks,
And wash them with thy tears, and say: 'My son!'   720
Quick! quick! for numbered are my sands of life,
And swift; for like the lightning to this field
I came, and like the wind I go away—
Sudden, and swift, and like a passing wind.
But it was writ in Heaven that this should be."   725
    So said he, and his voice released the heart
Of Rustum, and his tears broke forth; he cast
His arms round his son's neck, and wept aloud,
And kissed him. And awe fell on both the hosts,
When they saw Rustum's grief: and Ruksh, the
        horse,   730
With his head bowing to the ground and mane
Sweeping the dust, came near, and in mute woe
First to the one, then to the other moved
His head, as if inquiring what their grief
Might mean; and from his dark, compassionate eyes, 735
The big warm tears rolled down, and caked the sand.
But Rustum chid him with stern voice, and said:—
    "Ruksh, now thou grievest; but O Ruksh, thy feet
Should first have rotted on their nimble joints,
Or ere they brought thy master to this field!"   740
    But Sohrab looked upon the horse and said:—
"Is this, then, Ruksh? How often, in past days,
My mother told me of thee, thou brave steed,
My terrible father's terrible horse! and said,
That I should one day find thy lord and thee.   745
Come, let me lay my hand upon thy mane!
O Ruksh, thou art more fortunate than I;
For thou hast gone where I shall never go,
And snuffed the breezes of my father's home.
And thou hast trod the sands of Seistan,   750
And seen the River of Helmund, and the Lake
Of Zirrah; and the aged Zal himself
Has often stroked thy neck, and given thee food,
Corn in a golden platter soaked with wine,
And said: 'O Ruksh! bear Rustum well!'—but I   755
Have never known my grandsire's furrowed face,
Nor seen his lofty house in Seistan,
Nor slaked my thirst at the clear Helmund stream;
But lodged among my father's foes, and seen
Afrasiab's cities only, Samarcand,   760
Bokhara, and lone Khiva in the waste,
And the black Toorkmun tents; and only drunk
The desert rivers, Moorghab and Tejend,
Kohik, and where the Kalmuks feed their sheep,
The northern Sir; and this great Oxus stream—   765
The yellow Oxus, by whose brink I die."
    Then, with a heavy groan, Rustum bewailed:—
"Oh, that its waves were flowing over me!
Oh, that I saw its grains of yellow silt
Roll tumbling in the current o'er my head!"   770
    But, with a grave mild voice, Sohrab replied:—
"Desire not that, my father! thou must live.
For some are born to do great deeds, and live,
As some are born to be obscured, and die.
Do thou the deeds I die too young to do,   775
And reap a second glory in thine age;
Thou art my father, and thy gain is mine.
But come! thou seest this great host of men
Which follow me; I pray thee, slay not these!
Let me entreat for them; what have they done?   780
They followed me, my hope, my fame, my star.
Let them all cross the Oxus back in peace.
But me thou must bear hence, not send with them,
But carry me with thee to Seistan,
And place me on a bed, and mourn for me,   785
Thou, and the snow-haired Zal, and all thy friends.
And thou must lay me in that lovely earth,
And heap a stately mound above my bones,
And plant a far-seen pillar over all.
That so the passing horseman on the waste   790
May see my tomb a great way off, and cry:
'Sohrab, the mighty Rustum's son, lies there,
Whom his great father did in ignorance kill'!
And I be not forgotten in my grave."
    And, with a mournful voice, Rustum replied:—   795
"Fear not! as thou hast said, Sohrab, my son,

So shall it be; for I will burn my tents,
And quit the host, and bear thee hence with me,
And carry thee away to Seistan,
And place thee on a bed, and mourn for thee,   800
With the snow-headed Zal, and all my friends.
And I will lay thee in that lovely earth,
And heap a stately mound above thy bones,
And plant a far-seen pillar over all,
And men shall not forget thee in thy grave.   805
And I will spare thy host; yea, let them go!
Let them all cross the Oxus back in peace!
What should I do with slaying any more?
For would that all whom I have ever slain
Might be once more alive; my bitterest foes,   810
And they who were called champions in their time,
And through whose death I won that fame I have—
And I were nothing but a common man,
A poor, mean soldier, and without renown,
So thou mightest live too, my son, my son!   815
Or rather would that I, even I myself,
Might now be lying on this bloody sand,
Near death, and by an ignorant stroke of thine,
Not thou of mine! and I might die, not thou;
And I, not thou, be borne to Seistan;   820
And Zal might weep above my grave, not thine;
And say: 'O son, I weep thee not too sore,
For willingly, I know, thou met'st thine end!'
But now in blood and battles was my youth,
And full of blood and battles is my age,   825
And I shall never end this life of blood."

    Then, at the point of death, Sohrab replied:—
"A life of blood indeed, thou dreadful man!
But thou shalt yet have peace; only not now,
Not yet! but thou shalt have it on that day,   830
When thou shalt sail in a high-masted ship,
Thou and the other peers of Kai-Khosroo,
Returning home over the salt blue sea,
From laying thy dear master in his grave."

    And Rustum gazed on Sohrab's face, and said:—   835
"Soon be that day, my son, and deep that sea!
Till then, if fate so wills, let me endure."

    He spoke; and Sohrab smiled on him, and took
The spear, and drew it from his side, and eased
His wound's imperious anguish; but the blood   840
Came welling from the open gash, and life
Flowed with the stream;—all down his cold white side
The crimson torrent ran, dim now and soiled
Like the soiled tissue of white violets
Left, freshly gathered, on their native bank,   845
By children, whom their nurses call with haste
Indoors from the sun's eye; his head drooped low,
His limbs grew slack; motionless, white, he lay—
White, with eyes closed; only when heavy gasps,

Deep heavy gasps quivering through all his frame,   850
Convulsed him back to life, he opened them,
And fixed them feebly on his father's face;
Till now all strength was ebbed, and from his limbs
Unwillingly the spirit fled away,
Regretting the warm mansion which it left,   855
And youth, and bloom, and this delightful world.

    So, on the bloody sand, Sohrab lay dead;
And the great Rustum drew his horseman's cloak
Down o'er his face, and sate by his dead son.
As those black granite pillars, once high-reared   860
By Jemshid in Persepolis,[14] to bear
His house, now 'mid their broken flights of steps
Lie prone, enormous, down the mountain side—
So in the sand lay Rustum by his son.

    And night came down over the solemn waste,   865
And the two gazing hosts, and that sole pair,
And darkened all; and a cold fog, with night,
Crept from the Oxus. Soon a hum arose,
As of a great assembly loosed, and fires
Began to twinkle through the fog: for now   870
Both armies moved to camp, and took their meal;
The Persians took it on the open sands
Southward, the Tartars by the river marge;
And Rustum and his son were left alone.

    But the majestic river floated on,   875
Out of the mist and hum of that low land,
Into the frosty starlight, and there moved,
Rejoicing, through the hushed Chorasmian waste,[15]
Under the solitary moon;—he flowed
Right for the polar star, past Orgunjè,[16]   880
Brimming, and bright, and large; then sands begin
To hem his watery march, and dam his streams,
And split his currents; that for many a league
The shorn and parcelled Oxus strains along
Through beds of sand and matted rushy isles—   885
Oxus, forgetting the bright speed he had
In his high mountain cradle in Pamere,
A foiled circuitous wanderer—till at last
The longed-for dash of waves is heard, and wide
His luminous home of waters opens, bright   890
And tranquil, from whose floor the new-bathed stars
Emerge, and shine upon the Aral Sea.[17]

---

[14] Capital city of ancient Persia, of which Jemshid was a legendary
king.   [15] Khiva in Turkestan.   [16] Village on the Oxus.
[17] The function of the final paragraph, which is to create a feeling
of quiet peace and reassurance after the tragedy, is achieved
partly on the direct level by an image of natural beauty, partly
on a symbolic level by the suggestion—it is only a suggestion—
that the Oxus stands for the stream of human life, which begins
with the bright strength of youth, has to endure being shorn of
its potentialities and foiled of its hopes, but finally reaches its
"luminous home."

REQUIESCAT[18]

Strew on her roses, roses,
    And never a spray of yew!
In quiet she reposes;
    Ah, would that I did too!

Her mirth the world required;   5
    She bathed it in smiles of glee.
But her heart was tired, tired,
    And now they let her be.

Her life was turning, turning,
    In mazes of heat and sound.   10
But for peace her soul was yearning,
    And now peace laps her round.

Her cabined, ample spirit,
    It fluttered and failed for breath.
To-night it doth inherit   15
    The vasty hall of death.

THE SCHOLAR–GIPSY[1]

Go, for they call you, shepherd, from the hill;
    Go, shepherd, and untie the wattled cotes![2]
    No longer leave thy wistful flock unfed,
    Nor let thy bawling fellows rack their throats,
    Nor the cropped herbage shoot another head.   5
        But when the fields are still,
    And the tired men and dogs all gone to rest,
        And only the white sheep are sometimes seen
    Cross and recross the strips of moon-blanched green,
    Come, shepherd, and again begin the quest![3]   10

18 "May she rest [in peace]."

1 There was very lately a lad in the University of Oxford, who was by his poverty forced to leave his studies there; and at last to join himself to a company of vagabond gipsies. Among these extravagant people, by the insinuating subtilty of his carriage, he quickly got so much of their love and esteem as that they discovered to him their mystery. After he had been a pretty while exercised in the trade, there chanced to ride by a couple of scholars, who had formerly been of his acquaintance. They quickly spied out their old friend among the gipsies; and he gave them an account of the necessity which drove him to that kind of life, and told them that the people he went with were not such impostors as they were taken for, but that they had a traditional kind of learning among them, and could do wonders by the power of imagination, their fancy binding that of others: that himself had learned much of their art, and when he had compassed the whole secret, he intended, he said, to leave their company, and give the world an account of what he had learned.—Glanvil's *Vanity of Dogmatizing*, 1661. (Affixed to the poem by Arnold himself.)

2 Sheepfolds made of interwoven twigs.

3 The search for the Scholar-Gipsy (see line 63).

Here, where the reaper was at work of late—
    In this high field's dark corner, where he leaves
    His coat, his basket, and his earthen cruse,
    And in the sun, all morning binds the sheaves,
    Then here, at noon, comes back his stores to
        use—   15
        Here will I sit and wait,
    While to my ear from uplands far away
    The bleating of the folded flocks is borne,
    With distant cries of reapers in the corn—
    All the live murmur of a summer's day.   20

Screened is this nook o'er the high, half-reaped field,
    And here till sun-down, shepherd! will I be.
    Through the thick corn the scarlet poppies peep,
    And round green roots and yellowing stalks, I see
    Pale pink convolvulus in tendrils creep;   25
        And air-swept lindens yield
    Their scent, and rustle down their perfumed showers
    Of bloom on the bent grass where I am laid,
    And bower me from the August sun with shade;
    And the eye travels down to Oxford's towers.   30

And near me on the grass lies Glanvil's book—
    Come, let me read the oft-read tale again!
    The story of the Oxford scholar poor,
    Of pregnant parts and quick inventive brain,
    Who, tired of knocking at preferment's door,   35
        One summer morn forsook
    His friends, and went to learn the gipsy-lore,
    And roamed the world with that wild brotherhood,
    And came, as most men deemed, to little good,
    But came to Oxford and his friends no more.   40

But once, years after, in the country-lanes,
    Two scholars, whom at college erst he knew,
    Met him, and of his way of life enquired;
    Whereat he answered that the gipsy-crew,
    His mates, had arts to rule as they desired   45
        The workings of men's brains,
    And they can bind them to what thoughts they
        will.[4]
    "And I," he said, "the secret of their art,
    When fully learned, will to the world impart;
    But it needs heaven-sent moments for this skill." 50

This said, he left them, and returned no more.—
    But rumors hung about the countryside,
    That the lost Scholar long was seen to stray,
    Seen by rare glimpses, pensive and tongue-tied,

4 Cf. note 1. The arts are those of hypnotism, as the rest of the passage from Glanvil, not quoted by Arnold, makes clear.

In hat of antique shape, and cloak of grey,   55
    The same the gipsies wore.
Shepherds had met him on the Hurst[5] in spring;
    At some lone alehouse in the Berkshire moors,
    On the warm ingle-bench,[6] the smock-frocked
        boors[7]
Had found him seated at their entering,   60

But, 'mid their drink and clatter, he would fly.
    And I myself seem half to know thy looks,
        And put the shepherds, wanderer! on thy trace;
    And boys who in lone wheatfields scare the rooks
        I ask if thou hast passed their quiet place;   65
            Or in my boat I lie
    Moored to the cool bank in the summer-heats,
        'Mid wide grass meadows which the sunshine fills,
    And watch the warm, green-muffled Cumner hills,
    And wonder if thou haunt'st their shy retreats.   70

For most, I know, thou lov'st retired ground:
    Thee, at the ferry, Oxford riders blithe,
        Returning home on summer-nights, have met
    Crossing the stripling Thames at Bablock-hithe,
        Trailing in the cool stream thy fingers wet,   75
            As the punt's rope chops round;[8]
    And leaning backward in a pensive dream,
        And fostering in thy lap a heap of flowers
    Plucked in shy fields and distant Wychwood
        bowers,
    And thine eyes resting on the moonlit stream.   80

And then they land, and thou art seen no more!—
    Maidens, who from the distant hamlets come
        To dance around the Fyfield elm in May,
    Oft through the darkening fields have seen thee roam,
        Or cross a stile into the public way.   85
            Oft thou hast given them store
    Of flowers—the frail-leafed white anemony,
        Dark bluebells drenched with dews of summer eves,
    And purple orchises with spotted leaves—
    But none hath words she can report of thee.   90

And, above Godstow Bridge, when hay-time's here
    In June, and many a scythe in sunshine flames,
        Men who through those wide fields of breezy grass
    Where black-winged swallows haunt the glittering
        Thames,

To bathe in the abandoned lasher pass,[9]   95
    Have often passed thee near
Sitting upon the river bank o'ergrown;
    Marked thine outlandish garb, thy figure spare,
    Thy dark vague eyes, and soft abstracted air—
But, when they came from bathing, thou wast
    gone!   100

At some lone homestead in the Cumner hills,
    Where at her open door the housewife darns,
        Thou hast been seen, or hanging on a gate
    To watch the threshers in the mossy barns.
        Children, who early range these slopes and late   105
            For cresses from the rills,
    Have known thee eying, all an April-day,
        The springing pastures and the feeding kine;
    And marked thee, when the stars come out and
        shine,
    Through the long dewy grass move slow away.   110

In autumn, on the skirts of Bagley Wood—
    Where most the gipsies by the turf-edged way
        Pitch their smoked tents, and every bush you see
    With scarlet patches tagged and shreds of grey,
        Above the forest-ground called Thessaly—   115
            The blackbird, picking food,
    Sees thee, nor stops his meal, nor fears at all;
        So often has he known thee past him stray,
    Rapt, twirling in thy hand a withered spray,
    And waiting for the spark from heaven to fall.   120

And once, in winter, on the causeway chill
    Where home through flooded fields foot-travellers go,
        Have I not passed thee on the wooden bridge,
    Wrapt in thy cloak and battling with the snow,
        Thy face toward Hinksey and its wintry ridge?   125
            And thou hast climbed the hill,
    And gained the white brow of the Cumner range;
        Turned once to watch, while thick the snowflakes
            fall,
    The line of festal light in Christ-Church hall[10]—
Then sought thy straw in some sequestered grange.   130

But what—I dream! Two hundred years are flown
    Since first thy story ran through Oxford halls,
        And the grave Glanvil did the tale inscribe
    That thou wert wandered from the studious walls
        To learn strange arts, and join a gipsy-tribe;   135
            And thou from earth art gone
    Long since, and in some quiet churchyard laid—

---

[5] A hill outside Oxford. All the proper names in the following stanzas are of places in the environs of Oxford.
[6] Bench in the chimney corner.   [7] Peasants.
[8] The rope which pulls the ferryboat across the Thames is shaken about by the wind.

[9] Pool below a dam.
[10] The dining hall at Christ Church College.

Some country-nook, where o'er thy unknown grave
Tall grasses and white flowering nettles wave,
Under a dark, red-fruited yew-tree's shade.   140

—No, no, thou hast not felt the lapse of hours!
For what wears out the life of mortal men?
'Tis that from change to change their being rolls;
'Tis that repeated shocks, again, again,
Exhaust the energy of strongest souls   145
And numb the elastic powers.
Till, having used our nerves with bliss and teen,[11]
And tired upon a thousand schemes our wit,
To the just-pausing Genius[12] we remit
Our worn-out life, and are—what we have been.   150

Thou hast not lived, why shouldst thou perish, so?
Thou hadst *one* aim, *one* business, *one* desire;
Else wert thou long since numbered with the dead!
Else hadst thou spent, like other men, thy fire!
The generations of thy peers are fled,   155
And we ourselves shall go;
But thou possessest an immortal lot,
And we imagine thee exempt from age
And living as thou liv'st on Glanvil's page,
Because thou hadst—what we, alas! have not.   160

For early didst thou leave the world, with powers
Fresh, undiverted to the world without,
Firm to their mark, not spent on other things;
Free from the sick fatigue, the languid doubt,
Which much to have tried, in much been baffled,
brings.   165
O life unlike to ours!
Who fluctuate idly without term or scope,
Of whom each strives, nor knows for what he
strives,
And each half lives a hundred different lives;
Who wait like thee, but not, like thee, in hope.   170

Thou waitest for the spark from heaven! and we,
Light half-believers of our casual creeds,
Who never deeply felt, nor clearly willed,
Whose insight never has borne fruit in deeds,
Whose vague resolves never have been fulfilled;   175
For whom each year we see
Breeds new beginnings, disappointments new;
Who hesitate and falter life away,
And lose to-morrow the ground won to-day—
Ah! do not we, wanderer! await it too?   180

Yes, we await it!—but it still delays,
And then we suffer! and amongst us one,
Who most has suffered, takes dejectedly
His seat upon the intellectual throne;
And all his store of sad experience he   185
Lays bare of wretched days;
Tells us his misery's birth and growth and signs,
And how the dying spark of hope was fed,
And how the breast was soothed, and how the head,
And all his hourly varied anodynes.[13]   190

This for our wisest![14] and we others pine,
And wish the long unhappy dream would end,
And waive all claim to bliss, and try to bear;
With close-lipped patience for our only friend,
Sad patience, too near neighbor to despair—   195
But none has hope like thine!
Thou through the fields and through the woods dost
stray,
Roaming the country-side, a truant boy,
Nursing thy project in unclouded joy,
And every doubt long blown by time away.   200

O born in days when wits were fresh and clear,
And life ran gaily as the sparkling Thames;
Before this strange disease of modern life,
With its sick hurry, its divided aims,
Its heads o'ertaxed, its palsied hearts, was rife—   205
Fly hence, our contact fear!
Still fly, plunge deeper in the bowering wood!
Averse, as Dido did with gesture stern
From her false friend's approach in Hades turn,[15]
Wave us away, and keep thy solitude!   210

Still nursing the unconquerable hope,[16]
Still clutching the inviolable shade,
With a free, onward impulse brushing through,
By night, the silvered branches of the glade—
Far on the forest-skirts, where none pursue,   215
On some mild pastoral slope
Emerge, and resting on the moonlit pales
Freshen thy flowers as in former years
With dew, or listen with enchanted ears,
From the dark dingles,[17] to the nightingales!   220

[11] Sorrow.
[12] A genius is a guardian spirit. The general reference is to death, but the meaning of "just-pausing" is uncertain.

[13] Palliatives as distinguished from curative drugs.
[14] The reference is either to Goethe or to Tennyson. Lines 185–190 fit *In Memoriam* perfectly, and line 184 could refer to the laureateship. It is true that Arnold did not consider Tennyson "our wisest," but the last phrase may simply mean, "the one who is thought or called our wisest" (since he has been placed on the intellectual throne).
[15] Dido, who had killed herself when Aeneas deserted her, turned away from him scornfully when he visited Hades.
[16] Cf. line 120.   [17] Wooded dells.

But fly our paths, our feverish contact fly!
  For strong the infection of our mental strife,
    Which, though it gives no bliss, yet spoils for rest;
  And we should win thee from thy own fair life,
    Like us distracted, and like us unblest.   225
      Soon, soon thy cheer would die,
  Thy hopes grow timorous, and unfixed thy powers,
    And thy clear aims be cross and shifting made;
  And then thy glad perennial youth would fade,
  Fade, and grow old at last, and die like ours.   230

Then fly our greetings, fly our speech and smiles!
  —As some grave Tyrian[18] trader, from the sea,
    Descried at sunrise an emerging prow
  Lifting the cool-haired creepers stealthily,[19]
    The fringes of a southward-facing brow   235
      Among the Aegaean isles;
  And saw the merry Grecian coaster come,
    Freighted with amber grapes, and Chian wine,
    Green, bursting figs, and tunnies[20] steeped in brine—
  And knew the intruders on his ancient home,   240

The young light-hearted masters of the waves—
  And snatched his rudder, and shook out more sail;
    And day and night held on indignantly
  O'er the blue Midland waters with the gale,
    Betwixt the Syrtes[21] and soft Sicily,   245
      To where the Atlantic raves
  Outside the western straits;[22] and unbent sails
    There, where down cloudy cliffs, through sheets
        of foam,
    Shy traffickers, the dark Iberians[23] come;
  And on the beach undid his corded bales.[24]   250

---

[18] Tyre, in Asia Minor, was the chief city of the Phoenicians, who controlled the Mediterranean trade until the rise of the Greeks.
[19] The foliage overhanging a cliff at the entrance to a harbor.
[20] Fish.   [21] Gulf of Sidra on the northern coast of Africa.
[22] Beyond the straits of Gibraltar.
[23] Early inhabitants of the Spanish peninsula.
[24] The appropriateness of this famous simile is somewhat dubious. The analogies between the Tyrian trader and the Scholar-Gipsy, and between the Greeks and either the Oxford scholars of Glanvil's time or the modern Victorians who have just been described, are less obvious than their differences. The best that can be said is that the Tyrian trader has "one aim, one business, one desire" which he can achieve if he turns away from "civilization" and flies to the dark Iberians (the gipsies). But his (commercial) aim is definite where the Scholar-Gipsy's aim is indefinite; and the trader shows no interest whatever in the beauties of nature, which, in point of fact, the Scholar-Gipsy flies to.

STANZAS FROM
THE GRANDE CHARTREUSE[1]

Through Alpine meadows soft-suffused
With rain, where thick the crocus blows,
Past the dark forges long disused,
The mule-track from Saint Laurent[2] goes.
The bridge is crossed, and slow we ride,   5
Through forest, up the mountain-side.

The autumnal evening darkens round,
The wind is up, and drives the rain;
While hark! far down, with strangled sound
Doth the Dead Guier's[3] stream complain,   10
Where that wet smoke, among the woods,
Over his boiling cauldron broods.

Swift rush the spectral vapors white
Past limestone scars with ragged pines,
Showing—then blotting from our sight!—   15
Halt—through the cloud-drift something shines!
High in the valley, wet and drear,
The huts of Courrerie[4] appear.

Strike leftward! cries our guide; and higher
Mounts up the stony forest-way.   20
At last the encircling trees retire;
Look! through the showery twilight gray
What pointed roofs are these advance?—
A palace of the kings of France?

Approach, for what we seek is here.
Alight, and sparely sup, and wait   25
For rest in this outbuilding near;
Then cross the sward and reach that gate.
Knock; pass the wicket! Thou art come
To the Carthusians' world-famed home.   30

The silent courts, where night and day
Into their stone-carved basins cold
The splashing icy fountains play—
The humid corridors behold!   35
Where, ghostlike in the deepening night,
Cowled forms brush by in gleaming white.

The chapel, where no organ's peal
Invests the stern and naked prayer—
With penitential cries they kneel
And wrestle; rising then, with bare   40

---

[1] Carthusian monastery in the Alps which Arnold visited in 1851.
[2] Village near the monastery.   [3] River near the monastery.
[4] Another mountain village.

And white uplifted faces stand,
Passing the Host[5] from hand to hand;

Each takes, and then his visage wan
Is buried in his cowl once more.
The cells!—the suffering Son of Man   45
Upon the wall—the knee-worn floor—
And where they sleep, that wooden bed,
Which shall their coffin be, when dead!

The library, where tract and tome
Not to feed priestly pride are there,   50
To hymn the conquering march of Rome,
Nor yet to amuse, as ours are!
They paint of souls the inner strife,
Their drops of blood, their death in life.

The garden, overgrown—yet mild,   55
See, fragrant herbs are flowering there!
Strong children of the Alpine wild
Whose culture is the brethren's care;
Of human tasks their only one,
And cheerful works beneath the sun.   60

Those halls, too, destined to contain
Each its own pilgrim-host of old,
From England, Germany, or Spain—
All are before me! I behold
The House, the Brotherhood austere!   65
—And what am I, that I am here?

For rigorous teachers seized my youth,
And purged its faith, and trimmed its fire,
Showed me the high, white star of Truth,
There bade me gaze, and there aspire.[6]   70
Even now their whispers pierce the gloom:
What dost thou in this living tomb?

Forgive me, masters of the mind!
At whose behest I long ago
So much unlearnt, so much resigned—   75
I come not here to be your foe!
I seek these anchorites, not in ruth,
To curse and to deny your truth;[7]

Not as their friend, or child, I speak!
But, as on some far northern strand,   80
Thinking of his own Gods, a Greek
In pity and mournful awe might stand
Before some fallen Runic stone—
For both were faiths, and both are gone.[8]

Wandering between two worlds, one dead,   85
The other powerless to be born,[9]
With nowhere yet to rest my head,
Like these, on earth I wait forlorn.
Their faith, my tears, the world deride—
I come to shed them at their side.   90

Oh, hide me in your gloom profound,
Ye solemn seats of holy pain!
Take me, cowled forms, and fence me round,
Till I possess my soul again;
Till free my thoughts before me roll,   95
Not chafed by hourly false control!

For the world cries your faith is now
But a dead time's exploded dream;
My melancholy, sciolists[10] say,
Is a pass'd mode, an outworn theme—   100
As if the world had ever had
A faith, or sciolists been sad![11]

Ah, if it *be* pass'd, take away,[12]
At least, the restlessness, the pain;
Be man henceforth no more a prey   105
To these out-dated stings again!
The nobleness of grief is gone—
Ah, leave us not the fret alone!

But—if you cannot give us ease—
Last of the race of them who grieve   110
Here leave us to die out with these
Last of the people who believe!
Silent, while years engrave the brow;
Silent—the best are silent now.

---

5 The consecrated bread in the service of the Mass. But since it is never passed from hand to hand, Arnold must have confused the Host with the Pax (a crucifix).

6 The rationalists (Goethe in one way, Mill and the scientists in another) who insisted he follow the truth of fact and reason to the exclusion not only of Catholic Christianity, Roman and Anglican, but even of his father's Liberal Protestantism (cf. lines 74–75).

7 Not in repentance for my faith in reason.

8 A runic stone is a religious tablet written in early Germanic characters. Arnold likens himself to a rational Greek who has lost his faith in the gods (as Arnold has lost his in Liberal Protestantism) and who therefore feels "pity and mournful awe" before another exploded superstition, German paganism (as Arnold does before Roman Catholicism).

9 In the age of transition (cf. General Introduction, opening section), when the old religious philosophy of life is dead, and no new one has yet been formulated.

10 Men of superficial knowledge.

11 The world and the sciolists can talk this way only because the one has never known the real meaning of faith and the other has never known sadness.

12 In this stanza and the next Arnold is again addressing his "rigorous teachers" (see lines 67–78 and note 6).

Achilles ponders in his tent,[13]   115
The kings of modern thought are dumb;
Silent they are, though not content,
And wait to see the future come.
They have the grief men had of yore,
But they contend and cry no more.   120

Our fathers watered with their tears[14]
This sea of time whereon we sail,
Their voices were in all men's ears
Who passed within their puissant hail.
Still the same ocean round us raves,   125
But we stand mute, and watch the waves.

For what availed it, all the noise
And outcry of the former men?—
Say, have their sons achieved more joys,
Say, is life lighter now than then?   130
The sufferers died, they left their pain—
The pangs which tortured them remain.

What helps it now, that Byron bore,
With haughty scorn which mocked the smart,
Through Europe to the Aetolian shore[15]   135
The pageant of his bleeding heart?
That thousands counted every groan,
And Europe made his woe her own?

What boots it, Shelley! that the breeze
Carried thy lovely wail away,   140
Musical through Italian trees
Which fringe thy soft blue Spezzian bay?[16]
Inheritors of thy distress
Have restless hearts one throb the less?

Or are we easier, to have read,   145
O Obermann![17] the sad, stern page,
Which tells us how thou hidd'st thy head
From the fierce tempest of thine age
In the lone brakes of Fontainebleau,
Or chalets near the Alpine snow?   150

Ye slumber in your silent grave!—
The world, which for an idle day
Grace to your mood of sadness gave,

Long since hath flung her weeds away.
The eternal trifler breaks your spell;   155
But we—we learnt your lore[18] too well!

Years hence, perhaps, may dawn an age,
More fortunate, alas! than we,
Which without hardness will be sage,
And gay without frivolity.   160
Sons of the world, oh, speed those years;
But, while we wait, allow our tears!

Allow them! We admire with awe
The exulting thunder of your race;
You give the universe your law,   165
You triumph over time and space!
Your pride of life, your tireless powers,
We laud them, but they are not ours.

We are like children reared in shade
Beneath some old-world abbey wall,   170
Forgotten in a forest-glade,
And secret from the eyes of all.
Deep, deep the greenwood round them waves,
Their abbey, and its close of graves!

But, where the road runs near the stream,   175
Oft through the trees they catch a glance
Of passing troops in the sun's beam—
Pennon, and plume, and flashing lance!
Forth to the world those soldiers fare,
To life, to cities, and to war!   180

And through the wood, another way,
Faint bugle-notes from far are borne,
Where hunters gather, staghounds bay,
Round some fair forest-lodge at morn.
Gay dames are there, in sylvan green;   185
Laughter and cries—those notes between!

The banners flashing through the trees
Make their blood dance and chain their eyes;
That bugle-music on the breeze
Arrests them with a charmed surprise.   190
Banner by turns and bugle woo:
Ye shy recluses, follow too!

O children, what do ye reply?—
"Action and pleasure, will ye roam
Through these secluded dells to cry   195
And call us?—but too late ye come!

---

13 Whom Achilles stands for, if anyone in particular, is unknown.
He symbolizes the "kings of modern thought" who have withdrawn from the struggle to solve the religious problem.
14 The melancholy romantics of the previous age.
15 To the shore of the Greek province where Byron died.
16 Shelley spent his last days on the shore of the Gulf of Spezia.
17 Étienne Pivert de Sénancour (1770–1846), author of a philosophic romance called *Obermann*. He died at Fontainebleau near
Paris.

18 Your melancholy grief.

Too late for us your call ye blow,
Whose bent was taken long ago.

"Long since we pace this shadowed nave;
We watch those yellow tapers shine,   200
Emblems of hope over the grave,
In the high altar's depth divine;
The organ carries to our ear
Its accents of another sphere.

"Fenced early in this cloistral round   205
Of reverie, of shade, of prayer,
How should we grow in other ground?
How can we flower in foreign air?
—Pass, banners, pass, and bugles, cease;
And leave our desert to its peace!"   210

ISOLATION. TO MARGUERITE[1]

We were apart; yet, day by day,
I bade my heart more constant be.
I bade it keep the world away,
And grow a home for only thee;
Nor feared but thy love likewise grew,   5
Like mine, each day, more tried, more true.

The fault was grave! I might have known,
What far too soon, alas! I learned—
The heart can bind itself alone,
And faith may oft be unreturned.   10
Self-swayed our feelings ebb and swell—
Thou lov'st no more;—Farewell! Farewell!

Farewell!—and thou, thou lonely heart,
Which never yet without remorse
Even for a moment didst depart   15
From thy remote and sphered course
To haunt the place where passions reign—
Back to thy solitude again!

Back! with the conscious thrill of shame
Which Luna felt, that summer night,   20
Flash through her pure immortal frame,
When she forsook the starry height
To hang over Endymion's sleep
Upon the pine-grown Latmian steep.[2]

Yet she, chaste queen, had never proved   25
How vain a thing is mortal love,
Wandering in heaven, far removed;
But thou hast long had place to prove
This truth—to prove, and make thine own:
"Thou hast been, shalt be, art, alone."   30

Or, if not quite alone, yet they
Which touch thee are unmating things—
Ocean and clouds and night and day;
Lorn autumns and triumphant springs;
And life, and others' joy and pain,   35
And love, if love, of happier men.

Of happier men—for they, at least,
Have *dreamed* two human hearts might blend
In one, and were through faith released
From isolation without end   40
Prolonged; nor knew, although not less
Alone than thou, their loneliness.

TO MARGUERITE—CONTINUED

Yes! in the sea of life enisled,
With echoing straits between us thrown,
Dotting the shoreless watery wild,
We mortal millions live *alone*.
The islands feel the enclasping flow,   5
And then their endless bounds they know.

But when the moon their hollows lights,
And they are swept by balms of spring,
And in their glens, on starry nights,
The nightingales divinely sing;   10
And lovely notes, from shore to shore,
Across the sounds and channels pour—

Oh! then a longing like despair
Is to their farthest caverns sent;
For surely once, they feel, we were   15
Parts of a single continent!
Now round us spreads the watery plain—
Oh, might our marges meet again!

Who ordered that their longing's fire
Should be, as soon as kindled, cooled?   20
Who renders vain their deep desire?—
A god, a god their severance ruled!
And bade betwixt their shores to be
The unplumbed, salt, estranging sea.

---

[1] This poem and the following one are taken from a series of seven poems published under the heading *Switzerland*. Who Marguerite was is not known. Arnold's pronunciation was *Margueritè*.
[2] Diana, goddess of the moon and of chastity, fell in love with the shepherd Endymion, whom she found sleeping on Mt. Latmos.

THE BETTER PART[3]

Long fed on boundless hopes, O race of man,
How angrily thou spurn'st all simpler fare!
"Christ," some one says, "was human as we are;
No judge eyes us from Heaven, our sin to scan;

"We live no more, when we have done our span."— 5
"Well, then, for Christ," thou answerest, "who can care?
From sin, which Heaven records not, why forbear?
Live we like brutes our life without a plan!"

So answerest thou; but why not rather say:
"Hath man no second life?—*Pitch this one high!*   10
Sits there no judge in Heaven, our sin to see?—

"*More strictly, then, the inward judge obey!*
Was Christ a man like us? Ah! let us try
If we then, too, can be such men as he!"

DOVER BEACH

The sea is calm to-night.
The tide is full, the moon lies fair
Upon the straits;—on the French coast the light
Gleams and is gone; the cliffs of England stand,
Glimmering and vast, out in the tranquil bay.   5
Come to the window, sweet is the night-air!
Only, from the long line of spray
Where the sea meets the moon-blanched land,
Listen! you hear the grating roar
Of pebbles which the waves draw back, and fling,   10
At their return, up the high strand,
Begin, and cease, and then again begin,
With tremulous cadence slow, and bring
The eternal note of sadness in.

Sophocles long ago   15
Heard it on the Aegaean, and it brought
Into his mind the turbid ebb and flow
Of human misery;[4] we
Find also in the sound a thought,
Hearing it by this distant northern sea.   20

The Sea of Faith
Was once, too, at the full, and round earth's shore
Lay like the folds of a bright girdle furled.
But now I only hear
Its melancholy, long, withdrawing roar,   25

---

[3] Originally called "Anti-Desperation."
[4] The reference is to a passage in the *Antigone*, lines 583 ff.

Retreating, to the breath
Of the night wind, down the vast edges drear
And naked shingles of the world.[5]

Ah, love, let us be true
To one another! for the world, which seems   30
To lie before us like a land of dreams,
So various, so beautiful, so new,
Hath really neither joy, nor love, nor light,
Nor certitude, nor peace, nor help for pain;
And we are here as on a darkling plain,   35
Swept with confused alarms of struggle and flight,
Where ignorant armies clash by night.[6]

THE LAST WORD

Creep into thy narrow bed,
Creep, and let no more be said!
Vain thy onset! all stands fast.
Thou thyself must break at last.

Let the long contention cease!
Geese are swans, and swans are geese.   5
Let them have it how they will!
Thou art tired; best be still.

They out-talked thee, hissed thee, tore thee?
Better men fared thus before thee;   10
Fired their ringing shot and passed,
Hotly charged—and sank at last.

Charge once more, then, and be dumb!
Let the victors, when they come,
When the forts of folly fall,   15
Find thy body by the wall!

---

[5] Shingles are pebbled beaches. Though what is retreating is mainly religious faith, it is also faith of any kind, any coherent philosophy of the world which can make life meaningful.
[6] Cf. J. A. Symonds in his diary for 1865: "Scepticism is my spirit. In my sorest needs I have had no actual faith, and have said to destruction, 'Thou art my sister.' To the skirts of human love I have clung, and I cling blindly. But all else is chaos—a mountain chasm filled with tumbling mists."
It should be noticed that the moonlit scene of stanza one takes on symbolic meaning in the final stanza. The world that lies before him from the Dover cliffs is a beautiful world but it is not the real world. It is a world clothed in moonlight, a land of dreams. The real world is a land of darkness where ignorant armies clash by night.

IN TWO small volumes of Poems, published anonymously, one in 1849, the other in 1852, many of the Poems which compose the present volume have already appeared. The rest are now published for the first time.

I have, in the present collection, omitted the poem from which the volume published in 1852 took its title.[1] I have done so, not because the subject of it was a Sicilian Greek born between two and three thousand years ago, although many persons would think this a sufficient reason. Neither have I done so because I had, in my own opinion, failed in the delineation which I intended to effect. I intended to delineate the feelings of one of the last of the Greek religious philosophers, one of the family of Orpheus and Musaeus,[2] having survived his fellows, living on into a time when the habits of Greek thought and feeling had begun fast to change, character to dwindle, the influence of the Sophists[3] to prevail. Into the feelings of a man so situated there entered much that we are accustomed to consider as exclusively modern, how much, the fragments of Empedocles himself which remain to us are sufficient at least to indicate. What those who are familiar only with the great monuments of early Greek genius suppose to be its exclusive characteristics, have disappeared; the calm, the cheerfulness, the disinterested objectivity have disappeared; the dialogue of the mind with itself has commenced; modern problems have presented themselves; we hear already the doubts, we witness the discouragement, of Hamlet and of Faust.

The representation of such a man's feelings must be interesting, if consistently drawn. We all naturally take pleasure, says Aristotle,[4] in any imitation or representation whatever: this is the basis of our love of poetry: and we take pleasure in them, he adds, because all knowledge is naturally agreeable to us; not to the philosopher only, but to mankind at large. Every representation therefore which is consistently drawn may be supposed to be interesting, inasmuch as it gratifies this natural interest in knowledge of all kinds. What is *not* interesting, is that which does not add to our knowledge of any kind; that which is vaguely conceived and loosely drawn; a representation which is general, indeterminate, and faint, instead of being particular, precise, and firm.

Any accurate representation may therefore be expected to be interesting; but, if the representation be a poetical one, more than this is demanded. It is demanded, not only that it shall interest, but also that it shall inspirit and rejoice the reader: that it shall convey a charm, and infuse delight. For the Muses, as Hesiod says,[5] were born that they might be "a forgetfulness of evils, and a truce from cares": and it is not enough that the poet should add to the knowledge of men, it is required of him also that he should add to their happiness. "All art," says Schiller, "is dedicated to Joy, and there is no higher and no more serious problem, than how to make men happy. The right art is that alone, which creates the highest enjoyment."

A poetical work, therefore, is not yet justified when it has been shown to be an accurate, and therefore interesting representation; it has to be shown also that it is a representation from which men can derive enjoyment. In presence of the most tragic circumstances represented in a work of art, the feeling of enjoyment, as is well known, may still subsist: the representation of the most utter calamity, of the liveliest anguish, is not sufficient to destroy it: the more tragic the situation, the deeper becomes the enjoyment; and the situation is more tragic in proportion as it becomes more terrible.

What then are the situations, from the representation of which, though accurate, no poetical enjoyment can be derived? They are those in which the suffering finds no vent in action; in which a continuous state of mental distress is prolonged, unrelieved by incident, hope, or resistance; in which there is everything to be endured, nothing to be done. In such situations there is inevitably something morbid, in the description of them something monotonous. When they occur in actual life, they are painful, not tragic; the representation of them in poetry is painful also.

To this class of situations, poetically faulty as it appears to me, that of Empedocles, as I have endeavoured to represent him, belongs; and I have therefore excluded the poem from the present collection.

And why, it may be asked, have I entered into this explanation respecting a matter so unimportant as the

[1] "Empedocles on Etna."
[2] Legendary Greek poets and musicians. Orpheus was the father of Musaeus.
[3] Greek teachers of philosophy and rhetoric whose influence led to the placing of greater emphasis on ingenious argument than on the substance of truth.   [4] *Poetics*, IV, 2–5.

[5] Early Greek poet in his *Theogony*.

admission or exclusion of the poem in question? I have done so, because I was anxious to avow that the sole reason for its exclusion was that which has been stated above; and that it has not been excluded in deference to the opinion which many critics of the present day appear to entertain against subjects chosen from distant times and countries: against the choice, in short, of any subjects but modern ones.

"The poet," it is said,[6] and by an intelligent critic, "the poet who would really fix the public attention must leave the exhausted past, and draw his subjects from matters of present import, and *therefore* both of interest and novelty."

Now this view I believe to be completely false. It is worth examining, inasmuch as it is a fair sample of a class of critical dicta everywhere current at the present day, having a philosophical form and air, but no real basis in fact; and which are calculated to vitiate the judgement of readers of poetry, while they exert, so far as they are adopted, a misleading influence on the practice of those who make it.

What are the eternal objects of poetry, among all nations and at all times? They are actions; human actions; possessing an inherent interest in themselves, and which are to be communicated in an interesting manner by the art of the poet. Vainly will the latter imagine that he has everything in his own power; that he can make an intrinsically inferior action equally delightful with a more excellent one by his treatment of it: he may indeed compel us to admire his skill, but his work will possess, within itself, an incurable defect.

The poet, then, has in the first place to select an excellent action; and what actions are the most excellent? Those, certainly, which most powerfully appeal to the great primary human affections: to those elementary feelings which subsist permanently in the race, and which are independent of time. These feelings are permanent and the same; that which interests them is permanent and the same also. The modernness or antiquity of an action, therefore, has nothing to do with its fitness for poetical representation; this depends upon its inherent qualities. To the elementary part of our nature, to our passions, that which is great and passionate is eternally interesting; and interesting solely in proportion to its greatness and to its passion. A great human action of a thousand years ago is more interesting to it than a smaller human action of today, even though upon the repre-

sentation of this last the most consummate skill may have been expended, and though it has the advantage of appealing by its modern language, familiar manners, and contemporary allusions, to all our transient feelings and interests. These, however, have no right to demand of a poetical work that it shall satisfy them; their claims are to be directed elsewhere. Poetical works belong to the domain of our permanent passions: let them interest these, and the voice of all subordinate claims upon them is at once silenced.

Achilles, Prometheus, Clytemnestra, Dido—what modern poem presents personages as interesting, even to us moderns, as these personages of an "exhausted past"? We have the domestic epic dealing with the details of modern life, which pass daily under our eyes; we have poems representing modern personages in contact with the problems of modern life, moral, intellectual, and social; these works have been produced by poets the most distinguished of their nation and time; yet I fearlessly assert that *Hermann and Dorothea, Childe Harold, Jocelyn,* the *Excursion,*[7] leave the reader cold in comparison with the effect produced upon him by the latter books of the *Iliad,* by the *Oresteia,* or by the episode of Dido.[8] And why is this? Simply because in the three last-named cases the action is greater, the personages nobler, the situations more intense: and this is the true basis of the interest in a poetical work, and this alone.

It may be urged, however, that past actions may be interesting in themselves, but that they are not to be adopted by the modern poet, because it is impossible for him to have them clearly present to his own mind, and he cannot therefore feel them deeply, nor represent them forcibly. But this is not necessarily the case. The externals of a past action, indeed, he cannot know with the precision of a contemporary; but his business is with its essentials. The outward man of Oedipus[9] or of Macbeth, the houses in which they lived, the ceremonies of their courts, he cannot accurately figure to himself; but neither do they essentially concern him. His business is with their inward man; with their feelings and behaviour in certain tragic situations, which engage their passions as men; these have in them nothing local and casual; they are as accessible to the modern poet as to a contemporary.

---

6 "In the *Spectator* of April 2, 1853. The words quoted were not used with reference to poems of mine." (Arnold)

7 Narrative and philosophical poems by Goethe, Byron, Lamartine, and Wordsworth.

8 Cf. the opening sentence of this paragraph. Clytemnestra, the wife of Agamemnon, is in Aeschylus's *Oresteia.*

9 King of Thebes and hero of Sophocles's *Oedipus Tyrannus.*

The date of an action, then, signifies nothing: the action itself, its selection and construction, this is what is all-important. This the Greeks understood far more clearly than we do. The radical difference between their poetical theory and ours consists, as it appears to me, in this: that, with them, the poetical character of the action in itself, and the conduct of it, was the first consideration; with us, attention is fixed mainly on the value of the separate thoughts and images which occur in the treatment of an action. They regarded the whole; we regard the parts. With them, the action predominated over the expression of it; with us, the expression predominates over the action. Not that they failed in expression, or were inattentive to it; on the contrary, they are the highest models of expression, the unapproached masters of the *grand style:*[10] but their expression is so excellent because it is so admirably kept in its right degree of prominence; because it is so simple and so well subordinated; because it draws its force directly from the pregnancy of the matter which it conveys. For what reason was the Greek tragic poet confined to so limited a range of subjects? Because there are so few actions which united in themselves, in the highest degree, the conditions of excellence; and it was not thought that on any but an excellent subject could an excellent poem be constructed. A few actions, therefore, eminently adapted for tragedy, maintained almost exclusive possession of the Greek tragic stage. Their significance appeared inexhaustible; they were as permanent problems, perpetually offered to the genius of every fresh poet. This too is the reason of what appears to us moderns a certain baldness of expression in Greek tragedy; of the triviality with which we often reproach the remarks of the chorus, where it takes part in the dialogue: that the action itself, the situation of Orestes, or Merope, or Alcmaeon,[11] was to stand the central point of interest, unforgotten, absorbing, principal; that no accessories were for a moment to distract the spectator's attention from this, that the tone of the parts was to be perpetually kept down, in order not to impair the grandiose effect of the whole. The terrible old mythic story on which the drama was founded stood, before he entered the theatre, traced in its bare outlines upon the spectator's mind; it stood in his memory, as a group of statuary, faintly seen, at the end of a long and dark vista: then came the poet, embodying outlines, developing situations, not a word wasted, not a sentiment capriciously thrown in: stroke upon stroke, the drama proceeded: the light deepened upon the group; more and more it revealed itself to the rivetted gaze of the spectator: until at last, when the final words were spoken, it stood before him in broad sunlight, a model of immortal beauty.

This was what a Greek critic demanded; this was what a Greek poet endeavoured to effect. It signified nothing to what time an action belonged. We do not find that the *Persae* occupied a particularly high rank among the dramas of Aeschylus because it represented a matter of contemporary interest: this was not what a cultivated Athenian required. He required that the permanent elements of his nature should be moved; and dramas of which the action, though taken from a long-distant mythic time, yet was calculated to accomplish this in a higher degree than that of the *Persae*, stood higher in his estimation accordingly. The Greeks felt, no doubt, with their exquisite sagacity of taste, that an action of present times was too near them, too much mixed up with what was accidental and passing, to form a sufficiently grand, detached, and self-subsistent object for a tragic poem. Such objects belonged to the domain of the comic poet, and of the lighter kinds of poetry. For the more serious kinds, for *pragmatic* poetry, to use an excellent expression of Polybius,[12] they were more difficult and severe in the range of subjects which they permitted. Their theory and practice alike, the admirable treatise of Aristotle, and the unrivalled works of their poets, exclaim with a thousand tongues—"All depends upon the subject; choose a fitting action, penetrate yourself with the feeling of its situations; this done, everything else will follow."

But for all kinds of poetry alike there was one point on which they were rigidly exacting; the adaptability of the subject to the kind of poetry selected, and the careful construction of the poem.

How different a way of thinking from this is ours! We can hardly at the present day understand what Menander[13] meant, when he told a man who inquired as to the progress of his comedy that he had finished it, not having yet written a single line, because he had constructed the action of it in his mind. A modern critic would have assured him that

---

10 That is, great art. Cf. Arnold's definition in his *On Translating Homer: Last Words:* "The grand style arises in poetry, when a noble nature, poetically gifted, treats with simplicity or with severity a serious subject."

11 Three heroic characters in Greek tragedies, each of whom was involved in avenging a family murder.

12 The Greek historian of the second century B.C. Pragmatic poetry means poetry concerned with the business of life, social and personal.

13 The Greek comic dramatist (342?–292 B.C.).

the merit of his piece depended on the brilliant things which arose under his pen as he went along. We have poems which seem to exist merely for the sake of single lines and passages; not for the sake of producing any total impression. We have critics who seem to direct their attention merely to detached expressions, to the language about the action, not to the action itself. I verily think that the majority of them do not in their hearts believe that there is such a thing as a total-impression to be derived from a poem at all, or to be demanded from a poet; they think the term a commonplace of metaphysical criticism. They will permit the poet to select any action he pleases, and to suffer that action to go as it will, provided he gratifies them with occasional bursts of fine writing, and with a shower of isolated thoughts and images. That is, they permit him to leave their poetical sense ungratified, provided that he gratifies their rhetorical sense and their curiosity. Of his neglecting to gratify these, there is little danger; he needs rather to be warned against the danger of attempting to gratify these alone; he needs rather to be perpetually reminded to prefer his action to everything else; so to treat this, as to permit its inherent excellences to develop themselves, without interruption from the intrusion of his personal peculiarities: most fortunate when he most entirely succeeds in effacing himself, and in enabling a noble action to subsist as it did in nature.

But the modern critic not only permits a false practice: he absolutely prescribes false aims. "A true allegory of the state of one's own mind in a representative history," the poet is told, "is perhaps the highest thing that one can attempt in the way of poetry." And accordingly he attempts it. An allegory of the state of one's own mind, the highest problem of an art which imitates actions! No, assuredly, it is not, it never can be so: no great poetical work has ever been produced with such an aim. *Faust* itself, in which something of the kind is attempted, wonderful passages as it contains, and in spite of the unsurpassed beauty of the scenes which relate to Margaret, *Faust* itself, judged as a whole, and judged strictly as a poetical work, is defective: its illustrious author, the greatest poet of modern times, the greatest critic of all times, would have been the first to acknowledge it; he only defended his work, indeed, by asserting it to be "something incommensurable."

The confusion of the present times is great, the multitude of voices counselling different things bewildering, the number of existing works capable of attracting a young writer's attention and of becoming his models, immense: what he wants is a hand to guide him through the confusion, a voice to prescribe to him the aim which he should keep in view, and to explain to him that the value of the literary works which offer themselves to his attention is relative to their power of helping him forward on his road towards this aim. Such a guide the English writer at the present day will nowhere find. Failing this, all that can be looked for, all indeed that can be desired, is, that his attention should be fixed on excellent models; that he may reproduce, at any rate, something of their excellence, by penetrating himself with their works and by catching their spirit, if he cannot be taught to produce what is excellent independently.

Foremost among these models for the English writer stands Shakespeare: a name the greatest perhaps of all poetical names; a name never to be mentioned without reverence. I will venture, however, to express a doubt whether the influence of his works, excellent and fruitful for the readers of poetry, for the great majority, has been an unmixed advantage to the writers of it. Shakespeare indeed chose excellent subjects—the world could afford no better than *Macbeth,* or *Romeo and Juliet,* or *Othello:* he had no theory respecting the necessity of choosing subjects of present import, or the paramount interest attaching to allegories of the state of one's own mind; like all great poets, he knew well what constituted a poetical action; like them, wherever he found such an action, he took it; like them, too, he found his best in past times. But to these general characteristics of all great poets he added a special one of his own; a gift, namely, of happy, abundant, and ingenious expression, eminent and unrivalled; so eminent as irresistibly to strike the attention first in him and even to throw into comparative shade his other excellences as a poet. Here has been the mischief. These other excellences were his fundamental excellences *as a poet;* what distinguishes the artist from the mere amateur, says Goethe, is *Architectonicè* in the highest sense; that power of execution which creates, forms, and constitutes: not the profoundness of single thoughts, not the richness of imagery, not the abundance of illustration. But these attractive accessories of a poetical work being more easily seized than the spirit of the whole, and these accessories being possessed by Shakespeare in an unequalled degree, a young writer having recourse to Shakespeare as his model runs great risk of being vanquished and absorbed by them, and, in consequence, of reproducing, according to the measure of his power, these, and these alone. Of this preponderring quality of Shakespeare's genius, accordingly, almost the whole of modern English poetry has, it appears to me, felt the influence. To the exclusive attention on the part of his imitators to this, it is in a great degree owing that of the majority of modern poetical works the details alone are valuable, the composition worthless. In reading them one is perpetually reminded of that terrible sentence on a modern French poet,—*il dit tout ce qu'il veut, mais malheureusement il n'a rien à dire.*[14]

Let me give an instance of what I mean. I will take it from the works of the very chief among those who seem to have been formed in the school of Shakespeare; of one whose exquisite genius and pathetic death render him forever interesting. I will take the poem of *Isabella, or the Pot of Basil,* by Keats. I choose this rather than the *Endymion,* because the latter work (which a modern critic has classed with the *Faery Queen!*), although undoubtedly there blows through it the breath of genius, is yet as a whole so utterly incoherent, as not strictly to merit the name of a poem at all. The poem of *Isabella,* then, is a perfect treasure-house of graceful and felicitous words and images: almost in every stanza there occurs one of those vivid and picturesque turns of expression, by which the object is made to flash upon the eye of the mind, and which thrill the reader with a sudden delight. This one short poem contains, perhaps, a greater number of happy single expressions which one could quote than all the extant tragedies of Sophocles. But the action, the story? The action in itself is an excellent one; but so feebly is it conceived by the poet, so loosely constructed, that the effect produced by it, in and for itself, is absolutely null. Let the reader, after he has finished the poem of Keats, turn to the same story in the *Decameron:*[15] he will then feel how pregnant and interesting the same action has become in the hands of a great artist, who above all things delineates his object; who subordinates expression to that which it is designed to express.

I have said that the imitators of Shakespeare, fixing their attention on his wonderful gift of expression, have directed their imitation to this, neglecting his other excellences. These excellences, the fundamental excellences of poetical art, Shakespeare no doubt possessed them—possessed many of them in a splendid degree; but it may perhaps be doubted whether even he himself did not sometimes give scope to his faculty of expression to the prejudice of a higher poetical duty. For we must never forget that Shakespeare is the great poet he is from his skill in discerning and firmly conceiving an excellent action, from his power of intensely feeling a situation, of intimately associating himself with a character; not from his gift of expression, which rather even leads him astray, degenerating sometimes into a fondness for curiosity of expression, into an irritability of fancy, which seems to make it impossible for him to say a thing plainly, even when the press of the action demands the very directest language, or its level character the very simplest. Mr. Hallam,[16] than whom it is impossible to find a saner and more judicious critic, has had the courage (for at the present day it needs courage) to remark, how extremely and faultily difficult Shakespeare's language often is. It is so: you may find main scenes in some of his greatest tragedies, *King Lear,* for instance, where the language is so artificial, so curiously tortured, and so difficult, that every speech has to be read two or three times before its meaning can be comprehended. This over-curiousness of expression is indeed but the excessive employment of a wonderful gift—of the power of saying a thing in a happier way than any other man; nevertheless, it is carried so far that one understands what M. Guizot[17] meant when he said that Shakespeare appears in his language to have tried all styles except that of simplicity. He has not the severe and scrupulous self-restraint of the ancients, partly, no doubt, because he had a far less cultivated and exacting audience. He has indeed a far wider range than they had, a far richer fertility of thought; in this respect he rises above them. In his strong conception of his subject, in the genuine way in which he is penetrated with it, he resembles them, and is unlike the moderns. But in the accurate limitation of it, the conscientious rejection of superfluities, the simple and rigorous development of it from the first line of his work to the last, he falls below them, and comes nearer to the moderns. In his chief works, besides what he has of his own, he has the elementary soundness of the ancients; he has their important action and their large and broad manner; but he has not their purity of method. He is therefore a less safe model; for what he has of his own is personal, and inseparable from his own rich nature; it may be imitated and exaggerated, it cannot be learned or applied as an art. He is above

---

14 "He says all he wishes to, but unfortunately he has nothing to say." The poet referred to is Théophile Gautier (1811–72), the leader of the French school of Art for Art's Sake.
15 By Boccaccio: the fifth novel of the fourth day.

16 Henry Hallam (1777–1859) in his *Introduction to the Literature of Europe in the Fifteenth, Sixteenth, and Seventeenth Centuries,* chap. 23.
17 The French historian (1787–1874) in his preface to *Shakespeare and His Times.*

all suggestive; more valuable, therefore, to young writers as men than as artists. But clearness of arrangement, rigour of development, simplicity of style—these may to a certain extent be learned: and these may, I am convinced, be learned best from the ancients, who, although infinitely less suggestive than Shakespeare, are thus, to the artist, more instructive.

What then, it will be asked, are the ancients to be our sole models? the ancients with their comparatively narrow range of experience, and their widely different circumstances? Not, certainly, that which is narrow in the ancients, nor that in which we can no longer sympathize. An action like the action of the *Antigone* of Sophocles, which turns upon the conflict between the heroine's duty to her brother's corpse and that to the laws of her country, is no longer one in which it is possible that we should feel a deep interest. I am speaking too, it will be remembered, not of the best sources of intellectual stimulus for the general reader, but of the best models of instruction for the individual writer. This last may certainly learn of the ancients, better than anywhere else, three things which it is vitally important for him to know:—the all-importance of the choice of a subject; the necessity of accurate construction; and the subordinate character of expression. He will learn from them how unspeakably superior is the effect of the one moral impression left by a great action treated as a whole, to the effect produced by the most striking single thought or by the happiest image. As he penetrates into the spirit of the great classical works, as he becomes gradually aware of their intense significance, their noble simplicity, and their calm pathos, he will be convinced that it is this effect, unity and profoundness of moral impression, at which the ancient poets aimed; that it is this which constitutes the grandeur of their works, and which makes them immortal. He will desire to direct his own efforts towards producing the same effect. Above all, he will deliver himself from the jargon of modern criticism, and escape the danger of producing poetical works conceived in the spirit of the passing time, and which partake of its transitoriness.

The present age makes great claims upon us: we owe it service, it will not be satisfied without our admiration. I know not how it is, but their commerce with the ancients appears to me to produce, in those who constantly practise it, a steadying and composing effect upon their judgement, not of literary works only, but of men and events in general. They are like persons who have had a very weighty and impressive experience; they are more truly than others under the empire of facts, and more independent of the language current among those with whom they live. They wish neither to applaud nor to revile their age: they wish to know what it is, what it can give them, and whether this is what they want. What they want, they know very well; they want to educe and cultivate what is best and noblest in themselves: they know, too, that this is no easy task—χαλεπὸν, as Pittacus said, χαλεπὸν ἐσθλὸν ἔμμεναι[18]—and they ask themselves sincerely whether their age and its literature can assist them in the attempt. If they are endeavouring to practise any art, they remember the plain and simple proceedings of the old artists, who attained their grand results by penetrating themselves with some noble and significant action, not by inflating themselves with a belief in the pre-eminent importance and greatness of their own times. They do not talk of their mission, nor of interpreting their age, nor of the coming poet; all this, they know, is the mere delirium of vanity; their business is not to praise their age, but to afford to the men who live in it the highest pleasure which they are capable of feeling. If asked to afford this by means of subjects drawn from the age itself, they ask what special fitness the present age has for supplying them. They are told that it is an era of progress, an age commissioned to carry out the great ideas of industrial development and social amelioration. They reply that with all this they can do nothing; that the elements they need for the exercise of their art are great actions, calculated powerfully and delightfully to affect what is permanent in the human soul; that so far as the present age can supply such actions, they will gladly make use of them; but that an age wanting in moral grandeur can with difficulty supply such, and an age of spiritual discomfort with difficulty be powerfully and delightfully affected by them.

A host of voices will indignantly rejoin that the present age is inferior to the past neither in moral grandeur nor in spiritual health. He who possesses the discipline I speak of will content himself with remembering the judgements passed upon the present age, in this respect, by the men of strongest head and widest culture whom it has produced; by Goethe and by Niebuhr.[19] It will be sufficient for him that he knows the opinions held by these two great men respecting the present age and its literature; and that he feels assured in his own mind that their aims and demands upon life were such as he would wish, at

---

18 "It is hard to be excellent." Pittacus was one of the Seven Sages of Greece.
19 A German historian of Rome, contemporary with Goethe.

any rate, his own to be; and their judgement as to what is impeding and disabling such as he may safely follow. He will not, however, maintain a hostile attitude towards the false pretensions of his age; he will content himself with not being overwhelmed by them. He will esteem himself fortunate if he can succeed in banishing from his mind all feelings of contradiction, and irritation, and impatience; in order to delight himself with the contemplation of some noble action of a heroic time, and to enable others, through his representation of it, to delight in it also.

I am far indeed from making any claim, for myself, that I possess this discipline; or for the following poems, that they breathe its spirit. But I say, that in the sincere endeavour to learn and practise, amid the bewildering confusion of our times, what is sound and true in poetical art, I seemed to myself to find the only sure guidance, the only solid footing, among the ancients. They, at any rate, knew what they wanted in art, and we do not. It is this uncertainty which is disheartening, and not hostile criticism. How often have I felt this when reading words of disparagement or of cavil: that it is the uncertainty as to what is

really to be aimed at which makes our difficulty, not the dissatisfaction of the critic, who himself suffers from the same uncertainty. *Non me tua fervida terrent Dicta; . . . Dii me terrent, et Jupiter hostis.*[20]

Two kinds of *dilettanti,* says Goethe, there are in poetry: he who neglects the indispensable mechanical part, and thinks he has done enough if he shows spirituality and feeling; and he who seeks to arrive at poetry merely by mechanism, in which he can acquire an artisan's readiness, and is without soul and matter. And he adds, that the first does most harm to art, and the last to himself. If we must be *dilettanti:* if it is impossible for us, under the circumstances amidst which we live, to think clearly, to feel nobly, and to delineate firmly: if we cannot attain to the mastery of the great artists—let us, at least, have so much respect for our art as to prefer it to ourselves. Let us not bewilder our successors: let us transmit to them the practice of poetry, with its boundaries and wholesome regulative laws, under which excellent works may again, perhaps, at some future time, be produced, not yet fallen into oblivion through our neglect, not yet condemned and cancelled by the influence of their eternal enemy, caprice.

from ESSAYS IN CRITICISM, FIRST SERIES

I

from THE FUNCTION OF CRITICISM
AT THE PRESENT TIME[1]

MANY objections have been made to a proposition which, in some remarks of mine on translating Homer, I ventured to put forth; a proposition about criticism, and its importance at the present day. I said that "of the literature of France and Germany, as of the intellect of Europe in general, the main effort, for now many years, has been a critical effort; the endeavor, in all branches of knowledge, theology, philosophy, history, art, science, to see the object as in itself it really is." I added, that owing to the operation in English literature of certain causes, "almost the last thing for which one would come to English literature is just that very thing which now Europe most desires—criticism"; and that the power and value of English literature was thereby impaired. More than one rejoinder declared that the importance I here assigned to criticism was excessive, and asserted

the inherent superiority of the creative effort of the human spirit over its critical effort. And the other day, having been led by an excellent notice of Wordsworth, published in the *North British Review,* to turn again to his biography, I found, in the words of this great man, whom I, for one, must always listen to with the profoundest respect, a sentence passed on the critic's business, which seems to justify every possible disparagement of it. Wordsworth says in one of his letters:

"The writers in these publications" (the Reviews), "while they prosecute their inglorious employment, cannot be supposed to be in a state of mind very favorable for being affected by the finer influences of a thing so pure as genuine poetry."

And a trustworthy reporter of his conversation quotes a more elaborate judgment to the same effect:

"Wordsworth holds the critical power very low, infinitely lower than the inventive; and he said to-day that if the quantity of time consumed in writing critiques on the works of others were given to original

---

[1] First published in November, 1864.

[20] Vergil's *Aeneid,* XII, 894–5: "Your hot words do not frighten me. . . . The gods frighten me, and Jupiter as my enemy."

composition, of whatever kind it might be, it would be much better employed; it would make a man find out sooner his own level, and it would do infinitely less mischief. A false or malicious criticism may do much injury to the minds of others; a stupid invention, either in prose or verse, is quite harmless."

It is almost too much to expect of poor human nature, that a man capable of producing some effect in one line of literature, should, for the greater good of society, voluntarily doom himself to impotence and obscurity in another. Still less is this to be expected from men addicted to the composition of the "false or malicious criticism" of which Wordsworth speaks. However, everybody would admit that a false or malicious criticism had better never have been written. Everybody, too, would be willing to admit, as a general proposition, that the critical faculty is lower than the inventive. But is it true that criticism is really, in itself, a baneful and injurious employment; is it true that all time given to writing critiques on the works of others would be much better employed if it were given to original composition of whatever kind this may be? Is it true that Johnson had better have gone on producing more *Irenes*[2] instead of writing his *Lives of the Poets;* nay, is it certain that Wordsworth himself was better employed in making his Ecclesiastical Sonnets than when he made his celebrated Preface,[3] so full of criticism, and criticism of the works of others? Wordsworth was himself a great critic, and it is to be sincerely regretted that he has not left us more criticism; Goethe was one of the greatest of critics, and we may sincerely congratulate ourselves that he has left us so much criticism. Without wasting time over the exaggeration which Wordsworth's judgment on criticism clearly contains, or over an attempt to trace the causes—not difficult, I think, to be traced —which may have led Wordsworth to this exaggeration, a critic may with advantage seize an occasion for trying his own conscience, and for asking himself of what real service, at any given moment, the practice of criticism either is, or may be made, to his own mind and spirit, and to the minds and spirits of others.

The critical power is of lower rank than the creative. True; but in assenting to this proposition, one or two things are to be kept in mind. It is undeniable that the exercise of a creative power, that a free creative activity, is the true function of man; it is proved to be so by man's finding in it his true happiness. But it is undeniable, also, that men may have the sense of exercising this free creative activity in other ways than in producing great works of literature or art; if it were not so, all but a very few men would be shut out from the true happiness of all men. They may have it in well-doing, they may have it in learning, they may have it even in criticizing. This is one thing to be kept in mind. Another is, that the exercise of the creative power in the production of great works of literature or art, however high this exercise of it may rank, is not at all epochs and under all conditions possible; and that therefore labor may be vainly spent in attempting it, which might with more fruit be used in preparing for it, in rendering it possible. This creative power works with elements, with materials; what if it has not those materials, those elements, ready for its use? In that case it must surely wait till they are ready. Now, in literature—I will limit myself to literature, for it is about literature that the question arises—the elements with which the creative power works are ideas; the best ideas on every matter which literature touches, current at the time. At any rate we may lay it down as certain that in modern literature no manifestation of the creative power not working with these can be very important or fruitful. And I say *current* at the time, not merely accessible at the time; for creative literary genius does not principally show itself in discovering new ideas, that is rather the business of the philosopher. The grand work of literary genius is a work of synthesis and exposition, not of analysis and discovery; its gift lies in the faculty of being happily inspired by a certain intellectual and spiritual atmosphere, by a certain order of ideas, when it finds itself in them; of dealing divinely with these ideas, presenting them in the most effective and attractive combinations, making beautiful works with them, in short. But it must have the atmosphere, it must find itself amidst the order of ideas, in order to work freely; and these it is not so easy to command. This is why great creative epochs in literature are so rare; this is why there is so much that is unsatisfactory in the productions of many men of real genius; because, for the creation of a master-work of literature two powers must concur, the power of the man and the power of the moment, and the man is not enough without the moment; the creative power has, for its happy exercise, appointed elements, and those elements are not in its own control.

Nay, they are more within the control of the critical power. It is the business of the critical power, as I said in the words already quoted, "in all branches of knowledge, theology, philosophy, history, art,

---

[2] Dr. Johnson's *Irene* (1749) was an unsuccessful play.
[3] To the second edition of *Lyrical Ballads* (pp. 69–78, above).

science, to see the object as in itself it really is." Thus it tends, at last, to make an intellectual situation of which the creative power can profitably avail itself. It tends to establish an order of ideas, if not absolutely true, yet true by comparison with that which it displaces; to make the best ideas prevail. Presently these new ideas reach society, the touch of truth is the touch of life, and there is a stir and growth everywhere; out of this stir and growth come the creative epochs of literature.

Or, to narrow our range, and quit these considerations of the general march of genius and of society—considerations which are apt to become too abstract and impalpable—every one can see that a poet, for instance, ought to know life and the world before dealing with them in poetry; and life and the world being in modern times very complex things, the creation of a modern poet, to be worth much, implies a great critical effort behind it; else it would be a comparatively poor, barren, and short-lived affair. This is why Byron's poetry had so little endurance in it, and Goethe's so much; both Byron and Goethe had a great productive power, but Goethe's was nourished by a great critical effort providing the true materials for it, and Byron's was not; Goethe knew life and the world, the poet's necessary subjects, much more comprehensively and thoroughly than Byron. He knew a great deal more of them, and he knew them much more as they really are.

It has long seemed to me that the burst of creative activity in our literature, through the first quarter of this century, had about it in fact something premature; and that from this cause its productions are doomed, most of them, in spite of the sanguine hopes which accompanied and do still accompany them, to prove hardly more lasting than the productions of far less splendid epochs. And this prematureness comes from its having proceeded without having its proper data, without sufficient materials to work with. In other words, the English poetry of the first quarter of this century, with plenty of energy, plenty of creative force, did not know enough. This makes Byron so empty of matter, Shelley so incoherent, Wordsworth even, profound as he is, yet so wanting in completeness and variety. Wordsworth cared little for books, and disparaged Goethe. I admire Wordsworth, as he is, so much that I cannot wish him different; and it is vain, no doubt, to imagine such a man different from what he is, to suppose that he could have been different. But surely the one thing wanting to make Wordsworth an even greater poet than he is—his thought richer, and his influence of wider application—was that he should have read

more books, among them, no doubt, those of that Goethe whom he disparaged without reading him.

But to speak of books and reading may easily lead to a misunderstanding here. It was not really books and reading that lacked to our poetry at this epoch; Shelley had plenty of reading, Coleridge had immense reading. Pindar and Sophocles—as we all say so glibly, and often with so little discernment of the real import of what we are saying—had not many books; Shakespeare was no deep reader. True; but in the Greece of Pindar and Sophocles, in the England of Shakespeare, the poet lived in a current of ideas in the highest degree animating and nourishing to the creative power; society was, in the fullest measure, permeated by fresh thought, intelligent and alive. And this state of things is the true basis for the creative power's exercise, in this it finds its data, its materials, truly ready for its hand; all the books and reading in the world are only valuable as they are helps to this. Even when this does not actually exist, books and reading may enable a man to construct a kind of semblance of it in his own mind, a world of knowledge and intelligence in which he may live and work. This is by no means an equivalent to the artist for the nationally diffused life and thought of the epochs of Sophocles or Shakespeare; but, besides that it may be a means of preparation for such epochs, it does really constitute, if many share in it, a quickening and sustaining atmosphere of great value. Such an atmosphere the many-sided learning and the long and widely-combined critical effort of Germany formed for Goethe, when he lived and worked. There was no national glow of life and thought there, as in the Athens of Pericles or the England of Elizabeth. That was the poet's weakness. But there was a sort of equivalent for it in the complete culture and unfettered thinking of a large body of Germans. That was his strength. In the England of the first quarter of this century there was neither a national glow of life and thought, such as we had in the age of Elizabeth, nor yet a culture and a force of learning and criticism such as were to be found in Germany. Therefore the creative power of poetry wanted, for success in the highest sense, materials and a basis; a thorough interpretation of the world was necessarily denied to it.

At first sight it seems strange that out of the immense stir of the French Revolution and its age should not have come a crop of works of genius equal to that which came out of the stir of the great productive time of Greece, or out of that of the Renaissance, with its powerful episode the Reformation. But the truth is that the stir of the French Revolution took a character which essentially distinguished it from such movements as these. These were, in the main, disinterestedly intellectual and spiritual movements; movements in which the human spirit looked for its satisfaction in itself and in the increased play of its own activity. The French Revolution took a political, practical character. The movement which went on in France under the old régime, from 1700 to 1789, was far more really akin than that of the Revolution itself to the movement of the Renaissance; the France of Voltaire and Rousseau told far more powerfully upon the mind of Europe than the France of the Revolution. Goethe reproached this last expressly with having "thrown quiet culture back." Nay, and the true key to how much in our Byron, even in our Wordsworth, is this!—that they had their source in a great movement of feeling, not in a great movement of mind. The French Revolution, however, that object of so much blind love and so much blind hatred, found undoubtedly its motive-power in the intelligence of men, and not in their practical sense;—this is what distinguishes it from the English Revolution of Charles the First's time. This is what makes it a more spiritual event than our Revolution, an event of much more powerful and world-wide interest, though practically less successful—it appeals to an order of ideas which are universal, certain, permanent. 1789 asked of a thing, Is it rational? 1642 asked of a thing, Is it legal? or, when it went furthest, Is it according to conscience? This is the English fashion, a fashion to be treated, within its own sphere, with the highest respect; for its success, within its own sphere, has been prodigious. But what is law in one place is not law in another; what is law here to-day is not law even here to-morrow; and as for conscience, what is binding on one man's conscience is not binding on another's. The old woman who threw her stool at the head of the surpliced minister in the Tron Church at Edinburgh[4] obeyed an impulse to which millions of the human race may be permitted to remain strangers. But the prescriptions of reason are absolute, unchanging, of universal validity; *to count by tens is the easiest way of counting*—that is a proposition of which every one, from here to the Antipodes, feels the force; at least I should say so if we did not live in a country where it is not impossible that any morning we may find a letter in the *Times* declaring that a decimal coinage is an absurdity. That a whole nation should have been penetrated with an enthusiasm for pure

reason, and with an ardent zeal for making its prescriptions triumph, is a very remarkable thing, when we consider how little of mind or anything so worthy and quickening as mind, comes into the motives which alone, in general, *impel* great masses of men. In spite of the extravagant direction given to this enthusiasm, in spite of the crimes and follies in which it lost itself, the French Revolution derives from the force, truth, and universality of the ideas which it took for its law, and from the passion with which it could inspire a multitude for these ideas, a unique and still living power; it is—it will probably long remain—the greatest, the most animating event in history. And as no sincere passion for the things of the mind, even though it turn out in many respects an unfortunate passion, is ever quite thrown away and quite barren of good, France has reaped from hers one fruit—the natural and legitimate fruit, though not precisely the grand fruit she expected: she is the country in Europe where *the people* is most alive.

But the mania for giving an immediate political and practical application to all these fine ideas of the reason was fatal. Here an Englishman is in his element: on this theme we can all go for hours. And all we are in the habit of saying on it has undoubtedly a great deal of truth. Ideas cannot be too much prized in and for themselves, cannot be too much lived with; but to transport them abruptly into the world of politics and practice, violently to revolutionize this world to their bidding—that is quite another thing. There is the world of ideas and there is the world of practice; the French are often for suppressing the one and the English the other; but neither is to be suppressed. A member of the House of Commons said to me the other day: "That a thing is an anomaly, I consider to be no objection to it whatever." I venture to think he was wrong; that a thing is an anomaly *is* an objection to it, but absolutely and in the sphere of ideas: it is not necessarily, under such and such circumstances, or at such and such a moment, an objection to it in the sphere of politics and practice. Joubert[5] has said beautifully: "C'est la force et le droit qui règlent toutes choses dans le monde; la force en attendant le droit." Force and right are the governors of this world; force till right is ready. *Force till right is ready;* and till right is ready, force, the existing order of things, is justified, is the legitimate ruler. But right is something moral, and implies inward recognition, free assent of the will; we are not ready for right—*right,* so far as we are concerned,

---

[4] Janet Geddes thus protested against the imposition of the English liturgy on the Scotch Church by Charles I in 1637.

[5] French moralist of the nineteenth century.

is not ready—until we have attained this sense of seeing it and willing it. The way in which for us it may change and transform force, the existing order of things, and become, in its turn, the legitimate ruler of the world, will depend on the way in which, when our time comes, we see it and will it. Therefore for other people enamored of their own newly discerned right, to attempt to impose it upon us as ours, and violently to substitute their right for our force, is an act of tyranny, and to be resisted. It sets at nought the second great half of our maxim, *force till right is ready*. This was the grand error of the French Revolution; and its movement of ideas, by quitting the intellectual sphere and rushing furiously into the political sphere, ran, indeed, a prodigious and memorable course, but produced no such intellectual fruit as the movement of ideas of the Renaissance, and created, in opposition to itself, what I may call an *epoch of concentration*. The great force of that epoch of concentration was England; and the great voice of that epoch of concentration was Burke. It is the fashion to treat Burke's writings on the French Revolution as superannuated and conquered by the event; as the eloquent but unphilosophical tirades of bigotry and prejudice. I will not deny that they are often disfigured by the violence and passion of the moment, and that in some directions Burke's view was bounded, and his observation therefore at fault. But on the whole, and for those who can make the needful corrections, what distinguishes these writings is their profound, permanent, fruitful, philosophical truth. They contain the true philosophy of an epoch of concentration, dissipate the heavy atmosphere which its own nature is apt to engender round it, and make its resistance rational instead of mechanical.

But Burke is so great because, almost alone in England, he brings thought to bear upon politics, he saturates politics with thought. It is his accident that his ideas were at the service of an epoch of concentration, not of an epoch of expansion; it is his characteristic that he so lived by ideas, and had such a source of them welling up within him, that he could float even an epoch of concentration and English Tory politics with them. It does not hurt him that Dr. Price[6] and the Liberals were displeased with him; it does not even hurt him that George the Third and the Tories were enchanted with him. His greatness is that he lived in a world which neither English Liberalism nor English Toryism is apt to enter;—the

world of ideas, not the world of catchwords and party habits. So far is it from being really true of him that he "to party gave up what was meant for mankind," that at the very end of his fierce struggle with the French Revolution, after all his invectives against its false pretensions, hollowness, and madness, with his sincere conviction of its mischievousness, he can close a memorandum on the best means of combating it, some of the last pages he ever wrote—the *Thoughts on French Affairs,* in December 1791—with these striking words:

"The evil is stated, in my opinion, as it exists. The remedy must be where power, wisdom, and information, I hope, are more united with good intentions than they can be with me. I have done with this subject, I believe, for ever. It has given me many anxious moments for the last two years. *If a great change is to be made in human affairs, the minds of men will be fitted to it; the general opinions and feelings will draw that way. Every fear, every hope will forward it; and then they who persist in opposing this mighty current in human affairs, will appear rather to resist the decrees of Providence itself, than the mere designs of men. They will not be resolute and firm, but perverse and obstinate.*"

That return of Burke upon himself has always seemed to me one of the finest things in English literature, or indeed in any literature. That is what I call living by ideas: when one side of a question has long had your earnest support, when all your feelings are engaged, when you hear all round you no language but one, when your party talks this language like a steam-engine and can imagine no other—still to be able to think, still to be irresistibly carried, if so it be, by the current of thought to the opposite side of the question, and, like Balaam, to be unable to speak anything *but what the Lord has put in your mouth*.[7] I know nothing more striking, and I must add that I know nothing more un-English.

For the Englishman in general is like my friend the Member of Parliament, and believes, point-blank, that for a thing to be an anomaly is absolutely no objection to it whatever. He is like the Lord Auckland of Burke's day, who, in a memorandum on the French Revolution, talks of "certain miscreants, assuming the name of philosophers, who have presumed themselves capable of establishing a new system of society." The Englishman has been called a political animal, and he values what is political and practical so much that ideas easily become objects of dislike in his eyes, and thinkers "miscreants," because ideas and thinkers have rashly meddled with politics

---

[6] The nonconformist Richard Price, who supported both the American and French revolutions.

[7] Numbers 22:35, 38.

and practice. This would be all very well if the dislike and neglect confined themselves to ideas transported out of their own sphere, and meddling rashly with practice; but they are inevitably extended to ideas as such, and to the whole life of intelligence; practice is everything, a free play of the mind is nothing. The notion of the free play of the mind upon all subjects being a pleasure in itself, being an object of desire, being an essential provider of elements without which a nation's spirit, whatever compensations it may have for them, must, in the long run, die of inanition, hardly enters into an Englishman's thoughts. It is noticeable that the word *curiosity*, which in other languages is used in a good sense, to mean, as a high and fine quality of man's nature, just this disinterested love of a free play of the mind on all subjects, for its own sake,—it is noticeable, I say, that this word has in our language no sense of the kind, no sense but a rather bad and disparaging one. But criticism, real criticism, is essentially the exercise of this very quality. It obeys an instinct prompting it to try to know the best that is known and thought in the world, irrespectively of practice, politics, and everything of the kind; and to value knowledge and thought as they approach this best, without the intrusion of any other considerations whatever. This is an instinct for which there is, I think, little original sympathy in the practical English nature, and what there was of it has undergone a long benumbing period of blight and suppression in the epoch of concentration which followed the French Revolution.

But epochs of concentration cannot well endure for ever; epochs of expansion, in the due course of things, follow them. Such an epoch of expansion seems to be opening in this country. In the first place all danger of a hostile forcible pressure of foreign ideas upon our practice has long disappeared; like the traveller in the fable,[8] therefore, we begin to wear our cloak a little more loosely. Then, with a long peace, the ideas of Europe steal gradually and amicably in, and mingle, though in infinitesimally small quantities at a time, with our own notions. Then, too, in spite of all that is said about the absorbing and brutalizing influence of our passionate material progress, it seems to be indisputable that this progress is likely, though not certain, to lead in the end to an apparition of intellectual life; and that man, after he has made himself perfectly comfortable and has now to determine what to do with himself next, may be-

gin to remember that he has a mind, and that the mind may be made the source of great pleasure. I grant it is mainly the privilege of faith, at present, to discern this end to our railways, our business, and our fortune-making; but we shall see if, here as elsewhere, faith is not in the end the true prophet. Our ease, our travelling, and our unbounded liberty to hold just as hard and securely as we please to the practice to which our notions have given birth, all tend to beget an inclination to deal a little more freely with these notions themselves, to canvass them a little, to penetrate a little into their real nature. Flutterings of curiosity, in the foreign sense of the word, appear amongst us, and it is in these that criticism must look to find its account. Criticism first; a time of true creative activity, perhaps—which, as I have said, must inevitably be preceded amongst us by a time of criticism—hereafter, when criticism has done its work.

It is of the last importance that English criticism should clearly discern what rule for its course, in order to avail itself of the field now opening to it, and to produce fruit for the future, it ought to take. The rule may be summed up in one word—disinterestedness. And how is criticism to show disinterestedness? By keeping aloof from what is called "the practical view of things"; by resolutely following the law of its own nature, which is to be a free play of the mind on all subjects which it touches. By steadily refusing to lend itself to any of those ulterior, political, practical considerations about ideas, which plenty of people will be sure to attach to them, which perhaps ought often to be attached to them, which in this country at any rate are certain to be attached to them quite sufficiently, but which criticism has really nothing to do with. Its business is, as I have said, simply to know the best that is known and thought in the world, and by in its turn making this known, to create a current of true and fresh ideas. Its business is to do this with inflexible honesty, with due ability; but its business is to do no more, and to leave alone all questions of practical consequences and applications, questions which will never fail to have due prominence given to them. Else criticism, besides being really false to its own nature, merely continues in the old rut which it has hitherto followed in this country, and will certainly miss the chance now given to it.

For what is at present the bane of criticism in this country? It is that practical considerations cling to it and stifle it. It subserves interests not its own. Our organs of criticism are organs of men and parties having practical ends to serve, and with them those

---

8 Of the wind and the sun in Aesop.

practical ends are the first thing and the play of mind the second; so much play of mind as is compatible with the prosecution of those practical ends is all that is wanted. An organ like the *Revue des Deux Mondes,* having for its main function to understand and utter the best that is known and thought in the world, existing, it may be said, as just an organ for a free play of the mind, we have not. But we have the *Edinburgh Review,* existing as an organ of the old Whigs, and for as much play of the mind as may suit its being that; we have the *Quarterly Review,* existing as an organ of the Tories, and for as much play of mind as may suit its being that; we have the *British Quarterly Review,* existing as an organ of the political Dissenters, and for as much play of mind as may suit its being that; we have the *Times,* existing as an organ of the common, satisfied, well-to-do Englishman, and for as much play of mind as may suit its being that. And so on through all the various fractions, political and religious, of our society; every fraction has, as such, its organ of criticism, but the notion of combining all fractions in the common pleasure of a free disinterested play of mind meets with no favor. Directly this play of mind wants to have more scope, and to forget the pressure of practical considerations a little, it is checked, it is made to feel the chain. We saw this the other day in the extinction, so much to be regretted, of the *Home and Foreign Review.* Perhaps in no organ of criticism in this country was there so much knowledge, so much play of mind; but these could not save it. The *Dublin Review* subordinates play of mind to the practical business of English and Irish Catholicism, and lives. It must needs be that men should act in sects and parties, that each of these sects and parties should have its organ, and should make this organ subserve the interests of its action; but it would be well, too, that there should be a criticism, not the minister of these interests, not their enemy, but absolutely and entirely independent of them. No other criticism will ever attain any real authority or make any real way towards its end,—the creating a current of true and fresh ideas.

It is because criticism has so little kept in the pure intellectual sphere, has so little detached itself from practice, has been so directly polemical and controversial, that it has so ill accomplished, in this country, its best spiritual work; which is to keep man from a self-satisfaction which is retarding and vulgarizing, to lead him towards perfection, by making his mind dwell upon what is excellent in itself, and the absolute beauty and fitness of things. A polemical practical criticism makes men blind even to the ideal imperfection of their practice, makes them willingly

assert its ideal perfection, in order the better to secure it against attack; and clearly this is narrowing and baneful for them. If they were reassured on the practical side, speculative considerations of ideal perfection they might be brought to entertain, and their spiritual horizon would thus gradually widen. Sir Charles Adderley[9] says to the Warwickshire farmers:

Talk of the improvement of breed! Why, the race we ourselves represent, the men and women, the old Anglo-Saxon race, are the best breed in the whole world. . . . The absence of a too enervating climate, too unclouded skies, and a too luxurious nature, has produced so vigorous a race of people, and has rendered us so superior to all the world.

Mr. Roebuck[10] says to the Sheffield cutlers:

I look around me and ask what is the state of England? Is not property safe? Is not every man able to say what he likes? Can you not walk from one end of England to the other in perfect security? I ask you whether, the world over or in past history, there is anything like it? Nothing. I pray that our unrivalled happiness may last.

Now obviously there is a peril for poor human nature in words and thoughts of such exuberant self-satisfaction, until we find ourselves safe in the streets of the Celestial City.

Das wenige verschwindet leicht dem Blicke
Der vorwärts sieht, wie viel noch übrig bleibt—

says Goethe: "the little that is done seems nothing when we look forward and see how much we have yet to do." Clearly this is a better line of reflection for weak humanity, so long as it remains on this earthly field of labor and trial.

But neither Sir Charles Adderley nor Mr. Roebuck is by nature inaccessible to considerations of this sort. They only lose sight of them owing to the controversial life we all lead, and the practical form which all speculation takes with us. They have in view opponents whose aim is not ideal, but practical; and in their zeal to uphold their own practice against these innovators, they go so far as even to attribute to this practice an ideal perfection. Somebody has been wanting to introduce a six-pound franchise,[11] or to abolish church-rates,[12] or to collect agricultural statistics by force, or to diminish local self-govern-

---

9 A Tory politician.
10 John Arthur Roebuck, a prominent radical and Utilitarian. On p. 761, below, Arnold refers again to his argument.
11 A law allowing all men to vote who own land or buildings whose rental value amounts to at least £6 per annum. The 1832 Reform Bill established the £10 franchise.
12 Taxes legally imposed by the state Church of England.

ment. How natural, in reply to such proposals, very likely improper or ill-timed, to go a little beyond the mark and to say stoutly, "such a race of people as we stand, so superior to all the world! The old Anglo-Saxon race, the best breed in the whole world! I pray that our unrivalled happiness may last! I ask you whether, the world over or in past history, there is anything like it?" And so long as criticism answers this dithyramb by insisting that the old Anglo-Saxon race would be still more superior to all others if it had no church-rates, or that our unrivalled happiness would last yet longer with a six-pound franchise, so long will the strain, "The best breed in the whole world!" swell louder and louder, everything ideal and refining will be lost out of sight, and both the assailed and their critics will remain in a sphere, to say the truth, perfectly unvital, a sphere in which spiritual progression is impossible. But let criticism leave church-rates and the franchise alone, and in the most candid spirit, without a single lurking thought of practical innovation, confront with our dithyramb this paragraph on which I stumbled in a newspaper immediately after reading Mr. Roebuck:

A shocking child murder has just been committed at Nottingham. A girl named Wragg left the workhouse there on Saturday morning with her young illegitimate child. The child was soon afterwards found dead on Mapperly Hills, having been strangled. Wragg is in custody.

Nothing but that; but, in juxtaposition with the absolute eulogies of Sir Charles Adderley and Mr. Roebuck, how eloquent, how suggestive are those few lines! "Our old Anglo-Saxon breed, the best in the whole world!"—how much that is harsh and ill-favored there is in this best! Wragg! If we are to talk of ideal perfection, of "the best in the whole world," has any one reflected what a touch of grossness in our race, what an original shortcoming in the more delicate spiritual perceptions, is shown by the natural growth amongst us of such hideous names—Higginbottom, Stiggins, Bugg! In Ionia and Attica they were luckier in this respect than "the best race in the world"; by the Ilissus there was no Wragg, poor thing! And "our unrivalled happiness";—what an element of grimness, bareness, and hideousness mixes with it and blurs it; the workhouse, the dismal Mapperly Hills—how dismal those who have seen them will remember;—the gloom, the smoke, the cold, the strangled illegitimate child! "I ask you whether, the world over or in past history, there is anything like it?" Perhaps not, one is inclined to answer; but at any rate, in that case, the world is very much to be pitied. And the final touch—short,

bleak and inhuman: *Wragg is in custody*. The sex lost in the confusion of our unrivalled happiness; or (shall I say?) the superfluous Christian name lopped off by the straightforward vigor of our old Anglo-Saxon breed! There is profit for the spirit in such contrasts as this; criticism serves the cause of perfection by establishing them. By eluding sterile conflict, by refusing to remain in the sphere where alone narrow and relative conceptions have any worth and validity, criticism may diminish its momentary importance, but only in this way has it a chance of gaining admittance for those wider and more perfect conceptions to which all its duty is really owed. Mr. Roebuck will have a poor opinion of an adversary who replies to his defiant songs of triumph only by murmuring under his breath, *Wragg is in custody;* but in no other way will these songs of triumph be induced gradually to moderate themselves, to get rid of what in them is excessive and offensive, and to fall into a softer and truer key.

It will be said that it is a very subtle and indirect action which I am thus prescribing for criticism, and that, by embracing in this manner the Indian virtue of detachment and abandoning the sphere of practical life, it condemns itself to a slow and obscure work. Slow and obscure it may be, but it is the only proper work of criticism. The mass of mankind will never have any ardent zeal for seeing things as they are; very inadequate ideas will always satisfy them. On these inadequate ideas reposes, and must repose, the general practice of the world. That is as much as saying that whoever sets himself to see things as they are will find himself one of a very small circle; but it is only by this small circle resolutely doing its own work that adequate ideas will ever get current at all. The rush and roar of practical life will always have a dizzying and attracting effect upon the most collected spectator, and tend to draw him into its vortex; most of all will this be the case where that life is so powerful as it is in England. But it is only by remaining collected, and refusing to lend himself to the point of view of the practical man, that the critic can do the practical man any service; and it is only by the greatest sincerity in pursuing his own course, and by at last convincing even the practical man of his sincerity, that he can escape misunderstandings which perpetually threaten him.

For the practical man is not apt for fine distinctions, and yet in these distinctions truth and the highest culture greatly find their account. But it is not easy to lead a practical man—unless you reassure him as to your practical intentions, you have no chance of leading him—to see that a thing which he has always been used to look at from one side only, which he greatly values, and which, looked at from that side, quite deserves, perhaps, all the prizing and admiring which he bestows upon it—that this thing, looked at from another side, may appear much less beneficent and beautiful, and yet retain all its claims to our practical allegiance. Where shall we find language innocent enough, how shall we make the spotless purity of our intentions evident enough, to enable us to say to the political Englishman that the British constitution itself, which, seen from the practical side, looks such a magnificent organ of progress and virtue, seen from the speculative side—with its compromises, its love of facts, its horror of theory, its studied avoidance of clear thoughts—that, seen from this side, our august constitution sometimes looks—forgive me, shade of Lord Somers![13]—a colossal machine for the manufacture of Philistines?[14] How is Cobbett[15] to say this and not be misunderstood, blackened as he is with the smoke of a lifelong conflict in the field of political practice? how is Mr. Carlyle to say it and not be misunderstood, after his furious raid into this field with his *Latter-day Pamphlets?* how is Mr. Ruskin, after his pugnacious political economy? I say, the critic must keep out of the region of immediate practice in the political, social, humanitarian sphere, if he wants to make a beginning for that more free speculative treatment of things, which may perhaps one day make its benefits felt even in this sphere, but in a natural and thence irresistible manner.

Do what he will, however, the critic will still remain exposed to frequent misunderstandings, and nowhere so much as in this country. For here people are particularly indisposed even to comprehend that without this free disinterested treatment of things, truth and the highest culture are out of the question. So immersed are they in practical life, so accustomed to take all their notions from this life and its processes, that they are apt to think that truth and culture themselves can be reached by the processes of this life, and that it is an impertinent singularity to think of reaching them in any other. "We are all *terrae filii*,"[16] cries their eloquent advocate; "all Philistines together. Away with the notion of proceeding by any other

way than the way dear to the Philistines; let us have a social movement, let us organize and combine a party to pursue truth and new thought, let us call it *the liberal party,* and let us all stick to each other, and back each other up. Let us have no nonsense about independent criticism, and intellectual delicacy, and the few and the many. Don't let us trouble ourselves about foreign thought; we shall invent the whole thing for ourselves as we go along. If one of us speaks well, applaud him; if one of us speaks ill, applaud him too; we are all in the same movement, we are all liberals, we are all in pursuit of truth." In this way the pursuit of truth becomes really a social, practical, pleasurable affair, almost requiring a chairman, a secretary, and advertisements; with the excitement of a little resistance, an occasional scandal, to give the happy sense of difficulty overcome; but, in general, plenty of bustle and very little thought. To act is so easy, as Goethe says; to think is so hard! It is true that the critic has many temptations to go with the stream, to make one of the party movement, one of these *terrae filii;* it seems ungracious to refuse to be a *terrae filius,* when so many excellent people are; but the critic's duty is to refuse, or, if resistance is vain, at least to cry with Obermann: *Périssons en résistant.*[17] . . .

I lately heard a man of thought and energy contrasting the want of ardor and movement which he now found amongst young men in this country with what he remembered in his own youth, twenty years ago. "What reformers we were then!" he exclaimed; "what a zeal we had! how we canvassed every institution in Church and State, and were prepared to remodel them all on first principles!" He was inclined to regret, as a spiritual flagging, the lull which he saw. I am disposed rather to regard it as a pause in which the turn to a new mode of spiritual progress is being accomplished. Everything was long seen, by the young and ardent amongst us, in inseparable connection with politics and practical life. We have pretty well exhausted the benefits of seeing things in this connection, we have got all that can be got by so seeing them. Let us try a more disinterested mode of seeing them; let us betake ourselves more to the serener life of the mind and spirit. This life, too, may have its excesses and dangers; but they are not for us at present. Let us think of quietly enlarging our stock of true and fresh ideas, and not, as soon as we get an idea or half an idea, be running out with it into the street, and trying to make it rule there. Our ideas will, in the end, shape the world all the better for

---

13 The chairman of the committee that drew up the Declaration of Rights in 1689.
14 The enemies of the Israelites in the Old Testament. This is Arnold's famous term for the Victorian middle classes, the enemies of culture, neither possessing nor respecting "sweetness and light."   15 Radical journalist (1762–1835).
16 "Sons of the earth."

17 "Let us die resisting," from *Obermann* (1804) by the French romantic Étienne de Sénancour.

maturing a little. Perhaps in fifty years' time it will in the English House of Commons be an objection to an institution that it is an anomaly, and my friend the Member of Parliament will shudder in his grave. But let us in the meanwhile rather endeavor that in twenty years' time it may, in English literature, be an objection to a proposition that it is absurd. That will be a change so vast, that the imagination almost fails to grasp it. *Ab integro saeclorum nascitur ordo.*[18]

If I have insisted so much on the course which criticism must take where politics and religion are concerned, it is because, where these burning matters are in question, it is most likely to go astray. I have wished, above all, to insist on the attitude which criticism should adopt towards things in general, on its right tone and temper of mind. But then comes another question as to the subject-matter which literary criticism should seek. Here in general, its course is determined for it by the idea which is the law of its being; the idea of a disinterested endeavor to learn and propagate the best that is known and thought in the world, and thus to establish a current of fresh and true ideas. By the very nature of things, as England is not all the world, much of the best that is known and thought in the world cannot be of English growth, must be foreign; by the nature of things, again, it is just this that we are least likely to know, while English thought is streaming in upon us from all sides, and takes excellent care that we shall not be ignorant of its existence. The English critic, therefore, must dwell much on foreign thought, and with particular heed on any part of it, which, while significant and fruitful in itself, is for any reason specially likely to escape him. Again, judging is often spoken of as the critic's one business, and so in some sense it is; but the judgment which almost insensibly forms itself in a fair and clear mind, along with fresh knowledge, is the valuable one; and thus knowledge, and ever fresh knowledge, must be the critic's great concern for himself. And it is by communicating fresh knowledge, and letting his own judgment pass along with it—but insensibly, and in the second place, not the first, as a sort of companion and clue, not as an abstract lawgiver—that he will generally do most good to his readers. Sometimes, no doubt, for the sake of establishing an author's place in literature, and his relation to a central standard (and if this is not done, how are we to get at our *best in the world?*) criticism may have to deal with a subject-matter so

familiar that fresh knowledge is out of the question, and then it must be all judgment; an enunciation and detailed application of principles. Here the great safeguard is never to let oneself become abstract, always to retain an intimate and lively consciousness of the truth of what one is saying, and, the moment this fails us, to be sure that something is wrong. Still, under all circumstances, this mere judgment and application of principles is, in itself, not the most satisfactory work to the critic; like mathematics, it is tautological, and cannot well give us, like fresh learning, the sense of creative activity.

But stop, someone will say; all this talk is of no practical use to us whatever; this criticism of yours is not what we have in our minds when we speak of criticism; when we speak of critics and criticism, we mean critics and criticism of the current English literature of the day; when you offer to tell criticism of its function, it is to this criticism that we expect you to address yourself. I am sorry for it for I am afraid I must disappoint these expectations. I am bound by my own definition of criticism: *a disinterested endeavor to learn and propagate the best that is known and thought in the world.* How much of current English literature comes into this "best that is known and thought in the world"? Not very much, I fear; certainly less, at this moment, than of the current literature of France or Germany. Well, then, am I to alter my definition of criticism, in order to meet the requirements of a number of practising English critics, who, after all, are free in their choice of a business? that would be making criticism lend itself to one of those alien practical considerations, which, I have said, are so fatal to it. One may say, indeed, to those who have to deal with the mass—so much better disregarded—of current English literature, that they may at all events endeavor, in dealing with this, to try it, so far as they can, by the standard of the best that is known and thought in the world: one may say, that to get anywhere near this standard, every critic should try and possess one great literature, at least, besides his own; and the more unlike his own, the better. But, after all, the criticism I am really concerned with—the criticism which alone can much help us for the future, the criticism which, throughout Europe, is at the present moment meant, when so much stress is laid on the importance of criticism and the critical spirit—is a criticism which regards Europe as being, for intellectual and spiritual purposes, one great confederation, bound to a joint action and working to a common result; and whose members have, for their proper outfit, a knowledge of Greek, Roman, and Eastern antiquity, and of one

---

[18] "From the renewal of the generations order is born" (from Vergil's fourth *Eclogue*).

another. Special, local, and temporary advantages being put out of account, that modern nation will in the intellectual and spiritual sphere make most progress, which most thoroughly carries out this programme. And what is that but saying that we too, all of us, as individuals, the more thoroughly we carry it out, shall make the more progress?

There is so much inviting us!—what are we to take? what will nourish us in growth towards perfection? That is the question which, with the immense field of life and literature lying before him, the critic has to answer: for himself first, afterwards for others. In this idea of the critic's business the essays brought together in the following pages have had their origin; in this idea, widely different as are their subjects, they have, perhaps, their unity.

I conclude with what I said at the beginning: to have the sense of creative activity is the great happiness and the great proof of being alive, and it is not denied to criticism to have it; but then criticism must be sincere, simple, flexible, ardent, ever widening its knowledge. Then it may have, in no contemptible

measure, a joyful sense of creative activity; a sense which a man of insight and conscience will prefer to what he might derive from a poor, starved, fragmentary, inadequate creation. And at some epochs no other creation is possible.

Still, in full measure, the sense of creative activity belongs only to genuine creation; in literature we must never forget that. But what true man of letters ever can forget it? It is no such common matter for a gifted nature to come into possession of a current of true and living ideas, and to produce amidst the inspiration of them, that we are likely to underrate it. The epochs of Aeschylus and Shakespeare make us feel their pre-eminence. In an epoch like those is, no doubt, the true life of literature; there is the promised land, towards which criticism can only beckon. That promised land it will not be ours to enter, and we shall die in the wilderness: but to have desired to enter it, to have saluted it from afar, is already, perhaps, the best distinction among contemporaries; it will certainly be the best title to esteem with posterity.

from CULTURE AND ANARCHY[1]

Chapter I

SWEETNESS AND LIGHT

THE disparagers of culture make its motive curiosity: sometimes, indeed, they make its motive mere exclusiveness and vanity. The culture which is supposed to plume itself on a smattering of Greek and Latin is a culture which is begotten by nothing so intellectual as curiosity; it is valued either out of sheer vanity and ignorance or else as an engine of social and class distinction, separating its holder, like a badge or title, from other people who have not got it. No serious man would call this *culture*, or attach any value to it, as culture, at all. To find the real ground for the very different estimate which serious people will set upon culture, we must find some motive for culture in the terms of which may lie a real ambiguity; and such a motive the word *curiosity* gives us.

I have before now pointed out[2] that we English do not, like the foreigners, use this word in a good sense as well as in a bad sense. With us the word is always used in a somewhat disapproving sense. A

liberal and intelligent eagerness about the things of the mind may be meant by a foreigner when he speaks of curiosity, but with us the word always conveys a certain notion of frivolous and unedifying activity. In the *Quarterly Review,* some little time ago, was an estimate of the celebrated French critic, M. Sainte-Beuve, and a very inadequate estimate it in my judgment was. And its inadequacy consisted chiefly in this: that in our English way it left out of sight the double sense really involved in the word *curiosity,* thinking enough was said to stamp M. Sainte-Beuve with blame if it was said that he was impelled in his operations as a critic by curiosity, and omitting either to perceive that M. Sainte-Beuve himself, and many other people with him, would consider that this was praiseworthy and not blameworthy, or to point out why it ought really to be accounted worthy of blame and not of praise. For as there is a curiosity about intellectual matters which is futile, and merely a disease, so there is certainly a curiosity,—a desire after the things of the mind simply for their own sakes and for the pleasure of seeing them as they are,—which is, in an intelligent being, natural and laudable. Nay, and the very desire to see things as they are implies a balance and regulation of mind which is not often attained without

1 Published in 1869.   2 See p. 753, above.

fruitful effort, and which is the very opposite of the blind and diseased impulse of mind which is what we mean to blame when we blame curiosity. Montesquieu says: "The first motive which ought to impel us to study is the desire to augment the excellence of our nature, and to render an intelligent being yet more intelligent." This is the true ground to assign for the genuine scientific passion, however manifested, and for culture, viewed simply as a fruit of this passion; and it is a worthy ground, even though we let the term *curiosity* stand to describe it.

But there is of culture another view, in which not solely the scientific passion, the sheer desire to see things as they are, natural and proper in an intelligent being, appears as the ground of it. There is a view in which all the love of our neighbour, the impulses towards action, help, and beneficence, the desire for removing human error, clearing human confusion, and diminishing human misery, the noble aspiration to leave the world better and happier than we found it,—motives eminently such as are called social,—come in as part of the grounds of culture, and the main and pre-eminent part. Culture is then properly described not as having its origin in curiosity, but as having its origin in the love of perfection; it is *a study of perfection*. It moves by the force, not merely or primarily of the scientific passion for pure knowledge, but also of the moral and social passion for doing good. As, in the first view of it, we took for its worthy motto Montesquieu's words: "To render an intelligent being yet more intelligent!" so, in the second view of it, there is no better motto which it can have than these words of Bishop Wilson:[3] "To make reason and the will of God prevail!"

Only, whereas the passion for doing good is apt to be overhasty in determining what reason and the will of God say, because its turn is for acting rather than thinking and it wants to be beginning to act; and whereas it is apt to take its own conceptions, which proceed from its own state of development and share in all the imperfections and immaturities of this, for a basis of action; what distinguishes culture is, that it is possessed by the scientific passion as well as by the passion of doing good; that it demands worthy notions of reason and the will of God, and does not readily suffer its own crude conceptions to substitute themselves for them. And knowing that no action or institution can be salutary and stable which is not based on reason and the will of God, it is not so bent on acting and instituting,

even with the great aim of diminishing human error and misery ever before its thoughts, but that it can remember that acting and instituting are of little use, unless we know how and what we ought to act and to institute.

This culture is more interesting and more far-reaching than that other, which is founded solely on the scientific passion for knowing. But it needs times of faith and ardour, times when the intellectual horizon is opening and widening all round us, to flourish in. And is not the close and bounded intellectual horizon within which we have long lived and moved now lifting up, and are not new lights finding free passage to shine in upon us? For a long time there was no passage for them to make their way in upon us, and then it was of no use to think of adapting the world's action to them. Where was the hope of making reason and the will of God prevail among people who had a routine which they had christened reason and the will of God, in which they were inextricably bound, and beyond which they had no power of looking? But now the iron force of adhesion to the old routine,—social, political, religious,—has wonderfully yielded; the iron force of exclusion of all which is new has wonderfully yielded. The danger now is, not that people should obstinately refuse to allow anything but their old routine to pass for reason and the will of God, but either that they should allow some novelty or other to pass for these too easily, or else that they should underrate the importance of them altogether, and think it enough to follow action for its own sake, without troubling themselves to make reason and the will of God prevail therein. Now, then, is the moment for culture to be of service, culture which believes in making reason and the will of God prevail, believes in perfection, is the study and pursuit of perfection, and is no longer debarred, by a rigid invincible exclusion of whatever is new, from getting acceptance for its ideas, simply because they are new.

The moment this view of culture is seized, the moment it is regarded not solely as the endeavour to see things as they are, to draw towards a knowledge of the universal order which seems to be intended and aimed at in the world, and which it is a man's happiness to go along with or his misery to go counter to,—to learn, in short, the will of God,—the moment, I say, culture is considered not merely as the endeavour to *see* and *learn* this, but as the endeavour, also, to make it *prevail*, the moral, social, and beneficent character of culture becomes manifest. The mere endeavour to see and learn the truth for our own personal satisfaction is indeed a commence-

---

[3] Thomas Wilson (1663–1755) in his *Sacra Privata*.

ment for making it prevail, a preparing the way for this, which always serves this, and is wrongly, therefore, stamped with blame absolutely in itself and not only in its caricature and degeneration. But perhaps it has got stamped with blame, and disparaged with the dubious title of curiosity, because in comparison with this wider endeavour of such great and plain utility it looks selfish, petty, and unprofitable.

And religion, the greatest and most important of the efforts by which the human race has manifested its impulse to perfect itself,—religion, that voice of the deepest human experience,—does not only enjoin and sanction the aim which is the great aim of culture, the aim of setting ourselves to ascertain what perfection is and to make it prevail; but also, in determining generally in what human perfection consists, religion comes to a conclusion identical with that which culture,—culture seeking the determination of this question through *all* the voices of human experience which have been heard upon it, of art, science, poetry, philosophy, history, as well as of religion, in order to give a greater fulness and certainty to its solution,—likewise reaches. Religion says: *The kingdom of God is within you;* and culture, in like manner, places human perfection in an *internal* condition, in the growth and predominance of our humanity proper, as distinguished from our animality. It places it in the ever-increasing efficacy and in the general harmonious expansion of those gifts of thought and feeling, which make the peculiar dignity, wealth, and happiness of human nature. As I have said on a former occasion: "It is in making endless additions to itself, in the endless expansion of its powers, in endless growth in wisdom and beauty, that the spirit of the human race finds its ideal. To reach this ideal, culture is an indispensable aid, and that is the true value of culture." Not a having and a resting, but a growing and a becoming, is the character of perfection as culture conceives it; and here, too, it coincides with religion.

And because men are all members of one great whole, and the sympathy which is in human nature will not allow one member to be indifferent to the rest or to have a perfect welfare independent of the rest, the expansion of our humanity, to suit the idea of perfection which culture forms, must be a *general* expansion. Perfection, as culture conceives it, is not possible while the individual remains isolated. The individual is required, under pain of being stunted and enfeebled in his own development if he disobeys, to carry others along with him in his march towards perfection, to be continually doing all he can to enlarge and increase the volume of the human stream sweeping thitherward. And here, once more, culture lays on us the same obligation as religion which says, as Bishop Wilson has admirably put it, that "to promote the kingdom of God is to increase and hasten one's own happiness."

But, finally, perfection,—as culture from a thorough disinterested study of human nature and human experience learns to conceive it,—is a harmonious expansion of *all* the powers which make the beauty and worth of human nature, and is not consistent with the over-development of any one power at the expense of the rest. Here culture goes beyond religion, as religion is generally conceived by us.

If culture, then, is a study of perfection, and of harmonious perfection, general perfection, and perfection which consists in becoming something rather than in having something, in an inward condition of the mind and spirit, not in an outward set of circumstances,—it is clear that culture, instead of being the frivolous and useless thing which Mr. Bright, and Mr. Frederic Harrison, and many other Liberals are apt to call it, has a very important function to fulfil for mankind. And this function is particularly important in our modern world, of which the whole civilisation is, to a much greater degree than the civilisation of Greece and Rome, mechanical and external, and tends constantly to become more so. But above all in our own country has culture a weighty part to perform, because here that mechanical character, which civilisation tends to take everywhere, is shown in the most eminent degree. Indeed nearly all the characters of perfection, as culture teaches us to fix them, meet in this country with some powerful tendency which thwarts them and sets them at defiance. The idea of perfection as an *inward* condition of the mind and spirit is at variance with the mechanical and material civilisation in esteem with us, and nowhere, as I have said, so much in esteem as with us. The idea of perfection as a *general* expansion of the human family is at variance with our strong individualism, our hatred of all limits to the unrestrained swing of the individual's personality, our maxim of "every man for himself." Above all, the idea of perfection as a *harmonious* expansion of human nature is at variance with our want of flexibility, with our inaptitude for seeing more than one side of a thing, with our intense energetic absorption in the particular pursuit we happen to be following. So culture has a rough task to achieve in this country. Its preachers have, and are likely long to have, a hard time of it, and they will much oftener be regarded, for a great while to come, as elegant or spurious Jeremiahs than as friends and benefactors. That, however, will not prevent their doing in the end good service if they persevere. And, meanwhile, the mode of action they have to pursue, and the sort of habits they must fight against, ought to be made quite clear for every one to see, who may be willing to look at the matter attentively and dispassionately.

Faith in machinery, is, I said, our besetting danger; often in machinery most absurdly disproportioned to the end which this machinery, if it is to do any good at all, is to serve; but always in machinery, as if it had a value in and for itself. What is freedom but machinery? what is population but machinery? what is coal but machinery? what are railroads but machinery? what is wealth but machinery? what are, even, religious organisations but machinery? Now almost every voice in England is accustomed to speak of these things as if they were precious ends in themselves, and therefore had some of the characters of perfection indisputably joined to them. I have before now noticed Mr. Roebuck's stock argument for proving the greatness and happiness of England as she is,[4] and for quite stopping the mouths of all gainsayers. Mr. Roebuck is never weary of reiterating this argument of his, so I do not know why I should be weary of noticing it. "May not every man in England say what he likes?"—Mr. Roebuck perpetually asks; and that, he thinks, is quite sufficient, and when every man may say what he likes, our aspirations ought to be satisfied. But the aspirations of culture, which is the study of perfection, are not satisfied, unless what men say, when they may say what they like, is worth saying,—has good in it, and more good than bad. In the same way the *Times,* replying to some foreign strictures on the dress, looks, and behaviour of the English abroad, urges that the English ideal is that every one should be free to do and to look just as he likes. But culture indefatigably tries, not to make what each raw person may like the rule by which he fashions himself; but to draw ever nearer to a sense of what is indeed beautiful, graceful, and becoming, and to get the raw person to like that.

And in the same way with respect to railroads and coal. Every one must have observed the strange language current during the late discussions as to the possible failures of our supplies of coal. Our coal, thousands of people were saying, is the real basis of our national greatness; if our coal runs short, there is an end of the greatness of England. But what *is*

greatness?—culture makes us ask. Greatness is a spiritual condition worthy to excite love, interest, and admiration; and the outward proof of possessing greatness is that we excite love, interest, and admiration. If England were swallowed up by the sea tomorrow, which of the two, a hundred years hence, would most excite the love, interest, and admiration of mankind,—would most, therefore, show the evidences of having possessed greatness,—the England of the last twenty years, or the England of Elizabeth, of a time of splendid spiritual effort, but when our coal, and our industrial operations depending on coal, were very little developed? Well, then, what an unsound habit of mind it must be which makes us talk of things like coal or iron as constituting the greatness of England, and how salutary a friend is culture, bent on seeing things as they are, and thus dissipating delusions of this kind and fixing standards of perfection that are real!

Wealth, again, that end to which our prodigious works for material advantage are directed,—the commonest of commonplaces tells us how men are always apt to regard wealth as a precious end in itself; and certainly they have never been so apt thus to regard it as they are in England at the present time. Never did people believe anything more firmly than nine Englishmen out of ten at the present day believe that our greatness and welfare are proved by our being so very rich. Now, the use of culture is that it helps us, by means of its spiritual standard of perfection, to regard wealth as but machinery, and not only to say as a matter of words that we regard wealth as but machinery, but really to perceive and feel that it is so. If it were not for this purging effect wrought upon our minds by culture, the whole world, the future as well as the present, would inevitably belong to the Philistines. The people who believe most that our greatness and welfare are proved by our being very rich, and who most give their lives and thoughts to becoming rich, are just the very people whom we call Philistines. Culture says: "Consider these people, then, their way of life, their habits, their manners, the very tones of their voice; look at them attentively; observe the literature they read, the things which give them pleasure, the words which come forth out of their mouths, the thoughts which make the furniture of their minds; would any amount of wealth be worth having with the condition that one was to become just like these people by having it?" And thus culture begets a dissatisfaction which is of the highest possible value in stemming the common tide of men's thoughts in a wealthy and industrial community, and which saves

4 See p. 754, above.

the future, as one may hope, from being vulgarised, even if it cannot save the present.

Population, again, and bodily health and vigour, are things which are nowhere treated in such an unintelligent, misleading, exaggerated way as in England. Both are really machinery; yet how many people all around us do we see rest in them and fail to look beyond them! Why, one has heard people, fresh from reading certain articles of the *Times* on the Registrar-General's returns of marriages and births in this country, who would talk of our large English families in quite a solemn strain, as if they had something in itself beautiful, elevating, and meritorious in them; as if the British Philistine would have only to present himself before the Great Judge with his twelve children, in order to be received among the sheep as a matter of right!

But bodily health and vigour, it may be said, are not to be classed with wealth and population as mere machinery; they have a more real and essential value. True; but only as they are more intimately connected with a perfect spiritual condition than wealth or population are. The moment we disjoin them from the idea of a perfect spiritual condition, and pursue them, as we do pursue them, for their own sake and as ends in themselves, our worship of them becomes as mere worship of machinery, as our worship of wealth or population, and as unintelligent and vulgarising a worship as that is. Every one with anything like an adequate idea of human perfection has distinctly marked this subordination to higher and spiritual ends of the cultivation of bodily vigour and activity. "Bodily exercise profiteth little; but godliness is profitable unto all things," says the author of the Epistle to Timothy. And the utilitarian Franklin says just as explicitly:—"Eat and drink such an exact quantity as suits the constitution of thy body, *in reference to the services of the mind.*" But the point of view of culture, keeping the mark of human perfection simply and broadly in view, and not assigning to this perfection, as religion or utilitarianism assigns to it, a special and limited character, this point of view, I say, of culture is best given by these words of Epictetus:[5]—"It is a sign of ἀφυΐα," says he,—that is, of a nature not finely tempered,— "to give yourselves up to things which relate to the body; to make, for instance, a great fuss about exercise, a great fuss about eating, a great fuss about drinking, a great fuss about walking, a great fuss about riding. All these things ought to be done

merely by the way: the formation of the spirit and character must be our real concern." This is admirable; and, indeed, the Greek word εὐφυΐα, a finely tempered nature, gives exactly the notion of perfection as culture brings us to conceive it: a harmonious perfection, a perfection in which the characters of beauty and intelligence are both present, which unites "the two noblest of things,"—as Swift, who of one of the two, at any rate, had himself all too little, most happily calls them in his *Battle of the Books*,—"the two noblest of things, *sweetness and light.*" The εὐφυής is the man who tends towards sweetness and light; the ἀφυής, on the other hand, is our Philistine. The immense spiritual significance of the Greeks is due to their having been inspired with this central and happy idea of the essential character of human perfection; and Mr. Bright's[6] misconception of culture, as a smattering of Greek and Latin, comes itself, after all, from this wonderful significance of the Greeks having affected the very machinery of our education, and is in itself a kind of homage to it.

In thus making sweetness and light to be characters of perfection, culture is of like spirit with poetry, follows one law with poetry. Far more than on our freedom, our population, and our industrialism, many amongst us rely upon our religious organisations to save us. I have called religion a yet more important manifestation of human nature than poetry, because it has worked on a broader scale for perfection, and with greater masses of men. But the idea of beauty and of a human nature perfect on all its sides, which is the dominant idea of poetry, is a true and invaluable idea, though it has not yet had the success that the idea of conquering the obvious faults of our animality, and of a human nature perfect on the moral side,—which is the dominant idea of religion,—has been enabled to have; and it is destined, adding to itself the religious idea of a devout energy, to transform and govern the other.

The best art and poetry of the Greeks, in which religion and poetry are one, in which the idea of beauty and of a human nature perfect on all sides adds to itself a religious and devout energy, and works in the strength of that, is on this account of such surpassing interest and instructiveness for us, though it was,—as, having regard to the human race in general, and, indeed, having regard to the Greeks themselves, we must own,—a premature attempt,

---

[5] The Roman Stoic philosopher (60?–120?).

[6] John Bright, "that fine speaker and famous Liberal," as Arnold calls him, in a political speech.

an attempt which for success needed the moral and religious fibre in humanity to be more braced and developed than it had yet been. But Greece did not err in having the idea of beauty, harmony, and complete human perfection, so present and paramount. It is impossible to have this idea too present and paramount; only, the moral fibre must be braced too. And we, because we have braced the moral fibre, are not on that account in the right way, if at the same time the idea of beauty, harmony, and complete human perfection, is wanting or misapprehended amongst us; and evidently it *is* wanting or misapprehended at present. And when we rely as we do on our religious organisations, which in themselves do not and cannot give us this idea, and think we have done enough if we make them spread and prevail, then, I say, we fall into our common fault of overvaluing machinery.

Nothing is more common than for people to confound the inward peace and satisfaction which follows the subduing of the obvious faults of our animality with what I may call absolute inward peace and satisfaction,—the peace and satisfaction which are reached as we draw near to complete spiritual perfection, and not merely to moral perfection, or rather to relative moral perfection. No people in the world have done more and struggled more to attain this relative moral perfection than our English race has. For no people in the world has the command to *resist the devil*, to *overcome the wicked one*, in the nearest and most obvious sense of those words, had such a pressing force and reality. And we have had our reward, not only in the great worldly prosperity which our obedience to this command has brought us, but also, and far more, in great inward peace and satisfaction. But to me few things are more pathetic than to see people, on the strength of the inward peace and satisfaction which their rudimentary efforts towards perfection have brought them, employ, concerning their incomplete perfection and the religious organisations within which they have found it, language which properly applies only to complete perfection, and is a far-off echo of the human soul's prophecy of it. Religion itself, I need hardly say, supplies them in abundance with this grand language. And very freely do they use it; yet it is really the severest possible criticism of such an incomplete perfection as alone we have yet reached through our religious organisations.

The impulse of the English race towards moral development and self-conquest has nowhere so powerfully manifested itself as in Puritanism. Nowhere has Puritanism found so adequate an expression as in the religious organisation of the Independents.[7] The modern Independents have a newspaper, the *Nonconformist,* written with great sincerity and ability. The motto, the standard, the profession of faith which this organ of theirs carries aloft, is: "The Dissidence of Dissent and the Protestantism of the Protestant religion." There is sweetness and light, and an ideal of complete harmonious human perfection! One need not go to culture and poetry to find language to judge it. Religion, with its instinct for perfection, supplies language to judge it, language, too, which is in our mouths every day. "Finally, be of one mind, united in feeling," says St. Peter.[8] There is an ideal which judges the Puritan ideal: "The Dissidence of Dissent and the Protestantism of the Protestant religion!" And religious organisations like this are what people believe in, rest in, would give their lives for! Such, I say, is the wonderful virtue of even the beginnings of perfection, of having conquered even the plain faults of our animality, that the religious organisation which has helped us to do it can seem to us something precious, salutary, and to be propagated, even when it wears such a brand of imperfection on its forehead as this. And men have got such a habit of giving to the language of religion a special application, of making it a mere jargon, that for the condemnation which religion itself passes on the shortcomings of their religious organisations they have no ear; they are sure to cheat themselves and to explain this condemnation away. They can only be reached by the criticism which culture, like poetry, speaking a language not to be sophisticated, and resolutely testing these organisations by the ideal of a human perfection complete on all sides, applies to them.

But men of culture and poetry, it will be said, are again and again failing, and failing conspicuously, in the necessary first stage to a harmonious perfection, in the subduing of the great obvious faults of our animality, which it is the glory of these religious organisations to have helped us to subdue. True, they do often so fail. They have often been without the virtues as well as the faults of the Puritan; it has been one of their dangers that they so felt the Puritan's faults that they too much neglected the practice of his virtues. I will not, however, exculpate them at the Puritan's expense. They have often failed in morality, and morality is indispensable. And they have been punished for their failure, as the Puritan has been

---

[7] The Congregationalists, who believed in the right of each congregation to govern itself independently.
[8] 1 Peter 3:8.

rewarded for his performance. They have been punished wherein they erred; but their ideal of beauty, of sweetness and light, and a human nature complete on all its sides, remains the true ideal of perfection still; just as the Puritan's ideal of perfection remains narrow and inadequate, although for what he did well he has been richly rewarded. Notwithstanding the mighty results of the Pilgrim Fathers' voyage, they and their standard of perfection are rightly judged when we figure to ourselves Shakspeare or Virgil,—souls in whom sweetness and light, and all that in human nature is most humane, were eminent, —accompanying them on their voyage, and think what intolerable company Shakspeare and Virgil would have found them! In the same way let us judge the religious organisations which we see all around us. Do not let us deny the good and the happiness which they have accomplished; but do not let us fail to see clearly that their idea of human perfection is narrow and inadequate, and that the Dissidence of Dissent and the Protestantism of the Protestant religion will never bring humanity to its true goal. As I said with regard to wealth: Let us look at the life of those who live in and for it,—so I say with regard to the religious organisations. Look at the life imaged in such a newspaper as the *Nonconformist,*—a life of jealousy of the Establishment,[9] disputes, tea-meetings, openings of chapels, sermons; and then think of it as an ideal of a human life completing itself on all sides, and aspiring with all its organs after sweetness, light, and perfection!

Another newspaper, representing, like the *Nonconformist,* one of the religious organisations of this country, was a short time ago giving an account of the crowd at Epsom on the Derby day,[10] and of all the vice and hideousness which was to be seen in that crowd; and then the writer turned suddenly round upon Professor Huxley,[11] and asked him how he proposed to cure all this vice and hideousness without religion. I confess I felt disposed to ask the asker this question: and how do you propose to cure it with such a religion as yours? How is the ideal of a life so unlovely, so unattractive, so incomplete, so narrow, so far removed from a true and satisfying ideal of human perfection, as is the life of your religious organisation as you yourself reflect it, to conquer and transform all this vice and hideousness? Indeed, the strongest plea for the study of perfection

as pursued by culture, the clearest proof of the actual inadequacy of the idea of perfection held by the religious organisations,—expressing, as I have said, the most widespread effort which the human race has yet made after perfection,—is to be found in the state of our life and society with these in possession of it, and having been in possession of it I know not how many hundred years. We are all of us included in some religious organisation or other; we all call ourselves, in the sublime and aspiring language of religion which I have before noticed, *children of God.* Children of God;—it is an immense pretension!—and how are we to justify it? By the works which we do, and the words which we speak. And the work which we collective children of God do, our grand centre of life, our *city* which we have builded for us to dwell in, is London! London, with its unutterable external hideousness, and with its internal canker of *publicè egestas, privatim opulentia,*[12]—to use the words which Sallust puts into Cato's mouth about Rome,— unequalled in the world! The word, again, which we children of God speak, the voice which most hits our collective thought, the newspaper with the largest circulation in England, nay, with the largest circulation in the whole world, is the *Daily Telegraph!*[13] I say that when our religious organisations, —which I admit to express the most considerable effort after perfection that our race has yet made,— land us in no better result than this, it is high time to examine carefully their idea of perfection, to see whether it does not leave out of account sides and forces of human nature which we might turn to great use; whether it would not be more operative if it were more complete. And I say that the English reliance on our religious organisations and on their ideas of human perfection just as they stand, is like our reliance on freedom, on muscular Christianity, on population, on coal, on wealth,—mere belief in machinery, and unfruitful; and that it is wholesomely counteracted by culture, bent on seeing things as they are, and on drawing the human race onwards to a more complete, a harmonious perfection.

Culture, however, shows its single-minded love of perfection, its desire simply to make reason and the will of God prevail, its freedom from fanaticism, by its attitude towards all this machinery, even while it insists that it *is* machinery. Fanatics, seeing the mischief men do themselves by their blind belief in

---

9 The Church of England.
10 The day of the horse races.
11 The scientist and agnostic. See p. 596, above.

12 "Publicly, for most people, privation; privately, for a few, great wealth." From the *Catiline* of Sallust, the Roman historian (86–35 B.C.).
13 The first penny newspaper in England, founded in 1855.

some machinery or other,—whether it is wealth and industrialism, or whether it is the cultivation of bodily strength and activity, or whether it is a political organisation,—or whether it is a religious organisation,—oppose with might and main the tendency to this or that political and religious organisation, or to games and athletic exercises, or to wealth and industrialism, and try violently to stop it. But the flexibility which sweetness and light give, and which is one of the rewards of culture pursued in good faith, enables a man to see that a tendency may be necessary, and even, as a preparation for something in the future, salutary, and yet that the generations or individuals who obey this tendency are sacrificed to it, that they fall short of the hope of perfection by following it; and that its mischiefs are to be criticised, lest it should take too firm a hold and last after it has served its purpose.

Mr. Gladstone well pointed out, in a speech at Paris,—and others have pointed out the same thing,— how necessary is the present great movement towards wealth and industrialism, in order to lay broad foundations of material well-being for the society of the future. The worst of these justifications is, that they are generally addressed to the very people engaged, body and soul, in the movement in question; at all events, that they are always seized with the greatest avidity by these people, and taken by them as quite justifying their life; and that thus they tend to harden them in their sins. Now, culture admits the necessity of the movement towards fortune-making and exaggerated industrialism, readily allows that the future may derive benefit from it; but insists, at the same time, that the passing generations of industrialists,—forming, for the most part, the stout main body of Philistinism,—are sacrificed to it. In the same way, the result of all the games and sports which occupy the passing generation of boys and young men may be the establishment of a better and sounder physical type for the future to work with. Culture does not set itself against the games and sports; it congratulates the future, and hopes it will make a good use of its improved physical basis; but it points out that our passing generation of boys and young men is, meantime, sacrificed. Puritanism was perhaps necessary to develop the moral fibre of the English race, Nonconformity to break the yoke of ecclesiastical domination over men's minds and to prepare the way for freedom of thought in the distant future; still, culture points out that the harmonious perfection of generations of Puritans and Nonconformists has been, in consequence, sacrificed. Freedom of speech may be

necessary for the society of the future, but the young lions of the *Daily Telegraph* in the meanwhile are sacrificed. A voice for every man in his country's government may be necessary for the society of the future, but meanwhile Mr. Beales and Mr. Bradlaugh are sacrificed.[14]

Oxford, the Oxford of the past, has many faults; and she has heavily paid for them in defeat, in isolation, in want of hold upon the modern world. Yet we in Oxford, brought up amidst the beauty and sweetness of that beautiful place, have not failed to seize one truth,—the truth that beauty and sweetness are essential characters of a complete human perfection. When I insist on this, I am all in the faith and tradition of Oxford. I say boldly that this our sentiment for beauty and sweetness, our sentiment against hideousness and rawness, has been at the bottom of our attachment to so many beaten causes, of our opposition to so many triumphant movements. And the sentiment is true, and has never been wholly defeated, and has shown its power even in its defeat. We have not won our political battles, we have not carried our main points, we have not stopped our adversaries' advance, we have not marched victoriously with the modern world; but we have told silently upon the mind of the country, we have prepared currents of feeling which sap our adversaries' position when it seems gained, we have kept up our own communications with the future. Look at the course of the great movement which shook Oxford to its centre some thirty years ago! It was directed, as any one who reads Dr. Newman's *Apology* may see, against what in one word may be called "Liberalism."[15] Liberalism prevailed; it was the appointed force to do the work of the hour; it was necessary, it was inevitable that it should prevail. The Oxford movement was broken, it failed; our wrecks are scattered on every shore:—

Quae regio in terris nostri non plena laboris?[16]

But what was it, this liberalism, as Dr. Newman saw it, and as it really broke the Oxford movement? It was the great middle-class liberalism, which had for the cardinal points of its belief the Reform Bill of

---

[14] The young writers of the *Daily Telegraph* were often loud asserters of freedom of speech in the extreme form which rejects all authority and claims that the individual should think and speak whatever he considers true. Like them, Edmond Beales and Charles Bradlaugh were examples of extreme and unbalanced supporters of liberalism, in this case of manhood suffrage in particular.

[15] See Newman's "Note on Liberalism," pp. 492 ff., above.

[16] "What country in the world is not full [does not know] of our toil and trouble?" (Vergil's *Aeneid,* I, 460)

1832, and local self-government, in politics; in the social sphere, free-trade, unrestricted competition, and the making of large industrial fortunes; in the religious sphere, the Dissidence of Dissent and the Protestantism of the Protestant religion. I do not say that other and more intelligent forces than this were not opposed to the Oxford movement: but this was the force which really beat it; this was the force which Dr. Newman felt himself fighting with; this was the force which till only the other day seemed to be the paramount force in this country, and to be in possession of the future; this was the force whose achievements fill Mr. Lowe[17] with such inexpressible admiration, and whose rule he was so horror-struck to see threatened. And where is this great force of Philistinism now? It is thrust into the second rank, it is become a power of yesterday, it has lost the future. A new power has suddenly appeared,[18] a power which it is impossible yet to judge fully, but which is certainly a wholly different force from middle-class liberalism; different in its cardinal points of belief, different in its tendencies in every sphere. It loves and admires neither the legislation of middle-class Parliaments, nor the local self-government of middle-class vestries,[19] nor the unrestricted competition of middle-class industrialists, nor the dissidence of middle-class Dissent and the Protestantism of middle-class Protestant religion. I am not now praising this new force, or saying that its own ideals are better; all I say is, that they are wholly different. And who will estimate how much the currents of feeling created by Dr. Newman's movements, the keen desire for beauty and sweetness which it nourished, the deep aversion it manifested to the hardness and vulgarity of middle-class liberalism, the strong light it turned on the hideous and grotesque illusions of middle-class Protestantism,—who will estimate how much all these contributed to swell the tide of secret dissatisfaction which has mined the ground under self-confident liberalism of the last thirty years, and has prepared the way for its sudden collapse and supersession? It is in this manner that the sentiment of Oxford for beauty and sweetness conquers, and in this manner long may it continue to conquer!

In this manner it works to the same end as culture, and there is plenty of work for it yet to do. I have said that the new and more democratic force which is now superseding our old middle-class liberalism cannot yet be rightly judged. It has its main tendencies still to form. We hear promises of its giving us administrative reform, law reform, reform of education, and I know not what; but those promises come rather from its advocates, wishing to make a good plea for it and to justify it for superseding middle-class liberalism, than from clear tendencies which it has itself yet developed. But meanwhile it has plenty of well-intentioned friends against whom culture may with advantage continue to uphold steadily its ideal of human perfection; that this is an inward spiritual activity, having for its characters increased sweetness, increased light, increased life, increased sympathy. Mr. Bright, who has a foot in both worlds, the world of middle-class liberalism and the world of democracy, but who brings most of his ideas from the world of middle-class liberalism in which he was bred, always inclines to inculcate that faith in machinery to which, as we have seen, Englishmen are so prone, and which has been the bane of middle-class liberalism. He complains with a sorrowful indignation of people who "appear to have no proper estimate of the value of the franchise"; he leads his disciples to believe,—what the Englishman is always too ready to believe,—that the having a vote, like the having a large family, or a large business, or large muscles, has in itself some edifying and perfecting effect upon human nature. Or else he cries out to the democracy,—"the men," as he calls them, "upon whose shoulders the greatness of England rests,"—he cries out to them: "See what you have done! I look over this country and see the cities you have built, the railroads you have made, the manufactures you have produced, the cargoes which freight the ships of the greatest mercantile navy the world has ever seen! I see that you have converted by your labours what was once a wilderness, these islands, into a fruitful garden; I know that you have created this wealth, and are a nation whose name is a word of power throughout all the world." Why, this is just the very style of laudation with which Mr. Roebuck or Mr. Lowe debauches the minds of the middle classes, and makes such Philistines of them. It is the same fashion of teaching a man to value himself not on what he *is*, not on his progress in sweetness and light, but on the number of the railroads he has constructed, or the bigness of the tabernacle he has built. Only the middle classes are told they have done it all with their energy, self-reliance, and capital, and the democracy are told they have done it all with their hands and sinews. But teaching

---

[17] Robert Lowe was a middle-class liberal who was horrified by the extension of the suffrage (by the 1867 Reform Bill) to the proletariat in the towns.   [18] The town democracy.
[19] The vestry in Anglican churches is a group of members who manage its temporal affairs.

the democracy to put its trust in achievements of this kind is merely training them to be Philistines to take the place of the Philistines whom they are superseding; and they too, like the middle class, will be encouraged to sit down at the banquet of the future without having on a wedding garment, and nothing excellent can then come from them. Those who know their besetting faults, those who have watched them and listened to them, or those who will read the instructive account recently given of them by one of themselves, the *Journeyman Engineer*,[20] will agree that the idea which culture sets before us of perfection,—an increased spiritual activity, having for its characters increased sweetness, increased light, increased life, increased sympathy,—is an idea which the new democracy needs far more than the idea of the blessedness of the franchise, or the wonderfulness of its own industrial performances.

Other well-meaning friends of this new power are for leading it, not in the old ruts of middle-class Philistinism, but in ways which are naturally alluring to the feet of democracy, though in this country they are novel and untried ways. I may call them the ways of Jacobinism.[21] Violent indignation with the past, abstract systems of renovation applied wholesale, a new doctrine drawn up in black and white for elaborating down to the very smallest details a rational society for the future,—these are the ways of Jacobinism. Mr. Frederic Harrison and other disciples of Comte,[22]—one of them, Mr. Congreve, is an old friend of mine, and I am glad to have an opportunity of publicly expressing my respect for his talents and character,—are among the friends of democracy who are for leading it in paths of this kind. Mr. Frederic Harrison is very hostile to culture, and from a natural enough motive; for culture is the eternal opponent of the two things which are the signal marks of Jacobinism,—its fierceness, and its addiction to an abstract system. Culture is always assigning to system-makers and systems a smaller share in the bent of human destiny than their friends like. A current in people's minds sets towards new ideas; people are dissatisfied with their old narrow stock of Philistine ideas, Anglo-Saxon ideas, or any other; and some man, some Bentham or Comte, who has the real

merit of having early and strongly felt and helped the new current, but who brings plenty of narrowness and mistakes of his own into his feeling and help of it, is credited with being the author of the whole current, the fit person to be entrusted with its regulation and to guide the human race.

The excellent German historian of the mythology of Rome, Preller, relating the introduction at Rome under the Tarquins of the worship of Apollo, the god of light, healing, and reconciliation, will have us observe that it was not so much the Tarquins who brought to Rome the new worship of Apollo, as a current in the mind of the Roman people which set powerfully at that time towards a new worship of this kind, and away from the old run of Latin[23] and Sabine religious ideas. In a similar way, culture directs our attention to the natural current there is in human affairs, and to its continual working, and will not let us rivet our faith upon any one man and his doings. It makes us see not only his good side, but also how much in him was of necessity limited and transient; nay, it even feels a pleasure, a sense of an increased freedom and of an ampler future, in so doing.

I remember, when I was under the influence of a mind to which I feel the greatest obligations, the mind of a man who was the very incarnation of sanity and clear sense, a man the most considerable, it seems to me, whom America has yet produced,—Benjamin Franklin,—I remember the relief with which, after long feeling the sway of Franklin's imperturbable common-sense, I came upon a project of his for a new version of the Book of Job, to replace the old version, the style of which, says Franklin, has become obsolete, and thence less agreeable. "I give," he continues, "a few verses, which may serve as a sample of the kind of version I would recommend." We all recollect the famous verse in our translation: "Then Satan answered the Lord and said: 'Doth Job fear God for nought?'" Franklin makes this: "Does your Majesty imagine that Job's good conduct is the effect of mere personal attachment and affection?" I well remember how, when first I read that, I drew a deep breath of relief, and said to myself: "After all, there is a stretch of humanity beyond Franklin's victorious good sense!" So, after hearing Bentham cried loudly up as the renovator of modern society, and Bentham's mind and ideas proposed as the rulers of our future, I open the *Deontology*.[24] There I read: "While Xenophon was writing his history and Euclid teaching geometry, Socrates and

---

[20] The pseudonym of Thomas Wright, who wrote a book on *Some Habits and Customs of the Working Classes* (1867).

[21] Of the extreme party in the French Revolution, the Jacobins.

[22] The French philosopher (1798–1857) who also influenced Mill. He advocated a strong centralized government in the hands of industrialists which would organize all phases of economic life, and a Religion of Humanity founded on the worship of great men. Both schemes illustrate Arnold's previous sentence.

[23] I.e., of Latium, the district of Italy which included Rome. The Sabine district was northeast of Latium.

[24] Bentham's *Deontology*, or *The Science of Morality* (1834).

Plato were talking nonsense under pretence of talking wisdom and morality. This morality of theirs consisted in words; this wisdom of theirs was the denial of matters known to every man's experience."[25] From the moment of reading that, I am delivered from the bondage of Bentham! the fanaticism of his adherents can touch me no longer. I feel the inadequacy of his mind and ideas for supplying the rule of human society, for perfection.

Culture tends always thus to deal with the men of a system, of disciples, of a school; with men like Comte, or the late Mr. Buckle, or Mr. Mill.[26] However much it may find to admire in these personages, or in some of them, it nevertheless remembers the text: "Be not ye called Rabbi!"[27] and it soon passes on from any Rabbi. But Jacobinism loves a Rabbi; it does not want to pass on from its Rabbi in pursuit of a future and still unreached perfection; it wants its Rabbi and his ideas to stand for perfection, that they may with the more authority recast the world; and for Jacobinism, therefore, culture,—eternally passing onwards and seeking,—is an impertinence and an offence. But culture, just because it resists this tendency of Jacobinism to impose on us a man with limitations and errors of his own along with the true ideas of which he is the organ, really does the world and Jacobinism itself a service.

So, too, Jacobinism, in its fierce hatred of the past and of those whom it makes liable for the sins of the past, cannot away with the inexhaustible indulgence proper to culture, the consideration of circumstances, the severe judgment of actions joined to the merciful judgment of persons. "The man of culture is in politics," cries Mr. Frederic Harrison, "one of the poorest mortals alive!" Mr. Frederic Harrison wants to be doing business, and he complains that the man of culture stops him with a "turn for small fault-finding, love of selfish ease, and indecision in action." Of what use is culture, he asks, except for "a critic of new books or a professor of *belles-lettres?*" Why, it is of use because, in presence of the fierce exasperation which breathes, or rather, I may say, hisses through the whole production in which Mr. Frederic Harrison asks that question, it reminds us that the perfection of human nature is sweetness and light. It is of use because, like religion,—that other

effort after perfection,—it testifies, that, where bitter envying and strife are, there is confusion and every evil work.

The pursuit of perfection, then, is the pursuit of sweetness and light. He who works for sweetness and light, works to make reason and the will of God prevail. He who works for machinery, he who works for hatred, works only for confusion. Culture looks beyond machinery, culture hates hatred; culture has one great passion, the passion for sweetness and light. It has one even yet greater!—the passion for making them *prevail*. It is not satisfied till we *all* come to a perfect man; it knows that the sweetness and light of the few must be imperfect until the raw and unkindled masses of humanity are touched with sweetness and light. If I have not shrunk from saying that we must work for sweetness and light, so neither have I shrunk from saying that we must have a broad basis, must have sweetness and light for as many as possible. Again and again I have insisted how those are the happy moments of humanity, how those are the marking epochs of a people's life, how those are the flowering times for literature and art and all the creative power of genius, when there is a *national* glow of life and thought, when the whole of society is in the fullest measure permeated by thought, sensible to beauty, intelligent and alive. Only it must be *real* thought and *real* beauty; *real* sweetness and *real* light. Plenty of people will try to give the masses, as they call them, an intellectual food prepared and adapted in the way they think proper for the actual condition of the masses. The ordinary popular literature is an example of this way of working on the masses. Plenty of people will try to indoctrinate the masses with the set of ideas and judgments constituting the creed of their own profession or party. Our religious and political organisations give an example of this way of working on the masses. I condemn neither way; but culture works differently. It does not try to teach down to the level of inferior classes; it does not try to win them for this or that sect of its own, with ready-made judgments and watchwords. It seeks to do away with classes; to make the best that has been thought and known in the world current everywhere; to make all men live in an atmosphere of sweetness and light, where they may use ideas, as it uses them itself, freely,—nourished, and not bound by them.

This is the *social idea;* and the men of culture are the true apostles of equality. The great men of culture are those who have had a passion for diffusing, for making prevail, for carrying from one end of society to the other, the best knowledge, the best ideas of

---

[25] Cf. Macaulay's remark on p. 464, above.

[26] John Stuart Mill, the disciple of Bentham. Thomas Henry Buckle wrote a *History of Civilization in England* (1857, 1861) which attempted to put history on a scientific basis and to explain the social laws that determine the character and progress of institutions and beliefs.

[27] Matthew 23:8. *Rabbi* means Master.

their time; who have laboured to divest knowledge of all that was harsh, uncouth, difficult, abstract, professional, exclusive; to humanise it, to make it efficient outside the clique of the cultivated and learned, yet still remaining the *best* knowledge and thought of the time, and a true source, therefore, of sweetness and light. Such a man was Abelard in the Middle Ages, in spite of all his imperfections; and thence the boundless emotion and enthusiasm which Abelard excited. Such were Lessing and Herder in Germany, at the end of the last century; and their services to Germany were in this way inestimably precious. Generations will pass, and literary monuments will accumulate, and works far more perfect than the works of Lessing and Herder will be produced in Germany; and yet the names of these two men will fill a German with a reverence and enthusiasm such as the names of the most gifted masters will hardly awaken. And why? Because they *humanised* knowledge; because they broadened the basis of life and intelligence; because they worked powerfully to diffuse sweetness and light, to make reason and the will of God prevail. With Saint Augustine they said: "Let us not leave thee alone to make in the secret of thy knowledge, as thou didst before the creation of the firmament, the division of light from darkness; let the children of thy spirit, placed in their firmament, make their light shine upon the earth, mark the division of night and day, and announce the revolution of the times; for the old order is passed, and the new arises; the night is spent, the day is come forth; and thou shalt crown the year with thy blessing, when thou shalt send forth labourers into thy harvest sown by other hands than theirs; when thou shalt send forth new labourers to new seed-times, whereof the harvest shall be not yet."

Dante Gabriel Rossetti

1828–1882

DANTE GABRIEL ROSSETTI was a rarely endowed individual, having to a high degree the gift not only of poetic but also of pictorial expression. Indeed, so evenly balanced were these two sides of his artistic temperament that his pictures sometimes seem the plastic expression of his poetic inspiration, and his poems often create the impression of paintings. Actually he often dealt with the same subject in both media, writing sonnets for his pictures or depicting the subjects of his poems on canvas. A contemporary critic notes that Rossetti, "the poet-painter," was unable to dissever his pictorial from his poetic faculty, and Rossetti himself all but identified the two arts when he declared, "If any man has any poetry in him he should paint it," which is essentially what he strove to do with both color and words.

Born in London in 1828, the son of an exiled Italian patriot, this doubly talented youth grew up in a household where culture and politics, mainly Italian, were the major preoccupations: the simple home welcomed sooner or later almost all the Italians who had fled to England to escape Austrian tyranny, and was at the same time a meeting place for those of literary, musical, and artistic interests. The father, who had both musical and poetic talents, was a devoted student of Dante. As his political hopes grew dim, he gradually gave himself up almost exclusively to the interpretation of the great Florentine, who became, we are told, a kind of familiar spirit in the house, "a sacred and benign, though mysteriously invisible visitor."

Dante's influence upon young Dante Gabriel did not remain completely ethereal, for the son in turn began to pore over the *Divina Commedia* and more especially over the *Vita Nuova*. At first it was no doubt the pictorial qualities that appealed to his sensuous imagination, but there was also a strain of mysticism in him which responded to Dante's conception of the final fulfillment of human love and beauty in the divine. Moreover, he was at the same time discovering with delight the glowing and picturesque character of the Middle Ages as portrayed in Malory, in Scott, and in Keats. Here was a world to which he, like William Morris, instinctively felt he belonged, with all its wealth of color and romance and its chivalric tradition of courtly love. Thus stirred, it is small wonder that when he decided to bend his main efforts to painting, he should find the drab tones and academic conventionalism of contemporary art both lifeless and intolerable, "wishy-washy to the last degree." It was primarily "in the Italian painters from Giotto to Leonardo, and in certain early Flemish and German painters," that he recognized some of the qualities which had exerted such a spell over him in poetry, "a manifest emotional sincerity, expressed sometimes in a lofty and solemn way, and sometimes with a candid *naïveté*; . . . strong evidences of grace, decorative charm." To rescue English painting from its worn-out traditions by returning to the spirit of those early painters, he joined in 1848 with Holman Hunt and Edward Millais to form the Pre-Raphaelite Brotherhood (see the General Introduction, p. 387). His brother William asserted that the basis of their new start was to be "serious and elevated invention of subject, along with earnest scrutiny of visible facts, and an earnest endeavour to present them veraciously and exactly." This careful observation and reproduction of visible facts was what Morris had in mind years later when he singled out naturalism as the "special and particular doctrine" of the school. (See p. 792, below.) To spread their ideas the group started in 1850 a short-lived magazine, *The Germ.* Nearly a dozen poems were contributed by Rossetti, chief among which was "The Blessed Damozel," the very epitome of his Pre-Raphaelite ideals. The subject is elevated, but at the same time heaven and its inhabitants are depicted in the most candid and naturalistic terms; the details are earnestly studied and accurately presented, while the color and imagery are full of decorative charm. Whatever the immediate occasion for the poem, it is clearly a reflection of Rossetti's deep and lifelong preoccupation with Dante and with the story of his semimystical devotion to Beatrice, for the blessed damozel is certainly an echo of Dante's portrayal of his lady in Paradise. But the echo, by its very nature, has undergone transformation. The lady who leaned out from the gold bar of heaven has retained far more of her earthly attributes than the Beatrice of the "Paradiso." With all of his appreciation of Dante's transcendentally spiritualized love, Rossetti remained a man whose sensuous perceptions could not be separated from his spiritual ideals, so that the poem conveys an atmosphere of almost opulent beauty that contrasts markedly with Dante's austerity. Indeed, so striking are the plastic elements that the reader may well ask himself whether he has been reading a poem or looking at a picture, an effect which attains to what Rossetti once proclaimed to be the supreme perfection: "the point of meeting where the two [picture and poem] are most identical."

The same plastic effect tends to dominate in other poems where he is depicting more contemporary and more earthly scenes. "My Sister's Sleep" describes one of those incidents which William Morris termed distinctive of the naturalistic painting of the Pre-Raphaelite group (see p. 793, below), an incident taken from ordinary modern life; but again the poem is a picture, with the same conscientious attention to accurate presentment of physical detail. Rossetti painted another contemporary scene in his dramatic monologue "Jenny," written under the influence of Robert Browning, for whom at one period he experienced an intense admiration. Here again, although the emotional and psychological factors are much more

in evidence, it is still the pictorial impression that is dominant.

These, however, are scenes and incidents such as Rossetti usually eschewed; his love of beauty and color and romance, coupled to his fascination with Dante and with the semimystical traditions of chivalry, led him more often to medieval subjects. One of the earliest and best of his poems on such subjects is "Sister Helen." Though the same pictorial imagination is recognizable in this study of the almost demoniacal cruelty engendered by unrequited love and jealousy, there is a comparative lack of either decorative or colorful detail. The power of the narrative is enforced by the austerity of diction and image that perfectly reflect the stark scene and the grim emotions, as well as by the skillful use of the refrain to communicate Helen's inner excitement and final despair.

With his mind thus filled with themes and images of the Middle Ages in general and of Dante in particular, it is hardly surprising that when, in 1850, Rossetti fell in love with Elizabeth Siddal, he should have identified himself and her with Dante and Beatrice, an identity which was emphasized by Lizzie's posing for his pictures of the latter. Nor is it too surprising that during the next ten years Rossetti, although mainly busied with his painting, and distracted by his troubled and prolonged engagement and subsequent marriage (1860) to the beautiful but difficult Miss Siddal—a union which was soon terminated by her death under circumstances which did not preclude the possibility of suicide—should still have found time to translate the *Vita Nuova* and some of Dante's sonnets, as well as poems by various of his predecessors and contemporaries. These he published in 1861 as *The Early Italian Poets,* later revising and rearranging them under the title of *Dante and His Circle* (1874).

He had planned to publish his own poetry separately shortly after the volume of Italian translations, but the project was temporarily halted when, in 1862, in a fit of remorse he put his manuscripts into his wife's coffin. This impulsive and somewhat histrionic gesture was an attempt to attone to Lizzie for the unhappiness he felt he had caused her. In the first flush of his attachment he had viewed her in an aura of Dantesque mysticism, but as the stress of their personalities and circumstances revealed with ever-increasing clarity that he was no Dante and Lizzie no Beatrice, he tasted keen disillusionment and frustration, and finally, bitter self-reproach. No doubt the galling realization of the gulf between his earlier dream and the actuality is responsible for the tone of desolation and vain regret that sounds in many of the sonnets which he was writing during this period and which eventually formed part of his sequence, *The House of Life.* But Rossetti, whatever his bitterness and disillusionment, could not escape the influence that had been such a dominating force from his earliest years. He was still "half lost in medievalism and Dante," as Ruskin complained to the Brownings in 1859. He still dreamed of love as he had found it in the *Vita Nuova,* "love sublimed to heavenly mood," although time had proved it so foreign to his own experience and nature. The mystical fulfillment that had been so signally wanting in his relations with Lizzie, he now looked for in his love for Jane Morris, the wife of his friend and one-time disciple William Morris. Thus, joined with vain regret for the past, there is in these sonnets an equally vain hope for the future, and that hope, by the very nature of the case, led full circle round to vain regret for what might have been.

Written over a period of more than thirty years, the completed series of a hundred and one sonnets makes no attempt to present a consecutive story or to trace an ordered psychological development; rather, as the poet himself explains, each sonnet is "a moment's monument." For obvious personal reasons both Rossetti and later his brother and editor, William, made every effort to obscure the exact autobiographical bearing of the sonnets; it is nevertheless quite clear that the sonnets do reflect for the most part Rossetti's experiences and moods, and are attempts to translate these into a semi-Platonic and allegorical idiom. While there are lines which do recapture momentarily the naturalistic and pictorial qualities of some of his other poems, specifically descriptions of nature or natural settings, the sonnets are on the whole noticeably abstract and stylized, full of symbolic imagery and elaborate personification. But occasionally, when the intensity of the underlying mood of remorse or long-ing does break through the conventionalized expression of the medieval tradition, we can recognize and respond to the emotions of a living man.

It was not until 1869, when he feared that his eyesight might be failing, that Rossetti took the necessary steps to have the manuscripts of his poems recovered from Lizzie's grave. After some revision and addition, he published in April, 1870, the first collection of his own work, *Poems.* The publication gave rise in October to a scurrilous denunciation by Robert Buchanan in the *Contemporary Review,* entitled "The Fleshly School of Poetry—Mr. D. G. Rossetti," which lashed out at the sensualism of Rossetti's poems, designating *The House of Life* a very hotbed of offensive ideas and nasty phrases. To a man in a less morbidly sensitive state, the attack might have proved irritating enough, but to Rossetti, whose mind was already showing signs of paranoia and a persecution complex, it seemed "the first symptom in a widespread conspiracy for crushing his fair fame as an artist and a man, and for hounding him out of honest society." He suffered a breakdown the following May, and his brother tells us that henceforth till the close of his life Rossetti was a changed man, although during his last ten years he did work actively at his painting and in 1881 published his *Ballads and Sonnets* and a revised edition of his *Poems.*

The standard edition is *Collected Works of Dante Gabriel Rossetti,* edited by his brother William (1887–8). The most recent and exhaustive biography is *A Victorian Romantic: Dante Gabriel Rossetti,* by Oswald Doughty (1949). There is a good essay by Graham Hough in *The Last Romantics* (1949).

Dante Gabriel Rossetti

THE BLESSED DAMOZEL[1]

The blessed damozel leaned out
  From the gold bar of Heaven;
Her eyes were deeper than the depth
  Of waters stilled at even;
She had three lilies in her hand,
  And the stars in her hair were seven.

Her robe, ungirt from clasp to hem,
  No wrought flowers did adorn,
But a white rose of Mary's gift,
  For service meetly worn;[2]   10
Her hair that lay along her back
  Was yellow like ripe corn.[3]

Herseemed[4] she scarce had been a day
  One of God's choristers;
The wonder was not yet quite gone   15
  From that still look of hers;

---

[1] The word "damozel" is an early form of the French "demoiselle" or English "damsel." Rossetti, many years after writing the poem, attributed its origin to his admiration for Poe's "Raven." "I saw," he is reported to have said, "that Poe had done the utmost it was possible to do with grief of the lover on earth, and I determined to reverse the conditions."

[2] The white rose is a symbol of virginity and therefore a fitting flower to be worn by one in the service of Mary.

[3] In England *corn* is a general term for grain.

[4] It seemed to her.

Albeit, to them she left, her day
  Had counted as <u>ten years</u>.

(To one, it is ten years of years.
  . . . Yet now, and in this place,   20
Surely she leaned o'er me—her hair
  Fell all about my face. . . .
Nothing: the autumn-fall of leaves.
  The whole year sets apace.)

It was the rampart of God's house   25
  That she was standing on;
By God built over the sheer depth
  The which is Space begun;
So high, that looking downward thence
  She scarce could see the sun.   30

It lies in Heaven, across the flood
  Of ether, as a bridge.
Beneath, the tides of day and night
  With flame and darkness ridge
The void, as low as where this earth   35
  Spins like a fretful midge.

<u>Around her, lovers, newly met</u>
  <u>'Mid deathless love's acclaims,</u>
Spoke evermore among themselves
  Their heart-remembered names;   40
And the souls mounting up to God
  Went by her like thin flames.

And still she bowed herself and stooped
  Out of the circling charm;
<u>Until her bosom must have made</u>   45
  The bar she leaned on warm,
And the lilies lay as if asleep
  Along her bended arm.

From the fixed place of Heaven she saw
  Time like a pulse shake fierce   50
Through all the worlds. Her gaze still strove
  Within the gulf to pierce
Its path; and now she spoke as when
  The stars sang in their spheres.[5]

The sun was gone now; the <u>curled moon</u>
  <u>Was like a little feather</u>
Fluttering far down the gulf; and now
  She spoke through the still weather.

Her voice was like the voice the stars
  Had when they sang together.   60

(Ah, sweet! Even now, in that bird's song,
  Strove not her accents there,
Fain to be harkened? When those bells
  Possessed the midday air,
Strove not her steps to <u>reach my side</u>   65
  <u>Down all the echoing stair</u>?)

"<u>I wish that he were come to me</u>,
  <u>For he will come</u>," she said.
"Have I not prayed in Heaven?—on earth,
  Lord, Lord, has he not prayed?   70
<u>Are not two prayers a perfect strength?</u>
  And shall I feel afraid?

"When round his head the aureole clings,
  And he is clothed in white,
I'll take his hand and go with him   75
  To the deep wells of light;
As unto a stream we will step down,
  And bathe there in God's sight.

"We two will stand beside that shrine,
  Occult, withheld, untrod,   80
Whose lamps are stirred continually
  With prayer sent up to God;
And see our old prayers, granted, melt
  Each like a little cloud.

"We two will lie i' the shadow of   85
  That living mystic tree[6]
Within whose secret growth the Dove[7]
  Is sometimes felt to be,
While every leaf that His plumes touch
  Saith His Name audibly.   90

"And I myself will teach to him,
  I myself, lying so,
The songs I sing here; which his voice
  Shall pause in, hushed and slow,
And find some knowledge at each pause,   95
  Or some new thing to know."

(Alas! We two, we two, thou say'st!
  Yea, one wast thou with me
That once of old. But shall God lift
  <u>To endless unity</u>   100
The soul whose likeness with thy soul
  Was but its love for thee?)

---

[5] It was a common belief in ancient times that the stars made a
singing noise as they moved in their spheres.

[6] Cf. Revelation 22:2.   [7] The Holy Spirit.

"We two," she said, "will seek the groves
  Where the lady Mary is,
With her five handmaidens, whose names   105
  Are five sweet symphonies,
Cecily, Gertrude, Magdalen,
  Margaret, and Rosalys.[8]   *musical effect*

"Circlewise sit they, with bound locks
  And foreheads garlanded;   110
Into the fine cloth white like flame
  Weaving the golden thread,
To fashion the birth-robes for them
  Who are just born, being dead.

"He shall fear, haply, and be dumb;   115
  Then will I lay my cheek
To his, and tell about our love,
  Not once abashed or weak;
And the dear Mother will approve
  My pride, and let me speak.   120

"Herself shall bring us, hand in hand,
  To Him round whom all souls
Kneel, the clear-ranged unnumbered heads
  Bowed with their aureoles;
And angels meeting us shall sing   125
  To their citherns and citoles.[9]

"There will I ask of Christ the Lord
  Thus much for him and me:—
Only to live as once on earth
  With Love,—only to be,   130
As then awhile, forever now,
  Together, I and he."

She gazed and listened and then said,
  Less sad of speech than mild,—
"All this is when he comes." She ceased.   135
  The light thrilled toward her, filled
With angels in strong level flight.
  Her eyes prayed, and she smiled.

(I saw her smile.) But soon their path
  Was vague in distant spheres;   140
And then she cast her arms along   *Complete why?*
  The golden barriers,
And laid her face between her hands,
  And wept. (I heard her tears.)

---

[8] The names of the saints attending Mary are chosen purely for the musical effect.   [9] Medieval musical instruments.

MY SISTER'S SLEEP[1]

She fell asleep on Christmas Eve.
  At length the long-ungranted shade
  Of weary eyelids overweighed
The pain naught else might yet relieve.

Our mother, who had leaned all day   5
  Over the bed from chime to chime,
  Then raised herself for the first time,
And as she sat her down, did pray.

Her little work-table was spread
  With work to finish. For the glare   10
  Made by her candle, she had care
To work some distance from the bed.

Without, there was a cold moon up,   *nature*
  Of winter radiance sheer and thin;
  The hollow halo it was in   15
Was like an icy crystal cup.

Through the small room, with subtle sound
  Of flame, by vents the fireshine drove
  And reddened. In its dim alcove
The mirror shed a clearness round.   20

I had been sitting up some nights,
  And my tired mind felt weak and blank;
  Like a sharp strengthening wine it drank
The stillness and the broken lights.

Twelve struck. That sound, by dwindling years   25
  Heard in each hour,[2] crept off; and then
  The ruffled silence spread again,
Like water that a pebble stirs.

Our mother rose from where she sat;
  Her needles, as she laid them down,   30
  Met lightly, and her silken gown
Settled: no other noise than that.

"Glory unto the Newly Born!"
  So, as said angels, she did say,
  Because we were in Christmas Day,   35
Though it would still be long till morn.

---

[1] "This little poem, written in 1847, was printed in a periodical [*The Germ*] at the outset of 1850. The metre, which is used by several old English writers, became celebrated a month or two later on the publication of '*In Memoriam*.'" (Rossetti) The poem is not based upon any autobiographical facts.
[2] Because old people tend to sleep less than others, they hear the striking of all the hours.

Just then in the room over us
  There was a pushing back of chairs,
  As some who had sat unawares
So late, now heard the hour, and rose.   40

With anxious softly-stepping haste
  Our mother went where Margaret lay,
  Fearing the sounds o'erhead—should they
Have broken her long watched-for rest!

She stooped an instant, calm, and turned,   45
  But suddenly turned back again;
  And all her features seemed in pain
With woe, and her eyes gazed and yearned.

For my part, I but hid my face,
  And held my breath, and spoke no word: 50
  There was none spoken; but I heard
The silence for a little space.

Our mother bowed herself and wept;
  And both my arms fell, and I said,
  "God knows I knew that she was dead."   55
And there, all white, my sister slept.

Then kneeling, upon Christmas morn
  A little after twelve o'clock
  We said, ere the first quarter struck,
"Christ's blessing on the newly born!"   60

THE BALLAD OF DEAD LADIES[3]

(FROM FRANÇOIS VILLON)

Tell me now in what hidden way is
  Lady Flora the lovely Roman?
  Where's Hipparchia, and where is Thaïs,[4]
    Neither of them the fairer woman?
    Where is Echo, beheld of no man,   5
Only heard on river and mere—
  She whose beauty was more than human? . . .
But where are the snows of yester-year?

Where's Héloïse,[5] the learned nun,
  For whose sake Abeillard, I ween,   10
Lost manhood and put priesthood on?
  (From Love he won such dule and teen!)
  And where, I pray you, is the Queen[6]
Who willed that Buridan should steer
  Sewed in a sack's mouth down the Seine? . . .   15
But where are the snows of yester-year?

White Queen Blanche, like a queen of lilies,[7]
  With a voice like any mermaiden—
Bertha Broadfoot, Beatrice, Alice,[8]
  And Ermengarde the lady of Maine[9]—   20
  And that good Joan[10] whom Englishmen
At Rouen doomed and burned her there—
  Mother of God, where are they then? . . .
But where are the snows of yester-year?

Nay, never ask this week, fair lord,   25
  Where they are gone, nor yet this year,
Except with this for an overword—
  But where are the snows of yester-year?

SISTER HELEN[1]

"Why did you melt your waxen man,
                 Sister Helen?
Today is the third since you began."
  "The time was long, yet the time ran,
                Little brother."   5
        (O Mother, Mary Mother,
  Three days today, between Hell and Heaven!)

"But if you have done your work aright,
                 Sister Helen,
You'll let me play, for you said I might."   10

---

[5] Héloïse was the beautiful niece of a church official, who fell in love with her teacher, the famous philosopher and theologian, Abelard (1079-1142). They eloped, and the uncle was so incensed that he caused Abelard to be set upon and emasculated. As a result Abelard became a monk and Héloïse a nun, and the reward of their love was sorrow and pain.

[6] The Queen was Margaret of Burgundy, who used to have her lovers, among whom was the scholar Buridan, sewn in sacks and thrown into the Seine.

[7] Perhaps Blanche of Castille, or perhaps a figment of Villon's imagination.

[8] Bertha Broadfoot, in epic accounts, is the mother of Charlemagne. The identity of Beatrice and Alice is uncertain and immaterial. The poet may well not have had any specific ladies in mind.

[9] A countess of Anjou in France.   [10] Joan of Arc.

[1] The ballad is based on the superstition that melting the waxen image of a person will bring about his suffering and death.

---

[3] This is a translation of the "Ballade des Dames du Temps Jadis" by François Villon (b. 1431), whose irregular life and haunting songs captured the imaginations of many later writers. Rossetti was much attracted by medieval literary forms. The *ballade* is a French form composed of three eight-line stanzas and a concluding four-line "envoy," each ending with the same line by way of refrain. Strictly speaking, the same rimes should be employed throughout, in the order *ababbcbc* (*bcbc* for the envoy), but Rossetti introduces fresh *a* and *b* rimes in each stanza.

[4] Flora was a famous courtesan of Rome, Hipparchia a Greek courtesan, and Thaïs an Athenian lady of like profession.

"Be very still in your play tonight,
                    Little brother."
                    (*O Mother, Mary Mother,*
Third night, tonight, between Hell and Heaven!)

"You said it must melt ere vesper-bell,   15
                    Sister Helen;
If now it be molten, all is well."
"Even so—nay, peace! you cannot tell,
                    Little brother."
                    (*O Mother, Mary Mother,*   20
Oh, what is this, between Hell and Heaven?)

"Oh, the waxen knave was plump today,
                    Sister Helen;
How like dead folk he has dropped away!"
"Nay now, of the dead what can you say,   25
                    Little brother?"
                    (*O Mother, Mary Mother,*
What of the dead, between Hell and Heaven?)

"See, see, the sunken pile of wood,
                    Sister Helen,   30
Shines through the thinned wax red as blood!"
"Nay now, when looked you yet on blood,
                    Little brother?"
                    (*O Mother, Mary Mother,*
How pale she is, between Hell and Heaven!)   35

"Now close your eyes, for they're sick and sore,
                    Sister Helen,
And I'll play without the gallery door."
"Aye, let me rest—I'll lie on the floor,
                    Little brother."   40
                    (*O Mother, Mary Mother,*
What rest tonight, between Hell and Heaven?)

"Here high up in the balcony,
                    Sister Helen,
The moon flies face to face with me."   45
"Aye, look and say whatever you see,
                    Little brother."
                    (*O Mother, Mary Mother,*
What sight tonight, between Hell and Heaven?)

"Outside it's merry in the wind's wake,   50
                    Sister Helen;
In the shaken trees the chill stars shake."
"Hush, heard you a horse-tread as you spake,
                    Little brother?"
                    (*O Mother, Mary Mother,*   55
What sound tonight, between Hell and Heaven?)

"I hear a horse-tread, and I see,
                    Sister Helen,
Three horsemen that ride terribly."
"Little brother, whence come the three,   60
                    Little brother?"
                    (*O Mother, Mary Mother,*
Whence should they come, between Hell and Heaven?)

"They come by the hill-verge from Boyne Bar,[2]
                    Sister Helen,   65
And one draws nigh, but two are afar."
"Look, look, do you know them who they are,
                    Little brother?"
                    (*O Mother, Mary Mother,*
Who should they be, between Hell and Heaven?)   70

"Oh, it's Keith of Eastholm rides so fast,
                    Sister Helen,
For I know the white mane on the blast."
"The hour has come, has come at last,
                    Little brother!"   75
                    (*O Mother, Mary Mother,*
Her hour at last, between Hell and Heaven!)

"He has made a sign and called Halloo!
                    Sister Helen,
And he says that he would speak with you."   80
"Oh, tell him I fear the frozen dew,
                    Little brother."
                    (*O Mother, Mary Mother,*
Why laughs she thus, between Hell and Heaven?)

"The wind is loud, but I hear him cry,   85
                    Sister Helen,
That Keith of Ewern's like to die."
"And he and thou, and thou and I,
                    Little brother."
                    (*O Mother, Mary Mother,*   90
And they and we, between Hell and Heaven!)

"Three days ago, on his marriage-morn,
                    Sister Helen,
He sickened, and lies since then forlorn."
"For bridegroom's side is the bride a thorn,   95
                    Little brother?"
                    (*O Mother, Mary Mother,*
Cold bridal cheer, between Hell and Heaven!)

------

[2] At the mouth of the river of that name in Ireland.

"Three days and nights he has lain abed,
                              Sister Helen,   100
And he prays in torment to be dead."
"The thing may chance, if he have prayed,
                              Little brother!"
          (O Mother, Mary Mother,
If he have prayed, between Hell and Heaven!)   105

"But he has not ceased to cry today,
                              Sister Helen,
That you should take your curse away."
"My prayer was heard—he need but pray,
                              Little brother!"   110
          (O Mother, Mary Mother,
Shall God not hear, between Hell and Heaven?)

"But he says, till you take back your ban,
                              Sister Helen,
His soul would pass, yet never can."   115
"Nay then, shall I slay a living man,[3]
                              Little brother?"
          (O Mother, Mary Mother,
A living soul, between Hell and Heaven!)

"But he calls for ever on your name,   120
                              Sister Helen,
And says that he melts before a flame."
"My heart for his pleasure fared the same,
                              Little brother."
          (O Mother, Mary Mother, 125
Fire at the heart, between Hell and Heaven!)

"Here's Keith of Westholm riding fast,
                              Sister Helen,
For I know the white plume on the blast."
"The hour, the sweet hour I forecast,   130
                              Little brother!"
          (O Mother, Mary Mother,
Is the hour sweet, between Hell and Heaven?)

"He stops to speak, and he stills his horse,
                              Sister Helen;   135
But his words are drowned in the wind's course."
"Nay hear, nay hear, you must hear perforce,
                              Little brother!"
          (O Mother, Mary Mother,
What word now heard, between Hell and Heaven?)   140

"Oh, he says that Keith of Ewern's cry,
                              Sister Helen,
Is ever to see you ere he die."
"In all that his soul sees, there am I,
                              Little brother!"   145
          (O Mother, Mary Mother,
The soul's one sight, between Hell and Heaven!)

"He sends a ring and a broken coin,[4]
                              Sister Helen,
And bids you mind the banks of Boyne."   150
"What else he broke will he ever join,
                              Little brother?"
          (O Mother, Mary Mother,
No, never joined, between Hell and Heaven!)

"He yields you these and craves full fain,   155
                              Sister Helen,
You pardon him in his mortal pain."
"What else he took will he give again,
                              Little brother?"
          (O Mother, Mary Mother, 160
Not twice to give, between Hell and Heaven!)

"He calls your name in an agony,
                              Sister Helen,
That even dead Love must weep to see."
"Hate, born of Love, is blind as he,   165
                              Little brother!"
          (O Mother, Mary Mother,
Love turned to hate, between Hell and Heaven!)

"Oh, it's Keith of Keith now that rides fast,
                              Sister Helen,   170
For I know the white hair on the blast."
"The short short hour will soon be past,
                              Little brother!"
          (O Mother, Mary Mother,
Will soon be past, between Hell and Heaven!)   175

"He looks at me and he tries to speak,
                              Sister Helen,
But oh! his voice is sad and weak!"
"What here should the mighty Baron seek,
                              Little brother?"   180
          (O Mother, Mary Mother,
Is this the end, between Hell and Heaven?)

---

[3] A piece of sophistry: if Helen would retract her curse, her victim, Keith of Ewern, could die; but this, says Helen, would be to kill a living man. Like her other replies, this is merely to evade the pleas for help.

[4] Helen and Keith had pledged their troth by breaking a coin in two and each one retaining a half.

"Oh, his son still cries, if you forgive,
                    Sister Helen,
The body dies but the soul shall live."   185
"Fire shall forgive me as I forgive,[5]
                    Little brother!"
          (*O Mother, Mary Mother,*
As she forgives, between Hell and Heaven!)

"Oh, he prays you, as his heart would rive,[6]   190
                    Sister Helen,
To save his dear son's soul alive."
"Fire cannot slay it; it shall thrive,[7]
                    Little brother!"
          (*O Mother, Mary Mother,* 195
Alas, alas, between Hell and Heaven!)

"He cries to you, kneeling in the road,
                    Sister Helen,
To go with him for the love of God!"
"The way is long to his son's abode,   200
                    Little brother."
          (*O Mother, Mary Mother,*
The way is long, between Hell and Heaven!)

"A lady's here, by a dark steed brought,
                    Sister Helen,   205
So darkly clad, I saw her not."
"See her now or never see aught,
                    Little brother!"
          (*O Mother, Mary Mother,*
What more to see, between Hell and Heaven?)   210

"Her hood falls back, and the moon shines fair,
                    Sister Helen,
On the Lady of Ewern's golden hair."
"Blest hour of my power and her despair,
                    Little brother!"   215
          (*O Mother, Mary Mother,*
Hour blest and banned, between Hell and Heaven!)

"Pale, pale her cheeks, that in pride did glow,
                    Sister Helen,
'Neath the bridal-wreath three days ago."   220
"One morn for pride and three days for woe,
                    Little brother!"
          (*O Mother, Mary Mother,*
Three days, three nights, between Hell and Heaven!)

"Her clasped hands stretch from her bending head,   225
                    Sister Helen;
With the loud wind's wail her sobs are wed."
"What wedding-strains hath her bridal-bed,
                    Little brother?"
          (*O Mother, Mary Mother,* 230
What strain but death's, between Hell and Heaven!)

"She may not speak, she sinks in a swoon,
                    Sister Helen—
She lifts her lips and gasps on the moon."
"Oh! might I but hear her soul's blithe tune,   235
                    Little brother!"
          (*O Mother, Mary Mother,*
Her woe's dumb cry, between Hell and Heaven!)

"They've caught her to Westholm's saddlebow,
                    Sister Helen,   240
And her moonlit hair gleams white in its flow."
"Let it turn whiter than winter snow,
                    Little brother!"
          (*O Mother, Mary Mother,*
Woe-withered gold, between Hell and Heaven!)   245

"O Sister Helen, you heard the bell,
                    Sister Helen!
More loud than the vesper-chime it fell."
"No vesper-chime, but a dying knell,
                    Little brother!"   250
          (*O Mother, Mary Mother,*
His dying knell, between Hell and Heaven!)

"Alas! but I fear the heavy sound,
                    Sister Helen;
Is it in the sky or in the ground?"   255
"Say, have they turned their horses round,
                    Little brother?"
          (*O Mother, Mary Mother,*
What would she more, between Hell and Heaven?)

"They have raised the old man from his knee,   260
                    Sister Helen,
And they ride in silence hastily."
"More fast the naked soul doth flee,
                    Little brother!"
          (*O Mother, Mary Mother,* 265
The naked soul, between Hell and Heaven!)

---

[5] Hell fire will burn me as I burn this image. In neither case will
there be forgiveness.
[6] As if his heart would burst with sorrow.

[7] It shall thrive only in the sense that it will never die, for part of
the effect of the curse is that it shall never find peace but remain
between heaven and hell.

"Flank to flank are the three steeds gone,
                    Sister Helen,
But the lady's dark steed goes alone."
"And lonely her bridegroom's soul hath flown,   270
                    Little brother."
               (*O Mother, Mary Mother,*
The lonely ghost, between Hell and Heaven!)

"Oh, the wind is sad in the iron chill,
                    Sister Helen,   275
And weary sad they look by the hill."
"But he and I are sadder still,
                    Little brother!"
               (*O Mother, Mary Mother,*
Most sad of all, between Hell and Heaven!)   280

"See, see, the wax has dropped from its place,
                    Sister Helen,
And the flames are winning up apace!"
"Yet here they burn but for a space,[8]
                    Little brother!"   285
               (*O Mother, Mary Mother,*
Here for a space, between Hell and Heaven!)

"Ah! what white thing at the door has crossed,
                    Sister Helen?
Ah! what is this that sighs in the frost?"   290
"A soul that's lost as mine is lost,
                    Little brother!"
               (*O Mother, Mary Mother,*
Lost, lost, all lost, between Hell and Heaven!)

from THE HOUSE OF LIFE[1]

A Sonnet is a moment's monument,—
     Memorial from the Soul's eternity
     To one dead deathless hour. Look that it be,
Whether for lustral[2] rite or dire portent,
Of its own arduous fulness reverent: 5
     Carve it in ivory or in ebony,
     As Day or Night may rule; and let Time see
Its flowering crest impearled and orient.

A Sonnet is a coin: its face reveals
     The soul—its converse, to what Power 'tis due:—   10
Whether for tribute to the august appeals
     Of Life, or dower in Love's high retinue,

It serve; or, 'mid the dark wharf's cavernous breath,
In Charon's[3] palm it pay the toll to Death.

4. LOVESIGHT

When do I see thee most, beloved one?
     When in the light the spirits of mine eyes
     Before thy face, their altar, solemnize
The worship of that Love through thee made known?
Or when in the dusk hours (we two alone,)   5
     Close-kissed and eloquent of still replies
     Thy twilight-hidden glimmering visage lies,
And my soul only sees thy soul its own?

O love, my love! if I no more should see
Thyself, nor on the earth the shadow of thee,   10
     Nor image of thine eyes in any spring,—
How then should sound upon Life's darkening slope
The ground-whirl of the perished leaves of Hope,
     The wind of Death's imperishable wing?

19. SILENT NOON

Your hands lie open in the long fresh grass,—
     The finger-points look through like rosy blooms:
     Your eyes smile peace. The pasture gleams and glooms
'Neath billowing skies[4] that scatter and amass.
All round our nest, far as the eye can pass,   5
     Are golden kingcup-fields with silver edge
     Where the cow-parsley skirts the hawthorn-hedge.[5]
'Tis visible silence, still as the hour-glass.

Deep in the sun-searched growths the dragon-fly
Hangs like a blue thread loosened from the sky:—   10
     So this winged hour is dropt to us from above.
Oh! clasp we to our hearts, for deathless dower,
This close-companioned inarticulate hour
     When twofold silence was the song of love.

24. PRIDE OF YOUTH

Even as a child, of sorrow that we give
     The dead, but little in his heart can find,
     Since without need of thought to his clear mind
Their turn it is to die and his to live:—
Even so the winged New Love smiles to receive   5
     Along his eddying plumes the auroral wind,
     Nor, forward glorying, casts one look behind
Where night-rack shrouds the Old Love fugitive.

---

[8] The implication is that in hell they burn eternally.

[1] The title is derived from astrology, where the heavens are divided into houses, the chief of which is the House of Life. In other words, the sonnets purport to be a comment upon life. Actually they are primarily reflections on three subjects: life, love, and death.   [2] Purifying.

[3] Charon was the ferryman who, for a coin, rowed the dead across the Styx to the Underworld.   [4] I.e., clouds.
[5] Fields of buttercups, edged with silvery-leafed cow-parsley.

There is a change in every hour's recall,
  And the last cowslip in the fields we see   10
  On the same day with the first corn-poppy.
Alas for hourly change! Alas for all
The loves that from his hand proud Youth lets fall,
  Even as the beads of a told rosary!

51. WILLOWWOOD, 3 [6]

"O ye, all ye that walk in Willowwood,
  That walk with hollow faces burning white;
What fathom-depth of soul-struck widowhood,
  What long, what longer hours, one lifelong night,
Ere ye again, who so in vain have wooed   5
  Your last hope lost, who so in vain invite
Your lips to that their unforgotten food,
  Ere ye, ere ye again shall see the light.

Alas! the bitter banks in Willowwood,
  With tear-spurge wan, with blood-wort burning red:
Alas! if ever such a pillow could   11
  Steep deep the soul in sleep till she were dead,—
Better all life forget her than this thing,
That Willowwood should hold her wandering!"

56. TRUE WOMAN [7]

1. Herself

To be a sweetness more desired than Spring;
  A bodily beauty more acceptable
  Than the wild rose-tree's arch that crowns the fell; [8]
To be an essence more environing [9]
Than wine's drained juice; a music ravishing   5
  More than the passionate pulse of Philomel; [10]—
  To be all this 'neath one soft bosom's swell
That is the flower of life:—how strange a thing!

How strange a thing to be what Man can know
  But as a sacred secret! Heaven's own screen   10
Hides her soul's purest depth and loveliest glow;
  Closely withheld, as all things most unseen,—
  The wave-bowered pearl,—the heart-shaped seal of
      green
That flecks the snowdrop underneath the snow.

---

[6] There is a series of four sonnets under this title. The wood
indicated is one of weeping willows, symbolizing a period or
mood of mourning, not necessarily exclusively for Lizzie, but
rather, and more probably, for the years which Rossetti and
Janey had endured of separation, longing, and frustration.
[7] Three sonnets bear this title. The second has the subtitle "Her
Love"; the third, "Her Heaven."   [8] Cliff.
[9] Permeating.   [10] The nightingale.

69. AUTUMN IDLENESS

This sunlight shames November where he grieves
  In dead red leaves, and will not let him shun
  The day, though bough with bough be over-run.
But with a blessing every glade receives
High salutation; while from hillock-eaves   5
  The deer gaze calling, dappled white and dun,
  As if, being foresters of old, the sun
Had marked them with the shade of forest-leaves.

Here dawn today unveiled her magic glass; [11]
  Here noon now gives the thirst and takes the dew;   10
Till eve bring rest when other good things pass.
  And here the lost hours the lost hours renew [12]
While I still lead my shadow o'er the grass,
  Nor know, for longing, that which I should do.

77. SOUL'S BEAUTY [13]

Under the arch of Life, where love and death,
  Terror and mystery, guard her shrine, I saw
  Beauty enthroned; and though her gaze struck awe,
I drew it in as simply as my breath.
Hers are the eyes which, over and beneath,   5
  The sky and sea bend on thee,—which can draw,
  By sea or sky or woman, to one law,
The allotted bondman of her palm and wreath.

This is that Lady Beauty, in whose praise
  Thy voice and hand shake still,—long known to thee
    By flying hair and fluttering hem, [14]—the beat   11
    Following her daily of thy heart and feet,
  How passionately and irretrievably,
In what fond flight, how many ways and days!

78. BODY'S BEAUTY

Of Adam's first wife, Lilith, it is told
  (The witch he loved before the gift of Eve,)
  That, ere the snake's, her sweet tongue could deceive,
And her enchanted hair was the first gold.
And still she sits, young while the earth is old,   5

---

[11] Dew or frost reflecting the sunlight.
[12] I am now losing time as I live over in memory the past hours
which are lost. The second "lost" may mean merely past and
gone or may have the added sense of "wasted." The line may
be compared with the sonnet "Lost Days," printed below.
[13] This sonnet and the next, according to William Rossetti, were
written respectively for Rossetti's pictures entitled Sibylla
Palmifera and Lilith.
[14] Heretofore the poet has known beauty only through fleeting
glimpses.

And, subtly of herself contemplative,
   Draws men to watch the bright web she can weave,
Till heart and body and life are in its hold.

The rose and poppy are her flowers; for where
   Is he not found, O Lilith, whom shed scent   10
And soft-shed kisses and soft sleep shall snare?
   Lo! as that youth's eyes burned at thine, so went
   Thy spell through him, and left his straight neck bent
And round his heart one strangling golden hair.

86. LOST DAYS

The lost days of my life until to-day,
   What were they, could I see them on the street
   Lie as they fell? Would they be ears of wheat
Sown once for food but trodden into clay?
Or golden coins squandered and still to pay?   5
   Or drops of blood dabbling the guilty feet?
   Or such spilt water as in dreams must cheat
The undying throats of Hell, athirst alway?

I do not see them here; but after death
   God knows I know the faces I shall see,   10
Each one a murdered self, with low last breath.
   "I am thyself,—what hast thou done to me?"
"And I—and I—thyself," (lo! each one saith,)
   "And thou thyself to all eternity!"

97. A SUPERSCRIPTION[15]

Look in my face; my name is Might-have-been;
   I am also called No-more, Too-late, Fare-well;
   Unto thine ear I hold the dead-sea shell
Cast up thy Life's foam-fretted feet between;
Unto thine eyes the glass where that is seen   5
   Which had Life's form and Love's, but by my spell
   Is now a shaken shadow intolerable,
Of ultimate things unuttered the frail screen.

Mark me, how still I am! But should there dart
   One moment through thy soul the soft surprise   10
   Of that winged Peace which lulls the breath of sighs,[16]—
Then shalt thou see me smile, and turn apart
Thy visage to mine ambush at thy heart
   Sleepless with cold commemorative eyes.

---

[15] Mr. Doughty suggests that the title refers to the new love for Janey Morris " 'superscribed' as it were, upon his heart as on a palimpsest; written, that is, upon the old love." Certainly the sonnet is charged with a haunting sense of an old love that will not allow itself to be forgotten.

[16] I.e., of perfect love fulfilled.

101. THE ONE HOPE[17]

When vain desire at last and vain regret
   Go hand in hand to death, and all is vain,
   What shall assuage the unforgotten pain
And teach the unforgetful to forget?
Shall Peace be still a sunk stream long unmet,—   5
   Or may the soul at once in a green plain
   Stoop through the spray of some sweet life-fountain
And cull the dew-drenched flowering amulet?

Ah! when the wan soul in that golden air
   Between the scriptured petals softly blown   10
   Peers breathless for the gift of grace unknown,—
Ah! let none other alien spell soe'er
But only the one Hope's one name be there,—
   Not less nor more, but even that word alone.

THE WOODSPURGE

The wind flapped loose, the wind was still,
Shaken out dead from tree and hill:
I had walked on at the wind's will,—
I sat now, for the wind was still.

Between my knees my forehead was,—   5
My lips, drawn in, said not Alas!
My hair was over in the grass,
My naked ears heard the day pass.

My eyes, wide open, had the run
Of some ten weeds to fix upon;   10
Among those few, out of the sun,
The woodspurge flowered, three cups in one.

From perfect grief there need not be
Wisdom or even memory:
One thing then learnt remains to me,—   15
The woodspurge has a cup of three.

---

[17] The one hope is that of eternal union in the hereafter with "the woman supremely beloved upon earth," Janey Morris.

William Morris

1834–1896

WILLIAM MORRIS was born in 1834 and brought up on his father's country estate at Woodford in Essex. In his early years he developed what was to be a lifelong love of the Middle Ages, partly from reading Scott, partly from excursions to old Essex churches and a visit to Canterbury Cathedral at the age of eight which "left on his mind an ineffaceable impression of the glory of Gothic architecture." As a result, he was prepared to respond sympathetically to the High Church influence at Marlborough, where he went to boarding school, and before he entered Oxford in 1853 he had become an Anglo-Catholic. There he read church history, the *Tracts for the Times,* and masses of medieval chronicles; and he presently decided to enter the ministry. But the attraction of Anglo-Catholicism for him lay more in its ritual and its architecture than in its theology—more in its beauty than its truth. For at bottom Morris's temperament was strongly aesthetic; and it was only a matter of time before art displaced religion as his major interest.

The change was foreshadowed by his enthusiastic reading of Malory's *Morte d'Arthur,* of Keats and Shelley, along with Tennyson (especially the early Romantic poems), then Chaucer and Browning; and in prose, Ruskin's *Modern Painters* and *The Stones of Venice* and Carlyle's *Past and Present,* which were taken for "inspired and absolute truth" (though not so much for their social gospel—that influence came later—as for their medievalism, and in the case of Ruskin, for his enthusiastic account of Gothic). The plan to take orders was dropped, "art and literature were no longer thought of as handmaids to religion, but as ends to be pursued for their own sake" (Art for Art's Sake), and Morris decided to become an architect. Then, at London in 1856 as he was beginning the study of architecture, he met Rossetti and came into direct contact with the Pre-Raphaelite Movement. This crucial influence led him first to painting and then to poetry, with the result that in 1858 he published what is perhaps the finest volume of Pre-Raphaelite verse, *The Defence of Guenevere and Other Poems.*

The chief characteristics of this work are suggested by Morris's lecture on Pre-Raphaelitism (reprinted on pp. 791 ff.). Though the Naturalism which he first takes up applies mainly to painting, it is responsible for the sharp, pictorial detail in the poetry of both Rossetti and Morris. The very opening lines of "The Defence of Guenevere,"

> But, knowing now that they would have her speak,
> She threw her wet hair backward from her brow,
> Her hand close to her mouth touching her cheek,

are the lines of a painter trained to realistic observation, especially one who had read Ruskin's *Modern Painters,* and of a poet schooled in the Romantics, particularly in Keats (Arnold's description of Keats's imagery on p. 746 might apply equally well to Morris's). But as these lines suggest, and as Morris goes on to state in his lecture, Pre-Raphaelite art was primarily centered not on the description of natural facts, but on "telling some kind of a story." Many of the pictures present dramatic incidents taken from the Bible, or from medieval, Shakespearean, or Romantic literature. Half of Morris's volume consists of narrative poems like "The Haystack in the Floods"; or dramatic studies of character in the manner of Browning without his moralistic strain ("The Defence of Guenevere"); or poems where the lyrical and the dramatic are fused into a striking and original form, as in "The Eve of Crécy" with its combination of speaking voice and musical refrain. In this poetry there is nothing dreamy or remote from life. Its violent action and intense emotion brought into Victorian poetry a vitality and range of feeling which had been quite lacking in Tennyson and Arnold, and was just beginning to appear, at a lower emotional level, in Browning. Only in the minor sense that these poems portray medieval and not modern life can they be called escapist.

But side by side with them stood other poems which warrant that epithet. These illustrate the third characteristic of Pre-Raphaelitism which Morris speaks of, its decorative and ornamental art. A poem like "The Blue Closet" is a piece of tapestry. The figures are almost lifeless, the story hardly exists, dramatic speech is gone. What we have is a vague, intangible mood made out of color and sound, perfectly achieved and perfectly empty of human significance. It is simply a charming piece of decoration which draws the mind completely away, not only from the troubled and ugly world of the nineteenth century, but from life itself; and as such it is the forerunner of the "pure" aesthetic verse of Swinburne and the early Yeats.

Morris's interest in decorative art was not limited to poetry. In 1861 he founded Morris and Company, where he and a group of craftsmen made stained-glass windows, tapestries, carpets, furniture (he invented the Morris chair), and wallpapers. The impulse here was by no means merely aesthetic. It was also, if indirectly, social. In both respects its main source was Ruskin's chapter on "The Nature of Gothic" in *The Stones of Venice,* where the mechanical work devoid of pleasure which men had to do in the modern factory was contrasted with the joyous creative activity of the workmen who built the Gothic cathedrals. From this observation Morris, as well as Ruskin, drew two conclusions: that so far as possible handcrafts should be revived, and that the modern system of high-pressure competitive capitalism, which was turning out thousands of things which no one really needed at the cost of turning thousands of men into machines, should be replaced by some form of socialism. Both conclusions are found in the essay on "The Art of the People" (1879). A few years later, after reading Karl Marx, Morris became a communist. But he failed to realize that while the triumph of communism would transfer control of the machines from the bourgeoisie to the proletariat, it would leave the machines as powerful and as deadly to the human spirit as ever. His mistake came from imagining that everyone shared his own longing for a simple life of creative activity, and consequently that once the people came to power they would abandon the machines, except those necessary to perform disagreeable work. The Revolution, he thought, would usher in a happy society in which creative pleasure would be available to everyone, either directly in handiwork or indirectly as an avocation to fill one's leisure; and art would again "be made by the people and for the people, as a happiness to the maker and the user."

If we may dismiss Morris's socialism as Utopian, we must recognize the truth—and for our time as well as his—of what he says about the state of the arts. Indeed, perhaps the best thing in "The Art of the People" is his acute analysis of a society divided between a public, on the one hand, which thinks "Art as at best trifling" and whose very leaders of thought know nothing and feel nothing about it except a vague sense of repulsion, and on the other hand, as a consequence, a small group of artists who despise the common herd and hold themselves aloof from the major concerns of modern life, to live in a palace of art and write a poetry of faraway times or purely verbal beauty. This, of course, applies to Morris himself and his own poetry in the 50's and 60's (in *Jason* and *The Earthly Paradise* as well as *The Defence of Guenevere*). In those years he had turned away from "politico-social subjects" because "on the whole I see that things are in a muddle, and I have no power or vocation to set them right," and therefore made his work "the embodiment of dreams in one form or another" (cf. "An Apology"). But now that socialism offered a solution, Morris renounced his renunciation and became, in his later prose work, a late Victorian prophet. From that new perspective he could criticize the divorce between public and artist which grew up in his time and has grown even sharper in our own. Indeed, if we change only one aspect of his analysis, and substitute an esoteric, obscure art for a delicate, aesthetic art, his description of the state of affairs is as valid today as it was in 1879. For "the general tendency of civilisation," which he found responsible for the situation, is still the same, still industrial and scientific, still concerned not with art but with making "machines for carrying on the competition in buying and selling, . . . and machines for the violent destruction of life."

The standard edition of Morris is the *Collected Works*, edited by May Morris (24 vols., 1910–15). The best Life, and also a book which illuminates the whole Pre-Raphaelite Movement, is by J. W. Mackail (2 vols., 1899). There is a good chapter on Morris in Graham Hough's *The Last Romantics* (1949).

William Morris

AN APOLOGY[1]

Of Heaven or Hell I have no power to sing,
I cannot ease the burden of your fears,
Or make quick-coming death a little thing,
Or bring again the pleasure of past years,
Nor for my words shall ye forget your tears,   5
Or hope again for aught that I can say,
The idle singer of an empty day.

But rather, when aweary of your mirth,
From full hearts still unsatisfied ye sigh,
And, feeling kindly unto all the earth,   10
Grudge every minute as it passes by,
Made the more mindful that the sweet days die—

Remember me a little then I pray,
The idle singer of an empty day.

The heavy trouble, the bewildering care   15
That weighs us down who live and earn our bread,
These idle verses have no power to bear;
So let me sing of names rememberèd,
Because they, living not, can ne'er be dead,
Or long time take their memory quite away   20
From us poor singers of an empty day.

---

[1] The prefatory poem to *The Earthly Paradise* (1868–70), a collection of stories from Greek and Norse mythology. The four poems that follow it below are from *The Defence of Guenevere and Other Poems* (1858).

Dreamer of dreams, born out of my due time,
Why should I strive to set the crooked straight?
Let it suffice me that my murmuring rhyme
Beats with light wing against the ivory gate,[2]   25
Telling a tale not too importunate
To those who in the sleepy region stay,
Lulled by the singer of an empty day.

Folk say, a wizard to a northern king
At Christmas-tide such wondrous things did show,   30
That through one window men beheld the spring,
And through another saw the summer glow,
And through a third the fruited vines a-row,
While still, unheard, but in its wonted way,
Piped the drear wind of that December day.   35

So with this Earthly Paradise it is,
If ye will read aright, and pardon me,
Who strive to build a shadowy isle of bliss
Midmost the beating of the steely sea,
Where tossed about all hearts of men must be;   40
Whose ravening monsters mighty men shall slay,
Not the poor singer of an empty day.

THE HAYSTACK IN THE FLOODS[3]

Had she come all the way for this,
To part at last without a kiss?
Yea, had she borne the dirt and rain
That her own eyes might see him slain
Beside the haystack in the floods?   5

Along the dripping leafless woods,
The stirrup touching either shoe,
She rode astride as troopers do;
With kirtle kilted[4] to her knee,
To which the mud splashed wretchedly;   10
And the wet dripped from every tree
Upon her head and heavy hair,
And on her eyelids broad and fair;
The tears and rain ran down her face.
By fits and starts they rode apace,   15
And very often was his place
Far off from her; he had to ride

Ahead, to see what might betide
When the roads crossed; and sometimes, when
There rose a murmuring from his men,   20
Had to turn back with promises;
Ah me! she had but little ease;
And often for pure doubt and dread
She sobbed, made giddy in the head
By the swift riding; while, for cold,   25
Her slender fingers scarce could hold
The wet reins; yea, and scarcely, too,
She felt the foot within her shoe
Against the stirrup: all for this,
To part at last without a kiss   30
Beside the haystack in the floods.

For when they neared that old soaked hay,
They saw across the only way
That Judas, Godmar, and the three
Red running lions dismally   35
Grinned from his pennon,[5] under which
In one straight line along the ditch,
They counted thirty heads.
                         So then,
While Robert turned round to his men,
She saw at once the wretched end,   40
And, stooping down, tried hard to rend
Her coif the wrong way from her head,
And hid her eyes;[6] while Robert said:
"Nay, love, 'tis scarcely two to one;
At Poictiers where we made them run   45
So fast—why, sweet my love, good cheer,
The Gascon frontier is so near,
Nought after us."
                  But, "O!" she said,
"My God! my God! I have to tread
The long way back without you; then   50
The court at Paris; those six men;[7]
The gratings of the Chatelet;[8]
The swift Seine on some rainy day
Like this, and people standing by,
And laughing, while my weak hands try   55
To recollect how strong men swim.[9]
All this, or else a life with him,[10]
For which I should be damned at last;
Would God that this next hour were past!"

---

[2] According to Greek legend, the ivory gate was the gate through which false dreams issued. Morris's "rhyme" does not pretend to express truth, but only to create a dream world of shadowy bliss (cf. line 38).

[3] Sir Robert de Marny, an English knight, and his mistress, Jehane, are riding hard for Gascony, which was in British hands. The date is 1356, shortly after the English victory over the French at Poitiers.   [4] Tucked up.

[5] Godmar's banner bearing his family crest.

[6] She tried to turn her cap about so that the longer part (ordinarily at the back) would cover her eyes and prevent her from seeing Robert slain.   [7] The judges.

[8] The bars of the Châtelet prison in Paris.

[9] In the trial by water, she would be judged innocent of being a witch if she sank and drowned; if she swam, guilty, and then burned (cf. line 108).   [10] Godmar.

He answered not, but cried his cry,   60
"St. George[11] for Marny!" cheerily;
And laid his hand upon her rein.
Alas! no man of all his train
Gave back that cheery cry again;
And, while for rage his thumb beat fast   65
Upon his sword-hilt, some one cast
About his neck a kerchief long,
And bound him.
     Then they went along
To Godmar; who said: "Now, Jehane,
Your lover's life is on the wane   70
So fast, that, if this very hour
You yield not as my paramour,
He will not see the rain leave off—
Nay, keep your tongue from gibe and scoff,
Sir Robert, or I slay you now."   75

She laid her hand upon her brow,
Then gazed upon the palm, as though
She thought her forehead bled, and—"No!"
She said, and turned her head away,
As there were nothing else to say,   80
And everything were settled: red
Grew Godmar's face from chin to head:
"Jehane, on yonder hill there stands
My castle, guarding well my lands:
What hinders me from taking you,   85
And doing that I list to do
To your fair wilful body, while
Your knight lies dead?"
     A wicked smile
Wrinkled her face, her lips grew thin,
A long way out she thrust her chin: 90
"You know that I should strangle you
While you were sleeping; or bite through
Your throat, by God's help—ah!" she said,
"Lord Jesus, pity your poor maid!
For in such wise they hem me in,   95
I cannot choose but sin and sin,
Whatever happens: yet I think
They could not make me eat or drink,
And so should I just reach my rest."
"Nay, if you do not my behest,   100
O Jehane! though I love you well,"
Said Godmar, "would I fail to tell
All that I know?" "Foul lies," she said.
"Eh? lies, my Jehane? by God's head,
At Paris folks would deem them true!   105
Do you know, Jehane, they cry for you:

'Jehane the brown! Jehane the brown!
Give us Jehane to burn or drown!'—
Eh—gag me Robert!—sweet my friend,
This were indeed a piteous end   110
For those long fingers, and long feet,
And long neck, and smooth shoulders sweet;
An end that few men would forget
That saw it—So, an hour yet:
Consider, Jehane, which to take   115
Of life or death!"
     So, scarce awake,
Dismounting, did she leave that place,
And totter some yards: with her face
Turned upward to the sky she lay,
Her head on a wet heap of hay,   120
And fell asleep: and while she slept,
And did not dream, the minutes crept
Round to the twelve again; but she,
Being waked at last, sighed quietly,
And strangely childlike came, and said: 125
"I will not." Straightway Godmar's head,
As though it hung on strong wires, turned
Most sharply round, and his face burned.

For Robert—both his eyes were dry,
He could not weep, but gloomily   130
He seemed to watch the rain; yea, too,
His lips were firm; he tried once more
To touch her lips; she reached out, sore
And vain desire so tortured them,
The poor gray lips, and now the hem   135
Of his sleeve brushed them.
     With a start
Up Godmar rose, thrust them apart;
From Robert's throat he loosed the bands
Of silk and mail; with empty hands
Held out, she stood and gazed, and saw   140
The long bright blade without a flaw
Glide out from Godmar's sheath, his hand
In Robert's hair; she saw him bend
Back Robert's head; she saw him send
The thin steel down; the blow told well,   145
Right backward the knight Robert fell,
And moaned as dogs do, being half dead,
Unwitting, as I deem: so then
Godmar turned grinning to his men,
Who ran, some five or six, and beat   150
His head to pieces at their feet.

Then Godmar turned again and said:
"So, Jehane, the first fitte[12] is read!

11 Patron saint of England.

12 Part of a song or tale.

Take note, my lady, that your way
Lies backward to the Chatelet!"   155
She shook her head and gazed awhile
At her cold hands with a rueful smile,
As though this thing had made her mad.

This was the parting that they had
Beside the haystack in the floods.   160

THE DEFENCE OF GUENEVERE[1]

But, knowing now that they would have her speak,
She threw her wet hair backward from her brow,
Her hand close to her mouth touching her cheek,

As though she had had there a shameful blow,
And feeling it shameful to feel aught but shame   5
All through her heart, yet felt her cheek burned so,

She must a little touch it; like one lame
She walked away from Gauwaine, with her head
Still lifted up; and on her cheek of flame

The tears dried quick; she stopped at last and said: 10
"O knights and lords, it seems but little skill[2]
To talk of well-known things past now and dead.

"God wot[3] I ought to say, I have done ill,
And pray you all forgiveness heartily!
Because you must be right, such great lords—still   15

"Listen, suppose your time were come to die,
And you were quite alone and very weak;
Yea, laid a dying while very mightily

"The wind was ruffling up the narrow streak
Of river through your broad lands running well: 20
Suppose a hush should come, then some one speak:

" 'One of these cloths is heaven, and one is hell,
Now choose one cloth for ever; which they be,
I will not tell you, you must somehow tell

" 'Of your own strength and mightiness; here, see!'   25
Yea, yea, my lord,[4] and you to ope your eyes,
At foot of your familiar bed to see

"A great God's angel standing, with such dyes,
Not known on earth, on his great wings, and hands
Held out two ways, light from the inner skies   30

"Showing him well, and making his commands
Seem to be God's commands, moreover, too,
Holding within his hands the cloths on wands;

"And one of these strange choosing cloths was blue,
Wavy and long, and one cut short and red;   35
No man could tell the better of the two.

"After a shivering half-hour you said,
'God help! heaven's color, the blue'; and he said, 'hell.'[5]
Perhaps you then would roll upon your bed,

"And cry to all good men that loved you well,   40
'Ah Christ! if only I had known, known, known';
Launcelot went away, then I could tell,[6]

"Like wisest man how all things would be, moan,
And roll and hurt myself, and long to die,
And yet fear much to die for what was sown.   45

"Nevertheless you, O Sir Gauwaine, lie,
Whatever may have happened through these years,
God knows I speak truth, saying that you lie."[7]

Her voice was low at first, being full of tears,
But as it cleared, it grew full loud and shrill,   50
Growing a windy shriek in all men's ears,

---

[1] Guenevere is speaking in self-defense at her trial for adultery.
She and Launcelot had been trapped by Agravaine and Modred,
who had persuaded King Arthur on a hunting expedition to
send back word to his Queen that he could not return that
night. Thereupon, as the conspirators hoped, she had arranged
a rendezvous with Launcelot and they had been caught together
in her room. (Lines 242–281 give her account of the incident.)
One of the conspirators and her chief accuser at the trial is
Gauwaine, brother of Agravaine, who has just finished his
speech as the poem opens. To support his accusation of adultery,
he has cited not only the occasion just mentioned but a former
occasion at the castle of Mellyagraunce when some of Guenevere's knights who had been wounded were placed in her
chambers, and next morning blood was found on her bed—
which had provoked a previous charge of adultery, by Mellyagraunce (rightly enough, in fact, but it was not the blood of a
wounded knight, as Mellyagraunce thought, but that of Launcelot, who had cut his arm crawling through the barred window
of Guenevere's bedroom). At that time she had been saved by
Launcelot from being burnt at the stake, the punishment for
adultery (and therefore what she is now threatened with again).
He had defended her honor in trial by battle with Mellyagraunce
(see lines 167–221).   2 Use.   3 Knows.

[4] Gauwaine.
[5] Guenevere implies that her original choice of Launcelot instead
of Arthur as the object of her admiration and friendship was
just about as accidental (things being so evenly divided) and
certainly as innocent of evil intentions as the choice of a blue
cloth over a red cloth; and yet, through no fault of hers, it
turned out to be the wrong (because evil) choice.
[6] Because she then knew, for the first time, that she loved him
passionately and not merely as a friend, and had therefore, in
fact, though unwittingly, chosen "hell" when she found him
more attractive than Arthur.
[7] Whatever my relations with Launcelot have been, they have
not been adulterous.

A ringing in their startled brains, until
She said that Gauwaine lied, then her voice sunk,
And her great eyes began again to fill,

Though still she stood right up, and never shrunk,   55
But spoke on bravely, glorious lady fair!
Whatever tears her full lips may have drunk,

She stood, and seemed to think, and wrung her hair,
Spoke out at last with no more trace of shame,
With passionate twisting of her body there: 60

"It chanced upon a day that Launcelot came
To dwell at Arthur's court: at Christmastime
This happened; when the heralds sung his name,

" 'Son of King Ban of Benwick,' seemed to chime
Along with all the bells that rang that day,   65
O'er the white roofs, with little change of rhyme.

"Christmas and whitened winter passed away,
And over me the April sunshine came,
Made very awful with black hail-clouds, yea

"And in the Summer I grew white with flame,   70
And bowed my head down—Autumn, and the sick
Sure knowledge things would never be the same,

"However often Spring might be most thick
Of blossoms and buds, smote on me, and I grew
Careless of most things, let the clock tick, tick,   75

"To my unhappy pulse, that beat right through
My eager body: while I laughed out loud,
And let my lips curl up at false or true,

"Seemed cold and shallow without any cloud.
Behold my judges, then the cloths were brought: 80
While I was dizzied thus, old thoughts would crowd,

"Belonging to the time ere I was bought
By Arthur's great name and his little love;
Must I give up for ever then, I thought,

"That which I deemed would ever round me move   85
Glorifying all things; for a little word,
Scarce ever meant at all, must I now prove

"Stone-cold for ever?[8] Pray you, does the Lord
Will that all folks should be quite happy and good?
I love God now a little; if this cord   90

"Were broken,[9] once for all what striving could
Make me love anything in earth or heaven?
So day by day it grew, as if one should

"Slip slowly down some path worn smooth and
    even,
Down to a cool sea on a summer day;   95
Yet still in slipping was there some small leaven

"Of stretched hands catching small stones by the
    way,
Until one surely reached the sea at last,
And felt strange new joy as the worn head lay

"Back, with the hair like sea-weed; yea all past   100
Sweat of the forehead, dryness of the lips,
Washed utterly out by the dear waves o'ercast,

"In the lone sea, far off from any ships!
Do I not know now of a day in Spring?
No minute of that wild day ever slips   105

"From out my memory; I hear thrushes sing,
And wheresoever I may be, straightway
Thoughts of it all come up with most fresh sting;

"I was half mad with beauty on that day,
And went without my ladies all alone,   110
In a quiet garden walled round every way;

"I was right joyful of that wall of stone,
That shut the flowers and trees up with the sky,
And trebled all the beauty: to the bone,

"Yea right through to my heart, grown very shy   115
With weary thoughts, it pierced, and made me glad;
Exceedingly glad, and I knew verily,

"A little thing just then had made me mad;
I dared not think, as I was wont to do,
Sometimes, upon my beauty; if I had   120

"Held out my long hand up against the blue,
And, looking on the tenderly darkened fingers,
Thought that by rights one ought to see quite
    through,

"There, see you, where the soft still light yet
    lingers,
Round by the edges; what should I have done,   125
If this had joined with yellow spotted singers,

<hr />

[8] Must I give up love for ever just because I once said, but scarcely meant it, that I would "love, honor, and obey"?

[9] If this tie with Launcelot were severed, I could never love anything again, not even God.

"And startling green drawn upward by the sun?[10]
But shouting, loosed out, see now! all my hair,
And trancedly stood watching the west wind run

"With faintest half-heard breathing sound—why
  there   130
I lose my head e'en now in doing this;
But shortly listen—In that garden fair

"Came Launcelot walking; this is true, the kiss
Wherewith we kissed in meeting that spring day,
I scarce dare talk of the remembered bliss, 135

"When both our mouths went wandering in one way,
And aching sorely, met among the leaves;
Our hands being left behind strained far away.

"Never within a yard of my bright sleeves
Had Launcelot come before—and now, so nigh! 140
After that day why is it Guenevere grieves?

"Nevertheless you, O Sir Gauwaine, lie,
Whatever happened on through all those years,
God knows I speak truth, saying that you lie.

"Being such a lady could I weep these tears 145
If this were true? A great queen such as I
Having sinned this way, straight her conscience sears;

"And afterwards she liveth hatefully,
Slaying and poisoning, certes never weeps,—
Gauwaine, be friends now, speak me lovingly. 150

"Do I not see how God's dear pity creeps
All through your frame, and trembles in your mouth?[11]
Remember in what grave your mother sleeps,

"Buried in some place far down in the south,
Men are forgetting as I speak to you; 155
By her head severed in that awful drouth

"Of pity that drew Agravaine's fell blow,
I pray your pity![12] let me not scream out
For ever after, when the shrill winds blow

"Through half your castle-locks! let me not shout 160
For ever after in the winter night
When you ride out alone! in battle-rout

"Let not my rusting tears make your sword light![13]
Ah! God of mercy, how he turns away!
So, ever must I dress[14] me to the fight; 165

"So—let God's justice work! Gauwaine, I say,
See me hew down your proofs: yea, all men know
Even as you said how Mellyagraunce one day,

"One bitter day in la Fausse Garde,[15] for so
All good knights held it after, saw—   170
Yea, sirs, by cursed unknightly outrage;[16] though

"You, Gauwaine, held his word without a flaw,
This Mellyagraunce saw blood upon my bed—
Whose blood then pray you? is there any law

"To make a queen say why some spots of red 175
Lie on her coverlet? or will you say,
'Your hands are white, lady, as when you wed,

" 'Where did you bleed?' and must I stammer out,
 'Nay,
I blush indeed, fair lord, only to rend
My sleeve up to my shoulder, where there lay 180

" 'A knife-point last night': so must I defend
The honor of the lady Guenevere?
Not so, fair lords, even if the world should end

"This very day, and you were judges here
Instead of God. Did you see Mellyagraunce 185
When Launcelot stood by him? what white fear

"Curdled his blood, and how his teeth did dance,
His side sink in? as my knight cried and said,
'Slayer of unarmed men, here is a chance!

" 'Setter of traps,[17] I pray you guard your head, 190
By God I am so glad to fight with you,
Stripper of ladies, that my hand feels lead

---

[10] If the sight of the blue sky seen through or behind her uplifted
hand were joined with the further beauty of singing thrushes
(cf. line 106) and spring-green leaves.

[11] I.e., God's pity should creep, etc., for the reason which follows.

[12] In the name of another woman, your own mother and King
Arthur's sister, who was accused of infidelity and violently slain
by your brother Agravaine in an "awful drouth [lack] of pity,"
I beg of you to act otherwise—to pity me and spare my life.

[13] Be careful lest my tears of injured innocence rust your sword
and make it light (weak)—that is, lest your guilty conscience
paralyze your ability to fight. [14] Address.

[15] Literally, the False Prison, which is the name Guenevere gives
Mellyagraunce's castle because he had attacked her knights
when they were unarmed and had carried Guenevere off to his
castle as a prisoner.

[16] Coming to her bedside before she was up.

[17] After Launcelot had undertaken to defend Guenevere's honor in
trial by battle, Mellyagraunce had sprung a trap in the floor
and pitched him into a dungeon, from which he had escaped
just in time to rescue Guenevere.

" 'For driving weight; hurrah now! draw and do,
For all my wounds are moving in my breast,
And I am getting mad with waiting so.'   195

"He struck his hands together o'er the beast,
Who fell down flat and grovelled at his feet,
And groaned at being slain so young. 'At least,'

"My knight said, 'Rise you, sir, who are so fleet
At catching ladies, half-armed will I fight,   200
My left side all uncovered!' then I weet,[18]

"Up sprang Sir Mellyagraunce with great delight
Upon his knave's face; not until just then
Did I quite hate him, as I saw my knight

"Along the lists look to my stake and pen[19]   205
With such a joyous smile, it made me sigh
From agony beneath my waist-chain, when

"The fight began, and to me they drew nigh;
Ever Sir Launcelot kept him on the right,
And traversed warily, and ever high   210

"And fast leapt caitiff's sword, until my knight
Sudden threw up his sword to his left hand,
Caught it, and swung it; that was all the fight,

"Except a spout of blood on the hot land;
For it was hottest summer; and I know   215
I wondered how the fire,[20] while I should stand,

"And burn, against the heat, would quiver so,
Yards above my head; thus these matters went;
Which things were only warnings of the woe

"That fell on me. Yet Mellyagraunce was shent,[21]   220
For Mellyagraunce had fought against the Lord;
Therefore, my lords, take heed lest you be blent

"With all this wickedness;[22] say no rash word
Against me, being so beautiful; my eyes,
Wept all away to grey, may bring some sword   225

"To drown you in your blood; see my breast rise,
Like waves of purple sea, as here I stand;
And how my arms are moved in wonderful wise,

"Yea also at my full heart's strong command,
See through my long throat how the words go up   230
In ripples to my mouth; how in my hand

"The shadow lies like wine within a cup
Of marvellously colored gold; yea now
This little wind is rising, look you up,

"And wonder how the light is falling so   235
Within my moving tresses: will you dare,
When you have looked a little on my brow,

"To say this thing is vile? or will you care
For any plausible lies of cunning woof,
When you can see my face with no lie there   240

"For ever? am I not a gracious proof—
'But in your chamber Launcelot was found'—
Is there a good knight then would stand aloof,

"When a queen says with gentle queenly sound:
'O true as steel, come now and talk with me,   245
I love to see your step upon the ground

" 'Unwavering, also well I love to see
That gracious smile light up your face, and hear
Your wonderful words, that all mean verily

" 'The thing they seem to mean: good friend, so
          dear   250
To me in everything, come here to-night,
Or else the hours will pass most dull and drear;

" 'If you come not, I fear this time I might
Get thinking over much of times gone by,
When I was young, and green hope was in sight;   255

" 'For no man cares now to know why I sigh;
And no man comes to sing me pleasant songs,
Nor any brings me the sweet flowers that lie

" 'So thick in the gardens; therefore one so longs
To see you, Launcelot; that we may be   260
Like children once again, free from all wrongs

" 'Just for one night.' Did he not come to me?
What thing could keep true Launcelot away
If I said 'Come'? There was one less than three

"In my quiet room that night, and we were gay;   265
Till sudden I rose up, weak, pale, and sick,
Because a bawling broke our dream up, yea

---

[18] Know.   [19] Enclosure for a prisoner.
[20] She had been sentenced to be burned for adultery.
[21] Disgraced and destroyed.
[22] *Blent with* may mean either blended with (i.e., involved in) or
          blinded by.

"I looked at Launcelot's face and could not speak,
For he looked helpless too, for a little while;
Then I remembered how I tried to shriek,   270

"And could not, but fell down; from tile to tile
The stones they threw up rattled o'er my head
And made me dizzier; till within a while

"My maids were all about me, and my head
On Launcelot's breast was being soothed away   275
From its white chattering, until Launcelot said—

"By God! I will not tell you more to-day,
Judge any way you will—what matters it?
You know quite well the story of that fray,

"How Launcelot stilled their bawling, the mad fit   280
That caught up Gauwaine[23]—all, all, verily,
But just that which would save me; these things flit.

"Nevertheless you, O Sir Gauwaine, lie,
Whatever may have happened these long years,
God knows I speak truth, saying that you lie!   285

"All I have said is truth, by Christ's dear tears."
She would not speak another word, but stood
Turned sideways; listening, like a man who hears

His brother's trumpet sounding through the wood
Of his foes' lances. She leaned eagerly,   290
And gave a slight spring sometimes, as she could

At last hear something really; joyfully
Her cheek grew crimson, as the headlong speed
Of the roan charger drew all men to see,   294
The knight who came was Launcelot at good need.[24]

THE EVE OF CRÉCY[1]

Gold on her head, and gold on her feet,
And gold where the hems of her kirtle meet,
And a golden girdle round my sweet;—
　　Ah! qu'elle est belle La Marguerite.[2]

---

[23] The fit of mad suspicion which has made him accuse her.
[24] Just in the nick of time, to save her again from death at the stake.

[1] The poem is spoken by Sir Lambert du Bois, a French knight in impoverished circumstances, who is dreaming of the glory and the wealth which he imagines he will gain in the next day's battle of Crécy (1346), and which will enable him to marry Margaret. The pathos and the irony of the poem lie in the fact that the French were to be defeated in the battle.
[2] How beautiful is Margaret.

Margaret's maids are fair to see,   5
Freshly dressed and pleasantly;
Margaret's hair falls down to her knee;—
　　Ah! qu'elle est belle La Marguerite.

If I were rich I would kiss her feet,
I would kiss the place where the gold hems meet,   10
And the golden girdle round my sweet—
　　Ah! qu'elle est belle La Marguerite.

Ah me! I have never touched her hand;
When the arriere-ban[3] goes through the land,
Six basnets under my pennon stand;[4]—   15
　　Ah! qu'elle est belle La Marguerite.

And many an one grins under his hood:
"Sir Lambert du Bois, with all his men good,
Has neither food nor firewood."—
　　Ah! qu'elle est belle La Marguerite.   20

If I were rich I would kiss her feet,
And the golden girdle of my sweet,
And thereabouts where the gold hems meet;
　　Ah! qu'elle est belle La Marguerite.

Yet even now it is good to think,   25
While my few poor varlets grumble and drink
In my desolate hall, where the fires sink,—
　　Ah! qu'elle est belle La Marguerite.

Of Margaret sitting glorious there,
In glory of gold and glory of hair,
And glory of glorious face most fair;—   30
　　Ah! qu'elle est belle La Marguerite.

Likewise to-night I make good cheer,
Because this battle draweth near:
For what have I to lose or fear?—   35
　　Ah! qu'elle est belle La Marguerite.

For, look you, my horse is good to prance
A right fair measure in this war-dance,
Before the eyes of Philip of France;[5]—
　　Ah! qu'elle est belle La Marguerite.   40

And sometime it may hap, perdie,
While my new towers stand up three and three,
And my hall gets painted fair to see—
　　Ah! qu'elle est belle La Marguerite—

---

[3] Proclamation calling men to arms.
[4] Only six helmeted men stand under my banner.
[5] The King of France, Philip VI.

That folks may say: "Times change, by the rood,   45
For Lambert, banneret[6] of the wood,[7]
Has heaps of food and firewood;—
    Ah! qu'elle est belle La Marguerite.

"And wonderful eyes, too, under the hood
Of a damsel of right noble blood":   50
St. Ives, for Lambert of the wood!—
    Ah! qu'elle est belle La Marguerite.

THE BLUE CLOSET[1]

THE DAMOZELS

Lady Alice, Lady Louise,
Between the wash of the tumbling seas
We are ready to sing, if so ye please;
So lay your long hands on the keys;
    Sing, "*Laudate pueri.*"[2]   5

And ever the great bell overhead
Boomed in the wind a knell for the dead,
Though no one tolled it, a knell for the dead.

LADY LOUISE

Sister, let the measure swell
Not too loud; for you sing not well   10
If you drown the faint boom of the bell;
    He is weary, so am I.

And ever the chevron[3] overhead
Flapped on the banner of the dead.
(Was he asleep, or was he dead?)   15

LADY ALICE

Alice the Queen, and Louise the Queen,
Two damozels wearing purple and green,
Four lone ladies dwelling here
From day to day and year to year;

And there is none to let us go;   20
To break the locks of the doors below,
Or shovel away the heaped-up snow;
And when we die no man will know
That we are dead: but they give us leave,
Once every year on Christmas-eve,   25
To sing in the Closet Blue one song;
And we should be so long, so long,
If we dared, in singing; for dream on dream,
They float on in a happy stream;
Float from the gold strings, float from the keys,   30
Float from the opened lips of Louise;
But, alas! the sea-salt oozes through
The chinks of the tiles of the Closet Blue.

And ever the great bell overhead
Booms in the wind a knell for the dead,   35
The wind plays on it a knell for the dead.

    They sing all together

How long ago was it, how long ago,
He came to this tower with hands full of snow?

"Kneel down, O love Louise, kneel down!" he said,
And sprinkled the dusty snow over my head.   40

He watched the snow melting, it ran through my hair,
Ran over my shoulders, white shoulders and bare.

"I cannot weep for thee, poor love Louise,
For my tears are all hidden deep under the seas;

"In a gold and blue casket she keeps all my tears,   45
But my eyes are no longer blue, as in old years;

"Yea, they grow gray with time, grow small and dry;
I am so feeble now, would I might die."

And in truth the great bell overhead
Left off his pealing for the dead,   50
Perchance because the wind was dead.

Will he come back again, or is he dead?
O! is he sleeping, my scarf round his head?

Or did they strangle him as he lay there,
With the long scarlet scarf I used to wear?   55

Only I pray thee, Lord, let him come here!
Both his soul and his body to me are most dear.

Dear Lord, that loves me, I wait to receive
Either body or spirit this wild Christmas-eve.

---

[6] A knight who could lead vassals to battle under his own heraldic banner.

[7] This phrase is a translation of his name: cf. line 18.

[1] Lady Louise is in love with Arthur, who rode off wearing her scarf and was never heard of again. He returns, apparently, at the end of the poem as a ghost, and leads Lady Louise, her sister, Lady Alice, and their two damozels across the bridge to the land of death. But the situation is very vague and of no importance.

[2] "Let the children praise [the Lord]"—the opening words of a medieval hymn.

[3] Device of honor on Arthur's banner, which he has left in the Blue Closet.

Through the floor shot up a lily red, 60
With a patch of earth from the land of the dead,
For he was strong in the land of the dead.

What matter that his cheeks were pale,
  His kind kissed lips all gray?
"O love Louise, have you waited long?" 65
  "O my lord Arthur, yea."

What if his hair that brushed her cheek
  Was stiff with frozen rime?
His eyes were grown quite blue again,
  As in the happy time. 70

"O love Louise, this is the key
  Of the happy golden land!
O sisters, cross the bridge with me,
  My eyes are full of sand.
What matter that I cannot see, 75
  If ye take me by the hand?"

And ever the great bell overhead
And the tumbling seas mourned for the dead;
For their song ceased, and they were dead.

from ADDRESS ON THE COLLECTION OF PAINTINGS OF THE ENGLISH PRE-RAPHAELITE SCHOOL IN THE CITY OF BIRMINGHAM MUSEUM AND ART GALLERY ON FRIDAY, OCTOBER 24, 1891[1]

MR. KENRICK has said that I am going to address you on the subject of Art, but it is clear that that subject is a very wide one and that I must limit myself very considerably. Not only so, even if I were to speak about all the pictures exhibited here, the subject would be again such a very wide one, that there would be no end of it. So I must limit myself still further. Therefore I propose to speak to you almost entirely, according to the light I have, of that school of painters once called the pre-Raphaelites, and who perhaps should still be called pre-Raphaelites. There is all the more reason for my doing so because, as a matter of fact, their doctrines have been successful; they have impressed themselves upon the present generation, at any rate of the English people, and, I think to a certain extent, have influenced also the artists of France. In fact, they have exercised a very great influence on the works of art that are now current. I mean, even apart from the magnificent works that have been produced by the leaders of that School, the School itself has made its mark upon the age.

Let us consider what these pre-Raphaelites were. They were certainly a very small body of men. The three original leaders, the chief members of the pre-Raphaelite Brotherhood, as you probably know, were Dante Gabriel Rossetti, Everett Millais, and Holman Hunt; but there were others who belonged to the School, though they were not actually enrolled in the Brotherhood. The most noteworthy of these painters, in the early days of the School, were Ford Madox Brown and Arthur Hughes. Later on your fellow-townsman, Burne-Jones, became a friend and fellow-worker of the above named men. There were several others, but those named were not only the greatest, but also the most characteristic.

However, these few young men, wholly unknown till they *forced* the public to recognize them, began what must be called a really audacious attempt; a definite revolt against the Academical Art which brooded over all the Schools of civilized Europe at the time.[2] In point of fact I think, in considering the revolt of the pre-Raphaelites, one must look upon it as a portion of the general revolt against Academicism in Literature as well as in Art. In Literature the revolt had taken place much earlier. There were many reasons for that; but the principal one seems to me to be that the Art of Painting, being so much more technical than Literature, depends much more upon tradition than Literature does, and that tradition, however much it may have lost its original position, however poor a tradition may be, and however deficient in positive, in creative power, nevertheless retains the negative and conservative power, and keeps people from changing the general tendency of the Art; whereas the sister Art of Literature depends less on traditions, and is more individual than that of Painting, though less than many think, and consequently the necessity for a revolt is sooner felt, and the effect of it is more easily and plainly to be seen.

[1] Reprinted from *William Morris; Artist, Writer, Socialist,* edited by May Morris (Oxford, 1936), by permission of Basil Blackwell, the publisher.

[2] See the General Introduction, pp. 387–88.

Before I go further I may as well give something like an approximate date. If I am wrong I see at least one friend in this room who can correct me. It seems to me that somewhere about the year 1848 will cover the date for the first general appearance of the pre-Raphaelites before the public.

Well, let us consider, first of all, what their first and underlying doctrine was. What was the special and particular standpoint they took up? Because in all revolts there is one special and particular principle which, so to speak, swallows up all others, which is so engrossing that those who are carrying on the revolt can scarcely see any other side to what they are doing than that which embodies this particular doctrine. Well, I think that the special and particular doctrine of the pre-Raphaelites is not very far to seek. It is, in one word, Naturalism.

That is to say the pre-Raphaelites started by saying, "You have Nature before you, what you have to do is to copy Nature and you will produce something which at all events is worth people's attention." Now that at first sight seems a self-evident proposition. But you must not forget what I said just now as to that worn-out tradition which was dominating the whole of the artistic schools of Europe at the time. I remember distinctly myself, as a boy, that when I had pictures offered to my notice I could not understand what they were about at all. I said, "Oh, well, that is all right. It has got the sort of thing in it which there ought to be in a picture. There is nothing to be said against it, no doubt. I cannot say I would have it other than that, because it is clearly the proper thing to do." But really I took very little interest in it, and I should think that would be the case with nine hundred and ninety-nine out of every thousand of those people who had not received definite technical instruction in the art, who were not formally artists. I should have said, but just now my friend Mr. Wallis rather corrected me on that point, that even up to the present day the greater part of what I should call the laymen in these matters of the Arts do not feel any very great exultation when they see an Old Master. If they are suddenly introduced to an Old Master I venture to think they are more or less disappointed with the impression that it makes upon them.

Well, what the pre-Raphaelites really practically said was this, "We are going to break with this poor and worn-out tradition which has tyrannized over us so long. We are going in point of fact to present you with something that is natural." And I must say that they certainly did do so. They did paint fully intending to be, and fully succeeding in being naturalistic,

and I should have thought most people would have thought that the public would have received this attempt with acclamation, with joy, that they would have said: "Here at last is something we can understand. Here are visible sheep; here are such and such things as we have seen them, as we see them every day, exceedingly like the things in question. There may be short-comings here and there, very probably, but after all we understand what it means. This is addressed to us, the public, and not merely to artists prejudiced in favour of certain traditions."

But strange to say, the public did exactly the reverse of receiving these paintings with acclamation. What they really said was "These things are monsters. They are not like nature." They did not mean that; they meant to say "They are not like pictures." They certainly were not, as pictures then were, but they assuredly were like nature; you could not possibly get out of that. However as I tell you, the public received these attempts as revolutionary attempts of young men always are received, with jeers, because they also were under the influence of the academical tradition.

But there was one man, at all events, who although he had been brought up in a very different school from that of the pre-Raphaelites, in what I should call the old-fashioned Drawing Master School (I do not mean to use the word with any sort of contempt but merely as an explanatory word)—who although he was brought up in that school, and although his master was Mr. J. D. Harding—a name you know very well—really looked at these pre-Raphaelite paintings with open eyes. That man I need scarcely tell you was John Ruskin. He immediately came forward as the champion of those young men before the public. And no doubt they needed such a champion very badly.

However, they made way and they finally won, in the first place great personal reputation, thoroughly well deserved, and they also achieved success as a School; as far as their root doctrine, Naturalism, is concerned they destroyed the old feeble Academical tradition.

But now one has got to say a little more about what one means by the word Naturalism. I can conceive, I fancy most of you can conceive, a certain kind of Naturalism which would not be very interesting. There is a good deal of talk about such Naturalism as that nowadays. It means but very little more than bare statements of fact by means of the Art of painting, and it seems to me that pictures painted with that end in view, unless—as not very seldom happens by the bye—in spite of the theory they have other things to help them, will be scarcely works of Art. They will be rather something on the border-line between works of Art and scientific statements. Now the pre-Raphaelite pictures were not in the least like that, because besides the mere presentment of natural facts, they aimed at another kind of thing which was far more important. The painters aimed, some of them no doubt much more than others, at the conscientious presentment of incident. In other words they certainly had entirely come to the conclusion that not only was it necessary that they should paint well, but that this painting, this good painting, the excellent execution, the keen eyesight, the care, the skill, and so on, should be the instrument for telling some kind of story to the beholder. That you see completes the Naturalism. Granted that you have something to say, and that you say it well by means of the Art of Painting, you are then, and then only, a Naturalistic Painter.

No doubt in the early days of pre-Raphaelitism, in talk at all events, it was rather the fashion to decry the use of any sort of convention in dealing with the works of painting which were produced in the reaction against the aforesaid tyranny of a weak, poor and unworthy convention. But as a matter of fact every work of Art whether it is imitative or whether it is suggestive, must be founded on some convention or other. It seems to me that the real point of the thing—and that I think the pre-Raphaelites understood instinctively—is that that convention shall not be so to say, a conventional convention. It must be a convention that you have found out for yourself in some way or another, whether that has been deduced from history, or whether you yourself have been able to hit upon it by the light of nature. In any case, this you must understand, that it is absolutely impossible to give a really literal transcript of nature. You must have some convention. You know in the old story about Parrhasios and Zeuxis, Parrhasios says, "Zeuxis deceived the birds but I deceived Zeuxis."[3] This story, though instructive in some respects, makes a mistake. Zeuxis would never have deceived the birds: Zeuxis himself was very much easier to deceive than the birds, because Zeuxis was a man, and had an imagination, which was all his life telling him some kind of a story, which story was connected with the actual sights that passed before his eyes. Well the Naturalism of the pre-Raphaelites which did not stop

at the simple presentment of scientific fact but went further and conscientiously considered the due and proper incidents that were necessary in order to make a work of Art, was founded on a genuinely *natural* convention.

I have so far spoken of two sides of the qualities that go to make a great work of plastic Art: presentation of nature and the telling of a story. There is also however a third side necessary in a work of Art: and that third side was both less considered by the public, and was much more difficult to put before it: that side was the ornamental function of the Art. No picture it seems to me is complete unless it is something more than a representation of nature and the teller of a tale. It ought also to have a definite, harmonious, conscious beauty. It ought to be ornamental. It ought to be possible for it to be part of a beautiful whole in a room or church or hall. Now of the original pre-Raphaelites, Rossetti was the man who mostly felt that side of the Art of painting: all his pictures have a decorative quality as an essential, and not as a mere accident of them, and not unnaturally, because of all his fellows he had most sense of the historical connection of the Arts. His mind was formed on that looking into history which is such a marked feature of the general revolt against Academicism: and whoever looks into history will find living Art there always decorative.

But this decorative side of the school needed another man to complete its development, and did not fail to get him—your townsman, Burne-Jones—of whom, indeed, I feel some difficulty in speaking as the truth demands, because he is such a close friend of mine. But I must say that he added the element of *perfect* ornamentation, the completely decorative side of the Art. In fact, when the pre-Raphaelite School was completed by this representative man, it then became apparent that what pre-Raphaelitism was, was sufficiently indicated by its name. That is to say, it was the continuation of the art that had been current throughout Europe before Raphael marked the completion of the period when art became academical, i.e., inorganic; the so-called renaissance.

It has become clear that the "new" school which was received at one time with such volleys of scorn and has since made its way so vigorously, was really nothing more or less than a branch of the great Gothic Art which once pervaded all Europe. I will repeat that the characteristics of that Gothic Art were in the main three. The first was Love of Nature—not, mind you, of the mere dead surface of it—but Love of Nature as the only instrument for telling a tale of some sort or another. Love of nature is the first element

---

[3] Greek painters who strove to outdo each other in creating an illusion of actual reality. Zeuxis boasted that birds tried to eat the grapes in one of his pictures.

in the Gothic Art; next is the epical quality, and joined to those two things is what people very often think perhaps is the only quality it has got, and that is its ornamental quality. These qualities you may say it shares with the ancient organic Schools of Art, the Greek above all, (though it seems to me that it outgoes them in its epical and ornamental developments,) but at least one quality distinguishes it from them, the romantic quality, as I must call it for lack of a better word; and this quality is eminently characteristic of both Rossetti and Burne-Jones, but especially of the latter. It is an element of the epical quality (as notably in Homer), though it is not the whole of it; and is necessary to the utmost refinement, abundance and enduring interest of decoration; though I admit that it is rather to be felt than defined.

And I must say, that you will find throughout the whole of the history of the Arts, that when artists are thinking in the main of conscientiously telling a story their works are really much more beautiful, much more fitted for the ornamenting of public buildings than when they are only thinking of producing works of *mere* ornament. How this comes about it would take long to say, but so it is. Perhaps it may seem at first something like a paradox to you. I am afraid however I must add another paradox to it, and say, that when people talk most about Works of Art, generally speaking at that period they do least in art. Well we must take that home to ourselves for after all we are in that position. We must acknowledge that in these times of the world we have got a great deal of backway to make up. We are forced to talk about Art, clearly not because it is in a satisfactory condition, but because it is in a very unsatisfactory condition: or else why should we have to say anything about it?

A word or two of summing up the characteristics of the individual members of the pre-Raphaelite School. I should say that as a representative of its pure naturalism, not thinking so much about taletelling as about the presentment of natural form, Millais was the leader, and that the three, Dante Gabriel Rossetti, Holman Hunt and Ford Madox Brown were all of them equally concerned with the conscientious presentation of incident. You will find in looking at their pictures that they always want to knock in the nail hard on this point: that there is always something going on, there is something being done in the picture. They say, "Here is an event"; and at their best they are successful in doing what every genuine artist tries to do—in really convincing the beholder that the events they represent could have happened in no other way than the way in which they represent them. That is the end and aim of what, for want of a better word, I will call dramatic Art: perhaps epical Art would be a better word. And Rossetti and Burne-Jones are those members of the school whose conscientious presentation of events deals with romantic subjects in a romantic way, and *consequently* includes decoration as an essential.

Now I must just say one word about the fact that both Rossetti and Burne-Jones have had very little to do with representing the scenes of ordinary modern life as they go on before your eyes. One has often heard that brought against the "Romantic" artists, as a shortcoming. Now, quite plainly, I must say that I think it *is* a shortcoming. But is the shortcoming due to the individual artist, or is it due to the public at large? for my part I think the latter. When an artist has really a very keen sense of beauty, I venture to think that he can not literally represent an event that takes place in modern life. He must add something or another to qualify or soften the ugliness and sordidness of the surroundings of life in our generation. That is not only the case with pictures, if you please: it is the case also in literature. Two examples occur to my mind at this moment. Let us take the novels of such a man as Hardy, or the others who write more or less in the same way. They are supposed to represent scenes of modern life in their novels. But do they? I say they do not; because they take care to surround those modern scenes with an atmosphere of out-of-the-way country life, which we ourselves never by any chance see. If you go down into the country you won't see Mr. Hardy's heroes and heroines walking about, I assure you. You will see a very different kind of thing from that when you meet the ordinary British farmer or the ordinary British agricultural labourer walking about, and more especially—excuse me—more especially when you see their wives and daughters walking about. I am very sorry, but so it is. Well, I say the difficulty is even greater, perhaps, for the painter. In painting, you cannot get so far away from the facts as you can in literature. Nevertheless I think those of you who have seen Walker's pictures (and if you have seen them you must have admired them, for they are exceedingly beautiful and exceedingly skilful) will have perceived that his countrymen: his haymakers, his carters and all the rest of them: are really not modern English carters and haymakers: they are carters and haymakers that have stepped down from the frieze of the Parthenon.[4] The agricultural Briton

---

[4] That is, they have the idealized character of Phidias's statues, which adorned the Greek temple of the Parthenon at Athens.

is not built like that, or is built like that very rarely. Sometimes you may get people of that kind amongst waifs and strays: amongst, perhaps, the gipsies, but never amongst the ordinary working people of the country. Well, of course Art is free to everybody, and by all means, if anyone is really moved by the spirit to treat modern subjects, let him do so, and do it in the best way he can; but, on the other hand, I don't think he has a right, under the circumstances and considering the evasions he is absolutely bound to make, to lay any blame on his brother artist who turns back again to the life of past times; or who, shall we rather say, since his imagination must have some garb or another, naturally takes the raiment of some period in which the surroundings of life were not ugly but beautiful.

Well, I have tried as well as I could to give you some idea of the general principles of the pre-Raphaelite School. I say that those principles, so far as they inculcated pure naturalism, have more or less succeeded: I mean in producing a continuous School. So far as they inculcated the conscientious representation of incident—their special side—they have not succeeded so well, because, after all, for the production of works of that kind you want either artists of startling and stupendous genius, of whom very few can be born in one epoch, or else a great homo-geneous school of tradition, which is able to use up all the various qualities of the lesser men and combine them in a harmonious whole. On the other hand, the ornamental aim of the School has made less impression still upon the age. That cannot be wondered at, because, after all, the ornamental side of the Art is but a part of architecture, and architecture cannot flourish unless it is the spontaneous expression of the pleasure and the will of the whole people. In these days let us admit it at once: and that is one reason why these galleries hung with pictures, each one complete in itself, are interesting to us: whatever you can get out of Art can not be got out of the combined efforts of the people at large, but must be simply the work and the expression of individual genius, individual capacity, working towards a certain end. And I recur to what I was talking about just now, and say that I think one reason why there is much to be said for that Art which deals with the life of the past, or rather with the artist's imagination of it, is because only so can the artist have at his back in the form of history anything like that traditional combined idea of Art which once was common to the whole people. That, I think, is perhaps, after all, the real inner reason why it is so very difficult to represent the life which is round about us at the present day. . . .

from THE ART OF THE PEOPLE

DELIVERED BEFORE THE BIRMINGHAM SOCIETY OF ARTS AND SCHOOL OF DESIGN, FEBRUARY 19, 1879

"And the men of labour spent their strength in daily struggling for bread to maintain the vital strength they labour with: so living in a daily circulation of sorrow, living but to work, and working but to live, as if daily bread were the only end of a wearisome life, and a wearisome life the only occasion of daily bread."—DANIEL DEFOE

. . . TO ME, and I hope to you, Art is a very serious thing, and cannot by any means be dissociated from the weighty matters that occupy the thoughts of men; and there are principles underlying the practice of it, on which all serious-minded men may—nay, must—have their own thoughts. It is on some of these that I ask your leave to speak, and to address myself, not only to those who are consciously interested in the arts, but to all those also who have considered what the progress of civilization promises and threatens to those who shall come after us: what there is to hope and fear for the future of the arts, which were born with the birth of civilization and will only die with its death—what on this side of things, the present time of strife and doubt and change is preparing for the better time, when the change shall have come, the strife be lulled, and the doubt cleared: this is a question, I say, which is indeed weighty, and may well interest all thinking men. . . .

The aim of your Society and School of Arts is, as I understand it, to further those arts by education widely spread. A very great object is that, and well worthy of the reputation of this great city; but since Birmingham has also, I rejoice to know, a great reputation for not allowing things to go about shamming life when the brains are knocked out of them, I think you should know and see clearly what it is you have undertaken to further by these institutions, and whether you really care about it, or only languidly acquiesce in it—whether, in short, you know it to the heart, and are indeed part and parcel of it, with your own will, or against it; or else have heard say that it is a good thing if anyone care to meddle with it.

If you are surprised at my putting that question for your consideration, I will tell you why I do so. There are some of us who love Art most, and I may say most faithfully, who see for certain that such love is rare nowadays. We cannot help seeing, that besides a vast number of people, who (poor souls!) are sordid and brutal of mind and habits, and have had no chance or choice in the matter, there are many high-minded, thoughtful, and cultivated men who inwardly think the arts to be a foolish accident of civilization—nay, worse perhaps, a nuisance, a disease, a hindrance to human progress. Some of these, doubtless, are very busy about other sides of thought. They are, as I should put it, so *artistically* engrossed by the study of science, politics, or what not, that they have necessarily narrowed their minds by their hard and praiseworthy labours. But since such men are few, this does not account for a prevalent habit of thought that looks upon Art as at best trifling.

What is wrong, then, with us or the arts, since what was once accounted so glorious, is now deemed paltry?

The question is no light one; for, to put the matter in its clearest light, I will say that the leaders of modern thought do for the most part sincerely and single-mindedly hate and despise the arts; and you know well that as the leaders are, so must the people be; and that means that we who are met together here for the furthering of Art by wide-spread education are either deceiving ourselves and wasting our time, since we shall one day be of the same opinion as the best men among us, or else we represent a small minority that is right, as minorities sometimes are, while those upright men aforesaid, and the great mass of civilized men, have been blinded by untoward circumstances.

That we are of this mind—the minority that is right—is, I hope, the case. I hope we know assuredly that the arts we have met together to further are necessary to the life of man, if the progress of civilization is not to be as causeless as the turning of a wheel that makes nothing.

How, then, shall we, the minority, carry out the duty which our position thrusts upon us, of striving to grow into a majority?

If we could only explain to those thoughtful men, and the millions of whom they are the flower, what the thing is that we love, which is to us as the bread we eat, and the air we breathe, but about which they know nothing and feel nothing, save a vague instinct of repulsion, then the seed of victory might be sown.

This is hard indeed to do; yet if we ponder upon a chapter of ancient or mediaeval history, it seems to me some glimmer of a chance of doing so breaks in upon us. Take for example a century of the Byzantine Empire, weary yourselves with reading the names of the pedants, tyrants, and tax-gatherers to whom the terrible chain which long-dead Rome once forged, still gave the power of cheating people into thinking that they were necessary lords of the world. Turn then to the lands they governed, and read and forget a long string of the causeless murders of Northern and Saracen pirates and robbers. That is pretty much the sum of what so-called history has left us of the tale of those days—the stupid languor and the evil deeds of kings and scoundrels. Must we turn away then, and say that all was evil? How then did men live from day to day? How then did Europe grow into intelligence and freedom? It seems there were others than those of whom history (so called) has left us the names and the deeds. These, the raw material for the treasury and the slave-market, we now call "the people," and we know that they were working all that while. Yes, and that their work was not merely slaves' work, the meal-trough before them and the whip behind them; for though history (so called) has forgotten them, yet their work has not been forgotten, but has made another history—the history of Art. There is not an ancient city in the East or the West that does not bear some token of their grief, and joy, and hope. From Ispahan[1] to Northumberland, there is no building built between the seventh and seventeenth centuries that does not show the influence of the labour of that oppressed and neglected herd of men. No one of them, indeed, rose high above his fellows. There was no Plato, or Shakespeare, or Michael Angelo amongst them. Yet scattered as it was among many men, how strong their thought was, how long it abided, how far it travelled!

And so it was ever through all those days when Art was so vigorous and progressive. Who can say how little we should know of many periods, but for their art? History (so called) has remembered the kings and warriors, because they destroyed; Art has remembered the people, because they created.

I think, then, that this knowledge we have of the life of past times gives us some token of the way we should take in meeting those honest and single-hearted men who above all things desire the world's progress, but whose minds are, as it were, sick on this point of the arts. Surely you may say to them:

---

[1] A city in Iran, once the capital of Persia.

When all is gained that you (and we) so long for, what shall we do then? That great change which we are working for, each in his own way, will come like other changes, as a thief in the night, and will be with us before we know it; but let us imagine that its consummation has come suddenly and dramatically, acknowledged and hailed by all right-minded people; and what shall we do then, lest we begin once more to heap up fresh corruption for the woeful labour of ages once again? I say, as we turn away from the flagstaff where the new banner has been just run up; as we depart, our ears yet ringing with the blare of the heralds' trumpets that have proclaimed the new order of things, what shall we turn to then, what *must* we turn to then?

To what else, save to our work, our daily labour?

With what, then, shall we adorn it when we have become wholly free and reasonable? It is necessary toil, but shall it be toil only? Shall all we can do with it be to shorten the hours of that toil to the utmost, that the hours of leisure may be long beyond what men used to hope for? and what then shall we do with the leisure, if we say that all toil is irksome? Shall we sleep it all away?—Yes, and never wake up again, I should hope, in that case.

What shall we do then? what shall our necessary hours of labour bring forth?

That will be a question for all men in that day when many wrongs are righted, and when there will be no classes of degradation on whom the dirty work of the world can be shovelled; and if men's minds are still sick and loathe the arts, they will not be able to answer that question.

Once men sat under grinding tyrannies, amidst violence and fear so great, that nowadays we wonder how they lived through twenty-four hours of it, till we remember that then, as now, their daily labour was the main part of their lives, and that that daily labour was sweetened by the daily creation of Art; and shall we who are delivered from the evils they bore, live drearier days than they did? Shall men, who have come forth from so many tyrannies, bind themselves to yet another one, and become the slaves of nature, piling day upon day of hopeless, useless toil? Must this go on worsening till it comes to this at last—that the world shall have come into its inheritance, and with all foes conquered and nought to bind it, shall choose to sit down and labour for ever amidst grim ugliness? How, then, were all our hopes cheated, what a gulf of despair should we tumble into then!

In truth, it cannot be; yet if that sickness of repulsion to the arts were to go on hopelessly, nought else would be, and the extinction of the love of beauty and imagination would prove to be the extinction of civilization. But that sickness the world will one day throw off, yet will, I believe, pass through many pains in so doing, some of which will look very like the death-throes of Art, and some, perhaps, will be grievous enough to the poor people of the world; since hard necessity, I doubt, works many of the world's changes, rather than the purblind striving to see, which we call the foresight of man.

Meanwhile, remember that I asked just now, what was amiss in Art or in ourselves that this sickness was upon us. Nothing is wrong or can be with Art in the abstract—that must always be good for mankind, or we are all wrong together: but with Art as we of these latter days have known it, there is much wrong; nay, what are we here for to-night if that is not so? were not the schools of art founded all over the country some thirty years ago because we had found out that popular art was fading—or perhaps had faded out from amongst us?

As to the progress made since then in this country —and in this country only, if at all—it is hard for me to speak without being either ungracious or insincere, and yet speak I must. I say, then, that an apparent external progress in some ways is obvious, but I do not know how far that is hopeful, for time must try it, and prove whether it be a passing fashion or the first token of a real stir among the great mass of civilized men. To speak quite frankly, and as one friend to another, I must needs say that even as I say those words they seem too good to be true. And yet —who knows?—so wont are we to frame history for the future as well as for the past, so often are our eyes blind both when we look backward and when we look forward, because we have been gazing so intently at our own days, our own lines. May all be better than I think it!

At any rate let us count our gains, and set them against less hopeful signs of the times. In England, then—and as far as I know, in England only—painters of pictures have grown, I believe, more numerous, and certainly more conscientious in their work, and in some cases—and this more especially in England— have developed and expressed a sense of beauty which the world has not seen for the last three hundred years. This is certainly a very great gain, which is not easy to over-estimate, both for those who make the pictures and those who use them.

Furthermore, in England, and in England only, there has been a great improvement in architecture and the arts that attend it—arts which it was the special province of the afore-mentioned schools to revive and foster. This, also, is a considerable gain to the users of the works so made, but I fear a gain less important to most of those concerned in making them.

Against these gains we must, I am very sorry to say, set the fact not easy to be accounted for, that the rest of the civilized world (so called) seems to have done little more than stand still in these matters; and that among ourselves these improvements have concerned comparatively few people, the mass of our population not being in the least touched by them; so that the great bulk of our architecture—the art which most depends on the taste of the people at large—grows worse and worse every day.

I must speak also of another piece of discouragement before I go further. I daresay many of you will remember how emphatically those who first had to do with the movement of which the foundation of our art-schools was a part, called the attention of our pattern-designers to the beautiful works of the East. This was surely most well judged of them, for they bade us look at an art at once beautiful, orderly, living in our own day, and above all, popular. Now, it is a grievous result of the sickness of civilization that this art is fast disappearing before the advance of western conquest and commerce—fast, and every day faster. While we are met here in Birmingham to further the spread of education in art, Englishmen in India are, in their short-sightedness, actively destroying the very sources of that education—jewellery, metal-work, pottery, calico-printing, brocade-weaving, carpet-making—all the famous and historical arts of the great peninsula have been for long treated as matters of no importance, to be thrust aside for the advantage of any paltry scrap of so-called commerce; and matters are now speedily coming to an end there. . . .

I have just shown you for one thing that lovers of Indian and Eastern Art, including as they do the heads of our institutions for art education, and I am sure many among what are called the governing classes, are utterly powerless to stay its downward course. The general tendency of civilization is against them, and is too strong for them.

Again, though many of us love architecture dearly, and believe that it helps the healthiness both of the body and soul to live among beautiful things, we of the big towns are mostly compelled to live in houses which have become a by-word of contempt for their ugliness and inconvenience. The stream of civilization is against us, and we cannot battle against it.

Once more, those devoted men who have upheld the standard of truth and beauty amongst us, and whose pictures, painted amidst difficulties that none but a painter can know, show great qualities of mind unsurpassed in any age—these great men have but a narrow circle that can understand their works, and are utterly unknown to the great mass of the people: civilization is so much against them, that they cannot move the people.

Therefore, looking at all this, I cannot think that all is well with the root of the tree we are cultivating. Indeed, I believe that if other things were but to stand still in the world, this improvement before mentioned would lead to a kind of art which, in that impossible case, would be in a way stable, would perhaps stand still also. This would be an art cultivated professedly by a few, and for a few, who would consider it necessary—a duty, if they could admit duties—to despise the common herd, to hold themselves aloof from all that the world has been struggling for from the first, to guard carefully every approach to their palace of art. It would be a pity to waste many words on the prospect of such a school of art as this, which does in a way, theoretically at least, exist at present, and has for its watchword a piece of slang that does not mean the harmless thing it seems to mean—art for art's sake. Its fore-doomed end must be, that art at last will seem too delicate a thing for even the hands of the initiated to touch; and the initiated must at last sit still and do nothing— to the grief of no one.

Well, certainly, if I thought you were come here to further such an art as this I could not have stood up and called you *friends*; though such a feeble folk as I have told you of one could scarce care to call foes.

Yet, as I say, such men exist, and I have troubled you with speaking of them, because I know that those honest and intelligent people, who are eager for human progress, and yet lack part of the human senses and are anti-artistic, suppose that such men are artists, and that this is what art means, and what it does for people, and that such a narrow, cowardly life is what we, fellow-handicraftsmen, aim at. I see this taken for granted continually, even by many who, to say truth, ought to know better, and I long to put the slur from off us; to make people understand that we, least of all men, wish to widen the gulf between the classes, nay, worse still, to make new classes of elevation, and new classes of degradation—new lords and new slaves; that we, least of all men, want to cultivate the "plant called man" in different ways—here stingily, there wastefully: I wish people to understand that the art we are striving for is a good thing which all can share, which will elevate all; in good sooth, if all people do not soon share it there will soon be none to share; if all are not elevated by it, mankind will lose the elevation it has gained. Nor is such an art as we long for a vain dream; such an art once was in times that were worse than these, when there was less courage, kindness, and truth in the world than there is now; such an art there will be hereafter, when there will be more courage, kindness, and truth than there is now in the world.

Let us look backward in history once more for a short while, and then steadily forward till my words are done: I began by saying that part of the common and necessary advice given to Art students was to study antiquity; and no doubt many of you, like me, have done so; have wandered, for instance, through the galleries of the admirable museum of South Kensington, and, like me, have been filled with wonder and gratitude at the beauty which has been born from the brain of man. Now, consider, I pray you, what these wonderful works are, and how they were made; and indeed, it is neither in extravagance nor without due meaning that I use the word "wonderful" in speaking of them. Well, these things are just the common household goods of those past days, and that is one reason why they are so few and so carefully treasured. They were common things in their own day, used without fear of breaking or spoiling—no rarities then—and yet we have called them "wonderful."

And how were they made? Did a great artist draw the designs for them—a man of cultivation, highly paid, daintily fed, carefully housed, wrapped up in cotton wool, in short, when he was not at work? By no means. Wonderful as these works are, they were made by "common fellows," as the phrase goes, in the common course of their daily labour. Such were the men we honour in honouring those works. And their labour—do you think it was irksome to them? Those of you who are artists know very well that it was not; that it could not be. Many a grin of pleasure I'll be bound—and you will not contradict me—went to the carrying through of those mazes of mysterious beauty, to the invention of those strange beasts and birds and flowers that we ourselves have chuckled over at South Kensington. While they were at work, at least, these men were not unhappy, and I suppose they worked most days, and the most part of the day, as we do.

Or those treasures of architecture that we study so carefully nowadays—what are they? how were they made? There are great minsters among them, indeed, and palaces of kings and lords, but not many; and, noble and awe-inspiring as these may be, they differ only in size from the little grey church that still so often makes the common-place English landscape beautiful, and the little grey house that still, in some parts of the country at least, makes an English village a thing apart, to be seen and pondered on by all who love romance and beauty. These form the mass of our architectural treasures, the houses that everyday people lived in, the unregarded churches in which they worshipped.

And, once more, who was it that designed and ornamented them? The great architect, carefully kept for the purpose, and guarded from the common troubles of common men? By no means. Sometimes, perhaps, it was the monk, the ploughman's brother; oftenest his other brother, the village carpenter, smith, mason, what not—"a common fellow," whose common everyday labour fashioned works that are to-day the wonder and despair of many a hard-working "cultivated" architect. And did he loathe his work? No, it is impossible. I have seen, as we most of us have, work done by such men in some out-of-the-way hamlet—where to-day even few strangers ever come, and whose people seldom go five miles from their own doors; in such places, I say, I have seen work so delicate, so careful, and so inventive, that nothing in its way could go further. And I will assert, without fear of contradiction, that no human ingenuity can produce work such as this without pleasure being a third party to the brain that conceived and the hand that fashioned it. Nor are such works rare. The throne of the great Plantagenet, or the great Valois, was no more daintily carved than the seat of the village mass-john,[2] or the chest of the yeoman's good-wife.

So, you see, there was much going on to make life endurable in those times. Not every day, you may be sure, was a day of slaughter and tumult, though the histories read almost as if it were so; but every day the hammer chinked on the anvil, and the chisel played about the oak beam, and never without some beauty and invention being born of it, and consequently some human happiness.

That last word brings me to the very kernel and heart of what I have come here to say to you, and I pray you to think of it most seriously—not as to my words, but as to a thought which is stirring in the world, and will one day grow into something.

That thing which I understand by real art is the expression by man of his pleasure in labour. I do not believe he can be happy in his labour without ex-

---

[2] Priest, from Mas or Mass (Master) John, a name once applied contemptuously to a Scotch Presbyterian minister.

pressing that happiness; and especially is this so when he is at work at anything in which he specially excels. A most kind gift is this of nature, since all men, nay, it seems all things too, must labour; so that not only does the dog take pleasure in hunting, and the horse in running, and the bird in flying, but so natural does the idea seem to us, that we imagine to ourselves that the earth and the very elements rejoice in doing their appointed work; and the poets have told us of the spring meadows smiling, of the exultation of the fire, of the countless laughter of the sea.

Nor until these latter days has man ever rejected this universal gift, but always, when he has not been too much perplexed, too much bound by disease or beaten down by trouble, has striven to make his work at least happy. Pain he has too often found in his pleasure, and weariness in his rest, to trust to these. What matter if his happiness lie with what must be always with him—his work?

And, once more, shall we, who have gained so much, forgo this gain, the earliest, most natural gain of mankind? If we have to a great extent done so, as I verily fear we have, what strange foglights must have misled us; or rather let me say, how hard pressed we must have been in the battle with the evils we have overcome, to have forgotten the greatest of all evils. I cannot call it less than that. If a man has work to do which he despises, which does not satisfy his natural and rightful desire for pleasure, the greater part of his life must pass unhappily and without self-respect. Consider, I beg of you, what that means, and what ruin must come of it in the end.

If I could only persuade you of this, that the chief duty of the civilized world to-day is to set about making labour happy for all, to do its utmost to minimize the amount of unhappy labour—nay, if I could only persuade some two or three of you here present—I should have made a good night's work of it.

Do not, at any rate, shelter yourselves from any misgiving you may have behind the fallacy that the art-lacking labour of to-day is happy work: for the most of men it is not so. It would take long, perhaps, to show you, and make you fully understand that the would-be art which it produces is joyless. But there is another token of its being most unhappy work, which you cannot fail to understand at once—a grievous thing that token is—and I beg of you to believe that I feel the full shame of it, as I stand here speaking of it; but if we do not admit that we are sick, how can we be healed? This hapless token is, that the work done by the civilized world is mostly dishonest work. Look now: I admit that civilization does make certain things well, things which it knows, consciously or unconsciously, are necessary to its present unhealthy condition. These things, to speak shortly, are chiefly machines for carrying on the competition in buying and selling called falsely commerce; and machines for the violent destruction of life—that is to say, materials for two kinds of war; of which kinds the last is no doubt the worst, not so much in itself perhaps, but because on this point the conscience of the world is beginning to be somewhat pricked. But, on the other hand, matters for the carrying on of a dignified daily life, that life of mutual trust, forbearance, and help, which is the only real life of thinking men—these things the civilized world makes ill, and even increasingly worse and worse.

If I am wrong in saying this, you know well I am only saying what is widely thought, nay widely said too, for that matter. Let me give an instance, familiar enough, of that wide-spread opinion. There is a very clever book of pictures now being sold at the railway bookstalls, called *The British Working Man, by one who does not believe in him*—a title and a book which make me both angry and ashamed, because the two express much injustice, and not a little truth in their quaint, and necessarily exaggerated way. It is quite true, and very sad to say, that if any one nowadays wants a piece of ordinary work done by gardener, carpenter, mason, dyer, weaver, smith, what you will, he will be a lucky rarity if he get it well done. He will, on the contrary, meet on every side with evasion of plain duties, and disregard of other men's rights; yet I cannot see how the "British Working Man" is to be made to bear the whole burden of this blame, or indeed the chief part of it. I doubt if it be possible for a whole mass of men to do work to which they are driven, and in which there is no hope and no pleasure, without trying to shirk it—at any rate, shirked it has always been under such circumstances. On the other hand, I know that there are some men so right-minded, that they will, in despite of irksomeness and hopelessness, drive right through their work. Such men are the salt of the earth. But must there not be something wrong with a state of society which drives these into that bitter heroism, and the most part into shirking, into the depths often of half-conscious self-contempt and degradation? Be sure that there is, that the blindness and hurry of civilization as it now is, have to answer a heavy charge as to that enormous amount of pleasureless work—work that tries every muscle of the body and every atom of the brain, and which is done without pleasure and without aim—work which everybody who has to do with tries to shuffle off in the speediest way that dread of starvation or ruin will allow him.

I am as sure of one thing as that I am living and breathing, and it is this: that the dishonesty in the daily arts of life, complaints of which are in all men's mouths, and which I can answer for it does exist, is the natural and inevitable result of the world in the hurry of the war of the counting-house, and the war of the battlefield, having forgotten—of all men, I say, each for the other, having forgotten that pleasure in our daily labour which nature cries out for as its due.

Therefore, I say again, it is necessary to the further progress of civilization that men should turn their thoughts to some means of limiting, and in the end of doing away with, degrading labour.

I do not think my words hitherto spoken have given you any occasion to think that I mean by this either hard or rough labour; I do not pity men much for their hardships, especially if they be accidental; not necessarily attached to one class or one condition, I mean. Nor do I think (I were crazy or dreaming else) that the work of the world can be carried on without rough labour; but I have seen enough of that to know that it need not be by any means degrading. To plough the earth, to cast the net, to fold the flock —these, and such as these, which are rough occupations enough, and which carry with them many hardships, are good enough for the best of us, certain conditions of leisure, freedom, and due wages being granted. As to the bricklayer, the mason, and the like —these would be artists, and doing not only necessary, but beautiful, and therefore happy work, if art were anything like what it should be. No, it is not such labour as this which we need to do away with, but the toil which makes the thousand and one things which nobody wants, which are used merely as the counters for the competitive buying and selling, falsely called commerce, which I have spoken of before—I know in my heart, and not merely by my reason, that this toil cries out to be done away with. But, besides that, the labour which now makes things good and necessary in themselves, merely as counters for the commercial war aforesaid, needs regulating and reforming. Nor can this reform be brought about save by art; and if we were only come to our right minds, and could see the necessity for making labour sweet to all men, as it is now to very few—the necessity, I repeat; lest discontent, unrest, and despair should at last swallow up all society—If we, then, with our eyes cleared, could but make some sacrifice of things which do us no good, since we unjustly and uneasily possess them, then indeed I believe we should sow the seeds of a happiness which the world has not yet known, of a rest and content which would make it what I cannot help thinking it was meant to be: and with that seed would be sown also the seed of real art, the expression of man's happiness in his labour—an art made by the people, and for the people, as a happiness to the maker and the user.

That is the only real art there is, the only art which will be an instrument to the progress of the world, and not a hindrance. Nor can I seriously doubt that in your hearts you know that it is so, all of you, at any rate, who have in you an instinct for art. I believe that you agree with me in this, though you may differ from much else that I have said. I think assuredly that this is the art whose welfare we have met together to further, and the necessary instruction in which we have undertaken to spread as widely as may be.

Thus I have told you something of what I think is to be hoped and feared for the future of Art; and if you ask me what I expect as a practical outcome of the admission of these opinions, I must say at once that I know, even if we were all of one mind, and that what I think the right mind on this subject, we should still have much work and many hindrances before us; we should still have need of all the prudence, foresight, and industry of the best among us; and, even so, our path would sometimes seem blind enough. And, to-day, when the opinions which we think right, and which one day will be generally thought so, have to struggle sorely to make themselves noticed at all, it is early days for us to try to see our exact and clearly mapped road. I suppose you will think it too commonplace of me to say that the general education that makes men think, will one day make them think rightly upon art. Commonplace as it is, I really believe it, and am indeed encouraged by it, when I remember how obviously this age is one of transition from the old to the new, and what a strange confusion, from out of which we shall one day come, our ignorance and half-ignorance is like to make of the exhausted rubbish of the old and the crude rubbish of the new, both of which lie so ready to our hands.

But, if I must say, furthermore, any words that seem like words of practical advice, I think my task is hard, and I fear I shall offend some of you whatever I say; for this is indeed an affair of morality, rather than of what people call art.

However, I cannot forget that, in my mind, it is not possible to dissociate art from morality, politics, and religion. Truth in these great matters of principle is of one, and it is only in formal treatises that it can be split up diversely. I must also ask you to remember how I have already said, that though my mouth alone speaks, it speaks, however feebly and disjointedly, the thoughts of many men better than myself. And further, though when things are tending to the best, we shall still, as aforesaid, need our best men to lead us quite right; yet even now surely, when it is far from that, the least of us can do some yeoman's service to the cause, and live and die not without honour.

So I will say that I believe there are two virtues much needed in modern life, if it is ever to become sweet; and I am quite sure that they are absolutely necessary in the sowing the seed of an *art which is to be made by the people and for the people, as a happiness to the maker and the user*. These virtues are honesty, and simplicity of life. To make my meaning clearer I will name the opposing vice of the second of these —luxury to wit. Also I mean by honesty, the careful and eager giving his due to every man, the determination not to gain by any man's loss, which in my experience is not a common virtue.

But note how the practice of either of these virtues will make the other easier to us. For if our wants are few, we shall have but little chance of being driven by our wants into injustice; and if we are fixed in the principle of giving every man his due, how can our self-respect bear that we should give too much to ourselves?

And in art, and in that preparation for it without which no art that is stable or worthy can be, the raising, namely, of those classes which have heretofore been degraded, the practice of these virtues would make a new world of it. For if you are rich, your simplicity of life will both go towards smoothing over the dreadful contrast between waste and want, which is the great horror of civilized countries, and will also give an example and standard of dignified life to those classes which you desire to raise, who, as it is indeed, being like enough to rich people, are given both to envy and to imitate the idleness and waste that the possession of much money produces.

Nay, and apart from the morality of the matter, which I am forced to speak to you of, let me tell you that though simplicity in art may be costly as well as uncostly, at least it is not wasteful, and nothing is more destructive to art than the want of it. I have never been in any rich man's house which would not have looked the better for having a bonfire made outside of it of nine-tenths of all that it held. Indeed, our sacrifice on the side of luxury will, it seems to me, be little or nothing: for, as far as I can make out, what people usually mean by it, is either a gathering of possessions which are sheer vexations to the owner,

or a chain of pompous circumstance, which checks and annoys the rich man at every step. Yes, luxury cannot exist without slavery of some kind or other, and its abolition will be blessed, like the abolition of other slaveries, by the freeing both of the slaves and of their masters.

Lastly, if, besides attaining to simplicity of life, we attain also to the love of justice, then will all things be ready for the new springtime of the arts. For those of us that are employers of labour, how can we bear to give any man less money than he can decently live on, less leisure than his education and self-respect demand? or those of us who are workmen, how can we bear to fail in the contract we have undertaken, or to make it necessary for a foreman to go up and down spying out our mean tricks and evasions? or we the shopkeepers—can we endure to lie about our wares, that we may shuffle off our losses on to someone else's shoulders? or we the public—how can we bear to pay a price for a piece of goods which will help to trouble one man, to ruin another, and starve a third? Or, still more, I think, how can we bear to use, how can we enjoy something which has been a pain and a grief for the maker to make?

And now, I think, I have said what I came to say. I confess that there is nothing new in it, but you know the experience of the world is that a thing must be said over and over again before any great number of men can be got to listen to it. Let my words to-night, therefore, pass for one of the necessary times that the thought in them must be spoken out.

For the rest I believe that, however seriously these words may be gainsaid, I have been speaking to an audience in whom any words spoken from a sense of duty and in hearty good-will, as mine have been, will quicken thought and sow some good seed. At any rate, it is good for a man who thinks seriously to face his fellows, and speak out whatever really burns in him, so that men may seem less strange to one another, and misunderstanding, the fruitful cause of aimless strife, may be avoided.

But if to any of you I have seemed to speak hopelessly, my words have been lacking in art; and you must remember that hopelessness would have locked my mouth, not opened it. I am, indeed, hopeful, but can I give a date to the accomplishment of my hope, and say that it will happen in my life or yours?

But I will say at least, Courage! for things wonderful, unhoped-for, glorious, have happened even in this short while I have been alive.

Yes, surely these times are wonderful and fruitful of change, which, as it wears and gathers new life even in its wearing, will one day bring better things for the toiling days of men, who, with freer hearts and clearer eyes, will once more gain the sense of outward beauty, and rejoice in it.

Meanwhile, if these hours be dark, as, indeed, in many ways they are, at least do not let us sit deedless, like fools and fine gentlemen, thinking the common toil not good enough for us, and beaten by the muddle; but rather let us work like good fellows trying by some dim candle-light to set our workshop ready against to-morrow's daylight—that to-morrow, when the civilized world, no longer greedy, strifeful, and destructive, shall have a new art, a glorious art, made by the people and for the people, as a happiness to the maker and the user.

Algernon Charles Swinburne

1837–1909

SWINBURNE, who was of aristocratic stock, was slight and delicate in build, but was so fired with nervous energy that he was in a constant ferment of physical activity and intellectual excitement. Too restive to accept the usual restraints of university life, he left Oxford without a degree to take up a Bohemian existence in London. In the succeeding twenty years he wrote and published feverishly both poetry and criticism, until by 1879 his erratic and uncontrolled way of living had so burnt up his limited physique that he was on the verge of collapse, and was led to retire into seclusion and almost complete inactivity for the remaining thirty years of his life.

From 1859 to 1879, however, staid but troubled Victorian England had no more outspoken rebel than Swinburne, and his right-minded contemporaries regarded him with a mixture of horror and fear. They remembered Shelley's revolt some two generations before. Only, to make matters worse, this new outbreak was the more extravagant on the one hand because of the somewhat flamboyant temperament of Swinburne, and the more insidious on the other because the lyrical cadences of his verse were so charming that almost in spite of oneself one was attracted to poetry filled with noxious and revolutionary themes. The radical character of his mind was unnoticed at first in his brilliant reproduction of the form of Greek tragedy in *Atalanta in Calydon* (1865), but with the publication of *Poems and Ballads* (1866) it became clear that here was a threat to all that the Victorians were struggling to uphold. The representative "Hymn to Proserpine" not only extolled that goddess but likewise condemned the sway of the pale Galilean as gray, lifeless, sorrowful, and even worse, as transitory:

> Yet thy kingdom shall pass, Galilean, thy dead shall
> go down to thee dead.

Shocking as this scorn of Christianity was in itself, it provoked less of an outcry than the ideal which was exalted in its stead—no mere abstract Platonism, as in the case of Shelley, but an unabashed naturalism, a glorification of man's senses and the free expansion of his whole being, mental and physical. So violent, indeed, was Swinburne's rejection of the stultifying morality of his time that he could not resist the temptation to exaggerate those sensuous elements most likely to offend his readers, in such poems, for instance, as "Laus Veneris" and "Sapphics." It was, says Thomas Hardy, "as though a garland of red roses had fallen about the hood of some smug nun."

In addition to release from the gloom of Christian doctrine and escape from moral prudishness, there was yet a third freedom championed by Swinburne, as it had been by Shelley too, namely, political liberty. Under the influence of Mazzini, Swinburne pleaded for the cause of Italian nationalism; stirred by Victor Hugo, he bitterly denounced Louis Napoleon for betraying the French Republic. These were the preoccupations which later inspired his *Songs before Sunrise* (1871), although the challenge to the hierarchy in both church and state had already been clearly sounded in "A Song in Time of Order, 1852" (*Songs and Ballads*), in which Bonaparte was termed a bastard and the Pope was condemned to the galleys. Similarly, his admiration for freedom and democracy in the New World inspired "To Walt Whitman in America," which gave voice to his disgust with the discords of Europe and begged that the vivifying spirit of American liberty might "rise and remain and take station" in the Old World as well.

Just as he considered America the home of political freedom, so he saw the ancient world as the scene of moral and social freedom. This attitude, together with an unusually fine knowledge of both Greek and Latin literature, accounts for his fascination with classical models and themes. It was, he felt, primarily in pre-Christian times that man had been truly free, free of the bonds of a sorrowing asceticism and a hypocritical prudery. But in the Middle Ages, too, he found in such subjects as the Tannhäuser Venus and in such poets as Villon outspoken delight in sensuous enjoyment and defiance of conventional tabus; and it was only natural that he should have hailed his own contemporary, Charles Baudelaire, for these same qualities.

A corollary to his demand for freedom from the shackles of contemporary standards was his reaction against the current didactic and moralistic tendencies of Victorian poetry; and in his essay on Baudelaire (1862) he flares out, "Critical students . . . seem to have pretty well forgotten that a poet's business is presumably to write good verses, and by no means to redeem the age and remould society." Now this from a poet who in his own way was trying his best to remold society and redeem the age from tyranny as well as from cant and hypocrisy calls for an explanation. Aware of this, Swinburne in an essay on Victor Hugo attempted a reconciliation, defining his position in terms of the contemporary aesthetic movement: "The one primary requisite of art is artistic worth; art for art's sake first, and then all things shall be added to her—or if not, it is a matter of quite secondary importance. . . . On the other hand we refuse to admit that art of the highest kind may not ally itself with moral or religious passion, with the ethics or the politics of a nation or an age." This statement of Swinburne's poetic creed was in conformity with both his

temperament and his gifts. It allowed him to give free rein to his love of sound and pattern, of metrical brilliance, and of song for singing's sake, and thus to become, on the musical side, the leading poet of the Aesthetic Movement; yet it justified the intense expression of his moral, social, and political convictions.

There was, however, a fundamental flaw in Swinburne which kept him from realizing the ideal he had set up. He was too facile, too undisciplined. He allowed his thought to become blurred in a maze of beautiful sound and he let himself be floated away on a sea of words—words as such, in which even the image was sometimes lost or distorted. The result was a vagueness and diffusion, which, on occasion, almost nullifies meaning, and which, of course, accounts for the length of many of his poems, where he seems literally unable to set a term. He had a genius for words, but as Hopkins remarked, with Swinburne in mind, "words only are only words."

The standard edition is *The Complete Works of Algernon Charles Swinburne,* edited by Sir Edmund Gosse and T. J. Wise (20 vols., 1925–27). Perhaps the best Life is by H. Nicolson, *Swinburne* (1926). There is an interesting estimate by T. S. Eliot, "Swinburne as Poet," in *The Sacred Wood* (1920). E. M. W. Tillyard has published an essay on "Hertha" in *Five Poems* (1948).

Algernon Charles Swinburne

CHORUSES *from*
ATALANTA IN CALYDON

I

When the hounds of spring are on winter's traces,
   The mother of months[1] in meadow or plain
Fills the shadows and windy places
   With lisp of leaves and ripple of rain;
And the brown bright nightingale amorous   5
Is half assuaged for Itylus,
For the Thracian ships and the foreign faces,
   The tongueless vigil and all the pain.[2]

Come with bows bent and with emptying of quivers,
   Maiden most perfect, lady of light,   10
With a noise of winds and many rivers,
   With a clamor of waters, and with might;
Bind on thy sandals, O thou most fleet,
Over the splendor and speed of thy feet;
For the faint east quickens, the wan west shivers,   15
   Round the feet of the day and the feet of the night.

Where shall we find her, how shall we sing to her,
   Fold our hands round her knees, and cling?
O that man's heart were as fire and could spring to her,
   Fire, or the strength of the streams that spring!   20
For the stars and the winds are unto her
As raiment, as songs of the harp-player;
For the risen stars and the fallen cling to her,
   And the southwest-wind and the west-wind sing.

For winter's rains and ruins are over,   25
   And all the season of snows and sins;
The days dividing lover and lover,
   The light that loses, the night that wins;

---

[1] Diana or Artemis, mother of months because goddess of the moon.

[2] These lines refer to the rape of Philomela by her brother-in-law, Tereus, king of Thrace. To ensure silence about his misdeed, Tereus tore out his victim's tongue, but she still managed to inform her sister Procne. Procne in revenge killed her son Itylus and fed his body to his unsuspecting father. The sisters then fled, Procne in the shape of a swallow, Philomela in that of a nightingale.

And time remembered is grief forgotten,
And frosts are slain and flowers begotten, 30
And in green underwood and cover
  Blossom by blossom the spring begins.

The full streams feed on flower of rushes,
  Ripe grasses trammel a traveling foot,
The faint fresh flame of the young year flushes 35
  From leaf to flower and flower to fruit;
And fruit and leaf are as gold and fire,
And the oat[3] is heard above the lyre,
And the hoofèd heel of a satyr crushes
  The chestnut-husk at the chestnut-root. 40

And Pan by noon and Bacchus by night,
  Fleeter of foot than the fleet-foot kid,
Follows with dancing and fills with delight
  The Maenad and the Bassarid;[4]
And soft as lips that laugh and hide 45
The laughing leaves of the trees divide,
And screen from seeing and leave in sight
  The god pursuing, the maiden hid.

The ivy falls with the Bacchanal's hair
  Over her eyebrows hiding her eyes; 50
The wild vine slipping down leaves bare
  Her bright breast shortening into sighs;
The wild vine slips with the weight of its leaves,
But the berried ivy catches and cleaves
To the limbs that glitter, the feet that scare 55
  The wolf that follows, the fawn that flies.

2

Before the beginning of years
  There came to the making of man
Time, with a gift of tears;
  Grief, with a glass that ran; 60
Pleasure, with pain for leaven;
  Summer, with flowers that fell;
Remembrance fallen from heaven,
  And madness risen from hell;
Strength without hands to smite; 65
  Love that endures for a breath:
Night, the shadow of light,
  And life, the shadow of death.

And the high gods took in hand
  Fire, and the falling of tears, 70
And a measure of sliding sand
  From under the feet of the years;

---

[3] Straw pipe of the shepherd.
[4] Followers of Bacchus.

And froth and drift of the sea;
  And dust of the laboring earth;
And bodies of things to be 75
  In the houses of death and of birth;
And wrought with weeping and laughter,
  And fashioned with loathing and love
With life before and after
  And death beneath and above, 80
For a day and a night and a morrow,
  That his strength might endure for a span
With travail and heavy sorrow,
  The holy spirit of man.

From the winds of the north and the south 85
  They gathered as unto strife:
They breathed upon his mouth,
  They filled his body with life;
Eyesight and speech they wrought
  For the veils of the soul therein, 90
A time for labor and thought,
  A time to serve and to sin;
They gave him light in his ways,
  And love, and a space for delight,
And beauty and length of days, 95
  And night, and sleep in the night.
His speech is a burning fire;
  With his lips he travaileth;
In his heart is a blind desire,
  In his eyes foreknowledge of death; 100
He weaves, and is clothed with derision;
  Sows and he shall not reap;
His life is a watch or a vision
  Between a sleep and a sleep.

HYMN TO PROSERPINE

AFTER THE PROCLAMATION IN ROME OF THE CHRISTIAN FAITH[1]

Vicisti, Galilæe[2]

I have lived long enough, having seen one thing, that
  love hath an end;
Goddess and maiden and queen, be near me now and
  befriend.
Thou art more than the day or the morrow, the seasons
  that laugh or that weep;
For these give joy and sorrow; but thou, Proserpina,
  sleep.

---

[1] After Constantine's Edict of Milan (313), which proclaimed
official toleration of the Christian religion.
[2] "You have conquered, O Galilean"—reported to have been
the dying words of the Emperor Julian (d. 363), who in his
lifetime had denied Christianity.

Sweet is the treading of wine, and sweet the feet of the
    dove;   5
But a goodlier gift is thine than foam of the grapes or
    love.
Yea, is not even Apollo, with hair and harpstring of
    gold,
A bitter God to follow, a beautiful God to behold?
I am sick of singing: the bays[3] burn deep and chafe: I
    am fain
To rest a little from praise and grievous pleasure and
    pain.   10
For the Gods we know not of, who give us our daily
    breath,
We know they are cruel as love or life, and lovely as
    death.
O Gods dethroned and deceased, cast forth, wiped out
    in a day!
From your wrath is the world released, redeemed from
    your chains, men say.
New Gods[4] are crowned in the city; their flowers have
    broken your rods;   15
They are merciful, clothed with pity, the young com-
    passionate Gods.
But for me their new device is barren, the days are
    bare;
Things long past over suffice, and men forgotten that
    were.
Time and the Gods are at strife; ye dwell in the midst
    thereof,
Draining a little life from the barren breasts of love.   20
I say to you, cease, take rest; yea, I say to you all, be
    at peace,
Till the bitter milk of her breast and the barren bosom
    shall cease.
Wilt thou yet take all, Galilean? but these thou shalt
    not take,
The laurel, the palms and the paean, the breast of the
    nymphs in the brake;
Breasts more soft than a dove's that tremble with
    tenderer breath;   25
And all the wings of the Loves, and all the joy before
    death;
All the feet of the hours that sound as a single lyre,
Dropped and deep in the flowers, with strings that
    flicker like fire.
More than these wilt thou give, things fairer than all
    these things?
Nay, for a little we live, and life hath mutable wings.   30
A little while and we die; shall life not thrive as it may?
For no man under the sky lives twice, outliving his day.

And grief is a grievous thing, and a man hath enough
    of his tears:
Why should he labor, and bring fresh grief to blacken
    his years?
Thou hast conquered, O pale Galilean; the world has
    grown gray from thy breath;   35
We have drunken of things Lethean,[5] and fed on the
    fulness of death.
Laurel is green for a season, and love is sweet for a day;
But love grows bitter with treason, and laurel outlives
    not May.
Sleep, shall we sleep after all? for the world is not sweet
    in the end;
For the old faiths loosen and fall, the new years ruin
    and rend.   40
Fate is a sea without shore, and the soul is a rock that
    abides;
But her ears are vexed with the roar and her face with
    the foam of the tides.
O lips that the live blood faints in, the leavings of racks
    and rods!
O ghastly glories of saints, dead limbs of gibbeted Gods!
Though all men abase them before you in spirit, and
    all knees bend,   45
I kneel not neither adore you, but standing, look to the
    end.
All delicate days and pleasant, all spirits and sorrows
    are cast
Far out with the foam of the present that sweeps to the
    surf of the past:
Where beyond the extreme sea-wall, and between the
    remote sea-gates,
Waste water washes, and tall ships founder, and deep
    death waits: 50
Where, mighty with deepening sides, clad about with
    the seas as with wings,
And impelled of invisible tides, and fulfilled of unspeak-
    able things,
White-eyed and poisonous-finned, shark-toothed and
    serpentine-curled,
Rolls, under the whitening wind of the future, the wave
    of the world.
The depths stand naked in sunder behind it, the storms
    flee away;   55
In the hollow before it the thunder is taken and snared
    as a prey;
In its sides is the north-wind bound; and its salt is of
    all men's tears;
With light of ruin, and sound of changes, and pulse of
    years:

---

[3] The bay or laurel leaves forming the poet's crown.
[4] The Christian saints.

[5] Lethe, the river of forgetfulness, was crossed by the dead on
their way to the Underworld.

With travail of day after day, and with trouble of hour
    upon hour;
And bitter as blood is the spray; and the crests are as
    fangs that devour: 60
And its vapor and storm of its steam as the sighing of
    spirits to be;
And its noise as the noise in a dream; and its depth as
    the roots of the sea:
And the height of its heads as the height of the utmost
    stars of the air:
And the ends of the earth at the might thereof tremble,
    and time is made bare.
Will ye bridle the deep sea with reins, will ye chasten
    the high sea with rods?   65
Will ye take her to chain her with chains, who is older
    than all ye Gods?
All ye as a wind shall go by, as a fire shall ye pass and
    be past;
Ye are Gods, and behold, ye shall die, and the waves be
    upon you at last.
In the darkness of time, in the deeps of the years, in the
    changes of things,
Ye shall sleep as a slain man sleeps, and the world shall
    forget you for kings.   70
Though the feet of thine high priests tread where thy
    lords and our forefathers trod,
Though these that were Gods are dead, and thou being
    dead art a God,
Though before thee the throned Cytherean[6] be fallen,
    and hidden her head,
Yet thy kingdom shall pass, Galilean, thy dead shall go
    down to thee dead.
Of the maiden thy mother men sing as a goddess with
    grace clad around;   75
Thou art throned where another was king; where
    another was queen she is crowned.
Yea, once we had sight of another: but now she is
    queen, say these.
Not as thine, not as thine was our mother, a blossom
    of flowering seas,
Clothed round with the world's desire as with raiment,
    and fair as the foam,
And fleeter than kindled fire, and a goddess, and mother
    of Rome.[7]   80
For thine came pale and a maiden, and sister to sorrow;
    but ours,
Her deep hair heavily laden with odor and color of
    flowers,
White rose of the rose-white water, a silver splendor,
    a flame,

---

[6] Aphrodite, or Venus, reputedly born of the foam near Cythera.
[7] Aeneas was believed to have been the son of Aphrodite.

Bent down unto us that besought her, and earth grew
    sweet with her name.
For thine came weeping, a slave among slaves, and
    rejected; but she   85
Came flushed from the full-flushed wave, and imperial,
    her foot on the sea.
And the wonderful waters knew her, the winds and the
    viewless ways,
And the roses grew rosier, and bluer the sea-blue stream
    of the bays.
Ye are fallen, our lords, by what token? we wist that
    ye should not fall.
Ye were all so fair that are broken; and one more fair
    than ye all.   90
But I turn to her still, having seen she shall surely abide
    in the end;
Goddess and maiden and queen, be near me now and
    befriend.
O daughter of earth, of my mother, her crown and
    blossom of birth,
I am also, I also, thy brother; I go as I came unto earth.
In the night where thine eyes are as moons are in
    heaven, the night where thou art,   95
Where the silence is more than all tunes, where sleep
    overflows from the heart,
Where the poppies are sweet as the rose in our world,
    and the red rose is white,
And the wind falls faint as it blows with the fume of the
    flowers of the night,
And the murmur of spirits that sleep in the shadow of
    Gods from afar
Grows dim in thine ears and deep as the deep dim soul
    of a star,   100
In the sweet low light of thy face, under heavens untrod
    by the sun,
Let my soul with their souls find place, and forget what
    is done and undone.
Thou art more than the Gods who number the days of
    our temporal breath;
For these give labor and slumber; but thou, Proserpina,
    death.
Therefore now at thy feet I abide for a season in silence.
    I know   105
I shall die as my fathers died, and sleep as they sleep;
    even so.
For the glass of the years is brittle wherein we gaze
    for a span;
A little soul for a little bears up this corpse which
    is man.
So long I endure, no longer; and laugh not again,
    neither weep.
For there is no God found stronger than death; and
    death is a sleep.   110

THE GARDEN OF PROSERPINE[1]

Here, where the world is quiet;
 Here, where all trouble seems
Dead winds' and spent waves' riot
 In doubtful dreams of dreams;
I watch the green field growing   5
For reaping folk and sowing,
For harvest-time and mowing,
 A sleepy world of streams.

I am tired of tears and laughter,
 And men that laugh and weep; 10
Of what may come hereafter
 For men that sow to reap:
I am weary of days and hours,
Blown buds of barren flowers,
Desires and dreams and powers 15
 And everything but sleep.

Here life has death for neighbor,
 And far from eye or ear
Wan waves and wet winds labor,
 Weak ships and spirits steer; 20
They drive adrift, and whither
They wot not who make thither;
But no such winds blow hither,
 And no such things grow here.

No growth of moor or coppice, 25
 No heather-flower or vine,
But bloomless buds of poppies,
 Green grapes of Proserpine,
Pale beds of blowing rushes
Where no leaf blooms or blushes 30
Save this whereout she crushes
 For dead men deadly wine.

Pale, without name or number,
 In fruitless fields of corn,
They bow themselves and slumber 35
 All night till light is born;
And like a soul belated,
In hell and heaven unmated,
By cloud and mist abated
 Comes out of darkness morn. 40

Though one were strong as seven,
 He too with death shall dwell,
Nor wake with wings in heaven,

Nor weep for pains in hell;
Though one were fair as roses, 45
His beauty clouds and closes;
And well though love reposes,
 In the end it is not well.

Pale, beyond porch and portal,
 Crowned with calm leaves, she stands 50
Who gathers all things mortal
 With cold immortal hands;
Her languid lips are sweeter
Than love's who fears to greet her,
To men that mix and meet her 55
 From many times and lands.

She waits for each and other,
 She waits for all men born;
Forgets the earth her mother,
 The life of fruits and corn; 60
And spring and seed and swallow
Take wing for her and follow
Where summer song rings hollow
 And flowers are put to scorn.

There go the loves that wither, 65
 The old loves with wearier wings:
And all dead years draw thither,
 And all disastrous things;
Dead dreams of days forsaken,
Blind buds that snows have shaken, 70
Wild leaves that winds have taken,
 Red strays of ruined springs.

We are not sure of sorrow,
 And joy was never sure;
To-day will die to-morrow; 75
 Time stoops to no man's lure;
And love, grown faint and fretful,
With lips but half regretful
Sighs, and with eyes forgetful
 Weeps that no loves endure. 80

From too much love of living,
 From hope and fear set free,
We thank with brief thanksgiving
 Whatever gods may be
That no life lives for ever; 85
That dead men rise up never;
That even the weariest river
 Winds somewhere safe to sea.

Then star nor sun shall waken,
 Nor any change of light: 90

---

[1] The land of the dead, whose queen is Proserpine, goddess of sleep.

Nor sound of waters shaken,
    Nor any sound or sight:
Nor wintry leaves nor vernal,
Nor days nor things diurnal;
Only the sleep eternal   95
    In an eternal night.

A BALLAD OF FRANÇOIS VILLON[2]

PRINCE OF ALL BALLAD-MAKERS

Bird of the bitter bright gray golden morn
    Scarce risen upon the dusk of dolorous years,
First of us all the sweetest singer born,
    Whose far shrill note the world of new men hears
    Cleave the cold shuddering shade as twilight clears; 5
When song new-born put off the old world's attire[3]
And felt its tune on her changed lips expire,
    Writ foremost on the roll of them that came
Fresh girt for service of the latter lyre,
    Villon, our sad bad glad mad brother's name!   10

Alas, the joy, the sorrow, and the scorn,
    That clothed thy life with hopes and sins and fears,
And gave thee stones for bread and tares for corn
    And plume-plucked gaol-birds for thy starveling peers
    Till death clipped close their flight with shameful
        shears;   15
Till shifts came short[4] and loves were hard to hire,
When lilt of song nor twitch of twangling wire
    Could buy thee bread or kisses; when light fame
Spurned like a ball and haled through brake and briar,
    Villon, our sad bad glad mad brother's name!   20

Poor splendid wings so frayed and soiled and torn!
    Poor kind wild eyes so dashed with light quick tears!
Poor perfect voice, most blithe when most forlorn,
    That rings athwart the sea whence no man steers,
    Like joy-bells crossed with death-bells in our ears! 25
What far delight has cooled the fierce desire
That like some ravenous bird was strong to tire
    On that frail flesh and soul consumed with flame,
But left more sweet than roses to respire,
    Villon, our sad bad glad mad brother's name?   30

---

[2] Villon, the great fifteenth-century French poet, was also a
thief and a rascal who was more than once in prison and had a
narrow escape from the gallows. Swinburne's praise of such a
social reprobate naturally scandalized his critics, but the skill
with which he imitated Villon's favorite stanzaic form delighted
his admirers. On the ballade, see p. 774, note 3, above.

[3] Swinburne considers Villon the first of the modern, as distinguished from the medieval, poets.

[4] A shift was a woman's garment. The meaning is, "Till there
was a shortage of women."

ENVOI

Prince of sweet songs made out of tears and fire,
A harlot was thy nurse, a God thy sire;[5]
    Shame soiled thy song, and song assoiled thy shame,
But from thy feet now death has washed the mire,
Love reads out first at head of all our quire,   35
    Villon, our sad bad glad mad brother's name.

HERTHA[1]

I am that which began;
    Out of me the years roll;
Out of me God and man;
    I am equal[2] and whole;
God changes, and man, and the form of them bodily;
    I am the soul.   5

Before ever land was,
    Before ever the sea,
Or soft hair of the grass,
    Or fair limbs of the tree,
Or the flesh-colored fruit of my branches, I was, and
    thy soul was in me.   10

First life on my sources
    First drifted and swam;
Out of me are the forces
    That save it or damn;
Out of me man and woman, and wild-beast and bird;
    before God was, I am.[3]   15

Beside or above me
    Nought is there to go;
Love or unlove me,
    Unknow me or know,
I am that which unloves me and loves; I am stricken,
    and I am the blow.   20

I the mark that is missed
    And the arrows that miss,
I the mouth that is kissed
    And the breath in the kiss,
The search, and the sought, and the seeker, the soul and
    the body that is.   25

---

[5] Although baseborn, Villon was a son of Apollo, god of poetry.

[1] The speaker in this poem is the Germanic goddess of earth and
growth, whom Swinburne here makes the original source of
all being. He regarded this poem as one of his best in that it had
"lyric force and music" combined with "condensed and clarified
thought."   [2] All of one nature.

[3] Cf. the words of Jesus in John 8:58, "Before Abraham was, I
am," echoed here probably with satiric intent.

I am that thing which blesses
  My spirit elate;
That which caresses
  With hands uncreate[4]
My limbs unbegotten that measure the length of the
  measure of fate.   30

But what thing dost thou now,
  Looking Godward, to cry
"I am I, thou art thou,
  I am low, thou art high"?
I am thou, whom thou seekest to find him; find thou
  but thyself, thou art I.   35

I the grain and the furrow,
  The plough-cloven clod
And the ploughshare drawn thorough,
  The germ and the sod,
The deed and the doer, the seed and the sower, the dust
  which is God.   40

Hast thou known how I fashioned thee,
  Child, underground?
Fire that impassioned thee,
  Iron that bound,
Dim changes of water, what thing of all these hast thou
  known of or found?   45

Canst thou say in thine heart
  Thou hast seen with thine eyes
With what cunning of art
  Thou wast wrought in what wise,
By what force of what stuff thou wast shapen, and
  shown on my breast to the skies?   50

Who hath given, who hath sold it thee,
  Knowledge of me?
Hath the wilderness told it thee?
  Hast thou learnt of the sea?
Hast thou communed in spirit with night? have the
  winds taken counsel with thee?   55

Have I set such a star
  To show light on thy brow
That thou sawest from afar
  What I show to thee now?
Have ye spoken as brethren together, the sun and the
  mountains and thou?   60

What is here, dost thou know it?
  What was, hast thou known?
Prophet nor poet
  Nor tripod[5] nor throne
Nor spirit nor flesh can make answer, but only thy
  mother alone.   65

Mother, not maker,
  Born, and not made;
Though her children forsake her,
  Allured or afraid,
Praying prayers to the God of their fashion, she stirs
  not for all that have prayed.   70

A creed is a rod,
  And a crown is of night;
But this thing is God,
  To be man with thy might,
To grow straight in the strength of thy spirit, and live
  out thy life as the light.   75

I am in thee to save thee,
  As my soul in thee saith;
Give thou, as I gave thee,
  Thy life-blood and breath,
Green leaves of thy labor, white flowers of thy thought,
  and red fruit of thy death.   80

Be the ways of thy giving
  As mine were to thee;
The free life of thy living,
  Be the gift of it free;
Not as servant to lord, nor as master to slave, shalt thou
  give thee to me.   85

O children of banishment,
  Souls overcast,
Were the lights ye see vanish meant
  Always to last,
Ye would know not the sun overshining the shadows
  and stars overpast.   90

I that saw where ye trod
  The dim paths of the night
Set the shadow called God
  In your skies to give light;
But the morning of manhood is risen, and the shadow-
  less soul is in sight.   95

---

[4] Not created, but having always existed; cf. "unbegotten" in
the next line.

[5] The priestess at the famous oracular shrine of Apollo at Delphi
sat upon a tripod. The reference here is probably to the church
or priesthood.

Man over god

The tree many-rooted
 That swells to the sky
With frondage red-fruited
 The life-tree am I;[6]
In the buds of your lives is the sap of my leaves: ye
  shall live and not die.   100

But the Gods of your fashion
 That take and that give,
In their pity and passion
 That scourge and forgive,
They are worms that are bred in the bark that falls off;
  they shall die and not live. 105

My own blood is what stanches
 The wounds in my bark;
Stars caught in my branches
 Make day of the dark,
And are worshipped as suns till the sunrise shall tread
  out their fires as a spark. 110

Where dead ages hide under
 The live roots of the tree,
In my darkness the thunder
 Makes utterance of me;
In the clash of my boughs with each other ye hear the
  waves sound of the sea. 115

That noise is of Time,
 As his feathers are spread
And his feet set to climb
 Through the boughs overhead,
And my foliage rings round him and rustles, and
  branches are bent with his tread. 120

The storm-winds of ages
 Blow through me and cease,
The war-wind that rages,
 The spring-wind of peace,
Ere the breath of them roughen my tresses, ere one of
  my blossoms increase. 125

All sounds of all changes,
 All shadows and lights
On the world's mountain-ranges
 And stream-riven heights,
Whose tongue is the wind's tongue and language of
  storm-clouds on earth-shaking nights; 130

All forms of all faces,
 All works of all hands

---

[6] In Germanic mythology, the tree Igdrasil.

In unsearchable places
 Of time-stricken lands,
All death and all life, and all reigns and all ruins, drop
  through me as sands. 135

Though sore be my burden
 And more than ye know,
And my growth have no guerdon
 But only to grow,
Yet I fail not of growing for lightnings above me or
  deathworms below. 140

These too have their part in me,
 As I too in these;
Such fire is at heart in me,
 Such sap is this tree's,
Which hath in it all sounds and all secrets of infinite
  lands and of seas. 145

In the spring-colored hours
 When my mind was as May's,
There brake forth of me flowers
 By centuries of days,
Strong blossoms with perfume of manhood, shot out
  from my spirit as rays. 150

And the sound of them springing
 And smell of their shoots
Were as warmth and sweet singing
 And strength to my roots;
And the lives of my children made perfect with freedom
  of soul were my fruits. 155

I bid you but be;
 I have need not of prayer;
I have need of you free
 As your mouths of mine air;
That my heart may be greater within me, beholding
  the fruits of me fair. 160

More fair than strange fruit is
 Of faiths ye espouse;
In me only the root is
 That blooms in your boughs;
Behold now your God that ye made you, to feed him
  with faith of your vows. 165

In the darkening and whitening
 Abysses adored,
With dayspring and lightning
 For lamp and for sword,
God thunders in heaven, and his angels are red with
  the wrath of the Lord. 170

O my sons, O too dutiful
  Towards Gods not of me, —
Was not I enough beautiful?
  Was it hard to be free?
For behold, I am with you, am in you and of you;
    look forth now and see.   175

Lo, winged with world's wonders,
  With miracles shod,
With the fires of his thunders
  For raiment and rod,
God trembles in heaven, and his angels are white with
    the terror of God.   180

For his twilight[7] is come on him,
  His anguish is here;
And his spirits gaze dumb on him,
  Grown gray from his fear;
And his hour taketh hold on him stricken, the last of
    his infinite year.   185

Thought made him and breaks him,
  Truth slays and forgives;
But to you, as time takes him,
  This new thing it gives,
Even love, the beloved Republic, that feeds upon
    freedom and lives.   190

For truth only is living,
  Truth only is whole,
And the love of his giving
  Man's polestar and pole;
Man, pulse of my center, and fruit of my body, and
    seed of my soul.   195

One birth of my bosom;
  One beam of mine eye;
One topmost blossom
  That scales the sky;
Man, equal and one with me, man that is made of me,
    man that is I.   200

TO WALT WHITMAN IN AMERICA

Send but a song oversea for us,
  Heart of their hearts who are free,
Heart of their singer, to be for us
  More than our singing can be;

Ours, in the tempest at error,
With no light but the twilight of terror;[1]   5
  Send us a song oversea!

Sweet-smelling of pine-leaves and grasses,
  And blown as a tree through and through
With the winds of the keen mountain-passes,   10
  And tender as sun-smitten dew;
Sharp-tongued as the winter that shakes
The wastes of your limitless lakes,
  Wide-eyed as the sea-line's blue.

O strong-winged soul with prophetic   15
  Lips hot with the bloodbeats of song,
With tremor of heartstrings magnetic,
  With thoughts as thunders in throng,
With consonant ardors of chords
That pierce men's souls as with swords   20
  And hale them hearing along,

Make us too music, to be with us
  As a word from a world's heart warm,
To sail the dark as a sea with us,
  Full-sailed, outsinging the storm,   25
A song to put fire in our ears
Whose burning shall burn up tears,
  Whose sign bid battle reform;

A note in the ranks of a clarion,
  A word in the wind of cheer,   30
To consume as with lightning the carrion
  That makes time foul for us here;
In the air that our dead things[2] infest
A blast of the breath of the west,
  Till east way as west way is clear.   35

Out of the sun beyond sunset,
  From the evening whence morning shall be,
With the rollers in measureless onset,
  With the van of the storming sea,
With the world-wide wind, with the breath   40
That breaks ships driven upon death,
  With the passion of all things free,

With the sea-steeds footless and frantic,
  White myriads for death to bestride
In the charge of the ruining Atlantic   45

---

[7] Swinburne here adapts the Germanic myth that foretold the "twilight" and fall of the gods as a prelude to the emergence of a regenerated world.

[1] Europe, which is here as much in question as England, was in the early and middle years of the century in the throes of casting off the despotism of its ecclesiastical and political rulers.
[2] Contemporary heads of church and state and what they stood for.

Where deaths by regiments ride,
With clouds and clamors of waters,
With a long note shriller than slaughter's
    On the furrowless fields world-wide,

With terror, with ardor and wonder,   50
    With the soul of the season that wakes
When the weight of a whole year's thunder
    In the tidestream of autumn breaks,
Let the flight of the wide-winged word
Come over, come in and be heard,   55
    Take form and fire for our sakes.

For a continent bloodless with travail
    Here toils and brawls as it can,
And the web of it who shall unravel
    Of all that peer on the plan;   60
Would fain grow men, but they grow not,
And fain be free, but they know not
    One name for freedom and man.

One name, not twain for division;
    One thing, not twain, from the birth;   65
Spirit and substance and vision,
    Worth more than worship is worth;
Unbeheld, unadored, undivined,
The cause, the center, the mind,
    The secret and sense of the earth.   70

Here as a weakling in irons,
    Here as a weanling in bands,
As a prey that the stake-net[3] environs,
    Our life that we looked for stands;
And the man-child naked and dear,   75
Democracy, turns on us here
    Eyes trembling with tremulous hands.

It sees not what season shall bring to it
    Sweet fruit of its bitter desire;
Few voices it hears yet sing to it,   80
    Few pulses of hearts reaspire;
Foresees not time, nor forehears
The noises of imminent years,
    Earthquake, and thunder, and fire:

When crowned and weaponed and curbless   85
    It shall walk without helm or shield
The bare burnt furrows and herbless
    Of war's last flame-stricken field,

Till godlike, equal with time,
It stand in the sun sublime,   90
    In the godhead of man revealed.

Round your people and over them
    Light like raiment is drawn,
Close as a garment to cover them
    Wrought not of mail nor of lawn;[4]   95
Here, with hope hardly to wear,
Naked nations and bare
    Swim, sink, strike out for the dawn.

Chains are here, and a prison,
    Kings, and subjects, and shame;   100
If the God upon you be arisen,[5]
    How should our songs be the same?
How, in confusion of change,
How shall we sing, in a strange
    Land, songs praising his name?   105

God is buried and dead to us,
    Even the spirit of earth,
Freedom; so have they said to us,
    Some with mocking and mirth,
Some with heartbreak and tears;   110
And a God without eyes, without ears,
    Who shall sing of him, dead in the birth?[6]

The earth-god Freedom, the lonely
    Face lightening, the footprint unshod,
Not as one man crucified only,   115
    Nor scourged with but one life's rod;
The soul that is substance of nations,
Reincarnate with fresh generations:
    The great god Man, which is God.

But in weariest of years and obscurest   120
    Doth it live not at heart of all things,
The one God and one spirit, a purest
    Life, fed from unstanchable springs?
Within love, within hatred it is,
And its seed in the stripe[7] as the kiss,   125
    And in slaves is the germ, and in kings.

---

[3] Fishing net spread upon stakes as a kind of weir.

[4] These represent respectively the military and the ecclesiastical
hierarchies: mail is armor and lawn is the material out of which
bishops' sleeves are made.
[5] The god is identified below as Freedom or Man.
[6] They have told us that Freedom is dead and that in any event
an abstraction, as opposed to a personal god, is no god at all.
[7] Blow of a lash.

Freedom we call it, for holier
  Name of the soul's there is none;
Surelier its labors, if slowlier,
  Than the meters of star or of sun;   130
Slowlier than life into breath,
Surelier than time into death,
  It moves till its labor be done.

Till the motion be done and the measure
  Circling through season and clime,   135
Slumber and sorrow and pleasure,
  Vision of virtue and crime;
Till consummate with conquering eyes,
A soul disembodied, it rise
  From the body transfigured of time.   140

Till it rise and remain and take station
  With the stars of the worlds that rejoice;
Till the voice of its heart's exultation
  Be as theirs an invariable voice;
By no discord of evil estranged,   145
By no pause, by no breach in it changed,
  By no clash in the chord of its choice.

It is one with the world's generations,
  With the spirit, the star, and the sod;
With the kingless and king-stricken nations,   150
  With the cross, and the chain, and the rod;
The most high, the most secret, most lonely,
The earth-soul Freedom, that only
  Lives, and that only is God.

Walter Horatio Pater

1839–1894

PATER was born in the East End of London in 1839. When he was five, his father, who was a physician, died, and perhaps some of his aloofness from the world of practical action and his delicate sense for distinctions of feeling may be traced to the feminine influence of the three women (mother, aunt, and grandmother) who brought him up. After school in Canterbury, where the Gothic beauty of the cathedral impressed him as deeply as it did Morris, he went to Oxford in 1858, and after graduation became a Fellow of Brasenose College, where he spent most of his life teaching and writing. His principal works are *Studies in the History of the Renaissance* (1873), a collection of critical essays mainly on Italian painters of that period, and a philosophical biography of an imaginary Roman, *Marius the Epicurean* (1885). He died at Oxford in 1894.

Arnold and Pater are the two major critics of the Victorian period, but the contrast between them is more striking, and more significant historically, than any similarity. Where Arnold has the characteristic longing of the mid-Victorians for certitude, and their characteristic faith in the discovery of truth and the resolution of practical problems, Pater by contrast is far closer to the twentieth century in his radical skepticism. The study of history made him conscious of the vast and bewildering variety of conflicting beliefs which men had held and abandoned in the past. Were their present beliefs likely to be any more stable or true? Indeed, are not all institutions and all philosophies, secular or religious, simply manifestations of the particular state of civilization in any given time and place? And if so, then everything is "right" and "true" relative to its environment; nothing is Right and True absolutely. The philosopher, therefore, can hardly expect to arrive at final answers or to formulate positive creeds. He must be content "with suspension of judgment, at the end of the intellectual journey, to the very last asking: *Que scais-je?* Who knows?" Could anything be more alien to the hopes and ideals of Arnold and the other Victorians of the middle century, or more fatal to the whole concept of the artist as prophet?

What did Pater advocate instead? What was *his* philosophy of life? and of art? The answer to the first is latent in his skepticism. If thought is impotent, the alternative is feeling. Not to reason but to burn always with a hard, gemlike flame, to respond ecstatically to every manifestation of beauty, is success in life. This conclusion was reinforced for Pater by his acceptance of the mechanistic universe which the new science was describing, where all things, material and human, were determined by a vast network of cause and effect. In such a world purposeful action was a delusion. All that man could do was to live in and for the impressions of the moment, to be as alert and sensitive as possible to the "forms of nature and human nature," in life and in art, which give the finest quality of sensuous pleasure. Not that Pater rules out "ideas," but an idea has become for him not something to believe and live by, but something to taste, some new or strange notion to add to his store of experience, or else a new angle of vision which will enable him to see and respond to what otherwise he would not have noticed. In short, what Pater offered his generation was fundamentally not a new criticism but a new philosophy, the philosophy of aestheticism. He was the architect, you might say, who built the Ivory Tower in which Morris was a visitor, and in which the aesthetes of the 90's, Wilde and Symons and the young Yeats, made their home. "As Pater offered instead of moral earnestness life lived as 'a pure gem-like flame' all accepted him for master" (Yeats). And in doing so, he offered a refuge from the physical ugliness and intellectual futility of modern life.

Given this philosophy of aesthetic enjoyment, we can predict the attraction of the Renaissance not only for Pater but for his contemporaries. As a matter of fact, *Studies in the History of the Renaissance* (1873) was a pioneer work in England, followed presently by J. A. Symonds's *The Renaissance in Italy* (1875–1886) and Vernon Lee's *Euphorion, Essays in the Renaissance* (1884). Strange as it now seems, there was no article on the period in the *Encyclopaedia Britannica* until the ninth edition of 1885, where the author (Symonds) explained that it was only during the previous twenty-five years that the importance of the Renaissance had been recognized—that is to say, in the very years when the new aesthetic attitude was displacing the moral and religious attitude of the mid-Victorians. The passage from Ruskin to Pater marks the transition. For by Pater the Renaissance is no longer viewed as a "bad" period of sensual luxury and pagan thought, as it had been by Ruskin (see p. 590), but as a "good" period of revolt against the narrow bounds of the Christian ideal, a freeing of the heart and imagination to enjoy once more the beauty of man and nature. The obvious analogy with the aesthetic revolt against the bounds of mid-Victorianism is the inciting cause of the Renaissance studies and the Renaissance enthusiasm of the period from 1860 to 1914. After the first world war, the next reaction (against aestheticism itself) and the rise of modern metaphysical poetry shifted literary sympathy to the seventeenth century.

Pater's critical theory is a natural deduction from his philosophy. If the goal of life is the fullest enjoyment of lovely or curious sensations, the purpose of art is not profit (one is tempted to say, not prophet) but pleasure, and the artist's role is to record the most striking impressions, in their novelty or beauty, which his sensitive nature has experienced. In theory this did not rule out a defined content, psychological or even ideological, but the reaction against the Victorian poetry of ideas could very well lead, as it sometimes did in Morris and Swinburne and the early Yeats, to a "pure" poetry of mood and atmosphere, created out of image and rhythm. The critical rationale of this development is found in Pater's essay on "The School of Giorgione." There he suggests that "the highest and most complete form of poetry" is the lyric, where the very perfection depends, in part, "on a certain suppression or vagueness of mere subject,"

and argues that all art should strive "to be independent of the mere intelligence, to become a matter of pure perception, to get rid of its responsibilities to subject or material." This is the doctrine of Art for Art's Sake at its extreme, as we find it maintained by the artists of the 80's and 90's. Yeats is speaking for the poets of that period when he says that the revolt against Victorianism meant the revolt against introducing into poetry "curiosities about politics, about science, about religion . . . with moral purpose and educational fervour," and the determination, by reaction, to "purify poetry of all that is not poetry" by writing lyrical poems where music and color would suggest an "almost bodiless emotion."

Pater's defense of claiming that all the arts should "aspire towards the condition of music" is that there form and matter are so completely fused that they cannot be separated even by the critical intellect. But to demand that kind of fusion from poetry and painting is to sacrifice their special potentialities, which are different from those of music but no less expressive. In a top-notch poem or painting, form and matter *are* welded together, only not so tightly that analysis may not be able to disengage them. But this is inevitable, and entirely justified by the character of the mediums. One suspects that Pater was simply trying to find critical grounds on which to exalt the kind of "pure" poetry and painting which he wanted. At any rate, and however faulty the particular argument, Pater's general insistence on the organic character of art was completely valid and very much needed. For the tendency of Victorian criticism was to focus too exclusively either on the content (the moral or religious ideas of a poet-prophet) or on the form (the technique of the painter, or the artistry of the poet). Pater's reassertion of the organic principle, derived from Coleridge, was a significant contribution to modern aesthetics. And on the side of practical as well as theoretical criticism. When he rightly claims (in the Preface to *The Renaissance*) that the first concern of the critic must be with the essential quality of a work of art, with the particular kind and shade of experience it communicates by means of all of its elements working together, he is, in effect, demanding that we read a poem or look at a picture as an organic whole to which we respond with a unified sensibility (with what he calls, in "The School of Giorgione," the "imaginative reason"). And in doing so, he is making precisely the same protest against the twin errors of reading poetry with the mind (for its ideas) or with the feelings (for its emotions), which modern critics like Eliot and Richards have been hammering home, and offering the same corrective which they have constantly affirmed.

The Works of Walter Pater have been published in 10 vols. (1910). The standard Life is by Thomas Wright (2 vols., 1907). There is a good essay on Pater in Graham Hough's *The Last Romantics* (1949).

Walter Horatio Pater

from THE RENAISSANCE. STUDIES IN ART AND POETRY

PREFACE

MANY attempts have been made by writers on art and poetry to define beauty in the abstract, to express it in the most general terms, to find some universal formula for it. The value of these attempts has most often been in the suggestive and penetrating things said by the way. Such discussions help us very little to enjoy what has been well done in art or poetry, to discriminate between what is more and what is less excellent in them, or to use words like beauty, excellence, art, poetry, with a more precise meaning than they would otherwise have. Beauty, like all other qualities presented to human experience, is relative; and the definition of it becomes unmeaning and useless in proportion to its abstractness. To define beauty, not in the most abstract but in the most concrete terms possible, to find not its universal formula, but the formula which expresses most adequately this or that special manifestation of it, is the aim of the true student of aesthetics.

"To see the object as in itself it really is," has been justly said to be the aim of all true criticism whatever;[1] and in aesthetic criticism the first step towards seeing one's object as it really is, is to know one's own impression as it really is, to discriminate it, to realise it distinctly. The objects with which aesthetic criticism deals—music, poetry, artistic and accomplished forms of human life—are indeed receptacles of so many powers or forces: they possess, like the products of nature, so many virtues or qualities. What is this song or picture, this engaging personality presented in life or in a book, to *me*? What effect does it really produce on me? Does it give me pleasure? and if so, what sort or degree of pleasure? How is my nature modified by its presence, and under its influence? The answers to these questions are the original facts with which the aesthetic critic has to do; and, as in the study of light, of morals, of number, one must realise such primary data for one's self, or not at all. And he who experiences these impressions strongly, and drives directly at the discrimination and analysis of them, has no need to trouble himself with the abstract question what beauty is in itself, or what its exact relation to truth or experience—meta-physical questions, as unprofitable as metaphysical questions elsewhere. He may pass them all by as being, answerable or not, of no interest to him.

The aesthetic critic, then, regards all the objects with which he has to do, all works of art, and the fairer forms of nature and human life, as powers or forces producing pleasurable sensations, each of a more or less peculiar or unique kind. This influence he feels, and wishes to explain, by analysing and reducing it to its elements. To him, the picture, the landscape, the engaging personality in life or in a book, *La Gioconda,* the hills of Carrara, Pico of Mirandola,[2] are valuable for their virtues, as we say, in speaking of a herb, a wine, a gem; for the property each has of affecting one with a special, a unique, impression of pleasure. Our education becomes complete in proportion as our susceptibility to these impressions increases in depth and variety. And the function of the aesthetic critic is to distinguish, to analyse, and separate from its adjuncts, the virtue by which a picture, a landscape, a fair personality in life or in a book, produces this special impression of beauty or pleasure, to indicate what the source of that impression is, and under what conditions it is experienced. His end is reached when he has disengaged that virtue, and noted it, as a chemist notes some natural element, for himself and others; and the rule for those who would reach this end is stated with great exactness in the words of a recent critic of Sainte-Beuve:—*De se borner à connaître de près les belles choses, et à s'en nourrir en exquis amateurs, en humanistes accomplis.*[3]

What is important, then, is not that the critic should possess a correct abstract definition of beauty for the intellect, but a certain kind of temperament, the power of being deeply moved by the presence of beautiful objects. He will remember always that beauty exists in many forms. To him all periods, types, schools of taste, are in themselves equal. In all ages there have been some excellent workmen, and some excellent work done. The question he asks is always:—In whom did the stir, the genius, the

[1] By Arnold in "The Function of Criticism" (see p. 748).

[2] The picture is the *Mona Lisa* by Leonardo da Vinci, the landscape a hilly section of Italy, and the personality an Italian humanist of the fifteenth century.

[3] "To limit ourselves to knowing beautiful things at first hand, and to nourish ourselves by them like sensitive amateurs and accomplished humanists."

sentiment of the period find itself? where was the receptacle of its refinement, its elevation, its taste? "The ages are all equal," says William Blake, "but genius is always above its age."

Often it will require great nicety to disengage this virtue from the commoner elements with which it may be found in combination. Few artists, not Goethe or Byron even, work quite cleanly, casting off all *débris,* and leaving us only what the heat of their imagination has wholly fused and transformed. Take, for instance, the writings of Wordsworth. The heat of his genius, entering into the substance of his work, has crystallised a part, but only a part, of it; and in that great mass of verse there is much which might well be forgotten. But scattered up and down it, sometimes fusing and transforming entire compositions, like the Stanzas on *Resolution and Independence,* or the *Ode on the Recollections of Childhood,* sometimes, as if at random, depositing a fine crystal here or there, in a matter it does not wholly search through and transmute, we trace the action of his unique, incommunicable faculty, that strange, mystical sense of a life in natural things, and of man's life as a part of nature, drawing strength and colour and character from local influences, from the hills and streams, and from natural sights and sounds. Well! that is the *virtue,* the active principle in Wordsworth's poetry; and then the function of the critic of Wordsworth is to follow up that active principle, to disengage it, to mark the degree in which it penetrates his verse.

The subjects of the following studies are taken from the history of the *Renaissance,* and touch what I think the chief points in that complex, many-sided movement. I have explained in the first of them what I understand by the word, giving it a much wider scope than was intended by those who originally used it to denote that revival of classical antiquity in the fifteenth century which was only one of many results of a general excitement and enlightening of the human mind, but of which the great aim and achievements of what, as Christian art, is often falsely opposed to the Renaissance, were another result. This outbreak of the human spirit may be traced far into the middle age itself, with its motives already clearly pronounced, the care for physical beauty, the worship of the body, the breaking down of those limits which the religious system of the middle age imposed on the heart and the imagination. I have taken as an example of this movement, this earlier Renaissance within the middle age itself, and as an expression of its qualities, two little compositions in early French;[4]

not because they constitute the best possible expression of them, but because they help the unity of my series, inasmuch as the Renaissance ends also in France, in French poetry, in a phase of which the writings of Joachim du Bellay[5] are in many ways the most perfect illustration. The Renaissance, in truth, put forth in France an aftermath, a wonderful later growth, the products of which have to the full that subtle and delicate sweetness which belongs to a refined and comely decadence, just as its earliest phases have the freshness which belongs to all periods of growth in art, the charm of *ascêsis,*[6] of the austere and serious girding of the loins in youth.

But it is in Italy, in the fifteenth century, that the interest of the Renaissance mainly lies,—in that solemn fifteenth century which can hardly be studied too much, not merely for its positive results in the things of the intellect and the imagination, its concrete works of art, its special and prominent personalities, with their profound aesthetic charm, but for its general spirit and character, for the ethical qualities of which it is a consummate type.

The various forms of intellectual activity which together make up the culture of an age, move for the most part from different starting-points, and by unconnected roads. As products of the same generation they partake indeed of a common character, and unconsciously illustrate each other; but of the producers themselves, each group is solitary, gaining what advantage or disadvantage there may be in intellectual isolation. Art and poetry, philosophy and the religious life, and that other life of refined pleasure and action in the conspicuous places of the world, are each of them confined to its own circle of ideas, and those who prosecute either of them are generally little curious of the thoughts of others. There come, however, from time to time, eras of more favourable conditions, in which the thoughts of men draw nearer together than is their wont, and the many interests of the intellectual world combine in one complete type of general culture. The fifteenth century in Italy is one of these happier eras, and what is sometimes said of the age of Pericles is true of that of Lorenzo:[7]—it is an age productive in personalities, many-sided, centralised, complete. Here, artists and philosophers and those whom the action of the world has elevated and made keen, do not live in isolation, but breathe a

---

[4] *Amis and Amile* and *Aucassin and Nicolette.*

[5] French poet and critic of the sixteenth century, the subject of one of Pater's essays.

[6] Defined elsewhere by Pater as "self-restraint, a skilful economy of means."

[7] Pericles, the Athenian statesman of the fifth century B.C., and Lorenzo de' Medici, prince of Florence and patron of Renaissance art.

common air, and catch light and heat from each other's thoughts. There is a spirit of general elevation and enlightenment in which all alike communicate. The unity of this spirit gives unity to all the various products of the Renaissance; and it is to this intimate alliance with mind, this participation in the best thoughts which that age produced, that the art of Italy in the fifteenth century owes much of its grave dignity and influence.

I have added an essay on Winckelmann,[8] as not incongruous with the studies which precede it, because Winckelmann, coming in the eighteenth century, really belongs in spirit to an earlier age. By his enthusiasm for the things of the intellect and the imagination for their own sake, by his Hellenism, his life-long struggle to attain to the Greek spirit, he is in sympathy with the humanists of a previous century. He is the last fruit of the Renaissance, and explains in a striking way its motive and tendencies.

from THE SCHOOL OF GIORGIONE[9]

It is the mistake of much popular criticism to regard poetry, music, and painting—all the various products of art—as but translations into different languages of one and the same fixed quantity of imaginative thought, supplemented by certain technical qualities of color, in painting—of sound, in music —of rhythmical words, in poetry. In this way, the sensuous element in art, and with it almost everything in art that is essentially artistic, is made a matter of indifference; and a clear apprehension of the opposite principle—that the sensuous material of each art brings with it a special phase or quality of beauty, untranslatable into the forms of any other, an order of impressions distinct in kind—is the beginning of all true aesthetic criticism. For, as art addresses not pure sense, still less the pure intellect, but the "imaginative reason"[10] through the senses, there are differences of kind in aesthetic beauty, corresponding to the differences in kind of the gifts of sense themselves. Each art, therefore, having its own peculiar and incommunicable sensuous charm, has its own special mode of reaching the imagination, its own special responsibilities to its material. One of the functions of aesthetic criticism is to define these limitations; to estimate the degree in which a given work of art fulfils its responsibilities to its special material; to note in a picture that true pictorial charm, which is neither a mere poetical thought nor sentiment, on the one hand, nor a mere result of communicable technical skill in colour or design, on the other; to define in a poem that true poetical quality, which is neither descriptive nor meditative merely, but comes of an inventive handling of rhythmical language—the element of song in the singing; to note in music the musical charm—that essential music, which presents no words, no matter of sentiment or thought, separable from the special form in which it is conveyed to us.

To such a philosophy of the variations of the beautiful, Lessing's analysis of the spheres of sculpture and poetry, in the *Laocoon,* was a very important contribution.[11] But a true appreciation of these things is possible only in the light of a whole system of such art-casuistries.[12] And it is in the criticism of painting that this truth most needs enforcing, for it is in popular judgments on pictures that that false generalisation of all art into forms of poetry is most prevalent. To suppose that all is mere technical acquirement in delineation or touch, working through and addressing itself to the intelligence, on the one side, or a merely poetical, or what may be called literary interest, addressed also to the pure intelligence, on the other;—this is the way of most spectators, and of many critics, who have never caught sight, all the time, of that true pictorial quality which lies between (unique pledge of the possession of the pictorial gift) the inventive or creative handling of pure line and colour, which, as almost always in Dutch painting, as often also in the works of Titian or Veronese, is quite independent of anything definitely poetical in the subject it accompanies. It is the *drawing*—the design projected from that peculiar pictorial temperament or constitution, in which, while it may possibly be ignorant of true anatomical proportions, all things whatever, all poetry, every idea however abstract or obscure, floats up as a visible scene or image: it is the *colouring*—that weaving as of just perceptible gold threads of light through the dress, the flesh, the atmosphere, in Titian's *Lace-girl*—the staining of the whole fabric of the thing with a new, delightful physical quality. This *drawing,* then—the arabesque traced in the air by Tintoret's flying figures, by Titian's forest branches; this colouring—the magic conditions of light and hue in the atmosphere of Titian's *Lace-girl,* or Rubens's

---

[8] Eighteenth-century historian of classical art.

[9] Italian painter of the Renaissance.

[10] What would now be called the unified sensibility, or the total feeling-thinking man which responds directly to any object, in life or in art. In the next sentence Pater uses simply the term "imagination" for the same thing.

[11] Lessing was a German critic and dramatist of the eighteenth century.

[12] Casuistry is the application of general moral principles to particular cases of conscience or conduct.

Descent from the Cross:[13]—these essential pictorial qualities must first of all delight the sense, delight it as directly and sensuously as a fragment of Venetian glass; and through this delight only be the medium of whatever poetry or science may lie beyond them, in the intention of the composer. In its primary aspect, a great picture has no more definite message for us than an accidental play of sunlight and shadow for a moment, on the wall or floor: is itself, in truth, a space of such fallen light, caught as the colours are caught in an Eastern carpet, but refined upon, and dealt with more subtly and exquisitely than by nature itself. And this primary and essential condition fulfilled, we may trace the coming of poetry into painting, by fine gradations upwards; from Japanese fan-painting, for instance, where we get, first, only abstract colour; then, just a little interfused sense of the poetry of flowers; then, sometimes, perfect flower-painting; and so, onwards, until in Titian we have, as his poetry in the *Ariadne,* so actually a touch of true childlike humour in the diminutive, quaint figure with its silk gown, which ascends the temple stairs, in his picture of the *Presentation of the Virgin,* at Venice.

But although each art has thus its own specific order of impressions, and an untranslatable charm, while a just apprehension of the ultimate differences of the arts is the beginning of aesthetic criticism; yet it is noticeable that, in its special mode of handling its given material, each art may be observed to pass into the condition of some other art, by what German critics term an *Anders-streben*—a partial alienation from its own limitations, by which the arts are able, not indeed to supply the place of each other, but reciprocally to lend each other new forces.

Thus some of the most delightful music seems to be always approaching to figure, to pictorial definition. Architecture, again, though it has its own laws —laws esoteric enough, as the true architect knows only too well—yet sometimes aims at fulfilling the conditions of a picture, as in the *Arena* chapel;[14] or of sculpture, as in the flawless unity of Giotto's tower at Florence; and often finds a true poetry, as in those strangely twisted staircases of the *châteaux* of the country of the Loire,[15] as if it were intended that among their odd turnings the actors in a wild life might pass each other unseen: there being a poetry

also of memory and of the mere effect of time, by which it often profits greatly. Thus, again, sculpture aspires out of the hard limitation of pure form towards colour, or its equivalent; poetry also, in many ways, finding guidance from the other arts, the analogy between a Greek tragedy and a work of Greek sculpture, between a sonnet and a relief, of French poetry generally with the art of engraving, being more than mere figures of speech; and all the arts in common aspiring towards the principle of music; music being the typical, or ideally consummate art, the object of the great *Anders-streben* of all art, of all that is artistic, or partakes of artistic qualities.

All art constantly aspires towards the condition of music. For while in all other works of art it is possible to distinguish the matter from the form, and the understanding can always make this distinction, yet it is the constant effort of art to obliterate it. That the mere matter of a poem, for instance—its subject, its given incidents or situation; that the mere matter of a picture—the actual circumstances of an event, the actual topography of a landscape—should be nothing without the form, the spirit, of the handling; that this form, this mode of handling, should become an end in itself, should penetrate every part of the matter: —this is what all art constantly strives after, and achieves in different degrees.

This abstract language becomes clear enough, if we think of actual examples. In an actual landscape we see a long white road, lost suddenly on the hillverge. That is the matter of one of the etchings of M. Legros:[16] only, in this etching, it is informed by an indwelling solemnity of expression, seen upon it or half-seen, within the limits of an exceptional moment, or caught from his own mood perhaps, but which he maintains as the very essence of the thing, throughout his work. Sometimes a momentary tint of stormy light may invest a homely or too familiar scene with a character which might well have been drawn from the deep places of the imagination. Then we might say that this particular effect of light, this sudden inweaving of gold thread through the texture of the haystack, and the poplars, and the grass, gives the scene artistic qualities; that it is like a picture. And such tricks of circumstance are commonest in landscape which has little salient character of its own; because, in such scenery, all the material details are so easily absorbed by that informing expression of passing light, and elevated, throughout their whole extent, to a new and delightful effect by it. And hence the superiority, for most conditions of the picturesque,

---

[13] Titian, Veronese, and Tintoretto were Italian painters of the Renaissance; Rubens was a Flemish painter of the seventeenth century.

[14] In Padua, Italy.

[15] The valley of the Loire river in France.

[16] Alphonse Legros, a French artist of the nineteenth century.

of a river-side in France to a Swiss valley, because, on the French river-side, mere topography, the simple material, counts for so little, and, all being so pure, untouched, and tranquil in itself, mere light and shade have such easy work in modulating it to one dominant tone. The Venetian landscape, on the other hand, has in its material conditions much which is hard, or harshly definite; but the masters of the Venetian school have shown themselves little burdened by them. Of its Alpine background they retain certain abstracted elements only, of cool colour and tranquillising line; and they use its actual details, the brown windy turrets, the straw-coloured fields, the forest arabesques, but as the notes of a music which duly accompanies the presence of their men and women, presenting us with the spirit or essence only of a certain sort of landscape—a country of the pure reason or half-imaginative memory.

Poetry, again, works with words addressed in the first instance to the mere intelligence; and it deals, most often, with a definite subject or situation. Sometimes it may find a noble and quite legitimate function in the expression of moral or political aspiration, as often in the poetry of Victor Hugo.[17] In such instances it is easy enough for the understanding to distinguish between the matter and the form, however much the matter, the subject, the element which is addressed to the mere intelligence, has been penetrated by the informing, artistic spirit. But the ideal types of poetry are those in which this distinction is reduced to its *minimum*; so that lyrical poetry, precisely because in it we are least able to detach the matter from the form, without a deduction of something from that matter itself, is, at least artistically, the highest and most complete form of poetry. And the very perfection of such poetry often seems to depend, in part, on a certain suppression or vagueness of mere subject, so that the meaning reaches us through ways not distinctly traceable by the understanding, as in some of the most imaginative compositions of William Blake, and often in Shakspere's songs, as pre-eminently in that song of Mariana's page in *Measure for Measure,* in which the kindling force and poetry of the whole play seems to pass for a moment into an actual strain of music.

And this principle holds good of all things that partake in any degree of artistic qualities, of the furniture of our houses, and of dress, for instance, of life itself, of gesture and speech, and the details of daily intercourse; these also, for the wise, being susceptible of a suavity and charm, caught from the way in which they are done, which gives them a worth in themselves; wherein, indeed, lies what is valuable and justly attractive, in what is called the fashion of a time, which elevates the trivialities of speech, and manner, and dress, into "ends in themselves," and gives them a mysterious grace and attractiveness in the doing of them.

Art, then, is thus always striving to be independent of the mere intelligence, to become a matter of pure perception, to get rid of its responsibilities to its subject or material; the ideal examples of poetry and painting being those in which the constituent elements of the composition are so welded together, that the material or subject no longer strikes the intellect only; nor the form, the eye or the ear only; but form and matter, in their union or identity, present one single effect to the "imaginative reason," that complex faculty for which every thought and feeling is twin-born with its sensible analogue or symbol.

It is the art of music which most completely realises this artistic ideal, this perfect identification of form and matter. In its ideal, consummate moments, the end is not distinct from the means, the form from the matter, the subject from the expression; they inhere in and completely saturate each other; and to it, therefore, to the condition of its perfect moments, all the arts may be supposed constantly to tend and aspire. Music, then, and not poetry, as is so often supposed, is the true type or measure of perfected art. Therefore, although each art has its incommunicable element, its untranslatable order of impressions, its unique mode of reaching the "imaginative reason," yet the arts may be represented as continually struggling after the law or principle of music, to a condition which music alone completely realises; and one of the chief functions of aesthetic criticism, dealing with the products of art, new or old, is to estimate the degree in which each of those products approaches, in this sense, to musical law. . . .

CONCLUSION

Λέγει που Ἡράκλειτος ὅτι πάντα χωρεῖ καὶ οὐδὲν μένει.[18]

To regard all things and principles of things as inconstant modes or fashions has more and more become the tendency of modern thought. Let us

---

17 French novelist and poet (1802–85) who was a passionate liberal in politics.

18 "Heraclitus says, 'All things give way; nothing remaineth' " (Pater's translation of a remark by Socrates in Plato's *Cratylus*).

begin with that which is without—our physical life. Fix upon it in one of its more exquisite intervals, the moment, for instance, of delicious recoil from the flood of water in summer heat. What is the whole physical life in that moment but a combination of natural elements to which science gives their names? But those elements, phosphorus and lime and delicate fibres, are present not in the human body alone: we detect them in places most remote from it. Our physical life is a perpetual motion of them—the passage of the blood, the waste and repairing of the lenses of the eye, the modification of the tissues of the brain under every ray of light and sound—processes which science reduces to simpler and more elementary forces. Like the elements of which we are composed, the action of these forces extends beyond us: it rusts iron and ripens corn. Far out on every side of us those elements are broadcast, driven in many currents; and birth and gesture and death and the springing of violets from the grave are but a few out of ten thousand resultant combinations. That clear, perpetual outline of face and limb is but an image of ours, under which we group them—a design in a web, the actual threads of which pass out beyond it. This at least of flame-like our life has, that it is but the concurrence, renewed from moment to moment, of forces parting sooner or later on their ways.

Or, if we begin with the inward world of thought and feeling, the whirlpool is still more rapid, the flame more eager and devouring. There it is no longer the gradual darkening of the eye, the gradual fading of colour from the wall—movements of the shore-side, where the water flows down indeed, though in apparent rest—but the race of the mid-stream, a drift of momentary acts of sight and passion and thought. At first sight experience seems to bury us under a flood of external objects, pressing upon us with a sharp and importunate reality, calling us out of ourselves in a thousand forms of action. But when re-flexion begins to play upon those objects they are dissipated under its influence; the cohesive force seems suspended like some trick of magic; each object is loosed into a group of impressions—colour, odour, texture—in the mind of the observer. And if we continue to dwell in thought on this world, not of objects in the solidity with which language invests them, but of impressions, unstable, flickering, in-consistent, which burn and are extinguished with our consciousness of them, it contracts still further: the whole scope of observation is dwarfed into the narrow chamber of the individual mind. Experience, already reduced to a group of impressions, is ringed round for each one of us by that thick wall of per-

sonality through which no real voice has ever pierced on its way to us, or from us to that which we can only conjecture to be without. Every one of those impressions is the impression of the individual in his isolation, each mind keeping as a solitary prisoner its own dream of a world. Analysis goes a step farther still, and assures us that those impressions of the individual mind to which, for each one of us, experience dwindles down, are in perpetual flight; that each of them is limited by time, and that as time is infinitely divisible, each of them is infinitely divisible also; all that is actual in it being a single moment, gone while we try to apprehend it, of which it may ever be more truly said that it has ceased to be than that it is. To such a tremulous wisp constantly re-forming itself on the stream, to a single sharp impression, with a sense in it, a relic more or less fleeting, of such moments gone by, what is real in our life fines itself down. It is with this movement, with the passage and dissolution of impressions, images, sensations, that analysis leaves off—that continual vanishing away, that strange, perpetual weaving and unweaving of ourselves.

Philosophiren, says Novalis, *ist dephlegmatisiren, vivificiren.*[19] The service of philosophy, of speculative culture, towards the human spirit, is to rouse, to startle it to a life of constant and eager observation. Every moment some form grows perfect in hand or face; some tone on the hills or the sea is choicer than the rest; some mood of passion or insight or intellectual excitement is irresistibly real and attractive to us, —for that moment only. Not the fruit of experience, but experience itself, is the end. A counted number of pulses only is given to us of a variegated, dramatic life. How may we see in them all that is to be seen in them by the finest senses? How shall we pass most swiftly from point to point, and be present always at the focus where the greatest number of vital forces unite in their purest energy?

To burn always with this hard, gemlike flame, to maintain this ecstasy, is success in life. In a sense it might even be said that our failure is to form habits: for, after all, habit is relative to a stereotyped world, and meantime it is only the roughness of the eye that makes any two persons, things, situations, seem alike. While all melts under our feet, we may well grasp at any exquisite passion, or any contribution to knowl-edge that seems by a lifted horizon to set the spirit free for a moment, or any stirring of the senses, strange dyes, strange colours, and curious odours, or

---

19 "To philosophize is to cast off inertia, to make oneself alive." Novalis was a German writer of the Romantic school.

work of the artist's hands, or the face of one's friend. Not to discriminate every moment some passionate attitude in those about us, and in the very brilliancy of their gifts some tragic dividing of forces on their ways, is, on this short day of frost and sun, to sleep before evening. With this sense of the splendour of our experience and of its awful brevity, gathering all we are into one desperate effort to see and touch, we shall hardly have time to make theories about the things we see and touch. What we have to do is to be for ever curiously testing new opinions and courting new impressions, never acquiescing in a facile orthodoxy of Comte, or of Hegel,[20] or of our own. Philosophical theories or ideas, as points of view, instruments of criticism, may help us to gather up what might otherwise pass unregarded by us. "Philosophy is the microscope of thought." The theory or idea or system which requires of us the sacrifice of any part of this experience, in consideration of some interest into which we cannot enter, or some abstract theory we have not identified with ourselves, or of what is only conventional, has no real claim upon us.

One of the most beautiful passages of Rousseau is that in the sixth book of the *Confessions,* where he describes the awakening in him of the literary sense. An undefinable taint of death had clung always about

him, and now in early manhood he believed himself smitten by mortal disease. He asked himself how he might make as much as possible of the interval that remained; and he was not biassed by anything in his previous life when he decided that it must be by intellectual excitement, which he found just then in the clear, fresh writings of Voltaire. Well! we are all *condamnés,* as Victor Hugo says: we are all under sentence of death but with a sort of indefinite reprieve —*les hommes sont tous condamnés à mort avec des sursis indéfinis:* we have an interval, and then our place knows us no more. Some spend this interval in listlessness, some in high passions, the wisest, at least among "the children of this world," in art and song. For our one chance lies in expanding that interval, in getting as many pulsations as possible into the given time. Great passions may give us this quickened sense of life, ecstasy and sorrow of love, the various forms of enthusiastic activity, disinterested or otherwise, which come naturally to many of us. Only be sure it is passion—that it does yield you this fruit of a quickened, multiplied consciousness. Of such wisdom, the poetic passion, the desire of beauty, the love of art for its own sake, has most. For art comes to you proposing frankly to give nothing but the highest quality to your moments as they pass, and simply for those moments' sake.

Gerard Manley Hopkins

1844–1889

HOPKINS was born near London in 1844, the son of highly educated parents who had active interests in politics, philosophy, and art, and who were moderate Anglicans in religion. Early in life the boy's temperament showed the marked influence of Romanticism: a sensitive and almost ecstatic love of beauty, especially in nature, and a beauty full of rich and sensuous color; a fascinated interest in whatever was "counter, original, spare, strange" (see "Pied Beauty"); and a passion for individuality (he spoke later of "my consciousness and feeling of myself, that taste of myself, . . . more distinctive than the smell of walnutleaf or camphor"). We could predict a romantic poet of nature with a marked strain of originality in perception and in form.

After attending boarding school at Highgate, Hopkins matriculated at Balliol College, Oxford, in 1863, and was

plunged into the violent religious controversy of the time and the place. The rival parties were led by Benjamin Jowett, the Broad Church Liberal, and Dr. Pusey, the High Church Anglican who had joined Keble and Newman a generation earlier to support the Oxford Movement. As one could have anticipated, it was the latter that claimed Hopkins's allegiance, partly because of the aesthetic appeal of its ritual and architecture, but partly, one suspects, because its ascetic practices and its authoritarian principles offered his insistent ego exactly the discipline and control he felt it most needed. His reading in 1864 of Newman's *Apologia pro Vita Sua,* explaining and defending the famous conversion to Rome, and his subsequent conversations with Newman himself at Birmingham, prepared the way for Hopkins's own conversion in 1866. Two years later he entered the Society of Jesus. He spent the rest of his short life serving his Order in various ways, most notably by missionary work in the slums of Liverpool and by teaching at Dublin, where

---

[20] French and German philosophers who each erected a large philosophic system purporting to be all-inclusive and final.

he was Professor of Classics in the new Catholic university.

When Hopkins entered the Jesuit Order in 1868, he burned most of his early verse and "resolved to write no more, as not belonging to my profession, unless it were by the wish of my superiors." Seven years later when he was asked to write an ode in memory of five Franciscan nuns who had been drowned at sea, his "Wreck of the Deutschland" revealed an original poet of major quality—indeed, its style was so new and unconventional that the editors of *The Month*, a Jesuit periodical to which Hopkins sent his manuscript, "dared not print it." Since this was the first poem written in his highly personal manner (the early verse is largely derivative, from Keats and George Herbert), it seems likely that the rigidly disciplined life of his Order, which Hopkins welcomed, surely, as an imperative check to his own *self*-indulgence, produced an indirect reaction in his verse. When his romantic ego was brought to heel in his vocation, it asserted itself all the more strongly in his avocation. Moreover, when Bridges told him to imitate classical poetry, Hopkins answered that "the effect of studying masterpieces is to make me admire and do otherwise. So it must be on every original artist to some degree, on me to a marked degree. Perhaps then more reading would only *refine my singularity,* which is not what you want." But his religious life was marked by entire and willing submission to traditional authority.

The poems which he felt free to compose, after writing the "Deutschland," are few in number and short, a handful of sonnets and lyrics. He could not find it in his conscience to spend time on poetry, nor did the pressure of his clerical work leave him leisure or creative energy for much composition. None of his verse was published during his lifetime, but he sent the manuscripts to his friend Robert Bridges, so that "if anyone should like, they might be published after my death." But Bridges, concluding that the public would be as much offended as he was by Hopkins's lack of literary decorum, did not print the *Poems of Gerard Manley Hopkins* until 1918. Even then the edition of 750 copies took ten years to sell out. But when the next printing appeared in 1930, it was gone in five months, and Hopkins rose suddenly to the rank of major Victorian poet. Or rather, modern poet. He began to appear in anthologies of twentieth-century verse, to be discussed in studies of contemporary poetry. By 1934 he was being called the "forerunner of the postwar poets, the first 'modern' poet, and a most evident link between them and Donne."

But if this is true (in ways to be considered in a moment), it is also true that much of Hopkins's work seems far from modern. One of his most characteristic poems begins:

Earnest, earthless, equal, attuneable, vaulty, voluminous, . . . stupendous
Evening strains to be time's vast, womb-of-all, home-of-all, hearse-of-all night.
Her fond yellow hornlight wound to the west, her wild hollow hoarlight hung to the height
Waste; her earliest stars, earl-stars, stars principal, overbend us,
Fire-featuring heaven.

This is no more like Donne than it is like Eliot. If anything, it suggests the musical art of Swinburne with its pronounced play of assonance and rime. But fundamentally it is unlike anyone else, a thing all its own, curious and strange in both imagery and rhythm. The first and often unfavorable impression which Hopkins makes is that of a poet straining for originality and succeeding only in being eccentric. But we must remember his answer to a friend who protested against the singularity of his style, that it was the spontaneous expression of his poetical feeling.

This is largely, if not wholly, true. Hopkins by nature saw things in a highly individual way. He had a passion for what he called "inscape," for the special individualizing quality which distinguishes one particular object or person or emotion from all other similar objects, persons, or emotions; and at the same time, a passion for "instress," the special individual response which the inscape of that object, person, or emotion awakened in him. In both respects (illustrated in "Henry Purcell") this is a romantic passion for what is singular and unique—and therefore rightly and inevitably to be expressed in a highly original style. The proof of this is in the reading. What at first seems merely eccentric is discovered, on further study, to carry a strange but entirely accurate perception. One passes through the image to an "idea" one can imaginatively grasp. You must not, he told Bridges, dismiss novelty and boldness offhand as affectation; and again, if the meaning is dark on first reading, see if it does not presently explode.

But sometimes the explosion never occurs. That was certain to be the case, given Hopkins's desire to capture the special and ultimate quality of every experience. He knew that no ordinary word would do. He had to find a unique expression for a unique emotion. And sometimes he failed to match the two. The strange image or the strange rhythm is not the right one, or at any rate not one which the average reader can assimilate. Instead of passing through it to a valid perception, he is simply stopped. "It is the vice of distinctiveness to become queer. This vice I cannot have escaped." But the instances grow fewer on every reading; the sense of oddness disappears as one catches Hopkins's angle of vision and shares his intuition.

In a similar fashion we modify our first impression that his art is largely verbal. There is no doubt that Hopkins was much attracted to the sensuous diction and the musical harmonies of Tennyson and the Pre-Raphaelites. His letters praise the popular poets of the day for their "poetical impetus, and . . . richness of diction," and Swinburne in particular for the extraordinary music of his words and his mastery of "a poetical dialect so ornate and continuously beautiful." Just as Pater was saying that poetry should aspire "towards the condition of music" (see pp. 819 f.), Hopkins was writing in his *Notebooks,* "Poetry is speech framed for contemplation of the mind by the way of hearing, or speech framed to be heard for its own sake and interest over and above its interest of meaning." This tendency to make prosody a primary end instead of a functional part can be seen at the close of the octave of "Spring" and in the opening lines of "Spelt from Sibyl's Leaves." On the other hand, the letters criticize contemporary poetry not only for the use of archaic and Elizabethan diction but for weakness "in thought and insight." And Swinburne is blamed for "a perpetual functioning of genius without truth, feeling, or any adequate matter to be at function on." The effect is extraordinary, "but words only are only words." The fact is that Hopkins's serious concern with religious experience, together with his personal suffering during the final years of his life, made a primarily verbal art simply impossible. The depth and intensity of his feeling brought all his technical skill to bear organically on its expression.

At its best, indeed, his style is not musical but dramatic. The diction, though it departs widely from current idiom, as Shakespeare's does, is a living diction, capable of great psychological precision, and without sacrifice of the evocative and sensuous effects of a lyrical vocabulary. His Sprung Rhythm (an accentual verse in which the foot varies from one to four syllables) was founded on common speech, as he himself explained by citing nursery rimes like "*Díng, dóng, béll; Pússy's ín the wéll; Whó pút* her ín? Líttle Jóhnny Thín." But like that example, it retained the movement of song. What he wanted to achieve was a metric flexible enough to catch the shifting emotions of felt experience and yet rhythmical enough to retain an incantatory effect; or, in his own words, he wanted to combine "markedness of rhythm—that is rhythm's self— and naturalness of expression." If the first two lines of "Spring and Fall" are lyrical and the next two dramatic, those that follow are precisely the fusion which Hopkins aimed at, in which the speaking voice is mounted, so to speak, on a singing base. In the same way his pronounced use of alliteration, assonance, and internal rime serves a dramatic purpose over and above its musical effect. In the closing couplet of "Spring and Fall," both the "b" and the "m" alliterations, as well as the rime, enforce the irony.

When Hopkins spoke of masterly execution as the artist's most essential quality, he defined it as "the begetting one's thought on paper, on verse," and went on to insist that "the life must be conveyed into the work and displayed there, not suggested as having been in the artist's mind." It is this power of dramatic realization, which is only possible in a living speech, that makes his poetry superior to most Victorian verse, and connects it with modern art. Indeed, his ability to do this in a medium that retains the sensuous and evocative element in Elizabethan and Romantic poetry is found in various contemporary poets, notably Yeats, Frost, and MacNeice. Furthermore, his verse has a density and compression of meaning which is far more modern than Victorian. The merit of a work, he once said, "may lie for one thing in its terseness. It is like a mate which may be given, one way only, in three moves; otherwise, various ways, in many." Hopkins's three-move checkmates are achieved by multiple meaning (cf. note 1, on "God's Grandeur"); by ambiguity of reference, where a phrase is linked grammatically in one way to what precedes it, in another to what follows (cf. "leaves and blooms" in line 6 of "Spring," which are first verbs and then nouns); by the use of ellipsis to suggest the immediacy of actual speech, or to follow and reproduce the very movement of the mind in the act of thought, leaping from image to image, or in the act of perception seizing in a single unity the various facets of observation (a falcon drawn toward and etched against the dappled sky of the morning becomes a "dapple-dawn-drawn falcon"). All these techniques are characteristic of twentieth-century verse. Finally, apart from form, if Hopkins's focus on nature is dated, his concern "with inner division, friction, and psychological complexities in general" has spoken directly to our own time.

This concern is to be traced to his personal life. His last years were filled with intense, if intermittent, suffering. From about 1880, and with increasing frequency, the letters speak of "a wretched state of weakness and weariness," of "a deep fit of nervous prostration" in which "I did not know but I was dying," of "that coffin of weakness and dejection in which I live, without even the hope of change," of "fits of sadness" which, "though they do not affect my judgment, resemble madness." It is hardly surprising that when he caught typhoid fever in June, 1889, he made no effort for his life, and died at the age of forty-five.

The poems, especially the so-called "terrible sonnets" written in the last four years, not only express this suffering in metaphors and rhythms that make its pain tangible (see especially the superb "No worst, there is none");

they also reveal its focal point, an agonizing sense of frustration. "In the life I lead now," he says, "which is one of a continually jaded and harassed mind, if in any leisure I try to do anything [in poetry] I make no way." Or he cries out, "If I could but get on, if I could but produce work I should not mind its being buried, silenced, going no further; but it kills me to be time's eunuch and never to beget." It must not be supposed that it was only the poet who was frustrated. So, to a lesser degree, was the Jesuit priest: "I cannot produce anything at all, not only the luxuries like poetry, but the duties almost of my position." If the sonnet "To R. B." refers to his art, the previous sonnet ("Thou art indeed just, Lord") asks, "Why must disappointment *all* I endeavour end?" and closes with a passionate prayer for God to send his roots rain that he may "breed one work that wakes"—in this context, plainly a Christian work.

Frustration is the normal expression of neurosis, of an inner conflict that is unresolved. Here we are on dangerous ground, since no layman, at any rate, is competent to diagnose Hopkins's illness. One thing is certain. The conflict was not that of the natural man, with his imperious ego and his artistic drive, fighting hopelessly to be free of Catholic and Jesuit bondage. No one can read the letters and imagine for a moment that Hopkins was not a profoundly religious person and a devout Catholic. Indeed, however much he wanted to be himself and to be the poet he knew he was, he wanted far more deeply to be a Christian. If his profession demanded time and energy that he might have given to poetry, if it stood between him and the fame his published work might have won him, if it asked him to submit his mind to orthodox beliefs and ecclesiastical control, he gladly made the sacrifice. But not—much as he wished to—wholeheartedly. "I have never wavered in my vocation," he said, "but I have not lived up to it." In a revealing letter to Dixon, he confessed to the reluctance he had shown in giving up hopes of poetic fame, to "the backward glances I have given with my hand upon the plough," to the "thoughts of vain-glory" which his artistic ambitions had quickened. There was no conflict of decision between religion and art, between the Christian and the Romantic, but there was a conflict of desires. And it was intensified, as the above passage implies, by a sense of guilt. He would gladly have lived all his life, he said, in a monastery and been "busied only with God. But in the midst of outward occupations . . . unhappily the will is entangled, worldly interests freshen, and worldly ambitions revive." This tension, in one form or another, between the Christian-Jesuit and the natural man, either poet or individualist, underlies "The Windhover," where it is momentarily resolved; may well be central in "Spelt from Sibyl's Leaves" (see note 37); and is explicit in milder tones in "My own heart let me more have pity on." No doubt it is not the whole story behind his suffering, but it is plainly an important source of the frustration he felt so keenly and profoundly.

Finally, equally modern in its appeal, there is the subtle and sophisticated attitude toward his suffering which Hopkins adopts. On the one hand, he feels it to be terribly unjust. He who has given his life to God, who has sacrificed so much in His service (parents, wife and children, the career of an artist), is not only desperately unhappy, but thwarted, defeated, in all he endeavors to do. On the other hand, his suffering is rightly and wisely imposed upon him by a just God: it is punishment for his sins, or it is Christian purgation, cleansing him of evil. These attitudes are not held singly in alternation, but at one and the same time. In "Carrion Comfort" and "Thou art indeed just, Lord," this ambivalence, which is as true of human nature on the secular as on the religious level, is rendered with surpassing skill.

Hopkins's poetry is too small in bulk, too narrow in range of observation, perhaps a trifle too strained and highly wrought, to justify calling him a major poet. But nowhere else in the Victorian period, and rarely anywhere else outside *King Lear*, can one find suffering so intensely felt and so poignantly expressed.

The third edition of the *Poems*, edited by W. H. Gardner (1948), is the most complete, in text and notes. Hopkins's *Letters to Robert Bridges*, his *Correspondence* with R. W. Dixon, and the *Further Letters*, . . . *including his Correspondence with Coventry Patmore* (all edited by C. C. Abbott, the first two in 1935, the third in 1938) are not only an invaluable body of information about the man and the poet but also, filled as they are with illuminating observations about English poets and poetry, a distinct contribution to English criticism. Eleanor Ruggles's *Gerard Manley Hopkins* (1944) is a competent biography. *The Kenyon Review* (Summer and Autumn, 1944) published a series of articles by well-known American critics.

The poems below are reprinted by kind permission of the Oxford University Press.

Gerard Manley Hopkins

GOD'S GRANDEUR

The world is charged with the grandeur of God.
It will flame out, like shining from shook foil;[1]
It gathers to a greatness, like the ooze of oil
Crushed.[2] Why do men then now not reck his rod?
Generations have trod, have trod, have trod;   5
And all is seared with trade; bleared, smeared with toil;
And wears man's smudge and shares man's smell: the
      soil
Is bare now, nor can foot feel, being shod.

And for all this, nature is never spent;
There lives the dearest freshness deep down things;   10
And though the last lights off the black West went
Oh, morning, at the brown brink eastward, springs—
Because the Holy Ghost over the bent
World broods with warm breast and with ah! bright
      wings.

SPRING

Nothing is so beautiful as spring—
When weeds, in wheels, shoot long and lovely and lush;
Thrush's eggs look little low heavens, and thrush
Through the echoing timber does so rinse and wring
The ear, it strikes like lightning to hear him sing;   5
The glassy peartree leaves and blooms, they brush
The descending blue; that blue is all in a rush
With richness; the racing lambs too have fair their fling.

What is all this juice and all this joy?
A strain of the earth's sweet being in the beginning   10
In Eden garden.—Have, get, before it cloy,
Before it cloud,[3] Christ, lord,[4] and sour with sinning,
Innocent mind and Mayday in girl and boy,
Most, O maid's child, thy choice and worthy the
      winning.[5]

---

[1] "I mean," said Hopkins (*Letters to Bridges*, p. 169), "foil in its sense of leaf or tinsel. . . . Shaken goldfoil gives off broad glares like sheet lightning and also, . . . owing to its zigzag dints and creasings and network of small many-cornered facets, a sort of fork lightning too."
[2] Crushed from a berry or a leaf, but the simile does not apply very closely to "gathers to a greatness."
[3] The antecedent of "it" is line 10.
[4] These two words are vocatives.
[5] Cf. Newman's sermon on "The Second Spring" (1857), which Hopkins must have known: "How beautiful is the human heart, when it puts forth its first leaves, and opens and rejoices in its spring-tide. Fair as may be the bodily form, fairer far, in its

THE WINDHOVER:

TO CHRIST OUR LORD

I caught this morning morning's minion, king-
dom of daylight's dauphin, dapple-dawn-drawn Falcon,
      in his riding
Of the rolling level underneath him steady air, and
      striding
High there, how he rung upon the rein of a wimpling
      wing[6]
In his ecstasy! then off, off forth on swing,   5
As a skate's heel sweeps smooth on a bow-bend: the
      hurl and gliding
Rebuffed the big wind. My heart in hiding
Stirred for a bird,—the achieve of, the mastery of the
      thing![7]

Brute beauty and valour and act, oh, air, pride, plume,[8]
      here
Buckle! AND the fire that breaks from thee then, a
      billion   10
Times told lovelier, more dangerous, O my chevalier![9]

green foliage and bright blossoms, is natural virtue. It blooms in the young, like some rich flower, so delicate, so fragrant, and so dazzling. . . . And yet, as night follows upon day, as decrepitude follows upon health, so surely are failure, and overthrow, and annihilation, the issue of this natural virtue, if time only be allowed to it to run its course. . . . Let the course of life proceed, let the bright soul go through the fire and water of the world's temptations and seductions and corruptions and transformations; and, alas for the insufficiency of nature! Alas for its powerlessness to persevere, its waywardness in disappointing its own promise!"
[6] In falconry "to ring" means to rise in the air spirally, but this image is combined with that of "ringing a horse," i.e., guiding him in a circle on a long rein. "Wimpling" is turning and twisting.
[7] Cf. Hopkins's letter, written from a Jesuit monastery (*Letters to Dixon*, pp. 75–76): "My mind is here more at peace than it has ever been and I would gladly live all my life, if it were so to be, in as great or a greater seclusion from the world and be busied only with God. But in the midst of outward occupations not only the mind is drawn away from God, . . . but unhappily the will too is entangled, worldly interests freshen, and worldly ambitions revive." The image of the falcon suggests the natural life in all its energy and beauty and freedom.
[8] These terms, in general, carry on the chivalric imagery in lines 1–2, which reappears in line 11; it is particularly appropriate to the heroic Christian life he goes on to describe. "Air" is used in the sense of "peculiar or characteristic appearance, mien, manner," and here suggests the knightly or princely air of the falcon. I take "pride" to mean "proud, chivalric scorn" of everything mean or even earthly.
[9] The "thee" is Christ, my chevalier, but only the Christ that is "realized" in the lives of men, in Hopkins's own life. It therefore really means "one's self as he takes on, or myself as I take on, the heroic Christian character of Christ." (Cf. one of the

No wonder of it: shéer plód makes plough down
    sillion[10]
Shine, and blue-bleak embers, ah my dear,
    Fall, gall themselves, and gash gold-vermillion.[11]

PIED BEAUTY

Glory be to God for dappled things—
    For skies of couple-colour as a brinded[12] cow;
      For rose-moles all in stipple[13] upon trout that swim;
Fresh-firecoal chestnut-falls;[14] finches' wings;
    Landscape plotted and pieced—fold, fallow, and
      plough;   5
    And áll trádes, their gear and tackle and trim.

All things counter,[15] original, spare,[16] strange;
    Whatever is fickle, freckled (who knows how?)
      With swift, slow; sweet, sour; adazzle, dim;
He fathers-forth whose beauty is past change: 10
              Praise him.

---

sonnets—No. 57, 3rd edition—where the just man by the
grace of God
    "Acts in God's eye what in God's eye he is—
    Christ—for Christ plays in ten thousand places,
    Lovely in limbs, and lovely in eyes not his
    To the Father through the features of men's faces.")
"Buckle" is an imperative (Hopkins is talking to himself and
to us). Here in the Christian life, in the priestly vocation, let
one, or/and let me, buckle these heroic qualities together, and
then the Christlike life of spiritual conquest will be far lovelier,
though more dangerous, than any natural life they could inform.
Or, for another possible reading, here in this mortal life or in
the heart (in hiding), let one, or/and let me, buckle (in the
sense of fasten down) these natural energies (under the Christian-
Catholic rule), and then in sublimated form they will burst out
in a Christlike life far lovelier, though more dangerous. (The
second reading is suggested by Gardner, who quotes *Macbeth*:
"He cannot buckle his distempered cause Within the belt of
rule.")   10 The ridge between the furrows.
11 Both metaphors illustrate and apply the thesis of lines 9–11.
Though the Christian life seems to lack the "beauty and valour
and act" of the natural life, it requires and reveals these qualities
in far higher degree. The hard, plodding work of plowing (of
the priest) makes the plowshare shine as it goes down the row
turning up the sillion. When embers, blue-bleak on the outside,
fall and break open (the death of martyrdom is implied), they
show forth a magnificent brightness (in the glory of martyrdom,
"gold-vermillion" suggesting both the blood and the gold
crown of the martyr).
12 Streaked (an early form of "brindled").
13 Method in painting of applying colors in dots.
14 Chestnuts without their husks.
15 Opposite to what is expected, or to the ordinary run of things.
16 Rare.
17 Pronounced *Púr-cell*. An English composer, and a Protestant,
who died in 1695.
18 Hopkins explained (*Letters to Bridges*, p. 171) that he meant,
May fair fortune have befallen Henry Purcell.

HENRY PURCELL[17]

The poet wishes well to the divine genius of Purcell and praise
him that, whereas other musicians have given utterance to the
moods of man's mind, he has, beyond that, uttered in notes the
very make and species of man as created both in him and in all
men generally.

Have fair fallen, O fair, fair have fallen,[18] so dear
To me, so arch-especial a spirit as heaves in Henry
    Purcell,
An age is now since passed, since parted; with the
    reversal
Of the outward sentence low lays him, listed to a
    heresy, here.[19]

Not mood in him nor meaning, proud fire or sacred
    fear,   5
Or love or pity or all that sweet notes not his might
    nursle:
It is the forgèd feature finds me; it is the rehearsal
Of own, of abrúpt sélf there so thrusts on, so throngs
    the ear.

Let him oh! with his air of angels then lift me, lay me!
    only I'll
Have an eye to the sakes of him,[20] quaint moonmarks,
    to his pelted plumage under   10
Wings:[21] so some great stormfowl, whenever he has
    walked his while

The thunder-purple seabeach plumèd purple-of-thunder,
If a wuthering of his palmy snow-pinions scatter a
    colossal smile
Off him, but meaning motion fans fresh our wits with
    wonder.[22]

19 *Letters to Bridges*, pp. 170–171: "May Purcell, O may he have
died a good death and that soul which I love so much and
which breathes and stirs so unmistakably in his works have
parted from the body and passed away, centuries since though
I frame the wish, in peace with God! so that the heavy condemnation under which he outwardly or nominally lay for
being out of the true Church may in consequence of his good
intentions have been reversed. 'Low lays him' is merely '[which]
lays him low,' that is, strikes him heavily, weighs upon him. . . .
'Listed,' by the by, is 'enlisted.' "
20 The "sakes of him" is his "arch-especial" spirit, his "forgèd
feature," his "own" or "abrupt self," which Hopkins will listen
for, over and above responding to the musical meaning ("his
air of angels").
21 His special individuality is like the special markings, shaped like
a new moon, on the plumage of a stormfowl under his wings.
22 Just as the bird, intending only flight, reveals his moonmarks
(like a "colossal smile" because of their shape) by a wuthering
(fluttering) of his wings as he prepares to take off, so Purcell,
though aiming only to communicate "proud fire or sacred
fear," reveals his own unique character and personality in his
style.

blackened with the swarming ant: a creature so small, so far from us in the hierarchy of brutes, that we can scarce trace and scarce comprehend his doings; and here also, in his ordered polities and rigorous justice, we see confessed the law of duty and the fact of individual sin. Does it stop, then, with the ant? Rather this desire of well-doing and this doom of frailty run through all the grades of life: rather is this earth, from the frosty top of Everest to the next margin of the internal fire, one stage of ineffectual virtues and one temple of pious tears and perseverance. The whole creation groaneth and travaileth together. It is the common and the god-like law of life. The browsers, the biters, the barkers, the hairy coats of field and forest, the squirrel in the oak, the thousand-footed creeper in the dust, as they share with us the gift of life, share with us the love of an ideal: strive like us—like us are tempted to grow weary of the struggle—to do well; like us receive at times un-merited refreshment, visitings of support, returns of courage; and are condemned like us to be crucified between that double law of the members and the will.[7] Are they like us, I wonder, in the timid hope of some reward, some sugar with the drug? do they, too, stand aghast at unrewarded virtues, at the sufferings of those whom, in our partiality, we take to be just, and the prosperity of such as, in our blindness we call wicked? It may be, and yet God knows what they should look for. Even while they look, even while they repent, the foot of man treads them by thou-sands in the dust, the yelping hounds burst upon their trail, the bullet speeds, the knives are heating in the den of the vivisectionist; or the dew falls, and the generation of a day is blotted out. For these are creatures, compared with whom our weakness is strength, our ignorance wisdom, our brief span eternity.

And as we dwell, we living things, in our isle of terror and under the imminent hand of death, God forbid it should be man the erected, the reasoner, the wise in his own eyes—God forbid it should be man that wearies in well-doing, that despairs of un-rewarded effort, or utters the language of complaint. Let it be enough for faith, that the whole creation groans in mortal frailty, strives with unconquerable constancy: surely not all in vain.

THE LANTERN-BEARERS

THESE boys congregated every autumn about a certain easterly fisher-village, where they tasted in a high degree the glory of existence. The place was created seemingly on purpose for the diversion of young gentlemen. A street or two of houses, mostly red and many of them tiled; a number of fine trees clustered about the manse and the kirkyard, and turn-ing the chief street into a shady alley; many little gardens more than usually bright with flowers; nets a-drying, and fisher-wives scolding in the backward parts; a smell of fish, a genial smell of seaweed; whiffs of blowing sand at the street corners; shops with golf-balls and bottled lollipops; another shop with penny pickwicks (that remarkable cigar) and the *London Journal,* dear to me for its startling pic-tures, and a few novels, dear for their suggestive names: such, as well as memory serves me, were the ingredients of the town. These, you are to conceive posted on a spit between two sandy bays, and sparsely flanked with villas—enough for the boys to lodge in with their subsidiary parents, not enough (not yet enough) to cocknify[1] the scene: a haven in the rocks in front: in front of that, a file of grey islets: to the left, endless links[2] and sand-wreaths, a wilderness of hiding-holes, alive with popping rabbits and soaring gulls; to the right, a range of seaward crags, one rug-ged brow beyond another; the ruins of a mighty and ancient fortress on the brink of one; coves between—now charmed into sunshine quiet, now whistling with wind and clamorous with bursting surges; the dens and sheltered hollows redolent of thyme and southernwood, the air at the cliff's edge brisk and clean and pungent of the sea—in front of all, the Bass Rock, tilted seaward like a doubtful bather, the surf ringing it with white, the solan-geese hanging round its summit like a great and glittering smoke. This choice piece of sea-board was sacred, besides, to the wrecker; and the Bass, in the eye of fancy, still flew the colors of King James;[3] and in the ear of fancy the

---

[7] The law of the members is desire; that of the will is control. Cf. Romans 7:23.

[1] To fill with cockney or low-class tourists.

[2] Level or undulating sandy ground near the sea with turf or coarse grass—the type of ground on which golf was originally played and from which the modern golf course has borrowed various features.

[3] This islet at the entrance of the Firth of Forth was held by the followers of James II against William III, 1691–94.

arches of Tantallon[4] still rang with horse-shoe iron, and echoed to the commands of Bell-the-Cat.

There was nothing to mar your days, if you were a boy summering in that part, but the embarrassment of pleasure. You might golf if you wanted; but I seem to have been better employed. You might secrete yourself in the Lady's Walk, a certain sunless dingle of elders, all mossed over by the damp as green as grass, and dotted here and there by the stream-side with roofless walls, the cold homes of anchorites. To fit themselves for life, and with a special eye to acquire the art of smoking, it was even common for the boys to harbor there; and you might have seen a single penny pickwick, honestly shared in lengths with a blunt knife, bestrew the glen with these apprentices. Again, you might join our fishing-parties, where we sat perched as thick as solan-geese, a covey of little anglers, boy and girl, angling over each other's heads, to the much entanglement of lines and loss of podleys and consequent shrill recrimination—shrill as the geese themselves. Indeed, had that been all, you might have done this often; but though fishing be a fine pastime, the podley is scarce to be regarded as a dainty for the table; and it was a point of honor that a boy should eat all that he had taken. Or again, you might climb the Law, where the whale's jawbone stood landmark in the buzzing wind, and behold the face of many counties, and the smoke and spires of many towns, and the sails of distant ships. You might bathe, now in the flaws of fine weather, that we pathetically call our summer, now in a gale of wind, with the sand scourging your bare hide, your clothes thrashing abroad from underneath their guardian stone, the froth of the great breakers casting you headlong ere it had drowned your knees. Or you might explore the tidal rocks, above all in the ebb of spring, when the very roots of the hills were for the nonce discovered; following my leader from one group to another, groping in slippery tangle for the wreck of ships, wading in pools after the abominable creatures of the sea, and ever with an eye cast backward on the march of the tide and the menaced line of your retreat. And then you might go Crusoeing, a word that covers all extempore eating in the open air: digging perhaps a house under the margin of the links, kindling a fire of the sea-ware, and cooking apples there—if they were truly apples, for I sometimes suppose the merchant must have played us off with some inferior and quite local fruit,

capable of resolving, in the neighborhood of fire, into mere sand and smoke and iodine; or perhaps pushing to Tantallon, you might lunch on sandwiches and visions in the grassy court, while the wind hummed in the crumbling turrets; or clambering along the coast, eat geans[5] (the worst, I must suppose, in Christendom) from an adventurous gean-tree that had taken root under a cliff, where it was shaken with an ague of east wind, and silvered after gales with salt, and grew so foreign among its bleak surroundings that to eat of its produce was an adventure in itself.

There are mingled some dismal memories with so many that were joyous. Of the fisher-wife, for instance, who had cut her throat at Canty Bay; and of how I ran with the other children to the top of the Quadrant, and beheld a posse of silent people escorting a cart, and on the cart, bound in a chair, her throat bandaged, and the bandage all bloody— horror!—the fisher-wife herself, who continued thenceforth to hag-ride my thoughts, and even today (as I recall the scene) darkens daylight. She was lodged in the little old jail in the chief street; but whether or no she died there, with a wise terror of the worst, I never inquired. She had been tippling; it was but a dingy tragedy; and it seems strange and hard that, after all these years, the poor crazy sinner should be still pilloried on her cart in the scrap-book of my memory. Nor shall I readily forget a certain house in the Quadrant where a visitor died, and a dark old woman continued to dwell alone with the dead body; nor how this old woman conceived a hatred to myself and one of my cousins, and in the dread hour of the dusk, as we were clambering on the garden-walls, opened a window in that house of mortality and cursed us in a shrill voice and with a marrowy choice of language. It was a pair of very colorless urchins that fled down the lane from this remarkable experience! But I recall with a more doubtful sentiment, compounded out of fear and exultation, the coil of equinoctial tempests; trumpeting squalls, scouring flaws of rain; the boats with their reefed lug-sails scudding for the harbor mouth, where danger lay, for it was hard to make when the wind had any east in it; the wives clustered with blowing shawls at the pier-head, where (if fate was against them) they might see boat and husband and sons—their whole wealth and their whole family—engulfed under their eyes; and (what I saw but once) a troop of neighbors forcing such an unfortunate homeward, and she squalling and battling in their midst, a figure scarcely human, a tragic Maenad.[6]

---

[4] A stronghold of the Douglas family; one of its members, Archibald Douglas (d. 1514), was popularly known as Bell-the-Cat.

[5] Wild cherries.   [6] A frenzied priestess of Bacchus.

These are things that I recall with interest; but what my memory dwells upon the most I have been all this while withholding. It was a sport peculiar to the place, and indeed to a week or so of our two months' holiday there. Maybe it still flourishes in its native spot; for boys and their pastimes are swayed by periodic forces inscrutable to man; so that tops and marbles reappear in their due season, regular like the sun and moon; and the harmless art of knuckle-bones has seen the fall of the Roman Empire and the rise of the United States. It may still flourish in its native spot, but nowhere else, I am persuaded; for I tried myself to introduce it on Tweedside,[7] and was defeated lamentably; its charm being quite local, like a country wine that cannot be exported.

The idle manner of it was this:—

Toward the end of September, when schooltime was drawing near and the nights were already black, we would begin to sally from our respective villas, each equipped with a tin bull's-eye lantern. The thing was so well known that it had worn a rut in the commerce of Great Britain; and the grocers, about the due time, began to garnish their windows with our particular brand of luminary. We wore them buckled to the waist upon a cricket belt, and over them, such was the rigor of the game, a buttoned top-coat. They smelled noisomely of blistered tin; they never burned aright, though they would always burn our fingers; their use was naught; the pleasure of them merely fanciful; and yet a boy with a bull's-eye under his top-coat asked for nothing more. The fishermen used lanterns about their boats, and it was from them, I suppose, that we had got the hint; but theirs were not bull's-eyes, nor did we ever play at being fishermen. The police carried them at their belts, and we had plainly copied them in that; yet we did not pretend to be policemen. Burglars, indeed, we may have had some haunting thoughts of; and we had certainly an eye to past ages when lanterns were more common, and to certain story-books in which we had found them to figure very largely. But take it for all in all, the pleasure of the thing was substantive; and to be a boy with a bull's-eye under his top-coat was good enough for us.

When two of these asses met, there would be an anxious "Have you got your lantern?" and a gratified "Yes!" That was the shibboleth, and very needful too; for, as it was the rule to keep our glory contained, none could recognize a lantern-bearer, unless

(like the pole-cat) by the smell. Four or five would sometimes climb into the belly of a ten-man lugger, with nothing but the thwarts above them—for the cabin was usually locked; or choose out some hollow of the links where the wind might whistle overhead. There the coats would be unbuttoned and the bull's-eye discovered; and in the chequering glimmer, under the huge windy hall of the night, and cheered by a rich steam of toasting tinware, these fortunate young gentlemen would crouch together in the cold sand of the links or on the scaly bilges of the fishing-boat, and delight themselves with inappropriate talk. Woe is me that I may not give some specimens—some of their foresights of life, or deep inquiries into the rudiments of man and nature, these were so fiery and so innocent, they were so richly silly, so romantically young. But the talk, at any rate, was but a condiment; and these gatherings themselves only accidents in the career of the lantern-bearer. The essence of this bliss was to walk by yourself in the black night; the slide shut, the top-coat buttoned; not a ray escaping, whether to conduct your footsteps or to make your glory public; a mere pillar of darkness in the dark; and all the while, deep down in the privacy of your fool's heart, to know you had a bull's-eye at your belt, and to exult and sing over the knowledge.

2

It is said that a poet has died young in the breast of the most stolid. It may be contended, rather, that this (somewhat minor) bard in almost every case survives, and is the spice of life to his possessor. Justice is not done to the versatility and the unplumbed childishness of man's imagination. His life from without may seem but a rude mound of mud; there will be some golden chamber at the heart of it, in which he dwells delighted; and for as dark as his pathway seems to the observer, he will have some kind of a bull's-eye at his belt.

It would be hard to pick out a career more cheerless than that of Dancer, the miser, as he figures in the "Old Bailey Reports,"[8] a prey to the most sordid persecutions, the butt of his neighborhood, betrayed by his hired man, his house beleaguered by the impish school-boy, and he himself grinding and fuming and impotently fleeing to the law against these pin-pricks. You marvel at first that anyone should willingly prolong a life so destitute of charm and dignity; and then you call to memory that had he chosen, had he ceased to be a miser, he could have been freed at once from these trials, and might have

<hr>

[7] By the banks of the Tweed, i.e., even as little as thirty or forty miles away.

[8] Reports of the chief criminal court in London.

built himself a castle and gone escorted by a squadron. For the love of more recondite joys, which we cannot estimate, which, it may be, we should envy, the man had willingly forgone both comfort and consideration. "His mind to him a kingdom was"; and sure enough, digging into that mind, which seems at first a dust-heap, we unearth some priceless jewels. For Dancer must have had the love of power and the disdain of using it, a noble character in itself; disdain of many pleasures, a chief part of what is commonly called wisdom; disdain of the inevitable end, that finest trait of mankind; scorn of men's opinions, another element of virtue; and at the back of all, a conscience just like yours and mine, whining like a cur, swindling like a thimble-rigger,[9] but still pointing (there or thereabout) to some conventional standard. Here were a cabinet portrait to which Hawthorne perhaps had done justice; and yet not Hawthorne either, for he was mildly minded, and it lay not in him to create for us that throb of the miser's pulse, his fretful energy of gusto, his vast arms of ambition clutching in he knows not what: insatiable, insane, a god with a muck-rake. Thus, at least, looking in the bosom of the miser, consideration detects the poet in the full tide of life, with more, indeed, of the poetic fire than usually goes to epics; and tracing that mean man about his cold hearth, and to and fro in his discomfortable house, spies within him a blazing bonfire of delight. And so with others, who do not live by bread alone, but by some cherished and perhaps fantastic pleasure; who are meat salesmen to the external eye, and possibly to themselves are Shakespeares, Napoleons, or Beethovens; who have not one virtue to rub against another in the field of active life, and yet perhaps, in the life of contemplation, sit with the saints. We see them on the street, and we can count their buttons; but Heaven knows in what they pride themselves! Heaven knows where they have set their treasure!

There is one fable that touches very near the quick of life; the fable of the monk who passed into the woods, heard a bird break into song, hearkened for a trill or two, and found himself on his return a stranger at his convent gates; for he had been absent fifty years, and of all his comrades there survived but one to recognize him. It is not only in the woods that this enchanter carols, though perhaps he is native there. He sings in the most doleful places. The miser hears him and chuckles, and the days are moments.

With no more apparatus than an ill-smelling lantern I have evoked him on the naked links. All life that is not merely mechanical is spun out of two strands: seeking for that bird and hearing him. And it is just this that makes life so hard to value, and the delight of each so incommunicable. And just a knowledge of this, and a remembrance of those fortunate hours in which the bird has sung to us, that fills us with such wonder when we turn the pages of the realist. There, to be sure, we find a picture of life in so far as it consists of mud and of old iron, cheap desires and cheap fears, that which we are ashamed to remember and that which we are careless whether we forget; but of the note of that time-devouring nightingale we hear no news.

The case of these writers of romance is most obscure. They have been boys and youths; they have lingered outside the window of the beloved, who was then most probably writing to someone else; they have sat before a sheet of paper, and felt themselves mere continents of congested poetry, not one line of which would flow; they have walked alone in the woods, they have walked in cities under the countless lamps; they have been to sea, they have hated, they have feared, they have longed to knife a man, and maybe done it; the wild taste of life has stung their palate. Or, if you deny them all the rest, one pleasure at least they have tasted to the full—their books are there to prove it—the keen pleasure of successful literary composition. And yet they fill the globe with volumes, whose cleverness inspires me with despairing admiration, and whose consistent falsity to all I care to call existence, with despairing wrath. If I had no better hope than to continue to revolve among the dreary and petty businesses, and to be moved by the paltry hopes and fears with which they surround and animate their heroes, I declare I would die now. But there has never an hour of mine gone quite so dully yet; if it were spent waiting at a railway junction, I would have some scattering thoughts, I could count some grains of memory, compared to which the whole of one of these romances seems but dross.

These writers would retort (if I take them properly) that this was very true; that it was the same with themselves and other persons of (what they call) the artistic temperament; that in this we were exceptional, and should apparently be ashamed of ourselves; but that our works must deal exclusively with (what they call) the average man, who was a prodigious dull fellow, and quite dead to all but the paltriest considerations. I accept the issue. We can only know others by ourselves. The artistic tempera-

---

[9] A professional cheat at a betting game played with thimbles.

ment (a plague on the expression!) does not make us different from our fellowmen, or it would make us incapable of writing novels; and the average man (a murrain on the word!) is just like you and me, or he would not be average. It was Whitman who stamped a kind of Birmingham sacredness upon the latter phrase;[10] but Whitman knew very well, and showed very nobly, that the average man was full of joys and full of poetry of his own. And this harping on life's dulness and man's meanness is a loud profession of incompetence; it is one of two things; the cry of the blind eye, *I cannot see,* or the complaint of the dumb tongue, *I cannot utter.* To draw a life without delights is to prove I have not realized it. To picture a man without some sort of poetry—well, it goes near to prove my case, for it shows an author may have little enough. To see Dancer only as a dirty, old, small-minded, impotently fuming man, in a dirty house, besieged by Harrow boys, and probably beset by small attorneys, is to show myself as keen an observer as . . . the Harrow boys. But these young gentlemen (with a more becoming modesty) were content to pluck Dancer by the coat-tails; they did not suppose they had surprised his secret or could put him living in a book: and it is there my error would have lain. Or say that in the same romance—I continue to call these books romances, in the hope of giving pain— say that in the same romance, which now begins really to take shape, I should leave to speak of Dancer, and follow instead the Harrow boys; and say that I came on some such business as that of my lantern-bearers on the links; and described the boys as very cold, spat upon by flurries of rain, and drearily surrounded, all of which they were; and their talk as silly and indecent, which it certainly was. I might upon these lines, and had I Zola's[11] genius, turn out, in a page or so, a gem of literary art, render the lantern-light with the touches of a master, and lay on the indecency with the ungrudging hand of love; and when all was done, what a triumph would my picture be of shallowness and dulness! how it would have missed the point! how it would have belied the boys! To the ear of the stenographer, the talk is merely silly and indecent; but ask the boys themselves, and they are discussing (as it is highly proper they should) the possibilities of existence. To the eye of the observer they are wet and cold and drearily surrounded; but ask themselves, and they are in the heaven of

recondite pleasure, the ground of which is an ill-smelling lantern.

3

For, to repeat, the ground of a man's joy is often hard to hit. It may hinge at times upon a mere accessory, like the lantern, it may reside, like Dancer's, in the mysterious inwards of psychology. It may consist with perpetual failure, and find exercise in the continued chase. It has so little bond with externals (such as the observer scribbles in his note-book) that it may even touch them not; and the man's true life, for which he consents to live, lie altogether in the field of fancy. The clergyman, in his spare hours, may be winning battles, the farmer sailing ships, the banker reaping triumph in the arts: all leading another life, plying another trade from that they chose; like the poet's house-builder, who, after all, is cased in stone,

> By his fireside, as impotent fancy prompts,
> Rebuilds it to his liking.

In such a case the poetry runs underground. The observer (poor soul, with his documents!) is all abroad. For to look at the man is but to court deception. We shall see the trunk from which he draws his nourishment; but he himself is above and abroad in the green dome of foliage, hummed through by winds and nested in by nightingales. And the true realism were that of the poets, to climb up after him like a squirrel, and catch some glimpse of the heaven for which he lives. And the true realism, always and everywhere, is that of the poets to find out where joy resides, and give it a voice far beyond singing.

For to miss the joy is to miss all. In the joy of the actors lies the sense of any action. That is the explanation, that the excuse. To one who has not the secret of the lanterns, the scene upon the links is meaningless. And hence the haunting and truly spectral unreality of realistic books. Hence, when we read the English realists, the incredulous wonder with which we observe the hero's constancy under the submerging tide of dulness, and how he bears up with his jibbing sweetheart, and endures the chatter of idiot girls, and stands by his whole unfeatured wilderness of an existence, instead of seeking relief in drink or foreign travel. Hence in the French, in that meat-market of middle-aged sensuality, the disgusted surprise with which we see the hero drift sidelong, and practically quite untempted, into every description of misconduct and dishonor. In each, we miss the personal poetry, the enchanted atmosphere, that rainbow work of fancy that clothes what is

---

[10] Gave the phrase the sanction of middle-class respectability.
[11] Émile Zola (1840–1902), the principal figure in the French school of naturalism.

naked and seems to ennoble what is base; in each, life falls dead like dough, instead of soaring away like a balloon into the colors of the sunset; each is true, each inconceivable; for no man lives in the external truth, among salts and acids, but in the warm, phantasmagoric chamber of his brain, with the painted windows and the storied walls.

Of this falsity we have had a recent example from a man who knows far better—Tolstoy's *Powers of Darkness.* Here is a piece full of force and truth, yet quite untrue. For before Mikita was led into so dire a situation he was tempted, and temptations are beautiful at least in part; and a work which dwells on the ugliness of crime and gives no hint of any loveliness in the temptation, sins against the modesty of life, and even when a Tolstoy writes it, sinks to melodrama. The peasants are not understood; they saw their life in fairer colors; even the deaf girl was clothed in poetry for Mikita, or he had never fallen. And so, once again, even an Old Bailey melodrama, without some brightness of poetry and luster of existence, falls into the inconceivable and ranks with fairy tales.

4

In nobler books we are moved with something like the emotions of life; and this emotion is very variously provoked. We are so moved when Levine labors in the field,[12] when André sinks beyond emotion,[13] when Richard Feverel and Lucy Desborough meet beside the river,[14] when Antony, "not cowardly, puts off his helmet,"[15] when Kent has infinite pity on the dying Lear, when, in Dostoieffsky's *Despised and Rejected,* the uncomplaining hero drains his cup of suffering and virtue. These are notes that please the great heart of man. Not only love, and the fields, and the bright face of danger, but sacrifice and death and unmerited suffering humbly supported, touch in us the vein of the poetic. We love to think of them, we long to try them, we are humbly hopeful that we may prove heroes also.

We have heard, perhaps, too much of lesser matters. Here is the door, here is the open air.

Itur in antiquam silvam.[16]

---

12 In Tolstoy's *Anna Karenina.*
13 In Tolstoy's *War and Peace.*
14 In Meredith's *The Ordeal of Richard Feverel.*
15 In Shakespeare's *Antony and Cleopatra.*
16 Let us go into the ancient wood.

SING ME A SONG

Sing me a song of a lad that is gone,
  Say, could that lad be I?
Merry of soul he sailed on a day
  Over the sea to Skye.[1]

Mull was astern, Rum on the port,
  Egg on the starboard bow;
Glory of youth glowed in his soul:
  Where is that glory now?

Sing me a song of a lad that is gone,
  Say, could that lad be I?
Merry of soul he sailed on a day
  Over the sea to Skye.

Give me again all that was there,
  Give me the sun that shone!
Give me the eyes, give me the soul,
  Give me the lad that's gone!

Sing me a song of a lad that is gone,
  Say, could that lad be I?
Merry of soul he sailed on a day
  Over the sea to Skye.

Billow and breeze, islands and seas,
  Mountains of rain and sun,
All that was good, all that was fair,
  All that was me is gone.

REQUIEM[2]

Under the wide and starry sky,
Dig the grave and let me lie.
Glad did I live and gladly die,
  And I laid me down with a will.

This be the verse you grave for me:
*Here he lies where he longed to be;
Home is the sailor, home from sea,
  And the hunter home from the hill.*

---

1 Skye is an island off the west coast of Scotland. To reach it from the mainland one passes the islands of Mull, Rum, and Egg (Eigg).
2 This poem is inscribed on Stevenson's gravestone.

A Group of Lesser Victorians

Elizabeth Barrett Browning

1806–1861

THE tremendous acclaim with which the poetry of Elizabeth Barrett Browning was received during her lifetime—greater than that accorded to her husband—was undoubtedly due to a deep and widely felt desire of her contemporaries for moral inspiration and guidance. She herself felt keenly that the poet should be a person apart, the mouthpiece of divine wisdom and truth. In her poem "The Dead Pan" she explicitly outlines the proper subjects of poetry and the mission of the poet:

> What is true and just and honest,
> What is lovely, what is pure . . .
> O brave poets . . .
> Look up Godward; speak the truth in
> Worthy song from earnest soul!

In "A Musical Instrument" she implicitly describes the poet as the reed in the service of divinity. In similar vein she speaks of Wordsworth, in the sonnet on his portrait by Haydon, as "poet-priest."

Her own talent, which was early apparent, was fostered by an unusually fine education in both classical and modern literatures, and was further developed during years of invalidism by wide reading. All of this, quite naturally, is reflected in her poetry, but less to be expected from one who was so isolated, at least before her marriage to Robert Browning in 1846, was her passionate interest in various humanitarian causes of the period, such as the amelioration of child labor and the abolition of slavery. When she had married and was living in Italy, she fervently championed Italian liberation from Austria and unity under an Italian ruler, conceiving of herself as an anointed spokesman for justice.

However, it is not by her humanitarian and political poems that Mrs. Browning's reputation survives. They were too often marred by redundancy, a kind of patent overelaboration of ideas, and by a self-conscious didacticism which makes them seem to come more from the preacher than from the poet. Where she did excel was in the expression of personal experience, particularly in that series of sonnets where under the transparent fiction of a Portuguese troubadour she expressed her own feelings during the time of her courtship by Browning. Here where she was really addressing herself only to her lover—she had not originally intended the sonnets for publication—we find direct and moving expressions of her woman's love, analyzed with a detail and described with a freedom unusual for the age and untouched by any sense of poetic or moralistic mission. This is not to say that *Sonnets from the Portuguese* gives a realistic description of love; rather it is the characteristically idealized view of a period in which very gradually, and for the most part unconsciously, perfect love for another human being came to take the place of love for the Divine Being, who was becoming more and more remote.

Mrs. Browning's poetry appears in her *Complete Works,* edited by C. Porter and H. A. Clark (6 vols., 1900). For her biography one may consult Osbert Burdett, *The Brownings* (1929), and Virginia Woolf, *Flush: A Biography* (1933). A critical estimate of her work is given by Sir Henry Jones, "Robert Browning and Elizabeth Barrett Browning," in *The Cambridge History of English Literature,* vol. XIII (1917).

A MUSICAL INSTRUMENT

What was he doing, the great god Pan,
   Down in the reeds by the river?
Spreading ruin and scattering ban,
Splashing and paddling with hoofs of a goat,
And breaking the golden lilies afloat   5
   With the dragon-fly on the river.

He tore out a reed, the great god Pan
   From the deep cool bed of the river:
The limpid water turbidly ran,
And the broken lilies a-dying lay,   10
And the dragon-fly had fled away,
   Ere he brought it out of the river.

High on the shore sat the great god Pan
   While turbidly flowed the river;
And hacked and hewed as a great god can,   15
With his hard bleak steel at the patient reed,
Till there was not a sign of the leaf indeed
   To prove it fresh from the river.

He cut it short, did the great god Pan,
   (How tall it stood in the river!)   20
Then drew the pith, like the heart of a man,
Steadily from the outside ring,
And notched the poor dry empty thing
   In holes, as he sat by the river.

"This is the way," laughed the great god Pan   25
    (Laughed while he sat by the river),
"The only way, since gods began
To make sweet music, they could succeed."
Then, dropping his mouth to a hole in the reed,
    He blew in power by the river.   30

    Sweet, sweet, sweet, O Pan!
      Piercing sweet by the river!
Blinding sweet, O great god Pan!
The sun on the hill forgot to die,
And the lilies revived, and the dragon-fly   35
    Came back to dream on the river.

    Yet half a beast is the great god Pan,
      To laugh as he sits by the river,
Making a poet out of a man:
The true gods sigh for the cost and pain,—   40
For the reed which grows nevermore again
    As a reed with the reeds in the river.

ON A PORTRAIT OF WORDSWORTH
BY B. R. HAYDON[1]

Wordsworth upon Helvellyn![2] Let the cloud
Ebb audibly along the mountain-wind,
Then break against the rock, and show behind
The lowland valleys floating up to crowd
The sense with beauty. He with forehead bowed   5
And humble-lidded eyes, as one inclined
Before the sovran thought of his own mind,
And very meek with inspirations proud,
Takes here his rightful place as poet-priest
By the high altar, singing prayer and prayer   10
To the higher Heavens. A nobler vision free
Our Haydon's hand has flung out from the mist:
No portrait this, with Academic air!
This is the poet and his poetry.

GRIEF

I tell you, hopeless grief is passionless;
That only men incredulous of despair,
Half-taught in anguish, through the midnight air
Beat upward to God's throne in loud access

Of shrieking and reproach. Full desertness,   5
In souls as countries, lieth silent-bare
Under the blanching, vertical eye-glare
Of the absolute Heavens. Deep-hearted man, express
Grief for thy Dead in silence like to death—
Most like a monumental statue set   10
In everlasting watch and moveless woe
Till itself crumble to the dust beneath.
Touch it; the marble eyelids are not wet:
If it could weep, it could arise and go.

SONNETS FROM THE PORTUGUESE[3]

I

I thought once how Theocritus[4] had sung
Of the sweet years, the dear and wished-for years,
Who each one in a gracious hand appears
To bear a gift for mortals, old or young;
And, as I mused it in his antique tongue,   5
I saw, in gradual vision through my tears,
The sweet, sad years, the melancholy years,
Those of my own life, who by turns had flung
A shadow across me. Straightway I was 'ware,
So weeping, how a mystic Shape did move   10
Behind me, and drew me backward by the hair;
And a voice said in mastery, while I strove,—
"Guess now who holds thee?"—"Death," I said. But there,
The silver answer rang,—"Not Death, but Love."

3

Unlike are we, unlike, O princely Heart!
Unlike our uses and our destinies.
Our ministering two angels look surprise
On one another, as they strike athwart
Their wings in passing. Thou, bethink thee, art   5
A guest for queens to social pageantries,
With gages[5] from a hundred brighter eyes
Than tears even can make mine, to play thy part
Of chief musician. What hast thou to do
With looking from the lattice-lights at me,   10
A poor, tired, wandering singer, singing through
The dark, and leaning up a cypress tree?
The chrism[6] is on thine head,—on mine, the dew,—
And Death must dig the level where these agree.

---

[1] Benjamin Robert Haydon (1786–1846), English historical painter, a personal friend of Wordsworth.
[2] A peak in the English Lake Country, a frequent haunt of Wordsworth.

[3] Mrs. Browning was reluctant to publish these sonnets as being too intimate and autobiographical, but when she was persuaded to do so by her husband, she hoped to protect herself by the pretense that they were merely translations from some Portuguese originals.
[4] Greek writer of pastoral poetry in the third century B.C.
[5] Promises.   [6] Consecrated oil used in religious rites.

THE BLESSED DAMOZEL

This painting by D. G. Rossetti, illustrating his own poem (see pp. 771-73), has both the lushness and the story-telling characteristics of much Pre-Raphaelite painting. It was not completed until 1877, thirty years after the poem was written. (Fogg Art Museum, Harvard University, Grenville Lindall Winthrop Collection)

THE DAYS OF CREATION

Three of six panels designed for a church window by Sir Edward Burne-Jones. Burne-Jones's work as a member of William Morris's company of decorative arts had enormous influence on design of all kinds at the end of the nineteenth century. He wrote: "I mean by a picture a beautiful romantic dream of something that never was, never will be. . . ." (1) The creation of trees and plants; (2) of birds and fishes; (3) of Adam and Eve. (Fogg Art Museum, Harvard University, Grenville Lindall Winthrop Collection)

"THE DEFENCE OF GUENEVERE"

As a follower of Pugin and Ruskin in the Gothic revival, William Morris influenced all the decorative arts. His interest in printing and book design dominated his activities during the last years of his life. This edition of his own poem was printed at his private press, the Kelmscott Press, in 1892. (Harvard College Library)

HERE BEGINNETH THE DEFENCE OF GUENEVERE.

BUT, KNOWING NOW THAT THEY WOULD HAVE HER SPEAK, SHE THREW HER WET HAIR BACKWARD FROM HER BROW,
HER HAND CLOSE TO HER MOUTH TOUCHING HER CHEEK,
AS THOUGH SHE HAD HAD THERE A SHAMEFUL BLOW, AND FEELING IT SHAMEFUL TO FEEL OUGHT BUT SHAME ALL THROUGH HER HEART, YET FELT HER CHEEK BURNED SO,
SHE MUST A LITTLE TOUCH IT; LIKE ONE LAME SHE WALKED AWAY FROM GAUWAINE, WITH HER HEAD

WILLIAM MORRIS'S RED HOUSE, BEXLEY, KENT

The use of brick, the irregular plan, the steep roof were all unusual at the time the house was built (1860). The architect was Philip Webb. Furniture, decorations, and all household utensils were specially designed by Morris himself. Rossetti called the house "more a poem than a house." The location was unhealthy and Morris moved in 1865. (National Buildings Record)

4

Thou hast thy calling to some palace floor,
Most gracious singer of high poems! where
The dancers will break footing, from the care
Of watching up thy pregnant lips for more.
And dost thou lift this house's latch too poor   5
For hand of thine? and canst thou think and bear
To let thy music drop here unaware
In folds of golden fulness at my door?
Look up and see the casement broken in,
The bats and owlets builders in the roof!   10
My cricket chirps against thy mandolin.
Hush, call no echo up in further proof
Of desolation! there's a voice within
That weeps . . . as thou must sing . . . alone, aloof.

6

Go from me. Yet I feel that I shall stand
Henceforward in thy shadow. Nevermore
Alone upon the threshold of my door
Of individual life, I shall command
The uses of my soul, nor lift my hand   5
Serenely in the sunshine as before,
Without the sense of that which I forbore—
Thy touch upon the palm. The widest land
Doom takes to part us, leaves thy heart in mine
With pulses that beat double. What I do   10
And what I dream include thee, as the wine
Must taste of its own grapes. And when I sue
God for myself, He hears that name of thine,
And sees within my eyes the tears of two.

7

The face of all the world is changed, I think,
Since first I heard the footsteps of thy soul
Move still, oh, still, beside me, as they stole
Betwixt me and the dreadful outer brink
Of obvious death, where I, who thought to sink,   5
Was caught up into love, and taught the whole
Of life in a new rhythm. The cup of dole
God gave for baptism, I am fain to drink,
And praise its sweetness, Sweet, with thee anear.
The names of country, heaven, are changed away   10
For where thou art or shalt be, there or here;
And this . . . this lute and song . . . loved yesterday,
(The singing angels know) are only dear
Because thy name moves right in what they say.

14

If thou must love me, let it be for nought
Except for love's sake only. Do not say,
"I love her for her smile—her look—her way

Of speaking gently,—for a trick of thought
That falls in well with mine, and certes brought   5
A sense of pleasant ease on such a day"—
For these things in themselves, Belovèd, may
Be changed, or change for thee,—and love, so wrought,
May be unwrought so. Neither love me for
Thine own dear pity's wiping my cheeks dry,—   10
A creature might forget to weep, who bore
Thy comfort long, and lose thy love thereby!
But love me for love's sake, that evermore
Thou may'st love on, through love's eternity.

20

Belovèd, my Belovèd, when I think
That thou wast in the world a year ago,
What time I sat alone here in the snow
And saw no footprint, heard the silence sink
No moment at thy voice, but, link by link,   5
Went counting all my chains as if that so
They never could fall off at any blow
Struck by thy possible hand,—why, thus I drink
Of life's great cup of wonder! Wonderful,
Never to feel thee thrill the day or night   10
With personal act or speech,—nor ever cull
Some prescience of thee with the blossoms white
Thou sawest growing! Atheists are as dull,
Who cannot guess God's presence out of sight.

22

When our two souls stand up erect and strong,
Face to face, silent, drawing nigh and nigher,
Until the lengthening wings break into fire
At either curvèd point,—what bitter wrong
Can the earth do to us, that we should not long   5
Be here contented? Think. In mounting higher,
The angels would press on us and aspire
To drop some golden orb of perfect song
Into our deep, dear silence. Let us stay
Rather on earth, Belovèd,—where the unfit   10
Contrarious moods of men recoil away
And isolate pure spirits, and permit
A place to stand and love in for a day,
With darkness and the death-hour rounding it.

26

I lived with visions for my company,
Instead of men and women, years ago,
And found them gentle mates, nor thought to know
A sweeter music than they played to me.
But soon their trailing purple was not free   5
Of this world's dust, their lutes did silent grow,
And I myself grew faint and blind below

Their vanishing eyes. Then THOU didst come—to be,
Belovèd, what they seemed. Their shining fronts,
Their songs, their splendors (better, yet the same,   10
As river-water hallowed into fonts),
Met in thee, and from out thee overcame
My soul with satisfaction of all wants:
Because God's gifts put man's best dreams to shame.

35

If I leave all for thee, wilt thou exchange
And be all to me? Shall I never miss
Home-talk and blessing and the common kiss
That comes to each in turn, nor count it strange,
When I look up, to drop on a new range   5
Of walls and floors, another home than this?
Nay, wilt thou fill that place by me which is
Filled by dead eyes too tender to know change?
That's hardest. If to conquer love, has tried,
To conquer grief, tries more, as all things prove;   10
For grief indeed is love and grief beside.
Alas, I have grieved so I am hard to love.
Yet love me—wilt thou? Open thine heart wide,
And fold within the wet wings of thy dove.

43

How do I love thee? Let me count the ways.
I love thee to the depth and breadth and height
My soul can reach, when feeling out of sight
For the ends of Being and ideal Grace.
I love thee to the level of everyday's   5
Most quiet need, by sun and candlelight.
I love thee freely, as men strive for Right;
I love thee purely, as they turn from Praise.
I love thee with the passion put to use
In my old griefs, and with my childhood's faith.   10
I love thee with a love I seemed to lose
With my lost saints,—I love thee with the breath,
Smiles, tears, of all my life!—and, if God choose,
I shall but love thee better after death.

Arthur Hugh Clough

1819–1861

CLOUGH was born at Liverpool in 1819 and educated at Rugby, where he came under the powerful influence of Thomas Arnold and his Liberal Protestantism (see General Introduction, p. 378). But when he arrived at Oxford in 1836, his faith was disturbed by the rival claim of Newman's Anglo-Catholicism, and presently undermined by the impact of Benthamism, science, and Biblical criticism. As a result Clough was driven into a state of doubt—not denial, but profound uncertainty. Was the scientific or the religious view of man and the universe the truth? How could either be proved? Were old beliefs entirely wrong? Or new ones wholly true? Could anyone say for certain what we are or why we are here? And yet all around him Clough found his contemporaries rushing to one or another conclusion, and worse, defending their choice with dogmatic and sectarian zeal. The only sensible course, he thought, was to wait with suspended judgment for deeper knowledge. It is this attitude which makes Clough so unusual in his period and so modern today. In 1869 Henry Sidgwick pointed out the emergence of what might be called "the modern spirit," and traced its first manifestation to Clough:

His point of view and habit of mind are less singular in England in the year 1869 than they were in 1859, and much less than they were in 1849. We are growing year by year more introspective and self-conscious: the current philosophy leads us to a close, patient, and impartial observation and analysis of our mental processes. . . . We are growing also more sceptical in the proper sense of the word: we suspend our judgment much more than our predecessors, and much more contentedly: we see that there are many sides to many questions: the opinions that we do hold we hold if not more loosely, at least more at arm's length: we can imagine how they appear to others, and can conceive ourselves not holding them. We are losing in faith and confidence: if we are not failing in hope, our hopes at least are becoming more indefinite; and we are gaining in impartiality and comprehensiveness of sympathy. In each of these respects, Clough, if he were still alive, would find himself gradually more and more at home in the changing world.

When we add to this his trenchant satire of bourgeois society (seen in "The Latest Decalogue"), the intellectual character of his verse, and the plain, idiomatic style devoid of sensuous diction and incantatory rhythm, we recognize that Clough is perhaps the most modern of the Victorian poets. He often reminds one of Auden or MacLeish.

But often not. Clough was of his time in finding suspended judgment painful, and in longing both to deny the nightmare of a mechanistic universe and to cling somehow to some religious belief, however vague. His skepticism—that is, his doubt of any solutions, including those of science—offered him a way out. If nothing is certain, let us trust our religious hopes and desires. A similar attitude appears in *In Memoriam,* where Tennyson speaks of faintly trusting the larger hope (No. 55). What distinguishes Clough is his candid recognition that to do so may be to delude ourselves, to cling to a dream, to bury our head like an ostrich in the sand (see the sonnet on p. 852). And yet "It may be that indeed and not in fancy, A hand that is not ours upstays our steps." I suspect that for many Victorians the wish was father to the faith; but few recognized, and still fewer confessed, the real character of this fideism to which they were driven.

Clough's complete work is in his *Poems and Prose Remains*, edited by his wife (1869). This also contains a selection from his letters and a biographical memoir. A more detailed Life is J. I. Osborne's *Arthur Hugh Clough* (1920). Perhaps the best critical article is by Henry Sidgwick, "The Poems and Prose Remains of Arthur Hugh Clough," in his *Miscellaneous Essays and Addresses* (1904).

THE LATEST DECALOGUE

Thou shalt have one God only; who
Would be at the expense of two?
No graven images may be
Worshiped, except the currency:
Swear not at all; for, for thy curse   5
Thine enemy is none the worse:
At church on Sunday to attend
Will serve to keep the world thy friend:
Honor thy parents: that is, all
From whom advancement may befall;   10
Thou shalt not kill; but need'st not strive
Officiously to keep alive:
Do not adultery commit;
Advantage rarely comes of it:
Thou shalt not steal; an empty feat,   15
When it's so lucrative to cheat:
Bear not false witness; let the lie
Have time on its own wings to fly:
Thou shalt not covet, but tradition
Approves all forms of competition.   20

"WEN GOTT BETRÜGT, IST WOHL BETROGEN"[1]

Is it true, ye gods, who treat us
As the gambling fool is treated;
O ye, who ever cheat us,
And let us feel we're cheated!
Is it true that poetical power,   5
The gift of heaven, the dower
Of Apollo and the Nine,
The inborn sense, "the vision and the
    faculty divine,"[2]

All we glorify and bless
In our rapturous exaltation,   10
All invention, and creation,
Exuberance of fancy, and sublime
    imagination,
All a poet's fame is built on,
The fame of Shakespeare, Milton,
Of Wordsworth, Byron, Shelley,   15
Is in reason's grave precision,
Nothing more, nothing less,
Than a peculiar conformation,
Constitution, and condition
Of the brain and of the belly?[3]   20
Is it true, ye gods who cheat us?
And that's the way ye treat us?

Oh say it, all who think it,
Look straight, and never blink it!
If it is so, let it be so,   25
And we will all agree so;
But the plot has counterplot,
It may be, and yet be not.[4]

AH! YET CONSIDER IT AGAIN!

"Old things need not be therefore true,"
O brother men, nor yet the new;
Ah! still awhile the old thought retain,
And yet consider it again!

The souls of now two thousand years   5
Have laid up here their toils and fears,
And all the earnings of their pain,—
Ah, yet consider it again!

We! what do we see? each a space
Of some few yards before his face;   10
Does that the whole wide plan explain?
Ah, yet consider it again!

Alas! the great world goes its way,
And takes its truth from each new day;
They do not quit, nor can retain,   15
Far less consider it again.

---

[1] A German proverb translated by Clough as "Whom God deludes is well deluded."
[2] Wordsworth's description of the poetic imagination (*The Excursion*, I, 79).

[3] See the General Introduction, p. 382.
[4] Huxley himself admitted that since science could not explain the nexus between the molecular changes in the brain and the thoughts in consciousness which accompanied them, we could not be sure that the latter were determined by the former.

"PERCHÈ PENSA? PENSANDO S'INVECCHIA"[5]

To spend uncounted years of pain,
Again, again, and yet again,
In working out in heart and brain
   The problem of our being here;
To gather facts from far and near,   5
Upon the mind to hold them clear,
And, knowing more may yet appear,
Unto one's latest breath to fear,
The premature result to draw—
Is this the object, end and law,   10
   And purpose of our being here?

"THROUGH A GLASS DARKLY"

What we, when face to face we see
The Father of our souls, shall be,
John tells us, doth not yet appear;[6]
Ah! did he tell what we are here!

A mind for thoughts to pass into,   5
A heart for loves to travel through,
Five senses to detect things near,
Is this the whole that we are here?

Rules baffle instincts—instincts rules,
Wise men are bad—and good are fools,   10
Facts evil—wishes vain appear,
We cannot go, why are we here?

O may we for assurance' sake,
Some arbitrary judgment take,
And wilfully pronounce it clear,   15
For this or that 'tis we are here?

Or is it right, and will it do,
To pace the sad confusion through,
And say:—It doth not yet appear,
What we shall be, what we are here?   20

Ah yet, when all is thought and said,
The heart still overrules the head;
Still what we hope we must believe,
And what is given us receive;

Must still believe, for still we hope   25
That in a world of larger scope,
What here is faithfully begun
Will be completed, not undone.

My child, we still must think, when we
That ampler life together see,   30
Some true result will yet appear
Of what we are, together, here.

"O THOU OF LITTLE FAITH"[7]

   It may be true
That while we walk the troublous tossing sea,
That when we see the o'ertopping waves advance,
And when we feel our feet beneath us sink,
There are who walk beside us; and the cry   5
That rises so spontaneous to the lips,
The "Help us or we perish," is not nought,
An evanescent spectrum of disease.
It may be that indeed and not in fancy,
A hand that is not ours upstays our steps,   10
A voice that is not ours commands the waves;
Commands the waves, and whispers in our ear,
O thou of little faith, why didst thou doubt?
At any rate,
That there are beings above us, I believe,   15
And when we lift up holy hands of prayer,
I will not say they will not give us aid.

from SEVEN SONNETS
ON THE THOUGHT OF DEATH

4

But whether in the uncoloured light of truth,
This inward strong assurance be, indeed,
More than the self-willed arbitrary creed,
Manhood's inheritor to the dream of youth;
Whether to shut out fact because forsooth   5
To live were insupportable unfreed,[8]
Be not or be the service of untruth:
Whether this vital confidence be more
Than his who, upon death's immediate brink,
Knowing, perforce determines to ignore;   10
Or than the bird's, that when the hunter's near,
Burying her eyesight, can forget her fear;
Who about this shall tell us what to think?

---

[5] "Why think? By thinking one grows old."
[6] Cf. 1 John 3:2: "Beloved, now are we the sons of God, and it doth not yet appear what we shall be: but we know that, when he shall appear, we shall be like him; for we shall see him as he is."

[7] Christ's rebuke to his disciples when they came to him in the storm at sea and cried out, "Lord, save us: we perish" (Matthew 8:23–26).
[8] Chained or tied down to fact.

SAY NOT THE STRUGGLE NOUGHT AVAILETH

Say not the struggle nought availeth,
  The labor and the wounds are vain,
The enemy faints not, nor faileth,
  And as things have been they remain.

If hopes were dupes, fears may be liars;   5
  It may be, in yon smoke concealed,
Your comrades chase e'en now the fliers,
  And, but for you, possess the field.

For while the tired waves, vainly breaking,
  Seem here no painful inch to gain,   10
Far back, through creeks and inlets making,
  Comes silent, flooding in, the main.

And not by eastern windows only,
  When daylight comes, comes in the light,
In front, the sun climbs slow, how slowly,   15
  But westward, look, the land is bright.

Edward FitzGerald

1809–1883

IN 1859 appeared almost unnoticed *The Rubáiyát of Omar Khayyám,* rendered into English verse anonymously. By the turn of the century it had achieved a startling popularity. The rendering had been made by an unusually modest gentleman of adequate means and scholarly tastes, Edward FitzGerald, a friend from his days at Cambridge of Tennyson and Thackeray, who was primarily only indulging his own interest in Persian literature and his flair for verse translation. It was Fitz-Gerald's goal so to paraphrase this series of random quatrains, originally composed about the time of the Norman Conquest, as to transmit the spirit of the Persian poet rather than his words, and in this process the poem became in a sense his own creation. But its epicurean and skeptical tone could probably only have been accepted by the general reader in 1859—and then not enthusiastically—as that of some long-departed Oriental poet. However, as the century advanced the quatrains came increasingly to reflect the weariness of spirit and the expanding skepticism that followed the scientific revolution. As men came more and more to terms with the seemingly irrefutable facts of evolution and scientific materialism, the public found in the *Rubáiyát* what seemed the only wisdom left to it: we know not whence or whither, we are but dust, sentient, it is true, but hardly different from the grape and the rose. Why then trouble ourselves with seeking what we cannot find? Let us rather accept our ignorance and get what pleasure we can from our senses before we too pass. Brave words, but not even Horace or Omar, much less FitzGerald and his contemporaries, could escape the inevitable tinge of melancholy that rises from such a view, and the closing quatrains echo their sigh for a scheme of things nearer to man's deep desire for significance and value.

While it was almost certainly this correspondence to a mood of the time that primarily accounted for the tremendous popularity of the *Rubáiyát* at the turn of the century, the wealth of Oriental imagery and FitzGerald's haunting cadences then and now have appealed to the ears and imaginations of readers to whose thoughts and beliefs the message of Omar is indifferent or utterly hostile. For them it is a kind of magic carpet of gorgeous design and texture to waft them far away from the actual and its problems.

There is an elaborate edition of FitzGerald's work, both verse and prose, by Sir Edmund Gosse and G. Bentham (7 vols., 1902–3). The four somewhat different versions of the *Rubáiyát* published in FitzGerald's lifetime have been printed together (1921). The volume on FitzGerald in the English Men of Letters series is by A. C. Benson (1905); a more recent biography is by A. McK. Terhune (1947). For a critical discussion of the translation of the *Rubáiyát,* consult A. Platt, "Edward FitzGerald," in *Nine Essays* (1927).

THE RUBÁIYÁT OF OMAR KHAYYÁM OF NAISHÁPÚR

1

Wake! For the Sun, who scattered into flight
The Stars before him from the Field of Night,
  Drives Night along with them from Heav'n and strikes
The Sultán's Turret with a Shaft of Light.

2

Before the phantom of False morning[1] died,   5
Methought a Voice within the Tavern cried,
  "When all the Temple is prepared within,
Why nods the drowsy Worshiper outside?"

3

And, as the Cock crew, those who stood before
The Tavern shouted—"Open then the Door!   10

---

[1] "A transient Light on the Horizon about an hour before . . . the True Dawn; a well-known Phenomenon in the East." (FitzGerald)

You know how little while we have to stay,
And, once departed, may return no more."

4

Now the New Year[2] reviving old Desires,
The thoughtful Soul to Solitude retires,
 Where the WHITE HAND OF MOSES on the Bough 15
Puts out, and Jesus from the Ground suspires.[3]

5

Iram[4] indeed is gone with all his Rose,
And Jamshyd's[5] Sev'n-ringed Cup where no one knows;
 But still a Ruby kindles in the Vine,
And many a Garden by the Water blows. 20

6

And David's[6] lips are locked; but in divine
High-piping Pehleví,[7] with "Wine! Wine! Wine!
 Red Wine!"—the Nightingale cries to the Rose
That sallow cheek of hers to incarnadine.

7

Come, fill the Cup, and in the fire of Spring 25
Your Winter-garment of Repentance fling;
 The Bird of Time has but a little way
To flutter—and the Bird is on the Wing.

8

Whether at Naishápúr[8] or Babylon,
Whether the Cup with sweet or bitter run, 30
 The Wine of Life keeps oozing drop by drop,
The Leaves of Life keep falling one by one.

9

Each Morn a thousand Roses brings, you say;
Yes, but where leaves the Rose of Yesterday?
 And this first Summer month that brings the Rose 35
Shall take Jamshyd and Kaikobád[9] away.

10

Well, let it take them! What have we to do
With Kaikobád the Great, or Kaikhosrú?[10]
 Let Zál and Rustum[11] bluster as they will,
Or Hátim[12] call to Supper—heed not you. 40

11

With me along the strip of Herbage strown
That just divides the desert from the sown,
 Where name of Slave and Sultán is forgot—
And Peace to Mahmúd[13] on his golden Throne!

12

A Book of Verses underneath the Bough, 45
A Jug of Wine, a Loaf of Bread—and Thou
 Beside me singing in the Wilderness—
Oh, Wilderness were Paradise enow!

13

Some for the Glories of This World; and some
Sigh for the Prophet's[14] Paradise to come; 50
 Ah, take the Cash, and let the Credit go,
Nor heed the rumble of a distant Drum![15]

14

Look to the blowing Rose about us—"Lo,
Laughing," she says, "into the world I blow,
 At once the silken tassel of my Purse 55
Tear, and its Treasure[16] on the Garden throw."

15

And those who husbanded the Golden Grain,[17]
And those who flung it to the winds like Rain,
 Alike to no such aureate Earth are turned
As, buried once, Men want dug up again. 60

16

The Worldly Hope men set their Hearts upon
Turns Ashes—or it prospers; and anon,
 Like Snow upon the Desert's dusty Face,
Lighting a little hour or two—is gone.

---

2 "Beginning with the Vernal Equinox, it must be remembered."
(FitzGerald)
3 The white blossoms emerging upon the branches in spring are
likened to the hand of Moses when he withdrew it from his
bosom (Exodus 4:6); and the flowers springing from the earth
seem like an exhalation of the breath of Jesus.
4 An ancient Persian garden, "now sunk somewhere in the Sands
of Arabia."
5 A legendary king of Persia. His cup "was typical of the 7
Heavens, 7 Planets, 7 Seas, etc.," and had magic powers.
6 Author of the Psalms.
7 "The old Heroic Sanskrit of Persia." (FitzGerald)
8 The home of Omar Khayyám.
9 Founder of an ancient Persian dynasty.

10 Early Persian hero.
11 "The 'Hercules' of Persia, and Zál his Father." (FitzGerald) See
Matthew Arnold, Sohrab and Rustum, pp. 725 ff., above.
12 The typical figure of Oriental hospitality.
13 The Sultan.
14 Mohammed's.
15 "A Drum—beaten outside a Palace" (FitzGerald), signifying
regal and worldly affairs.
16 "The Rose's Golden Centre." (FitzGerald)
17 Money.

17

Think, in this battered Caravanserai[18]   65
Whose Portals are alternate Night and Day,
How Sultán after Sultán with his Pomp
Abode his destined Hour, and went his way.

18

They say the Lion and the Lizard keep
The Courts where Jamshyd gloried and drank deep;   70
And Bahrám,[19] that great hunter—the Wild Ass
Stamps o'er his Head, but cannot break his Sleep.

19

I sometimes think that never blows so red
The Rose as where some buried Caesar bled;
That every Hyacinth the Garden wears   75
Dropped in her Lap from some once lovely Head.

20

And this reviving Herb whose tender Green
Fledges the River-Lip on which we lean—
Ah, lean upon it lightly! for who knows
From what once lovely Lip it springs unseen!   80

21

Ah, my Belovéd, fill the Cup that clears
TODAY of past Regrets and future Fears:
Tomorrow!—Why, Tomorrow I may be
Myself with Yesterday's Sev'n Thousand Years.

22

For some we loved, the loveliest and the best   85
That from his Vintage rolling Time hath prest,
Have drunk their Cup a Round or two before,
And one by one crept silently to rest.

23

And we, that now make merry in the Room
They left, and Summer dresses in new bloom,   90
Ourselves must we beneath the Couch of Earth
Descend—ourselves to make a Couch—for whom?

24

Ah, make the most of what we yet may spend,
Before we too into the Dust descend;
Dust into Dust, and under Dust to lie,   95
Sans[20] Wine, sans Song, sans Singer, and—sans End!

___

[18] An Oriental inn, primarily for the use of caravans.
[19] A Persian ruler, lost in a swamp while pursuing a wild ass.
[20] Without.

25

Alike for those who for TODAY prepare,
And those that after some TOMORROW stare,
A Muezzín[21] from the Tower of Darkness cries,
"Fools, your Reward is neither Here nor There."   100

26

Why, all the Saints and Sages who discussed
Of the Two Worlds so wisely—they are thrust
Like foolish Prophets forth; their Words to Scorn
Are scattered, and their Mouths are stopped with Dust.

27

Myself when young did eagerly frequent   105
Doctor and Saint, and heard great argument
About it and about; but evermore
Came out by the same door where in I went.

28

With them the seed of Wisdom did I sow,
And with mine own hand wrought to make it grow;   110
And this was all the Harvest that I reaped—
"I came like Water, and like Wind I go."

29

Into this Universe, and Why not knowing
Nor Whence, like Water willy-nilly flowing;
And out of it, as Wind along the Waste,   115
I know not Whither, willy-nilly blowing.

30

What, without asking, hither hurried Whence?
And, without asking, Whither hurried hence!
Oh, many a Cup of this forbidden Wine[22]
Must drown the memory of that insolence!   120

31

Up from the Earth's Center through the Seventh Gate
I rose, and on the Throne of Saturn sate,[23]
And many a Knot unraveled by the Road;
But not the Master-knot of Human Fate.

___

[21] One who calls the Mohammedans to prayer from a tower of the mosque.
[22] The drinking of wine is forbidden to faithful Mohammedans.
[23] The sphere of Saturn was the seventh of the concentric circles surrounding the earth in early concepts of the universe. Omar means that his studies had extended as far as man's knowledge of the universe.

32

There was the Door to which I found no Key;   125
There was the Veil through which I might not see;
   Some little talk awhile of ME and THEE[24]
There was—and then no more of THEE and ME.

33

Earth could not answer; nor the Seas that mourn
In flowing Purple, of their Lord forlorn;   130
   Nor rolling Heaven, with all his Signs revealed
And hidden by the sleeve of Night and Morn.

34

Then of the THEE IN ME[25] who works behind
The Veil, I lifted up my hands to find
   A lamp amid the Darkness; and I heard,   135
As from Without—"THE ME WITHIN THEE BLIND!"

35

Then to the Lip of this poor earthen Urn
I leaned, the Secret of my Life to learn;
   And Lip to Lip it murmured—"While you live,
Drink!—for, once dead, you never shall return."   140

36

I think the Vessel, that with fugitive
Articulation answered, once did live,
   And drink;[26] and Ah! the passive Lip I kissed,
How many Kisses might it take—and give!

37

For I remember stopping by the way   145
To watch a Potter thumping his wet Clay;
   And with its all-obliterated Tongue
It murmured—"Gently, Brother, gently, pray!"

38

And has not such a Story from of Old
Down Man's successive generations rolled   150
   Of such a clod of saturated Earth
Cast by the Maker into Human mold?[27]

39

And not a drop that from our Cups we throw
For Earth to drink of, but may steal below
   To quench the fire of Anguish in some Eye   155
There hidden—far beneath, and long ago.[28]

40

As then the Tulip for her morning sup
Of Heav'nly Vintage from the soil looks up,
   Do you devoutly do the like, till Heav'n
To Earth invert you—like an empty Cup.   160

41

Perplexed no more with Human or Divine,
Tomorrow's tangle to the winds resign,
   And lose your fingers in the tresses of
The Cypress-slender Minister of Wine.[29]

42

And if the Wine you drink, the Lip you press,   165
End in what All begins and ends in—Yes;
   Think then you are TODAY what YESTERDAY
You were—TOMORROW you shall not be less.

43

So when that Angel of the darker Drink
At last shall find you by the river-brink,   170
   And, offering his Cup, invite your Soul
Forth to your Lips to quaff—you shall not shrink.

44

Why, if the Soul can fling the Dust aside,
And naked on the Air of Heaven ride,
   Were't not a Shame—were't not a Shame for him   175
In this clay carcass crippled to abide?

45

'Tis but a Tent where takes his one day's rest
A Sultán to the realm of Death addrest;
   The Sultán rises, and the dark Ferrásh[30]
Strikes, and prepares it for another Guest.   180

---

[24] "Some individual Existence or Personality distinct from the Whole." (FitzGerald)
[25] The universal spirit?
[26] In a note FitzGerald refers to a Persian tale in which a thirsty traveler is told by a supernatural voice that the clay of which his bowl is made was once man.
[27] As, indeed, in the Biblical story of creation.

[28] The first two lines of this quatrain refer to a common Persian practice. "The precious Liquor is not lost, but sinks into the ground to refresh the dust of some poor Wine-worshipper foregone." (FitzGerald)
[29] The maiden who passes the wine, later called Sákí.
[30] A servant charged with setting up and "striking" or taking down the tents.

46

And fear not lest Existence closing your
Account, and mine, should know the like no more;
   The Eternal Sákí from that Bowl has poured
Millions of Bubbles like us, and will pour.

47

When You and I behind the Veil are past,   185
Oh, but the long, long while the World shall last,
   Which of our Coming and Departure heeds
As the Sea's self should heed a pebble-cast.

48

A Moment's Halt—a momentary taste
Of Being from the Well amid the Waste—   190
   And Lo!—the phantom Caravan has reached
The Nothing it set out from—Oh, make haste!

49

Would you that spangle of Existence spend
About the secret—quick about it, Friend!
   A Hair perhaps divides the False and True—   195
And upon what, prithee, may life depend?

50

A Hair perhaps divides the False and True,
Yes; and a single Alif[31] were the clue—
   Could you but find it—to the Treasure-house,
And peradventure to The Master too;   200

51

Whose secret Presence, through Creation's veins
Running Quicksilver-like eludes your pains;
   Taking all shapes from Máh to Máhi;[32] and
They change and perish all—but He remains;

52

A moment guessed—then back behind the Fold   205
Immersed of Darkness round the Drama rolled
   Which, for the Pastime of Eternity,
He doth Himself contrive, enact, behold.

53

But if in vain, down on the stubborn floor
Of Earth, and up to Heav'n's unopening Door,   210
   You gaze Today, while You are You—how then
Tomorrow, when You shall be You no more?

54

Waste not your Hour, nor in the vain pursuit
Of This and That endeavor and dispute;
   Better be jocund with the fruitful Grape   215
Than sadden after none, or bitter, Fruit.

55

You know, my Friends, with what a brave Carouse
I made a Second Marriage in my house;
   Divorced old barren Reason from my Bed,
And took the Daughter of the Vine to Spouse.   220

56

For "Is" and "Is-not" though with Rule and Line
And "Up-and-down" by Logic I define,
   Of all that one should care to fathom, I
Was never deep in anything but—Wine.

57

Ah, but my Computations, People say,   225
Reduced the Year to better reckoning?[33]—Nay,
   'Twas only striking from the Calendar
Unborn Tomorrow, and dead Yesterday.

58

And lately, by the Tavern Door agape,
Came shining through the Dusk an Angel Shape   230
   Bearing a Vessel on his Shoulder; and
He bid me taste of it; and 'twas—the Grape!

59

The Grape that can with Logic absolute
The Two-and-Seventy jarring Sects confute;
   The sovereign Alchemist that in a trice   235
Life's leaden metal into Gold transmute;

60

The mighty Mahmúd, Allah-breathing Lord,
That all the misbelieving and black Horde
   Of Fears and Sorrows that infest the Soul
Scatters before him with his whirlwind Sword.[34]   240

61

Why, be this Juice the growth of God, who dare
Blaspheme the twisted tendril as a Snare?

---

[31] A single stroke, the first letter of the Arabic alphabet.
[32] "From Fish to Moon." (FitzGerald)

[33] Omar was an astronomer and mathematician as well as a poet
and was instrumental in reforming the calendar.
[34] "Alluding to Sultan Mahmúd's Conquest of India and its dark
people." (FitzGerald) It was carried out in the name of Allah.

A Blessing, we should use it, should we not?
And if a Curse—why, then, Who set it there?

62

I must abjure the Balm of Life, I must,   245
Scared by some After-reckoning ta'en on trust,
   Or lured with Hope of some Diviner Drink,
To fill the Cup—when crumbled into Dust!

63

Oh threats of Hell and Hopes of Paradise!
One thing at least is certain—*This* Life flies;   250
   One thing is certain and the rest is Lies;
The Flower that once has blown for ever dies.

64

Strange, is it not? that of the myriads who
Before us passed the door of Darkness through,
   Not one returns to tell us of the Road,   255
Which to discover we must travel too.

65

The Revelations of Devout and Learned
Who rose before us, and as Prophets burned,
   Are all but Stories, which, awoke from Sleep
They told their comrades, and to Sleep returned.   260

66

I sent my Soul through the Invisible,
Some letter of that After-life to spell;
   And by and by my Soul returned to me,
And answered, "I Myself am Heav'n and Hell":

67

Heav'n but the Vision of fulfilled Desire,   265
And Hell the Shadow from a Soul on fire,
   Cast on the Darkness into which Ourselves,
So late emerged from, shall so soon expire.

68

We are no other than a moving row
Of Magic Shadow-shapes that come and go   270
   Round with the Sun-illumined Lantern held
In Midnight by the Master of the Show;

69

But helpless Pieces of the Game He plays
Upon this Checker-board of Nights and Days;
   Hither and thither moves, and checks, and slays,   275
And one by one back in the Closet lays.

70

The Ball no question makes of Ayes and Noes,
But Here or There as strikes the Player goes;
   And He that tossed you down into the Field,
He knows about it all—HE knows—HE knows!   280

71

The Moving Finger writes, and, having writ,
Moves on; nor all your Piety nor Wit
   Shall lure it back to cancel half a Line,
Nor all your Tears wash out a Word of it.

72

And that inverted Bowl they call the Sky,   285
Whereunder crawling cooped we live and die,
   Lift not your hands to *It* for help—for It
As impotently moves as you or I.

73

With Earth's first Clay They did the Last Man knead,
And there of the Last Harvest sowed the Seed;   290
   And the first Morning of Creation wrote
What the Last Dawn of Reckoning shall read.

74

YESTERDAY *This* Day's Madness did prepare;
Tomorrow's Silence, Triumph, or Despair:
   Drink! for you know not whence you came, nor
     why;   295
Drink! for you know not why you go, nor where.

75

I tell you this—When, started from the Goal,
Over the flaming shoulders of the Foal
   Of Heav'n Parwín and Mushtarí they flung,[35]
In my predestined Plot of Dust and Soul   300

76

The Vine had struck a fiber; which about
If clings my Being—let the Dervish[36] flout;
   Of my Base metal may be filed a Key,
That shall unlock the Door he howls without.

---

[35] When over the equatorial constellation known as the "Little Horse" they (the gods or supernatural forces; see stanza 73: "With Earth's first Clay They did the Last Man knead") flung or placed the Pleiades and the planet Jupiter.

[36] A Mohammedan fanatic.

77

And this I know: whether the one True Light 305
Kindle to Love, or Wrath-consume me quite,
   One Flash of It within the Tavern caught
Better than in the Temple lost outright.

78

What! out of senseless Nothing to provoke
A conscious Something to resent the yoke 310
   Of unpermitted Pleasure, under pain
Of Everlasting Penalties, if broke!

79

What! from his helpless Creature be repaid
Pure Gold for what he lent him dross-allayed—
   Sue for a Debt he never did contract, 315
And cannot answer—Oh the sorry trade!

80

Oh Thou, who didst with pitfall and with gin[37]
Beset the Road I was to wander in,
   Thou wilt not with Predestined Evil round
Enmesh, and then impute my Fall to Sin! 320

81

Oh Thou, who Man of Baser Earth didst make,
And ev'n with Paradise devise the Snake:
   For all the Sin wherewith the Face of Man
Is blackened—Man's forgiveness give—and take!

82

As under cover of departing Day 325
Slunk hunger-stricken Ramazán[38] away,
   Once more within the Potter's house alone
I stood, surrounded by the Shapes of Clay.

83

Shapes of all Sorts and Sizes, great and small,
That stood along the floor and by the wall; 330
   And some loquacious Vessels were; and some
Listened perhaps, but never talked at all.

84

Said one among them—"Surely not in vain
My substance of the common Earth was ta'en

85

   And to this Figure molded, to be broke, 335
Or trampled back to shapeless Earth again."

Then said a Second—"Ne'er a peevish Boy
Would break the Bowl from which he drank in joy;
   And He that with his hand the Vessel made
Will surely not in after Wrath destroy." 340

86

After a momentary silence spake
Some Vessel of a more ungainly Make;
   "They sneer at me for leaning all awry:
What! did the Hand, then, of the Potter shake?"

87

Whereat someone of the loquacious Lot— 345
I think a Súfi[39] pipkin—waxing hot—
   "All this of Pot and Potter—Tell me, then,
Who is the Potter, pray, and who the Pot?"

88

"Why," said another, "Some there are who tell
Of one who threatens he will toss to Hell 350
   The luckless Pots he marred in making—Pish!
He's a Good Fellow, and 'twill all be well."

89

"Well," murmured one, "Let whoso make or buy,
My Clay with long Oblivion is gone dry;
   But fill me with the old familiar Juice, 355
Methinks I might recover by and by."

90

So while the Vessels one by one were speaking,
The little Moon[40] looked in that all were seeking;
   And then they jogged each other, "Brother! Brother!
Now for the Porter's shoulder-knot[41] a-creaking!" 360

*   *   *   *   *   *

91

Ah, with the Grape my fading Life provide,
And wash the Body whence the Life has died,
   And lay me, shrouded in the living Leaf,
By some not unfrequented Garden-side.

---

[37] Trap.
[38] A month during which Mohammedans eat no food between
    sunrise and sunset.

[39] A Persian mystic, or pantheist.
[40] When the new moon appeared it signaled the end of Ramazán.
[41] The strap on which the jars were hung from the porter's shoulder.

That ev'n my buried Ashes such a snare   365
Of Vintage shall fling up into the Air
   As not a True-believer passing by
But shall be overtaken unaware.

93

Indeed the Idols I have loved so long
Have done my credit in this World much wrong: 370
   Have drowned my Glory in a shallow Cup,
And sold my Reputation for a Song.

94

Indeed, indeed, Repentance oft before
I swore—but was I sober when I swore?
   And then and then came Spring, and Rose-in-hand 375
My thread-bare Penitence apieces tore.

95

And much as Wine has played the Infidel,
And robbed me of my Robe of Honor—Well,
   I wonder often what the Vintners buy
One half so precious as the stuff they sell.   380

96

Yet Ah, that Spring should vanish with the Rose!
That Youth's sweet-scented manuscript should close!
   The Nightingale that in the branches sang,
Ah whence, and whither flown again, who knows!

97

Would but the Desert of the Fountain yield   385
One glimpse—if dimly, yet indeed, revealed,
   To which the fainting Traveler might spring,
As springs the trampled herbage of the field!

98

Would but some wingéd Angel ere too late
Arrest the yet unfolded Roll of Fate,   390
   And make the stern Recorder otherwise
Enregister, or quite obliterate!

99

Ah, Love! could you and I with Him conspire
To grasp this sorry Scheme of Things entire,
   Would not we shatter it to bits—and then   395
Remold it nearer to the Heart's Desire!

    *   *   *   *   *   *

Yon rising Moon that looks for us again—
How oft hereafter will she wax and wane;
   How oft hereafter rising look for us
Through this same Garden—and for *one* in vain!   400

101

And when like her, O Sákí, you shall pass
Among the Guests Star-scattered on the Grass,
   And in your joyous errand reach the spot
Where I made One—turn down an empty Glass!

TAMÁM[42]

George Meredith

1828–1909

IN an age when men were torn by doubt and anxiety as to the meaning of life, Meredith seems to stand curiously aloof, one somehow removed from the hopes and fears of his contemporaries, who can record from a lofty and purely intellectual viewpoint his observations of his fellow man. It is these observations which form the matter of his novels; they are primarily studies of character, as, indeed, their titles indicate: *The Ordeal of Richard Feverel* (1859), *The Adventures of Harry Richmond* (1871), *The Egoist* (1879), and *Diana of the Crossways* (1885), to name the best known.

Even in his verse novel, *Modern Love,* where his own unhappy first marriage is reflected, Meredith remains the cool and detached observer of human character. This perceptive study of the dissolution of married love is presented in a loosely connected series of sixteen-line sonnets, each providing a glimpse of the tragic progress toward a final collapse. But the poem is marred by Meredith's tendency to abandon the direct presentation of experience for an elaborate use of vague and abstract metaphor. In the first sonnet, for example, the contact with living emotions in the opening lines is half lost in the following passage with its "literary" and artificial language.

It is in his lyric poetry that Meredith comes to grips with the baffling questions posed by the conflict of the Christian tradition and scientific research, and yet here again his attitude seems relatively objective. His was essentially a naturalistic interpretation of the world and of man's role in it. For him the possibility of a personal God is ruled out in favor of nature itself, or Earth, as he

---

[42] It is ended.

prefers to call it. The only supernatural element of which he admits is the process of unalterable law, fulfilling itself in accord with the principles of evolution, without regard to individuals, but with some dimly perceived purpose of perfection for the human race. And it is characteristic of Meredith that this perfection is to be primarily that of the mind.

Fortunately for his poetry, abstract Earth and unalterable law had their concrete manifestations in sights and sounds and seasons that Meredith never tired of watching carefully, or of recording sharply in pastorals and lyrics which capture both the general impressions and the accurately noted details of his natural surroundings. Where the philosophical implications do appear, they seem secondary to the delight in nature for its own sake. Even in such poems as "The Lark Ascending" and "Hard Weather" the passages of natural description, while obviously intended as springboards into the philosophical exposition, still convey a keen awareness and enjoyment of the phenomena of nature.

The standard edition of Meredith's poems is the *Poetical Works* by G. M. Trevelyan (1928). Professor Trevelyan also provides a critical guide to the poems in *The Poetry and Philosophy of George Meredith* (1920). For a biography one may consult R. E. Sencourt, *The Life of George Meredith* (1929).

from MODERN LOVE[1]

I

By this he knew she wept with waking eyes:
That, at his hand's light quiver by her head,
The strange low sobs that shook their common bed
Were called into her with a sharp surprise,
And strangled mute, like little gaping snakes,   5
Dreadfully venomous to him. She lay
Stone-still, and the long darkness flowed away
With muffled pulses. Then, as midnight makes
Her giant heart of Memory and Tears
Drink the pale drug of silence, and so beat   10
Sleep's heavy measure, they from head to feet
Were moveless, looking through their dead black years,
By vain regret scrawled over the blank wall.
Like sculptured effigies they might be seen
Upon their marriage-tomb, the sword between;[2]   15
Each wishing for the sword that severs all.

16

In our old shipwrecked days there was an hour,
When in the firelight steadily aglow,
Joined slackly, we beheld the red chasm grow
Among the clicking coals. Our library-bower
That eve was left to us: and hushed we sat   5
As lovers to whom Time is whispering.
From sudden-opened doors we heard them sing;
The nodding elders mixed good wine with chat.
Well knew we that Life's greatest treasure lay
With us, and of it was our talk. "Ah, yes!   10
Love dies!" I said: I never thought it less.
She yearned to me that sentence to unsay.
Then when the fire domed blackening, I found
Her cheek was salt against my kiss, and swift
Up the sharp scale of sobs her breast did lift:—   15
Now am I haunted by that taste! that sound!

17

At dinner, she is hostess, I am host.
Went the feast ever cheerfuller? She keeps
The Topic over intellectual deeps
In buoyancy afloat. They see no ghost.
With sparkling surface-eyes we ply the ball;   5
It is in truth a most contagious game:
HIDING THE SKELETON shall be its name.
Such play as this the devils might appall!
But here's the greater wonder: in that we,
Enamored of an acting naught can tire,   10
Each other, like true hypocrites, admire;
Warm-lighted looks, Love's ephemerioe,[3]
Shoot gayly o'er the dishes and the wine.
We waken envy of our happy lot.
Fast, sweet, and golden, shows the marriage-knot.   15
Dear guests, you now have seen Love's corpse-light[4] shine.

43

Mark where the pressing wing shoots javelin-like
Its skeleton shadow on the broad-backed wave!
Here is a fitting spot to dig Love's grave;
Here where the ponderous breakers plunge and strike,
And dart their hissing tongues high up the sand: 5
In hearing of the ocean, and in sight
Of those ribbed wind-streaks running into white.
If I the death of Love had deeply planned,
I never could have made it half so sure,
As by the unblest kisses which upbraid   10
The full-waked senses; or failing that, degrade!

---

[1] Meredith's poems are reprinted from his *Selected Poems*, copyright 1897 by George Meredith, 1925 by William M. Meredith; used by permission of the publishers, Charles Scribner's Sons.
[2] In medieval legend, the sword dividing lovers signified chastity or honor. Here it symbolizes spiritual separation.

[3] Short-lived creatures.
[4] A flame sometimes seen in cemeteries, viewed as a portent of death.

'Tis morning: but no morning can restore
What we have forfeited. I see no sin:
The wrong is mixed. In tragic life, God wot,
No villain need be! Passions spin the plot: 15
We are betrayed by what is false within.

47

We saw the swallows gathering in the sky,
And in the osier-isle we heard them noise.
We had not to look back on summer joys,
Or forward to a summer of bright dye:
But in the largeness of the evening earth   5
Our spirits grew as we went side by side.
The hour became her husband and my bride.
Love, that had robbed us so, thus blessed our dearth!
The pilgrims of the year waxed very loud
In multitudinous chatterings, as the flood   10
Full brown came from the West, and like pale blood
Expanded to the upper crimson cloud.
Love, that had robbed us of immortal things,
This little moment mercifully gave,
Where I have seen across the twilight wave   15
The swan sail with her young beneath her wings.

50

Thus piteously Love closed what he begat:
The union of this ever-diverse pair!
These two were rapid falcons in a snare,
Condemned to do the flitting of the bat.
Lovers beneath the singing sky of May,   5
They wandered once; clear as the dew on flowers:
But they fed not on the advancing hours:
Their hearts held cravings for the buried day.
Then each applied to each that fatal knife,
Deep questioning, which probes to endless dole.   10
Ah, what a dusty answer gets the soul
When hot for certainties in this our life!—
In tragic hints here see what evermore
Moves dark as yonder midnight ocean's force,
Thundering like ramping hosts of warrior horse,   15
To throw that faint thin line upon the shore!

LUCIFER IN STARLIGHT

On a starred night Prince Lucifer[5] uprose.
Tired of his dark dominion swung the fiend
Above the rolling ball in cloud part screened,
Where sinners hugged their specter of repose.
Poor prey to his hot fit of pride were those.   5

---

[5] The angel who revolted against God and was exiled to rule over hell.

And now upon his western wing he leaned,
Now his huge bulk o'er Afric's sands careened,
Now the black planet shadowed Arctic snows.
Soaring through wider zones that pricked his scars
With memory of the old revolt from Awe,   10
He reached a middle height, and at the stars,
Which are the brain of heaven, he looked, and sank.
Around the ancient track marched, rank on rank,
The army of unalterable law.

HARD WEATHER

Bursts from a rending East in flaws[6]
The young green leaflet's harrier, sworn
To strew the garden, strip the shaws,[7]
And show our Spring with banner torn.
Was ever such virago morn?   5
The wind has teeth, the wind has claws.
All the wind's wolves through woods are loose,
The wild wind's falconry aloft.
Shrill underfoot the grassblade shrews,[8]
At gallop, clumped, and down the croft   10
Bestrid by shadows, beaten, tossed,
It seems a scythe, it seems a rod.
The howl is up at the howl's accost;
The shivers greet and the shivers nod.
Is the land ship? we are rolled, we drive   15
Tritonly, cleaving hiss and hum;
Whirl with the dead, or mount or dive,
Or down in dregs, or on in scum.
And drums the distant, pipes the near,
And vale and hill are gray in gray,   20
As when the surge is crumbling sheer,
And sea-mews wing the haze of spray.
Clouds—are they bony witches?—swarms,
Darting swift on the robber's flight,
Hurry an infant sky in arms: 25
It peeps, it becks; 'tis day, 'tis night.
Black while over the loop of blue
The swathe is closed, like shroud on corse.
Lo, as if swift the Furies flew,
The Fates at heel at a cry to horse!   30

Interpret me the savage whirr:
And is it Nature scourged, or she,
Her offspring's executioner,
Reducing land to barren sea?
But is there meaning in a day   35
When this fierce angel of the air,

---

[6] Squalls.
[7] Strips of woodland beside fields.
[8] Makes harsh noises.

Intent to throw, and haply slay,
Can for what breath of life we bear
Exact the wrestle? Call to mind
The many meanings glistening up   40
When Nature, to her nurslings kind,
Hands them the fruitage and the cup!
And seek we rich significance
Not otherwhere than with those tides
Of pleasure on the sunned expanse,   45
Whose flow deludes, whose ebb derides?

Look in the face of men who fare
Lock-mouthed, a match in lungs and thews
For this fierce angel of the air,
To twist with him and take his bruise.   50
That is the face beloved of old
Of Earth, young mother of her brood:
Nor broken for us shows the mold
When muscle is in mind renewed:
Though farther from her nature rude,   55
Yet nearer to her spirit's hold.
And though of gentler mood serene,
Still forceful of her fountain-jet.
So shall her blows be shrewdly met,
Be luminously read the scene   60
Where Life is at her grindstone set,
That she may give us edging keen,
String us for battle, till as play
The common strokes of fortune shower.
Such meaning in a dagger-day   65
Our wits may clasp to wax in power.
Yea, feel us warmer at her breast,
By spin of blood in lusty drill,
Than when her honeyed hands caressed,
And Pleasure, sapping, seemed to fill.   70

Behold the life at ease; it drifts.
The sharpened life commands its course.
She[9] winnows, winnows roughly; sifts,
To dip her chosen in her source:
Contention is the vital force,   75
Whence pluck they brain, her prize of gifts,
Sky of the senses! on which height,
Not disconnected, yet released,
They see how spirit comes to light,
Through conquest of the inner beast,   80
Which Measure tames to movement sane,
In harmony with what is fair.
Never is Earth misread by brain:
That is the welling of her, there

---

[9] Earth or nature.

The mirror: with one step beyond,   85
For likewise is it voice; and more,
Benignest kinship bids respond,
When wail the weak, and them restore
Whom days as fell as this may rive,
While Earth sits ebon in her gloom,   90
Us atomies of life alive
Unheeding, bent on life to come.
Her children of the laboring brain,
These are the champions of the race,
True parents, and the sole humane,   95
With understanding for their base.
Earth yields the milk, but all her mind
Is vowed to thresh for stouter stock.
Her passion for old giantkind,
That scaled the mount, uphurled the rock,   100
Devolves on them who read aright
Her meaning and devoutly serve;
Nor in her starlessness of night
Peruse her with the craven nerve:
But even as she from grass to corn,   105
To eagle high from grubbing mole,
Prove in strong brain her noblest born,
The station for the flight of soul.

Christina Georgina Rossetti

1830–1894

THE daughter of an exiled Italian patriot and the sister of
the gifted and exuberant Pre-Raphaelite painter and poet,
Christina Rossetti seems, so far as we may judge from the
expression she gave to her thoughts and feelings, to have
lived somewhat remote from the political and artistic
preoccupations which burned up so much of the energy
of the rest of the household. Aside from a very occasional
political utterance such as "To-day for me . . ." and a
relatively few poems such as "Goblin Market" and
"Paradise," her poetry is represented by a series of rather
simple and restrained lyrics, which if not always strictly
autobiographical, are certainly colored by her own
personal history. Because of her very restricted family
circumstances and her own rather frail health she had but
a limited knowledge of the world to draw upon, and she
used her gift mainly to express her inner emotional experience. She was the victim of an inner conflict: on the
one hand she responded eagerly to the beauties of nature
and the warmth of human affection, and on the other she
was almost tortured by a kind of religious asceticism,

which called upon her to reject these earthly pleasures and dedicate herself completely to God. So strong was this spiritual compulsion that she refused two suitors, one of whom she loved deeply, on religious grounds; but such was the pain of this rejection of one whole side of her nature that although she seems to have convinced herself of the wholeheartedness of her surrender, the dominant theme of her poetry is the relief and resolution that death, and death alone, will be able to bring to her frustration.

> Life is not sweet. One day it will be sweet
>   To shut our eyes and die

is her theme in "Life and Death," and the last poem she ever wrote tells of the peace that will come when she is sleeping at last. Aside from the subject matter, the distinguishing characteristics of the major part of her work are the simple diction and the wonderfully natural musical cadences, which combine to produce an impression of sincerity and spontaneity. "I question," wrote her brother William Michael, "her having ever once deliberated with herself whether or not she would write something or other. . . . Instead of this, something impelled her feelings, or 'came into her head,' and her hand obeyed the dictation."

Christina Rossetti's *Poetical Works* were edited by her brother, W. M. Rossetti, together with a memoir (1904). The most recent biography is by Marya Zaturenska, *Christina Rossetti: A Portrait with Background* (1949). C. M. Bowra discusses her poetry in *The Romantic Imagination* (1949).

SONG

When I am dead, my dearest,
  Sing no sad songs for me;
Plant thou no roses at my head,
  Nor shady cypress tree:
Be the green grass above me   5
  With showers and dewdrops wet;
And if thou wilt, remember,
  And if thou wilt, forget.

I shall not see the shadows,
  I shall not feel the rain;   10
I shall not hear the nightingale
  Sing on as if in pain:
And dreaming through the twilight
  That doth not rise nor set,
Haply I may remember,   15
  And haply may forget.

UP-HILL

Does the road wind up-hill all the way?
  Yes, to the very end.
Will the day's journey take the whole long day?
  From morn to night, my friend.

But is there for the night a resting-place?   5
  A roof for when the slow dark hours begin.
May not the darkness hide it from my face?
  You cannot miss that inn.

Shall I meet other wayfarers at night?
  Those who have gone before.   10
Then must I knock, or call when just in sight?
  They will not keep you standing at that door.

Shall I find comfort, travel-sore and weak?
  Of labour you shall find the sum.
Will there be beds for me and all who seek?   15
  Yea, beds for all who come.

A BETTER RESURRECTION

I have no wit, no words, no tears;
  My heart within me like a stone
Is numbered too much for hopes or fears.
  Look right, look left, I dwell alone;
I lift mine eyes, but dimmed with grief   5
  No everlasting hills I see;
My life is in the falling leaf;
  O Jesus, quicken me.

My life is like a faded leaf,
  My harvest dwindled to a husk;   10
Truly my life is void and brief
  And tedious in the barren dusk;
My life is like a frozen thing,
  No bud nor greenness can I see;
Yet rise it shall—the sap of Spring;   15
  O Jesus, rise in me.

My life is like a broken bowl,
  A broken bowl that cannot hold
One drop of water for my soul
  Or cordial in the searching cold;   20
Cast in the fire the perished thing;
  Melt and remold it, till it be
A royal cup for Him, my King;
  O Jesus, drink of me.

A BIRTHDAY

My heart is like a singing bird
  Whose nest is in a watered shoot;
My heart is like an apple-tree
  Whose boughs are bent with thickset fruit;
My heart is like a rainbow shell   5
  That paddles in a halcyon sea;
My heart is gladder than all these
  Because my love is come to me.

Raise me a dais of silk and down;
  Hang it with vair[1] and purple dyes;   10
Carve it in doves, and pomegranates,
  And peacocks with a hundred eyes;
Work it in gold and silver grapes,
  In leaves and silver fleurs-de-lys;
Because the birthday of my life   15
  Is come, my love is come to me.

LIFE AND DEATH

Life is not sweet. One day it will be sweet
  To shut our eyes and die;
Nor feel the wild flowers blow, nor birds dart by
  With flitting butterfly,
Nor grass grow long above our heads and feet,   5
Nor hear the happy lark that soars sky-high,
Nor sigh that spring is fleet and summer fleet,
  Nor mark the waxing wheat,
Nor know who sits in our accustomed seat.

Life is not good. One day it will be good   10
  To die, then live again;
To sleep meanwhile; so, not to feel the wane
  Of shrunk leaves dropping in the wood,
Nor hear the foamy lashing of the main,
Nor mark the blackened bean-fields, nor where stood 15
  Rich ranks of golden grain,
Only dead refuse stubble clothe the plain:
  Asleep from risk, asleep from pain.

SLEEPING AT LAST

Sleeping at last, the trouble and tumult over,
  Sleeping at last, the struggle and horror past,
Cold and white, out of sight of friend and of lover,
  Sleeping at last.

----

[1] A kind of squirrel fur.

No more a tired heart downcast or overcast,   5
No more pangs that wring or shifting fears that hover,
  Sleeping at last in a dreamless sleep locked fast.

Fast asleep. Singing birds in their leafy cover
  Cannot wake her, nor shake her the gusty blast.
Under the purple thyme and the purple clover   10
  Sleeping at last.

Francis Thompson

1859–1907

THOMPSON'S expressed wish to be known primarily as the poet of the return to God sets the tone of the major part of his work. Although he was unfitted to enter the Roman Catholic Church as a priest—as indeed he was unfitted both physically and morally to cope with practical existence—his poetic life was almost wholly spent in the service of religion. His outstanding achievement, "The Hound of Heaven," in a sense a spiritual autobiography, reflects his lamentable moral condition, closely paralleled by his physical collapse, before he was able in some degree to redeem himself and devote his time and what strength he could salvage to his religious and mystical bent. (He was a drug-addict in the last stages of tuberculosis, without roof, food, or friend, when he was rescued by the editor of a Catholic magazine and his poet-wife, Wilfred and Alice Meynell.)

By his own admission his temperament and poetic gift were allied to the tradition of seventeenth-century metaphysical poetry, particularly to Crashaw and Cowley; his love of paradox, of imagery, of conceit, all these, as well as his awareness of a spiritual world so close as to be almost tangible, are the tokens of his kinship, and are all to be found in "The Hound of Heaven." He fell at times, however, probably under the influence of Shelley in his less good passages, into extravagances of diction and lavishness of imagery which introduced irrelevant aesthetic emotions, and thus weakened the force and integrity of a poem and vitiated the intensity of his mysticism. However, these are but limitations which in large measure he was able to transcend in "The Hound of Heaven," where the primary theme of unrelenting pursuit is built up by a series of images, first of tremendous speed and immense space, then, for an interlude, of imagined escape, only to reach a kind of awful breathlessness in those which describe his worthlessness and impotency. Here the imagery is functional, not ornamental. The effect is tremendously heightened by the rhythm of the poem: the feeling of imminent pursuit is echoed in the rushing movement of the early section, in which the insistent beat of feet moves swiftly and inexorably onward; then as the chase nears its end and the stricken soul cowers before its Creator, the rhythm slows and slows as it comes to the final image of the shadow of God's caressing hand.

Wilfred Meynell edited Thompson's *Complete Poetical Works* (1913). M. A. Kelley has done a separate edition of "The Hound of Heaven" (1916). For biography, see *The Life of Francis Thompson* by Everard Meynell (1926); for criticism, the study by T. H. Wright, *Francis Thompson and His Poetry* (1927).

THE HOUND OF HEAVEN

I fled Him, down the nights and down the days;
　I fled Him, down the arches of the years;
　I fled Him, down the labyrinthine ways
　　Of my own mind; and in the mist of tears
I hid from Him, and under running laughter.　　　5
　　　Up vistaed hopes, I sped;
　　　And shot, precipitated,
Adown Titanic[1] glooms of chasmèd fears,
　From those strong Feet that followed, followed after.
　　　But with unhurrying chase,　　　10
　　　And unperturbèd pace,
Deliberate speed, majestic instancy,[2]
　　　They beat—and a Voice beat
　　　More instant than the Feet—
　　"All things betray thee, who betrayest Me."　　　15

　　　I pleaded, outlaw-wise,
By many a hearted casement, curtained red,
　Trellised with intertwining charities;[3]
(For, though I knew His Love Who followèd,
　　　Yet was I sore adread　　　20
Lest, having Him, I must have naught beside).
But, if one little casement parted wide,
　The gust of His approach would clash it to.
　Fear wist not to evade, as Love wist to pursue.
Across the margent[4] of the world I fled,　　　25
　And troubled the gold gateways of the stars,
　Smiting for shelter on their clangèd bars;
　　　Fretted to dulcet jars
And silvern chatter the pale ports o' the moon.[5]

I said to Dawn: Be sudden; to Eve: Be soon—　　　30
　With thy young skiey blossoms heap me over
　　From this tremendous Lover—
Float thy vague veil about me, lest He see!
　I tempted all His servitors, but to find
My own betrayal in their constancy,　　　35
In faith to Him their fickleness to me,
　Their traitorous trueness, and their loyal deceit.
To all swift things for swiftness did I sue;
　Clung to the whistling mane of every wind.
　　But whether they swept, smoothly fleet,　　　40
　The long savannahs of the blue;
　　Or whether, Thunder-driven,
　They clanged his chariot 'thwart a heaven,
Plashy with flying lightnings round the spurn o' their feet:—[6]
　Fear wist not to evade as Love wist to pursue.　　　45
　　　Still with unhurrying chase,
　　　And unperturbèd pace,
　Deliberate speed, majestic instancy,
　　　Came on the following Feet,
　　　And a Voice above their beat—　　　50
　"Naught shelters thee, who wilt not shelter Me."

I sought no more that after which I strayed
　　　In face of man or maid;
But still within the little children's eyes
　　Seems something, something that replies,　　　55
They at least are for me, surely for me!
I turned me to them very wistfully;
But just as their young eyes grew sudden fair
　　With dawning answers there,
Their angel plucked them from me by the hair.　　　60
"Come then, ye other children, Nature's—share
With me" (said I) "your delicate fellowship;
　　　Let me greet you lip to lip,
　　　Let me twine with you caresses,
　　　　Wantoning　　　65
　　　With our Lady-Mother's vagrant tresses,
　　　　Banqueting
　　With her in her wind-walled palace,
　　Underneath her azured daïs,
　　Quaffing, as your taintless way is,　　　70
　　　　From a chalice
Lucent-weeping[7] out of the dayspring."
　　　So it was done:
I in their delicate fellowship was one—
Drew the bolt of Nature's secrecies.　　　75

---

[1] Immense (the Titans were giants).　　　[2] Insistency.
[3] The poet fled like a fleeing outlaw to human love, to the human heart, hoping to find sympathy and kindness.
[4] Margin, boundary.
[5] Agitated or shook the portals of the moon until they gave forth sweet sounds.

[6] The sky was sparkling with the lightning-like sparks struck out by their hooves.
[7] Dripping luminous drops.

I knew all the swift importings[8]
On the wilful face of skies;
I knew how the clouds arise
Spumèd[9] of the wild sea-snortings;
    All that's born or dies   80
  Rose and drooped with; made them shapers
Of mine own moods, or wailful or divine;
  With them joyed and was bereaven.
  I was heavy with the even,
  When she lit her glimmering tapers   85
  Round the day's dead sanctities.
  I laughed in the morning's eyes.
I triumphed and I saddened with all weather,
  Heaven and I wept together,
And its sweet tears were salt with mortal mine;   90
Against the red throb of its sunset-heart
    I laid my own to beat,
    And share commingling heat;
But not by that, by that, was eased my human smart.
In vain my tears were wet on Heaven's gray cheek.   95
For ah! we know not what each other says,
  These things and I; in sound I speak—
Their sound is but their stir, they speak by silences.
Nature, poor stepdame, cannot slake my drouth;
  Let her, if she would owe[10] me,   100
Drop yon blue bosom-veil of sky, and show me
  The breasts o' her tenderness:
Never did any milk of hers once bless
    My thirsting mouth.
    Nigh and nigh draws the chase,   105
    With unperturbèd pace,
  Deliberate speed, majestic instancy,
    And past those noisèd Feet
    A Voice comes yet more fleet—
  "Lo! naught contents thee, who content'st not Me."

Naked I wait Thy love's uplifted stroke!   111
My harness piece by piece Thou hast hewn from me,
    And smitten me to my knee;
  I am defenseless utterly.
  I slept, methinks, and woke,   115
And, slowly gazing, find me stripped in sleep.
In the rash lustihead of my young powers,
  I shook the pillaring hours[11]
And pulled my life upon me; grimed with smears,
I stand amid the dust o' the mounded years—   120
My mangled youth lies dead beneath the heap.
My days have crackled and gone up in smoke,
Have puffed and burst as sun-starts[12] on a stream.

Yea, faileth now even dream
The dreamer, and the lute the lutanist;   125
Even the linked fantasies,[13] in whose blossomy twist
I swung the earth[14] a trinket at my wrist,
Are yielding; cords of all too weak account
For earth with heavy griefs so overplussed.
    Ah! is Thy love indeed   130
A weed, albeit an amaranthine[15] weed,
Suffering no flowers except its own to mount?
    Ah! must—
    Designer infinite!—
Ah! must Thou char the wood ere Thou canst limn with
    it?   135
My freshness spent its wavering shower i' the dust;
And now my heart is as a broken fount,
Wherein tear-drippings stagnate, spilt down ever
  From the dank thoughts that shiver
Upon the sighful branches of my mind.   140
    Such is; what is to be?
The pulp so bitter, how shall taste the rind?
I dimly guess what Time in mists confounds;
Yet ever and anon a trumpet sounds
From the hid battlements of Eternity;   145
Those shaken mists a space unsettle, then
Round the half-glimpsèd turrets slowly wash again.
    But not ere him who summoneth
    I first have seen, enwound
With glooming robes purpureal, cypress-crowned;[16] 150
His name I know, and what his trumpet saith.
Whether man's heart or life it be which yields
    Thee harvest, must Thy harvest-fields
    Be dunged with rotten death?[17]

    Now of that long pursuit   155
    Comes on at hand the bruit;[18]
That Voice is round me like a bursting sea:
    "And is thy earth so marred,
    Shattered in shard on shard?
Lo, all things fly thee, for thou fliest Me!   160
Strange, piteous, futile thing!
Wherefore should any set thee love apart?
Seeing none but I makes much of naught" (He said),
"And human love needs human meriting:
    How hast thou merited—   165
Of all man's clotted[19] clay the dingiest clot?

---

8 Meanings.
9 Made from the spray that is cast up by the waves.   10 Own.
11 Like Samson when he pulled the temple down.   12 Bubbles.

13 Poetic imaginings.   14 My world, my life.
15 Immortal, from the name of a flower that was reputed never to
    fade.
16 The cypress is associated with death and mourning.
17 Must man die spiritually as well as physically in order to nourish
    his salvation?
18 Noise, din.
19 Lumpish, without spark.

Alack, thou knowest not
How little worthy of any love thou art!
Whom wilt thou find to love ignoble thee,
    Save Me, save only Me?   170
All which I took from thee I did but take,
    Not for thy harms,
But just that thou might'st seek it in My arms.
    All which thy child's mistake
Fancies as lost, I have stored for thee at home: 175
    Rise, clasp My hand, and come!"

    Halts by me that footfall:
    Is my gloom, after all,
Shade of His hand, outstretched caressingly?
    "Ah, fondest, blindest, weakest,   180
    I am He Whom thou seekest!
Thou dravest love from thee, who dravest Me."

William Ernest Henley

1849–1903

HENLEY spent almost his entire life in a losing fight against tuberculosis, and much of his work reflects his reactions to the struggle. Primary among these is his preoccupation with death and suffering, which is lustily countered, and almost in the same breath, by his cry for life, life unflinching and lived to the full. The spirited defiance engendered by this battle, together with a strong sense of individuality, led him to revolt against the conventional attitudes and artistic forms of the mid-Victorians, giving him breadth of mind to appreciate in his critical essays the innovations made by others (he was among the first to recognize and admire Hardy, Swinburne, Meredith, and Conrad, among other writers, as well as Rodin and Whistler), and at the same time courage to experiment himself. He is the real founder of what came to be called "free verse," that is, verse free from any metrical pattern (and also, as a rule, from rime), so that shifting rhythms and changing lengths of line might fit more closely the successive emotional "units."

In content Henley's poetry is a curious mixture of new realism and old romanticism. "In Hospital," a series of poems written during a long stay in the Edinburgh Infirmary, is a sharp, graphic description of scenes and experiences in a big city hospital, acutely observed, and set down in the barest diction and in the most natural order of words. On the other hand, his passionate desire for dynamic life, extending sometimes into sheer worship of force, of the Strong Man, takes us back, in a poem like "Invictus," to Byron and the Byronic hero; while at the same time it links Henley with Kipling and British imperialism (besides explaining, incidentally, his blunt disgust with the aestheticism of the 90's). Equally romantic in a complementary way is the "I. M. Margaritae Sorori," where the longing to escape from the hard battle of life makes him imagine a lovely and painless death, and thus recalls a stanza in Keats's "Ode to a Nightingale" (pp. 334–5, above) and another in Shelley's "Stanzas Written in Dejection, near Naples" (pp. 293–4).

Henley's *Works* have been published in five volumes (1921); the *Poems* appear in a separate volume (1912). For biographical information consult John Connell, *W. E. Henley* (1949). For critical comments see John Drinkwater, "William Ernest Henley," in *The Muse in Council* (1925), or Arthur Symons, "Modernity in Verse," in *Studies in Two Literatures* (1924).

from IN HOSPITAL

I

ENTER PATIENT

The morning mists still haunt the stony street;
The northern summer air is shrill and cold;
And lo, the Hospital, gray, quiet, old,
Where Life and Death like friendly chafferers meet.
Thro' the loud spaciousness and draughty gloom   5
A small, strange child—so agèd yet so young!—
Her little arm besplinted and beslung,
Precedes me gravely to the waiting-room.
I limp behind, my confidence all gone.
The gray-haired soldier-porter waves me on,   10
And on I crawl, and still my spirits fail:
A tragic meanness seems so to environ
These corridors and stairs of stone and iron,
Cold, naked, clean—half-workhouse and half-jail.

4

BEFORE

Behold me waiting—waiting for the knife.
A little while, and at a leap I storm
The thick, sweet mystery of chloroform,
The drunken dark, the little death-in-life.
The gods are good to me: I have no wife,   5
No innocent child, to think of as I near
The fateful minute; nothing all-too dear
Unmans me for my bout of passive strife.
Yet I am tremulous and a trifle sick,
And, face to face with chance, I shrink a little: 10
My hopes are strong, my will is something weak.
Here comes the basket?[1] Thank you. I am ready.
But, gentlemen my porters, life is brittle:
You carry Caesar and his fortunes—steady!

---

[1] In which the patient is carried to the operating room.

Lived on one's back,
In the long hours of repose,
Life is a practical nightmare—
Hideous asleep or awake.

Shoulders and loins   5
Ache — — — !
Ache, and the mattress,
Run into boulders and hummocks,
Glows like a kiln, while the bedclothes—
Tumbling, importunate, daft—   10
Ramble and roll, and the gas,
Screwed to its lowermost,
An inevitable atom of light,
Haunts, and a stertorous sleeper
Snores me to hate and despair.   15

All the old time
Surges malignant before me;
Old voices, old kisses, old songs
Blossom derisive about me;
While the new days   20
Pass me in endless procession:
A pageant of shadows
Silently, leeringly wending
On . . . and still on . . . still on!

Far in the stillness a cat   25
Languishes loudly. A cinder[2]
Falls, and the shadows
Lurch to the leap of the flame. The next man to me
Turns with a moan; and the snorer,
The drug like a rope at his throat,   30
Gasps, gurgles, snorts himself free, as the night-nurse,
Noiseless and strange,
Her bull's eye half-lanterned in apron[3]
(Whispering me, "Are ye no' sleepin' yet?"),
Passes, list-slippered[4] and peering,   35
Round . . . and is gone.

Sleep comes at last—
Sleep full of dreams and misgivings—
Broken with brutal and sordid
Voices and sounds that impose on me,   40
Ere I can wake to it,
The unnatural, intolerable day.

---

[2] The ward is heated by a coal fire.
[3] A protected candlestick, the equivalent of a flashlight.
[4] With felt-soled slippers.

Carry me out
Into the wind and the sunshine,
Into the beautiful world.

O, the wonder, the spell of the streets!
The stature and strength of the horses,   5
The rustle and echo of footfalls,
The flat roar and rattle of wheels!
A swift tram floats huge on us . . .
It's a dream?
The smell of the mud in my nostrils   10
Blows brave—like a breath of the sea!

As of old,
Ambulant, undulant drapery,
Vaguely and strangely provocative,
Flutters and beckons. O, yonder—   15
Is it?—the gleam of a stocking!
Sudden, a spire

Wedged in the mist! O, the houses,
The long lines of lofty, gray houses,
Cross-hatched[5] with shadow and light!   20
These are the streets. . . .
Each is an avenue leading
Whither I will!

Free . . . !
Dizzy, hysterical, faint,   25
I sit, and the carriage rolls on with me
Into the wonderful world.

INVICTUS[6]

Out of the night that covers me,
    Black as the Pit from pole to pole,
I thank whatever gods may be
    For my unconquerable soul.

In the fell clutch of circumstance   5
    I have not winced nor cried aloud.
Under the bludgeonings of chance
    My head is bloody, but unbowed.

Beyond this place of wrath and tears
    Looms but the Horror of the shade,   10
And yet the menace of the years
    Finds, and shall find, me unafraid.

---

[5] A technique of etching.   [6] Unconquered.

It matters not how strait the gate,
　　How charged with punishments the scroll,
I am the master of my fate;　　　　　　　　15
　　I am the captain of my soul.

I. M.
MARGARITAE SORORI[7]

A late lark twitters from the quiet skies;
　　And from the west,
Where the sun, his day's work ended,
　　Lingers as in content,
There falls on the old, gray city　　　　　　5
An influence luminous and serene,
　　A shining peace.

The smoke ascends
In a rosy-and-golden haze. The spires
Shine, and are changed. In the valley　　　10
Shadows rise. The lark sings on. The sun,
Closing his benediction,
Sinks, and the darkening air
Thrills with a sense of the triumphing night—
Night with her train of stars　　　　　　　15
And her great gift of sleep.

So be my passing!
My task accomplished and the long day done,
My wages taken, and in my heart
Some late lark singing,　　　　　　　　　20
Let me be gathered to the quiet west,
The sundown splendid and serene,
Death.

SPACE AND DREAD AND THE DARK

Space and dread and the dark—
Over a livid stretch of sky
Cloud-monsters crawling, like a funeral train
Of huge, primeval presences
Stooping beneath the weight　　　　　　　5
Of some enormous, rudimentary grief;
While in the haunting loneliness
The far sea waits and wanders with a sound
As of the trailing skirts of Destiny,
Passing unseen　　　　　　　　　　　　10
To some immitigable end
With her gray henchman, Death.

What larve,[8] what specter is this
Thrilling the wilderness to life
As with the bodily shape of Fear?　　　　　15
What but a desperate sense,
A strong foreboding of those dim
Interminable continents, forlorn
And many-silenced, in a dusk
Inviolable utterly, and dead　　　　　　　20
As the poor dead it huddles and swarms and styes[9]
In hugger-mugger[10] through eternity?

Life—life—let there be life!
Better a thousand times the roaring hours
When wave and wind,　　　　　　　　　25
Like the Arch-Murderer in flight
From the Avenger at his heel,
Storms through the desolate fastnesses
And wild waste places of the world!

Life—give me life until the end,　　　　　30
That at the very top of being,
The battle-spirit shouting in my blood,
Out of the reddest hell of the fight
I may be snatched and flung
Into the everlasting lull,　　　　　　　　35
The immortal, incommunicable dream.

Rudyard Kipling
1865–1936

KIPLING was born in India and returned to it for his first job as a young man; he was thus especially fitted to interpret the natives, the British soldiery, and Anglo-Indian officialdom. And this, as a member of the staff of a local newspaper in Lahore, is what he first set out to do in 1882, writing a series of short stories and poems that dealt rather acidly with the manners and foibles (or worse) of English military and official society, portrayed native loyalty and superstition with sympathy, and described the life of the common soldier in an understanding, if somewhat uproarious, tone. The young Kipling was not a profound thinker, but he was a keen observer, with great vitality and a talent for brisk narrative. He also had an ear for pronounced rhythm which enabled him to translate into verse the vigor of his subjects, especially in the form of ballad or chanty.

These swinging rhythms, of course, were one source of the tremendous popularity of *Departmental Ditties* and

---

7 To the Memory of Sister Margaret.

8 Ghost.　　9 Herds into sties like pigs.　　10 Disorder.

Barrack-Room Ballads and Other Verses. But the underlying theme, too, had its own definite appeal, for the last twenty years of the century were the heyday of imperial expansion, and India and the soldiers and administrators who were forging this vast and mysterious territory into an English colony were subjects of great interest and pride at home. It is a credit to Kipling's integrity as man and artist that, while swept along with the current of imperial enthusiasm (see the dedication to *Barrack-Room Ballads*), with its concomitant exaltation of "Strong Men" and central authority, he could yet point the finger of satire at least at the minor evils of the situation, such as the shabby treatment of Tommy Atkins by his fellow-countrymen and the mean or bullying attitude of the average Anglo-Indian to the natives; and that at the very apex of the imperial fever he dared to intone the warning of his "Recessional."

But around 1900 success translated Kipling from an obscure reporter, very much in touch with the natives and with the common soldier, into a person of distinction, the friend of generals and top administrators. He still worshipped "Strong Men," but it was now the strength of autocratic dictation from above based on unquestioning submission from below, with utter condemnation for anyone who opposed the will of England. He could no longer have written "The Ballad of East and West" or admitted the valor of Fuzzy-Wuzzy. However, the great days of imperialism were drawing to a close and the English themselves were beginning to question the validity of "the White Man's burden." Kipling was out of tune with the new generation. It was no doubt some sense of his isolation that led him to withdraw into a retired country existence and to turn in his poetry from the wide world of Empire to England itself—England with its serenely beautiful countryside, its long historical tradition, and its sense of continuity with the past. This is the England which took hold of Kipling's imagination and which he delighted to honor in his later years in such a poem as "Sussex."

The standard edition is *Rudyard Kipling's Verse: Inclusive Edition, 1885-1932* (1934). For a biography one may consult Cecil Charles, *Rudyard Kipling: His Life and Works* (1911). In criticism there is the Introduction by T. S. Eliot to *A Choice of Kipling's Verse* (1942) and an essay by Edmund Wilson, "The Kipling That Nobody Read," in *The Wound and the Bow* (1941).

from BARRACK-ROOM BALLADS[1]

DEDICATION

Beyond the path of the outmost sun through utter
    darkness hurled—
Farther than ever comet flared or vagrant star-dust
    swirled—
Live such as fought and sailed and ruled and loved and
    made our world.

They are purged of pride because they died; they know
    the worth of their bays;
They sit at wine with the Maidens Nine[2] and the Gods
    of the Elder Days—   5
It is their will to serve or be still as fitteth Our Father's
    praise.

'Tis theirs to sweep through the ringing deep where
    Azrael's[3] outposts are,
Or buffet a path through the Pit's red wrath when
    God goes out to war,
Or hang with the reckless Seraphim on the rein of a
    red-maned star.

They take their mirth in the joy of the Earth—they
    dare not grieve for her pain.   10
They know of toil and the end of toil; they know God's
    Law is plain;
So they whistle the Devil to make them sport who
    know that Sin is vain.

And oft-times cometh our wise Lord God, master of
    every trade,
And tells them tales of His daily toil, of Edens newly
    made;
And they rise to their feet as He passes by, gentlemen
    unafraid.   15

To these who are cleansed of base Desire, Sorrow and
    Lust and Shame—
Gods for they knew the hearts of men, men for they
    stooped to Fame—
Borne on the breath that men call Death, my brother's
    spirit came.

---

[1] The first four poems are from *Departmental Ditties and Ballads and Barrack-Room Ballads* by Rudyard Kipling, reprinted by permission of Mrs. George Bambridge and Doubleday & Company, Inc. The last three are from *The Five Nations,* copyright 1903, 1931 by Rudyard Kipling; reprinted by permission of Mrs. George Bambridge and Doubleday & Company, Inc.   [2] The Muses.
[3] The angel in Jewish and Mohammedan mythology who severs body and soul at death.—The Pit (line 8) = hell.

He scarce had need to doff his pride or slough the dross
    of Earth—
E'en as he trod that day to God so walked he from his
    birth,   20
In simpleness and gentleness and honour and clean mirth.

So cup to lip in fellowship they gave him welcome high
And made him place at the banquet board—the Strong
    Men ranged thereby,
Who had done his work and held his peace and had no
    fear to die.

Beyond the loom of the last lone star, through open
    darkness hurled,   25
Further than rebel comet dared or hiving star-swarm
    swirled,
Sits he with those that praise our God for that they
    served His world.

THE BALLAD OF EAST AND WEST

1889

Oh, East is East, and West is West, and never the
    twain shall meet,
Till Earth and Sky stand presently at God's great
    Judgment Seat;
But there is neither East nor West, Border, nor Breed,
    nor Birth,
When two strong men stand face to face, though they
    come from the ends of the earth!

Kamal is out with twenty men to raise the Border
    side,   5
And he has lifted the Colonel's mare that is the Colonel's
    pride.
He has lifted her out of the stable-door between the dawn
    and the day,
And turned the calkins[4] upon her feet, and ridden her
    far away.
Then up spoke the Colonel's son that led a troop of
    the Guides:
"Is there never a man of all my men can say where
    Kamal hides?"   10
Then up and spoke Mohammed Khan, the son of the
    Ressaldar,
"If ye know the track of the morning-mist, ye know
    where his pickets are.
At dusk he harries the Abazai—at dawn he is into
    Bonair,

---

[4] Reversed the horseshoes.

But he must go by Fort Bukloh to his own place to
    fare,
So if ye gallop to Fort Bukloh as fast as a bird can
    fly,   15
By the favor of God ye may cut him off ere he win
    to the Tongue of Jagai.
But if he be passed the Tongue of Jagai, right swiftly
    turn ye then,
For the length and the breadth of that grisly plain is
    sown with Kamal's men.
There is rock to the left, and rock to the right, and low
    lean thorn between,
And ye may hear a breech-bolt snick where never a
    man is seen."   20
The Colonel's son has taken horse, and a raw rough
    dun was he,
With the mouth of a bell and the heart of Hell, and the
    head of the gallows-tree.
The Colonel's son to the Fort has won, they bid him
    stay to eat—
Who rides at the tail of a Border thief, he sits not long
    at his meat.
He's up and away from Fort Bukloh as fast as he can
    fly,   25
Till he was aware of his father's mare in the gut of the
    Tongue of Jagai,
Till he was aware of his father's mare with Kamal upon
    her back,
And when he could spy the white of her eye, he made
    the pistol crack.
He has fired once, he has fired twice, but the whistling
    ball went wide.
"Ye shoot like a soldier," Kamal said. "Show now if ye
    can ride!"   30
It's up and over the Tongue of Jagai, as blown dust-
    devils go,
The dun he fled like a stag of ten, but the mare like a
    barren doe.
The dun he leaned against the bit and slugged his head
    above,
But the red mare played with the snaffle-bars, as a
    maiden plays with a glove.
There was rock to the left and rock to the right, and
    low lean thorn between,   35
And thrice he heard a breech-bolt snick tho' never a
    man was seen.
They have ridden the low moon out of the sky, their
    hoofs drum up the dawn,
The dun he went like a wounded bull, but the mare
    like a new-roused fawn.
The dun he fell at a water-course—in a woeful heap
    fell he,

And Kamal has turned the red mare back, and pulled
    the rider free.   40
He has knocked the pistol out of his hand—small room
    was there to strive,
" 'Twas only by favor of mine," quoth he, "ye rode
    so long alive:
There was not a rock for twenty mile, there was not a
    clump of tree,
But covered a man of my own men with his rifle
    cocked on his knee.
If I had raised my bridle-hand, as I have held it low,   45
The little jackals that flee so fast were feasting all in a
    row.
If I had bowed my head on my breast, as I have held
    it high,
The kite that whistles above us now were gorged till
    she could not fly."
Lightly answered the Colonel's son: "Do good to
    bird and beast,
But count who come for the broken meats before
    thou makest a feast.   50
If there should follow a thousand swords to carry my
    bones away,
Belike the price of a jackal's meal were more than a
    thief could pay.
They will feed their horse on the standing crop, their
    men on the garnered grain,
The thatch of the byres will serve their fires when all
    the cattle are slain.
But if thou thinkest the price be fair,—thy brethren
    wait to sup,   55
The hound is kin to the jackal-spawn,—howl, dog, and
    call them up!
And if thou thinkest the price be high, in steer and
    gear and stack,
Give me my father's mare again, and I'll fight my own
    way back!"
Kamal has gripped him by the hand and set him upon
    his feet.
"No talk shall be of dogs," said he, "when wolf and
    gray wolf meet.   60
May I eat dirt if thou hast hurt of me in deed or breath;
What dam of lances brought thee forth to jest at the
    dawn with Death?"
Lightly answered the Colonel's son: "I hold by the
    blood of my clan:
Take up the mare for my father's gift—by God, she
    has carried a man!"
The red mare ran to the Colonel's son, and nuzzled
    against his breast;   65
"We be two strong men," said Kamal then, "but she
    loveth the younger best.

So she shall go with a lifter's dower, my turquoise-
    studded rein,
My 'broidered saddle and saddle-cloth, and silver
    stirrups twain."
The Colonel's son a pistol drew, and held it muzzle-end,
"Ye have taken the one from a foe," said he. "Will ye
    take the mate from a friend?"   70
"A gift for a gift," said Kamal straight; "a limb for the
    risk of a limb.
Thy father has sent his son to me, I'll send my son to
    him!"
With that he whistled his only son, that dropped from
    a mountain-crest—
He trod the ling[5] like a buck in spring, and he looked
    like a lance in rest.
"Now here is thy master," Kamal said, "who leads a
    troop of the Guides,   75
And thou must ride at his left side as shield on shoulder
    rides.
Till Death or I cut loose the tie, at camp and board and bed,
Thy life is his—thy fate it is to guard him with thy head.
So, thou must eat the White Queen's meat, and all her
    foes are thine,
And thou must harry thy father's hold for the peace of
    the Border-line.   80
And thou must make a trooper tough and hack thy
    way to power—
Belike they will raise thee to Ressaldar when I am
    hanged in Peshawur!"

They have looked each other between the eyes, and
    there they found no fault.
They have taken the Oath of the Brother-in-Blood on
    leavened bread and salt:
They have taken the Oath of the Brother-in-Blood on
    fire and fresh-cut sod,   85
On the hilt and the haft of the Khyber knife, and the
    Wondrous Names of God.
The Colonel's son he rides the mare and Kamal's boy
    the dun,
And two have come back to Fort Bukloh where there
    went forth but one.
And when they drew to the Quarter-Guard, full twenty
    swords flew clear—
There was not a man but carried his feud with the
    blood of the mountaineer.   90
"Ha' done! Ha' done!" said the Colonel's son. "Put up
    the steel at your sides!
Last night ye had struck at a Border thief—tonight 't is
    a man of the Guides!"

---

[5] Barren mountainside.

As a consequence of this mystic belief in the availability of the Infinite and in the ultimate unity of all impulses, the Symbolists could not be content merely to provide in their poetry accurate, recognizable copies of the visible world of natural appearances and social institutions. To do so would be to leave out all that was dazzling and eternal, all that was subtle and *true* in their vision. The hitherto inexpressible had somehow to be expressed, and it could only be done by the most subtle techniques of suggestion, by which each writer would attempt to render his own individual experience with the utmost fidelity. Symons urges his readers to remember Mallarmé's principle: that "to name is to destroy, to suggest is to create." Words must be used to suggest the poet's delicately apprehended sensation. They must be so selected and grouped that in their weight and rhythm and color, in their capacity to translate one sense impression into terms of another sense, they become symbols for the original perception. In this elaborate process there are obviously many points at which the poet and his reader will part company, and there is no poetry in English that for obscurity can rival what Symons calls the "frozen impenetrability" of Mallarmé's last sonnets.

The philosophical beliefs of the French Symbolists are not entirely easy to grasp, and they are far from easy to accept. Although their poetry seldom approximates the obscurity of Mallarmé's later verse, it sometimes betrays weaknesses—a bloodlessness, an exiguity, a preciousness, a remoteness—which are consequences of its very strengths. Yet these writers, both in their theory and in their practice, opened up to poetry domains of interest and power which lay at a wide remove from the areas habitually exploited by the Victorians in England. Few of the British writers who came under their spell went so far as to adopt their philosophic positions *in toto,* but for all who read them seriously and sympathetically the writing of poetry and the role of the poet were to be very different from what they had been in the fifty years between 1830 and 1880.

Symons insists that the artist's position is *outside* society, that

the artist . . . has no more part in society than a monk in domestic life: he cannot be judged by its rules, he can be neither praised nor blamed for his acceptance or rejection of its conventions. Social rules are made by normal people for normal people, and the man of genius is fundamentally abnormal. It is the poet against society, society against the poet, a direct antagonism. . . .

An extreme position, to be sure, involving for the artist who adheres to it a terrible loneliness, a denial of many sources of life and strength, for all its affirmation of his freedom to pursue and express his own individual perception and experience. The writers of the present century who inherit from the French Symbolists by way of the Aesthetic nineties have brought back into the subject matter of poetry large areas of political, social, and ethical experience which the extreme Symbolists had cast out. But at the same time they have preserved the ideal of a poetry which shall be as true to the poet's most subtle intuitions as he can possibly make it, rejecting completely the idea that the poet must coarsen his perceptions in order to make them more readily available to as large a group of readers as possible.

Much of the obscurity of poets like Mallarmé or Rimbaud derives from their attempt to use words as the symbolic equivalents of experiences which had quite simply never occurred to other men. Few contemporary poets have gone as far in their search for an expression of the well-nigh inexpressible as did Mallarmé, few have produced poetry as genuinely obscure, even to the patient reader, as his. " . . . But, apart from obscurity," Symons asks, at the end of his essay on Mallarmé, "which we may all be fortunate enough to escape, is it possible for a writer, at the present day, to be quite simple, with the old, objective simplicity, in either thought or expression?" This question, and the answer it implies, suggests the most profitable attitude to adopt when we approach for the first time the subtle, complex, and genuinely original poems and stories of our time:

To be naif, to be archaic, is not to be either natural or simple; I affirm that [it] is not natural to be what is called "natural" any longer. We have no longer the mental attitude of those to whom a story was but a story, and all stories good. . . . And, naturally, we can no longer write what we can no longer accept. Symbolism, implicit in all literature from the beginning, as it is implicit in the very words we use, comes to us now, at last quite conscious of itself, offering us the only escape from our many imprisonments. We find a new, an older, sense in the so worn out forms of things; the world, which we can no longer believe in as the satisfying material object it was to our grandparents, becomes transfigured with a new light; words, which long usage had darkened almost out of recognition, take fresh lustre. And it is on the lines of that spiritualising of the word, that perfecting of form in its capacity for allusion and suggestion, that confidence in the eternal correspondences between the visible and the invisible universe, which Mallarmé taught, and too intermittently practised, that literature must now move, if it is in any sense to move forward.

SYMONS dedicated *The Symbolist Movement in Literature* to Yeats as "the chief representative of that movement in our country." At that time Yeats was in his early thirties and had published three volumes of lyric poetry, *Crossways* (1889), *The Rose* (1893), and *The Wind among the Reeds* (1899), as well as a long narrative poem, *The Wanderings of Oisin* (1889), but the literary career which was to be the most remarkable that the twentieth century has thus far seen had no more than begun. In any account of twentieth-century literature Yeats's life and work demand a separate treatment, not only because of the intrinsic worth of the poetry itself, which is second to none in our time, but also because Yeats provides a link between the nineties and the developments of the new century. As a young man he had been closely associated with the figures whom we think of as typical of the nineties, sharing their views on art and the relation of art to life and their dissatisfaction with much that had been produced by the Victorians. But unlike the majority of the poets and painters of the Aesthetic Movement, Yeats lived beyond the nineties and continued to develop until his death in 1939. Thus we are able to see in his later work what the immediate heirs of the nineties were to make of their heritage.

In his *Autobiography*,[2] Yeats has described the forces and interests that shaped his life and art. We may read there of his childhood at Sligo, in Ireland, of his schooling and youth in London, from which he returned to Ireland for a part of every year. We learn of the influence exerted on him by his father, the painter John Yeats, who had at one time come under the influence of the pre-Raphaelites (writing of the late eighties, Yeats says, "I was in all things pre-Raphaelite") and to whom the Victorian poetry of ideas was distasteful. He marks out the early stages in the development of his interest in the occult, in theosophy, in Buddhism; the decline of his interest in science; his growing distrust of the vested interests of scientific thought and naturalistic art. But above all we see the great curve of his development from a poet wholly in key with the Aesthetic Movement to a poet wholly in key with the significant developments of the new century. He had begun by accepting the doctrine by which Pater and his followers had

attempted to purify literature of its concern with externalities. He went on, with no slightest sacrifice of the power of subtle evocation which the nineties had found in Symbolism, to bring back into poetry the directness of focus, the hard clarity of point, the reference to the world of actual human concern which the nineties had banished.

From the beginning, Yeats rejected the kind of poetry which the Victorians wrote. "I saw," he said, in describing the meetings of the Rhymers' Club in the late eighties and early nineties, " . . . that Swinburne in one way, Browning in another, and Tennyson in a third, had filled their work with what I called 'impurities,' curiosities about politics, about science, about history, about religion; and that we must create once more the pure work." There was no place in poetry for abstractions, for observation simply for observation's sake, for "mere reality." "I wanted the strongest passions, passions that had nothing to do with observation, and metrical forms that seemed old enough to have been sung by men half-asleep or riding upon a journey."

On these principles, he wrote the poems in his first three or four volumes, poems which he later described as "all picture, all association, all mythology." "The Falling of the Leaves," from his 1889 volume *Crossways* (see below, p. 902), may be taken as typical of many of these early poems. It has great beauty, which it offers up to the reader immediately. The frequent alliteration and the sway of the dactyls give an almost too palpable embodiment to the languorous autumn mood of the poem: for the poem is all mood. Yeats's early verse, like this, is superior to all but the best of the verse written by the other poets of the nineties, and it may be that we fail to do it justice because it is overshadowed by the poems in the later manner which he began to find as early as the first decade of the new century. The point is, however, that the passion, the beauty of the early poems exist in a vacuum, are summoned up for their own sake. In Yeats's later poems they exist side by side with intellect, and are evoked out of contact with the full world of active men.

There were many influences responsible for the particular line of development which Yeats's poetry took, away from a disembodied, wistful passion to the stern, hard beauty, the passionate responsibility, the unified sensibility of the later poems where intellect and passion feed one another. First of all, any such development would have been impossible without Yeats's great power of self-awareness and self-criticism. He saw, for instance, that a certain early habit of remorse "helped to spoil" his early

---

[2] The quotations below from *The Autobiography of W. B. Yeats*, copyright 1916 by The Macmillan Company, are used with their permission.

poetry, "giving it an element of sentimentality through my refusal to permit it any share of an intellect which I considered impure." A passage in the first section of his *Autobiography* describes his concern for qualities which are among the qualities of his later style:

. . . When I had finished *The Wanderings of Oisin,* dissatisfied with its yellow and dull green, with all that overcharged color inherited from the romantic movement, I deliberately reshaped my style, deliberately sought out an impression as of cold light and tumbling clouds. I cast off traditional metaphors and loosened my rhythm, and recognising that all the criticism of life known to me was alien and English, became as emotional as possible but with an emotion which I described to myself as cold.

We are reminded by the language of this passage of "The Fisherman" (pp. 902–3, below), from *The Wild Swans at Coole* (1919), which tells us much, when we compare it with an early poem like "The Falling of the Leaves," of the development Yeats's style had undergone.

Not only awareness of the limitations which the nineties had placed upon the writer and artist, but also certain contacts with the world of actuality were responsible for Yeats's growth. These contacts were chiefly of two sorts, political and theatrical, and Yeats owed both of them to his love of Ireland, his concern (however incompletely he might have been willing, at any given time, to identify himself with one Irish party or another) that Ireland should find herself as a nation and as a people. His *Autobiography* is full of political portraits—the Fenian leader John O'Leary, John Taylor, James Connolly, Padraic Pearce, Douglas Hyde—figures whom we encounter again, many of them, in the poems. Yeats was fond of quoting a statement of O'Leary which has the same ring of grand simplicity that we find in many a line of his own poetry—"There are things that a man must not do to save a nation." Describing the meetings of a Young Ireland Society, with O'Leary as president, Yeats said, "From these debates, from O'Leary's conversation, and from the Irish books he lent or gave me has come all I have set my hand to since." Yeats deplored the split between Catholic and Protestant Ireland and was aware of the inadequacies of both: "I thought we might bring the halves together if we had a national literature that made Ireland beautiful in the memory, and yet had been freed from provincialism by an exacting criticism, an European pose." There were various ways of contributing to this end. Most important, both for an Irish literature and for his own poetry, was his work in establishing an Irish theatre. With the help of Lady

Augusta Gregory he started around 1900 the Irish National Theatre Company, later to become the Abbey Theatre. The point has often been made that the discipline of writing plays for this group, imposing as it did the necessity for considering the demands and abilities of the actors and for aiming at bold, general effects which would not be lost on an audience, toughened the sinews of his style, helped to take his poetry out of the half-light of the Aesthetic Movement into the full light of day.

But for all the clarity and simplicity of line which these interests had brought into his poetry, Yeats was still a Symbolist with the Symbolist's distaste for the mere transcription of appearance for appearance's sake, the Symbolist's belief in a world of essences which is hinted at in the world of forms we know. Beside his remark about the importance to his later work of O'Leary's talk should be placed a passage about the influence of Arthur Symons:

My thoughts gained in richness and in clearness from his sympathy, nor shall I ever know how much my practice and my theory owe to the passages that he read me from Catullus and from Verlaine and Mallarmé. I had read *Axel* [an elaborate prose work in dramatic form by Villiers de l'Isle Adam, first published in Paris in 1890] to myself or was still reading it, so slowly, and with so much difficulty, that certain passages had an exaggerated importance, while all remained so obscure that I could without much effort imagine that here at last was the Sacred Book I longed for.

Beginning early, Yeats gradually built up—bit by bit from Irish folklore, from the visions of second-sighted servants, from the occult traditions of Europe and the East, from the philosophy of Plato and of the neo-Platonists—a private system of mystic, symbolic correspondences. Sooner or later in one's acquaintance with Yeats one must tackle *A Vision,* the work in which these doctrines are systematically presented. There one will encounter his description of the Great Wheel, with its fixed and recurrent arrangement of human types in harmony with the phases of the moon (the characteristics of an age are determined by the place that age occupies on the Wheel: all that has come and gone will come again). There and in other places he has described his belief in the "anima mundi," the soul of the world "which has a memory independent of embodied individual memories, though they constantly enrich it with their images and their thoughts." There also one encounters beliefs, political and religious, which are a consequence of his belief in this closed system: a determinism which makes nonsense of individual striving, a belief in the desirability of a hierarchical order based on wealth and power which resembles certain features of fascist doctrine and practice.

Yeats's private symbols would be a serious obstacle to reading his poetry if that poetry depended on them more centrally than is actually the case. At times, it is true, he is a Symbolist in the exact sense of the word. At such times, when he is using the full panoply of his esoteric symbols, his poems will reserve a part of their meaning for those who, having mastered his various doctrines, are able to give each symbol its proper place in the system. But two points need to be emphasized. In the first place, a given poem will often make its full effect upon us even when we accept in only a general sense statements in it which bear a different and more literal interpretation if they are referred to appropriate passages in *A Vision*. The opening of "The Second Coming," for example, involves Yeats's very definite conception of characteristics of the time he describes, which are a consequence and a sign of the place occupied by that time on the Great Wheel (see *A Vision* [London, 1927], pp. 210 ff.), but everything he says there has seemed a sufficiently accurate and powerful description of the state of the world at the end of the first World War to give the poem great force and meaning even without its being referred to *A Vision*. In the second place, the majority of Yeats's symbols are by no means esoteric. In "Sailing to Byzantium," for example, he is dealing with the conflicting claims of two approaches to human life: the one described in the many symbolic images of the first stanza, the other in the great symbol of Byzantium itself. All will recognize the direction of meaning that is common to the images in which he symbolizes the impermanence of the life of the flesh, the transitoriness of "that sensual music," and it takes very little more trouble to find out enough about Byzantine civilization of the fifth and sixth centuries, with its characteristically abstract, fleshless art and its fondness for artifice, to see why Yeats chose Byzantium as the symbol for the renunciation of the flesh in favor of the intellect. And once the direction and the import of these symbols have been grasped, it is impossible not to see how much of its essential quality the poem owes to their use.

Some of Yeats's political and religious doctrines may repel us or fill us with dismay. But even when they do, we can accept the poetry as the full, clear expression of a state of mind and soul which, though not ours, was indubitably the poet's. It is one of the chief glories of Yeats's mature poetry that he made it the vehicle for the most complete expression of *all*,

in mind and soul, that was relevant to the state of consciousness which sought expression in a particular poem. In his best poetry we encounter a marvelous blending of the firm control of art with complete freedom to say what is in his mind and to describe what he sees in the moment's outward circumstance. The poets of the nineties had sifted the subject matter of their poetry to exclude all that was not in their view strictly poetic. Yeats resembled other poets of the new century in seeing that *all* experience could provide subject matter for poetry, that to limit and exclude was to court a thin artificiality of tone and purpose. In "Among School Children," for example, the soaring appeal of the last stanza gains some of its power from the foundations laid for it in the opening stanzas, with their flat, unemphatic, deliberate—but never "unpoetic"—notation of all that Yeats saw in the schoolroom, described in his own voice.

For always it is Yeats's own voice, never a voice which we feel has been assumed, with pose and strain, for the purpose of poetic utterance. He describes in the *Autobiography* how he was led to formulate a poetic principle which is central to all that is best and most characteristic in his verse, from as early as *The Green Helmet* (1910) onwards:

We should write out our own thoughts in as nearly as possible the language we thought them in, as though in a letter to an intimate friend. We should not disguise them in any way; for our lives give them force as the lives of people in plays give force to their words. Personal utterance, which had almost ceased in English literature, could be as fine an escape from rhetoric and abstraction as drama itself. . . . I tried from that on to write out of my emotions exactly as they came to me in life, not changing them to make them more beautiful. "If I can be sincere and make my language natural, and without becoming discursive, like a novelist, and so indiscreet and prosaic," I said to myself, "I shall, if good luck or bad luck make my life interesting, be a great poet; for it will be no longer a matter of literature at all."

This principle of "personal utterance," the belief that the poet should write out of his life nor hesitate to bring his life's actuality into the poem, goes far to help us understand the quality that so compels and moves us in poems like "Easter, 1916," "Coole and Ballylee, 1931," or "At Algeciras." It is a principle of integrity and truth which makes it a small matter that (for example) we accept only poetically and temporarily the doctrine of reincarnation, referred to in "Sailing to Byzantium," which Yeats himself may have accepted literally.

IN Yeats we see how a man of great gifts made his own use of the doctrines and techniques of Symbolism. Those doctrines and techniques have touched, to one degree or another, the work of most of the twentieth-century writers whom we think of as writing for their own time rather than as being content to echo the late Victorians. In this respect, as in others, Yeats's development parallels the general development of poetry in the new century, yet he was in many ways (with the exception of his Irish interests and his place in the Irish Renaissance) an isolated figure, without attachment to programs and schools which seem, at least in retrospect, to have determined the direction taken by literature in the past few decades.

There has been no time in the present century when British poets and novelists have not produced valuable and significant work, and this is true even of the first decade of the century, a period which has sometimes struck the literary historian as a time of stagnation, when the comparative certainty of life in the Edwardian era produced a thickening of literary line and a dullness of spirit. Such generalizations are always dangerous, but they are not wholly meaningless if we take them not as objective descriptions of what writers were actually producing during the period in question but rather as expressions of the attitude of the younger writers who saw the techniques and interests of their elders as inadequate for their new purposes. Not every generation is a generation in revolt, of course, but the generation which came of age around the time of the first World War was as sharply in revolt against accepted literary conventions as any generation has ever been.

The shock of the war itself; the sense of monstrous futility which its suffering and destruction aroused; and, in the years following the war, the sense of bitter disillusionment as it became more and more obvious that the millions who had died in the war had died to no purpose: the difficult assimilation of these experiences was the major fact in the life of the European spirit from 1914 onwards. It was as if mankind had suddenly seen how deep a pit it was capable of digging for itself, how little it could trust itself to follow the modes of idealism, of humanistic purpose, and of human charity which earlier generations had taken for granted. Henry James, the great American novelist who, living for the most part in Europe, had for decades devoted a sensitive power of observation and understanding to analyzing the subtlest motives of European civilization, expressed the general dismay in a letter dated August 5, 1914:

The plunge of civilization into this abyss of blood and darkness by the wanton feat of those two infamous autocrats is a thing that so gives away the whole long age during which we have supposed the world to be, with whatever abatement, gradually bettering, that to have to take it all now for what the treacherous years were all the while really making for and *meaning* is too tragic for any words.

Nor, unhappily, did it long remain possible to attach sole blame for civilization's betrayal to the German and Austrian emperors.

The brutality of the war years themselves and the hitherto unparalleled suffering of the men who fought and died in the trenches was nowhere expressed with greater poignancy, dignity, or clear, hard force than in the poems of Wilfred Owen. Owen was killed on November 4, 1918, at the Sambre Canal, still in his twenties. A volume of his poems was first published in 1920, with an introduction by another distinguished war poet, Siegfried Sassoon; his complete poems, edited and with a memoir by Edmund Blunden, were published in 1931 and have been reprinted several times since, for Owen's verse has retained a strong hold on the imagination of succeeding generations, of poets as well as of readers of poetry. In some of his poems Owen used a new riming technique, off-rime or para-rime (some prefer the term "dissonance") where the riming words are similar in their consonants but dissimilar in their vowels (see, for example, in "Strange Meeting," p. 956, below, such rimes as *mystery-mastery, spoiled-spilled*), or in which rime is close but not exact. This device, which was particularly suitable for the wry pathos or bitterness of Owen's poems, also had the more general usefulness of allowing poets to retain the advantages of rime without the cramping disadvantages of the traditional English rime-schemes. W. H. Auden and other poets of the generation which began to publish around 1930 were to make considerable use of para-rime. But even more important than Owen's technique in winning the admiration and discipleship of the poets who came after him was the spirit of his poetry, the complete clarity and steadiness with which he fixed his regard on human suffering and human injustice. The few sentences with which he had thought to preface the volume of poems he was preparing at the time of his death have become famous. His book, he had warned, would not glorify conquest or salve the conscience of the English people by paying empty tribute to heroism. As to the heroes, "English poetry," he said, "is not yet fit to speak of them."

> Above all I am not concerned with Poetry.
> My subject is War and the pity of War.
> The Poetry is in the pity.

Owen's conviction that the poet's success is to be judged by his faithfulness to his subject, by the truthfulness he attains, finds at least a partial parallel in some of the critical positions of T. E. Hulme, also killed in the war, notably in Hulme's belief that the time was ripe for a kind of poetry which should be "classical" rather than "romantic," according to his definition of those vexed terms (pp. 964 f., below). Owen and Hulme were both protesting against what they saw as a grave weakness in much of the poetry of their time: the poet's willingness, inherited from the Romantic Movement, to abandon himself to an excess of feeling without sufficient regard for the object or situation which occasioned it, a habit which led to vagueness of the feeling itself and to a blunting of the instruments of expression. When Owen said he was "not concerned with Poetry," he meant that he was too gravely concerned with suffering, of which he wanted to make the English people bitterly aware, ever to be content with mere self-satisfied phrase-making about it. The truths he had seen were not to be the subject matter of poems which would receive their value from the poet's treatment; the poems were instruments for making the truth known, and the truth, if it were faithfully rendered, would give the poems their reason for being and their strength.

But such critical ideas were in the air, both during and after the war. An ideal of precision, of a controlling objectivity, of the greatest possible fidelity to the emotion or the appearance with which the poet was working: such an ideal figures in many of the critical programs of the time and has determined the direction taken by much of the most interesting poetry of the last few decades. In his autobiographical volume *The Innocent Eye,* Herbert Read says that around the time of the war "there was a general feeling that some new philosophy was necessary, much as it had been necessary when Wordsworth and Coleridge had published their *Lyrical Ballads* in 1798," and he cites as the clearest summation of this feeling the six "common principles" stated in the preface to a collection of Imagist poetry (including poems by Richard Aldington, H. D., and D. H. Lawrence) published in 1915. Everything in these principles (see below, p. 979) emphasizes the necessity for the poet of saying exactly what he himself sees or feels or thinks exactly as he himself sees or feels or thinks it, the necessity of finding his own rhythms, his own images, of being free from cramping conventions of experience or expression. Another statement of principles from the same period, recently reprinted (see "A Stray Document" in Ezra Pound's *Make It New,* 1934), insists on "direct treatment of the 'thing' whether subjective or objective."

Some of the work produced by poets who were too exclusively "imagist" (contenting themselves with fixing single images in two or three lines of verse) was so slight as to have retained no more than an antiquarian interest, just as much *vers libre,* or free verse, written with no more serious purpose than to celebrate a sense of escape from convention, is now wholly uninteresting and unreadable. But the principle of sharpness of image and the principle of correspondence of a poet's rhythms to his subject were of the greatest importance and usefulness in the hands of poets who had something to say, and who were capable of adapting these principles to produce their own characteristic techniques.

BETWEEN THE TWO WARS: EZRA POUND AND T. S. ELIOT; D. H. LAWRENCE

We sometimes talk of literary schools and programs and tendencies as if they had an existence of their own, as if they had produced the works which we cite in discussing them. In truth, of course, the most cogent declarations of literary principle would be no sooner framed than forgotten if it were not for the poems or plays or novels which make the program worth talking about in the first place. The critical ideas which we have just glanced at, and which began to be current around 1915, are still interesting to us, and still operative, because of the writers who entertained them and who demonstrated them in works of great intrinsic value. To those who followed the little magazines which provided a vehicle for young writers of the new school—*The Egoist, The Little Review,* and, in America, Harriet Monroe's *Poetry*— it may have been difficult to know which of the new movement's many adherents were its leaders. But in retrospect it is clear that—with the exception of D. H. Lawrence, who was a law unto himself—the chief figures, and certainly the most influential figures, were two Americans living in England, Ezra Pound and T. S. Eliot.

Ezra Pound, born in Idaho in 1885 and educated at the University of Pennsylvania and Hamilton College, first went to Europe in 1906, and lived abroad, except for brief visits to the United States, until 1945, chiefly in England and Italy. But unlike T. S. Eliot he has retained his American citizenship, and for that reason he is not represented in the following pages. His major work, on which a large part of his reputation must ultimately rest, is the *Cantos,* which have been appearing in various forms and in various groupings since 1916; the most recent collection, containing nearly a hundred cantos, was published in 1948. Pound's recent fate has been an unhappy one. In July, 1943, he was indicted for treason by the United States Government, as a consequence of his wartime broadcasts over Radio Roma, and in 1945 he was brought back to this country; having been declared of unsound mind, he has not faced trial. The award of the Bollingen Prize, in 1949, for the *Pisan Cantos* made him the center of a violent controversy, with distinguished writers and critics ranged on both sides of the question of whether he should have been given the award or not. That question need not be decided here, but it should be noted that many writers—among them T. S. Eliot, Edith Sitwell, Wyndham Lewis, and Ernest Hemingway—have provided warm testimony, both at this and at other times, to their admiration for Pound's work and, in some cases, to their recognition of his influence on their own work. Few names are more important in the literary history of our time.

Whether we admire the *Cantos* or not, and however much we may regret the shrillness as well as the direction of Pound's later critical and political utterances, we may still take pleasure in his early criticism and poetry. In his early essays he urged his readers to widen their horizons, to improve the *quality* of their attention to literature, to read valuable work which he thought was neglected or misunderstood: Provençal poetry, certain Scots and Elizabethan translations of the classics, French poetry of the nineteenth century and after. Some of these interests figured no less prominently in his poetry. Except for *A Lume Spento,* published in a limited edition in Venice, his first volume of poems, *Personae,* was published in London in 1909. These poems, and those which followed, were the focal point for many interests and influences. Many of them are dramatic, in the manner of Browning's dramatic monologues (Browning was the one Victorian poet whom Pound and his associates were able to admire or follow), and often Pound chose a Provençal or Italian poet, or a figure encountered in his reading of Provençal or Italian poetry, to be the *persona* or "mask" through which he spoke. Or at other times, in the course of a poem in which he gave direct voice to his own feelings or

thoughts, he would quote a phrase or a line or a brief passage from an earlier writer which would afford a commentary, by contrast or by similarity, on the situation he was describing. The fifteenth-century French poet François Villon, for example, begins one of his poems with these lines:

En l'an trentiesme de mon aage
Que toutes mes hontes j'ay beues . . .

(In the thirtieth year of my age
When I have drunk down all my shame . . .),

lines which Eliot was to use as the epigraph to "A Cooking Egg." The first section of a poem published in 1920, "E. P. Ode pour l'Election de son Sépulchre," in which Pound is describing with ironic detachment the divergence between his poetic ideals and those of the time in which he wrote, contains the following lines:

Unaffected by "the march of events,"
He passed from men's memory in *l'an trentiesme De son eage. . . .*

Here the use of Villon's phrase has the effect of adding to Pound's sardonic account of his own situation a swift comparison with the situation of an earlier poet with whom Pound feels a genial kinship; it could not have been done so deftly, or perhaps so effectively, in any other way, nor is it too much to expect that a reader will recognize a phrase from one of Villon's better-known poems. Pound's poem contains a number of other examples of the same technique, not all so easy to recognize as this, and in fact throughout his poetry Pound makes the fullest use of his reading in several languages, drawing on it for subject matter, for characters, for points of view, and for citations of the sort illustrated. Admittedly such a habit raises a barrier between Pound and the general reader, but—in the early poems at any rate—the barrier is by no means insurmountable, and the poems themselves, in point of beauty and wit, are worth the trouble.

Pound would be an important figure in the literary history of the early twentieth century if for no other reason than that of his services to letters at a time when young writers were seeking both new forms and some kind of outlet for their work. T. S. Eliot has recorded his own indebtedness to Pound in an essay dated 1946 (see *An Examination of Ezra Pound,* ed. Peter Russell, New Directions, 1950) in which, besides describing Pound's general personal influence on him and his contemporaries in the London literary scene between 1915 and 1922, he mentions that it was through Pound's efforts that his first volume of verse, *Prufrock and Other Observations,* was published by the Egoist Press in 1917. He has also told how in Paris, in 1922, he gave Pound "the manuscript of a sprawling chaotic poem called *The Waste Land* which left his hands, reduced to about half its size, in the form in which it appears in print." That poem is dedicated to Pound with a phrase (*il miglior fabbro,* "the better workman") in which Dante pays tribute to the Provençal poet, Arnaut Daniel.

The modesty of the small, buff-paper-covered pamphlet in which *Prufrock and Other Observations* originally appeared gave scant indication of its importance as a literary event. Here, as in Pound's poetry, influences crossed and blended, but the result was something new to English poetry. "The Love Song of J. Alfred Prufrock" is, among other things, a dramatic monologue, just as "My Last Duchess" is a dramatic monologue. But the character revealed is unlike any character Browning would have been interested in, just as the tone and technique of the revelation are unlike the tones or techniques of nineteenth-century English verse (after all, Arthur Hugh Clough was something of an anomaly). Prufrock's diffidence, his heart-gnawing awareness of his own insufficiency, his sardonic self-scrutiny are poles apart from the major tonalities of, say, Tennyson's Ulysses or Browning's Ferrarese Duke. We are more likely to encounter people like Prufrock in the poems of Jules Laforgue, where we also encounter the disabused clarity of view, the intent to undercut the old romantic effects by some sharp incongruity in the way in which they are presented, that we find in "Prufrock." Prufrock's description of the evening sky, in the opening lines of the poem, is arresting because it compares the sky to something with which we would have thought it had no single quality in common. But we immediately perceive that to a certain gaze, to a certain mood, there is a resemblance between the evening sky and "a patient etherized upon a table"; the effect of the image is above all to communicate that mood, Prufrock's mood, to us.

There are similar sunsets in Laforgue; indeed, in Eliot's early poems the tone of many passages reminds one of Laforgue, and occasionally one encounters single lines which are virtually translations from the French poet. More important than this, the structure and the movement of the verse in poems like "Prufrock" or "Portrait of a Lady" reproduce the structure of poems in Laforgue's *Derniers Vers,* just as the brisk, polysyllabic quatrains of poems like "Sweeney among the Nightingales" owe much to Laforgue's poems in the same form (see, for example, the

"Complainte de l'Organiste de Notre Dame de Nice"). But all this does not mean that Eliot was producing pastiche. If we recognize in his early verse many echoes of notes first struck by Laforgue, there are others which are traceable to his interest in other poetry, particularly Elizabethan dramatic verse, and the final result is entirely his own. His indebtedness to the French Symbolists, to Laforgue's particular use of *vers libre,* is to be understood in exactly the same light as the indebtedness of the Elizabethan sonneteers to the forms and conventions of their Italian masters. In this as in other respects Eliot and Pound must be credited with having brought English poetry once more into life-giving contact with Continental forms and movements from which it had been cut off by the insularity—in matters of literary influence, at least—of the Victorians.

Such difficulties as the reader may experience at his first acquaintance with Eliot's poetry may be overcome if he will keep in mind certain features of that poetry. First of all, one who comes to Eliot straight from the poets of the late nineteenth century may need a period of adjustment before he can see that the "Preludes," for instance, are poetry at all. But with familiarity the strong, desperate rhythms of those poems will begin to make their effect, the uncompromisingly realistic details will take on for him their wider character of symbols of the life of modern cities, and he will see that out of such things as the smells of meals being cooked and the descent of dusk over a wintry city street Eliot has created a poetic experience far more poignant and far more *responsible* as an account of the forms of life we see all about us than any evocation of conventional, neo-Victorian beauties could be. The sense of strangeness, the sense of straining to catch the music in the voice, will soon give way to the recognition of a highly controlled, highly individual poetic tone—Eliot is a master of his craft—and, what is more, the reader will gradually discover in himself a grateful awareness that he is reading poetry written for his own day, out of its moods, its sights and sounds, its life.

At first the new reader may be disturbed by the structural principle of a poem like "Prufrock." In it, and in his other poems, Eliot presents a character or a situation by establishing certain points in an experience, but he does not necessarily make the connections between those points: the reader is left to do that for himself. The various episodes in an Eliot poem, as C. Day Lewis has pointed out, are arranged according to a principle of emotional sequence, rather than of intellectual sequence, one image or one episode taking on its full meaning when it is confronted, for comparison or contrast, with the one that precedes or follows: it is a highly flexible and expressive technique, resembling that of the film-cutter. Or a phrase or a sentence may be given a thematic value, to which it refers whenever it recurs, in the manner of a Wagnerian leitmotiv.

At first, too, the reader may want to know things about a character or a situation in an Eliot poem which Eliot has no interest in telling him. In reading "Sweeney among the Nightingales," for instance, it is possible to establish the locale and the cast of characters with some precision, but it is *not* possible to say quite definitely what happens to Sweeney. We see him as a victim of sordid machinations which are not specified beyond a certain point: F. O. Matthiessen says that Eliot "once remarked that all he consciously set out to create in 'Sweeney among the Nightingales' was a sense of foreboding."

"Sweeney among the Nightingales" illustrates one more feature of Eliot's technique which may occasion some difficulty to the unwary: the technique of allusion which we have already noted in talking about Pound. The Greek epigraph—Agamemnon's cry when, in Aeschylus's tragedy, he is murdered by his wife, Clytemnestra ("Alas, I have been struck a most deadly blow!")—is an integral part of the poem. Through its use Eliot reminds us of another instance of victimization by treachery, and we are meant to see Agamemnon's fate as both different from and similar to Sweeney's: different in that it was the doom of a hero and a king, struck down by his faithless queen, different in the aura and significance of great tragedy that it carries with it as opposed to the meanness of Sweeney's falling victim to a tavern intrigue; similar in that baseness and treachery, of one kind or another, are present in both episodes. The commentary on the poem's present action which was begun by the epigraph is concluded and rounded off by the reference to Agamemnon in the concluding lines of the poem. It is neither possible nor necessary to sum up in a phrase or two the total effect that is produced by this juxtaposition of Agamemnon's murder and Sweeney's meaner fate, but it will be seen that the interplay between the two sets of events and values is central to the poem's meaning and purpose. In *The Waste Land* the system of allusions is much more complex than in "Sweeney among the Nightingales," but each particular allusion in that poem, as indeed in Eliot's poetry generally, will be found to depend on the technique we have noticed here.

The Waste Land is possibly the most celebrated poem of the twentieth century; it is certainly the most discussed. First published in 1922, it expressed the disillusionment, the sense of spiritual instability and inadequacy that the war had left behind it with devastating completeness, accuracy, and power. The essence of the various techniques that were employed in writing it is *concentration,* so that any commentary which aims at unfolding all it contains will be many times as long as the poem itself. It describes, in terms of symbolic characters and incidents, the spiritual aridity of our time. In his notes to the poem Eliot has pointed out that "not only the title, but the plan and a good deal of the incidental symbolism . . . were suggested by Miss Jessie L. Weston's book on the Grail Legend: *From Ritual to Romance. . . .*" In that book we find summarized the anthropological accounts of the myth by which, in various forms, primitive man accounted for the changing cycle of the year, particularly the return of the spring. The Waste Land is dry and sterile because the Fisher King, its ruler, is impotent; the life-giving waters will flow again when a Deliverer arrives who, after surviving a dangerous combat (in the Chapel Perilous of the medieval derivatives of the legend), will by sexual intercourse with the Woman restore the land to fertility. In Eliot's poem the Waste Land, its physical aridity powerfully suggested, becomes the symbol for the spiritually arid modern world of false values and misguided aims. All three characters of the legend appear many times, in many different guises: the Fisher King in lines 60–76, 173–214, 422–433, among other places; the Deliverer in the guise of the various men whose energies are devoted to pointless sexual or commercial activities; the Woman in the guise of all the women whose selfish, neurotic, or bewildered concerns and desires represent only a dead end. It is a world of fear, a world of dryness and emptiness that Eliot describes, and by means of allusions to other literary works he is able to set his world against an extraordinarily complex background of pertinent reminders of other worlds, other ideals: sometimes for contrast, at other times for comparison. The way out is clear—it is made clear in "What the Thunder Says," as well as by implication throughout the poem —but that way is not taken and as the poem ends the Fisher King sits upon the shore,

Fishing, with the arid plain behind me,

wondering what he can cling to in the general wreckage and failure.

Even in the early stages of one's acquaintance with *The Waste Land,* one is aware that new meanings are being expressed in new ways, that one has not read anything quite like it before. The opening lines, with their presentation of spring as cruelly disturbing, of winter as desirably negative and vegetative (these things viewed, of course, through the eyes of a generation whose emptiness causes it to see life as fear and death as a release from fear), make their compelling and characteristic impression long before we have begun to fit them into the total plan of the poem. It may be that much will escape us even after we have spent considerable time in studying the poem, in tracing out its allusions, in analyzing the exact position, as part of the poem's total statement, to which the basic questions are carried in each of the poem's five sections. But any labor thus spent will reward us by increasing our admiration for the poem's beauty and force, for its great distinction of thought and style, for the wealth of its tightly packed, detailed implications.

It seems evident, even in *The Waste Land* and *The Hollow Men* (1925), that Eliot's view of the plight of the western world in the twentieth century carries with it, by implication, the idea that the way of salvation lies through a return to religious faith. By the time Eliot published *Ash-Wednesday,* in 1930, he had himself joined the communion of the Church of England, and some of his later works have dealt with explicitly religious themes: for example, *The Rock* (1934), a pageant, and *Murder in the Cathedral* (1935), a verse play centering in the meaning, for the relations between Church and State, of the murder of Thomas à Becket in 1170. His most recent play, *The Cocktail Party,* which has had long commercial runs in London and New York, is in its own way concerned once more with the problem which has figured, directly or indirectly, in nearly all his work: the problem of helping our civilization to find a way out of the abyss. Nor has his later writing been limited to the verse drama; *Four Quartets,* a long reflective poem, with lyric episodes, whose four parts were first published collectively in 1943, reveals that his verse has undergone a marked development, since some of his earlier poems, in the direction of an increased resonance and suppleness.

Eliot has been no less important a force in criticism than in poetry, and many of the particular directions taken by the instructed literary taste of our time have been owing to his lead, either as the author of numerous critical essays or as editor of the *Criterion* or as one of the directors of a firm of London publishers. The first impetus to a revival of active interest in the metaphysical poets of the seventeenth century was probably given by Professor H. J. C. Grierson of the University of Edinburgh shortly before the first World War, but Eliot's essays have been greatly instrumental in furthering that interest, just as they have in making it seem desirable to read Dryden in a more receptive spirit than that in which he was customarily read in the nineteenth century. His criticism is essentially the criticism of an unusually acute reader —and a sensitive poet—who keeps his attention focused on the work before him, seeing it for what it is rather than for what it has always been said to be, but always aware of its position in relation to other works, from several literatures, of the same order. A number of reasons may be cited for Eliot's great current prestige—he was awarded the Nobel Prize in 1948 and made a member of the Order of Merit in the same year—but one need seek no further justification than the poetic power and skill, the acuity of mind, and the clear distinction of spirit which have been visible in his work at all points in his career.

If Eliot found the solution to the problems of the age in a return to established religion, D. H. Lawrence found his answer in quite other places. The insufficiencies, the grave errors of modern life were the consequence, he felt, of too much civilization, of too great a preoccupation with the false values of an industrialized urban society, of living too exclusively according to the dictates of the prudent, conscious mind. The way out lay in a return to the life of the instincts, to a recognition of the power and demands of the blood. Writing from Italy in 1913, Lawrence said, in a passage which finds echoes throughout his work:

My great religion is a belief in the blood, the flesh, as being wiser than the intellect. We can go wrong in our minds. But what our blood feels and believes and says, is always true. The intellect is only a bit and a bridle. What do I care about knowledge. All I want is to answer to my blood, direct, without fribbling intervention of mind, or moral, or what-not. I conceive a man's body as a kind of flame, like a candle flame, forever upright and yet flowing: and the intellect is just the light that is shed on to the things around—which is really mind—but with the mystery of the flame forever flowing, coming God knows how from out of practically nowhere, and being *itself,* whatever there is around it, that it lights up. We have got so ridiculously mindful, that we never know that we ourselves are anything—we think there are only the objects we shine upon. And there the poor flame goes on burning ignored, to produce this light. And instead of chasing the mystery in the fugitive, half-lighted things outside us, we ought to look at ourselves and say "My God, I am myself!" That is why I like to live in Italy. The people are so unconscious. They only feel and want: they don't know. We know too much. No, we only *think* we know such a lot. A flame isn't a flame because it lights up two, or twenty objects on a table. It's a flame because it is itself. And we have forgotten ourselves.

Lawrence's system of beliefs might seem, on the basis of such positions as are touched on in this passage, to be only a thoroughgoing and shallow anti-intellectualism. But it is the positive side of the statement, the belief in the blood, that gave Lawrence's ideas their depth and weight, that cut the channels in which his art was to flow. His belief that the dark gods of the blood may not be denied, that they will have their revenge if we attempt to deny them, reminds us inevitably of the teachings of the Viennese psychiatrist, Sigmund Freud ("I never did read Freud," Lawrence wrote in 1913, "but I have heard about him since I was in Germany"), and may at the same time remind us of the degree to which twentieth-century literature has been colored and shaped by the development of the techniques of psychoanalysis and indeed by the diffusion of psychological knowledge generally. One of the master-ideas of our time, an idea that has determined not only the content, the meaning, but also the very form of many important works in twentieth-century literature, has been the discovery that more is contained in a human mind than can be accounted for by exploring it at the level of consciously formulated thought. Lawrence believed that man should recognize and obey the dictates of the unconscious; other writers, without necessarily taking the same stand on this point, have believed that a character can be completely presented only by recording the content of his mind on all its levels, including the subconscious, and this belief has produced some striking technical developments, particularly in fiction and drama.

Alike because of health and inclination, Lawrence lived out of England for the greater part of his life, after his first visit to Germany and Italy in 1912. When he was in England he was often at odds with the authorities—some of his books were seized and banned, exhibitions of his paintings were closed—and he seemed to find something more nearly approaching contentment among other people than the English. "After us the Savage God," Yeats had said; Lawrence, for his part, sought out the savage god, the elements and forms of primitive belief, among the Indians of Mexico and New Mexico, among the natives in the Australian bush, in the records of Etruscan civilization which he found in Italy. But he also wrote about England, the life he had known as a child and as a young man in the Nottinghamshire mining country, or as a teacher on the outskirts of London. Although he is best known today as a novelist and storyteller, fiction did not suffice as an outlet for all that he was eager to record and describe: he wrote essays and pamphlets, more vehement as

his life neared its end; he wrote absorbing travel books; he occasionally wrote plays; and he was a painter. But he was also one of the three or four foremost poets of his generation.

There is a passage in one of his letters, dated 1916, which helps to place him, as a poet, against a background which includes Imagism and the critical ideas of Hulme, Herbert Read, and Ezra Pound:

The essence of poetry with us in this age of stark and unlovely actualities is a stark directness, without a shadow of a lie, or a shadow of deflection anywhere. Everything can go, but this stark, bare, rocky directness of statement, this alone makes poetry, to-day.

The directness and the truth are present in his poetry, but how much else is there that cannot be accounted for simply by saying "directness" or "truth"! Although it is often possible to feel, in reading Lawrence's letters or the accounts of his life, that he was at the mercy of tormented emotions, as a poet he is unsurpassed for an awareness and control of his own feeling which enabled him, as in a poem like "Nostalgia," to give frank and powerful expression to moods which in another poet would have become mawkish sentimentality. Or in a poem like "Ballad of Another Ophelia," the reader's admiration may be divided between the choice and arrangement of symbols around a common situation or theme, and the skill and beauty with which metrics (particularly line-lengths) are controlled. Lawrence's strong, vivid reactions to experience were matched by powers of expression that make his created world, whether in his fiction or his poetry, still burn with the color he saw in the real world, still beat with the pulse of his own life. Many readers who can scarcely pretend to accept his views, who might have been only abashed and overwhelmed by the man himself (for the man imposes himself as we read, we are as conscious of his presence as we are of Byron's), can in their degrees derive strength and solace from the energy with which he charged every line he wrote.

BETWEEN THE TWO WARS: FICTION

THE attention which the twentieth-century fiction writer has devoted to the short story, and particularly to the long, carefully integrated story which on the Continent is termed a *novella,* has made it possible to represent fiction in the present section of this book. While one cannot gain a complete idea of the work of any novelist simply from reading his short stories, many of his qualities and interests will be found to be common to both forms, and in fact some of the finest and most characteristic work of James Joyce, Aldous

Huxley, and E. M. Forster is to be found in their stories. Virginia Woolf, on the other hand, whose stories (contained in *Monday or Tuesday* and *A Haunted House*) do not seem, at least to the present editor, to measure up to her novels, is represented below not by a story but by an essay, "Mr. Bennett and Mrs. Brown," which is one of the key documents in the history of contemporary fiction.

The conviction which was common to the twentieth-century poets whom we have been discussing (in most respects so different one from another) that the problems as well as the insights and knowledge of their time demanded new emphases, new techniques of expression, was shared by a number of writers of fiction among their contemporaries. In the years immediately following the war the belief gained force that novelists like John Galsworthy, H. G. Wells, and Arnold Bennett were too preoccupied with the external forces and appearances of the life they described ever to capture and convey a sense of that life's true inwardness. It may be that Virginia Woolf, in her stirring essay on the state of fiction in the early twenties (see below, pp. 999 ff.), was so eager to state the claims of the psychological novelist that she did not do complete justice to the achievement of Galsworthy, Wells, and Bennett; and in the future the balance of judgment will probably have to be adjusted in their favor. Meanwhile, however, the most interesting developments in twentieth-century fiction have taken the directions described and defended in that essay.

The Georgian novelist, as Mrs. Woolf described him, was seeking a precedent to support his belief that what went on inside people's minds was more important than the physical and social circumstances in which they lived, but it is hard to believe that precedents were quite so far to seek as she seems to suggest. No novelist, before or since, has been more completely dedicated to tracing the life of the spirit than Henry James, whose later novels, particularly *The Wings of the Dove* (1902), *The Ambassadors* (1903), and *The Golden Bowl* (1904), may well seem to have formed the very portals of initiation for a number of the most distinguished twentieth-century novelists. Moreover, there was the example of the psychological cast given to fiction by the varied art of Joseph Conrad. And if these illustrious practices were not sufficiently close, it might be remembered that E. M. Forster had been an Edwardian before becoming a Georgian, his first novel, *Where Angels Fear to Tread,* having been published in 1905. But Mr. Forster, whose name is one of the first to occur to us when we think of what has been most essentially valuable in the development of the psychological novel, has had an amazing way of never, throughout a long career, being anything but contemporary with the best and liveliest minds of any given moment.

It is true, however, that Mrs. Woolf herself, in novels like *Mrs. Dalloway* (1925), *To the Lighthouse* (1927), and *The Waves* (1931), was more resolute and thorough in her insistence on taking up her stand in the minds of her characters than most other novelists had been. At her best she presents her characters, in terms of the mental and emotional reactions to certain crucial or typical sequences in their lives, with an unsurpassed purity and elegance. Beginning with *Mrs. Dalloway* it is almost as if the life of her novels were bathed in an entirely new medium of light and air. Her nervous, delicate prose gives to the threads of incident and plot which, crossing and recrossing, weave a day or a few months or several years in the lives of her characters, a lyric beauty which nothing else in fiction could quite prepare us for. At the time of her tragic early death in 1941 she enjoyed a higher prestige, both as novelist and as critical essayist, than any other woman in British letters, and it is only since her death that writers like Elizabeth Bowen and Ivy Compton-Burnett, who began their careers about the time she did, have begun to come into their own.

Nevertheless, hers is not perhaps the prime example to which we turn in estimating the range and success of the modern psychological novel; for that, we go to James Joyce. Joyce's early work—the volume of short stories called *Dubliners* (finally published, after many hazards, in 1914) and his first novel, *A Portrait of the Artist as a Young Man* (1916)—employs for the most part perfectly dependable techniques which Joyce had found ready to his hand in the work of the masters of French and Russian fiction. (It should be added that these techniques are employed with the utmost skill, sensitivity, and power, so that *Dubliners* may fairly claim to be the most perfect volume of short stories in English.) But with *Ulysses* it is a different story.

Each of the stories in *Dubliners* presents an episode in the life of some one citizen of Dublin, usually an incident which reveals that character and the meaning of his life not only to us but also to himself: Joyce thought of the stories as "Epiphanies." One of the stories, to be called "Mr. Bloom's Day," was to have followed a middle-class Dublin Jew, Leopold Bloom, through a typical (but also completely specific) day in his life. But this subject outgrew even the *novella* form, and became the subject for Joyce's second novel, *Ulysses* (Paris, 1922), in which we accompany Mr. Bloom through as nearly as possible *all* the events in a single day—June 16, 1904, to be exact. This book, each of whose main episodes parallels an episode in the *Odyssey,* each having its own prose style appropriate to the nature of the episode (for example, the chapter which refers itself to the Cave of the Winds episode in Homer takes place in a newspaper office and makes use of newspaper jargon and newspaper headlines), has demanded about as much critical explanation and analysis as *The Waste Land.* And for the same reasons: Joyce is describing a modern life, but he has felt impelled to base it in a structure of parallel reference to an earlier work (the *Odyssey* takes the place of the legend of the Fisher King), and again like Eliot, he has seen fit to pack his work with literary and historical allusions. Like *The Waste Land, Ulysses* rewards the reader who will make the effort to understand it with a rich and complex vision of the modern world.

Ulysses has been a significant work in twentieth-century literary history for a number of reasons. In the first place, because of the perfect frankness with which Joyce detailed the actions and thoughts of his characters, involving him in the representation of biological functions and erotic imagery which novelists had hitherto been accustomed to suppress. In 1933 Judge John M. Woolsey of the United States District Court rendered a notable decision lifting the ban on *Ulysses,* thus, as has been said, "making an honest book of it." This decision, printed as a preface to the American edition of the book, has established a precedent by which other honest, serious books may be relieved of the undeserved stigma of dishonesty.

Ulysses is important, too, for the thoroughness with which Joyce has utilized the technique of the interior monologue, reproducing as accurately and as completely as possible a character's "stream of consciousness," the whole flow of the waking mental process, in all its apparent inconsequentiality, formlessness, and detail. In the concluding section of the novel we follow, for some forty pages, the thoughts and fleeting impressions of Bloom's wife as she gradually drifts off to sleep. Although Joyce cannot be said to have "invented" the stream-of-consciousness technique, he carried it farther toward the limits of utter faithfulness than any other writer has done. In his last novel, *Finnegans Wake* (1939), he used a kind of dream-language to explore and present the dream-consciousness: the result is a work of enormous difficulty, of an inordinately closely-worked significance, and of great beauty and wit. (It is best approached in the form of the various sections which

were published separately while Joyce was working on it: particularly, perhaps, "Anna Livia Plurabelle.") Compared with such works, the stories in *Dubliners* may seem elementary, but Joyce's early work, since it sprang from the same sources of intelligence and compassion that produced *Ulysses,* and since it presents no difficulty of form, should have the effect of establishing for the reader the respect and understanding which will be helpful and appropriate when he first approaches the later books.

For the most part the writers whose careers form the history of English literature between the two wars believed in the mind, retained a faith in the validity of its most subtle workings even when they saw all about them the evidence that man was using his intellect to destroy himself. Aldous Huxley, who seemed to those who read his early novels and stories to have succeeded in taking all knowledge for his province, has been, with Evelyn Waugh and the late George Orwell as his chief competitors, the leading satirist of our time. His view of the world and of modern man's place in it has never been tinged with false optimism, but the surface gaiety and sparkle of the early work—novels like *Crome Yellow* (1921) or *Antic Hay* (1923) or *Point Counter Point* (1928)—has gradually given way to the uncompromising view of the future which he has set down in *Ape and Essence* (1949). This latter work, in its unflinchingly bitter revelation of its author's view of the ultimate consequences of man's present behavior, reminds us of the tone and purpose of the Fourth Book of *Gulliver's Travels.*

But mention of *Ape and Essence* has taken us away from the twenties, away from the whole period of between-the-two-wars to the years immediately following World War II. To return for a moment to the earlier period, it may be possible to point to one or two of its achievements even if it is not possible to "summarize" it. In the first place, its major writers stand for a consistent devotion to the principles of subtlety and intensity in literature, as well as to a principle of complexity which is a result not of mere fondness for complication of simple meanings but of the writer's having complex things to say. As we have seen, certain poetic developments involved more effective literary contacts with Continental forms and ideas than British literature had seen for almost a century. It was a period during which the intellectual life of men of letters was active and vivid, fed by an interest in new ideas, new forms and techniques, and stirred not infrequently by eager controversy. (The period supported two exciting and distinguished reviews, among its other periodicals: the *Criterion,* edited by T. S. Eliot, which was published between 1922 and 1939; and *Scrutiny,* edited by F. R. Leavis, which still appears.) The belief prevailed, and is easily seen in the writings of those who represent their time most faithfully, that nothing should be taken for granted, that all principles, and all values, aesthetic and otherwise, should be subjected to searching and recurrent examination. Finally, in spite of the defeatism, in spite of the disillusionment that grew as the shock of the War gave way to the realization that the Peace was doomed, these years produced work of the highest distinction and interest in all forms. In confirmation of this statement one might easily add a score or more of names to those already discussed: among them, certainly, Robert Graves, Edith Sitwell, Wyndham Lewis, Katherine Mansfield, Middleton Murry, Edmund Blunden, William Plomer, and Somerset Maugham.

W. H. AUDEN AND THE THIRTIES

IN 1930, a volume of poems was published by Faber and Faber in London which seems, in retrospect at least, to have heralded the most interesting poetry of the thirties as clearly as *Prufrock and Other Observations* had heralded that of the twenties. This volume, W. H. Auden's *Poems,* was not its author's first appearance in print; in 1928 another volume, also called *Poems,* had been hand-printed at Oxford by Stephen Spender, Auden's fellow poet, in an edition of about forty-five copies. Some of Auden's poems had also appeared in the annual collections of verse by Oxford undergraduates, *Oxford Poetry;* the volumes for 1926, 1927, and 1928 constitute a remarkable prediction of things to come in that they contain early poems not only by Auden but also by Stephen Spender, C. Day Lewis, Louis MacNeice, and Rex Warner, as well as by other writers who have since become only slightly less well known.

The poems in Auden's 1930 volume were various in kind, but all were wholly new both in manner and matter. It is true, they owed much to Eliot's exploration of important areas of thought and feeling; they owed certain features of their technique to Wilfred Owen, others to G. M. Hopkins (whose poems, it will be remembered, had first been published in 1918): which means merely that Auden built on the innovations and advances made by his immediate predecessors. But the total impression was of a new poetic voice whose tone and quality could not possibly have been predicted any more than it could henceforth be forgotten, an impression of an observed and created world whose problems and preoccupations differed widely from those of the immediate post-war world.

Just as it had taken readers some time to get used to the techniques of presentation and the subject matter of Eliot's early poems, so it took time to see beyond the apparent strangeness of poems like "Pur" or "Too Dear, Too Vague" (see below, pp. 943 f.) to the beauty which familiarity with them disclosed. In such poems as the two mentioned, with their arresting use of the two-beat line, Auden cultivated a compression, a deliberate suppression of links and transitions, which some readers were at first baffled by. But although Auden has produced poems and parts of poems which are rendered perfectly hermetic by their unexplained reference to private circumstances, private jokes, in general the way to "understand" his poetry lies in learning to see in it what is there and not to look for kinds of statement or explanation which we are accustomed to finding in other poetry but which Auden is not concerned with.

The way to "understand" a poem like "Pur," for example (this, like many of Auden's poems, was first given its title in *The Collected Poetry of W. H. Auden,* 1945), is not to try to paraphrase it, to reduce what it is saying to other terms, to prose, but to take it in *completely,* as it stands, to "get it by heart," in every sense of the word. Some parts of it would be difficult to paraphrase, but is it not an easy matter to apprehend what in general it is saying, about the way moonlight seems to change life, to give it a different meaning from that of our daylight existence, to give us a glimpse of life and the world free from time or change as it appears to be under the influence of moonlight? Or in "Too Dear, Too Vague," which like other of Auden's poems makes full use of what modern psychology, particularly as it involves psychoanalysis, has taught us about the human heart —do not lines like

> For no is not love: no is no

or

> Love is not there
> Love has moved to another chair

give in their measure an almost dazzlingly new verbal apprehension of old truths?

Auden and his contemporaries came of age during the economic slump of the thirties, and economic, political, and social questions form one of their major subjects, besides giving the tone to much of their imagery. In Auden's early poems the general interest of his time in finding a solution to grave social problems is frequently reflected in charade-like imagery, in references to an imaginary war with imaginary sides and campaigns. Later, as in the long poem "Spain, 1937" (see below, pp. 948 f.), the recognition of the necessity for political action became explicit. The special number of *New Verse* (November, 1937) which was devoted to Auden contained brief statements about him and his work by a number of writers of his and the preceding generation, among them one in which Stephen Spender says that at Oxford Auden had been interested not in politics but in "poetry, psychoanalysis and medicine," and that he " 'arrived at' politics by way of psychology."

His early poems begin by being preoccupied with neurosis in individuals, but this gradually extends (at the time when he had left Oxford and gone to live in Berlin) to an interest in the epoch and capitalist society.

Like so many thinking people of the thirties, these poets saw many places in the world where Communism offered an alternative to suffocation from the forces of reaction. Spender, who described the need for decisive political alignment in *Forward from Liberalism* (1937) and who has recently described his generation's disillusionment with Communism (in an essay in *The God That Failed*, 1950), goes on to show in the statement from which we have just quoted how the alternatives looked in the early thirties:

. . . In post-war and pre-Hitler Berlin, one began by noticing symptoms of decadence, suffering and unemployment; one looked further and one saw beneath the decay of the liberal state, the virulent reaction of the Nazis and the struggle for a new life of the Communists. The one side stood for the suppression of the very objectivity which the poet required, perhaps also his life, certainly his intellectual standards; the other, however painful and disillusioning its birth pangs, promised finally a world in which one could see and tell the truth.

We must remember in reading the poetry of the thirties that hopes and beliefs were then green which have since withered past all recognition. The tone and direction of much of that poetry are determined by a conviction that the sardonic disillusionment of the twenties should be swept away by forceful, positive action—by political action.

Since his first volume, Auden's poetry has been continually growing and changing. There have been many volumes since 1930: *The Orators, an English Study* (1932), a combination of verse and prose as exciting and unforgettable as it was bewildering; *Look, Stranger* (1936; called *On This Island* in

America), a collection of poems which to some readers represented the fulfillment of Auden's earlier promise, and which was in any case scarcely to be matched by any living poet for the perfect beauty, the wit, or the rich variety of its contents; *Another Time* (1940), with its remarkable poems about particular great men—Melville, Pascal, Voltaire, Yeats. Less interesting than the poems, but still sufficiently interesting, are experiments in the verse drama, either by Auden alone (*The Dance of Death*, 1933) or in collaboration with the novelist Christopher Isherwood (*The Dog beneath the Skin*, 1935, and *The Ascent of F-6*, 1936). Isherwood, by the way, whose stories and short novels about Berlin in the late twenties and early thirties offer a fascinating record of a tragic era, has included in his semifictional autobiographical volume, *Lions and Shadows*, a description of a young poet called Hugh Weston which will be of particular interest to readers of Auden.

In his more recent work, such as *For the Time Being* ("A Christmas Oratorio"), *The Sea and the Mirror* ("A Commentary on Shakespeare's *The Tempest*"), and *The Age of Anxiety* ("A Baroque Eclogue," whose meter is closely derived from Old English alliterative verse), Auden has continued to experiment with form. Wherever, in these works, he uses prose, it is no less brilliant than the verse. In two of his books (*Journey to a War*, written in collaboration with Isherwood and describing their journey to China in 1938, and *New Year Letter*, a long philosophical poem published in 1941) sonnet sequences are included. Some critics have felt that these sonnets (see below, pp. 946 f.), deriving in form and tone not from the English sonneteers but from Rainer Maria Rilke, the great German Symbolist poet who died in 1926, are the finest poetry Auden has yet written. But he has written too much verse of the first order of excellence to make such questions easy to decide.

If Auden is the most commanding poetic figure of his generation, by reason of the variety, the scope, and the consistent quality of his achievement, there are a number of other poets who nowise fall below him in quality or interest and who would repay full discussion if space were available. The publication of Stephen Spender's first volume of poems in 1933 was as significant and pleasurable an event as Auden's first appearance had been. Although Spender has written successfully in many forms, including the long poem, the verse drama, fiction, criticism, and reportage, he is best known for his several volumes of lyrics. Something of the sort might also be said of Louis MacNeice, whose books are as varied in scope, including as they do verse plays for theater and radio, a fine translation of Aeschylus's *Agamemnon,* criticism, and books of travel and observation: but it is to the successive collections of shorter poems that we return again and again. Either of these poets would confer distinction on the time in which he wrote, nor are they the only poets whom the thirties have to be proud of. Particularly one should mention C. Day Lewis and George Barker, as well as a number of Welsh poets—Dylan Thomas, Vernon Watkins, and Alun Lewis, to name only those who come first to mind.

But with these last-named poets we are in the forties, and that is closer than we can come without running the risk of losing a clear perspective by which to judge a writer and his achievement. We cannot tell what might have been produced during the last ten or twelve years if during that time so many lives, so much strength had not been taken up by the effort of the war and its ambiguous aftermath. Still, great works were produced during the war years by those who had already had a chance to begin: Eliot's *Four Quartets* first appeared together in 1943, and the poets of the thirties continued to publish. The new generation, scattered over the world on the fighting fronts, produced as it could, including much interesting writing, particularly in prose, describing the war's immediate impact on those who fought it. That generation is represented in the following pages by a story from the pen of Alun Lewis, the promising young Welsh poet who was killed in an accident in Burma in 1944. His work seems destined to live less for any influence it may have on later writers of the kind Owen has continued to exert, than for its own interest and merit, in which respects it stands as a tragic memorial to the waste of an era. Some of Lewis's work was published in Cyril Connolly's monthly review, *Horizon* (1940–50), and in John Lehmann's *Penguin New Writing;* one of the best and pleasantest ways to recapture the air and spirit of the forties is to read through the files of these two admirably interesting and unpretentious periodicals.

* * * * * * *

In the present section of this anthology, concerned as it is with writers who are close to us in time and in many cases still living, it is especially important to make clear the principles on which selections have been made. No matter how generous one's space, an anthology must be a selection, and one has a choice between offering a little of everything and giving an adequate representation of what seems centrally important. Our choice here has been the second one.

No attempt has been made to include every writer who has in some way distinguished himself during the past fifty years; instead, we have aimed at directing attention to work which it is essential to know if we are to understand what the twentieth century has made of the British literary tradition. There are of course many writers not mentioned here whose books might well be seen as parallel in importance to the books of those whom we include; the work of still others, while it is of great intrinsic interest and value, seems to be less strictly contemporary, less representative of the century than that of the writers we have chosen. Problems of bulk make it impracticable to include plays; add to this the late George Bernard Shaw's attitude to the anthologizing of his work, and you have the reason why that great figure is not represented, even though no one is apt to forget that the past half-century may someday be known as the Age of Shaw.

This claim is made: that the poems, critical documents, and stories which follow will in the most real sense of the word *introduce* the reader to twentieth-century British literature, that instead of offering a merely synoptic glance at names and samples they will enable the reader to form with some fullness an idea of the quality and direction of the writing which has been most nearly central to the literary developments of our time. The anthologist's aim, in the end, is to stir an impulse which will send his reader back to the volumes from which he has made selections. With each of the writers presented in the following pages it has been our aim to do just that, to send the reader to volumes which have offered all too embarrassing an array of riches. For an acquaintance with the writers represented here will, we believe, put the reader in possession of a key to what has been best and most distinctive in twentieth-century British literature.

GENERAL REFERENCES

Edwin Muir's *The Present Age from 1914* (1940), like the other volumes in the series of *Introductions to English Literature,* edited by Bonamy Dobrée, offers admirably full and convenient lists of authors and works, preceded by interesting critical chapters which survey the background and the achievement, in the several literary forms, of its period.

In no sense a handbook, Edmund Wilson's *Axel's Castle: A Study in the Imaginative Literature of 1870–1930* (1931, and later reissues) is undoubtedly one of the first books to which the student should turn for an account of the history and character of twentieth-century literature. It consists of an introductory chapter on Symbolism followed by chapters on—among others—Yeats, Eliot, and Joyce. In C. M. Bowra's *The Heritage of Symbolism* (1947), the introductory chapter and the chapter on Yeats will be of particular interest to the student of English literature.

F. R. Leavis's *New Bearings in English Poetry: A Study of the Contemporary Situation* (1932) offers the kind of general discussion suggested by its title as well as chapters on Eliot, Pound, and Hopkins. Another general study of twentieth-century literature, this time undertaken in support of a hypothesis which may be less readily acceptable than a number of the particular views it states, or than its analyses of particular works, is Stephen Spender's *The Destructive Element: A Study of Modern Writers and Beliefs* (1935). Even more personal, at times whimsical, but always lively and provocative is *Enemies of Promise* (1939), in which Cyril Connolly distributes rewards and punishments to contemporary writers on a system of his own devising.

C. Day Lewis's *A Hope for Poetry* (1934), after surveying the poetic practice of Owen, Hopkins, and Eliot, goes on to describe the aims of the generation of poets to which he, Auden, Spender, and MacNeice belong. Louis MacNeice's *Modern Poetry: A Personal Essay* (1938) is valuable not only for what it tells us of MacNeice's own development but also for its account of the demands and influences of which these poets were conscious at the beginning of their careers. Views of the function of poetry which were to some extent shared by these writers are brought out in a pamphlet by Stephen Spender, *Life and the Poet* (1942).

British, as well as Continental, literature up to the outbreak of World War II is surveyed in John Lehmann's *New Writing in Europe* (1940). The story is briefly recapitulated and then carried forward in a series of pamphlets (each illustrated with photographs of writers) published for the British Council in 1946: *Poetry since 1939*, by Stephen Spender; *The Novel since 1939*, by Henry Reed; *Prose Literature since 1939*, by John Hayward; and *Drama since 1939*, by Robert Speaight—the four later published together under the title *Since 1939*. Geoffrey Grigson's *Poetry of the Present: An Anthology of the 'Thirties and After* (1949) contains an introductory essay which carries the story of British poetry up through World War II.

The Novel and the Modern World (1939), by David Daiches, contains chapters on Galsworthy, Conrad, Katherine Mansfield, Joyce, Virginia Woolf, and Aldous Huxley. *The Modern Short Story: A Critical Survey* (1941), by H. E. Bates, provides a survey of the development of the short story in the twentieth century, as well as an account of its nineteenth-century origins.

William Butler Yeats

1865–1939

SINCE Yeats's development as a poet forms such an important chapter in twentieth-century literary history, that development and the events in his life which helped to determine it have been described with some fullness in the General Introduction. Here it may be added that Yeats was born at Sandymount, near Dublin, and was educated at schools in London and Dublin. The Yeats family moved to London in 1887, but Yeats was to move back and forth between England and Ireland throughout his life. "The Lake Isle of Innisfree," one of Yeats's best-known early poems, was inspired by a sudden fit of longing for the Irish countryside which overtook him in a crowded London street (*Autobiographies*, p. 134); he was in England when he heard the news of the Easter Rebellion which was the occasion of his magnificent tribute to the patriots, "Easter, 1916." But while it is sometimes easy (however mistaken it may be) to forget that Swift and Shaw were Irishmen, with Yeats we never for a moment do so. Nor is this simply a matter of the external events of his life: of his work in founding an Irish National Theatre, for instance, or of his having been a Senator of the Irish Free State from 1922 to 1928. For like James Joyce he accepted Ireland, Irish life, Irish questions of conscience as the subject matter and guiding inspirational force of his art, without ever descending to a superficial picturesqueness or to the special pleading that provincialism must supply in its own behalf. If he eagerly accepted his Irish inheritance, the orientation he gave it in his writing was effectively European and cosmopolitan.

Yeats's poems are at present most conveniently read in *The Collected Poems of W. B. Yeats* (1950), which includes the several volumes he published during his lifetime, beginning with *The Wanderings of Oisin* (1889), as well as the posthumous *Last Poems and Plays* (1940). Readers who are interested in the development of Yeats's style should notice that the texts of some of the earlier poems in this collected edition (as in the 1933 *Collected Poems*) incorporate the poet's later revisions, so that it is sometimes instructive to compare the text of a given poem as it appears in *The Collected Poems* with the original text: the most frequently cited instance is that of "The Sorrow of Love," first published in *The Rose* (1893). Yeats's plays, both in prose and verse, were last collected in 1934;

the next collection will presumably add *Wheels and Butterflies* (1935), which includes the remarkably interesting play about Swift, "The Words upon the Window-pane."

The volume of *Essays* (1924) incorporates three collections of Yeats's critical writings: *Ideas of Good and Evil* (1896–1903), *The Cutting of an Agate* (1903–15), and *Per Amica Silentia Lunae* (1916–17). The *Autobiography of William Butler Yeats* (1938), from which quotation is made several times in the General Introduction, is the first book which should be consulted by the reader who wishes to supplement the study of Yeats's poetry with a study of the forces and interests which lie behind it. The *Letters on Poetry from W. B. Yeats to Dorothy Wellesley* (1940), although somewhat specialized in point of view, are not without their interest, particularly as regards

Yeats's views of his contemporaries (see also his introductory essay to *The Oxford Book of Modern Verse,* which he edited). Closer in the nature of its interest to Yeats's own autobiographical writings than to the work of his critics or biographers is the volume of letters by the poet's father, *J. B. Yeats: Letters to His Son W. B. Yeats and Others, 1869–1922* (1934).

There is a vast body of critical and biographical writing about Yeats, both in essay and book form. Some of the most distinguished shorter pieces are conveniently collected in *The Permanence of Yeats: Selected Criticism,* edited by James Hall and Martin Steinmann (1950). Among the books, one would first want to recommend *Yeats, the Man and the Masks,* by Richard Ellmann (1948), and *The Poetry of W. B. Yeats,* by Louis MacNeice (1941).

William Butler Yeats

THE FALLING OF THE LEAVES[1]

Autumn is over the long leaves that love us,
And over the mice in the barley sheaves;
Yellow the leaves of the rowan above us,
And yellow the wet wild-strawberry leaves.

The hour of the waning of love has beset us,   5
And weary and worn are our sad souls now;
Let us part, ere the season of passion forget us,
With a kiss and a tear on thy drooping brow.

AN IRISH AIRMAN FORESEES HIS DEATH[2]

I know that I shall meet my fate
Somewhere among the clouds above;
Those that I fight I do not hate,
Those that I guard I do not love;

My country is Kiltartan Cross,[3]   5
My countrymen Kiltartan's poor,
No likely end could bring them loss
Or leave them happier than before.
Nor law, nor duty bade me fight,
Nor public men, nor cheering crowds,   10
A lonely impulse of delight
Drove to this tumult in the clouds;
I balanced all, brought all to mind,
The years to come seemed waste of breath,
A waste of breath the years behind   15
In balance with this life, this death.

THE FISHERMAN[4]

Although I can see him still,
The freckled man who goes
To a grey place on a hill
In grey Connemara clothes
At dawn to cast his flies,   5
It's long since I began
To call up to the eyes
This wise and simple man.
All day I'd looked in the face
What I had hoped 'twould be   10
To write for my own race
And the reality;

---

[1] The following poems are reprinted from *The Collected Poems of W. B. Yeats,* copyright 1950 by The Macmillan Company and used with their permission.—"The Falling of the Leaves" was printed in *Crossways* (1889).

[2] Yeats had in mind Major Robert Gregory, the son of Lady Augusta Gregory—
"... my dear friend's dear son,
 Our Sidney and our perfect man, ..."
as he calls him in the longer poem, "In Memory of Major Gregory," which precedes this one in *The Wild Swans at Coole* (1919). Lady Gregory's husband, Sir W. H. Gregory, had died in 1892; her only son, the *Dictionary of National Biography* tells us, "became a distinguished painter and was killed in action as an airman in Italy in January 1918."

[3] Kiltartan is a village near Coole Park, the Gregorys' estate, which is itself near Gort, County Galway, in the west of Ireland.

[4] Another poem from *The Wild Swans at Coole.* Connemara (line 4) is a district in County Galway.

The living men that I hate,
The dead man that I loved,
The craven man in his seat,   15
The insolent unreproved,
And no knave brought to book
Who has won a drunken cheer,
The witty man and his joke
Aimed at the commonest ear,   20
The clever man who cries
The catch-cries of the clown,
The beating down of the wise
And great Art beaten down.

Maybe a twelvemonth since   25
Suddenly I began,
In scorn of this audience,
Imagining a man,
And his sun-freckled face,
And grey Connemara cloth,   30
Climbing up to a place
Where stone is dark under froth,
And the down-turn of his wrist
When the flies drop in the stream;
A man who does not exist,   35
A man who is but a dream;
And cried, 'Before I am old
I shall have written him one
Poem maybe as cold
And passionate as the dawn.'   40

EASTER, 1916[5]

I have met them at close of day
Coming with vivid faces
From counter or desk among grey
Eighteenth-century houses.
I have passed with a nod of the head   5
Or polite meaningless words,
Or have lingered awhile and said
Polite meaningless words,
And thought before I had done
Of a mocking tale or a gibe   10
To please a companion
Around the fire at the club,
Being certain that they and I
But lived where motley is worn:
All changed, changed utterly: 15
A terrible beauty is born.

That woman's days were spent
In ignorant good-will,
Her nights in argument
Until her voice grew shrill.   20
What voice more sweet than hers
When, young and beautiful,
She rode to harriers?
This man had kept a school
And rode our wingèd horse;   25
This other his helper and friend
Was coming into his force;
He might have won fame in the end,
So sensitive his nature seemed,
So daring and sweet his thought.   30
This other man I had dreamed
A drunken, vainglorious lout.
He had done most bitter wrong
To some who are near my heart,
Yet I number him in the song;   35
He, too, has resigned his part
In the casual comedy;
He, too, has been changed in his turn,
Transformed utterly:
A terrible beauty is born.   40

Hearts with one purpose alone
Through summer and winter seem
Enchanted to a stone
To trouble the living stream.
The horse that comes from the road,   45
The rider, the birds that range
From cloud to tumbling cloud,
Minute by minute they change;
A shadow of cloud on the stream

5 A combination of Irish Nationalist groups had planned an insurrection for Easter Sunday, 1916. Despite attempts to postpone the uprising until a more favorable time (the ship which had been bringing arms from Germany had been intercepted on

April 20), it began on Easter Monday in Dublin. Seizing key points in the city, the insurgents proclaimed a republic, but by April 29, after the loss of three hundred lives, they had been forced to give in to the British. "The seven signatories of the republican proclamation, including Pearse and Connolly, and nine others were shot after court-martial between 3 and 12 May [see Yeats's poem, "Sixteen Dead Men," which follows "Easter, 1916" in the Collected Poems], 75 were reprieved and over 2,000 held prisoners." (For a fuller account of the Easter Rebellion and its place in the history of the Irish Republic see the article by D. B. Quinn in Chambers's Encyclopedia, New Edition [1950], VII, 728, from which the above facts are taken.)

The remembered scene, in the first section of the poem, is of course Dublin. The woman and the men enumerated in the second section may be identified as follows: lines 17–23, the Countess Markiewicz; lines 24–25, Pádraic Pearse; lines 26–30, MacDonagh; lines 31 ff., MacBride. In the third section Yeats establishes, as a symbol for the heart which is entirely dedicated to a high and harshly difficult political cause, the stone set in the midst of a stream, touched but unaffected by the accidental life and change of the stream—as the dedicated heart is unmoved by the other demands of its life.

This poem and the next are from Michael Robartes and the Dancer (1921).

Changes minute by minute; 50
A horse-hoof slides on the brim,
And a horse plashes within it;
The long-legged moor-hens dive,
And hens to moor-cocks call;
Minute by minute they live: 55
The stone's in the midst of all.

Too long a sacrifice
Can make a stone of the heart.
O when may it suffice?
That is Heaven's part, our part 60
To murmur name upon name,
As a mother names her child
When sleep at last has come
On limbs that had run wild.
What is it but nightfall? 65
No, no, not night but death;
Was it needless death after all?
For England may keep faith
For all that is done and said.
We know their dream; enough 70
To know they dreamed and are dead;
And what if excess of love
Bewildered them till they died?
I write it out in a verse—
MacDonagh and MacBride 75
And Connolly and Pearse
Now and in time to be,
Wherever green is worn,
Are changed, changed utterly:
A terrible beauty is born. 80

September 25, 1916

THE SECOND COMING[6]

Turning and turning in the widening gyre
The falcon cannot hear the falconer;
Things fall apart; the centre cannot hold;
Mere anarchy is loosed upon the world,
The blood-dimmed tide is loosed, and everywhere 5
The ceremony of innocence is drowned;
The best lack all conviction, while the worst
Are full of passionate intensity.

---

[6] For a note on this poem, and a reference to the relevant pages in Yeats's *A Vision,* see the General Introduction, p. 888, above. The scheme of the poem may be seen as follows: If the Second Coming were to occur in the present age, when evil is everywhere in power, it seems to the poet that it must take place under some such loathsome and terrible form as is described in the second part of the poem: not Christ, but some rough beast, an obscene and sphinxlike creature.

Surely some revelation is at hand;
Surely the Second Coming is at hand. 10
The Second Coming! Hardly are those words out
When a vast image out of *Spiritus Mundi*[7]
Troubles my sight: somewhere in sands of the desert
A shape with lion body and the head of a man,
A gaze blank and pitiless as the sun, 15
Is moving its slow thighs, while all about it
Reel shadows of the indignant desert birds.
The darkness drops again; but now I know
That twenty centuries of stony sleep
Were vexed to nightmare by a rocking cradle. 20
And what rough beast, its hour come round at last,
Slouches towards Bethlehem to be born?

SAILING TO BYZANTIUM[8]

I

That is no country for old men. The young
In one another's arms, birds in the trees,
—Those dying generations—at their song,
The salmon-falls, the mackerel-crowded seas,
Fish, flesh, or fowl, commend all summer long 5
Whatever is begotten, born, and dies.
Caught in that sensual music all neglect
Monuments of unageing intellect.

II

An aged man is but a paltry thing,
A tattered coat upon a stick, unless 10
Soul clap its hands and sing, and louder sing
For every tatter in its mortal dress,
Nor is there singing school but studying
Monuments of its own magnificence;
And therefore I have sailed the seas and come 15
To the holy city of Byzantium.

---

[7] *Spiritus Mundi,* like *Anima Mundi,* was for Yeats "the general mind," the soul of the wide world dreaming on things to come, the collective consciousness (or subconscious) which the individual can touch and draw upon by giving free rein to his power of intuition: the *Anima Mundi* has remarkable image-making power—"if you suspend the critical faculty, . . . images pass rapidly before you." These images, moreover, are not merely fortuitous or fanciful but have prophetic relevance. For a full discussion of the concept and its place in the thought of Henry More, the Cambridge Platonist (1614–87), see Yeats's essay, "Anima Mundi," in *Per Amica Silentia Lunae* (reprinted in *Essays by W. B. Yeats,* 1924).

[8] A word has been said in the General Introduction about the arrangement of symbolic values in this poem. It should be noted that (in the first stanzas) the poet imagines himself as having already reached Byzantium, the ancient city which symbolizes for him the triumph of intellect and spirit over the life of the body; from this vantage point he looks back on the world he has left—"*that* is no country for old men." Then the situation changes slightly in stanza 3, where his plea to be gathered "into the artifice

O sages standing in God's holy fire
As in the gold mosaic of a wall,
Come from the holy fire, perne in a gyre,[9]
And be the singing-masters of my soul.   20
Consume my heart away; sick with desire
And fastened to a dying animal
It knows not what it is; and gather me
Into the artifice of eternity.

IV

Once out of nature I shall never take   25
My bodily form from any natural thing,
But such a form as Grecian goldsmiths make
Of hammered gold and gold enamelling
To keep a drowsy Emperor awake;
Or set upon a golden bough to sing   30
To lords and ladies of Byzantium
Of what is past, or passing, or to come.

1927

AMONG SCHOOL CHILDREN[10]

I

I walk through the long schoolroom questioning;
A kind old nun in a white hood replies;
The children learn to cipher and to sing,
To study reading-books and history,
To cut and sew, be neat in everything   5
In the best modern way—the children's eyes
In momentary wonder stare upon
A sixty-year-old smiling public man.

II

I dream of a Ledaean body,[11] bent
Above a sinking fire, a tale that she   10
Told of a harsh reproof, or trivial event
That changed some childish day to tragedy—
Told, and it seemed that our two natures blent
Into a sphere from youthful sympathy,
Or else, to alter Plato's parable,[12]   15
Into the yolk and white of the one shell.

III

And thinking of that fit of grief or rage
I look upon one child or t' other there
And wonder if she stood so at that age—
For even daughters of the swan can share   20
Something of every paddler's heritage—
And had that colour upon cheek or hair,
And thereupon my heart is driven wild:
She stands before me as a living child.

IV

Her present image floats into the mind—   25
Did Quattrocento[13] finger fashion it

of eternity" is necessarily that of one who has not yet shaken off the "dying animal," the human body. In the fourth stanza he is frankly, completely, and calmly (after the fervor of stanza 3) in his own created being, in the world of nature, specifying a wish for future existences: never again to be a part of the natural world, to live in the flesh, but to exist only as spirit, symbolized by the goldsmith's artificial bird. In a note to stanza 4 Yeats says: "I have read somewhere that in the Emperor's palace at Byzantium was a tree made of gold and silver, and artificial birds that sang."—This poem and the next are from *The Tower* (1928).
[9] Both "pern" and "gyre" have special meanings for Yeats, but here it is enough to see them as combining to describe a kind of motion—"to pern," to descend spiral-wise, but including the individual light dancing or revolving motion of the object or body as well as the spiraling. The gyre (whatever it symbolizes in other places in Yeats of the confusion of earthly existence) may be seen here as a descending whirlpool-like structure.
[10] The first stanza describes the kind of school-visit which Yeats may have made when, in his sixties, he was a Senator of the Irish Free State. The sight of the children reminds him of a story told him in the past by a loved and beautiful woman of something that had happened to her as a child: a tale which, as it happened, had united them in sympathy. He tries then to see

her as she had been when a child—did she look like one or the other of the children in the school-room there?—and succeeds all too well: it is as if she were suddenly before him as a living child. He then thinks of her (stanza 4) as she is now, aged as he is aged, but at the end of the stanza it is as if, for the moment of the school-visit, he had put an end to the somber reflections which have occurred to him there. But these reflections have started a train of thought, about the harshness of man's lot who must pass from youth to age, and about what values may eventually be seen as giving life its meaning. What young mother, he asks in stanza 5, if she could see her son grown old, would think his latter state worth the pains of birth or the care of setting him on his way? It would seem that he was being forced into a position where it would be necessary to affirm that only the soul has value, that the body must be spurned—but no: in the last three stanzas he dismisses the abstractions and the asceticism of the philosophers, invoking instead the images, the Presences that hold human feelings in thrall, whether the feelings of nuns or mothers. These images—images of the human body which claim human affection—have the power to break hearts, they doom to disappointment all who worship them, and yet they must be worshiped. Even to the man "with sixty winters on his head," who knows how life ends, the meaning of life lies in accepting it, in the faith in beauty and in the body which the last stanza affirms, as no poet has ever more eloquently affirmed it.
[11] I.e., a body beautiful enough for a daughter of Leda, as Helen of Troy was. (In line 20 we are reminded that Helen was also the daughter of Zeus, who possessed Leda in the form of a swan.)
[12] In the *Symposium,* where Aristophanes tells how Zeus had decided that it was necessary to split the double-formed primeval men. "He . . . cut men in two, like a sorb-apple which is halved for pickling, or as you might divide an egg with a hair." Consequently "each of us when separated is but the indenture of a man, having one side only like a flat fish, and he is always looking for his other half." (Jowett's translation)
[13] The term used, from the Italian system of expressing dates, by art historians to describe the schools and style of fifteenth-century painting.

Hollow of cheek as though it drank the wind
And took a mess of shadows for its meat?
And I though never of Ledaean kind
Had pretty plumage once—enough of that,   30
Better to smile on all that smile, and show
There is a comfortable kind of old scarecrow.

V

What youthful mother, a shape upon her lap
Honey of generation had betrayed,[14]
And that must sleep, shriek, struggle to escape   35
As recollection or the drug decide,
Would think her son, did she but see that shape
With sixty or more winters on its head,
A compensation for the pang of his birth,
Or the uncertainty of his setting forth?   40

VI

Plato[15] thought nature but a spume that plays
Upon a ghostly paradigm of things;
Solider Aristotle played the taws
Upon the bottom of a king of kings;
World-famous golden-thighed Pythagoras   45
Fingered upon a fiddle-stick or strings
What a star sang and careless Muses heard:
Old clothes upon old sticks to scare a bird.

VII

Both nuns and mothers worship images,
But those the candles light are not as those   50
That animate a mother's reveries,
But keep a marble or a bronze repose.
And yet they too break hearts—O Presences
That passion, piety or affection knows,

And that all heavenly glory symbolise—   55
O self-born mockers of man's enterprise;

VIII

Labour is blossoming or dancing where
The body is not bruised to pleasure soul,
Nor beauty born out of its own despair,
Nor blear-eyed wisdom out of midnight oil.   60
O chestnut tree, great rooted blossomer,
Are you the leaf, the blossom or the bole?
O body swayed to music, O brightening glance,
How can we know the dancer from the dance?

COOLE AND BALLYLEE, 1931[16]

Under my window-ledge the waters race,
Otters below and moor-hens on the top,
Run for a mile undimmed in Heaven's face
Then darkening through "dark" Raftery's "cellar" drop,
Run underground, rise in a rocky place   5
In Coole demesne, and there to finish up
Spread to a lake and drop into a hole.
What's water but the generated soul?[17]

Upon the border of that lake's a wood
Now all dry sticks under a wintry sun,   10
And in a copse of beeches there I stood,
For Nature's pulled her tragic buskin on
And all the rant's a mirror of my mood:
At sudden thunder of the mounting swan
I turned about and looked where branches break   15
The glittering reaches of the flooded lake.

Another emblem there! That stormy white
But seems a concentration of the sky;

---

[14] Yeats has explained in a note that the phrase "honey of generation" was taken from Porphyry's essay on "The Cave of the
Nymphs"; but he adds, "[I] find no warrant in Porphyry for
considering it the 'drug' that destroys the 'recollection' of pre-
natal freedom. . . ." In his essay on "Shelley's Poetry" (*Essays
by W. B. Yeats,* especially p. 102) Yeats explains that for Porphyry, as for other of the ancients, "honey was the symbol . . . for
'pleasure arising from generation,' " the pleasure which had
betrayed the infant on her lap from the pre-natal world of non-
existence to the world of life.

[15] In this stanza Plato and his predecessor Pythagoras (*fl.* 532 B. C.)
serve to represent philosophical views which urge the freeing of
the soul from the trammels of the flesh. The followers of Pythagoras, for instance, are said to have "had much in common with
the Orphic communities which sought by rites and abstinences
to purify the believer's soul and enable it to escape from 'the
wheel of birth.' " "Solider Aristotle" (who for all his comparative
solidity is dismissed with the other two in the last line of the
stanza) was tutor to Alexander the Great, the "king of kings."
Taws = a whip.

[16] Coole demesne, or Coole Park, is the Gregorys' estate so often
referred to in Yeats's poems. At the time the poem describes,
Lady Gregory (who died the next year, 1932) was living there
old and alone, "a last inheritor" (stanza 4). The geographical
features mentioned in stanza 1 are described in "Dust Hath
Closed Helen's Eye," one of the chapters (dated 1900) of Yeats's
The Celtic Twilight, where he speaks of a visit to "a little group
of houses, not many enough to be called a village, in the barony
of Kiltartan in County Galway, whose name, Ballylee, is known
through all the west of Ireland." He mentions that Raftery, "a
famous poet" of the early nineteenth century, in an Irish poem
about Mary Hynes had said "there is a strong cellar in Ballylee."
Yeats's guide had told him that the cellar was "the great hole
where the river sank under ground, and he brought me to a deep
pool, where an otter hurried away under a grey boulder. . . . "
Raftery was nearly blind, hence "dark Raftery" (line 4).—This
poem and the next are from *The Winding Stair and Other Poems*
(1933); the last three are from *Last Poems and Plays* (1940).

[17] This idea, touched here only glancingly and incidentally,
Yeats derived from the philosophical writings of Henry More,
the seventeenth-century neo-Platonist.

And, like the soul, it sails into the sight
And in the morning's gone, no man knows why;   20
And is so lovely that it sets to right
What knowledge or its lack had set awry,
So arrogantly pure, a child might think
It can be murdered with a spot of ink.

Sound of a stick upon the floor, a sound   25
From somebody that toils from chair to chair;
Beloved books that famous hands have bound,
Old marble heads, old pictures everywhere;
Great rooms where travelled men and children found
Content or joy; a last inheritor   30
Where none has reigned that lacked a name and fame
Or out of folly into folly came.

A spot whereon the founders lived and died
Seemed once more dear than life; ancestral trees,
Or gardens rich in memory glorified   35
Marriages, alliances and families,
And every bride's ambition satisfied.
Where fashion or mere fantasy decrees
Man shifts about—all that great glory spent—
Like some poor Arab tribesman and his tent.   40

We were the last romantics—chose for theme
Traditional sanctity and loveliness;
Whatever's written in what poets name
The book of the people; whatever most can bless
The mind of man or elevate a rhyme;   45
But all is changed, that high horse riderless,
Though mounted in that saddle Homer rode
Where the swan drifts upon a darkening flood.

AT ALGECIRAS[18]—A MEDITATION UPON DEATH

The heron-billed pale cattle-birds
That feed on some foul parasite
Of the Moroccan flocks and herds
Cross the narrow Straits to light
In the rich midnight of the garden trees   5
Till the dawn break upon those mingled seas.[19]

Often at evening when a boy
Would I carry to a friend—
Hoping more substantial joy
Did an older mind commend—   10

---

[18] A Spanish city a few miles west of Gibraltar.
[19] In the Straits of Gibraltar, on which Algeciras faces, the waters of the Atlantic and Mediterranean meet.

Not such as are in Newton's metaphor,
But actual shells of Rosses' level shore.[20]

Greater glory in the sun,
An evening chill upon the air,
Bid imagination run   15
Much on the Great Questioner;
What He can question, what if questioned I
Can with a fitting confidence reply.

November 1928

LAPIS LAZULI[21]

(FOR HARRY CLIFTON)

I have heard that hysterical women say
They are sick of the palette and fiddle-bow,
Of poets that are always gay,
For everybody knows or else should know
That if nothing drastic is done   5
Aeroplane and Zeppelin will come out,
Pitch like King Billy bomb-balls in
Until the town lie beaten flat.

All perform their tragic play,
There struts Hamlet, there is Lear,   10
That's Ophelia, that Cordelia;
Yet they, should the last scene be there,
The great stage curtain about to drop,
If worthy their prominent part in the play,
Do not break up their lines to weep.   15

---

[20] For Yeats's description of Rosses, see "Drumcliff and Rosses" in *The Celtic Twilight,* where he calls it "a little sea-dividing, sandy plain, covered with short grass, like a green table-cloth, and lying in the foam mid-way between the round cairn-headed Knocknarea and 'Ben Bulben, famous for hawks. . . . '"

[21] I am told that the *objet d'art* which provides the central image of this poem is a large square of lapis lazuli carved to represent the scene here described; it is in the possession of Mrs. Yeats.

In the poem Yeats raises the question of whether the tragic mood is unseemly (as hysterical women say) at a time when civilization seems about to topple. In answer he says that tragic art is not to be seen as sniveling, weak, and self-indulgent: its essence is a salutary gaiety which provides the race with the strength and courage it needs. Civilizations have always fallen, nor can they be preserved in their individual physical manifestations. What matters, and what must be preserved through the kind of wisdom that tragic art recognizes and safeguards, is the spirit which enables mankind to go on building its civilization perpetually anew, with joy. It does not matter that of particular works by Callimachus, the Greek sculptor of the fifth century B. C., only the fame has come down to us; it is more important to have his name and his example, that each succeeding sculptor should obey the same impulse, than it would be to have a few specific works by a specific artist of the past. In the concluding section of the poem Yeats makes a little parable of his meaning from what he sees (and from what he imagines as following from what he sees) on the lapis lazuli plaque.

They know that Hamlet and Lear are gay;
Gaiety transfiguring all that dread.
All men have aimed at, found and lost;
Black out; Heaven blazing into the head:
Tragedy wrought to its uttermost.   20
Though Hamlet rambles and Lear rages,
And all the drop-scenes drop at once
Upon a hundred thousand stages,
It cannot grow by an inch or an ounce.

On their own feet they came, or on shipboard,   25
Camel-back, horse-back, ass-back, mule-back,
Old civilisations put to the sword.
Then they and their wisdom went to rack:
No handiwork of Callimachus,
Who handled marble as if it were bronze,   30
Made draperies that seemed to rise
When sea-wind swept the corner, stands;
His long lamp-chimney shaped like the stem
Of a slender palm, stood but a day;
All things fall and are built again,   35
And those that build them again are gay.

Two Chinamen, behind them a third,
Are carved in lapis lazuli,
Over them flies a long-legged bird,
A symbol of longevity;   40
The third, doubtless a serving-man,
Carries a musical instrument.

Every discoloration of the stone,
Every accidental crack or dent,
Seems a water-course or an avalanche,   45
Or lofty slope where it still snows
Though doubtless plum or cherry-branch
Sweetens the little half-way house
Those Chinamen climb towards, and I
Delight to imagine them seated there;   50
There, on the mountain and the sky,
On all the tragic scene they stare.
One asks for mournful melodies;
Accomplished fingers begin to play.
Their eyes mid many wrinkles, their eyes,   55
Their ancient, glittering eyes, are gay.

AN ACRE OF GRASS

Picture and book remain,
An acre of green grass
For air and exercise,
Now strength of body goes;
Midnight, an old house   5
Where nothing stirs but a mouse.

My temptation is quiet.
Here at life's end
Neither loose imagination,
Nor the mill of the mind   10
Consuming its rag and bone,
Can make the truth known.

Grant me an old man's frenzy,
Myself must I remake
Till I am Timon and Lear   15
Or that William Blake
Who beat upon the wall
Till Truth obeyed his call;

A mind Michael Angelo knew
That can pierce the clouds,   20
Or inspired by frenzy
Shake the dead in their shrouds;
Forgotten else by mankind,
An old man's eagle mind.

JOHN KINSELLA'S LAMENT FOR MRS. MARY MOORE

A bloody and a sudden end,
    Gunshot or a noose,
For Death who takes what man would keep,
    Leaves what man would lose.
He might have had my sister,   5
    My cousins by the score,
But nothing satisfied the fool
    But my dear Mary Moore,
None other knows what pleasures man
    At table or in bed.   10
What shall I do for pretty girls
    Now my old bawd is dead?

Though stiff to strike a bargain,
    Like an old Jew man,
Her bargain struck we laughed and talked   15
    And emptied many a can;
And O! but she had stories,
    Though not for the priest's ear,
To keep the soul of man alive,
    Banish age and care,   20
And being old she put a skin
    On everything she said.
What shall I do for pretty girls
    Now my old bawd is dead?

The priests have got a book that says   25
    But for Adam's sin

Eden's Garden would be there
  And I there within.
No expectation fails there,
  No pleasing habit ends,   30
No man grows old, no girl grows cold,

But friends walk by friends.
Who quarrels over halfpennies
  That plucks the trees for bread?
What shall I do for pretty girls   35
  Now my old bawd is dead?

THE SYMBOLISM OF POETRY[1]

'SYMBOLISM, as seen in the writers of our day, would have no value if it were not seen also, under one disguise or another, in every great imaginative writer,' writes Mr. Arthur Symons in *The Symbolist Movement in Literature,* a subtle book which I cannot praise as I would, because it has been dedicated to me; and he goes on to show how many profound writers have in the last few years sought for a philosophy of poetry in the doctrine of symbolism, and how even in countries where it is almost scandalous to seek for any philosophy of poetry, new writers are following them in their search. We do not know what the writers of ancient times talked of among themselves, and one bull is all that remains of Shakespeare's talk, who was on the edge of modern times; and the journalist is convinced, it seems, that they talked of wine and women and politics, but never about their art, or never quite seriously about their art. He is certain that no one, who had a philosophy of his art or a theory of how he should write, has ever made a work of art, that people have no imagination who do not write without forethought and afterthought as he writes his own articles. He says this with enthusiasm, because he has heard it at so many comfortable dinner-tables, where some one had mentioned through carelessness, or foolish zeal, a book whose difficulty had offended indolence, or a man who had not forgotten that beauty is an accusation. Those formulas and generalisations, in which a hidden sergeant has drilled the ideas of journalists and through them the ideas of all but all the modern world, have created in their turn a forgetfulness like that of soldiers in battle, so that journalists and their readers have forgotten, among many like events, that Wagner spent seven years arranging and explaining his ideas before he began his most characteristic music; that opera, and with it modern music, arose from certain talks at the house of one Giovanni Bardi of Florence; and that the Pleiade laid the foundations

of modern French literature with a pamphlet. Goethe has said, 'a poet needs all philosophy, but he must keep it out of his work,' though that is not always necessary; and almost certainly no great art, outside England, where journalists are more powerful and ideas less plentiful than elsewhere, has arisen without a great criticism, for its herald or its interpreter and protector, and it may be for this reason that great art, now that vulgarity has armed itself and multiplied itself, is perhaps dead in England.

All writers, all artists of any kind, in so far as they have had any philosophical or critical power, perhaps just in so far as they have been deliberate artists, at all, have had some philosophy, some criticism of their art; and it has often been this philosophy, or this criticism, that has evoked their most startling inspiration, calling into outer life some portion of the divine life, or of the buried reality, which could alone extinguish in the emotions what their philosophy or their criticism would extinguish in the intellect. They have sought for no new thing, it may be, but only to understand and to copy the pure inspiration of early times, but because the divine life wars upon our outer life, and must needs change its weapons and its movements as we change ours, inspiration has come to them in beautiful startling shapes. The scientific movement brought with it a literature, which was always tending to lose itself in externalities of all kinds, in opinion, in declamation, in picturesque writing, in word-painting, or in what Mr. Symons has called an attempt 'to build in brick and mortar inside the covers of a book'; and now writers have begun to dwell upon the element of evocation, of suggestion, upon what we call the symbolism in great writers.

II

In 'Symbolism in Painting,' I tried to describe the element of symbolism that is in pictures and sculpture, and described a little the symbolism in poetry, but did not describe at all the continuous indefinable symbolism which is the substance of all style.

There are no lines with more melancholy beauty than these by Burns—

---

[1] From W. B. Yeats, *Essays,* copyright 1924 by The Macmillan Company and used with their permission. The essay was written in 1900.

The white moon is setting behind the white wave,
And Time is setting with me, O!

and these lines are perfectly symbolical. Take from them the whiteness of the moon and of the wave, whose relation to the setting of Time is too subtle for the intellect, and you take from them their beauty. But, when all are together, moon and wave and whiteness and setting Time and the last melancholy cry, they evoke an emotion which cannot be evoked by any other arrangement of colours and sounds and forms. We may call this metaphorical writing, but it is better to call it symbolical writing, because metaphors are not profound enough to be moving, when they are not symbols, and when they are symbols they are the most perfect of all, because the most subtle, outside of pure sound, and through them one can the best find out what symbols are. If one begins the reverie with any beautiful lines that one can remember, one finds they are like those by Burns. Begin with this line by Blake—

The gay fishes on the wave when the moon
sucks up the dew;

or these lines by Nash—

Queens have died young and fair,
Brightness falls from the air,
Dust hath closed Helen's eye;

or these lines by Shakespeare—

Timon hath made his everlasting mansion
Upon the beached verge of the salt flood;
Who once a day with his embossed froth
The turbulent surge shall cover;

or take some line that is quite simple, that gets its beauty from its place in a story, and see how it flickers with the light of the many symbols that have given the story its beauty, as a sword-blade may flicker with the light of burning towers.

All sounds, all colours, all forms, either because of their pre-ordained energies or because of long association, evoke indefinable and yet precise emotions, or, as I prefer to think, call down among us certain disembodied powers, whose footsteps over our hearts we call emotions; and when sound, and colour, and form are in a musical relation, a beautiful relation to one another, they become as it were one sound, one colour, one form, and evoke an emotion that is made out of their distinct evocations and yet is one emotion. The same relation exists between all portions of every work of art, whether it be an epic or a song, and the more perfect it is, and the more various and numerous the elements that have flowed into its perfection, the more powerful will be the emotion, the power, the god it calls among us. Because an emotion does not exist, or does not become perceptible and active among us, till it has found its expression, in colour or in sound or in form, or in all of these, and because no two modulations or arrangements of these evoke the same emotion, poets and painters and musicians, and in a less degree because their effects are momentary, day and night and cloud and shadow, are continually making and un-making mankind. It is indeed only those things which seem useless or very feeble that have any power, and all those things that seem useful or strong, armies, moving wheels, modes of architecture, modes of government, speculations of the reason, would have been a little different if some mind long ago had not given itself to some emotion, as a woman gives herself to her lover, and shaped sounds or colours or forms, or all of these, into a musical relation, that their emotion might live in other minds. A little lyric evokes an emotion, and this emotion gathers others about it and melts into their being in the making of some great epic; and at last, needing an always less delicate body, or symbol, as it grows more powerful, it flows out, with all it has gathered, among the blind instincts of daily life, where it moves a power within powers, as one sees ring within ring in the stem of an old tree. This is maybe what Arthur O'Shaughnessy meant when he made his poets say they had built Nineveh with their sighing; and I am certainly never certain, when I hear of some war, or of some religious excitement or of some new manufacture, or of anything else that fills the ear of the world, that it has not all happened because of something that a boy piped in Thessaly. I remember once telling a seer to ask one among the gods who, as she believed, were standing about her in their symbolic bodies, what would come of a charming but seeming trivial labour of a friend, and the form answering, 'the devastation of peoples and the overwhelming of cities.' I doubt indeed if the crude circumstance of the world, which seems to create all our emotions, does more than reflect, as in multiplying mirrors, the emotions that have come to solitary men in moments of poetical contemplation; or that love itself would be more than an animal hunger but for the poet and his shadow the priest, for unless we believe that outer things are the reality, we must believe that the gross is the shadow of the subtle, that things are wise before they become foolish, and secret before they cry out in the market-place. Solitary men in moments of contemplation receive, as I think, the creative impulse from the lowest of the Nine Hierarchies, and so make and unmake mankind, and even the world itself, for does not 'the eye altering alter all'?

> Our towns are copied fragments from our breast;
> And all man's Babylons strive but to impart
> The grandeurs of his Babylonian heart.

III

The purpose of rhythm, it has always seemed to me, is to prolong the moment of contemplation, the moment when we are both asleep and awake, which is the one moment of creation, by hushing us with an alluring monotony, while it holds us waking by variety, to keep us in that state of perhaps real trance, in which the mind liberated from the pressure of the will is unfolded in symbols. If certain sensitive persons listen persistently to the ticking of a watch, or gaze persistently on the monotonous flashing of a light, they fall into the hypnotic trance; and rhythm is but the ticking of a watch made softer, that one must needs listen, and various, that one may not be swept beyond memory or grow weary of listening; while the patterns of the artist are but the monotonous flash woven to take the eyes in a subtler enchantment. I have heard in meditation voices that were forgotten the moment they had spoken; and I have been swept, when in more profound meditation, beyond all memory but of those things that came from beyond the threshold of waking life. I was writing once at a very symbolical and abstract poem, when my pen fell on the ground; and as I stooped to pick it up, I remembered some phantastic adventure that yet did not seem phantastic, and then another like adventure, and when I asked myself when these things had happened, I found that I was remembering my dreams for many nights. I tried to remember what I had done the day before, and then what I had done that morning; but all my waking life had perished from me, and it was only after a struggle that I came to remember it again, and as I did so that more powerful and startling life perished in its turn. Had my pen not fallen on the ground and so made me turn from the images that I was weaving into verse, I would never have known that meditation had become trance, for I would have been like one who does not know that he is passing through a wood because his eyes are on the pathway. So I think that in the making and in the understanding of a work of art, and the more easily if it is full of patterns and symbols and music, we are lured to the threshold of sleep, and it may be far beyond it, without knowing that we have ever set our feet upon the steps of horn or of ivory.

IV

Besides emotional symbols, symbols that evoke emotions alone,—and in this sense all alluring or hateful things are symbols, although their relations with one another are too subtle to delight us fully, away from rhythm and pattern,—there are intellectual symbols, symbols that evoke ideas alone, or ideas mingled with emotions; and outside the very definite traditions of mysticism and the less definite criticism of certain modern poets, these alone are called symbols. Most things belong to one or another kind, according to the way we speak of them and the companions we give them, for symbols, associated with ideas that are more than fragments of the shadows thrown upon the intellect by the emotions they evoke, are the playthings of the allegorist or the pedant, and soon pass away. If I say 'white' or 'purple' in an ordinary line of poetry, they evoke emotions so exclusively that I cannot say why they move me; but if I bring them into the same sentence with such obvious intellectual symbols as a cross or a crown of thorns, I think of purity and sovereignty. Furthermore, innumerable meanings, which are held to 'white' or to 'purple' by bonds of subtle suggestion, and alike in the emotions and in the intellect, move visibly through my mind, and move invisibly beyond the threshold of sleep, casting lights and shadows of an indefinable wisdom on what had seemed before, it may be, but sterility and noisy violence. It is the intellect that decides where the reader shall ponder over the procession of the symbols, and if the symbols are merely emotional, he gazes from amid the accidents and destinies of the world; but if the symbols are intellectual too, he becomes himself a part of pure intellect, and he is himself mingled with the procession. If I watch a rushy pool in the moonlight, my emotion at its beauty is mixed with memories of the man that I have seen ploughing by its margin, or of the lovers I saw there a night ago; but if I look at the moon herself and remember any of her ancient names and meanings, I move among divine people, and things that have shaken off our mortality, the tower of ivory, the queen of waters, the shining stag among enchanted woods, the white hare sitting upon the hilltop, the fool of faery with his shining cup full of dreams, and it may be 'make a friend of one of these images of wonder,' and 'meet the Lord in the air.' So, too, if one is moved by Shakespeare, who is content with emotional symbols that he may come the nearer to our sympathy, one is mixed with the whole spectacle of the world; while if one is moved by Dante, or by the myth of Demeter, one is mixed into the shadow of God or of a goddess. So too one is furthest from symbols when one is busy doing this or that, but the soul moves among symbols and unfolds in symbols when trance, or madness, or deep meditation has withdrawn it from every impulse but its own. 'I then saw,' wrote Gérard de Nerval of his madness, 'vaguely drifting into form, plastic images of antiquity, which outlined themselves, became definite, and seemed to represent symbols of which I only seized the idea with difficulty.' In an earlier time he would have been of that multitude, whose souls austerity withdrew, even more perfectly than madness could withdraw his soul, from hope and memory, from desire and regret, that they might reveal those processions of symbols that men bow to before altars, and woo with incense and offerings. But being of our time, he has been like Maeterlinck, like Villiers de l'Isle Adam in *Axël*, like all who are preoccupied with intellectual symbols in our time, a foreshadower of the new sacred book, of which all the arts, as somebody has said, are begging to dream. How can the arts overcome the slow dying of men's hearts that we call the progress of the world, and lay their hands upon men's heart-strings again, without becoming the garment of religion as in old times?

V

If people were to accept the theory that poetry moves us because of its symbolism, what change should one look for in the manner of our poetry? A return to the way of our fathers, a casting out of descriptions of nature for the sake of nature, of the moral law for the sake of the moral law, a casting out of all anecdotes and of that brooding over scientific opinion that so often extinguished the central flame in Tennyson, and

of that vehemence that would make us do or not do certain things; or, in other words, we should come to understand that the beryl stone was enchanted by our fathers that it might unfold the pictures in its heart, and not to mirror our own excited faces, or the boughs waving outside the window. With this change of substance, this return to imagination, this understanding that the laws of art, which are the hidden laws of the world, can alone bind the imagination, would come a change of style, and we would cast out of serious poetry those energetic rhythms, as of a man running, which are the invention of the will with its eyes always on something to be done or undone; and we would seek out those wavering, meditative, organic rhythms, which are the embodiment of the imagination, that neither desires nor hates, because it has done with time, and only wishes to gaze upon some reality, some beauty; nor would it be any longer possible for anybody to deny the importance of form, in all its kinds, for although you can expound an opinion, or describe a thing when your words are not quite well chosen, you cannot give a body to something that moves beyond the senses, unless your words are as subtle, as complex, as full of mysterious life, as the body of a flower or of a woman. The form of sincere poetry, unlike the form of the popular poetry, may indeed be sometimes obscure, or ungrammatical as in some of the best of the Songs of Innocence and Experience, but it must have the perfections that escape analysis, the subtleties that have a new meaning every day, and it must have all this whether it be but a little song made out of a moment of dreamy indolence, or some great epic made out of the dreams of one poet and of a hundred generations whose hands were never weary of the sword.

Thomas Stearns Eliot

T. S. ELIOT's place in the development of twentieth-century British literature has been described in the General Introduction, but one or two biographical facts must be added here. He was born in St. Louis, Missouri, in 1888, and was educated at Milton Academy and at Harvard, where he took his B. A. in three years and an M. A. in the fourth. He then spent a year in Paris, studying French literature and philosophy at the Sorbonne. He returned to Harvard for further graduate work in philosophy, and in 1914, unable because of the war to complete a projected stay in Germany on a traveling fellow-

ship, went to Merton College, Oxford. His stay in England prolonged itself into permanent residence, with various jobs: schoolteaching, working in a branch of Lloyd's bank, acting as assistant editor of *The Egoist* from 1917 to 1919, working for the distinguished publishing firm of Faber and Faber (formerly Faber and Gwyer), of which he is now a director. He acquired British citizenship in 1927. His most extended visit to the United States was made in 1932–33, when he held the Charles Eliot Norton Professorship of Poetry at Harvard, in which capacity he delivered the lectures since published under the title *The Use of Poetry and the Use of Criticism*. During the same season he delivered the Page Barbour Lectures at the University of Virginia, later published as *After Strange Gods: A Primer of Modern Heresy*.

Eliot's statement in the preface to *For Lancelot Andrewes* (1928) that the "general point of view" of the essays collected there "might be described as classicist in literature, royalist in politics, and anglo-catholic in religion" has a patness that has made for too frequent quotation, so that he has too often been "summed up" in terms of these phrases. The statement does, however, bring out his conservatism, not the least of the many apparent paradoxes that one encounters in studying this poet whose work has worn such a revolutionary air. But the early poetry, which to its first readers seemed to discard accepted poetic practices completely and abruptly, is seen to imply, when we look at it more closely, a greater regard for tradition than Eliot's immediate predecessors or many of his contemporaries had shown. The individual's present experience must be presented and scrutinized with reference to comparable experiences from the history and from the literature of the past: the whole technique of literary allusion is there to implement this principle. Not only as poet but as critic, much of Eliot's endeavor has been guided by an instinct for seeing the present against the background of the past which produced it: the individual writer, for example, as working within a tradition, a line of development, which his work, if it is valid, will alter to one degree or another (see *Tradition and the Individual Talent*, reprinted below).

Collected Poems: 1909–1935 (1936) includes all of Eliot's published verse up through the choruses from *The Rock*, a pageant published in 1934, and *Burnt Norton*, the first of the *Four Quartets;* to be read in its entirety, however, *Four Quartets* (consisting, besides *Burnt Norton*, of *East Coker*, *The Dry Salvages*, and *Little Gidding*) must be obtained separately. The three poetic dramas—*Murder in the Cathedral* (1935), *The Family Reunion* (1939), and *The Cocktail Party* (1950)—are likewise published separately. There is also a volume of delightful nonsense verse for children, *Old Possum's Book of Practical Cats* (1939), which should not be entirely overlooked by adults.

Eliot's literary criticism is most conveniently obtained in *Selected Essays* (New Edition, 1950). The original volumes from which this large selection is made have their fame, however, and since they are sometimes obtainable separately they should be listed: *The Sacred Wood* (1920), *Homage to John Dryden* (1924), *For Lancelot Andrewes* (1928), *Dante* (1929), *Essays Ancient and Modern* (1936). Like *The Use of Poetry* and *After Strange Gods*, both mentioned above, *The Idea of a Christian Society* (1939) and *Notes towards the Definition of Culture* (1948) must be obtained separately.

Of the numerous books about T. S. Eliot and his art, one of the earliest to give the beginning reader the help he needed was H. R. Williamson's *The Poetry of T. S. Eliot* (1933). F. O. Matthiessen's *The Achievement of T. S. Eliot* (1935) is detailed and authoritative. Helen Gardner's *The Art of T. S. Eliot* (1949) is likely to increase and refine any reader's insight into the work it analyzes.

In recent years a number of volumes have appeared which collect the numerous significant shorter critiques and essays on Eliot and his poetry. *T. S. Eliot: a Study of His Writings by Several Hands,* edited by B. Rajan (1947), includes essays by Cleanth Brooks, Helen Gardner, Philip Wheelwright, and M. C. Bradbrook, for instance. *T. S. Eliot: a Selected Critique,* edited by Leonard Unger (1948) gathers together many items which are not easily obtainable elsewhere. Nevertheless, there are two essays which the reader should not leave it to chance to come by: the chapter on Eliot in Edmund Wilson's *Axel's Castle* (1931) and C. M. Bowra's essay on *The Waste Land* in his book *The Creative Experiment* (1949).

T. S. Eliot: a Symposium (1949), compiled by Richard March and Tambimuttu, consists of interesting personal impressions by a number of writers who have known Eliot during one phase or another of his career.

THE LOVE SONG OF J. ALFRED PRUFROCK[1]

*S'io credesse che mia risposta fosse
A persona che mai tornasse al mondo,
Questa fiamma staria senza piu scosse.
Ma perciocche giammai di questo fondo
Non torno vivo alcun, s'i'odo il vero,
Senza tema d'infamia ti rispondo.*[2]

Let us go then, you and I,
When the evening is spread out against the sky
Like a patient etherised upon a table;
Let us go, through certain half-deserted streets,
The muttering retreats   5
Of restless nights in one-night cheap hotels
And sawdust restaurants with oyster-shells:

---

1 The following poems are reprinted from *Collected Poems: 1909–1935* by T. S. Eliot, copyright, 1936, by Harcourt, Brace and Company, Inc.

2 The epigraph, from Dante's *Inferno* (XXVII, 61–66), consists of the first six lines of the speech in which the spirit of Guido da Montefeltro (concealed, like the other spirits in this section of Hell, in the flame of its own sin) answers Dante's question as to his identity: "If I believed that my answer were given to anyone who would ever return to the world, this flame would stand without moving any more; but because no one ever returned alive from this depth, if what I hear is true, I answer you without fear of infamy."

Streets that follow like a tedious argument
Of insidious intent
To lead you to an overwhelming question . . .   10
Oh, do not ask, "What is it?"
Let us go and make our visit.

In the room the women come and go
Talking of Michelangelo.

The yellow fog that rubs its back upon the window-
    panes,   15
The yellow smoke that rubs its muzzle on the window-
    panes
Licked its tongue into the corners of the evening,
Lingered upon the pools that stand in drains,
Let fall upon its back the soot that falls from chimneys,
Slipped by the terrace, made a sudden leap,   20
And seeing that it was a soft October night,
Curled once about the house, and fell asleep.

And indeed there will be time
For the yellow smoke that slides along the street,
Rubbing its back upon the window-panes;   25
There will be time, there will be time
To prepare a face to meet the faces that you meet;
There will be time to murder and create,
And time for all the works and days[3] of hands
That lift and drop a question on your plate;   30
Time for you and time for me,
And time yet for a hundred indecisions,
And for a hundred visions and revisions,
Before the taking of a toast and tea.

In the room the women come and go   35
Talking of Michelangelo.

And indeed there will be time
To wonder, "Do I dare?" and, "Do I dare?"
Time to turn back and descend the stair,
With a bald spot in the middle of my hair—   40
[They will say: "How his hair is growing thin!"]
My morning coat, my collar mounting firmly to the
    chin,
My necktie rich and modest, but asserted by a simple
    pin—
[They will say: "But how his arms and legs are thin!"]
Do I dare   45
Disturb the universe?
In a minute there is time
For decisions and revisions which a minute will reverse.

For I have known them all already, known them all:—
Have known the evenings, mornings, afternoons,   50
I have measured out my life with coffee spoons;
I know the voices dying with a dying fall
Beneath the music from a farther room.
    So how should I presume?

And I have known the eyes already, known them all—   55
The eyes that fix you in a formulated phrase,
And when I am formulated, sprawling on a pin,
When I am pinned and wriggling on the wall,
Then how should I begin
To spit out all the butt-ends of my days and ways?   60
    And how should I presume?

And I have known the arms already, known them all—
Arms that are braceleted and white and bare
[But in the lamplight, downed with light brown hair!]
Is it perfume from a dress   65
That makes me so digress?
Arms that lie along a table, or wrap about a shawl.
    And should I then presume?
    And how should I begin?
        . . . .

Shall I say, I have gone at dusk through narrow streets   70
And watched the smoke that rises from the pipes
Of lonely men in shirt-sleeves, leaning out of
    windows? . . .
I should have been a pair of ragged claws
Scuttling across the floors of silent seas.
        . . . . .

And the afternoon, the evening, sleeps so peacefully!   75
Smoothed by long fingers,
Asleep . . . tired . . . or it malingers,
Stretched on the floor, here beside you and me.
Should I, after tea and cakes and ices,
Have the strength to force the moment to its crisis?   80
But though I have wept and fasted, wept and prayed,
Though I have seen my head [grown slightly bald]
    brought in upon a platter,[4]
I am no prophet—and here's no great matter;
I have seen the moment of my greatness flicker,
And I have seen the eternal Footman hold my coat, and
    snicker,   85
And in short, I was afraid.

And would it have been worth it, after all,
After the cups, the marmalade, the tea,
Among the porcelain, among some talk of you and me,
Would it have been worth while,   90
To have bitten off the matter with a smile,

[3] A reference, made with ironic intent, to the *Works and Days* of Hesiod (eighth century B.C.), in which the Greek poet describes the simple productive labors of his people.

[4] See the story of John the Baptist in Matthew 14.

To have squeezed the universe into a ball
To roll it toward some overwhelming question,
To say: "I am Lazarus, come from the dead,[5]
Come back to tell you all, I shall tell you all"—   95
If one, settling a pillow by her head,
    Should say: "That is not what I meant at all.
    That is not it, at all."

And would it have been worth it, after all,
Would it have been worth while,   100
After the sunsets and the dooryards and the sprinkled
    streets,
After the novels, after the teacups, after the skirts that
    trail along the floor—
And this, and so much more?—
It is impossible to say just what I mean!
But as if a magic lantern threw the nerves in patterns
    on a screen: 105
Would it have been worth while
If one, settling a pillow or throwing off a shawl,
And turning toward the window, should say:
    "That is not it at all,
    That is not what I meant, at all."   110

No! I am not Prince Hamlet, nor was meant to be;
Am an attendant lord, one that will do
To swell a progress, start a scene or two,
Advise the prince; no doubt, an easy tool,
Deferential, glad to be of use,   115
Politic, cautious, and meticulous;
Full of high sentence, but a bit obtuse;
At times, indeed, almost ridiculous—
Almost, at times, the Fool.

I grow old . . . I grow old . . .   120
I shall wear the bottoms of my trousers rolled.

Shall I part my hair behind? Do I dare to eat a peach?
I shall wear white flannel trousers, and walk upon the
    beach.
I have heard the mermaids singing, each to each.

I do not think that they will sing to me.   125

I have seen them riding seaward on the waves
Combing the white hair of the waves blown back
When the wind blows the water white and black.

We have lingered in the chambers of the sea
By sea-girls wreathed with seaweed red and brown   130
Till human voices wake us, and we drown.

_____
[5] For the resurrection of Lazarus, see John 11.

PRELUDES

I

The winter evening settles down
With smell of steaks in passageways.
Six o'clock.
The burnt-out ends of smoky days.
And now a gusty shower wraps   5
The grimy scraps
Of withered leaves about your feet
And newspapers from vacant lots;
The showers beat
On broken blinds and chimney-pots,   10
And at the corner of the street
A lonely cab-horse steams and stamps.
And then the lighting of the lamps.

II

The morning comes to consciousness
Of faint stale smells of beer
From the sawdust-trampled street
With all its muddy feet that press
To early coffee-stands.   5
With the other masquerades
That time resumes,
One thinks of all the hands
That are raising dingy shades
In a thousand furnished rooms.   10

III

You tossed a blanket from the bed,
You lay upon your back, and waited;
You dozed, and watched the night revealing
The thousand sordid images
Of which your soul was constituted;   5
They flickered against the ceiling.
And when all the world came back
And the light crept up between the shutters
And you heard the sparrows in the gutters,
You had such a vision of the street   10
As the street hardly understands;
Sitting along the bed's edge, where
You curled the papers from your hair,
Or clasped the yellow soles of feet
In the palms of both soiled hands.   15

IV

His soul stretched tight across the skies
That fade behind a city block,
Or trampled by insistent feet
At four and five and six o'clock;

THOMAS STEARNS ELIOT   915

And short square fingers stuffing pipes,   5
And evening newspapers, and eyes
Assured of certain certainties,
The conscience of a blackened street
Impatient to assume the world.

I am moved by fancies that are curled   10
Around these images, and cling:
The notion of some infinitely gentle
Infinitely suffering thing.

Wipe your hand across your mouth, and
    laugh;
The worlds revolve like ancient women   15
Gathering fuel in vacant lots.

A COOKING EGG[1]

*En l'an trentiesme de mon aage
Que toutes mes hontes j'ay beues . . .*[2]

Pipit sate upright in her chair
   Some distance from where I was sitting;
Views of the Oxford Colleges
   Lay on the table, with the knitting.

Daguerreotypes and silhouettes,   5
   Her grandfather and great great aunts,
Supported on the mantelpiece
   An *Invitation to the Dance.*

. . . . .

I shall not want Honour in Heaven
   For I shall meet Sir Philip Sidney   10
And have talk with Coriolanus
   And other heroes of that kidney.

I shall not want Capital in Heaven
   For I shall meet Sir Alfred Mond.
We two shall lie together, lapt   15
   In a five per cent. Exchequer Bond.

I shall not want Society in Heaven,
   Lucretia Borgia shall be my Bride;
Her anecdotes will be more amusing
   Than Pipit's experience could provide.   20

I shall not want Pipit in Heaven:
   Madame Blavatsky will instruct me
In the Seven Sacred Trances;
   Piccarda de Donati will conduct me.

. . . . .

But where is the penny world I bought   25
   To eat with Pipit behind the screen?
The red-eyed scavengers are creeping
   From Kentish Town and Golder's Green;

Where are the eagles and the trumpets?

   Buried beneath some snow-deep Alps.   30
Over buttered scones and crumpets
   Weeping, weeping multitudes
Droop in a hundred A.B.C.'s.

SWEENEY AMONG THE NIGHTINGALES[3]

ὤμοι, πέπληγμαι καιρίαν πληγὴν ἔσω.

Apeneck Sweeney spreads his knees
Letting his arms hang down to laugh,
The zebra stripes along his jaw
Swelling to maculate giraffe.

The circles of the stormy moon   5
Slide westward toward the River Plate,[4]
Death and the Raven drift above
And Sweeney guards the hornèd gate.[5]

---

[1] Different readers may have different views as to just who the "I" is, and just who Pipit is: for two such individual readings, see Elizabeth Drew, *Discovering Poetry* (1933), pp. 112 ff., and F. O. Matthiessen, *The Achievement of T. S. Eliot,* pp. 130-31 (Oxford Bookshelf Edition). To the "I" of the poem—the "cooking egg" of its title—Sir Philip Sidney represents the Elizabethan ideal of the perfect nobleman, as Shakespeare's Coriolanus represents that of the towering, assured hero. Sir Alfred Mond, the British financier, represents great wealth, and Lucrezia Borgia (1480-1519), the brilliant and deadly Renaissance intrigante, stands for exciting, romantic, willful relationships with women. Yeats has described his meetings with Madame Blavatsky (1831-91), the Russian theosophist, in various places: see especially his *Autobiography* (1938), p. 151.

Each of the figures evoked has been chosen for the extravagance with which it contrasts with the dull, limited actuality of the speaker's life. Kentish Town and Golder's Green are London workers' suburbs. In earlier editions of his *Poems,* Eliot included a note to the last line of the poem: "I.e. an endemic teashop, found in all parts of London. The initials signify: Aerated Bread Company, Limited."

[2] See p. 891, above.

[3] For an interpretative note (including translation of the epigraph) see p. 893, above.

[4] The River Plate (Río de la Plata) is the estuary of two South American rivers, between Paraguay and Argentina, which has led commentators to place the poem's otherwise unspecified scene in South America. Orion (line 9), in any event, is an equatorial constellation.

[5] Through the gates of ivory, in Homer and in various succeeding mythologies, come the dreams that are pleasant but untrue; through the gates of horn, the dreams that are unpleasant but true.

Gloomy Orion and the Dog
Are veiled; and hushed the shrunken seas;   10
The person in the Spanish cape
Tries to sit on Sweeney's knees

Slips and pulls the table cloth
Overturns a coffee-cup,
Reorganised upon the floor   15
She yawns and draws a stocking up;

The silent man in mocha brown
Sprawls at the window-sill and gapes;
The waiter brings in oranges
Bananas figs and hothouse grapes;   20

The silent vertebrate in brown
Contracts and concentrates, withdraws;
Rachel née Rabinovitch
Tears at the grapes with murderous paws;

She and the lady in the cape   25
Are suspect, thought to be in league;
Therefore the man with heavy eyes
Declines the gambit, shows fatigue,

Leaves the room and reappears
Outside the window, leaning in,   30
Branches of wistaria
Circumscribe a golden grin;

The host with someone indistinct
Converses at the door apart,
The nightingales are singing near   35
The Convent of the Sacred Heart,

And sang within the bloody wood
When Agamemnon cried aloud,
And let their liquid siftings fall
To stain the stiff dishonoured shroud.   40

THE WASTE LAND[1]

"*Nam Sibyllam quidem Cumis ego ipse oculis meis vidi in
ampulla pendere, et cum illi pueri dicerent: Σίβυλλα τί
θέλεις; respondebat illa: ἀποθανεῖν θέλω.*"[2]

FOR EZRA POUND
il miglior fabbro

I. THE BURIAL OF THE DEAD

April is the cruellest month, breeding
Lilacs out of the dead land, mixing
Memory and desire, stirring

Dull roots with spring rain.
Winter kept us warm, covering   5
Earth in forgetful snow, feeding
A little life with dried tubers.
Summer surprised us, coming over the Starnbergersee[3]
With a shower of rain; we stopped in the colonnade,
And went on in sunlight, into the Hofgarten,   10
And drank coffee, and talked for an hour.
Bin gar keine Russin, stamm' aus Litauen, echt deutsch.[4]
And when we were children, staying at the arch-duke's,
My cousin's, he took me out on a sled,
And I was frightened. He said, Marie,   15
Marie, hold on tight. And down we went.
In the mountains, there you feel free.
I read, much of the night, and go south in the winter.

What are the roots that clutch, what branches grow
Out of this stony rubbish? Son of man,   20

---

[1] It has occasionally been suggested (wrongly, I think) that in
providing notes to *The Waste Land* (reprinted in this volume
immediately following the poem) Eliot was in part guying the
reader, and that in any event his notes are not very helpful.
Now, a beginning reader who needs fundamental help with the
poem needs *more* help than can be provided by interlacing Eliot's
own notes with additional notes by the editor. For the reader
who is in a position to follow the suggestions for approaching
The Waste Land which have been made in the General Introduction, Eliot's notes should be taken seriously and literally and
will provide all the detailed help that is necessary once the right
directions have been taken. The technique of allusion which is
fundamental to the poem's structure depends on the reader's
knowing not merely where each of the quoted passages comes
from, as a simple fact, but something of the context of event,
meaning, or tone which each allusion calls up: if a passage is not
familiar to him, Eliot's notes will direct him, in most cases, to
its source so that he can build up for himself a sense of the passage's context which will enable him to see what values the poet
has hoped to summon up by citing it. The reader can easily see
how the process works by examining the effect of juxtaposing a
line (*Waste Land,* line 172) from Ophelia's speech in *Hamlet*,
IV, v, with the banal good nights of the Cockneys in the pub.
Nor is there any need to postpone "reading" the poem while one
undertakes an elaborate course of reading the works to which
allusion is made. Each reader should try to take in as much of the
background of reference as he can profitably absorb, and avoid
the pedantry which can so insidiously substitute itself for the
genuine poetic pleasure which the work can give at even an
early stage of one's acquaintance with it. I am above all anxious
not to give the impression that the "key" to an understanding and
appreciation of the poem lies in such notes on particular points
as are appended here. My chief aim has been to provide help
where the reader may not know the language in which the citation is made.

[2] The epigraph is taken from the *Satyricon* of Petronius, the Roman
satirist of the first century A.D.: "For indeed I myself, with my
own eyes, have seen the Cumaean Sibyl hanging in a bottle,
and when those boys would say to her, 'Sibyl, what do you
want?' she would reply, 'I want to die.'"

[3] A lake near Munich. The Hofgarten (line 10) was a pleasant
feature of Munich life before World War II.

[4] "I am no Russian, come from Lithuania, a real German."

You cannot say, or guess, for you know only
A heap of broken images, where the sun beats,
And the dead tree gives no shelter, the cricket no relief,
And the dry stone no sound of water. Only
There is shadow under this red rock,   25
(Come in under the shadow of this red rock),
And I will show you something different from either
Your shadow at morning striding behind you
Or your shadow at evening rising to meet you;
I will show you fear in a handful of dust.   30

     Frisch weht der Wind
     Der Heimat zu.
     Mein irisch Kind,
     Wo weilest du?[5]

"You gave me hyacinths first a year ago;   35
"They called me the hyacinth girl."
—Yet when we came back, late, from the Hyacinth
   garden,
Your arms full, and your hair wet, I could not
Speak, and my eyes failed, I was neither
Living nor dead, and I knew nothing,   40
Looking into the heart of light, the silence.
Oed' und leer das Meer.[6]

Madame Sosostris, famous clairvoyante,
Had a bad cold, nevertheless
Is known to be the wisest woman in Europe,   45
With a wicked pack of cards. Here, said she,
Is your card, the drowned Phoenician Sailor,
(Those are pearls that were his eyes. Look!)
Here is Belladonna, the Lady of the Rocks,
The lady of situations.   50
Here is the man with three staves, and here the Wheel,
And here is the one-eyed merchant, and this card,
Which is blank, is something he carries on his back,
Which I am forbidden to see. I do not find
The Hanged Man. Fear death by water.   55
I see crowds of people, walking round in a ring.
Thank you. If you see dear Mrs. Equitone,
Tell her I bring the horoscope myself:
One must be so careful these days.

Unreal City,[7]   60
Under the brown fog of a winter dawn,

A crowd flowed over London Bridge, so many,
I had not thought death had undone so many.[8]
Sighs, short and infrequent, were exhaled,[9]
And each man fixed his eyes before his feet.   65
Flowed up the hill and down King William Street,
To where Saint Mary Woolnoth kept the hours
With a dead sound on the final stroke of nine.
There I saw one I knew, and stopped him, crying:
   "Stetson!
"You who were with me in the ships at Mylae!   70
"That corpse you planted last year in your garden,
"Has it begun to sprout? Will it bloom this year?
"Or has the sudden frost disturbed its bed?
"Oh keep the Dog far hence, that's friend to men,[10]
"Or with his nails he'll dig it up again!   75
"You! hypocrite lecteur!—mon semblable,—mon
   frère!"[11]

II. A GAME OF CHESS

The Chair she sat in, like a burnished throne,
Glowed on the marble, where the glass
Held up by standards wrought with fruited vines
From which a golden Cupidon peeped out   80
(Another hid his eyes behind his wing)
Doubled the flames of sevenbranched candelabra
Reflecting light upon the table as
The glitter of her jewels rose to meet it,
From satin cases poured in rich profusion;   85
In vials of ivory and coloured glass
Unstoppered, lurked her strange synthetic perfumes,
Unguent, powdered, or liquid—troubled, confused
And drowned the sense in odours; stirred by the air
That freshened from the window, these ascended   90
In fattening the prolonged candle-flames,
Flung their smoke into the laquearia,[12]
Stirring the pattern on the coffered ceiling.
Huge sea-wood fed with copper
Burned green and orange, framed by the coloured
   stone,   95

8 (See Eliot's note.) " . . . Such a long train/ of people, that I would never have believed/ that death had undone so many."

9 (See Eliot's note.) "Here, as far as we could hear,/ there was no weeping, but such sighs/ as made the eternal air tremble."

10 For the dirge from Webster's *The White Devil* (1612) see I, 447, above.

11 The last line of Baudelaire's verse Preface to *Les Fleurs du Mal*. In this Preface Baudelaire has invoked *Ennui*, the spirit of boredom: "His eye charged with an involuntary tear, he dreams of scaffolds as he smokes his hookah. You know him, reader, this monster of delicate tastes,—hypocrite reader,—my counterpart,—my brother!"

12 The lines Eliot quotes from the *Aeneid* in his note may be translated as follows: "Glowing lamps hang from the gold-paneled ceiling, and the torches conquer the darkness with their flames."

5 (See Eliot's note.) The sailor's song from Wagner's *Tristan und Isolde:* "Fresh blows the wind/ towards the homeland./ My Irish child,/ where are you lingering?"

6 (See Eliot's note.) "Waste and empty the sea." (I.e., the ship bringing Isolde back to Tristan is nowhere in sight.)

7 (See Eliot's note.) The lines which Eliot cites from Baudelaire as providing the background of the phrase "Unreal City" are the opening lines of "Les Sept Vieillards" (The Seven Old Men) in *Les Fleurs du Mal* (1857): "Swarming city, city full of dreams,/ Where in broad daylight the specter accosts the passer-by!"

In which sad light a carvèd dolphin swam.
Above the antique mantel was displayed
As though a window gave upon the sylvan scene
The change of Philomel, by the barbarous king
So rudely forced; yet there the nightingale   100
Filled all the desert with inviolable voice
And still she cried, and still the world pursues,
"Jug Jug" to dirty ears.
And other withered stumps of time
Were told upon the walls; staring forms   105
Leaned out, leaning, hushing the room enclosed.
Footsteps shuffled on the stair.
Under the firelight, under the brush, her hair
Spread out in fiery points
Glowed into words, then would be savagely still.   110

"My nerves are bad to-night. Yes, bad. Stay with me.
"Speak to me. Why do you never speak. Speak.
"What are you thinking of? What thinking? What?
"I never know what you are thinking. Think."

I think we are in rats' alley   115
Where the dead men lost their bones.

"What is that noise?"
                    The wind under the door.
"What is that noise now? What is the wind doing?"
                    Nothing again nothing.   120
                                        "Do
"You know nothing? Do you see nothing? Do you
        remember
"Nothing?"

        I remember
Those are pearls that were his eyes.   125
"Are you alive, or not? Is there nothing in your head?"
                    But
O O O O that Shakespeherian Rag—
It's so elegant
So intelligent   130
"What shall I do now? What shall I do?
"I shall rush out as I am, and walk the street
"With my hair down, so. What shall we do tomorrow?
"What shall we ever do?"
                    The hot water at ten.   135
And if it rains, a closed car at four.
And we shall play a game of chess,
Pressing lidless eyes and waiting for a knock upon the
        door.

When Lil's husband got demobbed,[13] I said—
I didn't mince my words, I said to her myself,   140

HURRY UP PLEASE IT'S TIME[14]
Now Albert's coming back, make yourself a bit smart.
He'll want to know what you done with that money
        he gave you
To get yourself some teeth. He did, I was there.
You have them all out, Lil, and get a nice set,   145
He said, I swear, I can't bear to look at you.
And no more can't I, I said, and think of poor Albert,
He's been in the army four years, he wants a good time,
And if you don't give it him, there's others will, I said.
Oh is there, she said. Something o' that, I said.   150
Then I'll know who to thank, she said, and give me a
        straight look.
HURRY UP PLEASE IT'S TIME
If you don't like it you can get on with it, I said.
Others can pick and choose if you can't.
But if Albert makes off, it won't be for lack of
        telling.   155
You ought to be ashamed, I said, to look so antique.
(And her only thirty-one.)
I can't help it, she said, pulling a long face,
It's them pills I took, to bring it off, she said.
(She's had five already, and nearly died of young
        George.)   160
The chemist[15] said it would be all right, but I've never
        been the same.
You *are* a proper fool, I said.
Well, if Albert won't leave you alone, there it is, I said,
What you get married for if you don't want children?
HURRY UP PLEASE IT'S TIME   165
Well, that Sunday Albert was home, they had a hot
        gammon,
And they asked me in to dinner, to get the beauty of
        it hot—
HURRY UP PLEASE IT'S TIME
HURRY UP PLEASE IT'S TIME
Goonight Bill. Goonight Lou. Goonight May. Goonight.
Ta ta. Goonight. Goonight.   171
Good night, ladies, good night, sweet ladies, good night,
        good night.

III. THE FIRE SERMON

The river's tent is broken: the last fingers of leaf
Clutch and sink into the wet bank. The wind
Crosses the brown land, unheard. The nymphs are
        departed.   175

[14] The reiterated "Hurry up please it's time" is typical of the injunctions by which London barkeepers remind their customers
that it is closing time. Here, of course, it is used for symbolic
effect, as well as—in its literal sense—to set the scene.
[15] The British equivalent of our *druggist* or *pharmacist*.

[13] Demobilized.

Sweet Thames, run softly, till I end my song.
The river bears no empty bottles, sandwich papers,
Silk handkerchiefs, cardboard boxes, cigarette ends
Or other testimony of summer nights. The nymphs are
    departed.
And their friends, the loitering heirs of city directors; 180
Departed, have left no addresses.
By the waters of Leman I sat down and wept . . .[16]
Sweet Thames, run softly till I end my song,
Sweet Thames, run softly, for I speak not loud or
    long.
But at my back in a cold blast I hear   185
The rattle of the bones, and chuckle spread from ear
    to ear.
A rat crept softly through the vegetation
Dragging its slimy belly on the bank
While I was fishing in the dull canal
On a winter evening round behind the gashouse   190
Musing upon the king my brother's wreck
And on the king my father's death before him.
White bodies naked on the low damp ground
And bones cast in a little low dry garret,
Rattled by the rat's foot only, year to year.   195
But at my back from time to time I hear
The sound of horns and motors, which shall bring
Sweeney to Mrs. Porter in the spring.
O the moon shone bright on Mrs. Porter
And on her daughter   200
They wash their feet in soda water
Et O ces voix d'enfants, chantant dans la coupole![17]

Twit twit twit
Jug jug jug jug jug jug
So rudely forc'd.   205
Tereu

Unreal City[18]
Under the brown fog of a winter noon
Mr. Eugenides, the Smyrna merchant
Unshaven, with a pocket full of currants   210
C.i.f. London: documents at sight,
Asked me in demotic French
To luncheon at the Cannon Street Hotel
Followed by a weekend at the Metropole.

At the violet hour, when the eyes and back   215
Turn upward from the desk, when the human engine
    waits

Like a taxi throbbing waiting,
I Tiresias, though blind, throbbing between two lives,[19]
Old man with wrinkled female breasts, can see
At the violet hour, the evening hour that strives   220
Homeward, and brings the sailor home from sea,[20]
The typist home at teatime, clears her breakfast, lights
Her stove, and lays out food in tins.
Out of the window perilously spread
Her drying combinations touched by the sun's last
    rays,   225
On the divan are piled (at night her bed)
Stockings, slippers, camisoles, and stays.
I Tiresias, old man with wrinkled dugs
Perceived the scene, and foretold the rest—
I too awaited the expected guest.   230
He, the young man carbuncular, arrives,
A small house agent's clerk, with one bold stare,
One of the low on whom assurance sits
As a silk hat on a Bradford millionaire.
The time is now propitious, as he guesses,   235
The meal is ended, she is bored and tired,
Endeavours to engage her in caresses
Which still are unreproved, if undesired.

---

16 Cf. Psalm 137.
17 The concluding line of Verlaine's sonnet "Parsifal": "And oh
    those children's voices singing in the choir loft!"
18 Cf. lines 60–61, above.

19 The passage from Ovid (*Metamorphoses*, III, 322 ff.) which Eliot
    quotes in his note on this line reads as follows in Golding's
    translation (1567):
    They say that Jove, disposed to mirth as he and Juno sat
    A-drinking nectar after meat in sport and pleasant rate,
    Did fall a-jesting with his wife, and said: 'A greater pleasure
    In Venus' games ye women have than men beyond all measure.'
    She answered, no. To try the truth, they both of them agree
    The wise Tiresias in this case indifferent judge to be,
    Who both the man's and woman's joys by trial understood,
    For finding once two mighty snakes engend'ring in a wood,
    He struck them overthwart the backs, by means whereof behold
    (As strange a thing to be of truth as ever yet was told)
    He being made a woman straight, seven winter livèd so.
    The eighth he finding them again did say unto them tho:
    'And if to strike ye have such power as for to turn their shape
    That are the givers of the stripe, before you hence escape,
    One stripe now shall I lend you more.' He struck them as beforne
    And straight returned his former shape in which he first was born.
    Tiresias therefore being ta'en to judge this jesting strife,
    Gave sentence on the side of Jove; the which the queen his wife
    Did take a great deal more to heart than needed, and in spite
    To wreak her teen upon her judge, bereft him of his sight;
    But Jove (for to the gods it is unlawful to undo
    The things which other of the gods by any means have do)
    Did give him sight in things to come for loss of sight of eye,
    And so his grievous punishment with honour did supply.
20 The poem of Sappho in question in Eliot's note to this line is
    No. 120 in E. Diehl, *Anthologia Lyrica* (1922). It may be trans-
    lated as follows:
    Hesperus, all things you bring, as many as light-
      bringing morning has scattered abroad.
    You bring the sheep,
    You bring the goat, you bring the child to its mother.
    But see also R. L. Stevenson's "Requiem," line 7 (p. 846,
    above).

Flushed and decided, he assaults at once;
Exploring hands encounter no defence;   240
His vanity requires no response,
And makes a welcome of indifference.
(And I Tiresias have foresuffered all
Enacted on this same divan or bed;
I who have sat by Thebes below the wall   245
And walked among the lowest of the dead.)
Bestows one final patronising kiss,
And gropes his way, finding the stairs unlit . . .

She turns and looks a moment in the glass,
Hardly aware of her departed lover;   250
Her brain allows one half-formed thought to pass:
"Well now that's done: and I'm glad it's over."
When lovely woman stoops to folly and
Paces about her room again, alone,
She smoothes her hair with automatic hand,   255
And puts a record on the gramophone.

"This music crept by me upon the waters"
And along the Strand, up Queen Victoria Street.
O City city, I can sometimes hear
Beside a public bar in Lower Thames Street,   260
The pleasant whining of a mandoline
And a clatter and a chatter from within
Where fishmen lounge at noon: where the walls
Of Magnus Martyr hold
Inexplicable splendour of Ionian white and gold.   265

        The river sweats
        Oil and tar
        The barges drift
        With the turning tide
        Red sails   270
        Wide
        To leeward, swing on the heavy spar.
        The barges wash
        Drifting logs
        Down Greenwich reach   275
        Past the Isle of Dogs.
                Weialala leia
                Wallala leialala

        Elizabeth and Leicester
        Beating oars   280
        The stern was formed
        A gilded shell
        Red and gold
        The brisk swell
        Rippled both shores   285
        Southwest wind
        Carried down stream

        The peal of bells
        White towers
                Weialala leia   290
                Wallala leialala

"Trams and dusty trees.
Highbury bore me. Richmond and Kew[21]
Undid me. By Richmond I raised my knees
Supine on the floor of a narrow canoe."   295

"My feet are at Moorgate, and my heart
Under my feet. After the event
He wept. He promised 'a new start.'
I made no comment. What should I resent?"

"On Margate Sands.   300
I can connect
Nothing with nothing.
The broken fingernails of dirty hands.
My people humble people who expect
Nothing."   305
        la la

To Carthage then I came

Burning burning burning burning
O Lord Thou pluckest me out
O Lord Thou pluckest   310

burning

IV. DEATH BY WATER

Phlebas the Phoenician, a fortnight dead,
Forgot the cry of gulls, and the deep sea swell
And the profit and loss.
                A current under sea   315
Picked his bones in whispers. As he rose and fell
He passed the stages of his age and youth
Entering the whirlpool.
                Gentile or Jew
O you who turn the wheel and look to windward,   320
Consider Phlebas, who was once handsome and tall as
        you.

---

[21] The verses from the *Purgatorio* which Eliot quotes in his note to
this line are from the moving speech of La Pia, who says to
Dante: "Pray, when you have returned to the world and are
rested from your long journey, . . . remember me, who am La
Pia; Siena made me, the Maremma unmade me" (referring to
the manner of her death, possibly from being intentionally shut
up by her husband in the fever-ridden marshes around Siena
known as the Maremma).

V. WHAT THE THUNDER SAID

After the torchlight red on sweaty faces
After the frosty silence in the gardens
After the agony in stony places
The shouting and the crying   325
Prison and palace and reverberation
Of thunder of spring over distant mountains
He who was living is now dead
We who were living are now dying
With a little patience   330

Here is no water but only rock
Rock and no water and the sandy road
The road winding above among the mountains
Which are mountains of rock without water
If there were water we should stop and drink   335
Amongst the rock one cannot stop or think
Sweat is dry and feet are in the sand
If there were only water amongst the rock
Dead mountain mouth of carious teeth that cannot spit
Here one can neither stand nor lie nor sit   340
There is not even silence in the mountains
But dry sterile thunder without rain
There is not even solitude in the mountains
But red sullen faces sneer and snarl
From doors of mudcracked houses
                              If there were water   345
And no rock
If there were rock
And also water
And water
A spring   350
A pool among the rock
If there were the sound of water only
Not the cicada
And dry grass singing
But sound of water over a rock   355
Where the hermit-thrush sings in the pine trees
Drip drop drip drop drop drop drop
But there is no water

Who is the third who walks always beside you?
When I count, there are only you and I together   360
But when I look ahead up the white road
There is always another one walking beside you
Gliding wrapt in a brown mantle, hooded   *death?*
I do not know whether a man or a woman
—But who is that on the other side of you?   365

What is that sound high in the air[22]
Murmur of maternal lamentation
Who are those hooded hordes swarming

Over endless plains, stumbling in cracked earth
Ringed by the flat horizon only   370
What is the city over the mountains
Cracks and reforms and bursts in the violet air
Falling towers
Jerusalem Athens Alexandria
Vienna London   *cities - fake?*   375
Unreal

A woman drew her long black hair out tight
And fiddled whisper music on those strings
And bats with baby faces in the violet light
Whistled, and beat their wings   380
And crawled head downward down a blackened wall
And upside down in air were towers
Tolling reminiscent bells, that kept the hours
And voices singing out of empty cisterns and exhausted
    wells.

In this decayed hole among the mountains   385
In the faint moonlight, the grass is singing
Over the tumbled graves, about the chapel
There is the empty chapel, only the wind's home.   *to Religion*
It has no windows, and the door swings,
Dry bones can harm no one.   390
Only a cock stood on the rooftree
Co co rico co co rico
In a flash of lightning. Then a damp gust
Bringing rain

Ganga was sunken, and the limp leaves   395
Waited for rain, while the black clouds
Gathered far distant, over Himavant.
The jungle crouched, humped in silence.
Then spoke the thunder
Da   400
Datta: what have we given?
My friend, blood shaking my heart
The awful daring of a moment's surrender
Which an age of prudence can never retract
By this, and this only, we have existed   405
Which is not to be found in our obituaries
Or in memories draped by the beneficent spider
Or under seals broken by the lean solicitor   *will*
In our empty rooms
Da   410

---

[22] The passage from Hermann Hesse's *Blick ins Chaos* (*A Glance into Chaos*) which Eliot quotes in his note to this passage may be translated as follows: "Already half of Europe, already at least half of Eastern Europe is on the road to Chaos, drives drunkenly in holy madness along the abyss and sings the while, sings drunkenly a hymn as Dimitri Karamazov sang. The bourgeois laughs, insulted, over these songs, but the saint and prophet hear them with tears."

Dayadhvam: I have heard the key[23]
Turn in the door once and turn once only
We think of the key, each in his prison
Thinking of the key, each confirms a prison
Only at nightfall, aethereal rumours   415
Revive for a moment a broken Coriolanus[24]
Da
Damyata: The boat responded
Gaily, to the hand expert with sail and oar
The sea was calm, your heart would have responded 420
Gaily, when invited, beating obedient
To controlling hands

                      I sat upon the shore
Fishing, with the arid plain behind me
Shall I at least set my lands in order?   425
London Bridge is falling down falling down falling down
Poi s'ascose nel foco che gli affina[25]
Quando fiam uti chelidon—O swallow swallow[26]
Le Prince d'Aquitaine à la tour abolie[27]

---

[23] In his note to this line Eliot quotes a brief passage from the section of the *Inferno* in which Count Ugolino of Pisa recounts his imprisonment with his little sons in the Hunger Tower (Canto XXXII, lines 124–139, and Canto XXXIII, lines 1–90): "and I heard them below locking the entrance to the horrible tower."

[24] The hero of Shakespeare's tragedy, the symbol of the great man and hero who seeks, with tragic outcome, to be utterly self-sufficient.

[25] In his note to this line Eliot quotes part of the speech of the late twelfth-century poet Arnaut Daniel whom Dante encounters among the lustful in Purgatory: " 'I am Arnaut, who weep and go singing. In thought I see my past folly, and with joy I see the day I hope for before me. And so I pray you, by that Virtue which guides you to the top of the stair, be reminded in time of my grief.' Then he disappeared in the fire that refines them." Each of the fragments quoted in this last group of eleven lines has its purpose in representing one or another of the themes of the whole poem: this line brings in again the theme of pointless sexual lust which has loomed so large in the poem's picture of the values of a sick world, and to that theme it adds the idea of a solution through repentance and purgation.

[26] The first half of the line is from the conclusion of the *Pervigilium Veneris,* a Latin poem of some 90 lines, dating possibly from the late Empire, in praise of the power of Venus: "When shall I do as the swallow [i.e. sing] and cease to be silent?" The second half of the line is from Swinburne's "Itylus," and since to think of Itylus is to think of Philomela the line has the effect of reminding us yet again of a theme that has been touched on many times in the poem. (See Eliot's note to line 99, and see also the nightingale's song, lines 203–6.)

[27] Gérard de Nerval's sonnet *El Desdichado,* from which this line is taken, describes one who thinks of himself as in all senses "disinherited":
    Je suis le ténébreux,—le veuf,—l'inconsolé,
    Le prince d'Aquitaine à la tour abolie:
    Ma seule étoile est morte,—et mon luth constellé
    Porte le *Soleil noir* de la *Mélancholie.* . . .
"I am the shadowy one,—the widower,—the unconsoled, / The prince of Aquitania in the disused tower: / My only star is dead,—and my starred lute / Carries as its sign the black sun of Melancholy. . . ."

These fragments I have shored against my ruins   430
Why then Ile fit you. Hieronymo's mad againe.
Datta. Dayadhvam. Damyata.
      Shantih shantih shantih

NOTES ON THE WASTE LAND

Not only the title, but the plan and a good deal of the incidental symbolism of the poem were suggested by Miss Jessie L. Weston's book on the Grail legend: *From Ritual to Romance* (Cambridge). Indeed, so deeply am I indebted, Miss Weston's book will elucidate the difficulties of the poem much better than my notes can do; and I recommend it (apart from the great interest of the book itself) to any who think such elucidation of the poem worth the trouble. To another work of anthropology I am indebted in general, one which has influenced our generation profoundly; I mean *The Golden Bough;* I have used especially the two volumes *Adonis, Attis, Osiris.* Anyone who is acquainted with these works will immediately recognise in the poem certain references to vegetation ceremonies.

I. THE BURIAL OF THE DEAD

Line 20. Cf. Ezekiel II, i.
   23. Cf. Ecclesiastes XII, v.
   31. V. Tristan und Isolde, I, verses 5–8.
   42. Id. III, verse 24.
   46. I am not familiar with the exact constitution of the Tarot pack of cards, from which I have obviously departed to suit my own convenience. The Hanged Man, a member of the traditional pack, fits my purpose in two ways: because he is associated in my mind with the Hanged God of Frazer, and because I associate him with the hooded figure in the passage of the disciples to Emmaus in Part V. The Phoenician Sailor and the Merchant appear later; also the "crowds of people," and Death by Water is executed in Part IV. The Man with Three Staves (an authentic member of the Tarot pack) I associate, quite arbitrarily, with the Fisher King himself.
   60. Cf. Baudelaire:
"Fourmillante cité, cité pleine de rêves,
"Où le spectre en plein jour raccroche le passant."
   63. Cf. Inferno III, 55–57:
                   "si lunga tratta
      di gente, ch'io non avrei mai creduto
      che morte tanta n'avesse disfatta."
   64. Cf. Inferno IV, 25–27:
      "Quivi, secondo che per ascoltare,
      "non avea pianto, ma' che di sospiri,
      "che l'aura eterna facevan tremare."
   68. A phenomenon which I have often noticed.
   74. Cf. the Dirge in Webster's *White Devil.*
   76. V. Baudelaire, Preface to *Fleurs du Mal.*

II. A GAME OF CHESS

   77. Cf. *Antony and Cleopatra,* II, ii, l. 190.
   92. Laquearia. V. *Aeneid,* I, 726:
     dependant lychni laquearibus aureis incensi, et noctem flammis funalia vincunt.
   98. Sylvan scene. V. Milton, *Paradise Lost,* IV, 140.

99. V. Ovid, *Metamorphoses*, VI, Philomela.

100. Cf. Part III, l. 204.

115. Cf. Part III, l. 195.

118. Cf. Webster: "Is the wind in that door still?"

126. Cf. Part I, l. 37, 48.

138. Cf. the game of chess in Middleton's *Women beware Women*.

III. THE FIRE SERMON

176. V. Spenser, *Prothalamion*.

192. Cf. *The Tempest*, I, ii.

196. Cf. Marvell, *To His Coy Mistress*.

197. Cf. Day, *Parliament of Bees*:
"When of the sudden, listening, you shall hear,
"A noise of horns and hunting, which shall bring
"Actaeon to Diana in the spring,
"Where all shall see her naked skin . . ."

199. I do not know the origin of the ballad from which these lines are taken: it was reported to me from Sydney, Australia.

202. V. Verlaine, *Parsifal*.

210. The currants were quoted at a price "carriage and insurance free to London"; and the Bill of Lading etc. were to be handed to the buyer upon payment of the sight draft.

218. Tiresias, although a mere spectator and not indeed a "character," is yet the most important personage in the poem, uniting all the rest. Just as the one-eyed merchant, seller of currants, melts into the Phoenician Sailor, and the latter is not wholly distinct from Ferdinand Prince of Naples, so all the women are one woman, and the two sexes meet in Tiresias. What Tiresias *sees*, in fact, is the substance of the poem. The whole passage from Ovid is of great anthropological interest:
'. . . Cum Iunone iocos et maior vestra profecto est
Quam, quae contingit maribus,' dixisse, 'voluptas.'
Illa negat; placuit quae sit sententia docti
Quaerere Tiresiae: venus huic erat utraque nota.
Nam duo magnorum viridi coeuntia silva
Corpora serpentum baculi violaverat ictu
Deque viro factus, mirabile, femina septem
Egerat autumnos; octavo rursus eosdem
Vidit et 'est vestrae si tanta potentia plagae,'
Dixit 'ut auctoris sortem in contraria mutet,
Nunc quoque vos feriam!' percussis anguibus isdem
Forma prior rediit genetivaque venit imago.
Arbiter hic igitur sumptus de lite iocosa
Dicta Iovis firmat; gravius Saturnia iusto
Nec pro materia fertur doluisse suique
Iudicis aeterna damnavit lumina nocte,
At pater omnipotens (neque enim licet inrita cuiquam
Facta dei fecisse deo) pro lumine adempto
Scire futura dedit poenamque levavit honore.

221. This may not appear as exact as Sappho's lines, but I had in mind the "longshore" or "dory" fisherman, who returns at nightfall.

253. V. Goldsmith, the song in *The Vicar of Wakefield*.

257. V. *The Tempest*, as above.

264. The interior of St. Magnus Martyr is to my mind one of the finest among Wren's interiors. See *The Proposed Demolition of Nineteen City Churches*: (P. S. King & Son, Ltd.).

266. The Song of the (three) Thames-daughters begins here. From line 292 to 306 inclusive they speak in turn. V. *Götterdämmerung*, III, i: the Rhine-daughters.

279. V. Froude, *Elizabeth*, Vol. I, ch. iv, letter of De Quadra to Philip of Spain:
"In the afternoon we were in a barge, watching the games on the river. (The queen) was alone with Lord Robert and myself on the poop, when they began to talk nonsense, and went so far that Lord Robert at last said, as I was on the spot there was no reason why they should not be married if the queen pleased."

293. Cf. *Purgatorio*, V, 133:
"Ricorditi di me, che son la Pia;
"Siena mi fe', disfecemi Maremma."

307. V. St. Augustine's *Confessions*: "to Carthage then I came, where a cauldron of unholy loves sang all about mine ears."

308. The complete text of the Buddha's Fire Sermon (which corresponds in importance to the Sermon on the Mount) from which these words are taken, will be found translated in the late Henry Clarke Warren's *Buddhism in Translation* (Harvard Oriental Series). Mr. Warren was one of the great pioneers of Buddhist studies in the Occident.

309. From St. Augustine's *Confessions* again. The collocation of these two representatives of eastern and western asceticism, as the culmination of this part of the poem, is not an accident.

V. WHAT THE THUNDER SAID

In the first part of Part V three themes are employed: the journey to Emmaus, the approach to the Chapel Perilous (see Miss Weston's book) and the present decay of eastern Europe.

357. This is *Turdus aonalaschkae pallasii*, the hermit-thrush which I have heard in Quebec County. Chapman says (*Handbook of Birds of Eastern North America*) "it is most at home in secluded woodland and thickety retreats. . . . Its notes are not remarkable for variety or volume, but in purity and sweetness of tone and exquisite modulation they are unequalled." Its "water-dripping song" is justly celebrated.

360. The following lines were stimulated by the account of one of the Antarctic expeditions (I forget which, but I think one of Shackleton's): it was related that the party of explorers, at the extremity of their strength, had the constant delusion that there was *one more member* than could actually be counted.

366-76. Cf. Hermann Hesse, *Blick ins Chaos*: "Schon ist halb Europa, schon ist zumindest der halbe Osten Europas auf dem Wege zum Chaos, fährt betrunken im heiligem Wahn am Abgrund entlang und singt dazu, singt betrunken und hymnisch wie Dmitri Karamasoff sang. Ueber diese Lieder lacht der Bürger beleidigt, der Heilige und Seher hört sie mit Tränen."

401. "Datta, dayadhvam, damyata" (Give, sympathise, control). The fable of the meaning of the Thunder is found in the *Brihadaranyaka—Upanishad*, 5, 1. A translation is found in Deussen's *Sechzig Upanishads des Veda*, p. 489.

407. Cf. Webster, *The White Devil*, V, vi:
". . . they'll remarry
Ere the worm pierce your winding-sheet, ere the spider
Make a thin curtain for your epitaphs."

411. Cf. *Inferno*, XXXIII, 46:
"ed io sentii chiavar l'uscio di sotto
all' orribile torre."
Also F. H. Bradley, *Appearance and Reality*, p. 346.
"My external sensations are no less private to myself than are

my thoughts or my feelings. In either case my experience falls within my own circle, a circle closed on the outside; and, with all its elements alike, every sphere is opaque to the others which surround it. . . . In brief, regarded as an existence which appears in a soul, the whole world for each is peculiar and private to that soul."

424. V. Weston: *From Ritual to Romance;* chapter on the Fisher King.

427. V. *Purgatorio,* XXVI, 148.

" 'Ara vos prec per aquella valor
'que vos guida al som de l'escalina,
'sovegna vos a temps de ma dolor.'
Poi s'ascose nel foco che gli affina."

428. V. *Pervigilium Veneris.* Cf. Philomela in Parts II and III.

429. V. Gerard de Nerval, Sonnet *El Desdichado.*

431. V. Kyd's *Spanish Tragedy.*

433. Shantih. Repeated as here, a formal ending to an Upanishad. "The Peace which passeth understanding" is our equivalent to this word.

THE HOLLOW MEN

Mistah Kurtz—he dead

A penny for the Old Guy[1]

I

We are the hollow men
We are the stuffed men
Leaning together
Headpiece filled with straw. Alas!
Our dried voices, when   5
We whisper together
Are quiet and meaningless
As wind in dry grass
Or rats' feet over broken glass
In our dry cellar   10

Shape without form, shade without colour,
Paralysed force, gesture without motion;

---

[1] The first of the poem's two epigraphs comes from Joseph Conrad's *The Heart of Darkness;* perhaps here it may be taken as evoking the unspeakable horror and degradation of Kurtz's last days. Kurtz, the agent of a European company exploiting the resources and manpower of the African ivory district, had determined to stamp out savage beliefs and customs, but eventually he succumbs to their power—a power of darkness as opposed to the power of light that had been his inheritance as a European —and allows himself to be worshiped by the natives.

The second epigraph is typical of the phrases employed by English children on Guy Fawkes day, November 5, phrases which license them to solicit pennies from all comers. Such phrases, and the bonfires in which "the guy" is burnt in effigy, are all that remain of the conspiracy (and the religious zeal behind it, even though the conspiracy was traitorous) in which Guy Fawkes (1570-1606), a Roman Catholic, unsuccessfully attempted to blow up the Houses of Parliament.

Those who have crossed
With direct eyes, to death's other Kingdom
Remember us—if at all—not as lost   15
Violent souls, but only
As the hollow men
The stuffed men.

II

Eyes I dare not meet in dreams
In death's dream kingdom   20
These do not appear:
There, the eyes are
Sunlight on a broken column
There, is a tree swinging
And voices are   25
In the wind's singing
More distant and more solemn
Than a fading star.

Let me be no nearer
In death's dream kingdom   30
Let me also wear
Such deliberate disguises
Rat's coat, crowskin, crossed staves
In a field
Behaving as the wind behaves   35
No nearer—

Not that final meeting
In the twilight kingdom

III

This is the dead land
This is cactus land   40
Here the stone images
Are raised, here they receive
The supplication of a dead man's hand
Under the twinkle of a fading star.

Is it like this   45
In death's other kingdom
Waking alone
At the hour when we are
Trembling with tenderness
Lips that would kiss   50
Form prayers to broken stone.

IV

The eyes are not here
There are no eyes here
In this valley of dying stars

In this hollow valley   55
This broken jaw of our lost kingdoms

In this last of meeting places
We grope together
And avoid speech
Gathered on this beach of the tumid river   60

Sightless, unless
The eyes reappear
As the perpetual star
Multifoliate rose
Of death's twilight kingdom   65
The hope only
Of empty men.

                          V

Here we go round the prickly pear
Prickly pear prickly pear
Here we go round the prickly pear   70
At five o'clock in the morning.

Between the idea
And the reality
Between the motion
And the act   75
Falls the Shadow
          For Thine is the Kingdom

Between the conception
And the creation
Between the emotion   80
And the response
Falls the Shadow
          Life is very long

Between the desire
And the spasm   85
Between the potency
And the existence
Between the essence
And the descent
Falls the Shadow   90
          For Thine is the Kingdom

For Thine is
Life is
For Thine is the

This is the way the world ends   95
This is the way the world ends
This is the way the world ends
Not with a bang but a whimper.

ANIMULA[1]

'Issues from the hand of God, the simple soul'[2]
To a flat world of changing lights and noise,
To light, dark, dry or damp, chilly or warm;
Moving between the legs of tables and of chairs,
Rising or falling, grasping at kisses and toys,   5
Advancing boldly, sudden to take alarm,
Retreating to the corner of arm and knee,
Eager to be reassured, taking pleasure
In the fragrant brilliance of the Christmas tree,
Pleasure in the wind, the sunlight and the sea;   10
Studies the sunlit pattern on the floor
And running stags around a silver tray;
Confounds the actual and the fanciful,
Content with playing-cards and kings and queens,
What the fairies do and what the servants say.   15
The heavy burden of the growing soul
Perplexes and offends more, day by day;
Week by week, offends and perplexes more
With the imperatives of 'is and seems'
And may and may not, desire and control.   20
The pain of living and the drug of dreams
Curl up the small soul in the window seat
Behind the *Encyclopaedia Britannica.*
Issues from the hand of time the simple soul
Irresolute and selfish, misshapen, lame,   25
Unable to fare forward or retreat,
Fearing the warm reality, the offered good,
Denying the importunity of the blood,
Shadow of its own shadows, spectre in its own gloom,
Leaving disordered papers in a dusty room;   30
Living first in the silence after the viaticum.

---

1 The title recalls the opening lines of the Emperor Hadrian's
address to his soul: "Animula, vagula, blandula,/ Hospes,
comesque corporis . . . " (Little wandering, appealing soul,/
Guest and companion of the body . . .).
2 This line occurs in a passage in Dante's *Purgatorio* in which Marco
Lombardo explains to Dante the reason why "the world is
indeed so empty of all virtue" as we see it to be: reminding him
that mortals have Free Will, that heaven initiates their movements, giving them a light by which to recognize good and evil,
and that it is up to them to carry on the struggle against evil by
that light. Then follows a passage which has provided the first
line of the present poem ("Esce di mano a lui . . . l'anima/
semplicetta") as well as a part of its structural pattern: "There
issues from the hand of him who loves it before it exists, in the
shape of a little child which goes weeping and laughing on its
childish way, the simple soul, which knows nothing save that,
moved by its joyful maker, it turns willingly to whatever gives
it pleasure. First of all it experiences the savor of some trifling
good; then it is deceived and turns back to it, unless guide or
curb turn its love away. Wherefore it was suitable to erect law
as a curb. . . ."

Pray for Guiterriez, avid of speed and power,
For Boudin, blown to pieces,
For this one who made a great fortune,
And that one who went his own way.   35
Pray for Floret, by the boarhound slain between the
      yew trees,
Pray for us now and at the hour of our birth.

LANDSCAPES

I. NEW HAMPSHIRE

Children's voices in the orchard
Between the blossom- and the fruit-time:
Golden head, crimson head,
Between the green tip and the root.
Black wing, brown wing, hover over;   5
Twenty years and the spring is over;
To-day grieves, to-morrow grieves,
Cover me over, light-in-leaves;
Golden head, black wing,
Cling, swing,   10
Spring, sing,
Swing up into the apple-tree.

II. VIRGINIA

Red river, red river,
Slow flow heat is silence
No will is still as a river
Still. Will heat move
Only through the mocking-bird   5
Heard once? Still hills
Wait. Gates wait. Purple trees,
White trees, wait, wait,
Delay, decay. Living, living,
Never moving. Ever moving   10
Iron thoughts came with me
And go with me:
Red river, river, river.

III. USK

Do not suddenly break the branch, or
Hope to find
The white hart behind the white well.
Glance aside, not for lance, do not spell
Old enchantments. Let them sleep.   5
"Gently dip, but not too deep,"
Lift your eyes
Where the roads dip and where the roads rise
Seek only there
Where the grey light meets the green air   10
The hermit's chapel, the pilgrim's prayer.

IV. RANNOCH, BY GLENCOE

Here the crow starves, here the patient stag
Breeds for the rifle. Between the soft moor
And the soft sky, scarcely room
To leap or soar. Substance crumbles, in the thin air
Moon cold or moon hot. The road winds in   5
Listlessness of ancient war
Languor of broken steel,
Clamour of confused wrong, apt
In silence. Memory is strong
Beyond the bone. Pride snapped,   10
Shadow of pride is long, in the long pass
No concurrence of bone.

V. CAPE ANN

O quick quick quick, quick hear the song-sparrow,
Swamp-sparrow, fox-sparrow, vesper-sparrow
At dawn and dusk. Follow the dance
Of the goldfinch at noon. Leave to chance
The Blackburnian warbler, the shy one. Hail   5
With shrill whistle the note of the quail, the bob-white
Dodging by bay-bush. Follow the feet
Of the walker, the water-thrush. Follow the flight
Of the dancing arrow, the purple martin. Greet
In silence the bullbat. All are delectable. Sweet sweet
      sweet   10
But resign this land at the end, resign it
To its true owner, the tough one, the sea-gull.
The palaver is finished.

TRADITION AND THE INDIVIDUAL TALENT[1]

IN English writing we seldom speak of tradition, though we occasionally apply its name in deploring its absence. We cannot refer to "the tradition" or to "a tradition"; at most, we employ the adjective in saying that the poetry of So-and-so is "traditional" or even "too traditional." Seldom, perhaps, does the word appear except in a phrase of censure. If otherwise, it is vaguely approbative, with the implication, as to the work approved, of some pleasing archaeological reconstruction. You can hardly make the word agreeable to English ears without this comfortable reference to the reassuring science of archaeology.

Certainly the word is not likely to appear in our appreciations of living or dead writers. Every nation, every race, has not only its own creative, but its own critical turn of mind; and is even more oblivious of the shortcomings and limitations of its critical habits than of those of its creative genius. We know, or think we know, from the enormous mass of critical writing that has appeared in the French language the critical method or habit of the French; we only conclude (we are such unconscious people) that the French are "more critical" than we, and sometimes even plume ourselves a little with the fact, as if the French were the less spontaneous. Perhaps they are; but we might remind ourselves that criticism is as inevitable as breathing, and that we should be none the worse for articulating what passes in our minds when we read a book and feel an emotion about it, for criticizing our own minds in their work of criticism. One of the facts that might come to light in this process is our tendency to insist, when we praise a poet, upon those aspects of his work in which he least resembles any one else. In these aspects or parts of his work we pretend to find what is individual, what is the peculiar essence of the man. We dwell with satisfaction upon the poet's difference from his predecessors, especially his immediate predecessors; we endeavour to find something that can be isolated in order to be enjoyed. Whereas if we approach a poet without this prejudice we shall often find that not only the best, but the most individual parts of his work may be those in which the dead poets, his ancestors, assert their immortality most vigorously. And I do not mean the impressionable period of adolescence, but the period of full maturity.

Yet if the only form of tradition, of handing down, consisted in following the ways of the immediate generation before us in a blind or timid adherence to its successes, "tradition" should positively be discouraged. We have seen many such simple currents soon lost in the sand; and novelty is better than repetition. Tradition is a matter of much wider significance. It cannot be inherited, and if you want it you must obtain it by great labour. It involves, in the first place, the historical sense, which we may call nearly indispensable to any one who would continue to be a poet beyond his twenty-fifth year; and the historical sense involves a perception, not only of the pastness of the past, but of its presence; the historical sense compels a man to write not merely with his own generation in his bones, but with a feeling that the whole of the literature of Europe from Homer and within it the whole of the literature of his own country has a simultaneous existence and composes a simultaneous order. This historical sense, which is a sense of the timeless as well as of the temporal and of the timeless and of the temporal together, is what makes a writer traditional. And it is at the same time what makes a writer most acutely conscious of his place in time, of his own contemporaneity.

No poet, no artist of any art, has his complete meaning alone. His significance, his appreciation is the appreciation of his relation to the dead poets and artists. You cannot value him alone; you must set him, for contrast and comparison, among the dead. I mean this as a principle of aesthetic, not merely historical, criticism. The necessity that he shall conform, that he shall cohere, is not onesided; what happens when a new work of art is created is something that happens simultaneously to all the works of art which preceded it. The existing monuments form an ideal order among themselves, which is modified by the introduction of the new (the really new) work of art among them. The existing order is complete before the new work arrives; for order to persist after the supervention of novelty, the *whole* existing order must be, if ever so slightly, altered; and so the relations, proportions, values of each work of art toward the whole are readjusted; and this is conformity between the old and the new. Whoever has approved this idea of order, of the form of European, of English literature will not find it preposterous that the past should be altered by the present as much as the present is directed by the past. And the poet who is aware of this will be aware of great difficulties and responsibilities.

---

[1] From *Selected Essays* by T. S. Eliot, copyright, 1932, 1936, 1950, by Harcourt, Brace and Company, Inc.

In a peculiar sense he will be aware also that he must inevitably be judged by the standards of the past. I say judged, not amputated, by them; not judged to be as good as, or worse or better than, the dead; and certainly not judged by the canons of dead critics. It is a judgment, a comparison, in which two things are measured by each other. To conform merely would be for the new work not really to conform at all; it would not be new, and would therefore not be a work of art. And we do not quite say that the new is more valuable because it fits in; but its fitting in is a test of its value—a test, it is true, which can only be slowly and cautiously applied, for we are none of us infallible judges of conformity. We say: it appears to conform, and is perhaps individual, or it appears individual, and may conform; but we are hardly likely to find that it is one and not the other.

To proceed to a more intelligible exposition of the relation of the poet to the past: he can neither take the past as a lump, an indiscriminate bolus, nor can he form himself wholly on one or two private admirations, nor can he form himself wholly upon one preferred period. The first course is inadmissible, the second is an important experience of youth, and the third is a pleasant and highly desirable supplement. The poet must be very conscious of the main current, which does not at all flow invariably through the most distinguished reputations. He must be quite aware of the obvious fact that art never improves, but that the material of art is never quite the same. He must be aware that the mind of Europe—the mind of his own country—a mind which he learns in time to be much more important than his own private mind—is a mind which changes, and that this change is a development which abandons nothing *en route,* which does not superannuate either Shakespeare, or Homer, or the rock drawing of the Magdalenian draughtsmen. That this development, refinement perhaps, complication certainly, is not, from the point of view of the artist, any improvement. Perhaps not even an improvement from the point of view of the psychologist or not to the extent which we imagine; perhaps only in the end based upon a complication in economics and machinery. But the difference between the present and the past is that the conscious present is an awareness of the past in a way and to an extent which the past's awareness of itself cannot show.

Some one said: "The dead writers are remote from us because we *know* so much more than they did." Precisely, and they are that which we know.

I am alive to a usual objection to what is clearly part of my programme for the *métier* of poetry. The objection is that the doctrine requires a ridiculous amount of erudition (pedantry), a claim which can be rejected by appeal to the lives of poets in any pantheon. It will even be affirmed that much learning deadens or perverts poetic sensibility. While, however, we persist in believing that a poet ought to know as much as will not encroach upon his necessary receptivity and necessary laziness, it is not desirable to confine knowledge to whatever can be put into a useful shape for examinations, drawing-rooms, or the still more pretentious modes of publicity. Some can absorb knowledge, the more tardy must sweat for it. Shakespeare acquired more essential history from Plutarch than most men could from the whole British Museum. What is to be insisted upon is that the poet must develop or procure the consciousness of the past and that he should continue to develop this consciousness throughout his career.

What happens is a continual surrender of himself as he is at the moment to something which is more valuable. The progress of an artist is a continual self-sacrifice, a continual extinction of personality.

There remains to define this process of depersonalization and its relation to the sense of tradition. It is in this depersonalization that art may be said to approach the condition of science. I, therefore, invite you to consider, as a suggestive analogy, the action which takes place when a bit of finely filiated platinum is introduced into a chamber containing oxygen and sulphur dioxide.

II

Honest criticism and sensitive appreciation are directed not upon the poet but upon the poetry. If we attend to the confused cries of the newspaper critics and the *susurrus*[2] of popular repetition that follows, we shall hear the names of poets in great numbers; if we seek not Blue-book knowledge but the enjoyment of poetry, and ask for a poem, we shall seldom find it. I have tried to point out the importance of the relation of the poem to other poems by other authors, and suggested the conception of poetry as a living whole of all the poetry that has ever been written. The other aspect of this Impersonal theory of poetry is the relation of the poem to its author. And I hinted, by an analogy, that the mind of the mature poet differs from that of the immature one not precisely in any valuation of "personality," not being necessarily more interesting, or having "more to say," but rather by being a more finely

---

2 Whispering, buzzing, muttering (Latin).

perfected medium in which special, or very varied, feelings are at liberty to enter into new combinations.

The analogy was that of the catalyst. When the two gases previously mentioned are mixed in the presence of a filament of platinum, they form sulphurous acid. This combination takes place only if the platinum is present; nevertheless the newly formed acid contains no trace of platinum, and the platinum itself is apparently unaffected; has remained inert, neutral, and unchanged. The mind of the poet is the shred of platinum. It may partly or exclusively operate upon the experience of the man himself; but, the more perfect the artist, the more completely separate in him will be the man who suffers and the mind which creates; the more perfectly will the mind digest and transmute the passions which are its material.

The experience, you will notice, the elements which enter the presence of the transforming catalyst, are of two kinds: emotions and feelings. The effect of a work of art upon the person who enjoys it is an experience different in kind from any experience not of art. It may be formed out of one emotion, or may be a combination of several; and various feelings, inhering for the writer in particular words or phrases or images, may be added to compose the final result. Or great poetry may be made without the direct use of any emotion whatever: composed out of feelings solely. Canto XV of the *Inferno* (Brunetto Latini) is a working up of the emotion evident in the situation; but the effect, though single as that of any work of art, is obtained by considerable complexity of detail. The last quatrain gives an image, a feeling attaching to an image, which "came," which did not develop simply out of what precedes, but which was probably in suspension in the poet's mind until the proper combination arrived for it to add itself to. The poet's mind is in fact a receptacle for seizing and storing up numberless feelings, phrases, images, which remain there until all the particles which can unite to form a new compound are present together.

If you compare several representative passages of the greatest poetry you see how great is the variety of types of combination, and also how completely any semi-ethical criterion of "sublimity" misses the mark. For it is not the "greatness," the intensity, of the emotions, the components, but the intensity of the artistic process, the pressure, so to speak, under which the fusion takes place, that counts. The episode of Paolo and Francesca[3] employs a definite emotion,

but the intensity of the poetry is something quite different from whatever intensity in the supposed experience it may give the impression of. It is no more intense, furthermore, than Canto XXVI, the voyage of Ulysses, which has not the direct dependence upon an emotion. Great variety is possible in the process of transmutation of emotion: the murder of Agamemnon, or the agony of Othello, gives an artistic effect apparently closer to a possible original than the scenes from Dante. In the *Agamemnon,* the artistic emotion approximates to the emotion of an actual spectator; in *Othello* to the emotion of the protagonist himself. But the difference between art and the event is always absolute; the combination which is the murder of Agamemnon is probably as complex as that which is the voyage of Ulysses. In either case there has been a fusion of elements. The ode of Keats contains a number of feelings which have nothing particular to do with the nightingale, but which the nightingale, partly, perhaps, because of its attractive name, and partly because of its reputation, served to bring together.

The point of view which I am struggling to attack is perhaps related to the metaphysical theory of the substantial unity of the soul: for my meaning is, that the poet has, not a "personality" to express, but a particular medium, which is only a medium and not a personality, in which impressions and experiences combine in peculiar and unexpected ways. Impressions and experiences which are important for the man may take no place in the poetry, and those which become important in the poetry may play quite a negligible part in the man, the personality.

I will quote a passage[4] which is unfamiliar enough to be regarded with fresh attention in the light—or darkness—of these observations:

> And now methinks I could e'en chide myself
> For doating on her beauty, though her death
> Shall be revenged after no common action.
> Does the silkworm expend her yellow labours
> For thee? For thee does she undo herself?
> Are lordships sold to maintain ladyships
> For the poor benefit of a bewildering minute?
> Why does yon fellow falsify highways,
> And put his life between the judge's lips,
> To refine such a thing—keeps horse and men
> To beat their valours for her? . . .

In this passage (as is evident if it is taken in its context) there is a combination of positive and negative

---

[3] In Dante's *Inferno*, Canto V.

[4] From *The Revenger's Tragedy* (1607), by the Jacobean playwright Cyril Tourneur.

emotions: an intensely strong attraction toward beauty and an equally intense fascination by the ugliness which is contrasted with it and which destroys it. This balance of contrasted emotion is in the dramatic situation to which the speech is pertinent, but that situation alone is inadequate to it. This is, so to speak, the structural emotion, provided by the drama. But the whole effect, the dominant tone, is due to the fact that a number of floating feelings, having an affinity to this emotion by no means superficially evident, have combined with it to give us a new art emotion.

It is not in his personal emotions, the emotions provoked by particular events in his life, that the poet is in any way remarkable or interesting. His particular emotions may be simple, or crude, or flat. The emotion in his poetry will be a very complex thing, but not with the complexity of the emotions of people who have very complex or unusual emotions in life. One error, in fact, of eccentricity in poetry is to seek for new human emotions to express; and in this search for novelty in the wrong place it discovers the perverse. The business of the poet is not to find new emotions, but to use the ordinary ones and, in working them up into poetry, to express feelings which are not in actual emotions at all. And emotions which he has never experienced will serve his turn as well as those familiar to him. Consequently, we must believe that "emotion recollected in tranquillity" is an inexact formula. For it is neither emotion, nor recollection, nor, without distortion of meaning, tranquillity. It is a concentration, and a new thing resulting from the concentration, of a very great number of experiences which to the practical and active person would not seem to be experiences at all; it is a concentration which does not happen consciously or of deliberation. These experiences are not "recollected," and they finally unite in an atmosphere which is "tranquil" only in that it is a passive attending upon the event. Of course this is not quite the whole story. There is a great deal, in the writing of poetry, which must be conscious and deliberate. In fact, the bad poet is usually unconscious where he ought to be conscious, and conscious where he ought to be unconscious. Both errors tend to make him "personal." Poetry is not a turning loose of emotion, but an escape from emotion; it is not the expression of personality, but an escape from personality. But, of course, only those who have personality and emotions know what it means to want to escape from these things.

III

ὁ δὲ νοῦς ἴσως θειότερόν τι καὶ ἀπαθές ἐστιν[5]

This essay proposes to halt at the frontier of metaphysics or mysticism, and confine itself to such practical conclusions as can be applied by the responsible person interested in poetry. To divert interest from the poet to the poetry is a laudable aim: for it would conduce to a juster estimation of actual poetry, good and bad. There are many people who appreciate the expression of sincere emotion in verse, and there is a smaller number of people who can appreciate technical excellence. But very few know when there is an expression of *significant* emotion, emotion which has its life in the poem and not in the history of the poet. The emotion of art is impersonal. And the poet cannot reach this impersonality without surrendering himself wholly to the work to be done. And he is not likely to know what is to be done unless he lives in what is not merely the present, but the present moment of the past, unless he is conscious, not of what is dead, but of what is already living.

THE METAPHYSICAL POETS[1]

By collecting these poems[2] from the work of a generation more often named than read, and more often read than profitably studied, Professor Grierson has rendered a service of some importance. Certainly the reader will meet with many poems already preserved in other anthologies, at the same time that he discovers poems such as those of Aurelian Townshend or Lord Herbert of Cherbury here included. But the function of such an anthology as this is neither that of Professor Saintsbury's admirable edition of Caroline poets nor that of the *Oxford Book of English Verse*. Mr. Grierson's book is in itself a piece of criticism and a provocation of criticism; and we think that he was right in including so many

---

1 From *Selected Essays* by T. S. Eliot, copyright, 1932, 1936, 1950, by Harcourt, Brace and Company, Inc.

2 *Metaphysical Lyrics and Poems of the Seventeenth Century: Donne to Butler.* Selected and edited, with an Essay, by Herbert J. C. Grierson (Oxford: Clarendon Press. London: Milford). (Eliot's note)

5 Aristotle, *De Anima*, 408b, 29: ". . . The mind is at once something more divine and impassible."

poems of Donne, elsewhere (though not in many editions) accessible, as documents in the case of "metaphysical poetry." The phrase has long done duty as a term of abuse or as the label of a quaint and pleasant taste. The question is to what extent the so-called metaphysicals formed a school (in our own time we should say a "movement"), and how far this so-called school or movement is a digression from the main current.

Not only is it extremely difficult to define metaphysical poetry, but difficult to decide what poets practise it and in which of their verses. The poetry of Donne (to whom Marvell and Bishop King are sometimes nearer than any of the other authors) is late Elizabethan, its feeling often very close to that of Chapman. The "courtly" poetry is derivative from Jonson, who borrowed liberally from the Latin; it expires in the next century with the sentiment and witticism of Prior. There is finally the devotional verse of Herbert, Vaughan, and Crashaw (echoed long after by Christina Rossetti and Francis Thompson); Crashaw, sometimes more profound and less sectarian than the others, has a quality which returns through the Elizabethan period to the early Italians. It is difficult to find any precise use of metaphor, simile, or other conceit, which is common to all the poets and at the same time important enough as an element of style to isolate these poets as a group. Donne, and often Cowley, employ a device which is sometimes considered characteristically "metaphysical"; the elaboration (contrasted with the condensation) of a figure of speech to the farthest stage to which ingenuity can carry it. Thus Cowley develops the commonplace comparison of the world to a chess-board through long stanzas (To Destiny), and Donne, with more grace, in A Valediction, the comparison of two lovers to a pair of compasses. But elsewhere we find, instead of the mere explication of the content of a comparison, a development by rapid association of thought which requires considerable agility on the part of the reader.

> On a round ball
> A workman that hath copies by, can lay
> An Europe, Afrique, and an Asia,
> And quickly make that, which was nothing, All,
> So doth each teare,
> Which thee doth weare,
> A globe, yea, world by that impression grow,
> Till thy tears mixt with mine doe overflow
> This world, by waters sent from thee, my
> heaven dissolved so.[3]

Here we find at least two connexions which are not implicit in the first figure, but are forced upon it by the poet: from the geographer's globe to the tear, and the tear to the deluge. On the other hand, some of Donne's most successful and characteristic effects are secured by brief words and sudden contrasts:

> A bracelet of bright hair about the bone,[4]

where the most powerful effect is produced by the sudden contrast of associations of "bright hair" and of "bone." This telescoping of images and multiplied associations is characteristic of the phrase of some of the dramatists of the period which Donne knew: not to mention Shakespeare, it is frequent in Middleton, Webster, and Tourneur, and is one of the sources of the vitality of their language.

Johnson, who employed the term "metaphysical poets," apparently having Donne, Cleveland, and Cowley chiefly in mind, remarks of them that "the most heterogeneous ideas are yoked by violence together."[5] The force of this impeachment lies in the failure of the conjunction, the fact that often the ideas are yoked but not united; and if we are to judge of styles of poetry by their abuse, enough examples may be found in Cleveland to justify Johnson's condemnation. But a degree of heterogeneity of material compelled into unity by the operation of the poet's mind is omnipresent in poetry. We need not select for illustration such a line as:

> Notre âme est un trois-mâts cherchant son Icarie;[6]

we may find it in some of the best lines of Johnson himself (The Vanity of Human Wishes):

> His fate was destined to a barren strand,
> A petty fortress, and a dubious hand;
> He left a name at which the world grew pale,
> To point a moral, or adorn a tale.[7]

where the effect is due to a contrast of ideas, different in degree but the same in principle, as that which Johnson mildly reprehended. And in one of the finest poems of the age (a poem which could not have been written in any other age), the Exequy of Bishop King, the extended comparison is used with perfect success: the idea and the simile become one, in the passage in which the Bishop illustrates his impatience to see his dead wife, under the figure of a journey:

---

[3] Donne, "A Valediction: Of Weeping," lines 10–18.

[4] "The Relique," line 6.
[5] See the life of Cowley, in Johnson's Lives of the Poets.
[6] From Baudelaire's "Le Voyage" (in Les Fleurs du Mal): "Our soul is a three-master in quest of its Icaria."
[7] Lines 219 ff. (see I, 857, above).

Stay for me there; I will not faile
To meet thee in that hollow Vale.
And think not much of my delay;
I am already on the way,
And follow thee with all the speed
Desire can make, or sorrows breed.
Each minute is a short degree,
And ev'ry houre a step towards thee.
At night when I betake to rest,
Next morn I rise nearer my West
Of life, almost by eight houres sail,
Than when sleep breath'd his drowsy gale. . . .
But heark! My Pulse, like a soft Drum
Beats my approach, tells *Thee* I come;
And slow howere my marches be,
I shall at last sit down by Thee.

(In the last few lines there is that effect of terror which is several times attained by one of Bishop King's admirers, Edgar Poe.) Again, we may justly take these quatrains from Lord Herbert's Ode, stanzas which would, we think, be immediately pronounced to be of the metaphysical school:

So when from hence we shall be gone,
    And be no more, nor you, nor I,
    As one another's mystery,
Each shall be both, yet both but one.

This said, in her up-lifted face,
    Her eyes, which did that beauty crown,
    Were like two starrs, that having faln down,
Look up again to find their place:

While such a moveless silent peace
    Did seize on their becalmed sense,
    One would have thought some influence
Their ravished spirits did possess.

There is nothing in these lines (with the possible exception of the stars, a simile not at once grasped, but lovely and justified) which fits Johnson's general observations on the metaphysical poets in his essay on Cowley. A good deal resides in the richness of association which is at the same time borrowed from and given to the word "becalmed"; but the meaning is clear, the language simple and elegant. It is to be observed that the language of these poets is as a rule simple and pure; in the verse of George Herbert this simplicity is carried as far as it can go—a simplicity emulated without success by numerous modern poets. The *structure* of the sentences, on the other hand, is sometimes far from simple, but this is not a vice; it is a fidelity to thought and feeling. The effect, at its best, is far less artificial than that of an ode by Gray. And as this fidelity induces variety of thought

and feeling, so it induces variety of music. We doubt whether, in the eighteenth century, could be found two poems in nominally the same metre, so dissimilar as Marvell's *Coy Mistress* and Crashaw's *Saint Teresa;* the one producing an effect of great speed by the use of short syllables, and the other an ecclesiastical solemnity by the use of long ones:

Love, thou art absolute sole lord
    Of life and death.

If so shrewd and sensitive (though so limited) a critic as Johnson failed to define metaphysical poetry by its faults, it is worth while to inquire whether we may not have more success by adopting the opposite method: by assuming that the poets of the seventeenth century (up to the Revolution) were the direct and normal development of the precedent age; and, without prejudicing their case by the adjective "metaphysical," consider whether their virtue was not something permanently valuable, which subsequently disappeared, but ought not to have disappeared. Johnson has hit, perhaps by accident, on one of their peculiarities, when he observes that "their attempts were always analytic"; he would not agree that, after the dissociation, they put the material together again in a new unity.

It is certain that the dramatic verse of the later Elizabethan and early Jacobean poets expresses a degree of development of sensibility which is not found in any of the prose, good as it often is. If we except Marlowe, a man of prodigious intelligence, these dramatists were directly or indirectly (it is at least a tenable theory) affected by Montaigne. Even if we except also Jonson and Chapman, these two were notably erudite, and were notably men who incorporated their erudition into their sensibility: their mode of feeling was directly and freshly altered by their reading and thought. In Chapman especially there is a direct sensuous apprehension of thought, or a recreation of thought into feeling, which is exactly what we find in Donne:

in this one thing, all the discipline
Of manners and of manhood is contained;
A man to join himself with th' Universe
In his main sway, and make in all things fit
One with that All, and go on, round as it;
Not plucking from the whole his wretched part,
And into straits, or into nought revert,
Wishing the complete Universe might be
Subject to such a rag of it as he;
But to consider great Necessity.[8]

---

[8] George Chapman, *The Revenge of Bussy d'Ambois*, IV, i, 139 ff.

We compare this with some modern passage:

No, when the fight begins within himself,
A man's worth something. God stoops o'er his head,
Satan looks up between his feet—both tug—
He's left, himself, i' the middle; the soul wakes
And grows. Prolong that battle through his life![9]

It is perhaps somewhat less fair, though very tempting
(as both poets are concerned with the perpetuation of
love by offspring), to compare with the stanzas
already quoted from Lord Herbert's Ode the following from Tennyson:

> One walked between his wife and child,
> With measured footfall firm and mild,
> And now and then he gravely smiled.
>   The prudent partner of his blood
>   Leaned on him, faithful, gentle, good,
>   Wearing the rose of womanhood.
> And in their double love secure,
> The little maiden walked demure,
> Pacing with downward eyelids pure.
>   These three made unity so sweet,
>   My frozen heart began to beat,
>   Remembering its ancient heat.[10]

The difference is not a simple difference of degree
between poets. It is something which had happened
to the mind of England between the time of Donne
or Lord Herbert of Cherbury and the time of Tennyson and Browning; it is the difference between the
intellectual poet and the reflective poet. Tennyson and
Browning are poets, and they think; but they do not
feel their thought as immediately as the odour of a
rose. A thought to Donne was an experience; it
modified his sensibility. When a poet's mind is
perfectly equipped for its work, it is constantly
amalgamating disparate experience; the ordinary
man's experience is chaotic, irregular, fragmentary.
The latter falls in love, or reads Spinoza, and these
two experiences have nothing to do with each other,
or with the noise of the typewriter or the smell of
cooking; in the mind of the poet these experiences
are always forming new wholes.

We may express the difference by the following
theory: The poets of the seventeenth century, the
successors of the dramatists of the sixteenth, possessed
a mechanism of sensibility which could devour any
kind of experience. They are simple, artificial, difficult, or fantastic, as their predecessors were; no less
nor more than Dante, Guido Cavalcanti, Guinizelli,

or Cino. In the seventeenth century a dissociation of
sensibility set in, from which we have never recovered; and this dissociation, as is natural, was
aggravated by the influence of the two most powerful poets of the century, Milton and Dryden. Each of
these men performed certain poetic functions so
magnificently well that the magnitude of the effect
concealed the absence of others. The language went
on and in some respects improved; the best verse of
Collins, Gray, Johnson, and even Goldsmith satisfies
some of our fastidious demands better than that of
Donne or Marvell or King. But while the language
became more refined, the feeling became more crude.
The feeling, the sensibility, expressed in the *Country
Churchyard* (to say nothing of Tennyson and Browning) is cruder than that in the *Coy Mistress*.

The second effect of the influence of Milton and
Dryden followed from the first, and was therefore
slow in manifestation. The sentimental age began
early in the eighteenth century, and continued. The
poets revolted against the ratiocinative, the descriptive; they thought and felt by fits, unbalanced;
they reflected. In one or two passages of Shelley's
Triumph of Life, in the second *Hyperion,* there are
traces of a struggle toward unification of sensibility.
But Keats and Shelley died, and Tennyson and
Browning ruminated.

After this brief exposition of a theory—too brief,
perhaps, to carry conviction—we may ask, what
would have been the fate of the "metaphysical" had
the current of poetry descended in a direct line from
them, as it descended in a direct line to them? They
would not, certainly, be classified as metaphysical.
The possible interests of a poet are unlimited; the
more intelligent he is the better; the more intelligent
he is the more likely that he will have interests: our
only condition is that he turn them into poetry, and
not merely meditate on them poetically. A philosophical theory which has entered into poetry is
established, for its truth or falsity in one sense ceases
to matter, and its truth in another sense is proved. The
poets in question have, like other poets, various faults.
But they were, at best, engaged in the task of trying
to find the verbal equivalent for states of mind and
feeling. And this means both that they are more
mature, and that they wear better, than later poets of
certainly not less literary ability.

It is not a permanent necessity that poets should be
interested in philosophy, or in any other subject. We
can only say that it appears likely that poets in our
civilization, as it exists at present, must be *difficult.*
Our civilization comprehends great variety and
complexity, and this variety and complexity, playing

---

[9] Browning, "Bishop Blougram's Apology."
[10] "The Two Voices," lines 412 ff.

upon a refined sensibility, must produce various and complex results. The poet must become more and more comprehensive, more allusive, more indirect, in order to force, to dislocate if necessary, language into his meaning. (A brilliant and extreme statement of this view, with which it is not requisite to associate oneself, is that of M. Jean Epstein, *La Poésie d'aujourd-hui*.) Hence we get something which looks very much like the conceit—we get, in fact, a method curiously similar to that of the "metaphysical poets," similar also in its use of obscure words and of simple phrasing.

> O géraniums diaphanes, guerroyeurs sortilèges,
> Sacrilèges monomanes!
> Emballages, dévergondages, douches! O pressoirs
> Des vendanges des grands soirs!
> Layettes aux abois,
> Thyrses au fond des bois!
> Transfusions, représailles,
> Relevailles, compresses et l'éternelle potion,
> Angélus! n'en pouvoir plus
> De débâcles nuptiales! de débâcles nuptiales![11]

The same poet could write also simply:

> Elle est bien loin, elle pleure,
> Le grand vent se lamente aussi . . .[12]

Jules Laforgue, and Tristan Corbière in many of his poems, are nearer to the "school of Donne" than any modern English poet. But poets more classical than they have the same essential quality of transmuting ideas into sensations, of transforming an observation into a state of mind.

> Pour l'enfant, amoureux de cartes et d'estampes,
> L'univers est égal à son vaste appétit.
> Ah, que le monde est grand à la carté des lampes!
> Aux yeux du souvenir que le monde est petit![13]

In French literature the great master of the seventeenth century—Racine—and the great master of the nineteenth—Baudelaire—are in some ways more like each other than they are like any one else. The greatest two masters of diction are also the greatest two psychologists, the most curious explorers of the soul. It is interesting to speculate whether it is not a misfortune that two of the greatest masters of diction in our language, Milton and Dryden, triumph with a dazzling disregard of the soul. If we continued to produce Miltons and Drydens it might not so much matter, but as things are it is a pity that English poetry has remained so incomplete. Those who object to the "artificiality" of Milton or Dryden sometimes tell us to "look into our hearts and write." But that is not looking deep enough; Racine or Donne looked into a good deal more than the heart. One must look into the cerebral cortex, the nervous system, and the digestive tracts.

May we not conclude, then, that Donne, Crashaw, Vaughan, Herbert and Lord Herbert, Marvell, King, Cowley at his best, are in the direct current of English poetry, and that their faults should be reprimanded by this standard rather than coddled by antiquarian affection? They have been enough praised in terms which are implicit limitations because they are "metaphysical" or "witty," "quaint" or "obscure," though at their best they have not these attributes more than other serious poets. On the other hand, we must not reject the criticism of Johnson (a dangerous person to disagree with) without having mastered it, without having assimilated the Johnsonian canons of taste. In reading the celebrated passage in his essay on Cowley we must remember that by wit he clearly means something more serious than we usually mean today; in his criticism of their versification we must remember in what a narrow discipline he was trained, but also how well trained; we must remember that Johnson tortures chiefly the chief offenders, Cowley and Cleveland. It would be a fruitful work, and one requiring a substantial book, to break up the classification of Johnson (for there has been none since) and exhibit these poets in all their difference of kind and of degree, from the massive music of Donne to the faint, pleasing tinkle of Aurelian Townshend—whose *Dialogue between a Pilgrim and Time* is one of the few regrettable omissions from the excellent anthology of Professor Grierson.

---

[11] From Jules Laforgue, *Derniers Vers*, X, lines 1-10. Translation of these lines can only do them a grave injustice.

[12] From Laforgue, *Derniers Vers*, XI, "Sur une Défunte," lines 57 f.: "She is far away, she weeps, / The high wind too laments. . . ."

[13] The opening lines of Baudelaire's "Le Voyage": "For the child in love with maps and prints, / The universe is on a scale with his vast appetite. / Ah, how big the world is in the light of the study-lamp! / To the eyes of memory, how small!"

David Herbert Lawrence

1885-1930

D. H. LAWRENCE was born in the Midlands mining district of England, the son of a miner; the outward circumstances of his early life must fairly have resembled those of the miners' families depicted in his works—in *Sons and Lovers,* for instance, or in the story reprinted below (pp. 1032 ff.), *Odour of Chrysanthemums.* His first serious occupation was that of teacher; after taking his teaching certificate at Nottingham University College, he taught for a time at the Davidson Road School, Croydon, but in this life he felt cramped and stifled. The publication of his early books made it clear that another vocation awaited him, one that would allow him to seek the milder climates necessary to his frail health. His first novel, *The White Peacock* (1911), was followed by others, with a certain regularity: *The Trespasser* (1912), *Sons and Lovers* (1913), *The Rainbow* (1915), *Women in Love* (1921), *Aaron's Rod* (1922), *Kangaroo* (1923), *St. Mawr* (1925), *The Plumed Serpent* (1926), and—most widely discussed—*Lady Chatterley's Lover* (1928). His short stories and *novellen* appeared in four principal collections: *The Prussian Officer* (1914), *England, My England* (1922), *The Woman Who Rode Away* (1928), and *The Lovely Lady* (1933). In 1934 the whole of his shorter fiction, up to and including *The Man Who Died* (1931), was collected into one volume, *The Tales of D. H. Lawrence,* which has recently been reprinted. Whatever may be the case with other writers, with Lawrence it is wise to let first things come first and to begin the reading of his fiction with *The White Peacock* and *The Prussian Officer* (the volume in which *Odour of Chrysanthemums* originally appeared).

Lawrence has had his widest fame as a novelist, but it should not be forgotten that he was a complete man of letters, working at one time or another in virtually all forms. Above all, he was one of the three or four foremost poets of his time. His poetic voice is at once authoritative and completely individual: in any one of his poems we recognize the intensity with which life made its impression on him, the deep force of his convictions, and his unique power to create a seemingly palpable world by his words. *The Collected Poems of D. H. Lawrence* was first published in 1928 and last reprinted in 1933; since it does not include the separate volumes published in the last years of Lawrence's life (*Pansies,* 1929, and *Nettles,* 1930) or posthumously (*Last Poems,* 1933), it is to be hoped that a new, complete edition will be undertaken soon. At present his poems are most easily obtainable, in the United States, in *Selected Poems of D. H. Lawrence,* with an introduction by Kenneth Rexroth (1948).

After his first trip abroad, to Bavaria and Italy in 1912, he and his wife (he had married Frieda, Baroness von Richthofen, in 1914) traveled widely—in Germany, Italy, Ceylon, Australia, the United States and Mexico, the south of France and Switzerland—living abroad, particularly in Italy, for long periods. Certain of the qualities that made him a great poet and novelist are responsible for the interest, power, and vivacity of his travel books: *Twilight in Italy* (1916), *Sea and Sardinia* (1921), *Mornings in Mexico* (1927), *Etruscan Places* (1933). *The Fantasia of the Unconscious* (1923) is valuable as an explicit statement of many of the positions and beliefs which are close to the heart of everything Lawrence wrote. *Studies in Classic American Literature* (1924), despite its conventional title, is a most lively and unconventional book, revealing beneath its eccentric manner a profound insight into the American writers he treats, among them Cooper, Melville, Hawthorne, and Whitman. *Phoenix: The Posthumous Papers of D. H. Lawrence* (1936) gathers together a wide variety of nonfictional prose: critical papers and reviews, philosophical and psychological essays, sketches about people and places.

Lawrence died in the south of France, at Vence, Alpes Maritimes, on March 2, 1930; in a biographical note at the end of *The Letters of D. H. Lawrence* (1932), Aldous Huxley says: "No headstone is over his grave, save a phoenix (which was his own design), done in local stones by a peasant who loved him." There has been no shortage of books about Lawrence, but as often as not the biographers seem to have been chiefly occupied, consciously or unconciously, with the task of explaining their own respective relationships with him. It is not extravagant praise to say that the most recent full-length study of Lawrence, *Portrait of a Genius, But . . .* (1950), by Richard Aldington, is more satisfactory, for the general reader, than most of its predecessors. *The Letters of D. H. Lawrence,* edited and with an introductory essay by Aldous Huxley, is still indispensable to the reader who wishes to supplement his reading of Lawrence's work with the most direct possible insight into Lawrence's life. To the biographical note at the end of the *Letters* I am indebted for certain of the facts cited above.

LOVE ON THE FARM[1]

What large, dark hands are those at the window
Grasping in the golden light
Which weaves its way through the evening wind
  At my heart's delight?

Ah, only the leaves! But in the west   5
I see a redness suddenly come
Into the evening's anxious breast—
  'Tis the wound of love goes home!

The woodbine creeps abroad
Calling low to her lover: 10
  The sun-lit flirt who all the day
  Has poised above her lips in play
  And stolen kisses, shallow and gay
  Of pollen, now has gone away—
    She woos the moth with her sweet, low word;   15
And when above her his moth-wings hover
Then her bright breast she will uncover
And yield her honey-drop to her lover.

Into the yellow, evening glow
Saunters a man from the farm below;   20
Leans, and looks in at the low-built shed
Where the swallow has hung her marriage bed.
  The bird lies warm against the wall.
  She glances quick her startled eyes
  Towards him, then she turns away   25
  Her small head, making warm display
  Of red upon the throat. Her terrors sway
  Her out of the nest's warm, busy ball,
  Whose plaintive cry is heard as she flies
  In one blue stoop from out the sties   30
  Into the twilight's empty hall.

Oh, water-hen, beside the rushes
Hide your quaintly scarlet blushes,
Still your quick tail, lie still as dead,
Till the distance folds over his ominous tread!   35

The rabbit presses back her ears,
Turns back her liquid, anguished eyes
And crouches low; then with wild spring
Spurts from the terror of *his* oncoming;
To be choked back, the wire ring   40
Her frantic effort throttling:

[1] The following poems are from *Collected Poems of D. H. Lawrence,*
  copyright 1929 by Jonathan Cape & Harrison Smith, Inc.;
  reprinted by permission of The Viking Press, Inc., New York.

Piteous brown ball of quivering fears!
Ah, soon in his large, hard hands she dies,
And swings all loose from the swing of his walk!
Yet calm and kindly are his eyes   45
And ready to open in brown surprise
Should I not answer to his talk
Or should he my tears surmise.

I hear his hand on the latch, and rise from my chair
Watching the door open; he flashes bare   50
His strong teeth in a smile, and flashes his eyes
In a smile like triumph upon me; then careless-wise
He flings the rabbit soft on the table board
And comes towards me: ah! the uplifted sword
Of his hand against my bosom! and oh, the broad   55
Blade of his glance that asks me to applaud
His coming! With his hand he turns my face to him
And caresses me with his fingers that still smell grim
Of the rabbit's fur! God, I am caught in a snare!
I know not what fine wire is round my throat;   60
I only know I let him finger there
My pulse of life, and let him nose like a stoat
Who sniffs with joy before he drinks the blood.

And down his mouth comes to my mouth! and down
His bright dark eyes come over me, like a hood   65
Upon my mind! his lips meet mine, and a flood
Of sweet fire sweeps across me, so I drown
Against him, die, and find death good.

BABY RUNNING BAREFOOT

When the white feet of the baby beat across the grass
The little white feet nod like white flowers in a wind,
They poise and run like puffs of wind that pass
Over water where the weeds are thinned.

And the sight of their white playing in the grass   5
Is winsome as a robin's song, so fluttering;
Or like two butterflies that settle on a glass
Cup for a moment, soft little wing-beats uttering.

And I wish that the baby would tack across here to me
Like a wind-shadow running on a pond, so she could
    stand   10
With two little bare white feet upon my knee
And I could feel her feet in either hand

Cool as syringa buds in morning hours,
Or firm and silken as young peony flowers.

AWARE

Slowly the moon is rising out of the ruddy haze,
Divesting herself of her golden shift, and so
Emerging white and exquisite; and I in amaze
See in the sky before me, a woman I did not know
I loved, but there she goes, and her beauty hurts my
    heart;   5
I follow her down the night, begging her not to depart.

A WINTER'S TALE

Yesterday the fields were only grey with scattered snow,
And now the longest grass-leaves hardly emerge;
Yet her deep footsteps mark the snow, and go
On towards the pines at the hill's white verge.

I cannot see her, since the mist's pale scarf   5
Obscures the dark wood and the dull orange sky;
But she's waiting, I know, impatient and cold, half
Sobs struggling into her frosty sigh.

Why does she come so promptly, when she must know
She's only the nearer to the inevitable farewell?   10
The hill is steep, on the snow my steps are slow—
Why does she come, when she knows what I have to
    tell?

TROTH WITH THE DEAD

The moon is broken in twain, and half a moon
Beyond me lies on the low, still floor of the sky;
The other half of the broken coin of troth
Is buried away in the dark, where the dead all lie.

They buried her half in the grave when they laid her
    away;   5
Pushed gently away and hidden in the thick of her hair
Where it gathered towards the plait, on that very last
    day;
And like a moon unshowing it must still shine there.

So half lies on the sky, for a general sign
Of the troth with the dead that we are pledged to
    keep;   10
Turning its broken edge to the dark, its shine
Ends like a broken love, that turns to the dark of sleep.

And half lies there in the dark where the dead all lie
Lost and yet still connected; and between the two
Strange beams must travel still, for I feel that I   15
Am lit beneath my heart with a half-moon, weird and
    blue.

THE NORTH COUNTRY

In another country, black poplars shake themselves over
    a pond,
And rooks and the rising smoke-waves scatter and
    wheel from the works beyond:
The air is dark with north and with sulphur, the grass
    is a darker green,
And people darkly invested with purple move palpable
    through the scene.

Soundlessly down across the counties, out of the
    resonant gloom   5
That wraps the north in stupor and purple travels the
    deep, slow boom
Of the man-life north imprisoned, shut in the hum of
    the purpled steel
As it spins to sleep on its motion, drugged dense in the
    sleep of the wheel.

Out of the sleep, from the gloom of motion, sound-
    lessly, somnambule
Moans and booms the soul of a people imprisoned,
    asleep in the rule   10
Of the strong machine that runs mesmeric, booming
    the spell of its word
Upon them and moving them helpless, mechanic, their
    will to its will deferred.

Yet all the while comes the droning inaudible, out of
    the violet air,
The moaning of sleep-bound beings in travail that toil
    and are will-less there
In the spellbound north, convulsive now with a dream
    near morning, strong   15
With violent achings heaving to burst the sleep that is
    now not long.

A SNOWY DAY IN SCHOOL

All the long school-hours, round the irregular hum of
    the class
Have pressed immeasurable spaces of hoarse silence
Muffling my mind, as snow muffles the sounds that pass
Down the soiled street. We have pattered the lessons
    ceaselessly—

But the faces of the boys, in the brooding, yellow light 5
Have been for me like a dazed constellation of stars,
Like half-blown flowers dimly shaking at the night,
Like half-seen froth on an ebbing shore in the moon.

Out of each face, strange, dark beams that disquiet;
In the open depths of each flower, dark, restless drops; 10
Twin-bubbling challenge and mystery, in the foam's
  whispering riot.
—How can I answer the challenge of so many eyes?

The thick snow is crumpled on the roof, it plunges down
Awfully!—Must I call back a hundred eyes?—A voice
Falters a statement about an abstract noun— 15
What was my question?—My God, must I break this
  hoarse

Silence that rustles beyond the stars?—There!—
I have startled a hundred eyes, and now I must look
Them an answer back; it is more than I can bear.

The snow descends as if the slow sky shook 20
In flakes of shadow down; while through the gap
Between the schools sweeps one black rook.

In the playground, a shaggy snowball stands huge and
  still
With fair flakes lighting down on it. Beyond, the town
Is lost in this shadowed silence the skies distil. 25

And all things are in silence, they can brood
Alone within the dim and hoarse silence.
Only I and the class must wrangle; this work is a bitter
  rood!

BALLAD OF ANOTHER OPHELIA[1]

O the green glimmer of apples in the orchard,
Lamps in a wash of rain!
O the wet walk of my brown hen through the stack-
  yard!
O tears on the window-pane!

Nothing now will ripen the bright green apples 5
Full of disappointment and of rain;
Blackish they will taste, of tears, when the yellow
  dapples
Of autumn tell the withered tale again.

---

[1] In a letter to Harriet Monroe, July 31, 1914 (see *Letters of D. H. Lawrence*, p. 206), Lawrence wrote: "Why, oh why, do you want to cut off the tail of poor *Ophelia's* ballad? Don't you see the poor thing is cracked, and she used all those verses—apples and chickens and rat—according to true instinctive or *dream* symbolism? This poem—I am very proud of it—has the quality of a troublesome dream that seems incoherent but is selected by another sort of consciousness. The latter part is the waking up part, yet never really awake, because she is mad. No, you mustn't cut it in two. It is a good poem: I couldn't do it again to save my life."

All round the yard it is cluck! my brown hen.
Cluck! and the rain-wet wings; 10
Cluck! my marigold bird, and again
Cluck! for your yellow darlings.

For a grey rat found the gold thirteen
Huddled away in the dark.
Flutter for a moment, oh, the beast is quick and keen, 15
Extinct one yellow-fluffy spark!

Once I had a lover bright like running water,
Once his face was open like the sky,
Open like the sky looking down in all its laughter
On the buttercups, and the buttercups was I. 20

What then is there hidden in the skirts of all the
  blossom?
What is peeping from your skirts, O mother hen?
'Tis the sun that asks the question, in a lovely haste for
  wisdom;
What a lovely haste for wisdom is in men!

Yea, but it is cruel when undressed is all the blossom 25
And her shift is lying white upon the floor,
That a grey one, like a shadow, like a rat, a thief, a
  rainstorm
Creeps upon her then and ravishes her store!

O the grey garner that is full of half-grown apples!
O the golden sparkles laid extinct! 30
And O, behind the cloud-leaves, like yellow autumn
  dapples,
Did you see the wicked sun that winked?

READING A LETTER

She sits on the recreation ground
  Under an oak whose yellow buds dot the pale blue
    sky.
The young grass twinkles in the wind, and the sound
  Of the wind in the knotted buds makes a canopy.

So sitting under the knotted canopy 5
  Of the wind, she is lifted and carried away as in a
    balloon
Across the insensible void, till she stoops to see
  The sandy desert beneath her, the dreary platoon.

She knows the waste all dry beneath her, in one place
  Stirring with earth-coloured life, ever turning and
    stirring. 10
But never the motion has a human face
  Nor sound, only intermittent machinery whirring.

And so again, on the recreation ground
   She alights a stranger, wondering, unused to the scene;
Suffering at sight of the children playing around,   15
   Hurt at the chalk-coloured tulips, and the evening-
      green.

NOSTALGIA

The waning moon looks upward; this grey night
Slopes round the heavens in one smooth curve
Of easy sailing; odd red wicks serve
To show where the ships at sea move out of sight.

The place is palpable me, for here I was born   5
Of this self-same darkness. Yet the shadowy house
   below
Is out of bounds, and only the old ghosts know
I have come, I feel them whimper in welcome, and
   mourn.

My father suddenly died in the harvesting corn
And the place is no longer ours. Watching, I hear   10
No sound from the strangers, the place is dark, and fear
Opens my eyes till the roots of my vision seem torn.

Can I go no nearer, never towards the door?
The ghosts and I we mourn together, and shrink
In the shadow of the cart-shed. Must we hover on the
   brink   15
For ever, and never enter the homestead any more?

Is it irrevocable? Can I really not go
Through the open yard-way? Can I not go past the
   sheds
And through to the mowie?—Only the dead in their
   beds
Can know the fearful anguish that this is so.   20

I kiss the stones, I kiss the moss on the wall,
And wish I could pass impregnate into the place.
I wish I could take it all in a last embrace.
I wish with my breast I here could annihilate it all.

THE SHADOW OF DEATH

The earth again like a ship steams out of the dark sea
   over
The edge of the blue, and the sun stands up to see us
   glide
Slowly into another day; slowly the rover
Vessel of darkness takes the rising tide.

I, on the deck, am startled by this dawn confronting   5
Me who am issued amazed from the darkness, stripped
And quailing here in the sunshine, betrayed from
   haunting
The soundless night whereon our days are shipped.

Feeling myself undawning, the day's light playing upon
   me,
I who am substance of shadow, I all compact   10
Of the stuff of the night, finding myself all wrongly
Among crowds of things in the sunshine jostled and
   racked.

I with the night on my lips, I sigh with the silence of
   death;
And what do I care though the very stones should cry
   me unreal, though the clouds
Shine in conceit of substance upon me, who am less
   than the rain!   15
Do I not know the darkness within them? What are
   they but shrouds?

The clouds go down the sky with a wealthy ease,
Casting a shadow of scorn upon me for my share in
   death; but I
Hold my own in the midst of them, darkling defy
The whole of the day to extinguish the shadow I lift
   on the breeze.   20

Yea, though the very clouds have vantage over me
Enjoying their glancing flight, though love is dead,
I still am not homeless here, I've a tent by day
Of darkness whereon she sleeps on her perfect bed.

SONG OF A MAN WHO HAS COME THROUGH

Not I, not I, but the wind that blows through me!
A fine wind is blowing the new direction of Time.
If only I let it bear me, carry me, if only it carry me!
If only I am sensitive, subtle, oh, delicate, a winged gift!
If only, most lovely of all, I yield myself and am
   borrowed   5
By the fine, fine wind that takes its course through the
   chaos of the world
Like a fine, an exquisite chisel, a wedge-blade inserted;
If only I am keen and hard like the sheer tip of a wedge
Driven by invisible blows,
The rock will split, we shall come at the wonder, we
   shall find the Hesperides.   10

Oh, for the wonder that bubbles into my soul,
I would be a good fountain, a good well-head,
Would blur no whisper, spoil no expression.

What is the knocking?
What is the knocking at the door in the night?   15
It is somebody wants to do us harm.

No, no, it is the three strange angels.
Admit them, admit them.

BAT

At evening, sitting on this terrace,
When the sun from the west, beyond Pisa, beyond the
          mountains of Carrara
Departs, and the world is taken by surprise . . .

When the tired flower of Florence is in gloom beneath
          the glowing
Brown hills surrounding . . .   5

When under the arches of the Ponte Vecchio
A green light enters against stream, flush from the west,
Against the current of obscure Arno . . .

Look up, and you see things flying
Between the day and the night;   10
Swallows with spools of dark thread sewing the
          shadows together.

A circle swoop, and a quick parabola under the
          bridge arches
Where light pushes through;
A sudden turning upon itself of a thing in the air.
A dip to the water.   15

And you think:
"The swallows are flying so late!"

Swallows?

Dark air-life looping
Yet missing the pure loop . . .   20
A twitch, a twitter, an elastic shudder in flight
And serrated wings against the sky,
Like a glove, a black glove thrown up at the light,
And falling back.

Never swallows!   25
Bats!
The swallows are gone.

At a wavering instant the swallows give way to bats
By the Ponte Vecchio . . .
Changing guard.   30

Bats, and an uneasy creeping in one's scalp
As the bats swoop overhead!
Flying madly.

Pipistrello![1]
Black piper on an infinitesimal pipe.   35
Little lumps that fly in air and have voices indefinite,
          wildly vindictive;

Wings like bits of umbrella.

Bats!

Creatures that hang themselves up like an old rag, to
          sleep;
And disgustingly upside down.   40
Hanging upside down like rows of disgusting old rags
And grinning in their sleep.
Bats!

In China the bat is symbol of happiness.

Not for me!   45

SNAKE

A snake came to my water-trough
On a hot, hot day, and I in pyjamas for the heat,
To drink there.

In the deep, strange-scented shade of the great dark
          carob-tree
I came down the steps with my pitcher   5
And must wait, must stand and wait, for there he was
          at the trough before me.

He reached down from a fissure in the earth-wall in
          the gloom
And trailed his yellow-brown slackness soft-bellied
          down, over the edge of the stone trough
And rested his throat upon the stone bottom,
And where the water had dripped from the tap, in a
          small clearness,   10
He sipped with his straight mouth,
Softly drank through his straight gums, into his slack
          long body,
Silently.

_____

[1] The Italian word for bat ("little piper").

Someone was before me at my water-trough,
And I, like a second comer, waiting.   15

He lifted his head from his drinking, as cattle do,
And looked at me vaguely, as drinking cattle do,
And flickered his two-forked tongue from his lips, and
    mused a moment,
And stooped and drank a little more,
Being earth-brown, earth-golden from the burning
    bowels of the earth   20
On the day of Sicilian July, with Etna smoking.

The voice of my education said to me
He must be killed,
For in Sicily the black, black snakes are innocent, the
    gold are venomous.

And voices in me said, If you were a man   25
You would take a stick and break him now, and finish
    him off.

But must I confess how I liked him,
How glad I was he had come like a guest in quiet, to
    drink at my water-trough
And depart peaceful, pacified, and thankless,
Into the burning bowels of this earth?   30

Was it cowardice, that I dared not kill him?
Was it perversity, that I longed to talk to him?
Was it humility, to feel so honoured?
I felt so honoured.

And yet those voices: 35
If you were not afraid, you would kill him!

And truly I was afraid, I was most afraid,
But even so, honoured still more
That he should seek my hospitality
From out the dark door of the secret earth.   40

He drank enough
And lifted his head, dreamily, as one who has drunken,
And flickered his tongue like a forked night on the air,
    so black,
Seeming to lick his lips,
And looked around like a god, unseeing, into the air,   45
And slowly turned his head,
And slowly, very slowly, as if thrice adream,
Proceeded to draw his slow length curving round
And climb again the broken bank of my wall-face.

And as he put his head into that dreadful hole,   50
And as he slowly drew up, snake-easing his shoulders,
    and entered farther,

A sort of horror, a sort of protest against his with-
    drawing into that horrid black hole,
Deliberately going into the blackness, and slowly draw-
    ing himself after,
Overcame me now his back was turned.

I looked round, I put down my pitcher,   55
I picked up a clumsy log
And threw it at the water-trough with a clatter.

I think it did not hit him,
But suddenly that part of him that was left behind
    convulsed in undignified haste,
Writhed like lightning, and was gone   60
Into the black hole, the earth-lipped fissure in the wall-
    front,
At which, in the intense still noon, I stared with
    fascination.

And immediately I regretted it.
I thought how paltry, how vulgar, what a mean act!
I despised myself and the voices of my accursed human
    education.   65

And I thought of the albatross,
And I wished he would come back, my snake.

For he seemed to me again like a king,
Like a king in exile, uncrowned in the underworld,
Now due to be crowned again.   70

And so, I missed my chance with one of the lords
Of life.
And I have something to expiate;
A pettiness.

                Taormina.

THE ENGLISH ARE SO NICE

The English are so nice
so awfully nice
they are the nicest people in the world.

And what's more, they're very nice about being nice
about your being nice as well!   5
If you're not nice they soon make you feel it.

Americans and French and Germans and so on
they're all very well
but they're not *really* nice, you know.   9
They're not nice in *our* sense of the word, are they now?

That's why one doesn't have to take them seriously.
We must be nice to them, of course,
of course, naturally.
But it doesn't really matter what you say to them,
they don't really understand   15
you can just say anything to them:
be nice, you know, just nice

but you must never take them seriously, they
    wouldn't understand,
just be nice, you know! oh, fairly nice,
not too nice of course, they take advantage   20
but nice enough, just nice enough
to let them feel they're not quite as nice as they
    might be.

Wystan Hugh Auden

WHEN W. H. Auden's second collection of poems, *On This Island,* appeared in this country in 1937, it was reviewed in the *New York Herald Tribune Books* section by the young American poet Frederick Prokosch with an enthusiasm that must have struck many readers who had been following Auden's development as echoing their own excitement and pleasure. Auden's earlier books had been interesting and often wholly delightful, but *On This Island* displayed a variety of accomplishment and degrees of beauty and skill which the earlier volumes had not reached, or had not reached quite so often: all promises had been fulfilled, and Auden emerged, as Prokosch put it, "as a poet of spectacular and exciting powers." And while different readers may have different preferences among the books Auden has published since that time (for an account of his several volumes see the General Introduction), all will agree that he has continued to exercise those powers in ways that are both varied and highly engaging: to such an extent, indeed, that he seems quite clearly to be the leading poet of a generation that is not wanting in distinguished poets.

Auden was born in York in 1907, the son of a doctor. He offers a certain amount of biographical information in the verse "Letter to Lord Byron" in the travel book on which he collaborated with Louis MacNeice, *Letters from Iceland* (1941). There, or in other places (Isherwood's *Lions and Shadows,* for instance), we learn of his early scientific leanings, of the Icelandic strain in his family background, and of his interest in Icelandic saga and folklore. He was educated at St. Edmund's School and Gresham's School, Holt, and went as an exhibitioner to Christ Church, Oxford. After leaving Oxford he was a schoolmaster for a time, and in more recent years has taught at various institutions in the United States. In 1935 he wrote a short verse commentary ("This is the night mail crossing the border") for the British Post Office film *Night Mail.* In 1936 he went to Spain, in support of his sympathies for the republican side in the civil war; his role there is described in Stephen Spender's recent autobiography, *World within World* (1951), which is also valuable for its picture of Auden as Spender knew

him at Oxford. In 1937 he won the King's Gold Medal for Poetry. He left England in 1939 to take up permanent residence in America and is now an American citizen.

Auden's poems were first collected into one volume in 1945, under the title of *The Collected Poetry of W. H. Auden.* The poems in that volume are arranged alphabetically by first lines rather than chronologically, and some have undergone revision since their first publication in separate volumes. *Nones,* his first collection of shorter poems since *Another Time* (1940), appeared in 1951.

Aside from the various books in which Spender has discussed Auden's poetry, the works mentioned in the General References (p. 901, above) in which his work is treated, and the Auden number of *New Verse* (October, 1937), there are few critical items which one would feel bound to recommend. One might list: Francis Scarfe, *Auden and After: The Liberation of Poetry, 1930–1941* (1942), and the same writer's essay, *W. H. Auden* (Monaco, 1949); and G. Rostrevor Hamilton, *The Tell-tale Article: A Critical Approach to Modern Poetry* (1949).

PUR[1]

This lunar beauty
Has no history,
Is complete and early;
If beauty later
Bear any feature,   5
It had a lover
And is another.

This like a dream
Keeps other time,
And daytime is   10
The loss of this;

---

[1] Auden's poems are reprinted by permission of Random House, Inc. "In Memory of W. B. Yeats," "Spain 1937," "As I Walked Out One Evening," and "The Unknown Citizen" are from *Another Time,* copyright, 1940, by W. H. Auden; the others are from *Collected Poetry of W. H. Auden,* copyright, 1945, by W. H. Auden.

For time is inches
And the heart's changes,
Where ghost has haunted,
Lost and wanted.   15

But this was never
A ghost's endeavour
Nor, finished this,
Was ghost at ease;
And till it pass   20
Love shall not near
The sweetness here,
Nor sorrow take
His endless look.

TOO DEAR, TOO VAGUE

Love by ambition
Of definition
Suffers partition
And cannot go
From yes to no   5
For no is not love; no is no
The shutting of a door
The tightening jaw
A conscious sorrow;
And saying yes   10
Turns love into success,
Views from the rail
Of land and happiness,
Assured of all
The sofas creak   15
And were this all, love were
But cheek to cheek
And dear to dear.

Voices explain
Love's pleasure and love's pain,   20
Still tap the knee
And cannot disagree,
Hushed for aggression
Of full confession,
Likeness to likeness   25
Of each old weakness;
Love is not there
Love has moved to another chair.
Aware already
Of who stands next   30
And is not vexed
And is not giddy,
Leaves the North in place
With a good grace
And would not gather   35

Another to another,
Designs his own unhappiness
Foretells his own death and is faithless.

A SUMMER NIGHT 1933

(TO GEOFFREY HOYLAND)

Out on the lawn I lie in bed,
Vega conspicuous overhead
    In the windless nights of June,
As congregated leaves complete
Their day's activity; my feet   5
    Point to the rising moon.

Lucky, this point in time and space
Is chosen as my working-place,
    Where the sexy airs of summer,
The bathing hours and the bare arms,   10
The leisured drives through a land of farms
    Are good to the newcomer.

Equal with colleagues in a ring
I sit on each calm evening
    Enchanted as the flowers   15
The opening light draws out of hiding
With all its gradual dove-like pleading,
    Its logic and its powers

That later we, though parted then,
May still recall these evenings when   20
    Fear gave his watch no look;
The lion griefs loped from the shade
And on our knees their muzzles laid,
    And Death put down his book

Now north and south and east and west   25
Those I love lie down to rest;
    The moon looks on them all,
The healers and the brilliant talkers
The eccentrics and the silent walkers,
    The dumpy and the tall.   30

She climbs the European sky,
Churches and power-station lie
    Alike among earth's fixtures:
Into the galleries she peers
And blankly as a butcher stares   35
    Upon the marvellous pictures

To gravity attentive, she
Can notice nothing here, though we
    Whom hunger does not move,

From gardens where we feel secure   40
Look up and with a sigh endure
    The tyrannies of love:

And, gentle, do not care to know,
Where Poland draws her eastern bow,
    What violence is done,   45
Nor ask what doubtful act allows
Our freedom in this English house,
    Our picnics in the sun.

Soon, soon, through dykes of our content
The crumpling flood will force a rent   50
    And, taller than a tree,
Hold sudden death before our eyes
Whose river dreams long hid the size
    And vigours of the sea.

But when the waters make retreat   55
And through the black mud first the wheat
    In shy green stalks appears,
When stranded monsters gasping lie,
And sounds of riveting terrify
    Their whorled unsubtle ears,   60

May these delights we dread to lose,
This privacy, need no excuse
    But to that strength belong,
As through a child's rash happy cries
The drowned parental voices rise   65
    In unlamenting song.

After discharges of alarm
All unpredicted let them calm
    The pulse of nervous nations,
Forgive the murderer in his glass,   70
Tough in their patience to surpass
    The tigress her swift motions.

IN MEMORY OF W. B. YEATS

(D. JAN. 1939)

He disappeared in the dead of winter:
The brooks were frozen, the airports almost deserted,
And snow disfigured the public statues;
The mercury sank in the mouth of the dying day.
O all the instruments agree   5
The day of his death was a dark cold day.

Far from his illness
The wolves ran on through the evergreen forests,

The peasant river was untempted by the fashionable
    quays;
By mourning tongues   10
The death of the poet was kept from his poems.

But for him it was his last afternoon as himself,
An afternoon of nurses and rumours;
The provinces of his body revolted,
The squares of his mind were empty,   15
Silence invaded the suburbs,
The current of his feeling failed: he became his
    admirers.

Now he is scattered among a hundred cities
And wholly given over to unfamiliar affections:
To find his happiness in another kind of wood   20
And be punished under a foreign code of conscience.
The words of a dead man
Are modified in the guts of the living.

But in the importance and noise of tomorrow
When the brokers are roaring like beasts on the floor
    of the Bourse,   25
And the poor have the sufferings to which they are
    fairly accustomed,
And each in the cell of himself is almost convinced of
    his freedom;
A few thousand will think of this day
As one thinks of a day when one did something slightly
    unusual.
O all the instruments agree   30
The day of his death was a dark cold day.

2

You were silly like us: your gift survived it all;
The parish of rich women, physical decay,
Yourself; mad Ireland hurt you into poetry.
Now Ireland has her madness and her weather
    still,   35
For poetry makes nothing happen: it survives
In the valley of its saying where executives
Would never want to tamper; it flows south
From ranches of isolation and the busy griefs,
Raw towns that we believe and die in; it sur-
    vives,   40
A way of happening, a mouth.

3

Earth, receive an honoured guest;
    William Yeats is laid to rest:
Let the Irish vessel lie
Emptied of its poetry.   45

Time that is intolerant
Of the brave and innocent,
And indifferent in a week
To a beautiful physique,

Worships language and forgives   50
Everyone by whom it lives;
Pardons cowardice, conceit,
Lays its honours at their feet.

Time that with this strange excuse
Pardoned Kipling and his views,   55
And will pardon Paul Claudel,[2]
Pardons him for writing well.

In the nightmare of the dark
All the dogs of Europe bark,
And the living nations wait,   60
Each sequestered in its hate;

Intellectual disgrace
Stares from every human face,
And the seas of pity lie
Locked and frozen in each eye.   65

Follow, poet, follow right
To the bottom of the night,
With your unconstraining voice
Still persuade us to rejoice;

With the farming of a verse   70
Make a vineyard of the curse,
Sing of human unsuccess
In a rapture of distress;

In the deserts of the heart
Let the healing fountain start,   75
In the prison of his days
Teach the free man how to praise.

OUR BIAS

The hour-glass whispers to the lion's paw,
The clock-towers tell the gardens day and night,
How many errors Time has patience for,
How wrong they are in being always right.

Yet Time, however loud its chimes or deep,   5
However fast its falling torrent flows,
Has never put the lion off his leap
Nor shaken the assurance of the rose.

For they, it seems, care only for success:
While we choose words according to their sound   10
And judge a problem by its awkwardness;

And Time with us was always popular.
When have we not preferred some going round
To going straight to where we are?

from IN TIME OF WAR[3]

16

Here war is simple like a monument:
A telephone is speaking to a man;
Flags on a map assert that troops were sent;
A boy brings milk in bowls. There is a plan

For living men in terror of their lives,   5
Who thirst at nine who were to thirst at noon,
And can be lost and are, and miss their wives,
And, unlike an idea, can die too soon.

But ideas can be true although men die,
And we can watch a thousand faces   10
Made active by one lie:

And maps can really point to places
Where life is evil now:
Nanking; Dachau.[4]

---

2 Perhaps there is no need to be too dogmatic about just what it is
that time has to pardon Kipling and Claudel for, but a couple of
guesses may be hazarded. In Anthony Powell's novel, *A Question
of Upbringing* (1951), a not entirely unsympathetic Frenchman
says, "I like Kipling. That is, I like him up to a point. Naturally
one finds annoying this—this stress on nationalism. Almost
blatant nationalism, I should say." And Ezra Pound, in his
admirable essay, *Some French Poets,* speaks of "the deliquescence
of French Catholicism in Claudel, who (as I think it is James
Stephens has said) 'is merely lying on his back kicking his heels
in it.' "
3 The sonnets in this sequence originally appeared in *Journey to a
War,* the book in which Auden and Isherwood recorded what
they saw in China during their trip there in 1938. The Sino-

Japanese War, one of the earliest outcroppings of the general
fascist aggression which was later to bring on World War II,
had broken out in July, 1937. (Earlier hostilities beginning with
the Japanese invasion of Manchuria in September, 1931, had
come to a temporary end with the Tangku truce in May, 1933.)
4 Gilbert Ernest Hubbard, in his article on Chinese History in
Chambers's *Encyclopedia* (1950), points out that by the end of
1937 the Japanese were in Nanking, so that the Chinese government had had to move to Hankow, and adds: " . . . The troops
at Nanking sullied Japan's reputation by committing the grossest
excesses against the civilian population and disarmed soldiery, of
whom some 40,000 were massacred." Dachau was the site of one
of the German concentration camps.

17

They are and suffer; that is all they do;
A bandage hides the place where each is living,
His knowledge of the world restricted to
The treatment that the instruments are giving.

And lie apart like epochs from each other   5
—Truth in their sense is how much they can bear;
It is not talk like ours, but groans they smother—
And are remote as plants; we stand elsewhere.

For who when healthy can become a foot?
Even a scratch we can't recall when cured,   10
But are boist'rous in a moment and believe

In the common world of the uninjured, and cannot
Imagine isolation. Only happiness is shared,
And anger, and the idea of love.

18

Far from the heart of culture he was used:
Abandoned by his general and his lice,
Under a padded quilt he closed his eyes
And vanished. He will not be introduced

When this campaign is tidied into books: 5
No vital knowledge perished in his skull;
His jokes were stale; like wartime, he was dull;
His name is lost for ever like his looks.

He neither knew nor chose the Good, but taught us,
And added meaning like a comma, when   10
He turned to dust in China that our daughters

Be fit to love the earth, and not again
Disgraced before the dogs; that, where are waters,
Mountains and houses, may be also men.

23

When all the apparatus of report
Confirms the triumph of our enemies;
Our bastion pierced, our army in retreat,
Violence successful like a new disease,

And Wrong a charmer everywhere invited;   5
When we regret that we were ever born:
Let us remember all who seemed deserted.
Tonight in China let me think of one,[5]

Who through ten years of silence worked and waited,
Until in Muzot all his powers spoke,   10
And everything was given once for all:

And with the gratitude of the Completed
He went out in the winter night to stroke
That little tower like a great animal.

27

Wandering lost upon the mountains of our choice,
Again and again we sigh for an ancient South,
For the warm nude ages of instinctive poise,
For the taste of joy in the innocent mouth.

Asleep in our huts, how we dream of a part   5
In the glorious balls of the future; each intricate maze
Has a plan, and the disciplined movements of the heart
Can follow for ever and ever its harmless ways.

We envy streams and houses that are sure:
But we are articled to error; we   10
Were never nude and calm like a great door,

And never will be perfect like the fountains;
We live in freedom by necessity,
A mountain people dwelling among mountains.

AS I WALKED OUT ONE EVENING

As I walked out one evening,
    Walking down Bristol Street,
The crowds upon the pavement
    Were fields of harvest wheat.

Down by the brimming river   5
    I heard a lover sing
Under an arch of the railway:
    "Love has no ending.

I'll love you, dear, I'll love you
    Till China and Africa meet,   10
And the river jumps over the mountain
    And the salmon sing in the street.

---

[5] Writing in the days when the meaning of fascism and fascist
aggression was becoming more and more painfully apparent,
Auden thinks of one who stood in his life and art for everything
that totalitarianism would suppress: the great German symbolist
poet Rilke (d. 1926). On February 11, 1922, Rilke wrote to a
friend from the Château de Muzot sur Sierre, Valais, Switzerland, "At this moment . . . I lay my pen aside behind the last
completed Elegy, the tenth. . . . This is what I have been struggling for. Through everything. Miracle. Grace.—All in a few
days. . . . " And later in the same letter, "I have gone out and
stroked my little Muzot for having guarded all this for me and at
last granted it to me, stroked it like a great shaggy beast."
(*Selected Letters of Rainer Maria Rilke: 1902–1926,* trans. by
R. F. C. Hull, 1947.)

I'll love you till the ocean
  Is folded and hung up to dry,
And the seven stars go squawking   15
  Like geese about the sky.

The years shall run like rabbits,
  For in my arms I hold
The Flower of the Ages,
  And the first love of the world."   20

But all the clocks in the city
  Began to whirr and chime:
"O let not Time deceive you,
  You cannot conquer Time.

In the burrows of the Nightmare   25
  Where Justice naked is,
Time watches from the shadow
  And coughs when you would kiss.

In headaches and in worry
  Vaguely life leaks away,   30
And Time will have his fancy
  Tomorrow or today.

Into many a green valley
  Drifts the appalling snow;
Time breaks the threaded dances   35
  And the diver's brilliant bow.

O plunge your hands in water,
  Plunge them in up to the wrist;
Stare, stare in the basin
  And wonder what you've missed.   40

The glacier knocks in the cupboard,
  The desert sighs in the bed,
And the crack in the tea-cup opens
  A lane to the land of the dead.

Where the beggars raffle the banknotes   45
  And the Giant is enchanting to Jack,
And the Lily-white Boy is a Roarer,
  And Jill goes down on her back.

O look, look in the mirror,
  O look in your distress;   50
Life remains a blessing
  Although you cannot bless.

O stand, stand at the window
  As the tears scald and start;
You shall love your crooked neighbor   55
  With your crooked heart."

It was late, late in the evening,
  The lovers they were gone;
The clocks had ceased their chiming,
  And the deep river ran on.   60

SPAIN 1937[6]

Yesterday all the past. The language of size
Spreading to China along the trade-routes; the diffusion
        Of the counting-frame and the cromlech;
Yesterday the shadow-reckoning in the sunny climates.

Yesterday the assessment of insurance by cards,   5
The divination of water; yesterday the invention
        Of cart-wheels and clocks, the taming of
Horses; yesterday the bustling world of the navigators.

Yesterday the abolition of fairies and giants;
The fortress like a motionless eagle eyeing the valley,   10
        The chapel built in the forest;
Yesterday the carving of angels and of frightening
        gargoyles.

The trial of heretics among the columns of stone;
Yesterday the theological feuds in the taverns
        And the miraculous cure at the fountain;   15
Yesterday the Sabbath of Witches. But today the
        struggle.

Yesterday the installation of dynamos and turbines;
The construction of railways in the colonial desert;
        Yesterday the classic lecture
On the origin of Mankind. But today the struggle.   20

Yesterday the belief in the absolute value of Greek;
The fall of the curtain upon the death of a hero;
        Yesterday the prayer to the sunset,
And the adoration of madmen. But today the struggle.

As the poet whispers, startled among the pines   25
Or, where the loose waterfall sings, compact, or upright
        On the crag by the leaning tower:
"O my vision. O send me the luck of the sailor."

------

6 During the civil war which went on in Spain from 1936 to
1939, and which ended with the defeat of the republicans by the
rebels under General Franco and the establishment of yet
another totalitarian régime, liberals throughout the world saw
the struggle as a crucial one for the whole principle of human
liberty. The republicans were helped by Russia, Mexico, and
the band of international volunteers known as the International
Brigade; the rebels were helped by Hitler and Mussolini. This
struggle, Auden says in his poem, must be decided, men must see
that freedom wins out over oppression before mankind can
return to the endeavors by which it has advanced in the past or
to the gratifications of the individual life lived for its own sake.

And the investigator peers through his instruments
At the inhuman provinces, the virile bacillus   30
  Or enormous Jupiter finished:
"But the lives of my friends. I inquire, I inquire."

And the poor in their fireless lodgings dropping the
  sheets
Of the evening paper: "Our day is our loss. O show us
  History the operator, the   35
Organiser, Time the refreshing river."

And the nations combine each cry, invoking the life
That shapes the individual belly and orders
  The private nocturnal terror:
"Did you not found once the city state of the sponge,   40

"Raise the vast military empires of the shark
And the tiger, establish the robin's plucky canton?
  Intervene. O descend as a dove or
A furious papa or a mild engineer: but descend."

And the life, if it answers at all, replies from the
  heart   45
And the eyes and the lungs, from the shops and squares
  of the city:
  "O no, I am not the Mover,
Not today, not to you. To you I'm the

"Yes-man, the bar-companion, the easily-duped:
I am whatever you do; I am your vow to be   50
  Good, your humorous story;
I am your business voice; I am your marriage.

"What's your proposal? To build the Just City? I will.
I agree. Or is it the suicide pact, the romantic
  Death? Very well, I accept, for   55
I am your choice, your decision: yes, I am Spain."

Many have heard it on remote peninsulas,
On sleepy plains, in the aberrant fishermen's islands,
  In the corrupt heart of the city;
Have heard and migrated like gulls or the seeds of a
  flower.   60

They clung like burrs to the long expresses that lurch
Through the unjust lands, through the night, through
  the alpine tunnel;
  They floated over the oceans;
They walked the passes: they came to present their lives.

On that arid square, that fragment nipped off from hot   65
Africa, soldered so crudely to inventive Europe,
  On that tableland scored by rivers,
Our fever's menacing shapes are precise and alive.

Tomorrow, perhaps, the future: the research on fatigue
And the movements of packers; the gradual exploring
  of all the   70
  Octaves of radiation;
Tomorrow the enlarging of consciousness by diet and
  breathing.

Tomorrow the rediscovery of romantic love;
The photographing of ravens; all the fun under
  Liberty's masterful shadow;   75
Tomorrow the hour of the pageant-master and the
  musician.

Tomorrow, for the young, the poets exploding like
  bombs,
The walks by the lake, the winter of perfect communion;
  Tomorrow the bicycle races
Through the suburbs on summer evenings: but today
  the struggle.   80

Today the inevitable increase in the chances of death;
The conscious acceptance of guilt in the fact of murder;
  Today the expending of powers
On the flat ephemeral pamphlet and the boring meeting.

Today the makeshift consolations; the shared
  cigarette;   85
The cards in the candle-lit barn and the scraping concert,
  The masculine jokes; today the
Fumbled and unsatisfactory embrace before hurting.

The stars are dead; the animals will not look:
We are left alone with our day, and the time is short
  and   90
  History to the defeated
May say Alas but cannot help or pardon.

CASINO

Only the hands are living; to the wheel attracted,
Are moved as deer trek desperately towards a creek
 Through the dust and scrub of the desert, or gently
 As sunflowers turn to the light.

And, as the night takes up the cries of feverish
 children,   5
The cravings of lions in dens, the loves of dons,
 Gathers them all and remains the night, the
 Great room is full of their prayers.

To the last feast of isolation self-invited
They flock, and in the rite of disbelief are joined;   10
 From numbers all their stars are recreated,
 The enchanted, the world, the sad.

Without, the rivers flow among the wholly living,
Quite near their trysts; and the mountains part them;
   and the bird
  Deep in the greens and moistures of summer   15
  Sings towards their work.

But here no nymph comes naked to the youngest
   shepherd;
The fountain is deserted; the laurel will not grow;
  The labyrinth is safe but endless, and broken
  Is Ariadne's thread.   20

As deeper in these hands is grooved their fortune;
   "Lucky
Were few, and it is possible that none was loved;
  And what was godlike in this generation
  Was never to be born."

THE UNKNOWN CITIZEN

(TO JS/07/M/378
This Marble Monument
Is Erected by the State)

He was found by the Bureau of Statistics to be
One against whom there was no official complaint,
And all the reports on his conduct agree
That, in the modern sense of an old-fashioned word,
   he was a saint,
For in everything he did he served the Greater
   Community.   5
Except for the War till the day he retired
He worked in a factory and never got fired,
But satisfied his employers, Fudge Motors Inc.
Yet he wasn't a scab or odd in his views,
For his Union reports that he paid his dues,   10
(Our report on his Union shows it was sound)
And our Social Psychology workers found
That he was popular with his mates and liked a drink.
The Press are convinced that he bought a paper every
   day
And that his reactions to advertisements were normal
   in every way.   15
Policies taken out in his name prove that he was fully
   insured,
And his Health-card shows he was once in hospital
   but left it cured.
Both Producers Research and High-Grade Living declare
He was fully sensible to the advantages of the
   Instalment Plan
And had everything necessary to the Modern Man,   20
A phonograph, a radio, a car and a frigidaire.
Our researchers into Public Opinion are content
That he held the proper opinions for the time of year;

When there was peace, he was for peace; when there
   was war, he went.
He was married and added five children to the
   population,   25
Which our Eugenist says was the right number for a
   parent of his generation,
And our teachers report that he never interfered with
   their education.
Was he free? Was he happy? The question is absurd:
Had anything been wrong, we should certainly have
   heard.

from THE SEA AND THE MIRROR

PREFACE [7]

(The Stage Manager to the Critics)

The aged catch their breath,
For the nonchalant couple go
Waltzing across the tightrope
As if there were no death
Or hope of falling down;   5
The wounded cry as the clown
Doubles his meaning, and O
How the dear little children laugh
When the drums roll and the lovely
Lady is sawn in half.   10

O what authority gives
Existence its surprise?
Science is happy to answer
That the ghosts who haunt our lives
Are handy with mirrors and wire,   15
That song and sugar and fire,
Courage and come-hither eyes
Have a genius for taking pains.
But how does one think up a habit?
Our wonder, our terror remains.   20

---

[7] The following view of the poem's over-all scheme of significance
may offer the reader a plan on which he can rear a superior structure of his own, one that is closer to the poem:
   Stanza 1 seems to say, "To any given phenomenon or spectacle
—life itself or a given work of art, perhaps—there are as many
typical reactions as there are types of spectators, each reacting
according to the dictates of his interests or needs." Stanza 2
asks, "What is the meaning behind the whole spectacle of
existence?" and dismisses the answers of science as glib and inadequate. Stanza 3 points out that art pretends to be able to
satisfy our doubts and questionings about moral problems by
being above them, to have its own way of solving them: but
when we are faced with actual moral choices, art's "metaphorical"
solutions do not help. Stanza 4 returns, by way of answer, to
certain intuitions about the nature of life and truth. At the end
it juxtaposes certain well-known statements from Shakespeare's
plays: see (lines 36-37) *The Tempest*, IV, i; (line 38) *Hamlet*, V,
ii; (line 41) *King Lear*, IV, vii.

Art opens the fishiest eye
To the Flesh and the Devil who heat
The Chamber of Temptation
Where heroes roar and die.
We are wet with sympathy now;   25
Thanks for the evening; but how
Shall we satisfy when we meet,
Between Shall-I and I-Will,
The lion's mouth whose hunger
No metaphors can fill?   30

Well, who in his own backyard
Has not opened his heart to the smiling
Secret he cannot quote?
Which goes to show that the Bard
Was sober when he wrote   35
That this world of fact we love
Is insubstantial stuff:
All the rest is silence
On the other side of the wall;
And the silence ripeness,   40
And the ripeness all.

A Group of Modern Poets

Alfred Edward Housman

1859–1936

A. E. HOUSMAN led the austere life of a classics scholar, having been Professor of Latin at University College, London, from 1892 until, in 1911, he went to Cambridge as Professor of Latin and Fellow of Trinity College: he remained at Cambridge for the rest of his life. Although he may have seen his editions of Manilius, Juvenal, and Lucan as the main work of his life, he also published two small volumes of verse for which he will be known and remembered by *more* people, at any rate. *A Shropshire Lad* appeared in 1896 and *Last Poems* twenty-six years later (1922). In 1936 a further volume, *More Poems,* was published posthumously under the care of Laurence Housman, the poet's brother, and in 1939 *The Collected Poems* gathered together the contents of these three volumes plus a number of poems which had not appeared in them. Housman's Leslie Stephen Lecture, *The Name and Nature of Poetry,* delivered at Cambridge on May 9, 1933, and published later in the same year, has much to say that is memorable and individual about the poetic situation, as well as much that is interesting about Housman's own habits of composition.

Housman the poet was not an innovator, in the sense in which we use the term of poets who produce changes in poetic form and technique which their contemporaries and successors will be able to make use of: no subsequent poet can write "like Housman" except at the cost of being frankly imitative. To say this, however, is not to detract from the intrinsic value of his own verse: using conventional forms, coloring them by his classical training and his own highly individual moral temper, he produced

a collection of poems which at their frequent best are both flawless and thrilling.

Since his death a number of memoirs have appeared, of which that by Percy Withers, *A Buried Life: Personal Recollections of A. E. Housman* (1940) is among the more interesting. Others are Laurence Housman's *A. E. H.: Some Poems, Some Letters and a Personal Memoir by His Brother* (1937), and A. S. F. Gow's *A. E. Housman, a Sketch* (1936). Edmund Wilson's *The Triple Thinkers* (1938) contains a critical essay.

FROM FAR, FROM EVE AND MORNING[1]

From far, from eve and morning
    And yon twelve-winded sky,
The stuff of life to knit me
    Blew hither: here am I.

Now—for a breath I tarry   5
    Nor yet disperse apart—
Take my hand quick and tell me,
    What have you in your heart.

Speak now, and I will answer;
    How shall I help you, say;   10
Ere to the wind's twelve quarters
    I take my endless way.

[1] The following poems are reprinted from *The Collected Poems of A. E. Housman,* copyright, 1940, by Henry Holt and Company, Inc.; copyright, 1936, by Barclays Bank Ltd.; used by permission of the publisher. The first two were included in *A Shropshire Lad,* the last three in *More Poems.*

FAR IN A WESTERN BROOKLAND

Far in a western brookland
    That bred me long ago
The poplars stand and tremble
    By pools I used to know.

There, in the windless night-time,   5
    The wanderer, marvelling why,
Halts on the bridge to hearken
    How soft the poplars sigh.

He hears: no more remembered
    In fields where I was known,   10
Here I lie down in London
    And turn to rest alone.

There, by the starlit fences,
    The wanderer halts and hears
My soul that lingers sighing   15
    About the glimmering weirs.

I PROMISE NOTHING: FRIENDS WILL PART

I promise nothing: friends will part;
    All things may end, for all began;
And truth and singleness of heart
    Are mortal even as is man.

But this unlucky love should last   5
    When answered passions thin to air;
Eternal fate so deep has cast
    Its sure foundation of despair.

DIFFUGERE NIVES

HORACE. ODES IV. 7.

The snows are fled away, leaves on the shaws
    And grasses in the mead renew their birth,
The river to the river-bed withdraws,
    And altered is the fashion of the earth.

The Nymphs and Graces three put off their fear   5
    And unapparelled in the woodland play.
The swift hour and the brief prime of the year
    Say to the soul, *Thou wast not born for aye.*

Thaw follows frost; hard on the heel of spring
    Treads summer sure to die, for hard on hers   10

Comes autumn with his apples scattering;
    Then back to wintertide, when nothing stirs.

But oh, whate'er the sky-led seasons mar,
    Moon upon moon rebuilds it with her beams;
Come *we* where Tullus and where Ancus[2] are   15
    And good Aeneas,[3] we are dust and dreams.

Torquatus,[4] if the gods in heaven shall add
    The morrow to the day, what tongue has told?
Feast then thy heart, for what the heart has had
    The fingers of no heir will ever hold.   20

When thou descendest once the shades among,
    The stern assize and equal judgment o'er,
Not thy long lineage nor thy golden tongue,
    No, nor thy righteousness, shall friend thee more.

Night holds Hippolytus the pure of stain,   25
    Diana steads him nothing, he must stay;
And Theseus leaves Pirithous in the chain[5]
    The love of comrades cannot take away.

CROSSING ALONE THE NIGHTED FERRY

Crossing alone the nighted ferry
    With the one coin for fee,[6]
Whom, on the wharf of Lethe waiting,
    Count you to find? Not me.

The brisk fond lackey to fetch and carry,   5
    The true, sick-hearted slave,
Expect him not in the just city
    And free land of the grave.

---

[2] Legendary kings of Rome.

[3] Aeneas, a member of one of the branches of the Trojan royal house, was the son of Anchises and Aphrodite; in some legends, and of course in Vergil's *Aeneid,* he is the founder of the Roman State, from having founded a Trojan colony in Latium after his escape at the fall of Troy.

[4] A friend of Horace.

[5] *Line 27.* Theseus, son of Aegeus, legendary king of Athens, was the hero of a series of adventures (slaying the Minotaur, etc.). Pirithous, king of the Lapiths, was his faithful friend. Hippolytus (line 25) was Theseus' son: see, for his story, the tragedy by Euripides (produced 429 B.C.), or *Phèdre* by the French dramatist Racine, produced in 1677.

[6] In Greek mythology the shades of the dead were ferried across the rivers of the underworld by the aged boatman, Charon, who received a single coin, an obolus, for his charge: this coin was put in the mouths of the dead.

Rupert Brooke

1887–1915

THAT most readers have found intense satisfaction in the poetry of Rupert Brooke when they were young does not mean that he offers nothing for the same readers when they have grown older, or that he does not have his place in the history of twentieth-century literature. As a war poet he is not to be compared to Wilfred Owen, yet a number of his war poems (particularly the five sonnets which include "If I should die, think only this of me") were part and parcel of the time which produced them, as they have since become a significant and permanent feature of the memories of that time. It is hoped, however, that the poems which are reprinted below will remind readers that Brooke had other sides, that he could on occasion be astringently satiric and was capable of turning a completely disabused eye on the universe and man's place in it.

Rupert Brooke was educated at Rugby and at King's College, Cambridge. He traveled in Germany in 1912, and in 1913 made a journey which took him to the United States and to Samoa and Tahiti. He was on his way to the Dardanelles, on military service, when on April 23, 1915, he died of septicemia on board a French hospital ship in the Aegean; he was buried on the island of Skyros. His *Poems* appeared in 1911; *1914 and Other Poems* was published posthumously in 1915, and *Collected Poems* in 1918. *The Poetical Works of Rupert Brooke*, edited by Geoffrey Keynes, was published in 1946.

TOWN AND COUNTRY[1]

Here, where love's stuff is body, arm and side
    Are stabbing-sweet 'gainst chair and lamp and wall.
In every touch more intimate meanings hide;
    And flaming brains are the white heart of all.

Here, million pulses to one centre beat: 5
    Closed in by men's vast friendliness, alone,
Two can be drunk with solitude, and meet
    On the sheer point where sense with knowing's one.

Here the green-purple clanging royal night,
    And the straight lines and silent walls of town,   10
And roar, and glare, and dust, and myriad white
    Undying passers, pinnacle and crown

Intensest heavens between close-lying faces
    By the lamp's airless fierce ecstatic fire;
And we've found love in little hidden places,   15
    Under great shades, between the mist and mire.

Stay! though the woods are quiet, and you've heard
    Night creep along the hedges. Never go
Where tangled foliage shrouds the crying bird,
    And the remote winds sigh, and waters flow!   20

Lest—as our words fall dumb on windless noons,
    Or hearts grow hushed and solitary, beneath
Unheeding stars and unfamiliar moons,
    Or boughs bend over, close and quiet as death,—

Unconscious and unpassionate and still,   25
    Cloud-like we lean and stare as bright leaves stare,
And gradually along the stranger hill
    Our unwalled loves thin out on vacuous air,

And suddenly there's no meaning in our kiss,
    And your lit upward face grows, where we lie,   30
Lonelier and dreadfuller than sunlight is,
    And dumb and mad and eyeless like the sky.

c. 1909

MENELAUS AND HELEN[2]

i

Hot through Troy's ruin Menelaus broke
    To Priam's palace, sword in hand, to sate
    On that adulterous whore a ten years' hate
And a king's honour. Through red death, and smoke,
And cries, and then by quieter ways he strode,   5
    Till the still innermost chamber fronted him.
    He swung his sword, and crashed into the dim
Luxurious bower, flaming like a god.

High sat white Helen, lonely and serene.
    He had not remembered that she was so fair,   10
And that her neck curved down in such a way;
And he felt tired. He flung the sword away,
    And kissed her feet, and knelt before her there,
The perfect Knight before the perfect Queen.

---

[1] The following poems are reprinted by permission of Dodd, Mead & Company from *The Collected Poems of Rupert Brooke*, copyright, 1915, by Dodd, Mead & Company; copyright renewed 1943.

[2] According to the *Iliad*, the ten-year war waged by the Greeks against the Trojans was undertaken to recover Helen, the wife of Agamemnon's brother Menelaus, who had been abducted by Paris and taken to Priam's court at Troy. The *Odyssey* pictures Menelaus as having won his way safely back to Lacedaemon, where he lived out his days with Helen; Paris had been killed at the siege of Troy.

So far the poet. How should he behold   15
   That journey home, the long connubial years?
He does not tell you how white Helen bears
Child on legitimate child, becomes a scold,
Haggard with virtue. Menelaus bold
   Waxed garrulous, and sacked a hundred Troys   20
'Twixt noon and supper. And her golden voice
Got shrill as he grew deafer. And both were old.

Often he wonders why on earth he went
   Troyward, or why poor Paris ever came.
Oft she weeps, gummy-eyed and impotent;   25
   Her dry shanks twitch at Paris' mumbled name.
So Menelaus nagged; and Helen cried;
And Paris slept on by Scamander[3] side.

1909

THE JOLLY COMPANY

The stars, a jolly company,
   I envied, straying late and lonely;
And cried upon their revelry:
   'O white companionship! You only
In love, in faith unbroken dwell,   5
Friends radiant and inseparable!'

Light-heart and glad they seemed to me
   And merry comrades (*even so*
God out of Heaven may laugh to see
   The happy crowds; and never know   10
That in his lone obscure distress
Each walketh in a wilderness).

But I, remembering, pitied well
   And loved them, who, with lonely light,
In empty infinite spaces dwell,   15
   Disconsolate. For, all the night,
I heard the thin gnat-voices cry,
Star to faint star, across the sky.

November 1908

Walter De la Mare

It would be a grave mistake to assume that because Walter De la Mare has characteristically dealt in his writing with the worlds of childhood, of dream, and of fantasy, he has nothing to say to those who inhabit the adult world of daylight and gross fact: for it is precisely that latter world which he has illumined by bringing to it his sense of beauty, his grasp of human truth and his deep understanding of life.

Mr. De la Mare, who was born in 1873, published his first volume of poems, *Songs of Childhood,* in 1902. In the forty-odd volumes he has published since that time, including poetry, short stories and novels, criticism and essays, there is pleasure for a lifetime. His poems are most conveniently obtained in the *Collected Poems* (1942); *Collected Rhymes and Verses* (1944) gathers together his poems for children. Three further volumes of verse have appeared since 1942, *The Burning Glass* (1945), *The Traveller* (1946), and *Inward Companion* (1950).

From the various volumes of short stories and tales, one might single out *On the Edge* (1930) and *The Wind Blows Over* (1936) as good places to begin. It seems to the present editor, moreover, that Mr. De la Mare's stories form a better introduction to his fiction than do his novels, such as *Henry Brocken* (1904) or *Memoirs of a Midget* (1921). A number of his essays, including those on *Rupert Brooke and the Intellectual Imagination* and *Poetry in Prose,* have been collected under the title *Pleasures and Speculations* (1940). Mr. De la Mare is also the author of four extremely interesting and beautiful books which for want of a more accurate term one may describe as anthologies, with the richest kind of introductory and interspersed commentary: *Desert Islands* (1930); *Early One Morning* (1935), a book about childhood and records of childhood; *Behold, This Dreamer!* (1939); and *Love* (1943).

There have been two full-length studies of him and his work, the first by R. L. Mégroz, *Walter De la Mare: A Biographical and Critical Study* (1924), and the second by Forrest Reid, *Walter De la Mare* (1949).

THE BOTTLE[1]

Of green and hexagonal glass,
   With sharp, fluted sides—
Vaguely transparent these walls,
   Wherein motionless hides
A simple so potent it can   5
   To oblivion lull
The weary, the racked, the bereaved,
   The miserable.

Flowers in silent desire
   Their life-breath exhale—   10

---

[3] A river that flowed past Troy.

[1] The following poems are from *Collected Poems* by Walter De la Mare, copyright, 1920, by Henry Holt and Company, Inc.; copyright, 1948, by Walter De la Mare; used by permission of the publishers.

Self-heal, hellebore, aconite,
  Chamomile, dwale:
Sharing the same gentle heavens,
  The sun's heat and light,
And, in the dust at their roots,   15
  The same shallow night.

Each its own livelihood hath,
  Shape, pattern, hue;
Age on to age unto these
  Keeping steadfastly true;   20
And, musing amid them, there moves
  A stranger, named Man,
Who of their ichor distils
  What virtue he can;

Plucks them ere seed-time to blazon   25
  His house with their radiant dyes;
Prisons their attar in wax;
  Candies their petals; denies
Them freedom to breed in their wont;
  Buds, fecundates, grafts them at will; 30
And with cunningest leechcraft compels
  Their good to his ill.

Intrigue fantastic as this
  Where shall we find?
Mute in their beauty they serve him,   35
  Body and mind.
And one—but a weed in his wheat—
  Is the poppy—frail, pallid, whose juice
With its saplike and opiate fume
  Strange dreams will induce   40

Of wonder and horror. And none
  Can silence the soul,
Wearied of self and of life,
  Earth's darkness and dole,
Most secretly, deeply. But finally?—   45
  Waste not thy breath;
The words that are scrawled on this phial
  Have for synonym, *death*—

Wicket out into the dark
  That swings but one way;   50
Infinite hush in an ocean of silence
  Aeons away—
Thou forsaken!—even thou!—
  The dread good-bye;
The abandoned, the thronged,
    the watched, the unshared—   55
  Awaiting me—I!

WINTER DUSK

Dark frost was in the air without,
  The dusk was still with cold and gloom,
When less than even a shadow came
  And stood within the room.

But of the three around the fire,   5
  None turned a questioning head to look,
Still read a clear voice, on and on,
  Still stooped they o'er their book.

The children watched their mother's eyes
  Moving on softly line to line;   10
It seemed to listen too—that shade,
  Yet made no outward sign.

The fire-flames crooned a tiny song,
  No cold wind stirred the wintry tree;
The children both in Faerie dreamed   15
  Beside their mother's knee.

And nearer yet that spirit drew
  Above that heedless one, intent
Only on what the simple words
  Of her small story meant.   20

No voiceless sorrow grieved her mind,
  No memory her bosom stirred,
Nor dreamed she, as she read to two,
  'Twas surely three who heard.

Yet when, the story done, she smiled   25
  From face to face, serene and clear,
A love, half dread, sprang up, as she
  Leaned close and drew them near.

NOD

Softly along the road of evening,
  In a twilight dim with rose,
Wrinkled with age, and drenched with dew,
  Old Nod, the shepherd, goes.

His drowsy flock streams on before him,   5
  Their fleeces charged with gold,
To where the sun's last beam leans low
  On Nod the shepherd's fold.

The hedge is quick and green with brier,
  From their sand the conies creep;   10
And all the birds that fly in heaven
  Flock singing home to sleep.

His lambs outnumber a noon's roses,
 Yet, when night's shadows fall,
His blind old sheep-dog, Slumber-soon,   15
 Misses not one of all.

His are the quiet steeps of dreamland,
 The waters of no-more-pain,
His ram's bell rings 'neath an arch of stars,
 "Rest, rest, and rest again."   20

ALONE

A very old woman
Lives in yon house.
The squeak of the cricket,
The stir of the mouse,
Are all she knows   5
Of the earth and us.

Once she was young,
Would dance and play,
Like many another
Young popinjay;   10
And run to her mother
At dusk of day.

And colours bright
She delighted in;
The fiddle to hear,   15
And to lift her chin,
And sing as small
As a twittering wren.

But age apace
Comes at last to all;   20
And a lone house filled
With the cricket's call;
And the scampering mouse
In the hollow wall.

Wilfred Owen

1893–1918

FOR an account of Wilfred Owen's life and his place in
the literary history of his time, see the General Introduction, pp. 889 f., above.

STRANGE MEETING[1]

It seemed that out of battle I escaped
Down some profound dull tunnel, long since scooped
Through granites which titanic wars had groined.

Yet also there encumbered sleepers groaned,
Too fast in thought or death to be bestirred.   5
Then, as I probed them, one sprang up, and stared
With piteous recognition in fixed eyes,
Lifting distressful hands as if to bless.
And by his smile, I knew that sullen hall,
By his dead smile I knew we stood in Hell.   10
With a thousand pains that vision's face was grained;
Yet no blood reached there from the upper ground,
And no guns thumped, or down the flues made moan.
"Strange friend," I said, "here is no cause to mourn."
"None," said the other, "save the undone years,   15
The hopelessness. Whatever hope is yours,
Was my life also; I went hunting wild
After the wildest beauty in the world,
Which lies not calm in eyes, or braided hair,
But mocks the steady running of the hour,   20
And if it grieves, grieves richlier than here.
For by my glee might many men have laughed,
And of my weeping something had been left,
Which must die now. I mean the truth untold,
The pity of war, the pity war distilled.   25
Now men will go content with what we spoiled.
Or, discontent, boil bloody, and be spilled.
They will be swift with swiftness of the tigress,
None will break ranks, though nations trek from
          progress.
Courage was mine, and I had mystery,   30
Wisdom was mine, and I had mastery;
To miss the march of this retreating world
Into vain citadels that are not walled.
Then, when much blood had clogged their chariot-
          wheels
I would go up and wash them from sweet wells,   35
Even with truths that lie too deep for taint.
I would have poured my spirit without stint
But not through wounds; not on the cess of war.
Foreheads of men have bled where no wounds were.
I am the enemy you killed, my friend.   40
I knew you in this dark; for so you frowned
Yesterday through me as you jabbed and killed.
I parried; but my hands were loath and cold.
Let me sleep now. . . ."

MINERS

There was a whispering in my hearth,
 A sigh of the coal,
Grown wistful of a former earth
 It might recall.

---

[1] The following selections are reprinted from *The Poems of Wilfred
Owen* by permission of New Directions.

I listened for a tale of leaves   5
   And smothered ferns;
Frond-forests; and the low, sly lives
   Before the fawns.

My fire might show steam-phantoms simmer
   From Time's old cauldron,   10
Before the birds made nests in summer,
   Or men had children.

But the coals were murmuring of their mine,
   And moans down there
Of boys that slept wry sleep, and men   15
   Writhing for air.

And I saw white bones in the cinder-shard,
   Bones without number;
For many hearts with coal are charred
   And few remember.   20

I thought of some who worked dark pits
   Of war, and died
Digging the rock where Death reputes
   Peace lies indeed.

Comforted years will sit soft-chaired   25
   In rooms of amber;
The years will stretch their hands, well-cheered
   By our lives' ember.

The centuries will burn rich loads
   With which we groaned,   30
Whose warmth shall lull their dreaming lids
   While songs are crooned.
But they will not dream of us poor lads
   Lost in the ground.

ANTHEM FOR DOOMED YOUTH

What passing-bells for these who die as cattle?
   Only the monstrous anger of the guns.
   Only the stuttering rifles' rapid rattle
Can patter out their hasty orisons.
No mockeries for them from prayers or bells,   5
   Nor any voice of mourning save the choirs,—
The shrill, demented choirs of wailing shells;
   And bugles calling for them from sad shires.

What candles may be held to speed them all?
   Not in the hands of boys, but in their eyes   10
Shall shine the holy glimmers of good-byes.
   The pallor of girls' brows shall be their pall;
Their flowers the tenderness of silent minds,
And each slow dusk a drawing-down of blinds.

FUTILITY

Move him into the sun—
Gently its touch awoke him once,
At home, whispering of fields unsown.
Always it woke him, even in France,
Until this morning and this snow.   5
If anything might rouse him now
The kind old sun will know.

Think how it wakes the seeds,—
Woke, once, the clays of a cold star.
Are limbs, so dear-achieved, are sides,   10
Full-nerved—still warm—too hard to stir?
Was it for this the clay grew tall?
—O what made fatuous sunbeams toil
To break earth's sleep at all?

Stephen Spender

It has been impossible to write about twentieth-century
literature in the General Introduction without mentioning
Stephen Spender's various critical works, just as it has
been impossible to discuss the poets of the thirties without
giving him a prominent place. Here it may be added that
he was born in 1909 and was educated at University
College School and at University College, Oxford; that
he was a co-editor of Cyril Connolly's *Horizon* during its
first year or two, and that his occasional comprehensive
surveys of new poetry were among the most interesting
features of that review during its later years. For twenty
years Spender has been not only a distinguished and
delightful poet but also a keen, fair-minded observer
on the side of reason and humanity wherever he has gone:
at Oxford and in literary London, in Germany during
the early thirties and in Spain during the civil war, in
London as a member of the Auxiliary (later National)
Fire Service from 1942 to 1944, in Germany in 1945. His
separate volumes of poems, his critical works, and his
political essays have been mentioned in the General Introduction (they are listed below in chronological order for
the sake of convenience), but one must not conclude this
note without mentioning his recently published autobiography, *World within World* (1951). In it he describes
the milieux, the movements, and the people he has known,
and traces his own development as a man and as a writer.
There are many things about the book which make it
an intensely interesting one, but its freedom from cant
or falsity, its author's willingness and ability to tell the
truth about himself and his world without altering it to
accord with any pose or wish or *parti pris* whatever—
these things make it a noble one, with power to save,

even from the temptation to achieve an ordered certainty about matters where no certainty is possible.

Spender's principal volumes of poems are: *Poems* (Second Edition, Revised and Enlarged, 1934); *Vienna* (1934); *The Still Centre* (1939); *Ruins and Visions* (1942); *Poems of Dedication* (1946); and *The Edge of Being* (1949). A verse drama, *Trial of a Judge,* was published in 1938.

In prose, he has written *The Destructive Element* (1936) and *Life and the Poet* (1942), both works of criticism; *The Backward Son* (1940), a novel, and *The Burning Cactus* (1936), a volume of short stories; *Forward from Liberalism* (1937), an essay in political analysis and prescription which should be supplemented by his essay in *The God That Failed* (ed. Richard Crossman, 1950); and *European Witness* (1946), an account of what he saw in Europe, particularly in Germany, immediately after the end of World War II.

HE WILL WATCH THE HAWK WITH AN INDIFFERENT EYE[1]

He will watch the hawk with an indifferent eye
    Or pitifully;
Nor on those eagles that so feared him, now
    Will strain his brow;
Weapons men use, stone, sling and strong-thewed bow 5
    He will not know.

This aristocrat, superb of all instinct,
    With death close linked
Had paced the enormous cloud, almost had won
    War on the sun;   10
Till now, like Icarus mid-ocean-drowned,
    Hands, wings, are found.

IN RAILWAY HALLS, ON PAVEMENTS NEAR THE TRAFFIC

In railway halls, on pavements near the traffic,
They beg, their eyes made big by empty staring
And only measuring Time, like the blank clock.

No, I shall weave no tracery of pen-ornament
To make them birds upon my singing-tree: 5
Time merely drives these lives which do not live
As tides push rotten stuff along the shore.

—There is no consolation, no, none
In the curving beauty of that line
Traced on our graphs through history, where the
    oppressor   10
Starves and deprives the poor.

Paint here no draped despairs, no saddening clouds
Where the soul rests, proclaims eternity.
But let the wrong cry out as raw as wounds
That Time forgets and never heals, far less transcends. 15

THE DOUBLE SHAME[2]

You must live through the time when everything hurts
When the space of the ripe, loaded afternoon
Expands to a landscape of white heat frozen
And trees are weighed down with hearts of stone
And green stares back where you stare alone,   5
And the walking eyes throw flinty comments
And the words which carry most knives are the blind
Phrases searching to be kind.

Solid and usual objects are ghosts
The furniture carries cargoes of memory,   10
The staircase has corners which remember
As fire blows red in gusty embers,
And each empty dress cuts out an image
In fur and evening and summer and gold
Of her who was different in each.   15

Pull down the blind and lie on the bed
And clasp the hour in the glass of one room
Against your mouth like a crystal doom.
Take up the book and look at the letters
Hieroglyphs on sand and as meaningless—   20
Here birds crossed once and cries were uttered
In a mist where sight and sound are blurred.

For the story of those who made mistakes
Of one whose happiness pierced like a star
Eludes and evades between sentences   25
And the letters break into eyes which read
What the blood is now writing in your head,
As though the characters sought for some clue
To their being so perfectly living and dead
In your story, worse than theirs, but true.   30

Set in the mind of their poet, they compare
Their tragic bliss with your trivial despair
And they have fingers which accuse
You of the double way of shame.

---

[1] This poem and the next are from *Poems,* copyright, 1934, by Modern Library. Reprinted by permission of Random House, Inc.

[2] From *Ruins and Visions,* copyright, 1942, by Stephen Spender. Reprinted by permission of Random House, Inc.

At first you did not love enough 35
And afterwards you loved too much
And you lacked the confidence to choose
And you have only yourself to blame.

SEASCAPE[3]

There are some days the happy ocean lies
Like an unfingered harp, below the land.
Afternoon gilds all the silent wires
Into a burning music of the eyes.
On mirroring paths, between those fine-strung fires 5
The shore, laden with roses, horses, spires,
Wanders in water, imaged above ribbed sand.

The azure ecstasy of the air tires,
And a sigh, like a woman's, from inland
Brushes the vibrant wires with shading hand, 10
Drawing across the waves some bird's sharp cries,
A bell, a gasp, from distant hidden shires:
These, deep as anchors, the gilded wave buries.

Then, from the shore, two zig-zag butterflies,
Like errant dog roses, cross the warm strand 15
And on the ocean face search the salt byres
For foam flowers growing in reflected skies.
They drown. Witnesses understand
Such wings torn in such ritual sacrifice,

Remembering ships, treasures and cities, 20
Legendary heroes, plumed with flame like pyres,
Whose flesh-winged day was that bewildering island
The timeless sea engulfed. Their coins and eyes
Twisted by tides of the waves' desires,
Through the strong loving water are scarce scanned 25
Where, above them, the harp sighs with their sighs.

Louis MacNeice

LOUIS MACNEICE was born in Belfast, Ireland, in 1907.
He was educated at Marlborough and at Merton College,
Oxford. From 1930 to 1936 he was Lecturer in Classics
at the University of Birmingham, and from 1936 to 1940
Lecturer in Greek at Bedford College for Women. Since
1941 he has been associated with the British Broadcasting
Corporation as feature-writer and producer; *Christopher
Columbus* (1944), a play for radio, and *The Dark Tower*
(1946), a collection of radio scripts, reflect this latter

interest. His first volume of poems, *Blind Fireworks,* was
published in 1929; his second volume, *Poems* (1935),
attracted attention from those who were reading Auden
and Spender, and his reputation as a lyric and reflective
poet of great individuality and distinction has grown
steadily in the past fifteen years. Since 1935 he has published four volumes of poems, *The Earth Compels* (1938),
Plant and Phantom (1941), *Springboard* (1944), and *Holes
in the Sky* (1948). *Collected Poems: 1925–1948* was published in 1949. *Autumn Journal* (1939) is a long reflective
poem, in twenty-four sections, written between August
and December, 1938, "a record of the author's intellectual and emotional experience during that time." Mr.
MacNeice has also published a verse translation of the
Agamemnon of Aeschylus (1936), a critical study of W.
B. Yeats (1941), and a book called *Modern Poetry: A
Personal Essay* (1938), which describes the development
of modern poetry from the point of view afforded by
his own experience. With Auden he made a trip to Iceland
which is recorded, in prose and verse, in their jointly
written *Letters from Iceland* (1937). To Volume II of John
Lehmann's *Orpheus: A Symposium of the Arts* (1949), he
contributed an article called *Experiences with Images*
which offers some clear and helpful insights into his
poetic method.

SUNDAY MORNING[1]

Down the road someone is practising scales,
The notes like little fishes vanish with a wink of tails,
Man's heart expands to tinker with his car
For this is Sunday morning, Fate's great bazaar,
Regard these means as ends, concentrate on this Now, 5
And you may grow to music or drive beyond Hindhead
    anyhow,
Take corners on two wheels until you go so fast
That you can clutch a fringe or two of the windy past,
That you can abstract this day and make it to the week
    of time
A small eternity, a sonnet self-contained in rhyme. 10

But listen, up the road, something gulps, the church
    spire
Opens its eight bells out, skulls' mouths which will
    not tire
To tell how there is no music or movement which
    secures
Escape from the weekday time. Which deadens and
    endures.

LONDON RAIN

The rain of London pimples
The ebony street with white
And the neon-lamps of London
Stain the canals of night
And the park becomes a jungle 5
In the alchemy of night.

My wishes turn to violent
Horses black as coal—
The randy mares of fancy,
The stallions of the soul— 10
Eager to take the fences
That fence about my soul.

Across the countless chimneys
The horses ride and across
The country to the channel 15
Where warning beacons toss,
To a place where God and No-God
Play at pitch and toss.

Whichever wins I am happy
For God will give me bliss 20
But No-God will absolve me
From all I do amiss
And I need not suffer conscience
If the world was made amiss.

Under God we can reckon 25
On pardon when we fall
But if we are under No-God
Nothing will matter at all,
Adultery and murder
Will count for nothing at all. 30

So reinforced by logic
As having nothing to lose
My lust goes riding horseback
To ravish where I choose,
To burgle all the turrets 35
Of beauty as I choose.

But now the rain gives over
Its dance upon the town
Logic and lust together
Come dimly tumbling down, 40
And neither God nor No-God
Is either up or down.

The argument was wilful,
The alternatives untrue,
We need no metaphysics 45

To sanction what we do
Or to muffle us in comfort
From what we did not do.

Whether the living river
Began in bog or lake, 50
The world is what was given,
The world is what we make.
And we only can discover
Life in the life we make.

So let the water sizzle 55
Upon the gleaming slates,
There will be sunshine after
When the rain abates
And rain returning duly
When the sun abates. 60

My wishes now come homeward,
Their gallopings in vain,
Logic and lust are quiet
And again it starts to rain;
Falling asleep I listen 65
To the falling London rain.

July, 1939

EXPLORATIONS[2]

The whale butting through scarps of moving marble,
The tapeworm probing the intestinal darkness,
The swallows drawn collectively to their magnet,
  These are our prototypes and yet,
Though we may envy them still, they are merely
    patterns 5
  To wonder at—and forget.

For the ocean-carver, cumbrous but unencumbered,
Who tired of land looked for his freedom and frolic
    in water,
Though he succeeded, has failed; it is only instinct
  That plots his graph and he, 10
Though appearing to us a free and a happy monster,
    is merely
  An appanage of the sea.

And the colourless blind worm, triumphantly self-
    degraded,
Who serves as an image to men of the worst
    adjustment—

Oxymoron of parasitical glory— 15
  Cannot even be cursed,
Lacking the only pride of his way of life, not knowing
  That he has chosen the worst.

So even that legion of birds who appear so gladly
Purposeful, with air in their bones, enfranchised 20
Citizens of the sky and never at odds with
  The season or out of line,
Can be no model to us; their imputed purpose
  Is a foregone design—

And ours is not. For we are unique, a conscious 25
Hoping and therefore despairing creature, the final
Anomaly of the world, we can learn no method
  From whales or birds or worms;
Our end is our own to be won by our own endeavour
  And held on our own terms. 30

HIATUS³

The years that did not count—Civilians in the towns
Remained at the same age as in Nineteen-Thirty-Nine,
Saying last year, meaning the last of peace;
Yet eyes began to pucker, mouth to crease,
The hiatus was too packed with fears and frowns, 5
The would-be absent heart came forth a magnetic mine.

As if the weekly food queue were to stretch,
Absorb all future Europe. Or as if
The sleepers in the Tube had come from Goya's Spain
Or Thucydides' Corcyra⁴—a long way to fetch 10
People to prove that civilization is vain,
Wrapped in old quilts; no wonder they wake stiff.

Yes, we wake stiff and older; especially when
The schoolboys of the Thirties reappear,
Fledged in the void, indubitably men, 15
Having kept vigil on the Unholy Mount
And found some dark and tentative things made clear,
Some clear made dark, in the years that did not count.

³ From *Holes in the Sky,* copyright, 1948, by Louis MacNeice.
  Reprinted by permission of Random House, Inc.
⁴ The great Spanish painter Francisco Goya y Lucientes (1746–
  1828) recorded his bitter impressions of the Napoleonic armies'
  invasion of Spain in a series of etchings called "The Disasters of
  War," disasters and disruptions of human lives of which the
  poet is reminded by the sight of the London subway stations
  filled with sleepers seeking refuge from bombing attacks during
  the Battle of Britain. He is also reminded of the varying fortunes of the island of Corcyra (modern Corfu) during the
  Peloponnesian War (431–404 B.C.), described by Thucydides
  in his *History* of that war (I, 24–55; III, 70–85; IV, 46–48).

Dylan Thomas

ALTHOUGH he is not in any limiting sense a member of a
regional school, Dylan Thomas (who was born in
Swansea, Wales, in 1914) is one of the writers who have
done most to give Wales its prominent place in recent
British literature. His poetry is as powerful and rich as
any now being written; certain features which on first
acquaintance are apt to strike us as strangeness will later
be seen as contributing directly to a wholly unique kind
of beauty and force. His principal volumes of poetry
have been *18 Poems* (1934), *25 Poems* (1936), and *Deaths
and Entrances* (1946). Good as his poems are, they can
scarcely have given more immediate or lasting pleasure
than that afforded by the stories which make up *A
Portrait of the Artist as a Young Dog* (1940). These stories
of Welsh life and character as seen through the sharp,
frank, unflinching eyes of childhood and boyhood are
as warmhearted, as imaginative, and very often as funny
as any stories in English. Other prose, of a different order,
is included along with verse in *The Map of Love* (1939).
Selected Writings of Dylan Thomas (1947), with an introduction by John L. Sweeney, offers American readers a
full and convenient introduction to this writer.

FERN HILL¹

Now as I was young and easy under the apple boughs
About the lilting house and happy as the grass was
          green,
    The night above the dingle starry,
      Time let me hail and climb
    Golden in the heydays of his eyes, 5
And honoured among wagons I was prince of the apple
          towns
And once below a time I lordly had the trees and leaves
      Trail with daisies and barley
    Down the rivers of the windfall light.

And as I was green and carefree, famous among the
          barns 10
About the happy yard and singing as the farm was home,
    In the sun that is young once only,
      Time let me play and be
    Golden in the mercy of his means,
And green and golden I was huntsman and herdsman,
          the calves 15
Sang to my horn, the foxes on the hills barked clear
          and cold,

¹ The following poems are reprinted from *Selected Writings of
Dylan Thomas,* by permission of New Directions.

And the sabbath rang slowly
In the pebbles of the holy streams.

All the sun long it was running, it was lovely, the hay-
Fields high as the house, the tunes from the chimneys,
      it was air   20
  And playing, lovely and watery
    And fire green as grass.
And nightly under the simple stars
As I rode to sleep the owls were bearing the farm away,
All the moon long I heard, blessed among stables, the
      night-jars   25
  Flying with the ricks, and the horses
    Flashing into the dark.

And then to awake, and the farm, like a wanderer white
With the dew, come back, the cock on his shoulder: it
      was all
  Shining, it was Adam and maiden,   30
    The sky gathered again
  And the sun grew round that very day.
So it must have been after the birth of the simple light
In the first, spinning place, the spellbound horses
      walking warm
  Out of the whinnying green stable   35
  On to the fields of praise.

And honoured among foxes and pheasants by the gay
      house
Under the new made clouds and happy as the heart
      was long,
  In the sun born over and over,
    I ran my heedless ways,
My wishes raced through the house-high hay   40
And nothing I cared, at my sky blue trades, that time
    allows
In all his tuneful turning so few and such morning
      songs
  Before the children green and golden
    Follow him out of grace,   45

Nothing I cared, in the lamb white days, that time
      would take me
Up to the swallow thronged loft by the shadow of my
      hand,
  In the moon that is always rising,
    Nor that riding to sleep
I should hear him fly with the high fields   50
And wake to the farm forever fled from the childless
    land.
Oh as I was young and easy in the mercy of his means,
    Time held me green and dying
  Though I sang in my chains like the sea.

THE HAND THAT SIGNED THE PAPER FELLED A CITY

The hand that signed the paper felled a city;
Five sovereign fingers taxed the breath,
Doubled the globe of dead and halved a country;
These five kings did a king to death.

The mighty hand leads to a sloping shoulder,   5
The finger joints are cramped with chalk;
A goose's quill has put an end to murder
That put an end to talk.

The hand that signed the treaty bred a fever,
And famine grew, and locusts came;   10
Great is the hand that holds dominion over
Man by a scribbled name.

The five kings count the dead but do not soften
The crusted wound nor pat the brow;
A hand rules pity as a hand rules heaven;   15
Hands have no tears to flow.

THE HUNCHBACK IN THE PARK

The hunchback in the park
A solitary mister
Propped between trees and water
From the opening of the garden lock
That lets the trees and water enter   5
Until the Sunday sombre bell at dark

Eating bread from a newspaper
Drinking water from the chained cup
That the children filled with gravel
In the fountain basin where I sailed my ship   10
Slept at night in a dog kennel
But nobody chained him up.

Like the park birds he came early
Like the water he sat down
And Mister they called Hey mister   15
The truant boys from the town
Running when he had heard them clearly
On out of sound

Past lake and rockery
Laughing when he shook his paper   20
Hunchbacked in mockery
Through the loud zoo of the willow groves
Dodging the park keeper
With his stick that picked up leaves.

And the old dog sleeper   25
Alone between nurses and swans
While the boys among willows
Made the tigers jump out of their eyes
To roar on the rockery stones
And the groves were blue with sailors   30

Made all day until bell time
A woman figure without fault
Straight as a young elm

Straight and tall from his crooked bones
That she might stand in the night   35
After the locks and chains

All night in the unmade park
After the railings and shrubberies
The birds the grass the trees the lake
And the wild boys innocent as strawberries   40
Had followed the hunchback
To his kennel in the dark.

Thomas Ernest Hulme

1883–1917

DURING his short lifetime Hulme's principal publications were two translations: Bergson's *Introduction to Metaphysics* (1913) and Sorel's *Reflections on Violence* (1916). (The five little poems, afterwards so strangely celebrated, had first been published in *The New Age* in 1911; in 1915 they appeared again as an appendix to Ezra Pound's *Ripostes*.) Yet after his death, as a result of the posthumous publication of his notes and papers, arranged and edited by Herbert Read, under the title *Speculations* (1924), Hulme seems to have exerted a continuous and decisive influence on the development of English poetry and critical thought between the two wars. At the very least it may be said that his critical principles and beliefs, particularly those outlined in the chapter from *Speculations* here reprinted, affirmed and paralleled the critical principles and poetic practice of writers who, in the years following World War I, were to determine the directions taken by English poetry of their time. It may be that

some of Hulme's statements are overstatements, that in the form in which we have them they are understandably oversimplified; nevertheless they have their vitality and their clarity, and they are extremely interesting.

Of Hulme's life there is little to tell. He was born in Staffordshire and educated at the High School, Newcastle-under-Lyme, and at St. John's College, Cambridge. After being sent down from Cambridge in 1904 (he was readmitted in 1912) he traveled, worked, and studied independently, living at one time or another in London, in Canada, and on the Continent. He joined the Army in 1914 and was commissioned in 1916; he was killed in September, 1917.

A photograph of the portrait bust by Jacob Epstein forms the frontispiece to *Speculations,* which also contains a Foreword by Epstein and an Introduction by Herbert Read. A book-length study by Michael Roberts, *T. E. Hulme,* was published in 1938.

ROMANTICISM AND CLASSICISM[1]

I WANT to maintain that after a hundred years of romanticism, we are in for a classical revival, and that the particular weapon of this new classical spirit, when it works in verse, will be fancy. And in this I imply the superiority of fancy—not superior generally or   5
absolutely, for that would be obvious nonsense, but superior in the sense that we use the word good in empirical ethics—good for something, superior for something. I shall have to prove then two things, first that a classical revival is coming, and, secondly,   10

for its particular purposes, fancy will be superior to imagination.

So banal have the terms Imagination and Fancy become that we imagine they must have always been in the language. Their history as two differing terms in the vocabulary of criticism is comparatively short. Originally, of course, they both mean the same thing; they first began to be differentiated by the German writers on aesthetics in the eighteenth century.

I know that in using the words "classic" and "romantic" I am doing a dangerous thing. They represent five or six different kinds of antitheses, and while I may be using them in one sense you may be

---

[1] From *Speculations* by T. E. Hulme, reprinted by kind permission of Messrs. Routledge and Kegan Paul, Ltd.

interpreting them in another. In this present connection I am using them in a perfectly precise and limited sense. I ought really to have coined a couple of new words, but I prefer to use the ones I have used, as I then conform to the practice of the group of polemical writers who make most use of them at the present day, and have almost succeeded in making them political catchwords. I mean Maurras, Lasserre and all the group connected with *L'Action Française*.

At the present time this is the particular group with which the distinction is most vital. Because it has become a party symbol. If you asked a man of a certain set whether he preferred the classics or the romantics, you could deduce from that what his politics were.

The best way of gliding into a proper definition of my terms would be to start with a set of people who are prepared to fight about it—for in them you will have no vagueness. (Other people take the infamous attitude of the person with catholic tastes who says he likes both.)

About a year ago, a man whose name I think was Fauchois gave a lecture at the Odéon on Racine, in the course of which he made some disparaging remarks about his dullness, lack of invention and the rest of it. This caused an immediate riot: fights took place all over the house; several people were arrested and imprisoned, and the rest of the series of lectures took place with hundreds of gendarmes and detectives scattered all over the place. These people interrupted because the classical ideal is a living thing to them and Racine is the great classic. That is what I call a real vital interest in literature. They regard romanticism as an awful disease from which France had just recovered.

The thing is complicated in their case by the fact that it was romanticism that made the revolution. They hate the revolution, so they hate romanticism.

I make no apology for dragging in politics here; romanticism both in England and France is associated with certain political views, and it is in taking a concrete example of the working out of a principle in action that you can get its best definition.

What was the positive principle behind all the other principles of '89? I am talking here of the revolution in as far as it was an idea; I leave out material causes—they only produce the forces. The barriers which could easily have resisted or guided these forces had been previously rotted away by ideas. This always seems to be the case in successful changes; the privileged class is beaten only when it has lost faith in itself, when it has itself been penetrated with the ideas which are working against it.

It was not the rights of man—that was a good solid practical war-cry. The thing which created enthusiasm, which made the revolution practically a new religion, was something more positive than that. People of all classes, people who stood to lose by it, were in a positive ferment about the idea of liberty. There must have been some idea which enabled them to think that something positive could come out of so essentially negative a thing. There was, and here I get my definition of romanticism. They had been taught by Rousseau that man was by nature good, that it was only bad laws and customs that had suppressed him. Remove all these and the infinite possibilities of man would have a chance. This is what made them think that something positive could come out of disorder, this is what created the religious enthusiasm. Here is the root of all romanticism: that man, the individual, is an infinite reservoir of possibilities; and if you can so rearrange society by the destruction of oppressive order then these possibilities will have a chance and you will get Progress.

One can define the classical quite clearly as the exact opposite to this. Man is an extraordinarily fixed and limited animal whose nature is absolutely constant. It is only by tradition and organisation that anything decent can be got out of him.

This view was a little shaken at the time of Darwin. You remember his particular hypothesis, that new species came into existence by the cumulative effect of small variations—this seems to admit the possibility of future progress. But at the present day the contrary hypothesis makes headway in the shape of De Vries's mutation theory, that each new species comes into existence, not gradually by the accumulation of small steps, but suddenly in a jump, a kind of sport, and that once in existence it remains absolutely fixed. This enables me to keep the classical view with an appearance of scientific backing.

Put shortly, these are the two views, then. One, that man is intrinsically good, spoilt by circumstance; and the other that he is intrinsically limited, but disciplined by order and tradition to something fairly decent. To the one party man's nature is like a well, to the other like a bucket. The view which regards man as a well, a reservoir full of possibilities, I call the romantic; the one which regards him as a very finite and fixed creature, I call the classical.

One may note here that the Church has always taken the classical view since the defeat of the Pelagian heresy and the adoption of the sane classical dogma of original sin.

It would be a mistake to identify the classical view with that of materialism. On the contrary it is absolutely identical with the normal religious attitude. I should put it in this way: That part of the fixed nature of man is the belief in the Deity. This should be as fixed and true for every man as belief in the existence of matter and in the objective world. It is parallel to appetite, the instinct of sex, and all the other fixed qualities. Now at certain times, by the use of either force or rhetoric, these instincts have been suppressed—in Florence under Savonarola, in Geneva under Calvin, and here under the Roundheads. The inevitable result of such a process is that the repressed instinct bursts out in some abnormal direction. So with religion. By the perverted rhetoric of Rationalism, your natural instincts are suppressed and you are converted into an agnostic. Just as in the case of the other instincts, Nature has her revenge. The instincts that find their right and proper outlet in religion must come out in some other way. You don't believe in a God, so you begin to believe that man is a god. You don't believe in Heaven, so you begin to believe in a heaven on earth. In other words, you get romanticism. The concepts that are right and proper in their own sphere are spread over, and so mess up, falsify and blur the clear outlines of human experience. It is like pouring a pot of treacle over the dinner table. Romanticism then, and this is the best definition I can give of it, is spilt religion.

I must now shirk the difficulty of saying exactly what I mean by romantic and classical in verse. I can only say that it means the result of these two attitudes towards the cosmos, towards man, in so far as it gets reflected in verse. The romantic, because he thinks man infinite, must always be talking about the infinite; and as there is always the bitter contrast between what you think you ought to be able to do and what man actually can, it always tends, in its later stages at any rate, to be gloomy. I really can't go any further than to say it is the reflection of these two temperaments, and point out examples of the different spirits. On the one hand I would take such diverse people as Horace, most of the Elizabethans and the writers of the Augustan age, and on the other side Lamartine, Hugo, parts of Keats, Coleridge, Byron, Shelley and Swinburne.

I know quite well that when people think of classical and romantic in verse, the contrast at once comes into their mind between, say, Racine and Shakespeare. I don't mean this; the dividing line that I intend is here misplaced a little from the true middle. That Racine is on the extreme classical side I agree, but if you call Shakespeare romantic, you are using a different definition to the one I give. You are thinking of the difference between classic and romantic as being merely one between restraint and exuberance. I should say with Nietzsche that there are two kinds of classicism, the static and the dynamic. Shakespeare is the classic of motion.

What I mean by classical in verse, then, is this. That even in the most imaginative flights there is always a holding back, a reservation. The classical poet never forgets this finiteness, this limit of man. He remembers always that he is mixed up with earth. He may jump, but he always returns back; he never flies away into the circumambient gas.

You might say if you wished that the whole of the romantic attitude seems to crystallise in verse round metaphors of flight. Hugo is always flying, flying over abysses, flying up into the eternal gases. The word infinite in every other line.

In the classical attitude you never seem to swing right along to the infinite nothing. If you say an extravagant thing which does exceed the limits inside which you know man to be fastened, yet there is always conveyed in some way at the end an impression of yourself standing outside it, and not quite believing it, or consciously putting it forward as a flourish. You never go blindly into an atmosphere more than the truth, an atmosphere too rarefied for man to breathe for long. You are always faithful to the conception of a limit. It is a question of pitch; in romantic verse you move at a certain pitch of rhetoric which you know, man being what he is, to be a little high-falutin. The kind of thing you get in Hugo or Swinburne. In the coming classical reaction that will feel just wrong. For an example of the opposite thing, a verse written in the proper classical spirit, I can take the song from Cymbeline beginning with "Fear no more the heat of the sun." I am just using this as a parable. I don't quite mean what I say here. Take the last two lines:

> "Golden lads and lasses must,
> Like chimney sweepers come to dust."

Now, no romantic would have ever written that. Indeed, so ingrained is romanticism, so objectionable is this to it, that people have asserted that these were not part of the original song.

Apart from the pun, the thing that I think quite classical is the word lad. Your modern romantic could never write that. He would have to write golden youth, and take up the thing at least a couple of notes in pitch.

I want now to give the reasons which make me think that we are nearing the end of the romantic movement.

The first lies in the nature of any convention or

tradition in art. A particular convention or attitude in art has a strict analogy to the phenomena of organic life. It grows old and decays. It has a definite period of life and must die. All the possible tunes get played on it and then it is exhausted; moreover its best period is its youngest. Take the case of the extraordinary efflorescence of verse in the Elizabethan period. All kinds of reasons have been given for this—the discovery of the new world and all the rest of it. There is a much simpler one. A new medium had been given them to play with—namely, blank verse. It was new and so it was easy to play new tunes on it.

The same law holds in other arts. All the masters of painting are born into the world at a time when the particular tradition from which they start is imperfect. The Florentine tradition was just short of full ripeness when Raphael came to Florence, the Bellinesque was still young when Titian was born in Venice. Landscape was still a toy or an appanage of figure-painting when Turner and Constable arose to reveal its independent power. When Turner and Constable had done with landscape they left little or nothing for their successors to do on the same lines. Each field of artistic activity is exhausted by the first great artist who gathers a full harvest from it.

This period of exhaustion seems to me to have been reached in romanticism. We shall not get any new efflorescence of verse until we get a new technique, a new convention, to turn ourselves loose in.

Objection might be taken to this. It might be said that a century as an organic unity doesn't exist, that I am being deluded by a wrong metaphor, that I am treating a collection of literary people as if they were an organism or state department. Whatever we may be in other things, an objector might urge, in literature in as far as we are anything at all—in as far as we are worth considering—we are individuals, we are persons, and as distinct persons we cannot be subordinated to any general treatment. At any period at any time, an individual poet may be a classic or a romantic just as he feels like it. You at any particular moment may think that you can stand outside a movement. You may think that as an individual you observe both the classic and the romantic spirit and decide from a purely detached point of view that one is superior to the other.

The answer to this is that no one, in a matter of judgment of beauty, can take a detached standpoint in this way. Just as physically you are not born that abstract entity, man, but the child of particular parents, so you are in matters of literary judgment. Your opinion is almost entirely of the literary history that came just before you, and you are governed by that whatever you may think. Take Spinoza's example of a stone falling to the ground. If it had a conscious mind it would, he said, think it was going to the ground because it wanted to. So you with your pretended free judgment about what is and what is not beautiful. The amount of freedom in man is much exaggerated. That we are free on certain rare occasions, both my religion and the views I get from metaphysics convince me. But many acts which we habitually label free are in reality automatic. It is quite possible for a man to write a book almost automatically. I have read several such products. Some observations were recorded more than twenty years ago by Robertson on reflex speech, and he found that in certain cases of dementia, where the people were quite unconscious so far as the exercise of reasoning went, that very intelligent answers were given to a succession of questions on politics and such matters. The meaning of these questions could not possibly have been understood. Language here acted after the manner of a reflex. So that certain extremely complex mechanisms, subtle enough to imitate beauty, can work by themselves—I certainly think that this is the case with judgments about beauty.

I can put the same thing in slightly different form. Here is a question of a conflict of two attitudes, as it might be of two techniques. The critic, while he has to admit that changes from one to the other occur, persists in regarding them as mere variations to a certain fixed normal, just as a pendulum might swing. I admit the analogy of the pendulum as far as movement, but I deny the further consequence of the analogy, the existence of the point of rest, the normal point.

When I say that I dislike the romantics, I dissociate two things: the part of them in which they resemble all the great poets, and the part in which they differ and which gives them their character as romantics. It is this minor element which constitutes the particular note of a century, and which, while it excites contemporaries, annoys the next generation. It was precisely that quality in Pope which pleased his friends, which we detest. Now, anyone just before the romantics who felt that, could have predicted that a change was coming. It seems to me that we stand just in the same position now. I think that there is an increasing proportion of people who simply can't stand Swinburne.

When I say that there will be another classical revival I don't necessarily anticipate a return to Pope. I say merely that now is the time for such a revival. Given people of the necessary capacity, it may be a vital thing; without them we may get a formalism something like Pope. When it does come we may not even recognise it as classical. Although it will be classical it will be different because it has passed through a romantic period. To take a parallel example: I remember being very surprised, after seeing the Post Impressionists, to find in Maurice Denis's account of the matter that they consider themselves classical in the sense that they were trying to impose the same order on the mere flux of new material provided by the impressionist movement, that existed in the more limited materials of the painting before.

There is something now to be cleared away before I get on with my argument, which is that while romanticism is dead in reality, yet the critical attitude appropriate to it still continues to exist. To make this a little clearer: For every kind of verse, there is a corresponding receptive attitude. In a romantic period we demand from verse certain qualities. In a classical period we demand others. At the present time I should say that this receptive attitude has outlasted the thing from which it was formed. But while the romantic tradition has run dry, yet the critical attitude of mind, which demands romantic qualities from verse, still survives. So that if good classical verse were to be written to-morrow very few people would be able to stand it.

I object even to the best of the romantics. I object still more to the receptive attitude. I object to the sloppiness which doesn't consider that a poem is a poem unless it is moaning or whining about something or other. I always think in this connection of the last line of a poem of John Webster's which ends with a request I cordially endorse:

"End your moan and come away."

The thing has got so bad now that a poem which is all dry and hard, a properly classical poem, would not be considered poetry at all. How many people now can lay their hands on their hearts and say they like either Horace or Pope? They feel a kind of chill when they read them.

The dry hardness which you get in the classics is absolutely repugnant to them. Poetry that isn't damp isn't poetry at all. They cannot see that accurate description is a legitimate object of verse. Verse to them always means a bringing in of some of the emotions that are grouped round the word infinite.

The essence of poetry to most people is that it must lead them to a beyond of some kind. Verse strictly confined to the earthly and the definite (Keats is full of it) might seem to them to be excellent writing, excellent craftsmanship, but not poetry. So much has

romanticism debauched us, that, without some form of vagueness, we deny the highest.

In the classic it is always the light of ordinary day, never the light that never was on land or sea. It is always perfectly human and never exaggerated: man is always man and never a god.

But the awful result of romanticism is that, accustomed to this strange light, you can never live without it. Its effect on you is that of a drug.

There is a general tendency to think that verse means little else than the expression of unsatisfied emotion. People say: "But how can you have verse without sentiment?" You see what it is: the prospect alarms them. A classical revival to them would mean the prospect of an arid desert and the death of poetry as they understand it, and could only come to fill the gap caused by that death. Exactly why this dry classical spirit should have a positive and legitimate necessity to express itself in poetry is utterly inconceivable to them. What this positive need is, I shall show later. It follows from the fact that there is another quality, not the emotion produced, which is at the root of excellence in verse. Before I get to this I am concerned with a negative thing, a theoretical point, a prejudice that stands in the way and is really at the bottom of this reluctance to understand classical verse.

It is an objection which ultimately I believe comes from a bad metaphysic of art. You are unable to admit the existence of beauty without the infinite being in some way or another dragged in.

I may quote for purposes of argument, as a typical example of this kind of attitude made vocal, the famous chapters in Ruskin's *Modern Painters*, Vol. II, on the imagination. I must say here, parenthetically, that I use this word without prejudice to the other discussion with which I shall end the paper. I only use the word here because it is Ruskin's word. All that I am concerned with just now is the attitude behind it, which I take to be the romantic.

"Imagination cannot but be serious; she sees too far, too darkly, too solemnly, too earnestly, ever to smile. There is something in the heart of everything, if we can reach it, that we shall not be inclined to laugh at. . . . Those who have so pierced and seen the melancholy deeps of things, are filled with intense passion and gentleness of sympathy." (Part III, Chap. III, §9.)

"There is in every word set down by the imaginative mind an awful undercurrent of meaning, and evidence and shadow upon it of the deep places out of which it has come. It is often obscure, often half-told; for he who wrote it, in his clear seeing of the things beneath, may have been impatient of detailed interpretation; for if we choose to dwell upon it and trace it, it will lead us always securely back to that metropolis of the soul's dominion from which we may follow out all the ways and tracks to its farthest coasts." (Part III, Chap. III, §5.)

Really in all these matters the act of judgment is an instinct, an absolutely unstateable thing akin to the art of the tea taster. But you must talk, and the only language you can use in this matter is that of analogy. I have no material clay to mould to the given shape; the only thing which one has for the purpose, and which acts as a substitute for it, a kind of mental clay, are certain metaphors modified into theories of aesthetic and rhetoric. A combination of these, while it cannot state the essentially unstateable intuition, can yet give you a sufficient analogy to enable you to see what it was and to recognise it on condition that you yourself have been in a similar state. Now these phrases of Ruskin's convey quite clearly to me his taste in the matter.

I see quite clearly that he thinks the best verse must be serious. That is a natural attitude for a man in the romantic period. But he is not content with saying that he prefers this kind of verse. He wants to deduce his opinion like his master, Coleridge, from some fixed principle which can be found by metaphysic.

Here is the last refuge of this romantic attitude. It proves itself to be not an attitude but a deduction from a fixed principle of the cosmos.

One of the main reasons for the existence of philosophy is not that it enables you to find truth (it can never do that) but that it does provide you a refuge for definitions. The usual idea of the thing is that it provides you with a fixed basis from which you can deduce the things you want in aesthetics. The process is the exact contrary. You start in the confusion of the fighting line, you retire from that just a little to the rear to recover, to get your weapons right. Quite plainly, without metaphor this—it provides you with an elaborate and precise language in which you really can explain definitely what you mean, but what you want to say is decided by other things. The ultimate reality is the hurly-burly, the struggle; the metaphysic is an adjunct to clear-headedness in it.

To get back to Ruskin and his objection to all that is not serious. It seems to me that involved in this is a bad metaphysical aesthetic. You have the metaphysic which in defining beauty or the nature of art always drags in the infinite. Particularly in Germany, the land where theories of aesthetics were first created, the romantic aesthetes collated all beauty to an impression of the infinite involved in the identification of our being in absolute spirit. In the least element of beauty we have a total intuition of the whole world. Every artist is a kind of pantheist.

Now it is quite obvious to anyone who holds this kind of theory that any poetry which confines itself to the finite can never be of the highest kind. It seems a contradiction in terms to them. And as in metaphysics you get the last refuge of a prejudice, so it is now necessary for me to refute this.

Here follows a tedious piece of dialectic, but it is necessary for my purpose. I must avoid two pitfalls in discussing the idea of beauty. On the one hand there is the old classical view which is supposed to define it as lying in conformity to certain standard fixed forms; and on the other hand there is the romantic view which drags in the infinite. I have got to find a metaphysic between these two which will enable me to hold consistently that a neo-classic verse of the type I have indicated involves no contradiction in terms. It is essential to prove that beauty may be in small, dry things.

The great aim is accurate, precise and definite description. The first thing is to recognise how extraordinarily difficult this is. It is no mere matter of carefulness; you have to use language, and language is by its very nature a communal thing; that is, it expresses never the exact thing but a compromise—that which is common to you, me and everybody. But each man sees a little differently, and to get out clearly and exactly what he does see, he must have a terrific struggle with language, whether it be with words or the technique of other arts. Language has its own special nature, its own conventions and communal ideas. It is only by a concentrated effort of the mind that you can hold it fixed to your own purpose. I always think that the fundamental process at the back of all the arts might be represented by the following metaphor. You know what I call architect's curves—flat pieces of wood with all different kinds of curvature. By a suitable selection from these you can draw approximately any curve you like. The artist I take to be the man who simply can't bear the idea of that 'approximately.' He will get the exact curve of what he sees whether it be an object or an idea in the mind. I shall here have to change my metaphor a little to get the process in his mind. Suppose that instead of your curved pieces of wood you have a springy piece of steel of the same types of curvature as the wood. Now the state of tension or concentration of mind, if he is doing anything really good in this struggle against the ingrained habit of the technique, may be represented by a man employing all his fingers to bend the steel out of its own curve and into the exact curve which you want. Something different to what it would assume naturally.

There are then two things to distinguish, first the particular faculty of mind to see things as they really are, and apart from the conventional ways in which you have been trained to see them. This is itself rare enough in all consciousness. Second, the concentrated state of mind, the grip over oneself which is necessary in the actual expression of what one sees. To prevent one falling into the conventional curves of ingrained technique, to hold on through infinite detail and trouble to the exact curve you want. Wherever you get this sincerity, you get the fundamental quality of good art without dragging in infinite or serious.

I can now get at that positive fundamental quality of verse which constitutes excellence, which has nothing to do with infinity, with mystery or with emotions.

This is the point I aim at, then, in my argument. I prophesy that a period of dry, hard, classical verse is coming. I have met the preliminary objection founded on the bad romantic aesthetic that in such verse, from which the infinite is excluded, you cannot have the essence of poetry at all.

After attempting to sketch out what this positive quality is, I can get on to the end of my paper in this way: That where you get this quality exhibited in the realm of the emotions you get imagination, and that where you get this quality exhibited in the contemplation of finite things you get fancy.

In prose as in algebra concrete things are embodied in signs or counters which are moved about according to rules, without being visualised at all in the process. There are in prose certain type situations and arrangements of words, which move as automatically into certain other arrangements as do functions in algebra. One only changes the X's and the Y's back into physical things at the end of the process. Poetry, in one aspect at any rate, may be considered as an effort to avoid this characteristic of prose. It is not a counter language, but a visual concrete one. It is a compromise for a language of intuition which would hand over sensations bodily. It always endeavours to arrest you, and to make you continuously see a physical thing, to prevent you gliding through an abstract process. It chooses fresh epithets and fresh metaphors, not so much because they are new, and we are tired of the old, but because the old cease to convey a physical thing and become abstract counters. A poet says a ship 'coursed the seas' to get a physical image, instead of the counter word 'sailed.' Visual meanings can only be transferred by the new bowl of metaphor; prose is an old pot that lets them leak out. Images in verse are not mere decoration, but the very essence of an intuitive language. Verse is a pedestrian taking you over the ground, prose—a train which delivers you at a destination.

I can now get on to a discussion of two words often used in this connection, "fresh" and "unexpected." You praise a thing for being "fresh." I understand what you mean, but the word besides conveying the truth conveys a secondary something which is certainly false. When you say a poem or drawing is fresh, and so good, the impression is somehow conveyed that the essential element of goodness is freshness, that it is good because it is fresh. Now this is cetainly wrong, there is nothing particularly desirable about freshness *per se*. Works of art aren't eggs. Rather the contrary. It is simply an unfortunate necessity due to the nature of language and technique that the only way the element which does constitute goodness, the only way in which its presence can be detected externally, is by freshness. Freshness convinces you, you feel at once that the artist was in an actual physical state. You feel that for a minute. Real communication is so very rare, for plain speech is unconvincing. It is in this rare fact of communication that you get the root of aesthetic pleasure.

I shall maintain that wherever you get an extraordinary interest in a thing, a great zest in its contemplation which carries on the contemplator to accurate description in the sense of the word accurate I have just analysed, there you have sufficient justification for poetry. It must be an intense zest which heightens a thing out of the level of prose. I am using contemplation here just in the same way that Plato used it, only applied to a different subject; it is a detached interest. "The object of aesthetic contemplation is something framed apart by itself and regarded without memory or expectation, simply as being itself, as end not means, as individual not universal."

To take a concrete example. I am taking an extreme case. If you are walking behind a woman in the street, you notice the curious way in which the skirt rebounds from her heels. If that peculiar kind of motion becomes of such interest to you that you will search about until you can get the exact epithet which hits it off, there you have a properly aesthetic emotion. But it is the zest with which you look at the thing which decides you to make the effort. In this sense the feeling that was in Herrick's mind when he wrote "the tempestuous petticoat" was exactly the same as that which in bigger and vaguer matters makes the best romantic verse. It doesn't matter an atom that the emotion produced is not of dignified vagueness, but on the contrary amusing; the point is that exactly the same activity is at work as in the highest verse. That is the avoidance of conventional language in order to get the exact curve of the thing.

I have still to show that in the verse which is to come, fancy will be the necessary weapon of the classical school. The positive quality I have talked about can be manifested in ballad verse by extreme directness and simplicity, such as you get in "On Fair Kirkconnel Lea." But the particular verse we are going to get will be cheerful, dry and sophisticated, and here the necessary weapon of the positive quality must be fancy.

Subject doesn't matter; the quality in it is the same as you get in the more romantic people.

It isn't the scale or kind of emotion produced that decides, but this one fact: Is there any real zest in it? Did the poet have an actually realised visual object before him in which he delighted? It doesn't matter if it were a lady's shoe or the starry heavens.

Fancy is not mere decoration added on to plain speech. Plain speech is essentially inaccurate. It is only by new metaphors, that is, by fancy, that it can be made precise.

When the analogy has not enough connection with the thing described to be quite parallel with it, where it overlays the thing it described and there is a certain excess, there you have the play of fancy—that I grant is inferior to imagination.

But where the analogy is every bit of it necessary for accurate description in the sense of the word accurate I have previously described, and your only objection to this kind of fancy is that it is not serious in the effect it produces, then I think the objection to be entirely invalid. If it is sincere in the accurate sense, when the whole of the analogy is necessary to get out the exact curve of the feeling or thing you want to express—there you seem to me to have the highest verse, even though the subject be trivial and the emotions of the infinite far away.

It is very difficult to use any terminology at all for this kind of thing. For whatever word you use is at once sentimentalised. Take Coleridge's word "vital." It is used loosely by all kinds of people who talk about art, to mean something vaguely and mysteriously significant. In fact, vital and mechanical is to them exactly the same antithesis as between good and bad.

Nothing of the kind; Coleridge uses it in a perfectly definite and what I call dry sense. It is just this: A mechanical complexity is the sum of its parts. Put them side by side and you get the whole. Now vital or organic is merely a convenient metaphor for a complexity of a different kind, that in which the parts cannot be said to be elements as each one is modified by the other's presence, and each one to a certain extent is the whole. The leg of a chair by itself is still a leg. My leg by itself wouldn't be.

Now the characteristic of the intellect is that it can only represent complexities of the mechanical kind. It can only make diagrams, and diagrams are essentially things whose parts are separate one from another. The intellect always analyses—when there is a synthesis it is baffled. That is why the artist's work seems mysterious. The intellect can't represent it. This is a necessary consequence of the particular nature of the intellect and the purposes for which it is formed. It doesn't mean that your synthesis is ineffable, simply that it can't be definitely stated.

Now this is all worked out in Bergson, the central feature of his whole philosophy. It is all based on the clear conception of these vital complexities which he calls "intensive" as opposed to the other kind which he calls "extensive," and the recognition of the fact that the intellect can only deal with the extensive multiplicity. To deal with the intensive you must use intuition.

Now, as I said before, Ruskin was perfectly aware of all this, but he had no such metaphysical background which would enable him to state definitely what he meant. The result is that he has to flounder about in a series of metaphors. A powerfully imaginative mind seizes and combines at the same instant all the important ideas of its poem or picture, and while it works with one of them, it is at the same instant working with and modifying all in their relation to it and never losing sight of their bearings on each other—as the motion of a snake's body goes through all parts at once and its volition acts at the same instant in coils which go contrary ways.

A romantic movement must have an end of the very nature of the thing. It may be deplored, but it can't be helped—wonder must cease to be wonder.

I guard myself here from all the consequences of the analogy, but it expresses at any rate the inevitableness of the process. A literature of wonder must have an end as inevitably as a strange land loses its strangeness when one lives in it. Think of the lost ecstasy of the Elizabethans. "Oh my America, my new found land," think of what it meant to them and of what it means to us. Wonder can only be the attitude of a man passing from one stage to another, it can never be a permanently fixed thing.

Herbert Read

It is not easy to think of another writer in our time who has achieved such clear distinction in both the criticism of art and the criticism of literature as Herbert Read. Mr. Read has held important posts in the world of fine arts—he was Assistant Keeper of the Victoria and Albert Museum from 1922 to 1931, he has taught fine arts at the universities of Edinburgh, Liverpool, and London, he was editor of the *Burlington Magazine* from 1933 to 1939, and he has written a number of books about art, particularly modern art, and its place in the social structure: *The Meaning of Art* (1931), *Art Now* (1933), *Art and Industry* (1934), *Art and Society* (1936), and *Education through Art* (1943). He has been if anything even more prolific as a literary critic, and here again, as in his art criticism, he has done work of the first order of usefulness not only in exhibiting the literature of the past in its potential relation to present-day needs, but also in teaching the present to look at the work of its own writers with sympathy and understanding. In books like *Reason and Romanticism* (1926), *Wordsworth* (1930), *Coleridge as Critic* (1949), or the long title essay in *In Defence of Shelley* (1935), he has done more than any other critic of comparable stature to assure a fair appraisal and re-appraisal of the Romantic poets in a time that has produced some formidable dissenting voices. His studies of literary form—*English Prose Style* (1928), *Phases of English Poetry* (1928), and *Form in Modern Poetry* (1932)—have all been reprinted since their original publication. Some of Read's longer essays, including those on Malory, Vauvenargues, Swift, Hawthorne, and Henry James, were brought together in *Collected Essays* (1938): a revised edition of this work, under the title *Collected Essays in Literary Criticism*, is to appear shortly. *A Coat of Many Colors* (1945) consists of some seventy short occasional essays which cover a wide range of interests.

Nor should it be forgotten that Mr. Read has written on politics—*The Politics of the Unpolitical* (1943), for example; that he has written a novel, *The Green Child*, in a vein of fantasy; and that he is a good and original poet. The chapter from *The Innocent Eye* (1947) reprinted below has something to say about Read's early development as a poet, but it also has something to say (and this has been a primary reason for including it) about his development as a reader, as a man in whose life literature was to hold an honored, powerful, and happy place. For each of us the first discovery of literature must come about as it will; but later, when we have become more articulate and purposeful in ordering our approach to literature, it is interesting to see what the experience of others has been, to compare it with our own. One further word about *The Innocent Eye* (published in England as *Annals of Innocence and Experience* in 1940 and 1946): it is certainly one of the best and most delightful essays in autobiography that have appeared in some time, and deserves to be read in its entirety. The opening section, originally published separately under the title which has since been given to the American edition of the whole work, describes the author's childhood (he was born in 1893) on a Yorkshire farm. Other chapters describe his experiences as an infantry officer in France and Belgium from 1915 to 1918, with an objectivity that all but a few of those who have written about the two World Wars can only envy; still other chapters, like the one below, analyze his own spiritual and intellectual development.

THE DISCOVERY OF POETRY[1]

It was not until my seventeenth year that I became conscious of the art of poetry. At school we read and even acted Shakespeare, and there were 'recitations' which must have included some verse. But I never read a volume of poems for choice. It was only later, when I began to read for my matriculation, that I also began to listen more intently to the sound of what I was reading: words and phrases would now

linger insistently in my mind. At the evening school I attended there was a teacher who had a genuine enthusiasm for his subject; he read aloud to us with feeling and expressiveness. He communicated his pleasure in poetry to at least one of his pupils. About the same time I made the acquaintance of one who was for many years to be my only confidant and my devoted patron. My brother, eighteen months younger than myself, had left school and found employment with a tailor in the city, who bore our family name—even the same Christian name as my brother—and childless himself, henceforth was to

---

[1] From *The Innocent Eye* by Herbert Read, copyright, 1947, by Herbert Read. Reprinted by permission of Henry Holt and Company, Inc.

take a great interest in all of us. He belonged to a good Quaker family settled for many generations in the Isle of Axholme. Orphaned at an early age, he had been given into the care of two rich and cultured maiden aunts, who gave him a good education and destined him for a post in the British Museum. But at the age of sixteen or so he had suddenly revolted against the smug religious atmosphere in which he was being brought up, and he had run away. After various adventures he had been compelled to take whatever employment he could get, and this happened to be tailoring, a craft for which he had no liking, but which he was to follow for more than forty years with a quiet stoicism. He was a man of small proportions, gentle manners, and in physiognomy bore a close resemblance to the portraits of William Blake. He had two passions—the reading of poetry and the cultivation of flowers. His reading in every direction was wide, and it was in his house that I first made the acquaintance, not only of innumerable volumes of verse, but of the works of writers like Ibsen, Turgenev, Dostoevsky and Chekhov.

Hitherto my reading had been confined to what could be borrowed from the public library, and what I could buy out of an allowance of one shilling a week which I made to myself out of my meagre earnings as a bank-clerk. But now I not only had an enthusiast's library to draw from, but I rarely visited this friend without coming away with a gift of two or three volumes. It was probably to my advantage then that the blessings thus showered on me were indiscriminate. My friend praised with equal zest W. B. Yeats and Fiona Macleod, Browning and William Cullen Bryant, Francis Thompson and Sir Edwin Arnold. If I failed to share his enthusiasm—as in the case of Emerson—he did not question or complain: he was convinced that I should one day see the light.

I cannot now be certain whether my own first poems preceded this fruitful friendship: I think they did. But I cannot forget the emotion with which my mentor learned for the first time that I was writing verses, and with what eagerness he received my efforts when I offered them for his criticism. His criticism was not very severe, though it did check my absurdities. But for the most part he encouraged me with his praise and was for a long time the only audience I had, but a sufficing one. It is to his memory that I have dedicated my collected poems.

It is difficult to recapture the first access of composition. It descended on me like a frenzy, and a day was not perfect unless it gave birth to a poem. Of one thing I am certain: the breath that first fanned my smouldering tinder was Tennyson's. I soon outgrew Tennyson, and for many years affected to despise him—it was a natural reaction, for we tend to turn on all our adolescent enthusiasms. Now that I have balanced my reactions, and can judge Tennyson with a detached mind, I find that I admire him for qualities which must have appealed, however unconsciously, to my awakening sensibility: for the ease and simplicity of his diction, for a broad if not a very profound intelligence, and for an exact rendering of a special landscape—the watery fens and long dim wolds which were not so remote from my own dales and moors. At times he seems to describe the actual scenes of my own childhood:

> The seven elms, the poplars four,
> That stand beside my father's door,
> . . . . . . the brook that loves
> To purl o'er matted cress and ribbed sand,
> Or dimple in the dark of rushy coves,
> Drawing into his narrow earthen urn,
> In every elbow and turn,
> The filter'd tribute of the rough woodland.[2]

There would be more to say in adequate appreciation of this poet—more to discover, perhaps, of poetic merit than we generally admit; and a very curious personality to analyse. But now I only seek to relate my own sensibility to his, and to explain why he in particular should have been the reagent in the first poems precipitated from my mind. It would have been much more normal if my enthusiasm at this time had been for Shelley: but the very abstractness of Shelley's poetry kept him at a distance. Shelley, I would now say, demands a degree of intellectual development which I had not reached by the age of seventeen or eighteen. Tennyson had a more objective appeal and was therefore more open to my simple sensibility.

Even so, there were limits to my powers of absorption, and neither then, nor since, could I read the *Idylls of the King*. Romantic as I was, and am, this particular brand of archaism has always been repugnant to me. I hate every kind of literary fustian, every affectation of an earlier style, every exercise or experiment in an old measure. Such a whimsy attitude to the art of writing is impossible to anyone who believes in the immediacy of expression, in the automatism of inspiration, in the creative nature of even poetic evolution: and these are the doctrines of a true romanticism. The rest is dilettantism: not the vital function, but an academic diversion.

The compositions which came to me so easily in these adolescent days were destroyed long ago, and I

---

2 From the early "Ode to Memory," lines 56–63.

have no very precise recollection of their nature. They were, I think, mostly short lyrics about flowers, birds, atmospheric moods; the more realistic of them may have attempted to catch something of the poetry of foggy, gas-lit streets, the glow of furnaces by night, the clatter of clogs on the stone pavements. There were no love poems, for my heart was not yet engaged.

It was then that the poetry of William Blake descended on me like an apocalypse. Tennyson had chimed in with my moods, and shown me felicity. Blake shook me to the depths of my awakening mind, scattered the world of my objective vision, and left me floundering in subjective fantasy. I did not, at that time, venture far into the Prophetic Books; but the Songs of Innocence and Experience, and the poems from the Rossetti and Pickering manuscripts, pierced me like gleaming steel, and their meaning was annealed to my mind. Their meaning?—I should rather say their mystery, for many of these poems were not easy to understand, and indeed I did not seek to understand them. From the beginning I was content with the incantation of a poem, and I still maintain that this is the quality essential to poetry.

Blake kept his ascendancy in my mind for many years—indeed, though I have submitted to many influences and have been fired to more than one enthusiasm in the intervening years, there is no poet with whom to-day I would more readily identify the poetic essence. For me, Blake is absolute. Shakespeare is richer, Milton is more sonorous, Hopkins is more sensuous—one could make many more comparative statements; but Blake has no need of qualifying epithets: he is simply poetic, in imagination and in expression.

A discovery which I then made with some of the same emotional excitement that Blake had aroused was of a contemporary poet. There was published about this time a series of small yellow chapbooks, and in it appeared the first poems of Ralph Hodgson. The poems were in harmony with the archaic style of the production: they seemed to come from a world of gypsies and highwaymen, they were sometimes sentimental, and they had a simple insistent rhythm which haunted the mind:

> Eve with her basket, was
> Deep in the bells and grass,
> Wading in bells and grass
> Up to her knees,
> Picking a dish of sweet
> Berries and plums to eat,
> Down in the bells and grass
> Under the trees.

Ralph Hodgson is a genuine poet, and I think that in spite of his sentimentality and whimsicality he has a permanent place in our literature. But he was the worst, because the most superficial kind of influence. To be influenced by Shakespeare, Milton or Wordsworth cannot do a young poet any harm: at least, it is only a very poor creature who would be influenced by their idiosyncrasies without at the same time being profitably stirred by their profundities. There is nothing profound in the poetry of Ralph Hodgson, and I am far from implying that all poetry should be profound. But just as one would feel a little silly if one found oneself unconsciously imitating the antics or gestures of another man, and tend to blame the other man for having antics and gestures of an imitable kind, so I feel inclined to criticize Hodgson's verse for its pretty jingle and infectious rhythm. These are qualities to be enjoyed by non-poetic people: the poet must go his own gait.

It is easy to retort that if a poet's genius is strong enough, his diction will be independent enough. But a poet has to undergo a process of birth and growth: he does not discover himself until he has rejected the alternative selves represented by the poetry already existing in the world. Here, perhaps, I am advancing a romantic doctrine. It is possible to conceive of poetry as an established form, and of the poet's duty as merely to add to the general fund. That is the classical conception of the poet. But my conception was, and still is, of poetry as a unique experience: the individual, with his particular moods, emotions, thoughts, trying to express himself integrally, in his own choice of words. It is true that he has to use words which are common to all his countrymen; but there is an infinite number of ways of selecting and combining these words, and from these infinite possibilities one exact, original correspondence of idea and expression must emerge, or the poem will be an affectation and a failure.

To discover what other influences were at work in this early phase of my poetic awakening, I should have to examine the verses themselves, and as I have already related, they no longer exist. But this acquisitive age actually continues until the end of my twentieth year, and for the later stage of it there is the evidence of a small 'brochure' published by Elkin Mathews in 1915 and entitled *Songs of Chaos*. An epigraph from Nietzsche—'One must have chaos within one to give birth to a dancing star'—explains the title, but this sentence which I had printed on the title-page really belongs to a later phase of my development, and the poems in the modest little volume have none of the tremendous implications of such a motto. When, in January, 1915, I joined the Army, I was posted to a battalion stationed in Dorset. I had to travel via London and arrived in that city for the first time in my life. I carried, besides my military baggage, a large bundle of poems, and at King's Cross I told the taxi-driver to go to Waterloo via Cork Street. All I knew about Mr. Mathews was that he had been publishing the kind of poetry I was interested in: I had no introduction to him nor any means of obtaining one. However, he received me very kindly in the back of his shop and undertook to consider the publication of my poems if I would pay a reader's fee, which I willingly did. A few weeks later he sent me the reader's report, which was to the effect that though the poems were too slight and imitative to be published in bulk, a small selection that would pass might be made, and he indicated the ones he thought best. I was not so much dashed by his general criticism as angry at the selection he had made. I insisted on making my own selection, and Mr. Mathews published them at my expense—I do not remember what it cost me, but it was not exorbitant. Six months later twenty-two copies had been sold: but I had already regretted my rash and inexperienced venture, and at my request the remainder of the edition was pulped.

This abortive volume has been out of my mind for many years now, but I still possess a copy and I have unearthed it. It has the musty smell of forgotten books, but as I turn its pages I wonder if I have been too harsh with its simple conceits. I reprinted four of the poems in the 1926 edition of my *Collected Poems,* but in 1935 suppressed even these. The intensity with which I wrote some of these poems is still a vivid memory—it was not an intensity of emotion leading to expression, but an emotion generated by the act of creation. The intensity was due to the discovery that an image could be matched with exact words. The triviality of the image did not seem to matter. Even now, with all my literary and critical experience, I cannot be sure that it matters. I cannot be sure, for example, that a poem which now costs me a qualm to quote is not nevertheless a valid poem and therefore a good poem. It was called 'A Little Girl':

> I pluck a daisy here and there—
>   O many a daisy do I take!
> And I string them together in a ring,
>   But it's seldom the ring doesn't break.
>
> O daisies rosy, daisies white!
>   If I could string them in a ring
> They'd make a bonny daisy chain—
>   O why is a daisy a delicate thing?

If, as a very childlike youth, I succeeded in evoking the simplicity of a child's outlook, even a child's insight, then the result is valid. It is only sentimental if as an adult I am trying to exploit childish things.

In looking through this booklet (it ran to no more than thirty-seven pages), the only other influence besides those of Blake and Hodgson which I can now discern is that of Yeats:

> When Niordr arose from the burning deep
> And bade the waves no longer weep:—
> Niordr arose with a golden harp
> And touched the strings that never warp,
> Bidding the angry waves be still,
> And the Vanir gather to obey his will.

Niordr and the Vanir are no longer my familiar spirits, but I am reminded that at this time, at the instigation of the friend to whom I already owed so much, I read many of the Northern myths and sagas, and played with the idea of writing a Viking epic. But other influences, and other ambitions, were to intervene.

At the beginning of the Michaelmas Term, in the year 1912, I enrolled myself as a student at the University of Leeds. I was still not very certain of my intentions: ostensibly I was to become a lawyer of some kind, but secretly (it was half a secret to myself) I was determined on a literary career. I already saw myself as a novelist, a dramatist, or perhaps a journalist—the future would decide which. I was conscious of the scrappiness of my general education, and therefore resolved to spend a year in a way which was not strictly utilitarian: I took the first year course for the B. A. degree. The following year I switched over to my proper studies, which I had decided were Law and Economics, and I was rash enough to attempt to take the two degrees (LL. B. and B. Sc. Econ.) simultaneously. I do not think the prescribed limits of these two curricula would have been too much for me; but I never for a day kept within these limits. I was an anomalous figure among my fellow-undergraduates, whose careers were already determined: they were going to be school-teachers, or clergymen, or practical scientists and technicians in the local industries. Not a single soul, so far as I ever discovered, was there for the disinterested purpose of acquiring a 'liberal' education. It is true that I too had my purpose; but it was vague and self-selected, and not dependent on a grant or scholarship. I could pick and choose my subjects to suit my own idea of a career; and I did in fact choose my subjects with an abandon which ought undoubtedly to have been restrained. English and French literature, Latin, Logic, Roman

Law, Jurisprudence, Common Law, Constitutional Law and History, Political Economy, Social Economics, European History, Geology—the mere list now makes me dizzy. The result was complete mental congestion and over-work. My days were filled with lectures and I read till the small hours every night. But this is not half the toll. I had at the same time been let loose in a library of seemingly infinite dimensions. I used to seat myself at a table in this library in every spare interval between the lectures. By a chance which was almost perverse, the seat to which my instinct first directed me, and which I continued to use whenever I found it free, was sheltered by a high bookcase which contained, like a mountain veined with shining gold, the very names with which my intellectual curiosity was now engaged—Dostoevsky, Ibsen and Nietzsche. I would open my *Gaius* or *Justinian,* Welton's *Logic* or Marshall's *Political Economy;* but soon my eyes would be caught by the tempting titles at my side, and one by one the volumes were drawn out and only the closing bell awakened me from my absorption. With Dostoevsky and Ibsen I was already partly acquainted, but Nietzsche was a new world, and since my discovery of Blake, the most cataclysmic. It was Nietzsche who first introduced me to philosophy—I read far more than I could understand in his pages, but I did not let my ignorance rest. From Nietzsche I passed to Schopenhauer, to Kant, Hegel, Hume, Pascal, Plato —in very much this indiscriminate order. It was as though I had tapped a central exchange of intellectual tendencies; from Nietzsche communications ran in every direction and for at least five years he, and none of my professors or friends, was my real teacher.

These years at the university were thus an orgy of acquisitiveness: what basis of disciplined education had been devised by the university authorities was completely swamped by my own proclivities. It must be remembered that these new universities have no such institution as the tutor—perhaps their greatest failing; and though I could have consulted the lecturers and professors, the very oddness of my position and the indeterminateness of my aims made this, however desirable, not strictly necessary. And this educational machine is so rigid in its workings that any action which is not strictly necessary is almost impossible. I remember that in my second year I did venture to send to the professor of English Literature, F. W. Moorman, two poetic dramas which I had written in North Riding dialect—I ventured to do this because he was a great enthusiast for the dialect, and perhaps the most inspiring teacher

in the university. He was completely taken by surprise—though he had, some weeks earlier, been impressed by an essay I had written on Witchcraft and the Elizabethan Drama. It had never occurred to him that one of the hundred odd students who scribbled away taking notes as he lectured should attempt an original composition. He began to take a special interest in me and encouraged me to show him more of my efforts; but then came the war and before I could renew contact with this possible mentor, he had been accidentally drowned whilst bathing.

The experience of these years raises in its acutest form the whole question of disciplined education. Up to the age of fifteen my education had been perhaps more than usually disciplined, but from that age to the present day I have followed my own bent; the order has been of my own devising, and generally the order of my strongest inclinations. This is the kind of education which most authorities find reprehensible. 'I hold very strongly,' wrote Cardinal Newman in the best of all treatises on the subject, 'that the first step in intellectual training is to impress upon a boy's mind the idea of science, method, order, principle, and system; of rule and exception, of richness and harmony. . . . Let him once gain this habit of method, of starting from fixed points, of making his ground good as he goes, of distinguishing what he knows from what he does not know, and I conceive he will be gradually initiated into the largest and truest philosophical views, and will feel nothing but impatience and disgust at the random theories and imposing sophistries and dashing paradoxes, which carry away half-formed and superficial intellects.' These words, in which I recognize a large measure of truth, are a complete condemnation of the method of education which I pursued, and yet I am not entirely repentant. Admittedly I had some good habits: what I read I tended to read thoroughly; I made notes and to the best of my unaided ability made the ground good as I went on my way. Nietzsche is not a starting-point that Newman would have approved—he would almost certainly have included his works among 'the random theories and imposing sophistries and dashing paradoxes' which he scorns, and my intellect among the half-formed and superficial which are carried away by such theories and sophistries. Nevertheless, Nietzsche *was* a starting-point and all the circumstances considered, not one which I regret. He gave me vistas which were quite outside the range of formal education; he introduced me to the ferment of contemporary ideas. In his company I knew the excitement of an intellectual adventure, that highest exaltation which only comes when truth is conceived as a fleeting quarry in whose pursuit the whole mind must be engaged.

In my subsequent years I was often to come into contact with great men whose intellects had been formed in the gradual and disciplined manner indicated by Newman. Let me admit that I have always felt in their presence a sense of weakness; but it is the weakness of the runner who has returned from the chase and found the imperturbable god of reason still changeless in his niche. I had felt the earth spinning underneath my feet, and the clouds racing me in the sky; beauty had stirred like an animal in the covert and my senses had been assailed from a thousand directions. The flush on my features was a reflexion of the animation in my mind, where the images were as vivid as nature and as restless as the sea. If my ideal had been a static form, then I should have withered like a wreath at the feet of this impassive god; but my ideal was a labile green shoot, an emergent new world, a manifestation of the unknown in the desert of dead facts.

I have found that most people whose minds have responded to a formal university education are like monoliths. They are bodies at rest. They have acquired during their university years a choice armoury of information, and they assume that it will serve them for the rest of their lives. Many of them sell their classics to the second-hand bookseller before they 'come down' from Oxford or Cambridge; or if they keep them, it is for the sake of sentimental associations. They are stored in a glazed bookcase behind the 'chesterfield,' with a college shield on the wall above and a tobacco-jar on the ledge. In a few years the once proud possessor of a first in Greats will have forgotten all but a few tags of his Greek and Latin, and will be reduced to defending a classical education for its supposed disciplinary virtues. He can boast of having 'done' his Plato or his Aristotle, his Aeschylus or his Euripides; but these are names now, mingled with his sentimental recollections of professors and dons. They had not become a part of his life, a continuing influence and ever-present inspiration. They and the whole galaxy of classical poets and philosophers are dead and distant worlds.

There is another side to the argument. Some of these formally educated young men, on leaving the universities, have gone into the Civil Service or business, and have become very efficient administrators. Between their present efficiency and their education there is a very direct relation: not the relation of a vocational training to the vocation pursued (which is much more the ideal of the modern universities and technical colleges), but a relation

sanctioned by the intangible virtues of 'character'—in Newman's words, 'the force, the steadiness, the comprehensiveness and the versatility of intellect, the command over our own powers, the instinctive just estimate of things as they pass before us, which sometimes indeed is a natural gift, but commonly is not gained without much effort and the exercise of years.' These are the virtues which are needed in the upper ranks of any social hierarchy—these virtues rather than specialized knowledge or technical skill—and the Civil Service has quite rightly rejected the notion of a particularized training such as the Army, the Navy and the professions require. Its flexibility, its adaptability, its very humanity depend on this paradox in its recruitment.

The ideals of this kind of education are generally summed up in the word 'character,' though latterly the more equivocal word 'leadership' has been used. But administration is not the only function of an educated man, nor is leadership a necessity in a community of free individuals. There is an alternative ideal of education, for which I have always attempted to reserve the word 'personality.' Character is the product of a disciplined education: discipline inculcates habits of mind as well as of body, and the result is a firm, dependable set of ideas and reactions upon which a definite type of society can be based. A character is not necessarily conservative: rather it is constructive, and in a time of stress or disintegration might well seem revolutionary. It is moral, though its morality is not necessarily conventional. It cultivates a 'taste,' but this taste is rational rather than aesthetic, retrospective and historical rather than experimental and contemporary.

A personality, on the other hand, is distinguished by immediacy and by what I would call lability, or the capacity to change without loss of integrity. Keats, who discerned the quality in himself, gave it the name of Negative Capability; and in Hamlet Shakespeare depicted the type in all its mutability.

Character is only attained by limitation. The senses, which would otherwise be open to the impact of every phenomenal event, must be canalized, protected by a hard cortex or shell, and only allowed to operate when they have been directed by the conscious will; and it can be argued that sensations and their attendant emotions are all the finer for being thus restricted. But the personality will have none of this arbitrary interference with the natural process of selectivity: the senses are open to every impression which falls upon them, and the mind surrenders to its environment. Admittedly, from a moral and social point of view, there is a danger that such a passive attitude will lead to instability and disintegration. But the values of the personality are neither moral nor social: they are religious or aesthetic. Here the word 'religious,' put in contrast to 'moral,' may cause some surprise; but I would be prepared to maintain that the essentially religious experience described by the great mystics of the East as well as the West, and now generally known in modern theology as the Kierkegaardian 'instant,' the Barthian 'crisis' or 'leap,' is a surrender of the existential being only possible to a personality, a man of negative capability.

To question the values of the personality, therefore, is to question the values of mysticism and of art. The greatest mistake would be to suppose that a society can be based exclusively on one type of human being. Society needs for vitality, and for effective progress, the contrast and opposition of types, more particularly of these two fundamental types which I have called characters and personalities. The tautness of the social fabric depends on their dialectical counterplay.

It would seem to follow from these considerations that there should be two systems of education, one for character and one for personality. That would obviously be impracticable, and the most we can hope for is an elasticity in the general system which would provide for both types of individual. The present system is directed almost exclusively to the creation of character, and at its best is very successful in this aim. The survival of personality in this system is a matter of chance: sometimes an understanding teacher will give his protection to a boy obviously not made for the mould; but more often the boy revolts and escapes from the system (as Shelley did), or by some chance is never submitted to it—is *privately* educated, as we say. My own case was still more exceptional: I entered the system as a casual and undirected unit, a misfit. I did not consciously reject the system: rather, it rejected me. I played the game, but I did not obey the rules. I did not conform to a regular routine, and before I could be punished for my dilettantism, the war had taken me to another and a more realistic school.

During the whole of this subsequent period I read avidly. Even in the most difficult circumstances—in the most desperate trench warfare—I was never without a book in my pocket. It was necessarily very unsystematic reading, but it included Henry James and Flaubert, Baudelaire and Rimbaud, Plato and Berkeley. But it is not really necessary to isolate this period: I would rather say that the process of self-education was uninterrupted by the war, the only

difference being that before and after that event I was better equipped to find or refer to the books of which day by day I became conscious.

* * * * * * *

I have not lost sight of the original purpose of this chapter, which was to relate my gradual discovery of the world of poetry. But a divagation has been necessary to show what part was played in the process by my education. I think I have shown that it was mainly negative. When I look back on this period of my life, and when I compare my experience with that of other people, my strongest feeling is one of relief. It is so easy to crush a nascent sensibility, or if not to crush it, then to deform it. The poetic sensibility is especially vulnerable, and especially in England. Socially the poet is despised: for the great majority of people he is merely a comic figure, the butt of *Punch* and the music-halls. Poetry as an art has become a secret and shame-faced activity: people are even shy of being seen reading poetry in a train, whereas the public declamation of poetry, as it was practised even in the nineteenth century, and as it is still practised in Russia, is quite unknown.[3] Attempts to reintroduce the art through the very suitable medium of broadcasting have so far been very disappointing.

If this social opposition to poetry is reinforced by what one might call a process of academic sterilization, it is very difficult to retain any trace of free sensibility. Actually the attempt to reduce an art to materia paedagogii is always fatal: poetry cannot be dissected unless it is first killed. I do not imply, however, that poetry—or art in general—should be excluded from the curriculum of our schools and universities. On the contrary, I think that the arts should play a greater part in education. But they should be treated as arts and not as 'subjects,' still less as sciences. This is not the place to enlarge on the

3 "A few years ago I was one of a group of English poets invited to the Russian Embassy to meet three Russian poets (Lugovskoy, Selvinsky and one whose name I have forgotten). After tea and vodka, we adjourned to a drawing-room where our Russian colleagues recited in turn their own poems, magnificently. Though few, if any, of us knew the language, we were made to feel its music and its passion, and even the meaning penetrated by virtue of the poets' mime and rhetoric. When they had finished, they turned to us and asked us to recite some of our famous English poetry to them. We looked at each other in nervous embarrassment. After much shuffling and modest protestation, an elderly poet began to pipe out Shelley's 'Ode to the West Wind' in a high monotonous voice; faltered and broke down. Someone else recited a little poem about a little bird. There were a few other irrelevancies and then we parted, feeling that we had betrayed, not only our country, but also the art for which our country is respected even when all our other qualities are despised." (Read)

question, but as a general indication of what I mean, I would say that it is necessary to make a clear separation of the historical and the technical aspects of each art. The history of literature or the history of painting (including, of course, the history of their technical development) would be distinct subjects, taught like the history of any other aspect of social evolution. But the technique of literature, like the technique of painting, would be encouraged as a practical activity. Poetry and plays would be written, recited or produced, and the creative artist would be elevated above the academic scholar. It would, of course, revolutionize educational standards if marks were to be awarded, or even a degree granted, on the artistic merits of an original composition; but that, I contend, is the only way in which the arts can be brought into organic relation with a vital system of education.

Otherwise, it is better to let the aesthetic impulse develop unaided, as it did in my own case. Once I had become aware of this creative impulse in myself, I needed no encouragement to educate myself in the subject. I was filled with an insatiable curiosity which extended to all the poetry of the past, to the poetry of other languages, and to the poetry of my contemporaries. In a few years I had raced through all the poetry in my own language which I thought likely to appeal to me, and was then eager to discover the poetry of France, of Italy and of Germany. I doubt if I should ever have attempted to learn the languages of these countries but for the curiosity engendered by my poetic impulse. Latin poetry had been almost completely destroyed for me by the education I had received in this subject, but a measure of enjoyment was preserved in poets who by chance had never been 'set,' such as Catullus and Lucretius. But I must confess that Latin poetry in general has played an insignificant part in my poetic experience. I have excused myself by supposing a lack of sympathy, but this lack may have been due to a deficiency of knowledge. For Greek poetry, however, I have felt much sympathy on the basis of no knowledge at all. I have never had the time, nor perhaps the will, to teach myself Greek, and Greek poetry, in its essential nature, remains unknown to me. I say 'in its essential nature' because it is only in translation that I have read the great classics of Greek poetry: and though this may have given me a certain insight into the Greek spirit, it is futile, as I know from my experience with foreign poetry in general, to pretend that my lips have even touched the rim of the hippocrene fountain. I console myself with the thought that I am still far from the age at which Cato first learned the language.

In this account of my discovery of poetry I have so far not gone beyond Blake and Yeats. I have mentioned Ralph Hodgson, but his influence was short-lived and superficial. The next stage is represented by Donne and Browning among the poets of the past, and by a group of contemporary poets known as the Imagists. Together, these two influences may be said to have completed my poetic education. The years to follow held such surprises as Rimbaud and Apollinaire, Hölderlin and Rilke, but though such poets have deepened my conception of the content of poetry, they have not altered the attitude to the problems of technique which I formed under the influence of the Imagists.

Donne is an influence apart—not in any sense a technical influence, but rather an extension of sensibility, an education in emotional rectitude. The conceits which so disgusted Johnson appealed to me because they were an attempt to bridge the separate worlds of intellect and feeling, and I began to conceive of poetry as an intermediary between these conflicting forces. But it never occurred to me that poets of the twentieth century should use the language and diction of the seventeenth century—they might, with as good reason, dress in the costumes of that period. There was something even in this respect to learn from Donne: he did, after all, refuse to sacrifice his meaning to a conventional ideal of smoothness (which is not the same thing as felicity). Browning's technique I found entirely relevant. He too was occupied by this problem—the expression of intellectual concepts in the language of feeling—though his intelligence was historical and ethical rather than experimental and aesthetic, and his emotions were distorted by the moral conventions of his age. His technique, however, was free: a reaction against the Parnassian polish of Tennyson and Arnold, a return to the rugged exactitude of Donne. Until Hopkins was discovered (in 1918, though odd poems had appeared earlier) Browning was the only English poet of the immediate past who worked as anything like a ferment in the minds of the poets of the decade 1906–1915 (the decisive years in the formation of the modern poetic tradition in England). There was also Yeats, but he did not then appear as of the past: he was one of our contemporaries, himself subject to some of the same influences. But even Yeats can to a great extent be discounted—his real influence came later, when his later poems grew realistic and political, and as such appealed to a still later generation. Even before the outbreak of the war, we distrusted Yeats's romanticism. Only the Irish could move freely in the Celtic twilight, though the Americans might assimilate it like any other foreign tradition, and it was the

Americans among us, particularly Ezra Pound, who paid most respect to it. For the Anglo-Saxons it might be a fashionable craze, but as a poetic style it was racially foreign to us, only to be adopted as a mannerism and an affectation. The war finally killed it. An epigraph which appeared next to the title-page of the first edition of my war-poems, *Naked Warriors,* was intended as a parody of Yeats, and as a cynical expression of my own disillusionment:

> War through my soul has driven
> its jagged blades:
> The riven
> dream fades
> So you'd better grieve, heart, in the gathering night,
> Grieve, heart, in the loud twilight.

What I wish to insist on is the importance of Browning in the pre-war years. It is only necessary to turn to the poems published by Ezra Pound—'il miglior fabbro' of us all—particularly the volumes *Personae* and *Exultations,* to see that influence predominant. Even when Pound is writing a poem with a Provençal or Romantic theme, it may be given the manner or diction of Browning. The same influence is not absent from the earlier poems of his friend T. S. Eliot.

Mr. Pound, I know, has many other gods—Fenollosa and Rémy de Gourmont, for example—and he is very jealous on their behalf. But I am not writing about critical influences, which were very various, but of direct mentors of the technique and diction of verse. The modification of Browning's influence came from France—from Rimbaud and Laforgue, and from the early verse of Duhamel, Jules Romains, Jean de Bosschère, André Spire and Appollinaire. There was also T. E. Hulme, but by now his five short poems have begun to assume rather too much prominence in the history of this period. They were certainly good textbook examples of imagist technique, but if Hulme had written fifty or a hundred poems as good, we should not have heard so much about them.

This explanation has been long enough, and I must pick up the residue of my own impressions. If Browning was the last of my historical discoveries, it will now be seen how he came to be fused in my imagination with the activities of a contemporary school which was at that time learning from Browning and applying his technique to the expression of a modern sensibility. I had now reached the vanguard of the art for which I had felt an affinity in my own being. Henceforth my discovery of poetry was to be directed by my passionate participation in its immediate destiny. Hitherto I had read for enjoyment and understanding: I was now to read as if I drew in the substance of life itself, creatively manifested in the minds of living poets.

From this experience, which lasted from the year 1913 to 1917, I quickly evolved what I would have called my philosophy of composition. There was a general feeling then that some new philosophy was necessary, much as it had been necessary when Wordsworth and Coleridge published their *Lyrical Ballads* in 1798, and several attempts to formulate one had been made by the young poets for whom I felt such a strong sympathy. The clearest statement of these years is the Preface to *Some Imagist Poets,* an anthology published in 1915 which included the work of Richard Aldington, H. D., F. S. Flint, and D. H. Lawrence. That preface still remains the locus classicus for the doctrines of the imagist school, and since it is not now generally available, I will quote the six 'common principles'[4] which it set forth:

1. To use the language of common speech, but to employ always the *exact* word, not the nearly-exact, nor the merely decorative word.

2. To create new rhythms—as the expression of new moods—and not to copy old rhythms, which merely echo old moods. We do not insist upon 'free-verse' as the only method of writing poetry. We fight for it as for a principle of liberty. We believe that the individuality of a poet may often be better expressed in free-verse than in conventional forms. In poetry, a new cadence means a new idea.

3. To allow absolute freedom in the choice of subject. It is not good art to write badly about aeroplanes and automobiles; nor is it necessarily bad art to write about the past. We believe passionately in the artistic value of modern life, but we wish to point out that there is nothing so uninspiring nor so old-fashioned as an aeroplane of the year 1911.

4. To present an image (hence the name: 'Imagist'). We are not a school of painters, but we believe that poetry should render particulars exactly and not deal in vague generalities, however magnificent and sonorous. It is for this reason that we oppose the cosmic poet, who seems to us to shirk the real difficulties of his art.

5. To produce poetry that is hard and clear, never blurred nor indefinite.

6. Finally, most of us believe that concentration is of the very essence of poetry.

---

4 "The best *defence* of these principles is F. S. Flint's Preface to *Otherworld,* a volume of 'cadences' published in 1920 (Poetry Bookshop) and dedicated, I am proud to recall, to me. Flint had far more to do with the development of the Imagist school than has generally been acknowledged." (Read)

Three years later, in the third number of *Art and Letters,* I published my own 'Definitions towards a Modern Theory of Poetry.' I began with the following 'axioms':

1. Form is determined by the emotion which requires expression.

Corollary: Form is not an unchanging mould into which any emotion can be poured.

2. The poem is an artistic whole demanding strict unity.

3. The criterion of the poem is the quality of the vision expressed, granted that the expression is adequate.

Corollary: Rhyme, metre, cadence, alliteration, are various decorative devices to be used as the vision demands, and are not formal quantities pre-ordained.

I was evidently reading Spinoza at the time, and the whole essay is written in a dry analytical style. Terms like 'vision,' 'emotion,' 'value,' 'unity,' and 'form' are defined with the aid of a psychological jargon which I should now try to avoid; but the essay, differently worded, would still represent my views on the theory of poetry. What interests me now is to find myself criticizing my friends the Imagists. I admitted that they were the only modern school of poets which showed 'any clarity of creative intention'; but I criticized them because 'in their manifestoes they had renounced the decorative word, but their sea-violets and wild hyacinths tend to become as decorative as the beryls and jades of Oscar Wilde.' I also accused them of lacking 'that aesthetic selection which is the artist's most peculiar duty'—by which I meant, as far as I can now make out, that they thought any passing mood or emotion worthy of poetic expression—they did not apply an aesthetic (or did I mean intellectual?) judgment to the quality of the emotion itself. I concluded: 'Modern England may be "a nest of singing birds," but it is well for us to realize that the poem is still rather a primitive affair, and to make it otherwise there is a call for stern artistic devotion. We must shrink from the exotic and the decadent, and from the sheltered garden of cultivated beauties. Beauty is a discipline, demanding all the intensity of a man's intelligence to present clear and undefiled the infinite quality in things. The artist's vision is the supreme value; the expression of it is the supreme difficulty.'

This essay must have been written early in 1918, that is to say, before the end of the war, though I cannot remember where or in what circumstances I wrote it. I can look back with amusement on its earnest solemnity now, but I think it reflects something of the contradiction that was being forced on us by our daily experience. We were trying to maintain an abstract aesthetic ideal in the midst of terrorful and inhuman events. In my own case I am certain that this devotion to abstract notions and intellectual reveries saved me from a raw reaction to these events. But as the war went on, year after year, and there seemed no escape from its indignity except death, some compromise between dream and reality became necessary. The only worthy compromise, I even then dimly realized, was a synthesis—some higher reality in which the freedom of the mind and the necessity of experience became reconciled. If I had been older that solution might have been a philosophy; but I was not contemplative enough for that, nor wise enough. I therefore sought the solution in art: in a poetry which would represent my aesthetic ideals and yet at the same time deal with the experience that threatened to overwhelm me. The result was a series of war poems, some of which I afterwards destroyed, but most of which I published in a small volume to which I gave the title *Naked Warriors*. (Incidentally, I am sure that I had not at that time seen Pollaiuolo's engraving which so perfectly illustrates the title and the epigraph which I put on the title-page: 'And there were some that went into the battle naked and unarmed, fighting only with the fervour of their spirit, dying and getting many wounds.') It may seem that this was but a feeble response to such an immense event. In a later chapter I shall discuss my reactions to war in more detail, but on this level of aesthetic response, I would ask the reader to reflect on the millions who were engaged in that conflict and then to examine its poetic aftermath in any of the languages of the nations engaged. It is infinitesimal in quantity and almost negligible in poetic quality. Many years later, in his Introduction to the *Oxford Book of Modern Verse,* Yeats was to offer a reason for this strange disparity—'the same reason that made Arnold withdraw his "Empedocles on Etna" from circulation; passive suffering is not a theme for poetry'; and for the same reason Yeats decided to exclude war poetry from his anthology. It was a judgment that was to arouse a good deal of resentment among the young poets of to-day, and I am not sure that I myself accept it—at least, not for the reason given. Another sentence in the same paragraph of Yeats's Introduction, though it is metaphorical, seems to me to be nearer the truth of the matter: 'When man has withdrawn into the quicksilver at the back of the mirror no great event becomes luminous in his mind. . . .' In other words, the necessary element is the time-lapse implicit in Wordsworth's phrase, 'recollected in tranquillity,' an element of 'aesthetic distance.' Even passive suffering can be a fit theme for poetry if it is seen objectively enough, against a wide background. The direct expression of suffering is an animal cry; poetry, too, is an animal cry, but of another kind. There is a difference which is the difference between the scream of a slaughtered pig and the song of a nightingale, and this is perhaps the difference between passive suffering and passive joy. But art begins—and I think this was Yeats's meaning—when the joy is purposive, an active sublimation even of suffering and tragedy.

In 1917 and 1918, in the intervals of leave from the Front, I gradually made the acquaintance of the poets whose work I admired—Flint, Aldington, Pound and Eliot—and met other writers with whom I was in sympathy, such as A. R. Orage and P. Wyndham Lewis. Influences which had been literary and indirect now became personal, and the cold communication of the page was exchanged for the intimate give-and-take of conversation. Some of these friendships were to endure without interruption to the present day, some became intermittent, some never developed at all. It is not my intention to discuss my personal relationships in this book, but I cannot avoid a reference to my friendship with Eliot, because it has certainly had a considerable effect on my intellectual development, perhaps just because we are so divergent in origin, education, character and ideals. He has called himself royalist, classicist, and anglo-catholic, whereas I (with qualifications similar to those he made) would call myself anarchist, romanticist and agnostic. A long and uninterrupted friendship has been possible because in spite of these divergences, we have always agreed about things which are perhaps finally more important: the sense of beauty in poetry, the quality of the expression of ideas, and the priority to be given to natural goodness even when the intelligence seems perverse. I think our friendship has a certain general significance, because too much importance, in history and criticism, is given to ideological similarities and not enough to human sympathies. Life, even in its intimate or arcane recesses, is still dialectical.

These friendships no doubt modified my poetic outlook, but I think I may say that by the end of the war I had discovered myself and my style—that is to say, I had made an equation between emotion and image, between feeling and expression. So long as I was true to this equation, I need not be afraid of influences or acquired mannerisms. Poetry was reduced to an instrument of precision. 'Reduced' will imply, of course, a lack of bulk: from that time my output of verse was to be severely restricted. But what I wrote I tended to keep: I no longer destroyed a large part of my writing. Criticism had become innate, composition an instinctive language; and though I am very far from claiming perfection or permanence for the poems I have retained, I do not think it will be necessary for a reader of the future to approach my work with squared shoulders: he can accept or reject me on the instant. By this statement I lay myself open to the charge that there is nothing in my poetry to detain the reader; but that, of course, is not what I mean. One of the essential characteristics of poetry is what Coleridge called 'the power of reducing multitude into unity of effect.' Whatever the nature of poetry, be it lyrical or dramatic, meditative or philosophical, this unity of effect should exist, and be immediately apparent. If that unity is achieved, the poem has that quality which is possessed by all true works of art—the quality of retaining our interest in spite of familiarity.

Here I will break off this account of my discovery of poetry—'break off' because it is an enterprise which still continues. I am not now likely to modify my own technique, and I have reached that becalmed stage of life, midway between youth and old age, in which the poetic impulse is often dormant. But I still retain the zest, the insatiable thirst for this pellucid essence of experience. All other sensuous experiences are as nothing to this perception of poetic beauty. A few years ago I took my son, then aged about eleven, to an open-air performance of *A Midsummer Night's Dream*. It was a brilliant sunny day, and everywhere, not least on the green and leafy stage, the atmosphere was gay. But time after time the impact of Shakespeare's words—the words themselves and not their meaning—would send a gush of tears to my eyes, and there was no darkness to hide my paradoxical visage from my neighbours. But they too were absorbed in the play—some in the antics, some in the atmosphere; some few in the cadence of the words that came winged with inexplicable sorrow through the summer air.

Ivor Armstrong Richards

I. A. RICHARDS, who was born in 1893 and educated at Clifton and Magdalene College, Cambridge, has an international reputation as an educator, having taught at Cambridge, at Tsinghua University in Peking as visiting professor in 1929–30, and at Harvard, where he was visiting lecturer in 1931 and where, since 1944, he has held a University Professorship. His first book, *The Foundations of Aesthetics,* written in collaboration with C. K. Ogden and James Wood, was published in 1921; two years later he published *The Meaning of Meaning: A Study of the Influence of Language upon Thought and of the Science of Symbolism,* again written in collaboration with C. K. Ogden. Between 1924 and 1929 he published the three books to which those who are interested in him primarily as a literary critic most frequently find themselves turning back.

The Principles of Literary Criticism: A Study of Literary Judgment (1924) presents a psychological account of the literary situation, basing a theory of literary criticism and its attendant problems on what happens as we read, particularly as we read poetry. At least a preliminary notion of the theory of literature put forth in that book may be obtained from section 2 of *Science and Poetry,* the long essay published as a separate volume in 1925 and reprinted in its entirety below. Whether or not Professor Richards still adheres to all the positions which he advanced in *Science and Poetry,* it is still an important statement, both because of the comparison it challenges

with Matthew Arnold's *The Study of Poetry* (1880) and also because it represents an important and influential strain in the early twentieth century's consciousness of itself. The third of the books referred to above, *Practical Criticism* (1929), grew out of Professor Richards's habit of distributing to his students at Cambridge sheets of poems which bore no indication of authorship and asking his students to express their reactions and judgments with complete freedom; the results were interpreted and collated in an attempt to discover the factors which condition and which sometimes warp our responses to poetry. Even today when for twenty-five years other teachers have been free to check the Richards method by putting it into practice themselves, and when some of its limitations are more apparent than they were at first, it is still an engrossing and extraordinarily useful book, and has been responsible for many of the directions taken in the teaching of literature and in literary criticism since it was published. *Interpretation in Teaching* (1938) undertakes to apply the same method to prose.

Among Richards's other books are: *Mencius on the Mind: Experiments in Multiple Definition* (1931); *Coleridge on Imagination* (1934); *How to Read a Page* (1942); *Basic English and Its Uses* (1943); and *The Pocket Book of Basic English* (1945). T. S. Eliot has some interesting things to say about Richards's criticism (though perhaps not the last word) in the chapter on "The Modern Mind" in *The Use of Poetry and the Use of Criticism.*

SCIENCE AND POETRY[1]

THE future of poetry is immense, because in poetry, where it is worthy of its high destinies, our race, as time goes on, will find an ever surer and surer stay. There is not a creed which is not shaken, not an accredited dogma which is not shown to be questionable, not a received tradition which does not threaten to dissolve. Our religion has materialised itself in the fact, in the supposed fact; it has attached its emotion to the fact, and now the fact is failing it. But for poetry the idea is everything.

—MATTHEW ARNOLD

I

THE GENERAL SITUATION

MAN'S prospects are not at present so rosy that he can neglect any means of improving them. He has recently made a number of changes in his customs and ways of life, partly with intention, partly by

5

10

15

accident. These changes are involving such widespread further changes that the fairly near future is likely to see an almost complete reorganisation of our lives, in their intimate aspects as much as in their public. Man himself is changing, together with his circumstances; he has changed in the past, it is true, but never perhaps so swiftly. His circumstances are not known ever to have changed so much or so suddenly before, with psychological as well as with economic, social and political dangers. This suddenness threatens us. Some parts of human nature resist change more than others. We risk disaster if some

---

[1] Reprinted from *Science and Poetry* by I. A. Richards, by permission of W. W. Norton & Company, Inc. Copyright 1926 by W. W. Norton & Company, Inc.

of our customs change while others which should change with them stay as they are.

Habits that have endured for many thousands of years are not easy to throw off—least of all when they are habits of thought, and when they do not come into open conflict with changing circumstances, or do not clearly involve us in loss or inconvenience. Yet the loss may be great without our knowing anything about it. Before 1590 no one knew how inconvenient were our natural habits of thought about the ways in which a stone may fall; yet the modern world began when Galileo discovered what really happens. Before 1800 only persons thought to be crazy knew that ordinary traditional ideas as to cleanliness are dangerously inadequate. The infant's average "expectation of life" has increased by about 30 years since Lister upset them. Nobody before Sir Ronald Ross knew what were the consequences of thinking about malaria in terms of influences and miasmas instead of in terms of mosquitoes. The Roman Empire might perhaps have still been flourishing if some one had found this out before A.D. 100.

With such examples all about us we can no longer, in any department of life, so easily accept what was good enough for our fathers as good enough for ourselves or for our children. We are forced to wonder whether our ideas, even upon subjects apparently of little practical importance, such as poetry, may not be dangerously inadequate. It becomes indeed somewhat alarming to recognise, as we must, that our habits of thought remain, as regards most of our affairs, much as they were 5,000 years ago. The Sciences are, of course, simply the exceptions to this rule. Outside the Sciences—and the greater part of our thinking still goes on outside the Sciences—we think very much as our ancestors thought a hundred or two hundred generations ago. Certainly this is so as regards official views about poetry. Is it not possible that these are wrong, as wrong as most ideas of an equally hoary antiquity? Is it not possible that to the men of the future our life to-day will seem a continual, ceaseless disaster due only to our own stupidity, to the nervelessness with which we accept and transmit ideas which do not apply and never have applied to anything?

The average educated man is growing more conscious, an extraordinarily significant change. It is probably due to the fact that his life is becoming more complex, more intricate, his desires and needs more varied and more apt to conflict. And as he becomes more conscious he can no longer be content to drift in unreflecting obedience to custom. He is forced to reflect. And if reflection often takes the form of inconclusive

worrying, that is no more than might be expected in view of the unparalleled difficulty of the task. To live reasonably is much more difficult to-day than it was in Dr. Johnson's time, and even then, as Boswell shows, it was difficult enough.

To live reasonably is not to live by reason alone—the mistake is easy, and, if carried far, disastrous—but to live in a way of which reason, a clear full sense of the whole situation, would approve. And the most important part of the whole situation, as always, is ourselves, our own psychological make-up. The more we learn about the physical world, about our bodies, for example, the more points we find at which our ordinary behaviour is out of accord with the facts, inapplicable, wasteful, disadvantageous, dangerous or absurd. Witness our habit of boiling our vegetables. We have still to learn how to feed ourselves satisfactorily. Similarly, the little that is yet known about the mind already shows that our ways of thinking and feeling about very many of the things with which we concern ourselves are out of accord with the facts. This is pre-eminently true of our ways of thinking and feeling about poetry. We think and talk in terms of states of affairs which have never existed. We attribute to ourselves and to things, powers which neither we nor they possess. And equally we overlook or misuse powers which are all-important to us.

Day by day, in recent years, man is getting more out of place in Nature. Where he is going to he does not yet know, he has not yet decided. As a consequence he finds life more and more bewildering, more and more difficult to live coherently. Thus he turns to consider himself, his own nature. For the first step towards a reasonable way of life is a better understanding of human nature.

It has long been recognised that if only something could be done in psychology remotely comparable to what has been achieved in physics, practical consequences might be expected even more remarkable than any that the engineer can contrive. The first positive steps in the science of the mind have been slow in coming, but already they are beginning to change man's whole outlook.

2

THE POETIC EXPERIENCE

Extraordinary claims have often been made for poetry—Matthew Arnold's words quoted at the head of this essay are an example—claims which very many people are inclined to view with astonishment or with the smile which tolerance gives to the are so used to having their responses propped up by beliefs, however vague, that when these shadowy supports are removed they are no longer able to respond. Their attitudes to so many things have been forced in the past, over-encouraged. And when the world-picture ceases to assist there is a collapse. Over whole tracts of natural emotional response we are to-day like a bed of dahlias whose sticks have been removed. And this effect of the neutralisation of nature is only in its beginnings. Consider the probable effects upon love-poetry in the near future of the kind of enquiry into basic human constitution exemplified by psycho-analysis.

A sense of desolation, of uncertainty, of futility, of the groundlessness of aspirations, of the vanity of endeavour, and a thirst for a life-giving water which seems suddenly to have failed, are the signs in consciousness of this necessary reorganisation of our lives.[11] Our attitudes and impulses are being compelled to become self-supporting; they are being driven back upon their biological justification, made once again sufficient to themselves. And the only impulses which seem strong enough to continue unflagging are commonly so crude that, to more finely developed individuals, they hardly seem worth having. Such people cannot live by warmth, food, fighting, drink, and sex alone. Those who are least affected by the change are those who are emotionally least removed from the animals. As we shall see at the close of this essay, even a considerable poet may attempt to find relief by a reversion to primitive mentality.

It is important to diagnose the disease correctly and to put the blame in the right quarter. Usually it is some alleged "materialism" of science which is denounced. This mistake is due partly to clumsy thinking, but chiefly to relics of the Magical View. For even if the Universe were "spiritual" all through (whatever that assertion might mean; all such assertions are probably nonsense), that would not make it any more accordant to human attitudes. It is not what the universe is made of but how it works,

the law it follows, which makes knowledge of it incapable of spurring on our emotional responses, and further the nature of knowledge itself makes it inadequate. The contact with things which we therein establish is too sketchy and indirect to help us. We are beginning to know too much about the bond which unites the mind to its object in knowledge for that old dream of a perfect knowledge which would guarantee perfect life to retain its sanction. What was thought to be pure knowledge, we see now to have been shot through with hope and desire, with fear and wonder, and these intrusive elements indeed gave it all its power to support our lives. In knowledge, in the "How?" of events, we can find hints by which to take advantage of circumstances in our favour and avoid mischances. But we cannot get from it a *raison d'être* or a justification of more than a relatively lowly kind of life.

The justification, or the reverse, of any attitude lies, not in the object, but in itself, in its serviceableness to the whole personality. Upon its place in the whole system of attitudes, which is the personality, all its worth depends. This is true equally for the subtle, finely compounded attitudes of the civilised individual as for the simpler attitudes of the child.

In brief, experience is its own justification; and this fact must be faced, although sometimes—by a lover, for example—it may be very difficult to accept. Once it is faced, it is apparent that all the attitudes to other human beings and to the world in all its aspects, which have been serviceable to humanity, remain as they were, as valuable as ever. Hesitation felt in admitting this is a measure of the strength of the evil habit we have described. But many of these attitudes, valuable as ever, are, now that they are being set free, more difficult to maintain, because we still hunger after a basis in belief.

7

SOME CONTEMPORARY POETS

It is time to turn to those living poets through study of whose work these reflections have arisen. Mr. Hardy is for every reason the poet with whom it is most natural to begin. Not only does his work span the whole period in which what I have called the neutralisation of nature was finally effected, but it has throughout definitely reflected that change. Short essays in verse are fairly frequent among his *Collected Poems,* essays almost always dealing with this very topic; but these, however suggestive, are not the ground for singling him out as the poet who has most fully and courageously accepted the contem-

---

11 To those familiar with Mr. Eliot's *The Waste Land,* my indebtedness to it at this point will be evident. He seems to me by this poem, to have performed two considerable services for this generation. He has given a perfect emotive description of a state of mind which is probably inevitable for a while to all meditative people. Secondly, by effecting a complete severance between his poetry and *all* beliefs, and this without any weakening of the poetry, he has realised what might otherwise have remained largely a speculative possibility, and has shown the way to the only solution of these difficulties. "In the destructive element immerse. That is the way." (Richards)

porary background; nor are the poems which are most definitely *about* the neutrality of nature the ground for the assertion. There is an opportunity for a misunderstanding at this point. The ground is the tone, the handling and the rhythm of poems which treat other subjects, for example *The Self Unseeing, The Voice, A Broken Appointment,* and pre-eminently *After a Journey.* A poem does not necessarily accept the situation because it gives it explicit recognition, but only through the precise mutation of the attitudes of which it is composed. Mr. Middleton Murry, against whose recent positions parts of this essay may be suspected by the reader to be aimed, has best pointed out, in his *Aspects of Literature,* how peculiarly "adequate to what we know and have suffered" Mr. Hardy's poetry is. "His reaction to an episode has behind it and within it a reaction to the universe." This is not as I should put it were I making a statement; but read as a pseudo-statement, emotively, it is excellent; it makes us remember how we felt. Actually it describes just what Hardy, at his best, does not do. He makes no reaction to the universe, recognising it as something to which no reaction is more relevant than another. Mr. Murry is again well inspired, this time both emotively and scientifically, when he says: "Mr. Hardy stands high above all other modern poets by the deliberate purity of his responsiveness. The contagion of the world's slow stain has not touched him; from the first he held aloof from the general conspiracy to forget in which not only those who are professional optimists take a part." These extracts (from a writer more agonisingly aware than others that some strange change has befallen man in this generation, though his diagnosis is, I believe, mistaken) indicate very well Mr. Hardy's place and rank in English poetry. He is the poet who has most steadily refused to be comforted. The comfort of forgetfulness, the comfort of beliefs, he has put both these away. Hence his singular preoccupation with death; because it is in the contemplation of death that the necessity for human attitudes, in the face of an indifferent universe, to become self-supporting is felt most poignantly. Only the greatest tragic poets have achieved an equally self-reliant and immitigable acceptance.

From Mr. Hardy to Mr. De la Mare may seem a large transition, though readers of Mr. De la Mare's later work will agree that there are interesting resemblances—in *Who's That* and in other poems in *The Veil* where Mr. De la Mare is notably less himself than when writing at his best. In his best poetry, in *The Pigs and the Charcoal Burner,* in *John Mouldy,* no intimation of the contemporary situation sounds. He

is writing of, and from, a world which knows nothing of these difficulties, a world of pure phantasy for which the distinction between knowledge and feeling has not yet dawned. When in other poems, more reflective, in *The Tryst,* for example, Mr. De la Mare does seem to be directly facing the indifference of the universe towards "poor mortal longingness" a curious thing happens. His utterance, in spite of his words, becomes not at all a recognition of this indifference, but voices instead an impulse to turn away, to forget it, to seek shelter in the warmth of his own familiar thickets of dreams, not to stay out in the wind. His rhythm, that indescribable personal note which clings to all his best poetry, is a lulling rhythm, an anodyne, an opiate, it gives sleep and visions, phantasmagoria; but it does not give *vision*, it does not awaken. Even when he most appears to be contemplating the fate of the modern, "whom the words of the wise have made sad," the drift of his verse is still "seeking after that sweet golden clime" where the mental traveller's journey *begins*.

There is one exception to this charge (for in a sense it is an adverse criticism, though not one to be pressed except against a great poet), there is one poem in which there is no such reluctance to bear the blast— *The Mad Prince's Song* in *Peacock Pie.* But here the spirit of the poem, the impulse which gives it life, comes from a poet who more than most refused to take shelter; *The Mad Prince's Song* derives from *Hamlet.*

Mr. Yeats and Mr. Lawrence present two further ways of dodging those difficulties which come from being born into this generation rather than into some earlier age. Mr. De la Mare takes shelter in the dreamworld of the child, Mr. Yeats retires into black velvet curtains and the visions of the Hermetist, and Mr. Lawrence makes a magnificent attempt to reconstruct in himself the mentality of the Bushman. There are other modes of escape open to the poet. Mr. Blunden, to name one other poet only, goes into the country, but few people follow him there in his spirit, whereas Mr. Yeats and Mr. Lawrence, whether they are widely read or not, do represent tendencies among the defeated which are only too easily observable.

Mr. Yeats' work from the beginning was a repudiation of the most active contemporary interests. But at first the poet of *The Wanderings of Usheen, The Stolen Child* and *Innisfree* turned away from contemporary civilisation in favour of a world which he knew perfectly, the world of folk-lore as it is accepted, neither with belief nor disbelief, by the peasant. Folk-lore and the Irish landscape, its winds, woods, waters, islets, and seagulls, and for a while an unusually simple and direct kind of love poetry in which he became something more than a minor poet, these were his refuge. Later, after a drawn battle with the drama, he made a more violent repudiation, not merely of current civilisation but of life itself, in favour of a supernatural world. But the world of the "eternal moods," of supernal essences and immortal beings is not, like the Irish peasant stories and the Irish landscape, part of his natural and familiar experience. Now he turns to a world of symbolic phantasmagoria about which he is desperately uncertain. He is uncertain because he has adopted as a technique of inspiration the use of trance, of dissociated phases of consciousness, and the revelations given in these dissociated states are insufficiently connected with normal experience. This in part explains the weakness of Mr. Yeats' transcendental poetry. A deliberate reversal of the natural relations of thought and feeling is the rest of the explanation. Mr. Yeats takes certain feelings—feelings of conviction attaching to certain visions—as evidence for the thoughts which he supposes his visions to symbolise. To Mr. Yeats the value of *The Phases of the Moon* lies not in any attitudes which it arouses or embodies but in the doctrine which for an initiate it promulgates.

The resort to trance, and the effort to discover a new world-picture to replace that given by science are the two most significant points for our purpose in Mr. Yeats' work. A third might be the singularly bitter contempt for the generality of mankind which occasionally appears.

The doctrinal problem arises again, but in a clearer form, with Mr. Lawrence. But here (Mr. Yeats' promised treatise on the states of the soul has not yet appeared) we have the advantage of an elaborate prose exposition, *Phantasia of the Unconscious,* of the positions which so many of the poems advocate. It is not unfair to put the matter in this way, since there is little doubt possible that the bulk of Mr. Lawrence's published verse is prose, scientific prose too, jottings, in fact, from a psychologist's notebook, with a commentary interspersed. Due allowance being made for the extreme psychological interest of these observations, there remains the task of explaining how the poet who wrote the *Ballad of Another Ophelia* and *Aware,* and, above all, *The White Peacock,* should have wandered, through his own zeal misdirected, so far from the paths which once appeared to be his alone to open.

Mr. Lawrence's revolt against civilisation seems to have been originally spontaneous, an emotional revulsion free from *ad hoc* beliefs. It sprang directly from experience. He came to abhor all the attitudes men adopt, not through the direct prompting of their instincts, but because of the supposed nature of the objects to which they are directed. The conventions, the idealisations, which come between man and man and between man and woman, which often queer the pitch for the natural responses, seemed to him the source of all evil. Part of his revolt was certainly justified. These idealisations—representative examples are the dogma of the equality of man and the doctrine that Love is primarily sympathy—are beliefs illicitly interpolated in order to support and strengthen attitudes in the manner discussed at length above. And Mr. Lawrence's original rejection of a morality not self-supporting but based upon beliefs, makes his work an admirable illustration of my main thesis. But two simple and avoidable mistakes deprived his revolt of the greater part of its value. He overlooked the fact that such beliefs commonly arise because the attitudes they support are already existent. He assumed that a bad basis for an attitude meant a bad attitude. In general, it does mean a forced attitude, but that is another matter. Secondly, he tried to cure the disease by introducing other beliefs of his own manufacture in place of the conventional beliefs and in support of very different attitudes.

The genesis of these beliefs is extremely interesting as an illustration of primitive mentality. Since the attitudes on which he fell back are those of a very early stage of human development, it is not surprising that the means by which he has supported them should be of the same era, or that the world-picture which he has worked out should be similar to that described in *The Golden Bough.* The mental process at work is schematically as follows: First, undergo an intense emotion, located with unusual definiteness in the body, which can be described as "a feeling *as though* the solar plexus were connected by a current of dark passional energy with another person." Those whose emotions tend to be localised will be familiar with such feelings. The second step is to say "I must trust my feelings." The third is to call the feeling an intuition. The last is to say "*I know* that my solar plexus is, etc." By this means we arrive at indubitable knowledge that the sun's energy is recruited from the life on the earth and that the astronomers are wrong in what they say about the moon, and so on.

The illicit steps in the argument are not quite so evident as they appear to be in this analysis. To distinguish an intuition *of* an emotion from an intuition *by* it is not always easy, nor is a description of an emotion always in practice distinguishable from an emotion. Certainly we must trust our feelings—in the sense of acting upon them. We have nothing else to trust. And to confuse this trusting with believing an emotive description of them is a mistake which all traditional codes of morality encourage us to commit.

The significance of such similar disasters in the work of poets so unlike and yet so greatly gifted as Mr. Yeats and Mr. Lawrence is noteworthy. For each the traditional scaffolding of conventional beliefs has proved unsatisfying, unworkable as a basis for their attitudes. Each has sought, in very different directions it is true, a new set of beliefs as a remedy. For neither has the world-picture of science seemed a possible substitute. And neither seems to have envisaged the possibility of a poetry which is independent of all beliefs, probably because, however much they differ, both are very serious poets. A great deal of poetry can, of course, be written for which total independence of all beliefs is an easy matter. But it is never poetry of the more important kind, because the temptation to introduce beliefs is a sign and measure of the importance of the attitudes involved. At present it is not primarily religious beliefs, in the stricter sense of the word, which are most likely to be concerned. Emphases alter surprisingly. University societies founded fifteen years ago, for example, to discuss religion, are usually found to be discussing sex to-day. And serious love poetry, which is independent of beliefs of one kind or another, traditional or eccentric, is extremely rare.

Yet the necessity for independence is increasing. This is not to say that traditional poetry, into which beliefs readily enter, is becoming obsolete; it is merely becoming more and more difficult to approach without confusion; it demands a greater imaginative effort, a greater purity in the reader.

We must distinguish here, however. There are many feelings and attitudes which, though in the past supported by beliefs now untenable, can survive their removal because they have other, more natural, supports and spring directly from the necessities of existence. To the extent to which they have been undistorted by the beliefs which have gathered round them they will remain as before. But there are other attitudes which are very largely the product of belief

and have no other support. These will lapse if the changes here forecast continue. With their disappearance some forms of poetry—much minor devotional verse, for example—will become obsolete. And with the unravelling of the intellect *versus* emotion entanglement, there will be cases where even literature to which immense value has been assigned—the speculative portions of the work of Dostoevsky may be instanced—will lose much of its interest, except for the history of the mind. It was because he belonged to our age that Dostoevsky had to wrestle so terribly in these toils. A poet to-day, whose integrity is equal to that of the greater poets of the past, is inevitably plagued by the problem of thought and feeling as poets have never been plagued before.

A pioneer in modern research upon the origins of culture was asked recently whether his work had any bearing upon religion. He replied that it had, but that at present he was engaged merely in "getting the guns into position." The same answer might be given with regard to the probable consequences of recent progress in psychology, not only for religion but for the whole fabric of our traditional beliefs about ourselves. In many quarters there is a tendency to suppose that the series of attacks upon received ideas which began, shall we say, with Galileo and rose to a climax with Darwinism, has over-reached itself with Einstein and Eddington, and that the battle is now due to die down. This view seems to be too optimistic. The most dangerous of the sciences is only now beginning to come into action. I am thinking less of Psycho-analysis or of Behaviourism than of the whole subject which includes them. It is very probable that the Hindenburg Line to which the defence of our traditions retired as a result of the onslaughts of the last century will be blown up in the near future. If this should happen a mental chaos such as man has never experienced may be expected. We shall then be thrown back, as Matthew Arnold foresaw, upon poetry. It is capable of saving us; it is a perfectly possible means of overcoming chaos. But whether man is capable of the reorientation required, whether he can loosen in time the entanglement with belief which now takes from poetry half its power and would then take all, is another question, and too large for the scope of this essay.

Virginia Woolf

1882–1941

MRS. WOOLF's contribution to the life of British letters was made both as a novelist and as a critic. Of her importance as a novelist a word has already been said in the Introduction above. Her first two books, *The Voyage Out* (1915) and *Night and Day* (1919), were comparatively conventional in form and spirit, but with *Jacob's Room* (1922) there began the series of novels in which she developed her own impressionistic technique for communicating the inner life of her characters, the novels on which her reputation chiefly rests: *Mrs. Dalloway* (1925), *To the Lighthouse* (1927), *The Waves* (1931), *The Years* (1937), and *Between the Acts* (1941). In 1928 she published *Orlando,* a fantasy whose protagonist (no other term is quite so convenient) lives from Elizabethan to modern times without aging but who changes from a young man to a young woman during the process.

As a critic she is best known for the two volumes of essays published during her lifetime, *The Common Reader* (1925) and *The Second Common Reader* (1932)—the two have recently been reprinted in one volume, *The Common Reader.* In these essays a remarkably sure and delicate personal taste ranges over a wide variety of subjects— "The Russian Point of View," "The Strange Elizabethans," "How Should One Read a Book?," "How It Strikes a Contemporary," for example—though the larger number of them deal with fiction and fiction writers. The biographical skill which found expression in certain of these essays was later utilized in a full-length biography of the painter Roger Fry (1940). Her claims that women be given the same opportunities and be taken as seriously as men were stated in *A Room of One's Own* (1929) and *Three Guineas* (1938). Since her death three volumes of hitherto uncollected essays have been published: *The Death of a Moth* (1942), *The Moment* (1947), and *The Captain's Death Bed* (1950). The essay printed below will be found in the last mentioned volume: originally a paper read to The Heretics at Cambridge on May 18, 1924, it was first published as one of the Hogarth Essays in the same year.

Virginia Woolf, who was the daughter of Leslie Stephen, the late Victorian critic, had married Leonard Woolf in 1912. In 1917 they had started the Hogarth Press, working with a hand press in Hogarth House, Richmond. *Monday or Tuesday* (1921), a collection of short stories and sketches by Mrs. Woolf, and *Kew Gardens,* a short fantasy, both illustrated with woodcuts by her sister, Vanessa Bell, are characteristic products of this interesting and important press in its early days. For several years now the Hogarth Press has operated on a full commercial scale, but it has never lost the reputation for integrity of taste which it earned when it was the Woolfs' personal enterprise.

Since Virginia Woolf's death on April 3, 1941, a number of studies of her work have appeared. None is better than an essay by E. M. Forster, *Virginia Woolf,* originally delivered as the Rede Lecture at Cambridge in 1942. Two full-length studies may also be mentioned, *Virginia Woolf: Her Art as a Novelist,* by Joan Bennett (1945), and *The Novels of Virginia Woolf,* by R. L. Chambers (1948).

MR. BENNETT AND MRS. BROWN[1]

IT seems to me possible, perhaps desirable, that I may be the only person in this room who has committed the folly of writing, trying to write, or failing to write, a novel. And when I asked myself, as your invitation to speak to you about modern fiction made me ask myself, what demon whispered in my ear and urged me to my doom, a little figure rose before me—the figure of a man, or of a woman, who said, "My name is Brown. Catch me if you can."

Most novelists have the same experience. Some Brown, Smith, or Jones comes before them and says in the most seductive and charming way in the world, "Come and catch me if you can." And so, led on by this will-o'-the-wisp, they flounder through volume after volume, spending the best years of their lives in the pursuit, and receiving for the most part very little cash in exchange. Few catch the phantom; most have to be content with a scrap of her dress or a wisp of her hair.

My belief that men and women write novels because they are lured on to create some character

[1] From *The Captain's Death Bed and Other Essays* by Virginia Woolf, copyright, 1950, by Harcourt, Brace and Company, Inc.

which has thus imposed itself upon them has the sanction of Mr. Arnold Bennett. In an article from which I will quote he says, "The foundation of good fiction is character-creating and nothing else. . . . Style counts; plot counts; originality of outlook counts. But none of these counts anything like so much as the convincingness of the characters. If the characters are real the novel will have a chance; if they are not, oblivion will be its portion. . . ." And he goes on to draw the conclusion that we have no young novelists of first-rate importance at the present moment, because they are unable to create characters that are real, true, and convincing.

These are the questions that I want with greater boldness than discretion to discuss to-night. I want to make out what we mean when we talk about "character" in fiction; to say something about the question of reality which Mr. Bennett raises; and to suggest some reasons why the younger novelists fail to create characters, if, as Mr. Bennett asserts, it is true that fail they do. This will lead me, I am well aware, to make some very sweeping and some very vague assertions. For the question is an extremely difficult one. Think how little we know about character—think how little we know about art. But, to make a clearance before I begin, I will suggest that we range Edwardians and Georgians into two camps; Mr. Wells, Mr. Bennett, and Mr. Galsworthy I will call the Edwardians; Mr. Forster, Mr. Lawrence, Mr. Strachey, Mr. Joyce, and Mr. Eliot I will call the Georgians. And if I speak in the first person, with intolerable egotism, I will ask you to excuse me. I do not want to attribute to the world at large the opinions of one solitary, ill-informed, and misguided individual.

My first assertion is one that I think you will grant—that every one in this room is a judge of character. Indeed it would be impossible to live for a year without disaster unless one practised character-reading and had some skill in the art. Our marriages, our friendships depend on it; our business largely depends on it; every day questions arise which can only be solved by its help. And now I will hazard a second assertion, which is more disputable perhaps, to the effect that in or about December, 1910, human character changed.

I am not saying that one went out, as one might into a garden, and there saw that a rose had flowered, or that a hen had laid an egg. The change was not sudden and definite like that. But a change there was, nevertheless; and, since one must be arbitrary, let us date it about the year 1910. The first signs of it are recorded in the books of Samuel Butler, in *The Way of All Flesh* in particular; the plays of Bernard Shaw continue to record it. In life one can see the change, if I may use a homely illustration, in the character of one's cook. The Victorian cook lived like a leviathan in the lower depths, formidable, silent, obscure, inscrutable; the Georgian cook is a creature of sunshine and fresh air; in and out of the drawing-room, now to borrow the *Daily Herald,* now to ask advice about a hat. Do you ask for more solemn instances of the power of the human race to change? Read the *Agamemnon,* and see whether, in process of time, your sympathies are not almost entirely with Clytemnestra. Or consider the married life of the Carlyles and bewail the waste, the futility, for him and for her, of the horrible domestic tradition which made it seemly for a woman of genius to spend her time chasing beetles, scouring saucepans, instead of writing books. All human relations have shifted—those between masters and servants, husbands and wives, parents and children. And when human relations change there is at the same time a change in religion, conduct, politics, and literature. Let us agree to place one of these changes about the year 1910.

I have said that people have to acquire a good deal of skill in character-reading if they are to live a single year of life without disaster. But it is the art of the young. In middle age and in old age the art is practised mostly for its uses, and friendships and other adventures and experiments in the art of reading character are seldom made. But novelists differ from the rest of the world because they do not cease to be interested in character when they have learnt enough about it for practical purposes. They go a step further, they feel that there is something permanently interesting in character in itself. When all the practical business of life has been discharged, there is something about people which continues to seem to them of overwhelming importance, in spite of the fact that it has no bearing whatever upon their happiness, comfort, or income. The study of character becomes to them an absorbing pursuit; to impart character an obsession. And this I find it very difficult to explain: what novelists mean when they talk about character, what the impulse is that urges them so powerfully every now and then to embody their view in writing.

So, if you will allow me, instead of analysing and abstracting, I will tell you a simple story which, however pointless, has the merit of being true, of a journey from Richmond to Waterloo, in the hope that I may show you what I mean by character in itself; that you may realize the different aspects it can wear; and the hideous perils that beset you directly you try to describe it in words.

One night some weeks ago, then, I was late for the train and jumped into the first carriage I came to. As I sat down I had the strange and uncomfortable feeling that I was interrupting a conversation between two people who were already sitting there. Not that they were young or happy. Far from it. They were both elderly, the woman over sixty, the man well over forty. They were sitting opposite each other, and the man, who had been leaning over and talking emphatically to judge by his attitude and the flush on his face, sat back and became silent. I had disturbed him, and he was annoyed. The elderly lady, however, whom I will call Mrs. Brown, seemed rather relieved. She was one of those clean, threadbare old ladies whose extreme tidiness—everything buttoned, fastened, tied together, mended and brushed up— suggests more extreme poverty than rags and dirt. There was something pinched about her—a look of suffering, of apprehension, and, in addition, she was extremely small. Her feet, in their clean little boots, scarcely touched the floor. I felt that she had nobody to support her; that she had to make up her mind for herself; that, having been deserted, or left a widow, years ago, she had led an anxious, harried life, bringing up an only son, perhaps, who, as likely as not, was by this time beginning to go to the bad. All this shot through my mind as I sat down, being uncomfortable, like most people, at travelling with fellow passengers unless I have somehow or other accounted for them. Then I looked at the man. He was no relation of Mrs. Brown's I felt sure; he was of a bigger, burlier, less refined type. He was a man of business I imagined, very likely a respectable corn-chandler from the North, dressed in good blue serge with a pocket-knife and a silk handkerchief, and a stout leather bag. Obviously, however, he had an unpleasant business to settle with Mrs. Brown; a secret, perhaps sinister business, which they did not intend to discuss in my presence.

"Yes, the Crofts have had very bad luck with their servants," Mr. Smith (as I will call him) said in a considering way, going back to some earlier topic, with a view to keeping up appearances.

"Ah, poor people," said Mrs. Brown, a trifle condescendingly. "My grandmother had a maid who came when she was fifteen and stayed till she was eighty" (this was said with a kind of hurt and aggressive pride to impress us both perhaps).

"One doesn't often come across that sort of thing nowadays," said Mr. Smith in conciliatory tones.

Then they were silent.

"It's odd they don't start a golf club there—I should have thought one of the young fellows would," said

Mr. Smith, for the silence obviously made him uneasy.

Mrs. Brown hardly took the trouble to answer.

"What changes they're making in this part of the world," said Mr. Smith looking out of the window, and looking furtively at me as he did so.

It was plain, from Mrs. Brown's silence, from the uneasy affability with which Mr. Smith spoke, that he had some power over her which he was exerting disagreeably. It might have been her son's downfall, or some painful episode in her past life, or her daughter's. Perhaps she was going to London to sign some document to make over some property. Obviously against her will she was in Mr. Smith's hands. I was beginning to feel a great deal of pity for her, when she said, suddenly and inconsequently:

"Can you tell me if an oak-tree dies when the leaves have been eaten for two years in succession by caterpillars?"

She spoke quite brightly, and rather precisely, in a cultivated, inquisitive voice.

Mr. Smith was startled, but relieved to have a safe topic of conversation given him. He told her a great deal very quickly about plagues of insects. He told her that he had a brother who kept a fruit farm in Kent. He told her what fruit farmers do every year in Kent, and so on, and so on. While he talked a very odd thing happened. Mrs. Brown took out her little white handkerchief and began to dab her eyes. She was crying. But she went on listening quite composedly to what he was saying, and he went on talking, a little louder, a little angrily, as if he had seen her cry often before; as if it were a painful habit. At last it got on his nerves. He stopped abruptly, looked out of the window, then leant towards her as he had been doing when I got in, and said in a bullying, menacing way, as if he would not stand any more nonsense:

"So about that matter we were discussing. It'll be all right? George will be there on Tuesday?"

"We shan't be late," said Mrs. Brown, gathering herself together with superb dignity.

Mr. Smith said nothing. He got up, buttoned his coat, reached his bag down, and jumped out of the train before it had stopped at Clapham Junction. He had got what he wanted, but he was ashamed of himself; he was glad to get out of the old lady's sight.

Mrs. Brown and I were left alone together. She sat in her corner opposite, very clean, very small, rather queer, and suffering intensely. The impression she made was overwhelming. It came pouring out like a draught, like a smell of burning. What was it composed of—that overwhelming and peculiar impression? Myriads of irrelevant and incongruous ideas crowd into one's head on such occasions; one sees the person, one sees Mrs. Brown, in the centre of all sorts of different scenes. I thought of her in a seaside house, among queer ornaments: sea-urchins, models of ships in glass cases. Her husband's medals were on the mantelpiece. She popped in and out of the room, perching on the edges of chairs, picking meals out of saucers, indulging in long, silent stares. The caterpillars and the oak-trees seemed to imply all that. And then, into this fantastic and secluded life, in broke Mr. Smith. I saw him blowing in, so to speak, on a windy day. He banged, he slammed. His dripping umbrella made a pool in the hall. They sat closeted together.

And then Mrs. Brown faced the dreadful revelation. She took her heroic decision. Early, before dawn, she packed her bag and carried it herself to the station. She would not let Smith touch it. She was wounded in her pride, unmoored from her anchorage; she came of gentlefolks who kept servants—but details could wait. The important thing was to realize her character, to steep oneself in her atmosphere. I had no time to explain why I felt it somewhat tragic, heroic, yet with a dash of the flighty, and fantastic, before the train stopped, and I watched her disappear, carrying her bag, into the vast blazing station. She looked very small, very tenacious; at once very frail and very heroic. And I have never seen her again, and I shall never know what became of her.

The story ends without any point to it. But I have not told you this anecdote to illustrate either my own ingenuity or the pleasure of travelling from Richmond to Waterloo. What I want you to see in it is this. Here is a character imposing itself upon another person. Here is Mrs. Brown making someone begin almost automatically to write a novel about her. I believe that all novels begin with an old lady in the corner opposite. I believe that all novels, that is to say, deal with character, and that it is to express character—not to preach doctrines, sing songs, or celebrate the glories of the British Empire, that the form of the novel, so clumsy, verbose, and undramatic, so rich, elastic, and alive, has been evolved. To express character, I have said; but you will at once reflect that the very widest interpretation can be put upon those words. For example, old Mrs. Brown's character will strike you very differently according to the age and country in which you happen to be born. It would be easy enough to write three different versions of that incident in the train, an English, a French, and a Russian. The English writer would make the old lady into a "character"; he would bring out her oddities and mannerisms; her buttons and wrinkles; her ribbons and warts. Her personality would dominate the book. A French writer would rub out all that; he would sacrifice the individual Mrs. Brown to give a more general view of human nature; to make a more abstract, proportioned, and harmonious whole. The Russian would pierce through the flesh; would reveal the soul—the soul alone, wandering out into the Waterloo Road, asking of life some tremendous question which would sound on and on in our ears after the book was finished. And then besides age and country there is the writer's temperament to be considered. You see one thing in character, and I another. You say it means this, and I that. And when it comes to writing, each makes a further selection on principles of his own. Thus Mrs. Brown can be treated in an infinite variety of ways, according to the age, country, and temperament of the writer.

But now I must recall what Mr. Arnold Bennett says. He says that it is only if the characters are real that the novel has any chance of surviving. Otherwise, die it must. But, I ask myself, what is reality? And who are the judges of reality? A character may be real to Mr. Bennett and quite unreal to me. For instance, in this article he says that Dr. Watson in *Sherlock Holmes* is real to him: to me Dr. Watson is a sack stuffed with straw, a dummy, a figure of fun. And so it is with character after character—in book after book. There is nothing that people differ about more than the reality of characters, especially in contemporary books. But if you take a larger view I think that Mr. Bennett is perfectly right. If, that is, you think of the novels which seem to you great novels—*War and Peace, Vanity Fair, Tristram Shandy, Madame Bovary, Pride and Prejudice, The Mayor of Casterbridge, Villette*—if you think of these books, you do at once think of some character who has seemed to you so real (I do not by that mean so lifelike) that it has the power to make you think not merely of it itself, but of all sorts of things through its eyes—of religion, of love, of war, of peace, of family life, of balls in country towns, of sunsets, moonrises, the immortality of the soul. There is hardly any subject of human experience that is left out of *War and Peace* it seems to me. And in all these novels all these great novelists have brought us to see whatever they wish us to see through some character. Otherwise, they would not be novelists; but poets, historians, or pamphleteers.

But now let us examine what Mr. Bennett went on to say—he said that there was no great novelist among the Georgian writers because they cannot create characters who are real, true, and convincing.

And there I cannot agree. There are reasons, excuses, possibilities which I think put a different colour upon the case. It seems so to me at least, but I am well aware that this is a matter about which I am likely to be prejudiced, sanguine, and near-sighted. I will put my view before you in the hope that you will make it impartial, judicial, and broad-minded. Why, then, is it so hard for novelists at present to create characters which seem real, not only to Mr. Bennett, but to the world at large? Why, when October comes round, do the publishers always fail to supply us with a master-piece?

Surely one reason is that the men and women who began writing novels in 1910 or thereabouts had this great difficulty to face—that there was no English novelist living from whom they could learn their business. Mr. Conrad is a Pole; which sets him apart, and makes him, however admirable, not very helpful. Mr. Hardy has written no novel since 1895. The most prominent and successful novelists in the year 1910 were, I suppose, Mr. Wells, Mr. Bennett, and Mr. Galsworthy. Now it seems to me that to go to these men and ask them to teach you how to write a novel—how to create characters that are real—is precisely like going to a bootmaker and asking him to teach you how to make a watch. Do not let me give you the impression that I do not admire and enjoy their books. They seem to me of great value, and indeed of great necessity. There are seasons when it is more important to have boots than to have watches. To drop metaphor, I think that after the creative activity of the Victorian age it was quite necessary, not only for literature but for life, that someone should write the books that Mr. Wells, Mr. Bennett, and Mr. Galsworthy have written. Yet what odd books they are! Sometimes I wonder if we are right to call them books at all. For they leave one with so strange a feeling of incompleteness and dissatisfaction. In order to complete them it seems necessary to do something—to join a society, or, more desperately, to write a cheque. That done, the restlessness is laid, the book finished; it can be put upon the shelf, and need never be read again. But with the work of other novelists it is different. *Tristram Shandy* or *Pride and Prejudice* is complete in itself; it is self-contained; it leaves one with no desire to do anything, except indeed to read the book again, and to understand it better. The difference perhaps is that both Sterne and Jane Austen were interested in things in themselves; in character in itself; in the book in itself. Therefore everything was inside the book, nothing outside. But the Edwardians were never interested in character in itself; or in the book in itself. They were interested in something outside. Their books, then, were incomplete as books, and required that the reader should finish them, actively and practically, for himself.

Perhaps we can make this clearer if we take the liberty of imagining a little party in the railway carriage—Mr. Wells, Mr. Galsworthy, Mr. Bennett are travelling to Waterloo with Mrs. Brown. Mrs. Brown, I have said, was poorly dressed and very small. She had an anxious harassed look. I doubt whether she was what you call an educated woman. Seizing upon all these symptoms of the unsatisfactory condition of our primary schools with a rapidity to which I can do no justice, Mr. Wells would instantly project upon the window-pane a vision of a better, breezier, jollier, happier, more adventurous and gallant world, where these musty railway carriages and fusty old women do not exist; where miraculous barges bring tropical fruit to Camberwell by eight o'clock in the morning; where there are public nurseries, fountains, and libraries, dining-rooms, drawing-rooms, and marriages; where every citizen is generous and candid, manly and magnificent, and rather like Mr. Wells himself. But nobody is in the least like Mrs. Brown. There are no Mrs. Browns in Utopia. Indeed I do not think that Mr. Wells, in his passion to make her what she ought to be, would waste a thought upon her as she is. And what would Mr. Galsworthy see? Can we doubt that the walls of Doulton's factory would take his fancy? There are women in that factory who make twenty-five dozen earthenware pots every day. There are mothers in the Mile End Road who depend upon the farthings which those women earn. But there are employers in Surrey who are even now smoking rich cigars while the nightingale sings. Burning with indignation, stuffed with information, arraigning civilization, Mr. Galsworthy would only see in Mrs. Brown a pot broken on the wheel and thrown into the corner.

Mr. Bennett, alone of the Edwardians, would keep his eyes in the carriage. He, indeed, would observe every detail with immense care. He would notice the advertisements; the pictures of Swanage and Portsmouth; the way in which the cushion bulged between the buttons; how Mrs. Brown wore a brooch which had cost three-and-ten-three at Whitworth's bazaar; and had mended both gloves—indeed the thumb of the left-hand glove had been replaced. And he would observe, at length, how this was the non-stop train from Windsor which calls at Richmond for the convenience of middle-class residents, who can afford to go to the theatre but have not reached the social rank which can afford motorcars, though it is true, there are occasions (he would tell us what) when they hire them from a company (he would tell us which). And so he would gradually sidle sedately towards Mrs. Brown, and would remark how she had been left a little copyhold, not freehold, property at Datchet, which, however, was mortgaged to Mr. Bungay the solicitor—but why should I presume to invent Mr. Bennett? Does not Mr. Bennett write novels himself? I will open the first book that chance puts in my way—*Hilda Lessways*. Let us see how he makes us feel that Hilda is real, true, and convincing, as a novelist should. She shut the door in a soft, controlled way, which showed the constraint of her relations with her mother. She was fond of reading *Maud;* she was endowed with the power to feel intensely. So far, so good; in his leisurely, surefooted way Mr. Bennett is trying in these first pages, where every touch is important, to show us the kind of girl she was.

But then he begins to describe, not Hilda Lessways, but the view from her bedroom window, the excuse being that Mr. Skellorn, the man who collects rents, is coming along that way. Mr. Bennett proceeds:

"The bailiwick of Turnhill lay behind her; and all the murky district of the Five Towns, of which Turnhill is the northern outpost, lay to the south. At the foot of Chatterley Wood the canal wound in large curves on its way towards the undefiled plains of Cheshire and the sea. On the canal-side, exactly opposite to Hilda's window, was a flour-mill, that sometimes made nearly as much smoke as the kilns and the chimneys closing the prospect on either hand. From the flour-mill a bricked path, which separated a considerable row of new cottages from their appurtenant gardens, led straight into Lessways Street, in front of Mrs. Lessway's house. By this path Mr. Skellorn should have arrived, for he inhabited the farthest of the cottages."

One line of insight would have done more than all those lines of description; but let them pass as the necessary drudgery of the novelist. And now—where is Hilda? Alas. Hilda is still looking out of the window. Passionate and dissatisfied as she was, she was a girl with an eye for houses. She often compared this old Mr. Skellorn with the villas she saw from her bedroom window. Therefore the villas must be described. Mr. Bennett proceeds:

"The row was called Freehold Villas: a consciously proud name in a district where much of the land was copyhold and could only change owners subject to the payment of 'fines,' and to the feudal consent of a 'court' presided over by the agent of a lord of the manor. Most of the dwellings were owned by their occupiers, who, each an absolute monarch of the soil, niggled in his sooty garden of an evening amid the flutter of drying shirts

and towels. Freehold Villas symbolized the final triumph of Victorian economics, the apotheosis of the prudent and industrious artisan. It corresponded with a Building Society Secretary's dream of paradise. And indeed it was a very real achievement. Nevertheless, Hilda's irrational contempt would not admit this."

Heaven be praised, we cry! At last we are coming to Hilda herself. But not so fast. Hilda may have been this, that, and the other; but Hilda not only looked at houses, and thought of houses; Hilda lived in a house. And what sort of a house did Hilda live in? Mr. Bennett proceeds:

"It was one of the two middle houses of a detached terrace of four houses built by her grandfather Lessways, the teapot manufacturer; it was the chief of the four, obviously the habitation of the proprietor of the terrace. One of the corner houses comprised a grocer's shop, and this house had been robbed of its just proportion of garden so that the seigneurial garden-plot might be triflingly larger than the other. The terrace was not a terrace of cottages, but of houses rated at from twenty-six to thirty-six pounds a year; beyond the means of artisans and petty insurance agents and rent-collectors. And further, it was well-built, generously built; and its architecture, though debased, showed some faint traces of Georgian amenity. It was admittedly the best row of houses in that newly-settled quarter of the town. In coming to it out of Freehold Villas Mr. Skellorn obviously came to something superior, wider, more liberal. Suddenly Hilda heard her mother's voice. . . ."

But we cannot hear her mother's voice, or Hilda's voice; we can only hear Mr. Bennett's voice telling us facts about rents and freeholds and copyholds and fines. What can Mr. Bennett be about? I have formed my own opinion of what Mr. Bennett is about—he is trying to make us imagine for him; he is trying to hypnotize us into the belief that, because he has made a house, there must be a person living there. With all his powers of observation, which are marvellous, with all his sympathy and humanity, which are great, Mr. Bennett has never once looked at Mrs. Brown in her corner. There she sits in the corner of the carriage —that carriage which is travelling, not from Richmond to Waterloo, but from one age of English literature to the next, for Mrs. Brown is eternal, Mrs. Brown is human nature, Mrs. Brown changes only on the surface, it is the novelists who get in and out— there she sits and not one of the Edwardian writers has so much as looked at her. They have looked very powerfully, searchingly, and sympathetically out of the window; at factories, at Utopias, even at the decoration and upholstery of the carriage; but never at her, never at life, never at human nature. And so they have developed a technique of novel-writing which suits their purpose; they have made tools and established conventions which do their business. But those tools are not our tools, and that business is not our business. For us those conventions are ruin, those tools are death.

You may well complain of the vagueness of my language. What is a convention, a tool, you may ask, and what do you mean by saying that Mr. Bennett's and Mr. Wells's and Mr. Galsworthy's conventions are the wrong conventions for the Georgians? The question is difficult: I will attempt a short cut. A convention in writing is not much different from a convention in manners. Both in life and in literature it is necessary to have some means of bridging the gulf between the hostess and her unknown guest on the one hand, the writer and his unknown reader on the other. The hostess bethinks her of the weather, for generations of hostesses have established the fact that this is a subject of universal interest in which we all believe. She begins by saying that we are having a wretched May, and, having thus got into touch with her unknown guest, proceeds to matters of greater interest. So it is in literature. The writer must get into touch with his reader by putting before him something which he recognizes, which therefore stimulates his imagination, and makes him willing to co-operate in the far more difficult business of intimacy. And it is of the highest importance that this common meeting-place should be reached easily, almost instinctively, in the dark, with one's eyes shut. Here is Mr. Bennett making use of this common ground in the passage which I have quoted. The problem before him was to make us believe in the reality of Hilda Lessways. So he began, being an Edwardian, by describing accurately and minutely the sort of house Hilda lived in, and the sort of house she saw from the window. House property was the common ground from which the Edwardians found it easy to proceed to intimacy. Indirect as it seems to us, the convention worked admirably, and thousands of Hilda Lessways were launched upon the world by this means. For that age and generation, the convention was a good one.

But now, if you will allow me to pull my own anecdote to pieces, you will see how keenly I felt the lack of a convention, and how serious a matter it is when the tools of one generation are useless for the next. The incident had made a great impression on me. But how was I to transmit it to you? All I could do was to report as accurately as I could what was said, to describe in detail what was worn, to say, despairingly, that all sorts of scenes rushed into my mind, to proceed to tumble them out pell-mell, and to describe this vivid, this overmastering impression by likening it to a draught or a smell of burning. To tell you the truth, I was also strongly tempted to manufacture a three-volume novel about the old lady's son, and his adventures crossing the Atlantic, and her daughter, and how she kept a milliner's shop in Westminster, the past life of Smith himself, and his house at Sheffield, though such stories seem to me the most dreary, irrelevant, and humbugging affairs in the world.

But if I had done that I should have escaped the appalling effort of saying what I meant. And to have got at what I meant I should have had to go back and back and back; to experiment with one thing and another; to try this sentence and that, referring each word to my vision, matching it as exactly as possible, and knowing that somehow I had to find a common ground between us, a convention which would not seem to you too odd, unreal, and farfetched to believe in. I admit that I shirked that arduous undertaking. I let my Mrs. Brown slip through my fingers. I have told you nothing whatever about her. But that is partly the great Edwardians' fault. I asked them—they are my elders and betters—How shall I begin to describe this woman's character? And they said: "Begin by saying that her father kept a shop in Harrogate. Ascertain the rent. Ascertain the wages of shop assistants in the year 1878. Discover what her mother died of. Describe cancer. Describe calico. Describe—" But I cried: "Stop! Stop!" And I regret to say that I threw that ugly, that clumsy, that incongruous tool out of the window, for I knew that if I began describing the cancer and the calico, my Mrs. Brown, that vision to which I cling though I know no way of imparting it to you, would have been dulled and tarnished and vanished for ever.

That is what I mean by saying that the Edwardian tools are the wrong ones for us to use. They have laid an enormous stress upon the fabric of things. They have given us a house in the hope that we may be able to deduce the human beings who live there. To give them their due, they have made that house much better worth living in. But if you hold that novels are in the first place about people, and only in the second about the houses they live in, that is the wrong way to set about it. Therefore, you see, the Georgian writer had to begin by throwing away the method that was in use at the moment. He was left alone there facing Mrs. Brown without any method of conveying her to the reader. But that is inaccurate. A writer is never alone. There is always the public with him— if not on the same seat, at least in the compartment next door. Now the public is a strange travelling companion. In England it is a very suggestible and docile creature, which, once you get it to attend, will believe implicitly what it is told for a certain number of years. If you say to the public with sufficient conviction: "All women have tails, and all men humps," it will actually learn to see women with tails and men with humps, and will think it very revolutionary and probably improper if you say: "Nonsense. Monkeys have tails and camels humps. But men and women have brains, and they have hearts; they think and they feel,"—that will seem to it a bad joke, and an improper one into the bargain.

But to return. Here is the British public sitting by the writer's side and saying in its vast and unanimous way, "Old women have houses. They have fathers. They have incomes. They have servants. They have hot-water bottles. That is how we know that they are old women. Mr. Wells and Mr. Bennett and Mr. Galsworthy have always taught us that this is the way to recognize them. But now with your Mrs. Brown—how are we to believe in her? We do not even know whether her villa was called Albert or Balmoral; what she paid for her gloves; or whether her mother died of cancer or of consumption. How can she be alive? No; she is a mere figment of your imagination."

And old women of course ought to be made of freehold villas and copyhold estates, not of imagination.

The Georgian novelist, therefore, was in an awkward predicament. There was Mrs. Brown protesting that she was different, quite different, from what people made out, and luring the novelist to her rescue by the most fascinating if fleeting glimpse of her charms; there were the Edwardians handing out tools appropriate to house building and house breaking; and there was the British public asseverating that they must see the hot-water bottle first. Meanwhile the train was rushing to that station where we must all get out.

Such, I think, was the predicament in which the young Georgians found themselves about the year 1910. Many of them—I am thinking of Mr. Forster and Mr. Lawrence in particular—spoilt their early work because, instead of throwing away those tools, they tried to use them. They tried to compromise. They tried to combine their own direct sense of the oddity and significance of some character with Mr. Galsworthy's knowledge of the Factory Acts, and Mr. Bennett's knowledge of the Five Towns. They tried it, but they had too keen, too overpowering a sense of Mrs. Brown and her peculiarities to go on trying it much longer. Something had to be done. At whatever cost of life, limb, and damage to valuable property Mrs. Brown must be rescued, expressed, and set in her high relations to the world

before the train stopped and she disappeared for ever. And so the smashing and the crashing began. Thus it is that we hear all round us, in poems and novels and biographies, even in newspaper articles and essays, the sound of breaking and falling, crashing and destruction. It is the prevailing sound of the Georgian age—rather a melancholy one if you think what melodious days there have been in the past, if you think of Shakespeare and Milton and Keats or even of Jane Austen and Thackeray and Dickens; if you think of the language, and the heights to which it can soar when free, and see the same eagle captive, bald, and croaking.

In view of these facts—with these sounds in my ears and these fancies in my brain—I am not going to deny that Mr. Bennett has some reason when he complains that our Georgian writers are unable to make us believe that our characters are real. I am forced to agree that they do not pour out three immortal masterpieces with Victorian regularity every autumn. But, instead of being gloomy, I am sanguine. For this state of things is, I think, inevitable whenever from hoar old age or callow youth the convention ceases to be a means of communication between writer and reader, and becomes instead an obstacle and an impediment. At the present moment we are suffering, not from decay, but from having no code of manners which writers and readers accept as a prelude to the more exciting intercourse of friendship. The literary convention of the time is so artificial —you have to talk about the weather and nothing but the weather throughout the entire visit—that, naturally, the feeble are tempted to outrage, and the strong are led to destroy the very foundations and rules of literary society. Signs of this are everywhere apparent. Grammar is violated; syntax disintegrated; as a boy staying with an aunt for the week-end rolls in the geranium bed out of sheer desperation as the solemnities of the sabbath wear on. The more adult writers do not, of course, indulge in such wanton exhibitions of spleen. Their sincerity is desperate, and their courage tremendous; it is only that they do not know which to use, a fork or their fingers. Thus, if you read Mr. Joyce and Mr. Eliot you will be struck by the indecency of the one, and the obscurity of the other. Mr. Joyce's indecency in *Ulysses* seems to me the conscious and calculated indecency of a desperate man who feels that in order to breathe he must break the windows. At moments, when the window is broken, he is magnificent. But what a waste of energy! And, after all, how dull indecency is, when it is not the overflowing of a superabundant energy or savagery, but the determined and public-spirited act of a man who needs fresh air! Again, with the obscurity of Mr. Eliot. I think that Mr. Eliot has written some of the loveliest single lines in modern poetry. But how intolerant he is of the old usages and politenesses of society—respect for the weak, consideration for the dull! As I sun myself upon the intense and ravishing beauty of one of his lines, and reflect that I must make a dizzy and dangerous leap to the next, and so on from line to line, like an acrobat flying precariously from bar to bar, I cry out, I confess, for the old decorums, and envy the indolence of my ancestors who, instead of spinning madly through mid-air, dreamt quietly in the shade with a book. Again, in Mr. Strachey's books, *Eminent Victorians* and *Queen Victoria,* the effort and strain of writing against the grain and current of the times is visible too. It is much less visible, of course, for not only is he dealing with facts, which are stubborn things, but he has fabricated, chiefly from eighteenth-century material, a very discreet code of manners of his own, which allows him to sit at table with the highest in the land and to say a great many things under cover of that exquisite apparel which, had they gone naked, would have been chased by the men-servants from the room. Still, if you compare *Eminent Victorians* with some of Lord Macaulay's essays, though you will feel that Lord Macaulay is always wrong, and Mr. Strachey always right, you will also feel a body, a sweep, a richness in Lord Macaulay's essays which show that his age was behind him; all his strength went straight into his work; none was used for purposes of concealment or of conversion. But Mr. Strachey has had to open our eyes before he made us see; he has had to search out and sew together a very artful manner of speech; and the effort, beautifully though it is concealed, has robbed his work of some of the force that should have gone into it, and limited his scope.

For these reasons, then, we must reconcile ourselves to a season of failures and fragments. We must reflect that where so much strength is spent on finding a way of telling the truth, the truth itself is bound to reach us in rather an exhausted and chaotic condition. Ulysses, Queen Victoria, Mr. Prufrock—to give Mrs. Brown some of the names she has made famous lately —is a little pale and dishevelled by the time her rescuers reach her. And it is the sound of their axes that we hear—a vigorous and stimulating sound in my ears—unless of course you wish to sleep, when, in the bounty of his concern, Providence has provided a host of writers anxious and able to satisfy your needs.

Thus I have tried, at tedious length, I fear, to answer some of the questions which I began by asking. I have given an account of some of the difficulties which in my view beset the Georgian writer in all his forms. I have sought to excuse him. May I end by venturing to remind you of the duties and responsibilities that are yours as partners in this business of writing books, as companions in the railway carriage, as fellow travellers with Mrs. Brown? For she is just as visible to you who remain silent as to us who tell stories about her. In the course of your daily life this past week you have had far stranger and more interesting experiences than the one I have tried to describe. You have overheard scraps of talk that filled you with amazement. You have gone to bed at night bewildered by the complexity of your feelings. In one day thousands of ideas have coursed through your brains; thousands of emotions have met, collided, and disappeared in astonishing disorder. Nevertheless, you allow the writers to palm off upon you a version of all this, an image of Mrs. Brown, which has no likeness to that surprising apparition whatsoever. In your modesty you seem to consider that writers are of different blood and bone from yourselves; that they know more of Mrs. Brown than you do. Never was there a more fatal mistake. It is this division between reader and writer, this humility on your part, these professional airs and graces on ours, that corrupt and emasculate the books which should be the healthy offspring of a close and equal alliance between us. Hence spring those sleek, smooth novels, those portentous and ridiculous biographies, that milk and watery criticism, those poems melodiously celebrating the innocence of roses and sheep which pass so plausibly for literature at the present time.

Your part is to insist that writers shall come down off their plinths and pedestals, and describe beautifully if possible, truthfully at any rate, our Mrs. Brown. You should insist that she is an old lady of unlimited capacity and infinite variety; capable of appearing in any place; wearing any dress; saying anything and doing heaven knows what. But the things she says and the things she does and her eyes and her nose and her speech and her silence have an overwhelming fascination, for she is, of course, the spirit we live by, life itself.

But do not expect just at present a complete and satisfactory presentment of her. Tolerate the spasmodic, the obscure, the fragmentary, the failure. Your help is invoked in a good cause. For I will make one final and surpassingly rash prediction—we are trembling on the verge of one of the great ages of English literature. But it can only be reached if we are determined never, never to desert Mrs. Brown.

James Joyce

1882–1941

JAMES JOYCE was born on February 2, 1882, in the Dublin suburb of Rathgar. Like Stephen Dedalus, the hero of his closely autobiographical first novel, *A Portrait of the Artist as a Young Man* (1916), he had his first schooling at Clongowes Wood College, where he was sent at the age of six and where he remained until 1891. In 1893 he went to Belvedere College, Dublin, another Jesuit school (Herbert Gorman remarks, in the biography of Joyce to which I am indebted for these facts about Joyce's early training, that he was to be educated by Jesuits until he was twenty), and in 1898 to University College, Dublin, where he studied for four years under the Faculty of Arts. *A Portrait of the Artist as a Young Man* gives a remarkably full and intensely wrought picture of Joyce's development up to the time he left Ireland for the first time in 1902, to go to Paris. "When the soul of a man is born in this country," Stephen Dedalus says, "there are nets flung at it to hold it back from flight. You talk to me of nationality, language, religion. I shall try to fly by those nets." Stephen's tutelary figure becomes an image of Daedalus fleeing from the Cretan labyrinth on the wings of his own artifice: ". . . He seemed to hear the noise of dim waves and to see a winged form flying above the waves and slowly climbing the air. What did it mean? Was it a quaint device opening a page of some medieval book of prophecies and symbols, a hawklike man flying sunward above the sea, a prophecy of the end he had been born to serve and had been following through the mists of childhood and boyhood, a symbol of the artist forging anew in his workshop out of the sluggish matter of the earth a new soaring impalpable imperishable being?" The novel ends as Stephen prepares to leave for Paris—"I go to encounter for the millionth time the reality of experience and to forge in the smithy of my soul the uncreated conscience of my race"; and its last sentence is a supplication to Daedalus—"Old father, old artificer, stand me now and ever in good stead."

The hand-to-mouth existence which Joyce led in Paris during the winter and spring of 1902–3 was brought to an end by a telegram—"Mother dying come home father"—received on Good Friday, 1903. He remained in Dublin until October 8, 1904, when he left it again, with his newly married wife, to take up a new life on the Continent. His life in Dublin during the interim is variously described, implied, or referred to in his second novel, *Ulysses* (Paris, 1922), whose entire action takes place in Dublin on June 16, 1904. With the exception of brief necessary visits to Ireland, the last of which ended in

September, 1912, the remaining years of Joyce's life were passed on the Continent: in Trieste; in Rome for a while; in Zurich, where he supported himself and his family by teaching languages; finally in Paris, where he was able to devote himself exclusively to writing. He died in 1941.

The commanding position which Joyce occupied in the world of letters between the two wars was first and foremost a result of the aims he realized, and the startling, varied techniques by which he realized them, in his two most ambitious novels, *Ulysses* and *Finnegans Wake* (1939). But these brilliant performances should not make us forget his earliest work of fiction, *Dubliners*, a collection of short stories ready for publication in 1905 which, because of unwarranted difficulties with censorship both in Dublin and in London, was not published until 1914. Each of these stories reveals the life of a citizen of Dublin, with the utmost economy and rightness of form: "My intention," Joyce said in a letter to Grant Richards, "was to write a chapter of the moral history of my country and I chose Dublin for the scene because that city seemed to me the centre of paralysis. . . . I have written it for the most part in a style of scrupulous meanness and with the conviction that he is a very bold man who dares to alter in the presentment, still more to deform, whatever he has seen and heard." The "scrupulous meanness," the precisely faithful rendering of Dublin life as he had seen and heard it, with no gratuitous false emphasis, produced a group of stories in which no word could be changed without damaging the taut fabric of the whole. Sometimes, as in the longest of the stories, "The Dead," reprinted below, an individual consciousness will soar in self-realization above the level inconscient mean, and then the prose soars with it, as at the end of "The Dead." The stories in *Dubliners* may be compared with the stories of Chekhov more appropriately than with those of any other writer, but in the end they are incomparable; there is a mood, experienced by the reader who has once come under the spell of their quiet power and precise beauty, when they seem, quite simply, to be the most perfect stories in English.

Herbert Gorman's *James Joyce* (1939) is invaluable as a fully detailed account of Joyce's life. The best and most generally useful of the critical studies is *James Joyce: A Critical Introduction* (1941), by Harry Levin. Stuart Gilbert's *James Joyce's "Ulysses": A Study* (1931) is still standard equipment for readers of *Ulysses,* especially for those approaching it for the first time.

THE DEAD[1]

LILY, the caretaker's daughter, was literally run off her feet. Hardly had she brought one gentleman into the little pantry behind the office on the ground floor and helped him off with his overcoat than the wheezy hall-door bell clanged again and she had to scamper along the bare hallway to let in another guest. It was well for her she had not to attend to the ladies also. But Miss Kate and Miss Julia had thought of that and had converted the bathroom upstairs into a ladies' dressing-room. Miss Kate and Miss Julia were there, gossiping and laughing and fussing, walking after each other to the head of the stairs, peering down over the banisters and calling down to Lily to ask her who had come.

It was always a great affair, the Misses Morkan's annual dance. Everybody who knew them came to it, members of the family, old friends of the family, the members of Julia's choir, any of Kate's pupils that were grown up enough, and even some of Mary Jane's pupils too. Never once had it fallen flat. For years and years it had gone off in splendid style, as long as anyone could remember; ever since Kate and Julia, after the death of their brother Pat, had left the house in Stoney Batter and taken Mary Jane, their only niece, to live with them in the dark, gaunt house on Usher's Island, the upper part of which they had rented from Mr. Fulham, the corn-factor on the ground floor. That was a good thirty years ago if it was a day. Mary Jane, who was then a little girl in short clothes, was now the main prop of the household, for she had the organ in Haddington Road. She had been through the Academy and gave a pupils' concert every year in the upper room of the Antient Concert Rooms. Many of her pupils belonged to the better-class families on the Kingstown and Dalkey line. Old as they were, her aunts also did their share. Julia, though she was quite grey, was still the leading soprano in Adam and Eve's, and Kate, being too feeble to go about much, gave music lessons to beginners on the old square piano in the back room. Lily, the caretaker's daughter, did housemaid's work for them. Though their life was modest, they believed in eating well; the best of everything: diamond-bone sirloins, three-shilling tea and the best bottled stout. But Lily seldom made a mistake in the orders, so that she got on well with her three mistresses. They were fussy, that was all. But the only thing they would not stand was back answers.

Of course, they had good reason to be fussy on such a night. And then it was long after ten o'clock and yet there was no sign of Gabriel and his wife. Besides they were dreadfully afraid that Freddy Malins might turn up screwed. They would not wish for worlds that any of Mary Jane's pupils should see him under the influence; and when he was like that it was sometimes very hard to manage him. Freddy Malins always came late, but they wondered what could be keeping Gabriel: and that was what brought them every two minutes to the banisters to ask Lily had Gabriel or Freddy come.

"O, Mr. Conroy," said Lily to Gabriel when she opened the door for him, "Miss Kate and Miss Julia thought you were never coming. Good-night, Mrs. Conroy."

"I'll engage they did," said Gabriel, "but they forget that my wife here takes three mortal hours to dress herself."

He stood on the mat, scraping the snow from his goloshes, while Lily led his wife to the foot of the stairs and called out:

"Miss Kate, here's Mrs. Conroy."

Kate and Julia came toddling down the dark stairs at once. Both of them kissed Gabriel's wife, said she must be perished alive, and asked was Gabriel with her.

"Here I am as right as the mail, Aunt Kate! Go on up. I'll follow," called out Gabriel from the dark.

He continued scraping his feet vigorously while the three women went upstairs, laughing, to the ladies' dressing-room. A light fringe of snow lay like a cape on the shoulders of his overcoat and like toecaps on the toes of his goloshes; and, as the buttons of his overcoat slipped with a squeaking noise through the snow-stiffened frieze, a cold, fragrant air from out-of-doors escaped from crevices and folds.

"Is it snowing again, Mr. Conroy?" asked Lily.

She had preceded him into the pantry to help him off with his overcoat. Gabriel smiled at the three syllables she had given his surname and glanced at her. She was a slim, growing girl, pale in complexion and with hay-coloured hair. The gas in the pantry made her look still paler. Gabriel had known her when she was a child and used to sit on the lowest step nursing a rag doll.

"Yes, Lily," he answered, "and I think we're in for a night of it."

[1] From *Dubliners,* now included in *The Portable James Joyce.* Copyright 1946, 1947 by The Viking Press, Inc. Reprinted by permission of The Viking Press, Inc., New York.

He looked up at the pantry ceiling, which was shaking with the stamping and shuffling of feet on the floor above, listened for a moment to the piano and then glanced at the girl, who was folding his overcoat carefully at the end of a shelf.

"Tell me, Lily," he said in a friendly tone, "do you still go to school?"

"O no, sir," she answered. "I'm done schooling this year and more."

"O, then," said Gabriel gaily, "I suppose we'll be going to your wedding one of these fine days with your young man, eh?"

The girl glanced back at him over her shoulder and said with great bitterness:

"The men that is now is only all palaver and what they can get out of you."

Gabriel coloured, as if he felt he had made a mistake and, without looking at her, kicked off his goloshes and flicked actively with his muffler at his patent-leather shoes.

He was a stout, tallish young man. The high colour of his cheeks pushed upwards even to his forehead, where it scattered itself in a few formless patches of pale red; and on his hairless face there scintillated restlessly the polished lenses and the bright gilt rims of the glasses which screened his delicate and restless eyes. His glossy black hair was parted in the middle and brushed in a long curve behind his ears where it curled slightly beneath the groove left by his hat.

When he had flicked lustre into his shoes he stood up and pulled his waistcoat down more tightly on his plump body. Then he took a coin rapidly from his pocket.

"O Lily," he said, thrusting it into her hands, "it's Christmas-time, isn't it? Just . . . here's a little. . . ."

He walked rapidly towards the door.

"O no, sir!" cried the girl, following him. "Really, sir, I wouldn't take it."

"Christmas-time! Christmas-time!" said Gabriel, almost trotting to the stairs and waving his hand to her in deprecation.

The girl, seeing that he had gained the stairs, called out after him:

"Well, thank you, sir."

He waited outside the drawing-room door until the waltz should finish, listening to the skirts that swept against it and to the shuffling of feet. He was still discomposed by the girl's bitter and sudden retort. It had cast a gloom over him which he tried to dispel by arranging his cuffs and the bows of his tie. He then took from his waistcoat pocket a little paper and glanced at the headings he had made for his speech. He was undecided about the lines from

Robert Browning, for he feared they would be above the heads of his hearers. Some quotation that they would recognise from Shakespeare or from the Melodies would be better. The indelicate clacking of the men's heels and the shuffling of their soles reminded him that their grade of culture differed from his. He would only make himself ridiculous by quoting poetry to them which they could not understand. They would think that he was airing his superior education. He would fail with them just as he had failed with the girl in the pantry. He had taken up a wrong tone. His whole speech was a mistake from first to last, an utter failure.

Just then his aunts and his wife came out of the ladies' dressing-room. His aunts were two small, plainly dressed old women. Aunt Julia was an inch or so the taller. Her hair, drawn low over the tops of her ears, was grey; and grey also, with darker shadows, was her large flaccid face. Though she was stout in build and stood erect, her slow eyes and parted lips gave her the appearance of a woman who did not know where she was or where she was going. Aunt Kate was more vivacious. Her face, healthier than her sister's, was all puckers and creases, like a shrivelled red apple, and her hair, braided in the same old-fashioned way, had not lost its ripe nut colour.

They both kissed Gabriel frankly. He was their favourite nephew, the son of their dead elder sister, Ellen, who had married T. J. Conroy of the Port and Docks.

"Gretta tells me you're not going to take a cab back to Monkstown tonight, Gabriel," said Aunt Kate.

"No," said Gabriel, turning to his wife, "we had quite enough of that last year, hadn't we? Don't you remember, Aunt Kate, what a cold Gretta got out of it? Cab windows rattling all the way, and the east wind blowing in after we passed Merrion. Very jolly it was. Gretta caught a dreadful cold."

Aunt Kate frowned severely and nodded her head at every word.

"Quite right, Gabriel, quite right," she said. "You can't be too careful."

"But as for Gretta here," said Gabriel, "she'd walk home in the snow if she were let."

Mrs. Conroy laughed.

"Don't mind him, Aunt Kate," she said. "He's really an awful bother, what with green shades for Tom's eyes at night and making him do the dumb-bells, and forcing Eva to eat the stirabout. The poor child! And she simply hates the sight of it! . . . O, but you'll never guess what he makes me wear now!"

She broke out into a peal of laughter and glanced at her husband, whose admiring and happy eyes had been wandering from her dress to her face and hair. The two aunts laughed heartily, too, for Gabriel's solicitude was a standing joke with them.

"Goloshes!" said Mrs. Conroy. "That's the latest. Whenever it's wet underfoot I must put on my goloshes. Tonight even, he wanted me to put them on, but I wouldn't. The next thing he'll buy me will be a diving suit."

Gabriel laughed nervously and patted his tie reassuringly, while Aunt Kate nearly doubled herself, so heartily did she enjoy the joke. The smile soon faded from Aunt Julia's face and her mirthless eyes were directed towards her nephew's face. After a pause she asked:

"And what are goloshes, Gabriel?"

"Goloshes, Julia!" exclaimed her sister. "Goodness me, don't you know what goloshes are? You wear them over your . . . over your boots, Gretta, isn't it?"

"Yes," said Mrs. Conroy. "Guttapercha things. We both have a pair now. Gabriel says everyone wears them on the continent."

"O, on the continent," murmured Aunt Julia, nodding her head slowly.

Gabriel knitted his brows and said, as if he were slightly angered:

"It's nothing very wonderful, but Gretta thinks it very funny because she says the word reminds her of Christy Minstrels."

"But tell me, Gabriel," said Aunt Kate, with brisk tact. "Of course, you've seen about the room. Gretta was saying . . ."

"O, the room is all right," replied Gabriel. "I've taken one in the Gresham."

"To be sure," said Aunt Kate, "by far the best thing to do. And the children, Gretta, you're not anxious about them?"

"O, for one night," said Mrs. Conroy. "Besides, Bessie will look after them."

"To be sure," said Aunt Kate again. "What a comfort it is to have a girl like that, one you can depend on! There's that Lily, I'm sure I don't know what has come over her lately. She's not the girl she was at all."

Gabriel was about to ask his aunt some questions on this point, but she broke off suddenly to gaze after her sister, who had wandered down the stairs and was craning her neck over the banisters.

"Now, I ask you," she said almost testily, "where is Julia going? Julia! Julia! Where are you going?"

Julia, who had gone half way down one flight, came back and announced blandly:

"Here's Freddy."

At the same moment a clapping of hands and a final flourish of the pianist told that the waltz had ended. The drawing-room door was opened from within and some couples came out. Aunt Kate drew Gabriel aside hurriedly and whispered into his ear:

"Slip down, Gabriel, like a good fellow and see if he's all right, and don't let him up if he's screwed. I'm sure he's screwed. I'm sure he is."

Gabriel went to the stairs and listened over the banisters. He could hear two persons talking in the pantry. Then he recognised Freddy Malins' laugh. He went down the stairs noisily.

"It's such a relief," said Aunt Kate to Mrs. Conroy, "that Gabriel is here. I always feel easier in my mind when he's here. . . . Julia, there's Miss Daly and Miss Power will take some refreshment. Thanks for your beautiful waltz, Miss Daly. It made lovely time."

A tall wizen-faced man, with a stiff grizzled moustache and swarthy skin, who was passing with his partner, said:

"And may we have some refreshment, too, Miss Morkan?"

"Julia," said Aunt Kate summarily, "and here's Mr. Browne and Miss Furlong. Take them in, Julia, with Miss Daly and Miss Power."

"I'm the man for the ladies," said Mr. Browne, pursing his lips until his moustache bristled and smiling in all his wrinkles. "You know, Miss Morkan, the reason they are so fond of me is—"

He did not finish his sentence, but, seeing that Aunt Kate was out of earshot, at once led the three young ladies into the back room. The middle of the room was occupied by two square tables placed end to end, and on these Aunt Julia and the caretaker were straightening and smoothing a large cloth. On the sideboard were arrayed dishes and plates, and glasses and bundles of knives and forks and spoons. The top of the closed square piano served also as a sideboard for viands and sweets. At a smaller sideboard in one corner two young men were standing, drinking hop-bitters.

Mr. Browne led his charges thither and invited them all, in jest, to some ladies' punch, hot, strong and sweet. As they said they never took anything strong, he opened three bottles of lemonade for them. Then he asked one of the young men to move aside, and, taking hold of the decanter, filled out for himself a goodly measure of whisky. The young men eyed him respectfully while he took a trial sip.

"God help me," he said, smiling, "it's the doctor's orders."

His wizened face broke into a broader smile, and

Edward Morgan Forster

OF E. M. Forster's five novels, four were published in the first decade of the century (*Where Angels Fear to Tread*, 1905; *The Longest Journey*, 1907; *A Room with a View*, 1908; *Howard's End*, 1910) and the fifth, *A Passage to India*, in 1927. A number of short stories which had first appeared in periodicals were collected in 1911 under the title of *The Celestial Omnibus*, and another such collection, *The Eternal Moment*, was published in 1928 (the stories in both volumes are at present obtainable in a single volume, *The Collected Tales of E. M. Forster*). Yet it would be a mistake to assume from glancing at these dates that one must approach E. M. Forster as an Edwardian, or perhaps even as a Georgian, for he has had a faculty for seeming to be exactly contemporary with the moment at which one reads him. Or one might put it this way: his works are shaped by a clear intelligence, by an ability to see through cant and sham and stuffiness, by a warmth of heart, and by a recognition of the difficulties inherent in the human situation, which must always strike us as pointing to the way out of the particular impasse in which at a given moment stupidity and hatred have succeeded in placing us. To follow the way out demands, of course, the same courage and bold faith which are demanded of his characters by the crucial situations in which he places them; like some of them, we do not often find the courage, or even know that it is demanded, until too late.

Forster, who was born in 1879, was educated at Tonbridge and at King's College, Cambridge. At the time of the first World War he spent three years in Egypt, commemorated in *Alexandria: A History and a Guide* (1922) and in a collection of essays on Alexandrian history, *Pharos and Pharillon* (1923). He had traveled in India in 1912, and was there again in 1922. In 1927 he gave the Clark Lectures at Cambridge, published in the same year as *Aspects of the Novel*. Among his other books are a biography of Goldsworthy Lowes Dickinson (1934); a collection of critical essays, reviews, and shorter biographical sketches, *Abinger Harvest* (1936); a pamphlet entitled *What I Believe* (1939); and an essay on Virginia Woolf, originally delivered as the Rede Lecture at Cambridge in May, 1942.

There have been two full-length studies of his work, *The Writings of E. M. Forster*, by Rose Macaulay (1938), and *E. M. Forster: A Study*, by Lionel Trilling (1944). An admirable introduction to his work is offered by Rex Warner's pamphlet, *E. M. Forster* (1950), in the series currently being published for the British Council and the National Book League by Longmans, Green; it is illustrated with a portrait and contains a select bibliography.

THE ROAD FROM COLONUS[1]

I

FOR no very intelligible reason, Mr Lucas had hurried ahead of his party. He was perhaps reaching the age at which independence becomes valuable, because it is so soon to be lost. Tired of attention and consideration, he liked breaking away from the younger members, to ride by himself, and to dismount unassisted. Perhaps he also relished that more subtle pleasure of being kept waiting for lunch, and of telling the others on their arrival that it was of no consequence.

So, with childish impatience, he battered the animal's sides with his heels, and made the muleteer bang it with a thick stick and prick it with a sharp one, and jolted down the hillsides through clumps of flowering shrubs and stretches of anemones and asphodel, till he heard the sound of running water, and came in sight of the group of plane trees where they were to have their meal.

Even in England those trees would have been remarkable, so huge were they, so interlaced, so magnificently clothed in quivering green. And here in Greece they were unique, the one cool spot in that hard brilliant landscape, already scorched by the heat of an April sun. In their midst was hidden a tiny Khan or country inn, a frail mud building with a broad wooden balcony in which sat an old woman spinning, while a small brown pig, eating orange peel, stood beside her. On the wet earth below squatted two children, playing some primaeval game with their

---

[1] Reprinted from *The Celestial Omnibus* by E. M. Forster, by permission of Alfred A. Knopf, Inc. Copyright 1947 by Alfred A. Knopf, Inc.—Colonus, which was the birthplace of Sophocles, "is a hill a mile north of Athens, where Oedipus [the protagonist of Sophocles's best-known tragedies, the *Oedipus Tyrannus* and the *Oedipus at Colonus*] found refuge and was buried" (*Oxford Classical Dictionary*). "In *Oedipus at Colonus* he is a wandering beggar, faithfully tended by Antigone," his daughter.

fingers; and their mother, none too clean either, was messing with some rice inside. As Mrs Forman would have said, it was all very Greek, and the fastidious Mr Lucas felt thankful that they were bringing their own food with them, and should eat it in the open air.

Still, he was glad to be there—the muleteer had helped him off—and glad that Mrs Forman was not there to forestall his opinions—glad even that he should not see Ethel for quite half an hour. Ethel was his youngest daughter, still unmarried. She was unselfish and affectionate, and it was generally understood that she was to devote her life to her father, and be the comfort of his old age. Mrs Forman always referred to her as Antigone, and Mr Lucas tried to settle down to the role of Oedipus, which seemed the only one that public opinion allowed him.

He had this in common with Oedipus, that he was growing old. Even to himself it had become obvious. He had lost interest in other people's affairs, and seldom attended when they spoke to him. He was fond of talking himself but often forgot what he was going to say, and even when he succeeded, it seldom seemed worth the effort. His phrases and gestures had become stiff and set, his anecdotes, once so successful, fell flat, his silence was as meaningless as his speech. Yet he had led a healthy, active life, had worked steadily, made money, educated his children. There was nothing and no one to blame: he was simply growing old.

At the present moment, here he was in Greece, and one of the dreams of his life was realized. Forty years ago he had caught the fever of Hellenism, and all his life he had felt that could he but visit that land, he would not have lived in vain. But Athens had been dusty, Delphi wet, Thermopylae flat, and he had listened with amazement and cynicism to the rapturous exclamations of his companions. Greece was like England: it was a man who was growing old, and it made no difference whether that man looked at the Thames or the Eurotas. It was his last hope of contradicting that logic of experience, and it was failing.

Yet Greece had done something for him, though he did not know it. It had made him discontented, and there are stirrings of life in discontent. He knew that he was not the victim of continual ill-luck. Something great was wrong, and he was pitted against no mediocre or accidental enemy. For the last month a strange desire had possessed him to die fighting.

'Greece is the land for young people,' he said to himself as he stood under the plane trees, 'but I will enter into it, I will possess it. Leaves shall be green

again, water shall be sweet, the sky shall be blue. They were so forty years ago, and I will win them back. I do mind being old, and I will pretend no longer.'

He took two steps forward, and immediately cold waters were gurgling over his ankle.

'Where does the water come from?' he asked himself. 'I do not even know that.' He remembered that all the hillsides were dry; yet here the road was suddenly covered with flowing streams.

He stopped still in amazement, saying: 'Water out of a tree—out of a hollow tree? I never saw nor thought of that before.'

For the enormous plane that leant towards the Khan was hollow—it had been burnt out for charcoal—and from its living trunk there gushed an impetuous spring, coating the bark with fern and moss, and flowing over the mule track to create fertile meadows beyond. The simple country folk had paid to beauty and mystery such tribute as they could, for in the rind of the tree a shrine was cut, holding a lamp and a little picture of the Virgin, inheritor of the Naiad's and Dryad's joint abode.

'I never saw anything so marvellous before,' said Mr Lucas. 'I could even step inside the trunk and see where the water comes from.'

For a moment he hesitated to violate the shrine. Then he remembered with a smile his own thought —'the place shall be mine; I will enter it and possess it'—and leapt almost aggressively on to a stone within.

The water pressed up steadily and noiselessly from the hollow roots and hidden crevices of the plane, forming a wonderful amber pool ere it spilt over the lip of bark on to the earth outside. Mr Lucas tasted it and it was sweet, and when he looked up the black funnel of the trunk he saw sky which was blue, and some leaves which were green; and he remembered, without smiling, another of his thoughts.

Others had been before him—indeed he had a curious sense of companionship. Little votive offerings to the presiding Power were fastened on to the bark—tiny arms and legs and eyes in tin, grotesque models of the brain or the heart—all tokens of some recovery of strength or wisdom or love. There was no such thing as the solitude of nature, for the sorrows and joys of humanity had pressed even into the bosom of a tree. He spread out his arms and steadied himself against the soft charred wood, and then slowly leant back, till his body was resting on the trunk behind. His eyes closed, and he had the strange feeling of one who is moving, yet at peace—

the feeling of the swimmer, who, after long struggling with chopping seas, finds that after all the tide will sweep him to his goal.

So he lay motionless, conscious only of the stream below his feet, and that all things were a stream, in which he was moving.

He was aroused at last by a shock—the shock of an arrival perhaps, for when he opened his eyes, something unimagined, indefinable, had passed over all things, and made them intelligible and good.

There was meaning in the stoop of the old woman over her work, and in the quick motions of the little pig, and in her diminishing globe of wool. A young man came singing over the streams on a mule, and there was beauty in his pose and sincerity in his greeting. The sun made no accidental patterns upon the spreading roots of the trees, and there was intention in the nodding clumps of asphodel, and in the music of the water. To Mr Lucas, who, in a brief space of time, had discovered not only Greece, but England and all the world and life, there seemed nothing ludicrous in the desire to hang within the tree another votive offering—a little model of an entire man.

'Why, here's papa, playing at being Merlin.'

All unnoticed they had arrived—Ethel, Mrs Forman, Mr Graham, and the English-speaking dragoman. Mr Lucas peered out at them suspiciously. They had suddenly become unfamiliar, and all that they did seemed strained and coarse.

'Allow me to give you a hand,' said Mr Graham, a young man who was always polite to his elders.

Mr Lucas felt annoyed. 'Thank you, I can manage perfectly well by myself,' he replied. His foot slipped as he stepped out of the tree, and went into the spring.

'Oh papa, my papa!' said Ethel, 'what are you doing? Thank goodness I have got a change for you on the mule.'

She tended him carefully, giving him clean socks and dry boots, and then sat him down on the rug beside the lunch basket, while she went with the others to explore the grove.

They came back in ecstasies, in which Mr Lucas tried to join. But he found them intolerable. Their enthusiasm was superficial, commonplace, and spasmodic. They had no perception of the coherent beauty that was flowering around them. He tried at least to explain his feelings, and what he said was:

'I am altogether pleased with the appearance of this place. It impresses me very favourably. The trees are fine, remarkably fine for Greece, and there is something very poetic in the spring of clear running water. The people too seem kindly and civil. It is decidedly an attractive place.'

Mrs Forman upbraided him for his tepid praise. 'Oh, it is a place in a thousand!' she cried, 'I could live and die here! I really would stop if I had not to be back at Athens! It reminds me of the Colonus of Sophocles.'

'Well, I must stop,' said Ethel. 'I positively must.'

'Yes, do! You and your father! Antigone and Oedipus. Of course you must stop at Colonus!'

Mr Lucas was almost breathless with excitement. When he stood within the tree, he had believed that his happiness would be independent of locality. But these few minutes' conversation had undeceived him. He no longer trusted himself to journey through the world, for old thoughts, old wearinesses might be waiting to rejoin him as soon as he left the shade of the planes, and the music of the virgin water. To sleep in the Khan with the gracious, kind-eyed country people, to watch the bats flit about within the globe of shade, and see the moon turn the golden patterns into silver—one such night would place him beyond relapse, and confirm him for ever in the kingdom he had regained. But all his lips could say was: 'I should be willing to put in a night here.'

'You mean a week, papa! It would be sacrilege to put in less.'

'A week then, a week,' said his lips, irritated at being corrected, while his heart was leaping with joy. All through lunch he spoke to them no more, but watched the place he should know so well, and the people who would so soon be his companions and friends. The inmates of the Khan only consisted of an old woman, a middle-aged woman, a young man and two children, and to none of them had he spoken, yet he loved them as he loved everything that moved or breathed or existed beneath the benedictory shade of the planes.

'En route!' said the shrill voice of Mrs Forman. 'Ethel! Mr Graham! The best of things must end.'

'To-night,' thought Mr Lucas, 'they will light the little lamp by the shrine. And when we all sit together on the balcony, perhaps they will tell me which offerings they put up.'

'I beg your pardon, Mr Lucas,' said Graham, 'but they want to fold up the rug you are sitting on.'

Mr Lucas got up, saying to himself: 'Ethel shall go to bed first, and then I will try to tell them about my offering too—for it is a thing I must do. I think they will understand if I am left with them alone.'

Ethel touched him on the cheek. 'Papa! I've called you three times. All the mules are here.'

'Mules? What mules?'

'Our mules. We're all waiting. Oh, Mr Graham, do help my father on.'

'I don't know what you're talking about, Ethel.'

'My dearest papa, we must start. You know we have to get to Olympia to-night.'

Mr Lucas in pompous, confident tones replied: 'I always did wish, Ethel, that you had a better head for plans. You know perfectly well that we are putting in a week here. It is your own suggestion.'

Ethel was startled into impoliteness. 'What a perfectly ridiculous idea. You must have known I was joking. Of course I meant I wished we could.'

'Ah! if we could only do what we wished!' sighed Mrs Forman, already seated on her mule.

'Surely,' Ethel continued in calmer tones, 'you didn't think I meant it.'

'Most certainly I did. I have made all my plans on the supposition that we are stopping here, and it will be extremely inconvenient, indeed, impossible for me to start.'

He delivered this remark with an air of great conviction, and Mrs Forman and Mr Graham had to turn away to hide their smiles.

'I am sorry I spoke so carelessly; it was wrong of me. But, you know, we can't break up our party, and even one night here would make us miss the boat at Patras.'

Mrs Forman, in an aside, called Mr Graham's attention to the excellent way in which Ethel managed her father.

'I don't mind about the Patras boat. You said that we should stop here, and we are stopping.'

It seemed as if the inhabitants of the Khan had divined in some mysterious way that the altercation touched them. The old woman stopped her spinning, while the young man and the two children stood behind Mr Lucas, as if supporting him.

Neither arguments nor entreaties moved him. He said little, but he was absolutely determined, because for the first time he saw his daily life aright. What need had he to return to England? Who would miss him? His friends were dead or cold. Ethel loved him in a way, but, as was right, she had other interests. His other children he seldom saw. He had only one other relative, his sister Julia, whom he both feared and hated. It was no effort to struggle. He would be a fool as well as a coward if he stirred from the place which brought him happiness and peace.

At last Ethel, to humour him, and not disinclined to air her modern Greek, went into the Khan with the astonished dragoman to look at the rooms. The woman inside received them with loud welcomes, and the young man, when no one was looking, began to lead Mr Lucas' mule to the stable.

'Drop it, you brigand!' shouted Graham, who always declared that foreigners could understand English if they chose. He was right, for the man obeyed, and they all stood waiting for Ethel's return.

She emerged at last, with close-gathered skirts, followed by the dragoman bearing the little pig, which he had bought at a bargain.

'My dear papa, I will do all I can for you, but stop in that Khan—no.'

'Are there—fleas?' asked Mrs Forman.

Ethel intimated that 'fleas' was not the word.

'Well, I am afraid that settles it,' said Mrs Forman, 'I know how particular Mr Lucas is.'

'It does not settle it,' said Mr Lucas. 'Ethel, you go on. I do not want you. I don't know why I ever consulted you. I shall stop here alone.'

'That is absolute nonsense,' said Ethel, losing her temper. 'How can you be left alone at your age? How would you get your meals or your bath? All your letters are waiting for you at Patras. You'll miss the boat. That means missing the London operas, and upsetting all your engagements for the month. And as if you could travel by yourself!'

'They might knife you,' was Mr Graham's contribution.

The Greeks said nothing; but whenever Mr Lucas looked their way, they beckoned him towards the Khan. The children would even have drawn him by the coat, and the old woman on the balcony stopped her almost completed spinning, and fixed him with mysterious appealing eyes. As he fought, the issue assumed gigantic proportions, and he believed that he was not merely stopping because he had regained youth or seen beauty or found happiness, but because in that place and with those people a supreme event was awaiting him which would transfigure the face of the world. The moment was so tremendous that he abandoned words and arguments as useless, and rested on the strength of his mighty unrevealed allies: silent men, murmuring water, and whispering trees. For the whole place called with one voice, articulate to him, and his garrulous opponents became every minute more meaningless and absurd. Soon they would be tired and go chattering away into the sun, leaving him to the cool grove and the moonlight and the destiny he foresaw.

Mrs Forman and the dragoman had indeed already started, amid the piercing screams of the little pig, and the struggle might have gone on indefinitely if Ethel had not called in Mr Graham.

'Can you help me?' she whispered. 'He is absolutely unmanageable.'

'I'm no good at arguing—but if I could help you in any other way—' and he looked down complacently at his well-made figure.

Ethel hesitated. Then she said: 'Help me in any way you can. After all, it is for his good that we do it.'

'Then have his mule led up behind him.'

So when Mr Lucas thought he had gained the day, he suddenly felt himself lifted off the ground, and sat sideways on the saddle, and at the same time the mule started off at a trot. He said nothing, for he had nothing to say, and even his face showed little emotion as he felt the shade pass and heard the sound of the water cease. Mr Graham was running at his side, hat in hand, apologizing.

'I know I had no business to do it, and I do beg your pardon awfully. But I do hope that some day you too will feel that I was—damn!'

A stone had caught him in the middle of the back. It was thrown by the little boy, who was pursuing them along the mule track. He was followed by his sister, also throwing stones.

Ethel screamed to the dragoman, who was some way ahead with Mrs Forman, but before he could rejoin them, another adversary appeared. It was the young Greek, who had cut them off in front, and now dashed down at Mr Lucas' bridle. Fortunately Graham was an expert boxer, and it did not take him a moment to beat down the youth's feeble defence, and to send him sprawling with a bleeding mouth into the asphodel. By this time the dragoman had arrived, the children, alarmed at the fate of their brother, had desisted, and the rescue party, if such it is to be considered, retired in disorder to the trees.

'Little devils!' said Graham, laughing with triumph. 'That's the modern Greek all over. Your father meant money if he stopped, and they consider we were taking it out of their pocket.'

'Oh, they are terrible—simple savages! I don't know how I shall ever thank you. You've saved my father.'

'I only hope you didn't think me brutal.'

'No,' replied Ethel with a little sigh. 'I admire strength.'

Meanwhile the cavalcade reformed, and Mr Lucas, who, as Mrs Forman said, bore his disappointment wonderfully well, was put comfortably on to his mule. They hurried up the opposite hillside, fearful of another attack, and it was not until they had left the eventful place far behind that Ethel found an opportunity to speak to her father and ask his pardon for the way she had treated him.

'You seemed so different, dear father, and you quite frightened me. Now I feel that you are your old self again.'

He did not answer, and she concluded that he was not unnaturally offended at her behaviour.

By one of those curious tricks of mountain scenery, the place they had left an hour before suddenly reappeared far below them. The Khan was hidden under the green dome, but in the open there still stood three figures, and through the pure air rose up a faint cry of defiance or farewell.

Mr Lucas stopped irresolutely, and let the reins fall from his hand.

'Come, father dear,' said Ethel gently.

He obeyed, and in another moment a spur of the hill hid the dangerous scene for ever.

II

It was breakfast time, but the gas was alight, owing to the fog. Mr Lucas was in the middle of an account of a bad night he had spent. Ethel, who was to be married in a few weeks, had her arms on the table, listening.

'First the door bell rang, then you came back from the theatre. Then the dog started, and after the dog the cat. And at three in the morning a young hooligan passed by singing. Oh yes: then there was the water gurgling in the pipe above my head.'

'I think that was only the bath water running away,' said Ethel, looking rather worn.

'Well, there's nothing I dislike more than running water. It's perfectly impossible to sleep in the house. I shall give it up. I shall give notice next quarter. I shall tell the landlord plainly, "The reason I am giving up the house is this: it is perfectly impossible to sleep in it." If he says—says—well, what has he got to say?'

'Some more toast, father?'

'Thank you, my dear.' He took it, and there was an interval of peace.

But he soon recommenced. 'I'm not going to submit to the practising next door as tamely as they think. I wrote and told them so—didn't I?'

'Yes,' said Ethel, who had taken care that the letter should not reach. 'I have seen the governess, and she has promised to arrange it differently. And Aunt Julia hates noise. It will be sure to be all right.'

Her aunt, being the only unattached member of the family, was coming to keep house for her father when she left him. The reference was not a happy one, and Mr Lucas commenced a series of half articulate sighs, which was only stopped by the arrival of the post.

'Oh, what a parcel!' cried Ethel. 'For me! What can it be! Greek stamps. This is most exciting!'

It proved to be some asphodel bulbs, sent by Mrs Forman from Athens for planting in the conservatory.

'Doesn't it bring it all back! You remember the asphodels, father. And all wrapped up in Greek newspapers. I wonder if I can read them still. I used to be able to, you know.'

She rattled on, hoping to conceal the laughter of the children next door—a favorite source of querulousness at breakfast time.

'Listen to me! "A rural disaster." Oh, I've hit on something sad. But never mind. "Last Tuesday at Plataniste, in the province of Messenia, a shocking tragedy occurred. A large tree"—aren't I getting on well?—"blew down in the night and"—wait a minute —oh, dear! "crushed to death the five occupants of the little Khan there, who had apparently been sitting in the balcony. The bodies of Maria Rhomaides, the aged proprietress, and of her daughter, aged forty-six, were easily recognizable, whereas that of her grandson"—oh, the rest is really too horrid; I wish I had never tried it, and what's more I feel to have heard the name Plataniste before. We didn't stop there, did we, in the spring?'

'We had lunch,' said Mr Lucas, with a faint expression of trouble on his vacant face. 'Perhaps it was where the dragoman bought the pig.'

'Of course,' said Ethel in a nervous voice. 'Where the dragoman bought the little pig. How terrible!'

'Very terrible!' said her father, whose attention was wandering to the noisy children next door. Ethel suddenly started to her feet with genuine interest.

'Good gracious!' she exclaimed. 'This is an old paper. It happened not lately but in April—the night of Tuesday the eighteenth—and we—we must have been there in the afternoon.'

'So we were,' said Mr Lucas. She put her hand to her heart, scarcely able to speak.

'Father, dear father, I must say it: you wanted to stop there. All those people, those poor half savage people, tried to keep you, and they're dead. The whole place, it says, is in ruins, and even the stream has changed its course. Father, dear, if it had not been for me, and if Arthur had not helped me, you must have been killed.'

Mr Lucas waved his hand irritably. 'It is not a bit of good speaking to the governess, I shall write to the landlord and say, "The reason I am giving up the house is this: the dog barks, the children next door are intolerable, and I cannot stand the noise of running water." '

Ethel did not check his babbling. She was aghast at the narrowness of the escape, and for a long time kept silence. At last she said: 'Such a marvellous deliverance does make one believe in Providence.'

Mr Lucas, who was still composing his letter to the landlord, did not reply.

David Herbert Lawrence[1]

1885–1930

ODOUR OF CHRYSANTHEMUMS[2]

THE small locomotive engine, Number 4, came clanking, stumbling down from Selston with seven full waggons. It appeared round the corner with loud threats of speed, but the colt that it startled from among the gorse, which still flickered indistinctly in the raw afternoon, outdistanced it at a canter. A woman, walking up the railway line to Underwood, drew back into the hedge, held her basket aside, and watched the footplate of the engine advancing. The trucks thumped heavily past, one by one, with slow inevitable movement, as she stood insignificantly trapped between the jolting black waggons and the hedge; then they curved away towards the coppice where the withered oak leaves dropped noiselessly, while the birds, pulling at the scarlet hips beside the track, made off into the dusk that had already crept into the spinney. In the open, the smoke from the engine sank and cleaved to the rough grass. The fields were dreary and forsaken, and in the marshy strip that led to the whimsey, a reedy pit-pond, the fowls

[1] For a biographical and bibliographical note on Lawrence, see p. 936, above.
[2] From *The Prussian Officer* by D. H. Lawrence. Reprinted by permission of The Viking Press, Inc., New York.

had already abandoned their run among the alders, to roost in the tarred fowl-house. The pit-bank loomed up beyond the pond, flames like red sores licking its ashy sides, in the afternoon's stagnant light. Just beyond rose the tapering chimneys and the clumsy black headstocks of Brinsley Colliery. The two wheels were spinning fast up against the sky, and the winding-engine rapped out its little spasms. The miners were being turned up.

The engine whistled as it came into the wide bay of railway lines beside the colliery, where rows of trucks stood in harbour.

Miners, single, trailing and in groups, passed like shadows diverging home. At the edge of the ribbed level of sidings squat a low cottage, three steps down from the cinder track. A large bony vine clutched at the house, as if to claw down the tiled roof. Round the bricked yard grew a few wintry primroses. Beyond, the long garden sloped down to a bush-covered brook course. There were some twiggy apple trees, winter-crack trees, and ragged cabbages. Beside the path hung dishevelled pink chrysanthemums, like pink cloths hung on bushes. A woman came stooping out of the felt-covered fowl-house, half-way down the garden. She closed and padlocked the door, then drew herself erect, having brushed some bits from her white apron.

She was a tall woman of imperious mien, handsome, with definite black eyebrows. Her smooth black hair was parted exactly. For a few moments she stood steadily watching the miners as they passed along the railway: then she turned towards the brook course. Her face was calm and set, her mouth was closed with disillusionment. After a moment she called:

"John!" There was no answer. She waited, and then said distinctly:

"Where are you?"

"Here!" replied a child's sulky voice from among the bushes. The woman looked piercingly through the dusk.

"Are you at that brook?" she asked sternly.

For answer the child showed himself before the raspberry-canes that rose like whips. He was a small, sturdy boy of five. He stood quite still, defiantly.

"Oh!" said the mother conciliated. "I thought you were down at that wet brook—and you remember what I told you—"

The boy did not move or answer.

"Come, come on in," she said more gently, "it's getting dark. There's your grandfather's engine coming down the line!"

The lad advanced slowly, with resentful, taciturn movement. He was dressed in trousers and waistcoat of cloth that was too thick and hard for the size of the garments. They were evidently cut down from a man's clothes.

As they went slowly towards the house he tore at the ragged wisps of chrysanthemums and dropped the petals in handfuls along the path.

"Don't do that—it does look nasty," said his mother. He refrained, and she, suddenly pitiful, broke off a twig with three or four wan flowers and held them against her face. When mother and son reached the yard her hand hesitated, and instead of laying the flower aside, she pushed it in her apron-band. The mother and son stood at the foot of the three steps looking across the bay of lines at the passing home of the miners. The trundle of the small train was imminent. Suddenly the engine loomed past the house and came to a stop opposite the gate.

The engine-driver, a short man with round grey beard, leaned out of the cab high above the woman.

"Have you got a cup of tea?" he said in a cheery, hearty fashion.

It was her father. She went in, saying she would mash. Directly, she returned.

"I didn't come to see you on Sunday," began the little grey-bearded man.

"I didn't expect you," said his daughter.

The engine-driver winced; then, reassuming his cheery, airy manner, he said:

"Oh, have you heard then? Well, and what do you think—?"

"I think it is soon enough," she replied.

At her brief censure the little man made an impatient gesture, and said coaxingly, yet with dangerous coldness:

"Well, what's a man to do? It's no sort of life for a man of my years, to sit at my own hearth like a stranger. And if I'm going to marry again it may as well be soon as late—what does it matter to anybody?"

The woman did not reply, but turned and went into the house. The man in the engine-cab stood assertive, till she returned with a cup of tea and a piece of bread and butter on a plate. She went up the steps and stood near the footplate of the hissing engine.

"You needn't 'a brought me bread and butter," said her father. "But a cup of tea"—he sipped appreciatively—"it's very nice." He sipped for a moment or two, then: "I hear as Walter's got another bout on," he said.

"When hasn't he?" said the woman bitterly.

"I heered tell of him in the 'Lord Nelson' braggin'

as he was going to spend that b— afore he went: half a sovereign that was."

"When?" asked the woman.

"A' Sat'day night—I know that's true."

"Very likely," she laughed bitterly. "He gives me twenty-three shillings."

"Aye, it's a nice thing, when a man can do nothing with his money but make a beast of himself!" said the grey-whiskered man. The woman turned her head away. Her father swallowed the last of his tea and handed her the cup.

"Aye," he sighed, wiping his mouth. "It's a settler, it is—"

He put his hand on the lever. The little engine strained and groaned, and the train rumbled towards the crossing. The woman again looked across the metals. Darkness was settling over the spaces of the railway and trucks: the miners, in grey sombre groups, were still passing home. The winding-engine pulsed hurriedly, with brief pauses. Elizabeth Bates looked at the dreary flow of men, then she went indoors. Her husband did not come.

The kitchen was small and full of firelight; red coals piled glowing up the chimney mouth. All the life of the room seemed in the white, warm hearth and the steel fender reflecting the red fire. The cloth was laid for tea; cups glinted in the shadows. At the back, where the lowest stairs protruded into the room, the boy sat struggling with a knife and a piece of whitewood. He was almost hidden in the shadow. It was half-past four. They had but to await the father's coming to begin tea. As the mother watched her son's sullen little struggle with the wood, she saw herself in his silence and pertinacity; she saw the father in her child's indifference to all but himself. She seemed to be occupied by her husband. He had probably gone past his home, slunk past his own door, to drink before he came in, while his dinner spoiled and wasted in waiting. She glanced at the clock, then took the potatoes to strain them in the yard. The garden and fields beyond the brook were closed in uncertain darkness. When she rose with the saucepan, leaving the drain steaming into the night behind her, she saw the yellow lamps were lit along the high road that went up the hill away beyond the space of the railway lines and the field.

Then again she watched the men trooping home, fewer now and fewer.

Indoors the fire was sinking and the room was dark red. The woman put her saucepan on the hob, and set a batter pudding near the mouth of the oven. Then she stood unmoving. Directly, gratefully, came quick young steps to the door. Someone hung on the latch a moment, then a little girl entered and began pulling off her outdoor things, dragging a mass of curls, just ripening from gold to brown, over her eyes with her hat.

Her mother chid her for coming late from school, and said she would have to keep her at home the dark winter days.

"Why, mother, it's hardly a bit dark yet. The lamp's not lighted, and my father's not home."

"No, he isn't. But it's a quarter to five! Did you see anything of him?"

The child became serious. She looked at her mother with large, wistful blue eyes.

"No, mother, I've never seen him. Why? Has he come up an' gone past, to Old Brinsley? He hasn't, mother, 'cos I never saw him."

"He'd watch that," said the mother bitterly, "he'd take care as you didn't see him. But you may depend upon it, he's seated in the 'Prince o' Wales.' He wouldn't be this late."

The girl looked at her mother piteously.

"Let's have our teas, mother, should we?" said she.

The mother called John to table. She opened the door once more and looked out across the darkness of the lines. All was deserted: she could not hear the winding-engines.

"Perhaps," she said to herself, "he's stopped to get some ripping done."

They sat down to tea. John, at the end of the table near the door, was almost lost in the darkness. Their faces were hidden from each other. The girl crouched against the fender slowly moving a thick piece of bread before the fire. The lad, his face a dusky mark on the shadow, sat watching her who was transfigured in the red glow.

"I do think it's beautiful to look in the fire," said the child.

"Do you?" said her mother. "Why?"

"It's so red, and full of little caves—and it feels so nice, and you can fair smell it."

"It'll want mending directly," replied her mother, "and then if your father comes he'll carry on and say there never is a fire when a man comes home sweating from the pit. A public-house is always warm enough."

There was silence till the boy said complainingly: "Make haste, our Annie."

"Well, I am doing! I can't make the fire do it no faster, can I?"

"She keeps wafflin' it about so's to make 'er slow," grumbled the boy.

"Don't have such an evil imagination, child," replied the mother.

Soon the room was busy in the darkness with the crisp sound of crunching. The mother ate very little. She drank her tea determinedly, and sat thinking. When she rose her anger was evident in the stern unbending of her head. She looked at the pudding in the fender, and broke out:

"It is a scandalous thing as a man can't even come home to his dinner! If it's crozzled up to a cinder I don't see why I should care. Past his very door he goes to get to a public-house, and here I sit with his dinner waiting for him—"

She went out. As she dropped piece after piece of coal on the red fire, the shadows fell on the walls, till the room was almost in total darkness.

"I canna see," grumbled the invisible John. In spite of herself, the mother laughed.

"You know the way to your mouth," she said. She set the dustpan outside the door. When she came again like a shadow on the hearth, the lad repeated, complaining sulkily:

"I canna see."

"Good gracious!" cried the mother irritably, "you're as bad as your father if it's a bit dusk!"

Nevertheless she took a paper spill from a sheaf on the mantelpiece and proceeded to light the lamp that hung from the ceiling in the middle of the room. As she reached up, her figure displayed itself just rounding with maternity.

"Oh, mother—!" exclaimed the girl.

"What?" said the woman, suspended in the act of putting the lamp glass over the flame. The copper reflector shone handsomely on her, as she stood with uplifted arm, turning to face her daughter.

"You've got a flower in your apron!" said the child, in a little rapture at this unusual event.

"Goodness me!" exclaimed the woman, relieved. "One would think the house was afire." She replaced the glass and waited a moment before turning up the wick. A pale shadow was seen floating vaguely on the floor.

"Let me smell!" said the child, still rapturously, coming forward and putting her face to her mother's waist.

"Go along, silly!" said the mother, turning up the lamp. The light revealed their suspense so that the woman felt it almost unbearable. Annie was still bending at her waist. Irritably, the mother took the flowers out from her apron-band.

"Oh, mother—don't take them out!" Annie cried, catching her hand and trying to replace the sprig.

"Such nonsense!" said the mother, turning away. The child put the pale chrysanthemums to her lips, murmuring:

"Don't they smell beautiful!"

Her mother gave a short laugh.

"No," she said, "not to me. It was chrysanthemums when I married him, and chrysanthemums when you were born, and the first time they ever brought him home drunk, he'd got brown chrysanthemums in his button-hole."

She looked at the children. Their eyes and their parted lips were wondering. The mother sat rocking in silence for some time. Then she looked at the clock.

"Twenty minutes to six!" In a tone of fine bitter carelessness she continued: "Eh, he'll not come now till they bring him. There he'll stick! But he needn't come rolling in here in his pit-dirt, for I won't wash him. He can lie on the floor—Eh, what a fool I've been, what a fool! And this is what I came here for, to this dirty hole, rats and all, for him to slink past his very door. Twice last week—he's begun now—"

She silenced herself, and rose to clear the table.

While for an hour or more the children played, subduedly intent, fertile of imagination, united in fear of the mother's wrath, and in dread of their father's home-coming, Mrs. Bates sat in her rocking-chair making a "singlet" of thick cream-coloured flannel, which gave a dull wounded sound as she tore off the grey edge. She worked at her sewing with energy, listening to the children, and her anger wearied itself, lay down to rest, opening its eyes from time to time and steadily watching, its ears raised to listen. Sometimes even her anger quailed and shrank, and the mother suspended her sewing, tracing the footsteps that thudded along the sleepers outside; she would lift her head sharply to bid the children "hush," but she recovered herself in time, and the footsteps went past the gate, and the children were not flung out of their play-world.

But at last Annie sighed, and gave in. She glanced at her waggon of slippers, and loathed the game. She turned plaintively to her mother.

"Mother!"—but she was inarticulate.

John crept out like a frog from under the sofa. His mother glanced up.

"Yes," she said, "just look at those shirt-sleeves!"

The boy held them out to survey them, saying nothing. Then somebody called in a hoarse voice away down the line, and suspense bristled in the room, till two people had gone by outside, talking.

"It is time for bed," said the mother.

"My father hasn't come," wailed Annie plaintively. But her mother was primed with courage.

"Never mind. They'll bring him when he does come—like a log." She meant there would be no scene. "And he may sleep on the floor till he wakes himself. I know he'll not go to work to-morrow after this!"

The children had their hands and faces wiped with a flannel. They were very quiet. When they had put on their nightdresses, they said their prayers, the boy mumbling. The mother looked down at them, at the brown silken bush of intertwining curls in the nape of the girl's neck, at the little black head of the lad, and her heart burst with anger at their father who caused all three such distress. The children hid their faces in her skirts for comfort.

When Mrs. Bates came down, the room was strangely empty, with a tension of expectancy. She took up her sewing and stitched for some time without raising her head. Meantime her anger was tinged with fear.

II

The clock struck eight and she rose suddenly, dropping her sewing on her chair. She went to the stairfoot door, opened it, listening. Then she went out, locking the door behind her.

Something scuffled in the yard, and she started, though she knew it was only the rats with which the place was overrun. The night was very dark. In the great bay of railway lines, bulked with trucks, there was no trace of light, only away back she could see a few yellow lamps at the pit-top, and the red smear of the burning pit-bank on the night. She hurried along the edge of the track, then, crossing the converging lines, came to the stile by the white gates, whence she emerged on the road. Then the fear which had led her shrank. People were walking up to New Brinsley; she saw the lights in the houses; twenty yards further on were the broad windows of the "Prince of Wales," very warm and bright, and the loud voices of men could be heard distinctly. What a fool she had been to imagine that anything had happened to him! He was merely drinking over there at the "Prince of Wales." She faltered. She had never yet been to fetch him, and she never would go. So she continued her walk towards the long straggling line of houses, standing blank on the highway. She entered a passage between the dwellings.

"Mr. Rigley?—Yes! Did you want him? No, he's not in at this minute."

The raw-boned woman leaned forward from her dark scullery and peered at the other, upon whom fell a dim light through the blind of the kitchen window.

"Is it Mrs. Bates?" she asked in a tone tinged with respect.

"Yes. I wondered if your Master was at home. Mine hasn't come yet."

" 'Asn't 'e! Oh, Jack's been 'ome an' 'ad 'is dinner an' gone out. 'E's just gone for 'alf an hour afore bed-time. Did you call at the 'Prince of Wales'?"

"No—"

"No, you didn't like—! It's not very nice." The other woman was indulgent. There was an awkward pause. "Jack never said nothink about—about your Mester," she said.

"No!—I expect he's stuck in there!"

Elizabeth Bates said this bitterly, and with recklessness. She knew that the woman across the yard was standing at her door listening, but she did not care. As she turned:

"Stop a minute! I'll just go an' ask Jack if 'e knows anythink," said Mrs. Rigley.

"Oh, no—I wouldn't like to put—!"

"Yes, I will, if you'll just step inside an' see as th' childer doesn't come downstairs and set theirselves afire."

Elizabeth Bates, murmuring a remonstrance, stepped inside. The other woman apologized for the state of the room.

The kitchen needed apology. There were little frocks and trousers and childish undergarments on the squab and on the floor, and a litter of playthings everywhere. On the black American cloth of the table were pieces of bread and cake, crusts, slops, and a teapot with cold tea.

"Eh, ours is just as bad," said Elizabeth Bates, looking at the woman, not at the house. Mrs. Rigley put a shawl over her head and hurried out, saying:

"I shanna be a minute."

The other sat, noting with faint disapproval the general untidiness of the room. Then she fell to counting the shoes of various sizes scattered over the floor. There were twelve. She sighed and said to herself, "No wonder!"—glancing at the litter. There came the scratching of two pairs of feet on the yard, and the Rigleys entered. Elizabeth Bates rose. Rigley was a big man, with very large bones. His head looked particularly bony. Across his temple was a blue scar, caused by a wound got in the pit, a wound in which the coal-dust remained blue like tattooing.

" 'Asna 'e come whoam yit?" asked the man, without any form of greeting, but with deference and sympathy. "I couldna say wheer he is—'e's non ower theer!"—he jerked his head to signify the "Prince of Wales."

" 'E's 'appen gone up to th' 'Yew,' " said Mrs. Rigley.

There was another pause. Rigley had evidently something to get off his mind:

"Ah left 'im finishin' a stint," he began. "Loose-all

'ad bin gone about ten minutes when we com'n away, an' I shouted, 'Are ter comin', Walt?' an' 'e said, 'Go on, Ah shanna be but a'ef a minnit,' so we com'n ter th' bottom, me an' Bowers, thinkin' as 'e wor just behint, an' 'ud come up i' th' next bantle—"

He stood perplexed, as if answering a charge of deserting his mate. Elizabeth Bates, now again certain of disaster, hastened to reassure him:

"I expect 'e's gone up to th' 'Yew Tree,' as you say. It's not the first time. I've fretted myself into a fever before now. He'll come home when they carry him."

"Ay, isn't it too bad!" deplored the other woman.

"I'll just step up to Dick's an' see if 'e *is* theer," offered the man, afraid of appearing alarmed, afraid of taking liberties.

"Oh, I wouldn't think of bothering you that far," said Elizabeth Bates, with emphasis, but he knew she was glad of his offer.

As they stumbled up the entry, Elizabeth Bates heard Rigley's wife run across the yard and open her neighbour's door. At this, suddenly all the blood in her body seemed to switch away from her heart.

"Mind!" warned Rigley. "Ah've said many a time as Ah'd fill up them ruts in this entry, sumb'dy 'll be breakin' their legs yit."

She recovered herself and walked quickly along with the miner.

"I don't like leaving the children in bed, and nobody in the house," she said.

"No, you dunna!" he replied courteously. They were soon at the gate of the cottage.

"Well, I shanna be many minnits. Dunna you be frettin' now, 'e'll be all right," said the butty.

"Thank you very much, Mr. Rigley," she replied.

"You're welcome!" he stammered, moving away. "I shanna be many minnits."

The house was quiet. Elizabeth Bates took off her hat and shawl, and rolled back the rug. When she had finished, she sat down. It was a few minutes past nine. She was startled by the rapid chuff of the winding-engine at the pit, and the sharp whirr of the brakes on the rope as it descended. Again she felt the painful sweep of her blood, and she put her hand to her side, saying aloud, "Good gracious!—it's only the nine o'clock deputy going down," rebuking herself.

She sat still, listening. Half an hour of this, and she was wearied out.

"What am I working myself up like this for?" she said pitiably to herself. "I s'll only be doing myself some damage."

She took out her sewing again.

At a quarter to ten there were footsteps. One person! She watched for the door to open. It was an elderly woman, in a black bonnet and a black woollen shawl—his mother. She was about sixty years old, pale, with blue eyes, and her face all wrinkled and lamentable. She shut the door and turned to her daughter-in-law peevishly.

"Eh, Lizzie, whatever shall we do, whatever shall we do!" she cried.

Elizabeth drew back a little, sharply.

"What is it, mother?" she said.

The elder woman seated herself on the sofa.

"I don't know, child, I can't tell you!"—she shook her head slowly. Elizabeth sat watching her, anxious and vexed.

"I don't know," replied the grandmother, sighing very deeply. "There's no end to my troubles, there isn't. The things I've gone through, I'm sure it's enough—!" She wept without wiping her eyes, the tears running.

"But, mother," interrupted Elizabeth, "what do you mean? What is it?"

The grandmother slowly wiped her eyes. The fountains of her tears were stopped by Elizabeth's directness. She wiped her eyes slowly.

"Poor child! Eh, you poor thing!" she moaned. "I don't know what we're going to do, I don't and you as you are—it's a thing, it is indeed!"

Elizabeth waited.

"Is he dead?" she asked, and at the words her heart swung violently, though she felt a slight flush of shame at the ultimate extravagance of the question. Her words sufficiently frightened the old lady, almost brought her to herself.

"Don't say so, Elizabeth! We'll hope it's not as bad as that; no, may the Lord spare us that, Elizabeth. Jack Rigley came just as I was sittin' down to a glass afore going to bed, an' 'e said, ' 'Appen you'll go down th' line, Mrs. Bates. Walt's had an accident. 'Appen you'll go an' sit wi' 'er till we can get him home.' I hadn't time to ask him a word afore he was gone. An' I put my bonnet on an' come straight down, Lizzie. I thought to myself, 'Eh, that poor blessed child, if anybody should come an' tell her of a sudden, there's no knowin' what'll 'appen to 'er.' You mustn't let it upset you, Lizzie—or you know what to expect. How long is it, six months—or is it five, Lizzie? Ay!"—the old woman shook her head— "time slips on, it slips on! Ay!"

Elizabeth's thoughts were busy elsewhere. If he was killed—would she be able to manage on the little pension and what she could earn?—she counted up rapidly. If he was hurt—they wouldn't take him to the hospital—how tiresome he would be to nurse!— but perhaps she'd be able to get him away from the drink and his hateful ways. She would—while he was ill. The tears offered to come to her eyes at the picture. But what sentimental luxury was this she was beginning? She turned to consider the children. At any rate she was absolutely necessary for them. They were her business.

"Ay!" repeated the old woman, "it seems but a week or two since he brought me his first wages. Ay—he was a good lad, Elizabeth, he was, in his way. I don't know why he got to be such a trouble, I don't. He was a happy lad at home, only full of spirits. But there's no mistake he's been a handful of trouble, he has! I hope the Lord'll spare him to mend his ways. I hope so, I hope so. You've had a sight o' trouble with him, Elizabeth, you have indeed. But he was a jolly enough lad wi' me, he was, I can assure you. I don't know how it is. . . ."

The old woman continued to muse aloud, a monotonous irritating sound, while Elizabeth thought concentratedly, startled once, when she heard the winding-engine chuff quickly, and the brakes skirr with a shriek. Then she heard the engine more slowly, and the brakes made no sound. The old woman did not notice. Elizabeth waited in suspense. The mother-in-law talked, with lapses into silence.

"But he wasn't your son, Lizzie, an' it makes a difference. Whatever he was, I remember him when he was little, an' I learned to understand him and to make allowances. You've got to make allowances for them—"

It was half-past ten, and the old woman was saying: "But it's trouble from beginning to end; you're never too old for trouble, never too old for that—" when the gate banged back, and there were heavy feet on the steps.

"I'll go, Lizzie, let me go," cried the old woman, rising. But Elizabeth was at the door. It was a man in pit-clothes.

"They're bringin' 'im, Missis," he said. Elizabeth's heart halted a moment. Then it surged on again, almost suffocating her.

"Is he—is it bad?" she asked.

The man turned away, looking at the darkness: "The doctor says 'e'd been dead hours. 'E saw 'im i' th' lamp-cabin."

The old woman, who stood just behind Elizabeth, dropped into a chair, and folded her hands, crying: "Oh, my boy, my boy!"

"Hush!" said Elizabeth, with a sharp twitch of a frown. "Be still, mother, don't waken th' children: I wouldn't have them down for anything!"

The old woman moaned softly, rocking herself. The man was drawing away. Elizabeth took a step forward.

"How was it?" she asked.

"Well, I couldn't say for sure," the man replied, very ill at ease. "'E wor finishin' a stint an' th' butties 'ad gone, an' a lot o' stuff come down atop 'n 'im."

"And crushed him?" cried the widow, with a shudder.

"No," said the man, "it fell at th' back of 'im. 'E wor under th' face, an' it niver touched 'im. It shut 'im in. It seems 'e wor smothered."

Elizabeth shrank back. She heard the old woman behind her cry:

"What?—what did 'e say it was?"

The man replied, more loudly: "'E wor smothered!"

Then the old woman wailed aloud, and this relieved Elizabeth.

"Oh, mother," she said, putting her hand on the old woman, "don't waken th' children, don't waken th' children."

She wept a little, unknowing, while the old mother rocked herself and moaned. Elizabeth remembered that they were bringing him home, and she must be ready. "They'll lay him in the parlour," she said to herself, standing a moment pale and perplexed.

Then she lighted a candle and went into the tiny room. The air was cold and damp, but she could not make a fire, there was no fireplace. She set down the candle and looked round. The candlelight glittered on the lustre-glasses, on the two vases that held some of the pink chrysanthemums, and on the dark mahogany. There was a cold, deathly smell of chrysanthemums in the room. Elizabeth stood looking at the flowers. She turned away, and calculated whether there would be room to lay him on the floor, between the couch and the chiffonier. She pushed the chairs aside. There would be room to lay him down and to step round him. Then she fetched the old red tablecloth, and another old cloth, spreading them down to save her bit of carpet. She shivered on leaving the parlour; so, from the dresser-drawer she took a clean shirt and put it at the fire to air. All the time her mother-in-law was rocking herself in the chair and moaning.

"You'll have to move from there, mother," said Elizabeth. "They'll be bringing him in. Come in the rocker."

The old mother rose mechanically, and seated herself by the fire, continuing to lament. Elizabeth went into the pantry for another candle, and there, in the little penthouse under the naked tiles, she heard them coming. She stood still in the pantry doorway, listening. She heard them pass the end of the house, and come awkwardly down the three steps, a jumble of shuffling footsteps and muttering voices. The old woman was silent. The men were in the yard.

Then Elizabeth heard Matthews, the manager of the pit, say: "You go in first, Jim. Mind!"

The door came open, and the two women saw a collier backing into the room, holding one end of a stretcher, on which they could see the nailed pit-boots of the dead man. The two carriers halted, the man at the head stooping to the lintel of the door.

"Wheer will you have him?" asked the manager, a short, white-bearded man.

Elizabeth roused herself and came from the pantry carrying the unlighted candle.

"In the parlour," she said.

"In there, Jim!" pointed the manager, and the carriers backed round into the tiny room. The coat with which they had covered the body fell off as they awkwardly turned through the two doorways, and the women saw their man, naked to the waist, lying stripped for work. The old woman began to moan in a low voice of horror.

"Lay th' stretcher at th' side," snapped the manager, "an' put 'im on th' cloths. Mind now, mind! Look you now—!"

One of the men had knocked off a vase of chrysanthemums. He stared awkwardly, then they set down the stretcher. Elizabeth did not look at her husband. As soon as she could get in the room, she went and picked up the broken vase and the flowers.

"Wait a minute!" she said.

The three men waited in silence while she mopped up the water with a duster.

"Eh, what a job, what a job, to be sure!" the manager was saying, rubbing his brow with trouble and perplexity. "Never knew such a thing in my life, never! He'd no business to ha' been left. I never knew such a thing in my life! Fell over him clean as a whistle, an' shut him in. Not four foot of space, there wasn't—yet it scarce bruised him."

He looked down at the dead man, lying prone, half naked, all grimed with coal-dust.

"'Sphyxiated,' the doctor said. It *is* the most terrible job I've ever known. Seems as if it was done o' purpose. Clean over him, an' shut 'im in, like a mouse-trap"—he made a sharp, descending gesture with his hand.

The colliers standing by jerked aside their heads in hopeless comment.

The horror of the thing bristled upon them all.

Then they heard the girl's voice upstairs calling shrilly: "Mother, mother—who is it? Mother, who is it?"

Elizabeth hurried to the foot of the stairs and opened the door:

"Go to sleep!" she commanded sharply. "What are you shouting about? Go to sleep at once—there's nothing—"

Then she began to mount the stairs. They could hear her on the boards, and on the plaster floor of the little bedroom. They could hear her distinctly:

"What's the matter now?—what's the matter with you, silly thing?"—her voice was much agitated, with an unreal gentleness.

"I thought it was some men come," said the plaintive voice of the child. "Has he come?"

"Yes, they've brought him. There's nothing to make a fuss about. Go to sleep now, like a good child."

They could hear her voice in the bedroom, they waited whilst she covered the children under the bedclothes.

"Is he drunk?" asked the girl, timidly, faintly.

"No! No—he's not! He—he's asleep."

"Is he asleep downstairs?"

"Yes—and don't make a noise."

There was silence for a moment, then the men heard the frightened child again:

"What's that noise?"

"It's nothing, I tell you, what are you bothering for?"

The noise was the grandmother moaning. She was oblivious of everything, sitting on her chair rocking and moaning. The manager put his hand on her arm and bade her "Sh—sh!!"

The old woman opened her eyes and looked at him. She was shocked by this interruption, and seemed to wonder.

"What time is it?"—the plaintive thin voice of the child, sinking back unhappily into sleep, asked this last question.

"Ten o'clock," answered the mother more softly. Then she must have bent down and kissed the children.

Matthews beckoned to the men to come away. They put on their caps and took up the stretcher. Stepping over the body, they tiptoed out of the house. None of them spoke till they were far from the wakeful children.

When Elizabeth came down she found her mother alone on the parlour floor, leaning over the dead man, the tears dropping on him.

"We must lay him out," the wife said. She put on the kettle, then returning knelt at the feet, and began to unfasten the knotted leather laces. The room was clammy and dim with only one candle, so that she had to bend her face almost to the floor. At last she got off the heavy boots and put them away.

"You must help me now," she whispered to the old woman. Together they stripped the man.

When they arose, saw him lying in the naive dignity of death, the women stood arrested in fear and respect. For a few moments they remained still, looking down, the old mother whimpering. Elizabeth felt countermanded. She saw him, how utterly inviolable he lay in himself. She had nothing to do with him. She could not accept it. Stooping, she laid her hand on him, in claim. He was still warm, for the mine was hot where he had died. His mother had his face between her hands, and was murmuring incoherently. The old tears fell in succession as drops from wet leaves; the mother was not weeping, merely her tears flowed. Elizabeth embraced the body of her husband, with cheek and lips. She seemed to be listening, inquiring, trying to get some connection. But she could not. She was driven away. He was impregnable.

She rose, went into the kitchen, where she poured warm water into a bowl, brought soap and flannel and a soft towel.

"I must wash him," she said.

Then the old mother rose stiffly, and watched Elizabeth as she carefully washed his face, carefully brushing the big blond moustache from his mouth with the flannel. She was afraid with a bottomless fear, so she ministered to him. The old woman, jealous, said:

"Let me wipe him!"—and she kneeled on the other side drying slowly as Elizabeth washed, her big black bonnet sometimes brushing the dark head of her daughter-in-law. They worked thus in silence for a long time. They never forgot it was death, and the touch of the man's dead body gave them strange emotions, different in each of the women; a great dread possessed them both, the mother felt the lie was given to her womb, she was denied; the wife felt the utter isolation of the human soul, the child within her was a weight apart from her.

At last it was finished. He was a man of handsome body, and his face showed no traces of drink. He was blond, full-fleshed, with fine limbs. But he was dead.

"Bless him," whispered his mother, looking always at his face, and speaking out of sheer terror. "Dear lad—bless him!" She spoke in a faint, sibilant ecstasy of fear and mother love.

Elizabeth sank down again to the floor, and put her face against his neck, and trembled and shuddered. But she had to draw away again. He was dead, and her living flesh had no place against his. A great dread and weariness held her: she was so unavailing. Her life was gone like this.

"White as milk he is, clear as a twelve-month baby, bless him, the darling!" the old mother murmured to herself. "Not a mark on him, clear and clean and white, beautiful as ever a child was made," she murmured with pride. Elizabeth kept her face hidden.

"He went peaceful, Lizzie—peaceful as sleep. Isn't he beautiful, the lamb? Ay—he must ha' made his peace, Lizzie. 'Appen he made it all right, Lizzie, shut in there. He'd have time. He wouldn't look like this if he hadn't made his peace. The lamb, the dear lamb. Eh, but he had a hearty laugh. I loved to hear it. He had the heartiest laugh, Lizzie, as a lad—"

Elizabeth looked up. The man's mouth was fallen back, slightly open under the cover of the moustache. The eyes, half shut, did not show glazed in the obscurity. Life with its smoky burning gone from him, had left him apart and utterly alien to her. And she knew what a stranger he was to her. In her womb was ice of fear, because of this separate stranger with whom she had been living as one flesh. Was this what it all meant—utter, intact separateness, obscured by heat of living? In dread she turned her face away. The fact was too deadly. There had been nothing between them, and yet they had come together, exchanging their nakedness repeatedly. Each time he had taken her, they had been two isolated beings, far apart as now. He was no more responsible than she. The child was like ice in her womb. For as she looked at the dead man, her mind, cold and detached, said clearly: "Who am I? What have I been doing? I have been fighting a husband who did not exist. *He* existed all the time. What wrong have I done? What was that I have been living with? There lies the reality, this man." And her soul died in her for fear: she knew she had never seen him, he had never seen her, they had met in the dark and had fought in the dark, not knowing whom they met nor whom they fought. And now she saw, and turned silent in seeing. For she had been wrong. She had said he was something he was not; she had felt familiar with him. Whereas he was apart all the while, living as she never lived, feeling as she never felt.

In fear and shame she looked at his naked body, that she had known falsely. And he was the father of her children. Her soul was torn from her body and stood apart. She looked at his naked body and was ashamed, as if she had denied it. After all, it was itself. It seemed awful to her. She looked at his face, and she turned her own face to the wall. For his look was other than hers, his way was not her way. She had denied him what he was—she saw it now. She had refused him as himself. And this had been her life, and his life. She was grateful to death, which restored the truth. And she knew she was not dead.

And all the while her heart was bursting with grief and pity for him. What had he suffered? What stretch of horror for this helpless man! She was rigid with agony. She had not been able to help him. He had been cruelly injured, this naked man, this other being, and she could make no reparation. There were the children—but the children belonged to life. This dead man had nothing to do with them. He and she were only channels through which life had flowed to issue in the children. She was a mother—but how awful she knew it now to have been a wife. And he, dead now, how awful he must have felt it to be a husband. She felt that in the next world he would be a stranger to her. If they met there, in the beyond, they would only be ashamed of what had been before. The children had come, for some mysterious reason, out of both of them. But the children did not unite them. Now he was dead, she knew how eternally he was apart from her, how eternally he had nothing more to do with her. She saw this episode of her life closed. They had denied each other in life. Now he had withdrawn. An anguish came over her. It was finished then: it had become hopeless between them long

before he died. Yet he had been her husband. But how little!

"Have you got his shirt, 'Lizabeth?"

Elizabeth turned without answering, though she strove to weep and behave as her mother-in-law expected. But she could not, she was silenced. She went into the kitchen and returned with the garment.

"It is aired," she said, grasping the cotton shirt here and there to try. She was almost ashamed to handle him; what right had she or any one to lay hands on him; but her touch was humble on his body. It was hard work to clothe him. He was so heavy and inert. A terrible dread gripped her all the while: that he could be so heavy and utterly inert, unresponsive, apart. The horror of the distance between them was almost too much for her—it was so infinite a gap she must look across.

At last it was finished. They covered him with a sheet and left him lying, with his face bound. And she fastened the door of the little parlour, lest the children should see what was lying there. Then, with peace sunk heavy on her heart, she went about making tidy the kitchen. She knew she submitted to life, which was her immediate master. But from death, her ultimate master, she winced with fear and shame.

Aldous Huxley

Despite the formidable competition of Evelyn Waugh and the late George Orwell, Aldous Huxley still holds the place which he won in the twenties and thirties as leading satirist of the first half of the present century. Born in 1894, the grandson of Thomas Henry Huxley and, on his mother's side, the great-grandson of Thomas Arnold, he might have seemed destined to reconcile in his own person intellectual forces which to the Victorians must sometimes have seemed irreconcilable. He was educated at Eton and Balliol. For a time in the early twenties he was engaged in journalistic activities in London, serving at one time or another as co-editor of the *Athenaeum* and as dramatic critic for the *Westminster Gazette*. From 1923 to 1930 he lived in Italy, and he has traveled widely throughout the world. At present he lives in California.

Huxley began his literary career with the publication of two volumes of poems, *The Burning Wheel* (1916) and *The Defeat of Youth* (1918). His first work of fiction, *Limbo,* consisting of six stories and a play, was published in 1920, and his first novel, *Crome Yellow,* in 1921. After that there was scarcely a year, throughout the twenties

and thirties, that did not witness the appearance of at least one new book from his pen. Of these many books, the novels undoubtedly form the center of his achievement, from *Crome Yellow* and *Antic Hay* (1923)—the latter presenting, among the many characters who move in little patterned groups or singly through its dancelike structure, a number of figures who seem almost the prototypes of all that we mean when we speak of the postwar "lost generation"—up through *Those Barren Leaves* (1925), *Point Counter Point* (1928), and *Brave New World* (1932)—these last two still the most widely read—to *Eyeless in Gaza* (1936), *After Many a Summer* (1939), *Time Must Have a Stop* (1944), and, the most recent to date, *Ape and Essence* (1949), a novel written, perhaps disconcertingly, in the form of a movie scenario. Huxley's satiric vision has grown steadily deeper and more intense; nevertheless certain qualities of mind and art which made for unmixed delight in the early novels and stories have persisted against the darkening background: his brilliant wit, his easily worn and widely varied learning, the clarity, force, and pungency of his style.

If the novels are the heart of his achievement, they are

still only a part of it: Huxley is a complete man of letters and has done distinguished work in many forms. Close to the novels in interest and theme are the several volumes of short stories, a number of the best, like the one printed below, set against a vividly evoked Italian background: *Mortal Coils* (1922), *Little Mexican* (1924), *Two or Three Graces* (1926), and *Brief Candles* (1930). He has written full-length travel books, like *Jesting Pilate* (1926), which grew out of a trip around the world and deals particularly with Asia, or *Beyond the Mexique Bay* (1934), and essays on travel and on particular places he has known, like those collected in *Along the Road* (1925). His philosophical and socio-political views have been set forth in such books as *Proper Studies* (1927) and *Ends and Means* (1937), or in the long essays in *Music at Night* (1931) and *The Olive Tree* (1936).

There is a volume-length critical essay, *Aldous Huxley*, by Alexander Henderson (1935).

GREEN TUNNELS[1]

"IN the Italian gardens of the thirteenth century . . ." Mr. Buzzacott interrupted himself to take another helping of the risotto which was being offered him. "Excellent risotto this," he observed. "Nobody who was not born in Milan can make it properly. So they say."

"So they say," Mr. Topes repeated in his sad, apologetic voice, and helped himself in his turn.

"Personally," said Mrs. Topes, with decision, "I find all Italian cooking abominable. I don't like the oil—especially hot. No, thank you." She recoiled from the proffered dish.

After the first mouthful Mr. Buzzacott put down his fork. "In the Italian gardens of the thirteenth century," he began again, making with his long, pale hand a curved and flowery gesture that ended with a clutch at his beard, "a frequent and most felicitous use was made of green tunnels."

"Green tunnels?" Barbara woke up suddenly from her tranced silence. "Green tunnels?"

"Yes, my dear," said her father. "Green tunnels. Arched alleys covered with vines or other creeping plants. Their length was often very considerable."

But Barbara had once more ceased to pay attention to what he was saying. Green tunnels—the word had floated down to her, through profound depths of reverie, across great spaces of abstraction, startling her like the sound of a strange-voiced bell. Green tunnels —what a wonderful idea. She would not listen to her father explaining the phrase into dullness. He made everything dull; an inverted alchemist, turning gold into lead. She pictured caverns in a great aquarium, long vistas between rocks and scarcely swaying weeds and pale, discoloured corals; endless dim green corridors with huge lazy fishes loitering aimlessly along them. Green-faced monsters with goggling eyes and mouths that slowly opened and shut. Green tunnels. . .

"I have seen them illustrated in illuminated manuscripts of the period," Mr. Buzzacott went on; once more he clutched his pointed brown beard— clutched and combed it with his long fingers.

Mr. Topes looked up. The glasses of his round owlish spectacles flashed as he moved his head. "I know what you mean," he said.

"I have a very good mind to have one planted in my garden here."

"It will take a long time to grow," said Mr. Topes. "In this sand, so close to the sea, you will only be able to plant vines. And they come up very slowly—very slowly indeed." He shook his head and the points of light danced wildly in his spectacles. His voice drooped hopelessly, his grey moustache drooped, his whole person drooped. Then, suddenly, he pulled himself up. A shy, apologetic smile appeared on his face. He wriggled uncomfortably. Then, with a final rapid shake of the head, he gave vent to a quotation:

"But at my back I always hear
Time's winged chariot hurrying near."[2]

He spoke deliberately, and his voice trembled a little. He always found it painfully difficult to say something choice and out of the ordinary; and yet what a wealth of remembered phrase, what apt new coinages were always surging through his mind!

"They don't grow so slowly as all that," said Mr. Buzzacott confidently. He was only just over fifty, and looked a handsome thirty-five. He gave himself at least another forty years; indeed, he had not yet begun to contemplate the possibility of ever concluding.

[1] From *Mortal Coils* by Aldous Huxley, copyright 1922 by Aldous Huxley. Reprinted by permission of Harper & Brothers.

[2] Andrew Marvell's "To His Coy Mistress," lines 21 f. (see I, 528 f., above).

"Miss Barbara will enjoy it, perhaps—your green tunnel." Mr. Topes sighed and looked across the table at his host's daughter.

Barbara was sitting with her elbows on the table, her chin in her hands, staring in front of her. The sound of her own name reached her faintly. She turned her head in Mr. Topes's direction and found herself confronted by the glitter of his round, convex spectacles. At the end of the green tunnel—she stared at the shining circles—hung the eyes of a goggling fish. They approached, floating, closer and closer, along the dim submarine corridor.

Confronted by this fixed regard, Mr. Topes looked away. What thoughtful eyes! He couldn't remember ever to have seen eyes so full of thought. There were certain Madonnas of Montagna, he reflected, very like her: mild little blonde Madonnas with slightly snub noses and very, very young. But he was old; it would be many years, in spite of Buzzacott, before the vines grew up into a green tunnel. He took a sip of wine; then, mechanically, sucked his drooping grey moustache.

"Arthur!"

At the sound of his wife's voice Mr. Topes started, raised his napkin to his mouth. Mrs. Topes did not permit the sucking of moustaches. It was only in moments of absentmindedness that he ever offended, now.

"The Marchese Prampolini is coming here to take coffee," said Mr. Buzzacott suddenly. "I almost forgot to tell you."

"One of these Italian marquises, I suppose," said Mrs. Topes, who was no snob, except in England. She raised her chin with a little jerk.

Mr. Buzzacott executed an upward curve of the hand in her direction. "I assure you, Mrs. Topes, he belongs to a very old and distinguished family. They are Genoese in origin. You remember their palace, Barbara? Built by Alessi."

Barbara looked up. "Oh yes," she said vaguely. "Alessi. I know." Alessi: Aleppo—where a malignant and a turbaned Turk.[3] *And* a turbaned; that had always seemed to her very funny.

"Several of his ancestors," Mr. Buzzacott went on, "distinguished themselves as viceroys of Corsica. They did good work in the suppression of rebellion. Strange, isn't it"—he turned parenthetically to Mr. Topes—"the way in which sympathy is always on the side of rebels? What a fuss people made of Corsica! That ridiculous book of Gregorovius, for

---

[3] See Othello's final speech.

example. And the Irish, and the Poles, and all the rest of them. It always seems to me very superfluous and absurd."

"Isn't it, perhaps, a little natural?" Mr. Topes began timorously and tentatively; but his host went on without listening.

"The present marquis," he said, "is the head of the local Fascisti. They have done no end of good work in this district in the way of preserving law and order and keeping the lower classes in their place."

"Ah, the Fascisti," Mrs. Topes repeated approvingly. "One would like to see something of the kind in England. What with all these strikes . . ."

"He has asked me for a subscription to the funds of the organisation. I shall give him one, of course."

"Of course." Mrs. Topes nodded. "My nephew, the one who was a major during the war, volunteered in the last coal strike. He was sorry, I know, that it didn't come to a fight. 'Aunt Annie,' he said to me, when I saw him last, 'if there had been a fight we should have knocked them out completely—completely.'"

In Aleppo, the Fascisti, malignant *and* turbaned, were fighting, under the palm trees. Weren't they palm trees, those tufted green plumes?

"What, no ice to-day? *Niente gelato?*" inquired Mr. Buzzacott as the maid put down the compote of peaches on the table.

Concetta apologised. The ice-making machine in the village had broken down. There would be no ice till to-morrow.

"Too bad," said Mr. Buzzacott. "*Troppo male,* Concetta."

Under the palm trees, Barbara saw them: they pranced about, fighting. They were mounted on big dogs, and in the trees were enormous many-coloured birds.

"Goodness me, the child's asleep." Mrs. Topes was proffering the dish of peaches. "How much longer am I to hold this in front of your nose, Barbara?"

Barbara felt herself blushing. "I'm so sorry," she mumbled, and took the dish clumsily.

"Day-dreaming. It's a bad habit."

"It's one we all succumb to sometimes," put in Mr. Topes deprecatingly, with a little nervous tremble of the head.

"You may, my dear," said his wife. "I do not."

Mr. Topes lowered his eyes to his plate and went on eating.

"The *marchese* should be here at any moment now," said Mr. Buzzacott, looking at his watch. "I hope he won't be late. I find I suffer so much from any postponement of my siesta. This Italian heat," he added, with growing plaintiveness, "one can't be too careful."

"Ah, but when I was with my father in India," began Mrs. Topes in a tone of superiority: "he was an Indian civilian, you know . . ."

Aleppo, India—always the palm trees. Cavalcades of big dogs, and tigers too.

Concetta ushered in the marquis. Delighted. Pleased to meet. Speak English? Yés, yéss. *Pocchino*.[4] Mrs. Topes: and Mr. Topes, the distinguished antiquarian. Ah, of course; know his name very well. My daughter. Charmed. Often seen the signorina bathing. Admired the way she dives. Beautiful—the hand made a long, caressing gesture. These athletic English signorine. The teeth flashed astonishingly white in the brown face, the dark eyes glittered. She felt herself blushing again, looked away, smiled foolishly. The marquis had already turned back to Mr. Buzzacott.

"So you have decided to settle in our Carrarese."

Well, not settled exactly; Mr. Buzzacott wouldn't go so far as to say settled. A villino for the summer months. The winter in Rome. One was forced to live abroad. Taxation in England . . . Soon they were all talking. Barbara looked at them. Beside the marquis they all seemed half dead. His face flashed as he talked; he seemed to be boiling with life. Her father was limp and pale, like something long buried from the light; and Mr. Topes was all dry and shrivelled; and Mrs. Topes looked more than ever like something worked by clockwork. They were talking about Socialism and Fascisti, and all that. Barbara did not listen to what they were saying; but she looked at them, absorbed.

Good-bye, good-bye. The animated face with its flash of a smile was turned like a lamp from one to another. Now it was turned on her. Perhaps one evening she would come, with her father, and the Signora Topes. He and his sister gave little dances sometimes. Only the gramophone, of course. But that was better than nothing, and the signorina must dance divinely—another flash—he could see that. He pressed her hand again. Good-bye.

It was time for the siesta.

"Don't forget to pull down the mosquito netting, my dear," Mr. Buzzacott exhorted. "There is always a danger of anophylines."

"All right, father." She moved towards the door without turning round to answer him. He was always terribly tiresome about mosquito nets. Once

---

[4] A little.

they had driven through the Campagna in a hired cab, completely enclosed in an improvised tent of netting. The monuments along the Appian Way had loomed up mistily as through bridal veils. And how everyone had laughed. But her father, of course, hadn't so much as noticed it. He never noticed anything.

"Is it at Berlin, that charming little Madonna of Montagna's?" Mr. Topes abruptly asked. "The one with the Donor kneeling in the left-hand corner as if about to kiss the foot of the Child." His spectacles flashed in Mr. Buzzacott's direction.

"Why do you ask?"

"I don't know. I was just thinking of it."

"I think you must mean the one in the Mond Collection."

"Ah yes; very probably. In the Mond . . ."

Barbara opened the door and walked into the twilight of her shuttered room. It was hot even here; for another three hours it would hardly be possible to stir. And that old idiot, Mrs. Topes, always made a fuss if one came in to lunch with bare legs and one's after-bathing tunic. "In India we always made a point of being properly and adequately dressed. An Englishwoman must keep up her position with natives, and to all intents and purposes Italians *are* natives." And so she always had to put on shoes and stockings and a regular frock just at the hottest hour of the day. What an old ass that woman was! She slipped off her clothes as fast as she could. That was a little better.

Standing in front of the long mirror in the wardrobe door she came to the humiliating conclusion that she looked like a piece of badly toasted bread. Brown face, brown neck and shoulders, brown arms, brown legs from the knee downwards; but all the rest of her was white, silly, effeminate, townish white. If only one could run about with no clothes on till one was like those little coppery children who rolled and tumbled in the burning sand! Now she was just underdone, half-baked, and wholly ridiculous. For a long time she looked at her pale image. She saw herself running, bronzed all over, along the sand; or through a field of flowers, narcissus and wild tulips; or in soft grass under grey olive trees. She turned round with a sudden start. There, in the shadows behind her . . . No, of course there was nothing. It was that awful picture in a magazine she had looked at, so many years ago, when she was a child. There was a lady sitting at her dressing-table, doing her hair in front of the glass; and a huge, hairy black monkey creeping up behind her. She always got the creeps when she looked at herself in a mirror. It was very silly. But still. She turned away from the mirror, crossed the room, and, without lowering the mosquito curtains, lay down on her bed. The flies buzzed about her, settled incessantly on her face. She shook her head, flapped at them angrily with her hands. There would be peace if she let down the netting. But she thought of the Appian Way seen mistily through the bridal veil and preferred to suffer the flies. In the end she had to surrender; the brutes were too much for her. But, at any rate, it wasn't the fear of anophylines that made her lower the netting.

Undisturbed now and motionless, she lay stretched stiffly out under the transparent bell of gauze. A specimen under a glass case. The fancy possessed her mind. She saw a huge museum with thousands of glass cases, full of fossils and butterflies and stuffed birds and mediaeval spoons and armour and Florentine jewellery and mummies and carved ivory and illuminated manuscripts. But in one of the cases was a human being, shut up there alive.

All of a sudden she became horribly miserable. "Boring, boring, boring," she whispered, formulating the words aloud. Would it never stop being boring? The tears came into her eyes. How awful everything was! And perhaps it would go on being as bad as this all her life. Seventeen from seventy was fifty-three. Fifty-three years of it. And if she lived to a hundred there would be more than eighty.

The thought depressed her all the evening. Even her bath after tea did her no good. Swimming far out, far out, she lay there, floating on the warm water. Sometimes she looked at the sky, sometimes she turned her head towards the shore. Framed in their pinewoods, the villas looked as small and smug as the advertisement of a seaside resort. But behind them, across the level plain, were the mountains. Sharp, bare peaks of limestone, green woodland slopes and grey-green expanses of terraced olive trees—they seemed marvellously close and clear in this evening light. And beautiful, beautiful beyond words. But that, somehow, only made things worse. And Shelley had lived a few miles farther up the coast, there, behind the headland guarding the Gulf of Spezia. Shelley had been drowned in this milk-warm sea. That made it worse too.

The sun was getting very low and red over the sea. She swam slowly in. On the beach Mrs. Topes waited, disapprovingly. She had known somebody, a strong man, who had caught cramp from staying in too long. He sank like a stone. Like a stone. The queer people Mrs. Topes had known! And the funny things they did, the odd things that happened to them! Dinner that evening was duller than ever. Barbara

went early to bed. All night long the same old irritating cicada scraped and scraped among the pine trees, monotonous and regular as clockwork. Zip zip, zip zip zip. Boring, boring, Was the animal never bored by its own noise? It seemed odd that it shouldn't be. But, when she came to think of it, nobody ever did get bored with their own noise. Mrs. Topes, for example; she never seemed to get bored. Zip zip, zip zip zip. The cicada went on without pause.

Concetta knocked at the door at half-past seven. The morning was as bright and cloudless as all the mornings were. Barbara jumped up, looked from one window at the mountains, from the other at the sea; all seemed to be well with them. All was well with her, too, this morning. Seated at the mirror, she did not so much as think of the big monkey in the far obscure corner of the room. A bathing dress and a bath-gown, sandals, a handkerchief round her head, and she was ready. Sleep had left no recollection of last night's mortal boredom. She ran downstairs.

"Good morning, Mr. Topes."

Mr. Topes was walking in the garden among the vines. He turned round, took off his hat, smiled a greeting.

"Good morning, Miss Barbara." He paused. Then, with an embarrassed wriggle of introduction he went on; a queer little falter came into his voice. "A real Chaucerian morning, Miss Barbara. A May-day morning—only it happens to be September. Nature is fresh and bright, and there is at least one specimen in this dream garden"—he wriggled more uncomfortably than ever, and there was a tremulous glitter in his round spectacle lenses—"of the poet's 'yonge fresshe folkes.'" He bowed in her direction, smiled deprecatingly, and was silent. The remark, it seemed to him, now that he had finished speaking, was somehow not as good as he had thought it would be.

Barbara laughed. "Chaucer! They used to make us read the *Canterbury Tales* at school. But they always bored me. Are you going to bathe?"

"Not before breakfast." Mr. Topes shook his head. "One is getting a little too old for that."

"Is one?" Why did the silly old man always say 'one' when he meant 'I'? She couldn't help laughing at him. "Well, I must hurry, or else I shall be late for breakfast again, and you know how I catch it."

She ran out, through the gate in the garden wall, across the beach, to the striped red-and-white bathing cabin that stood before the house. Fifty yards away she saw the Marchese Prampolini, still dripping from the sea, running up towards his bathing hut. Catching sight of her, he flashed a smile in her direction, gave a military salute. Barbara waved her hand, then thought that the gesture had been too familiar—but at this hour of the morning it was difficult not to have bad jolly manners—and added the corrective of a stiff bow. After all, she had only met him yesterday. Soon she was swimming out to sea, and, ugh! what a lot of horrible huge jelly-fish there were.

Mr. Topes had followed her slowly through the gate and across the sand. He watched her running down from the cabin, slender as a boy, with long, bounding strides. He watched her go jumping with great splashes through the deepening water, then throw herself forward and begin to swim. He watched her till she was no more than a small dark dot far out.

Emerging from his cabin, the marquis met him walking slowly along the beach, his head bent down and his lips slightly moving as though he were repeating something, a prayer or a poem, to himself.

"Good morning, signore." The marquis shook him by the hand with a more than English cordiality.

"Good morning," replied Mr. Topes, allowing his hand to be shaken. He resented this interruption of his thoughts.

"She swims very well, Miss Buzzacott."

"Very," assented Mr. Topes, and smiled to himself to think what beautiful, poetical things he might have said, if he had chosen.

"Well, so, so," said the marquis, too colloquial by half. He shook hands again, and the two men went their respective ways.

Barbara was still a hundred yards from the shore when she heard the crescendo and dying boom of the gong floating out from the villa. Damn! she'd be late again. She quickened her stroke and came splashing out through the shallows, flushed and breathless. She'd be ten minutes late, she calculated; it would take her at least that to do her hair and dress. Mrs. Topes would be on the warpath again; though what business that old woman had to lecture her as she did, goodness only knew. She always succeeded in making herself horribly offensive and unpleasant.

The beach was quite deserted as she trotted, panting, across it, empty to right and left as far as she could see. If only she had a horse to go galloping at the water's edge, miles and miles. Right away down to Bocca d'Arno she'd go, swim the river—she saw herself crouching on the horse's back, as he swam, with legs tucked up on the saddle, trying not to get her feet wet—and gallop on again, goodness only knew where.

In front of the cabin she suddenly halted. There in the ruffled sand she had seen a writing. Big letters, faintly legible, sprawled across her path.

O CLARA D'ELLÉBEUSE.[5]

She pieced the dim letters together. They hadn't been there when she started out to bathe. Who? . . . She looked round. The beach was quite empty. And what was the meaning? "O Clara d'Ellébeuse." She took her bath-gown from the cabin, slipped on her sandals, and ran back towards the house as fast as she could. She felt most horribly frightened.

It was a sultry, headachey sort of morning, with a hot sirocco that stirred the bunting on the flagstaffs. By midday the thunderclouds had covered half the sky. The sun still blazed on the sea, but over the mountains all was black and indigo. The storm broke noisily overhead just as they were drinking their after-luncheon coffee.

"Arthur," said Mrs. Topes, painfully calm, "shut the shutters, please."

She was not frightened, no. But she preferred not to see the lightning. When the room was darkened, she began to talk, suavely and incessantly.

Lying back in her deep arm-chair, Barbara was thinking of Clara d'Ellébeuse. What did it mean and who was Clara d'Ellébeuse? And why had he written it there for her to see? He—for there could be no doubt who had written it. The flash of teeth and eyes, the military salute; she knew she oughtn't to have waved to him. He had written it there while she was swimming out. Written it and then run away. She rather liked that—just an extraordinary word on the sand, like the footprint in *Robinson Crusoe*.

[5] The reader should know, even if Barbara doesn't, that the words traced in the sand are from a poem by Francis Jammes (1868–1938), beginning:

> J'aime dans les temps Clara d'Ellébeuse,
> l'écolière des anciens pensionnats,
> qui allait, les soirs chauds, sous les tilleuls
> lire les *magazines* d'autrefois.

> (I love in the old time Clara d'Ellébeuse,
> the scholar of the boarding-schools of that old time,
> who on warm evenings used to go under the lime trees
> to read the magazines of that day.)

After three more stanzas of evocation of Clara d'Ellébeuse and her world, it ends:

> Viens, viens, ma chère Clara d'Ellébeuse;
> aimons nous encore si tu existes.
> Le vieux jardin a de vieilles tulipes.
> Viens toute nue, ô Clara d'Ellébeuse.

> (Come, come, my dear Clara d'Ellébeuse;
> let us love again if you are on earth.
> The old garden has old tulips.
> Come quite naked, O Clara d'Ellébeuse.)

"Personally," Mrs. Topes was saying, "I prefer Harrod's."

The thunder crashed and rattled. It was rather exhilarating, Barbara thought; one felt, at any rate, that something was happening for a change. She remembered the little room half-way up the stairs at Lady Thingumy's house, with the bookshelves and the green curtains and the orange shade on the light; and that awful young man like a white slug who had tried to kiss her there, at the dance last year. But that was different—not at all serious; and the young man had been so horribly ugly. She saw the marquis running up the beach, quick and alert. Copper coloured all over, with black hair. He was certainly very handsome. But as for being in love, well . . . what did that exactly mean? Perhaps when she knew him better. Even now she fancied she detected something. O Clara d'Ellébeuse. What an extraordinary thing it was!

With his long fingers Mr. Buzzacott combed his beard. This winter, he was thinking, he would put another thousand into Italian money when the exchange was favourable. In the spring it always seemed to drop back again. One could clear three hundred pounds on one's capital if the exchange went down to seventy. The income on three hundred was fifteen pounds a year, and fifteen pounds was now fifteen hundred lire. And fifteen hundred lire, when you came to think of it, was really sixty pounds. That was to say that one would make an addition of more than one pound a week to one's income by this simple little speculation. He became aware that Mrs. Topes had asked him a question.

"Yes, yes, perfectly," he said.

Mrs. Topes talked on; she was keeping up her morale. Was she right in believing that the thunder sounded a little less alarmingly loud and near?

Mr. Topes sat, polishing his spectacles with a white silk handkerchief. Vague and myopic between their puckered lids, his eyes seemed lost, homeless, unhappy. He was thinking about beauty. There were certain relations between the eyelids and the temples, between the breast and the shoulder; there were certain successions of sounds. But what about them? Ah, that was the problem—that was the problem. And there was youth, there was innocence. But it was all very obscure, and there were so many phrases, so many remembered pictures and melodies; he seemed to get himself entangled among them. And he was after all so old and so ineffective.

He put on his spectacles again, and definition came into the foggy world beyond his eyes. The shuttered room was very dark. He could distinguish the Renaissance profile of Mr. Buzzacott, bearded and delicately featured. In her deep arm-chair Barbara appeared, faintly white, in an attitude relaxed and brooding. And Mrs. Topes was nothing more than a voice in the darkness. She had got on to the marriage of the Prince of Wales. Who would they eventually find for him?

Clara d'Ellébeuse, Clara d'Ellébeuse. She saw herself so clearly as the *marchesa*. They would have a house in Rome, a palace. She saw herself in the Palazzo Spada—it had such a lovely vaulted passage leading from the courtyard to the gardens at the back. "MARCHESA PRAMPOLINI, PALAZZO SPADA, ROMA"—a great big visiting-card beautifully engraved. And she would go riding every day in the Pincio. "*Mi porta il mio cavallo,*"[6] she would say to the footman, who answered the bell. *Porta?* Would that be quite correct? Hardly. She'd have to take some proper Italian lessons to talk to the servants. One must never be ridiculous before servants. "*Voglio il mio cavallo.*" Haughtily one would say it sitting at one's writing-table in a riding-habit, without turning round. It would be a green riding-habit, with a black tricorne hat, braided with silver.

"*Prendero la mia collazione al letto.*"[7] Was that right for breakfast? Because she would have breakfast in bed, always. And when she got up there would be lovely looking-glasses with three panels where one could see oneself sideface. She saw herself leaning forward, powdering her nose, carefully, scientifically. With the monkey creeping up behind? Ooh! Horrible! *Ho paura di questa scimmia, questo scimmione.*[8]

She would come back to lunch after her ride. Perhaps Prampolini would be there; she had rather left him out of the picture so far. "*Dov' è il Marchese?*" "*Nella sala di pranza, signora.*"[9] I began without you, I was so hungry. *Pasta asciutta.*[10] Where have you been, my love? Riding, my dove. She supposed they'd get into the habit of saying that sort of thing. Everyone seemed to. And you? I have been out with the Fascisti.

Oh, these Fascisti! Would life be worth living when he was always going out with pistols and bombs and

---

6 Barbara *thinks* she is saying, "Bring me my horse," just as she next thinks she is saying, "I want my horse."
7 "I shall take my breakfast in bed."
8 "I am afraid of this monkey, of this great ape."
9 "Where is the Marchese?" "In the dining room, signora."
10 Literally, dried paste, the generic term of which macaroni, spaghetti, etc., are particular species.

things? They would bring him back one day on a stretcher. She saw it. Pale, pale, with blood on him. *Il signore è ferito. Nel petto. Gravamente. E morto.*[11]

How could she bear it? It was too awful; too, too terrible. Her breath came in a kind of sob; she shuddered as though she had been hurt. *E morto. E morto.* The tears came into her eyes.

She was roused suddenly by a dazzling light. The storm had receded far enough into the distance to permit of Mrs. Topes's opening the shutters.

"It's quite stopped raining."

To be disturbed in one's intimate sorrow and self-abandonment at a death-bed by a stranger's intrusion, an alien voice . . . Barbara turned her face away from the light and surreptitiously wiped her eyes. They might see and ask her why she had been crying. She hated Mrs. Topes for opening the shutters; at the inrush of the light something beautiful had flown, an emotion had vanished, irrecoverably. It was a sacrilege.

Mr. Buzzacott looked at his watch. "Too late, I fear, for a siesta now," he said. "Suppose we ring for an early tea."

"An endless succession of meals," said Mr. Topes, with a tremolo and a sigh. "That's what life seems to be—real life."

"I have been calculating"—Mr. Buzzacott turned his pale green eyes towards his guest—"that I may be able to afford that pretty little *cinque* cassone,[12] after all. It would be a bit of a squeeze." He played with his beard. "But still . . ."

After tea, Barbara and Mr. Topes went for a walk along the beach. She didn't much want to go, but Mrs. Topes thought it would be good for her; so she had to. The storm had passed and the sky over the sea was clear. But the waves were still breaking with an incessant clamour on the outer shallows, driving wide sheets of water high up the beach, twenty or thirty yards above the line where, on a day of calm, the ripples ordinarily expired. Smooth, shining expanses of water advanced and receded like steel surfaces moved out and back by a huge machine. Through the rain-washed air the mountains appeared with an incredible clarity. Above them hung huge masses of cloud.

"Clouds over Carrara," said Mr. Topes, deprecating his remark with a little shake of the head and a movement of the shoulders. "I like to fancy sometimes that the spirits of the great sculptors lodge among these marble hills, and that it is their unseen hands that carve the clouds into these enormous splendid shapes. I imagine their ghosts"—his voice trembled—"feeling about among superhuman conceptions, planning huge groups and friezes and monumental figures with blowing draperies; planning, conceiving, but never quite achieving. Look, there's something of Michelangelo in that white cloud with the dark shadows underneath it." Mr. Topes pointed, and Barbara nodded and said, "Yes, yes," though she wasn't quite sure which cloud he meant. "It's like Night on the Medici tomb; all the power and passion are brooding inside it, pent up. And there, in that sweeping, gesticulating piece of vapour—you see the one I mean—there's a Bernini. All the passion's on the surface, expressed; the gesture's caught at its most violent. And that sleek, smug white fellow over there, that's a delicious absurd Canova." Mr. Topes chuckled.

"Why do you always talk about art?" said Barbara. "You bring these dead people into everything. What do I know about Canova or whoever it is?" They were none of them alive. She thought of that dark face, bright as a lamp with life. He at least wasn't dead. She wondered whether the letters were still there in the sand before the cabin. No, of course not; the rain and the wind would have blotted them out.

Mr. Topes was silent; he walked with slightly bent knees and his eyes were fixed on the ground; he wore a speckled black-and-white straw hat. He always thought of art; that was what was wrong with him. Like an old tree he was; built up of dead wood, with only a few fibres of life to keep him from rotting away. They walked on for a long time in silence.

"Here's the river," said Mr. Topes at last.

A few steps more and they were on the bank of a wide stream that came down slowly through the plain to the sea. Just inland from the beach it was fringed with pine trees; beyond the trees one could see the plain, and beyond the plain were the mountains. In this calm light after the storm everything looked strange. The colours seemed deeper and more intense than at ordinary times. And though all was so clear, there was a mysterious air of remoteness about the whole scene. There was no sound except the continuous breathing of the sea. They stood for a little while, looking; then turned back.

Far away along the beach two figures were slowly approaching. White flannel trousers, a pink skirt.

"Nature," Mr. Topes enunciated, with a shake of the head. "One always comes back to nature. At a

---

[11] "The signore is wounded. In the breast. Seriously. He is dead."

[12] Sixteenth-century chest (*cinque* for *cinquecento*, the term used to designate the sixteenth century as a period in the development of Italian art).

moment such as this, in surroundings like these, one realises it. One lives now—more quietly, perhaps, but more profoundly. Deep waters. Deep waters . . ."

The figures drew closer. Wasn't it the marquis? And who was with him? Barbara strained her eyes to see.

"Most of one's life," Mr. Topes went on, "is one prolonged effort to prevent oneself thinking. Your father and I, we collect pictures and read about the dead. Other people achieve the same results by drinking, or breeding rabbits, or doing amateur carpentry. Anything rather than think calmly about the important things."

Mr. Topes was silent. He looked about him, at the sea, at the great clouds, at his companion. A frail Montagna madonna, with the sea and the westering sun, the mountains and the storm, all eternity as a background. And he was sixty, with all a life, immensely long and yet timelessly short, behind him, an empty life. He thought of death and the miracles of beauty; behind his round, glittering spectacles he felt inclined to weep.

The approaching couple were quite near now.

"What a funny old walrus," said the lady.

"Walrus? Your natural history is quite wrong." The marquis laughed. "He's much too dry to be a walrus. I should suggest some sort of an old cat."

"Well, whatever he is, I'm sorry for that poor little girl. Think of having nobody better to go about with!"

"Pretty, isn't she?"

"Yes, but too young, of course."

"I like innocence."

"Innocence? Cher ami! These English girls. Oh, la la! They may look innocent. But, believe me . . ."

"Sh, sh. They'll hear you."

"Pooh, they don't understand Italian."

The marquis raised his hand. "The old walrus . . ." he whispered; then addressed himself loudly and jovially to the newcomers.

"Good evening, signorina. Good evening, Mr. Topes. After a storm the air is always the purest, don't you find, eh?"

Barbara nodded, leaving Mr. Topes to answer. It wasn't his sister. It was the Russian woman, the one of whom Mrs. Topes used to say that it was a disgrace she should be allowed to stay at the hotel. She had turned away, dissociating herself from the

conversation; Barbara looked at the line of her averted face. Mr. Topes was saying something about the Pastoral Symphony. Purple face powder in the daylight; it looked hideous.

"Well, au revoir."

The flash of the marquis's smile was directed at them. The Russian woman turned back from the sea, slightly bowed, smiled languidly. Her heavy white eyelids were almost closed; she seemed the prey of an enormous ennui.

"They jar a little," said Mr. Topes when they were out of earshot—"they jar on the time, on the place, on the emotion. They haven't the innocence for this . . . this . . . "—he wriggled and tremoloed out the just, the all too precious word—"this prelapsarian landscape."

He looked sideways at Barbara and wondered what she was so thoughtfully frowning over. Oh, lovely and delicate young creature! What could he adequately say of death and beauty and tenderness? Tenderness . . .

"All this," he went on desperately, and waved his hand to indicate the sky, the sea, the mountains, "this scene is like something remembered, clear and utterly calm; remembered across great gulfs of intervening time."

But that was not really what he wanted to say.

"You see what I mean?" he asked dubiously. She made no reply. How could she see? "This scene is so clear and pure and remote; you need the corresponding emotion. Those people were out of harmony. They weren't clear and pure enough." He seemed to be getting more muddled than ever. "It's an emotion of the young and of the old. You could feel it, I could feel it. Those people couldn't." He was feeling his way through obscurities. Where would he finally arrive? "Certain poems express it. You know Francis Jammes? I have thought so much of his work lately. Art instead of life, as usual; but then I'm made that way. I can't help thinking of Jammes. Those delicate, exquisite things he wrote about Clara d'Ellébeuse."

"Clara d'Ellébeuse?" She stopped and stared at him.

"You know the lines?" Mr. Topes smiled delightedly. "This makes me think, you make me think of them. 'J'aime dans les temps Clara d'Ellébeuse . . . ' But, my dear Barbara, what is the matter?"

She had started crying, for no reason whatever.

Alun Lewis

1915–1944

To the many who know this young writer's poems and stories, it seems altogether likely that his death by accident while on active duty in Burma was the heaviest loss sustained by British letters during the recent war. His published work consists of four volumes: two volumes of poetry, *Raiders' Dawn* (1942) and *Ha! Ha! among the Trumpets* (1945); a volume of short stories, *The Last Inspection* (1942); and a volume jointly composed of further short stories and a selection of letters written during the war to his parents and his wife, *In the Green Tree* (1949). Everything he wrote, whether in prose or verse, is marked by a sanity, an integrity, a clarity and power of imaginative vision, an unassuming, simple dignity which are beyond praise. Also, as will be clear to anyone who reads the story from *The Last Inspection* reprinted below, by a warm humor and by deep and compelling human compassion.

The letters in *In the Green Tree,* written from India and Burma, provide an interesting and moving revelation of the writer, his interests, and his aims. They describe the newness of a strange continent, they express the tensions of training and the larger tension of the war itself, they articulate Lewis's profoundly serious questionings about himself and his art. Many themes might be disengaged in discussing them: his sense of fatality, his sense of being a Welsh writer, his observations of the way the creative process worked for him in particular instances, his reactions to India, his reactions to the army life and to the men who lived it with him. Yet there is one theme, touched on in the following passage, which is more central and revelatory than any of the others: indeed, it includes many of the others. After attending staff-school at Karachi in the late summer of 1943, Lewis refused the assignment offered him ("a job which meant 900 rupees a month and a real mental and physical challenge") in order to return to his own Welsh troops:

And yet I want to be away, too. It's time I took a harder job in a way. Yet I'm frightened of leaving them. They

seem to have some secret knowledge that I want and will never find out until I go into action with them and war really happens to them. I dread missing such a thing; it seems desertion to something more than either me or them. When I was leaving Karachi, one of the instructors said to me, "You're the most selfish man I've ever met, Lewis. You think the war exists for you to write books about it."

I didn't deny it, though it's all wrong. I hadn't the strength to explain what is instinctive and categorical in me, the need to experience. The writing is only a proof of the sincerity of the experience, that's all.

Lewis's receptivity to experience, his reverence for it when it commanded reverence: in these respects, even if in no other, there is a fitness in the comparison with Keats which suggests itself. "I'm writing out of clarity of spirit, and letting Life have a chance," he says on one occasion, and it does not seem too much to say that, to judge from his poems and stories and letters, whatever life passed before him had its due. Even the snake his party killed on a trip into the jungle:

We . . . started a ten-foot snake from the long grass and G. had three shots at it as it flickered across the clearing. He got it: and it curled up slowly and raised its fine little head above its shattered body and stared at us inscrutably till the colonel slashed it with his stick and it was dead.

We know that he spoke the truth when he said, after remarking "I don't think I'll stop writing as long as I live," in a letter of June 18, 1943, "I feel as if there's a steady fountain with a good head of water in me, and without trying to be pretentious, I think I can do my duty to thought and work and life." And the sense of the truth in this statement is, for those of us who know him only through his books, the sense of the tragedy of his loss.

In the Green Tree contains a brief critical preface by A. L. Rowse and a postscript-memoir by Gwyn Jones. A fine brief glimpse of Lewis is provided by J. Maclaren-Ross in "Second Lieutenant Lewis," originally published in *Penguin New Writing,* No. 27 (April, 1946).

PRIVATE JONES[1]

DAFIS the post came down the lane to Siencyn's cottage earlier to-day than usual. He walked his bicycle through the stony muddy ruts, ringing his bell to call them out. Siencyn was still in bed, but Marged, his wife, had been up a couple of hours, feeding the wild chickens that nested in the apple trees and gorse bushes and mixing some swill for Granny the sow.

"It's come, Marged fach,[2] it's come," Dafis shouted, his excitement at a gleeful pitch, "Siencyn's notice is come."

He brandished a small brown envelope.

Marged straightened her heavy body, wiped her wet hands in her sack apron, showed nothing.

"Diw mawr,"[3] she said to herself, thinking that something important was happening inside her.

"Siencyn!" Dafis called, leaning his bicycle with its tied-on parcels against the crumbled wall of the cottage. "Your calling-up notice I got for you. Look alive, boy."

Siencyn poked his long head out of the tiny bedroom window, his hair the colour of swedes.[4] He was in his flannel nightshirt.

"Coming now, Dafis," he said cheerily and withdrew. He pulled his trousers and clogs on, and came downstairs buckling his leather belt across a handful of trousers, very excited.

Dafis opened the letter, Marged looking over his shoulder. She was twice his size.

"Printed matter," Dafis said. "There for you. Instructions, look. Railway travel voucher. Free trip, see?"

"In the train?" Siencyn asked.

"Third class," Dafis said. "From Cardigan station, Great Western Railway, to Talcen station, ditto. East Wales Fusiliers it is for you, Siencyn bach, poor dab. Plenty of V. C.'s[5] they got already. Watch out, you."

"East Wales Fusiliers, is it?" Siencyn repeated. "Well, well. Third class?"

"When is it?" Marged asked.

"Friday next, 21st inst.," Dafis said. "Take your identity card, Siencyn bach, don't forget that, now. Or it's C. B.[6] you'll be right from the word go."

"Jawch," said Siencyn, "there's a lot to remember, Dafis. Where's my identity card, Marged? In the poe in the spare room, is it?"

"And your birth certificate is there," she said, knowing where to put her hands on things. "You'll have to find somewhere else to keep your things from now on, Siencyn bach."

"Aye, that's true," he said, rubbing his tangled hair. "Well, I better go round and tell everybody."

"Don't trouble," Dafis said. "I'll tell them on my round. Stay you, my boy. I'll come down to-night and give you a bit of wisdom, see? Four years of it in the last war I had, and no more for me thank you." He looked at his right hand, from which three fingers were missing. "German sniper did that," he said proudly, and then screwed up his red bunioned face into a wink. "Held it up above the parapet, see, Siencyn, and got a nice little blighty. But there, you don't know what a parapet is yet, I don't doubt."

"I'll learn," Siencyn said, with all the good will in the world.

"You will," Dafis said, speaking with the sardonic finality of experience. "Solong both."

"Solong Dafis, thank you," Siencyn said.

Dafis pushed his bicycle off, the cycle clips pulling his small trousers up nearly to his knees. He wore a straw boater all the year round, Dafis did.

The third winter of the war was just relaxing its grip on this closed corner of Cardiganshire; six weeks of frost had held up the winter ploughing and the spring sowing, and Siencyn had been having a soft time of it, lying in bed in the mornings, chopping a bit of firewood, mending a few broken scythes and shafts, patching up the cowsheds of his employer, cutting enough hay for the dray-horses, and a pint or two some nights. He had been medically examined and registered a whole year back, but his call-up was deferred for the summer harvest and the autumn trapping,—Siencyn was the official trapper of the parish and sent four hundred and thirty-seven rabbits to Cardigan station, Great Western, in five weeks,—and then the winter ploughing. He had got tired of waiting, restless and unable to merge himself in his work and the weather and the requirements of the horses and of Marged. He was a good natured man, but out of patience with things. He had quarrelled

---

[1] From *The Last Inspection* by Alun Lewis, copyright 1943 by The Macmillan Company and used with their permission.

[2] *Bach*, or its mutated variant *fach*, the Welsh word for "little," is often added to proper names in familiar address.

[3] An exclamation of surprise or dismay, actually more neutral in force than its literal meaning ("great God").

[4] Rutabagas.

[5] Victoria Crosses, British military decorations for acts of outstanding bravery.

[6] Confined to barracks.

with Marged a lot this winter, beating her once, leaping out of bed on a Sunday morning when the cracked church bell was tolling, and beating her for calling him an idle heathen. And she used her tongue on him for that. Said that people were saying things about them. What things? She shrugged her shoulders. Once he'd cleared out of the way, they were saying, perhaps they'd discover before a year was out whose fault it was there were no babies coming in their house. Well, that wasn't a nice thing to say, and it says a lot for Siencyn's good nature that he only shrugged his shoulders and said pity they hadn't got more important things to think about than that. She didn't use the rough edge of her tongue on him again, but she was very secretive and moody all the winter. He didn't worry about her; he'd go and she'd stay behind; she was his wife; there you are; nobody is indispensable; she wouldn't want to leave the place she'd been born in, whether he went or not. It was different with him. He wanted to see the world. Lots of the boys from round about went into the merchant navy; either the sea or the land it was with all the boys. And he held it a grudge that his widowed mother had kept him home to work at odd jobs instead of letting him go to sea. His father must have been an old soft, too; he wasn't wounded and he wasn't ill in the last war. He just died. Ran home three times from the army, and then died in detention barracks. Heart-broken, his mother said. Well, what a complaint for a man!

Nobody had a bad word for Siencyn, except that he was idle and fond of his drink and irregular as a christian and not reliable for doing a job or fetching you something from market or being prompt at the chapel concert rehearsals. So, when he went round to say solong, everybody was sorry to see him go and genuinely hoped the army would make a man of him before it got him killed. Old Mari Siop, who had a soft spot for anybody in trousers, said she thought strong men like him ought to stay at home in case the Irish attacked us. And he had a real good walk-round, ending up at the Ship hotel, saying good-bye and drinking basin after basin of tea in the cottages and then a pint all round on the house. This was on his last night, and you wouldn't believe the offers he had to knit comforts for him, and old drovers and flannel vests fetched out of the cupboards where they had lain since their wearers had died. He took them all, and all that he didn't drop on the way down from the pub he carried into the kitchen where Marged was sitting doing nothing by the wood fire. She was cross with him for taking them; they'd be saying now she couldn't look after

her husband's pants even. She was always seeing the worst side of everything these days. She was almost fit to cry with desperation over a little thing like that.

So they had a bit of bread and milk for supper, not saying anything at all. Then he fetched the money from under the bed upstairs and counted it out, five pounds thirteen and four, and divided it into two piles, three pounds thirteen for her and two pounds for himself. And then he got up and very clumsily and hesitantly smoothed her hair back. She was vexed, and said what a mess she was, all untidy and fat-getting, and she bent her head forward as if she was feeling bad; and she was all white and her eyes were yellow and suffused with watery blood. He was shifting from one foot to the other, uneasy about what to do, and she wouldn't say a thing one way or the other. Dumb she was.

And he was thinking how happy everything and everybody had been when he went round the farms this afternoon, and now Marged spoiling it all. But when she looked up at him, raised her head to him slowly as if there was a millstone round her neck, and then stood up with her arms raised a little, and said that Welsh word to him that she hadn't said since they were courting, then he knew it was a million times better to feel black and torn in pieces like this than to be laughing and drinking tea and saying the Germans wouldn't last long now he was in it too. He picked her up, and she wasn't heavy any more; and carried her up the creaking stairs as if she was a young virgin. Only she was better than a virgin, her fine big body which his big shivering hands slowly divested of the red jersey and thick skirt and woollen stocking and flannel vests that she wore on it winter and summer. The moon was out and the river ringing on the stones and the old jollyboy owls crying goodywhoo in the wood, and he knew he'd been waiting for this for a whole year, to say good-bye to Marged like this. And she lay warm and silken and trembling under his huge hands and she heard neither the river nor the owls but only him grunting and breathing in her mouth and in her ears and something gentle at last opening inside her, like a baby begging her to receive it in.

Onions she boiled for his breakfast the next morning, and two hard-boiled eggs and a whole small loaf uncut for his pocket, and off he set, six miles to walk to Cardigan station. Dafis the postman had forgotten to bring him some stamped addressed envelopes, but he had found a letter in the grandfather clock with their address on it. He didn't know how to write the address himself, but somebody would copy it off this old letter for him when he got there, no doubt. So everything was alright. Plenty of wood left for the fire and Marged walking to the crossroads with him, and the weather crisp and young, the cockerels crowing all the way in to Cardigan station, and Dai Pencwm passing him on the road giving him the benediction of the big pew. His heart was like a feather, walking like this through his own countryside, seeing the sea through gates in the sandy hedges, and singing Dr. Parry's *Jerusalem* to himself which was this year's test piece at the Eisteddfod, and feeling a free man, as if he owned the place and no need to pick up a shovel nor a scythe nor the handles of the plough . . .

There were other men like him on the train the last part of the journey, from Swansea. But they were different to him, smoking cigarettes and wearing posh navy suits and pointy shoes, with white silk scarves and grease on their hair. He sat a long way from them and he felt hot and uneasy. But when they got there it was all in together and fags out and form up in threes with a soldier showing you how with a silver-knobbed cane, and march through the streets into the barracks. Then he lost direction and control, there were so many things and people. He knew how to sign his name, S. Jones, where they told him, but they wouldn't give him enough time to do it in, and he had to keep on signing in every room they went into, whereas he had never signed his name more than twice a week before, on the dole that was. But he was doing pretty well out of it; same as last night everybody was giving him things—mug, knife, fork, spoon, blankets, bag for straw, khaki suit, leggings, boots, cap, and lots of straps that he didn't know what for. And then a rifle and a bayonet. You didn't take long to become a soldier, for a fact. Then they had a good meal in the cookhouse, with girls in khaki doing for them, and then the most of them went out for a booze, and cursing everything they were when there were no corporals about. But Siencyn didn't open his mouth, and he was frightened a bit because he'd lost count of what was happening, and he wanted to lie down and sleep, being suddenly very weak and shaky and yawning all the time. As for Marged and all them at home, they didn't exist any more. It was all up with them, there was no doubt.

"You're looking buggered, Jack," a dark man said, sitting on the floor cleaning his rifle in the empty barrack room.

Siencyn, like a frightened animal, watched him suspiciously.

"Yes," he said. "Yes."

"It isn't worth worrying about this lot here," the man said. "They don't count in this war. They're all peace-time soldiers. They don't know what the war's about, they only want to stay here and shout on the square and take the tarts out. You keep your head up. Don't pay any attention to them."

"Yes," said Siencyn not understanding much except that the man was friendly, "that is so for a fact."

The man began cleaning his buttons with a button stick and silvo. "I'll learn you how to do things," he said. "They don't mean anything, all the things they do here, but you might as well do them properly, just to show them there's nothing in it, and then get on out somewhere where there *is* a war."

"You been a soldier before, is it?" Siencyn asked, friendly with him now, like a dog that barks first, then growls, then wags its tail and sidles up.

"Not in this army, mate. I fought two years in Spain, though. Seen a bit of it then, like."

"For a living, is it?" Siencyn asked, shifting up, willing to listen.

"No, not for a living," the man laughed. "A collier I am for a living, when the pits are open. Collier, stay-in striker, party member, anything's better than keeping a greyhound, chum."

"Spanish they speak in Spain?" Siencyn asked.

"No, not much now. German and Italian they speak there now. But it doesn't matter much there now."

"*This* war will do for me alright," Siencyn said. "Farm labourer I am, see, and trapper."

"That's right. You keep to the plough, mate. It's only a knife in your back or a few years in jail or no work and no friends you'll get if you start doing what you believe in. I've never had time to marry a wife, and yet I've never done nothing I can show."

"I'm married," Siencyn said. "It isn't very much of a thing; only down our way you got to get married if you want any peace, see." The man smiled, and Siencyn smiled back, and then sat thinking of the thing he'd just said.

"No girl in the valleys would take me on," the man said. "They want a steady man, see. I'm an anarchist. I won't go and live in two rooms and feed my kids on bread and dripping and make them sell the *Football Echo* and read the race results in the paper and shout hooray in the park on Labour Day."

Well, well, thought Siencyn, this is a different life to mine, and what it all is I don't know. But I wouldn't like to be on the wrong side of this man, because he is like the prophet Ezekiel, and he can kill people by seizing their wickedness in his hands and squeezing it till they choke.

And Siencyn became devoted to this man, and he wasn't afraid of all the things that happened to him in the next few weeks.